CRIMINAL PROCEDURE: CASES, MATERIALS, AND QUESTIONS
Fourth Edition

LexisNexis Law School Publishing Advisory Board

CRIMINAL PROCEDURE: CASES, MATERIALS, AND QUESTIONS

Fourth Edition

Arnold H. Loewy
George Killam Professor of Criminal Law
Texas Tech University School of Law

ISBN: 978-1-6328-1540-8
Looseleaf ISBN: 978-1-6328-1599-6
Ebook ISBN: 978-1-6328-1541-5

Library of Congress Cataloging-in-Publication Data

Loewy, Arnold H., author.
Criminal procedure : cases, materials, and questions / Arnold H. Loewy, George Killam Professor of Criminal Law, Texas Tech University School of Law. -- Fourth Edition.
    pages cm
Includes index.
ISBN 978-1-63281-540-8 (hardbound)
1. Criminal procedure--United States--Cases. 2. Criminal procedure--United States. I. Title.
KF9619.L64 2015
345.73'05--dc23
                                                                                                    2014048959

NOTE TO USERS
To ensure that you are using the latest materials available in this area, please be sure to periodically check the LexisNexis Law School web site for downloadable updates and supplements at www.lexisnexis.com/lawschool.

Editorial Offices
630 Central Ave., New Providence, NJ 07974 (908) 464-6800
201 Mission St., San Francisco, CA 94105-1831 (415) 908-3200
www.lexisnexis.com

MATTHEW♦BENDER

DEDICATION

To the Texas Tech School of Law that has provided me with an incredibly nurturing and sustaining environment for the past nine years, my former Dean, Walter Huffman, whose gentle persuasion helped convince me to come to Texas Tech, and my current Dean, Darby Dickerson.

Fourth Edition Preface

This book is designed for a complete criminal procedure course. It can be covered tightly in four hours or quite leisurely in five hours. In my judgment, much of criminal procedure is the sort of material that ought to be part of a good citizen/lawyer's repertoire. Consequently, this book and course are not designed exclusively for future criminal law practitioners. Rather, the book and course are designed as a roadmap for those who wish to learn about governmental limitations on police and/or trial procedures in the criminal context.

The presentation of the materials is focused, rather than scatter-gun. That is, each case is presented, lightly edited (deletions not usually noted in the material), with a series of focused questions and notes (mostly questions) following it. It is contemplated that the students will read the case, focus on the question, reread the case, and be prepared to discuss some or all of the questions in class. Because the cases are lightly edited, the total number of pages per class might seem unusually long. However, most classes will involve studying only three or four cases. Because of this precise focus, the material should be manageable.

As a matter of editing style, law review articles and other collateral material are usually not cited in the questions and notes. This is not because of the author's belief that they are unimportant. My primary reason for generally not including collateral sources is to ensure that the student's focus will not be directed away from the precise questions in the book.

There are many people to thank: John Fischer for research assistance in the 1st edition, William Cross for research assistance in the second edition, Clint Buck for research assistance on the third edition, and Ronald Miller for research assistance on the fourth edition. The UNC Law Center for financial assistance for the first and second edition, the Texas Tech School of Law for its incredible support in preparing the third edition, and my wife, Judy, for emotional assistance. A number of colleagues across the country have contributed to my understanding of criminal procedure, but I would like to particularly acknowledge two of them. Arthur LaFrance, of Lewis and Clark, who, coauthored my first criminal procedure casebook with me. Undoubtedly some of his influence remains in this book. The late Professor Laura Webster of Mercer Law School, a former Philadelphia Public Defender, taught me much about, among other things, criminal procedure.

Arnold H. Loewy
George Killam Professor of Criminal Law
Texas Tech School of Law
Lubbock, Texas
February 9, 2015

TABLE OF CONTENTS

Chapter 1   **THE PROTECTIONS OF AND RATIONALE FOR THE FOURTH AMENDMENT** 1

Brinegar v. United States 2
Questions and Notes 3
Draper v. United States 3
Questions and Notes 4

Chapter 2   **PROBABLE CAUSE** 5

Brinegar v. United States 5
Questions and Notes 12
Draper v. United States 13
Questions and Notes 18
Spinelli v. United States 18
Questions and Notes 27
Illinois v. Gates 28
Questions and Notes 46
Massachusetts v. Upton 47
Questions and Notes 51
Commonwealth v. Upton 52
Questions and Notes 55
Maryland v. Pringle 56
Questions and Notes 59
Florida v. Harris 59
Questions and Notes 65

Chapter 3   **THE NEED FOR A WARRANT** 67

A.   IS THE WARRANT REQUIREMENT THE EXCEPTION OR THE RULE? 67
    Vale v. Louisiana 67
    Questions and Notes 71
    Chambers v. Maroney 71
    Questions and Notes 76
    United States v. Chadwick 76
    Questions and Notes 79
B.   THE ANATOMY OF A WARRANT 80
    Groh v. Ramirez 80
    Questions and Notes 88
C.   WHO CAN ISSUE A WARRANT? 88
    Shadwick v. Tampa 88
    Questions and Notes 91

Table of Contents

Chapter 4	**ARRESTS**	**93**
A.	ARRESTS IN THE HOME	93
	United States v. Santana	94
	Questions and Notes	95
	Payton v. New York	96
	Questions and Notes	109
	Steagald v. United States	109
	Questions and Notes	118
	Welsh v. Wisconsin	119
	Questions and Notes	124
	Minnesota v. Olson	124
	Questions and Notes	126
	Problem	127
B.	FORCE IN EFFECTUATING AN ARREST	128
	Tennessee v. Garner	128
	Questions and Notes	138
	Graham v. Connor	139
	Questions and Notes	142
	Problem	142
	Scott v. Harris	142
	Questions and Notes	152
C.	DETENTION OF PERSONS PURSUANT TO A SEARCH WARRANT	153
	Michigan v. Summers	153
	Questions and Notes	158
	Muehler v. Mena	158
	Questions and Notes	165
	Problem	166
D.	SEARCH INCIDENT TO ARREST	167
	Chimel v. California	167
	Questions and Notes	176
	Maryland v. Buie	176
	Questions and Notes	183
Chapter 5	**PLAIN VIEW**	**185**
	Horton v. California	185
	Questions and Notes	194
	Arizona v. Hicks	194
	Questions and Notes	202

Table of Contents

Chapter 6   AUTOMOBILES 203

A.   THE RULE AND ITS RATIONALE 203

       California v. Carney 203

       Questions and Notes 211

B.   CARS AND CONTAINERS 211

       California v. Acevedo 212

       Questions and Notes 226

       Problem 226

C.   SEARCH INCIDENT TO ARREST IN AN AUTOMOBILE 228

       Arizona v. Gant 228

       Questions and Notes 243

D.   SUSPICIONLESS HIGHWAY STOPS 243

       Delaware v. Prouse 244

       Questions and Notes 250

       Michigan v. Sitz 250

       Questions and Notes 263

       City of Indianapolis v. Edmond 263

       Questions and Notes 274

       Illinois v. Lidster 274

       Questions and Notes 278

E.   INVENTORY SEARCHES 278

       Colorado v. Bertine 278

       Questions and Notes 287

       Florida v. Wells 288

       Questions and Notes 289

Chapter 7   SEARCHING COMPUTERS AND CELL PHONES 291

       Riley v. California 291

       Questions and Notes 306

Chapter 8   LIMITED SEARCHES ON LESS THAN
                      PROBABLE CAUSE 309

A.   PROTECTION OF THE OFFICER 309

       Terry v. Ohio 309

       Questions and Notes 322

       Sibron v. New York 323

       Questions and Notes 325

       Problem 325

       Michigan v. Long 326

       Questions and Notes 336

       Ybarra v. Illinois 336

Table of Contents

	Questions and Notes	342
B.	WHAT IS REASONABLE SUSPICION? HOW IS IT DIFFERENT FROM PROBABLE CAUSE?	342
	Adams v. Williams	343
	Questions and Notes	349
	United States v. Cortez	349
	Questions and Notes	355
	Florida v. Royer	355
	Questions and Notes	363
	United States v. Sokolow	363
	Questions and Notes	370
	Alabama v. White	371
	Questions and Notes	375
	Florida v. J.L.	375
	Questions and Notes	379
	Prado Navarette v. California	380
	Questions and Notes	389
	Illinois v. Wardlow	390
	Questions and Notes	399
	Ornelas v. United States	400
	Questions and Notes	407
	United States v. Arvizu	408
	Questions and Notes	413
C.	LIMITS ON *TERRY*-TYPE STOPS	414
	Florida v. Royer	414
	Questions and Notes	421
	United States v. Place	421
	Questions and Notes	428
	United States v. Sharpe	429
	Questions and Notes	440
	Hiibel v. Sixth Judicial District Court	440
	Questions and Notes	446
Chapter 9	**SEIZURES**	**447**
	United States v. Mendenhall	447
	Questions and Notes	455
	Florida v. Royer	456
	Questions and Notes	459
	Problem	460
	I.N.S. v. Delgado	460
	Florida v. Bostick	461
	Questions and Notes	472
	California v. Hodari D.	472

Table of Contents

	Questions and Notes	482
	Brendlin v. California	482
	Questions and Notes	487
	Problem	487

Chapter 10   SEARCHES   491

A.   THE DIVINING ROD THEORY OF THE
     FOURTH AMENDMENT 491

Arnold H. Loewy, *The Fourth Amendment as a Device for
Protecting the Innocent* 491

Questions and Notes 494

United States v. Place 494

Questions and Notes 496

United States v. Jacobsen 496

Questions and Notes 500

Illinois v. Caballes 501

Questions and Notes 509

B.   REASONABLE EXPECTATION OF PRIVACY 509

Lewis v. United States 509

Questions and Notes 511

Hoffa v. United States 512

Questions and Notes 515

Katz v. United States 515

Questions and Notes 518

Oliver v. United States 519

Questions and Notes 530

Problem 532

Florida v. Riley 533

Questions and Notes 541

Bond v. United States 542

Questions and Notes 546

Kyllo v. United States 546

Questions and Notes 558

United States v. Jones 558

Questions and Notes 571

Florida v. Jardines 571

Questions and Notes 583

Problem 583

Chapter 11   CONSENT   585

Schneckloth v. Bustamonte 585

Questions and Notes 596

Table of Contents

Illinois v. Rodriguez 597
Questions and Notes 604
Problem 604

Chapter 12   ARE WE MOVING TOWARD OPEN SEASON ON AUTOMOBILES IN THE 21ST CENTURY? 607

Whren v. United States 607
Questions and Notes 613
Ohio v. Robinette 613
Questions and Notes 619
Maryland v. Wilson 619
Questions and Notes 627
Knowles v. Iowa 627
Questions and Notes 629
Problem 630
Atwater v. City of Lago Vista 630
Questions and Notes 647
Arkansas v. Sullivan 648
Questions and Notes 650
Virginia v. Moore 650
Questions and Notes 656
Closing Note 657

Chapter 13   UNUSUAL SITUATIONS 659

A.   ESPECIALLY INTRUSIVE SEARCHES 659
Winston v. Lee 659
Questions and Notes 665
B.   TAKING DNA 666
Maryland v. King 666
Questions and Notes 684
C.   BORDER AND INTERNATIONAL SEARCHES 685
D.   ADMINISTRATIVE AND OTHER NONCRIMINAL SEARCHES 685

Chapter 14   THE EXCLUSIONARY RULE 687

A.   THE RATIONALE FOR THE EXCLUSIONARY RULE 687
Mapp v. Ohio 687
Questions and Notes 692
United States v. Calandra 693
Questions and Notes 700
Problem 701
Hudson v. Michigan 701
Questions and Notes 715
B.   THE GOOD FAITH EXCEPTION TO THE EXCLUSIONARY RULE 715

Table of Contents

United States v. Leon 715

Questions and Notes 734

Problem 735

Commonwealth v. Edmunds 736

Questions and Notes 747

Arizona v. Evans 747

Questions and Notes 758

Herring v. United States 758

Questions and Notes 769

Davis v. United States 770

Questions and Notes 783

C.   STANDING 783

Rakas v. Illinois 784

Questions and Notes 800

United States v. Salvucci 800

Questions and Notes 804

Rawlings v. Kentucky 804

Questions and Notes 812

Minnesota v. Carter 812

Questions and Notes 823

Problem 823

Chapter 15   CONFESSIONS, VOLUNTARINESS 825

Brown v. Mississippi 825

Questions and Notes 828

Watts v. Indiana 829

Questions and Notes 834

Crooker v. California 834

Questions and Notes 839

Spano v. New York 840

Questions and Notes 845

Chapter 16   RIGHT TO COUNSEL 847

Massiah v. United States 847

Questions and Notes 853

Escobedo v. State of Illinois 854

Questions and Notes 864

Chapter 17   MIRANDA 865

A.   THE CASE ITSELF 865

Miranda v. Arizona 865

Questions and Notes 900

B.   THE NATURE OF THE WARNINGS 901

Table of Contents

Duckworth v. Eagan 901

Questions and Notes 909

Problem 910

Colorado v. Spring 911

Questions and Notes 919

C.   INVOKING MIRANDA 920

  1.   Invoking Silence 920

     Michigan v. Mosley 920

     Questions and Notes 929

  2.   Invoking Counsel 930

     Edwards v. Arizona 930

     Questions and Notes 935

     Arizona v. Roberson 935

     Questions and Notes 941

     Minnick v. Mississippi 941

     Questions and Notes 951

     Maryland v. Shatzer 951

     Questions and Notes 962

     Davis v. United States 962

     Questions and Notes 969

     Problem 969

     Problem 970

D.   WAIVER 971

     North Carolina v. Butler 971

     Questions and Notes 975

     Tague v. Louisiana 975

     Questions and Notes 976

     Connecticut v. Barrett 977

     Questions and Notes 981

     Berghuis v. Thompkins 981

     Question and Notes 997

E.   CUSTODY 997

     Oregon v. Mathiason 998

     Questions and Notes 1002

     Problem 1002

     J.D.B. v. North Carolina 1003

     Questions and Notes 1019

     Problem 1019

     Illinois v. Perkins 1021

     Questions and Notes 1029

     Maryland v. Shatzer 1029

Table of Contents

	Questions and Notes	1032
	Howes v. Fields	1032
	Questions and Notes	1040
F.	INTERROGATION	1040
	Rhode Island v. Innis	1040
	Questions and Notes	1050
	Problem	1051
G.	THE PUBLIC SAFETY EXCEPTION	1052
	New York v. Quarles	1052
	Questions and Notes	1064

Chapter 18   THE RIGHT TO COUNSEL AND CONFESSIONS 1067

A.	*MASSIAH* REVISITED	1067
	Brewer v. Williams	1067
	Questions and Notes	1079
	Maine v. Moulton	1080
	Questions and Notes	1090
	Kuhlmann v. Wilson	1090
	Questions and Notes	1096
B.	CONTRASTING *MASSIAH* AND *MIRANDA*	1097
	Michigan v. Jackson	1097
	Questions and Notes	1102
	McNeil v. Wisconsin	1103
	Questions and Notes	1111
	Texas v. Cobb	1111
	Questions and Notes	1123
	Patterson v. Illinois	1124
	Questions and Notes	1133
	Problem	1134
	Problem	1134
C.	THE SIXTH AMENDMENT AND THE ROBERTS COURT: THE TIMES THEY ARE A CHANGING	1135
	Kansas v. Ventris	1135
	Questions and Notes	1139
	Montejo v. Louisiana	1140
	Questions and Notes	1157

Chapter 19   VOLUNTARINESS REVISITED 1159

	Mincey v. Arizona	1159
	Questions and Notes	1165
	Colorado v. Connelly	1165
	Questions and Notes	1172

Table of Contents

Problem 1173

Arizona v. Fulminante 1174

Questions and Notes 1183

Problem 1183

Chapter 20　　**MIRANDA REVISITED** **1211**

Dickerson v. United States 1211

Questions and Notes 1228

Chavez v. Martinez 1228

Questions and Notes 1244

Chapter 21　　**DUE PROCESS OUTSIDE OF THE**
　　　　　　　　　　CONFESSION CONTEXT **1245**

A.　　DUE PROCESS AND THE FOURTH OR FIFTH
　　　AMENDMENT 1245

Rochin v. California 1245

Questions and Notes 1249

Irvine v. California 1249

Questions and Notes 1254

Schmerber v. California 1254

Questions and Notes 1260

B.　　DUE PROCESS AND IDENTIFICATION 1260

Manson v. Brathwaite 1261

Questions and Notes 1276

Problem 1277

Chapter 22　　**ATTENUATION** **1279**

A.　　FOURTH AMENDMENT 1279

Wong Sun v. United States 1279

Questions and Notes 1284

Taylor v. Alabama 1284

Questions and Notes 1289

New York v. Harris 1289

Questions and Notes 1296

United States v. Ceccolini 1297

Questions and Notes 1305

B.　　MIRANDA 1306

New York v. Quarles 1306

Questions and Notes 1309

Oregon v. Elstad 1310

Questions and Notes 1328

Missouri v. Seibert 1328

Table of Contents

Questions and Notes 1339

United States v. Patane 1339

Questions and Notes 1344

Problem 1345

Problem 1346

Chapter 23	**INEVITABLE DISCOVERY**	**1347**

Nix v. Williams 1347

Questions and Notes 1356

Murray v. United States 1357

Questions and Notes 1365

Chapter 24	**ENTRAPMENT**	**1367**

A.   THE RELEVANCE OF PREDISPOSITION 1367

Sherman v. United States 1367

Questions and Notes 1374

Jacobson v. United States 1374

Questions and Notes 1384

B.   THE DUE PROCESS DEFENSE 1385

United States v. Gamble 1385

Questions and Notes 1390

Table of Cases TC-1

Index I-1

THE FOURTH AMENDMENT

The Right of the People to be Secure in their Persons, Papers, Houses, and Effects Against Unreasonable Searches and Seizures Shall Not be Violated, and no Warrant Shall Issue But upon Probable Cause Supported By Oath or Affirmation Specifically Describing the Place to be Searched and the Person or Thing to be Seized.

THE FIFTH AMENDMENT

No person shall be held to answer for a capital, or otherwise infamous crime, unless on a presentment or indictment of a Grand Jury, except in cases arising in the land or naval forces, or in the Militia, when in active service in time of War or public danger; nor shall any person be subject for the same offense to be twice put in jeopardy of life or limb; nor shall be compelled in ant criminal case to be a witness against himself, nor be deprived of life, liberty, or property, without due process; nor shall private property be taken for public use, without just compensation.

THE SIXTH AMENDMENT

In all criminal prosecutions, the accused shall enjoy the right to a speedy and public trial, by an impartial jury of the State and district wherein the crime shall have been committed, which district shall have been previously ascertained by law, and to be informed of the nature and cause of the accusation; to be confronted with the witnesses against him, to have compulsory process for obtaining witnesses in his favor, and to have Assistance of Counsel for his defense.

THE FOURTEENTH AMENDMENT

SECTION 1

All persons born or naturalized in the United States, and subject to the jurisdictions thereof, are citizens of the United States and of the State wherein they reside. No State shall make or enforce any law which shall abridge the privileges and immunities of citizens of the United States; nor shall any State deprive any person of life, liberty, or property without due process of law; nor deny to any person within its jurisdiction the equal protection of the laws.

Chapter 1

THE PROTECTIONS OF AND RATIONALE FOR THE FOURTH AMENDMENT

The Fourth Amendment offers two major protections — one substantive, and the other procedural. The primary substantive protection is probable cause. The primary procedural protection is a requirement that a warrant be issued by an independent magistrate prior to the search or seizure.

Before assessing the wisdom of these, or other ancillary, protections of the fourth amendment, it is helpful to ask why we should limit searches and seizures at all. Any limit on a policeman's power to conduct searches and seizures would ordinarily impact adversely on police efficiency.[1] Although some might argue that a limitation on police efficiency is desirable for its own sake, it is probably more realistic to think of it as an incidental detriment in order to ensure the security of us all.

How, you might ask, does rendering the police more inefficient ensure our security? One possible answer is that the Fourth Amendment strikes a balance between our need to be secure from criminals and our need to be secure from the police. To the extent that police are free to conduct unlimited searches and seizures, more criminals are likely to be caught, but at the same time, more innocent citizens are likely to be subjected to the embarrassment and/or offense of a search or seizure. On the other hand, if police are totally precluded from conducting searches or seizures (as I have heard anecdotally was suggested for the new Russian Republic), an unacceptably high amount of crime would go undetected, and perhaps undeterred. Under the Fourth Amendment compromise, police are free to conduct a search and/or seizure, but only if they have been approved in advance by an independent magistrate, who has determined that the police have probable cause to conduct the search (unless the particular search or seizure is one that is an exception to the warrant and/or probable cause requirement).

There are possible alternative rules that a government might set up. In the extreme, it could provide that all searches conducted by policemen in the line of duty (perhaps limited by a good faith belief that evidence would be found) are valid. Alternatively, a government could uphold all searches that in fact yielded evidence.

---

[1] Arguably there could be instances when a search is so unlikely to turn up evidence of crime that it would be inefficient for the police to invest the time necessary to conduct it. Presumably, internal police procedures would eliminate most such searches. In any event, the Fourth Amendment is hardly necessary for that purpose.

If you were in a position to enact any rules that you thought desirable upon your society, what rules would you enact? Do you think that you would want to increase or decrease the number of searches permitted? Is it such a bad thing to be searched, relative to the good that can come from finding evidence or dispelling suspicion? What is the point of the warrant requirement?

As you think about these questions, consider the following excerpts:

BRINEGAR v. UNITED STATES
338 U.S. 160 (1949)

MR. JUSTICE JACKSON, dissenting.

When this Court recently has promulgated a philosophy that some rights derived from the Constitution are entitled to "a preferred position," I have not agreed. We cannot give some constitutional rights a preferred position without relegating others to a deferred position; we can establish no firsts without thereby establishing seconds. Indications are not wanting that Fourth Amendment freedoms are tacitly marked as secondary rights, to be relegated to a deferred position. The Fourth Amendment states: "The right of the people to be secure in their persons, houses, papers, and effects, against unreasonable searches and seizures, shall not be violated, and no Warrants shall issue, but upon probable cause, supported by Oath or affirmation, and particularly describing the place to be searched, and the persons or things to be seized."

These, I protest, are not mere second-class rights but belong in the catalog of indispensable freedoms. Among deprivations of rights, none is so effective in cowing a population, crushing the spirit of the individual and putting terror in every heart. Uncontrolled search and seizure is one of the first and most effective weapons in the arsenal of every arbitrary government. And one need only briefly to have dwelt and worked among a people possessed of many admirable qualities but deprived of these rights to know that the human personality deteriorates and dignity and self-reliance disappear where homes, persons and possessions are subject at any hour to unheralded search and seizure by the police.

But the right to be secure against searches and seizures is one of the most difficult to protect. Since the officers are themselves the chief invaders, there is no enforcement outside of court.

Only occasional and more flagrant abuses come to the attention of the courts, and then only those where the search and seizure yields incriminating evidence and the defendant is at least sufficiently compromised to be indicted. If the officers raid a home, an office, or stop and search an automobile but find nothing incriminating, this invasion of the personal liberty of the innocent too often finds no practical redress. There may be, and I am convinced that there are, many unlawful searches of homes and automobiles of innocent people which turn up nothing incriminating, in which no arrest is made, about which courts do nothing, and about which we never hear.

Courts can protect the innocent against such invasions indirectly and through the medium of excluding evidence obtained against those who frequently are guilty. Federal courts have used this method of enforcement of the Amendment, in spite of its unfortunate consequences on law enforcement, although many state courts do not. This inconsistency does not disturb me, for local excesses or invasions of liberty are more amenable to political correction, the Amendment was directed only against the new and centralized government, and any really dangerous threat to the general liberties of the people can come only from this source. We must therefore look upon the exclusion of evidence in federal prosecutions if obtained in violation of the Amendment as a means of extending protection against the central government's agencies. So a search against Brinegar's car must be regarded as a search of the car of Everyman.

We must remember that the extent of any privilege of search and seizure without warrant which we sustain, the officers interpret and apply themselves and will push to the limit. We must remember, too, that freedom from unreasonable search differs from some of the other rights of the Constitution in that there is no way the innocent citizen can invoke advance protection. For example, any effective interference with freedom of the press, or free speech, or religion, usually requires a course of suppressions against which the citizen can and often does go to the court and obtain an injunction. Other rights, such as that to an impartial jury or the aid of counsel, are within the supervisory power of the courts themselves. Such a right as just compensation for the taking of private property may be vindicated after the act in terms of money.

But an illegal search and seizure usually is a single incident, perpetrated by surprise, conducted in haste, kept purposely beyond the court's supervision and limited only by the judgment and moderation of officers whose own interests and records are often at stake in the search. There is no opportunity for injunction or appeal to disinterested intervention. The citizen's choice is quietly to submit to whatever the officers undertake or to resist at risk of arrest or immediate violence.

And we must remember that the authority which we concede to conduct searches and seizures without warrant may be exercised by the most unfit and ruthless officers as well as by the fit and responsible, and resorted to in case of petty misdemeanors as well as in the case of the gravest felonies.

NOTE

One reason for the Fourth Amendment's being taken less seriously than other Amendments is suggested by Justice Douglas's dissenting opinion in *Draper*.

DRAPER v. UNITED STATES
358 U.S. 307 (1959)

Mr. Justice Douglas, dissenting.

Decisions under the Fourth Amendment, taken in the long view, have not given the protection to the citizen which the letter and spirit of the Amendment would seem to require. One reason, I think, is that wherever a culprit is caught red-handed, as in leading Fourth Amendment cases, it is difficult to adopt and enforce a rule that would turn him loose. A rule protective of law-abiding citizens is not apt to flourish where its advocates are usually criminals. Yet the rule we fashion is for the innocent and guilty alike. If the word of the informer on which the present arrest was made is sufficient to make the arrest legal, his word would also protect the police who, acting on it, hauled the innocent citizen off to jail.

Of course, the education we receive from mystery stories and television shows teaches that what happened in this case is efficient police work. The police are tipped off that a man carrying narcotics will step off the morning train. A man meeting the precise description does alight from the train. No warrant for his arrest has been — or, as I see it, could then be — obtained. Yet he is arrested; and narcotics are found in his pocket and a syringe in the bag he carried. This is the familiar pattern of crime detection which has been dinned into public consciousness as the correct and efficient one. It is, however, a distorted reflection of the constitutional system under which we are supposed to live.

QUESTION AND NOTE

Has anything that you have read thus far affected your answers to the questions preceding them? We will examine both *Brinegar* and *Draper* in greater depth in the next chapter which explores probable cause.

Chapter 2

PROBABLE CAUSE

Probable cause, the substantive heart of the Fourth Amendment, is the standard by which the legality of most searches is measured. In assessing what the term means, the relevant inquiry is whether the police ought to be allowed to search on the basis of the information they had *before* the search occurred. Consider how well the Court evaluated probable cause in the following cases in light of that purpose.

BRINEGAR v. UNITED STATES
338 U.S. 160 (1949)

Mr. Justice Rutledge delivered the opinion of the Court.

Brinegar was convicted of importing intoxicating liquor into Oklahoma from Missouri in violation of the federal statute which forbids such importation contrary to the laws of any state. His conviction was based in part on the use in evidence against him of liquor seized from his automobile in the course of the alleged unlawful importation.

The facts are substantially undisputed. At about six o'clock on the evening of March 3, 1947, Malsed, an investigator of the Alcohol Tax Unit, and Creehan, a special investigator, were parked in a car beside a highway near the Quapaw Bridge in northeastern Oklahoma. The point was about five miles west of the Missouri-Oklahoma line. Brinegar drove past headed west in his Ford coupe. Malsed had arrested him about five months earlier for illegally transporting liquor; had seen him loading liquor into a car or truck in Joplin, Missouri, on at least two occasions during the preceding six months; and knew him to have a reputation for hauling liquor. As Brinegar passed, Malsed recognized both him and the Ford. He told Creehan, who was driving the officers' car, that Brinegar was the driver of the passing car. Both agents later testified that the car, but not especially its rear end, appeared to be "heavily loaded" and "weighted down with something." Brinegar increased his speed as he passed the officers. They gave chase. After pursuing him for about a mile at top speed, they gained on him as his car skidded on a curve, sounded their siren, overtook him, and crowded his car to the side of the road by pulling across in front of it. The highway was one leading from Joplin, Missouri, toward Vinita, Oklahoma, Brinegar's home.

As the agents got out of their car and walked back toward petitioner, Malsed said, "Hello, Brinegar, how much liquor have you got in the car?" or "How much liquor have you got in the car this time?" Petitioner replied, "Not too much," or "Not so much." After further questioning he admitted that he had twelve cases in the car. Malsed testified that one case, which was on the front seat, was visible from outside the car, but petitioner testified that it was covered by a lap robe. Twelve

5

more cases were found under and behind the front seat. The agents then placed Brinegar under arrest and seized the liquor. The district judge, after a hearing on the motion to suppress at which the facts stated above appeared in evidence, was of the opinion that "the mere fact that the agents knew that this defendant was engaged in hauling whiskey, even coupled with the statement that the car appeared to be weighted, would not be probable cause for the search of this car." Therefore, he thought, there was no probable cause when the agents began the chase. He held, however, that the voluntary admission made by petitioner after his car had been stopped constituted probable cause for a search, regardless of the legality of the arrest and detention, and that therefore the evidence was admissible. At the trial, as has been said, the court overruled petitioner's renewal of the objection.

The crucial question is whether there was probable cause for Brinegar's arrest, in the light of prior adjudications on this problem, more particularly *Carroll v. United States*, 267 U.S. 132, which on its face most closely approximates the situation presented here.

In this case, the record shows that Brinegar had used Joplin, Missouri, to Malsed's personal knowledge derived from direct observation, not merely from hearsay as seems to be suggested, as a source of supply on other occasions within the preceding six months. It also discloses that Brinegar's home was in Vinita, Oklahoma, and that Brinegar when apprehended was traveling in a direction leading from Joplin to Vinita, at a point about four or five miles west of the Missouri-Oklahoma line.

Joplin, like Detroit in the *Carroll* case, was a ready source of supply. But unlike Detroit it was not an illegal source. So far as appears, Brinegar's purchases there were entirely legal. And so, we may assume for present purposes, was his transportation of the liquor in Missouri, until he reached and crossed the state line into Oklahoma.

This difference, however, is insubstantial. For the important thing here is not whether Joplin was an illegal source of a supply; it is rather that Joplin was a ready, convenient and probable one for persons disposed to violate the Oklahoma and federal statutes. That fact was demonstrated fully, not only by the geographic facts, but by Malsed's direct and undisputed testimony of his personal observation of Brinegar's use of liquor dispensing establishments in Joplin for procuring his whiskey.

The situation relating to the probable place of market, as bearing on the probability of unlawful importation, is somewhat different. Broadly on the facts this may well have been taken to be the State of Oklahoma as a whole or its populous northeastern region. From the facts of record we know, as the agents knew, that Oklahoma was a "dry" state. At the time of the search, its law forbade the importation of intoxicating liquors from other states, except under a permit not generally procurable and which there is no pretense Brinegar had secured or attempted to secure. This fact, taken in connection with the known "wet" status of Missouri and the location of Joplin close to the Oklahoma line, affords a very natural situation for persons inclined to violate the Oklahoma and federal statutes to ply their trade. The proof therefore concerning the source of supply, the place of probable destination and illegal market, and hence the probability that Brinegar was using the highway for the forbidden transportation, was certainly no less strong than the showing in these respects in the *Carroll* case.[9]

Finally, as for the most important potential distinction, namely, that concerning the primary and ultimate fact that the petitioner was engaging in liquor running, Malsed's personal observation of Brinegar's recent activities established that he was so engaged quite as effectively as did the agent's prior bargaining with the defendants in the *Carroll* case.[*] He saw Brinegar loading liquor, in larger quantities than would be normal for personal consumption, into a car or a truck in Joplin on other occasions during the six months prior to the search. He saw the car Brinegar was using in this case in use by him at least once in Joplin within that period and followed it. And several months prior to the search he had arrested Brinegar for unlawful transportation of liquor and this arrest had resulted in an indictment which was pending at the time of this trial. Moreover Malsed instantly recognized Brinegar's Ford coupe and Brinegar as the driver when he passed the parked police car. And at that time Brinegar was moving in a direction from Joplin toward Vinita only a short distance inside Oklahoma from the state line.

All these facts are undisputed. Wholly apart from Malsed's knowledge that Brinegar bore the general reputation of being engaged in liquor running, they constitute positive and convincing evidence that Brinegar was engaged in that activity, no less convincing than the evidence in *Carroll* that the defendants had offered to sell liquor to the officers. The evidence here is undisputed, is admissible on the issue of probable cause, and clearly establishes that the agent had good ground for believing that Brinegar was engaged regularly throughout the period in illicit liquor running and dealing.

In dealing with probable cause as the very name implies, we deal with probabilities. These are not technical; they are the factual and practical considerations of everyday life on which reasonable and prudent men, not legal technicians, act. The standard of proof is accordingly correlative to what must be proved.

"The substance of all the definitions" of probable cause "is a reasonable ground for belief of guilt." And this "means less than evidence which would justify condemnation" or conviction, as Marshall, C.J., said for the Court more than a century ago in *Locke v. United States*, 3 L. Ed. 364, 7 Cranch 339, 348. Since Marshall's time, at any rate,[14] it has come to mean more than bare suspicion: Probable cause exists where "the facts and circumstances within their (the officers') knowledge and of which they had reasonably trustworthy information (are) sufficient in themselves to warrant a man of reasonable caution in the belief that"

---

[9] On the present record judicial notice is hardly needed to give us cognizance of the differing laws of Missouri and Oklahoma, or of Joplin's proximity to the state line, and its ready convenience to one living as nearby as Vinita who might be disposed to use it as a base of supply for importing liquor into Oklahoma in violation of the state and federal statutes.

[*] In *Carroll*, the agents knew that Carroll was in the business of selling illegal liquor because he had previously offered to sell some to them.

[14] Marshall's full statement in *Locke* was: "It may be added, that the term 'probable cause,' according to its usual acceptation, means less than evidence which would justify condemnation; and, in all cases of seizure, has a fixed, and well known meaning. It imports a seizure made under circumstances which warrant suspicion."

an offense has been or is being committed.

These long-prevailing standards seek to safeguard citizens from rash and unreasonable interferences with privacy and from unfounded charges of crime. They also seek to give fair leeway for enforcing the law in the community's protection. Because many situations which confront officers in the course of executing their duties are more or less ambiguous, room must be allowed for some mistakes on their part. But the mistakes must be those of reasonable men, acting on facts leading sensibly to their conclusions of probability. The rule of probable cause is a practical, nontechnical conception affording the best compromise that has been found for accommodating these often opposing interests. Requiring more would unduly hamper law-enforcement. To allow less would be to leave law-abiding citizens at the mercy of the officers' whim or caprice.

The troublesome line posed by the facts in the *Carroll* case and this case is one between mere suspicion and probable cause. That line necessarily must be drawn by an act of judgment formed in the light of the particular situation and with account taken of all the circumstances. No problem of searching the home or any other place of privacy was presented either in *Carroll* or here. Both cases involve freedom to use public highways in swiftly moving vehicles for dealing in contraband, and to be unmolested by investigation and search in those movements. In such a case the citizen who has given no good cause for believing he is engaged in that sort of activity is entitled to proceed on his way without interference. But one who recently and repeatedly has given substantial ground for believing that he is engaging in the forbidden transportation in the area of his usual operations has no such immunity, if the officer who intercepts him in that region knows that fact at the time he makes the interception and the circumstances under which it is made are not such as to indicate the suspect going about legitimate affairs.

This does not mean, as seems to be assumed, that every traveler along the public highways may be stopped and searched at the officers' whim, caprice or mere suspicion.[17] The question presented in the *Carroll* case lay on the border between suspicion and probable cause. But the Court carefully considered that problem and resolved it by concluding that the facts within the officers' knowledge when they intercepted the *Carroll* defendants amounted to more than mere suspicion and constituted probable cause for their action. We cannot say this conclusion was wrong, or was so lacking in reason and consistency with the Fourth Amendment's purposes that it should now be overridden.

Accordingly the judgment is affirmed.

---

[17] "It would be intolerable and unreasonable if a prohibition agent were authorized to stop every automobile on the chance of finding liquor, and thus subject all persons lawfully using the highways to the inconvenience and indignity of such a search. Travelers may be so stopped in crossing an international boundary because of national self-protection reasonably requiring one entering the country to identify himself as entitled to come in, and his belongings as effects which may be lawfully brought in. But those lawfully within the country, entitled to use the public highways, have a right to free passage without interruption or search unless there is known to a competent official, authorized to search, probable cause for believing that their vehicles are carrying contraband or illegal merchandise." *Carroll.*

Mr. Justice Burton, concurring.

Whether or not the necessary probable cause for a search of the petitioner's car existed before the government agents caught up with him and said to him, "How much liquor have you got in the car this time?" and he replied, "Not too much," it is clear, and each of the lower courts found, that, under all of the circumstances of this case, the necessary probable cause for the search of the petitioner's car then existed. If probable cause for the search existed at that point, the search which then was begun was lawful without a search warrant as is demonstrated in the opinion of the Court. That search disclosed that a crime was in the course of its commission in the presence of the arresting officers, precisely as those officers had good reason to believe was the fact. The ensuing arrest of the petitioner was lawful and the subsequent denial of his motion to suppress the evidence obtained by the search was properly sustained.

It is my view that it is not necessary, for the purposes of this case, to establish probable cause for the search at any point earlier than that of the above colloquy. The earlier events, recited in the opinion of the Court, disclose at least ample grounds to justify the chase and official interrogation of the petitioner by the government agents in the manner adopted. This interrogation quickly disclosed indisputable probable cause for the search and for the arrest. In my view, these earlier events not only justified the steps taken by the government agents but those events imposed upon the government agents a positive duty to investigate further, in some such manner as they adopted. It is only by alertness to proper occasions for prompt inquiries and investigations that effective prevention of crime and enforcement of law is possible. Government agents are commissioned to represent the interests of the public in the enforcement of the law and this requires affirmative action not only when there is reasonable ground for an arrest or probable cause for a search but when there is reasonable ground for an investigation. This is increasingly true when the facts point directly to a crime in the course of commission in the presence of the agent. Prompt investigation may then not only discover but, what is still more important may interrupt the crime and prevent some or all of its damaging consequences.

In the present case, from the moment that the agents saw this petitioner driving his heavily laden car in Oklahoma, evidently en route from Missouri, the events justifying and calling for an interrogation of him rapidly gained cumulative force. Nothing occurred that even tended to lessen the reasonableness of the original basis for the suspicion of the agents that a crime within their particular line of duty was being committed in their presence. Nothing occurred to make it unlawful for them, in line of duty, to make the interrogation which suggested itself to them. When their interrogation of the petitioner to his voluntary response as quoted above, that response demonstrated ample probable cause for an immediate search of the petitioner's car for the contraband liquor which he had indicated might be found there. The interrogation of the petitioner, thus made by the agents in their justifiable investigation of a crime reasonably suspected by them to be in the course of commission in their presence, cannot now be resorted to by the petitioner in support of a motion to suppress the evidence of that crime. Government agents have duties of crime prevention and crime detection as well as the duty of arresting offenders caught in the commission of a crime or later identified as having committed a crime. The performance of the first duties is as important as the performance of the last. In this case the performance of the first halted the commission of the crime and also resulted in the arrest of the offender.

Mr. Justice Jackson, dissenting.

With this prologue [referring to the portion of his opinion reproduced in Chapter 1] I come to the case of Brinegar. His automobile was one of his "effects" and hence within the express protection of the Fourth Amendment. Undoubtedly the automobile presents peculiar problems for enforcement agencies, is frequently a facility for the perpetration of crime and an aid in the escape of criminals. But if we are to make judicial exceptions to the Fourth Amendment for these reasons, it seems to me they should depend somewhat upon the gravity of the offense. If we assume, for example, that a child is kidnaped and the officers throw a roadblock about the neighborhood and search every outgoing car, it would be a drastic and undiscriminating use of the search. The officers might be unable to show probable cause for searching any particular car. However, I should candidly strive hard to sustain such an action, executed fairly and in good faith, because it might be reasonable to subject travelers to that indignity if it was the only way to save a threatened life and detect a vicious crime. But I should not strain to sustain such a roadblock and universal search to salvage a few bottles of bourbon and catch a bootlegger.

The Court sustains this search as an application of *Carroll*. I dissent because I regard it as an extension of the *Carroll* case, which already has been too much taken by enforcement officers as blanket authority to stop and search cars on suspicion.

While the Court sustained the search without warrant in the *Carroll* case, it emphatically declined to dispense with the necessity for evidence of probable cause for making such a search. It said: "It would be intolerable and unreasonable if a prohibition agent were authorized to stop every automobile on the chance of finding liquor, and thus subject all persons lawfully using the highways to the inconvenience and indignity of such a search. Travelers may be so stopped in crossing an international boundary because of national self-protection reasonably requiring one entering the country to identify himself as entitled to come in, and his belongings as effects which may be lawfully brought in. But those lawfully within the country, entitled to use the public highways, have a right to free passage without interruption or search unless there is known to a competent official, authorized to search, probable cause for believing that their vehicles are carrying contraband or illegal merchandise."

Analysis of the *Carroll* facts shows that while several facts are common to the two cases, the setting from which those facts take color and meaning differ in essential respects.

In the *Carroll* case the primary and the ultimate fact that the accused was engaged in liquor running was not surmise or hearsay, as it is here. Carroll and his companion, some time before their arrest, had come to meet the two arresting officers, not then known as officials, upon the understanding that they were customers wanting liquor. Carroll promised to sell and deliver them three cases at $130 a case. For some reason there was a failure to deliver, but when the officers arrested them they had this positive and personal knowledge that these men were trafficking in liquor. Also, it is to be noted that the officers, when bargaining for liquor, saw and learned the number of the car these bootleggers were using in the business and, at the time of the arrest, recognized it as the same car.

Then this Court took judicial notice that the place whence Carroll, when stopped, was coming, on the international boundary, "is one of the most active centers for introducing illegally into this country spiritous liquors for distribution into the interior." These facts provided the very foundation of the opinion of this Court on the subject of probable cause, which it summed up as follows:

"The partners in the original combination to sell liquor in Grand Rapids were together in the same automobile they had been in the night when they tried to furnish the whisky to the officers, which was thus identified as part of the firm equipment. They were coming from the direction of the great source of supply for their stock to Grand Rapids, where they plied their trade. That the officers, when they saw the defendants, believed that they were carrying liquor, we can have no doubt, and we think it is equally clear that they had reasonable cause for thinking so."

Not only did the Court rely almost exclusively on information gained in personal negotiations of the officers to buy liquor from defendants to show probable cause, but the dissenting members asserted it to be the only circumstance which could have subjected the accused to any reasonable suspicion. And that is the sort of direct evidence on personal knowledge that is lacking here.

In contrast, the proof that Brinegar was trafficking in illegal liquor rests on inferences from two circumstances, neither one of which would be allowed to be proved at a trial: One, it appears that the same officers previously had arrested Brinegar on the same charge. But there had been no conviction and it does not appear whether the circumstances of the former arrest indicated any strong probability of it. In any event, this evidence of a prior arrest of the accused would not even be admissible in a trial to prove his guilt on this occasion.

As a second basis for inference, the officers also say that Brinegar had the reputation of being a liquor runner. The weakness of this hearsay evidence is revealed by contrasting it with the personal negotiations which proved that Carroll was one. The officers' testimony of reputation would not be admissible in a trial of defendant unless he was unwise enough to open the subject himself by offering character testimony.

I do not say that no evidence which would be inadmissible to prove guilt at a trial may be considered in weighing probable cause, but I am surprised that the Court is ready to rule that inadmissible evidence alone, as to vital facts without which other facts give little indication of guilt, establish probable cause as matter of law. The only other fact is that officer Malsed stated that twice, on September 23 and on September 30, about six months before this arrest, he saw Brinegar in a Missouri town where liquor is lawful, loading liquor into a truck, not the car in this case. That is all. The Court from that draws the inference which the courts below, familiar we presume with the local conditions, refused to draw, viz., that to be seen loading liquor into a truck where it is lawful is proof that defendant is unlawfully trafficking in liquor some distance away. There is not, as in the *Carroll* case, evidence that he was offering liquor for sale to anybody at any time. In the *Carroll* case, the offer to sell liquor to the officers would itself have been a law violation. It seems rather foggy reasoning to say that the courts are obliged to draw the same conclusion from legal conduct as from illegal conduct.

I think we cannot say the lower courts were wrong as matter of law in holding that there was no probable cause up to the time the car was put off the road and stopped, and that we cannot say it was proper to consider the deficiency supplied by what followed. When these officers engaged in a chase at speeds dangerous to those who participated, and to other lawful wayfarers, and ditched the defendant's car, they were either taking the initial steps in arrest, search and seizure, or they were committing a completely lawless and unjustifiable act. That they intended to set out on a search is unquestioned, and there seems no reason to doubt that in their own minds they thought there was cause and right to search. They have done exactly what they would have done, and done rightfully, if they had been executing a warrant. At all events, whatever it may have lacked technically of arrest, search and seizure, it was a form of coercion and duress under color of official authority — and a very formidable type of duress at that.

I do not, of course, contend that officials may never stop a car on the highway without the halting being considered an arrest or a search. Regulations of traffic, identifications where proper, traffic census, quarantine regulations, and many other causes give occasion to stop cars in circumstances which do not imply arrest or charge of crime. And to trail or pursue a suspected car to its destination, to observe it and keep it under surveillance, is not in itself an arrest nor a search. But when a car is forced off the road, summoned to stop by a siren, and brought to a halt under such circumstances as are here disclosed, we think the officers are then in the position of one who has entered a home: the search at its commencement must be valid and cannot be saved by what it turns up.

The findings of the two courts below make it clear that this search began and proceeded through critical and coercive phases without the justification of probable cause. What it yielded cannot save it. I would reverse the judgment.

Mr. Justice Frankfurter and Mr. Justice Murphy join in this opinion.

QUESTIONS AND NOTES

1. Do you believe that the police had probable cause to stop Brinegar? On what basis?

2. According to *Brinegar*, what does probable cause mean? More likely than not? Reasonable suspicion? Substantial probability? Some probability? Remote probability?

3. At the time that Brinegar was stopped, did the police have any reason to believe that he was not returning from an ordinary shopping trip? Presumably even bootleggers (if you believe that the evidence showed that he was regularly in that business) travel a short distance to a "source city" for things other than contraband.

4.   Doesn't the fact that Brinegar was close to home support the "shopping trip" theory rather than the "bootlegger" theory? Why didn't the Court see it that way? Does one incident of bootlegging make one a perpetual outlaw on the highways?

5.   Should probable cause vary according to the severity of the crime as Justice Jackson seems to suggest? Why? Isn't the constitutional standard the same?

6.   Should probable cause be less stringent in regard to automobiles than to homes (compare *Spinelli, infra*)? Why? Why not?

7.   Justice Burton's suggestion that reasonable suspicion (short of probable cause) may justify a brief stop, and that if probable cause develops from the stop, a search may be undertaken is a concept of some currency (*see* Chapter 8, *infra*). Even on that theory, however, one would have to establish reasonable suspicion.

8.   As you read *Draper*, consider whether the Court was applying a tougher, more lenient, or identical standard of probable cause as compared to *Brinegar*.

DRAPER v. UNITED STATES
358 U.S. 307 (1959)

MR. JUSTICE WHITTAKER delivered the opinion of the Court.

Petitioner was convicted of knowingly concealing and transporting narcotic drugs in Denver, Colorado, in violation of 35 Stat. 614. His conviction was based in part on the use in evidence against him of two "envelopes containing [865 grains of] heroin" and a hypodermic syringe that had been taken from his person, following his arrest, by the arresting officer.

The evidence offered at the hearing on the motion to suppress was not substantially disputed. It established that one Marsh, a federal narcotic agent with 29 years' experience, was stationed at Denver; that one Hereford had been engaged as a "special employee" of the Bureau of Narcotics at Denver for about six months, and from time to time gave information to Marsh regarding violations of the narcotic laws, for which Hereford was paid small sums of money, and that Marsh had always found the information given by Hereford to be accurate and reliable. On September 3, 1956, Hereford told Marsh that James Draper (petitioner) recently had taken up abode at a stated address in Denver and "was peddling narcotics to several addicts" in that city. Four days later, on September 7, Hereford told Marsh "that Draper had gone to Chicago the day before [September 6] by train [and] that he was going to bring back three ounces of heroin [and] that he would return to Denver either on the morning of the 8th of September or the morning of the 9th of September also by train." Hereford also gave Marsh a detailed physical description of Draper and of the clothing he was wearing,[2] and said that he would be carrying "a tan zipper bag," and that he habitually "walked real fast."

---

[2] Hereford told Marsh that Draper was a Negro of light brown complexion, 27 years of age, 5 feet 8 inches tall, weighed about 160 pounds, and that he was wearing a light colored raincoat, brown slacks and black shoes.

On the morning of September 8, Marsh and a Denver police officer went to the Denver Union Station and kept watch over all incoming trains from Chicago, but they did not see anyone fitting the description that Hereford had given. Repeating the process on the morning of September 9, they saw a person, having the exact physical attributes and wearing the precise clothing described by Hereford, alight from an incoming Chicago train and start walking "fast" toward the exit. He was carrying a tan zipper bag in his right hand and the left was thrust in his raincoat pocket. Marsh, accompanied by the police officer, overtook, stopped and arrested him. They then searched him and found the two "envelopes containing heroin" clutched in his left hand in his raincoat pocket, and found the syringe in the tan zipper bag. Marsh then took him (petitioner) into custody. Hereford died four days after the arrest and therefore did not testify at the hearing on the motion.

The crucial question for us then is whether knowledge of the related facts and circumstances gave Marsh "probable cause" within the meaning of the Fourth Amendment to believe that petitioner had committed or was committing a violation of the narcotic laws. If it did, the arrest, though without a warrant, was lawful and the subsequent search of petitioner's person and the seizure of the found heroin were validly made incident to a lawful arrest, and therefore the motion to suppress was properly overruled and the heroin was competently received in evidence at the trial.

Petitioner does not dispute this analysis of the question for decision. Rather, he contends (1) that the information given by Hereford to Marsh was "hearsay" and, because hearsay is not legally competent evidence in a criminal trial, could not legally have been considered, but should have been put out of mind, by Marsh in assessing whether he had "probable cause" and "reasonable grounds" to arrest petitioner without a warrant, and (2) that, even if hearsay could lawfully have been considered, Marsh's information should be held insufficient to show "probable cause" and "reasonable grounds" to believe that petitioner had violated or was violating the narcotic laws and to justify his arrest without a warrant.

Considering the first contention, we find petitioner entirely in error. *Brinegar* has settled the question the other way. There, in a similar situation, the convict contended "that the factors relating to inadmissibility of the evidence [for] *purposes of proving guilt at the trial*, deprive[d] the evidence as a whole of sufficiency to show probable cause for the search." (Emphasis added.) But this Court, rejecting that contention, said: "The so-called distinction places a wholly unwarranted emphasis upon the criterion of admissibility in evidence, to prove the accused's guilt, of the facts relied upon to show probable cause. That emphasis, we think, goes much too far in confusing and disregarding the difference between what is required to prove guilt in a criminal case and what is required to show probable cause for arrest or search. It approaches requiring (if it does not in practical effect require) proof sufficient to establish guilt in order to substantiate the existence of probable cause. There is a large difference between the two things to be proved [guilt and probable cause], as well as between the tribunals which determine them, and therefore a like difference in the *quanta* and modes of proof required to establish them."

Nor can we agree with petitioner's second contention that Marsh's information was insufficient to show probable cause and reasonable grounds to believe that petitioner had violated or was violating the narcotic laws and to justify his arrest without a warrant. The information given to narcotic agent Marsh by "special employee" Hereford may have been hearsay to Marsh, but coming from one employed for that purpose and whose information had always been found accurate and reliable, it is clear that Marsh would have been derelict in his duties had he not pursued it. And when, in pursuing that information, he saw a man, having the exact physical attributes and wearing the precise clothing and carrying the tan zipper bag that Hereford had described, alight from one of the very trains from the very place stated by Hereford and start to walk at a "fast" pace toward the station exit, Marsh had personally verified every facet of the information given him by Hereford except whether petitioner had accomplished his mission and had the three ounces of heroin on his person or in his bag. And surely, with every other bit of Hereford's information being thus personally verified, Marsh had "reasonable grounds" to believe that the remaining unverified bit of Hereford's information — that Draper would have the heroin with him — was likewise true.

"In dealing with probable cause, . . . as the very name implies, we deal with probabilities. These are not technical; they are the factual and practical consider-ations of everyday life on which reasonable and prudent men, not legal technicians, act." *Brinegar*. Probable cause exists where "the facts and circumstances within [the arresting officers'] knowledge and of which they had reasonably trustworthy information [are] sufficient in themselves to warrant a man of reasonable caution in the belief that" an offense has been or is being committed.

We believe that, under the facts and circumstances here, Marsh had probable cause to believe that petitioner was committing a violation of the laws of the United States relating to narcotic drugs at the time he arrested him. The arrest was therefore lawful, and the subsequent search and seizure, having been made incident to that lawful arrest, were likewise valid. It follows that petitioner's motion to suppress was properly denied and that the seized heroin was competent evidence lawfully received at the trial.

Affirmed.

MR. JUSTICE DOUGLAS, dissenting. [After beginning with the excerpt quoted in Chapter 1.]

With all due deference, the arrest made here on the mere word of an informer violated the spirit of the Fourth Amendment. If an arrest is made without a warrant, the offense must be committed in the presence of the officer or the officer must have "reasonable grounds to believe that the person to be arrested has committed or is committing" a violation of the narcotics law. The arresting officers did not have a bit of evidence, known to them and as to which they could take an oath had they gone to a magistrate for a warrant, that petitioner had committed any crime. The arresting officers did not know the grounds on which the informer based his conclusion; nor did they seek to find out what they were. They acted solely on the informer's word. In my view that was not enough.

The Virginia Declaration of Rights, adopted June 12, 1776, included the forerunner of the Fourth Amendment:

"That general warrants, whereby an officer or messenger may be commanded to search suspected places without evidence of a fact committed, or to seize any person or persons not named, or whose offence is not particularly described and *supported by evidence*, are grievous and oppressive, and ought not to be granted." (Italics added.)

The requirement that a warrant of arrest be "supported by evidence" was by then deeply rooted in history. And it is inconceivable that in those days, when the right of privacy was so greatly cherished, the mere word of an informer — such as we have in the present case — would be enough. For whispered charges and accusations, used in lieu of evidence of unlawful acts, were the main complaint of the age. *Frisbie v. Butler*, Kirby's Rep. (Conn.) 1785–1788, p. 213, decided in 1787, illustrates, I think, the mood of the day in the matter of arrests on suspicion. A warrant of arrest and search was issued by a justice of the peace on the oath of a citizen who had lost some pork from a cellar, the warrant stating, "said Butler suspects one Benjamin Frisbie, of Harwinton, to be the person that hath taken said pork." The court on appeal reversed the judgment of conviction, holding *inter alia* that the complaint "contained no direct charge of the theft, but only an averment that the defendant was suspected to be guilty." Nothing but suspicion is shown in the instant case — suspicion of an informer, not that of the arresting officers. Nor did they seek to obtain from the informer any information on which he based his belief. The arresting officers did not have a bit of *evidence* that the petitioner had committed or was committing a crime before the arrest. The only *evidence* of guilt was provided by the arrest itself.

The determination that arrests and searches on mere suspicion would find no place in American law enforcement did not abate following the adoption of a Bill of Rights applicable to the Federal Government. In *Conner v. Commonwealth*, 3 Binn. (Pa.) 38, an arrest warrant issued by a magistrate stating his "strong reason to suspect" that the accused had committed a crime because of "common rumor and report" was held illegal under a constitutional provision identical in relevant part to the Fourth Amendment. "It is true, that by insisting on an oath, felons may sometimes escape. This must have been very well known to the framers of our constitution; but they thought it better that the guilty should sometimes escape, than that every individual should be subject to vexation and oppression."

It was against this long background that Professors Hogan and Snee of Georgetown University recently wrote:

". . . it must be borne in mind that any arrest based on suspicion alone is illegal. This indisputable rule of law has grave implications for a number of traditional police investigative practices. The round-up or dragnet arrest, the arrest on suspicion, for questioning, for investigation or on an open charge all are prohibited by the law. It is undeniable that if those arrests were sanctioned by law, the police would be in a position to investigate a crime and to detect the real culprit much more easily, much more efficiently, much more economically, and with much more dispatch. It is equally true, however, that society cannot confer such power on the police without ripping away much of the fabric of a way of life which seeks to give the maximum of liberty to the individual citizen. The finger of suspicion is a long one. In an individual case it may point to all of a certain race, age group or locale.

Commonly it extends to any who have committed similar crimes in the past. Arrest on mere suspicion collides violently with the basic human right of liberty. It can be tolerated only in a society which is willing to concede to its government powers which history and experience teach are the inevitable accoutrements of tyranny." 47 Geo. L. J. 1, 22.

Down to this day our decisions have closely heeded that warning. So far as I can ascertain the mere word of an informer, not bolstered by some evidence a crime had been or was being committed, has never been approved by this Court as "reasonable grounds" for making an arrest without a warrant. Whether the act complained of be seizure of goods, search of premises, or the arrest of the citizen, the judicial inquiry has been directed toward the reasonableness of inferences to be drawn from suspicious circumstances attending the action thought to be unlawful. Evidence required to prove guilt is not necessary. But the attendant circumstances must be sufficient to give rise in the mind of the arresting officer at least to inferences of guilt.

The Court is quite correct in saying that proof of "reasonable grounds" for believing a crime was being committed need not be proof admissible at the trial. It could be inferences from suspicious acts, *e.g.*, consort with known peddlers, the surreptitious passing of a package, an intercepted message suggesting criminal activities, or any number of such events coming to the knowledge of the officer. But, if he takes the law into his own hands and does not seek the protection of a warrant, he must act on some evidence known to him. The law goes far to protect the citizen. Even suspicious acts observed by the officers may be as consistent with innocence as with guilt. That is not enough, for even the guilty may not be implicated on suspicion alone. The reason is, as I have said, that the standard set by the Constitution and by the statute is one that will protect both the officer and the citizen. For if the officer acts with "probable cause" or on "reasonable grounds," he is protected even though the citizen is innocent. This important requirement should be strictly enforced, lest the whole process of arrest revert once more to whispered accusations by people. When we lower the guards as we do today, we risk making the role of the informer — odious in our history — once more supreme.

Here the officers had no evidence — apart from the mere word of an informer — that petitioner was committing a crime. The fact that petitioner walked fast and carried a tan zipper bag was not evidence of any crime. The officers knew nothing except what they had been told by the informer. If they went to a magistrate to get a warrant of arrest and relied solely on the report of the informer, it is not conceivable to me that one would be granted. For they could not present to the magistrate any of the facts which the informer may have had. They could swear only to the fact that the informer had made the accusation. They could swear to no evidence that lay in their own knowledge. They could present, on information and belief, no facts which the informer disclosed. No magistrate could issue a warrant on the mere word of an officer, without more. We are not justified in lowering the standard when an arrest is made without a warrant and allowing the officers more leeway than we grant the magistrate.

With all deference I think we break with tradition when we sustain this arrest. "[A] search is not to be made legal by what it turns up. In law it is good or bad when it starts and does not change character from its success." In this case it was only after the arrest and search were made that there was a shred of evidence known to the officers that a crime was in the process of being committed.

QUESTIONS AND NOTES

1. At what point in this case was there probable cause? When Hereford provided the information, or when the officers corroborated the information by spotting Draper?

2. If your answer to Question 1 was when the officers spotted Draper, is Justice Douglas correct in saying that at the time that the information was received, no warrant could issue?

3. Justice Douglas (who concurred in *Brinegar*) seems particularly repulsed by the informer (whom he describes as "odious"). Do you share that distrust? Given the informant's information, wasn't Draper far more likely than Brinegar to have been engaged in criminal activity?

4. Should the fact that Hereford was revealed by name be relevant? Frequently informants, even when known by the police, do not have their names revealed. Because of the danger to informants in releasing their names (one can speculate about the cause of Hereford's death), coupled with the value that at least some Justices believe they serve, the practice of not naming informants was upheld in *McCray v. Illinois*, 386 U.S. 300 (1967).

5. Are there any special dangers of allowing arrests of this type without a warrant? Assuming that there was no probable cause to believe that Draper was carrying drugs until he alighted from the train, is there any way that a warrant could have been obtained?

6. As you read *Spinelli* consider whether there was more or less probable cause there than in *Draper*.

SPINELLI v. UNITED STATES
393 U.S. 410 (1969)

MR. JUSTICE HARLAN delivered the opinion of the Court.

William Spinelli was convicted of traveling to St. Louis, Missouri, from a nearby Illinois suburb with the intention of conducting gambling activities proscribed by Missouri law. At every appropriate stage in the proceedings in the lower courts, the petitioner challenged the constitutionality of the warrant which authorized the FBI search that uncovered the evidence necessary for his conviction.

In *Aguilar v. Texas*, 378 U.S. 1 (1964), a search warrant had issued upon an affidavit of police officers who swore only that they had "received reliable information from a credible person and do believe" that narcotics were being illegally stored on the described premises. While recognizing that the constitutional requirement of probable cause can be satisfied by hearsay information, this Court held the affidavit inadequate for two reasons. First, the application failed to set forth any of the "underlying circumstances" necessary to enable the magistrate independently to judge of the validity of the informant's conclusion that the narcotics were where he said they were. Second, the affiant-officers did not attempt to support their claim that their informant was "'credible' or his information 'reliable.'" The Government is, however, quite right in saying that the FBI affidavit in the present case is more ample than that in Aguilar. Not only does it contain a report from an anonymous informant, but it also contains a report of an independent FBI investigation which is said to corroborate the informant's tip. We are, then, required to delineate the manner in which Aguilar's two-pronged test should be applied in these circumstances.

In essence, the affidavit contained the following allegations:

1. The FBI had kept track of Spinelli's movements on five days during the month of August 1965. On four of these occasions, Spinelli was seen crossing one of two bridges leading from Illinois into St. Louis, Missouri, between 11 a.m. and 12:15 p.m. On four of the five days, Spinelli was also seen parking his car in a lot used by residents of an apartment house at 1108 Indian Circle Drive in St. Louis, between 3:30 p.m. and 4:45 p.m.[4] On one day, Spinelli was followed further and seen to enter a particular apartment in the building.

2. An FBI check with the telephone company revealed that this apartment contained two telephones listed under the name of Grace P. Hagen, and carrying the numbers WYdown 4-0029 and WYdown 4-0136.

3. The application stated that "William Spinelli is known to this affiant and to federal law enforcement agents and local law enforcement agents as a bookmaker, an associate of bookmakers, a gambler, and an associate of gamblers."

4. Finally, it was stated that the FBI "has been informed by a confidential reliable informant that William Spinelli is operating a handbook and accepting wagers and disseminating wagering information by means of the telephones which have been assigned the numbers WYdown 4-0029 and WYdown 4-0136."

There can be no question that the last item mentioned, detailing the informant's tip, has a fundamental place in this warrant application. Without it, probable cause could not be established. The first two items reflect only innocent-seeming activity and data. Spinelli's travels to and from the apartment building and his entry into a particular apartment on one occasion could hardly be taken as bespeaking gambling activity; and there is surely nothing unusual about an apartment containing two separate telephones. Many a householder indulges himself in this petty luxury. Finally, the allegation that Spinelli was "known" to the affiant and to other federal and local law enforcement officers as a gambler and an associate of gamblers is but a bald and unilluminating assertion of suspicion that is entitled to no weight in appraising the magistrate's decision.

So much indeed the Government does not deny. Rather, following the reasoning of the Court of Appeals, the Government claims that the informant's tip gives a

---

[4] No report was made as to Spinelli's movements during the period between his arrival in St. Louis at noon and his arrival at the parking lot in the late afternoon. In fact, the evidence at trial indicated that Spinelli frequented the offices of his stockbroker during this period.

suspicious color to the FBI's reports detailing Spinelli's innocent-seeming conduct and that, conversely, the FBI's surveillance corroborates the informant's tip, thereby entitling it to more weight. It is true, of course, that the magistrate is obligated to render a judgment based upon a common-sense reading of the entire affidavit. We believe, however, that the "totality of circumstances" approach taken by the Court of Appeals paints with too broad a brush. Where, as here, the informer's tip is a necessary element in a finding of probable cause, its proper weight must be determined by a more precise analysis.

The informer's report must first be measured against *Aguilar*'s standards so that its probative value can be assessed. If the tip is found inadequate under *Aguilar*, the other allegations which corroborate the information contained in the hearsay report should then be considered. At this stage as well, however, the standards enunciated in *Aguilar* must inform the magistrate's decision. He must ask: Can it fairly be said that the tip, even when certain parts of it have been corroborated by independent sources, is as trustworthy as a tip which would pass *Aguilar*'s tests without independent corroboration?

Applying these principles to the present case, we first consider the weight to be given the informer's tip when it is considered apart from the rest of the affidavit. It is clear that a Commissioner could not credit it without abdicating his constitutional function. Though the affiant swore that his confidant was "reliable," he offered the magistrate no reason in support of this conclusion. Perhaps even more important is the fact that *Aguilar*'s other test has not been satisfied. The tip does not contain a sufficient statement of the underlying circumstances from which the informer concluded that Spinelli was running a bookmaking operation. We are not told how the FBI's source received his information — it is not alleged that the informant personally observed Spinelli at work or that he had ever placed a bet with him. Moreover, if the informant came by the information indirectly, he did not explain why his sources were reliable. In the absence of a statement detailing the manner in which the information was gathered, it is especially important that the tip describe the accused's criminal activity in sufficient detail that the magistrate may know that he is relying on something more substantial than a casual rumor circulating in the underworld or an accusation based merely on an individual's general reputation.

The detail provided by the informant in *Draper*, provides a suitable benchmark. While Hereford, the Government's informer in that case, did not state the way in which he had obtained his information, he reported that Draper had gone to Chicago the day before by train and that he would return to Denver by train with three ounces of heroin on one of two specified mornings. Moreover, Hereford went on to describe, with minute particularity, the clothes that Draper would be wearing upon his arrival at the Denver station. A magistrate, when confronted with such detail, could reasonably infer that the informant had gained his information in a reliable way.[5] Such an inference cannot be made in the present case. Here, the only facts supplied were that Spinelli was using two specified telephones and that these

---

[5] While *Draper* involved the question whether the police had probable cause for an arrest without a warrant, the analysis required for an answer to this question is basically similar to that demanded of a magistrate when he considers whether a search warrant should issue.

phones were being used in gambling operations. This meager report could easily have been obtained from an offhand remark heard at a neighborhood bar.

Nor do we believe that the patent doubts *Aguilar* raises as to the report's reliability are adequately resolved by a consideration of the allegations detailing the FBI's independent investigative efforts. At most, these allegations indicated that Spinelli could have used the telephones specified by the informant for some purpose. This cannot by itself be said to support both the inference that the informer was generally trustworthy and that he had made his charge against Spinelli on the basis of information obtained in a reliable way. Once again, *Draper* provides a relevant comparison. Independent police work in that case corroborated much more than one small detail that had been provided by the informant. There, the police, upon meeting the inbound Denver train on the second morning specified by informer Hereford, saw a man whose dress corresponded precisely to Hereford's detailed description. It was then apparent that the informant had not been fabricating his report out of whole cloth; since the report was of the sort which in common experience may be recognized as having been obtained in a reliable way, it was perfectly clear that probable cause had been established.

We conclude, then, that in the present case the informant's tip — even when corroborated to the extent indicated — was not sufficient to provide the basis for a finding of probable cause. This is not to say that the tip was so insubstantial that it could not properly have counted in the magistrate's determination. Rather, it needed some further support. When we look to the other parts of the application, however, we find nothing alleged which would permit the suspicions engendered by the informant's report to ripen into a judgment that a crime was probably being committed. As we have already seen, the allegations detailing the FBI's surveillance of Spinelli and its investigation of the telephone company records contain no suggestion of criminal conduct when taken by themselves — and they are not endowed with an aura of suspicion by virtue of the informer's tip. Nor do we find that the FBI's reports take on a sinister color when read in light of common knowledge that bookmaking is often carried on over the telephone and from premises ostensibly used by others for perfectly normal purposes. Such an argument would carry weight in a situation in which the premises contain an unusual number of telephones or abnormal activity is observed, but it does not fit this case where neither of these factors is present.[6] All that remains to be considered is the flat statement that Spinelli was "known" to the FBI and others as a gambler. But just as a simple assertion of police suspicion is not itself a sufficient basis for a magistrate's finding of probable cause, we do not believe it may be used to give additional weight to allegations that would otherwise be insufficient.

The affidavit, then, falls short of the standards set forth in *Aguilar, Draper*, and our other decisions that give content to the notion of probable cause. In holding as we have done, we do not retreat from the established propositions that only the probability, and not a prima facie showing, of criminal activity is the standard of probable cause, that affidavits of probable cause are tested by much less rigorous standards than those governing the admissibility of evidence at trial, that in judging

---

[6] A box containing three uninstalled telephones was found in the apartment, but only after execution of the search warrant.

probable cause issuing magistrates are not to be confined by niggardly limitations or by restrictions on the use of their common sense, and that their determination of probable cause should be paid great deference by reviewing courts. But we cannot sustain this warrant without diluting important safeguards that assure that the judgment of a disinterested judicial officer will interpose itself between the police and the citizenry.

Mr. Justice White, concurring.

An investigator's affidavit that he has seen gambling equipment being moved into a house at a specified address will support the issuance of a search warrant. The oath affirms the honesty of the statement and negatives the lie or imagination. Personal observation attests to the facts asserted — that there is gambling equipment on the premises at the named address.

But if the officer simply avers, without more, that there is gambling paraphernalia on certain premises, the warrant should not issue, even though the belief of the officer is an honest one, as evidenced by his oath, and even though the magistrate knows him to be an experienced, intelligent officer who has been reliable in the past.

Neither should the warrant issue if the officer states that there is gambling equipment in a particular apartment and that his information comes from an informant, named or unnamed, since the honesty of the informant and the basis for his report are unknown. Nor would the missing elements be completely supplied by the officer's oath that the informant has often furnished reliable information in the past. This attests to the honesty of the informant, but *Aguilar* requires something more — did the information come from observation, or did the informant in turn receive it from another? Absent additional facts for believing the informant's report, his assertion stands no better than the oath of the officer to the same effect. Indeed, if the affidavit of an officer, known by the magistrate to be honest and experienced, stating that gambling equipment is located in a certain building is unacceptable, it would be quixotic if a similar statement from an honest informant were found to furnish probable cause. A strong argument can be made that both should be acceptable under the Fourth Amendment, but under our cases neither is. The past reliability of the informant can no more furnish probable cause for believing his current report than can previous experience with the officer himself.

If the affidavit rests on hearsay — an informant's report — what is necessary under *Aguilar* is one of two things: the informant must declare either (1) that he has himself seen or perceived the fact or facts asserted; or (2) that his information is hearsay, but there is good reason for believing it — perhaps one of the usual grounds for crediting hearsay information. The first presents few problems: since the report, although hearsay, purports to be first-hand observation, remaining doubt centers on the honesty of the informant, and that worry is dissipated by the officer's previous experience with the informant. The other basis for accepting the informant's report is more complicated. But if, for example, the informer's hearsay comes from one of the actors in the crime in the nature of admission against interest, the affidavit giving this information should be held sufficient.

I am inclined to agree with the majority that there are limited special circumstances in which an "honest" informant's report, if sufficiently detailed, will in effect verify itself — that is, the magistrate when confronted with such detail could reasonably infer that the informant had gained his information in a reliable way. Detailed information may sometimes imply that the informant himself has observed the facts. Suppose an informant with whom an officer has had satisfactory experience states that there is gambling equipment in the living room of a specified apartment and describes in detail not only the equipment itself but also the appointments and furnishings in the apartment. Detail like this, if true at all, must rest on personal observation either of the informant or of someone else. If the latter, we know nothing of the third person's honesty or sources; he may be making a wholly false report. But it is arguable that on these facts it was the informant himself who has perceived the facts, for the information reported is not usually the subject of casual, day-to-day conversation. Because the informant is honest and it is probable that he has viewed the facts, there is probable cause for the issuance of a warrant.

So too in the special circumstances of *Draper*, the kind of information related by the informant is not generally sent ahead of a person's arrival in a city except to those who are intimately connected with making careful arrangements for meeting him. The informant, posited as honest, somehow had the reported facts, very likely from one of the actors in the plan, or as one of them himself. The majority's suggestion is that a warrant could have been obtained based only on the informer's report. I am inclined to agree, although it seems quite plain that if it may be so easily inferred from the affidavit that the informant has himself observed the facts or has them from an actor in the event, no possible harm could come from requiring a statement to that effect, thereby removing the difficult and recurring questions which arise in such situations.

Of course, *Draper* itself did not proceed on this basis. Instead, the Court pointed out that when the officer saw a person getting off the train at the specified time, dressed and conducting himself precisely as the informant had predicted, all but the critical fact with respect to possessing narcotics had then been verified and for that reason the officer had "reasonable grounds" to believe also that Draper was carrying narcotics. Unquestionably, verification of arrival time, dress, and gait reinforced the honesty of the informant — he had not reported a made-up story. But if what *Draper* stands for is that the existence of the tenth and critical fact is made sufficiently probable to justify the issuance of a warrant by verifying nine other facts coming from the same source, I have my doubts about that case.

In the first place, the proposition is not that the tenth fact may be logically inferred from the other nine or that the tenth fact is usually found in conjunction with the other nine. No one would suggest that just anyone getting off the 10:30 train dressed as Draper was, with a brisk walk and carrying a zipper bag, should be arrested for carrying narcotics. The thrust of *Draper* is not that the verified facts have independent significance with respect to proof of the tenth. The argument instead relates to the reliability of the source: because an informant is right about some things, he is more probably right about other facts, usually the critical, unverified facts.

But the Court's cases have already rejected for Fourth Amendment purposes the notion that the past reliability of an officer is sufficient reason for believing his current assertions. Nor would it suffice, I suppose, if a reliable informant states there is gambling equipment in Apartment 607 and then proceeds to describe in detail Apartment 201, a description which is verified before applying for the warrant. He was right about 201, but that hardly makes him more believable about the equipment in 607. But what if he states that there are narcotics locked in a safe in Apartment 300, which is described in detail, and the apartment manager verifies everything but the contents of the safe? I doubt that the report about the narcotics is made appreciably more believable by the verification. The informant could still have gotten his information concerning the safe from others about whom nothing is known or could have inferred the presence of narcotics from circumstances which a magistrate would find unacceptable.

The tension between *Draper* and the *Aguilar* line of cases is evident from the course followed by the majority opinion. First, it is held that the report from a reliable informant that Spinelli is using two telephones with specified numbers to conduct a gambling business plus Spinelli's reputation in police circles as a gambler does not add up to probable cause. This is wholly consistent with *Aguilar*: the informant did not reveal whether he had personally observed the facts or heard them from another and, if the latter, no basis for crediting the hearsay was presented. Nor were the facts, as Mr. Justice Harlan says, of such a nature that they normally would be obtainable only by the personal observation of the informant himself. The police, however, did not stop with the informant's report. Independently, they established the existence of two phones having the given numbers and located them in an apartment house which Spinelli was regularly frequenting away from his home. There remained little question but that Spinelli was using the phones, and it was a fair inference that the use was not for domestic but for business purposes. The informant had claimed the business involved gambling. Since his specific information about Spinelli using two phones with particular numbers had been verified, did not his allegation about gambling thereby become sufficiently more believable if the *Draper* principle is to be given any scope at all? I would think so, particularly since the information from the informant which was verified was not neutral, irrelevant information but was material to proving the gambling allegation: two phones with different numbers in an apartment used away from home indicates a business use in an operation, like bookmaking, where multiple phones are needed. The *Draper* approach would reasonably justify the issuance of a warrant in this case, particularly since the police had some awareness of Spinelli's past activities. The majority, however, while seemingly embracing *Draper*, confines that case to its own facts. Pending full-scale reconsideration of that case, on the one hand, or of *Aguilar* on the other, I join the opinion of the Court and the judgment of reversal, especially since a vote to affirm would produce an equally divided Court.

MR. JUSTICE BLACK, dissenting.

In my view, this Court's decision in *Aguilar* was bad enough. That decision went very far toward elevating the magistrate's hearing for issuance of a search warrant to a full-fledged trial, where witnesses must be brought forward to attest personally to all the facts alleged. But not content with this, the Court today expands *Aguilar* to almost unbelievable proportions. Of course, it would strengthen the probable-cause presentation if eyewitnesses could testify that they saw the defendant commit the crime. It would be stronger still if these witnesses could explain in detail the nature of the sensual perceptions on which they based their "conclusion" that the person they had seen was the defendant and that he was responsible for the events they observed. Nothing in our Constitution, however, requires that the facts be established with that degree of certainty and with such elaborate specificity before a policeman can be authorized by a disinterested magistrate to conduct a carefully limited search.

The Fourth Amendment provides that "no Warrants shall issue, but upon probable cause, supported by Oath or affirmation, and particularly describing the place to be searched, and the persons or things to be seized." In this case a search warrant was issued supported by an oath and particularly describing the place to be searched and the things to be seized. The supporting oath was three printed pages and the full text of it is included in an Appendix to the Court's opinion. The magistrate, I think properly, held the information set forth sufficient facts to show "probable cause" that the defendant was violating the law. Six members of the Court of Appeals also agreed that the affidavit was sufficient to show probable cause. A majority of this Court today holds, however, that the magistrate and all of these judges were wrong. In doing so, they substitute their own opinion for that of the local magistrate and the circuit judges, and reject the *en banc* factual conclusion of the Eighth Circuit and reverse the judgment based upon that factual conclusion. I cannot join in any such disposition of an issue so vital to the administration of justice, and dissent as vigorously as I can.

I repeat my belief that the affidavit given the magistrate was more than ample to show probable cause of the petitioner's guilt. The affidavit meticulously set out facts sufficient to show the following:

1. The petitioner had been shown going to and coming from a room in an apartment which contained two telephones listed under the name of another person. Nothing in the record indicates that the apartment was of that large and luxurious type which could only be occupied by a person to whom it would be a "petty luxury" to have two separate telephones, with different numbers, both listed under the name of a person who did not live there.

2. The petitioner's car had been observed parked in the apartment's parking lot. This fact was, of course, highly relevant in showing that the petitioner was extremely interested in some enterprise which was located in the apartment.

3. The FBI had been informed by a reliable informant that the petitioner was accepting wagering information by telephones — the particular telephones located in the apartment the defendant had been repeatedly visiting. Unless the Court, going beyond the requirements of the Fourth Amendment, wishes to require magistrates to hold trials before issuing warrants, it is not necessary — as the Court holds — to have the affiant explain "the underlying circumstances from which the informer concluded that Spinelli was running a bookmaking operation."

4. The petitioner was known by federal and local law enforcement agents as a bookmaker and an associate of gamblers. I cannot agree with the Court that this knowledge was only a "bald and unilluminating assertion of suspicion that is entitled to no weight in appraising the magistrate's decision." Although the statement is hearsay that might not be admissible in a regular trial, everyone knows, unless he shuts his eyes to the realities of life, that this is a relevant fact which, together with other circumstances, might indicate a factual probability that gambling is taking place.

The foregoing facts should be enough to constitute probable cause for anyone who does not believe that the only way to obtain a search warrant is to prove beyond a reasonable doubt that a defendant is guilty.

Notwithstanding the Court's belief to the contrary, I think that in holding as it does, the Court does:

"retreat from the established propositions that only the probability, and not a prima facie showing, of criminal activity is the standard of probable cause, that affidavits of probable cause are tested by much less rigorous standards than those governing the admissibility of evidence at trial, that in judging probable cause issuing magistrates are not to be confined by niggardly limitations or by restrictions on the use of their common sense, and that their determination of probable cause should be paid great deference by reviewing courts."

In fact, I believe the Court is moving rapidly, through complex analyses and obfuscatory language, toward the holding that no magistrate can issue a warrant unless according to some unknown standard of proof he can be persuaded that the suspect defendant is actually guilty of a crime. I would affirm this conviction.

Mr. Justice Fortas, dissenting.

While I do not subscribe to the criticism of the majority expressed by my Brother Black in dissent, I believe — with all respect — that the majority is in error in holding that the affidavit supporting the warrant in this case is constitutionally inadequate.

The affidavit is unusually long and detailed. In fact, it recites so many minute and detailed facts developed in the course of the investigation of Spinelli that its substance is somewhat obscured. It is paradoxical that this very fullness of the affidavit may be the source of the constitutional infirmity that the majority finds. Stated in language more direct and less circumstantial than that used by the FBI agent who executed the affidavit, it sets forth that the FBI has been informed that Spinelli is accepting wagers by means of telephones numbered WY 4-0029 and WY 4-0136; that Spinelli is known to the affiant agent and to law enforcement agencies as a bookmaker; that telephones numbered WY 4-0029 and WY 4-0136 are located in a certain apartment; that Spinelli was placed under surveillance and his observed movements were such as to show his use of that apartment and to indicate that he frequented the apartment on a regular basis.

Aguilar holds that the reference in an affidavit to information described only as received from "a confidential reliable informant," standing alone, is not an adequate basis for issuance of a search warrant. The majority agrees that the "FBI affidavit in the present case is more ample than that in *Aguilar*," but concludes that it is nevertheless constitutionally inadequate. The majority states that the present affidavit fails to meet the "two-pronged test" of *Aguilar* because (a) it does not set forth the basis for the assertion that the informer is "reliable" and (b) it fails to state the "underlying circumstances" upon which the informant based his conclusion that Spinelli was engaged in bookmaking.

The majority acknowledges, however, that its reference to a "two-pronged test" should not be understood as meaning that an affidavit deficient in these respects is necessarily inadequate to support a search warrant. Other facts and circumstances may be attested which will supply the evidence of probable cause needed to support the search warrant. On this general statement we are agreed. Our difference is that I believe such facts and circumstances are present in this case, and the majority arrives at the opposite conclusion.

Aguilar expressly recognized that if, in that case, the affidavit's conclusory report of the informant's story had been supplemented by "the fact and results of . . . a surveillance . . . this would, of course, present an entirely different case." In the present case, as I view it, the affidavit showed not only relevant surveillance, entitled to some probative weight for purposes of the issuance of a search warrant, but also additional, specific facts of significance and adequate reliability: that Spinelli was using two telephone numbers, identified by an "informant" as being used for bookmaking, in his illegal operations; that these telephones were in an identified apartment; and that Spinelli, a known bookmaker,[5] frequented the apartment. Certainly, this is enough.

A policeman's affidavit should not be judged as an entry in an essay contest. As the majority recognizes, a policeman's affidavit is entitled to common-sense evaluation. So viewed, I conclude that the judgment of the Court of Appeals for the Eighth Circuit should be affirmed.

[Mr. Justice Stewart also dissented.]

QUESTIONS AND NOTES

1.   Do you agree with Harlan, White, Black, or Fortas? Why?

2.   Of the cases that we have read so far, *Brinegar*, *Draper*, and *Spinelli*, the Court failed to find probable cause only in *Spinelli*. Do you think that *Spinelli* was the weakest of the three cases for finding probable cause? Do you think it was the strongest?

3.   Did (should) it matter that *Spinelli* was the only case of the three in which a warrant was obtained?

---

[5] Although Spinelli's reputation standing alone would not, of course, justify the search, this Court has held that such a reputation may make the informer's report "much less subject to scepticism than would be such a charge against one without such a history." *Jones v. United States*, 362 U.S. 257, 271 (1960).

4.   Did (should) it matter that *Spinelli* involved a search whereas *Draper* involved an arrest?

5.   Did (should) it matter that *Spinelli* involved a home whereas *Brinegar* involved a car, and *Draper* involved a public area?

6.   Do you see the two telephones as a petty luxury or an indicator of criminal activity? Does it matter that we are speaking of 1965, not post-2000?

7.   Should we assume (as Justice Black suggests) that Grace Hagen is a nonexistent person, or should we assume that she was a friend of Spinelli's whom he frequently visited? Does the answer to that question impact on your assessment of probable cause?

8.   As a police attorney with the benefit of hindsight, what additional information would you have put in the warrant?

9.   In *Gates*, we will see that some of the specificity required by *Spinelli* has not survived. As you read *Gates*, see if you can ascertain why this is so?

ILLINOIS v. GATES
462 U.S. 213 (1983)

JUSTICE REHNQUIST delivered the opinion of the Court.

Respondents Lance and Susan Gates were indicted for violation of state drug laws after police officers, executing a search warrant, discovered marijuana and other contraband in their automobile and home. Prior to trial the Gates' moved to suppress evidence seized during this search. The Illinois Supreme Court affirmed the decisions of lower state courts granting the motion. It held that the affidavit submitted in support of the State's application for a warrant to search the Gateses' property was inadequate under this Court's decisions in *Aguilar* and *Spinelli*.

A chronological statement of events usefully introduces the issues at stake. Bloomingdale, Ill., is a suburb of Chicago located in DuPage County. On May 3, 1978, the Bloomingdale Police Department received by mail an anonymous handwritten letter which read as follows:

"This letter is to inform you that you have a couple in your town who strictly make their living on selling drugs. They are Sue and Lance Gates, they live on Greenway, off Bloomingdale Rd. in the condominiums. Most of their buys are done in Florida. Sue his wife drives their car to Florida, where she leaves it to be loaded up with drugs, then Lance flys down and drives it back. Sue flys back after she drops the car off in Florida. May 3 she is driving down there again and Lance will be flying down in a few days to drive it back. At the time Lance drives the car back he has the trunk loaded with over $100,000.00 in drugs. Presently they have over $100,000.00 worth of drugs in their basement.

"They brag about the fact they never have to work, and make their entire living on pushers.

"I guarantee if you watch them carefully you will make a big catch. They are friends with some big drugs dealers, who visit their house often.

"Lance & Susan Gates

"Greenway

"in Condominiums"

The letter was referred by the Chief of Police of the Bloomingdale Police Department to Detective Mader, who decided to pursue the tip. Mader learned, from the office of the Illinois Secretary of State, that an Illinois driver's license had been issued to one Lance Gates, residing at a stated address in Bloomingdale. He contacted a confidential informant, whose examination of certain financial records revealed a more recent address for the Gates, and he also learned from a police officer assigned to O'Hare Airport that "L. Gates" had made a reservation on Eastern Airlines flight 245 to West Palm Beach, Fla., scheduled to depart from Chicago on May 5 at 4:15 p.m.

Mader then made arrangements with an agent of the Drug Enforcement Administration for surveillance of the May 5 Eastern Airlines flight. The agent later reported to Mader that Gates had boarded the flight, and that federal agents in Florida had observed him arrive in West Palm Beach and take a taxi to the nearby Holiday Inn. They also reported that Gates went to a room registered to one Susan Gates and that, at 7:00 a.m. the next morning, Gates and an unidentified woman left the motel in a Mercury bearing Illinois license plates and drove northbound on an interstate frequently used by travelers to the Chicago area. In addition, the DEA agent informed Mader that the license plate number on the Mercury registered to a Hornet station wagon owned by Gates. The agent also advised Mader that the driving time between West Palm Beach and Bloomingdale was approximately 22 to 24 hours.

Mader signed an affidavit setting forth the foregoing facts, and submitted it to a judge of the Circuit Court of DuPage County, together with a copy of the anonymous letter. The judge of that court thereupon issued a search warrant for the Gateses' residence and for their automobile. The judge, in deciding to issue the warrant, could have determined that the *modus operandi* of the Gates had been substantially corroborated. As the anonymous letter predicted, Lance Gates had flown from Chicago to West Palm Beach late in the afternoon of May 5th, had checked into a hotel room registered in the name of his wife, and, at 7:00 a.m. the following morning, had headed north, accompanied by an unidentified woman, out of West Palm Beach on an interstate highway used by travelers from South Florida to Chicago in an automobile bearing a license plate issued to him.

At 5:15 a.m. on March 7th, only 36 hours after he had flown out of Chicago, Lance Gates, and his wife, returned to their home in Bloomingdale, driving the car in which they had left West Palm Beach some 22 hours earlier. The Bloomingdale police were awaiting them, searched the trunk of the Mercury, and uncovered approximately 350 pounds of marijuana. A search of the Gateses' home revealed marijuana, weapons, and other contraband.

The Illinois Supreme Court concluded — and we are inclined to agree — that, standing alone, the anonymous letter sent to the Bloomingdale Police Department would not provide the basis for a magistrate's determination that there was probable cause to believe contraband would be found in the Gates' car and home. The letter provides virtually nothing from which one might conclude that its author is either honest or his information reliable; likewise, the letter gives absolutely no indication of the basis for the writer's predictions regarding the Gates' criminal activities. Something more was required, then, before a magistrate could conclude that there was probable cause to believe that contraband would be found in the Gates' home and car.

The Illinois Supreme Court also properly recognized that Detective Mader's affidavit might be capable of supplementing the anonymous letter with information sufficient to permit a determination of probable cause. In holding that the affidavit in fact did not contain sufficient additional information to sustain a determination of probable cause, the Illinois court applied a "two-pronged test," derived from our decision in *Spinelli*. The Illinois Supreme Court, like some others, apparently understood *Spinelli* as requiring that the anonymous letter satisfy each of two independent requirements before it could be relied on. According to this view, the letter, as supplemented by Mader's affidavit, first had to adequately reveal the "basis of knowledge" of the letter writer — the particular means by which he came by the information given in his report. Second, it had to provide facts sufficiently establishing either the "veracity" of the affiant's informant, or, alternatively, the "reliability" of the informant's report in this particular case.

The Illinois court, alluding to an elaborate set of legal rules that have developed among various lower courts to enforce the "two-pronged test,"[4] found that the test had not been satisfied. First, the "veracity" prong was not satisfied because, "there was simply no basis [for] . . . conclud[ing] that the anonymous person [who wrote the letter to the Bloomingdale Police Department] was credible." The court indicated that corroboration by police of details contained in the letter might never satisfy the "veracity" prong, and in any event, could not do so if, as in the present case, only "innocent" details are corroborated. In addition, the letter gave no indication of the basis of its writer's knowledge of the Gateses' activities. The Illinois court understood *Spinelli* as permitting the detail contained in a tip to be

---

[4] See, *e.g., Stanley v. State*, 19 Md. App. 507, 313 A.2d 847 (Md. App. 1974). In summary, these rules posit that the "veracity" prong of the *Spinelli* test has two "spurs" — the informant's "credibility" and the "reliability" of his information. Various interpretations are advanced for the meaning of the "reliability" spur of the "veracity" prong. Both the "basis of knowledge" prong and the "veracity" prong are treated as entirely separate requirements, which must be independently satisfied in every case in order to sustain a determination of probable cause. See n. 5, *infra*. Some ancillary doctrines are relied on to satisfy certain of the foregoing requirements. For example, the "self-verifying detail" of a tip may satisfy the "basis of knowledge" requirement, although not the "credibility" spur of the "veracity" prong. Conversely, corroboration would seem not capable of supporting the "basis of knowledge" prong, but only the "veracity" prong.

The decision in *Stanley*, while expressly approving and conscientiously attempting to apply the "two-pronged test" observes that "[t]he built-in subtleties [of the test] are such, however, that a slipshod application calls down upon us the fury of Murphy's Law." The decision also suggested that it is necessary "to evolve analogous guidelines [to hearsay rules employed in trial settings] for the reception of hearsay in a probable cause setting."

used to infer that the informant had a reliable basis for his statements, but it thought that the anonymous letter failed to provide sufficient detail to permit such an inference. Thus, it concluded that no showing of probable cause had been made.

We agree with the Illinois Supreme Court that an informant's "veracity," "reliability" and "basis of knowledge" are all highly relevant in determining the value of his report. We do not agree, however, that these elements should be understood as entirely separate and independent requirements to be rigidly exacted in every case,[5] which the opinion of the Supreme Court of Illinois would imply. Rather, as detailed below, they should be understood simply as closely intertwined issues that may usefully illuminate the commonsense, practical question whether there is "probable cause" to believe that contraband or evidence is located in a particular place.

III

This totality of the circumstances approach is far more consistent with our prior treatment of probable cause than is any rigid demand that specific "tests" be satisfied by every informant's tip. Perhaps the central teaching of our decisions bearing on the probable cause standard is that it is a "practical, nontechnical conception." *Brinegar.* "In dealing with probable cause, . . . as the very name implies, we deal with probabilities. These are not technical; they are the factual and practical considerations of everyday life on which reasonable and prudent men, not legal technicians, act." Our observation in *United States v. Cortez*, 449 U.S. 411, 418 (1981), regarding "particularized suspicion," is also applicable to the probable cause standard:

"The process does not deal with hard certainties, but with probabilities. Long before the law of probabilities was articulated as such, practical people formulated certain common-sense conclusions about human behavior; jurors as factfinders are permitted to do the same — and so are law enforcement officers. Finally, the evidence thus collected must be seen and weighed not in terms of library analysis by scholars, but as understood by those versed in the field of law enforcement."

As these comments illustrate, probable cause is a fluid concept — turning on the assessment of probabilities in particular factual contexts — not readily, or even usefully, reduced to a neat set of legal rules. Informants' tips doubtless come in many shapes and sizes from many different types of persons. As we said in *Adams v. Williams*, "Informants' tips, like all other clues and evidence coming to a policeman on the scene may vary greatly in their value and reliability." Rigid legal rules are ill-suited to an area of such diversity. "One simple rule will not cover every situation."

Moreover, the "two-pronged test" directs analysis into two largely independent channels — the informant's "veracity" or "reliability" and his "basis of knowledge."

---

[5] The entirely independent character that the *Spinelli* prongs have assumed is indicated both by the opinion of the Illinois Supreme Court in this case, and by decisions of other courts. One frequently cited decision, *Stanley v. State*, remarks that "the dual requirements represented by the 'two-pronged test' are 'analytically severable' and an 'overkill' on one prong will not carry over to make up for a deficit on the other prong."

There are persuasive arguments against according these two elements such independent status. Instead, they are better understood as relevant considerations in the totality of circumstances analysis that traditionally has guided probable cause determinations: a deficiency in one may be compensated for, in determining the overall reliability of a tip, by a strong showing as to the other, or by some other indicia of reliability.

If, for example, a particular informant is known for the unusual reliability of his predictions of certain types of criminal activities in a locality, his failure, in a particular case, to thoroughly set forth the basis of his knowledge surely should not serve as an absolute bar to a finding of probable cause based on his tip. Likewise, if an unquestionably honest citizen comes forward with a report of criminal activity — which if fabricated would subject him to criminal liability — we have found rigorous scrutiny of the basis of his knowledge unnecessary. Conversely, even if we entertain some doubt as to an informant's motives, his explicit and detailed description of alleged wrongdoing, along with a statement that the event was observed first-hand, entitles his tip to greater weight than might otherwise be the case. Unlike a totality of circumstances analysis, which permits a balanced assessment of the relative weights of all the various indicia of reliability (and unreliability) attending an informant's tip, the "two-pronged test" has encouraged an excessively technical dissection of informants' tips,[9] with undue attention being focused on isolated issues that cannot sensibly be divorced from the other facts presented to the magistrate.

As early as *Locke v. United States*, 7 Cranch. 339, 348 (1813), Chief Justice Marshall observed, in a closely related context, that "the term 'probable cause,' according to its usual acceptation, means less than evidence which would justify condemnation . . . . It imports a seizure made under circumstances which warrant suspicion." More recently, we said that "the *quanta* . . . of proof" appropriate in ordinary judicial proceedings are inapplicable to the decision to issue a warrant. *Brinegar*. Finely-tuned standards such as proof beyond a reasonable doubt or by a preponderance of the evidence, useful in formal trials, have no place in the magistrate's decision. While an effort to fix some general, numerically precise degree of certainty corresponding to "probable cause" may not be helpful, it is clear that "only the probability, and not a prima facie showing, of criminal activity is the standard of probable cause." *Spinelli*.

We also have recognized that affidavits "are normally drafted by nonlawyers in the midst and haste of a criminal investigation. Technical requirements of elaborate specificity once exacted under common law pleading have no proper place in this area." Likewise, search and arrest warrants long have been issued by persons who are neither lawyers nor judges, and who certainly do not remain abreast of each judicial refinement of the nature of "probable cause." See *Shadwick v. City of*

---

[9] Some lower court decisions, brought to our attention by the State, reflect a rigid application of such rules. In *Bridger v. State*, 503 S.W.2d 801 (Tex. Crim. App. 1974), the affiant had received a confession of armed robbery from one of two suspects in the robbery; in addition, the suspect had given the officer $800 in cash stolen during the robbery. The suspect also told the officer that the gun used in the robbery was hidden in the other suspect's apartment. A warrant issued on the basis of this was invalidated on the ground that the affidavit did not satisfactorily describe how the accomplice had obtained his information regarding the gun.

Tampa, chapter III, *infra*. The rigorous inquiry into the *Spinelli* prongs and the complex superstructure of evidentiary and analytical rules that some have seen implicit in our *Spinelli* decision, cannot be reconciled with the fact that many warrants are — quite properly, — issued on the basis of nontechnical, common-sense judgments of laymen applying a standard less demanding than those used in more formal legal proceedings. Likewise, given the informal, often hurried context in which it must be applied, the "built-in subtleties" of the "two-pronged test" are particularly unlikely to assist magistrates in determining probable cause.

Similarly, we have repeatedly said that after-the-fact scrutiny by courts of the sufficiency of an affidavit should not take the form of *de novo* review. A magistrate's "determination of probable cause should be paid great deference by reviewing courts." "A grudging or negative attitude by reviewing courts toward warrants" is inconsistent with the Fourth Amendment's strong preference for searches conducted pursuant to a warrant "courts should not invalidate . . . warrant[s] by interpreting affidavit[s] in a hypertechnical, rather than a commonsense, manner."

If the affidavits submitted by police officers are subjected to the type of scrutiny some courts have deemed appropriate, police might well resort to warrantless searches, with the hope of relying on consent or some other exception to the warrant clause that might develop at the time of the search. In addition, the possession of a warrant by officers conducting an arrest or search greatly reduces the perception of unlawful or intrusive police conduct, by assuring "the individual whose property is searched or seized of the lawful authority of the executing officer, his need to search, and the limits of his power to search." Reflecting this preference for the warrant process, the traditional standard for review of an issuing magistrate's probable cause determination has been that so long as the magistrate had a "substantial basis for . . . conclud[ing]" that a search would uncover evidence of wrongdoing, the Fourth Amendment requires no more. We think reaffirmation of this standard better serves the purpose of encouraging recourse to the warrant procedure and is more consistent with our traditional deference to the probable cause determinations of magistrates than is the "two-pronged test."

Finally, the direction taken by decisions following Spinelli poorly serves "the most basic function of any government": "to provide for the security of the individual and of his property." The strictures that inevitably accompany the "two-pronged test" cannot avoid seriously impeding the task of law enforcement, see, *e.g.*, n. 9, *supra*. If, as the Illinois Supreme Court apparently thought, that test must be rigorously applied in every case, anonymous tips seldom would be of greatly diminished value in police work. Ordinary citizens, like ordinary witnesses, generally do not provide extensive recitations of the basis of their everyday observations. Likewise, as the Illinois Supreme Court observed in this case, the veracity of persons supplying anonymous tips is by hypothesis largely unknown, and unknowable. As a result, anonymous tips seldom could survive a rigorous application of either of the *Spinelli* prongs. Yet, such tips, particularly when supplemented by independent police investigation, frequently contribute to the solution of otherwise "perfect crimes." While a conscientious assessment of the basis for crediting such tips is required by the Fourth Amendment, a standard that leaves virtually no place for anonymous citizen informants is not.

For all these reasons, we conclude that it is wiser to abandon the "two-pronged test" established by our decisions in *Aguilar* and *Spinelli*.[11] In its place we reaffirm the totality of the circumstances analysis that traditionally has informed probable cause determinations. The task of the issuing magistrate is simply to make a practical, common-sense decision whether, given all the circumstances set forth in the affidavit before him, including the "veracity" and "basis of knowledge" of persons supplying hearsay information, there is a fair probability that contraband or evidence of a crime will be found in a particular place. And the duty of a reviewing court is simply to ensure that the magistrate had a "substantial basis for . . . conclud[ing]" that probable cause existed. We are convinced that this flexible, easily applied standard will better achieve the accommodation of public and private interests that the Fourth Amendment requires than does the approach that has developed from *Aguilar* and *Spinelli*.

Our earlier cases illustrate the limits beyond which a magistrate may not venture in issuing a warrant. A sworn statement of an affiant that "he has cause to suspect and does believe that" liquor illegally brought into the United States is located on certain premises will not do. *Nathanson v. United States*, 290 U.S. 41 (1933). An affidavit must provide the magistrate with a substantial basis for determining the existence of probable cause, and the wholly conclusory statement at issue in *Nathanson* failed to meet this requirement. An officer's statement that "affiants have received reliable information from a credible person and believe" that heroin is stored in a home, is likewise inadequate. *Aguilar*. As in *Nathanson*, this is a mere conclusory statement that gives the magistrate virtually no basis at all for making a judgment regarding probable cause. Sufficient information must be presented to the magistrate to allow that official to determine probable cause; his action cannot be a mere ratification of the bare conclusions of others. In order to ensure that such an abdication of the magistrate's duty does not occur, courts must continue to conscientiously review the sufficiency of affidavits on which warrants are issued. But when we move beyond the "bare bones" affidavits present in cases such as *Nathanson* and *Aguilar*, this area simply does not lend itself to a prescribed set of rules, like that which had developed from *Spinelli*. Instead, the flexible, common-sense standard articulated in *Brinegar* better serves the purposes of the Fourth Amendment's probable cause requirement.

Justice Brennan's dissent suggests in several places that the approach we take today somehow downgrades the role of the neutral magistrate, because *Aguilar* and *Spinelli* "preserve the role of magistrates as independent arbiters of probable cause . . . ." Quite the contrary, we believe, is the case. Nothing in our opinion in any way lessens the authority of the magistrate to draw such reasonable inferences as he will from the material supplied to him by applicants for a warrant; indeed, he is freer than under the regime of *Aguilar* and *Spinelli* to draw such inferences, or to refuse to draw them if he is so minded.

---

[11] Whether the allegations submitted to the magistrate in *Spinelli* would, under the view we now take, have supported a finding of probable cause, we think it would not be profitable to decide. There are so many variables in the probable cause equation that one determination will seldom be a useful "precedent" for another. Suffice it to say that while we in no way abandon *Spinelli*'s concern for the trustworthiness of informers and for the principle that it is the magistrate who must ultimately make a finding of probable cause, we reject the rigid categorization suggested by some of its language.

The real gist of Justice Brennan's criticism seems to be a second argument, somewhat at odds with the first, that magistrates should be restricted in their authority to make probable cause determinations by the standards laid down in *Aguilar* and *Spinelli*, and that such findings "should not be authorized unless there is some assurance that the information on which they are based has been obtained in a reliable way by an honest or credible person." However, under our opinion magistrates remain perfectly free to exact such assurances as they deem necessary, as well as those required by this opinion, in making probable cause determinations. Justice Brennan would apparently prefer that magistrates be restricted in their findings of probable cause by the development of an elaborate body of case law dealing with the "veracity" prong of the *Spinelli* test, which in turn is broken down into two "spurs" — the informant's "credibility" and the "reliability" of his information, together with the "basis of knowledge" prong of the Spinelli test. That such a labyrinthine body of judicial refinement bears any relationship to familiar definitions of probable cause is hard to imagine. Probable cause deals "with probabilities. These are not technical; they are the factual and practical consider-ations of everyday life on which reasonable and prudent men, not legal technicians, act," *Brinegar*.

Justice Brennan's dissent also suggests that "words such as 'practical,' 'nontech-nical,' and 'common sense,' as used in the Court's opinion, are but code words for an overly-permissive attitude towards police practices in derogation of the rights secured by the Fourth Amendment." An easy, but not a complete, answer to this rather florid statement would be that nothing we know about Justice Rutledge suggests that he would have used the words he chose in *Brinegar* in such a manner. More fundamentally, no one doubts that "under our Constitution only measures consistent with the Fourth Amendment may be employed by government to cure [the horrors of drug trafficking]," but this agreement does not advance the inquiry as to which measures are, and which measures are not, consistent with the Fourth Amendment. "Fidelity" to the commands of the Constitution suggests balanced judgment rather than exhortation. The highest "fidelity" is achieved neither by the judge who instinctively goes furthest in upholding even the most bizarre claim of individual constitutional rights, any more than it is achieved by a judge who instinctively goes furthest in accepting the most restrictive claims of governmental authorities. The task of this Court, as of other courts, is to "hold the balance true," and we think we have done that in this case.

IV

Our decisions applying the totality of circumstances analysis outlined above have consistently recognized the value of corroboration of details of an informant's tip by independent police work. *Draper* is the classic case. There, an informant named Hereford reported that Draper would arrive in Denver on a train from Chicago on one of two days, and that he would be carrying a quantity of heroin. The informant also supplied a fairly detailed physical description of Draper, and predicted that he would be wearing a light colored raincoat, brown slacks and black shoes, and would be walking "real fast." Hereford gave no indication of the basis for his information.[12]

On one of the stated dates police officers observed a man matching this description exit a train arriving from Chicago; his attire and luggage matched Hereford's report and he was walking rapidly. We explained in Draper that, by this point in his investigation, the arresting officer "had personally verified every facet of the information given him by Hereford except whether petitioner had accomplished his mission and had the three ounces of heroin on his person or in his bag. And surely, with every other bit of Hereford's information being thus personally verified, [the officer] had 'reasonable grounds' to believe that the remaining unverified bit of Hereford's information — that Draper would have the heroin with him — was likewise true."

The showing of probable cause in the present case was fully as compelling as that in Draper. Even standing alone, the facts obtained through the independent investigation of Mader and the DEA at least suggested that the Gates were involved in drug trafficking. In addition to being a popular vacation site, Florida is well-known as a source of narcotics and other illegal drugs. Lance Gates' flight to Palm Beach, his brief, overnight stay in a motel, and apparent immediate return north to Chicago in the family car, conveniently awaiting him in West Palm Beach, is as suggestive of a pre-arranged drug run, as it is of an ordinary vacation trip. In addition, the magistrate could rely on the anonymous letter, which had been corroborated in major part by Mader's efforts — just as had occurred in Draper.[13] The Supreme Court of Illinois reasoned that Draper involved an informant who had given reliable information on previous occasions, while the honesty and reliability of the anonymous informant in this case were unknown to the Bloomingdale police. While this distinction might be an apt one at the time the police department received the anonymous letter, it became far less significant after Mader's independent investigative work occurred. The corroboration of the letter's predictions that the Gates' car would be in Florida, that Lance Gates would fly to Florida in the next day or so, and that he would drive the car north toward Bloomingdale all indicated, albeit not with certainty, that the informant's other assertions also were true. "Because an informant is right about some things, he is more probably right about other facts," Spinelli (White, J., concurring) — including the claim regarding the Gateses' illegal activity. This may well not be the type of "reliability" or "veracity" necessary to satisfy some views of the "veracity prong" of Spinelli, but we think it suffices for the practical, common-sense judgment called for in making

---

[12] The tip in Draper might well not have survived the rigid application of the "two-pronged test" that developed following Spinelli. The only reference to Hereford's reliability was that he had "been engaged as a 'special employee' of the Bureau of Narcotics at Denver for about six months, and from time to time gave information to [the police] for small sums of money, and that [the officer] had always found the information given by Hereford to be accurate and reliable." Likewise, the tip gave no indication of how Hereford came by his information. At most, the detailed and accurate predictions in the tip indicated that, however Hereford obtained his information, it was reliable.

[13] The Illinois Supreme Court thought that the verification of details contained in the anonymous letter in this case amounted only to "the corroboration of innocent activity," and that this was insufficient to support a finding of probable cause. We are inclined to agree, however, with the observation of Justice Moran in his dissenting opinion that "In this case, just as in Draper, seemingly innocent activity became suspicious in the light of the initial tip." And it bears noting that all of the corroborating detail established in Draper was of entirely innocent activity.

a probable cause determination. It is enough, for purposes of assessing probable cause, that "corroboration through other sources of information reduced the chances of a reckless or prevaricating tale," thus providing "a substantial basis for crediting the hearsay."

Finally, the anonymous letter contained a range of details relating not just to easily obtained facts and conditions existing at the time of the tip, but to future actions of third parties ordinarily not easily predicted. The letter writer's accurate information as to the travel plans of each of the Gateses was of a character likely obtained only from the Gateses themselves, or from someone familiar with their not entirely ordinary travel plans. If the informant had access to accurate information of this type a magistrate could properly conclude that it was not unlikely that he also had access to reliable information of the Gates' alleged illegal activities.[14] Of course, the Gateses' travel plans might have been learned from a talkative neighbor or travel agent; under the "two-pronged test" developed from *Spinelli*, the character of the details in the anonymous letter might well not permit a sufficiently clear inference regarding the letter writer's "basis of knowledge." But, as discussed previously, probable cause does not demand the certainty we associate with formal trials. It is enough that there was a fair probability that the writer of the anonymous letter had obtained his entire story either from the Gateses or someone they trusted. And corroboration of major portions of the letter's predictions provides just this probability. It is apparent, therefore, that the judge issuing the warrant had a "substantial basis for . . . conclud[ing]" that probable cause to search the Gateses' home and car existed. The judgment of the Supreme Court of Illinois therefore must be reversed.

JUSTICE WHITE, concurring in the judgment.

Abandoning the "two-pronged test" of *Aguilar* and *Spinelli*, the Court upholds the validity of the warrant under a new "totality of the circumstances" approach.

---

[14] The dissent seizes on one inaccuracy in the anonymous informant's letter — its statement that Sue Gates would fly from Florida to Illinois, when in fact she drove — and argues that the probative value of the entire tip was undermined by this allegedly "material mistake." We have never required that informants used by the police be infallible, and can see no reason to impose such a requirement in this case. Probable cause, particularly when police have obtained a warrant, simply does not require the perfection the dissent finds necessary.

Likewise, there is no force to the dissent's argument that the Gates' action in leaving their home unguarded undercut the informant's claim that drugs were hidden there. Indeed, the line-by-line scrutiny that the dissent applies to the anonymous letter is akin to that we find inappropriate in reviewing magistrate's decisions. The dissent apparently attributes to the magistrate who issued the warrant in this case the rather implausible notion that persons dealing in drugs always stay at home, apparently out of fear that to leave might risk intrusion by criminals. If accurate, one could not help sympathizing with the self-imposed isolation of people so situated. In reality, however, it is scarcely likely that the magistrate ever thought that the anonymous tip "kept one spouse" at home, much less that he relied on the theory advanced by the dissent. The letter simply says that Sue would fly from Florida to Illinois, without indicating whether the Gateses made the bitter choice of leaving the drugs in their house, or those in their car, unguarded. The magistrate's determination that there might be drugs or evidence of criminal activity in the Gateses' home was well-supported by the less speculative theory, noted in text, that if the informant could predict with considerable accuracy the somewhat unusual travel plans of the Gateses, he probably also had a reliable basis for his statements that the Gateses' kept a large quantity of drugs in their home and frequently were visited by other drug traffickers there.

Although I agree that the warrant should be upheld, I reach this conclusion in accordance with the *Aguilar-Spinelli* framework.

For present purposes, the *Aguilar-Spinelli* rules can be summed up as follows. First, an affidavit based on an informer's tip, standing alone, cannot provide probable cause for issuance of a warrant unless the tip includes information that apprises the magistrate of the informant's basis for concluding that the contraband is where he claims it is (the "basis of knowledge" prong), *and* the affiant informs the magistrate of his basis for believing that the informant is credible (the "veracity" prong).[20] Second, if a tip fails under either or both of the two prongs, probable cause may yet be established by independent police investigatory work that corroborates the tip to such an extent that it supports "both the inference that the informer was generally trustworthy and that he made his charge on the basis of information obtained in a reliable way." In instances where the officers rely on corroboration, the ultimate question is whether the corroborated tip "is as trustworthy as a tip which would pass *Aguilar*'s tests without independent corroboration."

In the present case, it is undisputed that the anonymous tip, by itself, did not furnish probable cause. The question is whether those portions of the affidavit describing the results of the police investigation of the respondents, when considered in light of the tip, "would permit the suspicions engendered by the informant's report to ripen into a judgment that a crime was probably being committed." The Illinois Supreme Court concluded that the corroboration was insufficient to permit such a ripening. The court reasoned as follows: "[T]he nature of the corroborating evidence in this case would satisfy neither the 'basis of knowledge' nor the 'veracity' prong of *Aguilar*. Looking to the affidavit submitted as support for Detective Mader's request that a search warrant issue, we note that the corroborative evidence here was only of innocent activity. Mader's independent investigation revealed only that Lance and Sue Gates lived on Greenway Drive; that Lance Gates booked passage on a flight to Florida; that upon arriving he entered a room registered to his wife; and that he and his wife left the hotel together by car. The corroboration of innocent activity is insufficient to support a finding of probable cause."

In my view, the lower court's characterization of the Gates' activity here as totally "innocent" is dubious. In fact, the behavior was quite suspicious. I agree with the Court that Lance Gates' flight to Palm Beach, an area known to be a source of narcotics, the brief overnight stay in a motel, and apparent immediate return North, suggest a pattern that trained law enforcement officers have recognized as indicative of illicit drug-dealing activity.

---

[20] The "veracity" prong is satisfied by a recitation in the affidavit that the informant previously supplied accurate information to the police, or by proof that the informant gave his information against his penal interest. The "basis of knowledge" prong is satisfied by a statement from the informant that he personally observed the criminal activity, or, if he came by the information indirectly, by a satisfactory explanation of why his sources were reliable, or, in the absence of a statement detailing the manner in which the information was gathered, by a description of the accused's criminal activity in sufficient detail that the magistrate may infer that the informant is relying on something more substantial than casual rumor or an individual's general reputation.

Even, however, had the corroboration related only to completely innocuous activities, this fact alone would not preclude the issuance of a valid warrant. The critical issue is not whether the activities observed by the police are innocent or suspicious. Instead, the proper focus should be on whether the actions of the suspects, whatever their nature, give rise to an inference that the informant is credible and that he obtained his information in a reliable manner.

Thus, in *Draper*, an informant stated on Sept. 7 that Draper would be carrying narcotics when he arrived by train in Denver on the morning of Sept. 8 or Sept. 9. The informant also provided the police with a detailed physical description of the clothes Draper would be wearing when he alighted from the train. The police observed Draper leaving a train on the morning of Sept. 9, and he was wearing the precise clothing described by the informant. The Court held that the police had probable cause to arrest Draper at this point, even though the police had seen nothing more than the totally innocent act of a man getting off a train carrying a briefcase. As we later explained in *Spinelli*, the important point was that the corroboration showed both that the informant was credible, *i.e.* that he "had not been fabricating his report out of whole cloth," and that he had an adequate basis of knowledge for his allegations, "since the report was of the sort which in common experience may be recognized as having been obtained in a reliable way." The fact that the informer was able to predict, two days in advance, the exact clothing Draper would be wearing dispelled the possibility that his tip was just based on rumor or "an off-hand remark heard at a neighborhood bar." Probably Draper had planned in advance to wear these specific clothes so that an accomplice could identify him. A clear inference could therefore be drawn that the informant was either involved in the criminal scheme himself or that he otherwise had access to reliable, inside information.[22]

As in *Draper*, the police investigation in the present case satisfactorily demonstrated that the informant's tip was as trustworthy as one that would alone satisfy the *Aguilar* tests. The tip predicted that Sue Gates would drive to Florida, that Lance Gates would fly there a few days after May 3, and that Lance would then drive the car back. After the police corroborated these facts, the magistrate could

---

[22] Thus, as interpreted in *Spinelli*, the Court in *Draper* held that there was probable cause because "the kind of information related by the informant [was] not generally sent ahead of a person's arrival in a city except to those who are intimately connected with making careful arrangements for meeting him." *Spinelli* (White, J., concurring). As I said in Spinelli, the conclusion that Draper itself was based on this fact is far from inescapable. Prior to *Spinelli*, *Draper* was susceptible to the interpretation that it stood for the proposition that "the existence of the tenth and critical fact is made sufficiently probable to justify the issuance of a warrant by verifying nine other facts coming from the same source." But it now seems clear that the Court in Spinelli rejected this reading of *Draper*.

Justice Brennan erroneously interprets my *Spinelli* concurrence as espousing the view that "corroboration of certain details in a tip may be sufficient to satisfy the veracity, but not the basis of knowledge, prong of *Aguilar*." Others have made the same mistake. I did not say that corroboration could *never* satisfy the basis of knowledge prong. My concern was, and still is, that the prong might be deemed satisfied on the basis of corroboration of information that does not in any way suggest that the informant had an adequate basis of knowledge for his report. If, however, as in *Draper*, the police corroborate information from which it can be inferred that the informant's tip was grounded on inside information, this corroboration is sufficient to satisfy the basis of knowledge prong. The rules would indeed be strange if, as Justice Brennan suggests, the basis of knowledge prong could be satisfied by detail in the tip alone, but not by independent police work.

reasonably have inferred, as he apparently did, that the informant, who had specific knowledge of these unusual travel plans, did not make up his story and that he obtained his information in a reliable way. It is theoretically possible, as respondents insist, that the tip could have been supplied by a "vindictive travel agent" and that the Gateses' activities, although unusual, might not have been unlawful.[24] But *Aguilar* and *Spinelli*, like our other cases, do not require that certain guilt be established before a warrant may properly be issued. "[O]nly the probability, and not a prima facie showing, of criminal activity is the standard of probable cause." I therefore conclude that the judgment of the Illinois Supreme Court invalidating the warrant must be reversed.

The Court agrees that the warrant was valid, but, in the process of reaching this conclusion, it overrules the *Aguilar-Spinelli* tests and replaces them with a "totality of the circumstances" standard. As shown above, it is not at all necessary to overrule Aguilar-Spinelli in order to reverse the judgment below. Therefore, because I am inclined to believe that, when applied properly, the *Aguilar-Spinelli* rules play an appropriate role in probable cause determinations, and because the Court's holding may foretell an evisceration of the probable cause standard, I do not join the Court's holding. The Court reasons that the "veracity" and "basis of knowledge" tests are not independent, and that a deficiency as to one can be compensated for by a strong showing as to the other. Thus, a finding of probable cause may be based on a tip from an informant "known for the unusual reliability of his predictions" or from "an unquestionably honest citizen," even if the report fails thoroughly to set forth the basis upon which the information was obtained. If this is so, then it must follow *a fortiori* that "the affidavit of an officer, known by the magistrate to be honest and experienced, stating that [contraband] is located in a certain building" must be acceptable. It would be "quixotic" if a similar statement from an honest informant, but not one from an honest officer, could furnish probable cause. But we have repeatedly held that the unsupported assertion or belief of an officer does not satisfy the probable cause requirement. Thus, this portion of today's holding can be read as implicitly rejecting the teachings of these prior holdings.

The Court may not intend so drastic a result. Indeed, the Court expressly reaffirms the validity of cases such as *Nathanson* that have held that, no matter how reliable the affiant-officer may be, a warrant should not be issued unless the affidavit discloses supporting facts and circumstances. The Court limits these cases to situations involving affidavits containing only "bare conclusions" and holds that, if an affidavit contains anything more, it should be left to the issuing magistrate to decide, based solely on "practical[ity]" and "common-sense," whether there is a fair probability that contraband will be found in a particular place. Thus, as I read the majority opinion, it appears that the question whether the probable cause standard is to be diluted is left to the common-sense judgments of issuing magistrates. I am reluctant to approve any standard that does not expressly require, as a prerequisite to issuance of a warrant, some showing of facts from which an inference may be drawn that the informant is credible and that his information was obtained in a

---

[24] It is also true, as Justice Stevens points out, that the fact that respondents were last seen leaving West Palm Beach on a northbound interstate highway is far from conclusive proof that they were heading directly to Bloomingdale.

reliable way. The Court is correctly concerned with the fact that some lower courts have been applying *Aguilar-Spinelli* in an unduly rigid manner. I believe, however, that with clarification of the rule of corroborating information, the lower courts are fully able to properly interpret *Aguilar-Spinelli* and avoid such unduly rigid applications. I may be wrong; it ultimately may prove to be the case that the only profitable instruction we can provide to magistrates is to rely on common sense. But the question whether a particular anonymous tip provides the basis for issuance of a warrant will often be a difficult one, and I would at least attempt to provide more precise guidance by clarifying *Aguilar-Spinelli* and the relationship of those cases with *Draper* before totally abdicating our responsibility in this area. Hence, I do not join the Court's opinion rejecting the *Aguilar-Spinelli* rules.

JUSTICE BRENNAN, with whom JUSTICE MARSHALL joins, dissenting.

Although I join Justice Stevens' dissenting opinion and agree with him that the warrant is invalid even under the Court's newly announced "totality of the circumstances" test, I write separately to dissent from the Court's unjustified and ill-advised rejection of the two-prong test for evaluating the validity of a warrant based on hearsay.

I

The Court's current Fourth Amendment jurisprudence, as reflected by today's unfortunate decision, patently disregards Justice Jackson's admonition in *Brinegar*: "[Fourth Amendment rights] . . . are not mere second-class rights but belong in the catalog of indispensable freedoms. Among deprivations of rights, none is so effective in cowing a population, crushing the spirit of the individual and putting terror in every heart. Uncontrolled search and seizure is one of the first and most effective weapons in the arsenal of every arbitrary government. . . .

"But the right to be secure against searches and seizures is one of the most difficult to protect. Since the officers are themselves the chief invaders, there is no enforcement outside of court."

In recognition of the judiciary's role as the only effective guardian of Fourth Amendment rights, this Court has developed over the last half century a set of coherent rules governing a magistrate's consideration of a warrant application and the showings that are necessary to support a finding of probable cause.

In order to emphasize the magistrate's role as an independent arbiter of probable cause and to insure that searches or seizures are not effected on less than probable cause, the Court has insisted that police officers provide magistrates with the underlying facts and circumstances that support the officers' conclusions.

Although the rules drawn from the cases discussed above are cast in procedural terms, they advance an important underlying substantive value: Findings of probable cause, and attendant intrusions, should not be authorized unless there is some assurance that the information on which they are based has been obtained in a reliable way by an honest or credible person. As applied to police officers, the rules focus on the way in which the information was acquired. As applied to informants, the rules focus both on the honesty or credibility of the informant and on the reliability of the way in which the information was acquired. Insofar as it is more complicated, an evaluation of affidavits based on hearsay involves a more difficult inquiry. This suggests a need to structure the inquiry in an effort to insure greater accuracy. The standards announced in *Aguilar*, as refined by *Spinelli*, fulfill that need. The standards inform the police of what information they have to provide and magistrates of what information they should demand. The standards also inform magistrates of the subsidiary findings they must make in order to arrive at an ultimate finding of probable cause. *Spinelli*, properly understood, directs the magistrate's attention to the possibility that the presence of self-verifying detail might satisfy *Aguilar*'s basis of knowledge prong and that corroboration of the details of a tip might satisfy *Aguilar*'s veracity prong. By requiring police to provide certain crucial information to magistrates and by structuring magistrates' probable cause inquiries, *Aguilar* and *Spinelli* assure the magistrate's role as an independent arbiter of probable cause, insure greater accuracy in probable cause determinations, and advance the substantive value identified above.

Until today the Court has never squarely addressed the application of the *Aguilar* and *Spinelli* standards to tips from anonymous informants. Both *Aguilar* and *Spinelli* dealt with tips from informants known at least to the police. And surely there is even more reason to subject anonymous informants' tips to the tests established by *Aguilar* and *Spinelli*. By definition nothing is known about an anonymous informant's identity, honesty, or reliability. One commentator has suggested that anonymous informants should be treated as presumptively unreliable. In any event, there certainly is no basis for treating anonymous informants as presumptively reliable. Nor is there any basis for assuming that the information provided by an anonymous informant has been obtained in a reliable way. If we are unwilling to accept conclusory allegations from the police, who are presumptively reliable, or from informants who are known, at least to the police, there cannot possibly be any rational basis for accepting conclusory allegations from anonymous informants.

To suggest that anonymous informants' tips are subject to the tests established by *Aguilar* and *Spinelli* is not to suggest that they can never provide a basis for a finding of probable cause. It is conceivable that police corroboration of the details of the tip might establish the reliability of the informant under *Aguilar*'s veracity prong, as refined in *Spinelli*, and that the details in the tip might be sufficient to qualify under the "self-verifying detail" test established by *Spinelli* as a means of satisfying *Aguilar*'s basis of knowledge prong. The *Aguilar* and *Spinelli* tests must be applied to anonymous informants' tips, however, if we are to continue to insure that findings of probable cause, and attendant intrusions, are based on information provided by an honest or credible person who has acquired the information in a reliable way.

II

In rejecting the *Aguilar-Spinelli* standards, the Court suggests that a "totality of the circumstances approach is far more consistent with our prior treatment of probable cause than is any rigid demand that specific 'tests' be satisfied by every informant's tip." In support of this proposition the Court relies on the "practical, nontechnical" nature of probable cause.

[O]ne can concede that probable cause is a "practical, nontechnical" concept without betraying the values that *Aguilar* and *Spinelli* reflect. *Aguilar* and *Spinelli* require the police to provide magistrates with certain crucial information. They also provide structure for magistrates' probable cause inquiries. In so doing, *Aguilar* and *Spinelli* preserve the role of magistrates as independent arbiters of probable cause, insure greater accuracy in probable cause determinations, and advance the substantive value of precluding findings of probable cause, and attendant intrusions, based on anything less than information from an honest or credible person who has acquired his information in a reliable way. Neither the standards nor their effects are inconsistent with a "practical, nontechnical" conception of probable cause. Once a magistrate has determined that he has information before him that he can reasonably say has been obtained in a reliable way by a credible person, he has ample room to use his common sense and to apply a practical, nontechnical conception of probable cause.

The Court also insists that the *Aguilar-Spinelli* standards must be abandoned because they are inconsistent with the fact that non-lawyers frequently serve as magistrates. To the contrary, the standards help to structure probable cause inquiries and, properly interpreted, may actually help a non-lawyer magistrate in making a probable cause determination.

At the heart of the Court's decision to abandon *Aguilar* and *Spinelli* appears to be its belief that "the direction taken by decisions following *Spinelli* poorly serves 'the most basic function of any government: to provide for the security of the individual and of his property.' " This conclusion rests on the judgment that *Aguilar* and *Spinelli* "seriously imped[e] the task of law enforcement," and render anonymous tips valueless in police work. Surely, the Court overstates its case. But of particular concern to all Americans must be that the Court gives virtually no consideration to the value of insuring that findings of probable cause are based on information that a magistrate can reasonably say has been obtained in a reliable way by an honest or credible person. I share Justice WHITE's fear that the Court's rejection of *Aguilar* and *Spinelli* and its adoption of a new totality of the circumstances test "may foretell an evisceration of the probable cause standard . . . ."

III

The Court's complete failure to provide any persuasive reason for rejecting *Aguilar* and *Spinelli* doubtlessly reflects impatience with what it perceives to be "overly technical" rules governing searches and seizures under the Fourth Amendment. Words such as "practical," "nontechnical," and "commonsense," as used in the Court's opinion, are but code words for an overly permissive attitude towards police practices in derogation of the rights secured by the Fourth Amendment. Everyone shares the Court's concern over the horrors of drug trafficking, but under our Constitution only measures consistent with the Fourth Amendment may be employed by government to cure this evil. We must be ever mindful of Justice Stewart's admonition in *Coolidge v. New Hampshire*, 403 U.S. 443 (1971), that "[i]n times of unrest, whether caused by crime or racial conflict or fear of internal subversion, this basic law and the values that it represents may appear unrealistic or 'extravagant' to some. But the values were those of the authors of our fundamental constitutional concepts."

Rights secured by the Fourth Amendment are particularly difficult to protect because their "advocates are usually criminals." But the rules "we fashion [are] for the innocent and guilty alike." By replacing *Aguilar* and *Spinelli* with a test that provides no assurance that magistrates, rather than the police, or informants, will make determinations of probable cause; imposes no structure on magistrates' probable cause inquiries; and invites the possibility that intrusions may be justified on less than reliable information from an honest or credible person, today's decision threatens to "obliterate one of the most fundamental distinctions between our form of government, where officers are under the law, and the police-state where they are the law."

JUSTICE STEVENS, with whom JUSTICE BRENNAN joins, dissenting.

The fact that Lance and Sue Gates made a 22-hour nonstop drive from West Palm Beach, Florida, to Bloomingdale, Illinois, only a few hours after Lance had flown to Florida provided persuasive evidence that they were engaged in illicit activity. That fact, however, was not known to the magistrate when he issued the warrant to search their home.

What the magistrate did know at that time was that the anonymous informant had not been completely accurate in his or her predictions. The informant had indicated that "Sue drives their car to Florida *where she leaves it to be loaded up with drugs. . . . Sue flies back after she drops the car off in Florida*." (emphasis added). Yet Detective Mader's affidavit reported that she "left the West Palm Beach area driving the Mercury northbound."

The discrepancy between the informant's predictions and the facts known to Detective Mader is significant for three reasons. First, it cast doubt on the informant's hypothesis that the Gates already had "over $100,000 worth of drugs in their basement." The informant had predicted an itinerary that always kept one spouse in Bloomingdale, suggesting that the Gates did not want to leave their home unguarded because something valuable was hidden within. That inference obviously could not be drawn when it was known that the pair was actually together over a thousand miles from home.

Second, the discrepancy made the Gates' conduct seem substantially less unusual than the informant had predicted it would be. It would have been odd if, as predicted, Sue had driven down to Florida on Wednesday, left the car, and flown right back to Illinois. But the mere facts that Sue was in West Palm Beach with the car,[1] that she was joined by her husband at the Holiday Inn on Friday,[2] and that the

---

[1] The anonymous note suggested that she was going down on Wednesday, but for all the officers knew she had been in Florida for a month.

[2] Lance does not appear to have behaved suspiciously in flying down to Florida. He made a reservation in his own name and gave an accurate home phone number to the airlines. Cf. *Florida v.*

couple drove north together the next morning[3] are neither unusual nor probative of criminal activity.

Third, the fact that the anonymous letter contained a material mistake undermines the reasonableness of relying on it as a basis for making a forcible entry into a private home.[4]

Of course, the activities in this case did not stop when the magistrate issued the warrant. The Gates drove all night to Bloomingdale, the officers searched the car and found 400 pounds of marijuana, and then they searched the house. However, none of these subsequent events may be considered in evaluating the warrant, and the search of the house was legal only if the warrant was valid. I cannot accept the Court's casual conclusion that, *before the Gates arrived in Bloomingdale*, there was probable cause to justify a valid entry and search of a private home. No one knows who the informant in this case was, or what motivated him or her to write the note. Given that the note's predictions were faulty in one significant respect, and were corroborated by nothing except ordinary innocent activity, I must surmise that the Court's evaluation of the warrant's validity has been colored by subsequent events.[7]

Although the foregoing analysis is determinative as to the house search, the car search raises additional issues because "there is a constitutional difference between houses and cars." An officer who has probable cause to suspect that a highly movable automobile contains contraband does not need a valid warrant in order to search it. In a fact-bound inquiry of this sort, the judgment of three levels of state courts, all of whom are better able to evaluate the probable reliability of anonymous informants in Bloomingdale, Illinois, than we are, should be entitled to at least a presumption of accuracy.[8] I would simply vacate the judgment of the Illinois

---

Royer, 460 U.S. 491, 493 (1983); *United States v. Mendenhall*, 446 U.S. 544, 548 (1980) (Stewart, J., announcing the judgment). And Detective Mader's affidavit does not report that he did any of the other things drug couriers are notorious for doing, such as paying for the ticket in cash, *Royer*, dressing casually, *ibid.*, looking pale and nervous, *ibid.*; *Mendenhall*, improperly filling out baggage tags, *Royer*, carrying American Tourister luggage, ibid., not carrying any luggage, *Mendenhall* (Powell, J., concurring in part and concurring in the judgment), or changing airlines en route, *ibid.*

[3] Detective Mader's affidavit hinted darkly that the couple had set out upon "that interstate highway commonly used by travelers to the Chicago area." But the same highway is also commonly used by travelers to Disney World, Sea World, and Ringling Brothers and Barnum and Bailey Circus World. It is also the road to Cocoa Beach, Cape Canaveral, and Washington, D.C. I would venture that each year dozens of perfectly innocent people fly to Florida, meet a waiting spouse, and drive off together in the family car.

[4] The Court purports to rely on the proposition that "if the [anonymous] informant could predict with *considerable accuracy the somewhat unusual travel plans* of the Gateses, he probably also had a reliable basis for his statements that the Gateses kept a large quantity of drugs in their home." (emphasis added). Even if this syllogism were sound, but see *Spinelli* (White, J., concurring), its premises are not met in this case.

[7] *Draper* affords no support for today's holding. That case did not involve an anonymous informant. On the contrary, as the Court twice noted, Mr. Hereford was "employed for that purpose and [his] information had always been found accurate and reliable." In this case, the police had no prior experience with the informant, and some of his or her information in this case was unreliable and inaccurate.

[8] The Court holds that what were heretofore considered two independent "prongs" — "veracity" and "basis of knowledge" — are now to be considered together as circumstances whose totality must be appraised. "A deficiency in one may be compensated for, in determining the overall reliability of a tip, by a strong showing as to the other, or by some other indicia of reliability." Yet in this case, the lower

Supreme Court and remand the case for reconsideration in the light of our intervening decision in *United States v. Ross*, 476 U.S. 798 (1982).

QUESTIONS AND NOTES

1. Of the four opinions, two (Rehnquist and Stevens) would discard *Spinelli*, and two (White and Brennan) would retain it. One of each group found probable cause in *Gates* (Rehnquist and White), and one of each group found no probable cause (Brennan and Stevens). Does this breakdown suggest that whether to retain *Spinelli* is much ado about nothing?

2. Which of the four opinions (if any) would you have joined had you been on the Court? Why?

3. Do you agree with Justice Rehnquist's admonition that the most important job of a constitutional jurist is "to hold the balance true?" Which Justice do you think did the best job of that?

4. What does probable cause mean after *Gates*? Did it mean something different before *Gates*?

5. Does (should) probable cause mean more likely than not? Why? Why not?

6. Should *Draper* control *Gates*? Why? Why not?

7. Should anonymous (in the sense of unknown) informants be entitled to much weight in the probable cause determination? Would (should) the adoption of a test that severely circumscribed their weight be subject to criticism on that account?

8. If the magistrate had not found probable cause in *Gates*, what could the police have done? Does your answer suggest that a warrant should not have been issued in this case?

9. Are we more or less secure as a populace after *Gates* than we were before? Explain.

10. The breadth of the *Gates* decision is explored in *Upton*.

Author's Note: While teaching the *Gates* case, Professor David Harris (then at Toledo law School, now at the University of Pittsburgh Law School) suggested to his class that the case might make a great country song. Seizing on that invitation, one of his students, Kate Munger, wrote one. With her permission, here it is:

The Ballad of Lance and Susie

(Sung to the tune of "The Beverly Hillbillies" Theme Song)

Listen to a story 'bout Lance and Sue

---

courts found neither factor present. And the supposed "other indicia" in the affidavit take the form of activity that is not particularly remarkable. I do not understand how the Court can find that the "totality" so far exceeds the sum of its "circumstances."

Windy City kids who had a secret or two.
They didn't have to work, life just couldn't be better
'Til they were ratted out by an anonymous letter
Snitch, that is
Finger-pointin', betrayed

Well the next thing you know the detective tracked their flight
And the Sunshine State hosted our perps for the night.
Corroborated details, just like in the note
Enough to get a warrant that the magistrate wrote.
Too coincidental, that is,

Modus operandi
Well, Lance and Susie drove on home and didn't know
That the cops would soon be searchin' their happy bungalow.
Reefer in the trunk of their shiny Mercury
Sending Sue and Lance to the penitentiary.
Jail that is.

Hard time, orange pants.

Now the small Gates gang thought they might get off scot free
Cause the warrant was invalid to search their Mercury,
But the highest court shouted out a new decree,
The circumstances would be viewed in their totality.
Probable cause, that is
Case-by-case, big picture.

MASSACHUSETTS v. UPTON
466 U.S. 727 (1984)

Per Curiam.

Last Term, in *Gates*, we held that the Fourth Amendment's requirement of probable cause for the issuance of a warrant is to be applied, not according to a fixed and rigid formula, but rather in the light of the "totality of the circumstances" made known to the magistrate. We also emphasized that the task of a reviewing court is not to conduct a *de novo* determination of probable cause, but only to determine whether there is substantial evidence in the record supporting the magistrate's decision to issue the warrant. In this case, the Supreme Judicial Court of Massachusetts, interpreting the probable cause requirement of the Fourth Amendment to the United States Constitution, continued to rely on the approach set forth in cases such as *Aguilar* and *Spinelli*. Since this approach was rejected in *Gates*, we grant the petition for certiorari in this case and reverse the judgment of the Supreme Judicial Court.

At noon on September 11, 1980, Lt. Beland of the Yarmouth Police Department assisted in the execution of a search warrant for a motel room reserved by one Richard Kelleher at the Snug Harbor Motel in West Yarmouth. The search produced several items of identification, including credit cards, belonging to two persons whose homes had recently been burglarized. Other items taken in the burglaries, such as jewelry, silver and gold, were not found at the motel.

At 3:20 p.m. on the same day, Lt. Beland received a call from an unidentified female who told him that there was "a motor home full of stolen stuff" parked behind # 5 Jefferson Ave., the home of respondent George Upton and his mother. She stated that the stolen items included jewelry, silver and gold. As set out in Lt. Beland's affidavit in support of a search warrant:

"She further stated that George Upton was going to move the motor home any time now because of the fact that Ricky Kelleher's motel room was raided and that George Upton had purchased these stolen items from Ricky Kelleher. This unidentified female stated that she had seen the stolen items but refused to identify herself because 'he'll kill me,' referring to George Upton. I then told this unidentified female that I knew who she was, giving her the name of Lynn Alberico, who I had met on May 16, 1980, at George Upton's repair shop off Summer St., in Yarmouthport. She was identified to me by George Upton as being his girlfriend, Lynn Alberico. The unidentified female admitted that she was the girl that I had named, stating that she was surprised that I knew who she was. She then told me that she'd broken up with George Upton and wanted to burn him. She also told me that she wouldn't give me her address or phone number but that she would contact me in the future, if need be."

Following the phone call, Lt. Beland went to Upton's house to verify that a motor home was parked on the property. Then, while other officers watched the premises, Lt. Beland prepared the application for a search warrant, setting out all the information noted above in an accompanying affidavit. He also attached the police reports on the two prior burglaries, along with lists of the stolen property. A magistrate issued the warrant, and a subsequent search of the motor home produced the items described by the caller and other incriminating evidence. The discovered evidence led to Upton's conviction on multiple counts of burglary, receiving stolen property, and related crimes. On appeal to the Supreme Judicial Court, respondent argued that the search warrant was not supported by a sufficient showing of "probable cause" under the Fourth Amendment. With respect to our *Gates* opinion, that court said:

"It is not clear that the *Gates* opinion has announced a significant change in the appropriate Fourth Amendment treatment of applications for search warrants. Looking at what the Court did on the facts before it, and rejecting an expansive view of certain general statements not essential to the decision, we conclude that the *Gates* opinion deals principally with what corroboration of an informant's tip, not adequate by itself, will be sufficient to meet probable cause standards."

Prior to *Gates*, the Fourth Amendment was understood by many courts to require strict satisfaction of a "two-pronged test" whenever an affidavit supporting the issuance of a search warrant relies on an informant's tip. It was thought that the affidavit, first, must establish the "basis of knowledge" of the informant — the particular means by which he came by the information given in his report; and, second, that it must provide facts establishing either the general "veracity" of the informant or the specific "reliability" of his report in the particular case. The Massachusetts court apparently viewed *Gates* as merely adding a new wrinkle to this two-pronged test: where an informant's veracity and/or basis of knowledge are not sufficiently clear, substantial corroboration of the tip may save an otherwise invalid warrant.

"We do not view the *Gates* opinion as decreeing a standardless 'totality of the circumstances' test. The informant's veracity and the basis of his knowledge are still important but, where the tip is adequately corroborated, they are not elements indispensible [sic] to a finding of probable cause. It seems that, in a given case, the corroboration may be so strong as to satisfy probable cause in the absence of any other showing of the informant's 'veracity' and any direct statement of the 'basis of [his] knowledge.' "

Turning to the facts of this case, the Massachusetts court reasoned, first, that the basis of the informant's knowledge was not "forcefully apparent" in the affidavit. Although the caller stated that she had seen the stolen items and that they were in the motor home, she did not specifically state that she saw them in the motor home. Second, the court concluded that "[n]one of the common bases for determining the credibility of an informant or the reliability of her information is present here." The caller was not a "tried and true" informant, her statement was not against penal interest, and she was not an "ordinary citizen" providing information as a witness to a crime. "She was an anonymous informant, and her unverified assent to the suggestion that she was Lynn Alberico does not take her out of that category."

Finally, the court felt that there was insufficient corroboration of the informant's tip to make up for its failure to satisfy the two-pronged test. The facts that tended to corroborate the informant's story were that the motor home was where it was supposed to be, that the caller knew of the motel raid which took place only three hours earlier, and that the caller knew the name of Upton and his girlfriend. But, much as the Supreme Court of Illinois did in the opinion we reviewed in *Gates*, the Massachusetts court reasoned that each item of corroborative evidence either related to innocent, nonsuspicious conduct or related to an event that took place in public. To sustain the warrant, the court concluded, more substantial corroboration was needed. The court therefore held that the warrant violated the Fourth Amendment to the United States Constitution and reversed respondent's convictions.

We think that the Supreme Judicial Court of Massachusetts misunderstood our decision in *Gates*. We did not merely refine or qualify the "two-pronged test." We rejected it as hypertechnical and divorced from "the factual and practical considerations of everyday life on which reasonable and prudent men, not legal technicians, act." Our statement on that score was explicit. "[W]e conclude that it is wiser to abandon the 'two-pronged test' established by our decisions in *Aguilar* and *Spinelli*. In its place we reaffirm the totality of the circumstances analysis that traditionally has informed probable cause determinations." *Gates*. This "totality of the circumstances" analysis is more in keeping with the "practical, common-sense decision" demanded of the magistrate.

We noted in *Gates* that "the 'two-pronged test' has encouraged an excessively technical dissection of informants' tips, with undue attention being focused on isolated issues that cannot sensibly be divorced from the other facts presented to the magistrate." This, we think, is the error of the Massachusetts court in this case. The court did not consider Lt. Beland's affidavit in its entirety, giving significance to each relevant piece of information and balancing the relative weights of all the various indicia of reliability (and unreliability) attending the tip. Instead, the court insisted on judging bits and pieces of information in isolation against the artificial standards provided by the two-pronged test.

The Supreme Judicial Court also erred in failing to grant any deference to the decision of the magistrate to issue a warrant. Instead of merely deciding whether the evidence viewed as a whole provided a "substantial basis" for the magistrate's finding of probable cause, the court conducted a *de novo* probable cause determination. We rejected just such after-the-fact, *de novo* scrutiny in *Gates*.

Examined in light of *Gates*, Lt. Beland's affidavit provides a substantial basis for the issuance of the warrant. No single piece of evidence in it is conclusive. But the pieces fit neatly together and, so viewed, support the magistrate's determination that there was "a fair probability that contraband or evidence of crime" would be found in Upton's motor home. The informant claimed to have seen the stolen goods and gave a description of them which tallied with the items taken in recent burglaries. She knew of the raid on the motel room — which produced evidence connected to those burglaries — and that the room had been reserved by Kelleher. She explained the connection between Kelleher's motel room and the stolen goods in Upton's motor home. And she provided a motive both for her attempt at anonymity — fear of Upton's retaliation — and for furnishing the information — her recent breakup with Upton and her desire "to burn him."

The Massachusetts court dismissed Lt. Beland's identification of the caller as a mere "unconfirmed guess." But "probable cause does not demand the certainty we associate with formal trials." Lt. Beland noted that the caller "admitted that she was the girl I had named, stating that she was surprised that I knew who she was." It is of course possible that the caller merely adopted Lt. Beland's suggestion as "a convenient cover for her true identity." But given the caller's admission, her obvious knowledge of who Alberico was and how she was connected with Upton, and her explanation of her motive in calling, Lt. Beland's inference appears stronger than a mere uninformed and unconfirmed guess. It is enough that the inference was a reasonable one and conformed with the other pieces of evidence making up the total showing of probable cause.

In concluding that there was probable cause for the issuance of this warrant, the magistrate can hardly be accused of approving a mere "hunch" or a bare recital of legal conclusions. The informant's story and the surrounding facts possessed an internal coherence that gave weight to the whole. Accordingly, we conclude that the information contained in Lt. Beland's affidavit provided a sufficient basis for the "practical, common-sense decision" of the magistrate. "Although in a particular case it may not be easy to determine when an affidavit demonstrates the existence of probable cause, the resolution of doubtful or marginal cases in this area should be largely determined by the preference to be accorded warrants."

The judgment of the Supreme Judicial Court of Massachusetts is reversed, and the case is remanded for further proceedings not inconsistent with this opinion.

JUSTICE STEVENS, concurring in the judgment.

In my opinion the judgment of the Supreme Judicial Court of Massachusetts reflects an error of a more fundamental character than the one this Court corrects today. It rested its decision on the Fourth Amendment to the United States Constitution without telling us whether the warrant was valid as a matter of Massachusetts law.[1] It has thereby increased its own burdens as well as ours. For when the case returns to that court, it must then review the probable cause issue once again and decide whether or not a violation of the state constitutional protection against unreasonable searches and seizures has occurred. If such a violation did take place, much of that court's first opinion and all of this Court's opinion are for naught. If no such violation occurred, the second proceeding in that court could have been avoided by a ruling to that effect when the case was there a year ago.

It must be remembered that for the first century of this nation's history, the Bill of Rights of the Constitution of the United States was solely a protection for the individual in relation to federal authorities. State constitutions protected the liberties of the people of the several States from abuse by state authorities. The Bill of Rights is now largely applicable to state authorities and is the ultimate guardian of individual rights. The States in our federal system, however, remain the primary guardian of the liberty of the people. The Massachusetts court, I believe, ignored this fundamental premise of our constitutional system of government. In doing so, it made an ill-advised entry into the federal domain.

Accordingly, I concur in the Court's judgment.

JUSTICE BRENNAN and JUSTICE MARSHALL dissent from the summary disposition of this case and would deny the petition for certiorari.

QUESTIONS AND NOTES

1. Was *Upton* a stronger or weaker case for probable cause than *Gates*?

2. Was the potential mobility of the motor home a factor in finding probable cause? Should it have been?

3. Was the fact that the caller claimed to want to "burn" George, a point in favor of or against the finding of probable cause?

4. As we shall now see, *Upton* was ultimately resolved in accordance with

---

[1] Indeed, that court rather pointedly refused to consider whether the search violated the provisions of Art. 14 of the Massachusetts Declaration of Rights. It stated, in part:

"If we have correctly construed the significance of *Gates*, the Fourth Amendment standards for determining probable cause to issue a search warrant have not been made so much less clear and so relaxed as to compel us to try our hand at a definition of standards under art. 14. If we have misassessed the consequences of the *Gates* opinion and in fact the *Gates* standard proves to be unacceptably shapeless and permissive, this court may have to define the protections guaranteed to the people against unreasonable searches and seizures by art. 14, and the consequences of the violation of those protections."

Justice Stevens suggestion: the State Constitution. Although *Upton* presents us with our first opportunity to consider state constitutions or state laws as providing more protection than the Federal Constitution, it is a possibility that no good defense attorney should overlook and of which no good prosecutor should be unaware. Indeed, as Justice Stevens suggested, perhaps it should be the first resort of state courts and defense attorneys.

COMMONWEALTH v. UPTON
476 N.E.2d 548 (Mass. 1985)

WILKINS, JUSTICE.

We consider the defendant's State law challenges to the denial of his motions to suppress evidence seized pursuant to a search warrant. When this case was before us for the first time, we concluded that the search was unreasonable in violation of the Fourth Amendment to the Constitution of the United States because there was no demonstrated probable cause to issue the search warrant. In a per curiam opinion, the Supreme Court of the United States reversed our judgment, concluding that there was a proper showing of probable cause under the "totality of the circumstances" test articulated in *Gates*. The Supreme Court remanded the case to us for further proceedings consistent with its opinion.

We must now consider what standard art. 14 of the Declaration of Rights of the Constitution of the Commonwealth prescribes for determining the existence of probable cause.[6] We have equated the word "cause" in art. 14 with the words "probable cause." *Commonwealth v. Dana*, 2 Met. 329 (1841). In each case, the basic question for the magistrate is whether he has a substantial basis for concluding that any of the articles described in the warrant are probably in the place to be searched. Strong reason to suspect is not adequate.[7] Concerning search warrants for allegedly stolen property, we have said that the affidavit must "contain enough information for an issuing magistrate to determine that the items sought are related to the criminal activity under investigation, and that they reasonably may be expected to be located in the place to be searched."

The Commonwealth argues that art. 14 requires no more than is required by the Fourth Amendment as construed and implemented by the Supreme Court of the United States in *Gates* and *Upton*. By this view, the question whether probable cause exists is to be determined according to the "totality of the circumstances." The defendant, on the other hand, urges us to express a stricter standard for the determination of probable cause, specifically arguing that under art. 14 we should

---

[6] Article 14 provides: "Every subject has a right to be secure from all unreasonable searches, and seizures, of his person, his houses, his papers, and all his possessions. All warrants, therefore, are contrary to this right, if the cause or foundation of them be not previously supported by oath or affirmation; and if the order in the warrant to a civil officer, to make search in suspected places, or to arrest one or more suspected persons, or to seize their property, be not accompanied with a special designation of the persons or objects of search, arrest, or seizure: and no warrant ought to be issued but in cases, and with the formalities prescribed by the laws."

[7] We do not know whether the Supreme Court of the United States intended a lower definition of probable cause when in *Gates*, it used words such as "fair probability" and "substantial chance."

require a showing similar to that required by the Supreme Court of the United States before its adoption of the "flexible" standard of the *Gates* case.

This court has understandably had little occasion to determine what art. 14 requires be shown to a magistrate in order to constitute probable cause. As our earlier discussion shows, Massachusetts has not had an exclusionary rule as part of its common law or under art. 14, and, consequently, there has been little incentive for defendants to challenge the existence of probable cause on State common law or constitutional grounds. When the Fourth Amendment became applicable to the States through the Fourteenth Amendment, the battle over the existence of probable cause to issue a warrant came to be fought on Federal constitutional turf. Defendants simply raised the Federal issues to the substantial exclusion of arguments based on the State law.

As a practical matter, therefore, cases involving probable cause questions did not call for consideration of any State constitutional question. Nor did our earlier opinion in this case appear to call for such a consideration. There we erroneously concluded that the Federal constitutional principles expressed in *Gates* required the exclusion of the seized evidence. We simply failed to perceive that the Supreme Court could permit a test for probable cause as " 'flexible' and 'easily applied' " as the fluid *Gates* standard has turned out to be.

The Constitution of the Commonwealth preceded and is independent of the Constitution of the United States. In fact, portions of the Constitution of the United States are based on provisions in the Constitution of the Commonwealth, and this has been thought to be particularly true of the relationship between the Fourth Amendment and art. 14. In particular situations, on similar facts, we have reached different results under the State Constitution from those that were reached by the Supreme Court of the United States under the Federal Constitution. On occasion, the differences can be explained because of different language in the two Constitutions. On the other hand, in deciding similar constitutional questions, the two courts have reached contrary results based on differences of opinion concerning the application of similar constitutional principles.

Although we have never afforded more substantive protection to criminal defendants under art. 14 of the Declaration of Rights than prevails under the Constitution of the United States, on several occasions we have recognized the possibility of doing so. [W]e have had no appropriate occasion to consider what standard of probable cause is required by art. 14.

We conclude that art. 14 provides more substantive protection to criminal defendants than does the Fourth Amendment in the determination of probable cause. We reject the "totality of the circumstances" test now espoused by a majority of the United States Supreme Court. That standard is flexible, but is also "unacceptably shapeless and permissive." The Federal test lacks the precision that we believe can and should be articulated in stating a test for determining probable cause. The "totality of the circumstances" test is used in deciding several constitutional questions, but it has been applied where no more definite, universal standard could reasonably be developed.

In the area of probable cause to issue a search warrant, specific and worthwhile standards can be articulated, as opinions of the Supreme Court prior to *Gates* have demonstrated. "Clear lines defining constitutionally permissible conduct are most desirable to guide the police, magistrates, prosecutors, defense counsel, and judges." We thus reject the "totality of the circumstances" test as the appropriate standard for determining that probable cause which must be shown under art. 14.

We conclude instead that the principles developed under *Aguilar* and *Spinelli*, if not applied hypertechnically, provide a more appropriate structure for probable cause inquiries under art. 14. Under the *Aguilar-Spinelli* standard, if an affidavit is based on information from an unknown informant, the magistrate must "be informed of (1) some of the underlying circumstances from which the informant concluded that the contraband was where he claimed it was (the basis of knowledge test), and (2) some of the underlying circumstances from which the affiant concluded that the informant was 'credible' or his information 'reliable' (the veracity test). If the informant's tip does not satisfy each aspect of the *Aguilar* test, other allegations in the affidavit that corroborate the information could support a finding of probable cause."

Each prong of the *Aguilar-Spinelli* test — the basis of knowledge and the veracity of the informant — presents an independently important consideration. We have said that independent police corroboration can make up for deficiencies in either or both prongs of the *Aguilar-Spinelli* test. We reiterate today, however, that each element of the test must be separately considered and satisfied or supplemented in some way.

The test we adopt has been followed successfully by the police in this Commonwealth for approximately twenty years. It is a test that aids lay people, such as the police and certain magistrates, in a way that the "totality of the circumstances" test never could. We believe it has encouraged and will continue to encourage more careful police work and thus will tend to reduce the number of unreasonable searches conducted in violation of art. 14. We reject the argument that the higher standard will cause police to avoid seeking search warrants. We have no sense, and certainly we have no factual support for the proposition, that in recent years police in this Commonwealth have risked conducting warrantless searches because of the unreasonable strictures of the *Aguilar-Spinelli* test.

We also do not believe that the *Aguilar-Spinelli* test has interfered or will interfere with the deference that a reviewing court should show to the issuing magistrate's determination. "Once a magistrate has determined that he has information before him that he can reasonably say has been obtained in a reliable way by a credible person, he has ample room to use his common sense and to apply a practical, nontechnical conception of probable cause." In this Commonwealth, we have always urged reviewing courts to "be slow to jettison" warrants which exhibit such a commonsense approach.

Finally, we note that the number of cases in which evidence has been suppressed because of a failure to follow the requirements of the *Aguilar-Spinelli* test has not been substantial in relation to the number of challenges made to the adequacy of applications for search warrants. And, of course, there is no way to document the salutary circumstance that numerous unreasonable searches were never made because of the application of the *Aguilar-Spinelli* test. We conclude, therefore, that the *Aguilar-Spinelli* test, as modified by our earlier decision in this case, is the standard for determining probable cause under art. 14.

Probable cause in this case.

Pursuant to the appropriate standard, we must undertake an analysis of the affidavit presented in support of the warrant to search the motor home. We apply the *Aguilar-Spinelli* standard, with the modification we thought had been made in the *Gates* opinion. We also acknowledge that our attitude is not and should not be a grudging or negative one and that we should give great deference to the magistrate's determination of probable cause. We grant that the question is a close one.

Probable cause was not shown on the affidavit in this case. In our earlier opinion we concluded that the basis of the informant's knowledge was narrowly established, even though the reason why she believed the stolen property to be in the motor home was not presented. The veracity of the informant, however, was not shown. Anyone who might conclude that the veracity of the informant was demonstrated would have to place substantial credence in the unknown informant's uncorroborated statements as self-verifying. To paraphrase our earlier opinion, "[i]f the affidavit in the case before us were to be upheld, [art. 14 of the Declaration of Rights] would be weakened to the level of permitting the search of any person's premises based on a telephone tip from an anonymous informer who told a story connecting those premises with the fact of a recent police search of a third person's room on premises to which the public had access." The probability of a link between the search of the motel room and the motor home was not shown, as it could have been if other information known to the police had been set forth in the affidavit (particularly the fact that a wallet containing identification of Upton's wife had been found in the motel room).

Conclusion.

In our earlier opinion, we noted that, apart from the evidence seized from the motor home, "there was other evidence to support the defendant's conviction on at least some of the charges against him." The case is, therefore, remanded to the Superior Court subject to the same orders that we previously entered.

QUESTIONS AND NOTES

1.   Is there anything in the language of the two constitutional provisions (Mass. & U.S.) that warrants a different result?

2.   Is the fact that the Massachusetts Constitution predated the U.S. Constitution relevant to the resolution of the case? Suppose the Massachusetts provision had been adopted in 1900? In 1980?

3.   Is the Massachusetts Supreme Court essentially thumbing its nose at the U.S. Supreme Court? Is that anyway for a state court to act? Explain your thinking fully.

4. We continue this section with *Maryland v. Pringle*.

MARYLAND v. PRINGLE
540 U.S. 366 (2003)

CHIEF JUSTICE REHNQUIST delivered the opinion of the Court.

At 3:16 a.m. on August 7, 1999, a Baltimore County Police officer stopped a Nissan Maxima for speeding. There were three occupants in the car: Donte Partlow, the driver and owner, respondent Pringle, the front-seat passenger, and Otis Smith, the back-seat passenger. The officer asked Partlow for his license and registration. When Partlow opened the glove compartment to retrieve the vehicle registration, the officer observed a large amount of rolled-up money in the glove compartment. The officer returned to his patrol car with Partlow's license and registration to check the computer system for outstanding violations. The computer check did not reveal any violations. The officer returned to the stopped car, had Partlow get out, and issued him an oral warning.

After a second patrol car arrived, the officer asked Partlow if he had any weapons or narcotics in the vehicle. Partlow indicated that he did not. Partlow then consented to a search of the vehicle. The search yielded $763 from the glove compartment and five plastic glassine baggies containing cocaine from behind the back-seat armrest. When the officer began the search the armrest was in the upright position flat against the rear seat. The officer pulled down the armrest and found the drugs, which had been placed between the armrest and the back seat of the car.

The officer questioned all three men about the ownership of the drugs and money, and told them that if no one admitted to ownership of the drugs he was going to arrest them all. The men offered no information regarding the ownership of the drugs or money. All three were placed under arrest and transported to the police station.

Later that morning, Pringle waived his rights under *Miranda v. Arizona*, 384 U.S. 436 (1966), and gave an oral and written confession in which he acknowledged that the cocaine belonged to him, that he and his friends were going to a party, and that he intended to sell the cocaine or "[u]se it for sex." Pringle maintained that the other occupants of the car did not know about the drugs, and they were released.

The trial court denied Pringle's motion to suppress his confession as the fruit of an illegal arrest, holding that the officer had probable cause to arrest Pringle. A jury convicted Pringle of possession with intent to distribute cocaine and possession of cocaine. He was sentenced to 10 years' incarceration without the possibility of parole.

The Court of Appeals of Maryland, by divided vote, reversed, holding that, absent specific facts tending to show Pringle's knowledge and dominion or control over the drugs, "the mere finding of cocaine in the back armrest when [Pringle] was a front seat passenger in a car being driven by its owner is insufficient to establish probable cause for an arrest for possession." We granted certiorari, and now reverse.

Under the Fourth Amendment the people are "to be secure in their persons, houses, papers, and effects, against unreasonable searches and seizures, . . . and no Warrants shall issue, but upon probable cause . . . ." U.S. Const., Amdt. 4. Maryland law authorizes police officers to execute warrantless arrests, *inter alia*, for felonies committed in an officer's presence or where an officer has probable cause to believe that a felony has been committed or is being committed in the officer's presence. A warrantless arrest of an individual in a public place for a felony, or a misdemeanor committed in the officer's presence, is consistent with the Fourth Amendment if the arrest is supported by probable cause.

It is uncontested in the present case that the officer, upon recovering the five plastic glassine baggies containing suspected cocaine, had probable cause to believe a felony had been committed. The sole question is whether the officer had probable cause to believe that Pringle committed that crime.[8]

The long-prevailing standard of probable cause protects "citizens from rash and unreasonable interferences with privacy and from unfounded charges of crime," while giving "fair leeway for enforcing the law in the community's protection." *Brinegar*. On many occasions, we have reiterated that the probable-cause standard is a " 'practical, nontechnical conception' " that deals with " 'the factual and practical considerations of everyday life on which reasonable and prudent men, not legal technicians, act.' " *Illinois v. Gates*. "[P]robable cause is a fluid concept — turning on the assessment of probabilities in particular factual contexts — not readily, or even usefully, reduced to a neat set of legal rules." *Gates*.

The probable-cause standard is incapable of precise definition or quantification into percentages because it deals with probabilities and depends on the totality of the circumstances. We have stated, however, that "[t]he substance of all the definitions of probable cause is a reasonable ground for belief of guilt" and that the belief of guilt must be particularized with respect to the person to be searched or seized. In *Gates*, we noted:

"As early as *Locke v. United States*, 3 L. Ed. 364, 7 Cranch 339, 348 (1813), Chief Justice Marshall observed, in a closely related context: '[T]he term "probable cause," according to its usual acceptation, means less than evidence which would justify condemnation . . . . It imports a seizure made under circumstances which warrant suspicion.' More recently, we said that 'the *quanta* . . . of proof' appropriate in ordinary judicial proceedings are inapplicable to the decision to issue a warrant. *Brinegar*. Finely tuned standards such as proof beyond a reasonable doubt or by a preponderance of the evidence, useful in formal trials, have no place in the [probable-cause] decision."

To determine whether an officer had probable cause to arrest an individual, we examine the events leading up to the arrest, and then decide "whether these historical facts, viewed from the standpoint of an objectively reasonable police officer, amount to" probable cause.

---

[8] Maryland law defines "possession" as "the exercise of actual or constructive dominion or control over a thing by one or more persons."

In this case, Pringle was one of three men riding in a Nissan Maxima at 3:16 a.m. There was $763 of rolled-up cash in the glove compartment directly in front of Pringle.[9] Five plastic glassine baggies of cocaine were behind the back-seat armrest and accessible to all three men. Upon questioning, the three men failed to offer any information with respect to the ownership of the cocaine or the money.

We think it an entirely reasonable inference from these facts that any or all three of the occupants had knowledge of, and exercised dominion and control over, the cocaine. Thus a reasonable officer could conclude that there was probable cause to believe Pringle committed the crime of possession of cocaine, either solely or jointly.

Pringle's attempt to characterize this case as a guilt-by-association case is unavailing. His reliance on *Ybarra v. Illinois* and *United States v. Di Re* is misplaced. In *Ybarra*, police officers obtained a warrant to search a tavern and its bartender for evidence of possession of a controlled substance. Upon entering the tavern, the officers conducted patdown searches of the customers present in the tavern, including Ybarra. Inside a cigarette pack retrieved from Ybarra's pocket, an officer found six tinfoil packets containing heroin. We stated:

"[A] person's mere propinquity to others independently suspected of criminal activity does not, without more, give rise to probable cause to search that person. Where the standard is probable cause, a search or seizure of a person must be supported by probable cause particularized with respect to that person. This requirement cannot be undercut or avoided by simply pointing to the fact that coincidentally there exists probable cause to search or seize another or to search the premises where the person may happen to be."

We held that the search warrant did not permit body searches of all of the tavern's patrons and that the police could not pat down the patrons for weapons, absent individualized suspicion.

This case is quite different from *Ybarra*. Pringle and his two companions were in a relatively small automobile, not a public tavern. In *Wyoming v. Houghton*, 526 U.S. 295 (1999), we noted that "a car passenger — unlike the unwitting tavern patron in *Ybarra* — will often be engaged in a common enterprise with the driver, and have the same interest in concealing the fruits or the evidence of their wrongdoing." Here we think it was reasonable for the officer to infer a common enterprise among the three men. The quantity of drugs and cash in the car indicated the likelihood of drug dealing, an enterprise to which a dealer would be unlikely to admit an innocent person with the potential to furnish evidence against him.

In *Di Re*, a federal investigator had been told by an informant, Reed, that he was to receive counterfeit gasoline ration coupons from a certain Buttitta at a particular place. The investigator went to the appointed place and saw Reed, the sole occupant

---

[9] The Court of Appeals of Maryland dismissed the $763 seized from the glove compartment as a factor in the probable-cause determination, stating that "[m]oney, without more, is innocuous." The court's consideration of the money in isolation, rather than as a factor in the totality of the circumstances, is mistaken in light of our precedents. We think it is abundantly clear from the facts that this case involves more than money alone.

of the rear seat of the car, holding gasoline ration coupons. There were two other occupants in the car: Buttitta in the driver's seat and Di Re in the front passenger's seat. Reed informed the investigator that Buttitta had given him counterfeit coupons. Thereupon, all three men were arrested and searched. After noting that the officers had no information implicating Di Re and no information pointing to Di Re's possession of coupons, unless presence in the car warranted that inference, we concluded that the officer lacked probable cause to believe that Di Re was involved in the crime. We said "[a]ny inference that everyone on the scene of a crime is a party to it must disappear if the Government informer singles out the guilty person." No such singling out occurred in this case; none of the three men provided information with respect to the ownership of the cocaine or money.

We hold that the officer had probable cause to believe that Pringle had committed the crime of possession of a controlled substance. Pringle's arrest therefore did not contravene the Fourth and Fourteenth Amendments. Accordingly, the judgment of the Court of Appeals of Maryland is reversed, and the case is remanded for further proceedings not inconsistent with this opinion.

QUESTIONS AND NOTES

1. What was the probability that Pringle possessed drugs? Was it greater than 50%? Greater than 25%? Explain. How great should the probability be?

2. Was it less probable that Pringle possessed drugs than that Partlow possessed them? What about Smith? Assuming that it was more probable that either Partlow or Smith possessed the drugs, was *Pringle* necessarily wrongly decided? Why? Why not?

3. Should the cash in the glove compartment have been relevant in assessing probable cause? Why? Why not?

4. Was it fair to infer a common enterprise among the three men? Is it relevant that in fact, only Pringle was connected to the drugs and the others were innocent?

5. How did the Court distinguish *Di Re*? Do you find the distinction persuasive? Explain.

6. We conclude this section with *Florida v. Harris*, the Supreme Court's most recent exegesis on probable cause.

FLORIDA v. HARRIS
568 U.S. ___, 133 S. Ct. 1050 (2013)

JUSTICE KAGAN delivered the opinion of the Court.

In this case, we consider how a court should determine if the "alert" of a drug-detection dog during a traffic stop provides probable cause to search a vehicle. The Florida Supreme Court held that the State must in every case present an exhaustive set of records, including a log of the dog's performance in the field, to establish the dog's reliability. We think that demand inconsistent with the "flexible, common-sense standard" of probable cause. *Illinois v. Gates.*

I

William Wheetley is a K-9 Officer in the Liberty County, Florida Sheriff's Office. On June 24, 2006, he was on a routine patrol with Aldo, a German shepherd trained to detect certain narcotics (methamphetamine, marijuana, cocaine, heroin, and ecstasy). Wheetley pulled over respondent Clayton Harris's truck because it had an expired license plate. On approaching the driver's-side door, Wheetley saw that Harris was "visibly nervous," unable to sit still, shaking, and breathing rapidly. Wheetley also noticed an open can of beer in the truck's cup holder. Wheetley asked Harris for consent to search the truck, but Harris refused. At that point, Wheetley retrieved Aldo from the patrol car and walked him around Harris's truck for a "free air sniff." Aldo alerted at the driver's-side door handle — signaling, through a distinctive set of behaviors, that he smelled drugs there.

Wheetley concluded, based principally on Aldo's alert, that he had probable cause to search the truck. His search did not turn up any of the drugs Aldo was trained to detect. But it did reveal 200 loose pseudoephedrine pills, 8,000 matches, a bottle of hydrochloric acid, two containers of antifreeze, and a coffee filter full of iodine crystals — all ingredients for making methamphetamine. Wheetley accordingly arrested Harris, who admitted after proper *Miranda* warnings that he routinely "cooked" methamphetamine at his house and could not go "more than a few days without using" it. State charged Harris with possessing pseudoephedrine for use in manufacturing methamphetamine.

While out on bail, Harris had another run-in with Wheetley and Aldo. This time, Wheetley pulled Harris over for a broken brake light. Aldo again sniffed the truck's exterior, and again alerted at the driver's-side door handle. Wheetley once more searched the truck, but on this occasion discovered nothing of interest.

Harris moved to suppress the evidence found in his truck on the ground that Aldo's alert had not given Wheetley probable cause for a search. At the hearing on that motion, Wheetley testified about both his and Aldo's training in drug detection. In 2004, Wheetley (and a different dog) completed a 160-hour course in narcotics detection offered by the Dothan, Alabama Police Department, while Aldo (and a different handler) completed a similar, 120-hour course given by the Apopka, Florida Police Department. That same year, Aldo received a one-year certification from Drug Beat, a private company that specializes in testing and certifying K-9 dogs. Wheetley and Aldo teamed up in 2005 and went through another, 40-hour refresher course in Dothan together. They also did four hours of training exercises each week to maintain their skills. Wheetley would hide drugs in certain vehicles or buildings while leaving others "blank" to determine whether Aldo alerted at the right places. According to Wheetley, Aldo's performance in those exercises was "really good." The State introduced "Monthly Canine Detection Training Logs" consistent with that testimony: They showed that Aldo always found hidden drugs and that he performed "satisfactorily" (the higher of two possible assessments) on each day of training.

On cross-examination, Harris's attorney chose not to contest the quality of Aldo's or Wheetley's training. She focused instead on Aldo's certification and his performance in the field, particularly the two stops of Harris's truck. Wheetley conceded that the certification (which, he noted, Florida law did not require) had expired the year before he pulled Harris over. Wheetley also acknowledged that he did not keep complete records of Aldo's performance in traffic stops or other field work; instead, he maintained records only of alerts resulting in arrests. But Wheetley defended Aldo's two alerts to Harris's seemingly narcotics-free truck: According to Wheetley, Harris probably transferred the odor of methamphetamine to the door handle, and Aldo responded to that "residual odor."

The trial court concluded that Wheetley had probable cause to search Harris's truck and so denied the motion to suppress. Harris then entered a no-contest plea while reserving the right to appeal the trial court's ruling. An intermediate state court summarily affirmed.

The Florida Supreme Court reversed, holding that Wheetley lacked probable cause to search Harris's vehicle under the Fourth Amendment. "[W]hen a dog alerts," the court wrote, "the fact that the dog has been trained and certified is simply not enough to establish probable cause." To demonstrate a dog's reliability, the State needed to produce a wider array of evidence:

> "[T]he State must present . . . the dog's training and certification records, an explanation of the meaning of the particular training and certification, field performance records (including any unverified alerts), and evidence concerning the experience and training of the officer handling the dog, as well as any other objective evidence known to the officer about the dog's reliability."

The court particularly stressed the need for "evidence of the dog's performance history," including records showing "how often the dog has alerted in the field without illegal contraband having been found." That data, the court stated, could help to expose such problems as a handler's tendency (conscious or not) to "cue [a] dog to alert" and "a dog's inability to distinguish between residual odors and actual drugs." Accordingly, an officer like Wheetley who did not keep full records of his dog's field performance could never have the requisite cause to think "that the dog is a reliable indicator of drugs."

Judge Canady dissented, maintaining that the majority's "elaborate and inflexible evidentiary requirements" went beyond the demands of probable cause. He would have affirmed the trial court's ruling on the strength of Aldo's training history and Harris's "fail[ure] to present any evidence challenging" it.

We granted certiorari, and now reverse.

II

A police officer has probable cause to conduct a search when "the facts available to [him] would 'warrant a [person] of reasonable caution in the belief'" that contraband or evidence of a crime is present. The test for probable cause is not reducible to "precise definition or quantification." *Maryland v. Pringle*. "Finely tuned standards such as proof beyond a reasonable doubt or by a preponderance of the evidence . . . have no place in the [probable-cause] decision." *Gates*. All we have required is the kind of "fair probability" on which "reasonable and prudent [people,] not legal technicians, act."

In evaluating whether the State has met this practical and common-sensical standard, we have consistently looked to the totality of the circumstances. See, *e.g.*, *Pringle, Gates*, and *Brinegares*. We have rejected rigid rules, bright-line tests, and mechanistic inquiries in favor of a more flexible, all-things-considered approach. In *Gates*, for example, we abandoned our old test for assessing the reliability of informants' tips because it had devolved into a "complex superstructure of evidentiary and analytical rules," any one of which, if not complied with, would derail a finding of probable cause. 462 U.S., at 235. We lamented the development of a list of "inflexible, independent requirements applicable in every case." Probable cause, we emphasized, is "a fluid concept — turning on the assessment of probabilities in particular factual contexts — not readily, or even usefully, reduced to a neat set of legal rules." *Id.*, at 232.

The Florida Supreme Court flouted this established approach to determining probable cause. To assess the reliability of a drug-detection dog, the court created a strict evidentiary checklist, whose every item the State must tick off.[1] Most prominently, an alert cannot establish probable cause under the Florida court's decision unless the State introduces comprehensive documentation of the dog's prior "hits" and "misses" in the field. (One wonders how the court would apply its test to a rookie dog.) No matter how much other proof the State offers of the dog's reliability, the absent field performance records will preclude a finding of probable cause. That is the antithesis of a totality-of-the-circumstances analysis. It is, indeed, the very thing we criticized in *Gates* when we overhauled our method for assessing the trustworthiness of an informant's tip. A gap as to any one matter, we explained, should not sink the State's case; rather, that "deficiency . . . may be compensated for, in determining the overall reliability of a tip, by a strong showing as to . . . other indicia of reliability." *Id.*, at 233. So too here, a finding of a drug-detection dog's reliability cannot depend on the State's satisfaction of multiple, independent evidentiary requirements. No more for dogs than for human informants is such an inflexible checklist the way to prove reliability, and thus establish probable cause.

Making matters worse, the decision below treats records of a dog's field performance as the gold standard in evidence, when in most cases they have relatively limited import. Errors may abound in such records. If a dog on patrol fails to alert to a car containing drugs, the mistake usually will go undetected because the officer will not initiate a search. Field data thus may not capture a dog's false negatives. Conversely (and more relevant here), if the dog alerts to a car in which the officer finds no narcotics, the dog may not have made a mistake at all. The dog may have detected substances that were too well hidden or present in quantities too small for the officer to locate. Or the dog may have smelled the residual odor of drugs previously in the vehicle or on the driver's person.[2] Field data thus may

---

[1] By the time of oral argument in this case, even Harris declined to defend the idea that the Fourth Amendment compels the State to produce each item of evidence the Florida Supreme Court enumerated. ("I don't believe the Constitution requires [that list]"). Harris instead argued that the court's decision, although "look[ing] rather didactic," in fact did not impose any such requirement. ("[I]t's not a specific recipe that can't be deviated from"). But in reading the decision below as establishing a mandatory checklist, we do no more than take the court at its (oft-repeated) word. See, *e.g.*, 71 So. 3d 756, 758, 759, 771, 775 (Fla. 2011) (holding that the State "must" present the itemized evidence).

[2] See U.S. Dept. of Army, Military Working Dog Program 30 (Pamphlet 190-12, 1993) ("The odor of

markedly overstate a dog's real false positives. By contrast, those inaccuracies — in either direction — do not taint records of a dog's performance in standard training and certification settings. There, the designers of an assessment know where drugs are hidden and where they are not — and so where a dog should alert and where he should not. The better measure of a dog's reliability thus comes away from the field, in controlled testing environments.

For that reason, evidence of a dog's satisfactory performance in a certification or training program can itself provide sufficient reason to trust his alert. If a bona fide organization has certified a dog after testing his reliability in a controlled setting, a court can presume (subject to any conflicting evidence offered) that the dog's alert provides probable cause to search. The same is true, even in the absence of formal certification, if the dog has recently and successfully completed a training program that evaluated his proficiency in locating drugs. After all, law enforcement units have their own strong incentive to use effective training and certification programs, because only accurate drug-detection dogs enable officers to locate contraband without incurring unnecessary risks or wasting limited time and resources.

A defendant, however, must have an opportunity to challenge such evidence of a dog's reliability, whether by cross-examining the testifying officer or by introducing his own fact or expert witnesses. The defendant, for example, may contest the adequacy of a certification or training program, perhaps asserting that its standards are too lax or its methods faulty. So too, the defendant may examine how the dog (or handler) performed in the assessments made in those settings. Indeed, evidence of the dog's (or handler's) history in the field, although susceptible to the kind of misinterpretation we have discussed, may sometimes be relevant, as the Solicitor General acknowledged at oral argument. ("[T]he defendant can ask the handler, if the handler is on the stand, about field performance, and then the court can give that answer whatever weight is appropriate"). And even assuming a dog is generally reliable, circumstances surrounding a particular alert may undermine the case for probable cause — if, say, the officer cued the dog (consciously or not), or if the team was working under unfamiliar conditions.

In short, a probable-cause hearing focusing on a dog's alert should proceed much like any other. The court should allow the parties to make their best case, consistent with the usual rules of criminal procedure. And the court should then evaluate the proffered evidence to decide what all the circumstances demonstrate. If the State has produced proof from controlled settings that a dog performs reliably in

---

a substance may be present in enough concentration to cause the dog to respond even after the substance has been removed. Therefore, when a detector dog responds and no drug or explosive is found, do not assume the dog has made an error"); S. Bryson, Police Dog Tactics 257 (2d ed. 2000) ("Four skiers toke up in the parking lot before going up the mountain. Five minutes later a narcotic detector dog alerts to the car. There is no dope inside. However, the dog has performed correctly"). The Florida Supreme Court treated a dog's response to residual odor as an error, referring to the "inability to distinguish between [such] odors and actual drugs" as a "facto[r] that call[s] into question Aldo's reliability." But that statement reflects a misunderstanding. A detection dog recognizes an odor, not a drug, and should alert whenever the scent is present, even if the substance is gone (just as a police officer's much inferior nose detects the odor of marijuana for some time after a joint has been smoked). In the usual case, the mere chance that the substance might no longer be at the location does not matter; a well-trained dog's alert establishes a fair probability — all that is required for probable cause — that either drugs or evidence of a drug crime (like the precursor chemicals in Harris's truck) will be found.

detecting drugs, and the defendant has not contested that showing, then the court should find probable cause. If, in contrast, the defendant has challenged the State's case (by disputing the reliability of the dog overall or of a particular alert), then the court should weigh the competing evidence. In all events, the court should not prescribe, as the Florida Supreme Court did, an inflexible set of evidentiary requirements. The question — similar to every inquiry into probable cause — is whether all the facts surrounding a dog's alert, viewed through the lens of common sense, would make a reasonably prudent person think that a search would reveal contraband or evidence of a crime. A sniff is up to snuff when it meets that test.

III

And here, Aldo's did. The record in this case amply supported the trial court's determination that Aldo's alert gave Wheetley probable cause to search Harris's truck.

The State, as earlier described, introduced substantial evidence of Aldo's training and his proficiency in finding drugs. The State showed that two years before alerting to Harris's truck, Aldo had successfully completed a 120-hour program in narcotics detection, and separately obtained a certification from an independent company. And although the certification expired after a year, the Sheriff's Office required continuing training for Aldo and Wheetley. The two satisfied the requirements of another, 40-hour training program one year prior to the search at issue. And Wheetley worked with Aldo for four hours each week on exercises designed to keep their skills sharp. Wheetley testified, and written records confirmed, that in those settings Aldo always performed at the highest level.

Harris, as also noted above, declined to challenge in the trial court any aspect of Aldo's training. To be sure, Harris's briefs in *this* Court raise questions about that training's adequacy — for example, whether the programs simulated sufficiently diverse environments and whether they used enough blind testing (in which the handler does not know the location of drugs and so cannot cue the dog). Similarly, Harris here queries just how well Aldo performed in controlled testing. But Harris never voiced those doubts in the trial court, and cannot do so for the first time here. As the case came to the trial court, Aldo had successfully completed two recent drug-detection courses and maintained his proficiency through weekly training exercises. Viewed alone, that training record — with or without the prior certification — sufficed to establish Aldo's reliability.

And Harris's cross-examination of Wheetley, which focused on Aldo's field performance, failed to rebut the State's case. Harris principally contended in the trial court that because Wheetley did not find any of the substances Aldo was trained to detect, Aldo's two alerts must have been false. But we have already described the hazards of inferring too much from the failure of a dog's alert to lead to drugs, and here we doubt that Harris's logic does justice to Aldo's skills. Harris cooked and used methamphetamine on a regular basis; so as Wheetley later surmised, Aldo likely responded to odors that Harris had transferred to the driver's-side door handle of his truck. A well-trained drug-detection dog *should* alert to such odors; his response to them might appear a mistake, but in fact is not.

And still more fundamentally, we do not evaluate probable cause in hindsight, based on what a search does or does not turn up. For the reasons already stated, Wheetley had good cause to view Aldo as a reliable detector of drugs. And no special circumstance here gave Wheetley reason to discount Aldo's usual dependability or distrust his response to Harris's truck.

Because training records established Aldo's reliability in detecting drugs and Harris failed to undermine that showing, we agree with the trial court that Wheetley had probable cause to search Harris's truck. We accordingly reverse the judgment of the Florida Supreme Court.

QUESTIONS AND NOTES

1.   How relevant to the question of probable cause was the dog's training?

2.   How relevant should it have been? If the dog can detect residual odors, wouldn't that mean that a car rented by a totally innocent person (such as a Supreme Court Justice or a Law Professor) could be stopped if the previous renter had used it to manufacture drugs?

3.   Should the Court have taken that possibility more seriously or was the Court fixated on the fact that Harris, a meth manufacturer, was the person caught?

4.   How would you have decided this case? Why?

Chapter 3

THE NEED FOR A WARRANT

In Chapter 1, we briefly examined the importance of having a Fourteenth Amendment that limits the power of the police. In Chapter 2, we examined probable cause which can be conceived as the substantive heart of the Fourth Amendment. In this chapter, our focus is on the need for a warrant which is procedurally what the fourth amendment is (sometimes) about.

The first question which we will address is the procedural value of requiring a warrant *before* a policeman commences a search. Before considering the cases, try to think of all of the values served by requiring a warrant.

A. IS THE WARRANT REQUIREMENT THE EXCEPTION OR THE RULE?

It is sometimes not easy to determine whether the Court requires a warrant subject to a limited number of exceptions, or whether it permits warrantless searches unless the particular search is singled out as one subject to the warrant requirement. *Vale*, *Chambers*, and *Chadwick* are three substantially contemporaneous efforts to deal with the problem. Understanding the Court's thinking in these cases is a good starting point for comprehending that which follows.

VALE v. LOUISIANA
399 U.S. 30 (1970)

Mr. Justice Stewart delivered the opinion of the Court.

The appellant, Donald Vale, was convicted in a Louisiana court on a charge of possessing heroin and was sentenced as a multiple offender to 15 years' imprisonment at hard labor. The Louisiana Supreme Court affirmed the conviction, rejecting the claim that evidence introduced at the trial was the product of an unlawful search and seizure.

The evidence adduced at the pretrial hearing on a motion to suppress showed that on April 24, 1967, officers possessing two warrants for Vale's arrest and having information that he was residing at a specified address proceeded there in an unmarked car and set up a surveillance of the house. The evidence of what then took place was summarized by the Louisiana Supreme Court as follows:

"After approximately 15 minutes the officers observed a green 1958 Chevrolet drive up and sound the horn and after backing into a parking place, again blew the horn. At this juncture Donald Vale, who was well known to Officer Brady having arrested him twice in the previous month, was seen coming out of the house and walk up to the passenger side of the Chevrolet where he had a close brief conversation with the driver; and after looking up and down the street returned inside of the house. Within a few minutes he reappeared on the porch, and again cautiously looked up and down the street before proceeding to the passenger side of the Chevrolet, leaning through the window. From this the officers were convinced a narcotics sale had taken place. They returned to their car and immediately drove toward Donald Vale, and as they reached within approximately three cars lengths from the accused, (Donald Vale) he looked up and, obviously recognizing the officers, turned around, walking quickly toward the house. At the same time the driver of the Chevrolet started to make his get away when the car was blocked by the police vehicle. The three officers promptly alighted from the car, whereupon Officers Soule and Laumann called to Donald Vale to stop as he reached the front steps of the house, telling him he was under arrest. Officer Brady at the same time, seeing the driver of the Chevrolet, Arizzio Saucier, whom the officers knew to be a narcotic addict, place something hurriedly in his mouth, immediately placed him under arrest and joined his co-officers. Because of the transaction they had just observed they, informed Donald Vale they were going to search the house, and thereupon advised him of his constitutional rights. After they all entered the front room, Officer Laumann made a cursory inspection of the house to ascertain if anyone else was present and within about three minutes Mrs. Vale and James Vale, mother and brother of Donald Vale, returned home carrying groceries and were informed of the arrest and impending search."

The search of a rear bedroom revealed a quantity of narcotics.

"Belief, however well founded, that an article sought is concealed in a dwelling house furnishes no justification for a search of that place without a warrant." That basic rule "has never been questioned in this Court."

The Louisiana Supreme Court thought the search independently supportable because it involved narcotics, which are easily removed, hidden, or destroyed. It would be unreasonable, the Louisiana court concluded, "to require the officers under the facts of the case to first secure a search warrant before searching the premises, as time is of the essence inasmuch as the officers never know whether there is anyone on the premises to be searched who could very easily destroy the evidence." Such a rationale could not apply to the present case, since by their own account the arresting officers satisfied themselves that no one else was in the house when they first entered the premises. But entirely apart from that point, our past decisions make clear that only in "a few specifically established and well-delineated" situations, may a warrantless search of a dwelling withstand constitutional scrutiny, even though the authorities have probable cause to conduct it. The burden rests on the State to show the existence of such an exceptional situation. And the record before us discloses none.

There is no suggestion that anyone consented to the search. The officers were not responding to an emergency. They were not in hot pursuit of a fleeing felon. The goods ultimately seized were not in the process of destruction. Nor were they about to be removed from the jurisdiction.

The officers were able to procure two warrants for Vale's arrest. They also had information that he was residing at the address where they found him. There is thus no reason, so far as anything before us appears, to suppose that it was impracticable for them to obtain a search warrant as well. We decline to hold that an arrest on the street can provide its own "exigent circumstance" so as to justify a warrantless search of the arrestee's house.

Accordingly, the judgment is reversed and the case is remanded to the Louisiana Supreme Court for further proceedings not inconsistent with this opinion.

MR. JUSTICE BLACK, with whom THE CHIEF JUSTICE joins, dissenting.

The Fourth Amendment to the United States Constitution prohibits only "unreasonable searches." A warrant has never been thought to be an absolute requirement for a constitutionally proper search. Searches, whether with or without a warrant, are to be judged by whether they are reasonable, and, as I said, speaking for the Court in *Preston v. United States*, 376 U.S. 364, 366–367 (1964), common sense dictates that reasonableness varies with the circumstances of the search. The Louisiana Supreme Court held not only that the police action here was reasonable but also that failure to conduct an immediate search would have been unreasonable. With that view I am in complete agreement, for the following reasons.

The police, having warrants for Vale's arrest, were watching his mother's house from a short distance away. Not long after they began their vigil a car arrived, sounded its horn, and backed into a parking space near the house. The driver did not get out, but instead honked the car horn again. Vale, who had been arrested twice the month before and against whom an indictment for a narcotics offense was then pending, came out of his mother's house and talked to the driver of the car. At the conclusion of the conversation Vale looked both ways, up and down the street, and then went back inside the house. When he reappeared he stopped before going to the car and stood, as one of the officers testified, "(l)ooking back and forth like to see who might be coming or who was in the neighborhood." He then walked to the car and leaned in.

From this behavior the officers were convinced that a narcotics transaction was taking place at that very moment. They drove down the street toward Vale and the parked car. When they came within a few car lengths of the two men Vale saw them and began to walk quickly back toward the house. At the same time the driver of the car attempted to pull away. The police brought both parties to the transaction to a stop. They then saw that the driver of the car was one Saucier, a known narcotics addict. He hurriedly placed something in his mouth, and apparently swallowed it. The police placed both Vale and Saucier under arrest.

At this point the police had probable cause to believe that Vale was engaged in a narcotics transfer, and that a supply of narcotics would be found in the house, to which Vale had returned after his first conversation, from which he had emerged furtively bearing what the police could readily deduce was a supply of narcotics, and toward which he hurried after seeing the police. But the police did not know then who else might be in the house. Vale's arrest took place near the house, and anyone observing from inside would surely have been alerted to destroy the stocks of contraband which the police believed Vale had left there. The police had already seen Saucier, the narcotics addict, apparently swallow what Vale had given him.

Believing that some evidence had already been destroyed and that other evidence might well be, the police were faced with the choice of risking the immediate destruction of evidence or entering the house and conducting a search. I cannot say that their decision to search was unreasonable. Delay in order to obtain a warrant would have given an accomplice just the time he needed.

That the arresting officers did, in fact, believe that others might be in the house is attested to by their actions upon entering the door left open by Vale. The police at once checked the small house to determine if anyone else was present. Just as they discovered the house was empty, however, Vale's mother and brother arrived. Now what had been a suspicion became a certainty: Vale's relatives were in possession and knew of his arrest. To have abandoned the search at this point, and left the house with Vale, would not have been the action of reasonable police officers.

[T]he circumstances here were sufficiently exceptional to justify a search. The Court recognizes that searches to prevent the destruction or removal of evidence have long been held reasonable by this Court.

The Court, however, finds the search here unreasonable. First, the Court suggests that the contraband was not "in the process of destruction." None of the cases cited by the Court supports the proposition that "exceptional circumstances" exist only when the process of destruction has already begun. On the contrary we implied that those circumstances did exist when "evidence or contraband was threatened with removal or destruction."

Second, the Court seems to argue that the search was unreasonable because the police officers had time to obtain a warrant. I agree that the opportunity to obtain a warrant is one of the factors to be weighed in determining reasonableness. But the record conclusively shows that there was no such opportunity here. As I noted above, once the officers had observed Vale's conduct in front of the house they had probable cause to believe that a felony had been committed and that immediate action was necessary. At no time after the events in front of Mrs. Vale's house would it have been prudent for the officers to leave the house in order to secure a warrant.

The Court asserts, however, that because the police obtained two warrants for Vale's arrest there is "no reason . . . to suppose that it was impracticable for them to obtain a search warrant as well." The difficulty is that the two arrest warrants on which the Court seems to rely so heavily were not issued because of any present misconduct of Vale's; they were issued because the bond had been increased for an earlier narcotics charge then pending against Vale. When the police came to arrest Vale, they knew only that his bond had been increased. There is nothing in the record to indicate that, absent the increased bond, there would have been probable cause for an arrest, much less a search. Probable cause for the search arose for the first time when the police observed the activity of Vale and Saucier in and around the house.

I do not suggest that all arrests necessarily provide the basis for a search of the arrestee's house. In this case there is far more than a mere street arrest. The police also observed Vale's use of the house as a base of operations for his commercial business, his attempt to return hurriedly to the house on seeing the officers, and the apparent destruction of evidence by the man with whom Vale was dealing.

Furthermore the police arrival and Vale's arrest were plainly visible to anyone within the house, and the police had every reason to believe that someone in the house was likely to destroy the contraband if the search were postponed.

This case raises most graphically the question how does a policeman protect evidence necessary to the State if he must leave the premises to get a warrant, allowing the evidence he seeks to be destroyed. The Court's answer to that question makes unnecessarily difficult the conviction of those who prey upon society.

QUESTIONS AND NOTES

1.   Is the Court saying that search warrants are (nearly) always required, or only that they are (nearly) always required when dealing with houses? If the latter, what is so special about a house?

2.   Do you think that there were exigent circumstances in this case? As between Stewart and Black, who has the more powerful argument on this point?

3.   What should the police have done to secure the situation? Would it have been better if they had denied Vale's relatives access to their own home pending a warrant? Why? Why not?

4.   *Could* the police deny access to Vale's relatives? *Cf. Illinois v. McArthur*, 531 U.S. 326 (2001) upholding the denial of access to the suspect, against whom the police had probable cause.

5.   If it were possible to radio for a warrant (as it is in some locales), should the police have been required to do that? (note: *Vale* seems predicated on the assumption that the police would have to drive downtown to obtain a warrant.)

6.   *Chambers*, decided the same day as *Vale*, clearly indicates that the importance of a warrant may well depend on what is being searched.

CHAMBERS v. MARONEY
399 U.S. 43 (1970)

MR. JUSTICE WHITE delivered the opinion of the Court.

The principal question in this case concerns the admissibility of evidence seized from an automobile, in which petitioner was riding at the time of his arrest, after the automobile was taken to a police station and was there thoroughly searched without a warrant. The Court of Appeals for the Third Circuit found no violation of petitioner's Fourth Amendment rights. We affirm.

I

During the night of May 20, 1963, a Gulf service station in North Braddock, Pennsylvania, was robbed by two men, each of whom carried and displayed a gun. The robbers took the currency from the cash register; the service station attendant, one Stephen Kovacich, was directed to place the coins in his right-hand glove, which was then taken by the robbers. Two teen-agers, who had earlier noticed a blue compact station wagon circling the block in the vicinity of the Gulf station, then saw the station wagon speed away from a parking lot close to the Gulf station. About the same time, they learned that the Gulf station had been robbed. They reported to police, who arrived immediately, that four men were in the station wagon and one was wearing a green sweater. Kovacich told the police that one of the men who robbed him was wearing a green sweater and the other was wearing a trench coat. A description of the car and the two robbers was broadcast over the police radio. Within an hour, a light blue compact station wagon answering the description and carrying four men was stopped by the police about two miles from the Gulf station. Petitioner was one of the men in the station wagon. He was wearing a green sweater and there was a trench coat in the car. The occupants were arrested and the car was driven to the police station. In the course of a thorough search of the car at the station, the police found concealed in a compartment under the dashboard two .38-caliber revolvers (one loaded with dumdum bullets), a right-hand glove containing small change, and certain cards bearing the name of Raymond Havicon, the attendant at a Boron service station in McKeesport, Pennsylvania, who had been robbed at gunpoint on May 13, 1963. In the course of a warrant-authorized search of petitioner's home the day after petitioner's arrest, police found and seized certain .38-caliber ammunition, including some dumdum bullets similar to those found in one of the guns taken from the station wagon.

Petitioner was indicted for both robberies. His first trial ended in a mistrial but he was convicted of both robberies at the second trial. Both Kovacich and Havicon identified petitioner as one of the robbers. The materials taken from the station wagon were introduced into evidence, Kovacich identifying his glove and Havicon the cards taken in the May 13 robbery. The bullets seized at petitioner's house were also introduced over objections of petitioner's counsel.

II

We pass quickly the claim that the search of the automobile was the fruit of an unlawful arrest. Both the courts below thought the arresting officers had probable cause to make the arrest. We agree. Having talked to the teen-age observers and to the victim Kovacich, the police had ample cause to stop a light blue compact station wagon carrying four men and to arrest the occupants, one of whom was wearing a green sweater and one of whom had a trench coat with him in the car.[6]

Here the police had probable cause to believe that the robbers, carrying guns and the fruits of the crime, had fled the scene in a light blue compact station wagon which would be carrying four men, one wearing a green sweater and another wearing a trench coat. As the state courts correctly held, there was probable cause to arrest the occupants of the station wagon that the officers stopped; just as obviously was there probable cause to search the car for guns and stolen money.

In terms of the circumstances justifying a warrantless search, the Court has long distinguished between an automobile and a home or office. In *Carroll v. United*

---

[6] In any event, as we point out below, the validity of an arrest is not necessarily determinative of the right to search a car if there is probable cause to make the search. Here as will be true in many cases, the circumstances justifying the arrest are also those furnishing probable cause for the search.

States, 267 U.S. 132 (1925), the issue was the admissibility in evidence of contraband liquor seized in a warrantless search of a car on the highway. After surveying the law from the time of the adoption of the Fourth Amendment onward, the Court held that automobiles and other conveyances may be searched without a warrant in circumstances that would not justify the search without a warrant of a house or an office, provided that there is probable cause to believe that the car contains articles that the officers are entitled to seize. The Court expressed its holding as follows:

"We have made a somewhat extended reference to these statutes to show that the guaranty of freedom from unreasonable searches and seizures by the Fourth Amendment has been construed, practically since the beginning of the government, as recognizing a necessary difference between a search of a store, dwelling house, or other structure in respect of which a proper official warrant readily may be obtained and a search of a ship, motor boat, wagon, or automobile for contraband goods, where it is not practicable to secure a warrant, because the vehicle can be quickly moved out of the locality or jurisdiction in which the warrant must be sought.

"Having thus established that contraband goods concealed and illegally transported in an automobile or other vehicle may be searched for without a warrant, we come now to consider under what circumstances such search may be made. (T)hose lawfully within the country, entitled to use the public highways, have a right to free passage without interruption or search unless there is known to a competent official, authorized to search, probable cause for believing that their vehicles are carrying contraband or illegal merchandise.

"The measure of legality of such a seizure is, therefore, that the seizing officer shall have reasonable or probable cause for believing that the automobile which he stops and seizes has contraband liquor therein which is being illegally transported."

Finding that there was probable cause for the search and seizure at issue before it, the Court affirmed the convictions.

Neither *Carroll* nor other cases in this Court require or suggest that in every conceivable circumstance the search of an auto even with probable cause may be made without the extra protection for privacy that a warrant affords. But the circumstances that furnish probable cause to search a particular auto for particular articles are most often unforeseeable; moreover, the opportunity to search is fleeting since a car is readily movable. Where this is true, as in *Carroll* and the case before us now, if an effective search is to be made at any time, either the search must be made immediately without a warrant or the car itself must be seized and held without a warrant for whatever period is necessary to obtain a warrant for the search.[9]

In enforcing the Fourth Amendment's prohibition against unreasonable searches and seizures, the Court has insisted upon probable cause as a minimum requirement for a reasonable search permitted by the Constitution. As a general

---

[9] Following the car until a warrant can be obtained seems an impractical alternative since, among other things, the car may be taken out of the jurisdiction. Tracing the car and searching it hours or days later would of course permit instruments or fruits of crime to be removed from the car before the search.

rule, it has also required the judgment of a magistrate on the probable-cause issue and the issuance of a warrant before a search is made. Only in exigent circumstances will the judgment of the police as to probable cause serve as a sufficient authorization for a search. *Carroll* holds a search warrant unnecessary where there is probable cause to search an automobile stopped on the highway; the car is movable, the occupants are alerted, and the car's contents may never be found again if a warrant must be obtained. Hence an immediate search is constitutionally permissible.

Arguably, because of the preference for a magistrate's judgment, only the immobilization of the car should be permitted until a search warrant is obtained; arguably, only the "lesser" intrusion is permissible until the magistrate authorizes the "greater." But which is the "greater" and which the "lesser" intrusion is itself a debatable question and the answer may depend on a variety of circumstances. For constitutional purposes, we see no difference between on the one hand seizing and holding a car before presenting the probable cause issue to a magistrate and on the other hand carrying out an immediate search without a warrant. Given probable cause to search, either course is reasonable under the Fourth Amendment.

On the facts before us, the blue station wagon could have been searched on the spot when it was stopped since there was probable cause to search and it was a fleeting target for a search. The probable-cause factor still obtained at the station house and so did the mobility of the car unless the Fourth Amendment permits a warrantless seizure of the car and the denial of its use to anyone until a warrant is secured. In that event there is little to choose in terms of practical consequences between an immediate search without a warrant and the car's immobilization until a warrant is obtained.[10] The same consequences may not follow where there is unforeseeable cause to search a house. Compare *Vale*. But as *Carroll* held, for the purposes of the Fourth Amendment there is a constitutional difference between houses and cars.

MR. JUSTICE HARLAN, dissenting in part.

In sustaining the search of the automobile I believe the Court ignores the framework of our past decisions circumscribing the scope of permissible search without a warrant. The Court has long read the Fourth Amendment's proscription of "unreasonable" searches as imposing a general principle that a search without a warrant is not justified by the mere knowledge by the searching officers of facts showing probable cause. The "general requirement that a search warrant be obtained" is basic to the Amendment's protection of privacy, and "the burden is on those seeking (an) exemption . . . to show the need for it."

Fidelity to this established principle requires that, where exceptions are made to accommodate the exigencies of particular situations, those exceptions be no broader than necessitated by the circumstances presented. For example, the Court has

---

[10] It was not unreasonable in this case to take the car to the station house. All occupants in the car were arrested in a dark parking lot in the middle of the night. A careful search at that point was impractical and perhaps not safe for the officers, and it would serve the owner's convenience and the safety of his car to have the vehicle and the keys together at the station house.

recognized that an arrest creates an emergency situation justifying a warrantless search of the arrestee's person and of "the area from within which he might gain possession of a weapon or destructible evidence;" however, because the exigency giving rise to this exception extends only that far, the search may go no further. Similarly we held in *Terry v. Ohio*, 392 U.S. 1 (1968), that a warrantless search in a "stop and frisk" situation must "be strictly circumscribed by the exigencies which justify its initiation." Any intrusion beyond what is necessary for the personal safety of the officer or others nearby is forbidden.

Where officers have probable cause to search a vehicle on a public way, a further limited exception to the warrant requirement is reasonable because "the vehicle can be quickly moved out of the locality or jurisdiction in which the warrant must be sought." Because the officers might be deprived of valuable evidence if required to obtain a warrant before effecting any search or seizure, I agree with the Court that they should be permitted to take the steps necessary to preserve evidence and to make a search possible. The Court holds that those steps include making a warrantless search of the entire vehicle on the highway — a conclusion reached by the Court in *Carroll* without discussion — and indeed appears to go further and to condone the removal of the car to the police station for a warrantless search there at the convenience of the police. I cannot agree that this result is consistent with our insistence in other areas that departures from the warrant requirement strictly conform to the exigency presented.

The Court concedes that the police could prevent removal of the evidence by temporarily seizing the car for the time necessary to obtain a warrant. It does not dispute that such a course would fully protect the interests of effective law enforcement; rather it states that whether temporary seizure is a "lesser" intrusion than warrantless search "is itself a debatable question and the answer may depend on a variety of circumstances."[8] I believe it clear that a warrantless search involves the greater sacrifice of Fourth Amendment values.

The Fourth Amendment proscribes, to be sure, unreasonable "seizures" as well as "searches." However, in the circumstances in which this problem is likely to occur, the lesser intrusion will almost always be the simple seizure of the car for the period — perhaps a day — necessary to enable the officers to obtain a search warrant. In the first place, as this case shows, the very facts establishing probable cause to search will often also justify arrest of the occupants of the vehicle. Since the occupants themselves are to be taken into custody, they will suffer minimal further inconvenience from the temporary immobilization of their vehicle. Even where no arrests are made, persons who wish to avoid a search — either to protect their privacy or to conceal incriminating evidence — will almost certainly prefer a brief loss of the use of the vehicle in exchange for the opportunity to have a magistrate pass upon the justification for the search. To be sure, one can conceive of instances

---

[8] The Court, unable to decide whether search or temporary seizure is the "lesser" intrusion, in this case authorizes both. The Court concludes that it was reasonable for the police to take the car to the station, where they searched it once to no avail. The searching officers then entered the station, interrogated petitioner and the car's owner, and returned later for another search of the car — this one successful. At all times the car and its contents were secure against removal or destruction. Nevertheless the Court approves the searches without even an inquiry into the officers' ability promptly to take their case before a magistrate.

in which the occupant, having nothing to hide and lacking concern for the privacy of the automobile, would be more deeply offended by a temporary immobilization of his vehicle than by a prompt search of it. However, such a person always remains free to consent to an immediate search, thus avoiding any delay. Where consent is not forthcoming, the occupants of the car have an interest in privacy that is protected by the Fourth Amendment even where the circumstances justify a temporary seizure. The Court's endorsement of a warrantless invasion of that privacy where another course would suffice is simply inconsistent with our repeated stress on the Fourth Amendment's mandate of "adherence to judicial processes."[9]

QUESTIONS AND NOTES

1.   Is the Court saying that an automobile on the highway is *per se* exigent, or is it saying that exigency is not necessary in regard to automobiles?

2.   Assuming that there would have been an exigency had the search been undertaken on the highway, how could there have been one when the car was locked in the impound lot? Are we to take seriously the Court's concern about denying access of the car to anyone pending a warrant? To whom did the Court think access was denied?

3.   Might the Court have had some other concern? If so, what?

4.   Were *Vale* and *Chambers* both wrongly decided in that the police overlooked a real exigency in *Vale* and made up a phony exigency in *Chambers*?

5.   The question of whether *Vale* or *Chambers* was the basic rule was answered, at least temporarily, in *Chadwick*.

UNITED STATES v. CHADWICK
433 U.S. 1 (1977)

Mr. Chief Justice Burger delivered the opinion of the Court.

We granted certiorari in this case to decide whether a search warrant is required before federal agents may open a locked footlocker which they have lawfully seized at the time of the arrest of its owners, when there is probable cause to believe the footlocker contains contraband.

On May 8, 1973, Amtrak railroad officials in San Diego observed respondents Gregory Machado and Bridget Leary load a brown footlocker onto a train bound for Boston. Their suspicions were aroused when they noticed that the trunk was unusually heavy for its size, and that it was leaking talcum powder, a substance often used to mask the odor of marihuana or hashish. Because Machado matched a

---

[9] Circumstances might arise in which it would be impracticable to immobilize the car for the time required to obtain a warrant — for example, where a single police officer must take arrested suspects to the station, and has no way of protecting the suspects' car during his absence. In such situations it might be wholly reasonable to perform an on-the-spot search based on probable cause. However, where nothing in the situation makes impracticable the obtaining of a warrant, I cannot join the Court in shunting aside that vital Fourth Amendment safeguard.

profile used to spot drug traffickers, the railroad officials reported these circumstances to federal agents in San Diego, who in turn relayed the information,
together with detailed descriptions of Machado and the footlocker, to their
counterparts in Boston.

When the train arrived in Boston two days later, federal narcotics agents were
on hand. Though the officers had not obtained an arrest or search warrant, they had
with them a police dog trained to detect marihuana. The agents identified Machado
and Leary and kept them under surveillance as they claimed their suitcases and the
footlocker, which had been transported by baggage cart from the train to the
departure area. Machado and Leary lifted the footlocker from the baggage cart,
placed it on the floor and sat down on it. The agents then released the dog near the
footlocker. Without alerting respondents, the dog signaled the presence of a
controlled substance inside. Respondent Chadwick then joined Machado and Leary,
and they engaged an attendant to move the footlocker outside to Chadwick's
waiting automobile. Machado, Chadwick, and the attendant together lifted the
200-pound footlocker into the trunk of the car, while Leary waited in the front seat.
At that point, while the trunk of the car was still open and before the car engine had
been started, the officers arrested all three. A search disclosed no weapons, but the
keys to the footlocker were apparently taken from Machado. Respondents were
taken to the Federal Building in Boston; the agents followed with Chadwick's car
and the footlocker. As the Government concedes, from the moment of respondents'
arrests at about 9 p. m., the footlocker remained under the exclusive control of law
enforcement officers at all times. The footlocker and luggage were placed in the
Federal Building, where, as one of the agents later testified, "there was no risk that
whatever was contained in the footlocker trunk would be removed by the
defendants or their associates." The agents had no reason to believe that the
footlocker contained explosives or other inherently dangerous items, or that it
contained evidence which would lose its value unless the footlocker were opened at
once. Facilities were readily available in which the footlocker could have been
stored securely; it is not contended that there was any exigency calling for an
immediate search.

At the Federal Building an hour and a half after the arrests, the agents opened
the footlocker and luggage. They did not obtain respondents' consent; they did not
secure a search warrant. The footlocker was locked with a padlock and a regular
trunk lock. It is unclear whether it was opened with the keys taken from respondent
Machado, or by other means. Large amounts of marihuana were found in the
footlocker.

Respondents were indicted for possession of marihuana with intent to distribute
it, in violation of 21 U.S.C. § 841(a)(1), and for conspiracy, in violation of 21 U.S.C.
§ 846. Before trial, they moved to suppress the marihuana obtained from the
footlocker.

In this Court the Government contends that the Fourth Amendment Warrant
Clause protects only interests traditionally identified with the home. Recalling the
colonial writs of assistance, which were often executed in searches of private
dwellings, the Government claims that the Warrant Clause was adopted primarily,
if not exclusively, in response to unjustified intrusions into private homes on the

authority of general warrants. The Government argues there is no evidence that the Framers of the Fourth Amendment intended to disturb the established practice of permitting warrantless searches outside the home, or to modify the initial clause of the Fourth Amendment by making warrantless searches supported by probable cause *per se* unreasonable.

Drawing on its reading of history, the Government argues that only homes, offices, and private communications implicate interests which lie at the core of the Fourth Amendment. Accordingly, it is only in these contexts that the determination whether a search or seizure is reasonable should turn on whether a warrant has been obtained. In all other situations, the Government contends, less significant privacy values are at stake, and the reasonableness of a government intrusion should depend solely on whether there is probable cause to believe evidence of criminal conduct is present. Where personal effects are lawfully seized outside the home on probable cause, the Government would thus regard searches without a warrant as not "unreasonable."

We do not agree that the Warrant Clause protects only dwellings and other specifically designated locales. As we have noted before, the Fourth Amendment "protects people, not places," *Katz v. United States*, 389 U.S. 347, 351 (1967); more particularly, it protects people from unreasonable government intrusions into their legitimate expectations of privacy. In this case, the Warrant Clause makes a significant contribution to that protection. The question, then, is whether a warrantless search in these circumstances was unreasonable.

It cannot be doubted that the Fourth Amendment's commands grew in large measure out of the colonists' experience with the writs of assistance and their memories of the general warrants formerly in use in England. These writs, which were issued on executive rather than judicial authority, granted sweeping power to customs officials and other agents of the King to search at large for smuggled goods. Though the authority to search granted by the writs was not limited to the home, searches conducted pursuant to them often were carried out in private residences. Although the searches and seizures which deeply concerned the colonists, and which were foremost in the minds of the Framers, were those involving invasions of the home, it would be a mistake to conclude, as the Government contends, that the Warrant Clause was therefore intended to guard only against intrusions into the home. First, the Warrant Clause does not in terms distinguish between searches conducted in private homes and other searches. There is also a strong historical connection between the Warrant Clause and the initial clause of the Fourth Amendment, which draws no distinctions among "persons, houses, papers, and effects" in safeguarding against unreasonable searches and seizures.

Moreover, if there is little evidence that the Framers intended the Warrant Clause to operate outside the home, there is no evidence at all that they intended to exclude from protection of the Clause all searches occurring outside the home. The absence of a contemporary outcry against warrantless searches in public places was because, aside from searches incident to arrest, such warrantless searches were not a large issue in colonial America. Thus, silence in the historical record tells us little about the Framers' attitude toward application of the Warrant Clause to the search of respondents' footlocker. What we do know is that the Framers were men who focused on the wrongs of that day but who intended the Fourth Amendment to safeguard fundamental values which would far outlast the specific abuses which gave it birth.

The judicial warrant has a significant role to play in that it provides the detached scrutiny of a neutral magistrate, which is a more reliable safeguard against improper searches than the hurried judgment of a law enforcement officer "engaged in the often competitive enterprise of ferreting out crime." *Johnson v. United States*, 333 U.S. 10, 14 (1948). Once a lawful search has begun, it is also far more likely that it will not exceed proper bounds when it is done pursuant to a judicial authorization "particularly describing the place to be searched and the persons or things to be seized." Further, a warrant assures the individual whose property is searched or seized of the lawful authority of the executing officer, his need to search, and the limits of his power to search. *Camara v. Municipal Court*, 387 U.S. 523 (1967).

Just as the Fourth Amendment "protects people, not places," the protections a judicial warrant offers against erroneous governmental intrusions are effective whether applied in or out of the home. Accordingly, we have held warrantless searches unreasonable, and therefore unconstitutional, in a variety of settings; *e.g.* electronic interception of conversation in public telephone booth, automobile on private premises, automobile in custody, hotel room, office. These cases illustrate the applicability of the Warrant Clause beyond the narrow limits suggested by the Government. They also reflect the settled constitutional principle that a fundamental purpose of the Fourth Amendment is to safeguard individuals from unreasonable government invasions of legitimate privacy interests, and not simply those interests found inside the four walls of the home.

In this case, important Fourth Amendment privacy interests were at stake. By placing personal effects inside a double-locked footlocker, respondents manifested an expectation that the contents would remain free from public examination. No less than one who locks the doors of his home against intruders, one who safeguards his personal possessions in this manner is due the protection of the Fourth Amendment Warrant Clause. There being no exigency, it was unreasonable for the Government to conduct this search without the safeguards a judicial warrant provides.

QUESTIONS AND NOTES

1.   Why wasn't this a simple automobile case controlled by *Chambers*?

2.   Does the text of the Fourth Amendment support a heavy presumption in favor of warrants? Why? Why not?

3.   Assuming that the text and history is ambiguous, do policy reasons support an expansive or restrictive view of the warrant requirement? What are the relevant policy reasons?

4.   As will become apparent, the *Chadwick* dicta, if not its holding, no longer fully represents the state of the law. *See California v. Acevedo*, Chapter 6, *infra*.

B. THE ANATOMY OF A WARRANT

GROH v. RAMIREZ
540 U.S. 551 (2004)

JUSTICE STEVENS delivered the opinion of the Court.

Petitioner conducted a search of respondents' home pursuant to a warrant that failed to describe the "persons or things to be seized." U.S. Const., Amdt. 4. The questions presented are (1) whether the search violated the Fourth Amendment, and (2) if so, whether petitioner nevertheless is entitled to qualified immunity, given that a Magistrate Judge (Magistrate), relying on an affidavit that particularly described the items in question, found probable cause to conduct the search.

I

Respondents, Joseph Ramirez and members of his family, live on a large ranch in Butte-Silver Bow County, Montana. Petitioner, Jeff Groh has been a Special Agent for the Bureau of Alcohol, Tobacco and Firearms (ATF) since 1989. In February 1997, a concerned citizen informed petitioner that on a number of visits to respondents' ranch the visitor had seen a large stock of weaponry, including an automatic rifle, grenades, a grenade launcher, and a rocket launcher. Based on that information, petitioner prepared and signed an application for a warrant to search the ranch. The application stated that the search was for "any automatic firearms or parts to automatic weapons, destructive devices to include but not limited to grenades, grenade launchers, rocket launchers, and any and all receipts pertaining to the purchase or manufacture of automatic weapons or explosive devices or launchers." Petitioner supported the application with a detailed affidavit, which he also prepared and executed, that set forth the basis for his belief that the listed items were concealed on the ranch. Petitioner then presented these documents to a Magistrate, along with a warrant form that petitioner also had completed. The Magistrate signed the warrant form.

Although the application particularly described the place to be searched and the contraband petitioner expected to find, the warrant itself was less specific; it failed to identify any of the items that petitioner intended to seize. In the portion of the form that called for a description of the "person or property" to be seized, petitioner typed a description of respondents' two-story blue house rather than the alleged stockpile of firearms.[2] The warrant did not incorporate by reference the itemized list contained in the application. It did, however, recite that the Magistrate was satisfied the affidavit established probable cause to believe that contraband was concealed on the premises, and that sufficient grounds existed for the warrant's issuance.[3]

---

[2] The warrant stated: "[T]here is now concealed [on the specified premises] a certain person or property, namely [a] single dwelling residence two story in height which is blue in color and has two additions attached to the east. The front entrance to the residence faces in a southerly direction."

[3] The affidavit was sealed. Its sufficiency is not disputed.

The day after the Magistrate issued the warrant, petitioner led a team of law enforcement officers, including both federal agents and members of the local sheriff's department, in the search of respondents' premises. Although respondent Joseph Ramirez was not home, his wife and children were. Petitioner states that he orally described the objects of the search to Mrs. Ramirez in person and to Mr. Ramirez by telephone. According to Mrs. Ramirez, however, petitioner explained only that he was searching for " 'an explosive device in a box.' " At any rate, the officers' search uncovered no illegal weapons or explosives. When the officers left, petitioner gave Mrs. Ramirez a copy of the search warrant, but not a copy of the application, which had been sealed. The following day, in response to a request from respondents' attorney, petitioner faxed the attorney a copy of the page of the application that listed the items to be seized. No charges were filed against the Ramirezes.

Respondents sued petitioner and the other officers, raising eight claims, including violation of the Fourth Amendment. The District Court entered summary judgment for all defendants. The court found no Fourth Amendment violation, because it considered the case comparable to one in which the warrant contained an inaccurate address, and in such a case, the court reasoned, the warrant is sufficiently detailed if the executing officers can locate the correct house. The court added that even if a constitutional violation occurred, the defendants were entitled to qualified immunity because the failure of the warrant to describe the objects of the search amounted to a mere "typographical error."

The Court of Appeals affirmed the judgment with respect to all defendants and all claims, with the exception of respondents' Fourth Amendment claim against petitioner. On that claim, the court held that the warrant was invalid because it did not "describe with particularity the place to be searched and the items to be seized," and that oral statements by petitioner during or after the search could not cure the omission. The court observed that the warrant's facial defect "increased the likelihood and degree of confrontation between the Ramirezes and the police" and deprived respondents of the means "to challenge officers who might have exceeded the limits imposed by the magistrate." The court also expressed concern that "permitting officers to expand the scope of the warrant by oral statements would broaden the area of dispute between the parties in subsequent litigation."

II

The warrant was plainly invalid. The Fourth Amendment states unambiguously that "no Warrants shall issue, but upon probable cause, supported by Oath or affirmation, and *particularly describing* the place to be searched, and *the persons or things to be seized*." (Emphasis added.) The warrant in this case complied with the first three of these requirements: It was based on probable cause and supported by a sworn affidavit, and it described particularly the place of the search. On the fourth requirement, however, the warrant failed altogether. Indeed, petitioner concedes that "the warrant . . . was deficient in particularity because it provided no description of the type of evidence sought."

The fact that the application adequately described the "things to be seized" does not save the warrant from its facial invalidity. The Fourth Amendment by its terms requires particularity in the warrant, not in the supporting documents. *See Massachusetts v. Sheppard*, 468 U.S. 981, 988, n. 5, (1984) ("[A] warrant that fails to conform to the particularity requirement of the Fourth Amendment is unconstitutional"); And for good reason: "The presence of a search warrant serves a high function," *McDonald v. United States*, 335 U.S. 451, 455 (1948), and that high function is not necessarily vindicated when some other document, somewhere, says something about the objects of the search, but the contents of that document are neither known to the person whose home is being searched nor available for her inspection. We do not say that the Fourth Amendment forbids a warrant from cross-referencing other documents. Indeed, most Courts of Appeals have held that a court may construe a warrant with reference to a supporting application or affidavit if the warrant uses appropriate words of incorporation, and if the supporting document accompanies the warrant. But in this case the warrant did not incorporate other documents by reference, nor did either the affidavit or the application (which had been placed under seal) accompany the warrant. Hence, we need not further explore the matter of incorporation.

Petitioner argues that even though the warrant was invalid, the search nevertheless was "reasonable" within the meaning of the Fourth Amendment. He notes that a Magistrate authorized the search on the basis of adequate evidence of probable cause, that petitioner orally described to respondents the items to be seized, and that the search did not exceed the limits intended by the Magistrate and described by petitioner. Thus, petitioner maintains, his search of respondents' ranch was functionally equivalent to a search authorized by a valid warrant.

We disagree. This warrant did not simply omit a few items from a list of many to be seized, or misdescribe a few of several items. Nor did it make what fairly could be characterized as a mere technical mistake or typographical error. Rather, in the space set aside for a description of the items to be seized, the warrant stated that the items consisted of a "single dwelling residence . . . blue in color." In other words, the warrant did not describe the items to be seized at all. In this respect the warrant was so obviously deficient that we must regard the search as "warrantless" within the meaning of our case law. "We are not dealing with formalities." Because " 'the right of a man to retreat into his own home and there be free from unreasonable governmental intrusion' " stands " '[a]t the very core' of the Fourth Amendment," our cases have firmly established the " 'basic principle of Fourth Amendment law' that searches and seizures inside a home without a warrant are presumptively unreasonable." Thus, "absent exigent circumstances, a warrantless entry to search for weapons or contraband is unconstitutional even when a felony has been committed and there is probable cause to believe that incriminating evidence will be found within."

We have clearly stated that the presumptive rule against warrantless searches applies with equal force to searches whose only defect is a lack of particularity in the warrant. In Sheppard, for instance, the petitioner argued that even though the warrant was invalid for lack of particularity, "the search was constitutional because it was reasonable within the meaning of the Fourth Amendment." In squarely rejecting that position, we explained:

"The uniformly applied rule is that a search conducted pursuant to a warrant that fails to conform to the particularity requirement of the Fourth Amendment is unconstitutional. That rule is in keeping with the well-established principle that 'except in certain carefully defined classes of cases, a search of private property without proper consent is "unreasonable" unless it has been authorized by a valid search warrant.' "

Petitioner asks us to hold that a search conducted pursuant to a warrant lacking particularity should be exempt from the presumption of unreasonableness if the goals served by the particularity requirement are otherwise satisfied. He maintains that the search in this case satisfied those goals — which he says are "to prevent general searches, to prevent the seizure of one thing under a warrant describing another, and to prevent warrants from being issued on vague or dubious information," because the scope of the search did not exceed the limits set forth in the application. But unless the particular items described in the affidavit are also set forth in the warrant itself (or at least incorporated by reference, and the affidavit present at the search), there can be no written assurance that the Magistrate actually found probable cause to search for, and to seize, every item mentioned in the affidavit. In this case, for example, it is at least theoretically possible that the Magistrate was satisfied that the search for weapons and explosives was justified by the showing in the affidavit, but not convinced that any evidentiary basis existed for rummaging through respondents' files and papers for receipts pertaining to the purchase or manufacture of such items. Or, conceivably, the Magistrate might have believed that some of the weapons mentioned in the affidavit could have been lawfully possessed and therefore should not be seized. The mere fact that the Magistrate issued a warrant does not necessarily establish that he agreed that the scope of the search should be as broad as the affiant's request. Even though petitioner acted with restraint in conducting the search, "the inescapable fact is that this restraint was imposed by the agents themselves, not by a judicial officer."[4]

We have long held, moreover, that the purpose of the particularity requirement is not limited to the prevention of general searches. A particular warrant also "assures the individual whose property is searched or seized of the lawful authority of the executing officer, his need to search, and the limits of his power to search." *See also Illinois v. Gates*, 462 U.S. 213, (1983) ("[P]ossession of a warrant by officers conducting an arrest or search greatly reduces the perception of unlawful or intrusive police conduct").[5]

---

[4] For this reason petitioner's argument that any constitutional error was committed by the Magistrate, not petitioner, is misplaced. In *Massachusetts v. Sheppard*, 468 U.S. 981 (1984), we suggested that "the judge, not the police officers," may have committed "[a]n error of constitutional dimension," because the judge had assured the officers requesting the warrant that he would take the steps necessary to conform the warrant to constitutional requirements. Thus, "it was not unreasonable for the police in [that] case to rely on the judge's assurances that the warrant authorized the search they had requested." In this case, by contrast, petitioner did not alert the Magistrate to the defect in the warrant that petitioner had drafted, and we therefore cannot know whether the Magistrate was aware of the scope of the search he was authorizing. Nor would it have been reasonable for petitioner to rely on a warrant that was so patently defective, even if the Magistrate was aware of the deficiency.

[5] It is true, as petitioner points out, that neither the Fourth Amendment nor Rule 41 of the Federal Rules of Criminal Procedure requires the executing officer to serve the warrant on the owner before commencing the search. Rule 41(f)(3) provides that "[t]he officer executing the warrant must: (A) give

Petitioner argues that even if the goals of the particularity requirement are broader than he acknowledges, those goals nevertheless were served because he orally described to respondents the items for which he was searching. Thus, he submits, respondents had all of the notice that a proper warrant would have accorded. But this case presents no occasion even to reach this argument, since respondents, as noted above, dispute petitioner's account. According to Mrs. Ramirez, petitioner stated only that he was looking for an " 'explosive device in a box.' " Because this dispute is before us on petitioner's motion for summary judgment, "[t]he evidence of the nonmovant is to be believed, and all justifiable inferences are to be drawn in [her] favor." The posture of the case therefore obliges us to credit Mrs. Ramirez's account, and we find that petitioner's description of " 'an explosive device in a box' " was little better than no guidance at all. *See Stefonek*, 179 F.3d, at 1032–1033 (holding that a search warrant for " 'evidence of crime' " was "[s]o open-ended" in its description that it could "only be described as a general warrant").

It is incumbent on the officer executing a search warrant to ensure the search is lawfully authorized and lawfully conducted.[6] Because petitioner did not have in his possession a warrant particularly describing the things he intended to seize, proceeding with the search was clearly "unreasonable" under the Fourth Amendment. The Court of Appeals correctly held that the search was unconstitutional.

JUSTICE THOMAS, with whom JUSTICE SCALIA joins, dissenting.

The Fourth Amendment provides: "The right of the people to be secure in their persons, houses, papers, and effects, against unreasonable searches and seizures, shall not be violated, and no Warrants shall issue, but upon probable cause, supported by Oath or affirmation, and particularly describing the place to be searched, and the persons or things to be seized." The precise relationship between the Amendment's Warrant Clause and Unreasonableness Clause is unclear. But neither Clause explicitly requires a warrant. While "it is of course textually possible to consider [a warrant requirement] implicit within the requirement of reasonableness," text of the Fourth Amendment certainly does not mandate this result. Nor does the Amendment's history, which is clear as to the Amendment's principal target (general warrants), but not as clear with respect to when warrants were required, if ever. Indeed, because of the very different nature and scope of federal

---

a copy of the warrant and a receipt for the property taken to the person from whom, or from whose premises, the property was taken; or (B) leave a copy of the warrant and receipt at the place where the officer took the property." Quite obviously, in some circumstances — a surreptitious search by means of a wiretap, for example, or the search of empty or abandoned premises — it will be impracticable or imprudent for the officers to show the warrant in advance. Whether it would be unreasonable to refuse a request to furnish the warrant at the outset of the search when, as in this case, an occupant of the premises is present and poses no threat to the officers' safe and effective performance of their mission, is a question that this case does not present.

[6] The Court of Appeals' decision is consistent with this principle. Petitioner mischaracterizes the court's decision when he contends that it imposed a novel proofreading requirement on officers executing warrants. The court held that officers leading a search team must "mak[e] sure that they have a proper warrant that in fact authorizes the search and seizure they are about to conduct." 298 F.3d 1022, 1027 (C.A.9 2002). That is not a duty to proofread; it is, rather, a duty to ensure that the warrant conforms to constitutional requirements.

authority and ability to conduct searches and arrests at the founding, it is possible that neither the history of the Fourth Amendment nor the common law provides much guidance.

As a result, the Court has vacillated between imposing a categorical warrant requirement and applying a general reasonableness standard. That is, our cases stand for the illuminating proposition that warrantless searches are per se unreasonable, except, of course, when they are not.

Today the Court holds that the warrant in this case was "so obviously deficient" that the ensuing search must be regarded as a warrantless search and thus presumptively unreasonable. However, the text of the Fourth Amendment, its history, and the sheer number of exceptions to the Court's categorical warrant requirement seriously undermine the bases upon which the Court today rests its holding. Instead of adding to this confusing jurisprudence, as the Court has done, I would turn to first principles in order to determine the relationship between the Warrant Clause and the Unreasonableness Clause. But even within the Court's current framework, a search conducted pursuant to a defective warrant is constitutionally different from a "warrantless search." Consequently, despite the defective warrant, I would still ask whether this search was unreasonable and would conclude that it was not. Furthermore, even if the Court were correct that this search violated the Constitution (and in particular, respondents' Fourth Amendment rights), given the confused state of our Fourth Amendment jurisprudence and the reasonableness of petitioner's actions, I cannot agree with the Court's conclusion that petitioner is not entitled to qualified immunity. For these reasons, I respectfully dissent.

I

"[A]ny Fourth Amendment case may present two separate questions: whether the search was conducted pursuant to a warrant issued in accordance with the second Clause, and, if not, whether it was nevertheless 'reasonable' within the meaning of the first." By categorizing the search here to be a "warrantless" one, the Court declines to perform a reasonableness inquiry and ignores the fact that this search is quite different from searches that the Court has considered to be "warrantless" in the past. Our cases involving "warrantless" searches do not generally involve situations in which an officer has obtained a warrant that is later determined to be facially defective, but rather involve situations in which the officers neither sought nor obtained a warrant. By simply treating this case as if no warrant had even been sought or issued, the Court glosses over what should be the key inquiry: whether it is always appropriate to treat a search made pursuant to a warrant that fails to describe particularly the things to be seized as presumptively unreasonable.

The Court bases its holding that a defect in the particularity of the warrant by itself renders a search "warrantless" on a citation of a single footnote in *Massachusetts v. Sheppard*, 468 U.S. 981, (1984). In *Sheppard*, the Court, after noting that "the sole issue . . . in th[e] case is whether the officers reasonably believed that the search they conducted was authorized by a valid warrant," rejected the petitioner's argument that despite the invalid warrant, the otherwise reasonable search was constitutional. The Court recognized that under its case law a reasonableness inquiry would be appropriate if one of the exceptions to the warrant requirement applied. But the Court declined to consider whether such an exception applied and whether the search actually violated the Fourth Amendment because that question presented merely a "fact-bound issue of little importance." Because the Court in *Sheppard* did not conduct any sort of inquiry into whether a Fourth Amendment violation actually occurred, it is clear that the Court assumed a violation for the purposes of its analysis. Rather than rely on dicta buried in a footnote in *Sheppard*, the Court should actually analyze the arguably dispositive issue in this case.

The Court also rejects the argument that the details of the warrant application and affidavit save the warrant, because " '[t]he presence of a search warrant serves a high function.' " But it is not only the physical existence of the warrant and its typewritten contents that serve this high function. The Warrant Clause's principal protection lies in the fact that the "Fourth Amendment has interposed a magistrate between the citizen and the police . . . so that an objective mind might weigh the need to invade [the searchee's] privacy in order to enforce the law." The Court has further explained,

"The point of the Fourth Amendment . . . is not that it denies law enforcement the support of the usual inferences which reasonable men draw from evidence. Its protection consists in requiring that those inferences be drawn by a neutral and detached magistrate instead of being judged by the officer engaged in the often competitive enterprise of ferreting out crime. Any assumption that evidence sufficient to support a magistrate's disinterested determination to issue a search warrant will justify the officers in making a search without a warrant would reduce the Amendment to a nullity and leave the people's homes secure only in the discretion of police officers. . . . When the right of privacy must reasonably yield to the right of search is, as a rule, to be decided by a judicial officer, not by a policeman or government enforcement agent." *Johnson v. United States*, 333 U.S. 10, 13–14, (1948).

But the actual contents of the warrant are simply manifestations of this protection. Hence, in contrast to the case of a truly warrantless search, a warrant (due to a mistake) does not specify on its face the particular items to be seized but the warrant application passed on by the magistrate judge contains such details, a searchee still has the benefit of a determination by a neutral magistrate that there is probable cause to search a particular place and to seize particular items. In such a circumstance, the principal justification for applying a rule of presumptive unreasonableness falls away.

In the instant case, the items to be seized were clearly specified in the warrant application and set forth in the affidavit, both of which were given to the Judge (Magistrate). The Magistrate reviewed all of the documents and signed the warrant application and made no adjustment or correction to this application. It is clear that respondents here received the protection of the Warrant Clause, as described in *Johnson* and *McDonald*. Under these circumstances, I would not hold that any ensuing search constitutes a presumptively unreasonable warrantless search. Instead, I would determine whether, despite the invalid warrant, the resulting search was reasonable and hence constitutional.

II

Because the search was not unreasonable, I would conclude that it was constitutional. Prior to execution of the warrant, petitioner briefed the search team and provided a copy of the search warrant application, the supporting affidavit, and the warrant for the officers to review. Petitioner orally reviewed the terms of the warrant with the officers, including the specific items for which the officers were authorized to search. Petitioner and his search team then conducted the search entirely within the scope of the warrant application and warrant; that is, within the scope of what the Magistrate had authorized. Finding no illegal weapons or explosives, the search team seized nothing. When petitioner left, he gave respondents a copy of the search warrant. Upon request the next day, petitioner faxed respondent a copy of the more detailed warrant application. Indeed, putting aside the technical defect in the warrant, it is hard to imagine how the actual search could have been carried out any more reasonably.

The Court argues that this eminently reasonable search is nonetheless unreasonable because "there can be no written assurance that the Magistrate actually found probable cause to search for, and to seize, every item mentioned in the affidavit" "unless the particular items described in the affidavit are also set forth in the warrant itself." The Court argues that it was at least possible that the Magistrate intended to authorize a much more limited search than the one petitioner requested. As a theoretical matter, this may be true. But the more reasonable inference is that the Magistrate intended to authorize everything in the warrant application, as he signed the application and did not make any written adjustments to the application or the warrant itself.

The Court also attempts to bolster its focus on the faulty warrant by arguing that the purpose of the particularity requirement is not only to prevent general searches, but also to assure the searchee of the lawful authority for the search. But as the Court recognizes, neither the Fourth Amendment nor Federal Rule of Criminal Procedure 41 requires an officer to serve the warrant on the searchee before the search. Thus, a search should not be considered per se unreasonable for failing to apprise the searchee of the lawful authority prior to the search, especially where, as here, the officer promptly provides the requisite information when the defect in the papers is detected. Additionally, unless the Court adopts the Court of Appeals' view that the Constitution protects a searchee's ability to "be on the lookout and to challenge officers," while the officers are actually carrying out the search, petitioner's provision of the requisite information the following day is sufficient to satisfy this interest.

Justice Kennedy and Chief Justice Rehnquist agreed with the Court that the search was unconstitutional, but would have immunized the officers from liability based on their good faith.

Compare Chapter 14 B, *infra.*

QUESTIONS AND NOTES

1. Reconsider the reasons for requiring a warrant. Which of those reasons were met by the procedure in *Groh*? Which were not?

2. Should a defective warrant (as in *Groh*) be treated like a warrantless search? Or should it be treated as a partially warranted search? If the latter, should it have been held reasonable?

3. Which opinion was more persuasive? Why?

4. Which opinion was truer to the text of the Fourth Amendment? Explain.

C. WHO CAN ISSUE A WARRANT?

On several occasions, the Court has been confronted with the question of who can qualify as a neutral magistrate. The general rule is that a potential conflict of interest will disqualify. For example, in *Coolidge v. New Hampshire*, 403 U.S. 443 (1971), the Court ruled that the Justice of the Peace who was involved in prosecuting the case, upon which the warrant was issued could not qualify as a neutral and detached magistrate. In *Coolidge* itself, it was the Attorney General of New Hampshire, who while personally prosecuting the case, assumed the role of issuing magistrate. In the course of overturning the warrant, the Court indicated that New Hampshire's, by then abandoned, practice of allowing Justices of the Peace/Police Officers to issue warrants was unconstitutional.

Several years later, in *Connally v. Georgia*, 429 U.S. 245 (1977), the Court held that a Georgia scheme that paid a Justice of the Peace $5 for each warrant he issued, but nothing for each warrant he reviewed and turned down, was unconstitutional. Emphasizing the built-in incentive to find probable cause, the Court had no difficulty in invalidating the scheme as inconsistent with judicial neutrality.

We close this section, with *Shadwick v. Tampa*, a case emphasizing that neutrality, not special training, is the hallmark of magisterial competence.

SHADWICK v. TAMPA
407 U.S. 345 (1972)

MR. JUSTICE POWELL delivered the opinion of the Court.

The charter of Tampa, Florida, authorizes the issuance of certain arrest warrants by clerks of the Tampa Municipal Court. The sole question in this case is whether these clerks qualify as neutral and detached magistrates for purposes of the Fourth Amendment. We hold that they do.

Appellant was arrested for impaired driving on a warrant issued by a clerk of the municipal court. He moved the court to quash the warrant on the ground that it was issued by a nonjudicial officer in violation of the Fourth and Fourteenth Amendment.

I

A clerk of the municipal court is appointed by the city clerk from a classified list of civil servants and assigned to work in the municipal court. The statute does not specify the qualifications necessary for this job, but no law degree or special legal training is required. The clerk's duties are to receive traffic fines, prepare the court's dockets and records, fill out commitment papers and perform other routine clerical tasks. Apparently he may issue subpoenas. He may not, however, sit as a judge, and he may not issue a search warrant or even a felony or misdemeanor arrest warrant for violations of state laws. The only warrants he may issue are for the arrest of those charged with having breached municipal ordinances of the city of Tampa.

Appellant, contending that the Fourth Amendment requires that warrants be issued by "judicial officers," argues that even this limited warrant authority is constitutionally invalid. He reasons that warrant applications of whatever nature cannot be assured the discerning, independent review compelled by the Fourth Amendment when the review is performed by less than a judicial officer. It is less than clear, however, as to who would qualify as a "judicial officer" under appellant's theory. There is some suggestion in appellant's brief that a judicial officer must be a lawyer or the municipal court judge himself. A more complete portrayal of appellant's position would be that the Tampa clerks are disqualified as judicial officers not merely because they are not lawyers or judges, but because they lack the institutional independence associated with the judiciary in that they are members of the civil service, appointed by the city clerk, "an executive official," and enjoy no statutorily specified tenure in office.

II

Past decisions of the Court have mentioned review by a "judicial officer" prior to issuance of a warrant. In some cases the term "judicial officer" appears to have been used interchangeably with that of "magistrate." In others, it was intended simply to underscore the now accepted fact that someone independent of the police and prosecution must determine probable cause. The very term "judicial officer" implies, of course, some connection with the judicial branch. But it has never been held that only a lawyer or judge could grant a warrant, regardless of the court system or the type of warrant involved. [T]he Court [has] implied that United States Commissioners, many of whom were not lawyers or judges, were nonetheless "independent judicial officers."

The Court frequently has employed the term "magistrate" to denote those who may issue warrants. Historically, a magistrate has been defined broadly as "a public civil officer, possessing such power — legislative, executive, or judicial — as the government appointing him may ordain," or, in a narrower sense "an inferior judicial officer, such as a justice of the peace." More recent definitions have not much changed.

An examination of the Court's decisions reveals that the terms "magistrate" and "judicial officer" have been used interchangeably. Little attempt was made to define either term, to distinguish the one from the other, or to advance one as the definitive

Fourth Amendment requirement. We find no commendment in either term, however, that all warrant authority must reside exclusively in a lawyer or judge. Such a requirement would have been incongruous when even within the federal system warrants were until recently widely issued by nonlawyers.

To attempt to extract further significance from the above terminology would be both unnecessary and futile. The substance of the Constitution's warrant requirements does not turn on the labeling of the issuing party. The warrant traditionally has represented an independent assurance that a search and arrest will not proceed without probable cause to believe that a crime has been committed and that the person or place named in the warrant is involved in the crime. Thus, an issuing magistrate must meet two tests. He must be neutral and detached, and he must be capable of determining whether probable cause exists for the requested arrest or search. This Court long has insisted that inferences of probable cause be drawn by "a neutral and detached magistrate instead of being judged by the officer engaged in the often competitive enterprise of ferreting out crime." In *Coolidge*, the Court last Term voided a search warrant issued by the state attorney general "who was actively in charge of the investigation and later was to be chief prosecutor at trial." If, on the other hand, detachment and capacity do conjoin, the magistrate has satisfied the Fourth Amendment's purpose.

III

The requisite detachment is present in the case at hand. Whatever else neutrality and detachment might entail, it is clear that they require severance and disengagement from activities of law enforcement. There has been no showing whatever here of partiality, or affiliation of these clerks with prosecutors or police. The record shows no connection with any law enforcement activity or authority which would distort the independent judgment the Fourth Amendment requires. Appellant himself expressly refused to allege anything to that effect. The municipal court clerk is assigned not to the police or prosecutor but to the municipal court judge for whom he does much of his work. In this sense, he may well be termed a "judicial officer." While a statutorily specified term of office and appointment by someone other than "an executive authority" might be desirable, the absence of such features is hardly disqualifying. Judges themselves take office under differing circumstances. Some are appointed, but many are elected by legislative bodies or by the people. Many enjoy but limited terms and are subject to re-appointment or re-election. Most depend for their salary level upon the legislative branch. We will not elevate requirements for the independence of a municipal clerk to a level higher than that prevailing with respect to many judges. The clerk's neutrality has not been impeached: he is removed from prosecutor or police and works within the judicial branch subject to the supervision of the municipal court judge.

Appellant likewise has failed to demonstrate that these clerks lack capacity to determine probable cause. The clerk's authority extends only to the issuance of arrest warrants for breach of municipal ordinances. We presume from the nature of the clerk's position that he would be able to deduce from the facts on an affidavit before him whether there was probable cause to believe a citizen guilty of impaired driving, breach of peace, drunkenness, trespass, or the multiple other common offenses covered by a municipal code. There has been no showing that this is too difficult a task for a clerk to accomplish. Our legal system has long entrusted nonlawyers to evaluate more complex and significant factual data than that in the case at hand. Grand juries daily determine probable cause prior to rendering indictments, and trial juries assess whether guilt is proved beyond a reasonable doubt. The significance and responsibility of these lay judgments betray any belief that the Tampa clerks could not determine probable cause for arrest.

Nor need we determine whether a State may lodge warrant authority in someone entirely outside the sphere of the judicial branch. Many persons may not qualify as the kind of "public civil officers" we have come to associate with the term "magistrate." Had the Tampa clerk been entirely divorced from a judicial position, this case would have presented different considerations. Here, however, the clerk is an employee of the judicial branch of the city of Tampa, disassociated from the role of law enforcement. On the record in this case, the independent status of the clerk cannot be questioned.

What we do reject today is any *per se* invalidation of a state or local warrant system on the ground that the issuing magistrate is not a lawyer or judge. Communities may have sound reasons for delegating the responsibility of issuing warrants to competent personnel other than judges or lawyers. Many municipal courts face stiff and unrelenting caseloads. A judge pressured with the docket before him may give warrant applications more brisk and summary treatment than would a clerk. All this is not to imply that a judge or lawyer would not normally provide the most desirable review of warrant requests. But our federal system warns of converting desirable practice into constitutional commandment. It recognizes in plural and diverse state activities one key to national innovation and vitality. States are entitled to some flexibility and leeway in their designation of magistrates, so long as all are neutral and detached and capable of the probable-cause determination required of them.

We affirm the judgment of the Florida Supreme Court.

QUESTIONS AND NOTES

1. Would (should) it matter these clerks are limited to issuing misdemeanor warrants? Would you expect the same result if they could issue a search warrant in felony cases? Why? Why Not?

2. How does (should) the educational non-requirement of these magistrates affect the *Gates* debate about the desirability of specific guidelines to constrain magistrates?

3. How close can the relationship be between magistrate and police officer? Suppose they are located in the same building? The same suite of offices? They regularly go to lunch together?

4. If the magistrate doesn't read the warrant before signing it, should it be invalid *per se*?

Chapter 4

ARRESTS

At common law, arrests made in public with probable cause did not require a warrant. In *United States v. Watson*, 423 U.S. 411 (1976), a divided Supreme Court constitutionalized this rule. The majority, per Justice White, upheld the rule on the basis of its long history of use, coupled with the presumption of constitutionality. Justice Powell's concurring opinion would have reached the same result on the need for police flexibility. As Powell saw it, a policeman often is unsure of the precise moment that an arrest is appropriate. If the policeman fails to get a warrant, he cannot make the arrest. If he gets the warrant, postpones the arrest, and subsequently makes it, it is possible that the warrant would have grown stale, but that new probable cause would justify the arrest. Thus Powell would adhere to the common law rule.

Justice Marshall, joined by Brennan dissented on the legal issue on the ground that a non-emergency arrest should require a warrant. On the other hand, he concurred in result in the case because the police did not have probable cause until the very moment that they sought to make the arrest.

In Part A of this chapter, we examine the need for a warrant in effectuating an in-the-house arrest. Part B looks at the force that the police may use in effectuating an arrest. Part C explores the police ability to detain residents of a home pursuant to a search warrant. Finally, Part D examines the items that may be seized in the course of an arrest.

A. ARRESTS IN THE HOME

Arrests in the home involve a clash of principles. *Watson* suggests that ordinarily arrests do not require a warrant. *Vale*, on the other hand, suggests that warrants are ordinarily required before entering one's home. The question of whether a warrant is required, and if so, what must the warrant allege, was ultimately resolved in *Payton v. New York* and somewhat embellished in *Steagald v. United States*. Shortly, we will examine those cases. However, we will begin with *United States v. Santana*, a classic law professor's case, which involves a woman standing at the door of her home, one foot in and one foot out.

UNITED STATES v. SANTANA
427 U.S. 38 (1976)

Mr. Justice Rehnquist delivered the opinion of the Court.

On August 16, 1974, Michael Gilletti, an undercover officer with the Philadelphia Narcotics Squad arranged a heroin "buy" with one Patricia McCafferty (from whom he had purchased narcotics before). McCafferty told him it would cost $115 "and we will go down to Mom Santana's for the dope."

Gilletti notified his superiors of the impending transaction, recorded the serial numbers of $110 (*sic*) in marked bills, and went to meet McCafferty at a prearranged location. She got in his car and directed him to drive to 2311 North Fifth Street, which, as she had previously informed him, was respondent Santana's residence.

McCafferty took the money and went inside the house, stopping briefly to speak to respondent Alejandro who was sitting on the front steps. She came out shortly afterwards and got into the car. Gilletti asked for the heroin; she thereupon extracted from her bra several glassine envelopes containing a brownish-white powder and gave them to him.

Gilletti then stopped the car, displayed his badge, and placed McCafferty under arrest. He told her that the police were going back to 2311 North Fifth Street and that he wanted to know where the money was. She said, "Mom has the money." At this point Sergeant Pruitt and other officers came up to the car. Gilletti showed them the envelope and said "Mom Santana has the money." Gilletti then took McCafferty to the police station.

Pruitt and the others then drove approximately two blocks back to 2311 North Fifth Street. They saw Santana standing in the doorway of the house[1] with a brown paper bag in her hand. They pulled up to within 15 feet of Santana and got out of their van, shouting "police," and displaying their identification. As the officers approached, Santana retreated into the vestibule of her house.

The officers followed through the open door, catching her in the vestibule. As she tried to pull away, the bag tilted and "two bundles of glazed paper packets with a white powder" fell to the floor.

The District Court granted respondents' motion [to suppress]. In an oral opinion the court found that "(t)here was strong probable cause that Defendant Santana had participated in the transaction with Defendant McCafferty." However, the court continued:

"One of the police officers . . . testified that the mission was to arrest Defendant Santana. Another police officer testified that the mission was to recover the bait money. Either one would require a warrant, one a warrant of arrest under ordinary circumstances and one a search warrant."

---

[1] An Officer Strohm testified that he recognized Santana, whom he had seen before. He also indicated that she was standing directly in the doorway one step forward would have put her outside, one step backward would have put her in the vestibule of her residence.

The court further held that Santana's "reentry from the doorway into the house" did not support allowing the police to make a warrantless entry into the house on the grounds of "hot pursuit," because it took "hot pursuit" to mean "a chase in and about public streets." The court did find, however, that the police acted under "extreme emergency" conditions. The Court of Appeals affirmed this decision without opinion.

In *Watson*, we held that the warrantless arrest of an individual in a public place upon probable cause did not violate the Fourth Amendment. Thus the first question we must decide is whether, when the police first sought to arrest Santana, she was in a public place.

While it may be true that under the common law of property the threshold of one's dwelling is "private," as is the yard surrounding the house, it is nonetheless clear that under the cases interpreting the Fourth Amendment Santana was in a "public" place. She was not in an area where she had any expectation of privacy. "What a person knowingly exposes to the public, even in his own house or office, is not a subject of Fourth Amendment protection." She was not merely visible to the public but was as exposed to public view, speech, hearing, and touch as if she had been standing completely outside her house. Thus, when the police, who concededly had probable cause to do so, sought to arrest her, they merely intended to perform a function which we have approved in *Watson*.

The only remaining question is whether her act of retreating into her house could thwart an otherwise proper arrest. We hold that it could not. In *Warden v. Hayden*, 387 U.S. 294 (1967), we recognized the right of police, who had probable cause to believe that an armed robber had entered a house a few minutes before, to make a warrantless entry to arrest the robber and to search for weapons. This case, involving a true "hot pursuit," is clearly governed by *Warden* ; the need to act quickly here is even greater than in that case while the intrusion is much less. The District Court was correct in concluding that "hot pursuit" means some sort of a chase, but it need not be an extended hue and cry "in and about (the) public streets." The fact that the pursuit here ended almost as soon as it began did not render it any the less a "hot pursuit" sufficient to justify the warrantless entry into Santana's house. Once Santana saw the police, there was likewise a realistic expectation that any delay would result in destruction of evidence. See *Vale*. Once she had been arrested the search, incident to that arrest, which produced the drugs and money was clearly justified.

We thus conclude that a suspect may not defeat an arrest which has been set in motion in a public place, and is therefore proper under *Watson*, by the expedient of escaping to a private place. The judgment of the Court of Appeals is reversed.

(Concurring and Dissenting opinions omitted.)

QUESTIONS AND NOTES

1. Was the Court playing fast and loose with the facts in analogizing *Santana* to *Watson*?

2. Would (should) the result have been different if "Mom" Santana had been totally inside the house, but visible from the street?

3. Could the police have avoided this entire problem by getting a warrant after arresting McCafferty, and before arresting Santana? If so, why should we excuse their failure to do so?

4. Does the Court's citation to *Vale*, strengthen or weaken its argument?

5. In *Payton*, the Court finally resolved the need for a warrant for an arrest in the home.

Can give someone more rights but cannot take rights away

PAYTON v. NEW YORK
445 U.S. 573 (1980)

Mr. Justice Stevens delivered the opinion of the Court.

These appeals challenge the constitutionality of New York statutes that authorize police officers to enter a private residence without a warrant and with force, if necessary, to make a routine felony arrest.

The important constitutional question presented by this challenge has been expressly left open in a number of our prior opinions. In *Watson*, we upheld a warrantless "midday public arrest," expressly noting that the case did not pose "the still unsettled question . . . 'whether and under what circumstances an officer may enter a suspect's home to make a warrantless arrest.'"

I

On January 14, 1970, after two days of intensive investigation, New York detectives had assembled evidence sufficient to establish probable cause to believe that Theodore Payton had murdered the manager of a gas station two days earlier. At about 7:30 a.m. on January 15, six officers went to Payton's apartment in the Bronx, intending to arrest him. They had not obtained a warrant. Although light and music emanated from the apartment, there was no response to their knock on the metal door. They summoned emergency assistance and, about 30 minutes later, used crowbars to break open the door and enter the apartment. No one was there. In plain view, however, was a .30-caliber shell casing that was seized and later admitted into evidence at Payton's murder trial.

In due course Payton surrendered to the police, was indicted for murder, and moved to suppress the evidence taken from his apartment. The trial judge held that the warrantless and forcible entry was authorized by the New York Code of Criminal Procedure, and that the evidence in plain view was properly seized. He had no occasion to decide whether those circumstances also would have justified the failure to obtain a warrant, because he concluded that the warrantless entry was adequately supported by the statute without regard to the circumstances.

The New York Court of Appeals affirmed the conviction of Payton. The court recognized that the question whether and under what circumstances an officer may enter a suspect's home to make a warrantless arrest had not been settled either by that court or by this Court. In answering that question, the majority of four judges relied primarily on its perception that there is a

". . . substantial difference between the intrusion which attends an entry for the purpose of searching the premises and that which results from an entry for the purpose of making an arrest, and [a] significant difference in the governmental interest in achieving the objective of the intrusion in the two instances."

The majority supported its holding by noting the "apparent historical acceptance" of warrantless entries to make felony arrests, both in the English common law and in the practice of many American States.

Three members of the New York Court of Appeals dissented on this issue because they believed that the Constitution requires the police to obtain a "warrant to enter a home in order to arrest or seize a person, unless there are exigent circumstances." Starting from the premise that, except in carefully circumscribed instances, "the Fourth Amendment forbids police entry into a private home to search for and seize an object without a warrant," the dissenters reasoned that an arrest of the person involves an even greater invasion of privacy and should therefore be attended with at least as great a measure of constitutional protection. The dissenters noted "the existence of statutes and the American Law Institute imprimatur codifying the common-law rule authorizing warrantless arrests in private homes" and acknowledged that "the statutory authority of a police officer to make a warrantless arrest in this State has been in effect for almost 100 years," but concluded that "neither antiquity nor legislative unanimity can be determinative of the grave constitutional question presented" and "can never be a substitute for reasoned analysis."

Before addressing the narrow question presented by these appeals, we put to one side other related problems that are not presented today. Although it is arguable that the warrantless entry to effect Payton's arrest might have been justified by exigent circumstances, none of the New York courts relied on any such justification. The Court of Appeals majority treated Payton's case as involving routine arrests in which there was ample time to obtain a warrant, and we will do the same. Accordingly, we have no occasion to consider the sort of emergency or dangerous situation, described in our cases as "exigent circumstances," that would justify a warrantless entry into a home for the purpose of either arrest or search.

II

It is familiar history that indiscriminate searches and seizures conducted under the authority of "general warrants" were the immediate evils that motivated the framing and adoption of the Fourth Amendment. Indeed, as originally proposed in the House of Representatives, the draft contained only one clause, which directly imposed limitations on the issuance of warrants, but imposed no express restrictions on warrantless searches or seizures. As it was ultimately adopted, however, the Amendment contained two separate clauses, the first protecting the basic right to be free from unreasonable searches and seizures and the second requiring that warrants be particular and supported by probable cause. The Amendment provides:

"The right of the people to be secure in their persons, houses, papers, and effects, against unreasonable searches and seizures, shall not be violated, and no Warrants shall issue, but upon probable cause, supported by Oath or affirmation, and particularly describing the place to be searched, and the persons or things to be seized."

It is thus perfectly clear that the evil the Amendment was designed to prevent was broader than the abuse of a general warrant. Unreasonable searches or seizures conducted without any warrant at all are condemned by the plain language of the first clause of the Amendment. Almost a century ago the Court stated in resounding terms that the principles reflected in the Amendment "reached farther than the concrete form" of the specific cases that gave it birth, and "apply to all invasions on the part of the government and its employes of the sanctity of a man's home and the privacies of life." *Boyd v. United States*, 116 U.S. 616. Without pausing to consider whether that broad language may require some qualification, it is sufficient to note that the warrantless arrest of a person is a species of seizure required by the Amendment to be reasonable. Indeed, as Mr. Justice Powell noted in his concurrence in *Watson*, the arrest of a person is "quintessentially a seizure."

The simple language of the Amendment applies equally to seizures of persons and to seizures of property. Our analysis in this case may therefore properly commence with rules that have been well established in Fourth Amendment litigation involving tangible items. As the Court reiterated just a few years ago, the "physical entry of the home is the chief evil against which the wording of the Fourth Amendment is directed." And we have long adhered to the view that the warrant procedure minimizes the danger of needless intrusions of that sort.

It is a "basic principle of Fourth Amendment law" that searches and seizures inside a home without a warrant are presumptively unreasonable. Yet it is also well settled that objects such as weapons or contraband found in a public place may be seized by the police without a warrant. The seizure of property in plain view involves no invasion of privacy and is presumptively reasonable, assuming that there is probable cause to associate the property with criminal activity. The distinction between a warrantless seizure in an open area and such a seizure on private premises was plainly stated in *G. M. Leasing Corp. v. United States*, 429 U.S. 338, 354.

As the late Judge Leventhal recognized, this distinction has equal force when the seizure of a person is involved. Writing on the constitutional issue now before us for the United States Court of Appeals for the District of Columbia Circuit sitting en banc, *Dorman v. United States*, 435 F.2d 385 (1970), Judge Leventhal first noted the settled rule that warrantless arrests in public places are valid. He immediately recognized, however, that "[a] greater burden is placed . . . on officials who enter a home or dwelling without consent. Freedom from intrusion into the home or dwelling is the archetype of the privacy protection secured by the Fourth Amendment."

His analysis of this question then focused on the long-settled premise that, absent exigent circumstances, a warrantless entry to search for weapons or contraband is unconstitutional even when a felony has been committed and there is probable cause to believe that incriminating evidence will be found within. He reasoned that the constitutional protection afforded to the individual's interest in the privacy of his own home is equally applicable to a warrantless entry for the purpose of arresting a resident of the house; for it is inherent in such an entry that a search for the suspect may be required before he can be apprehended. Judge Leventhal concluded that an entry to arrest and an entry to search for and to seize property implicate the same interest in preserving the privacy and the sanctity of the home, and justify the same level of constitutional protection.

We find this reasoning to be persuasive and in accord with this Court's Fourth Amendment decisions.

The majority of the New York Court of Appeals, however, suggested that there is a substantial difference in the relative intrusiveness of an entry to search for property and an entry to search for a person. It is true that the area that may legally be searched is broader when executing a search warrant than when executing an arrest warrant in the home. This difference may be more theoretical than real, however, because the police may need to check the entire premises for safety reasons, and sometimes they ignore the restrictions on searches incident to arrest.

But the critical point is that any differences in the intrusiveness of entries to search and entries to arrest are merely ones of degree rather than kind. The two intrusions share this fundamental characteristic: the breach of the entrance to an individual's home. The Fourth Amendment protects the individual's privacy in a variety of settings. In none is the zone of privacy more clearly defined than when bounded by the unambiguous physical dimensions of an individual's home — a zone that finds its roots in clear and specific constitutional terms: "The right of the people to be secure in their . . . houses . . . shall not be violated." That language unequivocally establishes the proposition that "[a]t the very core [of the Fourth Amendment] stands the right of a man to retreat into his own home and there be free from unreasonable governmental intrusion." In terms that apply equally to seizures of property and to seizures of persons, the Fourth Amendment has drawn a firm line at the entrance to the house. Absent exigent circumstances, that threshold may not reasonably be crossed without a warrant.

III

Without contending that *Watson*, decided the question presented by these appeals, New York argues that the reasons that support the *Watson* holding require a similar result here. In *Watson* the Court relied on (a) the well-settled common-law rule that a warrantless arrest in a public place is valid if the arresting officer had probable cause to believe the suspect is a felon; (b) the clear consensus among the States adhering to that well-settled common-law rule; and (c) the expression of the judgment of Congress that such an arrest is "reasonable." We consider each of these reasons as it applies to a warrantless entry into a home for the purpose of making a routine felony arrest.

A

An examination of the common-law understanding of an officer's authority to arrest sheds light on the obviously relevant, if not entirely dispositive, consideration of what the Framers of the Amendment might have thought to be reasonable.

A study of the common law on the question whether a constable had the authority to make warrantless arrests in the home on mere suspicion of a felony — as distinguished from an officer's right to arrest for a crime committed in his presence — reveals a surprising lack of judicial decisions and a deep divergence among scholars.

The common-law commentators disagreed sharply on the subject. Three distinct views were expressed. Lord Coke, widely recognized by the American colonists "as the greatest authority of his time on the laws of England," clearly viewed a warrantless entry for the purpose of arrest to be illegal. Burn, Foster, and Hawkins agreed, as did East and Russell, though the latter two qualified their opinions by stating that if an entry to arrest was made without a warrant, the officer was perhaps immune from liability for the trespass if the suspect was actually guilty. Blackstone, Chitty, and Stephen took the opposite view, that entry to arrest without a warrant was legal, though Stephen relied on Blackstone who, along with Chitty, in turn relied exclusively on Hale. But Hale's view was not quite so unequivocally expressed.[41]

It is obvious that the common-law rule on warrantless home arrests was not as clear as the rule on arrests in public places. Indeed, particularly considering the prominence of Lord Coke, the weight of authority as it appeared to the Framers was to the effect that a warrant was required, or at the minimum that there were substantial risks in proceeding without one. The common-law sources display a sensitivity to privacy interests that could not have been lost on the Framers. The zealous and frequent repetition of the adage that a "man's house is his castle," made it abundantly clear that both in England and in the Colonies "the freedom of one's house" was one of the most vital elements of English liberty.

Thus, our study of the relevant common law does not provide the same guidance that was present in *Watson*. Whereas the rule concerning the validity of an arrest in a public place was supported by cases directly in point and by the unanimous views of the commentators, we have found no direct authority supporting forcible entries into a home to make a routine arrest and the weight of the scholarly opinion is somewhat to the contrary. Indeed, the absence of any 17th- or 18th-century English cases directly in point, together with the unequivocal endorsement of the tenet that "a man's house is his castle," strongly suggests that the prevailing practice was not to make such arrests except in hot pursuit or when authorized by a warrant. In all events, the issue is not one that can be said to have been

---

[41] Hale writes that in the case where the constable suspects a person of a felony, "if the supposed offender fly and take house, and the door will not be opened upon demand of the constable and notification of his business, the constable may break the door, tho he have no warrant." Although it would appear that Hale might have meant to limit warrantless home arrests to cases of hot pursuit, the quoted passage has not typically been read that way.

definitively settled by the common law at the time the Fourth Amendment was adopted.

B

A majority of the States that have taken a position on the question permit warrantless entry into the home to arrest even in the absence of exigent circumstances. At this time, 24 States permit such warrantless entries; 15 States clearly prohibit them, though 3 States do so on federal constitutional grounds alone; and 11 States have apparently taken no position on the question.

But these current figures reflect a significant decline during the last decade in the number of States permitting warrantless entries for arrest. Recent dicta in this Court raising questions about the practice, and Federal Courts of Appeals' decisions on point have led state courts to focus on the issue. Virtually all of the state courts that have had to confront the constitutional issue directly have held warrantless entries into the home to arrest to be invalid in the absence of exigent circumstances. Three state courts have relied on Fourth Amendment grounds alone, while seven have squarely placed their decisions on both federal and state constitutional grounds. A number of other state courts, though not having had to confront the issue directly, have recognized the serious nature of the constitutional question. Apparently, only the Supreme Court of Florida and the New York Court of Appeals in this case have expressly upheld warrantless entries to arrest in the face of a constitutional challenge.

A longstanding, widespread practice is not immune from constitutional scrutiny. But neither is it to be lightly brushed aside. This is particularly so when the constitutional standard is as amorphous as the word "reasonable," and when custom and contemporary norms necessarily play such a large role in the constitutional analysis. In this case, although the weight of state-law authority is clear, there is by no means the kind of virtual unanimity on this question that was present in *Watson*, with regard to warrantless arrests in public places.

C

No congressional determination that warrantless entries into the home are "reasonable" has been called to our attention. None of the federal statutes cited in the Watson opinion reflects any such legislative judgment. Thus, that support for the *Watson* holding finds no counterpart in this case.

Mr. Justice Powell, concurring in *Watson*, stated: "But logic sometimes must defer to history and experience. The Court's opinion emphasizes the historical sanction accorded warrantless felony arrests [in public places]." In this case, however, neither history nor this Nation's experience requires us to disregard the overriding respect for the sanctity of the home that has been embedded in our traditions since the origins of the Republic.[54]

---

[54] There can be no doubt that Pitt's address in the House of Commons in March 1763 echoed and re-echoed throughout the Colonies: "The poorest man may in his cottage bid defiance to all the forces of the Crown. It may be frail; its roof may shake; the wind may blow through it; the storm may enter; the

IV

The parties have argued at some length about the practical consequences of a warrant requirement as a precondition to a felony arrest in the home.[55] In the absence of any evidence that effective law enforcement has suffered in those States that already have such a requirement, we are inclined to view such arguments with skepticism. More fundamentally, however, such arguments of policy must give way to a constitutional command that we consider to be unequivocal.

Finally, we note the State's suggestion that only a search warrant based on probable cause to believe the suspect is at home at a given time can adequately protect the privacy interests at stake, and since such a warrant requirement is manifestly impractical, there need be no warrant of any kind. We find this ingenious argument unpersuasive. It is true that an arrest warrant requirement may afford less protection than a search warrant requirement, but it will suffice to interpose the magistrate's determination of probable cause between the zealous officer and the citizen. If there is sufficient evidence of a citizen's participation in a felony to persuade a judicial officer that his arrest is justified, it is constitutionally reasonable to require him to open his doors to the officers of the law. Thus, for Fourth Amendment purposes, an arrest warrant founded on probable cause implicitly carries with it the limited authority to enter a dwelling in which the suspect lives when there is reason to believe the suspect is within.

Because no arrest warrant was obtained in either of these cases, the judgments must be reversed and the cases remanded to the New York Court of Appeals for further proceedings not inconsistent with this opinion.

MR. JUSTICE BLACKMUN, concurring.

I joined the Court's opinion in *Watson*, upholding, on probable cause, the warrantless arrest in a public place. I, of course, am still of the view that the decision in *Watson* is correct. The Court's balancing of the competing governmental and individual interests properly occasioned that result. Where, however, the warrantless arrest is in the suspect's home, that same balancing requires that, absent exigent circumstances, the result be the other way. The suspect's interest in the sanctity of his home then outweighs the governmental interests.

I therefore join the Court's opinion, firm in the conviction that the result in *Watson* and the result here, although opposite, are fully justified by history and by

---

rain may enter; but the King of England cannot enter — all his force dares not cross the threshold of the ruined tenement!" *Miller v. United States,* 357 U.S., at 307.

[55] The State of New York argues that the warrant requirement will pressure police to seek warrants and make arrests too hurriedly, thus increasing the likelihood of arresting innocent people; that it will divert scarce resources thereby interfering with the police's ability to do thorough investigations; that it will penalize the police for deliberate planning; and that it will lead to more injuries. Appellants counter that careful planning is possible and that the police need not rush to get a warrant, because if an exigency arises necessitating immediate arrest in the course of an orderly investigation, arrest without a warrant is permissible; that the warrant procedure will decrease the likelihood that an innocent person will be arrested; that the inconvenience of obtaining a warrant and the potential for diversion of resources is exaggerated by the State; and that there is no basis for the assertion that the time required to obtain a warrant would create peril.

the Fourth Amendment.

MR. JUSTICE WHITE, with whom THE CHIEF JUSTICE and MR. JUSTICE REHNQUIST join, dissenting.

The Court today holds that absent exigent circumstances officers may never enter a home during the daytime to arrest for a dangerous felony unless they have first obtained a warrant. This hard-and-fast rule, founded on erroneous assumptions concerning the intrusiveness of home arrest entries, finds little or no support in the common law or in the text and history of the Fourth Amendment. I respectfully dissent.

I

As the Court notes, the common law of searches and seizures, as evolved in England, as transported to the Colonies, and as developed among the States, is highly relevant to the present scope of the Fourth Amendment. Today's decision virtually ignores these centuries of common-law development, and distorts the historical meaning of the Fourth Amendment, by proclaiming for the first time a rigid warrant requirement for all nonexigent home arrest entries.

As the Court notes, commentators have differed as to the scope of the constable's inherent authority, when not acting under a warrant, to break doors in order to arrest. Probably the majority of commentators would permit arrest entries on probable suspicion even if the person arrested were not in fact guilty. Blackstone, Burn 87–88, Dalton, [and] Hale 583 would have permitted the type of home arrest entries that occurred in the present cases. The inclusion of Blackstone in this list is particularly significant in light of his profound impact on the minds of the colonists at the time of the framing of the Constitution and the ratification of the Bill of Rights. And Coke is flatly contrary to the Court's rule requiring a warrant, since he believed that even a warrant would not justify an arrest entry until the suspect had been indicted.

Finally, it bears noting that the doctrine against home entries on bare suspicion developed in a period in which the validity of *any* arrest on bare suspicion — even one occurring outside the home — was open to question. Not until Lord Mansfield's decision in *Samuel v. Payne*, 1 Doug. 359, 99 Eng. Rep. 230 (K.B.1780), was it definitively established that the constable could arrest on suspicion even if it turned out that no felony had been committed. To the extent that the commentators relied on by the Court reasoned from any general rule against warrantless arrests based on bare suspicion, the rationale for their position did not survive *Samuel v. Payne*.

B

The history of the Fourth Amendment does not support the rule announced today. At the time that Amendment was adopted the constable possessed broad inherent powers to arrest. The limitations on those powers derived, not from a warrant "requirement," but from the generally ministerial nature of the constable's office at common law. Far from restricting the constable's arrest power, the institution of the warrant was used to expand that authority by giving the constable delegated powers of a superior officer such as a justice of the peace. Hence at the time of the Bill of Rights, the warrant functioned as a powerful tool of law enforcement rather than as a protection for the rights of criminal suspects.

In fact, it was the abusive use of the warrant power, rather than any excessive zeal in the discharge of peace officers' inherent authority, that precipitated the Fourth Amendment. That Amendment grew out of colonial opposition to the infamous general warrants known as writs of assistance, which empowered customs officers to search at will, and to break open receptacles or packages, wherever they suspected uncustomed goods to be.

That the Framers were concerned about warrants, and not about the constable's inherent power to arrest, is also evident from the text and legislative history of the Fourth Amendment. That provision first reaffirms the basic principle of common law, that "[t]he right of the people to be secure in their persons, houses, papers, and effects, against unreasonable searches and seizures, shall not be violated . . . ." The Amendment does not here purport to limit or restrict the peace officer's inherent power to arrest or search, but rather assumes an existing right against actions in excess of that inherent power and ensures that it remain inviolable. As I have noted, it was not generally considered "unreasonable" at common law for officers to break doors in making warrantless felony arrests. The Amendment's second clause is directed at the actions of officers taken in their ministerial capacity pursuant to writs of assistance and other warrants. In contrast to the first Clause, the second Clause does purport to alter colonial practice: "and no Warrants shall issue, but upon probable cause, supported by Oath or affirmation, and particularly describing the place to be searched, and the persons or things to be seized."

In sum, the background, text, and legislative history of the Fourth Amendment demonstrate that the purpose was to restrict the abuses that had developed with respect to warrants; the Amendment preserved common-law rules of arrest. Because it was not considered generally unreasonable at common law for officers to break doors to effect a warrantless felony arrest, I do not believe that the Fourth Amendment was intended to outlaw the types of police conduct at issue in the present cases.

C

Probably because warrantless arrest entries were so firmly accepted at common law, there is apparently no recorded constitutional challenge to such entries in the 19th-century cases. Common-law authorities on both sides of the Atlantic, however, continued to endorse the validity of such arrests.

This Court apparently first questioned the reasonableness of warrantless nonexigent entries to arrest in *Jones v. United States*, 357 U.S. 493, 499–500 (1958), noting in dictum that such entries would pose a "grave constitutional question" if carried out at night. In *Coolidge v. New Hampshire*, 403 U.S. 443, (1971), the Court stated, again in dictum:

"[I]f [it] is correct that it has generally been assumed that the Fourth Amendment is not violated by the warrantless entry of a man's house for purposes of arrest, it might be wise to re-examine the assumption. Such a re-examination 'would confront us with a grave constitutional question, namely, whether the forcible nighttime entry into a dwelling to arrest a person reasonably believed within, upon probable cause that he has committed a felony, under circumstances where no reason appears why an arrest warrant could not have been sought, is consistent with the Fourth Amendment.' "

Although *Coolidge* and *Jones* both referred to the special problem of warrantless entries during the nighttime, it is not surprising that state and federal courts have tended to read those dicta as suggesting a broader infirmity applying to daytime entries also, and that the majority of recent decisions have been against the constitutionality of all types of warrantless, nonexigent home arrest entries. As the Court concedes, however, even despite *Coolidge* and *Jones* it remains the case that "[a] majority of the States that have taken a position on the question permit warrantless entry into the home to arrest even in the absence of exigent circumstances. At this time, 24 States permit such warrantless entries; 15 States clearly prohibited them, though 3 States do so on federal constitutional grounds alone; and 11 States have apparently taken no position on the question." This consensus, in the face of seemingly contrary dicta from this Court, is entitled to more deference than the Court today provides. Cf. *Watson*.

D

In the present cases, as in *Watson*, the applicable federal statutes are relevant to the reasonableness of the type of arrest in question. Under 18 U.S.C. § 3052, specified federal agents may "make arrests without warrants for any offense against the United States committed in their presence, or for any felony cognizable under the laws of the United States, if they have reasonable grounds to believe that the person to be arrested has committed or is committing such felony." On its face this provision authorizes federal agents to make warrantless arrests anywhere, including the home. Particularly in light of the accepted rule at common law and among the States permitting warrantless home arrests, the absence of any explicit exception for the home from § 3052 is persuasive evidence that Congress intended to authorize warrantless arrests there as well as elsewhere.

Further, Congress has not been unaware of the special problems involved in police entries into the home. In 18 U.S.C. § 3109, it provided that "[t]he officer may break open any outer or inner door or window of a house, or any part of a house, or anything therein, to execute a search warrant, if, after notice of its authority and purpose, he is refused admittance . . . ." In explicitly providing authority to enter when executing a search warrant, Congress surely did not intend to derogate from the officers' power to effect an arrest entry either with or without a warrant. Rather, Congress apparently assumed that this power was so firmly established either at common law or by statute that no explicit grant of arrest authority was required in § 3109. In short, although the Court purports to find no guidance in the relevant federal statutes, I believe that fairly read they authorize the type of police conduct at issue in these cases.

II

A

Today's decision rests, in large measure, on the premise that warrantless arrest entries constitute a particularly severe invasion of personal privacy. I do not dispute that the home is generally a very private area or that the common law displayed a special "reverence . . . for the individual's right of privacy in his house." However, the Fourth Amendment is concerned with protecting people, not places, and no talismanic significance is given to the fact that an arrest occurs in the home rather than elsewhere. It is necessary in each case to assess realistically the actual extent of invasion of constitutionally protected privacy. Further, as Mr. Justice POWELL observed in *Watson*, all arrests involve serious intrusions into an individual's privacy and dignity. Yet we settled in *Watson* that the intrusiveness of a public arrest is not enough to mandate the obtaining of a warrant. The inquiry in the present case, therefore, is whether the incremental intrusiveness that results from an arrest's being made in the dwelling is enough to support an inflexible constitutional rule requiring warrants for such arrests whenever exigent circumstances are not present.

Today's decision ignores the carefully crafted restrictions on the common-law power of arrest entry and thereby overestimates the dangers inherent in that practice. At common law, absent exigent circumstances, entries to arrest could be made only for felony. Even in cases of felony, the officers were required to announce their presence, demand admission, and be refused entry before they were entitled to break doors. Further, it seems generally accepted that entries could be made only during daylight hours. And, in my view, the officer entering to arrest must have reasonable grounds to believe, not only that the arrestee has committed a crime, but also that the person suspected is present in the house at the time of the entry.

These four restrictions on home arrests — felony, knock and announce, daytime, and stringent probable cause — constitute powerful and complementary protections for the privacy interests associated with the home. The felony requirement guards against abusive or arbitrary enforcement and ensures that invasions of the home occur only in case of the most serious crimes. The knock-and- announce and daytime requirements protect individuals against the fear, humiliation, and embarrassment of being aroused from their beds in states of partial or complete undress. And these requirements allow the arrestee to surrender at his front door, thereby maintaining his dignity and preventing the officers from entering other rooms of the dwelling. The stringent probable-cause requirement would help ensure against the possibility that the police would enter when the suspect was not home, and, in searching for him, frighten members of the family or ransack parts of the house, seizing items in plain view. In short, these requirements, taken together, permit an individual suspected of a serious crime to surrender at the front door of his dwelling and thereby avoid most of the humiliation and indignity that the Court seems to believe necessarily accompany a house arrest entry. Such a front-door arrest, in my view, is no more intrusive on personal privacy than the public warrantless arrests which we found to pass constitutional muster in *Watson*.[14]

All of these limitations on warrantless arrest entries are satisfied on the facts of the present case. The arrests here were for serious felonies — murder and armed robbery — and occurred during daylight hours. The authorizing statutes required that the police announce their business and demand entry. And it is not argued that the police had no probable cause to believe that Payton [was] in [his] dwelling at the time of the entry. Today's decision, therefore, sweeps away any possibility that warrantless home entries might be permitted in some limited situations other than those in which exigent circumstances are present. The Court substitutes, in one sweeping decision, a rigid constitutional rule in place of the common-law approach, evolved over hundreds of years, which achieved a flexible accommodation between the demands of personal privacy and the legitimate needs of law enforcement.

A rule permitting warrantless arrest entries would not pose a danger that officers would use their entry power as a pretext to justify an otherwise invalid warrantless search. A search pursuant to a warrantless arrest entry will rarely, if ever, be as complete as one under authority of a search warrant. If the suspect surrenders at the door, the officers may not enter other rooms. Of course, the suspect may flee or hide, or may not be at home, but the officers cannot anticipate the first two of these possibilities and the last is unlikely given the requirement of probable cause to believe that the suspect is at home. Even when officers are justified in searching other rooms, they may seize only items within the arrestee's position or immediate control or items in plain view discovered during the course of a search reasonably directed at discovering a hiding suspect. Hence a warrantless home entry is likely to uncover far less evidence than a search conducted under authority of a search warrant. Furthermore, an arrest entry will inevitably tip off the suspects and likely result in destruction or removal of evidence not uncovered during the arrest. I therefore cannot believe that the police would take the risk of losing valuable evidence through a pretextual arrest entry rather than applying to a magistrate for a search warrant.

B

While exaggerating the invasion of personal privacy involved in home arrests, the Court fails to account for the danger that its rule will "severely hamper effective law enforcement." The policeman on his beat must now make subtle discriminations that perplex even judges in their chambers. As Mr. Justice POWELL noted, concurring *Watson*, police will sometimes delay making an arrest, even after probable cause is established, in order to be sure that they have enough evidence to convict. Then, if they suddenly have to arrest, they run the risk that the subsequent exigency will not excuse their prior failure to obtain a warrant. This problem cannot effectively be cured by obtaining a warrant as soon as probable cause is established because of the chance that the warrant will go stale before the arrest is made.

---

[14] If the suspect flees or hides, of course, the intrusiveness of the entry will be somewhat greater; but the policeman's hands should not be tied merely because of the possibility that the suspect will fail to cooperate with legitimate actions by law enforcement personnel.

Further, police officers will often face the difficult task of deciding whether the circumstances are sufficiently exigent to justify their entry to arrest without a warrant. This is a decision that must be made quickly in the most trying of circumstances. If the officers mistakenly decide that the circumstances are exigent, the arrest will be invalid and any evidence seized incident to the arrest or in plain view will be excluded at trial. On the other hand, if the officers mistakenly determine that exigent circumstances are lacking, they may refrain from making the arrest, thus creating the possibility that a dangerous criminal will escape into the community. The police could reduce the likelihood of escape by staking out all possible exits until the circumstances become clearly exigent or a warrant is obtained. But the costs of such a stakeout seem excessive in an era of rising crime and scarce police resources.

The uncertainty inherent in the exigent-circumstances determination burdens the judicial system as well. In the case of searches, exigent circumstances are sufficiently unusual that this Court has determined that the benefits of a warrant outweigh the burdens imposed, including the burdens on the judicial system. In contrast, arrests recurringly involve exigent circumstances, and this Court has heretofore held that a warrant can be dispensed with without undue sacrifice in Fourth Amendment values. The situation should be no different with respect to arrests in the home. Under today's decision, whenever the police have made a warrantless home arrest there will be the possibility of "endless litigation with respect to the existence of exigent circumstances, whether it was practicable to get a warrant, whether the suspect was about to flee, and the like."

Our cases establish that the ultimate test under the Fourth Amendment is one of "reasonableness." I cannot join the Court in declaring unreasonable a practice which has been thought entirely reasonable by so many for so long. It would be far preferable to adopt a clear and simple rule: after knocking and announcing their presence, police may enter the home to make a daytime arrest without a warrant when there is probable cause to believe that the person to be arrested committed a felony and is present in the house. This rule would best comport with the common-law background, with the traditional practice in the States, and with the history and policies of the Fourth Amendment. Accordingly, I respectfully dissent.

Mr. Justice Rehnquist, dissenting.

I fully concur in and join the dissenting opinion of Mr. Justice White. There is significant historical evidence that we have over the years misread the history of the Fourth Amendment in connection with searches, elevating the warrant requirement over the necessity for probable cause in a way which the Framers of that Amendment did not intend. See T. Taylor, Two Studies in Constitutional Interpretation 38–50 (1969). But one may accept all of that as *stare decisis*, and still feel deeply troubled by the transposition of these same errors into the area of actual arrests of felons within their houses with respect to whom there is probable cause to suspect guilt of the offense in question.

QUESTIONS AND NOTES

1.   Do you perceive history and deference to Congress to have played the same role in *Payton* that it did in *Watson*? If not, why not?

2.   Are the policy reasons for not requiring a warrant significantly different in *Payton* than they were in *Watson*?

3.   To some extent, *Payton* involves a clash between flexibility and certainty (bright line). The Court's rule provides certainty. Justice White would allow more flexibility. In general, which of those values ought to predominate? Why? In the context of this case, who reached the better result? Why?

4.   In Justice White's four-part standard, is there a difference between "stringent probable cause" and ordinary probable cause? If so, do we want judges determining what constitutes stringent probable cause as opposed to ordinary probable cause? What kind of guidance would such a standard provide the police?

5.   Do you agree with the Court that an arrest warrant, as opposed to a search warrant, adequately protects the homeowners' interest? In regard thereto, contrast the *Payton* situation to *Steagald*.

STEAGALD v. UNITED STATES
451 U.S. 204 (1981)

JUSTICE MARSHALL delivered the opinion of the Court.

The issue in this case is whether, under the Fourth Amendment, a law enforcement officer may legally search for the subject of an arrest warrant in the home of a third party without first obtaining a search warrant. Concluding that a search warrant must be obtained absent exigent circumstances or consent, we reverse the judgment of the United States Court of Appeals for the Fifth Circuit affirming petitioner's conviction.

In early January 1978, an agent of the Drug Enforcement Administration (DEA) was contacted in Detroit, Mich., by a confidential informant who suggested that he might be able to locate Ricky Lyons, a federal fugitive wanted on drug charges. On January 14, 1978, the informant called the agent again, and gave him a telephone number in the Atlanta, Ga., area where, according to the informant, Ricky Lyons could be reached during the next 24 hours. On January 16, 1978, the agent called fellow DEA Agent Kelly Goodowens in Atlanta and relayed the information he had obtained from the informant. Goodowens contacted Southern Bell Telephone Co., and secured the address corresponding to the telephone number obtained by the informant. Goodowens also discovered that Lyons was the subject of a 6-month-old arrest warrant.

Two days later, Goodowens and 11 other officers drove to the address supplied by the telephone company to search for Lyons. The officers observed two men standing outside the house to be searched. These men were Hoyt Gaultney and petitioner Gary Steagald. The officers approached with guns drawn, frisked both men, and, after demanding identification, determined that neither man was Lyons.

Several agents proceeded to the house. Gaultney's wife answered the door, and informed the agents that she was alone in the house. She was told to place her hands against the wall and was guarded in that position while one agent searched the house. Ricky Lyons was not found, but during the search of the house the agent observed what he believed to be cocaine. Upon being informed of this discovery, Agent Goodowens sent an officer to obtain a search warrant and in the meantime conducted a second search of the house, which uncovered additional incriminating evidence. During a third search conducted pursuant to a search warrant, the agents uncovered 43 pounds of cocaine. Petitioner was arrested and indicted on federal drug charges.

Prior to trial, petitioner moved to suppress all evidence uncovered during the various searches on the ground that it was illegally obtained because the agents had failed to secure a search warrant before entering the house. Agent Goodowens testified at the suppression hearing that there had been no "physical hinderance" preventing him from obtaining a search warrant and that he did not do so because he believed that the arrest warrant for Ricky Lyons was sufficient to justify the entry and search. Because the issue presented by this case is an important one that has divided the Circuits, we granted certiorari.

The question before us is a narrow one.[6] The search at issue here took place in the absence of consent or exigent circumstances. Except in such special situations, we have consistently held that the entry into a home to conduct a search or make an arrest is unreasonable under the Fourth Amendment unless done pursuant to a warrant. Thus, as we recently observed: "[I]n terms that apply equally to seizures of property and to seizures of persons, the Fourth Amendment has drawn a firm line at the entrance to the house. Absent exigent circumstances, that threshold may not reasonably be crossed without a warrant." *Payton*. Here, of course, the agents had a warrant — one authorizing the arrest of Ricky Lyons. However, the Fourth Amendment claim here is not being raised by Ricky Lyons. Instead, the challenge to the search is asserted by a person not named in the warrant who was convicted on the basis of evidence uncovered during a search of his residence for Ricky Lyons. Thus, the narrow issue before us is whether an arrest warrant — as opposed to a search warrant — is adequate to protect the Fourth Amendment interests of persons not named in the warrant, when their homes are searched without their consent and in the absence of exigent circumstances.

The purpose of a warrant is to allow a neutral judicial officer to assess whether the police have probable cause to make an arrest or conduct a search. As we have often explained, the placement of this checkpoint between the Government and the citizen implicitly acknowledges that an "officer engaged in the often competitive enterprise of ferreting out crime," may lack sufficient objectivity to weigh correctly the strength of the evidence supporting the contemplated action against the individual's interests in protecting his own liberty and the privacy of his home. However, while an arrest warrant and a search warrant both serve to subject the probable-cause determination of the police to judicial review, the interests pro-

---

[6] Initially, we assume without deciding that the information relayed to Agent Goodowens concerning the whereabouts of Ricky Lyons would have been sufficient to establish probable cause to believe that Lyons was at the house searched by the agents.

tected by the two warrants differ. An arrest warrant is issued by a magistrate upon a showing that probable cause exists to believe that the subject of the warrant has committed an offense and thus the warrant primarily serves to protect an individual from an unreasonable seizure. A search warrant, in contrast is issued upon a showing of probable cause to believe that the legitimate object of a search is located in a particular place, and therefore safeguards an individual's interest in the privacy of his home and possessions against the unjustified intrusion of the police.

Thus, whether the arrest warrant issued in this case adequately safeguarded the interests protected by the Fourth Amendment depends upon what the warrant authorized the agents to do. To be sure, the warrant embodied a judicial finding that there was probable cause to believe the Ricky Lyons had committed a felony, and the warrant therefore authorized the officers to seize Lyons. However, the agents sought to do more than use the warrant to arrest Lyons in a public place or in his home; instead, they relied on the warrant as legal authority to enter the home of a third person based on their belief that Ricky Lyons might be a guest there. Regardless of how reasonable this belief might have been, it was never subjected to the detached scrutiny of a judicial officer. Thus, while the warrant in this case may have protected Lyons from an unreasonable seizure, it did absolutely nothing to protect petitioner's privacy interest in being free from an unreasonable invasion and search of his home. Instead, petitioner's only protection from an illegal entry and search was the agent's personal determination of probable cause. In the absence of exigent circumstances, we have consistently held that such judicially untested determinations are not reliable enough to justify an entry into a person's home to arrest him without a warrant, or a search of a home for objects in the absence of a search warrant. We see no reason to depart from this settled course when the search of a home is for a person rather than an object.[7]

---

[7] Indeed, the plain wording of the Fourth Amendment admits of no exemption from the warrant requirement when the search of a home is for a person rather than for a thing. As previously noted, absent exigent circumstances or consent, an entry into a private dwelling to conduct a search or effect an arrest is unreasonable without a warrant. The second clause of the Fourth Amendment, which governs the issuance of such warrants, provides that "no Warrants shall issue but upon probable cause, supported by Oath or affirmation, and particularly describing the place to be searched, and the persons or things to be seized." This language plainly suggests that the same sort of judicial determination must be made when the search of a person's home is for another person as is necessary when the search is for an object. Specifically, absent exigent circumstances the magistrate, rather than the police officer, must make the decision that probable cause exists to believe that the person or object to be seized is within a particular place.

In *Payton*, of course, we recognized that an arrest warrant alone was sufficient to authorize the entry into a person's home to effect his arrest. We reasoned: "If there is sufficient evidence of a citizen's participation in a felony to persuade a judicial officer that his arrest is justified, it is constitutionally reasonable to require him to open his doors to the officers of the law. Thus, for Fourth Amendment purposes, an arrest warrant founded on probable cause implicitly carries with it the limited authority to enter a dwelling in which the suspect lives when there is reason to believe the suspect is within." Because an arrest warrant authorizes the police to deprive a person of his liberty, it necessarily also authorizes a limited invasion of that person's privacy interest when it is necessary to arrest him in his home. This analysis, however, is plainly inapplicable when the police seek to use an arrest warrant as legal authority to enter the home of a third party to conduct a search. Such a warrant embodies no judicial determination whatsoever regarding the person whose home is to be searched. Because it does not authorize the police to deprive the third person of his liberty, it cannot embody any derivative authority to deprive this person of his interest in the privacy of his home. Such a deprivation must instead be based

A contrary conclusion — that the police, acting alone and in the absence of exigent circumstances, may decide when there is sufficient justification for searching the home of a third party for the subject of an arrest warrant — would create a significant potential for abuse. Armed solely with an arrest warrant for a single person, the police could search all the homes of that individual's friends and acquaintances. See, *e.g.*, *Lankford v. Gelston*, 364 F.2d 197 (CA4 1966) (enjoining police practice under which 300 homes were searched pursuant to arrest warrants for two fugitives). Moreover, an arrest warrant may serve as the pretext for entering a home in which the police have a suspicion, but not probable cause to believe, that illegal activity is taking place. The Government recognizes the potential for such abuses,[8] but contends that existing remedies — such as motions to suppress illegally procured evidence and damages actions for Fourth Amendment violations — provide adequate means of redress. We do not agree. As we observed on a previous occasion, "[t]he [Fourth] Amendment is designed to prevent, not simply to redress, unlawful police action." Indeed, if suppression motions and damages actions were sufficient to implement the Fourth Amendment's prohibition against unreasonable searches and seizures, there would be no need for the constitutional requirement that in the absence of exigent circumstances a warrant must be obtained for a home arrest or a search of a home for objects. We have instead concluded that in such cases the participation of a detached magistrate in the probable-cause determination is an essential element of a reasonable search or seizure, and we believe that the same conclusion should apply here.

In sum, two distinct interests were implicated by the search at issue here — Ricky Lyons' interest in being free from an unreasonable seizure and petitioner's interest in being free from an unreasonable search of his home. Because the arrest warrant for Lyons addressed only the former interest, the search of petitioner's home was no more reasonable from petitioner's perspective than it would have been if conducted in the absence of any warrant. Since warrantless searches of a home are impermissible absent consent or exigent circumstances, we conclude that the instant search violated the Fourth Amendment.

The Government concedes that this view is "apparently logical," that it furthers the general policies underlying the Fourth Amendment, and that it "has the virtue of producing symmetry between the law of entry to conduct a search for things to be seized and the law of entry to conduct a search for persons to be seized." Yet we are informed that this conclusion is "not without its flaws" in that it is contrary to common-law precedent and creates some practical problems of law enforcement. We treat these contentions in turn.

---

on an independent showing that a legitimate object of a search is located in the third party's home. We have consistently held, however, that such a determination is the province of the magistrate, and not that of the police officer.

[8] The Government concedes that "an arrest warrant may be thought to have some of the undesirable attributes of a general warrant if it authorizes entry into third party premises." Similarly, the Government agrees that "the potential for abuse is much less if the implicit entry authorization of an arrest warrant is confined to the suspect's own residence and is not held to make the police free to search for the suspect in anyone else's house without obtaining a particularized judicial determination that the suspect is present."

The common law may, within limits,[10] be instructive in determining what sorts of searches the Framers of the Fourth Amendment regarded as reasonable. The Government contends that at common law an officer could forcibly enter the home of a third party to execute an arrest warrant. To be sure, several commentators do suggest that a constable could "break open doors" to effect such an arrest. As support for this proposition, these commentators all rely on a single decision, *Semayne's Case*, 5 Co. Rep. 91a, 92b–93a, 77 Eng. Rep. 194, 198 (K.B.1603). Although that case involved only the authority of a sheriff to effect civil service on a person within his own home, the court noted in dictum that a person could not "escape the ordinary process of law" by seeking refuge in the home of a third party. However, the language of the decision, while not free from ambiguity, suggests that forcible entry into a third party's house was permissible only when the person to be arrested was pursued to the house. The decision refers to a person who "flies" to another's home, and the annotation notes that "in order to justify the breaking of the outer door; after denial on request to take a person . . . in the house of a stranger, it must be understood . . . that the person upon a pursuit taketh refuge in the house of another." The common-law commentators appear to have adopted this limitation. We have long recognized that such "hot pursuit" cases fall within the exigent-circumstances exception to the warrant requirement, see *Warden v. Hayden*, 387 U.S. 294 (1967), and therefore are distinguishable from the routine search situation presented here.

More important, the general question addressed by the common-law commentators was very different from the issue presented by this case. The authorities on which the Government relies were concerned with whether the *subject* of the arrest warrant could claim sanctuary from arrest by hiding in the home of a third party. The issue here, however, is not whether the subject of an arrest warrant can object to the absence of a search warrant when he is apprehended in another person's home, but rather whether the residents of that home can complain of the search. Because the authorities relied on by the Government focus on the former question without addressing the latter, we find their usefulness limited. Indeed, if anything, the little guidance that can be gleaned from common-law authorities undercuts the Government's position. The language of *Semayne's Case* quoted above, for example, suggests that although the subject of an arrest warrant could not find sanctuary in the home of the third party, the home remained a "castle or privilege" for its residents. Similarly, several commentators suggested that a search warrant, rather than an arrest warrant, was necessary to fully insulate a constable from an action for trespass brought by a party whose home was searched.

While the common law thus sheds relatively little light on the narrow question before us, the history of the Fourth Amendment strongly suggests that its Framers

---

[10] The significance accorded to such authority, however, must be kept in perspective, for our decisions in this area have not "simply frozen into constitutional law those enforcement practices that existed at the time of the Fourth Amendment's passage." The common-law rules governing searches and arrests evolved in a society far simpler than ours is today. Crime has changed, as have the means of law enforcement, and it would therefore be naive to assume that those actions a constable could take in an English or American village three centuries ago should necessarily govern what we, as a society, now regard as proper. Instead, the Amendment's prohibition against "unreasonable searches and seizures" must be interpreted "in light of contemporary norms and conditions."

would not have sanctioned the instant search. The Fourth Amendment was intended partly to protect against the abuses of the general warrants that had occurred in England and of the writs of assistance used in the Colonies. The general warrant specified only an offense — typically seditious libel — and left to the discretion of the executing officials the decision as to which persons should be arrested and which places should be searched. Similarly, the writs of assistance used in the Colonies noted only the object of the search — any uncustomed goods — and thus left customs officials completely free to search any place where they believed such goods might be. The central objectionable feature of both warrants was that they provided no judicial check on the determination of the executing officials that the evidence available justified an intrusion into any particular home. An arrest warrant, to the extent that it is invoked as authority to enter the homes of third parties, suffers from the same infirmity. Like a writ of assistance, it specifies only the object of a search — in this case, Ricky Lyons — and leaves to the unfettered discretion of the police the decision as to which particular homes should be searched. We do not believe that the Framers of the Fourth Amendment would have condoned such a result.

The Government also suggests that practical problems might arise if law enforcement officers are required to obtain a search warrant before entering the home of a third party to make an arrest. The basis of this concern is that persons, as opposed to objects, are inherently mobile, and thus officers seeking to effect an arrest may be forced to return to the magistrate several times as the subject of the arrest warrant moves from place to place. We are convinced, however, that a search warrant requirement will not significantly impede effective law enforcement efforts.

First, the situations in which a search warrant will be necessary are few. As noted in *Payton*, an arrest warrant alone will suffice to enter a suspect's own residence to effect his arrest. Furthermore, if probable cause exists, no warrant is required to apprehend a suspected felon in a public place. *Watson*. Thus, the subject of an arrest warrant can be readily seized before entering or after leaving the home of a third party.[14] Finally, the exigent-circumstances doctrine significantly limits the situations in which a search warrant would be needed. For example, a warrantless entry of a home would be justified if the police were in "hot pursuit" of a fugitive. Thus, to the extent that searches for persons pose special problems, we believe that the exigent-circumstances doctrine is adequate to accommodate legitimate law enforcement needs.

Moreover, in those situations in which a search warrant is necessary, the inconvenience incurred by the police is simply not that significant. First, if the police know of the location of the felon when they obtain an arrest warrant, the additional burden of obtaining a search warrant at the same time is miniscule. The inconvenience of obtaining such a warrant does not increase significantly when an outstanding arrest warrant already exists. In this case, for example, Agent Goodowens knew the address of the house to be searched two days in advance, and planned the raid from the federal courthouse in Atlanta where, we are informed,

---

[14] Indeed, the "inherent mobility" of persons noted by the Government suggests that in most situations the police may avoid altogether the need to obtain a search warrant simply by waiting for a suspect to leave the third person's home before attempting to arrest that suspect.

three full-time magistrates were on duty. In routine search cases such as this, the short time required to obtain a search warrant from a magistrate will seldom hinder efforts to apprehend a felon. Finally, if a magistrate is not nearby, a telephonic search warrant can usually be obtained.

Whatever practical problems remain, however, cannot outweigh the constitutional interests at stake. Any warrant requirement impedes to some extent the vigor with which the Government can seek to enforce its laws, yet the Fourth Amendment recognizes that this restraint is necessary in some cases to protect against unreasonable searches and seizures. We conclude that this is such a case. The additional burden imposed on the police by a warrant requirement is minimal. In contrast, the right protected — that of presumptively innocent people to be secure in their homes from unjustified, forcible intrusions by the Government — is weighty. Thus, in order to render the instant search reasonable under the Fourth Amendment, a search warrant was required.

Accordingly, the judgment of the Court of Appeals is reversed, and the case is remanded to that court for further proceedings consistent with this opinion.

JUSTICE REHNQUIST, with whom JUSTICE WHITE joins, dissenting.

The Court's opinion reversing petitioner's conviction proceeds in a pristinely simple manner: Steagald had a Fourth Amendment privacy interest in the dwelling entered by the police, and even though the police entered the premises for the sole purpose of executing a valid arrest warrant for Lyons, a fugitive from justice, whom they had probable cause to believe was within, the arrest warrant was not sufficient absent exigent circumstances to justify invading Steagald's privacy interest in the dwelling. Petitioner Steagald's privacy interest is different from Lyons' interest in being free from an unreasonable seizure, according to the Court, and the arrest warrant only validated the invasion of the latter. In the words of the Court:

"[T]he search of petitioner's home was no more reasonable from petitioner's perspective than it would have been if conducted in the absence of any warrant. Since warrantless searches of a home are impermissible absent consent or exigent circumstances, we conclude that the instant search violated the Fourth Amendment."

This "reasoning" not only assumes the answer to the question presented — whether the search of petitioner's dwelling could be undertaken without a search warrant — but also conveniently ignores the critical fact in this case, the existence of an arrest warrant for a fugitive believed on the basis of probable cause to be in the dwelling. The Court assumes that because the arrest warrant did not specifically address petitioner's privacy interest it is of no further relevance to the case. Incidental infringements of distinct Fourth Amendment interests may, however, be reasonable when they occur in the course of executing a valid warrant addressed to other interests. In *Dalia v. United States*, 441 U.S. 238 (1979), the Court rejected the argument that a separate search warrant was required before police could enter a business office to install an eavesdropping device when a warrant authorizing the eavesdropping itself had already been obtained. As the Court put it: "This view of the Warrant Clause parses too finely the interests protected by the Fourth Amendment. *Often in executing a warrant the police may find it necessary to interfere with privacy rights not explicitly considered by the judge who issued the warrant.*" (emphasis supplied). In *Payton*, the Court rejected the suggestion that a separate search warrant was required before police could execute an arrest warrant by entering the home of the subject of the warrant. Although the subject of the warrant had a Fourth Amendment interest in the privacy of his dwelling quite distinct from the interest in being free from unreasonable seizures addressed by the arrest warrant, the Court concluded that it was "constitutionally reasonable to require him to open his doors to the officers of the law."

This case, therefore, cannot be resolved by the simple Aristotelian syllogism which the Court employs. Concluding as it does that the arrest warrant did not address the privacy interest affected by the search by no means ends the matter; it simply presents the issue for decision. Resolution of that issue depends upon a balancing of the "need to search against the invasion which the search entails." Here, as in all Fourth Amendment cases, "reasonableness is still the ultimate standard." In determining the reasonableness of dispensing with the requirement of a separate search warrant in this case, I believe that the existence of a valid arrest warrant is highly relevant.

The government's interests in the warrantless entry of a third-party dwelling to execute an arrest warrant are compelling. The basic problem confronting police in such situations is the inherent mobility of the fugitive. By definition, the police have probable cause to believe that the fugitive is in a dwelling which is not his home. He may stay there for a week, a day, or 10 minutes. Fugitives from justice tend to be mobile, and police officers will generally have no way of knowing whether the subject of an arrest warrant will be at the dwelling when they return from seeking a search warrant. Imposition of a search warrant requirement in such circumstances will frustrate the compelling interests of the government and indeed the public in the apprehension of those subject to outstanding arrest warrants.

The Court's responses to these very real concerns are singularly unpersuasive. It first downplays them by stating that "the situations in which a search warrant will be necessary are few," because no search warrant is necessary to arrest a suspect at his home and, if the suspect is at another's home, the police need only wait until he leaves, since no search warrant is needed to arrest him in a public place. These beguilingly simple answers to a serious law enforcement problem simply will not wash. Criminals who know or suspect they are subject to arrest warrants would not be likely to return to their homes, and while "[t]he police could reduce the likelihood of escape by staking out all possible exits . . . the costs of such a stakeout seems excessive in an era of rising crime and scarce police resources." The Court's ivory tower misconception of the realities of the apprehension of fugitives from justice reaches its apogee when it states: "In routine search cases such as this, the short time required to obtain a search warrant from a magistrate will seldom hinder efforts to apprehend a felon." The cases we are considering are not "routine search cases." They are cases of attempted arrest, pursuant to a warrant, when the object of the arrest may flee at any time — including the "short time" during which the police are endeavoring to obtain a search warrant.

At the same time the interference with the Fourth Amendment privacy interests of those whose homes are entered to apprehend the felon is not nearly as significant as suggested by the Court. The arrest warrant serves some of the functions a separate search warrant would. It assures the occupants that the police officer is present on official business. The arrest warrant also limits the scope of the search, specifying what the police may search for — i.e., the subject of the arrest warrant. No general search is permitted, but only a search of those areas in which the object of the search might hide. Indeed there may be no intrusion on the occupant's privacy at all, since if present the suspect will have the opportunity to voluntarily surrender at the door. Even if the suspect does not surrender but secretes himself within the house, the occupant can limit the search by pointing him out to the police. It is important to remember that the contraband discovered during the entry and search for Lyons was in plain view, and was discovered during a "sweep search" for Lyons, not a probing of drawers or cabinets for contraband.

Because the burden on law enforcement officers to obtain a separate search warrant before entering the dwelling of a third party to execute a concededly valid arrest warrant is great, and carries with it a high possibility that the fugitive named in the arrest warrant will escape apprehension, I would conclude that the application of the traditional "reasonableness" standard of the Fourth Amendment does not require a separate search warrant in a case such as this.

This conclusion is supported by the common law as it existed at the time of the framing of the Fourth Amendment, which incorporated the standard of "reasonableness." As the Court noted last Term in Payton: "An examination of the common-law understanding of an officer's authority to arrest sheds light on the obviously relevant, if not entirely dispositive, consideration of what the Framers of the Amendment might have thought to be reasonable." The duty of the populace to aid in the apprehension of felons was well established at common law, and in light of the overriding interest in apprehension, the common law permitted officers to enter the dwelling of third parties when executing an arrest warrant.

The Court argues that the common-law authorities are not relevant because they do not consider the rights of third parties whose dwellings were entered but only the rights of the arrestee. This is not so. The authorities typically concern the right of the third party to resist the officer's attempted entry or the offense committed by the officer against the third party in entering.

The basic error in the Court's treatment of the common law is its reliance on the adage that "a man's home is his castle." Though there is undoubtedly early case support for this in the common law, it cannot be accepted as an uncritical statement of black letter law which answers all questions in this area. William Pitt, when he was Prime Minister of England, used it with telling effect in a speech on the floor of the House of Commons; but parliamentary speaking ability and analytical legal ability ought not to be equated with one another. It is clear that the privilege of the home did not extend when the King was a party, *i.e.*, when a warrant in a criminal case had been issued. The suggestion in the Court's opinion, ante, at 1651, that "[t]he language of *Semayne's Case* . . . suggests that although the subject of an arrest warrant could not find sanctuary in the home of the third party, the home remained a 'castle or privilege' for its residents," is thus completely unfounded in the present context.

An officer could break into one's own home to execute an arrest warrant for the owner, and "so much more may he break open the house of another person to take him." Entry into the house of a third party to effect arrest was considered to follow a fortiori from the accepted entry into the home of the subject of the arrest warrant himself. This was because those in the home of a third party had no protection against civil process, let alone criminal process. At common law the Sovereign's key — criminal process — unlocked all doors, whether to apprehend the owner or someone else.

While I cannot subscribe to the Court's decision today, I will not falsely cry "wolf" in this dissent. The decision rests on a very special set of facts, and with a change in one or more of them it is clear that no separate search warrant would be required even under the reasoning of the Court.

On the one side *Payton* makes clear that an arrest warrant is all that is needed to enter the suspect's "home" to effect the arrest. If a suspect has been living in a particular dwelling for any significant period, say a few days, it can certainly be considered his "home" for Fourth Amendment purposes, even if the premises are owned by a third party and others are living there, and even if the suspect concurrently maintains a residence elsewhere as well. In such a case the police could enter the premises with only an arrest warrant. On the other side, the more fleeting a suspect's connection with the premises, such as when he is a mere visitor, the more likely that exigent circumstances will exist justifying immediate police action without departing to obtain a search warrant. The practical damage done to effective law enforcement by today's decision, without any basis in the Constitution, may well be minimal if courts carefully consider the various congeries of facts in the actual case before them.

The genuinely unfortunate aspect of today's ruling is not that fewer fugitives will be brought to book, or fewer criminals apprehended, though both of these consequences will undoubtedly occur; the greater misfortune is the increased uncertainty imposed on police officers in the field, committing magistrates, and trial judges, who must confront variations and permutations of this factual situation on a day-to-day basis. They will, in their various capacities, have to weigh the time during which a suspect for whom there is an outstanding arrest warrant has been in the building, whether the dwelling is the suspect's home, how long he has lived there, whether he is likely to leave immediately, and a number of related and equally imponderable questions. Certainty and repose, as Justice Holmes said, may not be the destiny of man, but one might have hoped for a higher degree of certainty in this one narrow but important area of the law than is offered by today's decision.

QUESTIONS AND NOTES

1. Is it always easy to determine one's residence? Suppose that Lyons had been visiting for a week? A month? Suppose that the police reasonably thought that he was such a visitor?

2.   In any of the Question 1 hypotheticals, should it matter whether Lyons has a permanent address elsewhere?

3.   In the case of a crime lord who owns several mansions, should the police be able to enter any of them to arrest him with only an arrest warrant? Should it matter whether they have probable cause to believe that he is present at the particular one being searched? Suppose that they have no idea where he is?

4.   Could a smart criminal increase her chances of beating a charge by floating from friend to friend rather than staying at home?

5.   What harm did the Court see in allowing an arrest without a search warrant in a home other than the arrestees? Could that harm be ameliorated requirement that there be probable cause to find the arrestee there?

6.   How would you advise a police department that is not sure whether the potential arrestee lives at the address at which they expect to find her? Would you advise them to get an arrest warrant? A search warrant? Or both?

7.   As you read *Welsh*, consider whether the special protection given homes from warrantless entries should extend to some exigent circumstances?

WELSH v. WISCONSIN
466 U.S. 740 (1984)

Justice Brennan delivered the opinion of the Court.

Shortly before 9:00 p.m. on the rainy night of April 24, 1978, a lone witness, Randy Jablonic, observed a car being driven erratically. After changing speeds and veering from side to side, the car eventually swerved off the road and came to a stop in an open field. No damage to any person or property occurred. Concerned about the driver and fearing that the car would get back on the highway, Jablonic drove his truck up behind the car so as to block it from returning to the road. Another passerby also stopped at the scene, and Jablonic asked her to call the police. Before the police arrived, however, the driver of the car emerged from his vehicle, approached Jablonic's truck, and asked Jablonic for a ride home. Jablonic instead suggested that they wait for assistance in removing or repairing the car. Ignoring Jablonic's suggestion, the driver walked away from the scene.

A few minutes later, the police arrived and questioned Jablonic. He told one officer what he had seen, specifically noting that the driver was either very inebriated or very sick. The officer checked the motor vehicle registration of the abandoned car and learned that it was registered to the petitioner, Edward G. Welsh. In addition, the officer noted that the petitioner's residence was a short distance from the scene, and therefore easily within walking distance.

Without securing any type of warrant, the police proceeded to the petitioner's home, arriving about 9:00 p.m. When the petitioner's stepdaughter answered the door, the police gained entry into the house. Proceeding upstairs to the petitioner's bedroom, they found him lying naked in bed. At this point, the petitioner was placed under arrest for driving or operating a motor vehicle while under the influence of an intoxicant, in violation of Wis. Stat. s 346.63(1) (1977). The petitioner was taken to the police station, where he refused to submit to a Breathalyzer test.

It is axiomatic that "the physical entry of the home is the chief evil against which the wording of the Fourth Amendment is directed." And a principal protection against unnecessary intrusions into private dwellings is the warrant requirement imposed by the Fourth Amendment on agents of the government who seek to enter the home for purposes of search or arrest. It is not surprising, therefore, that the Court has recognized, as "a 'basic principle of Fourth Amendment law,' that searches and seizures inside a home without a warrant are presumptively unreasonable."

Consistently with these long-recognized principles, the Court decided in *Payton*, that warrantless felony arrests in the home are prohibited by the Fourth Amendment, absent probable cause and exigent circumstances. At the same time, the Court declined to consider the scope of any exception for exigent circumstances that might justify warrantless home arrests, thereby leaving to the lower courts the initial application of the exigent-circumstances exception. Prior decisions of this Court, however, have emphasized that exceptions to the warrant requirement are "few in number and carefully delineated," and that the police bear a heavy burden when attempting to demonstrate an urgent need that might justify warrantless searches or arrests. Indeed, the Court has recognized only a few such emergency conditions, and has actually applied only the "hot pursuit" doctrine to arrests in the home, see *Santana*.

Our hesitation in finding exigent circumstances, especially when warrantless arrests in the home are at issue, is especially appropriate when the underlying offense for which there is probable cause to arrest is relatively minor. Before agents of the government may invade the sanctity of the home, the burden is on the government to demonstrate exigent circumstances that overcome the presumption of unreasonableness that attaches to all warrantless home entries. When the government's interest is only to arrest for a minor offense,[12] that presumption of unreasonableness is difficult to rebut, and the government usually should be allowed to make such arrests only with a warrant issued upon probable cause by a neutral and detached magistrate.

This is not a novel idea. Writing in concurrence in *McDonald v. United States*, 335 U.S. 451 (1948), Justice Jackson explained why a finding of exigent circumstances to justify a warrantless home entry should be severely restricted when only a minor offense has been committed:

"Even if one were to conclude that urgent circumstances might justify a forced entry without a warrant, no such emergency was present in this case. This method of law enforcement displays a shocking lack of all sense of proportion. Whether there is reasonable necessity for a search without waiting to obtain a warrant certainly depends somewhat upon the gravity of the offense thought to be in progress as well as the hazards of the method of attempting to reach it . . . . It is

---

[12] Even the dissenters in *Payton*, although believing that warrantless home arrests are not prohibited by the Fourth Amendment, recognized the importance of the felony limitation on such arrests.

to me a shocking proposition that private homes, even quarters in a tenement, may be indiscriminately invaded at the discretion of any suspicious police officer engaged in following up offenses that involve no violence or threats of it. While I should be human enough to apply the letter of the law with some indulgence to officers acting to deal with threats or crimes of violence which endanger life or security, it is notable that few of the searches found by this Court to be unlawful dealt with that category of crime . . . . While the enterprise of parting fools from their money by the 'numbers' lottery is one that ought to be suppressed, I do not think that its suppression is more important to society than the security of the people against unreasonable searches and seizures. When an officer undertakes to act as his own magistrate, he ought to be in a position to justify it by pointing to some real immediate and serious consequences if he postponed action to get a warrant."

Consistently with this approach, the lower courts have looked to the nature of the underlying offense as an important factor to be considered in the exigent-circumstances calculus. In a leading federal case defining exigent circumstances, for example, the en banc United States Court of Appeals for the District of Columbia recognized that the gravity of the underlying offense was a principal factor to be weighed. Without approving all of the factors included in the standard adopted by that court, it is sufficient to note that many other lower courts have also considered the gravity of the offense an important part of their constitutional analysis.

For example, courts have permitted warrantless home arrests for major felonies if identifiable exigencies, independent of the gravity of the offense, existed at the time of the arrest. But of those courts addressing the issue, most have refused to permit warrantless home arrests for nonfelonious crimes. The approach taken in these cases should not be surprising. Indeed, without necessarily approving any of these particular holdings or considering every possible factual situation, we note that it is difficult to conceive of a warrantless home arrest that would not be unreasonable under the Fourth Amendment when the underlying offense is extremely minor.

We therefore conclude that the commonsense approach utilized by most lower courts is required by the Fourth Amendment prohibition on "unreasonable searches and seizures," and hold that an important factor to be considered when determining whether any exigency exists is the gravity of the underlying offense for which the arrest is being made. Moreover, although no exigency is created simply because there is probable cause to believe that a serious crime has been committed, application of the exigent-circumstances exception in the context of a home entry should rarely be sanctioned when there is probable cause to believe that only a minor offense, such as the kind at issue in this case, has been committed.

Application of this principle to the facts of the present case is relatively straightforward. The petitioner was arrested in the privacy of his own bedroom for a noncriminal, traffic offense. The State attempts to justify the arrest by relying on the hot-pursuit doctrine, on the threat to public safety, and on the need to preserve evidence of the petitioner's blood-alcohol level. On the facts of this case, however, the claim of hot pursuit is unconvincing because there was no immediate or continuous pursuit of the petitioner from the scene of a crime. Moreover, because the petitioner had already arrived home, and had abandoned his car at the scene of the accident, there was little remaining threat to the public safety. Hence, the only potential emergency claimed by the State was the need to ascertain the petitioner's blood-alcohol level.

Even assuming, however, that the underlying facts would support a finding of this exigent circumstance, mere similarity to other cases involving the imminent destruction of evidence is not sufficient. The State of Wisconsin has chosen to classify the first offense for driving while intoxicated as a noncriminal, civil forfeiture offense for which no imprisonment is possible. This is the best indication of the state's interest in precipitating an arrest, and is one that can be easily identified both by the courts and by officers faced with a decision to arrest. Given this expression of the state's interest, a warrantless home arrest cannot be upheld simply because evidence of the petitioner's blood-alcohol level might have dissipated while the police obtained a warrant.[14] To allow a warrantless home entry on these facts would be to approve unreasonable police behavior that the principles of the Fourth Amendment will not sanction.

The Supreme Court of Wisconsin let stand a warrantless, nighttime entry into the petitioner's home to arrest him for violation of a civil traffic offense. Such an arrest, however, is clearly prohibited by the special protection afforded the individual in his home by the Fourth Amendment. The petitioner's arrest was therefore invalid, the judgment of the Supreme Court of Wisconsin is vacated, and the case is remanded for further proceedings not inconsistent with this opinion.

JUSTICE WHITE, with whom JUSTICE REHNQUIST joins, Dissenting

It follows from *Payton*, that warrantless nonfelony arrests in the home are prohibited by the Fourth Amendment absent probable cause and exigent circumstances. Although I continue to believe that the Court erred in *Payton* in requiring exigent circumstances to justify warrantless in-home felony arrests, I do not reject the obvious logical implication of the Court's decision. But I see little to commend an approach that looks to "the nature of the underlying offense as an important factor to be considered in the exigent-circumstances calculus."

The gravity of the underlying offense is, I concede, a factor to be considered in determining whether the delay that attends the warrant-issuance process will endanger officers or other persons. The seriousness of the offense with which a suspect may be charged also bears on the likelihood that he will flee and escape apprehension if not arrested immediately. But if, under all the circumstances of a particular case, an officer has probable cause to believe that the delay involved in procuring an arrest warrant will gravely endanger the officer or other persons or will result in the suspect's escape, I perceive no reason to disregard those

---

[14] Nor do we mean to suggest that the prevention of drunk driving is not properly of major concern to the States. The State of Wisconsin, however, along with several other States, has chosen to limit severely the penalties that may be imposed after a first conviction for driving while intoxicated. Given that the classification of state crimes differs widely among the States, the penalty that may attach to any particular offense seems to provide the clearest and most consistent indication of the state's interest in arresting individuals suspected of committing that offense.

exigencies on the ground that the offense for which the suspect is sought is a "minor" one.

As a practical matter, I suspect, the Court's holding is likely to have a greater impact in cases where the officer acted without a warrant to prevent the imminent destruction or removal of evidence. If the evidence the destruction or removal of which is threatened documents only the suspect's participation in a "minor" crime, the Court apparently would preclude a finding that exigent circumstances justified the warrantless arrest. I do not understand why this should be so.

A warrantless home entry to arrest is no more intrusive when the crime is "minor" than when the suspect is sought in connection with a serious felony. The variable factor, if there is one, is the governmental interest that will be served by the warrantless entry. Wisconsin's Legislature and its Supreme Court have both concluded that warrantless in-home arrests under circumstances like those present here promote valid and substantial state interests. In determining whether the challenged governmental conduct was reasonable, we are not bound by these determinations. But nothing in our previous decisions suggests that the fact that a State has defined an offense as a misdemeanor for a variety of social, cultural, and political reasons necessarily requires the conclusion that warrantless in-home arrests designed to prevent the imminent destruction or removal of evidence of that offense are always impermissible. If anything, the Court's prior decisions support the opposite conclusion.

A test under which the existence of exigent circumstances turns on the perceived gravity of the crime would significantly hamper law enforcement and burden courts with pointless litigation concerning the nature and gradation of various crimes. The Court relies heavily on Justice Jackson's concurring opinion in *McDonald* which, in minimizing the gravity of the felony at issue there, illustrates that the need for an evaluation of the seriousness of particular crimes could not be confined to offenses defined by statute as misdemeanors. To the extent that the Court implies that the seriousness of a particular felony is a factor to be considered in deciding whether the need to preserve evidence of that felony constitutes an exigent circumstance justifying a warrantless in-home arrest, I think that its approach is misguided. The decision to arrest without a warrant typically is made in the field under less-than-optimal circumstances; officers have neither the time nor the competence to determine whether a particular offense for which warrantless arrests have been authorized by statute is serious enough to justify a warrantless home entry to prevent the imminent destruction or removal of evidence.

This problem could be lessened by creating a bright-line distinction between felonies and other crimes, but the Court — wisely in my view — does not adopt such an approach. There may have been a time when the line between misdemeanors and felonies marked off those offenses involving a sufficiently serious threat to society to justify warrantless in-home arrests under exigent circumstances. But the category of misdemeanors today includes enough serious offenses to call into question the desirability of such line drawing. If I am correct in asserting that a bright-line distinction between felonies and misdemeanors is untenable and that the need to prevent the imminent destruction or removal of evidence of some nonfelony crimes can constitute an exigency justifying warrantless in-home arrests under certain circumstances, the Court's approach will necessitate a case-by-case evaluation of the seriousness of particular crimes, a difficult task for which officers and courts are poorly equipped.

[T]he fact that Wisconsin has chosen to punish the first offense for driving under the influence with a fine rather than a prison term does not demand the conclusion that the State's interest in punishing first offenders is insufficiently substantial to justify warrantless in-home arrests under exigent circumstances. As the Supreme Court of Wisconsin observed, "[t]his is a model case demonstrating the urgency involved in arresting the suspect in order to preserve evidence of the statutory violation." We have previously recognized that "the percentage of alcohol in the blood begins to diminish shortly after drinking stops, as the body functions to eliminate it from the system." Moreover, a suspect could cast substantial doubt on the validity of a blood or breath test by consuming additional alcohol upon arriving at his home. In light of the promptness with which the officers reached Welsh's house, therefore, I would hold that the need to prevent the imminent and ongoing destruction of evidence of a serious violation of Wisconsin's traffic laws provided an exigent circumstance justifying the warrantless in-home arrest.

I respectfully dissent.

QUESTIONS AND NOTES

1. Ought Welsh's arrest have been justified under the *Santana* "hot pursuit" principle?

2. Is the Court adopting a *per se* rule about warrantless arrests for misdemeanors in the home, or is it only making that a factor?

3. Is *Brigham City v. Stewart*, 547 U.S. 398 (2006), where the Supreme Court unanimously held that upon witnessing a fracas taking place inside a home where a loud party was being held, the police were justified in making a warrantless entry relevant to the resolution of question 2?

4. Would (should) the case have been different if Wisconsin had made drunk driving a felony?

5. Suppose second offense drunk driving were a felony, and the police did not know whether Welsh had previously been convicted. What result? Why?

6. In *Olson*, we see The Court's unwillingness to allow a warrantless in-home arrest even for a very serious felony, unless the circumstances are truly exigent.

MINNESOTA v. OLSON
495 U.S. 91 (1990)

WHITE, J., delivered the opinion of the Court:

The police in this case made a warrantless, nonconsensual entry into a house where Olson was an overnight guest and arrested him. The issue is whether the arrest violated Olson's Fourth Amendment rights. We hold that it did.

Shortly before 6 a.m. on Saturday, July 18, 1987, a lone gunman robbed an Amoco gasoline station in Minneapolis, Minnesota, and fatally shot the station manager. A police officer heard the police dispatcher report and suspected Joseph Ecker. The officer and his partner drove immediately to Ecker's home, arriving at about the same time that an Oldsmobile arrived. The Oldsmobile took evasive action, spun out of control, and came to a stop. Two men fled the car on foot. Ecker, who was later identified as the gunman, was captured shortly thereafter inside his home. The second man escaped.

Inside the abandoned Oldsmobile, police found a sack of money and the murder weapon. They also found a title certificate with the name Rob Olson crossed out as a secured party, a letter addressed to a Roger R. Olson of 3151 Johnson Street, and a videotape rental receipt made out to Rob Olson and dated two days earlier. The police verified that a Robert Olson lived at 3151 Johnson Street.

The next morning, Sunday, July 19, a woman identifying herself as Dianna Murphy called the police and said that a man by the name of Rob drove the car in which the gas-station killer left the scene and that Rob was planning to leave town by bus. About noon, the same woman called again, gave her address and phone number, and said that a man named Rob had told a Maria and two other women, Louanne and Julie, that he was the driver in the Amoco robbery. The caller stated that Louanne was Julie's mother and that the two women lived at 2406 Fillmore Northeast. The detective-in-charge who took the second phone call sent police officers to 2406 Fillmore to check out Louanne and Julie. When police arrived they determined that the dwelling was a duplex and that Louanne Bergstrom and her daughter Julie lived in the upper unit but were not home. Police spoke to Louanne's mother, Helen Niederhoffer, who lived in the lower unit. She confirmed that a Rob Olson had been staying upstairs but was not then in the unit. She promised to call the police when Olson returned. At 2 p.m., a pickup order, or "probable cause arrest bulletin," was issued for Olson's arrest. The police were instructed to stay away from the duplex.

At approximately 2:45 p.m., Niederhoffer called police and said Olson had returned. The detective-in-charge instructed police officers to go to the house and surround it. He then telephoned Julie from headquarters and told her Rob should come out of the house. The detective heard a male voice say "tell them I left." Julie stated that Rob had left, whereupon at 3 p.m. the detective ordered the police to enter the house. Without seeking permission and with weapons drawn, the police entered the upper unit and found respondent hiding in a closet. Less than an hour after his arrest, respondent made an inculpatory statement at police headquarters.

The Hennepin County trial court held a hearing and denied respondent's motion to suppress his statement. The statement was admitted into evidence at Olson's trial, and he was convicted on one count of first degree murder, three counts of armed robbery, and three counts of second degree assault. On appeal, the Minnesota Supreme Court reversed. The court ruled that respondent had a sufficient interest in the Bergstrom home to challenge the legality of his warrantless arrest there, that the arrest was illegal because there were no exigent circumstances to justify a warrantless entry,[1] and that respondent's statement was tainted by that illegality and should have been suppressed.

In *Payton*, the Court had no occasion to "consider the sort of emergency or dangerous situation, described in our cases as 'exigent circumstances,' that would justify a warrantless entry into a home for the purpose of either arrest or search." This case requires us to determine whether the Minnesota Supreme Court was correct in holding that there were no exigent circumstances that justified the warrantless entry into the house to make the arrest.

The Minnesota Supreme Court applied essentially the correct standard in determining whether exigent circumstances existed. The court observed that "a warrantless intrusion may be justified by hot pursuit of a fleeing felon, or imminent destruction of evidence, *Welsh*, or the need to prevent a suspect's escape, or the risk of danger to the police or to other persons inside or outside the dwelling." The court also apparently thought that in the absence of hot pursuit there must be at least probable cause to believe that one or more of the other factors justifying the entry were present and that in assessing the risk of danger, the gravity of the crime and likelihood that the suspect is armed should be considered. Applying this standard, the state court determined that exigent circumstances did not exist.

We are not inclined to disagree with this fact-specific application of the proper legal standard. The court pointed out that although a grave crime was involved, respondent "was known not to be the murderer but thought to be the driver of the getaway car," and that the police had already recovered the murder weapon. "The police knew that Louanne and Julie were with the suspect in the upstairs duplex with no suggestion of danger to them. Three or four Minneapolis police squads surrounded the house. The time was 3 p.m., Sunday . . . . It was evident the suspect was going nowhere. If he came out of the house he would have been promptly apprehended." We do not disturb the state court's judgment that these facts do not add up to exigent circumstances.

We therefore affirm the judgment of the Minnesota Supreme Court.

JUSTICE KENNEDY, Concurring

I interpret the last two paragraphs of [the opinion] as deference to a State court's application of the exigent circumstances test to the facts of this case, and not as an endorsement of that particular application of the standard. With that understanding, I join in the opinion of the Court.

REHNQUIST, C.J. and BLACKMUN, J. dissented.

QUESTIONS AND NOTES

1. Do you agree with Justice Kennedy's reading of the majority?

---

[1] Because the absence of a warrant made respondent's arrest illegal, the court did not review the trial court's determination that the police had probable cause for the arrest. Hence, we judge the case on the assumption that there was probable cause.

2.   If he is correct, would the result have been different if the State Supreme Court had reached the opposite conclusion?

3.   Should constitutional principles turn on the happenstance of a particular state court opinion?

4.   How would you have voted if you had been on the Minnesota Supreme Court? The United States Supreme Court?

5.   Suppose that the police *did* have a warrant for Olson's arrest, but lacked a warrant to enter the Bergstroms' residence. Would Olson have a valid defense by relying on *Steagald*? Why? Why not?

PROBLEM

About 8 a.m. on March 17, 1962, an armed robber entered the business premises of the Diamond Cab Company in Baltimore, Maryland. He took some $363 and ran. Two cab drivers in the vicinity, attracted by shouts of "Holdup," followed the man to 2111 Cocoa Lane. One driver notified the company dispatcher by radio that the man was a Negro about 5'8" tall, wearing a light cap and dark jacket, and that he had entered the house on Cocoa Lane. The dispatcher relayed the information to police who were proceeding to the scene of the robbery. Within minutes, police arrived at the house in a number of patrol cars. An officer knocked and announced their presence. Mrs. Hayden answered, and the officers told her they believed that a robber had entered the house, and asked to search the house.

The officers spread out through the first and second floors and the cellar in search of the robber. Hayden was found in an upstairs bedroom feigning sleep. He was arrested when the officers on the first floor and in the cellar reported that no other man was in the house. Meanwhile an officer was attracted to an adjoining bathroom by the noise of running water, and discovered a shotgun and a pistol in a flush tank; another officer who, according to the District Court, "was searching the cellar for a man or the money" found in a washing machine a jacket and trousers of the type the fleeing man was said to have worn. A clip of ammunition for the pistol and a cap were found under the mattress of Hayden's bed, and ammunition for the shotgun was found in a bureau drawer in Hayden's room. All these items of evidence were introduced against him at his trial.

Should Hayden's warrantless arrest have been upheld? For the Supreme Court's pre-*Payton* answer, see *Warden v. Hayden*, 387 U.S. 294 (1967).

PROBLEM

In the Fayette County Circuit Court, a grand jury charged respondent with trafficking in marijuana, first-degree trafficking in a controlled substance, and second-degree persistent felony offender status. Respondent filed a motion to suppress the evidence from the warrantless search, but the Circuit Court denied the motion. The Circuit Court concluded that the officers had probable cause to investigate the marijuana odor and that the officers "properly conducted [the investigation] by initially knocking on the door of the apartment unit and awaiting the response or consensual entry." Exigent circumstances justified the warrantless entry, the court held, because "there was no response at all to the knocking," and because "Officer Cobb heard movement in the apartment which he reasonably concluded were persons in the act of destroying evidence, particularly narcotics because of the smell." Respondent then entered a conditional guilty plea, reserving his right to appeal the denial of his suppression motion. The court sentenced respondent to 11 years' imprisonment. The Kentucky Court of Appeals affirmed. It held that exigent circumstances justified the warrantless entry because the police reasonably believed that evidence would be destroyed. The police did not impermissibly create the exigency, the court explained, because they did not deliberately evade the warrant requirement.

The Supreme Court of Kentucky reversed. As a preliminary matter, the court observed that there was "certainly some question as to whether the sound of persons moving [inside the apartment] was sufficient to establish that evidence was being destroyed." but the court did not answer that question. Instead it "assume[d] for the purpose of argument that exigent circumstances existed."

To determine whether police impermissibly created the exigency, the supreme court of Kentucky announced a two-part test. First, the court held, police cannot "deliberately creat[e] the exigent circumstances with the bad faith intent to avoid the warrant requirement." Second, even absent bad faith, the court concluded, police may not rely on exigent circumstances if "it was reasonably foreseeable that the investigative tactics employed by the police would create the exigent circumstances." Although the Court found no evidence of bad faith, it held that exigent circumstances could not justify the search because it was reasonably foreseeable that the occupants would destroy evidence when the police knocked on the door and announced their presence.

1. Were there exigent circumstances? Explain.

2. If so, did they justify a warrantless entry? Why?

For the Supreme Court's partial answer, see Kentucky v. King, 563 U.S. ___, 131 S. Ct. 1849 (2011).

B. FORCE IN EFFECTUATING AN ARREST

For most of our history, the amount of force used in effectuating an arrest was not thought to raise any Fourth Amendment concerns. That changed abruptly in 1985 when the Supreme Court decided *Tennessee v. Garner.* As you read *Garner* consider whether the Court is giving the Fourth Amendment more weight than it can properly bear.

TENNESSEE v. GARNER
471 U.S. 1 (1985)

JUSTICE WHITE delivered the opinion of the Court

This case requires us to determine the constitutionality of the use of deadly force to prevent the escape of an apparently unarmed suspected felon. We conclude that such force may not be used unless it is necessary to prevent the escape and the officer has probable cause to believe that the suspect poses a significant threat of death or serious physical injury to the officer or others.

I

At about 10:45 p.m. on October 3, 1974, Memphis Police Officers Elton Hymon and Leslie Wright were dispatched to answer a "prowler inside call." Upon arriving at the scene they saw a woman standing on her porch and gesturing toward the adjacent house.[2] She told them she had heard glass breaking and that "they" or "someone" was breaking in next door. While Wright radioed the dispatcher to say that they were on the scene, Hymon went behind the house. He heard a door slam and saw someone run across the backyard. The fleeing suspect, who was appellee-respondent's decedent, Edward Garner, stopped at a 6-feet-high chain link fence at the edge of the yard. With the aid of a flashlight, Hymon was able to see Garner's face and hands. He saw no sign of a weapon, and, though not certain, was "reasonably sure" and "figured" that Garner was unarmed. He thought Garner was 17 or 18 years old and about 5'5" or 5'7" tall.[3] While Garner was crouched at the base of the fence, Hymon called out "police, halt" and took a few steps toward him. Garner then began to climb over the fence. Convinced that if Garner made it over the fence he would elude capture,[4] Hymon shot him. The bullet hit Garner in the back of the head. Garner was taken by ambulance to a hospital, where he died on the operating table. Ten dollars and a purse taken from the house were found on his body.[5]

In using deadly force to prevent the escape, Hymon was acting under the authority of a Tennessee statute and pursuant to Police Department policy. The statute provides that "[i]f, after notice of the intention to arrest the defendant, he either flee or forcibly resist, the officer may use all the necessary means to effect the arrest."[6] The Department policy was slightly more restrictive than the statute, but still allowed the use of deadly force in cases of burglary. The incident was reviewed

---

[2] The owner of the house testified that no lights were on in the house, but that a back door light was on. Officer Hymon, though uncertain, stated in his deposition that there were lights on in the house.

[3] In fact, Garner, an eighth-grader, was 15. He was 5' 4" tall and weighed somewhere around 100 or 110 pounds.

[4] When asked at trial why he fired, Hymon stated: "Well, first of all it was apparent to me from the little bit that I knew about the area at the time that he was going to get away because, number 1, I couldn't get to him. My partner then couldn't find where he was because, you know, he was late coming around. He didn't know where I was talking about. I couldn't get to him because of the fence here, I couldn't have jumped this fence and come up, consequently jumped this fence and caught him before he got away because he was already up on the fence, just one leap and he was already over the fence, and so there is no way that I could have caught him." He also stated that the area beyond the fence was dark, that he could not have gotten over the fence easily because he was carrying a lot of equipment and wearing heavy boots, and that Garner, being younger and more energetic, could have outrun him.

[5] Garner had rummaged through one room in the house, in which, in the words of the owner, "[a]ll the stuff was out on the floors, all the drawers was pulled out, and stuff was scattered all over." The owner testified that his valuables were untouched but that, in addition to the purse and the 10 dollars, one of his wife's rings was missing. The ring was not recovered.

[6] Although the statute does not say so explicitly, Tennessee law forbids the use of deadly force in the arrest of a misdemeanant. See Johnson v. State, 173 Tenn. 134, 114 S.W.2d 819 (1938).

by the Memphis Police Firearm's Review Board and presented to a grand jury. Neither took any action.

Garner's father then brought this action in the Federal District Court for the Western District of Tennessee, seeking damages under 42 U.S.C. s 1983 for asserted violations of Garner's constitutional rights. The Court of Appeals reasoned that the killing of a fleeing suspect is a "seizure" under the Fourth Amendment, and is therefore constitutional only if "reasonable." The Tennessee statute failed as applied to this case because it did not adequately limit the use of deadly force by distinguishing between felonies of different magnitudes — "the facts, as found, did not justify the use of deadly force under the Fourth Amendment." Officers cannot resort to deadly force unless they "have probable cause . . . to believe that the suspect [has committed a felony and] poses a threat to the safety of the officers or a danger to the community if left at large."

The State of Tennessee, which had intervened to defend the statute, appealed to this Court. The City filed a petition for certiorari.

II

Whenever an officer restrains the freedom of a person to walk away, he has seized that person. While it is not always clear just when minimal police interference becomes a seizure, there can be no question that apprehension by the use of deadly force is a seizure subject to the reasonableness requirement of the Fourth Amendment.

A

A police officer may arrest a person if he has probable cause to believe that person committed a crime. *Watson.* Petitioners and appellant argue that if this requirement is satisfied the Fourth Amendment has nothing to say about *how* that seizure is made. This submission ignores the many cases in which this Court, by balancing the extent of the intrusion against the need for it, has examined the reasonableness of the manner in which a search or seizure is conducted. To determine the constitutionality of a seizure "[w]e must balance the nature and quality of the intrusion on the individual's Fourth Amendment interests against the importance of the governmental interests alleged to justify the intrusion." We have described "the balancing of competing interests" as "the key principle of the Fourth Amendment." Because one of the factors is the extent of the intrusion, it is plain that reasonableness depends on not only when a seizure is made, but also how it is carried out.

B

The intrusiveness of a seizure by means of deadly force is unmatched. The suspect's fundamental interest in his own life need not be elaborated upon. The use of deadly force also frustrates the interest of the individual, and of society, in judicial determination of guilt and punishment. Against these interests are ranged governmental interests in effective law enforcement.[8] It is argued that overall violence will be reduced by encouraging the peaceful submission of suspects who know that they may be shot if they flee. Effectiveness in making arrests requires the resort to deadly force, or at least the meaningful threat thereof. "Being able to arrest such individuals is a condition precedent to the state's entire system of law enforcement."

Without in any way disparaging the importance of these goals, we are not convinced that the use of deadly force is a sufficiently productive means of accomplishing them to justify the killing of nonviolent suspects. The use of deadly force is a self-defeating way of apprehending a suspect and so setting the criminal justice mechanism in motion. If successful, it guarantees that that mechanism will not be set in motion. And while the meaningful threat of deadly force might be thought to lead to the arrest of more live suspects by discouraging escape attempts, the presently available evidence does not support this thesis. The fact is that a majority of police departments in this country have forbidden the use of deadly force against nonviolent suspects. If those charged with the enforcement of the criminal law have abjured the use of deadly force in arresting non-dangerous felons, there is a substantial basis for doubting that the use of such force is an essential attribute of the arrest power in all felony cases. Petitioners and appellant have not persuaded us that shooting non-dangerous fleeing suspects is so vital as to outweigh the suspect's interest in his own life.

The use of deadly force to prevent the escape of all felony suspects, whatever the circumstances, is constitutionally unreasonable. It is not better that all felony suspects die than that they escape. Where the suspect poses no immediate threat to the officer and no threat to others, the harm resulting from failing to apprehend him does not justify the use of deadly force to do so. It is no doubt unfortunate when a suspect who is in sight escapes, but the fact that the police arrive a little late or are a little slower afoot does not always justify killing the suspect. A police officer may not seize an unarmed, non-dangerous suspect by shooting him dead. The Tennessee statute is unconstitutional insofar as it authorizes the use of deadly force against such fleeing suspects.

It is not, however, unconstitutional on its face. Where the officer has probable cause to believe that the suspect poses a threat of serious physical harm, either to the officer or to others, it is not constitutionally unreasonable to prevent escape by using deadly force. Thus, if the suspect threatens the officer with a weapon or there is probable cause to believe that he has committed a crime involving the infliction or threatened infliction of serious physical harm, deadly force may be used if necessary to prevent escape, and if, where feasible, some warning has been given. As applied in such circumstances, the Tennessee statute would pass constitutional muster.

---

[8] The dissent emphasizes that subsequent investigation cannot replace immediate apprehension. We recognize that this is so, see n. 13, *infra*; indeed, that is the reason why there is any dispute. If subsequent arrest were assured, no one would argue that use of deadly force was justified. Thus, we proceed on the assumption that subsequent arrest is not likely. Nonetheless, it should be remembered that failure to apprehend at the scene does not necessarily mean that the suspect will never be caught.

III

A

It is insisted that the Fourth Amendment must be construed in light of the common-law rule, which allowed the use of whatever force was necessary to effect the arrest of a fleeing felon, though not a misdemeanant. As stated in Hale's posthumously published Pleas of the Crown: "[I]f persons that are pursued by these officers for felony or the just suspicion thereof . . . shall not yield themselves to these officers, but shall either resist or fly before they are apprehended or being apprehended shall rescue themselves and resist or fly, so that they cannot be otherwise apprehended, and are upon necessity slain therein, because they cannot be otherwise taken, it is no felony." Most American jurisdictions also imposed a flat prohibition against the use of deadly force to stop a fleeing misdemeanant, coupled with a general privilege to use such force to stop a fleeing felon.

The State and city argue that because this was the prevailing rule at the time of the adoption of the Fourth Amendment and for some time thereafter, and is still in force in some States, use of deadly force against a fleeing felon must be "reasonable." It is true that this Court has often looked to the common law in evaluating the reasonableness, for Fourth Amendment purposes, of police activity. On the other hand, it "has not simply frozen into constitutional law those law enforcement practices that existed at the time of the Fourth Amendment's passage." Because of sweeping change in the legal and technological context, reliance on the common-law rule in this case would be a mistaken literalism that ignores the purposes of a historical inquiry.

B

It has been pointed out many times that the common-law rule is best understood in light of the fact that it arose at a time when virtually all felonies were punishable by death. "Though effected without the protections and formalities of an orderly trial and conviction, the killing of a resisting or fleeing felon resulted in no greater consequences than those authorized for punishment of the felony of which the individual was charged or suspected." Courts have also justified the common-law rule by emphasizing the relative dangerousness of felons.

Neither of these justifications makes sense today. Almost all crimes formerly punishable by death no longer are or can be. And while in earlier times "the gulf between the felonies and the minor offences was broad and deep," today the distinction is minor and often arbitrary. Many crimes classified as misdemeanors, or nonexistent, at common law are now felonies. These changes have undermined the concept, which was questionable to begin with, that use of deadly force against a fleeing felon is merely a speedier execution of someone who has already forfeited his life. They have also made the assumption that a "felon" is more dangerous than a misdemeanant untenable. Indeed, numerous misdemeanors involve conduct more dangerous than many felonies.[12]

---

[12] White-collar crime, for example, poses a less significant physical threat than, say, drunken driving.

There is an additional reason why the common-law rule cannot be directly translated to the present day. The common-law rule developed at a time when weapons were rudimentary. Deadly force could be inflicted almost solely in a hand-to-hand struggle during which, necessarily, the safety of the arresting officer was at risk. Handguns were not carried by police officers until the latter half of the last century. Only then did it become possible to use deadly force from a distance as a means of apprehension. As a practical matter, the use of deadly force under the standard articulation of the common-law rule has an altogether different meaning — and harsher consequences — now than in past centuries.[13]

One other aspect of the common-law rule bears emphasis. It forbids the use of deadly force to apprehend a misdemeanant, condemning such action as disproportionately severe.

In short, though the common-law pedigree of Tennessee's rule is pure on its face, changes in the legal and technological context mean the rule is distorted almost beyond recognition when literally applied.

C

In evaluating the reasonableness of police procedures under the Fourth Amendment, we have also looked to prevailing rules in individual jurisdictions.

It cannot be said that there is a constant or overwhelming trend away from the common-law rule. In recent years, some States have reviewed their laws and expressly rejected abandonment of the common-law rule. Nonetheless, the long-term movement has been away from the rule that deadly force may be used against any fleeing felon, and that remains the rule in less than half the States.

This trend is more evident and impressive when viewed in light of the policies adopted by the police departments themselves. Overwhelmingly, these are more restrictive than the common-law rule. The Federal Bureau of Investigation and the New York City Police Department, for example, both forbid the use of firearms except when necessary to prevent death or grievous bodily harm. A 1974 study reported that the police department regulations in a majority of the large cities of the United States allowed the firing of a weapon only when a felon presented a threat of death or serious bodily harm. Overall, only 7.5% of departmental and municipal policies explicitly permit the use of deadly force against any felon; 86.8% explicitly do not. In light of the rules adopted by those who must actually administer them, the older and fading common-law view is a dubious indicium of the constitutionality of the Tennessee statute now before us.

---

[13] It has been argued that sophisticated techniques of apprehension and increased communication between the police in different jurisdictions have made it more likely that an escapee will be caught than was once the case, and that this change has also reduced the "reasonableness" of the use of deadly force to prevent escape. *E.g.*, Sherman, *Execution Without Trial: Police Homicide and the Constitution*, 33 Vand. L. Rev. 71, 76 (1980). We are unaware of any data that would permit sensible evaluation of this claim. Current arrest rates are sufficiently low, however, that we have some doubt whether in past centuries the failure to arrest at the scene meant that the police had missed their only chance in a way that is not presently the case. In 1983, 21% of the offenses in the Federal Bureau of Investigation crime index were cleared by arrest.

D

Actual departmental policies are important for an additional reason. We would hesitate to declare a police practice of long standing "unreasonable" if doing so would severely hamper effective law enforcement. But the indications are to the contrary. There has been no suggestion that crime has worsened in any way in jurisdictions that have adopted, by legislation or departmental policy, rules similar to that announced today. *Amici* noted that "[a]fter extensive research and consideration, [they] have concluded that laws permitting police officers to use deadly force to apprehend unarmed, non-violent fleeing felony suspects actually do not protect citizens or law enforcement officers, do not deter crime or alleviate problems caused by crime, and do not improve the crime-fighting ability of law enforcement agencies." The submission is that the obvious state interests in apprehension are not sufficiently served to warrant the use of lethal weapons against all fleeing felons.

Nor do we agree with petitioners and appellant that the rule we have adopted requires the police to make impossible, split-second evaluations of unknowable facts. We do not deny the practical difficulties of attempting to assess the suspect's dangerousness. However, similarly difficult judgments must be made by the police in equally uncertain circumstances. Nor is there any indication that in States that allow the use of deadly force only against dangerous suspects, the standard has been difficult to apply or has led to a rash of litigation involving inappropriate second-guessing of police officers' split-second decisions. Moreover, the highly technical felony/misdemeanor distinction is equally, if not more, difficult to apply in the field. An officer is in no position to know, for example, the precise value of property stolen, or whether the crime was a first or second offense. Finally, as noted above, this claim must be viewed with suspicion in light of the similar self-imposed limitations of so many police departments.

IV

The District Court concluded that Hymon was justified in shooting Garner because state law allows, and the Federal Constitution does not forbid, the use of deadly force to prevent the escape of a fleeing felony suspect if no alternative means of apprehension is available. This conclusion made a determination of Garner's apparent dangerousness unnecessary. The court did find, however, that Garner appeared to be unarmed, though Hymon could not be certain that was the case. Restated in Fourth Amendment terms, this means Hymon had no articulable basis to think Garner was armed.

In reversing, the Court of Appeals accepted the District Court's factual conclusions and held that "the facts, as found, did not justify the use of deadly force." We agree. Officer Hymon could not reasonably have believed that Garner — young, slight, and unarmed — posed any threat. Indeed, Hymon never attempted to justify his actions on any basis other than the need to prevent an escape. The District Court stated in passing that "[t]he facts of this case did not indicate to Officer Hymon that Garner was 'non-dangerous.' " This conclusion is not explained, and seems to be based solely on the fact that Garner had broken into a house at night. However, the fact that Garner was a suspected burglar could not, without regard to the other circumstances, automatically justify the use of deadly force. Hymon did not have probable cause to believe that Garner, whom he correctly believed to be unarmed, posed any physical danger to himself or others.

The dissent argues that the shooting was justified by the fact that Officer Hymon had probable cause to believe that Garner had committed a nighttime burglary. While we agree that burglary is a serious crime, we cannot agree that it is so dangerous as automatically to justify the use of deadly force. The FBI classifies burglary as a "property" rather than a "violent" crime. Although the armed burglar would present a different situation, the fact that an unarmed suspect has broken into a dwelling at night does not automatically mean he is physically dangerous. This case demonstrates as much. In fact, the available statistics demonstrate that burglaries only rarely involve physical violence. During the 10-year period from 1973–1982, only 3.8% of all burglaries involved violent crime.[23]

We hold that the statute is invalid insofar as it purported to give Hymon the authority to act as he did.

JUSTICE O'CONNOR, with whom THE CHIEF JUSTICE and JUSTICE REHNQUIST join, dissenting.

The Court today holds that the Fourth Amendment prohibits a police officer from using deadly force as a last resort to apprehend a criminal suspect who refuses to halt when fleeing the scene of a nighttime burglary. This conclusion rests on the majority's balancing of the interests of the suspect and the public interest in effective law enforcement. Notwithstanding the venerable common-law rule authorizing the use of deadly force if necessary to apprehend a fleeing felon, and continued acceptance of this rule by nearly half the States, the majority concludes that Tennessee's statute is unconstitutional inasmuch as it allows the use of such force to apprehend a burglary suspect who is not obviously armed or otherwise dangerous. Although the circumstances of this case are unquestionably tragic and unfortunate, our constitutional holdings must be sensitive both to the history of the Fourth Amendment and to the general implications of the Court's reasoning. By disregarding the serious and dangerous nature of residential burglaries and the longstanding practice of many States, the Court effectively creates a Fourth Amendment right allowing a burglary suspect to flee unimpeded from a police officer who has probable cause to arrest, who has ordered the suspect to halt, and who has no means short of firing his weapon to prevent escape. I do not believe that the Fourth Amendment supports such a right, and I accordingly dissent.

---

[23] The dissent points out that three-fifths of all rapes in the home, three-fifths of all home robberies, and about a third of home assaults are committed by burglars. Post, at 1709. These figures mean only that if one knows that a suspect committed a rape in the home, there is a good chance that the suspect is also a burglar. That has nothing to do with the question here, which is whether the fact that someone has committed a burglary indicates that he has committed, or might commit, a violent crime. The dissent also points out that this 3.8% adds up to 2.8 million violent crimes over a 10-year period, as if to imply that today's holding will let loose 2.8 million violent burglars. The relevant universe is, of course, far smaller. At issue is only that tiny fraction of cases where violence has taken place and an officer who has no other means of apprehending the suspect is unaware of its occurrence.

I

The facts below warrant brief review because they highlight the difficult, split-second decisions police officers must make in these circumstances. Memphis Police Officers Elton Hymon and Leslie Wright responded to a late-night call that a burglary was in progress at a private residence. When the officers arrived at the scene, the caller said that "they" were breaking into the house next door. The officers found the residence had been forcibly entered through a window and saw lights on inside the house. Officer Hymon testified that when he saw the broken window he realized "that something was wrong inside," but that he could not determine whether anyone — either a burglar or a member of the household — was within the residence. As Officer Hymon walked behind the house, he heard a door slam. He saw Edward Eugene Garner run away from the house through the dark and cluttered backyard. Garner crouched next to a 6-foot-high fence. Officer Hymon thought Garner was an adult and was unsure whether Garner was armed because Hymon "had no idea what was in the hand [that he could not see] or what he might have had on his person." Id., at 658–659. In fact, Garner was 15 years old and unarmed. Hymon also did not know whether accomplices remained inside the house. The officer identified himself as a police officer and ordered Garner to halt. Garner paused briefly and then sprang to the top of the fence. Believing that Garner would escape if he climbed over the fence, Hymon fired his revolver and mortally wounded the suspected burglar.

The precise issue before the Court deserves emphasis, because both the decision below and the majority obscure what must be decided in this case. The issue is not the constitutional validity of the Tennessee statute on its face or as applied to some hypothetical set of facts. Instead, the issue is whether the use of deadly force by Officer Hymon under the circumstances of this case violated Garner's constitutional rights. Thus, the majority's assertion that a police officer who has probable cause to seize a suspect "may not always do so by killing him" is unexceptionable but also of little relevance to the question presented here. The same is true of the rhetorically stirring statement that "[t]he use of deadly force to prevent the escape of all felony suspects, whatever the circumstances, is constitutionally unreasonable." The question we must address is whether the Constitution allows the use of such force to apprehend a suspect who resists arrest by attempting to flee the scene of a nighttime burglary of a residence.

II

For purposes of Fourth Amendment analysis, I agree with the Court that Officer Hymon "seized" Garner by shooting him. Whether that seizure was reasonable and therefore permitted by the Fourth Amendment requires a careful balancing of the important public interest in crime prevention and detection and the nature and quality of the intrusion upon legitimate interests of the individual. In striking this balance here, it is crucial to acknowledge that police use of deadly force to apprehend a fleeing criminal suspect falls within the "rubric of police conduct . . . necessarily [involving] swift action predicated upon the on-the-spot observations of the officer on the beat." The clarity of hindsight cannot provide the standard for judging the reasonableness of police decisions made in uncertain and often dangerous circumstances. Moreover, I am far more reluctant than is the Court to conclude that the Fourth Amendment proscribes a police practice that was accepted at the time of the adoption of the Bill of Rights and has continued to receive the support of many state legislatures. Although the Court has recognized that the requirements of the Fourth Amendment must respond to the reality of social and technological change, fidelity to the notion of *constitutional* — as opposed to purely judicial — limits on governmental action requires us to impose a heavy burden on those who claim that practices accepted when the Fourth Amendment was adopted are now constitutionally impermissible.

The public interest involved in the use of deadly force as a last resort to apprehend a fleeing burglary suspect relates primarily to the serious nature of the crime. Household burglaries not only represent the illegal entry into a person's home, but also "pos[e] real risk of serious harm to others." According to recent Department of Justice statistics, "[t]hree-fifths of all rapes in the home, three-fifths of all home robberies, and about a third of home aggravated and simple assaults are committed by burglars." During the period 1973–1982, 2.8 million such violent crimes were committed in the course of burglaries. Victims of a forcible intrusion into their home by a nighttime prowler will find little consolation in the majority's confident assertion that "burglaries only rarely involve physical violence." Moreover, even if a particular burglary, when viewed in retrospect, does not involve physical harm to others, the "harsh potentialities for violence" inherent in the forced entry into a home preclude characterization of the crime as "innocuous, inconsequential, minor, or 'nonviolent.'"

Because burglary is a serious and dangerous felony, the public interest in the prevention and detection of the crime is of compelling importance. Where a police officer has probable cause to arrest a suspected burglar, the use of deadly force as a last resort might well be the only means of apprehending the suspect. With respect to a particular burglary, subsequent investigation simply cannot represent a substitute for immediate apprehension of the criminal suspect at the scene. Indeed, the Captain of the Memphis Police Department testified that in his city, if apprehension is not immediate, it is likely that the suspect will not be caught. Although some law enforcement agencies may choose to assume the risk that a criminal will remain at large, the Tennessee statute reflects a legislative determination that the use of deadly force in prescribed circumstances will serve generally to protect the public. Such statutes assist the police in apprehending suspected perpetrators of serious crimes and provide notice that a lawful police order to stop and submit to arrest may not be ignored with impunity.

The Court unconvincingly dismisses the general deterrence effects by stating that "the presently available evidence does not support [the] thesis" that the threat of force discourages escape and that "there is a substantial basis for doubting that the use of such force is an essential attribute to the arrest power in all felony cases." There is no question that the effectiveness of police use of deadly force is arguable and that many States or individual police departments have decided not to authorize it in circumstances similar to those presented here. But it should go without saying that the effectiveness or popularity of a particular police practice does not determine its constitutionality.

Against the strong public interests justifying the conduct at issue here must be weighed the individual interests implicated in the use of deadly force by police officers. The majority declares that "[t]he suspect's fundamental interest in his own life need not be elaborated upon." This blithe assertion hardly provides an adequate substitute for the majority's failure to acknowledge the distinctive manner in which the suspect's interest in his life is even exposed to risk. For purposes of this case, we must recall that the police officer, in the course of investigating a nighttime burglary, had reasonable cause to arrest the suspect and ordered him to halt. The officer's use of force resulted because the suspected burglar refused to heed this command and the officer reasonably believed that there was no means short of firing his weapon to apprehend the suspect. Without questioning the importance of a person's interest in his life, I do not think this interest encompasses a right to flee unimpeded from the scene of a burglary. Cf. *Payton* (WHITE, J., dissenting) ("[T]he policeman's hands should not be tied merely because of the possibility that the suspect will fail to cooperate with legitimate actions by law enforcement personnel"). The legitimate interests of the suspect in these circumstances are adequately accommodated by the Tennessee statute: to avoid the use of deadly force and the consequent risk to his life, the suspect need merely obey the valid order to halt.

A proper balancing of the interests involved suggests that use of deadly force as a last resort to apprehend a criminal suspect fleeing from the scene of a nighttime burglary is not unreasonable within the meaning of the Fourth Amendment. Admittedly, the events giving rise to this case are in retrospect deeply regrettable. No one can view the death of an unarmed and apparently nonviolent 15-year-old without sorrow, much less disapproval. Nonetheless, the reasonableness of Officer Hymon's conduct for purposes of the Fourth Amendment cannot be evaluated by what later appears to have been a preferable course of police action. The officer pursued a suspect in the darkened backyard of a house that from all indications had just been burglarized. The police officer was not certain whether the suspect was alone or unarmed; nor did he know what had transpired inside the house. He ordered the suspect to halt, and when the suspect refused to obey and attempted to flee into the night, the officer fired his weapon to prevent escape. The reasonableness of this action for purposes of the Fourth Amendment is not determined by the unfortunate nature of this particular case; instead, the question is whether it is constitutionally impermissible for police officers, as a last resort, to shoot a burglary suspect fleeing the scene of the crime.

IV

The Court's opinion sweeps broadly to adopt an entirely new standard for the constitutionality of the use of deadly force to apprehend fleeing felons. Thus, the Court "lightly brushe[s] aside," a long-standing police practice that predates the Fourth Amendment and continues to receive the approval of nearly half of the state legislatures. I cannot accept the majority's creation of a constitutional right to flight for burglary suspects seeking to avoid capture at the scene of the crime. Whatever the constitutional limits on police use of deadly force in order to apprehend a fleeing felon, I do not believe they are exceeded in a case in which a police officer has probable cause to arrest a suspect at the scene of a residential burglary, orders the suspect to halt, and then fires his weapon as a last resort to prevent the suspect's escape into the night. I respectfully dissent.

QUESTIONS AND NOTES

1.   Should *Garner* have taken tradition and history more seriously, particularly when compared to *Watson*? All Watson asked for was a warrant when practicable prior to arrest, whereas Garner was functionally asking for the right to escape?

2.   Do you think that the amount of force used has much to do with Fourth Amendment values? Why?

3.   Assuming that the Court was correct on the relationship of force and the severity of the crime, do you agree that it properly categorized nighttime burglary? Explain your answer.

4.   In responding to question 3 is (ought) it (to be) relevant that Garner was responsible for creating the cruel choice of escape or death? Officer Hymon would have preferred that he simply submitted to arrest so that he wouldn't have to choose between death or escape.

5.   Arguably *Garner* could have been limited to cases of deadly force, however, in *Graham* any such limitation was explicitly rejected.

GRAHAM v. CONNOR
490 U.S. 386 (1989)

REHNQUIST C.J. delivered the opinion of the Court.

This case requires us to decide what constitutional standard governs a free citizen's claim that law enforcement officials used excessive force in the course of making an arrest, investigatory stop, or other "seizure" of his person. We hold that such claims are properly analyzed under the Fourth Amendment's "objective reasonableness" standard, rather than under a substantive due process standard.

In this action under 42 U.S.C. § 1983, petitioner Dethorne Graham seeks to recover damages for injuries allegedly sustained when law enforcement officers used physical force against him during the course of an investigatory stop. Because the case comes to us from a decision of the Court of Appeals affirming the entry of a directed verdict for respondents, we take the evidence hereafter noted in the light most favorable to petitioner. On November 12, 1984, Graham, a diabetic, felt the onset of an insulin reaction. He asked a friend, William Berry, to drive him to a nearby convenience store so he could purchase some orange juice to counteract the reaction. Berry agreed, but when Graham entered the store, he saw a number of people ahead of him in the checkout line. Concerned about the delay, he hurried out of the store and asked Berry to drive him to a friend's house instead.

Respondent Connor, an officer of the Charlotte, North Carolina, Police Department, saw Graham hastily enter and leave the store. The officer became suspicious that something was amiss and followed Berry's car. About one-half mile from the store, he made an investigative stop. Although Berry told Connor that Graham was simply suffering from a "sugar reaction," the officer ordered Berry and Graham to wait while he found out what, if anything, had happened at the convenience store. When Officer Connor returned to his patrol car to call for backup assistance, Graham got out of the car, ran around it twice, and finally sat down on the curb, where he passed out briefly.

In the ensuing confusion, a number of other Charlotte police officers arrived on the scene in response to Officer Connor's request for backup. One of the officers rolled Graham over on the sidewalk and cuffed his hands tightly behind his back, ignoring Berry's pleas to get him some sugar. Another officer said: "I've seen a lot of people with sugar diabetes that never acted like this. Ain't nothing wrong with the M.F. but drunk. Lock the S.B. up." Several officers then lifted Graham up from behind, carried him over to Berry's car, and placed him face down on its hood. Regaining consciousness, Graham asked the officers to check in his wallet for a diabetic decal that he carried. In response, one of the officers told him to "shut up" and shoved his face down against the hood of the car. Four officers grabbed Graham and threw him headfirst into the police car. A friend of Graham's brought some orange juice to the car, but the officers refused to let him have it. Finally, Officer Connor received a report that Graham had done nothing wrong at the convenience store, and the officers drove him home and released him.

At some point during his encounter with the police, Graham sustained a broken foot, cuts on his wrists, a bruised forehead, and an injured shoulder; he also claims to have developed a loud ringing in his right ear that continues to this day. He commenced this action against the individual officers involved in the incident, all of whom are respondents here, alleging that they had used excessive force in making the investigatory stop, in violation of "rights secured to him under the Fourteenth Amendment to the United States Constitution."

Where, as here, the excessive force claim arises in the context of an arrest or investigatory stop of a free citizen, it is most properly characterized as one invoking the protections of the Fourth Amendment, which guarantees citizens the right "to be secure in their persons . . . against unreasonable . . . seizures" of the person. This much is clear from our decision in *Garner*. In *Garner*, we addressed a claim that the use of deadly force to apprehend a fleeing suspect who did not appear to be armed or otherwise dangerous violated the suspect's constitutional rights, notwithstanding the existence of probable cause to arrest. Though the complaint alleged violations of both the Fourth Amendment and the Due Process Clause, we analyzed the constitutionality of the challenged application of force solely by reference to the Fourth Amendment's prohibition against unreasonable seizures of the person, holding that the "reasonableness" of a particular seizure depends not only on *when* it is made, but also on *how* it is carried out. Today we make explicit what was implicit in *Garner's* analysis, and hold that *all* claims that law enforcement officers have used excessive force — deadly or not — in the course of an arrest, investigatory stop, or other "seizure" of a free citizen should be analyzed under the Fourth Amendment and its "reasonableness" standard, rather than under a "substantive due process" approach. Because the Fourth Amendment provides an explicit textual source of constitutional protection against this sort of physically intrusive governmental conduct, that Amendment, not the more generalized notion of "substantive due process," must be the guide for analyzing these claims.

Determining whether the force used to effect a particular seizure is "reasonable" under the Fourth Amendment requires a careful balancing of " 'the nature and quality of the intrusion on the individual's Fourth Amendment interests' " against the countervailing governmental interests at stake. Our Fourth Amendment jurisprudence has long recognized that the right to make an arrest or investigatory stop necessarily carries with it the right to use some degree of physical coercion or threat thereof to effect it. Because "[t]he test of reasonableness under the Fourth Amendment is not capable of precise definition or mechanical application," however, its proper application requires careful attention to the facts and circumstances of each particular case, including the severity of the crime at issue, whether the suspect poses an immediate threat to the safety of the officers or others, and whether he is actively resisting arrest or attempting to evade arrest by flight.

The "reasonableness" of a particular use of force must be judged from the perspective of a reasonable officer on the scene, rather than with the 20/20 vision of hindsight. The Fourth Amendment is not violated by an arrest based on probable cause, even though the wrong person is arrested, nor by the mistaken execution of a valid search warrant on the wrong premises. With respect to a claim of excessive force, the same standard of reasonableness at the moment applies: "Not every push or shove, even if it may later seem unnecessary in the peace of a judge's chambers," violates the Fourth Amendment. The calculus of reasonableness must embody allowance for the fact that police officers are often forced to make split-second judgments — in circumstances that are tense, uncertain, and rapidly evolving — about the amount of force that is necessary in a particular situation.

As in other Fourth Amendment contexts, however, the "reasonableness" inquiry in an excessive force case is an objective one: the question is whether the officers' actions are "objectively reasonable" in light of the facts and circumstances confronting them, without regard to their underlying intent or motivation. An officer's evil intentions will not make a Fourth Amendment violation out of an objectively reasonable use of force; nor will an officer's good intentions make an objectively unreasonable use of force constitutional.

Because petitioner's excessive force claim is one arising under the Fourth Amendment, the Court of Appeals erred in analyzing it under the *Johnson v. Glick* [481 F.2d 1028 (2d. Cir. 1973)] test. That test, which requires consideration of whether the individual officers acted in "good faith" or "maliciously and sadistically for the very purpose of causing harm," is incompatible with a proper Fourth Amendment analysis. We do not agree with the Court of Appeals' suggestion that the "malicious and sadistic" inquiry is merely another way of describing conduct that is objectively unreasonable under the circumstances. Whatever the empirical correlations between "malicious and sadistic" behavior and objective unreasonableness may be, the fact remains that the "malicious and sadistic" factor puts in issue the subjective motivations of the individual officers, which our prior cases make clear has no bearing on whether a particular seizure is "unreasonable" under the Fourth Amendment. Nor do we agree with the Court of Appeals' conclusion that because the subjective motivations of the individual officers are of central importance in deciding whether force used against a convicted prisoner violates the Eighth Amendment, it cannot be reversible error to inquire into them in deciding whether force used against a suspect or arrestee violates the Fourth Amendment.

Differing standards under the Fourth and Eighth Amendments are hardly surprising: the terms "cruel" and "punishment" clearly suggest some inquiry into subjective state of mind, whereas the term "unreasonable" does not. Moreover, the less protective Eighth Amendment standard applies "only after the State has complied with the constitutional guarantees traditionally associated with criminal prosecutions." The Fourth Amendment inquiry is one of "objective reasonableness" under the circumstances, and subjective concepts like "malice" and "sadism" have no proper place in that inquiry.[12]

Because the Court of Appeals reviewed the District Court's ruling on the motion for directed verdict under an erroneous view of the governing substantive law, its judgment must be vacated and the case remanded to that court for reconsideration of that issue under the proper Fourth Amendment standard.

QUESTIONS AND NOTES

1.   Does *Garner* or *Graham* present a stronger Fourth Amendment claim? Explain your answer.

2.   On retrial, do you think that Graham will prevail? Why? Why not?

3.   Does *Graham* put an undue burden on the police? Does it put enough of a burden on them?

4.   In *Saucier v. Katz*, 533 U.S. 194 (2001), the Court emphasized that the allegation of a gratuitous shove is not enough to allow the jury to impose liability under the Fourth Amendment.

PROBLEM

Assume that the police engage a motorcyclist with a passenger in a high speed chase in order to issue a citation for a traffic offense. Assume further that the motorcyclist crashes while trying to elude the police officer, thereby killing his passenger. May the decedent's estate successfully sue the police officer under *Garner* and *Graham*. For the Supreme Court's resolution, see *County of Sacramento v. Lewis*, 523 U.S. 833 (1998). Nine years later, the Court decided *Scott v. Harris*.

---

[12] Of course, in assessing the credibility of an officer's account of the circumstances that prompted the use of force, a factfinder may consider, along with other factors, evidence that the officer may have harbored ill-will toward the citizen. Similarly, the officer's objective "good faith" — that is, whether he could reasonably have believed that the force used did not violate the Fourth Amendment — may be relevant to the availability of the qualified immunity defense to monetary liability under § 1983. Since no claim of qualified immunity has been raised in this case, however, we express no view on its proper application in excessive force cases that arise under the Fourth Amendment.

SCOTT v. HARRIS
550 U.S. 372 (2007)

JUSTICE SCALIA delivered the opinion of the Court. We consider whether a law enforcement official can, consistent with the Fourth Amendment, attempt to stop a fleeing motorist from continuing his public-endangering flight by ramming the motorist's car from behind. Put another way: Can an officer take actions that place a fleeing motorist at risk of serious injury or death in order to stop the motorist's flight from endangering the lives of innocent bystanders?

I

In March 2001, a Georgia county deputy clocked respondent's vehicle traveling at 73 miles per hour on a road with a 55-mile-per-hour speed limit. The deputy activated his blue flashing lights indicating that respondent should pull over. Instead, respondent sped away, initiating a chase down what is in most portions a two-lane road, at speeds exceeding 85 miles per hour. The deputy radioed his dispatch to report that he was pursuing a fleeing vehicle, and broadcast its license plate number. Petitioner, Deputy Timothy Scott, heard the radio communication and joined the pursuit along with other officers. In the midst of the chase, respondent pulled into the parking lot of a shopping center and was nearly boxed in by the various police vehicles. Respondent evaded the trap by making a sharp turn, colliding with Scott's police car, exiting the parking lot, and speeding off once again down a two lane highway.

Following respondent's shopping center maneuvering which resulted in slight damage to Scott's police car, Scott took over as the lead pursuit vehicle. Six minutes and nearly 10 miles after the chase h ad begun, Scott decided to attempt to terminate the episode by employing a "Precision Intervention Technique ('PIT') maneuver, which causes the fleeing vehicle to spin to a stop." Having radioed his supervisor for permission, Scott was told to " '[g]o ahead and take him out.' " Instead, Scott applied his push bumper to the rear of respondent's vehicle.[13] As a result, respondent lost control of his vehicle, which left the roadway, ran down an embankment, overturned, and crashed. Respondent was badly injured and was rendered a quadriplegic.

Respondent filed suit against Deputy Scott and others under Rev. Stat. § 1979, 42 U.S.C. § 1983, alleging *inter alia*, a violation of his federal constitutional rights, viz. use of excessive force resulting in an unreasonable seizure under the Fourth Amendment. In response, Scott filed a motion for summary judgment based on an assertion of qualified immunity. The District Court denied the motion, finding that "there are material issues of fact on which the issue of qualified immunity turns which present sufficient disagreement to require submission to a jury."

---

[13] Scott says he decided not to employ the PIT maneuver because he was "concerned that the vehicles were moving too quickly to safely execute the maneuver." Respondent agrees that the PIT maneuver could not have been safely employed. It is irrelevant to our analysis whether Scott had permission to take the precise action he took.

II

In resolving questions of qualified immunity, courts are required to resolve a "threshold question: Taken in the light most favorable to the party asserting the injury, do the facts alleged show the officer's conduct violated a constitutional right?" We therefore turn to the threshold inquiry: whether Deputy Scott's actions violated the Fourth Amendment.

III

A

The first step in assessing the constitutionality of Scott's actions is to determine the relevant facts. As this case was decided on summary judgment, there have not yet been factual findings by a judge or jury, and respondent's version of events (unsurprisingly) differs substantially from Scott's version. When things are in such a posture, courts are required to view the facts and draw reasonable inferences "in the light most favorable to the party opposing the [summary judgment] motion." In qualified immunity cases, this usually means adopting (as the Court of Appeals did here) the plaintiff's version of the facts.

There is, however, an added wrinkle in this case: existence in the record of a videotape capturing the events in question. There are no allegations or indications that this videotape was doctored or altered in any way, nor any contention that what it depicts differs from what actually happened. The videotape quite clearly contradicts the version of the story told by respondents and adopted by the Court of Appeals.[14] For example, the Court of Appeals adopted respondent's assertion that, during the chase, "there was little, if any, actual threat to pedestrians or other motorists, as the roads were mostly empty and [respondent] remained in control of his vehicle." Indeed, reading the lower court's opinion, one gets the impression that respondent, rather than fleeing from police, was attempting to pass his driving test:

> "[T]aking the facts from the non-movant's viewpoint, [respondent] remained in control of his vehicle, slowed for turns and intersections, and typically used his indicators for turns. He did not run any motorists off the road. Nor was he a threat to pedestrians in the shopping center parking lot, which was free from pedestrian and vehicular traffic as the center was closed. Significantly, by the time the parties were back on the highway and Scott rammed [respondent], the motorway had been cleared of motorists and pedestrians allegedly because of police blockades of the nearby intersections."

The videotape tells quite a different story. There we see respondent's vehicle racing down narrow, two-lane roads in the dead of night at speeds that are

---

[14] Justice STEVENS suggests that our reaction to the videotape is somehow idiosyncratic, and seems to believe we are misrepresenting its contents. (dissenting opinion) ("In sum, the factual statements by the Court of Appeals quoted by the Court . . . were entirely accurate"). We are happy to allow the videotape to speak for itself. See Record 36, Exh. A, available at http://www.supremecourtus.gov/opinions/vido/scott_v_harris.rmvb and in Clerk of Court's case file.

shockingly fast. We see it swerve around more than a dozen other cars, cross the double-yellow line, and force cars traveling in both directions to their respective shoulders to avoid being hit.[15] We see it run multiple red lights and travel for considerable periods of time in the occasional center left-turn-only lane, chased by numerous police cars forced to engage in the same hazardous maneuvers just to keep up. Far from being the cautious and controlled driver the lower court depicts, what we see on the video more closely resembles a Hollywood-style car chase of the most frightening sort, placing police officers and innocent bystanders alike at great risk of serious injury.[16]

At the summary judgment stage, facts must be viewed in the light most favorable to the nonmoving party only if there is a "genuine" dispute as to those facts. As we have emphasized, "[w]hen the moving party has carried its burden under Rule 56 C, its opponent must do more than simply show that there is some metaphysical doubt as to the material facts. . . . Where the record taken as a whole could not lead a rational trier of fact to find for the nonmoving party, there is no 'genuine issue for trial.' " When opposing parties tell two different stories, one of which is blatantly contradicted by the record, so that no reasonable jury could believe it, a court should not adopt that version of the facts for purposes of ruling on a motion for summary judgment.

That was the case here with regard to the factual issue whether respondent was driving in such fashion as to endanger human life. Respondent's version of events is so utterly discredited by the record that no reasonable jury could have believed him. The Court of Appeals should not have relied on such visible fiction; it should have viewed the facts in the light depicted by the videotape.

B

Judging the matter on that basis, we think it is quite clear that Deputy Scott did not violate the Fourth Amendment. Scott does not contest that his decision to terminate the car chase by ramming his bumper into respondent's vehicle constituted a "seizure." It is also conceded, by both sides, that a claim of "excessive force in the course of making [a] . . . 'seizure' of [the] person . . . [is] properly analyzed under the Fourth Amendment's 'objective reasonableness' standard." *Graham v.*

---

[15] Justice STEVENS hypothesizes that these cars "had already pulled to the side of the road or were driving along the shoulder because they heard the police sirens or saw the flashing lights," so that "[a] jury could certainly conclude that those motorists were exposed to no greater risk than persons who take the same action in response to a speeding ambulance." It is not our experience that ambulances and fire engines careen down two-lane roads at 85-plus miles per hour, with an unmarked scout car out in front of them. The risk they pose to the public is vastly less than what respondent created here. But even if that were not so, it would in no way lead to the conclusion that it was unreasonable to eliminate the threat to life that respondent posed. Society accepts the risk of speeding ambulances and fire engines in order to save life and property; it need not (and assuredly does not) accept a similar risk posed by a reckless motorist fleeing the police.

[16] This is not to say that each and every factual statement made by the Court of Appeals is inaccurate. For example, the videotape validates the court's statement that when Scott rammed respondent's vehicle it was not threatening any other vehicles or pedestrians. (Undoubtedly Scott *waited* for the road to be clear before executing his maneuver.)

Connor. The question we need to answer is whether Scott's actions were objectively reasonable.[17]

1

Respondent urges us to analyze this case as we analyzed *Garner.* We must first decide, he says, whether the actions Scott took constituted "deadly force." (He defines "deadly force" as "any use of force which creates a substantial likelihood of causing death or serious bodily injury.") If so, respondent claims that *Garner* prescribes certain preconditions that must be met before Scott's actions can survive Fourth Amendment scrutiny: (1) The suspect must have posed an immediate threat of serious physical harm to the officer or others; (2) deadly force must have been necessary to prevent escape;[18] and (3) where feasible, the officer must have given the suspect some warning. Since these *Garner* preconditions for using deadly force were not met in this case, Scott's actions were *per se* unreasonable. Respondent's argument falters at its first step; *Garner* did not establish a magical on/off switch that triggers rigid preconditions whenever an officer's actions constitute "deadly force." *Garner* was simply an application of the Fourth Amendment's "reasonableness" test, *Graham,* to the use of a particular type of force in a particular situation. *Garner* held that it was unreasonable to kill a "young, slight, and unarmed" burglary suspect, by shooting him "in the back of the head" while he was running away on foot, and when the officer "could not reasonably have believed that [the suspect] . . . posed any threat," and "never attempted to justify his actions on any basis other than the need to prevent an escape." Whatever *Garner* said about the factors that *might have* justified shooting the suspect in that case, such "preconditions" have scant applicability to this case, which has vastly different facts. "*Garner* had nothing to do with one car striking another or even with car chases in general . . . . A police car's bumping a fleeing car is, in fact, not much like a policeman's shooting a gun so as to hit a person." Nor is the threat posed by the flight on foot of an unarmed suspect even remotely comparable to the extreme danger to human life posed by respondent in this case. Although respondent's attempt to craft an easy-to-apply legal test in the Fourth Amendment context is admirable, in the end

---

[17] Justice STEVENS incorrectly declares this to be "a question of fact best reserved for a jury," and complains we are "usurp[ing] the jury's factfinding function." *Post,* at 7. At the summary judgment stage, however, once we have determined the relevant set of facts and drawn all inferences in favor of the nonmoving party *to the extent supportable by the record,* the reasonableness of Scott's actions — or, in Justice STEVENS' parlance, "[w]hether actions have risen to a level warranting deadly force," is a pure question of law.

[18] Respondent, like the Court of Appeals, defines this second precondition as " 'necessary to prevent escape,' " Brief for Respondent 17; *Harris v. Coweta County,* 433 F.3d 807, 813 (CA11 2005), quoting *Garner,* 471 U.S., at 11. But that quote from *Garner* is taken out of context. The necessity described in *Garner* was, in fact, the need to prevent "serious physical harm, either to the officer or to others." *Ibid.* By way of example only, *Garner* hypothesized that deadly force may be used "if necessary to prevent escape" when the suspect is known to have "committed a crime involving the infliction or threatened infliction of serious physical harm," *ibid.,* so that his mere being at large poses an inherent danger to society. Respondent did not pose that type of inherent threat to society, since (prior to the car chase) he had committed only a minor traffic offense and, as far as the police were aware, had no prior criminal record. But in this case, unlike in *Garner,* it was respondent's flight itself (by means of a speeding automobile) that posed the threat of "serious physical harm . . . to others."

we must still slosh our way through the factbound morass of "reasonableness." Whether or not Scott's actions constituted application of "deadly force," all that matters is whether Scott's actions were reasonable.

2

In determining the reasonableness of the manner in which a seizure is effected, "[w]e must balance the nature and quality of the intrusion on the individual's Fourth Amendment interests against the importance of governmental interests alleged to justify the intrusion." Scott defends his actions by pointing to the paramount governmental interest in ensuring public safety, and respondent nowhere suggests this was not the purpose motivating Scott's behavior. Thus, in judging whether Scott's actions were reasonable, we must consider the risk of bodily harm that Scott's actions posed to respondent in light of the threat to the public that Scott was trying to eliminate. Although there is no obvious way to quantify the risks on either side, it is clear from the videotape that respondent posed an actual and imminent threat to the lives of any pedestrians who might have been present, to other civilian motorists, and to officers involved in the chase. It is equally clear that Scott's actions posed a high likelihood of serious injury or death to respondent — though not the near *certainty* of death posed by, say, shooting a fleeing felon in the back of the head, see *Garner, supra*, at 4, or pulling alongside a fleeing motorist's car and shooting the motorist, cf. *Vaughan v. Cox*, 343 F.3d 1323, 1326–1337 (CA11 2003). So how does a court go about weighing the perhaps lesser probability of injuring or killing a single person? We think it appropriate in this process to take into account not only the number of lives at risk, but also their relative culpability. It was respondent, after all, who intentionally placed himself and the public in danger by unlawfully engaging in the reckless, high-speed flight that ultimately produced the choice between two evils that Scott confronted. Multiple police cars, with blue lights flashing and sirens blaring, had been chasing respondent for nearly 10 miles, but he ignored their warning to stop. By contrast, those who might have been h armed had Scott not taken the action he did were entirely innocent. We have little difficulty in concluding it was reasonable for Scott to take the action that he did.

But wait, says respondent: Couldn't the innocent public equally have been protected, and the tragic accident entirely avoided, if the police had simply ceased their pursuit? We think the police need not have taken that chance and hoped for the best. Whereas Scott's action — ramming respondent off the road — was *certain* to eliminate the risk that respondent posed to the public, ceasing pursuit was not. First of all, there would have been no way to convey convincingly to respondent that the chase was off, and that he was free to go. Had respondent looked in his rearview mirror and seen the police cars deactivate their flashing lights and turn around, he would have had no idea whether they were truly letting him get away, or simply devising a new strategy for capture. Perhaps the police knew a shortcut he didn't know, and would reappear down the road to intercept him; or perhaps they were setting up a roadblock in his path. Given such uncertainty, respondent might have been just as likely to respond by continuing to drive recklessly as by slowing down and wiping his brow.[19]

Second, we are loath to lay down a rule requiring the police to allow fleeing suspects to get away whenever they drive *so recklessly* that they put other people's lives in danger. It is obvious the perverse incentives such a rule would create: Every fleeing motorist would know that escape is within his grasp, if only he accelerates to 90 miles per hour, crosses the double-yellow line a few times, and runs a few red lights. The Constitution assuredly does not impose this invitation to impunity-earned-by-recklessness. Instead, we lay down a more sensible rule: A police officer's attempt to terminate a dangerous high speed car chase that threatens the lives of innocent bystanders does not violate the Fourth Amendment, even when it places the fleeing motorist at risk of serious injury or death.

*   *   *

The car chase that respondent initiated in this case posed a substantial and immediate risk of serious physical injury to others' no reasonable jury could conclude otherwise. Scott's attempt to terminate the chase by forcing respondent off the road was reasonable, and Scott is entitled to summary judgment. The Court of Appeals' decision to the contrary is reversed.

(The concurring opinions of Justices Ginsburg and Breyer are omitted.)

JUSTICE STEVENS, dissenting.

Today, the Court asks whether an officer may "take actions that place a fleeing motorist at risk of serious injury or death in order to stop the motorist's flight from endangering the lives of innocent bystanders. Depending on the circumstances, the answer may be an obvious "yes," an "obvious "no," or sufficiently doubtful that the question of reasonableness of the officer's actions should be decided by a jury, after a review of the degree of danger and the alternatives available to the officer. A high speed chase in a desert in Nevada is, after all, quite different from one that travels through the heart of Las Vegas.

Relying on a *de novo* review of a videotape of a portion of a nighttime chase on a lightly traveled road in Georgia where no pedestrians or other "bystanders" were present, buttressed by uninformed speculation about the possible consequences of discontinuing the chase, eight of the jurors on this Court reach a verdict that differs from the views of the judges on both the District Court and the Court of Appeals who are surely more familiar with the hazards of driving on Georgia roads than we are. The Court's justification for this unprecedented departure from our well-settled standard of review of factual determinations made by a district court and affirmed by a court of appeals is based on its mistaken view that the Court of Appeals' description of the facts was "blatantly contradicted by the record" and that

---

[19] Contrary to Justice STEVENS' assertions, we do not "assum[e] that dangers caused by flight from a police pursuit will continue after the pursuit ends," nor do we make any "factual assumptions," with respect to what would have happened if the police had gone home. We simply point out the *uncertainties* regarding what would have happened, in response to *respondent's* factual assumption that the high-speed flight would have ended.

respondent's version of the events was "so utterly discredited by the record that no reasonable jury could have believed him."

Rather than supporting the conclusion that we see on the video "resembles a Hollywood-style car chase of the most frightening sort,"[20] the tape actually confirms, rather than contradicts, the lower courts' appraisal of the factual questions at issue. More important, it surely does not provide a principle basis for depriving the respondent of his right to have a jury evaluate the question whether the police officers' decision to use deadly force to bring the chase to an end was reasonable.

Omitted from the Court's description of the initial speeding violation is the fact that respondent was on a four-lane portion of Highway 34 when the officer clocked his speed at 73 miles per hour and initiated the chase.[21] More significant — and contrary to the Court's assumption that respondent's vehicle "force[d] cars traveling in both directions to their respective shoulders to avoid being hit;" — a fact unmentioned in the text of the opinion explains why those cars pulled over prior to being passed by respondent. The sirens and flashing lights on the police cars following respondent gave the same warning that a speeding ambulance or fire engine would have provided. The 13 cars that respondent passed on his side of the road before entering the shopping center, and both of that cars that he passed on the right after leaving the center, no doubt had already pulled to the side of the road or were deriving along the shoulder because they heard the police sirens or saw the flashing lights before respondent or the police cruisers[22] approached. A jury could certainly conclude that those motorists were exposed to no greater risk than persons who take the same action in response to a speeding ambulance, and that their actions were fully consistent with the evidence that respondent, though speeding, retained full control of his vehicle.

The police sirens also minimized any risk that may have arisen from running "multiple red lights," *ibid.* In fact, respondent and his pursuers went through only two intersections with stop lights and in both cases all other vehicles in sight were stationary, presumably because they had been warned of the approaching speeders. Incidentally, the videos do show that the lights were red when the police cars passed through them but, because the cameras were farther away when respondent

---

[20] I can only conclude that my colleagues were unduly frightened by two or three images on the tape that looked like bursts of lightning or explosions, but were in fact merely the headlights of vehicles zooming by in the opposite lane. Had they learned to driven when most high speed driving took place on two-lane roads rather than on superhighways — when split second judgments about the risk passing a slowpoke in the face of oncoming traffic were routing — they might well have reacted to the videotape more dispassionately.

[21] According to the District Court record, when respondent was clocked at 73 miles per hour, the deputy who recorded his speed was sitting in his patrol car on Highway 34 between Lora Smith Road and Sullivan Road in Coweta County, Georgia. At that point, as well as at the point at which Highway 34 intersects with Highway 154 — where the deputy caught up with respondent and the videotape begins — Highway 34 is a four-lane road, consisting of two lanes in each direction with a wide grass divider separating the flow of traffic.

[22] Although perhaps understandable, because their volume on the sound recording is low (possibly due to sound proofing in the officer's vehicle), the Court appears to minimize the significance of the sirens audible throughout the tape recording of the pursuit.

did so and it is difficult to discern the color of the signal at that point, it is not entirely clear that he ran either or both of the red lights. In any event, the risk of harm to the stationary vehicles was minimized by the sirens, and there is no reason to believe that respondent would have disobeyed the signals if he were not being pursued.

My colleagues on the jury saw respondent "swerve around more than a dozen other cars," and "force cars traveling in both directions to their respective shoulders," but they apparently discounted the possibility that those cars were already out of the pursuit's path as a result of hearing the sirens. Even if that were not so, passing a slower vehicle on a two-lane road always involves some degree of swerving and is not especially dangerous if there are no cars coming from the opposite direction. At no point during the chase did respondent pull into the opposite lane other than to pass a car in front of him; he did the latter no more than five times and, on most of those occasions, used his turn signal. On none of these occasions was there a car traveling in the opposite direction. In fact, at one point, when respondent found himself behind a car in his own lane and there were cars traveling in the opposite direction. In fact, at one point, when respondent found himself behind a car in his own lane and there were cars traveling in the other direction, he slowed and waited for the cars traveling in the other direction to pass before overtaking the car in front of him while using his turn signal to do so. This is hardly the stuff of Hollywood. To the contrary, the video does not reveal any incidents that could even be remotely characterized as "close calls."

In sum, the factual statements by the Court of Appeals quoted by the Court, were entirely accurate. That court did not describe respondent as a "cautious" driver as my colleagues imply but it did correctly conclude that there is no evidence that he ever lost control of his vehicle. That court also correctly pointed out that the incident in the shopping center parking lot did not create any risk to the pedestrians or other vehicles because the chase occurred just before 11 p.m. or weekday night and the center was closed. It is apparent from the record (including the videotape) that local police had blocked off intersections to keep respondent from entering residential neighborhoods and possibly endangering other motorists. I would add that the videos also show that no pedestrians, parked cars, sidewalks, or residences were visible at any time during the chase. The only "innocent bystanders" who were placed "at great risk of serious injury," were the drivers who either pulled off the road in response to the sirens or passed respondent in the opposite direction when he was driving on his side of the road.

I recognize, of course, that even though respondent's original speeding violation on a four-lane highway was rather ordinary, his refusal to stop and subsequent flight was a serious offense that merited severe punishment. It was not, however, a capital offense, or even an offense that justified the use of deadly force rather than an abandonment of the chase. The Court's concern about the "imminent threat to the lives of any pedestrians who might have been present," while surely valid in an appropriate case, should be discounted in a case involving a nighttime chase in an area where no pedestrians were present.

What would have happened if the police had decided to abandon the chase? We now know that they could have apprehended respondent later because they his license plate number. Even if that were not true, and even if he would have escaped any punishment at all, the use of deadly force in this case was no more appropriate than the use of a deadly weapon against a fleeing felon in *Tennessee v. Garner.* In any event, any uncertainty about the result of abandoning the pursuit has not prevented the Court from basing its conclusions on its own factual assumptions.[23] The Court attempts to avoid the conclusion that deadly force was unnecessary by speculating that if the officers had let him go, respondent might have been "just as likely" to continue to drive recklessly as to slow down and wipe his brow. That speculation is unconvincing as a matter of common sense and improper as a matter of law. Our duty to view the evidence in the light most favorable to the nonmoving party would foreclose such speculation if the Court had not used its observation of the video as an excuse for replacing the rule of law with its ad hoc judgment. There is no evidentiary basis for an assumption that dangers caused by flight from a police pursuit will continue after the pursuit ends. Indeed, rules adopted by countless police departments throughout the country are based on a judgment that differs from the Court's.

Although *Garner*, may not as the Court suggests, "establish a magical on/off switch that triggers rigid preconditions" for the use of deadly force, it did set a threshold under which the use of deadly force would be considered constitutionally unreasonable:

> "Where the officer has probable cause to believe that the suspect poses a threat of serious physical harm either to the officer or to others, it is not constitutionally unreasonable to prevent escape by using deadly force. Thus, if the suspect threatens the officer with a weapon or there is probable cause to believe that he has committed a crime involving the infliction or threatened infliction of serious physical harm, deadly force may be used if necessary to prevent escape, and if, where feasible, some warning has been given."

Whether a person's actions have risen to a level warranting deadly force is a question of fact best reserved for a jury.[24] Here, the Court has usurped the jury's factfinding function and, in doing so, implicitly labeled the four other judges to review the case unreasonable. It chastises the Court of Appeals for failing to "vie[w] the facts in the light depicted by the videotape" and implies that no reasonable

---

[23] In noting that Scott's action "was *certain* to eliminate the risk that respondent posed to the public," while "ceasing pursuit was not," the Court prioritizes total elimination of the risk of harm to the public over the risk that respondent may be seriously injured or even killed. The Court is only able to make such a statement by assuming, based on its interpretation of events on the videotape, that the risk of harm posed in this case, and the type of harm involved, rose to a level warranting deadly force. These are the same types of questions that, when disputed, are typically resolved by a jury; this is why both the District Court and the Court of Appeals saw fit to have them be so decided. Although the Court claims only to have drawn factual inferences in respondent's favor "to the extent supportable by the record," (emphasis in original), its own view of the record has clearly precluded it from doing so to the same extent as the two courts through which this case has already traveled.

[24] In its opinion, the Court of Appeals correctly noted: "We reject the defendants' argument that Harris' driving must, as a matter of law, be considered sufficiently reckless to give Scott probable cause to believe that he posed a substantial threat of imminent physical harm to motorists and pedestrians. This is a disputed issue to be resolved by a jury."

person could view the videotape and come to the conclusion that deadly force was unjustified. However, the three judges on the Court of Appeals panel apparently did view the videotapes entered into evidence[25] and described a very different version of events:

"At the time of the ramming, apart from speeding and running two red lights, Harris was driving in a nonaggressive fashion (i.e., without trying to ram or run into the officers). Moreover, . . . Scott's path on the open highway was largely clear. The videos introduced into evidence show little to no vehicular (or pedestrian) traffic, allegedly because of the late hour and the police blockade of the nearby intersections. Finally, Scott issued absolutely no warning (e.g., over the loudspeaker or otherwise) prior to using deadly force."

If two groups of judges can disagree so vehemently about the nature of the pursuit and the circumstances surrounding that pursuit, it seems eminently likely that a reasonable juror could disagree with this Court's characterization of events. Moreover, under the standard set forth in *Garner*, it is certainly possible that "a jury could conclude that Scott unreasonably used deadly force to seize Harris by ramming him off the road under the instant circumstances." 433 F.3d, at 821.

The Court today sets forth a *per se* rule that presumes its own version of the facts: "A police officer's attempt to terminate a dangerous high-speed car chase *that threatens the lives of innocent bystanders* does not violate the Fourth Amendment, even when it places the fleeing motorist at risk of serious injury or death." (emphasis added). Not only does that rule fly in the face of the flexible and case-by-case "reasonableness" approach applied in *Garner* and *Graham* v. *Connor*, but is also arguably inapplicable to the case at hand, given that it is not clear that this chase threatened the life of any "innocent bystande[r]."[26] In my view, the risks inherent in justifying unwarranted police conduct on the basis of unfounded assumptions are unacceptable, particularly when less drastic measures — in this case, the use of stop sticks[27] or a simple warning issued from a loudspeaker — could have avoided such a tragic result. In my judgment, jurors in Georgia should be allowed to evaluate the reasonableness of the decision to ram respondent's speeding vehicle in a manner that created an obvious risk of death and has in fact made him a quadriplegic at the age of 19.

I respectfully dissent.

QUESTIONS AND NOTES

1. Does *Scott* seem to reflect the same values as *Garner* or a different set of value? Explain.

---

[25] In total, there are four police tapes which captured portions of the pursuit, all recorded from different officers' vehicles.

[26] It is unclear whether, in referring to "innocent bystanders," the Court is referring to the motorists driving unfazed in the opposite direction or to the drivers who pulled over to the side of the road, safely out of respondent's and petitioner's path.

[27] "Stop sticks" are a device which can be placed across the roadway and used to flatten a vehicle's tires slowly to safely terminate a pursuit.

2. Whose crime was more serious, Garner's or Harris's?

3. If you said Garner's, are the decisions actually perverse? Why? Why not?

4. Would it be worse to let Harris get away than it would have been to let Garner have gotten away? Explain.

5. Do you believe that Harris would have continued his reckless driving if the police had discontinued the chase? Where should the presumption lie on that question?

6. Does the *Scott* opinion appear to be more deferential to the police than the *Garner* opinion?

7. If so, do you think that 9/11 had anything to do with it?

8. Should the videotape have played such a major role in the result? Is it relevant that Justice Stevens and all of the judges on the two lower courts construed the videotape different from the majority of the Supreme Court?

C. DETENTION OF PERSONS PURSUANT TO A SEARCH WARRANT

MICHIGAN v. SUMMERS
452 U.S. 692 (1981)

JUSTICE STEVENS delivered the opinion of the Court.

As Detroit police officers were about to execute a warrant to search a house for narcotics, they encountered respondent descending the front steps. They requested his assistance in gaining entry and detained him while they searched the premises. After finding narcotics in the basement and ascertaining that respondent owned the house, the police arrested him, searched his person, and found in his coat pocket an envelope containing 8.5 grams of heroin.[28]

---

[28] The execution of the warrant is described in greater detail in Justice Moody's opinion for the Michigan Supreme Court:

"Upon arriving at the named address, Officer Roger Lehman saw the defendant go out the front door of the house and proceed across the porch and down the steps. When defendant was asked to open the door he replied that he could not because he left his keys inside, but he could ring someone over the intercom. Dwight Calhoun came to the door, but did not admit the police officers. As a result, the officers obtained entrance to the premises by forcing open the front door. Once admittance had been gained Officer Lehman instructed Officer Conant, previously stationed along the side of the house, to bring the defendant, still on the porch, into the house.

"After the eight occupants of the house were detained, a search of the premises revealed two plastic bags of suspected narcotics under the bar in the basement. After finding the suspected narcotics in the basement and upon determining that the defendant was the owner of the house, Officer Conant formally arrested the defendant for violation of the Controlled Substances Act of 1971. A custodial search conducted by Officer Conant revealed a plastic bag containing suspected heroin in the defendant's jacket pocket. It is this heroin, discovered on the person of the defendant, that forms the basis of the instant possession charge."

I

The dispositive question in this case is whether the initial detention of respondent violated his constitutional right to be secure against an unreasonable seizure of his person. The State attempts to justify the eventual search of respondent's person by arguing that the authority to search premises granted by the warrant implicitly included the authority to search persons on those premises, just as that authority included an authorization to search furniture and containers in which the particular things described might be concealed. But as the Michigan Court of Appeals correctly noted, even if otherwise acceptable, this argument could not justify the initial detention of respondent outside the premises described in the warrant. If that detention was permissible, there is no need to reach the question whether a search warrant for premises includes the right to search persons found there, because when the police searched respondent, they had probable cause to arrest him and had done so.[3] Our appraisal of the validity of the search of respondent's person therefore depends upon a determination whether the officers had the authority to require him to re-enter the house and to remain there while they conducted their search.[4]

III

Of prime importance in assessing the intrusion is the fact that the police had obtained a warrant to search respondent's house for contraband. A neutral and detached magistrate had found probable cause to believe that the law was being violated in that house and had authorized a substantial invasion of the privacy of the persons who resided there. The detention of one of the residents while the premises were searched, although admittedly a significant restraint on his liberty, was surely less intrusive than the search itself. Indeed, we may safely assume that most citizens — unless they intend flight to avoid arrest — would elect to remain in order to observe the search of their possessions. Furthermore, the type of detention imposed here is not likely to be exploited by the officer or unduly prolonged in order to gain more information, because the information the officers seek normally will be obtained through the search and not through the detention.[14] Moreover, because the detention in this case was in respondent's own residence, it could add only

---

[3] Because there were several other occupants of the house, under Michigan law the evidence that narcotics had been found in the basement of respondent's house would apparently be insufficient to support a conviction. Respondent does not challenge the conclusion that the evidence found in his home established probable cause to arrest him.

[4] The "seizure" issue in this case should not be confused with the "search" issue presented in *Ybarra v. Illinois*, 444 U.S. 85 (1979). In *Ybarra* the police executing a search warrant for a public tavern detained and searched all of the customers who happened to be present. No question concerning the legitimacy of the detention was raised. Rather, the Court concluded that the search of Ybarra was invalid because the police had no reason to believe he had any special connection with the premises, and the police had no other basis for suspecting that he was armed or in possession of contraband. In this case, only the detention is at issue. The police knew respondent lived in the house, and they did not search him until after they had probable cause to arrest and had done so.

[14] Professor LaFave has noted that the reasonableness of a detention may be determined in part by "whether the police are diligently pursuing a means of investigation which is likely to resolve the matter one way or another very soon . . . ."

minimally to the public stigma associated with the search itself and would involve neither the inconvenience nor the indignity associated with a compelled visit to the police station. In sharp contrast to the custodial interrogation in *Dunaway*, the detention of this respondent was "substantially less intrusive" than an arrest.[15]

In assessing the justification for the detention of an occupant of premises being searched for contraband pursuant to a valid warrant, both the law enforcement interest and the nature of the "articulable facts" supporting the detention are relevant. Most obvious is the legitimate law enforcement interest in preventing flight in the event that incriminating evidence is found. Less obvious, but sometimes of greater importance, is the interest in minimizing the risk of harm to the officers. Although no special danger to the police is suggested by the evidence in this record, the execution of a warrant to search for narcotics is the kind of transaction that may give rise to sudden violence or frantic efforts to conceal or destroy evidence. The risk of harm to both the police and the occupants is minimized if the officers routinely exercise unquestioned command of the situation. Finally, the orderly completion of the search may be facilitated if the occupants of the premises are present. Their self-interest may induce them to open locked doors or locked containers to avoid the use of force that is not only damaging to property but may also delay the completion of the task at hand.

It is also appropriate to consider the nature of the articulable and individualized suspicion on which the police base the detention of the occupant of a home subject to a search warrant. We have already noted that the detention represents only an incremental intrusion on personal liberty when the search of a home has been authorized by a valid warrant. The existence of a search warrant, however, also provides an objective justification for the detention. A judicial officer has determined that police have probable cause to believe that someone in the home is committing a crime. Thus a neutral magistrate rather than an officer in the field has made the critical determination that the police should be given a special authorization to thrust themselves into the privacy of a home. The connection of an occupant to that home gives the police officer an easily identifiable and certain basis for determining that suspicion of criminal activity justifies a detention of that occupant.

In *Payton*, we held that police officers may not enter a private residence to make a routine felony arrest without first obtaining a warrant. In that case we rejected the suggestion that only a search warrant could adequately protect the privacy interests at stake, noting that the distinction between a search warrant and an arrest warrant was far less significant than the interposition of the magistrate's determination of probable cause between the zealous officer and the citizen:

"It is true that an arrest warrant requirement may afford less protection than a search warrant requirement, but it will suffice to interpose the magistrate's determination of probable cause between the zealous officer and the citizen. If there is sufficient evidence of a citizen's participation in a felony to persuade a judicial

---

[15] We do not view the fact that respondent was leaving his house when the officers arrived to be of constitutional significance. The seizure of respondent on the sidewalk outside was no more intrusive than the detention of those residents of the house whom the police found inside.

officer that his arrest is justified, it is constitutionally reasonable to require him to open his doors to the officers of the law. Thus, for Fourth Amendment purposes, an arrest warrant founded on probable cause implicitly carries with it the limited authority to enter a dwelling in which the suspect lives when there is reason to believe the suspect is within."

That holding is relevant today. If the evidence that a citizen's residence is harboring contraband is sufficient to persuade a judicial officer that an invasion of the citizen's privacy is justified, it is constitutionally reasonable to require that citizen to remain while officers of the law execute a valid warrant to search his home. Thus, for Fourth Amendment purposes, we hold that a warrant to search for contraband[20] founded on probable cause implicitly carries with it the limited authority to detain the occupants of the premises while a proper search is conducted.[21]

Because it was lawful to require respondent to re-enter and to remain in the house until evidence establishing probable cause to arrest him was found, his arrest and the search incident thereto were constitutionally permissible. The judgment of the Supreme Court of Michigan must therefore be reversed.

JUSTICE STEWART, with whom JUSTICE BRENNAN and JUSTICE MARSHALL join, dissenting.

It seems clear that before a court can uphold a detention on less than probable cause on the ground that it is "reasonable" in the light of the competing interests, the government must demonstrate an important purpose beyond the normal goals of criminal investigation, or must demonstrate an extraordinary obstacle to such investigation.

II

What the Court approves today is justified by no such special governmental interest or law enforcement need. There were only two governmental purposes supporting the detention of the respondent.[1] One was "the legitimate law enforcement interest in preventing flight in the event that incriminating evidence is found." The other was that "the orderly completion of the search may be facilitated if the occupants of the premises are present." Unlike the law enforcement objectives that

---

[20] We do not decide whether the same result would be justified if the search warrant merely authorized a search for evidence.

[21] Although special circumstances, or possibly a prolonged detention, might lead to a different conclusion in an unusual case, we are persuaded that this routine detention of residents of a house while it was being searched for contraband pursuant to a valid warrant is not such a case.

[1] As the Court acknowledges, the record in this case presents no evidence whatsoever that the police feared any threat to their safety or that of others from the conduct of the respondent, or that they could reasonably have so feared. The Court says that this nevertheless was the "kind of transaction that may give rise to sudden violence . . . ." But where the police cannot demonstrate, on the basis of specific and articulable facts, a reasonable belief that a person threatens physical harm to them or others, the speculation that other persons in that circumstance might pose such a threat cannot justify a search or seizure. *Ybarra*.

justified the police conduct in *Terry* and the border stop cases, these objectives represented nothing more than the ordinary police interest in discovering evidence of crime and apprehending wrongdoers. And the Fourth and Fourteenth Amendments impose significant restraints upon these traditional police activities, even though the police and the courts may find those restraints unreasonably inconvenient.

If the police, acting without probable cause, can seize a person to make him available for arrest in case probable cause is later developed to arrest him, the requirement of probable cause for arrest has been turned upside down. And if the police may seize a person without probable cause in order to "facilitate" the execution of a warrant that did not authorize his arrest, the fundamental principle that the scope of a search and seizure can be justified only by the scope of the underlying warrant has suffered serious damage. There is no authority in this Court for the principle that the police can engage in searches and seizures without probable cause simply because to do so enhances their ability to conduct investigations which may eventually lead to probable cause.[2]

The explicit holding of the Court is that "a warrant to search for contraband founded on probable cause implicitly carries with it the limited authority to detain the occupants of the premises while a proper search is conducted." Though on superficial reading, this language may suggest a minor intrusion of brief duration, a detention "while a proper search is being conducted" can mean a detention of several hours.[3] The police thereby make the person a prisoner in his own home for a potentially very long period of time.[4] Moreover, because of the questionable

---

[2] In perplexing citation, the Court notes our holding in *Payton*, that an arrest warrant based on probable cause justifies entering a person's home to carry out the arrest, and declares that *Payton* "is relevant today." But I had thought that the very point of the passage of the Court quotes from *Payton*, is that the police would be justified in arresting a person in his own home because they had a warrant for his arrest based upon probable cause to believe that he had violated the criminal law. Since it is the absence of such probable cause that lies at the heart of this case, I fail to understand *Payton's* "relevance."

[3] The record does not clearly reveal the length of the search in this case. In *Harris v. United States*, 331 U.S. 145, a Federal Bureau of Investigation search of a one-bedroom apartment for burglar tools and a pair of checks consumed five hours.

[4] I also question the Court's confident assertions about the inoffensive nature of the detention in this case. First, the Court says the detention was innocuous because it was less intrusive than the search that was mandated by the warrant. This reasoning is, of course, circular, since the very question of the severity of the detention arises only because it was not based on a warrant or probable cause.

Second, the Court says that the intrusion was not a serious one because a reasonable-minded citizen would in fact want to be present at a search of his house unless he was fleeing to avoid arrest. But I must infer that the respondent here did not want to be present in his house during the search, else he would not have brought this claim, and the law cannot penalize him for "fleeing arrest" when the police did not have probable cause to arrest him. This second reason amounts to the view that a person cannot assert his rights under the exclusionary rule if he stands to benefit from the exclusion.

Finally, the Court observes that this sort of detention is not likely to be exploited or unduly prolonged by the police, since the officers are more likely to find the information they seek through the search than through the detention. I confess I do not understand this reason. It seems no more than a restatement of the view that the police may detain the person to have him available for arrest when they complete the search, but that view merely begs the question whether the potential duration of the search threatens the person with a lengthy detention.

nature of the governmental interest asserted by the State and acknowledged by the Court in this case, the requirement that the scope of the intrusion be reasonably related to its justification does not provide a limiting principle for circumscribing the detention. If the purpose of the detention is to help the police make the search, the detention can be as long as the police find it necessary to protract the search.[5]

In *Dunaway*, the Court reaffirmed that the " 'long-prevailing standards' of probable cause embodied 'the best compromise that has been found for accommodating [the] often opposing interests' in 'safeguard[ing] citizens from rash and unreasonable interferences with privacy' and in 'seek[ing] to give fair leeway for enforcing the law in the community's protection.' " Because the present case presents no occasion for departing from this principle, I respectfully dissent.

QUESTIONS AND NOTES

1.   How extensive of a detention did the Court authorize?

2.   In regard to question 1, how long do you think that a search would have lasted if the home owners were innocent, and there were in fact *no* drugs on the premises?

3.   What reasons does the Court give to justify this detention? How persuasive are they?

4.   Would (should) the Court's reasoning justify detaining a non-owner/resident of the house? What about a visitor to the house? How about a patron at a bar which was subject to a warranted search?

5.   The scope of a detention that the Court is prepared to tolerate is explored in *Muehler v. Mena*.

MUEHLER v. MENA
544 U.S. 93 (2005)

CHIEF JUSTICE REHNQUIST delivered the opinion of the Court.

Respondent Iris Mena was detained in handcuffs during a search of the premises that she and several others occupied. Petitioners were lead members of a police detachment executing a search warrant of these premises. She sued the officers under § 1983, and the District Court found in her favor. The Court of Appeals affirmed the judgment, holding that the use of handcuffs to detain Mena during the search violated the Fourth Amendment. We hold that Mena's detention in

---

[5] The Court adverts to this problem only by suggesting that "special circumstances, or possibly a prolonged detention, might lead to a different conclusion in an unusual case." But the Court provides no criteria for identifying "special circumstances" or for determining when a detention is "prolonged"; in particular, it fails to tell law enforcement officers whether a detention will always be permissible, however protracted, so long as it does not exceed the length of the search of the house. This ambiguity casts doubt on the Court's assertion, that its holding will not require individual police officers to engage in the sort of on-the-scene, ad hoc legal judgments which pose a serious threat to Fourth and Fourteenth Amendment protections.

handcuffs for the length of the search was consistent with our opinion in *Michigan v. Summers.*

* * *

Based on information gleaned from the investigation of a gang-related, driveby shooting, petitioners Muehler and Brill had reason to believe at least one member of a gang — the West Side Locos — lived at 1363 Patricia Avenue. They also suspected that the individual was armed and dangerous, since he had recently been involved in the driveby shooting. As a result, Muehler obtained a search warrant for 1363 Patricia Avenue that authorized a broad search of the house and premises for, among other things, deadly weapons and evidence of gang membership. In light of the high degree of risk involved in searching a house suspected of housing at least one, and perhaps multiple, armed gang members, a Special Weapons and Tactics (SWAT) team was used to secure the residence and grounds before the search.

At 7 a.m. on February 3, 1998, petitioners, along with the SWAT team and other officers, executed the warrant. Mena was asleep in her bed when the SWAT team, clad in helmets and black vests adorned with badges and the word "POLICE," entered her bedroom and placed her in handcuffs at gunpoint. The SWAT team also handcuffed three other individuals found on the property. The SWAT team then took those individuals and Mena into a converted garage, which contained several beds and some other bedroom furniture. While the search proceeded, one or two officers guarded the four detainees, who were allowed to move around the garage but remained in handcuffs.

The search of the premises yielded a .22 caliber handgun with .22 caliber ammunition, a box of .25 caliber ammunition, several baseball bats with gang writing, various additional gang paraphernalia, and a bag of marijuana. Before the officers left the area, Mena was released.

In her § 1983 suit against the officers she alleged that she was detained "for an unreasonable time and in an unreasonable manner" in violation of the Fourth Amendment. In addition, she claimed that the warrant and its execution were overbroad, that the officers failed to comply with the "knock and announce" rule, and that the officers had needlessly destroyed property during the search. The officers moved for summary judgment, asserting that they were entitled to qualified immunity, but the District Court denied their motion. The Court of Appeals affirmed that denial.

* * *

In *Summers* we held that officers executing a search warrant for contraband have the authority "to detain the occupants of the premises while a proper search is conducted." Such detentions are appropriate, we explained, because the character of the additional intrusion caused by detention is slight and because the justifications for detention are substantial. We made clear that the detention of an occupant is "surely less intrusive than the search itself," and the presence of a warrant assures that a neutral magistrate has determined that probable cause exists to search the home. Against this incremental intrusion, we posited three legitimate law enforcement interests that provide substantial justification for detaining an occupant: "preventing flight in the event that incriminating evidence is found"; "minimizing the risk of harm to the officers"; and facilitating "the orderly completion of the search," as detainees' "self-interest may induce them to open locked doors or locked containers to avoid the use of force."

Mena's detention was, under *Summers*, plainly permissible An officer's authority to detain incident to a search is categorical; it does not depend on the "quantum of proof justifying detention or the extent of the intrusion to be imposed by the seizure." Thus, Mena's detention for the duration of the search was reasonable under *Summers* because a warrant existed to search 1363 Patricia Avenue and she was an occupant of that address at the time of the search.

Inherent in *Summers'* authorization to detain an occupant of the place to be searched is the authority to use reasonable force to effectuate the detention. See *Graham v. Connor* ("Fourth Amendment jurisprudence has long recognized that the right to make an arrest or investigatory stop necessarily carries with it the right to use some degree of physical coercion or threat thereof to effect it"). Indeed, *Summers* itself stressed that the risk of harm to officers and occupants is minimized "if the officers routinely exercise unquestioned command of the situation."

The officers' use of force in the form of handcuffs to effectuate Mena's detention in the garage, as well as the detention of the three other occupants, was reasonable because the governmental interests outweigh the marginal intrusion. See *Graham*. The imposition of correctly applied handcuffs on Mena, who was already being lawfully detained during a search of the house, was undoubtedly a separate intrusion in addition to detention in the converted garage.[2] The detention was thus more intrusive than that which we upheld in *Summers*.

But this was no ordinary search. The governmental interests in not only detaining, but using handcuffs, are at their maximum when, as here, a warrant authorizes a search for weapons and a wanted gang member resides on the premises. In such inherently dangerous situations, the use of handcuffs minimizes the risk of harm to both officers and occupants. Cf. *Summers* (recognizing the execution of a warrant to search for drugs "may give rise to sudden violence or frantic efforts to conceal or destroy evidence"). Though this safety risk inherent in executing a search warrant for weapons was sufficient to justify the use of handcuffs, the need to detain multiple occupants made the use of handcuffs all the more reasonable.

Mena argues that, even if the use of handcuffs to detain her in the garage was reasonable as an initial matter, the duration of the use of handcuffs made the detention unreasonable. The duration of a detention can, of course, affect the

---

[2] In finding the officers should have released Mena from the handcuffs, the Court of Appeals improperly relied upon the fact that the warrant did not include Mena as a suspect. The warrant was concerned not with individuals but with locations and property. In particular, the warrant in this case authorized the search of 1363 Patricia Avenue and its surrounding grounds for, among other things, deadly weapons and evidence of street gang membership. In this respect, the warrant here resembles that at issue in *Summers* which allowed the search of a residence for drugs without mentioning any individual, including the owner of the home whom police ultimately arrested. *Summers* makes clear that when a neutral magistrate has determined police have probable cause to believe contraband exists, "[t]he connection of an occupant to [a] home" alone "justifies a detention of that occupant."

balance of interests under Graham. However, the 2- to 3-hour detention in handcuffs in this case does not outweigh the government's continuing safety interests. As we have noted, this case involved the detention of four detainees by two officers during a search of a gang house for dangerous weapons. We conclude that the detention of Mena in handcuffs during the search was reasonable.

Mena has advanced in this Court, as she did before the Court of Appeals, an alternative argument for affirming the judgment below. She asserts that her detention extended beyond the time the police completed the tasks incident to the search. Because the Court of Appeals did not address this contention, we too decline to address it.

The judgment of the Court of Appeals is therefore vacated, and the case is remanded for further proceedings consistent with this opinion.

JUSTICE KENNEDY, concurring.

I concur in the judgment and in the opinion of the Court. It does seem important to add this brief statement to help ensure that police handcuffing during searches becomes neither routine nor unduly prolonged.

The safety of the officers and the efficacy of the search are matters of first concern, but so too is it a matter of first concern that excessive force is not used on the persons detained, especially when these persons, though lawfully detained under *Michigan v. Summers* are not themselves suspected of any involvement in criminal activity. The use of handcuffs is the use of force, and such force must be objectively reasonable under the circumstances, *Graham v. Connor*.

The reasonableness calculation under *Graham* is in part a function of the expected and actual duration of the search. If the search extends to the point when the handcuffs can cause real pain or serious discomfort, provision must be made to alter the conditions of detention at least long enough to attend to the needs of the detainee. This is so even if there is no question that the initial handcuffing was objectively reasonable. The restraint should also be removed if, at any point during the search, it would be readily apparent to any objectively reasonable officer that removing the handcuffs would not compromise the officers' safety or risk interference or substantial delay in the execution of the search. The time spent in the search here, some two to three hours, certainly approaches, and may well exceed, the time beyond which a detainee's Fourth Amendment interests require revisiting the necessity of handcuffing in order to ensure the restraint, even if permissible as an initial matter, has not become excessive.

That said, under these circumstances I do not think handcuffing the detainees for the duration of the search was objectively unreasonable. As I understand the record, during much of this search 2 armed officers were available to watch over the 4 unarmed detainees, while the other 16 officers on the scene conducted an extensive search of a suspected gang safe house. Even if we accept as true — as we must — the factual assertions that these detainees posed no readily apparent danger and that keeping them handcuffed deviated from standard police procedure, it does not follow that the handcuffs were unreasonable. Where the detainees outnumber those supervising them, and this situation could not be remedied without diverting officers from an extensive, complex, and time-consuming search, the continued use of handcuffs after the initial sweep may be justified, subject to adjustments or temporary release under supervision to avoid pain or excessive physical discomfort. Because on this record it does not appear the restraints were excessive, I join the opinion of the Court.

JUSTICE STEVENS, with whom JUSTICE SOUTER, JUSTICE GINSBURG, and JUSTICE BREYER join, concurring in the judgment.

The jury in this case found that the two petitioners violated Iris Mena's Fourth Amendment right to be free from unreasonable seizure by detaining her with greater force and for a longer period of time than was reasonable under the circumstances.

In its opinion affirming the judgment, the Court of Appeals, instead of merely deciding whether there was sufficient evidence in the record to support the jury's verdict, appears to have ruled as a matter of law that the officers should have released her from the handcuffs sooner than they did. I agree that it is appropriate to remand the case to enable the Court of Appeals to consider whether the evidence supports Iris Mena's contention that she was held longer than the search actually lasted. In doing so, the Court of Appeals must of course accord appropriate deference to the jury's reasonable factual findings, while applying the correct legal standard. See *Ornelas v. United States.*

In my judgment, however, the Court's discussion of the amount of force used to detain Iris pursuant to *Michigan v. Summers* is analytically unsound. Although the Court correctly purports to apply the "objective reasonableness" test announced in *Graham v. Connor* it misapplies that test. Given the facts of this case — and the presumption that a reviewing court must draw all reasonable inferences in favor of supporting the verdict — I think it clear that the jury could properly have found that this 5-foot-2-inch young lady posed no threat to the officers at the scene, and that they used excessive force in keeping her in handcuffs for up to three hours. Although Summers authorizes the detention of any individual who is present when a valid search warrant is being executed, that case does not give officers carte blanche to keep individuals who pose no threat in handcuffs throughout a search, no matter how long it may last. On remand, I would therefore instruct the Court of Appeals to consider whether the evidence supports Mena's contention that the petitioners used excessive force in detaining her when it considers the length of the Summers detention.

I

As the Court notes, the warrant in this case authorized the police to enter the Mena home to search for a gun belonging to Raymond Romero that may have been used in a gang-related driveby shooting. Romero, a known member of the West Side Locos gang, rented a room from the Mena family. The house, described as a "'poor house,'" was home to several unrelated individuals who rented from the Menas. Each resident had his or her own bedroom, which could be locked with a padlock on the outside, and each had access to the living room and kitchen. In addition, several individuals lived in trailers in the back yard and also had access to the common spaces in the Mena home.

In addition to Romero, police had reason to believe that at least one other West Side Locos gang member had lived at the residence, although Romero's brother told police that the individual had returned to Mexico. The officers in charge of the search, petitioners Muehler and Brill, had been at the same residence a few months earlier on an unrelated domestic violence call, but did not see any other individuals they believed to be gang members inside the home on that occasion.

In light of the fact that the police believed that Romero possessed a gun and that there might be other gang members at the residence, petitioner Muehler decided to use a Special Weapons and Tactics (SWAT) team to execute the warrant. As described in the majority opinion, eight members of the SWAT team forcefully entered the home at 7 a.m. In fact, Iris Mena was the only occupant of the house and she was asleep in her bedroom. The police woke her up at gunpoint, and immediately handcuffed her. At the same time, officers served another search warrant at the home of Romero's mother, where Romero was known to stay several nights each week. In part because Romero's mother had previously cooperated with police officers, they did not use a SWAT team to serve that warrant. Romero was found at his mother's house; after being cited for possession of a small amount of marijuana, he was released.

Meanwhile, after the SWAT team secured the Mena residence and gave the "all clear," police officers transferred Iris and three other individuals (who had been in trailers in the back yard) to a converted garage.[4] To get to the garage, Iris, who was still in her bedclothes, was forced to walk barefoot through the pouring rain. The officers kept her and the other three individuals in the garage for up to three hours while they searched the home. Although she requested them to remove the handcuffs, they refused to do so. For the duration of the search, two officers guarded Iris and the other three detainees. A .22 caliber handgun, ammunition, and gang-related paraphernalia were found in Romero's bedroom, and other gang-related paraphernalia was found in the living room. Officers found nothing of significance in Iris' bedroom.[5]

II

In analyzing the quantum of force used to effectuate the Summers detention, the Court rightly employs the "objective reasonableness" test of Graham. Under Graham, the trier of fact must balance " 'the nature and quality of the intrusion on the individual's Fourth Amendment interests' against the countervailing govern-

---

[4] The other individuals were a 55-year-old Latina female, a 40-year-old Latino male who was removed from the scene by the Immigration and Naturalization Service (INS), and a white male who appears to be in his early 30's and who was cited for possession of a small amount of marijuana.

[5] One of the justifications for our decision in *Summers* was the fact that the occupants may be willing to "open locked doors or locked containers to avoid the use of force that is not only damaging to property but may also delay the completion of the task at hand." Iris, however, was never asked to assist the officers, although she testified that she was willing to do so. Instead, officers broke the locks on several cabinets and dressers to which Iris possessed the keys.

mental interests at stake." The District Court correctly instructed the jury to take into consideration such factors as " 'the severity of the suspected crime, whether the person being detained is the subject of the investigation, whether such person poses an immediate threat to the security of the police or others or to the ability of the police to conduct the search, and whether such person is actively resisting arrest or attempting to flee.' " The District Court also correctly instructed the jury to consider whether the detention was prolonged and whether Iris was detained in handcuffs after the search had ended. Many of these factors are taken from Graham itself, and the jury instruction reflects an entirely reasonable construction of the objective reasonableness test in the *Summers* context.

Considering those factors, it is clear that the SWAT team's initial actions were reasonable. When officers undertake a dangerous assignment to execute a warrant to search property that is presumably occupied by violence-prone gang members, it may well be appropriate to use both overwhelming force and surprise in order to secure the premises as promptly as possible. In this case the decision to use a SWAT team of eight heavily armed officers and to execute the warrant at 7 a.m. gave the officers maximum protection against the anticipated risk. As it turned out, there was only one person in the house — Iris Mena — and she was sound asleep. Nevertheless, "[t]he 'reasonableness' of a particular use of force must be judged from the perspective of a reasonable officer on the scene, rather than with the 20/20 vision of hindsight." At the time they first encountered Iris, the officers had no way of knowing her relation to Romero, whether she was affiliated with the West Side Locos, or whether she had any weapons on her person. Further, the officers needed to use overwhelming force to immediately take command of the situation; by handcuffing Iris they could more quickly secure her room and join the other officers. It would be unreasonable to expect officers, who are entering what they believe to be a high risk situation, to spend the time necessary to determine whether Iris was a threat before they handcuffed her. To the extent that the Court of Appeals relied on the initial actions of the SWAT team to find that there was sufficient evidence to support the jury's verdict, it was in error.

Whether the well-founded fears that justified the extraordinary entry into the house should also justify a prolonged interruption of the morning routine of a presumptively innocent person, however, is a separate question and one that depends on the specific facts of the case. This is true with respect both to how the handcuffs were used, and to the totality of the circumstances surrounding the detention, including whether Mena was detained in handcuffs after the search had concluded. With regard to the handcuffs, police may use them in different ways.[6] Here, the cuffs kept Iris' arms behind her for two to three hours. She testified that they were " 'real uncomfortable' " and that she had asked the officers to remove them, but that they had refused. Moreover, she was continuously guarded by two police officers who obviously made flight virtually impossible even if the cuffs had been removed.

---

[6] For instance, a suspect may be handcuffed to a fixed object, to a custodian, or her hands may simply be linked to one another. The cuffs may join the wrists either in the front or the back of the torso. They can be so tight that they are painful, particularly when applied for prolonged periods. While they restrict movement, they do not necessarily preclude flight if the prisoner is not kept under constant surveillance.

A jury could reasonably have found a number of facts supporting a conclusion that the prolonged handcuffing was unreasonable. No contraband was found in Iris' room or on her person. There were no indications suggesting she was or ever had been a gang member, which was consistent with the fact that during the police officers' last visit to the home, no gang members were present. She fully cooperated with the officers and the INS agent, answering all their questions. She was unarmed, and given her small size, was clearly no match for either of the two armed officers who were guarding her. In sum, there was no evidence that Mena posed any threat to the officers or anyone else.

The justifications offered by the officers are not persuasive. They have argued that at least six armed officers were required to guard the four detainees, even though all of them had been searched for weapons. Since there were 18 officers at the scene, and since at least 1 officer who at one point guarded Mena and the other three residents was sent home after offering to assist in the search, it seems unlikely that lack of resources was really a problem. While a court should not ordinarily question the allocation of police officers or resources, a jury could have reasonably found that this is a case where ample resources were available.

The Court suggests that officers are under "no duty to divert resources from the search to make a predictive judgment about whether a particular occupant can be freed from handcuffs." In reality, the officers did make such an inquiry when they filled out the field identification cards, the use of which is standard police practice and takes less than five minutes. Further, the armed officers who guarded Iris had, of course, already been diverted from other search activities. It is therefore difficult to see what additional resources would have been required to determine that she posed no threat to the officers that would justify handcuffing her for two to three hours.

The jury may also have been skeptical of testimony that the officers in fact feared for their safety given that the actual suspect of the shooting had been found at the other location and promptly released. Additionally, while the officers testified that as a general matter they would not release an individual from handcuffs while searching a residence, the SWAT team's tactical plan for this particular search arguably called for them to do just that, since it directed that "[a]ny subjects encountered will be handcuffed and detained until they can be patted down, their location noted, [field identified], and released by Officer Muehler or Officer R. Brill." The tactical plan suggests that they can, and often do, release individuals who are not related to the search. The SWAT team leader testified that handcuffs are not always required when executing a search.

In short, under the factors listed in Graham and those validly presented to the jury in the jury instructions, a jury could have reasonably found from the evidence that there was no apparent need to handcuff Iris for the entire duration of the search and that she was detained for an unreasonably prolonged period. She posed no threat whatsoever to the officers at the scene. She was not suspected of any crime and was not a person targeted by the search warrant. She had no reason to flee the scene and gave no indication that she desired to do so. Viewing the facts in the light most favorable to the jury's verdict, as we are required to do, there is certainly no obvious factual basis for rejecting the jury's verdict that the officers acted unreasonably, and no obvious basis for rejecting the conclusion that, on these facts, the quantum of force used was unreasonable as a matter of law.

III

Police officers' legitimate concern for their own safety is always a factor that should weigh heavily in balancing the relevant Graham factors. But, as Officer Brill admitted at trial, if that justification were always sufficient, it would authorize the handcuffing of every occupant of the premises for the duration of every Summers detention. Nothing in either the Summers or the Graham opinion provides any support for such a result. Rather, the decision of what force to use must be made on a case-by-case basis. There is evidence in this record that may well support the conclusion that it was unreasonable to handcuff Iris Mena throughout the search. On remand, therefore, I would instruct the Ninth Circuit to consider that evidence, as well as the possibility that Iris was detained after the search was completed, when deciding whether the evidence in the record is sufficient to support the jury's verdict.

QUESTIONS AND NOTES

1. Is *Mena* consistent with *Summers,* or a gross perversion of it? Explain.

2. On what basis did the Court conclude that two to three hours in handcuffs was not too long? Do you agree? Why? Why not?

3. If on remand, the Court of Appeals concludes that she was held for too long, how should the case be resolved?

4. Given Justice Kennedy's conclusion that handcuffing was not per se ok, why did he vote to uphold this continued handcuffing? Do you agree?

5. None of the Justices seemed to question the initial handcuffing. Why was that so clear? Did it follow from *Summers?*

6. Should anything have turned on the fact that the police did not try to minimize damages by asking Mena for help (one of the reasons given by *Summers* for allowing the detention in the first place)?

7. Why did Justice Stevens concur?

PROBLEM

At 8:45 p.m. on July 28, 2005, local police obtained a warrant to search a residence for a .380-caliber handgun. The residence was a basement apartment at 103 Lake Drive, in Wyandanch, New York. A confidential informant had told police he observed the gun when he was at the apartment to purchase drugs from "a heavy set black male with short hair" known as "Polo." As the search unit began preparations for executing the warrant, two officers, Detectives Richard Sneider and Richard Gorbecki, were conducting surveillance in an unmarked car outside the residence. About 9:56 p.m., Sneider and Gorbecki observed two men — later identified as petitioner Chunon Bailey and Bryant Middleton — leave the gated area above the basement apartment and enter a car parked in the driveway. Both matched the general physical description of "Polo" provided by the informant. There was no indication that the men were aware of the officers' presence or had any knowledge of the impending search. The detectives watched the car leave the driveway. They waited for it to go a few hundred yards down the street and followed. The detectives informed the search team of their intent to follow and detain the departing occupants. The search team then executed the search warrant at the apartment.

Detectives Sneider and Gorbecki tailed Bailey's car for about a mile — and for about five minutes — before pulling the vehicle over in a parking lot by a fire station. They ordered Bailey and Middleton out of the car and did a patdown search of both men. The officers found no weapons but discovered a ring of keys in Bailey's pocket. Bailey identified himself and said he was coming from his home at 103 Lake Drive. His driver's license, however, showed his address as Bayshore, New York, the town where the confidential informant told the police the suspect, "Polo," used to live. Bailey's passenger, Middleton, said Bailey was giving him a ride home and confirmed they were coming from Bailey's residence at 103 Lake Drive. The officers put both men in handcuffs. When Bailey asked why, Gorbecki stated that they were being detained incident to the execution of a search warrant at 103 Lake Drive. Bailey responded: "I don't live there. Anything you find there ain't mine, and I'm not cooperating with your investigation."

The detectives called for a patrol car to take Bailey and Middleton back to the Lake Drive apartment. Detective Sneider drove the unmarked car back, while Detective Gorbecki used Bailey's set of keys to drive Bailey's car back to the search scene. By the time the group returned to 103 Lake Drive, the search team had discovered a gun and drugs in plain view inside the apartment. Bailey and Middleton were placed under arrest, and Bailey's keys were seized incident to the arrest. Officers later discovered that one of Bailey's keys opened the door of the basement apartment.

Was the detention of Bailey lawful under *Summers* and *Mena*? Why? Why not? For the Court's resolution, see *Bailey v. United States*, 568 U.S. ___, 134 S. Ct. 484 (2013). _no_

once a person leaves a premises any detention must be justified by other means

D. SEARCH INCIDENT TO ARREST

From a police perspective, perhaps the single most important factor in the rules governing arrest is the right to search incident to arrest. Recall that in *Draper* (*supra* Chapter 2), the legality of the arrest was significant only insofar as it allowed the government to introduce into evidence the heroin seized from Draper's person. In *Chimel*, we will focus on the rationale for and limitations on a search incident to arrest.

CHIMEL v. CALIFORNIA
395 U.S. 752 (1969)

MR. JUSTICE STEWART delivered the opinion of the Court.

This case raises basic questions concerning the permissible scope under the Fourth Amendment of a search incident to a lawful arrest.

The relevant facts are essentially undisputed. Late in the afternoon of September 13, 1965, three police officers arrived at the Santa Ana, California, home of the petitioner with a warrant authorizing his arrest for the burglary of a coin shop. The officers knocked on the door, identified themselves to the petitioner's wife, and asked if they might come inside. She ushered them into the house, where they waited 10 or 15 minutes until the petitioner returned home from work. When the petitioner entered the house, one of the officers handed him the arrest warrant and asked for permission to 'look around.' The petitioner objected, but was advised that 'on the basis of the lawful arrest,' the officers would nonetheless conduct a search. No search warrant had been issued.

Accompanied by the petitioner's wife, the officers then looked through the entire three-bedroom house, including the attic, the garage, and a small workshop. In some rooms the search was relatively cursory. In the master bedroom and sewing room, however, the officers directed the petitioner's wife to open drawers and 'to physically move contents of the drawers from side to side so that (they) might view any items that would have come from (the) burglary.' After completing the search, they seized numerous items — primarily coins, but also several medals, tokens, and a few other objects. The entire search took between 45 minutes and an hour.

At the petitioner's subsequent state trial on two charges of burglary, the items taken from his house were admitted into evidence against him, over his objection that they had been unconstitutionally seized. He was convicted, and the judgments of conviction were affirmed by both the California Court of Appeal and the California Supreme Court.

Without deciding the question, we proceed on the hypothesis that the California courts were correct in holding that the arrest of the petitioner was valid under the Constitution. This brings us directly to the question whether the warrantless search of the petitioner's entire house can be constitutionally justified as incident to that arrest. The decisions of this Court bearing upon that question have been far from consistent, as even the most cursory review makes evident.

Approval of a warrantless search incident to a lawful arrest seems first to have been articulated by the Court in 1914 as dictum in *Weeks v. United States*, 232 U.S. 383, in which the Court stated:

"What then is the present case? Before answering that inquiry specifically, it may be well by a process of exclusion to state what it is not. It is not an assertion of the right on the part of the Government, always recognized under English and American law, to search the person of the accused when legally arrested to discover and seize the fruits or evidences of crime."

That statement made no reference to any right to search the place where an arrest occurs, but was limited to a right to search the 'person.' Eleven years later *Carroll* brought the following embellishment of the *Weeks* statement: "When a man is legally arrested for an offense, whatever is found upon his person or in his control which it is unlawful for him to have and which may be used to prove the offense may be seized and held as evidence in the prosecution." Still, that assertion too was far from a claim that the 'place' where one is arrested may be searched so long as the arrest is valid. Without explanation, however, the principle emerged in expanded form a few months later in *Agnello v. United States*, 269 U.S. 20 — although still by way of dictum: "The right without a search warrant contemporaneously to search persons lawfully arrested while committing crime and to search the place where the arrest is made in order to find and seize things connected with the crime as its fruits or as the means by which it was committed, as well as weapons and other things to effect an escape from custody, is not to be doubted." (citing *Carroll* and *Weeks*). And in *Marron v. United States*, 275 U.S. 192, two years later, the dictum of *Agnello* appeared to be the foundation of the Court's decision. In that case federal agents had secured a search warrant authorizing the seizure of liquor and certain articles used in its manufacture. When they arrived at the premises to be searched, they saw 'that the place was used for retailing and drinking intoxicating liquors.' They proceeded to arrest the person in charge and to execute the warrant. In searching a closet for the items listed in the warrant they came across an incriminating ledger, concededly not covered by the warrant, which they also seized. The Court upheld the seizure of the ledger by holding that since the agents had made a lawful arrest, '(t)hey had a right without a warrant contemporaneously to search the place in order to find and seize the things used to carry on the criminal enterprise.'

That the *Marron* opinion did not mean all that it seemed to say became evident, however, a few years later in *Go-Bart Importing Co. v. United States*, 282 U.S. 344, and *United States v. Lefkowitz*, 285 U.S. 452. In each of those cases the opinion of the Court was written by Mr. Justice Butler, the author of the opinion in Marron. In *Go-Bart*, agents had searched the office of persons whom they had lawfully arrested, and had taken several papers from a desk, a safe, and other parts of the office. The Court noted that no crime had been committed in the agents' presence, and that although the agent in charge 'had an abundance of information and time to swear out a valid (search) warrant, he failed to do so.' In holding the search and seizure unlawful, the Court stated:

'Plainly the case before us is essentially different from *Marron*. There, officers executing a valid search warrant for intoxicating liquors found and arrested one Birdsall who in pursuance of a conspiracy was actually engaged in running a saloon. As an incident to the arrest they seized a ledger in a closet where the liquor or some of it was kept and some bills beside the cash register. These things were visible and accessible and in the offender's immediate custody. There was no threat of force or general search or rummaging of the place.'

This limited characterization of Marron was reiterated in Lefkowitz, a case in which the Court held unlawful a search of desk drawers and a cabinet despite the fact that the search had accompanied a lawful arrest.

The limiting views expressed in *Go-Bart* and *Lefkowitz* were thrown to the winds, however, in *Harris v. United States*, 331 U.S. 145, decided in 1947. In that case, officers had obtained a warrant for Harris' arrest on the basis of his alleged involvement with the cashing and interstate transportation of a forged check. He was arrested in the living room of his four-room apartment, and in an attempt to recover two canceled checks thought to have been used in effecting the forgery, the officers undertook a thorough search of the entire apartment. Inside a desk drawer they found a sealed envelope marked 'George Harris, personal papers.' The envelope, which was then torn open, was found to contain altered Selective Service documents, and those documents were used to secure Harris' conviction for violating the Selective Training and Service Act of 1940. The Court rejected Harris' Fourth Amendment claim, sustaining the search as 'incident to arrest.'

Only a year after *Harris*, however, the pendulum swung again. In *Trupiano v. United States*, 334 U.S. 699, agents raided the site of an illicit distillery, saw one of several conspirators operating the still, and arrested him, contemporaneously 'seiz(ing) the illicit distillery.' The Court held that the arrest and others made subsequently had been valid, but that the unexplained failure of the agents to procure a search warrant — in spite of the fact that they had had more than enough time before the raid to do so — rendered the search unlawful. The opinion stated:

"It is a cardinal rule that, in seizing goods and articles, law enforcement agents must secure and use search warrants wherever reasonably practicable. . . . This rule rests upon the desirability of having magistrates rather than police officers determine when searches and seizures are permissible and what limitations should be placed upon such activities. . . . To provide the necessary security against unreasonable intrusions upon the private lives of individuals, the framers of the Fourth Amendment required adherence to judicial processes wherever possible. And subsequent history has confirmed the wisdom of that requirement . . . . A search or seizure without a warrant as an incident to a lawful arrest has always been considered to be a strictly limited right. It grows out of the inherent necessities of the situation at the time of the arrest. But there must be something more in the way of necessity than merely a lawful arrest."

In 1950, two years after *Trupiano*, came *United States v. Rabinowitz*, 339 U.S. 56, the decision upon which California primarily relies in the case now before us. In *Rabinowitz*, federal authorities had been informed that the defendant was dealing in stamps bearing forged overprints. On the basis of that information they secured a warrant for his arrest, which they executed at his one-room business office. At the time of the arrest, the officers 'searched the desk, safe, and file cabinets in the office for about an hour and a half,' and seized 573 stamps with forged overprints. The stamps were admitted into evidence at the defendant's trial, and this Court affirmed his conviction, rejecting the contention that the warrantless search had been unlawful. The Court held that the search in its entirety fell within the principle giving law enforcement authorities "(t)he right 'to search the place where the arrest is made in order to find and seize things connected with the crime . . . .' " *Harris* was regarded as 'ample authority' for that conclusion. The opinion rejected the rule of *Trupiano* that 'in seizing goods and articles, law enforcement agents must secure and use search warrants wherever reasonably practicable.' The test, said the Court, 'is not whether it is reasonable to procure a search warrant, but whether the search was reasonable.'

Rabinowitz has come to stand for the proposition, inter alia, that a warrantless search 'incident to a lawful arrest' may generally extend to the area that is considered to be in the 'possession' or under the 'control' of the person arrested. And it was on the basis of that proposition that the California courts upheld the search of the petitioner's entire house in this case. That doctrine, however, at least in the broad sense in which it was applied by the California courts in this case, can withstand neither historical nor rational analysis.

Even limited to its own facts, the *Rabinowitz* decision was, as we have seen, hardly founded on an unimpeachable line of authority. As Mr. Justice Frankfurter commented in dissent in that case, the 'hint' contained in Weeks was, without persuasive justification, 'loosely turned into dictum and finally elevated to a decision.' And the approach taken in cases such as *Go-Bart, Lefkowitz,* and *Trupiano* was essentially disregarded by the *Rabinowitz* Court.

Nor is the rationale by which the State seeks here to sustain the search of the petitioner's house supported by a reasoned view of the background and purpose of the Fourth Amendment. Mr. Justice Frankfurter wisely pointed out in his *Rabinowitz* dissent that the Amendment's proscription of 'unreasonable searches and seizures' must be read in light of 'the history that gave rise to the words' — a history of 'abuses so deeply felt by the Colonies as to be one of the potent causes of the Revolution . . . .' The Amendment was in large part a reaction to the general warrants and warrantless searches that had so alienated the colonists and had helped speed the movement for independence. In the scheme of the Amendment, therefore, the requirement that 'no Warrants shall issue, but upon probable cause,' plays a crucial part. As the Court put it in *McDonald v. United States,* 335 U.S. 451:

"We are not dealing with formalities. The presence of a search warrant serves a high function. Absent some grave emergency, the Fourth Amendment has interposed a magistrate between the citizen and the police. This was done not to shield criminals nor to make the home a safe haven for illegal activities. It was done so that an objective mind might weigh the need to invade that privacy in order to enforce the law. The right of privacy was deemed too precious to entrust to the discretion of those whose job is the detection of crime and the arrest of criminals. . . . And so the Constitution requires a magistrate to pass on the desires of the police before they violate the privacy of the home. We cannot be true to that constitutional requirement and excuse the absence of a search warrant without a showing by those who seek exemption from the constitutional mandate that the exigencies of the situation made that course imperative."

When an arrest is made, it is reasonable for the arresting officer to search the person arrested in order to remove any weapons that the latter might seek to use in order to resist arrest or effect his escape. Otherwise, the officer's safety might well be endangered, and the arrest itself frustrated. In addition, it is entirely reasonable for the arresting officer to search for and seize any evidence on the arrestee's person in order to prevent its concealment or destruction. And the area into which an arrestee might reach in order to grab a weapon or evidentiary items must, of course, be governed by a like rule. A gun on a table or in a drawer in front of one who is arrested can be as dangerous to the arresting officer as one concealed in the clothing of the person arrested. There is ample justification, therefore, for a search of the arrestee's person and the area 'within his immediate control' — construing that phrase to mean the area from within which he might gain possession of a weapon or destructible evidence.

There is no comparable justification, however, for routinely searching any room other than that in which an arrest occurs — or, for that matter, for searching through all the desk drawers or other closed or concealed areas in that room itself. Such searches in the absence of well-recognized exceptions, may be made only under the authority of a search warrant. The "adherence to the judicial process" mandated by the Fourth Amendment requires no less.

"The rule allowing contemporaneous seizures is justified by the need to seize weapons and other things which might be used to assault an officer or effect an escape, as well as by the need to prevent the destruction of evidence of the crime — things which might easily happen where the weapon or evidence is on the accused's person or under his immediate control. But these justifications are absent where a search is remote in time or place from the arrest."

It is argued in the present case that it is 'reasonable' to search a man's house when he is arrested in it. But that argument is founded on little more than a subjective view regarding the acceptability of certain sorts of police conduct, and not on consideration relevant to Fourth Amendment interests. Under such an unconfined analysis, Fourth Amendment protection in this area would approach the evaporation point. It is not easy to explain why, for instance, it is less subjectively 'reasonable' to search a man's house when he is arrested on his front lawn — or just down the street — than it is when he happens to be in the house at the time of arrest. As Mr. Justice Frankfurter put it:

"To say that the search must be reasonable is to require some criterion of reason. It is no guide at all either for a jury or for district judges or the police to say that an 'unreasonable search' is forbidden — that the search must be reasonable. What is the test of reason which makes a search reasonable? The test is the reason underlying and expressed by the Fourth Amendment: the history and experience which it embodies and the safeguards afforded by it against the evils to which it was a response." *Rabinowitz* (dissenting opinion).

Thus, although '(t)he recurring questions of the reasonableness of searches' depend upon 'the facts and circumstances — the total atmosphere of the case,' those facts and circumstances must be viewed in the light of established Fourth Amendment principles.

It would be possible, of course, to draw a line between *Rabinowitz* and *Harris* on the one hand, and this case on the other. For *Rabinowitz* involved a single room, and *Harris* a four-room apartment, while in the case before us an entire house was searched. But such a distinction would be highly artificial. The rationale that allowed the searches and seizures in *Rabinowitz* and *Harris* would allow the searches and seizures in this case. No consideration relevant to the Fourth Amendment suggests any point of rational limitation, once the search is allowed to go beyond the area from which the person arrested might obtain weapons or evidentiary items.[11] The only reasoned distinction is one between a search of the person arrested and the area within his reach on the one hand, and more extensive searches on the other.[12]

The petitioner correctly points out that one result of decisions such as Rabinowitz and Harris is to give law enforcement officials the opportunity to engage in searches not justified by probable cause, by the simple expedient of arranging to arrest suspects at home rather than elsewhere. We do not suggest that the petitioner is necessarily correct in his assertion that such a strategy was utilized here,[13] but the fact remains that had he been arrested earlier in the day, at his place of employment rather than at home, no search of his house could have been made without a search warrant. In any event, even apart from the possibility of such police tactics, the general point so forcefully made by Judge Learned Hand in *United States v. Kirschenblatt*, 16 F.2d 202 (2 Cir.), remains:

'After arresting a man in his house, to rummage at will among his papers in search of whatever will convict him, appears to us to be indistinguishable from what might be done under a general warrant; indeed, the warrant would give more protection, for presumably it must be issued by a magistrate. True, by hypothesis the power would not exist, if the supposed offender were not found on the premises; but it is small consolation to know that one's papers are safe only so long as one is not at home.'

Rabinowitz and *Harris* have been the subject of critical commentary for many years, and have been relied upon less and less in our own decisions. It is time, for the reasons we have stated, to hold that on their own facts, and insofar as the principles they stand for are inconsistent with those that we have endorsed today, they are no longer to be followed.

---

[11] *Cf.* Mr. Justice Jackson's dissenting comment in *Harris*: 'The difficulty with this problem for me is that once the search is allowed to go beyond the person arrested and the objects upon him or in his immediate physical control, I see no practical limit short of that set in the opinion of the Court — and that means to me no limit at all.'

[12] It is argued in dissent that so long as there is probable cause to search the place where an arrest occurs, a search of that place should be permitted even though no search warrant has been obtained. This position seems to be based principally on two premises: first, that once an arrest has been made, the additional invasion of privacy stemming from the accompanying search is 'relatively minor'; and second, that the victim of the search may 'shortly thereafter' obtain a judicial determination of whether the search was justified by probable cause. With respect to the second premise, one may initially question whether all of the States in fact provide the speedy suppression procedures the dissent assumes. More fundamentally, however, we cannot accept the view that Fourth Amendment interests are vindicated so long as 'the rights of the criminal' are 'protect(ed) . . . against introduction of evidence seized without probable cause.' The Amendment is designed to prevent, not simply to redress, unlawful police action. In any event, we cannot join in characterizing the invasion of privacy that results from a top-to-bottom search of a man's house as 'minor.' And we can see no reason why, simply because some interference with an individual's privacy and freedom of movement has lawfully taken place, further intrusions should automatically be allowed despite the absence of a warrant that the Fourth Amendment would otherwise require.

[13] Although the warrant was issued at 10:39 a.m. and the arrest was not made until late in the afternoon, the State suggests that the delay is accounted for by normal police procedures and by the heavy workload of the officer in charge. In addition, that officer testified that he and his colleagues went to the petitioner's house 'to keep from approaching him at his place of business to cause him any problem there.'

Application of sound Fourth Amendment principles to the facts of this case produces a clear result. The search here went far beyond the petitioner's person and the area from within which he might have obtained either a weapon or something that could have been used as evidence against him. There was no constitutional justification, in the absence of a search warrant, for extending the search beyond that area. The scope of the search was, therefore, 'unreasonable' under the Fourth and Fourteenth Amendments and the petitioner's conviction cannot stand.

Reversed.

(Justice Harlan wrote a brief concurring opinion)

MR. JUSTICE WHITE, with whom MR. JUSTICE BLACK joins, dissenting.

Few areas of the law have been as subject to shifting constitutional standards over the last 50 years as that of the search 'incident to an arrest.' There has been a remarkable instability in this whole area, which has seen at least four major shifts in emphasis. Today's opinion makes an untimely fifth. In my view, the Court should not now abandon the old rule.

The Court must decide whether a given search is reasonable. The Amendment does not proscribe 'warrantless searches' but instead it proscribes 'unreasonable searches' and this Court has never held nor does the majority today assert that warrantless searches are necessarily unreasonable.

Applying this reasonableness test to the area of searches incident to arrests, one thing is clear at the outset. Search of an arrested man and of the items within his immediate reach must in almost every case be reasonable. There is always a danger that the suspect will try to escape, seizing concealed weapons with which to overpower and injure the arresting officers, and there is a danger that he may destroy evidence vital to the prosecution. Circumstances in which these justifications would not apply are sufficiently rare that inquiry is not made into searches of this scope, which have been considered reasonable throughout.

The justifications which make such a search reasonable obviously do not apply to the search of areas to which the accused does not have ready physical access. This is not enough, however, to prove such searches unconstitutional. The Court has always held, and does not today deny, that when there is probable cause to search and it is 'impracticable' for one reason or another to get a search warrant, then a warrantless search may be reasonable. This is the case whether an arrest was made at the time of the search or not.

This is not to say that a search can be reasonable without regard to the probable cause to believe that seizable items are on the premises. But when there are exigent circumstances, and probable cause, then the search may be made without a warrant, reasonably. An arrest itself may often create an emergency situation making it impracticable to obtain a warrant before embarking on a related search. Again assuming that there is probable cause to search premises at the spot where a suspect is arrested, it seems to me unreasonable to require the police to leave the scene in order to obtain a search warrant when they are already legally there to make a valid arrest, and when there must almost always be a strong possibility that confederates of the arrested man will in the meanwhile remove the items for which the police have probable cause to search. This must so often be the case that it seems to me as unreasonable to require a warrant for a search of the premises as to require a warrant for search of the person and his very immediate surroundings.

This case provides a good illustration of my point that it is unreasonable to require police to leave the scene of an arrest in order to obtain a search warrant when they already have probable cause to search and there is a clear danger that the items for which they may reasonably search will be removed before they return with a warrant. Petitioner was arrested in his home after an arrest whose validity will be explored below, but which I will now assume was valid. There was doubtless probable cause not only to arrest petitioner, but also to search his house. He had obliquely admitted, both to a neighbor and to the owner of the burglarized store, that he had committed the burglary.[4] In light of this, and the fact that the neighbor had seen other admittedly stolen property in petitioner's house, there was surely probable cause on which a warrant could have issued to search the house for the stolen coins. Moreover, had the police simply arrested petitioner, taken him off to the station house, and later returned with a warrant,[5] it seems very likely that petitioner's wife, who in view of petitioner's generally garrulous nature must have known of the robbery, would have removed the coins. For the police to search the house while the evidence they had probable cause to search out and seize was still there cannot be considered unreasonable.

The majority today proscribes searches for which there is probable cause and which may prove fruitless unless carried out immediately. This rule will have no added effect whatsoever in protecting the rights of the criminal accused at trial against introduction of evidence seized without probable cause. Such evidence could not be introduced under the old rule. Nor does the majority today give any added protection to the right of privacy of those whose houses there is probable cause to search. A warrant would still be sworn out for those houses, and the privacy of their owners invaded. The only possible justification for the majority's rule is that in some

[4] Before the burglary of the coin store, petitioner had told its owner that he was planning a big robbery, had inquired about the alarm system in the store, the state of the owner's insurance, and the location of the owner's most valuable coins. Petitioner wandered about the store the day before the burglary. After the burglary, petitioner called the store's owner and accused him of robbing the store himself for the insurance proceeds on a policy which, as petitioner knew, had just been reduced from $50,000 to $10,000 coverage. On being told that the robbery had been sloppy, petitioner excitedly claimed that it had been 'real professional' but then denied the robbery. On the night of the robbery itself petitioner declined an invitation to a bicycle ride, saying he was 'going to knock over a place' and that a coin shop was 'all set.' After the robbery, he told the same neighbor that he had started to break into the coin shop, but had stopped, and then denied the whole incident. The neighbor had earlier seen stacks of typewriters in petitioner's house. Asked whether they were 'hot' petitioner replied, 'Hotter than a $3 bill.' On reading a newspaper description of the coin store burglary, the neighbor called the police.

[5] There were three officers at the scene of the arrest, one from the city where the coin burglary had occurred, and two from the city where the arrest was made. Assuming that one policeman from each city would be needed to bring the petitioner in and obtain a search warrant, one policeman could have been left to guard the house. However, if he not only could have remained in the house against petitioner's wife's will, but followed her about to assure that no evidence was being tampered with, the invasion of her privacy would be almost as great as that accompanying an actual search. Moreover, had the wife summoned an accomplice, one officer could not have watched them both.

instances arresting officers may search when they have no probable cause to do so and that such unlawful searches might be prevented if the officers first sought a warrant from a magistrate. Against the possible protection of privacy in that class of cases, in which the privacy of the house has already been invaded by entry to make the arrest — an entry for which the majority does not assert that any warrant is necessary — must be weighed the risk of destruction of evidence for which there is probable cause to search, as a result of delays in obtaining a search warrant. Without more basis for radical change than the Court's opinion reveals, I would not upset the balance of these interests which has been struck by the former decisions of this Court.

In considering searches incident to arrest, it must be remembered that there will be immediate opportunity to challenge the probable cause for the search in an adversary proceeding. The suspect has been apprised of the search by his very presence at the scene, and having been arrested, he will soon be brought into contact with people who can explain his rights. As Mr. Justice Brennan noted in a dissenting opinion, joined by The Chief Justice and Justices Black and Douglas, in *Abel v. United States*, 362 U.S. 217, 249–250, a search contemporaneous with a warrantless arrest is specially safeguarded since "(s)uch an arrest may constitutionally be made only upon probable cause, the existence of which is subject to judicial examination, and such an arrest demands the prompt bringing of the person arrested before a judicial officer, where the existence of probable cause is to be inquired into." And since that time the Court has imposed on state and federal officers alike the duty to warn suspects taken into custody, before questioning them, of their right to a lawyer.

An arrested man, by definition conscious of the police interest in him, and provided almost immediately with a lawyer and a judge, is in an excellent position to dispute the reasonableness of his arrest and contemporaneous search in a full adversary proceeding. I would uphold the constitutionality of this search contemporaneous with an arrest since there were probable cause both for the search and for the arrest, exigent circumstances involving the removal or destruction of evidence, and satisfactory opportunity to dispute the issues of probable cause shortly thereafter. In this case, the search was reasonable.

QUESTIONS AND NOTES

1.   Ought a search incident to an arrest be permissible in every case regardless of the likelihood of a weapon being present or evidence being destroyed? Why? Why not? For the Supreme Court's answer, see *United States v. Robinson*, 414 U.S. 218 (1973).

2.   Assuming that a search incident to an arrest is going to be permitted at all, are the *Chimel* limitations arbitrary?

3.   What values does *Chimel* serve?

4.   Could *Rabinowitz* be legitimately distinguished from *Chimel*? Could *Harris*?

5.   Given probable cause to search the Chimel home, what if anything is wrong with Justice White's suggestion that probable cause to search will be determined soon enough?

6.   In addition to a search incident to an arrest, it is sometimes argued that the police should be able to make a "protective sweep" of the house in which an arrest is effectuated. The Supreme Court resolved that issue in *Buie*. As you read *Buie* consider whether the Court gave the police too much power, too little power, or the right amount of power.

MARYLAND v. BUIE
494 U.S. 325 (1990)

JUSTICE WHITE delivered the opinion of the Court.

A "protective sweep" is a quick and limited search of a premises, incident to an arrest and conducted to protect the safety of police officers or others. It is narrowly confined to a cursory visual inspection of those places in which a person might be hiding. In this case we must decide what level of justification is required by the Fourth and Fourteenth Amendments before police officers, while effecting the arrest of a suspect in his home pursuant to an arrest warrant, may conduct a warrantless protective sweep of all or part of the premises. The Court of Appeals of Maryland held that a running suit seized in plain view during such a protective sweep should have been suppressed at respondent's armed robbery trial because the officer who conducted the sweep did not have probable cause to believe that a serious and demonstrable potentiality for danger existed. We conclude that the Fourth Amendment would permit the protective sweep undertaken here if the searching officer "possesse[d] a reasonable belief based on 'specific and articulable facts which, taken together with the rational inferences from those facts, reasonably warrant[ed]' the officer in believing," that the area swept harbored an individual posing a danger to the officer or others. We accordingly vacate the judgment below and remand for application of this standard.

I

On February 3, 1986, two men committed an armed robbery of a Godfather's Pizza restaurant in Prince George's County, Maryland. One of the robbers was wearing a red running suit. That same day, Prince George's County police obtained arrest warrants for respondent Jerome Edward Buie and his suspected accomplice in the robbery, Lloyd Allen. Buie's house was placed under police surveillance.

On February 5, the police executed the arrest warrant for Buie. They first had a police department secretary telephone Buie's house to verify that he was home. The secretary spoke to a female first, then to Buie himself. Six or seven officers proceeded to Buie's house. Once inside, the officers fanned out through the first and second floors. Corporal James Rozar announced that he would "freeze" the basement so that no one could come up and surprise the officers. With his service revolver drawn, Rozar twice shouted into the basement, ordering anyone down there to come out. When a voice asked who was calling, Rozar announced three times: "this is the police, show me your hands." Eventually, a pair of hands appeared around the bottom of the stairwell and Buie emerged from the basement. He was arrested, searched, and handcuffed by Rozar. Thereafter, Detective Joseph Frolich entered the basement "in case there was someone else" down there. He noticed a red running suit lying in plain view on a stack of clothing and seized it.

II

It is not disputed that until the point of Buie's arrest the police had the right, based on the authority of the arrest warrant, to search anywhere in the house that Buie might have been found, including the basement. "If there is sufficient evidence of a citizen's participation in a felony to persuade a judicial officer that his arrest is justified, it is constitutionally reasonable to require him to open his doors to the officers of the law." There is also no dispute that if Detective Frolich's entry into the basement was lawful, the seizure of the red running suit, which was in plain view and which the officer had probable cause to believe was evidence of a crime, was also lawful under the Fourth Amendment. The issue in this case is what level of justification the Fourth Amendment required before Detective Frolich could legally enter the basement to see if someone else was there.

Petitioner, the State of Maryland, argues that, under a general reasonableness balancing test, police should be permitted to conduct a protective sweep whenever they make an in-home arrest for a violent crime. As an alternative to this suggested bright-line rule, the State contends that protective sweeps may be conducted in conjunction with a valid in-home arrest whenever the police reasonably suspect a risk of danger to the officers or others at the arrest scene. Respondent argues that a protective sweep may not be undertaken without a warrant unless the exigencies of the situation render such warrantless search objectively reasonable. According to Buie, because the State has shown neither exigent circumstances to immediately enter Buie's house nor an unforeseen danger that arose once the officers were in the house, there is no excuse for the failure to obtain a search warrant to search for dangerous persons believed to be on the premises. Buie further contends that, even if the warrant requirement is inapplicable, there is no justification for relaxing the probable-cause standard. If something less than probable cause is sufficient, respondent argues that it is no less than individualized suspicion — specific, articulable facts supporting a reasonable belief that there are persons on the premises who are a threat to the officers. According to Buie, there were no such specific, articulable facts to justify the search of his basement.

III

It goes without saying that the Fourth Amendment bars only unreasonable searches and seizures. Our cases show that in determining reasonableness, we have balanced the intrusion on the individual's Fourth Amendment interests against its promotion of legitimate governmental interests. Under this test, a search of the house or office is generally not reasonable without a warrant issued on probable cause. There are other contexts, however, where the public interest is such that neither a warrant nor probable cause is required.

The *Terry* case (*Terry v. Ohio*, Chapter 7, *infra.*) is most instructive for present purposes. There we held that an on-the-street "frisk" for weapons must be tested by the Fourth Amendment's general proscription against unreasonable searches because such a frisk involves "an entire rubric of police conduct — necessarily swift action predicated upon the on-the-spot observations of the officer on the beat — which historically has not been, and as a practical matter could not be, subjected to the warrant procedure." We stated that there is " 'no ready test for determining reasonableness other than by balancing the need to search . . . against the invasion which the search . . . entails.' " Applying that balancing test, it was held that although a frisk for weapons "constitutes a severe, though brief, intrusion upon cherished personal security," such a frisk is reasonable when weighed against the "need for law enforcement officers to protect themselves and other prospective victims of violence in situations where they may lack probable cause for an arrest." We therefore authorized a limited patdown for weapons where a reasonably prudent officer would be warranted in the belief, based on "specific and articulable facts," and not on a mere "inchoate and unparticularized suspicion or 'hunch,' " "that he is dealing with an armed and dangerous individual."

In *Michigan v. Long*, (*infra* Chapter 8), the principles of Terry were applied in the context of a roadside encounter: "the search of the passenger compartment of an automobile, limited to those areas in which a weapon may be placed or hidden, is permissible if the police officer possesses a reasonable belief based on 'specific and articulable facts which, taken together with the rational inferences from those facts, reasonably warrant' the officer in believing that the suspect is dangerous and the suspect may gain immediate control of weapons." The *Long* Court expressly rejected the contention that Terry restricted preventative searches to the person of a detained suspect. In a sense, *Long* authorized a "frisk" of an automobile for weapons.

The ingredients to apply the balance struck in *Terry* and *Long* are present in this case. Possessing an arrest warrant and probable cause to believe Buie was in his home, the officers were entitled to enter and to search anywhere in the house in which Buie might be found. Once he was found, however, the search for him was over, and there was no longer that particular justification for entering any rooms that had not yet been searched.

That Buie had an expectation of privacy in those remaining areas of his house, however, does not mean such rooms were immune from entry. In *Terry* and *Long* we were concerned with the immediate interest of the police officers in taking steps to assure themselves that the persons with whom they were dealing were not armed with or able to gain immediate control of a weapon that could unexpectedly and fatally be used against them. In the instant case, there is an analogous interest of the officers in taking steps to assure themselves that the house in which a suspect is being or has just been arrested is not harboring other persons who are dangerous and who could unexpectedly launch an attack. The risk of danger in the context of an arrest in the home is as great as, if not greater than, it is in an on-the-street or roadside investigatory encounter. A *Terry* or *Long* frisk occurs before a police-citizen confrontation has escalated to the point of arrest. A protective sweep, in contrast, occurs as an adjunct to the serious step of taking a person into custody for the purpose of prosecuting him for a crime. Moreover, unlike an encounter on the street or along a highway, an in-home arrest puts the officer at the disadvantage of being on his adversary's "turf." An ambush in a confined setting of unknown configuration is more to be feared than it is in open, more familiar surroundings.

We recognized in *Terry* that "[e]ven a limited search of the outer clothing for weapons constitutes a severe, though brief, intrusion upon cherished personal security, and it must surely be an annoying, frightening, and perhaps humiliating experience." But we permitted the intrusion, which was no more than necessary to protect the officer from harm. Nor do we here suggest, as the State does, that entering rooms not examined prior to the arrest is a *de minimis* intrusion that may be disregarded. We are quite sure, however, that the arresting officers are permitted in such circumstances to take reasonable steps to ensure their safety after, and while making, the arrest. That interest is sufficient to outweigh the intrusion such procedures may entail.

We agree with the State, as did the court below, that a warrant was not required.[1] We also hold that as an incident to the arrest the officers could, as a precautionary matter and without probable cause or reasonable suspicion, look in closets and other spaces immediately adjoining the place of arrest from which an attack could be immediately launched. Beyond that, however, we hold that there must be articulable facts which, taken together with the rational inferences from those facts, would warrant a reasonably prudent officer in believing that the area to be swept harbors an individual posing a danger to those on the arrest scene. This is no more and no less than was required in Terry and Long, and as in those cases, we think this balance is the proper one.[2]

We should emphasize that such a protective sweep, aimed at protecting the arresting officers, if justified by the circumstances, is nevertheless not a full search of the premises, but may extend only to a cursory inspection of those spaces where a person may be found. The sweep lasts no longer than is necessary to dispel the reasonable suspicion of danger and in any event no longer than it takes to complete the arrest and depart the premises.

IV

Affirmance is not required by *Chimel*, where it was held that in the absence of a search warrant, the justifiable search incident to an in-home arrest could not

---

[1] Buie suggests that because the police could have sought a warrant to search for dangerous persons in the house, they were constitutionally required to do so. But the arrest warrant gave the police every right to enter the home to search for Buie. Once inside, the potential for danger justified a standard of less than probable cause for conducting a limited protective sweep.

[2] The State's argument that no level of objective justification should be required because of "the danger that inheres in the in-home arrest for a violent crime," is rebutted by *Terry* itself. The State argues that "[o]fficers facing the life threatening situation of arresting a violent criminal in the home should not be forced to pause and ponder the legal subtleties associated with a quantum of proof analysis." But despite the danger that inheres in on-the-street encounters and the need for police to act quickly for their own safety, the Court in Terry did not adopt a bright-line rule authorizing frisks for weapons in all confrontational encounters. Even in high crime areas, where the possibility that any given individual is armed is significant, Terry requires reasonable, individualized suspicion before a frisk for weapons can be conducted. That approach is applied to the protective sweep of a house.

extend beyond the arrestee's person and the area from within which the arrestee might have obtained a weapon. First, *Chimel* was concerned with a full-blown search of the entire house for evidence of the crime for which the arrest was made, not the more limited intrusion contemplated by a protective sweep. Second, the justification for the search incident to arrest considered in *Chimel* was the threat posed by the arrestee, not the safety threat posed by the house, or more properly by unseen third parties in the house. To reach our conclusion today, therefore, we need not disagree with the Court's statement in *Chimel*, that "the invasion of privacy that results from a top-to-bottom search of a man's house [cannot be characterized] as 'minor,' " nor hold that "simply because some interference with an individual's privacy and freedom of movement has lawfully taken place, further intrusions should automatically be allowed despite the absence of a warrant that the Fourth Amendment would otherwise require," The type of search we authorize today is far removed from the "top-to-bottom" search involved in *Chimel*; moreover, it is decidedly not "automati[c]," but may be conducted only when justified by a reasonable, articulable suspicion that the house is harboring a person posing a danger to those on the arrest scene.

V

We conclude that by requiring a protective sweep to be justified by probable cause to believe that a serious and demonstrable potentiality for danger existed, the Court of Appeals of Maryland applied an unnecessarily strict Fourth Amendment standard. The Fourth Amendment permits a properly limited protective sweep in conjunction with an in-home arrest when the searching officer possesses a reasonable belief based on specific and articulable facts that the area to be swept harbors an individual posing a danger to those on the arrest scene. We therefore vacate the judgment below and remand this case to the Court of Appeals of Maryland for further proceedings not inconsistent with this opinion.

Justice Stevens, concurring.

Today the Court holds that reasonable suspicion, rather than probable cause, is necessary to support a protective sweep while an arrest is in progress. I agree with that holding and with the Court's opinion, but I believe it is important to emphasize that the standard applies only to *protective* sweeps. Officers conducting such a sweep must have a reasonable basis for believing that their search will reduce the danger of harm to themselves or of violent interference with their mission; in short, the search must be protective.

In this case, to justify Officer Frolich's entry into the basement, it is the State's burden to demonstrate that the officers had a reasonable basis for believing not only that someone in the basement might attack them or otherwise try to interfere with the arrest, but also that it would be safer to go down the stairs instead of simply guarding them from above until respondent had been removed from the house. The fact that respondent offered no resistance when he emerged from the basement is somewhat inconsistent with the hypothesis that the danger of an attack by a hidden confederate persisted after the arrest. Moreover, Officer Rozar testified that he was not worried about any possible danger when he arrested Buie.[1] Officer Frolich, who conducted the search, supplied no explanation for why he might have thought another person was in the basement. He said only that he "had no idea who lived there." This admission is made telling by Officer Frolich's participation in the three-day pre-arrest surveillance of Buie's home. The Maryland Supreme Court was under the impression that the search took place after "Buie was safely outside the house, handcuffed and unarmed." All of this suggests that no reasonable suspicion of danger justified the entry into the basement.

Indeed, were the officers concerned about safety, one would expect them to do what Officer Rozar did before the arrest: guard the basement door to prevent surprise attacks. As the Court indicates, Officer Frolich might, at the time of the arrest, reasonably have "looked in" the already open basement door to ensure that no accomplice had followed Buie to the stairwell. But Officer Frolich did not merely "look in" the basement; he entered it.[2] That strategy is sensible if one wishes to search the basement. It is a surprising choice for an officer, worried about safety, who need not risk entering the stairwell at all.

The State may thus face a formidable task on remand. However, the Maryland courts are better equipped than are we to review the record. Moreover, the Maryland Court of Special Appeals suggested that Officer Frolich's search could survive a "reasonable suspicion" test, and the Maryland Court of Appeals has not reviewed this conclusion. I therefore agree that a remand is appropriate.

JUSTICE KENNEDY, concurring:

The Court adopts the prudent course of explaining the general rule and permitting the state court to apply it in the first instance. The concurrence by Justice STEVENS, however, makes the gratuitous observation that the State has a formidable task on remand. My view is quite to the contrary. Based on my present understanding of the record, I should think the officers' conduct here was in full accord with standard police safety procedure, and that the officers would have been remiss if they had not taken these precautions. This comment is necessary, lest by acquiescence the impression be left that Justice STEVENS' views can be interpreted as authoritative guidance for application of our ruling to the facts of the case.

JUSTICE BRENNAN, with whom JUSTICE MARSHALL joins, dissenting:

Today the Court for the first time extends *Terry*, into the home, dispensing with the Fourth Amendment's general requirements of a warrant and probable cause and carving a "reasonable suspicion" exception for protective sweeps in private dwellings.

---

[1] Buie's attorney asked, " 'You weren't worried about there being any danger or anything like that?' " Officer Rozar answered, " 'No.' "

[2] What more the officers might have done to protect themselves against threats from other places is obviously a question not presented on the facts of this case, and so is not one we can answer. Indeed, the peculiarity of Officer Frolich's search is that it appears to have concentrated upon the part of the house least likely to make the departing officers vulnerable to attack.

The Court today holds that *Terry's* "reasonable suspicion" standard "strikes the proper balance between officer safety and citizen privacy" for protective sweeps in private dwellings. I agree with the majority that officers executing an arrest warrant within a private dwelling have an interest in protecting themselves against potential ambush by third parties, but the majority offers no support for its assumption that the danger of ambush during planned home arrests approaches the danger of unavoidable "on-the-beat" confrontations in "the myriad daily situations in which policemen and citizens confront each other on the street."[2] In any event, the Court's implicit judgment that a protective sweep constitutes a "minimally intrusive" search akin to that involved in Terry markedly undervalues the nature and scope of the privacy interests involved.

While the Fourth Amendment protects a person's privacy interests in a variety of settings, "physical entry of the home is the chief evil against which the wording of the Fourth Amendment is directed." The Court discounts the nature of the intrusion because it believes that the scope of the intrusion is limited. The Court explains that a protective sweep's scope is "narrowly confined to a cursory visual inspection of those places in which a person might be hiding," and confined in duration to a period "no longer than is necessary to dispel the reasonable suspicion of danger and in any event no longer than it takes to complete the arrest and depart the premises."[4] But these spatial and temporal restrictions are not particularly limiting. A protective sweep would bring within police purview virtually all personal possessions within the house not hidden from view in a small enclosed space. Police officers searching for potential ambushers might enter every room including basements and attics; open up closets, lockers, chests, wardrobes, and cars; and peer under beds and behind furniture. The officers will view letters, documents and personal effects that are on tables or desks or are visible inside open drawers; books, records, tapes, and pictures on shelves; and clothing, medicines, toiletries and other paraphernalia not carefully stored in dresser drawers or bathroom cupboards. While perhaps not a "full-blown" or "top-to-bottom" search, a protective sweep is much closer to it than to a "limited patdown for weapons" or a " 'frisk' of an automobile."[5] Because the nature and scope of the intrusion sanctioned here are far greater than those upheld in *Terry* and *Long*, the Court's conclusion that "[t]he ingredients to apply the balance struck in *Terry* and *Long* are present in this case,"

---

[2] Individual police officers necessarily initiate street encounters without advance planning "for a wide variety of purposes." But officers choosing to execute an arrest warrant in the suspect's house may minimize any risk of ambush by, for example, a show of force; in this case, at least six armed officers secured the premises. And, of course, officers could select a safer venue for making their arrest.

[4] The protective sweep in this case may have exceeded the permissible temporal scope defined by the Court. The Court of Appeals of Maryland expressly noted that "at the time of the warrantless search, Buie was safely outside the house, handcuffed and unarmed." On remand, therefore, the state court need not decide whether the "reasonable suspicion" standard is satisfied in this case should it determine that the sweep of the basement took place after the police had sufficient time to "complete the arrest and depart the premises."

[5] Indeed, a protective sweep is sufficiently broad in scope that today's ruling might encourage police officers to execute arrest warrants in suspects' homes so as to take advantage of the opportunity to peruse the premises for incriminating evidence left in "plain view." This incentive runs directly counter to our central tenet that "in [no setting] is the zone of privacy more clearly defined than when bounded by the unambiguous physical dimensions of an individual's home — a zone that finds its roots in clear and specific constitutional terms."

is unwarranted. The "ingredient" of a minimally intrusive search is absent, and the Court's holding today therefore unpalatably deviates from Terry and its progeny.[6]

In light of the special sanctity of a private residence and the highly intrusive nature of a protective sweep, I firmly believe that police officers must have probable cause to fear that their personal safety is threatened by a hidden confederate of an arrestee before they may sweep through the entire home. Given the state-court determination that the officers searching Buie's home lacked probable cause to perceive such a danger and therefore were not lawfully present in the basement, I would affirm the state court's decision to suppress the incriminating evidence. I respectfully dissent.

QUESTIONS AND NOTES

1. How is the Court likely to rule on remand? How do you think that you would rule? Why?

2. How intrusive do you consider a "protective sweep" to be?

3. Would it be better to allow it as a matter of routine (similar to search incident to an arrest) rather than litigate every single case?

4. Conversely, would a probable cause standard be more consistent with sound Fourth Amendment theory?

5. If the police were suspicious of cohorts couldn't they have so indicated on their warrant application? Why should we let them decide on the spot?

---

[6] The Court's decision also to expand the "search incident to arrest" exception previously recognized in *Chimel*, allowing police officers without any requisite level of suspicion to look into "closets and other spaces immediately adjoining the place of arrest from which an attack could be immediately launched," is equally disquieting. *Chimel* established that police officers may presume as a matter of law, without need for factual support in a particular case, that arrestees might take advantage of weapons or destroy evidence in the area "within [their] immediate control"; therefore, a protective search of that area is *per se* reasonable under the Fourth Amendment. I find much less plausible the Court's implicit assumption today that arrestees are likely to sprinkle hidden allies throughout the rooms in which they might be arrested. Hence there is no comparable justification for permitting arresting officers to presume as a matter of law that they are threatened by ambush from "immediately adjoining" spaces.

Chapter 5

PLAIN VIEW

The concept of "plain view" is a recurring theme in Fourth Amendment jurisprudence. In *Buie*, for example, the importance of the right to make a protective sweep was not related to an abstract claim of right by the homeowner. Rather, it was to ascertain whether the red running suit, found in "plain view" during the course of the protective sweep, was admissible in evidence.

In this chapter, we will focus upon the rationale for the "plain view" doctrine, along with an analysis of its scope and limitations. The first case to really develop the doctrine was *Coolidge v. New Hampshire* (Chapter 3, *supra*). *Coolidge* involved the search of an automobile pursuant to a warrant that was defective because it was issued by the Attorney General. The State argued, *inter alia*, that the automobile, and evidence found therein, should have been admissible because it was found in "plain view." A plurality of the Court rejected that argument, in part, because finding the car was not "inadvertent." In *Texas v. Brown*, 460 U.S. 730 (1983), a different plurality concluded that the inadvertence requirement was unnecessary. The issue was finally resolved in *Horton v. California*. As you read *Horton*, consider which Court got it right.

HORTON v. CALIFORNIA
496 U.S. 128 (1990)

JUSTICE STEVENS delivered the opinion of the Court.

In this case we revisit an issue that was considered, but not conclusively resolved, in *Coolidge*: Whether the warrantless seizure of evidence of crime in plain view is prohibited by the Fourth Amendment if the discovery of the evidence was not inadvertent. We conclude that even though inadvertence is a characteristic of most legitimate "plain view" seizures, it is not a necessary condition.

I

Petitioner was convicted of the armed robbery of Erwin Wallaker, the treasurer of the San Jose Coin Club. When Wallaker returned to his home after the Club's annual show, he entered his garage and was accosted by two masked men, one armed with a machine gun and the other with an electrical shocking device, sometimes referred to as a "stun gun." The two men shocked Wallaker, bound and handcuffed him, and robbed him of jewelry and cash. During the encounter sufficient conversation took place to enable Wallaker subsequently to identify petitioner's distinctive voice. His identification was partially corroborated by a witness who saw the robbers leaving the scene, and by evidence that petitioner had attended the coin show.

Sergeant LaRault, an experienced police officer, investigated the crime and determined that there was probable cause to search petitioner's home for the proceeds of the robbery and for the weapons used by the robbers. His affidavit for a search warrant referred to police reports that described the weapons as well as the proceeds, but the warrant issued by the Magistrate only authorized a search for the proceeds, including three specifically described rings.

Pursuant to the warrant, LaRault searched petitioner's residence, but he did not find the stolen property. During the course of the search, however, he discovered the weapons in plain view and seized them. Specifically, he seized an Uzi machine gun, a .38 caliber revolver, two stun guns, a handcuff key, a San Jose Coin Club advertising brochure, and a few items of clothing identified by the victim.[1] LaRault testified that while he was searching for the rings, he also was interested in finding other evidence connecting petitioner to the robbery. Thus, the seized evidence was not discovered "inadvertently."

The trial court refused to suppress the evidence found in petitioner's home and, after a jury trial, petitioner was found guilty and sentenced to prison. The California Court of Appeal affirmed. It rejected petitioner's argument that our decision in Coolidge required suppression of the seized evidence that had not been listed in the warrant because its discovery was not inadvertent. The court relied on the California Supreme Court's decision in *North v. Superior Court*, 502 P.2d 1305 (1972). In that case the court noted that the discussion of the inadvertence limitation on the "plain view" doctrine in Justice Stewart's opinion in *Coolidge* had been joined by only three other Members of this Court and therefore was not binding on it. The California Supreme Court denied petitioner's request for review.

Because the California courts' interpretation of the "plain view" doctrine conflicts with the view of other courts, and because the unresolved issue is important, we granted certiorari.

II

The right to security in person and property protected by the Fourth Amendment may be invaded in quite different ways by searches and seizures. A search compromises the individual interest in privacy; a seizure deprives the individual of dominion over his or her person or property. The "plain view" doctrine is often considered an exception to the general rule that warrantless searches are presumptively unreasonable, but this characterization overlooks the important difference between searches and seizures.[5] If an article is already in plain view, neither its observation nor its seizure would involve any invasion of privacy. A seizure of the

---

[1] Although the officer viewed other handguns and rifles, he did not seize them because there was no probable cause to believe they were associated with criminal activity.

[5] "It is important to distinguish 'plain view,' as used in Coolidge to justify seizure of an object, from an officer's mere observation of an item left in plain view. Whereas the latter generally involves no Fourth Amendment search, the former generally does implicate the Amendment's limitations upon seizures of personal property."

article, however, would obviously invade the owner's possessory interest. If "plain view" justifies an exception from an otherwise applicable warrant requirement, therefore, it must be an exception that is addressed to the concerns that are implicated by seizures rather than by searches.

The criteria that generally guide "plain view" seizures were set forth in *Coolidge*. The Court held that the seizure of two automobiles parked in plain view on the defendant's driveway in the course of arresting the defendant violated the Fourth Amendment. Accordingly, particles of gun powder that had been subsequently found in vacuum sweepings from one of the cars could not be introduced in evidence against the defendant. The State endeavored to justify the seizure of the automobiles, and their subsequent search at the police station, on four different grounds, including the "plain view" doctrine.[6] The scope of that doctrine as it had developed in earlier cases was fairly summarized in these three paragraphs from Justice Stewart's opinion:

"It is well established that under certain circumstances the police may seize evidence in plain view without a warrant. But it is important to keep in mind that, in the vast majority of cases, any evidence seized by the police will be in plain view, at least at the moment of seizure. The problem with the 'plain view' doctrine has been to identify the circumstances in which plain view has legal significance rather than being simply the normal concomitant of any search, legal or illegal. An example of the applicability of the 'plain view' doctrine is the situation in which the police have a warrant to search a given area for specified objects, and in the course of the search come across some other article of incriminating character. Where the initial intrusion that brings the police within plain view of such an article is supported, not by a warrant, but by one of the recognized exceptions to the warrant requirement, the seizure is also legitimate. Thus the police may inadvertently come across evidence while in 'hot pursuit' of a fleeing suspect. And an object that comes into view during a search incident to arrest that is appropriately limited in scope under existing law may be seized without a warrant. Finally, the 'plain view' doctrine has been applied where a police officer is not searching for evidence against the accused, but nonetheless inadvertently comes across an incriminating object.

"What the 'plain view' cases have in common is that the police officer in each of them had a prior justification for an intrusion in the course of which he came inadvertently across a piece of evidence incriminating the accused. The doctrine serves to supplement the prior justification — whether it be a warrant for another object, hot pursuit, search incident to lawful arrest, or some other legitimate reason for being present unconnected with a search directed against the accused — and permits the warrantless seizure. Of course, the extension of the original justification is legitimate only where it is immediately apparent to the police that they have evidence before them; the 'plain view' doctrine may not be used to extend a general

---

[6] The State primarily contended that the seizures were authorized by a warrant issued by the Attorney General, but the Court held the warrant invalid because it had not been issued by "a neutral and detached magistrate." In addition, the State relied on three exceptions from the warrant requirement: (1) search incident to arrest; (2) the automobile exception; and (3) the "plain view" doctrine.

exploratory search from one object to another until something incriminating at last emerges."

Justice Stewart then described the two limitations on the doctrine that he found implicit in its rationale: First, "that plain view *alone* is never enough to justify the warrantless seizure of evidence, and second, "that the discovery of evidence in plain view must be inadvertent."

Justice Stewart's analysis of the "plain view" doctrine did not command a majority and a plurality of the Court has since made clear that the discussion is "not a binding precedent." *Brown* (opinion of REHNQUIST, J.). The decision nonetheless is a binding precedent. Before discussing the second limitation, which is implicated in this case, it is therefore necessary to explain why the first adequately supports the Court's judgment.

It is, of course, an essential predicate to any valid warrantless seizure of incriminating evidence that the officer did not violate the Fourth Amendment in arriving at the place from which the evidence could be plainly viewed. There are, moreover, two additional conditions that must be satisfied to justify the warrantless seizure. First, not only must the item be in plain view, its incriminating character must also be "immediately apparent." Thus, in *Coolidge*, the cars were obviously in plain view, but their probative value remained uncertain until after the interiors were swept and examined microscopically. Second, not only must the officer be lawfully located in a place from which the object can be plainly seen, but he or she must also have a lawful right of access to the object itself.[7] As the Solicitor General has suggested, Justice Harlan's vote in Coolidge may have rested on the fact that the seizure of the cars was accomplished by means of a warrantless trespass on the defendant's property. In all events, we are satisfied that the absence of inadvertence was not essential to the Court's rejection of the State's "plain view" argument in *Coolidge*.

III

Justice Stewart concluded that the inadvertence requirement was necessary to avoid a violation of the express constitutional requirement that a valid warrant must particularly describe the things to be seized. He explained:

"The rationale of the exception to the warrant requirement, as just stated, is that a plain-view seizure will not turn an initially valid (and therefore limited) search into a 'general' one, while the inconvenience of procuring a warrant to cover an inadvertent discovery is great. But where the discovery is anticipated, where the police know in advance the location of the evidence and intend to seize it, the situation is altogether different. The requirement of a warrant to seize imposes no inconvenience whatever, or at least none which is constitutionally cognizable in a

---

[7] "This is simply a corollary of the familiar principle discussed above, that no amount of probable cause can justify a warrantless search or seizure absent 'exigent circumstances.' Incontrovertible testimony of the senses that an incriminating object is on premises belonging to a criminal suspect may establish the fullest possible measure of probable cause. But even where the object is contraband, this Court has repeatedly stated and enforced the basic rule that the police may not enter and make a warrantless seizure."

legal system that regards warrantless searches as 'per se unreasonable' in the absence of 'exigent circumstances.' "If the initial intrusion is bottomed upon a warrant that fails to mention a particular object, though the police know its location and intend to seize it, then there is a violation of the express constitutional requirement of 'Warrants . . . particularly describing . . . [the] things to be seized.' "

We find two flaws in this reasoning. First, evenhanded law enforcement is best achieved by the application of objective standards of conduct, rather than standards that depend upon the subjective state of mind of the officer. The fact that an officer is interested in an item of evidence and fully expects to find it in the course of a search should not invalidate its seizure if the search is confined in area and duration by the terms of a warrant or a valid exception to the warrant requirement. If the officer has knowledge approaching certainty that the item will be found, we see no reason why he or she would deliberately omit a particular description of the item to be seized from the application for a search warrant.[8] Specification of the additional item could only permit the officer to expand the scope of the search. On the other hand, if he or she has a valid warrant to search for one item and merely a suspicion concerning the second, whether or not it amounts to probable cause, we fail to see why that suspicion should immunize the second item from seizure if it is found during a lawful search for the first. The hypothetical case put by Justice WHITE in his dissenting opinion in Coolidge is instructive:

"Let us suppose officers secure a warrant to search a house for a rifle. While staying well within the range of a rifle search, they discover two photographs of the murder victim, both in plain sight in the bedroom. Assume also that the discovery of the one photograph was inadvertent but finding the other was anticipated. The Court would permit the seizure of only one of the photographs. But in terms of the 'minor' peril to Fourth Amendment values there is surely no difference between these two photographs: the interference with possession is the same in each case and the officers' appraisal of the photograph they expected to see is no less reliable than their judgment about the other. And in both situations the actual inconvenience and danger to evidence remain identical if the officers must depart and secure a warrant."

Second, the suggestion that the inadvertence requirement is necessary to prevent the police from conducting general searches, or from converting specific warrants into general warrants, is not persuasive because that interest is already served by the requirements that no warrant issue unless it "particularly describ[es] the place to be searched and the persons or things to be seized," and that a warrantless search be circumscribed by the exigencies which justify its initiation. Scrupulous adherence to these requirements serves the interests in limiting the area and duration of the search that the inadvertence requirement inadequately protects. Once those commands have been satisfied and the officer has a lawful right

---

[8] "If the police have probable cause to search for a photograph as well as a rifle and they proceed to seek a warrant, they could have no possible motive for deliberately including the rifle but omitting the photograph. Quite the contrary is true. Only oversight or careless mistake would explain the omission in the warrant application if the police were convinced they had probable cause to search for the photograph." Coolidge (WHITE, J., dissenting).

of access, however, no additional Fourth Amendment interest is furthered by requiring that the discovery of evidence be inadvertent. If the scope of the search exceeds that permitted by the terms of a validly issued warrant or the character of the relevant exception from the warrant requirement, the subsequent seizure is unconstitutional without more. Thus, in the case of a search incident to a lawful arrest, "[i]f the police stray outside the scope of an authorized *Chimel* search they are already in violation of the Fourth Amendment, and evidence so seized will be excluded; adding a second reason for excluding evidence hardly seems worth the candle." Similarly, the object of a warrantless search of an automobile also defines its scope:

"The scope of a warrantless search of an automobile thus is not defined by the nature of the container in which the contraband is secreted. Rather, it is defined by the object of the search and the places in which there is probable cause to believe that it may be found. Just as probable cause to believe that a stolen lawnmower may be found in a garage will not support a warrant to search an upstairs bedroom, probable cause to believe that undocumented aliens are being transported in a van will not justify a warrantless search of a suitcase. Probable cause to believe that a container placed in the trunk of a taxi contains contraband or evidence does not justify a search of the entire cab." *United States v. Ross* (ch. 6, *infra*.)

In this case, the scope of the search was not enlarged in the slightest by the omission of any reference to the weapons in the warrant. Indeed, if the three rings and other items named in the warrant had been found at the outset — or if petitioner had them in his possession and had responded to the warrant by producing them immediately — no search for weapons could have taken place. Again, Justice WHITE's dissenting opinion in Coolidge is instructive: "Police with a warrant for a rifle may search only places where rifles might be and must terminate the search once the rifle is found; the inadvertence rule will in no way reduce the number of places into which they may lawfully look."

In this case the items seized from petitioner's home were discovered during a lawful search authorized by a valid warrant. When they were discovered, it was immediately apparent to the officer that they constituted incriminating evidence. He had probable cause, not only to obtain a warrant to search for the stolen property, but also to believe that the weapons and handguns had been used in the crime he was investigating. The search was authorized by the warrant, the seizure was authorized by the "plain view" doctrine. The judgment is affirmed.

JUSTICE BRENNAN, with whom JUSTICE MARSHALL joins, dissenting.

I remain convinced that Justice Stewart correctly articulated the plain view doctrine in *Coolidge*. The Fourth Amendment permits law enforcement officers to seize items for which they do not have a warrant when those items are found in plain view and (1) the officers are lawfully in a position to observe the items, (2) the discovery of the items is "inadvertent," and (3) it is immediately apparent to the officers that the items are evidence of a crime, contraband, or otherwise subject to seizure. In eschewing the inadvertent discovery requirement, the majority ignores the Fourth Amendment's express command that warrants particularly describe not only the places to be searched, but also the things to be seized. I respectfully dissent from this rewriting of the Fourth Amendment.

I

The Fourth Amendment protects two distinct interests. The prohibition against unreasonable searches and the requirement that a warrant "particularly describ[e] the place to be searched" protect an interest in privacy. The prohibition against unreasonable seizures and the requirement that a warrant "particularly describ[e] . . . the . . . things to be seized" protect a possessory interest in property. The Fourth Amendment, by its terms, declares the privacy and possessory interests to be equally important. As this Court recently stated, "Although the interest protected by the Fourth Amendment injunction against unreasonable searches is quite different from that protected by its injunction against unreasonable seizures, neither the one nor the other is of inferior worth or necessarily requires only lesser protection."

The Amendment protects these equally important interests in precisely the same manner: by requiring a neutral and detached magistrate to evaluate, before the search or seizure, the government's showing of probable cause and its particular description of the place to be searched and the items to be seized. Accordingly, just as a warrantless search is *per se* unreasonable absent exigent circumstances, so too a seizure of personal property is "*per se* unreasonable within the meaning of the Fourth Amendment unless it is accomplished pursuant to a judicial warrant issued upon probable cause and particularly describing the items to be seized." "Prior review by a neutral and detached magistrate is the time-tested means of effectuating Fourth Amendment rights." A decision to invade a possessory interest in property is too important to be left to the discretion of zealous officers "engaged in the often competitive enterprise of ferreting out crime." "The requirement that warrants shall particularly describe the things to be seized makes general searches under them impossible and prevents the seizure of one thing under a warrant describing another. As to what is to be taken, nothing is left to the discretion of the officer executing the warrant."

The plain view doctrine is an exception to the general rule that a seizure of personal property must be authorized by a warrant. As Justice Stewart explained in *Coolidge*, we accept a warrantless seizure when an officer is lawfully in a location and inadvertently sees evidence of a crime because of "the inconvenience of procuring a warrant" to seize this newly discovered piece of evidence. But "where the discovery is anticipated, where the police know in advance the location of the evidence and intend to seize it," the argument that procuring a warrant would be "inconvenient" loses much, if not all, of its force. Barring an exigency, there is no reason why the police officers could not have obtained a warrant to seize this evidence before entering the premises. The rationale behind the inadvertent discovery requirement is simply that we will not excuse officers from the general requirement of a warrant to seize if the officers know the location of evidence, have probable cause to seize it, intend to seize it, and yet do not bother to obtain a warrant particularly describing that evidence. To do so would violate "the express constitutional requirement of 'Warrants . . . particularly describing . . . [the] things to be seized,' " and would "fly in the face of the basic rule that no amount of probable cause can justify a warrantless seizure."

Although joined by only three other Members of the Court, Justice Stewart's discussion of the inadvertent discovery requirement has become widely accepted. See *Brown* (Powell, J., concurring in judgment) ("Whatever my view might have been when *Coolidge* was decided, I see no reason at this late date to imply criticism of its articulation of this exception. It has been accepted generally for over a decade"). Forty-six States and the District of Columbia and twelve United States Courts of Appeals now require plain view seizures to be inadvertent. There has been no outcry from law enforcement officials that the inadvertent discovery requirement unduly burdens their efforts. Given that the requirement is inescapably rooted in the plain language of the Fourth Amendment, I cannot fathom the Court's enthusiasm for discarding this element of the plain view doctrine.

The Court posits two "flaws" in Justice Stewart's reasoning that it believes demonstrate the inappropriateness of the inadvertent discovery requirement. But these flaws are illusory. First, the majority explains that it can see no reason why an officer who "has knowledge approaching certainty" that an item will be found in a particular location "would deliberately omit a particular description of the item to be seized from the application for a search warrant." But to the individual whose possessory interest has been invaded, it matters not why the police officer decided to omit a particular item from his application for a search warrant. When an officer with probable cause to seize an item fails to mention that item in his application for a search warrant — for whatever reason — and then seizes the item anyway, his conduct is per se unreasonable. Suppression of the evidence so seized will encourage officers to be more precise and complete in future warrant applications.

Furthermore, there are a number of instances in which a law enforcement officer might deliberately choose to omit certain items from a warrant application even though he has probable cause to seize them, knows they are on the premises, and intends to seize them when they are discovered in plain view. For example, the warrant application process can often be time-consuming, especially when the police attempt to seize a large number of items. An officer interested in conducting a search as soon as possible might decide to save time by listing only one or two hard-to-find items, such as the stolen rings in this case, confident that he will find in plain view all of the other evidence he is looking for before he discovers the listed items. Because rings could be located almost anywhere inside or outside a house, it is unlikely that a warrant to search for and seize the rings would restrict the scope of the search. An officer might rationally find the risk of immediately discovering the items listed in the warrant — thereby forcing him to conclude the search immediately — outweighed by the time saved in the application process.

The majority also contends that, once an officer is lawfully in a house and the scope of his search is adequately circumscribed by a warrant, "no additional Fourth Amendment interest is furthered by requiring that the discovery of evidence be inadvertent." Put another way, " 'the inadvertence rule will in no way reduce the number of places into which [law enforcement officers] may lawfully look.' " The majority is correct, but it has asked the wrong question. It is true that the inadvertent discovery requirement furthers no privacy interests. The requirement in no way reduces the scope of a search or the number of places into which officers may look. But it does protect possessory interests. Cf. *Illinois v. Andreas*, 463 U.S. 765, 771 (1983) ("The plain-view doctrine is grounded on the proposition that once police are lawfully in a position to observe an item first-hand, its owner's privacy interest in that item is lost; *the owner may retain the incidents of title and possession* but not privacy") (emphasis added). The inadvertent discovery requirement is essential if we are to take seriously the Fourth Amendment's protection of possessory interests as well as privacy interests. The Court today eliminates a rule designed to further possessory interests on the ground that it fails to further privacy interests. I cannot countenance such constitutional legerdemain.

II

Fortunately, this decision should have only a limited impact, for the Court is not confronted today with what lower courts have described as a "pretextual" search. For example, if an officer enters a house pursuant to a warrant to search for evidence of one crime when he is really interested only in seizing evidence relating to another crime, for which he does not have a warrant, his search is "pretextual" and the fruits of that search should be suppressed. See, e.g., *State v. Kelsey*, 592 S.W.2d 509 (Mo. App. 1979) (evidence suppressed because officers, who had ample opportunity to obtain warrant relating to murder investigation, entered the premises instead pursuant to a warrant relating to a drug investigation, and searched only the hiding place of the murder weapon, rather than conducting a "top to bottom" search for drugs). Similarly, an officer might use an exception to the generally applicable warrant requirement, such as "hot pursuit," as a pretext to enter a home to seize items he knows he will find in plain view. Such conduct would be a deliberate attempt to circumvent the constitutional requirement of a warrant "particularly describing the place to be searched, and the persons or things to be seized," and cannot be condoned.

The discovery of evidence in pretextual searches is not "inadvertent" and should be suppressed for that reason. But even state courts that have rejected the inadvertent discovery requirement have held that the Fourth Amendment prohibits pretextual searches. The Court's opinion today does not address pretextual searches, but I have no doubt that such searches violate the Fourth Amendment.[4]

III

The Fourth Amendment demands that an individual's possessory interest in property be protected from unreasonable governmental seizures, not just by requiring a showing of probable cause, but also by requiring a neutral and detached magistrate to authorize the seizure in advance. The Court today ignores the explicit language of the Fourth Amendment, which protects possessory interests in the

---

[4] The Court also does not dispute the unconstitutionality of a search that goes "so far astray of a search for the items mentioned in the warrant that it [becomes] a general exploratory search for any evidence of wrongdoing that might be found." Indeed, the Court reiterates that "converting specific warrants into general warrants" is unconstitutional and emphasizes the need for scrupulous adherence to the requirements that warrants particularly describe the place to be searched and the things to be seized and that a warrantless search "be circumscribed by the exigencies which justify its initiation."

same manner as it protects privacy interests, in order to eliminate a generally accepted element of the plain view doctrine that has caused no apparent difficulties for law enforcement officers. I am confident, however, that when confronted with more egregious police conduct than that found in this case, such as pretextual searches, the Court's interpretation of the Constitution will be less parsimonious than it is today. I respectfully dissent.

QUESTIONS AND NOTES

1.   What is the root justification for the "plain view" doctrine?

2.   Is "plain view" an exception to the law of "search" or the law of "seizure"? Does it matter?

3.   In general, do you see any Fourth Amendment values served by the inadvertence rule?

4.   Is Justice White's *Coolidge* hypothetical about the two photographs persuasive?

5.   Even if Justice Brennan's concerns were generally correct, would (should) they be applied to the facts of *Horton*, where the police *tried* to get a warrant for the items seized, but were turned down?

6.   We conclude this chapter with *Arizona v. Hicks*, a case refusing to move the plain view exception even a fraction of an inch.

ARIZONA v. HICKS
480 U.S. 321 (1987)

JUSTICE SCALIA delivered the opinion of the Court

In *Coolidge*, we said that in certain circumstances a warrantless seizure by police of an item that comes within plain view during their lawful search of a private area may be reasonable under the Fourth Amendment. We granted certiorari in the present case to decide whether this "plain view" doctrine may be invoked when the police have less than probable cause to believe that the item in question is evidence of a crime or is contraband.

I

On April 18, 1984, a bullet was fired through the floor of respondent's apartment, striking and injuring a man in the apartment below. Police officers arrived and entered respondent's apartment to search for the shooter, for other victims, and for weapons. They found and seized three weapons, including a sawed-off rifle, and in the course of their search also discovered a stocking-cap mask.

One of the policemen, Officer Nelson, noticed two sets of expensive stereo components, which seemed out of place in the squalid and otherwise ill-appointed four-room apartment. Suspecting that they were stolen, he read and recorded their serial numbers — moving some of the components, including a Bang and Olufsen turntable, in order to do so — which he then reported by phone to his headquarters. On being advised that the turntable had been taken in an armed robbery, he seized it immediately. It was later determined that some of the other serial numbers matched those on other stereo equipment taken in the same armed robbery, and a warrant was obtained and executed to seize that equipment as well. Respondent was subsequently indicted for the robbery.

The state trial court granted respondent's motion to suppress the evidence that had been seized. The Court of Appeals of Arizona affirmed. It was conceded that the initial entry and search, although warrantless, were justified by the exigent circumstance of the shooting. The Court of Appeals viewed the obtaining of the serial numbers, however, as an additional search, unrelated to that exigency. Relying upon a statement in *Mincey v. Arizona*, 437 U.S. 385, that a "warrantless search must be 'strictly circumscribed by the exigencies which justify its initiation,'" the Court of Appeals held that the police conduct violated the Fourth Amendment, requiring the evidence derived from that conduct to be excluded. Both courts — the trial court explicitly and the Court of Appeals by necessary implication — rejected the State's contention that Officer Nelson's actions were justified under the "plain view" doctrine of *Coolidge*. The Arizona Supreme Court denied review, and the State filed this petition.

II

As an initial matter, the State argues that Officer Nelson's actions constituted neither a "search" nor a "seizure" within the meaning of the Fourth Amendment. We agree that the mere recording of the serial numbers did not constitute a seizure. To be sure, that was the first step in a process by which respondent was eventually deprived of the stereo equipment. In and of itself, however, it did not "meaningfully interfere" with respondent's possessory interest in either the serial numbers or the equipment, and therefore did not amount to a seizure.

Officer Nelson's moving of the equipment, however, did constitute a "search" separate and apart from the search for the shooter, victims, and weapons that was the lawful objective of his entry into the apartment. Merely inspecting those parts of the turntable that came into view during the latter search would not have constituted an independent search, because it would have produced no additional invasion of respondent's privacy interest. But taking action, unrelated to the objectives of the authorized intrusion, which exposed to view concealed portions of the apartment or its contents, did produce a new invasion of respondent's privacy unjustified by the exigent circumstance that validated the entry. This is why, contrary to Justice POWELL's suggestion, the "distinction between 'looking' at a suspicious object in plain view and 'moving' it even a few inches" is much more than trivial for purposes of the Fourth Amendment. It matters not that the search uncovered nothing of any great personal value to respondent — serial numbers rather than (what might conceivably have been hidden behind or under the equipment) letters or photographs. A search is a search, even if it happens to disclose nothing but the bottom of a turntable.

III

The remaining question is whether the search was "reasonable" under the Fourth Amendment.

On this aspect of the case we reject, at the outset, the apparent position of the Arizona Court of Appeals that because the officers' action directed to the stereo equipment was unrelated to the justification for their entry into respondent's apartment, it was *ipso facto* unreasonable. That lack of relationship *always* exists with regard to action validated under the "plain view" doctrine; where action is taken for the purpose justifying the entry, invocation of the doctrine is superfluous. *Mincey*, in saying that a warrantless search must be "strictly circumscribed by the exigencies which justify its initiation," was addressing only the scope of the primary search itself, and was not overruling by implication the many cases acknowledging that the "plain view" doctrine can legitimate action beyond that scope.

We turn, then, to application of the doctrine to the facts of this case. "It is well established that under certain circumstances the police may *seize* evidence in plain view without a warrant," *Coolidge* (plurality opinion) (emphasis added). Those circumstances include situations "[w]here the initial intrusion that brings the police within plain view of such [evidence] is supported . . . by one of the recognized exceptions to the warrant requirement," such as the exigent-circumstances intrusion here. It would be absurd to say that an object could lawfully be seized and taken from the premises, but could not be moved for closer examination. It is clear, therefore, that the search here was valid if the "plain view" doctrine would have sustained a seizure of the equipment.

There is no doubt it would have done so if Officer Nelson had probable cause to believe that the equipment was stolen. The State has conceded, however, that he had only a "reasonable suspicion," by which it means something less than probable cause. We have not ruled on the question whether probable cause is required in order to invoke the "plain view" doctrine. Dicta in *Payton*, suggested that the standard of probable cause must be met, but our later opinions in *Brown*, explicitly regarded the issue as unresolved.

We now hold that probable cause is required. To say otherwise would be to cut the "plain view" doctrine loose from its theoretical and practical moorings. The theory of that doctrine consists of extending to nonpublic places such as the home, where searches and seizures without a warrant are presumptively unreasonable, the police's longstanding authority to make warrantless seizures in public places of such objects as weapons and contraband. And the practical justification for that extension is the desirability of sparing police, whose viewing of the object in the course of a lawful search is as legitimate as it would have been in a public place, the inconvenience and the risk — to themselves or to preservation of the evidence — of going to obtain a warrant. Dispensing with the need for a warrant is worlds apart from permitting a lesser standard of *cause* for the seizure than a warrant would require, *i.e.*, the standard of probable cause. No reason is apparent why an object should routinely be seizable on lesser grounds, during an unrelated search and seizure, than would have been needed to obtain a warrant for that same object if it had been known to be on the premises.

We do not say, of course, that a seizure can never be justified on less than probable cause. We have held that it can — where, for example, the seizure is minimally intrusive and operational necessities render it the only practicable means of detecting certain types of crime. No special operational necessities are relied on here, however — but rather the mere fact that the items in question came lawfully within the officer's plain view. That alone cannot supplant the requirement of probable cause.

The same considerations preclude us from holding that, even though probable cause would have been necessary for a *seizure*, the *search* of objects in plain view that occurred here could be sustained on lesser grounds. A dwelling-place search, no less than a dwelling-place seizure, requires probable cause, and there is no reason in theory or practicality why application of the "plain view" doctrine would supplant that requirement. Although the interest protected by the Fourth Amendment injunction against unreasonable searches is quite different from that protected by its injunction against unreasonable seizures, see *Brown* (STEVENS, J., concurring in judgment), neither the one nor the other is of inferior worth or necessarily requires only lesser protection. We have not elsewhere drawn a categorical distinction between the two insofar as concerns the degree of justification needed to establish the reasonableness of police action, and we see no reason for a distinction in the particular circumstances before us here. Indeed, to treat searches more liberally would especially erode the plurality's warning in *Coolidge* that "the 'plain view' doctrine may not be used to extend a general exploratory search from one object to another until something incriminating at last emerges." In short, whether legal authority to move the equipment could be found only as an inevitable concomitant of the authority to seize it, or also as a consequence of some independent power to search certain objects in plain view, probable cause to believe the equipment was stolen was required.

Justice O'CONNOR's dissent suggests that we uphold the action here on the ground that it was a "cursory inspection" rather than a "full-blown search," and could therefore be justified by reasonable suspicion instead of probable cause. As already noted, a truly cursory inspection — one that involves merely looking at what is already exposed to view, without disturbing it — is not a "search" for Fourth Amendment purposes, and therefore does not even require reasonable suspicion. We are unwilling to send police and judges into a new thicket of Fourth Amendment law, to seek a creature of uncertain description that is neither a "plain view" inspection nor yet a "full-blown search."

Justice POWELL's dissent reasonably asks what it is we would have had Officer Nelson do in these circumstances. The answer depends, of course, upon whether he had probable cause to conduct a search, a question that was not preserved in this case. If he had, then he should have done precisely what he did. If not, then he should have followed up his suspicions, if possible, by means other than a search — just as he would have had to do if, while walking along the street, he had noticed the same suspicious stereo equipment sitting inside a house a few feet away from him, beneath an open window. It may well be that, in such circumstances, no effective means short of a search exist. But there is nothing new in the realization that the Constitution sometimes insulates the criminality of a few in order to protect the privacy of us all. Our disagreement with the dissenters pertains to where the proper balance should be struck; we choose to adhere to the textual and traditional standard of probable cause.

For the reasons stated, the judgment of the Court of Appeals of Arizona is affirmed.

JUSTICE WHITE, concurring.

I write only to emphasize that this case does not present, and we have no occasion to address, the so-called "inadvertent discovery" prong of the plain-view exception to the Warrant Clause. This "requirement" of the plain-view doctrine has never been accepted by a judgment supported by a majority of this Court, and I therefore do not accept Justice O'CONNOR's dissent's assertion that evidence seized in plain view must have been inadvertently discovered in order to satisfy the dictates of the Fourth Amendment. I join the majority opinion today without regard to the inadvertence of the officers' discovery of the stereo components' serial numbers. The police officers conducted a search of respondent's stereo equipment absent probable cause that the equipment was stolen. It is for this reason that the judgment of the Court of Appeals of Arizona must be affirmed.

JUSTICE POWELL, with whom the CHIEF JUSTICE and JUSTICE O'CONNOR join, dissenting.

I join Justice O'CONNOR's dissenting opinion, and write briefly to highlight what seem to me the unfortunate consequences of the Court's decision.

Today the Court holds for the first time that the requirement of probable cause operates as a separate limitation on the application of the plain-view doctrine. The plurality opinion in *Coolidge*, required only that it be "immediately apparent to the police that they have evidence before them; the 'plain view' doctrine may not be used to extend a general exploratory search from one object to another until something incriminating at last emerges." There was no general exploratory search in this case, and I would not approve such a search. All the pertinent objects were in plain view and could be identified as objects frequently stolen. There was no looking into closets, opening of drawers or trunks, or other "rummaging around." Justice O'CONNOR properly emphasizes that the moving of a suspicious object in plain view results in a minimal invasion of privacy. The Court nevertheless holds that "merely looking at" an object in plain view is lawful, ante, at 1154, but "moving" or "disturbing" the object to investigate a reasonable suspicion is not. The facts of this case well illustrate the unreasonableness of this distinction.

The officers' suspicion that the stereo components at issue were stolen was both reasonable and based on specific, articulable facts. Indeed, the State was unwise to concede the absence of probable cause. The police lawfully entered respondent's apartment under exigent circumstances that arose when a bullet fired through the floor of the apartment struck a man in the apartment below. What they saw in the apartment hardly suggested that it was occupied by law-abiding citizens. A .25-caliber automatic pistol lay in plain view on the living room floor. During a concededly lawful search, the officers found a .45-caliber automatic, a .22-caliber, sawed-off rifle, and a stocking-cap mask. The apartment was littered with drug paraphernalia. The officers also observed two sets of expensive stereo components of a type that frequently was stolen.[2]

It is fair to ask what Officer Nelson should have done in these circumstances. Accepting the State's concession that he lacked probable cause, he could not have obtained a warrant to seize the stereo components. Neither could he have remained on the premises and forcibly prevented their removal. Officer Nelson's testimony indicates that he was able to read some of the serial numbers without moving the component.[3] To read the serial number on a Bang and Olufsen turntable, however, he had to "turn it around or turn it upside down." Officer Nelson noted the serial numbers on the stereo components and telephoned the National Crime Information Center to check them against the Center's computerized listing of stolen property. The computer confirmed his suspicion that at least the Bang and Olufsen turntable had been stolen. On the basis of this information, the officers obtained a warrant to seize the turntable and other stereo components that also proved to be stolen.

The Court holds that there was an unlawful search of the turntable. It agrees that the "mere recording of the serial numbers did not constitute a seizure." Thus, if the computer had identified as stolen property a component with a visible serial number, the evidence would have been admissible. But the Court further holds that "Officer Nelson's moving of the equipment . . . did constitute a 'search' . . . ." It perceives a constitutional distinction between reading a serial number on an object and moving or picking up an identical object to see its serial number. To make its position unmistakably clear, the Court concludes that a "search is a search, even if it happens to disclose nothing but the bottom of a turntable." With all respect, this distinction between "looking" at a suspicious object in plain view and "moving" it even a few inches trivializes the Fourth Amendment.[4] The Court's new rule will cause uncertainty, and could deter conscientious police officers from lawfully obtaining evidence necessary to convict guilty persons. Apart from the importance of rationality in the interpretation of the Fourth Amendment, today's decision may handicap law enforcement without enhancing privacy interests. Accordingly, I dissent.

---

[2] Responding to a question on cross-examination, Officer Nelson explained that his suspicion was "based on 12 years' worth of police experience. I have worked in different burglary crimes throughout that period of time and . . . I'm just very familiar with people converting stolen stereos and TV's into their own use."

[3] Officer Nelson testified that there was an opening of about a foot between the back of one set of stereo equipment and the wall. Presumably this opening was large enough to permit Officer Nelson to view serial numbers on the backs of the components without moving them.

[4] Numerous articles that frequently are stolen have identifying numbers, including expensive watches and cameras, and also credit cards. Assume for example that an officer reasonably suspects that two identical watches, both in plain view, have been stolen. Under the Court's decision, if one watch is lying face up and the other lying face down, reading the serial number on one of the watches would not be a search. But turning over the other watch to read its serial number would be a search. Moreover, the officer's ability to read a serial number may depend on its location in a room and light conditions at a particular time. Would there be a constitutional difference if an officer, on the basis of a reasonable suspicion, used a pocket flashlight or turned on a light to read a number rather than moving the object to a point where a serial number was clearly visible?

JUSTICE O'CONNOR, with whom the CHIEF JUSTICE and JUSTICE POWELL join, dissenting.

The Court today gives the right answer to the wrong question. The Court asks whether the police must have probable cause before either seizing an object in plain view or conducting a full-blown search of that object, and concludes that they must. I agree. In my view, however, this case presents a different question: whether police must have probable cause before conducting a cursory inspection of an item in plain view. Because I conclude that such an inspection is reasonable if the police are aware of facts or circumstances that justify a reasonable suspicion that the item is evidence of a crime, I would reverse the judgment of the Arizona Court of Appeals, and therefore dissent.

In *Coolidge*, Justice Stewart summarized three requirements that the plurality thought must be satisfied for a plain-view search or seizure. First, the police must lawfully make an initial intrusion or otherwise be in a position from which they can view a particular area. Second, the officer must discover incriminating evidence "inadvertently." Third, it must be "immediately apparent" to the police that the items they observe may be evidence of a crime, contraband, or otherwise subject to seizure. As another plurality observed in *Brown*, these three requirements have never been expressly adopted by a majority of this Court, but "as the considered opinion of four Members of this Court [the *Coolidge* plurality] should obviously be the point of reference for further discussion of the issue." There is no dispute in this case that the first two requirements have been satisfied. The officers were lawfully in the apartment pursuant to exigent circumstances, and the discovery of the stereo was inadvertent — the officers did not " 'know in advance the location of [certain] evidence and intend to seize it,' relying on the plain-view doctrine only as a pretext." Instead, the dispute in this case focuses on the application of the "immediately apparent" requirement; at issue is whether a police officer's reasonable suspicion is adequate to justify a cursory examination of an item in plain view.

The purpose of the "immediately apparent" requirement is to prevent "general, exploratory rummaging in a person's belongings." If an officer could indiscriminately search every item in plain view, a search justified by a limited purpose — such as exigent circumstances — could be used to eviscerate the protections of the Fourth Amendment. In order to prevent such a general search, therefore, we require that the relevance of the item be "immediately apparent."

Thus, I agree with the Court that even under the plain-view doctrine, probable cause is required before the police seize an item, or conduct a full-blown search of evidence in plain view. Such a requirement of probable cause will prevent the plain-view doctrine from authorizing general searches. This is not to say, however, that even a mere inspection of a suspicious item must be supported by probable cause. When a police officer makes a cursory inspection of a suspicious item in plain view in order to determine whether it is indeed evidence of a crime, there is no "exploratory rummaging." Only those items that the police officer "reasonably suspects" as evidence of a crime may be inspected, and perhaps more importantly, the scope of such an inspection is quite limited. In short, if police officers have a reasonable, articulable suspicion that an object they come across during the course of a lawful search is evidence of crime, in my view they may make a cursory examination of the object to verify their suspicion. If the officers wish to go beyond such a cursory examination of the object, however, they must have probable cause.

This distinction between a full-blown search and seizure of an item and a mere inspection of the item was first suggested by Justice Stewart. In his concurrence in *Stanley v. Georgia*, 394 U.S. 557 (1969), which is cited in *Coolidge*, Justice Stewart observed that the federal agents there had acted within the scope of a lawful warrant in opening the drawers of the defendant's desk. When they found in one of the drawers not the gambling material described in the warrant but movie films, they proceeded to exhibit the films on the defendant's projector, and thereafter arrested the defendant for possession of obscene matter. Justice Stewart agreed with the majority that the film had to be suppressed, but in doing so he suggested that a less intrusive inspection of evidence in plain view would present a different case: "This is not a case where agents in the course of a lawful search came upon contraband, criminal activity, or criminal evidence in plain view. For the record makes clear that the contents of the films could not be determined by *mere inspection*." (emphasis added).

Following Justice Stewart's suggestion, the overwhelming majority of both state and federal courts have held that probable cause is not required for a minimal inspection of an item in plain view. As Professor LaFave summarizes the view of these courts, "the minimal additional intrusion which results from an inspection or examination of an object in plain view is reasonable if the officer was first aware of some facts and circumstances which justify a reasonable suspicion (not probable cause, in the traditional sense) that the object is or contains a fruit, instrumentality, or evidence of crime." 2 W. LaFave, Search and Seizure s 6.7(b), p. 717 (2d ed. 1987); see also id., at 345 ("It is generally assumed that there is nothing improper in merely picking up an unnamed article for the purpose of noting its brand name or serial number or other identifying characteristics to be found on the surface"). Thus, while courts require probable cause for more extensive examination, cursory inspections — including picking up or moving objects for a better view — require only a reasonable suspicion.

This distinction between searches based on their relative intrusiveness — and its subsequent adoption by a consensus of American courts — is entirely consistent with our Fourth Amendment jurisprudence. We have long recognized that searches can vary in intrusiveness, and that some brief searches "may be so minimally intrusive of Fourth Amendment interests that strong countervailing governmental interests will justify a [search] based only on specific articulable facts" that the item in question is contraband or evidence of a crime.

In my view, the balance of the governmental and privacy interests strongly supports a reasonable-suspicion standard for the cursory examination of items in plain view. The additional intrusion caused by an inspection of an item in plain view for its serial number is minuscule. Weighed against this minimal additional invasion of privacy are rather major gains in law enforcement. The use of identification numbers in tracing stolen property is a powerful law enforcement tool. Serial numbers are far more helpful and accurate in detecting stolen property than simple police recollection of the evidence. Given the prevalence of mass produced goods in our national economy, a serial number is often the only sure method of detecting stolen property. The balance of governmental and private interests strongly supports the view accepted by a majority of courts that a standard of reasonable suspicion meets the requirements of the Fourth Amendment.

Unfortunately, in its desire to establish a "bright-line" test, the Court has taken a step that ignores a substantial body of precedent and that places serious roadblocks to reasonable law enforcement practices. Indeed, in this case no warrant to search the stereo equipment for its serial number could have been obtained by the officers based on reasonable suspicion alone, and in the Court's view the officers may not even move the stereo turntable to examine its serial number. The theoretical advantages of the "search is a search" approach adopted by the Court today are simply too remote to justify the tangible and severe damage it inflicts on legitimate and effective law enforcement.

Even if probable cause were the appropriate standard, I have little doubt that it was satisfied here. When police officers, during the course of a search inquiring into grievously unlawful activity, discover the tools of a thief (a sawed-off rifle and a stocking mask) and observe in a small apartment two sets of stereo equipment that are both inordinately expensive in relation to their surroundings and known to be favored targets of larcenous activity, the "flexible, common-sense standard" of probable cause has been satisfied. *Brown.*

Because the Court today ignores the existence of probable cause, and in doing so upsets a widely accepted body of precedent on the standard of reasonableness for the cursory examination of evidence in plain view, I respectfully dissent.

QUESTIONS AND NOTES

1. Do you think that Officer Nelson acted properly? If you were his superior, would you have praised or criticized him? What else could he have done?

2. Should the State have conceded the probable cause issue? Why do you suppose that it did?

3. Should "immediately apparent" mean (a) more than probable cause, (b) less than probable cause, (c) the same as probable cause, (d) something different from probable cause.

4. Is this the type of issue that ought to be decided by flexible standards (O'Connor) or a bright-line rule (Scalia)? What are the advantages either way?

5. Did the Court trivialize the Fourth Amendment, or announce a significant principle? Explain your answer.

6. After *Hicks* and *Horton,* is *Coolidge* still good law? Should it be?

Chapter 6

AUTOMOBILES

A. THE RULE AND ITS RATIONALE

Automobile searches are governed by sufficiently different rules from other types of searches that a substantial separate study of them is warranted. You should begin this section by reviewing and refamiliarizing yourself with *Chambers v. Maroney*, Chapter 3, *supra*. In contrast to *Chambers*, the ubiquitous *Coolidge* case developed an important limitation on the automobile exception to a warrant rule. When the warrant was held invalid, and the "plain view" exception failed, New Hampshire argued that it could seize the car without a warrant because it was an automobile. The Court responded by holding that an automobile in a private residence that was being guarded by the police was not inherently mobile and presented no justification for dispensing with a warrant. As the Court put it: "The word 'automobile' is not a talisman in whose presence the Fourth Amendment fades away and disappears."

Whether *Chambers* or *Coolidge* was to control intermediate cases was the question until *California v. Carney*.

CALIFORNIA v. CARNEY
471 U.S. 386 (1985)

CHIEF JUSTICE BURGER delivered the opinion of the Court.

We granted certiorari to decide whether law enforcement agents violated the Fourth Amendment when they conducted a warrantless search, based on probable cause, of a fully mobile "motor home" located in a public place.

I

On May 31, 1979, Drug Enforcement Agency Agent Robert Williams watched respondent, Charles Carney, approach a youth in downtown San Diego. The youth accompanied Carney to a Dodge Mini Motor Home parked in a nearby lot. Carney and the youth closed the window shades in the motor home, including one across the front window. Agent Williams had previously received uncorroborated information that the same motor home was used by another person who was exchanging marihuana for sex. Williams, with assistance from other agents, kept the motor home under surveillance for the entire one and one-quarter hours that Carney and the youth remained inside. When the youth left the motor home, the agents followed and stopped him. The youth told the agents that he had received marijuana in return for allowing Carney sexual contacts.

At the agents' request, the youth returned to the motor home and knocked on its door; Carney stepped out. The agents identified themselves as law enforcement officers. Without a warrant or consent, one agent entered the motor home and observed marihuana, plastic bags, and a scale of the kind used in weighing drugs on a table. Agent Williams took Carney into custody and took possession of the motor home. A subsequent search of the motor home at the police station revealed additional marihuana in the cupboards and refrigerator.

Respondent was charged with possession of marihuana for sale. At a preliminary hearing, he moved to suppress the evidence discovered in the motor home. The Magistrate denied the motion, upholding the initial search as a justifiable search for other persons, and the subsequent search as a routine inventory search.

The California Supreme Court reversed the conviction. The Supreme Court did not disagree with the conclusion of the trial court that the agents had probable cause to arrest respondent and to believe that the vehicle contained evidence of a crime; however, the court held that the search was unreasonable because no warrant was obtained, rejecting the State's argument that the vehicle exception to the warrant requirement should apply. That court reached its decision by concluding that the mobility of a vehicle "is no longer the prime justification for the automobile exception; rather, 'the answer lies in the diminished expectation of privacy which surrounds the automobile.' " The California Supreme Court held that the expectations of privacy in a motor home are more like those in a dwelling than in an automobile because the primary function of motor homes is not to provide transportation but to "provide the occupant with living quarters." We reverse.

II

The Fourth Amendment protects the "right of the people to be secure in their persons, houses, papers, and effects, against unreasonable searches and seizures." This fundamental right is preserved by a requirement that searches be conducted pursuant to a warrant issued by an independent judicial officer. There are, of course, exceptions to the general rule that a warrant must be secured before a search is undertaken; one is the so-called "automobile exception" at issue in this case. This exception to the warrant requirement was first set forth by the Court 60 years ago in *Carroll*. There, the Court recognized that the privacy interests in an automobile are constitutionally protected; however, it held that the ready mobility of the automobile justifies a lesser degree of protection of those interests. The Court rested this exception on a long-recognized distinction between stationary structures and vehicles: "[T]he guaranty of freedom from unreasonable searches and seizures by the Fourth Amendment has been construed, practically since the beginning of Government, as recognizing a necessary difference between a search of a store, dwelling house or other structure in respect of which a proper official warrant readily may be obtained, and a search of a ship, motor boat, wagon or automobile, for contraband goods, where it is not practicable to secure a warrant because the vehicle can be *quickly moved* out of the locality or jurisdiction in which the warrant must be sought." (emphasis added).

The capacity to be "quickly moved" was clearly the basis of the holding in *Carroll*, and our cases have consistently recognized ready mobility as one of the principal bases of the automobile exception. In *Chambers*, for example, commenting on the rationale for the vehicle exception, we noted that "the opportunity to search is fleeting since a car is readily movable." More recently, in *United States v. Ross* (sec. B, *infra*), we once again emphasized that "an immediate intrusion is necessary" because of "the nature of an automobile in transit . . . ." The mobility of automobiles, we have observed, "creates circumstances of such exigency that, as a practical necessity, rigorous enforcement of the warrant requirement is impossible."

However, although ready mobility alone was perhaps the original justification for the vehicle exception, our later cases have made clear that ready mobility is not the only basis for the exception. The reasons for the vehicle exception, we have said, are twofold. "Besides the element of mobility, less rigorous warrant requirements govern because the expectation of privacy with respect to one's automobile is significantly less than that relating to one's home or office."

Even in cases where an automobile was not immediately mobile, the lesser expectation of privacy resulting from its use as a readily mobile vehicle justified application of the vehicular exception. In some cases, the configuration of the vehicle contributed to the lower expectations of privacy; for example, we held in *Cardwell v. Lewis*, 417 U.S. 583 (1974) that, because the passenger compartment of a standard automobile is relatively open to plain view, there are lesser expectations of privacy. But even when enclosed "repository" areas have been involved, we have concluded that the lesser expectations of privacy warrant application of the exception. We have applied the exception in the context of a locked car trunk, a sealed package in a car trunk, a closed compartment under the dashboard, the interior of a vehicle's upholstery, or sealed packages inside a covered pickup truck.

These reduced expectations of privacy derive not from the fact that the area to be searched is in plain view, but from the pervasive regulation of vehicles capable of traveling on the public highways. As we explained in *South Dakota v. Opperman*, an inventory search case: "Automobiles, unlike homes, are subjected to pervasive and continuing governmental regulation and controls, including periodic inspection and licensing requirements. As an everyday occurrence, police stop and examine vehicles when license plates or inspection stickers have expired, or if other violations, such as exhaust fumes or excessive noise, are noted, or if headlights or other safety equipment are not in proper working order." 428 U.S., at 368.

The public is fully aware that it is accorded less privacy in its automobiles because of this compelling governmental need for regulation. Historically, "individuals always [have] been on notice that movable vessels may be stopped and searched on facts giving rise to probable cause that the vehicle contains contraband, without the protection afforded by a magistrate's prior evaluation of those facts." In short, the pervasive schemes of regulation, which necessarily lead to reduced expectations of privacy, and the exigencies attendant to ready mobility justify searches without prior recourse to the authority of a magistrate so long as the overriding standard of probable cause is met.

When a vehicle is being used on the highways, or if it is readily capable of such use and is found stationary in a place not regularly used for residential purposes — temporary or otherwise — the two justifications for the vehicle exception come into play. First, the vehicle is obviously readily mobile by the turn of an ignition key, if not actually moving. Second, there is a reduced expectation of privacy stemming from its use as a licensed motor vehicle subject to a range of police regulation inapplicable to a fixed dwelling. At least in these circumstances, the overriding societal interests in effective law enforcement justify an immediate search before the vehicle and its occupants become unavailable.

While it is true that respondent's vehicle possessed some, if not many of the attributes of a home, it is equally clear that the vehicle falls clearly within the scope of the exception laid down in *Carroll* and applied in succeeding cases. Like the automobile in *Carroll*, respondent's motor home was readily mobile. Absent the prompt search and seizure, it could readily have been moved beyond the reach of the police. Furthermore, the vehicle was licensed to "operate on public streets; [was] serviced in public places; . . . and [was] subject to extensive regulation and inspection." And the vehicle was so situated that an objective observer would conclude that it was being used not as a residence, but as a vehicle.

Respondent urges us to distinguish his vehicle from other vehicles within the exception because it was *capable of functioning as a home*. In our increasingly mobile society, many vehicles used for transportation can be and are being used not only for transportation but for shelter, i.e., as a "home" or "residence." To distinguish between respondent's motor home and an ordinary sedan for purposes of the vehicle exception would require that we apply the exception depending upon the size of the vehicle and the quality of its appointments. Moreover, to fail to apply the exception to vehicles such as a motor home ignores the fact that a motor home lends itself easily to use as an instrument of illicit drug traffic and other illegal activity. In *Ross*, we declined to distinguish between "worthy" and "unworthy" containers, noting that "the central purpose of the Fourth Amendment forecloses such a distinction." We decline today to distinguish between "worthy" and "unworthy" vehicles which are either on the public roads and highways, or situated such that it is reasonable to conclude that the vehicle is not being used as a residence.

Our application of the vehicle exception has never turned on the other uses to which a vehicle might be put. The exception has historically turned on the ready mobility of the vehicle, and on the presence of the vehicle in a setting that objectively indicates that the vehicle is being used for transportation.[3] These two requirements for application of the exception ensure that law enforcement officials are not unnecessarily hamstrung in their efforts to detect and prosecute criminal activity, and that the legitimate privacy interests of the public are protected. Applying the vehicle exception in these circumstances allows the essential purposes

---

[3] We need not pass on the application of the vehicle exception to a motor home that is situated in a way or place that objectively indicates that it is being used as a residence. Among the factors that might be relevant in determining whether a warrant would be required in such a circumstance is its location, whether the vehicle is readily mobile or instead, for instance, elevated on blocks, whether the vehicle is licensed, whether it is connected to utilities, and whether it has convenient access to a public road.

served by the exception to be fulfilled, while assuring that the exception will acknowledge legitimate privacy interests.

III

The question remains whether, apart from the lack of a warrant, this search was unreasonable. Under the vehicle exception to the warrant requirement, "[o]nly the prior approval of the magistrate is waived; the search otherwise [must be such] as the magistrate could authorize."

This search was not unreasonable; it was plainly one that the magistrate could authorize if presented with these facts. The DEA agents had fresh, direct, uncontradicted evidence that the respondent was distributing a controlled substance from the vehicle, apart from evidence of other possible offenses. The agents thus had abundant probable cause to enter and search the vehicle for evidence of a crime notwithstanding its possible use as a dwelling place.

The judgment of the California Supreme Court is reversed, and the case is remanded for further proceedings not inconsistent with this opinion.

JUSTICE STEVENS, with whom JUSTICE BRENNAN and JUSTICE MARSHALL join, dissenting.

The character of "the place to be searched" plays an important role in Fourth Amendment analysis. In this case, police officers searched a Dodge/Midas Mini Motor Home. The California Supreme Court correctly characterized this vehicle as a "hybrid" which combines "the mobility attribute of an automobile . . . with most of the privacy characteristics of a house."

The hybrid character of the motor home places it at the crossroads between the privacy interests that generally forbid warrantless invasions of the home, and the law enforcement interests that support the exception for warrantless searches of automobiles based on probable cause. By choosing to follow the latter route, the Court errs in three respects: it has entered new territory prematurely, it has accorded priority to an exception rather than to the general rule, and it has abandoned the limits on the exception imposed by prior cases.

II

The Fourth Amendment guarantees the "right of the people to be secure in their persons, houses, papers, and effects against unreasonable searches and seizures." We have interpreted this language to provide law enforcement officers with a bright-line standard: "searches conducted outside the judicial process, without prior approval by judge or magistrate, are *per se* unreasonable under the Fourth Amendment — subject only to a few specifically established and well delineated exceptions."

In *Ross*, the Court reaffirmed the primary importance of the general rule condemning warrantless searches, and emphasized that the exception permitting the search of automobiles without a warrant is a narrow one. We expressly endorsed "the general rule," stated in *Carroll*, that " '[i]n cases where the securing of a warrant is reasonably practicable, it must be used.' " Given this warning and the presumption of regularity that attaches to a warrant, it is hardly unrealistic to expect experienced law enforcement officers to obtain a search warrant when one can easily be secured.

The ascendancy of the warrant requirement in our system of justice must not be bullied aside by extravagant claims of necessity: " 'The warrant requirement . . . is not an inconvenience to be somehow "weighed" against the claims of police efficiency. It is, or should be, an important working part of our machinery of government, operating as a matter of course to check the "well-intentioned but mistakenly overzealous executive officers" who are a part of any system of law enforcement.' [*Coolidge*] ". . . By requiring that conclusions concerning probable cause and the scope of a search 'be drawn by a neutral and detached magistrate instead of being judged by the officer engaged in the often competitive enterprise of ferreting out crime', we minimize the risk of unreasonable assertions of executive authority." If the motor home were parked in the exact middle of the intersection between the general rule and the exception for automobiles, priority should be given to the rule rather than the exception.

III

The motor home, however, was not parked in the middle of that intersection. Our prior cases teach us that inherent mobility is not a sufficient justification for the fashioning of an exception to the warrant requirement, especially in the face of heightened expectations of privacy in the location searched. Motor homes, by their common use and construction, afford their owners a substantial and legitimate expectation of privacy when they dwell within. When a motor home is parked in a location that is removed from the public highway, I believe that society is prepared to recognize that the expectations of privacy within it are not unlike the expectations one has in a fixed dwelling. As a general rule, such places may only be searched with a warrant based upon probable cause. Warrantless searches of motor homes are only reasonable when the motor home is traveling on the public streets or highways, or when exigent circumstances otherwise require an immediate search without the expenditure of time necessary to obtain a warrant.

As we explained in *Ross*, the automobile exception is the product of a long history: "[S]ince its earliest days Congress had recognized the impracticability of securing a warrant in cases involving the transportation of contraband goods. It is this impracticability, viewed in historical perspective, that provided the basis for the *Carroll* decision. Given the nature of an automobile in transit, the Court recognized that an immediate intrusion is necessary if police officers are to secure the illicit substance. In this class of cases, the Court held that a warrantless search of an automobile is not unreasonable."

The automobile exception has been developed to ameliorate the practical problems associated with the search of vehicles that have been stopped on the streets or public highways because there was probable cause to believe they were transporting contraband. Until today, however, the Court has never decided whether the practical justifications that apply to a vehicle that is stopped in transit on a public way apply with the same force to a vehicle parked in a lot near a court house where it could easily be detained while a warrant is issued.[15]

In this case, the motor home was parked in an off-the-street lot only a few blocks from the courthouse in downtown San Diego where dozens of magistrates were available to entertain a warrant application.[16] The officers clearly had the element of surprise with them, and with curtains covering the windshield, the motor home offered no indication of any imminent departure. The officers plainly had probable cause to arrest the respondent and search the motor home, and on this record, it is inexplicable why they eschewed the safe harbor of a warrant.[17]

In the absence of any evidence of exigency in the circumstances of this case, the Court relies on the inherent mobility of the motor home to create a conclusive presumption of exigency. This Court, however, has squarely held that mobility of the place to be searched is not a sufficient justification for abandoning the warrant requirement. In *Chadwick*, the Court held that a warrantless search of a footlocker violated the Fourth Amendment even though there was ample probable cause to believe it contained contraband. The Government had argued that the rationale of the automobile exception applied to movable containers in general, and that the warrant requirement should be limited to searches of homes and other "core" areas of privacy. We categorically rejected the Government's argument, observing that there are greater privacy interests associated with containers than with automobiles,[18] and that there are less practical problems associated with the temporary detention of a container than with the detention of an automobile.

We again endorsed that analysis in *Ross*: "The Court in *Chadwick* specifically rejected the argument that the warrantless search was 'reasonable' because a

---

[15] In *Coolidge*, a plurality refused to apply the automobile exception to an automobile that was seized while parked in the driveway of the suspect's house, towed to a secure police compound, and later searched: "The word 'automobile' is not a talisman in whose presence the Fourth Amendment fades away and disappears. And surely there is nothing in this case to invoke the meaning and purpose of the rule of *Carroll* — no alerted criminal bent on flight, no fleeting opportunity on an open highway after a hazardous chase, no contraband or stolen goods or weapons, no confederates waiting to move the evidence, not even the inconvenience of a special police detail to guard the immobilized automobile. In short, by no possible stretch of the legal imagination can this be made into a case where 'it is not practicable to secure a warrant.' and the 'automobile exception' despite its label, is simply irrelevant." (opinion of Stewart, J., joined by Douglas, BRENNAN, and MARSHALL, JJ.). In *Cardwell*, a different plurality approved the seizure of an automobile from a public parking lot, and a later examination of its exterior. (opinion of BLACKMUN, J.). Here, of course, we are concerned with the reasonableness of the search, not the seizure. Even if the diminished expectations of privacy associated with an automobile justify the warrantless search of a parked automobile notwithstanding the diminished exigency, the heightened expectations of privacy in the interior of a motor home require a different result.

[16] In addition, a telephonic warrant was only 20 cents and the nearest phone booth away.

[17] This willingness to search first and later seek justification has properly been characterized as "a decision roughly comparable in prudence to determining whether an electrical wire is charged by grasping it."

[18] "The factors which diminish the privacy aspects of an automobile do not apply to respondent's footlocker. Luggage contents are not open to public view, except as a condition to a border entry or common carrier travel; nor is luggage subject to regular inspections and official scrutiny on a continuing basis. Unlike an automobile, whose primary function is transportation, luggage is intended as a repository of personal effects. In sum, a person's expectations of privacy in personal luggage are substantially greater than in an automobile."

footlocker has some of the mobile characteristics that support warrantless searches of automobiles. The Court recognized that 'a person's expectations of privacy in personal luggage are substantially greater than in an automobile,' and noted that the practical problems associated with the temporary detention of a piece of luggage during the period of time necessary to obtain a warrant are significantly less than those associated with the detention of an automobile." It is perfectly obvious that the citizen has a much greater expectation of privacy concerning the interior of a mobile home than of a piece of luggage such as a footlocker. If "inherent mobility" does not justify warrantless searches of containers, it cannot rationally provide a sufficient justification for the search of a person's dwelling place.

Unlike a brick bungalow or a frame Victorian, a motor home seldom serves as a permanent lifetime abode. The motor home in this case, however, was designed to accommodate a breadth of ordinary everyday living. Photographs in the record indicate that its height, length, and beam provided substantial living space inside: stuffed chairs surround a table; cupboards provide room for storage of personal effects; bunk beds provide sleeping space; and a refrigerator provides ample space for food and beverages. Moreover, curtains and large opaque walls inhibit viewing the activities inside from the exterior of the vehicle. The interior configuration of the motor home establishes that the vehicle's size, shape, and mode of construction should have indicated to the officers that it was a vehicle containing mobile living quarters.

The State contends that officers in the field will have an impossible task determining whether or not other vehicles contain mobile living quarters. It is not necessary for the Court to resolve every unanswered question in this area in a single case, but common English usage suggests that we already distinguish between a "motor home" which is "equipped as a self-contained traveling home," a "camper" which is only equipped for "casual travel and camping," and an automobile which is "designed for passenger transportation." Surely the exteriors of these vehicles contain clues about their different functions which could alert officers in the field to the necessity of a warrant.[21]

The California Vehicle Code also refutes the State's argument that the exclusion of "motor homes" from the automobile exception would be impossible to apply in practice. In its definitional section, the Code distinguishes campers and house cars from station wagons, and suggests that they are special categories of the more general terms — motor vehicles and passenger vehicles. A "house car" is "a motor vehicle originally designed, or permanently altered, and equipped for human habitation, or to which a camper has been permanently attached." Alcoholic beverages may not be opened or consumed in motor vehicles traveling on the highways, except in the "living quarters of a housecar or camper." The same definitions might not necessarily apply in the context of the Fourth Amendment,

---

[21] In refusing to extend the California Supreme Court's decision in *Carney* beyond its context, the California Court of Appeals have had no difficulty in distinguishing the motor home involved there from a Ford van, and a cab-high camper shell on the back of a pickup truck. There is no reason to believe that trained officers could not make similar distinctions between different vehicles, especially when state vehicle laws already require them to do so.

but they do indicate that descriptive distinctions are humanly possible. They also reflect the California Legislature's judgment that "house cars" entertain different kinds of activities than the ordinary passenger vehicle.

In my opinion, searches of places that regularly accommodate a wide range of private human activity are fundamentally different from searches of automobiles which primarily serve a public transportation function. Although it may not be a castle, a motor home is usually the functional equivalent of a hotel room, a vacation and retirement home, or a hunting and fishing cabin. These places may be as spartan as a humble cottage when compared to the most majestic mansion, but the highest and most legitimate expectations of privacy associated with these temporary abodes should command the respect of this Court. In my opinion, a warrantless search of living quarters in a motor home is "presumptively unreasonable absent exigent circumstances."

I respectfully dissent.

QUESTIONS AND NOTES

1.   Would (should) it have mattered if the motor home was Carney's *only* residence?

2.   In what sense wasn't the motor home being used as a home? It was parked, curtains were drawn across the front windshield, and the very reason that he was arrested was in part *because* he performed an unlawful intimate act in the motor home.

3.   Do you agree that police would have difficulty with a "worthy vehicle" rule?

4.   Should there be a special rule for states that designate certain vehicles as "house cars"?

5.   If there were a special rule for motor homes, should that rule extend to (some) vans and campers? What about a used Volkswagen in which a homeless person regularly sleeps?

6.   What could (should) the police have done a case like this if the Stevens opinion had prevailed? Would that have been unduly burdensome?

7.   Would it have been better to apply *Coolidge*, rather than *Chambers*, to parked vehicles? Why? Why not?

8.   After *Carney*, is the word "automobile" "a talisman in whose presence the Fourth Amendment disappears?"

9.   Would the automobile exception aspect of *Coolidge* be decided the same way if it arose today? Explain.

B.   CARS AND CONTAINERS

As we know from *Chambers* and *Carney*, searches of automobiles without a warrant, but with probable cause, will ordinarily be upheld. However, as *Chadwick*, Chapter 3, *supra*, tells us, the same deferential attitude does not extend to searches of containers, however movable they may be. This section concerns the problem of containers found within cars. The question is when do we apply *Chambers* and when do we apply *Chadwick*.

Initially it appeared as though *Chadwick* would carry the day. In *Arkansas v. Sanders*, 442 U.S. 753 (1979), the police had probable cause to arrest Sanders and search a green suitcase that he was carrying when he arrived at the Little Rock airport. Instead of arresting him, they allowed him and a companion to put the suitcase in the trunk of a cab, which drove off. The police stopped the car, had the cab driver open the trunk, and search the closed but unlocked suitcase. The government argued that the automobile exception applied and that the search should be valid. The Court rejected that argument, holding that *Chadwick*, rather than *Chambers*, controlled.

However, in *United States v. Ross*, 456 U.S. 798 (1982), it became clear that containers were not sacrosanct. There the police received reliable information that Ross was dealing drugs and had drugs and money in his car. The police stopped the car, searched the trunk, and found drugs in a paper bag and money in a zippered leather pouch. Ross argued that because police searched containers in his car, the case was controlled by *Chadwick* and *Sanders*. The Court disagreed, holding that because probable cause related to the whole car, and not simply packages found therein, *Chambers* controlled.

Thus the stage was set for *California v. Acevedo*.

CALIFORNIA v. ACEVEDO
500 U.S. 565 (1991)

JUSTICE BLACKMUN delivered the opinion of the Court.

This case requires us once again to consider the so-called "automobile exception" to the warrant requirement of the Fourth Amendment and its application to the search of a closed container in the trunk of a car.

I

On October 28, 1987, Officer Coleman of the Santa Ana, Cal., Police Department received a telephone call from a federal drug enforcement agent in Hawaii. The agent informed Coleman that he had seized a package containing marijuana which was to have been delivered to the Federal Express Office in Santa Ana and which was addressed to J.R. Daza at 805 West Stevens Avenue in that city. The agent arranged to send the package to Coleman instead. Coleman then was to take the package to the Federal Express office and arrest the person who arrived to claim it.

Coleman received the package on October 29, verified its contents, and took it to the Senior Operations Manager at the Federal Express office. At about 10:30 a.m. on October 30, a man, who identified himself as Jamie Daza, arrived to claim the package. He accepted it and drove to his apartment on West Stevens. He carried the package into the apartment.

At 11:45 a.m., officers observed Daza leave the apartment and drop the box and paper that had contained the marijuana into a trash bin. Coleman at that point left the scene to get a search warrant. About 12:05 p.m., the officers saw Richard St. George leave the apartment carrying a blue knapsack which appeared to be half full. The officers stopped him as he was driving off, searched the knapsack, and found 1 1/2 pounds of marijuana.

At 12:30 p.m., respondent Charles Steven Acevedo arrived. He entered Daza's apartment, stayed for about 10 minutes, and reappeared carrying a brown paper bag that looked full. The officers noticed that the bag was the size of one of the wrapped marijuana packages sent from Hawaii. Acevedo walked to a silver Honda in the parking lot. He placed the bag in the trunk of the car and started to drive away. Fearing the loss of evidence, officers in a marked police car stopped him. They opened the trunk and the bag, and found marijuana.[22]

Respondent was charged in state court with possession of marijuana for sale. He moved to suppress the marijuana found in the car. The motion was denied. He then pleaded guilty but appealed the denial of the suppression motion.

The California Court of Appeal, Fourth District, concluded that the marijuana found in the paper bag in the car's trunk should have been suppressed. The court concluded that the officers had probable cause to believe that the paper bag contained drugs but lacked probable cause to suspect that Acevedo's car, itself, otherwise contained contraband. Because the officers' probable cause was directed specifically at the bag, the court held that the case was controlled by *Chadwick*, rather than by *Ross*. Although the court agreed that the officers could seize the paper bag, it held that, under *Chadwick*, they could not open the bag without first obtaining a warrant for that purpose. The court then recognized "the anomalous nature" of the dichotomy between the rule in *Chadwick* and the rule in *Ross*. That dichotomy dictates that if there is probable cause to search a car, then the entire car — including any closed container found therein — may be searched without a warrant, but if there is probable cause only as to a container in the car, the container may be held but not searched until a warrant is obtained.

We granted certiorari to reexamine the law applicable to a closed container in an automobile, a subject that has troubled courts and law enforcement officers since it was first considered in *Chadwick*.

II

The Fourth Amendment protects the "right of the people to be secure in their persons, houses, papers, and effects, against unreasonable searches and seizures." Contemporaneously with the adoption of the Fourth Amendment, the First Congress, and, later, the Second and Fourth Congresses, distinguished between the need for a warrant to search for contraband concealed in "a dwelling house or

---

[22] When Officer Coleman returned with a warrant, the apartment was searched and bags of marijuana were found there. We are here concerned, of course, only with what was discovered in the automobile.

similar place" and the need for a warrant to search for contraband concealed in a movable vessel.

In *Ross*, we held that a warrantless search of an automobile under the *Carroll* doctrine could include a search of a container or package found inside the car when such a search was supported by probable cause. The warrantless search of Ross' car occurred after an informant told the police that he had seen Ross complete a drug transaction using drugs stored in the trunk of his car. The police stopped the car, searched it, and discovered in the trunk a brown paper bag containing drugs. We decided that the search of Ross' car was not unreasonable under the Fourth Amendment: "The scope of a warrantless search based on probable cause is no narrower — and no broader — than the scope of a search authorized by a warrant supported by probable cause." Thus, "[i]f probable cause justifies the search of a lawfully stopped vehicle, it justifies the search of every part of the vehicle and its contents that may conceal the object of the search." In *Ross*, therefore, we clarified the scope of the *Carroll* doctrine as properly including a "probing search" of compartments and containers within the automobile so long as the search is supported by probable cause.

In addition to this clarification, *Ross* endeavored to distinguish between *Carroll*, which governed the *Ross* automobile search, and *Chadwick*, which governed the *Sanders* automobile search. It held that the *Carroll* doctrine covered searches of automobiles when the police had probable cause to search an entire vehicle but that the *Chadwick* doctrine governed searches of luggage when the officers had probable cause to search only a container within the vehicle. Thus, in a *Ross* situation, the police could conduct a reasonable search under the Fourth Amendment without obtaining a warrant, whereas in a *Sanders* situation, the police had to obtain a warrant before they searched.

The dissent is correct, of course, that *Ross* involved the scope of an automobile search. *Ross* held that closed containers encountered by the police during a warrantless search of a car pursuant to the automobile exception could also be searched. Thus, this Court in *Ross* took the critical step of saying that closed containers in cars could be searched without a warrant because of their presence within the automobile. Despite the protection that *Sanders* purported to extend to closed containers, the privacy interest in those closed containers yielded to the broad scope of an automobile search.

III

The facts in this case closely resemble the facts in *Ross*. In *Ross*, the police had probable cause to believe that drugs were stored in the trunk of a particular car. Here, the California Court of Appeal concluded that the police had probable cause to believe that respondent was carrying marijuana in a bag in his car's trunk. Furthermore, for what it is worth, in *Ross*, as here, the drugs in the trunk were contained in a brown paper bag.

This Court in *Ross* rejected *Chadwick*'s distinction between containers and cars. It concluded that the expectation of privacy in one's vehicle is equal to one's expectation of privacy in the container, and noted that "the privacy interests in a car's trunk or glove compartment may be no less than those in a movable container." It also recognized that it was arguable that the same exigent circumstances that permit a warrantless search of an automobile would justify the warrantless search of a movable container. In deference to the rule of *Chadwick* and *Sanders*, however, the Court put that question to one side. It concluded that the time and expense of the warrant process would be misdirected if the police could search every cubic inch of an automobile until they discovered a paper sack, at which point the Fourth Amendment required them to take the sack to a magistrate for permission to look inside. We now must decide the question deferred in *Ross*: whether the Fourth Amendment requires the police to obtain a warrant to open the sack in a movable vehicle simply because they lack probable cause to search the entire car. We conclude that it does not.

IV

Dissenters in *Ross* asked why the suitcase in *Sanders* was "more private, less difficult for police to seize and store, or in any other relevant respect more properly subject to the warrant requirement, than a container that police discover in a probable-cause search of an entire automobile?" We now agree that a container found after a general search of the automobile and a container found in a car after a limited search for the container are equally easy for the police to store and for the suspect to hide or destroy. In fact, we see no principled distinction in terms of either the privacy expectation or the exigent circumstances between the paper bag found by the police in *Ross* and the paper bag found by the police here. Furthermore, by attempting to distinguish between a container for which the police are specifically searching and a container which they come across in a car, we have provided only minimal protection for privacy and have impeded effective law enforcement.

The line between probable cause to search a vehicle and probable cause to search a package in that vehicle is not always clear, and separate rules that govern the two objects to be searched may enable the police to broaden their power to make warrantless searches and disserve privacy interests. We noted this in *Ross* in the context of a search of an entire vehicle. Recognizing that under *Carroll*, the "entire vehicle itself . . . could be searched without a warrant," we concluded that "prohibiting police from opening immediately a container in which the object of the search is most likely to be found and instead forcing them first to comb the entire vehicle would actually exacerbate the intrusion on privacy interests." At the moment when officers stop an automobile, it may be less than clear whether they suspect with a high degree of certainty that the vehicle contains drugs in a bag or simply contains drugs. If the police know that they may open a bag only if they are actually searching the entire car, they may search more extensively than they otherwise would in order to establish the general probable cause required by *Ross*.

Such a situation is not far fetched. In *United States v. Johns*, 469 U.S. 478 (1985), customs agents saw two trucks drive to a private airstrip and approach two small planes. The agents drew near the trucks, smelled marijuana, and then saw in the backs of the trucks packages wrapped in a manner that marijuana smugglers customarily employed. The agents took the trucks to headquarters and searched the packages without a warrant. Relying on *Chadwick*, the defendants argued that the search was unlawful. The defendants contended that *Ross* was inapplicable because the agents lacked probable cause to search anything but the packages themselves and supported this contention by noting that a search of the entire vehicle never occurred. We rejected that argument and found *Chadwick* and *Sanders* inapposite because the agents had probable cause to search the entire body of each truck, although they had chosen not to do so. We cannot see the benefit of a rule that requires law enforcement officers to conduct a more intrusive search in order to justify a less intrusive one.

To the extent that the *Chadwick-Sanders* rule protects privacy, its protection is minimal. Law enforcement officers may seize a container and hold it until they obtain a search warrant. "Since the police, by hypothesis, have probable cause to seize the property, we can assume that a warrant will be routinely forthcoming in the overwhelming majority of cases." *Sanders* (dissenting opinion). And the police often will be able to search containers without a warrant, despite the *Chadwick-Sanders* rule, as a search incident to a lawful arrest. In *New York v. Belton* (Sec. C. *infra*), the Court said: "[W]e hold that when a policeman has made a lawful custodial arrest of the occupant of an automobile, he may, as a contemporaneous incident of that arrest, search the passenger compartment of that automobile. "It follows from this conclusion that the police may also examine the contents of any containers found within the passenger compartment." Under *Belton*, the same probable cause to believe that a container holds drugs will allow the police to arrest the person transporting the container and search it.

Finally, the search of a paper bag intrudes far less on individual privacy than does the incursion sanctioned long ago in *Carroll*. In that case, prohibition agents slashed the upholstery of the automobile. This Court nonetheless found their search to be reasonable under the Fourth Amendment. If destroying the interior of an automobile is not unreasonable, we cannot conclude that looking inside a closed container is. In light of the minimal protection to privacy afforded by the *Chadwick-Sanders* rule, and our serious doubt whether that rule substantially serves privacy interests, we now hold that the Fourth Amendment does not compel separate treatment for an automobile search that extends only to a container within the vehicle.

V

The *Chadwick-Sanders* rule not only has failed to protect privacy but it has also confused courts and police officers and impeded effective law enforcement. The conflict between the *Carroll* doctrine cases and the *Chadwick-Sanders* line has been criticized in academic commentary. One leading authority on the Fourth Amendment, after comparing *Chadwick* and *Sanders* with *Carroll* and its progeny, observed: "These two lines of authority cannot be completely reconciled, and thus how one comes out in the container-in-the-car situation depends upon which line of authority is used as a point of departure." 3 W. LaFave, Search & Seizure 53 (2d ed. 1987).

The discrepancy between the two rules has led to confusion for law enforcement officers. For example, when an officer, who has developed probable cause to believe that a vehicle contains drugs, begins to search the vehicle and immediately discovers a closed container, which rule applies? The defendant will argue that the fact that the officer first chose to search the container indicates that his probable cause extended only to the container and that *Chadwick* and *Sanders* therefore require a warrant. On the other hand, the fact that the officer first chose to search in the most obvious location should not restrict the propriety of the search. The *Chadwick* rule, as applied in *Sanders*, has devolved into an anomaly such that the more likely the police are to discover drugs in a container, the less authority they have to search it. We have noted the virtue of providing " ' "clear and unequivocal" guidelines to the law enforcement profession.' " The *Chadwick-Sanders* rule is the antithesis of a " 'clear and unequivocal' guideline."

The dissent argues that law enforcement has not been impeded because the Court has decided 29 Fourth Amendment cases since *Ross* in favor of the government. In each of these cases, the government appeared as the petitioner. The dissent fails to explain how the loss of 29 cases below, not to mention the many others which this Court did not hear, did not interfere with law enforcement. The fact that the state courts and the federal courts of appeals have been reversed in their Fourth Amendment holdings 29 times since 1982 further demonstrates the extent to which our Fourth Amendment jurisprudence has confused the courts.

The *Chadwick* dissenters predicted that the container rule would have "the perverse result of allowing fortuitous circumstances to control the outcome" of various searches. The rule also was so confusing that within two years after *Chadwick*, this Court found it necessary to expound on the meaning of that decision and explain its application to luggage in general. *Sanders*. Again, dissenters bemoaned the "inherent opaqueness" of the difference between the *Carroll* and *Chadwick* principles and noted "the confusion to be created for all concerned." Three years after *Sanders*, we returned in *Ross* to "this troubled area," in order to assert that Sanders had not cut back on Carroll.

Although we have recognized firmly that the doctrine of *stare decisis* serves profoundly important purposes in our legal system, this Court has overruled a prior case on the comparatively rare occasion when it has bred confusion or been a derelict or led to anomalous results. *Sanders* was explicitly undermined in Ross, and the existence of the dual regimes for automobile searches that uncover containers has proved as confusing as the *Chadwick* and *Sanders* dissenters predicted. We conclude that it is better to adopt one clear-cut rule to govern automobile searches and eliminate the warrant requirement for closed containers set forth in *Sanders*.

VI

The interpretation of the *Carroll* doctrine set forth in *Ross* now applies to all searches of containers found in an automobile. In other words, the police may search without a warrant if their search is supported by probable cause. The Court in *Ross* put it this way: "The scope of a warrantless search of an automobile . . . is not defined by the nature of the container in which the contraband is secreted. Rather, it is defined by the object of the search and the places in which there is probable cause to believe that it may be found." It went on to note: "Probable cause to believe that a container placed in the trunk of a taxi contains contraband or evidence does not justify a search of the entire cab." We reaffirm that principle. In the case before us, the police had probable cause to believe that the paper bag in the automobile's trunk contained marijuana. That probable cause now allows a warrantless search of the paper bag. The facts in the record reveal that the police did not have probable cause to believe that contraband was hidden in any other part of the automobile and a search of the entire vehicle would have been without probable cause and unreasonable under the Fourth Amendment.

Our holding today neither extends the *Carroll* doctrine nor broadens the scope of the permissible automobile search delineated in *Carroll, Chambers*, and *Ross*. It remains a "cardinal principle that 'searches conducted outside the judicial process, without prior approval by judge or magistrate, are per se unreasonable under the Fourth Amendment — subject only to a few specifically established and well-delineated exceptions.'" We held in *Ross*: "The exception recognized in *Carroll* is unquestionably one that is 'specifically established and well delineated.'"

Until today, this Court has drawn a curious line between the search of an automobile that coincidentally turns up a container and the search of a container that coincidentally turns up in an automobile. The protections of the Fourth Amendment must not turn on such coincidences. We therefore interpret *Carroll* as providing one rule to govern all automobile searches. The police may search an automobile and the containers within it where they have probable cause to believe contraband or evidence is contained.

The judgment of the California Court of Appeal is reversed and the case is remanded to that court for further proceedings not inconsistent with this opinion.

JUSTICE SCALIA, concurring in the judgment.

I agree with the dissent that it is anomalous for a briefcase to be protected by the "general requirement" of a prior warrant when it is being carried along the street, but for that same briefcase to become unprotected as soon as it is carried into an automobile. On the other hand, I agree with the Court that it would be anomalous for a locked compartment in an automobile to be unprotected by the "general requirement" of a prior warrant, but for an unlocked briefcase within the automobile to be protected. I join in the judgment of the Court because I think its holding is more faithful to the text and tradition of the Fourth Amendment, and if these anomalies in our jurisprudence are ever to be eliminated that is the direction in which we should travel.

The Fourth Amendment does not by its terms require a prior warrant for searches and seizures; it merely prohibits searches and seizures that are "unreasonable." What it explicitly states regarding warrants is by way of limitation upon their issuance rather than requirement of their use. For the warrant was a means of insulating officials from personal liability assessed by colonial juries. An officer who searched or seized without a warrant did so at his own risk; he would be liable for trespass, including exemplary damages, unless the jury found that his action was "reasonable." If, however, the officer acted pursuant to a proper warrant, he would be absolutely immune. By restricting the issuance of warrants, the Framers endeavored to preserve the jury's role in regulating searches and seizures.

Although the Fourth Amendment does not explicitly impose the requirement of a warrant, it is of course textually possible to consider that implicit within the requirement of reasonableness. For some years after the (still continuing) explosion in Fourth Amendment litigation that followed our announcement of the exclusionary rule in Weeks v. United States, 232 U.S. 383 (1914), our jurisprudence lurched back and forth between imposing a categorical warrant requirement and looking to reasonableness alone. By the late 1960's, the preference for a warrant had won out, at least rhetorically. See *Chimel; Coolidge.*

The victory was illusory. Even before today's decision, the "warrant requirement" had become so riddled with exceptions that it was basically unrecognizable. In 1985, one commentator cataloged nearly 20 such exceptions, including "searches incident to arrest . . . automobile searches . . . border searches . . . administrative searches of regulated businesses . . . exigent circumstances . . . search[es] incident to nonarrest when there is probable cause to arrest . . . boat boarding for document checks . . . welfare searches . . . inventory searches . . . airport searches . . . school search[es] . . . ." Bradley, Two Models of the Fourth Amendment, 83 Mich. L. Rev. 1468, 1473–1474 (1985). Since then, we have added at least two more. *Carney* (searches of mobile homes); *O'Connor v. Ortega*, 480 U.S. 709 (1987) (searches of offices of government employees). Our intricate body of law regarding "reasonable expectation of privacy" has been developed largely as a means of creating these exceptions, enabling a search to be denominated not a Fourth Amendment "search" and therefore not subject to the general warrant requirement.

Unlike the dissent, therefore, I do not regard today's holding as some momentous departure, but rather as merely the continuation of an inconsistent jurisprudence that has been with us for years. Cases like *Chadwick* and *Sanders* have taken the "preference for a warrant" seriously, while cases like *Ross* and *Carroll* have not. There can be no clarity in this area unless we make up our minds, and unless the principles we express comport with the actions we take.

In my view, the path out of this confusion should be sought by returning to the first principle that the "reasonableness" requirement of the Fourth Amendment affords the protection that the common law afforded. I have no difficulty with the proposition that that includes the requirement of a warrant, where the common law required a warrant; and it may even be that changes in the surrounding legal rules (for example, elimination of the common- law rule that reasonable, good-faith belief was no defense to absolute liability for trespass) may make a warrant indispensable to reasonableness where it once was not. But the supposed "general rule" that a warrant is always required does not appear to have any basis in the common law, and confuses rather than facilitates any attempt to develop rules of reasonableness in light of changed legal circumstances, as the anomaly eliminated and the anomaly created by today's holding both demonstrate.

And there are more anomalies still. Under our precedents (as at common law), a person may be arrested outside the home on the basis of probable cause, without an arrest warrant. *Watson.* Upon arrest, the person, as well as the area within his grasp, may be searched for evidence related to the crime. *Chimel.* Under these principles, if a known drug dealer is carrying a briefcase reasonably believed to contain marijuana (the unauthorized possession of which is a crime), the police may arrest him and search his person on the basis of probable cause alone. And, under our precedents, upon arrival at the station house, the police may inventory his possessions, including the briefcase, even if there is no reason to suspect that they contain contraband. *Illinois v. Lafayette*, 462 U.S. 640 (1983). According to our current law, however, the police may not, on the basis of the same probable cause, take the less intrusive step of stopping the individual on the street and demanding to see the contents of his briefcase. That makes no sense *a priori*, and in the absence of any common-law tradition supporting such a distinction, I see no reason to continue it.

*   *   *

I would reverse the judgment in the present case, not because a closed container carried inside a car becomes subject to the "automobile" exception to the general warrant requirement, but because the search of a closed container, outside a privately owned building, with probable cause to believe that the container contains contraband, and when it in fact does contain contraband, is not one of those searches whose Fourth Amendment reasonableness depends upon a warrant. For that reason I concur in the judgment of the Court.

JUSTICE STEVENS, with whom JUSTICE MARSHALL, joins; and with whom JUSTICE WHITE substantially joins, dissenting.

At the end of its opinion, the Court pays lip service to the proposition that should provide the basis for a correct analysis of the legal question presented by this case: It is " 'a cardinal principle that "searches conducted outside the judicial process, without prior approval by judge or magistrate, are *per se* unreasonable under the Fourth Amendment — subject only to a few specifically established and well-delineated exceptions." ' "

Relying on arguments that conservative judges have repeatedly rejected in past cases, the Court today — despite its disclaimer to the contrary, enlarges the scope of the automobile exception to this "cardinal principle," which undergirded our Fourth Amendment jurisprudence prior to the retirement of the author of the landmark opinion in *Chadwick*.* As a preface to my response to the Court's arguments, it is appropriate to restate the basis for the warrant requirement, the significance of the *Chadwick* case, and the reasons why the limitations on the automobile exception that were articulated in *Ross*, represent a fair accommodation between the basic rule requiring prior judicial approval of searches and the automobile exception.

I

The Fourth Amendment is a restraint on Executive power. The Amendment constitutes the Framers' direct constitutional response to the unreasonable law enforcement practices employed by agents of the British Crown. Over the years —

---

* [Justice Stevens reference is to Chief Justice Burger. — Ed.]

particularly in the period immediately after World War II and particularly in opinions authored by Justice Jackson after his service as a special prosecutor at the Nuremburg trials — the Court has recognized the importance of this restraint as a bulwark against police practices that prevail in totalitarian regimes.

This history is, however, only part of the explanation for the warrant requirement. The requirement also reflects the sound policy judgment that, absent exceptional circumstances, the decision to invade the privacy of an individual's personal effects should be made by a neutral magistrate rather than an agent of the Executive. In his opinion for the Court in *Johnson v. United States*, Justice Jackson explained: "The point of the Fourth Amendment, which often is not grasped by zealous officers, is not that it denies law enforcement the support of the usual inferences which reasonable men draw from evidence. Its protection consists in requiring that those inferences be drawn by a neutral and detached magistrate instead of being judged by the officer engaged in the often competitive enterprise of ferreting out crime."

Our decisions have always acknowledged that the warrant requirement imposes a burden on law enforcement. And our cases have not questioned that trained professionals normally make reliable assessments of the existence of probable cause to conduct a search. We have repeatedly held, however, that these factors are outweighed by the individual interest in privacy that is protected by advance judicial approval. The Fourth Amendment dictates that the privacy interest is paramount, no matter how marginal the risk of error might be if the legality of warrantless searches were judged only after the fact.

In the concluding paragraph of his opinion in *Chadwick*, Chief Justice Burger made the point this way: "Even though on this record the issuance of a warrant by a judicial officer was reasonably predictable, a line must be drawn. In our view, when no exigency is shown to support the need for an immediate search, the Warrant Clause places the line at the point where the property to be searched comes under the exclusive dominion of police authority. Respondents were therefore entitled to the protection of the Warrant Clause with the evaluation of a neutral magistrate, before their privacy interests in the contents of [their luggage] were invaded."

Two Terms after Chadwick, we decided [*Sanders*], a case in which the relevant facts were identical to those before the Court today.

Chief Justice Burger wrote separately to identify the distinction between cases in which police have probable cause to believe contraband is located somewhere in a vehicle — the typical automobile exception case — and cases like *Chadwick* and *Sanders* in which they had probable cause to search a particular container before it was placed in the car. He wrote: "Because the police officers had probable cause to believe that respondent's green suitcase contained marihuana before it was placed in the trunk of the taxicab, their duty to obtain a search warrant before opening it is clear under *Chadwick*. The essence of our holding in *Chadwick* is that there is a legitimate expectation of privacy in the contents of a trunk or suitcase accompanying or being carried by a person; that expectation of privacy is not diminished simply because the owner's arrest occurs in a public place. Whether arrested in a hotel lobby, an airport, a railroad terminal, or on a public street, as here, the owner has the right to expect that the contents of his luggage will not, without his consent, be exposed on demand of the police. . . . "The breadth of the Court's opinion and its repeated references to the 'automobile' from which respondent's suitcase was seized at the time of his arrest, however, might lead the reader to believe — as the dissenters apparently do — that this case involves the 'automobile' exception to the warrant requirement. It does not. Here, as in *Chadwick*, it was the *luggage* being transported by respondent at the time of the arrest, not the automobile in which it was being carried, that was the suspected locus of the contraband." (Burger, C.J., concurring in judgment).

Chief Justice Burger thus carefully explained that *Sanders*, which the Court overrules today, "simply d[id] not present the question of whether a warrant is required before opening luggage when the police have probable cause to believe contraband is located somewhere in the vehicle, but when they do not know whether, for example, it is inside a piece of luggage in the trunk, in the glove compartment, or concealed in some part of the car's structure."

We held in *Ross* that "the scope of the warrantless search authorized by [the automobile] exception is no broader and no narrower than a magistrate could legitimately authorize by warrant." The inherent mobility of the vehicle justified the immediate search without a warrant, but did not affect the scope of the search. Thus, the search could encompass containers, which might or might not conceal the object of the search, as well as the remainder of the vehicle.

Our conclusion was supported not only by prior cases defining the proper scope of searches authorized by warrant, as well as cases involving the automobile exception, but also by practical considerations that apply to searches in which the police have only generalized probable cause to believe that contraband is somewhere in a vehicle. We explained that, in such instances, "prohibiting police from opening immediately a container in which the object of the search is most likely to be found and instead forcing them first to comb the entire vehicle would actually exacerbate the intrusion on privacy interests." Indeed, because "the police could never be certain that the contraband was not secreted in a yet undiscovered portion of the vehicle," the most likely result would be that "the vehicle would need to be secured while a warrant was obtained."

These concerns that justified our holding in *Ross* are not implicated in cases like *Chadwick* and *Sanders* in which the police have probable cause to search a *particular* container rather than the *entire* vehicle. Because the police can seize the container which is the object of their search, they have no need either to search or to seize the entire vehicle. Indeed, as even the Court today recognizes, they have no authority to do so.

In reaching our conclusion in *Ross*, we therefore did not retreat at all from the holding in either *Chadwick* or *Sanders*. Instead, we expressly endorsed the reasoning in Chief Justice Burger's separate opinion in *Sanders*. We explained repeatedly that *Ross* involved the scope of the warrantless search authorized by the automobile exception, and, unlike *Chadwick* and *Sanders*, did not involve the applicability of the exception to closed containers.

Thus, we recognized in *Ross* that *Chadwick* and *Sanders* had not created a special rule for container searches, but rather had merely applied the cardinal principle that warrantless searches are per se unreasonable unless justified by an exception to the general rule.[8] *Ross* dealt with the scope of the automobile exception; *Chadwick* and *Sanders* were cases in which the exception simply did not apply.

II

In its opinion today, the Court recognizes that the police did not have probable cause to search respondent's vehicle and that a search of anything but the paper bag that respondent had carried from Daza's apartment and placed in the trunk of his car would have been unconstitutional. Moreover, as I read the opinion, the Court assumes that the police could not have made a warrantless inspection of the bag before it was placed in the car. Finally, the Court also does not question the fact that, under our prior cases, it would have been lawful for the police to seize the container and detain it (and respondent) until they obtained a search warrant. Thus, all of the relevant facts that governed our decisions in *Chadwick* and *Sanders* are present here whereas the relevant fact that justified the vehicle search in *Ross* is not present.

The Court does not attempt to identify any exigent circumstances that would justify its refusal to apply the general rule against warrantless searches. Instead, it advances these three arguments: First, the rules identified in the foregoing cases are confusing and anomalous. Second, the rules do not protect any significant interest in privacy. And, third, the rules impede effective law enforcement. None of these arguments withstands scrutiny.

The "Confusion"

In the case the Court decides today, the California Court of Appeal also had no difficulty applying the critical distinction. Relying on *Chadwick*, it explained that "the officers had probable cause to believe marijuana would be found only in a brown lunch bag and nowhere else in the car. We are compelled to hold they should have obtained a search warrant before opening it."

In the case in which the police had probable cause to search two vehicles, *Johns*, we rejected the respondent's reliance on *Chadwick* with a straightforward explanation of why that case, unlike *Ross*, did not involve an exception to the warrant requirement. We first expressed our agreement with the Court of Appeals that the Customs officers who had conducted the search had probable cause to search the vehicles. We then explained:

---

[8] Although the Court today purports to acknowledge that the warrant requirement is the general rule, it nonetheless inexplicably persists in referring to *Chadwick* and *Sanders* as announcing a "separate rule, unique to luggage and other closed packages, bags, and containers." Equally inexplicable is the Court's contention that, in overruling *Sanders*, it has not "extend[ed] the *Carroll* doctrine" that created the automobile exception.

"Under the circumstances of this case, respondents' reliance on *Chadwick* is misplaced. . . . *Chadwick* . . . did not involve the exception to the warrant requirement recognized in *Carroll* because the police had no probable cause to believe that the automobile, as contrasted to the footlocker, contained contraband. This point is underscored by our decision in *Ross*, which held that notwithstanding *Chadwick* police officers may conduct a warrantless search of containers discovered in the course of a lawful vehicle search. Given our conclusion that the Customs officers had probable cause to believe that the pickup trucks contained contraband, *Chadwick* is simply inapposite.

The decided cases thus provide no support for the Court's concern about "confusion." The Court instead relies primarily on predictions that were made by Justice BLACKMUN in his dissenting opinions in *Chadwick* and *Sanders*. The Court, however, cites no evidence that these predictions have in fact materialized or that anyone else has been unable to understand the "inherent opaqueness" of this uncomplicated issue. The only support offered by the Court, other than the unsubstantiated allegations of prior dissents, is three law review comments and a sentence from Professor LaFave's treatise. None of the law review pieces criticizes the holdings in *Chadwick* and *Sanders*. The sentence from Professor LaFave's treatise, at most, indicates that, as is often the case, there may be some factual situations at the margin of the relevant rules that are difficult to decide. Moreover, to the extent Professor LaFave criticizes our jurisprudence in this area, he is critical of *Ross* rather than *Chadwick* or *Sanders*. And he ultimately concludes that even *Ross* was correctly decided.

The Court summarizes the alleged "anomaly" created by the coexistence of *Ross*, *Chadwick*, and *Sanders* with the statement that "the more likely the police are to discover drugs in a container, the less authority they have to search it." This juxtaposition is only anomalous, however, if one accepts the flawed premise that the degree to which the police are likely to discover contraband is correlated with their authority to search *without a warrant*. Yet, even proof beyond a reasonable doubt will not justify a warrantless search that is not supported by one of the exceptions to the warrant requirement. And, even when the police have a warrant or an exception applies, once the police possess probable cause, the extent to which they are more or less certain of the contents of a container has no bearing on their authority to search it.

To the extent there was any "anomaly" in our prior jurisprudence, the Court has "cured" it at the expense of creating a more serious paradox. For, surely it is anomalous to prohibit a search of a briefcase while the owner is carrying it exposed on a public street yet to permit a search once the owner has placed the briefcase in the locked trunk of his car. One's privacy interest in one's luggage can certainly not be diminished by one's removing it from a public thoroughfare and placing it — out of sight — in a privately owned vehicle. Nor is the danger that evidence will escape increased if the luggage is in a car rather than on the street. In either location, if the police have probable cause, they are authorized to seize the luggage and to detain it until they obtain judicial approval for a search. Any line demarking an exception to the warrant requirement will appear blurred at the edges, but the Court has certainly erred if it believes that, by erasing one line and drawing another, it has drawn a clearer boundary.

The Privacy Argument

The Court's statement that *Chadwick* and *Sanders* provide only "minimal protection to privacy" is also unpersuasive. Every citizen clearly has an interest in the privacy of the contents of his or her luggage, briefcase, handbag or any other container that conceals private papers and effects from public scrutiny. That privacy interest has been recognized repeatedly in cases spanning more than a century.

Under the Court's holding today, the privacy interest that protects the contents of a suitcase or a briefcase from a warrantless search when it is in public view simply vanishes when its owner climbs into a taxicab. Unquestionably the rejection of the *Sanders* line of cases by today's decision will result in a significant loss of individual privacy.

To support its argument that today's holding works only a minimal intrusion on privacy, the Court suggests that "[i]f the police know that they may open a bag only if they are actually searching the entire car, they may search more extensively than they otherwise would in order to establish the general probable cause required by *Ross*." [T]his fear is unexplained and inexplicable. Neither evidence uncovered in the course of a search nor the scope of the search conducted can be used to provide *post hoc* justification for a search unsupported by probable cause at its inception.

The Court also justifies its claim that its holding inflicts only minor damage by suggesting that, under *Belton*, the police could have arrested respondent and searched his bag if respondent had placed the bag in the passenger compartment of the automobile instead of the trunk. In *Belton*, however, the justification for stopping the car and arresting the driver had nothing to do with the subsequent search, which was based on the potential danger to the arresting officer.

The Burden on Law Enforcement

The Court's suggestion that *Chadwick* and *Sanders* have created a significant burden on effective law enforcement is unsupported, inaccurate, and, in any event, an insufficient reason for creating a new exception to the warrant requirement.

Despite repeated claims that *Chadwick* and *Sanders* have "impeded effective law enforcement," the Court cites no authority for its contentions. Moreover, all evidence that does exist points to the contrary conclusion. In the years since *Ross* was decided, the Court has heard argument in 30 Fourth Amendment cases involving narcotics. In all but one, the government was the petitioner. All save two involved a search or seizure without a warrant or with a defective warrant. And, in all except three, the Court upheld the constitutionality of the search or seizure.

In the meantime, the flow of narcotics cases through the courts has steadily and dramatically increased. No impartial observer could criticize this Court for hindering the progress of the war on drugs. On the contrary, decisions like the one the Court makes today will support the conclusion that this Court has become a loyal foot soldier in the Executive's fight against crime.

Even if the warrant requirement does inconvenience the police to some extent, that fact does not distinguish this constitutional requirement from any other procedural protection secured by the Bill of Rights. It is merely a part of the price that our society must pay in order to preserve its freedom. Thus, in a unanimous opinion that relied on both *Johnson* and *Chadwick*, Justice Stewart wrote: "Moreover, the mere fact that law enforcement may be made more efficient can never by itself justify disregard of the Fourth Amendment. The investigation of crime would always be simplified if warrants were unnecessary. But the Fourth Amendment reflects the view of those who wrote the Bill of Rights that the privacy of a person's home and property may not be totally sacrificed in the name of maximum simplicity in enforcement of the criminal law." *Mincey v. Arizona* (1978).

It is too early to know how much freedom America has lost today. The magnitude of the loss is, however, not nearly as significant as the Court's willingness to inflict it without even a colorable basis for its rejection of prior law.

I respectfully dissent.

QUESTIONS AND NOTES

1.   Is *Chadwick* still good law?

2.   Would our jurisprudence be improved if the Court forthrightly adopted the Scalia approach? What, if anything, would be lost?

3.   Did Justice Scalia really mean to make anything turn on whether, *in fact*, evidence was found in the bag? Is Scalia suggesting that if the probable cause turned out to be wrong, and that Acevedo merely had lunch in his bag, that Acevedo could sue the police officer?

4.   If the Stevens opinion had prevailed, and the *Sanders-Ross* dichotomy had been maintained, what would (should) have been the result in a case in which a reliable informant tells a police officer that a particular individual has drugs in a suitcase, *currently* in the trunk of a particularly described car?

5.   Does the Court's opinion bring clarity to the area? Was it all that confused to begin with?

6.   What, if any, costs are associated with the Court's opinion?

7.   With which (if any) of the opinions would you have concurred? Explain.

8.   Having finally resolved the question of the right to search a driver's luggage, the Court tackled the issue of a passenger's luggage in *Wyoming v. Houghton.*

PROBLEM
WYOMING v. HOUGHTON

In the early morning hours of July 23, 1995, a Wyoming Highway Patrol officer stopped an automobile for speeding and driving with a faulty brake light. There were three passengers in the front seat of the car: David Young (the driver), his girlfriend, and respondent. While questioning Young, the officer noticed a hypodermic syringe in Young's shirt pocket. He left the occupants under the supervision of two backup officers as he went to get gloves from his patrol car. Upon his return, he instructed Young to step out of the car and place the syringe on the hood. The officer then asked Young why he had a syringe; with refreshing candor, Young replied that he used it to take drugs.

At this point, the backup officers ordered the two female passengers out of the car and asked them for identification. Respondent falsely identified herself as "Sandra James" and stated that she did not have any identification. Meanwhile, in light of Young's admission, the officer searched the passenger compartment of the car for contraband. On the back seat, he found a purse, which respondent claimed as hers. He removed from the purse a wallet containing respondent's driver's license, identifying her properly as Sandra K. Houghton. When the officer asked her why she had lied about her name, she replied: "In case things went bad."

Continuing his search of the purse, the officer found a brown pouch and a black wallet-type container. Respondent denied that the former was hers, and claimed ignorance of how it came to be there; it was found to contain drug paraphernalia and a syringe with 60 ccs of methamphetamine. Respondent admitted ownership of the black container, which was also found to contain drug paraphernalia, and a syringe (which respondent acknowledged was hers) with 10 ccs of methamphetamine — an amount insufficient to support the felony conviction at issue in this case. The officer also found fresh needle-track marks on respondent's arms. He placed her under arrest.

The State of Wyoming charged respondent with felony possession of methamphetamine in a liquid amount greater than three-tenths of a gram. See Wyo. Stat. Ann. 35-7-1031(c)(iii) (Supp. 1996). After a hearing, the trial court denied her motion to suppress all evidence obtained from the purse as the fruit of a violation of the Fourth and Fourteenth Amendments. The court held that the officer had probable cause to search the car for contraband, and, by extension, any containers therein that could hold such contraband. A jury convicted respondent as charged.

The Wyoming Supreme Court, by divided vote, reversed the conviction and announced the following rule:

> Generally, once probable cause is established to search a vehicle, an officer is entitled to search all containers therein which may contain the object of the search. However, if the officer knows or should know that a container is the personal effect of a passenger who is not suspected of criminal activity, then the container is outside the scope of the search unless someone had the opportunity to conceal the contraband within the personal effect to avoid detection.

The court held that the search of respondent's purse violated the Fourth and Fourteenth Amendments because the officer "knew or should have known that the purse did not belong to the driver, but to one of the passengers," and because "there was no probable cause to search the passengers' personal effects and no reason to believe that contraband had been placed within the purse."

Should Houghton's conviction be reinstated? Why? Why not? Would your answer be any different if Young were a bus driver? Why? Why not? Would it matter if Houghton's person were searched? If the bag were attached to her person? Explain. For the Supreme Court's resolution, see *Wyoming v. Houghton*, 526 U.S. 295 (1999).

C. SEARCH INCIDENT TO ARREST IN AN AUTOMOBILE

In addition to probable cause searches of automobiles (and containers within automobiles), a *Chimel* search incident to arrest can occur when an individual is arrested in or near his automobile (or presumably, motor home). For a time, it appeared that the scope of such a search might exceed the bounds set out by *Chimel*. In *New York v. Belton*, 453 U.S. 454 (1981), the Court held that a search incident to arrest of somebody arrested in his automobile can include the entire passenger compartment of the automobile. Then, in *Thornton v. United States*, 541 U.S. 615 (2004), the court expanded *Belton* to arrests outside of the car of which the arrestee was a recent occupant. But in *Arizona v. Gant*, the Court sharply limited (some would argue, overruled) the scope of those decisions.

ARIZONA v. GANT
556 U.S. 332 (2009)

JUSTICE STEVENS delivered the opinion of the Court.

After Rodney Gant was arrested for driving with a suspended license, handcuffed, and locked in the back of a patrol car, police officers searched his car and discovered cocaine in the pocket of a jacket on the backseat. Because Gant could not have accessed his car to retrieve weapons or evidence at the time of the search, the Arizona Supreme Court held that the search-incident-to-arrest exception to the Fourth Amendment's warrant requirement, as defined in *Chimel v. California*, and applied to vehicle searches in *New York v. Belton*, did not justify the search in this case. We agree with that conclusion.

Under *Chimel*, police may search incident to arrest only the space within an arrestee's " 'immediate control,' " meaning "the area from within which he might gain possession of a weapon or destructible evidence." The safety and evidentiary justifications underlying *Chimel*'s reaching-distance rule determine *Belton*'s scope. Accordingly, we hold that *Belton* does not authorize a vehicle search incident to a recent occupant's arrest after the arrestee has been secured and cannot access the interior of the vehicle. Consistent with the holding in *Thornton v. United States*, and following the suggestion in JUSTICE SCALIA's opinion concurring in the judgment in that case, we also conclude that circumstances unique to the automobile context justify a search incident to arrest when it is reasonable to believe that evidence of the offense of arrest might be found in the vehicle.

I

On August 25, 1999, acting on an anonymous tip that the residence at 2524 North Walnut Avenue was being used to sell drugs, Tucson police officers Griffith and Reed knocked on the front door and asked to speak to the owner. Gant answered the door and, after identifying himself, stated that he expected the owner to return later. The officers left the residence and conducted a records check, which revealed that Gant's driver's license had been suspended and there was an outstanding warrant for his arrest for driving with a suspended license. When the officers returned to the house that evening, they found a man near the back of the house and a woman in a car parked in front of it. After a third officer arrived, they arrested the man for providing a false name and the woman for possessing drug paraphernalia. Both arrestees were handcuffed and secured in separate patrol cars when Gant arrived. The officers recognized his car as it entered the driveway, and Officer Griffith confirmed that Gant was the driver by shining a flashlight into the car as it drove by him. Gant parked at the end of the driveway, got out of his car, and shut the door. Griffith, who was about 30 feet away, called to Gant, and they approached each other, meeting 10-to-12 feet from Gant's car. Griffith immediately arrested Gant and handcuffed him.

Because the other arrestees were secured in the only patrol cars at the scene, Griffith called for backup. When two more officers arrived, they locked Gant in the backseat of their vehicle. After Gant had been handcuffed and placed in the back of a patrol car, two officers searched his car: One of them found a gun, and the other discovered a bag of cocaine in the pocket of a jacket on the backseat.

Gant was charged with two offenses — possession of a narcotic drug for sale and possession of drug paraphernalia (*i.e.*, the plastic bag in which the cocaine was found). He moved to suppress the evidence seized from his car on the ground that the warrantless search violated the Fourth Amendment. Among other things, Gant argued that *Belton* did not authorize the search of his vehicle because he posed no threat to the officers after he was handcuffed in the patrol car and because he was arrested for a traffic offense for which no evidence could be found in his vehicle. When asked at the suppression hearing why the search was conducted, Officer Griffith responded: "Because the law says we can do it."

The trial court rejected the State's contention that the officers had probable cause to search Gant's car for contraband when the search began, but it denied the motion to suppress. Relying on the fact that the police saw Gant commit the crime of driving without a license and apprehended him only shortly after he exited his car, the court held that the search was permissible as a search incident to arrest. A jury found Gant guilty on both drug counts, and he was sentenced to a 3 year term of imprisonment.

After protracted state-court proceedings, the Arizona Supreme Court concluded that the search of Gant's car was unreasonable within the meaning of the Fourth Amendment. The court's opinion discussed at length our decision in *Belton*, which held that police may search the passenger compartment of a vehicle and any containers therein as a contemporaneous incident of an arrest of the vehicle's recent occupant. The court distinguished *Belton* as a case concerning the permissible scope of a vehicle search incident to arrest and concluded that it did not answer "the threshold question whether the police may conduct a search incident to arrest at all once the scene is secure." Relying on our earlier decision in *Chimel*, the court observed that the search-incident-to-arrest exception to the warrant requirement is justified by interests in officer safety and evidence preservation. When "the justifications underlying *Chimel* no longer exist because the scene is secure and the arrestee is handcuffed, secured in the back of a patrol car, and under the supervision of an officer," the court concluded, a "warrantless search of the arrestee's car cannot be justified as necessary to protect the officers at the scene or prevent the destruction of evidence." Accordingly, the court held that the search of Gant's car was unreasonable.

The dissenting justices would have upheld the search of Gant's car based on their view that "the validity of a *Belton* search . . . clearly does not depend on the presence of the *Chimel* rationales in a particular case." Although they disagreed with the majority's view of *Belton*, the dissenting justices acknowledged that "[t]he bright-line rule embraced in *Belton* has long been criticized and probably merits reconsideration." They thus "add[ed their] voice[s] to the others that have urged the Supreme Court to revisit *Belton*."

The chorus that has called for us to revisit *Belton* includes courts, scholars, and Members of this Court who have questioned that decision's clarity and its fidelity to Fourth Amendment principles. We therefore granted the State's petition for certiorari.

II

Consistent with our precedent, our analysis begins, as it should in every case addressing the reasonableness of a warrantless search, with the basic rule that "searches conducted outside the judicial process, without prior approval by judge or magistrate, are *per se* unreasonable under the Fourth Amendment — subject only to a few specifically established and well-delineated exceptions." Among the exceptions to the warrant requirement is a search incident to a lawful arrest. The exception derives from interests in officer safety and evidence preservation that are typically implicated in arrest situations.

In *Chimel*, we held that a search incident to arrest may only include "the arrestee's person and the area 'within his immediate control' — construing that phrase to mean the area from within which he might gain possession of a weapon or destructible evidence." That limitation, which continues to define the boundaries of the exception, ensures that the scope of a search incident to arrest is commensurate with its purposes of protecting arresting officers and safeguarding any evidence of the offense of arrest that an arrestee might conceal or destroy.

In *Belton*, we considered *Chimel*'s application to the automobile context. A lone police officer in that case stopped a speeding car in which Belton was one of four occupants. While asking for the driver's license and registration, the officer smelled burnt marijuana and observed an envelope on the car floor marked "Supergold" — a name he associated with marijuana. Thus having probable cause to believe the occupants had committed a drug offense, the officer ordered them out of the vehicle, placed them under arrest, and patted them down. Without handcuffing the arrestees,[9] the officer " 'split them up into four separate areas of the Thruway . . . so they would not be in physical touching area of each other' " and searched the vehicle, including the pocket of a jacket on the backseat, in which he found cocaine.

Focusing on the number of arrestees and their proximity to the vehicle, the State asserted that it was reasonable for the officer to believe the arrestees could have

---

[9] The officer was unable to handcuff the occupants because he had only one set of handcuffs.

accessed the vehicle and its contents, making the search permissible under *Chimel*. There was no suggestion by the parties or *amici* that *Chimel* authorizes a vehicle search incident to arrest when there is no realistic possibility that an arrestee could access his vehicle.

After considering these arguments, we held that when an officer lawfully arrests "the occupant of an automobile, he may, as a contemporaneous incident of that arrest, search the passenger compartment of the automobile" and any containers therein. That holding was based in large part on our assumption "that articles inside the relatively narrow compass of the passenger compartment of an automobile are in fact generally, even if not inevitably, within 'the area into which an arrestee might reach.' "

The Arizona Supreme Court read our decision in *Belton* as merely delineating "the proper scope of a search of the interior of an automobile" incident to an arrest. That is, *when* the passenger compartment is within an arrestee's reaching distance, *Belton* supplies the generalization that the entire compartment and any containers therein may be reached. On that view of *Belton*, the state court concluded that the search of Gant's car was unreasonable because Gant clearly could not have accessed his car at the time of the search. It also found that no other exception to the warrant requirement applied in this case.

Gant now urges us to adopt the reading of *Belton* followed by the Arizona Supreme Court.

III

Despite the textual and evidentiary support for the Arizona Supreme Court's reading of *Belton*, our opinion has been widely understood to allow a vehicle search incident to the arrest of a recent occupant even if there is no possibility the arrestee could gain access to the vehicle at the time of the search. This reading may be attributable to Justice Brennan's dissent in *Belton*, in which he characterized the Court's holding as resting on the "fiction . . . that the interior of a car is *always* within the immediate control of an arrestee who has recently been in the car." Under the majority's approach, he argued, "the result would presumably be the same even if [the officer] had handcuffed Belton and his companions in the patrol car" before conducting the search.

Since we decided *Belton*, Courts of Appeals have given different answers to the question whether a vehicle must be within an arrestee's reach to justify a vehicle search incident to arrest, but Justice Brennan's reading of the Court's opinion has predominated. As Justice O'Connor observed, "lower court decisions seem now to treat the ability to search a vehicle incident to the arrest of a recent occupant as a police entitlement rather than as an exception justified by the twin rationales of *Chimel*." *Thornton*. JUSTICE SCALIA has similarly noted that, although it is improbable that an arrestee could gain access to weapons stored in his vehicle after he has been handcuffed and secured in the backseat of a patrol car, cases allowing a search in "this precise factual scenario . . . are legion." Indeed, some courts have upheld searches under *Belton* "even when . . . the handcuffed arrestee has already left the scene."

Under this broad reading of *Belton*, a vehicle search would be authorized incident to every arrest of a recent occupant notwithstanding that in most cases the vehicle's passenger compartment will not be within the arrestee's reach at the time of the search. To read *Belton* as authorizing a vehicle search incident to every recent occupant's arrest would thus untether the rule from the justifications underlying the *Chimel* exception — a result clearly incompatible with our statement in *Belton* that it "in no way alters the fundamental principles established in the *Chimel* case regarding the basic scope of searches incident to lawful custodial arrests." Accordingly, we reject this reading of *Belton* and hold that the *Chimel* rationale authorizes police to search a vehicle incident to a recent occupant's arrest only when the arrestee is unsecured and within reaching distance of the passenger compartment at the time of the search.[4]

Although it does not follow from *Chimel*, we also conclude that circumstances unique to the vehicle context justify a search incident to a lawful arrest when it is "reasonable to believe evidence relevant to the crime of arrest might be found in the vehicle." *Thornton*, 541 U.S., at 632 (SCALIA, J., concurring in judgment). In many cases, as when a recent occupant is arrested for a traffic violation, there will be no reasonable basis to believe the vehicle contains relevant evidence. But in others, including *Belton* and *Thornton*, the offense of arrest will supply a basis for searching the passenger compartment of an arrestee's vehicle and any containers therein.

Neither the possibility of access nor the likelihood of discovering offense-related evidence authorized the search in this case. Unlike in *Belton*, which involved a single officer confronted with four unsecured arrestees, the five officers in this case outnumbered the three arrestees, all of whom had been handcuffed and secured in separate patrol cars before the officers searched Gant's car. Under those circumstances, Gant clearly was not within reaching distance of his car at the time of the search. An evidentiary basis for the search was also lacking in this case. Whereas Belton and Thornton were arrested for drug offenses, Gant was arrested for driving with a suspended license — an offense for which police could not expect to find evidence in the passenger compartment of Gant's car. Because police could not reasonably have believed either that Gant could have accessed his car at the time of the search or that evidence of the offense for which he was arrested might have been found therein, the search in this case was unreasonable.

IV

The State does not seriously disagree with the Arizona Supreme Court's conclusion that Gant could not have accessed his vehicle at the time of the search, but it nevertheless asks us to uphold the search of his vehicle under the broad reading of *Belton* discussed above. The State argues that *Belton* searches are

---

[4] Because officers have many means of ensuring the safe arrest of vehicle occupants, it will be the rare case in which an officer is unable to fully effectuate an arrest so that a real possibility of access to the arrestee's vehicle remains. Cf. 3 W. LaFave, Search and Seizure § 7.1(c), p. 525 (4th ed. 2004) (hereinafter LaFave) (noting that the availability of protective measures "ensur[es] the nonexistence of circumstances in which the arrestee's 'control' of the car is in doubt").But in such a case a search incident to arrest is reasonable under the Fourth Amendment.

reasonable regardless of the possibility of access in a given case because that expansive rule correctly balances law enforcement interests, including the interest in a bright-line rule, with an arrestee's limited privacy interest in his vehicle. For several reasons, we reject the State's argument. First, the State seriously under-values the privacy interests at stake. Although we have recognized that a motorist's privacy interest in his vehicle is less substantial than in his home, the former interest is nevertheless important and deserving of constitutional protection. It is particularly significant that *Belton* searches authorize police officers to search not just the passenger compartment but every purse, briefcase, or other container within that space. A rule that gives police the power to conduct such a search whenever an individual is caught committing a traffic offense, when there is no basis for believing evidence of the offense might be found in the vehicle, creates a serious and recurring threat to the privacy of countless individuals. Indeed, the character of that threat implicates the central concern underlying the Fourth Amendment — the concern about giving police officers unbridled discretion to rummage at will among a person's private effects.

At the same time as it undervalues these privacy concerns, the State exaggerates the clarity that its reading of *Belton* provides. Courts that have read *Belton* expansively are at odds regarding how close in time to the arrest and how proximate to the arrestee's vehicle an officer's first contact with the arrestee must be to bring the encounter within *Belton*'s purview[6] and whether a search is reason able when it commences or continues after the arrestee has been removed from the scene.[7] The rule has thus generated a great deal of uncertainty, particularly for a rule touted as providing a "bright line."

Contrary to the State's suggestion, a broad reading of *Belton* is also unnecessary to protect law enforcement safety and evidentiary interests. Under our view, *Belton* and *Thornton* permit an officer to conduct a vehicle search when an arrestee is within reaching distance of the vehicle or it is reasonable to believe the vehicle contains evidence of the offense of arrest. Other established exceptions to the warrant requirement authorize a vehicle search under additional circumstances when safety or evidentiary concerns demand. Unlike the searches permitted by JUSTICE SCALIA's opinion concurring in the judgment *Thornton*, which we conclude today are reasonable for purposes of the Fourth Amendment, *Ross* allows searches for evidence relevant to offenses other than the offense of arrest, and the scope of the search authorized is broader. Finally, there may be still other circumstances in

---

[6] Compare *United States* v. *Caseres*, 533 F.3d 1064, 1072 (CA9 2008) (declining to apply *Belton* when the arrestee was approached by police after he had exited his vehicle and reached his residence), with *Rainey* v. *Commonwealth*, 197 S.W.3d 89, 94–95 (Ky. 2006) (applying *Belton* when the arrestee was apprehended 50 feet from the vehicle), and *Black* v. *State*, 810 N.E.2d 713, 716 (Ind. 2004) (applying *Belton* when the arrestee was apprehended inside an auto repair shop and the vehicle was parked outside).

[7] Compare *McLaughlin*, 170 F. 3d, at 890–891 (upholding a search that commenced five minutes after the arrestee was removed from the scene), *United States* v. *Snook*, 88 F.3d 605, 608 (CA8 1996) (same), and *United States* v. *Doward*, 41 F.3d 789, 793 (CA1 1994) (upholding a search that continued after the arrestee was removed from the scene),with *United States* v. *Lugo*, 978 F.2d 631, 634 (CA10 1992) (holding invalid a search that commenced after the arrestee was removed from the scene), and *State* v. *Badgett*, 200 Conn. 412, 427–428, 512 A.2d 160, 169 (1986) (holding invalid a search that continued after the arrestee was removed from the scene).

which safety or evidentiary interests would justify a search. Cf. *Maryland* v. *Buie*, (holding that, incident to arrest, an officer may conduct a limited protective sweep of those areas of a house in which he reasonably suspects a dangerous person may be hiding).

These exceptions together ensure that officers may search a vehicle when genuine safety or evidentiary concerns encountered during the arrest of a vehicle's recent occupant justify a search. Construing *Belton* broadly to allow vehicle searches incident to any arrest would serve no purpose except to provide a police entitlement, and it is anathema to the Fourth Amendment to permit a warrantless search on that basis. For these reasons, we are unpersuaded by the State's arguments that a broad reading of *Belton* would meaningfully further law enforcement interests and justify a substantial intrusion on individuals' privacy.

V

Our dissenting colleagues argue that the doctrine of *stare decisis* requires adherence to a broad reading of *Belton* even though the justifications for searching a vehicle incident to arrest are in most cases absent.* The doctrine of *stare decisis* is of course "essential to the respect accorded to the judgments of the Court and to the stability of the law," but it does not compel us to follow a past decision when its rationale no longer withstands "careful analysis."

We have never relied on *stare decisis* to justify the continuance of an unconstitutional police practice. And we would be particularly loath to uphold an unconstitutional result in a case that is so easily distinguished from the decisions that arguably compel it. The safety and evidentiary interests that supported the search in *Belton* simply are not present in this case. Indeed, it is hard to imagine two cases that are factually more distinct, as *Belton* involved one officer confronted by four unsecured arrestees suspected of committing a drug offense and this case involves several officers confronted with a securely detained arrestee apprehended for driving with a suspended license. This case is also distinguishable from *Thornton*, in which the petitioner was arrested for a drug offense. It is thus unsurprising that Members of this Court who concurred in the judgments in *Belton* and *Thornton* also concur in the decision in this case.[10]

We do not agree with the contention in JUSTICE ALITO's dissent (hereinafter dissent) that consideration of police reliance interests requires a different result. Although I it appears that the State's reading of *Belton* has been widely taught in police academies and that law enforcement officers have relied on the rule in

---

* JUSTICE ALITO's dissenting opinion also accuses us of "overrul[ing]" *Belton* and *Thornton* v. *United States*, 541 U.S. 615 (2004), "even though respondent Gant has not asked us to do so." Contrary to that claim, the narrow reading of *Belton* we adopt today is precisely the result Gant has urged. That JUSTICE ALITO has chosen to describe this decision as overruling our earlier cases does not change the fact that the resulting rule of law is the one advocated by respondent.

[10] JUSTICE STEVENS concurred in the judgment in *Belton*, for the reasons stated in his dissenting opinion in *Robbins* v. *California*, JUSTICE THOMAS joined the Court's opinion in *Thornton*, and JUSTICE SCALIA and JUSTICE GINSBURG concurred in the judgment in that case.

conducting vehicle searches during the past 28 years,[11] many of these searches were not justified by the reasons underlying the *Chimel* exception. Countless individuals guilty of nothing more serious than a traffic violation have had their constitutional right to the security of their private effects violated as a result. The fact that the law enforcement community may view the State's version of the *Belton* rule as an entitlement does not establish the sort of reliance interest that could outweigh the countervailing interest that all individuals share in having their constitutional rights fully protected. If it is clear that a practice is unlawful, individuals' interest in its discontinuance clearly outweighs any law enforcement "entitlement" to its persistence. The dissent's reference in this regard to the reliance interests cited in *Dickerson* v. *United States*, 530 U.S. 428 (2000), is misplaced. In observing that "*Miranda* has become embedded in routine police practice to the point where the warnings have become part of our national culture," the Court was referring not to police reliance on a rule requiring them to provide warnings but to the broader societal reliance on that individual right.

The experience of the 28 years since we decided *Belton* has shown that the generalization underpinning the broad reading of that decision is unfounded. We now know that articles inside the passenger compartment are rarely "within the area, into which an arrestee might reach,'" 453 U.S., at 460, and blind adherence to *Belton*'s faulty assumption would authorize myriad unconstitutional searches. The doctrine of *stare decisis* does not require us to approve routine constitutional violations.

VI

Police may search a vehicle incident to a recent occupant's arrest only if the arrestee is within reaching distance of the passenger compartment at the time of the search or it is reasonable to believe the vehicle contains evidence of the offense of arrest. When these justifications are absent, a search of an arrestee's vehicle will be unreasonable unless police obtain a warrant or show that another exception to the warrant requirement applies. The Arizona Supreme Court correctly held that this case involved an unreasonable search. Accordingly, the judgment of the State Supreme Court is affirmed.

It is so ordered.

JUSTICE SCALIA, concurring.

To determine what is an "unreasonable" search within the meaning of the Fourth Amendment, we look first to the historical practices the Framers sought to preserve; if those provide inadequate guidance, we apply traditional standards of reasonableness. It is abundantly clear that those standards do not justify what I take to be the rule set forth in *Belton* and *Thornton*: that arresting officers may always search an arrestee's vehicle in order to protect themselves from hidden

---

[11] Because a broad reading of *Belton* has been widely accepted, the doctrine of qualified immunity will shield officers from liability for searches conducted in reasonable reliance on that understanding.

weapons. When an arrest is made in connection with a roadside stop, police virtually always have a less intrusive and more effective means of ensuring their safety — and a means that is virtually always employed: ordering the arrestee away from the vehicle, patting him down in the open, handcuffing him, and placing him in the squad car.

Law enforcement officers face a risk of being shot whenever they pull a car over. But that risk is at its height at the time of the initial confrontation; and it is *not at all* reduced by allowing a search of the stopped vehicle after the driver has been arrested and placed in the squad car. I observed in *Thornton* that the government had failed to provide a single instance in which a formerly restrained arrestee escaped to retrieve a weapon from his own vehicle; Arizona and its *amici* have not remedied that significant deficiency in the present case.

It must be borne in mind that we are speaking here only of a rule automatically permitting a search when the driver or an occupant is arrested. Where no arrest is made, we have held that officers may search the car if they reasonably believe "the suspect is dangerous and . . . may gain immediate control of weapons." *Michigan v. Long*, 463 U.S. 1032, 1049 (1983). In the no-arrest case, the possibility of access to weapons in the vehicle always exists, since the driver or passenger will be allowed to return to the vehicle when the interrogation is completed. The rule of *Michigan v. Long* is not at issue here.

JUSTICE STEVENS acknowledges that an officer-safety rationale cannot justify all vehicle searches incident to arrest, but asserts that that is not the rule *Belton* and *Thornton* adopted. (As described above, I read those cases differently). JUSTICE STEVENS would therefore retain the application of *Chimel*, in the car-search context but would apply in the future what he believes our cases held in the past: that officers making a roadside stop may search the vehicle so long as the "arrestee is within reaching distance of the passenger compartment at the time of the search." I believe that this standard fails to provide the needed guidance to arresting officers and also leaves much room for manipulation, inviting officers to leave the scene unsecured (at least where dangerous suspects are not involved) in order to conduct a vehicle search. In my view we should simply abandon the *Belton-Thornton* charade of officer safety and overrule those cases. I would hold that a vehicle search incident to arrest is *ipso facto* "reasonable" only when the object of the search is evidence of the crime for which the arrest was made, or of another crime that the officer has probable cause to believe occurred. Because respondent was arrested for driving without a license (a crime for which no evidence could be expected to be found in the vehicle), I would hold in the present case that the search was unlawful.

JUSTICE ALITO insists that the Court must demand a good reason for abandoning prior precedent. That is true enough, but it seems to me ample reason that the precedent was badly reasoned and produces erroneous (in this case unconstitutional) results. We should recognize *Belton*'s fanciful reliance upon officer safety for what it was: "a return to the broader sort of [evidence-gathering] search incident to arrest that we allowed before *Chimel*." *Thornton*, (SCALIA, J., concurring in judgment; citations omitted).

JUSTICE ALITO argues that there is no reason to adopt a rule limiting automobile-arrest searches to those cases where the search's object is evidence of the crime of arrest. I disagree. This formulation of officers' authority both preserves the outcomes of our prior cases and tethers the scope and rationale of the doctrine to the triggering event. *Belton*, by contrast, allowed searches precisely when its exigency-based rationale was least applicable: The fact of the arrest in the automobile context makes searches on exigency grounds less reasonable, not more. I also disagree with Justice Alito's conclusory assertion that this standard will be difficult to administer in practice; the ease of its application in this case would suggest otherwise.

No other Justice, however, shares my view that application of *Chimel* in this context should be entirely abandoned. It seems to me unacceptable for the Court to come forth with a 4-to-1-to-4 opinion that leaves the governing rule uncertain. I am therefore confronted with the choice of either leaving the current understanding of *Belton* and *Thornton* in effect, or acceding to what seems to me the artificial narrowing of those cases adopted by Justice Stevens. The latter, as I have said, does not provide the degree of certainty I think desirable in this field; but the former opens the field to what I think are plainly unconstitutional searches — which is the greater evil. I therefore join the opinion of the Court.

Justice Breyer, dissenting.

I agree with Justice Alito that *Belton* is best read as setting forth a bright-line rule that permits a warrantless search of the passenger compartment of an automobile incident to the lawful arrest of an occupant — regardless of the danger the arrested individual in fact poses. I also agree with Justice Stevens, however, that the rule can produce results divorced from its underlying Fourth Amendment rationale. For that reason I would look for a better rule — were the question before us one of first impression.

The matter, however, is not one of first impression, and that fact makes a substantial difference. The *Belton* rule has been followed not only by this Court in *Thornton*, but also by numerous other courts. Principles of *stare decisis* must apply, and those who wish this Court to change a well-established legal precedent — where, as here, there has been considerable reliance on the legal rule in question — bear a heavy burden. I have not found that burden met. Nor do I believe that the other considerations ordinarily relevant when determining whether to overrule a case are satisfied. I consequently join Justice Alito's dissenting opinion with the exception of Part II-E.

Justice Alito, with whom The Chief Justice and Justice Kennedy join, and with whom Justice Breyer joins except as to Part II-E, dissenting.

Twenty-eight years ago, in *New York* v. *Belton*, this Court held that "when a policeman has made a lawful custodial arrest of the occupant of an automobile, he may, as a contemporaneous incident of that arrest, search the passenger compartment of that automobile." Five years ago, in *Thornton* v. *United States*, 541 U.S. 615 (2004) — a case involving a situation not materially distinguishable from the situation here — the Court not only reaffirmed but extended the holding of *Belton*, making it applicable to recent occupants. Today's decision effectively overrules those important decisions, even though respondent Gant has not asked us to do so.

To take the place of the overruled precedents, the Court adopts a new two-part rule under which a police officer who arrests a vehicle occupant or recent occupant may search the passenger compartment if (1) the arrestee is within reaching distance of the vehicle at the time of the search or (2) the officer has reason to believe that the vehicle contains evidence of the offense of arrest.

The first part of this new rule may endanger arresting officers and is truly endorsed by only four Justices; Justice SCALIA joins solely for the purpose of avoiding a "4-to-1-to-4 opinion." The second part of the new rule is taken from Justice SCALIA's separate opinion in *Thornton* without any independent explanation of its origin or justification and is virtually certain to confuse law enforcement officers and judges for some time to come. The Court's decision will cause the suppression of evidence gathered in many searches carried out in good-faith reliance on well-settled case law, and although the Court purports to base its analysis on the landmark decision in *Chimel*, the Court's reasoning undermines *Chimel*. I would follow *Belton*, and I therefore respectfully dissent.

I

Although the Court refuses to acknowledge that it is overruling *Belton* and *Thornton*, there can be no doubt that it does so.

In *Belton*, an officer on the New York Thruway removed the occupants from a car and placed them under arrest but did not handcuff them. The officer then searched a jacket on the car's back seat and found drugs. By a divided vote, the New York Court of Appeals held that the search of the jacket violated *Chimel*, in which this Court held that an arresting officer may search the area within an arrestee's immediate control. The justices of the New York Court of Appeals disagreed on the factual question whether the *Belton* arrestees could have gained access to the car. The majority thought that they could not have done so, but the dissent thought that this was a real possibility.

Viewing this disagreement about the application of the *Chimel* rule as illustrative of a persistent and important problem, the *Belton* Court concluded that " '[a] single familiar standard' " was " 'essential to guide police officers' " who make roadside arrests. The Court acknowledged that articles in the passenger compartment of a car are not always within an arrestee's reach, but "[i]n order to establish the workable rule this category of cases requires," the Court adopted a rule that categorically permits the search of a car's passenger compartment incident to the lawful arrest of an occupant.

The precise holding in *Belton* could not be clearer. The Court stated unequivocally: "[W]e hold that when a policeman has made a lawful custodial arrest of the occupant of an automobile, he may, as a contemporaneous incident of that arrest, search the passenger compartment of that automobile."

Despite this explicit statement, the opinion of the Court in the present case curiously suggests that *Belton* may reasonably be read as adopting a holding that is narrower than the one explicitly set out in the *Belton* opinion, namely, that an officer arresting a vehicle occupant may search the passenger compartment *"when the passenger compartment is within an arrestee's reaching distance."* (emphasis in original). According to the Court, the broader reading of *Belton* that has gained wide acceptance "may be attributable to Justice Brennan's dissent."

Contrary to the Court's suggestion, however, Justice Brennan's *Belton* dissent did not mischaracterize the Court's holding in that case or cause that holding to be misinterpreted. As noted, the *Belton* Court explicitly stated precisely what it held. In *Thornton*, the Court recognized the scope of *Belton*'s holding.

So did Justice SCALIA's separate opinion. (opinion concurring in judgment) ("In *[Belton]* we set forth a bright-line rule for arrests of automobile occupants, holding that . . . a search of the whole [passenger] compartment is justified in every case"). This "bright-line rule" has now been interred.

II

Because the Court has substantially overruled *Belton* and *Thornton*, the Court must explain why its departure from the usual rule of *stare decisis* is justified. I recognize that stare decisis is not an "inexorable command," and applies less rigidly in constitutional cases. But the Court has said that a constitutional precedent should be followed unless there is a " 'special justification' " for its abandonment. Relevant factors identified in prior cases include whether the precedent has engendered reliance, whether there has been an important change in circumstances in the outside world, whether the precedent has proved to be unworkable, and whether the decision was badly reasoned. These factors weigh in favor of retaining the rule established in *Belton*.

A

Reliance. While reliance is most important in "cases involving property and contract rights," the Court has recognized that reliance by law enforcement officers is also entitled to weight. In *Dickerson*, the Court held that principles of *stare decisis* "weigh[ed]" heavily against overruling *Miranda* v. *Arizona*, because the *Miranda* rule had become "embedded in routine police practice."

If there was reliance in *Dickerson*, there certainly is substantial reliance here. The *Belton* rule has been taught to police officers for more than a quarter century. Many searches — almost certainly including more than a few that figure in cases now on appeal — were conducted in scrupulous reliance on that precedent. It is likely that, on the very day when this opinion is announced, numerous vehicle searches will be conducted in good faith by police officers who were taught the *Belton* rule.

The opinion of the Court recognizes that "*Belton* has been widely taught in police academies and that law enforcement officers have relied on the rule in conducting vehicle searches during the past 28 years." But for the Court, this seemingly counts for nothing. The Court states that "[w]e have never relied on *stare decisis* to justify the continuance of an unconstitutional police practice," but of course the Court routinely relies on decisions sustaining the constitutionality of police practices without doing what the Court has done here — *sua sponte* considering whether those decisions should be overruled. And the Court cites no authority for the proposition that *stare decisis* may be disregarded or provides only lesser protection when the precedent that is challenged is one that sustained the constitutionality of a law enforcement practice.

The Court also errs in arguing that the reliance interest that was given heavy weight in *Dickerson* was not "police reliance on a rule requiring them to provide warnings but to the broader societal reliance on that individual right." The *Dickerson* opinion makes no reference to "societal reliance," and petitioner in that case contended that there had been reliance on *Miranda* because, among other things, "[f]or nearly thirty-five years, *Miranda*'s requirements ha[d] shaped law enforcement training [and] police conduct."

B

Changed circumstances. Abandonment of the *Belton* rule cannot be justified on the ground that the dangers surrounding the arrest of a vehicle occupant are different today than they were 28 years ago. The Court claims that "[w]e now know that articles inside the passenger compartment are rarely 'within "the area into which an arrestee might reach," but surely it was well known in 1981 that a person who is taken from a vehicle, handcuffed, and placed in the back of a patrol car is unlikely to make it back into his own car to retrieve a weapon or destroy evidence.

C

Workability. The *Belton* rule has not proved to be unworkable. On the contrary, the rule was adopted for the express purpose of providing a test that would be relatively easy for police officers and judges to apply. The Court correctly notes that even the *Belton* rule is not perfectly clear in all situations. Specifically, it is sometimes debatable whether a search is or is not contemporaneous with an arrest, but that problem is small in comparison with the problems that the Court's new two-part rule will produce. The first part of the Court's new rule — which permits the search of a vehicle's passenger compartment if it is within an arrestee's reach at the time of the search — reintroduces the same sort of case-by-case, fact-specific decision making that the *Belton* rule was adopted to avoid. As the situation in *Belton* illustrated, there are cases in which it is unclear whether an arrestee could retrieve a weapon or evidence in the passenger compartment of a car.

Even more serious problems will also result from the second part of the Court's new rule, which requires officers making roadside arrests to determine whether there is reason to believe that the vehicle contains evidence of the crime of arrest. What this rule permits in a variety of situations is entirely unclear.

D

Consistency with later cases. The *Belton* bright-line rule has not been undermined by subsequent cases. On the contrary, that rule was reaffirmed and extended just five years ago in *Thornton*.

E

Bad reasoning. The Court is harshly critical of *Belton*'s reasoning, but the problem that the Court perceives cannot be remedied simply by overruling *Belton. Belton* represented only a modest — and quite defensible — extension of *Chimel,* as I understand that decision. Prior to *Chimel,* the Court's precedents permitted an arresting officer to search the area within an arrestee's "possession" and "control" for the purpose of gathering evidence. Based on this "abstract doctrine," the Court had sustained searches that extended far beyond an arrestee's grabbing area. See *United States v. Rabinowitz,* 339 U.S. 56 (1950) (search of entire office); *Harris v. United States,* 331 U.S. 145 (1947) (search of entire apartment). The *Chimel* Court, in an opinion written by Justice Stewart, overruled these cases. Concluding that there are only two justifications for a warrantless search incident to arrest — officer safety and the preservation of evidence — the Court stated that such a search must be confined to "the arrestee's person" and "the area from within which he might gain possession of a weapon or destructible evidence."

Unfortunately, *Chimel* did not say whether "the area from within which [an arrestee] might gain possession of a weapon or destructible evidence" is to be measured at the time of the arrest or at the time of the search, but unless the *Chimel* rule was meant to be a specialty rule, applicable to only a few unusual cases, the Court must have intended for this area to be measured at the time of arrest.

This is so because the Court can hardly have failed to appreciate the following two facts. First, in the great majority of cases, an officer making an arrest is able to handcuff the arrestee and remove him to a secure place before conducting a search incident to the arrest. Second, because it is safer for an arresting officer to secure an arrestee before searching, it is likely that this is what arresting officers do in the great majority of cases. (And it appears, not surprisingly, that this is in fact the prevailing practice.[1]) Thus, if the area within an arrestee's reach were assessed, not at the time of arrest, but at the time of the search, the *Chimel* rule would rarely come into play.

Moreover, if the applicability of the *Chimel* rule turned on whether an arresting officer chooses to secure an arrestee prior to conducting a search, rather than searching first and securing the arrestee later, the rule would "create a perverse incentive for an arresting officer to prolong the period during which the arrestee is kept in an area where he could pose a danger to the officer." If this is the law, the D. C. Circuit observed, "the law would truly be, as Mr. Bumble said, 'a ass.'" See *United States v. Tejada,* 524 F.3d 809, 812 (CA7 2008) ("[I]f the police could lawfully have searched the defendant's grabbing radius at the moment of arrest, he has no legitimate complaint if, the better to protect themselves from him, they first put him outside that radius").

I do not think that this is what the *Chimel* Court intended. Handcuffs were in use in 1969. The ability of arresting officers to secure arrestees before conducting a search — and their incentive to do so — are facts that can hardly have escaped the Court's attention. I therefore believe that the *Chimel* Court intended that its new

---

[1] *See* Moskovitz, *A Rule in Search of a Reason: An Empirical Reexamination of Chimel and Belton,* 2002 Wis. L. Rev. 657, 665.

rule apply in cases in which the arrestee is handcuffed before the search is conducted.

The *Belton* Court, in my view, proceeded on the basis of this interpretation of *Chimel*. Again speaking through Justice Stewart, the *Belton* Court reasoned that articles in the passenger compartment of a car are "generally, even if not inevitably" within an arrestee's reach. This is undoubtedly true at the time of the arrest of a person who is seated in a car but plainly not true when the person has been removed from the car and placed in handcuffs. Accordingly, the *Belton* Court must have proceeded on the assumption that the *Chimel* rule was to be applied at the time of arrest. And that is why the *Belton* Court was able to say that its decision "in no way alter[ed] the fundamental principles established in the *Chimel* case regarding the basic scope of searches incident to lawful custodial arrests." Viewing *Chimel* as having focused on the time of arrest, *Belton*'s only new step was to eliminate the need to decide on a case-by-case basis whether a particular person seated in a car actually could have reached the part of the passenger compartment where a weapon or evidence was hidden. For this reason, if we are going to reexamine *Belton*, we should also reexamine the reasoning in *Chimel* on which *Belton* rests.

F

The Court, however, does not reexamine *Chimel* and thus leaves the law relating to searches incident to arrest in a confused and unstable state. The first part of the Court's new two-part rule — which permits an arresting officer to search the area within an arrestee's reach at the time of the search — applies, at least for now, only to vehicle occupants and recent occupants, but there is no logical reason why the same rule should not apply to all arrestees. The second part of the Court's new rule, which the Court takes uncritically from Justice SCALIA's separate opinion in *Thornton*, raises doctrinal and practical problems that the Court makes no effort to address. Why, for example, is the standard for this type of evidence gathering search "reason to believe" rather than probable cause? And why is this type of search restricted to evidence of the offense of arrest? It is true that an arrestee's vehicle is probably more likely to contain evidence of the crime of arrest than of some other crime, but if reason-to believe is the governing standard for an evidence gathering search incident to arrest, it is not easy to see why an officer should not be able to search when the officer has reason to believe that the vehicle in question possesses evidence of a crime other than the crime of arrest. Nor is it easy to see why an evidence-gathering search incident to arrest should be restricted to the passenger compartment. The *Belton* rule was limited in this way because the passenger compartment was considered to be the area that vehicle occupants can generally reach, but since the second part of the new rule is not based on officer safety or the preservation of evidence, the ground for this limitation is obscure.[2]

---

[2] I do not understand the Court's decision to reach the following situations. First, it is not uncommon for an officer to arrest some but not all of the occupants of a vehicle. The Court's decision in this case does not address the question whether in such a situation a search of the passenger compartment may be justified on the ground that the occupants who are not arrested could gain access to the car and retrieve a weapon or destroy evidence. Second, there may be situations in which an arresting officer has

III

Respondent in this case has not asked us to overrule *Belton*, much less *Chimel*. Respondent's argument rests entirely on an interpretation of *Belton* that is plainly incorrect, an interpretation that disregards *Belton*'s explicit delineation of its holding. I would therefore leave any reexamination of our prior precedents for another day, if such a reexamination is to be undertaken at all. In this case, I would simply apply *Belton* and reverse the judgment below.

QUESTIONS AND NOTES

1.   What does "reasonable to believe that evidence of the offense of arrest might be found in the vehicle" mean? Does it mean probable cause? Reasonable suspicion? Less than either? Something different? Does the world need yet another Fourth Amendment standard?

2.   The Court suggests that warrants are the norm subject "only to a few specifically established and well-delineated exceptions." Do you believe that is the law? Should it be? Is the focus on warrants in this context misplaced?

3.   After *Gant*, will a search incident to an arrest in a home or office include the grabbing area at the time of an arrest if the arrestee is handcuffed and removed *before* the search? Should it?

4.   Is it clear that there was no evidence of Gant's liability for driving without a license in his car? Isn't it possible that he could have had a phony driver's license in his car? *Cf. United States v. Robinson*, 414 U.S. 218 (1973).

5.   Is the Court actually overruling anything in this case? Explain.

6.   How important is (should) stare decisis (be)?

7.   How important should police reliance on *Belton/Thornton* be? Is it enough that they have a good faith defense from suit for searches conducted prior *Gant*?

D.   SUSPICIONLESS HIGHWAY STOPS

In every automobile case that we have discussed thus far, the police had a particular reason to stop and search the vehicle. In none of those cases did the Government argue that the searchee was subject to a search or seizure simply because he was on the highway. In the cases that follow, that is precisely the Government's argument. It argues that because an individual is on the highway, she can be subject to a license or sobriety check. In *Prouse, Sitz, Edmond*, and *Lidster* we will see the extent to which, the Court finds this argument persuasive.

---

cause to fear that persons who were not passengers in the car might attempt to retrieve a weapon or evidence from the car while the officer is still on the scene. The decision in this case, as I understand it, does not address that situation either.

DELAWARE v. PROUSE
440 U.S. 648 (1979)

Mr. Justice White delivered the opinion of the Court.

The question is whether it is an unreasonable seizure to stop an automobile, being driven on a public highway, for the purpose of checking the driving license of the operator and the registration of the car, where there is neither probable cause nor reasonable suspicion that the car is being driven contrary to the laws governing the operation of motor vehicles or that either the car or any of its occupants is subject to seizure or detention in connection with the violation of any other applicable law.

I

At 7:20 p.m. on November 30, 1976, a New Castle County, Del., patrolman in a police cruiser stopped an automobile occupied by respondent. The patrolman smelled marihuana smoke as he was walking toward the stopped vehicle, and he seized marihuana in plain view on the car floor. Respondent was subsequently indicted for illegal possession of a controlled substance. At a hearing on respondent's motion to suppress the marihuana seized as a result of the stop, the patrolman testified that prior to stopping the vehicle he had observed neither traffic or equipment violations nor any suspicious activity, and that he made the stop only in order to check the driver's license and registration. The patrolman was not acting pursuant to any standards, guidelines, or procedures pertaining to document spot checks, promulgated by either his department or the State Attorney General. Characterizing the stop as "routine," the patrolman explained, "I saw the car in the area and wasn't answering any complaints, so I decided to pull them off." The trial court granted the motion to suppress, finding the stop and detention to have been wholly capricious and therefore violative of the Fourth Amendment.

The Delaware Supreme Court affirmed, noting first that "[t]he issue of the legal validity of systematic, roadblock-type stops of a number of vehicles for license and vehicle registration check is *not* now before the Court" (emphasis in original). The court held that "a random stop of a motorist in the absence of specific articulable facts which justify the stop by indicating a reasonable suspicion that a violation of the law has occurred is constitutionally impermissible and violative of the Fourth and Fourteenth Amendments to the United States Constitution." We granted certiorari to resolve the conflict between this decision, which is in accord with decisions in five other jurisdictions, and the contrary determination in six jurisdictions that the Fourth Amendment does not prohibit the kind of automobile stop that occurred here.

III

The Fourth and Fourteenth Amendments are implicated in this case because stopping an automobile and detaining its occupants constitute a "seizure" within the meaning of those Amendments, even though the purpose of the stop is limited and the resulting detention quite brief. The essential purpose of the proscriptions in the Fourth Amendment is to impose a standard of "reasonableness" upon the exercise of discretion by government officials, including law enforcement agents, in order "to safeguard the privacy and security of individuals against arbitrary invasions." Thus, the permissibility of a particular law enforcement practice is judged by balancing its intrusion on the individual's Fourth Amendment interests against its promotion of legitimate governmental interests. Implemented in this manner, the reasonableness standard usually requires, at a minimum, that the facts upon which an intrusion is based be capable of measurement against "an objective standard," whether this be probable cause or a less stringent test. In those situations in which the balance of interests precludes insistence upon "some quantum of individualized suspicion," other safeguards are generally relied upon to assure that the individual's reasonable expectation of privacy is not "subject to the discretion of the official in the field."

In this case, however, the State of Delaware urges that patrol officers be subject to no constraints in deciding which automobiles shall be stopped for a license and registration check because the State's interest in discretionary spot checks as a means of ensuring the safety of its roadways outweighs the resulting intrusion on the privacy and security of the persons detained.

V

Delaware urges that these stops are reasonable under the Fourth Amendment because the State's interest in the practice as a means of promoting public safety upon its roads more than outweighs the intrusion entailed. Although the record discloses no statistics concerning the extent of the problem of lack of highway safety, in Delaware or in the Nation as a whole, we are aware of the danger to life and property posed by vehicular traffic and of the difficulties that even a cautious and an experienced driver may encounter. We agree that the States have a vital interest in ensuring that only those qualified to do so are permitted to operate motor vehicles, that these vehicles are fit for safe operation, and hence that licensing, registration, and vehicle inspection requirements are being observed. Automobile licenses are issued periodically to evidence that the drivers holding them are sufficiently familiar with the rules of the road and are physically qualified to operate a motor vehicle. The registration requirement and, more pointedly, the related annual inspection requirement in Delaware are designed to keep dangerous automobiles off the road. Unquestionably, these provisions, properly administered, are essential elements in a highway safety program. Furthermore, we note that the State of Delaware requires a minimum amount of insurance coverage as a condition to automobile registration, implementing its legitimate interest in seeing to it that its citizens have protection when involved in a motor vehicle accident.[18]

The question remains, however, whether in the service of these important ends the discretionary spot check is a sufficiently productive mechanism to justify the

---

[18] It has been urged that additional state interests are the apprehension of stolen vehicles and of drivers under the influence of alcohol or narcotics. The latter interest is subsumed by the interest in roadway safety, as may the former to some extent. The remaining governmental interest in controlling automobile thefts is not distinguishable from the general interest in crime control.

intrusion upon Fourth Amendment interests which such stops entail. On the record before us, that question must be answered in the negative. Given the alternative mechanisms available, both those in use and those that might be adopted, we are unconvinced that the incremental contribution to highway safety of the random spot check justifies the practice under the Fourth Amendment.

The foremost method of enforcing traffic and vehicle safety regulations, it must be recalled, is acting upon observed violations. Vehicle stops for traffic violations occur countless times each day; and on these occasions, licenses and registration papers are subject to inspection and drivers without them will be ascertained. Furthermore, drivers without licenses are presumably the less safe drivers whose propensities may well exhibit themselves. Absent some empirical data to the contrary, it must be assumed that finding an unlicensed driver among those who commit traffic violations is a much more likely event than finding an unlicensed driver by choosing randomly from the entire universe of drivers. If this were not so, licensing of drivers would hardly be an effective means of promoting roadway safety. It seems common sense that the percentage of all drivers on the road who are driving without a license is very small and that the number of licensed drivers who will be stopped in order to find one unlicensed operator will be large indeed. The contribution to highway safety made by discretionary stops selected from among drivers generally will therefore be marginal at best. Furthermore, and again absent something more than mere assertion to the contrary, we find it difficult to believe that the unlicensed driver would not be deterred by the possibility of being involved in a traffic violation or having some other experience calling for proof of his entitlement to drive but that he would be deterred by the possibility that he would be one of those chosen for a spot check. In terms of actually discovering unlicensed drivers or deterring them from driving, the spot check does not appear sufficiently productive to qualify as a reasonable law enforcement practice under the Fourth Amendment.

Much the same can be said about the safety aspects of automobiles as distinguished from drivers. Many violations of minimum vehicle-safety requirements are observable, and something can be done about them by the observing officer, directly and immediately. Furthermore, in Delaware, as elsewhere, vehicles must carry and display current license plates, which themselves evidence that the vehicle is properly registered; and, under Delaware law, to qualify for annual registration a vehicle must pass the annual safety inspection and be properly insured. It does not appear, therefore, that a stop of a Delaware-registered vehicle is necessary in order to ascertain compliance with the State's registration requirements; and, because there is nothing to show that a significant percentage of automobiles from other States do not also require license plates indicating current registration, there is no basis for concluding that stopping even out-of-state cars for document checks substantially promotes the State's interest.

The marginal contribution to roadway safety possibly resulting from a system of spot checks cannot justify subjecting every occupant of every vehicle on the roads to a seizure — limited in magnitude compared to other intrusions but nonetheless constitutionally cognizable — at the unbridled discretion of law enforcement officials. To insist neither upon an appropriate factual basis for suspicion directed at a particular automobile nor upon some other substantial and objective standard or rule to govern the exercise of discretion "would invite intrusions upon constitutionally guaranteed rights based on nothing more substantial than inarticulate hunches." By hypothesis, stopping apparently safe drivers is necessary only because the danger presented by some drivers is not observable at the time of the stop. When there is not probable cause to believe that a driver is violating any one of the multitude of applicable traffic and equipment regulations — or other articulable basis amounting to reasonable suspicion that the driver is unlicensed or his vehicle unregistered — we cannot conceive of any legitimate basis upon which a patrolman could decide that stopping a particular driver for a spot check would be more productive than stopping any other driver. This kind of standardless and unconstrained discretion is the evil the Court has discerned when in previous cases it has insisted that the discretion of the official in the field be circumscribed, at least to some extent.

VI

The "grave danger" of abuse of discretion does not disappear simply because the automobile is subject to state regulation resulting in numerous instances of police-citizen contact. Only last Term we pointed out that "if the government intrudes . . . . the privacy interest suffers whether the government's motivation is to investigate violations of criminal laws or breaches of other statutory or regulatory standards." There are certain "relatively unique circumstances," in which consent to regulatory restrictions is presumptively concurrent with participation in the regulated enterprise. (federal regulation of firearms); (federal regulation of liquor). Otherwise, regulatory inspections unaccompanied by any quantum of individualized, articulable suspicion must be undertaken pursuant to previously specified "neutral criteria."

An individual operating or traveling in an automobile does not lose all reasonable expectation of privacy simply because the automobile and its use are subject to government regulation. Automobile travel is a basic, pervasive, and often necessary mode of transportation to and from one's home, workplace, and leisure activities. Many people spend more hours each day traveling in cars than walking on the streets. Undoubtedly, many find a greater sense of security and privacy in traveling in an automobile than they do in exposing themselves by pedestrian or other modes of travel. Were the individual subject to unfettered governmental intrusion every time he entered an automobile, the security guaranteed by the Fourth Amendment would be seriously circumscribed. [P]eople are not shorn of all Fourth Amendment protection when they step from their homes onto the public sidewalks. Nor are they shorn of those interests when they step from the sidewalks into their automobiles.

VII

Accordingly, we hold that except in those situations in which there is at least articulable and reasonable suspicion that a motorist is unlicensed or that an automobile is not registered, or that either the vehicle or an occupant is otherwise subject to seizure for violation of law, stopping an automobile and detaining the driver in order to check his driver's license and the registration of the automobile are unreasonable under the Fourth Amendment. This holding does not preclude the

State of Delaware or other States from developing methods for spot checks that involve less intrusion or that do not involve the unconstrained exercise of discretion.[26] Questioning of all oncoming traffic at roadblock-type stops is one possible alternative. We hold only that persons in automobiles on public roadways may not for that reason alone have their travel and privacy interfered with at the unbridled discretion of police officers. The judgment below is affirmed.

JUSTICE BLACKMUN, with whom JUSTICE POWELL joins, concurring.

The Court carefully protects from the reach of its decision other less intrusive spot checks "that do not involve the unconstrained exercise of discretion." The roadblock stop for all traffic is given as an example. I necessarily assume that the Court's reservation also includes other not purely random stops (such as every 10th car to pass a given point) that equate with, but are less intrusive than, a 100% roadblock stop. And I would not regard the present case as a precedent that throws any constitutional shadow upon the necessarily somewhat individualized and perhaps largely random examinations by game wardens in the performance of their duties. In a situation of that type, it seems to me, the Court's balancing process, and the value factors under consideration, would be quite different.

With this understanding, I join the Court's opinion and its judgment.

MR. JUSTICE REHNQUIST, dissenting.

The Court holds, in successive sentences, that absent an articulable, reasonable suspicion of unlawful conduct, a motorist may not be subjected to a random license check, but that the States are free to develop "methods for spot checks that . . . do not involve the unconstrained exercise of discretion," such as "[q]uestioning . . . all oncoming traffic at roadblock-type stops . . . ." Because motorists, apparently like sheep, are much less likely to be "frightened" or "annoyed" when stopped en masse, a highway patrolman needs neither probable cause nor articulable suspicion to stop all motorists on a particular thoroughfare, but he cannot without articulable suspicion stop *less* than all motorists. The Court thus elevates the adage "misery loves company" to a novel role in Fourth Amendment jurisprudence. The rule becomes "curiouser and curiouser" as one attempts to follow the Court's explanation for it.

As the Court correctly points out, people are not shorn of their Fourth Amendment protection when they step from their homes onto the public sidewalks or from the sidewalks into their automobiles. But a random license check of a motorist operating a vehicle on highways owned and maintained by the State is quite different from a random stop designed to uncover violations of laws that have nothing to do with motor vehicles. No one questions that the State may require the licensing of those who drive on its highways and the registration of vehicles which are driven on those highways. If it may insist on these requirements, it obviously

---

[26] Nor does our holding today cast doubt on the permissibility of roadside truck weigh-stations and inspection checkpoints, at which some vehicles may be subject to further detention for safety and regulatory inspection than are others.

may take steps necessary to enforce compliance. The reasonableness of the enforcement measure chosen by the State is tested by weighing its intrusion on the motorists' Fourth Amendment interests against its promotion of the State's legitimate interests.

In executing this balancing process, the Court concludes that given the alternative mechanisms available, discretionary spot checks are not a "sufficiently productive mechanism" to safeguard the State's admittedly "vital interest in ensuring that only those qualified to do so are permitted to operate motor vehicles, that these vehicles are fit for safe operation, and hence that licensing, registration, and vehicle inspection requirements are being observed." Foremost among the alternative methods of enforcing traffic and vehicle safety regulations, according to the Court, is acting upon observed violations, for "drivers without licenses are presumably the less safe drivers whose propensities may well exhibit themselves." Noting that "finding an unlicensed driver among those who commit traffic violations is a much more likely event than finding an unlicensed driver by choosing randomly from the entire universe of drivers," the Court concludes that the contribution to highway safety made by random stops would be marginal at best. The State's primary interest, however, is in traffic safety, not in apprehending unlicensed motorists for the sake of apprehending unlicensed motorists. The whole point of enforcing motor vehicle safety regulations is to remove from the road the unlicensed driver before he demonstrates why he is unlicensed. The Court would apparently prefer that the State check licenses and vehicle registrations as the wreckage is being towed away.

Nor is the Court impressed with the deterrence rationale, finding it inconceivable that an unlicensed driver who is not deterred by the prospect of being involved in a traffic violation or other incident requiring him to produce a license would be deterred by the possibility of being subjected to a spot check. The Court arrives at its conclusion without the benefit of a shred of empirical data in this record suggesting that a system of random spot checks would fail to deter violators. In the absence of such evidence, the State's determination that random stops would serve a deterrence function should stand.

On the other side of the balance, the Court advances only the most diaphanous of citizen interests. Indeed, the Court does not say that these interests can never be infringed by the State, just that the State must infringe them en masse rather than citizen by citizen. To comply with the Fourth Amendment, the State need only subject *all* citizens to the same "anxiety" and "inconvenien[ce]" to which it now subjects only a few.

For constitutional purposes, the action of an individual law enforcement officer is the action of the State itself, and state acts are accompanied by a presumption of validity until shown otherwise. Although a system of discretionary stops could conceivably be abused, the record before us contains no showing that such abuse is probable or even likely. Nor is there evidence in the record that a system of random license checks would fail adequately to further the State's interest in deterring and apprehending violators. Nevertheless, the Court concludes "[o]n the record before us" that the random spot check is not "a sufficiently productive mechanism to justify the intrusion upon Fourth Amendment interests which such stops entail." I think that the Court's approach reverses the presumption of constitutionality accorded acts of the States. The burden is not upon the State to demonstrate that its procedures are consistent with the Fourth Amendment, but upon respondent to demonstrate that they are not. "On this record" respondent has failed to make such a demonstration.

Neither the Court's opinion, nor the opinion of the Supreme Court of Delaware, suggests that the random stop made in this case was carried out in a manner inconsistent with the Equal Protection Clause of the Fourteenth Amendment. Absent an equal protection violation, the fact that random stops may entail "a possibly unsettling show of authority," and "may create substantial anxiety," seems an insufficient basis to distinguish for Fourth Amendment purposes between a roadblock stopping all cars and the random stop at issue here. Accordingly, I would reverse the judgment of the Supreme Court of Delaware.

QUESTIONS AND NOTES

1. Justice Rehnquist suggests that this seizure should be presumed constitutional and that the burden should be on Prouse to establish its unconstitutionality. Do you agree? Why? Why not?

2. Do you agree with Justice White that the balance of individual inconvenience to societal gain militates against allowing license checks?

3. If so, how would that be changed by inconveniencing everybody? Does misery really love company, and is that a constitutional principle?

4. Although *Prouse* referred to a roadblock license check as merely a "possible alternative," later cases have assumed that *Prouse* decided the issue in favor of their constitutionality.

The next step, sobriety roadblocks, was at issue in *Sitz*.

MICHIGAN v. SITZ
496 U.S. 444 (1990)

CHIEF JUSTICE REHNQUIST delivered the opinion of the Court.

This case poses the question whether a State's use of highway sobriety checkpoints violates the Fourth and Fourteenth Amendments to the United States Constitution. We hold that it does not and therefore reverse the contrary holding of the Court of Appeals of Michigan.

Petitioners, the Michigan Department of State Police and its Director, established a sobriety checkpoint pilot program in early 1986. The Director appointed a Sobriety Checkpoint Advisory Committee comprising representatives of the State Police force, local police forces, state prosecutors, and the University of Michigan Transportation Research Institute. Pursuant to its charge, the Advisory Committee created guidelines setting forth procedures governing checkpoint operations, site selection, and publicity.

Under the guidelines, checkpoints would be set up at selected sites along state roads. All vehicles passing through a checkpoint would be stopped and their drivers briefly examined for signs of intoxication. In cases where a checkpoint officer detected signs of intoxication, the motorist would be directed to a location out of the traffic flow where an officer would check the motorist's driver's license and car registration and, if warranted, conduct further sobriety tests. Should the field tests and the officer's observations suggest that the driver was intoxicated, an arrest would be made. All other drivers would be permitted to resume their journey immediately.

The first — and to date the only — sobriety checkpoint operated under the program was conducted in Saginaw County with the assistance of the Saginaw County Sheriff's Department. During the hour-and-fifteen-minute duration of the checkpoint's operation, 126 vehicles passed through the checkpoint. The average delay for each vehicle was approximately 25 seconds. Two drivers were detained for field sobriety testing, and one of the two was arrested for driving under the influence of alcohol. A third driver who drove through without stopping was pulled over by an officer in an observation vehicle and arrested for driving under the influence.

On the day before the operation of the Saginaw County checkpoint, respondents filed a complaint in the Circuit Court of Wayne County seeking declaratory and injunctive relief from potential subjection to the checkpoints. Each of the respondents "is a licensed driver in the State of Michigan . . . who regularly travels throughout the State in his automobile." During pretrial proceedings, petitioners agreed to delay further implementation of the checkpoint program pending the outcome of this litigation.

After the trial, at which the court heard extensive testimony concerning the "effectiveness" of highway sobriety checkpoint programs, the court ruled that the Michigan program violated the Fourth Amendment and Art. 1, § 11, of the Michigan Constitution. On appeal, the Michigan Court of Appeals affirmed the holding that the program violated the Fourth Amendment and, for that reason, did not consider whether the program violated the Michigan Constitution. After the Michigan Supreme Court denied petitioners' application for leave to appeal, we granted certiorari.

To decide this case the trial court performed a balancing test derived from our opinion in *Brown v. Texas*, 443 U.S. 47.[*] As described by the Court of Appeals, the test involved "balancing the state's interest in preventing accidents caused by drunk drivers, the effectiveness of sobriety checkpoints in achieving that goal, and the level of intrusion on an individual's privacy caused by the checkpoints."

As characterized by the Court of Appeals, the trial court's findings with respect to the balancing factors were that the State has "a grave and legitimate" interest in curbing drunken driving; that sobriety checkpoint programs are generally "inef-fective" and, therefore, do not significantly further that interest; and that the checkpoints' "subjective intrusion" on individual liberties is substantial. According to the court, the record disclosed no basis for disturbing the trial court's findings,

---

[*] [Not to be confused with *Texas v. Brown*, in Chapter 5, *supra*. — Ed.]

which were made within the context of an analytical framework prescribed by this Court for determining the constitutionality of seizures less intrusive than traditional arrests.

Petitioners concede, correctly in our view, that a Fourth Amendment "seizure" occurs when a vehicle is stopped at a checkpoint. The question thus becomes whether such seizures are "reasonable" under the Fourth Amendment.

It is important to recognize what our inquiry is *not* about. No allegations are before us of unreasonable treatment of any person after an actual detention at a particular checkpoint. As pursued in the lower courts, the instant action challenges only the use of sobriety checkpoints generally. We address only the initial stop of each motorist passing through a checkpoint and the associated preliminary questioning and observation by checkpoint officers. Detention of particular motorists for more extensive field sobriety testing may require satisfaction of an individualized suspicion standard.

No one can seriously dispute the magnitude of the drunken driving problem or the States' interest in eradicating it. Media reports of alcohol-related death and mutilation on the Nation's roads are legion. The anecdotal is confirmed by the statistical. "Drunk drivers cause an annual death toll of over 25,000 and in the same time span cause nearly one million personal injuries and more than five billion dollars in property damage."

Conversely, the weight bearing on the other scale — the measure of the intrusion on motorists stopped briefly at sobriety checkpoints — is slight. We reached a similar conclusion as to the intrusion on motorists subjected to a brief stop at a highway checkpoint for detecting illegal aliens. *See United States v. Martinez-Fuerte*, 428 U.S. 543 (1976). We see virtually no difference between the levels of intrusion on law-abiding motorists from the brief stops necessary to the effectuation of these two types of checkpoints, which to the average motorist would seem identical save for the nature of the questions the checkpoint officers might ask. The trial court and the Court of Appeals, thus, accurately gauged the "objective" intrusion, measured by the duration of the seizure and the intensity of the investigation, as minimal.

With respect to what it perceived to be the "subjective" intrusion on motorists, however, the Court of Appeals found such intrusion substantial. The court first affirmed the trial court's finding that the guidelines governing checkpoint operation minimize the discretion of the officers on the scene. But the court also agreed with the trial court's conclusion that the checkpoints have the potential to generate fear and surprise in motorists. This was so because the record failed to demonstrate that approaching motorists would be aware of their option to make U-turns or turnoffs to avoid the checkpoints. On that basis, the court deemed the subjective intrusion from the checkpoints unreasonable.

We believe the Michigan courts misread our cases concerning the degree of "subjective intrusion" and the potential for generating fear and surprise. The "fear and surprise" to be considered are not the natural fear of one who has been drinking over the prospect of being stopped at a sobriety checkpoint but, rather, the fear and surprise engendered in law abiding motorists by the nature of the stop. This was made clear in *Martinez-Fuerte*. Comparing checkpoint stops to roving patrol stops considered in prior cases, we said, "we view checkpoint stops in a different light because the subjective intrusion — the generating of concern or even fright on the part of lawful travelers — is appreciably less in the case of a checkpoint stop. " '[T]he circumstances surrounding a checkpoint stop and search are far less intrusive than those attending a roving-patrol stop. Roving patrols often operate at night on seldom-traveled roads, and their approach may frighten motorists. At traffic checkpoints the motorist can see that other vehicles are being stopped, he can see visible signs of the officers' authority, and he is much less likely to be frightened or annoyed by the intrusion.' " Here, checkpoints are selected pursuant to the guidelines, and uniformed police officers stop every approaching vehicle. The intrusion resulting from the brief stop at the sobriety checkpoint is for constitutional purposes indistinguishable from the checkpoint stops we upheld in *Martinez-Fuerte*.

The Court of Appeals went on to consider as part of the balancing analysis the "effectiveness" of the proposed checkpoint program. Based on extensive testimony in the trial record, the court concluded that the checkpoint program failed the "effectiveness" part of the test, and that this failure materially discounted petitioners' strong interest in implementing the program. We think the Court of Appeals was wrong on this point as well.

The actual language from *Brown v. Texas*, upon which the Michigan courts based their evaluation of "effectiveness," describes the balancing factor as "the degree to which the seizure advances the public interest." This passage from *Brown* was not meant to transfer from politically accountable officials to the courts the decision as to which among reasonable alternative law enforcement techniques should be employed to deal with a serious public danger. Experts in police science might disagree over which of several methods of apprehending drunken drivers is preferable as an ideal. But for purposes of Fourth Amendment analysis, the choice among such reasonable alternatives remains with the governmental officials who have a unique understanding of, and a responsibility for, limited public resources, including a finite number of police officers.

In *Prouse*, we disapproved random stops made by Delaware Highway Patrol officers in an effort to apprehend unlicensed drivers and unsafe vehicles. We observed that *no* empirical evidence indicated that such stops would be an effective means of promoting roadway safety and said that "[i]t seems common sense that the percentage of all drivers on the road who are driving without a license is very small and that the number of licensed drivers who will be stopped in order to find one unlicensed operator will be large indeed." We observed that the random stops involved the "kind of standardless and unconstrained discretion [which] is the evil the Court has discerned when in previous cases it has insisted that the discretion of the official in the field be circumscribed, at least to some extent." We went on to state that our holding did not "cast doubt on the permissibility of roadside truck weigh-stations and inspection checkpoints, at which some vehicles may be subject to further detention for safety and regulatory inspection than are others."

Unlike *Prouse*, this case involves neither a complete absence of empirical data nor a challenge to random highway stops. During the operation of the Saginaw

County checkpoint, the detention of each of the 126 vehicles that entered the checkpoint resulted in the arrest of two drunken drivers. Stated as a percentage, approximately 1.5 percent of the drivers passing through the checkpoint were arrested for alcohol impairment. In addition, an expert witness testified at the trial that experience in other States demonstrated that, on the whole, sobriety checkpoints resulted in drunken driving arrests of around 1 percent of all motorists stopped. By way of comparison, the record from one of the consolidated cases in *Martinez-Fuerte*, showed that in the associated checkpoint, illegal aliens were found in only 0.12 percent of the vehicles passing through the checkpoint. The ratio of illegal aliens detected to vehicles stopped (considering that on occasion two or more illegal aliens were found in a single vehicle) was approximately 0.5 percent. We concluded that this "record . . . provides a rather complete picture of the effectiveness of the San Clemente checkpoint," *ibid.*, and we sustained its constitutionality. We see no justification for a different conclusion here.

In sum, the balance of the State's interest in preventing drunken driving, the extent to which this system can reasonably be said to advance that interest, and the degree of intrusion upon individual motorists who are briefly stopped, weighs in favor of the state program. We therefore hold that it is consistent with the Fourth Amendment. The judgment of the Michigan Court of Appeals is accordingly reversed, and the cause is remanded for further proceedings not inconsistent with this opinion.

Reversed.

JUSTICE BRENNAN, with whom JUSTICE MARSHALL joins, dissenting.

Today, the Court rejects a Fourth Amendment challenge to a sobriety checkpoint policy in which police stop all cars and inspect all drivers for signs of intoxication without any individualized suspicion that a specific driver is intoxicated. The Court does so by balancing "the State's interest in preventing drunken driving, the extent to which this system can reasonably be said to advance that interest, and the degree of intrusion upon individual motorists who are briefly stopped." For the reasons stated by Justice STEVENS in Parts I and II of his dissenting opinion, I agree that the Court misapplies that test by undervaluing the nature of the intrusion and exaggerating the law enforcement need to use the roadblocks to prevent drunken driving. I write separately to express a few additional points.

The majority opinion creates the impression that the Court generally engages in a balancing test in order to determine the constitutionality of all seizures, or at least those "dealing with police stops of motorists on public highways." This is not the case. In most cases, the police must possess probable cause for a seizure to be judged reasonable. Only when a seizure is "substantially less intrusive," than a typical arrest is the general rule replaced by a balancing test. I agree with the Court that the initial stop of a car at a roadblock under the Michigan State Police sobriety checkpoint policy is sufficiently less intrusive than an arrest so that the reasonableness of the seizure may be judged, not by the presence of probable cause, but by balancing "the gravity of the public concerns served by the seizure, the degree to which the seizure advances the public interest, and the severity of the interference with individual liberty." But one searches the majority opinion in vain for any acknowledgment that the *reason* for employing the balancing test is that the seizure is minimally intrusive.

Indeed, the opinion reads as if the minimal nature of the seizure *ends* rather than begins the inquiry into reasonableness. Once the Court establishes that the seizure is "slight," it asserts without explanation that the balance "weighs in favor of the state program." The Court ignores the fact that in this class of minimally intrusive searches, we have generally required the Government to prove that it had reasonable suspicion for a minimally intrusive seizure to be considered reasonable. By holding that no level of suspicion is necessary before the police may stop a car for the purpose of preventing drunken driving, the Court potentially subjects the general public to arbitrary or harassing conduct by the police. I would have hoped that before taking such a step, the Court would carefully explain how such a plan fits within our constitutional framework.

Presumably, the Court purports to draw support from *Martinez-Fuerte*, which is the only case in which the Court has upheld a program that subjects the general public to suspicionless seizures. But as Justice STEVENS demonstrates, the Michigan State Police policy is sufficiently different from the program at issue in *Martinez-Fuerte* that such reliance is unavailing. Moreover, even if the policy at issue here were comparable to the program at issue in *Martinez-Fuerte*, it does not follow that the balance of factors in this case also justifies abandoning a requirement of individualized suspicion. In *Martinez-Fuerte*, the Court explained that suspicion-less stops were justified because "[a] requirement that stops . . . be based on reasonable suspicion would be impractical because the flow of traffic tends to be too heavy to allow the particularized study of a given car that would enable it to be identified as a possible carrier of illegal aliens." There has been no showing in this case that there is a similar difficulty in detecting individuals who are driving under the influence of alcohol, nor is it intuitively obvious that such a difficulty exists. That stopping every car might make it easier to prevent drunken driving, but is an insufficient justification for abandoning the requirement of individualized suspicion. "The needs of law enforcement stand in constant tension with the Constitution's protections of the individual against certain exercises of official power. It is precisely the predictability of these pressures that counsels a resolute loyalty to constitutional safeguards." Without proof that the police cannot develop individu-alized suspicion that a person is driving while impaired by alcohol, I believe the constitutional balance must be struck in favor of protecting the public against even the "minimally intrusive" seizures involved in this case.

I do not dispute the immense social cost caused by drunken drivers, nor do I slight the government's efforts to prevent such tragic losses. Indeed, I would hazard a guess that today's opinion will be received favorably by a majority of our society, who would willingly suffer the minimal intrusion of a sobriety checkpoint stop in order to prevent drunken driving. But consensus that a particular law enforcement technique serves a laudable purpose has never been the touchstone of constitutional analysis. "The Fourth Amendment was designed not merely to protect against official intrusions whose social utility was less as measured by some 'balancing test' than its intrusion on individual privacy; it was designed in addition to grant the individual a zone of privacy whose protections could be breached only where the 'reasonable' requirements of the probable cause standard were met.

Moved by whatever momentary evil has aroused their fears, officials — perhaps even supported by a majority of citizens — may be tempted to conduct searches that sacrifice the liberty of each citizen to assuage the perceived evil. But the Fourth Amendment rests on the principle that a true balance between the individual and society depends on the recognition of 'the right to be let alone — the most comprehensive of rights and the right most valued by civilized men.' "

In the face of the "momentary evil" of drunken driving, the Court today abdicates its role as the protector of that fundamental right. I respectfully dissent.

JUSTICE STEVENS, with whom JUSTICE MARSHALL join as to parts I and II, dissenting.

A sobriety checkpoint is usually operated at night at an unannounced location. Surprise is crucial to its method. The test operation conducted by the Michigan State Police and the Saginaw County Sheriff's Department began shortly after midnight and lasted until about 1 a.m. During that period, the 19 officers participating in the operation made two arrests and stopped and questioned 125 other unsuspecting and innocent drivers.[1] It is, of course, not known how many arrests would have been made during that period if those officers had been engaged in normal patrol activities. However, the findings of the trial court, based on an extensive record and affirmed by the Michigan Court of Appeals, indicate that the net effect of sobriety checkpoints on traffic safety is infinitesimal and possibly negative.

Indeed, the record in this case makes clear that a decision holding these suspicionless seizures unconstitutional would not impede the law enforcement community's remarkable progress in reducing the death toll on our highways.[2] Because the Michigan program was patterned after an older program in Maryland, the trial judge gave special attention to that State's experience. Over a period of several years, Maryland operated 125 checkpoints; of the 41,000 motorists passing through those checkpoints, only 143 persons (0.3%) were arrested.[3] The number of man-hours devoted to these operations is not in the record, but it seems inconceivable that a higher arrest rate could not have been achieved by more conventional means.[4] Yet, even if the 143 checkpoint arrests were assumed to involve a net increase in the number of drunk driving arrests per year, the figure would still be insignificant by comparison to the 71,000 such arrests made by Michigan State Police without checkpoints in 1984 alone.

Any relationship between sobriety checkpoints and an actual reduction in highway fatalities is even less substantial than the minimal impact on arrest rates.

---

[1] The 19 officers present at the sole Michigan checkpoint were not the standard detail; a few were observers. Nevertheless, the standard plan calls for having at least 8 and as many as 12 officers on hand.

[2] The fatality rate per 100 million miles traveled has steadily declined from 5.2 in 1968 to 2.3 in 1988.

[3] The figures for other States are roughly comparable.

[4] "The then sheriffs of Macomb County, Kalamazoo County, and Wayne County all testified as to other means used in their counties to combat drunk driving and as to their respective opinions that other methods currently in use, e.g., patrol cars, were more effective means of combating drunk driving and utilizing law enforcement resources than sobriety checkpoints."

As the Michigan Court of Appeals pointed out, "Maryland had conducted a study comparing traffic statistics between a county using checkpoints and a control county. The results of the study showed that alcohol-related accidents in the checkpoint county decreased by ten percent, whereas the control county saw an eleven percent decrease; and while fatal accidents in the control county fell from sixteen to three, fatal accidents in the checkpoint county actually doubled from the prior year."

In light of these considerations, it seems evident that the Court today misapplies the balancing test announced in *Brown v. Texas*. The Court overvalues the law enforcement interest in using sobriety checkpoints, undervalues the citizen's interest in freedom from random, unannounced investigatory seizures, and mistakenly assumes that there is "virtually no difference" between a routine stop at a permanent, fixed checkpoint and a surprise stop at a sobriety checkpoint. I believe this case is controlled by our several precedents condemning suspicionless random stops of motorists for investigatory purposes. [*E.g.*] *Prouse*.

I

There is a critical difference between a seizure that is preceded by fair notice and one that is effected by surprise. That is one reason why a border search, or indeed any search at a permanent and fixed checkpoint, is much less intrusive than a random stop. A motorist with advance notice of the location of a permanent checkpoint has an opportunity to avoid the search entirely, or at least to prepare for, and limit, the intrusion on her privacy.

No such opportunity is available in the case of a random stop or a temporary checkpoint, which both depend for their effectiveness on the element of surprise. A driver who discovers an unexpected checkpoint on a familiar local road will be startled and distressed. She may infer, correctly, that the checkpoint is not simply "business as usual," and may likewise infer, again correctly, that the police have made a discretionary decision to focus their law enforcement efforts upon her and others who pass the chosen point.

This element of surprise is the most obvious distinction between the sobriety checkpoints permitted by today's majority and the interior border checkpoints approved by this Court in *Martinez-Fuerte*. The distinction casts immediate doubt upon the majority's argument, for *Martinez-Fuerte* is the only case in which we have upheld suspicionless seizures of motorists. But the difference between notice and surprise is only one of the important reasons for distinguishing between permanent and mobile checkpoints. With respect to the former, there is no room for discretion in either the timing or the location of the stop — it is a permanent part of the landscape. In the latter case, however, although the checkpoint is most frequently employed during the hours of darkness on weekends (because that is when drivers with alcohol in their blood are most apt to be found on the road), the police have extremely broad discretion in determining the exact timing and placement of the roadblock.

There is also a significant difference between the kind of discretion that the officer exercises after the stop is made. A check for a driver's license, or for identification papers at an immigration checkpoint, is far more easily standardized than is a search for evidence of intoxication. A Michigan officer who questions a motorist at a sobriety checkpoint has virtually unlimited discretion to detain the driver on the basis of the slightest suspicion. A ruddy complexion, an unbuttoned shirt, bloodshot eyes or a speech impediment may suffice to prolong the detention. Any driver who had just consumed a glass of beer, or even a sip of wine, would almost certainly have the burden of demonstrating to the officer that her driving ability was not impaired.

Finally, it is significant that many of the stops at permanent checkpoints occur during daylight hours, whereas the sobriety checkpoints are almost invariably operated at night. A seizure followed by interrogation and even a cursory search at night is surely more offensive than a daytime stop that is almost as routine as going through a toll gate. Thus we thought it important to point out that the random stops at issue in *Ortiz* [*v. United States*] frequently occurred at night. 422 U.S. at 894.

These fears are not, as the Court would have it, solely the lot of the guilty. To be law abiding is not necessarily to be spotless, and even the most virtuous can be unlucky. Unwanted attention from the local police need not be less discomforting simply because one's secrets are not the stuff of criminal prosecutions. Moreover, those who have found — by reason of prejudice or misfortune — that encounters with the police may become adversarial or unpleasant without good cause will have grounds for worrying at any stop designed to elicit signs of suspicious behavior. Being stopped by the police is distressing even when it should not be terrifying, and what begins mildly may by happenstance turn severe.

For all these reasons, I do not believe that this case is analogous to *Martinez-Fuerte*. In my opinion, the sobriety checkpoints are instead similar to — and in some respects more intrusive than — the random investigative stops that the Court held unconstitutional in *Prouse*. In [that] case the Court explained:

> We cannot agree that stopping or detaining a vehicle on an ordinary city street is less intrusive than a roving-patrol stop on a major highway and that it bears greater resemblance to a permissible stop and secondary detention at a checkpoint near the border. In this regard, we note that *Brignoni-Ponce* [*v. United States*, a case invalidating suspicionless stops by roving border patrol officers] was not limited to roving-patrol stops on limited-access roads, but applied to any roving-patrol stop by Border Patrol agents on any type of roadway on less than reasonable suspicion. We cannot assume that the physical and psychological intrusion visited upon the occupants of a vehicle by a random stop to check documents is of any less moment than that occasioned by a stop by border agents on roving patrol. Both of these stops generally entail law enforcement officers signaling a moving automobile to pull over to the side of the roadway, by means of a possibly unsettling show of authority. Both interfere with freedom of movement, are inconvenient, and consume time. Both may create substantial anxiety.

We accordingly held that the State must produce evidence comparing the challenged seizure to other means of law enforcement, so as to show that the seizure

is a sufficiently productive mechanism to justify the intrusion upon Fourth
Amendment interests which such stops entail. On the record before us, that
question must be answered in the negative. Given the alternative mechanisms available, both those in use and those that might be adopted, we are
unconvinced that the incremental contribution to highway safety of the
random spot check justifies the practice under the Fourth Amendment.

II

The Court, unable to draw any persuasive analogy to *Martinez-Fuerte*, rests its
decision today on application of a more general balancing test taken from *Brown v.
Texas*. In that case the appellant, a pedestrian, had been stopped for questioning in
an area of El Paso, Texas, that had "a high incidence of drug traffic" because he
"looked suspicious." He was then arrested and convicted for refusing to identify
himself to police officers. We set aside his conviction because the officers stopped
him when they lacked any reasonable suspicion that he was engaged in criminal
activity. In our opinion, we stated: "Consideration of the constitutionality of such
seizures involves a weighing of the gravity of the public concerns served by the
seizure, the degree to which the seizure advances the public interest, and the
severity of the interference with individual liberty."

The gravity of the public concern with highway safety that is implicated by this
case is, of course, undisputed.[7] Yet, that same grave concern was implicated in
Prouse. Moreover, I do not understand the Court to have placed any lesser value on
the importance of the drug problem implicated in *Brown*, or on the need to control
the illegal border crossings that were at stake in *Almeida-Sanchez* and its
progeny.[8] A different result in this case must be justified by the other two factors
in the *Brown* formulation.

As I have already explained, I believe the Court is quite wrong in blithely
asserting that a sobriety checkpoint is no more intrusive than a permanent
checkpoint. In my opinion, unannounced investigatory seizures are, particularly
when they take place at night, the hallmark of regimes far different from ours;[9] the

---

[7] It is, however, inappropriate for the Court to exaggerate that concern.

[8] The dissents in those cases touted the relevant State interests in detail. In *Almeida-Sanchez*,
Justice WHITE, joined by the author of today's majority opinion, wrote:

> The fact is that illegal crossings at other than the legal ports of entry are numerous and
> recurring. If there is to be any hope of intercepting illegal entrants and of maintaining any
> kind of credible deterrent, it is essential that permanent or temporary checkpoints be
> maintained away from the borders, and roving patrols be conducted to discover and intercept
> illegal entrants as they filter to the established roads and highways and attempt to move away
> from the border area. It is for this purpose that the Border Patrol maintained the roving
> patrol involved in this case and conducted random, spot checks of automobiles and other
> vehicular traffic.

Almeida-Sanchez v. United States, 413 U.S. 266, 293 (1973). Justice REHNQUIST argued in a similar vein
in his dissent in *Prouse*, in which he observed that: "The whole point of enforcing motor vehicle safety
regulations is to remove from the road the unlicensed driver before he demonstrates why he is
unlicensed."

[9] "It is well to recall the words of Mr. Justice Jackson, soon after his return from the Nuremberg
Trials: 'These [Fourth Amendment rights], I protest, are not mere second-class rights but belong in the

surprise intrusion upon individual liberty is not minimal. On that issue, my difference with the Court may amount to nothing less than a difference in our respective evaluations of the importance of individual liberty, a serious albeit inevitable source of constitutional disagreement. On the degree to which the sobriety checkpoint seizures advance the public interest, however, the Court's position is wholly indefensible.

The Court's analysis of this issue resembles a business decision that measures profits by counting gross receipts and ignoring expenses. The evidence in this case indicates that sobriety checkpoints result in the arrest of a fraction of one percent of the drivers who are stopped,[11] but there is absolutely no evidence that this figure represents an increase over the number of arrests that would have been made by using the same law enforcement resources in conventional patrols.[12] Thus, although the *gross* number of arrests is more than zero, there is a complete failure of proof on the question whether the wholesale seizures have produced any *net* advance in the public interest in arresting intoxicated drivers.

Indeed, the position adopted today by the Court is not one endorsed by any of the law enforcement authorities to whom the Court purports to defer. The Michigan police do not rely, as the Court does, on the *arrest rate* at sobriety checkpoints to justify the stops made there. Colonel Hough, the commander of the Michigan State Police and a leading proponent of the checkpoints, admitted at trial that the arrest rate at the checkpoints was "very low." Instead, Colonel Hough and the State have maintained that the mere *threat* of such arrests is sufficient to deter drunk driving and so to reduce the accident rate. The Maryland police officer who testified at trial took the same position with respect to his State's program. There is, obviously, nothing wrong with a law enforcement technique that reduces crime by pure deterrence without punishing anybody; on the contrary, such an approach is highly commendable. One cannot, however, prove its efficacy by counting the arrests that were made. One must instead measure the number of crimes that were avoided. Perhaps because the record is wanting, the Court simply ignores this point.

The Court's sparse analysis of this issue differs markedly from Justice Powell's opinion for the Court in *Martinez-Fuerte*. He did not merely count the 17,000 arrests made at the San Clemente checkpoint in 1973; he also carefully explained why those arrests represented a net benefit to the law enforcement interest at stake.[15] Common sense, moreover, suggests that immigration checkpoints are more

---

catalog of indispensable freedoms. Among deprivations of rights, none is so effective in cowing a population, crushing the spirit of the individual and putting terror in every heart. Uncontrolled search and seizure is one of the first and most effective weapons in the arsenal of every arbitrary government.' *Brinegar* (Jackson, J., dissenting)."

[11] The Court refers to the expert testimony that the arrest rate is "around 1 percent," but a fair reading of the entire testimony of that witness, together with the other statistical evidence in the record, points to a significantly lower percentage.

[12] Indeed, a single officer in a patrol car parked at the same place as the sobriety checkpoint would no doubt have been able to make some of the arrests based on the officer's observation of the way the intoxicated driver was operating his vehicle.

[15] "These checkpoints are located on important highways; in their absence such highways would offer illegal aliens a quick and safe route into the interior. Routine checkpoint inquiries apprehend many smugglers and illegal aliens who succumb to the lure of such highways. And the prospect of such

necessary than sobriety checkpoints: there is no reason why smuggling illegal aliens should impair a motorist's driving ability, but if intoxication did not noticeably affect driving ability it would not be unlawful. Drunk driving, unlike smuggling, may thus be detected absent any checkpoints. A program that produces thousands of otherwise impossible arrests is not a relevant precedent for a program that produces only a handful of arrests which would be more easily obtained without resort to suspicionless seizures of hundreds of innocent citizens.

III

The most disturbing aspect of the Court's decision today is that it appears to give no weight to the citizen's interest in freedom from suspicionless unannounced investigatory seizures. Although the author of the opinion does not reiterate his description of that interest as "diaphanous," see *Prouse* (REHNQUIST, J., dissenting), the Court's opinion implicitly adopts that characterization. On the other hand, the Court places a heavy thumb on the law enforcement interest by looking only at gross receipts instead of net benefits. Perhaps this tampering with the scales of justice can be explained by the Court's obvious concern about the slaughter on our highways, and a resultant tolerance for policies designed to alleviate the problem by "setting an example" of a few motorists. This possibility prompts two observations.

First, my objections to random seizures or temporary checkpoints do not apply to a host of other investigatory procedures that do not depend upon surprise and are unquestionably permissible. These procedures have been used to address other threats to human life no less pressing than the threat posed by drunken drivers. It is, for example, common practice to require every prospective airline passenger, or every visitor to a public building, to pass through a metal detector that will reveal the presence of a firearm or an explosive. Permanent, nondiscretionary checkpoints could be used to control serious dangers at other publicly operated facilities. Because concealed weapons obviously represent one such substantial threat to public safety, I would suppose that all subway passengers could be required to pass through metal detectors, so long as the detectors were permanent and every passenger was subjected to the same search.[17] Likewise, I would suppose that a State could condition access to its toll roads upon not only paying the toll but also taking a uniformly administered Breathalyzer test. That requirement might well keep all drunken drivers off the highways that serve the fastest and most dangerous traffic. This procedure would not be subject to the constitutional objections that control this case: the checkpoints would be permanently fixed, the stopping procedure would apply to all users of the toll road in precisely the same

---

inquiries forces others onto less efficient roads that are less heavily traveled, slowing their movement and making them more vulnerable to detection by roving patrols.

"A requirement that stops on major routes inland always be based on reasonable suspicion would be impractical because the flow of traffic tends to be too heavy to allow the particularized study of a given car that would enable it to be identified as a possible carrier of illegal aliens. In particular, such a requirement would largely eliminate any deterrent to the conduct of well-disguised smuggling operations, even though smugglers are known to use these highways regularly."

[17] Permanent, nondiscretionary checkpoints are already a common practice at public libraries, which now often require every patron to submit to a brief search for books, or to leave by passing through a special detector.

way, and police officers would not be free to make arbitrary choices about which neighborhoods should be targeted or about which individuals should be more thoroughly searched. Random, suspicionless seizures designed to search for evidence of firearms, drugs, or intoxication belong, however, in a fundamentally different category. These seizures play upon the detained individual's reasonable expectations of privacy, injecting a suspicionless search into a context where none would normally occur. The imposition that seems diaphanous today may be intolerable tomorrow.

Second, sobriety checkpoints are elaborate, and disquieting, publicity stunts. The possibility that anybody, no matter how innocent, may be stopped for police inspection is nothing if not attention-getting. The shock value of the checkpoint program may be its most effective feature: Lieutenant Cotton of the Maryland State Police, a defense witness, testified that "the media coverage . . . has been absolutely overwhelming. . . . Quite frankly we got benefits just from the controversy of the sobriety checkpoints." Insofar as the State seeks to justify its use of sobriety checkpoints on the basis that they dramatize the public interest in the prevention of alcohol related accidents, the Court should heed Justice SCALIA's comment upon a similar justification for a drug screening program:

> The only plausible explanation, in my view, is what the Commissioner himself offered in the concluding sentence of his memorandum to Customs Service employees announcing the program: "Implementation of the drug screening program would set an important example in our country's struggle with this most serious threat to our national health and security." Or as respondent's brief to this Court asserted: "if a law enforcement agency and its employees do not take the law seriously, neither will the public on which the agency's effectiveness depends." What better way to show that the Government is serious about its "war on drugs" than to subject its employees on the front line of that war to this invasion of their privacy and affront to their dignity? To be sure, there is only a slight chance that it will prevent some serious public harm resulting from Service employee drug use, but it will show to the world that the Service is "clean," and — most important of all — will demonstrate the determination of the Government to eliminate this scourge of our society! I think it obvious that this justification is unacceptable; that the impairment of individual liberties cannot be the means of making a point; that symbolism, even symbolism for so worthy a cause as the abolition of unlawful drugs, cannot validate an otherwise unreasonable search.

Treasury Employees v. Von Raab, 109 S. Ct. 1384, 1401 (1989) (SCALIA, J., dissenting).

This is a case that is driven by nothing more than symbolic state action — an insufficient justification for an otherwise unreasonable program of random seizures. Unfortunately, the Court is transfixed by the wrong symbol — the illusory prospect of punishing countless intoxicated motorists — when it should keep its eyes on the road plainly marked by the Constitution.

I respectfully dissent.

QUESTIONS AND NOTES

1. Would you categorize the plaintiff's interest in *Sitz* as "diaphanous"? Why? Why not?

2. What exactly is the plaintiff's interest? Is it different from or greater than that alleged in *Martinez-Fuerte*?

3. Is the *Brown* balancing test; which balances the importance of the State's interest, the effectiveness of the seizure in implementing the State's interest, and the importance of the defendant's interest; a good way to decide cases like *Sitz*?

4. In deferring completely to the police in regard to effectiveness, did the Court shirk its Fourth Amendment responsibilities?

5. Where should the burden of proof lie in a question like this? Why?

6. Do you agree with Justice Stevens that the state could condition access to a toll road upon the passing of a Breathalyzer test? How about conditioning access to roads that don't charge a toll? Suppose the motorist doesn't know that she is breathing into a Breathalyzer?

7. Could the State require that all automobiles be equipped with Breathalyzer so that the car wouldn't start if the driver's alcohol content was too high? Would such a proposal raise more or less constitutional problems than the *Sitz* statute?

8. Any thoughts from *Sitz*, that the Court might approve *carte blanche* roadblocks was squelched in *Edmond*.

CITY OF INDIANAPOLIS v. EDMOND
531 U.S. 32 (2000)

JUSTICE O'CONNOR delivered the opinion of the Court.

In *Sitz* and *Martinez-Fuerte*, we held that brief, suspicionless seizures at highway checkpoints for the purposes of combating drunk driving and intercepting illegal immigrants were constitutional. We now consider the constitutionality of a highway checkpoint program whose primary purpose is the discovery and interdiction of illegal narcotics.

I

In August 1998, the city of Indianapolis began to operate vehicle checkpoints on Indianapolis roads in an effort to interdict unlawful drugs. The city conducted six such roadblocks between August and November that year, stopping 1,161 vehicles and arresting 104 motorists. Fifty-five arrests were for drug-related crimes, while 49 were for offenses unrelated to drugs. The overall "hit rate" of the program was thus approximately nine percent.

At each checkpoint location, the police stop a predetermined number of vehicles. Approximately 30 officers are stationed at the checkpoint. Pursuant to written directives issued by the chief of police, at least one officer approaches the vehicle, advises the driver that he or she is being stopped briefly at a drug checkpoint, and asks the driver to produce a license and registration. The officer also looks for signs of impairment and conducts an open-view examination of the vehicle from the outside. A narcotics-detection dog walks around the outside of each stopped vehicle.

The directives instruct the officers that they may conduct a search only by consent or based on the appropriate quantum of particularized suspicion. The officers must conduct each stop in the same manner until particularized suspicion develops, and the officers have no discretion to stop any vehicle out of sequence. The city agreed in the stipulation to operate the checkpoints in such a way as to ensure that the total duration of each stop, absent reasonable suspicion or probable cause, would be five minutes or less.

The affidavit of Indianapolis Police Sergeant Marshall DePew, although it is technically outside the parties' stipulation, provides further insight concerning the operation of the checkpoints. According to Sergeant DePew, checkpoint locations are selected weeks in advance based on such considerations as area crime statistics and traffic flow. The checkpoints are generally operated during daylight hours and are identified with lighted signs reading, "NARCOTICS CHECKPOINT ___ MILE AHEAD, NARCOTICS K-9 IN USE, BE PREPARED TO STOP." Once a group of cars has been stopped, other traffic proceeds without interruption until all the stopped cars have been processed or diverted for further processing. Sergeant DePew also stated that the average stop for a vehicle not subject to further processing lasts two to three minutes or less.

Respondents James Edmond and Joell Palmer were each stopped at a narcotics checkpoint in late September 1998. Respondents then filed a lawsuit on behalf of themselves and the class of all motorists who had been stopped or were subject to being stopped in the future at the Indianapolis drug checkpoints. Respondents claimed that the roadblocks violated the Fourth Amendment of the United States Constitution and the search and seizure provision of the Indiana Constitution. Respondents requested declaratory and injunctive relief for the class, as well as damages and attorney's fees for themselves.

II

The Fourth Amendment requires that searches and seizures be reasonable. A search or seizure is ordinarily unreasonable in the absence of individualized suspicion of wrongdoing. While such suspicion is not an "irreducible" component of reasonableness, *Martinez-Fuerte*, we have recognized only limited circumstances in which the usual rule does not apply. For example, we have upheld certain regimes of suspicionless searches where the program was designed to serve "special needs, beyond the normal need for law enforcement." *See, e.g., Vernonia School Dist. 47J v. Acton*, 515 U.S. 646 (1995) (random drug testing of student-athletes); *Treasury Employees v. Von Raab*, 489 U.S. 656 (1989) (drug tests for United States Customs Service employees seeking transfer or promotion to certain positions); *Skinner v. Railway Labor Executives' Assn.*, 489 U.S. 602 (1989) (drug and alcohol tests for railway employees involved in train accidents or found to be in violation of particular safety regulations). We have also allowed searches for certain administrative purposes without particularized suspicion of misconduct, provided that those searches are appropriately limited. *See, e.g., New York v. Burger*, 482 U.S. 691 (1987) (warrantless administrative inspection of premises of "closely regulated" business); *Michigan v. Tyler*, 436 U.S. 499, 507–509, 511–512, 56 L. Ed. 2d 486, 98 S. Ct. 1942 (1978) (administrative inspection of fire-damaged premises to determine cause of blaze); *Camara v. Municipal Court of City and County of San Francisco*, 387 U.S. 523 (1967) (administrative inspection to ensure compliance with city housing code).

We have also upheld brief, suspicionless seizures of motorists at a fixed Border Patrol checkpoint designed to intercept illegal aliens, *Martinez-Fuerte*, and at a sobriety checkpoint aimed at removing drunk drivers from the road, *Sitz*. In addition, in *Prouse*, we suggested that a similar type of roadblock with the purpose of verifying drivers' licenses and vehicle registrations would be permissible. In none of these cases, however, did we indicate approval of a checkpoint program whose primary purpose was to detect evidence of ordinary criminal wrongdoing.

In *Martinez-Fuerte*, we entertained Fourth Amendment challenges to stops at two permanent immigration checkpoints located on major United States highways less than 100 miles from the Mexican border. We noted at the outset the particular context in which the constitutional question arose, describing in some detail the "formidable law enforcement problems" posed by the northbound tide of illegal entrants into the United States.

We found that the balance tipped in favor of the Government's interests in policing the Nation's borders. 428 U.S. at 561–564. In so finding, we emphasized the difficulty of effectively containing illegal immigration at the border itself. 428 U.S. at 556. We also stressed the impracticality of the particularized study of a given car to discern whether it was transporting illegal aliens, as well as the relatively modest degree of intrusion entailed by the stops. 428 U.S. at 556–564.

In *Sitz*, we evaluated the constitutionality of a Michigan highway sobriety checkpoint program. The *Sitz* checkpoint involved brief suspicionless stops of motorists so that police officers could detect signs of intoxication and remove impaired drivers from the road. Motorists who exhibited signs of intoxication were diverted for a license and registration check and, if warranted, further sobriety tests. This checkpoint program was clearly aimed at reducing the immediate hazard posed by the presence of drunk drivers on the highways, and there was an obvious connection between the imperative of highway safety and the law enforcement practice at issue. The gravity of the drunk driving problem and the magnitude of the State's interest in getting drunk drivers off the road weighed heavily in our determination that the program was constitutional.

In *Prouse*, we invalidated a discretionary, suspicionless stop for a spot check of a motorist's driver's license and vehicle registration. The officer's conduct in that case was unconstitutional primarily on account of his exercise of "standardless and unconstrained discretion." We nonetheless acknowledged the States' "vital interest in ensuring that only those qualified to do so are permitted to operate motor vehicles, that these vehicles are fit for safe operation, and hence that licensing, registration, and vehicle inspection requirements are being observed." Accordingly, we suggested that "questioning of all oncoming traffic at roadblock-type stops" would be a lawful means of serving this interest in highway safety.

We further indicated in *Prouse* that we considered the purposes of such a hypothetical roadblock to be distinct from a general purpose of investigating crime. The State proffered the additional interests of "the apprehension of stolen motor vehicles and of drivers under the influence of alcohol or narcotics" in its effort to justify the discretionary spot check. We attributed the entirety of the latter interest to the State's interest in roadway safety. We also noted that the interest in apprehending stolen vehicles may be partly subsumed by the interest in roadway safety. We observed, however, that "the remaining governmental interest in controlling automobile thefts is not distinguishable from the general interest in crime control." Not only does the common thread of highway safety thus run through *Sitz* and *Prouse*, but *Prouse* itself reveals a difference in the Fourth Amendment significance of highway safety interests and the general interest in crime control.

III

It is well established that a vehicle stop at a highway checkpoint effectuates a seizure within the meaning of the Fourth Amendment. *See, e.g., Sitz.* The fact that officers walk a narcotics-detection dog around the exterior of each car at the Indianapolis checkpoints does not transform the seizure into a search. *See United States v. Place*, 462 U.S. 696 (1983) [Ch. 10, *infra*]. Just as in *Place*, an exterior sniff of an automobile does not require entry into the car and is not designed to disclose any information other than the presence or absence of narcotics. Like the dog sniff in *Place*, a sniff by a dog that simply walks around a car is "much less intrusive than a typical search." Rather, what principally distinguishes these checkpoints from those we have previously approved is their primary purpose.

As petitioners concede, the Indianapolis checkpoint program unquestionably has the primary purpose of interdicting illegal narcotics. In their stipulation of facts, the parties repeatedly refer to the checkpoints as "drug checkpoints" and describe them as "being operated by the City of Indianapolis in an effort to interdict unlawful drugs in Indianapolis." In addition, the first document attached to the parties' stipulation is entitled "DRUG CHECKPOINT CONTACT OFFICER DIRECTIVES BY ORDER OF THE CHIEF OF POLICE." These directives instruct officers to "advise the citizen that they are being stopped briefly at a drug checkpoint." The second document attached to the stipulation is entitled "1998 Drug Road Blocks" and contains a statistical breakdown of information relating to the checkpoints conducted. Further, according to Sergeant DePew, the checkpoints are identified with lighted signs reading, "NARCOTICS CHECKPOINT ___ MILE AHEAD, NARCOTICS K-9 IN USE, BE PREPARED TO STOP." Finally, both the District Court and the Court of Appeals recognized that the primary purpose of the roadblocks is the interdiction of narcotics.

We have never approved a checkpoint program whose primary purpose was to detect evidence of ordinary criminal wrongdoing. Rather, our checkpoint cases have recognized only limited exceptions to the general rule that a seizure must be accompanied by some measure of individualized suspicion. We suggested in *Prouse* that we would not credit the "general interest in crime control" as justification for a regime of suspicionless stops. Consistent with this suggestion, each of the checkpoint programs that we have approved was designed primarily to serve purposes closely related to the problems of policing the border or the necessity of ensuring roadway safety. Because the primary purpose of the Indianapolis narcotics checkpoint program is to uncover evidence of ordinary criminal wrongdoing, the program contravenes the Fourth Amendment.

Petitioners propose several ways in which the narcotics-detection purpose of the instant checkpoint program may instead resemble the primary purposes of the checkpoints in *Sitz* and *Martinez-Fuerte*. Petitioners state that the checkpoints in those cases had the same ultimate purpose of arresting those suspected of committing crimes. Securing the border and apprehending drunk drivers are, of course, law enforcement activities, and law enforcement officers employ arrests and criminal prosecutions in pursuit of these goals. If we were to rest the case at this high level of generality, there would be little check on the ability of the authorities to construct roadblocks for almost any conceivable law enforcement purpose. Without drawing the line at roadblocks designed primarily to serve the general interest in crime control, the Fourth Amendment would do little to prevent such intrusions from becoming a routine part of American life.

Petitioners also emphasize the severe and intractable nature of the drug problem as justification for the checkpoint program. There is no doubt that traffic in illegal narcotics creates social harms of the first magnitude. *Cf. Von Raab.* The law enforcement problems that the drug trade creates likewise remain daunting and complex, particularly in light of the myriad forms of spin-off crime that it spawns. The same can be said of various other illegal activities, if only to a lesser degree. But the gravity of the threat alone cannot be dispositive of questions concerning what means law enforcement officers may employ to pursue a given purpose. Rather, in determining whether individualized suspicion is required, we must consider the nature of the interests threatened and their connection to the particular law enforcement practices at issue. We are particularly reluctant to recognize exceptions to the general rule of individualized suspicion where governmental authorities primarily pursue their general crime control ends.

Nor can the narcotics-interdiction purpose of the checkpoints be rationalized in terms of a highway safety concern similar to that present in *Sitz*. The detection and punishment of almost any criminal offense serves broadly the safety of the community, and our streets would no doubt be safer but for the scourge of illegal drugs. Only with respect to a smaller class of offenses, however, is society confronted with the type of immediate, vehicle-bound threat to life and limb that the sobriety checkpoint in *Sitz* was designed to eliminate.

Petitioners also liken the anticontraband agenda of the Indianapolis checkpoints to the antismuggling purpose of the checkpoints in *Martinez-Fuerte*. Petitioners cite this Court's conclusion in *Martinez-Fuerte* that the flow of traffic was too heavy to permit "particularized study of a given car that would enable it to be identified as a possible carrier of illegal aliens," and claim that this logic has even more force here. The problem with this argument is that the same logic prevails any time a vehicle is employed to conceal contraband or other evidence of a crime. This type of connection to the roadway is very different from the close connection to roadway safety that was present in *Sitz* and *Prouse*. Further, the Indianapolis checkpoints are far removed from the border context that was crucial in *Martinez-Fuerte*. While the difficulty of examining each passing car was an important factor in validating the law enforcement technique employed in *Martinez-Fuerte*, this factor alone cannot justify a regime of suspicionless searches or seizures. Rather, we must look more closely at the nature of the public interests that such a regime is designed principally to serve.

The primary purpose of the Indianapolis narcotics checkpoints is in the end to advance "the general interest in crime control." We decline to suspend the usual requirement of individualized suspicion where the police seek to employ a checkpoint primarily for the ordinary enterprise of investigating crimes. We cannot sanction stops justified only by the generalized and ever-present possibility that interrogation and inspection may reveal that any given motorist has committed some crime.

Of course, there are circumstances that may justify a law enforcement checkpoint where the primary purpose would otherwise, but for some emergency, relate to ordinary crime control. For example, as the Court of Appeals noted, the Fourth Amendment would almost certainly permit an appropriately tailored roadblock set up to thwart an imminent terrorist attack or to catch a dangerous criminal who is likely to flee by way of a particular route. The exigencies created by these scenarios are far removed from the circumstances under which authorities might simply stop cars as a matter of course to see if there just happens to be a felon leaving the jurisdiction. While we do not limit the purposes that may justify a checkpoint program to any rigid set of categories, we decline to approve a program whose primary purpose is ultimately indistinguishable from the general interest in crime control.[1]

Petitioners argue that our prior cases preclude an inquiry into the purposes of the checkpoint program. For example, they cite *Whren v. United States*, 517 U.S. 806 (1996) [Ch. 12, *infra*], to support the proposition that "where the government articulates and pursues a legitimate interest for a suspicionless stop, courts should not look behind that interest to determine whether the government's 'primary purpose' is valid." These cases, however, do not control the instant situation.

In *Whren*, we held that an individual officer's subjective intentions are irrelevant to the Fourth Amendment validity of a traffic stop that is justified objectively by probable cause to believe that a traffic violation has occurred. We observed that our prior cases "foreclose any argument that the constitutional reasonableness of traffic stops depends on the actual motivations of the individual officers involved." In so holding, we expressly distinguished cases where we had addressed the validity of searches conducted in the absence of probable cause. (distinguishing *Florida v.*

---

[1] THE CHIEF JUSTICE's dissent erroneously characterizes our opinion as resting on the application of a "non-law-enforcement primary purpose test." Our opinion nowhere describes the purposes of the *Sitz* and *Martinez-Fuerte* checkpoints as being "not primarily related to criminal law enforcement." Rather, our judgment turns on the fact that the primary purpose of the Indianapolis checkpoints is to advance the general interest in crime Control. THE CHIEF JUSTICE's dissent also erroneously characterizes our opinion as holding that the "use of a drug-sniffing dog . . . annuls what is otherwise plainly constitutional under our Fourth Amendment jurisprudence." Again, the constitutional defect of the program is that its primary purpose is to advance the general interest in crime control.

Wells) (stating that "an inventory search must not be a ruse for a general rummaging in order to discover incriminating evidence"), *Colorado v. Bertine*, 479 U.S. 367 (1987) (suggesting that the absence of bad faith and the lack of a purely investigative purpose were relevant to the validity of an inventory search), and *Burger* (observing that a valid administrative inspection conducted with neither a warrant nor probable cause did not appear to be a pretext for gathering evidence of violations of the penal laws)).

Whren therefore reinforces the principle that, while "subjective intentions play no role in ordinary, probable-cause Fourth Amendment analysis," programmatic purposes may be relevant to the validity of Fourth Amendment intrusions undertaken pursuant to a general scheme without individualized suspicion. Accordingly, *Whren* does not preclude an inquiry into programmatic purpose in such contexts. It likewise does not preclude an inquiry into programmatic purpose here.

Petitioners argue that the Indianapolis checkpoint program is justified by its lawful secondary purposes of keeping impaired motorists off the road and verifying licenses and registrations. If this were the case, however, law enforcement authorities would be able to establish checkpoints for virtually any purpose so long as they also included a license or sobriety check. For this reason, we examine the available evidence to determine the primary purpose of the checkpoint program. While we recognize the challenges inherent in a purpose inquiry, courts routinely engage in this enterprise in many areas of constitutional jurisprudence as a means of sifting abusive governmental conduct from that which is lawful. As a result, a program driven by an impermissible purpose may be proscribed while a program impelled by licit purposes is permitted, even though the challenged conduct may be outwardly similar. While reasonableness under the Fourth Amendment is predominantly an objective inquiry, our special needs and administrative search cases demonstrate that purpose is often relevant when suspicionless intrusions pursuant to a general scheme are at issue.[2]

It goes without saying that our holding today does nothing to alter the constitutional status of the sobriety and border checkpoints that we approved in *Sitz* and *Martinez-Fuerte*, or of the type of traffic checkpoint that we suggested would be lawful in *Prouse*. The constitutionality of such checkpoint programs still depends on a balancing of the competing interests at stake and the effectiveness of the program. When law enforcement authorities pursue primarily general crime control purposes at checkpoints such as here, however, stops can only be justified by some quantum of individualized suspicion.

Our holding also does not affect the validity of border searches or searches at places like airports and government buildings, where the need for such measures to ensure public safety can be particularly acute. Nor does our opinion speak to other intrusions aimed primarily at purposes beyond the general interest in crime control. Our holding also does not impair the ability of police officers to act appropriately

---

[2] Because petitioners concede that the primary purpose of the Indianapolis checkpoints is narcotics detection, we need not decide whether the State may establish a checkpoint program with the primary purpose of checking licenses or driver sobriety and a secondary purpose of interdicting narcotics. Specifically, we express no view on the question whether police may expand the scope of a license or sobriety checkpoint seizure in order to detect the presence of drugs in a stopped car.

upon information that they properly learn during a checkpoint stop justified by a lawful primary purpose, even where such action may result in the arrest of a motorist for an offense unrelated to that purpose. Finally, we caution that the purpose inquiry in this context is to be conducted only at the programmatic level and is not an invitation to probe the minds of individual officers acting at the scene.

Because the primary purpose of the Indianapolis checkpoint program is ultimately indistinguishable from the general interest in crime control, the checkpoints violate the Fourth Amendment. The judgment of the Court of Appeals is accordingly affirmed.

CHIEF JUSTICE REHNQUIST, with whom JUSTICE THOMAS joins, and with whom JUSTICE SCALIA joins as to Part I, dissenting.

The State's use of a drug-sniffing dog, according to the Court's holding, annuls what is otherwise plainly constitutional under our Fourth Amendment jurisprudence: brief, standardized, discretionless, roadblock seizures of automobiles, seizures which effectively serve a weighty state interest with only minimal intrusion on the privacy of their occupants. Because these seizures serve the State's accepted and significant interests of preventing drunken driving and checking for driver's licenses and vehicle registrations, and because there is nothing in the record to indicate that the addition of the dog sniff lengthens these otherwise legitimate seizures, I dissent.

I

As it is nowhere to be found in the Court's opinion, I begin with blackletter roadblock seizure law. "The principal protection of Fourth Amendment rights at checkpoints lies in appropriate limitations on the scope of the stop." Roadblock seizures are consistent with the Fourth Amendment if they are "carried out pursuant to a plan embodying explicit, neutral limitations on the conduct of individual officers." *Brown v. Texas.* Specifically, the constitutionality of a seizure turns upon "a weighing of the gravity of the public concerns served by the seizure, the degree to which the seizure advances the public interest, and the severity of the interference with individual liberty."

We first applied these principles in *Martinez-Fuerte*, which approved highway checkpoints for detecting illegal aliens. In *Martinez-Fuerte*, we balanced the United States' formidable interest in checking the flow of illegal immigrants against the limited "objective" and "subjective" intrusion on the motorists. The objective intrusion — the stop itself,[1] the brief questioning of the occupants, and the visual inspection of the car — was considered "limited" because "neither the vehicle nor its occupants [were] searched." Likewise, the subjective intrusion, or the fear and surprise engendered in law-abiding motorists by the nature of the stop, was found to be minimal because the "regularized manner in which [the] established checkpoints [were] operated [was] visible evidence, reassuring to law-abiding motorists,

---

[1] The record from one of the consolidated cases indicated that the stops lasted between three and five minutes. *See United States v. Martinez-Fuerte*, 428 U.S. 543 (1976).

that the stops [were] duly authorized and believed to serve the public interest." Indeed, the standardized operation of the roadblocks was viewed as markedly different from roving patrols, where the unbridled discretion of officers in the field could result in unlimited interference with motorists' use of the highways. And although the decision in *Martinez-Fuerte* did not turn on the checkpoints' effectiveness, the record in one of the consolidated cases demonstrated that illegal aliens were found in 0.12 percent of the stopped vehicles.

In *Sitz*, we upheld the State's use of a highway sobriety checkpoint after applying the framework set out in *Martinez-Fuerte* and *Brown*. There, we recognized the gravity of the State's interest in curbing drunken driving and found the objective intrusion of the approximately 25-second seizure to be "slight." Turning to the subjective intrusion, we noted that the checkpoint was selected pursuant to guidelines and was operated by uniformed officers. Finally, we concluded that the program effectively furthered the State's interest because the checkpoint resulted in the arrest of two drunk drivers, or 1.6 percent of the 126 drivers stopped.

This case follows naturally from *Martinez-Fuerte* and *Sitz*. Petitioners acknowledge that the "primary purpose" of these roadblocks is to interdict illegal drugs, but this fact should not be controlling. Even accepting the Court's conclusion that the checkpoints at issue in *Martinez-Fuerte* and *Sitz* were not primarily related to criminal law enforcement,[2] the question whether a law enforcement purpose could support a roadblock seizure is not presented in this case. The District Court found that another "purpose of the checkpoints is to check driver's licenses and vehicle registrations," and the written directives state that the police officers are to "look for signs of impairment." The use of roadblocks to look for signs of impairment was validated by *Sitz*, and the use of roadblocks to check for driver's licenses and vehicle registrations was expressly recognized in *Prouse*. That the roadblocks serve these legitimate state interests cannot be seriously disputed, as the 49 people arrested for offenses unrelated to drugs can attest. And it would be speculative to conclude — given the District Court's findings, the written directives, and the actual arrests — that petitioners would not have operated these roadblocks but for the State's interest in interdicting drugs.

Because of the valid reasons for conducting these roadblock seizures, it is constitutionally irrelevant that petitioners also hoped to interdict drugs. In *Whren v. United States*, 517 U.S. 806 (1996) [Ch. 12, *infra*], we held that an officer's subjective intent would not invalidate an otherwise objectively justifiable stop of an automobile. The reasonableness of an officer's discretionary decision to stop an automobile, at issue in *Whren*, turns on whether there is probable cause to believe that a traffic violation has occurred. The reasonableness of highway checkpoints, at issue here, turns on whether they effectively serve a significant state interest with

---

[2] This gloss is not at all obvious. The respondents in *Martinez-Fuerte* were criminally prosecuted for illegally transporting aliens, and the Court expressly noted that "interdicting the flow of illegal entrants from Mexico poses formidable law enforcement problems." And the *Sitz* Court recognized that if an "officer's observations suggest that the driver was intoxicated, an arrest would be made." But however persuasive the distinction, the Court's opinion does not impugn the continuing validity of *Martinez-Fuerte* and *Sitz*.

minimal intrusion on motorists. The stop in *Whren* was objectively reasonable because the police officers had witnessed traffic violations; so too the roadblocks here are objectively reasonable because they serve the substantial interests of preventing drunken driving and checking for driver's licenses and vehicle registrations with minimal intrusion on motorists.

Once the constitutional requirements for a particular seizure are satisfied, the subjective expectations of those responsible for it, be it police officers or members of a city council, are irrelevant. Because the objective intrusion of a valid seizure does not turn upon anyone's subjective thoughts, neither should our constitutional analysis.

With these checkpoints serving two important state interests, the remaining prongs of the *Brown v. Texas* balancing test are easily met. The seizure is objectively reasonable as it lasts, on average, two to three minutes and does not involve a search. The subjective intrusion is likewise limited as the checkpoints are clearly marked and operated by uniformed officers who are directed to stop every vehicle in the same manner. The only difference between this case and *Sitz* is the presence of the dog. We have already held, however, that a "sniff test" by a trained narcotics dog is not a "search" within the meaning of the Fourth Amendment because it does not require physical intrusion of the object being sniffed and it does not expose anything other than the contraband items. *United States v. Place*, 462 U.S. 696 (1983) [Ch. 10, *infra*]. And there is nothing in the record to indicate that the dog sniff lengthens the stop. Finally, the checkpoints' success rate — 49 arrests for offenses unrelated to drugs — only confirms the State's legitimate interests in preventing drunken driving and ensuring the proper licensing of drivers and registration of their vehicles.[5]

These stops effectively serve the State's legitimate interests; they are executed in a regularized and neutral manner; and they only minimally intrude upon the privacy of the motorists. They should therefore be constitutional.

II

The Court, unwilling to adopt the straightforward analysis that these precedents dictate, adds a new non-law-enforcement primary purpose test lifted from a distinct area of Fourth Amendment jurisprudence relating to the *searches* of homes and businesses. As discussed above, the question that the Court answers is not even posed in this case given the accepted reasons for the seizures. But more fundamentally, whatever sense a non-law-enforcement primary purpose test may make in the search setting, it is ill suited to brief roadblock seizures, where we have consistently looked at "the scope of the stop" in assessing a program's constitutionality.

"One's expectation of privacy in an automobile and of freedom in its operation are significantly different from the traditional expectation of privacy and freedom in one's residence." The lowered expectation of privacy in one's automobile is coupled

---

[5] Put in statistical terms, 4.2 percent of the 1,161 motorists stopped were arrested for offenses unrelated to drugs.

with the limited nature of the intrusion: a brief, standardized, nonintrusive seizure.[6] The brief seizure of an automobile can hardly be compared to the intrusive search of the body or the home. Thus, just as the "special needs" inquiry serves to both define and limit the permissible scope of those searches, the *Brown v. Texas* balancing test serves to define and limit the permissible scope of automobile seizures.

Because of these extrinsic limitations upon roadblock seizures, the Court's newfound non-law-enforcement primary purpose test is both unnecessary to secure Fourth Amendment rights and bound to produce wide-ranging litigation over the "purpose" of any given seizure. Police designing highway roadblocks can never be sure of their validity, since a jury might later determine that a forbidden purpose exists. Roadblock stops identical to the one that we upheld in *Sitz* 10 years ago, or to the one that we upheld 24 years ago in *Martinez-Fuerte*, may now be challenged on the grounds that they have some concealed forbidden purpose.

Efforts to enforce the law on public highways used by millions of motorists are obviously necessary to our society. The Court's opinion today casts a shadow over what had been assumed, on the basis of *stare decisis*, to be a perfectly lawful activity. Conversely, if the Indianapolis police had assigned a different purpose to their activity here, but in no way changed what was done on the ground to individual motorists, it might well be valid. The Court's non-law-enforcement primary purpose test simply does not serve as a proxy for anything that the Fourth Amendment is, or should be, concerned about in the automobile seizure context.

Petitioners' program complies with our decisions regarding roadblock seizures of automobiles, and the addition of a dog sniff does not add to the length or the intrusion of the stop. Because such stops are consistent with the Fourth Amendment, I would reverse the decision of the Court of Appeals.

JUSTICE THOMAS, dissenting.

Taken together, our decisions in *Sitz* and *Martinez-Fuerte* stand for the proposition that suspicionless roadblock seizures are constitutionally permissible if conducted according to a plan that limits the discretion of the officers conducting the stops. I am not convinced that *Sitz* and *Martinez-Fuerte* were correctly decided. Indeed, I rather doubt that the Framers of the Fourth Amendment would have considered "reasonable" a program of indiscriminate stops of individuals not suspected of wrongdoing.

Respondents did not, however, advocate the overruling of *Sitz* and *Martinez-Fuerte*, and I am reluctant to consider such a step without the benefit of briefing and argument. For the reasons given by THE CHIEF JUSTICE, I believe that those cases compel upholding the program at issue here. I, therefore, join his opinion.

---

[6] This fact distinguishes the roadblock seizure of an automobile from an inventory search of an automobile. *Cf. Colorado v. Bertine* (automobile inventory search).

QUESTIONS AND NOTES

1.   Would the result in *Edmond* be different if instead of a drug checkpoint that also checked licenses and sobriety, it were a license and sobriety checkpoint that also employed drug sniffing dogs? What would O'Connor say? What would Rehnquist say?

2.   Is the distinction suggested by Question 1, one of form or substance?

3.   If Indianapolis wanted to continue its roadblock, what would you advise it to do?

4.   After *Edmond*, are *Sitz* and *Martinez-Fuerte* good law? Should they be?

5.   We conclude this section with *Illinois v. Lidster*, which establishes that not all suspicionless highway stops for the purpose of solving crime are unconstitutional.

ILLINOIS v. LIDSTER
540 U.S. 419 (2004)

JUSTICE BREYER delivered the opinion of the Court.

This Fourth Amendment case focuses upon a highway checkpoint where police stopped motorists to ask them for information about a recent hit-and-run accident. We hold that the police stops were reasonable, hence, constitutional.

I

The relevant background is as follows: On Saturday, August 23, 1997, just after midnight, an unknown motorist traveling eastbound on a highway in Lombard, Illinois, struck and killed a 70-year-old bicyclist. The motorist drove off without identifying himself. About one week later at about the same time of night and at about the same place, local police set up a highway checkpoint designed to obtain more information about the accident from the motoring public.

Police cars with flashing lights partially blocked the eastbound lanes of the highway. The blockage forced traffic to slow down, leading to lines of up to 15 cars in each lane. As each vehicle drew up to the checkpoint, an officer would stop it for 10 to 15 seconds, ask the occupants whether they had seen anything happen there the previous weekend, and hand each driver a flyer. The flyer said "ALERT . . . FATAL HIT & RUN ACCIDENT" and requested "assistance in identifying the vehicle and driver in this accident which killed a 70 year old bicyclist."

Robert Lidster, the respondent, drove a minivan toward the checkpoint. As he approached the checkpoint, his van swerved, nearly hitting one of the officers. The officer smelled alcohol on Lidster's breath. He directed Lidster to a side street where another officer administered a sobriety test and then arrested Lidster. Lidster was tried and convicted in Illinois state court of driving under the influence of alcohol.

II

The Illinois Supreme Court basically held that our decision in *Edmond* governs the outcome of this case. We do not agree. *Edmond* involved a checkpoint at which police stopped vehicles to look for evidence of drug crimes committed by occupants of those vehicles. After stopping a vehicle at the checkpoint, police would examine (from outside the vehicle) the vehicle's interior; they would walk a drug-sniffing dog around the exterior; and, if they found sufficient evidence of drug (or other) crimes, they would arrest the vehicle's occupants. We found that police had set up this checkpoint primarily for general "crime control" purposes, i.e., "to detect evidence of ordinary criminal wrongdoing." We noted that the stop was made without individualized suspicion. And we held that the Fourth Amendment forbids such a stop, in the absence of special circumstances.

The checkpoint stop here differs significantly from that in *Edmond*. The stop's primary law enforcement purpose was not to determine whether a vehicle's occupants were committing a crime, but to ask vehicle occupants, as members of the public, for their help in providing information about a crime in all likelihood committed by others. The police expected the information elicited to help them apprehend, not the vehicle's occupants, but other individuals.

Edmond's language, as well as its context, makes clear that the constitutionality of this latter, information-seeking kind of stop was not then before the Court. *Edmond* refers to the subject matter of its holding as "stops justified only by the generalized and ever-present possibility that interrogation and inspection may reveal that *any given motorist has committed some crime*." (emphasis added). We concede that *Edmond* describes the law enforcement objective there in question as a "general interest in crime control," but it specifies that the phrase "general interest in crime control" does not refer to every "law enforcement" objective. We must read this and related general language in *Edmond* as we often read general language in judicial opinions — as referring in context to circumstances similar to the circumstances then before the Court and not referring to quite different circumstances that the Court was not then considering.

Neither do we believe, *Edmond* aside, that the Fourth Amendment would have us apply an *Edmond*-type rule of automatic unconstitutionality to brief, information-seeking highway stops of the kind now before us. For one thing, the fact that such stops normally lack individualized suspicion cannot by itself determine the constitutional outcome. As in Edmond, the stop here at issue involves a motorist. The Fourth Amendment does not treat a motorist's car as his castle. And special law enforcement concerns will sometimes justify highway stops without individualized suspicion. Moreover, unlike *Edmond*, the context here (seeking information from the public) is one in which, by definition, the concept of individualized suspicion has little role to play. Like certain other forms of police activity, say, crowd control or public safety, an information-seeking stop is not the kind of event that involves suspicion, or lack of suspicion, of the relevant individual.

For another thing, information-seeking highway stops are less likely to provoke anxiety or to prove intrusive. The stops are likely brief. The police are not likely to ask questions designed to elicit self-incriminating information. And citizens will often react positively when police simply ask for their help as "responsible citizen[s]" to "give whatever information they may have to aid in law enforcement."

Further, the law ordinarily permits police to seek the voluntary cooperation of members of the public in the investigation of a crime. "[L]aw enforcement officers do not violate the Fourth Amendment by merely approaching an individual on the street or in another public place, by asking him if he is willing to answer some questions, [or] by putting questions to him if the person is willing to listen."

The importance of soliciting the public's assistance is offset to some degree by the need to stop a motorist to obtain that help — a need less likely present where a pedestrian, not a motorist, is involved. The difference is significant in light of our determinations that such an involuntary stop amounts to a "seizure" in Fourth Amendment terms. That difference, however, is not important enough to justify an *Edmond*-type rule here. After all, as we have said, the motorist stop will likely be brief. Any accompanying traffic delay should prove no more onerous than many that typically accompany normal traffic congestion. And the resulting voluntary questioning of a motorist is as likely to prove important for police investigation as is the questioning of a pedestrian. Given these considerations, it would seem anomalous were the law (1) ordinarily to allow police freely to seek the voluntary cooperation of pedestrians but (2) ordinarily to forbid police to seek similar voluntary cooperation from motorists.

Finally, we do not believe that an *Edmond*-type rule is needed to prevent an unreasonable proliferation of police checkpoints. Practical considerations — namely, limited police resources and community hostility to related traffic tie-ups — seem likely to inhibit any such proliferation. See Fell, Ferguson, Williams, & Fields, Why Aren't Sobriety Checkpoints Widely Adopted as an Enforcement Strategy in the United States?, 35 Accident Analysis & Prevention 897 (Nov. 2003) (finding that sobriety checkpoints are not more widely used due to the lack of police resources and the lack of community support). And, of course, the Fourth Amendment's normal insistence that the stop be reasonable in context will still provide an important legal limitation on police use of this kind of information-seeking checkpoint.

These considerations, taken together, convince us that an *Edmond*-type presumptive rule of unconstitutionality does not apply here. That does not mean the stop is automatically, or even presumptively, constitutional. It simply means that we must judge its reasonableness, hence, its constitutionality, on the basis of the individual circumstances. And as this Court said in *Brown v. Texas*, 443 U.S. 47, 51 (1979), in judging reasonableness, we look to "the gravity of the public concerns served by the seizure, the degree to which the seizure advances the public interest, and the severity of the interference with individual liberty."

III

We now consider the reasonableness of the checkpoint stop before us in light of the factors just mentioned, an issue that, in our view, has been fully argued here. We hold that the stop was constitutional.

The relevant public concern was grave. Police were investigating a crime that had resulted in a human death. No one denies the police's need to obtain more information at that time. And the stop's objective was to help find the perpetrator of a specific and known crime, not of unknown crimes of a general sort. *Cf. Edmond.*

The stop advanced this grave public concern to a significant degree. The police appropriately tailored their checkpoint stops to fit important criminal investigatory needs. The stops took place about one week after the hit-and-run accident, on the same highway near the location of the accident, and at about the same time of night. And police used the stops to obtain information from drivers, some of whom might well have been in the vicinity of the crime at the time it occurred. See App. 28–29 (describing police belief that motorists routinely leaving work after night shifts at nearby industrial complexes might have seen something relevant).

Most importantly, the stops interfered only minimally with liberty of the sort the Fourth Amendment seeks to protect. Viewed objectively, each stop required only a brief wait in line — a very few minutes at most. Contact with the police lasted only a few seconds. *Cf. Martinez-Fuerte,* (upholding stops of three-to-five minutes); *Sitz,* (upholding delays of 25 seconds). Police contact consisted simply of a request for information and the distribution of a flyer. Viewed subjectively, the contact provided little reason for anxiety or alarm. The police stopped all vehicles systematically. And there is no allegation here that the police acted in a discriminatory or otherwise unlawful manner while questioning motorists during stops.

For these reasons we conclude that the checkpoint stop was constitutional.

The judgment of the Illinois Supreme Court is

Reversed.

JUSTICE STEVENS, with whom JUSTICE SOUTER and JUSTICE GINSBURG join, concurring in part and dissenting in part.

There is a valid and important distinction between seizing a person to determine whether she has committed a crime and seizing a person to ask whether she has any information about an unknown person who committed a crime a week earlier. I therefore join Parts I and II of the Court's opinion explaining why our decision in *Edmond* is not controlling in this case. However, I find the issue discussed in Part III of the opinion closer than the Court does and believe it would be wise to remand the case to the Illinois state courts to address that issue in the first instance.

In contrast to pedestrians, who are free to keep walking when they encounter police officers handing out flyers or seeking information, motorists who confront a roadblock are required to stop, and to remain stopped for as long as the officers choose to detain them. Such a seizure may seem relatively innocuous to some, but annoying to others who are forced to wait for several minutes when the line of cars is lengthened — for example, by a surge of vehicles leaving a factory at the end of a shift. Still other drivers may find an unpublicized roadblock at midnight on a Saturday somewhat alarming.

On the other side of the equation, the likelihood that questioning a random sample of drivers will yield useful information about a hit-and-run accident that occurred a week earlier is speculative at best. To be sure, the sample in this case was not entirely random: The record reveals that the police knew that the victim had finished work at the Post Office shortly before the fatal accident, and hoped that other employees of the Post Office or the nearby industrial park might work on similar schedules and, thus, have been driving the same route at the same time the previous week. That is a plausible theory, but there is no evidence in the record that the police did anything to confirm that the nearby businesses in fact had shift changes at or near midnight on Saturdays, or that they had reason to believe that a roadblock would be more effective than, say, placing flyers on the employees' cars.

In short, the outcome of the multifactor test prescribed in *Brown v. Texas* is by no means clear on the facts of this case. Because the Illinois Appellate Court and the State Supreme Court held that the Lombard roadblock was per se unconstitutional under *Edmond*, neither court attempted to apply the *Brown* test. "We ordinarily do not decide in the first instance issues not resolved below." We should be especially reluctant to abandon our role as a court of review in a case in which the constitutional inquiry requires analysis of local conditions and practices more familiar to judges closer to the scene. I would therefore remand the case to the Illinois courts to undertake the initial analysis of the issue that the Court resolves in Part III of its opinion. To that extent, I respectfully dissent.

QUESTIONS AND NOTES

1. Among the procedures at issue in *Prouse, Sitz, Edmond,* and *Lidster*, which is likely to cause the least resentment among the populace?

2. Assuming that you said *Lidster* for Question 1, would that fact mean that the case was necessarily rightly decided?

3. Why did Justice Stevens think that a remand was necessary? Do you agree?

4. Even if one were to assume that the roadblock was invalid, should Lidster have a defense to drunk driving? Why? Why not?

E. INVENTORY SEARCHES

When the police impound a towed car, or impound the car of an arrestee, it is sometimes argued that the police should be permitted to inventory the contents of that car. In a couple of closely divided cases in the seventies, the Supreme Court upheld inventory searches under the special facts of the case. In *Bertine*, the state argued that inventory searches were always permitted, at least if conducted according to guidelines.

COLORADO v. BERTINE
479 U.S. 367 (1987)

CHIEF JUSTICE REHNQUIST delivered the opinion of the Court.

On February 10, 1984, a police officer in Boulder, Colorado, arrested respondent Steven Lee Bertine for driving while under the influence of alcohol. After Bertine was taken into custody and before the arrival of a tow truck to take Bertine's van to an impoundment lot,[1] a backup officer inventoried the contents of the van. The officer opened a closed backpack in which he found controlled substances, cocaine paraphernalia, and a large amount of cash. Bertine was subsequently charged with driving while under the influence of alcohol, unlawful possession of cocaine with intent to dispense, sell, and distribute, and unlawful possession of methaqualone. We are asked to decide whether the Fourth Amendment prohibits the State from proving these charges with the evidence discovered during the inventory of Bertine's van. We hold that it does not.

The backup officer inventoried the van in accordance with local police procedures, which require a detailed inspection and inventory of impounded vehicles. He found the backpack directly behind the front seat of the van. Inside the pack, the officer observed a nylon bag containing metal canisters. Opening the canisters, the officer discovered that they contained cocaine, methaqualone tablets, cocaine paraphernalia, and $700 in cash. In an outside zippered pouch of the backpack, he also found $210 in cash in a sealed envelope. After completing the inventory of the van, the officer had the van towed to an impound lot and brought the backpack, money, and contraband to the police station.

After Bertine was charged with the offenses described above, he moved to suppress the evidence found during the inventory search on the ground, *inter alia*, that the search of the closed backpack and containers exceeded the permissible scope of such a search under the Fourth Amendment. The Colorado trial court ruled that probable cause supported Bertine's arrest and that the police officers had made the decisions to impound the vehicle and to conduct a thorough inventory search in good faith. Although noting that the inventory of the vehicle was performed in a "somewhat slipshod" manner, the District Court concluded that "the search of the backpack was done for the purpose of protecting the owner's property, protection of the police from subsequent claims of loss or stolen property, and the protection of the police from dangerous instrumentalities."

[T]he Supreme Court of Colorado recognized that in *South Dakota v. Opperman*, 428 U.S. 364 (1976), we had held inventory searches of automobiles to be consistent with the Fourth Amendment, and that in *Illinois v. Lafayette*, 462 U.S. 640 (1983), we had held that the inventory search of personal effects of an arrestee at a police station was also permissible under that Amendment. The Supreme Court of Colorado felt, however, that our decisions in *Sanders* and *Chadwick*, holding searches of closed trunks and suitcases to violate the Fourth Amendment, meant that Opperman and Lafayette did not govern this case.

We granted certiorari to consider the important and recurring question of federal law decided by the Colorado Supreme Court. As that court recognized,

---

[1] Section 7-7-2(a)(4) of the Boulder Revised Code authorizes police officers to impound vehicles when drivers are taken into custody. Section 7-7-2(a)(4) provides:

> A peace officer is authorized to remove or cause to be removed a vehicle from any street, parking lot, or driveway when:

*   *   *

> (4) The driver of a vehicle is taken into custody by the police department.

BOULDER REV.CODE § 7-7-2(a)(4) (1981).

inventory searches are now a well-defined exception to the warrant requirement of the Fourth Amendment. The policies behind the warrant requirement are not implicated in an inventory search, nor is the related concept of probable cause: "The standard of probable cause is peculiarly related to criminal investigations, not routine, noncriminal procedures. . . . The probable-cause approach is unhelpful when analysis centers upon the reasonableness of routine administrative caretaking functions, particularly when no claim is made that the protective procedures are a subterfuge for criminal investigations." *Opperman.* For these reasons, the Colorado Supreme Court's reliance on *Sanders* and *Chadwick* was incorrect. Both of these cases concerned searches solely for the purpose of investigating criminal conduct, with the validity of the searches therefore dependent on the application of the probable-cause and warrant requirements of the Fourth Amendment.

By contrast, an inventory search may be "reasonable" under the Fourth Amendment even though it is not conducted pursuant to a warrant based upon probable cause. In *Opperman,* this Court assessed the reasonableness of an inventory search of the glove compartment in an abandoned automobile impounded by the police. We found that inventory procedures serve to protect an owner's property while it is in the custody of the police, to insure against claims of lost, stolen, or vandalized property, and to guard the police from danger. In light of these strong governmental interests and the diminished expectation of privacy in an automobile, we upheld the search. In reaching this decision, we observed that our cases accorded deference to police caretaking procedures designed to secure and protect vehicles and their contents within police custody.[4]

In our more recent decision, *Lafayette,* a police officer conducted an inventory search of the contents of a shoulder bag in the possession of an individual being taken into custody. In deciding whether this search was reasonable, we recognized that the search served legitimate governmental interests similar to those identified in *Opperman.* We determined that those interests outweighed the individual's Fourth Amendment interests and upheld the search.

In the present case, as in *Opperman* and *Lafayette,* there was no showing that the police, who were following standardized procedures, acted in bad faith or for the sole purpose of investigation. In addition, the governmental interests justifying the inventory searches in *Opperman* and *Lafayette* are nearly the same as those which obtain here. In each case, the police were potentially responsible for the property taken into their custody. By securing the property, the police protected the property from unauthorized interference. Knowledge of the precise nature of the property helped guard against claims of theft, vandalism, or negligence. Such knowledge also helped to avert any danger to police or others that may have been posed by the property.[5]

---

[4] The Colorado Supreme Court correctly stated that *Opperman* did not address the question whether the scope of an inventory search may extend to closed containers located in the interior of an impounded vehicle. We did note, however, that " 'when the police take custody of any sort of container [such as] an automobile . . . it is reasonable to search the container to itemize the property to be held by the police.' "

[5] In arguing that the latter two interests are not implicated here, the dissent overlooks the testimony of the backup officer who conducted the inventory of Bertine's van. According to the officer, the vehicle inventory procedures of the Boulder Police Department are designed for the "[p]rotection of the police

The Supreme Court of Colorado opined that *Lafayette* was not controlling here because there was no danger of introducing contraband or weapons into a jail facility. Our opinion in *Lafayette*, however, did not suggest that the station-house setting of the inventory search was critical to our holding in that case. Both in the present case and in *Lafayette*, the common governmental interests described above were served by the inventory searches.

The Supreme Court of Colorado also expressed the view that the search in this case was unreasonable because Bertine's van was towed to a secure, lighted facility and because Bertine himself could have been offered the opportunity to make other arrangements for the safekeeping of his property. But the security of the storage facility does not completely eliminate the need for inventorying; the police may still wish to protect themselves or the owners of the lot against false claims of theft or dangerous instrumentalities. And while giving Bertine an opportunity to make alternative arrangements would undoubtedly have been possible, we said in *Lafayette*: "[T]he real question is not what 'could have been achieved,' but whether the Fourth Amendment *requires* such steps . . . . The reasonableness of any particular governmental activity does not necessarily or invariably turn on the existence of alternative 'less intrusive' means." (emphasis in original). We conclude that here, as in *Lafayette*, reasonable police regulations relating to inventory procedures administered in good faith satisfy the Fourth Amendment, even though courts might as a matter of hindsight be able to devise equally reasonable rules requiring a different procedure.[6]

The Supreme Court of Colorado also thought it necessary to require that police, before inventorying a container, weigh the strength of the individual's privacy interest in the container against the possibility that the container might serve as a repository for dangerous or valuable items. We think that such a requirement is contrary to our decisions in *Opperman* and *Lafayette*, and by analogy to our decision in *Ross*: "When a legitimate search is under way, and when its purpose and its limits have been precisely defined, nice distinctions between closets, drawers, and containers, in the case of a home, or between glove compartments, upholstered seats, trunks, and wrapped packages, in the case of a vehicle, must give way to the interest in the prompt and efficient completion of the task at hand." *Ross*.

We reaffirm these principles here: " '[a] single familiar standard is essential to guide police officers, who have only limited time and expertise to reflect on and

---

department" in the event that an individual later claims that "there was something of value taken from within the vehicle." The officer added that inventories are also conducted in order to check "[f]or any dangerous items such as explosives [or] weapons." The officer testified that he had found such items in vehicles.

   [6] We emphasize that, in this case, the trial court found that the Police Department's procedures mandated the opening of closed containers and the listing of their contents. Our decisions have always adhered to the requirement that inventories be conducted according to standardized criteria. *See Lafayette, Opperman.*

   By quoting a portion of the Colorado Supreme Court's decision out of context, the dissent suggests that the inventory here was not authorized by the standard procedures of the Boulder Police Department. Yet that court specifically stated that the procedure followed here was "officially authorized." In addition, the court did not disturb the trial court's finding that the police procedures for impounding vehicles required a detailed inventory of Bertine's van.

balance the social and individual interests involved in the specific circumstances they confront.' "

Bertine finally argues that the inventory search of his van was unconstitutional because departmental regulations gave the police officers discretion to choose between impounding his van and parking and locking it in a public parking place. The Supreme Court of Colorado did not rely on this argument in reaching its conclusion, and we reject it. Nothing in *Opperman* or *Lafayette* prohibits the exercise of police discretion so long as that discretion is exercised according to standard criteria and on the basis of something other than suspicion of evidence of criminal activity. Here, the discretion afforded the Boulder police was exercised in light of standardized criteria, related to the feasibility and appropriateness of parking and locking a vehicle rather than impounding it.[7] There was no showing that the police chose to impound Bertine's van in order to investigate suspected criminal activity.

While both *Opperman* and *Lafayette* are distinguishable from the present case on their facts, we think that the principles enunciated in those cases govern the present one. The judgment of the Supreme Court of Colorado is therefore reversed.

JUSTICE BLACKMUN, with whom JUSTICE POWELL and JUSTICE O'CONNOR join, concurring.

The Court today holds that police officers may open closed containers while conducting a routine inventory search of an impounded vehicle. I join the Court's opinion, but write separately to underscore the importance of having such inventories conducted only pursuant to standardized police procedures. The underlying rationale for allowing an inventory exception to the Fourth Amendment warrant rule is that police officers are not vested with discretion to determine the scope of the inventory search. This absence of discretion ensures that inventory searches will not be used as a purposeful and general means of discovering evidence of crime. Thus, it is permissible for police officers to open closed containers in an inventory search only if they are following standard police procedures that mandate the opening of such containers in every impounded vehicle. As the Court emphasizes, the trial court in this case found that the Police Department's standard procedures did mandate the opening of closed containers and the listing of their contents.

---

[7] In arguing that the Boulder Police Department procedures set forth no standardized criteria guiding an officer's decision to impound a vehicle, the dissent selectively quotes from the police directive concerning the care and security of vehicles taken into police custody. The dissent fails to mention that the directive establishes several conditions that must be met before an officer may pursue the park-and-lock alternative. For example, police may not park and lock the vehicle where there is reasonable risk of damage or vandalism to the vehicle or where the approval of the arrestee cannot be obtained. Not only do such conditions circumscribe the discretion of individual officers, but they also protect the vehicle and its contents and minimize claims of property loss.

JUSTICE MARSHALL, with whom JUSTICE BRENNAN joins, dissenting.

Recognizing that "both *Opperman* and *Lafayette* are distinguishable from the present case on their facts," the majority applies the balancing test enunciated in those cases to uphold as reasonable the inventory of a closed container in a car impounded when its driver was placed under arrest. However, the distinctive facts of this case require a different result. This search — it cannot legitimately be labeled an inventory — was unreasonable and violated the Fourth Amendment. Unlike the inventories in *Opperman* and *Lafayette*, it was not conducted according to standardized procedures. Furthermore, the governmental interests justifying the intrusion are significantly weaker than the interests identified in either *Opperman* or *Lafayette* and the expectation of privacy is considerably stronger.

I

As the Court acknowledges, inventory searches are reasonable only if conducted according to standardized procedures. In both *Opperman* and *Lafayette*, the Court relied on the absence of police discretion in determining that the inventory searches in question were reasonable. Chief Justice Burger's opinion in *Opperman* repeatedly referred to this standardized nature of inventory procedures. Justice POWELL's concurring opinion in that case also stressed that "no significant discretion is placed in the hands of the individual officer: he usually has no choice as to the subject of the search or its scope." Similarly, the Court in *Lafayette* emphasized the standardized procedure under which the station-house inventory was conducted. In assessing the reasonableness of searches conducted in limited situations such as these, where we do not require probable cause or a warrant, we have consistently emphasized the need for such set procedures: "standardless and unconstrained discretion is the evil the Court has discerned when in previous cases it has insisted that the discretion of the official in the field be circumscribed, at least to some extent." *E.g. Prouse.*

The Court today attempts to evade these clear prohibitions on unfettered police discretion by declaring that "the discretion afforded the Boulder police was exercised in light of standardized criteria, related to the feasibility and appropriateness of parking and locking a vehicle rather than impounding it." This vital assertion is flatly contradicted by the record in this case. The officer who conducted the inventory, Officer Reichenbach, testified at the suppression hearing that the decision not to "park and lock" respondent's vehicle was his "own individual discretionary decision." Indeed, application of these supposedly standardized "criteria" upon which the Court so heavily relies would have yielded a different result in this case. Since there was ample public parking adjacent to the intersection where respondent was stopped, consideration of "feasibility" would certainly have militated in favor of the "park and lock" option, not against it. I do not comprehend how consideration of "appropriateness" serves to channel a field officer's discretion; nonetheless, the "park and lock" option would seem particularly appropriate in this case, where respondent was stopped for a traffic offense and was not likely to be in custody for a significant length of time.

Indeed, the record indicates that *no* standardized criteria limit a Boulder police officer's discretion. According to a departmental directive, after placing a driver under arrest, an officer has three options for disposing of the vehicle. First, he can allow a third party to take custody. Second, the officer or the driver (depending on the nature of the arrest) may take the car to the nearest public parking facility, lock it, and take the keys. Finally, the officer can do what was done in this case: impound the vehicle, and search and inventory its contents, including closed containers.

Under the first option, the police have no occasion to search the automobile. Under the "park and lock" option, "[c]losed containers that give no indication of containing either valuables or a weapon *may not be opened and the contents searched (i.e., inventoried)*." (emphasis added). Only if the police choose the third option are they entitled to search closed containers in the vehicle. Where the vehicle is not itself evidence of a crime,[5] as in this case, the police apparently have totally unbridled discretion as to which procedure to use. ("[T]he Boulder Police Department's regulations and rules do not require that an automobile be inventoried and searched in accordance with the procedures followed in this case"). Consistent with this conclusion, Officer Reichenbach testified that such decisions were left to the discretion of the officer on the scene.

Once a Boulder police officer has made this initial completely discretionary decision to impound a vehicle, he is given little guidance as to which areas to search and what sort of items to inventory. The arresting officer, Officer Toporek, testified at the suppression hearing as to what items would be inventoried: "That would I think be very individualistic as far as what an officer may or may not go into. I think whatever arouses his suspicious [*sic*] as far as what may be contained in any type of article in the car." In application, these so-called procedures left the breadth of the "inventory" to the whim of the individual officer. Clearly, "[t]he practical effect of this system is to leave the [owner] subject to the discretion of the official in the field."

Inventory searches are not subject to the warrant requirement because they are conducted by the government as part of a "community caretaking" function, "totally divorced from the detection, investigation, or acquisition of evidence relating to the violation of a criminal statute." Standardized procedures are necessary to ensure that this narrow exception is not improperly used to justify, after the fact, a warrantless investigative foray. Accordingly, to invalidate a search that is conducted without established procedures, it is not necessary to establish that the police actually acted in bad faith, or that the inventory was in fact a "pretext." By allowing the police unfettered discretion, Boulder's discretionary scheme, like the random spot checks in *Prouse*, is unreasonable because of the " 'grave danger' of abuse of discretion."

---

[5] Respondent's van was not evidence of a crime within the meaning of the departmental directive; Officer Reichenbach testified that it was not his practice to impound all cars following an arrest for driving while under the influence of alcohol. The Memorandum also requires the "approval of the arrestee" before the police can "park and lock" his car. In this case, however, respondent was never advised of this option and had no opportunity to consent. At the suppression hearing, he indicated that he would have consented to such a procedure.

II

In *Opperman* and *Lafayette*, both of which involved inventories conducted pursuant to standardized procedures, we balanced the individual's expectation of privacy against the government's interests to determine whether the search was reasonable. Even if the search in this case did constitute a legitimate inventory, it would nonetheless be unreasonable under this analysis.

A

The Court greatly overstates the justifications for the inventory exception to the Fourth Amendment. Chief Justice BURGER, writing for the majority in *Opperman*, relied on three governmental interests to justify the inventory search of an unlocked glove compartment in an automobile impounded for overtime parking: (i) "the protection of the owner's property while it remains in police custody"; (ii) "the protection of the police against claims or disputes over lost or stolen property"; and (iii) "the protection of the police from potential danger." The majority finds that "nearly the same" interests obtain in this case. As Justice POWELL's concurring opinion in *Opperman* reveals, however, only the first of these interests is actually served by an automobile inventory search.

The protection-against-claims interest did not justify the inventory search either in *Opperman*, or in this case. As the majority apparently concedes, the use of secure impoundment facilities effectively eliminates this concern.[6] As to false claims, "inventories are [not] a completely effective means of discouraging false claims, since there remains the possibility of accompanying such claims with an assertion that an item was stolen prior to the inventory or was intentionally omitted from the police records."

Officer Reichenbach's inventory in this case would not have protected the police against claims lodged by respondent, false or otherwise. Indeed, the trial court's characterization of the inventory as "slip-shod" is the height of understatement. For example, Officer Reichenbach failed to list $150 in cash found in respondent's wallet or the contents of a sealed envelope marked "rent," $210, in the relevant section of the property form. His reports make no reference to other items of value, including respondent's credit cards, and a converter, a hydraulic jack, and a set of tire chains, worth a total of $125. The $700 in cash found in respondent's backpack, along with the contraband, appeared only on a property form completed later by someone other than Officer Reichenbach. The interior of the vehicle was left in disarray, and the officer "inadvertently" retained respondent's keys — including his house keys — for two days following his arrest.

---

[6] The impoundment lot in *Opperman* was "the old county highway yard. It ha[d] a wooden fence partially around part of it, and kind of a dilapidated wire fence, a makeshift fence." *See also Cady v. Dombrowski*, 413 U.S. 433, 443 (1973) ("[T]he car was left outside, in a lot seven miles from the police station to which respondent had been taken, and no guard was posted over it"). By contrast, in the present case, respondent's vehicle was taken to a lighted, private storage lot with a locked 6-foot fence. The lot was patrolled by private security officers and police, and nothing had ever been stolen from a vehicle in the lot.

The third interest — protecting the police from potential danger — failed to receive the endorsement of a majority of the Court in *Opperman*. After noting that "there is little danger associated with impounding unsearched vehicles," Justice POWELL recognized that "there does not appear to be any effective way of identifying in advance those circumstances or classes of automobile impoundments which represent a greater risk." As with the charge of overtime parking in *Opperman*, there is nothing in the nature of the offense for which respondent was arrested that suggests he was likely to be carrying weapons, explosives, or other dangerous items. *Cf. Cady v. Dombrowski* (police reasonably believed that the defendant's service revolver was in the car). Not only is protecting the police from dangerous instrumentalities an attenuated justification for most automobile inventory searches, but opening closed containers to inventory the contents can only increase the risk. In the words of the District Court in *United States v. Cooper*, 428 F. Supp. 652, 654–655 (SD Ohio 1977): "The argument that the search was necessary to avoid a possible booby-trap is . . . easily refuted. No sane individual inspects for booby-traps by simply opening the container."

Thus, only the government's interest in protecting the owner's property actually justifies an inventory search of an impounded vehicle. While I continue to believe that preservation of property does not outweigh the privacy and security interests protected by the Fourth Amendment, I fail to see how preservation can even be asserted as a justification for the search in this case. In *Opperman*, the owner of the impounded car was not available to safeguard his possessions, and it could plausibly be argued that, in his absence, the police were entitled to act for his presumed benefit. See also *Cady* (comatose defendant). When the police conducted the inventory in *Opperman*, they could not predict how long the car would be left in their possession. ("[M]any owners might leave valuables in their automobiles temporarily that they would not leave there unattended for the several days that police custody may last"). In this case, however, the owner was "present to make other arrangements for the safekeeping of his belongings," yet the police made no attempt to ascertain whether in fact he wanted them to "safeguard" his property. Furthermore, since respondent was charged with a traffic offense, he was unlikely to remain in custody for more than a few hours. He might well have been willing to leave his valuables unattended in the locked van for such a short period of time. (Had he been given the choice, respondent indicated at the suppression hearing that he "would have parked [the van] in the lot across the street [and] [h]ad somebody come and get it").

Thus, the government's interests in this case are weaker than in *Opperman*, but the search here is much more intrusive. *Opperman* did not involve a search of closed containers or other items that " 'touch upon intimate areas of an individual's personal affairs.' " To expand the *Opperman* rationale to include containers in which the owner clearly has a reasonable expectation of privacy, the Court relies on *Lafayette*. Such reliance is fundamentally misplaced, however; the inventory in *Lafayette* was justified by considerations which are totally absent in this context.

In *Lafayette*, we upheld a station-house inventory search of an arrestee's shoulder bag. Notwithstanding the Court's assertions to the contrary, the inventory in that case *was* justified primarily by compelling governmental interests unique to the station house, preincarceration context. There is a powerful interest in preventing the introduction of contraband or weapons into a jail.[7] "Arrested persons have also been known to injure themselves — or others — with belts, knives, drugs, or other items on their person while being detained. Dangerous instrumentalities — such as razor blades, bombs, or weapons — can be concealed in innocent-looking articles taken from the arrestee's possession." Removing such items from persons about to be incarcerated is necessary to reasonable jail security; once these items have been identified and removed, "inventorying them is an entirely reasonable administrative procedure." Although *Lafayette* also involved the property justifications relied on in *Opperman*, I do not believe it can fairly be read to expand the scope of inventory searches where the pressing security concerns of the station house are absent.

III

In *Coolidge*, a plurality of this Court stated: "The word 'automobile' is not a talisman in whose presence the Fourth Amendment fades away and disappears." By upholding the search in this case, the Court not only ignores that principle, but creates another talisman to overcome the requirements of the Fourth Amendment — the term "inventory." Accordingly, I dissent.

QUESTIONS AND NOTES

1. What, if anything, can justify a routine inventory search?

2. Were any of those justifications present in *Bertine*?

3. Justice Rehnquist refers to the *Ross* statement about not allowing "nice distinctions" to determine the scope of the search. In view of the rationale for the search in *Ross* (finding evidence for which there is probable cause to look) as opposed to the *Bertine* rationale (protecting property and protecting the police from false claims), is Rehnquist's quotation an unjustifiable out-of-context lifting of a phrase?

4. Should the "slipshod" nature of the search have been relevant? Does it establish the insubstantiality of the inventory justification (excuse)?

5. Is there a difference between an *authorized* inventory, and a *mandated* inventory? If so, what is the difference? Did the Court essentially establish that the inventory was "authorized" and treat it as if it were "mandatory"?

6. In reading these opinions, do you come away with the sense that Officer Reichenbach would have been in trouble with his department if he had *not* conducted an inventory search of the van?

7. Did the police treat this inventory search as if the Fourth Amendment were no big deal? Is there anything in the court's language that invites such a view?

8. Is *Bertine* explicable because of the trial court's determination that the

---

[7] The importance of this justification to the outcome in *Lafayette* is amply demonstrated by the Court's direction on remand: "The record is unclear as to whether respondent was to have been incarcerated after being booked for disturbing the peace. That is an appropriate inquiry on remand."

search was mandated? (See particularly Justice Blackmun's concurring opinion.)

9. Any thought that *Bertine* allowed *carte blanche* automobile inventory searches was squelched in *Wells*.

FLORIDA v. WELLS
495 U.S. 1 (1990)

CHIEF JUSTICE REHNQUIST delivered the opinion of the Court.

A Florida Highway Patrol trooper stopped respondent Wells for speeding. After smelling alcohol on Wells' breath, the trooper arrested Wells for driving under the influence. Wells then agreed to accompany the trooper to the station to take a Breathalyzer test. The trooper informed Wells that the car would be impounded and obtained Wells' permission to open the trunk. At the impoundment facility, an inventory search of the car turned up two marijuana cigarette butts in an ashtray and a locked suitcase in the trunk. Under the trooper's direction, employees of the facility forced open the suitcase and discovered a garbage bag containing a considerable amount of marijuana.

Wells was charged with possession of a controlled substance. His motion to suppress the marijuana on the ground that it was seized in violation of the Fourth Amendment to the United States Constitution was denied by the trial court. He thereupon pleaded nolo contendere to the charge but reserved his right to appeal the denial of the motion to suppress. On appeal, the Florida District Court of Appeal for the Fifth District held, inter alia, that the trial court erred in denying suppression of the marijuana found in the suitcase. Over a dissent, the Supreme Court of Florida affirmed. We granted certiorari, and now affirm (although we disagree with part of the reasoning of the Supreme Court of Florida).

The Supreme Court of Florida relied on the opinions in *Bertine* (BLACKMUN, J., concurring). Referring to language in the *Bertine* concurrence and a footnote in the majority opinion, the court held that: "[i]n the absence of a policy specifically requiring the opening of closed containers found during a legitimate inventory search, *Bertine* prohibits us from countenancing the procedure followed in this instance." According to the court, the record contained no evidence of any Highway Patrol policy on the opening of closed containers found during inventory searches. The court added, however, that: "[t]he police under *Bertine* must mandate either that all containers will be opened during an inventory search, or that no containers will be opened. There can be no room for discretion."

While this latter statement of the Supreme Court of Florida derived support from a sentence in the *Bertine* concurrence taken in isolation, we think it is at odds with the thrust of both the concurrence and the opinion of the Court in that case. We said in *Bertine*: "[n]othing in *Opperman* or *Lafayette* prohibits the exercise of police discretion so long as that discretion is exercised according to standard criteria and on the basis of something other than suspicion of evidence of criminal activity." Our view that standardized criteria, or established routine, must regulate the opening of containers found during inventory searches is based on the principle that an inventory search must not be a ruse for a general rummaging in order to discover incriminating evidence. The policy or practice governing inventory searches should be designed to produce an inventory. The individual police officer must not be allowed so much latitude that inventory searches are turned into "a purposeful and general means of discovering evidence of crime."

But in forbidding uncanalized discretion to police officers conducting inventory searches, there is no reason to insist that they be conducted in a totally mechanical "all or nothing" fashion. "[I]nventory procedures serve to protect an owner's property while it is in the custody of the police, to insure against claims of lost, stolen, or vandalized property, and to guard the police from danger." A police officer may be allowed sufficient latitude to determine whether a particular container should or should not be opened in light of the nature of the search and characteristics of the container itself. Thus, while policies of opening all containers or of opening no containers are unquestionably permissible, it would be equally permissible, for example, to allow the opening of closed containers whose contents officers determine they are unable to ascertain from examining the containers' exteriors. The allowance of the exercise of judgment based on concerns related to the purposes of an inventory search does not violate the Fourth Amendment.

In the present case, the Supreme Court of Florida found that the Florida Highway Patrol had no policy whatever with respect to the opening of closed containers encountered during an inventory search. We hold that absent such a policy, the instant search was not sufficiently regulated to satisfy the Fourth Amendment and that the marijuana which was found in the suitcase, therefore, was properly suppressed by the Supreme Court of Florida. Its judgment is therefore Affirmed.

[BRENNAN, MARSHALL, BLACKMUN, and STEVENS, J.J., concurred only in the result.]

QUESTIONS AND NOTES

1. Would one who was worried about excessive police discretion after *Bertine* be more or less worried after *Wells*?

2. Do you see any difference between *Wells* and *Bertine*?

3. We will return to automobile cases later in the book, after studying other doctrines, especially consent, that bear on the extent of police power over citizens in automobiles.

Chapter 7

SEARCHING COMPUTERS AND CELL PHONES

RILEY v. CALIFORNIA
573 U.S. ___, 134 S. Ct. 2473 (2014)

CHIEF JUSTICE ROBERTS delivered the opinion of the Court.

These two cases raise a common question: whether the police may, without a warrant, search digital information on a cell phone seized from an individual who has been arrested.

I

A

In the first case, petitioner David Riley was stopped by a police officer for driving with expired registration tags. In the course of the stop, the officer also learned that Riley's license had been suspended. The officer impounded Riley's car, pursuant to department policy, and another officer conducted an inventory search of the car. Riley was arrested for possession of concealed and loaded firearms when that search turned up two handguns under the car's hood. See Cal. Penal Code Ann. §§ 12025(a)(1), 12031(a)(1) (West 2009).

An officer searched Riley incident to the arrest and found items associated with the "Bloods" street gang. He also seized a cell phone from Riley's pants pocket. According to Riley's uncontradicted assertion, the phone was a "smart phone," a cell phone with a broad range of other functions based on advanced computing capability, large storage capacity, and Internet connectivity. The officer accessed information on the phone and noticed that some words (presumably in text messages or a contacts list) were preceded by the letters "CK" — a label that, he believed, stood for "Crip Killers," a slang term for members of the Bloods gang.

At the police station about two hours after the arrest, a detective specializing in gangs further examined the contents of the phone. The detective testified that he "went through" Riley's phone "looking for evidence, because . . . gang members will often video themselves with guns or take pictures of themselves with the guns." Although there was "a lot of stuff" on the phone, particular files that "caught [the detective's] eye" included videos of young men sparring while someone yelled encouragement using the moniker "Blood." The police also found photographs of Riley standing in front of a car they suspected had been involved in a shooting a few weeks earlier.

Riley was ultimately charged, in connection with that earlier shooting, with firing at an occupied vehicle, assault with a semiautomatic firearm, and attempted murder. The State alleged that Riley had committed those crimes for the benefit of a criminal street gang, an aggravating factor that carries an enhanced sentence. Prior to trial, Riley moved to suppress all evidence that the police had obtained from his cell phone. He contended that the searches of his phone violated the Fourth Amendment, because they had been performed without a warrant and were not otherwise justified by exigent circumstances. The trial court rejected that argument. At Riley's trial, police officers testified about the photographs and videos found on the phone, and some of the photographs were admitted into evidence. Riley was convicted on all three counts and received an enhanced sentence of 15 years to life in prison.

B

In the second case, a police officer performing routine surveillance observed respondent Brima Wurie make an apparent drug sale from a car. Officers subsequently arrested Wurie and took him to the police station. At the station, the officers seized two cell phones from Wurie's person. The one at issue here was a "flip phone," a kind of phone that is flipped open for use and that generally has a smaller range of features than a smart phone. Five to ten minutes after arriving at the station, the officers noticed that the phone was repeatedly receiving calls from a source identified as "my house" on the phone's external screen. A few minutes later, they opened the phone and saw a photograph of a woman and a baby set as the phone's wallpaper. They pressed one button on the phone to access its call log, then another button to determine the phone number associated with the "my house" label. They next used an online phone directory to trace that phone number to an apartment building.

When the officers went to the building, they saw Wurie's name on a mailbox and observed through a window a woman who resembled the woman in the photograph on Wurie's phone. They secured the apartment while obtaining a search warrant and, upon later executing the warrant, found and seized 215 grams of crack cocaine, marijuana, drug paraphernalia, a firearm and ammunition, and cash.

Wurie was charged with distributing crack cocaine, possessing crack cocaine with intent to distribute, and being a felon in possession of a firearm and ammunition. See 18 U. S. C. § 922(g); 21 U. S. C. § 841(a). He moved to suppress the evidence obtained from the search of the apartment, arguing that it was the fruit of an unconstitutional search of his cell phone. The District Court denied the motion. Wurie was convicted on all three counts and sentenced to 262 months in prison.

A divided panel of the First Circuit reversed the denial of Wurie's motion to suppress and vacated Wurie's convictions for possession with intent to distribute and possession of a firearm as a felon. The court held that cell phones are distinct from other physical possessions that may be searched incident to arrest with-out a warrant, because of the amount of personal data cell phones contain and the negligible threat they pose to law enforcement interests.

We granted certiorari.

II

The Fourth Amendment provides:

> "The right of the people to be secure in their persons, houses, papers, and effects, against unreasonable searches and seizures, shall not be violated, and no Warrants shall issue, but upon probable cause, supported by Oath or affirmation, and particularly describing the place to be searched, and the persons or things to be seized."

As the text makes clear, "the ultimate touchstone of the Fourth Amendment is 'reasonableness.'" Our cases have determined that "[w]here a search is undertaken by law enforcement officials to discover evidence of criminal wrongdoing, . . . reasonableness generally requires the obtaining of a judicial warrant." Such a warrant ensures that the inferences to support a search are "drawn by a neutral and detached magistrate instead of being judged by the officer engaged in the often competitive enterprise of ferreting out crime." *Johnson v. United States*, 333 U.S. 10, 14 (1948). In the absence of a warrant, a search is reasonable only if it falls within a specific exception to the warrant requirement. See *Kentucky v. King*.

The two cases before us concern the reasonableness of a warrantless search incident to a lawful arrest. In 1914, this Court first acknowledged in dictum "the right on the part of the Government, always recognized under English and American law, to search the person of the accused when legally arrested to discover and seize the fruits or evidences of crime." *Weeks v. United States*, 232 U.S. 383, 392. Since that time, it has been well accepted that such a search constitutes an exception to the warrant requirement. Indeed, the label "exception" is something of a misnomer in this context, as warrantless searches incident to arrest occur with far greater frequency than searches conducted pursuant to a warrant.

Although the existence of the exception for such searches has been recognized for a century, its scope has been debated for nearly as long. See *Arizona v. Gant*. That debate has focused on the extent to which officers may search property found on or near the arrestee. Three related precedents set forth the rules governing such searches:

The first, *Chimel v. California*, laid the groundwork for most of the existing search incident to arrest doctrine. Police officers in that case arrested Chimel inside his home and proceeded to search his entire three-bedroom house, including the attic and garage. In particular rooms, they also looked through the contents of drawers.

The Court crafted the following rule for assessing the reasonableness of a search incident to arrest:

> "When an arrest is made, it is reasonable for the arresting officer to search the person arrested in order to remove any weapons that the latter might seek to use in order to resist arrest or effect his escape. Otherwise, the officer's safety might well be endangered, and the arrest itself frustrated. In addition, it is entirely reasonable for the arresting officer to search for and seize any evidence on the arrestee's person in order to prevent its concealment or destruction. . . . There is ample justification,

therefore, for a search of the arrestee's person and the area 'within his immediate control' — construing that phrase to mean the area from within which he might gain possession of a weapon or destructible evidence."

The extensive warrantless search of Chimel's home did not fit within this exception, because it was not needed to protect officer safety or to preserve evidence. *Id.*, at 763, 768.

Four years later, in *United States v. Robinson*, the Court applied the *Chimel* analysis in the context of a search of the arrestee's person. A police officer had arrested Robinson for driving with a revoked license. The officer conducted a patdown search and felt an object that he could not identify in Robinson's coat pocket. He removed the object, which turned out to be a crumpled cigarette package, and opened it. Inside were 14 capsules of heroin.

The Court of Appeals concluded that the search was unreasonable because Robinson was unlikely to have evidence of the crime of arrest on his person, and because it believed that extracting the cigarette package and opening it could not be justified as part of a protective search for weapons. This Court reversed, rejecting the notion that "case-by-case adjudication" was required to determine "whether or not there was present one of the reasons supporting the authority for a search of the person incident to a lawful arrest." As the Court explained, "[t]he authority to search the person incident to a lawful custodial arrest, while based upon the need to disarm and to discover evidence, does not depend on what a court may later decide was the probability in a particular arrest situation that weapons or evidence would in fact be found upon the person of the suspect." Instead, a "custodial arrest of a suspect based on probable cause is a reasonable intrusion under the Fourth Amendment; that intrusion being lawful, a search incident to the arrest requires no additional justification."

The Court thus concluded that the search of Robinson was reasonable even though there was no concern about the loss of evidence, and the arresting officer had no specific concern that Robinson might be armed. In doing so, the Court did not draw a line between a search of Robinson's person and a further examination of the cigarette pack found during that search. It merely noted that, "[h]aving in the course of a lawful search come upon the crumpled package of cigarettes, [the officer] was entitled to inspect it." A few years later, the Court clarified that this exception was limited to "personal property . . . immediately associated with the person of the arrestee." *United States v. Chadwick*, (200-pound, locked footlocker could not be searched incident to arrest), abrogated on other grounds by *California v. Acevedo*.

The search incident to arrest trilogy concludes with *Gant*, which analyzed searches of an arrestee's vehicle. *Gant*, like *Robinson*, recognized that the *Chimel* concerns for officer safety and evidence preservation underlie the search incident to arrest exception. As a result, the Court concluded that *Chimel* could authorize police to search a vehicle "only when the arrestee is unsecured and within reaching distance of the passenger compartment at the time of the search." *Gant* added, however, an independent exception for a warrantless search of a vehicle's passenger compartment "when it is 'reasonable to believe evidence relevant to the crime of arrest might be found in the vehicle.' " That exception stems not from *Chimel*, the

Court explained, but from "circumstances unique to the vehicle context."

III

These cases require us to decide how the search incident to arrest doctrine applies to modern cell phones, which are now such a pervasive and insistent part of daily life that the proverbial visitor from Mars might conclude they were an important feature of human anatomy. A smart phone of the sort taken from Riley was unheard of ten years ago; a significant majority of American adults now own such phones. Even less sophisticated phones like Wurie's, which have already faded in popularity since Wurie was arrested in 2007, have been around for less than 15 years. Both phones are based on technology nearly inconceivable just a few decades ago, when *Chimel* and *Robinson* were decided.

Absent more precise guidance from the founding era, we generally determine whether to exempt a given type of search from the warrant requirement "by assessing, on the one hand, the degree to which it intrudes upon an individual's privacy and, on the other, the degree to which it is needed for the promotion of legitimate governmental interests." Such a balancing of interests supported the search incident to arrest exception in *Robinson*, and a mechanical application of *Robinson* might well support the warrantless searches at issue here.

But while *Robinson's* categorical rule strikes the appropriate balance in the context of physical objects, neither of its rationales has much force with respect to digital content on cell phones. On the government interest side, *Robinson* concluded that the two risks identified in *Chimel* — harm to officers and destruction of evidence — are present in all custodial arrests. There are no comparable risks when the search is of digital data. In addition, *Robinson* regarded any privacy interests retained by an individual after arrest as significantly diminished by the fact of the arrest itself. Cell phones, however, place vast quantities of personal information literally in the hands of individuals. A search of the information on a cell phone bears little resemblance to the type of brief physical search considered in *Robinson*.

We therefore decline to extend *Robinson* to searches of data on cell phones, and hold instead that officers must generally secure a warrant before conducting such a search.

A

We first consider each *Chimel* concern in turn. In doing so, we do not overlook *Robinson's* admonition that searches of a person incident to arrest, "while based upon the need to disarm and to discover evidence," are reasonable regardless of "the probability in a particular arrest situation that weapons or evidence would in fact be found." Rather than requiring the "case-by-case adjudication" that *Robinson* rejected, we ask instead whether application of the search incident to arrest doctrine to this particular category of effects would "untether the rule from the justifications underlying the *Chimel* exception."

1

Digital data stored on a cell phone cannot itself be used as a weapon to harm an arresting officer or to effectuate the arrestee's escape. Law enforcement officers remain free to examine the physical aspects of a phone to ensure that it will not be used as a weapon — say, to determine whether there is a razor blade hidden between the phone and its case. Once an officer has secured a phone and eliminated any potential physical threats, however, data on the phone can endanger no one.

Perhaps the same might have been said of the cigarette pack seized from Robinson's pocket. Once an officer gained control of the pack, it was unlikely that Robinson could have accessed the pack's contents. But unknown physical objects may always pose risks, no matter how slight, during the tense atmosphere of a custodial arrest. The officer in *Robinson* testified that he could not identify the objects in the cigarette pack but knew they were not cigarettes. Given that, a further search was a reasonable protective measure. No such unknowns exist with respect to digital data. As the First Circuit explained, the officers who searched Wurie's cell phone "knew exactly what they would find therein: data. They also knew that the data could not harm them."

The United States and California both suggest that a search of cell phone data might help ensure officer safety in more indirect ways, for example by alerting officers that confederates of the arrestee are headed to the scene. There is undoubtedly a strong government interest in warning officers about such possibilities, but neither the United States nor California offers evidence to suggest that their concerns are based on actual experience. The proposed consideration would also represent a broadening of *Chimel's* concern that an *arrestee himself* might grab a weapon and use it against an officer "to resist arrest or effect his escape." And any such threats from outside the arrest scene do not "lurk[] in all custodial arrests." Accordingly, the interest in protecting officer safety does not justify dispensing with the warrant requirement across the board. To the extent dangers to arresting officers may be implicated in a particular way in a particular case, they are better addressed through consideration of case-specific exceptions to the warrant requirement, such as the one for exigent circumstances.

2

The United States and California focus primarily on the second *Chimel* rationale: preventing the destruction of evidence.

Both Riley and Wurie concede that officers could have seized and secured their cell phones to prevent destruction of evidence while seeking a warrant. That is a sensible concession. See *Illinois v. McArthur*, 531 U.S. 326, 331–333 (2001). And once law enforcement officers have secured a cell phone, there is no longer any risk that the arrestee himself will be able to delete incriminating data from the phone.

The United States and California argue that information on a cell phone may nevertheless be vulnerable to two types of evidence destruction unique to digital data — remote wiping and data encryption. Remote wiping occurs when a phone, connected to a wireless network, receives a signal that erases stored data. This can happen when a third party sends a remote signal or when a phone is preprogrammed to delete data upon entering or leaving certain geographic areas (so-called "geofencing"). Encryption is a security feature that some modern cell phones use in addition to password protection. When such phones lock, data becomes protected by sophisticated encryption that renders a phone all but "unbreakable" unless police know the password.

As an initial matter, these broader concerns about the loss of evidence are distinct from *Chimel's* focus on a defendant who responds to arrest by trying to conceal or destroy evidence within his reach. With respect to remote wiping, the Government's primary concern turns on the actions of third parties who are not present at the scene of arrest. And data encryption is even further afield. There, the Government focuses on the ordinary operation of a phone's security features, apart from *any* active attempt by a defendant or his associates to conceal or destroy evidence upon arrest.

We have also been given little reason to believe that either problem is prevalent. The briefing reveals only a couple of anecdotal examples of remote wiping triggered by an arrest. Similarly, the opportunities for officers to search a password-protected phone before data becomes encrypted are quite limited. Law enforcement officers are very unlikely to come upon such a phone in an unlocked state because most phones lock at the touch of a button or, as a default, after some very short period of inactivity. This may explain why the encryption argument was not made until the merits stage in this Court, and has never been considered by the Courts of Appeals.

Moreover, in situations in which an arrest might trigger a remote-wipe attempt or an officer discovers an unlocked phone, it is not clear that the ability to conduct a warrantless search would make much of a difference. The need to effect the arrest, secure the scene, and tend to other pressing matters means that law enforcement officers may well not be able to turn their attention to a cell phone right away. Cell phone data would be vulnerable to remote wiping from the time an individual anticipates arrest to the time any eventual search of the phone is completed, which might be at the station house hours later. Likewise, an officer who seizes a phone in an unlocked state might not be able to begin his search in the short time remaining before the phone locks and data becomes encrypted.

In any event, as to remote wiping, law enforcement is not without specific means to address the threat. Remote wiping can be fully prevented by disconnecting a phone from the network. There are at least two simple ways to do this: First, law enforcement officers can turn the phone off or remove its battery. Second, if they are concerned about encryption or other potential problems, they can leave a phone powered on and place it in an enclosure that isolates the phone from radio waves. Such devices are commonly called "Faraday bags," after the English scientist Michael Faraday. They are essentially sandwich bags made of aluminum foil: cheap, lightweight, and easy to use. They may not be a complete answer to the problem, but at least for now they provide a reasonable response. In fact, a number of law enforcement agencies around the country already encourage the use of Faraday bags.

To the extent that law enforcement still has specific concerns about the potential loss of evidence in a particular case, there remain more targeted ways to address those concerns. If "the police are truly confronted with a 'now or never' situation," — for example, circumstances suggesting that a defendant's phone will be the target of an imminent remote-wipe attempt — they may be able to rely on exigent circumstances to search the phone immediately. Or, if officers happen to seize a phone in an unlocked state, they may be able to disable a phone's automatic-lock feature in order to prevent the phone from locking and encrypting data. Such a preventive measure could be analyzed under the principles set forth in our decision in *McArthur*, 531 U.S. 326, which approved officers' reasonable steps to secure a scene to preserve evidence while they awaited a warrant.

B

The search incident to arrest exception rests not only on the heightened government interests at stake in a volatile arrest situation, but also on an arrestee's reduced privacy interests upon being taken into police custody. *Robinson* focused primarily on the first of those rationales. But it also quoted with approval then-Judge Cardozo's account of the historical basis for the search incident to arrest exception: "Search of the person becomes lawful when grounds for arrest and accusation have been discovered, and the law is in the act of subjecting the body of the accused to its physical dominion." See also (Powell, J., concurring) ("an individual lawfully subjected to a custodial arrest retains no significant Fourth Amendment interest in the privacy of his person"). Put simply, a patdown of Robinson's clothing and an inspection of the cigarette pack found in his pocket constituted only minor additional intrusions compared to the substantial government authority exercised in taking Robinson into custody.

The fact that an arrestee has diminished privacy interests does not mean that the Fourth Amendment falls out of the picture entirely. Not every search "is acceptable solely because a person is in custody." *Maryland v. King*, 569 U.S. ___, ___ (2013). To the contrary, when "privacy-related concerns are weighty enough" a "search may require a warrant, notwithstanding the diminished expectations of privacy of the arrestee." One such example, of course, is *Chimel*. *Chimel* refused to "characteriz[e] the invasion of privacy that results from a top-to-bottom search of a man's house as 'minor.'" Because a search of the arrestee's entire house was a substantial invasion beyond the arrest itself, the Court concluded that a warrant was required.

Robinson is the only decision from this Court applying *Chimel* to a search of the contents of an item found on an arrestee's person. In an earlier case, this Court had approved a search of a zipper bag carried by an arrestee, but the Court analyzed only the validity of the arrest itself. See *Draper v. United States*. Lower courts applying *Robinson* and *Chimel*, however, have approved searches of a variety of personal items carried by an arrestee.

The United States asserts that a search of all data stored on a cell phone is "materially indistinguishable" from searches of these sorts of physical items. That is like saying a ride on horseback is materially indistinguishable from a flight to the moon. Both are ways of getting from point A to point B, but little else justifies lumping them together. Modern cell phones, as a category, implicate privacy concerns far beyond those implicated by the search of a cigarette pack, a wallet, or a purse. A conclusion that inspecting the contents of an arrestee's pockets works no substantial additional intrusion on privacy beyond the arrest itself may make sense as applied to physical items, but any extension of that reasoning to digital data has to rest on its own bottom.

1

Cell phones differ in both a quantitative and a qualitative sense from other objects that might be kept on an arrestee's person. The term "cell phone" is itself misleading shorthand; many of these devices are in fact minicomputers that also happen to have the capacity to be used as a telephone. They could just as easily be called cameras, video players, rolodexes, calendars, tape recorders, libraries, diaries, albums, televisions, maps, or newspapers.

One of the most notable distinguishing features of modern cell phones is their immense storage capacity. Before cell phones, a search of a person was limited by physical realities and tended as a general matter to constitute only a narrow intrusion on privacy. Most people cannot lug around every piece of mail they have received for the past several months, every picture they have taken, or every book or article they have read — nor would they have any reason to attempt to do so. And if they did, they would have to drag behind them a trunk of the sort held to require a search warrant in *Chadwick*, rather than a container the size of the cigarette package in *Robinson*.

But the possible intrusion on privacy is not physically limited in the same way when it comes to cell phones. The current top-selling smart phone has a standard capacity of 16 gigabytes (and is available with up to 64 gigabytes). Sixteen gigabytes translates to millions of pages of text, thousands of pictures, or hundreds of videos. Cell phones couple that capacity with the ability to store many different types of information: Even the most basic phones that sell for less than $20 might hold photographs, picture messages, text messages, Internet browsing history, a calendar, a thousand-entry phone book, and so on. We expect that the gulf between physical practicability and digital capacity will only continue to widen in the future.

The storage capacity of cell phones has several interrelated consequences for privacy. First, a cell phone collects in one place many distinct types of information — an address, a note, a prescription, a bank statement, a video — that reveal much more in combination than any isolated record. Second, a cell phone's capacity allows even just one type of information to convey far more than previously possible. The sum of an individual's private life can be reconstructed through a thousand photographs labeled with dates, locations, and descriptions; the same cannot be said of a photograph or two of loved ones tucked into a wallet. Third, the data on a phone can date back to the purchase of the phone, or even earlier. A person might carry in his pocket a slip of paper reminding him to call Mr. Jones; he would not carry a record of all his communications with Mr. Jones for the past several months, as would routinely be kept on a phone.[1]

---

[1] Because the United States and California agree that these cases involve *searches* incident to arrest, these cases do not implicate the question whether the collection or inspection of aggregated digital information amounts to a search under other circumstances.

Finally, there is an element of pervasiveness that characterizes cell phones but not physical records. Prior to the digital age, people did not typically carry a cache of sensitive personal information with them as they went about their day. Now it is the person who is not carrying a cell phone, with all that it contains, who is the exception. According to one poll, nearly three-quarters of smart phone users report being within five feet of their phones most of the time, with 12% admitting that they even use their phones in the shower. A decade ago police officers searching an arrestee might have occasionally stumbled across a highly personal item such as a diary. But those discoveries were likely to be few and far between. Today, by contrast, it is no exaggeration to say that many of the more than 90% of American adults who own a cell phone keep on their person a digital record of nearly every aspect of their lives — from the mundane to the intimate. Allowing the police to scrutinize such records on a routine basis is quite different from allowing them to search a personal item or two in the occasional case.

Although the data stored on a cell phone is distinguished from physical records by quantity alone, certain types of data are also qualitatively different. An Internet search and browsing history, for example, can be found on an Internet-enabled phone and could reveal an individual's private interests or concerns — perhaps a search for certain symptoms of disease, coupled with frequent visits to WebMD. Data on a cell phone can also reveal where a person has been. Historic location information is a standard feature on many smart phones and can reconstruct someone's specific movements down to the minute, not only around town but also within a particular building. See *United States v. Jones*, (Sotomayor, J., concurring) ("GPS monitoring generates a precise, comprehensive record of a person's public movements that reflects a wealth of detail about her familial, political, professional, religious, and sexual associations.").

Mobile application software on a cell phone, or "apps," offer a range of tools for managing detailed information about all aspects of a person's life. There are apps for Democratic Party news and Republican Party news; apps for alcohol, drug, and gambling addictions; apps for sharing prayer requests; apps for tracking pregnancy symptoms; apps for planning your budget; apps for every conceivable hobby or pastime; apps for improving your romantic life. There are popular apps for buying or selling just about anything, and the records of such transactions may be accessible on the phone indefinitely. There are over a million apps available in each of the two major app stores; the phrase "there's an app for that" is now part of the popular lexicon. The average smart phone user has installed 33 apps, which together can form a revealing montage of the user's life.

In 1926, Learned Hand observed (in an opinion later quoted in *Chimel*) that it is "a totally different thing to search a man's pockets and use against him what they contain, from ransacking his house for everything which may incriminate him." *United States v. Kirschenblatt*, 16 F.2d 202, 203 (CA2). If his pockets contain a cell phone, however, that is no longer true. Indeed, a cell phone search would typically expose to the government far *more* than the most exhaustive search of a house: A phone not only contains in digital form many sensitive records previously found in the home; it also contains a broad array of private information never found in a home in any form — unless the phone is.

2

To further complicate the scope of the privacy interests at stake, the data a user views on many modern cell phones may not in fact be stored on the device itself. Treating a cell phone as a container whose contents may be searched incident to an arrest is a bit strained as an initial matter. But the analogy crumbles entirely when a cell phone is used to access data located elsewhere, at the tap of a screen. That is what cell phones, with increasing frequency, are designed to do by taking advantage of "cloud computing." Cloud computing is the capacity of Internet-connected devices to display data stored on remote servers rather than on the device itself. Cell phone users often may not know whether particular information is stored on the device or in the cloud, and it generally makes little difference. Moreover, the same type of data may be stored locally on the device for one user and in the cloud for another.

The United States concedes that the search incident to arrest exception may not be stretched to cover a search of files accessed remotely — that is, a search of files stored in the cloud. Such a search would be like finding a key in a suspect's pocket and arguing that it allowed law enforcement to unlock and search a house. But officers searching a phone's data would not typically know whether the information they are viewing was stored locally at the time of the arrest or has been pulled from the cloud.

Although the Government recognizes the problem, its proposed solutions are unclear. It suggests that officers could disconnect a phone from the network before searching the device — the very solution whose feasibility it contested with respect to the threat of remote wiping. Alternatively, the Government proposes that law enforcement agencies "develop protocols to address" concerns raised by cloud computing. Probably a good idea, but the Founders did not fight a revolution to gain the right to government agency protocols. The possibility that a search might extend well beyond papers and effects in the physical proximity of an arrestee is yet another reason that the privacy interests here dwarf those in *Robinson*.

C

Apart from their arguments for a direct extension of *Robinson*, the United States and California offer various fallback options for permitting warrantless cell phone searches under certain circumstances. Each of the proposals is flawed and contravenes our general preference to provide clear guidance to law enforcement through categorical rules. "[I]f police are to have workable rules, the balancing of the competing interests . . . 'must in large part be done on a categorical basis — not in an ad hoc, case-by-case fashion by individual police officers.'"

The United States first proposes that the *Gant* standard be imported from the vehicle context, allowing a warrantless search of an arrestee's cell phone whenever it is reasonable to believe that the phone contains evidence of the crime of arrest. But *Gant* relied on "circumstances unique to the vehicle context" to endorse a search solely for the purpose of gathering evidence. Justice Scalia's *Thornton* opinion, on which *Gant* was based, explained that those unique circumstances are "a reduced expectation of privacy" and "heightened law enforcement needs" when it comes to motor vehicles. For reasons that we have explained, cell phone searches bear neither of those characteristics.

At any rate, a *Gant* standard would prove no practical limit at all when it comes to cell phone searches. In the vehicle context, *Gant* generally protects against searches for evidence of past crimes. In the cell phone context, however, it is reasonable to expect that incriminating information will be found on a phone regardless of when the crime occurred. Similarly, in the vehicle context *Gant* restricts broad searches resulting from minor crimes such as traffic violations. That would not necessarily be true for cell phones. It would be a particularly inexperienced or unimaginative law enforcement officer who could not come up with several reasons to suppose evidence of just about any crime could be found on a cell phone. Even an individual pulled over for something as basic as speeding might well have locational data dispositive of guilt on his phone. An individual pulled over for reckless driving might have evidence on the phone that shows whether he was texting while driving. The sources of potential pertinent information are virtually unlimited, so applying the *Gant* standard to cell phones would in effect give "police officers unbridled discretion to rummage at will among a person's private effects."

The United States also proposes a rule that would restrict the scope of a cell phone search to those areas of the phone where an officer reasonably believes that information relevant to the crime, the arrestee's identity, or officer safety will be discovered. This approach would again impose few meaningful constraints on officers. The proposed categories would sweep in a great deal of information, and officers would not always be able to discern in advance what information would be found where.

We also reject the United States' final suggestion that officers should always be able to search a phone's call log, as they did in Wurie's case. The Government relies on *Smith v. Maryland*, which held that no warrant was required to use a pen register at telephone company premises to identify numbers dialed by a particular caller. The Court in that case, however, concluded that the use of a pen register was not a "search" at all under the Fourth Amendment. There is no dispute here that the officers engaged in a search of Wurie's cell phone. Moreover, call logs typically contain more than just phone numbers; they include any identifying information that an individual might add, such as the label "my house" in Wurie's case.

Finally, at oral argument California suggested a different limiting principle, under which officers could search cell phone data if they could have obtained the same information from a pre-digital counterpart. See Tr. of Oral Arg. in No. 13-132, at 38–43; see also *Flores-Lopez*, 670 F.3d, at 807 ("If police are entitled to open a pocket diary to copy the owner's address, they should be entitled to turn on a cell phone to learn its number."). But the fact that a search in the pre-digital era could have turned up a photograph or two in a wallet does not justify a search of thousands of photos in a digital gallery. The fact that someone could have tucked a paper bank statement in a pocket does not justify a search of every bank statement from the last five years. And to make matters worse, such an analogue test would allow law enforcement to search a range of items contained on a phone, even though people would be unlikely to carry such a variety of information in physical form. In Riley's case, for example, it is implausible that he would have strolled around with video tapes, photo albums, and an address book all crammed into his pockets. But because each of those items has a pre-digital analogue, police under California's proposal would be able to search a phone for all of those items — a significant diminution of privacy.

In addition, an analogue test would launch courts on a difficult line-drawing expedition to determine which digital files are comparable to physical records. Is an e-mail equivalent to a letter? Is a voicemail equivalent to a phone message slip? It is not clear how officers could make these kinds of decisions before conducting a search, or how courts would apply the proposed rule after the fact. An analogue test would "keep defendants and judges guessing for years to come."

IV

We cannot deny that our decision today will have an impact on the ability of law enforcement to combat crime. Cell phones have become important tools in facilitating coordination and communication among members of criminal enterprises, and can provide valuable incriminating information about dangerous criminals. Privacy comes at a cost.

Our holding, of course, is not that the information on a cell phone is immune from search; it is instead that a warrant is generally required before such a search, even when a cell phone is seized incident to arrest. Our cases have historically recognized that the warrant requirement is "an important working part of our machinery of government," not merely "an inconvenience to be somehow 'weighed' against the claims of police efficiency." *Coolidge v. New Hampshire.* Recent technological advances similar to those discussed here have, in addition, made the process of obtaining a warrant itself more efficient.

Moreover, even though the search incident to arrest exception does not apply to cell phones, other case-specific exceptions may still justify a warrantless search of a particular phone. "One well-recognized exception applies when " 'the exigencies of the situation" make the needs of law enforcement so compelling that [a] warrantless search is objectively reasonable under the Fourth Amendment.' " Such exigencies could include the need to prevent the imminent destruction of evidence in individual cases, to pursue a fleeing suspect, and to assist persons who are seriously injured or are threatened with imminent injury. In *Chadwick*, for example, the Court held that the exception for searches incident to arrest did not justify a search of the trunk at issue, but noted that "if officers have reason to believe that luggage contains some immediately dangerous instrumentality, such as explosives, it would be foolhardy to transport it to the station house without opening the luggage."

In light of the availability of the exigent circumstances exception, there is no reason to believe that law enforcement officers will not be able to address some of the more extreme hypotheticals that have been suggested: a suspect texting an accomplice who, it is feared, is preparing to detonate a bomb, or a child abductor who may have information about the child's location on his cell phone. The defendants here recognize — indeed, they stress — that such fact-specific threats may justify a warrantless search of cell phone data. The critical point is that, unlike the search incident to arrest exception, the exigent circumstances exception requires a court to examine whether an emergency justified a warrantless search in each particular case.[2]

* * *

Our cases have recognized that the Fourth Amendment was the founding generation's response to the reviled "general warrants" and "writs of assistance" of the colonial era, which allowed British officers to rummage through homes in an unrestrained search for evidence of criminal activity. Opposition to such searches was in fact one of the driving forces behind the Revolution itself. In 1761, the patriot James Otis delivered a speech in Boston denouncing the use of writs of assistance. A young John Adams was there, and he would later write that "[e]very man of a crowded audience appeared to me to go away, as I did, ready to take arms against writs of assistance." According to Adams, Otis's speech was "the first scene of the first act of opposition to the arbitrary claims of Great Britain. Then and there the child Independence was born."

Modern cell phones are not just another technological convenience. With all they contain and all they may reveal, they hold for many Americans "the privacies of life." The fact that technology now allows an individual to carry such information in his hand does not make the information any less worthy of the protection for which the Founders fought. Our answer to the question of what police must do before searching a cell phone seized incident to an arrest is accordingly simple — get a warrant.

JUSTICE ALITO, concurring in part and concurring in the judgment.

I agree with the Court that law enforcement officers, in conducting a lawful search incident to arrest, must generally obtain a warrant before searching information stored or accessible on a cell phone. I write separately to address two points.

I

A

First, I am not convinced at this time that the ancient rule on searches incident to arrest is based exclusively (or even primarily) on the need to protect the safety of arresting officers and the need to prevent the destruction of evidence. This rule antedates the adoption of the Fourth Amendment by at least a century. ("The power to search incident to arrest — a search of the arrested suspect's person . . . — was well established in the mid-eighteenth century, and nothing in . . . the Fourth Amendment changed that"). And neither in *Weeks* nor in any of the

---

[2] In Wurie's case, for example, the dissenting First Circuit judge argued that exigent circumstances could have justified a search of Wurie's phone. See 728 F.3d 1, 17 (2013) (opinion of Howard, J.) (discussing the repeated unanswered calls from "my house," the suspected location of a drug stash). But the majority concluded that the Government had not made an exigent circumstances argument. The Government acknowledges the same in this Court.

authorities discussing the old common-law rule have I found any suggestion that it was based exclusively or primarily on the need to protect arresting officers or to prevent the destruction of evidence.

On the contrary, when pre-*Weeks* authorities discussed the basis for the rule, what was mentioned was the need to obtain probative evidence. For example, an 1839 case stated that "it is clear, and beyond doubt, that . . . constables . . . are entitled, upon a lawful arrest by them of one charged with treason or felony, to take and detain property found in his possession which will form material evidence in his prosecution for that crime."

What ultimately convinces me that the rule is not closely linked to the need for officer safety and evidence preservation is that these rationales fail to explain the rule's well-recognized scope. It has long been accepted that written items found on the person of an arrestee may be examined and used at trial. But once these items are taken away from an arrestee (something that obviously must be done before the items are read), there is no risk that the arrestee will destroy them. Nor is there any risk that leaving these items unread will endanger the arresting officers.

The idea that officer safety and the preservation of evidence are the sole reasons for allowing a warrantless search incident to arrest appears to derive from the Court's reasoning in *Chimel v. California*, a case that involved the lawfulness of a search of the scene of an arrest, not the person of an arrestee. As I have explained, *Chimel's* reasoning is questionable, see *Arizona v. Gant*, (Alito, J., dissenting), and I think it is a mistake to allow that reasoning to affect cases like these that concern the search of the person of arrestees.

B

Despite my view on the point discussed above, I agree that we should not mechanically apply the rule used in the predigital era to the search of a cell phone. Many cell phones now in use are capable of storing and accessing a quantity of information, some highly personal, that no person would ever have had on his person in hard-copy form. This calls for a new balancing of law enforcement and privacy interests.

The Court strikes this balance in favor of privacy interests with respect to all cell phones and all information found in them, and this approach leads to anomalies. For example, the Court's broad holding favors information in digital form over information in hard-copy form. Suppose that two suspects are arrested. Suspect number one has in his pocket a monthly bill for his land-line phone, and the bill lists an incriminating call to a long-distance number. He also has in his a wallet a few snapshots, and one of these is incriminating. Suspect number two has in his pocket a cell phone, the call log of which shows a call to the same incriminating number. In addition, a number of photos are stored in the memory of the cell phone, and one of these is incriminating. Under established law, the police may seize and examine the phone bill and the snapshots in the wallet without obtaining a warrant, but under the Court's holding today, the information stored in the cell phone is out.

While the Court's approach leads to anomalies, I do not see a workable alternative. Law enforcement officers need clear rules regarding searches incident to arrest, and it would take many cases and many years for the courts to develop more nuanced rules. And during that time, the nature of the electronic devices that ordinary Americans carry on their persons would continue to change.

II

This brings me to my second point. While I agree with the holding of the Court, I would reconsider the question presented here if either Congress or state legislatures, after assessing the legitimate needs of law enforcement and the privacy interests of cell phone owners, enact legislation that draws reasonable distinctions based on categories of information or perhaps other variables.

The regulation of electronic surveillance provides an instructive example. After this Court held that electronic surveillance constitutes a search even when no property interest is invaded, see *Katz v. United States*, 389 U.S. 347, 353–359 (1967), Congress responded by enacting Title III of the Omnibus Crime Control and Safe Streets Act of 1968, 82 Stat. 211. Since that time, electronic surveillance has been governed primarily, not by decisions of this Court, but by the statute, which authorizes but imposes detailed restrictions on electronic surveillance.

Modern cell phones are of great value for both lawful and unlawful purposes. They can be used in committing many serious crimes, and they present new and difficult law enforcement problems. At the same time, because of the role that these devices have come to play in contemporary life, searching their contents implicates very sensitive privacy interests that this Court is poorly positioned to understand and evaluate. Many forms of modern technology are making it easier and easier for both government and private entities to amass a wealth of information about the lives of ordinary Americans, and at the same time, many ordinary Americans are choosing to make public much information that was seldom revealed to outsiders just a few decades ago.

In light of these developments, it would be very unfortunate if privacy protection in the 21st century were left primarily to the federal courts using the blunt instrument of the Fourth Amendment. Legislatures, elected by the people, are in a better position than we are to assess and respond to the changes that have already occurred and those that almost certainly will take place in the future.

QUESTIONS AND NOTES

1.   Were the searches of the cell phones in this case incident to an arrest in the first place, given that they occurred several minutes after the arrest?

2.   Do searches for evidence generally require a warrant as the opinion suggests at one point?

3.   Would a probable cause requirement rather than a warrant have been a reasonable compromise? If so, how would these cases have been decided?

4.   The Court emphasizes that *Chimel* was concerned with the officer's safety from the "arrestee himself." Is that too narrow a focus in these days of gang violence (particularly relevant in the *Riley* case)?

5.   Is it factually true that most cellphones lock at the touch of a button or in a very short time? If that were true, wouldn't the issues in this case be essentially irrelevant because there would never be an opportunity to search the contents of a cell phone?

6.   What do you make of footnote 1? When wouldn't an examination of a cell phone be a search?

7.   How important is a bright line rule?

8.   Should *Riley* and *Wurie* be analyzed as automobile searches? If so, are they too restrictive?

9.   Should the search of a wallet or a diary be allowed incident to arrest? How, if at all, are they different from the search of a cell phone?

10.   Should a search incident to arrest be allowed as a means of collecting evidence of a crime as Justice Alito suggests, or did *Chimel* have it right?

11.   What role, if any, should Congress have in resolving this issue? Do you agree with Justice Alito on that score?

Chapter 8

LIMITED SEARCHES ON LESS THAN PROBABLE CAUSE

A. PROTECTION OF THE OFFICER

During the sixties, it was frequently argued that a policeman ought to be able to frisk a suspect for weapons before talking to the suspect, in order to protect himself. In the leading case of *Terry v. Ohio*, the Supreme Court adopted that viewpoint. In *Terry* and its progeny, we will examine the scope and limitation of this power.

TERRY v. OHIO
392 U.S. 1 (1968)

Mr. Chief Justice Warren delivered the opinion of the Court.

This case presents serious questions concerning the role of the Fourth Amendment in the confrontation on the street between the citizen and the policeman investigating suspicious circumstances.

Petitioner Terry was convicted of carrying a concealed weapon and sentenced to the statutorily prescribed term of one to three years in the penitentiary. Following the denial of a pretrial motion to suppress, the prosecution introduced in evidence two revolvers and a number of bullets seized from Terry and a codefendant, Richard Chilton, by Cleveland Police Detective Martin McFadden. At the hearing on the motion to suppress this evidence, Officer McFadden testified that while he was patrolling in plain clothes in downtown Cleveland at approximately 2:30 in the afternoon of October 31, 1963, his attention was attracted by two men, Chilton and Terry, standing on the corner of Huron Road and Euclid Avenue. He had never seen the two men before, and he was unable to say precisely what first drew his eye to them. However, he testified that he had been a policeman for 39 years and a detective for 35 and that he had been assigned to patrol this vicinity of downtown Cleveland for shoplifters and pickpockets for 30 years. He explained that he had developed routine habits of observation over the years and that he would "stand and watch people or walk and watch people at many intervals of the day." He added: "Now, in this case when I looked over they didn't look right to me at the time."

His interest aroused, Officer McFadden took up a post of observation in the entrance to a store 300 to 400 feet away from the two men. "I get more purpose to watch them when I seen their movements," he testified. He saw one of the men leave the other one and walk southwest on Huron Road, past some stores. The man paused for a moment and looked in a store window, then walked on a short distance, turned around and walked back toward the corner, pausing once again to look in the same store window. He rejoined his companion at the corner, and the two conferred briefly. Then the second man went through the same series of motions, strolling down Huron Road, looking in the same window, walking on a short distance, turning back, peering in the store window again, and returning to confer with the first man at the corner. The two men repeated this ritual alternately between five and six times apiece — in all, roughly a dozen trips. At one point, while the two were standing together on the corner, a third man approached them and engaged them briefly in conversation. This man then left the two others and walked west on Euclid Avenue. Chilton and Terry resumed their measured pacing, peering and conferring. After this had gone on for 10 to 12 minutes, the two men walked off together, heading west on Euclid Avenue, following the path taken earlier by the third man.

By this time Officer McFadden had become thoroughly suspicious. He testified that after observing their elaborately casual and oft-repeated reconnaissance of the store window on Huron Road, he suspected the two men of "casing a job, a stick-up," and that he considered it his duty as a police officer to investigate further. He added that he feared "they may have a gun." Thus, Officer McFadden followed Chilton and Terry and saw them stop in front of Zucker's store to talk to the same man who had conferred with them earlier on the street corner. Deciding that the situation was ripe for direct action, Officer McFadden approached the three men, identified himself as a police officer and asked for their names. At this point his knowledge was confined to what he had observed. He was not acquainted with any of the three men by name or by sight, and he had received no information concerning them from any other source. When the men 'mumbled something' in response to his inquiries, Officer McFadden grabbed petitioner Terry, spun him around so that they were facing the other two, with Terry between McFadden and the others, and patted down the outside of his clothing. In the left breast pocket of Terry's overcoat Officer McFadden felt a pistol. He reached inside the overcoat pocket, but was unable to remove the gun. At this point, keeping Terry between himself and the others, the officer ordered all three men to enter Zucker's store. As they went in, he removed Terry's overcoat completely, removed a .38-caliber revolver from the pocket and ordered all three men to face the wall with their hands raised. Officer McFadden proceeded to pat down the outer clothing of Chilton and the third man, Katz. He discovered another revolver in the outer pocket of Chilton's overcoat, but no weapons were found on Katz. The officer testified that he only patted the men down to see whether they had weapons, and that he did not put his hands beneath the outer garments of either Terry or Chilton until he felt their guns. So far as appears from the record, he never placed his hands beneath Katz' outer garments. Officer McFadden seized Chilton's gun, asked the proprietor of the store to call a police wagon, and took all three men to the station, where Chilton and Terry were formally charged with carrying concealed weapons.

On the motion to suppress the guns the prosecution took the position that they had been seized following a search incident to a lawful arrest. The trial court rejected this theory, stating that it "would be stretching the facts beyond reasonable comprehension" to find that Officer McFadden had had probable cause to arrest the men before he patted them down for weapons. However, the court denied the defendants' motion on the ground that Officer McFadden, on the basis of his experience, "had reasonable cause to believe . . . that the defendants were conducting themselves suspiciously, and some interrogation should be made of their action." Purely for his own protection, the court held, the officer had the right to pat down the outer clothing of these men, who he had reasonable cause to believe might be armed. The court distinguished between an investigatory "stop" and an arrest, and between a "frisk" of the outer clothing for weapons and a full-blown search for evidence of crime. The frisk, it held, was essential to the proper performance of the officer's investigatory duties, for without it "the answer to the police officer may be a bullet, and a loaded pistol discovered during the frisk is admissible."

After the court denied their motion to suppress, Chilton and Terry waived jury trial and pleaded not guilty. The court adjudged them guilty, and the Court of Appeals for the Eighth Judicial District, Cuyahoga County, affirmed. We granted certiorari to determine whether the admission of the revolvers in evidence violated petitioner's rights under the Fourth Amendment. We affirm the conviction.

I.

We have recently held that "the Fourth Amendment protects people, not places," and wherever an individual may harbor a reasonable "expectation of privacy," he is entitled to be free from unreasonable governmental intrusion. Of course, the specific content and incidents of this right must be shaped by the context in which it is asserted. For "what the Constitution forbids is not all searches and seizures, but unreasonable searches and seizures." Unquestionably petitioner was entitled to the protection of the Fourth Amendment as he walked down the street in Cleveland. The question is whether in all the circumstances of this on-the-street encounter, his right to personal security was violated by an unreasonable search and seizure.

We would be less than candid if we did not acknowledge that this question thrusts to the fore difficult and troublesome issues regarding a sensitive area of police activity — issues which have never before been squarely presented to this Court. Reflective of the tensions involved are the practical and constitutional arguments pressed with great vigor on both sides of the public debate over the power of the police to "stop and frisk" — as it is sometimes euphemistically termed — suspicious persons.

On the one hand, it is frequently argued that in dealing with the rapidly unfolding and often dangerous situations on city streets the police are in need of an escalating set of flexible responses, graduated in relation to the amount of information they possess. For this purpose it is urged that distinctions should be made between a "stop" and an "arrest" (or a "seizure" of a person), and between a "frisk" and a "search." Thus, it is argued, the police should be allowed to "stop" a person and detain him briefly for questioning upon suspicion that he may be connected with criminal activity. Upon suspicion that the person may be armed, the police should have the power to "frisk" him for weapons. If the "stop" and the "frisk" give rise to probable cause to believe that the suspect has committed a crime, then the police should be empowered to make a formal "arrest," and a full incident "search" of the person. This scheme is justified in part upon the notion that a "stop" and a "frisk" amount to a mere "minor inconvenience and petty indignity," which can properly be imposed upon the citizen in the interest of effective law enforcement on the basis of a police officer's suspicion.

On the other side the argument is made that the authority of the police must be strictly circumscribed by the law of arrest and search as it has developed to date in the traditional jurisprudence of the Fourth Amendment. It is contended with some force that there is not — and cannot be — a variety of police activity which does not depend solely upon the voluntary cooperation of the citizen and yet which stops short of an arrest based upon probable cause to make such an arrest. The heart of the Fourth Amendment, the argument runs, is a severe requirement of specific justification for any intrusion upon protected personal security, coupled with a highly developed system of judicial controls to enforce upon the agents of the State the commands of the Constitution. Acquiescence by the courts in the compulsion inherent in the field interrogation practices at issue here, it is urged, would constitute an abdication of judicial control over, and indeed an encouragement of, substantial interference with liberty and personal security by police officers whose judgment is necessarily colored by their primary involvement in "the often competitive enterprise of ferreting out crime." This, it is argued, can only serve to exacerbate police-community tensions in the crowded centers of our Nation's cities.

In this context we approach the issues in this case mindful of the limitations of the judicial function in controlling the myriad daily situations in which policemen and citizens confront each other on the street. The State has characterized the issue here as "the right of a police officer . . . to make an on-the-street stop, interrogate and pat down for weapons (known in street vernacular as 'stop and frisk')." But this is only partly accurate. For the issue is not the abstract propriety of the police conduct, but the admissibility against petitioner of the evidence uncovered by the search and seizure. Ever since its inception, the rule excluding evidence seized in violation of the Fourth Amendment has been recognized as a principal mode of discouraging lawless police conduct. Thus in our system evidentiary rulings provide the context in which the judicial process of inclusion and exclusion approves some conduct as comporting with constitutional guarantees and disapproves other actions by state agents. A ruling admitting evidence in a criminal trial, we recognize, has the necessary effect of legitimizing the conduct which produced the evidence, while an application of the exclusionary rule withholds the constitutional imprimatur.

The exclusionary rule has its limitations, however, as a tool of judicial control. It cannot properly be invoked to exclude the products of legitimate police investigative techniques on the ground that much conduct which is closely similar involves unwarranted intrusions upon constitutional protections. Moreover, in some contexts the rule is ineffective as a deterrent. Street encounters between citizens and police officers are incredibly rich in diversity. They range from wholly friendly exchanges of pleasantries or mutually useful information to hostile confrontations of armed men involving arrests, or injuries, or loss of life. Moreover, hostile confrontations are not all of a piece. Some of them begin in a friendly enough manner, only to take a different turn upon the injection of some unexpected element into the conversation. Encounters are initiated by the police for a wide variety of purposes, some of which are wholly unrelated to a desire to prosecute for crime. Doubtless some police "field interrogation" conduct violates the Fourth Amendment. But a stern refusal by this Court to condone such activity does not necessarily render it responsive to the exclusionary rule. Regardless of how effective the rule may be where obtaining convictions is an important objective of the police, it is powerless to deter invasions of constitutionally guaranteed rights where the police either have no interest in prosecuting or are willing to forgo successful prosecution in the interest of serving some other goal.

Proper adjudication of cases in which the exclusionary rule is invoked demands a constant awareness of these limitations. The wholesale harassment by certain elements of the police community, of which minority groups, particularly Negroes, frequently complain,[11] will not be stopped by the exclusion of any evidence from any criminal trial. Yet a rigid and unthinking application of the exclusionary rule, in futile protest against practices which it can never be used effectively to control, may exact a high toll in human injury and frustration of efforts to prevent crime. No judicial opinion can comprehend the protean variety of the street encounter, and we can only judge the facts of the case before us. Nothing we say today is to be taken as indicating approval of police conduct outside the legitimate investigative sphere. Under our decision, courts still retain their traditional responsibility to guard against police conduct which is over-bearing or harassing, or which trenches upon personal security without the objective evidentiary justification which the Constitution requires. When such conduct is identified, it must be condemned by the judiciary and its fruits must be excluded from evidence in criminal trials. And, of course, our approval of legitimate and restrained investigative conduct undertaken on the basis of ample factual justification should in no way discourage the employment of other remedies than the exclusionary rule to curtail abuses for which that sanction may prove inappropriate.

Having thus roughly sketched the perimeters of the constitutional debate over the limits on police investigative conduct in general and the background against which this case presents itself, we turn our attention to the quite narrow question posed by the facts before us: whether it is always unreasonable for a policeman to seize a person and subject him to a limited search for weapons unless there is probable cause for an arrest. Given the narrowness of this question, we have no occasion to canvass in detail the constitutional limitations upon the scope of a policeman's power when he confronts a citizen without probable cause to arrest him.

II.

Our first task is to establish at what point in this encounter the Fourth Amendment becomes relevant. That is, we must decide whether and when Officer McFadden "seized" Terry and whether and when he conducted a "search." There is some suggestion in the use of such terms as "stop" and "frisk" that such police

---

[11] The President's Commission on Law Enforcement and Administration of Justice found that "[i]n many communities, field interrogations are a major source of friction between the police and minority groups." It was reported that the friction caused by "[m]isuse of field interrogations" increases "as more police departments adopt 'aggressive patrol' in which officers are encouraged routinely to stop and question persons on the street who are unknown to them, who are suspicious, or whose purpose for being abroad is not readily evident." While the frequency with which "frisking" forms a part of field interrogation practice varies tremendously with the locale, the objective of the interrogation, and the particular officer, it cannot help but be a severely exacerbating factor in police-community tensions. This is particularly true in situations where the "stop and frisk" of youths or minority group members is "motivated by the officers' perceived need to maintain the power image of the beat officer, an aim sometimes accomplished by humiliating anyone who attempts to undermine police control of the streets."

conduct is outside the purview of the Fourth Amendment because neither action rises to the level of a "search" or "seizure" within the meaning of the Constitution.[12] We emphatically reject this notion. It is quite plain that the Fourth Amendment governs "seizures" of the person which do not eventuate in a trip to the station house and prosecution for crime — "arrests" in traditional terminology. It must be recognized that whenever a police officer accosts an individual and restrains his freedom to walk away, he has "seized" that person. And it is nothing less than sheer torture of the English language to suggest that a careful exploration of the outer surfaces of a person's clothing all over his or her body in an attempt to find weapons is not a "search." Moreover, it is simply fantastic to urge that such a procedure performed in public by a policeman while the citizen stands helpless, perhaps facing a wall with his hands raised, is a "petty indignity."[13] It is a serious intrusion upon the sanctity of the person, which may inflict great indignity and arouse strong resentment, and it is not to be undertaken lightly.[14]

The danger in the logic which proceeds upon distinctions between a "stop" and an "arrest," or "seizure" of the person, and between a "frisk" and a "search" is twofold. It seeks to isolate from constitutional scrutiny the initial stages of the contact between the policeman and the citizen. And by suggesting a rigid all-or-nothing model of justification and regulation under the Amendment, it obscures the utility of limitations upon the scope, as well as the initiation, of police action as a means of constitutional regulation.[15] This Court has held in the past that a search which is reasonable at its inception may violate the Fourth Amendment by virtue of its intolerable intensity and scope. The scope of the search must be "strictly tied to and justified by" the circumstances which rendered its initiation permissible.

The distinctions of classical "stop-and-frisk" theory thus serve to divert attention from the central inquiry under the Fourth Amendment — the reasonableness in all the circumstances of the particular governmental invasion of a citizen's personal security. "Search" and "seizure" are not talismans. We therefore reject the notions that the Fourth Amendment does not come into play at all as a limitation upon

---

[12] In this case, for example, the Ohio Court of Appeals stated that "we must be careful to distinguish that the 'frisk' authorized herein includes only a 'frisk' for a dangerous weapon. It by no means authorizes a search for contraband, evidentiary material, or anything else in the absence of reasonable grounds to arrest. Such a search is controlled by the requirements of the Fourth Amendment, and probable cause is essential."

[13] Consider the following apt description: "[T]he officer must feel with sensitive fingers every portion of the prisoner's body. A through search must be made of the prisoner's arms and armpits, waistline and back, the groin and area about the testicles, and entire surface of the legs down to the feet." Priar & Martin, *Searching and Disarming Criminals*, 45 J. Crim. L.C. & P.S. 481 (1954).

[14] We have noted that the abusive practices which play a major, though by no means exclusive, role in creating this friction are not susceptible of control by means of the exclusionary rule, and cannot properly dictate our decision with respect to the powers of the police in genuine investigative and preventive situations. However, the degree of community resentment aroused by particular practices is clearly relevant to an assessment of the quality of the intrusion upon reasonable expectations of personal security caused by those practices.

[15] In our view the sounder course is to recognize that the Fourth Amendment governs all intrusions by agents of the public upon personal security, and to make the scope of the particular intrusion, in light of all the exigencies of the case, a central element in the analysis of reasonableness.

police conduct if the officers stop short of something called a "technical arrest" or a "full-blown search."

In this case there can be no question, then, that Officer McFadden "seized" petitioner and subjected him to a "search" when he took hold of him and patted down the outer surfaces of his clothing. We must decide whether at that point it was reasonable for Officer McFadden to have interfered with petitioner's personal security as he did.[16] And in determining whether the seizure and search were "unreasonable" our inquiry is a dual one — whether the officer's action was justified at its inception, and whether it was reasonably related in scope to the circumstances which justified the interference in the first place.

III.

If this case involved police conduct subject to the Warrant Clause of the Fourth Amendment, we would have to ascertain whether "probable cause" existed to justify the search and seizure which took place. However, that is not the case. We do not retreat from our holdings that the police must, whenever practicable, obtain advance judicial approval of searches and seizures through the warrant procedure, or that in most instances failure to comply with the warrant requirement can only be excused by exigent circumstances. But we deal here with an entire rubric of police conduct — necessarily swift action predicated upon the on-the-spot observations of the officer on the beat — which historically has not been, and as a practical matter could not be, subjected to the warrant procedure. Instead, the conduct involved in this case must be tested by the Fourth Amendment's general proscription against unreasonable searches and seizures.

Nonetheless, the notions which underlie both the warrant procedure and the requirement of probable cause remain fully relevant in this context. In order to assess the reasonableness of Officer McFadden's conduct as a general proposition, it is necessary "first to focus upon the governmental interest which allegedly justifies official intrusion upon the constitutionally protected interests of the private citizen," for there is "no ready test for determining reasonableness other than by balancing the need to search (or seize) against the invasion which the search (or seizure) entails." And in justifying the particular intrusion the police officer must be able to point to specific and articulable facts which, taken together with rational inferences from those facts, reasonably warrant that intrusion.[18] The scheme of the Fourth Amendment becomes meaningful only when it is assured that at some point the conduct of those charged with enforcing the laws can be subjected to the more

---

[16] We thus decide nothing today concerning the constitutional propriety of an investigative 'seizure' upon less than probable cause for purposes of 'detention' and/or interrogation. Obviously, not all personal intercourse between policemen and citizens involves 'seizures' of persons. Only when the officer, by means of physical force or show of authority, has in some way restrained the liberty of a citizen may we conclude that a 'seizure' has occurred. We cannot tell with any certainty upon this record whether any such "seizure" took place here prior to Officer McFadden's initiation of physical contact for purposes of searching Terry for weapons, and we may assume that up to that point no intrusion upon constitutionally protected rights had occurred.

[18] This demand for specificity in the information upon which this police action is predicated is the central teaching of this Court's Fourth Amendment jurisprudence.

detached, neutral scrutiny of a judge who must evaluate the reasonableness of a particular search or seizure in light of the particular circumstances. And in making that assessment it is imperative that the facts be judged against an objective standard: would the facts available to the officer at the moment of the seizure or the search "warrant a man of reasonable caution in the belief" that the action taken was appropriate? Anything less would invite intrusions upon constitutionally guaranteed rights based on nothing more substantial than inarticulate hunches, a result this Court has consistently refused to sanction.

Applying these principles to this case, we consider first the nature and extent of the governmental interests involved. One general interest is of course that of effective crime prevention and detection; it is this interest which underlies the recognition that a police officer may in appropriate circumstances and in an appropriate manner approach a person for purposes of investigating possibly criminal behavior even though there is no probable cause to make an arrest. It was this legitimate investigative function Officer McFadden was discharging when he decided to approach petitioner and his companions He had observed Terry, Chilton, and Katz go Through a series of acts, each of them perhaps innocent in itself, but which taken together warranted further investigation. There is nothing unusual in two men standing together on a street corner, perhaps waiting for someone. Nor is there anything suspicious about people in such circumstances strolling up and down the street, singly or in pairs. Store windows, moreover, are made to be looked in. But the story is quite different where, as here, two men hover about a street corner for an extended period of time, at the end of which it becomes apparent that they are not waiting for anyone or anything; where these men pace alternately along an identical route, pausing to stare in the same store window roughly 24 times; where each completion of this route is followed immediately by a conference between the two men on the corner; where they are joined in one of these conferences by a third man who leaves swiftly; and where the two men finally follow the third and rejoin him a couple of blocks away. It would have been poor police work indeed for an officer of 30 years' experience in the detection of thievery from stores in this same neighborhood to have failed to investigate this behavior further.

The crux of this case, however, is not the propriety of Officer McFadden's taking steps to investigate petitioner's suspicious behavior, but rather, whether there was justification for McFadden's invasion of Terry's personal security by searching him for weapons in the course of that investigation. We are now concerned with more than the governmental interest in investigating crime; in addition, there is the more immediate interest of the police officer in taking steps to assure himself that the person with whom he is dealing is not armed with a weapon that could unexpectedly and fatally be used against him. Certainly it would be unreasonable to require that police officers take unnecessary risks in the performance of their duties. American criminals have a long tradition of armed violence, and every year in this country many law enforcement officers are killed in the line of duty, and thousands more are wounded. Virtually all of these deaths and a substantial portion of the injuries are inflicted with guns and knives.

In view of these facts, we cannot blind ourselves to the need for law enforcement officers to protect themselves and other prospective victims of violence in situations where they may lack probable cause for an arrest. When an officer is justified in believing that the individual whose suspicious behavior he is investigating at close range is armed and presently dangerous to the officer or to others, it would appear to be clearly unreasonable to deny the officer the power to take necessary measures to determine whether the person is in fact carrying a weapon and to neutralize the threat of physical harm.

We must still consider, however, the nature and quality of the intrusion on individual rights which must be accepted if police officers are to be conceded the right to search for weapons in situations where probable cause to arrest for crime is lacking. Even a limited search of the outer clothing for weapons constitutes a severe, though brief, intrusion upon cherished personal security, and it must surely be an annoying, frightening, and perhaps humiliating experience. Petitioner contends that such an intrusion is permissible only incident to a lawful arrest, either for a crime involving the possession of weapons or for a crime the commission of which led the officer to investigate in the first place. However, this argument must be closely examined.

Petitioner does not argue that a police officer should refrain from making any investigation of suspicious circumstances until such time as he has probable cause to make an arrest; nor does he deny that police officers in properly discharging their investigative function may find themselves confronting persons who might well be armed and dangerous. Moreover, he does not say that an officer is always unjustified in searching a suspect to discover weapons. Rather, he says it is unreasonable for the policeman to take that step until such time as the situation evolves to a point where there is probable cause to make an arrest. When that point has been reached, petitioner would concede the officer's right to conduct a search of the suspect for weapons, fruits or instrumentalities of the crime, or 'mere' evidence, incident to the arrest.

There are two weaknesses in this line of reasoning however. First, it fails to take account of traditional limitations upon the scope of searches, and thus recognizes no distinction in purpose, character, and extent between a search incident to an arrest and a limited search for weapons. The former, although justified in part by the acknowledged necessity to protect the arresting officer from assault with a concealed weapon, is also justified on other grounds, and can therefore involve a relatively extensive exploration of the person. A search for weapons in the absence of probable cause to arrest, however, must, like any other search, be strictly circumscribed by the exigencies which justify its initiation.

A second, and related, objection to petitioner's argument is that it assumes that the law of arrest has already worked out the balance between the particular interests involved here — the neutralization of danger to the policeman in the investigative circumstance and the sanctity of the individual. But this is not so. An arrest is a wholly different kind of intrusion upon individual freedom from a limited search for weapons, and the interests each is designed to serve are likewise quite different. An arrest is the initial stage of a criminal prosecution. It is intended to vindicate society's interest in having its laws obeyed, and it is inevitably accompanied by future interference with the individual's freedom of movement, whether or not trial or conviction ultimately follows. The protective search for weapons, on the other hand, constitutes a brief, though far from inconsiderable, intrusion upon the sanctity of the person. It does not follow that because an officer may lawfully arrest a person only when he is apprised of facts sufficient to warrant a belief that the person has committed or is committing a crime, the officer is equally unjustified, absent that kind of evidence, in making any intrusions short of an arrest. Moreover, a perfectly reasonable apprehension of danger may arise long before the officer is possessed of adequate information to justify taking a person into custody for the purpose of prosecuting him for a crime. Petitioner's reliance on cases which have worked out standards of reasonableness with regard to "seizures" constituting arrests and searches incident thereto is thus misplaced. It assumes that the interests sought to be vindicated and the invasions of personal security may be equated in the two cases, and thereby ignores a vital aspect of the analysis of the reasonableness of particular types of conduct under the Fourth Amendment.

Our evaluation of the proper balance that has to be struck in this type of case leads us to conclude that there must be a narrowly drawn authority to permit a reasonable search for weapons for the protection of the police officer, where he has reason to believe that he is dealing with an armed and dangerous individual, regardless of whether he has probable cause to arrest the individual for a crime. The officer need not be absolutely certain that the individual is armed; the issue is whether a reasonably prudent man in the circumstances would be warranted in the belief that his safety or that of others was in danger. And in determining whether the officer acted reasonably in such circumstances, due weight must be given, not to his inchoate and unparticularized suspicion or "hunch," but to the specific reasonable inferences which he is entitled to draw from the facts in light of his experience.

IV.

We must now examine the conduct of Officer McFadden in this case to determine whether his search and seizure of petitioner were reasonable, both at their inception and as conducted. He had observed Terry, together with Chilton and another man, acting in a manner he took to be preface to a "stick-up." We think on the facts and circumstances Officer McFadden detailed before the trial judge a reasonably prudent man would have been warranted in believing petitioner was armed and thus presented a threat to the officer's safety while he was investigating his suspicious behavior. The actions of Terry and Chilton were consistent with McFadden's hypothesis that these men were contemplating a daylight robbery — which, it is reasonable to assume, would be likely to involve the use of weapons — and nothing in their conduct from the time he first noticed them until the time he confronted them and identified himself as a police officer gave him sufficient reason to negate that hypothesis. Although the trio had departed the original scene, there was nothing to indicate abandonment of an intent to commit a robbery at some point. Thus, when Officer McFadden approached the three men gathered before the display window at Zucker's store he had observed enough to make it quite reasonable to fear that they were armed; and nothing in their response to his hailing them, identifying himself as a police officer, and asking their names served to dispel that reasonable belief. We cannot say his decision at that point to seize Terry and pat his clothing for weapons was the product of a volatile or inventive imagination, or was undertaken simply as an act of harassment; the record evidences the tempered act of a policeman who in the course of an investigation had to make a quick decision as to how to protect himself and others from possible danger, and took limited steps to do so.

The manner in which the seizure and search were conducted is, of course, as vital a part of the inquiry as whether they were warranted at all. We need not develop at length in this case, however, the limitations which the Fourth Amendment places upon a protective seizure and search for weapons. These limitations will have to be developed in the concrete factual circumstances of individual cases. *See Sibron* [*infra*], decided today. Suffice it to note that such a search, unlike a search without a warrant incident to a lawful arrest, is not justified by any need to prevent the disappearance or destruction of evidence of crime. The sole justification of the search in the present situation is the protection of the police officer and others nearby, and it must therefore be confined in scope to an intrusion reasonably designed to discover guns, knives, clubs, or other hidden instruments for the assault of the police officer.

The scope of the search in this case presents no serious problem in light of these standards. Officer McFadden patted down the outer clothing of petitioner and his two companions. He did not place his hands in their pockets or under the outer surface of their garments until he had felt weapons, and then he merely reached for and removed the guns. He never did invade Katz' person beyond the outer surfaces of his clothes, since he discovered nothing in his patdown which might have been a weapon. Officer McFadden confined his search strictly to what was minimally necessary to learn whether the men were armed and to disarm them once he discovered the weapons. He did not conduct a general exploratory search for whatever evidence of criminal activity he might find.

V.

We conclude that the revolver seized from Terry was properly admitted in evidence against him. At the time he seized petitioner and searched him for weapons, Officer McFadden had reasonable grounds to believe that petitioner was armed and dangerous, and it was necessary for the protection of himself and others to take swift measures to discover the true facts and neutralize the threat of harm if it materialized. The policeman carefully restricted his search to what was appropriate to the discovery of the particular items which he sought. Such a search is a reasonable search under the Fourth Amendment, and any weapons seized may properly be introduced in evidence against the person from whom they were taken.

Affirmed.

MR. JUSTICE BLACK concurs in the judgment.

MR. JUSTICE HARLAN, concurring.

While I unreservedly agree with the Court's ultimate holding in this case, I am constrained to fill in a few gaps, as I see them, in its opinion. I do this because what is said by this Court today will serve as initial guidelines for law enforcement authorities and courts throughout the land as this important new field of law develops.

In the first place, if the frisk is justified in order to protect the officer during an encounter with a citizen, the officer must first have constitutional grounds to insist on an encounter, to make a *forcible* stop. Any person, including a policeman, is at liberty to avoid a person he considers dangerous. If and when a policeman has a right instead to disarm such a person for his own protection, he must first have a right not to avoid him but to be in his presence. That right must be more than the liberty (again, possessed by every citizen) to address questions to other persons, for ordinarily the person addressed has an equal right to ignore his interrogator and walk away; he certainly need not submit to a frisk for the questioner's protection. I would make it perfectly clear that the right to frisk in this case depends upon the reasonableness of a forcible stop to investigate a suspected crime.

Where such a stop is reasonable, however, the right to frisk must be immediate and automatic if the reason for the stop is, as here, an articulable suspicion of a crime of violence. Just as a full search incident to a lawful arrest requires no additional justification, a limited frisk incident to a lawful stop must often be rapid and routine. There is no reason why an officer, rightfully but forcibly confronting a person suspected of a serious crime, should have to ask one question and take the risk that the answer might be a bullet.

The facts of this case are illustrative of a proper stop and an incident frisk. Officer McFadden had no probable cause to arrest Terry for anything, but he had observed circumstances that would reasonably lead an experienced, prudent policeman to suspect that Terry was about to engage in burglary or robbery. His justifiable suspicion afforded a proper constitutional basis for accosting Terry, restraining his liberty of movement briefly, and addressing questions to him, and Officer McFadden did so. When he did, he had no reason whatever to suppose that Terry might be armed, apart from the fact that he suspected him of planning a violent crime. McFadden asked Terry his name, to which Terry "mumbled something." Whereupon McFadden, without asking Terry to speak louder and without giving him any chance to explain his presence or his actions, forcibly frisked him.

I would affirm this conviction for what I believe to be the same reasons the Court relies on. I would, however, make explicit what I think is implicit in affirmance on the present facts. Officer McFadden's right to interrupt Terry's freedom of movement and invade his privacy arose only because circumstances warranted forcing an encounter with Terry in an effort to prevent or investigate a crime. Once that forced encounter was justified, however, the officer's right to take suitable measures for his own safely followed automatically.

Upon the foregoing premises, I join the opinion of the Court.

[JUSTICE WHITE'S concurring opinion is omitted.]

MR. JUSTICE DOUGLAS, dissenting.

I agree that petitioner was "seized" within the meaning of the Fourth Amendment. I also agree that frisking petitioner and his companions for guns was a "search." But it is a mystery how that "search" and that "seizure" can be constitutional by Fourth Amendment standards, unless there was "probable cause"[1] to believe that (1) a crime had been committed or (2) a crime was in the process of being committed or (3) a crime was about to be committed.

The opinion of the Court disclaims the existence of "probable cause." If loitering were in issue and that was the offense charged, there would be "probable cause" shown. But the crime here is carrying concealed weapons; and there is no basis for concluding that the officer had "probable cause" for believing that that crime was being committed. Had a warrant been sought, a magistrate would, therefore, have been unauthorized to issue one, for he can act only if there is a showing of "probable cause." We hold today that the police have greater authority to make a "seizure" and conduct a "search" than a judge has to authorize such action. We have said precisely the opposite over and over again.

In other words, police officers up to today have been permitted to effect arrests or searches without warrants only when the facts within their personal knowledge would satisfy the constitutional standard of *probable cause*. At the time of their 'seizure' without a warrant they must possess facts concerning the person arrested that would have satisfied a magistrate that "probable cause" was indeed present. The term "probable cause" rings a bell of certainty that is not sounded by phrases such as "reasonable suspicion." Moreover, the meaning of "probable cause" is deeply imbedded in our constitutional history.

The infringement on personal liberty of any "seizure" of a person can only be "reasonable" under the Fourth Amendment if we require the police to possess "probable cause" before they seize him. Only that line draws a meaningful distinction between an officer's mere inkling and the presence of facts within the officer's personal knowledge which would convince a reasonable man that the person seized has committed, is committing, or is about to commit a particular crime. "In dealing with probable cause, . . . as the very name implies, we deal with probabilities. These are not technical; they are the factual and practical considerations of everyday life on which reasonable and prudent men, not legal technicians, act."

---

[1] The meaning of "probable cause" has been developed in cases where an officer has reasonable grounds to believe that a crime has been or is being committed. In such cases, of course, the officer may make an "arrest" which results in charging the individual with commission of a crime. But while arresting persons who have already committed crimes is an important task of law enforcement, an equally if not more important function is crime prevention and deterrence of would-be criminals. "[T]here is no war between the Constitution and common sense." Police officers need not wait until they see a person actually commit a crime before they are able to "seize" that person. Respect for our constitutional system and personal liberty demands in return, however, that such a "seizure" be made only upon "probable cause."

To give the police greater power than a magistrate is to take a long step down the totalitarian path. Perhaps such a step is desirable to cope with modern forms of lawlessness. But if it is taken, it should be the deliberate choice of the people through a constitutional amendment. Until the Fourth Amendment is rewritten, the person and the effects of the individual are beyond the reach of all government agencies until there are reasonable grounds to believe (probable cause) that a criminal venture has been launched or is about to be launched.

There have been powerful hydraulic pressures throughout our history that bear heavily on the Court to water down constitutional guarantees and give the police the upper hand. That hydraulic pressure has probably never been greater than it is today.

Yet if the individual is no longer to be sovereign, if the police can pick him up whenever they do not like the cut of his jib, if they can "seize" and "search" him in their discretion, we enter a new regime. The decision to enter it should be made only after a full debate by the people of this country.

QUESTIONS AND NOTES

1. Do you think that there was probable cause for the frisk?

2. If your answer to Question 1 was "no" and probable cause means (as *Gates* later said it meant) "fair probability," would you be concluding that McFadden's belief did not amount to a fair probability?

3. If McFadden lacked a fair probability, how can we say that his suspicion was reasonable?

4. Do you perceive a meaningful difference between reasonable suspicion and probable cause?

5. Do you see any good reason for dispensing with the probable cause requirement?

6. To what extent did Terry's "mumble" contribute to reasonable suspicion?

7. Is the Court analyzing this case as an "exclusionary rule" case? That is, is the Court saying that the exclusionary rule won't work when the police are concerned with protecting themselves so why bother to apply it? Put differently, would (should) the case have been decided differently if it were a lawsuit by Katz against McFadden for violating his Fourth Amendment rights?

8. Conversely, would it be reasonable to allow a protective frisk for the policeman's benefit, but disallow the evidence to be admitted?

9. The scope and limitation of *Terry* was fairly well fleshed out in the companion case of *Sibron v. New York*.

SIBRON v. NEW YORK
392 U.S. 40 (1968)

MR. CHIEF JUSTICE WARREN delivered the opinion of the Court.

Sibron was convicted of the unlawful possession of heroin. He moved before trial to suppress the heroin seized from his person by the arresting officer, Brooklyn Patrolman Anthony Martin. After the trial court denied his motion, Sibron pleaded guilty to the charge, preserving his right to appeal the evidentiary ruling. At the hearing on the motion to suppress, Officer Martin testified that while he was patrolling his beat in uniform on March 9, 1965, he observed Sibron "continually from the hours of 4:00 P.M. to 12:00, midnight . . . in the vicinity of 742 Broadway." He stated that during this period of time he saw Sibron in conversation with six or eight persons whom he (Patrolman Martin) knew from past experience to be narcotics addicts. The officer testified that he did not overhear any of these conversations, and that he did not see anything pass between Sibron and any of the others. Late in the evening Sibron entered a restaurant. Patrolman Martin saw Sibron speak with three more known addicts inside the restaurant. Once again, nothing was overheard and nothing was seen to pass between Sibron and the addicts. Sibron sat down and ordered pie and coffee, and, as he was eating Patrolman Martin approached him and told him to come outside. Once outside, the officer said to Sibron, "You know what I am after." According to the officer, Sibron "mumbled something and reached into his pocket." Simultaneously, Patrolman Martin thrust his hand into the same pocket, discovering several glassine envelopes, which, it turned out, contained heroin.

The prosecutor's theory at the hearing was that Patrolman Martin had probable cause to believe that Sibron was in possession of narcotics because he had seen him conversing with a number of known addicts over an eight-hour period. In the absence of any knowledge on Patrolman Martin's part concerning the nature of the intercourse between Sibron and the addicts, however, the trial court was inclined to grant the motion to suppress. As the judge stated, "All he knows about the unknown men: They are narcotics addicts. They might have been talking about the World Series. They might have been talking about prize fights." The prosecutor, however, reminded the judge that Sibron had admitted on the stand, in Patrolman Martin's absence, that he had been talking to the addicts about narcotics. Thereupon, the trial judge changed his mind and ruled that the officer had probable cause for an arrest.

Turning to the facts of Sibron's case, it is clear that the heroin was inadmissible in evidence against him. The prosecution has quite properly abandoned the notion that there was probable cause to arrest Sibron for any crime at the time Patrolman Martin accosted him in the restaurant, took him outside and searched him. The officer was not acquainted with Sibron and had no information concerning him. He merely saw Sibron talking to a number of known narcotics addicts over a period of eight hours. It must be emphasized that Patrolman Martin was completely ignorant regarding the content of these conversations, and that he saw nothing pass between Sibron and the addicts. So far as he knew, they might indeed "have been talking about the World Series." The inference that persons who talk to narcotics addicts are engaged in the criminal traffic in narcotics is simply not the sort of reasonable inference required to support an intrusion by the police upon an individual's personal security. Nothing resembling probable cause existed until after the search had turned up the envelopes of heroin. It is axiomatic that an incident search may not precede an arrest and serve as part of its justification. Thus the search cannot be justified as incident to a lawful arrest.

If Patrolman Martin lacked probable cause for an arrest, however, his seizure and search of Sibron might still have been justified at the outset if he had reasonable grounds to believe that Sibron was armed and dangerous. We are not called upon to decide in this case whether there was a "seizure" of Sibron inside the restaurant antecedent to the physical seizure which accompanied the search. The record is unclear with respect to what transpired between Sibron and the officer inside the restaurant. It is totally barren of any indication whether Sibron accompanied Patrolman Martin outside in submission to a show of force or authority which left him no choice, or whether he went voluntarily in a spirit of apparent cooperation with the officer's investigation. In any event, this deficiency in the record is immaterial, since Patrolman Martin obtained no new information in the interval between his initiation of the encounter in the restaurant and his physical seizure and search of Sibron outside.

Although the Court of Appeals of New York wrote no opinion in this case, it seems to have viewed the search here as a self-protective search for weapons and to have affirmed on the basis of § 180a, which authorizes such a search when the officer "reasonably suspects that he is in danger of life or limb." The Court of Appeals has, at any rate, justified searches during field interrogation on the ground that "[t]he answer to the question propounded by the policeman may be a bullet; in any case the exposure to danger could be very great." *People v. Rivera*, 201 N.E.2d 32, 35 (N.Y. 1964). But the application of this reasoning to the facts of this case proves too much. The police officer is not entitled to seize and search every person whom he sees on the street or of whom he makes inquiries. Before he places a hand on the person of a citizen in search of anything, he must have constitutionally adequate, reasonable grounds for doing so. In the case of the self-protective search for weapons, he must be able to point to particular facts from which he reasonably inferred that the individual was armed and dangerous. Patrolman Martin's testimony reveals no such facts. The suspect's mere act of talking with a number of known narcotics addicts over an eight-hour period no more gives rise to reasonable fear of life or limb on the part of the police officer than it justifies an arrest for committing a crime. Nor did Patrolman Martin urge that when Sibron put his hand in his pocket, he feared that he was going for a weapon and acted in self-defense. His opening statement to Sibron —"You know what I am after"— made it abundantly clear that he sought narcotics, and his testimony at the hearing left no doubt that he thought there were narcotics in Sibron's pocket.

Even assuming *arguendo* that there were adequate grounds to search Sibron for weapons, the nature and scope of the search conducted by Patrolman Martin were so clearly unrelated to that justification as to render the heroin inadmissible. The search for weapons approved in *Terry* consisted solely of a limited patting of the outer clothing of the suspect for concealed objects which might be used as instruments of assault. Only when he discovered such objects did the officer in

Terry place his hands in the pockets of the men he searched. In this case, with no attempt at an initial limited exploration for arms, Patrolman Martin thrust his hand into Sibron's pocket and took from him envelopes of heroin. His testimony shows that he was looking for narcotics, and he found them. The search was not reasonably limited in scope to the accomplishment of the only goal which might conceivably have justified its inception — the protection of the officer by disarming a potentially dangerous man. Such a search violates the guarantee of the Fourth Amendment, which protects the sanctity of the person against unreasonable intrusions on the part of all government agents.

[Concurring and dissenting opinions omitted.]

QUESTIONS AND NOTES

1. Was Officer Martin's search unjustified (a) because his search was not limited to a frisk for weapons, (b) because he lacked reasonable suspicion to believe that Sibron was armed, or (c) both?

2. Is a person who repeatedly converses with known drug users less likely to be armed than one who, as in *Terry* "cases a joint"? Would you answer be different in the 21st century than it was in 1968?

3. Was Sibron's behavior less suspicious than Terry's?

4. What lesson do you take from a composite of *Terry* and *Sibron*?

PROBLEM
MINNESOTA v. DICKERSON

On the evening of November 9, 1989, two Minneapolis police officers were patrolling an area on the city's north side in a marked squad car. At about 8:15 p.m., one of the officers observed respondent leaving a 12-unit apartment building on Morgan Avenue North. The officer, having previously responded to complaints of drug sales in the building's hallways and having executed several search warrants on the premises, considered the building to be a notorious "crack house." According to testimony credited by the trial court, respondent began walking toward the police but, upon spotting the squad car and making eye contact with one of the officers, abruptly halted and began walking in the opposite direction. His suspicion aroused, this officer watched as respondent turned and entered an alley on the other side of the apartment building. Based upon respondent's seemingly evasive actions and the fact that he had just left a building known for cocaine traffic, the officers decided to stop respondent and investigate further.

The officers pulled their squad car into the alley and ordered respondent to stop and submit to a patdown search. The search revealed no weapons, but the officer conducting the search did take an interest in a small lump in respondent's nylon jacket. The officer later testified: "[A]s I pat-searched the front of his body, I felt a lump, a small lump, in the front pocket. I examined it with my fingers and it slid and it felt to be a lump of crack cocaine in cellophane." The officer then reached into respondent's pocket and retrieved a small plastic bag containing one fifth of one gram of crack cocaine. Respondent was arrested and charged in Hennepin County

District Court with possession of a controlled substance.

Assuming that all parties concede that the stop was lawful and that a frisk for weapons was appropriate, should the crack cocaine be suppressed at respondent's trial. For the Supreme Court's resolution of this question, *see Minnesota v. Dickerson*, 508 U.S. 366 (1993).

Fifteen years after *Terry* and *Sibron*, in *Long*, a Court with different Justices expanded the potential scope of a "frisk."

MICHIGAN v. LONG
463 U.S. 1032 (1983)

Justice O'Connor delivered the opinion of the Court.

In *Terry*, we upheld the validity of a protective search for weapons in the absence of probable cause to arrest because it is unreasonable to deny a police officer the right "to neutralize the threat of physical harm," when he possesses an articulable suspicion that an individual is armed and dangerous. We did not, however, expressly address whether such a protective search for weapons could extend to an area beyond the person in the absence of probable cause to arrest. In the present case, respondent David Long was convicted for possession of marijuana found by police in the passenger compartment and trunk of the automobile that he was driving. The police searched the passenger compartment because they had reason to believe that the vehicle contained weapons potentially dangerous to the officers. We hold that the protective search of the passenger compartment was reasonable under the principles articulated in *Terry* and other decisions of this Court.

I

Deputies Howell and Lewis were on patrol in a rural area one evening when, shortly after midnight, they observed a car traveling erratically and at excessive speed.[1] The officers observed the car turning down a side road, where it swerved off into a shallow ditch. The officers stopped to investigate. Long, the only occupant of the automobile, met the deputies at the rear of the car, which was protruding from the ditch onto the road. The door on the driver's side of the vehicle was left open.

---

[1] It is clear, and the respondent concedes, that if the officers had arrested Long for speeding or for driving while intoxicated, they could have searched the passenger compartment under *Belton*, and the trunk under *Ross*, if they had probable cause to believe that the trunk contained contraband. However, at oral argument, the State informed us that while Long could have been arrested for a speeding violation under Michigan law, he was *not* arrested because "[a]s a matter of practice," police in Michigan do not arrest for speeding violations unless "more" is involved. The officers did issue Long an appearance ticket. The petitioner also confirmed that the officers could have arrested Long for driving while intoxicated but they "would have to go through a process to make a determination as to whether the party is intoxicated and then go from that point." The court below treated this case as involving a protective search, and not a search justified by probable cause to arrest for speeding, driving while intoxicated, or any other offense. Further, the petitioner does not argue that if probable cause to arrest exists, but the officers do not actually effect the arrest, *that* the police may nevertheless conduct a search as broad as those authorized by *Belton* and *Ross*. Accordingly, we do not address that issue.

Deputy Howell requested Long to produce his operator's license, but he did not respond. After the request was repeated, Long produced his license. Long again failed to respond when Howell requested him to produce the vehicle registration. After another repeated request, Long, whom Howell thought "appeared to be under the influence of something," turned from the officers and began walking toward the open door of the vehicle. The officers followed Long and both observed a large hunting knife on the floorboard of the driver's side of the car. The officers then stopped Long's progress and subjected him to a *Terry* protective pat-down, which revealed no weapons.

Long and Deputy Lewis then stood by the rear of the vehicle while Deputy Howell shined his flashlight into the interior of the vehicle, but did not actually enter it. The purpose of Howell's action was "to search for other weapons." The officer noticed that something was protruding from under the armrest on the front seat. He knelt in the vehicle and lifted the armrest. He saw an open pouch on the front seat, and upon flashing his light on the pouch, determined that it contained what appeared to be marijuana. After Deputy Howell showed the pouch and its contents to Deputy Lewis, Long was arrested for possession of marijuana. A further search of the interior of the vehicle, including the glovebox, revealed neither more contraband nor the vehicle registration. The officers decided to impound the vehicle. Deputy Howell opened the trunk, which did not have a lock, and discovered inside it approximately 75 pounds of marijuana.

The Barry County Circuit Court denied Long's motion to suppress the marijuana taken from both the interior of the car and its trunk. He was subsequently convicted of possession of marijuana. The Michigan Court of Appeals affirmed Long's conviction, holding that the search of the passenger compartment was valid as a protective search under *Terry*, and that the search of the trunk was valid as an inventory search under *Opperman*. The Michigan Supreme Court reversed. The court held that "the sole justification of the *Terry* search, protection of the police officers and others nearby, cannot justify the search in this case." The marijuana found in Long's trunk was considered by the court below to be the "fruit" of the illegal search of the interior, and was also suppressed.

We granted certiorari in this case to consider the important question of the authority of a police officer to protect himself by conducting a *Terry*-type search of the passenger compartment of a motor vehicle during the lawful investigatory stop of the occupant of the vehicle.

III

The court below held, and respondent Long contends, that Deputy Howell's entry into the vehicle cannot be justified under the principles set forth in *Terry* because "*Terry* authorized only a limited pat-down search of a *person* suspected of criminal activity" rather than a search of an area. Although *Terry* did involve the protective frisk of a person, we believe that the police action in this case is justified by the principles that we have already established in *Terry* and other cases.

Examining the reasonableness of the officer's conduct in *Terry*, we held that there is " 'no ready test for determining reasonableness other than by balancing the

need to search [or seize] against the invasion which the search [or seizure] entails.' "
Although the conduct of the officer in *Terry* involved a "severe, though brief,
intrusion upon cherished personal security," we found that the conduct was
reasonable when we weighed the interest of the individual against the legitimate
interest in "crime prevention and detection," and the "need for law enforcement
officers to protect themselves and other prospective victims of violence in situations
where they lack probable cause for an arrest." When the officer has a reasonable
belief "that the individual whose suspicious behavior he is investigating at close
range is armed and presently dangerous to the officer or to others, it would appear
to be clearly unreasonable to deny the officer the power to take necessary measures
to determine whether the person is in fact carrying a weapon and to neutralize the
threat of physical harm."

Although *Terry* itself involved the stop and subsequent pat-down search of a
person, we were careful to note that "[w]e need not develop at length in this case,
however, the limitations which the Fourth Amendment places upon a protective
search and seizure for weapons. These limitations will have to be developed in the
concrete factual circumstances of individual cases." Contrary to Long's view, *Terry*
need not be read as restricting the preventative search to the person of the detained
suspect.[12]

In two cases in which we applied *Terry* to specific factual situations, we
recognized that investigative detentions involving suspects in vehicles are especially
fraught with danger to police officers. In *Pennsylvania v. Mimms*, 434 U.S. 106
(1977), we held that police may order persons out of an automobile during a stop for
a traffic violation, and may frisk those persons for weapons if there is a reasonable
belief that they are armed and dangerous. Our decision rested in part on the
"inordinate risk confronting an officer as he approaches a person seated in an
automobile." In *Adams v. Williams*, 407 U.S. 143 (1972), we held that the police,
acting on an informant's tip, may reach into the passenger compartment of an
automobile to remove a gun from a driver's waistband even where the gun was not
apparent to police from outside the car and the police knew of its existence only
because of the tip. Again, our decision rested in part on our view of the danger
presented to police officers in "traffic stop" and automobile situations.[13]

Finally, we have also expressly recognized that suspects may injure police
officers and others by virtue of their access to weapons, even though they may not
themselves be armed. In the Term following *Terry*, we decided *Chimel*, which
involved the limitations imposed on police authority to conduct a search incident to
a valid arrest. Relying explicitly on *Terry*, we held that when an arrest is made, it
is reasonable for the arresting officer to search "the arrestee's person and the area
'within his immediate control' — construing that phrase to mean the area from

---

[12] As Chief Justice Coleman noted in her dissenting opinion in the present case: "The opinion in *Terry*
authorized the frisking of an overcoat worn by defendant because that was the issue presented by the
facts. One could reasonably conclude that a different result would not have been constitutionally
required if the overcoat had been carried, folded over the forearm, rather than worn. The constitutional
principles stated in *Terry* would still control."

[13] "According to one study, approximately 30% of police shootings occurred when a police officer
approached a suspect seated in an automobile."

within which he might gain possession of a weapon or destructible evidence." We reasoned that "[a] gun on a table or in a drawer in front of one who is arrested can be as dangerous to the arresting officer as one concealed in the clothing of the person arrested." In *Belton*, we determined that the lower courts "have found no workable definition of 'the area within the immediate control of the arrestee' when that area arguably includes the interior of an automobile and the arrestee is its recent occupant." In order to provide a "workable rule," we held that "articles inside the relatively narrow compass of the passenger compartment of an automobile are in fact generally, even if not inevitably, within 'the area into which an arrestee might reach in order to grab a weapon' . . . ." We also held that the police may examine the contents of any open or closed container found within the passenger compartment, "for if the passenger compartment is within the reach of the arrestee, so will containers in it be within his reach."

Our past cases indicate then that protection of police and others can justify protective searches when police have a reasonable belief that the suspect poses a danger, that roadside encounters between police and suspects are especially hazardous, and that danger may arise from the possible presence of weapons in the area surrounding a suspect. These principles compel our conclusion that the search of the passenger compartment of an automobile, limited to those areas in which a weapon may be placed or hidden, is permissible if the police officer possesses a reasonable belief based on "specific and articulable facts which, taken together with the rational inferences from those facts, reasonably warrant" the officers in believing that the suspect is dangerous and the suspect may gain immediate control of weapons.[14] "[T]he issue is whether a reasonably prudent man in the circumstances would be warranted in the belief that his safety or that of others was in danger." If a suspect is "dangerous," he is no less dangerous simply because he is not arrested. If, while conducting a legitimate *Terry* search of the interior of the automobile, the officer should, as here, discover contraband other than weapons, he clearly cannot be required to ignore the contraband, and the Fourth Amendment does not require its suppression in such circumstances.

The circumstances of this case clearly justified Deputies Howell and Lewis in their reasonable belief that Long posed a danger if he were permitted to reenter his vehicle. The hour was late and the area rural. Long was driving his automobile at excessive speed, and his car swerved into a ditch. The officers had to repeat their

---

[14] We stress that our decision does not mean that the police may conduct automobile searches *whenever* they conduct an investigative stop, although the "bright line" that we drew in *Belton* clearly authorizes such a search whenever officers effect a custodial arrest. An additional interest exists in the arrest context, *i.e.*, preservation of evidence, and this justifies an "automatic" search. However, that additional interest does not exist in the *Terry* context. A *Terry* search, "unlike a search without a warrant incident to a lawful arrest, is not justified by any need to prevent the disappearance or destruction of evidence of crime . . . . The sole justification of the search . . . is the protection of police officers and others nearby . . . ." What we borrow now from *Chimel* and *Belton* is merely the recognition that part of the reason to allow area searches incident to an arrest is that the arrestee, who may not himself be armed, may be able to gain access to weapons to injure officers or others nearby, or otherwise to hinder legitimate police activity. This recognition applies as well in the *Terry* context. However, because the interest in collecting and preserving evidence is not present in the *Terry* context, we require that officers who conduct area searches during investigative detentions must do so only when they have the level of suspicion identified in *Terry*.

questions to Long, who appeared to be "under the influence" of some intoxicant. Long was not frisked until the officers observed that there was a large knife in the interior of the car into which Long was about to reenter. The subsequent search of the car was restricted to those areas to which Long would generally have immediate control, and that could contain a weapon. The trial court determined that the leather pouch containing marijuana could have contained a weapon.[15] It is clear that the intrusion was "strictly circumscribed by the exigencies which justifi[ed] its initiation."

In evaluating the validity of an officer's investigative or protective conduct under *Terry*, the "[t]ouchstone of our analysis . . . is always 'the reasonableness in all circumstances of the particular governmental intrusion of a citizen's personal security.' " In this case, the officers did not act unreasonably in taking preventive measures to ensure that there were no other weapons within Long's immediate grasp before permitting him to reenter his automobile. Therefore, the balancing required by *Terry* clearly weighs in favor of allowing the police to conduct an area search of the passenger compartment to uncover weapons, as long as they possess an articulable and objectively reasonable belief that the suspect is potentially dangerous.

The Michigan Supreme Court appeared to believe that it was not reasonable for the officers to fear that Long could injure them, because he was effectively under their control during the investigative stop and could not get access to any weapons that might have been located in the automobile. This reasoning is mistaken in several respects. During any investigative detention, the suspect is "in the control" of the officers in the sense that he "may be briefly detained against his will . . . ." Just as a *Terry* suspect on the street may, despite being under the brief control of a police officer, reach into his clothing and retrieve a weapon, so might a *Terry* suspect in Long's position break away from police control and retrieve a weapon from his automobile. In addition, if the suspect is not placed under arrest, he will be permitted to reenter his automobile, and he will then have access to any weapons inside. Or, as here, the suspect may be permitted to reenter the vehicle before the *Terry* investigation is over, and again, may have access to weapons. In any event, we stress that a *Terry* investigation, such as the one that occurred here, involves a police investigation "at close range," when the officer remains particularly vulnerable in part because a full custodial arrest has not been effected, and the officer must make a "quick decision as to how to protect himself and others from possible danger . . . ." In such circumstances, we have not required that officers adopt alternate means to ensure their safety in order to avoid the intrusion involved in a *Terry* encounter.[16]

---

[15] Of course, our analysis would apply to justify the search of Long's person that was conducted by the officers after the discovery of the knife.

[16] Long makes a number of arguments concerning the invalidity of the search of the passenger compartment. The thrust of these arguments is that *Terry* searches are limited in scope and that an area search is fundamentally inconsistent with this limited scope. We have recognized that *Terry* searches are limited insofar as they may not be conducted in the absence of an articulable suspicion that the intrusion is justified, *see, e.g., Sibron,* and that they are protective in nature and limited to weapons, *see Ybarra v. Illinois* [*infra*]. However, neither of these concerns is violated by our decision. To engage in an area

The decision of the Michigan Supreme Court is reversed, and the case is remanded for further proceedings not inconsistent with this opinion.

JUSTICE BRENNAN, with whom JUSTICE MARSHALL joins, dissenting.

The Court today holds that "the protective search of the passenger compartment" of the automobile involved in this case "was reasonable under the principles articulated in *Terry* and other decisions of this Court." I disagree. *Terry* does not support the Court's conclusion and the reliance on "other decisions" is patently misplaced. Plainly, the Court is simply continuing the process of distorting *Terry* beyond recognition and forcing it into service as an unlikely weapon against the Fourth Amendment's fundamental requirement that searches and seizures be based on probable cause. I, therefore, dissent.

In *Terry*, the Court confronted the "quite narrow question" of "whether it is always unreasonable for a policeman to seize a person and subject him to a *limited* search for weapons unless there is probable cause for an arrest." (emphasis supplied). Because the Court was dealing "with an entire rubric of police conduct . . . which historically [had] not been, and as a practical matter could not be, subjected to the warrant procedure," the Court tested the conduct at issue "by the Fourth Amendment's general proscription against unreasonable searches and seizures." It deserves emphasis that in discussing the "invasion" at issue, the Court stated that "[e]ven *a limited search of the outer clothing for weapons* constitutes a severe, though brief, intrusion upon cherished personal security . . . ." (emphasis supplied). Ultimately, the Court concluded that "there must be *a narrowly drawn authority* to permit a reasonable search for weapons for the protection of the police officer, where he has reason to believe that he is dealing with an armed and dangerous individual, regardless of whether he has probable cause to arrest the individual for a crime."

---

search, which is limited to seeking weapons, the officer must have an articulable suspicion that the suspect is potentially dangerous.

Long also argues that there cannot be a legitimate *Terry* search based on the discovery of the hunting knife because Long possessed that weapon legally. Assuming arguendo that Long possessed the knife lawfully, we have expressly rejected the view that the validity of a *Terry* search depends on whether the weapon is possessed in accordance with state law. Contrary to Justice Brennan's suggestion in dissent, the reasoning of *Terry*, *Chimel*, and *Belton* point clearly to the direction that we have taken today. Although *Chimel* involved a full custodial arrest, the rationale for *Chimel* rested on the recognition in *Terry* that it is unreasonable to prevent the police from taking reasonable steps to protect their safety. Justice Brennan suggests that we are expanding the scope of a *Terry*-type search to include a search incident to a valid arrest. However, our opinion clearly indicates that the area search that we approve is limited to a search for weapons in circumstances where the officers have a reasonable belief that the suspect is potentially dangerous to them. Justice Brennan quotes at length from *Sibron*, but fails to recognize that the search in that case was a search for narcotics, and not a search for weapons.

Justice Brennan concedes that "police should not be exposed to unnecessary danger in the performance of their duties." but then would require that police officers, faced with having to make quick determinations about self-protection and the defense of innocent citizens in the area, must also decide instantaneously what "less intrusive" alternative exists to ensure that any threat presented by the suspect will be neutralized. For the practical reasons explained in *Terry*, we have not in the past, and do not now, require police to adopt alternate measures to avoid a legitimate *Terry*-type intrusion.

It is clear that *Terry* authorized only limited searches of the person for weapons. In light of what *Terry* said, relevant portions of which the Court neglects to quote, the Court's suggestion that *"Terry* need not be read as restricting the preventive search to the person of the detained suspect," can only be described as disingenuous. Nothing in *Terry* authorized police officers to search a suspect's car based on reasonable suspicion.

The Court's reliance on *Chimel* and *Belton* as support for its new "area search" rule within the context of a *Terry* stop is misplaced. In *Chimel*, the Court addressed the scope of a search incident to a lawful arrest, and held invalid the search at issue there because it "went far beyond the petitioner's person and the area from within which he might have obtained a weapon or something that could have been used as evidence against him." . . . *Chimel* stressed the need to limit the scope of searches incident to arrest and overruled two prior decisions of this Court validating overly broad searches.

In *Belton*, the Court considered the scope of a search incident to the lawful custodial arrest of an occupant of an automobile. In this "particular and problematic context," the Court held that "when a policeman has made a lawful custodial arrest of the occupant of an automobile, he may, as a contemporaneous incident of that arrest, search the passenger compartment of that automobile."

The critical distinction between this case and *Terry* on the one hand, and *Chimel* and *Belton* on the other, is that the latter two cases arose within the context of lawful custodial arrests supported by probable cause. The Court in *Terry* expressly recognized the difference between a search incident to arrest and the "limited search for weapons," involved in that case. The Court stated:

> . . . An arrest is a wholly different kind of intrusion upon individual freedom from a limited search for weapons, and the interests each is designed to serve are likewise quite different. An arrest is the initial stage of a criminal prosecution. It is intended to vindicate society's interest in having its laws obeyed, and it is inevitably accompanied by future interference with the individual's freedom of movement, whether or not trial or conviction ultimately follows. The protective search for weapons, on the other hand, constitutes a brief, though far from inconsiderable, intrusion upon the sanctity of the person.

In *United States v. Robinson*, 414 U.S. 218 (1973), the Court relied on the differences between searches incident to lawful custodial arrests and *Terry* "stop-and-frisk" searches to reject an argument that the limitations established in *Terry* should be applied to a search incident to arrest. The Court noted that *"Terry* clearly recognized the distinction between the two types of searches, and that a different rule governed one than governed the other," and described *Terry* as involving "stricter . . . standards," than those governing searches incident to arrest. The Court went on to state:

> A custodial arrest of a suspect based on probable cause is a reasonable intrusion under the Fourth Amendment; that intrusion being lawful, a search incident to the arrest requires no additional justification. It is the fact of the lawful arrest which establishes the authority to search, and we

hold that in the case of a lawful custodial arrest a full search of the person is not only an exception to the warrant requirement of the Fourth Amendment, but is also a "reasonable" search under that Amendment.

As these cases recognize, there is a vital difference between searches incident to lawful custodial arrests and *Terry* protective searches. The Court deliberately ignores that difference in relying on principles developed within the context of intrusions supported by probable cause to arrest to construct an "area search" rule within the context of a *Terry* stop.

The Court denies that an "area search" is fundamentally inconsistent with *Terry*, stating:

> We have recognized that *Terry* searches are limited insofar as they may not be conducted in the absence of an articulable suspicion that the intrusion is justified, and that they are protective in nature and limited to weapons. However, neither of these concerns is violated by our decision. To engage in an area search, which is limited to seeking weapons, the officer must have an articulable suspicion that the suspect is potentially dangerous.

This patently is no answer: respondent's argument relates to the *scope* of the search, not to the standard that justifies it. The Court flouts *Terry*'s holding that *Terry* searches must be carefully limited in scope. Indeed, the page in *Sibron* cited by the Court states:

> Even assuming *arguendo* that there were adequate grounds to search Sibron for weapons, the nature *and scope* of the search conducted by Patrolman Martin were so clearly unrelated to that justification as to render the heroin inadmissible. The search for weapons approved in *Terry* consisted *solely of a limited patting of the outer clothing of the suspect* for concealed objects which might be used as instruments of assault. Only when he discovered such objects did the officer in *Terry* place his hands in the pockets of the men he searched. In this case, with no attempt at an initial limited exploration for arms, Patrolman Martin thrust his hand into Sibron's pocket and took from him envelopes of heroin. His testimony shows that he was looking for narcotics, and he found them. The search was not reasonably limited in scope to the accomplishment of the only goal which might conceivably have justified its inception — the protection of the officer by disarming a potentially dangerous man.

(emphasis supplied). As this passage makes clear, the scope of a search is determined not only by reference to its purpose, but also by reference to its intrusiveness. Yet the Court today holds that a search of a car (and the containers within it) that is not even occupied by the suspect is only as intrusive as, or perhaps less intrusive than, thrusting a hand into a pocket after an initial patdown has suggested the presence of concealed objects that might be used as weapons.

The Court suggests no limit on the "area search" it now authorizes. The Court states that a

> search of the passenger compartment of an automobile, limited to those areas in which a weapon may be placed or hidden, is permissible if the

police officer possesses a reasonable belief based on "specific and articulable facts which, taken together with the rational inferences from those facts, reasonably warrant" the officers to believe that the suspect is dangerous and the suspect may gain immediate control of weapons.

Presumably a weapon "may be placed or hidden" anywhere in a car. A weapon also might be hidden in a container in the car. In this case, the Court upholds the officer's search of a leather pouch because it "could have contained a weapon." In addition, the Court's requirement that an officer have a reasonable suspicion that a suspect is armed and dangerous does little to check the initiation of an area search. In this case, the officers saw a hunting knife in the car, but the Court does not base its holding that the subsequent search was permissible on the ground that possession of the knife may have been illegal under state law. An individual can lawfully possess many things that can be used as weapons. A hammer, or a baseball bat, can be used as a very effective weapon. Finally, the Court relies on the following facts to conclude that the officers had a reasonable suspicion that respondent was presently dangerous: the hour was late; the area was rural; respondent had been driving at an excessive speed; he had been involved in an accident; he was not immediately responsive to the officers' questions; and he appeared to be under the influence of some intoxicant. Based on these facts, one might reasonably conclude that respondent was drunk. A drunk driver is indeed dangerous while driving, but not while stopped on the roadside by the police. Even when an intoxicated person lawfully has in his car an object that could be used as a weapon, it requires imagination to conclude that he is presently dangerous. Even assuming that the facts in this case justified the officers' initial "frisk" of respondent, they hardly provide adequate justification for a search of a suspect's car and the containers within it. This represents an intrusion not just different in degree, but in kind, from the intrusion sanctioned by *Terry*. In short, the implications of the Court's decision are frightening.

The Court also rejects the Michigan Supreme Court's view that it "was not reasonable for the officers to fear that [respondent] could injure them, because he was effectively under their control during the investigative stop and could not get access to any weapons that might have been located in the automobile." In this regard, the Court states:

> [W]e stress that a *Terry* investigation, such as the one that occurred here, involves a police investigation "at close range," . . . when the officer remains particularly vulnerable in part *because* a full custodial arrest has not been effected, and the officer must make a "quick decision as to how to protect himself and others from possible danger." . . . In such circumstances, we have not required that officers adopt alternate means to ensure their safety in order to avoid the intrusion involved in a *Terry* encounter.

(emphasis in original). Putting aside the fact that the search at issue here involved a far more serious intrusion than that "involved in a *Terry* encounter," and as such might suggest the need for resort to "alternate means," the Court's reasoning is perverse. The Court's argument in essence is that the *absence* of probable cause to arrest compels the conclusion that a broad search, traditionally associated in scope with a search incident to arrest, must be permitted based on reasonable suspicion.

But *United States v. Robinson* stated: "It is scarcely open to doubt that the danger to an officer is far greater in the case of the extended exposure which follows the taking of a suspect into custody and transporting him to the police station than in the case of the relatively fleeting contact resulting from the typical *Terry*-type stop." In light of *Robinson's* observation, today's holding leaves in grave doubt the question of whether the Court's assessment of the relative dangers posed by given confrontations is based on any principled standard.

[T]oday's decision reflects once again the threat to Fourth Amendment values posed by "balancing." As Justice Frankfurter stated in *United States v. Rabinowitz*: "To say that the search must be reasonable is to require some criterion of reason. It is no guide at all either for a jury or for district judges or the police to say that an 'unreasonable search' is forbidden — that the search must be reasonable. What is the test of reason which makes a search reasonable? The test is the reason underlying and expressed by the Fourth Amendment: the history and the experience which it embodies and the safeguards afforded by it against the evils to which it was a response." 339 U.S. 56, 83 (1950) (dissenting opinion). Hornbook law has been that "the police may not conduct a search unless they first convince a neutral magistrate that there is probable cause to do so." While under some circumstances the police may search a car without a warrant, "the exception to the warrant requirement established in *Carroll* . . . applies only to searches of vehicles that are supported by probable cause." *Ross.* Today the Court discards these basic principles and employs the very narrow exception established by *Terry* "to swallow the general rule that Fourth Amendment [searches of cars] are 'reasonable' only if based on probable cause."[6]

"The needs of law enforcement stand in constant tension with the Constitution's protections of the individual against certain exercises of official power. It is precisely the predictability of these pressures that counsels a resolute loyalty to constitutional safeguards." Of course, police should not be exposed to unnecessary danger in the performance of their duties. But a search of a car and the containers within it based on nothing more than reasonable suspicion, even under the circumstances present here, cannot be sustained without doing violence to the requirements of the Fourth Amendment. There is no reason in this case why the officers could not have pursued less intrusive, but equally effective, means of insuring their safety.[7] The Court takes a long step today toward "balancing" into oblivion the protections the Fourth Amendment affords. I dissent, for as Justice Jackson said in *Brinegar*:

> [Fourth Amendment rights] are not mere second-class rights but belong in
> the catalog of indispensable freedoms. Among deprivations of rights, none
> is so effective in cowing a population, crushing the spirit of the individual

---

[6] Of course, the Court's decision also swallows the general rule that searches of containers must be based on probable cause. Without probable cause to search the car, *Ross* does not apply. Moreover, in the absence of a lawful custodial arrest, *Belton* does not apply.

[7] The police, for example, could have continued to detain respondent outside the car and asked him to tell them where his registration was. The police then could have retrieved the registration themselves. This would have resulted in an intrusion substantially less severe than the one at issue here.

and putting terror in every heart. Uncontrolled search and seizure is one of the first and most effective weapons in the arsenal of every arbitrary government.

Id. at 180, 69 S. Ct. at 1313 (dissenting opinion).

[JUSTICE STEVENS' dissenting opinion is omitted.]

QUESTIONS AND NOTES

1.   Accepting the Court's contention that it is not approving generic "car frisks" simply because a car was stopped, what is there about *Long* that warrants the frisk?

2.   Did (should) the hunting knife influence (have influenced) the Court? Why? Why not?

3.   Would (should) the *Long* reasoning permit the police to look inside a knapsack in a *Terry situation*?

4.   Do you think that the *Brinegar* quote at the end of the Brennan opinion was overly apocalyptic?

5.   Would *Long* have seemed less threatening to libertarians if it were accompanied by a decision, like *Sibron*, disallowing an automobile frisk when the evidence for it was less persuasive than it was in *Long*?

6.   We close this section with *Ybarra*, a case clearly establishing that *Terry* "is not a talisman in whose presence the Fourth Amendment disappears.

YBARRA v. ILLINOIS
444 U.S. 85 (1979)

MR. JUSTICE STEWART delivered the opinion of the Court.

An Illinois statute authorizes law enforcement officers to detain and search any person found on premises being searched pursuant to a search warrant, to protect themselves from attack or to prevent the disposal or concealment of anything described in the warrant. The question before us is whether the application of this statute to the facts of the present case violated the Fourth and Fourteenth Amendments.

I

On March 1, 1976, a special agent of the Illinois Bureau of Investigation presented a "Complaint for Search Warrant" to a judge of an Illinois Circuit Court. The complaint recited that the agent had spoken with an informant known to the police to be reliable and:

> 3. The informant related . . . that over the weekend of 28 and 29 February he was in the [Aurora Tap Tavern, located in the city of Aurora, Ill.] and observed fifteen to twenty-five tin-foil packets on the person of the

bartender "Greg" and behind the bar. He also has been in the tavern on at least ten other occasions and has observed tin-foil packets on "Greg" and in a drawer behind the bar. The informant has used heroin in the past and knows that tin-foil packets are a common method of packaging heroin.

4. The informant advised . . . that over the weekend of 28 and 29 February he had a conversation with "Greg" and was advised that "Greg" would have heroin for sale on Monday, March 1, 1976. This conversation took place in the tavern described.

On the strength of this complaint, the judge issued a warrant authorizing the search of "the following person or place: . . . [T]he Aurora Tap Tavern . . . . Also the person of 'Greg', the bartender, a male white with blondish hair appx. 25 years." The warrant authorized the police to search for "evidence of the offense of possession of a controlled substance," to wit, "[h]eroin, contraband, other controlled substances, money, instrumentalities and narcotics, paraphernalia used in the manufacture, processing and distribution of controlled substances."

In the late afternoon of that day, seven or eight officers proceeded to the tavern. Upon entering it, the officers announced their purpose and advised all those present that they were going to conduct a "cursory search for weapons." One of the officers then proceeded to patdown each of the 9 to 13 customers present in the tavern, while the remaining officers engaged in an extensive search of the premises.

The police officer who frisked the patrons found the appellant, Ventura Ybarra, in front of the bar standing by a pinball machine. In his first patdown of Ybarra, the officer felt what he described as "a cigarette pack with objects in it." He did not remove this pack from Ybarra's pocket. Instead, he moved on and proceeded to patdown other customers. After completing this process the officer returned to Ybarra and frisked him once again. This second search of Ybarra took place approximately 2 to 10 minutes after the first. The officer relocated and retrieved the cigarette pack from Ybarra's pants pocket. Inside the pack he found six tinfoil packets containing a brown powdery substance which later turned out to be heroin.

II

There is no reason to suppose that, when the search warrant was issued on March 1, 1976, the authorities had probable cause to believe that any person found on the premises of the Aurora Tap Tavern, aside from "Greg," would be violating the law.[2] The search warrant complaint did not allege that the bar was frequented by persons illegally purchasing drugs. It did not state that the informant had ever seen a patron of the tavern purchase drugs from "Greg" or from any other person.

---

[2] The warrant issued on March 1, 1976, did not itself authorize the search of Ybarra or of any other patron found on the premises of the Aurora Tap Tavern. It directed the police to search "the following person or place: . . . the Aurora Tap Tavern . . . . Also the person of 'Greg' . . . ." Had the issuing judge intended that the warrant would or could authorize a search of every person found within the tavern, he would hardly have specifically authorized the search of "Greg" alone. "Greg" was an employee of the tavern, and the complaint upon which the search warrant was issued gave every indication that he would be present at the tavern on March 1.

Nowhere, in fact, did the complaint even mention the patrons of the Aurora Tap Tavern.

Not only was probable cause to search Ybarra absent at the time the warrant was issued, it was still absent when the police executed the warrant. Upon entering the tavern, the police did not recognize Ybarra and had no reason to believe that he had committed, was committing, or was about to commit any offense under state or federal law. Ybarra made no gestures indicative of criminal conduct, made no movements that might suggest an attempt to conceal contraband, and said nothing of a suspicious nature to the police officers. In short, the agents knew nothing in particular about Ybarra, except that he was present, along with several other customers, in a public tavern at a time when the police had reason to believe that the bartender would have heroin for sale.

It is true that the police possessed a warrant based on probable cause to search the tavern in which Ybarra happened to be at the time the warrant was executed. But, a person's mere propinquity to others independently suspected of criminal activity does not, without more, give rise to probable cause to search that person. *Sibron.* Where the standard is probable cause, a search or seizure of a person must be supported by probable cause particularized with respect to that person. This requirement cannot be undercut or avoided by simply pointing to the fact that coincidentally there exists probable cause to search or seize another or to search the premises where the person may happen to be. The Fourth and Fourteenth Amendments protect the "legitimate expectations of privacy" of persons, not places.

Each patron who walked into the Aurora Tap Tavern on March 1, 1976, was clothed with constitutional protection against an unreasonable search or an unreasonable seizure. That individualized protection was separate and distinct from the Fourth and Fourteenth Amendment protection possessed by the proprietor of the tavern or by "Greg." Although the search warrant, issued upon probable cause, gave the officers authority to search the premises and to search "Greg," it gave them no authority whatever to invade the constitutional protections possessed individually by the tavern's customers.[4]

Notwithstanding the absence of probable cause to search Ybarra, the State argues that the action of the police in searching him and seizing what was found in his pocket was nonetheless constitutionally permissible. We are asked to find that the first patdown search of Ybarra constituted a reasonable frisk for weapons under the doctrine of *Terry.* If this finding is made, it is then possible to conclude, the State argues, that the second search of Ybarra was constitutionally justified. The argument is that the patdown yielded probable cause to believe that Ybarra was carrying narcotics, and that this probable cause constitutionally supported the

---

[4] The Fourth Amendment directs that "no Warrants shall issue, but upon probable cause . . . and particularly describing the place to be searched, and the persons or things to be seized." Thus, "open-ended" or "general" warrants are constitutionally prohibited. It follows that a warrant to search a place cannot normally be construed to authorize a search of each individual in that place. The warrant for the Aurora Tap Tavern provided no basis for departing from this general rule. Consequently, we need not consider situations where the warrant itself authorizes the search of unnamed persons in a place and is supported by probable cause to believe that persons who will be in the place at the time of the search will be in possession of illegal drugs.

second search, no warrant being required in light of the exigencies of the situation coupled with the ease with which Ybarra could have disposed of the illegal substance.

We are unable to take even the first step required by this argument. The initial frisk of Ybarra was simply not supported by a reasonable belief that he was armed and presently dangerous, a belief which this Court has invariably held must form the predicate to a patdown of a person for weapons.[5] When the police entered the Aurora Tap Tavern on March 1, 1976, the lighting was sufficient for them to observe the customers. Upon seeing Ybarra, they neither recognized him as a person with a criminal history nor had any particular reason to believe that he might be inclined to assault them. Moreover, as Police Agent Johnson later testified, Ybarra, whose hands were empty, gave no indication of possessing a weapon, made no gestures or other actions indicative of an intent to commit an assault, and acted generally in a manner that was not threatening. At the suppression hearing, the most Agent Johnson could point to was that Ybarra was wearing a 3/4-length lumber jacket, clothing which the State admits could be expected on almost any tavern patron in Illinois in early March. In short, the State is unable to articulate any specific fact that would have justified a police officer at the scene in even suspecting that Ybarra was armed and dangerous.

Terry created an exception to the requirement of probable cause, an exception whose "narrow scope" this Court "has been careful to maintain." Under that doctrine a law enforcement officer, for his own protection and safety, may conduct a patdown to find weapons that he reasonably believes or suspects are then in the possession of the person he has accosted. Nothing in *Terry* can be understood to allow a generalized "cursory search for weapons" or indeed, any search whatever for anything but weapons. The "narrow scope" of the *Terry* exception does not permit a frisk for weapons on less than reasonable belief or suspicion directed at the person to be frisked, even though that person happens to be on premises where an authorized narcotics search is taking place.

[The Court then held that the state's interest in controlling narcotics did not justify an evidence search of everybody who happened to be at the place that was searched.]

For these reasons, we conclude that the searches of Ybarra and the seizure of what was in his pocket contravened the Fourth and Fourteenth Amendments.

MR. CHIEF JUSTICE BURGER, with whom MR. JUSTICE BLACKMUN and MR. JUSTICE REHNQUIST join, dissenting.

I join Mr. Justice Rehnquist's dissent since I cannot subscribe to the Court's unjustifiable narrowing of the rule of *Terry*. The Court would require a particularized and individualized suspicion that a person is armed and dangerous as a condition to a *Terry* search. This goes beyond the rationale of *Terry* and overlooks

---

[5] Since we conclude that the initial patdown of Ybarra was not justified under the Fourth and Fourteenth Amendments, we need not decide whether or not the presence on Ybarra's person of "a cigarette pack with objects in it" yielded probable cause to believe that Ybarra was carrying any illegal substance.

the practicalities of a situation which no doubt often confronts officers executing a valid search warrant.

These officers had validly obtained a warrant to search a named person and a rather small, one-room tavern for narcotics. Upon arrival, they found the room occupied by 12 persons. Were they to ignore these individuals and assume that all were unarmed and uninvolved? Given the setting and the reputation of those who trade in narcotics, it does not go too far to suggest that they might pay for such an easy assumption with their lives. The law does not require that those executing a search warrant must be so foolhardy. That is precisely what Mr. Chief Justice Warren's opinion in *Terry* stands for. Indeed, the *Terry* Court recognized that a balance must be struck between the privacy interest of individuals and the safety of police officers in performing their duty. I would hold that when police execute a search warrant for narcotics in a place of known narcotics activity they may protect themselves by conducting a *Terry* search. They are not required to assume that they will not be harmed by patrons of the kind of establishment shown here, something quite different from a ballroom at the Waldorf. "The officer need not be absolutely certain that the individual is armed; the issue is whether a reasonably prudent man in the circumstances would be warranted in the belief that his safety or that of others was in danger."

I do not find it controlling that the heroin was not actually retrieved from appellant until the officer returned after completing the first search. The "cigarette pack with objects in it" was noticed in the first search. In the "second search," the officer did no more than return to the appellant and retrieve the pack he had already discovered. That there was a delay of minutes between the search and the seizure is not dispositive in this context, where the searching officer made the on-the-spot judgment that he need not seize the suspicious package immediately. He could first reasonably make sure that none of the patrons was armed before returning to appellant. Thus I would treat the second search and its fruits just as I would had the officer taken the pack immediately upon noticing it, which plainly would have been permissible.

MR. JUSTICE REHNQUIST, with whom THE CHIEF JUSTICE and MR. JUSTICE BLACKMUN join, dissenting.

On March 1, 1976, agents of the Illinois Bureau of Investigation executed a search warrant in the Aurora Tap Tavern in Aurora, Ill. The warrant was based on information given by a confidential informant who said that he had seen heroin on the person of the bartender and in a drawer behind the bar on at least 10 occasions. Moreover, the informant advised the affiant that the bartender would have heroin for sale on March 1. The warrant empowered the police to search the Aurora Tap and the person of "Greg," the bartender.

When police arrived at the Aurora Tap, a drab, dimly lit tavern, they found about a dozen or so persons standing or sitting at the bar. The police announced their purpose and told everyone at the bar to stand for a patdown search. Agent Jerome Johnson, the only officer to testify in the proceedings below, explained that the initial search was a frisk for weapons to protect the officers executing the warrant. Johnson frisked several patrons, including appellant Ybarra. During this patdown,

Johnson felt "a cigarette pack with objects in it" in Ybarra's front pants pocket. He finished frisking the other patrons and then returned to Ybarra. At that time, he frisked Ybarra once again, reached into Ybarra's pocket, and removed the cigarette package that he had felt previously. The package, upon inspection, confirmed the officer's previously aroused suspicion that it contained not cigarettes but packets of heroin.

Confronted with these facts, the Court concludes that the police were without authority under the warrant to search any of the patrons in the tavern and that, absent probable cause to believe that Ybarra possessed contraband, the search of his person violated the Fourth and Fourteenth Amendments. Because I believe that this analysis is faulty, I dissent.

[JUSTICE REHNQUIST then concluded that the search of Ybarra was justified because a warrant to search the bar included all persons found therein.]

Viewed sequentially, the actions of the police in this case satisfy the scope/justification test of reasonableness established by the first clause of the Fourth Amendment as interpreted in *Terry*. The police entered the Aurora Tap pursuant to the warrant and found themselves confronting a dozen people, all standing or sitting at the bar, the suspected location of the contraband. Because the police were aware that heroin was being offered for sale in the tavern, it was quite reasonable to assume that any one or more of the persons at the bar could have been involved in drug trafficking. This assumption, by itself, might not have justified a full-scale search of all the individuals in the tavern. Nevertheless, the police also were quite conscious of the possibility that one or more of the patrons could be armed in preparation for just such an intrusion. In the narcotics business, "firearms are as much 'tools of the trade' as are most commonly recognized articles of narcotics paraphernalia." The potential danger to the police executing the warrant and to innocent individuals in this dimly lit tavern cannot be minimized. By conducting an immediate frisk of those persons at the bar, the police eliminated this danger and "froze" the area in preparation for the search of the premises.

Ybarra contends that *Terry* requires an "individualized" suspicion that a particular person is armed and dangerous. While this factor may be important in the case of an on-the-street stop, where the officer must articulate some reason for singling the person out of the general population, there are at least two reasons why it has less significance in the present situation, where execution of a valid warrant had thrust the police into a confrontation with a small but potentially dangerous, group of people. First, in place of the requirement of "individualized suspicion" as a guard against arbitrary exercise of authority, we have here the determination of a neutral and detached magistrate that a search was necessary. The question then becomes whether, given the initial decision to intrude, the scope of the intrusion is reasonable.

In addition, the task performed by the officers executing a search warrant is inherently more perilous than is a momentary encounter on the street. The danger is greater "not only because the suspect and officer will be in close proximity for a longer period of time, but also . . . because the officer's investigative responsibilities under the warrant require him to direct his attention to the premises rather than the person." To hold a police officer in such a situation to the same standard of "individualized suspicion" as might be required in the case of an on-the-street stop would defeat the purpose of gauging reasonableness in terms of all the circumstances surrounding an encounter.

Measured against the purpose for the initial search is the scope of that search. I do not doubt that a patdown for weapons is a substantial intrusion into one's privacy. Nevertheless, such an intrusion was more than justified, under the circumstances here, by the potential threat to the lives of the searching officers and innocent bystanders. In the rubric of *Terry* itself, a "man of reasonable caution" would have been warranted in the belief that it was appropriate to frisk the 12 or so persons in the vicinity of the bar for weapons.

I would conclude that Officer Johnson, acting under the authority of a valid search warrant, did not exceed the reasonable scope of that warrant in locating and retrieving the heroin secreted in Ybarra's pocket. This is not a case where Ybarra's Fourth Amendment rights were at the mercy of overly zealous officers "engaged in the often competitive enterprise of ferreting out crime." On the contrary, the need for a search was determined, as contemplated by the second clause of the Fourth Amendment, by a neutral and detached magistrate, and the officers performed their duties pursuant to their warrant in an appropriate fashion. The Fourth Amendment requires nothing more.

QUESTIONS AND NOTES

1.   Should the search of Ybarra have been upheld, as Justice Rehnquist suggested, on the ground that he was in the Aurora Tap and the warrant included the Aurora Tap as a place to be searched? Why? Why not?

2.   Did the Court show insufficient sensitivity to the fact that the Aurora Tap was not like "a ballroom at the Waldorf"? Or is the point of the Fourth Amendment that a person shouldn't be subject to a search because he frequents establishments that fail to meet a threshold standard of elegance?

3.   Is the danger of a weapon being found on Ybarra more like the danger of a weapon being found on *Terry*, the danger of a weapon being found on Sibron, or the danger of a weapon being found under the armrest of Long's car, or none of the above? Explain.

4.   What can the police now do to protect themselves in an *Ybarra*-type situation? Could they order all of the patrons to leave? Could they give the patrons an option to leave or be frisked? Could they order all of the patrons to stay?

B.   WHAT IS REASONABLE SUSPICION? HOW IS IT DIFFERENT FROM PROBABLE CAUSE?

In the questions following *Terry*, we saw the difficulty inherent in trying to distinguish reasonable suspicion from probable cause. While the Court's opinions have been less than perfectly clear, there are a series that have tried to define reasonable suspicion, sometimes, but not always, distinguishing it from probable cause. In this section, we examine those cases.

ADAMS v. WILLIAMS
407 U.S. 143 (1972)

Mr. Justice Rehnquist delivered the opinion of the Court.

Respondent Robert Williams was convicted in a Connecticut state court of illegal possession of a handgun found during a "stop and frisk," as well as of possession of heroin that was found during a full search incident to his weapons arrest. After respondent's conviction was affirmed by the Supreme Court of Connecticut, this Court denied certiorari. Williams' petition for federal habeas corpus relief was denied by the District Court and by a divided panel of the Second Circuit, but on rehearing *en banc* the Court of Appeals granted relief. That court held that evidence introduced at Williams' trial had been obtained by an unlawful search of his person and car, and thus the state court judgments of conviction should be set aside. Since we conclude that the policeman's actions here conformed to the standards this Court laid down in *Terry*, we reverse.

Police Sgt. John Connolly was alone early in the morning on car patrol duty in a high-crime area of Bridgeport, Connecticut. At approximately 2:15 a.m. a person known to Sgt. Connolly approached his cruiser and informed him that an individual seated in a nearby vehicle was carrying narcotics and had a gun at his waist.

After calling for assistance on his car radio, Sgt. Connolly approached the vehicle to investigate the informant's report. Connolly tapped on the car window and asked the occupant, Robert Williams to open the door. When Williams rolled down the window instead, the sergeant reached into the car and removed a fully loaded revolver from Williams' waistband. The gun had not been visible to Connolly from outside the car, but it was in precisely the place indicated by the informant. Williams was then arrested by Connolly for unlawful possession of the pistol. A search incident to that arrest was conducted after other officers arrived. They found substantial quantities of heroin on Williams' person and in the car, and they found a machete and a second revolver hidden in the automobile.

Respondent contends that the initial seizure of his pistol, upon which rested the later search and seizure of other weapons and narcotics, was not justified by the informant's tip to Sgt. Connolly. He claims that absent a more reliable informant, or some corroboration of the tip, the policeman's actions were unreasonable under the standards set forth in *Terry*.

In *Terry* this Court recognized that "a police officer may in appropriate circumstances and in an appropriate manner approach a person for purposes of investigating possibly criminal behavior even though there is no probable cause to make an arrest." The Fourth Amendment does not require a policeman who lacks the precise level of information necessary for probable cause to arrest to simply shrug his shoulders and allow a crime to occur or a criminal to escape. On the contrary, *Terry* recognizes that it may be the essence of good police work to adopt an intermediate response. A brief stop of a suspicious individual, in order to determine his identity or to maintain the status quo momentarily while obtaining more information, may be most reasonable in light of the facts known to the officer at the time.

The Court recognized in *Terry* that the policeman making a reasonable investigatory stop should not be denied the opportunity to protect himself from attack by a hostile suspect. "When an officer is justified in believing that the individual whose suspicious behavior he is investigating at close range is armed and presently dangerous to the officer or to others," he may conduct a limited protective search for concealed weapons. The purpose of this limited search is not to discover evidence of crime, but to allow the officer to pursue his investigation without fear of violence, and thus the frisk for weapons might be equally necessary and reasonable, whether or not carrying a concealed weapon violated any applicable state law. So long as the officer is entitled to make a forcible stop, and has reason to believe that the suspect is armed and dangerous, he may conduct a weapons search limited in scope to this protective purpose.

Applying these principles to the present case, we believe that Sgt. Connolly acted justifiably in responding to his informant's tip. The informant was known to him personally and had provided him with information in the past. This is a stronger case than obtains in the case of an anonymous telephone tip. The informant here came forward personally to give information that was immediately verifiable at the scene. Indeed, under Connecticut law, the informant might have been subject to immediate arrest for making a false complaint had Sgt. Connolly's investigation proved the tip incorrect.[2] Thus, while the Court's decisions indicate that this informant's unverified tip may have been insufficient for a narcotics arrest or search warrant, see, *e.g., Spinelli*, the information carried enough indicia of reliability to justify the officer's forcible stop of Williams.

In reaching this conclusion, we reject respondent's argument that reasonable cause for a stop and frisk can only be based on the officer's personal observation, rather than on information supplied by another person. Informants' tips, like all other clues and evidence coming to a policeman on the scene, may vary greatly in their value and reliability. One simple rule will not cover every situation. Some tips, completely lacking in indicia of reliability, would either warrant no police response or require further investigation before a forcible stop of a suspect would be authorized. But in some situations — for example, when the victim of a street crime seeks immediate police aid and gives a description of his assailant, or when a credible informant warns of a specific impending crime — the subtleties of the hearsay rule should not thwart an appropriate police response.

While properly investigating the activity of a person who was reported to be carrying narcotics and a concealed weapon and who was sitting alone in a car in a high-crime area at 2:15 in the morning, Sgt. Connolly had ample reason to fear for his safety. When Williams rolled down his window, rather than complying with the policeman's request to step out of the car so that his movements could more easily be seen, the revolver allegedly at Williams' waist became an even greater threat.

---

[2] Section 53-168 of the Connecticut General Statutes, in force at the time of these events, provided that a "person who knowingly makes to any police officer . . . a false report or a false complaint alleging that a crime or crimes have been committed" is guilty of a misdemeanor.

Under these circumstances the policeman's action in reaching to the spot where the gun was thought to be hidden constituted a limited intrusion designed to insure his safety, and we conclude that it was reasonable. The loaded gun seized as a result of this intrusion was therefore admissible at Williams' trial.

Under the circumstances surrounding Williams' possession of the gun seized by Sgt. Connolly, the arrest on the weapons charge was supported by probable cause, and the search of his person and of the car incident to that arrest was lawful. The fruits of the search were therefore properly admitted at Williams' trial, and the Court of Appeals erred in reaching a contrary conclusion.

Reversed.

JUSTICE BRENNAN, dissenting.

The crucial question on which this case turns, as the Court concedes, is whether, there being no contention that Williams acted voluntarily in rolling down the window of his car, the State had shown sufficient cause to justify Sgt. Connolly's "forcible" stop. I would affirm, believing, for the following reasons stated by Judge, now Chief Judge, Friendly, dissenting, 436 F.2d 30, 38–39, that the State did not make that showing:

> To begin, I have the gravest hesitancy in extending (*Terry*) to crimes like the possession of narcotics . . . . There is too much danger that, instead of the stop being the object and the protective frisk an incident thereto, the reverse will be true. Against that we have here the added fact of the report that Williams had a gun on his person . . . . [But] Connecticut allows its citizens to carry weapons, concealed or otherwise, at will, provided only they have a permit, CONN. GEN. STAT. §§ 29-35 and 29-38, and gives its police officers no special authority to stop for the purpose of determining whether the citizen has one.
>
> . . .
>
> If I am wrong in thinking that *Terry* should not be applied at all to mere possessory offenses, . . . I would not find the combination of Officer Connolly's almost meaningless observation and the tip in this case to sufficient justification for the intrusion. The tip suffered from a threefold defect, with each fold compounding the others. The informer was unnamed, he was not shown to have been reliable with respect to guns or narcotics, and he gave no information which demonstrated personal knowledge or — what is worse — could not readily have been manufactured by the officer after the event. To my mind, it has not been sufficiently recognized that the difference between this sort of tip and the accurate prediction of an unusual event is as important on the latter score as on the former. (In *Draper*) Narcotics Agent Marsh would hardly have been at the Denver Station at the exact moment of the arrival of the train Draper had taken from Chicago unless *someone* had told him *something* important, although the agent might later have embroidered the details to fit the observed facts . . . . There is no such guarantee of a patrolling officer's veracity when he testifies to a "tip" from an unnamed informer saying no more than that the

officer will find a gun and narcotics on a man across the street, as he later does. If the state wishes to rely on a tip of that nature to validate a stop and frisk, revelation of the name of the informer or demonstration that his name is unknown and could not reasonably have been ascertained should be the price.

Terry was intended to free a police officer from the rigidity of a rule that would prevent his doing anything to a man reasonably suspected of being about to commit or having just committed a crime of violence, no matter how grave the problem or impelling the need for swift action, unless the officer had what a court would later determine to be probable cause for arrest. It was meant for the serious cases of imminent danger or of harm recently perpetrated to persons or property, not the conventional ones of possessory offenses. If it is to be extended to the latter at all, this should be only where observation by the officer himself or well authenticated information shows "that criminal activity may be afoot." I greatly fear that if the (contrary view) should be followed, *Terry* will have opened the sluicegates for serious and unintended erosion of the protection of the Fourth Amendment.

MR. JUSTICE MARSHALL, with whom MR. JUSTICE DOUGLAS joins, dissenting.

Four years have passed since we decided *Terry* and *Sibron*. They were the first cases in which this Court explicitly recognized the concept of "stop and frisk" and squarely held that police officers may, under appropriate circumstances, stop and frisk persons suspected of criminal activity even though there is less than probable cause for an arrest. This case marks our first opportunity to give some flesh to the bones of *Terry et al*. Unfortunately, the flesh provided by today's decision cannot possibly be made to fit on *Terry's* skeletal framework.

In today's decision the Court ignores the fact that *Terry* begrudgingly accepted the necessity for creating an exception from the warrant requirement of the Fourth Amendment and treats this case as if warrantless searches were the rule rather than the "narrowly drawn" exception. This decision betrays the careful balance that *Terry* sought to strike between a citizen's right to privacy and his government's responsibility for effective law enforcement and expands the concept of warrantless searches far beyond anything heretofore recognized as legitimate. I dissent.

The Court erroneously attempts to describe the search for the gun as a protective search incident to a reasonable investigatory stop. But, as in *Terry* [and] *Sibron*, there is no occasion in this case to determine whether or not police officers have a right to seize and to restrain a citizen in order to interrogate him. The facts are clear that the officer intended to make the search as soon as he approached the respondent. He asked no questions; he made no investigation; he simply searched. There was nothing apart from the information supplied by the informant to cause the officer to search. Our inquiry must focus, therefore, as it did in *Terry* on whether the officer had sufficient facts from which he could reasonably infer that respondent was not only engaging in illegal activity, but also that he was armed and dangerous. The focus falls on the informant.

The only information that the informant had previously given the officer involved homosexual conduct in the local railroad station. The following colloquy took place between respondent's counsel and the officer at the hearing on respondent's motion to suppress the evidence that had been seized from him.

"Q.   Now, with respect to the information that was given you about homosexuals in the Bridgeport Police Station (*sic*), did that lead to an arrest?

A.   No.

Q.   An arrest was not made.

A.   No. There was no substantiating evidence.

Q.   There was no substantiating evidence?

A.   No.

Q.   And what do you mean by that?

A.   I didn't have occasion to witness these individuals committing any crime of any nature.

Q.   In other words, after this person gave you the information, you checked for corroboration before you made an arrest. Is that right?

A.   Well, I checked to determine the possibility of homosexual activity.

Q.   And since an arrest was made, I take it you didn't find any substantiating information.

A.   I'm sorry counselor, you say since an arrest was made.

Q.   Was not made. Since an arrest was not made, I presume you didn't find any substantiating information.

A.   No.

Q.   So that, you don't recall any other specific information given you about the commission of crimes by this informant.

A.   No.

Q.   And you still thought this person was reliable.

A.   Yes.

Assuming, *arguendo*, that this case truly involves, not an arrest and a search incident thereto, but a stop and frisk,[2] we must decide whether or not the information possessed by the officer justified this interference with respondent's liberty. *Terry*, our only case to actually uphold a stop and frisk, is not directly in point, because the police officer in that case acted on the basis of his own personal observations. No informant was involved. But the rational of *Terry* is still controlling, and it requires that we condemn the conduct of the police officer in encountering the respondent.

---

[2] *Terry* makes it clear that a stop and frisk is a search and seizure within the meaning of the Fourth Amendment. When I use the term stop and frisk herein, I merely intend to emphasize that it is, as *Terry* held, a lesser intrusion than a full-scale search and seizure.

Terry did not hold that whenever a policeman has a hunch that a citizen is engaging in criminal activity, he may engage in a stop and frisk. It held that if police officers want to stop and frisk, they must have specific facts from which they can reasonably infer that an individual is engaged in criminal activity and is armed and dangerous. It was central to our decision in *Terry* that the police officer acted on the basis of his own personal observations and that he carefully scrutinized the conduct of his suspects before interfering with them in any way. When we legitimated the conduct of the officer in *Terry* we did so because of the substantial *reliability* of the information on which the officer based his decision to act.

If the Court does not ignore the care with which we examined the knowledge possessed by the officer in *Terry* when he acted, then I cannot see how the actions of the officer in this case can be upheld. The Court explains what the officer knew about respondent before accosting him. But what is more significant is what he did not know. With respect to the scene generally, the officer had no idea how long respondent had been in the car, how long the car had been parked, or to whom the car belonged. With respect to the gun,[5] the officer did not know if or when the informant had ever seen the gun, or whether the gun was carried legally, as Connecticut law permitted, or illegally. And with respect to the narcotics, the officer did not know what kind of narcotics respondent allegedly had, whether they were legally or illegally possessed, what the basis of the informant's knowledge was, or even whether the informant was capable of distinguishing narcotics from other substances.

Unable to answer any of these questions, the officer nevertheless determined that it was necessary to intrude on respondent's liberty. I believe that his determination was totally unreasonable. As I read *Terry*, an officer may act on the basis of *reliable* information short of probable cause to make a stop, and ultimately a frisk, if necessary; but the officer may not use unreliable, unsubstantiated, conclusory hearsay to justify an invasion of liberty. *Terry* never meant to approve the kind of knee-jerk police reaction that we have before us in this case.

Even assuming that the officer had some legitimate reason for relying on the informant, *Terry* requires, before any stop and frisk is made, that the reliable information in the officer's possession demonstrate that the suspect is both armed and *dangerous*. The fact remains that Connecticut specifically authorizes persons to carry guns so long as they have a permit. Thus, there was no reason for the officer to infer from anything that the informant said that the respondent was dangerous. His frisk was, therefore, illegal under *Terry*.

Mr. Justice Douglas was the sole dissenter in *Terry*. He warned of the "powerful hydraulic pressures throughout our history that bear heavily on the Court to water down constitutional guarantees . . . ." While I took the position then that we were not watering down rights, but were hesitantly and cautiously striking a necessary balance between the rights of American citizens to be free from government intrusion into their privacy and their government's urgent need for a narrow

---

[5] The fact that the respondent carried his gun in a high-crime area is irrelevant. In such areas it is more probable than not that citizens would be more likely to carry weapons authorized by the State to protect themselves.

exception to the warrant requirement of the Fourth Amendment, today's decision demonstrates just how prescient Mr. Justice Douglas was.

It seems that the delicate balance that *Terry* struck was simply too delicate, too susceptible to the "hydraulic pressures" of the day. As a result of today's decision, the balance struck in *Terry* is now heavily weighted in favor of the government. And the Fourth Amendment, which was included in the Bill of Rights to prevent the kind of arbitrary and oppressive police action involved herein, is dealt a serious blow. Today's decision invokes the specter of a society in which innocent citizens may be stopped, searched, and arrested at the whim of police officers who have only the slightest suspicion of improper conduct.

QUESTIONS AND NOTES

1. If you had been Officer Connolly, would you have been suspicious of Williams? If so, would you have considered your suspicions reasonable? Why? Why not?

2. Do we want police officers to do what Connolly did in this case?

3. Is the Brennan/Friendly opinion insensitive to the need to combat drugs?

4. How important is it that the informant was known? Suppose that Connolly had been told by an anonymous phone call earlier in the day that at 2 a.m. someone meeting Williams description would be sitting in a car like the one in which Williams sat, and that he would have a gun in his waistband and narcotics in his glove compartment?

5. How, if at all, does *Adams* expand *Terry*? Wasn't it *more* likely that Williams was armed than that *Terry*, Chilton, and Katz were armed?

6. Should it have mattered that it is not necessarily unlawful to carry a concealed weapon in Connecticut? Even after finding the weapon, were the police justified in arresting Williams and searching his car incident thereto?

7. In *Cortez*, we see significantly more police affirmation prior to the stop.

UNITED STATES v. CORTEZ
449 U.S. 411 (1981)

CHIEF JUSTICE BURGER delivered the opinion of the Court.

We granted certiorari to consider whether objective facts and circumstantial evidence suggesting that a particular vehicle is involved in criminal activity may provide a sufficient basis to justify an investigative stop of that vehicle.

I

Late in 1976, Border Patrol officers patrolling a sparsely populated section of southern central Arizona found human footprints in the desert. In time, other sets of similar footprints were discovered in the same area. From these sets of footprints, it was deduced that, on a number of occasions, groups of from 8 to 20 persons had walked north from the Mexican border, across 30 miles of desert and mountains, over a fairly well-defined path, to an isolated point on Highway 86, an east-west road running roughly parallel to the Mexican border.

Officers observed that one recurring shoeprint bore a distinctive and repetitive V-shaped or chevron design. Because the officers knew from recorded experience that the area through which the groups passed was heavily trafficked by aliens illegally entering the country from Mexico, they surmised that a person, to whom they gave the case-name "Chevron," was guiding aliens illegally into the United States over the path marked by the tracks to a point where they could be picked up by a vehicle.

The tracks led into or over obstacles that would have been avoided in daylight. From this, the officers deduced that "Chevron" probably led his groups across the border and to the pickup point at night. Moreover, based upon the times when they had discovered the distinctive sets of tracks, they concluded that "Chevron" generally traveled during or near weekends and on nights when the weather was clear.

Their tracking disclosed that when "Chevron's" groups came within 50 to 75 yards of Highway 86, they turned right and walked eastward, parallel to the road. Then, approximately at highway milepost 122, the tracks would turn north and disappear at the road. From this pattern, the officers concluded that the aliens very likely were picked up by a vehicle — probably one approaching from the east, for after a long overland march the group was most likely to walk parallel to the highway *toward* the approaching vehicle. The officers also concluded that, after the pickup, the vehicle probably returned to the east, because it was unlikely that the group would be walking away from its ultimate destination.

On the Sunday night of January 30–31, 1977, Officers Gray and Evans, two Border Patrolmen who had been pursuing the investigation of "Chevron," were on duty in the Casa Grande area. The latest set of observed "Chevron" tracks had been made on Saturday night, January 15–16. January 30–31 was the first clear night after three days of rain. For these reasons, Gray and Evans decided there was a strong possibility that "Chevron" would lead aliens from the border to the highway that night.

The officers assumed that, if "Chevron" did conduct a group that night, he would not leave Mexico until after dark, that is, about 6 p. m. They knew from their experience that groups of this sort, traveling on foot, cover about two and a half to three miles an hour. Thus, the 30-mile journey would take from 8 to 12 hours. From this, the officers calculated that "Chevron" and his group would arrive at Highway 86 somewhere between 2 a. m. and 6 a. m. on January 31.

About 1 a. m., Gray and Evans parked their patrol car on an elevated location about 100 feet off Highway 86 at milepost 149, a point some 27 miles east of milepost 122. From their vantage point, the officers could observe the Altar Valley, an adjoining territory they had been assigned to watch that night, and they also could see vehicles passing on Highway 86. They estimated that it would take approximately one hour and a half for a vehicle to make a round trip from their vantage point to milepost 122. Working on the hypothesis that the pickup vehicle approached milepost 122 from the east and thereafter returned to its starting point, they focused upon vehicles that passed them from the east and, after about one hour and a half, passed them returning to the east.

Because "Chevron" appeared to lead groups of between 8 and 20 aliens at a time, the officers deduced that the pickup vehicle would be one that was capable of carrying that large a group without arousing suspicion. For this reason, and because they knew that certain types of vehicles were commonly used for smuggling sizable groups of aliens, they decided to limit their attention to vans, pickup trucks, other small trucks, campers, motor homes, and similar vehicles.

Traffic on Highway 86 at milepost 149 was normal on the night of the officers' surveillance. In the 5-hour period between 1 a. m. and 6 a. m., 15 to 20 vehicles passed the officers heading west, toward milepost 122. Only two of them — both pickup trucks with camper shells — were of the kind that the officers had concluded "Chevron" would likely use if he was to carry aliens that night. One, a distinctively colored pickup truck with a camper shell, passed for the first time at 4:30 a. m. Officer Gray was able to see and record only a partial license number, "GN 88 —."[1] At 6:12 a. m., almost exactly the estimated one hour and a half later, a vehicle looking like this same pickup passed them again, this time heading east.

The officers followed the pickup and were satisfied from its license plate, "GN 8804" that it was the same vehicle that had passed at 4:30 a. m. At that point, they flashed their police lights and intercepted the vehicle. Respondent Jesus Cortez was the driver and owner of the pickup; respondent Pedro Hernandez-Loera was sitting in the passenger's seat. Hernandez-Loera was wearing shoes with soles matching the distinctive "chevron" shoeprint.

The officers identified themselves and told Cortez they were conducting an immigration check. They asked if he was carrying any passengers in the camper. Cortez told them he had picked up some hitchhikers, and he proceeded to open the back of the camper. In the camper, there were six illegal aliens. The officers then arrested the respondents.

Cortez and Hernandez-Loera were charged with six counts of transporting illegal aliens. By pretrial motion, they sought to suppress the evidence obtained by Officers Gray and Evans as a result of stopping their vehicle. They argued that the officers did not have adequate cause to make the investigative stop. The District Court denied the motion. A jury found the respondents guilty as charged. They were sentenced to concurrent prison terms of five years on each of six counts. In addition, Hernandez-Loera was fined $12,000.

A divided panel of the Court of Appeals for the Ninth Circuit reversed, holding that the officers lacked a sufficient basis to justify the stop of the pickup. That court recognized that *United States v. Brignoni-Ponce*, 422 U.S. 873 (1975), provides a standard governing investigative stops of the kind involved in this case, stating: "The quantum of cause necessary in . . . cases [like this one] was established . . . in *Brignoni-Ponce* . . . "[O]fficers on roving patrol may stop vehicles only if they

---

[1] The second camper passed them 15 or 20 minutes later. As far as the record shows, it did not return.

are aware of specific articulable facts, together with rational inferences from those facts, that reasonably warrant suspicion that the vehicles contain aliens who may be illegally in the country." "The court also recognized that "the ultimate question on appeal is whether the trial judge's finding that founded suspicion was present here was clearly erroneous." Here, because, in the view of the facts of the two judges constituting the majority, "[t]he officers did not have a valid basis for singling out the Cortez vehicle," and because the circumstances admitted "far too many innocent inferences to make the officers' suspicions reasonably warranted," the panel concluded that the stop of Cortez' vehicle was a violation of the respondents' rights under the Fourth Amendment. In dissent, Judge Chambers was persuaded that *Brignoni-Ponce* recognized the validity of permitting an officer to assess the facts in light of his past experience.

II

A

The Fourth Amendment applies to seizures of the person, including brief investigatory stops such as the stop of the vehicle here. An investigatory stop must be justified by some objective manifestation that the person stopped is, or is about to be, engaged in criminal activity.[2]

Courts have used a variety of terms to capture the elusive concept of what cause is sufficient to authorize police to stop a person. Terms like "articulable reasons" and "founded suspicion" are not self-defining; they fall short of providing clear guidance dispositive of the myriad factual situations that arise. But the essence of all that has been written is that the totality of the circumstances — the whole picture — must be taken into account. Based upon that whole picture the detaining officers must have a particularized and objective basis for suspecting the particular person stopped of criminal activity.

The idea that an assessment of the whole picture must yield a particularized suspicion contains two elements, each of which must be present before a stop is permissible. First, the assessment must be based upon all the circumstances. The analysis proceeds with various objective observations, information from police reports, if such are available, and consideration of the modes or patterns of operation of certain kinds of lawbreakers. From these data, a trained officer draws inferences and makes deductions — inferences and deductions that might well elude an untrained person.

The process does not deal with hard certainties, but with probabilities. Long before the law of probabilities was articulated as such, practical people formulated certain common sense conclusions about human behavior; jurors as factfinders are permitted to do the same — and so are law enforcement officers. Finally, the evidence thus collected must be seen and weighed not in terms of library analysis by scholars, but as understood by those versed in the field of law enforcement.

---

[2] Of course, an officer may stop and question a person if there are reasonable grounds to believe that person is wanted for past criminal conduct.

The second element contained in the idea that an assessment of the whole picture must yield a particularized suspicion is the concept that the process just described must raise a suspicion that the particular individual being stopped is engaged in wrongdoing. Chief Justice Warren, speaking for the Court in *Terry*, said that, "[t]his demand for specificity in the information upon which police action is predicated is *the central teaching of this Court's Fourth Amendment jurisprudence*." (emphasis added).

B

This case portrays at once both the enormous difficulties of patrolling a 2,000-mile open border and the patient skills needed by those charged with halting illegal entry into this country. It implicates all of the principles just discussed — especially the imperative of recognizing that, when used by trained law enforcement officers, objective facts, meaningless to the untrained, can be combined with permissible deductions from such facts to form a legitimate basis for suspicion of a particular person and for action on that suspicion. We see here the kind of police work often suggested by judges and scholars as examples of appropriate and reasonable means of law enforcement. Here, fact on fact and clue on clue afforded a basis for the deductions and inferences that brought the officers to focus on "Chevron."

Of critical importance, the officers knew that the area was a crossing point for illegal aliens. They knew that it was common practice for persons to lead aliens through the desert from the border to Highway 86, where they could — by prearrangement — be picked up by a vehicle. Moreover, based upon clues they had discovered in the 2-month period prior to the events at issue here, they believed that one such guide, whom they designated "Chevron," had a particular pattern of operations.

By piecing together the information at their disposal, the officers tentatively concluded that there was a reasonable likelihood that "Chevron" would attempt to lead a group of aliens on the night of Sunday, January 30–31. Someone with chevron-soled shoes had led several groups of aliens in the previous two months, yet it had been two weeks since the latest crossing. "Chevron," they deduced, was therefore due reasonably soon. "Chevron" tended to travel on clear weekend nights. Because it had rained on the Friday and Saturday nights of the weekend involved here, Sunday was the only clear night of that weekend; the officers surmised it was therefore a likely night for a trip.

Once they had focused on that night, the officers drew upon other objective facts known to them to deduce a time frame within which "Chevron" and the aliens were likely to arrive. From what they knew of the practice of those who smuggle aliens, including what they knew of "Chevron's" previous activities, they deduced that the border crossing and journey through the desert would probably be at night. They knew the time when sunset would occur at the point of the border crossing; they knew about how long the trip would take. They were thus able to deduce that "Chevron" would likely arrive at the pickup point on Highway 86 in the time frame between 2 a. m. and 6 a. m.

From objective facts, the officers also deduced the probable point on the highway — milepost 122 — at which "Chevron" would likely rendezvous with a pickup vehicle. They deduced from the direction taken by the sets of "Chevron" footprints they had earlier discovered that the pickup vehicle would approach the aliens from, and return with them to, a point east of milepost 122. They therefore staked out a position east of milepost 122 (at milepost 149) and watched for vehicles that passed them going west and then, approximately one and a half hours later, passed them again, this time going east.

From what they had observed about the previous groups guided by the person with "chevron" shoes, they deduced that "Chevron" would lead a group of 8 to 20 aliens. They therefore focused their attention on enclosed vehicles of that passenger capacity.

The analysis produced by Officers Gray and Evans can be summarized as follows: if, on the night upon which they believed "Chevron" was likely to travel, sometime between 2 a. m. and 6 a. m., a large enclosed vehicle was seen to make an east-west-east round trip to and from a deserted point (milepost 122) on a deserted road (Highway 86), the officers would stop the vehicle on the return trip. In a 4-hour period the officers observed only one vehicle meeting that description. And it is not surprising that when they stopped the vehicle on its return trip it contained "Chevron" and several illegal aliens.

C

The limited purpose of the stop in this case was to question the occupants of the vehicle about their citizenship and immigration status and the reasons for the round trip in a short timespan in a virtually deserted area. No search of the camper or any of its occupants occurred until after respondent Cortez voluntarily opened the back door of the camper; thus, only the stop, not the search is at issue here. The intrusion upon privacy associated with this stop was limited and was "reasonably related in scope to the justification for [its] initiation."

We have recently held that stops by the Border Patrol may be justified under circumstances less than those constituting probable cause for arrest or search. *Brignoni-Ponce.* Thus, the test is not whether Officers Gray and Evans had probable cause to conclude that the vehicle they stopped would contain "Chevron" and a group of illegal aliens. Rather the question is whether, based upon the whole picture, they, as experienced Border Patrol officers, could reasonably surmise that the particular vehicle they stopped was engaged in criminal activity. On this record, they could so conclude.

Reversed.

JUSTICE STEWART, concurring in judgment

The Border Patrol officers in this case knew, or had rationally deduced, that "Chevron" had repeatedly shepherded illegal aliens up from the border; that his treks had commonly ended early in the morning around milepost 122 on Highway 86; that he usually worked on weekends; that he probably had made no trips for two weeks; and that trips were most likely when the weather was good. Knowing of this pattern, the officers could reasonably anticipate, even if they could not guarantee, the arrival of another group of aliens, led by Chevron, at milepost 122 on the first clear weekend night in late January 1977. Route 86 leads through almost uninhabited country, so little traveled in the hours of darkness that only 15 to 20 westbound vehicles passed the police during the five hours they watched that Sunday night. Only two vehicles capacious enough to carry a sizable group of illegal aliens went by. One of those two vehicles not only drove past them, but returned in the opposite direction after just enough time had elapsed for a journey to milepost 122 and back. This nocturnal round trip into "desolate desert terrain" would in any event have been puzzling. Coming when and as it did, surely the most likely explanation for it was that Chevron was again shepherding aliens.

In sum, the Border Patrol officers had discovered an abundance of "specific articulable facts" which, "together with rational inferences from [them]," entirely warranted a "suspicion that the vehicl[e] contain[ed] aliens who [might] be illegally in the country." Because the information possessed by the officers thus met the requirements established by the Brignoni-Ponce case for the kind of stop made here, I concur in the reversal of the judgment of the Court of Appeals

JUSTICE MARSHALL also concurred in result, only.

QUESTIONS AND NOTES

1.   If it were necessary, could the Court have found probable cause? Is *Cortez* a stronger or weaker case for probable cause than *Gates*?

2.   Is there any reason that the Court might *not* have wanted to find probable cause here?

3.   Does Justice Stewart's concurrence say something different from the majority? Why do you suppose that he only concurred in result?

4.   Do think that Cortez was (felt) compelled to open the camper? Should your answer effect the resolution of this case? Explain.

5.   Is footnote 2 as obvious as the Court makes it appear? Does (should) it accurately state the law?

6.   Distinctions between probable cause and reasonable suspicion were never more important than they were in *Royer*.

FLORIDA v. ROYER
460 U.S. 491 (1983)

JUSTICE WHITE announced the judgment of the Court and delivered an opinion in which JUSTICES MARSHALL, POWELL and STEVENS joined.

We are required in this case to determine whether the Court of Appeal of Florida, Third District, properly applied the precepts of the Fourth Amendment in holding that respondent Royer was being illegally detained at the time of his purported consent to a search of his luggage.

I

On January 3, 1978, Royer was observed at Miami International Airport by two plain-clothes detectives of the Dade County, Florida, Public Safety Department assigned to the County's Organized Crime Bureau, Narcotics Investigation Section. Detectives Johnson and Magdalena believed that Royer's appearance, mannerisms, luggage, and actions fit the so-called "drug courier profile."[2] Royer, apparently unaware of the attention he had attracted, purchased a one-way ticket to New York City and checked his two suitcases, placing on each suitcase an identification tag bearing the name "Holt" and the destination, "LaGuardia". As Royer made his way to the concourse which led to the airline boarding area, the two detectives approached him, identified themselves as policemen working out of the sheriff's office, and asked if Royer had a "moment" to speak with them; Royer said "Yes."

Upon request, but without oral consent, Royer produced for the detectives his airline ticket and his driver's license. The airline ticket, like the baggage identification tags, bore the name "Holt," while the driver's license carried respondent's correct name, "Royer." When the detectives asked about the discrepancy, Royer explained that a friend had made the reservation in the name of "Holt." Royer became noticeably more nervous during this conversation, whereupon the detectives informed Royer that they were in fact narcotics investigators and that they had reason to suspect him of transporting narcotics.

The detectives did not return his airline ticket and identification but asked Royer to accompany them to a room, approximately forty feet away, adjacent to the concourse. Royer said nothing in response but went with the officers as he had been asked to do. The room was later described by Detective Johnson as a "large storage closet," located in the stewardesses' lounge and containing a small desk and two chairs. Without Royer's consent or agreement, Detective Johnson, using Royer's baggage check stubs, retrieved the "Holt" luggage from the airline and brought it to the room where respondent and Detective Magdalena were waiting. Royer was asked if he would consent to a search of the suitcases. Without orally responding to this request, Royer produced a key and unlocked one of the suitcases, which the detective then opened without seeking further assent from Royer. Drugs were found in that suitcase. According to Detective Johnson, Royer stated that he did not know the combination to the lock on the second suitcase. When asked if he objected to the detective opening the second suitcase, Royer said "no, go ahead," and did not object when the detective explained that the suitcase might have to be broken open.

---

[2] The "drug courier profile" is an abstract of characteristics found to be typical of persons transporting illegal drugs. In Royer's case, the detectives' attention was attracted by the following facts which were considered to be within the profile: a) Royer was carrying American Tourister luggage, which appeared to be heavy, b) he was young, apparently between 25–35, c) he was casually dressed, d) Royer appeared pale and nervous, looking around at other people, e) Royer paid for his ticket in cash with a large number of bills, and f) rather than completing the airline identification tag to be attached to checked baggage, which had space for a name, address, and telephone number, Royer wrote only a name and the destination.

The suitcase was pried open by the officers and more marihuana was found. Royer was then told that he was under arrest. Approximately fifteen minutes had elapsed from the time the detectives initially approached respondent until his arrest upon the discovery of the contraband.

Prior to his trial for felony possession of marihuana, Royer made a motion to suppress the evidence obtained in the search of the suitcases. The trial court found that Royer's consent to the search was "freely and voluntarily given," and that, regardless of the consent, the warrantless search was reasonable because "the officer doesn't have the time to run out and get a search warrant because the plane is going to take off." Following the denial of the motion to suppress, Royer changed his plea from "not guilty" to "nolo contendere," specifically reserving the right to appeal the denial of the motion to suppress. Royer was convicted.

The District Court of Appeal reversed Royer's conviction. The court held that Royer had been involuntarily confined in a small room without probable cause; that the involuntary detention had exceeded the limited restraint permitted by *Terry*, at the time his consent to the search was obtained; and that the consent to search was therefor invalid because tainted by the unlawful confinement.[7]

Several factors led the court to conclude that respondent's confinement was tantamount to arrest. Royer had "found himself in a small enclosed area being confronted by two police officers — a situation which presents an almost classic definition of imprisonment." The detectives' statement to Royer that he was suspected of transporting narcotics also bolstered the finding that Royer was "in custody" at the time the consent to search was given. In addition, the detectives' possession of Royer's airline ticket and their retrieval and possession of his luggage made it clear, in the District Court of Appeal's view, that Royer was not free to leave.

At the suppression hearing Royer testified that he was under the impression that he was not free to leave the officers' presence. The Florida Court of Appeal found that this apprehension "was much more than a well-justified subjective belief," for the State had conceded at oral argument before that court that "the officers would not have permitted Royer to leave the room even if [Royer] had erroneously thought he could." The nomenclature used to describe Royer's confinement, the court found, was unimportant because under *Dunaway v. New York*, 442 U.S. 200 (1979), "[a] police confinement which . . . goes beyond the limited restraint of a *Terry* investigatory stop may be constitutionally justified only by probable cause." Detective Johnson, who conducted the search, had specifically stated at the suppression hearing that he did not have probable cause to arrest Royer until the suitcases were opened and their contents revealed.

---

[7] The Florida court was also of the opinion that "a mere similarity with the contents of the drug courier profile is insufficient even to constitute the articulable suspicion required to justify" the stop authorized by *Terry*. It went on to hold that even if it followed a contrary rule, or even if articulable suspicion occurred at some point prior to Royer's consent to search, the facts did not amount to probable cause that would justify the restraint imposed on Royer. As will become clear, we disagree on the reasonable-suspicion issue but do concur that probable cause to arrest was lacking.

II

Some preliminary observations are in order. First, it is unquestioned that without a warrant to search Royer's and in the absence of probable cause and exigent circumstances, the validity of the search depended on Royer's purported consent. Neither is it disputed that where the validity of a search rests on consent, the State has the burden of proving that the necessary consent was obtained and that it was freely and voluntarily given, a burden that is not satisfied by showing a mere submission to a claim of lawful authority.

[I]t is also clear that not all seizures of the person must be justified by probable cause to arrest for a crime. Prior to *Terry*, any restraint on the person amounting to a seizure for the purposes of the Fourth Amendment was invalid unless justified by probable cause. *Terry* created a limited exception to this general rule: certain seizures are justifiable under the Fourth Amendment if there is articulable suspicion that a person has committed or is about to commit a crime. In that case, a stop and a frisk for weapons were found unexceptionable. *Adams* applied the same approach in the context of an informant's report that an unnamed individual in a nearby vehicle was carrying narcotics and a gun. Although not expressly authorized in *Terry*, *Brignoni-Ponce* was unequivocal in saying that reasonable suspicion of criminal activity warrants a temporary seizure for the purpose of questioning limited to the purpose of the stop. Royer does not suggest, nor do we, that a similar rationale would not warrant temporary detention for questioning on less than probable cause where the public interest involved is the suppression of illegal transactions in drugs or of any other serious crime.

III

[T]he State submits that if Royer was seized, there existed reasonable, articulable suspicion to justify a temporary detention and that the limits of a *Terry*-type stop were never exceeded. We agree with the State that when the officers discovered that Royer was travelling under an assumed name, this fact, and the facts already known to the officers — paying cash for a one-way ticket, the mode of checking the two bags, and Royer's appearance and conduct in general — were adequate grounds for suspecting Royer of carrying drugs and for temporarily detaining him and his luggage while they attempted to verify or dispel their suspicions in a manner that did not exceed the limits of an investigative detention. We also agree that had Royer voluntarily consented to the search of his luggage while he was justifiably being detained on reasonable suspicion, the products of the search would be admissible against him. We have concluded, however, that at the time Royer produced the key to his suitcase, the detention to which he was then subjected was a more serious intrusion on his personal liberty than is allowable on mere suspicion of criminal activity.

IV

The State's final argument is that Royer was not being illegally held when he gave his consent because there was probable cause to arrest him at that time. Officer Johnson testified at the suppression hearing and the Florida Court of

Appeal held that there was no probable cause to arrest until Royer's bags were opened, but the fact that the officers did not believe there was probable cause and proceeded on a consensual or *Terry*-stop rationale would not foreclose the State from justifying Royer's custody by proving probable cause and hence removing any barrier to relying on Royer's consent to search. We agree with the Florida Court of Appeal, however, that probable cause to arrest Royer did not exist at the time he consented to the search of his luggage. The facts are that a nervous young man with two American Tourister bags paid cash for an airline ticket to a "target city". These facts led to inquiry, which in turn revealed that the ticket had been bought under an assumed name. The proffered explanation did not satisfy the officers. We cannot agree with the State, if this is its position, that every nervous young man paying cash for a ticket to New York City under an assumed name and carrying two heavy American Tourister bags may be arrested and held to answer for a serious felony charge.

V

Because we affirm the Florida Court of Appeal's conclusion that Royer was being illegally detained when he consented to the search of his luggage, we agree that the consent was tainted by the illegality and was ineffective to justify the search. The judgment of the Florida Court of Appeal is accordingly

Affirmed.

BRENNAN, J. Concurring in result

I dissent from the plurality's view that the initial stop of Royer was legal. Before *Terry*, only "seizures" of persons based on probable cause were held to satisfy the Fourth Amendment. As we stated in *Brignoni-Ponce*, however, *Terry* and *Adams* "establish that in appropriate circumstances the Fourth Amendment allows a properly limited 'search' or 'seizure' on facts that do not constitute probable cause to arrest or to search for contraband or evidence of crime." But to justify such a seizure an officer must have a reasonable suspicion of criminal activity based on "specific and articulable facts . . . [and] rational inferences from those facts . . . ." In this case, the officers decided to approach Royer because he was carrying American Tourister luggage, which appeared to be heavy; he was young; he was casually dressed; he appeared to be pale and nervous and was looking around at other people; he paid for his airline ticket in cash with a large number of bills; and he did not completely fill out the identification tags for his luggage, which was checked to New York. These facts clearly are not sufficient to provide the reasonable suspicion of criminal activity necessary to justify the officers' subsequent seizure of Royer. Indeed, considered individually or collectively, they are perfectly consistent with innocent behavior and cannot possibly give rise to any inference supporting a reasonable suspicion of criminal activity. The officers' seizure of Royer, therefore, was illegal.

Although I recognize that the traffic in illicit drugs is a matter of pressing national concern, that cannot excuse this Court from exercising its unflagging duty to strike down official activity that exceeds the confines of the Constitution. In discussing the Fourth Amendment in *Coolidge*, Justice Stewart stated: "In times of unrest, whether caused by crime or racial conflict or fear of internal subversion, this basic law and the values that it represents may appear unrealistic or 'extravagant' to some. But the values were those of the authors of our fundamental constitutional concepts." We must not allow our zeal for effective law enforcement to blind us to the peril to our free society that lies in this Court's disregard of the protections afforded by the Fourth Amendment.

JUSTICE BLACKMUN, dissenting.

[Justice Blackmun agreed with the plurality's holding that there was reasonable suspicion, but that there was not probable cause. For reasons that will appear, Section C, *infra*, he concluded that Royer was not unlawfully detained at the time that he consented to the opening of his suitcase.]

JUSTICE REHNQUIST, dissenting.

The plurality's meandering opinion contains in it a little something for everyone, and although it affirms the reversal of a judgment of conviction, it can scarcely be said to bespeak a total indifference to the legitimate needs of law enforcement agents seeking to curb trafficking in dangerous drugs. Indeed, in both manner and tone, the opinion brings to mind the old nursery rhyme: "The King of France With forty thousand men Marched up the hill And then marched back again."

The opinion nonetheless, in my view, betrays a mind-set more useful to those who officiate at shuffleboard games, primarily concerned with which particular square the disc has landed on, than to those who are seeking to administer a system of justice whose twin purposes are the conviction of the guilty and the vindication of the innocent. The plurality loses sight of the very language of the Amendment which it purports to interpret: "The right of the people to be secure in their persons, houses, papers, and effects, against *unreasonable* searches and seizures, shall not be violated . . . ." (Emphasis added).

Analyzed simply in terms of its "reasonableness" as that term is used in the Fourth Amendment, the conduct of the investigating officers toward Royer would pass muster with virtually all thoughtful, civilized persons not overly steeped in the mysteries of this Court's Fourth Amendment jurisprudence. Analyzed even in terms of the most meticulous regard for our often conflicting cases, it seems to me to pass muster equally well.

The facts of this case, which are doubtless typical of those facing narcotics officers in major airports throughout the country, may be usefully stated in a somewhat different manner than that followed in the opinion of the plurality. Officers Magdalena and Johnson, members of the "Smuggling Detail" of the Dade County Public Safety Department created in response to a growing drug problem at the Miami Airport, were on duty at that airport on January 3, 1978. Since this is one of the peak periods of the tourist season in South Florida and the Caribbean, we may presumably take judicial notice that the airport was in all probability very crowded and busy at that time.

The detectives first saw Royer walking through the airport concourse. He was a young man, casually dressed, carrying two heavily-laden suitcases. The officers described him as nervous in appearance, and looking around in a manner which suggested that he was trying to detect and avoid police officers. Before they approached him, the officers followed Royer to a ticket counter. He there requested a ticket for New York City, and in paying for it produced a large roll of cash in small denomination bills from which he peeled off the necessary amount. He then affixed two baggage tags to his luggage and checked it. Rather than filling out his full name, address, and phone number in the spaces provided on the tags, Royer merely wrote the words "Holt" and "La Guardia" on each tag.

At this point, the officers approached Royer, identified themselves, and asked if he had a moment to talk. He answered affirmatively, and the detectives then asked to see his airline ticket and some identification. Although his ticket was for the name "Holt," his driver's license was in the name of "Mark Royer." When asked to explain this discrepancy, he said that a friend named Holt had made the ticket reservation. This explanation, of course, did not account for his use of the name "Holt" on the baggage tags that he had just filled out.

By this time Royer had become all the more obviously nervous. The detectives told Royer that they suspected he was transporting narcotics, and asked if he would accompany them for further questioning to a room adjacent to the concourse "to get out of the general population of the Airport." Royer agreed to go.

The plurality concedes that after their initial conversation with Royer, the officers had "grounds for suspecting Royer of carrying drugs and for temporarily detaining him and his luggage while they attempted to verify or dispel their suspicions . . . ." I agree that their information reached at least this level. The detectives had learned, among other things, that (1) Royer was carrying two heavy suitcases; (2) he was visibly nervous, exhibiting the behavior of a person trying to identify and evade police officers; (3) at a ticket counter in a major import center for illicit drugs, he had purchased a ticket for a city that is a major distribution center for such drugs; (4) he paid for his ticket from a large roll of small denomination bills, avoiding the need to show identification; (5) in filling out his baggage tags, Royer listed only a last name and the airport of destination, failing to give his full name, address, and phone number in the provided spaces, and (6) he was traveling under an assumed name.

The Florida court felt that even these facts did not amount to articulable suspicion, reasoning that this behavior was "at least equally, and usually far more frequently, consistent with complete innocence."[5] This evaluation of the evidence seems to me singularly akin to observing that because a stranger who was loitering near a building shortly before an arsonist set fire to the building could not be detained against his will for questioning solely on the basis of that fact, the same

---

[5] The Florida District Court of Appeal took specific exception to the officers' conclusion that Royer appeared to be nervously attempting to evade police contact. The lower court said that since police officers are not psychiatrists, this conclusion "must be completely disregarded." This Court, however, has repeatedly emphasized that a trained police officer may draw inferences and make deductions that could elude any untrained person observing the same conduct. *See, e.g. Cortez.* We have noted as an example the behavior of a suspect who appears to the officer to be evading police contact.

conclusion would be reached even though the same stranger had been found loitering in the presence of four other buildings shortly before arsonists had likewise set them on fire. Any one of these factors relied upon by the Miami police may have been as consistent with innocence as with guilt; but the combination of several of these factors is the essence of both "articulable suspicion" and "probable cause."[6]

---

[6] While the plurality does not address the use of "drug courier profiles" in narcotics investigations, it affirms a decision where the Florida District Court of Appeal took the liberty to fashion a bright-line rule with regard to the use of these profiles. The state court concluded that conformity with a "drug courier profile," "without more," is insufficient to establish even reasonable suspicion that criminal activity is afoot. In 1974 the Department of Justice Drug Enforcement Administration instituted training programs for its narcotics officers wherein instruction was given on a "drug courier profile." A "profile" is, in effect, the collective or distilled experience of narcotics officers concerning characteristics repeatedly seen in drug smugglers. As one DEA agent explained: "Basically it's a number of characteristics which we attribute or which we believe can be used to pick out drug couriers. And these characteristics are basically things that normal travelers do not do . . . . Essentially, when we started this detail at the airport, we didn't really know what we were looking for. The majority of our cases, when we first started, involved cases we made based on information from law enforcement agencies or from airline personnel. And as these cases were made, certain characteristics were noted among the defendants. At a later time we began to see a pattern in these characteristics and began using them to pick out individuals we suspected as narcotic couriers without any prior information." Few statistics have been kept on the effectiveness of "profile" usage, but the data available suggests it has been a success. In the first few months of a "profile" program at the Detroit Metropolitan Airport, 141 persons were searched in 96 different encounters; drugs were discovered in 77 of the searches. A DEA agent working at the La Guardia Airport in New York City estimated that some 60% percent of the persons identified as having "profile" characteristics are found to be carrying drugs. Because of this success, state and local law enforcement agencies also have instructed narcotics officers according to "drug courier profiles." It was partly on the basis of "profile" characteristics that Detectives Johnson and Magdalena initially began surveillance of Royer. Certainly in this case the use of the "profile" proved effective. Use of "drug courier profiles" has played an important part in a number of lower court decisions. In fact, the function of the "profile" has been somewhat overplayed. Certainly, a law enforcement officer can rely on his own experience in detection and prevention of crime. Likewise, in training police officers, instruction focuses on what has been learned through the collective experience of law enforcers. The "drug courier profile" is an example of such instruction. It is not intended to provide a mathematical formula that automatically establishes grounds for a belief that criminal activity is afoot. By the same reasoning, however, simply because these characteristics are accumulated in a "profile," they are not to be given less weight in assessing whether a suspicion is well founded. While each case will turn on its own facts, sheer logic dictates that where certain characteristics repeatedly are found among drug smugglers, the existence of those characteristics in a particular case is to be considered accordingly in determining whether there are grounds to believe that further investigation is appropriate. Cf. Cortez. The "drug courier profile" is not unfamiliar to this Court. We have held that conformity with certain aspects of the "profile" does not automatically create a particularized suspicion which will justify an investigatory stop. Reid v. Georgia, 448 U.S. 438 (1980) (per curiam). Yet our decision in United States v. Mendenhall, 446 U.S. 544 (1980), made it clear that a police officer is entitled to assess the totality of the circumstances in the light of his own training and experience and that instruction on a "drug courier profile" would be a part of his accumulated knowledge. This process is not amenable to bright-line rules such as the Florida court tried to establish. We are not dealing "with hard certainties, but with probabilities. Long before the law of probabilities was articulated as such, practical people formulated certain common-sense conclusions about human behavior; jurors as factfinders are permitted to do the same — and so are law enforcement officers. Finally, the evidence thus collected must be seen and weighed not in terms of library analysis by scholars, but as understood by those versed in the field of law enforcement." Cortez.

QUESTIONS AND NOTES

1. Why did a majority of the Court fail to find probable cause? As between Mark Royer and Lance Gates (*See Gates*, Chapter 2, *supra*), who did more objective things to manifest guilt? If your answer is "Royer," why does the plurality wax so eloquently about not allowing every young, casually-dressed man with heavy luggage who pays for his ticket in cash and uses an alias to answer for a serious crime?

2. If you were on the Court, would you have found reasonable suspicion (like White), probable cause (like Rehnquist), or neither (like Brennan)? Explain.

3. The extent to which the "drug courier profile" can (should) play a part in reasonable suspicion is explored by both the majority and dissent in *Sokolow*. We will return to *Royer* in Section C, and Chapter 9, *infra*.

UNITED STATES v. SOKOLOW
490 U.S. 1 (1989)

CHIEF JUSTICE REHNQUIST delivered the opinion of the Court.

Respondent Andrew Sokolow was stopped by Drug Enforcement Administration (DEA) agents upon his arrival at Honolulu International Airport. The agents found 1,063 grams of cocaine in his carry-on luggage. When respondent was stopped, the agents knew, inter alia, that (1) he paid $2,100 for two airplane tickets from a roll of $20 bills; (2) he traveled under a name that did not match the name under which his telephone number was listed; (3) his original destination was Miami, a source city for illicit drugs; (4) he stayed in Miami for only 48 hours, even though a round-trip flight from Honolulu to Miami takes 20 hours; (5) he appeared nervous during his trip; and (6) he checked none of his luggage. A divided panel of the United States Court of Appeals for the Ninth Circuit held that the DEA agents did not have a reasonable suspicion to stop respondent, as required by the Fourth Amendment. We take the contrary view.

This case involves a typical attempt to smuggle drugs through one of the Nation's airports. On a Sunday in July 1984, respondent went to the United Airlines ticket counter at Honolulu Airport, where he purchased two round-trip tickets for a flight to Miami leaving later that day. The tickets were purchased in the names of "Andrew Kray" and "Janet Norian" and had open return dates. Respondent paid $2,100 for the tickets from a large roll of $20 bills, which appeared to contain a total of $4,000. He also gave the ticket agent his home telephone number. The ticket agent noticed that respondent seemed nervous; he was about 25 years old; he was dressed in a black jumpsuit and wore gold jewelry; and he was accompanied by a woman, who turned out to be Janet Norian. Neither respondent nor his companion checked any of their four pieces of luggage.

After the couple left for their flight, the ticket agent informed Officer John McCarthy of the Honolulu Police Department of respondent's cash purchase of tickets to Miami. Officer McCarthy determined that the telephone number respondent gave to the ticket agent was subscribed to a "Karl Herman," who resided at

348-A Royal Hawaiian Avenue in Honolulu. Unbeknownst to McCarthy (and later to the DEA agents), respondent was Herman's roommate. The ticket agent identified respondent's voice on the answering machine at Herman's number. Officer McCarthy was unable to find any listing under the name "Andrew Kray" in Hawaii. McCarthy subsequently learned that return reservations from Miami to Honolulu had been made in the names of Kray and Norian, with their arrival scheduled for July 25, three days after respondent and his companion had left. He also learned that Kray and Norian were scheduled to make stopovers in Denver and Los Angeles.

On July 25, during the stopover in Los Angeles, DEA agents identified respondent. He "appeared to be very nervous and was looking all around the waiting area." Later that day, at 6:30 p.m., respondent and Norian arrived in Honolulu. As before, they had not checked their luggage. Respondent was still wearing a black jumpsuit and gold jewelry. The couple proceeded directly to the street and tried to hail a cab, where Agent Richard Kempshall and three other DEA agents approached them. Kempshall displayed his credentials, grabbed respondent by the arm, and moved him back onto the sidewalk. Kempshall asked respondent for his airline ticket and identification; respondent said that he had neither. He told the agents that his name was "Sokolow," but that he was traveling under his mother's maiden name, "Kray."

Respondent and Norian were escorted to the DEA office at the airport. There, the couple's luggage was examined by "Donker," a narcotics detector dog, which alerted on respondent's brown shoulder bag. The agents arrested respondent. He was advised of his constitutional rights and declined to make any statements. The agents obtained a warrant to search the shoulder bag. They found no illicit drugs, but the bag did contain several suspicious documents indicating respondent's involvement in drug trafficking. The agents had Donker reexamine the remaining luggage, and this time the dog alerted on a medium sized Louis Vuitton bag. By now, it was 9:30 p.m., too late for the agents to obtain a second warrant. They allowed respondent to leave for the night, but kept his luggage. The next morning, after a second dog confirmed Donker's alert, the agents obtained a warrant and found 1,063 grams of cocaine inside the bag.

Respondent was indicted for possession with the intent to distribute cocaine. The United States District Court for Hawaii denied his motion to suppress the cocaine and other evidence seized from his luggage, finding that the DEA agents had a reasonable suspicion that he was involved in drug trafficking when they stopped him at the airport. Respondent then entered a conditional plea of guilty to the offense charged.

The United States Court of Appeals for the Ninth Circuit reversed respondent's conviction by a divided vote, holding that the DEA agents did not have a reasonable suspicion to justify the stop. The majority divided the facts bearing on reasonable suspicion into two categories. In the first category, the majority placed facts describing "ongoing criminal activity," such as the use of an alias or evasive movement through an airport; the majority believed that at least one such factor was always needed to support a finding of reasonable suspicion. In the second category, it placed facts describing "personal characteristics" of drug couriers, such as the cash payment for tickets, a short trip to a major source city for drugs, nervousness, type of attire, and unchecked luggage. The majority believed that such characteristics, "shared by drug couriers and the public at large," were only relevant if there was evidence of ongoing criminal behavior and the Government offered "[e]mpirical documentation" that the combination of facts at issue did not describe the behavior of "significant numbers of innocent persons." Applying this two-part test to the facts of this case, the majority found that there was no evidence of ongoing criminal behavior, and thus that the agents' stop was impermissible. The dissenting judge took the view that the majority's approach was "overly mechanistic" and "contrary to the case-by-case determination of reasonable articulable suspicion based on all the facts."

We granted certiorari to review the decision of the Court of Appeals because of its serious implications for the enforcement of the federal narcotics laws. We now reverse.

The Court of Appeals held that the DEA agents seized respondent when they grabbed him by the arm and moved him back onto the sidewalk. The Government does not challenge that conclusion, and we assume — without deciding — that a stop occurred here. Our decision, then, turns on whether the agents had a reasonable suspicion that respondent was engaged in wrongdoing when they encountered him on the sidewalk. In *Terry*, we held that the police can stop and briefly detain a person for investigative purposes if the officer has a reasonable suspicion supported by articulable facts that criminal activity "may be afoot," even if the officer lacks probable cause.

The officer, of course, must be able to articulate something more than an "inchoate and unparticularized suspicion or 'hunch.'" The Fourth Amendment requires "some minimal level of objective justification" for making the stop. That level of suspicion is considerably less than proof of wrongdoing by a preponderance of the evidence. We have held that probable cause means "a fair probability that contraband or evidence of a crime will be found," and the level of suspicion required for a *Terry* stop is obviously less demanding than that for probable cause.

The concept of reasonable suspicion, like probable cause, is not "readily, or even usefully, reduced to a neat set of legal rules." We think the Court of Appeals' effort to refine and elaborate the requirements of "reasonable suspicion" in this case creates unnecessary difficulty in dealing with one of the relatively simple concepts embodied in the Fourth Amendment. In evaluating the validity of a stop such as this, we must consider "the totality of the circumstances — the whole picture." As we said in *Cortez*: "The process does not deal with hard certainties, but with probabilities. Long before the law of probabilities was articulated as such, practical people formulated certain common-sense conclusions about human behavior; jurors as fact-finders are permitted to do the same — and so are law enforcement officers."

The rule enunciated by the Court of Appeals, in which evidence available to an officer is divided into evidence of "ongoing criminal behavior," on the one hand, and "probabilistic" evidence, on the other, is not in keeping with the quoted statements from our decisions. It also seems to us to draw a sharp line between types of evidence, the probative value of which varies only in degree. The Court of Appeals classified evidence of traveling under an alias, or evidence that the suspect took an evasive or erratic path through an airport, as meeting the test for showing "ongoing criminal activity." But certainly instances are conceivable in which traveling under an alias would not reflect ongoing criminal activity: for example, a person who wished to travel to a hospital or clinic for an operation and wished to concealed that fact. One taking an evasive path through an airport might be seeking to avoid a confrontation with an angry acquaintance or with a creditor. This is not to say that each of these types of evidence is not highly probative, but they do not have the sort of ironclad significance attributed to them by the Court of Appeals.

On the other hand, the factors in this case that the Court of Appeals treated as merely "probabilistic" also have probative significance. Paying $2,100 in cash for two airplane tickets is out of the ordinary, and it is even more out of the ordinary to pay that sum from a roll of $20 bills containing nearly twice that amount of cash. Most business travelers, we feel confident, purchase airline tickets by credit card or check so as to have a record for tax or business purposes, and few vacationers carry with them thousands of dollars in $20 bills. We also think the agents had a reasonable ground to believe that respondent was traveling under an alias; the evidence was by no means conclusive, but it was sufficient to warrant consideration.[3] While a trip from Honolulu to Miami, standing alone, is not a cause for any sort of suspicion, here there was more: surely few residents of Honolulu travel from that city for 20 hours to spend 48 hours in Miami during the month of July.

Any one of these factors is not by itself proof of any illegal conduct and is quite consistent with innocent travel. But we think taken together they amount to reasonable suspicion. *See Royer.* We said in *Reid v. Georgia*, 448 U.S. 438 (1980) (per curiam), "there could, of course, be circumstances in which wholly lawful conduct might justify the suspicion that criminal activity was afoot."[5] Indeed, *Terry* itself involved "a series of acts, each of them perhaps innocent" if viewed separately, "but which taken together warranted further investigation." We noted in *Gates* that "innocent behavior will frequently provide the basis for a showing of probable cause," and that "[i]n making a determination of probable cause the relevant inquiry is not whether particular conduct is 'innocent' or 'guilty,' but the degree of suspicion that attaches to particular types of noncriminal acts." That principle applies equally well to the reasonable suspicion inquiry.

We do not agree with respondent that our analysis is somehow changed by the agents' belief that his behavior was consistent with one of the DEA's "drug courier

---

[3] Respondent also claims that the agents should have conducted a further inquiry to resolve the inconsistency between the name he gave the airline and the name, "Karl Herman," under which his telephone number was listed. Brief for Respondent 26. This argument avails respondent nothing; had the agents done further checking, they would have discovered not only that respondent was Herman's roommate but also that his name was "Sokolow" and not "Kray," the name listed on his ticket.

[5] In *Reid*, the Court held that a DEA agent stopped the defendant without reasonable suspicion. At the time of the stop, the agent knew that (1) the defendant flew into Atlanta from Fort Lauderdale, a source city for cocaine; (2) he arrived early in the morning, when police activity was believed to be at a low ebb; (3) he did not check his luggage; and (4) the defendant and his companion appeared to be attempting to hide the fact that they were together. The Court held that the first three of these facts were not sufficient to supply reasonable suspicion, because they "describe a very large category of presumably innocent travelers," while the last fact was insufficient on the facts of that case to establish reasonable suspicion.

profiles."[6] A court sitting to determine the existence of reasonable suspicion must require the agent to articulate the factors leading to that conclusion, but the fact that these factors may be set forth in a "profile" does not somehow detract from their evidentiary significance as seen by a trained agent.

We hold that the agents had a reasonable basis to suspect that respondent was transporting illegal drugs on these facts. The judgment of the Court of Appeals is therefore reversed, and the case is remanded for further proceedings consistent with our decision.

JUSTICE MARSHALL, with whom JUSTICE BRENNAN joins, dissenting

Because the strongest advocates of Fourth Amendment rights are frequently criminals, it is easy to forget that our interpretations of such rights apply to the innocent and the guilty alike. In the present case, the chain of events set in motion when respondent Andrew Sokolow was stopped by Drug Enforcement Administration (DEA) agents at Honolulu International Airport led to the discovery of cocaine and, ultimately, to Sokolow's conviction for drug trafficking. But in sustaining this conviction on the ground that the agents reasonably suspected Sokolow of ongoing criminal activity, the Court diminishes the rights of all citizens "to be secure in their persons," as they traverse the Nation's airports. Finding this result constitutionally impermissible, I dissent.

The Fourth Amendment cabins government's authority to intrude on personal privacy and security by requiring that searches and seizures usually be supported by a showing of probable cause. The reasonable suspicion standard is a derivation of the probable-cause command, applicable only to those brief detentions which fall short of being full-scale searches and seizures and which are necessitated by law enforcement exigencies such as the need to stop ongoing crimes, to prevent imminent crimes, and to protect law enforcement officers in highly charged situations. By requiring reasonable suspicion as a prerequisite to such seizures, the Fourth Amendment protects innocent persons from being subjected to "overbearing or harassing" police conduct carried out solely on the basis of imprecise stereotypes of what criminals look like, or on the basis of irrelevant personal characteristics such as race.

To deter such egregious police behavior, we have held that a suspicion is not reasonable unless officers have based it on "specific and articulable facts." It is not enough to suspect that an individual has committed crimes in the past, harbors unconsummated criminal designs, or has the propensity to commit crimes. On the contrary, before detaining an individual, law enforcement officers must reasonably suspect that he is engaged in, or poised to commit, a criminal act at that moment. The rationale for permitting brief, warrantless seizures is, after all, that it is impractical to demand strict compliance with the Fourth Amendment's ordinary probable-cause requirement in the face of ongoing or imminent criminal activity demanding "swift action predicated upon the on-the-spot observations of the officer

---

[6] Agent Kempshall testified that respondent's behavior "had all the classic aspects of a drug courier." Since 1974, the DEA has trained narcotics officers to identify drug smugglers on the basis of the sort of circumstantial evidence at issue here.

on the beat." *Terry.* Observations raising suspicions of past criminality demand no such immediate action, but instead should appropriately trigger routine police investigation, which may ultimately generate sufficient information to blossom into probable cause.

Evaluated against this standard, the facts about Andrew Sokolow known to the DEA agents at the time they stopped him fall short of reasonably indicating that he was engaged at the time in criminal activity. It is highly significant that the DEA agents stopped Sokolow because he matched one of the DEA's "profiles" of a paradigmatic drug courier. In my view, a law enforcement officer's mechanistic application of a formula of personal and behavioral traits in deciding whom to detain can only dull the officer's ability and determination to make sensitive and fact-specific inferences "in light of his experience," *Terry*, particularly in ambiguous or borderline cases. Reflexive reliance on a profile of drug courier characteristics runs a far greater risk than does ordinary, case-by-case police work of subjecting innocent individuals to unwarranted police harassment and detention. This risk is enhanced by the profile's "chameleon-like way of adapting to any particular set of observations." Compare [the following different and sometimes contradictory standards: (suspect was first to deplane), (last to deplane), (deplaned from middle); (one-way tickets), (round-trip tickets), (nonstop flight), (changed planes); (no luggage), (gym bag), (new suitcases); (traveling alone), (traveling with companion); (acted nervously), (acted too calmly). In asserting that it is not "somehow" relevant that the agents who stopped Sokolow did so in reliance on a prefabricated profile of criminal characteristics, the majority thus ducks serious issues relating to a questionable law enforcement practice, to address the validity of which we granted certiorari in this case.[1]

That the factors comprising the drug courier profile relied on in this case are especially dubious indices of ongoing criminal activity is underscored by *Reid v. Georgia*, a strikingly similar case. There, four facts, encoded in a drug courier profile, were alleged in support of the DEA's detention of a suspect at the Atlanta Airport. First, Reid had arrived from Fort Lauderdale, Florida, a source city for cocaine. Second, he arrived in the early morning, when law enforcement activity is diminished. Third, he and his companion appeared to have no luggage other than their shoulder bags. And fourth, he and his companion appeared to be trying to conceal the fact that they were traveling together.

This collection of facts, we held, was inadequate to support a finding of reasonable suspicion. All but the last of these facts, we observed, "describe a very large category of presumably innocent travelers, who would be subject to virtually random seizures were the Court to conclude that as little foundation as there was in this case could justify a seizure." The sole fact that suggested criminal activity was that Reid "preceded another person and occasionally looked backward at him as they proceeded through the concourse." This observation did not of itself provide a reasonable basis for suspecting wrongdoing, for inferring criminal activity from

---

[1] Even if such profiles had reliable predictive value, their utility would be short lived, for drug couriers will adapt their behavior to sidestep detection from profile-focused officers.

such evidence reflected no more than an "inchoate and unparticularized suspicion or 'hunch.' "[2]

The facts known to the DEA agents at the time they detained the traveler in this case are scarcely more suggestive of ongoing criminal activity than those in Reid. Unlike traveler Reid, who sought to conceal the fact that he was traveling with a companion, and who even attempted to run away after being approached by a DEA agent, traveler Sokolow gave no indications of evasive activity. On the contrary, the sole behavioral detail about Sokolow noted by the DEA agents was that he was nervous. With news accounts proliferating of plane crashes, near collisions, and air terrorism, there are manifold and good reasons for being agitated while awaiting a flight, reasons that have nothing to do with one's involvement in a criminal endeavor.

The remaining circumstantial facts known about Sokolow, considered either singly or together, are scarcely indicative of criminal activity. Like the information disavowed in Reid as nonprobative, the fact that Sokolow took a brief trip to a resort city for which he brought only carry-on luggage also "describe[s] a very large category of presumably innocent travelers." That Sokolow embarked from Miami, "a source city for illicit drugs," is no more suggestive of illegality; thousands of innocent persons travel from "source cities" every day and, judging from the DEA's testimony in past cases, nearly every major city in the country may be characterized as a source or distribution city. That Sokolow had his phone listed in another person's name also does not support the majority's assertion that the DEA agents reasonably believed Sokolow was using an alias; it is commonplace to have one's phone registered in the name of a roommate, which, it later turned out, was precisely what Sokolow had done.[3] That Sokolow was dressed in a black jumpsuit and wore gold jewelry also provides no grounds for suspecting wrongdoing, the majority's repeated and unexplained allusions to Sokolow's style of dress notwithstanding. For law enforcement officers to base a search, even in part, on a pop guess that persons dressed in a particular fashion are likely to commit crimes not only stretches the concept of reasonable suspicion beyond recognition, but also is inimical to the self-expression which the choice of wardrobe may provide.

Finally, that Sokolow paid for his tickets in cash indicates no imminent or ongoing criminal activity. The majority "feel[s] confident" that "[m]ost business travelers . . . purchase airline tickets by credit card or check." Why the majority confines its focus only to "business travelers" I do not know, but I would not so lightly infer ongoing crime from the use of legal tender. Making major cash purchases, while surely less common today, may simply reflect the traveler's aversion to, or inability to obtain, plastic money. Conceivably, a person who spends

[2] Nor was Reid a close case: eight Members of the Court found the challenged detention insupportable, five of whom saw fit to dispose of the case by reversing the court below in a per curiam opinion. In a separate concurrence, Justice Powell, joined by Chief Justice Burger and Justice Blackmun, agreed that "the fragmentary facts apparently relied on by the DEA agents" provided "no justification" for Reid's detention. Only then-Justice Rehnquist, the author of today's majority opinion, dissented, on the ground that the police conduct involved did not implicate Reid's constitutional rights.

[3] That Sokolow was, in fact, using an alias was not known to the DEA agents until after they detained him. Thus, it cannot legitimately be considered as a basis for the seizure in this case.

large amounts of cash may be trying to launder his proceeds from past criminal enterprises by converting them into goods and services. But, as I have noted, investigating completed episodes of crime goes beyond the appropriately limited purview of the brief, *Terry*-style seizure. Moreover, it is unreasonable to suggest that, had Sokolow left the airport, he would have been gone forever and thus immune from subsequent investigation. Sokolow, after all, had given the airline his phone number, and the DEA, having ascertained that it was indeed Sokolow's voice on the answering machine at that number, could have learned from that information where Sokolow resided.

The fact is that, unlike the taking of patently evasive action, *Florida v. Rodriguez*, 469 U.S. 1 (1984), the use of an alias, *Royer*, the casing of a store, *Terry*, or the provision of a reliable report from an informant that wrongdoing is imminent, *Gates*, nothing about the characteristics shown by airport traveler Sokolow reasonably suggests that criminal activity is afoot. The majority's hasty conclusion to the contrary serves only to indicate its willingness, when drug crimes or antidrug policies are at issue, to give short shrift to constitutional rights. In requiring that seizures be based on at least some evidence of criminal conduct, the Court of Appeals was faithful to the Fourth Amendment principle that law enforcement officers must reasonably suspect a person of criminal activity before they can detain him. Because today's decision, though limited to its facts, disobeys this important constitutional command, I dissent.

QUESTIONS AND NOTES

1. Do you see the "drug courier profile" as a good thing or a bad thing?

2. Does Justice Marshall's rejection of the profile encourage the sort of unbridled discretion that he and Justice Brennan have abhorred in other areas of the Fourth Amendment? Doesn't the profile, compiled by somebody other than the "officer on the beat" at least channel discretion? Or is this profile just too amorphous?

3. Is Justice Marshall requiring too much probative value from each point? Might not the whole tell you more than the sum of its parts?

4. On the other hand, Justice Rehnquist says that certiorari was granted "because of (the lower court's decision's) serious implications for the enforcement of the federal narcotics laws." Does that statement skew the equation, when the Court's job is supposed to be (as Rehnquist said in *Gates*; "To hold the balance true"?

5. For an example of reasonable suspicion as little more than watered-down probable cause, we turn to *Alabama v. White*.

ALABAMA v. WHITE
496 U.S. 325 (1990)

JUSTICE WHITE delivered the opinion of the Court.

Based on an anonymous telephone tip, police stopped respondent's vehicle. A consensual search of the car revealed drugs. The issue is whether the tip, as corroborated by independent police work, exhibited sufficient indicia of reliability to provide reasonable suspicion to make the investigatory stop. We hold that it did.

On April 22, 1987, at approximately 3 p.m., Corporal B.H. Davis of the Montgomery Police Department received a telephone call from an anonymous person, stating that Vanessa White would be leaving 235-C Lynwood Terrace Apartments at a particular time in a brown Plymouth station wagon with the right taillight lens broken, that she would be going to Dobey's Motel, and that she would be in possession of about an ounce of cocaine inside a brown attaché case. Corporal Davis and his partner, Corporal P. A. Reynolds, proceeded to the Lynwood Terrace Apartments. The officers saw a brown Plymouth station wagon with a broken right taillight in the parking lot in front of the 235 building. The officers observed respondent leave the 235 building, carrying nothing in her hands, and enter the station wagon. They followed the vehicle as it drove the most direct route to Dobey's Motel. When the vehicle reached the Mobile Highway, on which Dobey's Motel is located, Corporal Reynolds requested a patrol unit to stop the vehicle. The vehicle was stopped at approximately 4:18 p.m., just short of Dobey's Motel. Corporal Davis asked respondent to step to the rear of her car, where he informed her that she had been stopped because she was suspected of carrying cocaine in the vehicle. He asked if they could look for cocaine and respondent said they could look. The officers found a locked brown attaché case in the car and, upon request, respondent provided the combination to the lock. The officers found marijuana in the attaché case and placed respondent under arrest. During processing at the station, the officers found three milligrams of cocaine in respondent's purse.

Respondent was charged in Montgomery County court with possession of marijuana and possession of cocaine. The trial court denied respondent's motion to suppress and she pleaded guilty to the charges, reserving the right to appeal the denial of her suppression motion. The Court of Criminal Appeals of Alabama held that the officers did not have the reasonable suspicion necessary under *Terry*, to justify the investigatory stop of respondent's car, and that the marijuana and cocaine were fruits of respondent's unconstitutional detention. The court concluded that respondent's motion to dismiss should have been granted and reversed her conviction. The Supreme Court of Alabama denied the State's petition for writ of certiorari, two justices dissenting. Because of differing views in the state and federal courts over whether an anonymous tip may furnish reasonable suspicion for a stop, we granted the State's petition for certiorari. We now reverse.

Adams sustained a *Terry* stop and frisk undertaken on the basis of a tip given in person by a known informant who had provided information in the past. We concluded that, while the unverified tip may have been insufficient to support an arrest or search warrant, the information carried sufficient "indicia of reliability" to justify a forcible stop. We did not address the issue of anonymous tips in *Adams*, except to say that "[t]his is a stronger case than obtains in the case of an anonymous telephone tip."

Gates dealt with an anonymous tip in the probable cause context. The Court there abandoned the "two-pronged test" of *Aguilar* and *Spinelli*, in favor of a "totality of the circumstances" approach to determining whether an informant's tip establishes probable cause. *Gates* made clear, however, that those factors that had been considered critical under *Aguilar* and *Spinelli* — an informant's "veracity," "reliability," and "basis of knowledge" — remain "highly relevant in determining the value of his report." These factors are also relevant in the reasonable suspicion context, although allowance must be made in applying them for the lesser showing required to meet that standard.

The opinion in *Gates* recognized that an anonymous tip alone seldom demonstrates the informant's basis of knowledge or veracity inasmuch as ordinary citizens generally do not provide extensive recitations of the basis of their everyday observations and given that the veracity of persons supplying anonymous tips is "by hypothesis largely unknown, and unknowable." This is not to say that an anonymous caller could never provide the reasonable suspicion necessary for a *Terry* stop. But the tip in *Gates* was not an exception to the general rule, and the anonymous tip in this case is like the one in *Gates*: "[it] provides virtually nothing from which one might conclude that [the caller] is either honest or his information reliable; likewise, the [tip] gives absolutely no indication of the basis for the [caller's] predictions regarding [Vanessa White's] criminal activities." By requiring "[s]omething more," as *Gates* did, we merely apply what we said in *Adams*: "Some tips, completely lacking in indicia of reliability, would either warrant no police response or require further investigation before a forcible stop of a suspect would be authorized." Simply put, a tip such as this one, standing alone, would not " 'warrant a man of reasonable caution in the belief' that [a stop] was appropriate."

As there was in *Gates*, however, in this case there is more than the tip itself. The tip was not as detailed, and the corroboration was not as complete, as in *Gates*, but the required degree of suspicion was likewise not as high. We discussed the difference in the two standards last Term in *Sokolow*: "The officer [making a *Terry* stop] . . . must be able to articulate something more than an 'inchoate and unparticularized suspicion or "hunch." ' " The Fourth Amendment requires 'some minimal level of objective justification' for making the stop. That level of suspicion is considerably less than proof of wrongdoing by a preponderance of the evidence. We have held that probable cause means 'a fair probability that contraband or evidence of a crime will be found,' and the level of suspicion required for a *Terry* stop is obviously less demanding than for probable cause."

Reasonable suspicion is a less demanding standard than probable cause not only in the sense that reasonable suspicion can be established with information that is different in quantity or content than that required to establish probable cause, but also in the sense that reasonable suspicion can arise from information that is less reliable than that required to show probable cause. *Adams* demonstrates as much. We there assumed that the unverified tip from the known informant might not have been reliable enough to establish probable cause, but nevertheless found it sufficiently reliable to justify a *Terry* stop. Reasonable suspicion, like probable cause, is dependent upon both the content of information possessed by police and its degree of reliability. Both factors — quantity and quality — are considered in the "totality of the circumstances — the whole picture," that must be taken into account when evaluating whether there is reasonable suspicion. Thus, if a tip has a relatively low degree of reliability, more information will be required to establish the requisite quantum of suspicion than would be required if the tip were more reliable. The *Gates* Court applied its totality of the circumstances approach in this manner, taking into account the facts known to the officers from personal observation, and giving the anonymous tip the weight it deserved in light of its indicia of reliability as established through independent police work. The same approach applies in the reasonable suspicion context, the only difference being the level of suspicion that must be established. Contrary to the court below, we conclude that when the officers stopped respondent, the anonymous tip had been sufficiently corroborated to furnish reasonable suspicion that respondent was engaged in criminal activity and that the investigative stop therefore did not violate the Fourth Amendment.

It is true that not every detail mentioned by the tipster was verified, such as the name of the woman leaving the building or the precise apartment from which she left; but the officers did corroborate that a woman left the 235 building and got into the particular vehicle that was described by the caller. With respect to the time of departure predicted by the informant, Corporal Davis testified that the caller gave a particular time when the woman would be leaving, but he did not state what that time was. He did testify that, after the call, he and his partner proceeded to the Lynwood Terrace Apartments to put the 235 building under surveillance. Given the fact that the officers proceeded to the indicated address immediately after the call and that respondent emerged not too long thereafter, it appears from the record before us that respondent's departure from the building was within the time frame predicted by the caller. As for the caller's prediction of respondent's destination, it is true that the officers stopped her just short of Dobey's Motel and did not know whether she would have pulled in or continued on past it. But given that the four-mile route driven by respondent was the most direct route possible to Dobey's Motel, but nevertheless involved several turns, we think respondent's destination was significantly corroborated.

The Court's opinion in *Gates* gave credit to the proposition that because an informant is shown to be right about some things, he is probably right about other facts that he has alleged, including the claim that the object of the tip is engaged in criminal activity. Thus, it is not unreasonable to conclude in this case that the independent corroboration by the police of significant aspects of the informer's predictions imparted some degree of reliability to the other allegations made by the caller.

We think it also important that, as in *Gates*, "the anonymous [tip] contained a range of details relating not just to easily obtained facts and conditions existing at the time of the tip, but to future actions of third parties ordinarily not easily predicted." The fact that the officers found a car precisely matching the caller's description in front of the 235 building is an example of the former. Anyone could have "predicted" that fact because it was a condition presumably existing at the time of the call. What was important was the caller's ability to predict respondent's *future behavior*, because it demonstrated inside information — a special familiarity with respondent's affairs. The general public would have had no way of knowing that respondent would shortly leave the building, get in the described car, and drive the most direct route to Dobey's Motel. Because only a small number of people are generally privy to an individual's itinerary, it is reasonable for police to believe that a person with access to such information is likely to also have access to reliable information about that individual's illegal activities. When significant aspects of the caller's predictions were verified, there was reason to believe not only that the caller was honest but also that he was well informed, at least well enough to justify the stop.

Although it is a close case, we conclude that under the totality of the circumstances the anonymous tip, as corroborated, exhibited sufficient indicia of reliability to justify the investigatory stop of respondent's car. We therefore reverse the judgment of the Court of Criminal Appeals of Alabama and remand for further proceedings not inconsistent with this opinion.

JUSTICE STEVENS, with whom JUSTICE BRENNAN and JUSTICE MARSHALL join, dissenting.

Millions of people leave their apartments at about the same time every day carrying an attaché case and heading for a destination known to their neighbors. Usually, however, the neighbors do not know what the briefcase contains. An anonymous neighbor's prediction about somebody's time of departure and probable destination is anything but a reliable basis for assuming that the commuter is in possession of an illegal substance — particularly when the person is not even carrying the attaché case described by the tipster.

The record in this case does not tell us how often respondent drove from the Lynwood Terrace Apartments to Dobey's Motel; for all we know, she may have been a room clerk or telephone operator working the evening shift. It does not tell us whether Officer Davis made any effort to ascertain the informer's identity, his reason for calling, or the basis of his prediction about respondent's destination. Indeed, for all that this record tells us, the tipster may well have been another police officer who had a "hunch" that respondent might have cocaine in her attaché case.

Anybody with enough knowledge about a given person to make her the target of a prank, or to harbor a grudge against her, will certainly be able to formulate a tip about her like the one predicting Vanessa White's excursion. In addition, under the Court's holding, every citizen is subject to being seized and questioned by any officer who is prepared to testify that the warrantless stop was based on an anonymous tip predicting whatever conduct the officer just observed. Fortunately, the vast majority of those in our law enforcement community would not adopt such a practice. But the Fourth Amendment was intended to protect the citizen from the overzealous and unscrupulous officer as well as from those who are conscientious and truthful. This decision makes a mockery of that protection.

I respectfully dissent.

QUESTIONS AND NOTES

1. Do you think that the police had reasonable suspicion in this case?

2. If your answer to Question 1 was "no," what would you have expected the police to do under these circumstances?

3. If your answer to Question 1 was "yes," how do you deal with the problem of nonexistent informants manufactured by the police out of whole cloth after the fact?

4. Does *White* undervalue the importance of a known informant risking criminal charges for lying (*see Adams, supra*) by according this much significance to an unknown informant?

5. Given *Gates* and *Sokolow*, does *White* almost inexorably follow?

6. In *Florida v. J.L.*, the Court explored the limits of *White*.

FLORIDA v. J.L.
529 U.S. 266 (2000)

JUSTICE GINSBURG delivered the opinion of the Court.

The question presented in this case is whether an anonymous tip that a person is carrying a gun is, without more, sufficient to justify a police officer's stop and frisk of that person. We hold that it is not.

I

On October 13, 1995, an anonymous caller reported to the Miami-Dade Police that a young black male standing at a particular bus stop and wearing a plaid shirt was carrying a gun. So far as the record reveals, there is no audio recording of the tip, and nothing is known about the informant. Sometime after the police received the tip — the record does not say how long — two officers were instructed to respond. They arrived at the bus stop about six minutes later and saw three black males "just hanging out [there]." One of the three, respondent J.L., was wearing a plaid shirt. Apart from the tip, the officers had no reason to suspect any of the three of illegal conduct. The officers did not see a firearm, and J.L. made no threatening or otherwise unusual movements. One of the officers approached J.L., told him to put his hands up on the bus stop, frisked him, and seized a gun from J.L.'s pocket. The second officer frisked the other two individuals, against whom no allegations had been made, and found nothing.

J.L., who was at the time of the frisk "10 days shy of his 16th birthday," was charged under state law with carrying a concealed firearm without a license and possessing a firearm while under the age of 18. He moved to suppress the gun as the fruit of an unlawful search, and the trial court granted his motion. The intermediate appellate court reversed, but the Supreme Court of Florida quashed that decision and held the search invalid under the Fourth Amendment.

Seeking review in this Court, the State of Florida noted that the decision of the State's Supreme Court conflicts with decisions of other courts declaring similar searches compatible with the Fourth Amendment. We granted certiorari and now affirm the judgment of the Florida Supreme Court.

II

Our "stop and frisk" decisions begin with *Terry v. Ohio* [where this Court held:]

> Where a police officer observes unusual conduct which leads him reasonably to conclude in light of his experience that criminal activity may be afoot and that the persons with whom he is dealing may be armed and presently dangerous, where in the course of investigating this behavior he identifies himself as a policeman and makes reasonable inquiries, and where nothing in the initial stages of the encounter serves to dispel his reasonable fear for his own or others' safety, he is entitled for the protection of himself and others in the area to conduct a carefully limited search of the outer clothing of such persons in an attempt to discover weapons which might be used to assault him.

In the instant case, the officers' suspicion that J.L. was carrying a weapon arose not from any observations of their own but solely from a call made from an unknown location by an unknown caller. Unlike a tip from a known informant whose reputation can be assessed and who can be held responsible if her allegations turn out to be fabricated, *see Adams v. Williams*, "an anonymous tip alone seldom demonstrates the informant's basis of knowledge or veracity," *Alabama v. White*. As we have recognized, however, there are situations in which an anonymous tip, suitably corroborated, exhibits "sufficient indicia of reliability to provide reasonable suspicion to make the investigatory stop." The question we here confront is whether the tip pointing to J.L. had those indicia of reliability.

In *White*, the police received an anonymous tip asserting that a woman was carrying cocaine and predicting that she would leave an apartment building at a specified time, get into a car matching a particular description, and drive to a named motel. Standing alone, the tip would not have justified a *Terry* stop. Only after police observation showed that the informant had accurately predicted the woman's movements, we explained, did it become reasonable to think the tipster had inside knowledge about the suspect and therefore to credit his assertion about the cocaine. Although the Court held that the suspicion in *White* became reasonable after police surveillance, we regarded the case as borderline. Knowledge about a person's future movements indicates some familiarity with that person's affairs, but having such knowledge does not necessarily imply that the informant knows, in particular, whether that person is carrying hidden contraband. We accordingly classified *White* as a "close case."

The tip in the instant case lacked the moderate indicia of reliability present in *White* and essential to the Court's decision in that case. The anonymous call concerning J.L. provided no predictive information and therefore left the police without means to test the informant's knowledge or credibility. That the allegation about the gun turned out to be correct does not suggest that the officers, prior to the frisks, had a reasonable basis for suspecting J.L. of engaging in unlawful conduct: The reasonableness of official suspicion must be measured by what the officers knew before they conducted their search. All the police had to go on in this case was the bare report of an unknown, unaccountable informant who neither explained how he knew about the gun nor supplied any basis for believing he had inside information about J.L. If *White* was a close case on the reliability of anonymous tips, this one surely falls on the other side of the line.

Florida contends that the tip was reliable because its description of the suspect's visible attributes proved accurate: There really was a young black male wearing a plaid shirt at the bus stop. The United States as *amicus curiae* makes a similar argument, proposing that a stop and frisk should be permitted "when (1) an anonymous tip provides a description of a particular person at a particular location illegally carrying a concealed firearm, (2) police promptly verify the pertinent details of the tip except the existence of the firearm, and (3) there are no factors that cast doubt on the reliability of the tip . . . ." These contentions misapprehend the reliability needed for a tip to justify a *Terry* stop.

An accurate description of a subject's readily observable location and appearance is of course reliable in this limited sense: It will help the police correctly identify the person whom the tipster means to accuse. Such a tip, however, does not show that the tipster has knowledge of concealed criminal activity. The reasonable suspicion here at issue requires that a tip be reliable in its assertion of illegality, not just in its tendency to identify a determinate person. *Cf.* 4 W. LaFave, Search and Seizure § 9.4(h), p. 213 (3d ed. 1996) (distinguishing reliability as to identification, which is often important in other criminal law contexts, from reliability as to the likelihood of criminal activity, which is central in anonymous-tip cases).

A second major argument advanced by Florida and the United States as *amicus* is, in essence, that the standard *Terry* analysis should be modified to license a "firearm exception." Under such an exception, a tip alleging an illegal gun would justify a stop and frisk even if the accusation would fail standard pre-search reliability testing. We decline to adopt this position.

Firearms are dangerous, and extraordinary dangers sometimes justify unusual precautions. Our decisions recognize the serious threat that armed criminals pose to public safety; *Terry's* rule, which permits protective police searches on the basis of reasonable suspicion rather than demanding that officers meet the higher standard of probable cause, responds to this very concern. But an automatic firearm exception to our established reliability analysis would rove too far. Such an exception would enable any person seeking to harass another to set in motion an intrusive, embarrassing police search of the targeted person simply by placing an anonymous call falsely reporting the target's unlawful carriage of a gun. Nor could one securely confine such an exception to allegations involving firearms. Several Courts of Appeals have held it *per se* foreseeable for people carrying significant amounts of illegal drugs to be carrying guns as well. If police officers may properly conduct *Terry* frisks on the basis of bare-boned tips about guns, it would be reasonable to maintain under the above-cited decisions that the police should similarly have discretion to frisk based on bare-boned tips about narcotics. As we clarified when we made indicia of reliability critical in *Adams* and *White*, the Fourth Amendment is not so easily satisfied. *Cf. Richards v. Wisconsin*, 520 U.S. 385, 393–394 (1997) (rejecting a *per se* exception to the "knock and announce" rule for narcotics cases partly because "the reasons for creating an exception in one category [of Fourth Amendment cases] can, relatively easily, be applied to others," thus allowing the exception to swallow the rule).[4]

The facts of this case do not require us to speculate about the circumstances under which the danger alleged in an anonymous tip might be so great as to justify a search even without a showing of reliability. We do not say, for example, that a report of a person carrying a bomb need bear the indicia of reliability we demand for a report of a person carrying a firearm before the police can constitutionally conduct a frisk. Nor do we hold that public safety officials in quarters where the reasonable expectation of Fourth Amendment privacy is diminished, such as airports, *see Florida v. Rodriguez*, 469 U.S. 1 (1984) (per curiam), and schools, *see New Jersey v. T.L.O.*, 469 U.S. 325 (1985), cannot conduct protective searches on the basis of information insufficient to justify searches elsewhere.

Finally, the requirement that an anonymous tip bear standard indicia of reliability in order to justify a stop in no way diminishes a police officer's prerogative, in accord with *Terry*, to conduct a protective search of a person who has already been legitimately stopped. We speak in today's decision only of cases in which the officer's authority to make the initial stop is at issue. In that context, we hold that an anonymous tip lacking indicia of reliability of the kind contemplated in *Adams* and *White* does not justify a stop and frisk whenever and however it alleges the illegal possession of a firearm.

The judgment of the Florida Supreme Court is affirmed.

It is so ordered.

JUSTICE KENNEDY, with whom THE CHIEF JUSTICE joins, concurring.

On the record created at the suppression hearing, the Court's decision is correct. The Court says all that is necessary to resolve this case, and I join the opinion in all respects. It might be noted, however, that there are many indicia of reliability respecting anonymous tips that we have yet to explore in our cases.

When a police officer testifies that a suspect aroused the officer's suspicion, and so justifies a stop and frisk, the courts can weigh the officer's credibility and admit evidence seized pursuant to the frisk even if no one, aside from the officer and defendant themselves, was present or observed the seizure. An anonymous telephone tip without more is different, however; for even if the officer's testimony about receipt of the tip is found credible, there is a second layer of inquiry

---

[4] At oral argument, petitioner also advanced the position that J.L.'s youth made the stop and frisk valid, because it is a crime in Florida for persons under the age of 21 to carry concealed firearms. *See* FLA. STAT. § 790.01 (1997) (carrying a concealed weapon without a license is a misdemeanor), § 790.06 (2)(b) (only persons aged 21 or older may be licensed to carry concealed weapons). This contention misses the mark. Even assuming that the arresting officers could be sure that J.L. was under 21, they would have had reasonable suspicion that J.L. was engaged in criminal activity only if they could be confident that he was carrying a gun in the first place. The mere fact that a tip, if true, would describe illegal activity does not mean that the police may make a *Terry* stop without meeting the reliability requirement, and the fact that J.L. was under 21 in no way made the gun tip more reliable than if he had been an adult.

respecting the reliability of the informant that cannot be pursued. If the telephone call is truly anonymous, the informant has not placed his credibility at risk and can lie with impunity. The reviewing court cannot judge the credibility of the informant and the risk of fabrication becomes unacceptable.

On this record, then, the Court is correct in holding that the telephone tip did not justify the arresting officer's immediate stop and frisk of respondent. There was testimony that an anonymous tip came in by a telephone call and nothing more. The record does not show whether some notation or other documentation of the call was made either by a voice recording or tracing the call to a telephone number. The prosecution recounted just the tip itself and the later verification of the presence of the three young men in the circumstances the Court describes.

It seems appropriate to observe that a tip might be anonymous in some sense yet have certain other features, either supporting reliability or narrowing the likely class of informants, so that the tip does provide the lawful basis for some police action. One such feature, as the Court recognizes, is that the tip predicts future conduct of the alleged criminal. There may be others. For example, if an unnamed caller with a voice which sounds the same each time tells police on two successive nights about criminal activity which in fact occurs each night, a similar call on the third night ought not be treated automatically like the tip in the case now before us. In the instance supposed, there would be a plausible argument that experience cures some of the uncertainty surrounding the anonymity, justifying a proportionate police response. In today's case, however, the State provides us with no data about the reliability of anonymous tips. Nor do we know whether the dispatcher or arresting officer had any objective reason to believe that this tip had some particular indicia of reliability.

If an informant places his anonymity at risk, a court can consider this factor in weighing the reliability of the tip. An instance where a tip might be considered anonymous but nevertheless sufficiently reliable to justify a proportionate police response may be when an unnamed person driving a car the police officer later describes stops for a moment and, face to face, informs the police that criminal activity is occurring. This too seems to be different from the tip in the present case.

Instant caller identification is widely available to police, and, if anonymous tips are proving unreliable and distracting to police, squad cars can be sent within seconds to the location of the telephone used by the informant. Voice recording of telephone tips might, in appropriate cases, be used by police to locate the caller. It is unlawful to make false reports to the police, and the ability of the police to trace the identity of anonymous telephone informants may be a factor which lends reliability to what, years earlier, might have been considered unreliable anonymous tips.

These matters, of course, must await discussion in other cases, where the issues are presented by the record.

QUESTIONS AND NOTES

1. Was *J.L.* an easy case? Should it have been? Explain.

2.   What should the police do when they get a call such as that in *J.L.*?

3.   What danger did the Court see in allowing the frisk of J.L.?

4.   In any event, were the police justified in frisking J.L.'s companions? Did (should) *that* frisk influence the *J.L.* result? Why? Why not?

5.   Did the Court hold that anonymous tips are *never* sufficient for reasonable suspicion? If not, what did it hold? Consider that question in conjunction with Prado Navarette.

PRADO NAVARETTE v. CALIFORNIA
572 U. S. ___, 134 S. Ct. 1683 (2014)

JUSTICE THOMAS delivered the opinion of the Court.

After a 911 caller reported that a vehicle had run her off the road, a police officer located the vehicle she identified during the call and executed a traffic stop. We hold that the stop complied with the Fourth Amendment because, under the totality of the circumstances, the officer had reasonable suspicion that the driver was intoxicated.

I

On August 23, 2008, a Mendocino County 911 dispatch team for the California Highway Patrol (CHP) received a call from another CHP dispatcher in neighboring Humboldt County. The Humboldt County dispatcher relayed a tip from a 911 caller, which the Mendocino County team recorded as follows: " 'Showing southbound Highway 1 at mile marker 88, Silver Ford 150 pickup. Plate of 8-David-94925. Ran the reporting party off the roadway and was last seen approximately five [minutes] ago.' " The Mendocino County team then broadcast that information to CHP officers at 3:47 p.m.

A CHP officer heading northbound toward the reported vehicle responded to the broadcast. At 4:00 p.m., the officer passed the truck near mile marker 69. At about 4:05 p.m., after making a U-turn, he pulled the truck over. A second officer, who had separately responded to the broadcast, also arrived on the scene. As the two officers approached the truck, they smelled marijuana. A search of the truck bed revealed 30 pounds of marijuana. The officers arrested the driver, petitioner Lorenzo Prado Navarette, and the passenger, petitioner José Prado Navarette.

Petitioners moved to suppress the evidence, arguing that the traffic stop violated the Fourth Amendment because the officer lacked reasonable suspicion of criminal activity. Both the magistrate who presided over the suppression hearing and the Superior Court disagreed.[1] Petitioners pleaded guilty to transporting marijuana

---

[1] At the suppression hearing, counsel for petitioners did not dispute that the reporting party identified herself by name in the 911 call recording. Because neither the caller nor the Humboldt County dispatcher who received the call was present at the hearing, however, the prosecution did not introduce the recording into evidence. The prosecution proceeded to treat the tip as anonymous, and the lower courts followed suit.

and were sentenced to 90 days in jail plus three years of probation.

The California Court of Appeal affirmed, concluding that the officer had reasonable suspicion to conduct an investigative stop. The court reasoned that the content of the tip indicated that it came from an eyewitness victim of reckless driving, and that the officer's corroboration of the truck's description, location, and direction established that the tip was reliable enough to justify a traffic stop. Finally, the court concluded that the caller reported driving that was sufficiently dangerous to merit an investigative stop without waiting for the officer to observe additional reckless driving himself. We granted certiorari and now affirm.

II

The Fourth Amendment permits brief investigative stops — such as the traffic stop in this case — when a law enforcement officer has "a particularized and objective basis for suspecting the particular person stopped of criminal activity." *Cortez*; see also *Terry*. The "reasonable suspicion" necessary to justify such a stop "is dependent upon both the content of information possessed by police and its degree of reliability." *Alabama v. White*. The standard takes into account "the totality of the circumstances — the whole picture." Although a mere "hunch" does not create reasonable suspicion, the level of suspicion the standard requires is "considerably less than proof of wrongdoing by a preponderance of the evidence," and "obviously less" than is necessary for probable cause. *Sokolow*.

A

These principles apply with full force to investigative stops based on information from anonymous tips. We have firmly rejected the argument "that reasonable cause for a[n investigative stop] can only be based on the officer's personal observation, rather than on information supplied by another person." *Adams v. Williams*. Of course, "an anonymous tip *alone* seldom demonstrates the informant's basis of knowledge or veracity." *White* (emphasis added). That is because "ordinary citizens generally do not provide extensive recitations of the basis of their everyday observations," and an anonymous tipster's veracity is " 'by hypothesis largely unknown, and unknowable.' " But under appropriate circumstances, an anonymous tip can demonstrate "sufficient indicia of reliability to provide reasonable suspicion to make [an] investigatory stop."

Our decisions in *Alabama v. White* and *Florida v. J.L.* are useful guides. In *White*, an anonymous tipster told the police that a woman would drive from a particular apartment building to a particular motel in a brown Plymouth station wagon with a broken right tail light. The tipster further asserted that the woman would be transporting cocaine. After confirming the innocent details, officers stopped the station wagon as it neared the motel and found cocaine in the vehicle. We held that the officers' corroboration of certain details made the anonymous tip sufficiently reliable to create reasonable suspicion of criminal activity. By accurately predicting future behavior, the tipster demonstrated "a special familiarity with respondent's affairs," which in turn implied that the tipster had "access to reliable information about that individual's illegal activities." We also recognized that an informant who is proved to tell the truth about some things is more likely to tell the truth about other things, "including the claim that the object of the tip is engaged in criminal activity." (citing *Illinois v. Gates*).

In *J.L.*, by contrast, we determined that no reasonable suspicion arose from a bare-bones tip that a young black male in a plaid shirt standing at a bus stop was carrying a gun. The tipster did not explain how he knew about the gun, nor did he suggest that he had any special familiarity with the young man's affairs. As a result, police had no basis for believing "that the tipster ha[d] knowledge of concealed criminal activity." Furthermore, the tip included no predictions of future behavior that could be corroborated to assess the tipster's credibility. We accordingly concluded that the tip was insufficiently reliable to justify a stop and frisk.

B

The initial question in this case is whether the 911 call was sufficiently reliable to credit the allegation that petitioners' truck "ran the [caller] off the roadway." Even assuming for present purposes that the 911 call was anonymous, see n. 1, *supra*, we conclude that the call bore adequate indicia of reliability for the officer to credit the caller's account. The officer was therefore justified in proceeding from the premise that the truck had, in fact, caused the caller's car to be dangerously diverted from the highway.

By reporting that she had been run off the road by a specific vehicle — a silver Ford F-150 pickup, license plate 8D94925 — the caller necessarily claimed eyewitness knowledge of the alleged dangerous driving. That basis of knowledge lends significant support to the tip's reliability. See *Gates*, ("[An informant's] explicit and detailed description of alleged wrongdoing, along with a statement that the event was observed firsthand, entitles his tip to greater weight than might otherwise be the case"); *Spinelli*, (a tip of illegal gambling is less reliable when "it is not alleged that the informant personally observed [the defendant] at work or that he had ever placed a bet with him"). This is in contrast to *J.L.*, where the tip provided no basis for concluding that the tipster had actually seen the gun. Even in *White*, where we upheld the stop, there was scant evidence that the tipster had actually observed cocaine in the station wagon. We called *White* a " 'close case' " because "[k]nowledge about a person's future movements indicates some familiarity with that person's affairs, but having such knowledge does not necessarily imply that the informant knows, in particular, whether that person is carrying hidden contraband." A driver's claim that another vehicle ran her off the road, however, necessarily implies that the informant knows the other car was driven dangerously.

There is also reason to think that the 911 caller in this case was telling the truth. Police confirmed the truck's location near mile marker 69 (roughly 19 highway miles south of the location reported in the 911 call) at 4:00 p.m. (roughly 18 minutes after the 911 call). That timeline of events suggests that the caller reported the incident soon after she was run off the road. That sort of contemporaneous report has long been treated as especially reliable. In evidence law, we generally credit the proposition that statements about an event and made soon after perceiving that event are especially trustworthy because "substantial contemporaneity of event and statement negate the likelihood of deliberate or conscious misrepresentation." A similar rationale applies to a "statement relating to a startling event" — such as getting run off the road — "made while the declarant was under the stress of excitement that it caused." Unsurprisingly, 911 calls that would otherwise be inadmissible hearsay have often been admitted on those grounds. See D. Binder, Hearsay Handbook (911 calls admitted as excited utterances). There was no indication that the tip in *J.L.* (or even in *White*) was contemporaneous with the observation of criminal activity or made under the stress of excitement caused by a startling event, but those considerations weigh in favor of the caller's veracity here.

Another indicator of veracity is the caller's use of the 911 emergency system. A 911 call has some features that allow for identifying and tracing callers, and thus provide some safeguards against making false reports with immunity. See *J.L.*, (Kennedy, J., concurring). As this case illustrates, see n. 1, *supra*, 911 calls can be recorded, which provides victims with an opportunity to identify the false tipster's voice and subject him to prosecution. The 911 system also permits law enforcement to verify important information about the caller. In 1998, the Federal Communications Commission (FCC) began to require cellular carriers to relay the caller's phone number to 911 dispatchers. Beginning in 2001, carriers have been required to identify the caller's geographic location with increasing specificity. And although callers may ordinarily block call recipients from obtaining their identifying information, FCC regulations exempt 911 calls from that privilege. None of this is to suggest that tips in 911 calls are *per se* reliable. Given the foregoing technological and regulatory developments, however, a reasonable officer could conclude that a false tipster would think twice before using such a system. The caller's use of the 911 system is therefore one of the relevant circumstances that, taken together, justified the officer's reliance on the information reported in the 911 call.

C

Even a reliable tip will justify an investigative stop only if it creates reasonable suspicion that "criminal activity may be afoot." We must therefore determine whether the 911 caller's report of being run off the roadway created reasonable suspicion of an ongoing crime such as drunk driving as opposed to an isolated episode of past recklessness. ("An investigatory stop must be justified by some objective manifestation that the person stopped is, or is about to be, engaged in criminal activity"). We conclude that the behavior alleged by the 911 caller, "viewed from the standpoint of an objectively reasonable police officer, amount[s] to reasonable suspicion" of drunk driving. *Ornelas v. United States*. The stop was therefore proper.[2]

Reasonable suspicion depends on "the factual and practical considerations of everyday life on which reasonable and prudent men, not legal technicians, act." Under that commonsense approach, we can appropriately recognize certain driving behaviors as sound indicia of drunk driving. Indeed, the accumulated experience of

---

[2] Because we conclude that the 911 call created reasonable suspicion of an ongoing crime, we need not address under what circumstances a stop is justified by the need to investigate completed criminal activity. Cf. *United States v. Hensley*, 469 U.S. 221, 229 (1985).

thousands of officers suggests that these sorts of erratic behaviors are strongly correlated with drunk driving. Of course, not all traffic infractions imply intoxication. Unconfirmed reports of driving without a seatbelt or slightly over the speed limit, for example, are so tenuously connected to drunk driving that a stop on those grounds alone would be constitutionally suspect. But a reliable tip alleging the dangerous behaviors discussed above generally would justify a traffic stop on suspicion of drunk driving.

The 911 caller in this case reported more than a minor traffic infraction and more than a conclusory allegation of drunk or reckless driving. Instead, she alleged a specific and dangerous result of the driver's conduct: running another car off the highway. That conduct bears too great a resemblance to paradigmatic manifestations of drunk driving to be dismissed as an isolated example of recklessness. Running another vehicle off the road suggests lane-positioning problems, decreased vigilance, impaired judgment, or some combination of those recognized drunk driving cues. And the experience of many officers suggests that a driver who almost strikes a vehicle or another object — the exact scenario that ordinarily causes "running [another vehicle] off the roadway" — is likely intoxicated. As a result, we cannot say that the officer acted unreasonably under these circumstances in stopping a driver whose alleged conduct was a significant indicator of drunk driving.

Petitioners' attempts to second-guess the officer's reasonable suspicion of drunk driving are unavailing. It is true that the reported behavior might also be explained by, for example, a driver responding to "an unruly child or other distraction." But we have consistently recognized that reasonable suspicion "need not rule out the possibility of innocent conduct." *United States v. Arvizu.*

Nor did the absence of additional suspicious conduct, after the vehicle was first spotted by an officer, dispel the reasonable suspicion of drunk driving. It is hardly surprising that the appearance of a marked police car would inspire more careful driving for a time. Cf. *Arvizu* (" '[s]lowing down after spotting a law enforcement vehicle' " does not dispel reasonable suspicion of criminal activity). Extended observation of an allegedly drunk driver might eventually dispel a reasonable suspicion of intoxication, but the 5-minute period in this case hardly sufficed in that regard. Of course, an officer who already has such a reasonable suspicion need not surveil a vehicle at length in order to personally observe suspicious driving. See *Adams v. Williams,* (repudiating the argument that "reasonable cause for a[n investigative stop] can only be based on the officer's personal observation"). Once reasonable suspicion of drunk driving arises, "[t]he reasonableness of the officer's decision to stop a suspect does not turn on the availability of less intrusive investigatory techniques." *Sokolow.* This would be a particularly inappropriate context to depart from that settled rule, because allowing a drunk driver a second chance for dangerous conduct could have disastrous consequences.

III

Like *White,* this is a "close case." As in that case, the indicia of the 911 caller's reliability here are stronger than those in *J.L.,* where we held that a bare-bones tip was unreliable. Although the indicia present here are different from those we found sufficient in *White,* there is more than one way to demonstrate "a particularized and objective basis for suspecting the particular person stopped of criminal activity." Under the totality of the circumstances, we find the indicia of reliability in this case sufficient to provide the officer with reasonable suspicion that the driver of the reported vehicle had run another vehicle off the road. That made it reasonable under the circumstances for the officer to execute a traffic stop. We accordingly affirm.

JUSTICE SCALIA, with whom JUSTICE GINSBURG, JUSTICE SOTOMAYOR, and JUSTICE KAGAN join, dissenting.

The California Court of Appeal in this case relied on jurisprudence from the California Supreme Court (adopted as well by other courts) to the effect that "an anonymous and uncorroborated tip regarding a possibly intoxicated highway driver" provides without more the reasonable suspicion necessary to justify a stop. Today's opinion does not explicitly adopt such a departure from our normal Fourth Amendment requirement that anonymous tips must be corroborated; it purports to adhere to our prior cases, such as *Florida v. J.L.* and *Alabama v. White*. Be not deceived.

Law enforcement agencies follow closely our judgments on matters such as this, and they will identify at once our new rule: So long as the caller identifies where the car is, anonymous claims of a single instance of possibly careless or reckless driving, called in to 911, will support a traffic stop. This is not my concept, and I am sure would not be the Framers', of a people secure from unreasonable searches and seizures. I would reverse the judgment of the Court of Appeal of California.

I

The California Highway Patrol in this case knew nothing about the tipster on whose word — and that alone — they seized Lorenzo and José Prado Navarette. They did not know her name.[1] They did not know her phone number or address. They did not even know where she called from (she may have dialed in from a neighboring county).

The tipster said the truck had "[run her] off the roadway," but the police had no reason to credit that charge and many reasons to doubt it, beginning with the peculiar fact that the accusation was anonymous. "[E]liminating accountability . . . is ordinarily the very purpose of anonymity." The unnamed tipster "can lie with impunity," *J.L.*, (Kennedy, J., concurring). Anonymity is especially suspicious with respect to the call that is the subject of the present case. When does a victim complain to the police about an arguably criminal act (running the victim off the road) without giving his identity, so that he can accuse and testify when the culprit is caught?

The question before us, the Court agrees, is whether the "content of information possessed by police and its degree of reliability" gave the officers reasonable suspicion that the driver of the truck (Lorenzo) was committing an ongoing crime.

---

[1] There was some indication below that the tipster was a woman. Beyond that detail, we must, as the Court notes, n. 1, assume that the identity of the tipster was unknown.

When the only source of the government's information is an informant's tip, we ask whether the tip bears sufficient " 'indicia of reliability' " to establish "a particularized and objective basis for suspecting the particular person stopped of criminal activity." *Cortez*.

The most extreme case, before this one, in which an anonymous tip was found to meet this standard was *White*. There the reliability of the tip was established by the fact that it predicted the target's behavior in the finest detail — a detail that could be known only by someone familiar with the target's business: She would, the tipster said, leave a particular apartment building, get into a brown Plymouth station wagon with a broken right tail light, and drive immediately to a particular motel. Very few persons would have such intimate knowledge, and hence knowledge of the unobservable fact that the woman was carrying unlawful drugs was plausible. Here the Court makes a big deal of the fact that the tipster was dead right about the fact that a silver Ford F-150 truck (license plate 8D94925) was traveling south on Highway 1 somewhere near mile marker 88. But everyone in the world who saw the car would have that knowledge, and anyone who wanted the car stopped would have to provide that information. Unlike the situation in *White*, that generally available knowledge in no way makes it plausible that the tipster saw the car run someone off the road.

The Court says that "[b]y reporting that she had been run off the road by a specific vehicle . . . the caller necessarily claimed eyewitness knowledge." So what? The issue is not how she claimed to know, but whether what she claimed to know was true. The claim to "eyewitness knowledge" of being run off the road supports *not at all* its veracity; nor does the amazing, mystifying prediction (so far short of what existed in *White*) that the petitioners' truck *would be heading south on Highway 1*.

The Court finds "reason to think" that the informant "was telling the truth" in the fact that police observation confirmed that the truck had been driving near the spot at which, and at the approximate time at which, the tipster alleged she had been run off the road. According to the Court, the statement therefore qualifies as a "present sense impression" or "excited utterance," kinds of hearsay that the law deems categorically admissible given their low likelihood of reflecting "deliberate or conscious misrepresentation." So, the Court says, we can fairly suppose that the accusation was true.

No, we cannot. To begin with, it is questionable whether either the "present sense impression" or the "excited utterance" exception to the hearsay rule applies here. The classic "present sense impression" is the recounting of an event that is occurring before the declarant's eyes, as the declarant is speaking ("I am watching the Hindenburg explode!"). And the classic "excited utterance" is a statement elicited, almost involuntarily, by the shock of what the declarant is immediately witnessing ("My God, those people will be killed!"). It is the immediacy that gives the statement some credibility; the declarant has not had time to dissemble or embellish. There is no such immediacy here. The declarant had time to observe the license number of the offending vehicle, 8D94925 (a difficult task if she was forced off the road and the vehicle was speeding away), to bring her car to a halt, to copy down the observed license number (presumably), and (if she was using her own cell phone) to dial a call to the police from the stopped car. Plenty of time to dissemble or embellish.

Moreover, even assuming that less than true immediacy will suffice for these hearsay exceptions to apply, the tipster's statement would run into additional barriers to admissibility and acceptance. According to the very Advisory Committee's Notes from which the Court quotes, cases addressing an unidentified declarant's present sense impression "indicate hesitancy in upholding the statement alone as sufficient" proof of the reported event. In sum, it is unlikely that the law of evidence would deem the mystery caller in this case "especially trustworthy."

Finally, and least tenably, the Court says that another "indicator of veracity" is the anonymous tipster's mere "use of the 911 emergency system." Because, you see, recent "technological and regulatory developments" suggest that the identities of unnamed 911 callers are increasingly less likely to remain unknown. Indeed, the systems are able to identify "the caller's geographic location with increasing specificity." *Amici* disagree with this, see Brief for National Association of Criminal Defense Lawyers, and the present case surely suggests that *amici* are right — since we know neither the identity of the tipster nor even the county from which the call was made. But assuming the Court is right about the ease of identifying 911 callers, it proves absolutely nothing in the present case unless the anonymous caller was *aware* of that fact. "It is the tipster's *belief* in anonymity, not its *reality*, that will control his behavior." (emphasis added). There is no reason to believe that your average anonymous 911 tipster is aware that 911 callers are readily identifiable.[2]

II

All that has been said up to now assumes that the anonymous caller made, at least in effect, an accusation of drunken driving. But in fact she did not. She said that the petitioners' truck " '[r]an [me] off the roadway.' " That neither asserts that the driver was drunk nor even raises the *likelihood* that the driver was drunk. The most it conveys is that the truck did some apparently nontypical thing that forced the tipster off the roadway, whether partly or fully, temporarily or permanently. Who really knows what (if anything) happened? The truck might have swerved to avoid an animal, a pothole, or a jaywalking pedestrian.

But let us assume the worst of the many possibilities: that it was a careless, reckless, or even intentional maneuver that forced the tipster off the road. Lorenzo might have been distracted by his use of a hands-free cell phone or distracted by an intense sports argument with José. Or, indeed, he might have intentionally forced the tipster off the road because of some personal animus, or hostility to her "Make Love, Not War" bumper sticker. I fail to see how reasonable suspicion of a *discrete instance* of irregular or hazardous driving generates a reasonable suspicion of *ongoing intoxicated driving*. What proportion of the hundreds of thousands — perhaps millions — of careless, reckless, or intentional traffic violations committed

---

[2] The Court's discussion of reliable 911 traceability has so little relevance to the present case that one must surmise it has been included merely to assure officers in the future that anonymous 911 accusations — even untraced ones — are not as suspect (and hence as unreliable) as other anonymous accusations. That is unfortunate.

each day is attributable to drunken drivers? I say 0.1 percent. I have no basis for that except my own guesswork. But unless the Court has some basis in reality to believe that the proportion is many orders of magnitude above that — say 1 in 10 or at least 1 in 20 — it has no grounds for its unsupported assertion that the tipster's report in this case gave rise to a *reasonable suspicion* of drunken driving.

Bear in mind that that is the only basis for the stop that has been asserted in this litigation. The stop required suspicion of an ongoing crime, not merely suspicion of having run someone off the road earlier. And driving while being a careless or reckless person, unlike driving while being a drunk person, is not an ongoing crime. In other words, in order to stop the petitioners the officers here not only had to assume without basis the accuracy of the anonymous accusation but also had to posit an unlikely reason (drunkenness) for the accused behavior.

In sum, at the moment the police spotted the truck, it was more than merely *"possib[le]"* that the petitioners were not committing an ongoing traffic crime. *United States v. Arvizu*, (emphasis added). It was overwhelmingly likely that they were not.

III

It gets worse. Not only, it turns out, did the police have no good reason *at first* to believe that Lorenzo was driving drunk, they had very good reason *at last* to know that he was not. The Court concludes that the tip, plus confirmation of the truck's location, produced reasonable suspicion that the truck not only had been *but still* was barreling dangerously and drunkenly down Highway 1. In fact, alas, it was not, and the officers knew it. They followed the truck for five minutes, presumably to see if it was being operated recklessly. And *that* was good police work. While the anonymous tip was not enough to support a stop for drunken driving under *Terry v. Ohio*, it was surely enough to counsel observation of the truck to see if it was driven by a drunken driver. But the pesky little detail left out of the Court's reasonable-suspicion equation is that, for the five minutes that the truck was being followed (five minutes is a *long* time), Lorenzo's driving was irreproachable. Had the officers witnessed the petitioners violate a single traffic law, they would have had cause to stop the truck, and this case would not be before us. And not only was the driving *irreproachable*, but the State offers no evidence to suggest that the petitioners even did anything *suspicious*, such as suddenly slowing down, pulling off to the side of the road, or turning somewhere to see whether they were being followed. Cf. *Arvizu*. Consequently, the tip's suggestion of ongoing drunken driving (if it could be deemed to suggest that) not only went uncorroborated; it was affirmatively undermined.?

A hypothetical variation on the facts of this case illustrates the point. Suppose an anonymous tipster reports that, while following near mile marker 88 a silver Ford F-150, license plate 8D949925, traveling southbound on Highway 1, she saw in the truck's open cab several five-foot-tall stacks of what was unmistakably baled cannabis. Two minutes later, a highway patrolman spots the truck exactly where the tip suggested it would be, begins following it, but sees nothing in the truck's cab. It is not enough to say that the officer's observation merely failed to corroborate the tipster's accusation. It is more precise to say that the officer's observation *discredited* the informant's accusation: The crime was supposedly occurring (and would continue to occur) in plain view, but the police saw nothing. Similarly, here, the crime supposedly suggested by the tip was ongoing intoxicated driving, the hallmarks of which are many, readily identifiable, and difficult to conceal. That the officers witnessed nary a minor traffic violation nor any other "sound indici[um] of drunk driving," strongly suggests that the suspected crime was *not* occurring after all. The tip's implication of continuing criminality, already weak, grew even weaker.

Resisting this line of reasoning, the Court curiously asserts that, since drunk drivers who see marked squad cars in their rearview mirrors may evade detection simply by driving "more careful[ly]," the "absence of additional suspicious conduct" is "hardly surprising" and thus largely irrelevant. Whether a drunk driver drives drunkenly, the Court seems to think, is up to him. That is not how I understand the influence of alcohol. I subscribe to the more traditional view that the dangers of intoxicated driving are the intoxicant's impairing effects on the body — effects that no mere act of the will can resist.

Consistent with this view, I take it as a fundamental premise of our intoxicated-driving laws that a driver soused enough to swerve once can be expected to swerve again — and soon. If he does not, and if the only evidence of his first episode of irregular driving is a mere inference from an uncorroborated, vague, and nameless tip, then the Fourth Amendment requires that he be left alone.

*   *   *

The Court's opinion serves up a freedom-destroying cocktail consisting of two parts patent falsity: (1) that anonymous 911 reports of traffic violations are reliable so long as they correctly identify a car and its location, and (2) that a single instance of careless or reckless driving necessarily supports a reasonable suspicion of drunkenness. All the malevolent 911 caller need do is assert a traffic violation, and the targeted car will be stopped, forcibly if necessary, by the police. If the driver turns out not to be drunk (which will almost always be the case), the caller need fear no consequences, even if 911 knows his identity. After all, he never alleged drunkenness, but merely called in a traffic violation — and on that point his word is as good as his victim's.

Drunken driving is a serious matter, but so is the loss of our freedom to come and go as we please without police interference. To prevent and detect murder we do not allow searches without probable cause or targeted *Terry* stops without reasonable suspicion. We should not do so for drunken driving either. After today's opinion all of us on the road, and not just drug dealers, are at risk of having our freedom of movement curtailed on suspicion of drunkenness, based upon a phone tip, true or false, of a single instance of careless driving. I respectfully dissent.

QUESTIONS AND NOTES

1.   Do you think that there was reasonable suspicion of drunk driving? Does Thomas overstate the probability? Does Scalia understate it? How high should the probability be?

2. Is your answer to question 1 effected by the fact that Prado Navarrete drove perfectly while being followed for five minutes? Why? Why not?

3. Apart from possible intoxication, is there any basis for this stop? Explain.

4. Consider footnote 1. The Court appears to concede that the case treats the name of the caller as unknown. At the same time, the footnote emphasizes that the caller was in fact identified by name. Does (should) that make a difference.

5. In regard to question 4, if the caller had somehow managed to hide her identity entirely, would (should) the result have been the same?

6. Was this case more like *White* or more like *J.L.*? Was it stronger than both? Weaker than both? Explain.

7. This case was the second time in two terms (*see Maryland v. King, infra*) where the Court rejected a Fourth Amendment case by a 5-4 vote with Scalia and the three women dissenting.

8. In *Illinois v. Wardlow*, the Court upheld a stop when the suspect appeared to run at the sight of an approaching police officer, but refrained from adopting a *per se* rule.

ILLINOIS v. WARDLOW
528 U.S. 119 (2000)

CHIEF JUSTICE REHNQUIST delivered the opinion of the Court.

Respondent Wardlow fled upon seeing police officers patrolling an area known for heavy narcotics trafficking. Two of the officers caught up with him, stopped him and conducted a protective pat-down search for weapons. Discovering a .38-caliber handgun, the officers arrested Wardlow. We hold that the officers' stop did not violate the Fourth Amendment to the United States Constitution.

On September 9, 1995, Officers Nolan and Harvey were working as uniformed officers in the special operations section of the Chicago Police Department. The officers were driving the last car of a four car caravan converging on an area known for heavy narcotics trafficking in order to investigate drug transactions. The officers were traveling together because they expected to find a crowd of people in the area, including lookouts and customers.

As the caravan passed 4035 West Van Buren, Officer Nolan observed respondent Wardlow standing next to the building holding an opaque bag. Respondent looked in the direction of the officers and fled. Nolan and Harvey turned their car southbound, watched him as he ran through the gangway and an alley, and eventually cornered him on the street. Nolan then exited his car and stopped respondent. He immediately conducted a protective pat-down search for weapons because in his experience it was common for there to be weapons in the near vicinity of narcotics transactions. During the frisk, Officer Nolan squeezed the bag respondent was carrying and felt a heavy, hard object similar to the shape of a gun. The officer then opened the bag and discovered a .38-caliber handgun with five live rounds of ammunition. The officers arrested Wardlow.

This case, involving a brief encounter between a citizen and a police officer on a public street, is governed by the analysis we first applied in *Terry v. Ohio*. In *Terry*, we held that an officer may, consistent with the Fourth Amendment, conduct a brief, investigatory stop when the officer has a reasonable, articulable suspicion that criminal activity is afoot. While "reasonable suspicion" is a less demanding standard than probable cause and requires a showing considerably less than preponderance of the evidence, the Fourth Amendment requires at least a minimal level of objective justification for making the stop. *United States v. Sokolow*. The officer must be able to articulate more than an "inchoate and unparticularized suspicion or 'hunch' " of criminal activity.[2]

Nolan and Harvey were among eight officers in a four car caravan that was converging on an area known for heavy narcotics trafficking, and the officers anticipated encountering a large number of people in the area, including drug customers and individuals serving as lookouts. It was in this context that Officer Nolan decided to investigate Wardlow after observing him flee. An individual's presence in an area of expected criminal activity, standing alone, is not enough to support a reasonable, particularized suspicion that the person is committing a crime. *Brown v. Texas*, 443 U.S. 47 (1979). But officers are not required to ignore the relevant characteristics of a location in determining whether the circumstances are sufficiently suspicious to warrant further investigation. Accordingly, we have previously noted the fact that the stop occurred in a "high crime area" among the relevant contextual considerations in a *Terry* analysis. *Adams v. Williams*.

In this case, moreover, it was not merely respondent's presence in an area of heavy narcotics trafficking that aroused the officers' suspicion but his unprovoked flight upon noticing the police. Our cases have also recognized that nervous, evasive behavior is a pertinent factor in determining reasonable suspicion. *United States v. Brignoni-Ponce*, 422 U.S. 873, 885 (1975); *Florida v. Rodriguez*, 469 U.S. 1, 6 (1984) (per curiam); *United States v. Sokolow*. Headlong flight — wherever it occurs — is the consummate act of evasion: it is not necessarily indicative of wrongdoing, but it is certainly suggestive of such. In reviewing the propriety of an officer's conduct, courts do not have available empirical studies dealing with inferences drawn from suspicious behavior, and we cannot reasonably demand scientific certainty from judges or law enforcement officers where none exists. Thus, the determination of reasonable suspicion must be based on commonsense judgments and inferences about human behavior. *See United States v. Cortez*. We conclude Officer Nolan was justified in suspecting that Wardlow was involved in criminal activity, and, therefore, in investigating further.

Such a holding is entirely consistent with our decision in *Florida v. Royer*, where we held that when an officer, without reasonable suspicion or probable cause, approaches an individual, the individual has a right to ignore the police and go about his business. And any "refusal to cooperate, without more, does not furnish the minimal level of objective justification needed for a detention or seizure." *Florida v. Bostick*, 501 U.S. 429, 437 (1991). But unprovoked flight is simply not a mere refusal to cooperate. Flight, by its very nature, is not "going about one's business"; in fact,

---

[2] We granted certiorari solely on the question of whether the initial stop was supported by reasonable suspicion. Therefore, we express no opinion as to the lawfulness of the frisk independently of the stop.

it is just the opposite. Allowing officers confronted with such flight to stop the fugitive and investigate further is quite consistent with the individual's right to go about his business or to stay put and remain silent in the face of police questioning.

Respondent and *amici* also argue that there are innocent reasons for flight from police and that, therefore, flight is not necessarily indicative of ongoing criminal activity. This fact is undoubtedly true, but does not establish a violation of the Fourth Amendment. Even in *Terry*, the conduct justifying the stop was ambiguous and susceptible of an innocent explanation. The officer observed two individuals pacing back and forth in front of a store, peering into the window and periodically conferring. All of this conduct was by itself lawful, but it also suggested that the individuals were casing the store for a planned robbery. *Terry* recognized that the officers could detain the individuals to resolve the ambiguity.

In allowing such detentions, *Terry* accepts the risk that officers may stop innocent people. Indeed, the Fourth Amendment accepts that risk in connection with more drastic police action; persons arrested and detained on probable cause to believe they have committed a crime may turn out to be innocent. The *Terry* stop is a far more minimal intrusion, simply allowing the officer to briefly investigate further. If the officer does not learn facts rising to the level of probable cause, the individual must be allowed to go on his way. But in this case the officers found respondent in possession of a handgun, and arrested him for violation of an Illinois firearms statute. No question of the propriety of the arrest itself is before us.

The judgment of the Supreme Court of Illinois is reversed, and the cause is remanded for further proceedings not inconsistent with this opinion.

It is so ordered.

JUSTICE STEVENS, with whom JUSTICE SOUTER, JUSTICE GINSBURG, and JUSTICE BREYER join, concurring in part and dissenting in part.

The State of Illinois asks this Court to announce a "bright-line rule" authorizing the temporary detention of anyone who flees at the mere sight of a police officer. Respondent counters by asking us to adopt the opposite *per se* rule — that the fact that a person flees upon seeing the police can never, by itself, be sufficient to justify a temporary investigative stop of the kind authorized by *Terry*.

The Court today wisely endorses neither *per se* rule. Instead, it rejects the proposition that "flight is . . . necessarily indicative of ongoing criminal activity," adhering to the view that "the concept of reasonable suspicion . . . is not readily, or even usefully, reduced to a neat set of legal rules," but must be determined by looking to "the totality of the circumstances — the whole picture." Abiding by this framework, the Court concludes that "Officer Nolan was justified in suspecting that Wardlow was involved in criminal activity."

Although I agree with the Court's rejection of the *per se* rules proffered by the parties, unlike the Court, I am persuaded that in this case the brief testimony of the officer who seized respondent does not justify the conclusion that he had reasonable suspicion to make the stop. Before discussing the specific facts of this case, I shall comment on the parties' requests for a *per se* rule.

I

In *Terry v. Ohio*, we first recognized "that a police officer may in appropriate circumstances and in an appropriate manner approach a person for purposes of investigating possibly criminal behavior even though there is no probable cause to make an arrest," an authority permitting the officer to "stop and briefly detain a person for investigative purposes." We approved as well "a reasonable search for weapons for the protection of the police officer, where he has reason to believe that he is dealing with an armed and dangerous individual, regardless of whether he has probable cause to arrest the individual for a crime." Cognizant that such police intrusion had never before received constitutional imprimatur on less than probable cause, we reflected upon the magnitude of the departure we were endorsing. "Even a limited search," we said, "constitutes a severe, though brief, intrusion upon cherished personal security, and it must be an annoying, frightening, and perhaps humiliating experience."

Accordingly, we recognized only a "narrowly drawn authority" that is "limited to that which is necessary for the discovery of weapons." An officer conducting an investigatory stop, we further explained, must articulate "a particularized and objective basis for suspecting the particular person stopped of criminal activity." *Cortez*. That determination, we admonished, "becomes meaningful only when it is assured that at some point the conduct of those charged with enforcing the laws can be subjected to the more detached, neutral scrutiny of a judge who must evaluate the reasonableness of a particular search or seizure in light of the particular circumstances." In undertaking that neutral scrutiny "based on all of the circumstances," a court relies on "certain commonsense conclusions about human behavior." "The relevant inquiry" concerning the inferences and conclusions a court draws "is not whether particular conduct is 'innocent' or 'guilty,' but the degree of suspicion that attaches to particular types of noncriminal acts." *Sokolow*.

The question in this case concerns "the degree of suspicion that attaches to" a person's flight — or, more precisely, what "commonsense conclusions" can be drawn respecting the motives behind that flight. A pedestrian may break into a run for a variety of reasons — to catch up with a friend a block or two away, to seek shelter from an impending storm, to arrive at a bus stop before the bus leaves, to get home in time for dinner, to resume jogging after a pause for rest, to avoid contact with a bore or a bully, or simply to answer the call of nature — any of which might coincide with the arrival of an officer in the vicinity. A pedestrian might also run because he or she has just sighted one or more police officers. In the latter instance, the State properly points out "that the fleeing person may be, *inter alia*, (1) an escapee from jail; (2) wanted on a warrant, (3) in possession of contraband, (*i.e.* drugs, weapons, stolen goods, etc.); or (4) someone who has just committed another type of crime."[2] In short, there are unquestionably circumstances in which

---

[2] If the fleeing person exercises his or her right to remain silent after being stopped, only in the third of the State's four hypothetical categories is the stop likely to lead to probable cause to make an arrest. And even in the third category, flight does not necessarily indicate that the officer is "dealing with an armed and dangerous individual." *Terry*.

a person's flight is suspicious, and undeniably instances in which a person runs for entirely innocent reasons.[3]

Given the diversity and frequency of possible motivations for flight, it would be profoundly unwise to endorse either *per se* rule. The inference we can reasonably draw about the motivation for a person's flight, rather, will depend on a number of different circumstances. Factors such as the time of day, the number of people in the area, the character of the neighborhood, whether the officer was in uniform, the way the runner was dressed, the direction and speed of the flight, and whether the person's behavior was otherwise unusual might be relevant in specific cases. This number of variables is surely sufficient to preclude either a bright-line rule that always justifies, or that never justifies, an investigative stop based on the sole fact that flight began after a police officer appeared nearby.[4]

Still, Illinois presses for a *per se* rule regarding "unprovoked flight upon seeing a clearly identifiable police officer." The phrase "upon seeing," as used by Illinois, apparently assumes that the flight is motivated by the presence of the police officer.[5] Illinois contends that unprovoked flight is "an extreme reaction" because innocent people simply do not "flee at the mere sight of the police." To be sure, Illinois concedes, an innocent person — even one distrustful of the police — might "avoid eye contact or even sneer at the sight of an officer," and that would not justify a *Terry* stop or any sort of *per se* inference. But, Illinois insists, unprovoked flight is altogether different. Such behavior is so "aberrant" and "abnormal" that a *per se* inference is justified.

Even assuming we know that a person runs because he sees the police, the inference to be drawn may still vary from case to case. Flight to escape police detection, we have said, may have an entirely innocent motivation:

---

[3] Compare, *e.g.*, Proverbs 28:1 ("The wicked flee when no man pursueth: but the righteous are as bold as a lion") with Proverbs 22:3 ("A shrewd man sees trouble coming and lies low; the simple walk into it and pay the penalty").

I have rejected reliance on the former proverb in the past, because its "ivory-towered analysis of the real world" fails to account for the experiences of many citizens of this country, particularly those who are minorities. *See California v. Hodari D.*, 499 U.S. 621, 630, n. 4 (1991) (Stevens, J., dissenting). That this pithy expression fails to capture the total reality of our world, however, does not mean it is inaccurate in all instances.

[4] Of course, *Terry* itself recognized that sometimes behavior giving rise to reasonable suspicion is entirely innocent, but it accepted the risk that officers may stop innocent people. And as the Court correctly observes, it is "undoubtedly true" that innocent explanations for flight exist, but they do not "establish a violation of the Fourth Amendment." It is equally true, however, that the innocent explanations make the single act of flight sufficiently ambiguous to preclude the adoption of a *per se* rule.

In *Terry*, furthermore, reasonable suspicion was supported by a concatenation of acts, each innocent when viewed in isolation, that when considered collectively amounted to extremely suspicious behavior. Flight alone, however, is not at all like a "series of acts, each of them perhaps innocent in itself, but which taken together warrant further investigation." Nor is flight similar to evidence which in the aggregate provides "fact on fact and clue on clue affording a basis for the deductions and inferences," supporting reasonable suspicion. *Cortez.*

[5] Nowhere in Illinois' briefs does it specify what it means by "unprovoked." At oral argument, Illinois explained that if officers precipitate a flight by threats of violence, that flight is "provoked." But if police officers in a patrol car — with lights flashing and siren sounding — descend upon an individual for the sole purpose of seeing if he or she will run, the ensuing flight is "unprovoked."

[I]t is a matter of common knowledge that men who are entirely innocent do sometimes fly from the scene of a crime through fear of being apprehended as the guilty parties, or from an unwillingness to appear as witnesses. Nor is it true as an accepted axiom of criminal law that "the wicked flee when no man pursueth, but the righteous are as bold as a lion." Innocent men sometimes hesitate to confront a jury — not necessarily because they fear that the jury will not protect them, but because they do not wish their names to appear in connection with criminal acts, are humiliated at being obliged to incur the popular odium of an arrest and trial, or because they do not wish to be put to the annoyance or expense of defending themselves.

Alberty v. United States, 162 U.S. 499, 511 (1896).

In addition to these concerns, a reasonable person may conclude that an officer's sudden appearance indicates nearby criminal activity. And where there is criminal activity there is also a substantial element of danger — either from the criminal or from a confrontation between the criminal and the police. These considerations can lead to an innocent and understandable desire to quit the vicinity with all speed.[6]

Among some citizens, particularly minorities and those residing in high crime areas, there is also the possibility that the fleeing person is entirely innocent, but, with or without justification, believes that contact with the police can itself be dangerous, apart from any criminal activity associated with the officer's sudden presence.[7] For such a person, unprovoked flight is neither "aberrant" nor "abnormal."[8] Moreover, these concerns and fears are known to the police officers

---

[6] Statistical studies of bystander victimization are rare. One study attributes this to incomplete recordkeeping and a lack of officially compiled data. *See* Sherman, Steele, Laufersweiler, Hooper & Julian, *Stray Bullets and "Mushrooms": Random Shootings of Bystanders in Four Cities, 1977–1988*, 5 JOURNAL OF QUANTITATIVE CRIMINOLOGY 297, 303 (1989). Nonetheless, that study, culling data from newspaper reports in four large cities over an 11-year period, found "substantial increases in reported bystander killings and woundings in all four cities." From 1986 to 1988, for example, the study identified 250 people who were killed or wounded in bystander shootings in the four survey cities. Most significantly for the purposes of the present case, the study found that such incidents "rank at the top of public outrage." The saliency of this phenomenon, in turn, "violate[s] the routine assumptions" of day-to-day affairs, and, "[w]ith enough frequency . . . it shapes the conduct of daily life."

[7] *See* Casimir, *Minority Men: We Are Frisk Targets*, N.Y. DAILY NEWS, Mar. 26, 1999, p. 34 (informal survey of 100 young black and Hispanic men living in New York City; 81 reported having been stopped and frisked by police at least once; none of the 81 stops resulted in arrests); Brief for NAACP Legal Defense & Educational Fund as *Amicus Curiae* 17–19 (reporting figures on disproportionate street stops of minority residents in Pittsburgh and Philadelphia, Pennsylvania, and St. Petersburg, Florida); U.S. Dept. of Justice, Bureau of Justice Statistics, S. Smith, Criminal Victimization and Perceptions of Community Safety in 12 Cities 25 (June 1998) (African-American residents in 12 cities are more than twice as likely to be dissatisfied with police practices than white residents in same community).

[8] *See, e.g.*, Kotlowitz, *Hidden Casualties: Drug War's Emphasis on Law Enforcement Takes a Toll on Police*, Wall Street Journal, Jan. 11, 1991, p. A2, col. 1 ("Black leaders complained that innocent people were picked up in the drug sweeps . . . . Some teen-agers were so scared of the task force they ran even if they weren't selling drugs").

Many stops never lead to an arrest, which further exacerbates the perceptions of discrimination felt by racial minorities and people living in high crime areas. *See* Goldberg, *The Color of Suspicion*, N.Y. TIMES MAGAZINE, June 20, 1999, p. 85 (reporting that in 2-year period, New York City Police Department Street Crimes Unit made 45,000 stops, only 9,500, or 20%, of which resulted in arrest); Casimir, *supra*,

themselves,[9] and are validated by law enforcement investigations into their own practices.[10] Accordingly, the evidence supporting the reasonableness of these beliefs is too pervasive to be dismissed as random or rare, and too persuasive to be disparaged as inconclusive or insufficient.[11] In any event, just as we do not require "scientific certainty" for our commonsense conclusion that unprovoked flight can sometimes indicate suspicious motives, neither do we require scientific certainty to conclude that unprovoked flight can occur for other, innocent reasons.[12]

The probative force of the inferences to be drawn from flight is a function of the varied circumstances in which it occurs. Sometimes those inferences are entirely consistent with the presumption of innocence, sometimes they justify further investigation, and sometimes they justify an immediate stop and search for

---

n.7 (reporting that in 1997, New York City's Street Crimes Unit conducted 27,061 stop-and-frisks, only 4,647 of which, 17%, resulted in arrest). Even if these data were race neutral, they would still indicate that society as a whole is paying a significant cost in infringement on liberty by these virtually random stops.

[9] The Chief of the Washington, D.C., Metropolitan Police Department, for example, confirmed that "sizeable percentages of Americans today — especially Americans of color — still view policing in the United States to be discriminatory, if not by policy and definition, certainly in its day-to-day application."

[10] New Jersey's Attorney General, in a recent investigation into allegations of racial profiling on the New Jersey Turnpike, concluded that "minority motorists have been treated differently [by New Jersey State Troopers] than non-minority motorists during the course of traffic stops on the New Jersey Turnpike." "The problem of disparate treatment is real — not imagined," declared the Attorney General. Not surprisingly, the report concluded that this disparate treatment "engenders feelings of fear, resentment, hostility, and mistrust by minority citizens."

Likewise, the Massachusetts Attorney General investigated similar allegations of egregious police conduct toward minorities. The report stated:

> We conclude that Boston police officers engaged in improper, and unconstitutional, conduct in the 1989–90 period with respect to stops and searches of minority individuals . . . . Although we cannot say with precision how widespread this illegal conduct was, we believe that it was sufficiently common to justify changes in certain Department practices.
>
> Perhaps the most disturbing evidence was that the scope of a number of *Terry* searches went far beyond anything authorized by that case and indeed, beyond anything that we believe would be acceptable under the federal and state constitutions even where probable cause existed to conduct a full search incident to an arrest. Forcing young men to lower their trousers, or otherwise searching inside their underwear, on public streets or in public hallways, is so demeaning and invasive of fundamental precepts of privacy that it can only be condemned in the strongest terms. The fact that not only the young men themselves, but independent witnesses complained of strip searches, should be deeply alarming to all members of this community.

[11] Taking into account these and other innocent motivations for unprovoked flight leads me to reject Illinois' requested *per se* rule in favor of adhering to a totality-of-the-circumstances test. This conclusion does not, as Illinois suggests, "establish a separate *Terry* analysis based on the individual characteristics of the person seized." My rejection of a *per se* rule, of course, applies to members of all races.

It is true, as Illinois points out, that *Terry* approved of the stop and frisk procedure notwithstanding "the wholesale harassment by certain elements of the police community, of which minority groups, particularly Negroes, frequently complain." But in this passage, *Terry* simply held that such concerns would not preclude the use of the stop and frisk procedure altogether. Nowhere did *Terry* suggest that such concerns cannot inform a court's assessment of whether reasonable suspicion sufficient to justify a particular stop existed.

[12] As a general matter, local courts often have a keener and more informed sense of local police practices and events that may heighten these concerns at particular times or locations. Thus, a reviewing court may accord substantial deference to a local court's determination that fear of the police is especially acute in a specific location or at a particular time.

weapons. These considerations have led us to avoid categorical rules concerning a person's flight and the presumptions to be drawn therefrom:

> Few things . . . distinguish an enlightened system of judicature from a rude and barbarous one more than the manner in which they deal with evidence. The former weighs testimony, whilst the latter, conscious perhaps of its inability to do so or careless of the consequences of error, at times rejects whole portions *en masse*, and at others converts pieces of evidence into rules of law by investing with conclusive effect some whose probative force has been found to be in general considerable . . . . Our ancestors, observing that guilty persons usually fled from justice, adopted the hasty conclusion that it was only the guilty who did so . . . so that under the old law, a man who fled to avoid being tried for felony forfeited all his goods even though he were acquitted . . . . In modern times more correct views have prevailed, and the evasion of or flight from justice seems now nearly reduced to its true place in the administration of the criminal law, namely, that of a circumstance — a fact which it is always of importance to take into consideration, and combined with others may afford strong evidence of guilt, but which, like any other piece of presumptive evidence, it is equally absurd and dangerous to invest with infallibility.

Hickory v. United States, 160 U.S. 408, 419–420 (1896) (internal quotation marks omitted).

"Unprovoked flight," in short, describes a category of activity too broad and varied to permit a *per se* reasonable inference regarding the motivation for the activity. While the innocent explanations surely do not establish that the Fourth Amendment is always violated whenever someone is stopped solely on the basis of an unprovoked flight, neither do the suspicious motivations establish that the Fourth Amendment is never violated when a *Terry* stop is predicated on that fact alone. For these reasons, the Court is surely correct in refusing to embrace either *per se* rule advocated by the parties. The totality of the circumstances, as always, must dictate the result.

II

Guided by that totality-of-the-circumstances test, the Court concludes that Officer Nolan had reasonable suspicion to stop respondent. In this respect, my view differs from the Court's. The entire justification for the stop is articulated in the brief testimony of Officer Nolan. Some facts are perfectly clear; others are not. This factual insufficiency leads me to conclude that the Court's judgment is mistaken.

Respondent Wardlow was arrested a few minutes after noon on September 9, 1995. Nolan was part of an eight-officer, four-car caravan patrol team. The officers were headed for "one of the areas in the 11th District [of Chicago] that's high [in] narcotics traffic."[15] The reason why four cars were in the caravan was that "normally in these different areas there's an enormous amount of people, sometimes lookouts, customers." Officer Nolan testified that he was in uniform on that

---

[15] The population of the 11th district is over 98,000 people.

day, but he did not recall whether he was driving a marked or an unmarked car.

Officer Nolan and his partner were in the last of the four patrol cars that "were all caravanning eastbound down Van Buren." Nolan first observed respondent "in front of 4035 West Van Buren." Wardlow "looked in our direction and began fleeing." Nolan then "began driving southbound down the street observing [respondent] running through the gangway and the alley southbound," and observed that Wardlow was carrying a white, opaque bag under his arm. After the car turned south and intercepted respondent as he "ran right towards us," Officer Nolan stopped him and conducted a "protective search," which revealed that the bag under respondent's arm contained a loaded handgun.

This terse testimony is most noticeable for what it fails to reveal. Though asked whether he was in a marked or unmarked car, Officer Nolan could not recall the answer. He was not asked whether any of the other three cars in the caravan were marked, or whether any of the other seven officers were in uniform. Though he explained that the size of the caravan was because "normally in these different areas there's an enormous amount of people, sometimes lookouts, customers," Officer Nolan did not testify as to whether *anyone* besides Wardlow was nearby 4035 West Van Buren. Nor is it clear that that address was the intended destination of the caravan. As the Appellate Court of Illinois interpreted the record, "it appears that the officers were simply driving by, on their way to some unidentified location, when they noticed defendant standing at 4035 West Van Buren."[16] Officer Nolan's testimony also does not reveal how fast the officers were driving. It does not indicate whether he saw respondent notice the other patrol cars. And it does not say whether the caravan, or any part of it, had already passed Wardlow by before he began to run.

Indeed, the Appellate Court thought the record was even "too vague to support the inference that . . . defendant's flight was related to his expectation of police focus on him." Presumably, respondent did not react to the first three cars, and we cannot even be sure that he recognized the occupants of the fourth as police officers. The adverse inference is based entirely on the officer's statement: "He looked in our direction and began fleeing."[17]

No other factors sufficiently support a finding of reasonable suspicion. Though respondent was carrying a white, opaque bag under his arm, there is nothing at all suspicious about that. Certainly the time of day — shortly after noon — does not support Illinois' argument. Nor were the officers "responding to any call or report of suspicious activity in the area." Officer Nolan did testify that he expected to find "an enormous amount of people," including drug customers or lookouts, and the Court points out that "it was in this context that Officer Nolan decided to investigate Wardlow after observing him flee." This observation, in my view, lends insufficient weight to the reasonable suspicion analysis; indeed, in light of the

---

[16] Of course, it would be a different case if the officers had credible information respecting that specific street address which reasonably led them to believe that criminal activity was afoot in that narrowly defined area.

[17] Officer Nolan also testified that respondent "was looking *at* us," (emphasis added), though this minor clarification hardly seems sufficient to support the adverse inference.

absence of testimony that anyone else was nearby when respondent began to run, this observation points in the opposite direction.

The State, along with the majority of the Court, relies as well on the assumption that this flight occurred in a high crime area. Even if that assumption is accurate, it is insufficient because even in a high crime neighborhood unprovoked flight does not invariably lead to reasonable suspicion. On the contrary, because many factors providing innocent motivations for unprovoked flight are concentrated in high crime areas, the character of the neighborhood arguably makes an inference of guilt less appropriate, rather than more so. Like unprovoked flight itself, presence in a high crime neighborhood is a fact too generic and susceptible to innocent explanation to satisfy the reasonable suspicion inquiry. *See Brown v. Texas.*

It is the State's burden to articulate facts sufficient to support reasonable suspicion. In my judgment, Illinois has failed to discharge that burden. I am not persuaded that the mere fact that someone standing on a sidewalk looked in the direction of a passing car before starting to run is sufficient to justify a forcible stop and frisk.

I therefore respectfully dissent from the Court's judgment to reverse the court below.

QUESTIONS AND NOTES

1. Although the Court stopped short of announcing a *per se* rule that flight at the sight of an officer equals reasonable suspicion, did the Court adopt a rule that flight in a high crime area *per se* creates reasonable suspicion? If not, why was this stop permissible? If so, why should people in high crime areas be any less free to flee the police than folks in tree-lined suburbs?

2. How suspicious is flight? Is it more or less suspicious in a high crime area?

3. Do we know Wardlow's race? Should that have been relevant? Why? Why not?

4. Justice Stevens presents a much more detailed description of the facts than the Chief Justice. Is it possible (likely) that this difference in focus contributed to their different results?

5. Where should the burden of proof lie in a case like this? How significant is it that Officer Nolan didn't even know whether his car was marked? That nobody asked about whether the other cars were marked or if the other officers were in uniform?

6. How would you have decided this case? Why?

7. We continue this subsection with *Ornelas v. United States*, a case that focuses on whether questions of reasonable suspicion and probable cause are questions of fact or law.

ORNELAS v. UNITED STATES
517 U.S. 690 (1996)

CHIEF JUSTICE REHNQUIST delivered the opinion of the Court.

Petitioners each pleaded guilty to possession of cocaine with intent to distribute. They reserved their right to appeal the District Court's denial of their motion to suppress the cocaine found in their car. The District Court had found reasonable suspicion to stop and question petitioners as they entered their car, and probable cause to remove one of the interior panels where a package containing two kilos of cocaine was found. The Court of Appeals opined that the findings of reasonable suspicion to stop, and probable cause to search, should be reviewed "deferentially," and "for clear error." We hold that the ultimate questions of reasonable suspicion and probable cause to make a warrantless search should be reviewed *de novo*.

The facts are not disputed. In the early morning of a December day in 1992, Detective Michael Pautz, a 20-year veteran of the Milwaukee County Sheriff's Department with 2 years specializing in drug enforcement, was conducting drug-interdiction surveillance in downtown Milwaukee. Pautz noticed a 1981 two-door Oldsmobile with California license plates in a motel parking lot. The car attracted Pautz's attention for two reasons: because older model, two-door General Motors cars are a favorite with drug couriers because it is easy to hide things in them; and because California is a "source State" for drugs. Detective Pautz radioed his dispatcher to inquire about the car's registration. The dispatcher informed Pautz that the owner was either Miguel Ledesma Ornelas or Miguel Ornelas Ledesma from San Jose, California; Pautz was unsure which name the dispatcher gave. Detective Pautz checked the motel registry and learned that an Ismael Ornelas accompanied by a second man had registered at 4:00 a.m., without reservations.

Pautz called for his partner, Donald Hurrle, a detective with approximately 25 years of law enforcement experience, assigned for the past 6 years to the drug enforcement unit. When Hurrle arrived at the scene, the officers contacted the local office of the Drug Enforcement Administration (DEA) and asked DEA personnel to run the names Miguel Ledesma Ornelas and Ismael Ornelas through the Narcotics and Dangerous Drugs Information System (NADDIS), a federal database of known and suspected drug traffickers. Both names appeared in NADDIS. The NADDIS report identified Miguel Ledesma Ornelas as a heroin dealer from El Centro, California, and Ismael Ornelas, Jr. as a cocaine dealer from Tucson, Arizona. The officers then summoned Deputy Luedke and the department's drug-sniffing dog, Merlin. Upon their arrival, Detective Pautz left for another assignment. Detective Hurrle informed Luedke of what they knew and together they waited.

Sometime later, petitioners emerged from the motel and got into the Oldsmobile. Detective Hurrle approached the car, identified himself as a police officer, and inquired whether they had any illegal drugs or contraband. Petitioners answered "No." Hurrle then asked for identification and was given two California driver's licenses bearing the names Saul Ornelas and Ismael Ornelas. Hurrle asked them if he could search the car and petitioners consented. The men appeared calm, but

Ismael was shaking somewhat. Deputy Luedke, who over the past nine years had searched approximately 2,000 cars for narcotics, searched the Oldsmobile's interior. He noticed that a panel above the right rear passenger armrest felt somewhat loose and suspected that the panel might have been removed and contraband hidden inside. Luedke would testify later that a screw in the door jamb adjacent to the loose panel was rusty, which to him meant that the screw had been removed at some time. Luedke dismantled the panel and discovered two kilograms of cocaine. Petitioners were arrested.

Petitioners filed pretrial motions to suppress, alleging that the police officers violated their Fourth Amendment rights when the officers detained them in the parking lot and when Deputy Luedke searched inside the panel without a warrant.[1] The Government conceded in the court below that when the officers approached petitioners in the parking lot, a reasonable person would not have felt free to leave, so the encounter was an investigatory stop. An investigatory stop is permissible under the Fourth Amendment if supported by reasonable suspicion, *Terry*, and a warrantless search of a car is valid if based on probable cause, *California v. Acevedo*.

After conducting an evidentiary hearing, the Magistrate Judge concluded that the circumstances gave the officers reasonable suspicion, but not probable cause. The Magistrate found, as a finding of fact, that there was no rust on the screw and hence concluded that Deputy Luedke had an insufficient basis to conclude that drugs would be found within the panel. The Magistrate nonetheless recommended that the District Court deny the suppression motions because he thought, given the presence of the drug-sniffing dog, that the officers would have found the cocaine by lawful means eventually and therefore the drugs were admissible under the inevitable discovery doctrine. *See Nix v. Williams*.

The District Court adopted the Magistrate's recommendation with respect to reasonable suspicion, but not its reasoning as to probable cause. The District Court thought that the model, age, and source-State origin of the car, and the fact that two men traveling together checked into a motel at 4 o'clock in the morning without reservations, formed a drug-courier profile and that this profile together with the NADDIS reports gave rise to reasonable suspicion of drug-trafficking activity; in the court's view, reasonable suspicion became probable cause when Deputy Luedke found the loose panel. Accordingly, the court ruled that the cocaine need not be excluded.[2]

---

[1] Petitioners also alleged that they had not given their consent to search the interior of the car. The Magistrate Judge rejected this claim, finding that the record "clearly establishe[d] consent to search the Oldsmobile" and that "neither [petitioner] placed any restrictions on the areas the officers could search." The Magistrate ruled that this consent did not give the officers authority to search inside the panel, however, because under Seventh Circuit precedent the police may not dismantle the car body during an otherwise valid search unless the police have probable cause to believe the car's panels contain narcotics. *See United States v. Garcia*, 897 F.2d 1413, 1419–1420 (1990). We assume correct the Circuit's limitation on the scope of consent only for purposes of this decision.

[2] The District Court emphasized twice that it did not reject the Magistrate's recommendation with respect to the inevitable discovery doctrine. But on appeal the Government did not defend the seizure on this alternative ground and the Seventh Circuit considered the argument waived.

The Court of Appeals reviewed deferentially the District Court's determinations of reasonable suspicion and probable cause; it would reverse only upon a finding of "clear error."[3] The court found no clear error in the reasonable-suspicion analysis and affirmed that determination. With respect to the probable-cause finding, however, the court remanded the case for a determination on whether Luedke was credible when testifying about the loose panel.

On remand, the Magistrate Judge expressly found the testimony credible. The District Court accepted the finding, and once again ruled that probable cause supported the search. The Seventh Circuit held that determination not clearly erroneous.

We granted certiorari to resolve the conflict among the Circuits over the applicable standard of appellate review.[4]

Articulating precisely what "reasonable suspicion" and "probable cause" mean is not possible. They are commonsense, nontechnical conceptions that deal with " 'the factual and practical considerations of everyday life on which reasonable and prudent men, not legal technicians, act.' " *Gates* (quoting *Brinegar*); *see Sokolow*. As such, the standards are "not readily, or even usefully, reduced to a neat set of legal rules." We have described reasonable suspicion simply as "a particularized and objective basis" for suspecting the person stopped of criminal activity, *Cortez*, and probable cause to search as existing where the known facts and circumstances are sufficient to warrant a man of reasonable prudence in the belief that contraband or evidence of a crime will be found, *see Brinegar; Gates*. We have cautioned that these two legal principles are not "finely-tuned standards," comparable to the standards of proof beyond a reasonable doubt or of proof by a preponderance of the evidence. *Gates*. They are instead fluid concepts that take their substantive content from the particular contexts in which the standards are being assessed. ("This Cour[t] [has a] long-established recognition that standards of reasonableness under the Fourth Amendment are not susceptible of Procrustean application"; "[e]ach case is to be decided on its own facts and circumstances" *Terry* (the limitations imposed by the Fourth Amendment "will have to be developed in the concrete factual circumstances of individual cases").

The principal components of a determination of reasonable suspicion or probable cause will be the events which occurred leading up to the stop or search, and then the decision whether these historical facts, viewed from the standpoint of an

---

[3] While the Seventh Circuit uses the term "clear error" to denote the deferential standard applied when reviewing determinations of reasonable suspicion or probable cause, we think the preferable term is "abuse of discretion." "Clear error" is a term of art derived from Rule 52(a) of the Federal Rules of Civil Procedure, and applies when reviewing questions of fact.

[4] *Compare, e.g., United States v. Puerta*, 982 F.2d 1297, 1300 (9th Cir. 1992) (*de novo* review); *United States v. Ramos*, 933 F.2d 968, 972 (11th Cir. 1991) (*de novo* review), *cert. denied*, 503 U.S. 908 (1992); *United States v. Patrick*, 899 F.2d 169, 171 (2d Cir. 1990) (*de novo* review) with *United States v. Spears*, 965 F.2d 262, 268–271 (7th Cir. 1992) (clear error).

The United States, in accord with petitioners, contends that a *de novo* standard of review should apply to determinations of probable cause and reasonable suspicion. We therefore invited Peter D. Isakoff to brief and argue this case as *amicus curiae* in support of the judgment below. Mr. Isakoff accepted the appointment and has well fulfilled his assigned responsibility.

objectively reasonable police officer, amount to reasonable suspicion or to probable cause. The first part of the analysis involves only a determination of historical facts, but the second is a mixed question of law and fact: "[T]he historical facts are admitted or established, the rule of law is undisputed, and the issue is whether the facts satisfy the [relevant] statutory [or constitutional] standard, or to put it another way, whether the rule of law as applied to the established facts is or is not violated."

We think independent appellate review of these ultimate determinations of reasonable suspicion and probable cause is consistent with the position we have taken in past cases. We have never, when reviewing a probable-cause or reasonable-suspicion determination ourselves, expressly deferred to the trial court's determination. *See, e.g., Brinegar* (rejecting district court's conclusion that the police lacked probable cause); *Alabama v. White* (conducting independent review and finding reasonable suspicion). A policy of sweeping deference would permit, "[i]n the absence of any significant difference in the facts," "the Fourth Amendment's incidence [to] tur[n] on whether different trial judges draw general conclusions that the facts are sufficient or insufficient to constitute probable cause." Such varied results would be inconsistent with the idea of a unitary system of law. This, if a matter-of-course, would be unacceptable.

In addition, the legal rules for probable cause and reasonable suspicion acquire content only through application. Independent review is therefore necessary if appellate courts are to maintain control of, and to clarify the legal principles. *See Miller v. Fenton*, 474 U.S. 104, 114 (1985) (where the "relevant legal principle can be given meaning only through its application to the particular circumstances of a case, the Court has been reluctant to give the trier of fact's conclusions presumptive force and, in so doing, strip a federal appellate court of its primary function as an expositor of law").

Finally, *de novo* review tends to unify precedent and will come closer to providing law enforcement officers with a defined " 'set of rules which, in most instances, makes it possible to reach a correct determination beforehand as to whether an invasion of privacy is justified in the interest of law enforcement.' " ("[T]he law declaration aspect of independent review potentially may guide police, unify precedent, and stabilize the law," and those effects "serve legitimate law enforcement interests").

It is true that because the mosaic which is analyzed for a reasonable-suspicion or probable-cause inquiry is multi-faceted, "one determination will seldom be a useful 'precedent' for another." But there are exceptions. For instance, the circumstances in *Brinegar* and *Carroll v. United States* were so alike that we concluded that reversing the Circuit Court's decision in *Brinegar* was necessary to be faithful to *Carroll*. We likewise recognized the similarity of facts in *Sokolow* and *Royer* (in both cases, the defendant traveled under an assumed name; paid for an airline ticket in cash with a number of small bills; traveled from Miami, a source city for illicit drugs; and appeared nervous in the airport). The same was true both in *Ross* and *Acevedo* ("The facts in this case closely resemble the facts in Ross"); and in *United States v. Mendenhall*, 446 U.S. 544 (1980), and *Reid v. Georgia*, 448 U.S. 438 (1980) ("facts [in *Mendenhall*] [are] remarkably similar to those in the present case"). And even where one case may not squarely control another one, the two decisions when viewed together may usefully add to the body of law on the subject.

The Court of Appeals, in adopting its deferential standard of review here, reasoned that *de novo* review for warrantless searches would be inconsistent with the " 'great deference' " paid when reviewing a decision to issue a warrant. We cannot agree. The Fourth Amendment demonstrates a "strong preference for searches conducted pursuant to a warrant," *Gates*, and the police are more likely to use the warrant process if the scrutiny applied to a magistrate's probable-cause determination to issue a warrant is less than that for warrantless searches. Were we to eliminate this distinction, we would eliminate the incentive.

We therefore hold that as a general matter determinations of reasonable suspicion and probable cause should be reviewed *de novo* on appeal. Having said this, we hasten to point out that a reviewing court should take care both to review findings of historical fact only for clear error and to give due weight to inferences drawn from those facts by resident judges and local law enforcement officers.

A trial judge views the facts of a particular case in light of the distinctive features and events of the community; likewise a police officer views the facts through the lens of his police experience and expertise. The background facts provide a context for the historical facts, and when seen together yield inferences that deserve deference. For example, what may not amount to reasonable suspicion at a motel located alongside a transcontinental highway at the height of the summer tourist season may rise to that level in December in Milwaukee. That city is unlikely to have been an overnight stop selected at the last minute by a traveler coming from California to points east. The 85-mile width of Lake Michigan blocks any further eastward progress. And while the city's salubrious summer climate and seasonal attractions bring many tourists at that time of year, the same is not true in December. Milwaukee's average daily high temperature in that month is 31 degrees and its average daily low is 17 degrees; the percentage of possible sunshine is only 38 percent. It is a reasonable inference that a Californian stopping in Milwaukee in December is either there to transact business or to visit family or friends. The background facts, though rarely the subject of explicit findings, inform the judge's assessment of the historical facts.

In a similar vein, our cases have recognized that a police officer may draw inferences based on his own experience in deciding whether probable cause exists. To a layman the sort of loose panel below the back seat arm rest in the automobile involved in this case may suggest only wear and tear, but to Officer Luedke, who had searched roughly 2,000 cars for narcotics, it suggested that drugs may be secreted inside the panel. An appeals court should give due weight to a trial court's finding that the officer was credible and the inference was reasonable.

We vacate the judgments and remand the case to the Court of Appeals to review de novo the District Court's determinations that the officer had reasonable suspicion and probable cause in this case.

It is so ordered.

JUSTICE SCALIA, dissenting.

The Court today decides that a district court's determinations whether there was probable cause to justify a warrantless search and reasonable suspicion to make an investigatory stop should be reviewed *de novo*. We have in the past reviewed some mixed questions of law and fact on a *de novo* basis, and others on a deferential basis, depending upon essentially practical considerations. Because, with respect to the questions at issue here, the purpose of the determination and its extremely fact-bound nature will cause *de novo* review to have relatively little benefit, it is in my view unwise to require courts of appeals to undertake the searching inquiry that standard requires. I would affirm the judgment of the Court of Appeals.

As the Court recognizes, determinations of probable cause and reasonable suspicion involve a two-step process. First, a court must identify all of the relevant historical facts known to the officer at the time of the stop or search; and second, it must decide whether, under a standard of objective reasonableness, those facts would give rise to a reasonable suspicion justifying a stop or probable cause to search. Because this second step requires application of an objective legal standard to the facts, it is properly characterized as a mixed question of law and fact.

Merely labeling the issues "mixed questions," however, does not establish that they receive *de novo* review. While it is well settled that appellate courts "accep[t] findings of fact that are not 'clearly erroneous' but decid[e] questions of law de novo," there is no rigid rule with respect to mixed questions. We have said that "deferential review of mixed questions of law and fact is warranted when it appears that the district court is 'better positioned' than the appellate court to decide the issue in question or that probing appellate scrutiny will not contribute to the clarity of legal doctrine."

These primary factors that counsel in favor of deferential review of some mixed questions of law and fact-expertise of the district court and lack of law-clarifying value in the appellate decision-are ordinarily present with respect to determinations of reasonable suspicion and probable cause. The factual details bearing upon those determinations are often numerous and (even when supported by uncontroverted police testimony) subject to credibility determinations. An appellate court never has the benefit of the district court's intimate familiarity with the details of the case-nor the full benefit of its hearing of the live testimony, unless the district court makes specific findings on the "totality of the circumstances" bearing upon the stop or search.

Moreover, as the Court acknowledges, "reasonable suspicion" and "probable cause" are "commonsense, nontechnical conceptions that deal with" " 'the factual and practical considerations of everyday life on which reasonable and prudent men, not legal technicians, act.' " Where a trial court makes such commonsense determinations based on the totality of circumstances, it is ordinarily accorded deference. What we said in a case concerning the question whether certain payments were a "gift" excludable from income under the Internal Revenue Code, is equally pertinent here.

"Decision of the issue presented in these cases must be based ultimately on the application of the fact-finding tribunal's experience with the mainsprings of human conduct to the totality of the facts of each case. The nontechnical nature of the . . . standard, the close relationship of it to the data of practical human experience, and the multiplicity of relevant factual elements, with their various combinations, creating the necessity of ascribing the proper force to each, confirm us in our conclusion that primary weight in this area must be given to the conclusions of the trier of fact." *Commissioner v. Duberstein*, 363 U.S. 278, 289 (1960).

With respect to the second factor counseling in favor of deferential review, level of law-clarifying value in the appellate decision: Law clarification requires generalization, and some issues lend themselves to generalization much more than others. Thus, in *Pierce v. Underwood*, 487 U.S. 552, 562 (1988), a principal basis for our applying an abuse-of-discretion standard to a district court's determination that the United States' litigating position was "substantially justified" within the meaning of the Equal Access to Justice Act, 28 U.S.C. § 2412(d), was that the question was "a multifarious and novel question, little susceptible, for the time being at least, of useful generalization." Probable cause and reasonable suspicion determinations are similarly resistant to generalization. As the Court recognizes, these are "fluid concepts," " 'not readily, or even usefully, reduced to a neat set of legal rules' "; and "because the mosaic which is analyzed for a reasonable-suspicion or probable-cause inquiry is multifaceted, 'one determination will seldom be a useful "precedent" for another.' " The Court maintains that there will be exceptions to this-that fact-patterns will occasionally repeat themselves, so that a prior de novo appellate decision will provide useful guidance in a similar case. I do not dispute that, but I do not understand why we should allow the exception to frame the rule.

The facts of this very case illustrate the futility of attempting to craft useful precedent from the fact-intensive review demanded by determinations of probable cause and reasonable suspicion. On remand, in conducting *de novo* review, the Seventh Circuit might consider, *inter alia*, the following factors relevant to its determination whether there was probable cause to conduct a warrantless search and reasonable suspicion justifying the investigatory stop: (i) the two NADDIS tips; (ii) that the car was a 1981 two-door General Motors product; (iii) that the car was from California, a source state; (iv) that the car was in Milwaukee; (v) that it was December; (vi) that one suspect checked into the hotel at 4 a.m.; (vii) that he did not have reservations; (viii) that he had one traveling companion; (ix) that one suspect appeared calm but shaking; and (x) that there was a loose panel in the car door. If the Seventh Circuit were to find that this unique confluence of factors supported probable cause and reasonable suspicion, the absence of any one of these factors in the next case would render the precedent inapplicable.

Of course, even when all of the factors *are* replicated, use of a *de novo* standard as opposed to a deferential standard will provide greater clarity only where the latter would not suffice to set the trial court's conclusion aside. For where the appellate court holds, on the basis of deferential review, that it was reversible error for a district court to find probable cause or reasonable suspicion in light of certain facts, it advances the clarity of the law just as much as if it had reversed the district court after conducting plenary review.

In the present case, an additional factor counseling against *de novo* review must be mentioned: The prime benefit of *de novo* appellate review in criminal cases is, of course, to prevent a miscarriage of justice that might result from permitting the verdict of guilty to rest upon the legal determinations of a single judge. But the issue in these probable-cause and reasonable-suspicion cases is not innocence but deterrence of unlawful police conduct. That deterrence will not be *at all* lessened if the trial judge's determination, right or wrong, is subjected to only deferential review.

The Court is wrong in its assertion, that unless there is a dual standard of review-deferential review of a magistrate's decision to issue a warrant, and *de novo* review of a district court's *ex post facto* approval of a warrantless search-the incentive to obtain a warrant would be eliminated. In *United States v. Leon*, we held that "reliable physical evidence seized by officers reasonably relying on a warrant issued by a detached and neutral magistrate . . . should be admissible in the prosecutor's case in chief." Only a warrant can provide this assurance that the fruits of even a technically improper search will be admissible. Law enforcement officers would still have ample incentive to proceed by warrant.

Finally, I must observe that the Court does not appear to have the courage of its conclusions. In an apparent effort to reduce the unproductive burden today's decision imposes upon appellate courts, or perhaps to salvage some of the trial court's superior familiarity with the facts that it has cast aside, the Court suggests that an appellate court should give "due weight" to a trial court's finding that an officer's inference of wrongdoing (*i.e.*, his assessment of probable cause to search), was reasonable. The Court cannot have it both ways. This finding of "reasonableness" is precisely what it has told us the appellate court must review *de novo*; and in *de novo* review, the "weight due" to a trial court's finding is zero. In the last analysis, there-fore, the Court's opinion seems to me not only wrong but contra-dictory.

I would affirm the judgment of the Seventh Circuit on the ground that it correctly applied a deferential standard of review to the District Court's findings of probable cause and reasonable suspicion.

QUESTIONS AND NOTES

1. The Court says that reasonable suspicion and probable cause are incapable of precise definition. Do you agree? Didn't *Gates* define probable cause as "fair probability"?

2. Why do you suppose that the Government joined Ornelas in asking for reversal of the Circuit Court's decision? (*See* fn. 4). Isn't the Government risking reversal of its conviction?

3. If the Court can't define reasonable suspicion or probable cause anyway, does it make sense to treat it as a question of law? Explain.

4. Do you agree with Justice Scalia that the Court is trying to have it both ways in calling for *de novo* review, while urging the appellate court to give "due weight" to a trial court's finding of special police officer expertise?

5. If the facts of *Ornelas* had been an exam question, would you have (1) found reasonable suspicion, (2) found probable cause? How would you have resolved the

case? Why?

6. We conclude this section with *Arvizu*, a case which arguably gives more deference to the trial court than *Ornelas* had suggested.

UNITED STATES v. ARVIZU
534 U.S. 266 (2002)

CHIEF JUSTICE REHNQUIST delivered the opinion of the Court.

Respondent Ralph Arvizu was stopped by a border patrol agent while driving on an unpaved road in a remote area of southeastern Arizona. A search of his vehicle turned up more than 100 pounds of marijuana. The District Court for the District of Arizona denied respondent's motion to suppress, but the Court of Appeals for the Ninth Circuit reversed. In the course of its opinion, it categorized certain factors relied upon by the District Court as simply out of bounds in deciding whether there was "reasonable suspicion" for the stop. We hold that the Court of Appeals' methodology was contrary to our prior decisions and that it reached the wrong result in this case.

On an afternoon in January 1998, Agent Clinton Stoddard was working at a border patrol checkpoint along U.S. Highway 191 approximately 30 miles north of Douglas, Arizona. Douglas has a population of about 13,000 and is situated on the United States-Mexico border in the southeastern part of the State. Only two highways lead north from Douglas. Highway 191 leads north to Interstate 10, which passes through Tucson and Phoenix. State Highway 80 heads northeast through less populated areas toward New Mexico, skirting south and east of the portion of the Coronado National Forest that lies approximately 20 miles northeast of Douglas.

The checkpoint is located at the intersection of 191 and Rucker Canyon Road, an unpaved east-west road that connects 191 and the Coronado National Forest. When the checkpoint is operational, border patrol agents stop the traffic on 191 as part of a coordinated effort to stem the flow of illegal immigration and smuggling across the international border. Agents use roving patrols to apprehend smugglers trying to circumvent the checkpoint by taking the backroads, including those roads through the sparsely populated area between Douglas and the national forest. Magnetic sensors, or "intrusion devices," facilitate agents' efforts in patrolling these areas. Directionally sensitive, the sensors signal the passage of traffic that would be consistent with smuggling activities.

Sensors are located along the only other northbound road from Douglas besides Highways 191 and 80: Leslie Canyon Road. Leslie Canyon Road runs roughly parallel to 191, about halfway between 191 and the border of the Coronado National Forest, and ends when it intersects Rucker Canyon Road. It is unpaved beyond the 10-mile stretch leading out of Douglas and is very rarely traveled except for use by local ranchers and forest service personnel. Smugglers commonly try to avoid the 191 checkpoint by heading west on Rucker Canyon Road from Leslie Canyon Road and thence to Kuykendall Cutoff Road, a primitive dirt road that leads north approximately 12 miles east of 191. From there, they can gain access to Tucson and Phoenix.

Around 2:15 p.m., Stoddard received a report via Douglas radio that a Leslie Canyon Road sensor had triggered. This was significant to Stoddard for two reasons. First, it suggested to him that a vehicle might be trying to circumvent the checkpoint. Second, the timing coincided with the point when agents begin heading back to the checkpoint for a shift change, which leaves the area unpatrolled. Stoddard knew that alien smugglers did extensive scouting and seemed to be most active when agents were en route back to the checkpoint. Another border patrol agent told Stoddard that the same sensor had gone off several weeks before and that he had apprehended a minivan using the same route and witnessed the occupants throwing bundles of marijuana out the door.

Stoddard drove eastbound on Rucker Canyon Road to investigate. As he did so, he received another radio report of sensor activity. It indicated that the vehicle that had triggered the first sensor was heading westbound on Rucker Canyon Road. He continued east, passing Kuykendall Cutoff Road. He saw the dust trail of an approaching vehicle about a half mile away. Stoddard had not seen any other vehicles and, based on the timing, believed that this was the one that had tripped the sensors. He pulled off to the side of the road at a slight slant so he could get a good look at the oncoming vehicle as it passed by.

It was a minivan, a type of automobile that Stoddard knew smugglers used. As it approached, it slowed dramatically, from about 50–55 to 25–30 miles per hour. He saw five occupants inside. An adult man was driving, an adult woman sat in the front passenger seat, and three children were in the back. The driver appeared stiff and his posture very rigid. He did not look at Stoddard and seemed to be trying to pretend that Stoddard was not there. Stoddard thought this suspicious because in his experience on patrol most persons look over and see what is going on, and in that area most drivers give border patrol agents a friendly wave. Stoddard noticed that the knees of the two children sitting in the very back seat were unusually high, as if their feet were propped up on some cargo on the floor.

At that point, Stoddard decided to get a closer look, so he began to follow the vehicle as it continued westbound on Rucker Canyon Road toward Kuykendall Cutoff Road. Shortly thereafter, all of the children, though still facing forward, put their hands up at the same time and began to wave at Stoddard in an abnormal pattern. It looked to Stoddard as if the children were being instructed. Their odd waving continued on and off for about four to five minutes.

Several hundred feet before the Kuykendall Cutoff Road intersection, the driver signaled that he would turn. At one point, the driver turned the signal off, but just as he approached the intersection he put it back on and abruptly turned north onto Kuykendall. The turn was significant to Stoddard because it was made at the last place that would have allowed the minivan to avoid the checkpoint. Also, Kuykendall, though passable by a sedan or van, is rougher than either Rucker Canyon or Leslie Canyon roads, and the normal traffic is four-wheel-drive vehicles. Stoddard did not recognize the minivan as part of the local traffic agents encounter on patrol, and he did not think it likely that the minivan was going to or coming from a picnic outing. He was not aware of any picnic grounds on Turkey Creek, which could be reached by following Kuykendall Cutoff all the way up. He knew of picnic grounds and a Boy Scout camp east of the intersection of Rucker Canyon and Leslie Canyon roads, but the minivan had turned west at that intersection. And he had never seen anyone picnicking or sightseeing near where the first sensor went off. Stoddard radioed for a registration check and learned that the minivan was registered to an address in Douglas that was four blocks north of the border in an area notorious for alien and narcotics smuggling. After receiving the information, Stoddard decided to make a vehicle stop. He approached the driver and learned that his name was Ralph Arvizu. Stoddard asked if respondent would mind if he looked inside and searched the vehicle. Respondent agreed, and Stoddard discovered marijuana in a black duffel bag under the feet of the two children in the back seat. Another bag containing marijuana was behind the rear seat. In all, the van contained 128.85 pounds of marijuana, worth an estimated $99,080.

Respondent was charged with possession with intent to distribute marijuana. He moved to suppress the marijuana, arguing among other things that Stoddard did not have reasonable suspicion to stop the vehicle as required by the Fourth Amendment. After holding a hearing where Stoddard and respondent testified, the District Court for the District of Arizona ruled otherwise. It pointed to a number of the facts described above and noted particularly that any recreational areas north of Rucker Canyon would have been accessible from Douglas via 191 and another paved road, making it unnecessary to take a 40-to-50-mile trip on dirt roads.

The Court of Appeals for the Ninth Circuit reversed. In its view, fact-specific weighing of circumstances or other multifactor tests introduced "a troubling degree of uncertainty and unpredictability" into the Fourth Amendment analysis. It therefore "attempt[ed] . . . to describe and clearly delimit the extent to which certain factors may be considered by law enforcement officers in making stops such as the stop involv[ing]" respondent. After characterizing the District Court's analysis as relying on a list of 10 factors, the Court of Appeals proceeded to examine each in turn. It held that 7 of the factors, including respondent's slowing down, his failure to acknowledge Stoddard, the raised position of the children's knees, and their odd waving carried little or no weight in the reasonable-suspicion calculus. The remaining factors — the road's use by smugglers, the temporal proximity between respondent's trip and the agents' shift change, and the use of minivans by smugglers — were not enough to render the stop permissible. We granted certiorari to review the decision of the Court of Appeals because of its importance to the enforcement of federal drug and immigration laws.

The Fourth Amendment prohibits "unreasonable searches and seizures" by the Government, and its protections extend to brief investigatory stops of persons or vehicles that fall short of traditional arrest. *Terry, Cortez*. Because the "balance between the public interest and the individual's right to personal security tilts in favor of a standard less than probable cause in such cases, the Fourth Amendment is satisfied if the officer's action is supported by reasonable suspicion to believe that criminal activity " 'may be afoot.' "

When discussing how reviewing courts should make reasonable-suspicion determinations, we have said repeatedly that they must look at the "totality of the circumstances" of each case to see whether the detaining officer has a "particularized and objective basis" for suspecting legal wrongdoing. This process allows officers to draw on their own experience and specialized training to make inferences from and deductions about the cumulative information available to them that "might well elude an untrained person." Although an officer's reliance on a mere " 'hunch' " is insufficient to justify a stop, the likelihood of criminal activity need not rise to the level required for probable cause, and it falls considerably short of satisfying a preponderance of the evidence standard.

Our cases have recognized that the concept of reasonable suspicion is somewhat abstract. *Ornelas, Cortez.* But we have deliberately avoided reducing it to " 'a neat set of legal rules,' " *Ornelas* (quoting *Gates*). In *Sokolow*, for example, we rejected a holding by the Court of Appeals that distinguished between evidence of ongoing criminal behavior and probabilistic evidence because it "create[d] unnecessary difficulty in dealing with one of the relatively simple concepts embodied in the Fourth Amendment."

We think that the approach taken by the Court of Appeals here departs sharply from the teachings of these cases. The court's evaluation and rejection of seven of the listed factors in isolation from each other does not take into account the "totality of the circumstances," as our cases have understood that phrase. The court appeared to believe that each observation by Stoddard that was by itself readily susceptible to an innocent explanation was entitled to "no weight." *Terry*, however, precludes this sort of divide-and-conquer analysis. The officer in *Terry* observed the petitioner and his companions repeatedly walk back and forth, look into a store window, and confer with one another. Although each of the series of acts was "perhaps innocent in itself," we held that, taken together, they "warranted further investigation." See also *Sokolow* (holding that factors which by themselves were "quite consistent with innocent travel" collectively amounted to reasonable suspicion).

The Court of Appeals' view that it was necessary to "clearly delimit" an officer's consideration of certain factors to reduce "troubling . . . uncertainty" also runs counter to our cases and underestimates the usefulness of the reasonable-suspicion standard in guiding officers in the field. In *Ornelas*, we held that the standard for appellate review of reasonable-suspicion determinations should be *de novo*, rather than for "abuse of discretion." There, we reasoned that de novo review would prevent the affirmance of opposite decisions on identical facts from different judicial districts in the same circuit, which would have been possible under the latter standard, and would allow appellate courts to clarify the legal principles. Other benefits of the approach, we said, were its tendency to unify precedent and greater capacity to provide law enforcement officers with the tools to reach correct determinations beforehand: Even if in many instances the factual "mosaic" analyzed for a reasonable-suspicion determination would preclude one case from squarely controlling another, "two decisions when viewed together may usefully add to the body of law on the subject."

But the Court of Appeals' approach would go considerably beyond the reasoning of *Ornelas* and seriously undercut the "totality of the circumstances" principle which governs the existence *vel non* of "reasonable suspicion." Take, for example, the court's positions that respondent's deceleration could not be considered because "slowing down after spotting a law enforcement vehicle is an entirely normal response that is in no way indicative of criminal activity" and that his failure to acknowledge Stoddard's presence provided no support because there were "no 'special circumstances' rendering 'innocent avoidance . . . improbable.' " We think it quite reasonable that a driver's slowing down, stiffening of posture, and failure to acknowledge a sighted law enforcement officer might well be unremarkable in one instance (such as a busy San Francisco highway) while quite unusual in another (such as a remote portion of rural southeastern Arizona). Stoddard was entitled to make an assessment of the situation in light of his specialized training and familiarity with the customs of the area's inhabitants. To the extent that a totality of the circumstances approach may render appellate review less circumscribed by precedent than otherwise, it is the nature of the totality rule. In another instance, the Court of Appeals chose to dismiss entirely the children's waving on grounds that odd conduct by children was all too common to be probative in a particular case. ("If every odd act engaged in by one's children . . . could contribute to a finding of reasonable suspicion, the vast majority of American parents might be stopped regularly within a block of their homes"). Yet this case did not involve simply any odd act by children. At the suppression hearing, Stoddard testified about the children's waving several times, and the record suggests that he physically demonstrated it as well.[14] The District Court Judge, who saw and heard Stoddard, then characterized the waving as "methodical," "mechanical," "abnormal," and "certainly . . . a fact that is odd and would lead a reasonable officer to wonder why they are doing this." Though the issue of this case does not turn on the children's idiosyncratic actions, the Court of Appeals should not have casually rejected this factor in light of the District Court's superior access to the evidence and the well-recognized inability of reviewing courts to reconstruct what happened in the courtroom.

Having considered the totality of the circumstances and given due weight to the factual inferences drawn by the law enforcement officer and District Court Judge, we hold that Stoddard had reasonable suspicion to believe that respondent was engaged in illegal activity. It was reasonable for Stoddard to infer from his observations, his registration check, and his experience as a border patrol agent that respondent had set out from Douglas along a little-traveled route used by smugglers to avoid the 191 checkpoint. Stoddard's knowledge further supported a commonsense inference that respondent intended to pass through the area at a time when officers would be leaving their backroads patrols to change shifts. The likelihood that respondent and his family were on a picnic outing was diminished by the fact that the minivan had turned away from the known recreational areas accessible to the east on Rucker Canyon Road. Corroborating this inference was the fact that recreational areas farther to the north would have been easier to reach by taking 191, as opposed to the 40-to-50-mile trip on unpaved and primitive roads. The children's elevated knees suggested the existence of concealed cargo in the passenger compartment. Finally, for the reasons we have given, Stoddard's assessment of respondent's reactions upon seeing him and the children's

---

[14] At one point during the hearing, Stoddard testified that "[the children's waving] wasn't in a normal pattern. It looked like they were instructed to do so. They kind of stuck their hands up and began waving to me like this."

mechanical-like waving, which continued for a full four to five minutes, were entitled to some weight.

Respondent argues that we must rule in his favor because the facts suggested a family in a minivan on a holiday outing. A determination that reasonable suspicion exists, however, need not rule out the possibility of innocent conduct. See *Illinois v. Wardlow* (that flight from police is not necessarily indicative of ongoing criminal activity does not establish Fourth Amendment violation). Undoubtedly, each of these factors alone is susceptible to innocent explanation, and some factors are more probative than others. Taken together, we believe they sufficed to form a particularized and objective basis for Stoddard's stopping the vehicle, making the stop reasonable within the meaning of the Fourth Amendment.

The judgment of the Court of Appeals is therefore reversed, and the case is remanded for further proceedings consistent with this opinion.

It is so ordered.

JUSTICE SCALIA, concurring.

I join the opinion of the Court, because I believe it accords with our opinion in *Ornelas* requiring de novo review which nonetheless gives "due weight to inferences drawn from [the] facts by resident judges . . . ." As I said in my dissent in *Ornelas*, however, I do not see how deferring to the District Court's factual inferences (as opposed to its findings of fact) is compatible with *de novo* review.

The Court today says that "due weight" should have been given to the District Court's determinations that the children's waving was " 'methodical,' 'mechanical,' 'abnormal,' and 'certainly . . . a fact that is odd and would lead a reasonable officer to wonder why they are doing this.' " "Methodical," "mechanical," and perhaps even "abnormal" and "odd," are findings of fact that deserve respect. But the inference that this "would lead a reasonable officer to wonder why they are doing this," amounts to the conclusion that their action was suspicious, which I would have thought (if *de novo* review is the standard) is the prerogative of the Court of Appeals. So we have here a peculiar sort of de novo review. I may add that, even holding the Ninth Circuit to no more than the traditional methodology of *de novo* review, its judgment here would have to be reversed.

QUESTIONS AND NOTES

1.   Suppose the trial judge had not found reasonable suspicion for essentially the reasons given by the appellate court. Would the Supreme Court result have been the same? Why? Why not?

2.   If your answer to Question 1 was no, what does that say about *Ornelas* and the importance of developing precedent?

3.   Does *Arvizu* add anything to *Cortez*? Explain.

4.   After *Arvizu*, does the average traveler have to worry about unruly children and either waving to, or not acknowledging, police officers?

5.   The Court said: "We granted certiorari to review the decision of the Court of Appeals because of its importance to the enforcement of drug and immigration laws." Did that statement influence its decision? Suppose it had said: "We granted certiorari because of the importance of American families' right to picnic off the beaten path without being subjected to being stopped by suspicious officers"?

C.   LIMITS ON *TERRY*-TYPE STOPS

Having explored the distinction between probable cause and reasonable suspicion, we will now examine the limitations on stops based on reasonable suspicion. The case most clearly developing those limitations is our old friend from Section B, *Royer*. Following *Royer*, we will consider *Place* and *Sharpe*, two cases that, when taken together, put some flesh on the *Royer* skeletal framework. We conclude with *Hiibel*, a case requiring identification from a person who did not know why he was stopped.

FLORIDA v. ROYER

460 U.S. 491 (1983)

JUSTICE WHITE announced the judgment of the Court and delivered an opinion in which JUSTICES MARSHALL, POWELL and STEVENS joined.

[For a statement of the facts, *see* Section B, *supra*.]

Terry and its progeny created only limited exceptions to the general rule that seizures of the person require probable cause to arrest. Detentions may be "investigative" yet violative of the Fourth Amendment absent probable cause. In the name of investigating a person who is no more than suspected of criminal activity, the police may not carry out a full search of the person or of his automobile or other effects. Nor may the police seek to verify their suspicions by means that approach the conditions of arrest. *Dunaway v. New York* made this clear. There, the suspect was taken to the police station from his home and, without being formally arrested, interrogated for an hour. The resulting incriminating statements were held inadmissible: reasonable suspicion of crime is insufficient to justify custodial interrogation even though the interrogation is investigative.

The Fourth Amendment's prohibition against unreasonable searches and seizures has always been interpreted to prevent a search that is not limited to the particularly described "place to be searched, and the persons or things to be seized," even if the search is made pursuant to a warrant and based upon probable cause. The Amendment's protection is not diluted in those situations where it has been determined that legitimate law enforcement interests justify a warrantless search: the search must be limited in scope to that which is justified by the particular purposes served by the exception. For example, a warrantless search is permissible incident to a lawful arrest because of legitimate concerns for the safety of the officer and to prevent the destruction of evidence by the arrestee. Nevertheless, such a search is limited to the person of the arrestee and the area immediately within his control. *Terry* also embodies this principle: "The scope of the search must be 'strictly tied to and justified by' the circumstances which rendered its initiation permissible."

The predicate permitting seizures on suspicion short of probable cause is that law enforcement interests warrant a limited intrusion on the personal security of the suspect. The scope of the intrusion permitted will vary to some extent with the particular facts and circumstances of each case. This much, however, is clear: an investigative detention must be temporary and last no longer than is necessary to effectuate the purpose of the stop. Similarly, the investigative methods employed should be the least intrusive means reasonably available to verify or dispel the officer's suspicion in a short period of time. It is the State's burden to demonstrate that the seizure it seeks to justify on the basis of a reasonable suspicion was sufficiently limited in scope and duration to satisfy the conditions of an investigative seizure.

The Florida Court of Appeal in the case before us, however, concluded not only that Royer had been seized when he gave his consent to search his luggage but also that the bounds of an investigative stop had been exceeded. In its view the "confinement" in this case went beyond the limited restraint of a *Terry* investigative stop, and Royer's consent was thus tainted by the illegality, a conclusion that required reversal in the absence of probable cause to arrest. The question before us is whether the record warrants that conclusion. We think that it does.

We also think that the officers' conduct was more intrusive than necessary to effectuate an investigative detention otherwise authorized by the *Terry* line of cases. First, by returning his ticket and driver's license, and informing him that he was free to go if he so desired, the officers may have obviated any claim that the encounter was anything but a consensual matter from start to finish.* Second, there are undoubtedly reasons of safety and security that would justify moving a suspect from one location to another during an investigatory detention, such as from an airport concourse to a more private area. There is no indication in this case that such reasons prompted the officers to transfer the site of the encounter from the concourse to the interrogation room. It appears, rather, that the primary interest of the officers was not in having an extended conversation with Royer but in the contents of his luggage, a matter which the officers did not pursue orally with Royer until after the encounter was relocated to the police room. The record does not reflect any facts which would support a finding that the legitimate law enforcement purposes which justified the detention in the first instance were furthered by removing Royer to the police room prior to the officer's attempt to gain his consent to a search of his luggage. As we have noted, had Royer consented to a search on the spot, the search could have been conducted with Royer present in the area where the bags were retrieved by Officer Johnson and any evidence recovered would have been admissible against him. If the search proved negative, Royer would have been free to go much earlier and with less likelihood of missing his flight, which in itself can be a very serious matter in a variety of circumstances.

[T]he State has not touched on the question whether it would have been feasible to investigate the contents of Royer's bags in a more expeditious way. The courts

---

* A point dealt with more clearly in Chapter 9, *infra*.

are not strangers to the use of trained dogs to detect the presence of controlled substances in luggage.[10] There is no indication here that this means was not feasible and available. If it had been used, Royer and his luggage could have been momentarily detained while this investigative procedure was carried out. Indeed, it may be that no detention at all would have been necessary. A negative result would have freed Royer in short order; a positive result would have resulted in his justifiable arrest on probable cause.

We do not suggest that there is a litmus-paper test for distinguishing a consensual encounter from a seizure or for determining when a seizure exceeds the bounds of an investigative stop. Even in the discrete category of airport encounters, there will be endless variations in the facts and circumstances, so much variation that it is unlikely that the courts can reduce to a sentence or a paragraph a rule that will provide unarguable answers to the question whether there has been an unreasonable search or seizure in violation of the Fourth Amendment. Nevertheless, we must render judgment, and we think that the Florida Court of Appeal cannot be faulted in concluding that the limits of a *Terry*-stop had been exceeded.

JUSTICE BRENNAN, concurring in result.

[E]ven assuming the legality of the initial stop, the plurality correctly holds, and I agree, that the officers' subsequent actions clearly exceeded the permissible bounds of a *Terry* "investigative" stop. "[A]ny 'exception' that could cover a seizure as intrusive as that in this case would threaten to swallow the general rule that Fourth Amendment seizures are 'reasonable' only if based on probable cause." *Dunaway*. Thus, most of the plurality's discussion of the permissible scope of *Terry* investigative stops is also unnecessary to the decision.

I emphasize that *Terry* was a very limited decision that expressly declined to address the "constitutional propriety of an investigative 'seizure' upon less than probable cause for purposes of 'detention' and/or interrogation." *Terry* simply held that under certain carefully defined circumstances a police officer "is entitled for the protection of himself and others in the area to conduct a carefully limited search of the outer clothing . . . in an attempt to discover weapons which might be used to assault him." *Adams* endorsed "brief" investigative stops based on reasonable suspicion, but the search for weapons upheld in that case was very limited and was based on *Terry's* safety rationale. In *Adams*, we stated that the purpose of the "limited" weapons search was "not to discover evidence of crime, but to allow the

---

[10] Courts of Appeals are in disagreement as to whether using a dog to detect drugs in luggage is a search, but no Court of Appeals has held that more than an articulable suspicion is necessary to justify this kind of a warrantless search if indeed it is a search. [A point discussed in Chapter 11, *infra*. — Ed.] Furthermore, the law of the circuit from which this case comes was and is that "use of [drug-detecting canines] constitute[s] neither a search nor a seizure under the Fourth Amendment."

In any event, we hold here that the officers had reasonable suspicion to believe that Royer's luggage contained drugs, and we assume that the use of dogs in the investigation would not have entailed any prolonged detention of either Royer or his luggage which may involve other Fourth Amendment concerns. In the case before us, the officers, with founded suspicion, could have detained Royer for the brief period during which Florida authorities at busy airports seem able to carry out the dog-sniffing procedure.

officer to pursue his investigation without fear of violence . . . ." In *Brignoni-Ponce*, we held that "when an officer's observations lead him reasonably to suspect that a particular vehicle may contain aliens who are illegally in the country, he may stop the car briefly and investigate the circumstances that provoke suspicion." We based this holding on the importance of the governmental interest in stemming the flow of illegal aliens, on the minimal intrusion of a brief stop, and on the absence of practical alternatives for policing the border. We noted the limited holdings of *Terry* and *Adams* and while authorizing the police to "question the driver and passengers about their citizenship and immigration status, and . . . ask them to explain suspicious circumstances," we expressly stated that "any further detention or search must be based on consent or probable cause."

The scope of a *Terry*-type "investigative" stop and any attendant search must be extremely limited or the *Terry* exception would "swallow the general rule that Fourth Amendment seizures [and searches] are 'reasonable' only if based on probable cause." In my view, any suggestion that the *Terry* reasonable-suspicion standard justifies anything but the briefest of detentions or the most limited of searches finds no support in the *Terry* line of cases.[1]

JUSTICE BLACKMUN, dissenting.

In my view, the police conduct in this case was minimally intrusive. Given the strength of society's interest in overcoming the extraordinary obstacles to the detection of drug traffickers, such conduct should not be subjected to a requirement of probable cause. Because the Court holds otherwise, I dissent.

I

The dispositive issue is whether the officers needed probable cause to arrest before they could take the actions that led to Royer's consent and the subsequent discovery of the contraband. I conclude that they did not.

A

"[T]he key principle of the Fourth Amendment is reasonableness — the balancing of competing interests." Previous cases suggest a two-step analysis to

---

[1] I interpret the plurality's requirement that the investigative methods employed pursuant to a *Terry* stop be "the least intrusive means reasonably available to verify or dispel the officer's suspicion in a short period of time" to mean that the availability of a less intrusive means may make an otherwise reasonable stop unreasonable. I do not interpret it to mean that the absence of a less intrusive means can make an otherwise unreasonable stop reasonable.

In addition, contrary to the plurality's apparent suggestion, I am not at all certain that the use of trained narcotics dogs constitutes a less intrusive means of conducting a lawful *Terry* investigative stop. Such a suggestion finds no support in our cases and any question concerning the use of trained dogs to detect the presence of controlled substances in luggage is clearly not before us.

In any event, the relevance of a least intrusive means requirement within the context of a *Terry* investigative stop is not clear to me. As I have discussed, a lawful stop must be so strictly limited that it is difficult to conceive of a less intrusive means that would be effective to accomplish the purpose of the stop.

distinguish seizures requiring probable cause from those requiring reasonable suspicion. On the one hand, any formal arrest, and any seizure "having the essential attributes of a formal arrest, is unreasonable unless it is supported by probable cause." On the other hand, a more limited intrusion, if supported by a special law enforcement need for greater flexibility, may be justifiable under the lesser "reasonable suspicion" standard. These lesser seizures are "not confined to the momentary, on-the-street detention accompanied by a frisk for weapons." In the case of a seizure less intrusive than a formal arrest, determining whether the less demanding reasonable suspicion standard will be applied requires balancing the amount of intrusion upon individual privacy against the special law enforcement interests that would be served by permitting such an intrusion on less than probable cause.

B

At the suppression hearing in this case, Royer agreed that he was not formally arrested until after his suitcases were opened. In my view, it cannot fairly be said that, prior to the formal arrest, the functional equivalent of an arrest had taken place. The encounter had far more in common with automobile stops justifiable on reasonable suspicion than with the detention deemed the functional equivalent of a formal arrest in *Dunaway*. In *Dunaway*, the suspect was taken from his neighbor's home and involuntarily transported to the police station in a squad car. At the precinct house, he was placed in an interrogation room and subjected to extended custodial interrogation. Here, Royer was not taken from a private residence, where reasonable expectations of privacy perhaps are at their greatest. Instead, he was approached in a major international airport where, due in part to extensive anti-hijacking surveillance and equipment, reasonable privacy expectations are of significantly lesser magnitude, certainly no greater than the reasonable privacy expectations of travelers in automobiles. As in the automobile stop cases, and indeed as in every case in which the Court has upheld seizures upon reasonable suspicion, Royer was questioned where he was found, and all questions were directly related to the purpose of the stop. Thus, the officers asked about Royer's identity, the purposes of his travel, and the suspicious circumstances they had noted. As the plurality appears to concede, probable cause was certainly not required at this point, and the officers' conduct was fully supported by reasonable suspicion.

What followed was within the scope of the lesser intrusions approved on less than probable cause in our prior cases, and was far removed from the circumstances of *Dunaway*. In the context of automobile stops, the Court has held that an officer "may question the driver and passengers about their citizenship and immigration status, and he may ask them to explain suspicious circumstances, but any further detention or search must be based on consent or probable cause." Here, Royer was not subjected to custodial interrogation, for which probable cause is required.

II

The officers in this case began their encounter with Royer with reasonable suspicion. They continued their questioning and requested further cooperation only as more facts, heightening their suspicion, came to their attention. Certainly, as any such detention continues or escalates, a greater degree of reasonable suspicion is necessary to sustain it, and at some point probable cause will be required. But here, the intrusion was short-lived and minimal. Only 15 minutes transpired from the initial approach to the opening of the suitcases. The officers were polite, and sought and immediately obtained Royer's consent at each significant step of the process.[3] Royer knew that if the search of the suitcases did not turn up contraband, he would be free to go on his way.[4] Thus, it seems clear to me that "the police [were] diligently pursuing a means of investigation which [was] likely to resolve the matter one way or another very soon . . . ."[5]

The special need for flexibility in uncovering illicit drug couriers is hardly debatable. Surely the problem is as serious, and as intractable, as the problem of illegal immigration. In light of the extraordinary and well-documented difficulty of identifying drug couriers, the minimal intrusion in this case, based on particularized suspicion, was eminently reasonable.

I dissent.

JUSTICE REHNQUIST, with whom THE CHIEF JUSTICE and JUSTICE O'CONNOR join, dissenting.

The point at which I part company with the plurality's opinion is in the assessment of the reasonableness of the officers' conduct following their initial conversation with Royer. The plurality focuses on the transfer of the place of the interview from the main concourse of the airport to the room off the concourse and observes that Royer "found himself in a small room — a large closet — equipped with a desk and two chairs. He was alone with two police officers who again told him that they thought he was carrying narcotics. He also found that the officers, without his consent, had retrieved his checked luggage from the airlines."

Obviously, this quoted language is intended to convey stern disapproval of the described conduct of the officers. To my mind, it merits no such disapproval and was eminently reasonable. Would it have been preferable for the officers to have detained Royer for further questioning, as they concededly had a right to do, without paying any attention to the fact that his luggage had already been checked on the flight to New York, and might be put aboard the flight even though Royer

---

[3] The officers acted reasonably in taking Royer's baggage stubs and bringing his luggage to the police room without his consent. Royer had already surrendered the suitcases to a third party, the airline. The officers brought the suitcases to him immediately, and their contents were not revealed until Royer gave his consent. Thus, Royer's privacy was not substantially invaded. At that time, moreover, Royer himself was validly detained, the object of the encounter had become the securing of Royer's consent to search his luggage, and the luggage would otherwise have been loaded onto the airplane.

[4] The fact that Royer knew the search was likely to turn up contraband is of course irrelevant; the potential intrusiveness of the officers' conduct must be judged from the viewpoint of an innocent person in Royer's position.

[5] Like Justice Rehnquist, I cannot accept the "least intrusive" alternative analysis the plurality would impose on the law of the Fourth Amendment. Prior cases do establish that "an investigative detention must be temporary and last no longer than is necessary to effectuate the purpose of the stop." The detention at issue fully met that standard.

himself was not on the plane? Would it have been more "reasonable" to interrogate Royer about the contents of his suitcases, and to seek his permission to open the suitcases when they were retrieved, in the busy main concourse of the Miami Airport, rather than to find a room off the concourse where the confrontation would surely be less embarrassing to Royer? If the room had been large and spacious, rather than small, if it had possessed three chairs rather than two, would the officers' conduct have been made reasonable by these facts?

The plurality's answers to these questions, to the extent that it attempts any, are scarcely satisfying. It commences with the observation that "the officers' conduct was more intrusive than necessary to effectuate an investigative detention otherwise authorized by the *Terry* line of cases." Earlier in its opinion, the plurality set the stage for this standard when the familiar "least intrusive means" principle of First Amendment law is suddenly carried over into Fourth Amendment law by the citation of two cases, *Brignoni-Ponce* and *Adams*, neither one of which lends any support to the principle as a part of Fourth Amendment law. The plurality goes on to say that had the officers returned Royer's ticket and driver's license, the encounter clearly would have been consensual. The plurality also states that while there were good reasons to justify moving Royer from one location to another, the officers' motives in seeking to examine his luggage renders these reasons unavailing — a conclusion the reason for which wholly escapes me. Finally, the plurality suggests that the officers might have examined Royer's bags in a more expeditious way, such as the use of trained dogs.

All of this to my mind adds up to little more than saying that if my aunt were a man, she would be my uncle. The officers might have taken different steps than they did to investigate Royer, but the same may be said of virtually every investigative encounter that has more than one step to it. The question we must decide is what was *unreasonable* about the steps which *these officers* took with respect to *this* suspect in the Miami Airport on this particular day. On this point, the plurality stutters, fudges, and hedges:

> What had begun as a consensual inquiry in a public place had escalated into an investigatory procedure in a police interrogation room, where the police, unsatisfied with previous explanations, sought to confirm their suspicions.

But since even the plurality concedes that there was articulable suspicion warranting an investigatory detention, the fact that the inquiry had become an "investigatory procedure in a police interrogation room" would seem to have little bearing on the proper disposition of a claim that the officers violated the Fourth Amendment. The plurality goes on to say:

> At least as of that moment, any consensual aspects of the encounter had evaporated, and we cannot fault the Florida Court of Appeal in concluding that *Terry* and the cases following it did not justify the restraint to which Royer was then subjected. As a practical matter, Royer was under arrest.

Does the plurality intimate that if the Florida Court of Appeal had reached the opposite conclusion with respect to the holdings of *Terry* and the cases which follow it, it would affirm that holding? Does it mean that the 15-minute duration of the total encounter, and the even lesser amount of elapsed time during which Royer was in the "interrogation room," was more than a *Terry* investigative stop can ever consume? These possible conclusions are adumbrated, but not stated; if the plurality's opinion were to be judged by standards appropriate to Impressionist paintings, it would perhaps receive a high grade, but the same cannot be said if it is to be judged by the standards of a judicial opinion.

Since the plurality concedes the existence of "articulable suspicion" at least after the initial conversation with Royer, the only remaining question is whether the detention of Royer during that period of time was permissible under the rule enunciated in *Terry*. Although *Terry* itself involved only a protective pat down for weapons, subsequent cases have expanded the permissible scope of such a "seizure." In *Adams*, we upheld both a search and seizure of a pistol being carried by a suspect seated in a parked automobile. In *Martinez-Fuerte*, we allowed government officials to stop, and divert for visual inspection and questioning, automobiles which were suspected of harboring illegal aliens. These stops, including waiting time, could clearly have approximated in length the time which Royer was detained, and yet *Martinez-Fuerte* allowed them to be made "in the absence of *any individualized suspicion* at reasonably located checkpoints." 428 U.S. at 562 (emphasis supplied). Unless we are to say that commercial drug trafficking is somehow quantitatively less weighty on the Fourth Amendment scale than trafficking in the illegal aliens, I think the articulable suspicion which concededly focused upon Royer justified the length and nature of his detention.

QUESTIONS AND NOTES

1.   The Court split 5-4 in favor of the least intrusive means test. This is contrary to the position that it has taken in other areas, notably "inventory searches." Is there something about *Terry*-stops that warrants such a stringent standard?

2.   As a practical matter, does the "least intrusive means" test practically insure defeat for the government in that a reasonably competent attorney can ordinarily think of something "less intrusive" than what the police actually did do? (We will consider this point further in conjunction with *Sharpe*.)

3.   Would (should) the result have been different if the Florida Court of Appeal had found the detention to be proper?

4.   In regard to Justice Rehnquist's questions, what exactly did the DEA agents do wrong? Is fifteen minutes too long *per se*? Were they insufficiently expeditious? Did they interview Royer in the wrong place?

5.   These questions are somewhat clarified in *Place*.

UNITED STATES v. PLACE
462 U.S. 696 (1983)

JUSTICE O'CONNOR delivered the opinion of the Court.

This case presents the issue whether the Fourth Amendment prohibits law enforcement authorities from temporarily detaining personal luggage for exposure to a trained narcotics detection dog on the basis of reasonable suspicion that the luggage contains narcotics. Given the enforcement problems associated with the detection of narcotics trafficking and the minimal intrusion that a properly limited detention would entail, we conclude that the Fourth Amendment does not prohibit such a detention. On the facts of this case, however, we hold that the police conduct exceeded the bounds of a permissible investigative detention of the luggage.

I

Respondent Raymond J. Place's behavior aroused the suspicions of law enforcement officers as he waited in line at the Miami International Airport to purchase a ticket to New York's LaGuardia Airport. As Place proceeded to the gate for his flight, the agents approached him and requested his airline ticket and some identification. Place complied with the request and consented to a search of the two suitcases he had checked. Because his flight was about to depart, however, the agents decided not to search the luggage.

Prompted by Place's parting remark that he had recognized that they were police, the agents inspected the address tags on the checked luggage and noted discrepancies in the two street addresses. Further investigation revealed that neither address existed and that the telephone number Place had given the airline belonged to a third address on the same street. On the basis of their encounter with Place and this information, the Miami agents called Drug Enforcement Administration (DEA) authorities in New York to relay their information about Place.

Two DEA agents waited for Place at the arrival gate at LaGuardia Airport in New York. There again, his behavior aroused the suspicion of the agents. After he had claimed his two bags and called a limousine, the agents decided to approach him. They identified themselves as federal narcotics agents, to which Place responded that he knew they were "cops" and had spotted them as soon as he had deplaned. One of the agents informed Place that, based on their own observations and information obtained from the Miami authorities, they believed that he might be carrying narcotics. After identifying the bags as belonging to him, Place stated that a number of police at the Miami Airport had surrounded him and searched his baggage. The agents responded that their information was to the contrary. The agents requested and received identification from Place — a New Jersey driver's license, on which the agents later ran a computer check that disclosed no offenses, and his airline ticket receipt. When Place refused to consent to a search of his luggage, one of the agents told him that they were going to take the luggage to a federal judge to try to obtain a search warrant and that Place was free to accompany them. Place declined, but obtained from one of the agents telephone numbers at which the agents could be reached.

The agents then took the bags to Kennedy Airport, where they subjected the bags to a "sniff test" by a trained narcotics detection dog. The dog reacted positively to the smaller of the two bags but ambiguously to the larger bag. Approximately 90 minutes had elapsed since the seizure of respondent's luggage. Because it was late on a Friday afternoon, the agents retained the luggage until Monday morning, when they secured a search warrant from a magistrate for the smaller bag. Upon opening that bag, the agents discovered 1,125 grams of cocaine.

II

In this case, the Government asks us to recognize the reasonableness under the Fourth Amendment of warrantless seizures of personal luggage from the custody of the owner on the basis of less than probable cause, for the purpose of pursuing a limited course of investigation, short of opening the luggage, that would quickly confirm or dispel the authorities' suspicion. Specifically, we are asked to apply the principles of *Terry* to permit such seizures on the basis of reasonable, articulable suspicion, premised on objective facts, that the luggage contains contraband or evidence of a crime. In our view, such application is appropriate.

The exception to the probable-cause requirement for limited seizures of the person recognized in *Terry* and its progeny rests on a balancing of the competing interests to determine the reasonableness of the type of seizure involved within the meaning of "the Fourth Amendment's general proscription against unreasonable searches and seizures." We must balance the nature and quality of the intrusion on the individual's Fourth Amendment interests against the importance of the governmental interests alleged to justify the intrusion. When the nature and extent of the detention are minimally intrusive of the individual's Fourth Amendment interests, the opposing law enforcement interests can support a seizure based on less than probable cause.

We examine first the governmental interest offered as a justification for a brief seizure of luggage from the suspect's custody for the purpose of pursuing a limited course of investigation. The Government contends that, where the authorities possess specific and articulable facts warranting a reasonable belief that a traveler's luggage contains narcotics, the governmental interest in seizing the luggage briefly to pursue further investigation is substantial. We agree. As observed in *United States v. Mendenhall* [Chapter 10, *infra*], "[t]he public has a compelling interest in detecting those who would traffic in deadly drugs for personal profit."

Respondent suggests that, absent some special law enforcement interest such as officer safety, a generalized interest in law enforcement cannot justify an intrusion on an individual's Fourth Amendment interests in the absence of probable cause. Our prior cases, however, do not support this proposition. In *Terry*, we described the governmental interests supporting the initial seizure of the person as "effective crime prevention and detection; it is this interest which underlies the recognition that a police officer may in appropriate circumstances and in an appropriate manner approach a person for purposes of investigating possibly criminal behavior even though there is no probable cause to make an arrest." Similarly, in *Michigan v. Summers* (*infra*), we identified three law enforcement interests that justified limited detention of the occupants of the premises during execution of a valid search warrant: "preventing flight in the event that incriminating evidence is found," "minimizing the risk of harm" both to the officers and the occupants, and "orderly completion of the search." *Cf. Royer.* The test is whether those interests are sufficiently "substantial," not whether they are independent of the interest in investigating crimes effectively and apprehending suspects. The context of a particular law enforcement practice, of course, may affect the determination whether a brief intrusion on Fourth Amendment interests on less than probable cause is essential to effective criminal investigation. Because of the inherently transient nature of drug courier activity at airports, allowing police to make brief investigative stops of persons at airports on reasonable suspicion of drug-trafficking substantially enhances the likelihood that police will be able to prevent the flow of narcotics into distribution channels.[6]

Against this strong governmental interest, we must weigh the nature and extent of the intrusion upon the individual's Fourth Amendment rights when the police briefly detain luggage for limited investigative purposes. On this point, respondent Place urges that the rationale for a *Terry* stop of the person is wholly inapplicable to investigative detentions of personalty. Specifically, the *Terry* exception to the probable-cause requirement is premised on the notion that a *Terry*-type stop of the person is substantially less intrusive of a person's liberty interests than a formal arrest. In the property context, however, Place urges, there are no degrees of intrusion. Once the owner's property is seized, the dispossession is absolute.

We disagree. The intrusion on possessory interests occasioned by a seizure of one's personal effects can vary both in its nature and extent. The seizure may be made after the owner has relinquished control of the property to a third party or, as here, from the immediate custody and control of the owner. Moreover, the police may confine their investigation to an on-the-spot inquiry — for example, immediate exposure of the luggage to a trained narcotics detection dog — or transport the property to another location. Given the fact that seizures of property can vary in intrusiveness, some brief detentions of personal effects may be so minimally intrusive of Fourth Amendment interests that strong countervailing governmental interests will justify a seizure based only on specific articulable facts that the property contains contraband or evidence of a crime.

III

There is no doubt that the agents made a "seizure" of Place's luggage for purposes of the Fourth Amendment when, following his refusal to consent to a search, the agent told Place that he was going to take the luggage to a federal judge to secure issuance of a warrant. As we observed in *Terry*, "[t]he manner in which the seizure . . . [was] conducted is, of course, as vital a part of the inquiry as whether [it was] warranted at all."

At the outset, we must reject the Government's suggestion that the point at which probable cause for seizure of luggage from the person's presence becomes necessary is more distant than in the case of a *Terry* stop of the person himself. The premise of the Government's argument is that seizures of property are generally less intrusive than seizures of the person. While true in some circumstances, that

---

[6] Referring to the problem of intercepting drug couriers in the nation's airports, Justice Powell has observed:

> Much of the drug traffic is highly organized and conducted by sophisticated criminal syndicates. The profits are enormous. And many drugs . . . may be easily concealed. As a result, the obstacles to detection of illegal conduct may be unmatched in any other area of law enforcement.

United States v. Mendenhall, 446 U.S., at 561–562 (opinion of Powell, J.) [Chapter 10, *infra*]. *See Royer* (Blackmun, J., dissenting) ("The special need for flexibility in uncovering illicit drug couriers is hardly debatable") (airport context).

premise is faulty on the facts we address in this case. The precise type of detention we confront here is seizure of personal luggage from the immediate possession of the suspect for the purpose of arranging exposure to a narcotics detection dog. Particularly in the case of detention of luggage within the traveler's immediate possession, the police conduct intrudes on both the suspect's possessory interest in his luggage as well as his liberty interest in proceeding with his itinerary. The person whose luggage is detained is technically still free to continue his travels or carry out other personal activities pending release of the luggage. Moreover, he is not subjected to the coercive atmosphere of a custodial confinement or to the public indignity of being personally detained. Nevertheless, such a seizure can effectively restrain the person since he is subjected to the possible disruption of his travel plans in order to remain with his luggage or to arrange for its return.[8] Therefore, when the police seize luggage from the suspect's custody, we think the limitations applicable to investigative detentions of the person should define the permissible scope of an investigative detention of the person's luggage on less than probable cause. Under this standard, it is clear that the police conduct here exceeded the permissible limits of a *Terry*-type investigative stop.

The length of the detention of respondent's luggage alone precludes the conclusion that the seizure was reasonable in the absence of probable cause. Although we have recognized the reasonableness of seizures longer than the momentary ones involved in *Terry, Adams*, and *Brignoni-Ponce*, the brevity of the invasion of the individual's Fourth Amendment interests is an important factor in determining whether the seizure is so minimally intrusive as to be justifiable on reasonable suspicion. Moreover, in assessing the effect of the length of the detention, we take into account whether the police diligently pursue their investigation. We note that here the New York agents knew the time of Place's scheduled arrival at LaGuardia, had ample time to arrange for their additional investigation at that location, and thereby could have minimized the intrusion on respondent's Fourth Amendment interests.[9] Thus, although we decline to adopt any outside time limitation for a permissible *Terry* stop,[10] we have never approved a seizure of the person for the prolonged 90-minute period involved here and cannot do so on the facts presented by this case. *See Dunaway.*

Although the 90-minute detention of respondent's luggage is sufficient to render the seizure unreasonable, the violation was exacerbated by the failure of the agents to accurately inform respondent of the place to which they were transporting his

---

[8] "At least when the authorities do not make it absolutely clear how they plan to reunite the suspect and his possessions at some future time and place, seizure of the object is tantamount to seizure of the person. This is because that person must either remain on the scene or else seemingly surrender his effects permanently to the police."

[9] *Cf. Royer* (plurality opinion) ("If [trained narcotics detection dogs] had been used, Royer and his luggage could have been momentarily detained while this investigative procedure was carried out"). This course of conduct also would have avoided the further substantial intrusion on respondent's possessory interests caused by the removal of his luggage to another location.

[10] *Cf.* ALI, Model Code of Pre-Arraignment Procedure § 110.2(1) (1975) (recommending a maximum of 20 minutes for a *Terry* stop). We understand the desirability of providing law enforcement authorities with a clear rule to guide their conduct. Nevertheless, we question the wisdom of a rigid time limitation. Such a limit would undermine the equally important need to allow authorities to graduate their responses to the demands of any particular situation.

luggage, of the length of time he might be dispossessed, and of what arrangements would be made for return of the luggage if the investigation dispelled the suspicion. In short, we hold that the detention of respondent's luggage in this case went beyond the narrow authority possessed by police to detain briefly luggage reasonably suspected to contain narcotics.

IV

We conclude that, under all of the circumstances of this case, the seizure of respondent's luggage was unreasonable under the Fourth Amendment. Consequently, the evidence obtained from the subsequent search of his luggage was inadmissible, and Place's conviction must be reversed. The judgment of the Court of Appeals, accordingly, is affirmed.

JUSTICE BRENNAN, with whom JUSTICE MARSHALL joins, concurring in result.

In some respects the Court's opinion in this case can be seen as the logical successor of the plurality opinion in *Royer*. The plurality opinion in *Royer* contained considerable language, which was unnecessary to the judgment regarding the permissible scope of *Terry* investigative stops. Even assuming, however, that the Court finds some support in *Royer* for its discussion of the scope of *Terry* stops, the Court today goes well beyond *Royer* in endorsing the notion that the principles of *Terry* permit "warrantless seizures of personal luggage from the custody of the owner on the basis of less than probable cause, for the purpose of pursuing a limited course of investigation, short of opening the luggage, that would quickly confirm or dispel the authorities' suspicion." In addition to being unnecessary to the Court's judgment, this suggestion finds no support in *Terry* or its progeny and significantly dilutes the Fourth Amendment's protections against government interference with personal property. In short, it represents a radical departure from settled Fourth Amendment principles.

As noted, *Terry* and the cases that followed it authorize a brief "investigative" stop of an individual based on reasonable suspicion and a limited search for weapons if the officer reasonably suspects that the individual is armed and presently dangerous. The purpose of this brief stop is "to determine [the individual's] identity or to maintain the status quo momentarily while obtaining more information . . . ." *Adams*. Anything more than a brief stop "must be based on consent or probable cause." *Brignoni-Ponce*. During the course of this stop, "the suspect must not be moved or asked to move more than a short distance; physical searches are permitted only to the extent necessary to protect the police officers involved during the encounter; and, most importantly, the suspect must be free to leave after a short time and to decline to answer the questions put to him." It is true that *Terry* stops may involve seizures of personal effects incidental to the seizure of the person involved. Obviously, an officer cannot seize a person without also seizing the personal effects that the individual has in his possession at the time. But there is a difference between incidental seizures of personal effects and seizures of property independent of the seizure of the person.

The officers did not develop probable cause to arrest respondent during their encounter with him. Therefore, they had to let him go. But despite the absence of probable cause to arrest respondent, the officers seized his luggage and deprived him of possession. Respondent, therefore, was subjected not only to an invasion of his personal security and privacy, but also to an independent dispossession of his personal effects based simply on reasonable suspicion. It is difficult to understand how this intrusion is not more severe than a brief stop for questioning or even a limited, on-the-spot patdown search for weapons.

In my view, as soon as the officers seized respondent's luggage, independent of their seizure of him, they exceeded the scope of a permissible *Terry* stop and violated respondent's Fourth Amendment rights. In addition, the officers' seizure of respondent's luggage violated the established rule that seizures of personal effects must be based on probable cause. Their actions, therefore, should not be upheld.

The Court acknowledges that seizures of personal property must be based on probable cause. Despite this recognition, the Court employs a balancing test drawn from *Terry* to conclude that personal effects may be seized based on reasonable suspicion. In *Dunaway*, the Court stated that "[t]he narrow intrusions involved in [*Terry* and its progeny] were judged by a balancing test rather than by the general principle that Fourth Amendment seizures must be supported by the 'long-prevailing standards' of probable cause . . . only because these intrusions fell far short of the kind of intrusion associated with an arrest." As *Dunaway* suggests, the use of a balancing test in this case is inappropriate. First, the intrusion involved in this case is no longer the "narrow" one contemplated by the *Terry* line of cases. In addition, the intrusion involved in this case involves not only the seizure of a person, but also the seizure of property. *Terry* and its progeny did not address seizures of property. Those cases left unchanged the rule that seizures of property must be based on probable cause. The *Terry* balancing test should not be wrenched from its factual and conceptual moorings.

Justice Douglas was the only dissenter in *Terry*. He stated that "[t]here have been powerful hydraulic pressures throughout our history that bear heavily on the Court to water down constitutional guarantees and give the police the upper hand." Today, the Court uses *Terry* as a justification for submitting to these pressures. Their strength is apparent, for even when the Court finds that an individual's Fourth Amendment rights have been violated it cannot resist the temptation to weaken the protections the Amendment affords.

JUSTICE BLACKMUN, with whom JUSTICE MARSHALL joins, concurring in result.

In providing guidance to other courts, we often include in our opinions material that, technically, constitutes dictum. I cannot fault the Court's desire to set guidelines for *Terry* seizures of luggage based on reasonable suspicion. I am concerned, however, with what appears to me to be an emerging tendency on the part of the Court to convert the *Terry* decision into a general statement that the Fourth Amendment requires only that any seizure be reasonable.[1]

---

[1] The Court states that the applicability of the *Terry* exception "rests on a balancing of the competing

I pointed out in dissent in *Royer*, that our prior cases suggest a two-step evaluation of seizures under the Fourth Amendment. The Amendment generally prohibits a seizure unless it is pursuant to a judicial warrant issued upon probable cause and particularly describing the items to be seized. The Court correctly observes that a warrant may be dispensed with if the officer has probable cause and if some exception to the warrant requirement, such as exigent circumstances, is applicable. While the Fourth Amendment speaks in terms of freedom from unreasonable seizures, the Amendment does not leave the reasonableness of most seizures to the judgment of courts or government officers: the Framers of the Amendment balanced the interests involved and decided that a seizure is reasonable only if supported by a judicial warrant based on probable cause.

Terry, however, teaches that in some circumstances a limited seizure that is less restrictive than a formal arrest may constitutionally occur upon mere reasonable suspicion, if "supported by a special law enforcement need for greater flexibility." When this exception to the Fourth Amendment's warrant and probable cause requirements is applicable, a reviewing court must balance the individual's interest in privacy against the Government's law enforcement interest and determine whether the seizure was reasonable under the circumstances. Only in this limited context is a court entitled to engage in any balancing of interests in determining the validity of a seizure.

Because I agree with the Court that there is a significant law enforcement interest in interdicting illegal drug traffic in the Nation's airports, a limited intrusion caused by a temporary seizure of luggage for investigative purposes could fall within the *Terry* exception. The critical threshold issue is the intrusiveness of the seizure.[2] In this case, the seizure went well beyond a minimal intrusion and therefore cannot fall within the *Terry* exception.

QUESTIONS AND NOTES

1.   Is the Court holding that 90 minutes is *per se* too long? Isn't the Court trying to avoid *per se* time limits?

---

interests to determine the reasonableness of the type of seizure involved within the meaning of 'the Fourth Amendment's general proscription against unreasonable searches and seizures.' " As the context of the quotation from *Terry* makes clear, however, this balancing to determine reasonableness occurs only under the exceptional circumstances that justify the *Terry* exception:

> But we deal here with an entire rubric of police conduct — necessarily swift action predicated upon the on-the-spot observations of the officer on the beat — which historically has not been, and as a practical matter could not be, subjected to the warrant procedure. Instead, the conduct involved in this case must be tested by the Fourth Amendment's general proscription against unreasonable searches and seizures.

[2] I cannot agree with the Court's assertion that the diligence of the police in acting on their suspicion is relevant to the extent of the intrusion on Fourth Amendment interests. It makes little difference to a traveler whose luggage is seized whether the police conscientiously followed a lead or bungled the investigation. The duration and intrusiveness of the seizure is not altered by the diligence the police exercise. Of course, diligence may be relevant to a court's determination of the reasonableness of the seizure once it is determined that the seizure is sufficiently nonintrusive as to be eligible for the *Terry* exception.

2. If you had been on the Court would you have allowed luggage to have been detained at all? Why? Why not?

3. Assuming that your answer to Question 2 is "yes," should it be subject to detention for less time, more time, or the same time that a person is subject to detention?

4. Did all nine Justices adopt the "least intrusive means" test?

5. A fairly extreme version of the "least intrusive means" test was rejected in *Sharpe*. As you read the case, see if you can ascertain the reason for that rejection.

UNITED STATES v. SHARPE
470 U.S. 675 (1985)

CHIEF JUSTICE BURGER delivered the opinion of the Court.

We granted certiorari to decide whether an individual reasonably suspected of engaging in criminal activity may be detained for a period of 20 minutes, when the detention is necessary for law enforcement officers to conduct a limited investigation of the suspected criminal activity.

I

On the morning of June 9, 1978, Agent Cooke of the Drug Enforcement Administration (DEA) was on patrol in an unmarked vehicle on a coastal road near Sunset Beach, North Carolina, an area under surveillance for suspected drug trafficking. At approximately 6:30 a.m., Cooke noticed a blue pickup truck with an attached camper shell traveling on the highway in tandem with a blue Pontiac Bonneville. Respondent Savage was driving the pickup, and respondent Sharpe was driving the Pontiac. The Pontiac also carried a passenger, Davis, the charges against whom were later dropped. Observing that the truck was riding low in the rear and that the camper did not bounce or sway appreciably when the truck drove over bumps or around curves, Agent Cooke concluded that it was heavily loaded. A quilted material covered the rear and side windows of the camper.

Cooke's suspicions were sufficiently aroused to follow the two vehicles for approximately 20 miles as they proceeded south into South Carolina. He then decided to make an "investigative stop" and radioed the State Highway Patrol for assistance. Officer Thrasher, driving a marked patrol car, responded to the call. Almost immediately after Thrasher caught up with the procession, the Pontiac and the pickup turned off the highway and onto a campground road.[1] Cooke and Thrasher followed the two vehicles as the latter drove along the road at 55 to 60 miles an hour, exceeding the speed limit of 35 miles an hour. The road eventually looped back to the highway, onto which Savage and Sharpe turned and continued to drive south.

---

[1] Officer Thrasher testified that the respondents' vehicles turned off the highway "[a]bout one minute" after he joined the procession.

At this point, all four vehicles were in the middle lane of the three right-hand lanes of the highway. Agent Cooke asked Officer Thrasher to signal both vehicles to stop. Thrasher pulled alongside the Pontiac, which was in the lead, turned on his flashing light, and motioned for the driver of the Pontiac to stop. As Sharpe moved the Pontiac into the right lane, the pickup truck cut between the Pontiac and Thrasher's patrol car, nearly hitting the patrol car, and continued down the highway. Thrasher pursued the truck while Cooke pulled up behind the Pontiac.

Cooke approached the Pontiac and identified himself. He requested identification, and Sharpe produced a Georgia driver's license bearing the name of Raymond J. Pavlovich. Cooke then attempted to radio Thrasher to determine whether he had been successful in stopping the pickup truck, but he was unable to make contact for several minutes, apparently because Thrasher was not in his patrol car. Cooke radioed the local police for assistance, and two officers from the Myrtle Beach Police Department arrived about 10 minutes later. Asking the two officers to "maintain the situation," Cooke left to join Thrasher.

In the meantime, Thrasher had stopped the pickup truck about one-half mile down the road. After stopping the truck, Thrasher had approached it with his revolver drawn, ordered the driver, Savage, to get out and assume a "spread eagled" position against the side of the truck, and patted him down. Thrasher then holstered his gun and asked Savage for his driver's license and the truck's vehicle registration. Savage produced his own Florida driver's license and a bill of sale for the truck bearing the name of Pavlovich. In response to questions from Thrasher concerning the ownership of the truck, Savage said that the truck belonged to a friend and that he was taking it to have its shock absorbers repaired. When Thrasher told Savage that he would be held until the arrival of Cooke, whom Thrasher identified as a DEA agent, Savage became nervous, said that he wanted to leave, and requested the return of his driver's license. Thrasher replied that Savage was not free to leave at that time.

Agent Cooke arrived at the scene approximately 15 minutes after the truck had been stopped. Thrasher handed Cooke Savage's license and the bill of sale for the truck; Cooke noted that the bill of sale bore the same name as Sharpe's license. Cooke identified himself to Savage as a DEA agent and said that he thought the truck was loaded with marihuana. Cooke twice sought permission to search the camper, but Savage declined to give it, explaining that he was not the owner of the truck. Cooke then stepped on the rear of the truck and, observing that it did not sink any lower, confirmed his suspicion that it was probably overloaded. He put his nose against the rear window, which was covered from the inside, and reported that he could smell marihuana. Without seeking Savage's permission, Cooke removed the keys from the ignition, opened the rear of the camper, and observed a large number of burlap-wrapped bales resembling bales of marihuana that Cooke had seen in previous investigations. Agent Cooke then placed Savage under arrest and left him with Thrasher.

Cooke returned to the Pontiac and arrested Sharpe and Davis. Approximately 30 to 40 minutes had elapsed between the time Cooke stopped the Pontiac and the time he returned to arrest Sharpe and Davis. Cooke assembled the various parties and vehicles and led them to the Myrtle Beach police station. That evening, DEA agents took the truck to the Federal Building in Charleston, South Carolina. Several days later, Cooke supervised the unloading of the truck, which contained 43 bales weighing a total of 2,629 pounds. Acting without a search warrant, Cooke had eight randomly selected bales opened and sampled. Chemical tests showed that the samples were marihuana.

II

A

The Fourth Amendment is not, of course, a guarantee against *all* searches and seizures, but only against *unreasonable* searches and seizures. The authority and limits of the Amendment apply to investigative stops of vehicles such as occurred here. In *Terry*, we adopted a dual inquiry for evaluating the reasonableness of an investigative stop. Under this approach, we examine

> whether the officer's action was justified at its inception, and whether it was reasonably related in scope to the circumstances which justified the interference in the first place.

As to the first part of this inquiry, the Court of Appeals assumed that the police had an articulable and reasonable suspicion that Sharpe and Savage were engaged in marihuana trafficking, given the setting and all the circumstances when the police attempted to stop the Pontiac and the pickup. That assumption is abundantly supported by the record.[3] As to the second part of the inquiry, however, the court concluded that the 30- to 40-minute detention of Sharpe and the 20-minute detention of Savage "failed to meet the [Fourth Amendment's] requirement of brevity."

It is not necessary for us to decide whether the length of Sharpe's detention was unreasonable, because that detention bears no causal relation to Agent Cooke's discovery of the marihuana. The marihuana was in Savage's pickup, not in Sharpe's Pontiac; the contraband introduced at respondents' trial cannot logically be considered the "fruit" of Sharpe's detention. The only issue in this case, then, is whether it was reasonable under the circumstances facing Agent Cooke and Officer Thrasher to detain Savage, whose vehicle contained the challenged evidence, for approximately 20 minutes. We conclude that the detention of Savage clearly meets the Fourth Amendment's standard of reasonableness.

In *Royer*, government agents stopped the defendant in an airport, seized his luggage, and took him to a small room used for questioning, where a search of the luggage revealed narcotics. The Court held that the defendant's detention consti-

---

[3] Agent Cooke had observed the vehicles traveling in tandem for 20 miles in an area near the coast known to be frequented by drug traffickers. Cooke testified that pickup trucks with camper shells were often used to transport large quantities of marihuana. Savage's pickup truck appeared to be heavily loaded, and the windows of the camper were covered with a quilted bed-sheet material rather than curtains. Finally, both vehicles took evasive actions and started speeding as soon as Officer Thrasher began following them in his marked car. Perhaps none of these facts, standing alone, would give rise to a reasonable suspicion; but taken together as appraised by an experienced law enforcement officer, they provided clear justification to stop the vehicles and pursue a limited investigation.

tuted an arrest. As in *Dunaway*, though, the focus was primarily on facts other than the duration of the defendant's detention — particularly the fact that the police confined the defendant in a small airport room for questioning.

The plurality in *Royer* did note that "an investigative detention must be temporary and last no longer than is necessary to effectuate the purpose of the stop." The Court followed a similar approach in *Place*. In that case, law enforcement agents stopped the defendant after his arrival in an airport and seized his luggage for 90 minutes to take it to a narcotics detection dog for a "sniff test." We decided that an investigative seizure of personal property could be justified under the *Terry* doctrine, but that "[t]he length of the detention of respondent's luggage alone precludes the conclusion that the seizure was reasonable in the absence of probable cause." However, the rationale underlying that conclusion was premised on the fact that the police knew of respondent's arrival time for several hours beforehand, and the Court assumed that the police could have arranged for a trained narcotics dog in advance and thus avoided the necessity of holding respondent's luggage for 90 minutes. "[I]n assessing the effect of the length of the detention, we take into account whether the police diligently pursue their investigation."

Here, the Court of Appeals did not conclude that the police acted less than diligently, or that they *unnecessarily* prolonged Savage's detention. *Place* and *Royer* thus provide no support for the Court of Appeals' analysis.

Admittedly, *Terry, Dunaway, Royer*, and *Place*, considered together, may in some instances create difficult line-drawing problems in distinguishing an investigative stop from a *de facto* arrest. Obviously, if an investigative stop continues indefinitely, at some point it can no longer be justified as an investigative stop. But our cases impose no rigid time limitation on *Terry* stops. While it is clear that "the brevity of the invasion of the individual's Fourth Amendment interests is an important factor in determining whether the seizure is so minimally intrusive as to be justifiable on reasonable suspicion," we have emphasized the need to consider the law enforcement purposes to be served by the stop as well as the time reasonably needed to effectuate those purposes. Much as a "bright line" rule would be desirable, in evaluating whether an investigative detention is unreasonable, common sense and ordinary human experience must govern over rigid criteria.

The Court of Appeals' decision would effectively establish a *per se* rule that a 20-minute detention is too long to be justified under the *Terry* doctrine. Such a result is clearly and fundamentally at odds with our approach in this area.

B

In assessing whether a detention is too long in duration to be justified as an investigative stop, we consider it appropriate to examine whether the police diligently pursued a means of investigation that was likely to confirm or dispel their suspicions quickly, during which time it was necessary to detain the defendant. A court making this assessment should take care to consider whether the police are acting in a swiftly developing situation, and in such cases the court should not indulge in unrealistic second-guessing. A creative judge engaged in *post hoc* evaluation of police conduct can almost always imagine some alternative means by which the objectives of the police might have been accomplished. But "[t]he fact that the protection of the public might, in the abstract, have been accomplished by 'less intrusive' means does not, itself, render the search unreasonable." *Cady v. Dombrowski*, 413 U.S. 433, 447 (1973); *see also United States v. Martinez-Fuerte*, 428 U.S. 543, 557, n.12 (1976). The question is not simply whether some other alternative was available, but whether the police acted unreasonably in failing to recognize or to pursue it.

We readily conclude that, given the circumstances facing him, Agent Cooke pursued his investigation in a diligent and reasonable manner. During most of Savage's 20-minute detention, Cooke was attempting to contact Thrasher and enlisting the help of the local police who remained with Sharpe while Cooke left to pursue Officer Thrasher and the pickup. Once Cooke reached Officer Thrasher and Savage,[4] he proceeded expeditiously: within the space of a few minutes, he examined Savage's driver's license and the truck's bill of sale, requested (and was denied) permission to search the truck, stepped on the rear bumper and noted that the truck did not move, confirming his suspicion that it was probably overloaded. He then detected the odor of marihuana.

Clearly this case does not involve any delay unnecessary to the legitimate investigation of the law enforcement officers. Respondents presented no evidence that the officers were dilatory in their investigation. The delay in this case was attributable almost entirely to the evasive actions of Savage, who sought to elude the police as Sharpe moved his Pontiac to the side of the road.[5] Except for Savage's maneuvers, only a short and certainly permissible pre-arrest detention would likely have taken place. The somewhat longer detention was simply the result of a "graduate[d] . . . respons[e] to the demands of [the] particular situation."

We reject the contention that a 20-minute stop is unreasonable when the police have acted diligently and a suspect's actions contribute to the added delay about which he complains. The judgment of the Court of Appeals is reversed, and the case is remanded for further proceedings consistent with this opinion.

JUSTICE MARSHALL, concurring in the judgment.

I join the result in this case because only the evasive actions of the defendants here turned what otherwise would have been a permissibly brief *Terry* stop into the prolonged encounter now at issue. I write separately, however, because in my view

---

[4] It was appropriate for Officer Thrasher to hold Savage for the brief period pending Cooke's arrival. Thrasher could not be certain that he was aware of all of the facts that had aroused Cooke's suspicions; and, as a highway patrolman, he lacked Cooke's training and experience in dealing with narcotics investigations. In this situation, it cannot realistically be said that Thrasher, a state patrolman called in to assist a federal agent in making a stop, acted unreasonably because he did not release Savage based solely on his own limited investigation of the situation and without the consent of Agent Cooke.

[5] Even if it could be inferred that Savage was not attempting to elude the police when he drove his car *between* Thrasher's patrol car and Sharpe's Pontiac — in the process nearly hitting the patrol car — such an assumption would not alter our analysis or our conclusion. The significance of Savage's actions is that, whether innocent or purposeful, they made it necessary for Thrasher and Cooke to split up, placed Thrasher and Cooke out of contact with each other, and required Cooke to enlist the assistance of local police before he could join Thrasher and Savage.

the Court understates the importance of *Terry's* brevity requirement to the constitutionality of *Terry* stops.

I

Terry recognized a "narrowly drawn" exception to the probable-cause requirement of the Fourth Amendment for certain seizures of the person that do not rise to the level of full arrests. Two justifications supported this "major development in Fourth Amendment jurisprudence." First, a legitimate *Terry* stop — brief and narrowly circumscribed — was said to involve a "wholly different kind of intrusion upon individual freedom" than a traditional arrest. Second, under some circumstances, the government's interest in preventing imminent criminal activity could be substantial enough to outweigh the still-serious privacy interests implicated by a limited *Terry* stop. Thus, when the intrusion on the individual is minimal, and when law enforcement interests outweigh the privacy interests infringed in a *Terry* encounter, a stop based on objectively reasonable and articulable suspicions, rather than upon probable cause, is consistent with the Fourth Amendment.

To those who rank zealous law enforcement above all other values, it may be tempting to divorce *Terry* from its rationales and merge the two prongs of *Terry* into the single requirement that the police act reasonably under all the circumstances when they stop and investigate on less than probable cause. As long as the police are acting diligently to complete their investigation, it is difficult to maintain that law enforcement goals would better be served by releasing an individual after a brief stop than by continuing to detain him for as long as necessary to discover whether probable cause can be established. But while the preservation of order is important to any society, the "needs of law enforcement stand in constant tension with the Constitution's protections of the individual against certain exercises of official power. It is precisely the predictability of these pressures that counsels a resolute loyalty to constitutional safeguards." *Terry* must be justified, not because it makes law enforcement easier, but because a *Terry* stop does not constitute the sort of arrest that the Constitution requires be made only upon probable cause.

For this reason, in reviewing any *Terry* stop, the "critical threshold issue is the intrusiveness of the seizure." *Place* (Blackmun, J., concurring in judgment). Regardless how efficient it may be for law enforcement officials to engage in prolonged questioning to investigate a crime, or how reasonable in light of law enforcement objectives it may be to detain a suspect until various inquiries can be made and answered, a seizure that in duration, scope, or means goes beyond the bounds of *Terry* cannot be reconciled with the Fourth Amendment in the absence of probable cause. Legitimate law enforcement interests that do not rise to the level of probable cause simply cannot turn an overly intrusive seizure into a constitutionally permissible one.

In my view, the length of the stop in and of itself may make the stop sufficiently intrusive to be unjustifiable in the absence of probable cause to arrest.[2] *Terry*

---

[2] A stop can also be unduly intrusive if the individual is moved or asked to move more than a short distance, if a search is more extensive than necessary to protect the police from an objective fear of danger, or if tactics amounting to custodial interrogation are used.

"stops" are justified, in part, because they are stops, rather than prolonged seizures. "[A] stopping differs from an arrest not in the incompleteness of the seizure but in the brevity of it."

Consistent with the rationales that make *Terry* stops legitimate, we have recognized several times that the requirement that *Terry* stops be brief imposes an independent and *per se* limitation on the extent to which officials may seize an individual on less than probable cause. The Court explicitly so held in *Place*, where we invalidated a search that was the product of a lengthy detention; as the Court said: "The length of the detention . . . alone precludes the conclusion that the seizure was reasonable in the absence of probable cause . . . . [T]he 90-minute detention . . . is sufficient to render the seizure unreasonable . . . ."[3] A *Terry* stop valid in its inception may become unduly intrusive on personal liberty and privacy simply by lasting too long. That remains true even if valid law enforcement objectives account for the length of the seizure.

The requirement that *Terry* stops be brief no matter what the needs of law enforcement in the particular case is buttressed by several sound pragmatic considerations. First, if the police know they must structure their *Terry* encounters so as to confirm or dispel the officer's reasonable suspicion in a brief time, police practices will adapt to minimize the intrusions worked by these encounters. *Cf. Place* (to assure brevity of *Terry* airport stops, narcotic detection dogs must, under some circumstances, be kept in same airport to which suspect is arriving). Firm adherence to the requirement that stops be brief forces law enforcement officials to take into account from the start the serious and constitutionally protected liberty and privacy interests implicated in *Terry* stops, and to alter official conduct accordingly.

Second, a *per se* ban on stops that are not brief yields the sort of objective standards mandated by our Fourth Amendment precedents, standards that would avoid placing courts in the awkward position of second-guessing police as to what constitutes reasonable police practice. We have recognized that the methods employed in a *Terry* stop "should be the least intrusive means reasonably available to verify or dispel the officer's suspicion in a short period of time." *Royer*.[6] Yet in the absence of a *per se* requirement that stops be brief, defining what means are "least intrusive" is a virtually unmanageable and unbounded task. Whether the police have acted with due diligence is a function not just of how quickly they

---

[3] The majority suggests that the 90-minute detention in *Place* was held too long only because the police had not acted diligently enough. In my view, the statements quoted in text adequately demonstrate that the length of the detention "alone" was "sufficient" to invalidate the seizure.

[6] At least we have until today. The language from *Cady v. Dombrowski*, quoted to the effect that full-scale Fourth Amendment searches may be reasonable even if not accomplished in the least intrusive means is of course wholly inconsistent with the holding of *Royer*. *Cady*, quite obviously, has nothing to do with the *Terry* stop issue here; there the question was whether a search that the Court found legitimate had to be accomplished in any particular way, while here the issue is whether the police have intruded on an individual so substantially as to need probable cause. I assume *Royer's* holding remains the law on this point, and that the Court's mere quotation out of context of *Cady*, unsupported by any argument or reasoned discussion, is not meant to overrule *Royer*. Legal reasoning hardly consists of finding isolated sentences in wholly different contexts and using them to overrule *sub silentio* prior holdings.

completed their investigation, but of an almost limitless set of alternative ways in which the investigation *might* have been completed. For example, in this case the Court posits that the officers acted with due diligence, but they might have acted with more diligence had Cooke summoned two rather than one highway patrolman to assist him, or had Cooke, who had the requisite "training and experience," stopped the pickup truck — the vehicle thought to be carrying the marihuana. And if due diligence takes as fixed the amount of resources a community is willing to devote to law enforcement, officials in one community may act with due diligence in holding an individual at an airport for 35 minutes while waiting for the sole narcotics detection dog they possess, while officials who have several dogs readily available may be dilatory in prolonging an airport stop to even 10 minutes.

Constitutional rights should not vary in this manner. Yet in the absence of a brevity standard that is independent of the actions or needs of the police, that variance is one of two inescapable results. The other is that the Court will have to take seriously its requirement that the police act with due diligence, which will require the Court to inject itself into such issues as whether this or that alternative investigative method ought to have been employed.[7] The better and judicially more manageable rule would be a *per se* requirement that *Terry* stops be brief, for that rule would avoid the Court's measuring police conduct according to a virtually standardless yardstick.

Finally, dissolving the brevity requirement into the general standard that the seizure simply be reasonable will "inevitably produce friction and resentment [among the police], for there are bound to be inconsistent and confusing decisions." The police themselves may have done nothing unreasonable in holding a motorist for one hour while waiting for a registration computer to come back on line, but surely such a prolonged detention would be unlawful. Indeed, in my view, as soon as a patrolman called in and learned that the computer was down, the suspect would have to be released. That is so not because waiting for information in this circumstance is unreasonable, but simply because the stop must be brief if it is to be constitutional on less than probable cause. A "balancing" test suggests that a stop is invalid only if officials have crossed over some line they should have avoided; the finding that such a "balance" has been struck improperly casts a certain moral opprobrium on official conduct. A brevity requirement makes clear that the Constitution imposes certain limitations on police powers no matter how reasonably those powers have been exercised. "[H]air-splitting distinctions that currently plague our Fourth Amendment jurisprudence" serve nobody's interest, but measuring the legitimacy of a *Terry* stop by the reasonableness and diligence of the official's actions, rather than by the intrusiveness of the stop, would proliferate such distinctions. Maintaining the clarity of *Terry's* brevity requirement will instead breed respect for the law among both police and citizens.

---

[7] It is clear from the Court's distaste for the task of "second-guessing" the police, and from Justice Brennan's critique of the cursory way in which the Court analyzes the investigative methods employed in this case, that the Court has little intention of choosing this option and taking seriously the requirement that the police act with "due diligence." That demonstrated lack of will makes a strict brevity requirement all the more important.

For these reasons, fidelity to the rationales that justify *Terry* stops requires that the intrusiveness of the stop be measured independently of law enforcement needs. A stop must first be found not unduly intrusive, particularly in its length, before it is proper to consider whether law enforcement aims warrant limited investigation.

In my view, the record demonstrates that the lengthy stop at issue in this case would have been permissibly brief but for the respondents' efforts to evade law enforcement officials. Accordingly, I agree with the Court's judgment. But because there is no way to fathom the extent to which the majority's holding rests on this basis, and because the majority acts with unseemly haste to decide other issues not presented [particularly referring to the Court's footnote 3, where it concluded that there was clearly reasonable suspicion to justify this stop. Justice Marshall thought that this resolution should only be assumed, and not resolved.], I join only its judgment.

JUSTICE BRENNAN, dissenting.

The respondent William Sharpe and his passenger were pulled over to the side of the highway, concededly without probable cause, and held for more than 30 minutes, much of that time in the back seat of a police cruiser, before they ultimately were arrested and informed of the charges against them. In the meantime, the respondent Donald Savage was stopped one-half mile down the road, also according to the Court without probable cause. He was ordered out of his pickup truck at gunpoint, spread-eagled and frisked, and questioned by the detaining patrolman, Kenneth Thrasher, about a suspected shipment of marihuana in his vehicle. Although Savage repeatedly asked to be released, Thrasher held him for almost 15 minutes until DEA Agent Luther Cooke, the officer who had stopped Sharpe back up the road, could arrive and sniff the vehicle's windows to determine whether he could smell the suspected marihuana. As Thrasher later conceded, Savage "was under custodial arrest" the entire time.

The Court today concludes that these lengthy detentions constituted reasonable investigative stops within the meaning of *Terry*. It explains that, although the length of an investigative stop made without probable cause may at some point become so excessive as to violate the Fourth Amendment, the primary inquiry must nevertheless be whether the investigating officers acted "diligently" in pursuing a stop that was no longer than "necessary" to the "legitimate investigation of the law enforcement officers." The Court reasons that *Terry's* brevity requirement is in fact an accordion-like concept that may be expanded outward depending on "the law enforcement purposes to be served by the stop." Applying this analysis to the instant case, the Court concludes that the lengthy detentions of Sharpe and Savage were reasonable because the delay was the fault of Savage, whom the Court contends "sought to elude the police" by speeding away when signaled to stop; had Savage not taken these "evasive actions," Agent Cooke could have questioned Sharpe and Savage together and "only a short and certainly permissible pre-arrest detention would likely have taken place."

I dissent. [T]he Court in criminal cases increasingly has evaded the plain requirements of our precedents where they would stand in the way of a judgment for the government. For a *Terry* stop to be upheld, for example, the government must show at a minimum that the "least intrusive means reasonably available" were used in carrying out the stop. *Royer* (opinion of White, J.).[1] The Government has made no such showing here, and the Court's bald assertion that "[c]learly this case does not involve any delay unnecessary" to "legitimate" law enforcement is completely undermined by the record before us.

The Court's discussion of Savage's purported attempt "to elude the police" amounts to nothing more than a *de novo* factual finding made on a record that is, at best, hopelessly ambiguous. Neither the District Court nor the Court of Appeals ever found that Savage's actions constituted evasion or flight. If we are nevertheless to engage in *de novo* factfinding, I submit the Court has taken insufficient account of several factors.

First, Savage's actions in continuing to drive down the highway could well have been entirely consistent with those of any driver who sees the police hail someone in front of him over to the side of the road. Sharpe's Pontiac was at least several car lengths in front of Savage's pickup truck; Thrasher thought there was a separation of "a car length or two," while Cooke testified that the distance was anywhere from between 30–50 and 100–150 feet. Approaching in the far-left lane, Thrasher pulled even with Sharpe's lead vehicle, "turned the blue light on," "blew the siren," and "motioned for *him* to pull over." (emphasis added). Savage moved into the right lane so as to avoid hitting Thrasher, who was slowing along with Sharpe, and continued on his way. Neither Cooke nor Thrasher ever testified that Savage "sought to elude" them, and there is nothing here that is necessarily inconsistent with the actions of any motorist who happens to be behind a vehicle that is being pulled over to the side of the road.

Because it has not been shown that Savage "sought to elude" the police, I agree with the Court that the constitutional propriety of these detentions is governed by *Terry* and its progeny. These precedents lead inexorably to the conclusion that the investigative actions at issue here violated the Fourth Amendment.

If the officers believed that the suspected marihuana was in Savage's pickup truck, and if only Cooke was capable of investigating for the presence of marihuana, I am at a loss why Cooke did not follow the truck and leave Thrasher with the Pontiac, rather than vice versa.

The Government has offered no plausible explanation why Thrasher, a trained South Carolina highway patrolman, could not have carried out the limited *Terry* investigation of Savage and the pickup truck. Once he had stopped Savage, Thrasher not only "held" him, but carried out his own investigation of the situation. He pointed out that the truck had been riding low and asked Savage what was inside. He inspected the exterior and even jumped up on the bumper to test how loaded down the camper might be. Moreover, although Cooke certainly had more drug enforcement experience than Thrasher, there is no reason why Thrasher could not have conducted the simple sniffing investigation that Cooke later did: Thrasher, like all South Carolina highway patrolmen, had received basic narcotics detection

---

[1] Concurring in the plurality's result in *Royer*, I argued that the Fourth Amendment requires an even more stringent standard: "a lawful stop must be so strictly limited that it is difficult to conceive of a less intrusive means that would be effective to accomplish the purpose of the stop."

training and knew exactly what marihuana smells like. He did not even attempt to smell the windows of the camper shell for two reasons: first, that was not his assigned "job"; and second, "[m]y sinuses were stopped up that morning." Thrasher's sinuses apparently cleared up several hours later, however, because once the pickup was at the police station he decided, "[j]ust as a matter of curiosity," to "get right up on the window" of the vehicle, and reported decisively that "I smelled some marijuana up around the windows." I would have thought that, before the Court chose to uphold a lengthy detention of a citizen without probable cause based on the "reasonable" ignorance of the detaining officer, it would have taken the time to get its facts straight.[19]

Finally, the record strongly suggests that the delay may have been attributable in large measure to the poor investigative coordination and botched communications on the part of the DEA. Drug enforcement agents were swarming throughout the immediate area on the morning that Savage and Sharpe were detained, conducting numerous roadblocks and "profile stops" of campers and recreational vehicles similar to Savage's. Even accepting the Court's dubious premise that a highway patrolman is somehow incapable of carrying out a simple investigative stop, it is clear that Cooke had followed Sharpe and Savage for over 30 minutes and, knowing that a multiple-vehicle stop was in the offing, should have obtained assistance from other DEA agents. This was, in fact, precisely what he attempted to do. He repeatedly tried to contact the area DEA headquarters but complained over his police radio that "I can't raise anybody else right now." He asked the local police dispatcher to telephone the DEA office to "ask them if anybody there has any contact with me on my DEA frequency." The dispatcher reported that the line was busy; local police units had to be sent out to headquarters "to tell these people to get off the telephone." Once the units arrived, it was learned that "[t]here's no one there. They're all down at the Mar Vista Motel." Additional units had to be sent to the motel to "get those people out of the sack." Agents apparently were eventually located at the motel and at Don's Pancake House, for by the time that Cooke returned to the Pontiac to complete the arrests there were several other DEA agents waiting to assist him. In the meantime, of course, Cooke had had to request Thrasher as a local backup.

Far from demonstrating that these investigative stops were carried out in the most "expeditious way" using all "reasonably available" investigative methods, the record in this case therefore strongly suggests custodial detentions more accurately characterized as resulting from hopelessly bungled communications and from Thrasher's unwillingness to tread on Cooke's investigative turf. I do not mean to suggest that Cooke and Thrasher bore the entire blame for these delays; it was not Cooke's fault that his DEA backups apparently were sleeping or eating breakfast rather than monitoring their radios for his calls, and Thrasher might well have felt that it was not his place to carry out an investigation he apparently was fully

---

[19] The Court has responded by insisting that Thrasher "could not be certain that he was aware" of all the facts and therefore was justified in detaining Savage indefinitely. The Court has not pointed to anything that would support this bald *de novo* finding, which is squarely contradicted by the record. In addition, the Court's reasoning flies directly in the face of the Fourth Amendment, which requires the authorities to ground their conduct on what is known at the time of their actions rather than on what might subsequently turn up.

capable of conducting. But constitutional rights should not so easily be balanced away simply because the individual officers may have subjectively been acting in good faith, especially where an objective evaluation of the facts suggests an unnecessarily intrusive exercise of police power.[20]

QUESTIONS AND NOTES

1.   What is the status of the "least intrusive means" test in regard to *Terry* stops after *Sharpe*? What should it be?

2.   After *Royer, Place*, and *Sharpe* is there an outside limit on *Terry* stops? Should there be? Why? Why not?

3.   Do you think that Savage was evasive? Should that matter?

4.   If the issue were before the Court, should the Court have found reasonable suspicion on this record?

5.   We conclude with *Hiibel*, a case that requires a suspect, reasonably stopped under *Terry*, to identify himself, even though he does not know why he was stopped.

HIIBEL v. SIXTH JUDICIAL DISTRICT COURT
542 U.S. 177 (2004)

JUSTICE KENNEDY delivered the opinion of the Court.

The petitioner was arrested and convicted for refusing to identify himself during a stop allowed by *Terry*. He challenges his conviction under the Fourth and Fifth Amendments to the United States Constitution, applicable to the States through the Fourteenth Amendment.

I

The sheriff's department in Humboldt County, Nevada, received an afternoon telephone call reporting an assault. The caller reported seeing a man assault a

---

[20] In response to this dissent, the Court offers several justifications for its failure to consult the record in making its *de novo* factual determinations. First, the Court asserts that judges "should not indulge in unrealistic second-guessing" of police conduct. There is nothing "unrealistic" about requiring police officers to pursue the "least intrusive means reasonably available" when detaining citizens on less than probable cause, and it is the *duty* of courts in every Fourth Amendment case to determine whether police conduct satisfied constitutional standards. Moreover, the public will understandably be perplexed why the Court ignores the record and refuses to engage in "second-guessing" where police conduct is challenged while it simultaneously engages in second-guessing of a defendant's conduct where necessary to ensure a verdict for the Government.

In addition, the Court attempts to slip into a footnote the astonishing assertion that *even if its textual discussion of Savage's actions is completely untrue*, this "would not alter our analysis or our conclusion." n.5 (emphasis added). The Court contends that, *"whether innocent* or purposeful," *Savage's* conduct "made . . . necessary" the length of these detentions. *Ibid.* (emphasis added). If the authorities did not reasonably carry out the stops, however, and if Savage's continued driving was "innocent" conduct, it is logically and constitutionally intolerable to hold that Savage waived important Fourth Amendment rights because the events were his "innocent" fault.

woman in a red and silver GMC truck on Grass Valley Road. Deputy Sheriff Lee Dove was dispatched to investigate. When the officer arrived at the scene, he found the truck parked on the side of the road. A man was standing by the truck, and a young woman was sitting inside it. The officer observed skid marks in the gravel behind the vehicle, leading him to believe it had come to a sudden stop.

The officer approached the man and explained that he was investigating a report of a fight. The man appeared to be intoxicated. The officer asked him if he had "any identification on [him]," which we understand as a request to produce a driver's license or some other form of written identification. The man refused and asked why the officer wanted to see identification. The officer responded that he was conducting an investigation and needed to see some identification. The unidentified man became agitated and insisted he had done nothing wrong. The officer explained that he wanted to find out who the man was and what he was doing there. After continued refusals to comply with the officer's request for identification, the man began to taunt the officer by placing his hands behind his back and telling the officer to arrest him and take him to jail. This routine kept up for several minutes: the officer asked for identification 11 times and was refused each time. After warning the man that he would be arrested if he continued to refuse to comply, the officer placed him under arrest.

We now know that the man arrested on Grass Valley Road is Larry Dudley Hiibel. Hiibel was charged with "willfully resist[ing], delay[ing], or obstruct[ing] a public officer in discharging or attempting to discharge any legal duty of his office." The government reasoned that Hiibel had obstructed the officer in carrying out his duties under § 171.123, a Nevada statute that defines the legal rights and duties of a police officer in the context of an investigative stop. Section 171.123 provides in relevant part:

"1. Any peace officer may detain any person whom the officer encounters under circumstances which reasonably indicate that the person has committed, is committing or is about to commit a crime.

. . . .

"3. The officer may detain the person pursuant to this section only to ascertain his identity and the suspicious circumstances surrounding his presence abroad. Any person so detained shall identify himself, but may not be compelled to answer any other inquiry of any peace officer."

Hiibel was tried in the Justice Court of Union Township. The court agreed that Hiibel's refusal to identify himself as required by § 171.123 "obstructed and delayed Dove as a public officer in attempting to discharge his duty." Hiibel was convicted and fined $250.

II

NRS § 171.123(3) is an enactment sometimes referred to as a "stop and identify" statute. Stop and identify statutes often combine elements of traditional vagrancy laws with provisions intended to regulate police behavior in the course of investigatory stops. The statutes vary from State to State, but all permit an officer to ask or require a suspect to disclose his identity. A few States model their statutes on the Uniform Arrest Act, a model code that permits an officer to stop a person reasonably suspected of committing a crime and "demand of him his name, address, business abroad and whither he is going." The provision, originally designated § 250.12, provides that a person who is loitering "under circumstances which justify suspicion that he may be engaged or about to engage in crime commits a violation if he refuses the request of a peace officer that he identify himself and give a reasonably credible account of the lawfulness of his conduct and purposes." In some States, a suspect's refusal to identify himself is a misdemeanor offense or civil violation; in others, it is a factor to be considered in whether the suspect has violated loitering laws. In other States, a suspect may decline to identify himself without penalty.

Stop and identify statutes have their roots in early English vagrancy laws that required suspected vagrants to face arrest unless they gave "a good Account of themselves," a power that itself reflected common-law rights of private persons to "arrest any suspicious night-walker, and detain him till he give a good account of himself . . . ." In recent decades, the Court has found constitutional infirmity in traditional vagrancy laws. In *Papachristou v. Jacksonville*, 405 U.S. 156, (1972), the Court held that a traditional vagrancy law was void for vagueness. Its broad scope and imprecise terms denied proper notice to potential offenders and permitted police officers to exercise unfettered discretion in the enforcement of the law.

The Court has recognized similar constitutional limitations on the scope and operation of stop and identify statutes. In *Brown v. Texas*, 443 U.S. 47, 52, (1979), the Court invalidated a conviction for violating a Texas stop and identify statute on Fourth Amendment grounds. The Court ruled that the initial stop was not based on specific, objective facts establishing reasonable suspicion to believe the suspect was involved in criminal activity. Absent that factual basis for detaining the defendant, the Court held, the risk of "arbitrary and abusive police practices" was too great and the stop was impermissible. Four Terms later, the Court invalidated a modified stop and identify statute on vagueness grounds. *See Kolender v. Lawson*, 461 U.S. 352, (1983). The California law in *Kolender* required a suspect to give an officer " 'credible and reliable' " identification when asked to identify himself. The Court held that the statute was void because it provided no standard for determining what a suspect must do to comply with it, resulting in " 'virtually unrestrained power to arrest and charge persons with a violation.' "

The present case begins where our prior cases left off. Here there is no question that the initial stop was based on reasonable suspicion, satisfying the Fourth Amendment requirements noted in *Brown*. Further, the petitioner has not alleged that the statute is unconstitutionally vague, as in *Kolender*. Here the Nevada statute is narrower and more precise. The statute in *Kolender* had been interpreted to require a suspect to give the officer "credible and reliable" identification. In contrast, the Nevada Supreme Court has interpreted NRS § 171.123(3) to require only that a suspect disclose his name. See 118 Nev., at 875, 59 P.3d, at 1206 (opinion of Young, C.J.) ("The suspect is not required to provide private details about his background, but merely to state his name to an officer when reasonable suspicion exists"). As we understand it, the statute does not require a suspect to give the officer a driver's license or any other document. Provided that the suspect either states his name or communicates it to the officer by other means — a choice, we assume, that the suspect may make — the statute is satisfied and no violation occurs.

III

Hiibel argues that his conviction cannot stand because the officer's conduct violated his Fourth Amendment rights. We disagree.

Asking questions is an essential part of police investigations. In the ordinary course a police officer is free to ask a person for identification without implicating the Fourth Amendment. "[I]nterrogation relating to one's identity or a request for identification by the police does not, by itself, constitute a Fourth Amendment seizure." *INS v. Delgado*, 466 U.S. 210, 216, (1984). Beginning with *Terry*, the Court has recognized that a law enforcement officer's reasonable suspicion that a person may be involved in criminal activity permits the officer to stop the person for a brief time and take additional steps to investigate further. To ensure that the resulting seizure is constitutionally reasonable, a *Terry* stop must be limited. The officer's action must be " 'justified at its inception, and . . . reasonably related in scope to the circumstances which justified the interference in the first place.' " *Sharpe* (quoting *Terry, supra,* at 20. For example, the seizure cannot continue for an excessive period of time, *see Place*, or resemble a traditional arrest, see *Dunaway v. New York*, 442 U.S. 200 (1979).

Our decisions make clear that questions concerning a suspect's identity are a routine and accepted part of many Terry stops. See *United States v. Hensley*, 469 U.S. 221, 229, (1985) ("[T]he ability to briefly stop [a suspect], ask questions, or check identification in the absence of probable cause promotes the strong government interest in solving crimes and bringing offenders to justice"); *Hayes v. Florida*, 470 U.S. 811, 816 (1985) ("[I]f there are articulable facts supporting a reasonable suspicion that a person has committed a criminal offense, that person may be stopped in order to identify him, to question him briefly, or to detain him briefly while attempting to obtain additional information"); *Adams v. Williams*, 407 U.S. 143, (1972) ("A brief stop of a suspicious individual, in order to determine his identity or to maintain the status quo momentarily while obtaining more information, may be most reasonable in light of the facts known to the officer at the time").

Obtaining a suspect's name in the course of a *Terry* stop serves important government interests. Knowledge of identity may inform an officer that a suspect is wanted for another offense, or has a record of violence or mental disorder. On the other hand, knowing identity may help clear a suspect and allow the police to concentrate their efforts elsewhere. Identity may prove particularly important in cases such as this, where the police are investigating what appears to be a domestic assault. Officers called to investigate domestic disputes need to know whom they are dealing with in order to assess the situation, the threat to their own safety, and possible danger to the potential victim.

Although it is well established that an officer may ask a suspect to identify himself in the course of a *Terry* stop, it has been an open question whether the suspect can be arrested and prosecuted for refusal to answer. Petitioner draws our attention to statements in prior opinions that, according to him, answer the question in his favor. In *Terry*, Justice White stated in a concurring opinion that a person detained in an investigative stop can be questioned but is "not obliged to answer, answers may not be compelled, and refusal to answer furnishes no basis for an arrest." The Court cited this opinion in dicta in Berkemer *v. McCarty*, 468 U.S. 420, 439 (1984), a decision holding that a routine traffic stop is not a custodial stop requiring the protections of *Miranda v. Arizona*, 384 U.S. 436 (1966). In the course of explaining why *Terry* stops have not been subject to *Miranda*, the Court suggested reasons why Terry stops have a "nonthreatening character," among them the fact that a suspect detained during a *Terry* stop "is not obliged to respond" to questions. According to petitioner, these statements establish a right to refuse to answer questions during a *Terry* stop.

We do not read these statements as controlling. The passages recognize that the Fourth Amendment does not impose obligations on the citizen but instead provides rights against the government. As a result, the Fourth Amendment itself cannot require a suspect to answer questions. This case concerns a different issue, however. Here, the source of the legal obligation arises from Nevada state law, not the Fourth Amendment. Further, the statutory obligation does not go beyond answering an officer's request to disclose a name. As a result, we cannot view the dicta in *Berkemer* or Justice White's concurrence in *Terry* as answering the question whether a State can compel a suspect to disclose his name during a *Terry* stop.

The principles of *Terry* permit a State to require a suspect to disclose his name in the course of a Terry stop. The reasonableness of a seizure under the Fourth Amendment is determined "by balancing its intrusion on the individual's Fourth Amendment interests against its promotion of legitimate government interests." The Nevada statute satisfies that standard. The request for identity has an immediate relation to the purpose, rationale, and practical demands of a *Terry* stop. The threat of criminal sanction helps ensure that the request for identity does not become a legal nullity. On the other hand, the Nevada statute does not alter the nature of the stop itself: it does not change its duration or its location. A state law requiring a suspect to disclose his name in the course of a valid *Terry* stop is consistent with Fourth Amendment prohibitions against unreasonable searches and seizures.

Petitioner argues that the Nevada statute circumvents the probable cause requirement, in effect allowing an officer to arrest a person for being suspicious. According to petitioner, this creates a risk of arbitrary police conduct that the Fourth Amendment does not permit. These are familiar concerns; they were central to the opinion in *Papachristou*, and also to the decisions limiting the operation of stop and identify statutes in *Kolender* and *Brown*. Petitioner's concerns are met by the requirement that a *Terry* stop must be justified at its inception and "reasonably related in scope to the circumstances which justified" the initial stop. Under these principles, an officer may not arrest a suspect for failure to identify himself if the request for identification is not reasonably related to the circumstances justifying the stop. The Court noted a similar limitation in *Hayes*, where it suggested that *Terry* may permit an officer to determine a suspect's identity by compelling the suspect to submit to fingerprinting only if there is "a reasonable basis for believing that fingerprinting will establish or negate the suspect's connection with that crime." It is clear in this case that the request for identification was "reasonably related in scope to the circumstances which justified" the stop. The officer's request was a commonsense inquiry, not an effort to obtain an arrest for failure to identify after a *Terry* stop yielded insufficient evidence. The stop, the request, and the State's requirement of a response did not contravene the guarantees of the Fourth Amendment.

JUSTICE BREYER, with whom JUSTICE SOUTER and JUSTICE GINSBURG join, dissenting.

Notwithstanding the vagrancy statutes to which the majority refers, this Court's Fourth Amendment precedents make clear that police may conduct a *Terry* stop only within circumscribed limits. And one of those limits invalidates laws that compel responses to police questioning.

In *Terry*, the Court considered whether police, in the absence of probable cause, can stop, question, or frisk an individual at all. The Court recognized that the Fourth Amendment protects the " 'right of every individual to the possession and control of his own person.' " At the same time, it recognized that in certain circumstances, public safety might require a limited "seizure," or stop, of an individual against his will. The Court consequently set forth conditions circumscribing when and how the police might conduct a *Terry* stop. They include what has become known as the "reasonable suspicion" standard. Justice White, in a separate concurring opinion, set forth further conditions. Justice White wrote: "Of course, the person stopped is not obliged to answer, answers may not be compelled, and refusal to answer furnishes no basis for an arrest, although it may alert the officer to the need for continued observation."

About 10 years later, the Court, in *Brown v. Texas*, held that police lacked "any reasonable suspicion" to detain the particular petitioner and require him to identify himself. The Court noted that the trial judge had asked the following: "I'm sure [officers conducting a *Terry* stop] should ask everything they possibly could find out. *What I'm asking is what's the State's interest in putting a man in jail because he doesn't want to answer . . . .*" (Appendix to opinion of the Court) (emphasis in original). The Court referred to Justice White's *Terry* concurrence. And it said that it "need not decide" the matter.

Then, five years later, the Court wrote that an "officer may ask the [*Terry*] detainee a moderate number of questions to determine his identity and to try to obtain information confirming or dispelling the officer's suspicions. *But the detainee is not obliged to respond.*" *Berkemer v. McCarty*, 468 U.S. 420, 439 (1984) (emphasis added). See also *Kolender v. Lawson*, 461 U.S. 352, 365 (1983) (Brennan, J., concurring) (*Terry* suspect "must be free to . . . decline to answer the questions put to him"); *Illinois v. Wardlow*, 528 U.S. 119, 125 (2000) (stating that allowing officers to stop and question a fleeing person "is quite consistent with the individual's right to go about his business or to stay put and remain silent in the face of police questioning").

This lengthy history — of concurring opinions, of references, and of clear explicit statements — means that the Court's statement in *Berkemer*, while technically dicta, is the kind of strong dicta that the legal community typically takes as a statement of the law. And that law has remained undisturbed for more than 20 years.

There is no good reason now to reject this generation-old statement of the law.

I consequently dissent.

(JUSTICE STEVENS dissented on Fifth Amendment grounds.)

QUESTIONS AND NOTES

1.   When can the police ask for identification after *Hiibel* and *Brown v. Texas*?

2.   How does a suspect in Hiibel's position know whether the police have reasonable suspicion? *Compare Florida v. J.L.* Would J.L. have been required to identify himself if requested to by the police?

3.   If he does not know whether the police have reasonable suspicion, how can he assess his duty to respond?

4.   Even with reasonable suspicion, how does knowing Hiibel's identity help the police resolve the question of whether he assaulted his daughter?

5.   In *Illinois v. Wardlow*, would Wardlow have been required to identify himself (provide an I.D.) if after the police frisked him, he had turned out to be unarmed? Why?

6.   Should the police at least be required to explain to the suspect why they want his identification?

7.   Suppose that he just said: "My name is Dudley Hiibel" but refused to give any other identification. Would (should) he be subject to prosecution?

8.   Did 9/11, and the concomitant need to track suspicious persons contribute to *the Hiibel* result? Should it have? Explain. *See* Loewy: *The Cowboy and the Cop: The Saga of Dudley Hiibel, 9/11, and the Vanishing Fourth Amendment*, 109 PENN ST. L. REV. 929 (2005).

Chapter 9

SEIZURES

Heretofore, we have assumed that we have been dealing with a search or seizure, and have sought to determine the circumstances under which that search or seizure was justified. In this chapter (seizure) and the next (search), we shall attempt to define those terms. The question is significant, because if the police conduct does not constitute a search or seizure, the Fourth Amendment is not implicated. The first opinion to seriously attempt to define "seizure" was Justice Stewart's opinion (for only himself and Justice Rehnquist) in *Mendenhall*.

UNITED STATES v. MENDENHALL
446 U.S. 544 (1980)

MR. JUSTICE STEWART delivered the opinion of the Court with respect to parts I, II-B, II-C, and III, and a judgment including Justice Rehnquist with respect to part II-A:

The respondent was brought to trial in the United States District Court for the Eastern District of Michigan on a charge of possessing heroin with intent to distribute it. She moved to suppress the introduction at trial of the heroin as evidence against her on the ground that it had been acquired from her through an unconstitutional search and seizure by agents of the Drug Enforcement Administration (DEA). The District Court denied the respondent's motion, and she was convicted after a trial upon stipulated facts. The Court of Appeals reversed, finding the search of the respondent's person to have been unlawful. We granted certiorari to consider whether any right of the respondent guaranteed by the Fourth Amendment was violated in the circumstances presented by this case.

I

At the hearing in the trial court on the respondent's motion to suppress, it was established how the heroin she was charged with possessing had been obtained from her. The respondent arrived at the Detroit Metropolitan Airport on a commercial airline flight from Los Angeles early in the morning on February 10, 1976. As she disembarked from the airplane, she was observed by two agents of the DEA, who were present at the airport for the purpose of detecting unlawful traffic in narcotics. After observing the respondent's conduct, which appeared to the agents to be characteristic of persons unlawfully carrying narcotics,[1] the agents approached her as she was walking through the concourse, identified themselves as federal agents, and asked to see her identification and airline ticket. The respondent produced her driver's license, which was in the name of Sylvia Mendenhall, and, in answer to a question of one of the agents, stated that she resided at the address appearing on the license. The airline ticket was issued in the name of "Annette Ford." When asked why the ticket bore a name different from her own, the respondent stated that she "just felt like using that name." In response to a further question, the respondent indicated that she had been in California only two days. Agent Anderson then specifically identified himself as a federal narcotics agent and, according to his testimony, the respondent "became quite shaken, extremely nervous. She had a hard time speaking."

After returning the airline ticket and driver's license to her, Agent Anderson asked the respondent if she would accompany him to the airport DEA office for further questions. She did so, although the record does not indicate a verbal response to the request. The office, which was located up one flight of stairs about 50 feet from where the respondent had first been approached, consisted of a reception area adjoined by three other rooms. At the office the agent asked the respondent if she would allow a search of her person and handbag and told her that she had the right to decline the search if she desired. She responded: "Go ahead." She then handed Agent Anderson her purse, which contained a receipt for an airline ticket that had been issued to "F. Bush" three days earlier for a flight from Pittsburgh through Chicago to Los Angeles. The agent asked whether this was the ticket that she had used for her flight to California, and the respondent stated that it was.

A female police officer then arrived to conduct the search of the respondent's person. She asked the agents if the respondent had consented to be searched. The agents said that she had, and the respondent followed the policewoman into a private room. There the policewoman again asked the respondent if she consented to the search, and the respondent replied that she did. The policewoman explained that the search would require that the respondent remove her clothing. The respondent stated that she had a plane to catch and was assured by the policewoman that if she were carrying no narcotics, there would be no problem. The respondent then began to disrobe without further comment. As the respondent removed her clothing, she took from her undergarments two small packages, one of which appeared to contain heroin, and handed both to the policewoman. The agents then arrested the respondent for possessing heroin.

---

[1] The agent testified that the respondent's behavior fit the so-called "drug courier profile" — an informally compiled abstract of characteristics thought typical of persons carrying illicit drugs. In this case the agents thought it relevant that (1) the respondent was arriving on a flight from Los Angeles, a city believed by the agents to be the place of origin for much of the heroin brought to Detroit; (2) the respondent was the last person to leave the plane, "appeared to be very nervous," and "completely scanned the whole area where [the agents] were standing"; (3) after leaving the plane the respondent proceeded past the baggage area without claiming any luggage; and (4) the respondent changed airlines for her flight out of Detroit.

II

The Fourth Amendment provides that "the right of the people to be secure in their persons, houses, papers, and effects, against unreasonable searches and seizures, shall not be violated . . . ." There is no question in this case that the respondent possessed this constitutional right of personal security as she walked through the Detroit Airport, for "the Fourth Amendment protects people, not places." Here the Government concedes that its agents had neither a warrant nor probable cause to believe that the respondent was carrying narcotics when the agents conducted a search of the respondent's person. It is the Government's position, however, that the search was conducted pursuant to the respondent's consent, and thus was excepted from the requirements of both a warrant and probable cause. *See Schneckloth v. Bustamonte* [Chapter 11, *infra*]. Evidently, the Court of Appeals concluded that the respondent's apparent consent to the search was in fact not voluntarily given and was in any event the product of earlier official conduct violative of the Fourth Amendment. We must first consider, therefore, whether such conduct occurred, either on the concourse or in the DEA office at the airport.

A

The Fourth Amendment's requirement that searches and seizures be founded upon an objective justification, governs all seizures of the person, "including seizures that involve only a brief detention short of traditional arrest. Accordingly, if the respondent was "seized" when the DEA agents approached her on the concourse and asked questions of her, the agents' conduct in doing so was constitutional only if they reasonably suspected the respondent of wrongdoing. But "[o]bviously, not all personal intercourse between policemen and citizens involves 'seizures' of persons. Only when the officer, by means of physical force or show of authority, has in some way restrained the liberty of a citizen may we conclude that a 'seizure' has occurred."

The distinction between an intrusion amounting to a "seizure" of the person and an encounter that intrudes upon no constitutionally protected interest is illustrated by the facts of *Terry*, which the Court recounted as follows: "Officer McFadden approached the three men, identified himself as a police officer and asked for their names . . . . When the men 'mumbled something' in response to his inquiries, Officer McFadden grabbed petitioner Terry, spun him around so that they were facing the other two, with Terry between McFadden and the others, and patted down the outside of his clothing." Obviously the officer "seized" Terry and subjected him to a "search" when he took hold of him, spun him around, and patted down the outer surfaces of his clothing. What was not determined in that case, however, was that a seizure had taken place before the officer physically restrained Terry for purposes of searching his person for weapons. The Court "assume[d] that up to that point no intrusion upon constitutionally protected rights had occurred." The Court's assumption appears entirely correct in view of the fact, noted in the concurring opinion of Mr. Justice WHITE, that "[t]here is nothing in the Constitution which prevents a policeman from addressing questions to anyone on the streets." Police officers enjoy "the liberty (again, possessed by every citizen) to address questions to other persons" (Harlan, J., concurring), although "ordinarily the person addressed has an equal right to ignore his interrogator and walk away."

Similarly, the Court in *Sibron*, a case decided the same day as *Terry*, indicated that not every encounter between a police officer and a citizen is an intrusion requiring an objective justification. In that case, a police officer, before conducting what was later found to have been an unlawful search, approached Sibron in a restaurant and told him to come outside, which Sibron did. The Court had no occasion to decide whether there was a "seizure" of Sibron inside the restaurant antecedent to the seizure that accompanied the search. The record was "barren of any indication whether Sibron accompanied [the officer] outside in submission to a show of force or authority which left him no choice, or *whether he went voluntarily in a spirit of apparent cooperation* with the officer's investigation." (emphasis added). Plainly, in the latter event, there was no seizure until the police officer in some way demonstrably curtailed Sibron's liberty.

We adhere to the view that a person is "seized" only when, by means of physical force or a show of authority, his freedom of movement is restrained. Only when such restraint is imposed is there any foundation whatever for invoking constitutional safeguards. The purpose of the Fourth Amendment is not to eliminate all contact between the police and the citizenry, but "to prevent arbitrary and oppressive interference by enforcement officials with the privacy and personal security of individuals." As long as the person to whom questions are put remains free to disregard the questions and walk away, there has been no intrusion upon that person's liberty or privacy as would under the Constitution require some particularized and objective justification.

Moreover, characterizing every street encounter between a citizen and the police as a "seizure," while not enhancing any interest secured by the Fourth Amendment, would impose wholly unrealistic restrictions upon a wide variety of legitimate law enforcement practices. The Court has on other occasions referred to the acknowledged need for police questioning as a tool in the effective enforcement of the criminal laws. "Without such investigation, those who were innocent might be falsely accused, those who were guilty might wholly escape prosecution, and many crimes would go unsolved. In short, the security of all would be diminished.

We conclude that a person has been "seized" within the meaning of the Fourth Amendment only if, in view of all of the circumstances surrounding the incident, a reasonable person would have believed that he was not free to leave.[6] Examples of circumstances that might indicate a seizure, even where the person did not attempt to leave, would be the threatening presence of several officers, the display of a weapon by an officer, some physical touching of the person of the citizen, or the use of language or tone of voice indicating that compliance with the officer's request might be compelled. In the absence of some such evidence, otherwise inoffensive contact between a member of the public and the police cannot, as a matter of law, amount to a seizure of that person.

---

[6] We agree with the District Court that the subjective intention of the DEA agent in this case to detain the respondent, had she attempted to leave, is irrelevant except insofar as that may have been conveyed to the respondent.

On the facts of this case, no "seizure" of the respondent occurred. The events took place in the public concourse. The agents wore no uniforms and displayed no weapons. They did not summon the respondent to their presence, but instead approached her and identified themselves as federal agents. They requested, but did not demand to see the respondent's identification and ticket. Such conduct without more, did not amount to an intrusion upon any constitutionally protected interest. The respondent was not seized simply by reason of the fact that the agents approached her, asked her if she would show them her ticket and identification, and posed to her a few questions. Nor was it enough to establish a seizure that the person asking the questions was a law enforcement official. In short, nothing in the record suggests that the respondent had any objective reason to believe that she was not free to end the conversation in the concourse and proceed on her way, and for that reason we conclude that the agents' initial approach to her was not a seizure.

Our conclusion that no seizure occurred is not affected by the fact that the respondent was not expressly told by the agents that she was free to decline to cooperate with their inquiry, for the voluntariness of her responses does not depend upon her having been so informed. We also reject the argument that the only inference to be drawn from the fact that the respondent acted in a manner so contrary to her self-interest is that she was compelled to answer the agents' questions. It may happen that a person makes statements to law enforcement officials that he later regrets, but the issue in such cases is not whether the statement was self-protective, but rather whether it was made voluntarily.

The Court's decision last Term in *Brown v. Texas*, 443 U.S. 47, on which the respondent relies, is not apposite. It could not have been plainer under the circumstances there presented that Brown was forcibly detained by the officers. In that case, two police officers approached Brown in an alley, and asked him to identify himself and to explain his reason for being there. Brown "refused to identify himself and angrily asserted that the officers had no right to stop him." Up to this point there was no seizure. But after continuing to protest the officers' power to interrogate him, Brown was first frisked, and then arrested for violation of a state statute making it a criminal offense for a person to refuse to give his name and address to an officer "who has lawfully stopped him and requested the information." The Court simply held in that case that because the officers had no reason to suspect Brown of wrongdoing, there was no basis for detaining him, and therefore no permissible foundation for applying the state statute in the circumstances there presented.

The Court's decisions involving investigatory stops of automobiles do not point in any different direction. In *Brignoni-Ponce*, the Court held that a roving patrol of law enforcement officers could stop motorists in the general area of an international border for brief inquiry into their residence status only if the officers reasonably suspected that the vehicle might contain aliens who were illegally in the country. The Government did not contend in that case that the persons whose automobiles were detained were not seized. Indeed, the Government acknowledged that the occupants of a detained vehicle were required to respond to the officers' questions and on some occasions to produce documents evidencing their eligibility to be in the United States. Moreover, stopping or diverting an automobile in transit, with the attendant opportunity for a visual inspection of areas of the passenger compartment not otherwise observable, is materially more intrusive than a question put to a passing pedestrian, and the fact that the former amounts to a seizure tells very little about the constitutional status of the latter.

B

Although we have concluded that the initial encounter between the DEA agents and the respondent on the concourse at the Detroit Airport did not constitute an unlawful seizure, it is still arguable that the respondent's Fourth Amendment protections were violated when she went from the concourse to the DEA office. Such a violation might in turn infect the subsequent search of the respondent's person.

The District Court specifically found that the respondent accompanied the agents to the office " 'voluntarily in a spirit of apparent cooperation,' " quoting *Sibron*. Notwithstanding this determination by the trial court, the Court of Appeals evidently concluded that the agents' request that the respondent accompany them converted the situation into an arrest requiring probable cause in order to be found lawful. But because the trial court's finding was sustained by the record, the Court of Appeals was mistaken in substituting for that finding its view of the evidence.

The question whether the respondent's consent to accompany the agents was in fact voluntary or was the product of duress or coercion, express or implied, is to be determined by the totality of all the circumstances, and is a matter which the Government has the burden of proving. The respondent herself did not testify at the hearing. The Government's evidence showed that the respondent was not told that she had to go to the office, but was simply asked if she would accompany the officers. There were neither threats nor any show of force. The respondent had been questioned only briefly, and her ticket and identification were returned to her before she was asked to accompany the officers.

On the other hand, it is argued that the incident would reasonably have appeared coercive to the respondent, who was 22 years old and had not been graduated from high school. It is additionally suggested that the respondent, a female and a Negro, may have felt unusually threatened by the officers, who were white males. While these factors were not irrelevant, neither were they decisive, and the totality of the evidence in this case was plainly adequate to support the District Court's finding that the respondent voluntarily consented to accompany the officers to the DEA office.

Mr. Justice Powell, with whom The Chief Justice and Mr. Justice Blackmun join, concurring in part and concurring in judgment.

I join Parts I, II-B, II-C, and III of the Court's opinion. Because neither of the courts below considered the question, I do not reach the Government's contention that the agents did not "seize" the respondent within the meaning of the Fourth Amendment. In my view, we may assume for present purposes that the stop did constitute a seizure.[1] I would hold — as did the District Court — that the federal agents had reasonable suspicion that the respondent was engaging in criminal activity, and, therefore, that they did not violate the Fourth Amendment by stopping the respondent for routine questioning.

MR. JUSTICE WHITE, with whom MR. JUSTICE BRENNAN, MR. JUSTICE MARSHALL, and MR. JUSTICE STEVENS join, dissenting.

Mr. Justice STEWART believes that a "seizure" within the meaning of the Fourth Amendment occurs when an individual's freedom of movement is restrained by means of physical force or a show of authority. Although it is undisputed that Ms. Mendenhall was not free to leave after the DEA agents stopped her and inspected her identification, Mr. Justice STEWART concludes that she was not "seized" because he finds that, under the totality of the circumstances, a reasonable person would have believed that she was free to leave. While basing this finding on an alleged absence from the record of objective evidence indicating that Ms. Mendenhall was not free to ignore the officer's inquiries and continue on her way, Mr. Justice STEWART's opinion brushes off the fact that this asserted evidentiary deficiency may be largely attributable to the fact that the "seizure" question was never raised below. In assessing what the record does reveal, the opinion discounts certain objective factors that would tend to support a "seizure" finding,[3] while relying on contrary factors inconclusive even under its own illustrations of how a "seizure" may be established.[4] Moreover, although Mr. Justice STEWART's opinion purports to make its "seizure" finding turn on objective factors known to the person accosted, in distinguishing prior decisions holding that investigatory stops constitute "seizures," it does not rely on differences in the extent to which persons accosted could reasonably believe that they were free to leave.[5] Even if one believes the Government should be permitted to raise the "seizure" question in this Court, the

---

[1] Mr. Justice STEWART concludes in Part II-A that there was no "seizure" within the meaning of the Fourth Amendment. He reasons that such a seizure occurs "only if, in view of all of the circumstances surrounding the incident, a reasonable person would have believed that he was not free to leave." Mr. Justice STEWART also notes that " '[t]here is nothing in the Constitution which prevents a policeman from addressing questions to anyone on the streets.' " I do not necessarily disagree with the views expressed in Part II-A. For me, the question whether the respondent in this case reasonably could have thought she was free to "walk away" when asked by two Government agents for her driver's license and ticket is extremely close.

[3] Not the least of these factors is the fact that the DEA agents for a time took Ms. Mendenhall's plane ticket and driver's license from her. It is doubtful that any reasonable person about to board a plane would feel free to leave when law enforcement officers have her plane ticket.

[4] Mr. Justice STEWART notes, for example, that a "seizure" might be established even if the suspect did not attempt to leave, by the nature of the language or tone of voice used by the officers, factors that were never addressed at the suppression hearing, very likely because the "seizure" question was not raised.

[5] In *Brown v. Texas* and *Brignoni-Ponce*, the prosecution, as here, did not question whether the suspects who had been stopped had been "seized," given its concessions that the suspects would not have been permitted to leave without responding to the officers' requests for identification. In each case the Court recognized that a "seizure" had occurred without inquiring into whether a reasonable person would have believed that he was not free to leave. Mr. Justice STEWART's present attempt to distinguish the fact that stops of automobiles constitute "seizures," on the ground that it is more intrusive to visually inspect the passenger compartment of a car, confuses the question of the quantum of reasonable suspicion necessary to justify such "seizures" with the question whether a "seizure" has occurred.

proper course would be to direct a remand to the District Court for an evidentiary hearing on the question, rather than to decide it in the first instance in this Court.

III

Whatever doubt there may be concerning whether Ms. Mendenhall's Fourth Amendment interests were implicated during the initial stages of her confrontation with the DEA agents, she undoubtedly was "seized" within the meaning of the Fourth Amendment when the agents escorted her from the public area of the terminal to the DEA office for questioning and a strip-search of her person. In *Dunaway*, we held that a person who accompanied police officers to a police station for purposes of interrogation undoubtedly "was 'seized' in the Fourth Amendment sense," even though "he was not told he was under arrest." We found it significant that the suspect was taken to a police station, "was never informed that he was 'free to go,' " and "would have been physically restrained if he had refused to accompany the officers or had tried to escape their custody." Like the "seizure" in Dunaway, the nature of the intrusion to which Ms. Mendenhall was subjected when she was escorted by DEA agents to their office and detained there for questioning and a strip-search was so great that it "was in important respects indistinguishable from a traditional arrest." Although Ms. Mendenhall was not told that she was under arrest, she in fact was not free to refuse to go to the DEA office and was not told that she was.[12] Furthermore, once inside the office, Ms. Mendenhall would not have been permitted to leave without submitting to a strip-search.[13] Thus, as in Dunaway, "[t]he mere facts that [the suspect] was not told he was under arrest, was not 'booked,' and would not have had an arrest record if the interrogation had proved fruitless, while not insignificant for all purposes, . . . obviously do not make [the suspect's] seizure even roughly analogous to the narrowly defined intrusions involved in *Terry* and its progeny." Because the intrusion to which Ms. Mendenhall was subjected when she was escorted to the DEA office is of the same character as

---

[12] Agent Anderson testified on cross-examination at the suppression hearing:

> Q. All right. Now, when you asked her to accompany you to the DEA office for further questioning, if she had wanted to walk away, would you have stopped her?
>
> A. Once I asked her to accompany me?
>
> Q. Yes.
>
> A. Yes, I would have stopped her.
>
> Q. She was not free to leave, was she?
>
> A. Not at that point.

[13] Agent Anderson testified:

> Q. Had she tried to leave that room when she was being accompanied by the female officer, would you have known?
>
> A. If she had attempted to leave the room?
>
> Q. Yes.
>
> A. Well yes, I could say that I would have known.
>
> Q. And if she had tried to leave prior to being searched by the female officer, would you have stopped her?
>
> A. Yes.

that involved in *Dunaway*, probable cause, which concededly was absent, was required to support the intrusion.

The Court's suggestion that no Fourth Amendment interest possessed by Ms. Mendenhall was implicated because she consented to go to the DEA office is inconsistent with *Dunaway* and unsupported in the record. There was no evidence in the record to support the District Court's speculation, made before *Dunaway* was decided, that Ms. Mendenhall accompanied "Agent Anderson to the airport DEA Office 'voluntarily in a spirit of apparent cooperation with the [agent's] investigation,' *Sibron*." Ms. Mendenhall did not testify at the suppression hearing and the officers presented no testimony concerning what she said, if anything, when informed that the officers wanted her to come with them to the DEA office. Indeed, the only testimony concerning what occurred between Agent Anderson's "request" and Ms. Mendenhall's arrival at the DEA office is the agent's testimony that if Ms. Mendenhall had wanted to leave at that point she would have been forcibly restrained. The evidence of consent here is even flimsier than that we rejected in *Dunaway* where it was claimed that the suspect made an affirmative response when asked if he would accompany the officers to the police station. Also in *Sibron*, from which the District Court culled its description of Ms. Mendenhall's "consent," we described a record in a similar state as "totally barren of any indication whether Sibron accompanied Patrolman Martin outside in submission to a show of force or authority which left him no choice, or whether he went voluntarily in a spirit of apparent cooperation with the officer's investigation."

The Court recognizes that the Government has the burden of proving that Ms. Mendenhall consented to accompany the officers, but it nevertheless holds that the "totality of evidence was plainly adequate" to support a finding of consent. On the record before us, the Court's conclusion can only be based on the notion that consent can be assumed from the absence of proof that a suspect resisted police authority. This is a notion that we have squarely rejected. While the Government need not prove that Ms. Mendenhall knew that she had a right to refuse to accompany the officers, it cannot rely solely on acquiescence to the officers' wishes to establish the requisite consent. The Court of Appeals properly understood this in rejecting the District Court's "findings" of consent.

Since the defendant was not present to testify at the suppression hearing, we can only speculate about her state of mind as her encounter with the DEA agents progressed from surveillance, to detention, to questioning, to seclusion in a private office, to the female officer's command to remove her clothing. Nevertheless, it is unbelievable[15] that this sequence of events involved no invasion of a citizen's constitutionally protected interest in privacy. The rule of law requires a different conclusion.

QUESTIONS AND NOTES

1. A majority of the Court concluded that Mendenhall was not seized when she "voluntarily" accompanied the officers to the DEA office. Only Justice Stewart and

---

[15] "Will you walk into my parlour?" said the spider to a fly. (You may find you have consented, without ever knowing why.)

Rehnquist, however, concluded that the initial encounter was voluntary (see fn.1 of Justice Powell's opinion).

2. Do you think that Mendenhall was seized at either or both times? Why? Why not?

3. Is the Court saying that even if (1) Agent Anderson thought that Mendenhall was not free to leave, and (2) Sylvia Mendenhall thought that she was not free to leave, a seizure did not occur because a reasonable person would have felt free to leave? If so, does something seem amiss?

4. Because the Government did not claim that there was no initial seizure, shouldn't the Court have at least remanded the case for a factual hearing to determine the extent to which the police may have coerced Mendenhall's compliance? *Compare Bostick, infra.*

5. If Mendenhall had been seized either in the concourse or when she "consented" to be searched, would either (both) of the seizures have been justified?

6. Did she ever actually consent to the strip search?

7. We now revisit *Royer*, where on arguably similar facts, the Court, applying Justice Stewart's definition, concluded that Royer *had* been seized.

FLORIDA v. ROYER
460 U.S. 491 (1983)

JUSTICE WHITE announced the judgment of the Court and delivered an opinion in which JUSTICES MARSHALL, POWELL and STEVENS joined.

[For a recounting of the facts (which are important), turn to this case in Chapter 8, Section B, *supra.*]

[L]aw enforcement officers do not violate the Fourth Amendment by merely approaching an individual on the street or in another public place, by asking him if he is willing to answer some questions, by putting questions to him if the person is willing to listen, or by offering in evidence in a criminal prosecution his voluntary answers to such questions. Nor would the fact that the officer identifies himself as a police officer, without more, convert the encounter into a seizure requiring some level of objective justification. *Mendenhall* (opinion of Stewart, J.). The person approached, however, need not answer any question put to him; indeed, he may decline to listen to the questions at all and may go on his way. *Terry* (Harlan, J., concurring); (White, J., concurring). He may not be detained even momentarily without reasonable, objective grounds for doing so; and his refusal to listen or answer does not, without more, furnish those grounds. *Mendenhall* (opinion of Stewart, J.). If there is no detention — no seizure within the meaning of the Fourth Amendment — then no constitutional rights have been infringed.

The State [contends] that the entire encounter was consensual and hence Royer was not being held against his will at all. We find this submission untenable. Asking for and examining Royer's ticket and his driver's license were no doubt permissible in themselves, but when the officers identified themselves as narcotics agents, told

Royer that he was suspected of transporting narcotics, and asked him to accompany them to the police room, while retaining his ticket and driver's license and without indicating in any way that he was free to depart, Royer was effectively seized for the purposes of the Fourth Amendment. These circumstances surely amount to a show of official authority such that "a reasonable person would have believed he was not free to leave." *Mendenhall* (Opinion of Stewart, J.).

By the time Royer was informed that the officers wished to examine his luggage, he had identified himself when approached by the officers and had attempted to explain the discrepancy between the name shown on his identification and the name under which he had purchased his ticket and identified his luggage. The officers were not satisfied, for they informed him they were narcotics agents and had reason to believe that he was carrying illegal drugs. They requested him to accompany them to the police room. Royer went with them. He found himself in a small room — a large closet — equipped with a desk and two chairs. He was alone with two police officers who again told him that they thought he was carrying narcotics. He also found that the officers, without his consent, had retrieved his checked luggage from the airlines. What had begun as a consensual inquiry in a public place had escalated into an investigatory procedure in a police interrogation room, where the police, unsatisfied with previous explanations, sought to confirm their suspicions. The officers had Royer's ticket, they had his identification, and they had seized his luggage. Royer was never informed that he was free to board his plane if he so chose, and he reasonably believed that he was being detained. At least as of that moment, any consensual aspects of the encounter had evaporated, and we cannot fault the Florida Court of Appeal for concluding that *Terry* and the cases following it did not justify the restraint to which Royer was then subjected. As a practical matter, Royer was under arrest. Consistent with this conclusion, the State conceded in the Florida courts that Royer would not have been free to leave the interrogation room had he asked to do so.[8] Furthermore, the state's brief in this Court interprets the testimony of the officers at the suppression hearing as indicating that had Royer refused to consent to a search of his luggage, the officers would have held the luggage and sought a warrant to authorize the search.[9]

---

[8] In its brief and at oral argument before this Court, the State contests whether this concession was ever made. We have no basis to question the statement of the Florida court.

[9] Our decision here is consistent with the Court's judgment in *Mendenhall*. In *Mendenhall*, the respondent was walking along an airport concourse when she was approached by two federal Drug Enforcement Agency (DEA) officers. As in the present case, the officers asked for Mendenhall's airline ticket and some identification; the names on the ticket and identification did not match. When one of the agents specifically identified himself as attached to the DEA, Mendenhall became visibly shaken and nervous. After returning the ticket and identification, one officer asked Mendenhall if she would accompany him to the DEA airport office, 50 feet away for further questions. Once in the office, Mendenhall was asked to consent to a search of her person and her handbag; she was advised of her right to decline. In a private room following further assurance from Mendenhall that she consented to the search, a policewoman began the search of Mendenhall's person by requesting that Mendenhall disrobe. As she began to undress, Mendenhall removed two concealed packages that appeared to contain heroin and handed them to the policewoman. The Court of Appeals determined that the initial "stop" of Mendenhall was unlawful because not based upon a reasonable suspicion of criminal activity. In the alternative, the court found that even if the initial stop was permissible, the officer's request that Mendenhall accompany him to the DEA office constituted an arrest without probable cause. This Court reversed. Two Justices were of the view that the entire encounter was consensual and that no seizure had

JUSTICE POWELL, concurring.

This case, however, differs strikingly from *Mendenhall* in the circumstances following the lawful initial questioning and the request that the suspect accompany the officers to a more private place. Royer then found himself in a small, windowless room — described as a "large closet" — alone with two officers who, without his consent, already had obtained possession of his checked luggage. In addition, they had retained his driver's license and airline ticket. Neither the evidence in this case nor common sense suggests that Royer was free to walk away. I agree with the plurality that as a practical matter he then was under arrest, and his surrender of the luggage key to the officers cannot be viewed as consensual.

JUSTICE BRENNAN, concurring in result.

[P]lainly Royer was "seized" for purposes of the Fourth Amendment when the officers asked him to produce his driver's license and airline ticket. *Terry* stated that "whenever a police officer accosts an individual and restrains his freedom to walk away, he has 'seized' that person." Although I agree that "not all personal intercourse between policemen and citizens involves 'seizures' of persons," and that policemen may approach citizens on the street and ask them questions without 'seizing' them for purposes of the Fourth Amendment, once an officer has identified himself and asked a traveller for identification and his airline ticket, the traveller has been "seized" within the meaning of the Fourth Amendment. By identifying themselves and asking for Royer's airline ticket and driver's license the officers, as a practical matter, engaged in a "show of authority" and "restrained [Royer's] liberty." It is simply wrong to suggest that a traveller feels free to walk away when he has been approached by individuals who have identified themselves as police officers and asked for, and received, his airline ticket and driver's license.

JUSTICE BLACKMUN, dissenting.

I concur in the plurality's adoption of the Fourth Amendment "seizure" standard proposed by Justice Stewart in *Mendenhall*: Fourth Amendment protections apply when "official authority" is exercised "such that 'a reasonable person would have believed he was not free to leave.'" I do not quarrel with the plurality's conclusion that at some point in this encounter, that threshold was passed.

---

taken place. Three other Justices assumed that there had been a seizure but would have held that there was reasonable suspicion to warrant it; hence a voluntary consent to search was a valid basis for the search. Thus, the five Justices voting to reverse appeared to agree that Mendenhall was not being illegally detained when she consented to be searched. The four dissenting Justices also assumed that there had been a detention but were of the view that reasonable grounds for suspecting Mendenhall did not exist and concluded that Mendenhall was thus being illegally detained at the time of her consent. The case before us differs in important respects. Here, Royer's ticket and identification remained in the possession of the officers throughout the encounter; the officers also seized and had possession of his luggage. As a practical matter, Royer could not leave the airport without them. In *Mendenhall*, no luggage was involved, the ticket and identification were immediately returned, and the officers were careful to advise that the suspect could decline to be searched. Here, the officers had seized Royer's luggage and made no effort to advise him that he need not consent to the search.

JUSTICE REHNQUIST, with whom THE CHIEF JUSTICE and JUSTICE O'CONNOR join, dissenting.

The facts are similar to those addressed in *Mendenhall*, where a majority of the Court determined that consent to accompany police officers had been voluntary. Royer was not told that he had to go to the room, but was simply asked, after a brief period of questioning, if he would accompany the detectives to the room. Royer was informed as to why the officers wished to question him further. There were neither threats nor any show of force. Detectives Johnson and Magdelena were not in uniform and did not display weapons. The detectives did not touch Royer and made no demands. In fact, Royer admits that the detectives were quite polite.[9]

The plurality concludes that somewhere between the beginning of the 40 foot journey and the resumption of conversation in the room the investigation became so intrusive that Royer's consent "evaporated" leaving him "[a]s a practical matter . . . under arrest." But if Royer was legally approached in the first instance and consented to accompany the detectives to the room, it does not follow that his consent went up in smoke and he was "arrested" upon entering the room. As we made clear in *Mendenhall*, logical analysis would focus on whether the environment in the room rendered the subsequent consent to a search of the luggage involuntary.

As we said in *Mendenhall*, "the fact that she was [in the room] is little or no evidence that she was in any way coerced." Other than the size of the room, described as "a large storage closet,[10] there is nothing in the record which would indicate that Royer's resistance was overborne by anything about the room. Royer, who was in his fourth year of study at Ithaca College at the time and has since graduated with a degree in *communications*, simply continued to cooperate with the detectives as he had from the beginning of the encounter. Absent any evidence of objective indicia of coercion, and even absent any claim of such indicia by Royer, the size of the room itself does not transform a voluntary consent to search into a coerced consent.

QUESTIONS AND NOTES

1. Are you persuaded that a meaningful distinction can be drawn between *Royer* and *Mendenhall* in regard to the question of seizure?

---

[9] Contrary to the Florida court's view, this phase of the encounter contrasts sharply with the circumstances we examined in *Dunaway*. In that case, police officers deliberately sought out the suspect at a neighbor's house and, with a show of force, brought the suspect to police headquarters in a police car, placed him in an interrogation room, and questioned him extensively after giving him a *Miranda* warning. Unlike in *Dunaway*, Royer, after brief questioning, was asked to cooperate by accompanying the officers to a room no more than 40 feet away, so that the questioning could proceed out of the view of the general public.

[10] The characterization of the room as a "closet" is quite misleading. The room contained one desk and two chairs. It was large enough to allow three persons to enter with two heavy suitcases. It also is relevant that it was the Florida court, not Royer, who focused on the size of the room. It was during rehearing by the court en banc that the conviction was reversed with the court finding that when Royer was taken into the private room he was in effect placed under arrest.

2. In that regard, should Royer's status as a near-graduate in communications as contrasted to Mendenhall's 11th grade education have cut in the opposite direction?

3. How persuasive is Justice Brennan's observation that "[i]t is simply wrong to suggest that a traveler feels free to walk away when he has been approached by individuals who have identified themselves as police officers and have asked for, and received, his airline ticket and driver's license"?

4. Would Brennan's statement be significantly less persuasive if the phrase "and received" were deleted?

I.N.S. v. DELGADO
466 U.S. 210 (1984)

JUSTICE REHNQUIST delivered the opinion of the Court.

In the course of enforcing the immigration laws, petitioner Immigration and Naturalization Service (INS) enters employers' worksites to determine whether any illegal aliens may be present as employees. The Court of Appeals for the Ninth Circuit held that the "factory surveys" involved in this case amounted to a seizure of the entire work forces, and further held that the INS could not question individual employees during any of these surveys unless its agents had a reasonable suspicion that the employee to be questioned was an illegal alien. We conclude that these factory surveys did not result in the seizure of the entire work forces, and that the individual questioning of the respondents in this case by INS agents concerning their citizenship did not amount to a detention or seizure under the Fourth Amendment. Accordingly, we reverse the judgment of the Court of Appeals.

Acting pursuant to two warrants, in January and September, 1977, the INS conducted a survey of the work force at Southern California Davis Pleating Company (Davis Pleating) in search of illegal aliens. The warrants were issued on a showing of probable cause by the INS that numerous illegal aliens were employed at Davis Pleating, although neither of the search warrants identified any particular illegal aliens by name. A third factory survey was conducted with the employer's consent in October, 1977, at Mr. Pleat, another garment factory.

At the beginning of the surveys several agents positioned themselves near the buildings' exits, while other agents dispersed throughout the factory to question most, but not all, employees at their work stations. The agents displayed badges, carried walkie-talkies, and were armed, although at no point during any of the surveys was a weapon ever drawn. Moving systematically through the factory, the agents approached employees and, after identifying themselves, asked them from one to three questions relating to their citizenship. If the employee gave a credible reply that he was a United States citizen, the questioning ended, and the agent moved on to another employee. If the employee gave an unsatisfactory response or admitted that he was an alien, the employee was asked to produce his immigration papers. During the survey, employees continued with their work and were free to walk around within the factory.

Respondents are four employees questioned in one of the three surveys.[1] In 1978 respondents and their union representative, the International Ladies Garment Workers' Union, filed two actions, later consolidated, in United States District Court for the Central District of California challenging the constitutionality of INS factory surveys and seeking declaratory and injunctive relief. Respondents argued that the factory surveys violated their Fourth Amendment right to be free from unreasonable searches or seizures.

The Court of Appeals, [a]pplying the standard first enunciated by a Member of this Court in *Mendenhall* (opinion of Stewart, J.), concluded that the entire work forces were seized for the duration of each survey, which lasted from one to two hours, because the stationing of agents at the doors to the buildings meant that "a reasonable worker 'would have believed that he was not free to leave.' " Although the Court of Appeals conceded that the INS had statutory authority to question any alien or person believed to be an alien as to his right to be or remain in the United States, it further held that under the Fourth Amendment individual employees could be questioned only on the basis of a reasonable suspicion that a particular employee being questioned was an alien illegally in the country. A reasonable suspicion or probable cause to believe that a number of illegal aliens were working at a particular factory site was insufficient to justify questioning any individual employee. Consequently, it also held that the individual questioning of respondents violated the Fourth Amendment because there had been no such reasonable suspicion or probable cause as to any of them.

How should the Supreme Court resolve this case. If you wished to find for the government should it be on the ground that there was no seizure or that the seizure was reasonable? For the Court's resolution, see *I.N.S. v. Delgado*, 466 U.S. 210 (1984).

In *Bostick*, the Court elaborated upon, and arguably expanded, what does *not* constitute a seizure.

FLORIDA v. BOSTICK
501 U.S. 429 (1991)

JUSTICE O'CONNOR delivered the opinion of the Court.

We have held that the Fourth Amendment permits police officers to approach individuals at random in airport lobbies and other public places to ask them questions and to request consent to search their luggage, so long as a reasonable person would understand that he or she could refuse to cooperate. This case requires us to determine whether the same rule applies to police encounters that take place on a bus.

---

[1] Respondents Herman Delgado, Ramona Correa, and Francisca Labonte worked at Davis Pleating, while Marie Miramontes, the fourth respondent, was employed by Mr. Pleat. Both Delgado and Correa are United States citizens, while Labonte and Miramontes are permanent resident aliens.

I

Drug interdiction efforts have led to the use of police surveillance at airports, train stations, and bus depots. Law enforcement officers stationed at such locations routinely approach individuals, either randomly or because they suspect in some vague way that the individuals may be engaged in criminal activity, and ask them potentially incriminating questions. Broward County has adopted such a program. County Sheriff's Department officers routinely board buses at scheduled stops and ask passengers for permission to search their luggage.

In this case, two officers discovered cocaine when they searched a suitcase belonging to Terrance Bostick. The underlying facts of the search are in dispute, but the Florida Supreme Court, whose decision we review here, stated explicitly the factual premise for its decision:

> Two officers, complete with badges, insignia and one of them holding a recognizable zipper pouch, containing a pistol, boarded a bus bound from Miami to Atlanta during a stopover in Fort Lauderdale. Eyeing the passengers, the officers admittedly without articulable suspicion, picked out the defendant passenger and asked to inspect his ticket and identification. The ticket, from Miami to Atlanta, matched the defendant's identification and both were immediately returned to him as unremarkable. However, the two police officers persisted and explained their presence as narcotics agents on the lookout for illegal drugs. In pursuit of that aim, they then requested the defendant's consent to search his luggage. Needless to say, there is a conflict in the evidence about whether the defendant consented to the search of the second bag in which the contraband was found and as to whether he was informed of his right to refuse consent. However, any conflict must be resolved in favor of the state, it being a question of fact decided by the trial judge.

Two facts are particularly worth noting. First, the police specifically advised Bostick that he had the right to refuse consent. Bostick appears to have disputed the point, but, as the Florida Supreme Court noted explicitly, the trial court resolved this evidentiary conflict in the State's favor. Second, at no time did the officers threaten Bostick with a gun. The Florida Supreme Court indicated that one officer carried a zipper pouch containing a pistol — the equivalent of carrying a gun in a holster — but the court did not suggest that the gun was ever removed from its pouch, pointed at Bostick, or otherwise used in a threatening manner. The dissent's characterization of the officers as "gun-wielding inquisitor[s]," is colorful, but lacks any basis in fact.

Bostick was arrested and charged with trafficking in cocaine. He moved to suppress the cocaine on the grounds that it had been seized in violation of his Fourth Amendment rights. The trial court denied the motion but made no factual findings. Bostick subsequently entered a plea of guilty, but reserved the right to appeal the denial of the motion to suppress.

The Florida Supreme Court reasoned that Bostick had been seized because a reasonable passenger in his situation would not have felt free to leave the bus to avoid questioning by the police. It rephrased and answered the certified question so as to make the bus setting dispositive in every case. It ruled categorically that " 'an impermissible seizure result[s] when police mount a drug search on buses during scheduled stops and question boarded passengers without articulable reasons for doing so, thereby obtaining consent to search the passengers' luggage.' " The Florida Supreme Court thus adopted a per se rule that the Broward County Sheriff's practice of "working the buses" is unconstitutional.[1] The result of this decision is that police in Florida, as elsewhere, may approach persons at random in most public places, ask them questions and seek consent to a search, but they may not engage in the same behavior on a bus. We granted certiorari to determine whether the Florida Supreme Court's per se rule is consistent with our Fourth Amendment jurisprudence.

II

The sole issue presented for our review is whether a police encounter on a bus of the type described above necessarily constitutes a "seizure" within the meaning of the Fourth Amendment. The State concedes, and we accept for purposes of this decision, that the officers lacked the reasonable suspicion required to justify a seizure and that, if a seizure took place, the drugs found in Bostick's suitcase must be suppressed as tainted fruit.

Our cases make it clear that a seizure does not occur simply because a police officer approaches an individual and asks a few questions. So long as a reasonable person would feel free "to disregard the police and go about his business," the encounter is consensual and no reasonable suspicion is required. The encounter will not trigger Fourth Amendment scrutiny unless it loses its consensual nature.

Since *Terry*, we have held repeatedly that mere police questioning does not constitute a seizure. In *Florida v. Royer*, 460 U.S. 491 (1983) (plurality opinion), for example, we explained that "law enforcement officers do not violate the Fourth Amendment by merely approaching an individual on the street or in another public place, by asking him if he is willing to answer some questions, by putting questions to him if the person is willing to listen, or by offering in evidence in a criminal prosecution his voluntary answers to such questions."

There is no doubt that if this same encounter had taken place before Bostick boarded the bus or in the lobby of the bus terminal, it would not rise to the level of a seizure. The Court has dealt with similar encounters in airports and has found them to be "the sort of consensual encounter[s] that implicat[e] no Fourth Amendment interest." We have stated that even when officers have no basis for suspecting a particular individual, they may generally ask questions of that individual, ask to examine the individual's identification, and request consent to search his or her luggage — as long as the police do not convey a message that

---

[1] The dissent acknowledges that the Florida Supreme Court's answer to the certified question reads like a *per se* rule, but dismisses as "implausible" the notion that the court would actually apply this rule to "trump" a careful analysis of all the relevant facts. Implausible as it may seem, that is precisely what the Florida Supreme Court does. It routinely grants review in bus search cases and quashes denials of motions to suppress *expressly on the basis of its answer to the certified question in this case*. (Citations omitted.)

compliance with their requests is required.

Bostick insists that this case is different because it took place in the cramped confines of a bus. A police encounter is much more intimidating in this setting, he argues, because police tower over a seated passenger and there is little room to move around. Bostick claims to find support in language from cases, indicating that a seizure occurs when a reasonable person would believe that he or she is not "free to leave." Bostick maintains that a reasonable bus passenger would not have felt free to leave under the circumstances of this case because there is nowhere to go on a bus. Also, the bus was about to depart. Had Bostick disembarked, he would have risked being stranded and losing whatever baggage he had locked away in the luggage compartment.

The Florida Supreme Court found this argument persuasive, so much so that it adopted a *per se* rule prohibiting the police from randomly boarding buses as a means of drug interdiction. The state court erred, however, in focusing on whether Bostick was "free to leave" rather than on the principle that those words were intended to capture. When police attempt to question a person who is walking down the street or through an airport lobby, it makes sense to inquire whether a reasonable person would feel free to continue walking. But when the person is seated on a bus and has no desire to leave, the degree to which a reasonable person would feel that he or she could leave is not an accurate measure of the coercive effect of the encounter.

Here, for example, the mere fact that Bostick did not feel free to leave the bus does not mean that the police seized him. Bostick was a passenger on a bus that was scheduled to depart. He would not have felt free to leave the bus even if the police had not been present. Bostick's movements were "confined" in a sense, but this was the natural result of his decision to take the bus; it says nothing about whether or not the police conduct at issue was coercive.

In this respect, the Court's decision in *Delgado* is dispositive. At issue there was the INS' practice of visiting factories at random and questioning employees to determine whether any were illegal aliens. Several INS agents would stand near the building's exits, while other agents walked through the factory questioning workers. The Court acknowledged that the workers may not have been free to leave their worksite, but explained that this was not the result of police activity: "Ordinarily, when people are at work their freedom to move about has been meaningfully restricted, not by the actions of law enforcement officials, but by the workers' voluntary obligations to their employers." We concluded that there was no seizure because, even though the workers were not free to leave the building without being questioned, the agents' conduct should have given employees "no reason to believe that they would be detained if they gave truthful answers to the questions put to them or if they simply refused to answer."

The present case is analytically indistinguishable from *Delgado*. Like the workers in that case, Bostick's freedom of movement was restricted by a factor independent of police conduct — *i.e.*, by his being a passenger on a bus. Accordingly, the "free to leave" analysis on which Bostick relies is inapplicable. In such a situation, the appropriate inquiry is whether a reasonable person would feel free to decline the officers' requests or otherwise terminate the encounter. This formulation follows logically from prior cases and breaks no new ground. We have said before that the crucial test is whether, taking into account all of the circumstances surrounding the encounter, the police conduct would "have communicated to a reasonable person that he was not at liberty to ignore the police presence and go about his business." Where the encounter takes place is one factor, but it is not the only one. And, as the Solicitor General correctly observes, an individual may decline an officer's request without fearing prosecution. We have consistently held that a refusal to cooperate, without more, does not furnish the minimal level of objective justification needed for a detention or seizure.

The facts of this case, as described by the Florida Supreme Court, leave some doubt whether a seizure occurred. Two officers walked up to Bostick on the bus, asked him a few questions, and asked if they could search his bags. As we have explained, no seizure occurs when police ask questions of an individual, ask to examine the individual's identification, and request consent to search his or her luggage — so long as the officers do not convey a message that compliance with their requests is required. Here, the facts recited by the Florida Supreme Court indicate that the officers did not point guns at Bostick or otherwise threaten him and that they specifically advised Bostick that he could refuse consent.

Nevertheless, we refrain from deciding whether or not a seizure occurred in this case. The trial court made no express findings of fact, and the Florida Supreme Court rested its decision on a single fact — that the encounter took place on a bus — rather than on the totality of the circumstances. We remand so that the Florida courts may evaluate the seizure question under the correct legal standard. We do reject, however, Bostick's argument that he must have been seized because no reasonable person would freely consent to a search of luggage that he or she knows contains drugs. This argument cannot prevail because the "reasonable person" test presupposes an *innocent person*. *See Royer* (BLACKMUN, J., dissenting) ("The fact that [respondent] knew the search was likely to turn up contraband is of course irrelevant; the potential intrusiveness of the officers' conduct must be judged from the viewpoint of an innocent person in [his] position").

The dissent characterizes our decision as holding that police may board buses and by an *"intimidating* show of authority," (emphasis added), demand of passengers their "voluntary" cooperation. That characterization is incorrect. Clearly, a bus passenger's decision to cooperate with law enforcement officers authorizes the police to conduct a search without first obtaining a warrant *only* if the cooperation is voluntary. "Consent" that is the product of official intimidation or harassment is not consent at all. Citizens do not forfeit their constitutional rights when they are coerced to comply with a request that they would prefer to refuse. The question to be decided by the Florida courts on remand is whether Bostick chose to permit the search of his luggage.

The dissent also attempts to characterize our decision as applying a lesser degree of constitutional protection to those individuals who travel by bus, rather than by other forms of transportation. This, too, is an erroneous characterization. Our Fourth Amendment inquiry in this case — whether a reasonable person would have felt free to decline the officers' requests or otherwise terminate the encounter — applies equally to police encounters that take place on trains, planes, and city streets. It is the dissent that would single out this particular mode of travel for differential treatment by adopting a *per se* rule that random bus searches are unconstitutional.

The dissent reserves its strongest criticism for the proposition that police officers can approach individuals as to whom they have no reasonable suspicion and ask them potentially incriminating questions. But this proposition is by no means novel; it has been endorsed by the Court any number of times. *Terry, Royer,* and *Delgado* are just a few examples. As we have explained, today's decision follows logically from those decisions and breaks no new ground. Unless the dissent advocates overruling a long, unbroken line of decisions dating back more than 20 years, its criticism is not well taken.

This Court, as the dissent correctly observes, is not empowered to suspend constitutional guarantees so that the Government may more effectively wage a "war on drugs." If that war is to be fought, those who fight it must respect the rights of individuals, whether or not those individuals are suspected of having committed a crime. By the same token, this Court is not empowered to forbid law enforcement practices simply because it considers them distasteful. The Fourth Amendment proscribes unreasonable searches and seizures; it does not proscribe voluntary cooperation. The cramped confines of a bus are one relevant factor that should be considered in evaluating whether a passenger's consent is voluntary. We cannot agree, however, with the Florida Supreme Court that this single factor will be dispositive in every case.

We adhere to the rule that, in order to determine whether a particular encounter constitutes a seizure, a court must consider all the circumstances surrounding the encounter to determine whether the police conduct would have communicated to a reasonable person that the person was not free to decline the officers' requests or otherwise terminate the encounter. That rule applies to encounters that take place on a city street or in an airport lobby, and it applies equally to encounters on a bus. The Florida Supreme Court erred in adopting a per se rule.

The judgment of the Florida Supreme Court is reversed, and the case remanded for further proceedings not inconsistent with this opinion.

JUSTICE MARSHALL, with whom JUSTICE BLACKMUN and JUSTICE STEVENS join, dissenting.

Our Nation, we are told, is engaged in a "war on drugs." No one disputes that it is the job of law-enforcement officials to devise effective weapons for fighting this war. But the effectiveness of a law-enforcement technique is not proof of its constitutionality. The general warrant, for example, was certainly an effective means of law enforcement. Yet it was one of the primary aims of the Fourth Amendment to protect citizens from the tyranny of being singled out for search and seizure without particularized suspicion *notwithstanding* the effectiveness of this method. In my view, the law-enforcement technique with which we are confronted in this case — the suspicionless police sweep of buses in intrastate or interstate travel — bears all of the indicia of coercion and unjustified intrusion associated with the general warrant. Because I believe that the bus sweep at issue in this case violates the core values of the Fourth Amendment, I dissent.

I

At issue in this case is a "new and increasingly common tactic in the war on drugs": the suspicionless police sweep of buses in interstate or intrastate travel. Typically under this technique, a group of state or federal officers will board a bus while it is stopped at an intermediate point on its route. Often displaying badges, weapons or other indicia of authority, the officers identify themselves and announce their purpose to intercept drug traffickers. They proceed to approach individual passengers, requesting them to show identification, produce their tickets, and explain the purpose of their travels. Never do the officers advise the passengers that they are free not to speak with the officers. An "interview" of this type ordinarily culminates in a request for consent to search the passenger's luggage.

These sweeps are conducted in "dragnet" style. The police admittedly act without an "articulable suspicion" in deciding which buses to board and which passengers to approach for interviewing.[1] By proceeding systematically in this fashion, the police are able to engage in a tremendously high volume of searches.

To put it mildly, these sweeps "are inconvenient, intrusive, and intimidating." They occur within cramped confines, with officers typically placing themselves in between the passenger selected for an interview and the exit of the bus. Because the bus is only temporarily stationed at a point short of its destination, the passengers are in no position to leave as a means of evading the officers' questioning. Undoubtedly, such a sweep holds up the progress of the bus. *Cf. United States v. Rembert*, 694 F. Supp. 163, 175 (WDNC 1988) (reporting testimony of officer that he makes " 'every effort in the world not to delay the bus' " but that the driver does not leave terminal until sweep is complete). Thus, this "new and increasingly common tactic," burdens the experience of traveling by bus with a degree of governmental interference to which, until now, our society has been proudly unaccustomed. *See, e.g., State ex rel. Ekstrom v. Justice Court*, 136 Ariz. 1, 6, 663 P.2d 992, 997 (1983) (Feldman, J., concurring) ("The thought that an American can be compelled to 'show his papers' before exercising his right to walk the streets, drive the highways or board the trains is repugnant to American institutions and ideals").

This aspect of the suspicionless sweep has not been lost on many of the lower courts called upon to review the constitutionality of this practice. Remarkably, the courts located at the heart of the "drug war" have been the most adamant in condemning this technique. As one Florida court put it:

[T]he evidence in this cause has evoked images of other days, under other flags, when no man traveled his nation's roads or railways without fear of

[1] That is to say, the police who conduct these sweeps decline to offer a reasonable, articulable suspicion of criminal wrongdoing sufficient to justify a warrantless "stop" or "seizure" of the confronted passenger. It does not follow, however, that the approach of passengers during a sweep is completely random. Indeed, at least one officer who routinely confronts interstate travelers candidly admitted that *race* is a factor influencing his decision whom to approach. Thus, the basis of the decision to single out particular passengers during a suspicionless sweep is less likely to be *inarticulable* than *unspeakable*.

unwarranted interruption, by individuals who held temporary power in the Government. The spectre of American citizens being asked, by badge-wielding police, for identification, travel papers — in short a *raison d'etre* — is foreign to any fair reading of the Constitution, and its guarantee of human liberties. This is not Hitler's Berlin, nor Stalin's Moscow, nor is it white supremacist South Africa. Yet in Broward County, Florida, these police officers approach every person on board buses and trains ("that time permits") and check identification [and] tickets, [and] ask to search luggage — all in the name of "voluntary cooperation" with law enforcement . . . .

The District Court for the District of Columbia spoke in equally pointed words:

> It seems rather incongruous at this point in the world's history that we find totalitarian states becoming more like our free society while we in this nation are taking on their former trappings of suppressed liberties and freedoms.

> . . . .

> The random indiscriminate stopping and questioning of individuals on interstate busses seems to have gone too far. If this Court approves such "bus stops" and allows prosecutions to be based on evidence seized as a result of such "stops," then we will have stripped our citizens of basic Constitutional protections. Such action would be inconsistent with what this nation has stood for during its 200 years of existence. If passengers on a bus passing through the Capital of this great nation cannot be free from police interference where there is absolutely no basis for the police officers to stop and question them, then the police will be free to accost people on our streets without any reason or cause. In this "anything goes" war on drugs, random knocks on the doors of our citizens' homes seeking "consent" to search for drugs cannot be far away. This is not America.

The question for this Court, then, is whether the suspicionless, dragnet-style sweep of buses in intrastate and interstate travel is consistent with the Fourth Amendment. The majority suggests that this latest tactic in the drug war is perfectly compatible with the Constitution. I disagree.

II

I have no objection to the manner in which the majority frames the test for determining whether a suspicionless bus sweep amounts to a Fourth Amendment "seizure." I agree that the appropriate question is whether a passenger who is approached during such a sweep "would feel free to decline the officers' requests or otherwise terminate the encounter." What I cannot understand is how the majority can possibly suggest an affirmative answer to this question.

The majority reverses what it characterizes as the Florida Supreme Court's *"per se* rule" against suspicionless encounters between the police and bus passengers, suggesting only in dictum its "doubt" that a seizure occurred on the facts of this case. However, the notion that the Florida Supreme Court decided this case on the basis of any *"per se* rule" *independent* of the facts of this case is wholly a product of the majority's imagination. As the majority acknowledges, the Florida Supreme Court "stated explicitly the factual premise for its decision." This factual premise contained *all* of the details of the encounter between respondent and the police. The lower court's analysis of whether respondent was seized drew heavily on these facts, and the court repeatedly emphasized that its conclusion was based on *"all the circumstances"* of this case. (emphasis added); (*"Here, the circumstances indicate* that the officers effectively 'seized' [respondent]" (emphasis added)).

The majority's conclusion that the Florida Supreme Court, contrary to all appearances, *ignored* these facts is based solely on the failure of the lower court to expressly incorporate all of the facts into its reformulation of the certified question on which respondent took his appeal.[2] The majority never explains the basis of its implausible assumption that the Florida Supreme Court intended its phrasing of the certified question to trump its opinion's careful treatment of the facts in this case. Certainly, when this Court issues an opinion, it does not intend lower courts and parties to treat as irrelevant the analysis of facts that the parties neglected to cram into the question presented in the petition for certiorari. But in any case, because the issue whether a seizure has occurred in any given factual setting is a question of law, nothing prevents this Court from deciding on its own whether a seizure occurred based on all of the facts of this case as they appear in the opinion of the Florida Supreme Court.

These facts exhibit all of the elements of coercion associated with a typical bus sweep. Two officers boarded the Greyhound bus on which respondent was a passenger while the bus, en route from Miami to Atlanta, was on a brief stop to pick up passengers in Fort Lauderdale. The officers made a visible display of their badges and wore bright green "raid" jackets bearing the insignia of the Broward County Sheriff's Department; one held a gun in a recognizable weapons pouch. These facts alone constitute an intimidating "show of authority." Once on board, the officers approached respondent, who was sitting in the back of the bus, identified themselves as narcotics officers and began to question him. One officer stood in front of respondent's seat, partially blocking the narrow aisle through which respondent would have been required to pass to reach the exit of the bus.

As far as is revealed by facts on which the Florida Supreme Court premised its decision, the officers did not advise respondent that he was free to break off this "interview." Inexplicably, the majority repeatedly stresses the trial court's implicit finding that the police officers advised respondent that he was free to refuse permission to search his travel bag. This aspect of the exchange between respondent and the police is completely irrelevant to the issue before us. For as the State concedes, and as the majority purports to "accept," *if* respondent was unlawfully seized when the officers approached him and initiated questioning, the resulting search was likewise unlawful no matter how well advised respondent was of his right to refuse it. *See Royer.* Consequently, the issue is not whether a passenger in respondent's position would have felt free to deny consent to the search of his bag, but whether such a passenger — without being apprised of his rights — would have

---

[2] As reformulated, this question read: "Does an impermissible seizure result when police mount a drug search on buses during scheduled stops and question boarded passengers without articulable reasons for doing so, thereby obtaining consent to search the passengers' luggage?"

felt free to terminate the antecedent encounter with the police.

Unlike the majority, I have no doubt that the answer to this question is no. Apart from trying to accommodate the officers, respondent had only two options. First, he could have remained seated while obstinately refusing to respond to the officers' questioning. But in light of the intimidating show of authority that the officers made upon boarding the bus, respondent reasonably could have believed that such behavior would only arouse the officers' suspicions and intensify their interrogation. Indeed, officers who carry out bus sweeps like the one at issue here frequently admit that this is the effect of a passenger's refusal to cooperate. The majority's observation that a mere refusal to answer questions, "without more," does not give rise to a reasonable basis for seizing a passenger is utterly beside the point, because a passenger unadvised of his rights and otherwise unversed in constitutional law has *no reason to know* that the police cannot hold his refusal to cooperate against him.

Second, respondent could have tried to escape the officers' presence by leaving the bus altogether. But because doing so would have required respondent to squeeze past the gun-wielding inquisitor who was blocking the aisle of the bus, this hardly seems like a course that respondent reasonably would have viewed as available to him.[3] The majority lamely protests that nothing in the stipulated facts shows that the questioning officer *"point[ed]* [his] gu[n] at [respondent] or otherwise *threatened* him" with the weapon. (emphasis added). Our decisions recognize the obvious point, however, that the choice of the police to "display" their weapons during an encounter exerts significant coercive pressure on the confronted citizen. We have never suggested that the police must go so far as to put a citizen in immediate apprehension of *being shot* before a court can take account of the intimidating effect of being questioned by an officer with weapon in hand.

Even if respondent had perceived that the officers would *let* him leave the bus, moreover, he could not reasonably have been expected to resort to this means of evading their intrusive questioning. For so far as respondent knew, the bus's departure from the terminal was imminent. Unlike a person approached by the police on the street, or at a bus or airport terminal after reaching his destination, a passenger approached by the police at an intermediate point in a long bus journey cannot simply leave the scene and repair to a safe haven to avoid unwanted probing by law-enforcement officials. The vulnerability that an intrastate or interstate traveler experiences when confronted by the police outside of his "own familiar territory" surely aggravates the coercive quality of such an encounter.

The case on which the majority primarily relies, *Delgado*, is distinguishable in every relevant respect. In *Delgado*, this Court held that workers approached by law-enforcement officials inside of a factory were not "seized" for purposes of the Fourth Amendment. The Court was careful to point out, however, that the presence of the agents did not furnish the workers with a reasonable basis for believing that they were not free to leave the factory, as at least some of them did. Unlike passengers confronted by law-enforcement officials on a bus stopped temporarily at

---

[3] As the majority's discussion makes plain, the officer questioning respondent clearly carried a weapons pouch during the interview.

an intermediate point in its journey, workers approached by law-enforcement officials at their workplace need not abandon personal belongings and venture into unfamiliar environs in order to avoid unwanted questioning. Moreover, the workers who did not leave the building in *Delgado* remained free to move about the entire factory, a considerably less confining environment than a bus. Finally, contrary to the officer who confronted respondent, the law-enforcement officials in *Delgado* did not conduct their interviews with guns in hand.

Rather than requiring the police to justify the coercive tactics employed here, the majority blames respondent for his own sensation of constraint. The majority concedes that respondent "did not feel free to leave the bus" as a means of breaking off the interrogation by the Broward County officers. But this experience of confinement, the majority explains, "was the natural result of *his* decision to take the bus." (emphasis added). Thus, in the majority's view, because respondent's "freedom of movement was restricted by a factor independent of police conduct — *i.e.*, by his being a passenger on a bus, "respondent was not seized for purposes of the Fourth Amendment.

This reasoning borders on sophism and trivializes the values that underlie the Fourth Amendment. Obviously, a person's "voluntary decision" to place himself in a room with only one exit does not authorize the police to force an encounter upon him by placing themselves in front of the exit. It is no more acceptable for the police to force an encounter on a person by exploiting his "voluntary decision" to expose himself to perfectly legitimate personal or social constraints. By consciously deciding to single out persons who have undertaken interstate or intrastate travel, officers who conduct suspicionless, dragnet-style sweeps put passengers to the choice of cooperating or of exiting their buses and possibly being stranded in unfamiliar locations. It is exactly because this "choice" is no "choice" at all that police engage this technique.

In my view, the Fourth Amendment clearly condemns the suspicionless, dragnet-style sweep of intrastate or interstate buses. Withdrawing this particular weapon from the government's drug-war arsenal would hardly leave the police without any means of combating the use of buses as instrumentalities of the drug trade. The police would remain free, for example, to approach passengers whom they have a reasonable, articulable basis to suspect of criminal wrongdoing.[4] Alternatively, they could continue to confront passengers without suspicion so long as they took simple steps, like advising the passengers confronted of their right to decline to be questioned, to dispel the aura of coercion and intimidation that pervades such encounters. There is no reason to expect that such requirements would render the Nation's buses law-enforcement-free zones.

III

The majority attempts to gloss over the violence that today's decision does to the Fourth Amendment with empty admonitions. "If th[e] [war on drugs] is to be fought," the majority intones, "those who fight it must respect the rights of

---

[4] Insisting that police officers explain their decision to single out a particular passenger for questioning would help prevent their reliance on impermissible criteria such as race.

individuals, whether or not those individuals are suspected of having committed a crime." The majority's actions, however, speak louder than its words.

I dissent.

QUESTIONS AND NOTES

1. How far apart are the majority and dissent? On remand, would it be appropriate for the Florida Supreme Court to determine that, under all of the circumstances, Bostick *was* seized?

2. If your answer to Question 1 was "yes," is the majority's approach (as opposed to the *"per se"* approach) nevertheless problematic because it invites swearing contests in which the truth may or may not ultimately prevail (*e.g.*, was the searchee told that he didn't have to permit the search)?

3. Is questioning a passenger on a bus inherently different from questioning him at a bus terminal?

4. Do you think that the police conducting bus sweeps are likely to make an effort to let the citizenry know that they do *not* have to consent? Or are they more likely to make an effort to convey the *opposite* message?

5. Is allowing "bus sweeps" unacceptably analogous to totalitarian practices? If so, is there anything in the Fourth Amendment that can fairly be read to condemn them?

6. The Court emphasizes the importance of focusing on a hypothetical "innocent" person. In what way, if at all, might an innocent person have been hurt by the conduct of the policemen in this case? (*See* Chapter 10, *infra*.)

7. We next consider *Hodari D.*, a case dealing with an attempted seizure.

CALIFORNIA v. HODARI D.
499 U.S. 621 (1991)

JUSTICE SCALIA delivered the opinion of the Court.

Late one evening in April 1988, Officers Brian McColgin and Jerry Pertoso were on patrol in a high-crime area of Oakland, California. They were dressed in street clothes but wearing jackets with "Police" embossed on both front and back. Their unmarked car proceeded west on Foothill Boulevard, and turned south onto 63rd Avenue. As they rounded the corner, they saw four or five youths huddled around a small red car parked at the curb. When the youths saw the officers' car approaching they apparently panicked, and took flight. The respondent here, Hodari D., and one companion ran west through an alley; the others fled south. The red car also headed south, at a high rate of speed.

The officers were suspicious and gave chase. McColgin remained in the car and continued south on 63rd Avenue; Pertoso left the car, ran back north along 63rd, then west on Foothill Boulevard, and turned south on 62nd Avenue. Hodari, meanwhile, emerged from the alley onto 62nd and ran north. Looking behind as he ran, he did not turn and see Pertoso until the officer was almost upon him, whereupon he tossed away what appeared to be a small rock. A moment later, Pertoso tackled Hodari, handcuffed him, and radioed for assistance. Hodari was found to be carrying $130 in cash and a pager; and the rock he had discarded was found to be crack cocaine.

In the juvenile proceeding brought against him, Hodari moved to suppress the evidence relating to the cocaine. The court denied the motion without opinion. The California Court of Appeal reversed, holding that Hodari had been "seized" when he saw Officer Pertoso running towards him, that this seizure was unreasonable under the Fourth Amendment, and that the evidence of cocaine had to be suppressed as the fruit of that illegal seizure. The California Supreme Court denied the State's application for review. We granted certiorari.

As this case comes to us, the only issue presented is whether, at the time he dropped the drugs, Hodari had been "seized" within the meaning of the Fourth Amendment.[1] If so, respondent argues, the drugs were the fruit of that seizure and the evidence concerning them was properly excluded. If not, the drugs were abandoned by Hodari and lawfully recovered by the police, and the evidence should have been admitted. (In addition, of course, Pertoso's seeing the rock of cocaine, at least if he recognized it as such, would provide reasonable suspicion for the unquestioned seizure that occurred when he tackled Hodari.

We have long understood that the Fourth Amendment's protection against "unreasonable . . . seizures" includes seizure of the person. From the time of the founding to the present, the word "seizure" has meant a "taking possession," 2 N. WEBSTER, AN AMERICAN DICTIONARY OF THE ENGLISH LANGUAGE 67 (1828); 2 J. BOUVIER, A LAW DICTIONARY 510 (6th ed. 1856); WEBSTER'S THIRD NEW INTERNATIONAL DICTIONARY 2057 (1981). For most purposes at common law, the word connoted not merely grasping, or applying physical force to, the animate or inanimate object in question, but actually bringing it within physical control. A ship still fleeing, even though under attack, would not be considered to have been seized as a war prize. To constitute an arrest, however — the quintessential "seizure of the person" under our Fourth Amendment jurisprudence — the mere grasping or application of physical force with lawful authority, whether or not it succeeded in subduing the arrestee, was sufficient. *See, e.g., Whithead v. Keyes*, 85 Mass. 495, 501 (1862) ("[A]n officer effects an arrest of a person whom he has authority to arrest, by laying his hand on him for the purpose of arresting him, though he may not succeed in stopping and holding him").

To say that an arrest is effected by the slightest application of physical force, despite the arrestee's escape, is not to say that for Fourth Amendment purposes there is a *continuing* arrest during the period of fugitivity. If, for example, Pertoso had laid his hands upon Hodari to arrest him, but Hodari had broken away and had *then* cast away the cocaine, it would hardly be realistic to say that that disclosure

[1] California conceded below that Officer Pertoso did not have the "reasonable suspicion" required to justify stopping Hodari. That it would be unreasonable to stop, for brief inquiry, young men who scatter in panic upon the mere sighting of the police is not self-evident, and arguably contradicts proverbial common sense. *See* Proverbs 28:1 ("The wicked flee when no man pursueth"). We do not decide that point here, but rely entirely upon the State's concession.

had been made during the course of an arrest. The present case, however, is even one step further removed. It does not involve the application of any physical force; Hodari was untouched by Officer Pertoso at the time he discarded the cocaine. His defense relies instead upon the proposition that a seizure occurs "when the officer, by means of physical force *or show of authority*, has in some way restrained the liberty of a citizen." *Terry* (emphasis added). Hodari contends (and we accept as true for purposes of this decision) that Pertoso's pursuit qualified as a "show of authority" calling upon Hodari to halt. The narrow question before us is whether, with respect to a show of authority as with respect to application of physical force, a seizure occurs even though the subject does not yield. We hold that it does not.

The language of the Fourth Amendment, of course, cannot sustain respondent's contention. The word "seizure" readily bears the meaning of a laying on of hands or application of physical force to restrain movement, even when it is ultimately unsuccessful. ("She seized the purse-snatcher, but he broke out of her grasp.") It does not remotely apply, however, to the prospect of a policeman yelling "Stop, in the name of the law!" at a fleeing form that continues to flee. That is no seizure.[2] Nor can the result respondent wishes to achieve be produced — indirectly, as it were — by suggesting that Pertoso's uncomplied-with show of authority was a common-law arrest, and then appealing to the principle that all common-law arrests are seizures. An arrest requires *either* physical force (as described above) *or*, where that is absent, *submission* to the assertion of authority.

> Mere words will not constitute an arrest, while, on the other hand, no actual, physical touching is essential. The apparent inconsistency in the two parts of this statement is explained by the fact that an assertion of authority and purpose to arrest followed by submission of the arrestee constitutes an arrest. There can be no arrest without either touching or submission.

Perkins, *The Law of Arrest*, 25 Iowa L. Rev. 201, 206 (1940).

We do not think it desirable, even as a policy matter, to stretch the Fourth Amendment beyond its words and beyond the meaning of arrest, as respondent urges. Street pursuits always place the public at some risk, and compliance with police orders to stop should therefore be encouraged. Only a few of those orders, we must presume, will be without adequate basis, and since the addressee has no ready means of identifying the deficient ones it almost invariably is the responsible course to comply. Unlawful orders will not be deterred, moreover, by sanctioning through the exclusionary rule those of them that are not obeyed. Since policemen do not command "Stop!" expecting to be ignored, or give chase hoping to be outrun, it fully suffices to apply the deterrent to their genuine, successful seizures.

---

[2] For this simple reason — which involves neither "logic-chopping," nor any arcane knowledge of legal history — it is irrelevant that English law proscribed "an unlawful *attempt* to take a presumptively innocent person into custody." We have consulted the common-law to explain the meaning of seizure — and, contrary to the dissent's portrayal, to expand rather than contract that meaning (since one would not normally think that the mere touching of a person would suffice). But neither usage nor common-law tradition makes an *attempted* seizure a seizure. The common-law may have made an attempted seizure unlawful in certain circumstances; but it made many things unlawful, very few of which were elevated to constitutional proscriptions.

Respondent contends that his position is sustained by the so-called *Mendenhall* test, formulated by Justice Stewart: "A person has been 'seized' within the meaning of the Fourth Amendment only if, in view of all the circumstances surrounding the incident, a reasonable person would have believed that he was not free to leave." In seeking to rely upon that test here, respondent fails to read it carefully. It says that a person has been seized "only if," not that he has been seized "whenever"; it states a *necessary*, but not a *sufficient* condition for seizure — or, more precisely, for seizure effected through a "show of authority." *Mendenhall* establishes that the test for existence of a "show of authority" is an objective one: not whether the citizen perceived that he was being ordered to restrict his movement, but whether the officer's words and actions would have conveyed that to a reasonable person. Application of this objective test was the basis for our decision in the other case principally relied upon by respondent, *Michigan v. Chesternut*, 486 U.S. 567 (1988), where we concluded that the police cruiser's slow following of the defendant did not convey the message that he was not free to disregard the police and go about his business. We did not address in *Chesternut*, however, the question whether, if the *Mendenhall* test was met — if the message that the defendant was not free to leave had been conveyed — a Fourth Amendment seizure would have occurred.

Quite relevant to the present case, however, was our decision in *Brower v. Inyo County*, 489 U.S. 593 (1989). In that case, police cars with flashing lights had chased the decedent for 20 miles — surely an adequate "show of authority" — but he did not stop until his fatal crash into a police-erected blockade. The issue was whether his death could be held to be the consequence of an unreasonable seizure in violation of the Fourth Amendment. We did not even consider the possibility that a seizure could have occurred during the course of the chase because, as we explained, that "show of authority" did not produce his stop. And we discussed an opinion of Justice Holmes, involving a situation not much different from the present case, where revenue agents had picked up containers dropped by moonshiners whom they were pursuing without adequate warrant. The containers were not excluded as the product of an unlawful seizure because "[t]he defendant's own acts, and those of his associates, disclosed the jug, the jar and the bottle — and there was no seizure in the sense of the law when the officers examined the contents of each after they had been abandoned." *Hester v. United States*, 265 U.S. 57, 58 (1924). The same is true here.

In sum, assuming that Pertoso's pursuit in the present case constituted a "show of authority" enjoining Hodari to halt, since Hodari did not comply with that injunction he was not seized until he was tackled. The cocaine abandoned while he was running was in this case not the fruit of a seizure, and his motion to exclude evidence of it was properly denied. We reverse the decision of the California Court of Appeal, and remand for further proceedings not inconsistent with this opinion.

JUSTICE STEVENS, with whom JUSTICE MARSHALL joins, dissenting.

The Court's narrow construction of the word "seizure" represents a significant, and in my view, unfortunate, departure from prior case law construing the Fourth Amendment. [T]he Court now adopts a definition of "seizure" that is unfaithful to a long line of Fourth Amendment cases. Even if the Court were defining seizure for the first time, which it is not, the definition that it chooses today is profoundly unwise. In its decision, the Court assumes, without acknowledging, that a police officer may now fire his weapon at an innocent citizen and not implicate the Fourth Amendment — as long as he misses his target.

For the purposes of decision, the following propositions are not in dispute. First, when Officer Pertoso began his pursuit of respondent,[4] the officer did not have a lawful basis for either stopping or arresting respondent. Second, the officer's chase amounted to a "show of force" as soon as respondent saw the officer nearly upon him. Third, the act of discarding the rock of cocaine was the direct consequence of the show of force. Fourth, as the Court correctly demonstrates, no common-law arrest occurred until the officer tackled respondent. Thus, the Court is quite right in concluding that the abandonment of the rock was not the fruit of a common-law arrest.

It is equally clear, however, that if the officer had succeeded in touching respondent before he dropped the rock — even if he did not subdue him — an arrest would have occurred. In that event (assuming the touching precipitated the abandonment), the evidence would have been the fruit of an unlawful common-law arrest. The distinction between the actual case and the hypothetical case is the same as the distinction between the common-law torts of assault and battery — a touching converts the former into the latter. Although the distinction between assault and battery was important for pleading purposes, the distinction should not take on constitutional dimensions. The Court mistakenly allows this common-law distinction to define its interpretation of the Fourth Amendment.

At the same time, the Court fails to recognize the existence of another, more telling, common-law distinction — the distinction between an arrest and an attempted arrest. As the Court teaches us, the distinction between battery and assault was critical to a correct understanding of the common law of arrest. However, the facts of this case do not describe an actual arrest, but rather, an unlawful *attempt* to take a presumptively innocent person into custody. Such an attempt was unlawful at common law.[7] Thus, if the Court wants to define the scope of the Fourth Amendment based on the common law, it should look, not to the common law of arrest, but to the common law of attempted arrest, according to the facts of this case.

The first question, then, is whether the common law should define the scope of the outer boundaries of the constitutional protection against unreasonable seizures. Even if, contrary to settled precedent, traditional common-law analysis were

---

[4] The Court's gratuitous quotation from Proverbs 28:1, mistakenly assumes that innocent residents have no reason to fear the sudden approach of strangers. We have previously considered, and rejected, this ivory-towered analysis of the real world for it fails to describe the experience of many residents, particularly if they are members of a minority. It has long been "a matter of common knowledge that men who are entirely innocent do sometimes fly from the scene of a crime through fear of being apprehended as the guilty parties, or from an unwillingness to appear as witnesses. Nor is it true as an accepted axiom of criminal law that 'the wicked flee when no man pursueth, but the righteous are as bold as a lion.'"

[7] "[E]ven without touching the other, the officer may subject himself to liability if he undertakes to make an arrest without being privileged by law to do so."

controlling, it would still be necessary to decide whether the unlawful attempt to make an arrest should be considered a seizure within the meaning of the Fourth Amendment, and whether the exclusionary rule should apply to unlawful attempts.

II

In *Terry*, in addition to stating that a seizure occurs "whenever a police officer accosts an individual and restrains his freedom to walk away," the Court noted that a seizure occurs "when the officer, by means of physical force or show of authority, has in some way restrained the liberty of a citizen . . . ." The touchstone of a seizure is the restraint of an individual's personal liberty *"in some way."* (emphasis added). Today the Court's reaction to respondent's reliance on *Terry* is to demonstrate that in "show of force" cases no common-law arrest occurs unless the arrestee *submits*. That answer, however, is plainly insufficient given the holding in Terry that the Fourth Amendment applies to stops that need not be justified by probable cause in the absence of a full-blown arrest.

In *Mendenhall*, the Court "adhere[d] to the view that a person is 'seized' only when, by means of physical force or a show of authority, his freedom of movement is restrained." The Court looked to whether the citizen who is questioned "remains free to disregard the questions and walk away," and if she is able to do so, then "there has been no intrusion upon that person's liberty or privacy" that would require some "particularized and objective justification" under the Constitution. The test for a "seizure," as formulated by the Court in *Mendenhall*, was whether, "in view of all of the circumstances surrounding the incident, a reasonable person would have believed that he was not free to leave." Examples of seizures include "the threatening presence of several officers, the display of a weapon by an officer, some physical touching of the person of the citizen, or the use of language or tone of voice indicating that compliance with the officer's request might be compelled." The Court's unwillingness today to adhere to the "reasonable person" standard, as formulated by Justice Stewart in *Mendenhall*, marks an unnecessary departure from Fourth Amendment case law.

The Court today draws the novel conclusion that even though no seizure can occur *unless* the Mendenhall reasonable person standard is met, the fact that the standard has been met does not necessarily mean that a seizure has occurred. (*Mendenhall* "states a *necessary*, but not a *sufficient* condition for seizure . . . effected through a 'show of authority' "). If it were true that a seizure requires more than whether a reasonable person felt free to leave, then the following passage from the Court's opinion in *Delgado*, is at best, seriously misleading:

> As we have noted elsewhere: 'Obviously, not all personal intercourse between policemen and citizens involves "seizures" of persons. Only when the officer, by means of physical force or show of authority, has restrained the liberty of a citizen may we conclude that a "seizure" has occurred.' While applying such a test is relatively straightforward in a situation resembling a traditional arrest, the protection against unreasonable seizures also extends to 'seizures that involve only a brief detention short of traditional arrest.' What has evolved from our cases is a determination that an initially consensual encounter between a police officer and a citizen can

be transformed into a seizure or detention within the meaning of the Fourth Amendment, 'if, in view of all the circumstances surrounding the incident, a reasonable person would have believed that he was not free to leave.'

More importantly, in *Royer*, a plurality of the Court adopted Justice Stewart's formulation in *Mendenhall* as the appropriate standard for determining when police questioning crosses the threshold from a consensual encounter to a forcible stop. In *Royer*, the Court held that an illegal seizure had occurred. As a predicate for that holding, Justice WHITE, in his opinion for the plurality, explained that the citizen "may not be detained *even momentarily* without reasonable, objective grounds for doing so; and his refusal to listen or answer does not, without more, furnish those grounds." (emphasis added). The rule looks, not to the subjective perceptions of the person questioned, but rather, to the objective characteristics of the encounter that may suggest whether a reasonable person would have felt free to leave.

Even though momentary, a seizure occurs whenever an objective evaluation of a police officer's show of force conveys the message that the citizen is not entirely free to leave — in other words, that his or her liberty is being restrained in a significant way. That the Court understood the *Mendenhall* definition as both necessary and sufficient to describe a Fourth Amendment seizure is evident from this passage in our opinion in *United States v. Jacobsen*, 466 U.S. 109 (1984) [Ch. 11, *infra*]: "While the concept of a 'seizure' of property is not much discussed in our cases, this definition follows from our oft-repeated definition of the 'seizure' of a person within the meaning of the Fourth Amendment — meaningful interference, however brief, with an individual's freedom of movement."

Finally, it is noteworthy that in *Chesternut*, the State asked us to repudiate the reasonable person standard developed in *Terry*, *Mendenhall*, *Delgado*, and *Royer*.[13] We decided, however, to "adhere to our traditional contextual approach." In our opinion, we described Justice Stewart's analysis in *Mendenhall* as "a test to be applied in determining whether 'a person has been "seized" within the meaning of the Fourth Amendment'" and noted that "[t]he Court has since embraced this test." Moreover, in commenting on the virtues of the test, we explained that it focused on the police officer's conduct: "The test's objective standard — looking to the reasonable man's interpretation of the conduct in question — allows the police to determine in advance whether the conduct contemplated will implicate the Fourth Amendment." Expressing his approval of the Court's rejection of Michigan's argument in *Chesternut*, Professor LaFave observed: "The 'free to leave' concept, in other words, has nothing to do with a particular suspect's choice to flee rather than submit or with his assessment of the probability of successful flight. Were it otherwise, police would be encouraged to utilize a very threatening but sufficiently slow chase as an evidence-gathering technique whenever they lack even the reasonable suspicion needed for a *Terry* stop."

---

[13] Petitioner argues that the Fourth Amendment is never implicated until an individual stops in response to the police's show of authority. Thus, petitioner would have us rule that a lack of objective and particularized suspicion would not poison police conduct, no matter how coercive, as long as the police did not succeed in actually apprehending the individual.

Whatever else one may think of today's decision, it unquestionably represents a departure from earlier Fourth Amendment case law. The notion that our prior cases contemplated a distinction between seizures effected by a touching on the one hand, and those effected by a show of force on the other hand, and that all of our repeated descriptions of the *Mendenhall* test stated only a necessary, but not a sufficient, condition for finding seizures in the latter category, is nothing if not creative lawmaking. Moreover, by narrowing the definition of the term seizure, instead of enlarging the scope of reasonable justifications for seizures, the Court has significantly limited the protection provided to the ordinary citizen by the Fourth Amendment. As we explained in *Terry*:

> The danger in the logic which proceeds upon distinctions between a "stop" and an "arrest," or "seizure" of the person, and between a "frisk" and a "search" is twofold. It seeks to isolate from constitutional scrutiny the initial stages of the contact between the policeman and the citizen. And by suggesting a rigid all-or-nothing model of justification and regulation under the Amendment, it obscures the utility of limitations upon the scope, as well as the initiation, of police action as a means of constitutional regulation.

III

In this case the officer's show of force — taking the form of a head-on chase — adequately conveyed the message that respondent was not free to leave.[14] Whereas in *Mendenhall*, there was "nothing in the record [to] sugges[t] that the respondent had any objective reason to believe that she was not free to end the conversation in the concourse and proceed on her way," here, respondent attempted to end "the conversation" before it began and soon found himself literally "not free to leave" when confronted by an officer running toward him head-on who eventually tackled him to the ground. There was an interval of time between the moment that respondent saw the officer fast approaching and the moment when he was tackled, and thus brought under the control of the officer. The question is whether the Fourth Amendment was implicated at the earlier or the later moment.

Because the facts of this case are somewhat unusual, it is appropriate to note that the same issue would arise if the show of force took the form of a command to "freeze," a warning shot, or the sound of sirens accompanied by a patrol car's flashing lights. In any of these situations, there may be a significant time interval between the initiation of the officer's show of force and the complete submission by the citizen. At least on the facts of this case, the Court concludes that the timing of the seizure is governed by the citizen's reaction, rather than by the officer's conduct. One consequence of this conclusion is that the point at which the interaction between citizen and police officer becomes a seizure occurs, not when a reasonable citizen believes he or she is no longer free to go, but rather, only after the officer exercises control over the citizen.

---

[14] The California Court of Appeal noted:

This case involves more than a pursuit, as Officer Pertoso did not pursue [respondent], but ran in such a fashion as to cut him off and confront him head on. Under the rationale of *Chesternut*, this action is reasonably perceived as an intrusion upon one's freedom of movement and as a maneuver intended to block or "otherwise control the direction or speed" of one's movement.

In my view, our interests in effective law enforcement and in personal liberty would be better served by adhering to a standard that "allows the police to determine in advance whether the conduct contemplated will implicate the Fourth Amendment." The range of possible responses to a police show of force, and the multitude of problems that may arise in determining whether, and at which moment, there has been "submission," can only create uncertainty and generate litigation.

In some cases, of course, it is immediately apparent at which moment the suspect submitted to an officer's show of force. For example, if the victim is killed by an officer's gunshot,[16] as in *Garner*[17] or by a hidden roadblock, as in *Brower v. Inyo County*, the submission is unquestionably complete. But what if, for example, William James Caldwell (Brower) had just been wounded before being apprehended? Would it be correct to say that no seizure had occurred and therefore the Fourth Amendment was not implicated even if the pursuing officer had no justification whatsoever for initiating the chase? The Court's opinion in *Brower* suggests that the officer's responsibility should not depend on the character of the victim's evasive action. The Court wrote:

> Brower's independent decision to continue the chase can no more eliminate respondents' responsibility for the termination of his movement effected by the roadblock than Garner's independent decision to flee eliminated the Memphis police officer's responsibility for the termination of his movement effected by the bullet.

It seems equally clear to me that the constitutionality of a police officer's show of force should be measured by the conditions that exist at the time of the officer's action. A search must be justified on the basis of the facts available at the time it is initiated; the subsequent discovery of evidence does not retroactively validate an unconstitutional search. The same approach should apply to seizures; the character of the citizen's response should not govern the constitutionality of the officer's conduct.

If an officer effects an arrest by touching a citizen, apparently the Court would accept the fact that a seizure occurred, even if the arrestee should thereafter break loose and flee. In such a case, the constitutionality of the seizure would be evaluated as of the time the officer acted. That category of seizures would then be analyzed in the same way as searches, namely, was the police action justified when it took place? It is anomalous, at best, to fashion a different rule for the subcategory of "show of force" arrests.

In cases within this new subcategory, there will be a period of time during which the citizen's liberty has been restrained, but he or she has not yet completely submitted to the show of force. A motorist pulled over by a highway patrol car

---

[16] Even under the common law, "If an officer shoots at an arrestee when he is not privileged to do so, he is guilty of an aggravated assault. And if death results from an arrest, or attempted arrest, which was not authorized at all, . . . the arrester is guilty of manslaughter or, in extreme cases, of murder." Perkins, 25 Iowa L. Rev. at 263–264.

[17] In *Garner*, even the dissent agreed with the majority that the police officer who shot at a fleeing suspect had "'seized' [the suspect] by shooting him." (O'Connor, J., dissenting).

cannot come to an immediate stop, even if the motorist intends to obey the patrol car's signal. If an officer decides to make the kind of random stop forbidden by *Prouse*, and, after flashing his lights, but before the vehicle comes to a complete stop, sees that the license plate has expired, can he justify his action on the ground that the seizure became lawful after it was initiated but before it was completed? In an airport setting, may a drug enforcement agent now approach a group of passengers with his gun drawn, announce a "baggage search," and rely on the passengers' reactions to justify his investigative stops? The holding of today's majority fails to recognize the coercive and intimidating nature of such behavior and creates a rule that may allow such behavior to go unchecked.

The deterrent purposes of the exclusionary rule focus on the conduct of law enforcement officers, and on discouraging improper behavior on their part, and not on the reaction of the citizen to the show of force. In the present case, if Officer Pertoso had succeeded in tackling respondent before he dropped the rock of cocaine, the rock unquestionably would have been excluded as the fruit of the officer's unlawful seizure. Instead, under the Court's logic-chopping analysis, the exclusionary rule has no application because an attempt to make an unconstitutional seizure is beyond the coverage of the Fourth Amendment, no matter how outrageous or unreasonable the officer's conduct may be.

It is too early to know the consequences of the Court's holding. If carried to its logical conclusion, it will encourage unlawful displays of force that will frighten countless innocent citizens into surrendering whatever privacy rights they may still have. It is not too soon, however, to note the irony in the fact that the Court's own justification for its result is its analysis of the rules of the common law of arrest that antedated *Terry*. Yet, even in those days the common law provided the citizen with protection against an attempt to make an unlawful arrest. The central message of *Terry* was that the protection the Fourth Amendment provides to the average citizen is not rigidly confined by ancient common-law precept. The message that today's literal-minded majority conveys is that the common law, rather than our understanding of the Fourth Amendment as it has developed over the last quarter of a century, defines, and limits, the scope of a seizure. The Court today defines a seizure as commencing, not with egregious police conduct, but rather, with submission by the citizen. Thus, it both delays the point at which "the Fourth Amendment becomes relevant" to an encounter and limits the range of encounters that will come under the heading of "seizure." Today's qualification of the Fourth Amendment means that innocent citizens may remain "secure in their persons . . . against unreasonable searches and seizures" only at the discretion of the police.

Some sacrifice of freedom always accompanies an expansion in the executive's unreviewable law enforcement powers. A court more sensitive to the purposes of the Fourth Amendment would insist on greater rewards to society before decreeing the sacrifice it makes today. Alexander Bickel presciently wrote that "many actions of government have two aspects: their immediate, necessarily intended, practical effects, and their perhaps unintended or unappreciated bearing on values we hold to have more general and permanent interest." The Court's immediate concern with containing criminal activity poses a substantial, though unintended, threat to values that are fundamental and enduring.

I respectfully dissent.

QUESTIONS AND NOTES

1. Do you think that the Scalia opinion may have been influenced by his attitude towards California's concession as reflected in his fn. 1? Should it have been?

2. If California had not made the fn. 1 concession, how would (should) that issue be decided?

3. Who has the better of the semantics, Scalia or Stevens? Explain.

4. If a criminal statute forbade rape, would (should) we imply that it intended to punish an attempted rapist?

5. Assume that a University forbade its employ racial criteria in placing students with roommates. Assume further that a University official had intentionally assigned a black student to room with another black student. Assume that upon the student's complaint, a higher University official placed the student with a roommate on a nonracial criterion. Would (should) the original University official be able to defend himself from being disciplined on the ground that he did *not* place the student on racial grounds, he only attempted to place the student on racial grounds?

6. Suppose that a City were to tax a particular church with the express purpose of taxing it out of business and preventing its free exercise of religion. Suppose further that the church paid the tax and continued to hold worship services. When the church sued for a tax refund on First Amendment grounds could the City defend on the ground that it only attempted to interfere with free exercise of religion, but did not succeed, and therefore no refund is appropriate? Does *Hodari D* present the same question or a different question?

7. As between Scalia and Stevens, who has the better of the policy argument? Explain.

8. We conclude this section with *Brendlin v. California*, a case that arguably takes the concept of seizure more seriously.

BRENDLIN v. CALIFORNIA
551 U.S. 249 (2007)

Justice Souter delivered the opinion of the Court.

When a police officer makes a traffic stop, the driver of the car is seized within the meaning of the Fourth Amendment. The question in this case is whether the same is true of a passenger. We hold that a passenger is seized as well and so may challenge the constitutionality of the stop.

I

Early in the morning of November 27, 2001, Deputy Sheriff Robert Brokenbrough and his partner saw a parked Buick with expired registration tags. In his ensuing conversation with the police dispatcher, Brokenbrough learned that an application for renewal of registration was being processed. The officers saw the car again on the road and this time Brokenbrough noticed its display of a temporary operating permit with the number "11," indicating it was legal to drive the car through November. The officers decided to pull the Buick over to verify that the permit matched the vehicle, even though, as Brokenbrough admitted later, there was nothing unusual about the permit or the way it was affixed. Brokenbrough asked the driver, Karen Simeroth, for her license and saw a passenger in the front seat, petitioner Bruce Brendlin, whom he recognized as "one of the Brendlin brothers." He recalled that either Scott or Bruce Brendlin had dropped out of parole supervision and asked Brendlin to identify himself. Brokenbrough returned to his cruiser, called for backup, and verified that Brendlin was a parole violator with an outstanding no-bail warrant for his arrest. While he was in the patrol car, Brokenbrough saw Brendlin briefly open and then close the passenger door of the Buick. Once reinforcements arrived, Brokenbrough went to the passenger side of the Buick, ordered him out of the car at gunpoint, and declared him under arrest. When the police searched Brendlin incident to arrest, they found an orange syringe cap on his person. A patdown search of Simeroth revealed syringes and a plastic bag of a green leafy substance, and she was also formally arrested. Officers then searched the car and found tubing, a scale, and other things used to produce methamphetamine.

Brendlin was charged with possession and manufacture of methamphetamine, and he moved to suppress the evidence obtained in the searches of his person and the car as fruits of an unconstitutional seizure, arguing that the officers lacked probable cause or reasonable suspicion to make the traffic stop. He did not assert that his Fourth Amendment rights were violated by the search of Simeroth's, cf. *Rakas* v. Illinois, but claimed only that the traffic stop was an unlawful seizure of his person. The trial court denied the suppression motion after finding that the stop was lawful and Brendlin was not seized until Brokenbrough order him out of the car and formally arrested him. Brendlin pleaded guilty, subject to appeal on the suppression issue, and was sentenced to four years in prison.

II

A

A person is seized by the police and thus entitled to challenge the government's action under the Fourth Amendment when the officer, " 'by means of physical force or show of authority,' " terminates or restrains his freedom of movement. *Bostick, "through means intentionally applied," Brower* v. *County of Inyo*, 489 U.S. 593, 597 (1989) (emphasis in original). Thus, an "unintended person . . . [may be] the object of the detention," so long as the detention is "willful" and not merely the consequence of "an unknowing act." cf. *County of Sacramento v. Lewis*, 523 U.S. 833, 844 (1998) (no seizure where a police officer accidentally struck and killed a motorcycle passenger during a high-speed pursuit). A police officer may make a seizure by a show of authority and without the use of physical force, but there is no seizure without actual submission; otherwise, there is at most an attempted seizure, so far as the Fourth Amendment is concerned. *Lewis.*

When the actions of the police do not show an unambiguous intent to restrain or when an individual's submission to a show of governmental authority takes the form of passive acquiescence, there needs to be some test for telling when a seizure occurs in response to authority, and when it does not. The test was devised by Justice Stewart in *Mendenhall,* who wrote that a seizure occurs if "in view of all the circumstances surrounding the incident, a reasonable person would have believed that he was not free to leave. Later on, the Court adopted Justice Stewart's touchstone, but added that when a person "has no desire to leave" for reasons unrelated to the police presence, the "coercive effect of the encounter" can be measured better by asking whether "a reasonable person would feel free to decline the officers' requests or otherwise terminate the encounter," *Bostick.*

The law is settled that in Fourth Amendment terms a traffic stop entails a seizure of the driver "even though the purpose of the stop is limited and the resulting detention quite brief." *Delaware v. Prouse.* And although we have not, until today, squarely answered the question whether a passenger is also seized, we have said over and over in dicta that during a traffic stop an officer seizes everyone in the vehicle, not just the driver.

We have come closest to the question here in two cases dealing with unlawful seizure of a passenger, and neither time did we indicate any distinction between driver and passenger that would affect the Fourth Amendment analysis. *Delaware v. Prouse* considered grounds for stopping a car on the road and held that Prouse's suppression motion was properly granted. We spoke of the arresting officer's testimony that Prouse was in the back seat when the car was pulled over. N.1, described Prouse as an occupant, not as the driver, and referred to the car's "occupants" as being seized. Justification for stopping a car was the issue again in *Whren v. U.S.,* where we passed upon a Fourth Amendment challenge by two petitioners who moved to suppress drug evidence found during the course of a traffic stop. Both driver and passenger claimed to have been seized illegally when the police stopped the car; we agreed and held suppression unwarranted only because the stop rested on probable cause.

B

The State concedes that the police had no adequate justification to pull the car over, but argues that the passenger was not seized and thus cannot claim that the evidence was tainted by an unconstitutional stop. We resolve this question by asking whether a reasonable person in Brendlin's position when the car stopped would have believed himself free to "terminate the encounter" between the police and himself. *Bostick.* We think that in these circumstances any reasonable passenger would have understood the police officers to be exercising control to the point that no one in the car was free to depart without police permission.

A traffic stop necessarily curtails the travel a passenger has chosen just as much as it halts the driver, diverting both from the stream of traffic to the side of the road, and the police activity that normally amounts to intrusion on "privacy and personal security" does not normally (and did not here) distinguish between passenger and driver. An officer who orders one particular car to pull over acts with an implicit claim of right based on fault of some sort, and a sensible person would not expect a police a police officer to allow people to come and go freely from the physical focal point of an investigation. If the likely wrongdoing is not the driving, the passenger will reasonably feel subject to suspicion owing to close association; but even when the wrongdoing is only bad driving, the passenger will expect to be subject to some scrutiny, and his attempt to leave the scene would be so obviously likely to prompt an objection from the officer that no passenger would feel free to leave in the first place.[18]

It is also reasonable for passengers to expect that a police officer at the scene of a crime, arrest, or investigation will not let people move around in ways that could jeopardize his safety. In *Maryland* v. *Wilson*, 519 U.S. 408 (1997), we held that during a lawful traffic stop an officer may order a passenger out of the car as a precautionary measure, without reasonable suspicion that the passenger poses a safety risk. cf. *Pennsylvania* v. *Mimms*, 434 U.S. 106 (1977) (*per curiam*) (driver may be order out of the car as a matter of course). In fashioning this rule, we invoked our earlier statement that " '[t]he risk of harm to both the police and the occupants is minimized if the officers routinely exercise unquestioned command of the situation.' " What we have said in these opinions probably reflects a societal expectation of " 'unquestioned [police] command' " at odds with any notion that a passenger would feel free to leave, or to terminate the personal encounter any other way, without advance permission.[19]

Our conclusion comports with the views of all nine Federal Courts of Appeals, and nearly every state court, to have ruled on the question.

C

The contrary conclusion drawn by the Supreme Court of California, that seizure came only with formal arrest, reflects three premises as to which we respectfully disagree. First, the State Supreme Court reasoned that Brendlin was not seized by the stop because Deputy Sheriff Brokenbrough only intended to investigate Simeroth and did not direct a show of authority toward Brendlin. The court saw Brokenbrough's "flashing lights [as] directed at the driver," and pointed to the lack of record evidence that Brokenbrough "was even aware [Brendlin] was in the car prior to the vehicle stop." But that view of the fact ignores the objective of *Mendenhall* test of what a reasonable passenger would understand. To the extent that there is anything ambiguous in the show of force (was it fairly seen as directed only at the driver or at the car and its occupants?), the test resolves the ambiguity,

---

[18] Of course, police may also stop a car solely to investigate a passenger's conduct. See, *e.g. United States v. Rodriguez-Diaz*, 161 F. Supp. 2d 627, 629, n. 1 (Md. 2001) (passenger's violation of local seatbelt law); *People v. Roth*, 85 P. 3d 571, 573 (Colo. App. 2003) (passenger's violation of littering ordinance). Accordingly, a passenger cannot assume, merely from the fact of a traffic stop, that the driver's conduct is the cause of the stop.

[19] Although the State Supreme Court inferred from Brendlin's decision to open and close the passenger door during the traffic stop that he was "awar[e] of the available options," this conduct could equally be taken to indicate that Brendlin felt compelled to remain inside the car. In any event, the test is not what Brendlin felt but what a reasonable passenger would have understood.

and here it leads to the intuitive conclusion that all the occupants were subject to like control by the successful display of authority. The State Supreme Court's approach on the contrary, shifts the issue from the intent of the police as objectively manifested to the motive of the police for taking the intentional action to stop the car, and we have repeatedly rejected attempts to introduce this kind of subjectivity into Fourth Amendment analysis.

California defends the State Supreme Court's ruling on this point by citing our cases holding that seizure requires a purposeful, deliberate act of detention. But *Chesternut, supra,* answers that argument. The intent that counts under the Fourth Amendment is the "intent [that] has been conveyed to the person confronted, and the criterion of willful restriction on freedom of movement is no invitation to look to subjective intent when determining who is seized. Our most recent cases are in accord on this point. In *Lewis*, we considered whether a seizure occurred when an officer accidentally ran over a passenger who had fallen off a motorcycle during a high-speed chase, and in holding that no seizure took place, we stressed that the officer stopped Lewis's movement by accidentally crashing, into him, not "through means intentionally applied." We did not even consider, let alone emphasize, the possibility that the officer had meant to detain the driver only and not the passenger. Nor is *Brower*, to the contrary, where it was dispositive that "Brower was meant to be stopped by the physical obstacle of the roadblock — and that he was stopped." California reads this language to suggest that for a specific occupant of the car to be seized he must be the motivating target of an officer's show of authority, see Brief for Respondent 12, as if the thrust of our observation were that Brower, and not someone else, was "meant to be stopped." But our point was not that Brower alone was the target but that officers detained him "through means intentionally applied"; if the car had had another occupant, it would have made sense to hold that he too had been seized when the car collided with the roadblock. Neither case, then, is at odds without our holding that the issue is whether a reasonable passenger would have perceived that the show of authority was at least partly directed at him, and that he was thus not free to ignore the police presence and go about his business.

Second, the Supreme Court of California assumed that Brendlin, "as the passenger, had no ability to submit to the deputy's show of authority" because only the driver was in control of the moving vehicle. But what may amount to submission depends on what a person was doing before the show of authority: a fleeing man is not seized until he is physically overpowered, but one sitting in a chair may submit to authority by not getting up to run away. Here, Brendlin had no effective way to signal submission while the car was still moving on the roadway, but once it came to a stop he could, and apparently did, submit by staying inside.

Third, the State Supreme Court shied away from the rule we apply today for fear that it "would encompass even those motorists following the vehicle subject to the traffic stop who, by virtue of the original detention, are forced to slow down and perhaps even come to a halt in order to accommodate that vehicle's submission to police authority." But an occupant of a car who knows that he is stuck in traffic because another car has been pulled over (like the motorist who can't even make out why the road is suddenly clogged) would not perceive a show of authority as directed at him or his car. Such incidental restrictions on freedom of movement would not tend to affect an individual's "sense of security and privacy in traveling in an automobile." Nor would the consequential blockage call for a precautionary rule to avoid the kind of "arbitrary and oppressive interference by [law] enforcement officials with the privacy and personal security of individuals" that the Fourth Amendment was intended to limit.[20]

Indeed, the consequence to worry about would not flow from our conclusion, but from the rule that almost all courts have rejected. Holding that the passenger in a private car is not (without more) seized in a traffic stop would invite police officers to stop cars with passengers regardless of probable cause or reasonable suspicion of anything illegal. The fact that evidence uncovered as a result of an arbitrary traffic stop would still be admissible against any passengers would be a powerful incentive to run the kind of "roving patrols" that would still violate the driver's Fourth Amendment right.

Brendlin was seized from the moment Simeroth's car came to a halt on the side of the road, and it was error to deny his suppression motion on the ground that seizure occurred only at the formal arrest. It will be for the state courts to consider in the first instance whether suppression turns on any other issue. The judgment of the Supreme Court of California is vacated, and the case is remanded for further proceedings not inconsistent with this opinion.

QUESTIONS AND NOTES

1.   Does *Brendlin* appear to be running against the tide of recent pro-police decision?

2.   If so, why do you suppose the Court unanimously let this drug manufacturer go (or at least made it harder to convict him) by excluding the evidence?

3.   Is there anything that could be said against the result? If so, what?

PROBLEM

On April 19, 2002, Officer Maria Trevizo and Detectives Machado and Gittings, all members of Arizona's gang task force, were on patrol in Tucson near a neighborhood associated with the Crips gang. At approximately 9 p.m., the officers pulled over an automobile after a license plate check revealed that the vehicle's registration had been suspended for an insurance-related violation. Under Arizona law, the violation for which the vehicle was stopped constituted a civil infraction warranting a citation. At the time of the stop, the vehicle had three occupants — the driver, a front-seat passenger, and a passenger in the back seat, Lemon Montrea Johnson, the respondent here. In making the stop the officers had no reason to suspect anyone in the vehicles of criminal activity.

---

[20]   California claims that, under today's rule, "all taxi cab and bus passengers would be 'seized' under the Fourth Amendment when the cab or bus driver is pulled over by the police for running a red light." But the relationship between driver and passenger is not the same in a common carrier as it is in a private vehicle, and the expectations of police officers and passengers differ accordingly. In those cases, as here, the crucial question would be whether a reasonable person in the passenger's position would feel free to take steps to terminate the encounter.

The three officers left their patrol car and approached the stopped vehicle. Machado instructed all of the occupants to keep their hands visible. He asked whether there were any weapons in the vehicle; all responded no. Machado then directed the driver to get out of the car. Gittings dealt with the front-seat passenger, who stayed in the vehicle throughout the stop. While Machado was getting the driver's license and information about the vehicle's registration and insurance, Trevizo attended to Johnson.

Trevizo noticed that, as the police approached, Johnson looked back and kept his eyes on the officers. When she drew near, she observed that Johnson was wearing clothing, including a blue bandana, that she considered consistent with Crips membership. She also noticed a scanner in Johnson's jacket pocket, which "struck [her] as highly unusual and cause [for] concern," because "most people" would not carry around a scanner that way "unless they're going to be involved in some kind of criminal activity or [are] going to try to evade the police by listening to the scanner." In response to Trevizo's questions, Johnson provided his name and date of birth but said he had no identification with him. He volunteered that he was from Elroy, Arizona, a place Trevizo knew was home to a Crips gang. Johnson further old Trevizo that he had served time in prison for burglary and had been out for about a year.

Trevizo wanted to question Johnson away from the front-seat passenger to gain "intelligence about the gang [Johnson] might be in." For that reason, she asked him to get out of the car. Johnson complied. Based on Trevizo's observations and Johnson's answers to her questions while he was still seated in the car, Trevizo suspected that "he might have a weapon on him." When he exited the vehicle, she therefore "patted him down for officer safety." During the patdown, Trevizo felt the butt of a gun near Johnson's waist. At that point Johnson began to struggle, and Trevizo placed him in handcuffs.

Johnson was charged in state court with, *inter alia*, possession of a weapon by a prohibited possessor. He moved to suppress the evidence as the fruit of an unlawful search. The trial court denied the motion, concluding that the stop was lawful and that Trevizo had cause to suspect Johnson was armed and dangerous.

A divided panel of the Arizona Court of Appeals reversed Johnson's conviction. Recognizing that "Johnson was [lawfully] seized when the officers stopped the car" the court nevertheless concluded that prior to the frisk the detention had "evolved into a separate, consensual encounter stemming from an unrelated investigation by Trevizo of Johnson's possible gang affiliation." Absent "reason to believe Johnson was involved in criminal activity," the Arizona appeals court held, Trevizo "had no right to pat him down for weapons, even if she had reason to suspect he was armed and dangerous."

Judge Espinosa dissented. He found it "highly unrealistic to conclude that merely because [Trevizo] was courteous and Johnson cooperative, the ongoing and virtually simultaneous chain of events [had] somehow 'evolved into a consensual encounter' in the few short moments involved." Throughout the episode, he stressed, Johnson remained "seized as part of [a] valid traffic stop." Further, he maintained, Trevizo "had a reasonable basis to consider [Johnson] dangerous, and could therefore ensure her own safety and that of others at the scene by patting down Johnson for weapons."

How should this case be resolved? For the Supreme Court's resolution, see *Arizona v. Johnson*, 555 U.S. 323 (2009).

Chapter 10

SEARCHES

In this Chapter, we shall attempt to define searches. As with seizures in Chapter 9, we have heretofore assumed that all of the alleged searches have in fact been such.

Perhaps a threshold question to ask is why we should care whether a particular police activity constitutes a search (or seizure). For example, why don't we just ask in a case like *Hodari D.* whether the police conduct was reasonable and not worry about whether it was a seizure? Would it be unduly burdensome for the police to *always* have to act reasonably? Why? Why not?

In fact, it is clear that (at least in the ordinary case) unreasonable police conduct, such as excessive questioning of friends and associates or excessive surveillance will not constitute a Fourth Amendment violation. So, for example, if after the DEA had questioned Mark Royer (*see Florida v. Royer*, Chapter 8, Section B, *supra*) and had *not* found evidence of crime, they went to Ithaca College and asked all of Royer's classmates and professors whether they had heard of Royer's drug activities, it is unlikely that the DEA would have been found to have violated the Fourth Amendment. (Whether they would have incurred any other tort or criminal liability is beyond the scope of this book.) Consequently, ascertaining whether particular activity constitutes a search is of critical importance to the Fourth Amendment.

A. THE DIVINING ROD THEORY OF THE FOURTH AMENDMENT

Your author has developed a theory of the Fourth Amendment which is presented in the following law review excerpt.

Arnold H. Loewy, *The Fourth Amendment as a Device for Protecting the Innocent*
81 Mich. L. Rev. 1229 (1983)

If the Fourth Amendment permits the government to search for and seize evidence of crime, it should follow that an individual has no inherent right to secrete such evidence. Consequently, the Fourth Amendment should be understood as a device to separate the wheat (evidence of crime) from the chaff (that which individuals may possess free from government prying). In a Utopian society,[69] each policeman would be equipped with an evidence-detecting divining rod. He would walk up and down the streets and whenever the divining rod detected evidence of

---

[69] Ignoring for the moment that nobody commits crime in a Utopia.

crime, it would locate the evidence. First, it would single out the house, then it would point to the room, then the drawer, and finally the evidence itself. Thus, all evidence of crime would be uncovered in the most efficient possible manner, and no innocent person would be subject to a search. In a real society (such as ours), the Fourth Amendment serves as an imperfect divining rod.

Consider the following hypothetical: Principal X of Y High School, because of a hunch that students A, B, and C each have marijuana in their respective lockers, opens the lockers with a passkey. In A's locker, he finds marijuana, which is subsequently given to the police and used to convict A of possession of marijuana, for which A receives a year's imprisonment. In B's locker he finds a picture of his (Principal X's) head attached to the rear end of a horse with the caption: "X is a Horse's Ass." In C's locker, he finds a picture of C's mother with the caption: "Mom."

Assuming that these searches were unlawful, conventional wisdom suggests that A's rights were violated more than the others since only he suffered a criminal conviction by virtue of the search. Yet B's and C's legitimate privacy interest were more seriously intruded upon. B had a fourth (and probably a first) amendment right to keep his opinion of the principal to himself. His belief that the principal's prying eyes would not see his crude, but arguably cute, caricature is a reasonable one which ought to be protected. Similarly, C's hanging his mother's picture in his locker (though along with apple pie and the flag, the paradigmatic affirmation of true-blue American values) could be a source of embarrassment if made known to the public.

Let us now vary the hypothetical. Assume that instead of searching the three lockers, X decides to confirm his suspicions by having a marijuana-sniffing dog sniff the three lockers. The dog determines that marijuana is present in A's locker, but is not present in either B's or C's locker. X then goes before a magistrate, who issues a search warrant to search A's locker for marijuana, which of course is found.

In this situation, neither B nor C has had his Fourth Amendment rights violated. Neither's privacy has been invaded. They have not been compelled to share secrets with others. The government has learned nothing about them except that they do not possess marijuana. Any interest they may have in keeping the authorities from learning of their innocence is surely too trivial to protect.

Have A's rights been violated? He would of course like to keep to himself the evidence of his crime. But his claim is not a powerful one. Indeed, in this case, an accurate dog[75] approaches the hypothetical divining rod by separating the innocent from the guilty.

Many students and colleagues with whom I have discussed the divining rod theory have objected to it because of its "1984" overtones. There is a major difference, however, between "Big Brother" watching *everything* and government being able to detect *only* evidence of crime.

I am not contending that any use of any device that in some ways resembles a divining rod is per se reasonable. For example, so innocuous a device as a

---

[75] Obviously, an inaccurate dog would present different problems.

magnetometer cannot distinguish permissible metals (coins, keys, etc.) from impermissible ones (guns, knives, etc.).[78] Furthermore, most magnetometers, such as the one in the United States Supreme Court Building, require that innocent people be herded like cattle and marched single file through the device. On the other hand, if a device could be invented that accurately detected weapons and did not disrupt the normal movement of people, there could be no Fourth Amendment objection to its use.[79]

Nor do I suggest carte blanche use of marijuana-sniffing dogs. To the extent that the dog is less than perfectly accurate, innocent people run the risk of being searched.[80] Additionally, the very act of being subjected to a body sniff by a German Shepherd may be offensive at best or harrowing at worst to the innocent sniffee.[81]

Another concern expressed about marijuana-sniffing dogs (and presumably other divining rods) is Professor Gardner's contention that people have a right to be free from unwarranted suspicion.[82] Thus, in our hypothetical locker search, A, B, and C could all argue that they had the right to be free from unwarranted suspicion. B and C, however, were benefitted by the dog (divining rod) because it was the dog that freed them from the unwarranted suspicion which otherwise would have continued in the principal's mind.

Student A might have an argument that he, along with students B and C, was singled out for special treatment. If he could introduce additional factors, for example, that half of the students were believed to have marijuana in their lockers and that A, B, and C were the only blacks in an otherwise all-white school, he might have a serious constitutional contention. Apart from this equal protection problem, however, there is no constitutional basis for holding that a person has a right to be free from unjustifiable suspicion.[85] Indeed, as noted, the beauty of the canine sniff

---

[78] Indeed, so innocent a person as the author of this Article was compelled to empty from his pockets metal-framed glasses, coins and keys in full view of his students after activating the magnetometer at the United States Supreme Court.

[79] This is not to say the use of a magnetometer is impermissible; rather, that it is only permissible when the interest in using it outweighs the offensiveness of the intrusion involved.

[80] For example, in *Doe v. Renfrow*, 475 F. Supp. 1012 (N.D. Ind. 1979), a drug-sniffing dog had "alerted" to a 13-year-old junior high school girl during a school-wide "sniff" of all the students. The dog continued to "alert" to her even after she emptied her pockets. Diane Doe was then subjected to a nude search by two women who examined her clothing and lifted her hair to look for drugs. No drugs were found but it was later discovered that she had been playing that morning with her dog, which was in heat.

To further highlight the inaccuracy of these particular dogs, they "alerted" to some fifty students, only seventeen of whom were found to be in possession of drugs.

[81] In *Doe v. Renfrow*, 475 F. Supp. at 1017, the Highland Town School District Board, the Superintendent of Schools (Omer Renfrow), members of the Highland Police Department and Patricia Little (owner of a dog training school) devised a plan to combat what they feared was a growing drug problem in the Highland Junior and Senior High Schools wherein all 2,780 students were required to remain seated at their desks while a dog sniffed at them as the dog and his trainer walked up and down the aisles. Thus approximately 2,763 innocent students were subjected to this potentially frightening and definitely degrading experience, and some 33 students were wrongly suspected of possessing contraband by the dogs' false alerts.

[82] Gardner, *Sniffing for Drugs in the Classroom — Perspectives on Fourth Amendment Scope*, 74 Nw. U. L. Rev. 803 (1980).

[85] Gardner cites no authority to support a constitutional basis for "the right to be free from unjust

is the ability to free one from unjustifiable suspicion.[86]

In sum, the Fourth Amendment exists to protect the innocent and may normally be invoked by the guilty only when necessary to protect the innocent.

QUESTIONS AND NOTES

1. At different times, both the "liberals" and "conservatives" seem to think of the Fourth Amendment as a device for protecting the innocent. For example, in *Bostick*, the conservatives emphasized that their only concern was whether an innocent person would have felt free to refrain from cooperating with the police. On the other hand, in other cases, the liberals have been concerned with the impact on hypothetically innocent people. *See, e.g., United States v. White* (n.6 after *Katz v. United States*). The "divining rod" theory suggests that we should always focus on the innocent, regardless of whose ox is gored.

2. We will first look at judicial attitudes towards the divining rod theory and then focus on its appropriateness as a Fourth Amendment measuring stick.

UNITED STATES v. PLACE
462 U.S. 696 (1983)

JUSTICE O'CONNOR delivered the opinion of the Court.

[For a statement of the facts, see Chapter 8, Section C, *supra*.]

The purpose for which respondent's luggage was seized, of course, was to arrange its exposure to a narcotics detection dog. Obviously, if this investigative procedure is itself a search requiring probable cause, the initial seizure of respondent's luggage for the purpose of subjecting it to the sniff test — no matter how brief — could not be justified on less than probable cause.

The Fourth Amendment "protects people from unreasonable government intrusions into their legitimate expectations of privacy." We have affirmed that a person possesses a privacy interest in the contents of personal luggage that is protected by the Fourth Amendment. A "canine sniff" by a well-trained narcotics detection dog,

---

suspicion." Furthermore, if there were such a rule, neither the principal nor the police could ask questions about students suspected of criminal activity as long as there were no probable cause (or at least no reasonable suspicion) for arrest or search. The result would be a catch-22 in which police could not search because they did not have probable cause and could not investigate in order to establish probable cause because suspicion would thereby be cast on the individual unjustly.

[86] A final objection to the divining rod theory is that if we had a device that would detect evidence of crimes whenever it existed, it would possibly precipitate enforcement of laws that we do not really want enforced. The following quote by Thurman W. Arnold expresses the idea sharply: "Most unenforced criminal laws survive in order to satisfy moral objections to established modes of conduct. They are unenforced because we want to continue our conduct, and unrepealed because we want to preserve our morals." Arnold, *Law Enforcement — An Attempt at Social Dissection*, 42 YALE L.J. 1, 14 (1932). Arguably certain drug laws (*e.g.*, possession of marijuana) are examples of such laws. If so, the better course of action is for the legislatures and perhaps the courts to rethink the propriety of marijuana laws. If the employment of crime-detecting devices such as marijuana-sniffing dogs causes us to rethink that which we outlaw, it is an argument in favor of, and not against, such a use.

however, does not require opening the luggage. It does not expose noncontraband items that otherwise would remain hidden from public view, as does, for example, an officer's rummaging through the contents of the luggage. Thus, the manner in which information is obtained through this investigative technique is much less intrusive than a typical search. Moreover, the sniff discloses only the presence or absence of narcotics, a contraband item. Thus, despite the fact that the sniff tells the authorities something about the contents of the luggage, the information obtained is limited. This limited disclosure also ensures that the owner of the property is not subjected to the embarrassment and inconvenience entailed in less discriminate and more intrusive investigative methods.

In these respects, the canine sniff is *sui generis*. We are aware of no other investigative procedure that is so limited both in the manner in which information is obtained and in the content of the information revealed by the procedure. Therefore, we conclude that the particular course of investigation that the agents intended to pursue here — exposure of respondent's luggage, which was located in a public place, to a trained canine — did not constitute a "search" within the meaning of the Fourth Amendment.

JUSTICE BRENNAN, with whom JUSTICE MARSHALL joins, concurring in result.

The Court suggests today, in a discussion unnecessary to the judgment, that exposure of respondent's luggage to a narcotics detection dog "did not constitute a 'search' within the meaning of the Fourth Amendment." In the District Court, respondent did "not contest the validity of sniff searches per se . . . ." The Court of Appeals did not reach or discuss the issue. It was not briefed or argued in this Court. In short, I agree with Justice Blackmun that the Court should not address the issue.

I also agree with Justice Blackmun's suggestion that the issue is more complex than the Court's discussion would lead one to believe. As Justice Stevens suggested in objecting to "unnecessarily broad dicta" in *United States v. Knotts*, 103 S. Ct. 1081 (1983), the use of electronic detection techniques that enhance human perception implicates "especially sensitive concerns." (opinion concurring in the judgment). Obviously, a narcotics detection dog is not an electronic detection device. Unlike the electronic "beeper" in *Knotts*, however, a dog does more than merely allow the police to do more efficiently what they could do using only their own senses. A dog adds a new and previously unobtainable dimension to human perception. The use of dogs, therefore, represents a greater intrusion into an individual's privacy. Such use implicates concerns that are at least as sensitive as those implicated by the use of certain electronic detection devices.

I have expressed the view that dog sniffs of people constitute searches. *See Doe v. Renfrow*, 451 U.S. 1022, 1025–1026 (1981) (Brennan, J., dissenting from denial of certiorari). In *Doe*, I suggested that sniffs of inanimate objects might present a different case. In any event, I would leave the determination of whether dog sniffs of luggage amount to searches, and the subsidiary question of what standards should govern such intrusions, to a future case providing an appropriate, and more informed, basis for deciding these questions.

QUESTIONS AND NOTES

1. Did the Court, in *Place*, adopt the divining rod theory?

2. If not, on what basis did it conclude that a dog sniff did not constitute a search?

3. The issue was more clearly joined in *Jacobsen.*

UNITED STATES v. JACOBSEN
466 U.S. 109 (1984)

JUSTICE STEVENS delivered the opinion of the Court.

A chemical test that merely discloses whether or not a particular substance is cocaine does not compromise any legitimate interest in privacy. This conclusion is not dependent on the result of any particular test. It is probably safe to assume that virtually all of the tests conducted under circumstances comparable to those disclosed by this record would result in a positive finding; in such cases, no legitimate interest has been compromised. But even if the results are negative — merely disclosing that the substance is something other than cocaine — such a result reveals nothing of special interest. Congress has decided — and there is no question about its power to do so — to treat the interest in "privately" possessing cocaine as illegitimate; thus governmental conduct that can reveal whether a substance is cocaine, and no other arguably "private" fact, compromises no legitimate privacy interest.[23]

This conclusion is dictated by *Place*, in which the Court held that subjecting luggage to a "sniff test" by a trained narcotics detection dog was not a "search" within the meaning of the Fourth Amendment: "A 'canine sniff' by a well-trained narcotics detection dog, however, does not require opening of the luggage. It does not expose noncontraband items that otherwise would remain hidden from public view, as does, for example, an officer's rummaging through the contents of the luggage. Thus, the manner in which information is obtained through this investigative technique is much less intrusive than a typical search. Moreover, the sniff discloses only the presence or absence of narcotics, a contraband item. Thus, despite the fact that the sniff tells the authorities something about the contents of the luggage, the information obtained is limited."[24]

Here, as in *Place*, the likelihood that official conduct of the kind disclosed by the record will actually compromise any legitimate interest in privacy seems much too remote to characterize the testing as a search subject to the Fourth Amendment.

---

[23] *See* Loewy, *The Fourth Amendment as a Device for Protecting the Innocent,* 81 MICH. L. REV. 1229 (1983). Our discussion, of course, is confined to possession of contraband.

[24] Respondents attempt to distinguish *Place* arguing that it involved no physical invasion of Place's effects, unlike the conduct at issue here. However, as the quotation makes clear, the reason this did not intrude upon any legitimate privacy interest was that the governmental conduct could reveal nothing about noncontraband items. That rationale is fully applicable here.

JUSTICE BRENNAN, with whom JUSTICE MARSHALL joins, dissenting.

The Court has reached this conclusion (legality of Government conduct) on a much broader ground, relying on two factors alone to support the proposition that the field test was not a search; first, the fact that the test revealed only whether or not the substance was cocaine, without providing any further information; and second, the assumption that an individual does not have a reasonable expectation of privacy in such a fact.

The Court asserts that its "conclusion is dictated by *Place*," in which the Court stated that a "canine sniff" of a piece of luggage did not constitute a search because it "is less intrusive than a typical search," and because it "discloses only the presence or absence of narcotics, a contraband item." Presumably, the premise of *Place* was that an individual could not have a reasonable expectation of privacy in the presence or absence of narcotics in his luggage. The validity of the canine sniff in that case, however, was neither briefed by the parties nor addressed by the courts below. Indeed, since the Court ultimately held that the defendant's luggage had been impermissibly seized, its discussion of the question was wholly unnecessary to its judgment. In short, as Justice Blackmun pointed out at the time, "the Court [was] certainly in no position to consider all the ramifications of this important issue."

Nonetheless, the Court concluded that "the canine sniff is *sui generis*. We are aware of no other investigative procedure that is so limited both in the manner in which the information is obtained and in the content of the information revealed by the procedure. Therefore, we conclude that the particular course of investigation that the agents intended to pursue here — exposure of respondent's luggage, which was located in a public place, to a trained canine — did not constitute a 'search' within the meaning of the Fourth Amendment." As it turns out, neither the Court's knowledge nor its imagination regarding criminal investigative techniques proved very sophisticated, for within one year we have learned of another investigative procedure that shares with the dog sniff the same defining characteristics that led the Court to suggest that the dog sniff was not a search.

Before continuing along the course that the Court so hastily charted in *Place*, it is only prudent to take this opportunity — in my view, the first real opportunity — to consider the implications of the Court's new Fourth Amendment jurisprudence. Indeed, in light of what these two cases have taught us about contemporary law-enforcement methods, it is particularly important that we analyze the basis upon which the Court has redefined the term "search" to exclude a broad class of surveillance techniques. In my view, such an analysis demonstrates that, although the Court's conclusion is correct in this case, its dictum in *Place* was dangerously incorrect. More important, however, the Court's reasoning in both cases is fundamentally misguided and could potentially lead to the development of a doctrine wholly at odds with the principles embodied in the Fourth Amendment.

Because the requirements of the Fourth Amendment apply only to "searches" and "seizures," an investigative technique that falls within neither category need not be reasonable and may be employed without a warrant and without probable cause, regardless of the circumstances surrounding its use. The prohibitions of the Fourth Amendment are not, however, limited to any preconceived conceptions of what constitutes a search or a seizure; instead we must apply the constitutional language to modern developments according to the fundamental principles that the Fourth Amendment embodies. Before excluding a class of surveillance techniques from the reach of the Fourth Amendment, therefore, we must be certain that none of the techniques so excluded threatens the areas of personal security and privacy that the Amendment is intended to protect.

What is most startling about the Court's interpretation of the term "search," both in this case and in *Place*, is its exclusive focus on the nature of the information or item sought and revealed through the use of a surveillance technique, rather than on the context in which the information or item is concealed. Combining this approach with the blanket assumption, implicit in *Place* and explicit in this case, that individuals in our society have no reasonable expectation of privacy in the fact that they have contraband in their possession, the Court adopts a general rule that a surveillance technique does not constitute a search if it reveals only whether or not an individual possesses contraband.

It is certainly true that a surveillance technique that identifies only the presence or absence of contraband is less intrusive than a technique that reveals the precise nature of an item regardless of whether it is contraband. But by seizing upon this distinction alone to conclude that the first type of technique, as a general matter, is not a search, the Court has foreclosed any consideration of the circumstances under which the technique is used, and may very well have paved the way for technology to override the limits of law in the area of criminal investigation.

For example, under the Court's analysis in these cases, law enforcement officers could release a trained cocaine-sensitive dog — to paraphrase the California Court of Appeal, a "canine cocaine connoisseur" — to roam the streets at random, alerting the officers to people carrying cocaine. Or, if a device were developed that, when aimed at a person, would detect instantaneously whether the person is carrying cocaine, there would be no Fourth Amendment bar, under the Court's approach, to the police setting up such a device on a street corner and scanning all passersby. In fact, the Court's analysis is so unbounded that if a device were developed that could detect, from the outside of a building, the presence of cocaine inside, there would be no constitutional obstacle to the police cruising through a residential neighborhood and using the device to identify all homes in which the drug is present. In short, under the interpretation of the Fourth Amendment first suggested in *Place* and first applied in this case, these surveillance techniques would not constitute searches and therefore could be freely pursued whenever and wherever law enforcement officers desire. Hence, at some point in the future, if the Court stands by the theory it has adopted today, search warrants, probable cause, and even "reasonable suspicion" may very well become notions of the past. Fortunately, we know from precedents such as *Katz v. United States* [Chapter 10, Section B, *infra*] that this Court ultimately stands ready to prevent this Orwellian world from coming to pass.

Although the Court accepts, as it must, the fundamental proposition that an investigative technique is a search within the meaning of the Fourth Amendment if it intrudes upon a privacy expectation that society considers to be reasonable, the Court has entirely omitted from its discussion the considerations that have always guided our decisions in this area. In determining whether a reasonable expectation of privacy has been violated, we have always looked to the context in which an item is concealed, not to the identity of the concealed item. Thus in cases involving searches for physical items, the Court has framed its analysis first in terms of the expectation of privacy that normally attends the location of the item and ultimately in terms of the legitimacy of that expectation. In *Chadwick*, for example, we held that "no less than one who locks the doors of his home against intruders, one who safeguards his possessions [by locking them in a footlocker] is due the protection of the Fourth Amendment . . . ." Our holding was based largely on the observation that, "[b]y placing personal effects inside a double-locked footlocker, respondents manifested an expectation that the contents would remain free from public examination." The Court made the same point in *Ross*, where it held that the "Fourth Amendment provides protection to the owner of every container that conceals its contents from plain view." The fact that a container contains contraband, which indeed it usually does in such cases, has never altered our analysis.

Similarly, in *Katz v. United States*, we held that electronic eavesdropping constituted a search under the Fourth Amendment because it violated a reasonable expectation of privacy. In reaching that conclusion, we focused upon the private context in which the conversation in question took place, stating that "[w]hat a person knowingly exposes to the public . . . is not a subject of Fourth Amendment protection. . . . But what he seeks to preserve as private, even in an area accessible to the public, may be constitutionally protected." Again, the fact that the conversations involved in *Katz* were incriminating did not alter our consideration of the privacy issue. Nor did such a consideration affect our analysis in *Payton*, in which we reaffirmed the principle that the home is private even though it may be used to harbor a fugitive.

In sum, until today this Court has always looked to the manner in which an individual has attempted to preserve the private nature of a particular fact before determining whether there is a reasonable expectation of privacy upon which the government may not intrude without substantial justification. And it has always upheld the general conclusion that searches constitute at least "those more extensive intrusions that significantly jeopardize the sense of security which is the paramount concern of Fourth Amendment liberties."

Nonetheless, adopting the suggestion in *Place*, the Court has veered away from this sound and well-settled approach and has focused instead solely on the product of the would-be search. In so doing, the Court has ignored the fundamental principle that "[a] search prosecuted in violation of the Constitution is not made lawful by what it brings to light." The unfortunate product of this departure from precedent is an undifferentiated rule allowing law enforcement officers free rein in utilizing a potentially broad range of surveillance techniques that reveal only whether or not contraband is present in a particular location. The Court's new rule has rendered irrelevant the circumstances surrounding the use of the technique, the accuracy of the technique, and the privacy interest upon which it intrudes. Furthermore, the Court's rule leaves no room to consider whether the surveillance technique is employed randomly or selectively, a consideration that surely implicates Fourth Amendment concerns. Although a technique that reveals only the presence or absence of illegal activity intrudes less into the private life of an individual under investigation than more conventional techniques, the fact remains that such a technique does intrude. In my view, when the investigation intrudes upon a domain over which the individual has a reasonable expectation of privacy, such as his home or a private container, it is plainly a search within the meaning of the Fourth Amendment. Surely it cannot be that the individual's reasonable expectation of privacy dissipates simply because a sophisticated surveillance technique is employed.

This is not to say that the limited nature of the intrusion has no bearing on the general Fourth Amendment inquiry. Although there are very few exceptions to the general rule that warrantless searches are presumptively unreasonable, the isolated exceptions that do exist are based on a "balancing [of] the need to search against the invasion which the search entails." *Camara*. Hence it may be, for example, that the limited intrusion effected by a given surveillance technique renders the employment of the technique, under particular circumstances, a "reasonable" search under the Fourth Amendment. *See Place*, (Blackmun, J., concurring in the judgment) ("a dog sniff may be a search, but a minimally intrusive one that could be justified in this situation under *Terry*"). At least under this well-settled approach, the Fourth Amendment inquiry would be broad enough to allow consideration of the method by which a surveillance technique is employed as well as the circumstances attending its use. More important, however, it is only under this approach that law enforcement procedures, like those involved in this case and in *Place*, may continue to be governed by the safeguards of the Fourth Amendment.

B

In sum, the question whether the employment of a particular surveillance technique constitutes a search depends on whether the technique intrudes upon a reasonable expectation of privacy. This inquiry, in turn, depends primarily on the private nature of the area or item subjected to the intrusion. In cases involving techniques used to locate or identify a physical item, the manner in which a person has attempted to shield the item's existence or identity from public scrutiny will usually be the key to determining whether a reasonable expectation of privacy has been violated. Accordingly, the use of techniques like the dog sniff at issue in *Place* constitutes a search whenever the police employ such techniques to secure any information about an item that is concealed in a container that we are prepared to view as supporting a reasonable expectation of privacy. The same would be true if a more technologically sophisticated method were developed to take the place of the dog.

QUESTIONS AND NOTES

1.   Justice Brennan sees an inconsistency between cases like *Chadwick, Ross,* and *Payton* and the divining rod theory of the Fourth Amendment because those cases were not concerned about the guilt of the defendant. Could a defender of the "divining rod" theory answer those objections? How?

2.   In *Chadwick* were we trying to protect the right to privately transport drugs? Or, were we trying to protect the right to transport other private things without the police discovering them? Put differently, are the criminals the *intended* beneficiaries of the Fourth Amendment, or necessary incidental beneficiaries of right of the innocent?

3.   Should it be permissible for the police to point an *accurate* cocaine detecting device at everybody who passes a particular (unannounced) street corner? How about some randomly selected people who pass that street corner? Why? Why not? Does *Caballes* affect your answer?

4.   The closest thing that I have heard of to an actual divining rod is a device that I have been told some cable companies have whereby they can drive through neighborhoods and the device can detect who is using cable and who is not. If they identify a house receiving cable that has not been paid for, they can take appropriate action. Is there anything wrong with using that device? Why? Why not?

ILLINOIS v. CABALLES
543 U.S. 405 (2005)

JUSTICE STEVENS delivered the opinion of the Court.

Illinois State Trooper Daniel Gillette stopped respondent for speeding on an interstate highway. When Gillette radioed the police dispatcher to report the stop, a second trooper, Craig Graham, a member of the Illinois State Police Drug Interdiction Team, overheard the transmission and immediately headed for the scene with his narcotics-detection dog. When they arrived, respondent's car was on the shoulder of the road and respondent was in Gillette's vehicle. While Gillette was in the process of writing a warning ticket, Graham walked his dog around respondent's car. The dog alerted at the trunk. Based on that alert, the officers searched the trunk, found marijuana, and arrested respondent. The entire incident lasted less than 10 minutes.

Respondent was convicted of a narcotics offense and sentenced to 12 years' imprisonment and a $256,136 fine. The trial judge denied his motion to suppress the seized evidence and to quash his arrest. He held that the officers had not unnecessarily prolonged the stop and that the dog alert was sufficiently reliable to provide probable cause to conduct the search. Although the Appellate Court affirmed, the Illinois Supreme Court reversed, concluding that because the canine sniff was performed without any " 'specific and articulable facts' " to suggest drug activity, the use of the dog "unjustifiably enlarg[ed] the scope of a routine traffic stop into a drug investigation."

The question on which we granted certiorari is narrow: "Whether the Fourth Amendment requires reasonable, articulable suspicion to justify using a drug-detection dog to sniff a vehicle during a legitimate traffic stop." Thus, we proceed on the assumption that the officer conducting the dog sniff had no information about respondent except that he had been stopped for speeding; accordingly, we have omitted any reference to facts about respondent that might have triggered a modicum of suspicion.

Here, the initial seizure of respondent when he was stopped on the highway was based on probable cause, and was concededly lawful. It is nevertheless clear that a seizure that is lawful at its inception can violate the Fourth Amendment if its manner of execution unreasonably infringes interests protected by the Constitution. *United States v. Jacobsen.* A seizure that is justified solely by the interest in issuing a warning ticket to the driver can become unlawful if it is prolonged beyond the time reasonably required to complete that mission. In an earlier case involving a dog sniff that occurred during an unreasonably prolonged traffic stop, the Illinois Supreme Court held that use of the dog and the subsequent discovery of contraband were the product of an unconstitutional seizure. *People v. Cox.* We may assume that a similar result would be warranted in this case if the dog sniff had been conducted while respondent was being unlawfully detained.

In the state-court proceedings, however, the judges carefully reviewed the details of Officer Gillette's conversations with respondent and the precise timing of his radio transmissions to the dispatcher to determine whether he had improperly extended the duration of the stop to enable the dog sniff to occur. We have not recounted those details because we accept the state court's conclusion that the duration of the stop in this case was entirely justified by the traffic offense and the ordinary inquiries incident to such a stop.

Despite this conclusion, the Illinois Supreme Court held that the initially lawful traffic stop became an unlawful seizure solely as a result of the canine sniff that occurred outside respondent's stopped car. That is, the court characterized the dog sniff as the cause rather than the consequence of a constitutional violation. In its view, the use of the dog converted the citizen-police encounter from a lawful traffic stop into a drug investigation, and because the shift in purpose was not supported by any reasonable suspicion that respondent possessed narcotics, it was unlawful. In our view, conducting a dog sniff would not change the character of a traffic stop that is lawful at its inception and otherwise executed in a reasonable manner, unless the dog sniff itself infringed respondent's constitutionally protected interest in privacy. Our cases hold that it did not.

Official conduct that does not "compromise any legitimate interest in privacy" is not a search subject to the Fourth Amendment. *Jacobsen.* We have held that any interest in possessing contraband cannot be deemed "legitimate," and thus, governmental conduct that only reveals the possession of contraband "compromises no legitimate privacy interest." This is because the expectation "that certain facts will not come to the attention of the authorities" is not the same as an interest in "privacy that society is prepared to consider reasonable." In *Place* we treated a canine sniff by a well-trained narcotics-detection dog as *"sui generis"* because it "discloses only the presence or absence of narcotics, a contraband item." see also *Indianapolis v. Edmond.* Respondent likewise concedes that "drug sniffs are designed, and if properly conducted are generally likely, to reveal only the presence of contraband." Although respondent argues that the error rates, particularly the existence of false positives, call into question the premise that drug-detection dogs alert only to contraband, the record contains no evidence or findings that support his argument. Moreover, respondent does not suggest that an erroneous alert, in and of itself, reveals any legitimate private information, and, in this case, the trial judge found that the dog sniff was sufficiently reliable to establish probable cause to conduct a full-blown search of the trunk.

Accordingly, the use of a well-trained narcotics-detection dog — one that "does not expose noncontraband items that otherwise would remain hidden from public view," *Place* — during a lawful traffic stop, generally does not implicate legitimate privacy interests. In this case, the dog sniff was performed on the exterior of respondent's car while he was lawfully seized for a traffic violation. Any intrusion on respondent's privacy expectations does not rise to the level of a constitutionally cognizable infringement.

This conclusion is entirely consistent with our recent decision that the use of a thermal-imaging device to detect the growth of marijuana in a home constituted an unlawful search. *Kyllo v. United States, infra.* Critical to that decision was the fact that the device was capable of detecting lawful activity — in that case, intimate details in a home, such as "at what hour each night the lady of the house takes her daily sauna and bath." The legitimate expectation that information about perfectly lawful activity will remain private is categorically distinguishable from respondent's hopes or expectations concerning the nondetection of contraband in the trunk of his car. A dog sniff conducted during a concededly lawful traffic stop that reveals no information other than the location of a substance that no individual has any right to possess does not violate the Fourth Amendment.

The judgment of the Illinois Supreme Court is vacated, and the case is remanded for further proceedings not inconsistent with this opinion.

THE CHIEF JUSTICE took no part in the decision of this case.

JUSTICE SOUTER, dissenting.

I would hold that using the dog for the purposes of determining the presence of marijuana in the car's trunk was a search unauthorized as an incident of the speeding stop and unjustified on any other ground. I would accordingly affirm the judgment of the Supreme Court of Illinois, and I respectfully dissent.

In *Place* we categorized the sniff of the narcotics-seeking dog as *"sui generis"* under the Fourth Amendment and held it was not a search. The classification rests not only upon the limited nature of the intrusion, but on a further premise that experience has shown to be untenable, the assumption that trained sniffing dogs do not err. What we have learned about the fallibility of dogs in the years since *Place* was decided would itself be reason to call for reconsidering Place's decision against treating the intentional use of a trained dog as a search. The portent of this very case, however, adds insistence to the call, for an uncritical adherence to Place would render the Fourth Amendment indifferent to suspicionless and indiscriminate sweeps of cars in parking garages and pedestrians on sidewalks; if a sniff is not preceded by a seizure subject to Fourth Amendment notice, it escapes Fourth Amendment review entirely unless it is treated as a search. We should not wait for these developments to occur before rethinking Place's analysis, which invites such untoward consequences.[25]

At the heart both of *Place* and the Court's opinion today is the proposition that sniffs by a trained dog are *sui generis* because a reaction by the dog in going alert is a response to nothing but the presence of contraband.[26] Hence, the argument goes, because the sniff can only reveal the presence of items devoid of any legal use, the sniff "does not implicate legitimate privacy interests" and is not to be treated as a search.

The infallible dog, however, is a creature of legal fiction. Although the Supreme Court of Illinois did not get into the sniffing averages of drug dogs, their supposed infallibility is belied by judicial opinions describing well-trained animals sniffing and alerting with less than perfect accuracy, whether owing to errors by their handlers, the limitations of the dogs themselves, or even the pervasive contamination of currency by cocaine. See, e.g., *United States v. Kennedy*, (describing a dog that had a 71% accuracy rate); *United States v. Scarborough*, (describing a dog that erroneously alerted 4 times out of 19 while working for the postal service and 8% of the time over its entire career); *United States v. Limares* (accepting as reliable a dog that gave false positives between 7 and 38% of the time); *Laime v. State* (speaking of a dog that made between 10 and 50 errors); *United States v. $242,484.00* (noting that because as much as 80% of all currency in circulation contains drug residue, a dog alert "is of little value") *United States v. Carr* (Becker, J., concurring in part and dissenting in part) ("[A] substantial portion of United States currency . . . is tainted with sufficient traces of controlled substances to cause a trained canine to alert to their presence"). Indeed, a study cited by Illinois in this case for the proposition that dog sniffs are "generally reliable" shows that dogs in artificial testing situations return false positives anywhere from 12.5 to 60% of the time, depending on the length of the search. In practical terms, the evidence is clear that the dog that alerts hundreds of times will be wrong dozens of times.

Once the dog's fallibility is recognized, however, that ends the justification claimed in *Place* for treating the sniff as *sui generis* under the Fourth Amendment: the sniff alert does not necessarily signal hidden contraband, and opening the container or enclosed space whose emanations the dog has sensed will not necessarily reveal contraband or any other evidence of crime. This is not, of course, to deny that a dog's reaction may provide reasonable suspicion, or probable cause, to search the container or enclosure; the Fourth Amendment does not demand certainty of success to justify a search for evidence or contraband. The point is simply that the sniff and alert cannot claim the certainty that *Place* assumed, both in treating the deliberate use of sniffing dogs as *sui generis* and then taking that characterization as a reason to say they are not searches subject to Fourth Amendment scrutiny. And when that aura of uniqueness disappears, there is no basis in *Place's* reasoning, and no good reason otherwise, to ignore the actual

---

[25] I also join Justice GINSBURG's dissent. Without directly reexamining the soundness of the Court's analysis of government dog sniffs in Place, she demonstrates that investigation into a matter beyond the subject of the traffic stop here offends the rule in *Terry v. Ohio*, the analysis I, too, adopt.

[26] Another proffered justification for *sui generis* status is that a dog sniff is a particularly nonintrusive procedure. I agree with Justice Ginsburg that the introduction of a dog to a traffic stop (let alone an encounter with someone walking down the street) can in fact be quite intrusive.

function that dog sniffs perform. They are conducted to obtain information about the contents of private spaces beyond anything that human senses could perceive, even when conventionally enhanced. The information is not provided by independent third parties beyond the reach of constitutional limitations, but gathered by the government's own officers in order to justify searches of the traditional sort, which may or may not reveal evidence of crime but will disclose anything meant to be kept private in the area searched. Thus in practice the government's use of a trained narcotics dog functions as a limited search to reveal undisclosed facts about private enclosures, to be used to justify a further and complete search of the enclosed area. And given the fallibility of the dog, the sniff is the first step in a process that may disclose "intimate details" without revealing contraband, just as a thermal-imaging device might do, as described in *Kyllo v. United States*.[27]

It makes sense, then, to treat a sniff as the search that it amounts to in practice, and to rely on the body of our Fourth Amendment cases, including *Kyllo*, in deciding whether such a search is reasonable. As a general proposition, using a dog to sniff for drugs is subject to the rule that the object of enforcing criminal laws does not, without more, justify suspicionless Fourth Amendment intrusions. See *Indianapolis v. Edmond*. Since the police claim to have had no particular suspicion that Caballes was violating any drug law, this sniff search must stand or fall on its being ancillary to the traffic stop that led up to it. It is true that the police had probable cause to stop the car for an offense committed in the officer's presence, which Caballes concedes could have justified his arrest. There is no occasion to consider authority incident to arrest, however, for the police did nothing more than detain Caballes long enough to check his record and write a ticket. As a consequence, the reasonableness of the search must be assessed in relation to the actual delay the police chose to impose, and as Justice Ginsburg points out in her opinion the Fourth Amendment consequences of stopping for a traffic citation are settled law.

In *Berkemer v. McCarty*, we held that the analogue of the common traffic stop was the limited detention for investigation authorized by *Terry v. Ohio*. While *Terry* authorized a restricted incidental search for weapons when reasonable suspicion warrants such a safety measure, the Court took care to keep a *Terry* stop from automatically becoming a foot in the door for all investigatory purposes; the permissible intrusion was bounded by the justification for the detention.[5] Although

---

[27] *Kyllo* was concerned with whether a search occurred when the police used a thermal-imaging device on a house to detect heat emanations associated with high-powered marijuana-growing lamps. In concluding that using the device was a search, the Court stressed that the "Government [may not] us[e] a device . . . to explore details of the home that would previously have been unknowable without physical intrusion." Any difference between the dwelling in *Kyllo* and the trunk of the car here may go to the issue of the reasonableness of the respective searches, but it has no bearing on the question of search or no search. Nor is it significant that *Kyllo's* imaging device would disclose personal details immediately, whereas they would be revealed only in the further step of opening the enclosed space following the dog's alert reaction; in practical terms the same values protected by the Fourth Amendment are at stake in each case. The justifications required by the Fourth Amendment may or may not differ as between the two practices, but if constitutional scrutiny is in order for the imager, it is in order for the dog.

[5] Thus, in *Place* itself, the Government officials had independent grounds to suspect that the luggage in question contained contraband before they employed the dog sniff. (describing how Place had acted

facts disclosed by enquiry within this limit might give grounds to go further, the government could not otherwise take advantage of a suspect's immobility to search for evidence unrelated to the reason for the detention. That has to be the rule unless *Terry* is going to become an open-sesame for general searches, and that rule requires holding that the police do not have reasonable grounds to conduct sniff searches for drugs simply because they have stopped someone to receive a ticket for a highway offense. Since the police had no indication of illegal activity beyond the speed of the car in this case, the sniff search should be held unreasonable under the Fourth Amendment and its fruits should be suppressed.

Nothing in the case relied upon by the Court unsettled the limit of reasonable enquiry adopted in *Terry*. In *Jacobsen*, the Court found that no Fourth Amendment search occurred when federal agents analyzed powder they had already lawfully obtained. The Court noted that because the test could only reveal whether the powder was cocaine, the owner had no legitimate privacy interest at stake. As already explained, however, the use of a sniffing dog in cases like this is significantly different and properly treated as a search that does indeed implicate Fourth Amendment protection.

In *Jacobsen*, once the powder was analyzed, that was effectively the end of the matter: either the powder was cocaine, a fact the owner had no legitimate interest in concealing, or it was not cocaine, in which case the test revealed nothing about the powder or anything else that was not already legitimately obvious to the police. But in the case of the dog sniff, the dog does not smell the disclosed contraband; it smells a closed container. An affirmative reaction therefore does not identify a substance the police already legitimately possess, but informs the police instead merely of a reasonable chance of finding contraband they have yet to put their hands on. The police will then open the container and discover whatever lies within, be it marijuana or the owner's private papers. Thus, while *Jacobsen* could rely on the assumption that the enquiry in question would either show with certainty that a known substance was contraband or would reveal nothing more, both the certainty and the limit on disclosure that may follow are missing when the dog sniffs the car.[6]

The Court today does not go so far as to say explicitly that sniff searches by dogs trained to sense contraband always get a free pass under the Fourth Amendment, since it reserves judgment on the constitutional significance of sniffs assumed to be more intrusive than a dog's walk around a stopped car. For this reason, I do not take the Court's reliance on *Jacobsen* as actually signaling recognition of a broad authority to conduct suspicionless sniffs for drugs in any parked car, about which Justice Ginsburg is rightly concerned or on the person of any pedestrian minding

---

suspiciously in line at the airport and had labeled his luggage with inconsistent and fictional addresses).

[6] It would also be error to claim that some variant of the plain-view doctrine excuses the lack of justification for the dog sniff in this case. When an officer observes an object left by its owner in plain view, no search occurs because the owner has exhibited "no intention to keep [the object] to himself." In contrast, when an individual conceals his possessions from the world, he has grounds to expect some degree of privacy. While plain view may be enhanced somewhat by technology, there are limits. If Fourth Amendment protections are to have meaning in the face of superhuman, yet fallible, techniques like the use of trained dogs, those techniques must be justified on the basis of their reasonableness, lest everything be deemed in plain view.

his own business on a sidewalk. But the Court's stated reasoning provides no apparent stopping point short of such excesses. For the sake of providing a workable framework to analyze cases on facts like these, which are certain to come along, I would treat the dog sniff as the familiar search it is in fact, subject to scrutiny under the Fourth Amendment.[7]

JUSTICE GINSBURG, with whom JUSTICE SOUTER joins, dissenting.

In applying *Terry*, the Court has several times indicated that the limitation on "scope" is not confined to the duration of the seizure; it also encompasses the manner in which the seizure is conducted.

"A routine traffic stop," the Court has observed, "is a relatively brief encounter and 'is more analogous to a so-called *Terry* stop . . . than to a formal arrest.' " I would apply *Terry's* reasonable-relation test, as the Illinois Supreme Court did, to determine whether the canine sniff impermissibly expanded the scope of the initially valid seizure of Caballes.

It is hardly dispositive that the dog sniff in this case may not have lengthened the duration of the stop. *Terry*, it merits repetition, instructs that any investigation must be "reasonably related in *scope* to the circumstances which justified the interference in the first place." (emphasis added). The unwarranted and nonconsensual expansion of the seizure here from a routine traffic stop to a drug investigation broadened the scope of the investigation in a manner that, in my judgment, runs afoul of the Fourth Amendment.[3]

The Court rejects the Illinois Supreme Court's judgment and, implicitly, the application of *Terry* to a traffic stop converted, by calling in a dog, to a drug search. The Court so rules, holding that a dog sniff does not render a seizure that is reasonable in time unreasonable in scope. Dog sniffs that detect only the possession of contraband may be employed without offense to the Fourth Amendment, the Court reasons, because they reveal no lawful activity and hence disturb no legitimate expectation of privacy.

In my view, the Court diminishes the Fourth Amendment's force by abandoning the second Terry inquiry (was the police action "reasonably related in scope to the circumstances [justifying] the [initial] interference"). A drug-detection dog is an intimidating animal. Cf. *United States v. Williams* (McKay, J., dissenting) ("drug dogs are not lap dogs"). Injecting such an animal into a routine traffic stop changes the character of the encounter between the police and the motorist. The stop becomes broader, more adversarial, and (in at least some cases) longer. Caballes —

---

[7] I should take care myself to reserve judgment about a possible case significantly unlike this one. All of us are concerned not to prejudge a claim of authority to detect explosives and dangerous chemical or biological weapons that might be carried by a terrorist who prompts no individualized suspicion. Suffice it to say here that what is a reasonable search depends in part on demonstrated risk. Unreasonable sniff searches for marijuana are not necessarily unreasonable sniff searches for destructive or deadly material if suicide bombs are a societal risk.

[3] The question whether a police officer inquiring about drugs without reasonable suspicion unconstitutionally broadens a traffic investigation is not before the Court. Cf. *Florida v. Bostick* (police questioning of a bus passenger, who might have just said "No," did not constitute a seizure).

who, as far as Troopers Gillette and Graham knew, was guilty solely of driving six miles per hour over the speed limit — was exposed to the embarrassment and intimidation of being investigated, on a public thoroughfare, for drugs. Even if the drug sniff is not characterized as a Fourth Amendment "search," cf. *Place*, the sniff surely broadened the scope of the traffic-violation-related seizure.

The Court has never removed police action from Fourth Amendment control on the ground that the action is well calculated to apprehend the guilty. Under today's decision, every traffic stop could become an occasion to call in the dogs, to the distress and embarrassment of the law-abiding population.

The Illinois Supreme Court, it seems to me, correctly apprehended the danger in allowing the police to search for contraband despite the absence of cause to suspect its presence. Today's decision, in contrast, clears the way for suspicionless, dog-accompanied drug sweeps of parked cars along sidewalks and in parking lots. Compare, e.g., *United States v. Ludwig* (upholding a search based on a canine drug sniff of a parked car in a motel parking lot conducted without particular suspicion), with *United States v. Quinn* (officers must have reasonable suspicion that a car contains narcotics at the moment a dog sniff is performed), and *Place* (Fourth Amendment not violated by a dog sniff of a piece of luggage that was seized, pre-sniff, based on suspicion of drugs). Nor would motorists have constitutional grounds for complaint should police with dogs, stationed at long traffic lights, circle cars waiting for the red signal to turn green.

Today's decision also undermines this Court's situation-sensitive balancing of Fourth Amendment interests in other contexts. For example, in *Bond v. United States*, the Court held that a bus passenger had an expectation of privacy in a bag placed in an overhead bin and that a police officer's physical manipulation of the bag constituted an illegal search. If canine drug sniffs are entirely exempt from Fourth Amendment inspection, a sniff could substitute for an officer's request to a bus passenger for permission to search his bag, with this significant difference: The passenger would not have the option to say "No."

The dog sniff in this case, it bears emphasis, was for drug detection only. A dog sniff for explosives, involving security interests not presented here, would be an entirely different matter.

The use of bomb-detection dogs to check vehicles for explosives without doubt has a closer kinship to the sobriety checkpoints in Sitz than to the drug checkpoints in Edmond. As the Court observed in *Edmond*: "[T]he Fourth Amendment would almost certainly permit an appropriately tailored roadblock set up to thwart an imminent terrorist attack . . . ." Even if the Court were to change course and characterize a dog sniff as an independent Fourth Amendment search, the immediate, present danger of explosives would likely justify a bomb sniff under the special needs doctrine.

*   *   *

For the reasons stated, I would hold that the police violated Caballes' Fourth Amendment rights when, without cause to suspect wrongdoing, they conducted a dog sniff of his vehicle. I would therefore affirm the judgment of the Illinois Supreme Court.

QUESTIONS AND NOTES

1.   Does Justice Souter dissent primarily because of his disagreement with the divining rod theory or because he does not believe that dogs are divining rods? What about Justice Ginsburg?

2.   Does the extent that dogs are less than perfectly reliable argue for considering a dog sniff a search, or for questioning whether a positive dog sniff creates probable cause?

3.   Would it be better or worse if the police regularly patrolled downtown streets and parking lots with dogs? Why? *Cf. Delaware v. Prouse.*

4.   Is (should it be) it relevant that police dogs aren't lap dogs?

5.   Would you (assuming your total innocence) be alarmed if another policeman brought a dog to sniff your car while the policeman who stopped you was issuing his warning? Explain.

6.   While the impact of the police practice on the innocent has appeared to motivate the Court in some cases, the rhetoric that has dominated this area of the law is "reasonable expectation of privacy." As you read the next series of cases, consider whether the police practices involved therein interfere with what you would have thought to have been a legitimate expectation of privacy.

B.   REASONABLE EXPECTATION OF PRIVACY

LEWIS v. UNITED STATES
385 U.S. 206 (1966)

MR. CHIEF JUSTICE WARREN delivered the opinion of the Court.

The question for resolution here is whether the Fourth Amendment was violated when a federal narcotics agent, by misrepresenting his identity and stating his willingness to purchase narcotics, was invited into petitioner's home where an unlawful narcotics transaction was consummated and the narcotics were thereafter introduced at petitioner's criminal trial over his objection. We hold that under the facts of this case it was not. Those facts are not disputed and may be briefly stated as follows:

On December 3, 1964, Edward Cass, an undercover federal narcotics agent, telephoned petitioner's home to inquire about the possibility of purchasing mari-huana. Cass, who previously had not met or dealt with petitioner, falsely identified himself as one "Jimmy the Pollack [sic]" and stated that a mutual friend had told him petitioner might be able to supply marihuana. In response, petitioner said, "Yes. I believe, Jimmy, I can take care of you," and then directed Cass to his home where, it was indicated, a sale of marihuana would occur. Cass drove to petitioner's home, knocked on the door, identified himself as "Jim," and was admitted. After discussing the possibility of regular future dealings at a discounted price, petitioner led Cass to a package located on the front porch of his home. Cass gave petitioner $50, took the package, and left the premises. The package contained five bags of marihuana. On December 17, 1964, a similar transaction took place, beginning with a phone conversation in which Cass identified himself as "Jimmy the Pollack" and ending with an invited visit by Cass to petitioner's home where a second sale of marihuana occurred. Once again, Cass paid petitioner $50, but this time he received in return a package containing six bags of marihuana.

Petitioner does not argue that he was entrapped, as he could not on the facts of this case; nor does he contend that a search of his home was made or that anything other than the purchased narcotics was taken away. His only contentions are that, in the absence of a warrant, any official intrusion upon the privacy of a home constitutes a Fourth Amendment violation and that the fact the suspect invited the intrusion cannot be held a waiver when the invitation was induced by fraud and deception.

Petitioner argues that the Government overstepped the constitutional bounds in this case and places principal reliance on *Gouled v. United States*, 255 U.S. 298 (1921). But a short statement of that case will demonstrate how misplaced his reliance is. There, a business acquaintance of the petitioner, acting under orders of federal officers, obtained entry into the petitioner's office by falsely representing that he intended only to pay a social visit. In the petitioner's absence, however, the intruder secretly ransacked the office and seized certain private papers of an incriminating nature. This Court had no difficulty concluding that the Fourth Amendment had been violated by the secret and general ransacking, notwithstanding that the initial intrusion was occasioned by a fraudulently obtained invitation rather than by force or stealth.

In the instant case, on the other hand, the petitioner invited the undercover agent to his home for the specific purpose of executing a felonious sale of narcotics. Petitioner's only concern was whether the agent was a willing purchaser who could pay the agreed price. Indeed, in order to convince the agent that his patronage at petitioner's home was desired, petitioner told him that, if he became a regular customer there, he would in the future receive an extra bag of marihuana at no additional cost; and in fact petitioner did hand over an extra bag at a second sale which was consummated at the same place and in precisely the same manner. During neither of his visits to petitioner's home did the agent see, hear, or take anything that was not contemplated, and in fact intended, by petitioner as a necessary part of his illegal business. Were we to hold the deceptions of the agent in this case constitutionally prohibited, we would come near to a rule that the use of undercover agents in any manner is virtually unconstitutional *per se*. Such a rule would, for example, severely hamper the Government in ferreting out those organized criminal activities that are characterized by covert dealings with victims who either cannot or do not protest.[6] A prime example is provided by the narcotics traffic.

---

[6] "Particularly, in the enforcement of vice, liquor or narcotics laws, it is all but impossible to obtain evidence for prosecution save by the use of decoys. There are rarely complaining witnesses. The participants in the crime enjoy themselves. Misrepresentation by a police officer or agent concerning the identity of the purchaser of illegal narcotics is a practical necessity . . . . Therefore, the law must attempt to distinguish between those deceits and persuasions which are permissible and those which are not." Model Penal Code § 2.10, comment, p. 16 (Tent. Draft No. 9, 1959).

The fact that the undercover agent entered petitioner's home does not compel a different conclusion. Without question, the home is accorded the full range of Fourth Amendment protections. But when, as here, the home is converted into a commercial center to which outsiders are invited for purposes of transacting unlawful business, that business is entitled to no greater sanctity than if it were carried on in a store, a garage, a car, or on the street. A government agent, in the same manner as a private person, may accept an invitation to do business and may enter upon the premises for the very purposes contemplated by the occupant. Of course, this does not mean that, whenever entry is obtained by invitation and the locus is characterized as a place of business, an agent is authorized to conduct a general search for incriminating materials; a citation to the *Gouled* case is sufficient to dispose of that contention.

Mr. Justice Douglas, dissenting.

Entering another's home in disguise to obtain evidence is a "search" that should bring into play all the protective features of the Fourth Amendment. When the agent had reason for believing that petitioner possessed narcotics, a search warrant should have been obtained.

Mr. Justice Brennan, with whom Mr. Justice Fortas joins, concurring.

While I concur in the Court's judgment, I vote to affirm solely on the reasoning on which the Court ultimately relies, namely that petitioner's apartment was not an area protected by the Fourth Amendment as related to the transactions in the present case.

The Fourth Amendment protects against governmental intrusion upon "the sanctity of a man's home and the privacies of life." However, the occupant can break the seal of sanctity and waive his right to privacy in the premises. Plainly he does this to the extent that he opens his home to the transaction of business and invites anyone willing to enter to come in to trade with him. When his customer turns out to be a government agent, the seller cannot, then, complain that his privacy has been invaded so long as the agent does no more than buy his wares. Thus the corner grocery with the living quarters in the rear would not be protected with respect to the area set aside for the purchase of groceries, although the living quarters to which shoppers are not privy retain the constitutional immunity.

The petitioner in this case opened his apartment for the conduct of a business, the sale of narcotics; the agent, in the same manner as any private person, entered the premises for the very purpose contemplated by the occupant and took nothing away except what would be taken away by any willing purchaser. There was therefore no intrusion upon the "sanctity" of petitioner's home or the "privacies of life."

QUESTIONS AND NOTES

1.　Do you agree with Justice Douglas' assertion that a disguised government agent attempting to find evidence of crime constitutes a search? Why? Why not?

2.   What do you perceive to be the distinction between *Lewis* and *Gouled*? Do you find it persuasive?

3.   Could an innocent person be hurt by the *Lewis* procedure? How? Could an innocent person be hurt by the *Gouled* procedure? How?

4.   Consider whether *Lewis* principles should control *Hoffa.*

HOFFA v. UNITED STATES
385 U.S. 293 (1966)

Mr. Justice Stewart delivered the opinion of the Court.

Over a period of several weeks in the late autumn of 1962 there took place in a federal court in Nashville, Tennessee, a trial by jury in which James Hoffa was charged with violating a provision of the Taft-Hartley Act. That trial, known in the present record as the Test Fleet trial, ended with a hung jury. The petitioners now before us — James Hoffa, Thomas Parks, Larry Campbell, and Ewing King — were tried and convicted in 1964 for endeavoring to bribe members of that jury. The convictions were affirmed by the Court of Appeals. A substantial element in the Government's proof that led to the convictions of these four petitioners was contributed by a witness named Edward Partin, who testified to several incriminating statements which he said petitioners Hoffa and King had made in his presence during the course of the Test Fleet trial.

The controlling facts can be briefly stated. The Test Fleet trial, in which James Hoffa was the sole individual defendant, was in progress between October 22 and December 23, 1962, in Nashville, Tennessee. James Hoffa was president of the International Brotherhood of Teamsters. During the course of the trial he occupied a three-room suite in the Andrew Jackson Hotel in Nashville. One of his constant companions throughout the trial was the petitioner King, president of the Nashville local of the Teamsters Union. Edward Partin, a resident of Baton Rouge, Louisiana, and a local Teamsters Union official there, made repeated visits to Nashville during the period of the trial. On these visits he frequented the Hoffa hotel suite, and was continually in the company of Hoffa and his associates, including King, in and around the hotel suite, the hotel lobby, the courthouse, and elsewhere in Nashville. During this period Partin made frequent reports to a federal agent named Sheridan concerning conversations he said Hoffa and King had had with him and with each other, disclosing endeavors to bribe members of the Test Fleet jury. Partin's reports and his subsequent testimony at the petitioners' trial unquestionably contributed, directly or indirectly, to the convictions of all four of the petitioners.

The chain of circumstances which led Partin to be in Nashville during the Test Fleet trial extended back at least to September of 1962. At that time Partin was in jail in Baton Rouge on a state criminal charge. He was also under a federal indictment for embezzling union funds, and other indictments for state offenses were pending against him. Between that time and Partin's initial visit to Nashville on October 22 he was released on bail on the state criminal charge, and proceedings under the federal indictment were postponed. On October 8, Partin telephoned Hoffa in Washington, D.C., to discuss local union matters and Partin's difficulties with the authorities. In the course of this conversation Partin asked if he could see Hoffa to confer about these problems, and Hoffa acquiesced. Partin again called Hoffa on October 18 and arranged to meet him in Nashville. During this period Partin also consulted on several occasions with federal law enforcement agents, who told him that Hoffa might attempt to tamper with the Test Fleet jury, and asked him to be on the lookout in Nashville for such attempts and to report to the federal authorities any evidence of wrongdoing that he discovered. Partin agreed to do so.

After the Test Fleet trial was completed, Partin's wife received four monthly installment payments of $300 from government funds, and the state and federal charges against Partin were either dropped or not actively pursued.

[W]hether or not the Government "placed" Partin with Hoffa in Nashville during the Test Fleet trial, we proceed upon the premise that Partin was a government informer from the time he first arrived in Nashville on October 22, and that the Government compensated him for his services as such. It is upon that premise that we consider the constitutional issues presented.

I.

It is contended that only by violating the petitioner's rights under the Fourth Amendment was Partin able to hear the petitioner's incriminating statements in the hotel suite. The argument is that Partin's failure to disclose his role as a government informer vitiated the consent that the petitioner gave to Partin's repeated entries into the suite, and that by listening to the petitioner's statements Partin conducted an illegal "search" for verbal evidence.

The preliminary steps of this argument are on solid ground. A hotel room can clearly be the object of Fourth Amendment protection as much as a home or an office. *United States v. Jeffers*, 342 U.S. 48. The Fourth Amendment can certainly be violated by guileful as well as by forcible intrusions into a constitutionally protected area. *Gouled v. United States*, 255 U.S. 298. And the protections of the Fourth Amendment are surely not limited to tangibles, but can extend as well to oral statements. *Silverman v. United States*, 365 U.S. 505.

Where the argument falls is in its misapprehension of the fundamental nature and scope of Fourth Amendment protection. What the Fourth Amendment protects is the security a man relies upon when he places himself or his property within a constitutionally protected area, be it his home or his office, his hotel room or his automobile. There he is protected from unwarranted governmental intrusion. And when he puts something in his filing cabinet, in his desk drawer, or in his pocket, he has the right to know it will be secure from an unreasonable search or an unreasonable seizure. So it was that the Fourth Amendment could not tolerate the warrantless search of the hotel room in *Jeffers*, the purloining of the petitioner's private papers in *Gouled*, or the surreptitious electronic surveillance in *Silverman*. Countless other cases which have come to this Court over the years have involved a myriad of differing factual contexts in which the protections of the Fourth Amendment have been appropriately invoked. No doubt the future will bring countless others. By nothing we say here do we either foresee or foreclose factual situations to which the Fourth Amendment may be applicable.

In the present case, however, it is evident that no interest legitimately protected by the Fourth Amendment is involved. It is obvious that the petitioner was not relying on the security of his hotel suite when he made the incriminating statements to Partin or in Partin's presence. Partin did not enter the suite by force or by stealth. He was not a surreptitious eavesdropper. Partin was in the suite by invitation, and every conversation which he heard was either directed to him or knowingly carried on in his presence. The petitioner, in a word, was not relying on the security of the hotel room; he was relying upon his misplaced confidence that Partin would not reveal his wrongdoing. As counsel for the petitioner himself points out, some of the communications with Partin did not take place in the suite at all, but in the "hall of the hotel," in the "Andrew Jackson Hotel lobby," and "at the courthouse."

Neither this Court nor any member of it has ever expressed the view that the Fourth Amendment protects a wrongdoer's misplaced belief that a person to whom he voluntarily confides his wrongdoing will not reveal it. Indeed, the Court unanimously rejected that very contention less than four years ago in *Lopez v. United States*, 373 U.S. 427. In that case the petitioner had been convicted of attempted bribery of an internal revenue agent named Davis. The Court was divided with regard to the admissibility in evidence of a surreptitious electronic recording of an incriminating conversation Lopez had had in his private office with Davis. But there was no dissent from the view that testimony about the conversation by Davis himself was clearly admissible.

As the Court put it, "Davis was not guilty of an unlawful invasion of petitioner's office simply because his apparent willingness to accept a bribe was not real. He was in the office with petitioner's consent, and while there he did not violate the privacy of the office by seizing something surreptitiously without petitioner's knowledge. The only evidence obtained consisted of statements made by Lopez to Davis, statements which Lopez knew full well could be used against him by Davis if he wished . . . ." In the words of the dissenting opinion in *Lopez*, "The risk of being overheard by an eavesdropper or betrayed by an informer or deceived as to the identity of one with whom one deals is probably inherent in the conditions of human society. It is the kind of risk we necessarily assume whenever we speak."

Adhering to these views, we hold that no right protected by the Fourth Amendment was violated in the present case.

[Mr. Chief Justice Warren, dissented on the ground that under the Court's Federal supervisory powers it should reverse the conviction because of the inherent unreliability of one whose motivations and propensity to lie is as strong as those of Mr. Partin.]

[Mr. Justice Clark, joined by Mr. Justice Douglas would have dismissed the writs of certiorari as improvidently granted on the ground that the trial and appellate courts' conclusion that Partin was not placed in Hoffa's hotel room by the government was not clearly erroneous.]

QUESTIONS AND NOTES

1. Is the risk that a friend has been planted by the government as a spy, a different risk than the risk that one who has not been planted by the government will nevertheless decided to turn state's evidence? Explain.

2. Does an innocent person run any risk in the *Hoffa* situation? If so, what are they?

3. The term reasonable expectation of privacy, which informs so much of our Fourth Amendment jurisprudence was first developed in *Katz*.

KATZ v. UNITED STATES
389 U.S. 347 (1967)

Mr. Justice Stewart delivered the opinion of the Court.

The petitioner was convicted in the District Court for the Southern District of California under an eight-count indictment charging him with transmitting wagering information by telephone from Los Angeles to Miami and Boston in violation of a federal statute. At trial the Government was permitted, over the petitioner's objection, to introduce evidence of the petitioner's end of telephone conversations, overheard by FBI agents who had attached an electronic listening and recording device to the outside of the public telephone booth from which he had placed his calls. In affirming his conviction, the Court of Appeals rejected the contention that the recordings had been obtained in violation of the Fourth Amendment, because "[t]here was no physical entrance into the area occupied by, [the petitioner]." We granted certiorari in order to consider the constitutional questions thus presented.

The petitioner had phrased those questions as follows:

A. Whether a public telephone booth is a constitutionally protected area so that evidence obtained by attaching an electronic listening recording device to the top of such a booth is obtained in violation of the right to privacy of the user of the booth.

B. Whether physical penetration of a constitutionally protected area is necessary before a search and seizure can be said to be violative of the Fourth Amendment to the United States Constitution.

We decline to adopt this formulation of the issues. In the first place the correct solution of Fourth Amendment problems is not necessarily promoted by incantation of the phrase "constitutionally protected area." Secondly, the Fourth Amendment cannot be translated into a general constitutional "right to privacy." That Amendment protects individual privacy against certain kinds of governmental intrusion, but its protections go further, and often have nothing to do with privacy at all. Other provisions of the Constitution protect personal privacy from other forms of governmental invasion. But the protection of a person's *general* right to privacy — his right to be let alone by other people — is, like the protection of his property and of his very life, left largely to the law of the individual States.

Because of the misleading way the issues have been formulated, the parties have attached great significance to the characterization of the telephone booth from which the petitioner placed his calls. The petitioner has strenuously argued that the booth was a "constitutionally protected area." The Government has maintained with equal vigor that it was not. But this effort to decide whether or not a given "area," viewed in the abstract, is "constitutionally protected" deflects attention from the problem presented by this case. For the Fourth Amendment protects people, not places. What a person knowingly exposes to the public, even in his own home or office, is not a subject of Fourth Amendment protection. *See Lewis.* But what he seeks to preserve as private, even in an area accessible to the public, may be constitutionally protected.

The Government stresses the fact that the telephone booth from which the petitioner made his calls was constructed partly of glass, so that he was as visible after he entered it as he would have been if he had remained outside. But what he sought to exclude when he entered the booth was not the intruding eye — it was the uninvited ear. He did not shed his right to do so simply because he made his calls from a place where he might be seen. No less than an individual in a business office, in a friend's apartment, or in a taxicab, a person in a telephone booth may rely upon the protection of the Fourth Amendment. One who occupies it, shuts the door behind him, and pays the toll that permits him to place a call is surely entitled to assume that the words he utters into the mouthpiece will not be broadcast to the world. To read the Constitution more narrowly is to ignore the vital role that the public telephone has come to play in private communication.

The Government contends, however, that the activities of its agents in this case should not be tested by Fourth Amendment requirements, for the surveillance technique they employed involved no physical penetration of the telephone booth from which the petitioner placed his calls. It is true that the absence of such penetration was at one time thought to foreclose further Fourth Amendment inquiry, for that Amendment was thought to limit only searches and seizures of tangible property. But "[t]he premise that property interests control the right of the Government to search and seize has been discredited." *Warden v. Hayden*, 387 U.S. 294.

The fact that the electronic device did not happen to penetrate the wall of the booth can have no constitutional significance.

The question remaining for decision, then, is whether the search and seizure conducted in this case complied with constitutional standards. [The Court then held that the government had probable cause to electronically eavesdrop, but that it did not have a good excuse for dispensing with a warrant. Consequently, it reversed the conviction because of the lack of a warrant.]

Mr. Justice Harlan, concurring.

I join the opinion of the Court, which I read to hold only (a) that an enclosed telephone booth is an area where, like a home, *Weeks v. United States*, 232 U.S. 383, and unlike a field, *Hester v. United States*, 265 U.S. 57, a person has a constitutionally protected reasonable expectation of privacy; (b) that electronic as well as physical intrusion into a place that is in this sense private may constitute a violation of the Fourth Amendment; and (c) that the invasion of a constitutionally protected area by federal authorities is, as the Court has long held, presumptively unreasonable in the absence of a search warrant.

As the Court's opinion states, "the Fourth Amendment protects people, not places." The question, however, is what protection it affords to those people. Generally, as here, the answer to that question requires reference to a "place." My understanding of the rule that has emerged from prior decisions is that there is a twofold requirement, first that a person have exhibited an actual (subjective) expectation of privacy and, second, that the expectation be one that society is prepared to recognize as "reasonable." Thus a man's home is, for most purposes, a place where he expects privacy, but objects, activities, or statements that he exposes to the "plain view" of outsiders are not "protected" because no intention to keep them to himself has been exhibited. On the other hand, conversations in the open would not be protected against being overheard, for the expectation of privacy under the circumstances would be unreasonable.

The critical fact in this case is that "[o]ne who occupies it, [a telephone booth] shuts the door behind him, and pays the toll that permits him to place a call is surely entitled to assume" that his conversation is not being intercepted. The point is not that the booth is "accessible to the public" at other times, but that it is a temporarily private place whose momentary occupants' expectations of freedom from intrusion are recognized as reasonable.

Mr. Justice Black, dissenting.

If I could agree with the Court that eavesdropping carried on by electronic means (equivalent to wiretapping) constitutes a "search" or "seizure," I would be happy to join the Court's opinion. For on that premise my Brother Stewart sets out methods in accord with the Fourth Amendment to guide States in the enactment and enforcement of laws passed to regulate wiretapping by government.

My basic objection is twofold: (1) I do not believe that the words of the Amendment will bear the meaning given them by today's decision, and (2) I do not believe that it is the proper role of this Court to rewrite the Amendment in order "to bring it into harmony with the times" and thus reach a result that many people believe to be desirable.

While I realize that an argument based on the meaning of words lacks the scope, and no doubt the appeal, of broad policy discussions and philosophical discourses on such nebulous subjects as privacy, for me the language of the Amendment is the crucial place to look in construing a written document such as our Constitution. The Fourth Amendment says that

> The right of the people to be secure in their persons, houses, papers, and effects, against unreasonable searches and seizures, shall not be violated, and no Warrants shall issue, but upon probable cause, supported by Oath or affirmation, and particularly describing the place to be searched, and the persons or things to be seized.

The first clause protects "persons, houses, papers, and effects, against unreasonable searches and seizures . . . ." These words connote the idea of tangible things with size, form, and weight, things capable of being searched, seized, or both. The second clause of the Amendment still further establishes its Framers' purpose to limit its protection to tangible things by providing that no warrants shall issue but those "particularly describing the place to be searched, and the persons or things to be seized." A conversation overheard by eavesdropping, whether by plain snooping or wiretapping, is not tangible and, under the normally accepted meanings of the words, can neither be searched nor seized. In addition the language of the second clause indicates that the Amendment refers not only to something tangible so it can be seized but to something already in existence so it can be described. Yet the Court's interpretation would have the Amendment apply to overhearing future conversations which by their very nature are nonexistent until they take place. How can one "describe" a future conversation, and, if one cannot, how can a magistrate issue a warrant to eavesdrop one in the future? It is argued that information showing what is expected to be said is sufficient to limit the boundaries of what later can be admitted into evidence; but does such general information really meet the specific language of the Amendment which says "particularly describing?" Rather than using language in a completely artificial way, I must conclude that the Fourth Amendment simply does not apply to eavesdropping.

Tapping telephone wires, of course, was an unknown possibility at the time the Fourth Amendment was adopted. But eavesdropping (and wiretapping is nothing more than eavesdropping by telephone) was recognized, "an ancient practice which at common law was condemned as a nuisance. In those days the eavesdropper listened by naked ear under the eaves of houses or their windows, or beyond their walls seeking out private discourse." There can be no doubt that the Framers were aware of this practice, and if they had desired to outlaw or restrict the use of evidence obtained by eavesdropping, I believe that they would have used the appropriate language to do so in the Fourth Amendment.

Since I see no way in which the words of the Fourth Amendment can be construed to apply to eavesdropping, that closes the matter for me. In interpreting the Bill of Rights, I willingly go as far as a liberal construction of the language takes me, but I simply cannot in good conscience give a meaning to words which they have never before been thought to have and which they certainly do not have in common ordinary usage. I will not distort the words of the Amendment in order to "keep the Constitution up to date" or "to bring it into harmony with the times." It was never meant that this Court have such power, which in effect would make us a continuously functioning constitutional convention.

For these reasons I respectfully dissent.

QUESTIONS AND NOTES

1. Is Justice Black's reliance on history, a defensible way to analyze Fourth Amendment issues? A desirable way?

2. Whose opinion is best supported by the text of the Fourth Amendment?

3. Should subjective expectation of privacy be at all relevant? Why? Why not?

4. If reasonable expectation of privacy is the key, how is it to be measured? Should empiric data of societal attitudes be relevant? Determinative?

5. Is it meaningful to talk about the Fourth Amendment as protecting people rather than places? Isn't the amount of protection that a person gets dependent on where she is? Isn't that inherent in the Fourth Amendment?

6. In *United States v. White*, 401 U.S. 745 (1971), a closely divided Court held that, even in a post-*Katz* world, a person did not have a reasonable expectation of privacy that a confederate overhearing his conversations would not record his conversations for, or transmit them to, a police officer.

7. In another sharply divided post *Katz* case, *Smith v. Maryland*, 442 U.S. 735 (1979), the Court held that the installation (at the phone company) and monitoring of a pen register, a device that can monitor numbers called from a home, did not violate one's reasonable expectation of privacy. This decision was partly predicated on the belief that only the numbers dialed was revealed to the police and that was not a significant invasion of privacy, and partly predicated on the theory that individuals know that the numbers they dial is communicated to the phone company, therefore they do not retain an expectation of privacy.

8. In *Oliver*, we see that even if the Fourth Amendment protects people rather than places, the place still matters.

OLIVER v. UNITED STATES
466 U.S. 170 (1984)

JUSTICE POWELL delivered the opinion of the Court.

The "open fields" doctrine, first enunciated by this Court in *Hester v. United States*, 265 U.S. 57, 44 S. Ct. 445, 68 L. Ed. 898 (1924), permits police officers to enter and search a field without a warrant. We granted certiorari in these cases to clarify confusion that has arisen as to the continued vitality of the doctrine.

I

No. 82-15. Acting on reports that marijuana was being raised on the farm of petitioner Oliver, two narcotics agents of the Kentucky State Police went to the farm to investigate.[2] Arriving at the farm, they drove past petitioner's house to a locked gate with a "No Trespassing" sign. A footpath led around one side of the gate. The agents walked around the gate and along the road for several hundred yards, passing a barn and a parked camper. At that point, someone standing in front of the camper shouted, "No hunting is allowed, come back here." The officers shouted back that they were Kentucky State Police officers, but found no one when they returned to the camper. The officers resumed their investigation of the farm and found a field of marijuana over a mile from petitioner's home.

---

[2] It is conceded that the police did not have a warrant authorizing the search, that there was no probable cause for the search and that no exception to the warrant requirement is applicable.

Petitioner was arrested and indicted for "manufactur[ing]" a "controlled substance." After a pretrial hearing, the District Court suppressed evidence of the discovery of the marijuana fields. Applying *Katz*, the court found that petitioner had a reasonable expectation that the fields would remain private because petitioner "had done all that could be expected of him to assert his privacy in the area of farm that was searched." He had posted no trespassing signs at regular intervals and had locked the gate at the entrance to the center of the farm. Further, the court noted that the fields themselves are highly secluded: they are bounded on all sides by woods, fences and embankments and cannot be seen from any point of public access. The court concluded that this was not an "open" field that invited casual intrusion.

The Court of Appeals for the Sixth Circuit, sitting en banc, reversed the district court. The court concluded that *Katz*, upon which the District Court relied, had not impaired the vitality of the open fields doctrine of *Hester*. Rather, the open fields doctrine was entirely compatible with *Katz's* emphasis on privacy. The court reasoned that the "human relations that create the need for privacy do not ordinarily take place" in open fields, and that the property owner's common law right to exclude trespassers is insufficiently linked to privacy to warrant the Fourth Amendment's protection. *Id.* at 360.[3] We granted certiorari.

II

The rule announced in *Hester v. United States* was founded upon the explicit language of the Fourth Amendment. That Amendment indicates with some precision the places and things encompassed by its protections. As Justice Holmes explained for the Court in his characteristically laconic style: "[T]he special protection accorded by the Fourth Amendment to the people in their 'persons, houses, papers, and effects,' is not extended to the open fields. The distinction between the latter and the house is as old as the common law."[6]

Nor are the open fields "effects" within the meaning of the Fourth Amendment. In this respect, it is suggestive that James Madison's proposed draft of what became the Fourth Amendment preserves "[t]he rights of the people to be secured

---

[3] The four dissenting judges contended that the open fields doctrine did not apply where, as in this case, "reasonable efforts have been made to exclude the public." 686 F.2d at 372. To that extent, the dissent considered that *Katz v. United States, supra,* implicitly had overruled previous holdings of this Court. The dissent then concluded that petitioner had established a "reasonable expectation of privacy" under the *Katz* standard. Judge Lively also wrote separately to argue that the open fields doctrine applied only to lands that could be viewed by the public.

[6] The dissent offers no basis for its suggestion that *Hester* rests upon some narrow, unarticulated principle rather than upon the reasoning enunciated by the Court's opinion in that case. Nor have subsequent cases discredited *Hester's* reasoning. This Court frequently has relied on the explicit language of the Fourth Amendment as delineating the scope of its affirmative protections. *Katz's* "reasonable expectation of privacy" standard did not sever Fourth Amendment doctrine from the Amendment's language. *Katz* itself construed the Amendment's protection of the person against unreasonable searches to encompass electronic eavesdropping of telephone conversations sought to be kept private; and *Katz's* fundamental recognition that "the Fourth Amendment protects people — and not simply 'areas' — against unreasonable searches and seizures" is faithful to the Amendment's language. As *Katz* demonstrates, the Court fairly may respect the constraints of the Constitution's language without wedding itself to a unreasoning literalism. In contrast, the dissent's approach would ignore the language of the Constitution itself as well as overturn this Court's governing precedent.

in their persons, their houses, their papers, and their other property, from all unreasonable searches and seizures . . . ." Although Congress' revisions of Madison's proposal broadened the scope of the Amendment in some respects, the term "effects" is less inclusive than "property" and cannot be said to encompass open fields.[7] We conclude, as did the Court in deciding *Hester*, that the government's intrusion upon the open fields is not one of those "unreasonable searches" proscribed by the text of the Fourth Amendment.

III

This interpretation of the Fourth Amendment's language is consistent with the understanding of the right to privacy expressed in our Fourth Amendment jurisprudence. Since *Katz*, the touchstone of Amendment analysis has been the question whether a person has a "constitutionally protected reasonable expectation of privacy." The Amendment does not protect the merely subjective expectation of privacy, but only "those expectations that society is prepared to recognize as 'reasonable.'" *See also Smith.*

A

No single factor determines whether an individual legitimately may claim under the Fourth Amendment that a place should be free of government intrusion not authorized by warrant. In assessing the degree to which a search infringes upon individual privacy, the Court has given weight to such factors as the intention of the Framers of the Fourth Amendment, the *Chadwick* test, 433 U.S. 1, 7–8 (1977), the uses to which the individual has put a location, and our societal understanding that certain areas deserve the most scrupulous protection from government invasion, the *Payton* test. These factors are equally relevant to determining whether the government's intrusion upon open fields without a warrant or probable cause violates reasonable expectations of privacy and is therefore a search proscribed by the Amendment.

In this light, the rule of *Hester* that we reaffirm today, may be understood as providing that an individual may not legitimately demand privacy for activities conducted out of doors in fields, except in the area immediately surrounding the home. This rule is true to the conception of the right to privacy embodied in the Fourth Amendment. The Amendment reflects the recognition of the Founders that certain enclaves should be free from arbitrary government interference. For example, the Court since the enactment of the Fourth Amendment has stressed "the overriding respect for the sanctity of the home that has been embedded in our traditions since the origins of the Republic."[8]

---

[7] The Framers would have understood the term "effects" to be limited to personal, rather than real, property.

[8] The Fourth Amendment's protection of offices and commercial buildings, in which there may be legitimate expectations of privacy, is also based upon societal expectations that have deep roots in the history of the Amendment.

In contrast, open fields do not provide the setting for those intimate activities that the Amendment is intended to shelter from government interference or surveillance. There is no societal interest in protecting the privacy of those activities, such as the cultivation of crops, that occur in open fields. Moreover, as a practical matter these lands usually are accessible to the public and the police in ways that a home, an office or commercial structure would not be. It is not generally true that fences or no trespassing signs effectively bar the public from viewing open fields in rural areas. And petitioner Oliver concede[s] that the public and police lawfully may survey lands from the air.[9] For these reasons, the asserted expectation of privacy in open fields is not an expectation that "society recognizes as reasonable."[10]

The historical underpinnings of the "open fields" doctrine also demonstrate that the doctrine is consistent with respect for "reasonable expectations of privacy." As Justice Holmes, writing for the Court, observed in *Hester*, the common law distinguished "open fields" from the "curtilage," the land immediately surrounding and associated with the home. The distinction implies that only the curtilage, not the neighboring open fields, warrants the Fourth Amendment protections that attach to the home. At common law, the curtilage is the area to which extends the intimate activity associated with the "sanctity of a man's home and the privacies of life," and therefore has been considered part of home itself for Fourth Amendment purposes. Thus, courts have extended Fourth Amendment protection to the curtilage; and they have defined the curtilage, as did the common law, by reference to the factors that determine whether an individual reasonably may expect that an area immediately adjacent to the home will remain private. Conversely, the common law implies, as we reaffirm today, that no expectation of privacy legitimately attaches to open fields.[11]

---

[9] In practical terms, Oliver's analysis merely would require law enforcement officers, in most situations, to use aerial surveillance to gather the information necessary to obtain a warrant or to justify warrantless entry onto the property. It is not easy to see how such a requirement would advance legitimate privacy interests.

[10] The dissent conceives of open fields as bustling with private activity as diverse as lovers' trysts and worship services. But in most instances police will disturb no one when they enter upon open fields. These fields, by their very character as open and unoccupied, are unlikely to provide the setting for activities whose privacy is sought to be protected by the Fourth Amendment. One need think only of the vast expanse of some western ranches or of the undeveloped woods of the Northwest to see the unreality of the dissent's conception. Further, the Fourth Amendment provides ample protection to activities in the open fields that might implicate an individual's privacy. An individual who enters a place defined to be "public" for Fourth Amendment analysis does not lose all claims to privacy or personal security. For example, the Fourth Amendment's protections against unreasonable arrest or unreasonable seizure of effects upon the person remain fully applicable. *See, e.g., United States v. Watson*, 423 U.S. 411, 96 S. Ct. 820, 46 L. Ed. 2d 598 (1976).

[11] Oliver has [not] contended that the property searched was within the curtilage. Nor is it necessary in [this case] to consider the scope of the curtilage exception to the open fields doctrine or the degree of Fourth Amendment protection afforded the curtilage, as opposed to the home itself. It is clear, however, that the term "open fields" may include any unoccupied or undeveloped area outside of the curtilage. An open field need be neither "open" nor a "field" as those terms are used in common speech. For example, a thickly wooded area nonetheless may be an open field as that term is used in construing the Fourth Amendment.

We conclude, from the text of the Fourth Amendment and from the historical and contemporary understanding of its purposes, that an individual has no legitimate expectation that open fields will remain free from warrantless intrusion by government officers.

B

Oliver contend[s], to the contrary, that the circumstances of a search sometimes may indicate that reasonable expectations of privacy were violated; and that courts therefore should analyze these circumstances on a case-by-case basis. The language of the Fourth Amendment itself answers their contention.

Nor would a case-by-case approach provide a workable accommodation between the needs of law enforcement and the interests protected by the Fourth Amendment. Under this approach, police officers would have to guess before every search whether landowners had erected fences sufficiently high, posted a sufficient number of warning signs, or located contraband in an area sufficiently secluded to establish a right of privacy. The lawfulness of a search would turn on "[a] highly sophisticated set of rules, qualified by all sorts of ifs, ands, and buts and requiring the drawing of subtle nuances and hairline distinctions . . . ." This Court repeatedly has acknowledged the difficulties created for courts, police and citizens by an ad hoc, case-by-case definition of Fourth Amendment standards to be applied in differing factual circumstances. *Belton.* The ad hoc approach not only makes it difficult for the policeman to discern the scope of his authority, it also creates a danger that constitutional rights will be arbitrarily and inequitably enforced.[12]

IV

In any event, while the factors that Oliver urge[s] the courts to consider may be relevant to Fourth Amendment analysis in some contexts, these factors cannot be decisive on the question whether the search of an open field is subject to the Amendment. Initially, we reject the suggestion that steps taken to protect privacy establish that expectations of privacy in an open field are legitimate. It is true, of course, that Oliver, in order to conceal his criminal activities, planted the marijuana upon secluded land and erected fences and no trespassing signs around the property. And it may be that because of such precautions, few members of the public stumbled upon the marijuana crops seized by the police. Neither of these suppositions demonstrates, however, that the expectation of privacy was *legitimate* in the sense required by the Fourth Amendment. The test of legitimacy is not

[12] The clarity of the open fields doctrine that we reaffirm today is not sacrificed, as the dissent suggests, by our recognition that the curtilage remains within the protections of the Fourth Amendment. Most of the many millions of acres that are "open fields" are not close to any structure and so not arguably within the curtilage. And, for most homes, the boundaries of the curtilage will be clearly marked; and the conception defining the curtilage — as the area around the home to which the activity of home life extends — is a familiar one easily understood from our daily experience. The occasional difficulties that courts might have in applying this, like other, legal concepts, do not argue for the unprecedented expansion of the Fourth Amendment advocated by the dissent.

whether the individual chooses to conceal assertedly "private" activity.[13] Rather, the correct inquiry is whether the government's intrusion infringes upon the personal and societal values protected by the Fourth Amendment. As we have explained, we find no basis for concluding that a police inspection of open fields accomplishes such an infringement.

Nor is the government's intrusion upon an open field a "search" in the constitutional sense because that intrusion is a trespass at common law. The existence of a property right is but one element in determining whether expectations of privacy are legitimate. " '[T]he premise that property interests control the right of the Government to search and seize has been discredited.' " *Katz.* "[E]ven a property interest in premises may not be sufficient to establish a legitimate expectation of privacy with respect to particular items located on the premises or activity conducted thereon."

The common law may guide consideration of what areas are protected by the Fourth Amendment search by defining areas whose invasion by others is wrongful. The law of trespass, however, forbids intrusions upon land that the Fourth Amendment would not proscribe. For trespass law extends to instances where the exercise of the right to exclude vindicates no legitimate privacy interest.[15] Thus, in the case of open fields, the general rights of property protected by the common law of trespass have little or no relevance to the applicability of the Fourth Amendment.

V

We conclude that the open fields doctrine, as enunciated in *Hester*, is consistent with the plain language of the Fourth Amendment and its historical purposes. Moreover, Justice Holmes' interpretation of the Amendment in *Hester* accords with the "reasonable expectation of privacy" analysis developed in subsequent decisions of this Court.

JUSTICE WHITE, concurring in part and in the judgment.

I concur in the judgment and join Parts I and II of the Court's opinion. These parts dispose of the issue before us; there is no need to go further and deal with the expectation of privacy matter. However reasonable a landowner's expectations of

---

[13] Certainly the Framers did not intend that the Fourth Amendment should shelter criminal activity wherever persons with criminal intent choose to erect barriers and post no trespassing signs.

[15] The law of trespass recognizes the interest in possession and control of one's property and for that reason permits exclusion of unwanted intruders. But it does not follow that the right to exclude conferred by trespass law embodies a privacy interest also protected by the Fourth Amendment. To the contrary, the common law of trespass furthers a range of interests that have nothing to do with privacy and that would not be served by applying the strictures of trespass law to public officers. Criminal laws against trespass are prophylactic: they protect against intruders who poach, steal livestock and crops or vandalize property. And the civil action of trespass serves the important function of authorizing an owner to defeat claims of prescription by asserting his own title. In any event, unlicensed use of property by others is presumptively unjustified, as anyone who wishes to use the property is free to bargain for the right to do so with the property owner. For these reasons, the law of trespass confers protections from intrusion by others far broader than those required by Fourth Amendment interests.

privacy may be, those expectations cannot convert a field into a "house" or an "effect."

JUSTICE MARSHALL, with whom JUSTICE BRENNAN and JUSTICE STEVENS join, dissenting.

I

The first ground on which the Court rests its decision is that the Fourth Amendment "indicates with some precision the places and things encompassed by its protections," and that real property is not included in the list of protected spaces and possessions. This line of argument has several flaws. Most obviously, it is inconsistent with the results of many of our previous decisions, none of which the Court purports to overrule. For example, neither a public telephone booth nor a conversation conducted therein can fairly be described as a person, house, paper, or effect;[1] yet we have held that the Fourth Amendment forbids the police without a warrant to eavesdrop on such a conversation. Nor can it plausibly be argued that an office or commercial establishment is covered by the plain language of the Amendment; yet we have held that such premises are entitled to constitutional protection if they are marked in a fashion that alerts the public to the fact that they are private.[2]

Indeed, the Court's reading of the plain language of the Fourth Amendment is incapable of explaining even its own holding in this case. The Court rules that the curtilage, a zone of real property surrounding a dwelling, is entitled to constitutional protection. We are not told, however, whether the curtilage is a "house" or an "effect" — or why, if the curtilage can be incorporated into the list of things and spaces shielded by the Amendment, a field cannot.

The Court's inability to reconcile its parsimonious reading of the phrase "persons, houses, papers, and effects" with our prior decisions or even its own holding is a symptom of a more fundamental infirmity in the Court's reasoning. The Fourth Amendment, like the other central provisions of the Bill of Rights that loom large in our modern jurisprudence, was designed, not to prescribe with "precision" permissible and impermissible activities, but to identify a fundamental human liberty that should be shielded forever from government intrusion. We do not construe constitutional provisions of this sort the way we do statutes, whose drafters can be expected to indicate with some comprehensiveness and exactitude the conduct they wish to forbid or control and to change those prescriptions when they become obsolete.[4] Rather, we strive, when interpreting these seminal consti-

---

[1] The Court informs us that the Framers would have understood the term "effects" to encompass only personal property. Such a construction of the term would exclude both a public phone booth and spoken words.

[2] On the other hand, an automobile surely does constitute an "effect." Under the Court's theory, cars should therefore stand on the same constitutional footing as houses. Our cases establish, however, that car owners' diminished expectations that their cars will remain free from prying eyes warrants a corresponding reduction in the constitutional protection accorded cars.

[4] Cf. *McCulloch v. Maryland*, 17 U.S. 316, 407, 4 L. Ed. 579, 4 Wheat. 316, 407 (1819) ("[W]e must

tutional provisions, to effectuate their purposes — to lend them meanings that ensure that the liberties the Framers sought to protect are not undermined by the changing activities of government officials.

The liberty shielded by the Fourth Amendment, as we have often acknowledged, is freedom "from unreasonable government intrusions into . . . legitimate expectations of privacy." That freedom would be incompletely protected if only government conduct that impinged upon a person, house, paper, or effect were subject to constitutional scrutiny. Accordingly, we have repudiated the proposition that the Fourth Amendment applies only to a limited set of locales or kinds of property. In *Katz*, we expressly rejected a proffered locational theory of the coverage of the Amendment, holding that it "protects people, not places." Since that time we have consistently adhered to the view that the applicability of the provision depends solely upon "whether the person invoking its protection can claim a 'justifiable,' a 'reasonable,' or a 'legitimate expectation of privacy' that has been invaded by government action." *Smith*. The Court's contention that, because a field is not a house or effect, it is not covered by the Fourth Amendment is inconsistent with this line of cases and with the understanding of the nature of constitutional adjudication from which it derives.[7]

II

The second ground for the Court's decision is its contention that any interest a landowner might have in the privacy of his woods and fields is not one that "society is prepared to recognize as 'reasonable.'" The mode of analysis that underlies this assertion is certainly more consistent with our prior decisions than that discussed above. But the Court's conclusion cannot withstand scrutiny.

As the Court acknowledges, we have traditionally looked to a variety of factors in determining whether an expectation of privacy asserted in a physical space is "reasonable." Though those factors do not lend themselves to precise taxonomy, they may be roughly grouped into three categories. First, we consider whether the expectation at issue is rooted in entitlements defined by positive law. Second, we consider the nature of the uses to which spaces of the sort in question can be put. Third, we consider whether the person claiming a privacy interest manifested that interest to the public in a way that most people would understand and respect. When the expectation of privacy asserted by Oliver[9] [is] examined through these

---

never forget, that it is a constitution we are expounding." Such a document cannot be as detailed as a "legal code"; "[i]ts nature . . . requires, that only its great outlines should be marked, its important objects designated, and the minor ingredients which compose those objects be deduced from the nature of the objects themselves.") (emphasis in original).

[7] Sensitive to the weakness of its argument that the "persons and things" mentioned in the Fourth Amendment exhaust the coverage of the provision, the Court goes on to analyze at length the privacy interests that might legitimately be asserted in "open fields." The inclusion of Parts III and IV in the opinion, coupled with the Court's reaffirmation of *Katz* and its progeny, strongly suggest that the plain-language theory sketched in Part II of the Court's opinion will have little or no effect on our future decisions in this area.

[9] The Court does not dispute that Oliver and Thornton had subjective expectations of privacy, not could it in view of the lower courts' findings on that issue. *See United States v. Oliver*, No. CR80-00005-01-BG (W.D. Ky. Nov. 14, 1980), App. to Pet. for Cert. A 22–23; *Maine v. Thornton*, No.

lenses, it becomes clear that [it is] entitled to constitutional protection.

A

We have frequently acknowledged that privacy interests are not coterminous with property rights. However, because "property rights reflect society's explicit recognition of a person's authority to act as he wishes in certain areas, [they] should be considered in determining whether an individual's expectations of privacy are reasonable."[10] Indeed, the Court has suggested that, insofar as "[o]ne of the main rights attaching to property is the right to exclude others, . . . one who owns or lawfully possesses or controls property will in all likelihood have a legitimate expectation of privacy by virtue of this right to exclude."

It is undisputed that Oliver owned the land into which the police intruded. That fact alone provides considerable support for their assertion of legitimate privacy interests in their woods and fields. But even more telling is the nature of the sanctions that Oliver could invoke, under local law, for violation of [his] property rights. In Kentucky, a knowing entry upon fenced or otherwise enclosed land, or upon unenclosed land conspicuously posted with signs excluding the public, constitutes criminal trespass. Thus, positive law not only recognizes the legitimacy of Oliver's insistence that strangers keep off [his] land, but subjects those who refuse to respect [his] wishes to the most severe of penalties — criminal liability. Under these circumstances, it is hard to credit the Court's assertion that Oliver's expectation of privacy [was] not of a sort that society is prepared to recognize as reasonable.

B

The uses to which a place is put are highly relevant to the assessment of a privacy interest asserted therein. If, in light of our shared sensibilities, those activities are of a kind in which people should be able to engage without fear of intrusion by private persons or government officials, we extend the protection of the Fourth Amendment to the space in question, even in the absence of any entitlement derived from positive law. *E.g.*, *Katz*.[13]

CR82-10 (Me. Super. Ct. April 16, 1982), App. to Pet. for Cert. B 4–5.

[10] The Court today seeks to evade the force of this principle by contending that the law of property is designed to serve various "prophylactic" and "economic" purposes unrelated to the protection of privacy. Such efforts to rationalize the distribution of entitlements under state law are interesting and may have some explanatory power, but cannot support the weight the Court seeks to place upon them. The Court surely must concede that one of the purposes of the law of real property (and specifically the law of criminal trespass) is to define and enforce privacy interests — to empower some people to make whatever use they wish of certain tracts of land without fear that other people will intrude upon their activities. The views of commentators, old and new, as to other functions served by positive law are thus insufficient to support the Court's sweeping assertion that "in the case of open fields, the general rights of property . . . have little or no relevance to the applicability of the Fourth Amendment."

[13] In most circumstances, this inquiry requires analysis of the sorts of uses to which a given space is susceptible, not the manner in which the person asserting an expectation of privacy in the space was in fact employing it. Thus, the majority's contention that, because the cultivation of marijuana is not an activity that society wishes to protect, Oliver had no legitimate privacy interest in [his] fields, reflects a

Privately-owned woods and fields that are not exposed to public view regularly are employed in a variety of ways that society acknowledges deserve privacy. Many landowners like to take solitary walks on their property, confident that they will not be confronted in their rambles by strangers or policemen. Others conduct agricultural businesses on their property.[14] Some landowners use their secluded spaces to meet lovers, others to gather together with fellow worshippers, still others to engage in sustained creative endeavor. Private land is sometimes used as a refuge for wildlife, where flora and fauna are protected from human intervention of any kind.[15] Our respect for the freedom of landowners to use their posted "open fields" in ways such as these partially explains the seriousness with which the positive law regards deliberate invasions of such spaces, and substantially reinforces the landowners' contention that their expectations of privacy are "reasonable."

C

Whether a person "took normal precautions to maintain his privacy" in a given space affects whether his interest is one protected by the Fourth Amendment. The reason why such precautions are relevant is that we do not insist that a person who has a right to exclude others exercise that right. A claim to privacy is therefore strengthened by the fact that the claimant somehow manifested to other people his desire that they keep their distance.

Certain spaces are so presumptively private that signals of this sort are unnecessary; a homeowner need not post a "do not enter" sign on his door in order to deny entrance to uninvited guests.[17] Privacy interests in other spaces are more ambiguous, and the taking of precautions is consequently more important; placing a lock on one's footlocker strengthens one's claim that an examination of its contents is impermissible. See *Chadwick*. Still other spaces are, by positive law and social convention, presumed accessible to members of the public unless the owner manifests his intention to exclude them.

Undeveloped land falls into the last-mentioned category. If a person has not marked the boundaries of his fields or woods in a way that informs passersby that they are not welcome, he cannot object if members of the public enter onto the property. There is no reason why he should have any greater rights as against government officials. Accordingly, we have held that an official may, without a warrant, enter private land from which the public is not excluded and make observations from that vantage point. *Air Pollution Variance Board v. Western*

---

misunderstanding of the level of generality on which the constitutional analysis must proceed.

[14] We accord constitutional protection to businesses conducted in office buildings; it is not apparent why businesses conducted in fields that are not open to the public are less deserving of the benefit of the Fourth Amendment.

[15] This last mentioned use implicates a kind of privacy interest somewhat different from those to which we are accustomed. It involves neither a person's interest in immunity from observation nor a person's interest in shielding from scrutiny the residues and manifestations of his personal life. It derives, rather, from a person's desire to preserve inviolate a portion of his world. The idiosyncrasy of this interest does not, however, render it less deserving of constitutional protection.

[17] However, if the homeowner acts affirmatively to invite someone into his abode, he cannot later insist that his privacy interests have been violated. *Lewis*.

Alfalfa Corp., 416 U.S. 861, 865, 94 S. Ct. 2114, 2115, 40 L. Ed. 2d 607 (1974). Fairly read, the case on which the majority so heavily relies, *Hester*, affirms little more than the foregoing unremarkable proposition. From aught that appears in the opinion in that case, the defendants, fleeing from revenue agents who had observed them committing a crime, abandoned incriminating evidence on private land from which the public had not been excluded. Under such circumstances, it is not surprising that the Court was unpersuaded by the defendants' argument that the entry onto their fields by the agents violated the Fourth Amendment.[18]

A very different case is presented when the owner of undeveloped land has taken precautions to exclude the public. As indicated above, a deliberate entry by a private citizen onto private property marked with "no trespassing" signs will expose him to criminal liability. I see no reason why a government official should not be obliged to respect such unequivocal and universally understood manifestations of a landowner's desire for privacy.[19]

III

A clear, easily administrable rule emerges from the analysis set forth above: Private land marked in a fashion sufficient to render entry thereon a criminal trespass under the law of the state in which the land lies is protected by the Fourth Amendment's proscription of unreasonable searches and seizures. One of the advantages of the foregoing rule is that it draws upon a doctrine already familiar to both citizens and government officials. In each jurisdiction, a substantial body of statutory and case law defines the precautions a landowner must take in order to avail himself of the sanctions of the criminal law. The police know that body of law, because they are entrusted with responsibility for enforcing it against the public; it therefore would not be difficult for the police to abide by it themselves.

By contrast, the doctrine announced by the Court today is incapable of determinate application. Police officers, making warrantless entries upon private land, will be obliged in the future to make on-the-spot judgments as to how far the curtilage extends, and to stay outside that zone. In addition, we may expect to see a spate of litigation over the question of how much improvement is necessary to remove private land from the category of "unoccupied or undeveloped area" to which the "open fields exception" is now deemed applicable.

The Court's holding not only ill serves the need to make constitutional doctrine "workable for application by rank and file, trained police officers," it withdraws the

---

[18] An argument supportive of the position taken by the Court today might be constructed on the basis of an examination of the record in *Hester*. It appears that, in his approach to the house, one of the agents crossed a pasture fence. However, the Court, in its opinion, placed no weight upon — indeed, did not even mention — that circumstance. In any event, to the extent that Hester may be read to support a rule any broader than that stated in *Air Pollution Variance Board, supra*, it is undercut by our decision in *Katz*, which repudiated the locational theory of the coverage of the Fourth Amendment.

[19] Indeed, important practical considerations suggest that the police should not be empowered to invade land closed to the public. In many parts of the country, landowners feel entitled to use self-help in expelling trespassers from their posted property. There is thus a serious risk that police officers, making unannounced, warrantless searches of "open fields," will become involved in violent confrontations with irate landowners, with potentially tragic results.

shield of the Fourth Amendment from privacy interests that clearly deserve protection. By exempting from the coverage of the Amendment large areas of private land, the Court opens the way to investigative activities we would all find repugnant. *Cf., e.g., United States v. Lace*, 669 F.2d 46, 54 (CA2 1982) (Newman, J., concurring in the result) ("[W]hen police officers execute military maneuvers on residential property for three weeks of round-the-clock surveillance, can that be called 'reasonable'?"); *Florida v. Brady*, 406 So.2d 1093, 1094–1095 (Fla. 1981) ("In order to position surveillance groups around the ranch's airfield, deputies were forced to cross a dike, ram through one gate and cut the chain lock on another, cut across posted fences, and proceed several hundred yards to their hiding places").[21]

The Fourth Amendment, properly construed, embodies and gives effect to our collective sense of the degree to which men and women, in civilized society, are entitled "to be let alone" by their governments. The Court's opinion bespeaks and will help to promote an impoverished vision of that fundamental right.

I dissent.

QUESTIONS AND NOTES

1. Your author wrote an article in which he commented on the *Oliver* Court's invitation to police officers to stop taking the Fourth Amendment so seriously. Arnold H. Loewy, *A Modest Proposal for Fighting Organized Crime: Stop Taking the Fourth Amendment So Seriously*, 16 RUTGERS L.J. 831. In the course thereof, he imagined the following dialogue between two different police officers and their respective chief of police:

Captain: Officer A, what did you do last month?

Officer A: Last month while on duty I saw thirty heavily wooded fenced-in areas with "no trespassing" signs. Because they sought privacy, I was somewhat concerned that they might be growing marijuana. So I blasted a hole in each fence, like the Supreme Court said I could, and carefully searched the whole fenced-in area. Fortunately, things were slow last month, so I had plenty of time for these operations.

Captain: Did you find anything?

Officer A: I sure did. In two of the thirty fields, I found marijuana growing. One of them even turned out to be owned by an organized crime leader. I think that we're going to be able to put him away.

Captain: What about the other twenty-eight?

Officer A: Well, in twenty of them, I found nothing. Except for the hole in the fence, nobody would even know I was there. In two other searches,

---

[21] Perhaps the most serious danger in the decision today is that, if the police are permitted routinely to engage in such behavior, it will gradually become less offensive to us all. As Justice Brandeis once observed: "Our Government is the potent, the omnipresent teacher. For good or for ill, it teaches the whole people by its example. Crime is contagious. If the Government becomes a lawbreaker, it breeds contempt for the law; . . ." *Olmstead v. United States*, 277 U.S. 438, 485, 48 S. Ct. 564, 575, 72 L. Ed. 944 (1928) (dissenting opinion).

I found couples making love. Unfortunately, they were married, so I couldn't arrest them. [footnote omitted] In three other searches, I found people meeting at a hideout that they had hoped to keep secret. In another search, I found a group of scientists conducting experiments that they had hoped to keep secret. In the remaining two searches, I just found the owners seeking peace and repose in their woods. I don't think they minded my being there, especially since they couldn't do anything about it.

Captain: Officer B, what did you do last month?

Officer B: I also saw thirty heavily wooded fenced-in areas with "no trespassing" signs. I figured that while one or two of these areas might contain evidence of crime, most would not. Since the owners obviously sought privacy, and since most were innocent and had no outward indicia of guilt, I decided to respect their privacy and not search any of them. Consequently, I have neither made any arrests nor uncovered any evidence this month.

    Each police officer reading this article can of course determine for himself whether his department would be more pleased with the performance of Officer A or Officer B. To the extent that I am correct, however, in thinking that most police departments would reward Officer A's performance more than Officer B's, there is a powerful incentive for a police officer to join the Supreme Court in not taking the Fourth Amendment seriously.

Id. at 846–847.

In your opinion, is the foregoing fair commentary on *Oliver*?

2. Which rule is more manageable, Justice Powell's opinion of the Court, or Justice Marshall's dissent?

3. If you think that Marshall's rule is more manageable, how do you deal with the problem of the uncertainty of height of fences or size and visibility of no trespassing signs?

4. On the other hand, if you think that the Court's rule is more manageable, how do you deal with the problem of distinguishing open fields from curtilage? (*See Dunn, infra.*)

5. Justice Marshall contends that freedom protected by the Fourth Amendment would be incomplete "if only government conduct that impinged upon a person, paper, house, or effect were subject to constitutional scrutiny." Is he saying that the Fourth Amendment, as written, incompletely protects Fourth Amendment values? If not, what is he saying?

6. Justice Powell says that "[a]n open field need be neither 'open' nor a 'field' as those terms are used in common speech." By that same logic, why do "persons, papers, houses, and effects" have to be defined in the dictionary sense?

7. How would you have decided this case? Why?

PROBLEM

Respondent Ronald Dale Dunn and a codefendant, Robert Lyle Carpenter, were convicted by a jury of conspiring to manufacture phenylacetone and amphetamine, and to possess amphetamine with intent to distribute. Respondent was also convicted of manufacturing these two controlled substances and possessing amphetamine with intent to distribute.

Respondent's ranch comprised approximately 198 acres and was completely encircled by a perimeter fence. The property also contained several interior fences, constructed mainly of posts and multiple strands of barbed wire. The ranch residence was situated 1/2 mile from a public road. A fence encircled the residence and a nearby small greenhouse. Two barns were located approximately 50 yards from this fence. The front of the larger of the two barns was enclosed by a wooden fence and had an open overhang. Locked, waist-high gates barred entry into the barn proper, and netting material stretched from the ceiling to the top of the wooden gates.

On the evening of November 5, 1980, law enforcement officials made a warrantless entry onto respondent's ranch property. A DEA agent accompanied by an officer from the Houston Police Department crossed over the perimeter fence and one interior fence. Standing approximately midway between the residence and the barns, the DEA agent smelled what he believed to be phenylacetic acid, the odor coming from the direction of the barns. The officers approached the smaller of the barns — crossing over a barbed wire fence — and, looking into the barn, observed only empty boxes. The officers then proceeded to the larger barn, crossing another barbed wire fence as well as a wooden fence that enclosed the front portion of the barn. The officers walked under the barn's overhang to the locked wooden gates and, shining a flashlight through the netting on top of the gates, peered into the barn. They observed what the DEA agent thought to be a phenylacetone laboratory. The officers did not enter the barn. At this point the officers departed from respondent's property, but entered it twice more on November 6 to confirm the presence of the phenylacetone laboratory.

On November 6, 1980, at 8:30 p.m., a Federal Magistrate issued a warrant authorizing a search of respondent's ranch. DEA agents and state law enforcement officials executed the warrant on November 8, 1980. The officers arrested respondent and seized chemicals and equipment, as well as bags of amphetamines they discovered in a closet in the ranch house.

Assuming that the warrant would have been valid if the police had validly discovered the lab, but otherwise would have been invalid, should the Court have sustained the warrant? For the United States Supreme Court's solution, see *United States v. Dunn*, 480 U.S. 294 (1987).

In the next case, *Riley*, we consider the extent to which even curtilage activities can be observed without a Fourth Amendment search.

FLORIDA v. RILEY
488 U.S. 445 (1989)

JUSTICE WHITE announced the judgment of the Court and delivered an opinion, in which THE CHIEF JUSTICE, JUSTICE SCALIA and JUSTICE KENNEDY join.

On certification to it by a lower state court, the Florida Supreme Court addressed the following question: "Whether surveillance of the interior of a partially covered greenhouse in a residential backyard from the vantage point of a helicopter located 400 feet above the greenhouse constitutes a 'search' for which a warrant is required under the Fourth Amendment. The court answered the question in the affirmative, and we granted the State's petition for certiorari challenging that conclusion. 484 U.S. 1058 (1988).

Respondent Riley lived in a mobile home located on five acres of rural property. A greenhouse was located 10 to 20 feet behind the mobile home. Two sides of the greenhouse were enclosed. The other two sides were not enclosed but the contents of the greenhouse were obscured from view from surrounding property by trees, shrubs and the mobile home. The greenhouse was covered by corrugated roofing panels, some translucent and some opaque. At the time relevant to this case, two of the panels, amounting to approximately 10% of the roof area, were missing. A wire fence surrounded the mobile home and the greenhouse, and the property was posted with a "DO NOT ENTER" sign.

This case originated with an anonymous tip to the Pasco County Sheriff's office that marijuana was being grown on respondent's property. When an investigating officer discovered that he could not see the contents of the greenhouse from the road, he circled twice over respondent's property in a helicopter at the height of 400 feet. With his naked eye, he was able to see through the openings in the roof and one or more of the open sides of the greenhouse and to identify what he thought was marijuana growing in the structure. A warrant was obtained based on these observations, and the ensuing search revealed marijuana growing in the greenhouse. Respondent was charged with possession of marijuana under Florida law. The trial court granted his motion to suppress; the Florida Court of Appeals reversed but certified the case to the Florida Supreme Court, which quashed the decision of the Court of Appeals and reinstated the trial court's suppression order.

We agree with the State's submission that our decision in *California v. Ciraolo*, 476 U.S. 207 (1986), controls this case. There, acting on a tip, the police inspected the back yard of a particular house while flying in a fixed-wing aircraft at 1,000 feet. With the naked eye the officers saw what they concluded was marijuana growing in the yard. A search warrant was obtained on the strength of this airborne inspection, and marijuana plants were found. The trial court refused to suppress this evidence, but a state appellate court held that the inspection violated the Fourth and Fourteenth Amendments of the United States Constitution and that the warrant was therefore invalid. We in turn reversed, holding that the inspection was not a search subject to the Fourth Amendment. We recognized that the yard was within the curtilage of the house, that a fence shielded the yard from observation from the street and that the occupant had a subjective expectation of privacy. We held, however, that such an expectation was not reasonable and not one "that society is prepared to honor." Our reasoning was that the home and its curtilage are not necessarily protected from inspection that involves no physical invasion. " 'What a person knowingly exposes to the public, even in his own home or office, is not a subject of Fourth Amendment protection.' " As a general proposition, the police may see what may be seen "from a public vantage point where [they have] a right to be." Thus the police, like the public, would have been free to inspect the backyard garden from the street if their view had been unobstructed. They were likewise, free to inspect the yard from the vantage point of an aircraft flying in the navigable airspace as this plane was. "In an age where private and commercial flight in the public airways is routine, it is unreasonable for respondent to expect that his marijuana plants were constitutionally protected from being observed with the naked eye from an altitude of 1,000 feet. The Fourth Amendment simply does not require the police traveling in the public airways at this altitude to obtain a warrant in order to observe what is visible to the naked eye."

We arrive at the same conclusion in the present case. In this case, as in *Ciraolo*, the property surveyed was within the curtilage of respondent's home. Riley no doubt intended and expected that his greenhouse would not be open to public inspection, and the precautions he took protected against ground-level observation. Because the sides and roof of his greenhouse were left partially open, however, what was growing in the greenhouse was subject to viewing from the air. Under the holding in *Ciraolo*, Riley could not reasonably have expected the contents of his greenhouse to be immune from examination by an officer seated in a fixed-wing aircraft flying in navigable airspace at an altitude of 1,000 feet or, as the Florida Supreme Court seemed to recognize, at an altitude of 500 feet, the lower limit of the navigable airspace for such an aircraft. Here, the inspection was made from a helicopter, but as is the case with fixed-wing planes, "private and commercial flight [by helicopter] in the public airways is routine" in this country, *supra*, at 215, and there is no indication that such flights are unheard of in Pasco County, Florida. Riley could not reasonably have expected that his greenhouse was protected from public or official observation from a helicopter had it been flying within the navigable airspace for fixed-wing aircraft.

Nor on the facts before us, does it make a difference for Fourth Amendment purposes that the helicopter was flying at 400 feet when the officer saw what was growing in the greenhouse through the partially open roof and sides of the structure. We would have a different case if flying at that altitude had been contrary to law or regulation. But helicopters are not bound by the lower limits of the navigable airspace allowed to other aircraft. Any member of the public could legally have been flying over Riley's property in a helicopter at the altitude of 400 feet and could have observed Riley's greenhouse. The police officer did no more. This is not to say that an inspection of the curtilage of a house from an aircraft will always pass muster under the Fourth Amendment simply because the plane is within the navigable airspace specified by law. But it is of obvious importance that the helicopter in this case was *not* violating the law, and there is nothing in the record or before us to suggest that helicopters flying at 400 feet are sufficiently rare in this country to lend substance to respondent's claim that he reasonably anticipated that his greenhouse would not be subject to observation from that altitude. Neither is there any intimation here that the helicopter interfered with respondent's normal use of the greenhouse or of other parts of the curtilage. As far as this record reveals, no intimate details connected with the use of the home or curtilage were observed, and there was no undue noise, no wind, dust, or threat of injury. In these circumstances, there was no violation of the Fourth Amendment.

The judgment of the Florida Supreme Court is accordingly reversed.

SO ORDERED.

JUSTICE O'CONNOR, concurring in the judgment.

I concur in the judgment reversing the Supreme Court of Florida because I agree that police observation of the greenhouse in Riley's curtilage from a helicopter passing at an altitude of 400 feet did not violate an expectation of privacy "that society is prepared to recognize as 'reasonable.'" I write separately, however, to clarify the standard I believe follows from *Ciraolo*. In my view, the plurality's approach rests the scope of Fourth Amendment protection too heavily on compliance with FAA regulations whose purpose is to promote air safety not to protect "[t]he right of the people to be secure in their persons, houses, papers, and effects, against unreasonable searches and seizures."

Ciraolo involved observation of curtilage by officers flying in an airplane at an altitude of 1,000 feet. In evaluating whether this observation constituted a search for which a warrant was required, we acknowledged the importance of curtilage in Fourth Amendment doctrine: "The protection afforded the curtilage is essentially a protection of families and personal privacy in an area intimately linked to the home, both physically and psychologically, where privacy expectations are most heightened." Although the curtilage is an area to which the private activities of the home extend, all police observation of the curtilage is not necessarily barred by the Fourth Amendment. As we observed: "The Fourth Amendment protection of the home has never been extended to require law enforcement officers to shield their eyes when passing by a home on public thoroughfares." In *Ciraolo*, we likened observation from a plane traveling in "public navigable airspace" at 1,000 feet to observation by police "passing by a home on public thoroughfares." We held that "[i]n an age where private and commercial flight in the public airways is routine," it is unreasonable to expect curtilage to be constitutionally protected from aerial observation with the naked eye from an altitude of 1,000 feet.

Ciraolo's expectation of privacy was unreasonable not because the airplane was operating where it had a "right to be," but because public air travel at 1,000 feet is a sufficiently routine part of modern life that it is unreasonable for persons on the ground to expect that their curtilage will not be observed from the air at that altitude. Although "helicopters are not bound by the lower limits of the navigable airspace allowed to other aircraft," there is no reason to assume that compliance with FAA regulations alone determines "'whether the government's intrusion infringes upon the personal and societal values protected by the Fourth Amendment.'" Because the FAA has decided that helicopters can lawfully operate at virtually any altitude so long as they pose no safety hazard, it does not follow that the expectations of privacy "society is prepared to recognize as 'reasonable'" simply mirror the FAA's safety concerns.

Observations of curtilage from helicopters at very low altitudes are not perfectly analogous to ground-level observations from public roads or sidewalks. While in both cases the police may have a legal right to occupy the physical space from which their observations are made, the two situations are not necessarily comparable in terms of whether expectations of privacy from such vantage points should be considered reasonable. Public roads, even those less traveled by, are clearly demarked public thoroughfares. Individuals who seek privacy can take precautions, tailored to the location of the road, to avoid disclosing private activities to those who pass by. They can build a tall fence, for example, and thus ensure private enjoyment of the curtilage without risking public observation from the road or sidewalk. If they do not take such precautions, they cannot reasonably expect privacy from public observation. In contrast, even individuals who have taken effective precautions to ensure against ground-level observations cannot block off all conceivable aerial views of their outdoor patios and yards without entirely giving up their enjoyment of those areas. To require individuals to completely cover and enclose their curtilage is to demand more than the "precautions customarily taken by those seeking privacy." The fact that a helicopter could conceivably observe the curtilage at virtually any altitude or angle, without violating FAA regulations, does not in itself mean that an individual has no reasonable expectation of privacy from such observation.

In determining whether Riley had a reasonable expectation of privacy from aerial observation, the relevant inquiry after *Ciraolo* is not whether the helicopter was where it had a right to be under FAA regulations. Rather, consistent with *Katz*, we must ask whether the helicopter was in the public airways at an altitude at which members of the public travel with sufficient regularity that Riley's expectation of privacy from aerial observation was not "one that society is prepared to recognize as 'reasonable.'" Thus, in determining "'whether the government's intrusion infringes upon the personal and societal values protected by the Fourth Amendment,'" it is not conclusive to observe, as the plurality does, that "[a]ny member of the public could legally have been flying over Riley's property in a helicopter at the altitude of 400 feet and could have observed Riley's greenhouse." Nor is it conclusive that police helicopters may often fly at 400 feet. If the public rarely, if ever, travels overhead at such altitudes, the observation cannot be said to be from a vantage point generally used by the public and Riley cannot be said to have "knowingly expose[d]" his greenhouse to public view. However, if the public can generally be expected to travel over residential backyards at an altitude of 400 feet, Riley cannot reasonably expect his curtilage to be free from such aerial observation.

In my view, the defendant must bear the burden of proving that his expectation of privacy was a reasonable one, and thus that a "search" within the meaning of the Fourth Amendment even took place.

Because there is reason to believe that there is considerable public use of airspace at altitudes of 400 feet and above, and because Riley introduced no evidence to the contrary before the Florida courts, I conclude that Riley's expectation that his curtilage was protected from naked-eye aerial observation from that altitude was not a reasonable one. However, public use of altitudes lower than that — particularly public observations from helicopters circling over the curtilage of a home — may be sufficiently rare that police surveillance from such altitudes would violate reasonable expectations of privacy, despite compliance with FAA air safety regulations.

JUSTICE BRENNAN, with whom JUSTICE MARSHALL and JUSTICE STEVENS, join, dissenting.

The plurality undertakes no inquiry into whether low-level helicopter surveillance by the police of activities in an enclosed backyard is consistent with the "aims of a free and open society." Instead, it summarily concludes that Riley's expectation of privacy was unreasonable because "[a]ny member of the public could legally have been flying over Riley's property in a helicopter at the altitude of 400 feet and could have observed Riley's greenhouse." This observation is, in turn, based solely on the fact that the police helicopter was within the airspace within which such craft are allowed by federal safety regulations to fly.

I agree, of course, that "[w]hat a person knowingly exposes to the public . . . is not a subject of Fourth Amendment protection." But I cannot agree that one "knowingly exposes [an area] to the public" solely because a helicopter may legally fly above it. Under the plurality's exceedingly grudging Fourth Amendment theory, the expectation of privacy is defeated if a single member of the public could conceivably position herself to see into the area in question without doing anything illegal. It is defeated whatever the difficulty a person would have in so positioning herself, and however infrequently anyone would in fact do so. In taking this view the plurality ignores the very essence of *Katz*. The reason why there is no reasonable expectation of privacy in an area that is exposed to the public is that little diminution in "the amount of privacy and freedom remaining to citizens" will result from police surveillance of something that any passerby readily sees. To pretend, as the plurality opinion does, that the same is true when the police use a helicopter to peer over high fences is, at best, disingenuous. Notwithstanding the plurality's statistics about the number of helicopters registered in this country, can it seriously be questioned that Riley enjoyed virtually complete privacy in his backyard greenhouse, and that that privacy was invaded solely by police helicopter surveillance? Is the theoretical possibility that any member of the public (with sufficient means) could also have hired a helicopter and looked over Riley's fence of any relevance at all in determining whether Riley suffered a serious loss of privacy and personal security through the police action?

In *Ciraolo*, we held that whatever might be observed from the window of an airplane flying at 1000 feet could be deemed unprotected by any reasonable expectation of privacy. That decision was based on the belief that airplane traffic at that altitude was sufficiently common that no expectation of privacy could inure in anything on the ground observable with the naked eye from so high. Indeed, we compared those airways to "public thoroughfares," and made the obvious point that police officers passing by a home on such thoroughfares were not required by the Fourth Amendment to "shield their eyes." Seizing on a reference in *Ciraolo* to the fact that the police officer was in a position "where he ha[d] a right to be," today's plurality professes to find this case indistinguishable because FAA regulations do not impose a minimum altitude requirement on helicopter traffic; thus, the officer in this case too made his observations from a vantage point where he had a right to be.

It is a curious notion that the reach of the Fourth Amendment can be so largely defined by administrative regulations issued for purposes of flight safety.[2] It is more curious still that the plurality relies to such an extent on the legality of the officer's act, when we have consistently refused to equate police violation of the law with infringement of the Fourth Amendment.[3] But the plurality's willingness to end its inquiry when it finds that the officer was in a position he had a right to be in is misguided for an even more fundamental reason. Finding determinative the fact that the officer was where he had a right to be is, at bottom, an attempt to analogize surveillance from a helicopter to surveillance by a police officer standing on a public road and viewing evidence of crime through an open window or a gap in a fence. In such a situation, the occupant of the home may be said to lack any reasonable expectation of privacy in what can be seen from that road — even if, in fact, people rarely pass that way.

The police officer positioned 400 feet above Riley's backyard was not, however, standing on a public road. The vantage point he enjoyed was not one any citizen could readily share. His ability to see over Riley's fence depended on his use of a very expensive and sophisticated piece of machinery to which few ordinary citizens have access. In such circumstances it makes no more sense to rely on the legality of the officer's position in the skies than it would to judge the constitutionality of the wiretap in *Katz* by the legality of the officer's position outside the telephone booth. The simple inquiry whether the police officer had the legal right to be in the position from which he made his observations cannot suffice, for we cannot assume that Riley's curtilage was so open to the observations of passersby in the skies that he retained little privacy or personal security to be lost to police surveillance. The question before us must be not whether the police were where they had a right to be, but whether public observation of Riley's curtilage was so commonplace that Riley's expectation of privacy in his backyard could not be considered reasonable. To say that an invasion of Riley's privacy from the skies was not impossible is most emphatically not the same as saying that his expectation of privacy within his enclosed curtilage was not "one that society is prepared to recognize as 'reasonable.'" While, as we held in *Ciraolo*, air traffic at elevations of 1000 feet or more may be so common that whatever could be seen with the naked eye from that elevation is unprotected by the Fourth Amendment, it is a large step from there to say that the Amendment offers no protection against low-level helicopter surveillance of enclosed curtilage areas. To take this step is error enough. That the plurality does so with little analysis beyond its determination that the police complied with FAA regulations is particularly unfortunate.

---

[2] The plurality's use of the FAA regulations as a means for determining whether Riley enjoyed a reasonable expectation of privacy produces an incredible result. Fixed-wing aircraft may not be operated below 500 feet (1000 feet over congested areas), while helicopters may be operated below those levels. Therefore, whether Riley's expectation of privacy is reasonable turns on whether the police officer at 400 feet above his curtilage is seated in an airplane or a helicopter. This cannot be the law.

[3] In *Oliver*, for example, we held that police officers who trespassed upon posted and fenced private land did not violate the Fourth Amendment, despite the fact that their action was subject to criminal sanctions. We noted that the interests vindicated by the Fourth Amendment were not identical with those served by the common law of trespass.

III

Perhaps the most remarkable passage in the plurality opinion is its suggestion that the case might be a different one had any "intimate details connected with the use of the home or curtilage [been] observed." What, one wonders, is meant by "intimate details"? If the police had observed Riley embracing his wife in the backyard greenhouse, would we then say that his reasonable expectation of privacy had been infringed? Where in the Fourth Amendment or in our cases is there any warrant for imposing a requirement that the activity observed must be "intimate" in order to be protected by the Constitution?

It is difficult to avoid the conclusion that the plurality has allowed its analysis of Riley's expectation of privacy to be colored by its distaste for the activity in which he was engaged. It is indeed easy to forget, especially in view of current concern over drug trafficking, that the scope of the Fourth Amendment's protection does not turn on whether the activity disclosed by a search is illegal or innocuous. But we dismiss this as a "drug case" only at the peril of our own liberties. Justice Frankfurter once noted that "[i]t is a fair summary of history to say that the safeguards of liberty have frequently been forged in controversies involving not very nice people," *United States v. Rabinowitz*, 339 U.S. 56, 69 (1950) (dissenting opinion), and nowhere is this observation more apt than in the area of the Fourth Amendment, whose words have necessarily been given meaning largely through decisions suppressing evidence of criminal activity. The principle enunciated in this case determines what limits the Fourth Amendment imposes on aerial surveillance of any person, for any reason. If the Constitution does not protect Riley's marijuana garden against such surveillance, it is hard to see how it will forbid the Government from aerial spying on the activities of a law-abiding citizen on her fully enclosed outdoor patio. As Professor Amsterdam has eloquently written: "The question is not whether you or I must draw the blinds before we commit a crime. It is whether you and I must discipline ourselves to draw the blinds every time we enter a room, under pain of surveillance if we do not." Amsterdam, 58 MINN. L. REV. at 403.[6]

IV

I find little to disagree with in the concurring opinion of Justice O'Connor, apart from its closing paragraphs. A majority of the Court thus agrees that the fundamental inquiry is not whether the police were where they had a right to be under FAA regulations, but rather whether Riley's expectation of privacy was rendered illusory by the extent of public observation of his backyard from aerial traffic at 400 feet.

What separates me from Justice O'Connor is essentially an empirical matter concerning the extent of public use of the airspace at that altitude, together with the

---

[6] *See also White* (Harlan, J., dissenting):

> The interest [protected by the Fourth Amendment] is the expectation of the ordinary citizen, who has never engaged in illegal conduct in his life, that he may carry on his private discourse freely, openly, and spontaneously . . . . Interposition of a warrant requirement is designed not to shield "wrongdoers," but to secure a measure of privacy and a sense of personal security throughout our society.

question of how to resolve that issue. I do not think the constitutional claim should fail simply because "there is reason to believe" that there is "considerable" public flying this close to earth or because Riley "introduced no evidence to the contrary before the Florida courts." I think we could take judicial notice that, while there may be an occasional privately owned helicopter that flies over populated areas at an altitude of 400 feet, such flights are a rarity and are almost entirely limited to approaching or leaving airports or to reporting traffic congestion near major roadways. And, as the concurring opinion agrees, the extent of police surveillance traffic cannot serve as a bootstrap to demonstrate public use of the airspace.

If, however, we are to resolve the issue by considering whether the appropriate party carried its burden of proof, I again think that Riley must prevail. Because the State has greater access to information concerning customary flight patterns and because the coercive power of the State ought not be brought to bear in cases in which it is unclear whether the prosecution is a product of an unconstitutional, warrantless search. The State quite clearly has not carried this burden.

V

The issue in this case is, ultimately, "how tightly the Fourth Amendment permits people to be driven back into the recesses of their lives by the risk of surveillance." The Court today approves warrantless helicopter surveillance from an altitude of 400 feet. While Justice O'CONNOR'S opinion gives reason to hope that this altitude may constitute a lower limit, I find considerable cause for concern in the fact that a plurality of four Justices would remove virtually all constitutional barriers to police surveillance from the vantage point of helicopters. The Fourth Amendment demands that we temper our efforts to apprehend criminals with a concern for the impact on our fundamental liberties of the methods we use. I hope it will be a matter of concern to my colleagues that the police surveillance methods they would sanction were among those described forty years ago in George Orwell's dread vision of life in the 1980's: "The black-mustachioed face gazed down from every commanding corner. There was one on the house front immediately opposite. BIG BROTHER IS WATCHING YOU, the caption said. . . . In the far distance a helicopter skimmed down between the roofs, hovered for an instant like a bluebottle, and darted away again with a curving flight. It was the Police Patrol, snooping into people's windows." G. ORWELL, NINETEEN EIGHTY-FOUR 4 (1949).

Who can read this passage without a shudder, and without the instinctive reaction that it depicts life in some country other than ours? I respectfully dissent.

JUSTICE BLACKMUN, dissenting.

The question before the Court is whether the helicopter surveillance over Riley's property constituted a "search" within the meaning of the Fourth Amendment. Like Justice Brennan, Justice Marshall, Justice Stevens, and Justice O'Connor, I believe that answering this question depends upon whether Riley has a "reasonable expectation of privacy" that no such surveillance would occur, and does not depend upon the fact that the helicopter was flying at a lawful altitude under FAA regulations. A majority of this Court thus agrees to at least this much.

The inquiry then becomes how to determine whether Riley's expectation was a reasonable one. Both Justice Brennan, and the two Justices who have joined him, and Justice O'Connor believe that the reasonableness of Riley's expectation depends, in large measure, on the frequency of nonpolice helicopter flights at an altitude of 400 feet. Again, I agree.

How is this factual issue to be decided? Justice Brennan suggests that we may resolve it ourselves without any evidence in the record on this point. I am wary of this approach. While I, too, suspect that for most American communities it is a rare event when nonpolice helicopters fly over one's curtilage at an altitude of 400 feet, I am not convinced that we should establish a *per se* rule for the entire Nation based on judicial suspicion alone.

But we need not abandon our judicial intuition entirely. The opinions of both Justice BRENNAN and Justice O'Connor, by their use of *"cf."* citations, implicitly recognize that none of our prior decisions tells us who has the burden of proving whether Riley's expectation of privacy was reasonable. In the absence of precedent on the point, it is appropriate for us to take into account our estimation of the frequency of nonpolice helicopter flights. Thus, because I believe that private helicopters rarely fly over curtilages at an altitude of 400 feet, I would impose upon the prosecution the burden of proving contrary facts necessary to show that Riley lacked a reasonable expectation of privacy. Indeed, I would establish this burden of proof for any helicopter surveillance case in which the flight occurred below 1000 feet — in other words, for any aerial surveillance case not governed by the Court's decision in *Ciraolo*.

In this case, the prosecution did not meet this burden of proof, as Justice Brennan notes. This failure should compel a finding that a Fourth Amendment search occurred. But because our prior cases gave the parties little guidance on the burden of proof issue, I would remand this case to allow the prosecution an opportunity to meet this burden.

The order of this Court, however, is not to remand the case in this manner. Rather, because Justice O'Connor would impose the burden of proof on Riley and because she would not allow Riley an opportunity to meet this burden, she joins the plurality's view that no Fourth Amendment search occurred. The judgment of the Court, therefore, is to reverse outright on the Fourth Amendment issue. Accordingly, for the reasons set forth above, I respectfully dissent.

QUESTIONS AND NOTES

1. Are *Riley* and *Ciraolo* distinguishable in any meaningful way? Explain.

2. If your answer to question 1 was "no," were the cases rightly decided? Why? Why not?

3. How do the White, O'Connor, Brennan, and Blackmun opinions differ from each other? With which would you most closely align yourself? Why?

4. What is the law of the case? Explain.

5. Following *White, Smith, Oliver, Ciraolo,* and *Riley,* among others, it should come as no surprise that the Court found a search (as the dictionary defines the term) of trash left on the curb (outside of the curtilage) for collection to not be a search (as the law defines the term). *See California v. Greenwood,* 486 U.S. 35 (1988).

6. In *Bond,* however, the pendulum swung a little in the other direction.

BOND v. UNITED STATES
529 U.S. 334 (2000)

CHIEF JUSTICE REHNQUIST delivered the opinion of the Court.

This case presents the question whether a law enforcement officer's physical manipulation of a bus passenger's carry-on luggage violated the Fourth Amendment's proscription against unreasonable searches. We hold that it did.

Petitioner Steven Dewayne Bond was a passenger on a Greyhound bus that left California bound for Little Rock, Arkansas. The bus stopped, as it was required to do, at the permanent Border Patrol checkpoint in Sierra Blanca, Texas. Border Patrol Agent Cesar Cantu boarded the bus to check the immigration status of its passengers. After reaching the back of the bus, having satisfied himself that the passengers were lawfully in the United States, Agent Cantu began walking toward the front. Along the way, he squeezed the soft luggage which passengers had placed in the overhead storage space above the seats.

Petitioner was seated four or five rows from the back of the bus. As Agent Cantu inspected the luggage in the compartment above petitioner's seat, he squeezed a green canvas bag and noticed that it contained a "brick-like" object. Petitioner admitted that the bag was his and agreed to allow Agent Cantu to open it.[1] Upon opening the bag, Agent Cantu discovered a "brick" of methamphetamine. The brick had been wrapped in duct tape until it was oval-shaped and then rolled in a pair of pants.

The Fourth Amendment provides that "the right of the people to be secure in their persons, houses, papers, and effects, against unreasonable searches and seizures, shall not be violated . . . ." A traveler's personal luggage is clearly an "effect" protected by the Amendment. *See United States v. Place.* Indeed, it is undisputed here that petitioner possessed a privacy interest in his bag.

But the Government asserts that by exposing his bag to the public, petitioner lost a reasonable expectation that his bag would not be physically manipulated. The Government relies on our decisions in *California v. Ciraolo* and *Florida v. Riley* for the proposition that matters open to public observation are not protected by the Fourth Amendment. In *Ciraolo,* we held that police observation of a backyard from a plane flying at an altitude of 1,000 feet did not violate a reasonable expectation of privacy. Similarly, in *Riley,* we relied on *Ciraolo* to hold that police observation of

---

[1] The Government has not argued here that petitioner's consent to Agent Cantu's opening the bag is a basis for admitting the evidence.

a greenhouse in a home's curtilage from a helicopter passing at an altitude of 400 feet did not violate the Fourth Amendment. We reasoned that the property was "not necessarily protected from inspection that involves no physical invasion," and determined that because any member of the public could have lawfully observed the defendants' property by flying overhead, the defendants' expectation of privacy was "not reasonable and not one 'that society is prepared to honor.'"

But *Ciraolo* and *Riley* are different from this case because they involved only visual, as opposed to tactile, observation. Physically invasive inspection is simply more intrusive than purely visual inspection. For example, in *Terry v. Ohio*, we stated that a "careful [tactile] exploration of the outer surfaces of a person's clothing all over his or her body" is a "serious intrusion upon the sanctity of the person, which may inflict great indignity and arouse strong resentment, and is not to be undertaken lightly." Although Agent Cantu did not "frisk" petitioner's person, he did conduct a probing tactile examination of petitioner's carry-on luggage. Obviously, petitioner's bag was not part of his person. But travelers are particularly concerned about their carry-on luggage; they generally use it to transport personal items that, for whatever reason, they prefer to keep close at hand.

Here, petitioner concedes that, by placing his bag in the overhead compartment, he could expect that it would be exposed to certain kinds of touching and handling. But petitioner argues that Agent Cantu's physical manipulation of his luggage "far exceeded the casual contact [petitioner] could have expected from other passengers." The Government counters that it did not.

Our Fourth Amendment analysis embraces two questions. First, we ask whether the individual, by his conduct, has exhibited an actual expectation of privacy; that is, whether he has shown that "he [sought] to preserve [something] as private." *Smith v. Maryland*. Here, petitioner sought to preserve privacy by using an opaque bag and placing that bag directly above his seat. Second, we inquire whether the individual's expectation of privacy is "one that society is prepared to recognize as reasonable."[2] When a bus passenger places a bag in an overhead bin, he expects that other passengers or bus employees may move it for one reason or another. Thus, a bus passenger clearly expects that his bag may be handled. He does not expect that other passengers or bus employees will, as a matter of course, feel the bag in an exploratory manner. But this is exactly what the agent did here. We therefore hold that the agent's physical manipulation of petitioner's bag violated the Fourth Amendment.

The judgment of the Court of Appeals is

Reversed.

JUSTICE BREYER, with whom JUSTICE SCALIA joins, dissenting.

Does a traveler who places a soft-sided bag in the shared overhead storage compartment of a bus have a "reasonable expectation" that strangers will not push,

---

[2] The parties properly agree that the subjective intent of the law enforcement officer is irrelevant in determining whether that officer's actions violate the Fourth Amendment. This principle applies to the agent's acts in this case as well; the issue is not his state of mind, but the objective effect of his actions.

pull, prod, squeeze, or otherwise manipulate his luggage? Unlike the majority, I believe that he does not.

Petitioner argues — and the majority points out — that, even if bags in overhead bins are subject to general "touching" and "handling," this case is special because "Agent Cantu's physical manipulation of [petitioner's] luggage 'far exceeded the casual contact [he] could have expected from other passengers.'" But the record shows the contrary. Agent Cantu testified that border patrol officers (who routinely enter buses at designated checkpoints to run immigration checks) "conduct an inspection of the overhead luggage by squeezing the bags as we're going out." On the occasion at issue here, Agent Cantu "felt a green bag" which had "a brick-like object in it." He explained that he felt "the edges of the brick in the bag," and that it was a "brick-like object . . . that, when squeezed, you could feel an outline of something of a different mass inside of it." Although the agent acknowledged that his practice was to "squeeze [bags] very hard," he testified that his touch ordinarily was not "hard enough to break something inside that might be fragile." Petitioner also testified that Agent Cantu "reached for my bag, and he shook it a little, and squeezed it."

How does the "squeezing" just described differ from the treatment that overhead luggage is likely to receive from strangers in a world of travel that is somewhat less gentle than it used to be? I think not at all. ("'Any person who has travelled on a common carrier knows that luggage placed in an overhead compartment is always at the mercy of all people who want to rearrange or move previously placed luggage'"); Eagan, *Familiar Anger Takes Flight with Airline Tussles*, BOSTON HERALD, Aug. 15, 1999, p.8 ("It's dog-eat-dog trying to cram half your home into overhead compartments"); Massingill, *Airlines Ride on the Wings of High-Flying Economy and Travelers Pay Price in Long Lines, Cramped Airplanes*, KANSAS CITY STAR, May 9, 1999, p.F4 ("Hundreds of passengers fill overhead compartments with bulky carry-on bags that they have to cram, recram, and then remove"); Flynn, *Confessions of a Once-Only Carry-On Guy*, SAN FRANCISCO EXAMINER, Sept. 6, 1998, p.T2 (flight attendant "rearranged the contents of three different overhead compartments to free up some room" and then "shoved and pounded until [the] bag squeezed in"). The trial court, which heard the evidence, saw nothing unusual, unforeseeable, or special about this agent's squeeze. It found that Agent Cantu simply "felt the outside of Bond's softside green cloth bag," and it viewed the agent's activity as "minimally intrusive touching." The Court of Appeals also noted that, because "passengers often handle and manipulate other passengers' luggage," the substantially similar tactile inspection here was entirely "foreseeable."

The record and these factual findings are sufficient to resolve this case. The law is clear that the Fourth Amendment protects against government intrusion that upsets an "actual (subjective) expectation of privacy" that is objectively "'reasonable.'" Privacy itself implies the exclusion of uninvited strangers, not just strangers who work for the Government. Hence, an individual cannot reasonably expect privacy in respect to objects or activities that he "knowingly exposes to the public."

Indeed, the Court has said that it is not *objectively* reasonable to expect privacy if "any member of the public . . . could have" used his senses to detect "everything that the officers observed." *California v. Ciraolo.* Thus, it has held that the fact that strangers may look down at fenced-in property from an aircraft or sift through garbage bags on a public street can justify a similar police intrusion. *See Florida v. Riley; California v. Greenwood; cf. Texas v. Brown,* 460 U.S. 730, 740 (1983) (police not precluded from " 'bending down' " to see since "the general public could peer into the interior of [the car] from any number of angles"). The comparative likelihood that strangers will give bags in an overhead compartment a hard squeeze would seem far greater. *See Riley* (O'Connor, J., concurring in judgment) (reasonableness of privacy expectation depends on whether intrusion is a "sufficiently routine part of modern life"). Consider, too, the accepted police practice of using dogs to sniff for drugs hidden inside luggage. *See Place.* Surely it is less likely that non-governmental strangers will sniff at other's bags (or, more to the point, permit their dogs to do so) than it is that such actors will touch or squeeze another person's belongings in the process of making room for their own.

Of course, the agent's *purpose* here — searching for drugs — differs dramatically from the intention of a driver or fellow passenger who squeezes a bag in the process of making more room for another parcel. But in determining whether an expectation of privacy is reasonable, it is the *effect,* not the purpose, that matters. Few individuals with something to hide wish to expose that something to the police, however careless or indifferent they may be in respect to discovery by other members of the public. Hence, a Fourth Amendment rule that turns on purpose could prevent police alone from intruding where other strangers freely tread. And the added privacy protection achieved by such an approach would not justify the harm worked to law enforcement — at least that is what this Court's previous cases suggest. *See Greenwood,* 41 ("The police cannot reasonably be expected to avert their eyes from evidence of criminal activity that could have been observed by any member of the public"); *Ciraolo* (rejecting petitioner's argument that the police should be restricted solely because their actions are "motivated by a law enforcement purpose, and not the result of a causal, accidental observation").

Nor can I accept the majority's effort to distinguish "tactile" from "visual" interventions, even assuming that distinction matters here. Whether tactile manipulation (say, of the exterior of luggage) is more intrusive or less intrusive than visual observation (say, through a lighted window) necessarily depends on the particular circumstances.

If we are to depart from established legal principles, we should not begin here. At best, this decision will lead to a constitutional jurisprudence of "squeezes," thereby complicating further already complex Fourth Amendment law, increasing the difficulty of deciding ordinary criminal matters, and hindering the administrative guidance (with its potential for control of unreasonable police practices) that a less complicated jurisprudence might provide. At worst, this case will deter law enforcement officers searching for drugs near borders from using even the most non-intrusive touch to help investigate publicly exposed bags. At the same time, the ubiquity of *non*-governmental pushes, prods, and squeezes (delivered by driver, attendant, passenger, or some other stranger) means that this decision cannot do much to protect true privacy. Rather, the traveler who wants to place a bag in a shared overhead bin and yet safeguard its contents from public touch should plan to pack those contents in a suitcase with hard sides, irrespective of the Court's decision today.

For these reasons, I dissent.

QUESTIONS AND NOTES

1. Does *Bond* appear to be retrenching from *Riley*? If so, how do you account for Rehnquist's writing the opinion? If not, what are the differences?

2. When you travel on a crowded bus or plane, do you assume that your soft luggage will never be squeezed by a fellow passenger?

3. Should the answer to question 2 resolve this case? Why? Why not?

4. In *Kyllo* a sharply divided Court held that thermal imaging was a search.

KYLLO v. UNITED STATES
533 U.S. 27 (2001)

JUSTICE SCALIA delivered the opinion of the Court.

This case presents the question whether the use of a thermal-imaging device aimed at a private home from a public street to detect relative amounts of heat within the home constitutes a "search" within the meaning of the Fourth Amendment.

I

In 1991 Agent William Elliott of the United States Department of the Interior came to suspect that marijuana was being grown in the home belonging to petitioner Danny Kyllo, part of a triplex on Rhododendron Drive in Florence, Oregon. Indoor marijuana growth typically requires high-intensity lamps. In order to determine whether an amount of heat was emanating from petitioner's home consistent with the use of such lamps, at 3:20 a.m. on January 16, 1992, Agent Elliott and Dan Haas used an Agema Thermovision 210 thermal imager to scan the triplex. Thermal imagers detect infrared radiation, which virtually all objects emit but which is not visible to the naked eye. The imager converts radiation into images based on relative warmth — black is cool, white is hot, shades of gray connote relative differences; in that respect, it operates somewhat like a video camera showing heat images. The scan of Kyllo's home took only a few minutes and was performed from the passenger seat of Agent Elliott's vehicle across the street from the front of the house and also from the street in back of the house. The scan showed that the roof over the garage and a side wall of petitioner's home were relatively hot compared to the rest of the home and substantially warmer than neighboring homes in the triplex. Agent Elliott concluded that petitioner was using halide lights to grow marijuana in his house, which indeed he was. Based on tips from informants, utility bills, and the thermal imaging, a Federal Magistrate Judge issued a warrant authorizing a search of petitioner's home, and the agents found an indoor growing operation involving more than 100 plants. Petitioner was indicted on one count of manufacturing marijuana, in violation of 21 U.S.C. § 841(a)(1). He unsuccessfully moved to suppress the evidence seized from his home and then entered a conditional guilty plea.

The Court of Appeals for the Ninth Circuit remanded the case for an evidentiary hearing regarding the intrusiveness of thermal imaging. On remand the District Court found that the Agema 210 "is a non-intrusive device which emits no rays or beams and shows a crude visual image of the heat being radiated from the outside of the house"; it "did not show any people or activity within the walls of the structure"; "the device used cannot penetrate walls or windows to reveal conversations or human activities"; and "no intimate details of the home were observed." Based on these findings, the District Court upheld the validity of the warrant that relied in part upon the thermal imaging, and reaffirmed its denial of the motion to suppress. A divided Court of Appeals initially reversed, but that opinion was withdrawn and the panel (after a change in composition) affirmed, with Judge Noonan dissenting. The court held that petitioner had shown no subjective expectation of privacy because he had made no attempt to conceal the heat escaping from his home, and even if he had, there was no objectively reasonable expectation of privacy because the imager "did not expose any intimate details of Kyllo's life," only "amorphous 'hot spots' on the roof and exterior wall." We granted certiorari.

II

The Fourth Amendment provides that "the right of the people to be secure in their persons, houses, papers, and effects, against unreasonable searches and seizures, shall not be violated." "At the very core" of the Fourth Amendment "stands the right of a man to retreat into his own home and there be free from unreasonable governmental intrusion." With few exceptions, the question whether a warrantless search of a home is reasonable and hence constitutional must be answered no.

On the other hand, the antecedent question of whether or not a Fourth Amendment "search" has occurred is not so simple under our precedent. The permissibility of ordinary visual surveillance of a home used to be clear because, well into the 20th century, our Fourth Amendment jurisprudence was tied to common-law trespass. Visual surveillance was unquestionably lawful because " 'the eye cannot by the laws of England be guilty of a trespass.' " We have since decoupled violation of a person's Fourth Amendment rights from trespassory violation of his property, see *Rakas v. Illinois* [Chapter 14, *infra*], but the lawfulness of warrantless visual surveillance of a home has still been preserved. As we observed in *California v. Ciraolo*, 476 U.S. 207 (1986), "the Fourth Amendment protection of the home has never been extended to require law enforcement officers to shield their eyes when passing by a home on public thoroughfares."

One might think that the new validating rationale would be that examining the portion of a house that is in plain public view, while it is a "search"[3] despite the absence of trespass, is not an "unreasonable" one under the Fourth Amendment.

---

[3] When the Fourth Amendment was adopted, as now, to "search" meant "to look over or through for the purpose of finding something; to explore; to examine by inspection; as, to *search* the house for a book;

See Minnesota v. Carter, 525 U.S. 83 (1998) (Breyer, J., concurring in judgment). But in fact we have held that visual observation is no "search" at all — perhaps in order to preserve somewhat more intact our doctrine that warrantless searches are presumptively unconstitutional. In assessing when a search is not a search, we have applied somewhat in reverse the principle first enunciated in *Katz v. United States. Katz* involved eavesdropping by means of an electronic listening device placed on the outside of a telephone booth — a location not within the catalog ("persons, houses, papers, and effects") that the Fourth Amendment protects against unreasonable searches. We held that the Fourth Amendment nonetheless protected Katz from the warrantless eavesdropping because he "justifiably relied" upon the privacy of the telephone booth. As Justice Harlan's oft-quoted concurrence described it, a Fourth Amendment search occurs when the government violates a subjective expectation of privacy that society recognizes as reasonable. We have subsequently applied this principle to hold that a Fourth Amendment search does *not* occur — even when the explicitly protected location of a *house* is concerned — unless "the individual manifested a subjective expectation of privacy in the object of the challenged search," and "society [is] willing to recognize that expectation as reasonable." We have applied this test in holding that it is not a search for the police to use a pen register at the phone company to determine what numbers were dialed in a private home, *Smith v. Maryland,* and we have applied the test on two different occasions in holding that aerial surveillance of private homes and surrounding areas does not constitute a search, *Ciraolo; Riley.*

The present case involves officers on a public street engaged in more than naked-eye surveillance of a home. We have previously reserved judgment as to how much technological enhancement of ordinary perception from such a vantage point, if any, is too much. While we upheld enhanced aerial photography of an industrial complex in *Dow Chemical,* we noted that we found "it important that this is *not* an area immediately adjacent to a private home, where privacy expectations are most heightened," 476 U.S. at 237, n. 4 (emphasis in original).

III

It would be foolish to contend that the degree of privacy secured to citizens by the Fourth Amendment has been entirely unaffected by the advance of technology. For example, as the cases discussed above make clear, the technology enabling human flight has exposed to public view (and hence, we have said, to official observation) uncovered portions of the house and its curtilage that once were private. The question we confront today is what limits there are upon this power of technology to shrink the realm of guaranteed privacy.

The *Katz* test — whether the individual has an expectation of privacy that society is prepared to recognize as reasonable — has often been criticized as circular, and hence subjective and unpredictable. *See* 1 W. LaFave, Search and Seizure § 2.1(d), pp. 393–394 (3d ed. 1996); Posner, *The Uncertain Protection of Privacy by the Supreme Court,* 1979 S. Ct. Rev. 173, 188; *Carter* (Scalia, J., concurring). While it

---

to *search* the wood for a thief." N. Webster, An American Dictionary of the English Language 66 (1828) (reprint 6th ed. 1989).

may be difficult to refine *Katz* when the search of areas such as telephone booths, automobiles, or even the curtilage and uncovered portions of residences are at issue, in the case of the search of the interior of homes — the prototypical and hence most commonly litigated area of protected privacy — there is a ready criterion, with roots deep in the common law, of the minimal expectation of privacy that *exists*, and that is acknowledged to be *reasonable*. To withdraw protection of this minimum expectation would be to permit police technology to erode the privacy guaranteed by the Fourth Amendment. We think that obtaining by sense-enhancing technology any information regarding the interior of the home that could not otherwise have been obtained without physical "intrusion into a constitutionally protected area" constitutes a search — at least where (as here) the technology in question is not in general public use. This assures preservation of that degree of privacy against government that existed when the Fourth Amendment was adopted. On the basis of this criterion, the information obtained by the thermal imager in this case was the product of a search.[4]

The Government maintains, however, that the thermal imaging must be upheld because it detected "only heat radiating from the external surface of the house." The dissent makes this its leading point, contending that there is a fundamental difference between what it calls "off-the-wall" observations and "through-the-wall surveillance." But just as a thermal imager captures only heat emanating from a house, so also a powerful directional microphone picks up only sound emanating from a house-and a satellite capable of scanning from many miles away would pick up only visible light emanating from a house. We rejected such a mechanical interpretation of the Fourth Amendment in *Katz*, where the eavesdropping device picked up only sound waves that reached the exterior of the phone booth. Reversing that approach would leave the homeowner at the mercy of advancing technology — including imaging technology that could discern all human activity in the home. While the technology used in the present case was relatively crude, the rule we adopt must take account of more sophisticated systems that are already in use or in development.[5] The dissent's reliance on the distinction between "off-the-wall"

---

[4] The dissent's repeated assertion that the thermal imaging did not obtain information regarding the interior of the home is simply inaccurate. A thermal imager reveals the relative heat of various rooms in the home. The dissent may not find that information particularly private or important, but there is no basis for saying it is not information regarding the interior of the home. The dissent's comparison of the thermal imaging to various circumstances in which outside observers might be able to perceive, without technology, the heat of the home — for example, by observing snowmelt on the roof — is quite irrelevant. The fact that equivalent information could sometimes be obtained by other means does not make lawful the use of means that violate the Fourth Amendment. The police might, for example, learn how many people are in a particular house by setting up year-round surveillance; but that does not make breaking and entering to find out the same information lawful. In any event, on the night of January 16, 1992, no outside observer could have discerned the relative heat of Kyllo's home without thermal imaging.

[5] The ability to "see" through walls and other opaque barriers is a clear, and scientifically feasible, goal of law enforcement research and development. The National Law Enforcement and Corrections Technology Center, a program within the United States Department of Justice, features on its Internet Website projects that include a "Radar-Based Through-the-Wall Surveillance System," "Handheld Ultrasound Through the Wall Surveillance," and a "Radar Flashlight" that "will enable law officers to detect individuals through interior building walls." www.nlectc.org/techproj/ (visited May 3, 2001). Some devices may emit low levels of radiation that travel "through-the-wall," but others, such as more sophisticated thermal imaging devices, are entirely passive, or "off-the-wall" as the dissent puts it.

and "through-the-wall" observation is entirely incompatible with the dissent's belief, which we discuss below, that thermal-imaging observations of the intimate details of a home are impermissible. The most sophisticated thermal imaging devices continue to measure heat "off-the-wall" rather than "through-the-wall"; the dissent's disapproval of those more sophisticated thermal-imaging devices is an acknowledgement that there is no substance to this distinction. As for the dissent's extraordinary assertion that anything learned through "an inference" cannot be a search, that would validate even the "through-the-wall" technologies that the dissent purports to disapprove. Surely the dissent does not believe that the through-the-wall radar or ultrasound technology produces an 8-by-10 Kodak glossy that needs no analysis (*i.e.*, the making of inferences). And, of course, the novel proposition that inference insulates a search is blatantly contrary to *United States v. Karo*, 468 U.S. 705 (1984), where the police "inferred" from the activation of a beeper that a certain can of ether was in the home. The police activity was held to be a search, and the search was held unlawful.[6]

The Government also contends that the thermal imaging was constitutional because it did not "detect private activities occurring in private areas." It points out that in *Dow Chemical* we observed that the enhanced aerial photography did not reveal any "intimate details." *Dow Chemical*, however, involved enhanced aerial photography of an industrial complex, which does not share the Fourth Amendment sanctity of the home. The Fourth Amendment's protection of the home has never been tied to measurement of the quality or quantity of information obtained. In *Silverman*, for example, we made clear that any physical invasion of the structure of the home, "by even a fraction of an inch," was too much, and there is certainly no exception to the warrant requirement for the officer who barely cracks open the front door and sees nothing but the nonintimate rug on the vestibule floor. In the home, our cases show, *all* details are intimate details, because the entire area is held safe from prying government eyes. Thus, in *Karo*, the only thing detected was a can of ether in the home; and in *Arizona v. Hicks*, the only thing detected by a physical search that went beyond what officers lawfully present could observe in "plain view" was the registration number of a phonograph turntable. These were intimate details because they were details of the home, just as was the detail of how warm — or even how relatively warm — Kyllo was heating his residence.[7]

---

[6] The dissent asserts at n. 3 that we have misunderstood its point, which is not that inference *insulates* a search, but that inference alone is *not* a search. If we misunderstood the point, it was only in a good-faith effort to render the point germane to the case at hand. The issue in this case is not the police's allegedly unlawful inferencing, but their allegedly unlawful thermal-imaging measurement of the emanations from a house. We say such measurement is a search; the dissent says it is not, because an inference is not a search. We took that to mean that, since the technologically enhanced emanations had to be the basis of inferences before anything inside the house could be known, the use of the emanations could not be a search. But the dissent certainly knows better than we what it intends. And if it means only that an inference is not a search, we certainly agree. That has no bearing, however, upon whether hi-tech measurement of emanations from a house is a search.

[7] The Government cites our statement in *California v. Ciraolo*, 476 U.S. 207 (1986), noting apparent agreement with the State of California that aerial surveillance of a house's curtilage could become " 'invasive' " if " 'modern technology' " revealed " 'those intimate associations, objects or activities otherwise imperceptible to police or fellow citizens.' " (quoting brief of the State of California). We think the Court's focus in this second-hand dictum was not upon intimacy but upon otherwise-imperceptibility, which is precisely the principle we vindicate today.

Limiting the prohibition of thermal imaging to "intimate details" would not only be wrong in principle; it would be impractical in application, failing to provide "a workable accommodation between the needs of law enforcement and the interests protected by the Fourth Amendment," *Oliver v. United States.* To begin with, there is no necessary connection between the sophistication of the surveillance equipment and the "intimacy" of the details that it observes — which means that one cannot say (and the police cannot be assured) that use of the relatively crude equipment at issue here will always be lawful. The Agema Thermovision 210 might disclose, for example, at what hour each night the lady of the house takes her daily sauna and bath — a detail that many would consider "intimate"; and a much more sophisticated system might detect nothing more intimate than the fact that someone left a closet light on. We could not, in other words, develop a rule approving only that through-the-wall surveillance which identifies objects no smaller than 36 by 36 inches, but would have to develop a jurisprudence specifying which home activities are "intimate" and which are not. And even when (if ever) that jurisprudence were fully developed, no police officer would be able to know *in advance* whether his through-the-wall surveillance picks up "intimate" details — and thus would be unable to know in advance whether it is constitutional.

The dissent's proposed standard — whether the technology offers the "functional equivalent of actual presence in the area being searched" — would seem quite similar to our own at first blush. The dissent concludes that *Katz* was such a case, but then inexplicably asserts that if the same listening device only revealed the volume of the conversation, the surveillance would be permissible. Yet if, without technology, the police could not discern volume without being actually present in the phone booth, Justice Stevens should conclude a search has occurred. Cf. *Karo* (Stevens, J., concurring in part and dissenting in part) ("I find little comfort in the Court's notion that no invasion of privacy occurs until a listener obtains some significant information by use of the device . . . . A bathtub is a less private area when the plumber is present even if his back is turned"). The same should hold for the interior heat of the home if only a person present in the home could discern the heat. Thus the driving force of the dissent, despite its recitation of the above standard, appears to be a distinction among different types of information — whether the "homeowner would even care if anybody noticed." The dissent offers no practical guidance for the application of this standard, and for reasons already discussed, we believe there can be none. The people in their houses, as well as the police, deserve more precision.[8]

We have said that the Fourth Amendment draws "a firm line at the entrance to the house," That line, we think, must be not only firm but also bright — which requires clear specification of those methods of surveillance that require a warrant. While it is certainly possible to conclude from the videotape of the thermal imaging

---

[8] The dissent argues that we have injected potential uncertainty into the constitutional analysis by noting that whether or not the technology is in general public use may be a factor. That quarrel, however, is not with us but with this Court's precedent. *See Ciraolo* ("In an age where private and commercial flight in the public airways is routine, it is unreasonable for respondent to expect that his marijuana plants were constitutionally protected from being observed with the naked eye from an altitude of 1,000 feet"). Given that we can quite confidently say that thermal imaging is not "routine," we decline in this case to reexamine that factor.

that occurred in this case that no "significant" compromise of the homeowner's privacy has occurred, we must take the long view, from the original meaning of the Fourth Amendment forward.

> The Fourth Amendment is to be construed in the light of what was deemed an unreasonable search and seizure when it was adopted, and in a manner which will conserve public interests as well as the interests and rights of individual citizens.

Where, as here, the Government uses a device that is not in general public use, to explore details of the home that would previously have been unknowable without physical intrusion, the surveillance is a "search" and is presumptively unreasonable without a warrant.

Since we hold the Thermovision imaging to have been an unlawful search, it will remain for the District Court to determine whether, without the evidence it provided, the search warrant issued in this case was supported by probable cause — and if not, whether there is any other basis for supporting admission of the evidence that the search pursuant to the warrant produced.

The judgment of the Court of Appeals is reversed; the case is remanded for further proceedings consistent with this opinion.

JUSTICE STEVENS, with whom THE CHIEF JUSTICE, JUSTICE O'CONNOR, and JUSTICE KENNEDY join, dissenting.

There is, in my judgment, a distinction of constitutional magnitude between "through-the-wall surveillance" that gives the observer or listener direct access to information in a private area, on the one hand, and the thought processes used to draw inferences from information in the public domain, on the other hand. The Court has crafted a rule that purports to deal with direct observations of the inside of the home, but the case before us merely involves indirect deductions from "off-the-wall" surveillance, that is, observations of the exterior of the home. Those observations were made with a fairly primitive thermal imager that gathered data exposed on the outside of petitioner's home but did not invade any constitutionally protected interest in privacy.[1] Moreover, I believe that the supposedly "bright-line" rule the Court has created in response to its concerns about future technological developments is unnecessary, unwise, and inconsistent with the Fourth Amendment.

I

There is no need for the Court to craft a new rule to decide this case, as it is controlled by established principles from our Fourth Amendment jurisprudence.

---

[1] After an evidentiary hearing, the District Court found:

> The use of the thermal imaging device here was not an intrusion into Kyllo's home. No intimate details of the home were observed, and there was no intrusion upon the privacy of the individuals within the home. The device used cannot penetrate walls or windows to reveal conversations or human activities. The device recorded only the heat being emitted from the home.

One of those core principles, of course, is that "searches and seizures *inside a home* without a warrant are presumptively unreasonable." But it is equally well settled that searches and seizures of property in plain view are presumptively reasonable.[2] Whether that property is residential or commercial, the basic principle is the same: " 'What a person knowingly exposes to the public, even in his own home or office, is not a subject of Fourth Amendment protection.' " That is the principle implicated here.

While the Court "takes the long view" and decides this case based largely on the potential of yet-to-be-developed technology that might allow "through-the-wall surveillance," this case involves nothing more than off-the-wall surveillance by law enforcement officers to gather information exposed to the general public from the outside of petitioner's home. All that the infrared camera did in this case was passively measure heat emitted from the exterior surfaces of petitioner's home; all that those measurements showed were relative differences in emission levels, vaguely indicating that some areas of the roof and outside walls were warmer than others. As still images from the infrared scans show, no details regarding the interior of petitioner's home were revealed. Unlike an x-ray scan, or other possible "through-the-wall" techniques, the detection of infrared radiation emanating from the home did not accomplish "an unauthorized physical penetration into the premises," nor did it "obtain information that it could not have obtained by observation from outside the curtilage of the house." *United States v. Karo.*

Indeed, the ordinary use of the senses might enable a neighbor or passerby to notice the heat emanating from a building, particularly if it is vented, as was the case here. Additionally, any member of the public might notice that one part of a house is warmer than another part or a nearby building if, for example, rainwater evaporates or snow melts at different rates across its surfaces. Such use of the senses would not convert into an unreasonable search if, instead, an adjoining neighbor allowed an officer onto her property to verify her perceptions with a sensitive thermometer. Nor, in my view, does such observation become an unreasonable search if made from a distance with the aid of a device that merely discloses that the exterior of one house, or one area of the house, is much warmer than another. Nothing more occurred in this case.

Thus, the notion that heat emissions from the outside of a dwelling is a private matter implicating the protections of the Fourth Amendment (the text of which guarantees the right of people "to be secure *in* their . . . houses" against unreasonable searches and seizures (emphasis added)) is not only unprecedented but also quite difficult to take seriously. Heat waves, like aromas that are generated in a kitchen, or in a laboratory or opium den, enter the public domain if and when they leave a building. A subjective expectation that they would remain private is not only implausible but also surely not "one that society is prepared to recognize as

---

[2] Thus, for example, we have found consistent with the Fourth Amendment, even absent a warrant, the search and seizure of garbage left for collection outside the curtilage of a home, *California v. Greenwood*, the aerial surveillance of a fenced-in backyard from an altitude of 1,000 feet, *California v. Ciraolo*, the aerial observation of a partially exposed interior of a residential greenhouse from 400 feet above, *Florida v. Riley*, the aerial photography of an industrial complex from several thousand feet above, *Dow Chemical Co. v. United States*, 476 U.S. 227 (1986), and the observation of smoke emanating from chimney stacks, *Air Pollution Variance Bd. of Colo. v. Western Alfalfa Corp*, 416 U.S. 861 (1974).

'reasonable.' " *Katz* (Harlan, J., concurring).

To be sure, the homeowner has a reasonable expectation of privacy concerning what takes place within the home, and the Fourth Amendment's protection against physical invasions of the home should apply to their functional equivalent. But the equipment in this case did not penetrate the walls of petitioner's home, and while it did pick up "details of the home" that were exposed to the public, it did not obtain "any information regarding the *interior* of the home" (emphasis added). In the Court's own words, based on what the thermal imager "showed" regarding the outside of petitioner's home, the officers "concluded" that petitioner was engaging in illegal activity inside the home. It would be quite absurd to characterize their thought processes as "searches," regardless of whether they inferred (rightly) that petitioner was growing marijuana in his house, or (wrongly) that "the lady of the house [was taking] her daily sauna and bath." In either case, the only conclusions the officers reached concerning the interior of the home were at least as indirect as those that might have been inferred from the contents of discarded garbage, *see Greenwood*, or pen register, *see Smith v. Maryland*, or, as in this case, subpoenaed utility records. For the first time in its history, the Court assumes that an inference can amount to a Fourth Amendment violation.[3]

Notwithstanding the implications of today's decision, there is a strong public interest in avoiding constitutional litigation over the monitoring of emissions from homes, and over the inferences drawn from such monitoring. Just as "the police cannot reasonably be expected to avert their eyes from evidence of criminal activity that could have been observed by any member of the public," so too public officials should not have to avert their senses or their equipment from detecting emissions in the public domain such as excessive heat, traces of smoke, suspicious odors, odorless gases, airborne particulates, or radioactive emissions, any of which could identify hazards to the community. In my judgment, monitoring such emissions with "sense-enhancing technology," and drawing useful conclusions from such monitoring, is an entirely reasonable public service.

On the other hand, the countervailing privacy interest is at best trivial. After all, homes generally are insulated to keep heat in, rather than to prevent the detection of heat going out, and it does not seem to me that society will suffer from a rule requiring the rare homeowner who both intends to engage in uncommon activities that produce extraordinary amounts of heat, and wishes to conceal that production from outsiders, to make sure that the surrounding area is well insulated. *Cf. United States v. Jacobsen* ("The concept of an interest in privacy that society is prepared to recognize as reasonable is, by its very nature, critically different from the mere expectation, however well justified, that certain facts will not come to the attention of the authorities"). The interest in concealing the heat escaping from one's house

---

[3] Although the Court credits us with the "novel proposition that inference insulates a search," our point simply is that an inference cannot *be* a search, contrary to the Court's reasoning. Thus, the Court's use of *United States v. Karo* to refute a point we do not make underscores the fact that the Court has no real answer (either in logic or in law) to the point we do make. Of course, *Karo* itself does not provide any support for the Court's view that inferences can amount to unconstitutional searches. The illegality in that case was "the monitoring of a beeper in a private residence" to obtain information that "could not have been obtained by observation from outside," rather than any thought processes that flowed from such monitoring.

pales in significance to the "the chief evil against which the wording of the Fourth Amendment is directed," the "physical entry of the home," and it is hard to believe that it is an interest the Framers sought to protect in our Constitution.

Since what was involved in this case was nothing more than drawing inferences from off-the-wall surveillance, rather than any "through-the-wall" surveillance, the officers' conduct did not amount to a search and was perfectly reasonable.

II

Instead of trying to answer the question whether the use of the thermal imager in this case was even arguably unreasonable, the Court has fashioned a rule that is intended to provide essential guidance for the day when "more sophisticated systems" gain the "ability to 'see' through walls and other opaque barriers." The newly minted rule encompasses "obtaining [1] by sense-enhancing technology [2] any information regarding the interior of the home [3] that could not otherwise have been obtained without physical intrusion into a constitutionally protected area . . . [4] at least where (as here) the technology in question is not in general public use." In my judgment, the Court's new rule is at once too broad and too narrow, and is not justified by the Court's explanation for its adoption. As I have suggested, I would not erect a constitutional impediment to the use of sense-enhancing technology unless it provides its user with the functional equivalent of actual presence in the area being searched.

Despite the Court's attempt to draw a line that is "not only firm but also bright," the contours of its new rule are uncertain because its protection apparently dissipates as soon as the relevant technology is "in general public use." Yet how much use is general public use is not even hinted at by the Court's opinion, which makes the somewhat doubtful assumption that the thermal imager used in this case does not satisfy that criterion.[5] In any event, putting aside its lack of clarity, this criterion is somewhat perverse because it seems likely that the threat to privacy will grow, rather than recede, as the use of intrusive equipment becomes more readily available.

It is clear, however, that the category of "sense-enhancing technology" covered by the new rule is far too broad. It would, for example, embrace potential mechanical substitutes for dogs trained to react when they sniff narcotics. But in *Place*, we held that a dog sniff that "discloses only the presence or absence of narcotics" does "not constitute a 'search' within the meaning of the Fourth Amendment," and it must follow that sense-enhancing equipment that identifies nothing but illegal activity is not a search either. Nevertheless, the use of such a device would be unconstitutional under the Court's rule, as would the use of other

---

[5] The record describes a device that numbers close to a thousand manufactured units; that has a predecessor numbering in the neighborhood of 4,000 to 5,000 units; that competes with a similar product numbering from 5,000 to 6,000 units; and that is "readily available to the public" for commercial, personal, or law enforcement purposes, and is just an 800-number away from being rented from "half a dozen national companies" by anyone who wants one. Since, by virtue of the Court's new rule, the issue is one of first impression, perhaps it should order an evidentiary hearing to determine whether these facts suffice to establish "general public use."

new devices that might detect the odor of deadly bacteria or chemicals for making a new type of high explosive, even if the devices (like the dog sniffs) are "so limited in both the manner in which" they obtain information and "in the content of the information" they reveal. If nothing more than that sort of information could be obtained by using the devices in a public place to monitor emissions from a house, then their use would be no more objectionable than the use of the thermal imager in this case.

The application of the Court's new rule to "any information regarding the interior of the home" is also unnecessarily broad. If it takes sensitive equipment to detect an odor that identifies criminal conduct and nothing else, the fact that the odor emanates from the interior of a home should not provide it with constitutional protection. The criterion, moreover, is too sweeping in that information "regarding" the interior of a home apparently is not just information obtained through its walls, but also information concerning the outside of the building that could lead to (however many) inferences "regarding" what might be inside. Under that expansive view, I suppose, an officer using an infrared camera to observe a man silently entering the side door of a house at night carrying a pizza might conclude that its interior is now occupied by someone who likes pizza, and by doing so the officer would be guilty of conducting an unconstitutional "search" of the home.

Because the new rule applies to information regarding the "interior" of the home, it is too narrow as well as too broad. Clearly, a rule that is designed to protect individuals from the overly intrusive use of sense-enhancing equipment should not be limited to a home. If such equipment did provide its user with the functional equivalent of access to a private place — such as, for example, the telephone booth involved in *Katz*, or an office building — then the rule should apply to such an area as well as to a home. *See Katz* ("The Fourth Amendment protects people, not places").

The final requirement of the Court's new rule, that the information "could not otherwise have been obtained without physical intrusion into a constitutionally protected area," also extends too far as the Court applies it. As noted, the Court effectively treats the mental process of analyzing data obtained from external sources as the equivalent of a physical intrusion into the home. As I have explained, however, the process of drawing inferences from data in the public domain should not be characterized as a search.

The two reasons advanced by the Court as justifications for the adoption of its new rule are both unpersuasive. First, the Court suggests that its rule is compelled by our holding in *Katz*, because in that case, as in this, the surveillance consisted of nothing more than the monitoring of waves emanating from a private area into the public domain. Yet there are critical differences between the cases. In *Katz*, the electronic listening device attached to the outside of the phone booth allowed the officers to pick up the content of the conversation inside the booth, making them the functional equivalent of intruders because they gathered information that was otherwise available only to someone inside the private area; it would be as if, in this case, the thermal imager presented a view of the heat-generating activity inside petitioner's home. By contrast, the thermal imager here disclosed only the relative amounts of heat radiating from the house; it would be as if, in *Katz*, the listening device disclosed only the relative volume of sound leaving the booth, which presumably was discernible in the public domain.[6] Surely, there is a significant difference between the general and well-settled expectation that strangers will not have direct access to the contents of private communications, on the one hand, and the rather theoretical expectation that an occasional homeowner would even care if anybody noticed the relative amounts of heat emanating from the walls of his house, on the other. It is pure hyperbole for the Court to suggest that refusing to extend the holding of *Katz* to this case would leave the homeowner at the mercy of "technology that could discern all human activity in the home."

Second, the Court argues that the permissibility of "through-the-wall surveillance" cannot depend on a distinction between observing "intimate details" such as "the lady of the house [taking] her daily sauna and bath," and noticing only "the nonintimate rug on the vestibule floor" or "objects no smaller than 36 by 36 inches." This entire argument assumes, of course, that the thermal imager in this case could or did perform "through-the-wall surveillance" that could identify any detail "that would previously have been unknowable without physical intrusion." In fact, the device could not, and did not enable its user to identify either the lady of the house, the rug on the vestibule floor, or anything else inside the house, whether smaller or larger than 36 by 36 inches. Indeed, the vague thermal images of petitioner's home that are reproduced in the Appendix were submitted by him to the District Court as part of an expert report raising the question whether the device could even take "accurate, consistent infrared images" of the *outside* of his house. Defendant's Exhibit 107, p. 4. But even if the device could reliably show extraordinary differences in the amounts of heat leaving his home, drawing the inference that there was something suspicious occurring inside the residence — a conclusion that officers far less gifted than Sherlock Holmes would readily draw — does not qualify as "through-the-wall surveillance," much less a Fourth Amendment violation.

III

Although the Court is properly and commendably concerned about the threats to privacy that may flow from advances in the technology available to the law enforcement profession, it has unfortunately failed to heed the tried and true counsel of judicial restraint. Instead of concentrating on the rather mundane issue that is actually presented by the case before it, the Court has endeavored to craft an all-encompassing rule for the future. It would be far wiser to give legislators an unimpeded opportunity to grapple with these emerging issues rather than to shackle them with prematurely devised constitutional constraints.

I respectfully dissent.

---

[6] The use of the latter device would be constitutional given *Smith v. Maryland*, which upheld the use of pen registers to record numbers dialed on a phone because, unlike "the listening device employed in *Katz* . . . pen registers do not acquire the *contents* of communications."

QUESTIONS AND NOTES

1.   The split on the Court seems unusual to say the least? Is Scalia consistent with his prior opinions? Is Stevens?

2.   Does *Kyllo* reject the divining rod theory of the Fourth Amendment?

3.   Is the question whether thermal imaging is a search at all, or whether it is a reasonable search? What does Scalia think? What does Stevens think? What should the question be?

4.   Given the Court's determination that thermal imaging is a search, does (should) it necessarily follow that a warrant is required? Explain.

5.   For thermal imagers to work, it is frequently necessary to measure heat from neighboring houses to ascertain whether a particularly large amount of heat is escaping. For example, the heat escaping from Danny Kyllo's house was contrasted to the relatively lesser amount of heat escaping from his neighbors' houses.

6.   Given Note 5, should thermal imaging of Kyllo's neighbors houses be forbidden, even if a warrant were obtained for Kyllo?

7.   If your answer to Question 6 was "yes," how, if at all, would it be proper to use thermal imaging?

8.   Is *Kyllo* more like *Katz* or *Smith*? Explain.

9.   Should there be a distinction between "off the wall" and "through the wall" technology? If so, should the distinction, be absolute or only one factor in assessing whether there was a search?

10.   In *Jones* the Court was faced with the installation and long-term monitoring of a GPS on defendant's car. The court split sharply as to why this was unconstitutional, although all nine Justices believed it was in fact unconstitutional. Some because of trespass, some because of invasion of reasonable expectation of privacy, and, at least one, both.

UNITED STATES v. JONES
565 U.S. ___, 132 S. Ct. 945 (2012)

JUSTICE SCALIA delivered the opinion of the Court.

We decide whether the attachment of a Global-Positioning System (GPS) tracking device to an individual's vehicle, and subsequent use of that device to monitor the vehicle's movements on public streets, constitutes a search or seizure within the meaning of the Fourth Amendment.

I

In 2004 respondent Antoine Jones, owner and operator of a nightclub in the District of Columbia, came under suspicion of trafficking in narcotics and was made the target of an investigation by a joint FBI and Metropolitan Police Department task force. Officers employed various investigative techniques, including visual surveillance of the nightclub, installation of a camera focused on the front door of the club, and a pen register and wiretap covering Jones's cellular phone.

Based in part on information gathered from these sources, in 2005 the Government applied to the United States District Court for the District of Columbia for a warrant authorizing the use of an electronic tracking device on the Jeep Grand Cherokee registered to Jones's wife. A warrant issued, authorizing installation of the device in the District of Columbia and within 10 days.

On the 11th day, and not in the District of Columbia but in Maryland,[1] agents installed a GPS tracking device on the undercarriage of the Jeep while it was parked in a public parking lot. Over the next 28 days, the Government used the device to track the vehicle's movements, and once had to replace the device's battery when the vehicle was parked in a different public lot in Maryland. By means of signals from multiple satellites, the device established the vehicle's location within 50 to 100 feet, and communicated that location by cellular phone to a Government computer. It relayed more than 2,000 pages of data over the 4-week period.

II

A

. . . The Fourth Amendment provides in relevant part that "[t]he right of the people to be secure in their persons, houses, papers, and effects, against unreasonable searches and seizures, shall not be violated." It is beyond dispute that a vehicle is an "effect" as that term is used in the Amendment. We hold that the Government's installation of a GPS device on a target's vehicle,[2] and its use of that device to monitor the vehicle's movements, constitutes a "search."

It is important to be clear about what occurred in this case: The Government physically occupied private property for the purpose of obtaining information. We have no doubt that such a physical intrusion would have been considered a "search" within the meaning of the Fourth Amendment when it was adopted. *Entick v. Carrington*, 95 Eng. Rep. 807 (C.P. 1765), is a "case we have described as a 'monument of English freedom' 'undoubtedly familiar' to 'every American statesman' at the time the Constitution was adopted, and considered to be 'the true and ultimate expression of constitutional law' " with regard to search and seizure. In that case, Lord Camden expressed in plain terms the significance of property rights in search-and-seizure analysis:

---

[1] In this litigation, the Government has conceded noncompliance with the warrant and has argued only that a warrant was not required.

[2] As we have noted, the Jeep was registered to Jones's wife. The Government acknowledged, however, that Jones was "the exclusive driver." If Jones was not the owner he had at least the property rights of a bailee. The Court of Appeals concluded that the vehicle's registration did not affect his ability to make a Fourth Amendment objection, and the Government has not challenged that determination here. We therefore do not consider the Fourth Amendment significance of Jones's status.

"[O]ur law holds the property of every man so sacred, that no man can set his foot upon his neighbour's close without his leave; if he does he is a trespasser, though he does no damage at all; if he will tread upon his neighbour's ground, he must justify it by law."

The text of the Fourth Amendment reflects its close connection to property, since otherwise it would have referred simply to "the right of the people to be secure against unreasonable searches and seizures"; the phrase "in their persons, houses, papers, and effects" would have been superfluous.

Consistent with this understanding, our Fourth Amendment jurisprudence was tied to common-law trespass, at least until the latter half of the 20th century. Thus, in *Olmstead v. United States*, 277 U.S. 438, we held that wiretaps attached to telephone wires on the public streets did not constitute a Fourth Amendment search because "[t]here was no entry of the houses or offices of the defendants.

Our later cases, of course, have deviated from that exclusively property-based approach. In *Katz*, we said that "the Fourth Amendment protects people, not places," and found a violation in attachment of an eavesdropping device to a public telephone booth. Our later cases have applied the analysis of Justice Harlan's concurrence in that case, which said that a violation occurs when government officers violate a person's "reasonable expectation of privacy," *id.*, at 360, 88 S. Ct. 507.

The Government contends that the Harlan standard shows that no search occurred here, since Jones had no "reasonable expectation of privacy" in the area of the Jeep accessed by Government agents (its underbody) and in the locations of the Jeep on the public roads, which were visible to all. But we need not address the Government's contentions, because Jones's Fourth Amendment rights do not rise or fall with the *Katz* formulation. At bottom, we must "assur[e] preservation of that degree of privacy against government that existed when the Fourth Amendment was adopted." *Kyllo.* As explained, for most of our history the Fourth Amendment was understood to embody a particular concern for government trespass upon the areas ("persons, houses, papers, and effects") it enumerates.[3] *Katz* did not repudiate that understanding. Less than two years later the Court upheld defendants' contention that the Government could not introduce against them conversations between *other* people obtained by warrantless placement of electronic surveillance devices in their homes. The opinion rejected the dissent's contention that there was no Fourth Amendment violation "unless the conversa-

---

[3] Justice ALITO's concurrence (hereinafter concurrence) doubts the wisdom of our approach because "it is almost impossible to think oflate-18th-century situations that are analogous to what took place in this case." But in fact it posits a situation that is not far afield — a constable's concealing himself in the target's coach in order to track its movements. There is no doubt that the information gained by that trespassory activity would be the product of an unlawful search — whether that information consisted of the conversations occurring in the coach, or of the destinations to which the coach traveled.

In any case, it is quite irrelevant whether there was an 18th-centuryanalog. Whatever new methods of investigation may be devised, our task, *at a minimum*, is to decide whether the action in question would have constituted a "search" within the original meaning of the Fourth Amendment. Where, as here, the Government obtains information by physically intruding on a constitutionally protected area, such a search has undoubtedly occurred.

tional privacy of the homeowner himself is invaded." *Alderman v. United States*, 394 U.S. 165 (1969). "[W]e [do not] believe that *Katz*, by holding that the Fourth Amendment protects persons and their private conversations, was intended to withdraw any of the protection which the Amendment extends to the home . . . ."

More recently, in *Soldal v. Cook County*, 506 U.S. 56 (1992), the Court unanimously rejected the argument that although a "seizure" had occurred "in a 'technical' sense" when a trailer home was forcibly removed, no Fourth Amendment violation occurred because law enforcement had not "invade[d] the [individuals'] privacy." *Katz*, the Court explained, established that "property rights are not the sole measure of Fourth Amendment violations," but did not "snuf[f] out the previously recognized protection for property." As Justice Brennan explained in his concurrence in *Knotts*, *Katz* did not erode the principle "that, when the Government *does* engage in physical intrusion of a constitutionally protected area in order to obtain information, that intrusion may constitute a violation of the Fourth Amendment." We have embodied that preservation of past rights in our very definition of "reasonable expectation of privacy" which we have said to be an expectation "that has a source outside of the Fourth Amendment, either by reference to concepts of real or personal property law or to understandings that are recognized and permitted by society." *Minnesota v. Carter*, 525 U.S. 83, 88 (1998). *Katz* did not narrow the Fourth Amendment's scope.[5]

The Government contends that several of our post-*Katz* cases foreclose the conclusion that what occurred here constituted a search. It relies principally on two cases in which we rejected Fourth Amendment challenges to "beepers," electronic tracking devices that represent another form of electronic monitoring. The first case, *Knotts*, upheld against Fourth Amendment challenge the use of a "beeper" that had been placed in a container of chloroform, allowing law enforcement to monitor the location of the container. We said that there had been no infringement of Knotts' reasonable expectation of privacy since the information obtained — the location of the automobile carrying the container on public roads, and the location of the off-loaded container in open fields near Knotts' cabin — had been voluntarily conveyed to the public.[6] But as we have discussed, the *Katz* reasonable-expectation-of-privacy test has been *added to*, not *substituted for*, the common-law trespassory test. The holding in *Knotts* addressed only the former, since the latter was not at

---

[5] The concurrence notes that post-*Katz* we have explained that " 'an actual trespass is neither necessary *nor sufficient* to establish a constitutional violation.' " (quoting *United States v. Karo*, 468 U.S. 705, 713 (1984)). That is undoubtedly true, and undoubtedly irrelevant. *Karo* was considering whether a seizure occurred, and as the concurrence explains, a seizure of property occurs, not when there is a trespass, but "when there is some meaningful interference with an individual's possessory interests in that property." Likewise with a search. Trespass alone does not qualify, but there must be conjoined with that what was present here: an attempt to find something or to obtain information. Related to this, and similarly irrelevant, is the concurrence's point that, if analyzed separately, neither the installation of the device nor its use would constitute a Fourth Amendment search. Of course not. A trespass on "houses" or "effects," or a *Katz* invasion of privacy, is not alone a search unless it is done to obtain information; and the obtaining of information is not alone a search unless it is achieved by such a trespass or invasion of privacy.

[6] *Knotts* noted the "limited use which the government made of the signals from this particular beeper," and reserved the question whether "different constitutional principles may be applicable" to "dragnet-type law enforcement practices" of the type that GPS tracking made possible here.

issue. The beeper had been placed in the container before it came into Knotts' possession, with the consent of the then-owner. Knotts did not challenge that installation, and we specifically declined to consider its effect on the Fourth Amendment analysis. *Knotts* would be relevant, perhaps, if the Government were making the argument that what would otherwise be an unconstitutional search is not such where it produces only public information. The Government does not make that argument, and we know of no case that would support it.

The second "beeper" case, *United States v. Karo*, does not suggest a different conclusion. There we addressed the question left open by *Knotts*, whether the installation of a beeper in a container amounted to a search or seizure. As in *Knotts*, at the time the beeper was installed the container belonged to a third party, and it did not come into possession of the defendant until later. Thus, the specific question we considered was whether the installation *"with the consent of the original owner* constitute[d] a search or seizure . . . when the container is delivered to a buyer having no knowledge of the presence of the beeper." (emphasis added). We held not. The Government, we said, came into physical contact with the container only before it belonged to the defendant Karo; and the transfer of the container with the unmonitored beeper inside did not convey any information and thus did not invade Karo's privacy. That conclusion is perfectly consistent with the one we reach here. Karo accepted the container as it came to him, beeper and all, and was therefore not entitled to object to the beeper's presence, even though it was used to monitor the container's location. Cf. *On Lee v. United States*, (no search or seizure where an informant, who was wearing a concealed microphone, was invited into the defendant's business). Jones, who possessed the Jeep at the time the Government trespassorily inserted the information-gathering device, is on much different footing.

Finally, the Government's position gains little support from our conclusion in *Oliver* that officers' information-gathering intrusion on an "open field" did not constitute a Fourth Amendment search even though it was a trespass at common law. Quite simply, an open field, unlike the curtilage of a home is not one of those protected areas enumerated in the Fourth Amendment. See also *Hester v. United States*, 265 U.S. 57, 59 (1924). The Government's physical intrusion on such an area — unlike its intrusion on the "effect" at issue here — is of no Fourth Amendment significance.

B

The concurrence begins by accusing us of applying "18th-century tort law." That is a distortion. What we apply is an 18th-century guarantee against unreasonable searches, which we believe must provide *at a minimum* the degree of protection it afforded when it was adopted. The concurrence does not share that belief. It would apply *exclusively Katz* 's reasonable-expectation-of-privacy test, even when that eliminates rights that previously existed.

The concurrence faults our approach for "present[ing] particularly vexing problems" in cases that do not involve physical contact, such as those that involve the transmission of electronic signals. We entirely fail to understand that point. For unlike the concurrence, which would make *Katz* the *exclusive* test, we do not make trespass the exclusive test. Situations involving merely the transmission of electronic signals without trespass would *remain* subject to *Katz* analysis.

In fact, it is the concurrence's insistence on the exclusivity of the *Katz* test that needlessly leads us into "particularly vexing problems" in the present case. This Court has to date not deviated from the understanding that mere visual observation does not constitute a search. See *Kyllo*. We accordingly held in *Knotts* that "[a] person traveling in an automobile on public thoroughfares has no reasonable expectation of privacy in his movements from one place to another." Thus, even assuming that the concurrence is correct to say that "[t]raditional surveillance" of Jones for a 4-week period "would have required a large team of agents, multiple vehicles, and perhaps aerial assistance," our cases suggest that such visual observation is constitutionally permissible. It may be that achieving the same result through electronic means, without an accompanying trespass, is an unconstitutional invasion of privacy, but the present case does not require us to answer that question.

And answering it affirmatively leads us needlessly into additional thorny problems. The concurrence posits that "relatively short-term monitoring of a person's movements on public streets" is okay, but that "the use of longer term GPS monitoring in investigations *of most offenses*" is no good. (emphasis added). That introduces yet another novelty into our jurisprudence. There is no precedent for the proposition that whether a search has occurred depends on the nature of the crime being investigated. And even accepting that novelty, it remains unexplained why a 4-week investigation is "surely" too long and why a drug-trafficking conspiracy involving substantial amounts of cash and narcotics is not an "extraordinary offens[e]" which may permit longer observation. What of a 2-day monitoring of a suspected purveyor of stolen electronics? Or of a 6-month monitoring of a suspected terrorist? We may have to grapple with these "vexing problems" in some future case where a classic trespassory search is not involved and resort must be had to *Katz* analysis; but there is no reason for rushing forward to resolve them here.

The judgment of the Court of Appeals for the D.C. Circuit is affirmed.

JUSTICE SOTOMAYOR, concurring.

I join the Court's opinion because I agree that a search within the meaning of the Fourth Amendment occurs, at a minimum, "[w]here, as here, the Government obtains information by physically intruding on a constitutionally protected area." In this case, the Government installed a Global Positioning System (GPS) tracking device on respondent Antoine Jones' Jeep without a valid warrant and without Jones' consent, then used that device to monitor the Jeep's movements over the course of four weeks. The Government usurped Jones' property for the purpose of conducting surveillance on him, thereby invading privacy interests long afforded, and undoubtedly entitled to, Fourth Amendment protection.

Of course, the Fourth Amendment is not concerned only with trespassory intrusions on property. Rather, even in the absence of a trespass, "a Fourth Amendment search occurs when the government violates a subjective expectation of privacy that society recognizes as reasonable." In *Katz*, this Court enlarged its then-prevailing focus on property rights by announcing that the reach of the Fourth Amendment does not "turn upon the presence or absence of a physical intrusion." As the majority's opinion makes clear, however, *Katz* 's reasonable-expectation-of-privacy test augmented, but did not displace or diminish, the common-law trespassory test that preceded it.

Nonetheless, as Justice Alito notes, physical intrusion is now unnecessary to many forms of surveillance. *Post*, at 961–963. With increasing regularity, the Government will be capable of duplicating the monitoring undertaken in this case by enlisting factory- or owner-installed vehicle tracking devices or GPS-enabled smartphones. As Justice Alito incisively observes, the same technological advances that have made possible nontrespassory surveillance techniques will also affect the *Katz* test by shaping the evolution of societal privacy expectations. *Post*, at 962–963. Under that rubric, I agree with Justice Alito that, at the very least, "longer term GPS monitoring in investigations of most offenses impinges on expectations of privacy."

In cases involving even short-term monitoring, some unique attributes of GPS surveillance relevant to the *Katz* analysis will require particular attention. GPS monitoring generates a precise, comprehensive record of a person's public movements that reflects a wealth of detail about her familial, political, professional, religious, and sexual associations. And because GPS monitoring is cheap in comparison to conventional surveillance techniques and, by design, proceeds surreptitiously, it evades the ordinary checks that constrain abusive law enforcement practices: "limited police resources and community hostility." *Illinois v. Lidster.*

More fundamentally, it may be necessary to reconsider the premise that an individual has no reasonable expectation of privacy in information voluntarily disclosed to third parties. *United States v. Miller*, 425 U.S. 435, 443 (1976). This approach is ill suited to the digital age, in which people reveal a great deal of information about themselves to third parties in the course of carrying out mundane tasks. People disclose the phone numbers that they dial or text to their cellular providers; the URLs that they visit and the e-mail addresses with which they correspond to their Internet service providers; and the books, groceries, and medications they purchase to online retailers. Perhaps, as Justice Alito notes, some people may find the "tradeoff" of privacy for convenience "worthwhile," or come to accept this "diminution of privacy" as "inevitable and perhaps not. I for one doubt that people would accept without complaint the warrantless disclosure to the Government of a list of every Web site they had visited in the last week, or month, or year. But whatever the societal expectations, they can attain constitutionally protected status only if our Fourth Amendment jurisprudence ceases to treat secrecy as a prerequisite for privacy. I would not assume that all information voluntarily disclosed to some member of the public for a limited purpose is, for that reason alone, disentitled to Fourth Amendment protection. See *Smith*, (Marshall, J., dissenting) ("Privacy is not a discrete commodity, possessed absolutely or not at all. Those who disclose certain facts to a bank or phone company for a limited business purpose need not assume that this information will be released to other persons for other purposes"); see also *Katz*, ("[W]hat [a person] seeks to preserve as private, even in an area accessible to the public, may be constitutionally protected").

Resolution of these difficult questions in this case is unnecessary, however, because the Government's physical intrusion on Jones' Jeep supplies a narrower basis for decision. I therefore join the majority's opinion.

JUSTICE ALITO, with whom JUSTICE GINSBURG, JUSTICE BREYER, and JUSTICE KAGAN join, concurring in the judgment

This case requires us to apply the Fourth Amendment's prohibition of unreasonable searches and seizures to a 21st-century surveillance technique, the use of a Global Positioning System (GPS) device to monitor a vehicle's movements for an extended period of time. Ironically, the Court has chosen to decide this case based on 18th-century tort law. By attaching a small GPS device[1] to the underside of the vehicle that respondent drove, the law enforcement officers in this case engaged in conduct that might have provided grounds in 1791 for a suit for trespass to chattels. And for this reason, the Court concludes, the installation and use of the GPS device constituted a search. This holding, in my judgment, is unwise. It strains the language of the Fourth Amendment; it has little if any support in current Fourth Amendment case law; and it is highly artificial.

I would analyze the question presented in this case by asking whether respondent's reasonable expectations of privacy were violated by the long-term monitoring of the movements of the vehicle he drove.

I

A

The Fourth Amendment prohibits "unreasonable searches and seizures," and the Court makes very little effort to explain how the attachment or use of the GPS device fits within these terms. The Court does not contend that there was a seizure. A seizure of property occurs when there is "some meaningful interference with an individual's possessory interests in that property," and here there was none. Indeed, the success of the surveillance technique that the officers employed was dependent on the fact that the GPS did not interfere in any way with the operation of the vehicle, for if any such interference had been detected, the device might have been discovered.

The Court does claim that the installation and use of the GPS constituted a search, but this conclusion is dependent on the questionable proposition that these two procedures cannot be separated for purposes of Fourth Amendment analysis. If these two procedures are analyzed separately, it is not at all clear from the Court's opinion why either should be regarded as a search. It is clear that the attachment of the GPS device was not itself a search; if the device had not

---

[1] Although the record does not reveal the size or weight of the device used in this case, there is now a device in use that weighs two ounces and is the size of a credit card.

functioned or if the officers had not used it, no information would have been obtained. And the Court does not contend that the use of the device constituted a search either. On the contrary, the Court accepts the holding in *United States v. Knotts*, that the use of a surreptitiously planted electronic device to monitor a vehicle's movements on public roads did not amount to a search.

The Court argues — and I agree — that "we must 'assur[e] preservation of that degree of privacy against government that existed when the Fourth Amendment was adopted.'" But it is almost impossible to think of late-18th-century situations that are analogous to what took place in this case. (Is it possible to imagine a case in which a constable secreted himself somewhere in a coach and remained there for a period of time in order to monitor the movements of the coach's owner?[3]) The Court's theory seems to be that the concept of a search, as originally understood, comprehended any technical trespass that led to the gathering of evidence, but we know that this is incorrect. At common law, any unauthorized intrusion on private property was actionable, but a trespass on open fields, as opposed to the "curtilage" of a home, does not fall within the scope of the Fourth Amendment because private property outside the curtilage is not part of a "hous[e]" within the meaning of the Fourth Amendment.

B

The Court's reasoning in this case is very similar to that in the Court's early decisions involving wiretapping and electronic eavesdropping, namely, that a technical trespass followed by the gathering of evidence constitutes a search. In the early electronic surveillance cases, the Court concluded that a Fourth Amendment search occurred when private conversations were monitored as a result of an "unauthorized physical penetration into the premises occupied" by the defendant. *Silverman v. United States*, 365 U.S. 505, 509 (1961). In *Silverman*, police officers listened to conversations in an attached home by inserting a "spike mike" through the wall that this house shared with the vacant house next door. This procedure was held to be a search because the mike made contact with a heating duct on the other side of the wall and thus "usurp[ed] . . . an integral part of the premises."

By contrast, in cases in which there was no trespass, it was held that there was no search. Thus, in *Olmstead v. United States*, the Court found that the Fourth Amendment did not apply because "[t]he taps from house lines were made in the streets near the houses." Similarly, the Court concluded that no search occurred in *Goldman v. United States*, 316 U.S. 129 (1942), where a "detectaphone" was placed on the outer wall of defendant's office for the purpose of overhearing conversations held within the room.

This trespass-based rule was repeated criticized.

Katz finally did away with the old approach, holding that a trespass was not required for a Fourth Amendment violation. *Katz* involved the use of a listening

---

[3] The Court suggests that something like this might have occurred in 1791, but this would have required either a gigantic coach, a very tiny constable, or both — not to mention a constable with incredible fortitude and patience.

device that was attached to the outside of a public telephone booth and that allowed police officers to eavesdrop on one end of the target's phone conversation. This procedure did not physically intrude on the area occupied by the target, but the *Katz* Court, "repudiate[ed]" the old doctrine and held that "[t]he fact that the electronic device employed . . . did not happen to penetrate the wall of the booth can have no constitutional significance. What mattered, the Court now held, was whether the conduct at issue "violated the privacy upon which [the defendant] justifiably relied while using the telephone booth." Under this approach, as the Court later put it when addressing the relevance of a technical trespass, "an actual trespass is neither necessary *nor sufficient* to establish a constitutional violation." ("Compar[ing] *Katz v. United States*, 389 U.S. 347 (1967) (no trespass, but Fourth Amendment violation), with *Oliver v. United States*, 466 U.S. 170 (1984) (trespass, but no Fourth Amendment violation)"). In *Oliver*, the Court wrote:

> "The existence of a property right is but one element in determining whether expectations of privacy are legitimate. 'The premise that property interests control the right of the Government to search and seize has been discredited.' "

II

The majority suggests that two post-*Katz* decisions — *Soldal v. Cook County*, 506 U.S. 56 (1992), and *Alderman v. United States*, 394 U.S. 165 (1969) — show that a technical trespass is sufficient to establish the existence of a search, but they provide little support.

In *Soldal*, the Court held that towing away a trailer home without the owner's consent constituted a seizure even if this did not invade the occupants' personal privacy. But in the present case, the Court does not find that there was a seizure, and it is clear that none occurred.

In *Alderman*, the Court held that the Fourth Amendment rights of homeowners were implicated by the use of a surreptitiously planted listening device to monitor third-party conversations that occurred within their home . . . *Alderman* is best understood to mean that the homeowners had a legitimate expectation of privacy in all conversations that took place under their roof.

In sum, the majority is hard pressed to find support in post-*Katz* cases for its trespass-based theory.

III

Disharmony with a substantial body of existing case law is only one of the problems with the Court's approach in this case.

I will briefly note four others. First, the Court's reasoning largely disregards what is really important (the *use* of a GPS for the purpose of long-term tracking) and instead attaches great significance to something that most would view as relatively minor (attaching to the bottom of a car a small, light object that does not interfere in any way with the car's operation). Attaching such an object is generally regarded as so trivial that it does not provide a basis for recovery under modern tort law. But under the Court's reasoning, this conduct may violate the Fourth Amendment. By contrast, if long-term monitoring can be accomplished without committing a technical trespass — suppose, for example, that the Federal Government required or persuaded auto manufacturers to include a GPS tracking device in every car — the Court's theory would provide no protection.

Second, the Court's approach leads to incongruous results. If the police attach a GPS device to a car and use the device to follow the car for even a brief time, under the Court's theory, the Fourth Amendment applies. But if the police follow the same car for a much longer period using unmarked cars and aerial assistance, this tracking is not subject to any Fourth Amendment constraints.

In the present case, the Fourth Amendment applies, the Court concludes, because the officers installed the GPS device after respondent's wife, to whom the car was registered, turned it over to respondent for his exclusive use. But if the GPS had been attached prior to that time, the Court's theory would lead to a different result. The Court proceeds on the assumption that respondent "had at least the property rights of a bailee," but a bailee may sue for a trespass to chattel only if the injury occurs during the term of the bailment. So if the GPS device had been installed before respondent's wife gave him the keys, respondent would have no claim for trespass — and, presumably, no Fourth Amendment claim either.

Third, under the Court's theory, the coverage of the Fourth Amendment may vary from State to State. If the events at issue here had occurred in a community property State[4] or a State that has adopted the Uniform Marital Property Act, respondent would likely be an owner of the vehicle, and it would not matter whether the GPS was installed before or after his wife turned over the keys. In non-community-property States, on the other hand, the registration of the vehicle in the name of respondent's wife would generally be regarded as presumptive evidence that she was the sole owner.

Fourth, the Court's reliance on the law of trespass will present particularly vexing problems in cases involving surveillance that is carried out by making electronic, as opposed to physical, contact with the item to be tracked. For example, suppose that the officers in the present case had followed respondent by surreptitiously activating a stolen vehicle detection system that came with the car when it was purchased. Would the sending of a radio signal to activate this system constitute a trespass to chattels? Trespass to chattels has traditionally required a physical touching of the property. In recent years, courts have wrestled with the application of this old tort in cases involving unwanted electronic contact with computer systems, and some have held that even the transmission of electrons that occurs when a communication is sent from one computer to another is enough. But may such decisions be followed in applying the Court's trespass theory? Assuming that what matters under the Court's theory is the law of trespass as it existed at the time of the adoption of the Fourth Amendment, do these recent decisions represent a change in the law or simply the application of the old tort to new situations?

---

[4] *See, e.g.,* CAL. FAMILY CODE ANN. §760 (West 2004).

IV

A

The *Katz* expectation-of-privacy test avoids the problems and complications noted above, but it is not without its own difficulties. It involves a degree of circularity and judges are apt to confuse their own expectations of privacy with those of the hypothetical reasonable person to which the *Katz* test looks. In addition, the *Katz* test rests on the assumption that this hypothetical reasonable person has a well-developed and stable set of privacy expectations. But technology can change those expectations. Dramatic technological change may lead to periods in which popular expectations are in flux and may ultimately produce significant changes in popular attitudes. New technology may provide increased convenience or security at the expense of privacy, and many people may find the tradeoff worthwhile. And even if the public does not welcome the diminution of privacy that new technology entails, they may eventually reconcile themselves to this development as inevitable.[6]

On the other hand, concern about new intrusions on privacy may spur the enactment of legislation to protect against these intrusions. This is what ultimately happened with respect to wiretapping. After *Katz*, Congress did not leave it to the courts to develop a body of Fourth Amendment case law governing that complex subject. Instead, Congress promptly enacted a comprehensive statute and since that time, the regulation of wiretapping has been governed primarily by statute and not by case law. In an ironic sense, although *Katz* overruled *Olmstead*, Chief Justice Taft's suggestion in the latter case that the regulation of wiretapping was a matter better left for Congress has been borne out.

B

Recent years have seen the emergence of many new devices that permit the monitoring of a person's movements. In some locales, closed-circuit television video monitoring is becoming ubiquitous. On toll roads, automatic toll collection systems create a precise record of the movements of motorists who choose to make use of that convenience. Many motorists purchase cars that are equipped with devices that permit a central station to ascertain the car's location at any time so that roadside assistance may be provided if needed and the car may be found if it is stolen.

Perhaps most significant, cell phones and other wireless devices now permit wireless carriers to track and record the location of users — and as of June 2011, it has been reported, there were more than 322 million wireless devices in use in the United States. For older phones, the accuracy of the location information depends on the density of the tower network, but new "smart phones," which are equipped with a GPS device, permit more precise tracking. For example, when a user activates the GPS on such a phone, a provider is able to monitor the phone's location

---

[6] See, *e.g.*, NPR, The End of Privacy http://www.npr.org/series/114250076/the-end-of-privacy (all Internet materials as visited Jan. 20, 2012, and available in Clerk of Court's case file); Time Magazine, Everything About You Is Being Tracked — Get Over It, Joel Stein, Mar. 21, 2011, Vol. 177, No. 11.

and speed of movement and can then report back real-time traffic conditions after combining ("crowdsourcing") the speed of all such phones on any particular road.[9] Similarly, phone-location-tracking services are offered as "social" tools, allowing consumers to find (or to avoid) others who enroll in these services. The availability and use of these and other new devices will continue to shape the average person's expectations about the privacy of his or her daily movements.

V

In the pre-computer age, the greatest protections of privacy were neither constitutional nor statutory, but practical. Traditional surveillance for any extended period of time was difficult and costly and therefore rarely undertaken. The surveillance at issue in this case — constant monitoring of the location of a vehicle for four weeks — would have required a large team of agents, multiple vehicles, and perhaps aerial assistance.[10] Only an investigation of unusual importance could have justified such an expenditure of law enforcement resources. Devices like the one used in the present case, however, make long-term monitoring relatively easy and cheap. In circumstances involving dramatic technological change, the best solution to privacy concerns may be legislative. A legislative body is well situated to gauge changing public attitudes, to draw detailed lines, and to balance privacy and public safety in a comprehensive way.

To date, however, Congress and most States have not enacted statutes regulating the use of GPS tracking technology for law enforcement purposes. The best that we can do in this case is to apply existing Fourth Amendment doctrine and to ask whether the use of GPS tracking in a particular case involved a degree of intrusion that a reasonable person would not have anticipated.

Under this approach, relatively short-term monitoring of a person's movements on public streets accords with expectations of privacy that our society has recognized as reasonable. But the use of longer term GPS monitoring in investigations of most offenses impinges on expectations of privacy. For such offenses, society's expectation has been that law enforcement agents and others would not — and indeed, in the main, simply could not — secretly monitor and catalogue every single movement of an individual's car for a very long period. In this case, for four weeks, law enforcement agents tracked every movement that respondent made in the vehicle he was driving. We need not identify with precision the point at which the tracking of this vehicle became a search, for the line was surely crossed before the 4-week mark. Other cases may present more difficult questions. But where uncertainty exists with respect to whether a certain period of GPS surveillance is

---

[9] See, e.g., The bright side of sitting in traffic: Crowdsourcing road congestion data, Google Blog, http://googleblog.blogspot.com/2009/08/bright-side-of-sitting-in-traffic.html.

[10] Even with a radio transmitter like those used in *United States v. Knotts*, 460 U.S. 276 (1983), or *United States v. Karo*, 468 U.S. 705 (1984), such long-term surveillance would have been exceptionally demanding. The beepers used in those cases merely "emit[ted] periodic signals that [could] be picked up by a radio receiver." *Knotts*, 460 U.S., at 277. The signal had a limited range and could be lost if the police did not stay close enough. Indeed, in *Knotts* itself, officers lost the signal from the beeper, and only "with the assistance of a monitoring device located in a helicopter [was] the approximate location of the signal . . . picked up again about one hour later."

long enough to constitute a Fourth Amendment search, the police may always seek a warrant. We also need not consider whether prolonged GPS monitoring in the context of investigations involving extraordinary offenses would similarly intrude on a constitutionally protected sphere of privacy. In such cases, long-term tracking might have been mounted using previously available techniques.

For these reasons, I conclude that the lengthy monitoring that occurred in this case constituted a search under the Fourth Amendment. I therefore agree with the majority that the decision of the Court of Appeals must be affirmed.

QUESTIONS AND NOTES

1.   The opinion begins by describing the following non-GPS surveillance devices: "visual surveillance of the nightclub, installation of a camera focused on the front door of the club, and a pen register and wiretapping covering Jones's cellular phone." Are any of these procedures constitutionally improper? Suspect? Explain.

2.   How important is (should) text (be)? Specifically does (should) the case turn on the meaning of "person, houses, papers, and effects?

3.   Is Scalia deciding this case on 18th century tort law?

4.   Is trespass simpliciter the test? If not, what more is required?

5.   Suppose that Jones had agreed to purchase a house under construction and the police had, with the permission of the builder, installed a listening device in the house. Permissible under *Jones* and *Knotts*?

6.   Is *Oliver* good law after *Jones*? Explain. Should it be?

7.   As you read *Jardines*, consider whether it logically follows from *Jones* or if it significantly expands it?

FLORIDA v. JARDINES
569 U.S. ___, 133 S. Ct. 1409 (2013)

JUSTICE SCALIA delivered the opinion of the Court.

We consider whether using a drug-sniffing dog on a homeowner's porch to investigate the contents of the home is a "search" within the meaning of the Fourth Amendment.

I

In 2006, Detective William Pedraja of the Miami-Dade Police Department received an unverified tip that marijuana was being grown in the home of respondent Joelis Jardines. One month later, the Department and the Drug Enforcement Administration sent a joint surveillance team to Jardines' home. Detective Pedraja was part of that team. He watched the home for fifteen minutes and saw no vehicles in the driveway or activity around the home, and could not see inside because the blinds were drawn. Detective Pedraja then approached Jardines' home accompanied by Detective Douglas Bartelt, a trained canine handler who had just arrived at the scene with his drug-sniffing dog. The dog was trained to detect the scent of marijuana, cocaine, heroin, and several other drugs, indicating the presence of any of these substances through particular behavioral changes recognizable by his handler.

Detective Bartelt had the dog on a six-foot leash, owing in part to the dog's "wild" nature, and tendency to dart around erratically while searching. As the dog approached Jardines' front porch, he apparently sensed one of the odors he had been trained to detect, and began energetically exploring the area for the strongest point source of that odor. As Detective Bartelt explained, the dog "began tracking that airborne odor by . . . tracking back and forth," engaging in what is called "bracketing," "back and forth, back and forth." Detective Bartelt gave the dog "the full six feet of the leash plus whatever safe distance [he could] give him" to do this — he testified that he needed to give the dog "as much distance as I can." And Detective Pedraja stood back while this was occurring, so that he would not "get knocked over" when the dog was "spinning around trying to find" the source.

After sniffing the base of the front door, the dog sat, which is the trained behavior upon discovering the odor's strongest point. Detective Bartelt then pulled the dog away from the door and returned to his vehicle. He left the scene after informing Detective Pedraja that there had been a positive alert for narcotics.

On the basis of what he had learned at the home, Detective Pedraja applied for and received a warrant to search the residence. When the warrant was executed later that day, Jardines attempted to flee and was arrested; the search revealed marijuana plants, and he was charged with trafficking in cannabis.

The Florida Supreme Court held that the use of the trained narcotics dog to investigate Jardines' home was a Fourth Amendment search unsupported by probable cause, rendering invalid the warrant based upon information gathered in that search.

We granted certiorari, limited to the question of whether the officers' behavior was a search within the meaning of the Fourth Amendment.

II

The Fourth Amendment provides in relevant part that the "right of the people to be secure in their persons, houses, papers, and effects, against unreasonable searches and seizures, shall not be violated." The Amendment establishes a simple baseline, one that for much of our history formed the exclusive basis for its protections: When "the Government obtains information by physically intruding" on persons, houses, papers, or effects, "a 'search' within the original meaning of the Fourth Amendment" has "undoubtedly occurred." *United States v. Jones.* By reason of our decision in *Katz*, property rights "are not the sole measure of Fourth Amendment violations," but though *Katz* may add to the baseline, it does not subtract anything from the Amendment's protections "when the Government *does* engage in [a] physical intrusion of a constitutionally protected area."

That principle renders this case a straightforward one. The officers were gathering information in an area belonging to Jardines and immediately surrounding his house — in the curtilage of the house, which we have held enjoys protection as part of the home itself. And they gathered that information by physically entering and occupying the area to engage in conduct not explicitly or implicitly permitted by the homeowner.

<h2 style="text-align:center">A</h2>

The Fourth Amendment "indicates with some precision the places and things encompassed by its protections": persons, houses, papers, and effects. *Oliver*. The Fourth Amendment does not, therefore, prevent all investigations conducted on private property; for example, an officer may (subject to *Katz*) gather information in what we have called "open fields" — even if those fields are privately owned — because such fields are not enumerated in the Amendment's text. *Hester v. United States*, 265 U.S. 57, 44 S. Ct. 445, 68 L. Ed. 898 (1924).

But when it comes to the Fourth Amendment, the home is first among equals. At the Amendment's "very core" stands "the right of a man to retreat into his own home and there be free from unreasonable governmental intrusion." This right would be of little practical value if the State's agents could stand in a home's porch or side garden and trawl for evidence with impunity; the right to retreat would be significantly diminished if the police could enter a man's property to observe his repose from just outside the front window.

We therefore regard the area "immediately surrounding and associated with the home" — what our cases call the curtilage — as "part of the home itself for Fourth Amendment purposes." That principle has ancient and durable roots. Just as the distinction between the home and the open fields is "as old as the common law," so too is the identity of home and what Blackstone called the "curtilage or homestall," for the "house protects and privileges all its branches and appurtenants." This area around the home is "intimately linked to the home, both physically and psychologically," and is where "privacy expectations are most heightened."

While the boundaries of the curtilage are generally "clearly marked," the "conception defining the curtilage" is at any rate familiar enough that it is "easily understood from our daily experience." *Oliver*. Here there is no doubt that the officers entered it: The front porch is the classic exemplar of an area adjacent to the home and "to which the activity of home life extends."

<h2 style="text-align:center">B</h2>

Since the officers' investigation took place in a constitutionally protected area, we turn to the question of whether it was accomplished through an unlicensed physical intrusion.[1] While law enforcement officers need not "shield their eyes" when passing by the home "on public thoroughfares," an officer's leave to gather

---

[1] At oral argument, the State and its *amicus* the Solicitor General argued that Jardines conceded in the lower courts that the officers had a right to be where they were. This misstates the record. Jardines conceded nothing more than the unsurprising proposition that the officers could have lawfully

information is sharply circumscribed when he steps off those thoroughfares and enters the Fourth Amendment's protected areas. In permitting, for example, visual observation of the home from "public navigable airspace," we were careful to note that it was done "in a physically nonintrusive manner." *Entick v. Carrington*, a case "undoubtedly familiar" to "every American statesman" at the time of the Founding, states the general rule clearly: "[O]ur law holds the property of every man so sacred, that no man can set his foot upon his neighbour's close without his leave." As it is undisputed that the detectives had all four of their feet and all four of their companion's firmly planted on the constitutionally protected extension of Jardines' home, the only question is whether he had given his leave (even implicitly) for them to do so. He had not.

"A license may be implied from the habits of the country," notwithstanding the "strict rule of the English common law as to entry upon a close." We have accordingly recognized that "the knocker on the front door is treated as an invitation or license to attempt an entry, justifying ingress to the home by solicitors, hawkers and peddlers of all kinds." *Breard v. Alexandria*, 341 U.S. 622, 626, 71 S. Ct. 920, 95 L. Ed. 1233 (1951). This implicit license typically permits the visitor to approach the home by the front path, knock promptly, wait briefly to be received, and then (absent invitation to linger longer) leave. Complying with the terms of that traditional invitation does not require fine-grained legal knowledge; it is generally managed without incident by the Nation's Girl Scouts and trick-or-treaters.[2] Thus, a police officer not armed with a warrant may approach a home and knock, precisely because that is "no more than any private citizen might do." *Kentucky v. King.*

But introducing a trained police dog to explore the area around the home in hopes of discovering incriminating evidence is something else. There is no customary invitation to do *that*. An invitation to engage in canine forensic investigation assuredly does not inhere in the very act of hanging a knocker.[3] To find a visitor knocking on the door is routine (even if sometimes unwelcome); to spot that same visitor exploring the front path with a metal detector, or marching his bloodhound into the garden before saying hello and asking permission, would inspire most of us to — well, call the police. The scope of a license — express or

---

approached his home to knock on the front door in hopes of speaking with him. Of course, that is not what they did.

[2] With this much, the dissent seems to agree — it would inquire into " 'the appearance of things,' " *post*, at 1422 (opinion of Alito, J.), what is "typica[l]" for a visitor, *ibid.*, what might cause "alarm" to a "resident of the premises," *ibid.*, what is "expected" of "ordinary visitors," *ibid.*, and what would be expected from a " 'reasonably respectful citizen,' " *post*, at 1423. These are good questions. But their answers are incompatible with the dissent's outcome, which is presumably why the dissent does not even try to argue that it would be customary, usual, reasonable, respectful, ordinary, typical, nonalarming, etc., for a stranger to explore the curtilage of the home with trained drug dogs.

[3] The dissent insists that our argument must rest upon "the particular instrument that Detective Bartelt used to detect the odor of marijuana" — the dog. It is not the dog that is the problem, but the behavior that here involved use of the dog. We think a typical person would find it " 'a cause for great alarm' " (the kind of reaction the dissent quite rightly relies upon to justify its no-night-visits rule) to find a stranger snooping about his front porch *with or without* a dog. The dissent would let the police do whatever they want by way of gathering evidence so long as they stay on the base-path, to use a baseball analogy — so long as they "stick to the path that is typically used to approach a front door, such as a paved walkway." From that vantage point they can presumably peer into the house through binoculars with impunity. That is not the law, as even the State concedes.

implied — is limited not only to a particular area but also to a specific purpose. Consent at a traffic stop to an officer's checking out an anonymous tip that there is a body in the trunk does not permit the officer to rummage through the trunk for narcotics. Here, the background social norms that invite a visitor to the front door do not invite him there to conduct a search.[4]

The State points to our decisions holding that the subjective intent of the officer is irrelevant. But those cases merely hold that a stop or search *that is objectively reasonable* is not vitiated by the fact that the officer's real reason for making the stop or search has nothing to do with the validating reason. Thus, the defendant will not be heard to complain that although he was speeding the officer's real reason for the stop was racial harassment. Here, however, the question before the court is precisely *whether* the officer's conduct was an objectively reasonable search. As we have described, that depends upon whether the officers had an implied license to enter the porch, which in turn depends upon the purpose for which they entered. Here, their behavior objectively reveals a purpose to conduct a search, which is not what anyone would think he had license to do.

III

The State argues that investigation by a forensic narcotics dog by definition cannot implicate any legitimate privacy interest. The State cites for authority our decisions in *Place, Jacobsen,* and *Caballes,* which held, respectively, that canine inspection of luggage in an airport, chemical testing of a substance that had fallen from a parcel in transit, and canine inspection of an automobile during a lawful traffic stop, do not violate the "reasonable expectation of privacy" described in *Katz.*

Just last Term, we considered an argument much like this. *Jones* held that tracking an automobile's whereabouts using a physically-mounted GPS receiver is a Fourth Amendment search. The Government argued that the *Katz* standard "show[ed] that no search occurred," as the defendant had "no 'reasonable expectation of privacy' " in his whereabouts on the public roads — a proposition with at least as much support in our case law as the one the State marshals here. But because the GPS receiver had been physically mounted on the defendant's automobile (thus intruding on his "effects"), we held that tracking the vehicle's movements was a search: a person's "Fourth Amendment rights do not rise or fall with the *Katz* formulation." The *Katz* reasonable-expectations test "has been *added to,* not *substituted for,*" the traditional property-based understanding of the Fourth Amendment, and so is unnecessary to consider when the government gains evidence by physically intruding on constitutionally protected areas.

Thus, we need not decide whether the officers' investigation of Jardines' home violated his expectation of privacy under *Katz.* One virtue of the Fourth Amend-

---

[4] The dissent argues, citing *King*, that "gathering evidence — even damning evidence — is a lawful activity that falls within the scope of the license to approach." That is a false generalization. What *King* establishes is that it is not a Fourth Amendment search to approach the home in order to speak with the occupant, *because all are invited to do that.* The mere "purpose of discovering information," in the course of engaging in that permitted conduct does not cause it to violate the Fourth Amendment. But no one is impliedly invited to enter the protected premises of the home in order to do nothing but conduct a search.

ment's property-rights baseline is that it keeps easy cases easy. That the officers learned what they learned only by physically intruding on Jardines' property to gather evidence is enough to establish that a search occurred.

For a related reason we find irrelevant the State's argument (echoed by the dissent) that forensic dogs have been commonly used by police for centuries. This argument is apparently directed to our holding in *Kyllo*, that surveillance of the home is a search where "the Government uses a device that is not in general public use" to "explore details of the home that would previously have been unknowable *without physical intrusion*." (emphasis added). But the implication of that state-ment (*inclusio unius est exclusio alterius*) is that when the government uses a physical intrusion to explore details of the home (including its curtilage), the antiquity of the tools that they bring along is irrelevant.

*   *   *

The government's use of trained police dogs to investigate the home and its immediate surroundings is a "search" within the meaning of the Fourth Amend-ment. The judgment of the Supreme Court of Florida is therefore affirmed.

JUSTICE KAGAN, with whom JUSTICE GINSBURG and JUSTICE SOTOMAYOR join, concur-ring.

For me, a simple analogy clinches this case — and does so on privacy as well as property grounds. A stranger comes to the front door of your home carrying super-high-powered binoculars. He doesn't knock or say hello. Instead, he stands on the porch and uses the binoculars to peer through your windows, into your home's furthest corners. It doesn't take long (the binoculars are really very fine): In just a couple of minutes, his uncommon behavior allows him to learn details of your life you disclose to no one. Has your "visitor" trespassed on your property, exceeding the license you have granted to members of the public to, say, drop off the mail or distribute campaign flyers? Yes, he has. And has he also invaded your "reasonable expectation of privacy," by nosing into intimacies you sensibly thought protected from disclosure? *Katz*. Yes, of course, he has done that too.

That case is this case in every way that matters. Here, police officers came to Joelis Jardines' door with a super-sensitive instrument, which they deployed to detect things inside that they could not perceive unassisted. The equipment they used was animal, not mineral. But contra the dissent, see *post*, at 1420 (opinion of Alito, J.) (noting the ubiquity of dogs in American households), that is of no significance in determining whether a search occurred. Detective Bartelt's dog was not your neighbor's pet, come to your porch on a leisurely stroll. As this Court discussed earlier this Term, drug-detection dogs are highly trained tools of law enforcement, geared to respond in distinctive ways to specific scents so as to convey clear and reliable information to their human partners. They are to the poodle down the street as high-powered binoculars are to a piece of plain glass. Like the binoculars, a drug-detection dog is a specialized device for discovering objects not in plain view (or plain smell). And as in the hypothetical above, that device was aimed here at a home — the most private and inviolate (or so we expect) of all the places and things the Fourth Amendment protects. Was this activity a trespass?

Yes, as the Court holds today. Was it also an invasion of privacy? Yes, that as well.

The Court today treats this case under a property rubric; I write separately to note that I could just as happily have decided it by looking to Jardines' privacy interests. A decision along those lines would have looked . . . well, much like this one. It would have talked about " 'the right of a man to retreat into his own home and there be free from unreasonable governmental intrusion.' " It would have insisted on maintaining the "practical value" of that right by preventing police officers from standing in an adjacent space and "trawl[ing] for evidence with impunity." It would have explained that " 'privacy expectations are most heightened' " in the home and the surrounding area. And it would have determined that police officers invade those shared expectations when they use trained canine assistants to reveal within the confines of a home what they could not otherwise have found there.

It is not surprising that in a case involving a search of a home, property concepts and privacy concepts should so align. The law of property "naturally enough influence[s]" our "shared social expectations" of what places should be free from governmental incursions. And so the sentiment "my home is my own," while originating in property law, now also denotes a common understanding — extending even beyond that law's formal protections — about an especially private sphere. Jardines' home was his property; it was also his most intimate and familiar space. The analysis proceeding from each of those facts, as today's decision reveals, runs mostly along the same path.

I can think of only one divergence: If we had decided this case on privacy grounds, we would have realized that *Kyllo v. United States*, 533 U.S. 27, 121 S. Ct. 2038, 150 L. Ed. 2d 94 (2001), already resolved it.[1] The *Kyllo* Court held that police officers conducted a search when they used a thermal-imaging device to detect heat emanating from a private home, even though they committed no trespass. Highlighting our intention to draw both a "firm" and a "bright" line at "the entrance to the house," we announced the following rule:

> "Where, as here, the Government uses a device that is not in general public use, to explore details of the home that would previously have been unknowable without physical intrusion, the surveillance is a 'search' and is presumptively unreasonable without a warrant."

That "firm" and "bright" rule governs this case: The police officers here conducted a search because they used a "device . . . not in general public use" (a trained drug-detection dog) to "explore details of the home" (the presence of certain substances) that they would not otherwise have discovered without entering the premises.

And again, the dissent's argument that the device is just a dog cannot change the equation. As *Kyllo* made clear, the "sense-enhancing" tool at issue may be "crude" or "sophisticated," may be old or new (drug-detection dogs actually go back not

---

[1] The dissent claims, alternatively, that *Illinois v. Caballes*, controls this case (or nearly does). But *Caballes* concerned a drug-detection dog's sniff of an automobile during a traffic stop. And we have held, over and over again, that people's expectations of privacy are much lower in their cars than in their homes.

"12,000 years" or "centuries," but only a few decades), may be either smaller or bigger than a breadbox; still, "at least where (as here)" the device is not "in general public use," training it on a home violates our "minimal expectation of privacy" — an expectation "that *exists*, and that is acknowledged to be *reasonable*."[2] That does not mean the device is off-limits, as the dissent implies, it just means police officers cannot use it to examine a home without a warrant or exigent circumstance.

With these further thoughts, suggesting that a focus on Jardines' privacy interests would make an "easy cas[e] easy" twice over, I join the Court's opinion in full.

JUSTICE ALITO, with whom THE CHIEF JUSTICE, JUSTICE KENNEDY, and JUSTICE BREYER join, dissenting.

The Court's decision in this important Fourth Amendment case is based on a putative rule of trespass law that is nowhere to be found in the annals of Anglo-American jurisprudence.

The law of trespass generally gives members of the public a license to use a walkway to approach the front door of a house and to remain there for a brief time. This license is not limited to persons who intend to speak to an occupant or who actually do so. (Mail carriers and persons delivering packages and flyers are examples of individuals who may lawfully approach a front door without intending to converse.) Nor is the license restricted to categories of visitors whom an occupant of the dwelling is likely to welcome; as the Court acknowledges, this license applies even to "solicitors, hawkers and peddlers of all kinds." And the license even extends to police officers who wish to gather evidence against an occupant (by asking potentially incriminating questions).

According to the Court, however, the police officer in this case, Detective Bartelt, committed a trespass because he was accompanied during his otherwise lawful visit to the front door of respondent's house by his dog, Franky. Where is the authority evidencing such a rule? Dogs have been domesticated for about 12,000 years; they were ubiquitous in both this country and Britain at the time of the adoption of the Fourth Amendment; and their acute sense of smell has been used in law enforcement for centuries. Yet the Court has been unable to find a single case — from the United States or any other common-law nation — that supports the rule

---

[2] The dissent's other principal reason for concluding that no violation of privacy occurred in this case — that police officers themselves might detect an aroma wafting from a house — works no better. If officers can smell drugs coming from a house, they can use that information; a human sniff is not a search, we can all agree. But it does not follow that a person loses his expectation of privacy in the many scents within his home that (his own nose capably tells him) are not usually detectible by humans standing outside. And indeed, *Kyllo* already decided as much. In response to an identical argument from the dissent in that case, (noting that humans can sometimes detect "heat emanating from a building"), the *Kyllo* Court stated: "The dissent's comparison of the thermal imaging to various circumstances in which outside observers might be able to perceive, without technology, the heat of the home . . . is quite irrelevant. The fact that equivalent information could sometimes be obtained by other means does not make lawful the use of means that violate the Fourth Amendment . . . . In any event, [at the time in question,] no outside observer could have discerned the relative heat of Kyllo's home without thermal imaging."

on which its decision is based. Thus, trespass law provides no support for the Court's holding today.

The Court's decision is also inconsistent with the reasonable-expectations-of-privacy test that the Court adopted in *Katz*. A reasonable person understands that odors emanating from a house may be detected from locations that are open to the public, and a reasonable person will not count on the strength of those odors remaining within the range that, while detectible by a dog, cannot be smelled by a human.

For these reasons, I would hold that no search within the meaning of the Fourth Amendment took place in this case, and I would reverse the decision below.

I

The opinion of the Court may leave a reader with the mistaken impression that Detective Bartelt and Franky remained on respondent's property for a prolonged period of time and conducted a far-flung exploration of the front yard. ("trawl for evidence with impunity"), ("marching his bloodhound into the garden"). But that is not what happened.

Detective Bartelt and Franky approached the front door via the driveway and a paved path — the route that any visitor would customarily use — and Franky was on the kind of leash that any dog owner might employ.[5] As Franky approached the door, he started to track an airborne odor. He held his head high and began "bracketing" the area (pacing back and forth) in order to determine the strongest source of the smell. Detective Bartelt knew "the minute [he] observed" this behavior that Franky had detected drugs. Upon locating the odor's strongest source, Franky sat at the base of the front door, and at this point, Detective Bartelt and Franky immediately returned to their patrol car.

A critical fact that the Court omits is that, as respondent's counsel explained at oral argument, this entire process — walking down the driveway and front path to the front door, waiting for Franky to find the strongest source of the odor, and walking back to the car — took approximately a minute or two. Thus, the amount of time that Franky and the detective remained at the front porch was even less. The Court also fails to mention that, while Detective Bartelt apparently did not personally smell the odor of marijuana coming from the house, another officer who subsequently stood on the front porch, Detective Pedraja, did notice that smell and was able to identify it.

II

The Court concludes that the conduct in this case was a search because Detective Bartelt exceeded the boundaries of the license to approach the house that is recognized by the law of trespass, but the Court's interpretation of the scope of that license is unfounded.

---

[5] The Court notes that Franky was on a 6-foot leash, but such a leash is standard equipment for ordinary dog owners.

A

It is said that members of the public may lawfully proceed along a walkway leading to the front door of a house because custom grants them a license to do so. This rule encompasses categories of visitors whom most homeowners almost certainly wish to allow to approach their front doors — friends, relatives, mail carriers, persons making deliveries. But it also reaches categories of visitors who are less universally welcome — "solicitors," "hawkers," "peddlers," and the like. The law might attempt to draw fine lines between categories of welcome and unwelcome visitors, distinguishing, for example, between tolerable and intolerable door-to-door peddlers (Girl Scouts selling cookies versus adults selling aluminum siding) or between police officers on agreeable and disagreeable missions (gathering information about a bothersome neighbor versus asking potentially incriminating questions). But the law of trespass has not attempted such a difficult taxonomy.

Of course, this license has certain spatial and temporal limits. A visitor must stick to the path that is typically used to approach a front door, such as a paved walkway. A visitor cannot traipse through the garden, meander into the backyard, or take other circuitous detours that veer from the pathway that a visitor would customarily use. ("[W]hen the police come on to private property to conduct an investigation or for some other legitimate purpose and restrict their movements to places visitors could be expected to go (e.g., walkways, driveways, porches), observations made from such vantage points are not covered by the Fourth Amendment").

Nor, as a general matter, may a visitor come to the front door in the middle of the night without an express invitation.

Similarly, a visitor may not linger at the front door for an extended period. ("[T]here is no such thing as squatter's rights on a front porch. A stranger may not plop down uninvited to spend the afternoon in the front porch rocking chair, or throw down a sleeping bag to spend the night, or lurk on the front porch, looking in the windows"). The license is limited to the amount of time it would customarily take to approach the door, pause long enough to see if someone is home, and (if not expressly invited to stay longer), leave.

As I understand the law of trespass and the scope of the implied license, a visitor who adheres to these limitations is not necessarily required to ring the doorbell, knock on the door, or attempt to speak with an occupant. For example, mail carriers, persons making deliveries, and individuals distributing flyers may leave the items they are carrying and depart without making any attempt to converse. A pedestrian or motorist looking for a particular address may walk up to a front door in order to check a house number that is hard to see from the sidewalk or road. A neighbor who knows that the residents are away may approach the door to retrieve an accumulation of newspapers that might signal to a potential burglar that the house is unoccupied.

As the majority acknowledges, this implied license to approach the front door extends to the police. ("It is not objectionable for an officer to come upon that part of the property which has been opened to public common use"). Even when the objective of a "knock and talk" is to obtain evidence that will lead to the homeowner's arrest and prosecution, the license to approach still applies. In other words, gathering evidence — even damning evidence — is a lawful activity that falls within the scope of the license to approach. And when officers walk up to the front door of a house, they are permitted to see, hear, and smell whatever can be detected from a lawful vantage point. ("[P]olice officers restricting their activity to [areas to which the public is impliedly invited] are permitted the same intrusion and the same level of observation as would be expected from a reasonably respectful citizen").

B

Detective Bartelt did not exceed the scope of the license to approach respondent's front door. He adhered to the customary path; he did not approach in the middle of the night; and he remained at the front door for only a very short period (less than a minute or two).

The Court concludes that Detective Bartelt went too far because he had the "*objectiv[e] . . . purpose* to conduct a search." (emphasis added). What this means, I take it, is that anyone aware of what Detective Bartelt did would infer that his subjective purpose was to gather evidence. But if this is the Court's point, then a standard "knock and talk" and most other police visits would likewise constitute searches. With the exception of visits to serve warrants or civil process, police almost always approach homes with a purpose of discovering information. That is certainly the objective of a "knock and talk." The Court offers no meaningful way of distinguishing the "objective purpose" of a "knock and talk" from the "objective purpose" of Detective Bartelt's conduct here.

The Court contends that a "knock and talk" is different because it involves talking, and "all are invited" to do that. But a police officer who approaches the front door of a house in accordance with the limitations already discussed may gather evidence by means other than talking. The officer may observe items in plain view and smell odors coming from the house. So the Court's "objective purpose" argument cannot stand.

What the Court must fall back on, then, is the particular instrument that Detective Bartelt used to detect the odor of marijuana, namely, his dog. But in the entire body of common-law decisions, the Court has not found a single case holding that a visitor to the front door of a home commits a trespass if the visitor is accompanied by a dog on a leash. On the contrary, the common law allowed even unleashed dogs to wander on private property without committing a trespass.

The Court responds that "[i]t is not the dog that is the problem, but the behavior that here involved use of the dog." But where is the support in the law of trespass for *this* proposition? Dogs' keen sense of smell has been used in law enforcement for centuries. The antiquity of this practice is evidenced by a Scottish law from 1318 that made it a crime to "disturb a tracking dog or the men coming with it for pursuing thieves or seizing malefactors." If bringing a tracking dog to the front door of a home constituted a trespass, one would expect at least one case to have arisen during the past 800 years. But the Court has found none.

For these reasons, the real law of trespass provides no support for the Court's holding today. While the Court claims that its reasoning has "ancient and durable roots," *ante*, at 1414, its trespass rule is really a newly struck counterfeit.

III

The concurring opinion attempts to provide an alternative ground for today's decision, namely, that Detective Bartelt's conduct violated respondent's reasonable expectations of privacy. But we have already rejected a very similar, if not identical argument, see *Illinois v. Caballes*, and in any event I see no basis for concluding that the occupants of a dwelling have a reasonable expectation of privacy in odors that emanate from the dwelling and reach spots where members of the public may lawfully stand.

It is clear that the occupant of a house has no reasonable expectation of privacy with respect to odors that can be smelled by human beings who are standing in such places. And I would not draw a line between odors that can be smelled by humans and those that are detectible only by dogs.

Consider the situation from the point of view of the occupant of a building in which marijuana is grown or methamphetamine is manufactured. Would such an occupant reason as follows? "I know that odors may emanate from my building and that atmospheric conditions, such as the force and direction of the wind, may affect the strength of those odors when they reach a spot where members of the public may lawfully stand. I also know that some people have a much more acute sense of smell than others,[6] and I have no idea who might be standing in one of the spots in question when the odors from my house reach that location. In addition, I know that odors coming from my building, when they reach these locations, may be strong enough to be detected by a dog. But I am confident that they will be so faint that they cannot be smelled by any human being." Such a finely tuned expectation would be entirely unrealistic, and I see no evidence that society is prepared to recognize it as reasonable.

In an attempt to show that respondent had a reasonable expectation of privacy in the odor of marijuana wafting from his house, the concurrence argues that this case is just like *Kyllo*, which held that police officers conducted a search when they used a thermal imaging device to detect heat emanating from a house. This Court, however, has already rejected the argument that the use of a drug-sniffing dog is the same as the use of a thermal imaging device. See *Caballes*. The very argument now advanced by the concurrence appears in Justice Souter's *Caballes* dissent. But the Court was not persuaded.

Contrary to the interpretation propounded by the concurrence, *Kyllo* is best understood as a decision about the use of new technology. The *Kyllo* Court focused on the fact that the thermal imaging device was a form of "sense-enhancing technology" that was "not in general public use," and it expressed concern that citizens would be "at the mercy of advancing technology" if its use was not restricted. A dog, however, is not a new form of "technology" or a "device." And, as noted, the use of dogs' acute sense of smell in law enforcement dates back many centuries.

---

[6] Some humans naturally have a much more acute sense of smell than others, and humans can be trained to detect and distinguish odors that could not be detected without such training. See E. Hancock, A Primer on Smell, http://www.jhu.edu/jhumag/996web/smell.html. Some individuals employed in the perfume and wine industries, for example, have an amazingly acute sense of smell.

The concurrence suggests that a *Kyllo*-based decision would be "much like" the actual decision of the Court, but that is simply not so. The holding of the Court is based on what the Court sees as a "'physical intrusion of a constitutionally protected area.'" As a result, it does not apply when a dog alerts while on a public sidewalk or street or in the corridor of a building to which the dog and handler have been lawfully admitted.

The concurrence's *Kyllo*-based approach would have a much wider reach. When the police used the thermal imaging device in *Kyllo*, they were on a public street, and "committed no trespass." Therefore, if a dog's nose is just like a thermal imaging device for Fourth Amendment purposes, a search would occur if a dog alerted while on a public sidewalk or in the corridor of an apartment building. And the same would be true if the dog was trained to sniff, not for marijuana, but for more dangerous quarry, such as explosives or for a violent fugitive or kidnapped child. I see no ground for hampering legitimate law enforcement in this way.

IV

The conduct of the police officer in this case did not constitute a trespass and did not violate respondent's reasonable expectations of privacy. I would hold that this conduct was not a search, and I therefore respectfully dissent.

QUESTIONS AND NOTES

1.   Do *Jones* and *Jardines* present the same or different issues? If the same, why did Roberts and Kennedy desert Scalia in *Jardines*? Why did Ginsburg and Kagan join him?

2.   If the issue is different, how is it different?

3.   Can *Jardines* be reconciled with *Place* and *Caballes*? If so, how? If not, can the majority opinion be defended?

4.   Who has the better argument in regard to trespass? Scalia or Alito?

5.   Would (should) it be permissible for a police officer without a dog to enter the area in issue for the sole purpose of smelling the outside of the house in the hopes of detecting the odor of marijuana? Would Scalia's answer be the same as Kagan's answer?

6.   What would be the result if this procedure had taken place in an apartment complex where people were free to walk all over the exterior and interior halls? Would it matter whether dogs were allowed in the complex?

7.   We conclude this section with a problem:

PROBLEM

(1) On the evening of May 15, 1994, an anonymous individual approached Officer Thielen, telling him that he had just walked by a nearby apartment window through which he had seen some people bagging drugs; (2) the apartment in question was a garden apartment that was partly below ground level; (3) families frequently used

the grassy area just outside the apartment's window for walking or for playing; (4) members of the public also used the area just outside the apartment's window to store bicycles; (5) in an effort to verify the tipster's information, Officer Thielen walked to a position about 1 to 1 ½ and one-half feet in front of the window; (6) Officer Thielen stood there for about 15 minutes looking down through a set of Venetian blinds; (7) what he saw, namely, people putting white powder in bags, verified the account he had heard; and (8) he then used that information to help obtain a search warrant. Should the Supreme Court find that Officer Thielen (A). Did not conduct a search, (B) Conducted a reasonable search, or (C) conducted an unreasonable search? For Justice Breyer's opinion, see *Minnesota v. Carter*, 525 U.S. 83, 104 (1998). The other eight Justices decided the case on other grounds, see Chapter 14, *infra*.

Chapter 11

CONSENT

It is beyond dispute that a consent search may be invalidated because the searchee is unconstitutionally detained. *See, e.g., Florida v. Royer* (*supra*). Conversely, a search conducted pursuant to a legally recognized consent is permitted by the Fourth Amendment. What constitutes a legally recognized consent is less clear. Also, less clear is whether consent searches are excepted from the Fourth Amendment because they are not searches at all, or because they are *per se* reasonable. Think about these questions as you read *Schneckloth* and *Rodriguez*.

SCHNECKLOTH v. BUSTAMONTE
412 U.S. 218 (1973)

MR. JUSTICE STEWART delivered the opinion of the Court.

I

While on routine patrol in Sunnyvale, California, at approximately 2:40 in the morning, Police Officer James Rand stopped an automobile when he observed that one headlight and its license plate light were burned out. Six men were in the vehicle. Joe Alcala and the respondent, Robert Bustamonte, were in the front seat with Joe Gonzales, the driver. Three older men were seated in the rear. When, in response to the policeman's question, Gonzales could not produce a driver's license, Officer Rand asked if any of the other five had any evidence of identification. Only Alcala produced a license, and he explained that the car was his brother's. After the six occupants had stepped out of the car at the officer's request and after two additional policemen had arrived, Officer Rand asked Alcala if he could search the car. Alcala replied, "Sure, go ahead." Prior to the search no one was threatened with arrest and, according to Officer Rand's uncontradicted testimony, it "was all very congenial at this time." Gonzales testified that Alcala actually helped in the search of the car, by opening the trunk and glove compartment. In Gonzales' words: "[T]he police officer asked Joe [Alcala], he goes, 'Does the trunk open?' And Joe said, 'Yes.' He went to the car and got the keys and opened up the trunk." Wadded up under the left rear seat, the police officers found three checks that had previously been stolen from a car wash.

II

It is important to make it clear at the outset what is not involved in this case. The respondent concedes that a search conducted pursuant to a valid consent is constitutionally permissible. And similarly the State concedes that "[w]hen a prosecutor seeks to rely upon consent to justify the lawfulness of a search, he has the burden of proving that the consent was, in fact, freely and voluntarily given."

The precise question in this case, then, is what must the prosecution prove to demonstrate that a consent was "voluntarily" given. And upon that question there is a square conflict of views between the state and federal courts that have reviewed the search involved in the case before us. The Court of Appeals for the Ninth Circuit concluded that it is an essential part of the State's initial burden to prove that a person knows he has a right to refuse consent. The California courts have followed the rule that voluntariness is a question of fact to be determined from the totality of all the circumstances, and that the state of a defendant's knowledge is only one factor to be taken into account in assessing the voluntariness of a consent.

A

The most extensive judicial exposition of the meaning of "voluntariness" has been developed in those cases in which the Court has had to determine the "voluntariness" of a defendant's confession for purposes of the Fourteenth Amendment. Almost 40 years ago, in *Brown v. Mississippi*, 297 U.S. 278, the Court held that a criminal conviction based upon a confession obtained by brutality and violence was constitutionally invalid under the Due Process Clause of the Fourteenth Amendment. In some 30 different cases decided during the era that intervened between *Brown* and *Escobedo v. Illinois*, 378 U.S. 478, the Court was faced with the necessity of determining whether in fact the confessions in issue had been "voluntarily" given. It is to that body of case law to which we turn for initial guidance on the meaning of "voluntariness" in the present context.

In determining whether a defendant's will was overborne in a particular case, the Court has assessed the totality of all the surrounding circumstances — both the characteristics of the accused and the details of the interrogation. Some of the factors taken into account have included the youth of the accused, his lack of education, or his low intelligence, the lack of any advice to the accused of his constitutional rights, the length of detention, the repeated and prolonged nature of the questioning, and the use of physical punishment such as the deprivation of food or sleep. In all of these cases, the Court determined the factual circumstances surrounding the confession, assessed the psychological impact on the accused, and evaluated the legal significance of how the accused reacted.

The significant fact about all of these decisions is that none of them turned on the presence or absence of a single controlling criterion; each reflected a careful scrutiny of all the surrounding circumstances. In none of them did the Court rule that the Due Process Clause required the prosecution to prove as part of its initial burden that the defendant knew he had a right to refuse to answer the questions that were put. While the state of the accused's mind, and the failure of the police to advise the accused of his rights, were certainly factors to be evaluated in assessing the "voluntariness" of an accused's responses, they were not in and of themselves determinative.

B

Similar considerations lead us to agree with the courts of California that the question whether a consent to a search was in fact "voluntary" or was the product of duress or coercion, express or implied, is a question of fact to be determined from the totality of all the circumstances. While knowledge of the right to refuse consent is one factor to be taken into account, the government need not establish such knowledge as the *sine qua non* of an effective consent. As with police questioning, two competing concerns must be accommodated in determining the meaning of a "voluntary" consent — the legitimate need for such searches and the equally important requirement of assuring the absence of coercion.

In situations where the police have some evidence of illicit activity, but lack probable cause to arrest or search, a search authorized by a valid consent may be the only means of obtaining important and reliable evidence. In the present case for example, while the police had reason to stop the car for traffic violations, the State does not contend that there was probable cause to search the vehicle or that the search was incident to a valid arrest of any of the occupants. Yet, the search yielded tangible evidence that served as a basis for a prosecution, and provided some assurance that others, wholly innocent of the crime, were not mistakenly brought to trial. And in those cases where there is probable cause to arrest or search, but where the police lack a warrant, a consent search may still be valuable. If the search is conducted and proves fruitless, that in itself may convince the police that an arrest with its possible stigma and embarrassment is unnecessary, or that a far more extensive search pursuant to a warrant is not justified. In short, a search pursuant to consent may result in considerably less inconvenience for the subject of the search, and, properly conducted, is a constitutionally permissible and wholly legitimate aspect of effective police activity.

The approach of the Court of Appeals for the Ninth Circuit finds no support in any of our decisions that have attempted to define the meaning of "voluntariness." Its ruling, that the State must affirmatively prove that the subject of the search knew that he had a right to refuse consent, would, in practice, create serious doubt whether consent searches could continue to be conducted. There might be rare cases where it could be proved from the record that a person in fact affirmatively knew of his right to refuse — such as a case where he announced to the police that if he didn't sign the consent form, "you [police] are going to get a search warrant;" or a case where by prior experience and training a person had clearly and convincingly demonstrated such knowledge. But more commonly where there was no evidence of any coercion, explicit or implicit, the prosecution would nevertheless be unable to demonstrate that the subject of the search in fact had known of his right to refuse consent.

One alternative that would go far toward proving that the subject of a search did know he had a right to refuse consent would be to advise him of that right before eliciting his consent. That, however, is a suggestion that has been almost universally repudiated by both federal and state courts, and, we think, rightly so. For it would be thoroughly impractical to impose on the normal consent search the detailed requirements of an effective warning. Consent searches are part of the standard investigatory techniques of law enforcement agencies. They normally occur on the highway, or in a person's home or office, and under informal and unstructured conditions. The circumstances that prompt the initial request to search may develop quickly or be a logical extension of investigative police questioning. The police may seek to investigate further suspicious circumstances or to follow up leads developed in questioning persons at the scene of a crime. These situations are a far cry from the structured atmosphere of a trial where, assisted by counsel if he chooses, a defendant is informed of his trial rights. And, while surely a closer question, these situations are still immeasurably, far removed from "custodial interrogation" where, in *Miranda v. Arizona*, 384 U.S. 436, we found that the Constitution required certain now familiar warnings as a prerequisite to police interrogation. Indeed, in language applicable to the typical consent search, we refused to extend the need for warnings:

> Our decision is not intended to hamper the traditional function of police officers in investigating crime . . . . When an individual is in custody on probable cause, the police may, of course, seek out evidence in the field to be used at trial against him. Such investigation may include inquiry of persons not under restraint. General on-the-scene questioning as to facts surrounding a crime or other general questioning of citizens in the fact-finding process is not affected by our holding. It is an act of responsible citizenship for individuals to give whatever information they may have to aid in law enforcement.

Consequently, we cannot accept the position of the Court of Appeals in this case that proof of knowledge of the right to refuse consent is a necessary prerequisite to demonstrating a "voluntary" consent. Rather it is only by analyzing all the circumstances of an individual consent that it can be ascertained whether in fact it was voluntary or coerced. It is this careful sifting of the unique facts and circumstances of each case that is evidenced in our prior decisions involving consent searches.

For example in *Davis v. United States*, 328 U.S. 582, federal agents enforcing wartime gasoline-rationing regulations, arrested a filling station operator and asked to see his rationing coupons. He eventually unlocked a room where the agents discovered the coupons that formed the basis for his conviction. The District Court found that the petitioner had consented to the search — that although he had at first refused to turn the coupons over, he had soon been persuaded to do so and that force or threat of force had not been employed to persuade him. Concluding that it could not be said that this finding was erroneous, this Court, in an opinion by Mr. Justice Douglas that looked to all the circumstances surrounding the consent, affirmed the judgment of conviction: "The public character of the property, the fact that the demand was made during business hours at the place of business where the coupons were required to be kept, the existence of the right to inspect, the nature of the request, the fact that the initial refusal to turn the coupons over was soon followed by acquiescence in the demand — these circumstances all support the conclusion of the District Court."

Conversely, if under all the circumstances it has appeared that the consent was not given voluntarily — that it was coerced by threats or force, or granted only in submission to a claim of lawful authority — then we have found the consent invalid and the search unreasonable. *See, e.g., Bumper v. North Carolina*, 391 U.S., at 548–549. In *Bumper*, a 66-year-old Negro widow, who lived in a house located in a rural area at the end of an isolated mile-long dirt road, allowed four white law enforcement officials to search her home after they asserted they had a warrant to search the house. We held the alleged consent to be invalid, noting that "[w]hen a law enforcement officer claims authority to search a home under a warrant, he announces in effect that the occupant has no right to resist the search. The situation is instinct with coercion — albeit colorably lawful coercion. Where there is coercion there cannot be consent."

Implicit in all of these cases is the recognition that knowledge of a right to refuse is not a prerequisite of a voluntary consent. If the prosecution were required to demonstrate such knowledge, *Davis* could not have found consent without evidence of that knowledge. And similarly if the failure to prove such knowledge were sufficient to show an ineffective consent, the *Bumper* opinion would surely have focused upon the subjective mental state of the person who consented. Yet it did not.

In short, neither this Court's prior cases, nor the traditional definition of "voluntariness" requires proof of knowledge of a right to refuse as the *sine qua non* of an effective consent to a search.

C

It is said, however, that a "consent" is a "waiver" of a person's rights under the Fourth and Fourteenth Amendments. The argument is that by allowing the police to conduct a search, a person "waives" whatever right he had to prevent the police from searching. It is argued that under the doctrine of *Johnson v. Zerbst*, 304 U.S. 458, 464, to establish such a "waiver" the State must demonstrate "an intentional relinquishment or abandonment of a known right or privilege."

But these standards were enunciated in *Johnson* in the context of the safeguards of a fair criminal trial. Our cases do not reflect an uncritical demand for a knowing and intelligent waiver in every situation where a person has failed to invoke a constitutional protection.

A strict standard of waiver has been applied to those rights guaranteed to a criminal defendant to insure that he will be accorded the greatest possible opportunity to utilize every facet of the constitutional model of a fair criminal trial. Any trial conducted in derogation of that model leaves open the possibility that the trial reached an unfair result precisely because all the protections specified in the Constitution were not provided. A prime example is the right to counsel. For without that right, a wholly innocent accused faces the real and substantial danger that simply because of his lack of legal expertise he may be convicted. As Mr. Justice Harlan once wrote: "The sound reason why [the right to counsel] is so freely extended for a criminal trial is the severe injustice risked by confronting an untrained defendant with a range of technical points of law, evidence, and tactics familiar to the prosecutor but not to himself." The Constitution requires that every effort be made to see to it that a defendant in a criminal case has not unknowingly relinquished the basic protections that the Framers thought indispensable to a fair trial.

The guarantees of the Fourth Amendment stand "as a protection of quite different constitutional values — values reflecting the concern of our society for the right of each individual to be let alone. To recognize this is no more than to accord those values undiluted respect."

Nor can it even be said that a search, as opposed to an eventual trial, is somehow "unfair" if a person consents to a search. While the Fourth and Fourteenth Amendments limit the circumstances under which the police can conduct a search, there is nothing constitutionally suspect in a person's voluntarily allowing a search. The actual conduct of the search may be precisely the same as if the police had obtained a warrant. And, unlike those constitutional guarantees that protect a defendant at trial, it cannot be said every reasonable presumption ought to be indulged against voluntary relinquishment. We have only recently stated: "[I]t is no part of the policy underlying the Fourth and Fourteenth Amendments to discourage citizens from aiding to the utmost of their ability in the apprehension of criminals." *Coolidge*. Rather, the community has a real interest in encouraging consent, for the resulting search may yield necessary evidence for the solution and prosecution of crime, evidence that may insure that a wholly innocent person is not wrongly charged with a criminal offense.

It would be unrealistic to expect that in the informal, unstructured context of a consent search, a policeman, upon pain of tainting the evidence obtained, could make the detailed type of examination demanded by *Johnson*.

D

Much of what has already been said disposes of the argument that the Court's decision in the *Miranda* case requires the conclusion that knowledge of a right to refuse is an indispensable element of a valid consent. The considerations that informed the Court's holding in *Miranda* are simply inapplicable in the present case. In *Miranda* the Court found that the techniques of police questioning and the nature of custodial surroundings produce an inherently coercive situation. The Court concluded that "[u]nless adequate protective devices are employed to dispel the compulsion inherent in custodial surroundings, no statement obtained from the defendant can truly be the product of his free choice." And at another point the Court noted that "without proper safeguards the process of in-custody interrogation of persons suspected or accused of crime contains inherently compelling pressures which work to undermine the individual's will to resist and to compel him to speak where he would not otherwise do so freely."

In this case, there is no evidence of any inherently coercive tactics — either from the nature of the police questioning or the environment in which it took place. Indeed, since consent searches will normally occur on a person's own familiar territory, the specter of incommunicado police interrogation in some remote station house is simply inapposite.[36] There is no reason to believe, under circumstances such as are present here, that the response to a policeman's question is presumptively coerced; and there is, therefore, no reason to reject the traditional test for determining the voluntariness of a person's response. *Miranda*, of course, did not reach investigative questioning of a person not in custody, which is most directly analogous to the situation of a consent search, and it assuredly did not indicate that such questioning ought to be deemed inherently coercive.

It is also argued that the failure to require the Government to establish knowledge as a prerequisite to a valid consent, will relegate the Fourth Amendment to the special province of "the sophisticated, the knowledgeable and the privileged." We cannot agree. The traditional definition of voluntariness we accept today has always taken into account evidence of minimal schooling, low intelligence, and the lack of any effective warnings to a person of his rights; and the voluntariness of any statement taken under those conditions has been carefully scrutinized to determine whether it was in fact voluntarily given.

E

Our decision today is a narrow one. We hold only that when the subject of a search is not in custody and the State attempts to justify a search on the basis of his consent, the Fourth and Fourteenth Amendments require that it demonstrate that the consent was in fact voluntarily given, and not the result of duress or coercion, express or implied. Voluntariness is a question of fact to be determined from all the circumstances, and while the subject's knowledge of a right to refuse is a factor to be taken into account, the prosecution is not required to demonstrate such knowledge as a prerequisite to establishing a voluntary consent. Because the California court followed these principles in affirming the respondent's conviction, and because the Court of Appeals for the Ninth Circuit in remanding for an evidentiary hearing required more, its judgment must be reversed.

It is so ordered.

[JUSTICE POWELL, joined by JUSTICE REHNQUIST and CHIEF JUSTICE BURGER, while concurring in the opinion, would have held that Bustamonte's claim was not cognizable on habeas corpus.]

MR. JUSTICE MARSHALL, dissenting.

I

I believe that the Court misstates the true issue in this case. That issue is not, as the Court suggests whether the police overbore Alcala's will in eliciting his consent, but rather, whether a simple statement of assent to search, without more, should be sufficient to permit the police to search and thus act as a relinquishment of Alcala's

---

[36] [T]he present case does not require a determination of what effect custodial conditions might have on a search authorized solely by an alleged consent.

constitutional right to exclude the police. This Court has always scrutinized with great care claims that a person has forgone the opportunity to assert constitutional rights. I see no reason to give the claim that a person consented to a search any less rigorous scrutiny. Every case in this Court involving this kind of search has heretofore spoken of consent as a waiver.[4]

A

The Court assumes that the issue in this case is: what are the standards by which courts are to determine that consent is voluntarily given? It then imports into the law of search and seizure standards developed to decide entirely different questions about coerced confessions.[6]

The Fifth Amendment, in terms, provides that no person "shall be compelled in any criminal case to be a witness against himself." Nor is the interest protected by the Due Process Clause of the Fourteenth Amendment any different. The inquiry in a case where a confession is challenged as having been elicited in an unconstitutional manner is, therefore, whether the behavior of the police amounted to compulsion of the defendant. Because of the nature of the right to be free of compulsion, it would be pointless to ask whether a defendant knew of it before he made a statement; no sane person would knowingly relinquish a right to be free of compulsion. Thus, the questions of compulsion and of violation of the right itself are inextricably intertwined. The cases involving coerced confessions, therefore, pass over the question of knowledge of that right as irrelevant, and turn directly to the question of compulsion.

B

In contrast, this case deals not with "coercion," but with "consent," a subtly different concept to which different standards have been applied in the past. Freedom from coercion is a substantive right, guaranteed by the Fifth and Fourteenth Amendments. Consent, however, is a mechanism by which substantive requirements, otherwise applicable, are avoided. In the context of the Fourth Amendment, the relevant substantive requirements are that searches be conducted only after evidence justifying them has been submitted to an impartial magistrate for a determination of probable cause. There are, of course, exceptions to these

---

[4] The Court reads *Davis v. United States*, 328 U.S. 582 (1946), as upholding a search like the one in this case on the basis of consent. But it was central to the reasoning of the Court in that case that the items seized were the property of the Government temporarily in Davis' custody. The agents of the Government were thus simply demanding that property to which they had a lawful claim be returned to them. Because of this, the Court held that "permissible limits of persuasion are not so narrow as where private papers are sought." The opinion of the Court therefore explicitly disclaimed stating a general rule for ordinary searches for evidence. That the distinction, for purposes of Fourth Amendment analysis, between mere evidence and contraband or instrumentalities has now been abolished, *Warden v. Hayden*, 387 U.S. 294 (1967), is no reason to disregard the fact that when *Davis* was decided, that distinction played an important role in shaping analysis.

[6] That this application of the "domino" method of adjudication is misguided is shown, I believe, by the fact that the phrase "voluntary consent" seems redundant in a way that the phrase "voluntary confession" does not.

requirements based on a variety of exigent circumstances that make it impractical to invalidate a search simply because the police failed to get a warrant. But none of the exceptions relating to the overriding needs of law enforcement are applicable when a search is justified solely by consent. On the contrary, the needs of law enforcement are significantly more attenuated, for probable cause to search may be lacking but a search permitted if the subject's consent has been obtained. Thus, consent searches are permitted, not because such an exception to the requirements of probable cause and warrant is essential to proper law enforcement, but because we permit our citizens to choose whether or not they wish to exercise their constitutional rights. Our prior decisions simply do not support the view that a meaningful choice has been made solely because no coercion was brought to bear on the subject.

For example, in *Bumper*, four law enforcement officers went to the home of Bumper's grandmother. They announced that they had a search warrant, and she permitted them to enter. Subsequently, the prosecutor chose not to rely on the warrant, but attempted to justify the search by the woman's consent. We held that consent could not be established "by showing no more than acquiescence to a claim of lawful authority." We did not there inquire into all the circumstances, but focused on a single fact, the claim of authority, even though the grandmother testified that no threats were made. It may be that, on the facts of that case, her consent was under all the circumstances involuntary, but it is plain that we did not apply the test adopted by the Court today. And, whatever the posture of the case when it reached this Court, it could not be said that the police in *Bumper* acted in a threatening or coercive manner, for they did have the warrant they said they had; the decision not to rely on it was made long after the search, when the case came into court.

That case makes it clear that police officers may not courteously order the subject of a search simply to stand aside while the officers carry out a search they have settled on. Yet there would be no coercion or brutality in giving that order. No interests that the Court today recognizes would be damaged in such a search. Thus, all the police must do is conduct what will inevitably be a charade of asking for consent. If they display any firmness at all, a verbal expression of assent will undoubtedly be forthcoming. I cannot believe that the protections of the Constitution mean so little.

II

If consent to search means that a person has chosen to forgo his right to exclude the police from the place they seek to search, it follows that his consent cannot be considered a meaningful choice unless he knew that he could in fact exclude the police. The Court appears, however, to reject even the modest proposition that, if the subject of a search convinces the trier of fact that he did not know of his right to refuse assent to a police request for permission to search, the search must be held unconstitutional. For it says only that "knowledge of the right to refuse consent is one factor to be taken into account." I find this incomprehensible. I can think of no other situation in which we would say that a person agreed to some course of action if he convinced us that he did not know that there was some other course he might have pursued. I would therefore hold, at a minimum, that the prosecution may not rely on a purported consent to search if the subject of the search did not know that he could refuse to give consent. That, I think, is the import of *Bumper*. Where the police claim authority to search yet in fact lack such authority, the subject does not know that he may permissibly refuse them entry, and it is this lack of knowledge that invalidates the consent.

If one accepts this view, the question then is a simple one: must the Government show that the subject knew of his rights, or must the subject show that he lacked such knowledge?

I think that any fair allocation of the burden would require that it be placed on the prosecution. On this question, the Court indulges in what might be called the "straw man" method of adjudication. The Court responds to this suggestion by overinflating the burden. And, when it is suggested that the *prosecution's* burden of proof could be easily satisfied if the police informed the subject of his rights, the Court responds by refusing to require the *police* to make a "detailed" inquiry. If the Court candidly faced the real question of allocating the burden of proof, neither of these maneuvers would be available to it. If the burden is placed on the defendant, all the subject can do is to testify that he did not know of his rights. And I doubt that many trial judges will find for the defendant simply on the basis of that testimony. Precisely because the evidence is very hard to come by, courts have traditionally been reluctant to require a party to prove negatives such as the lack of knowledge.

In contrast, there are several ways by which the subject's knowledge of his rights may be shown. The subject may affirmatively demonstrate such knowledge by his responses at the time the search took place. Where, as in this case, the person giving consent is someone other than the defendant, the prosecution may require him to testify under oath. Denials of knowledge may be disproved by establishing that the subject had, in the recent past, demonstrated his knowledge of his rights, for example, by refusing entry when it was requested by the police. The prior experience or training of the subject might in some cases support an inference that he knew of his right to exclude the police.

The burden on the prosecutor would disappear, of course, if the police, at the time they requested consent to search, also told the subject that he had a right to refuse consent and that his decision to refuse would be respected. The Court's assertions to the contrary notwithstanding, there is nothing impractical about this method of satisfying the prosecution's burden of proof. It must be emphasized that the decision about informing the subject of his rights would lie with the officers seeking consent. If they believed that providing such information would impede their investigation, they might simply ask for consent, taking the risk that at some later date the prosecutor would be unable to prove that the subject knew of his rights or that some other basis for the search existed.

The Court contends that if an officer paused to inform the subject of his rights, the informality of the exchange would be destroyed. I doubt that a simple statement by an officer of an individual's right to refuse consent would do much to alter the informality of the exchange, except to alert the subject to a fact that he surely is entitled to know. It is not without significance that for many years the agents of the Federal Bureau of Investigation have routinely informed subjects of their right to refuse consent, when they request consent to search. The reported cases in which the police have informed subjects of their right to refuse consent show, also, that the information can be given without disrupting the casual flow of events. What evidence there is, then, rather strongly suggests that nothing disastrous would happen if the police, before requesting consent, informed the subject that he had a right to refuse consent and that his refusal would be respected.[12]

I must conclude with some reluctance that when the Court speaks of practicality, what it really is talking of is the continued ability of the police to capitalize on the ignorance of citizens so as to accomplish by subterfuge what they could not achieve by relying only on the knowing relinquishment of constitutional rights. Of course it would be "practical" for the police to ignore the commands of the Fourth Amendment, if by practicality we mean that more criminals will be apprehended, even though the constitutional rights of innocent people also go by the board. But such a practical advantage is achieved only at the cost of permitting the police to disregard the limitations that the Constitution places on their behavior, a cost that a constitutional democracy cannot long absorb.

I find nothing in the opinion of the Court to dispel my belief that, in such a case, as the Court of Appeals for the Ninth Circuit said, "[u]nder many circumstances a reasonable person might read an officer's 'May I' as the courteous expression of a demand backed by force of law." Most cases, in my view, are akin to *Bumper*: consent is ordinarily given as acquiescence in an implicit claim of authority to search. Permitting searches in such circumstances, without any assurance at all that the subject of the search knew that, by his consent, he was relinquishing his constitutional rights, is something that I cannot believe is sanctioned by the Constitution.

III

The proper resolution of this case turns, I believe, on a realistic assessment of the nature of the interchange between citizens and the police, and of the practical import of allocating the burden of proof in one way rather than another. The Court seeks to escape such assessments by escalating its rhetoric to unwarranted heights, but no matter how forceful the adjectives the Court uses, it cannot avoid being judged by how well its image of these interchanges accords with reality. Although the Court says without real elaboration that it "cannot agree," the holding today confines the protection of the Fourth Amendment against searches conducted without probable cause to the sophisticated, the knowledgeable, and, I might add, the few.[13] In the final analysis, the Court now sanctions a game of blindman's buff,

---

[12] The Court's suggestion that it would be "unrealistic" to require the officers to make "the detailed type of examination" involved when a court considers whether a defendant has waived a trial right deserves little comment. The question before us relates to the inquiry to be made in court when the prosecution seeks to establish that consent was given. I therefore do not address the Court's strained argument that one may waive constitutional rights without making a knowing and intentional choice so long as the rights do not relate to the fairness of a criminal trial. I would suggest, however, that that argument is fundamentally inconsistent with the law of unconstitutional conditions. In any event, I do not understand how one can relinquish a right without knowing of its existence, and that is the only issue in this case.

[13] The Court's half-hearted defense, that lack of knowledge is to be "taken into account," rings rather

in which the police always have the upper hand, for the sake of nothing more than the convenience of the police. But the guarantees of the Fourth Amendment were never intended to shrink before such an ephemeral and changeable interest. The Framers of the Fourth Amendment struck the balance against this sort of convenience and in favor of certain basic civil rights. It is not for this Court to restrike that balance because of its own views of the needs of law enforcement officers. I fear that that is the effect of the Court's decision today.

It is regrettable that the obsession with validating searches like that conducted in this case, so evident in the Court's hyperbole, has obscured the Court's vision of how the Fourth Amendment was designed to govern the relationship between police and citizen in our society. I believe that experience and careful reflection show how narrow and inaccurate that vision is, and I respectfully dissent.

[JUSTICE DOUGLAS and BRENNAN also dissented.]

QUESTIONS AND NOTES

1.   Do you believe that the need for consent searches is especially important for the police? Does your answer to this question impact on your judgment about the correctness of the Court's decision?

2.   What percentage of the populace do you believe would feel free to decline consent in the *Schneckloth* situation? Would you have felt free to refuse consent before you entered law school? Would you feel free to decline consent now?

3.   If the Marshall opinion had prevailed, and you were a police attorney, could you devise a warning that would not break the informality of the police/citizen dialogue? If you can, would it follow that the majority reached the wrong result?

4.   Is the concept of "voluntary consent" redundant as Justice Marshall suggests in fn. 6? If so, is he correct in rejecting the voluntary confession cases as appropriate analogues?

5.   Is there a good reason for rejecting the *Johnson v. Zerbst* waiver standard?

6.   Assuming that your answer to Question 5 was "yes," can you still make an argument against the Court's result?

7.   Might it not be to an innocent citizen's advantage to consent to a search and thereby dispel suspicion? If so, did the majority reach the correct result?

8.   Is there a meaningful distinction between *Schneckloth* and *Bumper*?

9.   Would a good citizen consent to a search? Why? Why not?

10.   Does consent to search a car include consent to search containers within a car? The Supreme Court said yes in *Florida v. Jimeno*, 500 U.S. 248 (1991). *Jimeno* was not a case in which the searchee attempted to limit the scope of the search.

---

hollow, in light of the apparent import of the opinion that even a subject who proves his lack of knowledge may nonetheless have consented "voluntarily," under the Court's peculiar definition of voluntariness.

11. Can consent be spatially limit (*i.e.: You may search everything in the car except under the driver's floor mat and in the glove compartment.*)? What should a policeman do when given that type of consent

12. Can consent be withdrawn, once given? Why? Why not?

13. Consider the following quote from a 1964 Ninth Circuit case called *Martinez v. United States*: "While it may not be 'in accord with common experience' for a guilty person to consent to a search which, if successful, may help to prove his guilt, it may nevertheless occur. Happily, not all criminals are highly intelligent and use the most effective tactics in their contacts with the police. Again happily, sometimes their contacts with the police confuse them, and they say and do things which, after deliberation, they regret. To whatever extent stupidity or confusion on the part of the guilty person contributes to the prompt acquisition by the police of evidence of crime, so that the police can get back to work on the numerous cases which may remain unsolved, society is the gainer and nobody is the loser of anything to which he is constitutionally entitled." Does Justice Stewart's opinion in *Schneckloth* essentially embrace *Martinez*? If so is that a good thing or a bad thing? Explain.

14. In *Rodriguez*, we consider the problem of third party consent.

ILLINOIS v. RODRIGUEZ
497 U.S. 177 (1990)

JUSTICE SCALIA delivered the opinion of the Court.

In *United States v. Matlock*, 415 U.S. 164 (1974), this Court reaffirmed that a warrantless entry and search by law enforcement officers does not violate the Fourth Amendment's proscription of "unreasonable searches and seizures" if the officers have obtained the consent of a third party who possesses common authority over the premises. The present case presents an issue we expressly reserved in *Matlock*: whether a warrantless entry is valid when based upon the consent of a third party whom the police, at the time of the entry, reasonably believe to possess common authority over the premises, but who in fact does not do so.

I

On July 26, 1985, police were summoned to the residence of Dorothy Jackson on South Wolcott in Chicago. They were met by Ms. Jackson's daughter, Gail Fischer, who showed signs of a severe beating. She told the officers that she had been assaulted by respondent Edward Rodriguez earlier that day in an apartment on South California. Fischer stated that Rodriguez was then asleep in the apartment, and she consented to travel there with the police in order to unlock the door with her key so that the officers could enter and arrest him. During this conversation, Fischer several times referred to the apartment on South California as "our" apartment, and said that she had clothes and furniture there. It is unclear whether she indicated that she currently lived at the apartment, or only that she used to live there.

The police officers drove to the apartment on South California, accompanied by Fischer. They did not obtain an arrest warrant for Rodriguez, nor did they seek a search warrant for the apartment. At the apartment, Fischer unlocked the door with her key and gave the officers permission to enter. They moved through the door into the living room, where they observed in plain view drug paraphernalia and containers filled with white powder that they believed (correctly, as later analysis showed) to be cocaine. They proceeded to the bedroom, where they found Rodriguez asleep and discovered additional containers of white powder in two open attaché cases. The officers arrested Rodriguez and seized the drugs and related paraphernalia.

II

The Fourth Amendment generally prohibits the warrantless entry of a person's home, whether to make an arrest or to search for specific objects. *Payton*. The prohibition does not apply, however, to situations in which voluntary consent has been obtained, either from the individual whose property is searched, see *Schneckloth*, or from a third party who possesses common authority over the premises, see *Matlock*. The State of Illinois contends that that exception applies in the present case.

As we stated in *Matlock*, "[c]ommon authority" rests "on mutual use of the property by persons generally having joint access or control for most purposes . . . ." The burden of establishing that common authority rests upon the State. On the basis of this record, it is clear that burden was not sustained. The evidence showed that although Fischer, with her two small children, had lived with Rodriguez beginning in December 1984, she had moved out on July 1, 1985, almost a month before the search at issue here, and had gone to live with her mother. She took her and her children's clothing with her, though leaving behind some furniture and household effects. During the period after July 1 she sometimes spent the night at Rodriguez's apartment, but never invited her friends there, and never went there herself when he was not home. Her name was not on the lease nor did she contribute to the rent. She had a key to the apartment, which she said at trial she had taken without Rodriguez's knowledge (though she testified at the preliminary hearing that Rodriguez had given her the key). On these facts the State has not established that, with respect to the South California apartment, Fischer had "joint access or control for most purposes." To the contrary, the Appellate Court's determination of no common authority over the apartment was obviously correct.

III

[R]espondent asserts that permitting a reasonable belief of common authority to validate an entry would cause a defendant's Fourth Amendment rights to be "vicariously waived." We disagree.

What Rodriguez is assured by the trial right of the exclusionary rule, where it applies, is that no evidence seized in violation of the Fourth Amendment will be introduced at his trial unless he consents. What he is assured by the Fourth Amendment itself, however, is not that no government search of his house will occur unless he consents; but that no such search will occur that is "unreasonable." There are various elements, of course, that can make a search of a person's house "reasonable" — one of which is the consent of the person or his cotenant. The essence of respondent's argument is that we should impose upon this element a requirement that we have not imposed upon other elements that regularly compel government officers to exercise judgment regarding the facts: namely, the requirement that their judgment be not only responsible but correct.

The fundamental objective that alone validates all unconsented government searches is, of course, the seizure of persons who have committed or are about to commit crimes, or of evidence related to crimes. But "reasonableness," with respect to this necessary element, does not demand that the government be factually correct in its assessment that that is what a search will produce. Warrants need only be supported by "probable cause," which demands no more than a proper "assessment of probabilities in particular factual contexts . . . ." *Gates.* If a magistrate, based upon seemingly reliable but factually inaccurate information, issues a warrant for the search of a house in which the sought-after felon is not present, has never been present, and was never likely to have been present, the owner of that house suffers one of the inconveniences we all expose ourselves to as the cost of living in a safe society; he does not suffer a violation of the Fourth Amendment.

Another element often, though not invariably, required in order to render an unconsented search "reasonable" is, of course, that the officer be authorized by a valid warrant. Here also we have not held that "reasonableness" precludes error with respect to those factual judgments that law enforcement officials are expected to make. In *Maryland v. Garrison*, 480 U.S. 79 (1987) a warrant supported by probable cause with respect to one apartment was erroneously issued for an entire floor that was divided (though not clearly) into two apartments. We upheld the search of the apartment not properly covered by the warrant. We said:

> [T]he validity of the search of respondent's apartment pursuant to a warrant authorizing the search of the entire third floor depends on whether the officers' failure to realize the overbreadth of the warrant was objectively understandable and reasonable. Here it unquestionably was. The objective facts available to the officers at the time suggested no distinction between [the suspect's] apartment and the third-floor premises.

The ordinary requirement of a warrant is sometimes supplanted by other elements that render the unconsented search "reasonable." Here also we have not held that the Fourth Amendment requires factual accuracy. A warrant is not needed, for example, where the search is incident to an arrest. In *Hill v. California*, 401 U.S. 797 (1971), we upheld a search incident to an arrest, even though the arrest was made of the wrong person. We said:

> The upshot was that the officers in good faith believed Miller was Hill and arrested him. They were quite wrong as it turned out, and subjective good-faith belief would not in itself justify either the arrest or the subsequent search. But sufficient probability, not certainty, is the touchstone of reasonableness under the Fourth Amendment and on the record before us the officers' mistake was understandable and the arrest a

reasonable response to the situation facing them at the time.

Stoner v. California, 376 U.S. 483 (1964) is in our view not to the contrary. There, in holding that police had improperly entered the defendant's hotel room based on the consent of a hotel clerk, we stated that "the rights protected by the Fourth Amendment are not to be eroded . . . by unrealistic doctrines of 'apparent authority.'" It is ambiguous, of course, whether the word "unrealistic" is descriptive or limiting — that is, whether we were condemning as unrealistic all reliance upon apparent authority, or whether we were condemning only such reliance upon apparent authority as is unrealistic. Similarly ambiguous is the opinion's earlier statement that "there [is no] substance to the claim that the search was reasonable because the police, relying upon the night clerk's expressions of consent, had a reasonable basis for the belief that the clerk had authority to consent to the search." Was there no substance to it because it failed as a matter of law, or because the facts could not possibly support it? At one point the opinion does seem to speak clearly:

> It is important to bear in mind that it was the petitioner's constitutional right which was at stake here, and not the night clerk's nor the hotel's. It was a right, therefore, which only the petitioner could waive by word or deed, either directly or through an agent.

But as we have discussed, what is at issue when a claim of apparent consent is raised is not whether the right to be free of searches has been *waived*, but whether the right to be free of *unreasonable* searches has been *violated*. Even if one does not think the *Stoner* opinion had this subtlety in mind, the supposed clarity of its foregoing statement is immediately compromised, as follows:

> It is true that the night clerk clearly and unambiguously consented to the search. But there is nothing in the record to indicate that *the police had any basis whatsoever to believe that* the night clerk had been authorized by the petitioner to permit the police to search the petitioner's room.

(emphasis added). The italicized language should have been deleted, of course, if the statement two sentences earlier meant that an appearance of authority could never validate a search. In the last analysis, one must admit that the rationale of *Stoner* was ambiguous — and perhaps deliberately so. It is at least a reasonable reading of the case, and perhaps a preferable one, that the police could not rely upon the obtained consent because they knew it came from a hotel clerk, knew that the room was rented and exclusively occupied by the defendant, and could not reasonably have believed that the former had general access to or control over the latter.

As *Stoner* demonstrates, what we hold today does not suggest that law enforcement officers may always accept a person's invitation to enter premises. Even when the invitation is accompanied by an explicit assertion that the person lives there, the surrounding circumstances could conceivably be such that a reasonable person would doubt its truth and not act upon it without further inquiry. As with other factual determinations bearing upon search and seizure, determination of consent to enter must "be judged against an objective standard: would the facts available to the officer at the moment . . . 'warrant a man of reasonable caution in the belief'" that the consenting party had authority over the premises? If not, then warrantless entry without further inquiry is unlawful unless authority actually exists. But if so, the search is valid.

In the present case, the Appellate Court found it unnecessary to determine whether the officers reasonably believed that Fischer had the authority to consent, because it ruled as a matter of law that a reasonable belief could not validate the entry. Since we find that ruling to be in error, we remand for consideration of that question. The judgment of the Illinois Appellate Court is reversed and remanded for further proceedings not inconsistent with this opinion.

So ordered.

JUSTICE MARSHALL, with whom JUSTICE BRENNAN and JUSTICE STEVENS join, dissenting.

Dorothy Jackson summoned police officers to her house to report that her daughter Gail Fischer had been beaten. Fischer told police that Ed Rodriguez, her boyfriend, was her assaulter. During an interview with Fischer, one of the officers asked if Rodriguez dealt in narcotics. Fischer did not respond. Fischer did agree, however, to the officers' request to let them into Rodriguez's apartment so that they could arrest him for battery. The police, without a warrant and despite the absence of an exigency, entered Rodriguez's home to arrest him. As a result of their entry, the police discovered narcotics that the State subsequently sought to introduce in a drug prosecution against Rodriguez.

The baseline for the reasonableness of a search or seizure in the home is the presence of a warrant. Indeed, "searches and seizures inside a home without a warrant are presumptively unreasonable." Exceptions to the warrant requirement must therefore serve "compelling" law enforcement goals. Because the sole law enforcement purpose underlying third-party consent searches is avoiding the inconvenience of securing a warrant, a departure from the warrant requirement is not justified simply because an officer reasonably believes a third party has consented to a search of the defendant's home. In holding otherwise, the majority ignores our longstanding view that "the informed and deliberate determinations of magistrates . . . as to what searches and seizures are permissible under the Constitution are to be preferred over the hurried action of officers and others who may happen to make arrests."

I

The Court has tolerated departures from the warrant requirement only when an exigency makes a warrantless search imperative to the safety of the police and of the community. In the absence of an exigency, then, warrantless home searches and seizures are unreasonable under the Fourth Amendment. The weighty constitutional interest in preventing unauthorized intrusions into the home overrides any law enforcement interest in relying on the reasonable but potentially mistaken belief that a third party has authority to consent to such a search or seizure. Indeed, as the present case illustrates, only the minimal interest in avoiding the inconvenience of obtaining a warrant weighs in on the law enforcement side.

Unlike searches conducted pursuant to the recognized exceptions to the warrant requirement, third-party consent searches are not based on an exigency and therefore serve no compelling social goal. Police officers, when faced with the choice of relying on consent by a third party or securing a warrant, should secure a warrant, and must therefore accept the risk of error should they instead choose to rely on consent.

II

Our prior cases discussing searches based on third-party consent have never suggested that such searches are "reasonable." In *Matlock*, this Court upheld a warrantless search conducted pursuant to the consent of a third party who was living with the defendant. The Court rejected the defendant's challenge to the search, stating that a person who permits others to have "joint access or control for most purposes . . . assume[s] the risk that [such persons] might permit the common area to be searched." As the Court's assumption-of-risk analysis makes clear, third-party consent limits a person's ability to challenge the reasonableness of the search only because that person voluntarily has relinquished some of his expectation of privacy by sharing access or control over his property with another person.

A search conducted pursuant to an officer's reasonable but mistaken belief that a third party had authority to consent is thus on an entirely different constitutional footing from one based on the consent of a third party who in fact has such authority. Even if the officers reasonably believed that Fischer had authority to consent, she did not, and Rodriguez's expectation of privacy was therefore undiminished. Rodriguez accordingly can challenge the warrantless intrusion into his home as a violation of the Fourth Amendment. This conclusion flows directly from *Stoner*. There, the Court required the suppression of evidence seized in reliance on a hotel clerk's consent to a warrantless search of a guest's room. The Court reasoned that the guest's right to be free of unwarranted intrusion "was a right . . . which only [he] could waive by word or deed, either directly or through an agent." Accordingly, the Court rejected resort to "unrealistic doctrines of 'apparent authority' " as a means of upholding the search to which the guest had not consented.

III

Acknowledging that the third party in this case lacked authority to consent, the majority seeks to rely on cases suggesting that reasonable but mistaken factual judgments by police will not invalidate otherwise reasonable searches. The majority reads these cases as establishing a "general rule" that "what is generally demanded of the many factual determinations that must regularly be made by agents of the government — whether the magistrate issuing a warrant, the police officer executing a warrant, or the police officer conducting a search or seizure under one of the exceptions to the warrant requirement — is not that they always be correct, but that they always be reasonable."

The majority's assertion, however, is premised on the erroneous assumption that third-party consent searches are generally reasonable. Because reasonable factual errors by law enforcement officers will not validate unreasonable searches, the reasonableness of the officer's mistaken belief that the third party had authority to consent is irrelevant.

The majority's reliance on *Garrison* is also misplaced. In *Garrison*, the police obtained a valid warrant for the search of the "third floor apartment" of a building whose third floor in fact housed two apartments. Although the police had probable cause to search only one of the apartments, they entered both apartments because "[t]he objective facts available to the officers at the time suggested no distinction between [the apartment for which they legitimately had the warrant and the entire third floor]." The Court held that the officers' reasonable mistake of fact did not render the search unconstitutional. Because searches based on warrants are generally reasonable, the officers' reasonable mistake of fact did not render their search "unreasonable." This reasoning is evident in the Court's conclusion that little would be gained by adopting additional burdens "over and above the bedrock requirement that, with the exceptions we have traced in our cases, the police may conduct searches only pursuant to a reasonably detailed warrant."

Garrison thus tells us nothing about the reasonableness under the Fourth Amendment of a warrantless arrest in the home based on an officer's reasonable but mistaken belief that the third party consenting to the arrest was empowered to do so.

IV

Our cases demonstrate that third-party consent searches are free from constitutional challenge only to the extent that they rest on consent by a party empowered to do so. The majority's conclusion to the contrary ignores the legitimate expectations of privacy on which individuals are entitled to rely. That a person who allows another joint access over his property thereby limits his expectation of privacy does not justify trampling the rights of a person who has not similarly relinquished any of his privacy expectation.

Instead of judging the validity of consent searches, as we have in the past, based on whether a defendant has in fact limited his expectation of privacy, the Court today carves out an additional exception to the warrant requirement for third-party consent searches without pausing to consider whether " 'the exigencies of the situation' make the needs of law enforcement so compelling that the warrantless search is objectively reasonable under the Fourth Amendment." Where this free-floating creation of "reasonable" exceptions to the warrant requirement will end, now that the Court has departed from the balancing approach that has long been part of our Fourth Amendment jurisprudence, is unclear. But by allowing a person to be subjected to a warrantless search in his home without his consent and without exigency, the majority has taken away some of the liberty that the Fourth Amendment was designed to protect.

QUESTIONS AND NOTES

1. Is the theory of a consent search that it is not a search at all or that it is a reasonable search? What would Scalia say? What would Marshall say?

2. Does your answer to Question 1 affect the result in *Rodriguez*?

3. Are consent searches to be encouraged because they prevent (or reduce) adversarial police/citizen contact?

4. On the other hand, are consent searches to be discouraged because they circumvent the salutary principles of the Fourth Amendment?

5. Do your answers to Questions 3 and 4 affect your assessment of *Rodriguez*? Explain.

6. Had you been on the Court, how would you have resolved *Rodriguez*? Why?

7. We conclude this section with the following problem case:

PROBLEM

Respondent Scott Randolph and his wife, Janet, separated in late May 2001, when she left the marital residence in Americus, Georgia, and went to stay with her parents in Canada, taking their son and some belongings. In July, she returned to the Americus house with the child, though the record does not reveal whether her object was reconciliation or retrieval of remaining possessions.

On the morning of July 6, she complained to the police that after a domestic dispute her husband took their son away, and when officers reached the house she told them that her husband was a cocaine user whose habit had caused financial troubles. She mentioned the marital problems and said that she and their son had only recently returned after a stay of several weeks with her parents. Shortly after the police arrived, Scott Randolph returned and explained that he had removed the child to a neighbor's house out of concern that his wife might take the boy out of the country again; he denied cocaine use, and countered that it was in fact his wife who abused drugs and alcohol.

One of the officers, Sergeant Murray, went with Janet Randolph to reclaim the child, and when they returned she not only renewed her complaints about her husband's drug use, but also volunteered that there were "items of drug evidence' " in the house. Sergeant Murray asked Scott Randolph for permission to search the house, which he unequivocally refused.

The sergeant turned to Janet Randolph for consent to search, which she readily gave. She led the officer upstairs to a bedroom that she identified as Scott's, where the sergeant noticed a section of a drinking straw with a powdery residue he suspected was cocaine. He then left the house to get an evidence bag from his car and to call the district attorney's office, which instructed him to stop the search and apply for a warrant. When Sergeant Murray returned to the house, Janet Randolph withdrew her consent. The police took the straw to the police station, along with the Randolphs. After getting a search warrant, they returned to the house and seized further evidence of drug use, on the basis of which Scott Randolph was indicted for possession of cocaine.

He moved to suppress the evidence, as products of a warrantless search of his house unauthorized by his wife's consent over his express refusal. The trial court denied the motion, ruling that Janet Randolph had common authority to consent to the search.

We granted certiorari to resolve a split of authority on whether one occupant may give law enforcement effective consent to search shared premises, as against a co-tenant who is present and states a refusal to permit the search.

How should the Court resolve this case? Should it matter who spoke first? Should it matter whether Janet Randolph had relinquished common authority? Explain. For the Supreme Court's answer, see *Georgia v. Randolph* (2006).

Suppose after being refused permission by the suspect he is arrested and the police return to the premises and receive permission form the suspect's co-tenant? Is that the same problem as *Randolph*, or a different one? Explain. For the Court's answer, see *Fernandez v. California*, 134 S. Ct. 1126 (2014).

Chapter 12

ARE WE MOVING TOWARD OPEN SEASON ON AUTOMOBILES IN THE 21ST CENTURY?

Recall that in *Illinois v. Gates* (Ch. 2, *supra*), Justice Rehnquist suggested that a constitutional jurist should not accept extreme arguments on either side of the question, but should endeavor to "hold the balance true." In six of the seven cases in this Section (all except *Knowles v. Iowa*), the Court upheld the police officer, frequently on the broadest possible ground. Although, undoubtedly something could be said in favor of each of these decisions, their composite impact is such that the most marginally competent police officer could figure out how to search any car that he desired to search. Because most of the earlier automobile cases (80s and early 90s were not exactly anti-police, these cases raise the question of whether the Fourth Amendment is any limitation at all to a competent policeman.

We start with *Whren*, a case that, broadly construed, could significantly extend police power, and more importantly, unchanneled police power.

WHREN v. UNITED STATES
517 U.S. 806 (1996)

Justice Scalia delivered the opinion of the Court.

In this case we decide whether the temporary detention of a motorist who the police have probable cause to believe has committed a civil traffic violation is inconsistent with the Fourth Amendment's prohibition against unreasonable seizures unless a reasonable officer would have been motivated to stop the car by a desire to enforce the traffic laws.

I

On the evening of June 10, 1993, plainclothes vice-squad officers of the District of Columbia Metropolitan Police Department were patrolling a "high drug area" of the city in an unmarked car. Their suspicions were aroused when they passed a dark Pathfinder truck with temporary license plates and youthful occupants waiting at a stop sign, the driver looking down into the lap of the passenger at his right. The truck remained stopped at the intersection for what seemed an unusually long time — more than 20 seconds. When the police car executed a U-turn in order to head back toward the truck, the Pathfinder turned suddenly to its right, without signaling, and sped off at an "unreasonable" speed. The policemen followed, and in a short while overtook the Pathfinder when it stopped behind other traffic at a red light. They pulled up alongside, and Officer Ephraim Soto stepped out and approached the driver's door, identifying himself as a police officer and directing the driver, petitioner Brown, to put the vehicle in park. When Soto drew up to the driver's window, he immediately observed two large plastic bags of what appeared to be crack cocaine in petitioner Whren's hands. Petitioners were arrested, and quantities of several types of illegal drugs were retrieved from the vehicle.

II

The Fourth Amendment guarantees "[t]he right of the people to be secure in their persons, houses, papers, and effects, against unreasonable searches and seizures." Temporary detention of individuals during the stop of an automobile by the police, even if only for a brief period and for a limited purpose, constitutes a "seizure" of "persons" within the meaning of this provision. See *Delaware v. Prouse.* An automobile stop is thus subject to the constitutional imperative that it not be "unreasonable" under the circumstances. As a general matter, the decision to stop an automobile is reasonable where the police have probable cause to believe that a traffic violation has occurred. *See Prouse; Pennsylvania v. Mimms*, 434 U.S. 106, 109 (1977) (*per curiam*).

Petitioners accept that Officer Soto had probable cause to believe that various provisions of the District of Columbia traffic code had been violated. They argue, however, that "in the unique context of civil traffic regulations" probable cause is not enough. Since, they contend, the use of automobiles is so heavily and minutely regulated that total compliance with traffic and safety rules is nearly impossible, a police officer will almost invariably be able to catch any given motorist in a technical violation. This creates the temptation to use traffic stops as a means of investigating other law violations, as to which no probable cause or even articulable suspicion exists. Petitioners, who are both black, further contend that police officers might decide which motorists to stop based on decidedly impermissible factors, such as the race of the car's occupants. To avoid this danger, they say, the Fourth Amendment test for traffic stops should be, not the normal one (applied by the Court of Appeals) of whether probable cause existed to justify the stop; but rather, whether a police officer, acting reasonably, would have made the stop for the reason given.

A

Petitioners contend that the standard they propose is consistent with our past cases' disapproval of police attempts to use valid bases of action against citizens as pretexts for pursuing other investigatory agendas. We are reminded that in *Florida v. Wells*, we stated that "an inventory search must not be used as a ruse for a general rummaging in order to discover incriminating evidence"; that in *Colorado v. Bertine*, in approving an inventory search, we apparently thought it significant that there had been "no showing that the police, who were following standard procedures, acted in bad faith or for the sole purpose of investigation"; and that in *New York v. Burger*, 482 U.S. 691, 716–717, n. 27 (1987), we observed, in upholding the constitutionality of a warrantless administrative inspection, that the search did not appear to be "a 'pretext' for obtaining evidence of . . . violation of . . . penal laws." But only an undiscerning reader would regard these cases as endorsing the principle that ulterior motives can invalidate police conduct that is justifiable on the basis of probable cause to believe that a violation of law has occurred. In each case we were addressing the validity of a search conducted in the *absence* of probable cause. Our quoted statements simply explain that the exemption from the need for probable cause (and warrant), which is accorded to searches made for the purpose of inventory or administrative regulation, is not accorded to searches that are not made for those purposes.

Petitioners also rely upon *Colorado v. Bannister*, 449 U.S. 1 (1980) (*per curiam*), a case which, like this one, involved a traffic stop as the prelude to a plain-view sighting and arrest on charges wholly unrelated to the basis for the stop. Petitioners point to our statement that "there was no evidence whatsoever that the officer's presence to issue a traffic citation was a pretext to confirm any other previous suspicion about the occupants" of the car. That dictum *at most* demonstrates that the Court in *Bannister* found no need to inquire into the question now under discussion; not that it was certain of the answer. And it may demonstrate even less than that: if by "pretext" the Court meant that the officer really had not seen the car speeding, the statement would mean only that there was no reason to doubt probable cause for the traffic stop.

It would, moreover, be anomalous, to say the least, to treat a statement in a footnote in the *per curiam Bannister* opinion as indicating a reversal of our prior law. Petitioners' difficulty is not simply a lack of affirmative support for their position. Not only have we never held, outside the context of inventory search or administrative inspection (discussed above), that an officer's motive invalidates objectively justifiable behavior under the Fourth Amendment; but we have repeatedly held and asserted the contrary. In *United States v. Villamonte-Marquez*, 462 U.S. 579, 584, n. 3 (1983), we held that an otherwise valid warrantless boarding of a vessel by customs officials was not rendered invalid "because the customs officers were accompanied by a Louisiana state policeman, and were following an informant's tip that a vessel in the ship channel was thought to be carrying marihuana." We flatly dismissed the idea that an ulterior motive might serve to strip the agents of their legal justification. In *United States v. Robinson*, 414 U.S. 218 (1973), we held that a traffic-violation arrest (of the sort here) would not be rendered invalid by the fact that it was "a mere pretext for a narcotics search," and that a lawful postarrest search of the person would not be rendered invalid by the fact that it was not motivated by the officer-safety concern that justifies such searches. *See also Gustafson v. Florida*, 414 U.S. 260, 266 (1973). And in *Scott v. United States*, 436 U.S. 128, 138 (1978), in rejecting the contention that wiretap evidence was subject to exclusion because the agents conducting the tap had failed to make any effort to comply with the statutory requirement that unauthorized acquisitions be minimized, we said that "[s]ubjective intent alone . . . does not make otherwise lawful conduct illegal or unconstitutional." We described *Robinson* as having established that "the fact that the officer does not have the state of mind which is hypothecated by the reasons which provide the legal justification for the officer's action does not invalidate the action taken as long as the circumstances, viewed objectively, justify that action."

We think these cases foreclose any argument that the constitutional reasonableness of traffic stops depends on the actual motivations of the individual officers involved. We of course agree with petitioners that the Constitution prohibits selective enforcement of the law based on considerations such as race. But the constitutional basis for objecting to intentionally discriminatory application of laws is the Equal Protection Clause, not the Fourth Amendment. Subjective intentions play no role in ordinary, probable-cause Fourth Amendment analysis.

B

Recognizing that we have been unwilling to entertain Fourth Amendment challenges based on the actual motivations of individual officers, petitioners disavow any intention to make the individual officer's subjective good faith the touchstone of "reasonableness." They insist that the standard they have put forward — whether the officer's conduct deviated materially from usual police practices, so that a reasonable officer in the same circumstances would not have made the stop for the reasons given — is an "objective" one.

But although framed in empirical terms, this approach is plainly and indisputably driven by subjective considerations. Its whole purpose is to prevent the police from doing under the guise of enforcing the traffic code what they would like to do for different reasons. Petitioners' proposed standard may not use the word "pretext," but it is designed to combat nothing other than the perceived "danger" of the pretextual stop, albeit only indirectly and over the run of cases. Instead of asking whether the individual officer had the proper state of mind, the petitioners would have us ask, in effect, whether (based on general police practices) it is plausible to believe that the officer had the proper state of mind.

Why one would frame a test designed to combat pretext in such fashion that the court cannot take into account *actual and admitted pretext* is a curiosity that can only be explained by the fact that our cases have foreclosed the more sensible option. If those cases were based only upon the evidentiary difficulty of establishing subjective intent, petitioners' attempt to root out subjective vices through objective means might make sense. But they were not based only upon that, or indeed even principally upon that. Their principal basis — which applies equally to attempts to reach subjective intent through ostensibly objective means — is simply that the Fourth Amendment's concern with "reasonableness" allows certain actions to be taken in certain circumstances, *whatever* the subjective intent. *See, e.g., Robinson* ("Since it is the fact of custodial arrest which gives rise to the authority to search, it is of no moment that [the officer] did not indicate any subjective fear of the [arrestee] or that he did not himself suspect that [the arrestee] was armed"); *Gustafson* (same). But even if our concern had been only an evidentiary one, petitioners' proposal would by no means assuage it. Indeed, it seems to us somewhat easier to figure out the intent of an individual officer than to plumb the collective consciousness of law enforcement in order to determine whether a "reasonable officer" would have been moved to act upon the traffic violation. While police manuals and standard procedures may sometimes provide objective assistance, ordinarily one would be reduced to speculating about the hypothetical reaction of a hypothetical constable — an exercise that might be called virtual subjectivity.

Moreover, police enforcement practices, even if they could be practicably assessed by a judge, vary from place to place and from time to time. We cannot accept that the search and seizure protections of the Fourth Amendment are so variable, and can be made to turn upon such trivialities. The difficulty is illustrated by petitioners' arguments in this case. Their claim that a reasonable officer would not have made this stop is based largely on District of Columbia police regulations which permit plainclothes officers in unmarked vehicles to enforce traffic laws "only in the case of a violation that is so grave as to pose an *immediate threat* to the safety of others." Metropolitan Police Department-Washington, D. C., General Order 303.1, pt. 1, Objectives and Policies (A)(2)(4) (Apr. 30, 1992). This basis of invalidation would not apply in jurisdictions that had a different practice. And it would not have applied even in the District of Columbia, if Officer Soto had been wearing a uniform or patrolling in a marked police cruiser.

Petitioners argue that our cases support insistence upon police adherence to standard practices as an objective means of rooting out pretext. They cite no holding to that effect, and dicta in only two cases. In *Abel v. United States*, 362 U.S. 217 (1960), the petitioner had been arrested by the Immigration and Naturalization Service (INS), on the basis of an administrative warrant that, he claimed, had been issued on pretextual grounds in order to enable the Federal Bureau of Investigation (FBI) to search his room after his arrest. We regarded this as an allegation of "serious misconduct," but rejected Abel's claims on the ground that "[a] finding of bad faith is . . . not open to us on th[e] record" in light of the findings below, including the finding that "'the proceedings taken by the [INS] differed in no respect from what would have been done in the case of an individual concerning whom [there was no pending FBI investigation].'" But it is a long leap from the proposition that following regular procedures is some evidence of lack of pretext to the proposition that failure to follow regular procedures *proves* (or is an operational substitute for) pretext. *Abel*, moreover, did not involve the assertion that pretext could invalidate a search or seizure for which there was probable cause — and even what it said about pretext in other contexts is plainly inconsistent with the views we later stated in *Robinson, Gustafson, Scott,* and *Villamonte-Marquez.* In the other case claimed to contain supportive dicta, *United States v. Robinson,* in approving a search incident to an arrest for driving without a license, we noted that the arrest was "not a departure from established police department practice." That was followed, however, by the statement that "[w]e leave for another day questions which would arise on facts different from these." This is not even a dictum that purports to provide an answer, but merely one that leaves the question open.

III

In what would appear to be an elaboration on the "reasonable officer" test, petitioners argue that the balancing inherent in any Fourth Amendment inquiry requires us to weigh the governmental and individual interests implicated in a traffic stop such as we have here. That balancing, petitioners claim, does not support investigation of minor traffic infractions by plainclothes police in unmarked vehicles; such investigation only minimally advances the government's interest in traffic safety, and may indeed retard it by producing motorist confusion and alarm — a view said to be supported by the Metropolitan Police Department's own regulations generally prohibiting this practice. And as for the Fourth Amendment interests of the individuals concerned, petitioners point out that our cases acknowledge that even ordinary traffic stops entail "a possibly unsettling show of authority"; that they at best "interfere with freedom of movement, are inconvenient, and consume time" and at worst "may create substantial anxiety," *Prouse*. That anxiety is likely to be even more pronounced when the stop is conducted by plainclothes officers in unmarked cars.

It is of course true that in principle every Fourth Amendment case, since it turns upon a "reasonableness" determination, involves a balancing of all relevant factors. With rare exceptions not applicable here, however, the result of that balancing is not in doubt where the search or seizure is based upon probable cause. That is why petitioners must rely upon cases like *Prouse* to provide examples of actual "balancing" analysis. There, the police action in question was a random traffic stop for the purpose of checking a motorist's license and vehicle registration, a practice that — like the practices at issue in the inventory search and administrative inspection cases upon which petitioners rely in making their "pretext" claim — involves police intrusion without the probable cause that is its traditional justification. Our opinion in *Prouse* expressly distinguished the case from a stop based on precisely what is at issue here: "probable cause to believe that a driver is violating any one of the multitude of applicable traffic and equipment regulations." It noted approvingly that "[t]he foremost method of enforcing traffic and vehicle safety regulations . . . is acting upon observed violations," which afford the " 'quantum of individualized suspicion' " necessary to ensure that police discretion is sufficiently constrained.

Where probable cause has existed, the only cases in which we have found it necessary actually to perform the "balancing" analysis involved searches or seizures conducted in an extraordinary manner, unusually harmful to an individual's privacy or even physical interests — such as, for example, seizure by means of deadly force, *see Tennessee v. Garner*, unannounced entry into a home, *see Wilson v. Arkansas*, 514 U.S. 927 (1995), entry into a home without a warrant, *see Welsh v. Wisconsin*, or physical penetration of the body, *see Winston v. Lee* [Chapter 13, *infra*]. The making of a traffic stop out-of-uniform does not remotely qualify as such an extreme practice, and so is governed by the usual rule that probable cause to believe the law has been broken "outbalances" private interest in avoiding police contact.

Petitioners urge as an extraordinary factor in this case that the "multitude of applicable traffic and equipment regulations" is so large and so difficult to obey perfectly that virtually everyone is guilty of violation, permitting the police to single out almost whomever they wish for a stop. But we are aware of no principle that would allow us to decide at what point a code of law becomes so expansive and so commonly violated that infraction itself can no longer be the ordinary measure of the lawfulness of enforcement. And even if we could identify such exorbitant codes, we do not know by what standard (or what right) we would decide, as petitioners would have us do, which particular provisions are sufficiently important to merit enforcement.

For the run-of-the-mine case, which this surely is, we think there is no realistic alternative to the traditional common-law rule that probable cause justifies a search and seizure.

Here the District Court found that the officers had probable cause to believe that petitioners had violated the traffic code. That rendered the stop reasonable under the Fourth Amendment, the evidence thereby discovered admissible, and the upholding of the convictions by the Court of Appeals for the District of Columbia Circuit correct.

Judgment affirmed.

QUESTIONS AND NOTES

1.   Should a stop in violation of the local police manual be *per se* unreasonable? Why do you suppose that a unanimous Court was unwilling to so hold?

2.   Is there a middle ground between actually getting into each officer's subjective intentions and allowing any officer to stop anybody for a traffic violation? If so, why didn't the Court take it?

3.   To the extent that police engage in the (at least) constitutionally-suspect practice of racial profiling, does *Whren* practically give *carte blanche* approval to the practice? Should that problem have been a greater concern to the Court? Why? Why not?

4.   Later in this Chapter, we will examine whether *Whren* applies to a pretextual *arrest* as well as a pretextual stop for a traffic violation.

5.   Do you think that the police had reasonable suspicion to justify the stop here? If so, why wasn't the conviction affirmed on that ground?

6.   Now, we turn to *Robinette* to examine the scope of police power pursuant to a routine traffic stop.

OHIO v. ROBINETTE
519 U.S. 33 (1996)

CHIEF JUSTICE REHNQUIST delivered the opinion of the Court.

We are here presented with the question whether the Fourth Amendment requires that a lawfully seized defendant must be advised that he is "free to go" before his consent to search will be recognized as voluntary. We hold that it does not.

This case arose on a stretch of Interstate 70 north of Dayton, Ohio, where the posted speed limit was 45 miles per hour because of construction. Respondent Robert D. Robinette was clocked at 69 miles per hour as he drove his car along this stretch of road, and was stopped by Deputy Roger Newsome of the Montgomery

County Sheriff's office. Newsome asked for and was handed Robinette's driver's license, and he ran a computer check which indicated that Robinette had no previous violations. Newsome then asked Robinette to step out of his car, turned on his mounted video camera, issued a verbal warning to Robinette, and returned his license.

At this point, Newsome asked, "One question before you get gone: [A]re you carrying any illegal contraband in your car? Any weapons of any kind, drugs, anything like that?" Robinette answered "no" to these questions, after which Deputy Newsome asked if he could search the car. Robinette consented. In the car, Deputy Newsome discovered a small amount of marijuana and, in a film container, a pill which was later determined to be methylenedioxymethamphetamine (MDMA). Robinette was then arrested and charged with knowing possession of a controlled substance, MDMA, in violation of Ohio [law].

Before trial, Robinette unsuccessfully sought to suppress this evidence. He then pleaded "no contest," and was found guilty. On appeal, the Ohio Court of Appeals reversed, ruling that the search resulted from an unlawful detention. The Supreme Court of Ohio, by a divided vote, affirmed. In its opinion, that court established a bright-line prerequisite for consensual interrogation under these circumstances:

> The right, guaranteed by the federal and Ohio Constitutions, to be secure in one's person and property requires that citizens stopped for traffic offenses be clearly informed by the detaining officer when they are free to go after a valid detention, before an officer attempts to engage in a consensual interrogation. Any attempt at consensual interrogation must be preceded by the phrase "At this time you legally are free to go" or by words of similar import.

We granted certiorari to review this *per se* rule, and we now reverse.

We think that under our recent decision in *Whren* (decided after the Supreme Court of Ohio decided the present case), the subjective intentions of the officer did not make the continued detention of respondent illegal under the Fourth Amendment. As we made clear in *Whren*, " 'the fact that [an] officer does not have the state of mind which is hypothecated by the reasons which provide the legal justification for the officer's action does not invalidate the action taken as long as the circumstances, viewed objectively, justify that action.' . . . Subjective intentions play no role in ordinary, probable-cause Fourth Amendment analysis." And there is no question that, in light of the admitted probable cause to stop Robinette for speeding, Deputy Newsome was objectively justified in asking Robinette to get out of the car, subjective thoughts notwithstanding. *See Pennsylvania v. Mimms*, 434 U.S. 106, 111, n. 6 (1977) ("We hold . . . that once a motor vehicle has been lawfully detained for a traffic violation, the police officers may order the driver to get out of the vehicle without violating the Fourth Amendment's proscription of unreasonable searches and seizures").

We now turn to the merits of the question presented. We have long held that the "touchstone of the Fourth Amendment is reasonableness." Reasonableness, in turn, is measured in objective terms by examining the totality of the circumstances.

In applying this test we have consistently eschewed bright-line rules, instead emphasizing the fact-specific nature of the reasonableness inquiry. Thus, in *Florida v. Royer*, we expressly disavowed any "litmus-paper test" or single "sentence or . . . paragraph . . . rule," in recognition of the "endless variations in the facts and circumstances" implicating the Fourth Amendment. Then, in *Michigan v. Chesternut*, 486 U.S. 567 (1988), when both parties urged "bright-line rule[s] applicable to all investigatory pursuits," we rejected both proposed rules as contrary to our "traditional contextual approach." And again, in *Florida v. Bostick*, when the Florida Supreme Court adopted a *per se* rule that questioning aboard a bus always constitutes a seizure, we reversed, reiterating that the proper inquiry necessitates a consideration of "all the circumstances surrounding the encounter."

We have previously rejected a *per se* rule very similar to that adopted by the Supreme Court of Ohio in determining the validity of a consent to search. In *Schneckloth v. Bustamonte*, it was argued that such a consent could not be valid unless the defendant knew that he had a right to refuse the request. We rejected this argument: "While knowledge of the right to refuse consent is one factor to be taken into account, the government need not establish such knowledge as the *sine qua non* of an effective consent." And just as it "would be thoroughly impractical to impose on the normal consent search the detailed requirements of an effective warning," so too would it be unrealistic to require police officers to always inform detainees that they are free to go before a consent to search may be deemed voluntary.

The Fourth Amendment test for a valid consent to search is that the consent be voluntary, and "[v]oluntariness is a question of fact to be determined from all the circumstances." The Supreme Court of Ohio having held otherwise, its judgment is reversed, and the case is remanded for further proceedings not inconsistent with this opinion.

It is so ordered.

[JUSTICE GINSBURG's concurring opinion is omitted.]

JUSTICE STEVENS, dissenting.

The Court's holding today is narrow: The Federal Constitution does not require that a lawfully seized person be advised that he is "free to go" before his consent to search will be recognized as voluntary. I agree with that holding. Given the Court's reading of the opinion of the Supreme Court of Ohio, I also agree that it is appropriate for the Court to limit its review to answering the sole question presented in the State's certiorari petition.[1] As I read the state court opinion, however, the prophylactic rule announced in the second syllabus was intended as a guide to the decision of future cases rather than an explanation of the decision in this case. I would therefore affirm the judgment of the Supreme Court of Ohio

---

[1] "Whether the Fourth Amendment to the United States Constitution requires police officers to inform motorists, lawfully stopped for traffic violations, that the legal detention has concluded before any subsequent interrogation or search will be found to be consensual?"

because it correctly held that respondent's consent to the search of his vehicle was the product of an unlawful detention. Moreover, it is important to emphasize that nothing in the Federal Constitution-or in this Court's opinion-prevents a State from requiring its law enforcement officers to give detained motorists the advice mandated by the Ohio Court.

I

The relevant facts are undisputed.[2] Officer Newsome stopped respondent because he was speeding. Neither at the time of the stop nor at any later time prior to the search of respondent's vehicle did the officer have any basis for believing that there were drugs in the car. After ordering respondent to get out of his car, issuing a warning, and returning his driver's license, Newsome took no further action related to the speeding violation. He did, however, state: "One question before you get gone: are you carrying any illegal contraband in your car? Any weapons of any kind, drugs, anything like that?" Thereafter, he obtained respondent's consent to search the car.

These facts give rise to two questions of law: whether respondent was still being detained when the "one question" was asked, and, if so, whether that detention was unlawful. In my opinion the Ohio Appellate Court and the Ohio Supreme Court correctly answered both of those questions.

The Ohio Supreme Court correctly relied upon *United States v. Mendenhall* which stated that "a person has been 'seized' within the meaning of the Fourth Amendment . . . if, in view of all of the circumstances surrounding the incident, a reasonable person would have believed that he was not free to leave." (opinion of Stewart, J.); *see Michigan v. Chesternut*, 486 U.S. 567, 573 (1988) (noting that "[t]he Court has since embraced this test"). *See also Bostick*, (applying variant of this approach). The Ohio Court of Appeals applied a similar analysis.

Several circumstances support the Ohio courts' conclusion that a reasonable motorist in respondent's shoes would have believed that he had an obligation to answer the "one question" and that he could not simply walk away from the officer, get back in his car, and drive away. The question itself sought an answer *"before* you get gone."* In addition, the facts that respondent had been detained, had received no advice that he was free to leave, and was then standing in front of a television camera in response to an official command, are all inconsistent with an assumption that he could reasonably believe that he had no duty to respond. The Ohio Supreme Court was surely correct in stating: "Most people believe that they are validly in a police officer's custody as long as the officer continues to interrogate them. The police officer retains the upper hand and the accouterments of authority. That the officer lacks legal license to continue to detain them is unknown to most citizens, and a reasonable person would not feel free to walk away as the officer continues to address him."[6]

---

[2] This is in part because crucial portions of the exchange were videotaped; this recording is a part of the record.

[6] A learned commentator has expressed agreement on this point. *See* 4 W. LaFave, Search and

Moreover, as an objective matter it is fair to presume that most drivers who have been stopped for speeding are in a hurry to get to their destinations; such drivers have no interest in prolonging the delay occasioned by the stop just to engage in idle conversation with an officer, much less to allow a potentially lengthy search.[7] I also assume that motorists-even those who are not carrying contraband-have an interest in preserving the privacy of their vehicles and possessions from the prying eyes of a curious stranger. The fact that this particular officer successfully used a similar method of obtaining consent to search roughly 786 times in one year, *State v. Retherford*, 93 Ohio App. 3d 586, 591–592, 639 N.E. 2d 498, 502, *dism'd*, 69 Ohio St. 3d 1488, 635 N.E. 2d 43 (1994), indicates that motorists generally respond in a manner that is contrary to their self-interest. Repeated decisions by ordinary citizens to surrender that interest cannot satisfactorily be explained on any hypothesis other than an assumption that they believed they had a legal duty to do so.

The Ohio Supreme Court was therefore entirely correct to presume in the first syllabus preceding its opinion that a "continued detention" was at issue here.[8] The Ohio Court of Appeals reached a similar conclusion. In response to the State's contention that Robinette "was free to go" at the time consent was sought, that court held-after reviewing the record-that "a reasonable person in Robinette's position would not believe that the investigative stop had been concluded, and that he or she was free to go, so long as the police officer was continuing to ask investigative questions." As I read the Ohio opinions, these determinations were independent of the bright-line rule criticized by the majority.[9] I see no reason to disturb them.

In the first syllabus the Ohio Supreme Court also answered the question whether the officer's continued detention of respondent was lawful or unlawful. Although there is a possible ambiguity in the use of the word "motivation" in the Ohio Supreme Court's explanation of why the traffic officer's continued detention of

---

SEIZURE § 9.3(a), p. 112 (3d ed. 1996 and Supp. 1997) ("Given the fact that [defendant] quite clearly had been seized when his car was pulled over, the return of the credentials hardly manifests a change in status when it was immediately followed by interrogation concerning other criminal activity") (approving of Ohio Supreme Court's analysis in this case). We have indicated as much ourselves in the past. *See Berkemer v. McCarty* ("Certainly few motorists would feel free either to disobey a directive to pull over or to leave the scene of a traffic stop without being told they might do so").

[7] Though this search does not appear to have been particularly intrusive, that may not always be so. Indeed, our holding in *Florida v. Jimeno*, 500 U.S. 248 (1991), allowing police to open closed containers in the context of an automobile consent search where the "consent would reasonably be understood to extend to a particular container," ensures that many motorists will wind up "consenting" to a far broader search than they might have imagined. ("only objection that the police could have to" a rule requiring police to seek consent to search containers as well as the automobile itself "is that it would prevent them from exploiting the ignorance of a citizen who simply did not anticipate that his consent to search the car would be understood to authorize the police to rummage through his packages") (Marshall, J., dissenting).

[8] It is ordinarily the syllabus that precedes an Ohio Supreme Court opinion, rather than the opinion itself, that states the law of the case.

[9] Indeed, the first paragraph of the Ohio Supreme Court's opinion clearly indicates that the bright-line rule was meant to apply only in future cases. The Ohio Supreme Court first explained: "We find that the search was invalid since it was the product of an unlawful seizure." Only then did the court proceed to point out that it would "also use this case to establish a bright-line test . . . ."

respondent was an illegal seizure, the first syllabus otherwise was a correct statement of the relevant federal rule as well as the relevant Ohio rule. As this Court points out in its opinion, as a matter of federal law the subjective motivation of the officer does not determine the legality of a detention. Because I assume that the learned judges sitting on the Ohio Supreme Court were well aware of this proposition, we should construe the syllabus generously by replacing the ambiguous term "motivation behind" with the term "justification for" in order to make the syllabus unambiguously state the correct rule of federal law. So amended, the controlling proposition of federal law reads:

> When the [justification for] a police officer's continued detention of a person stopped for a traffic violation is not related to the purpose of the original, constitutional stop, and when that continued detention is not based on any articulable facts giving rise to a suspicion of some separate illegal activity justifying an extension of the detention, the continued detention constitutes an illegal seizure.

Notwithstanding that the subjective motivation for the officer's decision to stop respondent related to drug interdiction, the legality of the stop depended entirely on the fact that respondent was speeding. Of course, "[a]s a general matter, the decision to stop an automobile is reasonable where the police have probable cause to believe that a traffic violation has occurred." *Whren.* As noted above, however, by the time Robinette was asked for consent to search his automobile, the lawful traffic stop had come to an end; Robinette had been given his warning, and the speeding violation provided no further justification for detention. The continued detention was therefore only justifiable, if at all, on some other grounds.[10]

At no time prior to the search of respondent's vehicle did any articulable facts give rise to a reasonable suspicion of some separate illegal activity that would justify further detention. See *United States v. Sharpe; Terry v. Ohio.* As an objective matter, it inexorably follows that when the officer had completed his task of either arresting or reprimanding the driver of the speeding car, his continued detention of that person constituted an illegal seizure. This holding by the Ohio Supreme Court is entirely consistent with federal law.[11]

The proper disposition follows as an application of well-settled law. We held in *Royer,* that a consent obtained during an illegal detention is ordinarily ineffective to justify an otherwise invalid search. *See also Bostick* (noting that if consent was given during the course of an unlawful seizure, the results of the search "must be suppressed as tainted fruit"). Because Robinette's consent to the search was the product of an unlawful detention, "the consent was tainted by the illegality and was ineffective to justify the search." I would therefore affirm the judgment below.

---

[10] *Cf. Florida v. Royer,* (plurality opinion) ("[A]n investigative detention must be temporary and last no longer than is necessary to effectuate the purpose of the stop").

[11] Since "this Court reviews judgments, not opinions," the Ohio Supreme Court's holding that Robinette's continued seizure was illegal on these grounds provides a sufficient basis for affirming its judgment.

QUESTIONS AND NOTES

1. What did the Court perceive the issue to be in *Robinette*?

2. What did Justice Stevens perceive the issue to be in *Robinette*?

3. Who do you think more accurately perceived the issue? Why?

4. In the Court's view, at the time that Robinette consented, was he being lawfully held or not being held at all?

5. If the Court thought that Robinette was being unlawfully held, would it have reached the same result?

6. In a future case, is it open to one in Robinette's position to prove that he was being unlawfully held? If so, would (should) Justice Stevens' opinion prevail?

7. If your answers to Question 6 were both "yes," why didn't the Court see it that way in this case?

8. Are *per se* rules a bad thing? Are they different from bright line rules, which the Court frequently seems to like?

9. We now look at *Wilson*, where a *per se* (or bright line) rule didn't seem so bad to the to the Court.

MARYLAND v. WILSON
519 U.S. 408 (1997)

CHIEF JUSTICE REHNQUIST delivered the opinion of the Court.

In this case we consider whether the rule of *Pennsylvania v. Mimms*, 434 U.S. 106 (1977), that a police officer may as a matter of course order the driver of a lawfully stopped car to exit his vehicle, extends to passengers as well. We hold that it does.

At about 7:30 p.m. on a June evening, Maryland state trooper David Hughes observed a passenger car driving southbound on I-95 in Baltimore County at a speed of 64 miles per hour. The posted speed limit was 55 miles per hour, and the car had no regular license tag; there was a torn piece of paper reading "Enterprise Rent A Car" dangling from its rear. Hughes activated his lights and sirens, signaling the car to pull over, but it continued driving for another mile and a half until it finally did so.

During the pursuit, Hughes noticed that there were three occupants in the car and that the two passengers turned to look at him several times, repeatedly ducking below sight level and then reappearing. As Hughes approached the car on foot, the driver alighted and met him halfway. The driver was trembling and appeared extremely nervous, but nonetheless produced a valid Connecticut driver's license. Hughes instructed him to return to the car and retrieve the rental documents, and he complied. During this encounter, Hughes noticed that the front seat passenger, respondent Jerry Lee Wilson, was sweating and also appeared extremely nervous. While the driver was sitting in the driver's seat looking for the rental papers,

Hughes ordered Wilson out of the car.

When Wilson exited the car, a quantity of crack cocaine fell to the ground. Wilson was then arrested and charged with possession of cocaine with intent to distribute. Before trial, Wilson moved to suppress the evidence, arguing that Hughes' ordering him out of the car constituted an unreasonable seizure under the Fourth Amendment. The Circuit Court for Baltimore County agreed, and granted respondent's motion to suppress. On appeal, the Court of Special Appeals of Maryland affirmed, ruling that *Pennsylvania v. Mimms* does not apply to passengers. The Court of Appeals of Maryland denied certiorari. We granted certiorari and now reverse.

In *Mimms*, we considered a traffic stop much like the one before us today. There, Mimms had been stopped for driving with an expired license plate, and the officer asked him to step out of his car. When Mimms did so, the officer noticed a bulge in his jacket that proved to be a .38-caliber revolver, whereupon Mimms was arrested for carrying a concealed deadly weapon. Mimms, like Wilson, urged the suppression of the evidence on the ground that the officer's ordering him out of the car was an unreasonable seizure, and the Pennsylvania Supreme Court, like the Court of Special Appeals of Maryland, agreed.

We reversed, explaining that "[t]he touchstone of our analysis under the Fourth Amendment is always 'the reasonableness in all the circumstances of the particular governmental invasion of a citizen's personal security,' " and that reasonableness "depends 'on a balance between the public interest and the individual's right to personal security free from arbitrary interference by law officers.' " On the public interest side of the balance, we noted that the State "freely concede[d]" that there had been nothing unusual or suspicious to justify ordering Mimms out of the car, but that it was the officer's "practice to order all drivers [stopped in traffic stops] out of their vehicles as a matter of course" as a "precautionary measure" to protect the officer's safety. We thought it "too plain for argument" that this justification — officer safety — was "both legitimate and weighty." In addition, we observed that the danger to the officer of standing by the driver's door and in the path of oncoming traffic might also be "appreciable."

On the other side of the balance, we considered the intrusion into the driver's liberty occasioned by the officer's ordering him out of the car. Noting that the driver's car was already validly stopped for a traffic infraction, we deemed the additional intrusion of asking him to step outside his car "*de minimis.*" Accordingly, we concluded that "once a motor vehicle has been lawfully detained for a traffic violation, the police officers may order the driver to get out of the vehicle without violating the Fourth Amendment's proscription of unreasonable seizures."

Respondent urges, and the lower courts agreed, that this *per se* rule does not apply to Wilson because he was a passenger, not the driver.

We must now decide whether the rule of *Mimms* applies to passengers as well as to drivers.[1] On the public interest side of the balance, the same weighty interest

---

[1] Respondent argues that, because we have generally eschewed bright line rules in the Fourth Amendment context, *see, e.g., Ohio v. Robinette*, we should not here conclude that passengers may constitutionally be ordered out of lawfully stopped vehicles. But, that we typically avoid *per se* rules

in officer safety is present regardless of whether the occupant of the stopped car is a driver or passenger. Regrettably, traffic stops may be dangerous encounters. In 1994 alone, there were 5,762 officer assaults and 11 officers killed during traffic pursuits and stops. Federal Bureau of Investigation, Uniform Crime Reports: Law Enforcement Officers Killed and Assaulted 71, 33 (1994). In the case of passengers, the danger of the officer's standing in the path of oncoming traffic would not be present except in the case of a passenger in the left rear seat, but the fact that there is more than one occupant of the vehicle increases the possible sources of harm to the officer.[2]

On the personal liberty side of the balance, the case for the passengers is in one sense stronger than that for the driver. There is probable cause to believe that the driver has committed a minor vehicular offense, but there is no such reason to stop or detain the passengers. But as a practical matter, the passengers are already stopped by virtue of the stop of the vehicle. The only change in their circumstances which will result from ordering them out of the car is that they will be outside of, rather than inside of, the stopped car. Outside the car, the passengers will be denied access to any possible weapon that might be concealed in the interior of the passenger compartment. It would seem that the possibility of a violent encounter stems not from the ordinary reaction of a motorist stopped for a speeding violation, but from the fact that evidence of a more serious crime might be uncovered during the stop. And the motivation of a passenger to employ violence to prevent apprehension of such a crime is every bit as great as that of the driver.

We think that our opinion in *Michigan v. Summers* offers guidance by analogy here. There the police had obtained a search warrant for contraband thought to be located in a residence, but when they arrived to execute the warrant they found Summers coming down the front steps. The question in the case depended "upon a determination whether the officers had the authority to require him to reenter the house and to remain there while they conducted their search." In holding as it did, the Court said:

> Although no special danger to the police is suggested by the evidence in this record, the execution of a warrant to search for narcotics is the kind of transaction that may give rise to sudden violence or frantic efforts to conceal or destroy evidence. The risk of harm to both the police and the occupants is minimized if the officers routinely exercise unquestioned command of the situation.

In summary, danger to an officer from a traffic stop is likely to be greater when there are passengers in addition to the driver in the stopped car. While there is not the same basis for ordering the passengers out of the car as there is for ordering

concerning searches and seizures does not mean that we have always done so; *Mimms* itself drew a bright line, and we believe the principles that underlay that decision apply to passengers as well.

[2] Justice Stevens' dissenting opinion points out that these statistics are not further broken down as to assaults by passengers and assaults by drivers. It is, indeed, regrettable that the empirical data on a subject such as this are sparse, but we need not ignore the data which do exist simply because further refinement would be even more helpful. Justice Stevens agrees that there is "a strong public interest in minimizing" the number of assaults on law officers, and we believe that our holding today is more likely to accomplish that result than would be the case if his views were to prevail.

the driver out, the additional intrusion on the passenger is minimal. We therefore hold that an officer making a traffic stop may order passengers to get out of the car pending completion of the stop.[3]

The judgment of the Court of Special Appeals of Maryland is reversed, and the case is remanded for proceedings not inconsistent with this opinion.

It is so ordered.

JUSTICE STEVENS, with whom JUSTICE KENNEDY joins, dissenting.

In *Pennsylvania v. Mimms*, the Court answered the "narrow question" whether an "incremental intrusion" on the liberty of a person who had been lawfully seized was reasonable. This case, in contrast, raises a separate and significant question concerning the power of the State to make an initial seizure of persons who are not even suspected of having violated the law.

My concern is not with the ultimate disposition of this particular case, but rather with the literally millions of other cases that will be affected by the rule the Court announces. Though the question is not before us, I am satisfied that — under the rationale of *Terry v. Ohio* — if a police officer conducting a traffic stop has an articulable suspicion of possible danger, the officer may order passengers to exit the vehicle as a defensive tactic without running afoul of the Fourth Amendment. Accordingly, I assume that the facts recited in the majority's opinion provided a valid justification for this officer's order commanding the passengers to get out of this vehicle.[1] But the Court's ruling goes much farther. It applies equally to traffic stops in which there is not even a scintilla of evidence of any potential risk to the police officer. In those cases, I firmly believe that the Fourth Amendment prohibits routine and arbitrary seizures of obviously innocent citizens.

I

The majority suggests that the personal liberty interest at stake here, which is admittedly "stronger" than that at issue in *Mimms*, is outweighed by the need to ensure officer safety. The Court correctly observes that "traffic stops may be dangerous encounters." The magnitude of the danger to police officers is reflected in the statistic that, in 1994 alone, "there were 5,762 officer assaults and 11 officers killed during traffic pursuits and stops." There is, unquestionably, a strong public interest in minimizing the number of such assaults and fatalities. The Court's statistics, however, provide no support for the conclusion that its ruling will have any such effect.

---

[3] Maryland urges us to go further and hold that an officer may forcibly detain a passenger for the entire duration of the stop. But respondent was subjected to no detention based on the stopping of the car once he had left it; his arrest was based on probable cause to believe that he was guilty of possession of cocaine with intent to distribute. The question which Maryland wishes answered, therefore, is not presented by this case, and we express no opinion upon it.

[1] The Maryland Court of Special Appeals held, *inter alia*, that the State had not properly preserved this claim during the suppression hearing. The State similarly fails to press the point here. The issue is therefore not before us, and I am not free to concur in the Court's judgment on this alternate ground.

Those statistics do not tell us how many of the incidents involved passengers. Assuming that many of the assaults were committed by passengers, we do not know how many occurred after the passenger got out of the vehicle, how many took place while the passenger remained in the vehicle, or indeed, whether any of them could have been prevented by an order commanding the passengers to exit.[2] There is no indication that the number of assaults was smaller in jurisdictions where officers may order passengers to exit the vehicle without any suspicion than in jurisdictions where they were then prohibited from doing so. Indeed, there is no indication that any of the assaults occurred when there was a complete absence of any articulable basis for concern about the officer's safety — the only condition under which I would hold that the Fourth Amendment prohibits an order commanding passengers to exit a vehicle. In short, the statistics are as consistent with the hypothesis that ordering passengers to get out of a vehicle increases the danger of assault as with the hypothesis that it reduces that risk.

Furthermore, any limited additional risk to police officers must be weighed against the unnecessary invasion that will be imposed on innocent citizens under the majority's rule in the tremendous number of routine stops that occur each day. We have long recognized that "[b]ecause of the extensive regulation of motor vehicles and traffic . . . the extent of police citizen contact involving automobiles will be substantially greater than police citizen contact in a home or office." Most traffic stops involve otherwise law abiding citizens who have committed minor traffic offenses. A strong interest in arriving at a destination — to deliver a patient to a hospital, to witness a kick off, or to get to work on time — will often explain a traffic violation without justifying it. In the aggregate, these stops amount to significant law enforcement activity.

Indeed, the number of stops in which an officer is actually at risk is dwarfed by the far greater number of routine stops. If Maryland's share of the national total is about average, the State probably experiences about 100 officer assaults each year during traffic stops and pursuits. Making the unlikely assumption that passengers are responsible for one fourth of the total assaults, it appears that the Court's new rule would provide a potential benefit to Maryland officers in only roughly 25 stops a year.[4] These stops represent a minuscule portion of the total. In Maryland alone, there are something on the order of one million traffic stops each year. Assuming that there are passengers in about half of the cars stopped, the majority's rule is of some possible advantage to police in only about one out of every twenty thousand

---

[2] I am assuming that in the typical case the officer would not order passengers out of a vehicle until after he had stopped his own car, exited, and arrived at a position where he could converse with the driver. The only way to avoid all risk to the officer, I suppose, would be to adopt a routine practice of always issuing an order through an amplified speaker commanding everyone to get out of the stopped car before the officer exposed himself to the possibility of a shot from a hidden weapon. Given the predicate for the Court's ruling — that an articulable basis for suspecting danger to the officer provides insufficient protection against the possibility of a surprise assault — we must assume that every passenger, no matter how feeble or infirm, must be prepared to accept the "petty indignity" of obeying an arbitrary and sometimes demeaning command issued over a loud speaker.

[4] This figure may in fact be smaller. The majority's data aggregates assaults committed during "[t]raffic [p]ursuits and [s]tops." Federal Bureau of Investigation, Uniform Crime Reports: Law Enforcement Officers Killed and Assaulted 71 (1994). In those assaults that occur during the *pursuit* of a moving vehicle, it would obviously be impossible for an officer to order a passenger out of the car.

traffic stops in which there is a passenger in the car. And, any benefit is extremely marginal. In the overwhelming majority of cases posing a real threat, the officer would almost certainly have some ground to suspect danger that would justify ordering passengers out of the car.

In contrast, the potential daily burden on thousands of innocent citizens is obvious. That burden may well be "minimal" in individual cases. But countless citizens who cherish individual liberty and are offended, embarrassed, and sometimes provoked by arbitrary official commands may well consider the burden to be significant.[6] In all events, the aggregation of thousands upon thousands of petty indignities has an impact on freedom that I would characterize as substantial, and which in my view clearly outweighs the evanescent safety concerns pressed by the majority.

II

The Court concludes today that the balance of convenience and danger that supported its holding in *Mimms* applies to passengers of lawfully stopped cars as well as drivers. In *Mimms* itself, however, the Court emphasized the fact that the intrusion into the driver's liberty at stake was "occasioned not by the initial stop of the vehicle, which was admittedly justified, but by the order to get out of the car." The conclusion that "this additional intrusion can only be described as *de minimis*" rested on the premise that the "police have already lawfully decided that the driver shall be briefly detained."[7]

In this case as well, the intrusion on the passengers' liberty occasioned by the initial stop of the vehicle is not challenged. That intrusion was a necessary by product of the lawful detention of the driver. But the passengers had not yet been seized at the time the car was pulled over, any more than a traffic jam caused by construction or other state imposed delay not directed at a particular individual constitutes a seizure of that person. The question is whether a passenger in a lawfully stopped car may be seized, by an order to get out of the vehicle, without any evidence whatsoever that he or she poses a threat to the officer or has committed an offense.[8]

To order passengers about during the course of a traffic stop, insisting that they exit and remain outside the car, can hardly be classified as a *de minimis* intrusion. The traffic violation sufficiently justifies subjecting the driver to detention and some police control for the time necessary to conclude the business of the stop. The

---

[6] The number of cases in which the command actually protects the officer from harm may well be a good deal smaller than the number in which a passenger is harmed by exposure to inclement weather, as well as the number in which an ill-advised command is improperly enforced. Consider, for example, the harm caused to a passenger by an inadequately trained officer after a command was issued to exit the vehicle in *Board of Comm'rs of Bryan Cty. v. Brown*, [520 U.S. 397 (1996)].

[7] Dissenting in *Mimms*, I criticized the Court's reasoning and, indeed, predicted the result that the majority reaches today.

[8] The order to the passenger is unquestionably a "seizure" within the meaning of the Fourth Amendment . . . . "The Fourth Amendment applies to all seizures of the person, including seizures that involve only a brief detention short of traditional arrest."

restraint on the liberty of blameless passengers that the majority permits is, in contrast, entirely arbitrary.[9]

In my view, wholly innocent passengers in a taxi, bus, or private car have a constitutionally protected right to decide whether to remain comfortably seated within the vehicle rather than exposing themselves to the elements and the observation of curious bystanders. The Constitution should not be read to permit law enforcement officers to order innocent passengers about simply because they have the misfortune to be seated in a car whose driver has committed a minor traffic offense.

Unfortunately, the effect of the Court's new rule on the law may turn out to be far more significant than its immediate impact on individual liberty. Throughout most of our history the Fourth Amendment embodied a general rule requiring that official searches and seizures be authorized by a warrant, issued "upon probable cause, supported by Oath or affirmation, and particularly describing the place to be searched, and the persons or things to be seized." During the prohibition era, the exceptions for warrantless searches supported by probable cause started to replace the general rule. In 1968, in the landmark "stop and frisk" case *Terry v. Ohio*, the Court placed its stamp of approval on seizures supported by specific and articulable facts that did not establish probable cause. The Court crafted *Terry* as a narrow exception to the general rule that "the police must, whenever practicable, obtain advance judicial approval of searches and seizures through the warrant procedure." The intended scope of the Court's major departure from prior practice was reflected in its statement that the "demand for specificity in the information upon which police action is predicated is the central teaching of this Court's Fourth Amendment jurisprudence." In the 1970's, the Court twice rejected attempts to justify suspicionless seizures that caused only "modest" intrusions on the liberty of passengers in automobiles. *United States v. Brignoni-Ponce*, 422 U.S. 873, 879–880 (1975); *Delaware v. Prouse*.[10] Today, however, the Court takes the unprecedented step of authorizing seizures that are unsupported by any individualized suspicion whatsoever.

The Court's conclusion seems to rest on the assumption that the constitutional protection against "unreasonable" seizures requires nothing more than a hypothetically rational basis for intrusions on individual liberty. How far this ground breaking decision will take us, I do not venture to predict. I fear, however, that it may pose a more serious threat to individual liberty than the Court realizes.

I respectfully dissent.

JUSTICE KENNEDY, dissenting.

I join in the dissent by Justice Stevens and add these few observations.

---

[9] *Cf. Ybarra v. Illinois*, (" '[A] person's mere propinquity to others independently suspected of criminal activity does not, without more, give rise to probable cause to search that person' ").

[10] Dissenting in *Delaware v. Prouse*, 440 U.S. 648 (1979), then Justice Rehnquist characterized the motorist's interest in freedom from random stops as "only the most diaphanous of citizen interests."

The distinguishing feature of our criminal justice system is its insistence on principled, accountable decisionmaking in individual cases. If a person is to be seized, a satisfactory explanation for the invasive action ought to be established by an officer who exercises reasoned judgment under all the circumstances of the case. This principle can be accommodated even where officers must make immediate decisions to ensure their own safety.

Traffic stops, even for minor violations, can take upwards of 30 minutes. When an officer commands passengers innocent of any violation to leave the vehicle and stand by the side of the road in full view of the public, the seizure is serious, not trivial. As Justice Stevens concludes, the command to exit ought not to be given unless there are objective circumstances making it reasonable for the officer to issue the order. (We do not have before us the separate question whether passengers, who, after all are in the car by choice, can be ordered to remain there for a reasonable time while the police conduct their business.)

The requisite showing for commanding passengers to exit need be no more than the existence of any circumstance justifying the order in the interests of the officer's safety or to facilitate a lawful search or investigation. As we have acknowledged for decades, special latitude is given to the police in effecting searches and seizures involving vehicles and their occupants. Just last Term we adhered to a rule permitting vehicle stops if there is some objective indication that a violation has been committed, regardless of the officers real motives. See *Whren v. United States*. We could discern no other, workable rule. Even so, we insisted on a reasoned explanation for the stop.

The practical effect of our holding in *Whren*, of course, is to allow the police to stop vehicles in almost countless circumstances. When *Whren* is coupled with today's holding, the Court puts tens of millions of passengers at risk of arbitrary control by the police. If the command to exit were to become commonplace, the Constitution would be diminished in a most public way. As the standards suggested in dissent are adequate to protect the safety of the police, we ought not to suffer so great a loss.

Since a myriad of circumstances will give a cautious officer reasonable grounds for commanding passengers to leave the vehicle, it might be thought the rule the Court adopts today will be a little different in its operation than the rule offered in dissent. It does no disservice to police officers, however, to insist upon exercise of reasoned judgment. Adherence to neutral principles is the very premise of the rule of law the police themselves defend with such courage and dedication.

Most officers, it might be said, will exercise their new power with discretion and restraint; and no doubt this often will be the case. I might also be said that if some jurisdictions use today's ruling to require passengers to exit as a matter of routine in every stop, citizen complaints and political intervention will call for an end to the practice. These arguments, however, would miss the point. Liberty comes not from officials by grace but from the Constitution by right.

For these reasons, and with all respect for the opinion of the Court, I dissent.

QUESTIONS AND NOTES

1.   Why do you suppose that the Court opted for a *per se* rule in view of the ease of finding special circumstances? What are the advantages of a *per se* rule *vis-a-vis* a rule relying on special circumstances?

2.   In *Richards v. Wisconsin*, 520 U.S. 385 (1997), the Court eschewed a *per se* rule in favor of one depending on special circumstances. It then found those circumstances present, thereby holding in favor of the state.

3.   Do you think that it was wise of the state to predicate its entire case on the *per se* rule?

4.   Are there significant differences between *Mimms* and *Wilson*? What are they? Was *Mimms* correctly decided? Was *Wilson*? Explain.

5.   We now turn to a case that seems to suggest that it may not be open season on automobiles after all. As you read *Knowles*, think about the extent to which it limits police discretion.

KNOWLES v. IOWA
525 U.S. 113 (1998)

CHIEF JUSTICE REHNQUIST delivered the opinion of the Court.

An Iowa police officer stopped petitioner Knowles for speeding, but issued him a citation rather than arresting him. The question presented is whether such a procedure authorizes the officer, consistently with the Fourth Amendment, to conduct a full search of the car. We answer this question "no."

Knowles was stopped in Newton, Iowa, after having been clocked driving 43 miles per hour on a road where the speed limit was 25 miles per hour. The police officer issued a citation to Knowles, although under Iowa law he might have arrested him. The officer then conducted a full search of the car, and under the driver's seat he found a bag of marijuana and a "pot pipe." Knowles was then arrested and charged with violation of state laws dealing with controlled substances.

Before trial, Knowles moved to suppress the evidence so obtained. He argued that the search could not be sustained under the "search incident to arrest" exception recognized in *United States v. Robinson*, 414 U.S. 218 (1973), because he had not been placed under arrest. At the hearing on the motion to suppress, the police officer conceded that he had neither Knowles' consent nor probable cause to conduct the search. He relied on Iowa law dealing with such searches.

IOWA CODE ANN. § 321.485(1)(a) (1997) provides that Iowa peace officers having cause to believe that a person has violated any traffic or motor vehicle equipment law may arrest the person and immediately take the person before a magistrate. Iowa law also authorizes the far more usual practice of issuing a citation in lieu of arrest or in lieu of continued custody after an initial arrest.[1] Section 805.1(4) provides that the issuance of a citation in lieu of an arrest "does not affect the officer's authority to conduct an otherwise lawful search." The Iowa Supreme Court has interpreted this provision as providing authority to officers to conduct a full-blown search of an automobile and driver in those cases where police elect not to make a custodial arrest and instead issue a citation — that is, a search incident to citation.

Based on this authority, the trial court denied the motion to suppress and found Knowles guilty. The Supreme Court of Iowa, sitting en banc, affirmed by a divided vote. Relying on its earlier opinion in *State v. Doran*, 563 N.W.2d 620 (Iowa 1997), the Iowa Supreme Court upheld the constitutionality of the search under a bright-line "search incident to citation" exception to the Fourth Amendment's warrant requirement, reasoning that so long as the arresting officer had probable cause to make a custodial arrest, there need not in fact have been a custodial arrest. We granted certiorari, and we now reverse.

Knowles argued that "[b]ecause the officer had no probable cause and no search warrant, and the search cannot otherwise be justified under the Fourth Amendment, the search of the car was unconstitutional." Knowles did not argue below, and does not argue here, that the statute could never be lawfully applied. The question we therefore address is whether the search at issue, authorized as it was by state law, nonetheless violates the Fourth Amendment.

In *Robinson, supra*, we noted the two historical rationales for the "search incident to arrest" exception: (1) the need to disarm the suspect in order to take him into custody, and (2) the need to preserve evidence for later use at trial. But neither of these underlying rationales for the search incident to arrest exception is sufficient to justify the search in the present case.

We have recognized that the first rationale — officer safety — is "'both legitimate and weighty.'" The threat to officer safety from issuing a traffic citation, however, is a good deal less than in the case of a custodial arrest. In *Robinson*, we stated that a custodial arrest involves "danger to an officer" because of "the extended exposure which follows the taking of a suspect into custody and transporting him to the police station." We recognized that "[t]he danger to the police officer flows from the fact of the arrest, and its attendant proximity, stress, and uncertainty, and not from the grounds for arrest." A routine traffic stop, on the other hand, is a relatively brief encounter and "is more analogous to a so-called 'Terry stop' . . . than to a formal arrest." "Where there is no formal arrest . . . a person might well be less hostile to the police and less likely to take conspicuous, immediate steps to destroy incriminating evidence."

---

[1] Iowa law permits the issuance of a citation in lieu of arrest for most offenses for which an accused person would be "eligible for bail." *See* IOWA CODE ANN. §§ 805.1(1) (West Supp. 1997). In addition to traffic and motor vehicle equipment violations, this would permit the issuance of a citation in lieu of arrest for such serious felonies as second-degree burglary, and first-degree theft, both bailable offenses under Iowa law. The practice in Iowa of permitting citation in lieu of arrest is consistent with law reform efforts.

This is not to say that the concern for officer safety is absent in the case of a routine traffic stop. It plainly is not. But while the concern for officer safety in this context may justify the "minimal" additional intrusion of ordering a driver and passengers out of the car, it does not by itself justify the often considerably greater intrusion attending a full field-type search. Even without the search authority Iowa urges, officers have other, independent bases to search for weapons and protect themselves from danger. For example, they may order out of a vehicle both the driver and any passengers; perform a "patdown" of a driver and any passengers upon reasonable suspicion that they may be armed and dangerous, *Terry v. Ohio*; conduct a *"Terry* patdown" of the passenger compartment of a vehicle upon reasonable suspicion that an occupant is dangerous and may gain immediate control of a weapon, *Michigan v. Long*; and even conduct a full search of the passenger compartment, including any containers therein, pursuant to a custodial arrest, *New York v. Belton.*

Nor has Iowa shown the second justification for the authority to search incident to arrest — the need to discover and preserve evidence. Once Knowles was stopped for speeding and issued a citation, all the evidence necessary to prosecute that offense had been obtained. No further evidence of excessive speed was going to be found either on the person of the offender or in the passenger compartment of the car.

Iowa nevertheless argues that a "search incident to citation" is justified because a suspect who is subject to a routine traffic stop may attempt to hide or destroy evidence related to his identity (*e.g.*, a driver's license or vehicle registration), or destroy evidence of another, as yet undetected crime. As for the destruction of evidence relating to identity, if a police officer is not satisfied with the identification furnished by the driver, this may be a basis for arresting him rather than merely issuing a citation. As for destroying evidence of other crimes, the possibility that an officer would stumble onto evidence wholly unrelated to the speeding offense seems remote.

In *Robinson*, we held that the authority to conduct a full field search as incident to an arrest was a "bright-line rule," which was based on the concern for officer safety and destruction or loss of evidence, but which did not depend in every case upon the existence of either concern. Here we are asked to extend that "bright-line rule" to a situation where the concern for officer safety is not present to the same extent and the concern for destruction or loss of evidence is not present at all. We decline to do so. The judgment of the Supreme Court of Iowa is reversed, and the cause remanded for further proceedings not inconsistent with this opinion.

QUESTIONS AND NOTES

1.   Is there any good reason to allow the search in *Knowles*?

2.   Might any Supreme Court opinions have mislead the Iowa Court into thinking that the Fourth Amendment would allow the search at issue in *Knowles*?

3.   Before concluding that *Knowles* signals the end to any thought that it is "open season on automobiles," consider the following problem.

PROBLEM

Suppose that following Knowles' traffic citation, the following dialogue occurred:

Officer: Before you get gone, may I search your car?

Knowles: No.

Officer: Well then, I'm going to arrest you for speeding.

Knowles: So arrest me. You still can't search my car.

Officer: Yes I can. Once I arrest you, I can search your car incident to a valid arrest.

Knowles: But your only arresting me so that you can search my car.

Officer: True, but the Supreme Court says that I can do that.

Is the officer correct? Should he be correct? Reconsider your answer after reading *Atwater* and *Sullivan*.

ATWATER v. CITY OF LAGO VISTA
532 U.S. 318 (2001)

JUSTICE SOUTER delivered the opinion of the Court.

The question is whether the Fourth Amendment forbids a warrantless arrest for a minor criminal offense, such as a misdemeanor seatbelt violation punishable only by a fine. We hold that it does not.

I

In Texas, if a car is equipped with safety belts, a front-seat passenger must wear one, TEX. TRAN. CODE ANN. § 545.413(a) (1999), and the driver must secure any small child riding in front, § 545.413(b). Violation of either provision is "a misdemeanor punishable by a fine not less than $25 or more than $50." § 545.413(d). Texas law expressly authorizes "any peace officer [to] arrest without warrant a person found committing a violation" of these seatbelt laws, § 543.001, although it permits police to issue citations in lieu of arrest, §§ 543.003–543.005.

In March 1997, Petitioner Gail Atwater was driving her pickup truck in Lago Vista, Texas, with her 3-year-old son and 5-year-old daughter in the front seat. None of them was wearing a seatbelt. Respondent Bart Turek, a Lago Vista police officer at the time, observed the seatbelt violations and pulled Atwater over. According to Atwater's complaint (the allegations of which we assume to be true for present purposes), Turek approached the truck and "yelled" something to the effect of "we've met before" and "you're going to jail."[1] He then called for backup and asked to see Atwater's driver's license and insurance documentation, which state law required her to carry. TEX. TRAN. CODE ANN. §§ 521.025, 601.053 (1999). When

---

[1] Turek had previously stopped Atwater for what he had thought was a seatbelt violation, but had realized that Atwater's son, although seated on the vehicle's armrest, was in fact belted in. Atwater acknowledged that her son's seating position was unsafe, and Turek issued a verbal warning.

Atwater told Turek that she did not have the papers because her purse had been stolen the day before, Turek said that he had "heard that story two-hundred times."

Atwater asked to take her "frightened, upset, and crying" children to a friend's house nearby, but Turek told her, "you're not going anywhere." As it turned out, Atwater's friend learned what was going on and soon arrived to take charge of the children. Turek then handcuffed Atwater, placed her in his squad car, and drove her to the local police station, where booking officers had her remove her shoes, jewelry, and eyeglasses, and empty her pockets. Officers took Atwater's "mug shot" and placed her, alone, in a jail cell for about one hour, after which she was taken before a magistrate and released on $310 bond.

Atwater was charged with driving without her seatbelt fastened, failing to secure her children in seatbelts, driving without a license, and failing to provide proof of insurance. She ultimately pleaded no contest to the misdemeanor seatbelt offenses and paid a $50 fine; the other charges were dismissed.

II

The Fourth Amendment safeguards "the right of the people to be secure in their persons, houses, papers, and effects, against unreasonable searches and seizures." In reading the Amendment, we are guided by "the traditional protections against unreasonable searches and seizures afforded by the common law at the time of the framing," *Wilson v. Arkansas*, 514 U.S. 927 (1995), since "an examination of the common-law understanding of an officer's authority to arrest sheds light on the obviously relevant, if not entirely dispositive, consideration of what the Framers of the Amendment might have thought to be reasonable," *Payton v. New York*. Thus, the first step here is to assess Atwater's claim that peace officers' authority to make warrantless arrests for misdemeanors was restricted at common law (whether "common law" is understood strictly as law judicially derived or, instead, as the whole body of law extant at the time of the framing). Atwater's specific contention is that "founding-era common-law rules" forbade peace officers to make warrantless misdemeanor arrests except in cases of "breach of the peace," a category she claims was then understood narrowly as covering only those nonfelony offenses "involving or tending toward violence." Although her historical argument is by no means insubstantial, it ultimately fails.

[After canvassing in some detail the views of the early British commentators].

We thus find disagreement, not unanimity, among both the common-law jurists and the text-writers who sought to pull the cases together and summarize accepted practice. Having reviewed the relevant English decisions, as well as English and colonial American legal treatises, legal dictionaries, and procedure manuals, we simply are not convinced that Atwater's is the correct, or even necessarily the better, reading of the common-law history.

2

A second, and equally serious, problem for Atwater's historical argument is posed by the "divers Statutes," M. DALTON, COUNTRY JUSTICE ch. 170, § 4, p. 582

(1727), enacted by Parliament well before this Republic's founding that authorized warrantless misdemeanor arrests without reference to violence or turmoil. Quite apart from Hale and Blackstone, the legal background of any conception of reasonableness the Fourth Amendment's Framers might have entertained would have included English statutes, some centuries old, authorizing peace officers (and even private persons) to make warrantless arrests for all sorts of relatively minor offenses unaccompanied by violence. The so-called "nightwalker" statutes are perhaps the most notable examples. From the enactment of the Statute of Winchester in 1285, through its various readoptions and until its repeal in 1827, night watchmen were authorized and charged "as . . . in Times past" to "watch the Town continually all Night, from the Sun-setting unto the Sun-rising" and were directed that "if any Stranger do pass by them, he shall be arrested until Morning . . . ." 13 Edw. I, ch. 4, §§ 5–6, 1 Statutes at Large 232–233; see also 5 Edw. III, ch. 14, 1 Statutes at Large 448 (1331) (confirming and extending the powers of watchmen). Hawkins emphasized that the Statute of Winchester "was made" not in derogation but rather "in affirmance of the common law," for "every private person may by the common law arrest any suspicious night-walker, and detain him till he give good account of himself . . . ." 2 HAWKINS, ch. 13, § 6, p. 130. And according to Blackstone, these watchmen had virtually limitless warrantless nighttime arrest power: "Watchmen, either those appointed by the statute of Winchester . . . or such as are merely assistants to the constable, may *virtute officii* arrest all offenders, and particularly nightwalkers, and commit them to custody till the morning." 4 BLACKSTONE 289; see also 2 HALE, HISTORY OF THE PLEAS OF THE CROWN, at 97 (describing broad arrest powers of watchmen even over and above those conferred by the Statute of Winchester).[8] The Statute of Winchester, moreover, empowered peace officers not only to deal with nightwalkers and other nighttime "offenders," but periodically to "make Inquiry of all Persons being lodged in the Suburbs, or in foreign Places of the Towns." On that score, the Statute provided that "if they do find any that have lodged or received any Strangers or suspicious Person, against the Peace, the Bailiffs shall do Right therein," 13 Edw. I, ch. 4, §§ 3–4, 1 Statutes at Large 232–233, which Hawkins understood "surely" to mean that officers could "lawfully arrest and detain any such strangers," 2 HAWKINS, ch. 13, § 12, at 134.

Nor were the nightwalker statutes the only legislative sources of warrantless arrest authority absent real or threatened violence, as the parties and their *amici* here seem to have assumed. On the contrary, following the Edwardian legislation and throughout the period leading up to the framing, Parliament repeatedly extended warrantless arrest power to cover misdemeanor-level offenses not involving any breach of the peace. One 16th-century statute, for instance, authorized peace officers to arrest persons playing "unlawful games" like bowling, tennis, dice, and cards, and for good measure extended the authority beyond players to

---

[8] Atwater seeks to distinguish the nightwalker statutes by arguing that they "just reflected the reasonable notion that, in an age before lighting, finding a person walking about in the dead of night equaled probable suspicion that the person was a felon." Reply Brief for Petitioners 7, n. 6. Hale indicates, however, that nightwalkers and felons were not considered to be one and the same. 2 HALE, HISTORY OF THE PLEAS OF THE CROWN, at 97 ("And such a watchman may apprehend night-walkers and commit them to custody till the morning, and also felons and persons suspected of felony").

include persons "haunting" the "houses, places and alleys where such games shall be suspected to be holden, exercised, used or occupied." 33 Hen. VIII, ch. 9, §§ 11–16, 5 Statutes at Large 84–85 (1541). A 17th-century act empowered "any person . . . whatsoever to seize and detain any . . . hawker, pedlar, petty chapman, or other trading person" found selling without a license. 8 & 9 Wm. III, ch. 25, §§ 3, 8, 10 Statutes at Large 81–83 (1697). And 18th-century statutes authorized the warrantless arrest of "rogues, vagabonds, beggars, and other idle and disorderly persons" (defined broadly to include jugglers, palm-readers, and unlicensed play-actors), 17 Geo. II, ch. 5, §§ 1–2, 5, 18 Statutes at Large 144, 145–147 (1744); "horrid" persons who "profanely swear or curse," 19 Geo. II, ch. 21, § 3, 18 Statutes at Large 445 (1746); individuals obstructing "publick streets, lanes or open passages" with "pipes, butts, barrels, casks or other vessels" or an "empty cart, car, dray or other carriage," 30 Geo. II, ch. 22, §§ 5, 13, 22 Statutes at Large 107–108, 111 (1757); and, most significantly of all given the circumstances of the case before us, negligent carriage drivers, 27 Geo. II, ch. 16, § 7, 21 Statutes at Large 188 (1754). *See generally* S. BLACKERBY, THE JUSTICE OF PEACE: HIS COMPANION, OR A SUMMARY OF ALL THE ACTS OF PARLIAMENT (1723) (cataloguing statutes); S. WELCH, AN ESSAY ON THE OFFICE OF CONSTABLE 19–22 (1758) (describing same).

The significance of these early English statutes lies not in proving that any common-law rule barring warrantless misdemeanor arrests that might have existed would have been subject to statutory override; the sovereign Parliament could of course have wiped away any judge-made rule. The point is that the statutes riddle Atwater's supposed common-law rule with enough exceptions to unsettle any contention that the law of the mother country would have left the Fourth Amendment's Framers of a view that it would necessarily have been unreasonable to arrest without warrant for a misdemeanor unaccompanied by real or threatened violence.

B

An examination of specifically American evidence is to the same effect. Neither the history of the framing era nor subsequent legal development indicates that the Fourth Amendment was originally understood, or has traditionally been read, to embrace Atwater's position.

1

To begin with, Atwater has cited no particular evidence that those who framed and ratified the Fourth Amendment sought to limit peace officers' warrantless misdemeanor arrest authority to instances of actual breach of the peace, and our own review of the recent and respected compilations of framing-era documentary history has likewise failed to reveal any such design. *See* THE COMPLETE BILL OF RIGHTS 223–263 (N. Cogan ed. 1997) (collecting original sources); 5 THE FOUNDERS' CONSTITUTION 219–244 (P. Kurland & R. Lerner eds. 1987) (same). Nor have we found in any of the modern historical accounts of the Fourth Amendment's adoption any substantial indication that the Framers intended such a restriction. *See, e.g.*, L. LEVY, ORIGINS OF THE BILL OF RIGHTS 150–179 (1999); T. TAYLOR, TWO STUDIES IN CONSTITUTIONAL INTERPRETATION 19–93 (1969); J. LANDYNSKI, SEARCH AND SEIZURE AND

THE SUPREME COURT 19–48 (1966); N. LASSON, HISTORY AND DEVELOPMENT OF THE FOURTH AMENDMENT TO THE UNITED STATES CONSTITUTION 79–105 (1937); Davies, *Recovering the Original Fourth Amendment*, 98 MICH. L. REV. 547 (1999); Amar, *Fourth Amendment First Principles*, 107 HARV. L. REV. 757 (1994); Bradley, *Constitutional Theory of the Fourth Amendment*, 38 DEPAUL L. REV. 817 (1989). Indeed, to the extent these modern histories address the issue, their conclusions are to the contrary. *See* Landynski, *supra*, at 45 (Fourth Amendment arrest rules are "based on common-law practice," which "dispensed with" a warrant requirement for misdemeanors "committed in the presence of the arresting officer"); Davies, *supra*, at 551 ("The Framers did not address warrantless intrusions at all in the Fourth Amendment or in the earlier state provisions; thus, they never anticipated that 'unreasonable' might be read as a standard for warrantless intrusions").

The evidence of actual practice also counsels against Atwater's position. During the period leading up to and surrounding the framing of the Bill of Rights, colonial and state legislatures, like Parliament before them regularly authorized local peace officers to make warrantless misdemeanor arrests without conditioning statutory authority on breach of the peace. *See, e.g.*, FIRST LAWS OF THE STATE OF CONNECTICUT 214–215 (Cushing ed. 1982) (1784 compilation; exact date of Act unknown) (authorizing warrantless arrests of "all Persons unnecessarily travelling on the Sabbath or Lord's Day"); *id.* at 23 ("such as are guilty of Drunkenness, profane Swearing, Sabbath-breaking, also vagrant Persons [and] unseasonable Night-walkers"); DIGEST OF THE LAWS OF THE STATE OF GEORGIA 1755–1800, p. 411 (H. Marbury & W. Crawford eds. 1802) (1762 Act) (breakers of the Sabbath laws); *id.* at 252 (1764 Act) (persons "gaming . . . in any licensed public house, or other house selling liquors"); Colonial Laws of Massachusetts 139 (1889) (1646 Act) ("such as are overtaken with drink, swearing, Sabbath breaking, Lying, vagrant persons, [and] night-walkers"); Laws of the State of New Hampshire 549 (1800) (1799 Act) (persons "travelling unnecessarily" on Sunday); Digest of the Laws of New Jersey 1709–1838, pp. 585–586 (L. Elmer ed. 1838) (1799 Act) ("vagrants or vagabonds, common drunkards, common night-walkers, and common prostitutes," as well as fortune-tellers and other practitioners of "crafty science"); Laws of the State of New York, 1777–1784, pp. 358–359 (1886) (1781 Act) ("hawkers" and "pedlars"); Earliest Printed Laws of New York, 1665–1693, p. 133 (J. Cushing, ed., 1978) (Duke of York's Laws, 1665–1675) ("such as are overtaken with Drink, Swearing, Sabbath breaking, Vagrant persons or night walkers"); 3 Laws of the Commonwealth of Pennsylvania 177–183 (1810) (1794 Act) (persons "profanely cursing," drinking excessively, "cock-fighting," or "playing at cards, dice, billiards, bowls, shuffleboards, or any game of hazard or address, for money").

What we have here, then, is just the opposite of what we had in *Wilson v. Arkansas*. There, we emphasized that during the founding era a number of States had "enacted statutes specifically embracing" the common-law knock-and-announce rule, 514 U.S. at 933; here, by contrast, those very same States passed laws extending warrantless arrest authority to a host of nonviolent misdemeanors, and in so doing acted very much inconsistently with Atwater's claims about the Fourth Amendment's object. Of course, the Fourth Amendment did not originally apply to the States, *see Barron v. Mayor of Baltimore*, 7 Pet. 243 (1833), but that does not make state practice irrelevant in unearthing the Amendment's original meaning. A number of state constitutional search-and-seizure provisions served as models for the Fourth Amendment, and the fact that many of the original States with such constitutional limitations continued to grant their own peace officers broad warrantless misdemeanor arrest authority undermines Atwater's contention that the founding generation meant to bar federal law enforcement officers from exercising the same authority. Given the early state practice, it is likewise troublesome for Atwater's view that just one year after the ratification of the Fourth Amendment, Congress vested federal marshals with "the same powers in executing the laws of the United States, as sheriffs and their deputies in the several states have by law, in executing the laws of their respective states." Act of May 2, 1792, ch. 28, § 9, 1 Stat. 265. Thus, as we have said before in only slightly different circumstances, the Second Congress apparently "saw no inconsistency between the Fourth Amendment and legislation giving United States marshals the same power as local peace officers" to make warrantless arrests. *United States v. Watson.*

The record thus supports Justice Powell's observation that "there is no historical evidence that the Framers or proponents of the Fourth Amendment, outspokenly opposed to the infamous general warrants and writs of assistance, were at all concerned about warrantless arrests by local constables and other peace officers." We simply cannot conclude that the Fourth Amendment, as originally understood, forbade peace officers to arrest without a warrant for misdemeanors not amounting to or involving breach of the peace.

2

Nor does Atwater's argument from tradition pick up any steam from the historical record as it has unfolded since the framing, there being no indication that her claimed rule has ever become "woven . . . into the fabric" of American law. The story, on the contrary, is of two centuries of uninterrupted (and largely unchallenged) state and federal practice permitting warrantless arrests for misdemeanors not amounting to or involving breach of the peace.

The reports may well contain early American cases more favorable to Atwater's position than the ones she has herself invoked. But more to the point, we think, are the numerous early-and mid-19th-century decisions expressly sustaining (often against constitutional challenge) state and local laws authorizing peace officers to make warrantless arrests for misdemeanors not involving any breach of the peace.

Small wonder, then, that today statutes in all 50 States and the District of Columbia permit warrantless misdemeanor arrests by at least some (if not all) peace officers without requiring any breach of the peace, as do a host of congressional enactments. The American Law Institute has long endorsed the validity of such legislation, *see* AMERICAN LAW INSTITUTE, CODE OF CRIMINAL PROCEDURE § 21(a), p. 28 (1930); AMERICAN LAW INSTITUTE, MODEL CODE OF PRE-ARRAIGNMENT PROCEDURE § 120.1(1)(c), p. 13 (1975), and the consensus, as stated in the current literature, is that statutes "removing the breach of the peace limitation and thereby permitting arrest without warrant for *any* misdemeanor committed in the arresting officer's presence" have " 'never been successfully challenged and stand as the law of the land.' " This, therefore, simply is not a case in which the claimant can point to "a clear answer [that] existed in 1791 and has been generally adhered to by the traditions of our society ever since." *County of Riverside v. McLaughlin*, 500 U.S. 44, 60 (1991) (Scalia, J., dissenting).

III

While it is true here that history, if not unequivocal, has expressed a decided, majority view that the police need not obtain an arrest warrant merely because a misdemeanor stopped short of violence or a threat of it, Atwater does not wager all on history.[14] Instead, she asks us to mint a new rule of constitutional law on the understanding that when historical practice fails to speak conclusively to a claim grounded on the Fourth Amendment, courts are left to strike a current balance between individual and societal interests by subjecting particular contemporary circumstances to traditional standards of reasonableness. See *Wyoming v. Houghton.* Atwater accordingly argues for a modern arrest rule, one not necessarily requiring violent breach of the peace, but nonetheless forbidding custodial arrest, even upon probable cause, when conviction could not ultimately carry any jail time and when the government shows no compelling need for immediate detention.[15]

If we were to derive a rule exclusively to address the uncontested facts of this case, Atwater might well prevail. She was a known and established resident of Lago Vista with no place to hide and no incentive to flee, and common sense says she would almost certainly have buckled up as a condition of driving off with a citation. In her case, the physical incidents of arrest were merely gratuitous humiliations imposed by a police officer who was (at best) exercising extremely poor judgment. Atwater's claim to live free of pointless indignity and confinement clearly outweighs anything the City can raise against it specific to her case.

But we have traditionally recognized that a responsible Fourth Amendment balance is not well served by standards requiring sensitive, case-by-case determinations of government need, lest every discretionary judgment in the field be converted into an occasion for constitutional review. *See, e.g., United States v. Robinson*, 414 U.S. 218 (1973). Often enough, the Fourth Amendment has to be applied on the spur (and in the heat) of the moment, and the object in implementing its command of reasonableness is to draw standards sufficiently clear and simple to be applied with a fair prospect of surviving judicial second-guessing months and years after an arrest or search is made. Courts attempting to strike a reasonable Fourth Amendment balance thus credit the government's side with an essential

---

[14] And, indeed, the dissent chooses not to deal with history at all. *See* (O'Connor, J., dissenting). As is no doubt clear from the text, the historical record is not nearly as murky as the dissent suggests. History, moreover, is not just "one of the tools" relevant to a Fourth Amendment inquiry. Justice O'Connor herself has observed that courts must be "reluctant . . . to conclude that the Fourth Amendment proscribes a practice that was accepted at the time of adoption of the Bill of Rights and has continued to receive the support of many state legislatures," *Tennessee v. Garner*, 471 U.S. 1 (1985) (dissenting opinion), as the practice of making warrantless misdemeanor arrests surely was and has. Because here the dissent "claims that [a] practice[] accepted when the Fourth Amendment was adopted [is] now constitutionally impermissible," the dissent bears the "heavy burden" of justifying a departure from the historical understanding.

[15] Although it is unclear from Atwater's briefs whether the rule she proposes would bar custodial arrests for fine-only offenses even when made pursuant to a warrant, at oral argument Atwater's counsel "conceded that if a warrant were obtained, this arrest . . . would . . . be reasonable."

interest in readily administrable rules. *See Belton* (Fourth Amendment rules " 'ought to be expressed in terms that are readily applicable by the police in the context of the law enforcement activities in which they are necessarily engaged' " and not " 'qualified by all sorts of ifs, ands, and buts' ").[16]

At first glance, Atwater's argument may seem to respect the values of clarity and simplicity, so far as she claims that the Fourth Amendment generally forbids warrantless arrests for minor crimes not accompanied by violence or some demonstrable threat of it (whether "minor crime" be defined as a fine-only traffic offense, a fine-only offense more generally, or a misdemeanor[17]). But the claim is not ultimately so simple, nor could it be, for complications arise the moment we begin to think about the possible applications of the several criteria Atwater proposes for drawing a line between minor crimes with limited arrest authority and others not so restricted.

One line, she suggests, might be between "jailable" and "fine-only" offenses, between those for which conviction could result in commitment and those for which it could not. The trouble with this distinction, of course, is that an officer on the street might not be able to tell. It is not merely that we cannot expect every police officer to know the details of frequently complex penalty schemes, *see Berkemer v. McCarty*, 468 U.S. 420 (1984) [Chapter 17, *infra*] ("Officers in the field frequently 'have neither the time nor the competence to determine' the severity of the offense for which they are considering arresting a person"), but that penalties for ostensibly identical conduct can vary on account of facts difficult (if not impossible) to know at the scene of an arrest. Is this the first offense or is the suspect a repeat offender?[18] Is the weight of the marijuana a gram above or a gram below the fine-only line? Where conduct could implicate more than one criminal prohibition, which one will the district attorney ultimately decide to charge?[20] And so on.

But Atwater's refinements would not end there. She represents that if the line were drawn at nonjailable traffic offenses, her proposed limitation should be qualified by a proviso authorizing warrantless arrests where "necessary for enforcement of the traffic laws or when [an] offense would otherwise continue and pose a danger to others on the road." (Were the line drawn at misdemeanors

---

[16] *Terry*, upon which the dissent relies, is not to the contrary. *Terry* certainly supports a more finely tuned approach to the Fourth Amendment when police act without the traditional justification that either a warrant (in the case of a search) or probable cause (in the case of arrest) provides; but at least in the absence of "extraordinary" circumstances, *Whren*, there is no comparable cause for finicking when police act with such justification.

[17] *Compare, e.g.*, Brief for Petitioners 46 ("fine-only") *with, e.g.*, Tr. of Oral Arg. 11 (misdemeanors). Because the difficulties attendant to any major crime-minor crime distinction are largely the same, we treat them together.

[18] *See, e.g., Welsh* (first DUI offense subject to maximum fine of $200; subsequent offense punishable by one year's imprisonment); *Carroll v. United States*, 267 U.S. 132 (1925) (first offense of smuggling liquor subject to maximum fine of $500; subsequent offense punishable by 90 days' imprisonment); Tex. Penal Code Ann. §§ 42.01, 49.02, 12.23, 12.43 (1994 and Supp. 2001) (first public drunkenness or disorderly conduct offense subject to maximum $500 fine; third offense punishable by 180 days' imprisonment).

[20] For instance, the act of allowing a small child to stand unrestrained in the front seat of a moving vehicle at least arguably constitutes child endangerment, which under Texas law is a state jail felony.

generally, a comparable qualification would presumably apply.) The proviso only compounds the difficulties. Would, for instance, either exception apply to speeding? At oral argument, Atwater's counsel said that "it would not be reasonable to arrest a driver for speeding unless the speeding rose to the level of reckless driving." But is it not fair to expect that the chronic speeder will speed again despite a citation in his pocket, and should that not qualify as showing that the "offense would . . . continue" under Atwater's rule? And why, as a constitutional matter, should we assume that only reckless driving will "pose a danger to others on the road" while speeding will not?

There is no need for more examples to show that Atwater's general rule and limiting proviso promise very little in the way of administrability. It is no answer that the police routinely make judgments on grounds like risk of immediate repetition; they surely do and should. But there is a world of difference between making that judgment in choosing between the discretionary leniency of a summons in place of a clearly lawful arrest, and making the same judgment when the question is the lawfulness of the warrantless arrest itself. It is the difference between no basis for legal action challenging the discretionary judgment, on the one hand, and the prospect of evidentiary exclusion or (as here) personal § 1983 liability for the misapplication of a constitutional standard, on the other. Atwater's rule therefore would not only place police in an almost impossible spot but would guarantee increased litigation over many of the arrests that would occur.[21] For all these reasons, Atwater's various distinctions between permissible and impermissible arrests for minor crimes strike us as "very unsatisfactory lines" to require police officers to draw on a moment's notice.

One may ask, of course, why these difficulties may not be answered by a simple tie breaker for the police to follow in the field: if in doubt, do not arrest. The first answer is that in practice the tie breaker would boil down to something akin to a least-restrictive-alternative limitation, which is itself one of those "ifs, ands, and buts" rules, generally thought inappropriate in working out Fourth Amendment protection. *See, e.g., Skinner v. Railway Labor Executives' Assn.*, 489 U.S. 602 (1989) (collecting cases). Beyond that, whatever help the tie breaker might give would come at the price of a systematic disincentive to arrest in situations where even Atwater concedes that arresting would serve an important societal interest. An officer not quite sure that the drugs weighed enough to warrant jail time or not quite certain about a suspect's risk of flight would not arrest, even though it could perfectly well turn out that, in fact, the offense called for incarceration and the defendant was long gone on the day of trial. Multiplied many times over, the costs to society of such underenforcement could easily outweigh the costs to defendants of being needlessly arrested and booked, as Atwater herself acknowledges.[22]

---

[21] *See United States v. Watson* ("The judgment of the Nation and Congress has . . . long been to authorize warrantless public arrests on probable cause rather than to encumber criminal prosecutions with endless litigation with respect to the existence of exigent circumstances, whether it was practicable to get a warrant, whether the suspect was about to flee, and the like").

[22] The doctrine of qualified immunity is not the panacea the dissent believes it to be. As the dissent itself rightly acknowledges, even where personal liability does not ultimately materialize, the mere "specter of liability" may inhibit public officials in the discharge of their duties, for even those officers with airtight qualified immunity defenses are forced to incur "the expenses of litigation" and to endure

Just how easily the costs could outweigh the benefits may be shown by asking, as one Member of this Court did at oral argument, "how bad the problem is out there." The very fact that the law has never jelled the way Atwater would have it leads one to wonder whether warrantless misdemeanor arrests need constitutional attention, and there is cause to think the answer is no. So far as such arrests might be thought to pose a threat to the probable-cause requirement, anyone arrested for a crime without formal process, whether for felony or misdemeanor, is entitled to a magistrate's review of probable cause within 48 hours, *County of Riverside v. McLaughlin*, 500 U.S. at 55–58, and there is no reason to think the procedure in this case atypical in giving the suspect a prompt opportunity to request release, *see* TEX. TRAN. CODE ANN. § 543.002 (1999) (persons arrested for traffic offenses to be taken "immediately" before a magistrate). Many jurisdictions, moreover, have chosen to impose more restrictive safeguards through statutes limiting warrantless arrests for minor offenses. It is of course easier to devise a minor-offense limitation by statute than to derive one through the Constitution, simply because the statute can let the arrest power turn on any sort of practical consideration without having to subsume it under a broader principle. It is, in fact, only natural that States should resort to this sort of legislative regulation, for, as Atwater's own *amici* emphasize, it is in the interest of the police to limit petty-offense arrests, which carry costs that are simply too great to incur without good reason. See Brief for Institute on Criminal Justice at the University of Minnesota Law School and Eleven Leading Experts on Law Enforcement and Corrections Administration and Policy as *Amici Curiae* 11 (the use of custodial arrests for minor offenses "actually contradicts law enforcement interests"). Finally, and significantly, under current doctrine the preference for categorical treatment of Fourth Amendment claims gives way to individualized review when a defendant makes a colorable argument that an arrest, with or without a warrant, was "conducted in an extraordinary manner, unusually harmful to [his] privacy or even physical interests." *Whren v. United States; see also Graham v. Connor.*

The upshot of all these influences, combined with the good sense (and, failing that, the political accountability) of most local lawmakers and law-enforcement officials, is a dearth of horribles demanding redress. Indeed, when Atwater's counsel was asked at oral argument for any indications of comparably foolish, warrantless misdemeanor arrests, he could offer only one.[23] We are sure that there are others,[24] but just as surely the country is not confronting anything like an

---

the "diversion of [their] official energy from pressing public issues," *Harlow v. Fitzgerald*, 457 U.S. 800 (1982). Further, and somewhat perversely, the disincentive to arrest produced by Atwater's opaque standard would be most pronounced in the very situations in which police officers can least afford to hesitate: when acting "on the spur (and in the heat) of the moment." We could not seriously expect that when events were unfolding fast, an officer would be able to tell with much confidence whether a suspect's conduct qualified, or even "reasonably" qualified, under one of the exceptions to Atwater's general no-arrests rule.

[23] He referred to a newspaper account of a girl taken into custody for eating French fries in a Washington, D. C., subway station. Tr. of Oral Arg. 20–21; *see also* WASHINGTON POST, Nov. 16, 2000, p. A1 (describing incident). Not surprisingly, given the practical and political considerations discussed in text, the Washington Metro Transit Police recently revised their "zero-tolerance" policy to provide for citation in lieu of custodial arrest of subway snackers. Washington Post, Feb. 27, 2001, at B1.

[24] One of Atwater's *amici* described a handful in its brief. Brief for American Civil Liberties Union

epidemic of unnecessary minor-offense arrests.[25] That fact caps the reasons for rejecting Atwater's request for the development of a new and distinct body of constitutional law.

Accordingly, we confirm today what our prior cases have intimated: the standard of probable cause "applies to all arrests, without the need to 'balance' the interests and circumstances involved in particular situations." *Dunaway v. New York*, 442 U.S. 200 (1979). If an officer has probable cause to believe that an individual has committed even a very minor criminal offense in his presence, he may, without violating the Fourth Amendment, arrest the offender.

IV

Atwater's arrest satisfied constitutional requirements. There is no dispute that Officer Turek had probable cause to believe that Atwater had committed a crime in his presence. She admits that neither she nor her children were wearing seat belts, as required. Turek was accordingly authorized (not required, but authorized) to make a custodial arrest without balancing costs and benefits or determining whether or not Atwater's arrest was in some sense necessary.

Nor was the arrest made in an "extraordinary manner, unusually harmful to [her] privacy or . . . physical interests." As our citations in *Whren* make clear, the question whether a search or seizure is "extraordinary" turns, above all else, on the manner in which the search or seizure is executed. *See id.* at 818 (citing *Tennessee v. Garner* ("seizure by means of deadly force"); *Wilson v. Arkansas*, 514 U.S. 927 (1995) ("unannounced entry into a home"); *Welsh v. Wisconsin* ("entry into a home without a warrant"); and *Winston v. Lee*, 470 U.S. 753 (1985) [Chapter 13, *infra*] ("physical penetration of the body")). Atwater's arrest was surely "humiliating," as she says in her brief, but it was no more "harmful to . . . privacy or . . . physical interests" than the normal custodial arrest. She was handcuffed, placed in a squad car, and taken to the local police station, where officers asked her to remove her shoes, jewelry, and glasses, and to empty her pockets. They then took her photograph and placed her in a cell, alone, for about an hour, after which she was taken before a magistrate, and released on $310 bond. The arrest and booking were inconvenient and embarrassing to Atwater, but not so extraordinary as to violate the Fourth Amendment.

The Court of Appeals' en banc judgment is affirmed.

---

et al. as *Amici Curiae* 7–8 (reporting arrests for littering, riding a bicycle without a bell or gong, operating a business without a license, and "walking as to create a hazard").

[25] The dissent insists that a minor traffic infraction "may serve as an excuse" for harassment, and that fine-only misdemeanor prohibitions "may be enforced" in an arbitrary manner. Thus, the dissent warns, the rule that we recognize today "has potentially serious consequences for the everyday lives of Americans" and "carries with it grave potential for abuse." But the dissent's own language (*e.g.*, "may," "potentially") betrays the speculative nature of its claims. Noticeably absent from the parade of horribles is any indication that the "potential for abuse" has ever ripened into a reality. In fact, as we have pointed out in text, there simply is no evidence of widespread abuse of minor-offense arrest authority.

JUSTICE O'CONNOR, with whom JUSTICE STEVENS, JUSTICE GINSBURG, and JUSTICE BREYER join, dissenting.

The Fourth Amendment guarantees the right to be free from "unreasonable searches and seizures." The Court recognizes that the arrest of Gail Atwater was a "pointless indignity" that served no discernible state interest, and yet holds that her arrest was constitutionally permissible. Because the Court's position is inconsistent with the explicit guarantee of the Fourth Amendment, I dissent.

I

A full custodial arrest, such as the one to which Ms. Atwater was subjected, is the quintessential seizure. See *Payton*. When a full custodial arrest is effected without a warrant, the plain language of the Fourth Amendment requires that the arrest be reasonable. It is beyond cavil that "the touchstone of our analysis under the Fourth Amendment is always 'the reasonableness in all the circumstances of the particular governmental invasion of a citizen's personal security.'"

We have "often looked to the common law in evaluating the reasonableness, for Fourth Amendment purposes, of police activity." But history is just one of the tools we use in conducting the reasonableness inquiry. And when history is inconclusive, as the majority amply demonstrates it is in this case, we will "evaluate the search or seizure under traditional standards of reasonableness by assessing, on the one hand, the degree to which it intrudes upon an individual's privacy and, on the other, the degree to which it is needed for the promotion of legitimate governmental interests." In other words, in determining reasonableness, "each case is to be decided on its own facts and circumstances." *Go-Bart Importing Co. v. United States*, 282 U.S. 344 (1931).

The majority gives a brief nod to this bedrock principle of our Fourth Amendment jurisprudence, and even acknowledges that "Atwater's claim to live free of pointless indignity and confinement clearly outweighs anything the City can raise against it specific to her case." But instead of remedying this imbalance, the majority allows itself to be swayed by the worry that "every discretionary judgment in the field [will] be converted into an occasion for constitutional review." It therefore mints a new rule that "if an officer has probable cause to believe that an individual has committed even a very minor criminal offense in his presence, he may, without violating the Fourth Amendment, arrest the offender." This rule is not only unsupported by our precedent, but runs contrary to the principles that lie at the core of the Fourth Amendment.

As the majority tacitly acknowledges, we have never considered the precise question presented here, namely, the constitutionality of a warrantless arrest for an offense punishable only by fine. Indeed, on the rare occasions that members of this Court have contemplated such an arrest, they have indicated disapproval. *See, e.g., Gustafson v. Florida*, 414 U.S. 260, 266–267 (1973) (Stewart, J., concurring) ("[A] persuasive claim might have been made . . . that the custodial arrest of the petitioner for a minor traffic offense violated his rights under the Fourth and Fourteenth Amendments. But no such claim has been made"); *United States v. Robinson*, 414 U.S. 218 (1973) (Powell, J., concurring) (the validity of a custodial arrest for a minor traffic offense is not "self-evident").

To be sure, we have held that the existence of probable cause is a necessary condition for an arrest. *See Dunaway v. New York*, 442 U.S. 200 (1979). And in the case of felonies punishable by a term of imprisonment, we have held that the existence of probable cause is also a sufficient condition for an arrest. *See Watson.* In *Watson*, however, there was a clear and consistently applied common law rule permitting warrantless felony arrests. Accordingly, our inquiry ended there and we had no need to assess the reasonableness of such arrests by weighing individual liberty interests against state interests. *Cf. Wyoming v. Houghton; Tennessee v. Garner* (O'Connor, J., dissenting) (criticizing majority for disregarding undisputed common law rule).

Here, however, we have no such luxury. The Court's thorough exegesis makes it abundantly clear that warrantless misdemeanor arrests were not the subject of a clear and consistently applied rule at common law. We therefore must engage in the balancing test required by the Fourth Amendment. *See Wyoming v. Houghton.* While probable cause is surely a necessary condition for warrantless arrests for fine-only offenses, see *Dunaway v. New York*, any realistic assessment of the interests implicated by such arrests demonstrates that probable cause alone is not a sufficient condition.

Our decision in *Whren* is not to the contrary. The specific question presented there was whether, in evaluating the Fourth Amendment reasonableness of a traffic stop, the subjective intent of the police officer is a relevant consideration. We held that it is not, and stated that "the making of a traffic stop . . . is governed by the usual rule that probable cause to believe the law has been broken 'outbalances' private interest in avoiding police contact."

We of course did not have occasion in *Whren* to consider the constitutional preconditions for warrantless arrests for fine-only offenses. Nor should our words be taken beyond their context. There are significant qualitative differences between a traffic stop and a full custodial arrest. While both are seizures that fall within the ambit of the Fourth Amendment, the latter entails a much greater intrusion on an individual's liberty and privacy interests. As we have said, "[a] motorist's expectations, when he sees a policeman's light flashing behind him, are that he will be obliged to spend a short period of time answering questions and waiting while the officer checks his license and registration, that he may be given a citation, but that in the end he most likely will be allowed to continue on his way." *Berkemer v. McCarty*, 468 U.S. 420 (1984) [Chapter 17, *infra*]. Thus, when there is probable cause to believe that a person has violated a minor traffic law, there can be little question that the state interest in law enforcement will justify the relatively limited intrusion of a traffic stop. It is by no means certain, however, that where the offense is punishable only by fine, "probable cause to believe the law has been broken [will] 'outbalance' private interest in avoiding" a full custodial arrest. Justifying a full arrest by the same quantum of evidence that justifies a traffic stop — even though the offender cannot ultimately be imprisoned for her conduct — defies any sense of proportionality and is in serious tension with the Fourth Amendment's proscription of unreasonable seizures.

A custodial arrest exacts an obvious toll on an individual's liberty and privacy, even when the period of custody is relatively brief. The arrestee is subject to a full search of her person and confiscation of her possessions. *United States v. Robinson.* If the arrestee is the occupant of a car, the entire passenger compartment of the car, including packages therein, is subject to search as well. *See Belton.* The arrestee may be detained for up to 48 hours without having a magistrate determine whether there in fact was probable cause for the arrest. *See County of Riverside v. McLaughlin,* 500 U.S. 44 (1991). Because people arrested for all types of violent and nonviolent offenses may be housed together awaiting such review, this detention period is potentially dangerous. And once the period of custody is over, the fact of the arrest is a permanent part of the public record. *Cf. Paul v. Davis,* 424 U.S. 693 (1976).

We have said that "the penalty that may attach to any particular offense seems to provide the clearest and most consistent indication of the State's interest in arresting individuals suspected of committing that offense." *Welsh v. Wisconsin.* If the State has decided that a fine, and not imprisonment, is the appropriate punishment for an offense, the State's interest in taking a person suspected of committing that offense into custody is surely limited, at best. This is not to say that the State will never have such an interest. A full custodial arrest may on occasion vindicate legitimate state interests, even if the crime is punishable only by fine. Arrest is the surest way to abate criminal conduct. It may also allow the police to verify the offender's identity and, if the offender poses a flight risk, to ensure her appearance at trial. But when such considerations are not present, a citation or summons may serve the State's remaining law enforcement interests every bit as effectively as an arrest.

Because a full custodial arrest is such a severe intrusion on an individual's liberty, its reasonableness hinges on "the degree to which it is needed for the promotion of legitimate governmental interests." *Houghton.* In light of the availability of citations to promote a State's interests when a fine-only offense has been committed, I cannot concur in a rule which deems a full custodial arrest to be reasonable in every circumstance. Giving police officers constitutional carte blanche to effect an arrest whenever there is probable cause to believe a fine-only misdemeanor has been committed is irreconcilable with the Fourth Amendment's command that seizures be reasonable. Instead, I would require that when there is probable cause to believe that a fine-only offense has been committed, the police officer should issue a citation unless the officer is "able to point to specific and articulable facts which, taken together with rational inferences from those facts, reasonably warrant [the additional] intrusion" of a full custodial arrest. *Terry v. Ohio.*

The majority insists that a bright-line rule focused on probable cause is necessary to vindicate the State's interest in easily administrable law enforcement rules. Probable cause itself, however, is not a model of precision. "The quantum of information which constitutes probable cause — evidence which would 'warrant a man of reasonable caution in the belief' that a [crime] has been committed — must be measured by the facts of the particular case." The rule I propose — which merely requires a legitimate reason for the decision to escalate the seizure into a full custodial arrest — thus does not undermine an otherwise "clear and simple" rule.

While clarity is certainly a value worthy of consideration in our Fourth Amendment jurisprudence, it by no means trumps the values of liberty and privacy at the heart of the Amendment's protections. What the *Terry* rule lacks in precision it makes up for in fidelity to the Fourth Amendment's command of reasonableness and sensitivity to the competing values protected by that Amendment. Over the past 30 years, it appears that the *Terry* rule has been workable and easily applied by officers on the street.

At bottom, the majority offers two related reasons why a bright-line rule is necessary: the fear that officers who arrest for fine-only offenses will be subject to "personal § 1983 liability for the misapplication of a constitutional standard," and the resulting "systematic disincentive to arrest . . . where . . . arresting would serve an important societal interest." These concerns are certainly valid, but they are more than adequately resolved by the doctrine of qualified immunity.

Qualified immunity was created to shield government officials from civil liability for the performance of discretionary functions so long as their conduct does not violate clearly established statutory or constitutional rights of which a reasonable person would have known. *See Harlow v. Fitzgerald.* This doctrine is "the best attainable accommodation of competing values," namely, the obligation to enforce constitutional guarantees and the need to protect officials who are required to exercise their discretion.

In *Anderson v. Creighton*, 483 U.S. 635 (1987), we made clear that the standard of reasonableness for a search or seizure under the Fourth Amendment is distinct from the standard of reasonableness for qualified immunity purposes. If a law enforcement officer "reasonably but mistakenly concludes" that the constitutional predicate for a search or seizure is present, he "should not be held personally liable."

This doctrine thus allays any concerns about liability or disincentives to arrest. If, for example, an officer reasonably thinks that a suspect poses a flight risk or might be a danger to the community if released, he may arrest without fear of the legal consequences. Similarly, if an officer reasonably concludes that a suspect may possess more than four ounces of marijuana and thus might be guilty of a felony, the officer will be insulated from liability for arresting the suspect even if the initial assessment turns out to be factually incorrect. As we have said, "officials will not be liable for mere mistakes in judgment." Of course, even the specter of liability can entail substantial social costs, such as inhibiting public officials in the discharge of their duties. We may not ignore the central command of the Fourth Amendment, however, to avoid these costs.

II

The record in this case makes it abundantly clear that Ms. Atwater's arrest was constitutionally unreasonable. Atwater readily admits — as she did when Officer Turek pulled her over — that she violated Texas' seatbelt law. While Turek was justified in stopping Atwater, neither law nor reason supports his decision to arrest her instead of simply giving her a citation. The officer's actions cannot sensibly be viewed as a permissible means of balancing Atwater's Fourth Amendment interests with the State's own legitimate interests.

There is no question that Officer Turek's actions severely infringed Atwater's liberty and privacy. Turek was loud and accusatory from the moment he approached Atwater's car. Atwater's young children were terrified and hysterical. Yet when Atwater asked Turek to lower his voice because he was scaring the children, he responded by jabbing his finger in Atwater's face and saying, "You're going to jail." Having made the decision to arrest, Turek did not inform Atwater of her right to remain silent. He instead asked for her license and insurance information. *But cf. Miranda v. Arizona,* 384 U.S. 436 (1966).

Atwater asked if she could at least take her children to a friend's house down the street before going to the police station. But Turek — who had just castigated Atwater for not caring for her children — refused and said he would take the children into custody as well. Only the intervention of neighborhood children who had witnessed the scene and summoned one of Atwater's friends saved the children from being hauled to jail with their mother.

With the children gone, Officer Turek handcuffed Ms. Atwater with her hands behind her back, placed her in the police car, and drove her to the police station. Ironically, Turek did not secure Atwater in a seat belt for the drive. At the station, Atwater was forced to remove her shoes, relinquish her possessions, and wait in a holding cell for about an hour. A judge finally informed Atwater of her rights and the charges against her, and released her when she posted bond. Atwater returned to the scene of the arrest, only to find that her car had been towed.

Ms. Atwater ultimately pleaded no contest to violating the seatbelt law and was fined $50. Even though that fine was the maximum penalty for her crime, and even though Officer Turek has never articulated any justification for his actions, the city contends that arresting Atwater was constitutionally reasonable because it advanced two legitimate interests: "the enforcement of child safety laws and encouraging [Atwater] to appear for trial."

It is difficult to see how arresting Atwater served either of these goals any more effectively than the issuance of a citation. With respect to the goal of law enforcement generally, Atwater did not pose a great danger to the community. She had been driving very slowly — approximately 15 miles per hour — in broad daylight on a residential street that had no other traffic. Nor was she a repeat offender; until that day, she had received one traffic citation in her life — a ticket, more than 10 years earlier, for failure to signal a lane change. Although Officer Turek had stopped Atwater approximately three months earlier because he thought that Atwater's son was not wearing a seatbelt, Turek had been mistaken. Moreover, Atwater immediately accepted responsibility and apologized for her conduct. Thus, there was every indication that Atwater would have buckled herself and her children in had she been cited and allowed to leave.

With respect to the related goal of child welfare, the decision to arrest Atwater was nothing short of counterproductive. Atwater's children witnessed Officer Turek yell at their mother and threaten to take them all into custody. Ultimately, they were forced to leave her behind with Turek, knowing that she was being taken to jail. Understandably, the 3-year-old boy was "very, very, very traumatized." After the incident, he had to see a child psychologist regularly, who reported that the boy "felt very guilty that he couldn't stop this horrible thing . . . he was powerless to help his mother or sister." Both of Atwater's children are now terrified at the sight of any police car. According to Atwater, the arrest "just never leaves us. It's a conversation we have every other day, once a week, and it's — it raises its head constantly in our lives."

Citing Atwater surely would have served the children's interests well. It would have taught Atwater to ensure that her children were buckled up in the future. It also would have taught the children an important lesson in accepting responsibility and obeying the law. Arresting Atwater, though, taught the children an entirely different lesson: that "the bad person could just as easily be the policeman as it could be the most horrible person they could imagine."

Respondents also contend that the arrest was necessary to ensure Atwater's appearance in court. Atwater, however, was far from a flight risk. A 16-year resident of Lago Vista, population 2,486, Atwater was not likely to abscond. Although she was unable to produce her driver's license because it had been stolen, she gave Officer Turek her license number and address. In addition, Officer Turek knew from their previous encounter that Atwater was a local resident.

The city's justifications fall far short of rationalizing the extraordinary intrusion on Gail Atwater and her children. Measuring "the degree to which [Atwater's custodial arrest was] needed for the promotion of legitimate governmental interests," against "the degree to which it intruded upon [her] privacy," it can hardly be doubted that Turek's actions were disproportionate to Atwater's crime. The majority's assessment that "Atwater's claim to live free of pointless indignity and confinement clearly outweighs anything the City can raise against it specific to her case," is quite correct. In my view, the Fourth Amendment inquiry ends there.

III

The Court's error, however, does not merely affect the disposition of this case. The *per se* rule that the Court creates has potentially serious consequences for the everyday lives of Americans. A broad range of conduct falls into the category of fine-only misdemeanors. In Texas alone, for example, disobeying any sort of traffic warning sign is a misdemeanor punishable only by fine, as is failing to pay a highway toll, and driving with expired license plates. Nor are fine-only crimes limited to the traffic context. In several States, for example, littering is a criminal offense punishable only by fine.

To be sure, such laws are valid and wise exercises of the States' power to protect the public health and welfare. My concern lies not with the decision to enact or enforce these laws, but rather with the manner in which they may be enforced. Under today's holding, when a police officer has probable cause to believe that a fine-only misdemeanor offense has occurred, that officer may stop the suspect, issue a citation, and let the person continue on her way. Or, if a traffic violation, the officer may stop the car, arrest the driver, search the driver, search the entire passenger compartment of the car including any purse or package inside, and impound the car and inventory all of its contents, *see Bertine; Wells.* Although the Fourth Amendment expressly requires that the latter course be a reasonable and proportional response to the circumstances of the offense, the majority gives officers unfettered discretion to choose that course without articulating a single reason why such action is appropriate.

Such unbounded discretion carries with it grave potential for abuse. The majority takes comfort in the lack of evidence of "an epidemic of unnecessary minor-offense arrests." But the relatively small number of published cases dealing with such arrests proves little and should provide little solace. Indeed, as the recent debate over racial profiling demonstrates all too clearly, a relatively minor traffic infraction may often serve as an excuse for stopping and harassing an individual. After today, the arsenal available to any officer extends to a full arrest and the searches permissible concomitant to that arrest. An officer's subjective motivations for making a traffic stop are not relevant considerations in determining the reasonableness of the stop. *See Whren.* But it is precisely because these motivations are beyond our purview that we must vigilantly ensure that officers' poststop actions — which are properly within our reach — comport with the Fourth Amendment's guarantee of reasonableness.

The Court neglects the Fourth Amendment's express command in the name of administrative ease. In so doing, it cloaks the pointless indignity that Gail Atwater suffered with the mantle of reasonableness. I respectfully dissent.

QUESTIONS AND NOTES

1. How relevant was history to the resolution of this case? How relevant should it have been?

2. Is it fair to say that this arrest was not conducted in an unusual manner? Wouldn't it be accurate to say that prior to *Tennessee v. Garner*, it was more usual to seize a burglar by shooting him than to seize a seat belt violator by arresting her and holding her in jail for an hour with all of the indignities appurtenant thereto?

3. Had prior cases held that probable cause was *sufficient* to justify an arrest, or merely that it was *necessary* to justify an arrest? *Cf. Hodari D.*

4. Does the Court concede that Officer Turek's behavior was unreasonable, but that it is better to tolerate a few unreasonable searches than create a line that is too difficult for the police to administer in the heat of battle?

5. Does the fact that there have been so few similar type seizures (see fn. 23–25 and accompanying text) support the Court's position or does it support the argument that this particular seizure is unreasonable? Explain.

6. Is it possible (reasonable, likely) that the reason there have been so few arrests similar to *Atwater*, is that prior thereto, the legality of such an arrest was, *at best*, questionable? Consequently, prudent police officers may have feared to engage in such behavior?

7. Conversely, is it likely that now that custodial arrests for minor traffic offenses have been legitimated, that the police will engage in that tactic more frequently, and not exclusively (or even primarily) against soccer moms?

8. Indeed, as *Sullivan* so vividly demonstrates, we may have already started down that road.

ARKANSAS v. SULLIVAN
532 U.S. 769 (2001)

PER CURIAM.

In November 1998, Officer Joe Taylor of the Conway, Arkansas, Police Department stopped respondent Sullivan for speeding and for having an improperly tinted wind-shield. Taylor approached Sullivan' s vehicle, explained the reason for the stop, and requested Sullivan' s license, registration, and insurance documentation. Upon seeing Sullivan' s license, Taylor realized that he was aware of " 'intelligence on [Sullivan] regarding narcotics.' " When Sullivan opened his car door in an (unsuccessful) attempt to locate his registration and insurance papers, Taylor noticed a rusted roofing hatchet on the car' s floorboard. Taylor then arrested Sullivan for speeding, driving with-out his registration and insurance documentation, carrying a weapon (the roofing hatchet), and improper window tinting.

After another officer arrived and placed Sullivan in his squad car, Officer Taylor conducted an inventory search of Sullivan' s vehicle pursuant to the Conway Police Department's Vehicle Inventory Policy. Under the vehicle' s armrest, Taylor discovered a bag containing a substance that appeared to him to be methamphetamine as well as numerous items of suspected drug paraphernalia. As a result of the detention and search, Sullivan was charged with various state-law drug offenses, unlawful possession of a weapon, and speeding.

Sullivan moved to suppress the evidence seized from his vehicle on the basis that his arrest was merely a "pretext and sham to search" him and, therefore, violated the Fourth and Fourteenth Amendments to the United States Constitution. The trial court granted the suppression motion and, on the State's interlocutory appeal, the Arkansas Supreme Court affirmed. 340 Ark. 315, 11 S.W.3d 526 (2000). The State petitioned for rehearing, contending that the court had erred by taking into account Officer Taylor's subjective motivation, in disregard of this Court' s opinion in *Whren v. United States.* Over the dissent of three justices, the court rejected the State' s argument that *Whren* makes "the ulterior motives of police officers . . . irrelevant so long as there is probable cause for the traffic stop" and denied the State' s rehearing petition.

The Arkansas Supreme Court declined to follow *Whren* on the ground that "much of it is dicta." The court reiterated the trial judge's conclusion that "the arrest was pretextual and made for the purpose of searching Sullivan's vehicle for evidence of a crime," and observed that "we do not believe that *Whren* disallows" suppression on such a basis. Finally, the court asserted that, even if it were to conclude that *Whren* precludes inquiry into an arresting officer' s subjective motivation, "there is nothing that prevents this court from interpreting the U.S.

Constitution more broadly than the United States Supreme Court, which has the effect of providing more rights."

Because the Arkansas Supreme Court' s decision on rehearing is flatly contrary to this Court' s controlling precedent, we grant the State' s petition for a writ of certiorari and reverse. As an initial matter, we note that the Arkansas Supreme Court never questioned Officer Taylor's authority to arrest Sullivan for a fine-only traffic violation (speeding), and rightly so. *See Atwater.* Rather, the court affirmed the trial judge' s suppression of the drug-related evidence on the theory that Officer Taylor' s arrest of Sullivan, although supported by probable cause, nonetheless violated the Fourth Amendment because Taylor had an improper subjective motivation for making the stop. The Arkansas Supreme Court' s holding to that effect cannot be squared with our decision in *Whren*, in which we noted our "un-willing[ness] to entertain Fourth Amendment challenges based on the actual motivations of individual officers," and held unanimously that "[s]ubjective intentions play no role in ordinary, probable-cause Fourth Amendment analysis." That *Whren* involved a traffic stop, rather than a custodial arrest, is of no particular moment; indeed, *Whren* itself relied on *United States v. Robinson*, 414 U.S. 218 (1973), for the proposition that "a traffic-violation arrest . . . [will] not be rendered invalid by the fact that it was 'a mere pretext for a narcotics search.' "

The Arkansas Supreme Court' s alternative holding, that it may interpret the United States Constitution to provide greater protection than this Court' s own federal constitutional precedents provide, is foreclosed by *Oregon v. Hass*, 420 U.S. 714 (1975). There, we observed that the Oregon Supreme Court' s statement that it could " 'interpret the Fourth Amendment more restrictively than interpreted by the United States Supreme Court' " was "not the law and surely must be inadvertent error." We reiterated in *Hass* that while "a State is free *as a matter of its own law* to impose greater restrictions on police activity than those this Court holds to be necessary upon federal constitutional standards," it "may not impose such greater restrictions as a matter of *federal constitutional law* when this Court specifically refrains from imposing them."

The judgment of the Arkansas Supreme Court is reversed, and the case is remanded for further proceedings not inconsistent with this opinion.

JUSTICE GINSBURG, with whom JUSTICE STEVENS, JUSTICE O'CONNOR, and JUSTICE BREYER join, concurring.

The Arkansas Supreme Court was moved by a concern rooted in the Fourth Amendment. Validating Kenneth Sullivan's arrest, the Arkansas court feared, would accord police officers disturbing discretion to intrude on individuals' liberty and privacy. (expressing unwillingness "to sanction conduct where a police officer can trail a targeted vehicle with a driver merely suspected of criminal activity, wait for the driver to exceed the speed limit by one mile per hour, arrest the driver for speeding, and conduct a full-blown inventory search of the vehicle with impunity"). But this Court has held that such exercises of official discretion are unlimited by the Fourth Amendment. *See Atwater, Whren.* Given the Court' s current case law, I join the Court' s opinion.

In *Atwater*, which recognized no constitutional limitation on arrest for a fine-only misdemeanor offense, this Court relied in part on a perceived "dearth of horribles demanding redress." Although I joined a dissenting opinion questioning the relevance of the Court' s conclusion on that score, I hope the Court' s perception proves correct. But if it does not, if experience demonstrates "anything like an epidemic of unnecessary minor-offense arrests," I hope the Court will reconsider its recent precedent. *See Vasquez v. Hillery*, 474 U.S. 254, 266 (1986) (observing that Court has departed from *stare decisis* when necessary "to bring its opinions into agreement with experience and with facts newly ascertained") (quoting *Burnet v. Coronado Oil & Gas Co.*, 285 U.S. 393, 412 (1932) (Brandeis, J., dissenting)).

QUESTIONS AND NOTES

1.   Given that Sullivan was a professional roofer (which he was), should the arrest on the weapons charge be invalid? Assuming that it were, would it affect the validity of the traffic arrest?

2.   Would (should) a search incident to arrest (*Belton*) have been permitted here? Why do you suppose that the state decided to rely on an inventory search?

3.   Does this use of an inventory search undercut the rationale for allowing such searches? Compare *Bertine* and *Wells*?

4.   Do *Atwater* and *Sullivan* fundamentally shift the theretofore police/citizen balance? Are we a less secure people than we were before these decisions?

5.   Do you think that more cases like *Sullivan* will (should) cause the Court to rethink *Atwater*?

6.   *Virginia v. Moore* seems to suggest that the Court may be in no hurry to rethink *Atwater*.

VIRGINIA v. MOORE
553 U.S. 164 (2008)

JUSTICE SCALIA delivered the opinion of the Court.

We consider whether a police officer violates the Fourth Amendment by making an arrest based on probable cause but prohibited by state law.

I

On February 20, 2003, two City of Portsmouth police officers stopped a car driven by David Lee Moore. They had heard over the police radio that a person known as "Chubs" was driving with a suspended license, and one of the officers knew Moore by that nickname. The officers determined that Moore's license was in fact suspended, and arrested him for the misdemeanor of driving on a suspended license, which is punishable under Virginia law by a year in jail and a $2,500 fine. The officers subsequently searched Moore and found that he was carrying16 grams of crack cocaine and $516 in cash.[1]

Under state law, the officers should have issued Moore a summons instead of arresting him. Driving on a suspended license, like some other misdemeanors, is not an arrestable offense except as to those who "fail or refuse to discontinue" the violation, and those whom the officer reasonably believes to be likely to disregard a summons, or likely to harm themselves or others.

The intermediate appellate court found none of these circumstances applicable, and Virginia did not appeal that determination. Virginia also permits arrest for driving on a suspended license in jurisdictions where "prior general approval has been granted by order of the general district court." Virginia has never claimed such approval was in effect in the county where Moore was arrested.

Moore was charged with possessing cocaine with the intent to distribute it in violation of Virginia law. He filed a pretrial motion to suppress the evidence from the arrest search. Virginia law does not, as a general matter, require suppression of evidence obtained in violation of state law. Moore argued, however, that suppression was required by the Fourth Amendment. The trial court denied the motion, and after a bench trial found Moore guilty of the drug charge and sentenced him to a 5-year prison term, with one year and six months of the sentence suspended. The conviction was reversed by a panel of Virginia's intermediate court on Fourth Amendment grounds, reinstated by the intermediate court sitting en banc, and finally reversed again by the Virginia Supreme Court. The Court reasoned that since the arresting officers should have issued Moore a citation under state law, and the Fourth Amendment does not permit search incident to citation, the arrest search violated the Fourth Amendment. We granted certiorari.

II

[The Court found that history was inconclusive.]

III

A

When history has not provided a conclusive answer, we have analyzed a search or seizure in light of traditional standards of reasonableness "by assessing, on the one hand, the degree to which it intrudes upon an individual's privacy and, on the other, the degree to which it is needed for the promotion of legitimate governmental interests." That methodology provides no support for Moore's Fourth Amendment claim. In a long line of cases, we have said that when an officer has probable cause to believe a person committed even a minor crime in his presence, the balancing of

---

[1] The arresting officers did not perform a search incident to arrest immediately upon taking Moore into custody, because each of them mistakenly believed that the other had done so. They realized their mistake after arriving with Moore at Moore's hotel room, which they had obtained his consent to search, and they searched his person there. Moore does not contend that this delay violated the Fourth Amendment.

private and public interests is not in doubt. The arrest is constitutionally reasonable.

Our decisions counsel against changing this calculus when a State chooses to protect privacy beyond the level that the Fourth Amendment requires. We have treated additional protections exclusively as matters of state law. In *Cooper v. California*, 386 U.S. 58 (1967), we reversed a state court that had held the search of a seized vehicle to be in violation of the Fourth Amendment because state law did not explicitly authorize the search. We concluded that whether state law authorized the search was irrelevant. States, we said, remained free "to impose higher standards on searches and seizures than required by the Federal Constitution," but regardless of state rules, police could search a lawfully seized vehicle as a matter of federal constitutional law.

In *California v. Greenwood*, 486 U.S. 35 (1988), we held that search of an individual's garbage forbidden by California's Constitution was not forbidden by the Fourth Amendment. "[W]hether or not a search is reasonable within the meaning of the Fourth Amendment," we said, has never "depend[ed] on the law of the particular State in which the search occurs." While "[i]ndividual States may surely construe their own constitutions as imposing more stringent constraints on police conduct than does the Federal Constitution," state law did not alter the content of the Fourth Amendment.

We have applied the same principle in the seizure context. *Whren v. United States*, held that police officers had acted reasonably in stopping a car, even though their action violated regulations limiting the authority of plainclothes officers in unmarked vehicles. We thought it obvious that the Fourth Amendment's meaning did not change with local law enforcement practices — even practices set by rule. While those practices "vary from place to place and from time to time," Fourth Amendment protections are not "so variable" and cannot "be made to turn upon such trivialities."

Some decisions earlier than these excluded evidence obtained in violation of state law, but those decisions rested on our supervisory power over the federal courts, rather than the Constitution. In *Di Re*, 332 U.S. 581, federal and state officers collaborated in an investigation that led to an arrest for a federal crime. The Government argued that the legality of an arrest for a federal offense was a matter of federal law. We concluded, however, that since Congress had provided that arrests with warrants must be made in accordance with state law, the legality of arrests without warrants should also be judged according to state-law standards. This was plainly not a rule we derived from the Constitution, however, because we repeatedly invited Congress to change it by statute — saying that state law governs the validity of a warrantless arrest "in [the] absence of an applicable federal statute," and that the *Di Re* rule applies "except in those cases where Congress has enacted a federal rule."

B

We are convinced that the approach of our prior cases is correct, because an arrest based on probable cause serves interests that have long been seen as sufficient to justify the seizure. *Whren; Atwater.* Arrest ensures that a suspect appears to answer charges and does not continue a crime, and it safeguards evidence and enables officers to conduct an in-custody investigation.

Moore argues that a State has no interest in arrest when it has a policy against arresting for certain crimes. That is not so, because arrest will still ensure a suspect's appearance at trial, prevent him from continuing his offense, and enable officers to investigate the incident more thoroughly. State arrest restrictions are more accurately characterized as showing that the State values its interests in forgoing arrests more highly than its interests in making them, or as showing that the State places a higher premium on privacy than the Fourth Amendment requires.

A State is free to prefer one search-and-seizure policy among the range of constitutionally permissible options, but its choice of a more restrictive option does not render the less restrictive ones unreasonable, and hence unconstitutional.

If we concluded otherwise, we would often frustrate rather than further state policy. Virginia chooses to protect individual privacy and dignity more than the Fourth Amendment requires, but it also chooses not to attach to violations of its arrest rules the potent remedies that federal courts have applied to Fourth Amendment violations. Virginia does not, for example, ordinarily exclude from criminal trials evidence obtained in violation of its statutes. Moore would allow Virginia to accord enhanced protection against arrest only on pain of accompanying that protection with federal remedies for Fourth Amendment violations, which often include the exclusionary rule. States unwilling to lose control over the remedy would have to abandon restrictions on arrest altogether. This is an odd consequence of a provision designed to protect against searches and seizures.

Even if we thought that state law changed the nature of the Commonwealth's interests for purposes of the Fourth

Amendment, we would adhere to the probable-cause standard. In determining what is reasonable under the Fourth Amendment, we have given great weight to the "essential interest in readily administrable rules." In *Atwater*, we acknowledged that nuanced judgments about the need for warrantless arrest were desirable, but we nonetheless declined to limit to felonies and disturbances of the peace the Fourth Amendment rule allowing arrest based on probable cause to believe a law has been broken in the presence of the arresting officer. The rule extends even to minor misdemeanors, we concluded, because of the need for a bright-line constitutional standard. If the constitutionality of arrest for minor offenses turned in part on inquiries as to risk of flight and danger of repetition, officers might be deterred from making legitimate arrests. We found little to justify this cost, because there was no "epidemic of unnecessary minor-offense arrests," and hence "a dearth of horribles demanding redress."

Incorporating state-law arrest limitations into the Constitution would produce a constitutional regime no less vague and unpredictable than the one we rejected in *Atwater*. The constitutional standard would be only as easy to apply as the underlying state law, and state law can be complicated indeed. The Virginia statute in this case, for example, calls on law enforcement officers to weigh just the sort of case-specific factors that *Atwater* said would deter legitimate arrests if made part of the constitutional inquiry. It would authorize arrest if a misdemeanor suspect fails or refuses to discontinue the unlawful act, or if the officer believes the suspect to be likely to disregard a summons. *Atwater* specifically noted the "extremely poor judgment" displayed in arresting a local resident who would "almost certainly" have discontinued the offense and who had "no place to hide and no incentive to flee." It nonetheless declined to make those considerations part of the constitutional calculus. *Atwater* differs from this case in only one significant respect: It considered (and rejected) federal constitutional remedies for *all* minor-misdemeanor arrests; Moore seeks them in only that *subset* of minor-misdemeanor arrests in which there is the least to be gained — that is, where the State has already acted to constrain officers' discretion and prevent abuse. Here we confront fewer horribles than in *Atwater*, and less of a need for redress.

Finally, linking Fourth Amendment protections to state law would cause them to "vary from place to place and from time to time." Even at the same place and time, the Fourth Amendment's protections might vary if federal officers were not subject to the same statutory constraints as state officers. In *Elkins v. United States*, 364 U.S. 206, 210–212 (1960), we noted the practical difficulties posed by the "silver-platter doctrine," which had imposed more stringent limitations on federal officers than on state police acting independent of them. It would be strange to construe a constitutional provision that did not apply to the States at all when it was adopted to now restrict state officers more than federal officers, solely because the States have passed search-and-seizure laws that are the prerogative of independent sovereigns.

We conclude that warrantless arrests for crimes committed in the presence of an arresting officer are reasonable under the Constitution, and that while States are free to regulate such arrests however they desire, state restrictions do not alter the Fourth Amendment's protections.

IV

Moore argues that even if the Constitution allowed his arrest, it did not allow the arresting officers to search him. We have recognized, however, that officers may perform searches incident to constitutionally permissible arrests in order to ensure their safety and safeguard evidence. *United States v. Robinson*, 414 U.S. 218 (1973). We have described this rule as covering any "lawful arrest," with constitutional law as the reference point. That is to say, we have equated a lawful arrest with an arrest based on probable cause: "A custodial arrest of a suspect based on probable cause is a reasonable intrusion under the Fourth Amendment; *that intrusion being lawful*, a search incident to the arrest requires no additional justification." *Ibid.* (emphasis added). Moore correctly notes that several important state-court decisions have defined the lawfulness of arrest in terms of compliance with state law. But it is not surprising that States have used "lawful" as shorthand for compliance with state law, while our constitutional decision in *Robinson* used "lawful" as shorthand for compliance with constitutional constraints.

The interests justifying search are present whenever an officer makes an arrest. A search enables officers to safeguard evidence, and, most critically, to ensure their safety during "the extended exposure which follows the taking of a suspect into custody and transporting him to the police station." Officers issuing citations do not face the same danger, and we therefore held in *Knowles v. Iowa*, that they do not have the same authority to search. We cannot agree with the Virginia Supreme Court that *Knowles* controls here. The state officers *arrested* Moore, and therefore faced the risks that are "an adequate basis for treating all custodial arrests alike for purposes of search justification."

The Virginia Supreme Court may have concluded that *Knowles* required the exclusion of evidence seized from Moore because, under state law, the officers who arrested Moore should have issued him a citation instead. This argument might have force if the Constitution forbade Moore's arrest, because we have sometimes excluded evidence obtained through unconstitutional methods in order to deter constitutional violations. See *Wong Sun v. United States*, 371 U.S. 471, 484–485, 488 (1963). But the arrest rules that the officers violated were those of state law alone, and as we have just concluded, it is not the province of the Fourth Amendment to enforce state law. That Amendment does not require the exclusion of evidence obtained from a constitutionally permissible arrest.

We reaffirm against a novel challenge what we have signaled for more than half a century. When officers have probable cause to believe that a person has committed a crime in their presence, the Fourth Amendment permits them to make an arrest, and to search the suspect in order to safeguard evidence and ensure their own safety. The judgment of the Supreme Court of Virginia is reversed, and the case is remanded for further proceedings not inconsistent with this opinion.

JUSTICE GINSBURG, concurring in the judgment.

I find in the historical record more support for Moore's position than the Court does. Further, our decision in *United States v. Di Re*, 332 U.S. 581, 587–590 (1948), requiring suppression of evidence gained in a search incident to an unlawful arrest, seems to me pinned to the Fourth Amendment and not to our "supervisory power." And I am aware of no "long line of cases" holding that, regardless of state law, probable cause renders every warrantless arrest for crimes committed in the presence of an arresting officer "constitutionally reasonable."[3]

I agree with the Court's conclusion and its reasoning, however, to this extent. In line with the Court's decision in *Atwater*, Virginia could have made driving on a suspended license an arrestable offense. The Commonwealth chose not to do so. Moore asks us to credit Virginia law on a police officer's arrest authority, but only in part. He emphasizes Virginia's classification of driving on a suspended license as a nonarrestable misdemeanor. Moore would have us ignore, however, the limited consequences Virginia attaches to a police officer's failure to follow the Commonwealth's summons-only instruction. For such an infraction, the officer may be disciplined and the person arrested may bring a tort suit against the officer. But Virginia law does not demand the suppression of evidence seized by an officer who arrests when he should have issued a summons.

---

[3] The warrantless misdemeanor arrest in [all cases cited by the Court] were authorized by state law.

The Fourth Amendment, today's decision holds, does not put States to an all-or-nothing choice in this regard. A State may accord protection against arrest beyond what the Fourth Amendment requires, yet restrict the remedies available when police deny to persons they apprehend the extra protection state law orders. Because I agree that the arrest and search Moore challenges violated Virginia law, but did not violate the Fourth Amendment, I join the Court's judgment.

QUESTIONS AND NOTES

1.   Are you surprised that *Moore* was a unanimous decision? Had you been on the Court would you have agreed with Scalia? Ginsburg? Neither? Explain.

2.   Did the Court think that this was an easier case than *Atwater*? If so, do you agree?

3.   Did the police have better reasons for arresting Moore than for arresting Atwater? If your answer was yes, does that make *Moore* an easier case? Explain.

4.   The Court repeats its "dearth of horribles" analysis from *Atwater*. Given the police conduct in *Moore*, coupled with the police conduct in *Sullivan*, do you believe that there is still a dearth of horribles? If so, are they likely to increase after *Moore*?

5.   Do you think that the Court showed respect or disrespect for the Commonwealth of Virginia in upholding Moore's conviction? Explain.

6.   Why did Ginsburg concur?

7.   Is the following "Nightmare" accurate:

I. THE NIGHTMARE[*]

Imagine that you are a law student driving home to see your spouse and children after a hard day at school. As you drive down Oak Street towards your home, you see and wave to a police officer, glad that he is patrolling your street because of the frequency of people driving over forty-five mph on your twenty-five mph street. Shortly thereafter, you see his blue light behind you pulling you over. You pull over and engage in the following conversation:

You: I'm glad you're here. We've had a real problem with speeders in the neighborhood. But why did you stop me?

Police officer: You were going twenty-nine mph in a twenty-five mph zone.

You: The problem has been drivers driving over forty-five mph. That's why we asked you to step up neighborhood patrol. You aren't going to ticket me for going four miles over the speed limit, are you?

Police officer: Oh no, nothing like that, but I would like to search your car.

You: Sorry, I've got too many private items in my car. I can't let you do that.

---

[*] Taken from Arnold H. Loewy, *Cops, Cars and Citizens: Fixing the Broken Balance*, 76 St. Johns L. Rev. 535 (2002).

Police officer: Sorry you feel that way. In that case, I'm going to have to arrest you.

You: Now why would you want to do a thing like that?!

Police officer: Because I can search your car incident to the arrest. Then I can have it towed to the impound lot where pursuant to our normal procedures, your car, including its trunk can be inventoried. And, of course, I'll have to handcuff you to take you to the police station where you'll be held in a cell and fingerprinted before you are released. Then maybe the next time I ask to search your car, you won't be so uncooperative.

The police officer then carries out his threat, leaving your private items haphazardly thrown in a plastic garbage bag. As you leave the jail, the police officer hands you the bag, and the dialogue continues:

Police officer: Real sorry that I messed up your article on abusive police practices. Were you writing that for the law review?

You: As a matter of fact, I was.

Police officer: And that magazine on cross-dressing sure was interesting. Do your friends know that you're into that?

You (exasperated): I'm not into that! I have a cousin in Nebraska that's into that, and I got the magazine so I could understand it better.

Police officer: Sure, that's what they all say.

You: OK, Buster, that does it! I'm filing suit against you tomorrow.

Police officer: Don't bother. Everything I did is perfectly constitutional.

Just then you wake up and exclaim: "Thank God I live in America and this can't happen." You then breathe a sigh of relief, drink your morning coffee, and start reading your assignment for Criminal Procedure: *Atwater v. City of Lago Vista*, and *Arkansas v. Sullivan.* As you finish your assignment, you slam down the casebook in disgust and exclaim: "My God! The nightmare is real."

CLOSING NOTE

It would be unfair to close this section without noting a few very recent decisions that might suggest that the above section is overly apocalyptic. Several recent cases have suggested that searches of automobiles may not be as free as this section suggests. For example, *Brendlin v. California* held that any passenger in a car that is unlawfully stopped can challenge the seizure. *Arizona v. Gant* limited the right of search incident of a vehicle to cases where there is reason to believe that evidence of crime may be retrieved from the car (at least where the suspect was no longer in grabbing distance). Finally, *United States v. Jones* severely limited (arguably modifying prior precedent), government power to track a suspect's movement.

Yet, before one concludes that the worm has turned, or in Professor Orin Kerr's phrase, "We have returned to equilibrium,"(see Orin S. Kerr, *An Equilibrium-Adjustment Theory of the Fourth Amendment*, 125 HARV. L. REV. 476 (2011)), recall *Navarette v. California*, upholding the stopping of a vehicle on reasonable suspicion

ARE WE MOVING TOWARD OPEN SEASON ON AUTOMOBILES

of drunk driving because of a complaint from an unknown caller.

Chapter 13

UNUSUAL SITUATIONS

Handwritten margin note:

Not intrusive:
- *fingernail scrape*
- *hand scrape*
- *breathalizer*
- *urine sample*
- *vocal test*
- *writing sample*
- *walking back + forth*

In this Chapter, we focus on situations that do not comfortably fit the classic fourth Amendment mold.

A. ESPECIALLY INTRUSIVE SEARCHES

Some of the searches that we have considered heretofore have dispensed with the requirement of a warrant and/or probable cause, at least in part, because of the minor nature of the intrusion. In *Winston v. Lee*, the Court was compelled to determine whether a *more* than ordinarily intrusive search could be denied even *with* a warrant and probable cause.

WINSTON v. LEE
470 U.S. 753 (1985)

JUSTICE BRENNAN delivered the opinion of the Court.

Schmerber v. California (1966), held, inter alia, that a State may, over the suspect's protest, have a physician extract blood from a person suspected of drunken driving without violation of the suspect's right secured by the Fourth Amendment not to be subjected to unreasonable searches and seizures. However, *Schmerber* cautioned: "That we today hold that the Constitution does not forbid the States['] minor intrusions into an individual's body under stringently limited conditions in no way indicates that it permits more substantial intrusions, or intrusions under other conditions." In this case, the Commonwealth of Virginia seeks to compel the respondent Rudolph Lee, who is suspected of attempting to commit armed robbery, to undergo a surgical procedure under a general anesthetic for removal of a bullet lodged in his chest. Petitioners allege that the bullet will provide evidence of respondent's guilt or innocence. We conclude that the procedure sought here is an example of the "more substantial intrusion" cautioned against in *Schmerber*, and hold that to permit the procedure would violate respondent's right to be secure in his person guaranteed by the Fourth Amendment.

I

A

At approximately 1 a.m. on July 18, 1982, Ralph E. Watkinson was closing his shop for the night. As he was locking the door, he observed someone armed with a gun coming toward him from across the street. Watkinson was also armed and when he drew his gun, the other person told him to freeze. Watkinson then fired at the other person, who returned his fire. Watkinson was hit in the legs, while the other individual, who appeared to be wounded in his left side, ran from the scene. The police arrived on the scene shortly thereafter, and Watkinson was taken by ambulance to the emergency room of the Medical College of Virginia (MCV) Hospital.

Approximately 20 minutes later, police officers responding to another call found respondent eight blocks from where the earlier shooting occurred. Respondent was suffering from a gunshot wound to his left chest area and told the police that he had been shot when two individuals attempted to rob him. An ambulance took respondent to the MCV Hospital. Watkinson was still in the MCV emergency room and, when respondent entered that room, said "[t]hat's the man that shot me." After an investigation, the police decided that respondent's story of having been himself the victim of a robbery was untrue and charged respondent with attempted robbery, malicious wounding, and two counts of using a firearm in the commission of a felony.

B

The Commonwealth shortly thereafter moved in state court for an order directing respondent to undergo surgery to remove an object thought to be a bullet lodged under his left collarbone. The court conducted several evidentiary hearings on the motion. At the first hearing, the Commonwealth's expert testified that the surgical procedure would take 45 minutes and would involve a three to four percent chance of temporary nerve damage, a one percent chance of permanent nerve damage, and a one-tenth of one percent chance of death. At the second hearing, the expert testified that on reexamination of respondent, he discovered that the bullet was not "back inside close to the nerves and arteries," as he originally had thought. Instead, he now believed the bullet to be located "just beneath the skin." He testified that the surgery would require an incision of only one and one-half centimeters (slightly more than one-half inch), could be performed under local anesthesia, and would result in "no danger on the basis that there's no general anesthesia employed."

The state trial judge granted the motion to compel surgery. Respondent petitioned the Virginia Supreme Court for a writ of prohibition and/or a writ of habeas corpus, both of which were denied. Respondent then brought an action in the United States District Court for the Eastern District of Virginia to enjoin the pending operation on Fourth Amendment grounds. The court refused to issue a preliminary injunction, holding that respondent's cause had little likelihood of success on the merits.

On October 18, 1982, just before the surgery was scheduled, the surgeon ordered that X rays be taken of respondent's chest. The X rays revealed that the bullet was in fact lodged two and one-half to three centimeters (approximately one inch) deep in muscular tissue in respondent's chest, substantially deeper than had been thought when the state court granted the motion to compel surgery. The surgeon now believed that a general anesthetic would be desirable for medical reasons.

Respondent moved the state trial court for a rehearing based on the new evidence. After holding an evidentiary hearing, the state trial court denied the rehearing, and the Virginia Supreme Court affirmed. Respondent then returned to federal court, where he moved to alter or amend the judgment previously entered against him. After an evidentiary hearing, the District Court enjoined the threatened surgery. A divided panel of the Court of Appeals for the Fourth Circuit affirmed. We granted certiorari to consider whether a State may consistently with the Fourth Amendment compel a suspect to undergo surgery of this kind in a search for evidence of a crime.

II

The Fourth Amendment protects "expectations of privacy," — the individual's legitimate expectations that in certain places and at certain times he has "the right to be let alone — the most comprehensive of rights and the right most valued by civilized men." Putting to one side the procedural protections of the warrant requirement, the Fourth Amendment generally protects the "security" of "persons, houses, papers, and effects" against official intrusions up to the point where the community's need for evidence surmounts a specified standard, ordinarily "probable cause." Beyond this point, it is ordinarily justifiable for the community to demand that the individual give up some part of his interest in privacy and security to advance the community's vital interests in law enforcement; such a search is generally "reasonable" in the Amendment's terms.

A compelled surgical intrusion into an individual's body for evidence, however, implicates expectations of privacy and security of such magnitude that the intrusion may be "unreasonable" even if likely to produce evidence of a crime. In *Schmerber*, we addressed a claim that the State had breached the Fourth Amendment's protection of the "right of the people to be secure in their *persons* . . . against unreasonable searches and seizures" (emphasis added) when it compelled an individual suspected of drunken driving to undergo a blood test. Schmerber had been arrested at a hospital while receiving treatment for injuries suffered when the automobile he was driving struck a tree. Despite Schmerber's objection, a police officer at the hospital had directed a physician to take a blood sample from him. Schmerber subsequently objected to the introduction at trial of evidence obtained as a result of the blood test.

The authorities in *Schmerber* clearly had probable cause to believe that he had been driving while intoxicated, and to believe that a blood test would provide evidence that was exceptionally probative in confirming this belief. Because the case fell within the exigent — circumstances exception to the warrant requirement, no warrant was necessary. The search was not more intrusive than reasonably necessary to accomplish its goals. Nonetheless, Schmerber argued that the Fourth Amendment prohibited the authorities from intruding into his body to extract the blood that was needed as evidence.

Schmerber noted that "[t]he overriding function of the Fourth Amendment is to protect personal privacy and dignity against unwarranted intrusion by the State." [W]e observed that these values were "basic to a free society." We also noted that "[b]ecause we are dealing with intrusions into the human body rather than with state interferences with property relationships or private papers — 'houses, papers, and effects' — we write on a clean slate." The intrusion perhaps implicated Schmerber's most personal and deep-rooted expectations of privacy, and the Court recognized that Fourth Amendment analysis thus required a discerning inquiry into the facts and circumstances to determine whether the intrusion was justifiable. The Fourth Amendment neither forbids nor permits all such intrusions; rather, the Amendment's "proper function is to constrain, not against all intrusions as such, but against intrusions which are not justified in the circumstances, or which are made in an improper manner."

The reasonableness of surgical intrusions beneath the skin depends on a case-by-case approach, in which the individual's interests in privacy and security are weighed against society's interests in conducting the procedure. In a given case, the question whether the community's need for evidence outweighs the substantial privacy interests at stake is a delicate one admitting of few categorical answers. We believe that *Schmerber*, however, provides the appropriate framework of analysis for such cases.

Schmerber recognized that the ordinary requirements of the Fourth Amendment would be the threshold requirements for conducting this kind of surgical search and seizure. We noted the importance of probable cause. And we pointed out: "Search warrants are ordinarily required for searches of dwellings, and, absent an emergency, no less could be required where intrusions into the human body are concerned. . . . The importance of informed, detached and deliberate determinations of the issue whether or not to invade another's body in search of evidence of guilt is indisputable and great."

Beyond these standards, *Schmerber's* inquiry considered a number of other factors in determining the "reasonableness" of the blood test. A crucial factor in analyzing the magnitude of the intrusion in *Schmerber* is the extent to which the procedure may threaten the safety or health of the individual. "[F]or most people [a blood test] involves virtually no risk, trauma, or pain." Moreover, all reasonable medical precautions were taken and no unusual or untested procedures were employed in *Schmerber*; the procedure was performed "by a physician in a hospital environment according to accepted medical practices." Notwithstanding the existence of probable cause, a search for evidence of a crime may be unjustifiable if it endangers the life or health of the suspect.

Another factor is the extent of intrusion upon the individual's dignitary interests in personal privacy and bodily integrity. Intruding into an individual's living room, eavesdropping upon an individual's telephone conversations, or forcing an individual to accompany police officers to the police station, typically do not injure the physical person of the individual. Such intrusions do, however, damage the individual's sense of personal privacy and security and are thus subject to the Fourth Amendment's dictates. In noting that a blood test was "a commonplace in these days of periodic physical examinations," *Schmerber* recognized society's judgment that blood tests do not constitute an unduly extensive imposition on an individual's personal privacy and bodily integrity.

Weighed against these individual interests is the community's interest in fairly and accurately determining guilt or innocence. This interest is of course of great importance. We noted in *Schmerber* that a blood test is "a highly effective means of determining the degree to which a person is under the influence of alcohol." Moreover, there was "a clear indication that in fact [desired] evidence [would] be found" if the blood test were undertaken. Especially given the difficulty of proving drunkenness by other means, these considerations showed that results of the blood test were of vital importance if the State were to enforce its drunken driving laws. In *Schmerber*, we concluded that this state interest was sufficient to justify the intrusion, and the compelled blood test was thus "reasonable" for Fourth Amendment purposes.

III

Applying the *Schmerber* balancing test in this case, we believe that the Court of Appeals reached the correct result. The Commonwealth plainly had probable cause to conduct the search. In addition, all parties apparently agree that respondent has had a full measure of procedural protections and has been able fully to litigate the difficult medical and legal questions necessarily involved in analyzing the reasonableness of a surgical incision of this magnitude.[6] Our inquiry therefore must focus on the extent of the intrusion on respondent's privacy interests and on the State's need for the evidence.

The threats to the health or safety of respondent posed by the surgery are the subject of sharp dispute between the parties. Before the new revelations of October 18, the District Court found that the procedure could be carried out "with virtually no risk to [respondent]." On rehearing, however, with new evidence before it, the District Court held that "the risks previously involved have increased in magnitude even as new risks are being added."

The Court of Appeals examined the medical evidence in the record and found that respondent would suffer some risks associated with the surgical procedure.[7] One surgeon had testified that the difficulty of discovering the exact location of the bullet "could require extensive probing and retracting of the muscle tissue," carrying with it "the concomitant risks of injury to the muscle as well as injury to the nerves, blood vessels and other tissue in the chest and pleural cavity." The court further noted that "the greater intrusion and the larger incisions increase the risks of infection." Moreover, there was conflict in the testimony concerning the nature and the scope of the operation. One surgeon stated that it would take 15–20 minutes, while another predicted the procedure could take up to two and one-half hours. The court properly took the resulting uncertainty about the medical risks into account.[8]

---

[6] Because the State has afforded respondent the benefit of a full adversary presentation and appellate review, we do not reach the question whether the State may compel a suspect to undergo a surgical search of this magnitude for evidence absent such special procedural protections.

[7] The Court of Appeals concluded, however, that "the specific physical risks from putting [respondent] under general anesthesia may therefore be considered minimal." Testimony had shown that "the general risks of harm or death from general anesthesia are quite low, and that [respondent] was in the statistical group of persons with the lowest risk of injury from general anesthesia."

[8] One expert testified that this would be "minor" surgery. The question whether the surgery is to be characterized in medical terms as "major" or "minor" is not controlling. We agree with the Court of

Both lower courts in this case believed that the proposed surgery, which for purely medical reasons required the use of a general anesthetic,[9] would be an "extensive" intrusion on respondent's personal privacy and bodily integrity. When conducted with the consent of the patient, surgery requiring general anesthesia is not necessarily demeaning or intrusive. In such a case, the surgeon is carrying out the patient's own will concerning the patient's body and the patient's right to privacy is therefore preserved. In this case, however, the Court of Appeals noted that the Commonwealth proposes to take control of respondent's body, to "drug this citizen — not yet convicted of a criminal offense — with narcotics and barbiturates into a state of unconsciousness," and then to search beneath his skin for evidence of a crime. This kind of surgery involves a virtually total divestment of respondent's ordinary control over surgical probing beneath his skin.

The other part of the balance concerns the Commonwealth's need to intrude into respondent's body to retrieve the bullet. The Commonwealth claims to need the bullet to demonstrate that it was fired from Watkinson's gun, which in turn would show that respondent was the robber who confronted Watkinson. However, although we recognize the difficulty of making determinations in advance as to the strength of the case against respondent, petitioners' assertions of a compelling need for the bullet are hardly persuasive. The very circumstances relied on in this case to demonstrate probable cause to believe that evidence will be found tend to vitiate the Commonwealth's need to compel respondent to undergo surgery. The Commonwealth has available substantial additional evidence that respondent was the individual who accosted Watkinson on the night of the robbery. No party in this case suggests that Watkinson's entirely spontaneous identification of respondent at the hospital would be inadmissible. In addition, petitioners can no doubt prove that Watkinson (*sic*) [Lee? — Ed.] was found a few blocks from Watkinson's store shortly after the incident took place. And petitioners can certainly show that the location of the bullet (under respondent's left collarbone) seems to correlate with Watkinson's report that the robber "jerked" to the left. The fact that the Commonwealth has available such substantial evidence of the origin of the bullet restricts the need for the Commonwealth to compel respondent to undergo the contemplated surgery.[10]

Appeals and the District Court in this case that "there is no reason to suppose that the definition of a medical term of art should coincide with the parameters of a constitutional standard." This does not mean that the application of medical concepts in such cases is to be ignored. However, no specific medical categorization can control the multifaceted legal inquiry that the court must undertake.

[9] Somewhat different issues would be raised if the use of a general anesthetic became necessary because of the patient's refusal to cooperate.

[10] There are also some questions concerning the probative value of the bullet, even if it could be retrieved. The evidentiary value of the bullet depends on a comparison between markings, if any, on the bullet in respondent's shoulder and markings, if any, found on a test bullet that the police could fire from Watkinson's gun. However, the record supports some doubt whether this kind of comparison is possible. This is because the bullet's markings may have been corroded in the time that the bullet has been in respondent's shoulder, thus making it useless for comparison purposes. In addition, respondent argues that any given gun may be incapable of firing bullets that have a consistent set of markings. The record is devoid of any evidence that the police have attempted to test-fire Watkinson's gun, and there thus remains the additional possibility that a comparison of bullets is impossible because Watkinson's gun does not consistently fire bullets with the same markings. However, because the courts below made no findings on this point, we hesitate to give it significant weight in our analysis.

In weighing the various factors in this case, we therefore reach the same conclusion as the courts below. The operation sought will intrude substantially on respondent's protected interests. The medical risks of the operation, although apparently not extremely severe, are a subject of considerable dispute; the very uncertainty militates against finding the operation to be "reasonable." In addition, the intrusion on respondent's privacy interests entailed by the operation can only be characterized as severe. On the other hand, although the bullet may turn out to be useful to the Commonwealth in prosecuting respondent, the Commonwealth has failed to demonstrate a compelling need for it. We believe that in these circumstances the Commonwealth has failed to demonstrate that it would be "reasonable" under the terms of the Fourth Amendment to search for evidence of this crime by means of the contemplated surgery.

IV

The Fourth Amendment is a vital safeguard of the right of the citizen to be free from unreasonable governmental intrusions into any area in which he has a reasonable expectation of privacy. Where the Court has found a lesser expectation of privacy, or where the search involves a minimal intrusion on privacy interests, the Court has held that the Fourth Amendment's protections are correspondingly less stringent. Conversely, however, the Fourth Amendment's command that searches be "reasonable" requires that when the State seeks to intrude upon an area in which our society recognizes a significantly heightened privacy interest, a more substantial justification is required to make the search "reasonable." Applying these principles, we hold that the proposed search in this case would be "unreasonable" under the Fourth Amendment.

Justice Blackmun and Justice Rehnquist concur in the judgment.

Chief Justice Burger, concurring

I join because I read the Court's opinion as not preventing detention of an individual if there are reasonable grounds to believe that natural bodily functions will disclose the presence of contraband materials secreted internally.

QUESTIONS AND NOTES

1. Does the state lose because it has *too much probable cause*? If the state's case against Lee were weaker, would its need to retrieve the bullet be stronger, and perhaps successful? If so, doesn't the case turn the concept of probable cause on its head?

2. Should Lee's claim be discounted by the harm of *not* removing the bullet? Presumably leaving a bullet in a person carries its own risks?

3. Is the Court manufacturing an exception to the Fourth Amendment? Given a warrant (indeed an adversary hearing with multiple appeals) and probable cause, how can the Court conclude that Fourth Amendment standards were not met?

B. TAKING DNA

MARYLAND v. KING
569 U.S. ___, 133 S. Ct. 1958 (2013)

JUSTICE KENNEDY delivered the opinion of the Court.

In 2003 a man concealing his face and armed with a gun broke into a woman's home in Salisbury, Maryland. He raped her. The police were unable to identify or apprehend the assailant based on any detailed description or other evidence they then had, but they did obtain from the victim a sample of the perpetrator's DNA.

In 2009 Alonzo King was arrested in Wicomico County, Maryland, and charged with first- and second-degree assault for menacing a group of people with a shotgun. As part of a routine booking procedure for serious offenses, his DNA sample was taken by applying a cotton swab or filter paper — known as a buccal swab — to the inside of his cheeks. The DNA was found to match the DNA taken from the Salisbury rape victim. King was tried and convicted for the rape. Additional DNA samples were taken from him and used in the rape trial, but there seems to be no doubt that it was the DNA from the cheek sample taken at the time he was booked in 2009 that led to his first having been linked to the rape and charged with its commission.

The Court of Appeals of Maryland, on review of King's rape conviction, ruled that the DNA taken when King was booked for the 2009 charge was an unlawful seizure because obtaining and using the cheek swab was an unreasonable search of the person. It set the rape conviction aside. This Court granted certiorari and now reverses the judgment of the Maryland court.

II

The advent of DNA technology is one of the most significant scientific advancements of our era. The full potential for use of genetic markers in medicine and science is still being explored, but the utility of DNA identification in the criminal justice system is already undisputed. Since the first use of forensic DNA analysis to catch a rapist and murderer in England in 1986, law enforcement, the defense bar, and the courts have acknowledged DNA testing's "unparalleled ability both to exonerate the wrongly convicted and to identify the guilty. It has the potential to significantly improve both the criminal justice system and police investigative practices."

A

The Act authorizes Maryland law enforcement authorities to collect DNA samples from "an individual who is charged with . . . a crime of violence or an attempt to commit a crime of violence; or . . . burglary or an attempt to commit burglary." Maryland law defines a crime of violence to include murder, rape, first-degree assault, kidnaping, arson, sexual assault, and a variety of other serious crimes. Once taken, a DNA sample may not be processed or placed in a database before the individual is arraigned (unless the individual consents). It is at this point that a judicial officer ensures that there is probable cause to detain the arrestee on a qualifying serious offense. If "all qualifying criminal charges are determined to be unsupported by probable cause . . . the DNA sample shall be immediately destroyed." DNA samples are also destroyed if "a criminal action begun against the individual . . . does not result in a conviction," "the conviction is finally reversed or vacated and no new trial is permitted," or "the individual is granted an unconditional pardon."

The Act also limits the information added to a DNA database and how it may be used. Specifically, "[o]nly DNA records that directly relate to the identification of individuals shall be collected and stored." No purpose other than identification is permissible: "A person may not willfully test a DNA sample for information that does not relate to the identification of individuals as specified in this subtitle." Tests for familial matches are also prohibited. ("A person may not perform a search of the statewide DNA data base for the purpose of identification of an offender in connection with a crime for which the offender may be a biological relative of the individual from whom the DNA sample was acquired"). The officers involved in taking and analyzing respondent's DNA sample complied with the Act in all respects.

Respondent's DNA was collected in this case using a common procedure known as a "buccal swab." "Buccal cell collection involves wiping a small piece of filter paper or a cotton swab similar to a Q-tip against the inside cheek of an individual's mouth to collect some skin cells." The procedure is quick and painless. The swab touches inside an arrestee's mouth, but it requires no "surgical intrusio[n] beneath the skin," *Winston v. Lee*, and it poses no "threa[t] to the health or safety" of arrestees.

B

Respondent's identification as the rapist resulted in part through the operation of a national project to standardize collection and storage of DNA profiles. Authorized by Congress and supervised by the Federal Bureau of Investigation, the Combined DNA Index System (CODIS) connects DNA laboratories at the local, state, and national level. Since its authorization in 1994, the CODIS system has grown to include all 50 States and a number of federal agencies. CODIS collects DNA profiles provided by local laboratories taken from arrestees, convicted offenders, and forensic evidence found at crime scenes. To participate in CODIS, a local laboratory must sign a memorandum of understanding agreeing to adhere to quality standards and submit to audits to evaluate compliance with the federal standards for scientifically rigorous DNA testing.

One of the most significant aspects of CODIS is the standardization of the points of comparison in DNA analysis. The CODIS database is based on 13 loci at which the STR alleles are noted and compared. These loci make possible extreme accuracy in matching individual samples, with a "random match probability of approximately 1 in 100 trillion (assuming unrelated individuals)." The CODIS loci are from the non-protein coding junk regions of DNA, and "are not known to have any association with a genetic disease or any other genetic predisposition. Thus, the information in the database is only useful for human identity testing." STR information is recorded only as a "string of numbers"; and the DNA identification is accompanied only by information denoting the laboratory and the analyst responsible for the submission. In short, CODIS sets uniform national standards for DNA matching and then facilitates connections between local law enforcement agencies who can share more specific information about matched STR profiles.

All 50 States require the collection of DNA from felony convicts, and respondent does not dispute the validity of that practice. Twenty-eight States and the Federal Government have adopted laws similar to the Maryland Act authorizing the collection of DNA from some or all arrestees. Although those statutes vary in their particulars, such as what charges require a DNA sample, their similarity means that this case implicates more than the specific Maryland law. At issue is a standard, expanding technology already in widespread use throughout the Nation.

III

A

Although the DNA swab procedure used here presents a question the Court has not yet addressed, the framework for deciding the issue is well established. The Fourth Amendment provides that "[t]he right of the people to be secure in their persons, houses, papers, and effects, against unreasonable searches and seizures, shall not be violated." It can be agreed that using a buccal swab on the inner tissues of a person's cheek in order to obtain DNA samples is a search. Virtually any "intrusio[n] into the human body" will work an invasion of " 'cherished personal security' that is subject to constitutional scrutiny." The Court has applied the Fourth Amendment to police efforts to draw blood, scraping an arrestee's fingernails to obtain trace evidence, and even to "a Breathalyzer test, which generally requires the production of alveolar or 'deep lung' breath for chemical analysis."

A buccal swab is a far more gentle process than a venipuncture to draw blood. It involves but a light touch on the inside of the cheek; and although it can be deemed a search within the body of the arrestee, it requires no "surgical intrusions beneath the skin." The fact than an intrusion is negligible is of central relevance to determining reasonableness, although it is still a search as the law defines that term.

B

To say that the Fourth Amendment applies here is the beginning point, not the end of the analysis. "[T]he Fourth Amendment's proper function is to constrain, not against all intrusions as such, but against intrusions which are not justified in the circumstances, or which are made in an improper manner." In giving content to the inquiry whether an intrusion is reasonable, the Court has preferred "some quantum of individualized suspicion . . . [as] a prerequisite to a constitutional search or seizure. But the Fourth Amendment imposes no irreducible requirement of such suspicion."

In some circumstances, such as "[w]hen faced with special law enforcement needs, diminished expectations of privacy, minimal intrusions, or the like, the Court has found that certain general, or individual, circumstances may render a warrant-less search or seizure reasonable." Those circumstances diminish the need for a warrant, either because "the public interest is such that neither a warrant nor probable cause is required." or because an individual is already on notice, for instance because of his employment, or the conditions of his release from government custody, that some reasonable police intrusion on his privacy is to be expected. The need for a warrant is perhaps least when the search involves no discretion that could properly be limited by the "interpo[lation of] a neutral magistrate between the citizen and the law enforcement officer."

The instant case can be addressed with this background. The Maryland DNA Collection Act provides that, in order to obtain a DNA sample, all arrestees charged with serious crimes must furnish the sample on a buccal swab applied, as noted, to the inside of the cheeks. The arrestee is already in valid police custody for a serious offense supported by probable cause. The DNA collection is not subject to the judgment of officers whose perspective might be "colored by their primary involvement in 'the often competitive enterprise of ferreting out crime.'" As noted by this Court in a different but still instructive context involving blood testing, "[b]oth the circumstances justifying toxicological testing and the permissible limits of such intrusions are defined narrowly and specifically in the regulations that authorize them. . . . Indeed, in light of the standardized nature of the tests and the minimal discretion vested in those charged with administering the program, there are virtually no facts for a neutral magistrate to evaluate." Here, the search effected by the buccal swab of respondent falls within the category of cases this Court has analyzed by reference to the proposition that the "touchstone of the Fourth Amendment is reasonableness, not individualized suspicion."

Even if a warrant is not required, a search is not beyond Fourth Amendment scrutiny; for it must be reasonable in its scope and manner of execution. Urgent government interests are not a license for indiscriminate police behavior. To say that no warrant is required is merely to acknowledge that "rather than employing a *per se* rule of unreasonableness, we balance the privacy-related and law enforcement-related concerns to determine if the intrusion was reasonable." This application of "traditional standards of reasonableness" requires a court to weigh "the promotion of legitimate governmental interests" against "the degree to which [the search] intrudes upon an individual's privacy." An assessment of reasonableness to determine the lawfulness of requiring this class of arrestees to provide a DNA sample is central to the instant case.

IV

A

The legitimate government interest served by the Maryland DNA Collection Act is one that is well established: the need for law enforcement officers in a safe and accurate way to process and identify the persons and possessions they must take into custody. It is beyond dispute that "probable cause provides legal justification for arresting a person suspected of crime, and for a brief period of detention to take the administrative steps incident to arrest." Also uncontested is the "right on the part of the Government, always recognized under English and American law, to search the person of the accused when legally arrested."

The "routine administrative procedure[s] at a police station house incident to booking and jailing the suspect" derive from different origins and have different constitutional justifications than, say, the search of a place, for the search of a place not incident to an arrest depends on the "fair probability that contraband or evidence of a crime will be found in a particular place." The interests are further different when an individual is formally processed into police custody. Then "the law is in the act of subjecting the body of the accused to its physical dominion." When probable cause exists to remove an individual from the normal channels of society and hold him in legal custody, DNA identification plays a critical role in serving those interests.

First, "[i]n every criminal case, it is known and must be known who has been arrested and who is being tried." *Hiibel*. An individual's identity is more than just his name or Social Security number, and the government's interest in identification goes beyond ensuring that the proper name is typed on the indictment. An "arrestee may be carrying a false ID or lie about his identity," and "criminal history records . . . can be inaccurate or incomplete."

A suspect's criminal history is a critical part of his identity that officers should know when processing him for detention. It is a common occurrence that "[p]eople detained for minor offenses can turn out to be the most devious and dangerous criminals. Hours after the Oklahoma City bombing, Timothy McVeigh was stopped by a state trooper who noticed he was driving without a license plate. Police stopped serial killer Joel Rifkin for the same reason. One of the terrorists involved in the September 11 attacks was stopped and ticketed for speeding just two days before hijacking Flight 93." Police already seek this crucial identifying information. They use routine and accepted means as varied as comparing the suspect's booking photograph to sketch artists' depictions of persons of interest, showing his mugshot to potential witnesses, and of course making a computerized comparison of the arrestee's fingerprints against electronic databases of known criminals and un-solved crimes. In this respect the only difference between DNA analysis and the accepted use of fingerprint databases is the unparalleled accuracy DNA provides.

The task of identification necessarily entails searching public and police records based on the identifying information provided by the arrestee to see what is already known about him. The DNA collected from arrestees is an irrefutable identification of the person from whom it was taken. Like a fingerprint, the 13 CODIS loci are not themselves evidence of any particular crime, in the way that a drug test can by itself be evidence of illegal narcotics use. A DNA profile is useful to the police because it gives them a form of identification to search the records already in their valid possession. In this respect the use of DNA for identification is no different than matching an arrestee's face to a wanted poster of a previously unidentified suspect; or matching tattoos to known gang symbols to reveal a criminal affiliation; or matching the arrestee's fingerprints to those recovered from a crime scene. DNA is another metric of identification used to connect the arrestee with his or her public persona, as reflected in records of his or her actions that are available to the police. Those records may be linked to the arrestee by a variety of relevant forms of identification, including name, alias, date and time of previous convictions and the name then used, photograph, Social Security number, or CODIS profile. These data, found in official records, are checked as a routine matter to produce a more comprehensive record of the suspect's complete identity. Finding occurrences of the arrestee's CODIS profile in outstanding cases is consistent with this common practice. It uses a different form of identification than a name or fingerprint, but its function is the same.

Second, law enforcement officers bear a responsibility for ensuring that the custody of an arrestee does not create inordinate "risks for facility staff, for the existing detainee population, and for a new detainee." DNA identification can provide untainted information to those charged with detaining suspects and detaining the property of any felon. For these purposes officers must know the type of person whom they are detaining, and DNA allows them to make critical choices about how to proceed.

Third, looking forward to future stages of criminal prosecution, "the Government has a substantial interest in ensuring that persons accused of crimes are available for trials." A person who is arrested for one offense but knows that he has yet to answer for some past crime may be more inclined to flee the instant charges, lest continued contact with the criminal justice system expose one or more other serious offenses. For example, a defendant who had committed a prior sexual assault might be inclined to flee on a burglary charge, knowing that in every State a DNA sample would be taken from him after his conviction on the burglary charge that would tie him to the more serious charge of rape. In addition to subverting the administration of justice with respect to the crime of arrest, this ties back to the interest in safety; for a detainee who absconds from custody presents a risk to law enforcement officers, other detainees, victims of previous crimes, witnesses, and society at large.

Fourth, an arrestee's past conduct is essential to an assessment of the danger he poses to the public, and this will inform a court's determination whether the individual should be released on bail. "The government's interest in preventing crime by arrestees is both legitimate and compelling." DNA identification of a suspect in a violent crime provides critical information to the police and judicial officials in making a determination of the arrestee's future dangerousness. This inquiry always has entailed some scrutiny beyond the name on the defendant's driver's license. For example, Maryland law requires a judge to take into account not only "the nature and circumstances of the offense charged" but also "the defendant's family ties, employment status and history, financial resources, reputation, character and mental condition, length of residence in the community." Knowing that the defendant is wanted for a previous violent crime based on DNA identification is especially probative of the court's consideration of "the danger of the defendant to the alleged victim, another person, or the community."

Present capabilities make it possible to complete a DNA identification that provides information essential to determining whether a detained suspect can be released pending trial. Regardless of when the initial bail decision is made, release is not appropriate until a further determination is made as to the person's identity in the sense not only of what his birth certificate states but also what other records and data disclose to give that identity more meaning in the whole context of who the person really is. And even when release is permitted, the background identity of the suspect is necessary for determining what conditions must be met before release is allowed. If release is authorized, it may take time for the conditions to be met, and so the time before actual release can be substantial.

Even if an arrestee is released on bail, development of DNA identification revealing the defendant's unknown violent past can and should lead to the revocation of his conditional release. Pretrial release of a person charged with a dangerous crime is a most serious responsibility. It is reasonable in all respects for the State to use an accepted database to determine if an arrestee is the object of suspicion in other serious crimes, suspicion that may provide a strong incentive for the arrestee to escape and flee.

Finally, in the interests of justice, the identification of an arrestee as the perpetrator of some heinous crime may have the salutary effect of freeing a person wrongfully imprisoned for the same offense. "[P]rompt [DNA] testing . . . would speed up apprehension of criminals before they commit additional crimes, and prevent the grotesque detention of . . . innocent people." J. Dwyer, P. Neufeld, & B. Scheck, Actual Innocence 245 (2000).

Because proper processing of arrestees is so important and has consequences for every stage of the criminal process, the Court has recognized that the "governmental interests underlying a station-house search of the arrestee's person and possessions may in some circumstances be even greater than those supporting a search immediately following arrest." Thus, the Court has been reluctant to circumscribe the authority of the police to conduct reasonable booking searches. For example, "[t]he standards traditionally governing a search incident to lawful arrest are not . . . commuted to the stricter *Terry* standards." Nor are these interests in identification served only by a search of the arrestee himself. "[I]nspection of an arrestee's personal property may assist the police in ascertaining or verifying his identity."

B

DNA identification represents an important advance in the techniques used by law enforcement to serve legitimate police concerns for as long as there have been arrests, concerns the courts have acknowledged and approved for more than a century. Law enforcement agencies routinely have used scientific advancements in their standard procedures for the identification of arrestees. "Police had been using photography to capture the faces of criminals almost since its invention." Courts did not dispute that practice, concluding that a "sheriff in making an arrest for a felony on a warrant has the right to exercise a discretion . . . , [if] he should deem it necessary to the safe-keeping of a prisoner, and to prevent his escape, or to enable him the more readily to retake the prisoner if he should escape, to take his photograph." By the time that it had become "the daily practice of the police officers and detectives of crime to use photographic pictures for the discovery and identification of criminals," the courts likewise had come to the conclusion that "it would be [a] matter of regret to have its use unduly restricted upon any fanciful theory or constitutional privilege."

Perhaps the most direct historical analogue to the DNA technology used to identify respondent is the familiar practice of fingerprinting arrestees. From the advent of this technique, courts had no trouble determining that fingerprinting was a natural part of "the administrative steps incident to arrest." In the seminal case of *United States v. Kelly*, 55 F.2d 67 (C.A.2 1932), Judge Augustus Hand wrote that routine fingerprinting did not violate the Fourth Amendment precisely because it fit within the accepted means of processing an arrestee into custody:

> "Finger printing seems to be no more than an extension of methods of identification long used in dealing with persons under arrest for real or supposed violations of the criminal laws. It is known to be a very certain means devised by modern science to reach the desired end, and has become especially important in a time when increased population and vast aggregations of people in urban centers have rendered the notoriety of the individual in the community no longer a ready means of identification.
>
> . . .
>
> "We find no ground in reason or authority for interfering with a method of identifying persons charged with crime which has now become widely known and frequently practiced."

By the middle of the 20th century, it was considered "elementary that a person in lawful custody may be required to submit to photographing and fingerprinting as part of routine identification processes."

DNA identification is an advanced technique superior to fingerprinting in many ways, so much so that to insist on fingerprints as the norm would make little sense to either the forensic expert or a layperson. The additional intrusion upon the arrestee's privacy beyond that associated with fingerprinting is not significant, and DNA is a markedly more accurate form of identifying arrestees. A suspect who has changed his facial features to evade photographic identification or even one who has undertaken the more arduous task of altering his fingerprints cannot escape the revealing power of his DNA.

The respondent's primary objection to this analogy is that DNA identification is not as fast as fingerprinting, and so it should not be considered to be the 21st-century equivalent. But rapid analysis of fingerprints is itself of recent vintage. The FBI's vaunted Integrated Automated Fingerprint Identification System (IAFIS) was only "launched on July 28, 1999. Prior to this time, the processing of . . . fingerprint submissions was largely a manual, labor-intensive process, taking weeks or months to process a single submission." It was not the advent of this technology that rendered fingerprint analysis constitutional in a single moment. The question of how long it takes to process identifying information obtained from a valid search goes only to the efficacy of the search for its purpose of prompt identification, not the constitutionality of the search. Given the importance of DNA in the identification of police records pertaining to arrestees and the need to refine and confirm that identity for its important bearing on the decision to continue release on bail or to impose of new conditions, DNA serves an essential purpose despite the existence of delays such as the one that occurred in this case. Even so, the delay in processing DNA from arrestees is being reduced to a substantial degree by rapid technical advances.

In sum, there can be little reason to question "the legitimate interest of the government in knowing for an absolute certainty the identity of the person arrested, in knowing whether he is wanted elsewhere, and in ensuring his identification in the event he flees prosecution." DNA identification of arrestees, of the type approved by the Maryland statute here at issue, is "no more than an extension of methods of identification long used in dealing with persons under arrest." In the balance of reasonableness required by the Fourth Amendment, therefore, the Court must give great weight both to the significant government interest at stake in the identification of arrestees and to the unmatched potential of DNA identification to serve that interest.

V

A

By comparison to this substantial government interest and the unique effectiveness of DNA identification, the intrusion of a cheek swab to obtain a DNA sample is a minimal one. True, a significant government interest does not alone suffice to justify a search. The government interest must outweigh the degree to which the search invades an individual's legitimate expectations of privacy. In considering those expectations in this case, however, the necessary predicate of a valid arrest for a serious offense is fundamental. "Although the underlying command of the Fourth Amendment is always that searches and seizures be reasonable, what is reasonable depends on the context within which a search takes place."

The expectations of privacy of an individual taken into police custody "necessarily [are] of a diminished scope." *Bell*, 441 U.S., at 557, 99 S. Ct. 1861. "[B]oth the person and the property in his immediate possession may be searched at the station house." A search of the detainee's person when he is booked into custody may " 'involve a relatively extensive exploration,' " including "requir[ing] at least some detainees to lift their genitals or cough in a squatting position," *Florence*, 566 U.S., at ___.

When the police stop a motorist at a checkpoint, see *Indianapolis v. Edmond*, they intrude upon substantial expectations of privacy. So the Court has insisted on some purpose other than "to detect evidence of ordinary criminal wrongdoing" to justify these searches in the absence of individualized suspicion. *Edmond*. Once an individual has been arrested on probable cause for a dangerous offense that may require detention before trial, however, his or her expectations of privacy and freedom from police scrutiny are reduced. DNA identification like that at issue here thus does not require consideration of any unique needs that would be required to justify searching the average citizen. The special needs cases, though in full accord with the result reached here, do not have a direct bearing on the issues presented in this case, because unlike the search of a citizen who has not been suspected of a wrong, a detainee has a reduced expectation of privacy.

The reasonableness inquiry here considers two other circumstances in which the Court has held that particularized suspicion is not categorically required: "diminished expectations of privacy [and] minimal intrusions." This is not to suggest that any search is acceptable solely because a person is in custody. Some searches, such as invasive surgery, see *Winston,* or a search of the arrestee's home, see *Chimel,* involve either greater intrusions or higher expectations of privacy than are present in this case. In those situations, when the Court must "balance the privacy-related and law enforcement-related concerns to determine if the intrusion was reasonable," the privacy-related concerns are weighty enough that the search may require a warrant, notwithstanding the diminished expectations of privacy of the arrestee.

Here, by contrast to the approved standard procedures incident to any arrest detailed above, a buccal swab involves an even more brief and still minimal intrusion. A gentle rub along the inside of the cheek does not break the skin, and it "involves virtually no risk, trauma, or pain." "A crucial factor in analyzing the magnitude of the intrusion . . . is the extent to which the procedure may threaten the safety or health of the individual," and nothing suggests that a buccal swab poses any physical danger whatsoever. A brief intrusion of an arrestee's person is subject to the Fourth Amendment, but a swab of this nature does not increase the indignity already attendant to normal incidents of arrest.

B

In addition the processing of respondent's DNA sample's 13 CODIS loci did not intrude on respondent's privacy in a way that would make his DNA identification unconstitutional.

First, as already noted, the CODIS loci come from noncoding parts of the DNA that do not reveal the genetic traits of the arrestee. While science can always progress further, and those progressions may have Fourth Amendment consequences, alleles at the CODIS loci "are not at present revealing information beyond identification." The argument that the testing at issue in this case reveals any private medical information at all is open to dispute.

And even if non-coding alleles could provide some information, they are not in fact tested for that end. It is undisputed that law enforcement officers analyze DNA for the sole purpose of generating a unique identifying number against which future samples may be matched. This parallels a similar safeguard based on actual practice in the school drug-testing context, where the Court deemed it "significant that the tests at issue here look only for drugs, and not for whether the student is, for example, epileptic, pregnant, or diabetic." *Vernonia School Dist. 47J,* 515 U.S., at 658. If in the future police analyze samples to determine, for instance, an arrestee's predisposition for a particular disease or other hereditary factors not relevant to identity, that case would present additional privacy concerns not present here.

Finally, the Act provides statutory protections that guard against further invasion of privacy. As noted above, the Act requires that "[o]nly DNA records that directly relate to the identification of individuals shall be collected and stored." No purpose other than identification is permissible: "A person may not willfully test a

DNA sample for information that does not relate to the identification of individuals as specified in this subtitle." This Court has noted often that "a 'statutory or regulatory duty to avoid unwarranted disclosures' generally allays . . . privacy concerns." The Court need not speculate about the risks posed "by a system that did not contain comparable security provisions." In light of the scientific and statutory safeguards, once respondent's DNA was lawfully collected the STR analysis of respondent's DNA pursuant to CODIS procedures did not amount to a significant invasion of privacy that would render the DNA identification impermissible under the Fourth Amendment.

* * *

In light of the context of a valid arrest supported by probable cause respondent's expectations of privacy were not offended by the minor intrusion of a brief swab of his cheeks. By contrast, that same context of arrest gives rise to significant state interests in identifying respondent not only so that the proper name can be attached to his charges but also so that the criminal justice system can make informed decisions concerning pretrial custody. Upon these considerations the Court concludes that DNA identification of arrestees is a reasonable search that can be considered part of a routine booking procedure. When officers make an arrest supported by probable cause to hold for a serious offense and they bring the suspect to the station to be detained in custody, taking and analyzing a cheek swab of the arrestee's DNA is, like fingerprinting and photographing, a legitimate police booking procedure that is reasonable under the Fourth Amendment.

The judgment of the Court of Appeals of Maryland is reversed.

JUSTICE SCALIA, with whom JUSTICE GINSBURG, JUSTICE SOTOMAYOR, and JUSTICE KAGAN join, dissenting.

The Fourth Amendment forbids searching a person for evidence of a crime when there is no basis for believing the person is guilty of the crime or is in possession of incriminating evidence. That prohibition is categorical and without exception; it lies at the very heart of the Fourth Amendment. Whenever this Court has allowed a suspicionless search, it has insisted upon a justifying motive apart from the investigation of crime.

It is obvious that no such noninvestigative motive exists in this case. The Court's assertion that DNA is being taken, not to solve crimes, but to *identify* those in the State's custody, taxes the credulity of the credulous. And the Court's comparison of Maryland's DNA searches to other techniques, such as fingerprinting, can seem apt only to those who know no more than today's opinion has chosen to tell them about how those DNA searches actually work.

I

A

At the time of the Founding, Americans despised the British use of so-called "general warrants" — warrants not grounded upon a sworn oath of a specific infraction by a particular individual, and thus not limited in scope and application. The first Virginia Constitution declared that "general warrants, whereby any officer or messenger may be commanded to search suspected places without evidence of a fact committed," or to search a person "whose offence is not particularly described and supported by evidence," "are grievous and oppressive, and ought not be granted."

In the ratification debates, Antifederalists sarcastically predicted that the general, suspicionless warrant would be among the Constitution's "blessings." "Brutus" of New York asked why the Federal Constitution contained no provision like Maryland's, and Patrick Henry warned that the new Federal Constitution would expose the citizenry to searches and seizures "in the most arbitrary manner, without any evidence or reason."

Madison's draft of what became the Fourth Amendment answered these charges by providing that the "rights of the people to be secured in their persons . . . from all unreasonable searches and seizures, shall not be violated by warrants issued without probable cause . . . or not particularly describing the places to be searched." As ratified, the Fourth Amendment's Warrant Clause forbids a warrant to "issue" except "upon probable cause," and requires that it be "particula[r]" (which is to say, *individualized*) to "the place to be searched, and the persons or things to be seized." And we have held that, even when a warrant is not constitutionally necessary, the Fourth Amendment's general prohibition of "unreasonable" searches imports the same requirement of individualized suspicion.

Although there is a "closely guarded category of constitutionally permissible suspicionless searches," that has never included searches designed to serve "the normal need for law enforcement." Even the common name for suspicionless searches — "special needs" searches — itself reflects that they must be justified, *always*, by concerns "other than crime detection."

So while the Court is correct to note that there are instances in which we have permitted searches without individualized suspicion, "[i]n none of these cases . . . did we indicate approval of a [search] whose primary purpose was to detect evidence of ordinary criminal wrongdoing." *Indianapolis v. Edmond*. That limitation is crucial. It is only when a governmental purpose aside from crime-solving is at stake that we engage in the free-form "reasonableness" inquiry that the Court indulges at length today. To put it another way, both the legitimacy of the Court's method and the correctness of its outcome hinge entirely on the truth of a single proposition: that the primary purpose of these DNA searches is something other than simply discovering evidence of criminal wrongdoing. As I detail below, that proposition is wrong.

B

The Court alludes at several points to the fact that King was an arrestee, and arrestees may be validly searched incident to their arrest. But the Court does not really *rest* on this principle, and for good reason: The objects of a search incident to arrest must be either (1) weapons or evidence that might easily be destroyed, or (2) evidence relevant to the crime of arrest. See *Arizona v. Gant; Thornton v.*

United States (SCALIA, J., concurring in judgment). Neither is the object of the search at issue here.

The Court hastens to clarify that it does not mean to approve invasive surgery on arrestees or warrantless searches of their homes. That the Court feels the need to disclaim these consequences is as damning a criticism of its suspicionless-search regime as any I can muster. And the Court's attempt to distinguish those hypothetical searches from this real one is unconvincing. We are told that the "privacy-related concerns" in the search of a home "are weighty enough that the search may require a warrant, notwithstanding the diminished expectations of privacy of the arrestee." But why are the "privacy-related concerns" not also "weighty" when an intrusion into the *body* is at stake? (The Fourth Amendment lists "persons" *first* among the entities protected against unreasonable searches and seizures.) And could the police engage, without any suspicion of wrongdoing, in a "brief and . . . minimal" intrusion into the home of an arrestee — perhaps just peeking around the curtilage a bit? Obviously not.

At any rate, all this discussion is beside the point. No matter the degree of invasiveness, suspicionless searches are *never* allowed if their principal end is ordinary crime-solving. A search incident to arrest either serves other ends (such as officer safety, in a search for weapons) or is not suspicionless (as when there is reason to believe the arrestee possesses evidence relevant to the crime of arrest).

Sensing (correctly) that it needs more, the Court elaborates at length the ways that the search here served the special purpose of "identifying" King.[1] But that seems to me quite wrong — unless what one means by "identifying" someone is "searching for evidence that he has committed crimes unrelated to the crime of his arrest." At points the Court does appear to use "identifying" in that peculiar sense — claiming, for example, that knowing "an arrestee's past conduct is essential to an assessment of the danger he poses." If identifying someone means finding out what unsolved crimes he has committed, then identification is indistinguishable from the ordinary law-enforcement aims that have never been thought to justify a suspicion-less search. Searching every lawfully stopped car, for example, might turn up information about unsolved crimes the driver had committed, but no one would say that such a search was aimed at "identifying" him, and no court would hold such a search lawful. I will therefore assume that the Court means that the DNA search at issue here was useful to "identify" King in the normal sense of that word — in the sense that would identify the author of Introduction to the Principles of Morals and Legislation as Jeremy Bentham.

---

[1] The Court's insistence (*ante*, at 1978) that our special-needs cases "do not have a direct bearing on the issues presented in this case" is perplexing. Why spill so much ink on the special need of identification if a special need is not required? Why not just come out and say that any suspicionless search of an arrestee is allowed if it will be useful to solve crimes? The Court does not say that because most Members of the Court do not believe it. So whatever the Court's major premise — the opinion does not really contain what you would call a rule of decision — the *minor* premise is "this search was used to identify King." The incorrectness of that minor premise will therefore suffice to demonstrate the error in the Court's result.

1

The portion of the Court's opinion that explains the identification rationale is strangely silent on the actual workings of the DNA search at issue here. To know those facts is to be instantly disabused of the notion that what happened had anything to do with identifying King.

King was arrested on April 10, 2009, on charges unrelated to the case before us. That same day, April 10, the police searched him and seized the DNA evidence at issue here. What happened next? Reading the Court's opinion, particularly its insistence that the search was necessary to know "who [had] been arrested," one might guess that King's DNA was swiftly processed and his identity thereby confirmed — perhaps against some master database of known DNA profiles, as is done for fingerprints. After all, was not the suspicionless search here crucial to avoid "inordinate risks for facility staff" or to "existing detainee population"? Surely, then — *surely* — the State of Maryland got cracking on those grave risks immediately, by rushing to identify King with his DNA as soon as possible.

Nothing could be further from the truth. Maryland officials did not even begin the process of testing King's DNA that day. Or, actually, the next day. Or the day after that. And that was for a simple reason: Maryland law forbids them to do so. A "DNA sample collected from an individual charged with a crime . . . *may not* be tested or placed in the statewide DNA data base system prior to the first scheduled arraignment date." And King's first appearance in court was not until three days after his arrest. (I suspect, though, that they did not wait three days to ask his name or take his fingerprints.)

This places in a rather different light the Court's solemn declaration that the search here was necessary so that King could be identified at "every stage of the criminal process." I hope that the Maryland officials who read the Court's opinion do not take it seriously. Acting on the Court's misperception of Maryland law could lead to jail time. See Md. Pub. Saf. Code Ann. § 2-512(c)–(e) (punishing by up to five years' imprisonment anyone who obtains or tests DNA information except as provided by statute). Does the Court really believe that Maryland did not know whom it was arraigning? The Court's response is to imagine that release on bail could take so long that the DNA results are returned in time, or perhaps that bail could be revoked if the DNA test turned up incriminating information. That is no answer at all. If the purpose of this Act is to assess "whether [King] should be released on bail," why would it *possibly* forbid the DNA testing process to *begin* until King was arraigned? Why would Maryland resign itself to simply hoping that the bail decision will drag out long enough that the "identification" can succeed before the arrestee is released? The truth, known to Maryland and increasingly to the reader: this search had nothing to do with establishing King's identity.

It gets worse. King's DNA sample was not received by the Maryland State Police's Forensic Sciences Division until April 23, 2009 — two weeks after his arrest. It sat in that office, ripening in a storage area, until the custodians got around to mailing it to a lab for testing on June 25, 2009 — two months after it was received, and nearly *three* since King's arrest. After it was mailed, the data from the lab tests were not available for several more weeks, until July 13, 2009, which is when the test results were entered into Maryland's DNA database, *together with information identifying the person from whom the sample was taken.* Meanwhile, bail had been set, King had engaged in discovery, and he had requested a speedy trial — presumably not a trial of John Doe. It was not until August 4, 2009 — four months after King's arrest — that the forwarded sample transmitted (*without* identifying information) from the Maryland DNA database to the Federal Bureau of Investigation's national database was matched with a sample taken from the scene of an unrelated crime years earlier.

A more specific description of exactly what happened at this point illustrates why, by definition, King could not have been *identified* by this match. The FBI's DNA database (known as CODIS) consists of two distinct collections. FBI, CODIS and NDIS Fact Sheet. One of them, the one to which King's DNA was submitted, consists of DNA samples taken from known convicts or arrestees. I will refer to this as the "Convict and Arrestee Collection." The other collection consists of samples taken from crime scenes; I will refer to this as the "Unsolved Crimes Collection." The Convict and Arrestee Collection stores "no names or other personal identifiers of the offenders, arrestees, or detainees." Rather, it contains only the DNA profile itself, the name of the agency that submitted it, the laboratory personnel who analyzed it, and an identification number for the specimen. This is because the submitting state laboratories are expected *already* to know the identities of the convicts and arrestees from whom samples are taken. (And, of course, they do.)

Moreover, the CODIS system works by checking to see whether any of the samples in the Unsolved Crimes Collection match any of the samples in the Convict and Arrestee Collection. That is sensible, if what one wants to do is solve those cold cases, but note what it requires: that the identity of the people whose DNA has been entered in the Convict and Arrestee Collection *already be known.*[2] If one wanted to identify someone in custody using his DNA, the logical thing to do would be to compare that DNA against the Convict and Arrestee Collection: to search, in other words, the collection that could be used (by checking back with the submitting state agency) to identify people, rather than the collection of evidence from unsolved crimes, whose perpetrators are by definition unknown. But that is not what was done. And that is because this search had nothing to do with identification.

In fact, if anything was "identified" at the moment that the DNA database returned a match, it was not King — his identity was already known. (The docket for the original criminal charges lists his full name, his race, his sex, his height, his weight, his date of birth, and his address.) Rather, what the August 4 match "identified" was *the previously-taken sample from the earlier crime.* That sample was genuinely mysterious to Maryland; the State knew that it had probably been left by the victim's attacker, but nothing else. King was not identified by his association with the sample; rather, the sample was identified by its association with King. The Court effectively destroys its own "identification" theory when it acknowledges that the object of this search was "to see what [was] already known about [King]." King was who he was, and volumes of his biography could not make

---

[2] By the way, this procedure has nothing to do with exonerating the wrongfully convicted, as the Court soothingly promises. The FBI CODIS database includes DNA from *unsolved* crimes. I know of no indication (and the Court cites none) that it also includes DNA from all — or even any — crimes whose perpetrators have already been convicted.

him any more or any less King. No minimally competent speaker of English would say, upon noticing a known arrestee's similarity "to a wanted poster of a previously unidentified suspect," that the *arrestee* had thereby been identified. It was the previously unidentified suspect who had been identified — just as, here, it was the previously unidentified rapist.

2

That taking DNA samples from arrestees has nothing to do with identifying them is confirmed not just by actual practice (which the Court ignores) but by the enabling statute itself (which the Court also ignores). The Maryland Act at issue has a section helpfully entitled "Purpose of collecting and testing DNA samples." (One would expect such a section to play a somewhat larger role in the Court's analysis of the Act's purpose — which is to say, at least *some* role.) That provision lists five purposes for which DNA samples may be tested. By this point, it will not surprise the reader to learn that the Court's imagined purpose is not among them.

Instead, the law provides that DNA samples are collected and tested, as a matter of Maryland law, "as part of an official investigation into a crime." § 2-505(a)(2). (Or, as our suspicionless-search cases would put it: for ordinary law-enforcement purposes.) That is certainly how everyone has always understood the Maryland Act until today. The Governor of Maryland, in commenting on our decision to hear this case, said that he was glad, because "[a]llowing law enforcement to collect DNA samples . . . is absolutely critical to our efforts to continue driving down crime," and "bolsters our efforts to resolve open investigations and bring them to a resolution." The attorney general of Maryland remarked that he "look[ed] forward to the opportunity to defend this important crime-fighting tool," and praised the DNA database for helping to "bring to justice violent perpetrators." Even this Court's order staying the decision below states that the statute "provides a valuable tool for investigating unsolved crimes and thereby helping to remove violent offenders from the general population" — with, unsurprisingly, no mention of identity. (ROBERTS, C. J., in chambers).

More devastating still for the Court's "identification" theory, the statute *does* enumerate two instances in which a DNA sample may be tested for the purpose of identification: "to help identify *human remains*," § 2-505(a)(3) (emphasis added), and "to help identify *missing individuals*," (emphasis added). No mention of identifying arrestees. *Inclusio unius est exclusio alterius.* And note again that Maryland forbids using DNA records "for any purposes other than those specified" — it is actually a crime to do so.

The Maryland regulations implementing the Act confirm what is now monotonously obvious: These DNA searches have nothing to do with identification. For example, if someone is arrested and law enforcement determines that "a convicted offender Statewide DNA Data Base sample already exists" for that arrestee, "the agency is not required to obtain a new sample." But how could the State know if an arrestee has already had his DNA sample collected, if the point of the sample is to identify who he is? Of course, if the DNA sample is instead taken in order to investigate crimes, this restriction makes perfect sense: Having previously placed an identified someone's DNA on file to check against available crime-scene evidence, there is no sense in going to the expense of taking a new sample. Maryland's regulations further require that the "individual collecting a sample . . . verify the identity of the individual from whom a sample is taken by name and, if applicable, State identification (SID) number." (But how?) And after the sample is taken, it continues to be identified *by* the individual's name, fingerprints, etc., rather than (as the Court believes) being used *to identify* individuals.

So, to review: DNA testing does not even begin until after arraignment and bail decisions are already made. The samples sit in storage for months, and take weeks to test. When they are tested, they are checked against the Unsolved Crimes Collection — rather than the Convict and Arrestee Collection, which could be used to identify them. The Act forbids the Court's purpose (identification), but prescribes as its purpose what our suspicionless-search cases forbid ("official investigation into a crime"). Against all of that, it is safe to say that if the Court's identification theory is not wrong, there is no such thing as error.

II

The Court also attempts to bolster its identification theory with a series of inapposite analogies.

Is not taking DNA samples the same, asks the Court, as taking a person's photograph? No — because that is not a Fourth Amendment search at all. It does not involve a physical intrusion onto the person, and we have never held that merely taking a person's photograph invades any recognized "expectation of privacy," see *Katz*. Thus, it is unsurprising that the cases the Court cites as authorizing photo-taking do not even mention the Fourth Amendment.

It is on the fingerprinting of arrestees, however, that the Court relies most heavily. The Court does not actually say whether it believes that taking a person's fingerprints is a Fourth Amendment search, and our cases provide no ready answer to that question. Even assuming so, however, law enforcement's post-arrest use of fingerprints could not be more different from its post-arrest use of DNA. Fingerprints of arrestees are taken primarily to identify them (though that process sometimes solves crimes); the DNA of arrestees is taken to solve crimes (and nothing else). Contrast CODIS, the FBI's nationwide DNA database, with IAFIS, the FBI's Integrated Automated Fingerprint Identification System.

The Court asserts that the taking of fingerprints was "constitutional for generations prior to the introduction" of the FBI's rapid computer-matching system. This bold statement is bereft of citation to authority because there is none for it. The "great expansion in fingerprinting came before the modern era of Fourth Amendment jurisprudence," and so we were never asked to decide the legitimacy of the practice. As fingerprint databases expanded from convicted criminals, to arrestees, to civil servants, to immigrants, to everyone with a driver's license, Americans simply "became accustomed to having our fingerprints on file in some government database." But it is wrong to suggest that this was uncontroversial at the time, or that this Court blessed universal fingerprinting for "generations" before it was possible to use it effectively for identification.

The Court also assures us that "the delay in processing DNA from arrestees is being reduced to a substantial degree by rapid technical advances." The idea, presumably, is that the snail's pace in this case is atypical, so that DNA is now readily usable for identification. The Court's proof, however, is nothing but a pair of press releases — each of which turns out to undercut this argument. We learn in them that reductions in backlog have enabled Ohio and Louisiana crime labs to analyze a submitted DNA sample in twenty days. But that is *still longer* than the *eighteen* days that Maryland needed to analyze King's sample, once it worked its way through the State's labyrinthine bureaucracy. What this illustrates is that these times do not take into account the many other sources of delay. So if the Court means to suggest that Maryland is unusual, that may be right — it may qualify in this context as a paragon of efficiency. (Indeed, the Governor of Maryland was hailing the elimination of that State's backlog more than five years ago.

The Court also accepts uncritically the Government's representation at oral argument that it is developing devices that will be able to test DNA in mere minutes. At most, this demonstrates that it may one day be possible to design a program that uses DNA for a purpose other than crime-solving — not that Maryland has in fact designed such a program today. And that is the main point, which the Court's discussion of the brave new world of instant DNA analysis should not obscure. The issue before us is not whether DNA can *some day* be used for identification; nor even whether it can *today* be used for identification; but whether it *was used for identification here.*

Today, it can fairly be said that fingerprints really are used to identify people — so well, in fact, that there would be no need for the expense of a separate, wholly redundant DNA confirmation of the same information. What DNA adds — what makes it a valuable weapon in the law-enforcement arsenal — is the ability to solve unsolved crimes, by matching old crime-scene evidence against the profiles of people whose identities are already known. That is what was going on when King's DNA was taken, and we should not disguise the fact. Solving unsolved crimes is a noble objective, but it occupies a lower place in the American pantheon of noble objectives than the protection of our people from suspicionless law-enforcement searches. The Fourth Amendment must prevail.

* * *

The Court disguises the vast (and scary) scope of its holding by promising a limitation it cannot deliver. The Court repeatedly says that DNA testing, and entry into a national DNA registry, will not befall thee and me, dear reader, but only those arrested for "serious offense[s]." I cannot imagine what principle could possibly justify this limitation, and the Court does not attempt to suggest any. If one believes that DNA will "identify" someone arrested for assault, he must believe that it will "identify" someone arrested for a traffic offense. This Court does not base its judgments on senseless distinctions. At the end of the day, *logic will out.* When there comes before us the taking of DNA from an arrestee for a traffic violation, the Court will predictably (and quite rightly) say, "We can find no significant difference between this case and *King.*" Make no mistake about it: As an entirely predictable consequence of today's decision, your DNA can be taken and entered into a national DNA database if you are ever arrested, rightly or wrongly, and for whatever reason.

The most regrettable aspect of the suspicionless search that occurred here is that it proved to be quite unnecessary. All parties concede that it would have been entirely permissible, as far as the Fourth Amendment is concerned, for Maryland to take a sample of King's DNA as a consequence of his conviction for second-degree assault. So the ironic result of the Court's error is this: The only arrestees to whom the outcome here will ever make a difference are those who *have been acquitted* of the crime of arrest (so that their DNA could not have been taken upon conviction). In other words, this Act manages to burden uniquely the sole group for whom the Fourth Amendment's protections ought to be most jealously guarded: people who are innocent of the State's accusations.

Today's judgment will, to be sure, have the beneficial effect of solving more crimes; then again, so would the taking of DNA samples from anyone who flies on an airplane (surely the Transportation Security Administration needs to know the "identity" of the flying public), applies for a driver's license, or attends a public school. Perhaps the construction of such a genetic panopticon is wise. But I doubt that the proud men who wrote the charter of our liberties would have been so eager to open their mouths for royal inspection.

I therefore dissent, and hope that today's incursion upon the Fourth Amendment, like an earlier one,[6] will some day be repudiated.

QUESTIONS AND NOTES

1. Justice Thomas was the only member of the Court to be in the majority in both *Jardines* and *King.*

2. Is approaching universal collection of DNA (with limits on how it can be used) a good thing or a bad thing?

3. If you knew that the police (or CODIS) had your DNA on file, would you be alarmed? Explain.

4. How, if at all, could an innocent person be hurt by taking his/her DNA?

5. Is (should) DNA be justified, if at all, as a means of identifying an arrestee, or can (should) it also be available to detect past criminality?

6. Given that the police can strip search and body cavity search an arrestee just by the fact of arrest and temporary detention (see *Florence,* discussed in *King*) would it make any sense to deny the police the right to get DNA via a benign buccal swab?

7. Would the procedure be better if the police required the suspect to spit in a cup so that they did not have to enter his body at all?

---

[6] Compare, *New York v. Belton,* 453 U.S. 454, 101 S. Ct. 2860, 69 L. Ed. 2d 768 (1981) (suspicionless search of a car permitted upon arrest of the driver), with *Arizona v. Gant,* 556 U.S. 332, 129 S. Ct. 1710, 173 L. Ed. 2d 485 (2009) (on second thought, no).

8.   Do you think that the analogy to fingerprinting is sound?

9.   Does (should) it matter that it takes a long time for DNA results to be returned?

C.   BORDER AND INTERNATIONAL SEARCHES

The Court has long considered border searches special. Quite clearly ordinary rules do not apply to border searches. Indeed, the Court has allowed some extraordinary intrusions such as complete disassembly of a car's gas tank to look for drugs on nothing more than an officer's whim. *See United States v. Flores-Montano*, 541 U.S. 149 (2004). And, in *United States v. Montoya de Hernandez*, 473 U.S. 531 (1985), the Court permitted a warrantless 36 hour detention of a suspected drug smuggler, who refused to defecate into a waste basket on command.

In regard to international searches, the Court held that the Fourth Amendment did not apply to a search of a Mexican's home located in Mexico. In part the Court questioned whether he was one of the "people" alluded to in the Fourth Amendment. *See United States v. Verdugo-Urquidez*, 494 U.S. 259 (1990).

D.   ADMINISTRATIVE AND OTHER NONCRIMINAL SEARCHES

You will most likely focus more on administrative searches in other courses such as Administrative Law, or perhaps Health Law or School Law. For now, some familiarity with the Fourth Amendment in these contexts is helpful.

Typically an administrative search does require a warrant, although it does not require probable cause in the sense that we have come to know and love it. Rather, proof of a need to search all houses in the area for fire hazards is enough probable cause to justify a warrant. *See Camara v. Municipal Court*, 387 U.S. 523 (1967). Occasionally an area will be so heavily regulated that neither a warrant nor probable cause will be required; *e.g.*, guns, alcohol, or junk yards. *See United States v. Biswell*, 406 U.S. 311 (1972); *Colonnade Catering Corp. v. United States*, 397 U.S. 72 (1970); *New York v. Burger*, 482 U.S. 691 (1987).

Drug testing is a type of search that has occasionally been upheld. For example, in the *Skinner* and *Von Raab* cases, the Court upheld drug testing for railroad employees following an accident and certain DEA agents, seeking promotion, respectively. *Skinner v. Railway Labor Executives' Association*, 489 U.S. 602 (1989); *National Treasury Employees Union v. Von Raab*, 489 U.S. 656 (1989). And in *Vernonia School District 47J v. Acton*, 515 U.S. 646 (1995), the Court upheld drug testing for public school athletes, and later extended that rule to all students engaged in extra-curricular activity. *Board of Education of Pottawatomie County v. Earls*, 536 U.S. 822 (2002) But, it would not be accurate to think of suspicionless drug testing as the rule. Rather, the Court has refused to allow such testing for candidates for public office (*Chandler v. Miller*, 520 U.S. 305 (1997)) and for pregnant women treated at public hospitals (*Ferguson v. City of Charleston*, 532 U.S. 67 (2001)).

Public school teachers and principals are permitted to search without a warrant. But ordinarily reasonable suspicion will be required. *See T.L.O. v. New Jersey*, 469 U.S. 325 (1985).

In *Safford Unified School District v. Redding*, 557 U.S. 364 (2009), the Court clarified *T.L.O.*, by holding that reasonable suspicion was insufficient to warrant an in school strip search for the purpose of discovering extra strength ibuprofen, a substance forbidden by school rules, at least in the absence of reason to believe that the substance was present in a place likely to be revealed by a strip search.

Similarly, probationers and parolees are subject to a warrantless search of their home, if, but only if, reasonable suspicion is present. *See Griffin v. Wisconsin*, 483 U.S. 868 (1987). This is so even if the search is for criminal evidence and not merely to enforce parole or probation, if the parolee or probationer had previously agreed to those terms as a condition of his parole or probation. *United States v. Knights*, 534 U.S. 112 (2002) . In *Samson v. California* (2006), the Supreme Court upheld a suspicionless search of a parolee, who had previously agreed to such searches as a condition of his parole. The Court thought that California's prohibition on "arbitrary, capricious, or harassing" searches was a sufficient guarantee of reasonableness despite the fact that in the search at issue, the policeman searched the parolee on no basis other than that fact.

* 1-6 hours detention at border is not unreasonable
* Border officers can search virtually anything without RS
* can not destroy items but can dismantle

Chapter 14

THE EXCLUSIONARY RULE

We have postponed until now, an examination of the exclusionary rule. Heretofore, we have simply assumed that unconstitutionally obtained evidence may not be introduced against the victim of the unconstitutional search or seizure. Now that we know what it means to call something an unreasonable search or seizure, it is appropriate to consider whether or not (and under what circumstances) the exclusionary rule ought to apply.

A. THE RATIONALE FOR THE EXCLUSIONARY RULE

In analyzing the rationale for the exclusionary rule, we begin with a look at the opinion of the Court in the famous case of *Mapp v. Ohio*. At the time that *Mapp* was decided, not all provisions of the Bill of Rights were applicable to the states. Rather, the states were bound by only those provisions deemed fundamental. Bear that in mind, as you read *Mapp*.

MAPP v. OHIO
367 U.S. 643 (1961)

Mr. Justice Clark delivered the opinion of the Court.

Appellant stands convicted of knowingly having had in her possession and under her control certain lewd and lascivious books, pictures, and photographs in violation of § 2905.34 of Ohio's Revised Code. As officially stated in the syllabus to its opinion, the Supreme Court of Ohio found that her conviction was valid though "based primarily upon the introduction in evidence of lewd and lascivious books and pictures unlawfully seized during an unlawful search of defendant's home . . . ."

On May 23, 1957, three Cleveland police officers arrived at appellant's residence in that city pursuant to information that "a person [was] hiding out in the home, who was wanted for questioning in connection with a recent bombing, and that there was a large amount of policy paraphernalia being hidden in the home." Miss Mapp and her daughter by a former marriage lived on the top floor of the two-family dwelling. Upon their arrival at that house, the officers knocked on the door and demanded entrance but appellant, after telephoning her attorney, refused to admit them without a search warrant. They advised their headquarters of the situation and undertook a surveillance of the house.

The officers again sought entrance some three hours later when four or more additional officers arrived on the scene. When Miss Mapp did not come to the door immediately, at least one of the several doors to the house was forcibly opened and the policemen gained admittance. Meanwhile Miss Mapp's attorney arrived, but the officers, having secured their own entry, and continuing in their defiance of the law, would permit him neither to see Miss Mapp nor to enter the house. It appears that Miss Mapp was halfway down the stairs from the upper floor to the front door when the officers, in this highhanded manner, broke into the hall. She demanded to see the search warrant. A paper, claimed to be a warrant, was held up by one of the officers. She grabbed the "warrant" and placed it in her bosom. A struggle ensued in which the officers recovered the piece of paper and as a result of which they handcuffed appellant because she had been "belligerent" in resisting their official rescue of the "warrant" from her person. Running roughshod over appellant, a policeman "grabbed" her, "twisted [her] hand," and she "yelled [and] pleaded with him" because "it was hurting." Appellant, in handcuffs, was then forcibly taken upstairs to her bedroom where the officers searched a dresser, a chest of drawers, a closet and some suitcases. They also looked into a photo album and through personal papers belonging to the appellant. The search spread to the rest of the second floor including the child's bedroom, the living room, the kitchen and a dinette. The basement of the building and a trunk found therein were also searched. The obscene materials for possession of which she was ultimately convicted were discovered in the course of that widespread search.

The State says that even if the search were made without authority, or otherwise unreasonably, it is not prevented from using the unconstitutionally seized evidence at trial, citing *Wolf v. Colorado*, 338 U.S. 25 (1949), in which this Court did indeed hold "that in a prosecution in a State court for a State crime the Fourteenth Amendment does not forbid the admission of evidence obtained by an unreasonable search and seizure."

I.

This Court, in *Weeks v. United States*, 232 U.S. 383 (1914), stated that "the Fourth Amendment . . . put the courts of the United States and Federal officials, in the exercise of their power and authority, under limitations and restraints [and] . . . forever secure[d] the people, their persons, houses, papers, and effects, against all unreasonable searches and seizures under the guise of law . . . and the duty of giving to it force and effect is obligatory upon all entrusted under our Federal system with the enforcement of the laws." Specifically dealing with the use of the evidence unconstitutionally seized, the Court concluded:

> If letters and private documents can thus be seized and held and used in evidence against a citizen accused of an offense, the protection of the Fourth Amendment declaring his right to be secure against such searches and seizures is of no value, and, so far as those thus placed are concerned, might as well be stricken from the Constitution. The efforts of the courts and their officials to bring the guilty to punishment, praiseworthy as they are, are not to be aided by the sacrifice of those great principles established by years of endeavor and suffering which have resulted in their embodiment in the fundamental law of the land.

Finally, the Court in that case clearly stated that use of the seized evidence involved "a denial of the constitutional rights of the accused." Thus, in the year

1914, in the *Weeks* case, this Court "for the first time" held that "in a federal prosecution the Fourth Amendment barred the use of evidence secured through an illegal search and seizure." This Court has ever since required of federal law officers a strict adherence to that command which this Court has held to be a clear, specific, and constitutionally required — even if judicially implied — deterrent safeguard without insistence upon which the Fourth Amendment would have been reduced to "a form of words." Holmes J., *Silverthorne Lumber Co. v. United States*, 251 U.S. 385, 392 (1920). It meant, quite simply, that "conviction by means of unlawful seizures and enforced confessions . . . should find no sanction in the judgments of the courts . . . ," *Weeks*, and that such evidence "shall not be used at all." *Silverthorne*.

There are in the cases of this Court some passing references to the *Weeks* rule as being one of evidence. But the plain and unequivocal language of *Weeks* — and its later paraphrase in *Wolf* — to the effect that the *Weeks* rule is of constitutional origin, remains entirely undisturbed. In *Byars v. United States*, 273 U.S. 28 (1927), a unanimous Court declared that "the doctrine [cannot] . . . be tolerated *under our constitutional system*, that evidences of crime discovered by a federal officer in making a search without lawful warrant may be used against the victim of the unlawful search where a timely challenge has been interposed." (Emphasis added). The Court, in *Olmstead v. United States*, 277 U.S. 438 (1928), in unmistakable language restated the *Weeks* rule:

> The striking outcome of the Weeks case and those which followed it was the sweeping declaration that the Fourth Amendment, although not referring to or limiting the use of evidence in court, really forbade its introduction if obtained by government officers through a violation of the amendment.

II.

In 1949, 35 years after *Weeks* was announced, this Court, in *Wolf*, again for the first time, discussed the effect of the Fourth Amendment upon the States through the operation of the Due Process Clause of the Fourteenth Amendment. It said:

> [W]e have no hesitation in saying that were a State affirmatively to sanction such police incursion into privacy it would run counter to the guaranty of the Fourteenth Amendment.

Nevertheless, after declaring that the "security of one's privacy against arbitrary intrusion by the police" is "implicit in 'the concept of ordered liberty' and as such enforceable against the States through the Due Process Clause," and announcing that it "stoutly adhere[d]" to the *Weeks* decision, the Court decided that the Weeks exclusionary rule would not then be imposed upon the States as "an essential ingredient of the right." The Court's reasons for not considering essential to the right to privacy, as a curb imposed upon the States by the Due Process Clause, that which decades before had been posited as part and parcel of the Fourth Amendment's limitations upon federal encroachment of individual privacy, were bottomed on factual considerations.

The Court in *Wolf* first stated that "[t]he contrariety of views of the States" on the adoption of the exclusionary rule of *Weeks* was "particularly impressive" and, in this connection that it could not "brush aside the experience of States which deem the incidence of such conduct by the police too slight to call for a deterrent remedy . . . by overriding the [States'] relevant rules of evidence." While in 1949, prior to the *Wolf* case, almost two-thirds of the States were opposed to the use of the exclusionary rule, now, despite the *Wolf* case, more than half of those since passing upon it, by their own legislative or judicial decision, have wholly or partly adopted or adhered to the *Weeks* rule. Significantly, among those now following the rule is California, which, according to its highest court, was "compelled to reach that conclusion because other remedies have completely failed to secure compliance with the constitutional provisions . . . ." *People v. Cahan*, 282 P.2d 905, 911 (1955). In connection with this California case, we note that the second basis elaborated in *Wolf* in support of its failure to enforce the exclusionary doctrine against the States was that "other means of protection" have been afforded "the right to privacy."[7] The experience of California that such other remedies have been worthless and futile is buttressed by the experience of other States. The obvious futility of relegating the Fourth Amendment to the protection of other remedies has, moreover, been recognized by this Court since *Wolf.*

It, therefore, plainly appears that the factual considerations supporting the failure of the *Wolf* Court to include the *Weeks* exclusionary rule when it recognized the enforceability of the right to privacy against the States in 1949, while not basically relevant to the constitutional consideration, could not, in any analysis, now be deemed controlling.

IV.

Since the Fourth Amendment's right of privacy has been declared enforceable against the States through the Due Process Clause of the Fourteenth, it is enforceable against them by the same sanction of exclusion as is used against the Federal Government. Were it otherwise, then just as without the *Weeks* rule the assurance against unreasonable federal searches and seizures would be "a form of words," valueless and undeserving of mention in a perpetual charter of inestimable human liberties, so too, without that rule the freedom from state invasions of privacy would be so ephemeral and so neatly severed from its conceptual nexus with the freedom from all brutish means of coercing evidence as not to merit this Court's high regard as a freedom "implicit in 'the concept of ordered liberty.' " At the time that the Court held in *Wolf* that the Amendment was applicable to the States through the Due Process Clause, the cases of this Court, as we have seen, had steadfastly held that as to federal officers the Fourth Amendment included the exclusion of the evidence seized in violation of its provisions. Even Wolf "stoutly adhered" to that proposition. The right to privacy, when conceded operatively enforceable against the States, was not susceptible of destruction by avulsion of the sanction upon which its protection and enjoyment had always been deemed dependent under the *Weeks* and *Silverthorne* cases. Therefore, in extending the substantive protections of due process to all constitutionally unreasonable searches — state or federal — it was logically and constitutionally necessary that the

---

[7] Less than half of the States have any criminal provisions relating directly to unreasonable searches and seizures.

exclusion doctrine — an essential part of the right to privacy — be also insisted upon as an essential ingredient of the right newly recognized by the *Wolf* case. In short, the admission of the new constitutional right by *Wolf* could not consistently tolerate denial of its most important constitutional privilege, namely, the exclusion of the evidence which an accused had been forced to give by reason of the unlawful seizure. To hold otherwise is to grant the right but in reality to withhold its privilege and enjoyment. Only last year the Court itself recognized that the purpose of the exclusionary rule "is to deter — to compel respect for the constitutional guaranty in the only effectively available way — by removing the incentive to disregard it." *Elkins v. United States*, 364 U.S. 206 (1960).

Indeed, we are aware of no restraint, similar to that rejected today, conditioning the enforcement of any other basic constitutional right. The right to privacy, no less important than any other right carefully and particularly reserved to the people, would stand in marked contrast to all other rights declared as "basic to a free society." *Wolf*. This Court has not hesitated to enforce as strictly against the States as it does against the Federal Government the rights of free speech and of a free press, the rights to notice and to a fair, public trial, including, as it does, the right not to be convicted by use of a coerced confession, however logically relevant it be, and without regard to its reliability. *Rogers v. Richmond*, 365 U.S. 534 (1961). And nothing could be more certain that that when a coerced confession is involved, "the relevant rules of evidence" are overridden without regard to "the incidence of such conduct by the police," slight or frequent. Why should not the same rule apply to what is tantamount to coerced testimony by way of unconstitutional seizure of goods, papers, effect, documents, etc.? We find that, as to the Federal Government, the Fourth and Fifth Amendments and, as to the States, the freedom from unconscionable invasions of privacy and the freedom from convictions based upon coerced confessions do enjoy an "intimate relation" in their perpetuation of "principles of humanity and civil liberty [secured] . . . only after years of struggle." They express "supplementing phases of the same constitutional purpose — to maintain inviolate large areas of personal privacy." The philosophy of each Amendment and of each freedom is complementary to, although not dependent upon, that of the other in its sphere of influence — the very least that together they assure in either sphere is that no man is to be convicted on unconstitutional evidence.

V.

There are those who say, as did Justice (then Judge) Cardozo, that under our constitutional exclusionary doctrine "[t]he criminal is to go free because the constable has blundered." *People v. Defore*, 150 N.E. at page 587. In some cases this will undoubtedly be the result. But, as was said in *Elkins*, "there is another consideration — the imperative of judicial integrity." The criminal goes free, if he must, but it is the law that sets him free. Nothing can destroy a government more quickly than its failure to observe its own laws, or worse, its disregard of the charter of its own existence. As Mr. Justice Brandeis, dissenting, said in *Olmstead v. United States*, 277 U.S. 438 (1928): "Our government is the potent, the omnipresent teacher. For good or for ill, it teaches the whole people by its example . . . . If the government becomes a lawbreaker, it breeds contempt for law; it invites every man to become a law unto himself; it invites anarchy." Nor can it lightly be assumed that, as a practical matter, adoption of the exclusionary rule fetters law enforcement. Only last year this Court expressly considered that contention and found that "pragmatic evidence of a sort" to the contrary was not wanting. *Elkins*. The Court noted that

> The federal courts themselves have operated under the exclusionary rule of *Weeks* for almost half a century; yet it has not been suggested either that the Federal Bureau of Investigation has thereby been rendered ineffective, or that the administration of criminal justice in the federal courts has thereby been disrupted. Moreover, the experience of the states is impressive . . . . The movement towards the rule of exclusion has been halting but seemingly inexorable.

The ignoble shortcut to conviction left open to the State tends to destroy the entire system of constitutional restraints on which the liberties of the people rest. Having once recognized that the right to privacy embodied in the Fourth Amendment is enforceable against the States, and that the right to be secure against rude invasions of privacy by state officers is, therefore, constitutional in origin, we can no longer permit that right to remain an empty promise. Because it is enforceable in the same manner and to like effect as other basic rights secured by the Due Process Clause, we can no longer permit it to be revocable at the whim of any police officer who, in the name of law enforcement itself, chooses to suspend its enjoyment. Our decision, founded on reason and truth, gives to the individual no more than that which the Constitution guarantees him, to the police officer no less than that to which honest law enforcement is entitled, and, to the courts, that judicial integrity so necessary in the true administration of justice.

The judgment of the Supreme Court of Ohio is reversed and the cause remanded for further proceedings not inconsistent with this opinion.

Reversed and remanded.

[JUSTICES BLACK and DOUGLAS wrote separate concurring opinions. JUSTICE STEWART concurred in the result on other grounds.]

QUESTIONS AND NOTES

1.   Is there any logic to not *automatically* applying the exclusionary remedy if there has been a violation? Does it make any sense to say that the police violated your rights in obtaining evidence, but they can use it anyway?

2.   Which of the following factors influenced the Court's decision: A. The exclusionary rule creates a disincentive for the police to conduct unconstitutional searches, B. The exclusionary rule deters unconstitutional searches, C. The exclusionary rule is an inherent right of the victim of an unconstitutional search or seizure, D. Considerations of judicial integrity compel the exclusionary rule?

3.   Which of the factors in Question 2 do you find most persuasive?

4.   How, if at all, are factors A and B in Question 2 different? To the extent that they are different, which one ought to be deemed more significant?

5.   Under the exclusionary rule, is it fair to say that "the criminal goes free because the constable has blundered"? Explain.

6.   Does the benefit of the exclusionary rule necessarily redound solely to the benefit of criminals? If so, is that a good reason for abandoning it?

7.   In an ideal system of jurisprudence, would we have an exclusionary rule? Explain.

8.   As you read *Calandra*, consider whether it would change any of your answers to the preceding questions.

UNITED STATES v. CALANDRA
414 U.S. 338 (1973)

MR. JUSTICE POWELL delivered the opinion of the Court.

This case presents the question whether a witness summoned to appear and testify before a grand jury may refuse to answer questions on the ground that they are based on evidence obtained from an unlawful search and seizure. The issue is of considerable importance to the administration of criminal justice.

III

In the instant case, the Court of Appeals held that the exclusionary rule of the Fourth Amendment limits the grand jury's power to compel a witness to answer questions based on evidence obtained from a prior unlawful search and seizure. The exclusionary rule was adopted to effectuate the Fourth Amendment right of all citizens "to be secure in their persons, houses, papers, and effects, against unreasonable searches and seizures . . . ." Under this rule, evidence obtained in violation of the Fourth Amendment cannot be used in a criminal proceeding against the victim of the illegal search and seizure. This prohibition applies as well to the fruits of the illegally seized evidence.

The purpose of the exclusionary rule is not to redress the injury to the privacy of the search victim: "[T]he ruptured privacy of the victims' homes and effects cannot be restored. Reparation comes too late." *Linkletter v. Walker*, 381 U.S. 618, 637 (1965).

Instead, the rule's prime purpose is to deter future unlawful police conduct and thereby effectuate the guarantee of the Fourth Amendment against unreasonable searches and seizures: "The rule is calculated to prevent, not to repair. Its purpose is to deter — to compel respect for the constitutional guaranty in the only effectively available way — by removing the incentive to disregard it." *Elkins v. United States*, 364 U.S. 206, 217 (1960).

In sum, the rule is a judicially created remedy designed to safeguard Fourth Amendment rights generally through its deterrent effect, rather than a personal constitutional right of the party aggrieved.[5]

Despite its broad deterrent purpose, the exclusionary rule has never been interpreted to proscribe the use of illegally seized evidence in all proceedings or against all persons. As with any remedial device, the application of the rule has been restricted to those areas where its remedial objectives are thought most efficaciously served. The balancing process implicit in this approach is expressed in the contours of the standing requirement. Thus, standing to invoke the exclusionary rule has been confined to situations where the Government seeks to use such evidence to incriminate the victim of the unlawful search. This standing rule is premised on a recognition that the need for deterrence and hence the rationale for excluding the evidence are strongest where the Government's unlawful conduct would result in imposition of a criminal sanction on the victim of the search.

IV

In deciding whether to extend the exclusionary rule to grand jury proceedings, we must weigh the potential injury to the historic role and functions of the grand jury against the potential benefits of the rule as applied in this context. It is evident that this extension of the exclusionary rule would seriously impede the grand jury. Because the grand jury does not finally adjudicate guilt or innocence, it has traditionally been allowed to pursue its investigative and accusatorial functions unimpeded by the evidentiary and procedural restrictions applicable to a criminal trial. Permitting witnesses to invoke the exclusionary rule before a grand jury would precipitate adjudication of issues hitherto reserved for the trial on the merits and would delay and disrupt grand jury proceedings. Suppression hearings would halt the orderly progress of an investigation and might necessitate extended litigation of issues only tangentially related to the grand jury's primary objective.[7] The probable result would be "protracted interruption of grand jury proceedings," effectively transforming them into preliminary trials on the merits. In some cases the delay might be fatal to the enforcement of the criminal law.

In sum, we believe that allowing a grand jury witness to invoke the exclusionary rule would unduly interfere with the effective and expeditious discharge of the grand jury's duties.

Against this potential damage to the role and functions of the grand jury, we must weigh the benefits to be derived from this proposed extension of the exclusionary rule. Suppression of the use of illegally seized evidence against the search victim in a criminal trial is thought to be an important method of effectuating the Fourth Amendment. But it does not follow that the Fourth Amendment

---

[5] There is some disagreement as to the practical efficacy of the exclusionary rule, and as the Court noted in *Elkins v. United States*, relevant "[e]mpirical statistics are not available." *Cf.* Oaks, *Studying the Exclusionary Rule in Search and Seizure*, 37 U. CHI. L. REV. 665 (1970). We have no occasion in the present case to consider the extent of the rule's efficacy in criminal trials.

[7] The force of this argument is well illustrated by the facts of the present case. As of the date of this decision, almost two and one-half years will have elapsed since respondent was summoned to appear and testify before the grand jury. If respondent's testimony was vital to the grand jury's investigation in August 1971 of extortionate credit transactions, it is possible that this particular investigation has been completely frustrated.

requires adoption of every proposal that might deter police misconduct.

Any incremental deterrent effect which might be achieved by extending the rule to grand jury proceedings is uncertain at best. Whatever deterrence of police misconduct may result from the exclusion of illegally seized evidence from criminal trials, it is unrealistic to assume that application of the rule to grand jury proceedings would significantly further that goal. Such an extension would deter only police investigation consciously directed toward the discovery of evidence solely for use in a grand jury investigation. The incentive to disregard the requirement of the Fourth Amendment solely to obtain an indictment from a grand jury is substantially negated by the inadmissibility of the illegally seized evidence in a subsequent criminal prosecution of the search victim. For the most part, a prosecutor would be unlikely to request an indictment where a conviction could not be obtained. We therefore decline to embrace a view that would achieve a speculative and undoubtedly minimal advance in the deterrence of police misconduct at the expense of substantially impeding the role of the grand jury.

V

Respondent also argues that each and every question based on evidence obtained from an illegal search and seizure constitutes a fresh and independent violation of the witness' constitutional rights. Ordinarily, of course, a witness has no right of privacy before the grand jury. Absent some recognized privilege of confidentiality, every man owes his testimony. He may invoke his Fifth Amendment privilege against compulsory self-incrimination, but he may not decline to answer on the grounds that his responses might prove embarrassing or result in an unwelcome disclosure of his personal affairs. Respondent's claim must be, therefore, not merely that the grand jury's questions invade his privacy but that, because those questions are based on illegally obtained evidence, they somehow constitute distinct violations of his Fourth Amendment rights. We disagree.

The purpose of the Fourth Amendment is to prevent unreasonable governmental intrusions into the privacy of one's person, house, papers, or effects. The wrong condemned is the unjustified governmental invasion of these areas of an individual's life. That wrong, committed in this case, is fully accomplished by the original search without probable cause. Grand jury questions based on evidence obtained thereby involve no independent governmental invasion of one's person, house, papers, or effects, but rather the usual abridgment of personal privacy common to all grand jury questioning. Questions based on illegally obtained evidence are only a derivative use of the product of a past unlawful search and seizure. They work no new Fourth Amendment wrong. Whether such derivative use of illegally obtained evidence by a grand jury should be proscribed presents a question, not of rights, but of remedies.

In the usual context of a criminal trial, the defendant is entitled to the suppression of, not only the evidence obtained through an unlawful search and seizure, but also any derivative use of that evidence. The prohibition of the exclusionary rule must reach such derivative use if it is to fulfill its function of deterring police misconduct. In the context of a grand jury proceeding, we believe that the damage to that institution from the unprecedented extension of the exclusionary rule urged by respondent outweighs the benefit of any possible incremental deterrent effect. Our conclusion necessarily controls both the evidence seized during the course of an unlawful search and seizure and any question or evidence derived therefrom (the fruits of the unlawful search).[10] The same considerations of logic and policy apply to both the fruits of an unlawful search and seizure and derivative use of that evidence, and we do not distinguish between them.[11]

The judgment of the Court of Appeals is reversed.

MR. JUSTICE BRENNAN, with whom MR. JUSTICE DOUGLAS and MR. JUSTICE MARSHALL join, dissenting.

The Court holds that the exclusionary rule in search-and-seizure cases does not apply to grand jury proceedings because the principal objective of the rule is "to deter future unlawful police conduct," and "it is unrealistic to assume that application of the rule to grand jury proceedings would significantly further that goal." This downgrading of the exclusionary rule to a determination whether its application in a particular type of proceeding furthers deterrence of future police misconduct reflects a startling misconception, unless it is a purposeful rejection, of the historical objective and purpose of the rule.

The commands of the Fourth Amendment are, of course, directed solely to public officials. Necessarily, therefore, only official violations of those commands could have created the evil that threatened to make the Amendment a dead letter. But curtailment of the evil, if a consideration at all, was at best only a hoped-for effect of the exclusionary rule, not its ultimate objective. Indeed, there is no evidence that the possible deterrent effect of the rule was given any attention by the judges chiefly responsible for its formulation. Their concern as guardians of the Bill of Rights was to fashion an enforcement tool to give content and meaning to the Fourth Amendment's guarantees. They thus bore out James Madison's prediction in his address to the First Congress on June 8, 1789:

> If they [the rights] are incorporated into the Constitution, independent tribunals of justice will consider themselves in a peculiar manner the guardians of those rights; they will be an impenetrable bulwark against

---

[10] It should be noted that, even absent the exclusionary rule, a grand jury witness may have other remedies to redress the injury to his privacy and to prevent a further invasion in the future. He may be entitled to maintain a cause of action for damages against the officers who conducted the unlawful search. *Bivens v. Six Unknown Named Agents of Federal Bureau of Narcotics*, 403 U.S. 388 (1971). He may also seek return of the illegally seized property, and exclusion of the property and its fruits from being used as evidence against him in a criminal trial. *Go-Bart Importing Co. v. United States*, 282 U.S. 344 (1931). In these circumstances, we cannot say that such a witness is necessarily left remediless in the face of an unlawful search and seizure.

[11] The dissent voices concern that today's decision will betray "the imperative of judicial integrity," sanction "illegal government conduct," and even "imperil the very foundation of our people's trust in their Government." There is no basis for this alarm. "Illegal conduct" is hardly sanctioned, nor are the foundations of the Republic imperilled, by declining to make an unprecedented extension of the exclusionary rule to grand jury proceedings where the rule's objectives would not be effectively served and where other important and historic values would be unduly prejudiced.

every assumption of power in the Legislative or Executive; they will be naturally led to resist every encroachment upon rights expressly stipulated for in the Constitution by the declaration of rights.

1 Annals of Cong. 439 (1789). Since, however, those judges were without power to direct or control the conduct of law enforcement officers, the enforcement tool had necessarily to be one capable of administration by judges. The exclusionary rule, if not perfect, accomplished the twin goals of enabling the judiciary to avoid the taint of partnership in official lawlessness and of assuring the people — all potential victims of unlawful government conduct — that the government would not profit from its lawless behavior, thus minimizing the risk of seriously undermining popular trust in government.

That these considerations, not the rule's possible deterrent effect, were uppermost in the minds of the framers of the rule clearly emerges from the decision which fashioned it:

> The effect of the Fourth Amendment is to put the courts of the United States and Federal officials, in the exercise of their power and authority, under limitations and restraints as to the exercise of such power and authority, and to forever secure the people, their persons, houses, papers, and effects, against all unreasonable searches and seizures under the guise of law . . . . The tendency of those who execute the criminal laws of the country to obtain conviction by means of unlawful seizures . . . *should find no sanction in the judgments of the courts, which are charged at all times with the support of the Constitution, and to which people of all conditions have a right to appeal for the maintenance of such fundamental rights.* This protection is equally extended to the action of the government and officers of the law acting under it . . . . *To sanction such proceedings would be to affirm by judicial decision a manifest neglect, if not an open defiance, of the prohibitions of the Constitution, intended for the protection of the people against such unauthorized action.*

Weeks v. United States, 232 U.S. 383, 391–392, 394 (1914) (emphasis added).

Mr. Justice Brandeis and Mr. Justice Holmes added their enormous influence to these precepts in their notable dissents in *Olmstead v. United States*, 277 U.S. 438 (1928). Mr. Justice Brandeis said:

> In a government of laws, existence of the government will be imperiled if it fails to observe the law scrupulously. Our government is the potent, the omnipresent teacher. For good or for ill, it teaches the whole people by its example. Crime is contagious. If the government becomes a lawbreaker, it breeds contempt for law; it invites every man to become a law unto himself; it invites anarchy.

And Justice Holmes said:

> [W]e must consider the two objects of desire both of which we cannot have, and make up our minds which to choose. It is desirable that criminals should be detected, and to that end that all available evidence should be used. It also is desirable that the government should not itself foster and

pay for other crimes, when they are the means by which the evidence is to be obtained . . . . We have to choose, and for my part I think it a less evil that some criminals should escape than that the government should play an ignoble part.

. . . If the existing code does not permit district attorneys to have a hand in such dirty business it does not permit the judge to allow such iniquities to succeed.

The same principles were reiterated less than six years ago. In *Terry v. Ohio*, 392 U.S. 1, 12–13 (1968), Mr. Chief Justice Warren said for the Court:

The rule also serves another vital function — "the imperative of judicial integrity." Courts which sit under our Constitution cannot and will not be made party to lawless invasions of the constitutional rights of citizens by permitting unhindered governmental use of the fruits of such invasions.

It is true that deterrence was a prominent consideration in the determination whether *Mapp v. Ohio*, 367 U.S. 643 (1961), which applied the exclusionary rule to the States, should be given retrospective effect. *Linkletter v. Walker*, 381 U.S. 618 (1965). But that lends no support to today's holding that the application of the exclusionary rule depends solely upon whether its invocation in a particular type of proceeding will significantly further the goal of deterrence. The emphasis upon deterrence in *Linkletter* must be understood in the light of the crucial fact that the States had justifiably relied from 1949 to 1961 upon *Wolf*, and consequently, that application of *Mapp* would have required the wholesale release of innumerable convicted prisoners, few of whom could have been successfully retried. In that circumstance, *Linkletter* held not only that retrospective application of *Mapp* would not further the goal of deterrence but also that it would not further "the administration of justice and the integrity of the judicial process."

Thus, the Court seriously errs in describing the exclusionary rule as merely "a judicially created remedy designed to safeguard Fourth Amendment rights generally through its deterrent effect . . . ." Rather, the exclusionary rule is "part and parcel of the Fourth Amendment's limitation upon [governmental] encroachment of individual privacy" and "an essential part of both the Fourth and Fourteenth Amendments," that "gives to the individual no more than that which the Constitution guarantees him, to the police officer no less than that to which honest law enforcement is entitled, and, to the courts, that judicial integrity so necessary in the true administration of justice."

This *Mapp* summation crystallizes the series of decisions that developed the rule and with which today's holding is plainly at war. For the first time, the Court today discounts to the point of extinction the vital function of the rule to insure that the judiciary avoid even the slightest appearance of sanctioning illegal government conduct. This rejection of "the imperative of judicial integrity," openly invites "[t]he conviction that all government is staffed by . . . hypocrites, [a conviction] easy to instill and difficult to erase." When judges appear to become "accomplices in the willful disobedience of a Constitution they are sworn to uphold," we imperil the very foundation of our people's trust in their Government on which our democracy rests. The exclusionary rule is needed to make the Fourth Amendment something real; a guarantee that does not carry with it the exclusion of evidence obtained by its violation is a chimera. Moreover, "[I]nsistence on observance by law officers of traditional fair procedural requirements is, from the long point of view, best calculated to contribute to that end. However much in a particular case insistence upon such rules may appear as a technicality that inures to the benefit of a guilty person, the history of the criminal law proves that tolerance of shortcut methods in law enforcement impairs its enduring effectiveness."

The judges who developed the exclusionary rule were well aware that it embodied a judgment that it is better for some guilty persons to go free than for the police to behave in forbidden fashion.

[T]o allow Calandra to be subjected to questions derived from the illegal search of his office and seizure of his files is "to thwart the [Fourth and Fourteenth Amendments' protection] of . . . individual privacy . . . and to entangle the courts in the illegal acts of Government agents." "And for a court, on petition of the executive department, to sentence a witness who is [himself] the victim of the illegal [search and seizure], to jail for refusal to participate in the exploitation of that [conduct in violation of the explicit command of the Fourth Amendment] is to stand our whole system of criminal justice on its head."

It is no answer, to suggest as the Court does, that the grand jury witnesses' Fourth Amendment rights will be sufficiently protected "by the inadmissibility of the illegally seized evidence in a subsequent criminal prosecution of the search victim." This, of course, is no alternative for Calandra, since he was granted transactional immunity and cannot be criminally prosecuted. But the fundamental flaw of the alternative is that to compel Calandra to testify in the first place under penalty of contempt necessarily "thwarts" his Fourth Amendment protection and "entangle[s] the courts in the illegal acts of Government agents" — consequences that *Silverthorne* condemned as intolerable.

To be sure, the exclusionary rule does not "provide that illegally seized evidence is inadmissible against anyone for any purpose." But clearly there is a crucial distinction between withholding its cover from individuals whose Fourth Amendment rights have not been violated — as has been done in the "standing" cases, and withdrawing its cover from persons whose Fourth Amendment rights have in fact been abridged.

Respondent does not seek vicariously to assert another's Fourth Amendment rights. He himself has been the victim of an illegal search and desires "to mend no one's privacy [but his] own." Respondent is told that he must look to damages to redress the concededly unconstitutional invasion of his privacy. In other words, officialdom may profit from its lawlessness if it is willing to pay a price.

In *Mapp*, the Court thought it had "close[d] the only courtroom door remaining open to evidence secured by official lawlessness" in violation of Fourth Amendment rights. The door is again ajar. As a consequence, I am left with the uneasy feeling that today's decision may signal that a majority of my colleagues have positioned themselves to reopen the door still further and abandon altogether the exclusionary rule in search-and-seizure cases; for surely they cannot believe that application of the exclusionary rule at trial furthers the goal of deterrence, but that its application in grand jury proceedings will not "significantly" do so. Unless we are to shut our eyes to the evidence that crosses our desks every day, we must concede that official lawlessness has not abated and that no empirical data distinguishes trials from grand jury proceedings. I thus fear that when next we confront a case of a conviction rested on illegally seized evidence, today's decision will be invoked to sustained the conclusion in that case also, that "it is unrealistic to assume" that application of the rule at trial would "significantly further" the goal of deterrence — though, if the police are presently undeterred, it is difficult to see how removal of the sanction of exclusion will induce more lawful official conduct.

The exclusionary rule gave life to Madison's prediction that "independent tribunals of justice . . . will be naturally led to resist every encroachment upon rights expressly stipulated for in the Constitution by the declaration of rights." We betray the trust upon which that prediction rested by today's long step toward abandonment of the exclusionary rule. The observations of a recent commentator highlight the grievous error of the majority's retreat:

> If constitutional rights are to be anything more than pious pronouncements, then some measurable consequence must be attached to their violation. It would be intolerable if the guarantee against unreasonable search and seizure could be violated without practical consequence. It is likewise imperative to have a practical procedure by which courts can review alleged violations of constitutional rights and articulate the meaning of those rights. The advantage of the exclusionary rule — entirely apart from any direct deterrent effect — is that it provides an occasion for judicial review, and it gives credibility to the constitutional guarantees. By demonstrating that society will attach serious consequences to the violation of constitutional rights, the exclusionary rule invokes and magnifies the moral and educative force of the law. Over the long term this may integrate some fourth amendment ideals into the value system or norms of behavior of law enforcement agencies.

Oaks, *Studying the Exclusionary Rule in Search and Seizure*, 37 U. Chi. L. Rev. 665, 756 (1970). *See also* Dellinger, *Of Rights and Remedies: The Constitution as a Sword*, 85 Harv. L. Rev. 1532, 1562–1563 (1972).

I dissent and would affirm the judgment of the Court of Appeals.

QUESTIONS AND NOTES

1.   What does the *Calandra* Court perceive the purpose of the exclusionary rule to be? Is the Court's analysis consistent or in conflict with that employed in *Mapp*?

2.   Should the practical efficacy of the exclusionary rule matter (see fn. 5 of the Court's opinion)? Would (should) evidence that the exclusionary rule does not significantly deter police misconduct be relevant (determinative) of whether or not to retain the rule?

3.   Do you think that the exclusionary rule is likely to deter police conduct?

4.   Is *Calandra* too specific in the question it asks; *i.e.*, should we ask whether the exclusionary rule generally deters police misconduct, or should we ask (as

Calandra did) whether the exclusionary rule will deter the police from obtaining evidence that can be used to compel Calandra to testify before the grand jury against his friends?

5.   If the police knew before conducting the search against Calandra that what they found could not be used to convict him, but could be used to make him testify against the other criminals or alternatively be held in contempt, would the police have had an incentive to conduct the search?

6.   If your answer to Question 5 was "yes," does it follow that Calandra was wrongly decided?

7.   Do you believe that Calandra was subject to a continuing Fourth Amendment violation each time that he was questioned by the grand jury? Why? Why not?

8.   If you had been on the Court would you have voted with Powell or Brennan, or in some other way? Explain.

9.   Applying the *Calandra* cost benefit analysis, the Court has held that evidence unconstitutionally obtained by State police may be used in a Federal civil tax proceeding, *United States v. Janis*, 428 U.S. 433 (1976), and that evidence unconstitutionally obtained by the I.N.S. may be used in a civil deportation hearing against an allegedly deportable alien who was victimized by an unlawful search, *I.N.S. v. Lopez-Mendoza*, 468 U.S. 1032 (1984).

PROBLEM

Without probable cause, reasonable suspicion, a warrant, or consent (or so the Court assumed), three parole officers searched the home of Keith Scott, a parolee. The officers found weapons, the possession of which were in violation of his parole. The weapons were introduced at Scott's parole violation hearing and, because of the weapons, he was recommitted to serve three years in prison.

Assuming that the search constituted a violation of the Fourth amendment under *Griffin v. Wisconsin*, should the Supreme Court uphold the parole revocation? For the Supreme Court's actual resolution, *see Pennsylvania Board of Probation & Parole v. Scott*, 524 U.S. 357 (1998).

We conclude this section with *Michigan v. Hudson*, a case which may or may not portend the eventual demise of the exclusionary rule.

HUDSON v. MICHIGAN
547 U.S. 586 (2006)

JUSTICE SCALIA delivered the opinion of the Court, except as to Part IV.

We decide whether violation of the "knock-and-announce" rule requires the suppression of all evidence found in the search.

I Police obtained a warrant authorizing a search for drugs and firearms at the home of petitioner Booker Hudson. They discovered both. Large quantities of drugs were found, including cocaine rocks in Hudson's pocket. A loaded gun was lodged between the cushion and armrest of the chair in which he was sitting. Hudson was charged under Michigan law with unlawful drug and firearm possession.

This case is before us only because of the method of entry into the house. When the police arrived to execute the warrant, they announced their presence, but waited only a short time — perhaps "three to five seconds," — before turning the knob of the unlocked front door and entering Hudson's home. Hudson moved to suppress all the inculpatory evidence, arguing that the premature entry violated his Fourth Amendment rights.

The common-law principle that law enforcement officers must announce their presence and provide residents an opportunity to open the door is an ancient one. See *Wilson v. Arkansas*, 514 U.S. 927, 931–932 (1995).

We recognized that the new constitutional rule we had announced is not easily applied. *Wilson* and cases following it have noted the many situations in which it is not necessary to knock and announce. It is not necessary when "circumstances presen[t] a threat of physical violence," or if there is "reason to believe that evidence would likely be destroyed if advance notice were given," or if knocking and announcing would be "futile." We require only that police "have a reasonable suspicion . . . under the particular circumstances" that one of these grounds for failing to knock and announce exists, and we have acknowledged that "[t]his showing is not high."

When the knock-and-announce rule does apply, it is not easy to determine precisely what officers must do. How many seconds' wait are too few? Our "reasonable wait time" standard, see *United States v. Banks*, 540 U.S. 31, 41 (2003), is necessarily vague. *Banks* (a drug case, like this one) held that the proper measure was not how long it would take the resident to reach the door, but how long it would take to dispose of the suspected drugs — but that such a time (15 to 20 seconds in that case) would necessarily be extended when, for instance, the suspected contraband was not easily concealed. If our *ex post* evaluation is subject to such calculations, it is unsurprising that, *ex ante*, police officers about to encounter someone who may try to harm them will be uncertain how long to wait.

Happily, these issues do not confront us here. From the trial level onward, Michigan has conceded that the entry was a knock-and-announce violation. The issue here is remedy. *Wilson* specifically declined to decide whether the exclusionary rule is appropriate for violation of the knock-and-announce requirement. That question is squarely before us now.

In *Weeks v. United States*, we adopted the federal exclusionary rule for evidence that was unlawfully seized from a home without a warrant in violation of the Fourth Amendment. We began applying the same rule to the States, through the Fourteenth Amendment, in Mapp.

Suppression of evidence, however, has always been our last resort, not our first impulse. The exclusionary rule generates "substantial social costs," *United States v. Leon, infra*, which sometimes include setting the guilty free and the dangerous at large. We have there-fore been "cautio[us] against expanding" it, and "have repeatedly emphasized that the rule's 'costly toll' upon truth-seeking and law enforcement objectives presents a high obstacle for those urging [its] application."

We did not always speak so guardedly. ("[A]ll evidence obtained by searches and seizures in violation of the Constitution is, by that same authority, inadmissible in a state court"). But we have long since rejected that approach.

[E]xclusion may not be premised on the mere fact that a constitutional violation was a "but-for" cause of obtaining evidence. Our cases show that but-for causality is only a necessary, not a sufficient, condition for suppression. In this case, of course, the constitutional violation of an illegal *manner* of entry was *not* a but-for cause of obtaining the evidence. Whether that preliminary misstep had occurred *or not*, the police would have executed the warrant they had obtained, and would have discovered the gun and drugs inside the house. But even if the illegal entry here could be characterized as a but-for cause of discovering what was inside, we have "never held that evidence is 'fruit of the poisonous tree' simply because 'it would not have come to light but for the illegal actions of the police.' "

[C]ases excluding the fruits of unlawful warrantless searches, say nothing about the appropriateness of exclusion to vindicate the interests protected by the knock-and-announce requirement. Until a valid warrant has issued, citizens are entitled to shield "their persons, houses, papers, and effects" from the government's scrutiny. Exclusion of the evidence obtained by a warrantless search vindicates that entitlement. The interests protected by the knock-and-announce requirement are quite different — and do not include the shielding of potential evidence from the government's eyes.

One of those interests is the protection of human life and limb, because an unannounced entry may provoke violence in supposed self-defense by the surprised resident. Another interest is the protection of property. Breaking a house (as the old cases typically put it) absent an announcement would penalize someone who " 'did not know of the process, of which, if he had notice, it is to be presumed that he would obey it . . . .' " The knock-and-announce rule gives individuals "the opportunity to comply with the law and to avoid the destruction of property occasioned by a forcible entry." And thirdly, the knock-and-announce rule protects those elements of privacy and dignity that can be destroyed by a sudden entrance. It gives residents the "opportunity to prepare themselves for" the entry of the police. "The brief interlude between announcement and entry with a warrant may be the opportunity that an individual has to pull on clothes or get out of bed.". In other words, it assures the opportunity to collect oneself before answering the door.

What the knock-and-announce rule has never protected, however, is one's interest in preventing the government from seeing or taking evidence described in a warrant. Since the interests that *were* violated in this case have nothing to do with the seizure of the evidence, the exclusionary rule is inapplicable.

Quite apart from the requirement of unattenuated causation, the exclusionary rule has never been applied except "where its deterrence benefits outweigh its 'substantial social costs.' " The costs here are considerable. In addition to the grave adverse consequence that exclusion of relevant incriminating evidence always entails (viz., the risk of releasing dangerous criminals into society), imposing that massive remedy for a knock-and-announce violation would generate a constant flood of alleged failures to observe the rule, and claims that any asserted *Richards* justification for a no-knock entry, had inadequate support. The cost of entering this lottery would be small, but the jackpot enormous: suppression of all evidence, amounting in many cases to a get-out-of-jail-free card. Courts would experience as never before the reality that "[t]he exclusionary rule frequently requires extensive litigation to determine whether particular evidence must be excluded." Unlike the warrant or *Miranda* requirements, compliance with which is readily deter-mined (either there was or was not a warrant; either the *Miranda* warning was given, or it was not), what constituted a "reasonable wait time" in a particular case, (or, for that matter, how many seconds the police in fact waited), or whether there was "reasonable suspicion" of the sort that would invoke the *Richards* exceptions, is difficult for the trial court to determine and even more difficult for an appellate court to review.

Another consequence of the incongruent remedy Hudson proposes would be police officers' refraining from timely entry after knocking and announcing. As we have observed, the amount of time they must wait is necessarily uncertain. If the consequences of running afoul of the rule were so massive, officers would be inclined to wait longer than the law requires — producing preventable violence against officers in some cases, and the destruction of evidence in many others. We deemed these consequences severe enough to produce our unanimous agreement that a mere "reasonable suspicion" that knocking and announcing "under the particular circumstances, would be dangerous or futile, or that it would inhibit the effective investigation of the crime," will cause the requirement to yield. *Richards.*

Next to these "substantial social costs" we must consider the deterrence benefits, existence of which is a necessary condition for exclusion. (It is not, of course, a sufficient condition: "[I]t does not follow that the Fourth Amendment requires adoption of every proposal that might deter police misconduct." *Calandra.* To begin with, the value of deterrence depends upon the strength of the incentive to commit the forbidden act. Viewed from this perspective, deterrence of knock-and-announce violations is not worth a lot. Violation of the warrant requirement sometimes produces incriminating evidence that could not otherwise be obtained. But ignoring knock-and-announce can realistically be expected to achieve absolutely nothing except the prevention of destruction of evidence and the avoidance of life-threatening resistance by occupants of the premises — dangers which, if there is even "reasonable suspicion" of their existence, *suspend the knock-and-announce requirement anyway.* Massive deterrence is hardly required.

It seems to us not even true, as Hudson contends, that without suppression there will be no deterrence of knock-and-announce violations at all. Of course even if this assertion were accurate, it would not necessarily justify suppression. Assuming (as the assertion must) that civil suit is not an effective deterrent, one can think of many forms of police misconduct that are similarly "undeterred." When, for example, a confessed suspect in the killing of a police officer, arrested (along with incriminating evidence)in a lawful warranted search, is subjected to physical abuse at the station house, would it seriously be suggested that the evidence must be excluded, since that is the only "effective deterrent"? And what, other than civil suit, is the "effective deterrent" of police violation of an already-confessed suspect's Sixth Amendment rights by denying him prompt access to counsel? Many would regard these violated rights as more significant than the right not to be intruded upon in one's nightclothes — and yet nothing but "ineffective" civil suit is available as a deterrent. And the police incentive for those violations is arguably greater than the incentive for disregarding the knock-and-announce rule.

We cannot assume that exclusion in this context is necessary deterrence simply because we found that it was necessary deterrence in different contexts and long ago. That would be forcing the public today to pay for the sins and inadequacies of a legal regime that existed almost half a century ago. Dollree Mapp could not turn to 42 U. S. C. § 1983 for meaningful relief; *Monroe v. Pape*, 365 U.S. 167 (1961), which began the slow but steady expansion of that remedy, was decided the same Term as *Mapp*. It would be another 17 years before the § 1983 remedy was extended to reach the deep pocket of municipalities, *Monell v. New York City Dept. of Social Servs.*, 436 U.S. 658 (1978). Citizens whose Fourth Amendment rights were violated by federal officers could not bring suit until 10 years after *Mapp*, with this Court's decision in *Bivens v. Six Unknown Fed. Narcotics Agents*, 403 U.S. 388 (1971).

Hudson complains that "it would be very hard to find a lawyer to take a case such as this," but 42 U. S. C. § 1988(b) answers this objection. Since some civil-rights violations would yield damages too small to justify the expense of litigation, Congress has authorized attorney's fees for civil-rights plaintiffs. This remedy was unavailable in the heydays of our exclusionary-rule jurisprudence, because it is tied to the availability of a cause of action. For years after *Mapp*, "very few lawyers would even consider representation of persons who had civil rights claims against the police," but now "much has changed. Citizens and lawyers are much more willing to seek relief in the courts for police misconduct." M. Avery, D. Rudovsky, & K. Blum, Police Misconduct: Law and Litigation, p. v (3d ed. 2005); see generally N. Aron, Liberty and Justice for All: Public Interest Law in the 1980s and Beyond (1989) (describing the growth of public-interest law). The number of public-interest law firms and lawyers who specialize in civil-rights grievances has greatly expanded.

Hudson points out that few published decisions to date announce huge awards for knock-and-announce violations. But this is an unhelpful statistic. Even if we thought that only large damages would deter police misconduct (and that police somehow are deterred by "damages" but indifferent to the prospect of large § 1988 attorney's fees), we do not know how many claims have been settled, or indeed how many violations have occurred that produced any-thing more than nominal injury. It is clear, at least, that the lower courts are allowing colorable knock-and-announce suits to go forward, unimpeded by assertions of qualified immunity. See, *e.g.*, *Green v. Butler*, 420 F.3d 689, 700–701 (CA7 2005) (denying qualified immunity in a knock-and-announce civil suit); *Holland ex rel. Overdorff v. Harrington*, 268 F.3d 1179, 1193–1196 (CA10 2001) (same); *Mena v. Simi Valley*, 226 F.3d 1031, 1041–1042 (CA9 2000) (same); *Gould v. Davis*, 165 F.3d 265, 270–271 (CA4 1998) (same). As far as we know, civil liability is an effective deterrent here, as we have assumed it is in other contexts. See, *e.g.*, *Correctional Services Corp. v. Malesko*, 534 U.S. 61, 70 (2001) ("[T]he threat of litigation and liability will adequately deter federal officers for *Bivens* purposes no matter that they may enjoy qualified immunity."

Another development over the past half-century that deters civil-rights violations is the increasing professional-ism of police forces, including a new emphasis on internal police discipline. Even as long ago as 1980 we felt it proper to "assume" that unlawful police behavior would "be dealt with appropriately" by the authorities, *United States v. Payner*, 447 U.S. 727, 733–734, n. 5 (1980), but we now have increasing evidence that police forces across the United States take the constitutional rights of citizens seriously. There have been "wide-ranging reforms in the education, training, and supervision of police officers." S. Walker, Taming the System: The Control of Discretion in Criminal Justice 1950–1990, p.51 (1993). Numerous sources are now available to teach officers and their supervisors what is required of them under this Court's cases, how to respect constitutional guarantees in various situations, and how to craft an effective regime for internal discipline. See, *e.g.*, D. Waksman & D. Goodman, The Search and Seizure Handbook (2d ed. 2006); A. Stone & S. DeLuca, Police Administration: An Introduction (2d ed. 1994); E. Thibault, L. Lynch, & R. McBridge, Proactive Police Management (4th ed. 1998). Failure to teach and enforce constitutional requirements exposes municipalities to financial liability. Moreover, modern police forces are staffed with professionals; it is not credible to assert that internal discipline, which can limit successful careers, will not have a deterrent effect. There is also evidence that the increasing use of various forms of citizen review can enhance police accountability.

In sum, the social costs of applying the exclusionary rule to knock-and-announce violations are considerable; the incentive to such violations is minimal to begin with, and the extant deterrences against them are substantial — incomparably greater than the factors deterring warrantless entries when Mapp was decided. Resort to the massive remedy of suppressing evidence of guilt is unjustified.

For the foregoing reasons we affirm the judgment of the Michigan Court of Appeals.

It is so ordered.

JUSTICE KENNEDY, concurring in part and concurring in the judgment.

Two points should be underscored with respect to to-day's decision. First, the knock-and-announce requirement protects rights and expectations linked to ancient principles in our constitutional order. See *Wilson v. Arkansas.* The Court's decision should not be interpreted as suggesting that violations of the requirement are trivial or beyond the law's concern. Second, the continued operation of the exclusionary rule, as settled and defined by our precedents, is not in doubt. Today's decision determines only that in the specific con-text of the knock-and-announce requirement, a violation is not sufficiently related to the later discovery of evidence to justify suppression.

As to the basic right in question, privacy and security in the home are central to the Fourth Amendment's guarantees as explained in our decisions and as understood since the beginnings of the Republic. This common understanding ensures respect for the law and allegiance to our institutions, and it is an instrument for transmitting our Constitution to later generations undiminished in meaning and force. It bears repeating that it is a serious matter if law enforcement officers violate the sanctity of the home by ignoring the requisites of lawful entry. Security must not be subject to erosion by indifference or contempt.

Our system, as the Court explains, has developed procedures for training police officers and imposing discipline for failures to act competently and lawfully. If those measures prove ineffective, they can be fortified with more detailed regulations or legislation. Supplementing these safeguards are civil remedies, such as those available under 42 U. S. C. § 1983, that provide restitution for discrete harms. These remedies apply to all violations, including, of course, exceptional cases in which unannounced entries cause severe fright and humiliation.

Suppression is another matter. Under our precedents the causal link between a violation of the knock-and-announce requirement and a later search is too attenuated to allow suppression. When, for example, a violation results from want of a 20-second pause but an ensuing, lawful search lasting five hours discloses evidence of criminality, the failure to wait at the door cannot properly be described as having caused the discovery of evidence.

Today's decision does not address any demonstrated pattern of knock-and-announce violations. If a widespread pattern of violations were shown, and particularly if those violations were committed against persons who lacked the means or voice to mount an effective protest, there would be reason for grave concern. Even then, however, the Court would have to acknowledge that extending the remedy of exclusion to all the evidence seized following a knock-and-announce violation would mean revising the requirement of causation that limits our discretion in applying the exclusionary rule. That type of extension also would have significant practical implications, adding to the list of issues requiring resolution at the criminal trial questions such as whether police officers entered a home after waiting 10 seconds or 20.

In this case the relevant evidence was discovered not because of a failure to knock-and-announce, but because of a subsequent search pursuant to a lawful warrant. The Court in my view is correct to hold that suppression was not required. I accordingly concur in the judgment.

JUSTICE BREYER, with whom JUSTICE STEVENS, JUSTICE SOUTER, and JUSTICE GINSBURG join, dissenting.

In *Wilson v. Arkansas*, normally requires law enforcement officers to knock and announce their presence before entering a dwelling. Today's opinion holds that evidence seized from a home following a violation of this requirement need not be suppressed

As a result, the Court destroys the strongest legal incentive to comply with the Constitution's knock-and-announce requirement. And the Court does so without significant support in precedent. At least I can find no such support in the many Fourth Amendment cases the Court has decided in the near century since it first set forth the exclusionary principle in *Weeks v. United States*.

Today's opinion is thus doubly troubling. It represents a significant departure from the Court's precedents. And it weakens, perhaps destroys, much of the practical value of the Constitution's knock-and-announce protection.

This Court has set forth the legal principles that ought to have determined the outcome of this case in two sets of basic Fourth Amendment cases. I shall begin by describing that underlying case law.

The first set of cases describes the constitutional knock-and-announce requirement, a requirement that this Court initially set forth only 11 years ago in *Wilson*.

We noted that this "basic principle" was agreed upon by"[s]everal prominent founding-era commentators," and "was woven quickly into the fabric of early American law" via state constitutions and statutes. We further concluded that there was

> "little doubt that the Framers of the Fourth Amendment thought that the method of an officer's entry into a dwelling was among the factors to be considered in assessing the reasonableness of a search or seizure."

Wolf and *Mapp* considered whether *Weeks'* exclusionary rule applies to the States. In *Wolf*, the Court held that it did not. It said that "[t]he security of one's privacy against arbitrary intrusion by the police . . . is . . . implicit in 'the concept of ordered liberty' and as such enforceable against the States through the Due Process Clause." But the Court held that the exclusionary rule is not enforceable against the States as "an essential ingredient of the right." In *Mapp*, the Court overruled *Wolf*. Experience, it said, showed that alternative methods of enforcing the Fourth Amendment's requirements had failed.

Reading our knock-and-announce cases, in light of this foundational Fourth Amendment case law, it is clear that the exclusionary rule should apply. For one thing, elementary logic leads to that conclusion. We have held that a court must "con-side[r]" whether officers complied with the knock-and announce requirement "in assessing the reasonableness of a search or seizure." The Fourth Amendment insists that an unreasonable search or seizure is, constitutionally speaking, an illegal search or seizure. And ever since Weeks (in respect to federal prosecutions) and Mapp (in respect to state prosecutions), "the use of evidence secured through an illegal search and seizure" is "barred" in criminal trials.

For another thing, the driving legal purpose underlying the exclusionary rule, namely, the deterrence of unlawful government behavior, argues strongly for suppression.

Why is application of the exclusionary rule any the less necessary here? Without such a rule, as in *Mapp*, police know that they can ignore the Constitution's requirements without risking suppression of evidence discovered after an unreasonable entry. As in *Mapp*, some government officers will find it easier, or believe it less risky, to proceed with what they consider a necessary search immediately and without the requisite constitutional (say, war-rant or knock-and-announce) compliance. Cf. Mericli, The Apprehension of Peril Exception to the Knock and Announce Rule — Part I, 16 Search and Seizure L. Rep. 129,130 (1989) (hereinafter Mericili) (noting that some "[d]rug enforcement authorities believe that safety for the police lies in a swift, surprising entry with overwhelming force — not in announcing their official authority").

Of course, the State or the Federal Government may provide alternative remedies for knock-and-announce violations. But that circumstance was true of *Mapp* as well. What reason is there to believe that those remedies (such as private damages actions under 42 U. S. C. § 1983), which the Court found inadequate in *Mapp*, can adequately deter unconstitutional police behavior here?

The cases reporting knock-and-announce violations are legion. See, *e.g.*, 34 Geo. L. J. Ann. Rev. Crim. Proc. 31–35 (2005) (collecting court of appeals cases). Indeed, these cases of reported violations seem sufficiently frequent and serious as to indicate "a widespread pattern." (Kennedy, J., concurring in part and concurring in judgment). Yet the majority, like Michigan and the United States, has failed to cite a single reported case in which a plaintiff has collected more than nominal damages solely as a result of a knock-and-announce violation. Even Michigan concedes that, "in cases like the present one . . . , damages may be virtually non-existent."

As Justice Stewart, the author of a number of significant Fourth Amendment opinions, explained, the deter-rent effect of damage actions "can hardly be said to be great," as such actions are "expensive, time-consuming, not readily available, and rarely successful." Stewart, The Road to *Mapp v. Ohio* and Beyond: The Origins, Development and Future of the Exclusionary Rule in Search-and-Seizure Cases, 83 Colum. L. Rev. 1365, 1388 (1983). The upshot is that the need for deterrence — the critical factor driving this Court's Fourth Amendment cases for close to a century — argues with at least comparable strength for evidentiary exclusion here.

To argue, as the majority does, that new remedies, such as 42 U. S. C. § 1983 actions or better trained police, make suppression unnecessary is to argue that *Wolf*, not *Mapp*, *is* now the law. To argue that there may be few civil suits because violations may produce nothing "more than nominal injury" is to confirm, not to deny, the inability of civil suits to deter violations. And to argue without evidence (and despite myriad reported cases of violations, no reported case of civil damages, and Michigan's concession of their nonexistence) that civil suits may provide deterrence because claims *may* "have been settled" is, perhaps, to search in desperation for an argument. Rather, the majority, as it candidly admits, has simply "assumed" that, "[a]s far as [it] know[s], civil liability is an effective deterrent," a support-free assumption that *Mapp* and subsequent cases make clear does not embody the Court's normal approach to difficult questions of Fourth Amendment law.

It is not surprising, then, that after looking at virtually every pertinent Supreme Court case decided since *Weeks*, I can find no precedent that might offer the majority sup-port for its contrary conclusion. The Court has, of course, recognized that not every Fourth Amendment violation necessarily triggers the exclusionary rule. But the class of Fourth Amendment violations that do not result in suppression of the evidence seized, however, is limited.

The Court has declined to apply the exclusionary rule only:

(1) where there is a specific reason to believe that application of the rule would "not result in appreciable deterrence," *United States v. Janis*, 428

U.S. 433, 454 (1976); see, *e.g., United States v. Leon*, 468 U.S. 897, 919–920 (1984) (exception where searching officer exe-cutes defective search warrant in "good faith"); *Arizona v. Evans*, 514 U.S. 1, 14 (1995) (exception for clerical errors by court employees); *Walder v. United States*, 347 U.S. 62 (1954) (exception for impeachment purposes), or(2) where admissibility in proceedings other than criminal trials was at issue, see, *e.g., Pennsylvania Bd. of Probation and Parole v. Scott*, 524 U.S. 357, 364 (1998) (exception for parole revocation proceedings); *INS v. Lopez-Mendoza*, 468 U.S. 1032, 1050 (1984) (plurality opinion) (exception for deportation proceedings); *Janis, supra*, at 458 (exception for civil tax proceedings); *United States v. Calandra*, 414 U.S. 338, 348–350 (1974) (exception for grand jury proceedings); *Stone v. Powell*, 428 U.S. 465, 493–494 (1976) (exception for federal habeas proceedings).

Neither of these two exceptions applies here. The second does not apply because this case is an ordinary criminal trial. The first does not apply because (1) officers who violate the rule are not acting "as a reasonable officer would and should act in similar circumstances," *Leon*, (2) this case does not involve government employees other than police, *Evans*, and (3), most importantly, the key rationale for any exception, "lack of deterrence," is missing. That critical latter rationale, which underlies *every* exception, does not apply here, as there is no reason to think that, in the case of knock-and announce violations by the police, "the exclusion of evidence at trial would not sufficiently deter future errors," *Evans, supra*, at 14, or " 'further the ends of the exclusionary rule in any appreciable way." *Leon, supra* at 919–920.

I am aware of no other basis for an exception. The Court has decided more than 300 Fourth Amendment cases since *Weeks*. The Court has found constitutional violations in nearly a third of them. The nature of the constitutional violation varies. In most instances officers lacked a war-rant; in others, officers possessed a warrant based on false affidavits; in still others, the officers executed the search in an unconstitutional manner. But in every case involving evidence seized during an illegal search of a home (federally since *Weeks*, nationally since *Mapp*), the Court, with the exceptions mentioned, has either explicitly or implicitly upheld (or required) the suppression of the evidence at trial. See Appendix, *infra*. In not one of those cases did the Court "questio[n], in the absence of a more efficacious sanction, the continued application of the [ex-clusionary] rule to suppress evidence from the State's case" in a criminal trial.

[T]he majority [cannot] justify its failure to respect the need for deterrence, as set forth consistently in the Court's prior case law, through its claim of "substantial social costs" — at least if it means that those "social costs" are somehow special here. The only costs it mentions are those that typically accompany *any* use of the Fourth Amendment's exclusionary principle: (1) that where the constable blunders, a guilty defendant may be set free (consider *Mapp* itself); (2) that defendants may assert claims where Fourth Amendment rights are uncertain (consider the Court's qualified immunity jurisprudence), and (3) that sometimes it is difficult to decide the merits of those uncertain claims. In fact, the "no-knock" warrants that are provided by many States, by diminishing uncertainty, may make application of the knock-and-announce principle less "cost[ly]" on the whole than application of comparable

Fourth Amendment principles, such as determining whether a particular warrant-less search was justified by exigency. The majority's "substantial social costs" argument is an argument against the Fourth Amendment's exclusionary principle itself. And it is an argument that this Court, until now, has consistently rejected.

The majority, Michigan, and the United States make several additional arguments. In my view, those arguments rest upon misunderstandings of the principles underlying this Court's precedents.

The majority first argues that "the constitutional violation of an illegal *manner* of entry was *not* a but-for cause of obtaining the evidence." But taking causation as it is commonly understood in the law, I do not see how that can be so. Although the police might have entered Hudson's home lawfully, they did not in fact do so. Their unlawful behavior inseparably characterizes their actual entry; that entry was a necessary condition of their presence in Hudson's home; and their presence in Hudson's home was a necessary condition of their finding and seizing the evidence. At the same time, their discovery of evidence in Hudson's home was a readily foreseeable consequence of their entry and their unlawful presence within the home.

Moreover, separating the "manner of entry" from the related search slices the violation too finely. As noted, we have described a failure to comply with the knock-and-announce rule, not as an independently unlawful event, but as a factor that renders the *search* "constitutionally defective."

The Court nonetheless accepts Michigan's argument that the requisite but-for-causation is not satisfied in this case because, whether or not the constitutional violation occurred (what the Court refers to as a "preliminary mis-step"), "the police would have executed the warrant they had obtained, and would have discovered the gun and drugs inside the house.

Of course, had the police entered the house lawfully, they would have found the gun and drugs. But that fact is beside the point. The question is not what police might have done had they not behaved unlawfully. The question is what they did do. Was there set in motion an independent chain of events that would have inevitably led to the discovery and seizure of the evidence despite, and independent of, that behavior? The answer here is "no."

The majority, Michigan, and the United States point out that the officers here possessed a warrant authorizing a search. That fact, they argue, means that the evidence would have been discovered independently or somehow diminishes the need to suppress the evidence. But I do not see why that is so. The warrant in question was not a "no-knock" warrant, which many States (but not Michigan) issue to assure police that a prior knock is not necessary. It did not authorize a search that fails to comply with knock-and-announce requirements. Rather, it was an ordinary search warrant. It authorized a search that *complied with*, not a search that *disregarded*, the Constitution's knock-and-announce rule.

Would a warrant that authorizes entry into a home on Tuesday permit the police to enter on Monday? Would a warrant that authorizes entry during the day authorize the police to enter during the middle of the night? It is difficult for me to see how the presence of a warrant that does not authorize the entry in question has anything to do with the "inevitable discovery" exception or otherwise diminishes the need to enforce the knock-and-announce requirement through suppression.

The majority and the United States set forth a policy-related variant of the causal connection theme: The United States argues that the law should suppress evidence only insofar as a Fourth Amendment violation causes the kind of harm that the particular Fourth Amendment rule seeks to protect against. It adds that the constitutional purpose of the knock-and-announce rule is to prevent needless destruction of property (such as breaking down a door) and to avoid unpleasant surprise. And it concludes that the exclusionary rule should suppress evidence of, say, damage to property, the discovery of a defendant in an "intimate or compromising moment," or an excited utterance from the occupant caught by surprise, but nothing more.

The majority makes a similar argument. It says that evidence should not be suppressed once the causal connection between unlawful behavior and discovery of the evidence becomes too "attenuated." But the majority then makes clear that it is not using the word "attenuated" to mean what this Court's precedents have typically used that word to mean, namely, that the discovery of the evidence has come about long after the unlawful behavior took place or in an independent way, *i.e.*, through "means sufficiently distinguishable to be purged of the primary taint.' "

Rather, the majority gives the word "attenuation" a new meaning (thereby, in effect, making the same argument as the United States). "Attenuation," it says, "also occurs when, even given a direct causal connection, the interest protected by the constitutional guarantee that has been violated would not be served by suppression of the evidence obtained." The interests the knock-and-announce rule seeks to protect, the Court adds, are "human life" (at stake when a householder is "surprised"), "property" (such as the front door), and "those elements of privacy and dignity that can be destroyed by a sudden entrance," namely, "the opportunity to collect oneself before answering the door." Since none of those interests led to the discovery of the evidence seized here, there is no reason to suppress it.

There are three serious problems with this argument. First, it does not fully describe the constitutional values, purposes, and objectives underlying the knock-and-announce requirement. That rule does help to protect homeowners from damaged doors; it does help to protect occupants from surprise. But it does more than that. It protects the occupants' privacy by assuring them that government agents will not enter their home without complying with those requirements (among others) that diminish the offensive nature of any such intrusion. Many years ago, Justice Frankfurter wrote for the Court that the "knock at the door, . . . as a prelude to a search, with-out authority of law . . . [is] inconsistent with the conception of human rights enshrined in [our] history" and Constitution. How much the more offensive when the search takes place without any knock at all.

Over a century ago this Court wrote that "it is not the breaking of his doors" that is the "essence of the offence," but the "invasions on the part of the government . . . of the sanctity of a man's home and the privacies of life." *Boyd*, 116 U.S., at 630. And just this Term we have reiterated that "it is beyond dispute that the home is entitled to special protection as the center of the private lives of our people." *Georgia v. Randolph*, 547 U.S. ___, ___ (2006). The knock-and-announce requirement is no less a part of the "centuries-old principle" of special protection for the privacy of the home than the warrant requirement. ("[I]ndividual privacy interest[s]" protected by the rule are "not inconsequential" and "should not be unduly minimized").

Second, whether the interests underlying the knock-and-announce rule are implicated in any given case is, in a sense, beside the point. As we have explained, failure to comply with the knock-and-announce rule renders the related search unlawful. And where a search is unlawful, the law insists upon suppression of the evidence consequently discovered, even if that evidence or its possession has little or nothing to do with the reasons underlying the unconstitutionality of a search. The Fourth Amendment does not seek to protect contraband, yet we have required suppression of contraband seized in an unlawful search. That is because the exclusionary rule protects more general "privacy values through deterrence of future police misconduct." The same is true here.

Third, the majority's interest-based approach departs from prior law. Ordinarily a court will simply look to see if the unconstitutional search produced the evidence. The majority does not refer to any relevant case in which, beyond that, suppression turned on the far more detailed relation between, say, (1) a particular materially false statement made to the magistrate who issued a (consequently) invalid warrant and (2) evidence found after a search with that warrant. And the majority's failure does not surprise me, for such efforts to trace causal connections at retail could well complicate Fourth Amendment suppression law, threatening its workability.

The United States, in its brief and at oral argument, has argued that suppression is "an especially harsh remedy given the nature of the violation in this case.". This argument focuses upon the fact that entering a house after knocking and announcing can, in some cases, prove dangerous to a police officer. Perhaps someone inside has a gun, as turned out to be the case here. The majority adds that police officers about to encounter someone who may try to harm them will be "uncertain" as to how long to wait. It says that, "[i]f the consequences of running afoul" of the knock-and-announce "rule were so massive," *i.e.*, would lead to the exclusion of evidence, then "officers would be inclined to wait longer than the law requires — producing preventable violence against officers in some cases."

To argue that police efforts to assure compliance with the rule may prove dangerous, however, is not to argue against evidence suppression. It is to argue against the validity of the rule itself. Similarly, to argue that enforcement means uncertainty, which in turn means the potential for dangerous and longer-than-necessary delay, is (if true) to argue against meaningful compliance with the rule.

The answer to the first argument is that the rule itself does not require police to knock or to announce their presence where police have a "reasonable suspicion" that doing so "would be dangerous or futile" or "would inhibit the effective investigation of the crime by, for example, allowing the destruction of evidence." The answer to the second argument is that States can, and many do, reduce police uncertainty while assuring a neutral evaluation of concerns about risks to officers or the destruction of evidence by permitting police to obtain a "no-knock" search warrant from a magistrate judge, thereby assuring police that a prior announcement is not necessary. While such a procedure cannot remove all uncertainty, it does provide an easy way for officers to comply with the knock-and-announce rule.

Of course, even without such a warrant, police maintain the backup "authority to exercise independent judgment concerning the wisdom of a no-knock entry at the time the warrant is being executed." "[I]f circumstances support a reasonable suspicion of exigency when the officers arrive at the door, they may go straight in." And "[r]easonable suspicion is a less demanding standard that probably cause . . . ."

Consider this very case. The police obtained a search warrant that authorized a search, not only for drugs, but also for *guns*. If probable cause justified a search for guns, why would it not also have justified a no-knock warrant, thereby diminishing any danger to the officers? Why (in a State such as Michigan that lacks no-knock warrants) would it not have justified the very no-knock entry at issue here? Indeed, why did the prosecutor not argue in this very case that, given the likelihood of guns, the no-knock entry was lawful? From what I have seen in the record, he would have won. And had he won, there would have been no suppression here.

That is the right way to win. The very process of arguing the merits of the violation would help to clarify the contours of the knock-and-announce rule, contours that the majority believes are too fuzzy. That procedural fact, along with no-knock warrants, back up authority to enter without knocking regardless, and use of the "reasonable suspicion" standard for doing so should resolve the government's problems with the knock-and-announce rule while reducing the "uncertain[ty]" that the majority discusses to levels beneath that found elsewhere in Fourth Amendment law (*e.g.*, exigent circumstances). Regardless, if the Court fears that effective enforcement of a constitutional requirement will have harmful consequences, it should face those fears directly by addressing the requirement itself. It should not argue, "the requirement is fine, indeed, a serious matter, just don't enforce it."

There is perhaps one additional argument implicit in the majority's approach. The majority says, for example, that the "cost" to a defendant of "entering this lottery," *i.e.*, of claiming a "knock-and-announce" violation, "would be small, but the jackpot enormous" — namely, a potential "get-out-of-jail-free card." It adds that the "social costs" of applying the exclusionary rule here are not worth the deterrence benefits. Leaving aside what I believe are invalid arguments based on precedent or the majority's own estimate that suppression is not necessary to deter constitutional violations, one is left with a simple unvarnished conclusion, namely, that in this kind of case, a knock-and-announce case, "[r]esort to the massive remedy of suppressing evidence of guilt is unjustified." Why is that judicial judgment, taken on its own, inappropriate? Could it not be argued that the knock-and-announce rule, a subsidiary Fourth Amendment rule, is simply not important enough to warrant a suppression remedy? Could the majority not simply claim that the suppression game is not worth the candle?

The answer, I believe, is "no." That "no" reflects history, a history that shows the knock-and-announce rule is important. That "no" reflects precedent, precedent that shows there is no preexisting legal category of exceptions to the exclusionary rule into which the knock-and-announce cases might fit. That "no" reflects empirical fact, experience that provides confirmation of what common sense suggests: without suppression there is little to deter knock-and-announce violations.

There may be instances in the law where text or history or tradition leaves room for a judicial decision that rests upon little more than an unvarnished judicial instinct. But this is not one of them. Rather, our Fourth Amendment traditions place high value upon protecting privacy in the home. They emphasize the need to assure that its constitutional protections are effective, lest the Amendment 'sound the word of promise to the ear but break it to the hope.' They include an exclusionary principle, which since Weeks has formed the centerpiece of the criminal law's effort to ensure the practical reality of those promises. That is why the Court should assure itself that any departure from that principle is firmly grounded in logic, in history, in precedent, and in empirical fact. It has not done so. That is why, with respect, I dissent

QUESTIONS AND NOTES

1.   Is the Court hostile to the exclusionary rule, the knock and announce rule? Both? Neither?

2.   Does *Hudson* portend the end of the exclusionary rule (a return to *Wolf)* or is it limited to cases involving the knock and announce rule? Does the answer depend on Justice Kennedy?

3.   What, if anything, about the knock and announce rule warrants a different treatment under the exclusionary rule?

4.   Is the Court sufficiently concerned with the impact of its decision on suspects who happen to be innocent? Is its analysis entirely directed to those who are guilty? Is that appropriate? Why? Why not?

5.   If you had been on the Court, would have agreed with (a) Scalia, (B) Kennedy, (C) Breyer, or (D) None of the above. Explain.

B.   THE GOOD FAITH EXCEPTION TO THE EXCLUSIONARY RULE

In *Leon*, we consider when, and under what circumstances, the exclusionary rule can be avoided despite a violation of the Fourth Amendment.

UNITED STATES v. LEON
468 U.S. 897 (1984)

JUSTICE WHITE delivered the opinion of the Court.

This case presents the question whether the Fourth Amendment exclusionary rule should be modified so as not to bar the use in the prosecution's case-in-chief of evidence obtained by officers acting in reasonable reliance on a search warrant issued by a detached and neutral magistrate but ultimately found to be unsupported by probable cause. To resolve this question, we must consider once again the tension between the sometimes competing goals of, on the one hand, deterring official misconduct and removing inducements to unreasonable invasions of privacy and, on the other, establishing procedures under which criminal defendants are "acquitted or convicted on the basis of all the evidence which exposes the truth."

I

In August 1981, a confidential informant of unproven reliability informed an officer of the Burbank Police Department that two persons known to him as "Armando" and "Patsy" were selling large quantities of cocaine and methaqualone from their residence at 620 Price Drive in Burbank, Cal. The informant also indicated that he had witnessed a sale of methaqualone by "Patsy" at the residence approximately five months earlier and had observed at that time a shoe box containing a large amount of cash that belonged to "Patsy." He further declared that "Armando" and "Patsy" generally kept only small quantities of drugs at their residence and stored the remainder at another location in Burbank.

On the basis of this information, the Burbank police initiated an extensive investigation focusing first on the Price Drive residence and later on two other residences as well. Cars parked at the Price Drive residence were determined to belong to respondents Armando Sanchez, who had previously been arrested for possession of marihuana, and Patsy Stewart, who had no criminal record. During the course of the investigation, officers observed an automobile belonging to respondent Ricardo Del Castillo, who had previously been arrested for possession of 50 pounds of marihuana, arrive at the Price Drive residence. The driver of that car entered the house, exited shortly thereafter carrying a small paper sack, and drove away. A check of Del Castillo's probation records led the officers to respondent Alberto Leon, whose telephone number Del Castillo had listed as his employer's. Leon had been arrested in 1980 on drug charges, and a companion had informed the police at that time that Leon was heavily involved in the importation of drugs into this country. Before the current investigation began, the Burbank officers had learned that an informant had told a Glendale police officer that Leon stored a large quantity of methaqualone at his residence in Glendale. During the course of this investigation, the Burbank officers learned that Leon was living at 716 South Sunset Canyon in Burbank.

Subsequently, the officers observed several persons, at least one of whom had prior drug involvement, arriving at the Price Drive residence and leaving with small packages; observed a variety of other material activity at the two residences as well as at a condominium at 7902 Via Magdalena; and witnessed a variety of relevant activity involving respondents' automobiles. The officers also observed respondents Sanchez and Stewart board separate flights for Miami. The pair later returned to Los Angeles together, consented to a search of their luggage that revealed only a small amount of marihuana, and left the airport. Based on these and other observations summarized in the affidavit, Officer Cyril Rombach of the Burbank Police Department, an experienced and well-trained narcotics investigator, prepared an application for a warrant to search 620 Price Drive, 716 South Sunset Canyon, 7902 Via Magdalena, and automobiles registered to each of the respondents for an extensive list of items believed to be related to respondents' drug-trafficking activities. Officer Rombach's extensive application was reviewed by several Deputy District Attorneys.

A facially valid search warrant was issued in September 1981 by a state superior court judge. The ensuing searches produced large quantities of drugs at the Via Magdalena and Sunset Canyon addresses and a small quantity at the Price Drive residence. Other evidence was discovered at each of the residences and in Stewart's and Del Castillo's automobiles. Respondents were indicted by a grand jury in the District Court for the Central District of California and charged with conspiracy to possess and distribute cocaine and a variety of substantive counts.

The respondents then filed motions to suppress the evidence seized pursuant to the warrant. The District Court held an evidentiary hearing and, while recognizing that the case was a close one, granted the motions to suppress in part. It concluded that the affidavit was insufficient to establish probable cause,[2] but did not suppress all of the evidence as to all of the respondents because none of the respondents had standing to challenge all of the searches. In response to a request from the Government, the court made clear that Officer Rombach had acted in good faith, but it rejected the Government's suggestion that the Fourth Amendment exclusionary rule should not apply where evidence is seized in reasonable, good-faith reliance on a search warrant.

The Government's petition for certiorari expressly declined to seek review of the lower courts' determinations that the search warrant was unsupported by probable cause and presented only the question "[w]hether the Fourth Amendment exclusionary rule should be modified so as not to bar the admission of evidence seized in reasonable, good-faith reliance on a search warrant that is subsequently held to be defective." We granted certiorari to consider the propriety of such a modification. Although it undoubtedly is within our power to consider the question whether probable cause existed under the "totality of the circumstances" test announced last Term in *Illinois v. Gates*, 462 U.S. 213 (1983), that question has not been briefed or argued; and it is also within our authority, which we choose to exercise, to take the case as it comes to us, accepting the Court of Appeals' conclusion that probable cause was lacking under the prevailing legal standards.

We have concluded that, in the Fourth Amendment context, the exclusionary rule can be modified somewhat without jeopardizing its ability to perform its intended functions. Accordingly, we reverse the judgment of the Court of Appeals.

II

Language in opinions of this Court and of individual Justices has sometimes implied that the exclusionary rule is a necessary corollary of the Fourth Amendment, *Mapp*, or that the rule is required by the conjunction of the Fourth and Fifth Amendments. These implications need not detain us long. The Fifth Amendment

---

[2] I just cannot find this warrant sufficient for a showing of probable cause.

There is no question of the reliability and credibility of the informant as not being established. Some details given tended to corroborate, maybe, the reliability of [the informant's] information about the previous transaction, but if it is not a stale transaction, it comes awfully close to it; and all the other material I think is as consistent with innocence as it is with guilt.

So I just do not think this affidavit can withstand the test. I find, then, that there is no probable cause in this case for the issuance of the search warrant . . . .

theory has not withstood critical analysis or the test of time, see *Andresen*, and the Fourth Amendment "has never been interpreted to proscribe the introduction of illegally seized evidence in all proceedings or against all persons." *Stone v. Powell*, 428 U.S. 465, 486 (1976).

A

Whether the exclusionary sanction is appropriately imposed in a particular case, our decisions make clear, is "an issue separate from the question whether the Fourth Amendment rights of the party seeking to invoke the rule were violated by police conduct." Only the former question is currently before us, and it must be resolved by weighing the costs and benefits of preventing the use in the prosecution's case-in-chief of inherently trustworthy tangible evidence obtained in reliance on a search warrant issued by a detached and neutral magistrate that ultimately is found to be defective.

B

Close attention to remedial objectives has characterized our recent decisions concerning the scope of the Fourth Amendment exclusionary rule. The Court has, to be sure, not seriously questioned, "in the absence of a more efficacious sanction, the continued application of the rule to suppress evidence from the [prosecution's] case where a Fourth Amendment violation has been substantial and deliberate . . . ." Nevertheless, the balancing approach that has evolved in various contexts — including criminal trials — "forcefully suggest[s] that the exclusionary rule be more generally modified to permit the introduction of evidence obtained in the reasonable good-faith belief that a search or seizure was in accord with the Fourth Amendment."

In *Stone v. Powell, supra,* the Court emphasized the costs of the exclusionary rule, expressed its view that limiting the circumstances under which Fourth Amendment claims could be raised in federal habeas corpus proceedings would not reduce the rule's deterrent effect, and held that a state prisoner who has been afforded a full and fair opportunity to litigate a Fourth Amendment claim may not obtain federal habeas relief on the ground that unlawfully obtained evidence had been introduced at his trial. Proposed extensions of the exclusionary rule to proceedings other than the criminal trial itself have been evaluated and rejected under the same analytic approach.

As cases considering the use of unlawfully obtained evidence in criminal trials themselves make clear, it does not follow from the emphasis on the exclusionary rule's deterrent value that "anything which deters illegal searches is thereby commanded by the Fourth Amendment."

We have not required suppression of the fruits of a search incident to an arrest made in good-faith reliance on a substantive criminal statute that subsequently is declared unconstitutional. *Michigan v. DeFillippo*, 443 U.S. 31 (1979).[8] Similarly,

---

[8] We have held, however, that the exclusionary rule requires suppression of evidence obtained in

although the Court has been unwilling to conclude that new Fourth Amendment principles are always to have only prospective effect, *United States v. Johnson*, 457 U.S. 537, 560 (1982), no Fourth Amendment decision marking a "clear break with the past" has been applied retroactively. The propriety of retroactive application of a newly announced Fourth Amendment principle, moreover, has been assessed largely in terms of the contribution retroactivity might make to the deterrence of police misconduct.

As yet, we have not recognized any form of good-faith exception to the Fourth Amendment exclusionary rule. But the balancing approach that has evolved during the years of experience with the rule provides strong support for the modification currently urged upon us. As we discuss below, our evaluation of the costs and benefits of suppressing reliable physical evidence seized by officers reasonably relying on a warrant issued by a detached and neutral magistrate leads to the conclusion that such evidence should be admissible in the prosecution's case-in-chief.

III

A

Because a search warrant "provides the detached scrutiny of a neutral magistrate, which is a more reliable safeguard against improper searches than the hurried judgment of a law enforcement officer 'engaged in the often competitive enterprise of ferreting out crime,'" we have expressed a strong preference for warrants and declared that "in a doubtful or marginal case a search under a warrant may be sustainable where without one it would fail." Reasonable minds frequently may differ on the question whether a particular affidavit establishes probable cause, and we have thus concluded that the preference for warrants is most appropriately effectuated by according "great deference" to a magistrate's determination. *See Gates.*

Deference to the magistrate, however, is not boundless. It is clear, first, that the deference accorded to a magistrate's finding of probable cause does not preclude inquiry into the knowing or reckless falsity of the affidavit on which that determination was based. *Franks v. Delaware*, 438 U.S. 154 (1978).[12] Second, the courts must also insist that the magistrate purport to "perform his 'neutral and detached' function and not serve merely as a rubber stamp for the police." A

---

searches carried out pursuant to statutes, not yet declared unconstitutional, purporting to authorize searches and seizures without probable cause or search warrants. *See, e.g., Ybarra v. Illinois*, 444 U.S. 85 (1979); *Torres v. Puerto Rico*, 442 U.S. 465 (1979); *Almeida-Sanchez v. United States*, 413 U.S. 266 (1973); *Sibron v. New York*, 392 U.S. 40 (1968); *Berger v. New York*, 388 U.S. 41 (1967). "Those decisions involved statutes which, by their own terms, authorized searches under circumstances which did not satisfy the traditional warrant and probable-cause requirements of the Fourth Amendment." *Michigan v. DeFillippo*, 443 U.S. 31 (1979). The substantive Fourth Amendment principles announced in those cases are fully consistent with our holding here.

[12] Indeed, "it would be an unthinkable imposition upon [the magistrate's] authority if a warrant affidavit, revealed after the fact to contain a deliberately or recklessly false statement, were to stand beyond impeachment."

magistrate failing to "manifest that neutrality and detachment demanded of a judicial officer when presented with a warrant application" and who acts instead as "an adjunct law enforcement officer" cannot provide valid authorization for an otherwise unconstitutional search. *Lo-Ji Sales, Inc. v. New York*, 442 U.S. 319, 326–327 (1979).

Third, reviewing courts will not defer to a warrant based on an affidavit that does not "provide the magistrate with a substantial basis for determining the existence of probable cause." *Gates*. "Sufficient information must be presented to the magistrate to allow that official to determine probable cause; his action cannot be a mere ratification of the bare conclusions of others." Even if the warrant application was supported by more than a "bare bones" affidavit, a reviewing court may properly conclude that, notwithstanding the deference that magistrates deserve, the warrant was invalid because the magistrate's probable-cause determination reflected an improper analysis of the totality of the circumstances, *Gates*, or because the form of the warrant was improper in some respect.

Only in the first of these three situations, however, has the Court set forth a rationale for suppressing evidence obtained pursuant to a search warrant; in the other areas, it has simply excluded such evidence without considering whether Fourth Amendment interests will be advanced. To the extent that proponents of exclusion rely on its behavioral effects on judges and magistrates in these areas, their reliance is misplaced. First, the exclusionary rule is designed to deter police misconduct rather than to punish the errors of judges and magistrates. Second, there exists no evidence suggesting that judges and magistrates are inclined to ignore or subvert the Fourth Amendment or that lawlessness among these actors requires application of the extreme sanction of exclusion.[14]

Third, and most important, we discern no basis, and are offered none, for believing that exclusion of evidence seized pursuant to a warrant will have a significant deterrent effect on the issuing judge or magistrate. Many of the factors that indicate that the exclusionary rule cannot provide an effective "special" or "general" deterrent for individual offending law enforcement officers apply as well to judges or magistrates. And, to the extent that the rule is thought to operate as a "systemic" deterrent on a wider audience, it clearly can have no such effect on individuals empowered to issue search warrants. Judges and magistrates are not adjuncts to the law enforcement team; as neutral judicial officers, they have no stake in the outcome of particular criminal prosecutions. The threat of exclusion thus cannot be expected significantly to deter them. Imposition of the exclusionary sanction is not necessary meaningfully to inform judicial officers of their errors, and we cannot conclude that admitting evidence obtained pursuant to a warrant while at the same time declaring that the warrant was somehow defective will in any way reduce judicial officers' professional incentives to comply with the Fourth Amendment, encourage them to repeat their mistakes, or lead to the granting of all colorable warrant requests.

---

[14] Although there are assertions that some magistrates become rubber stamps for the police and others may be unable effectively to screen police conduct, we are not convinced that this is a problem of major proportions.

B

If exclusion of evidence obtained pursuant to a subsequently invalidated warrant is to have any deterrent effect, therefore, it must alter the behavior of individual law enforcement officers or the policies of their departments. One could argue that applying the exclusionary rule in cases where the police failed to demonstrate probable cause in the warrant application deters future inadequate presentations or "magistrate shopping" and thus promotes the ends of the Fourth Amendment. Suppressing evidence obtained pursuant to a technically defective warrant supported by probable cause also might encourage officers to scrutinize more closely the form of the warrant and to point out suspected judicial errors. We find such arguments speculative and conclude that suppression of evidence obtained pursuant to a warrant should be ordered only on a case-by-case basis and only in those unusual cases in which exclusion will further the purposes of the exclusionary rule.

We have frequently questioned whether the exclusionary rule can have any deterrent effect when the offending officers acted in the objectively reasonable belief that their conduct did not violate the Fourth Amendment. "No empirical researcher, proponent or opponent of the rule, has yet been able to establish with any assurance whether the rule has a deterrent effect . . . ." But even assuming that the rule effectively deters some police misconduct and provides incentives for the law enforcement profession as a whole to conduct itself in accord with the Fourth Amendment, it cannot be expected, and should not be applied, to deter objectively reasonable law enforcement activity.[20]

In short, where the officer's conduct is objectively reasonable,

> excluding the evidence will not further the ends of the exclusionary rule in any appreciable way; for it is painfully apparent that . . . the officer is acting as a reasonable officer would and should act under the circumstances. Excluding the evidence can in no way affect his future conduct unless it is to make him less willing to do his duty.

Stone v. Powell, 428 U.S., at 539–540 (White, J., dissenting).

This is particularly true, we believe, when an officer acting with objective good faith has obtained a search warrant from a judge or magistrate and acted within its scope. In most such cases, there is no police illegality and thus nothing to deter. It is the magistrate's responsibility to determine whether the officer's allegations establish probable cause and, if so, to issue a warrant comporting in form with the requirements of the Fourth Amendment. In the ordinary case, an officer cannot be expected to question the magistrate's probable-cause determination or his judgment that the form of the warrant is technically sufficient. "[O]nce the warrant issues, there is literally nothing more the policeman can do in seeking to comply with the law." Penalizing the officer for the magistrate's error, rather than his own,

---

[20] We emphasize that the standard of reasonableness we adopt is an objective one. Many objections to a good-faith exception assume that the exception will turn on the subjective good faith of individual officers. "Grounding the modification in objective reasonableness, however, retains the value of the exclusionary rule as an incentive for the law enforcement profession as a whole to conduct themselves in accord with the Fourth Amendment." The objective standard we adopt, moreover, requires officers to have a reasonable knowledge of what the law prohibits.

cannot logically contribute to the deterrence of Fourth Amendment violations.

C

We conclude that the marginal or nonexistent benefits produced by suppressing evidence obtained in objectively reasonable reliance on a subsequently invalidated search warrant cannot justify the substantial costs of exclusion. We do not suggest, however, that exclusion is always inappropriate in cases where an officer has obtained a warrant and abided by its terms. "[S]earches pursuant to a warrant will rarely require any deep inquiry into reasonableness," *Gates* (White, J., concurring in the judgment), for "a warrant issued by a magistrate normally suffices to establish" that a law enforcement officer has "acted in good faith in conducting the search." Nevertheless, the officer's reliance on the magistrate's probable-cause determination and on the technical sufficiency of the warrant he issues must be objectively reasonable,[23] and it is clear that in some circumstances the officer[24] will have no reasonable grounds for believing that the warrant was properly issued.

Suppression therefore remains an appropriate remedy if the magistrate or judge in issuing a warrant was misled by information in an affidavit that the affiant knew was false or would have known was false except for his reckless disregard of the truth. *Franks v. Delaware*, 438 U.S. 154 (1978). The exception we recognize today will also not apply in cases where the issuing magistrate wholly abandoned his judicial role in the manner condemned in *Lo-Ji Sales, Inc. v. New York*, 442 U.S. 319 (1979); in such circumstances, no reasonably well-trained officer should rely on the warrant. Nor would an officer manifest objective good faith in relying on a warrant based on an affidavit "so lacking in indicia of probable cause as to render official belief in its existence entirely unreasonable." Finally, depending on the circumstances of the particular case, a warrant may be so facially deficient — *i.e.*, in failing to particularize the place to be searched or the things to be seized — that the executing officers cannot reasonably presume it to be valid.

In so limiting the suppression remedy, we leave untouched the probable-cause standard and the various requirements for a valid warrant. Other objections to the modification of the Fourth Amendment exclusionary rule we consider to be insubstantial. The good-faith exception for searches conducted pursuant to warrants is not intended to signal our unwillingness strictly to enforce the requirements of the Fourth Amendment, and we do not believe that it will have this effect. As we have already suggested, the good-faith exception, turning as it does on

---

[23] Accordingly, our good-faith inquiry is confined to the objectively ascertainable question whether a reasonably well-trained officer would have known that the search was illegal despite the magistrate's authorization. In making this determination, all of the circumstances — including whether the warrant application had previously been rejected by a different magistrate — may be considered.

[24] References to "officer" throughout this opinion should not be read too narrowly. It is necessary to consider the objective reasonableness, not only of the officers who eventually executed a warrant, but also of the officers who originally obtained it or who provided information material to the probable-cause determination. Nothing in our opinion suggests, for example, that an officer could obtain a warrant on the basis of a "bare bones" affidavit and then rely on colleagues who are ignorant of the circumstances under which the warrant was obtained to conduct the search. *See Whiteley v. Warden*, 401 U.S. 560, 568, (1971).

objective reasonableness, should not be difficult to apply in practice. When officers have acted pursuant to a warrant, the prosecution should ordinarily be able to establish objective good faith without a substantial expenditure of judicial time.

Nor are we persuaded that application of a good-faith exception to searches conducted pursuant to warrants will preclude review of the constitutionality of the search or seizure, deny needed guidance from the courts, or freeze Fourth Amendment law in its present state.[25] There is no need for courts to adopt the inflexible practice of always deciding whether the officers' conduct manifested objective good faith before turning to the question whether the Fourth Amendment has been violated. Defendants seeking suppression of the fruits of allegedly unconstitutional searches or seizures undoubtedly raise live controversies which Article III empowers federal courts to adjudicate.

If the resolution of a particular Fourth Amendment question is necessary to guide future action by law enforcement officers and magistrates, nothing will prevent reviewing courts from deciding that question before turning to the good-faith issue.[26] Indeed, it frequently will be difficult to determine whether the officers acted reasonably without resolving the Fourth Amendment issue. Even if the Fourth Amendment question is not one of broad import, reviewing courts could decide in particular cases that magistrates under their supervision need to be informed of their errors and so evaluate the officers' good faith only after finding a violation. In other circumstances, those courts could reject suppression motions posing no important Fourth Amendment questions by turning immediately to a consideration of the officers' good faith. We have no reason to believe that our Fourth Amendment jurisprudence would suffer by allowing reviewing courts to exercise an informed discretion in making this choice.

IV

When the principles we have enunciated today are applied to the facts of this case, it is apparent that the judgment of the Court of Appeals cannot stand. The Court of Appeals applied the prevailing legal standards to Officer Rombach's warrant application and concluded that the application could not support the magistrate's probable-cause determination. In so doing, the court clearly informed the magistrate that he had erred in issuing the challenged warrant. This aspect of the court's judgment is not under attack in this proceeding.

---

[25] The argument that defendants will lose their incentive to litigate meritorious Fourth Amendment claims as a result of the good-faith exception we adopt today is unpersuasive. Although the exception might discourage presentation of insubstantial suppression motions, the magnitude of the benefit conferred on defendants by a successful motion makes it unlikely that litigation of colorable claims will be substantially diminished.

[26] It has been suggested, in fact, that "the recognition of a 'penumbral zone,' within which an inadvertent mistake would not call for exclusion, . . . will make it less tempting for judges to bend fourth amendment standards to avoid releasing a possibly dangerous criminal because of a minor and unintentional miscalculation by the police." Schroeder, *supra* n. 14, (footnote omitted); *see* Ashdown, *Good Faith, the Exclusionary Remedy, and Rule-Oriented Adjudication in the Criminal Process*, 24 WM. & MARY L. REV. 335, 383–384 (1983).

Having determined that the warrant should not have issued, the Court of Appeals understandably declined to adopt a modification of the Fourth Amendment exclusionary rule that this Court had not previously sanctioned. Although the modification finds strong support in our previous cases, the Court of Appeals' commendable self-restraint is not to be criticized. We have now re-examined the purposes of the exclusionary rule and the propriety of its application in cases where officers have relied on a subsequently invalidated search warrant. Our conclusion is that the rule's purposes will only rarely be served by applying it in such circumstances.

In the absence of an allegation that the magistrate abandoned his detached and neutral role, suppression is appropriate only if the officers were dishonest or reckless in preparing their affidavit or could not have harbored an objectively reasonable belief in the existence of probable cause. Only respondent Leon has contended that no reasonably well-trained police officer could have believed that there existed probable cause to search his house; significantly, the other respondents advance no comparable argument. Officer Rombach's application for a warrant clearly was supported by much more than a "bare bones" affidavit. The affidavit related the results of an extensive investigation and, as the opinions of the divided panel of the Court of Appeals make clear, provided evidence sufficient to create disagreement among thoughtful and competent judges as to the existence of probable cause. Under these circumstances, the officers' reliance on the magistrate's determination of probable cause was objectively reasonable, and application of the extreme sanction of exclusion is inappropriate.

Accordingly, the judgment of the Court of Appeals is Reversed.

JUSTICE BLACKMUN, concurring.

As the Court's opinion in this case makes clear, the Court has narrowed the scope of the exclusionary rule because of an empirical judgment that the rule has little appreciable effect in cases where officers act in objectively reasonable reliance on search warrants. Because I share the view that the exclusionary rule is not a constitutionally compelled corollary of the Fourth Amendment itself, I see no way to avoid making an empirical judgment of this sort, and I am satisfied that the Court has made the correct one on the information before it. Like all courts, we face institutional limitations on our ability to gather information about "legislative facts," and the exclusionary rule itself has exacerbated the shortage of hard data concerning the behavior of police officers in the absence of such a rule. Nonetheless, we cannot escape the responsibility to decide the question before us, however imperfect our information may be, and I am prepared to join the Court on the information now at hand.

What must be stressed, however, is that any empirical judgment about the effect of the exclusionary rule in a particular class of cases necessarily is a provisional one. By their very nature, the assumptions on which we proceed today cannot be cast in stone. To the contrary, they now will be tested in the real world of state and federal law enforcement, and this Court will attend to the results. If it should emerge from experience that, contrary to our expectations, the good faith exception to the exclusionary rule results in a material change in police compliance with the Fourth

Amendment, we shall have to reconsider what we have undertaken here. The logic of a decision that rests on untested predictions about police conduct demands no less.

If a single principle may be drawn from this Court's exclusionary rule decisions, from *Weeks* through *Mapp* to the decisions handed down today, it is that the scope of the exclusionary rule is subject to change in light of changing judicial understanding about the effects of the rule outside the confines of the courtroom. It is incumbent on the Nation's law enforcement officers, who must continue to observe the Fourth Amendment in the wake of today's decisions, to recognize the double-edged nature of that principle.

JUSTICE BRENNAN, with whom JUSTICE MARSHALL joins, dissenting.

Ten years ago in *Calandra.* I expressed the fear that the Court's decision "may signal that a majority of my colleagues have positioned themselves to reopen the door [to evidence secured by official lawlessness] still further and abandon altogether the exclusionary rule in search-and-seizure cases." Since then, in case after case, I have witnessed the Court's gradual but determined strangulation of the rule. It now appears that the Court's victory over the Fourth Amendment is complete. That today's decision represents the *piece de resistance* of the Court's past efforts cannot be doubted, for today the Court sanctions the use in the prosecution's case-in-chief of illegally obtained evidence against the individual whose rights have been violated — a result that had previously been thought to be foreclosed.

The Court seeks to justify this result on the ground that the "costs" of adhering to the exclusionary rule in cases like those before us exceed the "benefits." But the language of deterrence and of cost/benefit analysis, if used indiscriminately, can have a narcotic effect. It creates an illusion of technical precision and ineluctability. It suggests that not only constitutional principle but also empirical data supports the majority's result. When the Court's analysis is examined carefully, however, it is clear that we have not been treated to an honest assessment of the merits of the exclusionary rule, but have instead been drawn into a curious world where the "costs" of excluding illegally obtained evidence loom to exaggerated heights and where the "benefits" of such exclusion are made to disappear with a mere wave of the hand.

A proper understanding of the broad purposes sought to be served by the Fourth Amendment demonstrates that the principles embodied in the exclusionary rule rest upon a far firmer constitutional foundation than the shifting sands of the Court's deterrence rationale. But even if I were to accept the Court's chosen method of analyzing the question posed by these cases, I would still conclude that the Court's decision cannot be justified.

I

A

At bottom, the Court's decision turns on the proposition that the exclusionary rule is merely a "judicially created remedy designed to safeguard Fourth Amendment rights generally through its deterrent effect, rather than a personal constitutional right."

Such a reading appears plausible, because, as critics of the exclusionary rule never tire of repeating, the Fourth Amendment makes no express provision for the exclusion of evidence secured in violation of its commands. A short answer to this claim, of course, is that many of the Constitution's most vital imperatives are stated in general terms and the task of giving meaning to these precepts is therefore left to subsequent judicial decision-making in the context of concrete cases. The nature of our Constitution, as Chief Justice Marshall long ago explained, "requires that only its great outlines should be marked, its important objects designated, and the minor ingredients which compose those objects be deduced from the nature of the objects themselves." *McCulloch v. Maryland*, 4 Wheat. 316, 407 (1819).

A more direct answer may be supplied by recognizing that the Amendment, like other provisions of the Bill of Rights, restrains the power of the government as a whole; it does not specify only a particular agency and exempt all others. The judiciary is responsible, no less than the executive, for ensuring that constitutional rights are respected.

It is difficult to give any meaning at all to the limitations imposed by the Amendment if they are read to proscribe only certain conduct by the police but to allow other agents of the same government to take advantage of evidence secured by the police in violation of its requirements. The Amendment therefore must be read to condemn not only the initial unconstitutional invasion of privacy — which is done, after all, for the purpose of securing evidence — but also the subsequent use of any evidence so obtained.

The various arguments advanced by the Court in this campaign have only strengthened my conviction that the deterrence theory is both misguided and unworkable. First, the Court has frequently bewailed the "cost" of excluding reliable evidence. In large part, this criticism rests upon a refusal to acknowledge the function of the Fourth Amendment itself. If nothing else, the Amendment plainly operates to disable the government from gathering information and securing evidence in certain ways. In practical terms, of course, this restriction of official power means that some incriminating evidence inevitably will go undetected if the government obeys these constitutional restraints. It is the loss of that evidence that is the "price" our society pays for enjoying the freedom and privacy safeguarded by the Fourth Amendment. Thus, some criminals will go free *not*, in Justice (then Judge) Cardozo's misleading epigram, "because the constable has blundered," but rather because official compliance with Fourth Amendment requirements makes it more difficult to catch criminals. Understood in this way, the Amendment directly contemplates that some reliable and incriminating evidence will be lost to the government; therefore, it is not the exclusionary rule, but the

Amendment itself that has imposed this cost.[8]

In addition, the Court's decisions over the past decade have made plain that the entire enterprise of attempting to assess the benefits and costs of the exclusionary rule in various contexts is a virtually impossible task for the judiciary to perform honestly or accurately. Although the Court's language in those cases suggests that some specific empirical basis may support its analyses, the reality is that the Court's opinions represent inherently unstable compounds of intuition, hunches, and occasional pieces of partial and often inconclusive data. In *Calandra*, for example, the Court, in considering whether the exclusionary rule should apply in grand jury proceedings, had before it no concrete evidence whatever concerning the impact that application of the rule in such proceedings would have either in terms of the long-term costs or the expected benefits. To the extent empirical data is available regarding the general costs and benefits of the exclusionary rule, it has shown, on the one hand, as the Court acknowledges today, that the costs are not as substantial as critics have asserted in the past, and, on the other hand, that while the exclusionary rule may well have certain deterrent effects, it is extremely difficult to determine with any degree of precision whether the incidence of unlawful conduct by police is now lower than it was prior to *Mapp*. The Court has sought to turn this uncertainty to its advantage by casting the burden of proof upon proponents of the rule. "Obviously," however, "the assignment of the burden of proof on an issue where evidence does not exist and cannot be obtained is outcome determinative. [The] assignment of the burden is merely a way of announcing a predetermined conclusion."

III

Even if I were to accept the Court's general approach to the exclusionary rule, I could not agree with today's result.

At the outset, the Court suggests that society has been asked to pay a high price — in terms either of setting guilty persons free or of impeding the proper functioning of trials — as a result of excluding relevant physical evidence in cases where the police, in conducting searches and seizing evidence, have made only an "objectively reasonable" mistake concerning the constitutionality of their actions. But what evidence is there to support such a claim? Significantly, the Court points to none, and, indeed, as the Court acknowledges, recent studies have demonstrated

---

[8] Justice Stewart has explained this point in detail in a recent article:

Much of the criticism leveled at the exclusionary rule is misdirected; it is more properly directed at the Fourth Amendment itself. It is true that, as many observers have charged, the effect of the rule is to deprive the courts of extremely relevant, often direct evidence of the guilt of the defendant. But these same critics fail to acknowledge that, in many instances, the same extremely relevant evidence would not have been obtained had the police officer complied with the commands of the fourth amendment in the first place . . . .

The exclusionary rule places no limitations on the actions of the police. The fourth amendment does. The inevitable result of the Constitution's prohibition against unreasonable searches and seizures and its requirements that no warrant shall issue but upon probable cause is that police officers who obey its strictures will catch fewer criminals . . . . [T]hat is the price the framers anticipated and were willing to pay to ensure the sanctity of the person, home, and property against unrestrained governmental power.

that the "costs" of the exclusionary rule — calculated in terms of dropped prosecutions and lost convictions — are quite low.

What then supports the Court's insistence that this evidence be admitted? Apparently, the Court's only answer is that even though the costs of exclusion are not very substantial, the potential deterrent effect in these circumstances is so marginal that exclusion cannot be justified. The key to the Court's conclusion in this respect is its belief that the prospective deterrent effect of the exclusionary rule operates only in those situations in which police officers, when deciding whether to go forward with some particular search, have reason to know that their planned conduct will violate the requirements of the Fourth Amendment. If these officers in fact understand (or reasonably should understand because the law is well-settled) that their proposed conduct will offend the Fourth Amendment and that, conse- quently, any evidence they seize will be suppressed in court, they will refrain from conducting the planned search. In those circumstances, the incentive system created by the exclusionary rule will have the hoped-for deterrent effect. But in situations where police officers reasonably (but mistakenly) believe that their planned conduct satisfies Fourth Amendment requirements — presumably either (a) because they are acting on the basis of an apparently valid warrant, or (b) because their conduct is only later determined to be invalid as a result of a subsequent change in the law or the resolution of an unsettled question of law — then such officers will have no reason to refrain from conducting the search and the exclusionary rule will have no effect.

At first blush, there is some logic to this position. Undoubtedly, in the situation hypothesized by the Court, the existence of the exclusionary rule cannot be expected to have any deterrent effect on the particular officers at the moment they are deciding whether to go forward with the search. Indeed, the subsequent exclusion of any evidence seized under such circumstances appears somehow "unfair" to the particular officers involved. As the Court suggests, these officers have acted in what they thought was an appropriate and constitutionally authorized manner, but then the fruit of their efforts is nullified by the application of the exclusionary rule.

The flaw in the Court's argument, however, is that its logic captures only one comparatively minor element of the generally acknowledged deterrent purposes of the exclusionary rule. To be sure, the rule operates to some extent to deter future misconduct by individual officers who have had evidence suppressed in their own cases. But what the Court overlooks is that the deterrence rationale for the rule is not designed to be, nor should it be thought of as, a form of "punishment" of individual police officers for their failures to obey the restraints imposed by the Fourth Amendment. Instead, the chief deterrent function of the rule is its tendency to promote institutional compliance with Fourth Amendment requirements on the part of law enforcement agencies generally. Thus, as the Court has previously recognized, "over the long term, [the] demonstration [provided by the exclusionary rule] that our society attaches serious consequences to violation of constitutional rights is thought to encourage those who formulate law enforcement policies, and the officers who implement them, to incorporate Fourth Amendment ideals into their value system." It is only through such an institution-wide mechanism that information concerning Fourth Amendment standards can be effectively communicated to rank and file officers.[13]

If the overall educational effect of the exclusionary rule is considered, application of the rule to even those situations in which individual police officers have acted on the basis of a reasonable but mistaken belief that their conduct was authorized can still be expected to have a considerable long-term deterrent effect. If evidence is consistently excluded in these circumstances, police departments will surely be prompted to instruct their officers to devote greater care and attention to providing sufficient information to establish probable cause when applying for a warrant, and to review with some attention the form of the warrant that they have been issued, rather than automatically assuming that whatever document the magistrate has signed will necessarily comport with Fourth Amendment requirements.

After today's decision, however, that institutional incentive will be lost. Indeed, the Court's "reasonable mistake" exception to the exclusionary rule will tend to put a premium on police ignorance of the law. Armed with the assurance provided by today's decision that evidence will always be admissible whenever an officer has "reasonably" relied upon a warrant, police departments will be encouraged to train officers that if a warrant has simply been signed, it is reasonable, without more, to rely on it. Since in close cases there will no longer be any incentive to err on the side of constitutional behavior, police would have every reason to adopt a "let's-wait-until-its-decided" approach in situations in which there is a question about a warrant's validity or the basis for its issuance.

Although the Court brushes these concerns aside, a host of grave consequences can be expected to result from its decision to carve this new exception out of the exclusionary rule. A chief consequence of today's decision will be to convey a clear

---

[13] Although specific empirical data on the systemic deterrent effect of the rule is not conclusive, the testimony of those actually involved in law enforcement suggests that, at the very least, the *Mapp* decision had the effect of increasing police awareness of Fourth Amendment requirements and of prompting prosecutors and police commanders to work towards educating rank and file officers. For example, as former New York Police Commissioner Murphy explained the impact of the *Mapp* decision: "I can think of no decision in recent times in the field of law enforcement which had such a dramatic and traumatic effect . . . . I was immediately caught up in the entire program of reevaluating our procedures, which had followed the *Defore* rule, and modifying, amending, and creating new policies and new instructions for implementing *Mapp* . . . . Retraining sessions had to be held from the very top administrators down to each of the thousands of foot patrolmen." Murphy, *Judicial Review of Police Methods in Law Enforcement: The Problem of Compliance by Police Departments*, 44 TEX. L. REV. 939, 941 (1966).

Further testimony about the impact of the *Mapp* decision can be found in the statement of Deputy Commissioner Reisman: "The *Mapp* case was a shock to us. We had to reorganize our thinking, frankly. Before this, nobody bothered to take out search warrants. Although the U.S. Constitution requires warrants in most cases, the U.S. Supreme Court had ruled that evidence obtained without a warrant — illegally, if you will — was admissible in state courts. So the feeling was, why bother? Well, once that rule was changed we knew we had better start teaching our men about it." N.Y. TIMES, April 28, 1965, at 50, col. 1. A former United States Attorney and now Attorney General of Maryland, Stephen Sachs, has described the impact of the rule on police practices in similar terms: "I have watched the rule deter, routinely, throughout my years as a prosecutor . . . . [P]olice-prosecutor consultation is customary in all our cases when Fourth Amendment concerns arise . . . . In at least three Maryland jurisdictions, for example, prosecutors are on twenty-four hour call to field search and seizure questions presented by police officers."

and unambiguous message to magistrates that their decisions to issue warrants are now insulated from subsequent judicial review. Creation of this new exception for good faith reliance upon a warrant implicitly tells magistrates that they need not take much care in reviewing warrant applications, since their mistakes will from now on have virtually no consequence: If their decision to issue a warrant was correct, the evidence will be admitted; if their decision was incorrect but the police relied in good faith on the warrant, the evidence will also be admitted. Inevitably, the care and attention devoted to such an inconsequential chore will dwindle. Although the Court is correct to note that magistrates do not share the same stake in the outcome of a criminal case as the police, they nevertheless need to appreciate that their role is of some moment in order to continue performing the important task of carefully reviewing warrant applications. Today's decision effectively removes that incentive.

Finally, even if one were to believe, as the Court apparently does, that police are hobbled by inflexible and hypertechnical warrant procedures, today's decision cannot be justified. This is because, given the relaxed standard for assessing probable cause established just last Term in *Gates*, the Court's newly fashioned good faith exception, when applied in the warrant context, will rarely, if ever, offer any greater flexibility for police than the *Gates* standard already supplies. In *Gates*, the Court held that "the task of an issuing magistrate is simply to make a practical, common-sense decision whether, given all the circumstances set forth in the affidavit before him, . . . there is a fair probability that contraband or evidence of a crime will be found in a particular place." The task of a reviewing court is confined to determining whether "the magistrate had a 'substantial basis' for concluding that probable cause existed." Given such a relaxed standard, it is virtually inconceivable that a reviewing court, when faced with a defendant's motion to suppress, could first find that a warrant was invalid under the new *Gates* standard, but then, at the same time, find that a police officer's reliance on such an invalid warrant was nevertheless "objectively reasonable" under the test announced today. Because the two standards overlap so completely, it is unlikely that a warrant could be found invalid under *Gates* and yet the police reliance upon it could be seen as objectively reasonable; otherwise, we would have to entertain the mind-boggling concept of objectively reasonable reliance upon an objectively unreasonable warrant.

[T]he full impact of the Court's regrettable decision will not be felt until the Court attempts to extend this rule to situations in which the police have conducted a warrantless search solely on the basis of their own judgment about the existence of probable cause and exigent circumstances. When that question is finally posed, I for one will not be surprised if my colleagues decide once again that we simply cannot afford to protect Fourth Amendment rights.

IV

When the public, as it quite properly has done in the past as well as in the present, demands that those in government increase their efforts to combat crime, it is all too easy for those government officials to seek expedient solutions. In contrast to such costly and difficult measures as building more prisons, improving law enforcement methods, or hiring more prosecutors and judges to relieve the overburdened court systems in the country's metropolitan areas, the relaxation of Fourth Amendment standards seems a tempting, costless means of meeting the public's demand for better law enforcement. In the long run, however, we as a society pay a heavy price for such expediency, because as Justice Jackson observed, the rights guaranteed in the Fourth Amendment "are not mere second-class rights but belong in the catalog of indispensable freedoms." *Brinegar v. United States*, 338 U.S. 160, 180 (1949) (dissenting opinion). Once lost, such rights are difficult to recover. There is hope, however, that in time this or some later Court will restore these precious freedoms to their rightful place as a primary protection for our citizens against overreaching officialdom.

I dissent.

JUSTICE STEVENS dissenting.

The Court assumes that the searches in these cases violated the Fourth Amendment, yet refuses to apply the exclusionary rule because the Court concludes that it was "reasonable" for the police to conduct them. In my opinion an official search and seizure cannot be both "unreasonable" and "reasonable" at the same time. The doctrinal vice in the Court's holding is its failure to consider the separate purposes of the two prohibitory clauses in the Fourth Amendment.

The first clause prohibits unreasonable searches and seizures and the second prohibits the issuance of warrants that are not supported by probable cause or that do not particularly describe the place to be searched and the persons or things to be seized. We have, of course, repeatedly held that warrantless searches are presumptively unreasonable.

The notion that a police officer's reliance on a magistrate's warrant is automatically appropriate is one the Framers of the Fourth Amendment would have vehemently rejected. The precise problem that the Amendment was intended to address was *the unreasonable issuance of warrants*. As we have often observed, the Amendment was actually motivated by the practice of issuing general warrants — warrants which did not satisfy the particularity and probable cause requirements. The resentments which led to the Amendment were directed at the issuance of warrants unjustified by particularized evidence of wrongdoing. Those who sought to amend the Constitution to include a Bill of Rights repeatedly voiced the view that the evil which had to be addressed was the issuance of warrants on insufficient evidence. As Professor Taylor has written:

> [O]ur constitutional fathers were not concerned about warrantless searches, but about overreaching warrants. It is perhaps too much to say that they feared the warrant more than the search, but it is plain enough that the warrant was the prime object of their concern. Far from looking at the warrant as a protection against unreasonable searches, they saw it as an authority for unreasonable and oppressive searches . . . .

T. Taylor, Two Studies in Constitutional Interpretation 41 (1969).

In short, the Framers of the Fourth Amendment were deeply suspicious of warrants; in their minds the paradigm of an abusive search was the execution of a warrant not based on probable cause. The fact that colonial officers had magisterial authorization for their conduct when they engaged in general searches surely did not make their conduct "reasonable." The Court's view that it is consistent with our Constitution to adopt a rule that it is presumptively reasonable to rely on a defective warrant is the product of constitutional amnesia.[27]

IV

In *Brinegar*, Justice Jackson, after observing that "[i]ndications are not wanting that Fourth Amendment freedoms are tacitly marked as secondary rights, to be relegated to a deferred position," (dissenting opinion), continued:

> These, I protest, are not mere second-class rights but belong in the catalog of indispensable freedoms. Among deprivations of rights, none is so effective in cowing a population, crushing the spirit of the individual and putting terror in every heart. Uncontrolled search and seizure is one of the first and most effective weapons in the arsenal of every arbitrary government. And one need only briefly to have dwelt and worked among a people possessed of many admirable qualities but deprived of these rights to know that the human personality deteriorates and dignity and self-reliance disappear where homes, persons and possessions are subject at any hour to unheralded search and seizure by the police.
>
> Only occasional and more flagrant abuses come to the attention of the courts, and then only those where the search and seizure yields incriminating evidence and the defendant is at least sufficiently compromised to be indicted. If the officers raid a home, an office, or stop and search an automobile but find nothing incriminating, this invasion of the personal liberty of the innocent too often finds no practical redress. There may be, and I am convinced that there are, many unlawful searches of homes and automobiles of innocent people which turn up nothing incriminating, in which no arrest is made, about which courts do nothing, and about which we never hear.
>
> Courts can protect the innocent against such invasions only indirectly and through the medium of excluding evidence obtained against those who frequently are guilty . . . . So a search against Brinegar's car must be regarded as a search of the car of Everyman.

Justice Jackson's reference to his experience at Nuremberg should remind us of the importance of considering the consequences of today's decision for "Everyman."

---

[27] "It makes all the difference in the world whether one recognizes the central fact about the Fourth Amendment, namely, that it was a safeguard against recurrence of abuses so deeply felt by the Colonies as to be one of the potent causes of the Revolution, or one thinks of it as merely a requirement for a piece of paper." *United States v. Rabinowitz*, 339 U.S. 56, 69 (1950) (Frankfurter, J., dissenting).

The exclusionary rule is designed to prevent violations of the Fourth Amendment.[28] "Its purpose is to deter — to compel respect for the constitutional guaranty in the only effectively available way, by removing the incentive to disregard it." If the police cannot use evidence obtained through warrants issued on less than probable cause, they have less incentive to seek those warrants, and magistrates have less incentive to issue them.

Today's decisions do grave damage to that deterrent function. Under the majority's new rule, even when the police know their warrant application is probably insufficient, they retain an incentive to submit it to a magistrate, on the chance that he may take the bait. No longer must they hesitate and seek additional evidence in doubtful cases.

The Court is of course correct that the exclusionary rule cannot deter when the authorities have no reason to know that their conduct is unconstitutional. But when probable cause is lacking, then by definition a reasonable person under the circumstances would not believe there is a fair likelihood that a search will produce evidence of a crime. Under such circumstances well-trained professionals must know that they are violating the Constitution. The Court's approach — which, in effect, encourages the police to seek a warrant even if they know the existence of probable cause is doubtful — can only lead to an increased number of constitutional violations.

Today, for the first time, this Court holds that although the Constitution has been violated, no court should do anything about it at any time and in any proceeding.[35] In my judgment, the Constitution requires more. Courts simply cannot escape their responsibility for redressing constitutional violations if they admit evidence obtained through unreasonable searches and seizures, since the entire point of police conduct that violates the Fourth Amendment is to obtain evidence for use at trial. If such evidence is admitted, then the courts become not

---

[28] For at least two reasons, the exclusionary rule is a better remedy than a civil action against an offending officer. Unlike the fear of personal liability, it should not create excessive deterrence; moreover, it avoids the obvious unfairness of subjecting the dedicated officer to the risk of monetary liability for a misstep while endeavoring to enforce the law. Society, rather than the individual officer, should accept the responsibility for inadequate training or supervision of officers engaged in hazardous police work. What the Chief Justice wrote, some two decades ago, remains true today:

> It is the proud claim of a democratic society that the people are masters and all officials of the state are servants of the people. That being so, the ancient rule of *respondeat superior* furnishes us with a simple, direct and reasonable basis for refusing to admit evidence secured in violation of constitutional or statutory provisions. Since the policeman is society's servant, his acts in the execution of his duty are attributable to the master or employer. Society as a whole is thus responsible and society is "penalized" by refusing it the benefit of evidence secured by the illegal action. This satisfies me more than the other explanations because it seems to me that society — in a country like ours — *is* involved in and *is* responsible for what is done in its name and by its agents. Unlike the Germans of the 1930's and early '40's, we cannot say "it is all The Leader's doing. I am not responsible." In a representative democracy we are responsible, whether we like it or not. And so each of us is involved and each is in this sense responsible when a police officer breaks rules of law established for our common protection.

Burger, *Who Will Watch the Watchman?*, 14 Am. U.L. Rev. 1, 14 (1964) (emphasis in original) (footnote omitted).

[35] As the majority recognizes in all cases in which its "good faith" exception to the exclusionary rule would operate, there will also be immunity from civil damages.

merely the final and necessary link in an unconstitutional chain of events, but its actual motivating force. "If the existing code does not permit district attorneys to have a hand in such dirty business it does not permit the judge to allow such iniquities to succeed." *Olmstead v. United States*, 277 U.S 438, 470 (1928) (HOLMES, J., dissenting). Nor should we so easily concede the existence of a constitutional violation for which there is no remedy. To do so is to convert a Bill of *Rights* into an unenforced honor code that the police may follow in their discretion. The Constitution requires more; it requires a *remedy*. If the Court's new rule is to be followed, the Bill of Rights should be renamed.

It is of course true that the exclusionary rule exerts a high price — the loss of probative evidence of guilt. But that price is one courts have often been required to pay to serve important social goals. That price is also one the Fourth Amendment requires us to pay, assuming as we must that the Framers intended that its strictures "shall not be violated." For in all such cases, as Justice Stewart has observed, "the same extremely relevant evidence would not have been obtained had the police officer complied with the commands of the fourth amendment in the first place."

"[T]he forefathers thought this was not too great a price to pay for that decent privacy of home, papers and effects which is indispensable to individual dignity and self-respect. They may have overvalued privacy, but I am not disposed to set their command at naught." *Harris v. United States*, 331 U.S. 145, 198 (1947) (JACKSON, J., dissenting).

We could, of course, facilitate the process of administering justice to those who violate the criminal laws by ignoring the commands of the Fourth Amendment — indeed, by ignoring the entire Bill of Rights — but it is the very purpose of a Bill of Rights to identify values that may not be sacrificed to expediency. In a just society those who govern, as well as those who are governed, must obey the law.

I would vacate the judgment in *Leon* and remand the case to the Court of Appeals for reconsideration in the light of *Gates*. Accordingly, I respectfully dissent.

QUESTIONS AND NOTES

1. Do you think that the Court inappropriately balances the costs and benefits of the exclusionary rule?

2. Is the dispute between the Court and Justice Brennan anything more than a replay of *Calandra*?

3. Do you agree with the Court that indiscriminate application of the exclusionary rule brings the Court into disrespect?

4. Is the problem (if there is one) the exclusionary rule or the Fourth Amendment itself?

5. Is *Leon* likely to adversely impact on the magistrate's performance? Is it likely to change the manner in which police present warrants? Is it likely to lead to (more) magistrate shopping?

6.   Is it relevant, as Justice Stevens suggests, that one of the purposes of the Fourth Amendment was to strictly circumscribe the power of magistrates to issue warrants? If he is correct, is *Leon* necessarily wrongly decided?

7.   If the police are acting in objective good faith, is there anything more that we can expect of them?

8.   Can you imagine a case in which a warrant would have been invalid under *Gates*, but valid under *Leon*?

9.   If your answer to Question 7 was "no," does that suggest that *Leon* is a lot of fuss about nothing?

10.   Given that neither money damages nor exclusion of evidence is appropriate when police officer's act in good faith, is it meaningful to call the officer's action a violation of the Fourth Amendment at all?

11.   Given the implication of Question 10, would it have been better for the Court to hold that the Fourth Amendment is satisfied when the police act in good faith reliance on a warrant issued by a magistrate?

12.   In the companion case, *Massachusetts v. Sheppard*, 468 U.S. 981 (1984), the Court found the good faith exception applicable where the officers went to a judge's home on a Sunday with a warrant originally designed for drugs. The officers made some changes in the warrant for the evidence of murder warrant that they were seeking. They informed the judge of some of the problems they saw with relying on such a warrant. Upon assurance by the judge that he would make the necessary changes, the police accepted and relied on the warrant which turned out to be insufficient.

Believing that there was little else the police could do, the Court found the good faith exception applicable. Justice Stevens, in a concurring opinion, would have upheld the search on the ground that the technical errors in the warrant did not render the search unreasonable.

13.   Would (should) the good faith exception apply to a police officer's reasonable belief that an unconstitutional search authorized by an unconstitutional statute is constitutional. In a 5-4 decision, the Supreme Court answered that question "yes." *See Illinois v. Krull*, 480 U.S. 340 (1987).

PROBLEM

Recall *Groh v. Ramirez* (Ch. 3, *supra*). Groh raised a good faith defense. How should the Court resolve his defense? For the Court's resolution, see *Groh v. Ramirez*, 540 U.S. 551 (2004).

When considering questions such as those raised in this section (or for that matter, the entire book), the diligent attorney should not ignore state constitutions or state statutes. *Commonwealth v. Edmunds*, suggests both of those potential sources.

COMMONWEALTH v. EDMUNDS
586 A.2d 887 (Pa. 1991)

CAPPY, JUSTICE.

I. THE HISTORY OF THE CASE

The issue presented to this court is whether Pennsylvania should adopt the "good faith" exception to the exclusionary rule as articulated by the United States Supreme Court in *Leon*. We conclude that a "good faith" exception to the exclusionary rule would frustrate the guarantees embodied in Article I, Section 8, of the Pennsylvania Constitution. Accordingly, the decision of the Superior Court is reversed.

The defendant in the instant case was found guilty after a non-jury trial on August 18, 1987 of criminal conspiracy, simple possession, possession with intent to deliver, possession with intent to manufacture and manufacture of a controlled substance. The conviction was premised upon the admission into evidence of marijuana seized at the defendant's property pursuant to a search warrant, after information was received from two anonymous informants.

The trial court held that the search warrant failed to establish probable cause that the marijuana would be at the location to be searched on the date it was issued. The trial court found that the warrant failed to set forth with specificity the date upon which the anonymous informants observed the marijuana. *See Commonwealth v. Conner*, 452 Pa. 333, 305 A.2d 341 (1973). However, the trial court went on to deny the defendant's motion to suppress the marijuana. Applying the rationale of *Leon*, the trial court looked beyond the four corners of the affidavit, in order to establish that the officers executing the warrant acted in "good faith" in relying upon the warrant to conduct the search. In reaching this conclusion the trial court also decided that *Leon* permitted the court to undercut the language of Pa. R. Crim. P. 2003, which prohibits oral testimony outside the four corners of the written affidavit to supplement the finding of probable cause.

The Superior Court in a divided panel decision, opinion by Wieand J., dissent by Popovich J., affirmed the judgment of the trial court, specifically relying upon in *Leon*.

As a preliminary matter, we concur with the inevitable conclusion of the trial court and the Superior Court, that probable cause did not exist on the face of the warrant. In *Conner*, this Court made clear that a search warrant is defective if it is issued without reference to the time when the informant obtained his or her information. Coupled with Pa. R. Crim. P. 2003, which mandates that courts in Pennsylvania shall not consider oral testimony outside the four corners of the written affidavit to supplement the finding of probable cause for a search warrant, we are compelled to conclude that the affidavit of probable cause and warrant were facially invalid. As the Superior Court candidly stated, the affidavit in question "did not contain facts from which the date of the hunters' observations could be determined." Indeed, the dissenting opinion of Mr. Justice McDermott concedes that probable cause was lacking.

We are not at liberty to ignore the *Leon* issue as it has been injected into the case by the trial court, and expressly affirmed by the Superior Court. Both lower courts have acknowledged, correctly, that Rule 2003 and our decision in *Conner* render the warrant invalid on its face under Pennsylvania law. The only way to salvage the warrant from facial invalidity is to disregard Rule 2003 and consider oral testimony outside the four corners of the affidavit to establish probable cause, which we are not free to do; or to consider the same oral testimony to establish a "good faith" exception under the federal *Leon* test, which is precisely what the trial court sought to accomplish. The trial judge conducted a supplemental suppression hearing for the express purpose of bringing the *Leon* issue four-square into this case, and the Superior Court affirmed explicitly on that basis. The "good faith" exception issue having thus been joined by both courts below, we are now constrained to address it.

The sole question in this case, therefore, is whether the Constitution of Pennsylvania incorporates a "good faith" exception to the exclusionary rule, which permits the introduction of evidence seized where probable cause is lacking on the face of the warrant.

Put in other terms, the question is whether the federal *Leon* test circumvents the acknowledged deficiencies under Pennsylvania law, and prevents the suppression of evidence seized pursuant to an *invalid search warrant*. For the reasons that follow, we conclude that it does not.

[After analyzing *Leon, Sheppard*, and *Krull*, the Court continued.]

III. FACTORS TO CONSIDER IN UNDERTAKING PENNSYLVANIA CONSTITUTIONAL ANALYSIS

This Court has long emphasized that, in interpreting a provision of the Pennsylvania Constitution, we are not bound by the decisions of the United States Supreme Court which interpret similar (yet distinct) federal constitutional provisions.

As Mr. Chief Justice Nix aptly stated, the federal constitution establishes certain minimum levels which are "equally applicable to the [analogous] state constitutional provision." However, each state has the power to provide broader standards, and go beyond the minimum floor which is established by the federal Constitution. *Commonwealth v. Sell*, 470 A.2d at 467.

The United States Supreme Court has repeatedly affirmed that the states are not only free to, but also encouraged to engage in independent analysis in drawing meaning from their own state constitutions. *See PruneYard Shopping Center v. Robins*, 447 U.S. 74, 80–82 (1980) (Rehnquist, J.). Indeed, this is a positive expression of the jurisprudence which has existed in the United States since the founding of the nation. Alexander Hamilton, lobbying for the ratification of the U.S. Constitution in the Federalist Papers over two hundred years ago, made clear that the Supremacy Clause of the Federal Constitution was never designed to overshadow the states, or prevent them from maintaining their own pockets of autonomy. *See The Federalist No. 33* (A. Hamilton), *in* THE FEDERALIST PAPERS (The New American Library ed.) 204.

The past two decades have witnessed a strong resurgence of independent state constitutional analysis, in Pennsylvania and elsewhere.

Here in Pennsylvania, we have stated with increasing frequency that it is both important and necessary that we undertake an independent analysis of the Pennsylvania Constitution, each time a provision of that fundamental document is implicated. Although we may accord weight to federal decisions where they "are found to be logically persuasive and well reasoned, paying due regard to precedent and the policies underlying specific constitutional guarantees," we are free to reject the conclusions of the United States Supreme Court so long as we remain faithful to the minimum guarantees established by the United States Constitution.

Accordingly, as a general rule it is important that litigants brief and analyze at least the following four factors:

1) text of the Pennsylvania constitutional provision;

2) history of the provision, including Pennsylvania case-law;

3) related case-law from other states;

4) policy considerations, including unique issues of state and local concern, and applicability within modern Pennsylvania jurisprudence.

Depending upon the particular issue presented, an examination of related federal precedent may be useful as part of the state constitutional analysis, not as binding authority, but as one form of guidance. However, it is essential that courts in Pennsylvania undertake an independent analysis under the Pennsylvania Constitution. Utilizing the above four factors, and having reviewed *Leon*, we conclude that a "good faith" exception to the exclusionary rule would frustrate the guarantees embodied in Article I, Section 8 of our Commonwealth's constitution.

IV. ANALYSIS

A. Text

The text of Article 1, Section 8 of the Pennsylvania Constitution provides as follows:

Security from Searches and Seizures

Section 8. The people shall be secure in their persons, houses, papers and possessions from unreasonable searches and seizures, and no warrant to search any place or to seize any person or things shall issue without describing them as nearly as may be, nor without probable cause, supported by oath or affirmation subscribed to by the affiant.

Although the wording of the Pennsylvania Constitution is similar in language to the Fourth Amendment of the United States Constitution, we are not bound to interpret the two provisions as if they were mirror images, even where the text is similar or identical. Thus, we must next examine the history of Article I, Section 8, in order to draw meaning from that provision and consider the appropriateness of a "good faith" exception to the exclusionary rule in the Pennsylvania constitutional scheme.

B. History

We have made reference, on repeated occasions, to the unique history of Article 1, Section 8, as well as other provisions of the Pennsylvania Constitution. As we noted in *Sell*: "constitutional protection against unreasonable searches and seizures existed in Pennsylvania more than a decade before the adoption of the federal Constitution, and fifteen years prior to the promulgation of the Fourth Amendment."

Thus, contrary to the popular misconception that state constitutions are somehow patterned after the United States Constitution, the reverse is true. The federal Bill of Rights borrowed heavily from the Declarations of Rights contained in the constitutions of Pennsylvania and other colonies.

With respect to Article 1, Section 8 of the present Pennsylvania Constitution, which relates to freedom from unreasonable searches and seizures, that provision had its origin prior to the 4th Amendment, in Clause 10 of the original Constitution of 1776. Specifically, the original version of the search and seizure provision reads as follows:

The people have a right to hold themselves, their houses, papers and possessions free from search and seizure, and therefore warrants without oaths or affirmations first made, affording sufficient foundation for them, and whereby any officer or messenger may be commanded or required to search suspected places, or to seize any person or persons, his or their property, not particularly described, are contrary to that right and ought not be granted.

The requirement of probable cause in this Commonwealth thus traces its origin to its original Constitution of 1776, drafted by the first convention of delegates chaired by Benjamin Franklin. The primary purpose of the warrant requirement was to abolish "general warrants," which had been used by the British to conduct sweeping searches of residences and businesses, based upon generalized suspicions. Therefore, at the time the Pennsylvania Constitution was drafted in 1776, the issue of searches and seizures unsupported by probable cause was of utmost concern to the constitutional draftsmen.

Moreover, as this Court has stated repeatedly in interpreting Article 1, Section 8, that provision is meant to embody a strong notion of privacy, carefully safeguarded in this Commonwealth for the past two centuries. As we stated in *Sell*: "the survival of the language now employed in Article 1, Section 8 through over 200 years of profound change in other areas demonstrates that the paramount concern for privacy first adopted as part of our organic law in 1776 continues to enjoy the mandate of the people of this Commonwealth."

The history of Article I, Section 8, thus indicates that the purpose underlying the exclusionary rule in this Commonwealth is quite distinct from the purpose underlying the exclusionary rule under the 4th Amendment, as articulated by the majority in *Leon*.

The United States Supreme Court in *Leon* made clear that, in its view, the *sole purpose* for the exclusionary rule under the 4th Amendment was to deter police misconduct. The *Leon* majority also made clear that, under the Federal Constitution, the exclusionary rule operated as "a judicially created remedy designed to safeguard Fourth Amendment rights generally through its deterrent effect, rather than a personal constitutional right of the party aggrieved."

This reinterpretation differs from the way the exclusionary rule has evolved in Pennsylvania since the decision of *Mapp v. Ohio* in 1961 and represents a shift in judicial philosophy from the decisions of the United States Supreme Court dating back to *Weeks v. United States*.

Like many of its sister states, Pennsylvania did not adopt an exclusionary rule until the United States Supreme Court's decision in *Mapp* required it to do so. However, at the time the exclusionary rule was embraced in Pennsylvania, we clearly viewed it as a constitutional mandate. This interpretation was in keeping with a long line of federal cases, beginning with *Weeks* in 1914, which viewed the exclusionary rule as a necessary corollary to the prohibition against unreasonable searches and seizures.

During the first decade after *Mapp*, our decisions in Pennsylvania tended to parallel the cases interpreting the 4th Amendment. However, beginning in 1973, our case-law began to reflect a clear divergence from federal precedent. The United States Supreme Court at this time began moving towards a metamorphosed view, suggesting that the purpose of the exclusionary rule "is not to redress the injury to the *privacy* of the search victim (but, rather) to deter future *unlawful police conduct*." *Calandra*, 414 U.S. at 347 (emphasis added). At the same time this Court began to forge its own path under Article I, Section 8 of the Pennsylvania Constitution, declaring with increasing frequency that Article I, Section 8 of the Pennsylvania Constitution embodied a strong notion of privacy, notwithstanding federal cases to the contrary. In *Commonwealth v. Platou* and *Commonwealth v. DeJohn*, we made explicit that "the right to be free from unreasonable searches and seizures contained in Article I, Section 8 of the Pennsylvania Constitution is tied into the implicit right to privacy in this Commonwealth." In *DeJohn*, we specifically refused to follow the U.S. Supreme Court's decision in *U.S. v. Miller*, 425 U.S. 435 (1976), which had held that a citizen had no standing to object to the seizure of his or her bank records.

From *DeJohn* forward, a steady line of case-law has evolved under the Pennsylvania Constitution, making clear that Article I, Section 8 is unshakably linked to a right of privacy in this Commonwealth.

Most recently, in *Melilli*, 521 Pa. 405, 555 A.2d 1254 (1989), this Court held that Article I, Section 8 of the Pennsylvania Constitution was offended by the installation of a pen register device without probable cause. Mr. Justice Papadakos, in rejecting the holding of the United States Supreme Court in *Smith v. Maryland*, emphasized that "Article I, Section 8 of the Pennsylvania Constitution . . . may be employed to guard *individual privacy* rights against unreasonable searches and seizures more zealously than the federal government does under the Constitution of the United States by serving as an independent source of supplemental rights." Mr. Justice Papadakos went on to conclude that, because a pen register "is the equivalent of a search warrant in its operative effect where the intrusion involves a violation of a privacy interest," the affidavit and order "must comply with the requirements of probable cause required under Pa. Rules of Criminal Procedure Chapter 2000, Search Warrants."

Thus, the exclusionary rule in Pennsylvania has consistently served to bolster the twin aims of Article I, Section 8; to-wit, the safeguarding of privacy and the fundamental requirement that warrants shall only be issued upon probable cause.

Whether the United States Supreme Court has determined that the exclusionary rule does not advance the 4th Amendment purpose of deterring police conduct is irrelevant. Indeed, we disagree with that Court's suggestion in *Leon* that we in Pennsylvania have been employing the exclusionary rule all these years to deter police corruption. We flatly reject this notion. We have no reason to believe that police officers or district justices in the Commonwealth of Pennsylvania do not engage in "good faith" in carrying out their duties. What is significant, however, is that our Constitution has historically been interpreted to incorporate a strong right of privacy, and an equally strong adherence to the requirement of probable cause under Article 1, Section 8. Citizens in this Commonwealth possess such rights, even where a police officer in "good faith" carrying out his or her duties inadvertently invades the privacy or circumvents the strictures of probable cause. To adopt a "good faith" exception to the exclusionary rule, we believe, would virtually emasculate those clear safeguards which have been carefully developed under the Pennsylvania Constitution over the past 200 years.

C. Related Case-Law From Other States

A number of states other than Pennsylvania have confronted the issue of whether to apply a "good faith" exception to the exclusionary rule, under their own constitutions, in the wake of *Leon*.

The highest courts of at least two states — Arkansas and Missouri — have seemingly embraced the good faith exception under their own constitutions. Intermediary appellate courts in at least four other states — Indiana, Kansas, Maryland and Louisiana — have indicated their acceptance of the "good faith" exception. In virtually all of those states embracing the "good-faith" exception under their own constitutions, however, the reasoning is a simple affirmation of the logic of *Leon*, with little additional state constitutional analysis.[11]

On the other hand, the highest courts of at least four states — New Jersey, New York, North Carolina and Connecticut — have chosen to reject the "good-faith"

---

[11] For a complete list of those states which have adopted and rejected *Leon*, with or without analysis, *see* Uchida et al., *Acting In Good Faith: The Effects of* United States v. Leon *on the Police and Courts*, 30 Ariz. L. Rev. 467, 475–480 (1988).

exception under their own constitutions, with more detailed analysis of state constitutional principles. The intermediate appellate courts of at least four additional states — Tennessee, Wisconsin, Michigan, and Minnesota — have likewise eschewed the logic of *Leon* under their own state constitutions.

A mere scorecard of those states which have accepted and rejected *Leon* is certainly not dispositive of the issue in Pennsylvania. However, the logic of certain of those opinions bears upon our analysis under the Pennsylvania Constitution, particularly given the unique history of Article 1, Section 8.

In this respect, we draw support from other states which have declined to adopt a "good faith" exception, particularly New Jersey, Connecticut and North Carolina.

D. Policy Considerations

We recognize that, in analyzing any state constitutional provision, it is necessary to go beyond the bare text and history of that provision as it was drafted 200 years ago, and consider its application within the modern scheme of Pennsylvania jurisprudence. An assessment of various policy considerations, however, only supports our conclusion that the good faith exception to the exclusionary rule would be inconsistent with the jurisprudence surrounding Article 1, Section 8.

First, such a rule would effectively negate the judicially created mandate reflected in the Pennsylvania Rules of Criminal Procedure, in Rules 2003, 2005 and 2006. Specifically, Rule 2003 relates to the requirements for the issuance of a warrant, and provides in relevant part:

> (a) No search warrant shall issue but upon probable cause supported by one or more affidavits sworn to before the issuing authority. The issuing authority, in determining whether probable cause has been established, may not consider any evidence outside the affidavits.

> (b) At any hearing on a motion for the return or suppression of evidence, or for suppression of the fruits of evidence, obtained pursuant to a search warrant, no evidence shall be admissible to establish probable cause other than the affidavits provided for in paragraph (a).

Rule 2003 thus adopts a "four corners" requirement, and provides that only evidence contained within the four corners of the affidavit may be considered to establish probable cause. This Rule, along with Rules 2005 and 2006 which reiterate that probable cause must exist on the face of the affidavit, were promulgated by this Court following this Court's decision in *Commonwealth v. Milliken*, 450 Pa. 310, 300 A.2d 78 (1973). The decision in *Milliken* is significant, because it makes clear that the "four corners" requirement of Rule 2003 was carefully and deliberately established in this Commonwealth.

In *Milliken*, a police officer had obtained a warrant to search the defendant's home for evidence relating to a murder, based upon an informant's tip. The affidavit of probable cause failed to set forth sufficient facts to establish the "reliability" of the informant, under the prevailing *Aguilar-Spinelli* test, rendering the warrant defective. At the suppression hearing, however, the police officer testified that he had given additional sworn oral testimony to the magistrate at the time the warrant was issued, not reduced to writing, which established the informant's reliability. The magistrate admitted that his memory was "dimmed" by the fact the proceeding was "some time ago," but essentially corroborated the officer's story.

This Court in *Milliken* rejected the contention that Article I, Section 8 of the Pennsylvania Constitution itself mandated that all facts relied upon to establish probable cause be reduced to writing; the constitutional language itself contained no such requirement. We therefore held that the sworn oral testimony of the police officer in that case could be used to supplement the affidavit. However, we went on to express deep concern for the fact that "the 'passage of time' inevitably causes 'memories . . . [to] fade.'" We stated that without a transcribed record made contemporaneously with the issuance of the warrant, "subsequent review of the partially unwritten proceeding may become tainted by possible additions of relevant information initially omitted but later supplied by hindsight."

Recognizing this "troublesome" dilemma, this Court in a thoughtful opinion written by the late Mr. Justice Roberts (later Chief Justice Roberts) and joined by then Mr. Justice, now Chief Justice Nix, announced in *Milliken* that we would exercise our supervisory powers to formulate a rule of procedure mandating that "a sufficient written record (be) made contemporaneously with the issuance of search warrants." We held that since this rule was procedural in nature, it could not be applied retroactively to invalidate the warrant in Milliken's case. However, we made clear that: "After the effective date of the rule the determination of probable cause by a suppression hearing court and an appellate court upon review will be made *only* from the written record prepared contemporaneously with the issuance of the search warrant." The result was the adoption of Pa. R. Crim. P. 2003 on March 28, 1973, effective in 60 days, which made explicit that probable cause for search warrants in Pennsylvania may be based only upon materials contained within the four corners of the written affidavit.

A second policy consideration which bolsters our conclusion is that the underlying premise of *Leon* is still open to serious debate. Although it is clear that the exclusionary rule presents some cost to society, in allowing "some guilty defendants [to] . . . go free," the extent of the costs are far from clear. A number of recent studies have indicated that the exclusion of illegally seized evidence has had a marginal effect in allowing guilty criminals to avoid successful prosecution. Indeed, the *Leon* decision itself indicates relatively low statistics with respect to the impact of the exclusionary rule in thwarting legitimate prosecutions. Equally as important, the alternative to the exclusionary rule most commonly advanced — *i.e.*, allowing victims of improper searches to sue police officers directly — has raised serious concern among police officers.

A third policy consideration which compels our decisions is that, given the recent decision of the United States Supreme Court in *Gates*, adopting a "totality of the circumstances test" in assessing probable cause, there is far less reason to adopt a "good faith" exception to the exclusionary rule. We have adopted *Gates* as a matter of Pennsylvania law in the recent case of *Commonwealth v. Gray*. As a number of jurists have pointed out, the flexible *Gates* standard now eliminates much of the prior concern which existed with respect to an overly rigid application of the exclusionary rule.

Finally, the dangers of allowing magistrates to serve as "rubber stamps" and of fostering "magistrate-shopping," are evident under *Leon*. As the instant case illustrates, police officers and magistrates have historically worked closely together in this Commonwealth. Trooper Deise and District Justice Tlumac prepared the warrant and affidavit with Trooper Deise dictating the affidavit while the magistrate typed it verbatim.

There is no suggestion here that Trooper Deise and District Justice Tlumac acted other than in utmost "good faith" when preparing the warrant. Nevertheless, we are mindful of the fact that both state and federal interpretations of the 4th Amendment require a warrant to be issued by a "neutral and detached magistrate," because as Mr. Justice Papadakos noted, there is a requirement of "an independent determination of probable cause."

CONCLUSION

Thirty years ago, when the exclusionary rule was first introduced, police officers were perhaps plagued with ill-defined, unarticulated rules governing their conduct. However, the past thirty years have seen a gradual sharpening of the process, with police officers adapting well to the exclusionary rule.

The purpose of Rule 2003 is not to exclude *bona fide* evidence based upon technical errors and omissions by police officers or magistrates. Rather, Rule 2003 is meant to provide support for the probable cause requirement of Article I, Section 8, by assuring that there is an objective method for determining when probable cause exists, and when it does not.

In the instant case, the evidence seized from defendant Edmunds was the product of a constitutionally defective search warrant. Article I, Section 8 of the Pennsylvania Constitution does not incorporate a "good faith" exception to the exclusionary rule. Therefore, the marijuana seized from the white corrugated building, the marijuana seized from Edmund's home, and the written and oral statements obtained from Edmunds by the troopers, must be suppressed. We base our decision strictly upon the Pennsylvania Constitution; any reference to the United States Constitution is merely for guidance and does not compel our decision.

Although the exclusionary rule may place a duty of thoroughness and care upon police officers and district justices in this Commonwealth, in order to safeguard the rights of citizens under Article I, Section 8, that is a small price to pay, we believe, for a democracy.

JUDGMENT OF SENTENCE REVERSED. Jurisdiction relinquished.

PAPADAKOS, JUSTICE, concurring.

I am compelled to concur in the result because Rule 2003(a) of the Pa. Rules of Criminal Procedure is absolute in requiring that the affidavit of probable cause supporting the issuance of a search warrant must be complete on its face in every essential detail, and that no testimony is permitted after its execution to fill in the blanks. The affidavit of probable cause in this case clearly lacks the essential element of the date when the informants saw the contraband growing. Although the affiant orally related to the magistrate, before the preparation of the affidavit of probable cause, the date on which the informants had seen the contraband growing, the magistrate, in acting the role of the scribe in typing the affidavit of probable cause, neglected to include this crucial date and the affiant neglected to spot this omission.

The majority correctly quotes this court's prior pronouncement on the subject:

> After the effective date of the rule the determination of probable cause by a suppression hearing court and an appellate court upon review will be made only from the written record prepared contemporaneously with the issuance of the search warrant.

Commonwealth v. Milliken, quoted by the majority opinion.

In view of the clear, unequivocal command of Rule 2003(a), I see no reason for the majority to reinvent the wheel and re-express the rationale underpinning the judicially created rule of procedure. It's all been said before. I see no issue of a good faith exception applicable in this case. I see only a reaffirmation of the dictates of Rule 2003(a) by simple statement to that effect or a change in the rule to accommodate the error committed by the scribe. Since the majority apparently does not wish to change the rule to avoid the absurdity of excluding the evidence obtained by the police through no misconduct on their part, I see no need for the in-depth re-analysis given by the majority.

Were the rule not so absolute on its face, I would gladly join McDermott, J., in dissent, for my sympathies and reason lie in his expression of outrage in the result of cases such as this.

McDermott, Justice, dissenting.

Today we have abandoned the twenty seven (27) year history of this Court's restrictive use of the exclusionary rule to only those instances where its application would deter misconduct by law enforcement authorities. Now that we have ignored that history and have decided to employ it even in cases where police officers have fulfilled their every obligation to protect the individual constitutional rights of citizens, I dissent.

Until this day we have dutifully followed the canons of the Fourth Amendment prescribed by the Supreme Court of the United States through hundreds of cases. We accepted, as we must, their rationale that police procedures had overstepped constitutional bounds and we imposed the sanction of suppression to dissuade illegal search. To teach the lesson, we were obliged to ignore a mountain of illegal contraband that otherwise was palpable indicia of guilt. There is no doubt that the social cost has been more than criminals freed to try again. It has generated a disbelief and a growing disrespect in the efficacy of law that stands mute in the presence of incontrovertible evidence of fire and lets the house burn down because the fireman arrived before he was properly called. *Leon* does not open the gates to unauthorized search, it does not dissolve the need for probable cause. It simply and properly shifts the responsibility for determining probable cause to a neutral magistrate and frees the police of his or her mistakes. The police cannot search on a whim. They must present their cause to a neutral magistrate. The facts they present must be true, the magistrate must act within his bounds, and, as the final test, the police must employ their experience in recognizing whether a warrant is illegal despite the authorization of the magistrate. All of these contentions remain alive and subject to scrutiny at a suppression hearing. The instant case is a classic illustration. The defect in the affidavit of probable cause was that the time of the offense was not specified. What was told the magistrate was that the contraband was "growing," a clear indication of present tense. The informants told the police that they saw it growing and the magistrate was told that it was growing and he issued a search warrant on that premise. When the police arrived it was still growing. All concerned acted in good faith. To suppress the evidence because a date was not specified with exactitude under those circumstances dwindles into practiced absurdity.

The United States Supreme Court has made it abundantly clear that suppression of evidence seized without probable cause is not a constitutional right. This Court has made that clear as well. *See Commonwealth v. Miller*, 513 Pa. 118, 133–134, 518 A.2d 1187, 1195 (1986) ("[T]he exclusionary rule is a judicially created device designed to deter improper governmental action in the course of criminal investigations and prosecutions. It is not a personal right of the accused").

The United States Supreme Court has made it equally clear that suppression of evidence seized without probable cause is mandated to contain police action. Likewise, we have approved the suppression of evidence only where it will have the benefit of deterring similar police misconduct in the future.

In interpreting our Constitution we are, as are our sister states, always free to give more than that allowed under Federal Constitutional interpretation. I would choose to accept the rationale of the Supreme Court and recognize the "good faith exception" of *Leon* to the exclusionary rule as have eighteen of our sister states. My opinion is not merely grounded in the absurdity of excluding this evidence, nor only upon the persuasiveness of *Leon*, but also because it is firmly grounded in Pennsylvania jurisprudence.

[I]n *Commonwealth v. Melilli*, 521 Pa. 405, 555 A.2d 1254 (1989), we held that a pen register device could not be installed unless probable cause to do so was established. We concluded that evidence seized by the installation of pen registers without probable cause, even though the police reasonably relied upon the Federal standard, should nevertheless be suppressed. We explicitly did not disagree with the *Leon* decision. Instead, we determined that the evidence was appropriately suppressed because the judge who issued the order to install the pen registers never considered whether probable cause existed and thereby "wholly abandoned his judicial role," a situation "envisioned" by *Leon* as worthy of suppression.

To now reject the holding of *Leon* for Pennsylvania is mere fiat, an exercise of personal illumination about a need for protection not only from the police but from the judiciary. Like the United States Supreme Court, I find no evidence that the judiciary has run beyond its responsibilities, or that if they do we cannot correct them. The Supreme Court of the United States is a world landmark for the protection of constitutional rights. What they require we enforce; what they allow we ought not deter except upon clear evidence of positive need. The United States

Supreme Court has recognized a positive need to allow, under the canons of *Leon*, a good faith exception. To do otherwise is to provide a sanctuary for the lawless elements seeking profit, particularly in the growing human misery of addiction.

I would affirm the Superior Court.

QUESTIONS AND NOTES

1.   Given that the deficiency in the *Edmunds* warrant was the failure to put the time of the relevant observations in writing, and given further that the essential nature of both the time (substance) and the writing (procedure) have been the law of Pennsylvania since 1973, how could the police officer possibly claimed to have acted in objective good faith?

2.   How would you have decided this case if you had been on the Pennsylvania Supreme Court? Why?

3.   The lesson of *Edmunds* clearly transcends the case itself. The opinion indicates that some, though not all, other Supreme Court cases upholding searches despite the Fourth Amendment have been rejected by the Pennsylvania Supreme Court. One faced with such a question in state court should *never* overlook the possibility of excluding evidence on state constitutional *or statutory* grounds.

4.   Conversely, as the next case in this section, *Arizona v. Evans*, makes clear, the United States Supreme Court insists that a state court opinion purporting to rest on independent state grounds must do so clearly.

ARIZONA v. EVANS
514 U.S. 1 (1995)

CHIEF JUSTICE REHNQUIST delivered the opinion of the Court.

In January 1991, Phoenix police officer Bryan Sargent observed respondent Evans driving the wrong way on a one-way street in front of the police station. The officer stopped respondent and asked to see his driver's license. After respondent told him that his license had been suspended, the officer entered respondent's name into a computer data terminal located in his patrol car. The computer inquiry confirmed that respondent's license had been suspended and also indicated that there was an outstanding misdemeanor warrant for his arrest. Based upon the outstanding warrant, Officer Sargent placed respondent under arrest. While being handcuffed, respondent dropped a hand-rolled cigarette that the officers determined smelled of marijuana. Officers proceeded to search his car and discovered a bag of marijuana under the passenger's seat.

The State charged respondent with possession of marijuana. When the police notified the Justice Court that they had arrested him, the Justice Court discovered that the arrest warrant previously had been quashed and so advised the police. Respondent argued that because his arrest was based on a warrant that had been quashed 17 days prior to his arrest, the marijuana seized incident to the arrest should be suppressed as the fruit of an unlawful arrest. Respondent also argued that "[t]he 'good faith' exception to the exclusionary rule [was] inapplicable . . . because it was police error, not judicial error, which caused the invalid arrest."

At the suppression hearing, the Chief Clerk of the Justice Court testified that a Justice of the Peace had issued the arrest warrant on December 13, 1990, because respondent had failed to appear to answer for several traffic violations. On December 19, 1990, respondent appeared before a pro tem Justice of the Peace who entered a notation in respondent's file to "quash warrant."

The Chief Clerk also testified regarding the standard court procedure for quashing a warrant. Under that procedure a justice court clerk calls and informs the warrant section of the Sheriff's Office when a warrant has been quashed. The Sheriff's Office then removes the warrant from its computer records. After calling the Sheriff's Office, the clerk makes a note in the individual's file indicating the clerk who made the phone call and the person at the Sheriff's Office to whom the clerk spoke. The Chief Clerk testified that there was no indication in respondent's file that a clerk had called and notified the Sheriff's Office that his arrest warrant had been quashed. A records clerk from the Sheriff's Office also testified that the Sheriff's Office had no record of a telephone call informing it that respondent's arrest warrant had been quashed. At the close of testimony, respondent argued that the evidence obtained as a result of the arrest should be suppressed because "the purposes of the exclusionary rule would be served here by making the clerks for the court, or the clerk for the Sheriff's Office, whoever is responsible for this mistake, to be more careful about making sure that warrants are removed from the records."

We first must consider whether we have jurisdiction to review the Arizona Supreme Court's decision. Respondent argues that we lack jurisdiction under 28 U.S.C. § 1257 because the Arizona Supreme Court never passed upon the Fourth Amendment issue and instead based its decision on the Arizona good-faith statute, ARIZ. REV. STAT. ANN. § 13-3925 (1993), an adequate and independent state ground. In the alternative, respondent asks that we remand to the Arizona Supreme Court for clarification.

In *Michigan v. Long*, 463 U.S. 1032, we adopted a standard for determining whether a state-court decision rested upon an adequate and independent state ground. When "a state court decision fairly appears to rest primarily on federal law, or to be interwoven with the federal law, and when the adequacy and independence of any possible state law ground is not clear from the face of the opinion, we will accept as the most reasonable explanation that the state court decided the case the way it did because it believed that federal law required it to do so." We adopted this practice, in part, to obviate the "unsatisfactory and intrusive practice of requiring state courts to clarify their decisions to the satisfaction of this Court." We also concluded that this approach would "provide state judges with a clearer opportunity to develop state jurisprudence unimpeded by federal interference, and yet will preserve the integrity of federal law."

Justice GINSBURG would overrule *Long*, supra, because she believes that the rule of that case "impedes the States' ability to serve as laboratories for testing solutions to novel legal problems."

We believe that *Long* properly serves its purpose and should not be disturbed. Under it, state courts are absolutely free to interpret state constitutional provisions to accord greater protection to individual rights than do similar provisions of the United States Constitution.

Applying that standard here, we conclude that we have jurisdiction. In reversing the Court of Appeals, the Arizona Supreme Court stated that "[w]hile it may be inappropriate to invoke the exclusionary rule where a magistrate has issued a facially valid warrant (a discretionary judicial function) based on an erroneous evaluation of the facts, the law, or both, *Leon*, it is useful and proper to do so where negligent record keeping (a purely clerical function) results in an unlawful arrest." Thus, the Arizona Supreme Court's decision to suppress the evidence was based squarely upon its interpretation of federal law.

> The question whether the exclusionary rule's remedy is appropriate in a particular context has long been regarded as an issue separate from the question whether the Fourth Amendment rights of the party seeking to invoke the rule were violated by police conduct.

Where "the exclusionary rule does not result in appreciable deterrence, then, clearly, its use . . . is unwarranted."

In *Leon*, we applied these principles to the context of a police search in which the officers had acted in objectively reasonable reliance on a search warrant, issued by a neutral and detached Magistrate, that later was determined to be invalid. 468 U.S. at 905, 104 S. Ct. at 3411. On the basis of three factors, we determined that there was no sound reason to apply the exclusionary rule as a means of deterring misconduct on the part of judicial officers who are responsible for issuing warrants. First, we noted that the exclusionary rule was historically designed " 'to deter police misconduct rather than to punish the errors of judges and magistrates.' " Second, there was " 'no evidence suggesting that judges and magistrates are inclined to ignore or subvert the Fourth Amendment or that lawlessness among these actors requires the application of the extreme sanction of exclusion.' " Third, and of greatest importance, there was no basis for believing that exclusion of evidence seized pursuant to a warrant would have a significant deterrent effect on the issuing judge or magistrate.

The *Leon* Court then examined whether application of the exclusionary rule could be expected to alter the behavior of the law enforcement officers. We concluded:

> [W]here the officer's conduct is objectively reasonable, "excluding the evidence will not further the ends of the exclusionary rule in any appreciable way; for it is painfully apparent that . . . the officer is acting as a reasonable officer would and should act in similar circumstances. Excluding the evidence can in no way affect his future conduct unless it is to make him less willing to do his duty."

Respondent relies on *United States v. Hensley*, 469 U.S. 221 (1985), and argues that the evidence seized incident to his arrest should be suppressed because he was the victim of a Fourth Amendment violation. In *Hensley*, the Court determined that evidence uncovered as a result of a *Terry* stop was admissible because the officers who made the stop acted in objectively reasonable reliance on a flyer that had been issued by officers of another police department who possessed a reasonable suspicion to justify a *Terry* stop. Because the *Hensley* Court determined that there had been no Fourth Amendment violation, the Court never considered whether the seized evidence should have been excluded. *Hensley* does not contradict our earlier pronouncements that "[t]he question whether the exclusionary rule's remedy is appropriate in a particular context has long been regarded as an issue separate from the question whether the Fourth Amendment rights of the party seeking to invoke the rule were violated by police conduct."

Respondent also argues that *Whiteley v. Warden*, 401 U.S. 560 (1971), compels exclusion of the evidence. In *Whiteley*, the Court determined that the Fourth Amendment had been violated when police officers arrested Whiteley and recovered inculpatory evidence based upon a radio report that two suspects had been involved in two robberies. Although the "police were entitled to act on the strength of the radio bulletin," the Court determined that there had been a Fourth Amendment violation because the initial complaint, upon which the arrest warrant and subsequent radio bulletin were based, was insufficient to support an independent judicial assessment of probable cause. The Court concluded that "an otherwise illegal arrest cannot be insulated from challenge by the decision of the instigating officer to rely on fellow officers to make the arrest." Because the "arrest violated [Whiteley's] constitutional rights under the Fourth and Fourteenth Amendments; the evidence secured as an incident thereto should have been excluded from his trial."

Although *Whiteley* clearly retains relevance in determining whether police officers have violated the Fourth Amendment, its precedential value regarding application of the exclusionary rule is dubious. In *Whiteley*, the Court treated identification of a Fourth Amendment violation as synonymous with application of the exclusionary rule to evidence secured incident to that violation.

Subsequent case law has rejected this reflexive application of the exclusionary rule. *Sheppard, Leon*, and *Calandra*. These later cases have emphasized that the issue of exclusion is separate from whether the Fourth Amendment has been violated.

Applying the reasoning of *Leon* to the facts of this case, we conclude that the decision of the Arizona Supreme Court must be reversed. The Arizona Supreme Court determined that it could not "support the distinction drawn . . . between clerical errors committed by law enforcement personnel and similar mistakes by court employees," and that "even assuming . . . that responsibility for the error rested with the justice court, it does not follow that the exclusionary rule should be inapplicable to these facts."

This holding is contrary to the reasoning of *Leon* [and] *Sheppard*. If court employees were responsible for the erroneous computer record, the exclusion of evidence at trial would not sufficiently deter future errors so as to warrant such a severe sanction. First, as we noted in *Leon*, the exclusionary rule was historically designed as a means of deterring police misconduct, not mistakes by court employees. Second, respondent offers no evidence that court employees are inclined to ignore or subvert the Fourth Amendment or that lawlessness among these actors requires application of the extreme sanction of exclusion. To the contrary, the Chief Clerk of the Justice Court testified at the suppression hearing that this type of error occurred once every three or four years.

Finally, and most important, there is no basis for believing that application of the exclusionary rule in these circumstances will have a significant effect on court employees responsible for informing the police that a warrant has been quashed. Because court clerks are not adjuncts to the law enforcement team engaged in the often competitive enterprise of ferreting out crime they have no stake in the outcome of particular criminal prosecutions. The threat of exclusion of evidence could not be expected to deter such individuals from failing to inform police officials that a warrant had been quashed.

If it were indeed a court clerk who was responsible for the erroneous entry on the police computer, application of the exclusionary rule also could not be expected to alter the behavior of the arresting officer. As the trial court in this case stated: "I think the police officer [was] bound to arrest. I think he would [have been] derelict in his duty if he failed to arrest." Excluding the evidence can in no way affect [the officer's] future conduct unless it is to make him less willing to do his duty. The Chief Clerk of the Justice Court testified that this type of error occurred "on[c]e every three or four years." In fact, once the court clerks discovered the error, they immediately corrected it, and then proceeded to search their files to make sure that no similar mistakes had occurred. There is no indication that the arresting officer was not acting objectively reasonably when he relied upon the police computer record. Application of the *Leon* framework supports a categorical exception to the exclusionary rule for clerical errors of court employees.

The judgment of the Supreme Court of Arizona is therefore reversed, and the case is remanded to that court for proceedings not inconsistent with this opinion.

It is so ordered.

JUSTICE SOUTER, with whom JUSTICE BREYER joins, concurring.

In joining the Court's opinion, I share Justice O'CONNOR's understanding of the narrow scope of what we hold today. To her concurrence, which I join as well, I add only that we do not answer another question that may reach us in due course, that is, how far, in dealing with fruits of computerized error, our very concept of deterrence by exclusion of evidence should extend to the government as a whole, not merely the police, on the ground that there would otherwise be no reasonable expectation of keeping the number of resulting false arrests within an acceptable minimum limit.

JUSTICE O'CONNOR, with whom JUSTICE SOUTER and JUSTICE BREYER join, concurring.

The evidence in this case strongly suggests that it was a court employee's departure from established recordkeeping procedures that caused the record of respondent's arrest warrant to remain in the computer system after the warrant had been quashed. Prudently, then, the Court limits itself to the question whether a court employee's departure from such established procedures is the kind of error to which the exclusionary rule should apply. The Court holds that it is not such an error, and I agree with that conclusion and join the Court's opinion. The Court's holding reaffirms that the exclusionary rule imposes significant costs on society's law enforcement interests and thus should apply only where its deterrence purposes are "most efficaciously served."

In limiting itself to that single question, however, the Court does not hold that the court employee's mistake in this case was necessarily the only error that may have occurred and to which the exclusionary rule might apply. While the police were innocent of the court employee's mistake, they may or may not have acted reasonably in their reliance on the recordkeeping system itself. Surely it would not be reasonable for the police to rely, say, on a recordkeeping system, their own or some other agency's, that has no mechanism to ensure its accuracy over time and that routinely leads to false arrests, even years after the probable cause for any such arrest has ceased to exist (if it ever existed).

This is saying nothing new. We have said the same with respect to other information sources police use, informants being an obvious example. Certainly the reliability of recordkeeping systems deserves no less scrutiny than that of informants. Of course, the comparison to informants may be instructive the opposite way as well. So long as an informant's reliability does pass constitutional muster, a finding of probable cause may not be defeated by an after-the-fact showing that the information the informant provided was mistaken.

In recent years, we have witnessed the advent of powerful, computer-based recordkeeping systems that facilitate arrests in ways that have never before been possible. The police, of course, are entitled to enjoy the substantial advantages this technology confers. They may not, however, rely on it blindly. With the benefits of more efficient law enforcement mechanisms comes the burden of corresponding constitutional responsibilities.

JUSTICE STEVENS, dissenting.

The Court seems to assume that the Fourth Amendment — and particularly the exclusionary rule, which effectuates the Amendment's commands — has the limited purpose of deterring police misconduct. Both the constitutional text and the history of its adoption and interpretation identify a more majestic conception. The Amendment protects the fundamental "right of the people to be secure in their persons, houses, papers, and effects," against all official searches and seizures that are unreasonable. The Amendment is a constraint on the power of the sovereign, not merely on some of its agents. The remedy for its violation imposes costs on that sovereign, motivating it to train all of its personnel to avoid future violations. *See* Stewart, *The Road to* Mapp v. Ohio *and Beyond: The Origins, Development and Future of the Exclusionary Rule in Search-and-Seizure Cases*, 83 COLUM. L. REV. 1365, 1400 (1983).

The exclusionary rule is not fairly characterized as an "extreme sanction." As Justice Stewart cogently explained, the implementation of this constitutionally mandated sanction merely places the Government in the same position as if it had not conducted the illegal search and seizure in the first place.[1] Given the undisputed fact in this case that the Constitution prohibited the warrantless arrest of petitioner, there is nothing "extreme" about the Arizona Supreme Court's conclusion that the State should not be permitted to profit from its negligent misconduct.

Even if one accepts deterrence as the sole rationale for the exclusionary rule, the Arizona Supreme Court's decision is correct on the merits. The majority's reliance on *Leon* is misplaced. The search in that case had been authorized by a presumptively valid warrant issued by a California Superior Court Judge. In contrast, this case involves a search pursuant to an arrest made when no warrant at all was outstanding against petitioner. The holding in *Leon* rested on the majority's doubt "that exclusion of evidence seized pursuant to a warrant will have a significant deterrent effect on the issuing judge or magistrate." The reasoning in *Leon* assumed the existence of a warrant; it was, and remains, wholly inapplicable to warrantless searches and seizures.

The *Leon* Court's exemption of judges and magistrates from the deterrent ambit of the exclusionary rule rested, consistently with the emphasis on the warrant requirement, on those officials' constitutionally determined role in issuing warrants. Taken on its own terms, *Leon's* logic does not extend to the time after the warrant has issued; nor does it extend to court clerks and functionaries, some of whom work in the same building with police officers and may have more regular and direct contact with police than with judges or magistrates.

The Phoenix Police Department was part of the chain of information that resulted in petitioner's unlawful, warrantless arrest. We should reasonably presume that law enforcement officials, who stand in the best position to monitor such errors as occurred here, can influence mundane communication procedures in order to prevent those errors. That presumption comports with the notion that the exclusionary rule exists to deter future police misconduct systemically. The deterrent purpose extends to law enforcement as a whole, not merely to "the arresting officer." *Whiteley.* Consequently, the Phoenix officers' good faith does not diminish the deterrent value of invalidating their arrest of petitioner.

The Court seeks to minimize the impact of its holding on the security of the citizen by referring to the testimony of the chief clerk of the East Phoenix Number One Justice Court that in her "particular court" this type of error occurred " 'maybe [once] every three or four years.' " Apart from the fact that the clerk promptly contradicted herself,[22] this is slim evidence on which to base a conclusion that

---

[1] *See* Stewart, *The Road to* Mapp v. Ohio *and Beyond: The Origins, Development and Future of the Exclusionary Rule in Search-and-Seizure Cases*, 83 COLUM. L. REV. 1365, 1392 (1983). I am fully aware of the Court's statements that the question whether the exclusionary rule should be applied is distinct from the question whether the Fourth Amendment has been violated. I would note that such eminent members of this Court as Justices Holmes, Brandeis, Harlan, and Stewart have expressed the opposite view. The majority today candidly acknowledges that Justice Harlan's opinion for the Court in *Whiteley* "treated identification of a Fourth Amendment violation as synonymous with application of the exclusionary rule to evidence secured incident to that violation."

    Q. In your eight years as a chief clerk with the Justice of the Peace, have there been other occasions where a warrant was quashed but the police were not notified?

    A. That does happen on rare occasions.

computer error poses no appreciable threat to Fourth Amendment interests. The Court overlooks the reality that computer technology has changed the nature of threats to citizens' privacy over the past half century. What has not changed is the reality that only that fraction of Fourth Amendment violations held to have resulted in unlawful arrests is ever noted and redressed. As Justice Jackson observed: "There may be, and I am convinced that there are, many unlawful searches . . . of innocent people which turn up nothing incriminating, in which no arrest is made, about which courts do nothing, and about which we never hear." *Brinegar v. United States*, 338 U.S. 160 (1949) (dissenting opinion). Moreover, even if errors in computer records of warrants were rare, that would merely minimize the cost of enforcing the exclusionary rule in cases like this.

The use of general warrants to search for evidence of violations of the Crown's revenue laws understandably outraged the authors of the Bill of Rights. The offense to the dignity of the citizen who is arrested, handcuffed, and searched on a public street simply because some bureaucrat has failed to maintain an accurate computer data base strikes me as equally outrageous. In this case, of course, such an error led to the fortuitous detection of respondent's unlawful possession of marijuana, and the suppression of the fruit of the error would prevent the prosecution of his crime. That cost, however, must be weighed against the interest in protecting other, wholly innocent citizens from unwarranted indignity. In my judgment, the cost is amply offset by an appropriately "jealous regard for maintaining the integrity of individual rights." For this reason, as well as those set forth by Justice GINSBURG, I respectfully dissent.

JUSTICE GINSBURG, with whom JUSTICE STEVENS joins, dissenting.

This case portrays the increasing use of computer technology in law enforcement; it illustrates an evolving problem this Court need not, and in my judgment should not, resolve too hastily. The Arizona Supreme Court relied on "the principles of a free society" in reaching its decision. This Court reviews and reverses the Arizona decision on the assumption that Arizona's highest court sought assiduously to apply this Court's Fourth Amendment jurisprudence. The Court thus follows the presumption announced in *Michigan v. Long*: If it is unclear whether a state court's decision rests on state or federal law, *Long* dictates the assumption that the state court relied on federal law. On the basis of that assumption, the Court asserts jurisdiction to review the decision of the Arizona Supreme Court.

The *Long* presumption, as I see it, impedes the States' ability to serve as laboratories for testing solutions to novel legal problems. I would apply the opposite presumption and assume that Arizona's Supreme Court has ruled for its own State and people, under its own constitutional recognition of individual security against

---

Q. And when you say rare occasions, about how many times in your eight years as chief clerk?

A. In my particular court, they would be like maybe one every three or four years.

Q. When something like this happens, is anything done by your office to correct that problem?

A. Well, when this one happened, we searched all the files to make sure that there were no other ones in there, which there were three other ones on that same day that it happened. Fortunately, they weren't all arrested.

unwarranted state intrusion. Accordingly, I would dismiss the writ of certiorari.

I

Isaac Evans was arrested because a computer record erroneously identified an outstanding misdemeanor arrest warrant in his name. The Arizona Supreme Court's suppression of evidence obtained from this unlawful arrest did not rest on a close analysis of this Court's Fourth Amendment precedents. Indeed, the court found our most relevant decision, *Leon*, "not helpful." Instead, the Arizona court emphasized its comprehension of the severe curtailment of personal liberty inherent in arrest warrants.

Specifically, the Arizona Supreme Court saw the growing use of computerized records in law enforcement as a development presenting new dangers to individual liberty; excluding evidence seized as a result of incorrect computer data, the Arizona court anticipated, would reduce the incidence of uncorrected records:

> The dissent laments the "high costs" of the exclusionary rule, and suggests that its application here is "purposeless" and provides "no offsetting benefits." Such an assertion ignores the fact that arrest warrants result in a denial of human liberty, and are therefore among the most important of legal documents. It is repugnant to the principles of a free society that a person should ever be taken into police custody because of a computer error precipitated by government carelessness. As automation increasingly invades modern life, the potential for Orwellian mischief grows. Under such circumstances, the exclusionary rule is a "cost" we cannot afford to be without.

Thus, the Arizona court did not consider this case to involve simply and only a court employee's slip in failing to communicate with the police, or a police officer's oversight in failing to record information received from a court employee. That court recognized a "potential for Orwellian mischief" in the government's increasing reliance on computer technology in law enforcement. The Arizona Supreme Court concluded that *Leon's* distinction between police conduct and judicial conduct loses force where, as here, the error derives not from a discretionary judicial function, but from inattentive recordkeeping. Application of an exclusionary rule in the circumstances Evans' case presents, the Arizona court said, "will hopefully serve to improve the efficiency of those who keep records in our criminal justice system."

II

A

Widespread reliance on computers to store and convey information generates, along with manifold benefits, new possibilities of error, due to both computer malfunctions and operator mistakes. Most germane to this case, computerization greatly amplifies an error's effect, and correspondingly intensifies the need for prompt correction; for inaccurate data can infect not only one agency, but the many agencies that share access to the data-base. The computerized databases of the

FBI's National Crime Information Center (NCIC), to take a conspicuous example, contain over 23 million records, identifying, among other things, persons and vehicles sought by law enforcement agencies nationwide. Thus, any mistake entered into the NCIC spreads nationwide in an instant.

Isaac Evans' arrest exemplifies the risks associated with computerization of arrest warrants. Though his arrest was in fact warrantless — the warrant once issued having been quashed over two weeks before the episode in suit — the computer reported otherwise. Evans' case is not idiosyncratic. *Rogan v. Los Angeles*, 668 F. Supp. 1384 (CD Cal. 1987), similarly indicates the problem. There, the Los Angeles Police Department, in 1982, had entered into the NCIC computer an arrest warrant for a man suspected of robbery and murder. Because the suspect had been impersonating Terry Dean Rogan, the arrest warrant erroneously named Rogan. Compounding the error, the Los Angeles Police Department had failed to include a description of the suspect's physical characteristics. During the next two years, this incorrect and incomplete information caused Rogan to be arrested four times, three times at gunpoint, after stops for minor traffic infractions in Michigan and Oklahoma. In another case of the same genre, the District Court observed:

> Because of the inaccurate listing in the NCIC computer, defendant was a "marked man" for the five months prior to his arrest. . . . At any time . . . a routine check by the police could well result in defendant's arrest, booking, search and detention . . . . Moreover, this could happen anywhere in the United States where law enforcement officers had access to NCIC information. Defendant was subject to being deprived of his liberty at any time and without any legal basis.

United States v. Mackey, 387 F. Supp. 1121, 1124 (Nev. 1975).

In the instant case, the Court features testimony of the chief clerk of the justice court in East Phoenix to the effect that errors of the kind Evans encountered are reported only "on[c]e every three or four years." But the same witness also recounted that, when the error concerning Evans came to light, an immediate check revealed that three other errors of the very same kind had occurred on "that same day." [S]ee n. 3 (STEVENS, J., dissenting).

B

This Court and the Arizona Supreme Court hold diverse views on the question whether application of an exclusionary rule will reduce the incidence of erroneous computer data left without prompt correction. Observing that "court clerks are not adjuncts to the law enforcement team engaged in the often competitive enterprise of ferreting out crime," the Court reasons that "there is no basis for believing that application of the exclusionary rule in these circumstances will have a significant effect on court employees responsible for informing the police that a warrant has been quashed." In the Court's view, exclusion of evidence, even if capable of deterring police officer errors, cannot deter the carelessness of other governmental actors.[5] Whatever federal precedents may indicate — an issue on which I voice no

---

[5] It has been suggested that an exclusionary rule cannot deter carelessness, but can affect only

opinion — the Court's conclusion is not the lesson inevitably to be drawn from logic or experience.

In this electronic age, particularly with respect to recordkeeping, court personnel and police officers are not neatly compartmentalized actors. Instead, they serve together to carry out the State's information-gathering objectives. Whether particular records are maintained by the police or the courts should not be dispositive where a single computer database can answer all calls. Not only is it artificial to distinguish between court clerk and police clerk slips; in practice, it may be difficult to pinpoint whether one official, *e.g.*, a court employee, or another, *e.g.*, a police officer, caused the error to exist or to persist. Applying an exclusionary rule as the Arizona court did may well supply a powerful incentive to the State to promote the prompt updating of computer records. That was the Arizona Supreme Court's hardly unreasonable expectation. The incentive to update promptly would be diminished if court-initiated records were exempt from the rule's sway.

C

The debate over the efficacy of an exclusionary rule reveals that deterrence is an empirical question, not a logical one. "It is one of the happy incidents of the federal system that a single courageous State may, if its citizens choose, serve as a laboratory; and try novel social and economic experiments without risk to the rest of the country." *New State Ice Co. v. Liebmann*, 285 U.S. 262, 311 (1932) (Brandeis, J., dissenting). With that facet of our federalism in mind, this Court should select a jurisdictional presumption that encourages States to explore different means to secure respect for individual rights in modern times.

III

Under *Long*, when state courts engage in the essential process of developing state constitutional law, they may insulate their decisions from this Court's review by means of a plain statement of intent to rest upon an independent state ground. The plain statement option does not, however, make pleas for reconsideration of the *Long* presumption much ado about nothing. Both on a practical and on a symbolic level, the presumption chosen matters.

Application of the *Long* presumption has increased the incidence of nondispositive U.S. Supreme Court determinations — instances in which state courts, on

intentional or reckless misconduct. This suggestion runs counter to a premise underlying all of negligence law — that imposing liability for negligence, *i.e.*, lack of due care, creates an incentive to act with greater care.

That the mistake may have been made by a clerical worker does not alter the conclusion that application of the exclusionary rule has deterrent value. Just as the risk of respondeat superior liability encourages employers to supervise more closely their employees' conduct, so the risk of exclusion of evidence encourages policymakers and systems managers to monitor the performance of the systems they install and the personnel employed to operate those systems. In the words of the trial court, the mistake in Evans' case was "perhaps the negligence of the Justice Court, or the negligence of the Sheriff's Office. But it is still the negligence of the State."

remand, have reinstated their prior judgments after clarifying their reliance on state grounds.

The Arizona Supreme Court found it "repugnant to the principles of a free society," to take a person "into police custody because of a computer error precipitated by government carelessness." Few, I believe, would disagree. Whether, in order to guard against such errors, "the exclusionary rule is a 'cost' we cannot afford to be without," seems to me a question this Court should not rush to decide. The Court errs, as I see it, in presuming that Arizona rested its decision on federal grounds. I would abandon the *Long* presumption and dismiss the writ because the generally applicable obligation affirmatively to establish the Court's jurisdiction has not been satisfied.

QUESTIONS AND NOTES

1. Do you think that excluding the evidence against Evans would serve any deterrent purpose? If so, how?

2. On remand, is there any way that Evans could win on Federal Constitutional grounds? Explain.

3. Conversely, could the state win under *Atwater*?

4. Is it still open for the Arizona Supreme Court to release Evans on state grounds? Explain.

5. Is the *Long* presumption soundly premised? Why? Why not?

6. In *Herring v. United States*, the Court arguably expands the good faith exception even further than *Evans* suggested.

HERRING v. UNITED STATES
555 U.S. 135 (2009)

CHIEF JUSTICE ROBERTS delivered the opinion of the Court.

The Fourth Amendment forbids "unreasonable searches and seizures," and this usually requires the police to have probable cause or a warrant before making an arrest. What if an officer reasonably believes there is an outstanding arrest warrant, but that belief turns out to be wrong because of a negligent bookkeeping error by another police employee? The parties here agree that the ensuing arrest is still a violation of the Fourth Amendment, but dispute whether contraband found during a search incident to that arrest must be excluded in a later prosecution.

Our cases establish that such suppression is not an automatic consequence of a Fourth Amendment violation. Instead, the question turns on the culpability of the police and the potential of exclusion to deter wrongful police conduct. Here the error was the result of isolated negligence attenuated from the arrest. We hold that in these circumstances the jury should not be barred from considering all the evidence.

I

On July 7, 2004, Investigator Mark Anderson learned that Bennie Dean Herring had driven to the Coffee County Sheriff's Department to retrieve something from his impounded truck. Herring was no stranger to law enforcement, and Anderson asked the county's warrant clerk, Sandy Pope, to check for any outstanding warrants for Herring's arrest. When she found none, Anderson asked Pope to check with Sharon Morgan, her counterpart in neighboring Dale County. After checking Dale County's computer database, Morgan replied that there was an active arrest warrant for Herring's failure to appear on a felony charge. Pope relayed the information to Anderson and asked Morgan to fax over a copy of the warrant as confirmation. Anderson and a deputy followed Herring as he left the impound lot, pulled him over, and arrested him. A search incident to the arrest revealed methamphetamine in Herring's pocket, and a pistol (which as a felon he could not possess) in his vehicle.

There had, however, been a mistake about the warrant. The Dale County sheriff's computer records are supposed to correspond to actual arrest warrants, which the office also maintains. But when Morgan went to the files to retrieve the actual warrant to fax to Pope, Morgan was unable to find it. She called a court clerk and learned that the warrant had been recalled five months earlier. Normally when a warrant is recalled the court clerk's office or a judge's chambers calls Morgan, who enters the information in the sheriff's computer database and disposes of the physical copy. For whatever reason, the information about the recall of the warrant for Herring did not appear in the database. Morgan immediately called Pope to alert her to the mixup, and Pope contacted Anderson over a secure radio. This all unfolded in 10 to 15 minutes, but Herring had already been arrested and found with the gun and drugs, just a few hundred yards from the sheriff's office.

Herring was indicted in the District Court for the Middle District of Alabama for illegally possessing the gun and drugs. He moved to suppress the evidence on the ground that his initial arrest had been illegal because the warrant had been rescinded. The Magistrate Judge recommended denying the motion because the arresting officers had acted in a good-faith belief that the warrant was still outstanding. Thus, even if there were a Fourth Amendment violation, there was "no reason to believe that application of the exclusionary rule here would deter the occurrence of any future mistakes."

The Eleventh Circuit found that the arresting officers in Coffee County "were entirely innocent of any wrongdoing or carelessness." The court assumed that whoever failed to update the Dale County sheriff's records was also a law enforcement official, but noted that "the conduct in question [wa]s a negligent failure to act, not a deliberate or tactical choice to act." Because the error was merely negligent and attenuated from the arrest, the Eleventh Circuit concluded that the benefit of suppressing the evidence "would be marginal or nonexistent," and the evidence was therefore admissible under the good-faith rule of *United States v. Leon.*

Other courts have required exclusion of evidence obtained through similar police errors, *e.g.*, *Hoay v. State*, 348 Ark. 80, 86–87, 71 S.W.3d 573, 577 (2002), so we granted Herring's petition for certiorari to resolve the conflict. We now affirm the Eleventh Circuit's judgment.

II

When a probable-cause determination was based on reasonable but mistaken assumptions, the person subjected to a search or seizure has not necessarily been the victim of a constitutional violation. The very phrase "probable cause" confirms that the Fourth Amendment does not demand all possible precision. And whether the error can be traced to a mistake by a state actor or some other source may bear on the analysis. For purposes of deciding this case, however, we accept the parties' assumption that there was a Fourth Amendment violation. The issue is whether the exclusionary rule should be applied.

A

The Fourth Amendment protects "[t]he right of the people to be secure in their persons, houses, papers, and effects, against unreasonable searches and seizures," but "contains no provision expressly precluding the use of evidence obtained in violation of its commands," *Arizona v. Evans*, 514 U.S. 1, 10 (1995). Nonetheless, our decisions establish an exclusionary rule that, when applicable, forbids the use of improperly obtained evidence at trial. We have stated that this judicially created rule is "designed to safeguard Fourth Amendment rights generally through its deterrent effect." *United States v. Calandra.*

In analyzing the applicability of the rule, *Leon* admonished that we must consider the actions of all the police officers involved. ("It is necessary to consider the objective reasonableness, not only of the officers who eventually executed a warrant, but also of the officers who originally obtained it or who provided information material to the probable-cause determination.") The Coffee County officers did nothing improper. Indeed, the error was noticed so quickly because Coffee County requested a faxed confirmation of the warrant.

The Eleventh Circuit concluded, however, that somebody in Dale County should have updated the computer database to reflect the recall of the arrest warrant. The court also concluded that this error was negligent, but did not find it to be reckless or deliberate. That fact is crucial to our holding that this error is not enough by itself to require "the extreme sanction of exclusion."

B

1. The fact that a Fourth Amendment violation occurred — *i.e.*, that a search or arrest was unreasonable — does not necessarily mean that the exclusionary rule applies. *Illinois v. Gates*. Indeed, exclusion "has always been our last resort, not our first impulse," *Hudson v. Michigan*, and our precedents establish important principles that constrain application of the exclusionary rule.

First, the exclusionary rule is not an individual right and applies only where it " 'result[s] in appreciable deterrence.' " We have repeatedly rejected the argument that exclusion is a necessary consequence of a Fourth Amendment violation.

Instead we have focused on the efficacy of the rule in deterring Fourth Amendment violations in the future.[2]

In addition, the benefits of deterrence must outweigh the costs. *Leon, supra*, at 910. "We have never suggested that the exclusionary rule must apply in every circumstance in which it might provide marginal deterrence." "[T]o the extent that application of the exclusionary rule could provide some incremental deterrent, that possible benefit must be weighed against [its] substantial social costs." The principal cost of applying the rule is, of course, letting guilty and possibly dangerous defendants go free — something that "offends basic concepts of the criminal justice system." *Leon*. "[T]he rule's costly toll upon truth-seeking and law enforcement objectives presents a high obstacle for those urging [its] application."

These principles are reflected in the holding of *Leon*: When police act under a warrant that is invalid for lack of probable cause, the exclusionary rule does not apply if the police acted "in objectively reasonable reliance" on the subsequently invalidated search warrant. We (perhaps confusingly) called this objectively reasonable reliance "good faith." In a companion case, *Massachusetts v. Sheppard*, 468 U.S. 981 (1984), we held that the exclusionary rule did not apply when a warrant was invalid because a judge forgot to make "clerical corrections" to it. Shortly thereafter we extended these holdings to warrantless administrative searches performed in good-faith reliance on a statute later declared unconstitutional. *Krull*.

Finally, in *Evans*, 514 U.S. 1, we applied this good-faith rule to police who reasonably relied on mistaken information in a court's database that an arrest warrant was outstanding. We held that a mistake made by a judicial employee could not give rise to exclusion for three reasons: The exclusionary rule was crafted to curb police rather than judicial misconduct; court employees were unlikely to try to subvert the Fourth Amendment; and "most important, there [was] no basis for believing that application of the exclusionary rule in [those] circumstances" would have any significant effect in deterring the errors. *Evans* left unresolved "whether the evidence should be suppressed if police personnel were responsible for the error[3] an issue not argued by the State in that case, but one that we now confront.

2. The extent to which the exclusionary rule is justified by these deterrence principles varies with the culpability of the law enforcement conduct. As we said in *Leon*, "an assessment of the flagrancy of the police misconduct constitutes an important step in the calculus" of applying the exclusionary rule. 468 U.S. at 911.

---

[2] Justice GINSBURG's dissent champions what she describes as " 'a more majestic conception' of . . . the exclusionary rule," (quoting *Arizona v. Evans*, 514 U.S. 1, 18 (1995) (STEVENS, J., dissenting)), which would exclude evidence even where deterrence does not justify doing so. Majestic or not, our cases reject this conception, see, *e.g., United States v. Leon*, 468 U.S. 897, 921, n. 22 (1984), and perhaps for this reason, her dissent relies almost exclusively on previous dissents to support its analysis.

[3] We thus reject Justice BREYER's suggestion that *Evans* was entirely "premised on a distinction between judicial errors and police errors," *post*, at 1 (dissenting opinion). Were that the only rationale for our decision, there would have been no reason for us expressly and carefully to leave police error unresolved. In addition, to the extent *Evans* is viewed as presaging a particular result here, it is noteworthy that the dissent's view in that case was that the distinction Justice BREYER regards as determinative was instead "artificial." (GINSBURG, J., dissenting).

Anticipating the good-faith exception to the exclusionary rule, Judge Friendly wrote that "[t]he beneficent aim of the exclusionary rule to deter police misconduct can be sufficiently accomplished by a practice . . . outlawing evidence obtained by flagrant or deliberate violation of rights." The Bill of Rights as a Code of Criminal Procedure, 53 Calif. L. Rev. 929, 953 (1965) (footnotes omitted); see also *Brown v. Illinois*, 422 U.S. 590, 610–611 (1975) (Powell, J., concurring in part) ("[T]he deterrent value of the exclusionary rule is most likely to be effective" when "official conduct was flagrantly abusive of Fourth Amendment rights").

Indeed, the abuses that gave rise to the exclusionary rule featured intentional conduct that was patently unconstitutional. In *Weeks*, a foundational exclusionary rule case, the officers had broken into the defendant's home (using a key shown to them by a neighbor), confiscated incriminating papers, then returned again with a U. S. Marshal to confiscate even more. Not only did they have no search warrant, which the Court held was required, but they could not have gotten one had they tried. They were so lacking in sworn and particularized information that "not even an order of court would have justified such procedure." *Silverthorne Lumber Co. v. United States*, 251 U.S. 385 (1920), on which petitioner repeatedly relies, was similar; federal officials "without a shadow of authority" went to the defendants' office and "made a clean sweep" of every paper they could find. Even the Government seemed to acknowledge that the "seizure was an outrage."

Equally flagrant conduct was at issue in *Mapp v. Ohio*, which overruled *Wolf v. Colorado*, and extended the exclusionary rule to the States. Officers forced open a door to Ms. Mapp's house, kept her lawyer from entering, brandished what the court concluded was a false warrant, then forced her into handcuffs and canvassed the house for obscenity. ("[T]he situation in *Mapp*" featured a "flagrant or deliberate violation of rights"). An error that arises from nonrecurring and attenuated negligence is thus far removed from the core concerns that led us to adopt the rule in the first place. And in fact since *Leon*, we have never applied the rule to exclude evidence obtained in violation of the Fourth Amendment, where the police conduct was no more intentional or culpable than this.

3. To trigger the exclusionary rule, police conduct must be sufficiently deliberate that exclusion can meaningfully deter it, and sufficiently culpable that such deterrence is worth the price paid by the justice system. As laid out in our cases, the exclusionary rule serves to deter deliberate, reckless, or grossly negligent conduct, or in some circumstances recurring or systemic negligence. The error in this case does not rise to that level.[4]

The pertinent analysis of deterrence and culpability is objective, not an "inquiry into the subjective awareness of arresting officers." We have already held that "our good-faith inquiry is confined to the objectively ascertainable question whether a reasonably well trained officer would have known that the search was illegal" in light of "all of the circumstances." *Leon*. These circumstances frequently include a particular officer's knowledge and experience, but that does not make the test any

---

[4] We do not quarrel with Justice GINSBURG's claim that "liability for negligence . . . creates an incentive to act with greater care," and we do not suggest that the exclusion of this evidence could have no deterrent effect. But our cases require any deterrence to "be weighed against the 'substantial social costs exacted by the exclusionary rule,'" and here exclusion is not worth the cost.

more subjective than the one for probable cause, which looks to an officer's knowledge and experience, but not his subjective intent, *Whren v. United States.*

4. We do not suggest that all recordkeeping errors by the police are immune from the exclusionary rule. In this case, however, the conduct at issue was not so objectively culpable as to require exclusion. In *Leon* we held that "the marginal or nonexistent benefits produced by suppressing evidence obtained in objectively reasonable reliance on a subsequently invalidated search warrant cannot justify the substantial costs of exclusion." The same is true when evidence is obtained in objectively reasonable reliance on a subsequently recalled warrant.

If the police have been shown to be reckless in maintaining a warrant system, or to have knowingly made false entries to lay the groundwork for future false arrests, exclusion would certainly be justified under our cases should such misconduct cause a Fourth Amendment violation. We said as much in *Leon*, explaining that an officer could not "obtain a warrant on the basis of a 'bare bones' affidavit and then rely on colleagues who are ignorant of the circumstances under which the warrant was obtained to conduct the search." n. 24 (citing *Whiteley v. Warden, Wyo. State Penitentiary*, 401 U.S. 560, 568 (1971)). Petitioner's fears that our decision will cause police departments to deliberately keep their officers ignorant are thus unfounded.

The dissent also adverts to the possible unreliability of a number of databases not relevant to this case. *Post*, at 8–9. In a case where systemic errors were demonstrated, it might be reckless for officers to rely on an unreliable warrant system. But there is no evidence that errors in Dale County's system are routine or widespread. Officer Anderson testified that he had never had reason to question information about a Dale County warrant, and both Sandy Pope and Sharon Morgan testified that they could remember no similar miscommunication ever happening on their watch. That is even less error than in the database at issue in *Evans*, where we also found reliance on the database to be objectively reasonable (similar error "every three or four years"). Because no such showings were made here, the Eleventh Circuit was correct to affirm the denial of the motion to suppress.

*   *   *

Petitioner's claim that police negligence automatically triggers suppression cannot be squared with the principles underlying the exclusionary rule, as they have been explained in our cases. In light of our repeated holdings that the deterrent effect of suppression must be substantial and outweigh any harm to the justice system, we conclude that when police mistakes are the result of negligence such as that described here, rather than systemic error or reckless disregard of constitutional requirements, any marginal deterrence does not "pay its way." In such a case, the criminal should not "go free because the constable has blundered." *People v. Defore*, 242 N. Y. 13, 21, 150 N. E. 585, 587 (1926) (opinion of the Court by Cardozo, J.).

The judgment of the Court of Appeals for the Eleventh Circuit is affirmed.

It is so ordered.

JUSTICE GINSBURG, with whom JUSTICE STEVENS, JUSTICE SOUTER, and JUSTICE BREYER join, dissenting.

Petitioner Bennie Dean Herring was arrested, and subjected to a search incident to his arrest, although no warrant was outstanding against him, and the police lacked probable cause to believe he was engaged in criminal activity. The arrest and ensuing search therefore violated Herring's Fourth Amendment right "to be secure . . . against unreasonable searches and seizures." The Court of Appeals so determined, and the Government does not contend otherwise. The exclusionary rule provides redress for Fourth Amendment violations by placing the government in the position it would have been in had there been no unconstitutional arrest and search. The rule thus strongly encourages police compliance with the Fourth Amendment in the future. The Court, however, holds the rule inapplicable because careless recordkeeping by the police — not flagrant or deliberate misconduct — accounts for Herring's arrest.

I would not so constrict the domain of the exclusionary rule and would hold the rule dispositive of this case: "[I]f courts are to have any power to discourage [police] error of [the kind here at issue], it must be through the application of the exclusionary rule." The unlawful search in this case was contested in court because the police found methamphetamine in Herring's pocket and a pistol in his truck. But the "most serious impact" of the Court's holding will be on innocent persons "wrongfully arrested based on erroneous information [carelessly maintained] in a computer data base."

I

A warrant for Herring's arrest was recalled in February2004, apparently because it had been issued in error. The warrant database for the Dale County Sheriff's Department, however, does not automatically update to reflect such changes. A member of the Dale County Sheriff's Department — whom the parties have not identified — returned the hard copy of the warrant to the County Circuit Clerk's office, but did not correct the Department's database to show that the warrant had been recalled. The erroneous entry for the warrant remained in the database, undetected, for five months.

On a July afternoon in 2004, Herring came to the Coffee County Sheriff's Department to retrieve his belongings from a vehicle impounded in the Department's lot.

Investigator Mark Anderson, who was at the Department that day, knew Herring from prior interactions: Herring had told the district attorney, among others, of his suspicion that Anderson had been involved in the killing of a local teenager, and Anderson had pursued Herring to get him to drop the accusations. Informed that Herring was in the impoundment lot, Anderson asked the Coffee County warrant clerk whether there was an outstanding warrant for Herring's arrest. The clerk, Sandy Pope, found no warrant.

Anderson then asked Pope to call the neighboring Dale County Sheriff's Department to inquire whether a warrant to arrest Herring was outstanding there. Upon receiving Pope's phone call, Sharon Morgan, the warrant clerk for the Dale County Department, checked her computer database. As just recounted, that Department's database preserved an error. Morgan's check therefore showed — incorrectly — an active warrant for Herring's arrest. Morgan gave the misinformation to Pope, who relayed it to Investigator Anderson. Armed with the report that a warrant existed, Anderson promptly arrested Herring and performed an incident search minutes before detection of the error.

The Court of Appeals concluded, and the Government does not contest, that the "failure to bring the [Dale County Sheriff's Department] records up to date [was] 'at the very least negligent.'" And it is uncontested here that Herring's arrest violated his Fourth Amendment rights. The sole question presented, therefore, is whether evidence the police obtained through the unlawful search should have been suppressed. The Court holds that suppression was unwarranted because the exclusionary rule's "core concerns" are not raised by an isolated, negligent recordkeeping error attenuated from the arrest. In my view, the Court's opinion underestimates the need for a forceful exclusionary rule and the gravity of recordkeeping errors in law enforcement.

II

A

The Court states that the exclusionary rule is not a defendant's right; rather, it is simply a remedy applicable only when suppression would result in appreciable deterrence that outweighs the cost to the justice system ("[T]he exclusionary rule serves to deter deliberate, reckless, or grossly negligent conduct, or in some circumstances recurring or systemic negligence.").

The Court's discussion invokes a view of the exclusionary rule famously held by renowned jurists Henry J. Friendly and Benjamin Nathan Cardozo. Over 80 years ago, Cardozo, then seated on the New York Court of Appeals, commented critically on the federal exclusionary rule, which had not yet been applied to the States. He suggested that in at least some cases the rule exacted too high a price from the criminal justice system. In words often quoted, Cardozo questioned whether the criminal should "go free because the constable has blundered."

Judge Friendly later elaborated on Cardozo's query. "The sole reason for exclusion," Friendly wrote, "is that experience has demonstrated this to be the only effective method for deterring the police from violating the Constitution." The Bill of Rights as a Code of Criminal Procedure, 53 Calif. L. Rev. 929, 951 (1965). He thought it excessive, in light of the rule's aim to deter police conduct, to require exclusion when the constable had merely "blundered" — when a police officer committed a technical error in an on-the-spot judgment, or made a "slight and unintentional miscalculation." As the Court recounts, Judge Friendly suggested that deterrence of police improprieties could be "sufficiently accomplished" by confining the rule to "evidence obtained by flagrant or deliberate violation of rights."

B

Others have described "a more majestic conception" of the Fourth Amendment and its adjunct, the exclusionary rule. Protective of the fundamental "right of the people to be secure in their persons, houses, papers, and effects," the Amendment "is a constraint on the power of the sovereign, not merely on some of its agents." I share that vision of the Amendment.

The exclusionary rule is "a remedy necessary to ensure that" the Fourth Amendment's prohibitions "are observed in fact." The rule's service as an essential auxiliary to the Amendment earlier inclined the Court to hold the two inseparable.

Beyond doubt, a main objective of the rule "is to deter — to compel respect for the constitutional guaranty in the only effectively available way — by removing the incentive to disregard it." *Elkins v. United States*, 364 U.S. 206, 217 (1960). But the rule also serves other important purposes: It "enabl[es] the judiciary to avoid the taint of partnership in official lawlessness," and it "assur[es] the people — all potential victims of unlawful government conduct — that the government would not profit from its lawless behavior, thus minimizing the risk of seriously undermining popular trust in government." *United States v. Calandra*, 414 U.S. 338, 357 (1974) (BRENNAN, J., dissenting). See also *Terry v. Ohio*, 392 U.S. 1, 13 (1968) ("A rule admitting evidence in a criminal trial, we recognize, has the necessary effect of legitimizing the conduct which produced the evidence, while an application of the exclusionary rule withholds the constitutional imprimatur."); a principal reason for the exclusionary rule is that "the Court's aid should be denied 'in order to maintain respect for law [and] to preserve the judicial process from contamination.' "

The exclusionary rule, it bears emphasis, is often the only remedy effective to redress a Fourth Amendment violation.

III

The Court maintains that Herring's case is one in which the exclusionary rule could have scant deterrent effect and therefore would not "pay its way." I disagree.

A

The exclusionary rule, the Court suggests, is capable of only marginal deterrence when the misconduct at issue is merely careless, not intentional or reckless. The suggestion runs counter to a foundational premise of tort law — that liability for negligence, *i.e.*, lack of due care, creates an incentive to act with greater care. The Government so acknowledges.

That the mistake here involved the failure to make a computer entry hardly means that application of the exclusionary rule would have minimal value. "Just as the risk of *respondeat superior* liability encourages employers to supervise . . . their employees' conduct [more carefully],so the risk of exclusion of evidence encourages policymakers and systems managers to monitor the performance of the systems they install and the personnel employed to operate those systems." *Evans*, 514 U.S., at 29, n. 5 (GINSBURG, J., dissenting).

Consider the potential impact of a decision applying the exclusionary rule in this case. As earlier observed, the record indicates that there is no electronic connection between the warrant database of the Dale County Sheriff's Department and that of the County Circuit Clerk's office, which is located in the basement of the same building. When a warrant is recalled, one of the "many different people that have access to th[e] warrants," must find the hard copy of the warrant in the "two or three different places" where the department houses warrants, return it to the Clerk's office, and manually update the Department's database. The record reflects no routine practice of checking the database for accuracy, and the failure to remove the entry for Herring's warrant was not discovered until Investigator Anderson sought to pursue Herring five months later. Is it not altogether obvious that the Department could take further precautions to ensure the integrity of its database? The Sheriff's Department "is in a position to remedy the situation and might well do so if the exclusionary rule is there to remove the incentive to do otherwise."

B

Is the potential deterrence here worth the costs it imposes? In light of the paramount importance of accurate recordkeeping in law enforcement, I would answer yes, and next explain why, as I see it, Herring's motion presents a particularly strong case for suppression.

Electronic databases form the nervous system of contemporary criminal justice operations. In recent years, their breadth and influence have dramatically expanded. Police today can access databases that include not only the updated National Crime Information Center (NCIC), but also terrorist watchlists, the Federal Government's employee eligibility system, and various commercial databases. Moreover, States are actively expanding information sharing between jurisdictions. As a result, law enforcement has an increasing supply of information within its easy electronic reach.

The risk of error stemming from these databases is not slim. Herring's *amici* warn that law enforcement databases are insufficiently monitored and often out of date. Government reports describe, for example, flaws in NCIC databases, terrorist watchlist databases, and databases associated with the Federal Government's employment eligibility verification system.

Inaccuracies in expansive, interconnected collections of electronic information raise grave concerns for individual liberty. "The offense to the dignity of the citizen who is arrested, handcuffed, and searched on a public street simply because some bureaucrat has failed to maintain an accurate computer data base" is evocative of the use of general warrants that so outraged the authors of our Bill of Rights. *Evans*, 514 U.S., at 23 (STEVENS, J., dissenting).

C

The Court assures that "exclusion would certainly be justified" if "the police have been shown to be reckless in maintaining a warrant system, or to have knowingly made false entries to lay the groundwork for future false arrests." This concession provides little comfort.

First, by restricting suppression to bookkeeping errors that are deliberate or reckless, the majority leaves Herring, and others like him, with no remedy for violations of their constitutional rights. There can be no serious assertion that relief is available under 42 U. S. C. § 1983. The arresting officer would be sheltered by qualified immunity, see *Harlow v. Fitzgerald*, 457 U.S. 800 (1982), and the police department itself is not liable for the negligent acts of its employees, see *Monell v. New York City Dept. of Social Servs.*, 436 U.S. 658 (1978). Moreover, identifying the department employee who committed the error may be impossible.

Second, I doubt that police forces already possess sufficient incentives to maintain up-to-date records. The Government argues that police have no desire to send officers out on arrests unnecessarily, because arrests consume resources and place officers in danger. The facts of this case do not fit that description of police motivation. Here the officer wanted to arrest Herring and consulted the Department's records to legitimate his predisposition.[6]

Third, even when deliberate or reckless conduct is afoot, the Court's assurance will often be an empty promise: How is an impecunious defendant to make the required showing? If the answer is that a defendant is entitled to discovery (and if necessary, an audit of police databases), then the Court has imposed a considerable administrative burden on courts and law enforcement.[7]

IV

Negligent recordkeeping errors by law enforcement threaten individual liberty, are susceptible to deterrence by the exclusionary rule, and cannot be remedied effectively through other means. Such errors present no occasion to further erode the exclusionary rule.

JUSTICE BREYER, with whom JUSTICE SOUTER joins, dissenting.

I agree with JUSTICE GINSBURG and join her dissent. I write separately to note one additional supporting factor that I believe important. In *Arizona v. Evans*, 514 U.S. 1 (1995), we held that recordkeeping errors made by a court clerk do not trigger the exclusionary rule, so long as the police reasonably relied upon the court clerk's recordkeeping. The rationale for our decision was premised on a distinction

---

[6] It has been asserted that police departments have become sufficiently "professional" that they do not need external deterrence to avoid Fourth Amendment violations. See Tr. of Oral Arg. 24–25; cf. *Hudson v. Michigan*, 547 U.S. 586, 598–599 (2006). But professionalism is a sign of the exclusionary rule's efficacy — not of its superfluity.

[7] It is not clear how the Court squares its focus on deliberate conduct with its recognition that application of the exclusionary rule does not require inquiry into the mental state of the police. *Whren v. United States*, 517 U.S. 806, 812–813 (1996).

between judicial errors and police errors, and we gave several reasons for recognizing that distinction.

First, we noted that "the exclusionary rule was historically designed as a means of deterring *police* misconduct, not mistakes by court employees." (emphasis added). *Second,* we found "no evidence that court employees are inclined to ignore or subvert the Fourth Amendment or that lawlessness among these actors requires application of the extreme sanction of exclusion." *Third,* we recognized that there was "no basis for believing that application of the exclusionary rule . . . [would] have a significant effect on court employees responsible for informing the police that a warrant has been quashed. Because court clerks are not adjuncts to the law enforcement team engaged in the often competitive enterprise of ferreting out crime, they have no stake in the outcome of particular criminal prosecutions." Taken together, these reasons explain why police recordkeeping errors should be treated differently than judicial ones.

Other cases applying the "good faith" exception to the exclusionary rule have similarly recognized the distinction between police errors and errors made by others, such as judicial officers or legislatures. See *United States v. Leon,* 468 U.S. 897 (1984) (police reasonably relied on magistrate's issuance of warrant); *Massachusetts v. Sheppard,* 468 U.S. 981 (1984) (same); *Illinois v. Krull,* 480 U.S. 340 (1987) (police reasonably relied on statute's constitutionality).

Distinguishing between police recordkeeping errors and judicial ones not only is consistent with our precedent, but also is far easier for courts to administer than The Chief Justice's case-by-case, multifactored inquiry into the degree of police culpability. I therefore would apply the exclusionary rule when police personnel are responsible for a recordkeeping error that results in a Fourth Amendment violation.

The need for a clear line, and the recognition of such a line in our precedent, are further reasons in support of the outcome that JUSTICE GINSBURG'S dissent would reach.

QUESTIONS AND NOTES

1.   What if anything does *Herring* add to *Evans*?

2.   Do you think that Officer Anderson acted in complete good faith? What else could he have done?

3.   Is exclusion an extreme sanction? Why? Why not?

4.   If the exclusionary rule were applied in this case would the criminal go free because the constable had blundered or would he go free because he would have gone free because the constable hadn't blundered?

Does your answer to this question effect your analysis of question 3?

5.   Why did the Court cite *Gates* for the proposition that the exclusionary rule doesn't always apply when there has been a Fourth Amendment violation? Was there even a violation in *Gates.*

6.   Does *Herring* mean that Officer A could obtain a defective warrant, and rely on Officer B to execute it? *Cf. Whitely v. Warden?*

7.   If your answer to question 5 is "no," how is *Herring* different?

8.   If Herring were innocent, should he have a civil suit against anybody? If so, who?

9.   Do you agree with the Court that the exclusionary rule has not been applied to unintentional or non-culpable conduct since *Leon* was decided? What about *Florida v. J.L, Bond v United States, Kyllo v. United States, Florida v. Jardines?*

10.   Should the good faith exception apply whenever a police officer reasonably believes that he is not violating the Constitution, *e.g., Florida v. Royer?*

11.   We conclude this section with *Davis v. United States.*

DAVIS v. UNITED STATES
564 U.S. ___, 131 S. Ct. 2419 (2011)

JUSTICE ALITO delivered the opinion of the Court.

The Fourth Amendment protects the right to be free from "unreasonable searches and seizures," but it is silent about how this right is to be enforced. To supplement the bare text, this Court created the exclusionary rule, a deterrent sanction that bars the prosecution from introducing evidence obtained by way of a Fourth Amendment violation. The question here is whether to apply this sanction when the police conduct a search in compliance with binding precedent that is later overruled. Because suppression would do nothing to deter police misconduct in these circumstances, and because it would come at a high cost to both the truth and the public safety, we hold that searches conducted in objectively reasonable reliance on binding appellate precedent are not subject to the exclusionary rule.

I

The question presented arises in this case as a result of a shift in our Fourth Amendment jurisprudence on searches of automobiles incident to arrests of recent occupants.

A

(The Court explained the line of cases from Chimel to Belton to Thornton to Gant.)

B

The search at issue in this case took place a full two years before this Court announced its new rule in Gant. On an April evening in 2007, police officers in Greenville, Alabama, conducted a routine traffic stop that eventually resulted in the arrests of driver Stella Owens (for driving while intoxicated) and passenger Willie

Davis (for giving a false name to police). The police handcuffed both Owens and Davis, and they placed the arrestees in the back of separate patrol cars. The police then searched the passenger compartment of Owens's vehicle and found a revolver inside Davis's jacket pocket. Davis was indicted in the Middle District of Alabama on one count of possession of a firearm by a convicted felon.

In his motion to suppress the revolver, Davis acknowledged that the officers' search fully complied with "existing Eleventh Circuit precedent." Like most courts, the Eleventh Circuit had long read Belton to establish a bright-line rule authorizing substantially contemporaneous vehicle searches incident to arrests of recent occupants. *See United States v. Gonzalez* (upholding automobile search conducted after the defendant had been "pulled from the vehicle, handcuffed, laid on the ground, and placed under arrest"). Davis recognized that the District Court was obligated to follow this precedent, but he raised a Fourth Amendment challenge to preserve "the issue for review" on appeal. The District Court denied the motion, and Davis was convicted on the firearms charge.

While Davis's appeal was pending, this Court decided Gant. The Eleventh Circuit, in the opinion below, applied Gant's new rule and held that the vehicle search incident to Davis's arrest "violated [his] Fourth Amendment rights." As for whether this constitutional violation warranted suppression, the Eleventh Circuit viewed that as a separate issue that turned on "the potential of exclusion to deter wrongful police conduct." The court concluded that "penalizing the [arresting] officer" for following binding appellate precedent would do nothing to "dete[r] . . . Fourth Amendment violations." It therefore declined to apply the exclusionary rule and affirmed Davis's conviction. We granted certiorari.

II

The Fourth Amendment protects the "right of the people to be secure in their persons, houses, papers, and effects, against unreasonable searches and seizures." The Amendment says nothing about suppressing evidence obtained in violation of this command. That rule — the exclusionary rule — is a "prudential" doctrine, *Pennsylvania Bd. of Probation and Parole v. Scott*, 524 U.S. 357, created by this Court to "compel respect for the constitutional guaranty." Exclusion is "not a personal constitutional right," nor is it designed to "redress the injury" occasioned by an unconstitutional search. *See United States v. Janis*, 428 U.S. 433 (exclusionary rule "unsupportable as reparation or compensatory dispensation to the injured criminal"). The rule's sole purpose, we have repeatedly held, is to deter future Fourth Amendment violations. E.g., *Herring; Leon*. Our cases have thus limited the rule's operation to situations in which this purpose is "thought most efficaciously served." *Calandra*. Where suppression fails to yield "appreciable deterrence," exclusion is "clearly . . . unwarranted." *Janis*.

Real deterrent value is a "necessary condition for exclusion," but it is not "a sufficient" one. *Hudson v. Michigan*, 547 U.S. 586, 596 (2006). The analysis must also account for the "substantial social costs" generated by the rule. *Leon*, supra, at 907. Exclusion exacts a heavy toll on both the judicial system and society at large. *Stone*. It almost always requires courts to ignore reliable, trustworthy evidence bearing on guilt or innocence. And its bottom-line effect, in many cases, is to suppress the truth and set the criminal loose in the community without punishment. See Herring, supra, at 141. Our cases hold that society must swallow this bitter pill when necessary, but only as a "last resort." *Hudson.* For exclusion to be appropriate, the deterrence benefits of suppression must outweigh its heavy costs.

Admittedly, there was a time when our exclusionary-rule cases were not nearly so discriminating in their approach to the doctrine. "Expansive dicta" in several decisions, see Hudson, suggested that the rule was a self-executing mandate implicit in the Fourth Amendment itself. See *Olmstead v. United States*, 277 U.S. 438, 462 (1928) (remarking on the "striking outcome of the Weeks case" that "the Fourth Amendment, although not referring to or limiting the use of evidence in courts, really forbade its introduction"). As late as our 1971 decision in *Whiteley v. Warden, Wyo. State Penitentiary*, the Court "treated identification of a Fourth Amendment violation as synonymous with application of the exclusionary rule." *Arizona v. Evans.* In time, however, we came to acknowledge the exclusionary rule for what it undoubtedly is — a "judicially created remedy" of this Court's own making. *Calandra*, supra, at 348. We abandoned the old, "reflexive" application of the doctrine, and imposed a more rigorous weighing of its costs and deterrence benefits. *Evans.* In a line of cases beginning with *United States v. Leon*, 468 U.S. 897, we also recalibrated our cost-benefit analysis in exclusion cases to focus the inquiry on the "flagrancy of the police misconduct" at issue.

Other good-faith cases have sounded a similar theme. *Illinois v. Krull*, extended the good-faith exception to searches conducted in reasonable reliance on subsequently invalidated statutes. In *Arizona v. Evans*, the Court applied the good-faith exception in a case where the police reasonably relied on erroneous information concerning an arrest warrant in a database maintained by judicial employees. Most recently, in Herring, we extended Evans in a case where police employees erred in maintaining records in a war-rant database. "[I]solated," "nonrecurring" police negligence, we determined, lacks the culpability required to justify the harsh sanction of exclusion.

III

The question in this case is whether to apply the exclusionary rule when the police conduct a search in objectively reasonable reliance on binding judicial precedent. At the time of the search at issue here, we had not yet decided *Arizona v. Gant*, and the Eleventh Circuit had interpreted our decision in *New York v. Belton*, to establish a bright-line rule authorizing the search of a vehicle's passenger compartment incident to a recent occupant's arrest. The search incident to Davis's arrest in this case followed the Eleventh Circuit's Gonzalez precedent to the letter. Although the search turned out to be unconstitutional under Gant, all agree that the officers' conduct was in strict compliance with then-binding Circuit law and was not culpable in any way.

Under our exclusionary-rule precedents, this acknowledged absence of police culpability dooms Davis's claim. Police practices trigger the harsh sanction of exclusion only when they are deliberate enough to yield "meaningful" deterrence, and culpable enough to be "worth the price paid by the justice system." *Herring*, 555 U.S., at 144.The conduct of the officers here was neither of these things. The officers who conducted the search did not violate Davis's Fourth Amendment rights deliberately, recklessly, or with gross negligence. See ibid. Nor does this case involve any "recurring or systemic negligence" on the part of law enforcement. The police acted in strict compliance with binding precedent, and their behavior was not wrongful. Unless the exclusionary rule is to become a strict-liability regime, it can have no application in this case.

Indeed, in 27 years of practice under Leon's good-faith exception, we have "never applied" the exclusionary rule to suppress evidence obtained as a result of nonculpable, innocent police conduct. *Herring*, at 144. If the police in this case had reasonably relied on a warrant in conducting their search, *see Leon*, or on an erroneous warrant record in a government database, Herring, the exclusionary rule would not apply. And if Congress or the Alabama Legislature had enacted a statute codifying the precise holding of the Eleventh Circuit's decision in Gonzalez,[4] we would swiftly conclude that " '[p]enalizing the officer for the legislature's error . . . cannot logically contribute to the deterrence of Fourth Amendment violations.' " "The same should be true of Davis's attempt here to " '[p]enaliz[e] the officer for the [appellate judges'] error.' "

About all that exclusion would deter in this case is conscientious police work. Responsible law-enforcement officers will take care to learn "what is required of them" under Fourth Amendment precedent and will conform their conduct to these rules. *Hudson*, 547 U.S., at 599. But by the same token, when binding appellate precedent specifically authorizes a particular police practice, well-trained officers will and should use that tool to fulfill their crime-detection and public-safety responsibilities. An officer who conducts a search in reliance on binding appellate precedent does no more than " 'ac[t] as a reasonable officer would and should act' " under the circumstances. *Leon*, 468 U.S., at 920 (quoting Stone, 428 U.S., at 539–540 (WHITE, J., dissenting)). The deterrent effect of exclusion in such a case can only be to discourage the officer from " 'do[ing] his duty.' "

That is not the kind of deterrence the exclusionary rule seeks to foster. We have stated before, and we reaffirm today, that the harsh sanction of exclusion "should not be applied to deter objectively reasonable law enforcement activity." Evidence obtained during a search conducted in reasonable reliance on binding precedent is not subject to the exclusionary rule.

IV

JUSTICE BREYER'S dissent and Davis argue that, although the police conduct in this case was in no way culpable, other considerations should prevent the good-faith exception from applying. We are not persuaded.

---

[4] Cf. Kan. Stat. Ann. § 22–2501(c) (2007) ("When a lawful arrest is effected a law enforcement officer may reasonably search the person arrested and the area within such person's immediate presence for the purpose of . . . [d]iscovering the fruits, instrumentalities, or evidence of a crime"). The Kansas Supreme Court recently struck this provision down in light of *Arizona v. Gant*. But it has applied *Illinois v. Krull*, 480 U.S. 340 (1987), and the good-faith exception to searches conducted in reasonable reliance on the statute. *See State v. Daniel*.

A

1

The principal argument of both the dissent and Davis is that the exclusionary rule's availability to enforce new Fourth Amendment precedent is a retroactivity issue, *see Griffith v. Kentucky*, not a good-faith issue. They contend that applying the good-faith exception where police have relied on overruled precedent effectively revives the discarded retroactivity regime of *Linkletter*.

In *Linkletter*, we held that the retroactive effect of a new constitutional rule of criminal procedure should be determined on a case-by-case weighing of interests. For each new rule, Linkletter required courts to consider a three-factor balancing test that looked to the "purpose" of the new rule, "reliance" on the old rule by law enforcement and others, and the effect retroactivity would have "on the administration of justice." After "weigh[ing] the merits and demerits in each case," courts decided whether and to what extent a new rule should be given retroactive effect. In Linkletter itself, the balance of interests prompted this Court to conclude that *Mapp v. Ohio* — which incorporated the exclusionary rule against the States — should not apply retroactively to cases already final on direct review. The next year, we extended Linkletter to retroactivity determinations in cases on direct review. *See Johnson v. New Jersey* (holding that *Miranda v. Arizona*, and *Escobedo v. Illinois*, applied retroactively only to trials commenced after the decisions were released)

Over time, Linkletter proved difficult to apply in a consistent, coherent way. Individual applications of the standard "produced strikingly divergent results." Justice Harlan in particular, who had endorsed the Linkletter standard early on, offered a strong critique in which he argued that "basic judicial" norms required full retroactive application of new rules to all cases still subject to direct review. Eventually, and after more than 20 years of toil under Linkletter, the Court adopted Justice Harlan's view and held that newly announced rules of constitutional criminal procedure must apply "retroactively to all cases, state or federal, pending on direct review or not yet final, with no exception."

II

The dissent and Davis argue that applying the good-faith exception in this case is "incompatible" with our retroactivity precedent under Griffith. We think this argument conflates what are two distinct doctrines.

Our retroactivity jurisprudence is concerned with whether, as a categorical matter, a new rule is available on direct review as a potential ground for relief. Retroactive application under Griffith lifts what would otherwise be a categorical bar to obtaining redress for the government's violation of a newly announced constitutional rule. *See Danforth*, (noting that it may "make more sense to speak in terms of the 'redressability' of violations of new rules, rather than the 'retroactivity' of such new rules"). Retroactive application does not, however, determine what "appropriate remedy" (if any) the defendant should obtain. *See Powell v. Nevada*, 511 U.S. 79, 84 (1994) (noting that it "does not necessarily follow" from retroactive application of a new rule that the defendant will "gain . . . relief"). Remedy is a separate, analytically distinct issue. As a result, the retroactive application of a new rule of substantive Fourth Amendment law raises the question whether a suppression remedy applies; it does not answer that question. *See Leon,* 468 U.S., at 906 ("Whether the exclusionary sanction is appropriately imposed in a particular case . . . is 'an issue separate from the question whether the Fourth Amendment rights of the party seeking to invoke the rule were violated by police conduct' ").

When this Court announced its decision in Gant, Davis's conviction had not yet become final on direct review. Gant therefore applies retroactively to this case. Davis may invoke its newly announced rule of substantive Fourth Amendment law as a basis for seeking relief. *See Griffith.* The question, then, becomes one of remedy, and on that issue Davis seeks application of the exclusionary rule. But exclusion of evidence does not automatically follow from the fact that a Fourth Amendment violation occurred. See Evans, 514 U.S., at 13–14. The remedy is subject to exceptions and applies only where its "purpose is effectively advanced." *Krull,* 480 U.S., at 347.

The dissent and Davis recognize that at least some of the established exceptions to the exclusionary rule limit its availability in cases involving new Fourth Amendment rules. Suppression would thus be inappropriate, the dissent and Davis acknowledge, if the inevitable-discovery exception were applicable in this case. ("Doctrines such as inevitable discovery, independent source, attenuated basis, [and] standing . . . sharply limit the impact of newly-announced rules"). The good-faith exception, however, is no less an established limit on the remedy of exclusion than is inevitable discovery. Its application here neither contravenes Griffith nor denies retroactive effect to *Gant.*[5]

It is true that, under the old retroactivity regime of Linkletter, the Court's decisions on the "retroactivity problem in the context of the exclusionary rule" did take into account whether "law enforcement officers reasonably believed in good faith" that their conduct was in compliance with governing law. *Peltier.* As a matter of retroactivity analysis, that approach is no longer applicable. *See Griffith.* It does not follow, however, that reliance on binding precedent is irrelevant in applying the good-faith exception to the exclusionary rule. That reasonable reliance by police was once a factor in our retroactivity cases does not make it any less relevant under our Leon line of cases.[6]

---

[5] The dissent argues that the good-faith exception is "unlike . . . inevitable discovery" because the former applies in all cases where the police reasonably rely on binding precedent, while the latter "applies only upon occasion." We fail to see how this distinction makes any difference. The same could be said — indeed, the same was said — of searches conducted in reasonable reliance on statutes. *See Krull,* 480 U.S., at 368–369 (O'Connor, J., dissenting) (arguing that result in Krull was inconsistent with Griffith). When this Court strikes down a statute on Fourth Amendment grounds, the good-faith exception may prevent the exclusionary rule from applying "in every case pending when [the statute] is overturned." This result does not make the Court's newly announced rule of Fourth Amendment law any less retroactive. It simply limits the applicability of a suppression remedy. *See Krull.*

[6] Nor does *United States v. Johnson,* 457 U.S. 537 (1982), foreclose application of the good-faith exception in cases involving changing law. Johnson distinguished Peltier and held that all Fourth Amendment cases should be retroactive on direct review so long as the new decision is not a "clear break" from prior precedent. Johnson had no occasion to opine on the good-faith exception to the

B

Davis also contends that applying the good-faith exception to searches conducted in reliance on binding precedent will stunt the development of Fourth Amendment law. With no possibility of suppression, criminal defendants will have no incentive, Davis maintains, to request that courts overrule precedent.[7]

I

This argument is difficult to reconcile with our modern understanding of the role of the exclusionary rule. We have never held that facilitating the overruling of precedent is a relevant consideration in an exclusionary-rule case. Rather, we have said time and again that the sole purpose of the exclusionary rule is to deter misconduct by law enforcement. *See*, e.g., *Sheppard*, 468 U.S., at 990 (" 'adopted to deter unlawful searches by police' "); Evans, supra, at 14 ("historically designed as a means of deterring police misconduct").

We have also repeatedly rejected efforts to expand the focus of the exclusionary rule beyond deterrence of culpable police conduct. In *Leon*, for example, we made clear that that "the exclusionary rule is designed to deter police misconduct rather than to punish the errors of judges." 468 U.S., at 916; see id., at 918 ("If exclusion of evidence obtained pursuant to a subsequently invalidated warrant is to have any deterrent effect . . . it must alter the behavior of individual law enforcement officers or the policies of their departments"). *Krull* too noted that "legislators, like judicial officers, are not the focus" of the exclusionary rule. And in Evans, we said that the exclusionary rule was aimed at deterring "police misconduct, not mistakes by court employees." These cases do not suggest that the exclusionary rule should be modified to serve a purpose other than deterrence of culpable law-enforcement conduct.

II

And in any event, applying the good-faith exception in this context will not prevent judicial reconsideration of prior Fourth Amendment precedents. In most instances, as in this case, the precedent sought to be challenged will be a decision of a Federal Court of Appeals or State Supreme Court. But a good-faith exception for objectively reasonable reliance on binding precedent will not prevent review and correction of such decisions. This Court re-views criminal convictions from 12 Federal Courts of Appeals, 50 state courts of last resort, and the District of Columbia Court of Appeals. If one or even many of these courts uphold a particular type of search or seizure, defendants in jurisdictions in which the question remains open will still have an undiminished incentive to litigate the issue. This Court can

---

exclusionary rule, which we adopted two years later in Leon.

[7] Davis also asserts that a good-faith rule would permit "new Fourth Amendment decisions to be applied only prospectively," thus amounting to "a regime of rule-creation by advisory opinion." For reasons discussed in connection with Davis's argument that application of the good-faith exception here would revive the Linkletter regime, this argument conflates the question of retroactivity with the question of remedy.

then grant certiorari, and the development of Fourth Amendment law will in no way be stunted.[8]

Davis argues that Fourth Amendment precedents of this Court will be effectively insulated from challenge under a good-faith exception for reliance on appellate precedent. But this argument is overblown. For one thing, it is important to keep in mind that this argument applies to an exceedingly small set of cases. Decisions overruling this Court's Fourth Amendment precedents are rare. Indeed, it has been more than 40 years since the Court last handed down a decision of the type to which Davis refers. *Chimel v. California*, 395 U.S. 752 (overruling *United States v. Rabinowitz*, 339 U.S. 56 (1950), and *Harris v. United States*, 331 U.S. 145 (1947)). And even in those cases, Davis points out that no fewer than eight separate doctrines may preclude a defendant who successfully challenges an existing precedent from getting any relief. Moreover, as a practical matter, defense counsel in many cases will test this Court's Fourth Amendment precedents in the same way that Belton was tested in Gant — by arguing that the precedent is distinguishable.[9]

At most, Davis's argument might suggest that — to prevent Fourth Amendment law from becoming ossified — the petitioner in a case that results in the overruling of one of this Court's Fourth Amendment precedents should be given the benefit of the victory by permitting the suppression of evidence in that one case. Such a result would undoubtedly be a windfall to this one random litigant. But the exclusionary rule is "not a personal constitutional right." *Stone*, 428 U.S., at 486. It is a "judicially created" sanction, *Calandra*, 414 U.S., at 348, specifically designed as a "windfall" remedy to deter future Fourth Amendment violations. *See Stone*, supra, at 490. The good-faith exception is a judicially created exception to this judicially created rule. Therefore, in a future case, we could, if necessary, recognize a limited exception to the good-faith exception for a defendant who obtains a judgment overruling one of our Fourth Amendment precedents. Cf. Friendly, The Bill of Rights as a Code of Criminal Procedure, 53 Cal. L. Rev. 929, 952–953 (1965) ("[T]he same authority that empowered the Court to supplement the amendment by the exclusionary rule a hundred and twenty-five years after its adoption, likewise allows it to modify that rule as the lessons of experience may teach."[10]

---

[8] The dissent does not dispute this point, but it claims that the good-faith exception will prevent us from "rely[ing] upon lower courts to work out Fourth Amendment differences among themselves." If that is correct, then today's holding may well lead to more circuit splits in Fourth Amendment cases and a fuller docket of Fourth Amendment cases in this Court. See this Court's Rule 10. Such a state of affairs is unlikely to result in ossification of Fourth Amendment doctrine.

[9] Where the search at issue is conducted in accordance with a municipal "policy" or "custom," Fourth Amendment precedents may also be challenged, without the obstacle of the good-faith exception or qualified immunity, in civil suits against municipalities. *See* 42 U. S. C. § 1983; *Los Angeles County v. Humphries* (citing Monell v. New York City Dept. of Social Servs., 436 U.S. 658, 690–691 (1978)).

[10] Davis contends that a criminal defendant will lack Article III standing to challenge an existing Fourth Amendment precedent if the good-faith exception to the exclusionary rule precludes the defendant from obtaining relief based on police conduct that conformed to that precedent. This argument confuses weakness on the merits with absence of Article III standing. *See ASARCO Inc. v. Kadish* (standing does not " 'depen[d] on the merits of [a claim]' "). And as a practical matter, the argument is also overstated. In many instances, as in *Gant*, defendants will not simply concede that the police conduct conformed to the precedent; they will argue instead that the police conduct did not fall within the scope of the precedent. In any event, even if some criminal defendants will be unable to challenge some

But this is not such a case. Davis did not secure a decision overturning a Supreme Court precedent; the police in his case reasonably relied on binding Circuit precedent. See United States v. Gonzalez, 71 F.3d 819. That sort of blameless police conduct, we hold, comes within the good-faith exception and is not properly subject to the exclusionary rule.

It is one thing for the criminal "to go free because the constable has blundered." It is quite another to set the criminal free because the constable has scrupulously adhered to governing law. Excluding evidence in such cases deters no police misconduct and imposes substantial social costs. We therefore hold that when the police conduct a search in objectively reasonable reliance on binding appellate precedent, the exclusionary rule does not apply. The judgment of the Court of Appeals for the Eleventh Circuit is Affirmed.

JUSTICE SOTOMAYOR, concurring in the judgment.

Under our precedents, the primary purpose of the exclusionary rule is "to deter future Fourth Amendment violations." Accordingly, we have held, application of the exclusionary rule is unwarranted when it " 'does not result in appreciable deterrence.' *Arizona v. Evans*. In the circumstances of this case, where "binding appellate precedent specifically authorize[d] a particular police practice," — in accord with the holdings of nearly every other court in the country — application of the exclusionary rule cannot reasonably be expected to yield appreciable deterrence. I am thus compelled to conclude that the exclusionary rule does not apply in this case and to agree with the Court's disposition.

This case does not present the markedly different question whether the exclusionary rule applies when the law governing the constitutionality of a particular search is unsettled. As we previously recognized in deciding whether to apply a Fourth Amendment holding retroactively, when police decide to conduct a search or seizure in the absence of case law (or other authority) specifically sanctioning such action, exclusion of the evidence obtained may deter Fourth Amendment violations:

> "If, as the Government argues, all rulings resolving unsettled Fourth Amendment questions should be nonretroactive, then, in close cases, law enforcement officials would have little incentive to err on the side of constitutional behavior. Official awareness of the dubious constitutionality of a practice would be counterbalanced by official certainty that, so long as the Fourth Amendment law in the area remained unsettled, evidence obtained through the questionable practice would be excluded only in the one case definitively resolving the unsettled question." *United States v. Johnson*, 457 U.S. 537, 561 (1982).

---

precedents for the reason that Davis suggests, that provides no good reason for refusing to apply the good-faith exception. As noted, the exclusionary rule is not a personal right, *see Stone*, 428 U.S., at 486, 490, and therefore the rights of these defendants will not be impaired. And because (at least in almost all instances) the precedent can be challenged by others, Fourth Amendment case law will not be insulated from reconsideration.

The Court of Appeals recognized as much in limiting its application of the good-faith exception it articulated in this case to situations where its "precedent on a given point [is] unequivocal.". Whether exclusion would deter Fourth Amendment violations where appellate precedent does not specifically authorize a certain practice and, if so, whether the benefits of exclusion would outweigh its costs are questions unanswered by our previous decisions.

The dissent suggests that today's decision essentially answers those questions, noting that an officer who conducts a search in the face of unsettled precedent "is no more culpable than an officer who follows erroneous 'binding precedent.' The Court does not address this issue. In my view, whether an officer's conduct can be characterized as "culpable" is not itself dispositive. We have never refused to apply the exclusionary rule where its application would appreciably deter Fourth Amendment violations on the mere ground that the officer's conduct could be characterized as nonculpable. Rather, an officer's culpability is relevant because it may inform the overarching inquiry whether exclusion would result in appreciable deterrence. ("The basic insight of the Leon line of cases is that the deterrence benefits of exclusion var[y] with the culpability of the law enforcement conduct at issue" Whatever we have said about culpability, the ultimate questions have always been, one, whether exclusion would result in appreciable deterrence and, two, whether the benefits of exclusion outweigh its costs.

As stated, whether exclusion would result in appreciable deterrence in the circumstances of this case is a different question from whether exclusion would appreciably deter Fourth Amendment violations when the governing law is unsettled. The Court's answer to the former question in this case thus does not resolve the latter one.

JUSTICE BREYER, with whom JUSTICE GINSBURG joins, dissenting.

In 2009, in Arizona v. Gant, this Court held that a police search of an automobile without a warrant violates the Fourth Amendment if the police have previously removed the automobile's occupants and placed them securely in a squad car. The present case involves these same circumstances, and it was pending on appeal when this Court decided Gant. Because Gant represents a "shift" in the Court's Fourth Amendment jurisprudence, we must decide whether and how Gant's new rule applies here.

I

I agree with the Court about *whether Gant*'s new rule applies. It does apply. Between 1965, when the Court decided *Linkletter v. Walker*, and 1987, when it decided *Griffith v. Kentucky*, that conclusion would have been more difficult to reach. Under *Linkletter*, the Court determined a new rule's retroactivity by looking to several different factors, including whether the new rule represented a "clear break" with the past and the degree of "reliance by law enforcement authorities on the old standards." *Desist v. United States*, (also citing "the purpose to be served by the new standards" and "the effect on the administration of justice" as factors).

And the Court would often not apply the new rule to identical cases still pending on appeal.

After 22 years of struggling with its *Linkletter* approach, however, the Court decided in *Griffith* that *Linkletter* had proved unfair and unworkable. It then substituted a clearer approach, stating that "a new rule for the conduct of criminal prosecutions is to be applied retroactively to all cases, state or federal, pending on direct review or not yet final, with no exception for cases in which the new rule constitutes a 'clear break' with the past." The Court today, following *Griffith*, concludes that *Gant'* s new rule applies here. And to that extent I agree with its decision.

II

The Court goes on, however, to decide how Gant's new rule will apply. While conceding that, like the search in Gant, this search violated the Fourth Amendment, it holds that, unlike Gant, this defendant is not entitled to a remedy. That is because the Court finds a new "good faith" exception which prevents application of the normal remedy for a Fourth Amendment violation, namely, suppression of the illegally seized evidence. *Weeks v. United States; Mapp v. Ohio.* Leaving Davis with a right but not a remedy, the Court "keep[s] the word of promise to our ear" but "break[s] it to our hope."

A

At this point I can no longer agree with the Court. A new "good faith" exception and this Court's retroactivity decisions are incompatible. For one thing, the Court's distinction between (1) retroactive application of a new rule and (2) availability of a remedy is highly artificial and runs counter to precedent. To determine that a new rule is retroactive is to determine that, at least in the normal case, there is a remedy. As we have previously said, the "source of a 'new rule' is the Constitution itself, not any judicial power to create new rules of law"; hence, "[w]hat we are actually determining when we assess the 'retroactivity' of a new rule is not the temporal scope of a newly announced right, but whether a violation of the right that occurred prior to the announcement of the new rule will entitle a criminal defendant to the relief sought." The Court's "good faith" exception (unlike, say, inevitable discovery, a remedial doctrine that applies only upon occasion) creates "a categorical bar to obtaining redress" in every case pending when a precedent is overturned.

For another thing, the Court's holding re-creates the very problems that led the Court to abandon Linkletter's approach to retroactivity in favor of Griffith's. One such problem concerns workability. The Court says that its exception applies where there is "objectively reasonable" police "reliance on binding appellate precedent." But to apply the term "binding appellate precedent" often requires resolution of complex questions of degree. Davis conceded that he faced binding anti-Gant precedent in the Eleventh Circuit. But future litigants will be less forthcoming. Indeed, those litigants will now have to create distinctions to show that previous Circuit precedent was not "binding" lest they find relief foreclosed even if they win their constitutional claim.

At the same time, Fourth Amendment precedents frequently require courts to "slosh" their "way through the factbound morass of 'reasonableness.' " *Scott v. Harris*. Suppose an officer's conduct is consistent with the language of a Fourth Amendment rule that a court of appeals announced in a case with clearly distinguishable facts? Suppose the case creating the relevant precedent did not directly announce any general rule but involved highly analogous facts? What about a rule that all other jurisdictions, but not the defendant's jurisdiction, had previously accepted? What rules can be developed for determining when, where, and how these different kinds of precedents do, or do not, count as relevant "binding precedent"? The Linkletter-like result is likely complex legal argument and police force confusion.

Another such problem concerns fairness. Today's holding, like that in *Linkletter*, "violates basic norms of constitutional adjudication." It treats the defendant in a case announcing a new rule one way while treating similarly situated defendants whose cases are pending on appeal in a different way. Justice Harlan explained why this approach is wrong when he said:

> "We cannot release criminals from jail merely because we think one case is a particularly appropriate one [to announce a constitutional doctrine] . . . . Simply fishing one case from the stream of appellate review, using it as a vehicle for pronouncing new constitutional standards, and then permitting a stream of similar cases subsequently to flow by unaffected by that new rule constitute an indefensible departure from [our ordinary] model of judicial review."

And in Griffith, the Court "embraced to a significant extent the comprehensive analysis presented by Justice Harlan." Of course, the Court may, as it suggests, avoid this unfairness by refusing to apply the exclusionary rule even to the defendant in the very case in which it announces a "new rule." But that approach would make matters worse. What would then happen in the lower courts? How would courts of appeals, for example, come to reconsider their prior decisions when other circuits' cases lead them to believe those decisions may be wrong? Why would a defendant seek to overturn any such decision? After all, if the (incorrect) circuit precedent is clear, then even if the defendant wins (on the constitutional question), he loses (on relief). To what extent then could this Court rely upon lower courts to work out Fourth Amendment differences among themselves — through circuit reconsideration of a precedent that other circuits have criticized?

B

Perhaps more important, the Court's rationale for creating its new "good faith" exception threatens to undermine well-settled Fourth Amendment law. The Court correctly says that pre-Gant Eleventh Circuit precedent had held that a Gant-type search was constitutional; hence the police conduct in this case, consistent with that precedent was "innocent." But the Court then finds this fact sufficient to create a new "good faith" exception to the exclusionary rule. It reasons that the "sole purpose" of the exclusionary rule "is to deter future Fourth Amendment violations." Ante, at 6. The "deterrence benefits of exclusion vary with the culpability of the law enforcement conduct at issue." Those benefits are sufficient to justify exclusion where "police exhibit deliberate, reckless, or grossly negligent disregard for Fourth Amendment rights." But those benefits do not justify exclusion where, as here, the police act with "simple, isolated negligence" or an "objectively reasonable good-faith belief that their conduct is lawful."

If the Court means what it says, what will happen to the exclusionary rule, a rule that the Court adopted nearly a century ago for federal courts, *Weeks v. United States*, and made applicable to state courts a half century ago through the Fourteenth Amendment, *Mapp v. Ohio*? The Court has thought of that rule not as punishment for the individual officer or as reparation for the individual defendant but more generally as an effective way to secure enforcement of the Fourth Amendment's commands. *Weeks*, (without the exclusionary rule, the Fourth Amendment would be "of no value," and "might as well be stricken from the Constitution"). This Court has deviated from the "suppression" norm in the name of "good faith" only a handful of times and in limited, atypical circumstances: where a magistrate has erroneously issued a warrant, *Leon*, 468 U.S. 897 (1984) where a database has erroneously informed police that they have a warrant, *Arizona v. Evans*, 514 U.S. 1 (1995), *Herring v. United States*; and where an unconstitutional statute purported to authorize the search.

The fact that such exceptions are few and far between is understandable. Defendants frequently move to suppress evidence on Fourth Amendment grounds. In many, perhaps most, of these instances the police, uncertain of how the Fourth Amendment applied to the particular factual circumstances they faced, will have acted in objective good faith. Yet, in a significant percentage of these instances, courts will find that the police were wrong. And, unless the police conduct falls into one of the exceptions previously noted, courts have required the suppression of the evidence seized. 153 U. Pa. L. Rev. 1709, 1728 (2005) (suppression motions are filed in approximately 7% of criminal cases; approximately 12% of suppression motions are successful); LaFave, ("Surely many more Fourth Amendment violations result from carelessness than from intentional constitutional violations").

But an officer who conducts a search that he believes complies with the Constitution but which, it ultimately turns out, falls just outside the Fourth Amendment's bounds is no more culpable than an officer who follows erroneous "binding precedent." Nor is an officer more culpable where circuit precedent is simply suggestive rather than "binding," where it only describes how to treat roughly analogous instances, or where it just does not exist. Thus, if the Court means what it now says, if it would place determinative weight upon the culpability of an individual officer's conduct, and if it would apply the exclusionary rule only where a Fourth Amendment violation was "deliberate, reckless, or grossly negligent," then the "good faith" exception will swallow the exclusionary rule. Indeed, our broad dicta in Herring — dicta the Court repeats and expands upon today — may already be leading lower courts in this direction. *See United States v. Julius*, 610 F. 3d 60. (assuming warrantless search was unconstitutional and remanding for District Court to "perform the cost/benefit analysis required by Herring" and to consider "whether the degree of police culpability in this case rose beyond mere . . . negligence" before ordering suppression); *United States v. Master*, 614 F.3d 243 ("[T]he Herring Court's emphasis seems weighed more toward preserving evidence for use in obtaining convictions, even if illegally seized . . . unless the officers engage in 'deliberate, reckless, or grossly negligent conduct'" (quoting *Herring*)). Today's decision will doubtless accelerate this trend.

Any such change (which may already be underway) would affect not "an exceedingly small set of cases," but a very large number of cases, potentially many thousands each year. And since the exclusionary rule is often the only sanction available for a Fourth Amendment violation, the Fourth Amendment would no longer protect ordinary Americans from "unreasonable searches and seizures." *Herring*, (GINSBURG,., dissenting) (the exclusionary rule is "an essential auxiliary" to the Fourth Amendment). It would become a watered-down Fourth Amendment, offering its protection against only those searches and seizures that are egregiously unreasonable.

III

In sum, I fear that the Court's opinion will undermine the exclusionary rule. And I believe that the Court wrongly departs from Griffith regardless. Instead I would follow Griffith, apply Gant's rule retroactively to this case, and require suppression of the evidence. Such an approach is consistent with our precedent, and it would indeed affect no more than "an exceedingly small set of cases." For these reasons, with respect, I dissent.

QUESTIONS AND NOTES

1. Given *Herring*, is there any way that the police in *Davis* could be found not to have acted in good faith?

2. Should your answer to question 1 resolve the case? Why? Why not?

3. Is Justice Alito's claim that the *Gant* right is retroactive, but the *Gant* remedy is not, disingenuous? Explain.

4. Do you agree that in the 27 years since *Leon*, the Court has never applied the exclusionary rule to non-culpable conduct? What about *Gant* itself? *Kyllo*?

5. Do you think that Justice Sotomayor accurately read the limits of the majority opinion?

6. If a future case comes up in which the court is asked to resolve a previously unresolved question (*e.g.* like *Kyllo*) and the Court resolves it against the police, do you think the Court would (should) apply the good faith exception to the exclusionary rule? Why?

7. If *Arizona* had raised the question, should Gant have been allowed to benefit by the exclusionary rule?

C. STANDING

One limitation that the Court has always put on the exclusionary rule is "standing." That is, in addition to establishing a Fourth Amendment violation, the defendant must establish that he was the victim of the violation. How that rule developed, its scope and limitations, and the normative desirability of continuing to adhere to it, are all questions that you should think about as you read *Rakas, Salvucci, Rawlings*, and *Carter*.

RAKAS v. ILLINOIS
439 U.S. 128 (1978)

Mr. Justice Rehnquist delivered the opinion of the Court.

Petitioners were convicted of armed robbery in the Circuit Court of Kankakee County, Ill., and their convictions were affirmed on appeal. At their trial, the prosecution offered into evidence a sawed-off rifle and rifle shells that had been seized by police during a search of an automobile in which petitioners had been passengers. Neither petitioner is the owner of the automobile and neither has ever asserted that he owned the rifle or shells seized. The Illinois Appellate Court held that petitioners lacked standing to object to the allegedly unlawful search and seizure and denied their motion to suppress the evidence. We granted certiorari in light of the obvious importance of the issues raised to the administration of criminal justice, and now affirm.

I

Because we are not here concerned with the issue of probable cause, a brief description of the events leading to the search of the automobile will suffice. A police officer on a routine patrol received a radio call notifying him of a robbery of a clothing store in Bourbonnais, Ill., and describing the getaway car. Shortly thereafter, the officer spotted an automobile which he thought might be the getaway car. After following the car for some time and after the arrival of assistance, he and several other officers stopped the vehicle. The occupants of the automobile, petitioners and two female companions, were ordered out of the car and, after the occupants had left the car, two officers searched the interior of the vehicle. They discovered a box of rifle shells in the glove compartment, which had been locked, and a sawed-off rifle under the front passenger seat. After discovering the rifle and the shells, the officers took petitioners to the station and placed them under arrest.

Before trial petitioners moved to suppress the rifle and shells seized from the car on the ground that the search violated the Fourth and Fourteenth Amendments. They conceded that they did not own the automobile and were simply passengers; the owner of the car had been the driver of the vehicle at the time of the search. Nor did they assert that they owned the rifle or the shells seized. The prosecutor challenged petitioners' standing to object to the lawfulness of the search of the car because neither the car, the shells nor the rifle belonged to them. The trial court agreed that petitioners lacked standing and denied the motion to suppress the evidence. In view of this holding, the court did not determine whether there was probable cause for the search and seizure. On appeal after petitioners' conviction, the Appellate Court of Illinois, Third Judicial District, affirmed the trial court's denial of petitioners' motion to suppress because it held that "without a proprietary or other similar interest in an automobile, a mere passenger therein lacks standing to challenge the legality of the search of the vehicle." The court stated:

> We believe that defendants failed to establish any prejudice to their own constitutional rights because they were not persons aggrieved by the unlawful search and seizure . . . . They wrongly seek to establish prejudice only through the use of evidence gathered as a consequence of a search and seizure directed at someone else and fail to prove an invasion of their own privacy. *Alderman v. United States* (1969), 394 U.S. 165.

II

Petitioners first urge us to relax or broaden the rule of standing enunciated in *Jones v. United States*, 362 U.S. 257 (1960), so that any criminal defendant at whom a search was "directed" would have standing to contest the legality of that search and object to the admission at trial of evidence obtained as a result of the search. Alternatively, petitioners argue that they have standing to object to the search under *Jones* because they were "legitimately on [the] premises" at the time of the search.

The concept of standing discussed in *Jones* focuses on whether the person seeking to challenge the legality of a search as a basis for suppressing evidence was himself the "victim" of the search or seizure. Adoption of the so-called "target" theory advanced by petitioners would in effect permit a defendant to assert that a violation of the Fourth Amendment rights of a third party entitled him to have evidence suppressed at his trial. If we reject petitioners' request for a broadened rule of standing such as this, and reaffirm the holding of *Jones* and other cases that Fourth Amendment rights are personal rights that may not be asserted vicariously, we will have occasion to re-examine the "standing" terminology emphasized in *Jones*. For we are not at all sure that the determination of a motion to suppress is materially aided by labeling the inquiry identified in *Jones* as one of standing, rather than simply recognizing it as one involving the substantive question of whether or not the proponent of the motion to suppress has had his own Fourth Amendment rights infringed by the search and seizure which he seeks to challenge. We shall therefore consider in turn petitioners' target theory, the necessity for continued adherence to the notion of standing discussed in *Jones* as a concept that is theoretically distinct from the merits of a defendant's Fourth Amendment claim, and, finally, the proper disposition of petitioners' ultimate claim in this case.

A

We decline to extend the rule of standing in Fourth Amendment cases in the manner suggested by petitioners. As we stated in *Alderman*, "Fourth Amendment rights are personal rights which, like some other constitutional rights, may not be vicariously asserted." A person who is aggrieved by an illegal search and seizure only through the introduction of damaging evidence secured by a search of a third person's premises or property has not had any of his Fourth Amendment rights infringed. And since the exclusionary rule is an attempt to effectuate the guarantees of the Fourth Amendment, *Calandra*, it is proper to permit only defendants whose Fourth Amendment rights have been violated to benefit from the rule's protections.[3] There is no reason to think that a party whose rights have been infringed will not, if evidence is used against him, have ample motivation to move to suppress it. Even if such a person is not a defendant in the action, he may be able to recover damages for the violation of his Fourth Amendment rights, *see Monroe v. Pape*, 365 U.S. 167 (1961), or seek redress under state law for invasion of privacy or trespass.

In support of their target theory, petitioners rely on the following quotation from *Jones*:

> In order to qualify as a "person aggrieved by an unlawful search and seizure" one must have been a victim of a search or seizure, *one against whom the search was directed,* as distinguished from one who claims prejudice only through the use of evidence gathered as a consequence of a search or seizure directed at someone else.

(emphasis added). The above-quoted statement from *Jones* suggests that the italicized language was meant merely as a parenthetical equivalent of the previous phrase "a victim of a search or seizure." To the extent that the language might be read more broadly, it is dictum which was impliedly repudiated in *Alderman*, and which we now expressly reject. In *Jones*, the Court set forth two alternative holdings: It established a rule of "automatic" standing to contest an allegedly illegal search where the same possession needed to establish standing is an essential element of the offense charged; and second, it stated that "anyone legitimately on premises where a search occurs may challenge its legality by way of a motion to suppress." Had the Court intended to adopt the target theory now put forth by petitioners, neither of the above two holdings would have been necessary since Jones was the "target" of the police search in that case.[5]

In *Alderman*, Mr. Justice Fortas, in a concurring and dissenting opinion, argued that the Court should "include within the category of those who may object to the introduction of illegal evidence 'one against whom the search was directed.' " MR. JUSTICE HARLAN, concurring and dissenting, identified administrative problems posed by the target theory:

> [T]he [target] rule would entail very substantial administrative difficulties. In the majority of cases, I would imagine that the police plant a bug with the expectation that it may well produce leads to a large number of crimes. A lengthy hearing would, then, appear to be necessary in order to determine whether the police knew of an accused's criminal activity at the time the bug was planted and whether the police decision to plant a bug was

---

[3] The necessity for a showing of a violation of personal rights is not obviated by recognizing the deterrent purpose of the exclusionary rule. Despite the deterrent aim of the exclusionary rule, we never have held that unlawfully seized evidence is inadmissible in all proceedings or against all persons. "[T]he application of the rule has been restricted to those areas where its remedial objectives are thought most efficaciously served."

[5] The search of the apartment in *Jones* was pursuant to a search warrant naming Jones and another woman as occupants of the apartment. The affidavit submitted in support of the search warrant alleged that Jones and the woman were involved in illicit narcotics traffic and kept a supply of heroin and narcotics paraphernalia in the apartment.

motivated by an effort to obtain information against the accused or some other individual. I do not believe that this administrative burden is justified in any substantial degree by the hypothesized marginal increase in Fourth Amendment protection.

When we are urged to grant standing to a criminal defendant to assert a violation, not of his own constitutional rights but of someone else's, we cannot but give weight to practical difficulties such as those foreseen by Mr. Justice Harlan in the quoted language.

Conferring standing to raise vicarious Fourth Amendment claims would necessarily mean a more widespread invocation of the exclusionary rule during criminal trials. The Court's opinion in *Alderman* counseled against such an extension of the exclusionary rule:

> The deterrent values of preventing the incrimination of those whose rights the police have violated have been considered sufficient to justify the suppression of probative evidence even though the case against the defendant is weakened or destroyed. We adhere to that judgment. But we are not convinced that the additional benefits of extending the exclusionary rule to other defendants would justify further encroachment upon the public interest in prosecuting those accused of crime and having them acquitted or convicted on the basis of all the evidence which exposes the truth.

Each time the exclusionary rule is applied it exacts a substantial social cost for the vindication of Fourth Amendment rights. Relevant and reliable evidence is kept from the trier of fact and the search for truth at trial is deflected. Since our cases generally have held that one whose Fourth Amendment rights are violated may successfully suppress evidence obtained in the course of an illegal search and seizure, misgivings as to the benefit of enlarging the class of persons who may invoke that rule are properly considered when deciding whether to expand standing to assert Fourth Amendment violations.[6]

B

Had we accepted petitioners' request to allow persons other than those whose own Fourth Amendment rights were violated by a challenged search and seizure to suppress evidence obtained in the course of such police activity, it would be appropriate to retain *Jones'* use of standing in Fourth Amendment analysis. Under petitioners' target theory, a court could determine that a defendant had standing to invoke the exclusionary rule without having to inquire into the substantive question of whether the challenged search or seizure violated the Fourth Amendment rights of that particular defendant. However, having rejected petitioners' target theory

---

[6] For these same prudential reasons, the Court in *Alderman* rejected the argument that *any* defendant should be enabled to apprise the court of unconstitutional searches and seizures and to exclude all such unlawfully seized evidence from trial, regardless of whether his Fourth Amendment rights were violated by the search or whether he was the "target" of the search. This expansive reading of the Fourth Amendment also was advanced by the petitioner in *Jones* and implicitly rejected by the Court.

and reaffirmed the principle that the "rights assured by the Fourth Amendment are personal rights, [which] . . . may be enforced by exclusion of evidence only at the instance of one whose own protection was infringed by the search and seizure," the question necessarily arises whether it serves any useful analytical purpose to consider this principle a matter of standing, distinct from the merits of a defendant's Fourth Amendment claim. We can think of no decided cases of this Court that would have come out differently had we concluded, as we do now, that the type of standing requirement discussed in *Jones* and reaffirmed today is more properly subsumed under substantive Fourth Amendment doctrine. Rigorous application of the principle that the rights secured by this Amendment are personal, in place of a notion of "standing," will produce no additional situations in which evidence must be excluded. The inquiry under either approach is the same.[7] But we think the better analysis forthrightly focuses on the extent of a particular defendant's rights under the Fourth Amendment, rather than on any theoretically separate, but invariably intertwined concept of standing. The Court in *Jones* also may have been aware that there was a certain artificiality in analyzing this question in terms of standing because in at least three separate places in its opinion the Court placed that term within quotation marks.

It should be emphasized that nothing we say here casts the least doubt on cases which recognize that, as a general proposition, the issue of standing involves two inquiries: first, whether the proponent of a particular legal right has alleged "injury in fact," and, second, whether the proponent is asserting his own legal rights and interests rather than basing his claim for relief upon the rights of third parties. But this Court's long history of insistence that Fourth Amendment rights are personal in nature has already answered many of these traditional standing inquiries, and we think that definition of those rights is more properly placed within the purview of substantive Fourth Amendment law than within that of standing.[8]

Analyzed in these terms, the question is whether the challenged search or seizure violated the Fourth Amendment rights of a criminal defendant who seeks to exclude the evidence obtained during it. That inquiry in turn requires a determination of whether the disputed search and seizure has infringed an interest of the defendant which the Fourth Amendment was designed to protect. We are under no illusion that by dispensing with the rubric of standing used in *Jones* we have rendered any simpler the determination of whether the proponent of a motion to suppress is entitled to contest the legality of a search and seizure. But by frankly recognizing that this aspect of the analysis belongs more properly under the heading of substantive Fourth Amendment doctrine than under the heading of

---

[7] So, for example, in *Katz v. United States*, 389 U.S. 347, 352 (1967), the Court focused on substantive Fourth Amendment law, concluded that a person in a telephone booth "may rely upon the protection of the Fourth Amendment," and then proceeded to determine whether the search was "unreasonable." In *Mancusi v. DeForte*, 392 U.S. 364 (1968), on the other hand, the Court concentrated on the issue of standing, decided that the defendant possessed it, and with barely any mention of the threshold substantive question of whether the search violated DeForte's own Fourth Amendment rights, went on to decide whether the search was "unreasonable." In both cases, however, the first inquiry was much the same.

[8] This approach is consonant with that which the Court already has taken with respect to the Fifth Amendment privilege against self-incrimination, which also is a purely personal right.

standing, we think the decision of this issue will rest on sounder logical footing.

C

Here petitioners, who were passengers occupying a car which they neither owned nor leased, seek to analogize their position to that of the defendant in *Jones*. In *Jones*, petitioner was present at the time of the search of an apartment which was owned by a friend. The friend had given Jones permission to use the apartment and a key to it, with which Jones had admitted himself on the day of the search. He had a suit and shirt at the apartment and had slept there "maybe a night," but his home was elsewhere. At the time of the search, Jones was the only occupant of the apartment because the lessee was away for a period of several days. Under these circumstances, this Court stated that while one wrongfully on the premises could not move to suppress evidence obtained as a result of searching them, "anyone legitimately on premises where a search occurs may challenge its legality." Petitioners argue that their occupancy of the automobile in question was comparable to that of Jones in the apartment and that they therefore have standing to contest the legality of the search — or as we have rephrased the inquiry, that they, like Jones, had their Fourth Amendment rights violated by the search.

We do not question the conclusion in *Jones* that the defendant in that case suffered a violation of his personal Fourth Amendment rights if the search in question was unlawful. Nonetheless, we believe that the phrase "legitimately on premises" coined in *Jones* creates too broad a gauge for measurement of Fourth Amendment rights. For example, applied literally, this statement would permit a casual visitor who has never seen, or been permitted to visit, the basement of another's house to object to a search of the basement if the visitor happened to be in the kitchen of the house at the time of the search. Likewise, a casual visitor who walks into a house one minute before a search of the house commences and leaves one minute after the search ends would be able to contest the legality of the search. The first visitor would have absolutely no interest or legitimate expectation of privacy in the basement, the second would have none in the house, and it advances no purpose served by the Fourth Amendment to permit either of them to object to the lawfulness of the search.[11]

We think that *Jones* on its facts merely stands for the unremarkable proposition that a person can have a legally sufficient interest in a place other than his own home so that the Fourth Amendment protects him from unreasonable governmental intrusion into that place. In defining the scope of that interest, we adhere to the view expressed in *Jones* and echoed in later cases that arcane distinctions developed in property and tort law between guests, licensees, invitees, and the like, ought not to control. But the *Jones* statement that a person need only be "legitimately on premises" in order to challenge the validity of the search of a dwelling place cannot be taken in its full sweep beyond the facts of that case.

Katz provides guidance in defining the scope of the interest protected by the Fourth Amendment. [T]he Court in *Katz* held that capacity to claim the protection

---

[11] This is not to say that such visitors could not contest the lawfulness of the seizure of evidence or the search if their own property were seized during the search.

of the Fourth Amendment depends not upon a property right in the invaded place but upon whether the person who claims the protection of the Amendment has a legitimate expectation of privacy in the invaded place. Viewed in this manner, the holding in *Jones* can best be explained by the fact that Jones had a legitimate expectation of privacy in the premises he was using and therefore could claim the protection of the Fourth Amendment with respect to a governmental invasion of those premises, even though his "interest" in those premises might not have been a recognized property interest at common law.[12]

Our Brother WHITE in dissent expresses the view that by rejecting the phrase "legitimately on [the] premises" as the appropriate measure of Fourth Amendment rights, we are abandoning a thoroughly workable, "bright line" test in favor of a less certain analysis of whether the facts of a particular case give rise to a legitimate expectation of privacy. If "legitimately on premises" were the successful litmus test of Fourth Amendment rights that he assumes it is, his approach would have at least the merit of easy application, whatever it lacked in fidelity to the history and purposes of the Fourth Amendment. But a reading of lower court cases that have applied the phrase "legitimately on premises," and of the dissent itself, reveals that this expression is not a shorthand summary for a bright-line rule which somehow encapsulates the "core" of the Fourth Amendment's protections.

The dissent itself shows that the facile consistency it is striving for is illusory. The dissenters concede that "there comes a point when use of an area is shared with so many that one simply cannot reasonably expect seclusion." But surely the "point" referred to is not one demarcating a line which is black on one side and white on another; it is inevitably a point which separates one shade of gray from another. We are likewise told by the dissent that a person "legitimately on *private* premises . . . , though his privacy is *not absolute*, is entitled to expect that he is sharing it

---

[12] Obviously, however, a "legitimate" expectation of privacy by definition means more than a subjective expectation of not being discovered. A burglar plying his trade in a summer cabin during the off season may have a thoroughly justified subjective expectation of privacy, but it is not one which the law recognizes as "legitimate." His presence, in the words of *Jones*, 362 U.S. at 267, is "wrongful"; his expectation is not "one that society is prepared to recognize as 'reasonable.'" *Katz v. United States*, 389 U.S., at 361 (Harlan, J., concurring). And it would, of course, be merely tautological to fall back on the notion that those expectations of privacy which are legitimate depend primarily on cases deciding exclusionary-rule issues in criminal cases. Legitimation of expectations of privacy by law must have a source outside of the Fourth Amendment, either by reference to concepts of real or personal property law or to understandings that are recognized and permitted by society. One of the main rights attaching to property is the right to exclude others, and one who owns or lawfully possesses or controls property will in all likelihood have a legitimate expectation of privacy by virtue of this right to exclude. Expectations of privacy protected by the Fourth Amendment, of course, need not be based on a common-law interest in real or personal property, or on the invasion of such an interest. These ideas were rejected both in *Jones* and *Katz*. But by focusing on legitimate expectations of privacy in Fourth Amendment jurisprudence, the Court has not altogether abandoned use of property concepts in determining the presence or absence of the privacy interests protected by that Amendment. No better demonstration of this proposition exists than the decision in *Alderman*, where the Court held that an individual's property interest in his own home was so great as to allow him to object to electronic surveillance of conversations emanating from his home, even though he himself was not a party to the conversations. On the other hand, even a property interest in premises may not be sufficient to establish a legitimate expectation of privacy with respect to particular items located on the premises or activity conducted thereon. *See Katz, Lewis v. United States*, 385 U.S. 206, 210 (1966); *United States v. Lee*, 274 U.S. 559, 563 (1927); *Hester v. United States*, 265 U.S. 57, 58–59 (1924).

only with those persons [allowed there] and that governmental officials will intrude only with *consent* or by complying with the Fourth Amendment." (emphasis added). This single sentence describing the contours of the supposedly easily applied rule virtually abounds with unanswered questions: What are "private" premises? Indeed, what are the "premises?" It may be easy to describe the "premises" when one is confronted with a 1-room apartment, but what of the case of a 10-room house, or of a house with an attached garage that is searched? Also, if one's privacy is not absolute, how is it bounded? If he risks governmental intrusion "with consent," who may give that consent?

Again, we are told by the dissent that the Fourth Amendment assures that "*some* expectations of privacy are justified and will be protected from official intrusion." (emphasis added). But we are not told which of many possible expectations of privacy are embraced within this sentence. And our dissenting Brethren concede that "perhaps the Constitution provides some degree less protection for the personal freedom from unreasonable governmental intrusion when one does not have a possessory interest in the invaded private place." But how much "less" protection is available when one does not have such a possessory interest?

Our disagreement with the dissent is not that it leaves these questions unanswered, or that the questions are necessarily irrelevant in the context of the analysis contained in this opinion. Our disagreement is rather with the dissent's bland and self-refuting assumption that there will not be fine lines to be drawn in Fourth Amendment cases as in other areas of the law, and that its rubric, rather than a meaningful exegesis of Fourth Amendment doctrine, is more desirable or more easily resolves Fourth Amendment cases. In abandoning "legitimately on premises" for the doctrine that we announce today, we are not forsaking a time-tested and workable rule, which has produced consistent results when applied, solely for the sake of fidelity to the values underlying the Fourth Amendment. Rather, we are rejecting blind adherence to a phrase which at most has superficial clarity and which conceals underneath that thin veneer all of the problems of line drawing which must be faced in any conscientious effort to apply the Fourth Amendment. Where the factual premises for a rule are so generally prevalent that little would be lost and much would be gained by abandoning case-by-case analysis, we have not hesitated to do so. But the phrase "legitimately on premises" has not been shown to be an easily applicable measure of Fourth Amendment rights so much as it has proved to be simply a label placed by the courts on results which have not been subjected to careful analysis. We would not wish to be understood as saying that legitimate presence on the premises is irrelevant to one's expectation of privacy, but it cannot be deemed controlling.

D

Judged by the foregoing analysis, petitioners' claims must fail. They asserted neither a property nor a possessory interest in the automobile, nor an interest in the property seized. And as we have previously indicated, the fact that they were "legitimately on [the] premises" in the sense that they were in the car with the permission of its owner is not determinative of whether they had a legitimate expectation of privacy in the particular areas of the automobile searched. It is unnecessary for us to decide here whether the same expectations of privacy are warranted in a car as would be justified in a dwelling place in analogous circumstances. We have on numerous occasions pointed out that cars are not to be treated identically with houses or Apartments for Fourth Amendment purposes. But here petitioners' claim is one which would fail even in an analogous situation in a dwelling place, since they made no showing that they had any legitimate expectation of privacy in the glove compartment or area under the seat of the car in which they were merely passengers. Like the trunk of an automobile, these are areas in which a passenger *qua* passenger simply would not normally have a legitimate expectation of privacy.

Jones and *Katz* involved significantly different factual circumstances. Jones not only had permission to use the apartment of his friend, but also had a key to the apartment with which he admitted himself on the day of the search and kept possessions in the apartment. Except with respect to his friend, Jones had complete dominion and control over the apartment and could exclude others from it. Likewise in *Katz*, the defendant occupied the telephone booth, shut the door behind him to exclude all others and paid the toll, which "entitled [him] to assume that the words he utter[ed] into the mouthpiece [would] not be broadcast to the world."[16] Katz and Jones could legitimately expect privacy in the areas which were the subject of the search and seizure each sought to contest. No such showing was made by these petitioners with respect to those portions of the automobile which were searched and from which incriminating evidence was seized.[17]

III

The Illinois courts were therefore correct in concluding that it was unnecessary to decide whether the search of the car might have violated the rights secured to someone else by the Fourth and Fourteenth Amendments to the United States

---

[16] The dissent states that *Katz v. United States* expressly recognized protection for passengers of taxicabs and asks why that protection should not also extend to these petitioners. *Katz* relied on *Rios v. United States*, 364 U.S. 253 (1960), as support for that proposition. The question of Rios' right to contest the search was not presented to or addressed by the Court and the property seized appears to have belonged to Rios. Additionally, the facts of that case are quite different from those of the present case. Rios had hired the cab and occupied the rear passenger section. When police stopped the cab, he placed a package he had been holding on the floor of the rear section. The police saw the package and seized it after defendant was removed from the cab.

[17] For reasons which they do not explain, our dissenting Brethren repeatedly criticize our "holding" that unless one has a common-law property interest in the premises searched, one cannot object to the search. We have rendered no such "holding," however. To the contrary, we have taken pains to reaffirm the statements in *Jones* and *Katz* that "arcane distinctions developed in property . . . law . . . ought not to control." In a similar vein, the dissenters repeatedly state or imply that we now "hold" that a passenger lawfully in an automobile "may not invoke the exclusionary rule and challenge a search of that vehicle unless he happens to own or have a possessory interest in it." It is not without significance that these statements of today's "holding" come from the dissenting opinion, and not from the Court's opinion. The case before us involves the search of and seizure of property from the glove compartment and area under the seat of a car in which petitioners were riding as passengers. Petitioners claimed only that they were "legitimately on [the] premises" and did not claim that they had any legitimate expectation of privacy in the areas of the car which were searched. We cannot, therefore, agree with the dissenters' insistence that our decision will encourage the police to violate the Fourth Amendment.

Constitution. Since it did not violate any rights of these petitioners, their judgment of conviction is

Affirmed.

Mr. Justice Powell, with whom The Chief Justice joins, concurring.

I concur in the opinion of the Court, and add these thoughts. I do not believe my dissenting Brethren correctly characterize the rationale of the Court's opinion when they assert that it ties "the application of the Fourth Amendment . . . to property law concepts." On the contrary, I read the Court's opinion as focusing on whether there was a *legitimate* expectation of privacy protected by the Fourth Amendment.

The petitioners do not challenge the constitutionality of the police action in stopping the automobile in which they were riding; nor do they complain of being made to get out of the vehicle. Rather, petitioners assert that their constitutionally protected interest in privacy was violated when the police, after stopping the automobile and making them get out, searched the vehicle's interior, where they discovered a sawed-off rifle under the front seat and rifle shells in the locked glove compartment. The question before the Court, therefore, is a narrow one: Did the search of their friend's automobile after they had left it violate any Fourth Amendment right of the petitioners?

The dissenting opinion urges the Court to answer this question by considering only the talisman of legitimate presence on the premises.

This Court's decisions since *Jones* have emphasized a sounder standard for determining the scope of a person's Fourth Amendment rights: Only legitimate expectations of privacy are protected by the Constitution. As Mr. Justice Harlan pointed out in his concurrence [in *Katz*], however, it is not enough that an individual desired or anticipated that he would be free from governmental intrusion. Rather, for an expectation to deserve the protection of the Fourth Amendment, it must "be one that society is prepared to recognize as 'reasonable.'"

The ultimate question, therefore, is whether one's claim to privacy from government intrusion is reasonable in light of all the surrounding circumstances. As the dissenting opinion states, this standard "will not provide law enforcement officials with a bright line between the protected and the unprotected." Whatever the application of this standard may lack in ready administration, it is more faithful to the purposes of the Fourth Amendment than a test focusing solely or primarily on whether the defendant was legitimately present during the search.[1]

---

[1] Allowing anyone who is legitimately on the premises searched to invoke the exclusionary rule extends the rule far beyond the proper scope of Fourth Amendment protections, as not all who are legitimately present invariably have a reasonable expectation of privacy. And, as the Court points out, the dissenters' standard lacks even the advantage of easy application. I do not share the dissenters' concern that the Court's ruling will "invit[e] police to engage in patently unreasonable searches every time an automobile contains more than one occupant." A police officer observing an automobile carrying several passengers will not know the circumstances surrounding each occupant's presence in the automobile, and certainly will not know whether an occupant will be able to establish that he had a reasonable expectation of privacy. Thus, there will continue to be a significant incentive for the police to

The petitioners' Fourth Amendment rights were not abridged here because none of the factors relied upon by this Court on prior occasions supports petitioners' claim that their alleged expectation of privacy from government intrusion was *reasonable.*

We are concerned here with an automobile search. Nothing is better established in Fourth Amendment jurisprudence than the distinction between one's expectation of privacy in an automobile and one's expectation when in other locations.[2]

Here there were three passengers and a driver in the automobile searched. None of the passengers is said to have had control of the vehicle or the keys. It is unrealistic — as the shared experience of us all bears witness — to suggest that these passengers had any reasonable expectation that the car in which they had been riding would not be searched after they were lawfully stopped and made to get out. The minimal privacy that existed simply is not comparable to that, for example, of an individual in his place of abode, of one who secludes himself in a telephone booth, or of the traveler who secures his belongings in a locked suitcase or footlocker.[4]

This is not an area of the law in which any "bright line" rule would safeguard both Fourth Amendment rights and the public interest in a fair and effective criminal justice system. The range of variables in the fact situations of search and seizure is almost infinite. Rather than seek facile solutions, it is best to apply principles broadly faithful to Fourth Amendment purposes. I believe the Court has identified these principles.[5]

---

comply with the requirements of the Fourth Amendment, lest otherwise valid prosecutions be voided. Moreover, any marginal diminution in this incentive that might result from the Court's decision today is more than justified by society's interest in restricting the scope of the exclusionary rule to those cases where in fact there is a reasonable expectation of privacy.

[2] There are sound reasons for this distinction: Automobiles operate on public streets; they are serviced in public places; they stop frequently; they are usually parked in public places; their interiors are highly visible; and they are subject to extensive regulation and inspection. The rationale of the automobile distinction does not apply, of course, to objects on the person of an occupant.

[4] The sawed-off rifle in this case was merely pushed beneath the front seat, presumably by one of the petitioners. In that position, it could have slipped into full or partial view in the event of an accident, or indeed upon any sudden stop. As the rifle shells were in the locked glove compartment, this might have presented a closer case if it had been shown that one of the petitioners possessed the keys or if a rifle had not been found in the automobile. The dissenting opinion suggests that the petitioners here took the same actions to preserve their privacy as did the defendant in *Katz*: Just as Katz closed the door to the telephone booth after him, petitioners closed the doors to their automobile. Last Term, this Court determined in *Pennsylvania v. Mimms*, 434 U.S. 106 (1977), that passengers in automobiles have no Fourth Amendment right not to be ordered from their vehicle, once a proper stop is made. The dissenting opinion concedes that there is no question here of the propriety of the stopping of the automobile in which the petitioners were riding. Thus, the closing of the doors of a vehicle, even if there were only one occupant, cannot have the same significance as it might in other contexts.

[5] Even if one agreed with my dissenting Brethren that there was a Fourth Amendment violation in this case, the evidence seized would have been admissible under the modification of the exclusionary rule proposed by Mr. Justice WHITE in his dissenting opinion in *Stone v. Powell*, 428 U.S. 465, 538 (1976):

> [T]he rule should be substantially modified so as to prevent its application in those many circumstances where the evidence at issue was seized by an officer acting in the good-faith belief that his conduct comported with existing law and having reasonable grounds for this belief. These are recurring situations; and recurringly evidence is excluded without any

Mr. Justice White, with whom Mr. Justice Brennan, Mr. Justice Marshall, and Mr. Justice Stevens join, dissenting.

The Court today holds that the Fourth Amendment protects property, not people, and specifically that a legitimate occupant of an automobile may not invoke the exclusionary rule and challenge a search of that vehicle unless he happens to own or have a possessory interest in it. Though professing to acknowledge that the primary purpose of the Fourth Amendment's prohibition of unreasonable searches is the protection of privacy — not property — the Court nonetheless effectively ties the application of the Fourth Amendment and the exclusionary rule in this situation to property law concepts. Insofar as passengers are concerned, the Court's opinion today declares an "open season" on automobiles. However unlawful stopping and searching a car may be, absent a possessory or ownership interest, no "mere" passenger may object, regardless of his relationship to the owner. Because the majority's conclusion has no support in the Court's controlling decisions, in the logic of the Fourth Amendment, or in common sense, I must respectfully dissent. If the Court is troubled by the practical impact of the exclusionary rule, it should face the issue of that rule's continued validity squarely instead of distorting other doctrines in an attempt to reach what are perceived as the correct results in specific cases.

I

Two intersecting doctrines long established in this Court's opinions control here. The first is the recognition of some cognizable level of privacy in the interior of an automobile. Though the reasonableness of the expectation of privacy in a vehicle may be somewhat weaker than that in a home, "[a] search even of an automobile, is a substantial invasion of privacy. To protect that privacy from official arbitrariness, the Court always has regarded probable cause as the minimum requirement for a lawful search." *United States v. Ortiz*, 422 U.S. 891, 896 (1975). So far, the Court has not strayed from this application of the Fourth Amendment.[2]

The second tenet is that when a person is legitimately present in a private place, his right to privacy is protected from unreasonable governmental interference even if he does not own the premises. Just a few years ago, The Chief Justice, for a unanimous Court, wrote that the "[p]resence of the defendant at the search and seizure was held, in *Jones*, to be a sufficient source of standing in itself." The Court in *Jones* itself was unanimous in this regard, and its holding is not the less binding because it was an alternative one.

These two fundamental aspects of Fourth Amendment law demand that petitioners be permitted to challenge the search and seizure of the automobile in this case. It is of no significance that a car is different for Fourth Amendment purposes from a house, for if there is some protection for the privacy of an automobile then the only relevant analogy is between a person legitimately in someone else's vehicle and a person legitimately in someone else's home. If both strands of the Fourth

---

realistic expectation that its exclusion will contribute in the slightest to the purposes of the rule, even though the trial will be seriously affected or the indictment dismissed.

[2] *See Almeida-Sanchez v. United States*, 413 U.S. 266, 269 (1973) ("Automobile or no automobile, there must be probable cause for the search").

Amendment doctrine adumbrated above are valid, the Court must reach a different result. Instead, it chooses to eviscerate the *Jones* principle, an action in which I am unwilling to participate.

II

Though we had reserved the very issue over 50 years ago, *see Carroll v. United States*, 267 U.S. 132, 162 (1925), and never expressly dealt with it again until today, many of our opinions have assumed that a mere passenger in an automobile is entitled to protection against unreasonable searches occurring in his presence. In decisions upholding the validity of automobile searches, we have gone directly to the merits even though some of the petitioners did not own or possess the vehicles in question. *E.g., Schneckloth* (sole petitioner was not owner; in fact, owner was not in the automobile at all). Similarly, in *Preston v. United States*, 376 U.S. 364 (1964), the Court unanimously overturned a search though the single petitioner was not the owner of the automobile. The Court's silence on this issue in light of its actions can only mean that, until now, we, like most lower courts, had assumed that *Jones* foreclosed the answer now supplied by the majority. That assumption was perfectly understandable, since all private premises would seem to be the same for the purposes of the analysis set out in *Jones*.

III

The logic of Fourth Amendment jurisprudence compels the result reached by the above decisions. Our starting point is "[t]he established principle . . . that suppression of the product of a Fourth Amendment violation can be successfully urged only by those whose rights were violated by the search itself . . . ." Though the Amendment protects one's liberty and property interests against unreasonable seizures of self and effects, "the primary object of the Fourth Amendment [is] . . . the protection of privacy." And privacy is the interest asserted here, so the first step is to ascertain whether the premises searched "fall within a protected zone of privacy." My Brethren in the majority assertedly do not deny that automobiles warrant at least some protection from official interference with privacy. Thus, the next step is to decide who is entitled, vis-a-vis the State, to enjoy that privacy. The answer to that question must be found by determining "whether petitioner had an interest in connection with the searched premises that gave rise to 'a reasonable expectation [on his part] of freedom from governmental intrusion' upon those premises."

We have concluded on numerous occasions that the entitlement to an expectation of privacy does not hinge on ownership:

> What a person knowingly exposes to the public, even in his own home or office, is not a subject of Fourth Amendment protection . . . . But what he seeks to preserve as private, even in an area accessible to the public, may be constitutionally protected.

Katz.

Prior to *Jones*, the lower federal courts had based Fourth Amendment rights upon possession or ownership of the items seized or the premises searched. But *Jones* was foreshadowed by Mr. Justice Jackson's remark in 1948 that "even a guest may expect the shelter of the rooftree he is under against criminal intrusion." *McDonald v. United States*, 335 U.S. 451, 461 (1948) (Jackson, J., joined by Frankfurter, J., concurring).

In sum, one consistent theme in our decisions under the Fourth Amendment has been, until now, that "the Amendment does not shield only those who have title to the searched premises." Though there comes a point when use of an area is shared with so many that one simply cannot reasonably expect seclusion, short of that limit a person legitimately on private premises knows the others allowed there and, though his privacy is not absolute, is entitled to expect that he is sharing it only with those persons and that governmental officials will intrude only with consent or by complying with the Fourth Amendment.

It is true that the Court asserts that it is not limiting the Fourth Amendment bar against unreasonable searches to the protection of property rights, but in reality it is doing exactly that.[14] Petitioners were in a private place with the permission of the owner, but the Court states that that is not sufficient to establish entitlement to a legitimate expectation of privacy. But if that is not sufficient, what would be? We are not told, and it is hard to imagine anything short of a property interest that would satisfy the majority. Insofar as the Court's rationale is concerned, no passenger in an automobile, without an ownership or possessory interest and regardless of his relationship to the owner, may claim Fourth Amendment protection against illegal stops and searches of the automobile in which he is rightfully present. The Court approves the result in *Jones*, but it fails to give any explanation why the facts in *Jones* differ, in a fashion material to the Fourth Amendment, from the facts here.[15] More importantly, how is the Court able to avoid answering the question why presence in a private place with the owner's permission is insufficient? If it is "tautological to fall back on the notion that those expectations of privacy which are legitimate depend primarily on cases deciding exclusionary rule issues in criminal cases," then it surely must be tautological to decide that issue simply by unadorned fiat.

---

[14] The Court's reliance on property law concepts is additionally shown by its suggestion that visitors could "contest the lawfulness of the seizure of evidence or the search if their own property were seized during the search." What difference should that property interest make to constitutional protection against unreasonable searches, which is concerned with privacy? Contrary to the Court's suggestion, a legitimate passenger in a car expects to enjoy the privacy of the vehicle whether or not he happens to carry some item along for the ride. We have never before limited our concern for a person's privacy to those situations in which he is in possession of personal property. Even a person living in a barren room without possessions is entitled to expect that the police will not intrude without cause.

[15] Jones had permission to use the apartment, had slept in it one night, had a key, had left a suit and a shirt there, and was the only occupant at the time of the search. Petitioners here had permission to be in the car and were occupying it at the time of the search. Thus the only distinguishing fact is that Jones could exclude others from the apartment by using his friend's key. But petitioners and their friend the owner had excluded others by entering the automobile and shutting the doors. Petitioners did not need a key because the owner was present. Similarly, the Court attempts to distinguish *Katz* on the theory that Katz had "shut the door behind him to exclude all others," but petitioners here did exactly the same. The car doors remained closed until the police ordered them opened at gunpoint.

As a control on governmental power, the Fourth Amendment assures that some expectations of privacy are justified and will be protected from official intrusion. That should be true in this instance, for if protected zones of privacy can only be purchased or obtained by possession of property, then much of our daily lives will be unshielded from unreasonable governmental prying, and the reach of the Fourth Amendment will have been narrowed to protect chiefly those with possessory interests in real or personal property. I had thought that *Katz* firmly established that the Fourth Amendment was intended as more than simply a trespass law applicable to the government. Katz had no possessory interest in the public telephone booth, at least no more than petitioners had in their friend's car; Katz was simply legitimately present. And the decision in *Katz* was based not on property rights, but on the theory that it was essential to securing "conditions favorable to the pursuit of happiness" that the expectation of privacy in question be recognized.

At most, one could say that perhaps the Constitution provides some degree less protection for the personal freedom from unreasonable governmental intrusion when one does not have a possessory interest in the invaded private place. But that would only change the extent of the protection; it would not free police to do the unreasonable, as does the decision today. And since the accused should be entitled to litigate the application of the Fourth Amendment where his privacy interest is merely arguable, the failure to allow such litigation here is the more incomprehensible.

IV

The Court's holding is contrary not only to our past decisions and the logic of the Fourth Amendment but also to the everyday expectations of privacy that we all share. Because of that, it is unworkable in all the various situations that arise in real life. If the owner of the car had not only invited petitioners to join her but had said to them, "I give you a temporary possessory interest in my vehicle so that you will share the right to privacy that the Supreme Court says that I own," then apparently the majority would reverse. But people seldom say such things, though they may mean their invitation to encompass them if only they had thought of the problem.[19] If the nonowner were the spouse or child of the owner,[20] would the Court recognize a sufficient interest? If so, would distant relatives somehow have more of an expectation of privacy than close friends? What if the nonowner were driving with the owner's permission? Would nonowning drivers have more of an expectation of privacy than mere passengers? What about a passenger in a taxicab? *Katz* expressly recognized protection for such passengers. Why should Fourth Amendment rights be present when one pays a cabdriver for a ride but be absent when one is given a ride by a friend?

---

[19] So far as we know, the owner of the automobile in question might have expressly granted or intended to grant exactly such an interest. Apparently not contemplating today's radical change in the law, petitioners did not know at the suppression hearing that the precise form of the invitation extended by the owner to the petitioners would be dispositive of their rights against governmental intrusion.

[20] In fact, though it was not brought out at the suppression hearing, one of the petitioners is the former husband of the owner and driver of the car. He did testify at the suppression hearing that he was with her when she purchased it.

The distinctions the Court would draw are based on relationships between private parties, but the Fourth Amendment is concerned with the relationship of one of those parties to the government. Divorced as it is from the purpose of the Fourth Amendment, the Court's essentially property-based rationale can satisfactorily answer none of the questions posed above. That is reason enough to reject it. The *Jones* rule is relatively easily applied by police and courts; the rule announced today will not provide law enforcement officials with a bright line between the protected and the unprotected.[21] Only rarely will police know whether one private party has or has not been granted a sufficient possessory or other interest by another private party. Surely in this case the officers had no such knowledge. The Court's rule will ensnare defendants and police in needless litigation over factors that should not be determinative of Fourth Amendment rights.[22]

More importantly, the ruling today undercuts the force of the exclusionary rule in the one area in which its use is most certainly justified — the deterrence of bad-faith violations of the Fourth Amendment. This decision invites police to engage in patently unreasonable searches every time an automobile contains more than one occupant. Should something be found, only the owner of the vehicle, or of the item, will have standing to seek suppression, and the evidence will presumably be usable against the other occupants. The danger of such bad faith is especially high in cases such as this one where the officers are only after the passengers and can usually infer accurately that the driver is the owner. The suppression remedy for those owners in whose vehicles something is found and who are charged with crime is small consolation for all those owners *and* occupants whose privacy will be needlessly invaded by officers following mistaken hunches not rising to the level of probable cause but operated on in the knowledge that someone in a crowded car will probably be unprotected if contraband or incriminating evidence happens to be found. After this decision, police will have little to lose by unreasonably searching vehicles occupied by more than one person.

Of course, most police officers will decline the Court's invitation and will continue to do their jobs as best they can in accord with the Fourth Amendment. But the very purpose of the Bill of Rights was to answer the justified fear that governmental agents cannot be left totally to their own devices, and the Bill of Rights is enforceable in the courts because human experience teaches that not all such officials will otherwise adhere to the stated precepts. Some policemen simply do act in bad faith, even if for understandable ends, and some deterrent is needed. In the rush to limit the applicability of the exclusionary rule somewhere, anywhere, the Court ignores precedent, logic, and common sense to exclude the rule's operation

---

[21] Contrary to the assertions in the majority and concurring opinions, I do not agree that the Court's rule is faithful to the purposes of the Fourth Amendment but reject it only because it fails to provide a "bright line." As the discussion, *supra*, indicates, this dissent disagrees with the Court's view that petitioners lack a reasonable expectation of privacy. The Court's *ipse dixit* is not only unexplained but also is unjustified in light of what persons reasonably do, and should be entitled to, expect. My point in this portion of the opinion is that the Court's lack of faithfulness to the purposes of the Fourth Amendment does not have even the saving grace of providing an easily applied rule.

[22] To say that the Fourth Amendment goes beyond property rights, of course, is not to say that one not enjoying privacy in person would not be entitled to expect protection from unreasonable intrusions into the areas he owns, such as his house. *E.g., Alderman.*

from situations in which, paradoxically, it is justified and needed.

QUESTIONS AND NOTES

1. Should only those whose personal Fourth Amendment rights have been violated be permitted to invoke the exclusionary rule? Discuss all of the arguments that can be made on both sides of the question.

2. Assuming that you agree with (or at least accept) the Court's conclusion that Fourth Amendment rights are personal, should the Court adopt a broad view of standing (*Jones, Jeffers, Alderman*) or a narrower view (*Rakas*)? Explain.

3. Is *Rakas* an exclusionary rule case or a substantive Fourth Amendment case? If Rakas and King sued the officers who searched the car, would they win? Why? Why not?

4. Assuming that Fourth Amendment rights are personal, does merging the standing and substantive questions improve or retard analysis?

5. Why didn't Rakas and King have standing to challenge?

6. In view of Justice Powell's opinion, how would you assess defense counsel's performance?

7. Should the fact that this search involved an automobile rather than a house have been relevant to the resolution of the question in *Rakas*?

8. *Rakas* emphasizes that the defendant never alleged that he owned the guns or the shell casings. After *Salvucci* and *Rawlings*, it's doubtful that such an allegation would have done much good.

UNITED STATES v. SALVUCCI
448 U.S. 83 (1980)

MR. JUSTICE REHNQUIST delivered the opinion of the Court.

Relying on *Jones*, the Court of Appeals for the First Circuit held that since respondents were charged with crimes of possession, they were entitled to claim "automatic standing" to challenge the legality of the search which produced the evidence against them, without regard to whether they had an expectation of privacy in the premises searched. Today we hold that defendants charged with crimes of possession may only claim the benefits of the exclusionary rule if their own Fourth Amendment rights have in fact been violated. The automatic standing rule of *Jones* is therefore overruled.

I

Respondents, John Salvucci and Joseph Zackular, were charged in a federal indictment with 12 counts of unlawful possession of stolen mail. The 12 checks which formed the basis of the indictment had been seized by the Massachusetts police during the search of an apartment rented by respondent Zackular's mother. The search was conducted pursuant to a warrant.

Respondents filed a motion to suppress the checks on the ground that the affidavit supporting the application for the search warrant was inadequate to demonstrate probable cause. The District Court granted respondents' motions and ordered that the checks be suppressed.

II

[A]ttempts to vicariously assert violations of the Fourth Amendment rights of others have been repeatedly rejected by this Court. Most recently, in *Rakas*, we held that "it is proper to permit only defendants whose Fourth Amendment rights have been violated to benefit from the [exclusionary] rule's protections."

Even though the Court in *Jones* recognized that the exclusionary rule should only be available to protect defendants who have been the victims of an illegal search or seizure, the Court thought it necessary to establish an exception. In cases where possession of the seized evidence was an essential element of the offense charged, the Court held that the defendant was not obligated to establish that his own Fourth Amendment rights have been violated, but only that the search and seizure of the evidence was unconstitutional. Upon such a showing, the exclusionary rule would be available to prevent the admission of the evidence against the defendant.

The Court found that the prosecution of such possessory offenses presented a "special problem" which necessitated the departure from the then settled principles of Fourth Amendment "standing."[4] Two circumstances were found to require this exception. First, the Court found that in order to establish standing at a hearing on a motion to suppress, the defendant would often be "forced to allege facts the proof of which would tend, if indeed not be sufficient, to convict him," since several Courts of Appeals had "pinioned a defendant within this dilemma" by holding that evidence adduced at the motion to suppress could be used against the defendant at trial. The Court declined to embrace any rule which would require a defendant to assert his Fourth Amendment claims only at the risk of providing the prosecution with self-incriminating statements admissible at trial. The Court sought resolution of this dilemma by relieving the defendant of the obligation of establishing that his Fourth Amendment rights were violated by an illegal search or seizure.

The Court also commented that this rule would be beneficial for a second reason. Without a rule prohibiting a Government challenge to a defendant's "standing" to invoke the exclusionary rule in a possessory offense prosecution, the Government would be allowed the "advantage of contradictory positions." The Court reasoned that the Government ought not to be allowed to assert that the defendant possessed the goods for purposes of criminal liability, while simultaneously asserting that he did not possess them for the purposes of claiming the protections of the Fourth

---

[4] In *Rakas*, this Court discarded reliance on concepts of "standing" in determining whether a defendant is entitled to claim the protections of the exclusionary rule. The inquiry, after *Rakas*, is simply whether the defendant's rights were violated by the allegedly illegal search or seizure. Because *Jones* was decided at a time when "standing" was designated as a separate inquiry, we use that term for the purposes of re-examining that opinion.

Amendment. The Court found that "[i]t is not consonant with the amenities, to put it mildly, of the administration of criminal justice to sanction such squarely contradictory assertions of power by the Government." Thus in order to prevent both the risk that self-incrimination would attach to the assertion of Fourth Amendment rights, as well as to prevent the "vice of prosecutorial self-contradiction," the Court adopted the rule of "automatic standing."

In the 20 years which have lapsed since the Court's decision in *Jones*, the two reasons which led the Court to the rule of automatic standing have likewise been affected by time. This Court has held that testimony given by a defendant in support of a motion to suppress cannot be admitted as evidence of his guilt at trial. *Simmons v. United States*, 390 U.S. 377 (1968). Developments in the principles of Fourth Amendment standing, as well, clarify that a prosecutor may, with legal consistency and legitimacy, assert that a defendant charged with possession of a seized item did not have a privacy interest violated in the course of the search and seizure. We are convinced not only that the original tenets of the *Jones* decision have eroded, but also that no alternative principles exist to support retention of the rule.

B

We need not belabor the question of whether the "vice" of prosecutorial contradiction could alone support a rule countenancing the exclusion of probative evidence on the grounds that someone other than the defendant was denied a Fourth Amendment right. The simple answer is that the decisions of this Court, especially our most recent decision in *Rakas*, clearly establish that a prosecutor may simultaneously maintain that a defendant criminally possessed the seized good, but was not subject to a Fourth Amendment deprivation, without legal contradiction. To conclude that a prosecutor engaged in self-contradiction in *Jones*, the Court necessarily relied on the unexamined assumption that a defendant's possession of a seized good sufficient to establish criminal culpability was also sufficient to establish Fourth Amendment "standing." This assumption, however, even if correct at the time, is no longer so.[5]

The person in legal possession of a good seized during an illegal search has not necessarily been subject to a Fourth Amendment deprivation.[6] As we hold today in *Rawlings v. Kentucky*, legal possession of a seized good is not a proxy for determining whether the owner had a Fourth Amendment interest, for it does not invariably represent the protected Fourth Amendment interest. This Court has repeatedly repudiated the notion that "arcane distinctions developed in property and tort law" ought to control our Fourth Amendment inquiry. *Rakas*. In another

---

[5] Respondent Salvucci cites this Court's decision in *United States v. Jeffers*, 342 U.S. 48 (1951), as support for the view that legal ownership of the seized good was sufficient to confer Fourth Amendment "standing." In *Rakas*, however, we stated that "[s]tanding in *Jeffers* was based on Jeffers' possessory interest in *both* the premises searched and the property seized." 439 U.S. at 136. (Emphasis added.)

[6] Legal possession of the seized good may be sufficient in some circumstances to entitle a defendant to seek the return of the seized property if the seizure, as opposed to the search, was illegal. We need not explore this issue since respondents did not challenge the constitutionality of the seizure of the evidence.

section of the opinion in *Jones* itself, the Court concluded that, "it is unnecessary and ill-advised to import into the law surrounding the constitutional right to be free from unreasonable searches and seizures subtle distinctions, developed and refined by the common law in evolving the body of private property law . . . ."

While property ownership is clearly a factor to be considered in determining whether an individual's Fourth Amendment rights have been violated, property rights are neither the beginning nor the end of this Court's inquiry. In *Rakas*, this Court held that an illegal search only violates the rights of those who have "a legitimate expectation of privacy in the invaded place."

We simply decline to use possession of a seized good as a substitute for a factual finding that the owner of the good had a legitimate expectation of privacy in the area searched. In *Jones*, the Court held not only that automatic standing should be conferred on defendants charged with crimes of possession, but, alternatively, that Jones had actual standing because he was "legitimately on the premises" at the time of the search. In *Rakas*, this Court rejected the adequacy of this second *Jones* standard, finding that it was "too broad a gauge for measurement of Fourth Amendment rights." In language appropriate to our consideration of the automatic standing rule as well, we reasoned:

> In abandoning "legitimately on premises" for the doctrine that we an-
> nounce today, we are not forsaking a time-tested and workable rule, which
> has produced consistent results when applied, solely for the sake of fidelity
> to the values underlying the Fourth Amendment. Rather, we are rejecting
> blind adherence to a phrase which at most has superficial clarity and which
> conceals underneath that thin veneer all of the problems of line drawing
> which must be faced in any conscientious effort to apply the Fourth
> Amendment. Where the factual premises for a rule are so generally
> prevalent that little would be lost and much would be gained by abandoning
> case-by-case analysis, we have not hesitated to do so . . . . We would not
> wish to be understood as saying that legitimate presence on the premises
> is irrelevant to one's expectation of privacy, but it cannot be deemed
> controlling.

As in *Rakas*, we again reject "blind adherence" to the other underlying assumption in *Jones* that possession of the seized good is an acceptable measure of Fourth Amendment interests. As in *Rakas*, we find that the *Jones* standard "creates too broad a gauge for measurement of Fourth Amendment rights" and that we must instead engage in a "conscientious effort to apply the Fourth Amendment" by asking not merely whether the defendant had a possessory interest in the items seized, but whether he had an expectation of privacy in the area searched. Thus neither prosecutorial "vice," nor the underlying assumption of *Jones* that possession of a seized good is the equivalent of Fourth Amendment "standing" to challenge the search, can save the automatic standing rule.

C

This action comes to us as a challenge to a pretrial decision suppressing evidence. The respondents relied on automatic standing and did not attempt to establish that they had a legitimate expectation of privacy in the areas of Zackular's mother's home where the goods were seized. We therefore think it appropriate to remand so that respondents will have an opportunity to demonstrate, if they can, that their own Fourth Amendment rights were violated.

Reversed and remanded.

MR. JUSTICE MARSHALL, with whom MR. JUSTICE BRENNAN joins, dissenting.

Today the Court overrules the "automatic standing" rule of *Jones*, because it concludes that the rationale underpinning the rule has been "eroded." I do not share that view.

A ground for relieving the defendant charged with possession from the necessity of showing "an interest in the premises searched or the property seized" was that "to hold to the contrary . . . would be to permit the Government to have the advantage of contradictory positions as a basis for conviction," *Jones*. That is, since "possession both convicts and confers standing," the Government, which had charged the defendant with possession, would not be permitted to deny that he had standing. By holding today in *Rawlings*, that a person may assert a Fourth Amendment claim only if he has a privacy interest in the area that was searched, the Court has, to be sure, done away with that logical inconsistency. For reasons stated in my dissenting opinion in that case, I believe that holding is diametrically opposed to the meaning of the Fourth Amendment as it has always been understood.

The automatic standing rule is a salutary one which protects the rights of defendants and eliminates the wasteful requirement of making a preliminary showing of standing in pretrial proceedings involving possessory offenses, where the charge itself alleges an interest sufficient to support a Fourth Amendment claim. I dissent.

QUESTIONS AND NOTES

1. Explain how the government can consistently argue that the defendant possessed the items seized, but lacked standing to challenge the search?

2. Does *Rakas* support or oppose the *Salvucci* result?

RAWLINGS v. KENTUCKY
448 U.S. 98 (1980)

MR. JUSTICE REHNQUIST delivered the opinion of the Court.

I

In the middle of the afternoon on October 18, 1976, six police officers armed with a warrant for the arrest of one Lawrence Marquess on charges of drug distribution arrived at Marquess' house in Bowling Green, Ky. In the house at the time the police arrived were one of Marquess' housemates, Dennis Saddler, and four visitors, Keith Northern, Linda Braden, Vanessa Cox, and petitioner David Rawlings. While searching unsuccessfully in the house for Marquess, several police officers smelled marihuana smoke and saw marihuana seeds on the mantel in one of the bedrooms. After conferring briefly, Officers Eddie Railey and John Bruce left to obtain a search warrant. While Railey and Bruce were gone, the other four officers detained the occupants of the house in the living room, allowing them to leave only if they consented to a body search. Northern and Braden did consent to such a search and were permitted to depart. Saddler, Cox, and petitioner remained seated in the living room.

Approximately 45 minutes later, Railey and Bruce returned with a warrant authorizing them to search the house. Railey read the warrant to Saddler, Cox, and petitioner, and also read *"Miranda"* warnings from a card he carried in his pocket. At that time, Cox was seated on a couch with petitioner seated to her left. In the space between them was Cox's handbag.

After Railey finished his recitation, he approached petitioner and told him to stand. Officer Don Bivens simultaneously approached Cox and ordered her to empty the contents of her purse onto a coffee table in front of the couch. Among those contents were a jar containing 1,800 tablets of LSD and a number of smaller vials containing benzphetamine, methamphetamine, methyprylan, and pentobarbital, all of which are controlled substances under Kentucky law.

Upon pouring these objects out onto the coffee table, Cox turned to petitioner and told him "to take what was his." Petitioner, who was standing in response to Officer Railey's command, immediately claimed ownership of controlled substances. At that time, Railey searched petitioner's person and found $4,500 in cash in petitioner's shirt pocket and a knife in a sheath at petitioner's side. Railey then placed petitioner under formal arrest.

Petitioner was indicted for possession with intent to sell the various controlled substances recovered from Cox's purse. At the suppression hearing, he testified that he had flown into Bowling Green about a week before his arrest to look for a job and perhaps to attend the local university. He brought with him at that time the drugs later found in Cox's purse. Initially, petitioner stayed in the house where the arrest took place as the guest of Michael Swank, who shared the house with Marquess and Saddler. While at a party at that house, he met Cox and spent at least two nights of the next week on a couch at Cox's house.

On the morning of petitioner's arrest, Cox had dropped him off at Swank's house where he waited for her to return from class. At that time, he was carrying the drugs in a green bank bag. When Cox returned to the house to meet him, petitioner dumped the contents of the bank bag into Cox's purse. Although there is dispute over the discussion that took place, petitioner testified that he "asked her if she would carry this for me, and she said, 'yes' . . . ."[7] Petitioner then left the room to

---

[7] At petitioner's trial, Vanessa Cox described the transfer of possession quite differently. She testified that, as she and petitioner were getting ready to leave the house, petitioner asked "would you please carry this for me" and simultaneously dumped the drugs into her purse. According to Cox, she looked into her purse, saw the drugs, and said "would you please take this, I do not want this in my purse."

use the bathroom and, by the time he returned, discovered that the police had arrived to arrest Marquess.

The trial court denied petitioner's motion to suppress the drugs and the money and to exclude the statements made by petitioner when the police discovered the drugs. According to the trial court, the warrant obtained by the police authorized them to search Cox's purse. Moreover, even if the search of the purse was illegal, the trial court believed that petitioner lacked "standing" to contest that search. Finally, the trial court believed that the search that revealed the money and the knife was permissible "under the exigencies of the situation."

The Kentucky Court of Appeals affirmed. Disagreeing with the trial court, the appellate court held that petitioner did have "standing" to dispute the legality of the search of Cox's purse but that the detention of the five persons present in the house and the subsequent searches were legitimate because the police had probable cause to arrest all five people in the house when they smelled the marihuana smoke and saw the marihuana seeds.

The Supreme Court of Kentucky in turn affirmed, but again on a somewhat different rationale. According to the Supreme Court, petitioner had no "standing" because he had no "legitimate or reasonable expectation of freedom from governmental intrusion" into Cox's purse. *Rakas*. Moreover, according to the Supreme Court, the search uncovering the money in petitioner's pocket, which search followed petitioner's admission that he owned the drugs in Cox's purse, was justifiable as incident to a lawful arrest based on probable cause.

II

In this Court, petitioner claims that he did have a reasonable expectation of privacy in Cox's purse so as to allow him to challenge the legality of the search of that purse.[8]

In holding that petitioner could not challenge the legality of the search of Cox's purse, the Supreme Court of Kentucky looked primarily to our then recent decision in *Rakas* where we abandoned a separate inquiry into a defendant's "standing" to contest an allegedly illegal search in favor of an inquiry that focused directly on the

---

Petitioner allegedly replied "okay, just a minute, I will," and then went out of the room. At that point the police entered the house. David Saddler, who was in the next room at the time of the transfer, corroborated Cox's version of the events, testifying that he heard Cox say "I do not want this in my purse" and that he heard petitioner reply "don't worry" or something to that effect.

Although none of the lower courts specifically found that Cox did not consent to the bailment, the trial court clearly was skeptical about petitioner's version of events:

> The Court finds it unbelievable that just of his own volition, David Rawlings put the contraband in the purse of Mrs. Cox just a minute before the officers knocked on the door. He had been carrying these things around Bowling Green in a bank deposit sack for days, either on his person or in his pocket, and it is unworthy of belief that just immediately before the officers knocked on the door that he put them in the purse of Vanessa Cox. It is far more plausible to believe that he saw the officers pull up out front and then elected to "push them off" on Vanessa Cox, believing that search was probable, possible, and emminent [*sic*].

[8] Petitioner also claims that he is entitled to "automatic standing" to contest the legality of the search that uncovered the drugs. Our decision today in *Salvucci* disposes of this contention adversely to him.

substance of the defendant's claim that he or she possessed a "legitimate expectation of privacy" in the area searched. In the present case, the Supreme Court of Kentucky looked to the "totality of the circumstances," including petitioner's own admission at the suppression hearing that he did not believe that Cox's purse would be free from governmental intrusion,[9] and held that petitioner "[had] not made a sufficient showing that his legitimate or reasonable expectations of privacy were violated" by the search of the purse.

We believe that the record in this case supports that conclusion. Petitioner, of course, bears the burden of proving not only that the search of Cox's purse was illegal, but also that he had a legitimate expectation of privacy in that purse. At the time petitioner dumped thousands of dollars' worth of illegal drugs into Cox's purse, he had known her for only a few days. According to Cox's uncontested testimony, petitioner had never sought or received access to her purse prior to that sudden bailment. *Contrast Jones.* Nor did petitioner have any right to exclude other persons from access to Cox's purse. *See Rakas.* In fact, Cox testified that Bob Stallons, a longtime acquaintance and frequent companion of Cox's, had free access to her purse on the very morning of the arrest had rummaged through its contents in search of a hairbrush. Moreover, even assuming that petitioner's version of the bailment is correct and that Cox did consent to the transfer of possession, the precipitous nature of the transaction hardly supports a reasonable inference that petitioner took normal precautions to maintain his privacy. In addition to all the foregoing facts, the record also contains a frank admission by petitioner that he had no subjective expectation that Cox's purse would remain free from governmental intrusion, an admission credited by both the trial court and the Supreme Court of Kentucky.

Petitioner contends nevertheless that, because he claimed ownership of the drugs in Cox's purse, he should be entitled to challenge the search regardless of his expectation of privacy. We disagree. While petitioner's ownership of the drugs is undoubtedly one fact to be considered in this case, *Rakas* emphatically rejected the notion that "arcane" concepts of property law ought to control the ability to claim the protections of the Fourth Amendment. Had petitioner placed his drugs in plain view, he would still have owned them, but he could not claim any legitimate expectation of privacy. Prior to *Rakas*, petitioner might have been given "standing" in such a case to challenge a "search" that netted those drugs but probably would have lost his claim on the merits. After *Rakas*, the two inquiries merge into one: whether governmental officials violated any legitimate expectation of privacy held by petitioner.

In sum, we find no reason to overturn the lower court's conclusion that petitioner had no legitimate expectation of privacy in Cox's purse at the time of the search.

---

[9] Under questioning by his own counsel, petitioner testified as follows:

Q Did you feel that Vannessa [*sic*] Cox's purse would be free from the intrusion of the officers as you sat there? When you put the pills in her purse, did you feel that they would be free from governmental intrusion?

A No sir.

MR. JUSTICE BLACKMUN, concurring.

I join the Court's opinion, but I write separately to explain my somewhat different approach. In my view, *Rakas* recognized two analytically distinct but "invariably intertwined" issues of substantive Fourth Amendment jurisprudence. The first is "whether [a] disputed search or seizure has infringed an interest of the defendant which the Fourth Amendment was designed to protect;" the second is whether "the challenged search or seizure violated [that] Fourth Amendment righ[t]." The first of these questions is answered by determining whether the defendant has a "legitimate expectation of privacy" that has been invaded by a governmental search or seizure. The second is answered by determining whether applicable cause and warrant requirements have been properly observed.

I agree with the Court that these two inquiries "merge into one," in the sense that both are to be addressed under the principles of Fourth Amendment analysis developed in *Katz* and its progeny. But I do not read today's decision, or Rakas, as holding that it is improper for lower courts to treat these inquiries as distinct components of a Fourth Amendment claim. Indeed, I am convinced that it would invite confusion to hold otherwise. It remains possible for a defendant to prove that his legitimate interest of privacy was invaded, and yet fail to prove that the police acted illegally in doing so. And it is equally possible for a defendant to prove that the police acted illegally, and yet fail to prove that his own privacy interest was affected.

Nor do I read this Court's decisions to hold that property interests cannot be, in some circumstances at least, weighty factors in establishing the existence of fourth Amendment rights. Not every concept of ownership or possession is "arcane." Not every interest in property exists only in the desiccated atmosphere of ancient maxims and dusty books. Earlier this Term the Court recognized that "the right to exclude" is an essential element of modern property rights. *Kaiser Aetna v. United States*, 444 U.S. 164, at 179–180 (1979). In my view, that "right to exclude" often may be a principal determinant in the establishment of a legitimate Fourth Amendment interest. Accordingly, I would confine analysis to the facts of this case. On those facts, however, I agree that petitioner's possessory interest in the vials of controlled substances is not sufficient to create a privacy interest in Vanessa Cox's purse, and that such an interest was not otherwise conferred by any agreement between petitioner and Cox.

MR. JUSTICE MARSHALL, with whom MR. JUSTICE BRENNAN joins, dissenting.

The vials of pills found in Vanessa Cox's purse and petitioner's admission that they belonged to him established his guilt conclusively. The State concedes, as it must, that the search of the purse was unreasonable and in violation of the Fourth Amendment, *see Ybarra*, and the Court assumes that the detention which led to the search, the seizure, and the admissions also violated the Fourth Amendment. Nevertheless, the Court upholds the conviction. I dissent.

I

The Court holds first that petitioner may not object to the introduction of the pills into evidence because the unconstitutional actions of the police officers did not violate his personal Fourth Amendment rights. To reach this result, the Court holds that the Constitution protects an individual against unreasonable searches and seizures only if he has "a 'legitimate expectation of privacy' in the area searched." This holding cavalierly rejects the fundamental principle, unquestioned until today, that an interest in either the place searched or the property seized is sufficient to invoke the Constitution's protections against unreasonable searches and seizures.

The Court's examination of previous Fourth Amendment cases begins and ends — as it must if it is to reach its desired conclusion — with *Rakas*. Contrary to the Court's assertion, however, *Rakas* did not establish that the Fourth Amendment protects individuals against unreasonable searches and seizures only if they have a privacy interest in the place searched. The question before the Court in *Rakas* was whether the defendants could establish their right to Fourth Amendment protection simply by showing that they were "legitimately on [the] premises" searched. Overruling that portion of *Jones*, the Court held that when a Fourth Amendment objection is based on an interest in the place searched, the defendant must show an actual invasion of his personal privacy interest. The petitioners in *Rakas* did not claim that they had standing either under the *Jones* automatic standing rule for persons charged with possessory offenses, which the Court overrules today, see *Salvucci*, or because their possessory interest in the items seized gave them "actual standing." No Fourth Amendment claim based on an interest in the property seized was before the Court, and, consequently, the Court did not and could not have decided whether such a claim could be maintained. In fact, the Court expressly disavowed any intention to foreclose such a claim ("This is not to say that such [casual] visitors could not contest the lawfulness of the seizure of evidence or the search if their own property were seized during the search," and suggested its continuing validity ("[P]etitioners' claims must fail. They asserted neither a property nor a possessory interest in the automobile, *nor an interest in the property seized*," (emphasis supplied)).

The decision today, then, is not supported by the only case directly cited in its favor. Further, the Court has ignored a long tradition embodying the opposite view. *United States v. Jeffers*, 342 U.S. 48 (1951), for example, involved a seizure of contraband alleged to belong to the defendant from a hotel room occupied by his two aunts. The Court rejected the Government's argument that because the search of the room did not invade Jeffers' privacy he lacked standing to suppress the evidence. It held that standing to object to the seizure could not be separated from standing to object to the search, for "[t]he search and seizure are . . . incapable of being untied." The Court then concluded that Jeffers "unquestionably had standing . . . unless the contraband nature of the narcotics seized precluded his assertion, for purposes of the exclusionary rule, of *a property interest therein*." (emphasis supplied).

Similarly, *Jones* is quite plainly premised on the understanding that an interest in the seized property is sufficient to establish that the defendant "himself was the victim of an invasion of privacy." The Court observed that the "conventional standing requirement" required the defendant to "claim either to have *owned or possessed the seized property* or to have had a substantial possessory interest in the premises searched," (emphasis supplied). The Court relaxed that rule for defendants charged with possessory offenses because "[t]he same element . . . which has caused a dilemma, *i.e.,* that *possession both convicts and confers standing,* eliminates any necessity for a preliminary showing of an interest in the premises searched *or the property seized,* which ordinarily is required when standing is challenged." (emphasis supplied). Instead, "[t]he possession on the basis of which petitioner is to be and was convicted suffices to give him standing," *id.* at 264.

The Court's decision today is not wrong, however, simply because it is contrary to our previous cases. It is wrong because it is contrary to the Fourth Amendment, which guarantees that "[t]he right of the people to be secure in their persons, houses, papers, and effects, against unreasonable searches and seizures, shall not be violated." The Court's reading of the Amendment is far too narrow. The Court misreads the guarantee of security *"in* their persons, houses, papers, and effects, *against* unreasonable searches and seizures" to afford protection only against unreasonable searches and seizures *of* persons and places.

The Fourth Amendment, it seems to me, provides in plain language that if one's security in one's "effects" is disturbed by an unreasonable search and seizure, one has been the victim of a constitutional violation; and so it has always been understood. Therefore the Court's insistence that in order to challenge the legality of the search one must also assert a protected interest in the premises is misplaced. The interest in the item seized is quite enough to establish that the defendant's personal Fourth Amendment rights have been invaded by the government's conduct.

The idea that a person cannot object to a search unless he can show an interest in the premises, even though he is the owner of the seized property, was squarely rejected almost 30 years ago in *Jeffers.* There the Court stated:

> The Government argues . . . that the search did not invade respondent's privacy and that he, therefore, lacked the necessary standing to suppress the evidence seized. The significant act, it says, is the seizure of the goods of the respondent without a warrant. We do not believe the events are so easily isolable. Rather they are bound together by one sole purpose — to locate and seize the narcotics of respondent. The search and seizure are, therefore, incapable of being untied. To hold that this search and seizure were lawful as to the respondent would permit a quibbling distinction to overturn a principle which was designed to protect a fundamental right.

When the government seizes a person's property, it interferes with his constitutionally protected right to be secure in his effects. That interference gives him the right to challenge the reasonableness of the government's conduct, including the seizure. If the defendant's property was seized as the result of an unreasonable search, the seizure cannot be other than unreasonable.

In holding that the Fourth Amendment protects only those with a privacy interest in the place searched, and not those with an ownership or possessory interest in the things seized, the Court has turned the development of the law of search and seizure on its head. The history of the Fourth Amendment shows that it was designed to protect property interests as well as privacy interests; in fact, until *Jones* the question whether a person's Fourth Amendment rights had been violated turned on whether he had a property interest in the place searched or the items seized. *Jones* and *Katz* expanded our view of the protections afforded by the Fourth Amendment by recognizing that privacy interests are protected even if they do not arise from property rights. But that recognition was never intended to exclude interests that had historically been sheltered by the Fourth Amendment from its protection. Neither *Jones* nor *Katz* purported to provide an exclusive definition of the interests protected by the Fourth Amendment. Indeed, as *Katz* recognized: "That Amendment protects individual privacy against certain kinds of governmental intrusion, but its protections go further, and often have nothing to do with privacy at all." Those decisions freed Fourth Amendment jurisprudence from the constraints of "subtle distinctions, developed and refined by the common law in evolving the body of private property law which, more than almost any other branch of law, has been shaped by distinctions whose validity is largely historical." Rejection of those finely drawn distinctions as irrelevant to the concerns of the Fourth Amendment did not render property rights wholly outside its protection, however. Not every concept involving property rights, we should remember, is "arcane."

In fact, the Court rather inconsistently denies that property rights may, by themselves, entitle one to the protection of the Fourth Amendment, but simultaneously suggests that a person may claim such protection only if his expectation of privacy in the premises searched is so strong that he may exclude all others from that place. Such a harsh threshold requirement was not imposed even in the heyday of a property rights oriented Fourth Amendment.

III

In the words of Mr. Justice Frankfurter: "A decision [of a Fourth Amendment claim] may turn on whether one gives that Amendment a place second to none in the Bill of Rights, or considers it on the whole a kind of nuisance, a serious impediment in the war against crime." *Harris v. United States*, 331 U.S. 145, 157 (1947) (dissenting opinion). Today a majority of the Court has substantially cut back the protection afforded by the Fourth Amendment and the ability of the people to claim that protection, apparently out of concern lest the government's ability to obtain criminal convictions be impeded. A slow and steady erosion of the ability of victims of unconstitutional searches and seizures to obtain a remedy for the invasion of their rights saps the constitutional guarantee of its life just as surely as would a substantive limitation. Because we are called on to decide whether evidence should be excluded only when a search has been "successful," it is easy to forget that the standards we announce determine what government conduct is reasonable in searches and seizures directed at persons who turn out to be innocent as well as those who are guilty. I continue to believe that ungrudging application of the Fourth Amendment is indispensable to preserving the liberties of a democratic society. Accordingly, I dissent.

QUESTIONS AND NOTES

1.   Is it clear to you that the search which produced the drugs was unlawful? If you represented the government could you have made a case that the search was lawful?

2.   If the Government could have established that the search was lawful, why do you suppose that it didn't try?

3.   Why didn't Rawlings have a reasonable expectation of privacy in Cox's purse?

4.   Would (should) the case have been different if Rawlings had (with Cox's permission) placed a nude photograph of himself in her purse because he was embarrassed for a stranger to see it, and sued the police officer for violating his constitutional rights?

5.   We now turn to *Minnesota v. Carter*, where the Court further tightened the concept of standing.

MINNESOTA v. CARTER
525 U.S. 83 (1998)

CHIEF JUSTICE REHNQUIST delivered the opinion of the Court.

Respondents and the lessee of an apartment were sitting in one of its rooms, bagging cocaine. While so engaged they were observed by a police officer, who looked through a drawn window blind. The Supreme Court of Minnesota held that the officer's viewing was a search which violated respondents' Fourth Amendment rights. We hold that no such violation occurred.

James Thielen, a police officer in the Twin Cities' suburb of Eagan, Minnesota, went to an apartment building to investigate a tip from a confidential informant. The informant said that he had walked by the window of a ground-floor apartment and had seen people putting a white powder into bags. The officer looked in the same window through a gap in the closed blind and observed the bagging operation for several minutes. He then notified headquarters, which began preparing affidavits for a search warrant while he returned to the apartment building. When two men left the building in a previously identified Cadillac, the police stopped the car. Inside were respondents Carter and Johns. As the police opened the door of the car to let Johns out, they observed a black zippered pouch and a handgun, later determined to be loaded, on the vehicle's floor. Carter and Johns were arrested, and a later police search of the vehicle the next day discovered pagers, a scale, and 47 grams of cocaine in plastic sandwich bags.

After seizing the car, the police returned to Apartment 103 and arrested the occupant, Kimberly Thompson, who is not a party to this appeal. A search of the apartment pursuant to a warrant revealed cocaine residue on the kitchen table and plastic baggies similar to those found in the Cadillac. Thielen identified Carter, Johns, and Thompson as the three people he had observed placing the powder into baggies. The police later learned that while Thompson was the lessee of the apartment, Carter and Johns lived in Chicago and had come to the apartment for the sole purpose of packaging the cocaine. Carter and Johns had never been to the apartment before and were only in the apartment for approximately 2 1/2 hours. In return for the use of the apartment, Carter and Johns had given Thompson one-eighth of an ounce of the cocaine.

Carter and Johns were charged with conspiracy to commit controlled substance crime in the first degree and aiding and abetting in a controlled substance crime in the first degree, in violation of Minnesota [law]. They moved to suppress all evidence obtained from the apartment and the Cadillac, as well as to suppress several post-arrest incriminating statements they had made. They argued that Thielen's initial observation of their drug packaging activities was an unreasonable search in violation of the Fourth Amendment and that all evidence obtained as a result of this unreasonable search was inadmissible as fruit of the poisonous tree. The Minnesota trial court held that since, unlike the defendant in *Minnesota v. Olson*, 495 U.S. 91 (1990), Carter and Johns were not overnight social guests but temporary out-of-state visitors, they were not entitled to claim the protection of the Fourth Amendment against the government intrusion into the apartment. The trial court also concluded that Thielen's observation was not a search within the meaning of the Fourth Amendment. After a trial, Carter and Johns were each convicted of both offenses. The Minnesota Court of Appeals held that the respondent Carter did not have "standing" to object to Thielen's actions because his claim that he was predominantly a social guest was "inconsistent with the only evidence concerning his stay in the apartment, which indicates that he used it for a business purpose — to package drugs."

A divided Minnesota Supreme Court reversed, holding that respondents had "standing" to claim the protection of the Fourth Amendment because they had " 'a legitimate expectation of privacy in the invaded place.' " The court noted that even though "society does not recognize as valuable the task of bagging cocaine, we conclude that society does recognize as valuable the right of property owners or leaseholders to invite persons into the privacy of their homes to conduct a common task, be it legal or illegal activity. We, therefore, hold that [respondents] had standing to bring [their] motion to suppress the evidence gathered as a result of Thielen's observations." Based upon its conclusion that the respondents had "standing" to raise their Fourth Amendment claims, the court went on to hold that Thielen's observation constituted a search of the apartment under the Fourth Amendment, and that the search was unreasonable. We granted certiorari and now reverse.

The Minnesota courts analyzed whether respondents had a legitimate expectation of privacy under the rubric of "standing" doctrine, an analysis which this Court expressly rejected 20 years ago in *Rakas*. In that case, we held that automobile passengers could not assert the protection of the Fourth Amendment against the seizure of incriminating evidence from a vehicle where they owned neither the vehicle nor the evidence. Central to our analysis was the idea that in determining whether a defendant is able to show the violation of his (and not someone else's) Fourth Amendment rights, the "definition of those rights is more properly placed within the purview of substantive Fourth Amendment law than within that of standing." Thus, we held that in order to claim the protection of the Fourth

Amendment, a defendant must demonstrate that he personally has an expectation of privacy in the place searched, and that his expectation is reasonable; *i.e.*, one which has "a source outside of the Fourth Amendment, either by reference to concepts of real or personal property law or to understandings that are recognized and permitted by society."

The Fourth Amendment guarantees:

> The right of the people to be secure in their persons, houses, papers, and effects, against unreasonable searches and seizures, shall not be violated, and no Warrants shall issue, but upon probable cause, supported by Oath or affirmation, and particularly describing the place to be searched, and the persons or things to be seized.

The Amendment protects persons against unreasonable searches of "their persons [and] houses" and thus indicates that the Fourth Amendment is a personal right that must be invoked by an individual. *See Katz.* [T]he Fourth Amendment protects people, not places"). But the extent to which the Fourth Amendment protects people may depend upon where those people are. We have held that "capacity to claim the protection of the Fourth Amendment depends . . . upon whether the person who claims the protection of the Amendment has a legitimate expectation of privacy in the invaded place." *Rakas. See also Rawlings.*

The text of the Amendment suggests that its protections extend only to people in "their" houses. But we have held that in some circumstances a person may have a legitimate expectation of privacy in the house of someone else. In *Minnesota v. Olson*, 495 U.S. 91, (1990), for example, we decided that an overnight guest in a house had the sort of expectation of privacy that the Fourth Amendment protects. We said:

> To hold that an overnight guest has a legitimate expectation of privacy in his host's home merely recognizes the everyday expectations of privacy that we all share. Staying overnight in another's home is a long-standing social custom that serves functions recognized as valuable by society. We stay in others' homes when we travel to a strange city for business or pleasure, we visit our parents, children, or more distant relatives out of town, when we are in between jobs, or homes, or when we house-sit for a friend . . . . From the overnight guest's perspective, he seeks shelter in another's home precisely because it provides him with privacy, a place where he and his possessions will not be disturbed by anyone but his host and those his host allows inside. We are at our most vulnerable when we are asleep because we cannot monitor our own safety or the security of our belongings. It is for this reason that, although we may spend all day in public places, when we cannot sleep in our own home we seek out another private place to sleep, whether it be a hotel room, or the home of a friend.

In *Jones v. United States*, the defendant seeking to exclude evidence resulting from a search of an apartment had been given the use of the apartment by a friend. He had clothing in the apartment, had slept there " 'maybe a night,' " and at the time was the sole occupant of the apartment. But while the holding of *Jones* — that a search of the apartment violated the defendant's Fourth Amendment rights — is still valid, its statement that "anyone legitimately on the premises where a search occurs may challenge its legality," was expressly repudiated in *Rakas*. Thus an overnight guest in a home may claim the protection of the Fourth Amendment, but one who is merely present with the consent of the householder may not.

Respondents here were obviously not overnight guests, but were essentially present for a business transaction and were only in the home a matter of hours. There is no suggestion that they had a previous relationship with Thompson, or that there was any other purpose to their visit. Nor was there anything similar to the overnight guest relationship in *Olson* to suggest a degree of acceptance into the household.[1] While the apartment was a dwelling place for Thompson, it was for these respondents simply a place to do business.

Property used for commercial purposes is treated differently for Fourth Amendment purposes than residential property. "An expectation of privacy in commercial premises, however, is different from, and indeed less than, a similar expectation in an individual's home." And while it was a "home" in which respondents were present, it was not their home. Similarly, the Court has held that in some circumstances a worker can claim Fourth Amendment protection over his own workplace. *See, e.g., O'Connor v. Ortega*, 480 U.S. 709 (1987). But there is no indication that respondents in this case had nearly as significant a connection to Thompson's apartment as the worker in *O'Connor* had to his own private office.

If we regard the overnight guest in *Minnesota v. Olson* as typifying those who may claim the protection of the Fourth Amendment in the home of another, and one merely "legitimately on the premises" as typifying those who may not do so, the present case is obviously somewhere in between. But the purely commercial nature of the transaction engaged in here, the relatively short period of time on the premises, and the lack of any previous connection between respondents and the householder, all lead us to conclude that respondents' situation is closer to that of one simply permitted on the premises. We therefore hold that any search which may have occurred did not violate their Fourth Amendment rights.

Because we conclude that respondents had no legitimate expectation of privacy in the apartment, we need not decide whether the police officer's observation constituted a "search." The judgment of the Supreme Court of Minnesota is accordingly reversed, and the cause is remanded for proceedings not inconsistent with this opinion.

It is so ordered.

---

[1] Justice GINSBURG's dissent would render the operative language in *Minnesota v. Olson*, almost entirely superfluous. There, we explained the justification for extending Fourth Amendment protection to the overnight visitor: "Staying overnight in another's home is a long-standing social custom that serves functions recognized as valuable by society . . . . We are at our most vulnerable when we are asleep because we cannot monitor our own safety or the security of our belongings." If any short-term business visit by a stranger entitles the visitor to share the Fourth Amendment protection of the lease holder's home, the Court's explanation of its holding in *Olson* was quite unnecessary.

JUSTICE SCALIA, with whom JUSTICE THOMAS joins, concurring.

I join the opinion of the Court because I believe it accurately applies our recent case law, including *Minnesota v. Olson*. I write separately to express my view that that case law — like the submissions of the parties in this case — gives short shrift to the text of the Fourth Amendment, and to the well and long understood meaning of that text. Specifically, it leaps to apply the fuzzy standard of "legitimate expectation of privacy" — a consideration that is often relevant to whether a search or seizure covered by the Fourth Amendment is "unreasonable" — to the threshold question whether a search or seizure covered by the Fourth Amendment has occurred. If that latter question is addressed first and analyzed under the text of the Constitution as traditionally understood, the present case is not remotely difficult.

The Fourth Amendment protects "[t]he right of the people to be secure in *their* persons, houses, papers, and effects, against unreasonable searches and seizures . . . ." (emphasis added). It must be acknowledged that the phrase "their . . . houses" in this provision is, in isolation, ambiguous. It could mean "their respective houses," so that the protection extends to each person only in his *own* house. But it could also mean "their respective and each other's houses," so that each person would be protected even when visiting the house of someone else. As today's opinion for the Court suggests, however, it is not linguistically possible to give the provision the latter, expansive interpretation with respect to "houses" without giving it the same interpretation with respect to the nouns that are parallel to "houses" — "persons, . . . papers, and effects" — which would give me a constitutional right not to have your person unreasonably searched. This is so absurd that it has to my knowledge never been contemplated. The obvious meaning of the provision is that *each* person has the right to be secure against unreasonable searches and seizures in *his own* person, house, papers, and effects.

The Founding-era materials that I have examined confirm that this was the understood meaning. (Strangely, these materials went unmentioned by the State and its *amici* — unmentioned even in the State's reply brief, even though respondents had thrown down the gauntlet: "In briefs totaling over 100 pages, the State of Minnesota, the *amici* 26 attorneys general, and the Solicitor General of the United States of America have not mentioned one word about the history and purposes of the Fourth Amendment or the intent of the framers of that amendment.")

That "their . . . houses" was understood to mean "their respective houses" would have been clear to anyone who knew the English and early American law of arrest and trespass that underlay the Fourth Amendment. The people's protection against unreasonable search and seizure in their "houses" was drawn from the English common-law maxim, "A man's home is *his* castle." As far back as *Semayne's Case* of 1604, the leading English case for that proposition (and a case cited by Coke in his discussion of the proposition that Magna Carta outlawed general warrants based on mere surmise), the King's Bench proclaimed that "the house of any one is not a castle or privilege but for himself, and shall not extend to protect any person who flies to his house."

Of course this is not to say that the Fourth Amendment protects only the Lord of the Manor who holds his estate in fee simple. People call a house "their" home when legal title is in the bank, when they rent it, and even when they merely occupy it rent-free — *so long as they actually live there.* That this is the criterion of the people's protection against government intrusion into "their" houses is established by the leading American case of *Oystead v. Shed*, 13 Mass. 520 (1816), which held it a trespass for the sheriff to break into a dwelling to capture a boarder who lived there. The court reasoned that the "inviolability of dwelling-houses" described by Foster, Hale, and Coke extends to "the occupier or any of his family . . . who have their domicile or ordinary residence there," including "a boarder or a servant" "who have made the house *their* home." But, it added, "the house shall not be made a sanctuary" for one such as "a stranger, or perhaps a visitor," who "upon a pursuit, take[s] refuge in the house of another," for "the house is not *his* castle; and the officer may break open the doors or windows in order to execute his process."

Thus, in deciding the question presented today we write upon a slate that is far from clean. The text of the Fourth Amendment, the common-law background against which it was adopted, and the understandings consistently displayed after its adoption make the answer clear. We were right to hold in *Chapman v. United States*, 365 U.S. 610 (1961), that the Fourth Amendment protects an apartment tenant against an unreasonable search of his dwelling, even though he is only a leaseholder. And we were right to hold in *Bumper v. North Carolina*, 391 U.S. 543 (1968), that an unreasonable search of a grandmother's house violated her resident grandson's Fourth Amendment rights because the area searched "was *his* home." (emphasis added). We went to the absolute limit of what text and tradition permit in *Minnesota v. Olson*, when we protected a mere overnight guest against an unreasonable search of his hosts' apartment. But whereas it is plausible to regard a person's overnight lodging as at least his "temporary" residence, it is entirely impossible to give that characterization to an apartment that he uses to package cocaine. Respondents here were not searched in "their . . . hous[e]" under any interpretation of the phrase that bears the remotest relationship to the well understood meaning of the Fourth Amendment.

The dissent believes that "[o]ur obligation to produce coherent results" requires that we ignore this clear text and four-century-old tradition, and apply instead the notoriously unhelpful test adopted in a "benchmar[k]" decision that is 31 years old. [C]iting *Katz*. In my view, the only thing the past three decades have established about the *Katz* test (which has come to mean the test enunciated by Justice Harlan's separate concurrence in *Katz* is that, unsurprisingly, those "actual (subjective) expectation[s] of privacy" "that society is prepared to recognize as 'reasonable'" bear an uncanny resemblance to those expectations of privacy that this Court considers reasonable. When that self-indulgent test is employed (as the dissent would employ it here) to determine whether a "search or seizure" within the meaning of the Constitution has *occurred* (as opposed to whether that "search or seizure" is an "unreasonable" one), it has no plausible foundation in the text of the Fourth Amendment. That provision did not guarantee some generalized "right of privacy" and leave it to this Court to determine which particular manifestations of the value of privacy "society is prepared to recognize as 'reasonable.'" Rather, it enumerated ("persons, houses, papers, and effects") the objects of privacy protection to which the *Constitution* would extend, leaving further expansion to the good judgment, not of this Court, but of the people through their representatives in the legislature.[3]

The dissent may be correct that a person invited into someone else's house to engage in a common business (even common monkey-business, so to speak) *ought* to be protected against government searches of the room in which that business is conducted; and that persons invited in to deliver milk or pizza (whom the dissent dismisses as "classroom hypotheticals," as opposed, presumably, to flesh-and-blood hypotheticals) ought *not* to be protected against government searches of the rooms that they occupy. I am not sure of the answer to those policy questions. But I am sure that the answer is not remotely contained in the Constitution, which means that it is left — as *many*, indeed *most*, important questions are left — to the judgment of state and federal legislators. We go beyond our proper role as judges in a democratic society when we restrict the people's power to govern themselves over the full range of policy choices that the Constitution has left available to them.

JUSTICE KENNEDY, concurring.

I join the Court's opinion, for its reasoning is consistent with my view that almost all social guests have a legitimate expectation of privacy, and hence protection against unreasonable searches, in their host's home.

The Fourth Amendment protects "[t]he right of the people to be secure in their . . . houses," and it is beyond dispute that the home is entitled to special protection as the center of the private lives of our people. Security of the home must be guarded by the law in a world where privacy is diminished by enhanced surveillance and sophisticated communication systems. As is well established, however, Fourth Amendment protection, though dependent upon spatial definition, is in essence a personal right. Thus, as the Court held in *Rakas* there are limits on who may assert it.

The dissent, as I interpret it, does not question *Rakas* or the principle that not all persons in the company of the property owner have the owner's right to assert the spatial protection. *Rakas*, it is true, involved automobiles, where the necessities of law enforcement permit more latitude to the police than ought to be extended to houses. The analysis in *Rakas* was not conceived, however, as a utilitarian exception to accommodate the needs of law enforcement. The Court's premise was a more

---

[3] The dissent asserts that I ["undervalue"] the *Katz* Court's observation that "the Fourth Amendment protects people, not places." That catchy slogan would be a devastating response to someone who maintained that *a location* could claim protection of the Fourth Amendment — someone who asserted, perhaps, that "primeval forests have rights, too." *Cf.* Stone, *Should Trees Have Standing? — Toward Legal Rights For Natural Objects*, 45 S. CAL. L. REV. 450 (1972). The issue here, however, is the less druidical one of whether respondents (who are people) have suffered a violation of *their* right "to be secure in their persons, houses, papers, and effects, against unreasonable searches and seizures." That the Fourth Amendment does not protect places is simply unresponsive to the question whether the Fourth Amendment protects people in other people's homes. In saying this, I do not, as the dissent claims, clash with "the *leitmotif* of Justice Harlan's concurring opinion" in *Katz*, *au contraire* (or, to be more Wagnerian, *im Gegenteil*), in this regard I am entirely in harmony with that opinion, and it is the dissent that sings from another opera. "As the Court's opinion states, 'the Fourth Amendment protects people, not places.' The question, however, is what protection it affords to those people. Generally, as here, the answer to that question requires reference to a 'place.'"

fundamental one. Fourth Amendment rights are personal, and when a person objects to the search of a place and invokes the exclusionary rule, he or she must have the requisite connection to that place. The analysis in *Rakas* must be respected with reference to dwellings unless that precedent is to be overruled or so limited to its facts that its underlying principle is, in the end, repudiated.

As to the English authorities that were the historical basis for the Fourth Amendment, the Court has observed that scholars dispute their proper interpretation. See, *e.g., Payton. Semayne's Case*, says that "the house of every one is to him as his castle and fortress" and the home is privileged for the homeowner, "his family," and "his own proper goods." Read narrowly, the protections recognized in *Semayne's Case* might have been confined to the context of civil process, and so be of limited application to enforcement of the criminal law. Even if, at the time of *Semayne's Case*, a man's home was not his castle with respect to incursion by the King in a criminal matter, that would not be dispositive of the question before us. The axiom that a man's home is his castle, or the statement attributed to Pitt that the King cannot enter and all his force dares not cross the threshold has acquired over time a power and an independent significance justifying a more general assurance of personal security in one's home, an assurance which has become part of our constitutional tradition.

It is now settled, for example, that for a routine felony arrest and absent exigent circumstances, the police must obtain a warrant before entering a home to arrest the homeowner. *Payton.* So, too, the Court held in *Steagald v. United States*, that absent exigent circumstances or consent, the police cannot search for the subject of an arrest warrant in the home of a third party, without first obtaining a search warrant directing entry.

These cases strengthen and protect the right of the homeowner to privacy in his own home. They do not speak, however, to the right to claim such a privacy interest in the home of another. ([N]ot[e] that the issue in *Steagald* was the homeowner's right to privacy in his own home, and not the right to "claim sanctuary from arrest in the home of a third party"). *Steagald* itself affirmed that, in accordance with the common law, our Fourth Amendment precedents "recogniz[e] . . . that rights such as those conferred by the Fourth Amendment are personal in nature, and cannot bestow vicarious protection on those who do not have a reasonable expectation of privacy in the place to be searched."

The homeowner's right to privacy is not at issue in this case. The Court does not reach the question whether the officer's unaided observations of Thompson's apartment constituted a search. If there was in fact a search, however, then Thompson had the right to object to the unlawful police surveillance of her apartment and the right to suppress any evidence disclosed by the search. Similarly, if the police had entered her home without a search warrant to arrest respondents, Thompson's own privacy interests would be violated and she could presumably bring an action under 42 U.S.C. § 1983 or an action for trespass. Our cases establish, however, that respondents have no independent privacy right, the violation of which results in exclusion of evidence against them, unless they can establish a meaningful connection to Thompson's apartment.

The settled rule is that the requisite connection is an expectation of privacy that society recognizes as reasonable. *Katz* (HARLAN, J., concurring). The application of that rule involves consideration of the kind of place in which the individual claims the privacy interest and what expectations of privacy are traditional and well recognized. I would expect that most, if not all, social guests legitimately expect that, in accordance with social custom, the homeowner will exercise her discretion to include or exclude others for the guests' benefit. As we recognized in *Olson* where these social expectations exist — as in the case of an overnight guest — they are sufficient to create a legitimate expectation of privacy, even in the absence of any property right to exclude others. In this respect, the dissent must be correct that reasonable expectations of the owner are shared, to some extent, by the guest. This analysis suggests that, as a general rule, social guests will have an expectation of privacy in their host's home. That is not the case before us, however.

In this case respondents have established nothing more than a fleeting and insubstantial connection with Thompson's home. For all that appears in the record, respondents used Thompson's house simply as a convenient processing station, their purpose involving nothing more than the mechanical act of chopping and packing a substance for distribution. There is no suggestion that respondents engaged in confidential communications with Thompson about their transaction. Respondents had not been to Thompson's apartment before, and they left it even before their arrest. The Minnesota Supreme Court, which overturned respondents' convictions, acknowledged that respondents could not be fairly characterized as Thompson's "guests." (noting that Carter's only evidence — that he was there to package cocaine — was inconsistent with his claim that "he was predominantly a social guest" in Thompson's apartment).

If respondents here had been visiting twenty homes, each for a minute or two, to drop off a bag of cocaine and were apprehended by a policeman wrongfully present in the nineteenth home; or if they had left the goods at a home where they were not staying and the police had seized the goods in their absence, we would have said that *Rakas* compels rejection of any privacy interest respondents might assert. So it does here, given that respondents have established no meaningful tie or connection to the owner, the owner's home, or the owner's expectation of privacy.

We cannot remain faithful to the underlying principle in *Rakas* without reversing in this case, and I am not persuaded that we need depart from it to protect the homeowner's own privacy interests. Respondents have made no persuasive argument that we need to fashion a *per se* rule of home protection, with an automatic right for all in the home to invoke the exclusionary rule, in order to protect homeowners and their guests from unlawful police intrusion. With these observations, I join the Court's opinion.

JUSTICE BREYER, concurring in the judgment.

I agree with Justice GINSBURG that respondents can claim the Fourth Amendment's protection. [JUSTICE BREYER then concurred in result on the basis of his opinion reproduced in Chapter 11, *infra*.]

For these reasons, while agreeing with Justice GINSBURG, I also concur in the Court's judgment reversing the Minnesota Supreme Court.

JUSTICE GINSBURG, with whom JUSTICE STEVENS and JUSTICE SOUTER join, dissenting.

The Court's decision undermines not only the security of short-term guests, but also the security of the home resident herself. In my view, when a homeowner or lessor personally invites a guest into her home to share in a common endeavor, whether it be for conversation, to engage in leisure activities, or for business purposes licit or illicit, that guest should share his host's shelter against unreasonable searches and seizures.

I do not here propose restoration of the "legitimately on the premises" criterion stated in *Jones,* for the Court rejected that formulation in *Rakas* as it did the "automatic standing rule" in *Salvucci*. First, the disposition I would reach in this case responds to the unique importance of the home — the most essential bastion of privacy recognized by the law. Second, even within the home itself, the position to which I would adhere would not permit "a casual visitor who has never seen, or been permitted to visit, the basement of another's house to object to a search of the basement if the visitor happened to be in the kitchen of the house at the time of the search." *Rakas*. Further, I would here decide only the case of the homeowner who chooses to share the privacy of her home and her company with a guest, and would not reach classroom hypotheticals like the milkman or pizza deliverer.

My concern centers on an individual's choice to share her home and her associations there with persons she selects. Our decisions indicate that people have a reasonable expectation of privacy in their homes in part because they have the prerogative to exclude others. (legitimate expectation of privacy turns in large part on ability to exclude others from place searched). The power to exclude implies the power to include. *See, e.g.,* Coombs, *Shared Privacy and the Fourth Amendment, or the Rights of Relationships,* 75 CALIF. L. REV. 1593, 1618 (1987) ("One reason we protect the legal right to exclude others is to empower the owner to choose to share his home or other property with his intimates."); Alschuler, *Interpersonal Privacy and the Fourth Amendment,* 4 N. ILL. U.L. REV. 1, 13 (1983) ("[O]ne of the main rights attaching to property is the right to share its shelter, its comfort and its privacy with others."). Our Fourth Amendment decisions should reflect these complementary prerogatives.

A home dweller places her own privacy at risk, the Court's approach indicates, when she opens her home to others, uncertain whether the duration of their stay, their purpose, and their "acceptance into the household" will earn protection.[1] It remains textbook law that "[s]earches and seizures inside a home without a warrant are presumptively unreasonable absent exigent circumstances." The law in practice is less secure. Human frailty suggests that today's decision will tempt police to pry into private dwellings without warrant, to find evidence incriminating guests who do not rest there through the night. *See* Simien, *The Interrelationship of the Scope of*

---

[1] The oral argument, counsel for petitioner informed the Court that the lessee of the apartment was charged, tried, and convicted of the same crimes as respondents.

the Fourth Amendment and Standing to Object to Unreasonable Searches, 41 ARK. L. REV. 487, 539 (1988) "[I]f the police have no probable cause, they have everything to gain and nothing to lose if they search under circumstances where they know that at least one of the potential defendants will not have standing."). *Rakas* tolerates that temptation with respect to automobile searches. I see no impelling reason to extend this risk into the home. As I see it, people are not genuinely "secure in their . . . houses . . . against unreasonable searches and seizures," their invitations to others increase the risk of unwarranted governmental peering and prying into their dwelling places.

Through the host's invitation, the guest gains a reasonable expectation of privacy in the home. *Minnesota v. Olson*, so held with respect to an overnight guest. The logic of that decision extends to shorter term guests as well. One need not remain overnight to anticipate privacy in another's home, "a place where [the guest] and his possessions will not be disturbed by anyone but his host and those his host allows inside." In sum, when a homeowner chooses to share the privacy of her home and her company with a short-term guest, the twofold requirement "emerg[ing] from prior decisions" has been satisfied: Both host and guest "have exhibited an actual (subjective) expectation of privacy"; that "expectation [is] one [our] society is prepared to recognize as 'reasonable.' "[2]

As the Solicitor General acknowledged, the illegality of the host-guest conduct, the fact that they were partners in crime, would not alter the analysis. In *Olson*, for example, the guest whose security this Court's decision shielded stayed overnight while the police searched for him. The Court held that the guest had Fourth Amendment protection against a warrantless arrest in his host's home despite the guest's involvement in grave crimes (first-degree murder, armed robbery, and assault). Other decisions have similarly sustained Fourth Amendment pleas despite the criminality of the defendants' activities. Indeed, it must be this way. If the illegality of the activity made constitutional an otherwise unconstitutional search, such Fourth Amendment protection, reserved for the innocent only, would have little force in regulating police behavior toward either the innocent or the guilty.

Our leading decision in *Katz* is key to my view of this case. There, we ruled that the Government violated the petitioner's Fourth Amendment rights when it electronically recorded him transmitting wagering information while he was inside a public telephone booth. We were mindful that "the Fourth Amendment protects people, not places," and held that this electronic monitoring of a business call

---

[2] In his concurring opinion, Justice KENNEDY maintains that respondents here lacked "an expectation of privacy that society recognizes as reasonable," because they "established nothing more than a fleeting and insubstantial connection" with the host's home. As the Minnesota Supreme Court reported, however, the stipulated facts showed that respondents were inside the apartment with the host's permission, remained inside for at least 2 1/2 hours, and, during that time, engaged in concert with the host in a collaborative venture. These stipulated facts — which scarcely resemble a stop of a minute or two at the 19th of 20 homes to drop off a packet, securely demonstrate that the host intended to share her privacy with respondents, and that respondents, therefore, had entered into the homeland of Fourth Amendment protection. While I agree with the Minnesota Supreme Court that, under the rule settled since *Katz*, the reasonableness of the expectation of privacy controls, not the visitor's status as social guest, invitee, licensee, or business partner, I think it noteworthy that five Members of the Court would place under the Fourth Amendment's shield, at least, "almost all social guests" (KENNEDY, J., concurring).

"violated the privacy upon which [the caller] justifiably relied while using the telephone booth." Our obligation to produce coherent results in this often visited area of the law requires us to inform our current expositions by benchmarks already established.

The Court's decision in this case veers sharply from the path marked in *Katz*. I do not agree that we have a more reasonable expectation of privacy when we place a business call to a person's home from a public telephone booth on the side of the street, than when we actually enter that person's premises to engage in a common endeavor.[3]

For the reasons stated, I dissent from the Court's judgment, and would retain judicial surveillance over the warrantless searches today's decision allows.

QUESTIONS AND NOTES

1. Is *Carter* a logical extension of *Rakas* or a grotesque perversion of it (or something in between)? Explain.

2. Does denying a Fourth Amendment claim to Carter and Johns compromise Thompson's interest in her home? How?

3. In view of Kennedy's opinion, how would you describe the holding of the case?

4. Is the continuing vitality of *Olson* assured?

5. How important should Scalia's linguistic argument be to the case? Compare his *Hodari D* opinion (Ch. 10, *supra*).

We conclude this section with the following problem:

PROBLEM

Jack Payner was indicted in September 1976 on a charge of falsifying his 1972 federal income tax return. The indictment alleged that respondent denied maintaining a foreign bank account at a time when he knew that he had such an account at the Castle Bank and Trust Company of Nassau, Bahama Islands. The Government's case rested heavily on a loan guarantee agreement dated April 28, 1972, in which respondent pledged the funds in his Castle Bank account as security for a $100,000 loan. The court found, however, that the Government discovered the guarantee agreement by exploiting a flagrantly illegal search that occurred on January 15, 1973.

---

[3] Justice SCALIA's lively concurring opinion deplores our adherence to *Katz*. In suggesting that we have elevated Justice Harlan's concurring opinion in *Katz* to first place, Justice SCALIA undervalues the clear opinion of the Court that "the Fourth Amendment protects people, not places." That core understanding is the *leitmotif* of Justice Harlan's concurring opinion. One cannot avoid a strong sense of *deja vu* on reading Justice SCALIA's elaboration. It so vividly recalls the opinion of Justice Black *in dissent* in *Katz*. Again, as Justice Stewart emphasized in the majority opinion in *Katz*, which *stare decisis* and reason require us to follow, "the Fourth Amendment protects people, not places."

The events leading up to the 1973 search are not in dispute. In 1965, the Internal Revenue Service launched an investigation into the financial activities of American citizens in the Bahamas. The project, known as "Operation Trade Winds," was headquartered in Jacksonville, Fla. Suspicion focused on the Castle Bank in 1972, when investigators learned that a suspected narcotics trafficker had an account there. Special Agent Richard Jaffe of the Jacksonville office asked Norman Casper, a private investigator and occasional informant, to learn what he could about the Castle Bank and its depositors. To that end, Casper cultivated his friendship with Castle Bank vice president Michael Wolstencroft. Casper introduced Wolstencroft to Sybol Kennedy, a private investigator and former employee. When Casper discovered that the banker intended to spend a few days in Miami in January 1973, he devised a scheme to gain access to the bank records he knew Wolstencroft would be carrying in his briefcase. Agent Jaffe approved the basic outline of the plan.

Wolstencroft arrived in Miami on January 15 and went directly to Kennedy's apartment. At about 7:30 p. m., the two left for dinner at a Key Biscayne restaurant. Shortly thereafter, Casper entered the apartment using a key supplied by Kennedy. He removed the briefcase and delivered it to Jaffe. While the agent supervised the copying of approximately 400 documents taken from the briefcase, a "lookout" observed Kennedy and Wolstencroft at dinner. The observer notified Casper when the pair left the restaurant, and the briefcase was replaced. The documents photographed that evening included papers evidencing a close working relationship between the Castle Bank and the Bank of Perrine, Fla. Subpoenas issued to the Bank of Perrine ultimately uncovered the loan guarantee agreement at issue in this case.

The District Court found that the United States, acting through Jaffe, "knowingly and willfully participated in the unlawful seizure of Michael Wolstencroft's briefcase . . . ." According to that court, "the Government affirmatively counsels its agents that the Fourth Amendment standing limitation permits them to purposefully conduct an unconstitutional search and seizure of one individual in order to obtain evidence against third parties . . . ." The District Court also found that the documents seized from Wolstencroft provided the leads that ultimately led to the discovery of the critical loan guarantee agreement. Although the search did not impinge upon the respondent's Fourth Amendment rights, the District Court believed that the Due Process Clause of the Fifth Amendment and the inherent supervisory power of the federal courts required it to exclude evidence tainted by the Government's "knowing and purposeful *bad faith hostility* to any person's fundamental constitutional rights."

The Court of Appeals for the Sixth Circuit affirmed in a brief order endorsing the District Court's use of its supervisory power. The Court of Appeals did not decide the due process question. We granted certiorari.

How should the Supreme Court decide this case? For the Court's actual solution, see *United States v. Payner*, 447 U.S. 727 (1980).

Chapter 15

CONFESSIONS, VOLUNTARINESS

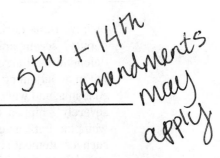

Although the privilege against self-incrimination precludes legal compulsion to testify, it was not available to invalidate coerced confessions for most of the nation's history for two reasons. First, until the 1960s, the privilege was thought to only apply to the Federal government. Second, the privilege was not thought to apply to interrogation because no *legal* process was applied to the arrestee to compel him to speak. Consequently, most of the coerced confession cases were analyzed under the due process clause. In this chapter, we analyze four of them, *Brown, Watts, Crooker,* and *Spano.*

BROWN v. MISSISSIPPI
297 U.S. 278 (1936)

Mr. Chief Justice Hughes delivered the opinion of the Court.

The question in this case is whether convictions, which rest solely upon confessions shown to have been extorted by officers of the state by brutality and violence, are consistent with the due process of law required by the Fourteenth Amendment of the Constitution of the United States.

Petitioners were indicted for the murder of one Raymond Stewart, whose death occurred on March 30, 1934. They were indicted on April 4, 1934, and were then arraigned and pleaded not guilty. Counsel were appointed by the court to defend them. Trial was begun the next morning and was concluded on the following day, when they were found guilty and sentenced to death.

> The crime with which these defendants, all ignorant negroes, are charged, was discovered about 1 o'clock p.m. on Friday, March 30, 1934. On that night one Dial, a deputy sheriff, accompanied by others, came to the home of Ellington, one of the defendants, and requested him to accompany them to the house of the deceased, and there a number of white men were gathered, who began to accuse the defendant of the crime. Upon his denial they seized him, and with the participation of the deputy they hanged him by a rope to the limb of a tree, and, having let him down, they hung him again, and when he was let down the second time, and he still protested his innocence, he was tied to a tree and whipped, and, still declining to accede to the demands that he confess, he was finally released, and he returned with some difficulty to his home, suffering intense pain and agony. The record of the testimony shows that the signs of the rope on his neck were

plainly visible during the so-called trial. A day or two thereafter the said deputy, accompanied by another, returned to the home of the said defendant and arrested him, and departed with the prisoner towards the jail in an adjoining county, but went by a route which led into the state of Alabama; and while on the way, in that state, the deputy stopped and again severely whipped the defendant, declaring that he would continue the whipping until he confessed, and the defendant then agreed to confess to such a statement as the deputy would dictate, and he did so, after which he was delivered to jail.

The other two defendants, Ed Brown and Henry Shields, were also arrested and taken to the same jail. On Sunday night, April 1, 1934, the same deputy, accompanied by a number of white men, one of whom was also an officer, and by the jailer, came to the jail, and the two last named defendants were made to strip and they were laid over chairs and their backs were cut to pieces with a leather strap with buckles on it, and they were likewise made by the said deputy definitely to understand that the whipping would be continued unless and until they confessed, and not only confessed, but confessed in every matter of detail as demanded by those present; and in this manner the defendants confessed the crime, and, as the whippings progressed and were repeated, they changed or adjusted their confession in all particulars of detail so as to conform to the demands of their torturers. When the confessions had been obtained in the exact form and contents as desired by the mob, they left with the parting admonition and warning that, if the defendants changed their story at any time in any respect from that last stated, the perpetrators of the outrage would administer the same or equally effective treatment.

Further details of the brutal treatment to which these helpless prisoners were subjected need not be pursued. It is sufficient to say that in pertinent respects the transcript reads more like pages torn from some medieval account than a record made within the confines of a modern civilization which aspires to an enlightened constitutional government.

All this having been accomplished, on the next day, that is, on Monday, April 2, when the defendants had been given time to recuperate somewhat from the tortures to which they had been subjected, the two sheriffs, one of the county where the crime was committed, and the other of the county of the jail in which the prisoners were confined, came to the jail, accompanied by eight other persons, some of them deputies, there to hear the free and voluntary confession of these miserable and abject defendants. The sheriff of the county of the crime admitted that he had heard of the whipping, but averred that he had no personal knowledge of it. He admitted that one of the defendants, when brought before him to confess, was limping and did not sit down, and that this particular defendant then and there stated that he had been strapped so severely that he could not sit down, and, as already stated, the signs of the rope on the neck of another of the defendants were plainly visible to all. Nevertheless the solemn farce of hearing the free and voluntary confessions was gone through with, and these two sheriffs and one other person then present were the three witnesses used in court to establish the so-called confessions, which were received by the court and admitted in evidence over the objections of the defendants duly entered of record as each of the said three witnesses delivered their alleged testimony. There was thus enough before the court when these confessions were first offered to make known to the court that they were not, beyond all reasonable doubt, free and voluntary; and the failure of the court then to exclude the confessions is sufficient to reverse the judgment, under every rule of procedure that has heretofore been prescribed, and hence it was not necessary subsequently to renew the objections by motion or otherwise.

The spurious confessions having been obtained — and the farce last mentioned having been gone through with on Monday, April 2d — the court, then in session, on the following day, Tuesday, April 3, 1934, ordered the grand jury to reassemble on the succeeding day, April 4, 1934, at 9 o'clock, and on the morning of the day last mentioned the grand jury returned an indictment against the defendants for murder. Late that afternoon the defendants were brought from the jail in the adjoining county and arraigned, when one or more of them offered to plead guilty, which the court declined to accept, and, upon inquiry whether they had or desired counsel, they stated that they had none, and did not suppose that counsel could be of any assistance to them. The court thereupon appointed counsel, and set the case for trial for the following morning at 9 o'clock, and the defendants were returned to the jail in the adjoining county about thirty miles away.

The defendants were brought to the courthouse of the county on the following morning, April 5th, and the so-called trial was opened, and was concluded on the next day, April 6, 1934, and resulted in a pretended conviction with death sentences. The evidence upon which the conviction was obtained was the so-called confessions. Without this evidence, a peremptory instruction to find for the defendants would have been inescapable. The defendants were put on the stand, and by their testimony the facts and the details thereof as to the manner by which the confessions were extorted from them were fully developed, and it is further disclosed by the record that the same deputy, Dial, under whose guiding hand and active participation the tortures to coerce the confessions were administered, was actively in the performance of the supposed duties of a court deputy in the courthouse and in the presence of the prisoners during what is denominated, in complimentary terms, the trial of these defendants. This deputy was put on the stand by the state in rebuttal, and admitted the whippings. It is interesting to note that in his testimony with reference to the whipping of the defendant Ellington, and in response to the inquiry as to how severely he was whipped, the deputy stated, 'Not too much for a negro; not as much as I would have done if it were left to me.' Two others who had participated in these whippings were introduced and admitted it — not a single witness was introduced who denied it. The facts are not only undisputed, they are admitted, and admitted to have been done by officers of the state, in conjunction with other participants, and all this was definitely well known to everybody connected with the trial, and during the trial, including the state's prosecuting attorney and the trial judge presiding.

1. The state stresses the statement in *Twining v. New Jersey*, 211 U.S. 78, 114, that "exemption from compulsory self-incrimination in the courts of the states is not secured by any part of the Federal Constitution," and the statement in *Snyder v. Massachusetts*, 291 U.S. 97, 105, that "the privilege against self-incrimination may be withdrawn and the accused put upon the stand as a witness for the state." But the question of the right of the state to withdraw the privilege against self-incrimination is not here involved. The compulsion to which the quoted statements refer is that of the processes of justice by which the accused may be called as a witness and required to testify. Compulsion by torture to extort a confession is a different matter.

The state is free to regulate the procedure of its courts in accordance with its own conceptions of policy, unless in so doing it "offends some principle of justice so rooted in the traditions and conscience of our people as to be ranked as fundamental." The state may abolish trial by jury. It may dispense with indictment by a grand jury and substitute complaint or information. But the freedom of the state in establishing its policy is the freedom of constitutional government and is limited by the requirement of due process of law. Because a state may dispense with a jury trial, it does not follow that it may substitute trial by ordeal. The rack and torture chamber may not be substituted for the witness stand. The state may not permit an accused to be hurried to conviction under mob domination — where the whole proceeding is but a mask — without supplying corrective process. The state may not deny to the accused the aid of counsel. Nor may a state, through the action of its officers, contrive a conviction through the pretense of a trial which in truth is "but used as a means of depriving a defendant of liberty through a deliberate deception of court and jury by the presentation of testimony known to be perjured." *Mooney v. Holohan*, 294 U.S. 103, 112. And the trial equally is a mere pretense where the state authorities have contrived a conviction resting solely upon confessions obtained by violence. The due process clause requires "that state action, whether through one agency or another, shall be consistent with the fundamental principles of liberty and justice which lie at the base of all our civil and political institutions." *Hebert v. Louisiana*, 272 U.S. 312, 316. It would be difficult to conceive of methods more revolting to the sense of justice than those taken to procure the confessions of these petitioners, and the use of the confessions thus obtained as the basis for conviction and sentence was a clear denial of due process.

Reversed.

QUESTIONS AND NOTES

1.   Are the convictions in this case reversed to compensate the victims for their torture, or because they never had a fair trial? Does it matter?

2.   Should there be a *per se* rule denying the admissibility of confessions where the arrestee had been beaten?

3.   If your answer to Question 2 was "yes," how should the Court determine from frequently conflicting stories whether or not a beating occurred?

4.   Can any conceivable argument be made in favor of the state in this case?

5.   Would (should) it matter if there was evidence derived from the confession that conclusively proved the defendant's guilt? (*E.g.*, defendant led police to a buried gun that turned out to be the murder weapon and the police did not previously know of its existence.)

6.   Without physical torture, the cases get much more difficult as will become apparent from reading *Watts.*

WATTS v. INDIANA
338 U.S. 49 (1949)

MR. JUSTICE FRANKFURTER announced the judgment of the Court and an opinion in which MR. JUSTICE MURPHY and MR. JUSTICE RUTLEDGE join.

In the application of so embracing a constitutional concept as "due process," it would be idle to expect at all times unanimity of views. Nevertheless, in all the cases that have come here during the last decade from the courts of the various States in which it was claimed that the admission of coerced confessions vitiated convictions for murder, there has been complete agreement that any conflict in testimony as to what actually led to a contested confession is not this Court's concern. Such conflict comes here authoritatively resolved by the State's adjudication. Therefore only those elements of the events and circumstances in which a confession was involved that are unquestioned in the State's version of what happened are relevant to the constitutional issue here. But if force has been applied, this Court does not leave to local determination whether or not the confession was voluntary. There is torture of mind as well as body; the will is as much affected by fear as by force. And there comes a point where this Court should not be ignorant as judges of what we know as men.

This brings us to the undisputed circumstances which must determine the issue of due process in this case. Thanks to the forthrightness of counsel for Indiana, these circumstances may be briefly stated.

On November 12, 1947, a Wednesday, petitioner was arrested and held as the suspected perpetrator of an alleged criminal assault earlier in the day. Later the same day, in the vicinity of this occurrence, a woman was found dead under conditions suggesting murder in the course of an attempted criminal assault. Suspicion of murder quickly turned towards petitioner and the police began to question him. They took him from the county jail to State Police Headquarters, where he was questioned by officers in relays from about eleven thirty that night until sometime between 2:30 and 3 o'clock the following morning. The same procedure of persistent interrogation from about 5:30 in the afternoon until about 3 o'clock the following morning, by a relay of six to eight officers, was pursued on Thursday the 13th, Friday the 14th, Saturday the 15th, Monday the 17th. Sunday was a day of rest from interrogation. About 3 o'clock on Tuesday morning, November 18, the petitioner made an incriminating statement after continuous questioning since 6 o'clock of the preceding evening. The statement did not satisfy the prosecutor who had been called in and he then took petitioner in hand. Petitioner, questioned by an interrogator of twenty years' experience as lawyer, judge and prosecutor, yielded a more incriminating document.

Until his inculpatory statements were secured, the petitioner was a prisoner in the exclusive control of the prosecuting authorities. He was kept for the first two days in solitary confinement in a cell aptly enough called "the hole" in view of its physical conditions as described by the State's witnesses. Apart from the five night sessions, the police intermittently interrogated Watts during the day and on three days drove him around town, hours at a time, with a view to eliciting identifications and other disclosures. Although the law of Indiana required that petitioner be given a prompt preliminary hearing before a magistrate, with all the protection a hearing was intended to give him, the petitioner was not only given no hearing during the entire period of interrogation but was without friendly or professional aid and without advice as to his constitutional rights. Disregard of rudimentary needs of life — opportunities for sleep and a decent allowance of food — are also relevant, not as aggravating elements of petitioner's treatment, but as part of the total situation out of which his confessions came and which stamped their character.

A confession by which life becomes forfeit must be the expression of free choice. A statement to be voluntary of course need not be volunteered. But if it is the product of sustained pressure by the police it does not issue from a free choice. When a suspect speaks because he is overborne, it is immaterial whether he has been subjected to a physical or a mental ordeal. Eventual yielding to questioning under such circumstances is plainly the product of the suction process of interrogation and therefore th reverse of voluntary. We would have to shut our minds to the plain significance of what here transpired to deny that this was a calculated endeavor to secure a confession through the pressure of unrelenting interrogation. The very relentlessness of such interrogation implies that it is better for the prisoner to answer than to persist in the refusal of disclosure which is his constitutional right. To turn the detention of an accused into a process of wrenching from him evidence which could not be extorted in open court with all its safeguards, is so grave an abuse of the power of arrest as to offend the procedural standards of due process.

This is so because it violates the underlying principle in our enforcement of the criminal law. Ours is the accusatorial as opposed to the inquisitorial system. Such has been the characteristic of Anglo-American criminal justice since it freed itself from practices borrowed by the Star Chamber from the Continent whereby an accused was interrogated in secret for hours on end. Under our system society carries the burden of proving its charge against the accused not out of his own mouth. It must establish its case, not by interrogation of the accused even under judicial safeguards, but by evidence independently secured through skillful investigation. "The law will not suffer a prisoner to be made the deluded instrument of his own conviction." 2 HAWKINS, PLEAS OF THE CROWN c. 46, § 34 (8th ed., 1824). The requirement of specific charges, their proof beyond a reasonable doubt, the protection of the accused from confessions extorted through whatever form of police pressures, the right to a prompt hearing before a magistrate, the right to assistance of counsel, to be supplied by government when circumstances make it necessary, the duty to advise an accused of his constitutional rights — these are all characteristics of the accusatorial system and manifestations of its demands. Protracted, systematic and uncontrolled subjection of an accused to interrogation by the police for the purpose of eliciting disclosures or confessions is subversive of the accusatorial system. It is the inquisitorial system without its safeguards. For while under that system the accused is subjected to judicial interrogation, he is protected by the disinterestedness of the judge in the presence of counsel. *See* Keedy, *The Preliminary Investigation of Crime in France*, 88 U. of PA. L. REV. 692, 708–712 (1940).

In holding that the Due Process Clause bars police procedure which violates the basic notions of our accusatorial mode of prosecuting crime and vitiates a conviction based on the fruits of such procedure, we apply the Due Process Clause to its historic function of assuring appropriate procedure before liberty is curtailed or life is taken. We are deeply mindful of the anguishing problems which the incidence of crime presents to the States. But the history of the criminal law proves overwhelmingly that brutal methods of law enforcement are essentially self-defeating, whatever may be their effect in a particular case. Law triumphs when the natural impulses aroused by a shocking crime yield to the safeguards which our civilization has evolved for an administration of criminal justice at once rational and effective.

We have examined petitioner's other contentions and do not sustain them.

Reversed

MR. JUSTICE BLACK concurs in the judgment of the Court on the authority of *Chambers v. Florida*, 309 U.S. 227; *Ashcraft v. Tennessee*, 322 U.S. 143.

On the record before us and in view of the consideration given by the states courts and the conclusion reached, THE CHIEF JUSTICE, Mr. Justice REED and Mr. Justice BURTON believe that the judgment should be affirmed.

MR. JUSTICE DOUGLAS, concurring.

It would be naive to think that this protective custody was less than the inquisition. The man was held until he broke. Then and only then was he arraigned and given the protection which the law provides all accused. Detention without arraignment is a time-honored method for keeping an accused under the exclusive control of the police. They can then operate at their leisure. The accused is wholly at their mercy. He is without the aid of counsel or friends; and he is denied the protection of the magistrate. We should unequivocally condemn the procedure and stand ready to outlaw any confession obtained during the period of the unlawful detention. The procedure breeds coerced confessions. It is the root of the evil. It is the procedure without which the inquisition could not flourish in the country.

MR. JUSTICE JACKSON concurring in the result in No. 610 and dissenting in Nos. 76 and 107.

These three cases, [*Watts, Harris v. South Carolina*, 338 U.S. 68 (1949), and *Turner v. Pennsylvania*, 338 U.S. 62 (1949)], from widely separated states, present essentially the same problem. Its recurrence suggests that it has roots in some condition fundamental and general to our criminal system.

In each case police were confronted with one or more brutal murders which the authorities were under the highest duty to solve. Each of these murders was unwitnessed, and the only positive knowledge on which a solution could be based was possessed by the killer. In each there was reasonable ground to *suspect* an individual but not enough legal evidence to *charge* him with guilt. In each the police attempted to meet the situation by taking the suspect into custody and interrogating him. This extended over varying periods. In each, confessions were made and received in evidence at the trial. Checked with external evidence, they are inherently believable, and were not shaken as to truth by anything that occurred at the trial. Each confessor was convicted by a jury and state courts affirmed. This Court sets all three convictions aside.

The seriousness of the Court's judgment is that no one suggests that any course held promise of solution of these murders other than to take the suspect into custody for questioning. The alternative was to close the books on the crime and forget it, with the suspect at large. This is a grave choice for a society in which two-thirds of the murders already are closed out as insoluble.

A concurring opinion, however, goes to the very limit and seems to declare for outlawing any confession, however freely given, if obtained during a period of custody between arrest and arraignment — which, in practice, means all of them.

Others would strike down these confessions because of conditions which they say make them "involuntary." In this, on only a printed record, they pit their judgment against that of the trial judge and the jury. Both, with the great advantage of hearing and seeing the confessor and also the officers whose conduct and bearing toward him is in question, have found that the confessions were voluntary. In addition, the majority overrule in each case one or more state appellate courts, which have the same limited opportunity to know the truth that we do.

Amid much that is irrelevant or trivial one serious situation seems to me to stand out in these cases. The suspect neither had nor was advised of his right to get counsel. This presents a real dilemma in a free society. To subject one without counsel to questioning which may and is intended to convict him, is a real peril to individual freedom. To bring in a lawyer means a real peril to solution of the crime because, under our adversary system, he deems that his sole duty is to protect his client — guilty or innocent — and that in such a capacity he owes no duty whatever to help society solve its crime problem. Under this conception of criminal procedure, any lawyer worth his salt will tell the suspect in no uncertain terms to make no statement to police under any circumstances.

If the State may arrest on suspicion and interrogate without counsel, there is no denying the fact that it largely negates the benefits of the constitutional guaranty of the right to assistance of counsel. Any lawyer who has ever been called into a case after his client has "told all" and turned any evidence he has over to the Government, knows how helpless he is to protect his client against the facts thus disclosed.

I suppose the view one takes will turn on what one thinks should be the right of an accused person against the State. Is it his right to have the judgment on the facts? Or is it his right to have a judgment based on only such evidence as he cannot conceal from the authorities, who cannot compel him to testify in court and also cannot question him before? Our system comes close to the latter by any interpretation, for the defendant is shielded by such safeguards as no system to law except the Anglo-American concedes to him.

Of course, no confession that has been obtained by any form of physical violence to the person is reliable and hence no conviction should rest upon one obtained in that manner. Such treatment not only breaks the will to conceal or lie, but may even break the will to stand by the truth. Nor is it questioned that the same result can sometimes be achieved by threats, promises, or inducements, which torture the mind but put no scar on the body. If the opinion of Mr. Justice FRANKFURTER in the *Watts* case were based solely on the State's admissions as to the treatment of Watts, I should not disagree. But if ultimate quest in a criminal trial is the truth and if the circumstances indicate no violence or threats of it, should society be deprived of the suspect's help in solving a crime merely because he was confined and questioned when uncounseled?

We must not overlook that in these, as in some previous cases, once a confession is obtained it supplies ways of verifying its trustworthiness. In these cases before us the verification is sufficient to leave me in no doubt that the admissions of guilt were genuine and truthful. Such corroboration consists in one case of finding a weapon where the accused has said he hid it, and in others that conditions which could only have been known to one who was implicated correspond with his story. It is possible, but it is rare, that a confession, if repudiated on the trial, standing alone will convict unless there is external proof of its verity.

In all such cases, along with other conditions criticized, the continuity and duration of the questioning is invoked and it is called an "inquiry", "inquest" or "inquisition," depending mainly on the emotional state of the writer. But as in some of the cases here, if interrogation is permissible at all, there are sound reasons for prolonging it — which the opinions here ignore. The suspect at first perhaps makes an effort to exculpate himself by alibis or other statements. These are verified, found false, and he is then confronted with his falsehood. Sometimes (though such cases do not reach us) verification proves them true or credible and the suspect is released. Sometimes, as here, more than one crime is involved. The duration of an interrogation may well depend on the temperament, shrewdness and cunning of the accused and the competence of the examiner. But assuming a right to examine at all, the right must include what is made reasonably necessary by the facts of the particular case.

If the right of interrogation be admitted, then it seems to me that we must leave it to trial judges and juries and state appellate courts to decide individual cases, unless they show some want of proper standards of decision.

I suppose no one would doubt that our Constitution and Bill of Rights, grounded in revolt against the arbitrary measures of George III and in the philosophy of the French Revolution, represent the maximum restrictions upon the power of organized society over the individual that are compatible with the maintenance of organized society itself. They were so intended and should be so interpreted. It cannot be denied that, even if construed as these provisions traditionally have been, they contain an aggregate of restrictions which seriously limit the power of society to solve such crimes as confront us in these cases. Those restrictions we should not for that reason cast aside, but that is good reason for indulging in no unnecessary expansion of them.

I doubt very much if they require us to hold that the State may not take into custody and question one suspected reasonably of an unwitnessed murder. If it does, the people of this country must discipline themselves to seeing their police stand by helplessly while those suspected of murder prowl about unmolested. Is it a necessary price to pay for the fairness which we know as "due process of law"? And if not a necessary one, should it be demanded by this Court? I do not know the ultimate answer to these questions; but, for the present, I should not increase the handicap on society.

QUESTIONS AND NOTES

1. Do you see anything wrong with the *Watts* procedure? Explain.

2. If one takes the Frankfurter opinion seriously, does it necessarily lead to the conclusion that Justice Douglas is correct?

3. The Court says: "The law will not suffer a prisoner to be made the deluded instrument of his own conviction." Do we really believe that? Should we really believe that?

4. How would you resolve the dilemma identified by Justice Jackson?

5. Do you think that the system is too pro-defendant? Why? Why not?

6. As you read *Crooker*, consider whether Justice Frankfurter's *Watts'* observations were taken seriously. It is worth noting that Frankfurter was necessary for a 5-4 majority in *Crooker*.

CROOKER v. CALIFORNIA
357 U.S. 433 (1958)

MR. JUSTICE CLARK delivered the opinion of the Court.

Petitioner, under sentence of death for the murder of his paramour, claims that his conviction in a California court violates Fourteenth Amendment due process of law because (1) the confession admitted into evidence over his objection had been coerced from him by state authorities, and (2) even if his confession was voluntary it occurred while he was without counsel because of the previous denial of his request therefor.

The record here clearly reveals that prior to petitioner's confession he asked for and was denied opportunity to call his lawyer. We first consider that denial in connection with petitioner's contention that his subsequent confession was involuntary in nature.

It is well established that the Fourteenth Amendment prohibits use of coerced confessions in state prosecutions. *E.g., Brown; Watts.*

The victim's son discovered her body the morning of July 5, 1955, stabbed and strangled to death in the bedroom of her Los Angeles home. She was last known to be alive about 1 a.m. the same day, when she talked with a friend by telephone.

Petitioner was arrested in his apartment at 1:30 that afternoon and subsequently was charged with the murder. He was then 31 years of age, a college graduate who had attended the first year of law school. While going to law school he had been a house boy in the home of the victim. That position led to an illicit relationship with her, which she had attempted several times to terminate in the month preceding her death. The week of her death, after telling petitioner they had been found out, she had requested, and he had agreed, that he would never see her again.

Despite this understanding, he returned to her house late in the afternoon of July 4. Finding no one at home, he did nearby for the ostensible purpose of discovering who was "threatening" her. From his hiding place he watched the victim return home with an escort around midnight. Shortly thereafter he saw the escort leave and watched the victim talk on the telephone. He claims that he then left the vicinity to return to his apartment, never having entered the house that evening.

At the time of his arrest, petitioner was questioned about scratches that were evident on his neck and hands. He attributed the former to shaving and the latter to a traffic mishap on his way to the beach on July 4. However he refused to reveal where the accident occurred. After his apartment was searched, petitioner was taken to the Los Angeles Police Station, where he was photographed and asked to take a lie detector test. He refused to submit to the test, and indicated that he wanted to call an attorney. At no time, however, does it appear that petitioner was offered the use of a telephone. Aside from sporadic questioning at his apartment, petitioner was interrogated for the first time from 8:30–9:30 p.m., the questioning being conducted by four officers and centering around his refusal of the lie detector test. During this time he asked for an opportunity to get a lawyer, naming a specific attorney whom he thought might represent him, but was told that "after [the] investigation was concluded he could call an attorney."

At 9:30 p.m. petitioner was transferred to the West Los Angeles Police Station, where five officers questioned him from 11 p.m. until shortly after midnight. He then was formally "booked," and given a physical examination by a police physician. The third and last questioning period was conducted by the same five men from approximately 1–2 a.m. July 6. For the next hour petitioner wrote and signed a detailed confession of the murder. Afterward, he was taken to the victim's home to re-enact the crime. At 5 a.m. he was put in jail and permitted to sleep.

That afternoon, a full day after his arrest, he was taken to the office of the Los Angeles County District Attorney to orally repeat the written confession. Petitioner balked at doing so and again asked that his attorney be called. Thereupon the District Attorney placed the call for him and listened to the conversation while petitioner talked on an extension phone with the attorney. Neither petitioner nor his attorney was aware that a tape recording was being made of everything that transpired in the office. The District Attorney interrupted at one point to deny that petitioner was forced to answer police questions, and later to advise that the most convenient time for the attorney to see petitioner would be at 7 p.m. back at the West Los Angeles Police Station. After the phone call, petitioner was returned to jail to meet his attorney that evening. From that time forward, through both arraignment and trial, he was represented by his own counsel.

In the 14 hours between his arrest and confession, petitioner was given coffee and allowed to smoke whenever he liked. He also was given milk and a sandwich a few hours after his arrest. Before being transferred to the West Los Angeles Police Station he was advised by a police lieutenant, "You don't have to say anything that you don't want to," and he in fact refused to answer many questions both before and after the transfer. At such times he simply stated he "would rather not answer, or rather not make a statement about that."

The bare fact of police "detention and police examination in private of one in official state custody" does not render involuntary a confession by the one so detained. Neither does an admonition by the police to tell the truth, nor the failure of state authorities to comply with local statutes requiring that an accused promptly be brought before a magistrate.[2]

Petitioner's claim of coercion, then, depends almost entirely on denial of his request to contact counsel.[3] This Court has not previously had occasion to determine the character of a confession obtained after such a denial. But we have held that confessions made by indigent defendants prior to state appointment of counsel are not thereby rendered involuntary, even in prosecutions where conviction without counsel would violate due process under the Fourteenth Amendment. To be sure, coercion seems more likely to result from state denial of a specific request for opportunity to engage counsel than it does from state failure to appoint counsel immediately upon arrest. That greater possibility, however, is not decisive. It is negated here by petitioner's age, intelligence, and education. While in law school he had studied criminal law; indeed, when asked to take the lie detector test, he informed the operator that the results of such a test would not be admissible at trial absent a stipulation by the parties. Supplementing that background is the police statement to petitioner well before his confession that he did not have to answer questions. Moreover, the manner of his refusals to answer indicates full awareness of the right to be silent. On this record we are unable to say that petitioner's confession was anything other than voluntary.

We turn now to the contention that even if the confession be voluntary, its use violates due process because it was obtained after denial of petitioner's request to

---

[2] Section 849 of the California Penal Code provides that a person arrested without a warrant must be brought before the nearest or most accessible magistrate in the county of arrest "without unnecessary delay." CAL. PENAL CODE, 1956, § 849.

[3] Even if within the scope of the limited grant of certiorari, claims of physical violence — "third degree" methods — were denied by witnesses for the State, and hence are not part of the undisputed portions of the record which we consider here. The ambiguous reply by one police officer, "I don't think we hurt you," in response to petitioner's assertion in the District Attorney's office that the officer struck him, cannot alter the contradicted state of the evidence when the same officer categorically denied the claim on cross-examination at the trial.

contact his attorney. Petitioner reaches this position by reasoning first that he has been denied a due process right to representation and advice from his attorney,[4] and secondly that the use of any confession obtained from him during the time of such a denial would itself be barred by the Due Process Clause, even though freely made. We think petitioner fails to sustain the first point, and therefore we do not reach the second.

In *House v. Mayo*, 324 U.S. 42 (1945), an uneducated man in his twenties, a stranger to the area, was brought before a court to be sentenced on two convictions previously returned against him. He was there presented for the first time with a burglary information filed by the State, asked for and was denied opportunity to engage counsel, and finally pleaded guilty to the information, thereby obviating any necessity for trial of the charge on the merits. We held that a due process right to counsel was denied.

In contrast, the sum total of the circumstances here during the time petitioner was without counsel is a voluntary confession by a college-educated man with law school training who knew of his right to keep silent. Such facts, while perhaps a violation of California law,[5] do not approach the prejudicial impact in *House v. Mayo*, and do not show petitioner to have been so "taken advantage of" as to violate due process of law.

Affirmed.

MR. JUSTICE DOUGLAS, with whom THE CHIEF JUSTICE, MR. JUSTICE BLACK and MR. JUSTICE BRENNAN concur, dissenting.

When petitioner was first arrested, and before any real interrogation took place, he asked that his attorney be present. "I had no objection to talking with them about whatever they had to talk about, but . . . I wanted counsel with me . . . . I wanted an attorney with me before I would talk with them."

That was petitioner's testimony; and it is verified by the testimony of Sergeant Gotch of the police.

A.   I stated to him that after our investigation was concluded he could call an attorney, and if he didn't have funds to hire an attorney, when he went to Court's public defender would be assigned to handle his case.

He then stated that he had a friend who had been an instructor at Pepperdine College that would probably handle the case for him. I

---

[4] At times petitioner appears to urge "a rule" barring use of a voluntary confession obtained after state denial of a request to contact counsel regardless of whether any violation of a due process right to counsel occurred. That contention is simply an appeal to the supervisory power of this Court over the administration of justice in the federal courts. *See McNabb v. United States*, 318 U.S. 332 (1943), which, significantly enough, petitioner cites. The short answer to such a contention here is that this conviction was had in a state, not a federal, court.

[5] Section 825 of the California Penal Code provides that after an arrest, an attorney "may at the request of the prisoner or any relative of such prisoner, visit the person so arrested." Any officer in charge of the prisoner who wilfully refuses to let the attorney see the prisoner is made guilty of a misdemeanor. CAL. PENAL CODE, 1956, § 825.

asked him who the name was, and he said it was a man by the name of Simpson, who lived in Long Beach.

Q.   He asked you if he could call an attorney at that time, and you told him that he could call after your investigation was completed, is that right?

A.   I told him, after I was through with the investigation, he could make a call.

This demand for an attorney was made over and again prior to the time a confession was extracted from the accused. Its denial was in my view a denial of that due process of law guaranteed the citizen by the Fourteenth Amendment.

The Court properly concedes that the right to counsel extends to pretrial proceedings as well as to the trial itself. The need is as great then as at any time. The right to have counsel at the pretrial stage is often necessary to give meaning and protection to the right to be heard at the trial itself. It may also be necessary as a restraint on the coercive power of the police. The pattern of the third degree runs through our cases: a lone suspect unrepresented by counsel against whom the full coercive force of a secret inquisition is brought to bear. *See Watts.* The third degree flourishes only in secrecy. One who feels the need of a lawyer and asks for one is asking for some protection which the law can give him against a coerced confession. No matter what care is taken innocent people are convicted of crimes they did not commit. We should not lower the barriers and deny the accused any procedural safeguard against coercive police practices. The trial of the issue of coercion is seldom helpful. Law officers usually testify one way, the accused another. The citizen who has been the victim of these secret inquisitions has little chance to prove coercion. The mischief and abuse of the third degree will continue as long as an accused can be denied the right to counsel at this the most critical period of his ordeal.[2] For what takes place in the secret confines of the police station may be more critical than what takes place at the trial.

---

[2] Dean Roscoe Pound wrote in 1934 as follows about this problem:

In the United States the feeling of police and prosecutors that they ought to be able to interrogate suspected persons long ago led to a systematic development of extra-legal or downright illegal examinations by officials, with every external appearance of legality. These examinations have become so much a matter of course that we may read in every morning paper how police or prosecutor examined (the word usually chosen is "grilled") so and so for anywhere from ten to forty-eight or more consecutive hours, going at him in relays to wear him out and break him down. They are now taken to be the established practice. Prosecutors often conduct them with a pretense of authority when those subjected to them are ignorant, unadvised as to their rights, insignificant, or without means of employing counsel. Indeed, so bold have those who resort to those practices become, that we now read in the newspapers how this man or that was held *"incommunicado"* in a police station or jail while the grilling process was going on . . . .

No amount of thundering against the third degree and its derivatives and analogues will achieve anything. The temper of the public will not permit of strengthening the constitutional safeguards of the accused. For some time to come the tendency is likely to be in the opposite direction. Indeed, a feeling that the public are with them is largely behind the boldness with which highhanded, secret, extra-legal interrogations of persons held *incommunicado* are constantly carried on.

My proposition is that the remedy for the third degree and its derivatives is to satisfy the reasonable demands of the police and the prosecutors for an interrogation of suspected persons and thus do away with the excuse for extralegal questionings.

[A]s stated by a Committee headed by Prof. Zechariah Chafee, "A person accused of crime needs a lawyer right after his arrest probably more than at any other time."

The Court speaks of the education of this petitioner and his ability to take care of himself. In an opinion written by Mr. Justice Sutherland the Court said, "Even the intelligent and educated layman has small and sometimes no skill in the science of law . . . . He requires the guiding hand of counsel at every step in the proceedings against him." *Powell v. Alabama*, 287 U.S. 45, 69. Mr. Justice Sutherland spoke of the trial itself. But what is true of the trial is true of the preparation for trial and of the period commencing with the arrest of the accused. No matter how well educated, and how well trained in the law an accused may be, he is sorely in need of legal advice once he is arrested for an offense that may exact his life. The innocent as well as the guilty may be caught in a web of circumstantial evidence that is difficult to break. A man may be guilty of indiscretions but not of the crime. He may be implicated by ambiguous circumstances difficult to explain away. He desperately needs a lawyer to help extricate him if he's innocent. He has the right to receive the benefit of the advice of his own counsel at the trial. That same right should extend to the pretrial stage.

QUESTIONS AND NOTES

1. Do you agree that the bare fact of detention, coupled with an admonition to tell the truth and a failure to bring the accused promptly before a magistrate does not render a confession involuntary? Was Frankfurter consistent with his *Watts* opinion in accepting that statement?

2. Should petitioner's education have been relevant? Would you have felt uncoerced under these circumstances? Explain.

3. How should the problem suggested by fn. 3 of the Court's opinion be resolved? Apparently if Crooker had been hit (even if not hurt too much) his confession would have been involuntary. However, the Court is willing to accept the findings of the lower court unless there is no evidence to support them.

I submit that there should be express provision for a legal examination of suspected or accused persons before a magistrate; that those to be examined should be allowed to have counsel present to safeguard their rights; that provision should be made for taking down the evidence so as to guarantee accuracy. As things are, it is not the least of the abuses of the system of extra-legal interrogation that there is a constant conflict of evidence as to what the accused said and as to the circumstances under which he said or was coerced into saying it.

24 J. CRIM. L. & C. 1014, 1016, 1017. As recently stated by T. B. Smith, a distinguished Scottish lawyer:

The opportunities for exerting pressure on a suspect to confess are greatest when there is no judicial supervision, no legal representation and no public scrutiny. If an accused at his trial seeks to retract a confession allegedly extorted If an accused at his trial seeks to stand alone against several police witnesses who may be expected to deny improper pressure. It is well known that in the totalitarian states extra-judicial pressure by brain-washing can eventually convince even the accused that he has committed the most improbable offenses, but when a confession has been extorted by less through third-degree methods it is likely to be retracted at the trial. The accused may, nevertheless, by then have damaged his position irreparably.

32 TULANE L. REV. 349, 354.

4. Should the fact that California violated its own statutes have been relevant? Why? Why not? *Cf. Virginia v. Moore.*

5. What do you understand to be the difference between supervisory powers and constitutional adjudication.

6. We conclude this section with *Spano*, where the entire Court appears to be growing impatient with, at least some aspects of police practices in obtaining confessions.

SPANO v. NEW YORK
360 U.S. 315 (1959)

MR. CHIEF JUSTICE WARREN delivered the opinion of the Court.

This is another in the long line of cases presenting the question whether a confession was properly admitted into evidence under the Fourteenth Amendment. As in all such cases, we are forced to resolve a conflict between two fundamental interests of society; its interest in prompt and efficient law enforcement, and its interest in preventing the rights of its individual members from being abridged by unconstitutional methods of law enforcement.

The State's evidence reveals the following: Petitioner Vincent Joseph Spano is a derivative citizen of this country, having been born in Messina, Italy. He was 25 years old at the time of the shooting in question and had graduated from junior high school. He had a record of regular employment. The shooting took place on January 22, 1957.

On that day, petitioner was drinking in a bar. The decedent, a former professional boxer weighing almost 200 pounds who had fought in Madison Square Garden, took some of petitioner's money from the bar. Petitioner followed him out of the bar to recover it. A fight ensued, with the decedent knocking petitioner down and then kicking him in the head three or four times. Shock from the force of these blow caused petitioner to vomit. After the bartender applied some ice to his head, petitioner left the bar, walked to his apartment, secured a gun, and walked eight or nine blocks to a candy store where the decedent was frequently to be found. He entered the store in which decedent, three friends of decedent, at least two of whom were ex-convicts, and a boy who was supervising the store were present. He fired five shots, two of which entered the decedent's body, causing his death. The boy was the only eyewitness; the three friends of decedent did not see the person who fired the shot. Petitioner then disappeared for the next week or so.

On February 1, 1957, the Bronx County Grand Jury returned an indictment for first-degree murder against petitioner. Accordingly, a bench warrant was issued for his arrest, commanding that he be forthwith brought before the court to answer the indictment, or, if the court had adjourned for the term, that he be delivered into the custody of the Sheriff of Bronx County.

On February 3, 1957, petitioner called one Gaspar Bruno, a close friend of 8 or 10 years' standing who had attended school with him. Bruno was a fledgling police officer, having at that time not yet finished attending police academy. According to

Bruno's testimony, petitioner told him "that he took a terrific beating, that the deceased hurt him real bad and he dropped him a couple of times and he was dazed; he didn't know what he was doing and that he went and shot at him." Petitioner told Bruno that he intended to get a lawyer and give himself up. Bruno relayed this information to his superiors.

The following day, February 4, at 7:10 p.m., petitioner, accompanied by counsel, surrendered himself to the authorities in front of the Bronx County Building, where both the office of the Assistant District Attorney who ultimately prosecuted his case and the court-room in which he was ultimately tried were located. His attorney had cautioned him to answer no questions, and left him in the custody of the officers. He was promptly taken to the office of the Assistant District Attorney and at 7:15 p.m. the questioning began, being conducted by Assistant District Attorney Goldsmith, Lt. Gannon, Detectives Farrell, Lehrer and Motta, and Sgt. Clarke. The record reveals that the questioning was both persistent and continuous. Petitioner, in accordance with his attorney's instructions, steadfastly refused to answer. Detective Motta testified: "He refused to talk to me." "He just looked up to the ceiling and refused to talk to me." Detective Farrell testified:

Q.   And you started to interrogate him?

A.   That is right.

Q.   What did he say?

A.   He said "you would have to see my attorney. I tell you nothing but my name."

Q.   Did you continue to examine him?

A.   Verbally, yes, sir.

He asked one officer, Detective Ciccone, if he could speak to his attorney, but that request was denied. Detective Ciccone testified that he could not find the attorney's name in the telephone book.[3] He was given two sandwiches, coffee and cake at 11 p.m.

At 12:15 a.m. on the morning of February 5, after five hours of questioning in which it became evident that petitioner was following his attorney's instructions, on the Assistant District Attorney's orders petitioner was transferred to the 46th Squad, Ryer Avenue Police Station. The Assistant District Attorney also went to the police station and to some extent continued to participate in the interrogation. Petitioner arrived at 12:30 and questioning was resumed at 12:40. The character of the questioning is revealed by the testimony of Detective Farrell:

Q.   Who did you leave him in the room with?

A.   With Detective Lehrer and Sergeant Clarke came in and Mr. Goldsmith came in or Inspector Halk came in. It was back and forth. People just came in, spoke a few words to the defendant or they listened a few minutes and they left.

---

[3] How this could be so when the attorney's name, Tobias Russo, was concededly in the telephone book does not appear. The trial judge sustained objections by the Assistant District Attorney to questions designed to delve into this mystery.

But petitioner persisted in his refusal to answer, and again requested permission to see his attorney, this time from Detective Lehrer. His request was again denied.

It was then that those in charge of the investigation decided that petitioner's close friend, Bruno, could be of use. He had been called out on the case around 10 or 11 p.m., although he was not connected with the 46th Squad or Precinct in any way. Although, in fact, his job was in no way threatened, Bruno was told to tell petitioner that petitioner's telephone call had gotten him "in a lot of trouble," and that he should seek to extract sympathy from petitioner for Bruno's pregnant wife and three children. Bruno developed this theme with petitioner without success, and petitioner, also without success, again sought to see his attorney, a request which Bruno relayed unavailingly to his superiors. After this first session with petitioner, Bruno was again directed by Lt. Gannon to play on petitioner's sympathies, but again no confession was forthcoming. But the Lieutenant a third time ordered Bruno falsely to importune his friend to confess but again petitioner clung to his attorney's advice. Inevitably, in the fourth such session directed by the Lieutenant, lasting a full hour, petitioner succumbed to his friend's prevarications and agreed to make a statement. Accordingly, at 3:25 a.m. the Assistant District Attorney, a stenographer, and several other law enforcement officials entered the room where petitioner was being questioned, and took his statement in question and answer form with the Assistant District Attorney asking the questions. The statement was completed at 4:05 a.m.

But this was not the end. At 4:30 a.m. three detectives took petitioner to Police Headquarters in Manhattan. On the way they attempted to find the bridge from which petitioner said he had thrown the murder weapon. They crossed the Triborough Bridge into Manhattan, arriving at Police Headquarters at 5 a.m., and left Manhattan for the Bronx at 5:40 a.m. via the Willis Avenue Bridge. When petitioner recognized neither bridge as the one from which he had thrown the weapon, they re-entered Manhattan via the Third Avenue Bridge, which petitioner stated was the right one, and then returned to the Bronx well after 6 a.m. During that trip the officers also elicited a statement from petitioner that the deceased was always "on [his] back," "always pushing" him and that he was "not sorry" he had shot the deceased. All three detectives testified to that statement at the trial.

Court opened at 10 a.m. that morning, and petitioner was arraigned at 10:15.

At the trial, the confession was introduced in evidence over appropriate objections. The jury was instructed that it could rely on it only if it was found to be voluntary. The jury returned a guilty verdict and petitioner was sentenced to death. The New York Court of Appeals affirmed the conviction over three dissents, and we granted certiorari to resolve the serious problem presented under the Fourteenth Amendment. 358 U.S. 919.

Petitioner's first contention is that his absolute right to counsel in a capital case became operative on the return of an indictment against him, for at that time he was in every sense a defendant in a criminal case, the grand jury having found sufficient cause to believe that he had committed the crime. He argues accordingly that following indictment no confession obtained in the absence of counsel can be used without violating the Fourteenth Amendment. He seeks to distinguish *Crooker* on the ground that in those cases no indictment had been returned. We find it unnecessary to reach that contention, for we find use of the confession obtained here inconsistent with the Fourteenth Amendment under traditional principles.

The abhorrence of society to the use of involuntary confessions does not turn alone on their inherent untrustworthiness. It also turns on the deep-rooted feeling that the police must obey the law while enforcing the law; that in the end life and liberty can be as much endangered from illegal methods used to convict those thought to be criminals as from the actual criminals themselves. Accordingly, the actions of police in obtaining confessions have come under scrutiny in a long series of cases. Those cases suggest that in recent years law enforcement officials have become increasingly aware of the burden which they share, along with our courts, in protecting fundamental rights of our citizenry, including that portion of our citizenry suspected of crime. The facts of no case recently in this Court have quite approached the brutal beatings in *Brown*, or the 36 consecutive hours of questioning present in *Ashcraft v. Tennessee*, 322 U.S. 143 (1944). But as law enforcement officers become more responsible, and the methods used to extract confessions more sophisticated, our duty to enforce federal constitutional protections does not cease. It only becomes more difficult because of the more delicate judgments to be made. Our judgment here is that, on all the facts, this conviction cannot stand.

Petitioner was a foreign-born young man of 25 with no past history of law violation or of subjection to official interrogation, at least insofar as the record shows. He had progressed only one-half year into high school and the record indicates that he had a history of emotional instability. He did not make a narrative statement, but was subject to the leading questions of a skillful prosecutor in a question and answer confession. He was subjected to questioning not by a few men, but by many. They included Assistant District Attorney Goldsmith, one Hyland of the District Attorney's Office, Deputy Inspector Halks, Lieutenant Gannon, Detective Ciccone, Detective Motta, Detective Lehrer, Detective Marshal, Detective Farrell, Detective Leira, Detective Murphy, Detective Murtha, Sergeant Clarke, Patrolman Bruno and Stenographer Baldwin. All played some part, and the effect of such massive official interrogation must have been felt. Petitioner was questioned for virtually eight straight hours before he confessed, with his only respite being a transfer to an arena presumably considered more appropriate by the police for the task at hand. Nor was the questioning conducted during normal business hours, but began in early evening, continued into the night, and did not bear fruition until the not-too-early morning. The drama was not played out, with the final admissions obtained, until almost sunrise. In such circumstances slowly mounting fatigue does, and is calculated to, play its part. The questioners persisted in the face of his repeated refusals to answer on the advice of his attorney, and they ignored his reasonable requests to contact the local attorney whom he had already retained and who had personally delivered him into the custody of these officers in obedience to the bench warrant.

The use of Bruno, characterized in this Court by counsel for the State as a "childhood friend" of petitioner's, is another factor which deserves mention in the totality of the situation. Bruno's was the one face visible to petitioner in which he could put some trust. There was a bond of friendship between them going back a decade into adolescence. It was with this material that the officers felt that they could overcome petitioner's will. They instructed Bruno falsely to state that petitioner's telephone call had gotten him into trouble, that his job was in jeopardy, and that loss of his job would be disastrous to his three children, his wife and his unborn child. And Bruno played this part of a worried father, harried by his superiors, in not one, but four different acts, the final one lasting an hour. Petitioner was apparently unaware of John Gay's famous couplet:

An open foe may prove a curse,

But a pretended friend is worse,

and he yielded to his false friend's entreaties.

We conclude that petitioner's will was overborne by official pressure, fatigue and sympathy falsely aroused after considering all the facts in their post-indictment setting. Here a grand jury had already found sufficient cause to require petitioner to face trial on a charge of first-degree murder, and the police had an eyewitness to the shooting. The police were not therefore merely trying to solve a crime, or even to absolve a suspect. Compare *Crooker*. They were rather concerned primarily with securing a statement from defendant on which they could convict him. The undeviating intent of the officers to extract a confession from petitioner is therefore patent. When such an intent is shown, this Court has held that the confession obtained must be examined with the most careful scrutiny, and has reversed a conviction on facts less compelling than these. Accordingly, we hold that petitioner's conviction cannot stand under the Fourteenth Amendment.

The judgment must be reversed.

MR. JUSTICE DOUGLAS, with whom MR. JUSTICE BLACK and MR. JUSTICE BRENNAN join, concurring.

While I join the opinion of the Court, I add what for me is an even more important ground of decision.

We have often divided on whether state authorities may question a suspect for hours on end when he has no lawyer present and when he has demanded that he have the benefit of legal advice. *See Crooker.* But here we deal not with a suspect but with a man who has been formally charged with a crime. The question is whether after the indictment and before the trial the Government can interrogate the accused *in secret* when he asked for his lawyer and when his request was denied.

Depriving a person, formally charged with a crime, of counsel during the period prior to trial may be more damaging than denial of counsel during the trial itself.

We do not have here mere suspects who are being secretly interrogated by the police as in *Crooker*. This is a case of an accused, who is scheduled to be tried by a judge and jury, being tried in a preliminary way by the police. This is a kangaroo court procedure whereby the police produce the vital evidence in the form of a confession which is useful or necessary to obtain a conviction. They in effect deny him effective representation by counsel. This seems to me to be a flagrant violation of the principle that the right of counsel extends to the preparation for trial, as well as to the trial itself. As Professor Chafee once said, "A person accused of crime needs a lawyer right after his arrest probably more than at any other time."

I join with Judges Desmond, Fuld, and Van Voorhis of the New York Court of Appeals in asking, what use is a defendant's right to effective counsel at every stage of a criminal case if, while he is held awaiting trial, he can be questioned in the absence of counsel until he confesses? In that event the secret trial in the police precincts effectively supplants the public trial guaranteed by the Bill of Rights.

MR. JUSTICE STEWART, whom MR. JUSTICE DOUGLAS and MR. JUSTICE BRENNAN join, concurring.

While I concur in the opinion of the Court, it is my view that the absence of counsel when this confession was elicited was alone enough to render it inadmissible under the Fourteenth Amendment.

Let it be emphasized at the outset that this is not a case where the police were questioning a suspect in the course of investigating an unsolved crime. *See Crooker.* When the petitioner surrendered to the New York authorities he was under indictment for first degree murder.

Under our system of justice an indictment is supposed to be followed by an arraignment and a trial.

[T]he right to the assistance of counsel whom the accused has himself retained is absolute.

What followed the petitioner's surrender in this case was not arraignment in a court of law, but an all-night inquisition in a prosecutor's office, a police station, and an automobile. Throughout the night the petitioner repeatedly asked to be allowed to send for his lawyer, and his requests were repeatedly denied. He finally was induced to make a confession. That confession was used to secure a verdict sending him to the electric chair.

Our Constitution guarantees the assistance of counsel to a man on trial for his life in an orderly courtroom, presided over by a judge, open to the public, and protected by all the procedural safeguards of the law. Surely a Constitution which promises that much can vouchsafe no less to the same man under midnight inquisition in the squad room of a police station.

QUESTIONS AND NOTES

1. Why do you suppose that the Court unanimously reversed this conviction?

2. Why do you suppose that the New York Court of Appeals affirmed it?

3. Should the police be permitted to lie (*e.g.*, Bruno could lose his job)? Why? Why not?

4. How significant is the indictment? How significant should it be? Why?

5. After this case, probably a majority of the Court (the four concurring Justices plus Warren, who had dissented in *Crooker*) believed that there was an absolute right to counsel after indictment.

6. Is there an inherent "Kangaroo Court" problem with police interrogation? Is there a solution? What might it be?

Chapter 16

RIGHT TO COUNSEL

The right to counsel was first used to invalidate a confession in *Massiah*, a 1963 decision. *Massiah's* fact pattern, on one level, does not appear to be about the right to counsel at all.

MASSIAH v. UNITED STATES
377 U.S. 201 (1964)

Mr. Justice Stewart delivered the opinion of the Court.

The petitioner was indicted for violating the federal narcotics laws. He retained a lawyer, pleaded not guilty, and was released on bail. While he was free on bail a federal agent succeeded by surreptitious means in listening to incriminating statements made by him. Evidence of these statements was introduced against the petitioner at his trial over his objection. He was convicted, and the Court of Appeals affirmed. We granted certiorari to consider whether, under the circumstances here presented, the prosecution's use at the trial of evidence of the petitioner's own incriminating statements deprived him of any right secured to him under the Federal Constitution.

The petitioner, a merchant seaman, was in 1958 a member of the crew of the S.S. *Santa Maria*. In April of that year federal customs officials in New York received information that he was going to transport a quantity of narcotics aboard that ship from South America to the United States. As a result of this and other information, the agents searched the *Santa Maria* upon its arrival in New York and found in the afterpeak of the vessel five packages containing about three and a half pounds of cocaine. They also learned of circumstances, not here relevant, tending to connect the petitioner with the cocaine. He was arrested, promptly arraigned, and subsequently indicted for possession of narcotics aboard a United States vessel. In July a superseding indictment was returned, charging the petitioner and a man named Colson with the same substantive offense, and in separate counts charging the petitioner, Colson, and others with having conspired to possess narcotics aboard a United States vessel, and to import, conceal, and facilitate the sale of narcotics. The petitioner, who had retained a lawyer, pleaded not guilty and was released on bail, along with Colson.

A few days later, and quite without the petitioner's knowledge, Colson decided to cooperate with the government agents in their continuing investigation of the narcotics activities in which the petitioner, Colson, and others had allegedly been engaged. Colson permitted an agent named Murphy to install a Schmidt radio transmitter under the front seat of Colson's automobile, by means of which Murphy, equipped with an appropriate receiving device, could overhear from some distance away conversations carried on in Colson's car.

On the evening of November 19, 1959, Colson and the petitioner held a lengthy conversation while sitting in Colson's automobile, parked on a New York street. By prearrangement with Colson, and totally unbeknown to the petitioner, the agent Murphy sat in a car parked out of sight down the street and listened over the radio to the entire conversation. The petitioner made several incriminating statements during the course of this conversation. At the petitioner's trial these incriminating statements were brought before the jury through Murphy's testimony, despite the insistent objection of defense counsel. The jury convicted the petitioner of several related narcotics offenses, and the convictions were affirmed by the Court of Appeals.

The petitioner argues that it was an error of constitutional dimensions to permit the agent Murphy at the trial to testify to the petitioner's incriminating statements which Murphy had overheard under the circumstances disclosed by this record. This argument is based upon two distinct and independent grounds. First, we are told that Murphy's use of the radio equipment violated the petitioner's rights under the Fourth Amendment, and, consequently, that all evidence which Murphy thereby obtained was inadmissible against the petitioner at the trial. Secondly, it is said that the petitioner's Fifth and Sixth Amendment rights were violated by the use in evidence against him of incriminating statements which government agents had deliberately elicited from him after he had been indicted and in the absence of his retained counsel. Because of the way we dispose of the case, we do not reach the Fourth Amendment issue.

In *Spano*, this Court reversed a state criminal conviction because a confession had been wrongly admitted into evidence against the defendant at his trial. In that case the defendant had already been indicted for first-degree murder at the time he confessed. The Court held that the defendant's conviction could not stand under the Fourteenth Amendment. While the Court's opinion relied upon the totality of the circumstances under which the confession had been obtained, four concurring Justices pointed out that the Constitution required reversal of the conviction upon the sole and specific ground that the confession had been deliberately elicited by the police after the defendant had been indicted, and therefore at a time when he was clearly entitled to a lawyer's help. It was pointed out that under our system of justice the most elemental concepts of due process of law contemplate that an indictment be followed by a trial, "in an orderly courtroom, presided over by a judge, open to the public, and protected by all the procedural safeguards of the law." (STEWART, J., concurring). It was said that a Constitution which guarantees a defendant the aid of counsel at such a trial could surely vouchsafe no less to an indicted defendant under interrogation by the police in a completely extrajudicial proceeding. Anything less, it was said, might deny a defendant "effective representation by counsel at the only stage when legal aid and advice would help him." (DOUGLAS, J., concurring).

Ever since this Court's decision in the *Spano* case, the New York courts have unequivocally followed this constitutional rule. "Any secret interrogation of the defendant, from and after the finding of the indictment, without the protection afforded by the presence of counsel, contravenes the basic dictates of fairness in the conduct of criminal causes and the fundamental rights of persons charged with crime." *People v. Waterman*, 9 N.Y.2d 561, 565, 216 N.Y.S.2d 70, 75, 175 N.E.2d 445, 448.

Here we deal not with a state court conviction, but with a federal case, where the specific guarantee of the Sixth Amendment directly applies.[6] *Johnson v. Zerbst*. We hold that the petitioner was denied the basic protections of that guarantee when there was used against him at his trial evidence of his own incriminating words, which federal agents had deliberately elicited from him after he had been indicted and in the absence of his counsel. It is true that in the *Spano* case the defendant was interrogated in a police station, while here the damaging testimony was elicited from the defendant without his knowledge while he was free on bail. But, as Judge Hays pointed out in his dissent in the Court of Appeals, "if such a rule is to have any efficacy it must apply to indirect and surreptitious interrogations as well as those conducted in the jailhouse. In this case, Massiah was more seriously imposed upon . . . because he did not even know that he was under interrogation by a government agent."

The Solicitor General, in his brief and oral argument, has strenuously contended that the federal law enforcement agents had the right, if not indeed the duty, to continue their investigation of the petitioner and his alleged criminal associates even though the petitioner had been indicted. He points out that the Government was continuing its investigation in order to uncover not only the source of narcotics found on the S.S. *Santa Maria*, but also their intended buyer. He says that the quantity of narcotics involved was such as to suggest that the petitioner was part of a large and well-organized ring, and indeed that the continuing investigation confirmed this suspicion, since it resulted in criminal charges against many defendants. Under these circumstances the Solicitor General concludes that the Government agents were completely "justified in making use of Colson's cooperation by having Colson continue his normal associations and by surveilling them."

We may accept and, at least for present purposes, completely approve all that this argument implies, Fourth Amendment problems to one side. We do not question that in this case, as in many cases, it was entirely proper to continue an investigation of the suspected criminal activities of the defendant and his alleged confederates, even though the defendant had already been indicted. All that we hold is that the defendant's own incriminating statements, obtained by federal agents under the circumstances here disclosed, could not constitutionally be used by the prosecution as evidence against *him* at his trial.

Reversed.

---

[6] "In all criminal prosecutions, the accused shall enjoy the right . . . to have the Assistance of Counsel for his defense."

MR. JUSTICE WHITE, with whom MR. JUSTICE CLARK and MR. JUSTICE HARLAN join, dissenting.

The current incidence of serious violations of the law represents not only an appalling waste of the potentially happy and useful lives of those who engage in such conduct but also an overhanging, dangerous threat to those unidentified and innocent people who will be the victims of crime today and tomorrow. This is a festering problem for which no adequate cures have yet been devised. At the very least there is much room for discontent with remedial measures so far undertaken. And admittedly there remains much to be settled concerning the disposition to be made of those who violate the law.

But dissatisfaction with preventive programs aimed at eliminating crime and profound dispute about whether we should punish, deter, rehabilitate or cure cannot excuse concealing one of our most menacing problems until the millennium has arrived. In my view, a civilized society must maintain its capacity to discover transgressions of the law and to identify those who flout it. This much is necessary even to know the scope of the problem, much less to formulate intelligent counter-measures. It will just not do to sweep these disagreeable matters under the rug or to pretend they are not there at all.

It is therefore a rather portentous occasion when a constitutional rule is established barring the use of evidence which is relevant, reliable and highly probative of the issue which the trial court has before it — whether the accused committed the act with which he is charged. Without the evidence, the quest for truth may be seriously impeded and in many cases the trial court, although aware of proof showing defendant's guilt, must nevertheless release him because the crucial evidence is deemed inadmissible. This result is entirely justified in some circumstances because exclusion serves other policies of overriding importance, as where evidence seized in an illegal search is excluded, not because of the quality of the proof, but to secure meaningful enforcement of the Fourth Amendment. *Weeks, Mapp.* But this only emphasizes that the soundest of reasons is necessary to warrant the exclusion of evidence otherwise admissible and the creation of another area of privileged testimony. With all due deference, I am not at all convinced that the additional barriers to the pursuit of truth which the Court today erects rest on anything like the solid foundations which decisions of this gravity should require.

The importance of the matter should not be underestimated, for today's rule promises to have wide application well beyond the facts of this case. The reason given for the result here — the admissions were obtained in the absence of counsel — would seem equally pertinent to statements obtained at any time after the right to counsel attaches, whether there has been an indictment or not; to admissions made prior to arraignment, at least where the defendant has counsel or asks for it; to the fruits of admissions improperly obtained under the new rule; to criminal proceedings in state courts; and to defendants long since convicted upon evidence including such admissions. The new rule will immediately do service in a great many cases.

Whatever the content or scope of the rule may prove to be, I am unable to see how this case presents an unconstitutional interference with Massiah's right to counsel. Massiah was not prevented from consulting with counsel as often as he wished. No meetings with counsel were disturbed or spied upon. Preparation for trial was in no way obstructed. It is only a sterile syllogism — an unsound one, besides — to say that because Massiah had a right to counsel's aid before and during the trial, his out-of-court conversations and admissions must be excluded if obtained without counsel's consent or presence. The right to counsel has never meant as much before, *Crooker*, and its extension in this case requires some further explanation, so far unarticulated by the Court.

Since the new rule would exclude all admissions made to the police, no matter how voluntary and reliable, the requirement of counsel's presence or approval would seem to rest upon the probability that counsel would foreclose any admissions at all. This is nothing more than a thinly disguised constitutional policy of minimizing or entirely prohibiting the use in evidence of voluntary out-of-court admissions and confessions made by the accused. Carried as far as blind logic may compel some to go, the notion that statements from the mouth of the defendant should not be used in evidence would have a severe and unfortunate impact upon the great bulk of criminal cases.

Viewed in this light, the Court's newly fashioned exclusionary principle goes far beyond the constitutional privilege against self-incrimination, which neither requires nor suggests the barring of voluntary pretrial admissions. The Fifth Amendment states that no person "shall be compelled in any criminal case to be a witness against himself . . . ." The defendant may thus not be compelled to testify at his trial, but he may if he wishes. Likewise he may not be compelled or coerced into saying anything before trial; but until today he could if he wished to, and if he did, it could be used against him. Whether as a matter of self-incrimination or of due process, the proscription is against compulsion — coerced incrimination. Under the prior law, announced in countless cases in this Court, the defendant's pretrial statements were admissible evidence if voluntarily made; inadmissible if not the product of his free will. Hardly any constitutional area has been more carefully patrolled by this Court, and until now the Court has expressly rejected the argument that admissions are to be deemed involuntary if made outside the presence of counsel.[*]

The Court presents no facts, no objective evidence, no reasons to warrant scrapping the voluntary-involuntary test for admissibility in this area. Without such evidence I would retain it in its present form.

This case cannot be analogized to the American Bar Association's rule forbidding an attorney to talk to the opposing party litigant outside the presence of his counsel. Aside from the fact that the Association's canons are not of constitutional dimensions, the specific canon argued is inapposite because it deals with the conduct of lawyers and not with the conduct of investigators. Lawyers are forbidden to

---

[*] Today's rule picks up where the Fifth Amendment ends and bars wholly voluntary admissions. I would assume, although one cannot be sure, that the new rule would not have a similar supplemental role in connection with the Fourth Amendment. While the Fifth Amendment bars only compelled incrimination, the Fourth Amendment bars only unreasonable searches. It could be argued, fruitlessly I would hope, that if the police must stay away from the defendant they must also stay away from his house once the right to counsel has attached and that a court must exclude the products of a reasonable search made pursuant to a properly issued warrant but without the consent or presence of the accused's counsel.

interview the opposing party because of the supposed imbalance of legal skill and acumen between the lawyer and the party litigant; the reason for the rule does not apply to non-lawyers and certainly not to Colson, Massiah's codefendant.

Applying the new exclusionary rule is peculiarly inappropriate in this case. At the time of the conversation in question, petitioner was not in custody but free on bail. He was not questioned in what anyone could call an atmosphere of official coercion. What he said was said to his partner in crime who had also been indicted. There was no suggestion or any possibility of coercion. What petitioner did not know was that Colson had decided to report the conversation to the police. Had there been no prior arrangements between Colson and the police, had Colson simply gone to the police after the conversation had occurred, his testimony relating Massiah's statements would be readily admissible at the trial, as would a recording which he might have made of the conversation. In such event, it would simply be said that Massiah risked talking to a friend who decided to disclose what he knew of Massiah's criminal activities. But, if, as occurred here, Colson had been cooperating with the police prior to his meeting with Massiah, both his evidence and the recorded conversation are somehow transformed into inadmissible evidence despite the fact that the hazard to Massiah remains precisely the same — the defection of a confederate in crime.

Reporting criminal behavior is expected or even demanded of the ordinary citizen. Friends may be subpoenaed to testify about friends, relatives about relatives and partners about partners. I therefore question the soundness of insulating Massiah from the apostasy of his partner in crime and of furnishing constitutional sanction for the strict secrecy and discipline of criminal organizations. Neither the ordinary citizen nor the confessed criminal should be discouraged from reporting what he knows to the authorities and from lending his aid to secure evidence of crime. Certainly after this case the Colsons will be few and far between; and the Massiahs can breathe much more easily, secure in the knowledge that the Constitution furnishes an important measure of protection against faithless compatriots and guarantees sporting treatment for sporting peddlers of narcotics.

Meanwhile, of course, the public will again be the loser and law enforcement will be presented with another serious dilemma. The general issue lurking in the background of the Court's opinion is the legitimacy of penetrating or obtaining confederates in criminal organizations. For the law enforcement agency, the answer for the time being can only be in the form of a prediction about the future application of today's new constitutional doctrine. More narrowly, and posed by the precise situation involved here, the question is this: when the police have arrested and released on bail one member of a criminal ring and another member, a confederate, is cooperating with the police, can the confederate be allowed to continue his association with the ring or must he somehow be withdrawn to avoid challenge to trial evidence on the ground that it was acquired after rather than before the arrest, after rather than before the indictment?

Defendants who are out on bail have been known to continue their illicit operations. That an attorney is advising them should not constitutionally immunize their statements made in furtherance of these operations and relevant to the question of their guilt at the pending prosecution. In this very case there is evidence that after indictment defendant Aiken tried to persuade Agent Murphy to go into the narcotics business with him. Under today's decision, Murphy may neither testify as to the content of this conversation nor seize for introduction in evidence any narcotics whose location Aiken may have made known.

Undoubtedly, the evidence excluded in this case would not have been available but for the conduct of Colson in cooperation with Agent Murphy, but is it this kind of conduct which should be forbidden to those charged with law enforcement? It is one thing to establish safeguards against procedures fraught with the potentiality of coercion and to outlaw "easy but self-defeating ways in which brutality is substituted for brains as an instrument of crime detection." But here there was no substitution of brutality for brains, no inherent danger of police coercion justifying the prophylactic effect of another exclusionary rule. Massiah was not being interrogated in a police station, was not surrounded by numerous officers or questioned in relays, and was not forbidden access to others. Law enforcement may have the elements of a contest about it, but it is not a game. Massiah and those like him receive ample protection from the long line of precedents in this Court holding that confessions may not be introduced unless they are voluntary. In making these determinations the courts must consider the absence of counsel as one of several factors by which voluntariness is to be judged. This is a wiser rule than the automatic rule announced by the Court, which requires courts and juries to disregard voluntary admissions which they might well find to be the best possible evidence in discharging their responsibility for ascertaining truth.

QUESTIONS AND NOTES

1. How would the Fourth Amendment question in *Massiah* have been decided if the case were before the Court today? Why?

2. The Court ends its opinion in seeming agreement with the Government's position that it did nothing wrong. If that is true, why should the evidence have been excluded?

3. Is it significant that Massiah's counsel was not present at the time he confessed? Would the case be significantly easier for the Government if Massiah's lawyer were with him in Colson's car when he made his incriminating statements? Why? Why not? Would it not have been more intrusive if the government had listened to or deliberately had reported to it, conversations among Colson, Massiah, and Massiah's lawyer? *Compare Weatherford v. Bursey*, 429 U.S. 545 (1977).

4. How did the Government deliberately elicit a confession? Didn't it simply overhear an incriminating statement?

5. Is Justice White overly apocalyptic in his view of *Massiah's* potential? Wasn't the fact of indictment a core part of the majority's opinion?

6. Justice White suggests that codefendant Aiken's attempt to recruit Officer Murphy into the drug smuggling business is inadmissible according to *Massiah*. Do you agree? Explain.

7. We now turn to *Escobedo*, which arguably constitutes the high water mark for the right to counsel during interrogation.

ESCOBEDO v. STATE OF ILLINOIS
378 U.S. 478 (1964)

Mr. Justice Goldberg delivered the opinion of the Court.

The critical question in this case is whether, under the circumstances, the refusal by the police to honor petitioner's request to consult with his lawyer during the course of an interrogation constitutes a denial of "the Assistance of Counsel" in violation of the Sixth Amendment to the Constitution as "made obligatory upon the States by the Fourteenth Amendment," *Gideon v. Wainwright*, 372 U.S. 335, 342, and thereby renders inadmissible in a state criminal trial any incriminating statement elicited by the police during the interrogation.

On the night of January 19, 1960, petitioner's brother-in-law was fatally shot. In the early hours of the next morning, at 2:30 a.m., petitioner was arrested without a warrant and interrogated. Petitioner made no statement to the police and was released at 5 that afternoon pursuant to a state court writ of habeas corpus obtained by Mr. Warren Wolfson, a lawyer who had been retained by petitioner.

On January 30, Benedict DiGerlando, who was then in police custody and who was later indicted for the murder along with petitioner, told the police that petitioner had fired the fatal shots. Between 8 and 9 that evening, petitioner and his sister, the widow of the deceased, were arrested and taken to police headquarters. En route to the police station, the police "had handcuffed the defendant behind his back," and "one of the arresting officers told defendant that DiGerlando had named him as the one who shot" the deceased. Petitioner testified, without contradiction, that the "detectives said they had us pretty well, up pretty tight, and we might as well admit to this crime," and that he replied, "I am sorry but I would like to have advice from my lawyer." A police officer testified that although petitioner was not formally charged "he was in custody' " and "couldn't walk out the door."

Shortly after petitioner reached police headquarters, his retained lawyer arrived. The lawyer described the ensuing events in the following terms:

> On that day I received a phone call [from "the mother of another defendant"] and pursuant to that phone call I went to the Detective Bureau at 11th and State. The first person I talked to was the Sergeant on duty at the Bureau Desk, Sergeant Pidgeon. I asked Sergeant Pidgeon for permission to speak to my client, Danny Escobedo . . . . Sergeant Pidgeon made a call to the Bureau lockup and informed me that the boy had been taken from the lockup to the Homicide Bureau. This was between 9:30 and 10:00 in the evening. Before I went anywhere, he called the Homicide Bureau and told them there was an attorney waiting to see Escobedo. He told me I could not see him. Then I went upstairs to the Homicide Bureau. There were several Homicide Detectives around and I talked to them. I identified myself as Escobedo's attorney and asked permission to see him. They said I could not . . . . The police officer told me to see Chief Flynn who was on duty. I identified myself to Chief Flynn and asked permission to see my client. He said I could not . . . . I think it was approximately 11:00 o'clock. He said I couldn't see him because they hadn't completed

questioning . . . . [F]or a second or two I spotted him in an office in the Homicide Bureau. The door was open and I could see through the office . . . . I waved to him and he waved back and then the door was closed, by one of the officers at Homicide.[2] There were four or five officers milling around the Homicide Detail that night. As to whether I talked to Captain Flynn any later that day, I waited around for another hour or two and went back again and renewed by (sic) request to see my client. He again told me I could not. . . . I filed an official complaint with Commissioner Phelan of the Chicago Police Department. I had a conversation with every police officer I could find. I was told at Homicide that I couldn't see him and I would have to get a writ of habeas corpus. I left the Homicide Bureau and from the Detective Bureau at 11th and State at approximately 1:00 A.M. [Sunday morning] I had no opportunity to talk to my client that night. I quoted to Captain Flynn the Section of the Criminal Code which allows an attorney the right to see his client."[3]

Petitioner testified that during the course of the interrogation he repeatedly asked to speak to his lawyer and that the police said that his lawyer "didn't want to see" him. The testimony of the police officers confirmed these accounts in substantial detail.

Notwithstanding repeated requests by each, petitioner and his retained lawyer were afforded no opportunity to consult during the course of the entire interrogation. At one point, as previously noted, petitioner and his attorney came into each other's view for a few moments but the attorney was quickly ushered away. Petitioner testified "that he heard a detective telling the attorney the latter would not be allowed to talk to [him] 'until they were done' " and that he heard the attorney being refused permission to remain in the adjoining room. A police officer testified that he had told the lawyer that he could not see petitioner until "we were through interrogating" him.

There is testimony by the police that during the interrogation, petitioner, a 22-year-old of Mexican extraction with no record of previous experience with the police, "was handcuffed" in a standing position and that he "was nervous, he had circles under his eyes and he was upset" and was "agitated" because "he had not slept well in over a week."

It is undisputed that during the course of the interrogation Officer Montejano, who "grew up" in petitioner's neighborhood, who knew his family, and who uses "Spanish language in [his] police work," conferred alone with petitioner "for about a quarter of an hour . . . ." Petitioner testified that the officer said to him "in Spanish that my sister and I could go home if I pinned it on Benedict DiGerlando," that "he would see to it that we would go home and be held only as witnesses, if

---

[2] Petitioner testified that this ambiguous gesture "could have meant most anything," but that he "took it upon [his] own to think that [the lawyer was telling him] not to say anything," and that the lawyer "wanted to talk" to him.

[3] The statute then in effect provided in pertinent part that: "All public officers . . . having the custody of any person . . . restrained of his liberty for any alleged cause whatever, shall, except in cases of imminent danger of escape, admit any practicing attorney . . . whom such person . . . may desire to see or consult . . . ." ILL. REV. STAT. (1959), c. 38, § 477.

anything, if we had made a statement against DiGerlando . . . , that we would be able to go home that night." Petitioner testified that he made the statement in issue because of this assurance. Officer Montejano denied offering any such assurance.

A police officer testified that during the interrogation the following occurred:

> I informed him of what DiGerlando told me and when I did, he told me that DiGerlando was [lying] and I said, "Would you care to tell DiGerlando that?" and he said, "Yes, I will." So, I brought . . . Escobedo in and he confronted DiGerlando and he told him that he was lying and said, "I didn't shoot Manuel, you did it."

In this way, petitioner, for the first time admitted to some knowledge of the crime. After that he made additional statements further implicating himself in the murder plot. At this point an Assistant State's Attorney, Theodore J. Cooper, was summoned "to take" a statement. Mr. Cooper, an experienced lawyer who was assigned to the Homicide Division to take "statements from some defendants and some prisoners that they had in custody," "took" petitioner's statement by asking carefully framed questions apparently designed to assure the admissibility into evidence of the resulting answers. Mr. Cooper testified that he did not advise petitioner of his constitutional rights, and it is undisputed that no one during the course of the interrogation so advised him.

Petitioner moved both before and during trial to suppress the incriminating statement, but the motions were denied. Petitioner was convicted of murder and he appealed the conviction.

The Supreme Court of Illinois, in its original opinion of February 1, 1963, held the statement inadmissible and reversed the conviction. The court said:

> [I]t seems manifest to us, from the undisputed evidence and the circumstances surrounding defendant at the time of his statement and shortly prior thereto, that the defendant understood he would be permitted to go home if he gave the statement and would be granted an immunity from prosecution.

The State petitioned for, and the court granted, rehearing. The court then affirmed the conviction. It said: "[T]he officer denied making the promise and the trier of fact believed him. We find no reason for disturbing the trial court's finding that the confession was voluntary."[4] The court also held, on the authority of this Court's decisions in *Crooker*, that the confession was admissible even though "it was

---

[4] Compare *Haynes v. Washington*, 373 U.S. 503, 515 (decided on the same day as the decision of the Illinois Supreme Court here), where we said:

> Our conclusion is in no way foreclosed, as the State contends, by the fact that the state trial judge or the jury may have reached a different result on this issue.

> It is well settled that the duty of constitutional adjudication resting upon this Court requires that the question whether the Due Process Clause of the Fourteenth Amendment has been violated by admission into evidence of a coerced confession be the subject of an *independent* determination here, see, e.g., *Ashcraft v. Tennessee*, 322 U.S. 143, 147–148; "we cannot escape the responsibility of making our own examination of the record," *Spano v. New York*, 360 U.S. 315, 316.

(Emphasis in original.)

obtained after he had requested the assistance of counsel, which request was denied."

In *Massiah*, this Court observed that "a Constitution which guarantees a defendant the aid of counsel at . . . trial could surely vouchsafe no less to an indicted defendant under interrogation by the police in a completely extrajudicial proceeding. Anything less . . . might deny a defendant 'effective representation by counsel at the only stage when legal aid and advice would help him." Quoting DOUGLAS, J., concurring in *Spano*.

The interrogation here was conducted before petitioner was formally indicted. But in the context of this case, that fact should make no difference. When petitioner requested, and was denied, an opportunity to consult with his lawyer, the investigation had ceased to be a general investigation of "an unsolved crime." *Spano* (STEWART, J., concurring). Petitioner had become the accused, and the purpose of the interrogation was to "get him" to confess his guilt despite his constitutional right not to do so. At the time of his arrest and throughout the course of the interrogation, the police told petitioner that they had convincing evidence that he had fired the fatal shots. Without informing him of his absolute right to remain silent in the face of this accusation, the police urged him to make a statement.[5] As this Court observed many years ago:

> It cannot be doubted that, placed in the position in which the accused was when the statement was made to him that the other suspected person had charged him with crime, the result was to produce upon his mind the fear that, if he remained silent, it would be considered an admission of guilt, and therefore render certain his being committed for trial as the guilty person, and it cannot be conceived that the converse impression would not also have naturally arisen that, by denying, there was hope of removing the suspicion from himself.

Bram v. United States, 168 U.S. 532, 562.

Petitioner, a layman, was undoubtedly unaware that under Illinois law an admission of "mere" complicity in the murder plot was legally as damaging as an admission of firing of the fatal shots. The "guiding hand of counsel" was essential to advise petitioner of his rights in this delicate situation. *Powell v. Alabama*, 287 U.S. 45, 69. This was the "stage when legal aid and advice" were most critical to petitioner. *Massiah*. It was a stage surely as critical as was the arraignment in *Hamilton v. Alabama*, 368 U.S. 52, and the preliminary hearing in *White v. Maryland*, 373 U.S. 59. What happened at this interrogation could certainly "affect the whole trial," since rights "may be as irretrievably lost, if not then and there asserted, as they are when an accused represented by counsel waives a right for strategic purposes." It would exalt form over substance to make the right to counsel, under these circumstances, depend on whether at the time of the interrogation, the authorities had secured a formal indictment. Petitioner had, for all practical purposes, already been charged with murder.

---

[5] Although there is testimony in the record that petitioner and his lawyer had previously discussed what petitioner should do in the event of interrogation, there is no evidence that they discussed what petitioner should, or could, do in the face of a false accusation that he had fired the fatal bullets.

In *Gideon v. Wainwright*, 372 U.S. 335, we held that every person accused of a crime, whether state or federal, is entitled to a lawyer at trial.[8] The rule sought by the State here, however, would make the trial no more than an appeal from the interrogation; and the "right to use counsel at the formal trial [would be] a very hollow thing [if], for all practical purposes, the conviction is already assured by pretrial examination." "One can imagine a cynical prosecutor saying: 'Let them have the most illustrious counsel, now. They can't escape the noose. There is nothing that counsel can do for them at the trial.'" *Ex parte Sullivan*, 107 F. Supp. 514, 517–518.[9]

It is argued that if the right to counsel is afforded prior to indictment, the number of confessions obtained by the police will diminish significantly, because most confessions are obtained during the period between arrest and indictment, and "any lawyer worth his salt will tell the suspect in no uncertain terms to make no statement to police under any circumstances." *Watts* (Jackson, J., concurring in part and dissenting in part). This argument, of course, cuts two ways. The fact that many confessions are obtained during this period points up its critical nature as a "stage when legal aid and advice" are surely needed. The right to counsel would indeed be hollow if it began at a period when few confessions were obtained. There is necessarily a direct relationship between the importance of a stage to the police in their quest for a confession and the criticalness of that stage to the accused in his need for legal advice. Our Constitution, unlike some others, strikes the balance in favor of the right of the accused to be advised by his lawyer of his privilege against self-incrimination.

We have learned the lesson of history, ancient and modern, that a system of criminal law enforcement which comes to depend on the "confession" will, in the long run, be less reliable and more subject to abuses than a system which depends on extrinsic evidence independently secured through skillful investigation. As Dean Wigmore so wisely said:

> (A)*ny system of administration which permits the prosecution to trust habitually to compulsory self-disclosure as a source of proof must itself suffer morally thereby.* The inclination develops to rely mainly upon such evidence, and to be satisfied with an incomplete investigation of the other sources. The exercise of the power to extract answers begets a forgetfulness of the just limitations of that power. — The simple and peaceful process of questioning breeds a readiness to resort to bullying and to physical force and torture. If there is a right to an answer, there soon seems to be a right to the expected answer, — that is, to a confession of guilt. Thus the legitimate use grows into the unjust abuse; ultimately, the innocent are jeopardized by the encroachments of a bad system. Such seems to have been the course of experience in those legal systems where the privilege was not recognized.

---

[8] Twenty-two States, including Illinois, urged us so to hold.

[9] The Soviet criminal code does not permit a lawyer to be present during the investigation. The Soviet Trial has thus been aptly described as "an appeal from the pretrial investigation." FEIFER, JUSTICE IN MOSCOW (1964), 86.

8 WIGMORE, EVIDENCE (3d ed. 1940), 309. (Emphasis in original.) This Court also has recognized that "history amply shows that confessions have often been extorted to save law enforcement officials the trouble and effort of obtaining valid and independent evidence . . . ."

We have also learned the companion lesson of history that no system of criminal justice can, or should, survive if it comes to depend for its continued effectiveness on the citizens' abdication through unawareness of their constitutional rights. No system worth preserving should have to *fear* that if an accused is permitted to consult with a lawyer, he will become aware of, and exercise, these rights.[13] If the exercise of constitutional rights will thwart the effectiveness of a system of law enforcement, then there is something very wrong with that system.[14]

We hold, therefore, that where, as here, the investigation is no longer a general inquiry into an unsolved crime but has begun to focus on a particular suspect, the suspect has been taken into police custody, the police carry out a process of interrogations that lends itself to eliciting incriminating statements, the suspect has requested and been denied an opportunity to consult with his lawyer, and the police have not effectively warned him of his absolute constitutional right to remain silent, the accused has been denied "The Assistance of Counsel" in violation of the Sixth Amendment to the Constitution as "made obligatory upon the States by the Fourteenth Amendment," *Gideon v. Wainwright*, 372 U.S. at 342, and that no statement elicited by the police during the interrogation may be used against him at a criminal trial.

Crooker does not compel a contrary result. In that case the Court merely rejected the absolute rule sought by petitioner, that "every state denial of a request to contact counsel [is] an infringement of the constitutional right *without regard to the circumstances of the case.*" (Emphasis in original.) In its place, the following rule was announced:

> [S]tate refusal of a request to engage counsel violates due process not only if the accused is deprived of counsel at trial on the merits, . . . *but also if he is deprived of counsel for any part of the pretrial proceedings*, provided that he is so prejudiced thereby as to infect his subsequent trial with an

---

[13] *Cf.* Report of Attorney General's Committee on Poverty and the Administration of Federal Criminal Justice (1963), 10–11:

> The survival of our system of criminal justice and the values which it advances depends upon a constant, searching, and creative questioning of official decisions and assertions of authority at all stages of the process . . . . Persons [denied access to counsel] are incapable of providing the challenges that are indispensable to satisfactory operation of the system. The loss to the interests of accused individuals, occasioned by these failures, are great and apparent. It is also clear that a situation in which persons are required to contest a serious accusation but are denied access to the tools of contest is offensive to fairness and equity. Beyond these considerations, however, is the fact that [this situation is] detrimental to the proper functioning of the system of justice and that the loss in vitality of the adversary system, thereby occasioned, significantly endangers the basic interests of a free community.

[14] The accused may, of course, intelligently and knowingly waive his privilege against self-incrimination and his right to counsel either at a pretrial stage or at the trial. But no knowing and intelligent waiver of any constitutional right can be said to have occurred under the circumstances of this case.

absence of "that fundamental fairness essential to the very concept of justice." . . . The latter determination necessarily depends upon all the circumstances of the case.

(Emphasis added.) The Court, applying "these principles" to "the sum total of the circumstances [there] during the time petitioner was without counsel," concluded that he had not been fundamentally prejudiced by the denial of his request for counsel. Among the critical circumstances which distinguish that case from this one are that the petitioner there, but not here, was explicitly advised by the police of his constitutional right to remain silent and not to "say anything" in response to the questions, and that petitioner there, but not here, was a well-educated man who had studied criminal law while attending law school for a year. The Court's opinion in *Cicenia v. Lagay*, 357 U.S. 504, decided the same day, merely said that the "contention that petitioner had a constitutional right to confer with counsel is disposed of by *Crooker v. California* . . . ." That case adds nothing, therefore, to Crooker. In any event, to the extent that *Cicenia* or *Crooker* may be inconsistent with the principles announced today, they are not to be regarded as controlling.

Nothing we have said today affects the powers of the police to investigate "an unsolved crime," *Spano* (STEWART, J., concurring), by gathering information from witnesses and by other "proper investigative efforts." We hold only that when the process shifts from investigatory to accusatory — when its focus is on the accused and its purpose is to elicit a confession — our adversary system begins to operate, and, under the circumstances here, the accused must be permitted to consult with his lawyer.

The judgment of the Illinois Supreme Court is reversed and the case remanded for proceedings not inconsistent with this opinion.

Reversed and remanded.

MR. JUSTICE HARLAN, dissenting.

I would affirm the judgment of the Supreme Court of Illinois on the basis of *Cicenia v. Lagay*, 357 U.S. 504, decided by this Court only six years ago. Like my Brother WHITE, I think the rule announced today is most ill-conceived and that it seriously and unjustifiably fetters perfectly legitimate methods of criminal law enforcement.

MR. JUSTICE STEWART, dissenting.

I think this case is directly controlled by *Cicenia v. Lagay*, 357 U.S. 504, and I would therefore affirm the judgment.

Massiah, is not in point here. In that case a federal grand jury had indicted Massiah. He had retained a lawyer and entered a formal plea of not guilty. Under our system of federal justice an indictment and arraignment are followed by a trial, at which the Sixth Amendment guarantees the defendant the assistance of counsel. But Massiah was released on bail, and thereafter agents of the Federal Government deliberately elicited incriminating statements from him in the absence of his lawyer. We held that the use of these statements against him at his trial denied him the basic protections of the Sixth Amendment guarantee. Putting to one side the fact that the case now before us is not a federal case, the vital fact remains that this case does not involve the deliberate interrogation of a defendant after the initiation of judicial proceedings against him. The Court disregards this basic difference between the present case and Massiah's, with the bland assertion that "that fact should make no difference."

It is "that fact," I submit, which makes all the difference. Under our system of criminal justice the institution of formal, meaningful judicial proceedings, by way of indictment, information, or arraignment, marks the point at which a criminal investigation has ended and adversary proceedings have commenced. It is at this point that the constitutional guarantees attach which pertain to a criminal trial. Among those guarantees are the right to a speedy trial, the right of confrontation, and the right to trial by jury. Another is the guarantee of the assistance of counsel.

The confession which the Court today holds inadmissible was a voluntary one. It was given during the course of a perfectly legitimate police investigation of an unsolved murder. The Court says that what happened during this investigation "affected" the trial. I had always supposed that the whole purpose of a police investigation of a murder was to "affect" the trial of the murderer, and that it would be only an incompetent, unsuccessful, or corrupt investigation which would not do so. The Court further says that the Illinois police officers did not advise the petitioner of his "constitutional rights" before he confessed to the murder. This Court has never held that the Constitution requires the police to give any "advice" under circumstances such as these.

Supported by no stronger authority than its own rhetoric, the Court today converts a routine police investigation of an unsolved murder into a distorted analogue of a judicial trial. It imports into this investigation constitutional concepts historically applicable only after the onset of formal prosecutorial proceedings. By doing so, I think the Court perverts those precious constitutional guarantees, and frustrates the vital interests of society in preserving the legitimate and proper function of honest and purposeful police investigation.

Like my Brother CLARK, I cannot escape the logic of my Brother WHITE's conclusions as to the extraordinary implications which emanate from the Court's opinion in this case, and I share their views as to the untold and highly unfortunate impact today's decision may have upon the fair administration of criminal justice. I can only hope we have completely misunderstood what the Court has said.

MR. JUSTICE WHITE, with whom MR. JUSTICE CLARK and MR. JUSTICE STEWART join, dissenting.

In *Massiah*, the Court held that as of the date of the indictment the prosecution is disentitled to secure admissions from the accused. The Court now moves that date back to the time when the prosecution begins to "focus" on the accused. Although the opinion purports to be limited to the facts of this case, it would be naive to think that the new constitutional right announced will depend upon whether the accused has retained his own counsel, or has asked to consult with counsel in the course of interrogation. At the very least the Court holds that once the accused becomes a suspect and, presumably, is arrested, any admission made to the police thereafter is inadmissible in evidence unless the accused has waived his right to counsel. The decision is thus another major step in the direction of the goal which the Court seemingly has in mind — to bar from evidence all admissions obtained from an individual suspected of crime, whether involuntarily made or not. It does of course put us one step "ahead" of the English judges who have had the good sense to leave the matter a discretionary one with the trial court. I reject this step and the invitation to go farther which the Court has now issued.

By abandoning the voluntary-involuntary test for admissibility of confessions, the Court seems driven by the notion that it is uncivilized law enforcement to use an accused's own admissions against him at his trial. It attempts to find a home for this new and nebulous rule of due process by attaching it to the right to counsel guaranteed in the federal system by the Sixth Amendment and binding upon the States by virtue of the due process guarantee of the Fourteenth Amendment. *Gideon*. The right to counsel now not only entitles the accused to counsel's advice and aid in preparing for trial but stands as an impenetrable barrier to any interrogation once the accused has become a suspect. From that very moment apparently his right to counsel attaches, a rule wholly unworkable and impossible to administer unless police cars are equipped with public defenders and undercover agents and police informants have defense counsel at their side. I would not abandon the Court's prior cases defining with some care and analysis the circumstances requiring the presence or aid of counsel and substitute the amorphous and wholly unworkable principle that counsel is constitutionally required whenever he would or could be helpful. Under this new approach one might just as well argue that a potential defendant is constitutionally entitled to a lawyer before, not after, he commits a crime, since it is then that crucial incriminating evidence is put within the reach of the Government by the would-be accused. Until now there simply has been no right guaranteed by the Federal Constitution to be free from the use at trial of a voluntary admission made prior to indictment.

It is incongruous to assume that the provision for counsel in the Sixth Amendment was meant to amend or supersede the self-incrimination provision of the Fifth Amendment, which is now applicable to the States. *Malloy v. Hogan*, 378 U.S. 1. That amendment addresses itself to the very issue of incriminating admissions of an accused and resolves it by proscribing only compelled statements. Neither the Framers, the constitutional language, a century of decisions of this Court nor Professor Wigmore provides an iota of support for the idea that an accused has an absolute constitutional right not to answer even in the absence of compulsion — the constitutional right not to incriminate himself by making voluntary disclosures.

Today's decision cannot be squared with other provisions of the Constitution which, in my view, define the system of criminal justice this Court is empowered to administer. The Fourth Amendment permits upon probable cause even compulsory searches of the suspect and his possessions and the use of the fruits of the search at trial, all in the absence of counsel. The Fifth Amendment and state constitutional provisions authorize, indeed require, inquisitorial grand jury proceedings at which a potential defendant, in the absence of counsel, is shielded against no more than compulsory incrimination. A grand jury witness, who may be a suspect, is interrogated and his answers, at least until today, are admissible in evidence at trial. And these provisions have been thought of as constitutional safeguards to persons suspected of an offense. Furthermore, until now, the Constitution has permitted the accused to be fingerprinted and to be identified in a line-up or in the courtroom itself.

The Court chooses to ignore these matters and to rely on the virtues and morality of a system of criminal law enforcement which does not depend on the "confession." No such judgment is to be found in the Constitution. It might be appropriate for a legislature to provide that a suspect should not be consulted during a criminal investigation; that an accused should never be called before a grand jury to answer, even if he wants to, what may well be incriminating questions; and that no person, whether he be a suspect, guilty criminal or innocent bystander, should be put to the ordeal of responding to orderly noncompulsory inquiry by the State. But this is not the system our Constitution requires. The only "inquisitions" the Constitution forbids are those which compel incrimination. Escobedo's statements were not compelled and the Court does not hold that they were.

This new American judges' rule, which is to be applied in both federal and state courts, is perhaps thought to be a necessary safeguard against the possibility of extorted confessions. To this extent it reflects a deep-seated distrust of law enforcement officers everywhere, unsupported by relevant data or current material based upon our own experience. Obviously law enforcement officers can make mistakes and exceed their authority, as today's decision shows that even judges can do, but I have somewhat more faith than the Court evidently has in the ability and desire of prosecutors and of the power of the appellate courts to discern and correct such violations of the law.

The Court may be concerned with a narrower matter: the unknowing defendant who responds to police questioning because he mistakenly believes that he must and that his admissions will not be used against him. But this worry hardly calls for the broadside the Court has now fired. The failure to inform an accused that he need not answer and that his answers may be used against him is very relevant indeed to whether the disclosures are compelled. Cases in this Court, to say the least, have never placed a premium on ignorance of constitutional rights. If an accused is told he must answer and does not know better, it would be very doubtful that the resulting admissions could be used against him. When the accused has not been informed of his rights at all the Court characteristically and properly looks very closely at the surrounding circumstances. I would continue to do so. But, in this case Danny Escobedo knew full well that he did not have to answer and knew full well that his lawyer had advised him not to answer.

I do not suggest for a moment that law enforcement will be destroyed by the rule announced today. The need for peace and order is too insistent for that. But it will be crippled and its task made a great deal more difficult, all in my opinion, for unsound, unstated reasons, which can find no home in any of the provisions of the Constitution.

QUESTIONS AND NOTES

1.   Prior to *Escobedo*, the Court had held that the right to counsel (*Gideon*), and the privilege against self-incrimination (*Malloy*) were both applicable to the states. Given that both of these decisions were rendered within a year of *Escobedo* does it surprise you that the Court opted for the Sixth Amendment right to counsel as the grounds for its decision? Why do you suppose the Court relied on the Sixth rather than the Fifth Amendment?

2.   Do you think that Escobedo's confession was (should have been) involuntary under traditional coerced confession law? Would (should) it matter whether Officer Montejano made the statements attributed to him by Escobedo? How and at what level should a question like that be resolved?

3.   Is the Court outlawing (or casting doubt upon) *all* confessions? Explain. Should it?

4.   Is the Court opting for a Utopian rule or a constitutionally mandated one?

5.   Is Justice Stewart's angry tone justified? Was his *Massiah* opinion justified by anything stronger than *his* own rhetoric? Put differently, why shouldn't arrest, rather than indictment, be conceived as the commencement of criminal proceedings against the defendant?

6.   When would a person be questioned under circumstances that are *not* accusatory?

7.   Do you agree with the Court that "if the exercise of constitutional rights will thwart the effectiveness of a system of law enforcement, then there is something very wrong with that system"?

8.   Should the Court have forthrightly overruled *Crooker* and its companion case, *Cicenia v. Lagay*, which involved a less sophisticated defendant than Crooker, rather than try to distinguish the cases?

Chapter 17

MIRANDA

If ever one case stood for an entire area of the law, it is *Miranda*. As we shall see over the next several classes, the text of *Miranda* has been construed as though it, itself, was constitutional language. We begin with the case itself.

A. THE CASE ITSELF

MIRANDA v. ARIZONA
384 U.S. 436 (1966)

MR. CHIEF JUSTICE WARREN delivered the opinion of the Court.

The cases before us raise questions which go to the roots of our concepts of American criminal jurisprudence: the restraints society must observe consistent with the Federal Constitution in prosecuting individuals for crime. More specifically, we deal with the admissibility of statements obtained from an individual who is subjected to custodial police interrogation and the necessity for procedures which assure that the individual is accorded his privilege under the Fifth Amendment to the Constitution not to be compelled to incriminate himself.

We dealt with certain phases of this problem recently in *Escobedo*. There, as in the four cases before us, law enforcement officials took the defendant into custody and interrogated him in a police station for the purpose of obtaining a confession. The police did not effectively advise him of his right to remain silent or of his right to consult with his attorney. Rather, they confronted him with an alleged accomplice who accused him of having perpetrated a murder. When the defendant denied the accusation and said "I didn't shoot Manuel, you did it," they handcuffed him and took him to an interrogation room. There, while handcuffed and standing, he was questioned for four hours until he confessed. During this interrogation, the police denied his request to speak to his attorney, and they prevented his retained attorney, who had come to the police station, from consulting with him. At his trial, the State, over his objection, introduced the confession against him. We held that the statements thus made were constitutionally inadmissible.

This case has been the subject of judicial interpretation and spirited legal debate since it was decided two years ago. Both state and federal courts, in assessing its implications, have arrived at varying conclusions. A wealth of scholarly material has been written tracing its ramifications and underpinnings.[2] Police and prosecutor

---

[2] *See, e.g.*, Enker & Elsen, *Counsel for the Suspect:* Massiah v. United States *and* Escobedo v. Illinois, 49 MINN. L. REV. 47 (1964); Herman, *The Supreme Court and Restrictions on Police Interrogation*, 25

have speculated on its range and desirability. We granted certiorari in these cases in order further to explore some facets of the problems, thus exposed, of applying the privilege against self-incrimination to in-custody interrogation, and to give concrete constitutional guidelines for law enforcement agencies and courts to follow.

We start here, as we did in *Escobedo*, with the premise that our holding is not an innovation in our jurisprudence, but is an application of principles long recognized and applied in other settings. We have undertaken a thorough re-examination of the *Escobedo* decision and the principles it announced, and we reaffirm it. That case was but an explication of basic rights that are enshrined in our Constitution — that "No person . . . shall be compelled in any criminal case to be a witness against himself," and that "the accused shall . . . have the Assistance of Counsel" — rights which were put in jeopardy in that case through official overbearing. These precious rights were fixed in our Constitution only after centuries of persecution and struggle. And in the words of Chief Justice Marshall, they were secured "for ages to come, and . . . designed to approach immortality as nearly as human institutions can approach it," *Cohens v. Virginia*, 6 Wheat. 264, 387 (1821).

This was the spirit in which we delineated, in meaningful language, the manner in which the constitutional rights of the individual could be enforced against overzealous police practices. It was necessary in *Escobedo*, as here, to insure that what was proclaimed in the Constitution had not become but a "form of words," *Silverthorn Lumber Co. v. United States*, 251 U.S. 385, 392 (1920), in the hands of government officials. And it is in this spirit, consistent with our role as judges, that we adhere to the principles of *Escobedo* today.

Our holding will be spelled out with some specificity in the pages which follow but briefly stated it is this: the prosecution may not use statements, whether exculpatory or inculpatory, stemming from custodial interrogation of the defendant unless it demonstrates the use of procedural safeguards effective to secure the privilege against self-incrimination. By custodial interrogation, we mean questioning initiated by law enforcement officers after a person has been taken into custody or otherwise deprived of his freedom of action in any significant way.[4] As for the procedural safeguards to be employed, unless other fully effective means are devised to inform accused persons of their right of silence and to assure a continuous opportunity to exercise it, the following measures are required. Prior to any questioning, the person must be warned that he has a right to remain silent, that any statement he does make may be used as evidence against him, and that he has a right to the presence of an attorney, either retained or appointed. The defendant may waive effectuation of these rights, provided the waiver is made voluntarily, knowingly and intelligently. If, however, he indicates in any manner

---

OHIO ST. L.J. 449 (1964); Kamisar, *Equal Justice in the Gatehouses and Mansions of American Criminal Procedure, in* CRIMINAL JUSTICE IN OUR TIME 1 (1965); Dowling, Escobedo *and Beyond: The Need for a Fourteenth Amendment Code of Criminal Procedure*, 56 J. CRIM. L., C. & P.S. 143, 156 (1965). The complex problems also prompted discussions by jurists. *Compare* Bazelon, *Law, Morality, and Civil Liberties*, 12 U.C.L.A.L. REV. 13 (1964), *with* Friendly, *The Bill of Rights as a Code of Criminal Procedure*, 53 CALIF. L. REV. 929 (1965).

[4] This is what we meant in *Escobedo* when we spoke of an investigation which had focused on an accused.

and at any stage of the process that he wishes to consult with an attorney before speaking there can be no questioning. Likewise, if the individual is alone and indicates in any manner that he does not wish to be interrogated, the police may not question him. The mere fact that he may have answered some questions or volunteered some statements on his own does not deprive him of the right to refrain from answering any further inquiries until he has consulted with an attorney and thereafter consents to be questioned.

I.

The constitutional issue we decide in each of these cases is the admissibility of statements obtained from a defendant questioned while in custody or otherwise deprived of his freedom of action in any significant way. In each, the defendant was questioned by police officers, detectives, or a prosecuting attorney in a room in which he was cut off from the outside world. In none of these cases was the defendant given a full and effective warning of his rights at the outset of the interrogation process. In all the cases, the questioning elicited oral admissions, and in three of them, signed statements as well which were admitted at their trials. They all thus share salient features — incommunicado interrogation of individuals in a police-dominated atmosphere, resulting in self-incriminating statements without full warnings of constitutional rights.

An understanding of the nature and setting of this in-custody interrogation is essential to our decisions today. The difficulty in depicting what transpires at such interrogations stems from the fact that in this country they have largely taken place incommunicado. From extensive factual studies undertaken in the early 1930's, including the famous Wickersham Report to Congress by a Presidential Commission, it is clear that police violence and the "third degree" flourished at that time. In a series of cases decided by this Court long after these studies, the police resorted to physical brutality — beatings, hanging, whipping — and to sustained and protracted questioning incommunicado in order to extort confessions. The Commission on Civil Rights in 1961 found much evidence to indicate that "some policemen still resort to physical force to obtain confessions." The use of physical brutality and violence is not, unfortunately, relegated to the past or to any part of the country. Only recently in Kings County, New York, the police brutally beat, kicked and placed lighted cigarette butts on the back of a potential witness under interrogation for the purpose of securing a statement incriminating a third party. *People v. Portelli*, 15 N.Y.2d 235, 257 N.Y.S.2d 931, 205 N.E.2d 857 (1965).[7]

---

[7] In addition, *see People v. Wakat*, 114 N.E.2d 706 (Ill. 1953); *Wakat v. Harlib*, 253 F.2d 59 (7th Cir. 1958) (defendant suffering from broken bones, multiple bruises and injuries sufficiently serious to require eight months' medical treatment after being manhandled by five policemen); *Kier v. State*, 132 A.2d 494 (Md. 1957) (police doctor told accused, who was strapped to a chair completely nude, that he proposed to take hair and skin scrapings from anything that looked like blood or sperm from various parts of his body); *Bruner v. People*, 156 P.2d 111 (Colo. 1945) (defendant held in custody over two months, deprived of food for 15 hours, forced to submit to a lie detector test when he wanted to go to the toilet); *People v. Matlock*, 336 P.2d 505 (Cal. 1959) (defendant questioned incessantly over an evening's time, made to lie on cold board and to answer questions whenever it appeared he was getting sleepy). Other cases are documented in AMERICAN CIVIL LIBERTIES UNION, ILLINOIS DIVISION, SECRET DETENTION BY THE CHICAGO POLICE (1959); Potts, *The Preliminary Examination and "The Third Degree,"* 2 BAYLOR L.

The examples given above are undoubtedly the exception now, but they are sufficiently widespread to be the object of concern. Unless a proper limitation upon custodial interrogation is achieved — such as these decisions will advance — there can be no assurance that practices of this nature will be eradicated in the foreseeable future.

Again we stress that the modern practice of in-custody interrogation is psychologically rather than physically oriented. As we have stated before, "Since *Chambers v. Florida*, 309 U.S. 227, this Court has recognized that coercion can be mental as well as physical, and that the blood of the accused is not the only hallmark of an unconstitutional inquisition." *Blackburn v. Alabama*, 361 U.S. 199, 206 (1960). Interrogation still takes place in privacy. Privacy results in secrecy and this in turn results in a gap in our knowledge as to what in fact goes on in the interrogation rooms. A valuable source of information about present police practices, however, may be found in various police manuals and texts which document procedures employed with success in the past, and which recommend various other effective tactics. These texts are used by law enforcement agencies themselves as guides. It should be noted that these texts professedly present the most enlightened and effective means presently used to obtain statements through custodial interrogation. By considering these texts and other data, it is possible to describe procedures observed and noted around the country.

The officers are told by the manuals that the "principal psychological factor contributing to a successful interrogation is privacy — being alone with the person under interrogation." The efficacy of this tactic has been explained as follows:

> If at all practicable, the interrogation should take place in the investigator's office or at least in a room of his own choice. The subject should be deprived of every psychological advantage. In his own home he may be confident, indignant, or recalcitrant. He is more keenly aware of his rights and more reluctant to tell of his indiscretions of criminal behavior within the walls of his home. Moreover his family and other friends are nearby, their presence lending moral support. In his office, the investigator possesses all the advantages. The atmosphere suggests the invincibility of the forces of the law.

To highlight the isolation and unfamiliar surroundings, the manuals instruct the police to display an air of confidence in the suspect's guilt and from outward appearance to maintain only an interest in confirming certain details. The guilt of the subject is to be posited as a fact. The interrogator should direct his comments toward the reasons why the subject committed the act, rather than court failure by asking the subject whether he did it. Like other men, perhaps the subject has had a bad family life, had an unhappy childhood, had too much to drink, had an unrequited desire for women. The officers are instructed to minimize the moral seriousness of the offense,[12] to cast blame on the victim or on society. These tactics are designed to put the subject in a psychological state where his story is but an

---

Rev. 131 (1950); Sterling, *Police Interrogation and the Psychology of Confession*, 14 J. Pub. L. 25 (1965).

[12] For example, in *Leyra v. Denno*, 347 U.S. 556 (1954), the interrogator-psychiatrist told the accused, "We do sometimes things that are not right, but in a fit of temper or anger we sometimes do

elaboration of what the police purport to know already — that he is guilty. Explanations to the contrary are dismissed and discouraged.

The texts thus stress that the major qualities an interrogator should possess are patience and perseverance. One writer describes the efficacy of these characteristics in this manner:

> In the preceding paragraphs emphasis has been placed on kindness and stratagems. The investigator will, however, encounter many situations where the sheer weight of his personality will be the deciding factor. Where emotional appeals and tricks are employed to no avail, he must rely on an oppressive atmosphere of dogged persistence. He must interrogate steadily and without relent, leaving the subject no prospect of surcease. He must dominate his subject and overwhelm him with his inexorable will to obtain the truth. He should interrogate for a spell of several hours pausing only for the subject's necessities in acknowledgment of the need to avoid a charge of duress that can be technically substantiated. In a serious case, the interrogation may continue for days, with the required intervals for food and sleep, but with no respite from the atmosphere of domination. It is possible in this way to induce the subject to talk without resorting to duress or coercion. The method should be used only when the guilt of the subject appears highly probable.

The manuals suggest that the suspect be offered legal excuses for his actions in order to obtain an initial admission of guilt. Where there is a suspected revenge-killing, for example, the interrogator may say:

> Joe, you probably didn't go out looking for this fellow with the purpose of shooting him. My guess is, however, that you expected something from him and that's why you carried a gun — for your own protection. You knew him for what he was, no good. Then when you met him he probably started using foul, abusive language and he gave some indication that he was about to pull a gun on you, and that's when you had to act to save your own life. That's about it, isn't it, Joe?

Having then obtained the admission of shooting, the interrogator is advised to refer to circumstantial evidence which negates the self-defense explanation. This should enable him to secure the entire story. One text notes that "Even if he fails to do so, the inconsistency between the subject's original denial of the shooting and his present admission of at least doing the shooting will serve to deprive him of a self-defense 'out' at the time of trial."

When the techniques described above prove unavailing, the texts recommend they be alternated with a show of some hostility. One ploy often used has been termed the "friendly-unfriendly" or the "Mutt and Jeff" act:

> . . . In this technique, two agents are employed. Mutt, the relentless investigator, who knows the subject is guilty and is not going to waste any time. He's sent a dozen men away for this crime and he's going to send the

---

things we aren't really responsible for," and again, "We know that morally you were just in anger. Morally, you are not to be condemned."

subject away for the full term. Jeff, on the other hand, is obviously a kindhearted man. He has a family himself. He has a brother who was involved in a little scrape like this. He disapproves of Mutt and his tactics and will arrange to get him off the case if the subject will cooperate. He can't hold Mutt off for very long. The subject would be wise to make a quick decision. The technique is applied by having both investigators present while Mutt acts out his role. Jeff may stand by quietly and demur at some of Mutt's tactics. When Jeff makes his plea for cooperation, Mutt is not present in the room.[17]

The interrogators sometimes are instructed to induce a confession out of trickery. The technique here is quite effective in crimes which require identification or which run in series. In the identification situation, the interrogator may take a break in his questioning to place the subject among a group of men in a line-up. "The witness or complainant (previously coached, if necessary) studies the line-up and confidently points out the subject as the guilty party." Then the questioning resumes "as though there were now no doubt about the guilt of the subject." A variation on this technique is called the "reverse line-up":

> The accused is placed in a line-up, but this time he is identified by several fictitious witnesses or victims who associated him with different offenses. It is expected that the subject will become desperate and confess to the offense under investigation in order to escape from the false accusations.

The manuals also contain instructions for police on how to handle the individual who refuses to discuss the matter entirely, or who asks for an attorney or relatives. The examiner is to concede him the right to remain silent. "This usually has a very undermining effect. First of all, he is disappointed in his expectation of an unfavorable reaction on the part of the interrogator. Secondly, a concession of this right to remain silent impresses the subject with the apparent fairness of his interrogator." After this psychological conditioning, however, the officer is told to point out the incriminating significance of the suspect's refusal to talk:

> Joe, you have a right to remain silent. That's your privilege and I'm the last person in the world who'll try to take it away from you. If that's the way you want to leave this, O.K. But let me ask you this. Suppose you were in my shoes and I were in yours and you called me in to ask me about this and I told you, "I don't want to answer any of your questions." You'd think I had something to hide, and you'd probably be right in thinking that. That's exactly what I'll have to think about you, and so will everybody else. So let's sit here and talk this whole thing over.

Few will persist in their initial refusal to talk, it is said, if this monologue is employed correctly.

---

[17] A variant on the technique of creating hostility is one of engendering fear. This is perhaps best described by the prosecuting attorney in *Malinski v. New York*, 324 U.S. 401, 407 (1945):

Why this talk about being undressed? Of course, they had a right to undress him to look for bullet scars, and keep the clothes off him. That was quite proper police procedure. That is some more psychology — let him sit around with a blanket on him, humiliate him there for a while; let him sit in the corner, let him think he is going to get a shellacking.

In the event that the subject wishes to speak to a relative or an attorney, the following advice is tendered:

> [T]he interrogator should respond by suggesting that the subject first tell the truth to the interrogator himself rather than get anyone else involved in the matter. If the request is for an attorney, the interrogator may suggest that the subject save himself or his family the expense of any such professional service, particularly if he is innocent of the offense under investigation. The interrogator may also add, "Joe, I'm only looking for the truth, and if you're telling the truth, that's it. You can handle this by yourself."

From these representative samples of interrogation techniques, the setting prescribed by the manuals and observed in practice becomes clear. In essence, it is this: To be alone with the subject is essential to prevent distraction and to deprive him of any outside support. The aura of confidence in his guilt undermines his will to resist. He merely confirms the preconceived story the police seek to have him describe. Patience and persistence, at times relentless questioning, are employed. To obtain a confession, the interrogator must "patiently maneuver himself or his quarry into a position from which the desired objective may be attained."[23] When normal procedures fail to produce the needed result, the police may resort to deceptive stratagems such as giving false legal advice. It is important to keep the subject off balance, for example, by trading on his insecurity about himself or his surroundings. The police then persuade, trick, or cajole him out of exercising his constitutional rights.

Even without employing brutality, the "third degree" or the specific stratagems described above, the very fact of custodial interrogation exacts a heavy toll on individual liberty and trades on the weakness of individuals.[24]

In the cases before us today, given this background, we concern ourselves primarily with this interrogation atmosphere and the evils it can bring. In *Miranda v. Arizona*, the police arrested the defendant and took him to a special interrogation room where they secured a confession. In *Vignera v. New York*, the defendant made oral admissions to the police after interrogation in the afternoon, and then signed an inculpatory statement upon being questioned by an assistant district attorney later the same evening. In *Westover v. United States*, the defendant was handed over to the Federal Bureau of Investigation by local authorities after they had detained and interrogated him for a lengthy period, both at night and the following morning. After some two hours of questioning, the federal officers had obtained signed statements from the defendant. Lastly, in *California v. Stewart*, the local police held the defendant five days in the station and interrogated him on nine separate occasions before they secured his inculpatory statement.

---

[23] Inbau & Reid, Lie Detection and Criminal Interrogation 185 (3d ed. 1953).

[24] Interrogation procedures may even give rise to a false confession. The most recent conspicuous example occurred in New York, in 1964, when a Negro of limited intelligence confessed to two brutal murders and a rape which he had not committed. When this was discovered, the prosecutor was reported as saying: "Call it what you want — brain-washing, hypnosis, fright. They made him give an untrue confession. The only thing I don't believe is that Whitmore was beaten." N.Y. Times, Jan. 28, 1965, p. 1, col. 5.

In these cases, we might not find the defendants' statements to have been involuntary in traditional terms. Our concern for adequate safeguards to protect precious Fifth Amendment rights is, of course, not lessened in the slightest. In each of the cases, the defendant was thrust into an unfamiliar atmosphere and run through menacing police interrogation procedures. The potentiality for compulsion is forcefully apparent, for example, in *Miranda*, where the indigent Mexican defendant was a seriously disturbed individual with pronounced sexual fantasies, and in *Stewart*, in which the defendant was an indigent Los Angeles Negro who had dropped out of school in the sixth grade. To be sure, the records do not evince overt physical coercion or patent psychological ploys. The fact remains that in none of these cases did the officers undertake to afford appropriate safeguards at the outset of the interrogation to insure that the statements were truly the product of free choice.

It is obvious that such an interrogation environment is created for no purpose other than to subjugate the individual to the will of his examiner. This atmosphere carries its own badge of intimidation. To be sure, this is not physical intimidation, but it is equally destructive of human dignity.[26] The current practice of incommunicado interrogation is at odds with one of our Nation's most cherished principles — that the individual may not be compelled to incriminate himself. Unless adequate protective devices are employed to dispel the compulsion inherent in custodial surroundings, no statement obtained from the defendant can truly be the product of his free choice.

From the foregoing, we can readily perceive an intimate connection between the privilege against self-incrimination and police custodial questioning.

III.

Today, there can be no doubt that the Fifth Amendment privilege is available outside of criminal court proceedings and serves to protect persons in all settings in which their freedom of action is curtailed in any significant way from being compelled to incriminate themselves. We have concluded that without proper safeguards the process of in-custody interrogation of persons suspected or accused of crime contains inherently compelling pressures which work to undermine the individual's will to resist and to compel him to speak where he would not otherwise do so freely. In order to combat these pressures and to permit a full opportunity to

[26] The absurdity of denying that a confession obtained under these circumstances is compelled is aptly portrayed by an example in Professor Sutherland's recent article, *Crime and Confession*, 79 HARV. L. REV. 21, 37 (1965):

Suppose a well-to-do testatrix says she intends to will her property to Elizabeth. John and James want her to bequeath it to them instead. They capture the testatrix, put her in a carefully designed room, out of touch with everyone but themselves and their convenient "witnesses," keep her secluded there for hours while they make insistent demands, weary her with contradictions of her assertions that she wants to leave her money to Elizabeth, and finally induce her to execute the will in their favor. Assume that John and James are deeply and correctly convinced that Elizabeth is unworthy and will make base use of the property if she gets her hands on it, whereas John and James have the noblest and most righteous intentions. Would any judge of probate accept the will so procured as the "voluntary" act of the testatrix?

exercise the privilege against self-incrimination, the accused must be adequately and effectively apprised of his rights and the exercise of those rights must be fully honored.

It is impossible for us to foresee the potential alternatives for protecting the privilege which might be devised by Congress or the States in the exercise of their creative rule-making capacities. Therefore we cannot say that the Constitution necessarily requires adherence to any particular solution for the inherent compulsions of the interrogation process as it is presently conducted. Our decision in no way creates a constitutional straitjacket which will handicap sound efforts at reform, nor is it intended to have this effect. We encourage Congress and the States to continue their laudable search for increasingly effective ways of protecting the rights of the individual while promoting efficient enforcement of our criminal laws. However, unless we are shown other procedures which are at least as effective in apprising accused persons of their right of silence and in assuring a continuous opportunity to exercise it, the following safeguards must be observed.

At the outset, if a person in custody is to be subjected to interrogation, he must first be informed in clear and unequivocal terms that he has the right to remain silent. For those unaware of the privilege, the warning is needed simply to make them aware of it — the threshold requirement for an intelligent decision as to its exercise. More important, such a warning is an absolute prerequisite in overcoming the inherent pressures of the interrogation atmosphere. It is not just the subnormal or woefully ignorant who succumb to an interrogator's imprecations, whether implied or expressly stated, that the interrogation will continue until a confession is obtained or that silence in the face of accusation is itself damning and will bode ill when presented to a jury.[37] Further, the warning will show the individual that his interrogators are prepared to recognize his privilege should he choose to exercise it.

The Fifth Amendment privilege is so fundamental to our system of constitutional rule and the expedient of giving an adequate warning as to the availability of the privilege so simple, we will not pause to inquire in individual cases whether the defendant was aware of his rights without a warning being given. Assessments of the knowledge the defendant possessed, based on information as to his age, education, intelligence, or prior contact with authorities, can never be more than speculation; a warning is a clear-cut fact. More important, whatever the background of the person interrogated, a warning at the time of the interrogation is indispensable to overcome its pressures and to insure that the individual knows he is free to exercise the privilege at that point in time.

---

[37] Lord Devlin has commented: "It is probable that even today, when there is much less ignorance about these matters than formerly, there is still a general belief that you must answer all questions put to you by a policeman, or at least that it will be the worse for you if you do not." DEVLIN, THE CRIMINAL PROSECUTION IN ENGLAND 32 (1958).

In accord with our decision today, it is impermissible to penalize an individual for exercising his Fifth Amendment privilege when he is under police custodial interrogation. The prosecution may not, therefore, use at trial the fact that he stood mute or claimed his privilege in the face of accusation. *Cf. Griffin v. California*, 380 U.S. 609 (1965).

The warning of the right to remain silent must be accompanied by the explanation that anything said can and will be used against the individual in court. This warning is needed in order to make him aware not only of the privilege, but also of the consequences of forgoing it. It is only through an awareness of these consequences that there can be any assurance of real understanding and intelligent exercise of the privilege. Moreover, this warning may serve to make the individual more acutely aware that he is faced with a phase of the adversary system — that he is not in the presence of persons acting solely in his interest.

The circumstances surrounding in-custody interrogation can operate very quickly to overbear the will of one merely made aware of his privilege by his interrogators. Therefore, the right to have counsel present at the interrogation is indispensable to the protection of the Fifth Amendment privilege under the system we delineate today. Our aim is to assure that the individual's right to choose between silence and speech remains unfettered throughout the interrogation process. A once-stated warning, delivered by those who will conduct the interrogation, cannot itself suffice to that end among those who most require knowledge of their rights. A mere warning given by the interrogators is not alone sufficient to accomplish that end. Prosecutors themselves claim that the admonishment of the right to remain silent without more "will benefit only the recidivist and the professional." Brief for the National District Attorneys Association as *amicus curiae*, p. 14. Even preliminary advice given to the accused by his own attorney can be swiftly overcome by the secret interrogation process. *Cf. Escobedo.* Thus, the need for counsel to protect the Fifth Amendment privilege comprehends not merely a right to consult with counsel prior to questioning, but also to have counsel present during any questioning if the defendant so desires.

The presence of counsel at the interrogation may serve several significant subsidiary functions as well. If the accused decides to talk to his interrogators, the assistance of counsel can mitigate the dangers of untrustworthiness. With a lawyer present the likelihood that the police will practice coercion is reduced, and if coercion is nevertheless exercised the lawyer can testify to it in court. The presence of a lawyer can also help to guarantee that the accused gives a fully accurate statement to the police and that the statement is rightly reported by the prosecution at trial.

An individual need not make a pre-interrogation request for a lawyer. While such request affirmatively secures his right to have one, his failure to ask for a lawyer does not constitute a waiver. No effective waiver of the right to counsel during interrogation can be recognized unless specifically made after the warnings we here delineate have been given. The accused who does not know his rights and therefore does not make a request may be the person who most needs counsel.

Accordingly we hold that an individual held for interrogation must be clearly informed that he has the right to consult with a lawyer and to have the lawyer with him during interrogation under the system for protecting the privilege we delineate today. As with the warnings of the right to remain silent and that anything stated can be used in evidence against him, this warning is an absolute prerequisite to interrogation. No amount of circumstantial evidence that the person may have been aware of this right will suffice to stand in its stead. Only through such a warning is there ascertainable assurance that the accused was aware of this right.

If an individual indicates that he wishes the assistance of counsel before any interrogation occurs, the authorities cannot rationally ignore or deny his request on the basis that the individual does not have or cannot afford a retained attorney. The financial ability of the individual has no relationship to the scope of the rights involved here. The privilege against self-incrimination secured by the Constitution applies to all individuals. The need for counsel in order to protect the privilege exists for the indigent as well as the affluent. In fact, were we to limit these constitutional rights to those who can retain an attorney, our decisions today would be of little significance. The cases before us as well as the vast majority of confession cases with which we have dealt in the past involve those unable to retain counsel. While authorities are not required to relieve the accused of his poverty, they have the obligation not to take advantage of indigence in the administration of justice. Denial of counsel to the indigent at the time of interrogation while allowing an attorney to those who can afford one would be no more supportable by reason or logic than the similar situation at trial and on appeal struck down in *Gideon v. Wainwright*, 372 U.S. 335 (1963), and *Douglas v. California*, 372 U.S. 353 (1963).

In order fully to apprise a person interrogated of the extent of his rights under this system then, it is necessary to warn him not only that he has the right to consult with an attorney, but also that if he is indigent a lawyer will be appointed to represent him. Without this additional warning, the admonition of the right to consult with counsel would often be understood as meaning only that he can consult with a lawyer if he has one or has the funds to obtain one. The warning of a right to counsel would be hollow if not couched in terms that would convey to the indigent — the person most often subjected to interrogation — the knowledge that he too has a right to have counsel present. As with the warnings of the right to remain silent and of the general right to counsel, only by effective and express explanation to the indigent of this right can there be assurance that he was truly in a position to exercise it.[43]

Once warnings have been given, the subsequent procedure is clear. If the individual indicates in any manner, at any time prior to or during questioning, that he wishes to remain silent, the interrogation must cease.[44] At this point he has shown that he intends to exercise his Fifth Amendment privilege; any statement taken after the person invokes his privilege cannot be other than the product of compulsion, subtle or otherwise. Without the right to cut off questioning, the setting of in-custody interrogation operates on the individual to overcome free choice in producing a statement after the privilege has been once invoked. If the individual states that he wants an attorney, the interrogation must cease until an attorney is

---

[43] While a warning that the indigent may have counsel appointed need not be given to the person who is known to have an attorney or is known to have ample funds to secure one, the expedient of giving a warning is too simple and the rights involved too important to engage in *ex post facto* inquiries into financial ability when there is any doubt at all on that score.

[44] If an individual indicates his desire to remain silent, but has an attorney present, there may be some circumstances in which further questioning would be permissible. In the absence of evidence of overbearing, statements them made in the presence of counsel might be free of the compelling influence of the interrogation process and might fairly be construed as a waiver of the privilege for purposes of these statements.

present. At that time, the individual must have an opportunity to confer with the attorney and to have him present during any subsequent questioning. If the individual cannot obtain an attorney and he indicates that he wants one before speaking to police, they must respect his decision to remain silent.

This does not mean, as some have suggested, that each police station must have a "station house lawyer" present at all times to advise prisoners. It does mean, however, that if police propose to interrogate a person they must make known to him that he is entitled to a lawyer and that if he cannot afford one, a lawyer will be provided for him prior to any interrogation. If authorities conclude that they will not provide counsel during a reasonable period of time in which investigation in the field is carried out, they may refrain from doing so without violating the person's Fifth Amendment privilege so long as they do not question him during that time.

If the interrogation continues without the presence of an attorney and a statement is taken, a heavy burden rests on the government to demonstrate that the defendant knowingly and intelligently waived his privilege against self-incrimination and his right to retained or appointed counsel. *Escobedo.* This Court has always set high standards of proof for the waiver of constitutional rights, *Johnson v. Zerbst*, 304 U.S. 458 (1938), and we reassert these standards as applied to in-custody interrogation. Since the State is responsible for establishing the isolated circumstances under which the interrogation takes place and has the only means of making available corroborated evidence of warnings given during incommunicado interrogation, the burden is rightly on its shoulders.

An express statement that the individual is willing to make a statement and does not want an attorney followed closely by a statement could constitute a waiver. But a valid waiver will not be presumed simply from the silence of the accused after warnings are given or simply from the fact that a confession was in fact eventually obtained. A statement we made in *Carnley v. Cochran*, 369 U.S. 506, 516 (1962), is applicable here:

> Presuming waiver from a silent record is impermissible. The record must show, or there must be an allegation and evidence which show, that an accused was offered counsel but intelligently and understandingly rejected the offer. Anything less is not waiver.

Moreover, where in-custody interrogation is involved, there is no room for the contention that the privilege is waived if the individual answers some questions or gives some information on his own prior to invoking his right to remain silent when interrogated.

Whatever the testimony of the authorities as to waiver of rights by an accused, the fact of lengthy interrogation or incommunicado incarceration before a statement is made is strong evidence that the accused did not validly waive his rights. In these circumstances the fact that the individual eventually made a statement is consistent with the conclusion that the compelling influence of the interrogation finally forced him to do so. It is inconsistent with any notion of a voluntary relinquishment of the privilege. Moreover, any evidence that the accused was threatened, tricked, or cajoled into a waiver will, of course, show that the defendant did not voluntarily waive his privilege. The requirement of warnings and waiver of rights is a fundamental with respect to the Fifth Amendment privilege and not simply a preliminary ritual to existing methods of interrogation.

The warnings required and the waiver necessary in accordance with our opinion today are, in the absence of a fully effective equivalent, prerequisites to the admissibility of any statement made by a defendant. No distinction can be drawn between statements which are direct confessions and statements which amount to "admissions" of part or all of an offense. The privilege against self-incrimination protects the individual from being compelled to incriminate himself in any manner; it does not distinguish degrees of incrimination. Similarly, for precisely the same reason, no distinction may be drawn between inculpatory statements and statements alleged to be merely "exculpatory." If a statement made were in fact truly exculpatory it would, of course, never be used by the prosecution. In fact, statements merely intended to be exculpatory by the defendant are often used to impeach his testimony at trial or to demonstrate untruths in the statement given under interrogation and thus to prove guilt by implication. These statements are incriminating in any meaningful sense of the word and may not be used without the full warnings and effective waiver required for any other statement. In *Escobedo* itself, the defendant fully intended his accusation of another as the slayer to be exculpatory as to himself.

The principles announced today deal with the protection which must be given to the privilege against self-incrimination when the individual is first subjected to police interrogation while in custody at the station or otherwise deprived of his freedom of action in any significant way. It is at this point that our adversary system of criminal proceedings commences, distinguishing itself at the outset from the inquisitorial system recognized in some countries. Under the system of warnings we delineate today or under any other system which may be devised and found effective, the safeguards to be erected about the privilege must come into play at this point.

Our decision is not intended to hamper the traditional function of police officers in investigating crime. When an individual is in custody on probable cause, the police may, of course, seek out evidence in the field to be used at trial against him. Such investigation may include inquiry of persons not under restraint. General on-the-scene questioning as to facts surrounding a crime or other general questioning of citizens in the fact-finding process is not affected by our holding. It is an act of responsible citizenship for individuals to give whatever information they may have to aid in law enforcement. In such situations the compelling atmosphere inherent in the process of in-custody interrogation is not necessarily present.[46]

In dealing with statements obtained through interrogation, we do not purport to find all confessions inadmissible. Confessions remain a proper element in law enforcement. Any statement given freely and voluntarily without any compelling

---

[46] The distinction and its significance has been aptly described in the opinion of a Scottish court:

In former times such questioning, if undertaken, would be conducted by police officers visiting the house or place of business of the suspect and there questioning him, probably in the presence of a relation or friend. However convenient the modern practice may be, it must normally create a situation very unfavourable to the suspect.

Chalmers v. H. M. Advocate, (1954) Sess. Cas. 66, 78 (J.C.).

influences is, of course, admissible in evidence. The fundamental import of the privilege while an individual is in custody is not whether he is allowed to talk to the police without the benefit of warnings and counsel, but whether he can be interrogated. There is no requirement that police stop a person who enters a police station and states that he wishes to confess to a crime, or a person who calls the police to offer a confession or any other statement he desires to make. Volunteered statements of any kind are not barred by the Fifth Amendment and their admissibility is not affected by our holding today.

To summarize, we hold that when an individual is taken into custody or otherwise deprived of his freedom by the authorities in any significant way and is subjected to questioning, the privilege against self-incrimination is jeopardized. Procedural safeguards must be employed to protect the privilege and unless other fully effective means are adopted to notify the person of his right of silence and to assure that the exercise of the right will be scrupulously honored, the following measures are required. He must be warned prior to any questioning that he has the right to remain silent, that anything he says can be used against him in a court of law, that he has the right to the presence of an attorney, and that if he cannot afford an attorney one will be appointed for him prior to any questioning if he so desires. Opportunity to exercise these rights must be afforded to him throughout the interrogation. After such warnings have been given, and such opportunity afforded him, the individual may knowingly and intelligently waive these rights and agree to answer questions or make a statement. But unless and until such warnings and waiver are demonstrated by the prosecution at trial, no evidence obtained as a result of interrogation can be used against him.[48]

IV.

A recurrent argument made in these cases is that society's need for interrogation outweighs the privilege. This argument is not unfamiliar to this Court. *See, e.g., Chambers v. Florida,* 309 U.S. 227, 240–241 (1940). The whole thrust of our foregoing discussion demonstrates that the Constitution has prescribed the rights of the individual when confronted with the power of government when it provided in the Fifth Amendment that an individual cannot be compelled to be a witness against himself. That right cannot be abridged. As Mr. Justice Brandeis once observed:

> Decency, security, and liberty alike demand that government officials shall be subjected to the same rules of conduct that are commands to the citizen. In a government of laws, existence of the government will be imperilled if it fails to observe the law scrupulously. Our government is the potent, the omnipresent teacher. For good or for ill, it teaches the whole people by its example. Crime is contagious. If the government becomes a lawbreaker, it breeds contempt for law; it invites every man to become a law unto himself; it invites anarchy. To declare that in the administration of the criminal law

---

[48] In accordance with our holdings today and in *Escobedo, Crooker v. California,* and *Cicenia* are not to be followed.

the end justifies the means . . . would bring terrible retribution. Against that pernicious doctrine this court should resolutely set its face.

Olmstead v. United States, 277 U.S. 438, 485 (1928) (dissenting opinion). In this connection, one of our country's distinguished jurists has pointed out: "The quality of a nation's civilization can be largely measured by the methods it uses in the enforcement of its criminal law."[50]

If the individual desires to exercise his privilege, he has the right to do so. This is not for the authorities to decide. An attorney may advise his client not to talk to police until he has had an opportunity to investigate the case, or he may wish to be present with his client during any police questioning. In doing so an attorney is merely exercising the good professional judgment he has been taught. This is not cause for considering the attorney a menace to law enforcement. He is merely carrying out what he is sworn to do under his oath — to protect to the extent of his ability the rights of his client. In fulfilling this responsibility the attorney plays a vital role in the administration of criminal justice under our Constitution.

In announcing these principles, we are not unmindful of the burdens which law enforcement officials must bear, often under trying circumstances. We also fully recognize the obligation of all citizens to aid in enforcing the criminal laws. This Court, while protecting individual rights, has always given ample latitude to law enforcement agencies in the legitimate exercise of their duties. The limits we have placed on the interrogation process should not constitute an undue interference with a proper system of law enforcement. As we have noted, our decision does not in any way preclude police from carrying out their traditional investigatory functions. Although confessions may play an important role in some convictions, the cases before us present graphic examples of the overstatement of the "need" for confessions. In each case authorities conducted interrogations ranging up to five days in duration despite the presence, through standard investigating practices, of considerable evidence against each defendant.[51] Further examples are chronicled in our prior cases.

It is also urged that an unfettered right to detention for interrogation should be allowed because it will often redound to the benefit of the person questioned. When police inquiry determines that there is no reason to believe that the person has committed any crime, it is said, he will be released without need for further formal procedures. The person who has committed no offense, however, will be better able to clear himself after warnings with counsel present than without. It can be assumed that in such circumstances a lawyer would advise his client to talk freely to police in order to clear himself.

Custodial interrogation, by contrast, does not necessarily afford the innocent an opportunity to clear themselves. A serious consequence of the present practice of the interrogation alleged to be beneficial for the innocent is that many arrests 'for investigation' subject large numbers of innocent persons to detention and interro-

---

[50] Schaefer, *Federalism and State Criminal Procedure*, 70 HARV. L. REV. 1, 26 (1956).

[51] Miranda, Vignera, and Westover were identified by eyewitnesses. Marked bills from the bank robbed were found in Westover's car. Articles stolen from the victim as well as from several other robbery victims were found in Stewart's home at the outset of the investigation.

gation. In one of the cases before us, *California v. Stewart*, police held four persons, who were in the defendant's house at the time of the arrest, in jail for five days until defendant confessed. At that time they were finally released. Police stated that there was "no evidence to connect them with any crime." Available statistics on the extent of this practice where it is condoned indicate that these four are far from alone in being subjected to arrest, prolonged detention, and interrogation without the requisite probable cause.[53]

Over the years the Federal Bureau of Investigation has compiled an exemplary record of effective law enforcement while advising any suspect or arrested person, at the outset of an interview, that he is not required to make a statement, that any statement may be used against him in court, that the individual may obtain the services of an attorney of his own choice and, more recently, that he has a right to free counsel if he is unable to pay.[54]

The practice of the FBI can readily be emulated by state and local enforcement agencies. The argument that the FBI deals with different crimes than are dealt with by state authorities does not mitigate the significance of the FBI experience.[56]

It is also urged upon us that we withhold decision on this issue until state legislative bodies and advisory groups have had an opportunity to deal with these problems by rule making. [H]owever, the issues presented are of constitutional dimensions and must be determined by the courts. The admissibility of a statement in the face of a claim that it was obtained in violation of the defendant's constitutional rights is an issue the resolution of which has long since been undertaken by this Court. Judicial solutions to problems of constitutional dimension have evolved decade by decade. As courts have been presented with the need to enforce constitutional rights, they have found means of doing so. That was our

---

[53] An extreme example of this practice occurred in the District of Columbia in 1958. Seeking three "stocky" young Negroes who had robbed a restaurant, police rounded up 90 persons of that general description. Sixth-three were held overnight before being released for lack of evidence. A man not among the 90 arrested was ultimately charged with the crime. WASHINGTON DAILY NEWS, January 21, 1958, p. 5, col. 1; Hearings before a Subcommittee of the Senate Judiciary Committee on H.R. 11477, S. 2970, S. 3325, and S. 3355, 85th Cong., 2d Sess. (July 1958), pp. 40, 78.

[54] In 1952, J. Edgar Hoover, Director of the Federal Bureau of Investigation, stated:

   Law enforcement, however, in defeating the criminal, must maintain inviolate the historic liberties of the individual. To turn back the criminal, yet, by so doing, destroy the dignity of the individual, would be a hollow victory.

   We can have the Constitution, the best laws in the land, and the most honest reviews by courts — but unless the law enforcement profession is steeped in the democratic tradition, maintains the highest in ethics, and makes its work a career of honor, civil liberties will continually — and without end be violated . . . . The best protection of civil liberties is an alert, intelligent and honest law enforcement agency. There can be no alternative.

   . . . Special Agents are taught that any suspect or arrested person, at the outset of an interview, must be advised that he is not required to make a statement and that any statement given can be used against him in court. Moreover, the individual must be informed that, if he desires, he may obtain the services of an attorney of his own choice.

Hoover, *Civil Liberties and Law Enforcement: The Role of the FBI*, 37 IOWA L. REV. 175, 177–182 (1952).

[56] Among the crimes within the enforcement jurisdiction of the FBI are kidnapping, white slavery, bank robbery, interstate transportation and sale of stolen property, all manner of conspiracies, and violations of civil rights. *See also* 18 U.S.C. § 1114 (1964 ed.) (murder of officer or employee of the United States).

responsibility when *Escobedo* was before us and it is our responsibility today. Where rights secured by the Constitution are involved, there can be no rule making or legislation which would abrogate them.

V.

Because of the nature of the problem and because of its recurrent significance in numerous cases, we have to this point discussed the relationship of the Fifth Amendment privilege to police interrogation without specific concentration on the facts of the cases before us. We turn now to these facts to consider the application to these cases of the constitutional principles discussed above. In each instance, we have concluded that statements were obtained from the defendant under circumstances that did not meet constitutional standards for protection of the privilege.

Miranda v. Arizona.

On March 13, 1963, petitioner, Ernesto Miranda, was arrested at his home and taken in custody to a Phoenix police station. He was there identified by the complaining witness. The police then took him to "Interrogation Room No. 2" of the detective bureau. There he was questioned by two police officers. The officers admitted at trial that Miranda was not advised that he had a right to have an attorney present. Two hours later, the officers emerged from the interrogation room with a written confession signed by Miranda. At the top of the statement was a typed paragraph stating that the confession was made voluntarily, without threats or promises of immunity and "with full knowledge of my legal rights, understanding any statement I make may be used against me."[67]

At his trial before a jury, the written confession was admitted into evidence over the objection of defense counsel, and the officers testified to the prior oral confession made by Miranda during the interrogation. Miranda was found guilty of kidnapping and rape. He was sentenced to 20 to 30 years' imprisonment on each count, the sentences to run concurrently. On appeal, the Supreme Court of Arizona held that Miranda's constitutional rights were not violated in obtaining the confession and affirmed the conviction. In reaching its decision, the court emphasized heavily the fact that Miranda did not specifically request counsel.

We reverse. From the testimony of the officers and by the admission of respondent, it is clear that Miranda was not in any way apprised of his right to consult with an attorney and to have one present during the interrogation, nor was his right not to be compelled to incriminate himself effectively protected in any other manner. Without these warnings the statements were inadmissible. The mere fact that he signed a statement which contained a typed-in clause stating that he had "full knowledge" of his "legal rights" does not approach the knowing and intelligent waiver required to relinquish constitutional rights.

---

[67] One of the officers testified that he read this paragraph to Miranda. Apparently, however, he did not do so until after Miranda had confessed orally.

Vignera v. New York.

Petitioner, Michael Vignera, was picked up by New York police on October 14, 1960, in connection with the robbery three days earlier of a Brooklyn dress shop. They took him to the 17th Detective Squad headquarters in Manhattan. Sometime thereafter he was taken to the 66th Detective Squad. There a detective questioned Vignera with respect to the robbery. Vignera orally admitted the robbery to the detective. The detective was asked on cross-examination at trial by defense counsel whether Vignera was warned of his right to counsel before being interrogated. The prosecution objected to the question and the trial judge sustained the objection. Thus, the defense was precluded from making any showing that warnings had not been given. While at the 66th Detective Squad, Vignera was identified by the store owner and a saleslady as the man who robbed the dress shop. At about 3 p.m. he was formally arrested. The police then transported him to still another station, the 70th Precinct in Brooklyn, "for detention." At 11 p.m. Vignera was questioned by an assistant district attorney in the presence of a hearing reporter who transcribed the questions and Vignera's answers. This verbatim account of these proceedings contains no statement of any warnings given by the assistant district attorney. At Vignera's trial on a charge of first degree robbery, the detective testified as to the oral confession. The transcription of the statement taken was also introduced in evidence. At the conclusion of the testimony, the trial judge charged the jury in part as follows:

> The law doesn't say that the confession is void or invalidated because the police officer didn't advise the defendant as to his rights. Did you hear what I said? I am telling you what the law of the State of New York is.

Vignera was found guilty of first degree robbery. He was subsequently adjudged a third-felony offender and sentenced to 30 to 60 years' imprisonment.

We reverse. The foregoing indicates that Vignera was not warned of any of his rights before the questioning by the detective and by the assistant district attorney. No other steps were taken to protect these rights. Thus he was not effectively apprised of his Fifth Amendment privilege or of his right to have counsel present and his statements are inadmissible.

Westover v. United States.

At approximately 9:45 p.m. on March 20, 1963, petitioner, Carl Calvin Westover, was arrested by local police in Kansas City as a suspect in two Kansas City robberies. A report was also received from the FBI that he was wanted on a felony charge in California. The local authorities took him to a police station and placed him in a line-up on the local charges, and at about 11:45 p.m. he was booked. Kansas City police interrogated Westover on the night of his arrest. He denied any knowledge of criminal activities. The next day local officers interrogated him again throughout the morning. Shortly before noon they informed the FBI that they were through interrogating Westover and that the FBI could proceed to interrogate him. There is nothing in the record to indicate that Westover was ever given any warning as to his rights by local police. At noon, three special agents of the FBI continued the interrogation in a private interview room of the Kansas City Police Department, this time with respect to the robbery of a savings and loan association and a bank in Sacramento, California. After two or two and one-half hours, Westover signed separate confessions to each of these two robberies which had been prepared by one of the agents during the interrogation. At trial one of the agents testified, and a paragraph on each of the statements states, that the agents advised Westover that he did not have to make a statement, that any statement he made could be used against him, and that he had the right to see an attorney.

On the facts of this case we cannot find that Westover knowingly and intelligently waived his right to remain silent and his right to consult with counsel prior to the time he made the statement. At the time the FBI agents began questioning Westover, he had been in custody for over 14 hours and had been interrogated at length during that period. The FBI interrogation began immediately upon the conclusion of the interrogation by Kansas City police and was conducted in local police headquarters. Although the two law enforcement authorities are legally distinct and the crimes for which they interrogated Westover were different, the impact on him was that of a continuous period of questioning. There is no evidence of any warning given prior to the FBI interrogation nor is there any evidence of an articulated waiver of rights after the FBI commenced its interrogation. The record simply shows that the defendant did in fact confess a short time after being turned over to the FBI following interrogation by local police. Despite the fact that the FBI agents gave warnings at the outset of their interview, from Westover's point of view the warnings came at the end of the interrogation process. In these circumstances an intelligent waiver of constitutional rights cannot be assumed.

We do not suggest that law enforcement authorities are precluded from questioning any individual who has been held for a period of time by other authorities and interrogated by them without appropriate warnings. A different case would be presented if an accused were taken into custody by the second authority, removed both in time and place from his original surroundings, and then adequately advised of his rights and given an opportunity to exercise them. But here the FBI interrogation was conducted immediately following the state inter-rogation in the same police station — in the same compelling surroundings. Thus, in obtaining a confession from Westover the federal authorities were the benefi-ciaries of the pressure applied by the local in-custody interrogation. In these circumstances the giving of warnings alone was not sufficient to protect the privilege.

California v. Stewart.

In the course of investigating a series of purse-snatch robberies in which one of the victims had died of injuries inflicted by her assailant, respondent, Roy Allen Stewart, was pointed out to Los Angeles police as the endorser of dividend checks taken in one of the robberies. At about 7:15 p.m., January 31, 1963, police officers went to Stewart's house and arrested him. One of the officers asked Stewart if they could search the house, to which he replied, "Go ahead." The search turned up various items taken from the five robbery victims. At the time of Stewart's arrest, police also arrested Stewart's wife and three other persons who were visiting him. These four were jailed along with Stewart and were interrogated. Stewart was taken to the University Station of the Los Angeles Police Department where he was placed in a cell. During the next five days, police interrogated Stewart on nine different occasions. Except during the first interrogation session, when he was confronted with an accusing witness, Stewart was isolated with his interrogators.

During the ninth interrogation session, Stewart admitted that he had robbed the deceased and stated that he had not meant to hurt her. Police then brought Stewart before a magistrate for the first time. Since there was no evidence to connect them with any crime, the police then released the other four persons arrested with him.

Nothing in the record specifically indicates whether Stewart was or was not advised of his right to remain silent or his right to counsel. In a number of instances, however, the interrogating officers were asked to recount everything that was said during the interrogations. None indicated that Stewart was ever advised of his rights.

Stewart was charged with kidnapping to commit robbery, rape, and murder. At his trial, transcripts of the first interrogation and the confession at the last interrogation were introduced in evidence. The jury found Stewart guilty of robbery and first degree murder and fixed the penalty as death. On appeal, the Supreme Court of California reversed. It held that under this Court's decision in *Escobedo*, Stewart should have been advised of his right to remain silent and of his right to counsel and that it would not presume in the face of a silent record that the police advised Stewart of his rights.[70]

We affirm. In dealing with custodial interrogation, we will not presume that a defendant has been effectively apprised of his rights and that his privilege against self-incrimination has been adequately safeguarded on a record that does not show that any warnings have been given or that any effective alternative has been employed. Nor can a knowing and intelligent waiver of these rights be assumed on a silent record. Furthermore, Stewart's steadfast denial of the alleged offenses through eight of the nine interrogations over a period of five days is subject to no other construction than that he was compelled by persistent interrogation to forgo his Fifth Amendment privilege.

Therefore, in accordance with the foregoing, the judgments of the Supreme Court of Arizona, of the New York Court of Appeals, and of the Court of Appeals for the Ninth Circuit are reversed. The judgment of the Supreme Court of California is affirmed. It is so ordered.

Mr. Justice Clark, dissenting in *Miranda*, *Vignera* and *Westover*, and concurring in the result in *Stewart*.

It is with regret that I find it necessary to write in these cases. However, I am unable to join the majority because its opinion goes too far on too little, while my dissenting brethren do not go quite far enough. Nor can I join in the Court's criticism of the present practices of police and investigatory agencies as to custodial

---

[70] Because of this disposition of the case, the California Supreme Court did not reach the claims that the confession was coerced by police threats to hold his ailing wife in custody until he confessed.

interrogation. The materials it refers to as "police manuals"[1] are, as I read them, merely writings in this filed by professors and some police officers. Not one is shown by the record here to be the official manual of any police department, much less in universal use in crime detection. Moreover the examples of police brutality mentioned by the Court are rare exceptions to the thousands of cases that appear every year in the law reports. The police agencies — all the way from municipal and state forces to the federal bureaus — are responsible for law enforcement and public safety in this country. I am proud of their efforts, which in my view are not fairly characterized by the Court's opinion.

I.

The *ipse dixit* of the majority has no support in our cases. Indeed, the Court admits that "we might not find the defendants' statements (here) to have been involuntary in traditional terms." The Court holds that failure to follow the new procedures requires inexorably the exclusion of any statement by the accused, as well as the fruits thereof. Such a strict constitutional specific inserted at the nerve center of crime detection may well kill the patient. Since there is at this time a paucity of information and an almost total lack of empirical knowledge on the practical operation of requirements truly comparable to those announced by the majority, I would be more restrained lest we go too far too fast.

II.

Custodial interrogation has long been recognized as "undoubtedly an essential tool in effective law enforcement." Recognition of this fact should put us on guard against the promulgation of doctrinaire rules. Especially is this true where the Court finds that "the Constitution has prescribed" its holding and where the light of our past cases is to the contrary. Indeed, even in *Escobedo* the Court never hinted that an affirmative "waiver" was a prerequisite to questioning; that the burden of proof as to waiver was on the prosecution; that the presence of counsel — absent a waiver — during interrogation was required; that a waiver can be withdrawn at the will of the accused; that counsel must be furnished during an accusatory stage to those unable to pay; nor that admissions and exculpatory statements are "confessions." To require all those things at one gulp should cause the Court to choke over more cases than *Crooker* and *Cicenia*, which it expressly overrules today.

The rule prior to today — as Mr. Justice Goldberg, the author of the Court's opinion in *Escobedo*, stated it in *Haynes v. Washington* — depended upon "a totality of circumstances evidencing an involuntary . . . admission of guilt." 373 U.S. at 514. And he concluded:

> Of course, detection and solution of crime is, at best, a difficult and arduous task requiring determination and persistence on the part of all responsible officers charged with the duty of law enforcement. And, certainly, we do not

---

[1] *E.g.*, INBAU & REID, CRIMINAL INTERROGATION AND CONFESSIONS (1962); O'HARA, FUNDAMENTALS OF CRIMINAL INVESTIGATION (1956); DIENSTEIN, TECHNICS FOR THE CRIME INVESTIGATOR (1952); MULBAR, INTERROGATION (1951); KIDD, POLICE INTERROGATION (1940).

mean to suggest that all interrogation of witnesses and suspects is impermissible. Such questioning is undoubtedly an essential took in effective law enforcement. The line between proper and permissible police conduct and techniques and methods offensive to due process is, at best, a difficult one to draw, particularly in cases such as this where it is necessary to make fine judgments as to the effect of psychologically coercive pressures and inducements on the mind and will of an accused. . . . We are here impelled to the conclusion, from all of the facts presented, that the bounds of due process have been exceeded.

III.

I would continue to follow that rule. Under the "totality of circumstances" rule of which my Brother Goldberg spoke in *Haynes*, I would consider in each case whether the police officer prior to custodial interrogation added the warning that the suspect might have counsel present at the interrogation and, further, that a court would appoint one at his request if he was too poor to employ counsel. In the absence of warnings, the burden would be on the State to prove that counsel was knowingly and intelligently waived or that in the totality of the circumstances, including the failure to give the necessary warnings, the confession was clearly voluntary.

Rather than employing the arbitrary Fifth Amendment rule which the Court lays down I would follow the more pliable dictates of the Due Process Clauses of the Fifth and Fourteenth Amendments which we are accustomed to administering and which we know from our cases are effective instruments in protecting persons in police custody. In this way we would not be acting in the dark nor in one full sweep changing the traditional rules of custodial interrogation which this Court has for so long recognized as a justifiable and proper tool in balancing individual rights against the rights of society. It will be soon enough to go further when we are able to appraise with somewhat better accuracy the effect of such a holding.

I would affirm the convictions in *Miranda*, *Vignera*, and *Westover*. In each of those cases I find from the circumstances no warrant for reversal. In *Stewart*, I would dismiss the writ of certiorari for want of a final judgment, but if the merits are to be reached I would affirm on the ground that the State failed to fulfill its burden, in the absence of a showing that appropriate warnings were given, of proving a waiver or a totality of circumstances showing voluntariness. Should there be a retrial, I would leave the State free to attempt to prove these elements.

MR. JUSTICE HARLAN, whom MR. JUSTICE STEWART and MR. JUSTICE WHITE join, dissenting.

I believe the decision of the Court represents poor constitutional law and entails harmful consequences for the country at large. How serious these consequences may prove to be only time can tell. But the basic flaws in the Court's justification seem to me readily apparent now once all sides of the problem are considered.

I. INTRODUCTION

At the outset, it is well to note exactly what is required by the Court's new constitutional code of rules for confessions. The foremost requirement, upon which later admissibility of a confession depends, is that a fourfold warning be given to a person in custody before he is questioned, namely, that he has a right to remain silent, that anything he says may be used against him, that he has a right to have present an attorney during the questioning, and that if indigent he has a right to a lawyer without charge. To forgo these rights, some affirmative statement of rejection is seemingly required, and threats, tricks, or cajolings to obtain this waiver are forbidden. If before or during questioning the suspect seeks to invoke his right to remain silent, interrogation must be forgone or cease; a request for counsel brings about the same result until a lawyer is procured. Finally, there are a miscellany of minor directives, for example, the burden of proof of waiver is on the State, admissions and exculpatory statements are treated just like confessions, withdrawal of a waiver is always permitted, and so forth.

While the fine points of this scheme are far less clear than the Court admits, the tenor is quite apparent. The new rules are not designed to guard against police brutality or other unmistakably banned forms of coercion. Those who use third-degree tactics and deny them in court are equally able and destined to lie as skillfully about warnings and waivers. Rather, the thrust of the new rules is to negate all pressures, to reinforce the nervous or ignorant suspect, and ultimately to discourage any confession at all. The aim in short is toward "voluntariness" in a utopian sense, or to view it from a different angle, voluntariness with a vengeance.

To incorporate this notion into the Constitution requires a strained reading of history and precedent and a disregard of the very pragmatic concerns that alone may on occasion justify such strains. I believe that reasoned examination will show that the Due Process Clauses provide an adequate tool for coping with confessions and that, even if the Fifth Amendment privilege against self-incrimination be invoked, its precedents taken as a whole do not sustain the present rules. Viewed as a choice based on pure policy, these new rules prove to be a highly debatable, if not one-sided, appraisal of the competing interests, imposed over widespread objection, at the very time when judicial restraint is most called for by the circumstances.

II. CONSTITUTIONAL PREMISES

It is most fitting to begin an inquiry into the constitutional precedents by surveying the limits on confessions the Court has evolved under the Due Process Clause of the Fourteenth Amendment. This is so because these cases show that there exists a workable and effective means of dealing with confessions in a judicial manner; because the cases are the baseline from which the Court now departs and so serve to measure the actual as opposed to the professed distance it travels; and because examination of them helps reveal how the Court has coasted into its present position.

The earliest confession cases in this Court emerged from federal prosecutions and were settled on a nonconstitutional basis, the Court adopting the common-law rule that the absence of inducements, promises, and threats made a confession voluntary and admissible. While a later case said the Fifth Amendment privilege controlled admissibility, this proposition was not itself developed in subsequent decisions.[2] The Court did, however, heighten the test of admissibility in federal trials to one of voluntariness "in fact," and then by and large left federal judges to apply the same standards the Court began to derive in a string of state court cases.

This new line of decisions, testing admissibility by the Due Process Clause, began in 1936 with *Brown v. Mississippi*, and must now embrace somewhat more than 30 full opinions of the Court. While the voluntariness rubric was repeated in many instances, the Court never pinned it down to a single meaning but on the contrary infused it with a number of different values. To travel quickly over the main themes, there was an initial emphasis on reliability, supplemented by concern over the legality and fairness of the police practices, in an "accusatorial" system of law enforcement, *Watts v. Indiana*, 338 U.S. 49, 54, and eventually by close attention to the individual's state of mind and capacity for effective choice. The outcome was a continuing re-evaluation on the facts of each case of *how much* pressure on the suspect was permissible.

Apart from direct physical coercion, however, no single default or fixed combination of defaults guaranteed exclusion, and synopses of the cases would serve little use because the overall gauge has been steadily changing, usually in the direction of restricting admissibility. But to mark just what point had been reached before the Court jumped the rails in *Escobedo*, it is worth capsulizing the then-recent case of *Haynes v. Washington*, 373 U.S. 503. There, Haynes had been held some 16 or more hours in violation of state law before signing the disputed confession, had received no warnings of any kind, and despite requests had been refused access to his wife or to counsel, the police indicating that access would be allowed after a confession. Emphasizing especially this last inducement and rejecting some contrary indicia of voluntariness, the Court in a 5-to-4 decision held the confession inadmissible.

There are several relevant lessons to be drawn from this constitutional history. The first is that with over 25 years of precedent the Court has developed an elaborate, sophisticated, and sensitive approach to admissibility of confessions. It is "judicial" in its treatment of one case at a time, flexible in its ability to respond to the endless mutations of fact presented, and ever more familiar to the lower courts. Of course, strict certainty is not obtained in this developing process, but this is often so with constitutional principles, and disagreement is usually confined to that borderland of close cases where it matters least.

The second point is that in practice and from time to time in principle, the Court has given ample recognition to society's interest in suspect questioning as an instrument of law enforcement. Cases countenancing quite significant pressures can be cited without difficulty,[5] and the lower courts may often have been yet more

---

[2] The case was *Bram v. United States*, 168 U.S. 532. Its historical premises were afterwards disproved by Wigmore, who concluded "that no assertions could be more unfounded."

[5] One not too distant example is *Stroble v. California*, 343 U.S. 181, in which the suspect was kicked and threatened after his arrest, questioned a little later for two hours, and isolated from a lawyer trying

tolerant. Of course the limitations imposed today were rejected by necessary implication in case after case, the right to warnings having been explicitly rebuffed in this Court many years ago.

Finally, the cases disclose that the language in many of the opinions overstates the actual course of decision. It has been said, for example, that an admissible confession must be made by the suspect "in the unfettered exercise of his own will," and that "a prisoner is not 'to be made the deluded instrument of his own conviction.'" Though often repeated, such principles are rarely observed in full measure. Even the word "voluntary" may be deemed somewhat misleading, especially when one considers many of the confessions that have been brought under its umbrella. The tendency to overstate may be laid in part to the flagrant facts often before the Court; but in any event one must recognize how it has tempered attitudes and lent some color of authority to the approach now taken by the Court.

I turn now to the Court's asserted reliance on the Fifth Amendment, an approach which I frankly regard as a *trompe l'oeil*. The Court's opinion in my view reveals no adequate basis for extending the Fifth Amendment's privilege against self-incrimination to the police station. Far more important, it fails to show that the Court's new rules are well supported, let alone compelled, by Fifth Amendment precedents. Instead, the new rules actually derive from quotation and analogy drawn from precedents under the Sixth Amendment, which should properly have no bearing on police interrogation.

The Court's opening contention, that the Fifth Amendment governs police station confessions, is perhaps not an impermissible extension of the law but it has little to commend itself in the present circumstances. Historically, the privilege against self-incrimination did not bear at all on the use of extra-legal confessions, for which distinct standards evolved; indeed, "the history of the two principles is wide apart, differing by one hundred years in origin, and derived through separate lines of precedents . . . ." Practice under the two doctrines has also differed in a number of important respects. Even those who would readily enlarge the privilege must concede some linguistic difficulties since the Fifth Amendment in terms proscribes only compelling any person "in any criminal case to be a witness against himself."

Though weighty, I do not say these points and similar ones are conclusive, for, as the Court reiterates, the privilege embodies basic principles always capable of expansion.[7] Certainly the privilege does represent a protective concern for the accused and an emphasis upon accusatorial rather than inquisitorial values in law enforcement, although this is similarly true of other limitations such as the grand jury requirement and the reasonable doubt standard. Accusatorial values, however, have openly been absorbed into the due process standard governing confessions; this indeed is why at present "the kinship of the two rules [governing confessions and self-incrimination] is too apparent for denial." Since extension of the general

---

to see him; the resulting confession was held admissible.

[7] Additionally, there are precedents and even historical arguments that can be arrayed in favor of bringing extra-legal questioning within the privilege.

principle has already occurred, to insist that the privilege applies as such serves only to carry over inapposite historical details and engaging rhetoric and to obscure the policy choices to be made in regulating confessions.

Having decided that the Fifth Amendment privilege does apply in the police station, the Court reveals that the privilege imposes more exacting restrictions than does the Fourteenth Amendment's voluntariness test. It then emerges from a discussion of *Escobedo* that the Fifth Amendment requires for an admissible confession that it be given by one distinctly aware of his right not to speak and shielded from "the compelling atmosphere" of interrogation. From these key premises, the Court finally develops the safeguards of warning, counsel, and so forth. I do not believe these premises are sustained by precedents under the Fifth Amendment.[9]

The more important premise is that pressure on the suspect must be eliminated though it be only the subtle influence of the atmosphere and surroundings. The Fifth Amendment, however, has never been thought to forbid *all* pressure to incriminate one's self in the situations covered by it. On the contrary, it has been held that failure to incriminate one's self can result in denial of removal of one's case from state to federal court, in refusal of a military commission, in denial of a discharge in bankruptcy, and in numerous other adverse consequences. This is not to say that short of jail or torture any sanction is permissible in any case; policy and history alike may impose sharp limits. However, the Court's unspoken assumption that *any* pressure violates the privilege is not supported by the precedents and it has failed to show why the Fifth Amendment prohibits that relatively mild pressure the Due Process Clause permits.

The Court appears similarly wrong in thinking that precise knowledge of one's rights is a settled prerequisite under the Fifth Amendment to the loss of its protections. A number of lower federal court cases have held that grand jury witnesses need not always be warned of their privilege, and Wigmore states this to be the better rule for trial witnesses. No Fifth Amendment precedent is cited for the Court's contrary view. There might of course be reasons apart from Fifth Amendment precedent for requiring warning or any other safeguard on questioning but that is a different matter entirely.

A closing word must be said about the Assistance of Counsel Clause of the Sixth Amendment, which is never expressly relied on by the Court but whose judicial precedents turn out to be linchpins of the confession rules announced today. To support its requirement of a knowing and intelligent waiver, the Court cites cases imparting glosses to the Sixth Amendment, concern[ing] counsel at trial or on appeal. While the Court finds no pertinent difference between judicial proceedings and police interrogation, I believe the differences are so vast as to disqualify wholly the Sixth Amendment precedents as suitable analogies in the present cases.

The only attempt in this Court to carry the right to counsel into the station house occurred in *Escobedo*, the Court repeating several times that that stage was no less

---

[9] I lay aside *Escobedo* itself; it contains no reasoning or even general conclusions addressed to the Fifth Amendment and indeed its citation in this regard seems surprising in view of *Escobedo's* primary reliance on the Sixth Amendment.

"critical" than trial itself. This is hardly persuasive when we consider that a grand jury inquiry, the filing of a certiorari petition, and certainly the purchase of narcotics by an undercover agent from a prospective defendant may all be equally "critical" yet provision of counsel and advice on the score have never been thought compelled by the Constitution in such cases. The sound reason why this right is so freely extended for a criminal trial is the severe injustice risked by confronting an untrained defendant with a range of technical points of law, evidence, and tactics familiar to the prosecutor but not to himself. This danger shrinks markedly in the police station where indeed the lawyer in fulfilling his professional responsibilities of necessity may become an obstacle to truthfinding. The Court's summary citation of the Sixth Amendment cases here seems to me best described as "the domino method of constitutional adjudication . . . wherein every explanatory statement in a previous opinion is made the basis for extension to a wholly different situation."

III. POLICY CONSIDERATIONS

Examined as an expression of public policy, the Court's new regime proves so dubious that there can be no due compensation for its weakness in constitutional law. The foregoing discussion has shown, I think, how mistaken is the Court in implying that the Constitution has struck the balance in favor of the approach the Court takes. Rather, precedent reveals that the Fourteenth Amendment in practice has been construed to strike a different balance, that the Fifth Amendment gives the Court little solid support in this context, and that the Sixth Amendment should have no bearing at all. Legal history has been stretched before to satisfy deep needs of society. In this instance, however, the Court has not and cannot make the powerful showing that its new rules are plainly desirable in the context of our society, something which is surely demanded before those rules are engrafted onto the Constitution and imposed on every State and county in the land.

Without at all subscribing to the generally black picture of police conduct painted by the Court, I think it must be frankly recognized at the outset that police questioning allowable under due process precedents may inherently entail some pressure on the suspect and may seek advantage in his ignorance or weaknesses. The atmosphere and questioning techniques, proper and fair though they be, can in themselves exert a tug on the suspect to confess, and in this light "[t]o speak of any confessions of crime made after arrest as being 'voluntary' or 'uncoerced' is somewhat inaccurate, although traditional. A confession is wholly and incontestably voluntary only if a guilty person gives himself up to the law and becomes his own accuser." Until today, the role of the Constitution has been only to sift out *undue* pressure, not to assure spontaneous confessions.

The Court's new rules aim to offset these minor pressures and disadvantages intrinsic to any kind of police interrogation. The rules do not serve due process interests in preventing blatant coercion since, as I noted earlier, they do nothing to contain the policeman who is prepared to lie from the start. The rules work for reliability in confessions almost only in the Pickwickian sense that they can prevent some from being given at all.[12] In short, the benefit of this new regime is simply to

---

[12] The Court's vision of a lawyer "mitigat[ing] the dangers of untrustworthiness" by witnessing

lessen or wipe out the inherent compulsion and inequalities to which the Court devotes some nine pages of description.

What the Court largely ignores is that its rules impair, if they will not eventually serve wholly to frustrate, an instrument of law enforcement that has long and quite reasonably been thought worth the price paid for it.[13] There can be little doubt that the Court's new code would markedly decrease the number of confessions. To warn the suspect that he may remain silent and remind him that his confession may be used in court are minor obstructions. To require also an express waiver by the suspect and an end to questioning whenever he demurs must heavily handicap questioning. And to suggest or provide counsel for the suspect simply invites the end of the interrogation.

How much harm this decision will inflict on law enforcement cannot fairly be predicted with accuracy. Evidence on the role of confessions is notoriously incomplete, and little is added by the Court's reference to the FBI experience and the resources believed wasted in interrogation. We do know that some crimes cannot be solved without confessions, that ample expert testimony attests to their importance in crime control, and that the Court is taking a real risk with society's welfare in imposing its new regime on the country. The social costs of crime are too great to call the new rules anything but a hazardous experimentation.

While passing over the costs and risks of its experiment, the Court portrays the evils of normal police questioning in terms which I think are exaggerated. Albeit stringently confined by the due process standards interrogation is no doubt often inconvenient and unpleasant for the suspect. However, it is no less so for a man to be arrested and jailed, to have his house searched, or to stand trial in court, yet all this may properly happen to the most innocent given probable cause, a warrant, or an indictment. Society has always paid a stiff price for law and order, and peaceful interrogation is not one of the dark moments of the law.

This brief statement of the competing considerations seems to me ample proof that the Court's preference is highly debatable at best and therefore not to be read into the Constitution. However, it may make the analysis more graphic to consider the actual facts of one of the four cases reversed by the Court. *Miranda v. Arizona* serves best, being neither the hardest nor easiest of the four under the Court's standards.[15]

On March 3, 1963, an 18-year-old girl was kidnapped and forcibly raped near Phoenix, Arizona. Ten days later, on the morning of March 13, petitioner Miranda

---

coercion and assisting accuracy in the confession is largely a fancy; for if counsel arrives, there is rarely going to be a police station confession. *Watts v. Indiana*, (separate opinion of Jackson, J.): "[A]ny lawyer worth his salt will tell the suspect in no uncertain terms to make no statement to police under any circumstances."

[13] This need is, of course, what makes so misleading the Court's comparison of a probate judge readily setting aside as involuntary the will of an old lady badgered and beleaguered by the new heirs. With wills, there is no public interest save in a totally free choice; with confessions, the solution of crime is a countervailing gain, however the balance is resolved.

[15] In *Westover*, a seasoned criminal was practically given the Court's full complement of warnings and did not heed them. The *Stewart* case, on the other hand, involves long detention and successive questioning. In *Vignera*, the facts are complicated and the record somewhat incomplete.

was arrested and taken to the police station. At this time Miranda was 23 years old, indigent, and educated to the extent of completing half the ninth grade. He had "an emotional illness" of the schizophrenic type, according to the doctor who eventually examined him; the doctor's report also stated that Miranda was "alert and oriented as to time, place, and person," intelligent within normal limits, competent to stand trial, and sane within the legal definition. At the police station, the victim picked Miranda out of a lineup, and two officers then took him into a separate room to interrogate him, starting about 11:30 a.m. Though at first denying his guilt, within a short time Miranda gave a detailed oral confession and then wrote out in his own hand and signed a brief statement admitting and describing the crime. All this was accomplished in two hours or less without any force, threats or promises and — I will assume this though the record is uncertain, — without any effective warnings at all.

Miranda's oral and written confessions are now held inadmissible under the Court's new rules. One is entitled to feel astonished that the Constitution can be read to produce this result. These confessions were obtained during brief, daytime questioning conducted by two officers and unmarked by any of the traditional indicia of coercion. They assured a conviction for a brutal and unsettling crime, for which the police had and quite possibly could obtain little evidence other than the victim's identifications, evidence which is frequently unreliable. There was, in sum, a legitimate purpose, no perceptible unfairness, and certainly little risk of injustice in the interrogation. Yet the resulting confessions, and the responsible course of police practice they represent, are to be sacrificed to the Court's own fine-spun conception of fairness which I seriously doubt is shared by many thinking citizens in this country.

The tenor of judicial opinion also falls well short of supporting the Court's new approach. Although *Escobedo* has widely been interpreted as an open invitation to lower courts to rewrite the law of confessions, a significant heavy majority of the state and federal decisions in point have sought quite narrow interpretations. Of the courts that have accepted the invitation, it is hard to know how many have felt compelled by their best guess as to this Court's likely construction; but none of the state decisions saw fit to rely on the state privilege against self-incrimination, and no decision at all has gone as far as this Court goes today.

In closing this necessarily truncated discussion of policy considerations attending the new confession rules, some reference must be made to their ironic untimeliness. There is now in progress in this country a massive re-examination of criminal law enforcement procedures on a scale never before witnessed. Participants in this undertaking include a Special Committee of the American Bar Association, under the chairmanship of Chief Judge Lumbard of the Court of Appeals for the Second Circuit; a distinguished study group of the American Law Institute, headed by Professors Vorenberg and Bator of the Harvard Law School; and the President's Commission on Law Enforcement and Administration of Justice, under the leadership of the Attorney General of the United States. Studies are also being conducted by the District of Columbia Crime Commission, the Georgetown Law Center, and by others equipped to do practical research. There are also signs that legislatures in some of the States may be preparing to re-examine the problem before us.

It is no secret that concern has been expressed lest long-range and lasting reforms be frustrated by this Court's too rapid departure from existing constitutional standards. Despite the Court's disclaimer, the practical effect of the decision made today must inevitably be to handicap seriously sound efforts at reform, not least by removing options necessary to a just compromise of competing interests. Of course legislative reform is rarely speedy or unanimous, though this Court has been more patient in the past.[25] But the legislative reforms when they come would have the vast advantage of empirical data and comprehensive study, they would allow experimentation and use of solutions not open to the courts, and they would restore the initiative in criminal law reform to those forums where it truly belongs.

MR. JUSTICE WHITE, with whom MR. JUSTICE HARLAN and MR. JUSTICE STEWART join, dissenting.

II.

That the Court's holding today is neither compelled nor even strongly suggested by the language of the Fifth Amendment, is at odds with American and English legal history, and involves a departure from a long line of precedent does not prove either that the Court has exceeded its powers or that the Court is wrong or unwise in its present reinterpretation of the Fifth Amendment. It does, however, underscore the obvious — that the Court has not discovered or found the law in making today's decision, nor has it derived it from some irrefutable sources; what it has done is to make new law and new public policy in much the same way that it has in the course of interpreting other great clauses of the Constitution. This is what the Court historically has done. Indeed, it is what it must do and will continue to do until and unless there is some fundamental change in the constitutional distribution of governmental powers.

But if the Court is here and now to announce new and fundamental policy to govern certain aspects of our affairs, it is wholly legitimate to examine the mode of this or any other constitutional decision in this Court and to inquire into the advisability of its end product in terms of the long-range interest of the country. At the very least, the Court's text and reasoning should withstand analysis and be a fair exposition of the constitutional provision which its opinion interprets. Decisions like these cannot rest alone on syllogism, metaphysics or some ill-defined notions of natural justice, although each will perhaps play its part. In proceeding to such constructions as it now announces, the Court should also duly consider all the factors and interests bearing upon the cases, at least insofar as the relevant materials are available; and if the necessary considerations are not treated in the record or obtainable from some other reliable source, the Court should not proceed to formulate fundamental policies based on speculation alone.

---

[25] The Court waited 12 years after *Wolf v. Colorado*, 338 U.S. 25, declared privacy against improper state intrusions to be constitutionally safeguarded before it concluded in *Mapp v. Ohio*, 367 U.S. 643, that adequate state remedies had not been provided to protect this interest so the exclusionary rule was necessary.

III.

First, we may inquire what are the textual and factual bases of this new fundamental rule. To reach the result announced on the grounds it does, the Court must stay within the confines of the Fifth Amendment, which forbids self-incrimination only if *compelled*. Hence the core of the Court's opinion is that because of the "compulsion inherent in custodial surroundings, no statement obtained from [a] defendant [in custody] can truly be the product of his free choice," absent the use of adequate protective devices as described by the Court. However, the Court does not point to any sudden inrush of new knowledge requiring the rejection of 70 years' experience. Nor does it assert that its novel conclusion reflects a changing consensus among state courts, *see Mapp*, or that a succession of cases had steadily eroded the old rule and proved it unworkable, *see Gideon v. Wainwright*, 372 U.S. 335. Rather than asserting new knowledge, the Court concedes that it cannot truly know what occurs during custodial questioning, because of the innate secrecy of such proceedings. It extrapolates a picture of what it conceives to be the norm from police investigatory manuals, published in 1959 and 1962 or earlier, without any attempt to allow for adjustments in police practices that may have occurred in the wake of more recent decisions of state appellate tribunals or this Court. But even if the relentless application of the described procedures could lead to involuntary confessions, it most assuredly does not follow that each and every case will disclose this kind of interrogation or this kind of consequence. Insofar as appears from the Court's opinion, it has not examined a single transcript of any police interrogation, let alone the interrogation that took place in any one of these cases which it decides today. Judged by any of the standards for empirical investigation utilized in the social sciences the factual basis for the Court's premise is patently inadequate.

Although in the Court's view in-custody interrogation is inherently coercive, the Court says that the spontaneous product of the coercion of arrest and detention is still to be deemed voluntary. An accused, arrested on probable cause, may blurt out a confession which will be admissible despite the fact that he is alone and in custody, without any showing that he had any notion of his right to remain silent or of the consequences of his admission. Yet, under the Court's rule, if the police ask him a single question such as "Do you have anything to say?" or "Did you kill your wife?" his response, if there is one, has somehow been compelled, even if the accused has been clearly warned of his right to remain silent. Common sense informs us to the contrary. While one may say that the response was "involuntary" in the sense the question provoked or was the occasion for the response and thus the defendant was induced to speak out when he might have remained silent if not arrested and not questioned, it is patently unsound to say the response is compelled.

The duration and nature of incommunicado custody, the presence or absence of advice concerning the defendant's constitutional rights, and the granting or refusal of requests to communicate with lawyers, relatives or friends have all been rightly regarded as important data bearing on the basic inquiry. But it has never been suggested, until today, that such questioning was so coercive and accused persons so lacking in hardihood that the very first response to the very first question following the commencement of custody must be conclusively presumed to be the product of an overborne will.

If the rule announced today were truly based on a conclusion that all confessions resulting from custodial interrogation are coerced, then it would simply have no rational foundation. *A fortiori* that would be true of the extension of the rule to exculpatory statements, which the Court effects after a brief discussion of why, in the Court's view, they must be deemed incriminatory but without any discussion of why they must be deemed coerced. Even if one were to postulate that the Court's concern is not that all confessions induced by police interrogation are coerced but rather that some such confessions are coerced and present judicial procedures are believed to be inadequate to identify the confessions that are coerced and those that are not, it would still not be essential to impose the rule that the Court has now fashioned. Transcripts or observers could be required, specific time limits, tailored to fit the cause, could be imposed, or other devices could be utilized to reduce the chances that otherwise indiscernible coercion will produce an inadmissible confession.

On the other hand, even if one assumed that there was an adequate factual basis for the conclusion that all confessions obtained during in-custody interrogation are the product of compulsion, the rule propounded by the Court will still be irrational, for, apparently, it is only if the accused is also warned of his right to counsel and waives both that right and the right against self-incrimination that the inherent compulsiveness of interrogation disappears. But if the defendant may not answer without a warning a question such as "Where were you last night?" without having his answer be a compelled one, how can the Court ever accept his negative answer to the question of whether he wants to consult his retained counsel or counsel whom the court will appoint? And why if counsel is present and the accused nevertheless confesses, or counsel tells the accused to tell the truth, and that is what the accused does, is the situation any less coercive insofar as the accused is concerned? The Court apparently realizes its dilemma of foreclosing questioning without the necessary warnings but at the same time permitting the accused, sitting in the same chair in front of the same policemen, to waive his right to consult an attorney. It expects, however, that the accused will not often waive the right; and if it is claimed that he has, the State faces a severe, if not impossible burden of proof.

All of this makes very little sense in terms of the compulsion which the Fifth Amendment proscribes. That amendment deals with compelling the accused himself. It is his free will that is involved. Confessions and incriminating admissions, as such, are not forbidden evidence; only those which are compelled are banned. I doubt that the Court observes these distinctions today. By considering any answers to any interrogation to be compelled regardless of the content and course of examination and by escalating the requirements to prove waiver, the Court not only prevents the use of compelled confessions but for all practical purposes forbids interrogation except in the presence of counsel. That is, instead of confining itself to protection of the right against compelled self-incrimination the Court has created a limited Fifth Amendment right to counsel — or, as the Court expresses it, a "need for counsel to protect the Fifth Amendment privilege . . . ." The focus then is not on the will of the accused but on the will of counsel and how much influence he can have on the accused. Obviously there is no warrant in the Fifth Amendment for thus installing counsel as the arbiter of the privilege.

In sum, for all the Court's expounding on the menacing atmosphere of police interrogation procedures, it has failed to supply any foundation for the conclusions it draws or the measures it adopts.

IV.

Criticism of the Court's opinion, however, cannot stop with a demonstration that the factual and textual bases for the rule it propounds are, at best, less than compelling. Equally relevant is an assessment of the rule's consequences measured against community values. The Court's duty to assess the consequences of its action is not satisfied by the utterance of the truth that a value of our system of criminal justice is "to respect the inviolability of the human personality" and to require government to produce the evidence against the accused by its own independent labors. More than the human dignity of the accused is involved; the human personality of others in the society must also be preserved. Thus the values reflected by the privilege are not the sole desideratum; society's interest in the general security is of equal weight.

The obvious underpinning of the Court's decision is a deep-seated distrust of all confessions. As the Court declares that the accused may not be interrogated without counsel present, absent a waiver of the right to counsel, and as the Court all but admonishes the lawyer to advise the accused to remain silent, the result adds up to a judicial judgment that evidence from the accused should not be used against him in any way, whether compelled or not. This is the not so subtle overtone of the opinion — that it is inherently wrong for the police to gather evidence from the accused himself. And this is precisely the nub of this dissent. I see nothing wrong or immoral, and certainly nothing unconstitutional, in the police's asking a suspect whom they have reasonable cause to arrest whether or not he killed his wife or in confronting him with the evidence on which the arrest was based, at least where he has been plainly advised that he may remain completely silent, *see Escobedo* (dissenting opinion). Until today, "the admissions or confessions of the prisoner, when voluntarily and freely made, have always ranked high in the scale of incriminating evidence." Particularly when corroborated, as where the police have confirmed the accused's disclosure of the hiding place of implements or fruits of the crime, such confessions have the highest reliability and significantly contribute to the certitude with which we may believe the accused is guilty. Moreover, it is by no means certain that the process of confessing is injurious to the accused. To the contrary it may provide psychological relief and enhance the prospects for rehabilitation.

This is not to say that the value of respect for the inviolability of the accused's individual personality should be accorded no weight or that all confessions should be indiscriminately admitted. This Court has long read the Constitution to proscribe compelled confessions, a salutary rule from which there should be no retreat. But I see no sound basis, factual or otherwise, and the Court gives none, for concluding that the present rule against the receipt of coerced confessions is inadequate for the task of sorting out inadmissible evidence and must be replaced by the *per se* rule which is now imposed. Even if the new concept can be said to have advantages of some sort over the present law, they are far outweighed by its likely undesirable impact on other very relevant and important interests.

The most basic function of any government is to provide for the security of the individual and of his property. These ends of society are served by the criminal laws which for the most part are aimed at the prevention of crime. Without the reasonably effective performance of the task of preventing private violence and retaliation, it is idle to talk about human dignity and civilized values.

The modes by which the criminal laws serve the interest in general security are many. First the murderer who has taken the life of another is removed from the streets, deprived of his liberty and thereby prevented from repeating his offense. In view of the statistics on recidivism in this country and of the number of instances in which apprehension occurs only after repeated offenses, no one can sensibly claim that this aspect of the criminal law does not prevent crime or contribute significantly to the personal security of the ordinary citizen.

Secondly, the swift and sure apprehension of those who refuse to respect the personal security and dignity of their neighbor unquestionably has its impact on others who might be similarly tempted. That the criminal law is wholly or partly ineffective with a segment of the population or with many of those who have been apprehended and convicted is a very faulty basis for concluding that it is not effective with respect to the great bulk of our citizens or for thinking that without the criminal laws, or in the absence of their enforcement, there would be no increase in crime. Arguments of this nature are not borne out by any kind of reliable evidence that I have been to this date.

Thirdly, the law concerns itself with those whom it has confined. The hope and aim of modern penology, fortunately, is as soon as possible to return the convict to society a better and more law-abiding man than when he left. Sometimes there is success, sometimes failure. But at least the effort is made, and it should be made to the very maximum extent of our present and future capabilities.

The rule announced today will measurably weaken the ability of the criminal law to perform these tasks. It is a deliberate calculus to prevent interrogations, to reduce the incidence of confessions and pleas of guilty and to increase the number of trials. Criminal trials, no matter how efficient the police are, are not sure bets for the prosecution, nor should they be if the evidence is not forthcoming. Under the present law, the prosecution fails to prove its case in about 30% of the criminal cases actually tried in the federal courts. But it is something else again to remove from the ordinary criminal case all those confessions which heretofore have been held to be free and voluntary acts of the accused and to thus establish a new constitutional barrier to the ascertainment of truth by the judicial process. There is, in my view, every reason to believe that a good many criminal defendants who otherwise would have been convicted on what this Court has previously thought to be the most satisfactory kind of evidence will now under this new version of the Fifth Amendment, either not be tried at all or will be acquitted if the State's evidence, minus the confession, is put to the test of litigation.

I have no desire whatsoever to share the responsibility for any such impact on the present criminal process.

In some unknown number of cases the Court's rule will return a killer, a rapist or other criminal to the streets and to the environment which produced him, to repeat his crime whenever it pleases him. As a consequence, there will not be a gain, but a loss, in human dignity. The real concern is not the unfortunate consequences of this new decision on the criminal law as an abstract, disembodied series of authoritative proscriptions, but the impact on those who rely on the public authority for protection and who without it can only engage in violent self-help with guns, knives and the help of their neighbors similarly inclined. There is, of course, a saving factor: the next victims are uncertain, unnamed and unrepresented in this case.

Nor can this decision do other than have a corrosive effect on the criminal laws as an effective device to prevent crime. A major component in its effectiveness in this regard is its swift and sure enforcement. The easier it is to get away with rape and murder, the less the deterrent effect on those who are inclined to attempt it. This is still good common sense. If it were not, we should posthaste liquidate the whole law enforcement establishment as a useless, misguided effort to control human conduct.

And what about the accused who has confessed or would confess in response to simple, noncoercive questioning and whose guilt could not otherwise be proved? Is it so clear that release is the best thing for him in every case? Has it so unquestionably been resolved that in each and every case it would be better for him not to confess and to return to his environment with no attempt whatsoever to help him? I think not. It may well be that in many cases it will be no less than a callous disregard for his own welfare as well as for the interests of his next victim.

There is another aspect to the effect of the Court's rule on the person whom the police have arrested on probable cause. The fact is that he may not be guilty at all and may be able to extricate himself quickly and simply if he were told the circumstances of his arrest and were asked to explain. This effort, and his release, must now await the hiring of a lawyer or his appointment by the court, consultation with counsel and then a session with the police or the prosecutor. Similarly, where probable cause exists to arrest several suspects, as where the body of the victim is discovered in a house having several residents, it will often be true that a suspect may be cleared only through the results of interrogation of other suspects. Here too the release of the innocent may be delayed by the Court's rule.

Much of the trouble with the Court's new rule is that it will operate indiscriminately in all criminal cases, regardless of the severity of the crime or the circumstances involved. It applies to every defendant, whether the professional criminal or one committing a crime of momentary passion who is not part and parcel of organized crime. It will slow down the investigation and the apprehension of confederates in those cases where time is of the essence, such as kidnapping, and some of those involving organized crime. In the latter context the lawyer who arrives may also be the lawyer for the defendant's colleagues and can be relied upon to insure that no breach of the organization's security takes place even though the accused may feel that the best thing he can do is to cooperate.

At the same time, the Court's *per se* approach may not be justified on the ground that it provides a "bright line" permitting the authorities to judge in advance whether interrogation may safely be pursued without jeopardizing the admissibility of any information obtained as a consequence. Nor can it be claimed that judicial time and effort, assuming that is a relevant consideration, will be conserved because of the ease of application of the new rule. Today's decision leaves open such questions as whether the accused was in custody, whether his statements were spontaneous or the product of interrogation, whether the accused has effectively waived his rights, and whether nontestimonial evidence introduced at trial is the fruit of statements made during a prohibited interrogation, all of which are certain to prove productive of uncertainty during investigation and litigation during prosecution. For all these reasons, if further restrictions on police interrogation are desirable at this time, a more flexible approach makes much more sense than the Court's constitutional straitjacket which forecloses more discriminating treatment by legislative or rule-making pronouncements.

Applying the traditional standards to the cases before the Court, I would hold these confessions voluntary.

QUESTIONS AND NOTES

1.   What were the available constitutional provisions upon which to predicate *Miranda*? Fourth Amendment? Fifth Amendment? Sixth Amendment? Fourteenth Amendment? Which did the Court choose? Why? If you wished to reach the Court's result, which would you have chosen? Why?

2.   Which opinion does the best job of balancing the interests that need to be balanced in cases like *Miranda*? Why?

3.   The majority is opting for a strict set of rules (bright-line, if you will) whereas the dissenters seem to prefer standards (*i.e.*, guidelines). What are the advantages and disadvantages of each approach? Which do you generally prefer? Why? Which do you prefer in this instance? Why?

4.   The Court begins by announcing that "our holding is not an innovation in our jurisprudence." Do you agree? Do you think that the quoted observation makes the opinion more or less persuasive to the neutral observer?

5.   Does fn.4 narrow *Escobedo*? If so, is it a desirable narrowing?

6.   Is *Miranda* likely to stop or significantly reduce the amount of police brutality? In that regard, what would be the post-*Miranda* result in *People v. Portelli* (text accompanying Court's fn. 7)?

7.   What, if any, relevance should the police manuals play? What relevance do they play?

8.   Was *Miranda* intended to stop the various psychological ploys (such as "Mutt and Jeff") referred to in the opinion? Do you think that it in fact stopped them?

9.   Do you think that the testatrix hypothetical in fn. 26 of the Court's opinion is a valid analogy? Is Justice Harlan's criticism of the analogy, in his dissent, well-taken?

10.   Is there any good reason to require the warnings for sophisticated defendants who know their rights?

11.   Is fn. 44 realistic? If you were representing a defendant under those circumstances would you permit him to speak? If so, when? If not, why not?

12.   In regard to Question 10, do you think that Justice Harlan got it right in dissent when he suggested that "the rules work for reliability only in the Pickwickian sense that they prevent some from being given at all?"

13.   What should (or could) the F.B.I. have done to legitimate the interrogation and subsequent confession in *Westover*?

14.   Justice White suggests that confessions may be good for a defendant psychologically and rehabilitatively. Are you persuaded? What, if any, impact should that possibility have had on the result in this case?

15.   Do you agree with Justice White's suggestions that *Miranda* might retard the achievement of some of the basic purposes of the criminal law?

16.   We now turn to cases examining particular aspects of *Miranda*, starting with the specificity of the warnings.

B.   THE NATURE OF THE WARNINGS

One of the many questions left open by *Miranda* was how closely the actual warnings must parallel the manner in which they were spelled out in *Miranda*. Like so much else about *Miranda*, it depends on which paragraph of the opinion one reads. The issue was joined in *Duckworth v. Eagan*, where a very different Court from the one that delivered *Miranda* split five to four.

DUCKWORTH v. EAGAN
492 U.S. 195 (1989)

CHIEF JUSTICE REHNQUIST delivered the opinion of the Court.

Respondent confessed to stabbing a woman nine times after she refused to have sexual relations with him, and he was convicted of attempted murder. Before confessing, respondent was given warnings by the police, which included the advice that a lawyer would be appointed "if and when you go to court." The United States Court of Appeals for the Seventh Circuit held that such advice did not comply with the requirements of *Miranda*. We disagree and reverse.

Late on May 16, 1982, respondent contacted a Chicago police officer he knew to report that he had seen the naked body of a dead woman lying on a Lake Michigan beach. Respondent denied any involvement in criminal activity. He then took several Chicago police officers to the beach, where the woman was crying for help. When she saw respondent, the woman exclaimed: "Why did you stab me? Why did you stab me?" Respondent told the officers that he had been with the woman earlier that night, but that they had been attacked by several men who abducted the woman in a van.

The next morning, after realizing that the crime had been committed in Indiana, the Chicago police turned the investigation over to the Hammond, Indiana, Police Department. Respondent repeated to the Hammond police officers his story that he had been attacked on the lakefront, and that the woman had been abducted by several men. After he filled out a battery complaint at a local police station, respondent agreed to go to the Hammond police headquarters for further questioning.

At about 11 a.m., the Hammond police questioned respondent. Before doing so, the police read to respondent a waiver form, entitled "Voluntary Appearance; Advice of Rights," and they asked him to sign it. The form provided:

> Before we ask you any questions, you must understand your rights. You have the right to remain silent. Anything you say can be used against you in court. *You have a right to talk to a lawyer for advice before we ask you any questions, and to have him with you during questioning.* You have this right to the advice and presence of a lawyer even if you cannot afford to hire one. *We have no way of giving you a lawyer, but one will be appointed for you, if you wish, if and when you go to court.* If you wish to answer questions now without a lawyer present, you have the right to stop answering questions at any time. You also have the right to stop answering at any time until you've talked to a lawyer.

(emphasis added).[1]

Respondent signed the form and repeated his exculpatory explanation for his activities of the previous evening.

Respondent was then placed in the "lock up" at the Hammond police headquarters. Some 29 hours later, at about 4 p.m. on May 18, the police again interviewed respondent. Before this questioning, one of the officers read the following waiver form to respondent:

> 1. Before making this statement, I was advised that I have the right to remain silent and that anything I might say may or will be used against me in a court of law.
>
> 2. That I have the right to consult with an attorney of my own choice before saying anything, and that an attorney may be present while I am making any statement or throughout the course of any conversation with any police officer if I so choose.

---

[1] The remainder of the form signed by respondent provided:

> I, [*Gary Eagan,*] have come to the Detective Bureau of the Hammond, Indiana Police Department, of my own choice to talk with Officers . . . . In [*sic*] regard to an investigation they are conducting. I know that I am not under arrest and that I can leave this office if I wish to do so.
>
> Prior to any questioning, I was furnished with the above statement of my rights . . . . I have (read) (had read to me) this statement of my rights. I understand what my rights are. I am willing to answer questions and make a statement. I do not want a lawyer. I understand and know what I am doing. No promises or threats have been made to me and no pressure of any kind has been used against me.

3. That I can stop and request an attorney at any time during the course of the taking of any statement or during the course of any such conversation.

4. That in the course of any conversation I can refuse to answer any further questions and remain silent, thereby terminating the conversation.

5. That if I do not hire an attorney, one will be provided for me."

Respondent read the form back to the officers and signed it. He proceeded to confess to stabbing the woman. The next morning, respondent led the officers to the Lake Michigan beach where they recovered the knife he had used in the stabbing and several items of clothing.

At trial, over respondent's objection, the state court admitted his confession, his first statement denying any involvement in the crime, the knife, and the clothing. The jury found respondent guilty of attempted murder, but acquitted him of rape. He was sentenced to 35 years' imprisonment. The conviction was upheld on appeal.

Respondent sought a writ of habeas corpus in the United States District Court for the Northern District of Indiana, claiming, *inter alia*, that his confession was inadmissible because the first waiver form did not comply with *Miranda*. The District Court denied the petition, holding that the record "clearly manifests adherence to *Miranda* . . . especially as to the so-called second statement."

A divided United States Court of Appeals for the Seventh Circuit reversed. The majority held that the advice that counsel would be appointed "if and when you go to court," which was included in the first warnings given to respondent, was "constitutionally defective because it denies an accused indigent a clear and unequivocal warning of the right to appointed counsel before any interrogation," and "link[s] an indigent's right to counsel before interrogation with a future event."

We then granted certiorari to resolve a conflict among the lower courts as to whether informing a suspect that an attorney would be appointed for him "if and when you go to court" renders *Miranda* warnings inadequate.[2] We agree with the majority of the lower courts that it does not.

In *Miranda*, the Court established certain procedural safeguards that require police to advise criminal suspects of their rights under the Fifth and Fourteenth Amendments before commencing custodial interrogation. In now-familiar words, the Court said that the suspect must be told that "he has the right to remain silent, that anything he says can be used against him in a court of law, that he has the right to the presence of an attorney, and that if he cannot afford an attorney one will be appointed for him prior to any questioning if he so desires." The Court in *Miranda* "presumed that interrogation in certain custodial circumstances is inherently coercive and . . . that statements made under those circumstances are inadmissible

---

[2] The majority of federal and state courts to consider the issue have held that warnings that contained "if and when you go to court" language satisfied *Miranda*. Other courts, although not using the precise "if and when you go to court" language, have held *Miranda* was satisfied by a warning that an attorney could not be appointed for a suspect until he appeared in court. On the other hand, a minority of federal and state courts, including the Seventh Circuit in this case, have held that "if and when you go to court" language did not satisfy *Miranda*.

unless the suspect is specifically warned of his *Miranda* rights and freely decides to forgo those rights."

We have never insisted that *Miranda* warnings be given in the exact form described in that decision.[4] In *Miranda* itself, the Court said that "[t]he warnings required and the waiver necessary in accordance with our opinion today are, *in the absence of a fully effective equivalent*, prerequisites to the admissibility of any statement made by a defendant." (emphasis added). In *California v. Prysock*, 453 U.S. 355 (1981) (*per curiam*), we stated that "the 'rigidity' of *Miranda* [does not] exten[d] to the precise formulation of the warnings given a criminal defendant," and that "no talismanic incantation [is] required to satisfy its strictures."

Miranda has not been limited to station house questioning, and the officer in the field may not always have access to printed *Miranda* warnings, or he may inadvertently depart from routine practice, particularly if a suspect requests an elaboration of the warnings. The prophylactic *Miranda* warnings are "not themselves rights protected by the Constitution but [are] instead measures to insure that the right against compulsory self-incrimination [is] protected." *Michigan v. Tucker*, 417 U.S. 433 (1974). Reviewing courts therefore need not examine *Miranda* warnings as if construing a will or defining the terms of an easement. The inquiry is simply whether the warnings reasonably "conve[y] to [a suspect] his rights as required by *Miranda*." *Prysock*.

We think the initial warnings given to respondent touched all of the bases required by *Miranda*. The police told respondent that he had the right to remain silent, that anything he said could be used against him in court, that he had the right to speak to an attorney before and during questioning, that he had "this right to the advice and presence of a lawyer even if [he could] not afford to hire one," and that he had the "right to stop answering at any time until [he] talked to a lawyer." As noted, the police also added that they could not provide respondent with a lawyer, but that one would be appointed "if and when you go to court." The Court of Appeals thought this "if and when you go to court" language suggested that "only those accused who can afford an attorney have the right to have one present before answering any questions," and "implie[d] that if the accused does not 'go to court,' *i.e.*[,] the government does not file charges, the accused is not entitled to [counsel] at all."

---

[4] For example, the standard *Miranda* warnings used by the Federal Bureau of Investigation provide as follows:

> Before we ask you any questions, you must understand your rights.
>
> You have the right to remain silent.
>
> Anything you say can be used against you in court.
>
> You have the right to talk to a lawyer for advice before we ask you any questions and to have a lawyer with you during questioning.
>
> If you cannot afford a lawyer, one will be appointed for you before any questioning if you wish.
>
> If you decide to answer questions now without a lawyer present, you will still have the right to stop answering at any time. You also have the right to stop answering at any time until you talk to a lawyer.

Brief for United States as *Amicus Curiae* 1–2, n. 1.

In our view, the Court of Appeals misapprehended the effect of the inclusion of "if and when you go to court" language in *Miranda* warnings. First, this instruction accurately described the procedure for the appointment of counsel in Indiana. Under Indiana law, counsel is appointed at the defendant's initial appearance in court, and formal charges must be filed at or before that hearing. We think it must be relatively commonplace for a suspect, after receiving *Miranda* warnings, to ask *when* he will obtain counsel. The "if and when you go to court" advice simply anticipates that question. Second, *Miranda* does not require that attorneys be producible on call, but only that the suspect be informed, as here, that he has the right to an attorney before and during questioning, and that an attorney would be appointed for him if he could not afford one.[7] The Court in *Miranda* emphasized that it was not suggesting that "each police station must have a 'station house lawyer' present at all times to advise prisoners." If the police cannot provide appointed counsel, *Miranda* requires only that the police not question a suspect unless he waives his right to counsel. Here, respondent did just that.

Respondent relies on language in *California v. Prysock*, where we suggested that *Miranda* warnings would not be sufficient "if the reference to the right to appointed counsel was linked [to a] future point in time *after* the police interrogation." (emphasis added). The Court of Appeals also referred to *Prysock* in finding deficient the initial warnings given to respondent. But the vice referred to in *Prysock* was that such warnings would not apprise the accused of his right to have an attorney present if he chose to answer questions. The warnings in this case did not suffer from that defect. Of the eight sentences in the initial warnings, one described respondent's right to counsel "before [the police] ask[ed] [him] questions," while another stated his right to "stop answering at any time until [he] talk[ed] to a lawyer." We hold that the initial warnings given to respondent, in their totality, satisfied *Miranda*, and therefore that his first statement denying his involvement in the crime, as well as the knife and the clothing, was properly admitted into evidence.

The Court of Appeals thought it necessary to remand this case for consideration of whether respondent's second statement was tainted by the first warnings. In view of our disposition of this case, we need not reach that question.[8] The judgment of the Court of Appeals is accordingly reversed, and the case is remanded for further proceedings not inconsistent with our decision.

It is so ordered.

---

[7] In *Miranda*, the Court stated that the FBI's then-current practice of informing suspects "of a right to free counsel *if* they are unable to pay, and the availability of such counsel from the Judge" was "consistent with the procedure which we delineate today."

[8] Respondent argues that the second set of *Miranda* warnings he received were deficient. These specific warnings have been upheld by the Seventh Circuit, and the Indiana Supreme Court, and we think they plainly comply with *Miranda*.

Justice Marshall, with whom Justice Brennan joins, and with whom Justice Blackmun and Justice Stevens join, dissenting.

The majority holds today that a police warning advising a suspect that he is entitled to an appointed lawyer only "if and when he goes to court" satisfies the requirements of *Miranda*. The majority reaches this result by seriously mischaracterizing that decision. Under *Miranda*, a police warning must *"clearly infor[m]"* a suspect taken into custody "that if he cannot afford an attorney one will be appointed for him *prior to any questioning* if he so desires." (emphasis added). A warning qualified by an "if and when you go to court" caveat does nothing of the kind; instead, it leads the suspect to believe that a lawyer will not be provided until some indeterminate time in the future *after questioning*.

In *Miranda*, the Court held that law enforcement officers who take a suspect into custody must inform the suspect of, among other things, his right to have counsel appointed to represent him before and during interrogation:

> In order fully to apprise a person interrogated of the extent of his rights . . . , it is necessary to warn him not only that he has the right to consult with an attorney, but also that if he is indigent a lawyer will be appointed to represent him. Without this additional warning, the admonition of the right to consult with counsel would often be understood as meaning only that he can consult with a lawyer if he has one or has the funds to obtain one. The warning of a right to counsel would be hollow if not couched in terms that would convey to the indigent — the person most often subjected to interrogation — the knowledge that he too has a right to have counsel present. As with the warning of the right to remain silent and of the general right to counsel, only by effective and express explanation to the indigent of this right can there be assurance that he was truly in a position to exercise it.

Miranda mandated no specific verbal formulation that police must use, but the Court, speaking through Chief Justice Warren, emphasized repeatedly that the offer of appointed counsel must be "effective and express." A clear and unequivocal offer to provide appointed counsel prior to questioning is, in short, an "absolute prerequisite to interrogation."

In concluding that the first warning given to respondent Eagan satisfies the dictates of *Miranda*, the majority makes a mockery of that decision. Eagan was initially advised that he had the right to the presence of counsel before and during questioning. But in the very next breath, the police informed Eagan that, if he could not afford a lawyer, one would be appointed to represent him only "if and when" he went to court. As the Court of Appeals found, Eagan could easily have concluded from the "if and when" caveat that only "those accused who can afford an attorney have the right to have one present before answering any questions; those who are not so fortunate must wait." Eagan was, after all, never told that questioning would be *delayed* until a lawyer was appointed "if and when" Eagan did, in fact, go to court. Thus, the "if and when" caveat may well have had the effect of negating the initial promise that counsel could be present. At best, a suspect like Eagan "would not know . . . whether or not he had a right to the services of a lawyer."

In lawyerlike fashion, THE CHIEF JUSTICE parses the initial warnings given Eagan and finds that the most plausible interpretation is that Eagan would not be questioned until a lawyer was appointed when he later appeared in court. What goes wholly overlooked in THE CHIEF JUSTICE'S analysis is that the recipients of police warnings are often frightened suspects unlettered in the law, not lawyers or judges or others schooled in interpreting legal or semantic nuance. Such suspects can hardly be expected to interpret, in as facile a manner as THE CHIEF JUSTICE, "the pretzel-like warnings here — intertwining, contradictory, and ambiguous as they are." The majority thus refuses to recognize that "[t]he warning of a right to counsel would be hollow if not couched in terms that would convey to the indigent — the person most often subjected to interrogation — the knowledge that he too has the right to have counsel present." *Miranda.*

Even if the typical suspect could draw the inference the majority does — that questioning will not commence until a lawyer is provided at a later court appearance — a warning qualified by an "if and when" caveat still fails to give a suspect any indication of *when* he will be taken to court. Upon hearing the warnings given in this case, a suspect would likely conclude that no lawyer would be provided until trial. In common parlance, "going to court" is synonymous with "going to trial." Furthermore, the negative implication of the caveat is that, if the suspect is never taken to court, he "is not entitled to an attorney at all." An unwitting suspect harboring uncertainty on this score is precisely the sort of person who may feel compelled to talk "voluntarily" to the police, without the presence of counsel, in an effort to extricate himself from his predicament:

"[The suspect] is effectively told that he can talk now or remain in custody — in an alien, friendless, harsh world — for an indeterminate length of time. To the average accused, still hoping at this stage to be home on time for dinner or to make it to work on time, the implication that his choice is to answer questions right away or remain in custody until that nebulous time 'if and when' he goes to court is a coerced choice of the most obvious kind." *Dickerson v. State*, 257 Ind. 562, 276 N.E.2d 845, 852 (1972) (DeBruler, J., concurring in result) (finding inadequate a warning identical to the one in this case). That the warning given to Eagan "accurately described the procedure for the appointment of counsel in Indiana," does nothing to mitigate the possibility that he would feel coerced into talking to the police. *Miranda*, it is true, does not require the police to have a "station house lawyer" ready at all times to counsel suspects taken into custody. But if a suspect does not understand that a lawyer will be made available within a reasonable period of time after he has been taken into custody and advised of his rights, the suspect may decide to talk to the police *for that reason alone.* The threat of an indefinite deferral of interrogation, in a system like Indiana's, thus constitutes an effective means by which the police can pressure a suspect to speak without the presence of counsel. Sanctioning such police practices simply because the warnings given do not misrepresent state law does nothing more than let the state-law tail wag the federal constitutional dog.[2]

---

[2] Nothing in *Miranda*, nor any of our other cases for that matter, supports the notion that the police may indefinitely delay the point at which counsel is appointed. On the contrary, the Court indicated in

The majority's misreading of *Miranda* — stating that police warnings need only "touc[h] all of the bases required by *Miranda*," that *Miranda* warnings need only be "reasonably 'conve[yed]'" to a suspect, and that *Miranda* warnings are to be measured not point by point but "in their totality," — is exacerbated by its interpretation of *California v. Prysock*, a decision that squarely supports Eagan's claim in this case. The juvenile suspect in *Prysock* was initially told that he had the right to have a lawyer present before and during questioning. He then was told that he had the right to have his parents present as well. At this point the suspect was informed that a lawyer would be appointed to represent him at no cost if he could not afford one. The California Court of Appeal ruled these warnings insufficient because the suspect was not expressly told of his right to an appointed attorney before and during questioning. This Court reversed, finding that "nothing in the warnings given respondent suggested any limitation on the right to the presence of appointed counsel."

In reaching this result, the *Prysock* Court pointedly distinguished a series of lower court decisions that had found inadequate warnings in which "the reference to the right to appointed counsel was linked with some future point in time." *Id.* at 360. In *United States v. Garcia*, 431 F.2d 134 (CA9 1970) (*per curiam*), for example, the suspect had been informed on one occasion that she had the right to appointed counsel "'when she answered any questions,'" and on another occasion that she could "'have an attorney appointed to represent [her] when [she] first appear[ed] before the U.S. Commissioner or the Court.'" Similarly, in *People v. Bolinski*, 260 Cal.App.2d 705, 718, 67 Cal. Rptr. 347, 355 (1968), the suspect was advised that counsel would be appointed "'if he was charged.'" These lower courts had correctly found these warnings defective, the *Prysock* Court explained, because "[i]n both instances the reference to appointed counsel was linked to a future point in time after police interrogation," and therefore did not clearly advise the suspect of his right to appointed counsel before such interrogation. The initial, conditional warning given Eagan suffers from precisely the same fatal defect. It is highly disingenuous for the majority to ignore this fact, characterizing *Prysock* as involving only the question whether a particular warning "apprise[d] the accused of his right to have an attorney present if he chose to answer questions."

It poses no great burden on law enforcement officers to eradicate the confusion stemming from the "if and when" caveat. Deleting the sentence containing the offending language is all that needs to be done. Purged of this language, the warning tells the suspect in a straightforward fashion that he has the right to the presence of a lawyer before and during questioning, and that a lawyer will be appointed if he cannot afford one. The suspect is given no reason to believe that the appointment of an attorney may come after interrogation. To the extent one doubts that it is the "if and when" caveat that is the source of the confusion, compare the initial warning given Eagan, and the crystal-clear warning currently used by the FBI, quoted at n.4. The majority's claim that the two warnings are indistinguishable in the message conveyed to a suspect defies belief. I dissent.[4]

Miranda that the police could detain a person without providing counsel for no more than "a reasonable period of time."

[4] With no analysis whatsoever, the majority also holds that the second set of warnings read to Eagan

QUESTIONS AND NOTES

1. Two of the Justices, O'Connor and Scalia, argued that *Miranda* claims should not be cognizable on habeas corpus. Two others, Marshall and Brennan, argued that they should be. The Court simply assumed that should be without deciding. Four years later, a sharply divided Supreme Court ruled that *Miranda* claims are cognizable in habeas corpus. *Withrow v. Williams*, 507 U.S. 680 (1993). Rehnquist, O'Connor, Scalia, and Thomas dissented. Do you think that the uncertain procedural status of Eagan's claim may have influenced the Court to decide against him?

2. Was the portion of the statement signed by Eagan indicating that he was not in custody obviously false (*see* fn. 1)? If so, should that have influenced the Court to have resolved the case against the state?

3. Which opinion (majority or dissent) comes closer to capturing the spirit of *Miranda*? Explain.

4. Which opinion comes closer to establishing the spirit of the Fifth Amendment? Explain.

5. Does the defendant have a *right* to an interview with the police so that he can get home for dinner or whatever?

6. If your answer to Question 5 is "no," is Marshall's dissent undercut to the extent that he suggests that the suspect will be coerced into talking to the police because he doesn't know when, if ever, he will be brought to trial?

7. Is the defendant entitled to counsel during questioning or just not to be questioned in the absence of counsel? Is there a difference between those two concepts? Is the difference significant in terms relevant to the resolution of this case?

8. Would somebody in Gary Eagan's position understand the difference between Rehnquist's reading of the warnings and Marshall's somewhat contrary reading of them? Would he understand the questions raised by your author? To the extent that your answer is "no," what does that tell us about the type of warning that he should be given.

9. Should the time of appointment of counsel according to Indiana law have been relevant? If so, should the police at least have been required to say that you

---

and included in a waiver form that he signed prior to his second interrogation, "plainly comply with *Miranda*." This proposition is subject to dispute given the presence of the "of my own choice" language. *See Sotelo v. State*, 342 N.E.2d 844, 851 (Ind. 1976) (DeBruler, J. concurring). But even assuming the second set of warnings complied with *Miranda*, it does not necessarily follow that Eagan's subsequent waiver of rights was knowing and intelligent. Given "the misapprehension caused by the initial warning," the issue is not whether the second warnings were adequate standing alone, but rather whether under the circumstances the mistaken impression Eagan was initially given was corrected. While various factors might inform this inquiry, such as the passage of time, the principal question must be whether the new warnings were sufficiently clear to correct the effect of the earlier, defective warning. As there is little in the record on "the factual circumstances surrounding these events because the state courts did not directly examine this issue," I agree with the Court of Appeals that "remand for a determination of whether [Eagan] knowingly and intelligently waived his right to the presence of an attorney during the second interrogation" is the appropriate course.

will

been required to say that counsel will be
urt" rather than "if and when you go to
atement should the fact that the form said
used against me" rather than simply "will
tes have made a differences.

DO?
I SHOULD
WHAT ELSE

LEM

officers in Tampa, Florida, seeking to
Powell in connection with a robbery
d by Powell's girlfriend. After spotting
searched the room and discovered a
ed.

ed him to the Tampa Police headquar-
Powell any questions, the officers read Powell
pa Police Department Consent and Release Form 310. The form
states:

"You have the right to remain silent. If you give up the right to remain silent, anything you say can be used against you in court. You have the right to talk to a lawyer before answering any of our questions. If you cannot afford to hire a lawyer, one will be appointed for you without cost and before any questioning. You have the right to use any of these rights at any time you want during this interview."

Acknowledging that he had been informed of his rights, that he "underst[oo]d them," and that he was "willing to talk" to the officers, Powell signed the form. He then admitted that he owned the handgun found in the apartment. Powell knew he was prohibited from possessing a gun because he had previously been convicted of a felony, but said he had nevertheless purchased and carried the firearm for his protection.

Powell was charged in state court with possession of a weapon by a prohibited possessor, in violation of Fla. Stat. Ann. '790.23(1) (West 2007). Contending that the *Miranda* warnings were deficient because they did not adequately convey his right to the presence of an attorney during questioning, he moved to suppress his inculpatory statements. The trial court denied the motion, concluding that the officers had properly notified Powell of his right to counsel. A jury convicted Powell of the gun-possession charge.

On appeal, the Florida Second District Court of Appeal held that the trial court should have suppressed Powell's statements. The *Miranda* warnings, the appellate court concluded, did not "adequately inform [Powell] of his . . . right to have an attorney present throughout [the] interrogation." Considering the issue to be "one of great public importance," the court certified the following question to the Florida Supreme Court:

"Does the failure to provide express advice of the right to the presence of counsel during questioning vitiate *Miranda* warnings which advise of both

(A) the right to talk to a lawyer 'before questioning' and (B) the 'right 'to use" the right to consult a lawyer 'at 'any time' during questioning?"

Surveying decisions of this Court as well as Florida precedent, the Florida Supreme Court answered the certified question in the affirmative. "Both *Miranda* and article I, section 9 of the Florida Constitution," the Florida High Court noted, "require that a suspect be clearly informed of the right to have a lawyer present during questioning." The court found that the advice Powell received was misleading because it suggested that Powell could "only consult with an attorney before questioning" and did not convey Powell's entitlement to counsel's presence throughout the interrogation. Nor, in the court's view, did the final catchall warning "[y]ou have the right to use any of these rights at any time you want during this interview" cure the defect the court perceived in the right-to-counsel advice: "The catch-all phrase did not supply the missing warning of the right to have counsel present during police questioning," the court stated, for "a right that has never been expressed cannot be reiterated."

Justice Wells dissented. He considered it "unreasonable to conclude that the broad, unqualified language read to Powell would lead a person of ordinary intelligence to believe that he or she had a limited right to consult with an attorney that could only be exercised before answering the *first* question posed by law enforcement." The final sentence of the warning, he stressed, "avoid[ed] the implication unreasonable as it may [have] be[en]C that advice concerning the right of access to counsel *before* questioning conveys the message that access to counsel is foreclosed *during* questioning." (Internal quotation marks omitted). Criticizing the majority's "technical adherence to language . . . that has no connection with whether the person who confessed understood his or her rights," he concluded that "[t]he totality of the warning reasonably conveyed to Powell his continuing right of access to counsel."

How should the Supreme Court resolve this case?

For the Court's answer, see Florida v. Powell, 559 U.S. 50 (2010).

In *Spring*, we will consider whether failure to inform the defendant as to what he is being questioned about can invalidate an otherwise effective waiver.

COLORADO v. SPRING
479 U.S. 564 (1987)

JUSTICE POWELL delivered the opinion of the Court.

In *Miranda v. Arizona*, 384 U.S. 436 (1966), the Court held that a suspect's waiver of the Fifth Amendment privilege against self-incrimination is valid only if it is made voluntarily, knowingly, and intelligently. This case presents the question whether the suspect's awareness of all the crimes about which he may be questioned is relevant to determining the validity of his decision to waive the Fifth Amendment privilege.

I

In February 1979, respondent John Leroy Spring and a companion shot and killed Donald Walker during a hunting trip in Colorado. Shortly thereafter, an informant told agents of the Bureau of Alcohol, Tobacco, and Firearms (ATF) that Spring was engaged in the interstate transportation of stolen firearms. The informant also told the agents that Spring had discussed his participation in the Colorado killing. At the time the ATF agents received this information, Walker's body had not been found and the police had received no report of his disappearance. Based on the information received from the informant relating to the firearms violations, the ATF agents set up an undercover operation to purchase firearms from Spring. On March 30, 1979, ATF agents arrested Spring in Kansas City, Missouri, during the undercover purchase.

An ATF agent on the scene of the arrest advised Spring of his *Miranda* rights. Spring was advised of his *Miranda* rights a second time after he was transported to the ATF office in Kansas City. At the ATF office, the agents also advised Spring that he had the right to stop the questioning at any time or to stop the questioning until the presence of an attorney could be secured. Spring then signed a written form stating that he understood and waived his rights, and that he was willing to make a statement and answer questions.

ATF agents first questioned Spring about the firearms transactions that led to his arrest. They then asked Spring if he had a criminal record. He admitted that he had a juvenile record for shooting his aunt when he was 10 years old. The agents asked if Spring had ever shot anyone else. Spring ducked his head and mumbled, "I shot another guy once." The agents asked Spring if he had ever been to Colorado. Spring said no. The agents asked Spring whether he had shot a man named Walker in Colorado and thrown his body into a snowbank. Spring paused and then ducked his head again and said no. The interview ended at this point.

On May 26, 1979, Colorado law enforcement officials visited Spring while he was in jail in Kansas City pursuant to his arrest on the firearms offenses. The officers gave Spring the *Miranda* warnings, and Spring again signed a written form indicating that he understood his rights and was willing to waive them. The officers informed Spring that they wanted to question him about the Colorado homicide. Spring indicated that he "wanted to get it off his chest." In an interview that lasted approximately 1 1/2 hours, Spring confessed to the Colorado murder. During that time, Spring talked freely to the officers, did not indicate a desire to terminate the questioning, and never requested counsel. The officers prepared a written statement summarizing the interview. Spring read, edited, and signed the statement.

Spring was charged in Colorado state court with first-degree murder. Spring moved to suppress both statements on the ground that his waiver of *Miranda* rights was invalid. The trial court found that the ATF agents' failure to inform Spring before the March 30 interview that they would question him about the Colorado murder did not affect his waiver of his *Miranda* rights:

> [T]he questions themselves suggested the topic of inquiry. The questions dealt with "shooting anyone" and specifically killing a man named Walker and throwing his body in a snowbank in Colorado. The questions were not

designed to gather information relating to a subject that was not readily evident or apparent to Spring. Spring had been advised of his right to remain silent, his right to stop answering questions, and to have an Attorney present during interrogation. He did not elect to exercise his right to remain silent or to refuse to answer questions relating to the homicide, nor did he request Counsel during interrogation.

Accordingly, the trial court concluded that the March 30 statement should not be suppressed on Fifth Amendment grounds. The trial court, however, subsequently ruled that Spring's statement that he "shot another guy once" was irrelevant, and that the context of the discussion did not support the inference that the statement related to the Walker homicide. For that reason, the March 30 statement was not admitted at Spring's trial. The court concluded that the May 26 statement "was made freely, voluntarily, and intelligently, after [Spring's] being properly and fully advised of his rights, and that the statement should not be suppressed, but should be admitted in evidence." The May 26 statement was admitted into evidence at trial, and Spring was convicted of first-degree murder.

Spring argued on appeal that his waiver of *Miranda* rights before the March 30 statement was invalid because he was not informed that he would be questioned about the Colorado murder. Although this statement was not introduced at trial, he claimed that its validity was relevant because the May 26 statement that was admitted against him was the illegal "fruit" of the March 30 statement, and therefore should have been suppressed. The Colorado Court of Appeals agreed with Spring, holding that the ATF agents "had a duty to inform Spring that he was a suspect, or to readvise him of his *Miranda* rights, before questioning him about the murder." Because they failed to do so before the March 30 interview, "any waiver of rights in regard to questions designed to elicit information about Walker's death was not given knowingly or intelligently." The court held that the March 30 statement was inadmissible and that the State had failed to meet its burden of proving that the May 26 statement was not the product of the prior illegal statement. The court reversed Spring's conviction and remanded the case for a new trial, directing that if the State sought to introduce the May 26 statement into evidence, the trial court should determine whether the "taint" of the March 30 statement was sufficiently attenuated to allow introduction of the May 26 statement.

The Colorado Supreme Court affirmed the judgment of the Court of Appeals, although its reasoning differed in some respects. The court found:

> [T]he validity of Spring's waiver of constitutional rights must be determined upon an examination of the totality of the circumstances surrounding the making of the statement to determine if the waiver was voluntary, knowing and intelligent. No one factor is always determinative in that analysis. Whether, and to what extent, a suspect has been informed or is aware of the subject matter of the interrogation prior to its commencement is simply one factor in the court's evaluation of the total circumstances, although it may be a major or even a determinative factor in some situations.

The court concluded:

Here, the absence of an advisement to Spring that he would be questioned about the Colorado homicide, and the lack of any basis to conclude that at the time of the execution of the waiver, he reasonably could have expected that the interrogation would extend to that subject, *are* determinative factors in undermining the validity of the waiver.

JUSTICE ERICKSON, joined by Justice Rovira, dissented as to the resolution of this issue, stating:

Law enforcement officers have no duty under *Miranda* to inform a person in custody of all charges being investigated prior to questioning him. All that *Miranda* requires is that the suspect be advised that he has the right to remain silent, that anything he says can and will be used against him in court, that he has the right to consult with a lawyer and to have the lawyer present during interrogation, and that if he cannot afford a lawyer one will be appointed to represent him.

The dissenting justices found "ample evidence to support the trial court's conclusion that Spring waived his *Miranda* rights" and rejected "the majority's conclusion that Spring's waiver of his *Miranda* rights on March 30, 1979 was invalid simply because he was not informed of all matters that would be reviewed when he was questioned by the police." The court remanded the case for further proceedings consistent with its opinion.

We granted certiorari and now reverse.

II

There is no dispute that the police obtained the May 26 confession after complete *Miranda* warnings and after informing Spring that he would be questioned about the Colorado homicide. The Colorado Supreme Court nevertheless held that the confession should have been suppressed because it was the illegal "fruit" of the March 30 statement. A confession cannot be "fruit of the poisonous tree" if the tree itself is not poisonous. Our inquiry, therefore, centers on the validity of the March 30 statement.

A

In this case, the law enforcement officials twice informed Spring of his Fifth Amendment privilege in precisely the manner specified by *Miranda*. As we have noted, Spring indicated that he understood the enumerated rights and signed a written form expressing his intention to waive his Fifth Amendment privilege. The trial court specifically found that "there was no element of duress or coercion used to induce Spring's statements [on March 30, 1978]." Despite the explicit warnings and the finding by the trial court, Spring argues that his March 30 statement was in effect compelled in violation of his Fifth Amendment privilege because he signed the waiver form without being aware that he would be questioned about the Colorado homicide. Spring's argument strains the meaning of compulsion past the breaking point.

B

A statement is not "compelled" within the meaning of the Fifth Amendment if an individual "voluntarily, knowingly and intelligently" waives his constitutional privilege. *Miranda*. The inquiry whether a waiver is coerced "has two distinct dimensions." *Moran v. Burbine*, 475 U.S. 412, 421 (1986):

> First the relinquishment of the right must have been voluntary in the sense that it was the product of a free and deliberate choice rather than intimidation, coercion, or deception. Second, the waiver must have been made with a full awareness both of the nature of the right being abandoned and the consequences of the decision to abandon it. Only if the "totality of the circumstances surrounding the interrogation" reveal both an uncoerced choice and the requisite level of comprehension may a court properly conclude that the *Miranda* rights have been waived.

There is no doubt that Spring's decision to waive his Fifth Amendment privilege was voluntary. He alleges no "coercion of a confession by physical violence or other deliberate means calculated to break [his] will," and the trial court found none. His allegation that the police failed to supply him with certain information does not relate to any of the traditional indicia of coercion: "the duration and conditions of detention . . . , the manifest attitude of the police toward him, his physical and mental state, the diverse pressures which sap or sustain his powers of resistance and self-control." *Culombe v. Connecticut*, 367 U.S. 568, 602 (1961) (opinion of Frankfurter, J.). Absent evidence that Spring's "will [was] overborne and his capacity for self-determination critically impaired" because of coercive police conduct, his waiver of his Fifth Amendment privilege was voluntary under this Court's decision in *Miranda*.

There also is no doubt that Spring's waiver of his Fifth Amendment privilege was knowingly and intelligently made: that is, that Spring understood that he had the right to remain silent and that anything he said could be used as evidence against him. The Constitution does not require that a criminal suspect know and understand every possible consequence of a waiver of the Fifth Amendment privilege. The Fifth Amendment's guarantee is both simpler and more fundamental: A defendant may not be compelled to be a witness against himself in any respect. The *Miranda* warnings protect this privilege by ensuring that a suspect knows that he may choose not to talk to law enforcement officers, to talk only with counsel present, or to discontinue talking at any time. The *Miranda* warnings ensure that a waiver of these rights is knowing and intelligent by requiring that the suspect be fully advised of this constitutional privilege, including the critical advice that whatever he chooses to say may be used as evidence against him.

In this case there is no allegation that Spring failed to understand the basic privilege guaranteed by the Fifth Amendment. Nor is there any allegation that he misunderstood the consequences of speaking freely to the law enforcement officials. In sum, we think that the trial court was indisputably correct in finding that Spring's waiver was made knowingly and intelligently within the meaning of *Miranda*.

III

A

Spring relies on this Court's statement in *Miranda* that "any evidence that the accused was threatened, tricked, or cajoled into a waiver will . . . show that the defendant did not voluntarily waive his privilege." He contends that the failure to inform him of the potential subjects of interrogation constitutes the police trickery and deception condemned in *Miranda*, thus rendering his waiver of *Miranda* rights invalid. Spring, however, reads this statement in *Miranda* out of context and without due regard to the constitutional privilege the *Miranda* warnings were designed to protect.

We note first that the Colorado courts made no finding of official trickery. In fact, as noted above, the trial court expressly found that "there was no element of duress or coercion used to induce Spring's statements." Spring nevertheless insists that the failure of the ATF agents to inform him that he would be questioned about the murder constituted official "trickery" sufficient to invalidate his waiver of his Fifth Amendment privilege, even if the official conduct did not amount to "coercion." Even assuming that Spring's proposed distinction has merit, we reject his conclusion. This Court has never held that mere silence by law enforcement officials as to the subject matter of an interrogation is "trickery" sufficient to invalidate a suspect's waiver of *Miranda* rights, and we expressly decline so to hold today.[8]

Once *Miranda* warnings are given, it is difficult to see how official silence could cause a suspect to misunderstand the nature of his constitutional right — "his right to refuse to answer any question which might incriminate him." "Indeed, it seems self-evident that one who is told he is free to refuse to answer questions is in a curious posture to later complain that his answers were compelled." We have held that a valid waiver does not require that an individual be informed of all information "useful" in making his decision or all information that "might . . . affec[t] his decision to confess." *Moran v. Burbine*, 475 U.S. at 422. "[W]e have never read the Constitution to require that the police supply a suspect with a flow of information to help him calibrate his self-interest in deciding whether to speak or stand by his rights."[9] Here, the additional information could affect only the wisdom of a *Miranda* waiver, not its essentially voluntary and knowing nature. Accordingly, the failure of the law enforcement officials to inform Spring of the subject matter of the

---

[8] In certain circumstances, the Court has found affirmative misrepresentations by the police sufficient to invalidate a suspect's waiver of the Fifth Amendment privilege. *See, e.g., Lynumn v. Illinois*, 372 U.S. 528 (1963) (misrepresentation by police officers that a suspect would be deprived of state financial aid for her dependent child if she failed to cooperate with authorities rendered the subsequent confession involuntary); *Spano v. New York*, 360 U.S. 315 (1959) (misrepresentation by the suspect's friend that the friend would lose his job as a police officer if the suspect failed to cooperate rendered his statement involuntary). In this case, we are not confronted with an affirmative misrepresentation by law enforcement officials as to the scope of the interrogation and do not reach the question whether a waiver of *Miranda* rights would be valid in such a circumstance.

[9] Such an extension of *Miranda* would spawn numerous problems of interpretation because any number of factors could affect a suspect's decision to waive his *Miranda* rights. The requirement would also vitiate to a great extent the *Miranda* rule's important "virtue of informing police and prosecutors with specificity" as to how a pretrial questioning of a suspect must be conducted.

interrogation could not affect Spring's decision to waive his Fifth Amendment privilege in a constitutionally significant manner.

B

This Court's holding in *Miranda* specifically required that the police inform a criminal suspect that he has the right to remain silent and that *anything* he says may be used against him. There is no qualification of this broad and explicit warning. The warning, as formulated in *Miranda*, conveys to a suspect the nature of his constitutional privilege and the consequences of abandoning it. Accordingly, we hold that a suspect's awareness of all the possible subjects of questioning in advance of interrogation is not relevant to determining whether the suspect voluntarily, knowingly, and intelligently waived his Fifth Amendment privilege.

IV

The judgment of the Colorado Supreme Court is reversed, and the case is remanded for further proceedings not inconsistent with this opinion.

It is so ordered.

JUSTICE MARSHALL, with whom JUSTICE BRENNAN joins, dissenting.

The Court asserts there is "no doubt" that respondent Spring's decision to waive his Fifth Amendment privilege was voluntarily, knowingly, and intelligently made. I agree, however, with the Colorado Supreme Court that a significant doubt exists in the circumstances of this case and thus the State has failed to carry the "heavy burden" recognized in *Miranda* for establishing the constitutional validity of Spring's alleged waiver.

Consistent with our prior decisions, the Court acknowledges that a suspect's waiver of fundamental constitutional rights, such as *Miranda's* protections against self-incrimination during a custodial interrogation, must be examined in light of the "totality of the circumstances." Nonetheless, the Court proceeds to hold that the specific crimes and topics of investigation known to the interrogating officers before questioning begins are "not relevant" to, and in this case "could not affect," the validity of the suspect's decision to waive his Fifth Amendment privilege. It seems to me self-evident that a suspect's decision to waive this privilege will necessarily be influenced by his awareness of the scope and seriousness of the matters under investigation.

To attempt to minimize the relevance of such information by saying that it "could affect only the wisdom of" the suspect's waiver, as opposed to the validity of that waiver, ventures an inapposite distinction. Wisdom and validity in this context are overlapping concepts, as circumstances relevant to assessing the validity of a waiver may also be highly relevant to its wisdom in any given context. Indeed, the admittedly "critical" piece of advice the Court recognizes today — that the suspect be informed that whatever he says may be used as evidence against him — is certainly relevant to the wisdom of any suspect's decision to submit to custodial interrogation without first consulting his lawyer. The Court offers no principled basis for concluding that this is a relevant factor for determining the validity of a waiver but that, under what it calls a *totality* of the circumstances analysis, a suspect's knowledge of the specific crimes and other topics previously identified for questioning can never be.

The Court quotes *Moran v. Burbine* as holding that "a valid waiver does not require that an individual be informed of all information 'useful' in making his decision or *all* information that 'might . . . affec[t] his decision to confess.'" (emphasis added). Noticeably similar is the Court's holding today: "[A] suspect's awareness of *all* the possible subjects of questioning in advance of interrogation is not relevant to determining" the validity of his waiver. (emphasis added). This careful phraseology avoids the important question whether the lack of *any* indication of the identified subjects for questioning *is* relevant to determining the validity of the suspect's waiver.

I would include among the relevant factors for consideration whether before waiving his Fifth Amendment rights the suspect was aware, either through the circumstances surrounding his arrest or through a specific advisement from the arresting or interrogating officers, of the crime or crimes he was suspected of committing and about which they intended to ask questions. To hold that such knowledge is relevant would not undermine the "'virtue of informing police and prosecutors with specificity' as to how a pretrial questioning of a suspect must be conducted," nor would it interfere with the use of legitimate interrogation techniques.

The interrogation tactics utilized in this case demonstrate the relevance of the information Spring did not receive. The agents evidently hoped to obtain from Spring a valid confession to the federal firearms charge for which he was arrested and then parlay this admission into an additional confession of first-degree murder. Spring could not have expected questions about the latter, separate offense when he agreed to waive his rights, as it occurred in a different State and was a violation of state law outside the normal investigative focus of federal Alcohol, Tobacco, and Firearms agents.

> Interrogators describe the point of the first admission as the "breakthrough" and the "beachhead," which once obtained will give them enormous "tactical advantages." The coercive aspects of the psychological ploy intended in this case, when combined with an element of surprise which may far too easily rise to a level of deception,[1] cannot be justified in light

---

[1] The Court rejects, for now, the notion that "mere silence" by law enforcement officials may deprive the suspect of information so relevant to his decision to waive his *Miranda* rights as to constitute deception, though it does acknowledge that circumstances can arise in which an affirmative misrepresentation by the officers will invalidate the suspect's waiver. In *Moran v. Burbine*, 475 U.S. 412, 453 (1986), I joined Justice STEVENS' dissenting opinion, which stated that "there can be no constitutional distinction . . . between a deceptive misstatement and the concealment by the police of the critical fact that an attorney retained by the accused or his family has offered assistance . . . ." I would hold the officers' failure in the present case to inform Spring of their intent to question him about the Colorado murder equally critical. *Miranda* places an especially heavy burden on the State to show that a suspect waived his privilege against self-incrimination: "[A]ny evidence that the accused was threatened, *tricked*, or cajoled into a waiver will, of course, show that the defendant did not voluntarily waive his privilege." (emphasis added). I would hold that the interrogating officers' preconceived plan in this case to obtain

of *Miranda's* strict requirements that the suspect's waiver and confession be voluntary, knowing, and intelligent. If a suspect has signed a waiver form with the intention of making a statement regarding a specifically alleged crime, the Court today would hold this waiver valid with respect to questioning about any other crime, regardless of its relation to the charges the suspect believes he will be asked to address. Yet once this waiver is given and the intended statement made, the protections afforded by *Miranda* against the "inherently compelling pressures" of the custodial interrogation have effectively dissipated. Additional questioning about entirely separate and more serious suspicions of criminal activity can take unfair advantage of the suspect's psychological state, as the unexpected questions cause the compulsive pressures suddenly to reappear. Given this technique of interrogation, a suspect's understanding of the topics planned for questioning is, therefore, at the very least "relevant" to assessing whether his decision to talk to the officers was voluntarily, knowingly, and intelligently made.

Not only is the suspect's awareness of the suspected criminal conduct relevant, its absence may be determinative in a given case. The State's burden of proving that a suspect's waiver was voluntary, knowing, and intelligent is a "heavy" one. We are to " 'indulge every reasonable presumption against waiver' of fundamental constitutional rights" and we shall " 'not presume acquiescence in the loss of fundamental rights.' " It is reasonable to conclude that, had Spring known of the federal agents' intent to ask questions about a murder unrelated to the offense for which he was arrested, he would not have consented to interrogation without first consulting his attorney. In this case, I would therefore accept the determination of the Colorado Supreme Court that Spring did not voluntarily, knowingly, and intelligently waive his Fifth Amendment rights.[2]

I dissent.

QUESTIONS AND NOTES

1.   The Colorado Supreme Court seems to prefer a "standard" to a "rule" in regard to ascertaining what warnings ought to be given. Apart from the issue of whether the warning was adequate in this case, do you think that this would be a good idea?

2.   If the dissent had prevailed, would the police have been deprived of a legitimate stratagem for bringing a murderer to justice? Explain.

3.   Should the fact that the defendant is free to stop questioning whenever he doesn't like the topic be a complete answer to the dissent?

---

a waiver from Spring with reference to a particular federal offense and then ask about a separate, unrelated state offense precludes the State from carrying that heavy burden.

[2] Nothing in the Court's decision today precludes the courts of Colorado from interpreting that State's Constitution as independently recognizing a suspect's knowledge of the intended scope of interrogation as a relevant factor for determining whether he validly waived his right against self-incrimination under state law. *See* COLO. CONST., Art. II, § 18.

4. In the context of this case, should "wisdom" and "validity" or "voluntariness" be separated from one another as the majority has done?

5. A competent defense attorney should carefully heed Justice Marshall's suggestion in fn. 2.

C. INVOKING MIRANDA

The Court has been clear that there are only two ways that *Miranda* can be invoked. One is by asking to remain silent; the other is by requesting counsel. As will soon be apparent different consequences follow depending on which of those requests is made. If one tries to invoke his rights by requesting something other than silence or counsel, the police are not required to honor it. For example, in *Fare v. Michael C.*, 443 U.S. 707 (1979), the Court held that a juvenile's request for a probation officer did not constitute the invocation of *Miranda*.

1.   Invoking Silence

MICHIGAN v. MOSLEY
423 U.S. 96 (1975)

MR. JUSTICE STEWART delivered the opinion of the Court.

The respondent, Richard Bert Mosley, was arrested in Detroit, Mich., in the early afternoon of April 8, 1971, in connection with robberies that had recently occurred at the Blue Goose Bar and the White Tower Restaurant on that city's lower east side. After effecting the arrest, Detective Cowie brought Mosley to the Robbery, Breaking and Entering Bureau of the Police Department, located on the fourth floor of the departmental headquarters building. The officer advised Mosley of his rights under this Court's decision in *Miranda*, and had him read and sign the department's constitutional rights notification certificate. After filling out the necessary arrest papers, Cowie began questioning Mosley about the robbery of the White Tower Restaurant. When Mosley said he did not want to answer any questions about the robberies, Cowie promptly ceased the interrogation. The completion of the arrest papers and the questioning of Mosley together took approximately 20 minutes. At no time during the questioning did Mosley indicate a desire to consult with a lawyer, and there is no claim that the procedures followed to this point did not fully comply with the strictures of the *Miranda* opinion. Mosley was then taken to a ninth-floor cell block.

Shortly after 6 p. m., Detective Hill of the Detroit Police Department Homicide Bureau brought Mosley from the cell block to the fifth-floor office of the Homicide Bureau for questioning about the fatal shooting of a man named Leroy Williams. Williams had been killed on January 9, 1971, during a holdup attempt outside the 101 Ranch Bar in Detroit. Mosley had not been arrested on this charge or interrogated about it by Detective Cowie.[2] Before questioning Mosley about this

---

[2] The original tip to Detective Cowie had, however, implicated Mosley in the Williams murder.

homicide, Detective Hill carefully advised him of his "*Miranda* rights." Mosley read the notification form both silently and aloud, and Detective Hill then read and explained the warnings to him and had him sign the form. Mosley at first denied any involvement in the Williams murder, but after the officer told him that Anthony Smith had confessed to participating in the slaying and had named him as the "shooter," Mosley made a statement implicating himself in the homicide.[3] The interrogation by Detective Hill lasted approximately 15 minutes, and at no time during its course did Mosley ask to consult with a lawyer or indicate that he did not want to discuss the homicide. In short, there is no claim that the procedures followed during Detective Hill's interrogation of Mosley, standing alone, did not fully comply with the strictures of the *Miranda* opinion.

Mosley was subsequently charged in a one-count information with first-degree murder. Before the trial he moved to suppress his incriminating statement on a number of grounds, among them the claim that under the doctrine of the *Miranda* case it was constitutionally impermissible for Detective Hill to question him about the Williams murder after he had told Detective Cowie that he did not want to answer any questions about the robberies.[5] The trial court denied the motion to suppress after an evidentiary hearing, and the incriminating statement was subsequently introduced in evidence against Mosley at his trial. The jury convicted Mosley of first-degree murder, and the court imposed a mandatory sentence of life imprisonment.

The appellate court reversed the judgment of conviction, holding that Detective Hill's interrogation of Mosley had been a *per se* violation of the *Miranda* doctrine. Accordingly, without reaching Mosley's other contentions, the Court remanded the case for a new trial with instructions that Mosley's statement be suppressed as evidence.

Neither party in the present case challenges the continuing validity of the *Miranda* decision, or of any of the so-called guidelines it established to protect what the Court there said was a person's constitutional privilege against compulsory self-incrimination. The issue in this case, rather, is whether the conduct of the Detroit police that led to Mosley's incriminating statement did in fact violate the *Miranda* "guidelines," so as to render the statement inadmissible in evidence against Mosley at his trial. Resolution of the question turns almost entirely on the interpretation of a single passage in the *Miranda* opinion, upon which the Michigan appellate court relied in finding a *per se* violation of *Miranda*:

> Once warnings have been given, the subsequent procedure is clear. If the individual indicates in any manner, at any time prior to or during questioning, that he wishes to remain silent, the interrogation must cease. At this point he has shown that he intends to exercise his Fifth Amendment

---

[3] During cross-examination by Mosley's counsel at the evidentiary hearing, Detective Hill conceded that Smith in fact had not confessed but had "denied a physical participation in the robbery."

[5] In addition to the claim that Detective Hill's questioning violated *Miranda*, Mosley contended that the statement was the product of an illegal arrest, that the statement was inadmissible because he had not been taken before a judicial officer without unnecessary delay, and that it had been obtained through trickery and promises of leniency. He argued that these circumstances, either independently or in combination, required the suppression of his incriminating statement.

privilege; any statement taken after the person invokes his privilege cannot be other than the product of compulsion, subtle or otherwise. Without the right to cut off questioning, the setting of in-custody interrogation operates on the individual to overcome free choice in producing a statement after the privilege has been once invoked.[7]

This passage states that "the interrogation must cease" when the person in custody indicates that "he wishes to remain silent." It does not state under what circumstances, if any, a resumption of questioning is permissible.[8] The passage could be literally read to mean that a person who has invoked his "right to silence" can never again be subjected to custodial interrogation by any police officer at any time or place on any subject. Another possible construction of the passage would characterize "any statement taken after the person invokes his privilege" as "the product of compulsion" and would therefore mandate its exclusion from evidence, even if it were volunteered by the person in custody without any further interrogation whatever. Or the passage could be interpreted to require only the immediate cessation of questioning, and to permit a resumption of interrogation after a momentary respite.

It is evident that any of these possible literal interpretations would lead to absurd and unintended results. To permit the continuation of custodial interrogation after a momentary cessation would clearly frustrate the purposes of *Miranda* by allowing repeated rounds of questioning to undermine the will of the person being questioned. At the other extreme, a blanket prohibition against the taking of voluntary statements or a permanent immunity from further interrogation, regardless of the circumstances, would transform the *Miranda* safeguards into wholly irrational obstacles to legitimate police investigative activity, and deprive suspects

---

[7] The present case does not involve the procedures to be followed if the person in custody asks to consult with a lawyer, since Mosley made no such request at any time. Those procedures are detailed in the *Miranda* opinion as follows:

  If the individual states that he wants an attorney, the interrogation must cease until an attorney is present. At that time, the individual must have an opportunity to confer with the attorney and to have him present during any subsequent questioning. If the individual cannot obtain an attorney and he indicates that he wants one before speaking to police, they must respect his decision to remain silent.

  This does not mean, as some have suggested, that each police station must have a "station house lawyer" present at all times to advise prisoners. It does mean, however, that if police propose to interrogate a person they must make known to him that he is entitled to a lawyer and that if he cannot afford one, a lawyer will be provided for him prior to any interrogation. If authorities conclude that they will not provide counsel during a reasonable period of time in which investigation in the field is carried out, they may refrain from doing so without violating the person's Fifth Amendment privilege so long as they do not question him during that time.

[8] The Court did state in a footnote:

  "If an individual indicates his desire to remain silent, but has an attorney present, there may be some circumstances in which further questioning would be permissible. In the absence of evidence of overbearing, statements then made in the presence of counsel might be free of the compelling influence of the interrogation process and might fairly be construed as a waiver of the privilege for purposes of these statements."

This footnote in the *Miranda* opinion is not relevant to the present case, since Mosley did not have an attorney present at the time he declined to answer Detective Cowie's questions, and the officer did not continue to question Mosley but instead ceased the interrogation in compliance with *Miranda's* dictates.

of an opportunity to make informed and intelligent assessments of their interests. Clearly, therefore, neither this passage nor any other passage in the *Miranda* opinion can sensibly be read to create a *per se* proscription of indefinite duration upon any further questioning by any police officer on any subject, once the person in custody has indicated a desire to remain silent.

A reasonable and faithful interpretation of the *Miranda* opinion must rest on the intention of the Court in that case to adopt "fully effective means . . . to notify the person of his right of silence and to assure that the exercise of the right will be scrupulously honored . . . ." The critical safeguard identified in the passage at issue is a person's "right to cut off questioning." Through the exercise of his option to terminate questioning he can control the time at which questioning occurs, the subjects discussed, and the duration of the interrogation. The requirement that law enforcement authorities must respect a person's exercise of that option counteracts the coercive pressures of the custodial setting. We therefore conclude that the admissibility of statements obtained after the person in custody has decided to remain silent depends under *Miranda* on whether his "right to cut off questioning" was "scrupulously honored."[10]

A review of the circumstances leading to Mosley's confession reveals that his "right to cut off questioning" was fully respected in this case. Before his initial interrogation, Mosley was carefully advised that he was under no obligation to answer any questions and could remain silent if he wished. He orally acknowledged that he understood the *Miranda* warnings and then signed a printed notification-of-rights form. When Mosley stated that he did not want to discuss the robberies, Detective Cowie immediately ceased the interrogation and did not try either to resume the questioning or in any way to persuade Mosley to reconsider his position. After an interval of more than two hours, Mosley was questioned by another police officer at another location about an unrelated holdup murder. He was given full and complete *Miranda* warnings at the outset of the second interrogation. He was thus reminded again that he could remain silent and could consult with a lawyer, and was carefully given a full and fair opportunity to exercise these options. The subsequent questioning did not undercut Mosley's previous decision not to answer Detective Cowie's inquiries. Detective Hill did not resume the interrogation about the White Tower Restaurant robbery or inquire about the Blue Goose Bar robbery, but instead focused exclusively on the Leroy Williams homicide, a crime different in nature and in time and place of occurrence from the robberies for which Mosley had been arrested and interrogated by Detective Cowie. Although it is not clear from the record how much Detective Hill knew about the earlier interrogation, his questioning of Mosley about an unrelated homicide was quite consistent with a reasonable interpretation of Mosley's earlier refusal to answer any questions about the robberies.

---

[10] The dissenting opinion asserts that *Miranda* established a requirement that once a person has indicated a desire to remain silent, questioning may be resumed only when counsel is present. But clearly the Court in *Miranda* imposed no such requirement, for it distinguished between the procedural safeguards triggered by a request to remain silent and a request for an attorney and directed that "the interrogation must cease until an attorney is present" only "[i]f the individual states that he wants an attorney."

This is not a case, therefore, where the police failed to honor a decision of a person in custody to cut off questioning, either by refusing to discontinue the interrogation upon request or by persisting in repeated efforts to wear down his resistance and make him change his mind. In contrast to such practices, the police here immediately ceased the interrogation, resumed questioning only after the passage of a significant period of time and the provision of a fresh set of warnings, and restricted the second interrogation to a crime that had not been a subject of the earlier interrogation.

The Michigan Court of Appeals viewed this case as factually similar to *Westover*, a companion case to *Miranda*. But the controlling facts of the two cases are strikingly different.

In *Westover*, the petitioner was arrested by the Kansas City police at 9:45 p.m. and taken to the police station. Without giving any advisory warnings of any kind to Westover, the police questioned him that night and throughout the next morning about various local robberies. At noon, three FBI agents took over, gave advisory warnings to Westover, and proceeded to question him about two California bank robberies. After two hours of questioning, the petitioner confessed to the California crimes. The Court held that the confession obtained by the FBI was inadmissible because the interrogation leading to the petitioner's statement followed on the heels of prolonged questioning that was commenced and continued by the Kansas City police without preliminary warnings to Westover of any kind. The Court found that "the federal authorities were the beneficiaries of the pressure applied by the local in-custody interrogation" and that the belated warnings given by the federal officers were "not sufficient to protect" Westover because from his point of view "the warnings came at the end of the interrogation process."

Here, by contrast, the police gave full "*Miranda* warnings" to Mosley at the very outset of each interrogation, subjected him to only a brief period of initial questioning, and suspended questioning entirely for a significant period before beginning the interrogation that led to his incriminating statement. The cardinal fact of *Westover* the failure of the police officers to give any warnings whatever to the person in their custody before embarking on an intense and prolonged interrogation of him was simply not present in this case. The Michigan Court of Appeals was mistaken, therefore, in believing that Detective Hill's questioning of Mosley was "not permitted" by the *Westover* decision.

For these reasons, we conclude that the admission in evidence of Mosley's incriminating statement did not violate the principles of *Miranda*. Accordingly, the judgment of the Michigan Court of Appeals is vacated, and the case is remanded to that court for further proceedings not inconsistent with this opinion.

It is so ordered.

Mr. Justice White, concurring.

I concur in the result and in much of the majority's reasoning. However, it appears to me that in an effort to make only a limited holding in this case, the majority has implied that some custodial confessions will be suppressed even though they follow an informed and voluntary waiver of the defendant's rights. The majority seems to say that a statement obtained within some unspecified time after an assertion by an individual of his "right to silence" is always inadmissible, even if it was the result of an informed and voluntary decision following, for example, a disclosure to such an individual of a piece of information bearing on his waiver decision which the police had failed to give him prior to his assertion of the privilege but which they gave him immediately thereafter. Indeed, the majority characterizes as "absurd" any contrary rule. I disagree. I do not think the majority's conclusion is compelled by *Miranda*, and I suspect that in the final analysis the majority will adopt voluntariness as the standard by which to judge the waiver of the right to silence by a properly informed defendant. I think the Court should say so now.

Miranda holds that custody creates an inherent compulsion on an individual to incriminate himself in response to questions, and that statements obtained under such circumstances are therefore obtained in violation of the Fifth Amendment privilege against compelled testimonial self-incrimination unless the privilege is "knowingly and intelligently waived." It also holds that an individual will not be deemed to have made a knowing and intelligent waiver of his "right to silence" unless the authorities have first informed him, *inter alia*, of that right "the threshold requirement for an intelligent decision as to its exercise." I am no more convinced that *Miranda* was required by the United States Constitution than I was when it was decided. However, there is at least some support in the law both before and after *Miranda* for the proposition that some rights will never be deemed waived unless the defendant is first expressly advised of their existence. There is little support in the law or in common sense for the proposition that an informed waiver of a right may be ineffective even where voluntarily made. Indeed, the law is exactly to the contrary. Unless an individual is incompetent, we have in the past rejected any paternalistic rule protecting a defendant from his intelligent and voluntary decisions about his own criminal case. To do so would be to "imprison a man in his privileges,"[1] and to disregard " 'that respect for the individual which is the lifeblood of the law.' " I am very reluctant to conclude that *Miranda* stands for such a proposition.

The language of *Miranda* no more compels such a result than does its basic rationale. As the majority points out, the statement in *Miranda* requiring interrogation to *cease* after an assertion of the "right to silence" tells us nothing because it does not indicate how soon this interrogation may resume. The Court showed in the very next paragraph, moreover, that when it wanted to create a *per se* rule against further interrogation after assertion of a right, it knew how to do so. The Court there said "[i]f the individual states that he wants an attorney, the

---

[1] The majority's rule may cause an accused injury. Although a recently arrested individual may have indicated an initial desire not to answer questions, he would nonetheless want to know immediately if it were true that his ability to explain a particular incriminating fact or to supply an alibi for a particular time period would result in his immediate release. Similarly, he might wish to know if it were true that (1) the case against him was unusually strong and that (2) his immediate cooperation with the authorities in the apprehension and conviction of others or in the recovery of property would redound to his benefit in the form of a reduced charge. Certainly the individual's lawyer, if he had one, would be interested in such information, even if communication of such information followed closely on an assertion of the "right to silence." Where the individual has not requested counsel and has chosen instead to make his own decisions regarding his conversations with the authorities, he should not be deprived even temporarily of any information relevant to the decision.

interrogation must cease *until an attorney is present.*"[2] However, when the individual indicates that he will decide unaided by counsel whether or not to assert his "right to silence" the situation is different. In such a situation, the Court in *Miranda* simply said: "If the interrogation continues without the presence of an attorney and a statement is taken, a heavy burden rests on the government to demonstrate that the defendant knowingly and intelligently waived his privilege against self-incrimination and his right to retained or appointed counsel." Apparently, although placing a heavy burden on the government, *Miranda* intended waiver of the "right to silence" to be tested by the normal standards. In any event, insofar as the *Miranda* decision might be read to require interrogation to cease for some magical and unspecified period of time following an assertion of the "right to silence," and to reject voluntariness as the standard by which to judge informed waivers of that right, it should be disapproved as inconsistent with otherwise uniformly applied legal principles.

In justifying the implication that questioning must inevitably cease for some unspecified period of time following an exercise of the "right to silence," the majority says only that such a requirement would be necessary to avoid "undermining" "the will of the person being questioned." Yet, surely a waiver of the "right to silence" obtained by "undermining the will" of the person being questioned would be considered an involuntary waiver. Thus, in order to achieve the majority's only stated purpose, it is sufficient to exclude all confessions which are the result of involuntary waivers. To exclude any others is to deprive the factfinding process of highly probative information for no reason at all. The "repeated rounds" of questioning following an assertion of the privilege, which the majority is worried about, would, of course, count heavily against the State in any determination of voluntariness particularly if no reason (such as new facts communicated to the accused or a new incident being inquired about) appeared for repeated questioning. There is no reason, however, to rob the accused of the choice to answer questions voluntarily for some unspecified period of time following his own previous contrary decision. The Court should now so state.

MR. JUSTICE BRENNAN, with whom MR. JUSTICE MARSHALL joins, dissenting.

The *Miranda* guidelines were necessitated by the inherently coercive nature of in-custody questioning. To assure safeguards that promised to dispel the "inherently compelling pressures" of in-custody interrogation, a prophylactic rule was fashioned to supplement the traditional determination of voluntariness on the facts of each case. *Miranda* held that any confession obtained when not preceded by the required warnings or an adequate substitute safeguard was *per se* inadmissible in evidence. Satisfaction of this prophylactic rule, therefore, was necessary, though

---

[2] The question of the proper procedure following expression by an individual of his desire to consult counsel is not presented in this case. It is sufficient to note that the reasons to keep the lines of communication between the authorities and the accused open when the accused has chosen to make his own decisions are not present when he indicates instead that he wishes legal advice with respect thereto. The authorities may then communicate with him through an attorney. More to the point, the accused having expressed his own view that he is not competent to deal with the authorities without legal advice, a later decision at the authorities' insistence to make a statement without counsel's presence may properly be viewed with skepticism.

not sufficient, for the admission of a confession.

The task that confronts the Court in this case is to satisfy the *Miranda* approach by establishing "concrete constitutional guidelines" governing the resumption of questioning a suspect who, while in custody, has once clearly and unequivocally "indicate[d] . . . that he wishes to remain silent . . . ." As the Court today continues to recognize, under *Miranda*, the cost of assuring voluntariness by procedural tests, independent of any actual inquiry into voluntariness, is that some voluntary statements will be excluded. Thus the consideration in the task confronting the Court is not whether voluntary statements will be excluded, but whether the procedures approved will be sufficient to assure with reasonable certainty that a confession is not obtained under the influence of the compulsion inherent in interrogation and detention. The procedures approved by the Court today fail to provide that assurance.

We observed in *Miranda*: "Whatever the testimony of the authorities as to waiver of rights by an accused, the fact of lengthy interrogation or incommunicado incarceration before a statement is made is strong evidence that the accused did not validly waive his rights. In these circumstances the fact that the individual eventually made a statement is consistent with the conclusion that the compelling influence of the interrogation finally forced him to do so. It is inconsistent with any notion of a voluntary relinquishment of the privilege." And, as that portion of *Miranda* which the majority finds controlling observed, "the setting of in-custody interrogation operates on the individual to overcome free choice in producing a statement after the privilege has been once invoked." Thus, as to statements which are the product of renewed questioning, *Miranda* established a virtually irrebuttable presumption of compulsion, and that presumption stands strongest where, as in this case, a suspect, having initially determined to remain silent, is subsequently brought to confess his crime. Only by adequate procedural safeguards could the presumption be rebutted.

In formulating its procedural safeguard, the Court skirts the problem of compulsion and thereby fails to join issue with the dictates of *Miranda*. The language which the Court finds controlling in this case teaches that renewed questioning itself is part of the process which invariably operates to overcome the will of a suspect. That teaching is embodied in the form of a proscription on any further questioning once the suspect has exercised his right to remain silent. Today's decision uncritically abandons that teaching. The Court assumes, contrary to the controlling language, that "scrupulously honoring" an initial exercise of the right to remain silent preserves the efficaciousness of initial and future warnings despite the fact that the suspect has once been subjected to interrogation and then has been detained for a lengthy period of time.

Observing that the suspect can control the circumstances of interrogation "[t]hrough the exercise of his option to terminate questioning," the Court concludes "that the admissibility of statements obtained after the person in custody has decided to remain silent depends . . . on whether his 'right to cut off questioning' was 'scrupulously honored.'" But scrupulously honoring exercises of the right to cut off questioning is only meaningful insofar as the suspect's will to exercise that right remains wholly unfettered. The Court's formulation thus assumes the very matter at issue here: whether renewed questioning following a lengthy period of detention acts to overbear the suspect's will, irrespective of giving the *Miranda* warnings a second time (and scrupulously honoring them), thereby rendering inconsequential any failure to exercise the right to remain silent. For the Court it is enough conclusorily to assert that "[t]he subsequent questioning did not undercut Mosley's previous decision not to answer Detective Cowie's inquiries." Under *Miranda*, however, Mosley's failure to exercise the right upon renewed questioning is presumptively the consequence of an overbearing in which detention and that subsequent questioning played central roles.

I agree that *Miranda* is not to be read, on the one hand, to impose an absolute ban on resumption of questioning "at any time or place on any subject," or on the other hand, "to permit a resumption of interrogation after a momentary respite." But this surely cannot justify adoption of a vague and ineffective procedural standard that falls somewhere between those absurd extremes, for *Miranda* in flat and unambiguous terms requires that questioning "cease" when a suspect exercises the right to remain silent. *Miranda's* terms, however, are not so uncompromising as to preclude the fashioning of guidelines to govern this case. Those guidelines must, of course, necessarily be sensitive to the reality that "[a]s a practical matter, the compulsion to speak in the isolated setting of the police station may well be greater than in courts or other official investigations, where there are often impartial observers to guard against intimidation or trickery."

The fashioning of guidelines for this case is an easy task. Adequate procedures are readily available. Michigan law requires that the suspect be arraigned before a judicial officer "without unnecessary delay,"[2] certainly not a burdensome requirement. Alternatively, a requirement that resumption of questioning should await appointment and arrival of counsel for the suspect would be an acceptable and readily satisfied precondition to resumption. *Miranda* expressly held that "[t]he presence of counsel . . . would be the adequate protective device necessary to make the process of police interrogation conform to the dictates of the privilege [against self-incrimination]." The Court expediently bypasses this alternative in its search for circumstances where renewed questioning would be permissible.[4]

Indeed, language in *Miranda* suggests that the presence of counsel is the only appropriate alternative. In categorical language we held in *Miranda*: "If the individual indicates in any manner, at any time prior to or during questioning, that he wishes to remain silent, the interrogation must cease." We then immediately observed:

---

[2] Detective Cowie's testimony indicated that a judge was available across the street from the police station in which Mosley was held from 2:15 p.m. until 4 p.m. or 4:30 p.m. The actual interrogation of Mosley, however, covered only 15 or 20 minutes of this time. The failure to comply with a simple state-law requirement in these circumstances is totally at odds with the holding that the police "scrupulously honored" Mosley's rights.

[4] I do not mean to imply that counsel may be forced on a suspect who does not request an attorney. I suggest only that either arraignment or counsel must be provided before resumption of questioning to eliminate the coercive atmosphere of in-custody interrogation. The Court itself apparently proscribes resuming questioning until counsel is present if an accused has exercised the right to have an attorney present at questioning.

> If an individual indicates his desire to remain silent, but has an attorney present, there *may* be some circumstances in which further questioning would be permissible. In the absence of evidence of overbearing, statements then made in the presence of counsel *might* be free of the compelling influence of the interrogation process and *might* fairly be construed as a waiver of the privilege for purposes of these statements.

(emphasis added). This was the only circumstance in which we at all suggested that questioning could be resumed, and even then, further questioning was not permissible in all such circumstances, for compulsion was still the presumption not easily dissipated.[5]

These procedures would be wholly consistent with the Court's rejection of a *"per se* proscription of indefinite duration,"* a rejection to which I fully subscribe. Today's decision, however, virtually empties *Miranda* of principle, for plainly the decision encourages police asked to cease interrogation to continue the suspect's detention until the police station's coercive atmosphere does its work and the suspect responds to resumed questioning.[6] I can only conclude that today's decision signals rejection of *Miranda's* basic premise.

QUESTIONS AND NOTES

1. Does the *Mosley* Court appear to be distancing itself from *Miranda*? Explain.

2. Do you agree that the alternatives suggested by Justice Stewart to his result are "absurd"? Are there any sensible alternatives other than his? Why do you suppose that he didn't opt for one of them?

3. Are you persuaded by the Court's distinction between *Mosley* and *Westover*? Why? Why not?

4. In regard to Justice White's opinion, is it meaningful to talk in terms of "rob[bing] the accused of the choice to answer questions . . ."? Is Justice White's fn. 1 helpful in analyzing this question?

5. Justice Brennan concluded in his dissent that "[i]n these circumstances the

---

[5] The Court asserts that this language is not relevant to the present case, for "Mosley did not have an attorney present at the time he declined to answer Detective Cowie's questions." The language, however, does not compel a reading that it is applicable only if counsel is present when the suspect initially exercises his right to remain silent. Even if it did, this would only indicate that *Miranda* placed even stiffer limits on the circumstances when questioning may be resumed than I suggest here. Moreover, since the concern in *Miranda* was with assuring the absence of compulsion upon renewed questioning, it makes little difference whether counsel is initially present. Thus, even if the language does not specifically address the situation where counsel is not initially present, it certainly contemplates that situation.

The Court also asserts that *Miranda* "directed that 'the interrogation must cease until an attorney is present' only '[i]f the individual states that he wants an attorney.'" This is patently inaccurate. The language from the quoted portion of *Miranda* actually reads: "If the individual states that he wants an attorney, the interrogation must cease until an attorney is present."

[6] I do not suggest that the Court's opinion is to be read as permitting unreasonably lengthy detention without arraignment so long as any exercise of rights by a suspect is "scrupulously honored."

fact that the individual made a statement is consistent with the conclusion that the compelling influences of the interrogation finally forced him to do so." Do you agree? How could interrogation have affected his decision at all, when he wasn't being interrogated until he agreed to it?

6. Is Justice Brennan's fn. 4 suggesting that after arraignment an accused, who has previously invoked her right to silence, can be questioned without counsel? If so, do you agree?

7. How would you have voted had you been on the Court? Why?

2. Invoking Counsel

EDWARDS v. ARIZONA
451 U.S. 477 (1981)

Justice White delivered the opinion of the Court.

I

On January 19, 1976, a sworn complaint was filed against Edwards in Arizona state court charging him with robbery, burglary, and first-degree murder. An arrest warrant was issued pursuant to the complaint, and Edwards was arrested at his home later that same day. At the police station, he was informed of his rights as required by *Miranda*. Petitioner stated that he understood his rights, and was willing to submit to questioning. After being told that another suspect already in custody had implicated him in the crime, Edwards denied involvement and gave a taped statement presenting an alibi defense. He then sought to "make a deal." The interrogating officer told him that he wanted a statement, but that he did not have the authority to negotiate a deal. The officer provided Edwards with the telephone number of a county attorney. Petitioner made the call, but hung up after a few moments. Edwards then said: "I want an attorney before making a deal." At that point, questioning ceased and Edwards was taken to county jail.

At 9:15 the next morning, two detectives, colleagues of the officer who had interrogated Edwards the previous night, came to the jail and asked to see Edwards. When the detention officer informed Edwards that the detectives wished to speak with him, he replied that he did not want to talk to anyone. The guard told him that "he had" to talk and then took him to meet with the detectives. The officers identified themselves, stated they wanted to talk to him, and informed him of his *Miranda* rights. Edwards was willing to talk, but he first wanted to hear the taped statement of the alleged accomplice who had implicated him.[2] After listening to the tape for several minutes, petitioner said that he would make a statement so long as it was not tape-recorded. The detectives informed him that the recording was irrelevant since they could testify in court concerning whatever he said. Edwards replied: "I'll tell you anything you want to know, but I don't want it on tape." He

---

[2] It appears from the record that the detectives had brought the tape-recording with them.

thereupon implicated himself in the crime.

Prior to trial, Edwards moved to suppress his confession on the ground that his *Miranda* rights had been violated when the officers returned to question him after he had invoked his right to counsel. The trial court initially granted the motion to suppress, but reversed its ruling when presented with a supposedly controlling decision of a higher Arizona court. The court stated without explanation that it found Edwards' statement to be voluntary. Edwards was tried twice and convicted.[5] Evidence concerning his confession was admitted at both trials.

On appeal, the Arizona Supreme Court held that Edwards had invoked both his right to remain silent and his right to counsel during the interrogation conducted on the night of January 19.[6] The court then went on to determine, however, that Edwards had waived both rights during the January 20 meeting when he voluntarily gave his statement to the detectives after again being informed that he need not answer questions and that he need not answer without the advice of counsel: "The trial court's finding that the waiver and confession were voluntarily and knowingly made is upheld."

II

We hold that an accused, such as Edwards, having expressed his desire to deal with the police only through counsel, is not subject to further interrogation by the authorities until counsel has been made available to him, unless the accused himself initiates further communication, exchanges, or conversations with the police.

Miranda itself indicated that the assertion of the right to counsel was a significant event and that once exercised by the accused, "the interrogation must cease until an attorney is present." Our later cases have not abandoned that view. In *Mosley*, the Court noted that *Miranda* had distinguished between the procedural safeguards triggered by a request to remain silent and a request for an attorney and had required that interrogation cease until an attorney was present only if the individual stated that he wanted counsel. In *Fare v. Michael C.*, the Court referred to Miranda's "rigid rule that an accused's request for an attorney is per se an invocation of his Fifth Amendment rights, requiring that all interrogation cease." We reconfirm these views and, to lend them substance, emphasize that it is inconsistent with *Miranda* and its progeny for the authorities, at their instance, to reinterrogate an accused in custody if he has clearly asserted his right to counsel.

In concluding that the fruits of the interrogation initiated by the police on January 20 could not be used against Edwards, we do not hold or imply that Edwards was powerless to countermand his election or that the authorities could in no event use any incriminating statements made by Edwards prior to his having access to counsel. Had Edwards initiated the meeting on January 20, nothing in the

---

[5] The jury in the first trial was unable to reach a verdict.

[6] This issue was disputed by the State. The court, while finding that the question was arguable, held that Edwards' request for an attorney to assist him in negotiating a deal was "sufficiently clear" within the context of the interrogation that it "must be interpreted as a request for counsel and as a request to remain silent until counsel was present."

Fifth and Fourteenth Amendments would prohibit the police from merely listening to his voluntary, volunteered statements and using them against him at the trial. The Fifth Amendment right identified in *Miranda* is the right to have counsel present at any custodial interrogation. Absent such interrogation, there would have been no infringement of the right that Edwards invoked and there would be no occasion to determine whether there had been a valid waiver.[9]

But this is not what the facts of this case show. Here, the officers conducting the interrogation on the evening of January 19 ceased interrogation when Edwards requested counsel as he had been advised he had the right to do. The Arizona Supreme Court was of the opinion that this was a sufficient invocation of his *Miranda* rights, and we are in accord. It is also clear that without making counsel available to Edwards, the police returned to him the next day. This was not at his suggestion or request. Indeed, Edwards informed the detention officer that he did not want to talk to anyone. At the meeting, the detectives told Edwards that they wanted to talk to him and again advised him of his *Miranda* rights. Edwards stated that he would talk, but what prompted this action does not appear. He listened at his own request to part of the taped statement made by one of his alleged accomplices and then made an incriminating statement, which was used against him at his trial. We think it is clear that Edwards was subjected to custodial interrogation on January 20 and that this occurred at the instance of the authorities. His statement made without having had access to counsel, did not amount to a valid waiver and hence was inadmissible.

Accordingly, the holding of the Arizona Supreme Court that Edwards had waived his right to counsel was infirm, and the judgment of that court is reversed.

So ordered.

CHIEF JUSTICE BURGER, concurring in the judgment.

I concur only in the judgment because I do not agree that either any constitutional standard or the holding of *Miranda* — as distinguished from its dicta — calls for a special rule as to how an accused in custody may waive the right to be free from interrogation. The extraordinary protections afforded a person in custody suspected of criminal conduct are not without a valid basis, but as with all "good" things they can be carried too far. The notion that any "prompting" of a person in custody is somehow evil *per se* has been rejected. For me, the inquiry in this setting is whether resumption of interrogation is a result of a voluntary waiver, and that inquiry should be resolved under the traditional standards established in *Johnson v. Zerbst*:

> A waiver is ordinarily an intentional relinquishment or abandonment of a known right or privilege. The determination of whether there has been an

---

[9] If, as frequently would occur in the course of a meeting initiated by the accused, the conversation is not wholly one-sided, it is likely that the officers will say or do something that clearly would be "interrogation." In that event, the question would be whether a valid waiver of the right to counsel and the right to silence had occurred, that is, whether the purported waiver was knowing and intelligent and found to be so under the totality of the circumstances, including the necessary fact that the accused, not the police, reopened the dialogue with the authorities.

intelligent waiver . . . must depend, in each case, upon the particular facts and circumstances surrounding that case, including the background, experience, and conduct of the accused.

In this case, the Supreme Court of Arizona described the situation as follows:

When the detention officer told Edwards that the detectives were there to see him, he told the officer that he did not wish to speak to anyone. The officer told him *that he had to.*

(emphasis added). This is enough for me, and on this record the Supreme Court of Arizona erred in holding that the resumption of interrogation was the product of a voluntary waiver.

JUSTICE POWELL, with whom Justice REHNQUIST joins, concurring in the result.

Although I agree that the judgment of the Arizona Supreme Court must be reversed, I do not join the Court's opinion because I am not sure what it means.

I can agree with much of the opinion. It states the settled rule:

It is reasonably clear under our cases that waivers of counsel must not only be voluntary, but must also constitute a knowing and intelligent relinquishment or abandonment of a known right or privilege, a matter which depends in each case "upon the particular facts and circumstances surrounding that case, including the background, experience and conduct of the accused."

I have thought it settled law that one accused of crime may waive *any* of the constitutional safeguards — including the right to remain silent, to jury trial, to call witnesses, to cross-examine one's accusers, to testify in one's own behalf, and — of course — to have counsel. Whatever the right, the standard for waiver is whether the actor fully understands the right in question and voluntarily intends to relinquish it.

In its opinion today, however, the Court — after reiterating the familiar principles of waiver — goes on to say:

We further hold that an accused, such as Edwards, having expressed his desire to deal with the police only through counsel, is not subject to further interrogation by the authorities until counsel has been made available to him, *unless the accused [has] himself initiate[d] further communication, exchanges, or conversations with the police.*

(emphasis added). In view of the emphasis placed on "initiation," I find the Court's opinion unclear. If read to create a new *per se* rule, requiring a threshold inquiry as to precisely who opened any conversation between an accused and state officials, I cannot agree. I would not superimpose a new element of proof on the established doctrine of waiver of counsel.

Perhaps the Court's opinion can be read as not departing from established doctrine. Accepting the formulation quoted above, two questions are identifiable: (i) was there in fact "interrogation," and (ii) did the police "initiate" it? Each of these questions is, of course, relevant to the admissibility of a confession. In this case, for example, it is clear that Edwards was taken from his cell against his will and subjected to renewed interrogation. Whether this is described as police-"initiated" interrogation or in some other way, it clearly was questioning under circumstances incompatible with a voluntary waiver of the fundamental right to counsel.

But few cases will be as clear as this one. Communications between police and a suspect in custody are common-place. It is useful to contrast the circumstances of this case with typical, and permissible, custodial communications between police and a suspect who has asked for counsel. For example, police do not impermissibly "initiate" renewed interrogation by engaging in routine conversations with suspects about unrelated matters. And police legitimately may inquire whether a suspect has changed his mind about speaking to them without an attorney. It is not unusual for a person in custody who previously has expressed an unwillingness to talk or a desire to have a lawyer, to change his mind and even welcome an opportunity to talk. Nothing in the Constitution erects obstacles that preclude police from ascertaining whether a suspect has reconsidered his original decision. As Justice WHITE has observed, this Court consistently has "rejected any paternalistic rule protecting a defendant from his intelligent and voluntary decisions about his own criminal case." *Mosley* (WHITE, J., concurring in result).[1]

In sum, once warnings have been given and the right to counsel has been invoked, the relevant inquiry — whether the suspect now desires to talk to police without counsel — is a question of fact to be determined in light of all of the circumstances. Who "initiated" a conversation may be relevant to the question of waiver, but it is not the *sine qua non* to the inquiry. The ultimate question is whether there was a free and knowing waiver of counsel before interrogation commenced.

If the Court's opinion does nothing more than restate these principles, I am in agreement with it. I hesitate to join the opinion only because of what appears to be an undue and undefined, emphasis on a single element: "initiation." As Justice WHITE has noted, the Court in *Miranda* imposed a general prophylactic rule that is not manifestly required by anything in the text of the Constitution. (WHITE, J., dissenting). *Miranda* itself recognized, moreover, that counsel's assistance can be waived. (opinion of WARREN, C. J.). Waiver always has been evaluated under the general formulation of the *Zerbst* standard quoted above. My concern is that the Court's opinion today may be read as "constitutionalizing" not the generalized *Zerbst* standard but a *single element of fact* among the various facts that may be relevant to determining whether there has been a valid waiver.

---

[1] In *Mosley*, of course, the question was whether a suspect who had invoked his right to *remain silent* later could change his mind and speak to police. The facts of *Mosley* differ somewhat from the present case because here petitioner had *requested counsel*. It is nevertheless true in both cases that "a blanket prohibition against the taking of voluntary statements or a permanent immunity from further interrogation, regardless of the circumstances, would transform the *Miranda* safeguards into wholly irrational obstacles to legitimate police investigative activity, and deprive suspects of an opportunity to make informed and intelligent assessments of their interests." (opinion of STEWART, J.).

QUESTIONS AND NOTES

1.   Whatever might be said of either *Edwards* or *Mosley* standing alone, do they make sense when considered together? Explain.

2.   If you were a suspect, would you think that you were invoking a different and superior right by invoking the right to counsel as opposed to the right to silence? If your answer is "no" would either *Mosley* or *Edwards* have to be wrong?

3.   May the police ask a suspect if he has changed his mind? Should they be able to? Why? Why not?

4.   Is Chief Justice Burger's opinion sounder than that of the majority? Explain.

5.   In *Oregon v. Bradshaw*, 462 U.S. 1039 (1983), the Court confronted the question of a suspect's "initiated" conversation with the police after having once invoked his right to counsel. There the suspect, after having invoked *Miranda*, while being transported from one jail to another, asked the policeman driver: "Well, what is going to happen to me now"? A badly fractured Court considered that sufficient to allow the policeman to readminister Miranda warnings, and upon the suspects waiver, renew questioning.

6.   In *Roberson*, the Court amplified and arguably expanded the *Edwards* right.

ARIZONA v. ROBERSON
486 U.S. 675 (1988)

JUSTICE STEVENS delivered the opinion of the Court.

In *Edwards*, we held that a suspect who has "expressed his desire to deal with the police only through counsel is not subject to further interrogation by the authorities until counsel has been made available to him, unless the accused himself initiates further communication, exchanges, or conversations with the police." In this case Arizona asks us to craft an exception to that rule for cases in which the police want to interrogate a suspect about an offense that is unrelated to the subject of their initial interrogation. Several years ago the Arizona Supreme Court considered, and rejected, a similar argument, stating:

> The only difference between Edwards and the appellant is that Edwards was questioned about the same offense after a request for counsel while the appellant was reinterrogated about an unrelated offense. We do not believe that this factual distinction holds any legal significance for fifth amendment purposes.

State v. Routhier, 137 Ariz. 90, 97, 669 P.2d 68, 75 (1983), *cert. denied*, 464 U.S. 1073, 104 S. Ct. 985, 79 L. Ed. 2d 221 (1984).

We agree with the Arizona Supreme Court's conclusion.

I

On April 16, 1985, respondent was arrested at the scene of a just-completed burglary. The arresting officer advised him that he had a constitutional right to remain silent and also the right to have an attorney present during any interrogation. Respondent replied that he "wanted a lawyer before answering any questions." This fact was duly recorded in the officer's written report of the incident. In due course, respondent was convicted of the April 16, 1985, burglary.

On April 19, 1985, while respondent was still in custody pursuant to the arrest three days earlier, a different officer interrogated him about a different burglary that had occurred on April 15. That officer was not aware of the fact that respondent had requested the assistance of counsel three days earlier. After advising respondent of his rights, the officer obtained an incriminating statement concerning the April 15 burglary. In the prosecution for that offense, the trial court suppressed that statement. In explaining his ruling, the trial judge relied squarely on the Arizona Supreme Court's opinion in *Routhier*, characterizing the rule of the *Edwards* case as "clear and unequivocal."

We now affirm.

III

Petitioner contends that the bright-line, prophylactic *Edwards* rule should not apply when the police-initiated interrogation following a suspect's request for counsel occurs in the context of a separate investigation. According to petitioner, both our cases and the nature of the factual setting compel this distinction. We are unpersuaded.

Petitioner points to our holding in *Mosley*, that when a suspect asserts his right to cut off questioning, the police may "scrupulously honor" that right by "immediately ceas[ing] the interrogation, resum[ing] questioning only after the passage of a significant period of time and the provision of a fresh set of warnings, and restrict[ing] the second interrogation to a crime that had not been a subject of the earlier interrogation." The police in this case followed precisely that course, claims the State. However, as *Mosley* made clear, a suspect's decision to cut off questioning, unlike his request for counsel, does not raise the presumption that he is unable to proceed without a lawyer's advice.

Petitioner argues that Roberson's request for counsel was limited to the investigation pursuant to which the request was made. This argument is flawed both factually and legally. As a matter of fact, according to the initial police report, respondent stated that "he wanted a lawyer before answering *any* questions." As a matter of law, the presumption raised by a suspect's request for counsel — that he considers himself unable to deal with the pressures of custodial interrogation without legal assistance — does not disappear simply because the police have approached the suspect, still in custody, still without counsel, about a separate investigation.

That a suspect's request for counsel should apply to any questions the police wish to pose follows, we think, not only from *Edwards* and *Miranda*, but also *Spring*. In

Spring, we held that "a suspect's awareness of all the possible subjects of questioning in advance of interrogation is not relevant to determining whether the suspect voluntarily, knowingly, and intelligently waived his Fifth Amendment privilege." In the face of the warning that anything he said could be used as evidence against him, Spring's willingness to answer questions, without limiting such a waiver, indicated that he felt comfortable enough with the pressures of custodial interrogation both to answer questions and to do so without an attorney. Since there is "no qualification of [the] broad and explicit warning" that *"anything* [a suspect] says may be used against him" (emphasis in original), Spring's decision to talk was properly considered to be equally unqualified. Conversely, Roberson's unwillingness to answer any questions without the advice of counsel, without limiting his request for counsel, indicated that he did not feel sufficiently comfortable with the pressures of custodial interrogation to answer questions without an attorney. This discomfort is precisely the state of mind that *Edwards* presumes to persist unless the suspect himself initiates further conversation about the investigation; unless he otherwise states, there is no reason to assume that a suspect's state of mind is in any way investigation-specific. *Spring*.

IV

Petitioner's attempts at distinguishing the factual setting here from that in *Edwards* are equally unavailing. Petitioner first relies on the plurality opinion in *Bradshaw*, (REHNQUIST, J.), which stated that *Edwards* laid down "a prophylactic rule, designed to protect an accused in police custody from being badgered by police officers in the manner in which the defendant in *Edwards* was." Petitioner reasons that "the chances that an accused will be questioned so repeatedly and in such quick succession that it will 'undermine the will' of the person questioned, or will constitute 'badger[ing],' are so minute as not to warrant consideration, if the officers are truly pursuing separate investigations." It is by no means clear, though, that police engaged in separate investigations will be any less eager than police involved in only one inquiry to question a suspect in custody. Further, to a suspect who has indicated his inability to cope with the pressures of custodial interrogation by requesting counsel, any further interrogation without counsel having been provided will surely exacerbate whatever compulsion to speak the suspect may be feeling. Thus, we also disagree with petitioner's contention that fresh sets of *Miranda* warnings will "reassure" a suspect who has been denied the counsel he has clearly requested that his rights have remained untrammeled. Especially in a case such as this, in which a period of three days elapsed between the unsatisfied request for counsel and the interrogation about a second offense, there is a serious risk that the mere repetition of the *Miranda* warnings would not overcome the presumption of coercion that is created by prolonged police custody.[6]

---

[6] The United States, as *amicus curiae* supporting petitioner, suggests similarly that "respondent's failure to reiterate his request for counsel to [the officer involved in the second investigation], even after [that officer] gave respondent complete *Miranda* warnings, could not have been the result of any doubt on respondent's part that the police would honor a request for counsel if one were made." This conclusion is surprising, considering that respondent had not been provided with the attorney he had already requested, despite having been subjected to police-initiated interrogation with respect to the first investigation as well. We reiterate here, though, that the "right" to counsel to protect the Fifth

The United States, as *amicus curiae* supporting petitioner, suggests that a suspect in custody might have "good reasons for wanting to speak with the police about the offenses involved in the new investigation, or at least to learn from the police what the new investigation is about so that he can decide whether it is in his interest to make a statement about that matter without the assistance of counsel." The simple answer is that the suspect, having requested counsel, can determine how to deal with the separate investigations with counsel's advice. Further, even if the police have decided temporarily not to provide counsel, they are free to inform the suspect of the facts of the second investigation as long as such communication does not constitute interrogation. As we have made clear, any "further communication, exchanges, or conversations with the police" that the suspect himself initiates, *Edwards*, are perfectly valid.

Finally, we attach no significance to the fact that the officer who conducted the second interrogation did not know that respondent had made a request for counsel. In addition to the fact that *Edwards* focuses on the state of mind of the suspect and not of the police, custodial interrogation must be conducted pursuant to established procedures, and those procedures in turn must enable an officer who proposes to initiate an interrogation to determine whether the suspect has previously requested counsel. In this case respondent's request had been properly memorialized in a written report but the officer who conducted the interrogation simply failed to examine that report. Whether a contemplated reinterrogation concerns the same or a different offense, or whether the same or different law enforcement authorities are involved in the second investigation, the same need to determine whether the suspect has requested counsel exists.[7] The police department's failure to honor that request cannot be justified by the lack of diligence of a particular officer.

The judgment of the Arizona Court of Appeals is *Affirmed.*

JUSTICE KENNEDY, with whom THE CHIEF JUSTICE joins, dissenting.

The majority frames the case as one in which we are asked to "craft an exception" to *Edwards*. The implication from this, it would seem, is that the burden of proof falls on those who say no constitutional or preventative purpose is served by prohibiting the police from asking a suspect, once he has requested counsel, if he chooses to waive that right in a new and independent investigation of a different crime. But the rule of *Edwards* is our rule, not a constitutional command; and it is our obligation to justify its expansion. Our justification must be consistent with the practical realities of suspects' rights and police investigations. With all respect, I suggest the majority does not have a convincing case. The majority's rule is not necessary to protect the rights of suspects, and it will in many instances deprive our

---

Amendment right against self-incrimination is not absolute; that is, "[i]f authorities conclude that they will not provide counsel during a reasonable period of time in which investigation in the field is carried out, they may refrain from doing so without violating the person's Fifth Amendment privilege so long as they do not question him during that time." *Miranda*.

[7] Indeed, the facts of this case indicate that different officers investigating the same offense are just as likely to bypass proper procedures as an officer investigating a different offense, inasmuch as the record discloses no less than five violations of the *Edwards* rule, four concerning the April 16 burglary and only one concerning the April 15 burglary. It is only the last violation that is at issue in this case.

nationwide law enforcement network of a legitimate investigative technique now routinely used to resolve major crimes.

When a suspect is in custody for even the most minor offense, his name and fingerprints are checked against master files. It is a frequent occurrence that the suspect is wanted for questioning with respect to crimes unrelated to the one for which he has been apprehended. The rule announced today will bar law enforcement officials, even those from some other city or other jurisdiction, from questioning a suspect about an unrelated matter if he is in custody and has requested counsel to assist in answering questions put to him about the crime for which he was arrested.

This is the first case in which we are asked to apply *Edwards* to separate and independent investigations. The statements deemed inadmissible in *Edwards* and in our later cases applying its doctrine were statements relating to the same investigation in which the right to counsel was invoked. The majority's extension of the *Edwards* rule to separate and independent investigations is unwarranted.

Our ultimate concern in *Edwards*, and in the cases which follow it, is whether the suspect knows and understands his rights and is willing to waive them, and whether courts can be assured that coercion did not induce the waiver. That concern does not dictate the result reached by the Court today, for the dangers present in *Edwards* and later cases are insubstantial here.

The rule in *Edwards* "was in effect a prophylactic rule, designed to protect an accused in police custody from being badgered by police officers in the manner in which the defendant in *Edwards* was." *Bradshaw*, (plurality opinion). Where the subsequent questioning is confined to an entirely independent investigation, there is little risk that the suspect will be badgered into submission.

The Court reasons that it is "by no means clear" that "police engaged in separate investigations will be any less eager than police involved in only one inquiry to question a suspect in custody." That misses the point. Unless there are so many separate investigations that fresh teams of police are regularly turning up to question the suspect, the danger of badgering is minimal, and insufficient to justify a rigid *per se* rule. Whatever their eagerness, the police in a separate investigation may not commence any questioning unless the suspect is readvised of his *Miranda* rights and consents to the interrogation, and they are required by *Edwards* to cease questioning him if he invokes his right to counsel. Consequently, the legitimate interest of the suspect in not being subjected to coercive badgering is already protected. The reason for the *Edwards* rule is not that confessions are disfavored but that coercion is feared. The rule announced today, however, prohibits the police from resuming questions, after a second *Miranda* warning, when there is no more likelihood of coercion than when the first interrogation began.

The Court suggests that the suspect may believe his rights are fictitious if he must assert them a second time, but the support for this suggestion is weak. The suspect, having observed that his earlier invocation of rights was effective in terminating questioning and having been advised that further questioning may not relate to that crime, would understand that he may invoke his rights again with respect to the new investigation, and so terminate questioning regarding that investigation as well. Indeed, the new warnings and explanations will reinforce his comprehension of a suspect's rights.

I note that the conduct of the police in this case was hardly exemplary; they reinitiated questioning of respondent regarding the first investigation after he had asserted his right to counsel in that investigation. The statements he gave in response, however, properly were excluded at trial for all purposes except impeachment. Any sense of coercion generated by this violation which carried over into the questioning on the second offense would of course be taken into account by a court reviewing whether the waiver of *Miranda* rights in the second investigation was voluntary, and the *per se* rule announced today is therefore not necessary to respond to such misconduct.

Allowing authorities who conduct a separate investigation to read the suspect his *Miranda* rights and ask him whether he wishes to invoke them strikes an appropriate balance, which protects the suspect's freedom from coercion without unnecessarily disrupting legitimate law enforcement efforts. Balance is essential when the Court fashions rules which are preventative and do not themselves stem from violations of a constitutional right. By contrast with the Fourth Amendment exclusionary rule, for instance, the rule here operates even absent constitutional violation, and we should be cautious in extending it. The Court expresses a preference for bright lines, but the line it draws here is far more restrictive than necessary to protect the interests at stake.

By prohibiting the police from questioning the suspect regarding a separate investigation, the Court chooses to presume that a suspect has made the decision that he does not wish to talk about that investigation without counsel present, although that decision was made when the suspect was unaware of even the existence of a separate investigation. The underlying premise seems to be that there are two types of people: those who never talk without a lawyer and those who always talk without a lawyer. The more realistic view of human nature suggests that a suspect will want the opportunity, when he learns of the separate investigations, to decide whether he wishes to speak to the authorities in a particular investigation with or without representation.

In other contexts, we have taken a more realistic approach to separate and independent investigations. [W]e held in *Mosley* that a suspect who had been arrested on charges of committing robbery and who had invoked his right to silence could be questioned later about an unrelated murder, if first read his *Miranda* rights. The Court correctly points out that *Mosley* involved the Fifth Amendment right to silence, while this case involves the Fifth Amendment right to counsel. *Mosley* nevertheless reflected an understanding that the invocation of a criminal suspect's constitutional rights could be respected, and the opportunities for unfair coercion restricted, without the establishment of a broad-brush rule by which the assertion of a right in one investigation is automatically applied to a separate and independent one.

In considering whether to extend the *Edwards* rule to this case, the choice is not between holding, as the Court does, that such statements will never be admissible, and holding that such statements will always be admissible. The choice is between the Court's absolute rule establishing an irrebuttable presumption of coercion, and one which relies upon known and tested warnings, applied to each investigation as required by *Edwards* and *Miranda v. Arizona*, to insure that a waiver is voluntary. The problems to which *Edwards* was addressed are not present here in any substantial degree. Today's rule will neither serve the interest of law enforcement nor give necessary protection to the rights of those suspected of crime. I respectfully dissent.

QUESTIONS AND NOTES

1. If when given his warnings, Roberson had said: "I want a lawyer before answering any questions about this burglary" would the result have been different? Should it have been different?

2. Do you think that this case is analogous to *Spring*? Explain.

3. Should this case be treated as an exception to *Edwards*, or as an exception to the voluntariness standard? Why? Would your conclusion likely be dictated by which of those premises you began the case?

4. Is the *Roberson* corollary to *Edwards* really necessary to prevent coercion? Why? Why not?

5. Explain the distinction between a prophylactic rule and a constitutional rule. Which is *Roberson*?

6. In *Minnick*, we explore what happens after a suspect who has invoked his right to counsel has an opportunity to speak with his attorney.

MINNICK v. MISSISSIPPI
498 U.S. 146 (1990)

JUSTICE KENNEDY delivered the opinion of the Court.

The issue in the case before us is whether *Edwards'* protection ceases once the suspect has consulted with an attorney.

Petitioner Robert Minnick and fellow prisoner James Dyess escaped from a county jail in Mississippi and, a day later, broke into a mobile home in search of weapons. In the course of the burglary they were interrupted by the arrival of the trailer's owner, Ellis Thomas, accompanied by Lamar Lafferty and Lafferty's infant son. Dyess and Minnick used the stolen weapons to kill Thomas and the senior Lafferty. Minnick's story is that Dyess murdered one victim and forced Minnick to shoot the other. Before the escapees could get away, two young women arrived at the mobile home. They were held at gunpoint, then bound hand and foot. Dyess and Minnick fled in Thomas' truck, abandoning the vehicle in New Orleans. The fugitives continued to Mexico, where they fought, and Minnick then proceeded alone to California. Minnick was arrested in Lemon Grove, California, on a Mississippi warrant, some four months after the murders.

The confession at issue here resulted from the last interrogation of Minnick while he was held in the San Diego jail, but we first recount the events which preceded it.

Minnick was arrested on Friday, August 22, 1986. Petitioner testified that he was mistreated by local police during and after the arrest. The day following the arrest, Saturday, two FBI agents came to the jail to interview him. Petitioner testified that he refused to go to the interview, but was told he would "have to go down or else." The FBI report indicates that the agents read petitioner his *Miranda* warnings, and that he acknowledged he understood his rights. He refused to sign a rights waiver form, however, and said he would not answer "very many" questions. Minnick told the agents about the jail break and the flight, and described how Dyess threatened and beat him. Early in the interview, he sobbed "[i]t was my life or theirs," but otherwise he hesitated to tell what happened at the trailer. The agents reminded him he did not have to answer questions without a lawyer present. According to the report, "Minnick stated 'Come back Monday when I have a lawyer,' and stated that he would make a more complete statement then with his lawyer present." The FBI interview ended.

After the FBI interview, an appointed attorney met with petitioner. Petitioner spoke with the lawyer on two or three occasions, though it is not clear from the record whether all of these conferences were in person.

On Monday, August 25, Deputy Sheriff J.C. Denham of Clarke County, Mississippi, came to the San Diego jail to question Minnick. Minnick testified that his jailers again told him he would "have to talk" to Denham and that he "could not refuse." Denham advised petitioner of his rights, and petitioner again declined to sign a rights waiver form. Petitioner told Denham about the escape and then proceeded to describe the events at the mobile home. According to petitioner, Dyess jumped out of the mobile home and shot the first of the two victims, once in the back with a shotgun and once in the head with a pistol. Dyess then handed the pistol to petitioner and ordered him to shoot the other victim, holding the shotgun on petitioner until he did so. Petitioner also said that when the two girls arrived, he talked Dyess out of raping or otherwise hurting them.

Minnick was tried for murder in Mississippi. He moved to suppress all statements given to the FBI or other police officers, including Denham. The trial court denied the motion with respect to petitioner's statements to Denham, but suppressed his other statements. Petitioner was convicted on two counts of capital murder and sentenced to death.

On appeal, petitioner argued that the confession to Denham was taken in violation of his rights to counsel under the Fifth and Sixth Amendments. The Mississippi Supreme Court rejected the claims. With respect to the Fifth Amendment aspect of the case, the court found "the *Edwards* bright-line rule as to initiation" inapplicable. Relying on language in *Edwards* indicating that the bar on interrogating the accused after a request for counsel applies "until counsel has been made available to him," the court concluded that "[s]ince counsel was made available to Minnick, his Fifth Amendment right to counsel was satisfied." We granted certiorari, and we decide that the Fifth Amendment protection of *Edwards* is not terminated or suspended by consultation with counsel.

Edwards is "designed to prevent police from badgering a defendant into waiving his previously asserted *Miranda* rights." The rule ensures that any statement made in subsequent interrogation is not the result of coercive pressures. *Edwards* conserves judicial resources which would otherwise be expended in making difficult determinations of voluntariness, and implements the protections of *Miranda* in practical and straightforward terms.

The merit of the *Edwards* decision lies in the clarity of its command and the certainty of its application. We have confirmed that the *Edwards* rule provides " 'clear and unequivocal' guidelines to the law enforcement profession." *Roberson.* Even before *Edwards*, we noted that *Miranda's* "relatively rigid requirement that interrogation must cease upon the accused's request for an attorney . . . has the virtue of informing police and prosecutors with specificity as to what they may do in conducting custodial interrogation, and of informing courts under what circumstances statements obtained during such interrogation are not admissible. This gain in specificity, which benefits the accused and the State alike, has been thought to outweigh the burdens that the decision in *Miranda* imposes on law enforcement agencies and the courts by requiring the suppression of trustworthy and highly probative evidence even though the confession might be voluntary under traditional Fifth Amendment analysis." *Fare v. Michael C.* This pre-*Edwards* explanation applies as well to *Edwards* and its progeny. *Roberson.*

The Mississippi Supreme Court relied on our statement in *Edwards* that an accused who invokes his right to counsel "is not subject to further interrogation by the authorities until counsel has been made available to him . . . ." We do not interpret this language to mean, as the Mississippi court thought, that the protection of *Edwards* terminates once counsel has consulted with the suspect. In context, the requirement that counsel be "made available" to the accused refers to more than an opportunity to consult with an attorney outside the interrogation room.

In *Edwards*, we focused on *Miranda's* instruction that when the accused invokes his right to counsel, "the interrogation must cease until an attorney is *present*," (emphasis added), agreeing with Edwards' contention that he had not waived his right "to have counsel *present* during custodial interrogation." (emphasis added). In the sentence preceding the language quoted by the Mississippi Supreme Court, we referred to the "right to have counsel *present* during custodial interrogation," and in the sentence following, we again quoted the phrase " 'interrogation must cease until an attorney is present.' " *Miranda* (emphasis added). The full sentence relied on by the Mississippi Supreme Court, moreover, says: "We further hold that an accused, such as Edwards, *having expressed his desire to deal with the police only through counsel*, is not subject to further interrogation by the authorities until counsel has been made available to him, unless the accused himself initiates further communication, exchanges, or conversations with the police." (emphasis added).

Our emphasis on counsel's *presence* at interrogation is not unique to *Edwards*. It derives from *Miranda*, where we said that in the cases before us "[t]he presence of counsel . . . would be the adequate protective device necessary to make the process of police interrogation conform to the dictates of the [Fifth Amendment] privilege. Writing for a plurality of the Court, for instance, then-Justice REHNQUIST described the holding of *Edwards* to be "that subsequent incriminating statements made *without [Edwards'] attorney present* violated the rights secured to the defendant by the Fifth and Fourteenth Amendments to the United States Constitution."

Bradshaw (emphasis added). In our view, a fair reading of *Edwards* and subsequent cases demonstrates that we have interpreted the rule to bar police-initiated interrogation unless the accused has counsel with him at the time of questioning. Whatever the ambiguities of our earlier cases on this point, we now hold that when counsel is requested, interrogation must cease, and officials may not reinitiate interrogation without counsel present, whether or not the accused has consulted with his attorney.

We consider our ruling to be an appropriate and necessary application of the *Edwards* rule. A single consultation with an attorney does not remove the suspect from persistent attempts by officials to persuade him to waive his rights, or from the coercive pressures that accompany custody and that may increase as custody is prolonged. The case before us well illustrates the pressures, and abuses, that may be concomitants of custody. Petitioner testified that though he resisted, he was required to submit to both the FBI and the Denham interviews. In the latter instance, the compulsion to submit to interrogation followed petitioner's unequivocal request during the FBI interview that questioning cease until counsel was present. The case illustrates also that consultation is not always effective in instructing the suspect of his rights. One plausible interpretation of the record is that petitioner thought he could keep his admissions out of evidence by refusing to sign a formal waiver of rights. If the authorities had complied with Minnick's request to have counsel present during interrogation, the attorney could have corrected Minnick's misunderstanding, or indeed counseled him that he need not make a statement at all. We decline to remove protection from police-initiated questioning based on isolated consultations with counsel who is absent when the interrogation resumes.

The exception to *Edwards* here proposed is inconsistent with *Edwards'* purpose to protect the suspect's right to have counsel present at custodial interrogation. It is inconsistent as well with *Miranda*, where we specifically rejected respondent's theory that the opportunity to consult with one's attorney would substantially counteract the compulsion created by custodial interrogation. We noted in *Miranda* that "[e]ven preliminary advice given to the accused by his own attorney can be swiftly overcome by the secret interrogation process. Thus the need for counsel to protect the Fifth Amendment privilege comprehends not merely a right to consult with counsel prior to questioning, but also to have counsel present during any questioning if the defendant so desires."

The exception proposed, furthermore, would undermine the advantages flowing from *Edwards'* "clear and unequivocal" character. Respondent concedes that even after consultation with counsel, a second request for counsel should reinstate the *Edwards* protection. We are invited by this formulation to adopt a regime in which *Edwards'* protection could pass in and out of existence multiple times prior to arraignment. Vagaries of this sort spread confusion through the justice system and lead to a consequent loss of respect for the underlying constitutional principle.

In addition, adopting the rule proposed would leave far from certain the sort of consultation required to displace *Edwards*. Consultation is not a precise concept, for it may encompass variations from a telephone call to say that the attorney is in route, to a hurried interchange between the attorney and client in a detention facility corridor, to a lengthy in-person conference in which the attorney gives full and adequate advice respecting all matters that might be covered in further interrogations. And even with the necessary scope of consultation settled, the officials in charge of the case would have to confirm the occurrence and, possibly, the extent of consultation to determine whether further interrogation is permissible. The necessary inquiries could interfere with the attorney-client privilege.

Added to these difficulties in definition and application of the proposed rule is our concern over its consequence that the suspect whose counsel is prompt would lose the protection of *Edwards*, while the one whose counsel is dilatory would not. There is more than irony to this result. There is a strong possibility that it would distort the proper conception of the attorney's duty to the client and set us on a course at odds with what ought to be effective representation.

Both waiver of rights and admission of guilt are consistent with the affirmation of individual responsibility that is a principle of the criminal justice system. It does not detract from this principle, however, to insist that neither admissions nor waivers are effective unless there are both particular and systemic assurances that the coercive pressures of custody were not the inducing cause. The *Edwards* rule sets forth a specific standard to fulfill these purposes, and we have declined to confine it in other instances. It would detract from the efficacy of the rule to remove its protections based on consultation with counsel.

Edwards does not foreclose finding a waiver of Fifth Amendment protections after counsel has been requested, provided the accused has initiated the conversation or discussions with the authorities; but that is not the case before us. There can be no doubt that the interrogation in question was initiated by the police; it was a formal interview which petitioner was compelled to attend. Since petitioner made a specific request for counsel before the interview, the police-initiated interrogation was impermissible. Petitioner's statement to Denham was not admissible at trial.

The judgment is reversed and the case remanded for further proceedings not inconsistent with this opinion.

JUSTICE SCALIA, with whom THE CHIEF JUSTICE joins, dissenting.

The Court today establishes an irrebuttable presumption that a criminal suspect, after invoking his *Miranda* right to counsel, can *never* validly waive that right during any police-initiated encounter, even after the suspect has been provided multiple *Miranda* warnings and has actually consulted his attorney. This holding builds on foundations already established in *Edwards*, but "the rule of *Edwards* is our rule, not a constitutional command; and it is our obligation to justify its expansion." *Roberson*. Because I see no justification for applying the *Edwards* irrebuttable presumption when a criminal suspect has actually consulted with his attorney, I respectfully dissent.

I

Some recapitulation of pertinent facts is in order, given the Court's contention that "[t]he case before us well illustrates the pressures, and abuses, that may be concomitants of custody." It is undisputed that the FBI agents who first interviewed Minnick on Saturday, August 23, 1986, advised him of his *Miranda* rights before any questioning began. Although he refused to sign a waiver form, he agreed to talk to the agents, and described his escape from prison in Mississippi and the ensuing events. When he came to what happened at the trailer, however, Minnick hesitated. The FBI agents then reminded him that he did not have to answer questions without a lawyer present. Minnick indicated that he would finish his account on Monday, when he had a lawyer, and the FBI agents terminated the interview forthwith.

Minnick was then provided with an attorney, with whom he consulted several times over the weekend. As Minnick testified at a subsequent suppression hearing:

> I talked to [my attorney] two different times and — it might have been three different times . . . . He told me that first day that he was my lawyer and that he was appointed to me and not to talk to nobody and not tell nobody nothing and to not sign no waivers and not sign no extradition papers or sign anything and that he was going to get a court order to have any of the police — I advised him of the FBI talking to me and he advised me not to tell anybody anything that he was going to get a court order drawn up to restrict anybody talking to me outside of the San Diego Police Department.

On Monday morning, Minnick was interviewed by Deputy Sheriff J.C. Denham, who had come to San Diego from Mississippi. Before the interview, Denham reminded Minnick of his *Miranda* rights. Minnick again refused to sign a waiver form, but he did talk with Denham, and did not ask for his attorney. As Minnick recalled at the hearing, he and Denham "went through several different conversations about — first, about how everybody was back in the county jail and what everybody was doing, had he heard from Mama and had he went and talked to Mama and had he seen my brother, Tracy, and several different other questions pertaining to such things as that. And, we went off into how the escape went down at the county jail . . . ." Minnick then proceeded to describe his participation in the double murder at the trailer.

Minnick was later extradited and tried for murder in Mississippi. Before trial, he moved to suppress the statements he had given the FBI agents and Denham in the San Diego jail. The trial court granted the motion with respect to the statements made to the FBI agents, but ordered a hearing on the admissibility of the statements made to Denham. After receiving testimony from both Minnick and Denham, the court concluded that Minnick's confession had been "freely and voluntarily given from the evidence beyond a reasonable doubt," and allowed Denham to describe Minnick's confession to the jury.

The Court today reverses the trial court's conclusion. It holds that, because Minnick had asked for counsel during the interview with the FBI agents, he could not — as a matter of law — validly waive the right to have counsel present during the conversation initiated by Denham. That Minnick's original request to see an attorney had been honored, that Minnick had consulted with his attorney on several occasions, and that the attorney had specifically warned Minnick not to speak to the authorities, are irrelevant. That Minnick was familiar with the criminal justice system in general or *Miranda* warnings in particular (he had previously been convicted of robbery in Mississippi and assault with a deadly weapon in California) is also beside the point. The confession must be suppressed, not because it was "compelled," nor even because it was obtained from an individual who could realistically be assumed to be unaware of his rights, but simply because this Court sees fit to prescribe as a "systemic assuranc[e]," that a person in custody who has once asked for counsel cannot thereafter be approached by the police unless counsel is present. Of course the Constitution's proscription of compelled testimony does not remotely authorize this incursion upon state practices; and even our recent precedents are not a valid excuse.

II

Notwithstanding our acknowledgment that *Miranda* rights are "not themselves rights protected by the Constitution but . . . instead measures to insure that the right against compulsory self-incrimination [is] protected," we have adhered to the principle that nothing less than the *Zerbst* standard for the waiver of constitutional rights applies to the waiver of *Miranda* rights. Until *Edwards*, however, we refrained from imposing on the States a *higher* standard for the waiver of *Miranda* rights. For example, in *Mosley*, we rejected a proposed irrebuttable presumption that a criminal suspect, after invoking the *Miranda* right to remain silent, could not validly waive the right during any subsequent questioning by the police. And in *Fare v. Michael C.*, we declined to hold that waivers of *Miranda* rights by juveniles are *per se* involuntary.

Edwards, however, broke with this approach, holding that a defendant's waiver of his *Miranda* right to counsel, made in the course of a police-initiated encounter after he had requested counsel but before counsel had been provided, was *per se* involuntary. The case stands as a solitary exception to our waiver jurisprudence. It does, to be sure, have the desirable consequences described in today's opinion. In the narrow context in which it applies, it provides 100% assurance against confessions that are "the result of coercive pressures," it "prevent[s] police from badgering a defendant," it "conserves judicial resources which would otherwise be expended in making difficult determinations of voluntariness," and it provides " 'clear and unequivocal' guidelines to the law enforcement profession." But so would a rule that simply excludes all confessions by all persons in police custody. The value of any prophylactic rule (assuming the authority to adopt a prophylactic rule) must be assessed not only on the basis of what is gained, but also on the basis of what is lost. In all other contexts we have thought the above-described consequences of abandoning *Zerbst* outweighed by "the need for police questioning as a tool for effective enforcement of criminal laws." "Admissions of guilt," we have said, "are more than merely 'desirable'; they are essential to society's compelling interest in finding, convicting, and punishing those who violate the law."

III

In this case, of course, we have not been called upon to reconsider *Edwards*, but simply to determine whether its irrebuttable presumption should continue after a suspect has actually consulted with his attorney. Whatever justifications might support *Edwards* are even less convincing in this context.

Most of the Court's discussion of *Edwards* — which stresses repeatedly, in various formulations, the case's emphasis upon "the 'right to have counsel *present* during custodial interrogation'" (emphasis added by the Court) — is beside the point. The existence and the importance of the *Miranda*-created right "to have counsel *present*" are unquestioned here. What *is* questioned is why a State should not be given the opportunity to prove (under *Zerbst*) that the right was *voluntarily waived* by a suspect who, after having been read his *Miranda* rights twice and having consulted with counsel at least twice, chose to speak to a police officer (and to admit his involvement in two murders) without counsel present.

Edwards did not assert the principle that no waiver of the *Miranda* right "to have counsel *present*" is possible. It simply adopted the presumption that no waiver is *voluntary* in certain circumstances, and the issue before us today is how broadly those circumstances are to be defined. They should not, in my view, extend beyond the circumstances present in *Edwards* itself — where the suspect in custody asked to consult an attorney, and was interrogated before that attorney had ever been provided. In those circumstances, the *Edwards* rule rests upon an assumption similar to that of *Miranda* itself: that when a suspect in police custody is first questioned he is likely to be ignorant of his rights and to feel isolated in a hostile environment. This likelihood is thought to justify special protection against unknowing or coerced waiver of rights. After a suspect has seen his request for an attorney honored, however, and has actually spoken with that attorney, the probabilities change. The suspect then knows that he has an advocate on his side, and that the police will permit him to consult that advocate. He almost certainly also has a heightened awareness (above what the *Miranda* warning itself will provide) of his right to remain silent — since at the earliest opportunity "any lawyer worth his salt will tell the suspect in no uncertain terms to make no statement to the police under any circumstances." *Watts v. Indiana* (Opinion of Jackson, J.).

Under these circumstances, an irrebuttable presumption that any police-prompted confession is the result of ignorance of rights, or of coercion, has no genuine basis in fact. After the first consultation, therefore, the *Edwards* exclusionary rule should cease to apply. Does this mean, as the Court implies, that the police will thereafter have license to "badger" the suspect? Only if all one means by "badger" is asking, without such insistence or frequency as would constitute coercion, whether he would like to reconsider his decision not to confess. Nothing in the Constitution (the only basis for our intervention here) prohibits such inquiry, which may often produce the desirable result of a voluntary confession. If and when post-consultation police inquiry becomes so protracted or threatening as to constitute coercion, the *Zerbst* standard will afford the needed protection.

One should not underestimate the extent to which the Court's expansion of *Edwards* constricts law enforcement. Today's ruling, that the invocation of a right to counsel permanently prevents a police-initiated waiver, makes it largely impossible for the police to urge a prisoner who has initially declined to confess to change his mind — or indeed, even to ask whether he has changed his mind. Many persons in custody will invoke the *Miranda* right to counsel during the first interrogation, so that the permanent prohibition will attach at once. Those who do not do so will almost certainly request or obtain counsel at arraignment. I presume that the perpetuality of prohibition announced in today's opinion applies in that context as well. "Perpetuality" is not too strong a term, since, although the Court rejects one logical moment at which the *Edwards* presumption might end, it suggests no alternative. In this case Minnick was reapproached by the police three days after he requested counsel, but the result would presumably be the same if it had been three months, or three years, or even three decades. This perpetual irrebuttable presumption will apply, I might add, not merely to interrogations involving the original crime but to those involving other subjects as well. *Roberson.*

Besides repeating the uncontroverted proposition that the suspect has a "right to have counsel *present*," the Court stresses the clarity and simplicity that are achieved by today's holding. Clear and simple rules are desirable, but only in pursuance of authority that we possess. We are authorized by the Fifth Amendment to exclude confessions that are "compelled," which we have interpreted to include confessions that the police obtain from a suspect in custody without a knowing and voluntary waiver of his right to remain silent. Undoubtedly some bright-line rules can be adopted to implement that principle, marking out the situations in which knowledge or voluntariness cannot possibly be established — for example, a rule excluding confessions obtained after five hours of continuous interrogation. But a rule excluding all confessions that follow upon even the slightest police inquiry cannot conceivably be justified on this basis. It does not rest upon a reasonable prediction that all such confessions, or even most such confessions, will be unaccompanied by a knowing and voluntary waiver.

It can be argued that the same is true of the category of confessions excluded by the *Edwards* rule itself. I think that is so, but, as I have discussed above, the presumption of involuntariness is at least more plausible for that category. There is, in any event, a clear and rational line between that category and the present one, and I see nothing to be said for expanding upon a past mistake. Drawing a distinction between police-initiated inquiry before consultation with counsel and police-initiated inquiry after consultation with counsel is assuredly more reasonable than other distinctions *Edwards* has already led us into — such as the distinction between police-initiated inquiry after assertion of the *Miranda* right to remain silent, and police-initiated inquiry after assertion of the *Miranda* right to counsel, *see* Kamisar, *The* Edwards *and* Bradshaw *Cases: The Court Giveth and the Court Taketh Away, in* 5 THE SUPREME COURT: TRENDS AND DEVELOPMENTS 157 (J. Choper, Y. Kamisar, & L. Tribe eds. 1984) ("[E]ither *Mosley* was wrongly decided or *Edwards* was"); or the distinction between what is needed to prove waiver of the *Miranda* right to have counsel present and what is needed to prove waiver of rights found in the Constitution.

The rest of the Court's arguments can be answered briefly. The suggestion that it will either be impossible or ethically impermissible to determine whether a "consultation" between the suspect and his attorney has occurred is alarmist. Since, as I have described above, the main purpose of the consultation requirement is to eliminate the suspect's feeling of isolation and to assure him the presence of legal assistance, any discussion between him and an attorney whom he asks to contact, or who is provided to him, in connection with his arrest, will suffice. The precise content of the discussion is irrelevant.

As for the "irony" that "the suspect whose counsel is prompt would lose the protection of *Edwards*, while the one whose counsel is dilatory would not:" There seems to me no irony in applying a special protection only when it is needed. The *Edwards* rule is premised on an (already tenuous) assumption about the suspect's psychological state, and when the event of consultation renders that assumption invalid the rule should no longer apply. One searching for ironies in the state of our law should consider, first, the irony created by *Edwards* itself: The suspect in custody who says categorically "I do not wish to discuss this matter" can be asked to change his mind; but if he should say, more tentatively, "I do not think I should discuss this matter without my attorney present" he can no longer be approached. To that there is added, by today's decision, the irony that it will be far harder for the state to establish a knowing and voluntary waiver of Fifth Amendment rights by a prisoner who has already consulted with counsel than by a newly arrested suspect.

Finally, the Court's concern that *"Edwards'* protection could pass in and out of existence multiple times," does not apply to the resolution of the matter I have proposed. *Edwards* would cease to apply, permanently, once consultation with counsel has occurred.

*   *   *

Today's extension of the *Edwards* prohibition is the latest stage of prophylaxis built upon prophylaxis, producing a veritable fairyland castle of imagined constitutional restriction upon law enforcement. This newest tower, according to the Court, is needed to avoid "inconsisten[cy] with [the] purpose" of *Edwards'* prophylactic rule, which was needed to protect *Miranda's* prophylactic right to have counsel present, which was needed to protect the right against *compelled self-incrimination* found (at last!) in the Constitution.

It seems obvious to me that, even in *Edwards* itself but surely in today's decision, we have gone far beyond any genuine concern about suspects who do not *know* their right to remain silent, or who have been *coerced* to abandon it. Both holdings are explicable, in my view, only as an effort to protect suspects against what is regarded as their own folly. The sharp-witted criminal would know better than to confess; why should the dull-witted suffer for his lack of mental endowment? Providing him an attorney at every stage where he might be induced or persuaded (though not coerced) to incriminate himself will even the odds. Apart from the fact that this protective enterprise is beyond our authority under the Fifth Amendment or any other provision of the Constitution, it is unwise. The procedural protections of the Constitution protect the guilty as well as the innocent, but it is not their objective to set the guilty free. That some clever criminals may employ those protections to their advantage is poor reason to allow criminals who have not done so to escape justice.

Thus, even if I were to concede that an honest confession is a foolish mistake, I would welcome rather than reject it; a rule that foolish mistakes do not count would leave most offenders not only unconvicted but undetected. More fundamentally, however, it is wrong, and subtly corrosive of our criminal justice system, to regard an honest confession as a "mistake." While every person is entitled to stand silent, it is more virtuous for the wrongdoer to admit his offense and accept the punishment he deserves. Not only for society, but for the wrongdoer himself, "admissio[n] of guilt . . . , if not coerced, [is] inherently desirable," because it advances the goals of both "justice *and* rehabilitation." (emphasis added). A confession is rightly regarded by the sentencing guidelines as warranting a reduction of sentence, because it "demonstrates a recognition and affirmative acceptance of personal responsibility for . . . criminal conduct," U.S. Sentencing Commission, Guidelines Manual § 3E1.1 (1988), which is the beginning of reform. We should, then, rejoice at an honest confession, rather than pity the "poor fool" who has made it; and we should regret the attempted retraction of that good act, rather than seek to facilitate and encourage it. To design our laws on premises contrary to these is to abandon belief in either personal responsibility or the moral claim of just government to obedience. Today's decision is misguided, it seems to me, in so readily exchanging, for marginal, super-*Zerbst* protection against genuinely compelled testimony, investigators' ability to urge, or even ask, a person in custody to do what is right.

QUESTIONS AND NOTES

1. Is Justice Kennedy consistent in dissenting in *Roberson* and writing *Minnick*? Conversely, is Justice Scalia consisting in dissenting in *Minnick* after having joined the *Roberson* majority? Explain.

2. Is there anything wrong with the dissent's approach to the case? Explain.

3. Is the dissent principally predicated on not wanting to expand a mistake? If the dissent thought that *Edwards* and *Miranda* were correctly decided, would it have reached the same result?

4. Would the dissent's rule reward dilatory counsel? Would it encourage counsel to be dilatory?

5. Apart from *Edwards*, should the statements in *Minnick* be inadmissible? Why? Why not?

6. *Maryland v. Shatzer* answers some of the questions raised by Justice Scalia's *Minnick* dissent.

MARYLAND v. SHATZER
559 U.S. 98 (2010)

JUSTICE SCALIA delivered the opinion of the Court.

We consider whether a break in custody ends the presumption of involuntariness established in *Edwards v. Arizona*, 451 U.S. 477 (1981).

I

In August 2003, a social worker assigned to the Child Advocacy Center in the Criminal Investigation Division of the Hagerstown Police Department referred to the department allegations that respondent Michael Shatzer, Sr., had sexually abused his 3-year-old son. At that time, Shatzer was incarcerated at the Maryland Correctional Institution-Hagerstown, serving a sentence for an unrelated child-sexual-abuse offense. Detective Shane Blankenship was assigned to the investigation and interviewed Shatzer at the correctional institution on August 7, 2003. Before asking any questions, Blankenship reviewed Shatzer's *Miranda* rights with him, and obtained a written waiver of those rights. When Blankenship explained that he was there to question Shatzer about sexually abusing his son, Shatzer expressed confusion — he had thought Blankenship was an attorney there to discuss the prior crime for which he was incarcerated. Blankenship clarified the purpose of his visit, and Shatzer declined to speak without an attorney. Accordingly, Blankenship ended the interview, and Shatzer was released back into the general prison population. Shortly thereafter, Blankenship closed the investigation.

Two years and six months later, the same social worker referred more specific allegations to the department about the same incident involving Shatzer. Detective Paul Hoover, from the same division, was assigned to the investigation. He and the social worker interviewed the victim, then eight years old, who described the incident in more detail. With this new information in hand, on March 2, 2006, they went to the Roxbury Correctional Institute, to which Shatzer had since been transferred, and interviewed Shatzer in a maintenance room outfitted with a desk and three chairs. Hoover explained that he wanted to ask Shatzer about the alleged incident involving Shatzer's son. Shatzer was surprised because he thought that the investigation had been closed, but Hoover explained they had opened a new file. Hoover then read Shatzer his *Miranda* rights and obtained a written waiver on a standard department form.

Hoover interrogated Shatzer about the incident for approximately 30 minutes. Shatzer denied ordering his son to perform fellatio on him, but admitted to masturbating in front of his son from a distance of less than three feet. Before the interview ended, Shatzer agreed to Hoover's request that he submit to a polygraph examination. At no point during the interrogation did Shatzer request to speak with an attorney or refer to his prior refusal to answer questions without one.

Five days later, on March 7, 2006, Hoover and another detective met with Shatzer at the correctional facility to administer the polygraph examination. After reading Shatzer his *Miranda* rights and obtaining a written waiver, the other detective administered the test and concluded that Shatzer had failed. When the detectives then questioned Shatzer, he became upset, started to cry, and incriminated himself by saying, " 'I didn't force him. I didn't force him.' " After making this inculpatory statement, Shatzer requested an attorney, and Hoover promptly ended the interrogation.

The State's Attorney for Washington County charged Shatzer with second-degree sexual offense, sexual child abuse, second-degree assault, and contributing to conditions rendering a child in need of assistance. Shatzer moved to suppress his March 2006 statements pursuant to *Edwards*. The trial court held a suppression hearing and later denied Shatzer's motion. The *Edwards* protections did not apply, it reasoned, because Shatzer had experienced a break in custody for *Miranda* purposes between the 2003 and 2006 interrogations. Shatzer pleaded not guilty, waived his right to a jury trial, and proceeded to a bench trial based on an agreed statement of facts. In accordance with the agreement, the State described the interview with the victim and Shatzer's 2006 statements to the detectives. Based on the proffered testimony of the victim and the "admission of the defendant as to the act of masturbation," the trial court found Shatzer guilty of sexual child abuse of his son.[1]

Over the dissent of two judges, the Court of Appeals of Maryland reversed and remanded. The court held that "the passage of time *alone* is insufficient to [end] the protections afforded by *Edwards*," and that, assuming, *arguendo*, a break-in-custody exception to *Edwards* existed, Shatzer's release back into the general prison population between interrogations did not constitute a break in custody. We granted certiorari.

II

In *Miranda v. Arizona*, the Court adopted a set of prophylactic measures to protect a suspect's Fifth Amendment right from the "inherently compelling pressures" of custodial interrogation. The Court observed that "incommunicado interrogation" in an "unfamiliar," "police-dominated atmosphere," involves psychological pressures "which work to undermine the individual's will to resist and to compel him to speak where he would not otherwise do so freely." Consequently, it reasoned, "[u]nless adequate protective devices are employed to dispel the compulsion inherent in custodial surroundings, no statement obtained from the defendant can truly be the product of his free choice."

In *Edwards*, the Court determined that *Zerbst's* traditional standard for waiver was not sufficient to protect a suspect's right to have counsel present at a subsequent interrogation if he had previously requested counsel; "additional safeguards" were necessary. The Court therefore superimposed a "second layer of prophylaxis." *Edwards* held:

> "[W]hen an accused has invoked his right to have counsel present during custodial interrogation, a valid waiver of that right cannot be established by showing only that he responded to further police-initiated custodial interrogation even if he has been advised of his rights . . . . [He] is not subject to further interrogation by the authorities until counsel has been made available to him, unless the accused himself initiates further communication, exchanges, or conversations with the police."

The rationale of *Edwards* is that once a suspect indicates that "he is not capable of undergoing [custodial] questioning without advice of counsel," "any subsequent waiver that has come at the authorities' behest, and not at the suspect's own instigation, is itself the product of the 'inherently compelling pressures' and not the purely voluntary choice of the suspect." *Roberson*. Under this rule, a voluntary *Miranda* waiver is sufficient at the time of an initial attempted interrogation to protect a suspect's right to have counsel present, but it is not sufficient at the time of subsequent attempts if the suspect initially requested the presence of counsel.

---

[1] The State filed a nolle prosequi to the second-degree sexual offense charge, and consented to dismissal of the misdemeanor charges as barred by the statute of limitations.

The implicit assumption, of course, is that the subsequent requests for interrogation pose a significantly greater risk of coercion. That increased risk results not only from the police's persistence in trying to get the suspect to talk, but also from the continued pressure that begins when the individual is taken into custody as a suspect and sought to be interrogated — pressure likely to "increase as custody is prolonged." *Minnick.* The *Edwards* presumption of involuntariness ensures that police will not take advantage of the mounting coercive pressures of "prolonged police custody," by repeatedly attempting to question a suspect who previously requested counsel until the suspect is "badgered into submission."

We have frequently emphasized that the *Edwards* rule is not a constitutional mandate, but judicially prescribed prophylaxis. Because *Edwards* is "our rule, not a constitutional command," "it is our obligation to justify its expansion." *Roberson,* (KENNEDY, J., dissenting). Lower courts have uniformly held that a break in custody ends the *Edwards* presumption.

A judicially crafted rule is "justified only by reference to its prophylactic purpose," and applies only where its benefits outweigh its costs. We begin with the benefits. *Edwards'* presumption of involuntariness has the incidental effect of "conserv[ing] judicial resources which would otherwise be expended in making difficult determinations of voluntariness." Its fundamental purpose, however, is to "[p]reserv[e] the integrity of an accused's choice to communicate with police only through counsel," by "prevent[ing] police from badgering a defendant into waiving his previously asserted *Miranda* rights." Thus, the benefits of the rule are measured by the number of coerced confessions it suppresses that otherwise would have been admitted.

It is easy to believe that a suspect may be coerced or badgered into abandoning his earlier refusal to be questioned without counsel in the paradigm *Edwards* case. That is a case in which the suspect has been arrested for a particular crime and is held in uninterrupted pretrial custody while that crime is being actively investigated. After the initial interrogation, and up to and including the second one, he remains cut off from his normal life and companions, "thrust into" and isolated in an "unfamiliar," "police-dominated atmosphere," where his captors "appear to control [his] fate." That was the situation confronted by the suspects in *Edwards, Roberson,* and *Minnick,* the three cases in which we have held the *Edwards* rule applicable. Edwards was arrested pursuant to a warrant and taken to a police station, where he was interrogated until he requested counsel. The officer ended the interrogation and took him to the county jail[2] but at 9:15 the next morning, two of the officer's colleagues reinterrogated Edwards at the jail. Roberson was arrested "at the scene of a just-completed burglary" and interrogated there until he requested a lawyer. A different officer interrogated him three days later while he "was still in custody pursuant to the arrest." Minnick was arrested by local police and taken to the San Diego jail, where two FBI agents interrogated him the next morning until he requested counsel. Two days later a Mississippi Deputy Sheriff reinterrogated him at the jail. None of these suspects regained a sense of control or

---

[2] Jail is a "local government's detention center where persons awaiting trial or those convicted of misdemeanors are confined." Black's Law Dictionary 910 (9th ed. 2009). Prison, by contrast, is a "state or federal facility of confinement for convicted criminals, esp. felons."

normalcy after they were initially taken into custody for the crime under investigation.

When, unlike what happened in these three cases, a suspect has been released from his pretrial custody and has returned to his normal life for some time before the later attempted interrogation, there is little reason to think that his change of heart regarding interrogation without counsel has been coerced. He has no longer been isolated. He has likely been able to seek advice from an attorney, family members, and friends.[3] And he knows from his earlier experience that he need only demand counsel to bring the interrogation to a halt; and that investigative custody does not last indefinitely. In these circumstances, it is far-fetched to think that a police officer's asking the suspect whether he would like to waive his *Miranda* rights will any more "wear down the accused," than did the first such request at the original attempted interrogation — which is of course not deemed coercive. His change of heart is less likely attributable to "badgering" than it is to the fact that further deliberation in familiar surroundings has caused him to believe (rightly or wrongly) that cooperating with the investigation is in his interest. Uncritical extension of *Edwards* to this situation would not significantly increase the number of genuinely coerced confessions excluded. The "justification for a conclusive presumption disappears when application of the presumption will not reach the correct result most of the time."

At the same time that extending the *Edwards* rule yields diminished benefits, extending the rule also increases its costs: the in-fact voluntary confessions it excludes from trial, and the voluntary confessions it deters law enforcement officers from even trying to obtain. Voluntary confessions are not merely "a proper element in law enforcement," *Miranda*, they are an "unmitigated good," *McNeil*, 501 U.S., at 181, " 'essential to society's compelling interest in finding, convicting, and punishing those who violate the law,' " (quoting *Moran* v. *Burbine*, 475 U.S. 412, 426 (1986)). The only logical endpoint of *Edwards* disability is termination of *Miranda* custody and any of its lingering effects. Without that limitation — and barring some purely arbitrary time-limit — every *Edwards* prohibition of custodial interrogation of a particular suspect would be eternal. The prohibition applies, of course, when the subsequent interrogation pertains to a different crime, *Roberson*, when it is conducted by a different law enforcement authority, *Minnick*, and even when the suspect has met with an attorney after the first interrogation. And it not only prevents questioning *ex ante*; it would render invalid *ex post*, confessions invited and obtained from suspects who (unbeknownst to the interrogators) have acquired *Edwards* immunity previously in connection with any offense in any jurisdiction. In a country that harbors a large number of repeat offenders, this consequence is disastrous.

---

[3] Justice STEVENS points out, (opinion concurring in judgment), that in Minnick, actual pre-reinterrogation consultation with an attorney during continued custody did not suffice to avoid application of Edwards. That does not mean that the ability to consult freely with attorneys and others does not reduce the level of coercion at all, or that it is "only questionably relevant," to whether termination of custody reduces the coercive pressure that is the basis for Edwards' super-prophylactic rule.

We conclude that such an extension of *Edwards* is not justified; we have opened its "protective umbrella" far enough. The protections offered by *Miranda*, which we have deemed sufficient to ensure that the police respect the suspect's desire to have an attorney present the first time police interrogate him, adequately ensure that result when a suspect who initially requested counsel is reinterrogated after a break in custody that is of sufficient duration to dissipate its coercive effects.

If Shatzer's return to the general prison population qualified as a break in custody (a question we address in Part III, *infra*), there is no doubt that it lasted long enough (2 1/2 years) to meet that durational requirement. But what about a break that has lasted only one year? Or only one week? It is impractical to leave the answer to that question for clarification in future case-by-case adjudication; law enforcement officers need to know, with certainty and beforehand, when renewed interrogation is lawful. And while it is certainly unusual for this Court to set forth precise time limits governing police action, it is not unheard-of. In *County of Riverside* v. *McLaughlin*, 500 U.S. 44 (1991), we specified 48 hours as the time within which the police must comply with the requirement of *Gerstein* v. *Pugh*, 420 U.S. 103 (1975), that a person arrested without a warrant be brought before a magistrate to establish probable cause for continued detention.

Like *McLaughlin*, this is a case in which the requisite police action (there, presentation to a magistrate; here, abstention from further interrogation) has not been prescribed by statute but has been established by opinion of this Court. We think it appropriate to specify a period of time to avoid the consequence that continuation of the *Edwards* presumption "will not reach the correct result most of the time." It seems to us that period is 14 days. That provides plenty of time for the suspect to get reacclimated to his normal life, to consult with friends and counsel, and to shake off any residual coercive effects of his prior custody.

The 14-day limitation meets Shatzer's concern that a break-in-custody rule lends itself to police abuse. He envisions that once a suspect invokes his *Miranda* right to counsel, the police will release the suspect briefly (to end the *Edwards* presumption) and then promptly bring him back into custody for reinterrogation. But once the suspect has been out of custody long enough (14 days) to eliminate its coercive effect, there will be nothing to gain by such gamesmanship — nothing, that is, except the entirely appropriate gain of being able to interrogate a suspect who has made a valid waiver of his *Miranda* rights.

IV

A few words in response to JUSTICE STEVENS' concurrence: It claims we ignore that "[w]hen police tell an indigent suspect that he has the right to an attorney" and then "reinterrogate" him without providing a lawyer, "the suspect is likely to feel that the police lied to him and that he really does not have any right to a lawyer." The fallacy here is that we are not talking about "reinterrogating" the suspect; we are talking about *asking his permission* to be interrogated. An officer has in no sense lied to a suspect when, after advising, as *Miranda* requires, "You have the right to remain silent, and if you choose to speak you have the right to the presence of an attorney," he promptly ends the attempted interrogation because the suspect declines to speak without counsel present, and then, two weeks later, reapproaches the suspect and asks, "Are you now willing to speak without a lawyer present?"

The "concer[n] that motivated the *Edwards* line of cases" is that the suspect will be coerced into saying yes. That concern guides our decision today. Contrary to the concurrence's conclusion, there is no reason to believe a suspect will view confession as " 'the only way to end his interrogation' " when, before the interrogation begins, he is told that he can avoid it by simply requesting that he not be interrogated without counsel present — an option that worked before. If, as the concurrence argues will often be the case, a break in custody does not change the suspect's mind, he need only say so.

The concurrence also accuses the Court of "ignor[ing] that when a suspect asks for counsel, until his request is answered, there are still the same 'inherently compelling' pressures of custodial interrogation on which the *Miranda* line of cases is based." We do not ignore these pressures; nor do we suggest that they disappear when custody is recommenced after a break. But if those pressures are merely "the same" as before, then *Miranda* provides sufficient protection — as it did before. The *Edwards* presumption of involuntariness is justified only in circumstances where the coercive pressures have increased so much that suspects' waivers of *Miranda* rights are likely to be involuntary most of the time. Contrary to the concurrence's suggestion, it is only in those narrow circumstances — when custody is unbroken — that the Court has concluded a "fresh se[t] of *Miranda* warnings" is not sufficient.

In the last analysis, it turns out that the concurrence accepts our principal points. It agrees that *Edwards* prophylaxis is not perpetual; it agrees that a break in custody reduces the inherently compelling pressure upon which *Edwards* was based; it agrees that Shatzer's release back into the general prison population constituted a break in custody; and it agrees that in this case the break was long enough to render *Edwards* inapplicable. We differ in two respects: Instead of terminating *Edwards* protection when the custodial pressures that were the basis for that protection dissipate, the concurrence would terminate it when the suspect would no longer "feel that he has 'been denied the counsel he has clearly requested.' " This is entirely unrelated to the rationale of *Edwards.* If confidence in the police's promise to provide counsel were the touchstone, *Edwards* would not have applied in *Minnick*, where the suspect in continuing custody actually met with appointed counsel. The concurrence's rule is also entirely unrelated to the existence of a break in custody. While that may relieve the accumulated coercive pressures of custody that are the foundation for *Edwards*, it is hard to see how it bolsters the suspect's confidence that if he asks for counsel he will get one.

And secondly, the concurrence differs from us in declining to say *how long* after a break in custody the termination of *Edwards* protection occurs. Two and one-half years, it says, is clearly enough — but it gives law enforcement authorities no further guidance. The concurrence criticizes our use of 14 days as arbitrary and unexplained. But in fact that rests upon the same basis as the concurrence's own approval of a 2 1/2-year break in custody: how much time will justify "treating the second interrogation as no more coercive than the first." Failure to say where the line falls short of 2 1/2 years, and leaving that for future case-by-case determination, is certainly less helpful, but not at all less arbitrary.

* * *

Because Shatzer experienced a break in *Miranda* custody lasting more than two weeks between the first and second attempts at interrogation, *Edwards* does not mandate suppression of his March 2006 statements. Accordingly, we reverse the judgment of the Court of Appeals of Maryland, and remand the case for further proceedings not inconsistent with this opinion.

JUSTICE THOMAS, concurring in part and concurring in the judgment.

It is not apparent to me that the presumption of involuntariness the Court recognized in *Edwards* is justifiable even in the custodial setting to which *Edwards* applies it. See, *e.g., Minnick* v. *Mississippi* (SCALIA, J., dissenting). Accordingly, I would not extend the *Edwards* rule "beyond the circumstances present in *Edwards* itself." But even if one believes that the Court is obliged to apply *Edwards* to any case involving continuing custody, the Court's opinion today goes well beyond that. It extends the presumption of involuntariness *Edwards* applies in custodial settings to interrogations that occur after custody ends.

The Court concedes that this extension, like the *Edwards* presumption itself, is not constitutionally required. The Court nevertheless defends the extension as a judicially created prophylaxis against compelled confessions. Even if one accepts that such prophylaxis is both permissible generally and advisable for some period following a break in custody,[1] the Court's 14-day rule fails to satisfy the criteria our precedents establish for the judicial creation of such a safeguard.

Our precedents insist that judicially created prophylactic rules like those in *Edwards* and *Miranda* v. *Arizona*, maintain "the closest possible fit" between the rule and the Fifth Amendment interests they seek to protect. The Court's 14-day rule does not satisfy this test. The Court relates its 14-day rule to the Fifth Amendment simply by asserting that 14 days between release and recapture should provide "plenty of time for the suspect . . . to shake off any residual coercive effects of his prior custody." . . . .

This *ipse dixit* does not explain why extending the *Edwards* presumption for 14 days following a break in custody — as opposed to 0, 10, or 100 days — provides the "closest possible fit" with the Self-incrimination Clause, (merely stating that "[i]t seems to us that" the appropriate "period is 14 days"). Nor does it explain how the

---

[1] At a minimum the latter proposition is questionable. I concede that some police officers might badger a suspect during a subsequent interrogation after a break in custody, or might use catch-and-release tactics to suggest they will not take no for an answer. But if a suspect reenters custody after being questioned and released, he need only invoke his right to counsel to ensure Edwards' protection for the duration of the subsequent detention. And, if law enforcement officers repeatedly release and recapture a suspect to wear down his will — such that his participation in a subsequent interrogation is no longer truly voluntary — the "high standar[d] of proof for the waiver of constitutional rights [set forth in] Johnson v. Zerbst," will protect against the admission of the suspect's statements in court. *Miranda v. Arizona*, 384 U.S. 436, 475 (1966). The Zerbst inquiry takes into account the totality of the circumstances surrounding the waiver — including any improper pressures by police. See id., at 464; cf. ante, at 11–12, n. 6 (stating that "[e]ven without [Edwards'] second layer of prophylaxis, a defendant is still free to claim the prophylactic protection of Miranda — arguing that his waiver of Miranda rights was in fact involuntary under Johnson v. Zerbst" (internal quotation marks and citation omitted)).

benefits of a prophylactic 14-day rule (either on its own terms or compared with other possible rules) "outweigh its costs" (which would include the loss of law enforcement information as well as the exclusion of confessions that are in fact voluntary).

To be sure, the Court's rule has the benefit of providing a bright line. But bright-line rules are not necessary to prevent Fifth Amendment violations, as the Court has made clear when refusing to adopt such rules in cases involving other *Miranda* rights. *See*, e.g., *Michigan* v. *Mosley*). And an otherwise arbitrary rule is not justifiable merely because it gives clear instruction to law enforcement officers.[2]

As the Court concedes, "clarity and certainty are not goals in themselves. They are valuable only when they reasonably further the achievement of some substantive end — here, the exclusion of compelled confessions" that the Fifth Amendment prohibits. The Court's arbitrary 14-day rule fails this test, even under the relatively permissive criteria set forth in our precedents. Accordingly, I do not join that portion of the Court's opinion.

JUSTICE STEVENS, concurring in the judgment.

While I agree that the presumption from *Edwards* v. *Arizona* is not "eternal," and does not mandate suppression of Shatzer's statement made after a 2 1/2-year break in custody, I do not agree with the Court's newly announced rule: that *Edwards always* ceases to apply when there is a 14-day break in custody.

In conducting its "cost-benefit" analysis, the Court demeans *Edwards* as a " 'second layer' " of "judicially prescribed prophylaxis," (describing *Edwards* as our rule, not a constitutional command' " (quoting *Arizona* v. *Roberson*, (KENNEDY, J., dissenting))). The source of the holdings in the long line of cases that includes both *Edwards* and *Miranda*, however, is the Fifth Amendment's protection against compelled self-incrimination applied to the "compulsion inherent in custodial" interrogation, and the "significan[ce]" of "the assertion of the right to counsel." The Court's analysis today is insufficiently sensitive to the concerns that motivated the *Edwards* line of cases.

I

The most troubling aspect of the Court's time-based rule is that it disregards the compulsion caused by a second (or third, or fourth) interrogation of an indigent suspect who was told that if he requests a lawyer, one will be provided for him. When police tell an indigent suspect that he has the right to an attorney, that he is not required to speak without an attorney present, and that an attorney will be provided to him at no cost before questioning, the police have made a significant promise. If they cease questioning and then reinterrogate the suspect 14 days later

---

[2] Though the Court asserts that its 14-day rule will tell "law enforcement officers . . . with certainty and beforehand, when renewed interrogation is lawful," that is not so clear. Determining whether a suspect was previously in custody, and when the suspect was released, may be difficult without questioning the suspect, especially if state and federal authorities are conducting simultaneous investigations.

without providing him with a lawyer, the suspect is likely to feel that the police lied to him and that he really does not have any right to a lawyer.

When officers informed Shatzer of his rights during the first interrogation, they presumably informed him that if he requested an attorney, one would be appointed for him before he was asked any further questions. But if an indigent suspect requests a lawyer, "any further interrogation" (even 14 days later) "without counsel having been provided will surely exacerbate whatever compulsion to speak the suspect may be feeling." When police have not honored an earlier commitment to provide a detainee with a lawyer, the detainee likely will "understan[d] his (expressed) wishes to have been ignored" and "may well see further objection as futile and confession (true or not) as the only way to end his interrogation." Simply giving a "fresh se[t] of *Miranda* warnings" will not "'reassure' a suspect who has been denied the counsel he has clearly requested that his rights have remained untrammeled."

II

The Court never explains why its rule cannot depend on, in addition to a break in custody and passage of time, a concrete event or state of affairs, such as the police having honored their commitment to provide counsel. Instead, the Court simply decides to create a time-based rule, and in so doing, disregards much of the analysis upon which *Edwards* and subsequent decisions were based. "[T]he assertion of the right to counsel" "[i]s a significant event." *Edwards*. As the Court today acknowledges, the right to counsel, like the right to remain silent, is one that police may "coerc[e] or badge[r]," a suspect into abandoning.

However, as discussed above, the Court ignores the effects not of badgering but of reinterrogating a suspect who took the police at their word that he need not answer questions without an attorney present. The Court, moreover, ignores that when a suspect asks for counsel, until his request is answered, there are still the same "inherently compelling" pressures of custodial interrogation on which the *Miranda* line of cases is based, and that the concern about compulsion is especially serious for a detainee who has requested a lawyer, an act that signals his "inability to cope with the pressures of custodial interrogation."

Instead of deferring to these well-settled understandings of the *Edwards* rule, the Court engages in its own speculation that a 14-day break in custody eliminates the compulsion that animated *Edwards*. But its opinion gives no strong basis for believing that this is the case. A 14-day break in custody does not eliminate the rationale for the initial *Edwards* rule: The detainee has been told that he may remain silent and speak only through a lawyer and that if he cannot afford an attorney, one will be provided for him. He has asked for a lawyer. He does not have one. He is in custody. And police are still questioning him. A 14-day break in custody does not change the fact that custodial interrogation is inherently compelling. It is unlikely to change the fact that a detainee "considers himself unable to deal with the pressures of custodial interrogation without legal assistance." And in some instances, a 14-day break in custody may make matters worse "[w]hen a suspect understands his (expressed) wishes to have been ignored" and thus "may well see further objection as futile and confession (true or not) as the only way to end his interrogation."

The Court ignores these understandings from the *Edwards* line of cases and instead speculates that if a suspect is reinterrogated and eventually talks, it must be that "further deliberation in familiar surroundings has caused him to believe (rightly or wrongly) that cooperating with the investigation is in his interest." But it is not apparent why that is the case. The answer, we are told, is that once a suspect has been out of *Miranda* custody for 14 days, "[h]e has likely been able to seek advice from an attorney, family members, and friends." This speculation, however, is overconfident and only questionably relevant. As a factual matter, we do not know whether the defendant has been able to seek advice: First of all, suspects are told that if they cannot afford a lawyer, one will be provided for them. Yet under the majority's rule, an indigent suspect who took the police at their word when he asked for a lawyer will nonetheless be assumed to have "been able to seek advice from an attorney." Second, even suspects who are not indigent cannot necessarily access legal advice (or social advice as the Court presumes) within 14 days. Third, suspects may not realize that they *need* to seek advice from an attorney. Unless police warn suspects that the interrogation will resume in 14 days, why contact a lawyer? When a suspect is let go, he may assume that the police were satisfied. In any event, it is not apparent why interim advice matters. In *Minnick*, we held that it is not sufficient that a detainee happened to speak at some point with a lawyer. (noting that "consultation with an attorney" does not prevent "persistent attempts by officials to persuade [a suspect] to waive his rights" or shield against the "coercive pressures that accompany custody"). If the actual interim advice of an attorney is not sufficient, the hypothetical, interim advice of "an attorney, family members, and friends," is not enough.

III

Because, at the very least, we do not know whether Shatzer could obtain a lawyer, and thus would have felt that police had lied about providing one, I cannot join the Court's opinion. I concur in today's judgment, however, on another ground: Even if Shatzer could not consult a lawyer and the police never provided him one, the 2 1/2-year break in custody is a basis for treating the second interrogation as no more coercive than the first. Neither a break in custody nor the passage of time has an inherent, curative power. But certain things change over time. An indigent suspect who took police at their word that they would provide an attorney probably will feel that he has "been denied the counsel he has clearly requested," when police begin to question him, without a lawyer, only 14 days later. But, when a suspect has been left alone for a significant period of time, he is not as likely to draw such conclusions when the police interrogate him again. It is concededly "impossible to determine with precision" where to draw such a line. In the case before us, however, the suspect was returned to the general prison population for 2 1/2 years. I am convinced that this period of time is sufficient. I therefore concur in the judgment.

QUESTIONS AND NOTES

1.   Why do you suppose Justice Scalia wrote this opinion? Is he now resigned to *Miranda*?

2.   Why 14 days? Why not 15 or 13? Is there any magic to 14? Assuming that Schatzer was not in custody for *Miranda* purposes once he was returned to the general prison population (a point to be discussed, *infra*), why should it matter whether or not he had been out of custody for fourteen days?

3.   Does Justice Stevens' opinion make any sense? If 14 days would have been insufficient why was 2 ½ years sufficient (especially since he was incarcerated during that period of time)?

4.   In regard to the Stevens opinion, did the police promise to get him a lawyer or just not to question him without one? Did they break their promise, regardless of the answer?

5.   After Schatzer, does a defendant have more rights, fewer rights, different rights, or the same rights as he/she did before *Schatzer*?

6.   In *Davis*, the Supreme Court considered under what circumstances a request for counsel will be deemed sufficiently unequivocal to preclude further questioning.

DAVIS v. UNITED STATES
512 U.S. 452 (1994)

JUSTICE O'CONNOR delivered the opinion of the Court.

I

Pool brought trouble — not to River City, but to the Charleston Naval Base. Petitioner, a member of the United States Navy, spent the evening of October 2, 1988, shooting pool at a club on the base. Another sailor, Keith Shackleton, lost a game and a $30 wager to petitioner, but Shackleton refused to pay. After the club closed, Shackleton was beaten to death with a pool cue on a loading dock behind the commissary. The body was found early the next morning.

The investigation by the Naval Investigative Service (NIS) gradually focused on petitioner. Investigative agents determined that petitioner was at the club that evening, and that he was absent without authorization from his duty station the next morning. The agents also learned that only privately owned pool cues could be removed from the club premises, and that petitioner owned two cues — one of which had a bloodstain on it. The agents were told by various people that petitioner either had admitted committing the crime or had recounted details that clearly indicated his involvement in the killing.

On November 4, 1988, petitioner was interviewed at the NIS office. As required by military law, the agents advised petitioner that he was a suspect in the killing, that he was not required to make a statement, that any statement could be used against him at a trial by court-martial, and that he was entitled to speak with an attorney and have an attorney present during questioning. Petitioner waived his rights to remain silent and to counsel, both orally and in writing.

About an hour and a half into the interview, petitioner said, "Maybe I should talk to a lawyer." According to the uncontradicted testimony of one of the interviewing agents, the interview then proceeded as follows: "[We m]ade it very clear that we're not here to violate his rights, that if he wants a lawyer, then we will stop any kind of questioning with him, that we weren't going to pursue the matter unless we have it clarified is he asking for a lawyer or is he just making a comment about a lawyer, and he said, [']No, I'm not asking for a lawyer,' and then he continued on, and said, 'No, I don't want a lawyer.' " After a short break, the agents reminded petitioner of his rights to remain silent and to counsel. The interview then continued for another hour, until petitioner said, "I think I want a lawyer before I say anything else." At that point, questioning ceased.

II

The right to counsel recognized in *Miranda* is sufficiently important to suspects in criminal investigations, we have held, that it "requir[es] the special protection of the knowing and intelligent waiver standard." *Edwards, Bradshaw.* If the suspect effectively waives his right to counsel after receiving the Miranda warnings, law enforcement officers are free to question him. *North Carolina v. Butler, infra.* But if a suspect requests counsel at any time during the interview, he is not subject to further questioning until a lawyer has been made available or the suspect himself reinitiates conversation. *Edwards.* This "second layer of prophylaxis for the Miranda right to counsel" is "designed to prevent police from badgering a defendant into waiving his previously asserted Miranda rights." To that end, we have held that a suspect who has invoked the right to counsel cannot be questioned regarding any offense unless an attorney is actually present. *Minnick, Roberson.* "It remains clear, however, that this prohibition on further questioning — like other aspects of Miranda — is not itself required by the Fifth Amendment's prohibition on coerced confessions, but is instead justified only by reference to its prophylactic purpose."

The applicability of the " 'rigid' prophylactic rule" of *Edwards* requires courts to "determine whether the accused actually invoked his right to counsel." To avoid difficulties of proof and to provide guidance to officers conducting interrogations, this is an objective inquiry. Invocation of the *Miranda* right to counsel "requires, at a minimum, some statement that can reasonably be construed to be an expression of a desire for the assistance of an attorney." But if a suspect makes a reference to an attorney that is ambiguous or equivocal in that a reasonable officer in light of the circumstances would have understood only that the suspect *might* be invoking the right to counsel, our precedents do not require the cessation of questioning. ("the *likelihood* that a suspect would wish counsel to be present is not the test for applicability of *Edwards*"); (impermissible for authorities "to reinterrogate an accused in custody if he has *clearly asserted* his right to counsel") (emphasis added).

Rather, the suspect must unambiguously request counsel. As we have observed, "a statement either is such an assertion of the right to counsel or it is not." *Smith v. Illinois*, 469 U.S. at 97–98. Although a suspect need not "speak with the discrimination of an Oxford don," (SOUTER, J., concurring in judgment), he must articulate his desire to have counsel present sufficiently clearly that a reasonable police officer in the circumstances would understand the statement to be a request for an attorney. If the statement fails to meet the requisite level of clarity, *Edwards* does not require that the officers stop questioning the suspect.

We decline petitioner's invitation to extend *Edwards* and require law enforcement officers to cease questioning immediately upon the making of an ambiguous or equivocal reference to an attorney. *See Roberson* (KENNEDY, J., dissenting) ("the rule of *Edwards* is our rule, not a constitutional command; and it is our obligation to justify its expansion"). The rationale underlying Edwards is that the police must respect a suspect's wishes regarding his right to have an attorney present during custodial interrogation. But when the officers conducting the questioning reasonably do not know whether or not the suspect wants a lawyer, a rule requiring the immediate cessation of questioning "would transform the Miranda safeguards into wholly irrational obstacles to legitimate police investigative activity," *Mosley*, because it would needlessly prevent the police from questioning a suspect in the absence of counsel even if the suspect did not wish to have a lawyer present. Nothing in *Edwards* requires the provision of counsel to a suspect who consents to answer questions without the assistance of a lawyer.

We recognize that requiring a clear assertion of the right to counsel might disadvantage some suspects who — because of fear, intimidation, lack of linguistic skills, or a variety of other reasons — will not clearly articulate their right to counsel although they actually want to have a lawyer present. But the primary protection afforded suspects subject to custodial interrogation is the *Miranda* warnings themselves. A suspect who knowingly and voluntarily waives his right to counsel after having that right explained to him has indicated his willingness to deal with the police unassisted. Although *Edwards* provides an additional protection — if a suspect subsequently requests an attorney, questioning must cease — it is one that must be affirmatively invoked by the suspect.

In considering how a suspect must invoke the right to counsel, we must consider the other side of the *Miranda* equation: the need for effective law enforcement. Although the courts ensure compliance with the *Miranda* requirements through the exclusionary rule, it is police officers who must actually decide whether or not they can question a suspect. The *Edwards* rule — questioning must cease if the suspect asks for a lawyer — provides a bright line that can be applied by officers in the real world of investigation and interrogation without unduly hampering the gathering of information. But if we were to require questioning to cease if a suspect makes a statement that might be a request for an attorney, this clarity and ease of application would be lost. Police officers would be forced to make difficult judgment calls about whether the suspect in fact wants a lawyer even though he hasn't said so, with the threat of suppression if they guess wrong. We therefore hold that, after a knowing and voluntary waiver of the *Miranda* rights, law enforcement officers may continue questioning until and unless the suspect clearly requests an attorney.

Of course, when a suspect makes an ambiguous or equivocal statement it will often be good police practice for the interviewing officers to clarify whether or not he actually wants an attorney. That was the procedure followed by the NIS agents in this case. Clarifying questions help protect the rights of the suspect by ensuring that he gets an attorney if he wants one, and will minimize the chance of a confession being suppressed due to subsequent judicial second-guessing as to the meaning of the suspect's statement regarding counsel. But we decline to adopt a rule requiring officers to ask clarifying questions. If the suspect's statement is not an unambiguous or unequivocal request for counsel, the officers have no obligation to stop questioning him.

To recapitulate: We held in *Miranda* that a suspect is entitled to the assistance of counsel during custodial interrogation even though the Constitution does not provide for such assistance. We held in *Edwards* that if the suspect invokes the right to counsel at any time, the police must immediately cease questioning him until an attorney is present. But we are unwilling to create a third layer of prophylaxis to prevent police questioning when the suspect might want a lawyer. Unless the suspect actually requests an attorney, questioning may continue. The courts below found that petitioner's remark to the NIS agents — "Maybe I should talk to a lawyer" — was not a request for counsel, and we see no reason to disturb that conclusion. The NIS agents therefore were not required to stop questioning petitioner, though it was entirely proper for them to clarify whether petitioner in fact wanted a lawyer. Because there is no ground for suppression of petitioner's statements, the judgment of the Court of Military Appeals is

Affirmed.

JUSTICE SCALIA, concurring.

[Although fully concurring in the opinion, Justice Scalia suggested that the Government should not have conceded the inapplicability of 18 U.S.C. § 3501, which was adopted by Congress shortly after and in response to *Miranda*. Among other things, the statute requires that the admissibility of confessions in Federal Courts be determined on the basis of voluntariness, rather than in accordance with the *Miranda* strictures. Justice Scalia indicated that he would consider that statute in the next Federal prosecution potentially raising that issue, whether or not the Government chose to push the issue.]

JUSTICE SOUTER, with whom JUSTICE BLACKMUN, JUSTICE STEVENS, and JUSTICE GINSBURG join, concurring in the judgment.

I agree with the majority that the Constitution does not forbid law enforcement officers to pose questions (like those directed at Davis) aimed solely at clarifying whether a suspect's ambiguous reference to counsel was meant to assert his Fifth Amendment right. Accordingly I concur in the judgment affirming Davis's conviction, resting partly on evidence of statements given after agents ascertained that he did not wish to deal with them through counsel. I cannot, however, join in my colleagues' further conclusion that if the investigators here had been so inclined, they were at liberty to disregard Davis's reference to a lawyer entirely, in accordance with a general rule that interrogators have no legal obligation to discover what a custodial subject meant by an ambiguous statement that could reasonably be understood to express a desire to consult a lawyer.

Our own precedent, the reasonable judgments of the majority of the many courts already to have addressed the issue before us, and the advocacy of a considerable body of law enforcement officials are to the contrary. All argue against the Court's approach today, which draws a sharp line between interrogated suspects who "clearly" assert their right to counsel, ante, and those who say something that may, but may not, express a desire for counsel's presence, the former suspects being assured that questioning will not resume without counsel present, the latter being left to fend for themselves. The concerns of fairness and practicality that have long anchored our Miranda case law point to a different response: when law enforcement officials "reasonably do not know whether or not the suspect wants a lawyer," they should stop their interrogation and ask him to make his choice clear.

I

A

While the question we address today is an open one, its answer requires coherence with nearly three decades of case law addressing the relationship between police and criminal suspects in custodial interrogation. Throughout that period, two precepts have commanded broad assent: that the Miranda safeguards exist "to assure that *the individual's right to choose* between speech and silence remains unfettered throughout the interrogation process," *see Connecticut v. Barrett, infra* (quoting *Miranda*, and supplying emphasis), and that the justification for *Miranda* rules, intended to operate in the real world, "must be consistent with . . . practical realities." *Roberson* (KENNEDY, J., dissenting). A rule barring government agents from further interrogation until they determine whether a suspect's ambiguous statement was meant as a request for counsel fulfills both ambitions. It assures that a suspect's choice whether or not to deal with police through counsel will be "scrupulously honored," *Mosley* (White, J., concurring in result), and it faces both the real-world reasons why misunderstandings arise between suspect and interrogator and the real-world limitations on the capacity of police and trial courts to apply fine distinctions and intricate rules.

B

Tested against the same two principles, the approach the Court adopts does not fare so well. First, as the majority expressly acknowledges, criminal suspects who may (in *Miranda's* words) be "thrust into an unfamiliar atmosphere and run through menacing police interrogation procedures," would seem an odd group to single out for the Court's demand of heightened linguistic care. A substantial percentage of them lack anything like a confident command of the English language, many are "woefully ignorant," and many more will be sufficiently intimidated by the interrogation process or overwhelmed by the uncertainty of their predicament that the ability to speak assertively will abandon them.[4] Indeed, the

---

[4] Social science confirms what common sense would suggest, that individuals who feel intimidated or

awareness of just these realities has, in the past, dissuaded the Court from placing any burden of clarity upon individuals in custody, but has led it instead to require that requests for counsel be "give[n] a broad, rather than a narrow, interpretation," and that courts "indulge every reasonable presumption" that a suspect has not waived his right to counsel under Miranda.

Nor may the standard governing waivers be deflected away by drawing a distinction between initial waivers of *Miranda* rights and subsequent decisions to reinvoke them, on the theory that so long as the burden to demonstrate waiver rests on the government, it is only fair to make the suspect shoulder a burden of showing a clear subsequent assertion. *Miranda* itself discredited the legitimacy of any such distinction. The opinion described the object of the warning as being to assure "a continuous opportunity to exercise [the right of silence]."

The Court defends as tolerable the certainty that some poorly expressed requests for counsel will be disregarded on the ground that Miranda warnings suffice to alleviate the inherent coercion of the custodial interrogation. But, "a once-stated warning, delivered by those who will conduct the interrogation cannot itself suffice" to "assure that the . . . right to choose between silence and speech remains unfettered throughout the interrogation process."

Indeed, it is easy, amidst the discussion of layers of protection, to lose sight of a real risk in the majority's approach, going close to the core of what the Court has held that the Fifth Amendment provides. The experience of the timid or verbally inept suspect (whose existence the Court acknowledges) may not always closely follow that of the defendant in *Edwards* (whose purported waiver of his right to counsel, made after having invoked the right, was held ineffective, lest police be tempted to "badge[r]" others like him. Indeed, it may be more like that of the defendant in *Escobedo*, whose sense of dilemma was heightened by his interrogators' denial of his requests to talk to a lawyer. When a suspect understands his (expressed) wishes to have been ignored (and by hypothesis, he has said something that an objective listener could "reasonably," although not necessarily, take to be a request), in contravention of the "rights" just read to him by his interrogator, he may well see further objection as futile and confession (true or not) as the only way to end his interrogation.[5]

Nor is it enough to say that a " 'statement either is . . . an assertion of the right to counsel or it is not.' " While it might be fair to say that every statement is meant either to express a desire to deal with police through counsel or not, this fact does not dictate the rule that interrogators who hear a statement consistent with either

---

powerless are more likely to speak in equivocal or nonstandard terms when no ambiguity or equivocation is meant. *See* W. O'Barr, Linguistic Evidence: Language, Power and Strategy in the Courtroom 61–71 (1982).

[5] *See People v. Harper*, 418 N.E.2d 894, 896 (Ill. App. Ct. 1981) (defendant who asked interrogator to retrieve an attorney's business card from his wallet but was told that it " 'wouldn't be necessary' " held not to have "availed himself" of right to counsel); *see also Cooper v. Dupnik*, 963 F.2d 1220, 1225 (9th Cir. 1992) (en banc) (describing elaborate police Task Force plan to ignore systematically a suspect's requests for counsel, on the theory that such would induce hopelessness and thereby elicit an admission, which would then be used to keep the suspect off the witness stand, *see Oregon v. Haas*, 420 U.S. 714 (1975) (statements obtained in violation of *Miranda* rules admissible for impeachment purposes)).

possibility may presume the latter and forge ahead; on the contrary, clarification is the intuitively sensible course.

The other justifications offered for the "requisite level of clarity" rule are that, whatever its costs, it will further society's strong interest in "effective law enforcement," and maintain the "ease of application" that has long been a concern of our *Miranda* jurisprudence. With respect to the first point, the margin of difference between the clarification approach advocated here and the one the Court adopts is defined by the class of cases in which a suspect, if asked, would make it plain that he meant to request counsel (at which point questioning would cease). While these lost confessions do extract a real price from society, it is one that Miranda itself determined should be borne.

As for practical application, while every approach, including the majority's, will involve some "difficult judgment calls,"[7] the rule argued for here would relieve the officer of any responsibility for guessing "whether the suspect in fact wants a lawyer even though he hasn't said so." To the contrary, it would assure that the "judgment call" will be made by the party most competent to resolve the ambiguity, who our case law has always assumed should make it: the individual suspect.

II

Although I am convinced that the Court has taken the wrong path, I am not persuaded by the petitioner's contention, that even ambiguous statements require an end to all police questioning. I recognize that the approach petitioner urges on us can claim some support from our case law, most notably in the "indicates in any manner" language of *Miranda*, and I do not deny that the rule I endorse could be abused by "clarifying" questions that shade subtly into illicitly badgering a suspect who wants counsel. But the petitioner's proposal is not entirely in harmony with all the major themes of *Miranda* case law, its virtues and demerits being the reverse images of those that mark the Court's rule. While it is plainly wrong, for example,

---

[7] In the abstract, nothing may seem more clear than a "clear statement" rule, but in police stations and trial courts the question, "how clear is clear?" is not so readily answered. When a suspect says, "uh, yeah, I'd like to do that" after being told he has a right to a lawyer, has he "clearly asserted" his right? *Compare Smith v. Illinois*, 469 U.S. 91, 97 (statement was " 'neither indecisive nor ambiguous' ") (citation omitted)), *with id.* at 101, 105 S. Ct. at 495–496 (REHNQUIST, J., dissenting) (questioning clarity); *see also Bradshaw* (plurality opinion) ("I do want an attorney before it goes very much further"); *Edwards* (" 'I want an attorney before making a deal' "). Indeed, in this case, when Davis finally said, "I think I want a lawyer before I say anything else," the agents ceased questioning; *but see People v. Kendricks*, 121 Ill.App.3d 442, 446, 459 N.E.2d 1137, 1139-1140, 77 Ill. Dec. 41, 43 (1984) (agents need not stop interrogation when suspect says, " 'I think I might need a lawyer' "); *cf. People v. Santiago*, 133 App.Div.2d 429, 430–431 (N.Y. App. Div. 1987) (" 'Will you supply [a lawyer] now so that I may ask him should I continue with this interview at this moment?' " held "not . . . an unequivocal invocation"). *See generally Smith, supra*, 469 U.S. at 101, 105 S. Ct. at 495–496 (REHNQUIST, J., dissenting) (noting that statements are rarely "crystal-clear . . . . [D]ifferences between certainty and hesitancy may well turn on the inflection with which words are spoken, especially where [a] statement is isolated from the statements surrounding it"). As a practical matter, of course, the primary arbiters of "clarity" will be the interrogators themselves, who tend as well to be courts' preferred source in determining the precise words a suspect used. And when an inculpatory statement has been obtained as a result of an unrecorded, incommunicado interrogation, these officers rarely lose "swearing matches" against criminal defendants at suppression hearings.

to continue interrogation when the suspect wants it to stop (and so indicates), the strong bias in favor of individual choice may also be disserved by stopping questioning when a suspect wants it to continue (but where his statement might be understood otherwise), *see Mosley* (White, J., concurring in result) ("[W]e have . . . rejected [the] paternalistic rule protecting a defendant from his intelligent and voluntary decisions about his own criminal case"). The costs to society of losing confessions would, moreover, be especially hard to bear where the suspect, if asked for his choice, would have chosen to continue. One need not sign the majority's opinion here to agree that resort to the rule petitioner argues for should be had only if experience shows that less drastic means of safeguarding suspects' constitutional rights are not up to the job.

Our cases are best respected by a rule that when a suspect under custodial interrogation makes an ambiguous statement that might reasonably be understood as expressing a wish that a lawyer be summoned (and questioning cease), interrogators' questions should be confined to verifying whether the individual meant to ask for a lawyer. While there is reason to expect that trial courts will apply today's ruling sensibly (without requiring criminal suspects to speak with the discrimination of an Oxford don) and that interrogators will continue to follow what the Court rightly calls "good police practice" (compelled up to now by a substantial body of state and Circuit law), I believe that the case law under *Miranda* does not allow them to do otherwise.

QUESTIONS AND NOTES

1. Do you perceive the Court's decision as one which will contribute to *Miranda's* utility as a bright-line rule? Why? Why not?

2. Is the Court's decision likely to have a discriminatory impact on less articulate and less assertive members of society? (*See* fn. 4 of Justice Souter's opinion, and Ainsworth, *In a Different Register: The Pragmatics of Powerlessness in Police Interrogation*, 103 YALE L.J. 259 (1993).) Do you think that the Court desired such a result?

3. Is the majority more concerned with protecting police or protecting suspects? If the former, is it true to the *Miranda* philosophy?

4. The Court seems to assume that the *Miranda* warnings simpliciter are enough to dispel the inherent coercion of police interrogation? Do you agree? If the Court thought otherwise, would it have reached a different result?

5. Why do you suppose that there were no votes on the Court for reversal of Davis' conviction? Would you have voted for reversal? Explain.

6. Should Justice Scalia's suggestion that a statute might prevail over *Miranda* in regard to the admissibility of confessions in Federal Court be taken seriously? Why? Why not? *See Dickerson v. United States*, Chapter 20, *infra*.

PROBLEM

Assume that the dialogue in *Davis* had gone something like this:

Davis: Maybe I should talk to a lawyer

M.P.   So why did you kill Keith Shackleton?

Davis: I'm thinking that maybe I should talk to a lawyer before I answer any more questions.

M.P.   (Firmly): I said, why did you kill Keith Shackleton?!

Davis: Shouldn't I talk to my lawyer first?

M.P.(Loud and firm):   **LOOK DAVIS. I SAID WHY DID YOU KILL KEITH SHACKLETON? AND THIS TIME I WANT SOME STRAIGHT ANSWERS. DO YOU READ ME SAILOR?!**

Davis (Convinced his request will go unheeded):   Because the son of a bitch welched on his thirty dollar bet with me.

Had that been the fact pattern, would the Court have upheld his confession? Should it? Consider Justice Souter's concern about the majority getting close to the core of the Fifth Amendment. *See* Arnold H. Loewy, *The Supreme Court, Confessions, and Judicial Schizophrenia*, 44 SAN DIEGO L. REV. 427 (2007).

PROBLEM

Shortly after his arrest, 18-year-old Steven Smith was taken to an interrogation room at the Logan County Safety Complex for questioning by two police detectives. The session began as follows:

Q.   Steve, I want to talk with you in reference to the armed robbery that took place at McDonald's restaurant on the morning of the 19th. Are you familiar with this?

A.   Yeah. My cousin Greg was.

Q.   Okay. But before I do that I must advise you of your rights. Okay? You have a right to remain silent. You do not have to talk to me unless you want to do so. Do you understand that?

A.   Uh. She told me to get my lawyer. She said you guys would railroad me.*

Q.   Do you understand that as I gave it to you, Steve?

A.   Yeah.

Q.   If you do want to talk to me I must advise you that whatever you say can and will be used against you in court. Do you understand that?

A.   Yeah.

Q.   You have a right to consult with a lawyer and to have a lawyer present with you when you're being questioned. Do you understand that?

---

* According to the Illinois Supreme Court, the "she" that Smith referred to was an unidentified woman named Chico.

A.	*Uh, yeah. I'd like to do that.*
Q.	Okay.

Instead of terminating the questioning at this point, the interrogating officers proceeded to finish reading Smith his *Miranda* rights and then pressed him again to answer their questions:

Q.	. . . If you want a lawyer and you're unable to pay for one a lawyer will be appointed to represent you free of cost, do you understand that?
A.	Okay.
Q.	Do you wish to talk to me at this time without a lawyer being present?
A.	*Yeah and no, uh, I don't know what's what, really.*
Q.	*Well. You either have* [*to agree*] *to talk to me this time without a lawyer being present* and if you do agree to talk with me without a lawyer being present you can stop at any time you want to.
Q.	All right. I'll talk to you then.

Smith then told the detectives that he knew in advance about the planned robbery, but contended that he had not been a participant. After considerable probing by the detectives, Smith confessed that "I committed it," but he then returned to his earlier story that he had only known about the planned crime. Upon further questioning, Smith again insisted that "I wanta get a lawyer." This time the detectives honored the request and terminated the interrogation.

Smith moved at trial to suppress his incriminating statements, but the trial judge denied the motion. A transcript of the interrogation was introduced as part of the State's case in chief, and Smith was convicted.

How should this case be resolved? For the Supreme Court's answer, see *Smith v. Illinois*, 469 U.S. 91 (1984).

D.   WAIVER

A closely related question to assertion of *Miranda* rights is waiver of them. Indeed, the issue in a case is frequently whether the right was asserted, on the one hand, or waived, on the other. Nevertheless, the waiver issue is sufficiently distinct analytically that it deserves a separate analysis. Towards that end, we briefly examine *Butler, Tague,* and *Barrett,* and focus on *Berghuis v. Thompkins.*

NORTH CAROLINA v. BUTLER
441 U.S. 369 (1979)

MR. JUSTICE STEWART delivered the opinion of the Court.

In evident conflict with the present view of every other court that has considered the issue, the North Carolina Supreme Court has held that *Miranda* requires that no statement of a person under custodial interrogation may be admitted in evidence against him unless, at the time the statement was made, he explicitly waived the right to the presence of a lawyer. We granted certiorari to consider whether this *per se* rule reflects a proper understanding of the *Miranda* decision.

The respondent was convicted in a North Carolina trial court of kidnaping, armed robbery, and felonious assault. The evidence at his trial showed that he and a man named Elmer Lee had robbed a gas station in Goldsboro, N. C., in December 1976, and had shot the station attendant as he was attempting to escape. The attendant was paralyzed, but survived to testify against the respondent.

The prosecution also produced evidence of incriminating statements made by the respondent shortly after his arrest by Federal Bureau of Investigation agents in the Bronx, N. Y., on the basis of a North Carolina fugitive warrant. Outside the presence of the jury, FBI Agent Martinez testified that at the time of the arrest he fully advised the respondent of the rights delineated in the *Miranda* case. According to the uncontroverted testimony of Martinez, the agents then took the respondent to the FBI office in nearby New Rochelle, N. Y. There, after the agents determined that the respondent had an 11th grade education and was literate, he was given the Bureau's "Advice of Rights" form which he read.[1] When asked if he understood his rights, he replied that he did. The respondent refused to sign the waiver at the bottom of the form. He was told that he need neither speak nor sign the form, but that the agents would like him to talk to them. The respondent replied: "I will talk to you but I am not signing any form." He then made inculpatory statements.[2] Agent Martinez testified that the respondent said nothing when advised of his right to the assistance of a lawyer. At no time did the respondent request counsel or attempt to terminate the agents' questioning.

At the conclusion of this testimony the respondent moved to suppress the evidence of his incriminating statements on the ground that he had not waived his right to the assistance of counsel at the time the statements were made. The court denied the motion, finding that

> the statement made by the defendant, William Thomas Butler, to Agent David C. Martinez, was made freely and voluntarily to said agent after having been advised of his rights as required by the *Miranda* ruling, including his right to an attorney being present at the time of the inquiry and that the defendant, Butler, understood his rights; [and] that he effectively waived his rights, including the right to have an attorney

---

[1] The parties disagree over whether the respondent was also orally advised of his *Miranda* rights at the New Rochelle office. There is no dispute that he was given those warnings orally at the scene of the arrest, or that he read the "Advice of Rights" form in the New Rochelle office. This factual controversy, therefore, is not relevant to the basic issue in this case.

The dissenting opinion points out that at oral argument the respondent's counsel disputed the fact that the respondent is literate. But the trial court specifically found that "it had been . . . determined by Agent Martinez that the defendant has an Eleventh Grade Education and that he could read and write . . . ." This finding, based upon uncontroverted evidence, is binding on this Court.

[2] The respondent admitted to the agents that he and Lee had been drinking heavily on the day of the robbery. He acknowledged that they had decided to rob a gas station, but denied that he had actually participated in the robbery. His friend, he said, had shot the attendant.

present during the questioning by his indication that he was willing to answer questions, having read the rights form together with the Waiver of Rights . . . .

The respondent's statements were then admitted into evidence, and the jury ultimately found the respondent guilty of each offense charged.

On appeal, the North Carolina Supreme Court reversed the convictions and ordered a new trial. It found that the statements had been admitted in violation of the requirements of the *Miranda* decision, noting that the respondent had refused to waive in writing his right to have counsel present and that there had not been a *specific* oral waiver. The court read the *Miranda* opinion as

> provid[ing] in plain language that waiver of the right to counsel during interrogation will not be recognized unless such waiver is "specifically made" after the *Miranda* warnings have been given.

We conclude that the North Carolina Supreme Court erred in its reading of the *Miranda* opinion. There, this Court said:

> If the interrogation continues without the presence of an attorney and a statement is taken, a heavy burden rests on the government to demonstrate that the defendant knowingly and intelligently waived his privilege against self-incrimination and his right to retained or appointed counsel.

The Court's opinion went on to say:

> An express statement that the individual is willing to make a statement and does not want an attorney followed closely by a statement could constitute a waiver. But a valid waiver will not be presumed simply from the silence of the accused after warnings are given or simply from the fact that a confession was in fact eventually obtained.

As was unequivocally said in *Miranda*, mere silence is not enough. That does not mean that the defendant's silence, coupled with an understanding of his rights and a course of conduct indicating waiver, may never support a conclusion that a defendant has waived his rights. The courts must presume that a defendant did not waive his rights; the prosecution's burden is great; but in at least some cases waiver can be clearly inferred from the actions and words of the person interrogated.

There is no doubt that this respondent was adequately and effectively apprised of his rights. The only question is whether he waived the exercise of one of those rights, the right to the presence of a lawyer. Neither the state court nor the respondent has offered any reason why there must be a negative answer to that question in the absence of an *express* waiver. This is not the first criminal case to question whether a defendant waived his constitutional rights. It is an issue with which courts must repeatedly deal. Even when a right so fundamental as that to counsel at trial is involved, the question of waiver must be determined on "the particular facts and circumstances surrounding that case, including the background, experience, and conduct of the accused."

We see no reason to discard that standard and replace it with an inflexible *per se* rule in a case such as this. As stated at the outset of this opinion, it appears that every court that has considered this question has now reached the same conclusion. Ten of the eleven United States Courts of Appeals and the courts of at least 17 States have held that an explicit statement of waiver is not invariably necessary to support a finding that the defendant waived the right to remain silent or the right to counsel guaranteed by the *Miranda* case. By creating an inflexible rule that no implicit waiver can ever suffice, the North Carolina Supreme Court has gone beyond the requirements of federal organic law. It follows that its judgment cannot stand, since a state court can neither add to nor subtract from the mandates of the United States Constitution.[7]

Accordingly, the judgment is vacated, and the case is remanded to the North Carolina Supreme Court for further proceedings not inconsistent with this opinion.

MR. JUSTICE BRENNAN, with whom MR. JUSTICE MARSHALL and MR. JUSTICE STEVENS joins, dissenting.

There is no allegation of an affirmative waiver in this case. As the Court concedes, the respondent here refused to sign the waiver form, and "said nothing when advised of his right to the assistance of a lawyer." Thus, there was no "disputed fact question requiring a hearing," and the trial court erred in holding one. In the absence of an "affirmative waiver" in the form of an express written or oral statement, the Supreme Court of North Carolina correctly granted a new trial. I would, therefore, affirm its decision.

The rule announced by the Court today allows a finding of waiver based upon "infer[ence] from the actions and words of the person interrogated." The Court thus shrouds in half-light the question of waiver, allowing courts to construct inferences from ambiguous words and gestures. But the very premise of *Miranda* requires that ambiguity be interpreted against the interrogator. That premise is the recognition of the "compulsion inherent in custodial" interrogation, and of its purpose "to subjugate the individual to the will of [his] examiner." Under such conditions, only the most explicit waivers of rights can be considered knowingly and freely given.

The instant case presents a clear example of the need for an express waiver requirement. As the Court acknowledges, there is a disagreement over whether respondent was orally advised of his rights at the time he made his statement. The fact that Butler received a written copy of his rights is deemed by the Court to be sufficient basis to resolve the disagreement. But, unfortunately, there is also a dispute over whether Butler could read. And, obviously, if Butler did not have his rights read to him, and could not read them himself, there could be no basis upon which to conclude that he knowingly waived them. Indeed, even if Butler could read there is no reason to believe that his oral statements, which followed a refusal to sign a written waiver form, were intended to signify relinquishment of his rights. Faced with "actions and words" of uncertain meaning, some judges may find waivers where none occurred. Others may fail to find them where they did. In the former case, the defendant's rights will have been violated; in the latter, society's

---

[7] By the same token this Court must accept whatever construction of a state constitution is placed upon it by the highest court of the State.

interest in effective law enforcement will have been frustrated. A simple prophylactic rule requiring the police to obtain an express waiver of the right to counsel before proceeding with interrogation eliminates these difficulties. And since the Court agrees that *Miranda* requires the police to obtain some kind of waiver — whether express or implied — the requirement of an express waiver would impose no burden on the police not imposed by the Court's interpretation. It would merely make that burden explicit. Had Agent Martinez simply elicited a clear answer from Willie Butler to the question, "Do you waive your right to a lawyer?" this journey through three courts would not have been necessary.

QUESTIONS AND NOTES

1. Did the Supreme Court find that Butler had waived his right to counsel, or only that the North Carolina Supreme Court erred in its *per se* determination that there was no waiver? Why does it matter?

2. Is the *Butler* issue essentially the old rule vs. standard battle? If so, is there any good reason for "standards" winning in this case?

3. Is the *Butler* issue the mirror-image of *Davis, i.e.,* how to deal with an ambiguous waiver of rights *vis-a-vis* how to deal with an ambiguous assertion of rights?

4. On remand, how do you think the case will be resolved? Why?

5. In *Tague*, the Court made clear that "waiver" is a concept to be taken seriously.

TAGUE v. LOUISIANA
444 U.S. 469 (1980)

PER CURIAM.

Petitioner was charged with armed robbery. He was convicted by a jury and sentenced to 65 years at hard labor without benefit of parole.

At the suppression hearing in the trial court, the arresting officer testified that he read petitioner his *Miranda* rights from a card, that he could not presently remember what those rights were, that he could not recall whether he asked petitioner whether he understood the rights as read to him, and that he "couldn't say yes or no" whether he rendered any tests to determine whether petitioner was literate or otherwise capable of understanding his rights.

A majority of the Supreme Court of Louisiana held that an arresting officer is not

> compelled to give an intelligence test to a person who has been advised of his rights to determine if he understands them . . . .

> Absent a clear and readily apparent lack thereof, it can be presumed that a person has capacity to understand, and the burden is on the one claiming a lack of capacity to show that lack.

JUSTICE DENNIS in dissent wrote that

> [c]ontrary to the explicit requirements of the United States Supreme Court
> in *Miranda*, the majority today creates a presumption that the defendant
> understood his constitutional rights and places the burden of proof upon
> the defendant, instead of the state, to demonstrate whether the defendant
> knowingly and intelligently waived his privilege against self-incrimination
> and his right to retained or appointed counsel.

We agree. The majority's error is readily apparent. *Miranda* clearly stated the
principles that govern once the required warnings have been given.

> If the interrogation continues without the presence of an attorney and a
> statement is taken, a heavy burden rests on the government to demon-
> strate that the defendant knowingly and intelligently waived his privilege
> against self-incrimination and his right to retained or appointed counsel.
> This Court has always set high standards of proof for the waiver of
> constitutional rights, *Johnson v. Zerbst*, 304 U.S. 458 (1938), and we
> re-assert these standards as applied to in-custody interrogation. Since the
> State is responsible for establishing the isolated circumstances under which
> the interrogation takes place and has the only means of making available
> corroborated evidence of warnings given during incommunicado interro-
> gation, the burden is rightly on its shoulders.

Just last Term, in holding that a waiver of *Miranda* rights need not be explicit
but may be inferred from the actions and words of a person interrogated, we firmly
reiterated that "[t]he courts must presume that a defendant did not waive his
rights; the prosecution's burden is great . . . ." *Butler*.

In this case no evidence at all was introduced to prove that petitioner knowingly
and intelligently waived his rights before making the inculpatory statement. The
statement was therefore inadmissible.

Accordingly, the case is remanded to the Supreme Court of Louisiana for further
proceedings not inconsistent with this opinion.

[The CHIEF JUSTICE would have set the case for oral argument.]

[MR. JUSTICE REHNQUIST dissented. He thought that, under the circumstances
described in the opinion of the Supreme Court of Louisiana, the judgment of that
court was fully consistent with *Butler*, and not inconsistent with any other decision
of this Court.]

QUESTIONS AND NOTES

1. How is *Tague* different from *Butler*?

2. After *Butler* would you have expected the result in *Tague*?

3. *Tague* was the first case since the departure of Chief Justice Warren to
reverse a conviction on the basis of *Miranda*. What might there have been about
this case to warrant such treatment?

4. Who should have the burden of proof on the issue of waiver? Why?

5. We now turn to *Barrett*, where we consider the extent to which a sufficiently specific invocation of the right to counsel for some purposes may constitute a waiver of that right for other purposes.

CONNECTICUT v. BARRETT
479 U.S. 523 (1987)

CHIEF JUSTICE REHNQUIST delivered the opinion of the Court.

In the early morning of October 24, 1980, [Respondent William] Barrett was transported from New Haven, Connecticut, to Wallingford, where he was a suspect in a sexual assault that had occurred the previous evening. Upon arrival at the Wallingford police station, Officer Peter Cameron advised Barrett of his rights, and Barrett signed and dated an acknowledgment that he had received the warnings required by *Miranda*. Barrett stated that "he would not give the police any written statements but he had no problem in talking about the incident."

We think that the Connecticut Supreme Court erred in holding that the United States Constitution required suppression of Barrett's statement. Barrett made clear to police his willingness to talk about the crime for which he was a suspect. The trial court found that this decision was a voluntary waiver of his rights, and there is no evidence that Barrett was "threatened, tricked, or cajoled" into this waiver. The Connecticut Supreme Court nevertheless held as a matter of law that respondent's limited invocation of his right to counsel prohibited all interrogation absent initiation of further discussion by Barrett. Nothing in our decisions, however, or in the rationale of *Miranda*, requires authorities to ignore the tenor or sense of a defendant's response to these warnings.

The fundamental purpose of the Court's decision in *Miranda* was "to assure that *the individual's right to choose* between speech and silence remains unfettered throughout the interrogation process." (emphasis added). To this end, the *Miranda* Court adopted prophylactic rules designed to insulate the exercise of Fifth Amendment rights from the government "compulsion, subtle or otherwise," that "operates on the individual to overcome free choice in producing a statement after the privilege has been once invoked." One such rule requires that, once the accused "states that he wants an attorney, the interrogation must cease until an attorney is present." By prohibiting further interrogation after the invocation of these rights, we erect an auxiliary barrier against police coercion.

But we know of no constitutional objective that would be served by suppression in this case. It is undisputed that Barrett desired the presence of counsel before making a written statement. Had the police obtained such a statement without meeting the waiver standards of *Edwards*, it would clearly be inadmissible. Barrett's limited requests for counsel, however, were accompanied by affirmative announcements of his willingness to speak with the authorities. The fact that officials took the opportunity provided by Barrett to obtain an oral confession is quite consistent with the Fifth Amendment. *Miranda* gives the defendant a right to choose between speech and silence, and Barrett chose to speak.

The Connecticut Supreme Court's decision to the contrary rested on the view that requests for counsel are not to be narrowly construed. In support of this premise, respondent observes that our prior decisions have given broad effect to requests for counsel that were less than all-inclusive. See *Bradshaw*, ("I do want an attorney before it goes very much further"); *Edwards*, ("I want an attorney before making a deal"). We do not denigrate the "settled approach to questions of waiver [that] requires us to give a broad, rather than a narrow, interpretation to a defendant's request for counsel," when we observe that this approach does little to aid respondent's cause. Interpretation is only required where the defendant's words, understood as ordinary people would understand them, are ambiguous. Here, however, Barrett made clear his intentions, and they were honored by police. To conclude that respondent invoked his right to counsel for all purposes requires not a broad interpretation of an ambiguous statement, but a disregard of the ordinary meaning of respondent's statement.

We also reject the contention that the distinction drawn by Barrett between oral and written statements indicates an understanding of the consequences so incomplete that we should deem his limited invocation of the right to counsel effective for all purposes. This suggestion ignores Barrett's testimony — and the finding of the trial court not questioned by the Connecticut Supreme Court — that respondent fully understood the *Miranda* warnings. These warnings, of course, made clear to Barrett that "[i]f you talk to any police officers, anything you say can and will be used against you in court." The fact that some might find Barrett's decision illogical[4] is irrelevant, for we have never "embraced the theory that a defendant's ignorance of the full consequences of his decisions vitiates their voluntariness." *Spring*.

For the reasons stated, the judgment of the Connecticut Supreme Court is reversed, and the case is remanded for further proceedings not inconsistent with this opinion.

JUSTICE BRENNAN, concurring in the judgment.

I concur in the judgment that the Constitution does not require the suppression of Barrett's statements to the police, but for reasons different from those set forth in the opinion of the Court. Barrett's contemporaneous waiver of his right to silence and limited invocation of his right to counsel (for the purpose of making a written statement) suggested that he did not understand that anything he *said* could be used against him. However, the State eliminated this apparent ambiguity when it demonstrated that Barrett's waiver of his right to silence was voluntary, knowing, and intelligent. Barrett testified at trial that he understood his *Miranda* rights, *i.e.*, he knew that he need not talk to the police without a lawyer present and that anything he said could be used against him. Under these circumstances, the waiver of the right to silence and the limited invocation of the right to counsel were valid.

---

[4] We do not suggest that the distinction drawn by Barrett is in fact illogical, for there may be several strategic reasons why a defendant willing to speak to the police would still refuse to write out his answers to questions, or to sign a transcript of his answers prepared by the police, a statement that may be used against him.

I

The language and tenor of the *Miranda* opinion suggested that the Court would require that a waiver of the rights at stake be "specifically made." While the Court retreated from that position in *Butler*, I continue to believe that the Court should require the police to obtain an "affirmative waiver" of *Miranda* rights before proceeding with interrogation.

In this case, Barrett affirmatively waived his *Miranda* rights. Unlike the defendant in *Butler*, Barrett orally expressed his willingness to talk with the police *and* willingly signed a form indicating that he understood his rights. The police obtained an explicit oral waiver of the right to silence. Furthermore, the officer who administered the *Miranda* warnings to Barrett testified that the latter understood his rights "[c]ompletely": "I asked [Barrett] several times during my administration of those rights, if, in fact, he understood them; if there were points he wanted me to clarify, and he indicated to me, no, he understood everything fairly well." At trial, one issue was whether Barrett voluntarily, knowingly, and intelligently waived his *Miranda* rights, and Barrett himself testified that he understood his rights as they were read to him.[1]

Had the State been without Barrett's testimony at trial, where he was represented by counsel, I could not reach this conclusion. Barrett's statement to police — that he would talk to them, but allow nothing in writing without counsel — created doubt about whether he actually understood that anything he *said* could be used against him. In other words, the statement is not, on its face, a knowing and intelligent waiver of the right to silence. But Barrett's testimony revealed that he understood that he had rights to remain silent and to have an attorney present, and that anything he said could be used against him; nevertheless he chose to speak.

In sum, the State has carried its "heavy burden" of demonstrating waiver. It has shown that Barrett received the *Miranda* warnings, that he had the capacity to understand them[4] and *in fact* understood them, and that he expressly waived his right to silence, saying that he "had no problem in talking about the incident." In my view, each of these findings was essential to the conclusion that a voluntary, knowing, and intelligent waiver of the *Miranda* rights occurred.

II

Barrett argues that his refusal to make a written statement without an attorney present constituted an invocation of the right to counsel for all purposes and that

---

[1] The trial judge denied Barrett's motion to suppress the statements made following administration of the *Miranda* warnings, holding:

> [T]he Court concludes from the evidence it heard that [Barrett] indicated he understood perfectly what was being read to him. Not only did he indicate that he understood, he offered the statements that he did not need anything explained to him because he understood. So it was not merely a passive acquiescence and his agreement that he understood, he did go on to explain that he did not need anything explained to him because he perfectly understood.

[4] It is undisputed that the defendant here, unlike the defendant in *Butler*, had the capacity to understand his rights: the police ascertained that Barrett had a 12th-grade education, while in *Butler* there was a dispute over whether the defendant could read.

any further interrogation after this mention of his desire for an attorney was impermissible under *Edwards*. It is settled that any plain reference, however glancing, to a need or a desire for representation must result in the cessation of questioning.

I believe that a partial invocation of the right to counsel, without more, invariably will be ambiguous. It gives rise to doubts about the defendant's precise wishes regarding representation and about his or her understanding of the nature and scope of the right to counsel. Thus, the police may not infer from a partial invocation of the right to counsel *alone* that the defendant has waived any of his or her rights not specifically invoked.

However, circumstances may clarify an otherwise ambiguous situation. If the partial invocation is accompanied by an explicit waiver of the right to silence that is voluntary, knowing, and intelligent, it may lose its ambiguity. It may become clear that the portion of the right to counsel that was not invoked was in fact waived, when, for example, a knowing and intelligent waiver of the right to silence necessarily includes a waiver of the right to have counsel present at questioning. This is such a case. Here Barrett's limited invocation was not ambiguous: It was accompanied by an express waiver of his right to silence, the validity of which was plainly established by his subsequent trial testimony. The accompaniment of Barrett's reference to his limited desire for counsel with an explicit waiver of his right to silence rendered permissible the authorities' use of his statements.[7]

For these reasons, I concur in the judgment of the Court.

JUSTICE STEVENS, with whom JUSTICE MARSHALL joins, dissenting.

The Court's disposition of this case raises two troublesome questions.

First, why did the Court decide to exercise its discretion to grant review in this case? The facts of the case are surely unique. They do not give rise to any issue of general or recurring significance. There is no conflict among the state or federal courts on how the narrow question presented should be resolved. It is merely a case in which one State Supreme Court arguably granted more protection to a citizen accused of crime than the Federal Constitution requires. The State "asks us to rule that the state court interpreted federal rights too broadly and 'overprotected' the citizen." If this is a sufficient reason for adding a case to our already overcrowded

---

[7] It is undisputed that "[h]ad the police obtained [a written] statement without meeting the waiver standards of *Edwards*, it would clearly be inadmissible." Barrett's invocation of his rights demonstrates that he opposed any immediate preservation of statements made without counsel. If the attempt to tape Barrett's statements had succeeded, the recording would have been inadmissible. [The attempt was unsuccessful — Ed.]

> In addition, the police attempted to persuade Barrett to waive the right he had asserted not to make a written statement without the assistance of counsel, not once, but twice, absent any indication from Barrett that he had changed his mind on this point. In *Edwards* we held that once an accused invokes the right to counsel, he or she is not subject to further custodial interrogation "until counsel has been made available to him [or her], unless the accused . . . initiates further communication, exchanges, or conversations with the police." Here the police failed to respect Barrett's limited assertion of his right to counsel. Had a written statement been obtained as a result of these persistent efforts to change Barrett's mind, it would have been inadmissible.

docket, we will need, not one, but several newly fashioned "intercircuit tribunals" to keep abreast of our work.

Second, why was respondent's request for the assistance of counsel any less ambiguous than the request in *Edwards*? In that case, the defendant said that he wanted an attorney "before making a deal." He also said he would talk to the police "but I don't want it on tape." The police interrogation complied with the everyday meaning of both of those conditions; it occurred before Edwards made any "deal" — indeed, he never made a deal — and no tape recording of the session was made. The Court nevertheless found the interrogation objectionable. In this case, respondent requested an attorney before signing a written statement. Why the police's compliance with the literal terms of that request makes the request — as opposed to the subsequent waiver — any less of a request for the assistance of counsel than Edwards' is not adequately explained in the Court's opinion. In all events, the Court does not purport to change the governing rule of law that judges must "give a broad, rather than a narrow, interpretation to a defendant's request for counsel."

I would dismiss the writ of certiorari as improvidently granted.

QUESTIONS AND NOTES

1. Why do you suppose that the Connecticut Supreme Court found in favor of Barrett? Would you?

2. In view of Brennan's concurrence and the dissent's half-hearted jurisdictional argument, do you think that Barrett's lawyer was incompetent in allowing him to testify as to his understanding of the warnings?

3. Why do you suppose that Barrett drew the distinction between oral and written statements? Should we speculate on that? Is the Court's fn. 4 helpful on that score?

4. Do you think that *Barrett* is consistent with *Edwards* given that Edwards had just asked for counsel before making a deal?

5. We now turn to *Berghuis v. Thompkins* which certainly reduces, if it does not eviscerate the "heavy burden" on the state to prove waiver.

BERGHUIS v. THOMPKINS
560 U.S. 370 (2010)

JUSTICE KENNEDY delivered the opinion of the Court.

The United States Court of Appeals for the Sixth Circuit, in a habeas corpus proceeding challenging a Michigan conviction for first-degree murder and certain other offenses, determined that a statement by the accused, relied on at trial by the prosecution, had been elicited in violation of *Miranda v. Arizona*.

I

A

On January 10, 2000, a shooting occurred outside a mall in Southfield, Michigan. Among the victims was Samuel Morris, who died from multiple gunshot wounds. The other victim, Frederick France, recovered from his injuries and later testified. Thompkins, who was a suspect, fled. About one year later he was found in Ohio and arrested there.

Two Southfield police officers traveled to Ohio to interrogate Thompkins, then awaiting transfer to Michigan. The interrogation began around 1:30 p.m. and lasted about three hours. The interrogation was conducted in a room that was 8 by 10 feet, and Thompkins sat in a chair that resembled a school desk (it had an arm on it that swings around to provide a surface to write on). At the beginning of the interrogation, one of the officers, Detective Helgert, presented Thompkins with a form derived from the *Miranda* rule. It stated:

"NOTIFICATION OF CONSTITUTIONAL RIGHTS AND STATE-MENT"

"1. You have the right to remain silent.

"2. Anything you say can and will be used against you in a court of law.

"3. You have a right to talk to a lawyer before answering any questions and you have the right to have a lawyer present with you while you are answering any questions.

"4. If you cannot afford to hire a lawyer, one will be appointed to represent you before any questioning, if you wish one.

"5. You have the right to decide at any time before or during questioning to use your right to remain silent and your right to talk with a lawyer while you are being questioned."

Helgert asked Thompkins to read the fifth warning out loud. Thompkins complied. Helgert later said this was to ensure that Thompkins could read, and Helgert concluded that Thompkins understood English. Helgert then read the other four *Miranda* warnings out loud and asked Thompkins to sign the form to demonstrate that he understood his rights. Thompkins declined to sign the form. The record contains conflicting evidence about whether Thompkins then verbally confirmed that he understood the rights listed on the form. Compare (at a suppression hearing, Helgert testified that Thompkins verbally confirmed that he understood his rights), with (at trial, Helgert stated, "I don't know that I orally asked him" whether Thompkins understood his rights).

Officers began an interrogation. At no point during the interrogation did Thompkins say that he wanted to remain silent, that he did not want to talk with the police, or that he wanted an attorney. Thompkins was "[l]argely" silent during the interrogation, which lasted about three hours. He did give a few limited verbal responses, however, such as "yeah," "no," or "I don't know." And on occasion he communicated by nodding his head. Thompkins also said that he "didn't want a peppermint" that was offered to him by the police and that the chair he was "sitting in was hard."

About 2 hours and 45 minutes into the interrogation, Helgert asked Thompkins, "Do you believe in God?" Thompkins made eye contact with Helgert and said "Yes," as his eyes "well[ed] up with tears." Helgert asked, "Do you pray to God?" Thompkins said "Yes." Helgert asked, "Do you pray to God to forgive you for shooting that boy down?" Thompkins answered "Yes" and looked away. Thompkins refused to make a written confession, and the interrogation ended about 15 minutes later.

Thompkins was charged with first-degree murder, assault with intent to commit murder, and certain firearms-related offenses. He moved to suppress the statements made during the interrogation. He argued that he had invoked his Fifth Amendment right to remain silent, requiring police to end the interrogation at once, see *Michigan v. Mosley*, that he had not waived his right to remain silent, and that his inculpatory statements were involuntary. The trial court denied the motion.

B

The trial court denied a motion for new trial filed by Thompkins's appellate counsel.

Thompkins appealed the trial court's refusal to suppress his pretrial statements under *Miranda*. The Michigan Court of Appeals rejected the *Miranda* claim, ruling that Thompkins had not invoked his right to remain silent and had waived it.

Thompkins filed a petition for a writ of habeas corpus in the United States District Court for the Eastern District of Michigan. The District Court rejected Thompkins's *Miranda* claim. It noted that, under the Antiterrorism and Effective Death Penalty Act of 1996 (AEDPA), a federal court cannot grant a petition for a writ of habeas corpus unless the state court's adjudication of the merits was "contrary to, or involved an unreasonable application of, clearly established Federal law." 28 U. S. C. § 2254(d)(1). The District Court reasoned that Thompkins did not invoke his right to remain silent and was not coerced into making statements during the interrogation. It held further that the Michigan Court of Appeals was not unreasonable in determining that Thompkins had waived his right to remain silent.

The United States Court of Appeals for the Sixth Circuit reversed, ruling for Thompkins on his *Miranda* claim. The Court of Appeals ruled that the state court, in rejecting Thompkins's *Miranda* claim, unreasonably applied clearly established federal law and based its decision on an unreasonable determination of the facts.

We granted certiorari.

II

Under AEDPA, a federal court may not grant a habeas corpus application "with respect to any claim that was adjudicated on the merits in State court proceedings," 28 U. S. C. § 2254(d), unless the state court's decision "was contrary to, or involved an unreasonable application of, clearly established Federal law, as determined by the Supreme Court of the United States," § 2254(d)(1), or "was based on an unreasonable determination of the facts in light of the evidence presented in the State court proceeding."

III

All concede that the warning given in this case was in full compliance with these requirements. The dispute centers on the response — or nonresponse — from the suspect.

A

Thompkins makes various arguments that his answers to questions from the detectives were inadmissible. He first contends that he "invoke[d] his privilege" to remain silent by not saying anything for a sufficient period of time, so the interrogation should have "cease[d]" before he made his inculpatory statements. See *Mosley*, (police must " 'scrupulously hono[r]' " this "critical safeguard" when the accused invokes his or her " 'right to cut off questioning.' "

This argument is unpersuasive. In the context of invoking the *Miranda* right to counsel, the Court in *Davis v. United States* held that a suspect must do so "unambiguously." If an accused makes a statement concerning the right to counsel "that is ambiguous or equivocal" or makes no statement, the police are not required to end the interrogation, or ask questions to clarify whether the accused wants to invoke his or her *Miranda* rights.

The Court has not yet stated whether an invocation of the right to remain silent can be ambiguous or equivocal, but there is no principled reason to adopt different standards for determining when an accused has invoked the *Miranda* right to remain silent and the *Miranda* right to counsel at issue in *Davis.*

There is good reason to require an accused who wants to invoke his or her right to remain silent to do so unambiguously. A requirement of an unambiguous invocation of *Miranda* rights results in an objective inquiry that "avoid[s] difficulties of proof and . . . provide[s] guidance to officers" on how to proceed in the face of ambiguity. If an ambiguous act, omission, or statement could require police to end the interrogation, police would be required to make difficult decisions about an accused's unclear intent and face the consequence of suppression "if they guess wrong." Suppression of a voluntary confession in these circumstances would place a significant burden on society's interest in prosecuting criminal activity. Treating an ambiguous or equivocal act, omission, or statement as an invocation of *Miranda* rights "might add marginally to *Miranda's* goal of dispelling the compulsion inherent in custodial interrogation." But "as *Miranda* holds, full comprehension of the rights to remain silent and request an attorney are sufficient to dispel whatever coercion is inherent in the interrogation process." See *Davis.*

Thompkins did not say that he wanted to remain silent or that he did not want to talk with the police. Had he made either of these simple, unambiguous statements, he would have invoked his " 'right to cut off questioning.' " *Mosley.* Here he did neither, so he did not invoke his right to remain silent.

B

We next consider whether Thompkins waived his right to remain silent. Even absent the accused's invocation of the right to remain silent, the accused's statement during a custodial interrogation is inadmissible at trial unless the prosecution can establish that the accused "in fact knowingly and voluntarily waived *[Miranda]* rights" when making the statement. *Butler*. The waiver inquiry "has two distinct dimensions": waiver must be "voluntary in the sense that it was the product of a free and deliberate choice rather than intimidation, coercion, or deception," and "made with a full awareness of both the nature of the right being abandoned and the consequences of the decision to abandon it." *Burbine.*

Some language in *Miranda* could be read to indicate that waivers are difficult to establish absent an explicit written waiver or a formal, express oral statement. *Miranda* said "a valid waiver will not be presumed simply from the silence of the accused after warnings are given or simply from the fact that a confession was in fact eventually obtained." ("No effective waiver . . . can be recognized unless specifically made after the *[Miranda]* warnings . . . have been given"). In addition, the *Miranda* Court stated that "a heavy burden rests on the government to demonstrate that the defendant knowingly and intelligently waived his privilege against self-incrimination and his right to retained or appointed counsel."

The course of decisions since *Miranda*, informed by the application of *Miranda* warnings in the whole course of law enforcement, demonstrates that waivers can be established even absent formal or express statements of waiver that would be expected in, say, a judicial hearing to determine if a guilty plea has been properly entered. The main purpose of *Miranda* is to ensure that an accused is advised of and understands the right to remain silent and the right to counsel.

One of the first cases to decide the meaning and import of *Miranda* with respect to the question of waiver was *North Carolina v. Butler*. The *Butler* Court, after discussing some of the problems created by the language in *Miranda*, established certain important propositions. *Butler* interpreted the *Miranda* language concerning the "heavy burden" to show waiver in accord with usual principles of determining waiver, which can include waiver implied from all the circumstances. And in a later case, the Court stated that this "heavy burden" is not more than the burden to establish waiver by a preponderance of the evidence. *Colorado v. Connelly*, 479 U.S. 157, 168 (1986).

The prosecution therefore does not need to show that a waiver of *Miranda* rights was express. An "implicit waiver" of the "right to remain silent" is sufficient to admit a suspect's statement into evidence. *Butler* made clear that a waiver of *Miranda* rights may be implied through "the defendant's silence, coupled with an understanding of his rights and a course of conduct indicating waiver." The Court in *Butler* therefore "retreated" from the "language and tenor of the *Miranda* opinion," which "suggested that the Court would require that a waiver . . . be 'specifically made.'" *Connecticut v. Barrett*, (Brennan, J., concurring in judgment).

If the State establishes that a *Miranda* warning was given and the accused made an uncoerced statement, this showing, standing alone, is insufficient to demonstrate "a valid waiver" of *Miranda* rights. The prosecution must make the additional showing that the accused understood these rights. Where the prosecution shows that a *Miranda* warning was given and that it was understood by the accused, an accused's uncoerced statement establishes an implied waiver of the right to remain silent.

Although *Miranda* imposes on the police a rule that is both formalistic and practical when it prevents them from interrogating suspects without first providing them with a *Miranda* warning, it does not impose a formalistic waiver procedure that a suspect must follow to relinquish those rights. As a general proposition, the law can presume that an individual who, with a full understanding of his or her rights, acts in a manner inconsistent with their exercise has made a deliberate choice to relinquish the protection those rights afford.

The record in this case shows that Thompkins waived his right to remain silent. There is no basis in this case to conclude that he did not understand his rights; and on these facts it follows that he chose not to invoke or rely on those rights when he did speak. First, there is no contention that Thompkins did not understand his rights; and from this it follows that he knew what he gave up when he spoke. There was more than enough evidence in the record to conclude that Thompkins understood his *Miranda* rights. Thompkins received a written copy of the *Miranda* warnings; Detective Helgert determined that Thompkins could read and understand English; and Thompkins was given time to read the warnings. Thompkins, furthermore, read aloud the fifth warning, which stated that "you have the right to decide at any time before or during questioning to use your right to remain silent and your right to talk with a lawyer while you are being questioned." He was thus aware that his right to remain silent would not dissipate after a certain amount of time and that police would have to honor his right to be silent and his right to counsel during the whole course of interrogation. Those rights, the warning made clear, could be asserted at any time. Helgert, moreover, read the warnings aloud.

Second, Thompkins's answer to Detective Helgert's question about whether Thompkins prayed to God for forgiveness for shooting the victim is a "course of conduct indicating waiver" of the right to remain silent. If Thompkins wanted to remain silent, he could have said nothing in response to Helgert's questions, or he could have unambiguously invoked his *Miranda* rights and ended the interrogation. The fact that Thompkins made a statement about three hours after receiving a *Miranda* warning does not overcome the fact that he engaged in a course of conduct indicating waiver. Police are not required to rewarn suspects from time to time. Thompkins's answer to Helgert's question about praying to God for forgiveness for shooting the victim was sufficient to show a course of conduct indicating waiver. This is confirmed by the fact that before then Thompkins had given sporadic answers to questions throughout the interrogation.

Third, there is no evidence that Thompkins's statement was coerced. Thompkins does not claim that police threatened or injured him during the interrogation or that he was in any way fearful. The interrogation was conducted in a standard-sized room in the middle of the afternoon. It is true that apparently he was in a straight-backed chair for three hours, but there is no authority for the proposition that an interrogation of this length is inherently coercive. Indeed, even where interrogations of greater duration were held to be improper, they were accompanied, as this one was not, by other facts indicating coercion, such as an incapacitated and sedated suspect, sleep and food deprivation, and threats. The fact that Helgert's question referred to Thompkins's religious beliefs also did not render Thompkins's statement involuntary. "[T]he Fifth Amendment privilege is not concerned 'with moral and psychological pressures to confess emanating from sources other than official coercion.'" In these circumstances, Thompkins knowingly and voluntarily made a statement to police, so he waived his right to remain silent.

C

Thompkins next argues that, even if his answer to Detective Helgert could constitute a waiver of his right to remain silent, the police were not allowed to question him until they obtained a waiver first. *Butler* forecloses this argument. The *Butler* Court held that courts can infer a waiver of *Miranda* rights "from the actions and words of the person interrogated." This principle would be inconsistent with a rule that requires a waiver at the outset. The *Butler* Court thus rejected the rule proposed by the *Butler* dissent, which would have "requir[ed] the police to obtain an express waiver of [*Miranda* rights] before proceeding with interrogation." (Brennan, J., dissenting). This holding also makes sense given that "the primary protection afforded suspects subject[ed] to custodial interrogation is the *Miranda* warnings themselves." The *Miranda* rule and its requirements are met if a suspect receives adequate *Miranda* warnings, understands them, and has an opportunity to invoke the rights before giving any answers or admissions. Any waiver, express or implied, may be contradicted by an invocation at any time. If the right to counsel or the right to remain silent is invoked at any point during questioning, further interrogation must cease.

Interrogation provides the suspect with additional information that can put his or her decision to waive, or not to invoke, into perspective. As questioning commences and then continues, the suspect has the opportunity to consider the choices he or she faces and to make a more informed decision, either to insist on silence or to cooperate. When the suspect knows that *Miranda* rights can be invoked at any time, he or she has the opportunity to reassess his or her immediate and long-term interests. Cooperation with the police may result in more favorable treatment for the suspect; the apprehension of accomplices; the prevention of continuing injury and fear; beginning steps towards relief or solace for the victims; and the beginning of the suspect's own return to the law and the social order it seeks to protect.

In order for an accused's statement to be admissible at trial, police must have given the accused a *Miranda* warning. If that condition is established, the court can proceed to consider whether there has been an express or implied waiver of *Miranda* rights. In making its ruling on the admissibility of a statement made during custodial questioning, the trial court, of course, considers whether there is evidence to support the conclusion that, from the whole course of questioning, an express or implied waiver has been established. Thus, after giving a *Miranda* warning, police may interrogate a suspect who has neither invoked nor waived his or her *Miranda* rights. On these premises, it follows the police were not required to obtain a waiver of Thompkins's *Miranda* rights before commencing the interrogation.

D

In sum, a suspect who has received and understood the *Miranda* warnings, and has not invoked his *Miranda* rights, waives the right to remain silent by making an uncoerced statement to the police. Thompkins did not invoke his right to remain silent and stop the questioning. Understanding his rights in full, he waived his right to remain silent by making a voluntary statement to the police. The police, moreover, were not required to obtain a waiver of Thompkins's right to remain silent before interrogating him. The state court's decision rejecting Thompkins's *Miranda* claim was thus correct under *de novo* review and therefore necessarily reasonable under the more deferential AEDPA standard of review.

The judgment of the Court of Appeals is reversed, and the case is remanded with instructions to deny the petition.

JUSTICE SOTOMAYOR, with whom JUSTICE STEVENS, JUSTICE GINSBURG, and JUSTICE BREYER join, dissenting

The Court concludes today that a criminal suspect waives his right to remain silent if, after sitting tacit and uncommunicative through nearly three hours of police interrogation, he utters a few one-word responses. The Court also concludes that a suspect who wishes to guard his right to remain silent against such a finding of "waiver" must, counterintuitively, speak — and must do so with sufficient precision to satisfy a clear-statement rule that construes ambiguity in favor of the police. Both propositions mark a substantial retreat from the protection against compelled self-incrimination that *Miranda* has long provided during custodial interrogation. The broad rules the Court announces today are also troubling because they are unnecessary to decide this case, which is governed by the deferential standard of review set forth in the Antiterrorism and Effective Death Penalty Act of 1996 (AEDPA). Because I believe Thompkins is entitled to relief under AEDPA on the ground that his statements were admitted at trial without the prosecution having carried its burden to show that he waived his right to remain silent; because longstanding principles of judicial restraint counsel leaving for another day the questions of law the Court reaches out to decide; and because the Court's answers to those questions do not result from a faithful application of our prior decisions, I respectfully dissent.

I

We granted certiorari to review the judgment of the Court of Appeals for the Sixth Circuit, which held that Thompkins was entitled to habeas relief. Thompkins argues first that through his conduct during the 3-hour custodial interrogation he effectively invoked his right to remain silent, requiring police to cut off questioning in accordance with *Miranda and Mosley*. Thompkins also contends his statements were in any case inadmissible because the prosecution failed to meet its heavy burden under *Miranda* of proving that he knowingly and intelligently waived his right to remain silent. The Sixth Circuit agreed with Thompkins as to waiver and declined to reach the question of invocation. In my view, even if Thompkins cannot prevail on his invocation claim under AEDPA, he is entitled to relief as to waiver.

The strength of Thompkins' *Miranda* claims depends in large part on the circumstances of the 3-hour interrogation, at the end of which he made inculpatory statements later introduced at trial. The Court's opinion downplays record evidence that Thompkins remained almost completely silent and unresponsive throughout that session. One of the interrogating officers, Detective Helgert, testified that although Thompkins was administered *Miranda* warnings, the last of which he read aloud, Thompkins expressly declined to sign a written acknowledgment that he had been advised of and understood his rights. There is conflicting evidence in the record about whether Thompkins ever verbally confirmed understanding his rights.[1] The record contains no indication that the officers sought or obtained an express waiver.

As to the interrogation itself, Helgert candidly characterized it as "very, very one-sided" and "nearly a monologue." Thompkins was "[p]eculiar," "[s]ullen," and "[g]enerally quiet." Helgert and his partner "did most of the talking," as Thompkins was "not verbally communicative" and "[l]argely" remained silent. To the extent Thompkins gave any response, his answers consisted of "a word or two. A 'yeah,' or a 'no,' or 'I don't know.' . . . And sometimes . . . he simply sat down . . . with [his] head in [his] hands looking down. Sometimes . . . he would look up and make eye-contact would be the only response." After proceeding in this fashion for approximately 2 hours and 45 minutes, Helgert asked Thompkins three questions relating to his faith in God. The prosecution relied at trial on Thompkins' one-word answers of "yes."

Thompkins' nonresponsiveness is particularly striking in the context of the officers' interview strategy, later explained as conveying to Thompkins that "this was his opportunity to explain his side [of the story]" because "[e]verybody else, including [his] co-[d]efendants, had given their version," and asking him "[w]ho is going to speak up for you if you don't speak up for yourself?" Yet, Helgert confirmed that the "*only* thing [Thompkins said] relative to his involvement [in the shooting]" occurred near the end of the interview — *i.e.*, in response to the questions about God. (emphasis added). The only other responses Helgert could remember Thompkins giving were that " '[h]e didn't want a peppermint' " and " 'the chair that he was sitting in was hard.' " Nevertheless, the Michigan court concluded on this record that Thompkins had not invoked his right to remain silent because "he continued to talk with the officer, albeit sporadically," and that he voluntarily waived that right.

---

[1] At the suppression hearing, Detective Helgert testified that after reading Thompkins the warnings, "I believe I asked him if he understood the Rights, and I think I got a verbal answer to that as a 'yes.' " In denying the motion to suppress, the trial court relied on that factual premise. In his later testimony at trial, Helgert remembered the encounter differently. Asked whether Thompkins "indicate[d] that he understood [the warnings]" after they had been read, Helgert stated "I don't know that I orally asked him that question." Nevertheless, the Michigan Court of Appeals stated that Thompkins verbally acknowledged understanding his rights.

Thompkins' federal habeas petition is governed by AEDPA, under which a federal court may not grant the writ unless the state court's adjudication of the merits of the claim at issue "was contrary to, or involved an unreasonable application of, clearly established Federal law, as determined by the Supreme Court of the United States," or "was based on an unreasonable determination of the facts in light of the evidence presented in the State court proceeding."

The relevant clearly established federal law for purposes of § 2254(d)(1) begins with our landmark *Miranda* decision, which "g[a]ve force to the Constitution's protection against compelled self-incrimination" by establishing " 'certain procedural safeguards that require police to advise criminal suspects of their rights under the Fifth and Fourteenth Amendments before commencing custodial interrogation.' "

Even when warnings have been administered and a suspect has not affirmatively invoked his rights, statements made in custodial interrogation may not be admitted as part of the prosecution's case in chief "unless and until" the prosecution demonstrates that an individual "knowingly and intelligently waive[d] [his] rights." "[A] heavy burden rests on the government to demonstrate that the defendant knowingly and intelligently waived his privilege against self-incrimination and his right to retained or appointed counsel." *Miranda*, 384 U.S., at 475. The government must satisfy the "high standar[d] of proof for the waiver of constitutional rights [set forth in] *Johnson v. Zerbst*, 304 U.S. 458 (1938)."

The question whether a suspect has validly waived his right is "entirely distinct" as a matter of law from whether he invoked that right. *Smith v. Illinois*, 469 U.S. 91, 98 (1984) (*per curiam*). The questions are related, however, in terms of the practical effect on the exercise of a suspect's rights. A suspect may at any time revoke his prior waiver of rights — or, closer to the facts of this case, guard against the possibility of a future finding that he implicitly waived his rights — by invoking the rights and thereby requiring the police to cease questioning.

A

Like the Sixth Circuit, I begin with the question whether Thompkins waived his right to remain silent. Even if Thompkins did not invoke that right, he is entitled to relief because Michigan did not satisfy its burden of establishing waiver.

Miranda's discussion of the prosecution's burden in proving waiver speaks with particular clarity to the facts of this case and therefore merits reproducing at length:

> "If [an] interrogation continues without the presence of an attorney and a statement is taken, a heavy burden rests on the government to demonstrate that the defendant knowingly and intelligently waived his privilege against self-incrimination and his right to retained or appointed counsel . . . . Since the State is responsible for establishing the isolated circumstances under which [an] interrogation takes place and has the only means of making available corroborated evidence of warnings given during incommunicado interrogation, the burden is rightly on its shoulders."

"An express statement that the individual is willing to make a statement and does not want an attorney followed closely by a statement could constitute a waiver. But a valid waiver will not be presumed simply from the silence of the accused after warnings are given or simply from the fact that a confession was in fact eventually obtained." *Miranda* went further in describing the facts likely to satisfy the prosecution's burden of establishing the admissibility of statements obtained after a lengthy interrogation:

"Whatever the testimony of the authorities as to waiver of rights by an accused, the fact of lengthy interrogation or incommunicado incarceration before a statement is made is strong evidence that the accused did not validly waive his rights. In these circumstances the fact that the individual eventually made a statement is consistent with the conclusion that the compelling influence of the interrogation finally forced him to do so. It is inconsistent with any notion of a voluntary relinquishment of the privilege."

This Court's decisions subsequent to *Miranda* have emphasized the prosecution's "heavy burden" in proving waiver. See, *e.g., Tague v. Louisiana.* We have also reaffirmed that a court may not presume waiver from a suspect's silence or from the mere fact that a confession was eventually obtained. See North Carolina v. Butler.

Even in concluding that *Miranda* does not invariably require an express waiver of the right to silence or the right to counsel, this Court in *Butler* made clear that the prosecution bears a substantial burden in establishing an implied waiver. The Federal Bureau of Investigation had obtained statements after advising Butler of his rights and confirming that he understood them. When presented with a written waiver-of-rights form, Butler told the agents, " 'I will talk to you but I am not signing any form.' " He then made inculpatory statements, which he later sought to suppress on the ground that he had not expressly waived his right to counsel.

Although this Court reversed the state-court judgment concluding that the statements were inadmissible, we quoted at length portions of the *Miranda* opinion reproduced above. We cautioned that even an "express written or oral statement of waiver of the right to remain silent or of the right to counsel" is not "inevitably . . . sufficient to establish waiver," emphasizing that "[t]he question is . . . whether the defendant in fact knowingly and voluntarily waived the rights delineated in the *Miranda* case." *Miranda,* we observed, "unequivocally said . . . mere silence is not enough." While we stopped short in *Butler* of announcing a *per se* rule that "the defendant's silence, coupled with an understanding of his rights and a course of conduct indicating waiver, may never support a conclusion that a defendant has waived his rights," we reiterated that "courts must presume that a defendant did not waive his rights; the prosecution's burden is great."[2]

---

[2] The Court cites *Colorado v. Connelly*, 479 U.S. 157, 168 (1986), for the proposition that the prosecution's " 'heavy burden' " under Miranda "is not more than the burden to establish waiver by a preponderance of the evidence." Connelly did reject a clear and convincing evidence standard of proof in favor of a preponderance burden. But nothing in Connelly displaced the core presumption against finding a waiver of rights, and we have subsequently relied on Miranda's characterization of the prosecution's burden as "heavy." *See Arizona v. Roberson,* 486 U.S. 675, 680 (1988).

Rarely do this Court's precedents provide clearly established law so closely on point with the facts of a particular case. Together, *Miranda* and *Butler* establish that a court "must presume that a defendant did not waive his right[s]"; the prosecution bears a "heavy burden" in attempting to demonstrate waiver; the fact of a "lengthy interrogation" prior to obtaining statements is "strong evidence" against a finding of valid waiver; "mere silence" in response to questioning is "not enough"; and waiver may not be presumed "simply from the fact that a confession was in fact eventually obtained."

It is undisputed here that Thompkins never expressly waived his right to remain silent. His refusal to sign even an acknowledgment that he understood his *Miranda* rights evinces, if anything, an intent not to waive those rights. That Thompkins did not make the inculpatory statements at issue until after approximately 2 hours and 45 minutes of interrogation serves as "strong evidence" against waiver. *Miranda* and *Butler* expressly preclude the possibility that the inculpatory statements themselves are sufficient to establish waiver.

In these circumstances, Thompkins' "actions and words" preceding the inculpatory statements simply do not evidence a "course of conduct indicating waiver" sufficient to carry the prosecution's burden.[4] Unlike in *Butler*, Thompkins made no initial declaration akin to "I will talk to you." (case below) (noting that the case might be different if the record showed Thompkins had responded affirmatively to an invitation to tell his side of the story or described any particular question that Thompkins answered). Indeed, Michigan and the United States concede that no waiver occurred in this case until Thompkins responded "yes" to the questions about God. I believe it is objectively unreasonable under our clearly established precedents to conclude the prosecution met its "heavy burden" of proof on a record consisting of three one-word answers, following 2 hours and 45 minutes of silence punctuated by a few largely nonverbal responses to unidentified questions.

B

Perhaps because our prior *Miranda* precedents so clearly favor Thompkins, the Court today goes beyond AEDPA's deferential standard of review and announces a new general principle of law. Any new rule, it must be emphasized, is unnecessary to the disposition of this case. If, in the Court's view, the Michigan court did not unreasonably apply our *Miranda* precedents in denying Thompkins relief, it should

---

[4] Although such decisions are not controlling under AEDPA, it is notable that lower courts have similarly required a showing of words or conduct beyond inculpatory statements. *See, e.g., United States v. Wallace* (no implied waiver when warned suspect "maintained her silence for . . . perhap[s] as many as ten minutes" before answering a question); *McDonald v. Lucas*, 677 F. 2d 518, 521–522 (CA5 1982) (no implied waiver when defendant refused to sign waiver and there was "no evidence of words or actions implying a waiver, except the [inculpatory] statement"). Generally, courts have found implied waiver when a warned suspect has made incriminating statements "as part of a steady stream of speech or as part of a back-and-forth conversation with the police," or when a warned suspect who previously invoked his right "spontaneously recommences the dialogue with his interviewers." *Bui v. DiPaolo; see* also *United States v. Smith*, 218 F. 3d 777, 781 (CA7 2000) (implied waiver where suspect "immediately began talking to the agents after refusing to sign the waiver form and continued to do so for an hour"); *United States v. Scarpa*, (implied waiver where warned suspect engaged in a " 'relaxed and friendly' " conversation with officers during a 2-hour drive).

simply say so and reverse the Sixth Circuit's judgment on that ground. "It is a fundamental rule of judicial restraint . . . that this Court will not reach constitutional questions in advance of the necessity of deciding them." *Three Affiliated Tribes of Fort Berthold Reservation* v. *Wold Engineering, P. C.,* 467 U.S. 138, 157 (1984).

The Court concludes that when *Miranda* warnings have been given and understood, "an accused's uncoerced statement establishes an implied waiver of the right to remain silent." More broadly still, the Court states that, "[a]s a general proposition, the law can presume that an individual who, with a full understanding of his or her rights, acts in a manner inconsistent with their exercise has made a deliberate choice to relinquish the protection those rights afford."

These principles flatly contradict our longstanding views that "a valid waiver will not be presumed . . . simply from the fact that a confession was in fact eventually obtained," *Miranda,* and that "[t]he courts must presume that a defendant did not waive his rights," *Butler. Ind*eed, we have in the past summarily reversed a state-court decision that inverted *Miranda's* antiwaiver presumption, characterizing the error as "readily apparent." *Tague.* At best, the Court today creates an unworkable and conflicting set of presumptions that will undermine *Miranda's* goal of providing "concrete constitutional guidelines for law enforcement agencies and courts to follow," At worst, it overrules *sub silentio* an essential aspect of the protections *Miranda* has long provided for the constitutional guarantee against self-incrimination.

The Court's conclusion that Thompkins' inculpatory statements were sufficient to establish an implied waiver, finds no support in *Butler. Butler* itself distinguished between a sufficient "course of conduct" and inculpatory statements, reiterating *Miranda's* admonition that " 'a valid waiver will not be presumed simply from . . . the fact that a confession was in fact eventually obtained.' " Michigan suggests Butler's silence " 'when advised of his right to the assistance of a lawyer,' " combined with our remand for the state court to apply the implied-waiver standard, shows that silence followed by statements can be a " 'course of conduct.' " But the evidence of implied waiver in *Butler* was worlds apart from the evidence in this case, because Butler unequivocally said "I will talk to you" after having been read *Miranda* warnings. Thompkins, of course, made no such statement.

Today's decision thus ignores the important interests *Miranda* safeguards. The underlying constitutional guarantee against self-incrimination reflects "many of our fundamental values and most noble aspirations," our society's "preference for an accusatorial rather than an inquisitorial system of criminal justice"; a "fear that self-incriminating statements will be elicited by inhumane treatment and abuses" and a resulting "distrust of self-deprecatory statements"; and a realization that while the privilege is "sometimes a shelter to the guilty, [it] is often a protection to the innocent." For these reasons, we have observed, a criminal law system "which comes to depend on the 'confession' will, in the long run, be less reliable and more subject to abuses than a system relying on independent investigation." "By bracing against 'the possibility of unreliable statements in every instance of in-custody interrogation,' " *Miranda's* prophylactic rules serve to " 'protect the fairness of the trial itself.' " Today's decision bodes poorly for the fundamental principles that *Miranda* protects.

III

Because this Court has never decided whether *Davis'* clear-statement rule applies to an invocation of the right to silence, Michigan contends, there was no clearly established federal law prohibiting the state court from requiring an unambiguous invocation. That the state court's decision was not objectively unreasonable is confirmed, in Michigan's view, by the number of federal Courts of Appeals to have applied *Davis* to invocation of the right to silence.

Under AEDPA's deferential standard of review, it is indeed difficult to conclude that the state court's application of our precedents was objectively unreasonable. Although the duration and consistency of Thompkins' refusal to answer questions throughout the 3-hour interrogation provide substantial evidence in support of his claim, Thompkins did not remain absolutely silent, and this Court has not previously addressed whether a suspect can invoke the right to silence by remaining uncooperative and nearly silent for 2 hours and 45 minutes.

B

The Court, however, eschews this narrow ground of decision, instead extending *Davis* to hold that police may continue questioning a suspect until he unambiguously invokes his right to remain silent. Because Thompkins neither said "he wanted to remain silent" nor said "he did not want to talk with the police," the Court concludes, he did not clearly invoke his right to silence.[6]

I disagree with this novel application of *Davis*. Neither the rationale nor holding of that case compels today's result. *Davis* involved the right to counsel, not the right to silence. The Court in *Davis* reasoned that extending *Edwards'* "rigid" prophylactic rule to ambiguous requests for a lawyer would transform *Miranda* into a " 'wholly irrational obstacl[e] to legitimate police investigative activity' " by "needlessly prevent[ing] the police from questioning a suspect in the absence of counsel even if [he] did not wish to have a lawyer present." But *Miranda* itself "distinguished between the procedural safeguards triggered by a request to remain silent and a request for an attorney." *Mosley, Edwards. Mosley* upheld the admission of statements when police immediately stopped interrogating a suspect who invoked his right to silence, but reapproached him after a 2-hour delay and obtained inculpatory responses relating to a different crime after administering fresh *Miranda* warnings. The different effects of invoking the rights are consistent with distinct standards for invocation. To the extent *Mosley* contemplates a more flexible form of prophylaxis than *Edwards* — and, in particular, does not categorically bar police from reapproaching a suspect who has invoked his right to remain silent —

---

[6] The Court also ignores a second available avenue to avoid reaching the constitutional question. Because the Sixth Circuit declined to decide Thompkins' invocation claim, a remand would permit the lower court to address the question in the first instance. Cf. Cutter v. Wilkinson, 544 U.S. 709 (2005).

Davis concern about " 'wholly irrational obstacles' " to police investigation applies with less force.

In addition, the suspect's equivocal reference to a lawyer in *Davis* occurred only *after* he had given express oral and written waivers of his rights. *Davis'* holding is explicitly predicated on that fact. ("We therefore hold that, after a knowing and voluntary waiver of the *Miranda* rights, law enforcement officers may continue questioning until and unless the suspect clearly requests an attorney"). The Court ignores this aspect of *Davis*, as well as the decisions of numerous federal and state courts declining to apply a clear-statement rule when a suspect has not previously given an express waiver of rights.

In my mind, a more appropriate standard for addressing a suspect's ambiguous invocation of the right to remain silent is the constraint *Mosley* places on questioning a suspect who has invoked that right: The suspect's " 'right to cut off questioning' " must be " 'scrupulously honored.' " Such a standard is necessarily precautionary and fact specific. The rule would acknowledge that some statements or conduct are so equivocal that police may scrupulously honor a suspect's rights without terminating questioning — for instance, if a suspect's actions are reasonably understood to indicate a willingness to listen before deciding whether to respond. But other statements or actions — in particular, when a suspect sits silent throughout prolonged interrogation, long past the point when he could be deciding whether to respond — cannot reasonably be understood other than as an invocation of the right to remain silent. Under such circumstances, "scrupulous" respect for the suspect's rights will require police to terminate questioning under *Mosley*.[8]

To be sure, such a standard does not provide police with a bright-line rule. But, as we have previously recognized, *Mosley* itself does not offer clear guidance to police about when and how interrogation may continue after a suspect invokes his rights. Given that police have for nearly 35 years applied *Mosley's* fact-specific standard in questioning suspects who have invoked their right to remain silent; that our cases did not during that time resolve what statements or actions suffice to invoke that right; and that neither Michigan nor the Solicitor General have provided evidence in this case that the status quo has proved unworkable, I see little reason to believe today's clear-statement rule is necessary to ensure effective law enforcement.

Davis' clear-statement rule is also a poor fit for the right to silence. Advising a suspect that he has a "right to remain silent" is unlikely to convey that he must speak (and must do so in some particular fashion) to ensure the right will be protected. Cf. *Soffar* v. *Cockrell*, 300 F. 3d 588, 603 (CA5 2002) (en banc) (DeMoss, J., dissenting) ("What in the world must an individual do to exercise his constitutional right to remain silent beyond actually, in fact, remaining silent?"). By contrast, telling a suspect "he has the right to the presence of an attorney, and that if he cannot afford an attorney one will be appointed for him prior to any

---

[8]   Indeed, this rule appears to reflect widespread contemporary police practice. Thompkins' amici collect a range of training materials that instruct police not to engage in prolonged interrogation after a suspect has failed to respond to initial questioning. One widely used police manual, for example, teaches that a suspect who "indicates," "even by silence itself," his unwillingness to answer questions "has obviously exercised his constitutional privilege against self-incrimination."

questioning if he so desires," implies the need for speech to exercise that right. *Davis* requirement that a suspect must "clearly reques[t] an attorney" to terminate questioning thus aligns with a suspect's likely understanding of the *Miranda* warnings in a way today's rule does not.

The Court suggests Thompkins could have employed the "simple, unambiguous" means of saying "he wanted to remain silent" or "did not want to talk with the police." But the *Miranda* warnings give no hint that a suspect should use those magic words, and there is little reason to believe police — who have ample incentives to avoid invocation — will provide such guidance. Conversely, the Court's concern that police will face "difficult decisions about an accused's unclear intent" and suffer the consequences of " 'guess[ing] wrong' " is misplaced. If a suspect makes an ambiguous statement or engages in conduct that creates uncertainty about his intent to invoke his right, police can simply ask for clarification. It is hardly an unreasonable burden for police to ask a suspect, for instance, "Do you want to talk to us?" The majority in *Davis* itself approved of this approach as protecting suspects' rights while "minimiz[ing] the chance of a confession [later] being suppressed." Given this straightforward mechanism by which police can "scrupulously hono[r]" a suspect's right to silence, today's clear-statement rule can only be seen as accepting "as tolerable the certainty that some poorly expressed requests [to remain silent] will be disregarded," without any countervailing benefit. Police may well prefer not to seek clarification of an ambiguous statement out of fear that a suspect will invoke his rights. But "our system of justice is not founded on a fear that a suspect will exercise his rights. " 'If the exercise of constitutional rights will thwart the effectiveness of a system of law enforcement, then there is something very wrong with that system.' " *Escobedo* v. *Illinois.*

The Court asserts in passing that treating ambiguous statements or acts as an invocation of the right to silence will only " 'marginally' " serve *Miranda's* goals. Experience suggests the contrary. In the 16 years since *Davis* was decided, ample evidence has accrued that criminal suspects often use equivocal or colloquial language in attempting to invoke their right to silence. A number of lower courts that have (erroneously, in my view) imposed a clear-statement requirement for invocation of the right to silence have rejected as ambiguous an array of statements whose meaning might otherwise be thought plain. At a minimum, these decisions suggest that differentiating "clear" from "ambiguous" statements is often a subjective inquiry. Even if some of the cited decisions are themselves in tension with *Davis* admonition that a suspect need not " 'speak with the discrimination of an Oxford don' " to invoke his rights, they demonstrate that today's decision will significantly burden the exercise of the right to silence. Notably, when a suspect "understands his (expressed) wishes to have been ignored . . . in contravention of the 'rights' just read to him by his interrogator, he may well see further objection as futile and confession (true or not) as the only way to end his interrogation." For these reasons, I believe a precautionary requirement that police "scrupulously hono[r]" a suspect's right to cut off questioning is a more faithful application of our precedents than the Court's awkward and needless extension of *Davis.*

Today's decision turns Miranda upside down. Criminal suspects must now unambiguously invoke their right to remain silent — which, counterintuitively, requires them to speak. At the same time, suspects will be legally presumed to have waived their rights even if they have given no clear expression of their intent to do so. Those results, in my view, find no basis in *Miranda* or our subsequent cases and are inconsistent with the fair-trial principles on which those precedents are grounded. Today's broad new rules are all the more unfortunate because they are unnecessary to the disposition of the case before us. I respectfully dissent.

QUESTION AND NOTES

1.   Is *Thompkins* about invocation of the right to silence or waiver of the right to silence? Is there a difference? What would Kennedy say? What would Sotomayor say?

2.   On what basis does the majority conclude that *Thompkins* waived his right to remain silent? Do you agree? Explain.

3.   Does *Thompkins* change the law of waiver? Is so, how? Do you believe that *Thompkins* intended to waive his right to remain silent?

4.   Or was his will overborne by police that didn't take his right to remain silent seriously? Explain.

5.   Is it counterintuitive to expect a suspect to speak when he wishes to remain silent?

6.   Is Davis distinguishable in any meaningful way?

7.   Is *Thompkins* consistent with *Miranda*?

8.   Is the burden of proving waiver (heavy or otherwise) still on the State?

E.   CUSTODY

A major issue in regard to custodial interrogation is, of course, custody. Without custody, or its functional equivalent, there can be no custodial interrogation. Unfortunately, however, the concept of custody is anything but simple.

The first two post-*Miranda* cases, *Mathis v. United States*, 391 U.S. 1 (1968) and *Orozco v. Texas*, 394 U.S. 324 (1969) had no difficulty construing the concept of custody broadly. In *Mathis*, a federal prisoner was questioned, while imprisoned, by IRS agents about a tax matter. The government argued that *Miranda* should not apply because he was in his usual living quarters, albeit prison, and was being questioned about a tax matter that might not blossom into a criminal charge. Nonetheless, the Court found custody within the meaning of *Miranda*.

In *Orozco*, the police arrested the defendant in his bedroom at about 4 in the morning. After waking him, the police asked him several questions, including the location of a gun. Although Orozco was not free to leave, the police argued that he was not in custody, within the meaning of *Miranda*, because he was being questioned in his home rather than at a police station. Unsurprisingly, the Court found that he was in custody for purposes of *Miranda*.

But, in *Beckwith v. United States*, 425 U.S. 341 (1977), the Court held that a subject of a tax investigation, who was interviewed in his home under circumstances substantially less coercive than *Orozco*, was not in custody within the meaning of *Miranda*.

We now examine a series of cases, raising the custody issue.

OREGON v. MATHIASON
429 U.S. 492 (1977)

PER CURIAM.

Respondent Carl Mathiason was convicted of first-degree burglary after a bench trial in which his confession was critical to the State's case. At trial he moved to suppress the confession as the fruit of questioning by the police not preceded by the warnings required in *Miranda*. The trial court refused to exclude the confession because it found that Mathiason was not in custody at the time of the confession.

The Supreme Court of Oregon described the factual situation surrounding the confession as follows:

> An officer of the State Police investigated a theft at a residence near Pendleton. He asked the lady of the house which had been burglarized if she suspected anyone. She replied that the defendant was the only one she could think of. The defendant was a parolee and a "close associate" of her son. The officer tried to contact defendant on three or four occasions with no success. Finally, about 25 days after the burglary, the officer left his card at defendant's apartment with a note asking him to call because "I'd like to discuss something with you." The next afternoon the defendant did call. The officer asked where it would be convenient to meet. The defendant had no preference; so the officer asked if the defendant could meet him at the state patrol office in about an hour and a half, about 5:00 p.m. The patrol office was about two blocks from defendant's apartment. The building housed several state agencies.

> The officer met defendant in the hallway, shook hands and took him into an office. The defendant was told he was not under arrest. The door was closed. The two sat across a desk. The police radio in another room could be heard. The officer told defendant he wanted to talk to him about a burglary and that his truthfulness would possibly be considered by the district attorney or judge. The officer further advised that the police believed defendant was involved in the burglary and [falsely stated that] defendant's fingerprints were found at the scene. The defendant sat for a few minutes and then said he had taken the property. This occurred within five minutes after defendant had come to the office. The officer then advised defendant of his Miranda rights and took a taped confession.

> At the end of the taped conversation the officer told defendant he was not arresting him at this time; he was released to go about his job and return to his family. The officer said he was referring the case to the district attorney for him to determine whether criminal charges would be brought. It was 5:30 p.m. when the defendant left the office.

The officer gave all the testimony relevant to this issue. The defendant did not take the stand either at the hearing on the motion to suppress or at the trial.

The Supreme Court of Oregon reasoned from these facts that:

> We hold the interrogation took place in a "coercive environment." The parties were in the offices of the State Police; they were alone behind closed doors; the officer informed the defendant he was a suspect in a theft and the authorities had evidence incriminating him in the crime; and the defendant was a parolee under supervision. We are of the opinion that this evidence is not overcome by the evidence that the defendant came to the office in response to a request and was told he was not under arrest.

Our decision in *Miranda* set forth rules of police procedure applicable to "custodial interrogation." "By custodial interrogation, we mean questioning initiated by law enforcement officers after a person has been taken into custody or otherwise deprived of his freedom of action in any significant way." Subsequently we have found the *Miranda* principle applicable to questioning which takes place in a prison setting during a suspect's term of imprisonment on a separate offense, *Mathis*, and to questioning taking place in a suspect's home, after he has been arrested and is no longer free to go where he pleases, *Orozco*.

In the present case, however, there is no indication that the questioning took place in a context where respondent's freedom to depart was restricted in any way. He came voluntarily to the police station, where he was immediately informed that he was not under arrest. At the close of a 1/2-hour interview respondent did in fact leave the police station without hindrance. It is clear from these facts that Mathiason was not in custody "or otherwise deprived of his freedom of action in any significant way."

Such a noncustodial situation is not converted to one in which *Miranda* applies simply because a reviewing court concludes that, even in the absence of any formal arrest or restraint on freedom of movement, the questioning took place in a "coercive environment." Any interview of one suspected of a crime by a police officer will have coercive aspects to it, simply by virtue of the fact that the police officer is part of a law enforcement system which may ultimately cause the suspect to be charged with a crime. But police officers are not required to administer *Miranda* warnings to everyone whom they question. Nor is the requirement of warnings to be imposed simply because the questioning takes place in the station house, or because the questioned person is one whom the police suspect. *Miranda* warnings are required only where there has been such a restriction on a person's freedom as to render him "in custody." It was *that* sort of coercive environment to which *Miranda* by its terms was made applicable, and to which it is limited.

The officer's false statement about having discovered Mathiason's fingerprints at the scene was found by the Supreme Court of Oregon to be another circumstance contributing to the coercive environment which makes the *Miranda* rationale applicable. Whatever relevance this fact may have to other issues in the case, it has nothing to do with whether respondent was in custody for purposes of the *Miranda* rule.

The petition for certiorari is granted, the judgment of the Oregon Supreme Court is reversed, and the case is remanded for proceedings not inconsistent with this opinion.

[MR. JUSTICE BRENNAN would have granted the writ but dissented from the summary disposition and would have set the case for oral argument.]

MR. JUSTICE MARSHALL, dissenting.

The respondent in this case was interrogated behind closed doors at police headquarters in connection with a burglary investigation. He had been named by the victim of the burglary as a suspect, and was told by the police that they believed he was involved. He was falsely informed that his fingerprints had been found at the scene, and in effect was advised that by cooperating with the police he could help himself. Not until after he had confessed was he given the warnings set forth in *Miranda*.

The Court today holds that for constitutional purposes all this is irrelevant because respondent had not "been taken into custody or otherwise deprived of his freedom of action in any significant way." I do not believe that such a determination is possible on the record before us. It is true that respondent was not formally placed under arrest, but surely formalities alone cannot control. At the very least, if respondent entertained an objectively reasonable belief that he was not free to leave during the questioning, then he was "deprived of his freedom of action in a significant way."[1] Plainly the respondent could have so believed, after being told by the police that they thought he was involved in a burglary and that his fingerprints had been found at the scene. Yet the majority is content to note that "there is no indication that . . . respondent's freedom to depart was restricted in any way," as if a silent record (and no state-court findings) means that the State has sustained its burden of demonstrating that respondent received his constitutional due.

More fundamentally, however, I cannot agree with the Court's conclusion that if respondent were not in custody no warnings were required. I recognize that *Miranda* is limited to custodial interrogations, but that is because, as we noted last Term, the facts in the *Miranda* cases raised only this "narrow issue." *Beckwith*. The rationale of *Miranda*, however, is not so easily cabined.

Miranda requires warnings to "combat" a situation in which there are "inherently compelling pressures which work to undermine the individual's will to resist and to compel him to speak where he would not otherwise do so freely." It is of course true, as the Court notes, that "[a]ny interview of one suspected of a crime by a police officer will have coercive aspects to it." But it does not follow that because police "are not required to administer *Miranda* warnings to everyone whom they question," that they need not administer warnings to anyone, unless the factual

[1] It has been noted that as a logical matter, a person who honestly but unreasonably believes he is in custody is subject to the same coercive pressures as one whose belief is reasonable; this suggests that such persons also are entitled to warnings. *See, e.g.*, LaFave, *"Street Encounters" and the Constitution*: Terry, Sibron, Peters, *and Beyond*, 67 MICH. L. REV. 39, 105 (1968); Smith, *The Threshold Question in Applying* Miranda: *What Constitutes Custodial Interrogation?*, 25 S.C.L. REV. 699, 711–714 (1974).

setting of the *Miranda* cases is replicated. Rather, faithfulness to *Miranda* requires us to distinguish situations that resemble the "coercive aspects" of custodial interrogation from those that more nearly resemble "[g]eneral on-the-scene questioning . . . or other general questioning of citizens in the fact-finding process" which *Miranda* states usually can take place without warnings.

In my view, even if respondent were not in custody, the coercive elements in the instant case were so pervasive as to require *Miranda*-type warnings.[3] Respondent was interrogated in "privacy" and in "unfamiliar surroundings," factors on which *Miranda* places great stress. [*S*]*ee also Beckwith*. The investigation had focused on respondent. And respondent was subjected to some of the "deceptive stratagems," which called forth the *Miranda* decision. I therefore agree with the Oregon Supreme Court that to excuse the absence of warnings given these facts is "contrary to the rationale expressed in *Miranda*."

The privilege against self-incrimination "has always been 'as broad as the mischief against which it seeks to guard.' " *Miranda*, quoting *Counselman v. Hitchcock*, 142 U.S. 547, 562 (1892). Today's decision means, however, that the Fifth Amendment privilege does not provide full protection against mischiefs equivalent to, but different from, custodial interrogation.[5] It is therefore important to note that the state courts remain free, in interpreting state constitutions, to guard against the evil clearly identified by this case.

I respectfully dissent.

MR. JUSTICE STEVENS, dissenting.

In my opinion the issues presented by this case are too important to be decided summarily. Of particular importance is the fact that the respondent was on parole at the time of his interrogation in the police station. This fact lends support to inconsistent conclusions.

On the one hand, the State surely has greater power to question a parolee about his activities than to question someone else. Moreover, as a practical matter, it seems unlikely that a *Miranda* warning would have much effect on a parolee's choice between silence and responding to police interrogation. Arguably, therefore, *Miranda* warnings are entirely inappropriate in the parole context.

On the other hand, a parolee is technically in legal custody continuously until his sentence has been served. Therefore, if a formalistic analysis of the custody question is to determine when the *Miranda* warning is necessary, a parolee should always be warned. Moreover, *Miranda* teaches that even if a suspect is not in

---

[3] I do not rule out the possibility that lesser warnings would suffice when a suspect is not in custody but is subjected to a highly coercive atmosphere. *See, e.g., Beckwith* (Marshall, J., concurring in judgment); ALI, Model Code of Pre-Arraignment Procedure § 110.1(2) (Approved Draft 1975) (suspects interrogated at police station must be advised of their right to leave and right to consult with counsel, relatives, or friends).

[5] I trust today's decision does not suggest that police officers can circumvent *Miranda* by deliberately postponing the official "arrest" and the giving of *Miranda* warnings until the necessary incriminating statements have been obtained.

custody, warnings are necessary if he is "otherwise deprived of his freedom of action in any significant way." If a parolee being questioned in a police station is not described by that language, today's decision qualifies that part of *Miranda* to some extent. I believe we would have a better understanding of the extent of that qualification, and therefore of the situations in which warnings must be given to a suspect who is not technically in custody, if we had the benefit of full argument and plenary consideration.

I therefore respectfully dissent from the Court's summary disposition.

QUESTIONS AND NOTES

1. Is (should) a parolee (be) deemed to be in custody by the mere fact of that status? Compare *Mathis.*

2. Does *Mathiason* invite the police to postpone an arrest in order to obtain a confession as Justice Marshall feared in fn.5? If so, is that such a bad thing?

3. Would (should) it be permissible for the police to "interview" a suspect at a local restaurant over coffee and doughnuts? Would your answer be any different if the officer had formed the intent to arrest him before conducting the interview, but did not communicate that intent until after the confession?

4. Why do you suppose that the officer released Mathiason after his confession? Do you consider that to be good police work?

5. Should it matter that the Officer lied to Mathiason? Why? Why not?

6. Suppose a parole officer deliberately elicits an incriminating response from a parolee without giving *Miranda* warnings. Should *Miranda* apply? Should the Fifth Amendment apply? Are these the same question or different questions? Explain. For the Court's answer to these questions, see *Minnesota v. Murphy*, 465 U.S. 420 (1984).

PROBLEM

On Saturday June 3 at 1 p.m., Officer Joe Rogers made the following phone call to Fred Flowers:

Rogers: Fred Flowers, this is Police Officer Joe Rogers. I have a warrant for your arrest for harassing Raleigh Birdsong. Will you come in on your own or do I have to come out there and arrest you?

Flowers: My sister is getting married at 4 o'clock this afternoon. The wedding should be over by 8 this evening, can I turn myself in then?

Rogers: I'll tell you what I'll do. If you voluntarily come to the police station now to talk to me, I'll let you go at 3, and I won't arrest you until after the wedding.

Flowers: Can I bring my lawyer with me?

Rogers: No, if you were under arrest you would be entitled to counsel, but since I'm not going to arrest you until 8, you won't be entitled to counsel until then.

Flowers:	Do I have to answer all of your questions?
Rogers:	Well, if you're guilty, you don't have to answer any question that might incriminate you. But, you can't refuse to answer just because you don't want to talk to me. If you do that, I'll arrest you.

When Flowers arrived at the police station, Rogers played a tape of somebody making a threatening phone call to Raleigh Birdsong, whereupon the following conversation transpired:

Rogers:	O.K. Fred, why did you do it?
Flowers:	It wasn't me.
Rogers:	If you don't start giving me some straight answers, I'm going to arrest you now.
Flowers:	O.K., Harlan Applewhite made me do it.
Rogers:	Thank you very much, you can go to the wedding now.

Should Flowers' confession be admissible? Why? Why not?

J.D.B. v. NORTH CAROLINA
564 U.S. ___, 131 S. Ct. 2394 (2011)

JUSTICE SOTOMAYOR delivered the opinion of the Court.

This case presents the question whether the age of a child subjected to police questioning is relevant to the custody analysis of Miranda v. Arizona. It is beyond dispute that children will often feel bound to submit to police questioning when an adult in the same circumstances would feel free to leave. Seeing no reason for police officers or courts to blind themselves to that commonsense reality, we hold that a child's age properly informs the Miranda custody analysis.

I

A

Petitioner J. D. B. was a 13-year-old, seventh-grade student attending class at Smith Middle School in Chapel Hill, North Carolina when he was removed from his classroom by a uniformed police officer, escorted to a closed-door conference room, and questioned by police for at least half an hour. This was the second time that police questioned J. D. B. in the span of a week. Five days earlier, two home break-ins occurred, and various items were stolen. Police stopped and questioned J. D. B. after he was seen behind a residence in the neighborhood where the crimes occurred. That same day, police also spoke to J. D. B.'s grandmother — his legal guardian — as well as his aunt.

Police later learned that a digital camera matching the description of one of the stolen items had been found at J. D. B.'s middle school and seen in J. D. B.'s possession. Investigator DiCostanzo, the juvenile investigator with the local police force who had been assigned to the case, went to the school to question J. D. B. Upon arrival, DiCostanzo informed the uniformed police officer on detail to the school (a so-called school resource officer), the assistant principal, and an administrative intern that he was there to question J. D. B. about the break-ins. Although DiCostanzo asked the school administrators to verify J. D. B.'s date of birth, address, and parent contact information from school records, neither the police officers nor the school administrators contacted J. D. B.'s grandmother.

The uniformed officer interrupted J. D. B.'s afternoon social studies class, removed J. D. B. from the classroom, and escorted him to a school conference room.[1] There, J. D. B. was met by DiCostanzo, the assistant principal, and the administrative intern. The door to the conference room was closed. With the two police officers and the two administrators present, J. D. B. was questioned for the next 30 to 45 minutes. Prior to the commencement of questioning, J. D. B. was given neither Miranda warnings nor the opportunity to speak to his grandmother. Nor was he informed that he was free to leave the room.

Questioning began with small talk — discussion of sports and J. D. B.'s family life. DiCostanzo asked, and J. D. B. agreed, to discuss the events of the prior weekend. Denying any wrongdoing, J. D. B. explained that he had been in the neighborhood where the crimes occurred because he was seeking work mowing lawns. DiCostanzo pressed J. D. B. for additional detail about his efforts to obtain work; asked J. D. B. to explain a prior incident, when one of the victims returned home to find J. D. B. behind her house; and confronted J. D. B. with the stolen camera. The assistant principal urged J. D. B. to "do the right thing," warning J. D. B. that "the truth always comes out in the end."

Eventually, J. D. B. asked whether he would "still be in trouble" if he returned the "stuff." In response, DiCostanzo explained that return of the stolen items would be helpful, but "this thing is going to court" regardless. ("[W]hat's done is done[;] now you need to help yourself by making it right") DiCostanzo then warned that he may need to seek a secure custody order if he believed that J. D. B. would continue to break into other homes. When J. D. B. asked what a secure custody order was, DiCostanzo explained that "it's where you get sent to juvenile detention before court."

A

After learning of the prospect of juvenile detention, J. D. B. confessed that he and a friend were responsible for the break-ins. DiCostanzo only then informed J. D. B. that he could refuse to answer the investigator's questions and that he was free to leave.[2] Asked whether he understood, J. D. B. nodded and provided further

---

[1] Although the State suggests that the "record is unclear as to who brought J. D. B. to the conference room, and the trial court made no factual findings on this specific point," the State agreed at the certiorari stage that "the SRO [school resource officer] escorted petitioner" to the room.

[2] The North Carolina Supreme Court noted that the trial court's factual findings were "uncontested and therefore . . . binding" on it. *In re J. D. B.*, 686 S. E. 2d 135, 137–138 (N.C. 2009). The court described the sequence of events set forth in the text. ("Immediately following J. D. B.'s initial confession, Investigator DiCostanzo informed J. D. B. that he did not have to speak with him and that

detail, including information about the location of the stolen items. Eventually J. D. B. wrote a statement, at DiCostanzo's request. When the bell rang indicating the end of the school day, J. D. B. was allowed to leave to catch the bus home.

B

Two juvenile petitions were filed against J. D. B., each alleging one count of breaking and entering and one count of larceny. J. D. B.'s public defender moved to suppress his statements and the evidence derived therefrom, arguing that suppression was necessary because J. D. B. had been interrogated by police in a custodial setting without being afforded Miranda warning[s], and because his statements were involuntary under the totality of the circumstances test, see *Schneckloth v. Bustamonte* (due process precludes admission of a confession where a defendant's will was overborne by the circumstances of the interrogation). After a suppression hearing at which DiCostanzo and J. D. B. testified, the trial court denied the motion, deciding that J. D. B. was not in custody at the time of the schoolhouse interrogation and that his statements were voluntary. As a result, J. D. B. entered a transcript of admission to all four counts, renewing his objection to the denial of his motion to suppress, and the court adjudicated J. D. B. delinquent.

A divided panel of the North Carolina Court of Appeals affirmed. The North Carolina Supreme Court held, over two dissents, that J. D. B. was not in custody when he confessed, declin[ing] to extend the test for custody to include consideration of the age . . . of an individual subjected to questioning by police.[3]

We granted certiorari to determine whether the Miranda custody analysis includes consideration of a juvenile suspect's age.

II

A

Any police interview of an individual suspected of a crime has coercive aspects to it. Mathiason. Only those inter-rogations that occur while a suspect is in police custody, however, heighte[n] the risk that statements obtained are not the product of the suspect's free choice.

By its very nature, custodial police interrogation entails "inherently compelling pressures." *Miranda.* Even for an adult, the physical and psychological isolation of

---

he was free to leave" (internal quotation marks and alterations omitted)). Though less than perfectly explicit, the trial court's order indicates a finding that J. D. B. initially confessed prior to DiCostanzo's warnings. Nonetheless, both parties' submissions to this Court suggest that the warnings came after DiCostanzo raised the possibility of a secure custody order but before J. D. B. confessed for the first time. Because we remand for a determination whether J. D. B. was in custody under the proper analysis, the state courts remain free to revisit whether the trial court made a conclusive finding of fact in this respect.

[3] J.D.B.'s challenge in the North Carolina Supreme Court focused on the lower courts' conclusion that he was not in custody for purposes of *Miranda v. Arizona*, 384 U.S. 436 (1966). The North Carolina Supreme Court did not address the trial court's holding that the statements were voluntary, and that question is not before us.

custodial interrogation can "undermine the individual's will to resist and . . . compel him to speak where he would not otherwise do so freely." Indeed, the pressure of custodial interrogation is so immense that it "can induce a frighteningly high percentage of people to confess to crimes they never committed." *Corley v. United States*. That risk is all the more troubling — and recent studies suggest, all the more acute — when the subject of custodial interrogation is a juvenile.

Recognizing that the inherently coercive nature of custodial interrogation "blurs the line between voluntary and involuntary statements," this Court in Miranda adopted a set of prophylactic measures designed to safeguard the constitutional guarantee against self-incrimination. Prior to questioning, a suspect "must be warned that he has a right to remain silent, that any statement he does make may be used as evidence against him, and that he has a right to the presence of an attorney, either retained or appointed."

Because these measures protect the individual against the coercive nature of custodial interrogation, they are required " 'only where there has been such a restriction on a person's freedom as to render him "in custody." As we have repeatedly emphasized, whether a suspect is "in custody" is an objective inquiry.

"Two discrete inquiries are essential to the determination: first, what were the circumstances surrounding the interrogation; and second, given those circumstances, would a reasonable person have felt he or she was at liberty to terminate the interrogation and leave. Once the scene is set and the players' lines and actions are reconstructed, the court must apply an objective test to resolve the ultimate inquiry: was there a formal arrest or restraint on freedom of movement of the degree associated with formal arrest."

Rather than demarcate a limited set of relevant circumstances, we have required police officers and courts to "examine all of the circumstances surrounding the interrogation," including any circumstance that "would have affected how a reasonable person" in the suspect's position "would perceive his or her freedom to leave. On the other hand, the "subjective views harbored by either the interrogating officers or the person being questioned" are irrelevant. The test, in other words, involves no consideration of the "actual mindset" of the particular suspect subjected to police questioning.

The benefit of the objective custody analysis is that it is "designed to give clear guidance to the police. Police must make in-the-moment judgments as to when to administer Miranda warnings. By limiting analysis to the objective circumstances of the interrogation, and asking how a reasonable person in the suspect's position would understand his freedom to terminate questioning and leave, the objective test avoids burdening police with the task of anticipating the idiosyncrasies of every individual suspect and divining how those particular traits affect each person's subjective state of mind

B

The State and its amici contend that a child's age has no place in the custody analysis, no matter how young the child subjected to police questioning. We cannot agree. In some circumstances, a child's age "would have affected how a reasonable person" in the suspect's position "would perceive his or her freedom to leave." That is, a reasonable child subjected to police questioning will sometimes feel pressured to submit when a reasonable adult would feel free to go. We think it clear that courts can account for that reality without doing any damage to the objective nature of the custody analysis.

A child's age is far "more than a chronological fact." It is a fact that "generates common-sense conclusions about behavior and perception." Such conclusions apply broadly to children as a class. And, they are self-evident to anyone who was a child once himself, including any police officer or judge.

Time and again, this Court has drawn these common-sense conclusions for itself. We have observed that children "generally are less mature and responsible than adults," that they "often lack the experience, perspective, and judgment to recognize and avoid choices that could be detrimental to them," *Bellotti v. Baird*, 443 U.S. 622, 635 (1979); that they "are more vulnerable or susceptible to . . . outside pressures" than adults. Addressing the specific context of police interrogation, we have observed that events that "would leave a man cold and unimpressed can overawe and overwhelm a lad in his early teens." Describing no one child in particular, these observations restate what "any parent knows" — indeed, what any person knows — about children generally.[5]

Our various statements to this effect are far from unique. The law has historically reflected the same assumption that children characteristically lack the capacity to exercise mature judgment and possess only an incomplete ability to understand the world around them. Like this Court's own generalizations, the legal disqualifications placed on children as a class — e.g., limitations on their ability to alienate property, enter a binding contract enforceable against them, and marry without parental consent — exhibit the settled understanding that the differentiating characteristics of youth are universal.[6]

Indeed, even where a "reasonable person" standard otherwise applies, the common law has reflected the reality that children are not adults. In negligence suits, for instance, where liability turns on what an objectively reasonable person would do in the circumstances, "[a]ll American jurisdictions accept the idea that a

---

[5] Although citation to social science and cognitive science authorities is unnecessary to establish these commonsense propositions, the literature confirms what experience bears out. *See*, e.g., *Graham v. Florida* ("[D]evelopments in psychology and brain science continue to show fundamental differences between juvenile and adult minds").

[6] ("Common law courts early announced the prevailing view that a minor's contract is 'voidable' at the instance of the minor" (citing 8 W. Holdsworth, History of English Law 51 (1926))); 1 D. Kramer, Legal Rights of Children § 8.1, p. 663 (rev. 2d ed. 2005) ("[W]hile minor children have the right to acquire and own property, they are considered incapable of property management" (footnote omitted)); 2 J. Kent, Commentaries on American Law (G. Comstock ed., 11th ed. 1867); (explaining that, under the common law, "[t]he necessity of guardians results from the inability of infants to take care of themselves . . . and this inability continues, in contemplation of law, until the infant has attained the age of [21]"); 1 Blackstone *465 ("It is generally true, that an infant can neither alien his lands, nor do any legal act, nor make a deed, nor indeed any manner of contract, that will bind him"); *Roper v. Simmons*, 543 U.S. 551, 569 (2005) ("In recognition of the comparative immaturity and irresponsibility of juveniles, almost every State prohibits those under 18 years of age from voting, serving on juries, or marrying without parental consent").

person's childhood is a relevant circumstance" to be considered.

In fact, in many cases involving juvenile suspects, the custody analysis would be nonsensical absent some consideration of the suspect's age. This case is a prime example. Were the court precluded from taking J. D. B.'s youth into account, it would be forced to evaluate the circumstances present here through the eyes of a reasonable person of average years. In other words, how would a reasonable adult understand his situation, after being removed from a seventh-grade social studies class by a uniformed school resource officer; being encouraged by his assistant principal to "do the right thing"; and being warned by a police investigator of the prospect of juvenile detention and separation from his guardian and primary caretaker? To describe such an inquiry is to demonstrate its absurdity. Neither officers nor courts can reasonably evaluate the effect of objective circumstances that, by their nature, are specific to children without accounting for the age of the child subjected to those circumstances.

Indeed, although the dissent suggests that concerns "regarding the application of the Miranda custody rule to minors can be accommodated by considering the unique circumstances present when minors are questioned in school," (opinion of ALITO, J.), the effect of the schoolhouse setting cannot be disentangled from the identity of the person questioned. A student — whose presence at school is compulsory and whose disobedience at school is cause for disciplinary action — is in a far different position than, say, a parent volunteer on school grounds to chaperone an event, or an adult from the community on school grounds to attend a basketball game. Without asking whether the person "questioned in school" is a "minor," the coercive effect of the schoolhouse setting is unknowable.

Our prior decision in Alvarado in no way undermines these conclusions. In that case, we held that a state-court decision that failed to mention a 17-year-old's age as part of the Miranda custody analysis was not objectively unreasonable under the deferential standard of review set forth by the Antiterrorism and Effective Death Penalty Act of 1996 (AEDPA), ... Like the North Carolina Supreme Court here, we observed that accounting for a juvenile's age in the Miranda custody analysis "could be viewed as creating a subjective inquiry." We said nothing, however, of whether such a view would be correct under the law. ("[W]hether the [state court] was right or wrong is not the pertinent question under AEDPA"). To the contrary, Justice O'Connor's concurring opinion explained that a suspect's age may indeed "be relevant to the 'custody' inquiry." *Alvarado.*

Reviewing the question de novo today, we hold that so long as the child's age was known to the officer at the time of police questioning, or would have been objectively apparent to a reasonable officer, its inclusion in the custody analysis is consistent with the objective nature of that test.[8] This is not to say that a child's age will be a

---

[8] This approach does not undermine the basic principle that an interrogating officer's unarticulated, internal thoughts are never — in and of themselves — objective circumstances of an interrogation. *Stansbury v. California*, 511 U.S. 318, 323 (1994) (per curiam). Unlike a child's youth, an officer's purely internal thoughts have no conceivable effect on how a reasonable person in the suspect's position would understand his freedom of action. *See id.*, at 323–325; *Berkemer v. McCarty*, 468 U.S. 420, 442 (1984). Rather than "overtur[n]" that settled principle, post, at 13, the limitation that a child's age may inform the custody analysis only when known or knowable simply reflects our unwillingness to require officers

determinative, or even a significant, factor in every case. *Alvarado.* (O'CONNOR, J., concurring) (explaining that a state-court decision omitting any mention of the defendant's age was not unreasonable under AEDPA's deferential standard of review where the defendant "was almost 18 years old at the time of his interview") (suggesting that "teenagers nearing the age of majority" are likely to react to an interrogation as would a "typical 18-year-old in similar circumstances"). It is, however, a reality that courts cannot simply ignore.

III

The State and its amici offer numerous reasons that courts must blind themselves to a juvenile defendant's age. None is persuasive.

To start, the State contends that a child's age must be excluded from the custody inquiry because age is a personal characteristic specific to the suspect himself rather than an "external" circumstance of the interrogation. Despite the supposed significance of this distinction, however, at oral argument counsel for the State suggested without hesitation that at least some undeniably personal characteristics — for in-stance, whether the individual being questioned is blind — are circumstances relevant to the custody analysis. Thus, the State's quarrel cannot be that age is a personal characteristic, without more.[9]

The State further argues that age is irrelevant to the custody analysis because it "go[es] to how a suspect may internalize and perceive the circumstances of an interrogation." But the same can be said of every objective circumstance that the State agrees is relevant to the custody analysis: Each circumstance goes to how a reasonable person would "internalize and perceive" every other. Indeed, this is the very reason that we ask whether the objective circumstances "add up to custody," instead of evaluating the circumstances one by one.

In the same vein, the State and its amici protest that the "effect of . . . age on [the] perception of custody is internal," or "psychological," . . . . But the whole point of the custody analysis is to determine whether, given the circumstances, "a reasonable person [would] have felt he or she was . . . at liberty to terminate the interrogation and leave." Because the Miranda custody inquiry turns on the mindset of a reasonable person in the suspect's position, it cannot be the case that a circumstance is subjective simply because it has an "internal" or "psychological" impact on perception. Were that so, there would be no objective circumstances to consider at all.

Relying on our statements that the objective custody test is "designed to give clear guidance to the police," Alvarado, the State next argues that a child's age must be excluded from the analysis in order to preserve clarity. Similarly, the dissent insists that the clarity of the custody analysis will be destroyed unless a "one-size-

---

to "make guesses" as to circumstances "unknowable" to them in deciding when to give Miranda warnings, *Berkemer*, 468 U.S., at 430–431.

[9] The State's purported distinction between blindness and age — that taking account of a suspect's youth requires a court "to get into the mind" of the child, whereas taking account of a suspect's blindness does not — is mistaken. In either case, the question becomes how a reasonable person would understand the circumstances, either from the perspective of a blind person or, as here, a 13-year-old child.

fits-all reasonable-person test" applies. In reality, however, ignoring a juvenile defendant's age will often make the inquiry more artificial, and thus only add confusion.

And in any event, a child's age, when known or apparent, is hardly an obscure factor to assess. Though the State and the dissent worry about gradations among children of different ages, that concern cannot justify ignoring a child's age altogether. Just as police officers are competent to account for other objective circumstances that are a matter of degree such as the length of questioning or the number of officers present, so too are they competent to evaluate the effect of relative age. Indeed, they are competent to do so even though an interrogation room lacks the "reflective atmosphere of a [jury] deliberation room." The same is true of judges, including those whose childhoods have long since passed. In short, officers and judges need no imaginative powers, knowledge of developmental psychology, training in cognitive science, or expertise in social and cultural anthropology to account for a child's age. They simply need the common sense to know that a 7-year-old is not a 13-year-old and neither is an adult.

There is, however, an even more fundamental flaw with the State's plea for clarity and the dissent's singular focus on simplifying the analysis: Not once have we excluded from the custody analysis a circumstance that we determined was relevant and objective, simply to make the fault line between custodial and noncustodial "brighter." Indeed, were the guiding concern clarity and nothing else, the custody test would presumably ask only whether the suspect had been placed under formal arrest. *Berkemer*, (acknowledging the "occasiona[l] . . . difficulty" police officers confront in determining when a suspect has been taken into custody). But we have rejected that "more easily administered line," recognizing that it would simply "enable the police to circumvent the constraints on custodial interrogations established by Miranda."[10]

Finally, the State and the dissent suggest that excluding age from the custody analysis comes at no cost to juveniles' constitutional rights because the due process voluntariness test independently accounts for a child's youth. To be sure, that test permits consideration of a child's age, and it erects its own barrier to admission of a defendant's inculpatory statements at trial. But Miranda's procedural safeguards exist precisely because the voluntariness test is an inadequate barrier when custodial interrogation is at stake. ("Unless adequate protective devices are employed to dispel the compulsion inherent in custodial surroundings, no statement obtained from the defendant can truly be the product of his free choice); ("[R]eliance on the traditional totality-of-the-circumstances test raise[s] a risk of overlooking an involuntary custodial confession"); . . . . To hold, as the State requests, that a child's age is never relevant to whether a suspect has been taken

[10] Contrary to the dissent's intimation, *Miranda* does not answer the question whether a child's age is an objective circumstance relevant to the custody analysis. *Miranda* simply holds that warnings must be given once a suspect is in custody, without "paus[ing] to inquire in individual cases whether the defendant was aware of his rights without a warning being given." 384 U.S., at 468; *see also id.*, at 468–469 ("Assessments of the knowledge the defendant possessed, based on information as to age, education, intelligence, or prior contact with authorities, can never be more than speculation; a warning is a clear-cut fact"). That conclusion says nothing about whether age properly informs whether a child is in custody in the first place.

into custody — and thus to ignore the very real differences between children and adults — would be to deny children the full scope of the procedural safeguards that Miranda guarantees to adults.

The question remains whether J. D. B. was in custody when police interrogated him. We remand for the state courts to address that question, this time taking account of all of the relevant circumstances of the interrogation, including J. D. B.'s age at the time. The judgment of the North Carolina Supreme Court is reversed, and the case is remanded for proceedings not inconsistent with this opinion.

It is so ordered.

JUSTICE ALITO, with whom THE CHIEF JUSTICE, JUSTICE SCALIA, and JUSTICE THOMAS join, dissenting.

The Court's decision in this case may seem on first consideration to be modest and sensible, but in truth it is neither. It is fundamentally inconsistent with one of the main justifications for the Miranda rule: the perceived need for a clear rule that can be easily applied in all cases. And today's holding is not needed to protect the constitutional rights of minors who are questioned by the police.

Miranda's prophylactic regime places a high value on clarity and certainty. Dissatisfied with the highly fact-specific constitutional rule against the admission of involuntary confessions, the Miranda Court set down rigid standards that often require courts to ignore personal characteristics that may be highly relevant to a particular suspect's actual susceptibility to police pressure. This rigidity, however, has brought with it one of Miranda's principal strengths — "the ease and clarity of its application" by law enforcement officials and courts. A key contributor to this clarity, at least up until now, has been *Miranda's* objective reasonable-person test for determining custody.

Miranda's custody requirement is based on the proposition that the risk of unconstitutional coercion is heightened when a suspect is placed under formal arrest or is subjected to some functionally equivalent limitation on freedom of movement. When this custodial threshold is reached, Miranda warnings must precede police questioning. But in the interest of simplicity, the custody analysis considers only whether, under the circumstances, a hypothetical reasonable person would consider himself to be confined.

Many suspects, of course, will differ from this hypothetical reasonable person. Some, including those who have been hardened by past interrogations, may have no need for Miranda warnings at all. And for other suspects — those who are unusually sensitive to the pressures of police questioning — Miranda warnings may come too late to be of any use. That is a necessary consequence of Miranda's rigid standards, but it does not mean that the constitutional rights of these especially sensitive suspects are left unprotected. A vulnerable defendant can still turn to the constitutional rule against actual coercion and contend that that his confession was extracted against his will.

Today's decision shifts the Miranda custody determination from a one-size-fits-all reasonable-person test into an inquiry that must account for at least one individualized characteristic — age — that is thought to correlate with susceptibility to coercive pressures. Age, however, is in no way the only personal characteristic that may correlate with pliability, and in future cases the Court will be forced to choose between two unpalatable alternatives. It may choose to limit today's decision by arbitrarily distinguishing a suspect's age from other personal characteristics — such as intelligence, education, occupation, or prior experience with law enforcement — that may also correlate with susceptibility to coercive pressures. Or, if the Court is unwilling to draw these arbitrary lines, it will be forced to effect a fundamental transformation of the Miranda custody test — from a clear, easily applied prophylactic rule into a highly fact-intensive standard resembling the voluntariness test that the Miranda Court found to be unsatisfactory.

For at least three reasons, there is no need to go down this road. First, many minors subjected to police interrogation are near the age of majority, and for these suspects the one-size-fits-all Miranda custody rule may not be a bad fit. Second, many of the difficulties in applying the Miranda custody rule to minors arise because of the unique circumstances present when the police conduct interrogations at school. The Miranda custody rule has always taken into account the setting in which questioning occurs, and accounting for the school setting in such cases will address many of these problems. Third, in cases like the one now before us, where the suspect is especially young, courts applying the constitutional voluntariness standard can take special care to ensure that incriminating statements were not obtained through coercion.

Safeguarding the constitutional rights of minors does not require the extreme makeover of Miranda that today's decision may portend.

I

In the days before Miranda, this Court's sole metric for evaluating the admissibility of confessions was a voluntariness standard rooted in both the Fifth Amendment's Self-Incrimination Clause and the Due Process Clause of the Fourteenth Amendment. The question in these voluntariness cases was whether the particular "defendant's will" had been "overborne."

Courts took into account both "the details of the interrogation" and "the characteristics of the accused," *Schneckloth v. Bustamonte*, and then "weigh[ed] . . . the circumstances of pressure against the power of resistance of the person confessing."

All manner of individualized, personal characteristics were relevant in this voluntariness inquiry. Among the most frequently mentioned factors were the defendant's education, physical condition, intelligence, and mental health. The suspect's age also received prominent attention in several cases, e.g., *Gallegos v. Colorado*, 370 U.S. 49, 54 (1962), especially when the suspect was a "mere child." *Haley v. Ohio*, 332 U.S. 596, 599 (1948). The weight assigned to any one consideration varied from case to case. But all of these factors, along with anything else that might have affected the "individual's . . . capacity for effective choice," were relevant in determining whether the confession was coerced or compelled. The all-encompassing nature of the voluntariness inquiry had its benefits. It allowed courts to accommodate a "complex of values," and to make a careful, highly individualized determination as to whether the police had wrung "a confession out of [the] accused against his will." But with this flexibility came a decrease in both certainty and predictability, and the voluntariness standard proved difficult "for law enforcement officers to conform to, and for courts to apply in a consistent manner."

In *Miranda*, the Court supplemented the voluntariness inquiry with a "set of prophylactic measures" designed to ward off the " 'inherently compelling pressures' of custodial interrogation." Miranda greatly simplified matters by requiring police to give suspects standard warnings before commencing any custodial interrogation.), and they often require courts to suppress "trustworthy and highly probative" statements that may be perfectly "voluntary under [a] traditional Fifth Amendment analysis. But with this rigidity comes increased clarity. Miranda provides "a workable rule to guide police officers," and an administrable standard for the courts. As has often been recognized, this gain in clarity and administrability is one of Miranda's "principal advantages."

No less than other facets of Miranda, the threshold requirement that the suspect be in "custody" is "designed to give clear guidance to the police." *Yarborough v. Alvarado*. Custody under Miranda attaches where there is a "formal arrest" or a "restraint on freedom of movement" akin to formal arrest. *California v. Beheler*. This standard is "objective" and turns on how a hypothetical "reasonable person in the position of the individual being questioned would gauge the breadth of his or her freedom of action.

Until today, the Court's cases applying this test have focused solely on the "objective circumstances of the inter-rogation. Relevant factors have included such things as where the questioning occurred,[2] how long it lasted,[3] what was said,[4] any physical restraints placed on suspect's movement,[5] and whether the suspect was allowed to leave when the questioning was through.[6]

The totality of these circumstances — the external circumstances, that is, of the interrogation itself — is what has mattered in this Court's cases. Personal characteristics of suspects have consistently been rejected or ignored as irrelevant under a one-size-fits-all reasonable-person standard. *Stansbury*. ("[C]ustody depends on the objective circumstances of the interrogation, not on the subjective views harbored by either the interrogating officers or the person being questioned").

For example, in *Berkemer v. McCarty*, police officers conducting a traffic stop questioned a man who had been drinking and smoking marijuana before he was pulled over. Although the suspect's inebriation was readily apparent to the officers at the scene, the Court's analysis did not advert to this or any other individualized consideration. Instead, the Court focused only on the external circumstances of the

---

[2] Maryland v. Shatzer, 559 U.S. 98, ___, ___ (2010).

[3] Berkemer v. McCarty, 468 U.S. 420, 437–438 (1984).

[4] Oregon v. Mathiason, 429 U.S. 492, 495 (1977) (per curiam).

[5] New York v. Quarles, 467 U.S. 649, 655 (1984).

[6] California v. Beheler, 463 U.S. 1121, 1122–1123 (1983) (per curiam).

interrogation itself. The opinion concluded that a typical "traffic stop" is akin to a "Terry stop" and does not qualify as the equivalent of "formal arrest."

California v. Beheler, supra, is another useful example. There, the circumstances of the interrogation were "remarkably similar" to the facts of the Court's earlier decision in *Oregon v. Mathiason*, — the suspect was "not placed under arrest," he "voluntarily [came] to the police station," and he was "allowed to leave unhindered by police after a brief inter-view." A California court in Beheler had nonetheless distinguished Mathiason because the police knew that Beheler "had been drinking earlier in the day" and was "emotionally distraught." In a summary reversal, this Court explained that the fact "[t]hat the police knew more" personal information about Beheler than they did about Mathiason was "irrelevant." Neither one of them was in custody under the objective reasonable-person standard. *See also Alvarado* (experience with law enforcement irrelevant to Miranda custody analysis "as a de novo matter").[8]

The glaring absence of reliance on personal characteristics in these and other custody cases should come as no surprise. To account for such individualized considerations would be to contradict Miranda's central premise. The Miranda Court's decision to adopt its inflexible prophylactic requirements was expressly based on the notion that "[a]ssessments of the knowledge the defendant possessed, based on information as to his age, education, intelligence, or prior contact with authorities, can never be more than speculation."

II

In light of this established practice, there is no denying that, by incorporating age into its analysis, the Court is embarking on a new expansion of the established custody standard. And since Miranda is this Court's rule, "not a constitutional command," it is up to the Court "to justify its expansion." *Arizona v. Roberson*, (KENNEDY, J., dissenting). This the Court fails to do.

In its present form, Miranda's prophylactic regime already imposes "high cost[s]" by requiring suppression of confessions that are often "highly probative" and "voluntary" by any traditional standard Nonetheless, a "core virtue" of Miranda has been the clarity and precision of its guidance to "police and courts." The Court has, however, repeatedly cautioned against upsetting the careful "balance" that Miranda struck, and it has "refused to sanction attempts to expand [the] Miranda holding" in ways that would reduce its "clarity." *See Quarles*, 467 U.S., at 658 (citing cases). Given this practice, there should be a "strong presumption" against the Court's new departure from the established custody test.

In my judgment, that presumption cannot be overcome here.

---

[8] The Court claims that "[n]ot once" have any of our cases "excluded from the custody analysis a circumstance that we determined was relevant and objective, simply to make the fault line between custodial and noncustodial 'brighter.' " Surely this is incorrect. The very act of adopting a reasonable-person test necessarily excludes all sorts of "relevant and objective" circumstances — for example, all the objective circumstances of a suspect's life history — that might otherwise bear on a custody determination.

A

The Court's rationale for importing age into the custody standard is that minors tend to lack adults' "capacity to exercise mature judgment" and that failing to account for that "reality" will leave some minors unprotected under Miranda in situations where they perceive themselves to be confined. I do not dispute that many suspects who are under 18 will be more susceptible to police pressure than the average adult. As the Court notes, our pre-Miranda cases were particularly attuned to this "reality" in applying the constitutional requirement of voluntariness in fact. It is no less a "reality," however, that many persons over the age of 18 are also more susceptible to police pressure than the hypothetical reasonable person. See *Payne* (fact that defendant was a "mentally dull 19-year-old youth" relevant in voluntariness inquiry). Yet the Miranda custody standard has never accounted for the personal characteristics of these or any other individual defendants.

Indeed, it has always been the case under Miranda that the unusually meek or compliant are subject to the same fixed rules, including the same custody requirement, as those who are unusually resistant to police pressure.

Miranda's rigid standards are both overinclusive and underinclusive. They are overinclusive to the extent that they provide a windfall to the most hardened and savvy of suspects, who often have no need for Miranda's protections. ("[N]o amount of circumstantial evidence that the person may have been aware of" his rights can overcome Miranda's requirements), with *Orozco v. Texas*, 394 U.S. 324, 329 (1969) (WHITE, J., dissenting) ("Where the defendant himself [w]as a lawyer, policeman, professional criminal, or otherwise has become aware of what his right to silence is, it is sheer fancy to assert that his answer to every question asked him is compelled unless he is advised of those rights with which he is already intimately familiar"). And Miranda's requirements are underinclusive to the extent that they fail to account for "frailties," "idiosyncrasies," and other individualized considerations that might cause a person to). But if it is, then the weakness is an inescapable consequence of the Miranda Court's decision to supplement the more holistic voluntariness requirement with a one-size-fits-all prophylactic rule.

That is undoubtedly why this Court's Miranda cases have never before mentioned "the suspect's age" or any other individualized consideration in applying the custody standard. And unless the Miranda custody rule is now to be radically transformed into one that takes into account the wide range of individual characteristics that are relevant in determining whether a confession is voluntary, the Court must shoulder the burden of explaining why age is different from these other personal characteristics.

Why, for example, is age different from intelligence? Suppose that an officer, upon going to a school to question a student, is told by the principal that the student has an I. Q. of 75 and is in a special-education class. Are those facts more or less important than the student's age in determining whether he or she "felt . . . at liberty to terminate the interrogation and leave"?

How about the suspect's cultural background? Suppose the police learn (or should have learned) that a suspect they wish to question is a recent immigrant from a country in which dire consequences often befall any person who dares to attempt to cut short any meeting with the police. Is this really less relevant than the fact that a suspect is a month or so away from his 18th birthday?

The defendant's education is another personal characteristic that may generate "conclusions about behavior and perception." Under today's decision, why should police officers and courts "blind themselves to the fact that a suspect has "only a fifth-grade education? Alternatively, what if the police know or should know that the suspect is "a college-educated man with law school training"? *See Crooker* overruled by *Miranda*. How are these individual considerations meaningfully different from age in their "relationship to a reasonable person's understanding of his freedom of action"? The Court proclaims that "[a] child's age . . . is different," but the basis for this ipse dixit is dubious.

I have little doubt that today's decision will soon be cited by defendants — and perhaps by prosecutors as well — for the proposition that all manner of other individual characteristics should be treated like age and taken into account in the Miranda custody calculus. Indeed, there are already lower court decisions that take this approach. See *United States v. Beraun-Panez*.

In time, the Court will have to confront these issues, and it will be faced with a difficult choice. It may choose to distinguish today's decision and adhere to the arbitrary proclamation that "age . . . is different." Or it may choose to extend today's holding and, in doing so, further undermine the very rationale for the Miranda regime.

B

If the Court chooses the latter course, then a core virtue of Miranda — the "ease and clarity of its application" — will be lost However, even today's more limited departure from Miranda's one-size-fits-all reasonable-person test will produce the very consequences that prompted the Miranda Court to abandon exclusive reliance on the voluntariness test in the first place: The Court's test will be hard for the police to follow, and it will be hard for judges to apply.

The Court holds that age must be taken into account when it "was known to the officer at the time of the interview," or when it "would have been objectively apparent" to a reasonable officer. The first half of this test overturns the rule that the "initial determination of custody" does not depend on the "subjective views harbored by . . . interrogating officers." The second half will generate time-consuming satellite litigation over a reasonable officer's perceptions. When, as here, the interrogation takes place in school, the inquiry may be relatively simple. But not all police questioning of minors takes place in schools. In many cases, courts will presumably have to make findings as to whether a particular suspect had a sufficiently youthful look to alert a reasonable officer to the possibility that the suspect was under 18, or whether a reasonable officer would have recognized that a suspect's I. D. was a fake. The inquiry will be both "time-consuming and disruptive" for the police and the courts. It will also be made all the more complicated by the fact that a suspect's dress and manner will often be different when the issue is litigated in court than it was at the time of the interrogation.

Even after courts clear this initial hurdle, further problems will likely emerge as judges attempt to put themselves in the shoes of the average 16-year-old, or 15-year-old, or 13-year-old, as the case may be. Consider, for example, a 60-year-old judge attempting to make a custody determination through the eyes of a hypothetical, average 15-year-old. Forty-five years of personal experience and societal change separate this judge from the days when he or she was 15 years old. And this judge may or may not have been an average 15-year-old. The Court's answer to these difficulties is to state that "no imaginative powers, knowledge of developmental psychology, [or] training in cognitive science" will be necessary. Judges "simply need the common sense," the Court assures, "to know that a 7-year-old is not a 13-year-old and neither is an adult." It is obvious, however, that application of the Court's new rule demands much more than this.

Take a fairly typical case in which today's holding may make a difference. A 16-year-old moves to suppress incriminating statements made prior to the administration of Miranda warnings. The circumstances are such that, if the defendant were at least 18, the court would not find that he or she was in custody, but the defendant argues that a reasonable 16-year-old would view the situation differently. The judge will not have the luxury of merely saying: "It is common sense that a 16-year-old is not an 18-year-old. Motion granted." Rather, the judge will be required to determine whether the differences between a typical 16-year-old and a typical 18-year-old with respect to susceptibility to the pressures of interrogation are sufficient to change the outcome of the custody determination. Today's opinion contains not a word of actual guidance as to how judges are supposed to go about making that determination.

C

Petitioner and the Court attempt to show that this task is not unmanageable by pointing out that age is taken into account in other legal contexts. In particular, the Court relies on the fact that the age of a defendant is a relevant factor under the reasonable-person standard applicable in negligence suits. But negligence is generally a question for the jury, the members of which can draw on their varied experiences with persons of different ages. It also involves a post hoc determination, in the reflective atmosphere of a deliberation room, about whether the defendant conformed to a standard of care. The Miranda custody determination, by contrast, must be made in the first instance by police officers in the course of an investigation that may require quick decision making

Equally inapposite are the Eighth Amendment cases the Court cites in support of its new rule. Those decisions involve the "judicial exercise of independent judgment" about the constitutionality of certain punishments. Like the negligence standard, they do not require on-the-spot judgments by the police.

Nor do state laws affording extra protection for juveniles during custodial interrogation provide any support for petitioner's arguments. States are free to enact additional restrictions on the police over and above those demanded by the Constitution or Miranda. In addition, these state statutes generally create clear, workable rules to guide police conduct. Today's decision, by contrast, injects a new, complicating factor into what had been a clear, easily applied prophylactic rule.[10]

III

The Court's decision greatly diminishes the clarity and administrability that have long been recognized as "principal advantages" of Miranda's prophylactic requirements. *See Moran.* But what is worse, the Court takes this step unnecessarily, as there are other, less disruptive tools available to ensure that minors are not coerced into confessing.

As an initial matter, the difficulties that the Court's standard introduces will likely yield little added protection for most juvenile defendants. Most juveniles who are subjected to police interrogation are teenagers nearing the age of majority. These defendants' reactions to police pressure are unlikely to be much different from the reaction of a typical 18-year-old in similar circumstances. A one-size-fits-all Miranda custody rule thus provides a roughly reasonable fit for these defendants.

In addition, many of the concerns that petitioner raises regarding the application of the Miranda custody rule to minors can be accommodated by considering the unique circumstances present when minors are questioned in school. The Miranda custody rule has always taken into account the setting in which questioning occurs, restrictions on a suspect's freedom of movement, and the presence of police officers or other authority figures. It can do so here as well. Finally, in cases like the one now before us, where the suspect is much younger than the typical juvenile defendant, courts should be instructed to take particular care to ensure that incriminating statements were not obtained involuntarily. The voluntariness inquiry is flexible and accommodating by nature, care" must be exercised in applying the voluntariness test where the confession of a "mere child" is at issue. If Miranda's rigid, one-size-fits-all standards fail to account for the unique needs of juveniles, the response should be to rigorously apply the constitutional rule against coercion to ensure that the rights of minors are protected. There is no need to run Miranda off the rails.

The Court rests its decision to inject personal characteristics into the Miranda custody inquiry on the principle that judges applying Miranda cannot "blind themselves to . . . commonsense reality." But the Court's shift is fundamentally at odds with the clear prophylactic rules that Miranda has long enforced. Miranda frequently requires judges to blind themselves to the reality that many un-Mirandized custodial confessions are "by no means involuntary" or coerced. It also requires police to provide a rote recitation of Miranda warnings that many suspects

---

[10] The Court also relies on North Carolina's concession at oral argument that a court could take into account a suspect's blindness as a factor relevant to the Miranda custody determination. This is a far-fetched hypothetical, and neither the parties nor their amici cite any case in which such a problem has actually arisen. Presumably such a case would involve a situation in which a blind defendant was given "a typed document advising him that he [was] free to leave." In such a case, furnishing this advice in a form calculated to be unintelligible to the suspect would be tantamount to failing to provide the advice at all. And advice by the police that a suspect is or is not free to leave at will has always been regarded as a circumstance regarding the conditions of the interrogation that must be taken into account in making the Miranda custody determination.

already know and could likely recite from memory.[13] Under today's new, "reality"-based approach to the doctrine, perhaps these and other principles of our Miranda jurisprudence will, like the custody standard, now be ripe for modification. Then, bit by bit, Miranda will lose the clarity and ease of application that has long been viewed as one of its chief justifications. I respectfully dissent.

QUESTIONS AND NOTES

1. Do you believe that J.D.B. will adversely affect Miranda's clarity? Why? Why not?

2. On remand will (should) J.D.B. prevail? Explain.

3. If the Alito opinion had prevailed, would (should) J.D.B. win on the merits. Explain.

4. Suppose a 30 year old soldier had been taken from his regular routine by a military officer and brought to the Captain's quarters. Suppose further that the Captain had told him that he should tell the truth. Would (should) that soldier be deemed in custody?

5. If your answer to 4 was "yes," would that indicate that J.D.B. unnecessarily resolved the question before it?

6. When, if ever, would a 13 year-old be in custody under circumstances that a 25 year-old would not? What about the Mathiason situation?

7. Given that custody is such a multi-factored fact bound determination anyway, is there any harm in a special rule for juveniles? Explain.

8. In *Berkemer v. McCarty*, 468 U.S. 420 (1984), the Court adopted a rather strict objective test for determining custody, holding that a traffic stop, even for drunk driving, did not constitute custody, because, like a *Terry* stop, and unlike an arrest, the stopped person expects to be gone in a few minutes. The Court, however, also held that *Miranda* was applicable to misdemeanors as well as felonies.

PROBLEM

Ten-year old Robyn Jackson disappeared from a playground in Baldwin Park, California, at around 6:30 p.m. on September 28, 1982. Early the next morning, about 10 miles away in Pasadena, Andrew Zimmerman observed a large man emerge from a turquoise American sedan and throw something into a nearby flood control channel. Zimmerman called the police, who arrived at the scene and discovered the girl's body in the channel. There was evidence that she had been raped, and the cause of death was determined to be asphyxia complicated by blunt force trauma to the head.

---

[13] Surveys have shown that "[l]arge majorities" of the public are aware that "individuals arrested for a crime" have a right to "remai[n] silent (81%)," a right to "a lawyer (95%)," and a right to have a lawyer "appointed" if the arrestee "cannot afford one (88%)." *See* Belden, Russonello & Stewart, Developing a National Message for Indigent Defense: online at http://www.nlada.org/DMS/Documents/1211996548.53/Polling%20results%20report.pdf.

Lieutenant Thomas Johnston, a detective with the Los Angeles County Sheriff's Department, investigated the homicide. From witnesses interviewed on the day the body was discovered, he learned that Robyn had talked to two ice cream truck drivers, one being petitioner Robert Edward Stansbury, in the hours before her disappearance. Given these contacts, Johnston thought Stansbury and the other driver might have some connection with the homicide or knowledge thereof, but for reasons unimportant here Johnston considered only the other driver to be a leading suspect. After the suspect driver was brought in for interrogation, Johnston asked Officer Lee of the Baldwin Park Police Department to contact Stansbury to see if he would come in for questioning as a potential witness.

Lee and three other plainclothes officers arrived at Stansbury's trailer home at about 11:00 that evening. The officers surrounded the door and Lee knocked. When Stansbury answered, Lee told him the officers were investigating a homicide to which Stansbury was a possible witness and asked if he would accompany them to the police station to answer some questions. Stansbury agreed to the interview and accepted a ride to the station in the front seat of Lee's police car.

At the station, Lieutenant Johnston, in the presence of another officer, questioned Stansbury about his whereabouts and activities during the afternoon and evening of September 28. Neither Johnston nor the other officer issued *Miranda* warnings. Stansbury told the officers (among other things) that on the evening of the 28th he spoke with the victim at about 6:00, returned to his trailer home after work at 9:00, and left the trailer at about midnight in his housemate's turquoise, American-made car. This last detail aroused Johnston's suspicions, as the turquoise car matched the description of the one Andrew Zimmerman had observed in Pasadena. When Stansbury, in response to a further question, admitted to prior convictions for rape, kidnaping and child molestation, Johnston terminated the interview and another officer advised Stansbury of his *Miranda* rights. Stansbury declined to make further statements, requested an attorney, and was arrested. Respondent State of California charged Stansbury with first-degree murder and other crimes.

Stansbury filed a pretrial motion to suppress all statements made at the station, and the evidence discovered as a result of those statements. The trial court denied the motion in relevant part, ruling that Stansbury was not "in custody" — and thus not entitled to *Miranda* warnings — until he mentioned that he had taken his housemate's turquoise car for a midnight drive. Before that stage of the interview, the trial court reasoned, "the focus in [Lieutenant Johnston's] mind certainly was on the other ice cream [truck] driver"; only "after Mr. Stansbury made the comment . . . describing the . . . turquoise-colored automobile" did Johnston's suspicions "shif[t] to Mr. Stansbury." Based upon its conclusion that Stansbury was not in custody until Johnston's suspicions had focused on him, the trial court permitted the prosecution to introduce in its case-in-chief the statements Stansbury made before that time. At trial, the jury convicted Stansbury of first-degree murder, rape, kidnaping, and lewd act on a child under the age of 14, and fixed the penalty for the first-degree murder at death.

The California Supreme Court affirmed. Before determining whether Stansbury was in custody during the interview at the station, the court set out what it viewed as the applicable legal standard: "In deciding the custody issue, the totality of the circumstances is relevant, and no one factor is dispositive. However, the most important considerations include (1) the site of the interrogation, (2) whether the investigation has focused on the subject, (3) whether the objective indicia of arrest are present, and (4) the length and form of questioning." The court proceeded to analyze the second factor in detail, in the end accepting the trial court's factual determination "that suspicion focused on [Stansbury] only when he mentioned that he had driven a turquoise car on the night of the crime." The court "conclude[d] that [Stansbury] was not subject to custodial interrogation before he mentioned the turquoise car," and thus approved the trial court's ruling that *Miranda* did not bar the admission of statements Stansbury made before that point.

How should the United States Supreme Court resolve this case? Why? Assuming that the Supreme Court remands the case to a California court, what factors should determine its resolution of the issue?

For the Supreme Court's resolution, see *Stansbury v. California*, 511 U.S. 318 (1994).

In *Perkins*, we see that not all forms of custodial interrogation are covered by *Miranda*.

ILLINOIS v. PERKINS
496 U.S. 292 (1990)

Justice Kennedy delivered the opinion of the Court.

An undercover government agent was placed in the cell of respondent Perkins, who was incarcerated on charges unrelated to the subject of the agent's investigation. Respondent made statements that implicated him in the crime that the agent sought to solve. Respondent claims that the statements should be inadmissible because he had not been given *Miranda* warnings by the agent. We hold that the statements are admissible. *Miranda* warnings are not required when the suspect is unaware that he is speaking to a law enforcement officer and gives a voluntary statement.

I

In November 1984, Richard Stephenson was murdered in a suburb of East St. Louis, Illinois. The murder remained unsolved until March 1986, when one Donald Charlton told police that he had learned about a homicide from a fellow inmate at the Graham Correctional Facility, where Charlton had been serving a sentence for burglary. The fellow inmate was Lloyd Perkins, who is the respondent here. Charlton told police that, while at Graham, he had befriended respondent, who told him in detail about a murder that respondent had committed in East St. Louis. On hearing Charlton's account, the police recognized details of the Stephenson murder that were not well known, and so they treated Charlton's story as a credible one.

By the time the police heard Charlton's account, respondent had been released from Graham, but police traced him to a jail in Montgomery County, Illinois, where he was being held pending trial on a charge of aggravated battery, unrelated to the Stephenson murder. The police wanted to investigate further respondent's connection to the Stephenson murder, but feared that the use of an eavesdropping device would prove impracticable and unsafe. They decided instead to place an undercover agent in the cellblock with respondent and Charlton. The plan was for Charlton and undercover agent John Parisi to pose as escapees from a work release program who had been arrested in the course of a burglary. Parisi and Charlton were instructed to engage respondent in casual conversation and report anything he said about the Stephenson murder.

Parisi, using the alias "Vito Bianco," and Charlton, both clothed in jail garb, were placed in the cellblock with respondent at the Montgomery County jail. The cellblock consisted of 12 separate cells that opened onto a common room. Respondent greeted Charlton who, after a brief conversation with respondent, introduced Parisi by his alias. Parisi told respondent that he "wasn't going to do any more time" and suggested that the three of them escape. Respondent replied that the Montgomery County jail was "rinky-dink" and that they could "break out." The trio met in respondent's cell later that evening, after the other inmates were asleep, to refine their plan. Respondent said that his girlfriend could smuggle in a pistol. Charlton said: "Hey, I'm not a murderer, I'm a burglar. That's your guys' profession." After telling Charlton that he would be responsible for any murder that occurred, Parisi asked respondent if he had ever "done" anybody. Respondent said that he had and proceeded to describe at length the events of the Stephenson murder. Parisi and respondent then engaged in some casual conversation before respondent went to sleep. Parisi did not give respondent *Miranda* warnings before the conversations.

II

In *Miranda*, the Court held that the Fifth Amendment privilege against self-incrimination prohibits admitting statements given by a suspect during "custodial interrogation" without a prior warning. Custodial interrogation means "questioning initiated by law enforcement officers after a person has been taken into custody . . . ." The warning mandated by *Miranda* was meant to preserve the privilege during "incommunicado interrogation of individuals in a police-dominated atmosphere." That atmosphere is said to generate "inherently compelling pressures which work to undermine the individual's will to resist and to compel him to speak where he would not otherwise do so freely." "Fidelity to the doctrine announced in *Miranda* requires that it be enforced strictly, but only in those types of situations in which the concerns that powered the decision are implicated." *McCarty.*

Conversations between suspects and undercover agents do not implicate the concerns underlying *Miranda*. The essential ingredients of a "police-dominated atmosphere" and compulsion are not present when an incarcerated person speaks freely to someone whom he believes to be a fellow inmate. Coercion is determined from the perspective of the suspect. *McCarty.* When a suspect considers himself in the company of cellmates and not officers, the coercive atmosphere is lacking. *Miranda* ("[T]he 'principal psychological factor contributing to a successful interrogation is *privacy* — being alone with the person under interrogation' "). There is no empirical basis for the assumption that a suspect speaking to those whom he assumes are not officers will feel compelled to speak by the fear of reprisal for remaining silent or in the hope of more lenient treatment should he confess.

It is the premise of *Miranda* that the danger of coercion results from the interaction of custody and official interrogation. We reject the argument that *Miranda* warnings are required whenever a suspect is in custody in a technical sense and converses with someone who happens to be a government agent. Questioning by captors, who appear to control the suspect's fate, may create mutually reinforcing pressures that the Court has assumed will weaken the suspect's will, but where a suspect does not know that he is conversing with a government agent, these pressures do not exist. The state court here mistakenly assumed that because the suspect was in custody, no undercover questioning could take place. When the suspect has no reason to think that the listeners have official power over him, it should not be assumed that his words are motivated by the reaction he expects from his listeners. "[W]hen the agent carries neither badge nor gun and wears not 'police blue,' but the same prison gray" as the suspect, there is no "*interplay* between police interrogation and police custody." Kamisar, Brewer v. Williams, Massiah *and* Miranda: *What is "Interrogation"? When Does it Matter?*, 67 Geo. L.J. 1, 67, 63 (1978).

Miranda forbids coercion, not mere strategic deception by taking advantage of a suspect's misplaced trust in one he supposes to be a fellow prisoner. As we recognized in *Miranda*, "[c]onfessions remain a proper element in law enforcement. Any statement given freely and voluntarily without any compelling influences is, of course, admissible in evidence." Ploys to mislead a suspect or lull him into a false sense of security that do not rise to the level of compulsion or coercion to speak are not within *Miranda's* concerns. *Cf. Mathiason.*

Miranda was not meant to protect suspects from boasting about their criminal activities in front of persons whom they believe to be their cellmates. This case is illustrative. Respondent had no reason to feel that undercover agent Parisi had any legal authority to force him to answer questions or that Parisi could affect respondent's future treatment. Respondent viewed the cellmate-agent as an equal and showed no hint of being intimidated by the atmosphere of the jail. In recounting the details of the Stephenson murder, respondent was motivated solely by the desire to impress his fellow inmates. He spoke at his own peril.

The tactic employed here to elicit a voluntary confession from a suspect does not violate the Self-Incrimination Clause. We held in *Hoffa*, that placing an undercover agent near a suspect in order to gather incriminating information was permissible under the Fifth Amendment. In *Hoffa*, while petitioner Hoffa was on trial, he met often with one Partin, who, unbeknownst to Hoffa, was cooperating with law enforcement officials. Partin reported to officials that Hoffa had divulged his attempts to bribe jury members. We approved using Hoffa's statements at his subsequent trial for jury tampering, on the rationale that "no claim ha[d] been or could [have been] made that [Hoffa's] incriminating statements were the product of any sort of coercion, legal or factual." In addition, we found that the fact that Partin had fooled Hoffa into thinking that Partin was a sympathetic colleague did not affect the voluntariness of the statements. *Cf. Mathiason* (officer's falsely telling suspect that suspect's fingerprints had been found at crime scene did not render interview "custodial" under *Miranda*). The only difference between this case and *Hoffa* is that the suspect here was incarcerated, but detention, whether or not for the crime in question, does not warrant a presumption that the use of an undercover agent to speak with an incarcerated suspect makes any confession thus obtained involuntary.

Our decision in *Mathis* is distinguishable. In *Mathis*, an inmate in a state prison was interviewed by an Internal Revenue Service agent about possible tax violations. No *Miranda* warning was given before questioning. The Court held that the suspect's incriminating statements were not admissible at his subsequent trial on tax fraud charges. The suspect in *Mathis* was aware that the agent was a Government official, investigating the possibility of non-compliance with the tax laws. The case before us now is different. Where the suspect does not know that he is speaking to a government agent there is no reason to assume the possibility that the suspect might feel coerced. (The bare fact of custody may not in every instance require a warning even when the suspect is aware that he is speaking to an official, but we do not have occasion to explore that issue here.)

Respondent can seek no help from his argument that a bright-line rule for the application of *Miranda* is desirable. Law enforcement officers will have little difficulty putting into practice our holding that undercover agents need not give *Miranda* warnings to incarcerated suspects. The use of undercover agents is a recognized law enforcement technique, often employed in the prison context to detect violence against correctional officials or inmates, as well as for the purposes served here. The interests protected by *Miranda* are not implicated in these cases, and the warnings are not required to safeguard the constitutional rights of inmates who make voluntary statements to undercover agents.

We hold that an undercover law enforcement officer posing as a fellow inmate need not give *Miranda* warnings to an incarcerated suspect before asking questions that may elicit an incriminating response. The statements at issue in this case were voluntary, and there is no federal obstacle to their admissibility at trial. We now reverse and remand for proceedings not inconsistent with our opinion.

JUSTICE BRENNAN, concurring in the judgment.

The Court holds that *Miranda* does not require suppression of a statement made by an incarcerated suspect to an undercover agent. Although I do not subscribe to the majority's characterization of *Miranda* in its entirety, I do agree that when a suspect does not know that his questioner is a police agent, such questioning does not amount to "interrogation" in an "inherently coercive" environment so as to require application of *Miranda*. Since the only issue raised at this stage of the litigation is the applicability of *Miranda*,[*] I concur in the judgment of the Court.

---

[*] As the case comes to us, it involves only the question whether *Miranda* applies to the questioning of an incarcerated suspect by an undercover agent. Nothing in the Court's opinion suggests that, had respondent previously invoked his Fifth Amendment right to counsel or right to silence, his statements would be admissible. If respondent had invoked either right, the inquiry would focus on whether he subsequently waived the particular right. *See Edwards v. Arizona*, 451 U.S. 477 (1981); *Michigan v.*

This is not to say that I believe the Constitution condones the method by which the police extracted the confession in this case. To the contrary, the deception and manipulation practiced on respondent raise a substantial claim that the confession was obtained in violation of the Due Process Clause.

The method used to elicit the confession in this case deserves close scrutiny. The police devised a ruse to lure respondent into incriminating himself when he was in jail on an unrelated charge. A police agent, posing as a fellow inmate and proposing a sham escape plot, tricked respondent into confessing that he had once committed a murder, as a way of proving that he would be willing to do so again should the need arise during the escape. The testimony of the undercover officer and a police informant at the suppression hearing reveal the deliberate manner in which the two elicited incriminating statements from respondent. We have recognized that "the mere fact of custody imposes pressures on the accused; confinement may bring into play subtle influences that will make him particularly susceptible to the ploys of undercover Government agents." As Justice Marshall points out, the pressures of custody make a suspect more likely to confide in others and to engage in "jailhouse bravado." The State is in a unique position to exploit this vulnerability because it has virtually complete control over the suspect's environment. Thus, the State can ensure that a suspect is barraged with questions from an undercover agent until the suspect confesses. The testimony in this case suggests the State did just that.

The deliberate use of deception and manipulation by the police appears to be incompatible "with a system that presumes innocence and assures that a conviction will not be secured by inquisitorial means," and raises serious concerns that respondent's will was overborne. It is open to the lower court on remand to determine whether, under the totality of the circumstances, respondent's confession was elicited in a manner that violated the Due Process Clause. That the confession was not elicited through means of physical torture, see *Brown*, or overt psychological pressure, does not end the inquiry. "[A]s law enforcement officers become more responsible, and the methods used to extract confessions more sophisticated, [a court's] duty to enforce federal constitutional protections does not cease. It only becomes more difficult because of the more delicate judgments to be made." *Spano.*

JUSTICE MARSHALL, dissenting.

This Court clearly and simply stated its holding in *Miranda*: "[T]he prosecution may not use statements, whether exculpatory or inculpatory, stemming from custodial interrogation of the defendant unless it demonstrates the use of procedural safeguards effective to secure the privilege against self-incrimination." The conditions that require the police to apprise a defendant of his constitutional rights — custodial interrogation conducted by an agent of the police — were present in this case. Because Lloyd Perkins received no *Miranda* warnings before he was

Mosley, 423 U.S. 96, 104 (1975). As the Court made clear in *Moran v. Burbine*, 475 U.S. 412, 421 (1986), the waiver of *Miranda* rights "must [be] voluntary in the sense that it [must be] the product of a free and deliberate choice rather than *intimidation, coercion or deception.*" (Emphasis added.) Since respondent was in custody on an unrelated charge when he was questioned, he may be able to challenge the admission of these statements if he previously had invoked his *Miranda* rights with respect to that charge. *See Arizona v. Roberson*, 486 U.S. 675 (1988); *Mosley.*

subjected to custodial interrogation, his confession was not admissible.

The Court reaches the contrary conclusion by fashioning an exception to the *Miranda* rule that applies whenever "an undercover law enforcement officer posing as a fellow inmate . . . ask[s] questions that may elicit an incriminating response" from an incarcerated suspect. This exception is inconsistent with the rationale supporting *Miranda* and allows police officers intentionally to take advantage of suspects unaware of their constitutional rights. I therefore dissent.

The Court does not dispute that the police officer here conducted a custodial interrogation of a criminal suspect. Perkins was incarcerated in county jail during the questioning at issue here; under these circumstances, he was in custody as that term is defined in *Miranda*. *Mathis* (holding that defendant incarcerated on charges different from the crime about which he is questioned was in custody for purposes of *Miranda*). The United States argues that Perkins was not in custody for purpose of *Miranda* because he was familiar with the custodial environment as a result of being in jail for two days and previously spending time in prison. Perkins' familiarity with confinement, however, does not transform his incarceration into some sort of noncustodial arrangement. Cf. *Orozco* (holding that suspect who had been arrested in his home and then questioned in his bedroom was in custody, notwithstanding his familiarity with the surroundings).

While Perkins was confined, an undercover police officer, with the help of a police informant, questioned him about a serious crime. Although the Court does not dispute that Perkins was interrogated, it downplays the nature of the 35-minute questioning by disingenuously referring to it as a "conversatio[n]." The officer's narration of the "conversation" at Perkins' suppression hearing however, reveals that it clearly was an interrogation.

[Agent:] You ever do anyone?

[Perkins:] Yeah, once in East St. Louis, in a rich white neighborhood.

Informant: I didn't know they had any rich white neighborhoods in East St. Louis.

Perkins: It wasn't in East St. Louis, it was by a race track in Fairview Heights . . . .

[Agent]: You did a guy in Fairview Heights?

Perkins: Yeah in a rich white section where most of the houses look the same.

[Informant]: If all the houses look the same, how did you know you had the right house?

Perkins: Me and two guys cased the house for about a week. I knew exactly which house, the second house on the left from the corner.

[Agent]: How long ago did this happen?

Perkins: Approximately about two years ago. I got paid $5,000 for that job.

[Agent]: How did it go down?

Perkins: I walked up [to] this guy['s] house with a sawed-off under my trench coat.

[Agent]:   What type gun[?]

Perkins: A .12 gauge Remmington [*sic*] Automatic Model 1100 sawed-off."

The police officer continued the inquiry, asking a series of questions designed to elicit specific information about the victim, the crime scene, the weapon, Perkins' motive, and his actions during and after the shooting. This interaction was not a "conversation"; Perkins, the officer, and the informant were not equal participants in a free-ranging discussion, with each man offering his views on different topics. Rather, it was an interrogation: Perkins was subjected to express questioning likely to evoke an incriminating response.

Because Perkins was interrogated by police while he was in custody, *Miranda* required that the officer inform him of his rights. In rejecting that conclusion, the Court finds that "conversations" between undercover agents and suspects are devoid of the coercion inherent in station house interrogations conducted by law enforcement officials who openly represent the State. *Miranda* was not, however, concerned solely with police *coercion*. It dealt with *any* police tactics that may operate to compel a suspect in custody to make incriminating statements without full awareness of his constitutional rights. Thus, when a law enforcement agent structures a custodial interrogation so that a suspect feels compelled to reveal incriminating information, he must inform the suspect of his constitutional rights and give him an opportunity to decide whether or not to talk.

The compulsion proscribed by *Miranda* includes deception by the police. *See Miranda* (indicting police tactics "to induce a confession out of trickery," such as using fictitious witnesses or false accusations); *McCarty* ("The purposes of the safeguards prescribed by *Miranda* are to ensure that the police do not coerce *or trick* captive suspects into confessing") (emphasis deleted and added). Although the Court did not find trickery by itself sufficient to constitute compulsion in *Hoffa*, the defendant in that case was not in custody. Perkins, however, was interrogated while incarcerated. As the Court has acknowledged in the Sixth Amendment context: "[T]he mere fact of custody imposes pressures on the accused; confinement may bring into play subtle influences that will make him particularly susceptible to the ploys of undercover Government agents." *See also Massiah* (holding, in the context of the Sixth Amendment, that defendant's constitutional privilege against self-incrimination was "more seriously imposed upon . . . because he did not even know that he was under interrogation by a government agent").

Custody works to the State's advantage in obtaining incriminating information. The psychological pressures inherent in confinement increase the suspect's anxiety, making him likely to seek relief by talking with others. The inmate is thus more susceptible to efforts by undercover agents to elicit information from him. Similarly, where the suspect is incarcerated, the constant threat of physical danger peculiar to the prison environment may make him demonstrate his toughness to other inmates by recounting or inventing past violent acts. "Because the suspect's ability to select people with whom he can confide is completely within their control, the police have a unique opportunity to exploit the suspect's vulnerability. In short, the police can insure that if the pressures of confinement lead the suspect to confide in anyone, it will be a police agent." In this case, the police deceptively took advantage of Perkins' psychological vulnerability by including him in a sham escape plot, a situation in which he would feel compelled to demonstrate his willingness to shoot a prison guard by revealing his past involvement in a murder. ([The] agent stressed that a killing might be necessary in the escape and then asked Perkins if he had ever murdered someone).

Thus, the pressures unique to custody allow the police to use deceptive interrogation tactics to compel a suspect to make an incriminating statement. The compulsion is not eliminated by the suspect's ignorance of his interrogator's true identity. The Court therefore need not inquire past the bare facts of custody and interrogation to determine whether *Miranda* warnings are required.

The Court's adoption of an exception to the *Miranda* doctrine is incompatible with the principle, consistently applied by this Court, that the doctrine should remain simple and clear. We explained the benefits of a bright-line rule in *Michael C.*: "*Miranda*'s holding has the virtue of informing police and prosecutors with specificity as to what they may do in conducting custodial interrogation, and of informing courts under what circumstances statements obtained during such interrogation are not admissible."

The Court's holding today complicates a previously clear and straightforward doctrine. The Court opines that "[l]aw enforcement officers will have little difficulty putting into practice our holding that undercover agents need not give *Miranda* warnings to incarcerated suspects." Perhaps this prediction is true with respect to fact patterns virtually identical to the one before the Court today. But the outer boundaries of the exception created by the Court are by no means clear. Would *Miranda* be violated, for instance, if an undercover police officer beat a confession out of a suspect, but the suspect thought the officer was another prisoner who wanted the information for his own purposes?

Even if *Miranda*, as interpreted by the Court, would not permit such obviously compelled confessions, the ramifications of today's opinion are still disturbing. The exception carved out of the *Miranda* doctrine today may well result in a proliferation of departmental policies to encourage police officers to conduct interrogations of confined suspects through undercover agents, thereby circumventing the need to administer *Miranda* warnings. Indeed, if *Miranda* now requires a police officer to issue warnings only in those situations in which the suspect might feel compelled "to speak by the fear of reprisal for remaining silent or in the hope of more lenient treatment should he confess," presumably it allows custodial interrogation by an undercover officer posing as a member of the clergy or a suspect's defense attorney. Although such abhorrent tricks would play on a suspect's need to confide in a trusted adviser, neither would cause the suspect to "think that the listeners have official power over him." The Court's adoption of the "undercover agent" exception to the *Miranda* rule thus is necessarily also the adoption of a substantial loophole in our jurisprudence protecting suspects' Fifth Amendment rights.

I dissent.

QUESTIONS AND NOTES

1. Does the Court find that Perkins was not in custody? Was not subject to interrogation? Something else? Explain.

2. Is the process by which the police obtained the confession in this case something that should be applauded or condemned? Why?

3. Does Justice Brennan's fn. make any sense? If the procedure to which Perkins was subjected does not constitute custodial interrogation, why should it matter whether he invoked his right to counsel *during custodial interrogation*?

4. Is Justice Marshall's concept of custody too wooden?

5. Conversely, is it fair to say that custody *per se*, even without interrogation, is inherently coercive?

6. Under the Court's opinion, would it be possible for the police to disguise one of their own as a priest or attorney and thereby obtain a confession? Should the Fifth Amendment forbid such a practice? Should any other amendment forbid such a practice? If so, which Amendment? Explain.

7. We now revisit *Maryland v. Shatzer*, which explores the difference between Miranda custody and ordinary prison custody.

MARYLAND v. SHATZER
559 U.S. 98 (2010)

JUSTICE SCALIA delivered the opinion of the Court.

(For the facts of the case see section C of this chapter.)

III

The facts of this case present an additional issue. No one questions that Shatzer was in custody for *Miranda* purposes during the interviews with Detective Blankenship in 2003 and Detective Hoover in 2006. Likewise, no one questions that Shatzer triggered the *Edwards* protections when, according to Detective Blankenship's notes of the 2003 interview, he stated that " 'he would not talk about this case without having an attorney present.' " After the 2003 interview, Shatzer was released back into the general prison population where he was serving an unrelated sentence. The issue is whether that constitutes a break in *Miranda* custody.

We have never decided whether incarceration constitutes custody for *Miranda* purposes, and have indeed explicitly declined to address the issue. See *Perkins*. Whether it does depends upon whether it exerts the coercive pressure that *Miranda* was designed to guard against — the "danger of coercion [that] results from the *interaction* of custody and official interrogation." *Perkins,* (emphasis added). To determine whether a suspect was in *Miranda* custody we have asked whether "there is a 'formal arrest or restraint on freedom of movement' of the degree associated with a formal arrest." This test, no doubt, is satisfied by all forms of incarceration. Our cases make clear, however, that the freedom-of-movement test identifies only a necessary and not a sufficient condition for *Miranda* custody. We have declined to accord it "talismanic power," because *Miranda* is to be enforced "only in those types of situations in which the concerns that powered the decision are implicated." *Berkemer* v. *McCarty*. Thus, the temporary and relatively non-threatening detention involved in a traffic stop or *Terry* stop, does not constitute *Miranda* custody.

Here, we are addressing the interim period during which a suspect was not interrogated, but was subject to a baseline set of restraints imposed pursuant to a prior conviction. Without minimizing the harsh realities of incarceration, we think lawful imprisonment imposed upon conviction of a crime does not create the coercive pressures identified in *Miranda*.

Interrogated suspects who have previously been convicted of crime live in prison. When they are released back into the general prison population, they return to their accustomed surroundings and daily routine — they regain the degree of control they had over their lives prior to the interrogation. Sentenced prisoners, in contrast to the *Miranda* paradigm, are not isolated with their accusers. They live among other inmates, guards, and workers, and often can receive visitors and communicate with people on the outside by mail or telephone.

Their detention, moreover, is relatively disconnected from their prior unwillingness to cooperate in an investigation. The former interrogator has no power to increase the duration of incarceration, which was determined at sentencing.[8] And even where the possibility of parole exists, the former interrogator has no apparent power to decrease the time served. This is in stark contrast to the circumstances faced by the defendants in *Edwards, Roberson*, and *Minnick*, whose continued detention as suspects rested with those controlling their interrogation, and who confronted the uncertainties of what final charges they would face, whether they would be convicted, and what sentence they would receive.

Shatzer's experience illustrates the vast differences between *Miranda* custody and incarceration pursuant to conviction. At the time of the 2003 attempted interrogation, Shatzer was already serving a sentence for a prior conviction. After that, he returned to the general prison population in the Maryland Correctional Institution-Hagerstown and was later transferred, for unrelated reasons, down the street to the Roxbury Correctional Institute. Both are medium-security state correctional facilities. Inmates in these facilities generally can visit the library each week, have regular exercise and recreation periods, can participate in basic adult education and occupational training, are able to send and receive mail, and are allowed to receive visitors twice a week. His continued detention after the 2003 interrogation did not depend on what he said (or did not say) to Detective Blankenship, and he has not alleged that he was placed in a higher level of security or faced any continuing restraints as a result of the 2003 interrogation. The

---

[8] We distinguish the duration of incarceration from the duration of what might be termed interrogative custody. When a prisoner is removed from the general prison population and taken to a separate location for questioning, the duration of *that separation* is assuredly dependent upon his interrogators. For which reason once he has asserted a refusal to speak without assistance of counsel *Edwards* prevents any efforts to get him to change his mind during that interrogative custody.

"inherently compelling pressures" of custodial interrogation ended when he returned to his normal life.

JUSTICE STEVENS, concurring in judgment.

The many problems with the Court's new rule are exacerbated in the very situation in this case: a suspect who is in prison. Even if, as the Court assumes, a trip to one's home significantly changes the *Edwards* calculus, a trip to one's prison cell is not the same. A prisoner's freedom is severely limited, and his entire life remains subject to government control. Such an environment is not conducive to "shak[ing] off any residual coercive effects of his prior custody."[12] Nor can a prisoner easily "seek advice from an attorney, family members, and friends," especially not within 14 days; prisoners are frequently subject to restrictions on communications. Nor, in most cases, can he live comfortably knowing that he cannot be badgered by police; prison is not like a normal situation in which a suspect "is in control, and need only shut his door or walk away to avoid police badgering." Indeed, for a person whose every move is controlled by the State, it is likely that "his sense of dependence on, and trust in, counsel as the guardian of his interests in dealing with government officials intensified."[13] The Court ignores these realities of prison, and instead rests its argument on the supposition that a prisoner's "detention . . . is relatively disconnected from their prior unwillingness to cooperate in an investigation." But that is not necessarily the case. Prisoners are uniquely vulnerable to the officials who control every aspect of their lives; prison guards may not look kindly upon a prisoner who refuses to cooperate with police. And cooperation frequently is relevant to whether the prisoner can obtain parole. Moreover, even if it is true as a factual matter that a prisoner's fate is not controlled by the police who come to interrogate him, how is the prisoner supposed to know that? As the Court itself admits, compulsion is likely when a suspect's "captors appear to control [his] fate." But when a guard informs a suspect that he must go speak with police, it will "appear" to the prisoner that the guard and police are not independent. "Questioning by captors, who *appear* to control the suspect's fate, may create mutually reinforcing pressures that the Court has assumed will weaken the suspect's will." *Illinois* v. *Perkins.*

---

[12] *Orozco v. Texas*, 394 U.S. 324, 326 (1969) (holding that a suspect was in custody while being held in own home, despite his comfort and familiarity with the surroundings); *Mathis v. United States*, 391 U.S. 1, 5 (1968) (holding that a person serving a prison sentence for one crime was in custody when he was interrogated in prison about another, unrelated crime).

[13] Prison also presents a troubling set of incentives for police. First, because investigators know that their suspect is also a prisoner, there is no need formally to place him under arrest. Thus, police generally can interview prisoners even without probable cause to hold them. This means that police can interrogate suspects with little or no evidence of guilt, and police can do so time after time, without fear of being sued for wrongful arrest. Second, because police know that their suspect is otherwise detained, there is no need necessarily to resolve the case quickly. Police can comfortably bide their time, interrogating and reinterrogating their suspect until he slips up. Third, because police need not hold their suspect, they do not need to arraign him or otherwise initiate formal legal proceedings that would trigger various protections.

QUESTIONS AND NOTES

1. Is Justice Stevens saying that Schatzer was in custody for *Miranda* purposes? If so, why did he vote to affirm the conviction? If not, what is he saying?

2. Is Scalia saying that Schatzer was not in custody or only that he was not in custody for *Miranda* purposes? If the latter, explain the difference?

3. We conclude this section with *Howes v. Fields*, which arguably makes it more difficult for a person questioned in prison to claim "custodial interrogation."

HOWES v. FIELDS
565 U.S. ___, 132 S. Ct. 1181 (2012)

JUSTICE ALITO delivered the opinion of the Court.

The United States Court of Appeals for the Sixth Circuit held that our precedents clearly establish that a prisoner is in custody within the meaning of *Miranda v. Arizona*, 384 U.S. 436, 86 S. Ct. 1602, 16 L. Ed. 2d 694 (1966), if the prisoner is taken aside and questioned about events that occurred outside the prison walls. Our decisions, however, do not clearly establish such a rule, and therefore the Court of Appeals erred in holding that this rule provides a permissible basis for federal habeas relief under the relevant provision of the Antiterrorism and Effective Death Penalty Act of 1996 (AEDPA), 28 U.S.C. § 2254(d)(1). Indeed, the rule applied by the court below does not represent a correct interpretation of our *Miranda* case law. We therefore reverse.

I

While serving a sentence in a Michigan jail, Randall Fields was escorted by a corrections officer to a conference room where two sheriff's deputies questioned him about allegations that, before he came to prison, he had engaged in sexual conduct with a 12-year-old boy. In order to get to the conference room, Fields had to go down one floor and pass through a locked door that separated two sections of the facility. Fields arrived at the conference room between 7 p.m. and 9 p.m. and was questioned for between five and seven hours.

At the beginning of the interview, Fields was told that he was free to leave and return to his cell. Later, he was again told that he could leave whenever he wanted. The two interviewing deputies were armed during the interview, but Fields remained free of handcuffs and other restraints. The door to the conference room was sometimes open and sometimes shut.

About halfway through the interview, after Fields had been confronted with the allegations of abuse, he became agitated and began to yell. Fields testified that one of the deputies, using an expletive, told him to sit down and said that "if [he] didn't want to cooperate, [he] could leave." Fields eventually confessed to engaging in sex acts with the boy. According to Fields' testimony at a suppression hearing, he said several times during the interview that he no longer wanted to talk to the deputies, but he did not ask to go back to his cell prior to the end of the interview.

When he was eventually ready to leave, he had to wait an additional 20 minutes or so because a corrections officer had to be summoned to escort him back to his cell, and he did not return to his cell until well after the hour when he generally retired. At no time was Fields given *Miranda* warnings or advised that he did not have to speak with the deputies.

The State of Michigan charged Fields with criminal sexual conduct. Relying on *Miranda*, Fields moved to suppress his confession, but the trial court denied his motion. Over the renewed objection of defense counsel, one of the interviewing deputies testified at trial about Fields' admissions. The jury convicted Fields of two counts of third-degree criminal sexual conduct, and the judge sentenced him to a term of 10 to 15 years of imprisonment. On direct appeal, the Michigan Court of Appeals affirmed, rejecting Fields' contention that his statements should have been suppressed because he was subjected to custodial interrogation without a *Miranda* warning. The court ruled that Fields had not been in custody for purposes of *Miranda* during the interview, so no *Miranda* warnings were required. The court emphasized that Fields was told that he was free to leave and return to his cell but that he never asked to do so. The Michigan Supreme Court denied discretionary review.

Fields then filed a petition for a writ of habeas corpus in Federal District Court, and the court granted relief. The Sixth Circuit affirmed, holding that the interview in the conference room was a "custodial interrogation" within the meaning of *Miranda* because isolation from the general prison population combined with questioning about conduct occurring outside the prison makes any such interrogation custodial *per se*. The Court of Appeals reasoned that this Court clearly established in *Mathis v. United States*, 391 U.S. 1, 88 S. Ct. 1503, 20 L. Ed. 2d 381 (1968), that "*Miranda* warnings must be administered when law enforcement officers remove an inmate from the general prison population and interrogate him regarding criminal conduct that took place outside the jail or prison." Because Fields was isolated from the general prison population and interrogated about conduct occurring in the outside world, the Court of Appeals found that the state court's decision was contrary to clearly established federal law as determined by this Court in *Mathis*.

We granted certiorari.

II

In this case, it is abundantly clear that our precedents do not clearly establish the categorical rule on which the Court of Appeals relied, *i.e.*, that the questioning of a prisoner is always custodial when the prisoner is removed from the general prison population and questioned about events that occurred outside the prison. On the contrary, we have repeatedly declined to adopt any categorical rule with respect to whether the questioning of a prison inmate is custodial.

In *Illinois v. Perkins*, where we upheld the admission of un-Mirandized statements elicited from an inmate by an undercover officer masquerading as another inmate, we noted that "[t]he bare fact of custody may not in every instance require a warning *even when the suspect is aware that he is speaking to an official, but we do not have occasion to explore that issue here.*" (emphasis added). Instead, we simply "reject[ed] the argument that *Miranda* warnings are required whenever a suspect is in custody in a technical sense and converses with someone who happens to be a government agent." *Id.*, at 297, 110 S. Ct. 2394.

Most recently, in *Maryland v. Shatzer*, we expressly declined to adopt a bright-line rule for determining the applicability of *Miranda* in prisons. *Shatzer* considered whether a break in custody ends the presumption of involuntariness established in *Edwards v. Arizona*, and, if so, whether a prisoner's return to the general prison population after a custodial interrogation constitutes a break in *Miranda* custody. In considering the latter question, we noted first that "[w]e have *never* decided whether incarceration constitutes custody for *Miranda* purposes, and have indeed explicitly declined to address the issue." The answer to this question, we noted, would "depen[d] upon whether [incarceration] exerts the coercive pressure that *Miranda* was designed to guard against — the 'danger of coercion [that] results from the *interaction* of custody and official interrogation.'"

In concluding that our precedents establish a categorical rule, the Court of Appeals placed great weight on the decision in *Mathis*, but the Court of Appeals misread the holding in that case. In *Mathis*, an inmate in a state prison was questioned by an Internal Revenue agent and was subsequently convicted for federal offenses. The Court of Appeals held that *Miranda* did not apply to this interview for two reasons: A criminal investigation had not been commenced at the time of the interview, and the prisoner was incarcerated for an "unconnected offense." This Court rejected both of those grounds for distinguishing *Miranda*, and thus the holding in *Mathis* is simply that a prisoner who otherwise meets the requirements for *Miranda* custody is not taken outside the scope of *Miranda* by either of the two factors on which the Court of Appeals had relied. *Mathis* did not hold that imprisonment, in and of itself, is enough to constitute *Miranda* custody.

The Court of Appeals purported to find support for its *per se* rule in *Shatzer*, relying on our statement that "[n]o one questions that Shatzer was in custody for *Miranda* purposes" when he was interviewed. But this statement means only that the issue of custody was not contested before us. It strains credulity to read the statement as constituting an "unambiguous conclusion" or "finding" by this Court that Shatzer was in custody.

Finally, contrary to respondent's suggestion, *Miranda* itself did not clearly establish the rule applied by the Court of Appeals. *Miranda* adopted a "set of prophylactic measures" designed to ward off the " 'inherently compelling pressures' of custodial interrogation," but *Miranda* did not hold that such pressures are always present when a prisoner is taken aside and questioned about events outside the prison walls. Indeed, *Miranda* did not even establish that police questioning of a suspect at the station house is always custodial. See *Mathiason*, (declining to find that *Miranda* warnings are required "simply because the questioning takes place in the station house, or because the questioned person is one whom the police suspect").

In sum, our decisions do not clearly establish that a prisoner is always in custody for purposes of *Miranda* whenever a prisoner is isolated from the general prison population and questioned about conduct outside the prison.

III

Not only does the categorical rule applied below go well beyond anything that is clearly established in our prior decisions, it is simply wrong. The three elements of that rule — (1) imprisonment, (2) questioning in private, and (3) questioning about events in the outside world — are not necessarily enough to create a custodial situation for *Miranda* purposes.

A

As used in our *Miranda* case law, "custody" is a term of art that specifies circumstances that are thought generally to present a serious danger of coercion. In determining whether a person is in custody in this sense, the initial step is to ascertain whether, in light of "the objective circumstances of the interrogation," a "reasonable person [would] have felt he or she was not at liberty to terminate the interrogation and leave." And in order to determine how a suspect would have "gauge[d]" his "freedom of movement," courts must examine "all of the circumstances surrounding the interrogation."

Determining whether an individual's freedom of movement was curtailed, however, is simply the first step in the analysis, not the last. Not all restraints on freedom of movement amount to custody for purposes of *Miranda*. We have "decline[d] to accord talismanic power" to the freedom-of-movement inquiry, *Berkemer* and have instead asked the additional question whether the relevant environment presents the same inherently coercive pressures as the type of station house questioning at issue in *Miranda*. "Our cases make clear . . . that the freedom-of-movement test identifies only a necessary and not a sufficient condition for *Miranda* custody."

It may be thought that the situation in *Berkemer* — the questioning of a motorist subjected to a brief traffic stop — is worlds away from those present when an inmate is questioned in a prison, but the same cannot be said of *Shatzer*, where we again distinguished between restraints on freedom of movement and *Miranda* custody. *Shatzer*, as noted, concerned the *Edwards* prophylactic rule, which limits the ability of the police to initiate further questioning of a suspect in *Miranda* custody once the suspect invokes the right to counsel. We held in *Shatzer* that this rule does not apply when there is a sufficient break in custody between the suspect's invocation of the right to counsel and the initiation of subsequent questioning. And, what is significant for present purposes, we further held that a break in custody may occur while a suspect is serving a term in prison. If a break in custody can occur while a prisoner is serving an uninterrupted term of imprisonment, it must follow that imprisonment alone is not enough to create a custodial situation within the meaning of *Miranda*.

There are at least three strong grounds for this conclusion. First, questioning a person who is already serving a prison term does not generally involve the shock that very often accompanies arrest. In the paradigmatic *Miranda* situation — a person is arrested in his home or on the street and whisked to a police station for questioning — detention represents a sharp and ominous change, and the shock may give rise to coercive pressures. A person who is "cut off from his normal life and companions," *Shatzer*, and abruptly transported from the street into a "police-dominated atmosphere," may feel coerced into answering questions.

By contrast, when a person who is already serving a term of imprisonment is questioned, there is usually no such change. "Interrogated suspects who have previously been convicted of crime live in prison." For a person serving a term of incarceration, we reasoned in *Shatzer*, the ordinary restrictions of prison life, while no doubt unpleasant, are expected and familiar and thus do not involve the same "inherently compelling pressures" that are often present when a suspect is yanked from familiar surroundings in the outside world and subjected to interrogation in a police station.

Second, a prisoner, unlike a person who has not been sentenced to a term of incarceration, is unlikely to be lured into speaking by a longing for prompt release. When a person is arrested and taken to a station house for interrogation, the person who is questioned may be pressured to speak by the hope that, after doing so, he will be allowed to leave and go home. On the other hand, when a prisoner is questioned, he knows that when the questioning ceases, he will remain under confinement.

Third, a prisoner, unlike a person who has not been convicted and sentenced, knows that the law enforcement officers who question him probably lack the authority to affect the duration of his sentence. And "where the possibility of parole exists," the interrogating officers probably also lack the power to bring about an early release. "When the suspect has no reason to think that the listeners have official power over him, it should not be assumed that his words are motivated by the reaction he expects from his listeners." Under such circumstances, there is little "basis for the assumption that a suspect . . . will feel compelled to speak by the fear of reprisal for remaining silent or in the hope of [a] more lenient treatment should he confess."

In short, standard conditions of confinement and associated restrictions on freedom will not necessarily implicate the same interests that the Court sought to protect when it afforded special safeguards to persons subjected to custodial interrogation. Thus, service of a term of imprisonment, without more, is not enough to constitute *Miranda* custody.

B

The two other elements included in the Court of Appeals' rule — questioning in private and questioning about events that took place outside the prison — are likewise insufficient.

Taking a prisoner aside for questioning — as opposed to questioning the prisoner in the presence of fellow inmates — does not necessarily convert a "noncustodial situation . . . to one in which *Miranda* applies." When a person who is not serving a prison term is questioned, isolation may contribute to a coercive atmosphere by preventing family members, friends, and others who may be sympathetic from providing either advice or emotional support. And without any such assistance, the person who is questioned may feel overwhelming pressure to speak and to refrain from asking that the interview be terminated.

By contrast, questioning a prisoner in private does not generally remove the prisoner from a supportive atmosphere. Fellow inmates are by no means necessarily friends. On the contrary, they may be hostile and, for a variety of reasons, may react negatively to what the questioning reveals. In the present case, for example, would respondent have felt more at ease if he had been questioned in the presence of other inmates about the sexual abuse of an adolescent boy? Isolation from the general prison population is often in the best interest of the interviewee and, in any event, does not suggest on its own the atmosphere of coercion that concerned the Court in *Miranda.*

It is true that taking a prisoner aside for questioning may necessitate some additional limitations on his freedom of movement. A prisoner may, for example, be removed from an exercise yard and taken, under close guard, to the room where the interview is to be held. But such procedures are an ordinary and familiar attribute of life behind bars. Escorts and special security precautions may be standard procedures regardless of the purpose for which an inmate is removed from his regular routine and taken to a special location. For example, ordinary prison procedure may require such measures when a prisoner is led to a meeting with an attorney.

Finally, we fail to see why questioning about criminal activity outside the prison should be regarded as having a significantly greater potential for coercion than questioning under otherwise identical circumstances about criminal activity within the prison walls. In both instances, there is the potential for additional criminal liability and punishment. If anything, the distinction would seem to cut the other way, as an inmate who confesses to misconduct that occurred within the prison may also incur administrative penalties, but even this is not enough to tip the scale in the direction of custody. "The threat to a citizen's Fifth Amendment rights that *Miranda* was designed to neutralize" is neither mitigated nor magnified by the location of the conduct about which questions are asked.

For these reasons, the Court of Appeals' categorical rule is unsound.

IV

A

When a prisoner is questioned, the determination of custody should focus on all of the features of the interrogation. These include the language that is used in summoning the prisoner to the interview and the manner in which the interrogation is conducted. An inmate who is removed from the general prison population for questioning and is "thereafter . . . subjected to treatment" in connection with the interrogation "that renders him 'in custody' for practical purposes . . . will be entitled to the full panoply of protections prescribed by *Miranda.*"

"Fidelity to the doctrine announced in *Miranda* requires that it be enforced strictly, but only in those types of situations in which the concerns that powered the decision are implicated." Confessions voluntarily made by prisoners in other situations should not be suppressed. "Voluntary confessions are not merely a proper element in law enforcement, they are an unmitigated good, essential to society's compelling interest in finding, convicting, and punishing those who violate the law."

B

The record in this case reveals that respondent was not taken into custody for purposes of *Miranda*. To be sure, respondent did not invite the interview or consent to it in advance, and he was not advised that he was free to decline to speak with the deputies. The following facts also lend some support to respondent's argument that *Miranda*'s custody requirement was met: The interview lasted for between five and seven hours in the evening and continued well past the hour when respondent generally went to bed; the deputies who questioned respondent were armed; and one of the deputies, according to respondent, "[u]sed a very sharp tone," and, on one occasion, profanity.

These circumstances, however, were offset by others. Most important, respondent was told at the outset of the interrogation, and was reminded again thereafter, that he could leave and go back to his cell whenever he wanted. Moreover, respondent was not physically restrained or threatened and was interviewed in a well-lit, average-sized conference room, where he was "not uncomfortable." He was offered food and water, and the door to the conference room was sometimes left open. "All of these objective facts are consistent with an interrogation environment in which a reasonable person would have felt free to terminate the interview and leave."

Because he was in prison, respondent was not free to leave the conference room by himself and to make his own way through the facility to his cell. Instead, he was escorted to the conference room and, when he ultimately decided to end the interview, he had to wait about 20 minutes for a corrections officer to arrive and escort him to his cell. But he would have been subject to this same restraint even if he had been taken to the conference room for some reason other than police questioning; under no circumstances could he have reasonably expected to be able to roam free. And while respondent testified that he "was told . . . if I did not want to cooperate, I needed to go back to my cell," these words did not coerce cooperation by threatening harsher conditions. ("I was told, if I didn't want to cooperate, I could leave"). Returning to his cell would merely have returned him to his usual environment.

Taking into account all of the circumstances of the questioning — including especially the undisputed fact that respondent was told that he was free to end the questioning and to return to his cell — we hold that respondent was not in custody within the meaning of *Miranda*.

The judgment of the Court of Appeals is *reversed*.

Justice Ginsburg, with whom Justice Breyer and Justice Sotomayor join, concurring in part and dissenting in part.

Given this Court's controlling decisions on what counts as "custody" for *Miranda* purposes, I agree that the law is not "clearly established" in respondent Fields's favor. But I disagree with the Court's further determination that Fields was not in custody under *Miranda*. Were the case here on direct review, I would vote to hold that *Miranda* precludes the State's introduction of Fields's confession as evidence against him.

Miranda reacted to police interrogation tactics that eroded the Fifth Amendment's ban on compulsory self-incrimination. The opinion did so by requiring interrogators to convey to suspects the now-familiar warnings.

Under what circumstances are *Miranda* warnings required? *Miranda* tells us "in all settings in which [a person's] freedom of action is curtailed in any significant way." Given the reality that police interrogators "trad[e] on the weakness of individuals," *i.e.*, their "insecurity about [themselves] or [their] surroundings," the Court found the preinterrogation warnings set out in the opinion "indispensable." Those warnings, the Court elaborated, are "an absolute prerequisite in overcoming the inherent pressures of the interrogation atmosphere," *id.*, at 468, 86 S. Ct. 1602; they "insure" that the suspect is timely told of his Fifth Amendment privilege, and his freedom to exercise it.

Fields, serving time for disorderly conduct, was, of course, "i[n] custody," but not "for purposes of *Miranda*," the Court concludes. I would not train, as the Court does, on the question whether there can be custody within custody. Instead, I would ask, as *Miranda* put it, whether Fields was subjected to "incommunicado interrogation . . . in a police-dominated atmosphere," whether he was placed, against his will, in an inherently stressful situation, and whether his "freedom of action [was] curtailed in any significant way." Those should be the key questions, and to each I would answer "Yes."

As the Court acknowledges, Fields did not invite or consent to the interview. He was removed from his cell in the evening, taken to a conference room in the sheriff's quarters, and questioned by two armed deputies long into the night and early morning. He was not told at the outset that he had the right to decline to speak with the deputies. Shut in with the armed officers, Fields felt "trapped." Although told he could return to his cell if he did not want to cooperate, Fields believed the deputies "would not have allowed [him] to leave the room." And with good reason. More than once, "he told the officers . . . he did not want to speak with them anymore." He was given water, but not his evening medications. Yet the Court concludes that Fields was in "an interrogation environment in which a reasonable person would have felt free to terminate the interview and leave."

Critical to the Court's judgment is "the undisputed fact that [Fields] was told that he was free to end the questioning and to return to his cell." Never mind the facts suggesting that Fields's submission to the overnight interview was anything but voluntary. Was Fields "held for interrogation"? Brought to, and left alone with, the gun-bearing deputies, he surely was in my judgment.

Miranda instructed that such a person "must be clearly informed that he has the right to consult with a lawyer and to have the lawyer with him during interrogation." Those warnings, along with "warnings of the right to remain silent and that anything stated can be used in evidence against [the speaker]," *Miranda* explained, are necessary "prerequisite[s] to [an] interrogation" compatible with the Fifth

Amendment. Today, for people already in prison, the Court finds it adequate for the police to say: "You are free to terminate this interrogation and return to your cell." Such a statement is no substitute for one ensuring that an individual is aware of his rights.

For the reasons stated, I would hold that the "incommunicado interrogation [of Fields] in a police-dominated atmosphere," without informing him of his rights, dishonored the Fifth Amendment privilege *Miranda* was designed to safeguard.

QUESTIONS AND NOTES

1. Should it matter that Fields said that he didn't want to talk to the officers? Why? Why not?

2. Is (should) *Perkins* (be) relevant? How?

3. Is the Court fairly reading *Schatzer*? Before you read this case, did you assume that Schatzer was in fact in custody?

4. Assuming, as the court correctly holds, that there is a difference between *Miranda* custody and the fact of imprisonment, what is the difference? On which side of the line was Fields?

5. What more is (should be) necessary to constitute *Miranda* custody for a prisoner?

6. Did Justice Ginsburg concede more than necessary in saying that the law was not "clearly established"?

7. In the next section, we will explore the Court's conception of "interrogation."

F.   INTERROGATION

RHODE ISLAND v. INNIS
446 U.S. 291 (1980)

MR. JUSTICE STEWART delivered the opinion of the Court.

In *Miranda*, the Court held that, once a defendant in custody asks to speak with a lawyer, all interrogation must cease until a lawyer is present. The issue in this case is whether the respondent was "interrogated" in violation of the standards promulgated in the *Miranda* opinion.

I

On the night of January 12, 1975, John Mulvaney, a Providence, R.I., taxicab driver, disappeared after being dispatched to pick up a customer. His body was discovered four days later buried in a shallow grave in Coventry, R.I. He had died from a shotgun blast aimed at the back of his head.

On January 17, 1975, shortly after midnight, the Providence police received a telephone call from Gerald Aubin, also a taxicab driver, who reported that he had just been robbed by a man wielding a sawed-off shotgun. Aubin further reported that he had dropped off his assailant near Rhode Island College in a section of Providence known as Mount Pleasant. While at the Providence police station waiting to give a statement, Aubin noticed a picture of his assailant on a bulletin board. Aubin so informed one of the police officers present. The officer prepared a photo array, and again Aubin identified a picture of the same person. That person was the respondent. Shortly thereafter, the Providence police began a search of the Mount Pleasant area.

At approximately 4:30 a.m. on the same date, Patrolman Lovell, while cruising the streets of Mount Pleasant in a patrol car, spotted the respondent standing in the street facing him. When Patrolman Lovell stopped his car, the respondent walked towards it. Patrolman Lovell then arrested the respondent, who was unarmed, and advised him of his so-called *Miranda* rights. While the two men waited in the patrol car for other police officers to arrive, Patrolman Lovell did not converse with the respondent other than to respond to the latter's request for a cigarette.

Within minutes, Sergeant Sears arrived at the scene of the arrest, and he also gave the respondent the *Miranda* warnings. Immediately thereafter, Captain Leyden and other police officers arrived. Captain Leyden advised the respondent of his *Miranda* rights. The respondent stated that he understood those rights and wanted to speak with a lawyer. Captain Leyden then directed that the respondent be placed in a "caged wagon," a four-door police car with a wire screen mesh between the front and rear seats, and be driven to the central police station. Three officers, Patrolmen Gleckman, Williams, and McKenna, were assigned to accompany the respondent to the central station. They placed the respondent in the vehicle and shut the doors. Captain Leyden then instructed the officers not to question the respondent or intimidate or coerce him in any way. The three officers then entered the vehicle, and it departed.

While en route to the central station, Patrolman Gleckman initiated a conversation with Patrolman McKenna concerning the missing shotgun.[1] As Patrolman Gleckman later testified:

> A. At this point, I was talking back and forth with Patrolman McKenna stating that I frequent this area while on patrol and [that because a school for handicapped children is located nearby,] there's a lot of handicapped children running around in this area, and God forbid one of them might find a weapon with shells and they might hurt themselves.

Patrolman McKenna apparently shared his fellow officer's concern:

> A. I more or less concurred with him [Gleckman] that it was a safety factor and that we should, you know, continue to search for the weapon and try to find it.

---

[1] Although there was conflicting testimony about the exact seating arrangements, it is clear that everyone in the vehicle heard the conversation.

While Patrolman Williams said nothing, he overheard the conversation between the two officers:

> A. He [Gleckman] said it would be too bad if the little — I believe he said a girl — would pick up the gun, maybe kill herself.

The respondent then interrupted the conversation, stating that the officers should turn the car around so he could show them where the gun was located. At this point, Patrolman McKenna radioed back to Captain Leyden that they were returning to the scene of the arrest and that the respondent would inform them of the location of the gun. At the time the respondent indicated that the officers should turn back, they had traveled no more than a mile, a trip encompassing only a few minutes.

The police vehicle then returned to the scene of the arrest where a search for the shotgun was in progress. There, Captain Leyden again advised the respondent of his *Miranda* rights. The respondent replied that he understood those rights but that he "wanted to get the gun out of the way because of the kids in the area in the school." The respondent then led the police to a nearby field, where he pointed out the shotgun under some rocks by the side of the road.

II

In the present case, the parties are in agreement that the respondent was fully informed of his *Miranda* rights and that he invoked his *Miranda* right to counsel when he told Captain Leyden that he wished to consult with a lawyer. It is also uncontested that the respondent was "in custody" while being transported to the police station.

The issue, therefore, is whether the respondent was "interrogated" by the police officers in violation of the respondent's undisputed right under *Miranda* to remain silent until he had consulted with a lawyer.[2] In resolving this issue, we first define the term "interrogation" under *Miranda* before turning to a consideration of the facts of this case.

A

The starting point for defining "interrogation" in this context is, of course, the Court's *Miranda* opinion. There the Court observed that "[b]y custodial interrogation, we mean *questioning* initiated by law enforcement officers after a person has been taken into custody or otherwise deprived of his freedom of action in any significant way." (emphasis added). This passage and other references throughout the opinion to "questioning" might suggest that the *Miranda* rules were to apply only to those police interrogation practices that involve express questioning of a defendant while in custody.

We do not, however, construe the *Miranda* opinion so narrowly. The concern of the Court in *Miranda* was that the "interrogation environment" created by the

---

[2] Since we conclude that the respondent was not "interrogated" for *Miranda* purposes, we do not reach the question whether the respondent waived his right under *Miranda* to be free from interrogation until counsel was present.

interplay of interrogation and custody would "subjugate the individual to the will of his examiner" and thereby undermine the privilege against compulsory self-incrimination. The police practices that evoked this concern included several that did not involve express questioning. For example, one of the practices discussed in *Miranda* was the use of line-ups in which a coached witness would pick the defendant as the perpetrator. This was designed to establish that the defendant was in fact guilty as a predicate for further interrogation. A variation on this theme discussed in *Miranda* was the so-called "reverse line-up" in which a defendant would be identified by coached witnesses as the perpetrator of a fictitious crime, with the object of inducing him to confess to the actual crime of which he was suspected in order to escape the false prosecution. The Court in *Miranda* also included in its survey of interrogation practices the use of psychological ploys, such as to "posi[t]" "the guilt of the subject," to "minimize the moral seriousness of the offense," and "to cast blame on the victim or on society." It is clear that these techniques of persuasion, no less than express questioning, were thought, in a custodial setting, to amount to interrogation.[3]

This is not to say, however, that all statements obtained by the police after a person has been taken into custody are to be considered the product of interrogation. As the Court in *Miranda* noted:

> Confessions remain a proper element in law enforcement. Any statement given freely and voluntarily without any compelling influences is, of course, admissible in evidence. *The fundamental import of the privilege while an individual is in custody is not whether he is allowed to talk to the police without the benefit of warnings and counsel, but whether he can be interrogated* . . . . Volunteered statements of any kind are not barred by the Fifth Amendment and their admissibility is not affected by our holding today.

(emphasis added). It is clear therefore that the special procedural safeguards outlined in *Miranda* are required not where a suspect is simply taken into custody, but rather where a suspect in custody is subjected to interrogation. "Interrogation," as conceptualized in the *Miranda* opinion, must reflect a measure of compulsion above and beyond that inherent in custody itself.

We conclude that the *Miranda* safeguards come into play whenever a person in custody is subjected to either express questioning or its functional equivalent. That is to say, the term "interrogation" under *Miranda* refers not only to express questioning, but also to any words or actions on the part of the police (other than those normally attendant to arrest and custody) that the police should know are reasonably likely to elicit an incriminating response[4] from the suspect.[5] The latter

---

[3] To limit the ambit of *Miranda* to express questioning would "place a premium on the ingenuity of the police to devise methods of indirect interrogation, rather than to implement the plain mandate of *Miranda*." *Commonwealth v. Hamilton*, 445 Pa. 292, 297, 285 A.2d 172, 175.

[4] By "incriminating response" we refer to any response — whether inculpatory or exculpatory — that the *prosecution* may seek to introduce at trial.

[5] One of the dissenting opinions seems totally to misapprehend this definition in suggesting that it "will almost certainly exclude every statement [of the police] that is not punctuated with a question mark."

portion of this definition focuses primarily upon the perceptions of the suspect, rather than the intent of the police. This focus reflects the fact that the *Miranda* safeguards were designed to vest a suspect in custody with an added measure of protection against coercive police practices, without regard to objective proof of the underlying intent of the police. A practice that the police should know is reasonably likely to evoke an incriminating response from a suspect thus amounts to interrogation.[6] But, since the police surely cannot be held accountable for the unforeseeable results of their words or actions, the definition of interrogation can extend only to words or actions on the part of police officers that they *should have known* were reasonably likely to elicit an incriminating response.[7]

B

Turning to the facts of the present case, we conclude that the respondent was not "interrogated" within the meaning of *Miranda*. It is undisputed that the first prong of the definition of "interrogation" was not satisfied, for the conversation between Patrolmen Gleckman and McKenna included no express questioning of the respondent. Rather, that conversation was, at least in form, nothing more than a dialogue between the two officers to which no response from the respondent was invited.

Moreover, it cannot be fairly concluded that the respondent was subjected to the "functional equivalent" of questioning. It cannot be said, in short, that Patrolmen Gleckman and McKenna should have known that their conversation was reasonably likely to elicit an incriminating response from the respondent. There is nothing in the record to suggest that the officers were aware that the respondent was peculiarly susceptible to an appeal to his conscience concerning the safety of handicapped children. Nor is there anything in the record to suggest that the police knew that the respondent was unusually disoriented or upset at the time of his arrest.[8]

The case thus boils down to whether, in the context of a brief conversation, the officers should have known that the respondent would suddenly be moved to make a self-incriminating response. Given the fact that the entire conversation appears to have consisted of no more than a few off hand remarks, we cannot say that the officers should have known that it was reasonably likely that Innis would so respond. This is not a case where the police carried on a lengthy harangue in the

---

[6] This is not to say that the intent of the police is irrelevant, for it may well have a bearing on whether the police should have known that their words or actions were reasonably likely to evoke an incriminating response. In particular, where a police practice is designed to elicit an incriminating response from the accused, it is unlikely that the practice will not also be one which the police should have known was reasonably likely to have that effect.

[7] Any knowledge the police may have had concerning the unusual susceptibility of a defendant to a particular form of persuasion might be an important factor in determining whether the police should have known that their words or actions were reasonably likely to elicit an incriminating response from the suspect.

[8] The record in no way suggests that the officers' remarks were *designed* to elicit a response. *See* n.7, *supra*. It is significant that the trial judge, after hearing the officers' testimony, concluded that it was "entirely understandable that [the officers] would voice their concern [for the safety of the handicapped children] to each other."

presence of the suspect. Nor does the record support the respondent's contention that, under the circumstances, the officers' comments were particularly "evocative." It is our view, therefore, that the respondent was not subjected by the police to words or actions that the police should have known were reasonably likely to elicit an incriminating response from him.

The Rhode Island Supreme Court erred, in short, in equating "subtle compulsion" with interrogation. That the officers' comments struck a responsive chord is readily apparent. Thus, it may be said, as the Rhode Island Supreme Court did say, that the respondent was subjected to "subtle compulsion." But that is not the end of the inquiry. It must also be established that a suspect's incriminating response was the product of words or actions on the part of the police that they should have known were reasonably likely to elicit an incriminating response.[9] This was not established in the present case.

For the reasons stated, the judgment of the Supreme Court of Rhode Island is vacated, and the case is remanded to that court for further proceedings not inconsistent with this opinion.

MR. CHIEF JUSTICE BURGER, concurring in the judgment.

Since the result is not inconsistent with *Miranda*, I concur in the judgment.

The meaning of *Miranda* has become reasonably clear and law enforcement practices have adjusted to its strictures; I would neither overrule *Miranda*, disparage it, nor extend it at this late date. I fear, however, that the rationale in Parts II-A and II-B, of the Court's opinion may introduce new elements of uncertainty; under the Court's test, a police officer, in the brief time available, apparently must evaluate the suggestibility and susceptibility of an accused. *See, e.g.*, n. 8. Few, if any, police officers are competent to make the kind of evaluation seemingly contemplated; even a psychiatrist asked to express an expert opinion on these aspects of a suspect in custody would very likely employ extensive questioning and observation to make the judgment now charged to police officers.

Trial judges have enough difficulty discerning the boundaries and nuances flowing from post-*Miranda* opinions, and we do not clarify that situation today.

MR. JUSTICE MARSHALL, with whom MR. JUSTICE BRENNAN joins, dissenting.

I am substantially in agreement with the Court's definition of "interrogation" within the meaning of *Miranda*. In my view, the *Miranda* safeguards apply whenever police conduct is intended or likely to produce a response from a suspect in custody. As I read the Court's opinion, its definition of "interrogation" for *Miranda* purposes is equivalent, for practical purposes, to my formulation, since it contemplates that "where a police practice is designed to elicit an incriminating

---

[9] By way of example, if the police had done no more than to drive past the site of the concealed weapon while taking the most direct route to the police station, and if the respondent, upon noticing for the first time the proximity of the school for handicapped children, had blurted out that he would show the officers where the gun was located, it could not seriously be argued that this "subtle compulsion" would have constituted "interrogation" within the meaning of the *Miranda* opinion.

response from the accused, it is unlikely that the practice will not also be one which the police should have known was reasonably likely to have that effect." Thus, the Court requires an objective inquiry into the likely effect of police conduct on a typical individual, taking into account any special susceptibility of the suspect to certain kinds of pressure of which the police know or have reason to know.

I am utterly at a loss, however, to understand how this objective standard as applied to the facts before us can rationally lead to the conclusion that there was no interrogation. Innis was arrested at 4:30 a.m., handcuffed, searched, advised of his rights, and placed in the back seat of a patrol car. Within a short time he had been twice more advised of his rights and driven away in a four-door sedan with three police officers. Two officers sat in the front seat and one sat beside Innis in the back seat. Since the car traveled no more than a mile before Innis agreed to point out the location of the murder weapon, Officer Gleckman must have begun almost immediately to talk about the search for the shotgun.

The Court attempts to characterize Gleckman's statements as "no more than a few off hand remarks" which could not reasonably have been expected to elicit a response. If the statements had been addressed to respondent, it would be impossible to draw such a conclusion. The simple message of the "talking back and forth" between Gleckman and McKenna was that they had to find the shotgun to avert a child's death.

One can scarcely imagine a stronger appeal to the conscience of a suspect — *any* suspect — than the assertion that if the weapon is not found an innocent person will be hurt or killed. And not just any innocent person, but an innocent child — a little girl — a helpless, handicapped little girl on her way to school. The notion that such an appeal could not be expected to have any effect unless the suspect were known to have some special interest in handicapped children verges on the ludicrous. As a matter of fact, the appeal to a suspect to confess for the sake of others, to "display some evidence of decency and honor," is a classic interrogation technique.

Gleckman's remarks would obviously have constituted interrogation if they had been explicitly directed to respondent, and the result should not be different because they were nominally addressed to McKenna. This is not a case where police officers speaking among themselves are accidentally overheard by a suspect. These officers were "talking back and forth" in close quarters with the handcuffed suspect, traveling past the very place where they believed the weapon was located. They knew respondent would hear and attend to their conversation, and they are chargeable with knowledge of and responsibility for the pressures to speak which they created.

I firmly believe that this case is simply an aberration, and that in future cases the Court will apply the standard adopted today in accordance with its plain meaning.

MR. JUSTICE STEVENS, dissenting.

I

As the Court recognizes, *Miranda* makes it clear that, once respondent requested an attorney, he had an absolute right to have any type of interrogation cease until an attorney was present. As it also recognizes, *Miranda* requires that the term "interrogation" be broadly construed to include "either express questioning or its functional equivalent."[4] In my view any statement that would normally be understood by the average listener as calling for a response is the functional equivalent of a direct question, whether or not it is punctuated by a question mark. The Court, however, takes a much narrower view. It holds that police conduct is not the "functional equivalent" of direct questioning unless the police should have known that what they were saying or doing was likely to elicit an incriminating response from the suspect.[5] This holding represents a plain departure from the principles set forth in *Miranda*.

[I]f after being told that he has a right to have an attorney present during interrogation, a suspect chooses to cut off questioning until counsel can be obtained, his choice must be "scrupulously honored" by the police. *See Mosley* (White, J., concurring in result). At the least this must mean that the police are prohibited from making deliberate attempts to elicit statements from the suspect. Yet the Court is unwilling to characterize all such attempts as "interrogation," noting only that "where a police practice is designed to elicit an incriminating response from the accused, it is unlikely that the practice will not also be one which the police should have known was reasonable likely to have that effect."[8]

From the suspect's, point of view, the effectiveness of the warnings depends on whether it appears that the police are scrupulously honoring his rights. Apparent attempts to elicit information from a suspect after he has invoked his right to cut off questioning necessarily demean that right and tend to reinstate the imbalance between police and suspect that the *Miranda* warnings are designed to correct. Thus, if the rationale for requiring those warnings in the first place is to be respected, any police conduct or statements that would appear to a reasonable person in the suspect's position to call for a response must be considered "interrogation."[10]

---

[4] As the Court points out, the Court in *Miranda* was acutely aware of the fact that police interrogation techniques are not limited to direct questioning.

[5] In limiting its test to police statements "likely to elicit an incriminating response," the Court confuses the scope of the exclusionary rule with the definition of "interrogation." Of course, any incriminating statement as defined in *Miranda*, must be excluded from evidence if it is the product of impermissible interrogation. But I fail to see how this rule helps in deciding whether a particular statement or tactic constitutes "interrogation." After all, *Miranda* protects a suspect in Innis' position not simply from interrogation that is likely to be successful, but from any interrogation at all.

[8] This factual assumption is extremely dubious. I would assume that police often interrogate suspects without any reason to believe that their efforts are likely to be successful in the hope that a statement will nevertheless be forthcoming.

[10] I would use an objective standard both to avoid the difficulties of proof inherent in a subjective

In short, in order to give full protection to a suspect's right to be free from any interrogation at all, the definition of "interrogation" must include any police statement or conduct that has the same purpose or effect as a direct question. Statements that appear to call for a response from the suspect, as well as those that are designed to do so, should be considered interrogation. By prohibiting only those relatively few statements or actions that a police officer should know are likely to elicit an incriminating response, the Court today accords a suspect considerably less protection. Indeed, since I suppose most suspects are unlikely to incriminate themselves even when questioned directly, this new definition will almost certainly exclude every statement that is not punctuated with a question mark from the concept of "interrogation."[11]

The difference between the approach required by a faithful adherence to *Miranda* and the stinted test applied by the Court today can be illustrated by comparing three different ways in which Officer Gleckman could have communicated his fears about the possible dangers posed by the shotgun to handicapped children. He could have:

(1) directly asked Innis:

  Will you please tell me where the shotgun is so we can protect handicapped school children from danger?

(2) announced to the other officers in the wagon:

  If the man sitting in the back seat with me should decide to tell us where the gun is, we can protect handicapped children from danger.

or (3) stated to the other officers:

  It would be too bad if a little handicapped girl would pick up the gun that this man left in the area and maybe kill herself.

In my opinion, all three of these statements should be considered interrogation because all three appear to be designed to elicit a response from anyone who in fact knew where the gun was located.[12] Under the Court's test, on the other hand, the form of the statements would be critical. The third statement would not be interrogation because in the Court's view there was no reason for Officer Gleckman to believe that Innis was susceptible to this type of an implied appeal, therefore, the statement would not be reasonably likely to elicit an incriminating response. Assuming that this is true, then it seems to me that the first two statements, which

---

standard and to give police adequate guidance in their dealings with suspects who have requested counsel.

[11] The Court's suggestion, n. 6, that I totally misapprehend the import of its definition is belied by its application of the new standard to the facts of this case.

[12] *See* White, Rhode Island v. Innis: *The Significance of a Suspect's Assertion of His Right to Counsel*, 17 AM. CRIM. L. REV. 53, 68 (1979), where the author proposes the same test and applies it to the facts of this case, stating:

  Under the proposed objective standard, the result is obvious. Since the conversation indicates a strong desire to know the location of the shotgun, any person with knowledge of the weapon's location would be likely to believe that the officers wanted him to disclose its location. Thus, a reasonable person in Innis's position would believe that the officers were seeking to solicit precisely the type of response that was given.

would be just as unlikely to elicit such a response, should also not be considered interrogation. But, because the first statement is clearly an express question, it *would* be considered interrogation under the Court's test. The second statement, although just as clearly a deliberate appeal to Innis to reveal the location of the gun, would presumably not be interrogation because (a) it was not in form a direct question and (b) it does not fit within the "reasonably likely to elicit an incriminating response" category that applies to indirect interrogation.

As this example illustrates, the Court's test creates an incentive for police to ignore a suspect's invocation of his rights in order to make continued attempts to extract information from him. If a suspect does not appear to be susceptible to a particular type of psychological pressure,[13] the police are apparently free to exert that pressure on him despite his request for counsel, so long as they are careful not to punctuate their statements with question marks. And if, contrary to all reasonable expectations, the suspect makes an incriminating statement, that statement can be used against him at trial. The Court thus turns *Miranda's* unequivocal rule against any interrogation at all into a trap in which unwary suspects may be caught by police deception.

II

I think the Court is clearly wrong in holding, as a matter of law, that Officer Gleckman should not have realized that his statement was likely to elicit an incriminating response. The Court implicitly assumes that, at least in the absence of a lengthy harangue, a criminal suspect will not be likely to respond to indirect appeals to his humanitarian impulses. It then goes on to state that the officers in this case had no reason to believe that respondent would be unusually susceptible to such appeals. Finally, although the significance of the officer's intentions is not clear under its objective test, the Court states in a footnote that the record "in no way suggests" that Officer Gleckman's remarks were designed to elicit a response.

The Court's assumption that criminal suspects are not susceptible to appeals to conscience is directly contrary to the teachings of police interrogation manuals, which recommend appealing to a suspect's sense of morality as a standard and often successful interrogation technique. Surely the practical experience embodied in such manuals should not be ignored in a case such as this in which the record is devoid of any evidence — one way or the other — as to the susceptibility of suspects in general or of Innis in particular.

Moreover, there is evidence in the record to support the view that Officer Gleckman's statement was intended to elicit a response from Innis. Officer Gleckman, who was not regularly assigned to the caged wagon, was directed by a police captain to ride with respondent to the police station. Although there is a dispute in the testimony, it appears that Gleckman may well have been riding in the

---

[13] As The Chief Justice points out in his concurring opinion, "[f]ew, if any, police officers are competent to make the kind of evaluation seemingly contemplated [by the Court's opinion]" except by close and careful observation. Under these circumstances, courts might well find themselves deferring to what appeared to be good-faith judgments on the part of the police.

back seat with Innis.[16] The record does not explain why, notwithstanding the fact that respondent was handcuffed, unarmed, and had offered no resistance when arrested by an officer acting alone, the captain ordered Officer Gleckman to ride with respondent.[17] It is not inconceivable that two professionally trained police officers concluded that a few well-chosen remarks might induce respondent to disclose the whereabouts of the shotgun.[18] This conclusion becomes even more plausible in light of the emotionally charged words chosen by Officer Gleckman ("God forbid" that a "little girl" should find the gun and hurt herself).[19]

III

Under my view of the correct standard, the judgment of the Rhode Island Supreme Court should be affirmed because the statements made within Innis' hearing were as likely to elicit a response as a direct question. However, even if I were to agree with the Court's much narrower standard, I would disagree with its disposition of this particular case because the Rhode Island courts should be given an opportunity to apply the new standard to the facts of this case.

QUESTIONS AND NOTES

1. Do you think that *Innis* takes a broad or narrow view of interrogation within the meaning of *Miranda*? Explain. If you think that it takes a broad view, how do you explain Justice Stewart's (a *Miranda* dissenter) authorship of the opinion, and Justice Rehnquist's concurrence?

2. If the police had *intentionally* driven out of the way to pass the suspected hiding place (compare n. 9) or had intentionally driven out of their way to pass the state's prison, would (should) that constitute interrogation?

3. Suppose the police left the items obtained from a burglary in front of the defendant's jail cell, and said nothing. Interrogation?

---

[16] Officer Gleckman testified that he was riding in the front seat with the driver. However, Officer McKenna, who had also ridden in the wagon, and the police captain both testified that Gleckman rode in the back seat with the suspect. Thereafter, the third officer in the wagon corroborated Gleckman's testimony.

[17] This was apparently a somewhat unusual procedure. Officer McKenna testified that:

> If I remember correctly, the vehicle — Innis was placed in it and the vehicle door was closed, and we were waiting for instructions from Captain Leyden . . . . At that point, Captain Leyden instructed Patrolman Gleckman to accompany us. There's usually two men assigned to the wagon, but in this particular case he wanted a third man to accompany us, and Gleckman got in the rear seat. In other words, the door was closed. Gleckman opened the door and got in the vehicle with the subject. Myself, I went over to the other side and got in the passenger's side in the front.

[18] Although Officer Gleckman testified that the captain told him not to interrogate, intimidate or coerce respondent on the way back, this does not rule out the possibility that either or both of them thought an indirect psychological ploy would be permissible.

[19] In his article quoted in n. 12, *supra*, Professor White also points out that the officers were probably aware that the chances of a handicapped child's finding the weapon at a time when police were not present were relatively slim. Thus, he concluded that it was unlikely that the true purpose of the conversation was to voice a genuine concern over the children's welfare. *See* 17 Am. Crim. L. Rev. at 68.

4.   Is interrogation *vel non* determined from the perspective of the policeman or the suspect? Explain.

5.   Does the Court adopt an objective or subjective view of interrogation? Which one should it have adopted?

6.   Was Officer Gleckman's professed concern reasonably *likely* to elicit an incriminating response? Was it reasonably *calculated* to elicit an incriminating response? Which of those questions was (should have been) the more relevant?

7.   Which (if any) of Justice Stevens three hypotheticals calls for a response? Which (if any) would be deemed interrogation by the majority? How (if at all) are they different from Gleckman's actual statements in the case?

PROBLEM

Police officers Jim Rogers and Joe Martin arrested Johnny Jones for burglary. After handcuffing him, placing him in the police car and driving him off to jail (Martin driving with Rogers sitting beside him in the front seat, and Jones sitting alone in the back seat), the following conversation transpired:

Rogers (looking at Jones): Johnny Jones: You have the right to remain silent; anything you say can and will be used against you in a court of law; you have the right to an attorney before I ask you any questions; if you cannot afford an attorney one will be appointed for you before any questions are asked if you so desire. Do you understand these rights?

Jones: Yes I do.

Rogers: What would you like to do?

Jones: I think that I better talk to my attorney before you ask me any questions.

Rogers (turning to Martin):   Thank goodness he invoked his right to counsel. If he talked to us the judge would probably go easy on him. Since we have him dead to rights anyway, we won't have to worry about the judge giving him a lighter sentence.

Jones: Maybe I should talk to you.

Rogers (looking back at Jones):   Not till you talk to your lawyer.

Jones: But wouldn't the judge go easier on me if I talked?

Rogers: That's not for me to say son; ask your lawyer. He's on your side. I'm out to get you.

Jones: But you think that the judge would go easier on me if I talked.

Rogers: True.

Jones: Then I want to talk to you.

Rogers: Sorry son, you waived your right to be questioned.

Jones: Couldn't I just waive my right to counsel?

Rogers: Yes, I suppose you could. Read this and sign right here.

Rogers then handed Jones a waiver of counsel and silence form which Jones (a college graduate who had no prior experience with the law) read and signed. The dialogue continued:

Rogers: Why did you burglarize Jewel's jewelry store?

Jones: Because Jewel ripped me off last week and I wanted to get back at her.

At Jones' trial for burglary, should his last statement be admissible? Explain thoroughly.

G.   THE PUBLIC SAFETY EXCEPTION

NEW YORK v. QUARLES
467 U.S. 649 (1984)

JUSTICE REHNQUIST delivered the opinion of the Court.

Respondent Benjamin Quarles was charged in the New York trial court with criminal possession of a weapon. The trial court suppressed the gun in question, and a statement made by respondent, because the statement was obtained by police before they read respondent his *"Miranda* rights." That ruling was affirmed on appeal through the New York Court of Appeals. We granted certiorari, and we now reverse. We conclude that under the circumstances involved in this case, overriding considerations of public safety justify the officer's failure to provide *Miranda* warnings before he asked questions devoted to locating the abandoned weapon.

On September 11, 1980, at approximately 12:30 a.m., Officer Frank Kraft and Officer Sal Scarring were on road patrol in Queens, New York, when a young woman approached their car. She told them that she had just been raped by a black male, approximately six feet tall, who was wearing a black jacket with the name "Big Ben" printed in yellow letters on the back. She told the officers that the man had just entered an A & P supermarket located nearby and that the man was carrying a gun.

The officers drove the woman to the supermarket, and Officer Kraft entered the store while Officer Scarring radioed for assistance. Officer Kraft quickly spotted respondent, who matched the description given by the woman, approaching a check-out counter. Apparently upon seeing the officer, respondent turned and ran toward the rear of the store, and Officer Kraft pursued him with a drawn gun. When respondent turned the corner at the end of an aisle, Officer Kraft lost sight of him for several seconds, and upon regaining sight of respondent, ordered him to stop and put his hands over his head.

Although more than three other officers had arrived on the scene by that time, Officer Kraft was the first to reach respondent. He frisked him and discovered that he was wearing a shoulder holster which was then empty. After handcuffing him, Officer Kraft asked him where the gun was. Respondent nodded in the direction of some empty cartons and responded, "the gun is over there." Officer Kraft thereafter retrieved a loaded .38-caliber revolver from one of the cartons, formally placed respondent under arrest, and read him his *Miranda* rights from a printed card. Respondent indicated that he would be willing to answer questions without an attorney present. Officer Kraft then asked respondent if he owned the gun and where he had purchased it. Respondent answered that he did own it and that he had purchased it in Miami, Florida.

In the subsequent prosecution of respondent for criminal possession of a weapon,[2] the judge excluded the statement, "the gun is over there," and the gun because the officer had not given respondent the warnings required by *Miranda* before asking him where the gun was located. The judge excluded the other statements about respondent's ownership of the gun and the place of purchase, as evidence tainted by the prior *Miranda* violation.

The Court of Appeals affirmed by a 4-3 vote. It concluded that respondent was in "custody" within the meaning of *Miranda* during all questioning and rejected the state's argument that the exigencies of the situation justified Officer Kraft's failure to read respondent his *Miranda* rights until after he had located the gun. The court declined to recognize an exigency exception to the usual requirements of *Miranda* because it found no indication from Officer Kraft's testimony at the suppression hearing that his subjective motivation in asking the question was to protect his own safety or the safety of the public. For the reasons which follow, we believe that this case presents a situation where concern for public safety must be paramount to adherence to the literal language of the prophylactic rules enunciated in *Miranda*.[3]

In this case we have before us no claim that respondent's statements were actually compelled by police conduct which overcame his will to resist. Thus the only issue before us is whether Officer Kraft was justified in failing to make available to respondent the procedural safeguards associated with the privilege against compulsory self-incrimination since *Miranda*.[5]

---

[2] The state originally charged respondent with rape, but the record provides no information as to why the state failed to pursue that charge.

[3] We have long recognized an exigent-circumstances exception to the warrant requirement in the Fourth Amendment context. We have found the warrant requirement of the Fourth Amendment inapplicable in cases where the "'exigencies of the situation' make the needs of law enforcement so compelling that the warrantless search is objectively reasonable under the Fourth Amendment." Although "the Fifth Amendment's strictures, unlike the Fourth's, are not removed by showing reasonableness," we conclude today that there are limited circumstances where the judicially imposed strictures of *Miranda* are inapplicable.

[5] The dissent curiously takes us to task for "endors[ing]" the introduction of coerced self-incriminating statements in criminal prosecutions," and for "sanctioning sub *silentio* criminal prosecutions based on compelled self-incriminating statements." Of course our decision today does nothing of the kind. As the *Miranda* Court itself recognized, the failure to provide *Miranda* warnings in and of itself does not render a confession involuntary, and respondent is certainly free on remand to argue that his statement was coerced under traditional due process standards. Today we merely reject the only argument that

The New York Court of Appeals was undoubtedly correct in deciding that the facts of this case come within the ambit of the *Miranda* decision as we have subsequently interpreted it. We agree that respondent was in police custody because we have noted that "the ultimate inquiry is simply whether there is a 'formal arrest or restraint on freedom of movement' of the degree associated with a formal arrest." *Mathiason*. Here Quarles was surrounded by at least four police officers and was handcuffed when the questioning at issue took place. As the New York Court of Appeals observed, there was nothing to suggest that any of the officers were any longer concerned for their own physical safety. The New York Court of Appeals' majority declined to express an opinion as to whether there might be an exception to the *Miranda* rule if the police had been acting to protect the public, because the lower courts in New York had made no factual determination that the police had acted with that motive.

We hold that on these facts there is a "public safety" exception to the requirement that *Miranda* warnings be given before a suspect's answers may be admitted into evidence, and that the availability of that exception does not depend upon the motivation of the individual officers involved. In a kaleidoscopic situation such as the one confronting these officers, where spontaneity rather than adherence to a police manual is necessarily the order of the day, the application of the exception which we recognize today should not be made to depend on *post hoc* findings at a suppression hearing concerning the subjective motivation of the arresting officer.[6] Undoubtedly most police officers, if placed in Officer Kraft's position, would act out of a host of different, instinctive, and largely unverifiable motives — their own safety, the safety of others, and perhaps as well the desire to obtain incriminating evidence from the suspect.

Whatever the motivation of individual officers in such a situation, we do not believe that the doctrinal underpinnings of *Miranda* require that it be applied in all its rigor to a situation in which police officers ask questions reasonably prompted by a concern for the public safety. The *Miranda* decision was based in large part on this Court's view that the warnings which it required police to give to suspects in custody would reduce the likelihood that the suspects would fall victim to constitutionally impermissible practices of police interrogation in the presumptively coercive environment of the station house. The dissenters warned that the requirement of *Miranda* warnings would have the effect of decreasing the number of suspects who respond to police questioning. The *Miranda* majority, however, apparently felt that whatever the cost to society in terms of fewer convictions of guilty suspects, that cost would simply have to be borne in the interest of enlarged protection for the Fifth Amendment privilege.

The police in this case, in the very act of apprehending a suspect, were confronted with the immediate necessity of ascertaining the whereabouts of a gun

---

respondent has raised to support the exclusion of his statement, that the statement must be *presumed* compelled because of Officer Kraft's failure to read him his *Miranda* warnings.

[6] Similar approaches have been rejected in other contexts. *See Innis* (officer's subjective intent to incriminate not determinative of whether "interrogation" occurred); *United States v. Mendenhall*, (opinion of Stewart, J.) (officer's subjective intent to detain not determinative of whether a "seizure" occurred within the meaning of the Fourth Amendment).

which they had every reason to believe the suspect had just removed from his empty holster and discarded in the supermarket. So long as the gun was concealed somewhere in the supermarket, with its actual whereabouts unknown, it obviously posed more than one danger to the public safety: an accomplice might make use of it, a customer or employee might later come upon it.

In such a situation, if the police are required to recite the familiar *Miranda* warnings before asking the whereabouts of the gun, suspects in Quarles' position might well be deterred from responding. Procedural safeguards which deter a suspect from responding were deemed acceptable in *Miranda* in order to protect the Fifth Amendment privilege; when the primary social cost of those added protections is the possibility of fewer convictions, the *Miranda* majority was willing to bear that cost. Here, had *Miranda* warnings deterred Quarles from responding to Officer Kraft's question about the whereabouts of the gun, the cost would have been something more than merely the failure to obtain evidence useful in convicting Quarles. Officer Kraft needed an answer to his question not simply to make his case against Quarles but to insure that further danger to the public did not result from the concealment of the gun in a public area.

We conclude that the need for answers to questions in a situation posing a threat to the public safety outweighs the need for the prophylactic rule protecting the Fifth Amendment's privilege against self-incrimination. We decline to place officers such as Officer Kraft in the untenable position of having to consider, often in a matter of seconds, whether it best serves society for them to ask the necessary questions without the *Miranda* warnings and render whatever probative evidence they uncover inadmissible, or for them to give the warnings in order to preserve the admissibility of evidence they might uncover but possibly damage or destroy their ability to obtain that evidence and neutralize the volatile situation confronting them.[7]

In recognizing a narrow exception to the *Miranda* rule in this case, we acknowledge that to some degree we lessen the desirable clarity of that rule. At least in part in order to preserve its clarity, we have over the years refused to sanction attempts to expand our *Miranda* holding. *See, e.g., Murphy* (refusal to extend *Miranda* requirements to interviews with probation officers); *Michael C.* (refusal to equate request to see a probation officer with request to see a lawyer for *Miranda* purposes); *Beckwith*, (refusal to extend *Miranda* requirements to questioning in non-custodial circumstances). As we have in other contexts, we recognize here the importance of a workable rule "to guide police officers, who have only limited time and expertise to reflect on and balance the social and individual interests involved in the specific circumstances they confront." But as we have pointed out, we believe that the exception which we recognize today lessens the necessity of that on-the-scene balancing process. The exception will not be difficult

---

[7] The dissent argues that a public safety exception to *Miranda* is unnecessary because in every case an officer can simply ask the necessary questions to protect himself or the public, and then the prosecution can decline to introduce any incriminating responses at a subsequent trial. But absent actual coercion by the officer, there is no constitutional imperative requiring the exclusion of the evidence that results from police inquiry of this kind; and we do not believe that the doctrinal underpinnings of *Miranda* require us to exclude the evidence, thus penalizing officers for asking the very questions which are the most crucial to their efforts to protect themselves and the public.

for police officers to apply because in each case it will be circumscribed by the exigency which justifies it. We think police officers can and will distinguish almost instinctively between questions necessary to secure their own safety or the safety of the public and questions designed solely to elicit testimonial evidence from a suspect.

The facts of this case clearly demonstrate that distinction and an officer's ability to recognize it. Officer Kraft asked only the question necessary to locate the missing gun before advising respondent of his rights. It was only after securing the loaded revolver and giving the warnings that he continued with investigatory questions about the ownership and place of purchase of the gun. The exception which we recognize today, far from complicating the thought processes and the on-the-scene judgments of police officers, will simply free them to follow their legitimate instincts when confronting situations presenting a danger to the public safety.[8]

We hold that the Court of Appeals in this case erred in excluding the statement, "the gun is over there," and the gun because of the officer's failure to read respondent his *Miranda* rights before attempting to locate the weapon. Accordingly we hold that it also erred in excluding the subsequent statements as illegal fruits of a *Miranda* violation.[9] We therefore reverse and remand for further proceedings not inconsistent with this opinion.

JUSTICE O'CONNOR, concurring in the judgment in part and dissenting in part.

Were the Court writing from a clean slate, I could agree with its holding. But *Miranda* is now the law and, in my view, the Court has not provided sufficient justification for departing from it or for blurring its now clear strictures. Accordingly, I would require suppression of the initial statement taken from respondent in this case. On the other hand, nothing in *Miranda* or the privilege itself requires exclusion of nontestimonial evidence derived from informal custodial interrogation, and I therefore agree with the Court that admission of the gun in evidence is proper.

---

[8] Although it involves police questions in part relating to the whereabouts of a gun, *Orozco*, is in no sense inconsistent with our disposition of this case. In *Orozco* four hours after a murder had been committed at a restaurant, four police officers entered the defendant's boardinghouse and awakened the defendant, who was sleeping in his bedroom. Without giving him *Miranda* warnings, they began vigorously to interrogate him about whether he had been present at the scene of the shooting and whether he owned a gun. The defendant eventually admitted that he had been present at the scene and directed the officers to a washing machine in the backroom of the boardinghouse where he had hidden the gun. We held that all the statements should have been suppressed. In *Orozco*, however, the questions about the gun were clearly investigatory; they did not in any way relate to an objectively reasonable need to protect the police or the public from any immediate danger associated with the weapon. In short there was no exigency requiring immediate action by the officers beyond the normal need expeditiously to solve a serious crime.

Innis also involved the whereabouts of a missing weapon, but our holding in that case depended entirely on our conclusion that no police interrogation took place so as to require consideration of the applicability of the *Miranda* prophylactic.

[9] Because we hold that there is no violation of *Miranda* in this case, we have no occasion to reach arguments made by the state and the United States as *amicus curiae* that the gun is admissible either because it is non-testimonial or because the police would inevitably have discovered it absent their questioning.

I

The *Miranda* Court itself considered objections akin to those raised by the Court today. In dissent, Justice White protested that the *Miranda* rules would "operate indiscriminately in all criminal cases, regardless of the severity of the crime or the circumstances involved." But the *Miranda* Court would not accept any suggestion "that society's need for interrogation [could] outweig[h] the privilege." To that Court, the privilege against self-incrimination was absolute and therefore could not be "abridged."

Since the time *Miranda* was decided, the Court has repeatedly refused to bend the literal terms of that decision. To be sure, the Court has been sensitive to the substantial burden the *Miranda* rules place on local law enforcement efforts, and consequently has refused to extend the decision or to increase its strictures on law enforcement agencies in almost any way.

In my view, a "public safety" exception unnecessarily blurs the edges of the clear line heretofore established and makes *Miranda's* requirements more difficult to understand. In some cases, police will benefit because a reviewing court will find that an exigency excused their failure to administer the required warnings. But in other cases, police will suffer because, though they thought an exigency excused their noncompliance, a reviewing court will view the "objective" circumstances differently and require exclusion of admissions thereby obtained. The end result will be a fine-spun new doctrine on public safety exigencies incident to custodial interrogation, complete with the hair-splitting distinctions that currently plague our Fourth Amendment jurisprudence. "While the rigidity of the prophylactic rules was a principal weakness in the view of dissenters and critics outside the Court, . . . that rigidity [has also been called a] strength of the decision. It [has] afforded police and courts clear guidance on the manner in which to conduct a custodial investigation: if it was rigid, it was also precise . . . . [T]his core virtue of *Miranda* would be eviscerated if the prophylactic rules were freely [ignored] by . . . courts under the guise of [reinterpreting] *Miranda* . . . ." *Fare v. Michael C.* (Rehnquist, J., in chambers on application for stay).

The justification the Court provides for upsetting the equilibrium that has finally been achieved — that police cannot and should not balance considerations of public safety against the individual's interest in avoiding compulsory testimonial self-incrimination — really misses the critical question to be decided. *Miranda* has never been read to prohibit the police from asking questions to secure the public safety. Rather, the critical question *Miranda* addresses is who shall bear the cost of securing the public safety when such questions are asked and answered: the defendant or the State. *Miranda*, for better or worse, found the resolution of that question implicit in the prohibition against compulsory self-incrimination and placed the burden on the State. When police ask custodial questions without administering the required warnings, *Miranda* quite clearly requires that the answers received be presumed compelled and that they be excluded from evidence at trial.

The Court concedes, as it must, both that respondent was in "custody" and subject to "interrogation" and that his statement "the gun is over there" was compelled within the meaning of our precedent. In my view, since there is nothing about an exigency that makes custodial interrogation any less compelling, a principled application of *Miranda* requires that respondent's statement be suppressed.

[Justice O'Connor then explained why, in her view, the gun was admissible. That issue will be discussed in Chapter 22, *infra*.]

JUSTICE MARSHALL, with whom JUSTICE BRENNAN and JUSTICE STEVENS join, dissenting.

The police in this case arrested a man suspected of possessing a firearm in violation of New York law. Once the suspect was in custody and found to be unarmed, the arresting officer initiated an interrogation. Without being advised of his right not to respond, the suspect incriminated himself by locating the gun. The majority concludes that the State may rely on this incriminating statement to convict the suspect of possessing a weapon. I disagree. The arresting officers had no legitimate reason to interrogate the suspect without advising him of his rights to remain silent and to obtain assistance of counsel. By finding on these facts justification for unconsented interrogation, the majority abandons the clear guidelines enunciated in *Miranda* and condemns the American judiciary to a new era of *post hoc* inquiry into the propriety of custodial interrogations. More significantly and in direct conflict with this Court's long-standing interpretation of the Fifth Amendment, the majority has endorsed the introduction of coerced self-incriminating statements in criminal prosecutions. I dissent.

I

The majority's entire analysis rests on the factual assumption that the public was at risk during Quarles' interrogation. This assumption is completely in conflict with the facts as found by New York's highest court. Before the interrogation began, Quarles had been "reduced to a condition of physical powerlessness." Contrary to the majority's speculations, Quarles was not believed to have, nor did he in fact have, an accomplice to come to his rescue. When the questioning began, the arresting officers were sufficiently confident of their safety to put away their guns. As Officer Kraft acknowledged at the suppression hearing, "the situation was under control." Based on Officer Kraft's own testimony, the New York Court of Appeals found: "Nothing suggests that any of the officers was by that time concerned for his own physical safety." The Court of Appeals also determined that there was no evidence that the interrogation was prompted by the arresting officers' concern for the public's safety.

The majority attempts to slip away from these unambiguous findings of New York's highest court by proposing that danger be measured by objective facts rather than the subjective intentions of arresting officers. Though clever, this ploy was anticipated by the New York Court of Appeals: "[T]here is no evidence in the record before us that there were exigent circumstances posing a risk to the public safety . . . ."

The New York court's conclusion that neither Quarles nor his missing gun posed a threat to the public's safety is amply supported by the evidence presented at the suppression hearing. Again contrary to the majority's intimations, no customers or employees were wandering about the store in danger of coming across Quarles' discarded weapon. Although the supermarket was open to the public, Quarles' arrest took place during the middle of the night when the store was apparently deserted except for the clerks at the checkout counter. The police could easily have cordoned off the store and searched for the missing gun. Had they done so, they would have found the gun forthwith. The police were well aware that Quarles had discarded his weapon somewhere near the scene of the arrest. As the State acknowledged before the New York Court of Appeals: "After Officer Kraft had handcuffed and frisked the defendant in the supermarket, *he knew with a high degree of certainty that the defendant's gun was within the immediate vicinity of the encounter.* He undoubtedly would have searched for it in the carton a few feet away without the defendant having looked in that direction and saying that it was there." Brief for Appellant, p.11 (emphasis added).

In this case, there was convincing, indeed almost overwhelming, evidence to support the New York court's conclusion that Quarles' hidden weapon did not pose a risk either to the arresting officers or to the public. The majority ignores this evidence and sets aside the factual findings of the New York Court of Appeals. More cynical observers might well conclude that a state court's findings of fact "deserv[e] a 'high measure of deference,' " only when deference works against the interests of a criminal defendant.

II

The majority's treatment of the legal issues presented in this case is no less troubling than its abuse of the facts. Before today's opinion, the Court had twice concluded that, under *Miranda*, police officers conducting custodial interrogations must advise suspects of their rights before any questions concerning the whereabouts of incriminating weapons can be asked. *Innis*, (dicta); *Orozco*, (holding).[2] Now the majority departs from these cases and rules that police may withhold *Miranda* warnings whenever custodial interrogations concern matters of public safety.

The majority contends that the law, as it currently stands, places police officers in a dilemma whenever they interrogate a suspect who appears to know of some threat to the public's safety. If the police interrogate the suspect without advising him of his rights, the suspect may reveal information that the authorities can use to defuse the threat, but the suspect's statements will be inadmissible at trial. If, on the other hand, the police advise the suspect of his rights, the suspect may be deterred from responding to the police's questions, and the risk to the public may continue unabated. According to the majority, the police must now choose between establishing the suspect's guilt and safeguarding the public from danger.

---

[2] The majority attempts to distinguish *Orozco* by stressing the fact that the interrogation in this case immediately followed the Quarles' arrest whereas the interrogation in *Orozco* occurred some four hours after the crime and was investigatory. I fail to comprehend the distinction. In both cases, a group of police officers had taken a suspect into custody and questioned the suspect about the location of a missing gun. In both cases a dangerous weapon was missing, and in neither case was there any direct evidence where the weapon was hidden.

The majority proposes to eliminate this dilemma by creating an exception to *Miranda* for custodial interrogations concerning matters of public safety. Under the majority's exception, police would be permitted to interrogate suspects about such matters before the suspects have been advised of their constitutional rights. Without being "deterred" by the knowledge that they have a constitutional right not to respond, these suspects will be likely to answer the questions. Should the answers also be incriminating, the State would be free to introduce them as evidence in a criminal prosecution. Through this "narrow exception to the *Miranda* rule," the majority proposes to protect the public's safety without jeopardizing the prosecution of criminal defendants. I find in this reasoning an unwise and unprincipled departure from our Fifth Amendment precedents.

Before today's opinion, the procedures established in *Miranda* had "the virtue of informing police and prosecutors with specificity as to what they may do in conducting custodial interrogation, and of informing courts under what circumstances statements obtained during such interrogations are not admissible." In a chimerical quest for public safety, the majority has abandoned the rule that brought eighteen years of doctrinal tranquility to the field of custodial interrogations. As the majority candidly concedes, a public-safety exception destroys forever the clarity of *Miranda* for both law enforcement officers and members of the judiciary. The Court's candor cannot mask what a serious loss the administration of justice has incurred.

This case is illustrative of the chaos the "public-safety" exception will unleash. The circumstances of Quarles' arrest have never been in dispute. After the benefit of briefing and oral argument, the New York Court of Appeals concluded that there was "no evidence in the record before us that there were exigent circumstances posing a risk to the public safety." Upon reviewing the same facts and hearing the same arguments, a majority of this Court has come to precisely the opposite conclusion: "So long as the gun was concealed somewhere in the supermarket, with its actual whereabouts unknown, it obviously posed more than one danger to the public safety . . . ."

If after plenary review two appellate courts so fundamentally differ over the threat to public safety presented by the simple and uncontested facts of this case, one must seriously question how law enforcement officers will respond to the majority's new rule in the confusion and haste of the real world. As The Chief Justice wrote in a similar context, "Few, if any, police officers are competent to make the kind of evaluation seemingly contemplated . . . ." *Innis* (concurring in the judgment). Not only will police officers have to decide whether the objective facts of an arrest justify an unconsented custodial interrogation; they will also have to remember to interrupt the interrogation and read the suspect his *Miranda* warnings once the focus of the inquiry shifts from protecting the public's safety to ascertaining the suspect's guilt. Disagreements of the scope of the "public-safety" exception and mistakes in its application are inevitable.[3]

---

[3] One of the peculiarities of the majority's decision is its suggestion that police officers can "distinguish almost instinctively" questions tied to public safety and questions designed to elicit testimonial evidence. Obviously, these distinctions are extraordinarily difficult to draw. In many cases — like this one — custodial questioning may serve both purposes. It is therefore wishful thinking for the

The end result, as Justice O'CONNOR predicts, will be "a fine-spun new doctrine of public safety exigencies incident to custodial interrogation, complete with the hair-splitting distinctions that currently plague our Fourth Amendment jurisprudence." In the meantime, the courts will have to dedicate themselves to spinning this new web of doctrines, and the country's law enforcement agencies will have to suffer patiently through the frustrations of another period of constitutional uncertainty.

III

Though unfortunate, the difficulty of administering the "public-safety" exception is not the most profound flaw in the majority's decision. The majority has lost sight of the fact that *Miranda* and our earlier custodial-interrogation cases all implemented a constitutional privilege against self-incrimination. The rules established in these cases were designed to protect criminal defendants against prosecutions based on coerced self-incriminating statements. The majority today turns its back on these constitutional considerations, and invites the government to prosecute through the use of what necessarily are coerced statements.

A

The majority's error stems from a serious misunderstanding of *Miranda* and of the Fifth Amendment upon which that decision was based. The majority implies that *Miranda* consisted of no more than a judicial balancing act in which the benefits of "enlarged protection for the Fifth Amendment privilege" were weighed against "the cost to society in terms of fewer convictions of guilty suspects." Supposedly because the scales tipped in favor of the privilege against self-incrimination, the *Miranda* Court erected a prophylactic barrier around statements made during custodial interrogations. The majority now proposes to return to the scales of social utility to calculate whether *Miranda's* prophylactic rule remains cost-effective when threats to public's safety are added to the balance. The results of the majority's "test" are announced with pseudoscientific precision:

> We conclude that the need for answers to questions in a situation posing a threat to the public safety outweighs the need for the prophylactic rule protecting the Fifth Amendment's privilege against self-incrimination.

The majority misreads *Miranda*. Though the *Miranda* dissent prophesized dire consequences, the *Miranda* Court refused to allow such concerns to weaken the protections of the Constitution:

> A recurrent argument made in these cases is that society's need for interrogation outweighs the privilege. This argument is not unfamiliar to this Court. The whole thrust of our foregoing discussion demonstrates that the Constitution has prescribed the rights of the individual when confronted with the power of government when it provided in the Fifth Amendment that an individual cannot be compelled to be a witness against himself. That right cannot be abridged.

---

majority to suggest that the intuitions of police officers will render its decision self-executing.

Whether society would be better off if the police warned suspects of their rights before beginning an interrogation or whether the advantages of giving such warnings would outweigh their costs did not inform the *Miranda* decision. On the contrary, the *Miranda* Court was concerned with the proscriptions of the Fifth Amendment, and, in particular, whether the Self-Incrimination Clause permits the government to prosecute individuals based on statements made in the course of custodial interrogations.

After a detailed examination of police practices and a review of its previous decisions in the area, the Court in *Miranda* determined that custodial interrogations are inherently coercive. The Court therefore created a constitutional presumption that statements made during custodial interrogations are compelled in violation of the Fifth Amendment and are thus inadmissible in criminal prosecutions. As a result of the Court's decision in *Miranda*, a statement made during a custodial interrogation may be introduced as proof of a defendant's guilt only if the prosecution demonstrates that the defendant knowingly and intelligently waived his constitutional rights before making the statement. The now-familiar *Miranda* warnings offer law-enforcement authorities a clear, easily administered device for ensuring that criminal suspects understand their constitutional rights well enough to waive them and to engage in consensual custodial interrogation.

In fashioning its "public-safety" exception to *Miranda*, the majority makes no attempt to deal with the constitutional presumption established by that case. The majority does not argue that police questioning about issues of public safety is any less coercive than custodial interrogations into other matters. The majority's only contention is that police officers could more easily protect the public if *Miranda* did not apply to custodial interrogations concerning the public's safety. But *Miranda* was not a decision about public safety; it was a decision about coerced confessions. Without establishing that interrogations concerning the public's safety are less likely to be coercive than other interrogations, the majority cannot endorse the "public-safety" exception and remain faithful to the logic of *Miranda*.

B

The majority's avoidance of the issue of coercion may not have been inadvertent. It would strain credulity to contend that Officer Kraft's questioning of respondent Quarles was not coercive.[8] In the middle of the night and in the back of an empty supermarket, Quarles was surrounded by four armed police officers. His hands were handcuffed behind his back. The first words out of the mouth of the arresting officer were: "Where is the gun?" In the majority's phrase, the situation was "kaleidoscopic." Police and suspect were acting on instinct. Officer Kraft's abrupt and pointed question pressured Quarles in precisely the way that the *Miranda* Court feared the custodial interrogations would coerce self-incriminating testimony.

---

[8] The majority's reliance on respondent's failure to claim that his testimony was compelled by police conduct can only be disingenuous. Before today's opinion, respondent had no need to claim actual compulsion. Heretofore, it was sufficient to demonstrate that the police had conducted nonconsensual custodial interrogation. But now that the law has changed, it is only fair to examine the facts of the case to determine whether coercion probably was involved.

That the application of the "public-safety" exception in this case entailed coercion is no happenstance. The majority's *ratio decidendi* is that interrogating suspects about matters of public safety *will* be coercive. In its cost-benefit analysis, the Court's strongest argument in favor of a public-safety exception to *Miranda* is that the police would be better able to protect the public's safety if they were not always required to give suspects their *Miranda* warnings. The crux of this argument is that, by deliberately withholding *Miranda* warnings, the police can get information out of suspects who would refuse to respond to police questioning were they advised of their constitutional rights. The "public-safety" exception is efficacious precisely because it permits police officers to coerce criminal defendants into making involuntary statements.

Indeed, in the efficacy of the "public-safety" exception lies a fundamental and constitutional defect. Until today, this Court could truthfully state that the Fifth Amendment is given "broad scope" "where there has been genuine compulsion of testimony." Coerced confessions were simply inadmissible in criminal prosecutions. The "public-safety" exception departs from this principle by expressly inviting police officers to coerce defendants into making incriminating statements, and then permitting prosecutors to introduce those statements at trial. Though the majority's opinion is cloaked in the beguiling language of utilitarianism, the Court has sanctioned *sub silentio* criminal prosecutions based on compelled self-incriminating statements. I find this result in direct conflict with the Fifth Amendment's dictate that "No person . . . shall be compelled in any criminal case to be a witness against himself."

The irony of the majority's decision is that the public's safety can be perfectly well protected without abridging the Fifth Amendment. If a bomb is about to explode or the public is otherwise imminently imperiled, the police are free to interrogate suspects without advising them of their constitutional rights. Such unconsented questioning may take place not only when police officers act on instinct but also when higher faculties lead them to believe that advising a suspect of his constitutional rights might decrease the likelihood that the suspect would reveal life-saving information. If trickery is necessary to protect the public, then the police may trick a suspect into confessing. While the Fourteenth Amendment sets limits on such behavior, nothing in the Fifth Amendment or our decision in *Miranda* proscribes this sort of emergency questioning. All the Fifth Amendment forbids is the introduction of coerced statements at trial. *Cf. Weatherford v. Bursey*, (Sixth Amendment violated only if trial affected).

To a limited degree, the majority is correct that there is a cost associated with the Fifth Amendment's ban on introducing coerced self-incriminating statements at trial. Without a "public-safety" exception, there would be occasions when a defendant incriminated himself by revealing a threat to the public, and the State was unable to prosecute because the defendant retracted his statement after consulting with counsel and the police cannot find independent proof of guilt. Such occasions would not, however, be common. The prosecution does not always lose the use of incriminating information revealed in these situations. After consulting with counsel, a suspect may well volunteer to repeat his statement in hopes of gaining a favorable plea bargain or more lenient sentence. The majority thus overstates its case when it suggests that a police officer must necessarily choose between public safety and admissibility.[9]

But however frequently or infrequently such cases arise, their regularity is irrelevant. The Fifth Amendment prohibits compelled self-incrimination.[10] As the Court has explained on numerous occasions, this prohibition is the mainstay of our adversarial system of criminal justice. Not only does it protect us against the inherent unreliability of compelled testimony, but it also ensures that criminal investigations will be conducted with integrity and that the judiciary will avoid the taint of official lawlessness. The policies underlying the Fifth Amendment's privilege against self-incrimination are not diminished simply because testimony is compelled to protect the public's safety. The majority should not be permitted to elude the Amendment's absolute prohibition simply by calculating special costs that arise when the public's safety is at issue. Indeed, were constitutional adjudication always conducted in such an ad hoc manner, the Bill of Rights would be a most unreliable protector of individual liberties.

QUESTIONS AND NOTES

1. Should the defense attorney have claimed that the confession was involuntary? Why do you suppose he failed to do so? Do you think that the confession was in fact involuntary? Explain.

2. Do you think that there was in fact an issue of public safety here? Why? Why not? Should the Supreme Court have substituted its judgment for that of the New York courts on this question?

3. If the concern is public safety, are we worried about the time that it takes to administer *Miranda* warnings? If that is not the concern, what is?

4. Do you think that the presumption of coercion that *Miranda* created is more or less valid in an emergency situation? Explain.

5. Even in the ordinary situation, does a police officer who fails to give *Miranda* warnings flout the Constitution, or is the Constitution only flouted by introducing the confessions at trial?

6. If the Constitution leaves room for the police officer to make a calculated choice between administering *Miranda* and using a subsequently obtained confes-

---

[9] I also seriously question how often a statement linking a suspect to the threat to the public ends up being the crucial and otherwise unprovable element of a criminal prosecution. The facts of the current case illustrate this point. The police arrested respondent Quarles not because he was suspected of carrying a gun, but because he was alleged to have committed rape. Had the State elected to prosecute on the rape count alone, petitioner's incriminating statement about the gun would have had no role in the prosecution. Only because the State dropped the rape count and chose to proceed to trial solely on the criminal-possession charge did respondent's answer to Officer Kraft's question become critical.

[10] In this sense, the Fifth Amendment differs fundamentally from the Fourth Amendment, which only prohibits unreasonable searches and seizures. Accordingly, the various exceptions to the Fourth Amendment permitting warrantless searches under various circumstances should have no analogy in the Fifth Amendment context. Curiously, the majority accepts this point, but persists in limiting the protections of the Fifth Amendment.

sion, or not administering *Miranda* and deriving the benefit of quickly finding the location of a gun, is it accurate (helpful) to think of the officer as being "penalized"?

7.   How do you calculate the costs and benefits of blurring the theretofore "bright line" *Miranda* rule? Explain.

Chapter 18

THE RIGHT TO COUNSEL AND CONFESSIONS

A. *MASSIAH* REVISITED

Although *Massiah*, along with *Escobedo*, was generally thought to have been relegated to the scrap heap of history by *Miranda*, in fact, as the following cases show, *Massiah* retains a good deal of vitality. As you read the cases in this chapter, think about what different values *Massiah* and *Miranda* serve. Also think about what triggers a *Massiah* as opposed to a *Miranda* violation, and how, if at all, are the results different. Obviously, if you have forgotten *Massiah*, or if your memory of it is a bit fuzzy, you would be well-advised to reread it. We start with *Brewer v. Williams*.

BREWER v. WILLIAMS
430 U.S. 387 (1977)

Mr. Justice Stewart delivered the opinion of the Court.

An Iowa trial jury found the respondent, Robert Williams, guilty of murder. The judgment of conviction was affirmed in the Iowa Supreme Court by a closely divided vote. In a subsequent habeas corpus proceeding a Federal District Court ruled that under the United States Constitution Williams is entitled to a new trial, and a divided Court of Appeals for the Eighth Circuit agreed. The question before us is whether the District Court and the Court of Appeals were wrong.

I

On the afternoon of December 24, 1968, a 10-year-old girl named Pamela Powers went with her family to the YMCA in Des Moines, Iowa, to watch a wrestling tournament in which her brother was participating. When she failed to return from a trip to the washroom, a search for her began. The search was unsuccessful.

Robert Williams, who had recently escaped from a mental hospital, was a resident of the YMCA. Soon after the girl's disappearance Williams was seen in the YMCA lobby carrying some clothing and a large bundle wrapped in a blanket. He obtained help from a 14-year-old boy in opening the street door of the YMCA and the door to his automobile parked outside. When Williams placed the bundle in the front seat of his car the boy "saw two legs in it and they were skinny and white." Before anyone could see what was in the bundle Williams drove away. His abandoned car was found the following day in Davenport, Iowa, roughly 160 miles east of Des Moines. A warrant was then issued in Des Moines for his arrest on a charge of abduction.

On the morning of December 26, a Des Moines lawyer named Henry McKnight went to the Des Moines police station and informed the officers present that he had just received a long-distance call from Williams, and that he had advised Williams to turn himself in to the Davenport police. Williams did surrender that morning to the police in Davenport, and they booked him on the charge specified in the arrest warrant and gave him the warnings required by *Miranda*. The Davenport police then telephoned their counterparts in Des Moines to inform them that Williams had surrendered. McKnight, the lawyer, was still at the Des Moines police headquarters, and Williams conversed with McKnight on the telephone. In the presence of the Des Moines chief of police and a police detective named Leaming, McKnight advised Williams that Des Moines police officers would be driving to Davenport to pick him up, that the officers would not interrogate him or mistreat him, and that Williams was not to talk to the officers about Pamela Powers until after consulting with McKnight upon his return to Des Moines. As a result of these conversations, it was agreed between McKnight and the Des Moines police officials that Detective Leaming and a fellow officer would drive to Davenport to pick up Williams, that they would bring him directly back to Des Moines, and that they would not question him during the trip.

In the meantime Williams was arraigned before a judge in Davenport on the outstanding arrest warrant. The judge advised him of his *Miranda* rights and committed him to jail. Before leaving the courtroom, Williams conferred with a lawyer named Kelly, who advised him not to make any statements until consulting with McKnight back in Des Moines.

Detective Leaming and his fellow officer arrived in Davenport about noon to pick up Williams and return him to Des Moines. Soon after their arrival they met with Williams and Kelly, who, they understood, was acting as Williams' lawyer. Detective Leaming repeated the *Miranda* warnings, and told Williams:

> [W]e both know that you're being represented here by Mr. Kelly and you're being represented by Mr. McKnight in Des Moines, and . . . I want you to remember this because we'll be visiting between here and Des Moines.

Williams then conferred again with Kelly alone, and after this conference Kelly reiterated to Detective Leaming that Williams was not to be questioned about the disappearance of Pamela Powers until after he had consulted with McKnight back in Des Moines. When Leaming expressed some reservations, Kelly firmly stated that the agreement with McKnight was to be carried out that there was to be no interrogation of Williams during the automobile journey to Des Moines. Kelly was denied permission to ride in the police car back to Des Moines with Williams and the two officers.

The two detectives, with Williams in their charge, then set out on the 160-mile drive. At no time during the trip did Williams express a willingness to be interrogated in the absence of an attorney. Instead, he stated several times that "[w]hen I get to Des Moines and see Mr. McKnight, I am going to tell you the whole story." Detective Leaming knew that Williams was a former mental patient, and knew also that he was deeply religious.

The detective and his prisoner soon embarked on a wide-ranging conversation covering a variety of topics, including the subject of religion. Then, not long after leaving Davenport and reaching the interstate highway, Detective Leaming delivered what has been referred to in the briefs and oral arguments as the "Christian burial speech." Addressing Williams as "Reverend," the detective said:

> I want to give you something to think about while we're traveling down the road . . . . Number one, I want you to observe the weather conditions, it's raining, it's sleeting, it's freezing, driving is very treacherous, visibility is poor, it's going to be dark early this evening. They are predicting several inches of snow for tonight, and I feel that you yourself are the only person that knows where this little girl's body is, that you yourself have only been there once, and if you get a snow on top of it you yourself may be unable to find it. And, since we will be going right past the area on the way into Des Moines, I feel that we could stop and locate the body, that the parents of this little girl should be entitled to a Christian burial for the little girl who was snatched away from them on Christmas [E]ve and murdered. And I feel we should stop and locate it on the way in rather than waiting until morning and trying to come back out after a snow storm and possibly not being able to find it at all.

Williams asked Detective Leaming why he thought their route to Des Moines would be taking them past the girl's body, and Leaming responded that he knew the body was in the area of Mitchellville a town they would be passing on the way to Des Moines.[1] Leaming then stated: "I do not want you to answer me. I don't want to discuss it any further. Just think about it as we're riding down the road."

As the car approached Grinnell, a town approximately 100 miles west of Davenport, Williams asked whether the police had found the victim's shoes. When Detective Leaming replied that he was unsure, Williams directed the officers to a service station where he said he had left the shoes; a search for them proved unsuccessful. As they continued towards Des Moines, Williams asked whether the police had found the blanket, and directed the officers to a rest area where he said he had disposed of the blanket. Nothing was found. The car continued towards Des Moines, and as it approached Mitchellville, Williams said that he would show the officers where the body was. He then directed the police to the body of Pamela Powers.

II

B

[T]here is no need to review in this case the doctrine of *Miranda*, a doctrine designed to secure the constitutional privilege against compulsory self-incrimination. It is equally unnecessary to evaluate the ruling of the District Court that Williams' self-incriminating statements were, indeed, involuntarily made. *Cf. Spano.* For it is clear that the judgment before us must in any event be affirmed

---

[1] The fact of the matter, of course, was that Detective Leaming possessed no such knowledge.

upon the ground that Williams was deprived of a different constitutional right — the right to the assistance of counsel.

There has occasionally been a difference of opinion within the Court as to the peripheral scope of this constitutional right. But its basic contours, which are identical in state and federal contexts, are too well established to require extensive elaboration here. Whatever else it may mean, the right to counsel granted by the Sixth and Fourteenth Amendments means at least that a person is entitled to the help of a lawyer at or after the time that judicial proceedings have been initiated against him "whether by way of formal charge, preliminary hearing, indictment, information, or arraignment." *Massiah.*

There can be no doubt in the present case that judicial proceedings had been initiated against Williams before the start of the automobile ride from Davenport to Des Moines. A warrant had been issued for his arrest, he had been arraigned on that warrant before a judge in a Davenport courtroom, and he had been committed by the court to confinement in jail. The State does not contend otherwise.

There can be no serious doubt, either, that Detective Leaming deliberately and designedly set out to elicit information from Williams just as surely as — and perhaps more effectively than — if he had formally interrogated him. Detective Leaming was fully aware before departing for Des Moines that Williams was being represented in Davenport by Kelly and in Des Moines by McKnight. Yet he purposely sought during Williams' isolation from his lawyers to obtain as much incriminating information as possible. Indeed, Detective Leaming conceded as much when he testified at Williams' trial:

Q.   In fact, Captain, whether he was a mental patient or not, you were trying to get all the information you could before he got to his lawyer, weren't you?

A.   I was sure hoping to find out where that little girl was, yes, sir.

Q.   Well, I'll put it this way: You was [*sic*] hoping to get all the information you could before Williams got back to McKnight, weren't you?

A.   Yes, sir.[2]

The state courts clearly proceeded upon the hypothesis that Detective Leaming's "Christian burial speech" had been tantamount to interrogation. Both courts recognized that Williams had been entitled to the assistance of counsel at the time he made the incriminating statements. Yet no such constitutional protection would

---

[2] Counsel for petitioner, in the course of oral argument in this Court, acknowledged that the "Christian burial speech" was tantamount to interrogation:

Q: But isn't the point, really, Mr. Attorney General, what you indicated earlier, and that is that the officer wanted to elicit information from Williams —

A: Yes, sir.

Q: — by whatever techniques he used, I would suppose a lawyer would consider that he were pursuing interrogation.

A: It is, but it was very brief.

have come into play if there had been no interrogation.

That the incriminating statements were elicited surreptitiously in the *Massiah* case, and otherwise here, is constitutionally irrelevant. Rather, the clear rule of *Massiah* is that once adversary proceedings have commenced against an individual, he has a right to legal representation when the government interrogates him.[8] It thus requires no wooden or technical application of the *Massiah* doctrine to conclude that Williams was entitled to the assistance of counsel guaranteed to him by the Sixth and Fourteenth Amendments.

III

The Iowa courts recognized that Williams had been denied the constitutional right to the assistance of counsel. They held, however, that he had waived that right during the course of the automobile trip from Davenport to Des Moines. The state trial court explained its determination of waiver as follows:

> The time element involved on the trip, the general circumstances of it, and more importantly the absence on the Defendant's part of any assertion of his right or desire not to give information absent the presence of his attorney, are the main foundations for the Court's conclusion that he voluntarily waived such right.

We conclude that the Court of Appeals was correct in holding that the record in this case falls far short of sustaining petitioner's burden [of proving waiver]. It is true that Williams had been informed of and appeared to understand his right to counsel. But waiver requires not merely comprehension but relinquishment, and Williams' consistent reliance upon the advice of counsel in dealing with the authorities refutes any suggestion that he waived that right. He consulted McKnight by long-distance telephone before turning himself in. He spoke with McKnight by telephone again shortly after being booked. After he was arraigned, Williams sought out and obtained legal advice from Kelly. Williams again consulted with Kelly after Detective Leaming and his fellow officer arrived in Davenport. Throughout, Williams was advised not to make any statements before seeing McKnight in Des Moines, and was assured that the police had agreed not to question him. His statements while in the car that he would tell the whole story *after* seeing McKnight in Des Moines were the clearest expressions by Williams himself that he desired the presence of an attorney before any interrogation took place. But even before making these statements, Williams had effectively asserted his right to counsel by having secured attorneys at both ends of the automobile trip, both of whom, acting as his agents, had made clear to the police that no

---

[8] The only other significant factual difference between the present case and *Massiah* is that here the police had *agreed* that they would not interrogate Williams in the absence of his counsel. This circumstances plainly provides petitioner with no argument for distinguishing away the protection afforded by *Massiah*.

It is argued that this agreement may not have been an enforceable one. But we do not deal here with notions of offer, acceptance, consideration, or other concepts of the law of contracts. We deal with constitutional law. And every court that has looked at this case has found an "agreement" in the sense of a commitment made by the Des Moines police officers that Williams would not be questioned about Pamela Powers in the absence of his counsel.

interrogation was to occur during the journey. Williams knew of that agreement and, particularly in view of his consistent reliance on counsel, there is no basis for concluding that he disavowed it.[10]

Despite Williams' express and implicit assertions of his right to counsel, Detective Leaming proceeded to elicit incriminating statements from Williams. Leaming did not preface this effort by telling Williams that he had a right to the presence of a lawyer, and made no effort at all to ascertain whether Williams wished to relinquish that right. The circumstances of record in this case thus provide no reasonable basis for finding that Williams waived his right to the assistance of counsel.

The Court of Appeals did not hold, nor do we, that under the circumstances of this case Williams *could not*, without notice to counsel, have waived his rights under the Sixth and Fourteenth Amendments. It only held, as do we, that he did not.

IV

The crime of which Williams was convicted was senseless and brutal, calling for swift and energetic action by the police to apprehend the perpetrator and gather evidence with which he could be convicted. No mission of law enforcement officials is more important. Yet "[d]isinterested zeal for the public good does not assure either wisdom or right in the methods it pursues." Although we do not lightly affirm the issuance of a writ of habeas corpus in this case, so clear a violation of the Sixth and Fourteenth Amendments as here occurred cannot be condoned. The pressures on state executive and judicial officers charged with the administration of the criminal law are great, especially when the crime is murder and the victim a small child. But it is precisely the predictability of those pressures that makes imperative a resolute loyalty to the guarantees that the Constitution extends to us all.

The judgment of the Court of Appeals is affirmed.[12]

---

[10] *Cf. Mosley*, (White, J., concurring in result):

[T]he reasons to keep the lines of communication between the authorities and the accused open when the accused has chosen to make his own decisions are not present when he indicates instead that he wishes legal advice with respect thereto. The authorities may then communicate with him through an attorney. More to the point, the accused having expressed his own view that he is not competent to deal with the authorities without legal advice, a later decision at the authorities' insistence to make a statement without counsel's presence may properly be viewed with skepticism.

[12] The District Court stated that its decision "does not touch upon the issue of what evidence, if any, beyond the incriminating statements themselves must be excluded as 'fruit of the poisonous tree.' " We, too, have no occasion to address this issue, and in the present posture of the case there is no basis for the view of our dissenting Brethren, that any attempt to retry the respondent would probably be futile. While neither Williams' incriminating statements themselves nor any testimony describing his having led the police to the victim's body can constitutionally be admitted into evidence, evidence of where the body was found and of its condition might well be admissible on the theory that the body would have been discovered in any event, even had incriminating statements not been elicited from Williams. *Cf. Killough v. United States*, 336 F.2d 929, 119 U.S. App. D.C. 10. In the event that a retrial is instituted, it will be for the state courts in the first instance to determine whether particular items of evidence may be admitted.

MR. JUSTICE MARSHALL, concurring.

I concur wholeheartedly in my Brother STEWART'S opinion for the Court, but add these words in light of the dissenting opinions filed today. The dissenters have, I believe, lost sight of the fundamental constitutional backbone of our criminal law. They seem to think that Detective Leaming's actions were perfectly proper, indeed laudable, examples of "good police work." In my view, good police work is something far different from catching the criminal at any price. It is equally important that the police, as guardians of the law, fulfill their responsibility to obey its commands scrupulously. For "in the end life and liberty can be as much endangered from illegal methods used to convict those thought to be criminals as from the actual criminals themselves." *Spano*.

In this case, there can be no doubt that Detective Leaming consciously and knowingly set out to violate Williams' Sixth Amendment right to counsel and his Fifth Amendment privilege against self-incrimination, as Leaming himself understood those rights. Leaming knew that Williams had been advised by two lawyers not to make any statements to police until he conferred in Des Moines with his attorney there, Mr. McKnight. Leaming surely understood, because he had overheard McKnight tell Williams as much, that the location of the body would be revealed to police. Undoubtedly Leaming realized the way in which that information would be conveyed to the police: McKnight would learn it from his client and then he would lead police to the body. Williams would thereby be protected by the attorney-client privilege from incriminating himself by directly demonstrating his knowledge of the body's location, and the unfortunate Powers child could be given a "Christian burial."

Of course, this scenario would accomplish all that Leaming sought from his investigation except that it would not produce incriminating statements or actions from Williams. Accordingly, Leaming undertook his charade to pry such evidence from Williams. After invoking the no-passengers rule to prevent attorney Kelly from accompanying the prisoner, Leaming had Williams at his mercy: during the three or four-hour trip he could do anything he wished to elicit a confession. The detective demonstrated once again "that the efficiency of the rack and the thumbscrew can be matched, given the proper subject by more sophisticated modes of 'persuasion.' "

Leaming knowingly isolated Williams from the protection of his lawyers and during that period he intentionally "persuaded" him to give incriminating evidence. It is this intentional police misconduct — not good police practice — that the Court rightly condemns. The heinous nature of the crime is no excuse, as the dissenters would have it, for condoning knowing and intentional police transgression of the constitutional rights of a defendant. If Williams is to go free — and given the ingenuity of Iowa prosecutors on retrial or in a civil commitment proceeding, I doubt very much that there is any chance a dangerous criminal will be loosed on the streets, the bloodcurdling cries of the dissents notwithstanding — it will hardly be because he deserves it. It will be because Detective Leaming, knowing full well that he risked reversal of Williams' conviction, intentionally denied Williams the right of *every* American under the Sixth Amendment to have the protective shield of a lawyer between himself and the awesome power of the State.

MR. JUSTICE POWELL, concurring.

As the dissenting opinion of THE CHIEF JUSTICE sharply illustrates, resolution of the issues in this case turns primarily on one's perception of the facts. There is little difference of opinion, among the several courts and numerous judges who have reviewed the case, as to the relevant constitutional principles: (i) Williams had the right to assistance of counsel; (ii) once that right attached (it is conceded that it had in this case), the State could not properly interrogate Williams in the absence of counsel unless he voluntarily and knowingly waive the right; and (iii) the burden was on the State to show that Williams in fact had waived the right before the police interrogated him.

After finding, upon a full review of the facts, that there had been "interrogation," the District Court addressed the ultimate issue of "waiver" and concluded not only that the State had failed to carry its burden but also that "there is *nothing* in the record to indicate that [Williams] waived his Fifth and Sixth Amendment rights *except* the fact that statements eventually were obtained." (Emphasis in original.)

The Court of Appeals stated affirmatively that "the facts as found by the District Court had substantial basis in the record."[1]

I join the opinion of the Court which also finds that the efforts of Detective Leaming "to elicit information from Williams," as conceded by counsel for petitioner at oral argument, were a skillful and effective form of interrogation. Moreover, the entire setting was conducive to the psychological coercion that was successfully exploited. Williams was known by the police to be a young man with quixotic religious convictions and a history of mental disorders. The date was the day after Christmas, the weather was ominous, and the setting appropriate for Detective Leaming's talk of snow concealing the body and preventing a "Christian burial." Williams was alone in the automobile with two police officers for several hours. It is clear from the record, as both of the federal courts below found, that there was no evidence of a knowing and voluntary waiver of the right to have counsel present beyond the fact that Williams ultimately confessed. It is settled law that an inferred waiver of a constitutional right is disfavored. I find no basis in the record of this case — or in the dissenting opinions — for disagreeing with the conclusion of the District Court that "the State has produced no affirmative evidence whatsoever to support its claim of waiver."

The dissenting opinion of THE CHIEF JUSTICE states that the Court's holding today "conclusively presumes a suspect is legally incompetent to change his mind

[1] Before concluding that the police had engaged in interrogation, the District Court summarized the factual background:

> Detective Leaming obtained statements from Petitioner in the absence of counsel (1) after making, and then breaking, an agreement with Mr. McKnight that Petitioner would not be questioned until he arrived in Des Moines and saw Mr. McKnight; (2) after being told by both Mr. McKnight and Mr. Kelly that Petitioner was not to be questioned until he reached Des Moines; (3) after refusing to allow Mr. Kelly, whom Detective Leaming himself regarded as Petitioner's co-counsel, to ride to Des Moines with Petitioner; and (4) after being told by Petitioner that he would talk *after* he reached Des Moines and Mr. McKnight. By violating or ignoring these several, clear indications that Petitioner was to have counsel during interrogation, Detective Leaming deprived Petitioner of his right to counsel in a way similar to, if not more objectionable than, that utilized against the defendant in *Massiah*.

and tell the truth until an attorney is present." I find no justification for this view. On the contrary, the opinion of the Court is explicitly clear that the right to assistance of counsel may be waived, after it has attached, without notice to or consultation with counsel. We would have such a case here if petitioner had proved that the police officers refrained from coercion and interrogation, as they had agreed, and that Williams freely on his own initiative had confessed the crime.

Mr. Justice Stevens, concurring.

Mr. Justice Stewart, in his opinion for the Court which I join, Mr. Justice Powell, and Mr. Justice Marshall have accurately explained the reasons why the law requires the result we reach today. Nevertheless, the strong language in the dissenting opinions prompts me to add this brief comment about the Court's function in a case such as this.

Nothing that we write, no matter how well reasoned or forcefully expressed, can bring back the victim of this tragedy or undo the consequences of the official neglect which led to the respondent's escape from a state mental institution. The emotional aspects of the case make it difficult to decide dispassionately, but do not qualify our obligation to apply the law with an eye to the future as well as with concern for the result in the particular case before us.

Underlying the surface issues in this case is the question whether a fugitive from justice can rely on his lawyer's advice given in connection with a decision to surrender voluntarily. The defendant placed his trust in an experienced Iowa trial lawyer who in turn trusted the Iowa law enforcement authorities to honor a commitment made during negotiations which led to the apprehension of a potentially dangerous person. Under any analysis, this was a critical stage of the proceeding in which the participation of an independent professional was of vital importance to the accused and to society. At this stage — as in countless others in which the law profoundly affects the life of the individual — the lawyer is the essential medium through which the demands and commitments of the sovereign are communicated to the citizen. If, in the long run, we are seriously concerned about the individuals effective representation by counsel, the State cannot be permitted to dishonor its promise to this lawyer.[*]

Mr. Chief Justice Burger, dissenting.

The result in this case ought to be intolerable in any society which purports to call itself an organized society. It continues the Court — by the narrowest margin — on the much-criticized course of punishing the public for the mistakes and misdeeds of law enforcement officers, instead of punishing the officer directly, if in fact he is guilty of wrongdoing. It mechanically and blindly keeps reliable evidence from juries whether the claimed constitutional violation involves gross police misconduct or honest human error.

---

[*] The importance of this point is emphasized by the State's refusal to permit counsel to accompany his client on the trip from Davenport to Des Moines.

Williams is guilty of the savage murder of a small child; no member of the Court contends he is not. While in custody, and after no fewer than *five* warnings of his rights to silence and to counsel, he led police to the concealed body of his victim. The Court concedes Williams was not threatened or coerced and that he spoke and acted voluntarily and with full awareness of his constitutional rights. In the face of all this, the Court now holds that because Williams was prompted by the detective's statement — not interrogation but a statement — the jury must not be told how the police found the body.

Today's holding fulfills Judge (later Mr. Justice) Cardozo's grim prophecy that someday some court might carry the exclusionary rule to the absurd extent that its operative effect would exclude evidence relating to the body of a murder victim because of the means by which it was found.[1] In so ruling the Court regresses to playing a grisly game of "hide and seek," once more exalting the sporting theory of criminal justice which has been experiencing a decline in our jurisprudence. With Justices White, Blackmun, and Rehnquist, I categorically reject the remarkable notion that the police in this case were guilty of unconstitutional misconduct, or any conduct justifying the bizarre result reached by the Court.

Under well-settled precedents which the Court freely acknowledges, it is very clear that Williams had made a valid waiver of his Fifth Amendment right to silence and his Sixth Amendment right to counsel when he led police to the child's body. Indeed, even under the Court's analysis I do not understand how a contrary conclusion is possible.

One plausible but unarticulated basis for the result reached is that once a suspect has asserted his right not to talk without the presence of an attorney, it becomes legally impossible for him to waive that right until he has seen an attorney. But constitutional rights are *personal*, and an otherwise valid waiver should not be brushed aside by judges simply because an attorney was not present. The Court's holding operates to "imprison a man in his privileges"; it conclusively presumes a suspect is legally incompetent to change his mind and tell the truth until an attorney is present. It denigrates an individual to a nonperson whose free will has become hostage to a lawyer so that until the lawyer consents, the suspect is deprived of any legal right or power to decide for himself that he wishes to make a disclosure. It denies that the rights to counsel and silence are personal, nondelegable, and subject to a waiver only by that individual. The opinions in support of the Court's judgment

---

[1] "The criminal is to go free because the constable has blundered . . . . A room is searched against the law, and the body of a murdered man is found . . . . The privacy of the home has been infringed, and the murderer goes free." *People v. Defore*, 242 N.Y. 13, 21, 23–24, 150 N.E. 585, 587, 588 (1926).

The Court protests, *ante*, n.12, that its holding excludes only "Williams' incriminating statements themselves [as well as] any testimony describing his having led the police to the victim's body," thus hinting that successful retrial of this palpably guilty felon is realistically possible. Even if this were all, and the *corpus delicti* could be used to establish the fact and manner of the victim's death, the Court's holding clearly bars all efforts to let the jury know how the police found the body. But the Court's further and remarkable statement that "evidence of where the body was found and of its condition" could be admitted *only* "on the theory that the body would have been discovered in any event" makes clear that the Court is determined to keep the truth from the jurors pledged to find the truth. If all use of the *corpus delicti* is to be barred by the Court as "fruit of the poisonous tree," except on the unlikely theory suggested by the Court, the Court renders the prospects of doing justice in this case exceedingly remote.

do not enlighten us as to why police conduct whether good or bad should operate to suspend Williams' right to change his mind and "tell all" at once rather than waiting until he reached Des Moines.

In any case, the Court assures us this is not at all what it intends, and that a valid waiver was *possible* in these circumstances, but was not quite made. Here, of course, Williams did not confess to the murder in so many words; it was his conduct in guiding police to the body, not his words, which incriminated him. And the record is replete with evidence that Williams knew precisely what he was doing when he guided police to the body. The human urge to confess wrongdoing is, of course, normal in all save hardened, professional criminals, as psychiatrists and analysts have demonstrated.

MR. JUSTICE WHITE, with whom MR. JUSTICE BLACKMUN and MR. JUSTICE REHN-QUIST join, dissenting.

The respondent in this case killed a 10-year-old child. The majority sets aside his conviction, holding that certain statements of unquestioned reliability were unconstitutionally obtained from him, and under the circumstances probably makes it impossible to retry him. Because there is nothing in the Constitution or in our previous cases which requires the Court's action, I dissent.

The majority recognizes that even after his "assertion" of his right to counsel, it would have found that respondent waived his right not to talk in counsel's absence if his waiver had been express — i.e., if the officers had asked him in the car whether he would be willing to answer questions in counsel's absence and if he had answered "yes."[1] But waiver is not a formalistic concept. Waiver is shown whenever the facts establish that an accused knew of a right and intended to relinquish it. Such waiver, even if not express, was plainly shown here. The only other conceivable basis for the majority's holding is the implicit suggestion that the right involved in *Massiah,* as distinguished from the right involved in *Miranda,* is a right not to be *asked* any questions in counsel's absence rather than a right not to *answer* any questions in counsel's absence, and that the right not to be *asked* questions must be waived *before* the questions are asked. Such wafer-thin distinctions cannot determine whether a guilty murderer should go free. The only conceivable purpose for the presence of counsel during questioning is to protect an accused from making incriminating *answers.* Questions, unanswered, have no significance at all. Absent coercion[6] — no matter how the right involved is defined — an accused is amply

---

[1] It does not matter whether the right not to make statements in the absence of counsel stems from *Massiah* or *Miranda.* In either case the question is one of waiver. Waiver was not addressed in *Massiah* because there the statements were being made to an informant and the defendant had no way of knowing that he had a right not to talk to him without counsel. [Footnote repositioned. — Ed.]

[6] There is a rigid prophylactic rule set forth in *Miranda* that once an arrestee requests presence of counsel at questioning, *questioning* must cease. The rule depends on an indication by the accused that he will be unable to handle the decision whether or not to answer questions without advice of counsel, *see Mosley,* (WHITE, J., concurring), and is inapplicable to this case for two reasons. First, at no time did *respondent* indicate a desire not to be asked questions outside the presence of his counsel — notwithstanding the fact that he was told that he and the officers would be "visiting in the car." The majority concludes, although studiously avoiding reliance on *Miranda,* that respondent *asserted* his

protected by a rule requiring waiver before or simultaneously with the giving by him of an answer or the making by him of a statement.

The consequence of the majority's decision is, as the majority recognizes, extremely serious. A mentally disturbed killer whose guilt is not in question may be released. Why? Apparently the answer is that the majority believes that the law enforcement officers acted in a way which involves some risk of injury to society and that such conduct should be deterred. However, the officers' conduct did not, and was not likely to, jeopardize the fairness of respondent's trial or in any way risk the conviction of an innocent man — the risk against which the Sixth Amendment guarantee of assistance of counsel is designed to protect. The police did nothing "wrong," let alone anything "unconstitutional." To anyone not lost in the intricacies of the prophylactic rules of *Miranda*, the result in this case seems utterly senseless; and for the reasons stated, *supra*, even applying those rules as well as the rule of *Massiah*, the statements made by respondent were properly admitted. In light of these considerations, the majority's protest that the result in this case is justified by a "clear violation" of the Sixth and Fourteenth Amendments has a distressing hollow ring. I respectfully dissent.

Mr. Justice Blackmun, with whom Mr. Justice White and Mr. Justice Rehnquist join, dissenting.

I disagree that respondent Williams' situation was in the mold of *Massiah*, that is, that it was dominated by a denial to Williams of his Sixth Amendment right to counsel after criminal proceedings had been instituted against him. The Court rules that the Sixth Amendment was violated because Detective Leaming "purposely sought during Williams' isolation from his lawyers to obtain as much incriminating information as possible." I cannot regard that as unconstitutional *per se*.

First, the police did not deliberately seek to isolate Williams from his lawyers so as to deprive him of the assistance of counsel. *Cf. Escobedo*. The isolation in this case was a necessary incident of transporting Williams to the county where the crime was committed.

Second, Leaming's purpose was not solely to obtain incriminating evidence. The victim had been missing for only two days, and the police could not be certain that she was dead. Leaming, of course, and in accord with his duty, was "hoping to find out where that little girl was," but such motivation does not equate with an intention to evade the Sixth Amendment. Moreover, the Court seems to me to place an undue emphasis and aspersion on what it and the lower courts have chosen to call the "Christian burial speech," and on Williams' "deeply religious" convictions.

---

right to counsel. This he did in some respects, but he never, himself, asserted a right not to be questioned in the absence of counsel. Second, as is noted in the dissenting opinion of Mr. Justice Blackmun, respondent was not questioned. The rigid prophylactic rule as the majority implicitly recognizes is designed solely to prevent involuntary waivers of the right against self-incrimination and is not to be applied to a statement by a law enforcement officer accompanied by a request by the officer that the accused make no response followed by more than an hour of silence and an apparently spontaneous statement on a subject — the victim's shoes — not broached in the "speech." Under such circumstances there is not even a small risk that the waiver will be involuntary.

Third, not every attempt to elicit information should be regarded as "tantamount to interrogation." I am not persuaded that Leaming's observations and comments, made as the police car traversed the snowy and slippery miles between Davenport and Des Moines that winter afternoon, were an interrogation, direct or subtle, of Williams. Contrary to this Court's statement, the Iowa Supreme Court appears to me to have thought and held otherwise, and I agree. Williams, after all, was counseled by lawyers, and warned by the arraigning judge in Davenport and by the police, and yet it was he who started the travel conversations and brought up the subject of the criminal investigation. Without further reviewing the circumstances of the trip, I would say it is clear there was no interrogation. In this respect, I am in full accord with Judge Webster in his vigorous dissent, and with the views implicitly indicated by Chief Judge Gibson and Judge Stephenson, who joined him in voting for rehearing en banc.

In summary, it seems to me that the Court is holding that *Massiah* is violated whenever police engage in any conduct, in the absence of counsel, with the subjective desire to obtain information from a suspect after arraignment. Such a rule is far too broad. Persons in custody frequently volunteer statements in response to stimuli other than interrogation. When there is no interrogation, such statements should be admissible as long as they are truly voluntary.[3]

The *Massiah* point thus being of no consequence, I would vacate the judgment of the Court of Appeals and remand the case for consideration of the issue of voluntariness, in the constitutional sense, of Williams' statements, an issue the Court of Appeals did not reach when the case was before it.

One final word: I can understand the discomfiture the Court obviously suffers and expresses in Part IV of its opinion. This was a brutal, tragic, and heinous crime inflicted upon a young girl on the afternoon of the day before Christmas. With the exclusionary rule operating as the Court effectuates it, the decision today probably means that, as a practical matter, no new trial will be possible at this date eight years after the crime, and that this respondent necessarily will go free. That, of course, is not the standard by which a case of this kind strictly is to be judged. But, as Judge Webster in dissent below observed, placing the case in sensible and proper perspective: "The evidence of Williams' guilt was overwhelming. No challenge is made to the reliability of the factfinding process." I am in full agreement with that observation.

QUESTIONS AND NOTES

1. Do you think that Leaming's course of conduct constituted good police work? Would your answer be any different if the dissent had prevailed?

2. Did Leaming break his promise to defense counsel? Explain. Should your answer to this question have any relevance to the resolution of the ultimate issue?

---

[3] With all deference to the Court, I do not agree that *Massiah* regarded it as "constitutionally irrelevant" that the statements in that case were surreptitiously obtained. The *Massiah* opinion quoted with approval the dissenting Circuit Judge's statement that "Massiah was more seriously imposed upon . . . because he did not even know that he was under interrogation by a government agent."

3.   In any event, should Williams' statements about the shoes and blanket be admissible? Why? Why not?

4.   How would (should) this case have been decided if it were a *Miranda* case? Explain.

5.   What makes this case a *Massiah* case?

6.   Is it clear that the "Christian burial speech" was a charade? Explain.

7.   Is it clear that Williams intended to confess to murder? Is it even clear that he was guilty? Explain. Should your answer to this question be relevant to the resolution of this case? Why? Why not?

8.   Do you think that Williams waived his right to counsel? Why? Why not?

9.   In conjunction with Question 8, consider Justice White's fn. 6, and surrounding and preceding text. Is Justice White or the Court more guilty of drawing wafer-thin distinctions?

10.   We will return to the next phase of this case later (*Nix v. Williams*, Chapter 22, *infra*) to examine the admissibility of the victim's body.

11.   We next turn to *Moulton*, which revives, and arguably expands, *Massiah*.

MAINE v. MOULTON
474 U.S. 159 (1985)

JUSTICE BRENNAN delivered the opinion of the Court.

The question presented in this case is whether respondent's Sixth Amendment right to the assistance of counsel was violated by the admission at trial of incriminating statements made by him to his codefendant, a secret government informant, after indictment and at a meeting of the two to plan defense strategy for the upcoming trial.

I

On the night of January 15, 1981, police officers in Belfast, Maine, responded to a fire call in the vicinity of the Belfast Dodge automobile dealership. Arriving at the scene, the officers discovered a burning Chevrolet dump truck which they recognized as a vehicle that had been reported stolen. After examining the burning truck, the officers searched a building located on the Belfast Dodge property. This building was not part of the dealership, but was leased to respondent Perley Moulton and his codefendant Gary Colson who were using the space to restore and sell old Ford Mustangs. Inside, the officers discovered evidence of several recent automobile and automobile-related thefts.

On April 7, 1981, a Waldo County grand jury returned indictments charging Moulton and Colson with four counts of theft. Specifically, the indictments alleged that Moulton and Colson received, retained, or disposed of a 1978 Ford pickup truck, a 1978 Chevrolet dump truck, a 1970 Ford Mustang automobile, and assorted

Ford Motor Company automotive parts knowing these to be stolen and intending to deprive the owners of possession. On April 9, Moulton and Colson, represented by retained counsel, appeared before the Maine Superior Court for Waldo County and entered pleas of not guilty. Both were enlarged on bail pending trial. Numerous proceedings, unnecessary to detail here, occurred during the ensuing year and a half.

On November 4, 1982, Colson complained by telephone to Robert Keating, Chief of the Belfast Police Department, that he had received anonymous threatening telephone calls regarding the charges pending against him and Moulton, and indicated that he wished to talk to the police about the charges. Keating told Colson to speak with his lawyer and to call back.

On November 6, Colson met with Moulton at a Belfast restaurant to plan for their upcoming trial. According to Colson, Moulton suggested the possibility of killing Gary Elwell, a State's witness, and they discussed how to commit the murder.

On November 9 and 10, Colson, accompanied by his lawyer, met with Police Chief Keating and State Police Detective Rexford Kelley. At these meetings, Colson gave full confessions of his participation with Moulton in committing the crimes for which they had been indicted. In addition, Colson admitted that he and Moulton had not merely received stolen automotive parts, but also had broken into the local Ford dealership to steal the parts. Colson also stated that he and Moulton had set fire to the dump truck and had committed other thefts. The officers offered Colson a deal: no further charges would be brought against him if he would testify against Moulton and otherwise cooperate in the prosecution of Moulton on the pending charges. Colson agreed to cooperate.[2]

Moulton asked Colson to set aside an entire day so that the two of them could meet and plan their defense. They agreed to meet on Sunday, December 26. [T]he police obtained Colson's consent to be equipped with a body wire transmitter to record what was said at the meeting. Chief Keating later testified that he did this for Colson's safety in case Moulton realized that Colson was cooperating with the police, and to record any further conversation concerning threats to witnesses. Keating also testified that he was aware that Moulton and Colson were meeting to discuss the charges for which Moulton was already under indictment. Colson was instructed "not to attempt to question Perley Moulton, just be himself in his conversation . . . ."

The December 26 meeting, as was to be expected, consisted of a prolonged discussion of the pending charges — what actually had occurred, what the State's evidence would show, and what Moulton and Colson should do to obtain a verdict of acquittal. The idea of eliminating witnesses was briefly mentioned early in the

---

[2] Seven months after the conclusion of Moulton's trial, Colson pleaded guilty to two counts of theft. The prosecutor recommended that Colson be sentenced to 2 years' imprisonment, all but 15 days to be suspended, and placed on probation for 2 years. Colson also agreed to make restitution up to $2,000 during the probationary period. The trial court accepted this recommendation and sentenced Colson accordingly.

conversation. After a short discussion, encouraged by Colson,[3] Moulton concluded that he did not think the plan would work. The remainder of the lengthy meeting was spent discussing the case. Moulton and Colson decided to create false alibis as their defense at trial. Because they sought to conform these alibis as closely as possible to what really happened, much of their discussion involved recounting the crimes. Although Colson had described what had happened in detail when he confessed to the police a month earlier, he now frequently professed to be unable to recall the events. Apologizing for his poor memory, he repeatedly asked Moulton to remind him about the details of what had happened, and this technique caused Moulton to make numerous incriminating statements.[4] Nor were all of Colson's memory lapses related to events that required discussion to fabricate convincing alibis. Colson also "reminisced" about events surrounding the various thefts, and this technique too elicited additional incriminating statements from Moulton. For example, Colson asked Moulton how many locks they had drilled to steal a truck, a fact obviously not relevant to developing an alibi. Similarly, Colson questioned Moulton about whether it was the Mustang or the pickup truck that did not have a heater. Later, Colson jokingly drew forth admissions from Moulton concerning the dumping of a stolen truck into a pond after it had been scavenged for parts, and the dumping of a load of potatoes from another stolen truck onto the road. Each of these statements was later admitted into evidence against Moulton at trial.

II

A

Once the right to counsel has attached and been asserted, the State must of course honor it. This means more than simply that the State cannot prevent the accused from obtaining the assistance of counsel. The Sixth Amendment also

---

[3] The exchange went as follows:

> [Moulton:] You know I thought of a way to eliminate them. Remember we were talking about it before?
>
> [Colson:] Yes, you thought of a way?
>
> [Moulton:] Yeah, but . . . I don't think we ought to go for it.
>
> [Colson:] Is it foolproof?
>
> [Moulton:] No.
>
> [Colson:] Is it, is it fairly foolproof?
>
> [Moulton:] I like it. I think it's just for the . . . .
>
> [Colson:] Well let me [hear it]."

Moulton explained that he had considered using air rifles to shoot poisoned darts and the conversation then turned to joking about a magazine that instructed readers how to build bombs to kill large numbers of people.

[4] Colson began doing this immediately after Moulton vetoed the plan to eliminate witnesses. Colson indicated that he did not have copies of all the discovery materials, and Moulton went outside to his car to get his copies. While Moulton was gone, Colson sighed heavily and whispered "[o]h boy, I just hope I can make it through this" into the microphone. Then, when Moulton returned moments later, Colson immediately stated, slowly and deliberately: "I want you to help me with some dates. One date I cannot remember Caps [Moulton's nickname], just can't remember, I know it was in December, what night did we break into Lothrop Ford? What date?"

imposes on the State an affirmative obligation to respect and preserve the accused's choice to seek this assistance. We have on several occasions been called upon to clarify the scope of the State's obligation in this regard, and have made clear that, at the very least, the prosecutor and police have an affirmative obligation not to act in a manner that circumvents and thereby dilutes the protection afforded by the right to counsel.

[In *Massiah*,] Massiah was indicted, along with a man named Colson,[8] for conspiracy to possess and to distribute cocaine. Massiah retained a lawyer, pleaded not guilty and was released on bail. Colson, meanwhile, decided to cooperate with Government agents in their continuing investigation of the narcotics activity in which Massiah and others were thought to be engaged. Colson permitted a Government agent to install a radio transmitter under the front seat of his automobile. Massiah held a lengthy conversation with Colson in this automobile while a Government agent listened over the radio. Massiah made several incriminating statements, and these were brought before the jury through the testimony of the Government agent. We reversed Massiah's conviction on the ground that the incriminating statements were obtained in violation of Massiah's rights under the Sixth Amendment. The Court stressed the fact that the interview took place after indictment, at a time when Massiah was clearly entitled to the assistance of counsel. Relying on Justice Douglas' *Spano* concurrence, the Court concluded that the need for, and consequently the right to, the assistance of counsel applied equally in this extrajudicial setting as at the trial itself. Consequently, the Court held:

> [Massiah] was denied the basic protections of [the right to the assistance of counsel] when there was used against him at trial evidence of his own incriminating words, which federal agents had deliberately elicited from him after he had been indicted and in the absence of his counsel.

B

The State contends that the decisive fact in *Massiah* and *United States v. Henry*, 447 U.S. 264 (1980), (discussed in *Kuhlmann v. Wilson*) was that the police set up the confrontation between the accused and a police agent at which incriminating statements were elicited. Supported by the United States as *amicus curiae*, the State maintains that the Sixth Amendment is violated only when police intentionally take this or some equivalent step. Because Moulton rather than Colson requested the December 26 meeting, the State concludes that Moulton's Sixth Amendment rights were not violated here.

[T]he State's attempt to limit our holdings in *Massiah* and *Henry* fundamentally misunderstands the nature of the right we recognized in those cases. The Sixth Amendment guarantees the accused, at least after the initiation of formal charges, the right to rely on counsel as a "medium" between him and the State. As noted above, this guarantee includes the State's affirmative obligation not to act in a manner that circumvents the protections accorded the accused by invoking this right. The determination whether particular action by state agents violates the

---

[8] The parties have taken pains to assure us that Massiah's friend Colson and Moulton's friend Colson are unrelated.

accused's right to the assistance of counsel must be made in light of this obligation. Thus, the Sixth Amendment is not violated whenever — by luck or happenstance — the State obtains incriminating statements from the accused after the right to counsel has attached. *See Henry*, (Powell, J., concurring). However, knowing exploitation by the State of an opportunity to confront the accused without counsel being present is as much a breach of the State's obligation not to circumvent the right to the assistance of counsel as is the intentional creation of such an opportunity. Accordingly, the Sixth Amendment is violated when the State obtains incriminating statements by knowingly circumventing the accused's right to have counsel present in a confrontation between the accused and a state agent.[12]

III

Applying this principle to the case at hand, it is clear that the State violated Moulton's Sixth Amendment right when it arranged to record conversations between Moulton and its undercover informant, Colson. It was the police who suggested to Colson that he record his telephone conversations with Moulton. Having learned from these recordings that Moulton and Colson were going to meet, the police asked Colson to let them put a body wire transmitter on him to record what was said. Police Chief Keating admitted that, when they made this request, the police knew — as they must have known from the recorded telephone conversations — that Moulton and Colson were meeting for the express purpose of discussing the pending charges and planning a defense for the trial.[13] The police thus knew that Moulton would make statements that he had a constitutional right not to make to their agent prior to consulting with counsel. As in *Henry*, the fact that the police were "fortunate enough to have an undercover informant already in close proximity to the accused" does not excuse their conduct under these circumstances. By concealing the fact that Colson was an agent of the State, the police denied Moulton the opportunity to consult with counsel and thus denied him the assistance of counsel guaranteed by the Sixth Amendment.

IV

The Solicitor General argues that the incriminating statements obtained by the Maine police nevertheless should not be suppressed because the police had other, legitimate reasons for listening to Moulton's conversations with Colson, namely, to investigate Moulton's alleged plan to kill Gary Elwell and to insure Colson's safety.

---

[12] Direct proof of the State's knowledge will seldom be available to the accused. However, as Henry makes clear, proof that the State "must have known" that its agent was likely to obtain incriminating statements from the accused in the absence of counsel suffices to establish a Sixth Amendment violation.

[13] Because Moulton thought of Colson only as his codefendant, Colson's engaging Moulton in active conversation about their upcoming trial was certain to elicit statements that Moulton would not intentionally reveal — and had a constitutional right not to reveal — to persons known to be police agents. Under these circumstances, Colson's merely participating in this conversation was "the functional equivalent of interrogation." In addition, the tapes disclose and the Supreme Judicial Court of Maine found that Colson "frequently pressed Moulton for details of various thefts and in so doing elicited much incriminating information that the State later used at trial." Thus, as in *Henry*, we need not reach the situation where the "listening post" cannot or does not participate in active conversation and prompt particular replies.

In *Massiah*, the Government also contended that incriminating statements obtained as a result of its deliberate efforts should not be excluded because law enforcement agents had "the right, if not indeed the duty, to continue their investigation of [Massiah] and his alleged criminal associates . . . ." There, as here, the Government argued that this circumstance justified its surveillance and cured any improper acts or purposes. We rejected this argument, and held:

> We do not question that in this case, as in many cases, it was entirely proper to continue an investigation of the suspected criminal activities of the defendant and his alleged confederates, even though the defendant had already been indicted. All that we hold is that the defendant's own incriminating statements, obtained by federal agents under the circumstances here disclosed, could not constitutionally be used by the prosecution as evidence against him at his trial.

We reaffirm this holding, which states a sensible solution to a difficult problem. The police have an interest in the thorough investigation of crimes for which formal charges have already been filed. They also have an interest in investigating new or additional crimes. Investigations of either type of crime may require surveillance of individuals already under indictment. Moreover, law enforcement officials investigating an individual suspected of committing one crime and formally charged with having committed another crime obviously seek to discover evidence useful at a trial of either crime. In seeking evidence pertaining to pending charges, however, the Government's investigative powers are limited by the Sixth Amendment rights of the accused. To allow the admission of evidence obtained from the accused in violation of his Sixth Amendment rights whenever the police assert an alternative, legitimate reason for their surveillance invites abuse by law enforcement personnel in the form of fabricated investigations and risks the evisceration of the Sixth Amendment right recognized in *Massiah*. On the other hand, to exclude evidence pertaining to charges as to which the Sixth Amendment right to counsel had not attached at the time the evidence was obtained, simply because other charges were pending at that time, would unnecessarily frustrate the public's interest in the investigation of criminal activities. Consequently, incriminating statements pertaining to pending charges are inadmissible at the trial of those charges, notwithstanding the fact that the police were also investigating other crimes, if, in obtaining this evidence, the State violated the Sixth Amendment by knowingly circumventing the accused's right to the assistance of counsel.[16]

Because we hold that the Maine police knowingly circumvented Moulton's right to have counsel present at a confrontation between Moulton and a police agent, the fact that the police had additional reasons for recording Moulton's meeting with Colson is irrelevant. The decision of the Supreme Judicial Court of Maine is affirmed.

---

[16] Incriminating statements pertaining to other crimes, as to which the Sixth Amendment right has not yet attached, are, of course, admissible at a trial of those offenses.

CHIEF JUSTICE BURGER, with whom JUSTICE WHITE and JUSTICE REHNQUIST join, and with whom JUSTICE O'CONNOR joins as to Parts I and III, dissenting.

Today the Court holds that the Sixth Amendment prohibits the use at trial of postindictment statements made to a government informant, even where those statements were recorded as part of a good-faith investigation of entirely separate crimes. Nothing whatever in the Constitution or our prior opinions supports this bizarre result, which creates a new "right" only for those possibly habitual offenders who persist in criminal activity even while under indictment for other crimes. I dissent and would reverse.

II

The Court today concludes that "[t]o allow the admission of evidence obtained from an accused in violation of his Sixth Amendment rights whenever the police assert an alternative, legitimate reason for their surveillance . . . risks the evisceration of the Sixth Amendment right recognized in *Massiah*." With all deference I am bound to state that this conclusion turns the Sixth Amendment on its head by first positing a constitutional violation and then asking whether "alternative, legitimate reasons" for the police surveillance are sufficient to justify that constitutional violation. As I see it, if "alternative, legitimate reasons" motivated the surveillance, then no Sixth Amendment violation has occurred. Indeed, if the police had failed to take the steps they took here knowing that Colson was endangering his life by talking to them, in my view they would be subject to censure.

Analysis of this issue must begin with *Hoffa*, not cited in the Court's opinion. In *Hoffa*, the Court held that postindictment statements obtained by a Government informant "relat[ing] to the commission of a quite separate offense" were properly admitted at a subsequent trial for the separate crime. Other courts have also held that *Massiah*, viewed in light of the later-decided *Hoffa* case, does not prohibit the introduction of incriminating statements obtained in good faith by the Government even after an indictment at a trial involving an offense different from that covered by the indictment.

Applying *Hoffa* to the facts of this case, it is clear that the statements obtained by Colson could have been introduced against respondent at a subsequent trial for crimes apart from those for which respondent had already been indicted, such as conspiracy to commit murder or to obstruct justice. The majority concedes as much: "Incriminating statements pertaining to other crimes, as to which the Sixth Amendment right has not yet attached, are, of course, admissible at a trial of those offenses." It follows from this that the State engaged in no impermissible conduct in its investigation of respondent based on Colson's revelations. By recording conversations between respondent and Colson, Chief Keating and Detective Kelley succeeded in obtaining evidence that the Court's opinion concedes could have been used to convict respondent of further crimes. In fact this record shows clearly that, based on the recordings, the State was able to obtain additional indictments against respondent for burglary, arson, and three more thefts. The Court's opinion notes that respondent pleaded guilty to several of the additional indictments secured as a result of pursuing Colson's leads.

Courts ought to applaud the kind of careful and diligent efforts of the police shown by this record. Indeed, the Court's opinion does not suggest that the police should have — or could have — conducted their investigation in any other way. Yet, inexplicably, the Court holds that the highly probative and reliable evidence produced by this wholly legitimate investigation must be excluded from respondent's trial for theft. The anomaly of this position, then, is that the evidence at issue in this case should have been excluded from respondent's theft trial even though the *same evidence* could have been introduced against *respondent himself* at a trial for separate crimes. Far from being "a sensible solution to a difficult problem," as the Court modestly suggests, it is a judicial aberration conferring a windfall benefit to those who are the subject of criminal investigations for one set of crimes while already under indictment for another. I can think of no reason to turn the Sixth Amendment into a "magic cloak" to protect criminals who engage in multiple offenses that are the subject of separate police investigations.

We have held that no Sixth Amendment violation occurs unless the State "deliberately elicit[s]" comments from the defendant. See *Massiah; Henry.* As the foregoing amply demonstrates, however, a finding of "deliberate elicitation" is not the end of the inquiry. In using the phrase "deliberate elicitation," we surely must have intended to denote elicitation for the purpose of using such statements against the defendant in connection with charges for which the Sixth Amendment right to counsel had attached. Here the State indeed set out to elicit information from a defendant, but it was an investigation with respect to crimes other than those for which the defendant then stood indicted. As two courts found, the State recorded the conversations "for legitimate purposes not related to the gathering of evidence concerning the crime for which [respondent] had been indicted."

No prior holding of this Court recognizes a Sixth Amendment violation in such circumstances. As one court has put it, the Sixth Amendment "speaks only to the situation where in the absence of retained counsel, statements are deliberately elicited from a defendant in connection with a crime for which he has already been indicted."[17] Thus, in *Henry, supra,* n. 14, we quoted Disciplinary Rule 7-104(A)(1) of the American Bar Association's Code of Professional Responsibility, which provides that "a lawyer shall not . . . [c]ommunicate or cause another to communicate *on the subject of the representation* with a party he knows to be represented by a lawyer in that matter" (emphasis added). Our reference in *Henry* to this rule

---

[17] The Court's opinion seems to read *Massiah* as if it definitively addresses situations where the police are investigating a separate crime. This reading is belied by the *Massiah* Court's statement of its own holding:

> We do not question that in this case, as in many cases, it was entirely proper to continue an investigation of the suspected criminal activities of the defendant and his alleged confederates, even though the defendant had already been indicted. All that we hold is that the defendant's own incriminating statements, obtained by federal agents *under the circumstances here disclosed*, could not constitutionally be used by the prosecution as evidence against *him* at his trial.

(first emphasis added).

The reference to the "circumstances here disclosed" must be to the fact that the Government, far from pursuing a good-faith investigation of different crimes, had "instructed the informant to engage [Massiah] in conversation relating to the crimes [for which he had already been indicted]." *Henry,* (Powell, J., concurring); Brief for Petitioner in *Massiah.*

illustrates that we have framed the Sixth Amendment issue in terms of whether the State deliberately circumvented counsel with regard to the "subject of representation." But where, as here, the incriminating statements are gathered for "an alternative, legitimate reason," wholly apart from the pending charges, no such deliberate circumvention exists.

The Court's opinion seems to rest on the notion that the evidence here is excludable because "the State 'must have known' that its agent was likely to obtain incriminating statements from the accused" with respect to the crimes for which he was already indicted. But the inquiry mandated by our holdings is whether the State recorded the statements not merely *in spite of*, but *because of* that consequence. If the State is not seeking to elicit information with respect to the crime for which the defendant is already indicted, it cannot rationally be said that the State has "planned an impermissible interference with the right to the assistance of counsel."

This case is a particularly inappropriate one for invoking the right to counsel. The right to counsel recognized in *Massiah* was designed to preserve the integrity of the trial. Here respondent was under investigation because of his plans to obstruct justice by killing an essential witness. There is no right to consult an attorney for advice on committing crimes. Indeed, any attorney who undertook to offer such advice would undoubtedly be subject to sanction. Thus there is no warrant for vindicating respondent's right to consult counsel. An observation of this Court in connection with the attorney-client evidentiary privilege bears mention here: "The privilege takes flight if the relation is abused. A client who consults an attorney for advice that will serve him in the commission of a fraud will have no help from the law. He must let the truth be told." I would let the truth be told in this case rather than exclude evidence that was the product of this police investigation into activities designed to thwart the judicial process.

Even though the *Massiah* rule is inapplicable to situations where the government is gathering information related to a separate crime, police misconduct need not be countenanced. Accordingly, evidence obtained through a separate crimes investigation should be admitted only "so long as investigating officers show no bad faith and do not institute the investigation of the separate offense as a pretext for avoiding the dictates of *Massiah*." Here the careful actions of Chief Keating and Detective Kelley steered well clear of these prohibitions.

Until today, the clearly prevailing view in the federal and state courts was that *Massiah* and its successors did not protect a defendant from the introduction of postindictment statements deliberately elicited when the police undertook an investigation of separate crimes. As two leading commentators have observed:

"Even before [*Brewer v.*] *Williams*, [430 U.S. 387 (1977),] it was generally accepted that the right to counsel did not bar contact with the defendant concerning *other offenses*, particularly if the offenses were clearly unrelated and it did not appear the charge was simply a pretext to gain custody in order to facilitate the investigation. The more recent cases recognize that [*Massiah* and its progeny do] not confer upon charged defendants immunity from investigation concerning other crimes. This is especially true when the offense under investigation is a new or ongoing one, such as illegal efforts to thwart the forthcoming prosecution." 1 W.

LaFave & J. Israel, Criminal Procedure § 6.4, p. 470 (1984) (emphasis added).

Rather than expand *Massiah* beyond boundaries currently recognized, I would take note of the observation that "*Massiah* certainly is the decision in which Sixth Amendment protections have been extended to their outermost point." *Henry* (Blackmun, J., dissenting). I would not expand them more and well beyond the limits of precedent and logic.

III

Even if I were prepared to join the Court in this enlargement of the protections of the Sixth Amendment, I would have serious doubts about also extending the reach of the exclusionary rule to cover this case. "Cases involving Sixth Amendment deprivations are subject to the general rule that remedies should be tailored to the injury suffered from the constitutional violation and should not unnecessarily infringe on competing interests." Application of the exclusionary rule here makes little sense, as demonstrated by "weighing the costs and benefits of preventing the use in the prosecution's case in chief of inherently trustworthy tangible evidence." *Leon*.

With respect to the costs, applying the rule to cases where the State deliberately elicits statements from a defendant in the course of investigating a separate crime excludes evidence that is "typically reliable and often the most probative information bearing on the guilt or innocence of the defendant." Moreover, because of the trustworthy nature of the evidence, its admission will not threaten "the fairness of a trial or . . . the integrity of the factfinding process." *Brewer*, (Powell, J., concurring). Hence, application of the rule to cases like this one "deflects the truthfinding process," "often frees the guilty," and may well "generat[e] disrespect for the law and [the] administration of justice."

Against these costs, applying the rule here appears to create precious little in the way of offsetting "benefits." Like searches in violation of the Fourth Amendment, the "wrong" that the Court condemns was "fully accomplished" by the elicitation of comments from the defendant and "the exclusionary rule is neither intended nor able to cure the invasion of the defendant's rights which he has already suffered." *Leon*.

The application of the exclusionary rule here must therefore be premised on deterrence of certain types of conduct by the police. We have explained, however, that "[t]he deterrent purpose of the exclusionary rule necessarily assumes that the police have engaged in willful, or at the very least negligent, conduct which has deprived the defendant of some right." Here the trial court found that the State obtained statements from respondent "for legitimate purposes not related to the gathering of evidence concerning the crime for which [respondent] had been indicted." Since the State was not trying to build its theft case against respondent in obtaining the evidence, excluding the evidence from the theft trial will not affect police behavior at all. The exclusion of evidence "cannot be expected, and should not be applied, to deter objectively reasonable law enforcement activity." *Leon*. Indeed, as noted above, it is impossible to identify any police "misconduct" to deter in this case. In fact, if anything, actions by the police of the type at issue here should be encouraged. The diligent investigation of the police in this case may have saved the lives of several potential witnesses and certainly led to the prosecution and conviction of respondent for additional serious crimes.

It seems, then, that the Sixth Amendment claims at issue here "closely parallel claims under the Fourth Amendment," where we have found the exclusionary rule to be inapplicable by weighing the costs and benefits of its applications. If anything, the argument for admission of the evidence here is even stronger because "[t]his is not a case where . . . 'the constable . . . blundered.' "

Because the Court today significantly and unjustifiably departs from our prior holdings, I respectfully dissent.

QUESTIONS AND NOTES

1.   Did the police perpetrate any wrong in obtaining the disputed evidence? Explain.

2.   If your answer to Question 1 was "no," does it necessarily follow that Chief Justice Burger's dissent was correct? Why? Why not?

3.   Is Chief Justice Burger's evaluation of the value of the exclusionary rule appropriate for this type of case? Explain.

4.   If *Moulton* were a *Miranda* case how would it have been decided? Why? If you concluded that it would have been decided differently, what is there about *Moulton* that warrants more protection than is afforded by *Miranda*?

5.   We conclude this section with *Kuhlmann v. Wilson*, a case that explores the impact of *Massiah* as applied to those confined in jail or prison.

KUHLMANN v. WILSON
477 U.S. 436 (1986)

JUSTICE POWELL announced the judgment of the Court and delivered the opinion of the Court with respect to Parts I, IV, and V, and an opinion with respect to Parts II and III in which THE CHIEF JUSTICE, JUSTICE REHNQUIST, and JUSTICE O'CONNOR join.

I

In the early morning of July 4, 1970, respondent and two confederates robbed the Star Taxicab Garage in the Bronx, New York, and fatally shot the night dispatcher. Shortly before, employees of the garage had observed respondent, a former employee there, on the premises conversing with two other men. They also witnessed respondent fleeing after the robbery, carrying loose money in his arms. After eluding the police for four days, respondent turned himself in. Respondent admitted that he had been present when the crimes took place, claimed that he had witnessed the robbery, gave the police a description of the robbers, but denied knowing them. Respondent also denied any involvement in the robbery or murder, claiming that he had fled because he was afraid of being blamed for the crimes.

After his arraignment, respondent was confined in the Bronx House of Detention, where he was placed in a cell with a prisoner named Benny Lee. Unknown to respondent, Lee had agreed to act as a police informant. Respondent made incriminating statements that Lee reported to the police. Prior to trial, respondent moved to suppress the statements on the ground that they were obtained in violation of his right to counsel. The trial court held an evidentiary hearing on the suppression motion, which revealed that the statements were made under the following circumstances.

Before respondent arrived in the jail, Lee had entered into an arrangement with Detective Cullen, according to which Lee agreed to listen to respondent's conversations and report his remarks to Cullen. Since the police had positive evidence of respondent's participation, the purpose of placing Lee in the cell was to determine the identities of respondent's confederates. Cullen instructed Lee not to ask respondent any questions, but simply to "keep his ears open" for the names of the other perpetrators. Respondent first spoke to Lee about the crimes after he looked out the cellblock window at the Star Taxicab Garage, where the crimes had occurred. Respondent said, "someone's messing with me," and began talking to Lee about the robbery, narrating the same story that he had given the police at the time of his arrest. Lee advised respondent that this explanation "didn't sound too good,"[1] but respondent did not alter his story. Over the next few days, however, respondent changed details of his original account. Respondent then received a visit from his brother, who mentioned that members of his family were upset because they believed that respondent had murdered the dispatcher. After the visit, respondent again described the crimes to Lee. Respondent now admitted that he and two other men, whom he never identified, had planned and carried out the robbery, and had murdered the dispatcher. Lee informed Cullen of respondent's statements and furnished Cullen with notes that he had written surreptitiously while sharing the cell with respondent.

After hearing the testimony of Cullen and Lee, the trial court found that Cullen had instructed Lee "to ask no questions of [respondent] about the crime but merely to listen as to what [respondent] might say in his presence." The court determined that Lee obeyed these instructions, that he "at no time asked any questions with respect to the crime," and that he "only listened to [respondent] and made notes regarding what [respondent] had to say." The trial court also found that respondent's statements to Lee were "spontaneous" and "unsolicited." Under state precedent, a defendant's volunteered statements to a police agent were admissible in evidence because the police were not required to prevent talkative defendants from making incriminating statements. The trial court accordingly denied the suppression motion.

The jury convicted respondent of common-law murder and felonious possession of a weapon. On May 18, 1972, the trial court sentenced him to a term of 20 years

---

[1] At the suppression hearing, Lee testified that, after hearing respondent's initial version of his participation in the crimes, "I think I remember telling him that the story wasn't — it didn't sound too good. Things didn't look too good for him." At trial, Lee testified to a somewhat different version of his remark: "Well, I said, look, you better come up with a better story than that because that one doesn't sound too cool to me, that's what I said."

to life on the murder count and to a concurrent term of up to 7 years on the weapons count. The Appellate Division affirmed without opinion, and the New York Court of Appeals denied respondent leave to appeal.

[Subsequently, on habeas corpus, the Second Circuit upheld Wilson's claim.]

IV

As the District Court observed, *Henry* left open the question whether the Sixth Amendment forbids admission in evidence of an accused's statements to a jailhouse informant who was "placed in close proximity but [made] no effort to stimulate conversations about the crime charged."[19] Our review of the line of cases beginning with *Massiah* shows that this question must, as the District Court properly decided, be answered negatively.

A

The Court in *Massiah* adopted the reasoning of the concurring opinions in *Spano* and held that, once a defendant's Sixth Amendment right to counsel has attached, he is denied that right when federal agents "deliberately elicit" incriminating statements from him in the absence of his lawyer. The Court adopted this test, rather than one that turned simply on whether the statements were obtained in an "interrogation," to protect accused persons from "indirect and surreptitious interrogations as well as those conducted in the jailhouse. In this case, Massiah was more seriously imposed upon . . . because he did not even know that he was under interrogation by a government agent." Thus, the Court made clear that it was concerned with interrogation or investigative techniques that were equivalent to interrogation, and that it so viewed the technique in issue in *Massiah*.

In *Henry*, the Court applied the *Massiah* test to incriminating statements made to a jailhouse informant. The Court of Appeals in that case found a violation of *Massiah* because the informant had engaged the defendant in conversations and "had developed a relationship of trust and confidence with [the defendant] such that [the defendant] revealed incriminating information." This Court affirmed, holding that the Court of Appeals reasonably concluded that the Government informant "deliberately used his position to secure incriminating information from [the defendant] when counsel was not present." Although the informant had not questioned the defendant, the informant had "stimulated" conversations with the defendant in order to "elicit" incriminating information. The Court emphasized that those facts, like the facts of *Massiah*, amounted to "indirect and surreptitious interrogatio[n]" of the defendant.

Earlier this Term, we applied the *Massiah* standard in a case involving incriminating statements made under circumstances substantially similar to the facts of *Massiah* itself. In *Moulton*, the defendant made incriminating statements in a meeting with his accomplice, who had agreed to cooperate with the police.

---

[19] In *Moulton*, we again reserved this question, declining to reach the situation where the informant acts simply as a "listening post" without "participat[ing] in active conversation and prompt[ing] particular replies."

During that meeting, the accomplice, who wore a wire transmitter to record the conversation, discussed with the defendant the charges pending against him, repeatedly asked the defendant to remind him of the details of the crime, and encouraged the defendant to describe his plan for killing witnesses. The Court concluded that these investigatory techniques denied the defendant his right to counsel on the pending charges. Significantly, the Court emphasized that, because of the relationship between the defendant and the informant, the informant's engaging the defendant "in active conversation about their upcoming trial was certain to elicit" incriminating statements from the defendant. Thus, the informant's participation "in this conversation was 'the functional equivalent of interrogation.' "

As our recent examination of this Sixth Amendment issue in *Moulton* makes clear, the primary concern of the *Massiah* line of decisions is secret interrogation by investigatory techniques that are the equivalent of direct police interrogation. Since "the Sixth Amendment is not violated whenever — by luck or happenstance — the State obtains incriminating statements from the accused after the right to counsel has attached," a defendant does not make out a violation of that right simply by showing that an informant, either through prior arrangement or voluntarily, reported his incriminating statements to the police. Rather, the defendant must demonstrate that the police and their informant took some action, beyond merely listening, that was designed deliberately to elicit incriminating remarks.

B

It is thus apparent that the Court of Appeals erred in concluding that respondent's right to counsel was violated under the circumstances of this case. Its error did not stem from any disagreement with the District Court over appropriate resolution of the question reserved in *Henry*, but rather from its implicit conclusion that this case did not present that open question. That conclusion was based on a fundamental mistake, namely, the Court of Appeals' failure to accord to the state trial court's factual findings the presumption of correctness expressly required by 28 U.S.C. § 2254(d).

The state court found that Officer Cullen had instructed Lee only to listen to respondent for the purpose of determining the identities of the other participants in the robbery and murder. The police already had solid evidence of respondent's participation.[22] The court further found that Lee followed those instructions, that he "at no time asked any questions" of respondent concerning the pending charges, and that he "only listened" to respondent's "spontaneous" and "unsolicited" statements. The only remark made by Lee that has any support in this record was his comment that respondent's initial version of his participation in the crimes "didn't sound too good." Without holding that any of the state court's findings were not entitled to the presumption of correctness under § 2254(d), the Court of Appeals focused on that one remark and gave a description of Lee's interaction with respondent that is completely at odds with the facts found by the trial court. In the

---

[22] Eyewitnesses had identified respondent as the man they saw fleeing from the garage with an armful of money.

Court of Appeals' view, "[s]ubtly and slowly, but surely, Lee's ongoing verbal intercourse with [respondent] served to exacerbate [respondent's] already troubled state of mind."[24] After thus revising some of the trial court's findings, and ignoring other more relevant findings, the Court of Appeals concluded that the police "deliberately elicited" respondent's incriminating statements. This conclusion conflicts with the decision of every other state and federal judge who reviewed this record, and is clear error in light of the provisions and intent of § 2254(d).

V

The judgment of the Court of Appeals is reversed, and the case is remanded for further proceedings consistent with this opinion.

CHIEF JUSTICE BURGER, concurring.

I agree fully with the Court's opinion and judgment. This case is clearly distinguishable from *Henry*. There is a vast difference between placing an "ear" in the suspect's cell and placing a voice in the cell to encourage conversation for the "ear" to record.

Furthermore, the abuse of the Great Writ needs to be curbed so as to limit, if not put a stop to, the "sporting contest" theory of criminal justice so widely practiced today.

JUSTICE BRENNAN, with whom JUSTICE MARSHALL joins, dissenting.

Because I believe that *Henry* directly controls the merits of this case, I dissent.

According to the Court, the Court of Appeals failed to accord § 2254(d)'s presumption of correctness to the state trial court's findings that respondent's cellmate, Lee, "at no time asked any questions" of respondent concerning the pending charges, and that Lee only listened to respondent's "spontaneous" and "unsolicited" statements. As a result, the Court concludes, the Court of Appeals failed to recognize that this case presents the question, reserved in *Henry*, whether the Sixth Amendment forbids the admission into evidence of an accused's statements to a jailhouse informant who was "placed in close proximity but [made] no effort to stimulate conversations about the crime charged." I disagree with the Court's characterization of the Court of Appeals' treatment of the state court's findings and, consequently, I disagree with the Court that the instant case presents the "listening post" question.

The state trial court simply found that Lee did not ask respondent any direct questions about the crime for which respondent was incarcerated. The trial court considered the significance of this fact only under state precedents, which the court interpreted to require affirmative "interrogation" by the informant as a prerequi-

---

[24] Curiously, the Court of Appeals expressed concern that respondent was placed in a cell that overlooked the scene of his crimes. For all the record shows, however, that fact was sheer coincidence. Nor do we perceive any reason to require police to isolate one charged with crime so that he cannot view the scene, whatever it may be, from his cell window.

site to a constitutional violation. The court did not indicate whether it referred to a Fifth Amendment or to a Sixth Amendment violation in identifying "interrogation" as a precondition to a violation; it merely stated that "the utterances made by [respondent] to Lee were unsolicited, and voluntarily made and did not violate the defendant's Constitutional rights."

The Court of Appeals did not disregard the state court's finding that Lee asked respondent no direct questions regarding the crime. Rather, the Court of Appeals *expressly* accepted that finding, but concluded that, as a matter of law, the deliberate elicitation standard of *Henry* and *Massiah* encompasses other, more subtle forms of stimulating incriminating admissions than overt questioning. The court suggested that the police deliberately placed respondent in a cell that overlooked the scene of the crime, hoping that the view would trigger an inculpatory comment to respondent's cellmate.[8] The court also observed that, while Lee asked respondent no questions, Lee nonetheless stimulated conversation concerning respondents' role in the Star Taxicab Garage robbery and murder by remarking that respondent's exculpatory story did not "sound too good" and that he had better come up with a better one. Thus, the Court of Appeals concluded that respondent's case did not present the situation reserved in *Henry*, where an accused makes an incriminating remark within the hearing of a jailhouse informant, who "makes no effort to stimulate conversations about the crime charged." Instead, the court determined this case to be virtually indistinguishable from *Henry*.

In *Henry*, we found that the Federal Government had "deliberately elicited" incriminating statements from Henry based on the following circumstances. The jailhouse informant, Nichols, had apparently followed instructions to obtain information without directly questioning Henry and without initiating conversations concerning the charges pending against Henry. We rejected the Government's argument that because Henry initiated the discussion of his crime, no Sixth Amendment violation had occurred. We pointed out that under *Massiah*, it is irrelevant whether the informant asks pointed questions about the crime or "merely engage[s] in general conversation about it." Nichols, we noted, "was not a passive listener; . . . he had 'some conversations with Mr. Henry' while he was in jail and Henry's incriminatory statements were 'the product of this conversation.'"

In deciding that Nichols' role in these conversations amounted to deliberate elicitation, we also found three other factors important. First, Nichols was to be paid for any information he produced and thus had an incentive to extract inculpatory admissions from Henry. Second, Henry was not aware that Nichols was acting as an informant. "Conversation stimulated in such circumstances," we observed, "may elicit information that an accused would not intentionally reveal to persons known to be Government agents." Third, Henry was in custody at the time he spoke with Nichols. This last fact is significant, we stated, because "custody imposes pressures on the accused [and] confinement may bring into play subtle influences that will make him particularly susceptible to the ploys of undercover Government agents." We concluded that by "intentionally creating a situation likely to induce Henry to make incriminating statements without the assistance of

---

[8] The Court of Appeals noted that "[a]s soon as Wilson arrived and viewed the garage, he became upset and stated that 'someone's messing with me.'"

counsel, the Government violated Henry's Sixth Amendment right to counsel."

In the instant case, as in *Henry*, the accused was incarcerated and therefore was "susceptible to the ploys of undercover Government agents." Like Nichols [in *Henry*], Lee was a secret informant, usually received consideration for the services he rendered the police, and therefore had an incentive to produce the information which he knew the police hoped to obtain. Just as Nichols had done, Lee obeyed instructions not to question respondent and to report to the police any statements made by the respondent in Lee's presence about the crime in question. And, like Nichols, Lee encouraged respondent to talk about his crime by conversing with him on the subject over the course of several days and by telling respondent that his exculpatory story would not convince anyone without more work. However, unlike the situation in *Henry*, a disturbing visit from respondent's brother, rather than a conversation with the informant, seems to have been the immediate catalyst for respondent's confession to Lee. While it might appear from this sequence of events that Lee's comment regarding respondent's story and his general willingness to converse with respondent about the crime were not the *immediate* causes of respondent's admission, I think that the deliberate-elicitation standard requires consideration of the entire course of government behavior.

The State intentionally created a situation in which it was foreseeable that respondent would make incriminating statements without the assistance of counsel — it assigned respondent to a cell overlooking the scene of the crime and designated a secret informant to be respondent's cellmate. The informant, while avoiding direct questions, nonetheless developed a relationship of cellmate camaraderie with respondent and encouraged him to talk about his crime. While the *coup de grace* was delivered by respondent's brother, the groundwork for respondent's confession was laid by the State. Clearly the State's actions had a sufficient nexus with respondent's admission of guilt to constitute deliberate elicitation within the meaning of *Henry*. I would affirm the judgment of the Court of Appeals.

JUSTICE STEVENS also dissented.

QUESTIONS AND NOTES

1. Do you think that *Kuhlmann*, and the earlier *Henry* case are consistent with one another? Explain. (Incidentally, Chief Justice Burger wrote *Henry*.)

2. If your answer to Question 1 was "no," which one got the right result? Explain.

3. Does (should) it matter whether Wilson was *intentionally* jailed overlooking the scene of his crime?

4. Do you think that Lee was merely a listening post? Explain.

5. Should a mere listening post be forbidden under the Sixth Amendment? Why is it not forbidden?

6. How would *Kuhlmann* and *Henry* be decided under *Miranda*? Why?

7.   In the next Section, we will specifically contrast *Massiah* and *Miranda* cases.

B.   CONTRASTING *MASSIAH* AND *MIRANDA*

MICHIGAN v. JACKSON
475 U.S. 625 (1986)

Justice Stevens delivered the opinion of the Court.

I

The relevant facts may be briefly stated. Respondent Bladel was convicted of the murder of three railroad employees at the Amtrak Station in Jackson, Michigan, on December 31, 1978. Bladel, a disgruntled former employee, was arrested on January 1, 1979, and, after being questioned on two occasions, was released on January 3. He was arrested again on March 22, 1979, and agreed to talk to the police that evening without counsel. On the following morning, Friday, March 23, 1979, Bladel was arraigned. He requested that counsel be appointed for him because he was indigent. The detective in charge of the Bladel investigation was present at the arraignment. A notice of appointment was promptly mailed to a law firm, but the law firm did not receive it until Tuesday, March 27. In the interim, on March 26, 1979, two police officers interviewed Bladel in the county jail and obtained a confession from him. Prior to that questioning, the officers properly advised Bladel of his *Miranda* rights. Although he had inquired about his representation several times since the arraignment, Bladel was not told that a law firm had been appointed to represent him.

Respondent Jackson was convicted of second-degree murder and conspiracy to commit second-degree murder. He was one of four participants in a wife's plan to have her husband killed on July 12, 1979. Arrested on an unrelated charge on July 30, 1979, he made a series of six statements in response to police questioning prior to his arraignment at 4:30 p.m. on August 1. During the arraignment, Jackson requested that counsel be appointed for him. The police involved in his investigation were present at the arraignment. On the following morning, before he had an opportunity to consult with counsel, two police officers obtained another statement from Jackson to "confirm" that he was the person who had shot the victim. As was true of the six prearraignment statements, the questioning was preceded by advice of his *Miranda* rights and Jackson's agreement to proceed without counsel being present.

The Michigan Supreme Court held that the postarraignment statements in both cases should have been suppressed. Noting that the Sixth Amendment right to counsel attached at the time of the arraignments, the court concluded that the *Edwards* rule "applies by analogy to those situations where an accused requests counsel before the arraigning magistrate. Once this request occurs, the police may not conduct further interrogations until counsel has been made available to the accused, unless the accused initiates further communications, exchanges, or conversations with the police. . . . The police cannot simply ignore a defendant's unequivocal request for counsel." We granted certiorari, and we now affirm.

II

The question is not whether respondents had a right to counsel at their postarraignment, custodial interrogations. The existence of that right is clear. It has two sources. The Fifth Amendment protection against compelled self-incrimination provides the right to counsel at custodial interrogations. *Edwards, Miranda.* The Sixth Amendment guarantee of the assistance of counsel also provides the right to counsel at postarraignment interrogations. The arraignment signals "the initiation of adversary judicial proceedings" and thus the attachment of the Sixth Amendment; thereafter, government efforts to elicit information from the accused, including interrogation, represent "critical stages" at which the Sixth Amendment applies. *Moulton, Henry, Brewer, Massiah.* The question in these cases is whether respondents validly waived their right to counsel at the postarraignment custodial interrogations.

The State contends that differences in the legal principles underlying the Fifth and Sixth Amendments compel the conclusion that the *Edwards* rule should not apply to a Sixth Amendment claim. *Edwards* flows from the Fifth Amendment's right to counsel at custodial interrogations, the State argues; its relevance to the Sixth Amendment's provision of the assistance of counsel is far less clear, and thus the *Edwards* principle for assessing waivers is unnecessary and inappropriate.

In our opinion, however, the reasons for prohibiting the interrogation of an uncounseled prisoner who has asked for the help of a lawyer are even stronger after he has been formally charged with an offense than before. Indeed, after a formal accusation has been made — and a person who had previously been just a "suspect" has become an "accused" within the meaning of the Sixth Amendment — the constitutional right to the assistance of counsel is of such importance that the police may no longer employ techniques for eliciting information from an uncounseled defendant that might have been entirely proper at an earlier stage of their investigation. Thus, the surreptitious employment of a cellmate, *see Henry*, or the electronic surveillance of conversations with third parties, *see Moulton, Massiah*, may violate the defendant's Sixth Amendment right to counsel even though the same methods of investigation might have been permissible before arraignment or indictment. Far from undermining the *Edwards* rule, the difference between the legal basis for the rule applied in *Edwards* and the Sixth Amendment claim asserted in these cases actually provides additional support for the application of the rule in these circumstances.

The State also relies on the factual differences between a request for counsel during custodial interrogation and a request for counsel at an arraignment. The State maintains that respondents may not have actually intended their request for counsel to encompass representation during any further questioning by the police. This argument, however, must be considered against the backdrop of our standard for assessing waivers of constitutional rights. Doubts must be resolved in favor of protecting the constitutional claim. This settled approach to questions of waiver requires us to give a broad, rather than a narrow, interpretation to a defendant's request for counsel — we presume that the defendant requests the lawyer's services at every critical stage of the prosecution.[6] We thus reject the State's suggestion that respondents' requests for the appointment of counsel should be construed to apply only to representation in formal legal proceedings.[7]

The State points to another factual difference: the police may not know of the defendant's request for attorney at the arraignment. That claimed distinction is similarly unavailing. In the cases at bar, in which the officers in charge of the investigations of respondents were present at the arraignments, the argument is particularly unconvincing. More generally, however, Sixth Amendment principles require that we impute the State's knowledge from one state actor to another. For the Sixth Amendment concerns the confrontation between the State and the individual. One set of state actors (the police) may not claim ignorance of defendants' unequivocal request for counsel to another state actor (the court).

Finally, the State maintains that each of the respondents made a valid waiver of his Sixth Amendment rights by signing a postarraignment confession after again being advised of his constitutional rights. In *Edwards*, however, we rejected the notion that, after a suspect's request for counsel, advice of rights and acquiescence in police-initiated questioning could establish a valid waiver. We find no warrant for a different view under a Sixth Amendment analysis. Just as written waivers are insufficient to justify police-initiated interrogations after the request for counsel in a Fifth Amendment analysis, so too they are insufficient to justify police-initiated interrogations after the request for counsel in a Sixth Amendment analysis.

III

Edwards is grounded in the understanding that "the assertion of the right to counsel [is] a significant event," and that "additional safeguards are necessary when the accused asks for counsel." We conclude that the assertion is no less significant, and the need for additional safeguards no less clear, when the request for counsel is made at an arraignment and when the basis for the claim is the Sixth Amendment. We thus hold that, if police initiate interrogation after a defendant's assertion, at an arraignment or similar proceeding, of his right to counsel, any waiver of the defendant's right to counsel for that police-initiated interrogation is invalid.

---

[6] In construing respondents' request for counsel, we do not, of course, suggest that the right to counsel turns on such a request. *See Brewer* ("[T]he right to counsel does not depend upon a request by the defendant"). Rather, we construe the defendant's request for counsel as an extremely important fact in considering the validity of a subsequent waiver in response to police-initiated interrogation.

[7] We also agree with the comments of the Michigan Supreme Court about the nature of an accused's request for counsel:

> Although judges and lawyers may understand and appreciate the subtle distinctions between the Fifth and Sixth Amendment rights to counsel, the average person does not. When an accused requests an attorney, either before a police officer or a magistrate, he does not know which constitutional right he is invoking; he therefore should not be expected to articulate exactly why or for what purposes he is seeking counsel. It makes little sense to afford relief from further interrogation to a defendant who asks a police officer for an attorney, but permit further interrogation to a defendant who makes an identical request to a judge. The simple fact that defendant has requested an attorney indicates that he does not believe that he is sufficiently capable of dealing with his adversaries singlehandedly.

The judgments are accordingly affirmed.

CHIEF JUSTICE BURGER, concurring in the judgment.

I concurred only in the judgment in *Edwards*, and in doing so I observed:

The extraordinary protections afforded a person in custody suspected of criminal conduct are not without a valid basis, but as with all "good" things they can be carried too far.

The urge for "bright-line" rules readily applicable to a host of varying situations would likely relieve this Court somewhat from more than a doubling of the Court's work in recent decades, but this urge seems to be leading the Court to an absolutist, mechanical treatment of the subject. At times, it seems, the judicial mind is in conflict with what behavioral — and theological — specialists have long recognized as a natural human urge of people to confess wrongdoing. *See, e.g.*, T. REIK, THE COMPULSION TO CONFESS (1959).

We must, of course, protect persons in custody from coercion, but step by step we have carried this concept well beyond sound, common-sense boundaries. The Court's treatment of this subject is an example of the infirmity of trying to perform the rulemaking function on a case-by-case basis, ignoring the reality that the criminal cases coming to this Court, far from typical, are the "hard" cases. This invokes the ancient axiom that hard cases can make bad law.

Stare decisis calls for my following the rule of *Edwards* in this context, but plainly the subject calls for reexamination. Increasingly, to borrow from Justice Cardozo, more and more "criminal[s] . . . go free because the constable has blundered."

JUSTICE REHNQUIST, with whom JUSTICE POWELL and JUSTICE O'CONNOR join, dissenting.

The Court's decision today rests on the following deceptively simple line of reasoning: *Edwards* created a bright-line rule to protect a defendant's Fifth Amendment rights; Sixth Amendment rights are even more important than Fifth Amendment rights; therefore, we must also apply the *Edwards* rule to the Sixth Amendment. The Court prefers this neat syllogism to an effort to discuss or answer the only relevant question: Does the *Edwards* rule make sense in the context of the Sixth Amendment? I think it does not, and I therefore dissent from the Court's unjustified extension of the *Edwards* rule to the Sixth Amendment.

My disagreement with the Court stems from our differing understandings of *Edwards*. In *Edwards*, this Court held that once a defendant has invoked his right under *Miranda* to have counsel present during custodial interrogation, "a valid waiver of that right cannot be established by showing only that he responded to further police-initiated custodial interrogation even if he has been advised of his rights." This "prophylactic rule" was deemed necessary to prevent the police from effectively "overriding" a defendant's assertion of his *Miranda* rights by "badgering" him into waiving those rights. In short, as we explained in later cases, "*Edwards* did not confer a substantive constitutional right that had not existed before; it 'created a protective umbrella serving to enhance a constitutional guarantee.'"

What the Court today either forgets or chooses to ignore is that the "constitutional guarantee" is the Fifth Amendment's prohibition on compelled self-incrimination. This prohibition, of course, is also the constitutional underpinning for the set of prophylactic rules announced in *Miranda* itself.[2] *Edwards*, like *Miranda*, imposes on the police a bright-line standard of conduct intended to help ensure that confessions obtained through custodial interrogation will not be "coerced" or "involuntary." Seen in this proper light, *Edwards* provides nothing more than a second layer of protection, in addition to those rights conferred by *Miranda*, for a defendant who might otherwise be compelled by the police to incriminate himself in violation of the Fifth Amendment.

The dispositive question in the instant cases, and the question the Court should address in its opinion, is whether the same kind of prophylactic rule is needed to protect a defendant's right to counsel under the Sixth Amendment. The answer to this question, it seems to me, is clearly "no." The Court does not even suggest that the police commonly deny defendants their Sixth Amendment right to counsel. Nor, I suspect, would such a claim likely be borne out by empirical evidence. Thus, the justification for the prophylactic rules this Court created in *Miranda* and *Edwards*, namely, the perceived widespread problem that the police were violating, and would probably continue to violate, the Fifth Amendment rights of defendants during the course of custodial interrogations, is conspicuously absent in the Sixth Amendment context. To put it simply, the prophylactic rule set forth in *Edwards* makes no sense at all except when linked to the Fifth Amendment's prohibition against compelled self-incrimination.

Not only does the Court today cut the *Edwards* rule loose from its analytical moorings, it does so in a manner that graphically reveals the illogic of the Court's position. The Court phrases the question presented in these cases as whether the *Edwards* rule applies "to a defendant who has been formally charged with a crime *and who has requested appointment of counsel at his arraignment*." (emphasis added). And the Court ultimately limits its holding to those situations where the police "initiate interrogation *after a defendant's assertion, at an arraignment or similar proceeding, of his right to counsel*." (emphasis added).

In other words, the Court most assuredly does *not* hold that the *Edwards per se* rule prohibiting all police-initiated interrogations applies from the moment the defendant's Sixth Amendment right to counsel attaches, with or without a request for counsel by the defendant. Such a holding would represent, after all, a shockingly dramatic restructuring of the balance this Court has traditionally struck between the rights of the defendant and those of the larger society. Applying the *Edwards* rule to situations in which a defendant has not made an explicit request for counsel would also render completely nugatory the extensive discussion of "waiver" in such

---

[2] The Court suggests, in dictum, that the Fifth Amendment also provides defendants with a "right to counsel." But our cases make clear that the Fifth Amendment itself provides no such "right." Instead, *Miranda* confers upon a defendant a "right to counsel," *but only when such counsel is requested during custodial interrogations*. Even under *Miranda*, the "right to counsel" exists solely as a means of protecting the defendant's Fifth Amendment right not to be compelled to incriminate himself.

prior Sixth Amendment cases as *Brewer*.

This leaves the Court, however, in an analytical straitjacket. The problem with the limitation the Court places on the Sixth Amendment version of the *Edwards* rule is that, unlike a defendant's "right to counsel" under *Miranda*, which does not arise until affirmatively invoked by the defendant during custodial interrogation, a defendant's Sixth Amendment right to counsel does not depend at all on whether the defendant has requested counsel. The Court acknowledges as much in footnote six of its opinion, where it stresses that "we do not, of course, suggest that the right to counsel turns on . . . a request [for counsel]."

The Court provides no satisfactory explanation for its decision to extend the *Edwards* rule to the Sixth Amendment, yet limit that rule to those defendants foresighted enough, or just plain lucky enough, to have made an explicit request for counsel which we have always understood to be completely unnecessary for Sixth Amendment purposes. The Court attempts to justify its emphasis on the otherwise legally insignificant request for counsel by stating that "we construe the defendant's request for counsel as an extremely important fact in considering the validity of a subsequent waiver in response to police-initiated interrogation." This statement sounds reasonable, but it is flatly inconsistent with the remainder of the Court's opinion, in which the Court holds that there can be no waiver of the Sixth Amendment right to counsel after a request for counsel has been made. It is obvious that, for the Court, the defendant's request for counsel is not merely an "extremely important fact"; rather, it is the *only* fact that counts.

The truth is that there is no satisfactory explanation for the position the Court adopts in these cases. The glaring inconsistencies in the Court's opinion arise precisely because the Court lacks a coherent, analytically sound basis for its decision. The prophylactic rule of *Edwards*, designed from its inception to protect a defendant's right under the Fifth Amendment not to be compelled to incriminate himself, simply does not meaningfully apply to the Sixth Amendment. I would hold that *Edwards* has no application outside the context of the Fifth Amendment, and would therefore reverse the judgment of the court below.

QUESTIONS AND NOTES

1. Do you think that the assertion of the right to counsel at the preliminary hearing necessarily, or even probably, meant that the suspects, who previously agreed to be questioned, no longer wished to be subject to custodial interrogation? Why?

2. Might *Jackson* discourage prompt arraignments in that once the defendant asserts his right to counsel at arraignment, the opportunity for interrogation will be gone?

3. If your answer to Question 2 is "yes," does it necessarily follow that *Jackson* was wrongly decided? Explain.

4. Should fn. 7 of the Court's opinion be taken seriously? If so, are all of the cases in this chapter that purport to draw a distinction between the Fifth and Sixth Amendment right to counsel, cases that are fundamentally flawed?

5.   In regard to Chief Justice Burger's opinion, is it accurate to think of this as a case in which the criminal goes free because the constable has blundered? Explain.

6.   Under the Court's opinion, is it possible for a suspect who has asserted her right to counsel to ever be questioned without counsel? If so, how?

7.   In *McNeil*, the Court explored some of the differences between *Jackson* and *Edwards*.

McNEIL v. WISCONSIN
501 U.S. 171 (1991)

JUSTICE SCALIA delivered the opinion of the Court.

This case presents the question whether an accused's invocation of his Sixth Amendment right to counsel during a judicial proceeding constitutes an invocation of his *Miranda* right to counsel.

I

Petitioner Paul McNeil was arrested in Omaha, Nebraska, in May 1987, pursuant to a warrant charging him with an armed robbery in West Allis, Wisconsin, a suburb of Milwaukee. Shortly after his arrest, two Milwaukee County deputy sheriffs arrived in Omaha to retrieve him. After advising him of his *Miranda* rights, the deputies sought to question him. He refused to answer any questions, but did not request an attorney. The deputies promptly ended the interview.

Once back in Wisconsin, petitioner was brought before a Milwaukee County court commissioner on the armed robbery charge. The Commissioner set bail and scheduled a preliminary examination. An attorney from the Wisconsin Public Defender's office represented petitioner at this initial appearance.

Later that evening, Detective Joseph Butts of the Milwaukee County Sheriff's Department visited petitioner in jail. Butts had been assisting the Racine County, Wisconsin, police in their investigation of a murder, attempted murder, and armed burglary in the town of Caledonia; petitioner was a suspect. Butts advised petitioner of his *Miranda* rights, and petitioner signed a form waiving them. In this first interview, petitioner did not deny knowledge of the Caledonia crimes, but said that he had not been involved.

Butts returned two days later with detectives from Caledonia. He again began the encounter by advising petitioner of his *Miranda* rights, and providing a waiver form. Petitioner placed his initials next to each of the warnings and signed the form. This time, petitioner admitted that he had been involved in the Caledonia crimes, which he described in detail. He also implicated two other men, Willie Pope and Lloyd Crowley. The statement was typed up by a detective and given to petitioner to review. Petitioner placed his initials next to every reference to himself and signed every page.

Butts and the Caledonia Police returned two days later, having in the meantime found and questioned Pope, who convinced them that he had not been involved in the Caledonia crimes. They again began the interview by administering the *Miranda* warnings, and obtaining petitioner's signature and initials on the waiver form. Petitioner acknowledged that he had lied about Pope's involvement to minimize his own role in the Caledonia crimes, and provided another statement recounting the events, which was transcribed, signed, and initialed as before.

The following day, petitioner was formally charged with the Caledonia crimes and transferred to that jurisdiction. His pretrial motion to suppress the three incriminating statements was denied. He was convicted of second-degree murder, attempted first-degree murder, and armed robbery, and sentenced to 60 years in prison.

On appeal, petitioner argued that the trial court's refusal to suppress the statements was reversible error. He contended that his courtroom appearance with an attorney for the West Allis crime constituted an invocation of the *Miranda* right to counsel, and that any subsequent waiver of that right during police-initiated questioning regarding *any* offense was invalid. Observing that the State's Supreme Court had never addressed this issue, the Court of Appeals certified to that court the following question:

> Does an accused's request for counsel at an initial appearance on a charged offense constitute an invocation of his fifth amendment right to counsel that precludes police interrogation on unrelated, uncharged offenses?

The Wisconsin Supreme Court answered "no." We granted certiorari.

II

The Sixth Amendment right is offense-specific. It cannot be invoked once for all future prosecutions, for it does not attach until a prosecution is commenced, that is, "at or after the initiation of adversary judicial criminal proceedings — whether by way of formal charge, preliminary hearing, indictment, information, or arraignment." And just as the right is offense-specific, so also its *Jackson* effect of invalidating subsequent waivers in police-initiated interviews is offense-specific.

The police have an interest . . . in investigating new or additional crimes [after an individual is formally charged with one crime.] . . . [T]o exclude evidence pertaining to charges as to which the Sixth Amendment right to counsel had not attached at the time the evidence was obtained, simply because other charges were pending at that time, would unnecessarily frustrate the public's interest in the investigation of criminal activities . . . .

Moulton.

> Incriminating statements pertaining to other crimes, as to which the Sixth Amendment right has not yet attached, are, of course, admissible at a trial of those offenses.

Because petitioner provided the statements at issue here before his Sixth Amendment right to counsel with respect to the *Caledonia offenses* had been (or even could have been) invoked, that right poses no bar to the admission of the statements in this case.

Petitioner relies, however, upon a different "right to counsel," found not in the text of the Sixth Amendment, but in this Court's jurisprudence relating to the Fifth Amendment guarantee that "[n]o person . . . shall be compelled in any criminal case to be a witness against himself." In *Miranda*, we established a number of prophylactic rights designed to counteract the "inherently compelling pressures" of custodial interrogation, including the right to have counsel present. *Miranda* did not hold, however, that those rights could not be waived. On the contrary, the opinion recognized that statements elicited during custodial interrogation would be admissible if the prosecution could establish that the suspect "knowingly and intelligently waived his privilege against self-incrimination and his right to retained or appointed counsel."

In *Edwards*, we established a second layer of prophylaxis for the *Miranda* right to counsel: once a suspect asserts the right, not only must the current interrogation cease, but he may not be approached for further interrogation "until counsel has been made available to him," — which means, we have most recently held, that counsel must be present, *Minnick*. If the police do subsequently initiate an encounter in the absence of counsel (assuming there has been no break in custody), the suspect's statements are presumed involuntary and therefore inadmissible as substantive evidence at trial, even where the suspect executes a waiver and his statements would be considered voluntary under traditional standards. This is "designed to prevent police from badgering a defendant into waiving his previously asserted *Miranda* rights." The *Edwards* rule, moreover, is *not* offense-specific: once a suspect invokes the *Miranda* right to counsel for interrogation regarding one offense, he may not be reapproached regarding *any* offense unless counsel is present. *Roberson*.

Having described the nature and effects of both the Sixth Amendment right to counsel and the *Miranda-Edwards* "Fifth Amendment" right to counsel, we come at last to the issue here: Petitioner seeks to prevail by combining the two of them. He contends that, although he expressly waived his *Miranda* right to counsel on every occasion he was interrogated, those waivers were the invalid product of impermissible approaches, because his prior invocation of the offense-specific Sixth Amendment right with regard to the West Allis burglary was also an invocation of the non-offense-specific *Miranda-Edwards* right. We think that is false as a matter of fact and inadvisable (if even permissible) as a contrary-to-fact presumption of policy.

As to the former: The purpose of the Sixth Amendment counsel guarantee — and hence the purpose of invoking it — is to "protec[t] the unaided layman at critical confrontations" with his "expert adversary," the government, *after* "the adverse positions of government and defendant have solidified" with respect to a particular alleged crime. The purpose of the *Miranda-Edwards* guarantee, on the other hand — and hence the purpose of invoking it — is to protect a quite different interest: the suspect's "desire to deal with the police only through counsel." This is in one respect narrower than the interest protected by the Sixth Amendment guarantee (because it relates only to custodial interrogation) and in another respect broader (because it relates to interrogation regarding *any* suspected crime and attaches whether or not the "adversarial relationship" produced by a pending prosecution has yet arisen). To invoke the Sixth Amendment interest is, as a matter of *fact, not* to invoke the *Miranda-Edwards* interest. One might be quite willing to speak to the police without counsel present concerning many matters, but not the matter under prosecution. It can be said, perhaps, that it is *likely* that one who has asked for counsel's assistance in defending against a prosecution would want counsel present for all custodial interrogation, even interrogation unrelated to the charge. That is not necessarily true, since suspects often believe that they can avoid the laying of charges by demonstrating an assurance of innocence through frank and unassisted answers to questions. But even if it were true, the *likelihood* that a suspect would wish counsel to be present is not the test for applicability of *Edwards*. The rule of that case applies only when the suspect "ha[s] *expressed*" his wish for the particular sort of lawyerly assistance that is the subject of *Miranda*. *Edwards* (emphasis added). It requires, at a minimum, some statement that can reasonably be construed to be expression of a desire for the assistance of an attorney *in dealing with custodial interrogation by the police*. Requesting the assistance of an attorney at a bail hearing does not bear that construction. "[T]o find that [the defendant] invoked his Fifth Amendment right to counsel on the present charges merely by requesting the appointment of counsel at his arraignment on the unrelated charge is to disregard the ordinary meaning of that request."

Our holding in *Jackson* does not, as petitioner asserts, contradict the foregoing distinction; to the contrary, it *rests* upon it. That case, it will be recalled, held that after the Sixth Amendment right to counsel attaches and is invoked, any statements obtained from the accused during subsequent police-initiated custodial questioning regarding the charge at issue (even if the accused purports to waive his rights) are inadmissible. The State in *Jackson* opposed that outcome on the ground that assertion of the Sixth Amendment right to counsel did not realistically constitute the *expression* (as *Edwards* required) of a wish to have counsel present during custodial interrogation. Our response to that contention was not that it *did* constitute such an expression, but that it *did not have to*, since the relevant question was not whether the *Miranda* "Fifth Amendment" right had been *asserted*, but whether the Sixth Amendment right to counsel had been *waived*. We said that since our "settled approach to questions of waiver requires us to give a broad, rather than a narrow, interpretation to a defendant's request for counsel, . . . we *presume* that the defendant requests the lawyer's services at every critical stage of the prosecution." (emphasis added). The holding of *Jackson* implicitly rejects any equivalence in fact between invocation of the Sixth Amendment right to counsel and the expression necessary to trigger *Edwards*. If such invocation constituted a real (as opposed to merely a legally presumed) request for the assistance of counsel in custodial interrogation, it would have been quite unnecessary for *Jackson* to go on to establish, as it did, a new Sixth Amendment rule of no police-initiated interrogation; we could simply have cited and relied upon *Edwards*.[1]

---

[1] A footnote in *Jackson* quoted with approval statements by the Michigan Supreme Court to the

There remains to be considered the possibility that, even though the assertion of the Sixth Amendment right to counsel does not *in fact* imply an assertion of the *Miranda* "Fifth Amendment" right, we should declare it to be such as a matter of sound policy. Assuming we have such an expansive power under the Constitution, it would not wisely be exercised. Petitioner's proposed rule has only insignificant advantages. If a suspect does not wish to communicate with the police except through an attorney, he can simply tell them that when they give him the *Miranda* warnings. There is not the remotest chance that he will feel "badgered" by their asking to talk to him without counsel present, since the subject will not be the charge on which he has already requested counsel's assistance (for in that event *Jackson* would preclude initiation of the interview) and he will not have rejected uncounseled interrogation on *any* subject before (for in that event *Edwards* would preclude initiation of the interview). The proposed rule would, however, seriously impede effective law enforcement. The Sixth Amendment right to counsel attaches at the first formal proceeding against an accused, and in most States, at least with respect to serious offenses, free counsel is made available at that time and ordinarily requested. Thus, if we were to adopt petitioner's rule, most persons in pretrial custody for serious offenses would be *unapproachable* by police officers suspecting them of involvement in other crimes, *even though they have never expressed any unwillingness to be questioned.* Since the ready ability to obtain uncoerced confessions is not an evil but an unmitigated good, society would be the loser. Admissions of guilt resulting from valid *Miranda* waivers "are more than merely 'desirable'; they are essential to society's compelling interest in finding, convicting, and punishing those who violate the law."[2]

Petitioner urges upon us the desirability of providing a "clear and unequivocal" guideline for the police: no police-initiated questioning of any person in custody who has requested counsel to assist him in defense or in interrogation. But the police do

---

effect that the average person does not "understand and appreciate the subtle distinctions between the Fifth and Sixth Amendment rights to counsel," that it "makes little sense to afford relief from further interrogation to a defendant who asks a police officer for an attorney, but permit further interrogation to a defendant who makes an identical request to a judge," and that "[t]he simple fact that defendant has requested an attorney indicates that he does not believe that he is sufficiently capable of dealing with his adversaries singlehandedly." Those observations were perhaps true in the context of deciding whether a request for the assistance of counsel in defending against a particular charge implied a desire to have that counsel serve as an "intermediary" for all further interrogation on that charge. They are assuredly not true in the quite different context of deciding whether such a request implies a desire never to undergo custodial interrogation, about anything, without counsel present.

[2] The dissent condemns these sentiments as "revealing a preference for an inquisitorial system of justice." We cannot imagine what this means. What makes a system adversarial rather than inquisitorial is not the presence of counsel, much less the presence of counsel where the defendant has not requested it; but rather, the presence of a judge who does not (as an inquisitor does) conduct the factual and legal investigation himself, but instead decides on the basis of facts and arguments pro and con adduced by the parties. In the inquisitorial criminal process of the civil law, the defendant ordinarily has counsel; and in the adversarial criminal process of the common law, he sometimes does not. Our system of justice is, and has always been, an inquisitorial one at the investigatory stage (even the grand jury is an inquisitorial body), and no other disposition is conceivable. Even if detectives were to bring impartial magistrates around with them to all interrogations, there would be no decision for the impartial magistrate to umpire. If all the dissent means by a "preference for an inquisitorial system" is a preference not to require the presence of counsel during an investigatory interview where the interviewee has not requested it — that is a strange way to put it, but we are guilty.

not need our assistance to establish such a guideline; they are free, if they wish, to adopt it on their own. Of course it *is* our task to establish guidelines for judicial review. We like *them* to be "clear and unequivocal," *see, e.g., Roberson*, but only when they guide sensibly, and in a direction we are authorized to go. Petitioner's proposal would in our view do much more harm than good, and is not contained within, or even in furtherance of, the Sixth Amendment's right to counsel or the Fifth Amendment's right against compelled self-incrimination.[3]

"This Court is forever adding new stories to the temples of constitutional law, and the temples have a way of collapsing when one story too many is added." *Douglas v. Jeannette*, 319 U.S. 157, 181 (1943) (opinion of JACKSON, J.). We decline to add yet another story to *Miranda*. The judgment of the Wisconsin Supreme Court is affirmed.

JUSTICE KENNEDY, concurring.

I join the opinion of the Court in all respects. Its sensible recognition that invocation of the Sixth Amendment right to counsel is specific to the offense in question should apply as well to requests for counsel under the Fifth Amendment. *See Roberson*, (KENNEDY, J., dissenting). For those in custody, *Edwards* and its progeny go far to protect an individual who desires the assistance of counsel during interrogation. Limiting the extraordinary protections of *Edwards* to a particular investigation would not increase the risk of confessions induced by official efforts to wear down the will of a suspect. Having adopted an offense-specific rule for invocation of the Sixth Amendment right to counsel, the Court should devote some attention to bringing its Fifth and Sixth Amendment jurisprudence into a logical alignment, and should give uniform, fair, and workable guidelines for the criminal justice system.

Even if petitioner had invoked his Fifth Amendment right with respect to the West Allis armed robbery, I do not believe the authorities should have been prohibited from questioning him in connection with the Caledonia offenses.

---

[3] The dissent predicts that the result in this case will routinely be circumvented when, "[i]n future preliminary hearings, competent counsel . . . make sure that they, or their clients, make a statement on the record" invoking the *Miranda* right to counsel. We have in fact never held that a person can invoke his *Miranda* rights anticipatorily, in a context other than "custodial interrogation" — which a preliminary hearing will not always, or even usually, involve. If the *Miranda* right to counsel can be invoked at a preliminary hearing, it could be argued, there is no logical reason why it could not be invoked by a letter prior to arrest, or indeed even prior to identification as a suspect. Most rights must be asserted when the government seeks to take the action they protect against. The fact that we have allowed the *Miranda* right to counsel, once asserted, to be effective with respect to future custodial interrogation does not necessarily mean that we will allow it to be asserted initially outside the context of custodial interrogation, with similar future effect. Assuming, however, that an assertion at arraignment would be effective, and would be routinely made, the mere fact that adherence to the principle of our decisions will not have substantial consequences is no reason to abandon that principle. It would remain intolerable that a person in custody who had expressed *no* objection to being questioned would be unapproachable.

JUSTICE STEVENS, with whom JUSTICE MARSHALL and JUSTICE BLACKMUN join, dissenting.

The Court's opinion demeans the importance of the right to counsel. As a practical matter, the opinion probably will have only a slight impact on current custodial interrogation procedures. As a theoretical matter, the Court's innovative development of an "offense-specific" limitation on the scope of the attorney-client relationship can only generate confusion in the law and undermine the protections that undergird our adversarial system of justice. As a symbolic matter, today's decision is ominous because it reflects a preference for an inquisitorial system that regards the defense lawyer as an impediment rather than a servant to the cause of justice.

I

The predicate for the Court's entire analysis is the failure of the defendant at the preliminary hearing to make a "statement that can reasonably be construed to be expression of a desire for the assistance of an attorney *in dealing with custodial interrogation by the police.*" If petitioner in this case had made such a statement indicating that he was invoking his Fifth Amendment right to counsel as well as his Sixth Amendment right to counsel, the entire offense-specific house of cards that the Court has erected today would collapse, pursuant to our holding in *Roberson*, that a defendant who invokes the right to counsel for interrogation on one offense may not be reapproached regarding any offense unless counsel is present.

In future preliminary hearings, competent counsel can be expected to make sure that they, or their clients, make a statement on the record that will obviate the consequences of today's holding. That is why I think this decision will have little, if any, practical effect on police practices.

II

The outcome of this case is determined by the Court's parsimonious "offense-specific" description of the right to counsel guaranteed by the Sixth Amendment. The Court's definition is inconsistent with the high value our prior cases have placed on this right, with the ordinary understanding of the scope of the right, and with the accepted practice of the legal profession.

In *Jackson*, we held that the defendant's invocation of his right to the assistance of counsel at arraignment prohibited the police from initiating a postarraignment custodial interrogation without notice to his lawyer. After explaining that our prior cases required us "to give a broad, rather than a narrow, interpretation to a defendant's request for counsel," we squarely rejected "the State's suggestion that respondents' requests for the appointment of counsel should be construed to apply only to representation in formal legal proceedings." Instead, we noted that "it is the State that has the burden of establishing a valid waiver [of the right to counsel]. Doubts must be resolved in favor of protecting the constitutional claim."

Today, however, the Court accepts a narrow, rather than a broad, interpretation of the same right. The Court's holding today moreover rejects the common sense evaluation of the nature of an accused's request for counsel that we expressly endorsed in *Jackson*:

We also agree with the comments of the Michigan Supreme Court about the nature of an accused's request for counsel:

> Although judges and lawyers may understand and appreciate the subtle distinctions between the Fifth and Sixth Amendment rights to counsel, the average person does not. When an accused requests an attorney, either before a police officer or a magistrate, he does not know which constitutional right he is invoking; he therefore should not be expected to articulate exactly why or for what purposes he is seeking counsel. It makes little sense to afford relief from further interrogation to a defendant who asks a police officer for an attorney, but permit further interrogation to a defendant who makes an identical request to a judge. The simple fact that defendant has requested an attorney indicates that he does not believe that he is sufficiently capable of dealing with his adversaries singlehandedly.

III

In the final analysis, the Court's decision is explained by its fear that making counsel available to persons held in custody would "seriously impede effective law enforcement." The magnitude of the Court's alarm is illuminated by its use of italics:

> Thus, if we were to adopt petitioner's rule, most persons in pretrial custody for serious offenses would be *unapproachable* by police officers suspecting them of involvement in other crimes, *even though they have never expressed any unwillingness to be questioned.*

Of course, the Court is quite wrong and its fears are grossly exaggerated. The fears are exaggerated because, as I have explained, today's holding will probably affect very few cases in the future. The fears are misguided because a contrary rule would not make all pretrial detainees "unapproachable"; it would merely serve to ensure that a suspect's statements during custodial interrogation are truly voluntary.

A contrary rule would also comport with respect to tradition. Undergirding our entire line of cases requiring the police to follow fair procedures when they interrogate presumptively innocent citizens suspected of criminal wrongdoing is the longstanding recognition that an adversarial system of justice can function effectively only when the adversaries communicate with one another through counsel and when laypersons are protected from overreaching by more experienced and skilled professionals. Whenever the Court ignores the importance of fair procedure in this context and describes the societal interest in obtaining "uncoerced confessions" from pretrial detainees as an "unmitigated good," the Court is revealing a preference for an inquisitorial system of justice. As I suggested in *Moran v. Burbine, infra*:

> This case turns on a proper appraisal of the role of the lawyer in our society. If a lawyer is seen as a nettlesome obstacle to the pursuit of wrongdoers — as in an inquisitorial society — then the Court's decision

today makes a good deal of sense. If a lawyer is seen as an aid to the understanding and protection of constitutional rights — as in an accusatorial society — then today's decision makes no sense at all.

The Court's refusal to acknowledge any "danger of 'subtle compulsion' " in a case of this kind evidences an inability to recognize the difference between an inquisitorial and an adversarial system of justice. Accordingly, I respectfully dissent.

QUESTIONS AND NOTES

1. How is the *McNeil* issue different from that presented in *Jackson*?

2. Do you agree that an uncoerced confession is an unmitigated good? If so, should we consider revamping all of the jurisprudence emanating from *Massiah*?

3. Assess fn. 3 of the majority opinion. Will lawyers routinely assert *Miranda* rights for their clients as soon as the attorney is appointed? Will (should) such an assertion be effective? Why? Why not?

4. The last paragraph of the Court's *McNeil* opinion looks very much like the nub of Justice Scalia's dissent in *Minnick*. Does he now have the votes to implement that viewpoint, or is *McNeil* just a different case from *Minnick*?

5. If the dissent had prevailed would suspects be essentially unapproachable to be questioned about any crime? Assuming that your answer is "yes," does it follow that the majority correctly decided the case?

6. The concept of separate offense was further explored in *Texas v. Cobb*. As you read *Cobb*, think about which side more accurately portrays the essence of *Jackson* and *McNeil*.

TEXAS v. COBB
532 U.S. 162 (2001)

CHIEF JUSTICE REHNQUIST delivered the opinion of the Court.

The Texas Court of Criminal Appeals held that a criminal defendant's Sixth Amendment right to counsel attaches not only to the offense with which he is charged, but to other offenses "closely related factually" to the charged offense. We hold that our decision in *McNeil* meant what it said, and that the Sixth Amendment right is "offense specific."

In December 1993, Lindsey Owings reported to the Walker County, Texas, Sheriff's Office that the home he shared with his wife, Margaret, and their 16-month-old daughter, Kori Rae, had been burglarized. He also informed police that his wife and daughter were missing. Respondent Raymond Levi Cobb lived across the street from the Owings. Acting on an anonymous tip that respondent was involved in the burglary, Walker County investigators questioned him about the events. He denied involvement. In July 1994, while under arrest for an unrelated offense, respondent was again questioned about the incident. Respondent then gave a written statement confessing to the burglary, but he denied knowledge relating to the disappearances. Respondent was subsequently indicted for the burglary, and Hal Ridley was appointed in August 1994 to represent respondent on that charge.

Shortly after Ridley's appointment, investigators asked and received his permission to question respondent about the disappearances. Respondent continued to deny involvement. Investigators repeated this process in September 1995, again with Ridley's permission and again with the same result.

In November 1995, respondent, free on bond in the burglary case, was living with his father in Odessa, Texas. At that time, respondent's father contacted the Walker County Sheriff's Office to report that respondent had confessed to him that he killed Margaret Owings in the course of the burglary. Walker County investigators directed respondent's father to the Odessa police station, where he gave a statement. Odessa police then faxed the statement to Walker County, where investigators secured a warrant for respondent's arrest and faxed it back to Odessa. Shortly thereafter, Odessa police took respondent into custody and administered warnings pursuant to *Miranda v. Arizona*. Respondent waived these rights.

After a short time, respondent confessed to murdering both Margaret and Kori Rae. Respondent explained that when Margaret confronted him as he was attempting to remove the Owings' stereo, he stabbed her in the stomach with a knife he was carrying. Respondent told police that he dragged her body to a wooded area a few hundred yards from the house. Respondent then stated:

> I went back to her house and I saw the baby laying on its bed. I took the baby out there and it was sleeping the whole time. I laid the baby down on the ground four or five feet away from its mother. I went back to my house and got a flat edge shovel. That's all I could find. Then I went back over to where they were and I started digging a hole between them. After I got the hole dug, the baby was awake. It started going toward its mom and it fell in the hole. I put the lady in the hole and I covered them up. I remember stabbing a different knife I had in the ground where they were. I was crying right then.

Respondent later led police to the location where he had buried the victims' bodies.

Respondent was convicted of capital murder for murdering more than one person in the course of a single criminal transaction. *See* TEXAS PENAL CODE ANN. § 19.03(a)(7)(A) (1994). He was sentenced to death. On appeal to the Court of Criminal Appeals of Texas, respondent argued, *inter alia*, that his confession should have been suppressed because it was obtained in violation of his Sixth Amendment right to counsel. Relying on *Michigan v. Jackson*, respondent contended that his right to counsel had attached when Ridley was appointed in the burglary case and that Odessa police were therefore required to secure Ridley's permission before proceeding with the interrogation.

The Court of Criminal Appeals reversed respondent's conviction by a divided vote and remanded for a new trial. The court held that "once the right to counsel attaches to the offense charged, it also attaches to any other offense that is very closely related factually to the offense charged." Finding the capital murder charge to be "factually interwoven with the burglary," the court concluded that respondent's Sixth Amendment right to counsel had attached on the capital murder charge even though respondent had not yet been charged with that offense. The court further found that respondent had asserted that right by accepting Ridley's appointment in the burglary case. Accordingly, it deemed the confession inadmissible and found that its introduction had not been harmless error. Three justices dissented, finding *Michigan v. Jackson* to be distinguishable and concluding that respondent had made a valid unilateral waiver of his right to counsel before confessing.

The State sought review in this Court, and we granted certiorari to consider first whether the Sixth Amendment right to counsel extends to crimes that are "factually related" to those that have actually been charged, and second whether respondent made a valid unilateral waiver of that right in this case. Because we answer the first question in the negative, we do not reach the second.

The Sixth Amendment provides that "in all criminal prosecutions, the accused shall enjoy the right . . . to have the Assistance of Counsel for his defence." In *McNeil*, we explained when this right arises:

> The Sixth Amendment right [to counsel] . . . is offense specific. It cannot be invoked once for all future prosecutions, for it does not attach until a prosecution is commenced, that is, at or after the initiation of adversary judicial criminal proceedings — whether by way of formal charge, preliminary hearing, indictment, information, or arraignment.

Accordingly, we held that a defendant's statements regarding offenses for which he had not been charged were admissible notwithstanding the attachment of his Sixth Amendment right to counsel on other charged offenses.

Some state courts and Federal Courts of Appeals, however, have read into *McNeil*'s offense-specific definition an exception for crimes that are "factually related" to a charged offense. Several of these courts have interpreted *Brewer v. Williams* and *Maine v. Moulton* — both of which were decided well before *McNeil* — to support this view, which respondent now invites us to approve. We decline to do so.

In *Brewer*, a suspect in the abduction and murder of a 10-year-old girl had fled from the scene of the crime in Des Moines, Iowa, some 160 miles east to Davenport, Iowa, where he surrendered to police. An arrest warrant was issued in Des Moines on a charge of abduction, and the suspect was arraigned on that warrant before a Davenport judge. Des Moines police traveled to Davenport, took the man into custody, and began the drive back to Des Moines. Along the way, one of the officers persuaded the suspect to lead police to the victim's body. The suspect ultimately was convicted of the girl's murder. This Court upheld the federal habeas court's conclusion that police had violated the suspect's Sixth Amendment right to counsel. We held that the officer's comments to the suspect constituted interrogation and that the suspect had not validly waived his right to counsel by responding to the officer.

Respondent suggests that *Brewer* implicitly held that the right to counsel attached to the factually related murder when the suspect was arraigned on the abduction charge. *See* Brief for Respondent 4. The Court's opinion, however, simply did not address the significance of the fact that the suspect had been arraigned only on the abduction charge, nor did the parties in any way argue this question. Constitutional rights are not defined by inferences from opinions which did not address the question at issue.

Moulton is similarly unhelpful to respondent. That case involved two individuals indicted for a series of thefts, one of whom had secretly agreed to cooperate with the police investigation of his codefendant, Moulton. At the suggestion of police, the informant recorded several telephone calls and one face-to-face conversation he had with Moulton during which the two discussed their criminal exploits and possible alibis. In the course of those conversations, Moulton made various incriminating statements regarding both the thefts for which he had been charged and additional crimes. In a superseding indictment, Moulton was charged with the original crimes as well as burglary, arson, and three additional thefts. At trial, the State introduced portions of the recorded face-to-face conversation, and Moulton ultimately was convicted of three of the originally charged thefts plus one count of burglary. Moulton appealed his convictions to the Supreme Judicial Court of Maine, arguing that introduction of the recorded conversation violated his Sixth Amendment right to counsel. That court agreed, holding:

> "Those statements may be admissible in the investigation or prosecution of charges for which, at the time the recordings were made, adversary proceedings had not yet commenced. But as to the charges for which Moulton's right to counsel had already attached, his incriminating statements should have been ruled inadmissible at trial, given the circumstances in which they were acquired."

We affirmed.

Respondent contends that, in affirming reversal of both the theft and burglary charges, the *Moulton* Court must have concluded that Moulton's Sixth Amendment right to counsel attached to the burglary charge. But the *Moulton* Court did not address the question now before us, and to the extent *Moulton* spoke to the matter at all, it expressly referred to the offense-specific nature of the Sixth Amendment right to counsel:

> The police have an interest in the thorough investigation of crimes for which *formal charges* have already been filed. They also have an interest in investigating new or additional crimes. Investigations of either type of crime may require surveillance of individuals already under indictment. Moreover, law enforcement officials investigating an individual suspected of committing one crime and *formally charged* with having committed another crime obviously seek to discover evidence useful at trial of either crime. In seeking evidence pertaining to *pending charges*, however, the Government's investigative powers are limited by the Sixth Amendment rights of the accused . . . . On the other hand, to exclude evidence pertaining to charges as to which the Sixth Amendment right to counsel had not attached at the time the evidence was obtained, simply because other charges were pending at that time, would unnecessarily frustrate the public's interest in the investigation of criminal activities.

("The purpose of their meeting was to discuss the *pending charges*"); ("The police knew . . . that Moulton and [the informant] were meeting for the express purpose of discussing the *pending charges* . . ." (emphasis added)). Thus, respondent's reliance on *Moulton* is misplaced and, in light of the language employed there and subsequently in *McNeil*, puzzling.

Respondent predicts that the offense-specific rule will prove "disastrous" to suspects' constitutional rights and will "permit law enforcement officers almost complete and total license to conduct unwanted and uncounseled interrogations." Besides offering no evidence that such a parade of horribles has occurred in those jurisdictions that have not enlarged upon *McNeil*, he fails to appreciate the significance of two critical considerations. First, there can be no doubt that a suspect must be apprised of his rights against compulsory self-incrimination and to consult with an attorney before authorities may conduct custodial interrogation. *See Miranda; Dickerson v. United States* [Chapter 19, *infra*] (quoting *Miranda*). In the present case, police scrupulously followed *Miranda's* dictates when questioning respondent.[2] Second, it is critical to recognize that the Constitution does not negate society's interest in the ability of police to talk to witnesses and suspects, even those who have been charged with other offenses.

"Since the ready ability to obtain uncoerced confessions is not an evil but an unmitigated good, society would be the loser. Admissions of guilt resulting from valid *Miranda* waivers 'are more than merely "desirable"; they are essential to society's compelling interest in finding, convicting, and punishing those who violate the law.' " *McNeil.*

See also Moulton ("To exclude evidence pertaining to charges as to which the Sixth Amendment right to counsel had not attached at the time the evidence was obtained, simply because other charges were pending at the time, would unnecessarily frustrate the public's interest in the investigation of criminal activities").

Although it is clear that the Sixth Amendment right to counsel attaches only to charged offenses, we have recognized in other contexts that the definition of an "offense" is not necessarily limited to the four corners of a charging instrument. In

---

[2] Curiously, while predicting disastrous consequences for the core values underlying the Sixth Amendment, (opinion of BREYER, J.), the dissenters give short shrift to the Fifth Amendment's role (as expressed in *Miranda* and *Dickerson*) in protecting a defendant's right to consult with counsel before talking to police. Even though the Sixth Amendment right to counsel has not attached to uncharged offenses, defendants retain the ability under *Miranda* to refuse any police questioning, and, indeed, charged defendants presumably have met with counsel and have had the opportunity to discuss whether it is advisable to invoke those Fifth Amendment rights. Thus, in all but the rarest of cases, the Court's decision today will have no impact whatsoever upon a defendant's ability to protect his Sixth Amendment right.

It is also worth noting that, contrary to the dissent's suggestion, there is no "background principle" of our Sixth Amendment jurisprudence establishing that there may be no contact between a defendant and police without counsel present. The dissent would expand the Sixth Amendment right to the assistance of counsel in a criminal prosecution into a rule which " 'exists to prevent lawyers from taking advantage of uncounseled laypersons and to preserve the integrity of the lawyer-client relationship.' " (quoting ABA Ann. Model Rule of Professional Conduct 4.2 (4th ed. 1999)). Every profession is competent to define the standards of conduct for its members, but such standards are obviously not controlling in interpretation of constitutional provisions. The Sixth Amendment right to counsel is personal to the defendant and specific to the offense.

Blockburger v. United States, 284 U.S. 299 (1932), we explained that "where the same act or transaction constitutes a violation of two distinct statutory provisions, the test to be applied to determine whether there are two offenses or only one, is whether each provision requires proof of a fact which the other does not." We have since applied the *Blockburger* test to delineate the scope of the Fifth Amendment's Double Jeopardy Clause, which prevents multiple or successive prosecutions for the "same offence." We see no constitutional difference between the meaning of the term "offense" in the contexts of double jeopardy and of the right to counsel. Accordingly, we hold that when the Sixth Amendment right to counsel attaches, it does encompass offenses that, even if not formally charged, would be considered the same offense under the *Blockburger* test.[3]

While simultaneously conceding that its own test "lacks the precision for which police officers may hope," the dissent suggests that adopting *Blockburger's* definition of "offense" will prove difficult to administer. But it is the dissent's vague iterations of the " 'closely related to' " or " 'inextricably intertwined with' " test that would defy simple application. The dissent seems to presuppose that officers will possess complete knowledge of the circumstances surrounding an incident, such that the officers will be able to tailor their investigation to avoid addressing factually related offenses. Such an assumption, however, ignores the reality that police often are not yet aware of the exact sequence and scope of events they are investigating — indeed, that is why police must investigate in the first place. Deterred by the possibility of violating the Sixth Amendment, police likely would refrain from questioning certain defendants altogether.

It remains only to apply these principles to the facts at hand. At the time he confessed to Odessa police, respondent had been indicted for burglary of the Owings residence, but he had not been charged in the murders of Margaret and Kori Rae. As defined by Texas law, burglary and capital murder are not the same offense under *Blockburger. Compare* TEXAS PENAL CODE ANN. § 30.02(a) (1994) (requiring entry into or continued concealment in a habitation or building) *with* § 19.03(a)(7)(A) (requiring murder of more than one person during a single criminal transaction). Accordingly, the Sixth Amendment right to counsel did not bar police from interrogating respondent regarding the murders, and respondent's confession was therefore admissible.

The judgment of the Court of Criminal Appeals of Texas is reversed.

JUSTICE KENNEDY, with whom JUSTICE SCALIA and JUSTICE THOMAS join, concurring.

The Court's opinion is altogether sufficient to explain why the decision of the Texas Court of Criminal Appeals should be reversed for failure to recognize the offense-specific nature of the Sixth Amendment right to counsel. It seems advisable, however, to observe that the Court has reached its conclusion without the necessity

---

[3] In this sense, we could just as easily describe the Sixth Amendment as "prosecution specific," insofar as it prevents discussion of charged offenses as well as offenses that, under *Blockburger*, could not be the subject of a later prosecution. And, indeed, the text of the Sixth Amendment confines its scope to "all criminal *prosecutions*."

to reaffirm or give approval to the decision in *Michigan v. Jackson*. This course is wise, in my view, for the underlying theory of *Jackson* seems questionable.

As the facts of the instant case well illustrate, it is difficult to understand the utility of a Sixth Amendment rule that operates to invalidate a confession given by the free choice of suspects who have received proper advice of their *Miranda* rights but waived them nonetheless. The *Miranda* rule, and the related preventative rule of *Edwards v. Arizona*, serve to protect a suspect's voluntary choice not to speak outside his lawyer's presence. The parallel rule announced in *Jackson*, however, supersedes the suspect's voluntary choice to speak with investigators. After *Jackson* had been decided, the Court made the following observation with respect to *Edwards*:

> Preserving the integrity of an accused's choice to communicate with police only through counsel is the essence of *Edwards* and its progeny — not barring an accused from making an *initial* election as to whether he will face the State's officers during questioning with the aid of counsel, or go it alone. If an accused "knowingly and intelligently" pursues the latter course, we see no reason why the uncounseled statements he then makes must be excluded at his trial.

Patterson v. Illinois, infra. There is little justification for not applying the same course of reasoning with equal force to the court-made preventative rule announced in *Jackson*; for *Jackson*, after all, was a wholesale importation of the *Edwards* rule into the Sixth Amendment.

In the instant case, Cobb at no time indicated to law enforcement authorities that he elected to remain silent about the double murder. By all indications, he made the voluntary choice to give his own account. Indeed, even now Cobb does not assert that he had no wish to speak at the time he confessed. While the *Edwards* rule operates to preserve the free choice of a suspect to remain silent, if *Jackson* were to apply it would override that choice.

There is further reason to doubt the wisdom of the *Jackson* holding. Neither *Miranda* nor *Edwards* enforces the Fifth Amendment right unless the suspect makes a clear and unambiguous assertion of the right to the presence of counsel during custodial interrogation. *Davis v. United States*. Where a required *Miranda* warning has been given, a suspect's later confession, made outside counsel's presence, is suppressed to protect the Fifth Amendment right of silence only if a reasonable officer should have been certain that the suspect expressed the unequivocal election of the right.

The Sixth Amendment right to counsel attaches quite without reference to the suspect's choice to speak with investigators after a *Miranda* warning. It is the commencement of a formal prosecution, indicated by the initiation of adversary judicial proceedings, that marks the beginning of the Sixth Amendment right. These events may be quite independent of the suspect's election to remain silent, the interest which the *Edwards* rule serves to protect with respect to *Miranda* and the Fifth Amendment, and it thus makes little sense for a protective rule to attach absent such an election by the suspect. We ought to question the wisdom of a judge-made preventative rule to protect a suspect's desire not to speak when it cannot be shown that he had that intent.

Even if *Jackson* is to remain good law, its protections should apply only where a suspect has made a clear and unambiguous assertion of the right not to speak outside the presence of counsel, the same clear election required under *Edwards*. Cobb made no such assertion here, yet Justice BREYER's dissent rests upon the assumption that the *Jackson* rule should operate to exclude the confession no matter. There would be little justification for this extension of a rule that, even in a more limited application, rests on a doubtful rationale.

Justice BREYER defends *Jackson* by arguing that, once a suspect has accepted counsel at the commencement of adversarial proceedings, he should not be forced to confront the police during interrogation without the assistance of counsel. But the acceptance of counsel at an arraignment or similar proceeding only begs the question: acceptance of counsel for what? It is quite unremarkable that a suspect might want the assistance of an expert in the law to guide him through hearings and trial, and the attendant complex legal matters that might arise, but nonetheless might choose to give on his own a forthright account of the events that occurred. A court-made rule that prevents a suspect from even making this choice serves little purpose, especially given the regime of *Miranda* and *Edwards*.

With these further remarks, I join in full the opinion of the Court.

JUSTICE BREYER, with whom JUSTICE STEVENS, JUSTICE SOUTER, and JUSTICE GINSBURG join, dissenting.

This case focuses upon the meaning of a single word, "offense," when it arises in the context of the Sixth Amendment. Several basic background principles define that context.

First, the Sixth Amendment right to counsel plays a central role in ensuring the fairness of criminal proceedings in our system of justice. *See Gideon v. Wainwright*, 372 U.S. 335 (1963); *Powell v. Alabama*, 287 U.S. 45 (1932).

Second, the right attaches when adversary proceedings, triggered by the government's formal accusation of a crime, begin. *See Brewer v. Williams; Kirby v. Illinois*, 406 U.S. 682 (1972); *Massiah v. United States*.

Third, once this right attaches, law enforcement officials are required, in most circumstances, to deal with the defendant through counsel rather than directly, even if the defendant has waived his Fifth Amendment rights. *See Michigan v. Jackson* (waiver of right to presence of counsel is assumed invalid unless accused initiates communication); *Maine v. Moulton* (Sixth Amendment gives defendant right "to rely on counsel as a 'medium' between him and the State"). *Cf.* ABA Model Rule of Professional Conduct 4.2 (2001) (lawyer is generally prohibited from communicating with a person known to be represented by counsel "about the subject of the representation" without counsel's "consent"); Green, *A Prosecutor's Communications with Defendants: What Are the Limits?*, 24 CRIM. L. BULL. 283, 284, and n. 5 (1988) (version of Model Rule 4.2 or its predecessor has been adopted by all 50 States).

Fourth, the particular aspect of the right here at issue — the rule that the police ordinarily must communicate with the defendant through counsel — has important limits. In particular, recognizing the need for law enforcement officials to investigate "new or additional crimes" not the subject of current proceedings, *Maine v. Moulton*, this Court has made clear that the right to counsel does not attach to any and every crime that an accused may commit or have committed, *see McNeil v. Wisconsin*. The right "cannot be invoked once for all future prosecutions," and it does not forbid "interrogation unrelated to the charge." In a word, as this Court previously noted, the right is "offense specific."

This case focuses upon the last-mentioned principle, in particular upon the meaning of the words "offense specific." These words appear in this Court's Sixth Amendment case law, not in the Sixth Amendment's text. *See* U.S. CONST., Amdt. 6 (guaranteeing right to counsel "in all criminal prosecutions"). The definition of these words is not self-evident. Sometimes the term "offense" may refer to words that are written in a criminal statute; sometimes it may refer generally to a course of conduct in the world, aspects of which constitute the elements of one or more crimes; and sometimes it may refer, narrowly and technically, just to the conceptually severable aspects of the latter. This case requires us to determine whether an "offense" — for Sixth Amendment purposes — includes factually related aspects of a single course of conduct other than those few acts that make up the essential elements of the crime charged.

We should answer this question in light of the Sixth Amendment's basic objectives as set forth in this Court's case law. At the very least, we should answer it in a way that does not undermine those objectives. But the Court today decides that "offense" means the crime set forth within "the four corners of a charging instrument," along with other crimes that "would be considered the same offense" under the test established by *Blockburger v. United States*, 284 U.S. 299 (1932). In my view, this unnecessarily technical definition undermines Sixth Amendment protections while doing nothing to further effective law enforcement.

For one thing, the majority's rule, while leaving the Fifth Amendment's protections in place, threatens to diminish severely the additional protection that, under this Court's rulings, the Sixth Amendment provides when it grants the right to counsel to defendants who have been charged with a crime and insists that law enforcement officers thereafter communicate with them through that counsel. *See, e.g., Michigan v. Jackson* (Sixth Amendment prevents police from questioning represented defendant through informants even when Fifth Amendment would not); *Rhode Island v. Innis* (Fifth Amendment right, unlike Sixth, applies only in custodial interrogation).

Justice KENNEDY, Justice SCALIA, and Justice THOMAS, if not the majority, apparently believe these protections constitutionally unimportant, for, in their view, "the underlying theory of *Jackson* seems questionable." Both the majority and concurring opinions suggest that a suspect's ability to invoke his Fifth Amendment right and "refuse any police questioning" offers that suspect adequate constitutional protection.

Jackson focuses upon a suspect — perhaps a frightened or uneducated suspect — who, hesitant to rely upon his own unaided judgment in his dealings with the police, has invoked his constitutional right to legal assistance in such matters. *See Michigan v. Jackson* n. 7 (" 'The simple fact that [a] defendant has requested an attorney indicates that he does not believe that he is sufficiently capable of dealing with his adversaries singlehandedly' "). *Jackson* says that, once such a request has been made, the police may not simply throw that suspect — who does not trust his own unaided judgment — back upon his own devices by requiring him to rely for protection upon that same unaided judgment that he previously rejected as inadequate. In a word, the police may not force a suspect who has asked for legal counsel to make a critical legal choice without the legal assistance that he has requested and that the Constitution guarantees. *See McNeil v. Wisconsin, supra,* at 177 ("The purpose of the Sixth Amendment counsel guarantee . . . is to 'protect the unaided layman at critical confrontations' with his 'expert adversary' ")); ABA Ann. Model Rule of Professional Conduct 4.2, p. 398, comment. (4th ed. 1999) ("Rule 4.2 . . . exists to prevent lawyers from taking advantage of uncounseled laypersons and to preserve the integrity of the lawyer-client relationship").

For these reasons, the Sixth Amendment right at issue is independent of the Fifth Amendment's protections; and the importance of this Sixth Amendment right has been repeatedly recognized in our cases. *See, e.g., Michigan v. Jackson* ("We conclude that the assertion [of the right to counsel] is no less significant, and the need for additional safeguards no less clear, when the request for counsel is made at an arraignment and when the basis for the claim is the Sixth Amendment").

Justice KENNEDY primarily relies upon *Patterson v. Illinois, infra,* in support of his conclusion that *Jackson* is not good law. He quotes *Patterson's* statement that the Constitution does " 'not bar an accused from making an *initial* election as to whether' " to speak with the police without counsel's assistance.

This statement, however, cannot justify the overruling of *Jackson*. That is because, in *Patterson* itself, this Court noted, "as a matter of some significance," that, at the time he was interrogated, *the defendant had neither retained nor accepted the appointment of counsel.* We characterized our holding in *Jackson* as having depended upon "the fact that the accused 'had asked for the help of a lawyer' in dealing with the police," and explained that, "once an accused has a lawyer, a distinct set of constitutional safeguards aimed at preserving the sanctity of the attorney-client relationship takes effect."

Justice KENNEDY also criticizes *Jackson* on the ground that it prevents a suspect "from . . . making the choice" to "give . . . a forthright account of the events that occurred." But that is not so. A suspect may initiate communication with the police, thereby avoiding the risk that the police induced him to make, unaided, the kind of critical legal decision best made with the help of counsel, whom he has requested.

Unlike Justice KENNEDY, the majority does not call *Jackson* itself into question. But the majority would undermine that case by significantly diminishing the Sixth Amendment protections that the case provides. That is because criminal codes are lengthy and highly detailed, often proliferating "overlapping and related statutory offenses" to the point where prosecutors can easily "spin out a startlingly numerous series of offenses from a single . . . criminal transaction." Thus, an armed robber who reaches across a store counter, grabs the cashier, and demands "your money or your life," may through that single instance of conduct have committed several "offenses," in the majority's sense of the term, including armed robbery, assault, battery, trespass, use of a firearm to commit a felony, and perhaps possession of a firearm by a felon, as well. A person who is using and selling drugs on a single occasion might be guilty of possessing various drugs, conspiring to sell drugs, being under the influence of illegal drugs, possessing drug paraphernalia, possessing a gun in relation to the drug sale, and, depending upon circumstances, violating various gun laws as well. A protester blocking an entrance to a federal building might also be trespassing, failing to disperse, unlawfully assembling, and obstructing Government administration all at one and the same time.

The majority's rule permits law enforcement officials to question those charged with a crime without first approaching counsel, through the simple device of asking questions about any other related crime not actually charged in the indictment. Thus, the police could ask the individual charged with robbery about, say, the assault of the cashier not yet charged, or about any other uncharged offense (unless under *Blockburger's* definition it counts as the "same crime"), all *without notifying counsel*. Indeed, the majority's rule would permit law enforcement officials to question anyone charged with any crime in any one of the examples just given about his or her conduct on the single relevant occasion without notifying counsel unless the prosecutor has charged every possible crime arising out of that same brief course of conduct. What Sixth Amendment sense — what common sense — does such a rule make? What is left of the "communicate through counsel" rule? The majority's approach is inconsistent with any common understanding of the scope of counsel's representation. It will undermine the lawyer's role as " 'medium' " between the defendant and the government. And it will, on a random basis, remove a significant portion of the protection that this Court has found inherent in the Sixth Amendment.

In fact, under the rule today announced by the majority, two of the seminal cases in our Sixth Amendment jurisprudence would have come out differently. In *Maine* v. *Moulton*, which the majority points out "expressly referred to the offense-specific nature of the Sixth Amendment right to counsel," we treated burglary and theft as the same offense for Sixth Amendment purposes. Despite the opinion's clear statement that "incriminating statements pertaining to other crimes, as to which the Sixth Amendment right has not yet attached, are, of course, admissible at a trial of those offenses," the Court affirmed the lower court's reversal of both burglary and theft charges even though, at the time that the incriminating statements at issue were made, Moulton had been charged only with theft by receiving. Under the majority's rule, in contrast, because theft by receiving and burglary each required proof of a fact that the other did not, only Moulton's theft convictions should have been overturned.

In *Brewer* v. *Williams*, the effect of the majority's rule would have been even more dramatic. Because first-degree murder and child abduction each required proof of a fact not required by the other, and because at the time of the impermissible interrogation Williams had been charged only with abduction of a child, Williams' murder conviction should have remained undisturbed. This is not to suggest that this Court has previously addressed and decided the question presented by this case. Rather, it is to point out that the Court's conception of the Sixth Amendment right at the time that *Moulton* and *Brewer* were decided naturally presumed that it extended to factually related but uncharged offenses.

At the same time, the majority's rule threatens the legal clarity necessary for effective law enforcement. That is because the majority, aware that the word "offense" ought to encompass something beyond "the four corners of the charging instrument," imports into Sixth Amendment law the definition of "offense" set forth in *Blockburger*, a case interpreting the Double Jeopardy Clause of the Fifth Amendment, which Clause uses the word "offence" but otherwise has no relevance here. Whatever Fifth Amendment virtues *Blockburger* may have, to import it into this Sixth Amendment context will work havoc.

In theory, the test says that two offenses are the "same offense" unless each requires proof of a fact that the other does not. That means that most of the different crimes mentioned above are not the "same offense." Under many States' laws, for example, the statute defining assault and the statute defining robbery each requires proof of a fact that the other does not. *Compare, e.g.*, CAL. PENAL CODE ANN. § 211 (West 1999) (robbery) (requiring taking of personal property of another) *with* § 240 (assault) (requiring attempt to commit violent injury). Hence the extension of the definition of "offense" that is accomplished by the use of the *Blockburger* test does nothing to address the substantial concerns about the circumvention of the Sixth Amendment right that are raised by the majority's rule.

But, more to the point, the simple-sounding *Blockburger* test has proved extraordinarily difficult to administer in practice. Judges, lawyers, and law professors often disagree about how to apply it. The test has emerged as a tool in an area of our jurisprudence that THE CHIEF JUSTICE has described as "a veritable Sargasso Sea which could not fail to challenge the most intrepid judicial navigator." *Albernaz v. United States*, 450 U.S. 333 (1981). Yet the Court now asks, not the lawyers and judges who ordinarily work with double jeopardy law, but police officers in the field, to navigate *Blockburger* when they question suspects. *Cf. New York v. Belton* (noting importance of clear rules to guide police behavior). Some will apply the test successfully; some will not. Legal challenges are inevitable. The result, I believe, will resemble not so much the Sargasso Sea as the criminal law equivalent of Milton's "Serbonian Bog . . . Where Armies whole have sunk."

There is, of course, an alternative. We can, and should, define "offense" in terms of the conduct that constitutes the crime that the offender committed on a particular occasion, including criminal acts that are "closely related to" or "inextricably intertwined with" the particular crime set forth in the charging instrument. This alternative is not perfect. The language used lacks the precision for which police officers may hope; and it requires lower courts to specify its meaning further as they apply it in individual cases. Yet virtually every lower court in the United States to consider the issue has defined "offense" in the Sixth Amendment context to encompass such closely related acts. These courts have found offenses "closely related" where they involved the same victim, set of acts, evidence, or motivation. They have found offenses unrelated where time, location, or factual circumstances significantly separated the one from the other.

One cannot say in favor of this commonly followed approach that it is perfectly clear — only that, because it comports with common sense, it is far easier to apply than that of the majority. One might add that, unlike the majority's test, it is consistent with this Court's assumptions in previous cases. *See Maine v. Moulton* (affirming reversal of both burglary and theft convictions); *Brewer v. Williams* (affirming grant of habeas which vacated murder conviction). And, most importantly, the "closely related" test furthers, rather than undermines, the Sixth Amendment's "right to counsel," a right so necessary to the realization in practice of that most "noble ideal," a fair trial. *Gideon v. Wainwright*, 372 U.S. at 344.

The Texas Court of Criminal Appeals, following this commonly accepted approach, found that the charged burglary and the uncharged murders were "closely related." All occurred during a short period of time on the same day in the same basic location. The victims of the murders were also victims of the burglary. Cobb committed one of the murders in furtherance of the robbery, the other to cover up the crimes. The police, when questioning Cobb, knew that he already had a lawyer representing him on the burglary charges and had demonstrated their belief that this lawyer also represented Cobb in respect to the murders by asking his permission to question Cobb about the murders on previous occasions. The relatedness of the crimes is well illustrated by the impossibility of questioning Cobb about the murders without eliciting admissions about the burglary. *See, e.g.*, Tr. 157 (Feb. 19, 1997) (testimony by police officer who obtained murder confession) ("Basically what he told us is he had gone over to the house to burglarize it and nobody was home"); (typed statement by Cobb) (admitting that he committed the murders after entering the house and stealing stereo parts). Nor, in my view, did Cobb waive his right to counsel. These considerations are sufficient. The police officers ought to have spoken to Cobb's counsel before questioning Cobb. I would affirm the decision of the Texas court.

Consequently, I dissent.

QUESTIONS AND NOTES

1.   What test does the Court adopt for "same offense"? How would it be applied?

2.   Which opinion does the best job of following precedent? Explain.

3.   Is *Michigan v. Jackson* on secure ground, or is it in serious danger of being overruled at the next appropriate opportunity? *See Montejo v. Louisiana, infra.*

4.   How would *Brewer v. Williams* be decided after *Cobb*? Why?

5.   Assuming that for Question 3, you answered: "Conviction affirmed," does it necessarily follow that *Cobb* was wrongly decided?

6.   We now turn to *Patterson v. Illinois*, referred to in *Cobb*, where a bare majority of the Court, to the benefit of the state, concluded that *Miranda* warnings were enough to protect a defendant's Sixth, as well as Fifth, Amendment interest in freedom from custodial interrogation.

PATTERSON v. ILLINOIS
487 U.S. 285 (1988)

JUSTICE WHITE delivered the opinion of the Court.

In this case, we are called on to determine whether the interrogation of petitioner after his indictment violated his Sixth Amendment right to counsel.

I

Before dawn on August 21, 1983, petitioner and other members of the "Vice Lords" street gang became involved in a fight with members of a rival gang, the "Black Mobsters." Sometime after the fight, a former member of the Black Mobsters, James Jackson, went to the home where the Vice Lords had fled. A second fight broke out there, with petitioner and three other Vice Lords beating Jackson severely. The Vice Lords then put Jackson into a car, drove to the end of a nearby street, and left him face down in a puddle of water. Later that morning, police discovered Jackson, dead, where he had been left.

That afternoon, local police officers obtained warrants for the arrest of the Vice Lords, on charges of battery and mob action, in connection with the first fight. One of the gang members who was arrested gave the police a statement concerning the first fight; the statement also implicated several of the Vice Lords (including petitioner) in Jackson's murder. A few hours later, petitioner was apprehended. Petitioner was informed of his rights under *Miranda* and volunteered to answer questions put to him by the police. Petitioner gave a statement concerning the initial fight between the rival gangs, but denied knowing anything about Jackson's death. Petitioner was held in custody the following day, August 22, as law enforcement authorities completed their investigation of the Jackson murder.

On August 23, a Cook County grand jury indicted petitioner and two other gang members for the murder of James Jackson. Police Officer Michael Gresham, who had questioned petitioner earlier, removed him from the lockup where he was being held, and told petitioner that because he had been indicted he was being transferred to the Cook County jail. Petitioner asked Gresham which of the gang members had been charged with Jackson's murder, and upon learning that one particular Vice Lord had been omitted from the indictments, asked: "[W]hy wasn't he indicted, he did everything." Petitioner also began to explain that there was a witness who would support his account of the crime.

At this point, Gresham interrupted petitioner, and handed him a *Miranda* waiver form. The form contained five specific warnings, as suggested by this Court's *Miranda* decision, to make petitioner aware of his right to counsel and of the consequences of any statement he might make to police. Gresham read the warnings aloud, as petitioner read along with him. Petitioner initialed each of the five warnings, and signed the waiver form. Petitioner then gave a lengthy statement to police officers concerning the Jackson murder; petitioner's statement described in detail the role of each of the Vice Lords — including himself — in the murder of James Jackson.

Later that day, petitioner confessed involvement in the murder for a second time. This confession came in an interview with Assistant State's Attorney (ASA) George Smith. At the outset of the interview, Smith reviewed with petitioner the *Miranda* waiver he had previously signed, and petitioner confirmed that he had signed the waiver and understood his rights. Smith went through the waiver procedure once again: reading petitioner his rights, having petitioner initial each one, and sign a waiver form. In addition, Smith informed petitioner that he was a lawyer working with the police investigating the Jackson case. Petitioner then gave another inculpatory statement concerning the crime.

Before trial, petitioner moved to suppress his statements, arguing that they were obtained in a manner at odds with various constitutional guarantees. The trial court denied these motions, and the statements were used against petitioner at his trial. The jury found petitioner guilty of murder, and petitioner was sentenced to a 24-year prison term.

On appeal, petitioner argued that he had not "knowingly and intelligently" waived his Sixth Amendment right to counsel before he gave his uncounseled postindictment confessions. Petitioner contended that the warnings he received, while adequate for the purposes of protecting his *Fifth* Amendment rights as guaranteed by *Miranda*, did not adequately inform him of his *Sixth* Amendment right to counsel. The Illinois Supreme Court, however, rejected this theory, [holding] that *Miranda* warnings were sufficient to make a defendant aware of his Sixth Amendment right to counsel during postindictment questioning.

In reaching this conclusion, the Illinois Supreme Court noted that this Court had reserved decision on this question on several previous occasions[2] and that the lower courts are divided on the issue. We granted this petition for certiorari to resolve this split of authority and to address the issues we had previously left open.

II

There can be no doubt that petitioner had the right to have the assistance of counsel at his postindictment interviews with law enforcement authorities. Our cases make it plain that the Sixth Amendment guarantees this right to criminal defendants. *Jackson; Brewer; Massiah*.[3] Petitioner asserts that the questioning that produced his incriminating statements violated his Sixth Amendment right to counsel in two ways.

---

[2] *See, e.g., Jackson; Burbine; Brewer.*

[3] We note as a matter of some significance that petitioner had not retained, or accepted by appointment, a lawyer to represent him at the time he was questioned by authorities. Once an accused has a lawyer, a distinct set of constitutional safeguards aimed at preserving the sanctity of the attorney-client relationship takes effect. *See Moulton.* The State conceded as much at argument.

Indeed, the analysis changes markedly once an accused even *requests* the assistance of counsel. *See Jackson.*

A

Petitioner's first claim is that because his Sixth Amendment right to counsel arose with his indictment, the police were thereafter barred from initiating a meeting with him. He equates himself with a preindictment suspect who, while being interrogated, asserts his Fifth Amendment right to counsel; under *Edwards*, such a suspect may not be questioned again unless he initiates the meeting.

Petitioner, however, at no time sought to exercise his right to have counsel present. The fact that petitioner's Sixth Amendment right came into existence with his indictment, *i.e.*, that he had such a right at the time of his questioning, does not distinguish him from the preindictment interrogatee whose right to counsel is in existence and available for his exercise while he is questioned. Had petitioner indicated he wanted the assistance of counsel, the authorities' interview with him would have stopped, and further questioning would have been forbidden (unless petitioner called for such a meeting). This was our holding in *Jackson*, which applied *Edwards* to the Sixth Amendment context. We observe that the analysis in *Jackson* is rendered wholly unnecessary if petitioner's position is correct: under petitioner's theory, the officers in *Jackson* would have been completely barred from approaching the accused in that case unless he called for them. Our decision in *Jackson*, however, turned on the fact that the accused "ha[d] asked for the help of a lawyer" in dealing with the police.

At bottom, petitioner's theory cannot be squared with our rationale in *Edwards*, the case he relies on for support. *Edwards* rested on the view that once "an accused . . . ha[s] expressed his desire to deal with the police only through counsel" he should "not [be] subject to further interrogation by the authorities until counsel has been made available to him, unless the accused himself initiates further communication." Preserving the integrity of an accused's choice to communicate with police only through counsel is the essence of *Edwards* and its progeny — not barring an accused from making an *initial* election as to whether he will face the State's officers during questioning with the aid of counsel, or go it alone. If an accused "knowingly and intelligently" pursues the latter course, we see no reason why the uncounseled statements he then makes must be excluded at his trial.

B

Petitioner's principal and more substantial claim is that questioning him without counsel present violated the Sixth Amendment because he did not validly waive his right to have counsel present during the interviews. Since it is clear that after the *Miranda* warnings were given to petitioner, he not only voluntarily answered questions without claiming his right to silence or his right to have a lawyer present to advise him but also executed a written waiver of his right to counsel during questioning, the specific issue posed here is whether this waiver was a "knowing and intelligent" waiver of his Sixth Amendment right.

In the past, this Court has held that a waiver of the Sixth Amendment right to counsel is valid only when it reflects "an intentional relinquishment or abandonment of a known right or privilege." In a case arising under the Fifth Amendment, we described this requirement as "a full awareness of both the nature of the right being abandoned and the consequences of the decision to abandon it." *Burbine*. Whichever of these formulations is used, the key inquiry in a case such as this one must be: Was the accused, who waived his Sixth Amendment rights during postindictment questioning, made sufficiently aware of his right to have counsel present during the questioning, and of the possible consequences of a decision to forgo the aid of counsel? In this case, we are convinced that by admonishing petitioner with the *Miranda* warnings, respondent has met this burden and that petitioner's waiver of his right to counsel at the questioning was valid.[5]

First, the *Miranda* warnings given petitioner made him aware of his right to have counsel present during the questioning. By telling petitioner that he had a right to consult with an attorney, to have a lawyer present while he was questioned, and even to have a lawyer appointed for him if he could not afford to retain one on his own, Officer Gresham and ASA Smith conveyed to petitioner the sum and substance of the rights that the Sixth Amendment provided him. "Indeed, it seems self-evident that one who is told he" has such rights to counsel "is in a curious posture to later complain" that his waiver of these rights was unknowing. There is little more petitioner could have possibly been told in an effort to satisfy this portion of the waiver inquiry.

Second, the *Miranda* warnings also served to make petitioner aware of the consequences of a decision by him to waive his Sixth Amendment rights during postindictment questioning. Petitioner knew that any statement that he made could be used against him in subsequent criminal proceedings. This is the ultimate adverse consequence petitioner could have suffered by virtue of his choice to make uncounseled admissions to the authorities. This warning also sufficed — contrary to petitioner's claim here — to let petitioner know what a lawyer could "do for him" during the postindictment questioning: namely, advise petitioner to refrain from making any such statements.[6] By knowing what could be done with any statements he might make, and therefore, what benefit could be obtained by having the aid of counsel while making such statements, petitioner was essentially informed of the possible consequences of going without counsel during questioning. If petitioner nonetheless lacked "a full and complete appreciation of all of the consequences flowing" from his waiver, it does not defeat the State's showing that the information it provided to him satisfied the constitutional minimum.

---

[5] We emphasize the significance of the fact that petitioner's waiver of counsel was only for this limited aspect of the criminal proceedings against him — only for postindictment questioning. Our decision on the validity of petitioner's waiver extends only so far.

Moreover, even within this limited context, we note that petitioner's waiver was binding on him *only* so long as he wished it to be. Under this Court's precedents, at any time during the questioning petitioner could have changed his mind, elected to have the assistance of counsel, and immediately dissolve the effectiveness of his waiver with respect to any subsequent statements. Our decision today does nothing to change this rule.

[6] An important basis for our analysis is our understanding that an attorney's role at postindictment questioning is rather limited, and substantially different from the attorney's role in later phases of criminal proceedings. At trial, an accused needs an attorney to perform several varied functions — some of which are entirely beyond even the most intelligent layman. Yet during postindictment questioning, a lawyer's role is rather unidimensional: largely limited to advising his client as to what questions to answer and which ones to decline to answer.

Our conclusion is supported by petitioner's inability, in the proceedings before this Court, to articulate with precision what additional information should have been provided to him before he would have been competent to waive his right to counsel. All that petitioner's brief and reply brief suggest is petitioner should have been made aware of his "right under the Sixth Amendment to the broad protection of counsel" — a rather nebulous suggestion — and the "gravity of [his] situation." But surely this latter "requirement" (if it is one) was met when Officer Gresham informed petitioner that he had been formally charged with the murder of James Jackson. Under close questioning on this same point at argument, petitioner likewise failed to suggest any meaningful additional information that he should have been, but was not, provided in advance of his decision to waive his right to counsel.[7]

The discussions found in favorable court decisions, on which petitioner relies, are similarly lacking.

As a general matter, then, an accused who is admonished with the warnings prescribed by this Court in *Miranda*, has been sufficiently apprised of the nature of his Sixth Amendment rights, and of the consequences of abandoning those rights, so that his waiver on this basis will be considered a knowing and intelligent one.[9] We

---

[7] Representative excerpts from the relevant portions of argument include the following:

QUESTION: [Petitioner] . . . was told that he had a right to counsel.

MR. HONCHELL [petitioner's counsel]: He was told — the word "counsel" was used. He was told he had a right to counsel. But not through information by which it would become meaningful to him, because the method that was used was not designed to alert the accused to the Sixth Amendment rights to counsel . . . .

QUESTION: . . . You mean they should have said you have a Sixth Amendment right to counsel instead of just, you have a right to counsel?
He knew he had a right to have counsel present before [he] made the confession. Now, what in addition did he have to know to make the waiver an intelligent one?

MR. HONCHELL: He had to meaningfully know he had a Sixth Amendment right to counsel present because —

QUESTION: What is the difference between meaningfully knowing and knowing?

MR. HONCHELL: Because the warning here used did not convey or express what counsel was intended to do for him after indictment.

QUESTION: So then you say . . . [that] he would have had to be told more about what counsel would do for him after indictment before he could intelligently waive?

MR. HONCHELL: That there is a right to counsel who would act on his behalf and represent him.

QUESTION: Well, okay. So it should have said, in addition to saying counsel, counsel who would act on your behalf and represent you? That would have been the magic solution?

MR. HONCHELL: That is a possible method, yes.

Tr. of Oral Arg. 7–8.

We do not believe that adding the words "who would act on your behalf and represent you" in Sixth Amendment cases would provide any meaningful improvement in the *Miranda* warnings.

[9] This does not mean, of course, that all Sixth Amendment challenges to the conduct of postindictment questioning will fail whenever the challenged practice would pass constitutional muster under *Miranda*. For example, we have permitted a *Miranda* waiver to stand where a suspect was not told that his lawyer was trying to reach him during questioning; in the Sixth Amendment context, this waiver would not be valid. *Burbine*. Likewise a surreptitious conversation between an undercover police officer and an unindicted suspect would not give rise to any *Miranda* violation as long as the "interrogation" was not

feel that our conclusion in a recent Fifth Amendment case is equally apposite here: "Once it is determined that a suspect's decision not to rely on his rights was uncoerced, that he at all times knew he could stand mute and request a lawyer, and that he was aware of the State's intention to use his statements to secure a conviction, the analysis is complete and the waiver is valid as a matter of law." *See Burbine.*

C

We consequently reject petitioner's argument, which has some acceptance from courts and commentators, that since "the sixth amendment right [to counsel] is far superior to that of the fifth amendment right" and since "[t]he greater the right the greater the loss from a waiver of that right," waiver of an accused's Sixth Amendment right to counsel should be "more difficult" to effectuate than waiver of a suspect's Fifth Amendment rights. While our cases have recognized a "difference" between the Fifth Amendment and Sixth Amendment rights to counsel, and the "policies" behind these constitutional guarantees, we have never suggested that one right is "superior" or "greater" than the other, nor is there any support in our cases for the notion that because a Sixth Amendment right may be involved, it is more difficult to waive than the Fifth Amendment counterpart.

Instead, we have taken a more pragmatic approach to the waiver question — asking what purposes a lawyer can serve at the particular stage of the proceedings in question, and what assistance he could provide to an accused at that stage — to determine the scope of the Sixth Amendment right to counsel, and the type of warnings and procedures that should be required before a waiver of that right will be recognized.

Applying this approach, it is our view that whatever warnings suffice for *Miranda's* purposes will also be sufficient in the context of postindictment questioning. The State's decision to take an additional step and commence formal adversarial proceedings against the accused does not substantially increase the value of counsel to the accused at questioning, or expand the limited purpose that an attorney serves when the accused is questioned by authorities. With respect to this inquiry, we do not discern a substantial difference between the usefulness of a lawyer to a suspect during custodial interrogation, and his value to an accused at postindictment questioning.

Thus, we require a more searching or formal inquiry before permitting an accused to waive his right to counsel at trial than we require for a Sixth Amendment waiver during postindictment questioning — *not* because postindictment questioning is "less important" than a trial (the analysis that petitioner's "hierarchical" approach would suggest) — but because the full "dangers and disadvantages of

---

in a custodial setting; however, once the accused is indicted, such questioning would be prohibited. *See Henry.*

Thus, because the Sixth Amendment's protection of the attorney-client relationship — "the right to rely on counsel as a 'medium' between [the accused] and the State" — extends beyond *Miranda's* protection of the Fifth Amendment right to counsel, see *Moulton,* there will be cases where a waiver which would be valid under *Miranda* will not suffice for Sixth Amendment purposes. *See also Jackson.*

self-representation," during questioning are less substantial and more obvious to an accused than they are at trial.[13] Because the role of counsel at questioning is relatively simple and limited, we see no problem in having a waiver procedure at that stage which is likewise simple and limited. So long as the accused is made aware of the "dangers and disadvantages of self-representation" during postindictment questioning, by use of the *Miranda* warnings, his waiver of his Sixth Amendment right to counsel at such questioning is "knowing and intelligent."

III

Before confessing to the murder of James Jackson, petitioner was meticulously informed by authorities of his right to counsel, and of the consequences of any choice not to exercise that right. On two separate occasions, petitioner elected to forgo the assistance of counsel, and speak directly to officials concerning his role in the murder. Because we believe that petitioner's waiver of his Sixth Amendment rights was "knowing and intelligent," we find no error in the decision of the trial court to permit petitioner's confessions to be used against him. Consequently, the judgment of the Illinois Supreme Court is affirmed.

JUSTICE BLACKMUN, dissenting.

I agree with most of what Justice STEVENS says in his dissenting opinion. I, however, merely would hold that after formal adversary proceedings against a defendant have been commenced, the Sixth Amendment mandates that the defendant not be " 'subject to further interrogation by the authorities until counsel has been made available to him, unless the accused himself initiates further communication, exchanges, or conversations with the police.' " *Jackson*, quoting *Edwards*.

The Court's majority concludes: "The fact that petitioner's Sixth Amendment right came into existence with his indictment . . . does not distinguish him from the preindictment interrogatee whose right to counsel is in existence and available for his exercise while he is questioned." I must disagree. "[W]hen the Constitution grants protection against criminal proceedings without the assistance of counsel, counsel must be furnished whether or not the accused requested the appointment of counsel." In my view, the Sixth Amendment does not allow the prosecution to take undue advantage of any gap between the commencement of the adversary process and the time at which counsel is appointed for a defendant.

JUSTICE STEVENS, with whom JUSTICE BRENNAN and JUSTICE MARSHALL join, dissenting.

The Court should not condone unethical forms of trial preparation by prosecutors or their investigators. In civil litigation it is improper for a lawyer to

---

[13] [A]n attorney's role at questioning is relatively limited. But at trial, counsel is required to help even the most gifted layman adhere to the rules of procedure and evidence, comprehend the subtleties of *voir dire*, examine and cross-examine witnesses effectively (including the accused), object to improper prosecution questions, and much more.

communicate with his or her adversary's client without either notice to opposing counsel or the permission of the court. An attempt to obtain evidence for use at trial by going behind the back of one's adversary would be not only a serious breach of professional ethics but also a manifestly unfair form of trial practice. In the criminal context, the same ethical rules apply and, in my opinion, notions of fairness that are at least as demanding should also be enforced.

The question that this case raises is at what point in the adversary process does it become impermissible for the prosecutor, or his or her agents, to conduct such private interviews with the opposing party? Several alternatives are conceivable: when the trial commences, when the defendant has actually met and accepted representation by his or her appointed counsel, when counsel is appointed, or when the adversary process commences. In my opinion, the Sixth Amendment right to counsel demands that a firm and unequivocal line be drawn at the point at which adversary proceedings commence.

In prior cases this Court has used strong language to emphasize the significance of the formal commencement of adversary proceedings. Such language has been employed to explain decisions denying the defendant the benefit of the protection of the Sixth Amendment in preindictment settings, but an evenhanded interpretation of the Amendment would support the view that additional protection should automatically attach the moment the formal proceedings begin. One such example is *Kirby v. Illinois*, 406 U.S. 682 (1972). JUSTICE Stewart's plurality opinion explained the significance of the formal charge:

> The initiation of judicial criminal proceedings is far from a mere formalism. It is the starting point of our whole system of adversary criminal justice. For it is only then that the government has committed itself to prosecute, and only then that the adverse positions of government and defendant have solidified. It is then that a defendant finds himself faced with the prosecutorial forces of organized society, and immersed in the intricacies of substantive and procedural criminal law. It is this point, therefore, that marks the commencement of the "criminal prosecutions" to which alone the explicit guarantees of the Sixth Amendment are applicable.

[R]ecently, in *Burbine*, the Court upheld a waiver of the right to counsel in a pretrial context even though the waiver "would not be valid" if the same situation had arisen after indictment. Today, however, in reaching a decision similarly favorable to the interest in law enforcement unfettered by process concerns, the Court backs away from the significance previously attributed to the initiation of formal proceedings. In the majority's view, the purported waiver of counsel in this case is properly equated with that of an unindicted suspect. Yet, as recognized in [our prior cases], important differences separate the two. The return of an indictment, or like instrument, substantially alters the relationship between the state and the accused. Only after a formal accusation has "the government . . . committed itself to prosecute, and only then [have] the adverse positions of government and defendant . . . solidified." Moreover, the return of an indictment also presumably signals the government's conclusion that it has sufficient evidence to establish a prima facie case. As a result, any further interrogation can only be designed to buttress the government's case; authorities are no longer simply attempting "to solve a crime." Given the significance of the initiation of formal proceedings and the concomitant shift in the relationship between the state and the accused, I think it quite wrong to suggest that *Miranda* warnings — or for that matter, any warnings offered by an adverse party — provide a sufficient basis for permitting the undoubtedly prejudicial — and, in my view, unfair — practice of permitting trained law enforcement personnel and prosecuting attorneys to communicate with as-of-yet unrepresented criminal defendants.

The majority premises its conclusion that *Miranda* warnings lay a sufficient basis for accepting a waiver of the right to counsel on the assumption that those warnings make clear to an accused "what a lawyer could 'do for him' during the postindictment questioning: namely, advise [him] to refrain from making any [incriminating] statements." Yet, this is surely a gross understatement of the disadvantage of proceeding without a lawyer and an understatement of what a defendant must understand to make a knowing waiver.[5] The *Miranda* warnings do not, for example, inform the accused that a lawyer might examine the indictment for legal sufficiency before submitting his or her client to interrogation or that a lawyer is likely to be considerably more skillful at negotiating a plea bargain and that such negotiations may be most fruitful if initiated prior to any interrogation. Rather, the warnings do not even go so far as to explain to the accused the nature of the charges pending against him — advice that a court would insist upon before allowing a defendant to enter a guilty plea with or without the presence of an attorney. Without defining precisely the nature of the inquiry required to establish a valid waiver of the Sixth Amendment right to counsel, it must be conceded that at least minimal advice is necessary — the accused must be told of the "dangers and disadvantages of self-representation."

Yet, once it is conceded that certain advice is required and that after indictment the adversary relationship between the state and the accused has solidified, it inescapably follows that a prosecutor may not conduct private interviews with a charged defendant. As at least one Court of Appeals has recognized, there are ethical constraints that prevent a prosecutor from giving legal advice to an uncounseled adversary. Thus, neither the prosecutor nor his or her agents can ethically provide the unrepresented defendant with the kind of advice that should precede an evidence-gathering interview after formal proceedings have been commenced. Indeed, in my opinion even the *Miranda* warnings themselves are a species of legal advice that is improper when given by the prosecutor after indictment.

---

[5] Respondent, and the United States as *amicus curiae*, argue that the comprehensive inquiry required by *Faretta v. California*, 422 U.S. 806 (1975), should not be extended to pretrial waivers because the role of counsel — and conversely the difficulty of proceeding without counsel — is more important at trial. I reject the premise that a lawyer's skills are more likely to sit idle at a pretrial interrogation than at trial. Both events require considerable experience and expertise and I would be reluctant to rank one over the other. Moreover, as we recognized in *Escobedo*:

> [T]he "right to use counsel at the formal trial [would be] a very hollow thing [if], for all practical purposes, the conviction is already assured by pretrial examination." "One can imagine a cynical prosecutor saying: 'Let them have the most illustrious counsel, now. They can't escape the noose. There is nothing that counsel can do for them at the trial.'"

Moreover, there are good reasons why such advice is deemed unethical, reasons that extend to the custodial, postindictment setting with unequaled strength. First, the offering of legal advice may lead an accused to underestimate the prosecuting authorities' true adversary posture. For an incarcerated defendant — in this case, a 17-year-old who had been in custody for 44 hours at the time he was told of the indictment — the assistance of someone to explain why he is being held, the nature of the charges against him, and the extent of his legal rights, may be of such importance as to overcome what is perhaps obvious to most, that the prosecutor is a foe and not a friend. Second, the adversary posture of the parties, which is not fully solidified until formal charges are brought, will inevitably tend to color the advice offered. As hard as a prosecutor might try, I doubt that it is possible for one to wear the hat of an effective adviser to a criminal defendant while at the same time wearing the hat of a law enforcement authority. Finally, regardless of whether or not the accused actually understands the legal and factual issues involved and the state's role as an adversary party, advice offered by a lawyer (or his or her agents) with such an evident conflict of interest cannot help but create a public perception of unfairness and unethical conduct.

In sum, without a careful discussion of the pitfalls of proceeding without counsel, the Sixth Amendment right cannot properly be waived. An adversary party, moreover, cannot adequately provide such advice. As a result, once the right to counsel attaches and the adversary relationship between the state and the accused solidifies, a prosecutor cannot conduct a private interview with an accused party without "dilut[ing] the protection afforded by the right to counsel," *Moulton*. Although this ground alone is reason enough to never permit such private interviews, the rule also presents the added virtue of drawing a clear and easily identifiable line at the point between the investigatory and adversary stages of a criminal proceeding. Such clarity in definition of constitutional rules that govern criminal proceedings is important to the law enforcement profession as well as to the private citizen. *See Roberson*. It is true, of course, that the interest in effective law enforcement would benefit from an opportunity to engage in incommunicado questioning of defendants who, for reasons beyond their control, have not been able to receive the legal advice from counsel to which they are constitutionally entitled. But the Court's single-minded concentration on that interest might also lead to the toleration of similar practices at any stage of the trial. I think it clear that such private communications are intolerable not simply during trial, but at any point after adversary proceedings have commenced.

I therefore respectfully dissent.

QUESTIONS AND NOTES

1. Is Patterson's argument that he was given insufficient warnings by the police, or that he should not have been approached by the police at all? Which of these arguments is more powerful? Explain.

2. Could you have developed more powerful answers to the questions put to Patterson's attorney in the Court's fn. 7? What might they have been?

3. Is the attorney's role as important during custodial interrogation as it is during trial? If your answer was "yes," is *Patterson* wrongly decided?

4. If counsel does no more for his client after indictment in regard to custodial interrogation than he did before such indictment, does it follow that *Miranda* should have been a Sixth Amendment case?

PROBLEM
FELLERS v. UNITED STATES

On February 24, 2000, after a grand jury indicted petitioner for conspiracy to distribute methamphetamine, Lincoln Police Sergeant Michael Garnett and Lancaster County Deputy Sheriff Jeff Bliemeister went to petitioner's home in Lincoln, Nebraska, to arrest him. The officers knocked on petitioner's door and, when petitioner answered, identified themselves and asked if they could come in. Petitioner invited the officers into his living room.

The officers advised petitioner they had come to discuss his involvement in methamphetamine distribution. They informed petitioner that they had a federal warrant for his arrest and that a grand jury had indicted him for conspiracy to distribute methamphetamine. The officers told petitioner that the indictment referred to his involvement with certain individuals, four of whom they named. Petitioner then told the officers that he knew the four people and had used methamphetamine during his association with them.

After spending about 15 minutes in petitioner's home, the officers transported petitioner to the Lancaster County jail. There, the officers advised petitioner for the first time of his rights under *Miranda* and *Patterson v. Illinois*. Petitioner and the two officers signed a Miranda waiver form, and petitioner then reiterated the inculpatory statements he had made earlier, admitted to having associated with other individuals implicated in the charged conspiracy and admitted to having loaned money to one of them even though he suspected that she was involved in drug transactions.

Before trial, petitioner moved to suppress the inculpatory statements he made at his home and at the county jail.

> Should petitioner's statements given at home be admissible? Should it matter whether he was interrogated or in custody at the time? For the Supreme Court's answer, see *Fellers v. United States*. 540 U.S. 519 (2004).

PROBLEM

After being informed of his rights pursuant to *Miranda*, and after executing a series of written waivers, respondent confessed to the murder of a young woman. At no point during the course of the interrogation, which occurred prior to arraignment, did he request an attorney. While he was in police custody, his sister attempted to retain a lawyer to represent him. The attorney telephoned the police station and received assurances that respondent would not be questioned further until the next day. In fact, the interrogation session that yielded the inculpatory statements began later that evening. The question presented is whether either the conduct of the police or respondent's ignorance of the attorney's efforts to reach him taints the validity of the waivers and therefore requires exclusion of the confessions.

Should the confession be inadmissible (A) under the Sixth Amendment? (B) under the Fifth Amendment? (C) as a violation of due process? For the supreme Court's resolution, see *Moran v. Burbine*, 475 U.S. 412 (1986).

C. THE SIXTH AMENDMENT AND THE ROBERTS COURT: THE TIMES THEY ARE A CHANGING

In 2009, the Roberts Court decided two cases, *Kansas v. Ventris*, and *Montejo v. Louisiana*, which fundamentally changed the way the Court thinks of the Sixth Amendment:

KANSAS v. VENTRIS
556 U.S. 586 (2009)

JUSTICE SCALIA delivered the opinion of the Court.

We address in this case the question whether a defendant's incriminating statement to a jailhouse informant, concededly elicited in violation of Sixth Amendment strictures, is admissible at trial to impeach the defendant's conflicting statement.

I

In the early hours of January 7, 2004, after two days of no sleep and some drug use, Rhonda Theel and respondent Donnie Ray Ventris reached an ill-conceived agreement to confront Ernest Hicks in his home. The couple testified that the aim of the visit was simply to investigate rumors that Hicks abused children, but the couple may have been inspired by the potential for financial gain: Theel had recently learned that Hicks carried large amounts of cash.

The encounter did not end well. One or both of the pair shot and killed Hicks with shots from a .38-caliber revolver, and the companions drove off in Hicks's truck with approximately $300 of his money and his cell phone. On receiving a tip from two friends of the couple who had helped transport them to Hicks's home, officers arrested Ventris and Theel and charged them with various crimes, chief among them murder and aggravated robbery. The State dropped the murder charge against Theel in exchange for her guilty plea to the robbery charge and her testimony identifying Ventris as the shooter.

Prior to trial, officers planted an informant in Ventris's holding cell, instructing him to "keep [his] ear open and listen" for incriminating statements. According to the informant, in response to his statement that Ventris appeared to have "something more serious weighing in on his mind," Ventris divulged that "[h]e'd shot this man in his head and in his chest" and taken "his keys, his wallet, about $350.00, and . . . a vehicle." At trial, Ventris took the stand and blamed the robbery and shooting entirely on Theel. The government sought to call the informant, to testify to Ventris's prior contradictory statement; Ventris objected. The State conceded that there was "probably a violation" of Ventris's Sixth Amendment right to counsel but nonetheless argued that the statement was admissible for impeachment purposes because the violation "doesn't give the Defendant . . . a license to just get on the stand and lie." The trial court agreed and allowed the informant's testimony, but instructed the jury to "consider with caution" all testimony given in exchange for benefits from the State. The jury ultimately acquitted Ventris of felony murder and misdemeanor theft but returned a guilty verdict on the aggravated burglary and aggravated robbery counts.

The Kansas Supreme Court reversed the conviction, holding that "[o]nce a criminal prosecution has commenced, the defendant's statements made to an undercover informant surreptitiously acting as an agent for the State are not admissible at trial for any reason, including the impeachment of the defendant's testimony." We granted the State's petition for certiorari.

II

The Sixth Amendment, applied to the States through the Fourteenth Amendment, guarantees that "[i]n all criminal prosecutions, the accused shall . . . have the Assistance of Counsel for his defence." The core of this right has historically been, and remains today, "the opportunity for a defendant to consult with an attorney and to have him investigate the case and prepare a defense for trial." *Michigan v. Harvey*, 494 U.S. 344, 348 (1990). We have held, however, that the right extends to having counsel present at various pretrial "critical" interactions between the defendant and the State, including the deliberate elicitation by law enforcement officers (and their agents) of statements pertaining to the charge, *Massiah v. United States*. The State has conceded throughout these proceedings that Ventris's confession was taken in violation of Massiah's dictates and was therefore not admissible in the prosecution's case in chief. Without affirming that this concession was necessary, see *Kuhlmann v. Wilson*, we accept it as the law of the case. The only question we answer today is whether the State must bear the additional consequence of inability to counter Ventris's contradictory testimony by placing the informant on the stand.

A

Whether otherwise excluded evidence can be admitted for purposes of impeachment depends upon the nature of the constitutional guarantee that is violated. Sometimes that explicitly mandates exclusion from trial, and sometimes it does not. The Fifth Amendment guarantees that no person shall be compelled to give evidence against himself, and so is violated whenever a truly coerced confession is introduced at trial, whether by way of impeachment or otherwise. *New Jersey v. Portash*, 440 U.S. 450, 458–459 (1979). The Fourth Amendment, on the other hand, guarantees that no person shall be subjected to unreasonable searches or seizures, and says nothing about excluding their fruits from evidence; exclusion comes by way of deterrent sanction rather than to avoid violation of the substantive guarantee. Inadmissibility has not been automatic, therefore, but we have instead applied an exclusionary-rule balancing test. See *Walder v. United States*, 347 U.S.

62, 65 (1954). The same is true for violations of the Fifth and Sixth Amendment prophylactic rules forbidding certain pretrial police conduct. See *Harris v. New York*, 401 U.S. 222, 225–226 (1971); *Harvey.*

Respondent argues that the Sixth Amendment's right to counsel is a "right an accused is to enjoy a[t] trial." The core of the right to counsel is indeed a trial right, ensuring that the prosecution's case is subjected to "the crucible of meaningful adversarial testing." But our opinions under the Sixth Amendment, as under the Fifth, have held that the right covers pretrial interrogations to ensure that police manipulation does not render counsel entirely impotent — depriving the defendant of " 'effective representation by counsel at the only stage when legal aid and advice would help him.' " *Massiah*; see also *Miranda v. Arizona.*

Our opinion in *Massiah*, to be sure, was equivocal on what precisely constituted the violation. It quoted various authorities indicating that the violation occurred at the moment of the postindictment interrogation because such questioning " 'contravenes the basic dictates of fairness in the conduct of criminal causes.' " But the opinion later suggested that the violation occurred only when the improperly obtained evidence was "used against [the defendant] at his trial." That question was irrelevant to the decision in *Massiah* in any event. Now that we are confronted with the question, we conclude that the *Massiah* right is a right to be free of uncounseled interrogation, and is infringed at the time of the interrogation. That, we think, is when the "Assistance of Counsel" is denied.

It is illogical to say that the right is not violated until trial counsel's task of opposing conviction has been undermined by the statement's admission into evidence. A defendant is not denied counsel merely because the prosecution has been permitted to introduce evidence of guilt — even evidence so overwhelming that the attorney's job of gaining an acquittal is rendered impossible. In such circumstances the accused continues to enjoy the assistance of counsel; the assistance is simply not worth much. The assistance of counsel has been denied, however, at the prior critical stage which produced the inculpatory evidence. Our cases acknowledge that reality in holding that the stringency of the warnings necessary for a waiver of the assistance of counsel varies according to "the usefulness of counsel to the accused at the particular [pretrial] proceeding." *Patterson v. Illinois*. It is *that* deprivation which demands a remedy.

The United States insists that "post-charge deliberate elicitation of statements without the defendant's counsel or a valid waiver of counsel is not intrinsically unlawful." That is true when the questioning is unrelated to charged crimes — the Sixth Amendment right is "offense specific," *McNeil v. Wisconsin*. We have never said, however, that officers may badger counseled defendants about charged crimes so long as they do not use information they gain. The constitutional violation occurs when the uncounseled interrogation is conducted.

B

This case does not involve, therefore, the prevention of a constitutional violation, but rather the scope of the remedy for a violation that has already occurred. Our precedents make clear that the game of excluding tainted evidence for impeachment purposes is not worth the candle. The interests safeguarded by such exclusion are "outweighed by the need to prevent perjury and to assure the integrity of the trial process."

On the other side of the scale, preventing impeachment use of statements taken in violation of *Massiah* would add little appreciable deterrence. Officers have significant incentive to ensure that they and their informants comply with the Constitution's demands, since statements lawfully obtained can be used for all purposes rather than simply for impeachment. And the *ex ante* probability that evidence gained in violation of *Massiah* would be of use for impeachment is exceedingly small. An investigator would have to anticipate both that the defendant would choose to testify at trial (an unusual occurrence to begin with) *and* that he would testify inconsistently despite the admissibility of his prior statement for impeachment. Not likely to happen — or at least not likely enough to risk squandering the opportunity of using a properly obtained statement for the prosecution's case in chief.

In any event, even if "the officer may be said to have little to lose and perhaps something to gain by way of possibly uncovering impeachment material," we have multiple times rejected the argument that this "speculative possibility" can trump the costs of allowing perjurious statements to go unchallenged. We have held in every other context that tainted evidence — evidence whose very introduction does not constitute the constitutional violation, but whose obtaining was constitutionally invalid — is admissible for impeachment. We see no distinction that would alter the balance here.[*]

*   *   *

We hold that the informant's testimony, concededly elicited in violation of the Sixth Amendment, was admissible to challenge Ventris's inconsistent testimony at trial. The judgment of the Kansas Supreme Court is reversed, and the case is remanded for further proceedings not inconsistent with this opinion.

It is so ordered.

JUSTICE STEVENS, with whom JUSTICE GINSBURG joins, dissenting.

Treating the State's actions in this case as a violation of a prophylactic right, the Court concludes that introducing the illegally obtained evidence at trial does not itself violate the Constitution. I strongly disagree. While the constitutional breach began at the time of interrogation, the State's use of that evidence at trial compounded the violation. The logic that compels the exclusion of the evidence

---

[*]   Respondent's *amicus* insists that jailhouse snitches are so inherently unreliable that this Court should craft a broader exclusionary rule for uncorroborated statements obtained by that means. Our legal system, however, is built on the premise that it is the province of the jury to weigh the credibility of competing witnesses, and we have long purported to avoid "establish[ing] this Court as a rule-making organ for the promulgation of state rules of criminal procedure." It would be especially inappropriate to fabricate such a rule in this case, where it appears the jury took to heart the trial judge's cautionary instruction on the unreliability of rewarded informant testimony by acquitting Ventris of felony murder.

during the State's case in chief extends to any attempt by the State to rely on the evidence, even for impeachment. The use of ill-gotten evidence during any phase of criminal prosecution does damage to the adversarial process — the fairness of which the Sixth Amendment was designed to protect. ("[The] procedural devices rooted in experience were written into the Bill of Rights not as abstract rubrics in an elegant code but in order to assure fairness and justice before any person could be deprived of 'life, liberty, or property' ").

When counsel is excluded from a critical pretrial interaction between the defendant and the State, she may be unable to effectively counter the potentially devastating, and potentially false,[7] evidence subsequently introduced at trial. Inexplicably, today's Court refuses to recognize that this is a constitutional harm.[8] Yet in *Massiah*, the Court forcefully explained that a defendant is "denied the basic protections of the [Sixth Amendment] guarantee when there [is] used against him at his trial evidence of his own incriminating words" that were "deliberately elicited from him after he had been indicted and in the absence of counsel." Sadly, the majority has retreated from this robust understanding of the right to counsel.

Today's decision is lamentable not only because of its flawed underpinnings, but also because it is another occasion in which the Court has privileged the prosecution at the expense of the Constitution. Permitting the State to cut corners in criminal proceedings taxes the legitimacy of the entire criminal process. "The State's interest in truth-seeking is congruent with the defendant's interest in representation by counsel, for it is an elementary premise of our system of criminal justice 'that partisan advocacy on both sides of a case will best promote the ultimate objective that the guilty be convicted and the innocent go free.' " Although the Court may not be concerned with the use of ill-gotten evidence in derogation of the right to counsel, I remain convinced that such shabby tactics are intolerable in all cases. I respectfully dissent.

QUESTIONS AND NOTES

1. Do you think the Court was ambiguous in *Massiah* as to when the right to counsel was violated? What about *Maine v. Moulton*, not even cited by the Court?

2. Could Massiah have sued Agent Murphy for listening to his conversations obtained without counsel even if those statements had never been introduced against him? Should he be able to so sue? What about Ventris? If his alleged statement to the jailhouse informant had never been introduced against him, could

---

[7] The likelihood that evidence gathered by self-interested jailhouse informants may be false cannot be ignored. Indeed, by deciding to acquit respondent of felony murder, the jury seems to have dismissed the informant's trial testimony as unreliable.

[8] In the majority's telling, "simply" having counsel whose help is "not worth much" is not a Sixth Amendment concern. Of course, the Court points to no precedent for this stingy view of the Counsel Clause, for we have never held that the Sixth Amendment only protects a defendant from actual denials of counsel. Indeed our venerable ineffective-assistance-of-counsel jurisprudence is built on a more realistic understanding of what the Constitution guarantees. See *Strickland v. Washington*, 466 U.S. 668 (1984); *McMann v. Richardson*, 397 U.S. 759, 771, n. 14 (1970) ("[T]he right to counsel is the right to the effective assistance of counsel").

(should) he have been able to sue the police for obtaining it? Why? Why not? Compare *Chavez v. Martinez, infra.*

3.   Even the dissent seemed to agree that the violation occurred at the time of obtaining the evidence? On that basis who do you think has the better of the argument? Explain.

4.   Do you think that Scalia treated Ventris' claim as a prophylactic right or a real right? Does it matter?

5.   Do you believe that Ventris' right to counsel was even violated under *Kuhlmann*? Why do you suppose that Kansas conceded the point?

6.   Is it irrelevant that Ventris retained his right to counsel at trial and that the only problem was that introduction of the statement made his job harder?

7.   As you read *Montejo*, think about whether the Court simplified or complicated the Sixth Amendment.

MONTEJO v. LOUISIANA
556 U.S. 778 (2009)

JUSTICE SCALIA delivered the opinion of the Court.

We consider in this case the scope and continued viability of the rule announced by this Court in *Michigan v. Jackson*, forbidding police to initiate interrogation of a criminal defendant once he has requested counsel at an arraignment or similar proceeding.

I

Petitioner Jesse Montejo was arrested on September 6, 2002, in connection with the robbery and murder of Lewis Ferrari, who had been found dead in his own home one day earlier. Suspicion quickly focused on Jerry Moore, a disgruntled former employee of Ferrari's dry cleaning business. Police sought to question Montejo, who was a known associate of Moore. Montejo waived his rights under *Miranda* and was interrogated at the sheriff's office by police detectives through the late afternoon and evening of September 6 and the early morning of September 7. During the interrogation, Montejo repeatedly changed his account of the crime, at first claiming that he had only driven Moore to the victim's home, and ultimately admitting that he had shot and killed Ferrari in the course of a botched burglary. These police interrogations were videotaped.

On September 10, Montejo was brought before a judge for what is known in Louisiana as a "72-hour hearing" — a preliminary hearing required under state law.[9] Although the proceedings were not transcribed, the minute record indicates what transpired: "The defendant being charged with First Degree Murder, Court

---

[9] "The sheriff or law enforcement officer having custody of an arrested person shall bring him promptly, and in any case within seventy-two hours from the time of the arrest, before a judge for the purpose of appointment of counsel." La. Code Crim. Proc. Ann., Art. 230.1(A) (West Supp. 2009).

ordered N[o] Bond set in this matter. Further, Court ordered the Office of Indigent Defender be appointed to represent the defendant."

Later that same day, two police detectives visited Montejo back at the prison and requested that he accompany them on an excursion to locate the murder weapon (which Montejo had earlier indicated he had thrown into a lake). After some back-and-forth, the substance of which remains in dispute, Montejo was again read his *Miranda* rights and agreed to go along; during the excursion, he wrote an inculpatory letter of apology to the victim's widow. Only upon their return did Montejo finally meet his court-appointed attorney, who was quite upset that the detectives had interrogated his client in his absence.

At trial, the letter of apology was admitted over defense objection. The jury convicted Montejo of first-degree murder, and he was sentenced to death.

The Louisiana Supreme Court affirmed the conviction and sentence. As relevant here, the court rejected Montejo's argument that under the rule of *Jackson* the letter should have been suppressed. *Jackson* held that "if police initiate interrogation after a defendant's assertion, at an arraignment or similar proceeding, of his right to counsel, any waiver of the defendant's right to counsel for that police-initiated interrogation is invalid."

Citing a decision of the United States Court of Appeals for the Fifth Circuit, *Montoya v. Collins*, 955 F.2d 279 (1992), the Louisiana Supreme Court reasoned that the prophylactic protection of *Jackson* is not triggered unless and until the defendant has actually requested a lawyer or has otherwise asserted his Sixth Amendment right to counsel. Because Montejo simply stood mute at his 72-hour hearing while the judge ordered the appointment of counsel, he had made no such request or assertion. So the proper inquiry, the court ruled, was only whether he had knowingly, intelligently, and voluntarily waived his right to have counsel present during the interaction with the police. And because Montejo had been read his *Miranda* rights and agreed to waive them, the Court answered that question in the affirmative and upheld the conviction.

We granted certiorari.

II

Montejo and his *amici* raise a number of pragmatic objections to the Louisiana Supreme Court's interpretation of *Jackson*. We agree that the approach taken below would lead either to an unworkable standard, or to arbitrary and anomalous distinctions between defendants in different States. Neither would be acceptable. Under the rule adopted by the Louisiana Supreme Court, a criminal defendant must request counsel, or otherwise "assert" his Sixth Amendment right at the preliminary hearing, before the *Jackson* protections are triggered. If he does so, the police may not initiate further interrogation in the absence of counsel. But if the court on its own appoints counsel, with the defendant taking no affirmative action to invoke his right to counsel, then police are free to initiate further interrogations provided that they first obtain an otherwise valid waiver by the defendant of his right to have counsel present.

This rule would apply well enough in States that require the indigent defendant formally to request counsel before any appointment is made, which usually occurs after the court has informed him that he will receive counsel if he asks for it. That is how the system works in Michigan, for example. Jackson, like all other represented indigent defendants in the State, had requested counsel in accordance with the applicable state law.

But many States follow other practices. In some two dozen, the appointment of counsel is automatic upon a finding of indigency, and in a number of others, appointment can be made either upon the defendant's request or *sua sponte* by the court. Nothing in our *Jackson* opinion indicates whether we were then aware that not all States require that a defendant affirmatively request counsel before one is appointed; and of course we had no occasion there to decide how the rule we announced would apply to these other States.

The Louisiana Supreme Court's answer to that unresolved question is troublesome. The central distinction it draws — between defendants who "assert" their right to counsel and those who do not — is exceedingly hazy when applied to States that appoint counsel absent request from the defendant. How to categorize a defendant who merely asks, prior to appointment, whether he will be appointed counsel? Or who inquires, after the fact, whether he has been? What treatment for one who thanks the court after the appointment is made? And if the court asks a defendant whether he would object to appointment, will a quick shake of his head count as an assertion of his right?

To the extent that the Louisiana Supreme Court's rule also permits a defendant to trigger *Jackson* through the "acceptance" of counsel, that notion is even more mysterious: How does one affirmatively accept counsel appointed by court order? An indigent defendant has no right to choose his counsel, so it is hard to imagine what his "acceptance" would look like, beyond the passive silence that Montejo exhibited.

In practice, judicial application of the Louisiana rule in States that do not require a defendant to make a request for counsel could take either of two paths. Courts might ask on a case-by-case basis whether a defendant has somehow invoked his right to counsel, looking to his conduct at the preliminary hearing — his statements and gestures — and the totality of the circumstances. Or, courts might simply determine as a categorical matter that defendants in these States — over half of those in the Union — simply have no opportunity to assert their right to counsel at the hearing and are therefore out of luck.

Neither approach is desirable. The former would be particularly impractical in light of the fact that, as *amici* describe, preliminary hearings are often rushed, and are frequently not recorded or transcribed. The sheer volume of indigent defendants would render the monitoring of each particular defendant's reaction to the appointment of counsel almost impossible. And sometimes the defendant is not even present. *E.g.*, La. Code Crim. Proc. Ann., Art. 230.1(A) (West Supp. 2009) (allowing court to appoint counsel if defendant is "unable to appear"). Police who did not attend the hearing would have no way to know whether they could approach a particular defendant; and for a court to adjudicate that question *ex post* would be a fact-intensive and burdensome task, even if monitoring were possible and transcription available. Because "clarity of . . . command" and "certainty of . . . application" are crucial in rules that govern law enforcement, *Minnick v. Mississippi*, this would be an unfortunate way to proceed.

The second possible course fares no better, for it would achieve clarity and certainty only at the expense of introducing arbitrary distinctions: Defendants in States that automatically appoint counsel would have no opportunity to invoke their rights and trigger *Jackson*, while those in other States, effectively instructed by the court to request counsel, would be lucky winners. That sort of hollow formalism is out of place in a doctrine that purports to serve as a practical safeguard for defendants' rights.

III

But if the Louisiana Supreme Court's application of *Jackson* is unsound as a practical matter, then Montejo's solution is untenable as a theoretical and doctrinal matter. Under his approach, once a defendant is *represented* by counsel, police may not initiate any further interrogation. Such a rule would be entirely untethered from the original rationale of *Jackson*.

A

It is worth emphasizing first what is *not* in dispute or at stake here. Under our precedents, once the adversary judicial process has been initiated, the Sixth Amendment guarantees a defendant the right to have counsel present at all "critical" stages of the criminal proceedings. Interrogation by the State is such a stage. *Massiah v. United States*, 377 U.S. 201, 204–205 (1964).

Our precedents also place beyond doubt that the Sixth Amendment right to counsel may be waived by a defendant, so long as relinquishment of the right is voluntary, knowing, and intelligent. The defendant may waive the right whether or not he is already represented by counsel; the decision to waive need not itself be counseled. And when a defendant is read his *Miranda* rights (which include the right to have counsel present during interrogation) and agrees to waive those rights, that typically does the trick, even though the *Miranda* rights purportedly have their source in the *Fifth* Amendment:

> "As a general matter . . . an accused who is admonished with the warnings prescribed by this Court in *Miranda* . . . has been sufficiently apprised of the nature of his Sixth Amendment rights, and of the consequences of abandoning those rights, so that his waiver on this basis will be considered a knowing and intelligent one." *Patterson*.

The *only* question raised by this case, and the only one addressed by the *Jackson* rule, is whether courts must *presume* that such a waiver is invalid under certain circumstances. We created such a presumption in *Jackson* by analogy to a similar prophylactic rule established to protect the Fifth Amendment based *Miranda* right to have counsel present at any custodial interrogation. *Edwards v. Arizona* decided that once "an accused has invoked his right to have counsel present during custodial interrogation . . . [he] is not subject to further interrogation by the authorities until counsel has been made available," unless he initiates the contact.

The *Edwards* rule is "designed to prevent police from badgering a defendant into waiving his previously asserted *Miranda* rights." It does this by presuming his postassertion statements to be involuntary, "even where the suspect executes a waiver and his statements would be considered voluntary under traditional standards." *McNeil v. Wisconsin*. This prophylactic rule thus "protect[s] a suspect's voluntary choice not to speak outside his lawyer's presence." *Texas v. Cobb* (KENNEDY, J., concurring).

Jackson represented a "wholesale importation of the *Edwards* rule into the Sixth Amendment." The *Jackson* Court decided that a request for counsel at an arraignment should be treated as an invocation of the Sixth Amendment right to counsel "at every critical stage of the prosecution" despite doubt that defendants "actually inten[d] their request for counsel to encompass representation during any further questioning" because doubts must be "resolved in favor of protecting the constitutional claim." Citing *Edwards*, the Court held that any subsequent waiver would thus be "insufficient to justify police initiated interrogation." In other words, we presume such waivers involuntary "based on the supposition that suspects who assert their right to counsel are unlikely to waive that right voluntarily" in subsequent interactions with police.

The dissent presents us with a revisionist view of *Jackson*. The defendants' *request* for counsel, it contends, was important only because it proved that counsel *had been appointed*. Such a non sequitur (nowhere alluded to in the case) hardly needs rebuttal. Proceeding from this fanciful premise, the dissent claims that the decision actually established "a rule designed to safeguard a defendant's right to rely on the assistance of counsel," (opinion of Stevens, J.), not one "designed to prevent police badgering." To safeguard the right to assistance of counsel from *what*? From a knowing and voluntary waiver by the defendant himself? Unless the dissent seeks to prevent a defendant altogether from waiving his Sixth Amendment rights, *i.e.*, to "imprison a man in his privileges and call it the Constitution," *Adams v. United States ex rel. McCann*, 317 U.S. 269, 280 (1942) — a view with zero support in reason, history or case law — the answer must be: from police pressure, *i.e.*, badgering. The antibadgering rationale is the only way to make sense of *Jackson's* repeated citations of *Edwards*, and the only way to reconcile the opinion with our waiver jurisprudence.[10]

B

With this understanding of what *Jackson* stands for and whence it came, it should be clear that Montejo's interpretation of that decision — that no *represented* defendant can ever be approached by the State and asked to consent to interroga-

---

[10] The dissent responds that *Jackson* also ensures that the defendant's counsel receives notice of any interrogation, n.2. But notice to what end? Surely not in order to protect some constitutional right to receive counsel's advice regarding waiver of the right to have counsel present. Contrary to the dissent's intimations, neither the advice nor the presence of counsel is needed in order to effectuate a knowing waiver of the Sixth Amendment right. Our cases make clear that the *Miranda* waivers typically suffice; indeed, even an *unrepresented* defendant can waive his right to counsel.

tion — is off the mark. When a court appoints counsel for an indigent defendant in the absence of any request on his part, there is no basis for a presumption that any subsequent waiver of the right to counsel will be involuntary. There is no "*initial election*" to exercise the right, *Patterson*, that must be preserved through a prophylactic rule against later waivers. No reason exists to assume that a defendant like Montejo, who has done *nothing at all* to express his intentions with respect to his Sixth Amendment rights, would not be perfectly amenable to speaking with the police without having counsel present.

And no reason exists to prohibit the police from inquiring. *Edwards* and *Jackson* are meant to prevent police from badgering defendants into changing their minds about their rights, but a defendant who never asked for counsel has not yet made up his mind in the first instance.

The dissent's argument to the contrary rests on a flawed *a fortiori:* "If a defendant is entitled to protection from police-initiated interrogation under the Sixth Amendment when he merely *requests* a lawyer, he is even more obviously entitled to such protection when he has *secured* a lawyer." The question in *Jackson*, however, was not whether respondents were entitled to counsel (they unquestionably were), but "whether respondents validly waived their right to counsel"; and even if it is reasonable to presume from a defendant's *request* for counsel that any subsequent waiver of the right was coerced, no such presumption can seriously be entertained when a lawyer was merely "secured" on the defendant's behalf, by the State itself, as a matter of course. Of course, reading the dissent's analysis, one would have no idea that Montejo executed any waiver at all.

In practice, Montejo's rule would prevent police-initiated interrogation entirely once the Sixth Amendment right attaches, at least in those States that appoint counsel promptly without request from the defendant. As the dissent in *Jackson* pointed out, with no expressed disagreement from the majority, the opinion "most assuredly [did] *not* hold that the *Edwards per se* rule prohibiting all police-initiated interrogations applies from the moment the defendant's Sixth Amendment right to counsel attaches, with or without a request for counsel by the defendant." That would have constituted a "shockingly dramatic restructuring of the balance this Court has traditionally struck between the rights of the defendant and those of the larger society."

Montejo's rule appears to have its theoretical roots in codes of legal ethics, not the Sixth Amendment. The American Bar Association's Model Rules of Professional Conduct (which nearly all States have adopted into law in whole or in part) mandate that "a lawyer shall not communicate about the subject of [a] representation with a party the lawyer knows to be represented by another lawyer in the matter, unless the lawyer has the consent of the other lawyer or is authorized to do so by law or a court order." Model Rule 4.2 (2008). But the Constitution does not codify the ABA's Model Rules, and does not make investigating police officers lawyers. Montejo's proposed rule is both broader and narrower than the Model Rule. Broader, because Montejo would apply it to all agents of the State, including the detectives who interrogated him, while the ethical rule governs only lawyers. And narrower, because he agrees that if a defendant initiates contact with the police, they may talk freely — whereas a lawyer could be sanctioned for interviewing a represented party even if that party "initiates" the communication and consents to the interview.

Montejo contends that our decisions support his interpretation of the *Jackson* rule. We think not. Many of the cases he cites concern the substantive scope of the Sixth Amendment — *e.g.*, whether a particular interaction with the State constitutes a "critical" stage at which counsel is entitled to be present — *not* the validity of a Sixth Amendment waiver. See *Moulton; Massiah*. Since everyone agrees that absent a valid waiver, Montejo was entitled to a lawyer during the interrogation, those cases do not advance his argument.

Montejo also points to descriptions of the *Jackson* holding in two later cases. In one, we noted that "analysis of the waiver issue changes" once a defendant "obtains or even requests counsel." *Harvey*. But elsewhere in the same opinion, we explained that *Jackson* applies "after a defendant requests assistance of counsel." The accuracy of the "obtains" language is thus questionable. Anyway, since *Harvey* held that evidence obtained in violation of the *Jackson* rule *could* be admitted to impeach the defendant's trial testimony, the Court's varying descriptions of when the rule was violated were dicta. The dictum from the other decision, *Patterson* is no more probative.[11]

The upshot is that even on *Jackson's* own terms, it would be completely unjustified to presume that a defendant's consent to police-initiated interrogation was involuntary or coerced simply because he had previously been appointed a lawyer.

IV

So on the one hand, requiring an initial "invocation" of the right to counsel in order to trigger the *Jackson* presumption is consistent with the theory of that decision, but would be unworkable in more than half the States of the Union. On the other hand, eliminating the invocation requirement would render the rule easy to apply but depart fundamentally from the *Jackson* rationale. We do not think that *stare decisis* requires us to expand significantly the holding of a prior decision — fundamentally revising its theoretical basis in the process — in order to cure its practical deficiencies. To the contrary, the fact that a decision has proved "unworkable" is a traditional ground for overruling it. Accordingly, we called for supplemental briefing addressed to the question whether *Michigan v. Jackson* should be overruled. Beyond workability, the relevant factors in deciding whether to adhere to the principle of *stare decisis* include the antiquity of the precedent, the reliance interests at stake, and of course whether the decision was well reasoned.

---

[11] In the cited passage, the Court noted that "[o]nce an accused has a lawyer, a distinct set of constitutional safeguards aimed at preserving the sanctity of attorney-client relationship takes effect." To support that proposition, the Court cited *Moulton*, which was not a case about waiver. The passage went on to observe that "the analysis changes markedly once an accused even *requests* the assistance of counsel," (emphasis in original), this time citing *Jackson*. Montejo infers from the "even *requests*" that having counsel is *more* conclusive of the invalidity of uncounseled waiver than the mere requesting of counsel. But the *Patterson* footnote did not suggest that the analysis "changes" in both these scenarios (having a lawyer, versus requesting one) with specific reference to the validity of waivers under the Sixth Amendment. The citation of *Moulton* (a nonwaiver case) for the first scenario suggests just the opposite.

The first two cut in favor of abandoning *Jackson:* the opinion is only two decades old, and eliminating it would not upset expectations. Any criminal defendant learned enough to order his affairs based on the rule announced in *Jackson* would also be perfectly capable of interacting with the police on his own. Of course it is likely true that police and prosecutors have been trained to comply with *Jackson*, but that is hardly a basis for retaining it as a constitutional requirement. If a State *wishes* to abstain from requesting interviews with represented defendants when counsel is not present, it obviously may continue to do so.[12]

Which brings us to the strength of *Jackson's* reasoning. When this Court creates a prophylactic rule in order to protect a constitutional right, the relevant "reasoning" is the weighing of the rule's benefits against its costs. "The value of any prophylactic rule . . . must be assessed not only on the basis of what is gained, but also on the basis of what is lost." *Minnick* (SCALIA, J., dissenting). We think that the marginal benefits of *Jackson* (viz., the number of confessions obtained coercively that are suppressed by its bright-line rule and would otherwise have been admitted) are dwarfed by its substantial costs (viz., hindering "society's compelling interest in finding, convicting, and punishing those who violate the law.")

What does the *Jackson* rule actually achieve by way of preventing unconstitutional conduct? Recall that the purpose of the rule is to preclude the State from badgering defendants into waiving their previously asserted rights. The effect of this badgering might be to coerce a waiver, which would render the subsequent interrogation a violation of the Sixth Amendment. See *Massiah*. Even though involuntary waivers are invalid even apart from *Jackson*, see *Patterson*, mistakes are of course possible when courts conduct case-by-case voluntariness review. A bright-line rule like that adopted in *Jackson* ensures that no fruits of interrogations made possible by badgering-induced involuntary waivers are ever erroneously admitted at trial.

But without *Jackson*, how many would be? The answer is few if any. The principal reason is that the Court has already taken substantial other, overlapping measures toward the same end. Under *Miranda's* prophylactic protection of the right against compelled self-incrimination, any suspect subject to custodial interrogation has the right to have a lawyer present if he so requests, and to be advised of that right. Under *Edwards'* prophylactic protection of the *Miranda* right, once such a defendant "has invoked his right to have counsel present," interrogation must stop. And under *Minnick's* prophylactic protection of the *Edwards* right, no subsequent interrogation may take place until counsel is present, "whether or not the accused has consulted with his attorney."

These three layers of prophylaxis are sufficient. Under the *Miranda-Edwards-Minnick* line of cases (which is not in doubt), a defendant who does not want to speak to the police without counsel present need only say as much when he is first

---

[12] The dissent posits a different reliance interest: "the public's interest in knowing that counsel, once secured, may be reasonably relied upon as a medium between the accused and the power of the State." We suspect the public would be surprised to learn that a criminal can freely sign away his right to a lawyer, confess his crimes, and then ask the courts to *assume* that the confession was coerced — on the ground that he had, at some earlier point in time, made a *pro forma* statement requesting that counsel be appointed on his behalf.

approached and given the *Miranda* warnings. At that point, not only must the immediate contact end, but "badgering" by later requests is prohibited. If that regime suffices to protect the integrity of "a suspect's voluntary choice not to speak outside his lawyer's presence" before his arraignment, it is hard to see why it would not also suffice to protect that same choice after arraignment, when Sixth Amendment rights have attached. And if so, then *Jackson* is simply superfluous.

It is true, as Montejo points out in his supplemental brief, that the doctrine established by *Miranda* and *Edwards* is designed to protect Fifth Amendment, not Sixth Amendment, rights. But that is irrelevant. What matters is that these cases, like *Jackson*, protect the right to have counsel during custodial interrogation — which right happens to be guaranteed (once the adversary judicial process has begun) by *two* sources of law. Since the right under both sources is waived using the same procedure, *Patterson*, doctrines ensuring voluntariness of the Fifth Amendment waiver simultaneously ensure the voluntariness of the Sixth Amendment waiver.

Montejo also correctly observes that the *Miranda-Edwards* regime is narrower than *Jackson* in one respect: The former applies only in the context of custodial interrogation. If the defendant is not in custody then those decisions do not apply; nor do they govern other, noninterrogative types of interactions between the defendant and the State (like pretrial lineups). However, those uncovered situations are the *least* likely to pose a risk of coerced waivers. When a defendant is not in custody, he is in control, and need only shut his door or walk away to avoid police badgering. And noninterrogative interactions with the State do not involve the "inherently compelling pressures" that one might reasonably fear could lead to involuntary waivers.

Jackson was policy driven, and if that policy is being adequately served through other means, there is no reason to retain its rule. *Miranda* and the cases that elaborate upon it already guarantee not simply noncoercion in the traditional sense, but what Justice Harlan referred to as "voluntariness with a vengeance." There is no need to take *Jackson's* further step of requiring voluntariness on stilts.

On the other side of the equation are the costs of adding the bright-line *Jackson* rule on top of *Edwards* and other extant protections. The principal cost of applying any exclusionary rule "is, of course, letting guilty and possibly dangerous criminals go free . . . ." *Herring v. United States. Jackson* not only "operates to invalidate a confession given by the free choice of suspects who have received proper advice of their *Miranda* rights but waived them nonetheless," but also deters law enforcement officers from even trying to obtain voluntary confessions. The "ready ability to obtain uncoerced confessions is not an evil but an unmitigated good." *McNeil.* Without these confessions, crimes go unsolved and criminals unpunished. These are not negligible costs, and in our view the *Jackson* Court gave them too short shrift.[13]

---

[13] The dissent claims that, in fact, few confessions have been suppressed by federal courts applying *Jackson*. If so, that is because, as the dissent boasts, "generations of police officers have been trained to refrain from approaching represented defendants." Anyway, if the rule truly does not hinder law enforcement or make much practical difference, then there is no reason to be particularly exercised about its demise.

Notwithstanding this calculus, Montejo and his *amici* urge the retention of *Jackson*. Their principal objection to its elimination is that the *Edwards* regime which remains will not provide an administrable rule. But this Court has praised *Edwards* precisely because it provides " 'clear and unequivocal' guidelines to the law enforcement profession." Our cases make clear which sorts of statements trigger its protections, see *Davis v. United States*, and once triggered, the rule operates as a bright line. Montejo expresses concern that courts will have to determine whether statements made at preliminary hearings constitute *Edwards* invocations — thus implicating all the practical problems of the Louisiana rule we discussed above. That concern is misguided. "We have in fact never held that a person can invoke his *Miranda* rights anticipatorily, in a context other than 'custodial interrogation' . . . ." *McNeil*. What matters for *Miranda* and *Edwards* is what happens when the defendant is approached for interrogation, and (if he consents) what happens during the interrogation — not what happened at any preliminary hearing.

In sum, when the marginal benefits of the *Jackson* rule are weighed against its substantial costs to the truth-seeking process and the criminal justice system, we readily conclude that the rule does not "pay its way," *United States v. Leon*, 468 U.S. 897, 907–908, n. 6 (1984). *Michigan v. Jackson* should be and now is overruled.

V

Although our holding means that the Louisiana Supreme Court correctly rejected Montejo's claim under *Jackson*, we think that Montejo should be given an opportunity to contend that his letter of apology should still have been suppressed under the rule of *Edwards*. If Montejo made a clear assertion of the right to counsel when the officers approached him about accompanying them on the excursion for the murder weapon, then no interrogation should have taken place unless Montejo initiated it. Even if Montejo subsequently agreed to waive his rights, that waiver would have been invalid had it followed an "unequivocal election of the right."

Montejo understandably did not pursue an *Edwards* objection, because *Jackson* served as the Sixth Amendment analogy to *Edwards* and offered broader protections. Our decision today, overruling *Jackson*, changes the legal landscape and does so in part based on the protections already provided by *Edwards*. Thus we think that a remand is appropriate so that Montejo can pursue this alternative avenue for relief. Montejo may also seek on remand to press any claim he might have that his Sixth Amendment waiver was not knowing and voluntary, *e.g.*, his argument that the waiver was invalid because it was based on misrepresentations by police as to whether he had been appointed a lawyer. These matters have heightened importance in light of our opinion today.

We do not venture to resolve these issues ourselves, not only because we are a court of final review, "not of first view," but also because the relevant facts remain unclear. Montejo and the police gave inconsistent testimony about exactly what took place on the afternoon of September 10, 2002, and the Louisiana Supreme Court did not make an explicit credibility determination. Moreover, Montejo's testimony came not at the suppression hearing, but rather only at trial, and we are unsure whether under state law that testimony came too late to affect the propriety of the admission of the evidence. These matters are best left for resolution on remand.

We do reject, however, the dissent's revisionist legal analysis of the "knowing and voluntary" issue. In determining whether a Sixth Amendment waiver was knowing and voluntary, there is no reason categorically to distinguish an unrepresented defendant from a represented one. It is equally true for each that, as we held in *Patterson*, the *Miranda* warnings adequately inform him "of his right to have counsel present during the questioning," and make him "aware of the consequences of a decision by him to waive his Sixth Amendment rights." Somewhat surprisingly for an opinion that extols the virtues of *stare decisis*, the dissent complains that our "treatment of the waiver question rests entirely on the dubious decision in *Patterson*." The Court in *Patterson* did not consider the result dubious, nor does the Court today.

* * *

This case is an exemplar of Justice Jackson's oft quoted warning that this Court "is forever adding new stories to the temples of constitutional law, and the temples have a way of collapsing when one story too many is added." *Douglas v. City of Jeannette*, 319 U.S. 157, 181 (1943) (opinion concurring in result). We today remove *Michigan v. Jackson's* fourth story of prophylaxis.

The judgment of the Louisiana Supreme Court is vacated, and the case is remanded for further proceedings not inconsistent with this opinion.

It is so ordered.

[JUSTICE ALITO (joined by JUSTICE KENNEDY), concurred, emphasizing that the Court's willingness to ignore *stare decisis* was amply justified by *Arizona v. Gant*, from which, of course, Alito, joined by Kennedy, dissented.]

JUSTICE STEVENS, with whom JUSTICE SOUTER and JUSTICE GINSBURG join, and with whom JUSTICE BREYER joins, except for footnote 5, dissenting.

Today the Court properly concludes that the Louisiana Supreme Court's parsimonious reading of our decision in *Michigan* v. *Jackson* is indefensible. Yet the Court does not reverse. Rather, on its own initiative and without any evidence that the longstanding Sixth Amendment protections established in *Jackson* have caused any harm to the workings of the criminal justice system, the Court rejects *Jackson* outright on the ground that it is "untenable as a theoretical and doctrinal matter." That conclusion rests on a misinterpretation of *Jackson's* rationale and a gross undervaluation of the rule of *stare decisis*. The police interrogation in this case clearly violated petitioner's Sixth Amendment right to counsel.

I

The Sixth Amendment provides that "[i]n all criminal prosecutions, the accused shall enjoy the right . . . to have the Assistance of Counsel for his defence." The right to counsel attaches during "the initiation of adversary judicial criminal proceedings," and it guarantees the assistance of counsel not only during in-court proceedings but during all critical stages, including postarraignment interviews with law enforcement officers.

In *Jackson*, this Court considered whether the Sixth Amendment bars police from interrogating defendants who have requested the appointment of counsel at arraignment. Applying the presumption that such a request constitutes an invocation of the right to counsel "at every critical stage of the prosecution," we held that "a defendant who has been formally charged with a crime and who has requested appointment of counsel at his arraignment" cannot be subject to uncounseled interrogation unless he initiates "exchanges or conversations with the police."

In this case, petitioner Jesse Montejo contends that police violated his Sixth Amendment right to counsel by interrogating him following his "72-hour hearing" outside the presence of, and without prior notice to, his lawyer. The Louisiana Supreme Court rejected Montejo's claim. Relying on the fact that the defendants in *Jackson* had "requested" counsel at arraignment, the state court held that *Jackson's* protections did not apply to Montejo because his counsel was appointed automatically; Montejo had not explicitly requested counsel or affirmatively accepted the counsel appointed to represent him before he submitted to police interrogation.

I agree with the majority's conclusion that the Louisiana Supreme Court's decision, if allowed to stand, "would lead either to an unworkable standard, or to arbitrary and anomalous distinctions between defendants in different States." Neither option is tolerable, and neither is compelled by *Jackson* itself.

Our decision in *Jackson* involved two consolidated cases, both arising in the State of Michigan. Under Michigan law in effect at that time, when a defendant appeared for arraignment the court was required to inform him that counsel would be provided if he was financially needy *and he requested representation*. It was undisputed that the *Jackson* defendants made such a "request" at their arraignment: one by completing an affidavit of indigency, and the other by responding affirmatively to a question posed to him by the court. In neither case, however, was it clear that counsel had actually been appointed at the arraignment. Thus, the defendants' requests for counsel were significant as a matter of state law because they served as evidence that the appointment of counsel had been effectuated even in the absence of proof that defense counsel had actual notice of the appointments.

Unlike Michigan, Louisiana does not require a defendant to make a request in order to receive court-appointed counsel. Consequently, there is no reason to place constitutional significance on the fact that Montejo neither voiced a request for counsel nor affirmatively embraced that appointment *post hoc*. Certainly our decision in *Jackson* did not mandate such an odd rule. If a defendant is entitled to protection from police-initiated interrogation under the Sixth Amendment when he merely *requests* a lawyer, he is even more obviously entitled to such protection when he has *secured* a lawyer. Indeed, we have already recognized as much. See *Michigan* v. *Harvey* (acknowledging that "once a defendant obtains or even requests counsel," *Jackson* alters the waiver analysis); *Patterson* (noting "as a matter of some significance" to the constitutional analysis that defendant had "not retained, or *accepted by appointment*, a lawyer to represent him at the time he was questioned by authorities" (emphasis added)).[14] Once an attorney-client relationship has been established through the appointment or retention of counsel, as a matter of federal law the method by which the relationship was created is irrelevant: The existence of a valid attorney-client relationship provides a defendant with the full constitutional protection afforded by the Sixth Amendment.

II

Today the Court correctly concludes that the Louisiana Supreme Court's holding is "troublesome," "impractical," and "unsound." Instead of reversing the decision of the state court by simply answering the question on which we granted certiorari in a unanimous opinion, however, the majority has decided to change the law. Acting on its own initiative, the majority overrules *Jackson* to correct a "theoretical and doctrinal" problem of its own imagining. A more careful reading of *Jackson* and the Sixth Amendment cases upon which it relied reveals that the rule announced in *Jackson* protects a fundamental right that the Court now dishonors. The majority's decision to overrule *Jackson* rests on its assumption that *Jackson's* protective rule was intended to "prevent police from badgering defendants into changing their minds about their rights," just as the rule adopted in *Edwards v. Arizona* was designed to prevent police from coercing unindicted suspects into revoking their requests for counsel at interrogation. Operating on that limited understanding of the purpose behind *Jackson's* protective rule, the Court concludes that *Jackson* provides no safeguard not already secured by this Court's Fifth Amendment jurisprudence.

The majority's analysis flagrantly misrepresents *Jackson's* underlying rationale and the constitutional interests the decision sought to protect. While it is true that the rule adopted in *Jackson* was patterned after the rule in *Edwards*, the *Jackson* opinion does not even mention the anti-badgering considerations that provide the basis for the Court's decision today. Instead, *Jackson* relied primarily on cases discussing the broad protections guaranteed by the Sixth Amendment right to counsel — not its Fifth Amendment counterpart. *Jackson* emphasized that the purpose of the Sixth Amendment is to " 'protec[t] the unaided layman at critical confrontations with his adversary.' " Underscoring that the commencement of criminal proceedings is a decisive event that transforms a suspect into an accused within the meaning of the Sixth Amendment, we concluded that arraigned defendants are entitled to "at least as much protection" during interrogation as the Fifth Amendment affords unindicted suspects. ("[T]he *difference* between the legal basis for the rule applied in *Edwards* and the Sixth Amendment claim asserted in these cases actually provides additional support for the application of the rule in these circumstances" (emphasis added)). Thus, although the rules adopted in *Edwards* and *Jackson* are similar, *Jackson* did not rely on the reasoning of *Edwards* but remained firmly rooted in the unique protections afforded to the

---

[14] In *Patterson v. Illinois*, we further explained, "[o]nce an accused has a lawyer," "a distinct set of constitutional safeguards aimed at preserving the sanctity of the attorney-client relationship takes effect."

attorney-client relationship by the Sixth Amendment.[15]

Once *Jackson* is placed in its proper Sixth Amendment context, the majority's justifications for overruling the decision crumble. Ordinarily, this Court is hesitant to disturb past precedent and will do so only when a rule has proven "outdated, ill-founded, unworkable, or otherwise legitimately vulnerable to serious reconsideration." While *stare decisis* is not "an inexorable command," we adhere to it as "the preferred course because it promotes the evenhanded, predictable, and consistent development of legal principles, fosters reliance on judicial decisions, and contributes to the actual and perceived integrity of the judicial process."

Most central to the Court's decision to overrule *Jackson*, is its assertion that *Jackson's* " 'reasoning' " — which the Court defines as "the weighing of the [protective] rule's benefits against its costs," — does not justify continued application of the rule it created. The balancing test the Court performs, however, depends entirely on its misunderstanding of *Jackson* as a rule designed to prevent police badgering, rather than a rule designed to safeguard a defendant's right to rely on the assistance of counsel.

Next, in order to reach the conclusion that the *Jackson* rule is unworkable, the Court reframes the relevant inquiry, asking not whether the *Jackson* rule as applied for the past quarter century has proved easily administrable, but instead whether the Louisiana Supreme Court's cramped interpretation of that rule is practically workable. The answer to that question, of course, is no. When framed more broadly, however, the evidence is overwhelming that *Jackson's* simple, bright-line rule has done more to advance effective law enforcement than to undermine it.

In a supplemental brief submitted by lawyers and judges with extensive experience in law enforcement and prosecution, *amici* Larry D. Thompson et al. argue persuasively that *Jackson's* bright-line rule has provided law enforcement officers with clear guidance, allowed prosecutors to quickly and easily assess whether confessions will be admissible in court, and assisted judges in determining whether a defendant's Sixth Amendment rights have been violated by police interrogation. While *amici* acknowledge that "*Jackson* reduces opportunities to interrogate defendants" and "may require exclusion of evidence that could support a criminal conviction," they maintain that "it is a rare case where this rule lets a guilty defendant go free." Notably, these representations are not contradicted by the State of Louisiana or other *amici*, including the United States. See United

---

[15] The majority insists that protection from police badgering is the only purpose the *Jackson* rule can plausibly serve. After all, it asks, from what other evil would the rule guard? There are two obvious answers. First, most narrowly, it protects the defendant from any police-initiated interrogation without notice to his counsel, not just from "badgering" which is not necessarily a part of police questioning. Second, and of prime importance, it assures that any waiver of counsel will be valid. The assistance offered by counsel protects a defendant from surrendering his rights with an insufficient appreciation of what those rights are and how the decision to respond to interrogation might advance or compromise his exercise of those rights throughout the course of criminal proceedings. A lawyer can provide her client with advice regarding the legal and practical options available to him; the potential consequences, both good and bad, of choosing to discuss his case with police; the likely effect of such a conversation on the resolution of the charges against him; and an informed assessment of the best course of action under the circumstances. Such assistance goes far beyond mere protection against police badgering.

States Brief 12 (conceding that the *Jackson* rule has not "resulted in the suppression of significant numbers of statements in federal prosecutions in the past").[4] In short, there is substantial evidence suggesting that *Jackson's* rule is not only workable, but also desirable from the perspective of law enforcement.

Turning to the reliance interests at stake in the case, the Court rejects the interests of criminal defendants with the flippant observation that any who are knowledgeable enough to rely on *Jackson* are too savvy to need its protections, and casts aside the reliance interests of law enforcement on the ground that police and prosecutors remain free to employ the *Jackson* rule if it suits them. Again as a result of its mistaken understanding of the purpose behind *Jackson's* protective rule, the Court fails to identify the real reliance interest at issue in this case: the public's interest in knowing that counsel, once secured, may be reasonably relied upon as a medium between the accused and the power of the State. That interest lies at the heart of the Sixth Amendment's guarantee, and is surely worthy of greater consideration than it is given by today's decision.

Finally, although the Court acknowledges that "antiquity" is a factor that counsels in favor of retaining precedent, it concludes that the fact *Jackson* is "only two decades old" cuts "in favor of abandoning" the rule it established. I would have thought that the 23-year existence of a simple bright-line rule would be a factor that cuts in the other direction.

Despite the fact that the rule established in *Jackson* remains relevant, well grounded in constitutional precedent, and easily administrable, the Court today rejects it *sua sponte*. Such a decision can only diminish the public's confidence in the reliability and fairness of our system of justice.[5]

III

Even if *Jackson* had never been decided, it would be clear that Montejo's Sixth Amendment rights were violated. Today's decision eliminates the rule that "any waiver of Sixth Amendment rights given in a discussion initiated by police is presumed invalid" once a defendant has invoked his right to counsel. Nevertheless, under the undisputed facts of this case, there is no sound basis for concluding that Montejo made a knowing and valid waiver of his Sixth Amendment right to counsel

---

[4] Further supporting the workability of the *Jackson* rule is the fact that it aligns with the professional standards and norms that already govern the behavior of police and prosecutors. Rules of Professional Conduct endorsed by the American Bar Association (ABA) and by every State Bar Association in the country prohibit prosecutors from making direct contact with represented defendants in all but the most limited of circumstances.

[5] In his concurrence, Justice ALITO assumes that my consideration of the rule of *stare decisis* in this case is at odds with the Court's recent rejection of his reliance on that doctrine in his dissent in *Arizona v. Gant*. While I agree that the reasoning in his dissent supports my position in this case, I do not agree with his characterization of our opinion in *Gant*. Contrary to his representation, the Court did not overrule our precedent in *New York v. Belton*. Rather, we affirmed the narrow interpretation of *Belton's* holding adopted by the Arizona Supreme Court, rejecting the broader interpretation adopted by other lower courts that had been roundly criticized by judges and scholars alike. By contrast, in this case the Court flatly overrules *Jackson* — a rule that has drawn virtually no criticism — on its own initiative. The two cases are hardly comparable. If they were, and if Justice ALITO meant what he said in *Gant*, I would expect him to join this opinion.

before acquiescing in police interrogation following his 72-hour hearing. Because police questioned Montejo without notice to, and outside the presence of, his lawyer, the interrogation violated Montejo's right to counsel even under pre-*Jackson* precedent.

Our pre-*Jackson* case law makes clear that "the Sixth Amendment is violated when the State obtains incriminating statements by knowingly circumventing the accused's right to have counsel present in a confrontation between the accused and a state agent." *Moulton.* The Sixth Amendment entitles indicted defendants to have counsel notified of and present during critical confrontations with the state throughout the pretrial process. Given the realities of modern criminal prosecution, the critical proceedings at which counsel's assistance is required more and more often occur outside the courtroom in pretrial proceedings "where the results might well settle the accused's fate and reduce the trial itself to a mere formality." *United States v. Wade*, 388 U.S. 218, 224 (1967).

In *Wade*, for instance, we held that because a postindictment lineup conducted for identification purposes is a critical stage of the criminal proceedings, a defendant and his counsel are constitutionally entitled to notice of the impending lineup. Accordingly, counsel's presence is a "requisite to conduct of the lineup, absent an intelligent waiver." The same reasoning applies to police decisions to interrogate represented defendants. For if the Sixth Amendment entitles an accused to such robust protection during a lineup, surely it entitles him to such protection during a custodial interrogation, when the stakes are as high or higher. Cf. *Spano v. New York*, (Douglas, J., concurring) ("[W]hat use is a defendant's right to effective counsel at every stage of a criminal case if, while he is held awaiting trial, he can be questioned in the absence of counsel until he confesses?").

The Court avoids confronting the serious Sixth Amendment concerns raised by the police interrogation in this case by assuming that Montejo validly waived his Sixth Amendment rights before submitting to interrogation.[6] It does so by summarily concluding that "doctrines ensuring voluntariness of the Fifth Amendment waiver simultaneously ensure the voluntariness of the Sixth Amendment waiver"; thus, because Montejo was given *Miranda* warnings prior to interrogation, his waiver was presumptively valid. Ironically, while the Court faults *Jackson* for blurring the line between this Court's Fifth and Sixth Amendment jurisprudence, it commits the same error by assuming that the *Miranda* warnings given in this case, designed purely to safeguard the Fifth Amendment right against self-incrimination, were somehow adequate to protect Montejo's more robust Sixth Amendment right to counsel.

The majority's cursory treatment of the waiver question rests entirely on the dubious decision in *Patterson*, in which we addressed whether, by providing *Miranda* warnings, police had adequately advised an indicted but unrepresented

---

[6] The majority leaves open the possibility that, on remand, Montejo may argue that his waiver was invalid because police falsely told him he had not been appointed counsel. While such police deception would obviously invalidate any otherwise valid waiver of Montejo's Sixth Amendment rights, Montejo has a strong argument that, given his status as a *represented* criminal defendant, the *Miranda* warnings given to him by police were insufficient to permit him to make a knowing waiver of his Sixth Amendment rights even absent police deception.

defendant of his Sixth Amendment right to counsel. The majority held that "[a]s a general matter . . . an accused who is admonished with the warnings prescribed . . . in *Miranda*, . . . has been sufficiently apprised of the nature of his Sixth Amendment rights, and of the consequences of abandoning those rights." The Court recognized, however, that "because the Sixth Amendment's protection of the attorney-client relationship . . . extends beyond *Miranda's* protection of the Fifth Amendment right to counsel, . . . there will be cases where a waiver which would be valid under *Miranda* will not suffice for Sixth Amendment purposes." This is such a case.

As I observed in *Patterson*, the conclusion that *Miranda* warnings ordinarily provide a sufficient basis for a knowing waiver of the right to counsel rests on the questionable assumption that those warnings make clear to defendants the assistance a lawyer can render during post-indictment interrogation. Because *Miranda* warnings do not hint at the ways in which a lawyer might assist her client during conversations with the police, I remain convinced that the warnings prescribed in *Miranda*, while sufficient to apprise a defendant of his Fifth Amendment right to remain silent, are inadequate to inform an unrepresented, indicted defendant of his Sixth Amendment right to have a lawyer present at all critical stages of a criminal prosecution. The inadequacy of those warnings is even more obvious in the case of a *represented* defendant. While it can be argued that informing an indicted but unrepresented defendant of his right to counsel at least alerts him to the fact that he is entitled to obtain something he does not already possess, providing that same warning to a defendant who has *already* secured counsel is more likely to confound than enlighten.[8] By glibly assuming that that the *Miranda* warnings given in this case were sufficient to ensure Montejo's waiver was both knowing and voluntary, the Court conveniently avoids any comment on the actual advice Montejo received, which did not adequately inform him of his relevant Sixth Amendment rights or alert him to the possible consequences of waiving those rights.

A defendant's decision to forgo counsel's assistance and speak openly with police is a momentous one. Given the high stakes of making such a choice and the potential value of counsel's advice and mediation at that critical stage of the criminal proceedings, it is imperative that a defendant possess "a full awareness of both the nature of the right being abandoned and the consequences of the decision to abandon it" before his waiver is deemed valid. Because the administration of *Miranda* warnings was insufficient to ensure Montejo understood the Sixth Amendment right he was being asked to surrender, the record in this case provides no basis for concluding that Montejo validly waived his right to counsel, even in the

---

[8] With respect to vulnerable defendants, such as juveniles and those with mental impairments of various kinds, *amici* National Association of Criminal Defense Lawyers et al. assert that "[o]verruling *Jackson* would be particularly detrimental . . . because of the confusing instructions regarding counsel that they would receive. At the initial hearing, they would likely learn that an attorney was being appointed for them, In a later custodial interrogation, however, they would be informed in the traditional manner of 'their right to counsel' and right to have counsel 'appointed' if they are indigent, notwithstanding that counsel had already been appointed in open court. These conflicting statements would be confusing to anyone, but would be especially baffling to defendants with mental disabilities or other impairments."

absence of *Jackson's* enhanced protections.

IV

The Court's decision to overrule *Jackson* is unwarranted. Not only does it rests on a flawed doctrinal premise, but the dubious benefits it hopes to achieve are far outweighed by the damage it does to the rule of law and the integrity of the Sixth Amendment right to counsel. Moreover, even apart from the protections afforded by *Jackson*, the police interrogation in this case violated Jesse Montejo's Sixth Amendment right to counsel.

I respectfully dissent.

JUSTICE BREYER, dissenting.

I join JUSTICE STEVENS' dissent except for footnote 5. Although the principles of *stare decisis* are not inflexible, I believe they bind the Court here. I reached a similar conclusion in *Arizona v. Gant*.

QUESTIONS AND NOTES

1. Which opinion was more "revisionist"? Scalia or Stevens? Explain. Is it relevant that Stevens wrote *Jackson* and Scalia was not even on the Court when it was decided?

2. Is there any need for the State to seek a confession after the onset of official judicial proceedings? Recall Justice Jackson's rationale for allowing interrogation at all in the *Watts* case, namely his concerned that society would not be able to solve crimes. Did the *Spano* concurrences and the *Massiah* opinion assume that there was no or little need for interrogation after the parties had become formally adversarial?

3. Do you think that the dissent intends to "imprison a man in his privileges" by precluding a voluntary waiver? Or would a voluntary waiver still be possible under the dissent's view of the case?

4. Is the dispute in this case over whether a person should be able to waive his Sixth Amendment rights without the advice of counsel, or is it over what the standards should be for determining waiver?

5. Was *Jackson* intended to prevent police badgering? Exclusively? Primarily? Partially?

6. Do you think that the dissent's rule "would have constituted a shockingly dramatic restructuring of the balance this Court has traditionally struck between the rights of the defendant and that of larger society? Why? Why not?

7. Do you believe that *Jackson* was a prophylactic rule? Why? Why not?

8. Is (should)the rule (be) less prophylactic where the defendant already has counsel as opposed to merely asking for it?

9. Was it prudent for Stevens to call the *Patterson* case dubious?

10. How important is stare decisis? How important ought it to be?

Chapter 19

VOLUNTARINESS REVISITED

With confessions being vulnerable under both *Miranda* and *Massiah*, it is easy to assume that plain old ordinary coerced or involuntary confessions (*e.g., Brown, Watts, Cooker*, and *Spano*) can be relegated to a legal history course. In fact, that is not the case.

Among other times when voluntariness is relevant are cases in which *Miranda* warnings are not required either because of an emergency (*e.g., Quarles*) or because the defendant was not in custody (*e.g., Mathiason, Perkins*). Other confessions might be deemed involuntary despite *Miranda* because of the police coercion exercised after the warnings were given and a waiver was obtained. Still other confessions might be inadmissible because of either the failure to give *Miranda* warnings, or the disregard of the warnings when given, but the subsequently obtained statements, if otherwise voluntary, could be admitted to impeach the defendant's credibility at trial. *Mincey* raised such a question.

MINCEY v. ARIZONA
437 U.S. 385 (1978)

MR. JUSTICE STEWART delivered the opinion of the Court.

On the afternoon of October 28, 1974, undercover police officer Barry Headricks of the Metropolitan Area Narcotics Squad knocked on the door of an apartment in Tucson, Ariz., occupied by the petitioner, Rufus Mincey. Earlier in the day, Officer Headricks had allegedly arranged to purchase a quantity of heroin from Mincey and had left, ostensibly to obtain money. On his return he was accompanied by nine other plainclothes policemen and a deputy county attorney. The door was opened by John Hodgman, one of three acquaintances of Mincey who were in the living room of the apartment. Officer Headricks slipped inside and moved quickly into the bedroom. Hodgman attempted to slam the door in order to keep the other officers from entering, but was pushed back against the wall. As the police entered the apartment, a rapid volley of shots was heard from the bedroom. Officer Headricks emerged and collapsed on the floor. When other officers entered the bedroom they found Mincey lying on the floor, wounded and semiconscious. Officer Headricks died a few hours later in the hospital.

The petitioner was indicted for murder, assault,[1] and three counts of narcotics offenses. He was tried at a single trial and convicted on all the charges. At his trial and on appeal, he contended that statements used to impeach his credibility were inadmissible because they had not been made voluntarily. The Arizona Supreme Court reversed the murder and assault convictions on state-law grounds,[2] but affirmed the narcotics convictions. It held that Mincey's statements were voluntary.

II

Since there will presumably be a new trial in this case, it is appropriate to consider the petitioner's contention that statements he made from a hospital bed were involuntary, and therefore could not constitutionally be used against him at his trial.

Mincey was brought to the hospital after the shooting and taken immediately to the emergency room where he was examined and treated. He had sustained a wound in his hip, resulting in damage to the sciatic nerve and partial paralysis of his right leg. Tubes were inserted into his throat to help him breathe, and through his nose into his stomach to keep him from vomiting; a catheter was inserted into his bladder. He received various drugs, and a device was attached to his arm so that he could be fed intravenously. He was then taken to the intensive care unit.

At about eight o'clock that evening, Detective Hust of the Tucson Police Department came to the intensive care unit to interrogate him. Mincey was unable to talk because of the tube in his mouth, and so he responded to Detective Hust's questions by writing answers on pieces of paper provided by the hospital.[11] Hust told Mincey he was under arrest for the murder of a police officer, gave him the warnings required by *Miranda*, and began to ask questions about the events that had taken place in Mincey's apartment a few hours earlier. Although Mincey asked repeatedly that the interrogation stop until he could get a lawyer, Hust continued to question him until almost midnight.

Statements made by a defendant in circumstances violating the strictures of *Miranda* are admissible for impeachment if their "trustworthiness . . . satisfies legal standards." *Harris v. New York*, 401 U.S. at 224; *Oregon v. Hass*, 420 U.S. at 722. But *any* criminal trial use against a defendant of his *involuntary* statement is a denial of due process of law, "even though there is ample evidence aside from the confession to support the conviction." If therefore, Mincey's statements to Detective Hust were not "the product of a rational intellect and a free will," his conviction

---

[1] The assault charge was based on the wounding of a person in the living room who was hit by a bullet that came through the wall.

[2] The state appellate court held that the jury had been improperly instructed on criminal intent. It appears from the record in this case that the retrial of the petitioner on the murder and assault charges was stayed by the trial court after certiorari was granted by this Court.

[11] Because of the way in which the interrogation was conducted, the only contemporaneous record consisted of Mincey's written answers. Hust testified that the next day he went over this document and made a few notes to help him reconstruct the conversation. In a written report dated about a week later, Hust transcribed Mincey's answers and added the questions he believed he had asked. It was this written report that was used to cross-examine Mincey at his subsequent trial.

cannot stand. In making this critical determination, we are not bound by the Arizona Supreme Court's holding that the statements were voluntary. Instead, this Court is under a duty to make an independent evaluation of the record.

It is hard to imagine a situation less conducive to the exercise of "a rational intellect and a free will" than Mincey's. He had been seriously wounded just a few hours earlier, and had arrived at the hospital "depressed almost to the point of coma," according to his attending physician. Although he had received some treatment, his condition at the time of Hust's interrogation was still sufficiently serious that he was in the intensive care unit.[14] He complained to Hust that the pain in his leg was "unbearable." He was evidently confused and unable to think clearly about either the events of that afternoon or the circumstances of his interrogation, since some of his written answers were on their face not entirely coherent.[15] Finally, while Mincey was being questioned he was lying on his back on a hospital bed, encumbered by tubes, needles, and breathing apparatus. He was, in short, "at the complete mercy" of Detective Hust, unable to escape or resist the thrust of Hust's interrogation.

In this debilitated and helpless condition, Mincey clearly expressed his wish not to be interrogated. As soon as Hust's questions turned to the details of the afternoon's events, Mincey wrote: "This is all I can say without a lawyer." Hust nonetheless continued to question him, and a nurse who was present suggested it would be best if Mincey answered. Mincey gave unresponsive or uninformative answers to several more questions, and then said again that he did not want to talk without a lawyer. Hust ignored that request and another made immediately thereafter.[16] Indeed, throughout the interrogation Mincey vainly asked Hust to desist. Moreover, he complained several times that he was confused or unable to

---

[14] A nurse testified at the suppression hearing that the device used to aid Mincey's respiration was reserved for "more critical" patients. Moreover, Mincey apparently remained hospitalized for almost a month after the shooting. According to docket entries in the trial court his arraignment was postponed several times because he was still in the hospital; he was not arraigned until November 26, 1974.

[15] For example, two of the answers written by Mincey were: "Do you me Did he give me some money [no]" and "Every body know Every body." And Mincey apparently believed he was being questioned by several different policemen, not Hust alone; although it was Hust who told Mincey he had killed a policeman, later in the interrogation Mincey indicated he thought it was someone else.

[16] In his reconstruction of the interrogation, see n. 11, *supra*, Hust stated that, after he asked Mincey some questions to try to identify one of the other victims, the following ensued:

HUST: . . . What do you remember that happened?

MINCEY: I remember somebody standing over me saying "move nigger, move." I was on the floor beside the bed.

HUST: Do you remember shooting anyone or firing a gun?

MINCEY: *This is all I can say without a lawyer.*

HUST: If you want a lawyer now, I cannot talk to you any longer, however, you don't have to answer any questions if you don't want to. Do you still want to talk to me?

MINCEY: (Shook his head in an affirmative manner.)

HUST: What else can you remember?

MINCEY: I'm going to have to put my head together. There are so many things that I don't remember I. Like how did they get into the apartment?

HUST: How did who get into the apartment?

MINCEY: Police.

think clearly, or that he could answer more accurately the next day. But despite Mincey's entreaties to be let alone, Hust ceased the interrogation only during intervals when Mincey lost consciousness or received medical treatment, and after each such interruption returned relentlessly to his task. The statements at issue were thus the result of virtually continuous questioning of a seriously and painfully wounded man on the edge of consciousness.

There were not present in this case some of the gross abuses that have led the Court in other cases to find confessions involuntary, such as beatings, *see Brown v. Mississippi*, or "truth serums," *see Townsend v. Sain*, 372 U.S. 293. But "the blood of the accused is not the only hallmark of an unconstitutional inquisition." *Blackburn v. Alabama*, 361 U.S. at 206. Determination of whether a statement is involuntary "requires more than a mere color-matching of cases." It requires careful evaluation of all the circumstances of the interrogation.

It is apparent from the record in this case that Mincey's statements were not "the product of his free and rational choice." To the contrary, the undisputed evidence makes clear that Mincey wanted *not* to answer Detective Hust. But Mincey was weakened by pain and shock, isolated from family, friends, and legal counsel, and barely conscious, and his will was simply overborne. Due process of law requires that statements obtained as these were cannot be used in any way against a defendant at his trial.

HUST: Did you sell some narcotics to the guy that was shot?

MINCEY: Do you mean, did he give me some money?

HUST: Yes.

MINCEY: No.

HUST: Did you give him a sample?

MINCEY: What do you call a sample?

HUST: A small amount of drug or narcotic to test?

MINCEY: *I can't say without a lawyer.*

HUST: Did anyone say police or narcs when they came into apartment?

MINCEY: Let me get myself together first. You see, I'm not for sure everything happened so fast. I can't answer at this time because I don't think so, but I can't say for sure. Some questions aren't clear to me at the present time.

HUST: Did you shoot anyone?

MINCEY: *I can't say, I have to see a lawyer.*" (Emphasis supplied.)

While some of Mincey's answers seem relatively responsive to the questions, it must be remembered that Hust added the questions at a later date, with the answers in front of him. *See* n. 11, *supra*. The reliability of Hust's report is uncertain. For example, Hust claimed that immediately after Mincey first expressed a desire to remain silent, Hust said Mincey need not answer any questions but Mincey responded by indicating that he wanted to continue. There is no contemporaneous record supporting Hust's statement that Mincey acted so inconsistently immediately after asserting his wish not to respond further, nor did the nurse who was present during the interrogation corroborate Hust. The Arizona Supreme Court apparently disbelieved Hust in this respect, since it stated that "after *each* indication from [Mincey] that he wanted to consult an attorney or that he wanted to stop answering questions, the police officer continued to question [him]." (emphasis supplied).

III

For the foregoing reasons, the judgment of the Arizona Supreme Court is reversed, and the case is remanded for further proceedings not inconsistent with this opinion.

MR. JUSTICE REHNQUIST, concurring in part and dissenting in part.

I dissent from the Court's holding that Mincey's statements were involuntary and thus inadmissible.

II

The Court in Part II of its opinion advises the Arizona courts on the admissibility of certain statements made by Mincey that are relevant only to the murder charge. Because Mincey's murder conviction was reversed by the Arizona Supreme Court, and it is not certain that there will be a retrial, I would not reach this issue. Since the Court addresses the issue, however, I must register my disagreement with its conclusion.

Before trial, Mincey moved to suppress as involuntary certain statements that he had made while confined in an intensive care unit some hours after the shooting. As the Court acknowledges, the trial court found "with unmistakable clarity" that the statements were voluntary, and the Supreme Court of Arizona, unanimously affirmed. This Court now disagrees and holds that "Mincey's statements were not 'the product of his free and rational choice'" and therefore "cannot be used in any way against [him] at his trial." Because I believe that the Court both has failed to accord the state-court finding the deference that the Court has always found such findings due and also misapplied our past precedents, I dissent.

The Court in this case ignores entirely some evidence of voluntariness and distinguishes away yet other testimony. There can be no discounting that Mincey was seriously wounded and laden down with medical equipment. Mincey was certainly not able to move about and, because of the breathing tube in his mouth, had to answer Detective Hust's questions on paper. But the trial court was certainly not required to find, as the Court would imply, that Mincey was "a seriously and painfully wounded man on the edge of consciousness." Nor is it accurate to conclude that Detective Hust "ceased the interrogation only during intervals when Mincey lost consciousness or received medical treatment, and after each such interruption returned relentlessly to his task."

As the Arizona Supreme Court observed in affirming the trial court's finding of voluntariness, Mincey's nurse

> testified that she had not given [Mincey] any medication and that [he] was alert and able to understand the officer's questions. . . . She said that [Mincey] was in moderate pain but was very cooperative with everyone. The interrogating officer also testified that [Mincey] did not appear to be

under the influence of drugs and that [his] answers were generally responsive to the questions.[1]

The uncontradicted testimony of Detective Hust also reveals a questioning that was far from "relentless." While the interviews took place over a three-hour time span, the interviews were not "very long; probably not more than an hour total for everything." Hust would leave the room whenever Mincey received medical treatment "or if it looked like he was getting a little bit exhausted." According to Detective Hust, Mincey never "los[t] consciousness at any time."

As the Court openly concedes, there were in this case none of the "gross abuses that have led the Court in other cases to find confessions involuntary, such as beatings . . . or 'truth serums.'" Neither is this a case, however, where the defendant's will was "simply overborne" by "mental coercion." As the Supreme Court of Arizona observed, it was the testimony of both Detective Hust and Nurse Graham "that neither mental or physical force nor abuse was used on [Mincey]. . . . Nor were any promises made." According to Mincey's own testimony, he wanted to help Hust "the best I could" and tried to answer each question "to the best of my recollection at the time that this was going on." Mincey did not claim that he felt compelled by Detective Hust to answer the questions propounded.[2]

By all of these standards enunciated in our previous cases, I think the Court today goes too far in substituting its own judgment for the judgment of a trial court and the highest court of a State, both of which decided these disputed issues differently than does this Court, and both of which were a good deal closer to the factual occurrences than is this Court. Admittedly we may not abdicate our duty to decide questions of constitutional law under the guise of wholly remitting to state courts the function of factfinding which is a necessary ingredient of the process of constitutional decision. But the authorities previously cited likewise counsel us against going to the other extreme, and attempting to extract from a cold record bits and pieces of evidence which we then treat as the "facts" of the case. I believe that the trial court was entitled to conclude that, notwithstanding Mincey's medical condition, his statements in the intensive care unit were admissible. The fact that the same court might have been equally entitled to reach the opposite conclusion does not justify this Court's adopting the opposite conclusion.

I therefore dissent from Part II of the Court's opinion.

---

[1] The Supreme Court of Arizona also emphasized "the fact that [Mincey] was able to write his answers in a legible and fairly sensible fashion." The Court concedes that "Mincey's answers seem relatively responsive to the questions," but chooses to ignore this evidence on the ground that the "reliability of Hust's report is uncertain." Despite the contrary impression given by the Court, the Arizona Supreme Court's opinion casts no doubt on the testimony or report of Detective Hust. The Court is thus left solely with its own conclusion as to the reliability of various witnesses based on a re-examination of the record on appeal.

[2] While Mincey asked at several points to see a lawyer, he also expressed his willingness to continue talking to Detective Hust even without a lawyer. As the Court notes, since Mincey's statements were not used as part of the prosecution's case in chief but only in impeachment, any violation of *Miranda* was irrelevant.

QUESTIONS AND NOTES

1. Should the voluntariness issue have been decided in this case? Why? Why not?

2. In your view, should factual doubts in a case such as *Mincey* be resolved against the state or against the defendant? Why?

3. Do you think that Mincey's statements were voluntarily given? Explain.

4. Sometimes, the involuntariness of a confession will not come from the state. In *Connelly*, the Court explored the question of how much of a difference that should make.

COLORADO v. CONNELLY
479 U.S. 157 (1986)

CHIEF JUSTICE REHNQUIST delivered the opinion of the Court.

In this case, the Supreme Court of Colorado held that the United States Constitution requires a court to suppress a confession when the mental state of the defendant, at the time he made the confession, interfered with his "rational intellect" and his "free will." Because this decision seemed to conflict with prior holdings of this Court, we granted certiorari. We conclude that the admissibility of this kind of statement is governed by state rules of evidence, rather than by our previous decisions regarding coerced confessions and *Miranda* waivers. We therefore reverse.

I

On August 18, 1983, Officer Patrick Anderson of the Denver Police Department was in uniform, working in an off-duty capacity in downtown Denver. Respondent Francis Connelly approached Officer Anderson and, without any prompting, stated that he had murdered someone and wanted to talk about it. Anderson immediately advised respondent that he had the right to remain silent, that anything he said could be used against him in court, and that he had the right to an attorney prior to any police questioning. *See Miranda.* Respondent stated that he understood these rights but he still wanted to talk about the murder. Understandably bewildered by this confession, Officer Anderson asked respondent several questions. Connelly denied that he had been drinking, denied that he had been taking any drugs, and stated that, in the past, he had been a patient in several mental hospitals. Officer Anderson again told Connelly that he was under no obligation to say anything. Connelly replied that it was "all right," and that he would talk to Officer Anderson because his conscience had been bothering him. To Officer Anderson, respondent appeared to understand fully the nature of his acts.

Shortly thereafter, Homicide Detective Stephen Antuna arrived. Respondent was again advised of his rights, and Detective Antuna asked him "what he had on his mind." Respondent answered that he had come all the way from Boston to confess to the murder of Mary Ann Junta, a young girl whom he had killed in

Denver sometime during November 1982. Respondent was taken to police head-quarters, and a search of police records revealed that the body of an unidentified female had been found in April 1983. Respondent openly detailed his story to Detective Antuna and Sergeant Thomas Haney, and readily agreed to take the officers to the scene of the killing. Under Connelly's sole direction, the two officers and respondent proceeded in a police vehicle to the location of the crime. Respondent pointed out the exact location of the murder. Throughout this episode, Detective Antuna perceived no indication whatsoever that respondent was suffering from any kind of mental illness.

Respondent was held overnight. During an interview with the public defender's office the following morning, he became visibly disoriented. He began giving confused answers to questions, and for the first time, stated that "voices" had told him to come to Denver and that he had followed the directions of these voices in confessing. Respondent was sent to a state hospital for evaluation. He was initially found incompetent to assist in his own defense. By March 1984, however, the doctors evaluating respondent determined that he was competent to proceed to trial.

At a preliminary hearing, respondent moved to suppress all of his statements. Dr. Jeffrey Metzner, a psychiatrist employed by the state hospital, testified that respondent was suffering from chronic schizophrenia and was in a psychotic state at least as of August 17, 1983, the day before he confessed. Metzner's interviews with respondent revealed that respondent was following the "voice of God." This voice instructed respondent to withdraw money from the bank, to buy an airplane ticket, and to fly from Boston to Denver. When respondent arrived from Boston, God's voice became stronger and told respondent either to confess to the killing or to commit suicide. Reluctantly following the command of the voices, respondent approached Officer Anderson and confessed.

Dr. Metzner testified that, in his expert opinion, respondent was experiencing "command hallucinations." This condition interfered with respondent's "volitional abilities; that is, his ability to make free and rational choices." Dr. Metzner further testified that Connelly's illness did not significantly impair his cognitive abilities. Thus, respondent understood the rights he had when Officer Anderson and Detective Antuna advised him that he need not speak. Dr. Metzner admitted that the "voices" could in reality be Connelly's interpretation of his own guilt, but explained that in his opinion, Connelly's psychosis motivated his confession.

II

Respondent relies on *Blackburn v. Alabama*, 361 U.S. 199 (1960), and *Townsend v. Sain*, 372 U.S. 293 (1963), for the proposition that the "deficient mental condition of the defendants in those cases was sufficient to render their confessions involuntary." But respondent's reading of *Blackburn* and *Townsend* ignores the integral element of police overreaching present in both cases. In *Blackburn*, the Court found that the petitioner was probably insane at the time of his confession and the police learned during the interrogation that he had a history of mental problems. The police exploited this weakness with coercive tactics: "the eight-to nine-hour sustained interrogation in a tiny room which was upon occasion literally filled with police officers; the absence of Blackburn's friends, relatives, or legal counsel; [and] the composition of the confession by the Deputy Sheriff rather than by Blackburn." These tactics supported a finding that the confession was involuntary. Indeed, the Court specifically condemned police activity that "wrings a confession out of an accused against his will." *Townsend* presented a similar instance of police wrongdoing. In that case, a police physician had given Townsend a drug with truth-serum properties. The subsequent confession, obtained by officers who knew that Townsend had been given drugs, was held involuntary. These two cases demonstrate that while mental condition is surely relevant to an individual's susceptibility to police coercion, mere examination of the confessant's state of mind can never conclude the due process inquiry.

Our "involuntary confession" jurisprudence is entirely consistent with the settled law requiring some sort of "state action" to support a claim of violation of the Due Process Clause of the Fourteenth Amendment. The Colorado trial court, of course, found that the police committed no wrongful acts, and that finding has been neither challenged by respondent nor disturbed by the Supreme Court of Colorado. The latter court, however, concluded that sufficient state action was present by virtue of the admission of the confession into evidence in a court of the State.

The difficulty with the approach of the Supreme Court of Colorado is that it fails to recognize the essential link between coercive activity of the State, on the one hand, and a resulting confession by a defendant, on the other. The flaw in respondent's constitutional argument is that it would expand our previous line of "voluntariness" cases into a far-ranging requirement that courts must divine a defendant's motivation for speaking or acting as he did even though there be no claim that governmental conduct coerced his decision.

The most outrageous behavior by a private party seeking to secure evidence against a defendant does not make that evidence inadmissible under the Due Process Clause. *See Walter v. United States*, 447 U.S. 649, 656 (1980); *Coolidge v. New Hampshire*, 403 U.S. 443, 487–488 (1971); *Burdeau v. McDowell*, 256 U.S. 465, 476 (1921). We have also observed that "[j]urists and scholars uniformly have recognized that the exclusionary rule imposes a substantial cost on the societal interest in law enforcement by its proscription of what concededly is relevant evidence." *United States v. Janis*, 428 U.S. 433, 448–449 (1976). *See also United States v. Havens*, 446 U.S. 620, 627 (1980); *Calandra*, 414 U.S. 338 (1974). Moreover, suppressing respondent's statements would serve absolutely no purpose in enforcing constitutional guarantees. The purpose of excluding evidence seized in violation of the Constitution is to substantially deter future violations of the Constitution. *See Leon*. Only if we were to establish a brand new constitutional right — the right of a criminal defendant to confess to his crime only when totally rational and properly motivated — could respondent's present claim be sustained.

We have previously cautioned against expanding "currently applicable exclusionary rules by erecting additional barriers to placing truthful and probative evidence before state juries . . . ." We abide by that counsel now. "[T]he central purpose of a criminal trial is to decide the factual question of the defendant's guilt or innocence," *Delaware v. Van Arsdall*, 475 U.S. 673, 681 (1986), and while we have previously held that exclusion of evidence may be necessary to protect constitutional guarantees, both the necessity for the collateral inquiry and the exclusion of evidence deflect a criminal trial from its basic purpose. Respondent would now have us require sweeping inquiries into the state of mind of a criminal defendant who has confessed, inquiries quite divorced from any coercion brought to bear on the defendant by the State. We think the Constitution rightly leaves this sort of inquiry to be resolved by state laws governing the admission of evidence and erects no standard of its own in this area. A statement rendered by one in the condition of respondent might be proved to be quite unreliable, but this is a matter to be governed by the evidentiary laws of the forum, and not by the Due Process Clause of the Fourteenth Amendment. "The aim of the requirement of due process is not to exclude presumptively false evidence, but to prevent fundamental unfairness in the use of evidence, whether true or false." *Lisenba v. California*, 314 U.S. 219, 236 (1941).

We hold that coercive police activity is a necessary predicate to the finding that a confession is not "voluntary" within the meaning of the Due Process Clause of the Fourteenth Amendment. We also conclude that the taking of respondent's statements, and their admission into evidence, constitute no violation of that Clause.

IV

The judgment of the Supreme Court of Colorado is accordingly reversed, and the cause is remanded for further proceedings not inconsistent with this opinion.

JUSTICE STEVENS, concurring in the judgment in part and dissenting in part.

Respondent made incriminatory statements both before and after he was handcuffed and taken into custody. The only question presented by the Colorado District Attorney in his certiorari petition concerned the admissibility of respondent's precustodial statements. I agree with the State of Colorado that the United States Constitution does not require suppression of those statements, but in reaching that conclusion, unlike the Court, I am perfectly willing to accept the state trial court's finding that the statements were involuntary.

The state trial court found that, in view of the "overwhelming evidence presented by the Defense," the prosecution did not meet its burden of demonstrating that respondent's initial statements to Officer Anderson were voluntary. Nevertheless, in my opinion, the use of these involuntary precustodial statements does not violate the Fifth Amendment because they were not the product of state compulsion. Although they may well be so unreliable that they could not support a conviction, at this stage of the proceeding I could not say that they have no probative force whatever. The fact that the statements were involuntary — just as the product of Lady Macbeth's nightmare was involuntary[2] — does not mean that their use for

---

[2] What, will these hands ne'er be clean?

      Here's the smell of the blood still: all the perfumes of Arabia will not sweeten this little hand.

W. SHAKESPEARE, MACBETH, Act V, scene 1, lines 41, 47.

      Lady Macbeth's "eyes are open," "but their sense is shut."

whatever evidentiary value they may have is fundamentally unfair or a denial of due process.

Accordingly, I concur in the judgment insofar as it applies to respondent's precustodial statements.

JUSTICE BRENNAN, with whom JUSTICE MARSHALL joins, dissenting.

Today the Court denies Mr. Connelly his fundamental right to make a vital choice with a sane mind, involving a determination that could allow the State to deprive him of liberty or even life. This holding is unprecedented: "Surely in the present stage of our civilization a most basic sense of justice is affronted by the spectacle of incarcerating a human being upon the basis of a statement he made while insane . . . ." *Blackburn.* Because I believe that the use of a mentally ill person's involuntary confession is antithetical to the notion of fundamental fairness embodied in the Due Process Clause, I dissent.

I

The respondent's seriously impaired mental condition is clear on the record of this case. At the time of his confession, Mr. Connelly suffered from a "longstanding severe mental disorder," diagnosed as chronic paranoid schizophrenia. He had been hospitalized for psychiatric reasons five times prior to his confession; his longest hospitalization lasted for seven months. Mr. Connelly heard imaginary voices and saw nonexistent objects. He believed that his father was God, and that he was a reincarnation of Jesus.

At the time of his confession, Mr. Connelly's mental problems included "grandiose and delusional thinking." He had a known history of "thought withdrawal and insertion." Although physicians had treated Mr. Connelly "with a wide variety of medications in the past including antipsychotic medications," he had not taken any antipsychotic medications for at least six months prior to his confession. Following his arrest, Mr. Connelly initially was found incompetent to stand trial because the court-appointed psychiatrist, Dr. Metzner, "wasn't very confident that he could consistently relate accurate information." Dr. Metzner testified that Mr. Connelly was unable "to make free and rational choices" due to auditory hallucinations: "[W]hen he was read his *Miranda* rights, he probably had the capacity to know that he was being read his *Miranda* rights [but] he wasn't able to use that information because of the command hallucinations that he had experienced." He achieved competency to stand trial only after six months of hospitalization and treatment with antipsychotic and sedative medications.

The state trial court found that the "overwhelming evidence presented by the Defense" indicated that the prosecution did not meet its burden of demonstrating by a preponderance of the evidence that the initial statement to Officer Anderson was voluntary. While the court found no police misconduct, it held:

[T]here's no question that the Defendant did not exercise free will in choosing to talk to the police. He exercised a choice both [sic] of which were mandated by auditory hallucination, had no basis in reality, and were the product of a psychotic break with reality. The Defendant at the time of the confession had absolutely in the Court's estimation no volition or choice to make.

The trial court also held that the State had not shown by clear and convincing evidence that the defendant had waived his *Miranda* right to counsel and to self-incrimination "voluntarily, knowingly and intelligently."

The Supreme Court of Colorado affirmed after evaluating "the totality of circumstances" surrounding the unsolicited confession and the waiver of *Miranda* rights.

II

The absence of police wrongdoing should not, by itself, determine the voluntariness of a confession by a mentally ill person. The requirement that a confession be voluntary reflects a recognition of the importance of free will and of reliability in determining the admissibility of a confession, and thus demands an inquiry into the totality of the circumstances surrounding the confession.

A

Today's decision restricts the application of the term "involuntary" to those confessions obtained by police coercion. Confessions by mentally ill individuals or by persons coerced by parties other than police officers are now considered "voluntary." The Court's failure to recognize all forms of involuntariness or coercion as antithetical to due process reflects a refusal to acknowledge free will as a value of constitutional consequence. But due process derives much of its meaning from a conception of fundamental fairness that emphasizes the right to make vital choices voluntarily.

This Court's assertion that we would be required "to establish a brand new constitutional right" to recognize the respondent's claim ignores 200 years of constitutional jurisprudence.[1] As we stated in *Culombe v. Connecticut*, 367 U.S. 568 (1961):

> The ultimate test remains that which has been the only clearly established test in Anglo-American courts for two hundred years: the test of voluntariness. Is the confession the product of an essentially free and unconstrained choice by its maker? . . . The line of distinction is that at which governing self-direction is lost *and compulsion, of whatever nature or however infused*, propels or helps to propel the confession.

---

[1] *Cf. Bram v. United States*, 168 U.S. 532, 547–548 (1897) (reviewing the "rule [of law] in England at the time of the adoption of the Constitution and of the Fifth Amendment" and citing W. HAWKINS, PLEAS OF THE CROWN: "[a] confession, therefore, whether made upon an official examination or *in discourse with private persons*, which is obtained from a defendant, either by the flattery of hope, or by the impressions of fear, however slightly the emotions may be implanted, . . . is not admissible evidence; for the law will not suffer a prisoner to be made the deluded instrument of his own conviction") (emphasis added).

(emphasis added). A true commitment to fundamental fairness requires that the inquiry be "not whether the conduct of state officers in obtaining the confession is shocking, but whether the confession was 'free and voluntary' . . . ." *Malloy v. Hogan*, 378 U.S. at 7.

This Court abandons this precedent in favor of the view that only confessions rendered involuntary by some state action are inadmissible, and that the only relevant form of state action is police conduct. But even if state action is required, police overreaching is not its only relevant form. The Colorado Supreme Court held that the trial court's admission of the involuntary confession into evidence is also state action. The state court's analysis is consistent with *Brown v. Mississippi* on which this Court so heavily relies. *Brown*, a case involving the use of confessions at trial, makes clear that "[t]he due process clause requires 'that state action, *whether through one agency or another*, shall be consistent with the fundamental principles of liberty and justice which lie at the base of all our civil and political institutions.' " Police conduct constitutes but one form of state action. "The objective of deterring improper police conduct is only part of the larger objective of safeguarding the integrity of our adversary system."

The only logical "flaw" which the Court detects in this argument is that it would require courts to "divine a defendant's motivation for speaking or acting as he did even though there be no claim that governmental conduct coerced his decision." Such a criticism, however, ignores the fact that we have traditionally examined the totality of the circumstances, including the motivation and competence of the defendant, in determining whether a confession is voluntary. Even today's Court admits that "as interrogators have turned to more subtle forms of psychological persuasion, courts have found the mental condition of the defendant a more significant factor in the 'voluntariness' calculus." The Court's holding that involuntary confessions are only those procured through police misconduct is thus inconsistent with the Court's historical insistence that only confessions reflecting an exercise of free will be admitted into evidence.

B

Since the Court redefines voluntary confessions to include confessions by mentally ill individuals, the reliability of these confessions becomes a central concern. A concern for reliability is inherent in our criminal justice system, which relies upon accusatorial rather than inquisitorial practices. While an inquisitorial system prefers obtaining confessions from criminal defendants, an accusatorial system must place its faith in determinations of "guilt by evidence independently and freely secured." In *Escobedo*, we justified our reliance upon accusatorial practices:

> We have learned the lesson of history, ancient and modern, that a system of criminal law enforcement which comes to depend on the "confession" will, in the long run, be less reliable and more subject to abuses than a system which depends on extrinsic evidence independently secured through skillful investigation.

Our distrust for reliance on confessions is due, in part, to their decisive impact upon the adversarial process. Triers of fact accord confessions such heavy weight in their determinations that "the introduction of a confession makes the other aspects of a trial in court superfluous, and the real trial, for all practical purposes, occurs when the confession is obtained."

Because the admission of a confession so strongly tips the balance against the defendant in the adversarial process, we must be especially careful about a confession's reliability. We have to date not required a finding of reliability for involuntary confessions only because *all* such confessions have been excluded upon a finding of involuntariness, regardless of reliability.[4] The Court's adoption today of a restrictive definition of an "involuntary" confession will require heightened scrutiny of a confession's reliability.

The instant case starkly highlights the danger of admitting a confession by a person with a severe mental illness. The trial court made no findings concerning the reliability of Mr. Connelly's involuntary confession, since it believed that the confession was excludable on the basis of involuntariness. However, the overwhelming evidence in the record points to the unreliability of Mr. Connelly's delusional mind. Mr. Connelly was found incompetent to stand trial because he was unable to relate accurate information, and the court-appointed psychiatrist indicated that Mr. Connelly was actively hallucinating and exhibited delusional thinking at the time of his confession. The Court, in fact, concedes that "[a] statement rendered by one in the condition of respondent might be proved to be quite unreliable . . . ."

Moreover, the record is barren of any corroboration of the mentally ill defendant's confession. No physical evidence links the defendant to the alleged crime. Police did not identify the alleged victim's body as the woman named by the defendant. Mr. Connelly identified the alleged scene of the crime, but it has not been verified that the unidentified body was found there or that a crime actually occurred there. There is not a shred of competent evidence in this record linking the defendant to the charged homicide. There is only Mr. Connelly's confession.

Minimum standards of due process should require that the trial court find substantial indicia of reliability, on the basis of evidence extrinsic to the confession itself, before admitting the confession of a mentally ill person into evidence. I would require the trial court to make such a finding on remand. To hold otherwise allows the State to imprison and possibly to execute a mentally ill defendant based solely upon an inherently unreliable confession.

QUESTIONS AND NOTES

1. Should the Constitution be concerned about the admission of an inaccurate confession? Is it satisfactory to say that it is merely a matter of state law?

2. Is the quote from *Lisenba* ("The aim of the requirement of due process is not to exclude presumptively false evidence, but to prevent fundamental unfairness in

---

[4] Prior to establishing this rule excluding all involuntary confessions, we held the view that the Fifth Amendment, at bottom, served as "a guarantee against conviction on inherently untrustworthy evidence." *Stein v. New York*, 346 U.S. 156, 192 (1953).

the use of evidence whether true or false.") decisive in answering Question 1?

3. Is it significant that most of the Court's exclusionary rule cites are Fourth Amendment cases? How? Why?

4. How should *Connelly* have been resolved? Why?

PROBLEM

On the morning of December 18, 1992, two brothers were shot and killed in their Houston home. There were no witnesses to the murders, but a neighbor who heard gunshots saw someone run out of the house and speed away in a dark-colored car. Police recovered six shotgun shell casings at the scene. The investigation led police to petitioner, who had been a guest at a party the victims hosted the night before they were killed. Police visited petitioner at his home, where they saw a dark blue car in the driveway. He agreed to hand over his shotgun for ballistics testing and to accompany police to the station for questioning.

Petitioner's interview with the police lasted approximately one hour. All agree that the interview was noncustodial, and the parties litigated this case on the assumption that he was not read *Miranda* warnings. For most of the interview, petitioner answered the officer's questions. But when asked whether his shotgun "would match the shells recovered at the scene of the murder," petitioner declined to answer. Instead, petitioner "[l]ooked down at the floor, shuffled his feet, bit his bottom lip, cl[e]nched his hands in his lap, [and] began to tighten up." After a few moments of silence, the officer asked additional questions, which petitioner answered.

Following the interview, police arrested petitioner on outstanding traffic warrants. Prosecutors soon concluded that there was insufficient evidence to charge him with the murders, and he was released. A few days later, police obtained a statement from a man who said he had heard petitioner confess to the killings. On the strength of that additional evidence, prosecutors decided to charge petitioner, but by this time he had absconded. In 2007, police discovered petitioner living in the Houston area under an assumed name.

Petitioner did not testify at trial. Over his objection, prosecutors used his reaction to the officer's question during the 1993 interview as evidence of his guilt. The jury found petitioner guilty, and he received a 20-year sentence. On direct appeal to the Court of Appeals of Texas, petitioner argued that prosecutors' use of his silence as part of their case in chief violated the Fifth Amendment. The Court of Appeals rejected that argument, reasoning that petitioner's prearrest, pre-*Miranda* silence was not "compelled" within the meaning of the Fifth Amendment. 369 S.W.3d 176 (Tex. Crim. App. 2012).

How should the Supreme Court resolve this case? For the Court's resolution, see *Salinas v. Texas*, 570 U.S. ___, 133 S. Ct. 2174 (2013).

Perhaps the most interesting post-*Miranda* case in regard to coerced confessions is *Fulminante*.

ARIZONA v. FULMINANTE
499 U.S. 279 (1991)

JUSTICE WHITE delivered the opinion of the Court.

The Arizona Supreme Court ruled in this case that respondent Oreste Fulminante's confession, received in evidence at his trial for murder, had been coerced and that its use against him was barred by the Fifth and Fourteenth Amendments to the United States Constitution. The court also held that the harmless-error rule could not be used to save the conviction. We affirm the judgment of the Arizona court, although for different reasons than those upon which that court relied.

I

Early in the morning of September 14, 1982, Fulminante called the Mesa, Arizona, Police Department to report that his 11-year-old stepdaughter, Jeneane Michelle Hunt, was missing. He had been caring for Jeneane while his wife, Jeneane's mother, was in the hospital. Two days later, Jeneane's body was found in the desert east of Mesa. She had been shot twice in the head at close range with a large caliber weapon, and a ligature was around her neck. Because of the decomposed condition of the body, it was impossible to tell whether she had been sexually assaulted.

Fulminante's statements to police concerning Jeneane's disappearance and his relationship with her contained a number of inconsistencies, and he became a suspect in her killing. When no charges were filed against him, Fulminante left Arizona for New Jersey. Fulminante was later convicted in New Jersey on federal charges of possession of a firearm by a felon.

Fulminante was incarcerated in the Ray Brook Federal Correctional Institution in New York. There he became friends with another inmate, Anthony Sarivola, then serving a 60-day sentence for extortion. The two men came to spend several hours a day together. Sarivola, a former police officer, had been involved in loansharking for organized crime but then became a paid informant for the Federal Bureau of Investigation. While at Ray Brook, he masqueraded as an organized crime figure. After becoming friends with Fulminante, Sarivola heard a rumor that Fulminante was suspected of killing a child in Arizona. Sarivola then raised the subject with Fulminante in several conversations, but Fulminante repeatedly denied any involvement in Jeneane's death. During one conversation, he told Sarivola that Jeneane had been killed by bikers looking for drugs; on another occasion, he said he did not know what had happened. Sarivola passed this information on to an agent of the Federal Bureau of Investigation, who instructed Sarivola to find out more.

Sarivola learned more one evening in October 1983, as he and Fulminante walked together around the prison track. Sarivola said that he knew Fulminante was "starting to get some tough treatment and whatnot" from other inmates because of the rumor. Sarivola offered to protect Fulminante from his fellow inmates, but told him, " 'You have to tell me about it,' you know. I mean, in other words, 'For me to give you any help.' " Fulminante then admitted to Sarivola that he had driven

Jeneane to the desert on his motorcycle, where he choked her, sexually assaulted her, and made her beg for her life, before shooting her twice in the head.

Sarivola was released from prison in November 1983. Fulminante was released the following May, only to be arrested the next month for another weapons violation. On September 4, 1984, Fulminante was indicted in Arizona for the first-degree murder of Jeneane.

Prior to trial, Fulminante moved to suppress the statement he had given Sarivola in prison, as well as a second confession he had given to Donna Sarivola, then Anthony Sarivola's fiancée and later his wife, following his May 1984 release from prison. He asserted that the confession to Sarivola was coerced, and that the second confession was the "fruit" of the first. Following the hearing, the trial court denied the motion to suppress, specifically finding that, based on the stipulated facts, the confessions were voluntary. The State introduced both confessions as evidence at trial, and on December 19, 1985, Fulminante was convicted of Jeneane's murder. He was subsequently sentenced to death.

Fulminante appealed, arguing, among other things, that his confession to Sarivola was the product of coercion and that its admission at trial violated his rights to due process under the Fifth and Fourteenth Amendments of the United States Constitution. After considering the evidence at trial as well as the stipulated facts before the trial court on the motion to suppress, the Arizona Supreme Court held that the confession was coerced, but initially determined that the admission of the confession at trial was harmless error, because of the overwhelming nature of the evidence against Fulminante. Upon Fulminante's motion for reconsideration, however, the court ruled that this Court's precedent precluded the use of the harmless-error analysis in the case of a coerced confession. The court therefore reversed the conviction and ordered that Fulminante be retried without the use of the confession to Sarivola.[1] Because of differing views in the state and federal courts over whether the admission at trial of a coerced confession is subject to a harmless-error analysis, we granted the State's petition for certiorari. Although a majority of this Court finds that such a confession is subject to a harmless-error analysis, for the reasons set forth below, we affirm the judgment of the Arizona court.

II

We deal first with the State's contention that the court below erred in holding Fulminante's confession to have been coerced. The State argues that it is the totality of the circumstances that determines whether Fulminante's confession was coerced, but contends that rather than apply this standard, the Arizona court applied a "but for" test, under which the court found that but for the promise given

---

[1] In its initial opinion, the Arizona Supreme Court had determined that the second confession, to Donna Sarivola was not the "fruit of the poisonous tree," because it was made six months after the confession to Sarivola; it occurred after Fulminante's need for protection from Sarivola presumably had ended; and it took place in the course of a casual conversation with someone who was not an agent of the State. This court adhered to this determination in its supplemental opinion. This aspect of the Arizona Supreme Court's decision is not challenged here.

by Sarivola, Fulminante would not have confessed. In support of this argument, the State points to the Arizona court's reference to *Bram v. United States*, 168 U.S. 532 (1897). Although the Court noted in *Bram* that a confession cannot be obtained by "any direct or implied promises, however slight, nor by the exertion of any improper influence," it is clear this passage from *Bram*, which under current precedent does not state the standard for determining the voluntariness of a confession, was not relied on by the Arizona court in reaching its conclusion. Rather, the court cited this language as part of a longer quotation from an Arizona case which accurately described the State's burden of proof for establishing voluntariness. Indeed, the Arizona Supreme Court stated that a "determination regarding the voluntariness of a confession . . . must be viewed in a totality of the circumstances," and under that standard plainly found that Fulminante's statement to Sarivola had been coerced.

In applying the totality of the circumstances test to determine that the confession to Sarivola was coerced, the Arizona Supreme Court focused on a number of relevant facts. First, the court noted that "because [Fulminante] was an alleged child murderer, he was in danger of physical harm at the hands of other inmates." In addition, Sarivola was aware that Fulminante had been receiving "rough treatment from the guys." Using his knowledge of these threats, Sarivola offered to protect Fulminante in exchange for a confession to Jeneane's murder, and "[i]n response to Sarivola's offer of protection, [Fulminante] confessed." Agreeing with Fulminante that "Sarivola's promise was 'extremely coercive,'" the Arizona Court declared: "[T]he confession was obtained as a direct result of extreme coercion and was tendered in the belief that the defendant's life was in jeopardy if he did not confess. This is a true coerced confession in every sense of the word."[2]

We normally give great deference to the factual findings of the state court. Nevertheless, "the ultimate issue of 'voluntariness' is a legal question requiring independent federal determination."

Although the question is a close one, we agree with the Arizona Supreme Court's conclusion that Fulminante's confession was coerced.[3] The Arizona Supreme Court found a credible threat of physical violence unless Fulminante confessed. Our cases have made clear that a finding of coercion need not depend upon actual violence by

---

[2] There are additional facts in the record, not relied upon by the Arizona Supreme Court, which also support a finding of coercion. Fulminante possesses low average to average intelligence; he dropped out of school in the fourth grade. He is short in stature and slight in build. Although he had been in prison before, he had not always adapted well to the stress of prison life. While incarcerated at the age of 26, he had "felt threatened by the [prison] population," and he therefore requested that he be placed in protective custody. Once there, however, he was unable to cope with the isolation and was admitted to a psychiatric hospital. The Court has previously recognized that factors such as these are relevant in determining whether a defendant's will has been overborne. In addition, we note that Sarivola's position as Fulminante's friend might well have made the latter particularly susceptible to the former's entreaties. *See Spano.*

[3] Our prior cases have used the terms "coerced confession" and "involuntary confession" interchangeably "by way of convenient shorthand." We use the former term throughout this opinion, as that is the term used by the Arizona Supreme Court.

a government agent;[4] a credible threat is sufficient. As in *Payne v. Arkansas*, 356 U.S. 560 (1958), where the Court found that a confession was coerced because the interrogating police officer had promised that if the accused confessed, the officer would protect the accused from an angry mob outside the jailhouse door, so too here, the Arizona Supreme Court found that it was fear of physical violence, absent protection from his friend (and Government agent) Sarivola, which motivated Fulminante to confess. Accepting the Arizona court's finding, permissible on this record, that there was a credible threat of physical violence, we agree with its conclusion that Fulminante's will was overborne in such a way as to render his confession the product of coercion.

III

[Justice White, speaking only for Justices Marshall, Blackmun, and Stevens, would have held that admission of a coerced confession can *never* be harmless error. However, they were outvoted by the other five Justices on this point.]

IV

Since five Justices have determined that harmless error analysis applies to coerced confessions, it becomes necessary to evaluate under that ruling the admissibility of Fulminante's confession to Sarivola. *Chapman v. California*, 386 U.S. at 24, made clear that "before a federal constitutional error can be held harmless, the court must be able to declare a belief that it was harmless beyond a reasonable doubt." The Court has the power to review the record *de novo* in order to determine an error's harmlessness. In so doing, it must be determined whether the State has met its burden of demonstrating that the admission of the confession to Sarivola did not contribute to Fulminante's conviction. Five of us are of the view that the State has not carried its burden and accordingly affirm the judgment of the court below reversing petitioner's conviction.

A confession is like no other evidence. Indeed, "the defendant's own confession is probably the most probative and damaging evidence that can be admitted against him. . . . [T]he admissions of a defendant come from the actor himself, the most knowledgeable and unimpeachable source of information about his past conduct. Certainly, confessions have profound impact on the jury, so much so that we may justifiably doubt its ability to put them out of mind even if told to do so." While some statements by a defendant may concern isolated aspects of the crime or may be incriminating only when linked to other evidence, a full confession in which the defendant discloses the motive for and means of the crime may tempt the jury to rely upon that evidence alone in reaching its decision. In the case of a coerced confession such as that given by Fulminante to Sarivola, the risk that the confession is unreliable, coupled with the profound impact that the confession has upon the jury, requires a reviewing court to exercise extreme caution before determining that the admission of the confession at trial was harmless.

---

[4] The parties agree that Sarivola acted as an agent of the Government when he questioned Fulminante about the murder and elicited the confession.

In the Arizona Supreme Court's initial opinion, in which it determined that harmless-error analysis could be applied to the confession, the court found that the admissible second confession to Donna Sarivola rendered the first confession to Anthony Sarivola cumulative. The court also noted that circumstantial physical evidence concerning the wounds, the ligature around Jeneane's neck, the location of the body, and the presence of motorcycle tracks at the scene corroborated the second confession. The court concluded that "due to the overwhelming evidence adduced from the second confession, if there had not been a first confession, the jury would still have had the same basic evidence to convict" Fulminante.

We have a quite different evaluation of the evidence. Our review of the record leads us to conclude that the State has failed to meet its burden of establishing, beyond a reasonable doubt, that the admission of Fulminante's confession to Anthony Sarivola was harmless error. Three considerations compel this result.

First, the transcript discloses that both the trial court and the State recognized that a successful prosecution depended on the jury believing the two confessions. Absent the confessions, it is unlikely that Fulminante would have been prosecuted at all, because the physical evidence from the scene and other circumstantial evidence would have been insufficient to convict. Indeed, no indictment was filed until nearly two years after the murder.[8] Although the police had suspected Fulminante from the beginning, as the prosecutor acknowledged in his opening statement to the jury, "[W]hat brings us to Court, what makes this case fileable, and prosecutable and triable is that later, Mr. Fulminante confesses this crime to Anthony Sarivola and later, to Donna Sarivola, his wife." After trial began, during a renewed hearing on Fulminante's motion to suppress, the trial court opined, "You know, I think from what little I know about this trial, the character of this man [Sarivola] for truthfulness or untruthfulness and his credibility is the centerpiece of this case, is it not?," to which the prosecutor responded, "It's very important, there's no doubt." Finally, in his closing argument, the prosecutor prefaced his discussion of the two confessions by conceding, "[W]e have a lot of [circumstantial] evidence that indicates that this is our suspect, this is the fellow that did it, but it's a little short as far as saying that it's proof that he actually put the gun to the girl's head and killed her. So it's a little short of that. We recognize that."

Second, the jury's assessment of the confession to Donna Sarivola could easily have depended in large part on the presence of the confession to Anthony Sarivola. Absent the admission at trial of the first confession, the jurors might have found Donna Sarivola's story unbelievable. Fulminante's confession to Donna Sarivola allegedly occurred in May 1984, on the day he was released from Ray Brook, as she and Anthony Sarivola drove Fulminante from New York to Pennsylvania. Donna Sarivola testified that Fulminante, whom she had never before met, confessed in detail about Jeneane's brutal murder in response to her casual question concerning why he was going to visit friends in Pennsylvania instead of returning to his family in Arizona. Although she testified that she was "disgusted" by Fulminante's

---

[8] Although Fulminante had allegedly confessed to Donna Sarivola several months previously, police did not yet know of this confession, which Anthony Sarivola did not mention to them until June 1985. They did, however, know of the first confession, which Fulminante had given to Anthony Sarivola nearly a year before.

disclosures, she stated that she took no steps to notify authorities of what she had learned. In fact, she claimed that she barely discussed the matter with Anthony Sarivola, who was in the car and overheard Fulminante's entire conversation with Donna. Despite her disgust for Fulminante, Donna Sarivola later went on a second trip with him. Although Sarivola informed authorities that he had driven Fulminante to Pennsylvania, he did not mention Donna's presence in the car or her conversation with Fulminante. Only when questioned by authorities in June 1985 did Anthony Sarivola belatedly recall the confession to Donna more than a year before, and only then did he ask if she would be willing to discuss the matter with authorities.

Although some of the details in the confession to Donna Sarivola were corroborated by circumstantial evidence, many, including details that Jeneane was choked and sexually assaulted, were not. As to other aspects of the second confession, including Fulminante's motive and state of mind, the only corroborating evidence was the first confession to Anthony Sarivola.[9] Thus, contrary to what the Arizona Supreme Court found, it is clear that the jury might have believed that the two confessions reinforced and corroborated each other. For this reason, one confession was *not* merely cumulative of the other. While in some cases two confessions, delivered on different occasions to different listeners, might be viewed as being independent of each other, it strains credulity to think that the jury so viewed the two confessions in this case, especially given the close relationship between Donna and Anthony Sarivola.

The jurors could also have believed that Donna Sarivola had a motive to lie about the confession in order to assist her husband. Anthony Sarivola received significant benefits from federal authorities, including payment for information, immunity from prosecution, and eventual placement in the federal Witness Protection Program. In addition, the jury might have found Donna motivated by her own desire for favorable treatment, for she, too, was ultimately placed in the Witness Protection Program.

Third, the admission of the first confession led to the admission of other evidence prejudicial to Fulminante. For example, the State introduced evidence that Fulminante knew of Sarivola's connections with organized crime in an attempt to explain why Fulminante would have been motivated to confess to Sarivola in seeking protection. Absent the confession, this evidence would have had no

---

[9] The inadmissible confession to Anthony Sarivola was itself subject to serious challenge. Sarivola's lack of moral integrity was demonstrated by his testimony that he had worked for organized crime during the time he was a uniformed police officer. His overzealous approach to gathering information for which he would be paid by authorities, was revealed by his admission that he had fabricated a tape recording in connection with an earlier, unrelated FBI investigation. He received immunity in connection with the information he provided. His eagerness to get in and stay in the federal Witness Protection Program provided a motive for giving detailed information to authorities. During his first report of the confession, Sarivola failed to hint at numerous details concerning an alleged sexual assault on Jeneane; he mentioned them for the first time more than a year later during further interrogation, at which he also recalled, for the first time, the confession to Donna Sarivola. The impeaching effect of each of these factors was undoubtedly undercut by the presence of the second confession, which, not surprisingly, recounted a quite similar story and thus corroborated the first confession. Thus, each confession, though easily impeachable if viewed in isolation, became difficult to discount when viewed in conjunction with the other.

relevance and would have been inadmissible at trial. The Arizona Supreme Court found that the evidence of Sarivola's connections with organized crime reflected on Sarivola's character, not Fulminante's, and noted that the evidence could have been used to impeach Sarivola. This analysis overlooks the fact that had the confession not been admitted, there would have been no reason for Sarivola to testify and thus no need to impeach his testimony. Moreover, we cannot agree that the evidence did not reflect on Fulminante's character as well, for it depicted him as someone who willingly sought out the company of criminals. It is quite possible that this evidence led the jury to view Fulminante as capable of murder.[10]

Although our concern here is with the effect of the erroneous admission of the confession on Fulminante's conviction, it is clear that the presence of the confession also influenced the sentencing phase of the trial. Under Arizona law, the trial judge is the sentencer. At the sentencing hearing, the admissibility of information regarding aggravating circumstances is governed by the rules of evidence applicable to criminal trials. In this case, "based upon admissible evidence produced at the trial," the judge found that only one aggravating circumstance existed beyond a reasonable doubt, *i.e.*, that the murder was committed in "an *especially* heinous, cruel, and depraved manner." In reaching this conclusion, the judge relied heavily on evidence concerning the manner of the killing and Fulminante's motives and state of mind which could only be found in the two confessions. For example, in labeling the murder "cruel," the judge focused in part on Fulminante's alleged statements that he choked Jeneane and made her get on her knees and beg before killing her. Although the circumstantial evidence was not inconsistent with this determination, neither was it sufficient to make such a finding beyond a reasonable doubt. Indeed, the sentencing judge acknowledged that the confessions were only partly corroborated by other evidence.

Finally, [i]n declaring that Fulminante "acted with an especially heinous and depraved state of mind," the sentencing judge relied solely on the two confessions. While the judge found that the statements in the confessions regarding the alleged sexual assault on Jeneane should not be considered on the issue of cruelty because they were not corroborated by other evidence, the judge determined that they were worthy of belief on the issue of Fulminante's state of mind. The judge then focused on Anthony Sarivola's statement that Fulminante had made vulgar references to Jeneane during the first confession, and on Donna Sarivola's statement that Fulminante had made similar comments to her. Finally, the judge stressed that Fulminante's alleged comments to the Sarivolas concerning torture, choking, and sexual assault, "whether they all occurred or not," depicted "a man who was bragging and relishing the crime he committed."

Because a majority of the Court has determined that Fulminante's confession to Anthony Sarivola was coerced and because a majority has determined that admitting this confession was not harmless beyond a reasonable doubt, we agree

---

[10] Fulminante asserts that other prejudicial evidence, including his prior felony convictions and incarcerations, and his prison reputation for untruthfulness, likewise would not have been admitted had the confession to Sarivola been excluded. Because we find that the admission of the confession was not harmless in any event, we express no opinion as to the effect any of this evidence might have had on Fulminante's conviction.

with the Arizona Supreme Court's conclusion that Fulminante is entitled to a new trial at which the confession is not admitted. Accordingly the judgment of the Arizona Supreme Court is affirmed.

CHIEF JUSTICE REHNQUIST, with whom JUSTICE O'CONNOR joins, JUSTICE KENNEDY and JUSTICE SOUTER join as to Parts I and II, and JUSTICE SCALIA joins as to Parts II and III, delivering the opinion of the Court as to Part II, and dissenting as to Parts I and III.

I

The question of whether respondent Fulminante's confession was voluntary is one of federal law. "Without exception, the Court's confession cases hold that the ultimate issue of 'voluntariness' is a legal question requiring independent federal determination." In *Mincey*, we overturned a determination by the Supreme Court of Arizona that a statement of the defendant was voluntary, saying "we are not bound by the Arizona Supreme Court's holding that the statements were voluntary. Instead, this Court is under a duty to make an independent evaluation of the record."

Exercising our responsibility to make the independent examination of the record necessary to decide this federal question, I am at a loss to see how the Supreme Court of Arizona reached the conclusion that it did. Fulminante offered no evidence that he believed that his life was in danger or that he in fact confessed to Sarivola in order to obtain the proffered protection. Indeed, he had stipulated that "[a]t no time did the defendant indicate he was in fear of other inmates nor did he ever seek Mr. Sarivola's 'protection.'" Sarivola's testimony that he told Fulminante that "if [he] would tell the truth, he could be protected," adds little if anything to the substance of the parties' stipulation. The decision of the Supreme Court of Arizona rests on an assumption that is squarely contrary to this stipulation, and one that is not supported by any testimony of Fulminante.

The facts of record in the present case are quite different from those present in cases where we have found confessions to be coerced and involuntary. Since Fulminante was unaware that Sarivola was an FBI informant, there existed none of "the danger of coercion result[ing] from the interaction of custody and official interrogation." *Perkins*. The fact that Sarivola was a government informant does not by itself render Fulminante's confession involuntary, since we have consistently accepted the use of informants in the discovery of evidence of a crime as a legitimate investigatory procedure consistent with the Constitution. The conversations between Sarivola and Fulminante were not lengthy, and the defendant was free at all times to leave Sarivola's company. Sarivola at no time threatened him or demanded that he confess; he simply requested that he speak the truth about the matter. Fulminante was an experienced habitué of prisons, and presumably able to fend for himself. In concluding on these facts that Fulminante's confession was involuntary, the Court today embraces a more expansive definition of that term than is warranted by any of our decided cases.

II

[This portion of the opinion is the opinion of the Court.]

Since this Court's landmark decision in *Chapman v. California*, 386 U.S. 18 (1967), in which we adopted the general rule that a constitutional error does not automatically require reversal of a conviction, the Court has applied harmless error analysis to a wide range of errors and has recognized that most constitutional errors can be harmless.

Of course an involuntary confession may have a more dramatic effect on the course of a trial than do other trial errors — in particular cases it may be devastating to a defendant — but this simply means that a reviewing court will conclude in such a case that its admission was not harmless error; it is not a reason for eschewing the harmless error test entirely. The Supreme Court of Arizona, in its first opinion in the present case, concluded that the admission of Fulminante's confession was harmless error. That court concluded that a second and more explicit confession of the crime made by Fulminante after he was released from prison was not tainted by the first confession, and that the second confession, together with physical evidence from the wounds (the victim had been shot twice in the head with a large caliber weapon at close range and a ligature was found around her neck) and other evidence introduced at trial rendered the admission of the first confession harmless beyond a reasonable doubt.

III

I would agree with the finding of the Supreme Court of Arizona in its initial opinion — in which it believed harmless-error analysis was applicable to the admission of involuntary confessions — that the admission of Fulminante's confession was harmless. Indeed, this seems to me to be a classic case of harmless error: a second confession giving more details of the crime than the first was admitted in evidence and found to be free of any constitutional objection. Accordingly, I would affirm the holding of the Supreme Court of Arizona in its initial opinion, and reverse the judgment which it ultimately rendered in this case.

JUSTICE KENNEDY, concurring in the judgment.

For the reasons stated by THE CHIEF JUSTICE, I agree that Fulminante's confession to Anthony Sarivola was not coerced. In my view, the trial court did not err in admitting this testimony. A majority of the Court, however, finds the confession coerced and proceeds to consider whether harmless-error analysis may be used when a coerced confession has been admitted at trial. With the case in this posture, it is appropriate for me to address the harmless-error issue.

Again for the reasons stated by THE CHIEF JUSTICE, I agree that harmless-error analysis should apply in the case of a coerced confession. That said, the court conducting a harmless-error inquiry must appreciate the indelible impact a full confession may have on the trier of fact, as distinguished, for instance, from the impact of an isolated statement that incriminates the defendant only when connected with other evidence. If the jury believes that a defendant has admitted the crime, it doubtless will be tempted to rest its decision on that evidence alone, without careful consideration of the other evidence in the case. Apart, perhaps, from a videotape of the crime, one would have difficulty finding evidence more damaging to a criminal defendant's plea of innocence. For the reasons given by Justice WHITE in Part IV of his opinion, I cannot with confidence find admission of Fulminante's confession to Anthony Sarivola to be harmless error.

The same majority of the Court does not agree on the three issues presented by the trial court's determination to admit Fulminante's first confession: whether the confession was inadmissible because coerced; whether harmless error analysis is appropriate; and if so whether any error was harmless here. My own view that the confession was not coerced does not command a majority.

In the interests of providing a clear mandate to the Arizona Supreme Court in this capital case, I deem it proper to accept in the case now before us the holding of five Justices that the confession was coerced and inadmissible. I agree with a majority of the Court that admission of the confession could not be harmless error when viewed in light of all the other evidence; and so I concur in the judgment to affirm the ruling of the Arizona Supreme Court.

QUESTIONS AND NOTES

1.   What three issues did the Court resolve? What was the breakdown of the Court on each of the issues? How many of the Justices were in the majority on all three issues?

2.   Why was the confession not invalidated because of *Miranda*?

3.   Do you think that the confession was coerced/involuntary? Explain. Do those terms have different legal meanings than factual meanings? Should they?

4.   Should the fact that Sarivola appeared to be a friend of Fulminante's cut for or against the voluntariness of his confession?

5.   Should a coerced confession ever be treated as harmless error? Why? Why not?

6.   Do you agree with the Court that admission of this confession (if it was involuntary) was not harmless beyond a reasonable doubt? Explain.

PROBLEM

The following dialogue comes from a case called *Miller v. Fenton*, 796 F.2d 598 (3d Cir. 1986) in which the third circuit, by a 2-1 vote, held the confession to be voluntary. Do you agree?

BOYCE: Testing 1 2 3. Testing 1 2 3. (Cough) Testing 1 2 3. Testing

BOYCE: Tuesday (cough), Tuesday, August 14, 1973, 1:47 A.M., Flemington State Police Barracks, Detectives' room, this is the start of an interrogation between Detective William Doyle, 1884, New Jersey State Police, Detective Boyce, 2097, also from the New Jersey State Police, and one Frank Melvin Miller, and this interrogation is in reference to the investigation now being conducted which involves the death of Miss Deborah Selma Margolin, white female, age 17, Brown Station Road, R.D. Ringoes, New Jersey. That's a correction, that's Bowne Station Road. This death occurring sometime approximately between 11:15 A.M., 8/13/73, and 5:45 P.M., 8/13/73.

BOYCE: Now, Mr. Miller, uh Frank, I talked to you earlier.

MILLER: Yeah, at PFD.

BOYCE: At PFD where you're employed. I was accompanied by Trooper Robert Scott at that time.

MILLER: Yes, sir.

BOYCE: We identified ourselves and we spoke to you on a voluntary basis in which you extended your cooperation to us, uh, in regards to this investigation of the death of the girl that I have just mentioned.

MILLER: Yes, sir.

BOYCE: You agreed at that time, voluntarily, to speak with us in regards to this matter . . .

MILLER: Yes, sir.

BOYCE: . . . also gave us permission while we were there to look at your vehicle . . .

MILLER: Yes, sir.

BOYCE: . . . to take clothing from your locker . . .

MILLER: Yes, sir.

BOYCE: . . . which is located inside the PFD plant, all of this being done, of course, with the cooperation that was extended to us from you on a voluntary basis.

MILLER: Right.

BOYCE: Now, Frank, you've been here since approximately 11, 11:49 P.M. which would actually be yesterday, 8/13/73. What I'm going to do at this time and, of course, let me just reiterate here, you, you, you came down, you accompanied Trooper Scott and myself here on a voluntary basis . . . that correct?

MILLER: Right.

BOYCE: Okay, and of your own free will?

MILLER: Yes, sir.

BOYCE: Without duress?

MILLER: Yes, sir.

BOYCE: Or having been threatened to do so.

MILLER: Right.

BOYCE: Okay, and while you were here you've been conversing again on a voluntary basis, with Trooper Scott, is that not right?

MILLER: Yes, sir.

BOYCE: Okay (cough). What I'm going to do at this time, as I've indicated already, you've been here for awhile, it is now almost 2:00 A.M. on the 14th, which puts you here approximately 2 hours. I'm going to advise you at this time of your constitutional rights, which you are entitled to, and start off by saying: Number 1, you have the right to remain silent and not to answer any questions, Number 2, if you decide to waive your right to remain silent, anything you say will be used against you if it is incriminating in nature. You have the right to be represented by an attorney before and during any questioning. If you want an attorney and cannot afford one, an attorney will be provided for you free by the State of New Jersey. Do you understand these rights, Frank?

MILLER: Yes, sir.

BOYCE: Are you willing to talk to us without having an attorney? In reference . . .

MILLER: Yes.

BOYCE: . . . to the, what we have talked about?

MILLER: Yes.

BOYCE: Okay, fine.

MILLER: But, at any time though, I can, uh, say no, right? I mean, you know . . .

BOYCE: Yes, Frank, let me go over that again.

MILLER: Yeah, I understand that, that . . .

BOYCE: You understand your rights, Frank?

MILLER: Yeah.

BOYCE: Okay. (cough). You may stop at anytime during this interrogation . . .

MILLER: Yeah.

BOYCE: . . . and request to remain silent and we will honor your request.

MILLER: Yes.

BOYCE: Okay?

MILLER: Yeah.

BOYCE: Now, we're talking about the death of a young girl, Frank, right?

MILLER: Yes, sir.

BOYCE: . . . very attractive, a very attractive young girl, who apparently at the time of her death was wearing nothing but a bathing suit, two piece bathing suit. We feel that there's a sexual aspect at this time is a good indication that there is some type of sexual assault that's associated with this crime. . . . Before we continue, Frank, what I would like to ask you to do is, I'm going to ask you to sign the back of this card, okay, with your rights on it, indicating that you in fact have been . . .

MILLER: Yeah, yeah.

BOYCE: . . . advised of your rights.

MILLER: I got a pen right here.

BOYCE: Just sign the back of that and date it. (Clanging noises.) Today's the 14th.

MILLER: You want it signed the 14th?

BOYCE: Yes, please.

MILLER: Alright.

BOYCE: Okay.

MILLER: Alright?

BOYCE: Thank you. Now, getting back to the, uh, the death of Miss Margolin, which we were discussing, you already related to me and Trooper Scott at the time in which you did it that as to where you were and what your activities were yesterday.

MILLER: Right, right.

BOYCE: You indicated you came back into the Ringoes area about 11:00 A.M., is that correct?

MILLER: It was somewheres in there, yeah, give or take a little bit of time.

BOYCE: Let's try and narrow that down, Frank. Can you think of anything that would give you any indication as to why you say now you came back into the area sometime around 11 o'clock.

MILLER: Well, this is what I told you at the barracks, or I mean at PFD. I figured it was between 11, uh, around 11 o'clock, because I figured I got home around 11:30, quarter to 12, back to my parents' house and I had stopped at the Post Office in Ringoes to mail a letter which I forgot to mail this morning, or yesterday morning.

BOYCE: Alright, but, in other words what I'm saying Frank is how can you substantiate in your mind, in your mind . . .

MILLER: Uh, huh.

BOYCE: . . . as to wh . . . how, why you feel a this time that you arrived in Ringoes, went to the Post Office around 11 o'clock, can you tell me how you come to this conclusion, or what was, what activity you were involved in prior to getting, getting into Ringoes that would come to your mind as, you know, making you think that you arrived in Ringoes at 11 o'clock?

MILLER: Well, because I was home around 11:30, quarter to 12, because, uh, so I figured, uh, it had to be somewheres around 11 o'clock that I was in Ringoes, that's about the only thing I can think of.

BOYCE: Alright, now, before, when I confronted you with the time element, you said that you were in Ringoes at 11, you got home around 12 o'clock, now, you say 11:30 or quarter to 12. Now, I'm going to ask you a question, how long does it take you to drive your vehicle from the Ringoes Post Office to your father's house?

MILLER: That depends on how fast you go.

BOYCE: Okay, let's say if you drive at a normal rate of speed.

MILLER: I'd say maybe 20 minutes.

BOYCE: 20 minutes. How far would you say it is, Frank?

MILLER: Oh, 6, 7 miles, maybe.

BOYCE: 6, 7 miles. Now, you've indicated once prior to this interrogation that you got home around 12. Now you've indicated 11:30, quarter to 12. Now, what time did you get home, Frank?

MILLER: I'm not exactly sure.

BOYCE: Now that, now you're not sure.

MILLER: Well, I, I say, uh, I figure anywheres from 11:30 to 12 o'clock, quarter to 12, somewheres around there . . .

BOYCE: Alright . . .

MILLER: . . . because I didn't look at the clock.

BOYCE: Okay. Why do you think it was somewhere around there?

MILLER: Because I got myself something to eat and, uh, got my stuff together to get ready to go to work, and I wanted to stop up the hospital to see how this fella was . . .

BOYCE: What time did you leave, how long were you, what time did you arrive at the Post Office? Approximately?

MILLER: I'd say around 11 o'clock.

BOYCE: Okay, how long were you in the Post Office, Frank?

MILLER: A few minutes is all.

BOYCE: A few minutes. What did you do when you walked outside, Frank?

MILLER: Got in my car.

BOYCE: And went where?

MILLER: Home.

BOYCE: Okay, Frank. You indicated it takes approximately 20 minutes to drive home.

MILLER: Approximately, yeah.

BOYCE: Therefore, you would have arrived home in the area of 11:15, 11:20 A.M., but you indicated to me on 4, 5, maybe 6, 7, 8, 9 occasions already that you arrived home between quarter to 12, 12 o'clock. Now, I'm . . . am I right?

MILLER: Yeah.

BOYCE: Okay, now, this is a problem.

MILLER: I realize this . . .

BOYCE: This creates a very serious problem.

MILLER: Times, I uh, you know, I uh . . .

BOYCE: Oh, well, you know, it's not so much times, knowing what time it is, but you do know how long it takes you to get from point A to point B, you've already indicated . . .

MILLER: Yeah, approximately.

BOYCE: Approximately 20 minutes.

MILLER: Right.

BOYCE: So that's 11:15, 11:20

MILLER: Right.

BOYCE: 12 o'clock comes to your mind and I see a 40 minute, anywhere from a half hour to a 40 minute period . . . where are we, where are you, is what I should say?

MILLER: Yeah.

BOYCE: And I, I just, you know, this, this, I have a big question mark in my mind right now.

MILLER: Right.

BOYCE: Do you see my point, Frank?

MILLER: Yes, sir.

BOYCE: That's point one. Your car, right now . . .

MILLER: Yeah.

BOYCE: . . . is dented on the right side?

MILLER: Right.

BOYCE: Your trunk is, I should, may be I should use the words sprang down, because this is some type of a metal spring . . .

MILLER: Right, yeah.

BOYCE: . . . securing the trunk of your vehicle. There is red dust on the vehicle, red dust that is visible to the naked eye . . .

MILLER: Yeah.

BOYCE: . . . when someone looks at it. It's got red clay or dirt in and around the wheel covers . . .

MILLER: Uh, huh.

BOYCE: . . . tires. I'll bet you right now, Frank, there is not another vehicle in Hunterdon County that fits the physical description that we, that Trooper Scott and I saw your vehicle in when we saw it up there tonight. I'll bet you, that I, I can call up a thousand people right now and there will not be another vehicle that fits the description of your vehicle. Am I right?

MILLER: There shouldn't be, no, not with the right side of it dented in like that.

BOYCE: That's the second point. You're with me now, right?

MILLER: Yeah.

BOYCE: Okay. Your vehicle was involved in an accident, was involved in two accidents.

MILLER: Two accidents.

BOYCE: There was blood found on the left front interior portion of your vehicle, tonight, fresh blood.

MILLER: Fresh blood?

BOYCE: Yes, sir. This is very, very serious.

MILLER: I realize this.

BOYCE: That's point 3. Now, you live a few miles from the scene where this young, innocent girl was found.

MILLER: Uh, huh.

BOYCE: You indicate that between 11 and 12 yesterday morning, between 11 and 12, one hour, 60 minutes, you went from, according to your statement . . .

MILLER: Right.

BOYCE: . . . the Ringoes Post Office to your house, a trip admitted to me by yourself that takes maybe 20 minutes.

MILLER: About 20 minutes, right.

BOYCE: You wear, and you have a lot of, dark blue trousers.

MILLER: Right.

BOYCE: You have a lot of light blue shirts.

MILLER: Right.

BOYCE: I know, I have a lot of them in my custody now. We went to your house last night and found blood stains on the front stoop.

MILLER: On the front stoop?

BOYCE: Yes, sir.

MILLER: Well, how did it get there?

BOYCE: I don't know Frank. Let me ask you, how did it get there?

MILLER: I have no idea.

BOYCE: We obtained a sample of the blood.

MILLER: Right.

BOYCE: Obtained a sample from the vehicle.

MILLER: Uh, huh.

BOYCE: We have a witness, Frank, now this is point 4. We have a witness who identified your car, who, no, I'm, I'm sorry, let me, I shouldn't say your car, who identified a vehicle that fits the description of your car, at this girl's home, speaking with her, telling her something about a cow being loose. Someone who was there who wanted to help her, they didn't want to hurt this girl, they didn't want to hurt this girl, Frank, they wanted to help her. You see, I know this, I know that, . . .

MILLER: Yeah.

BOYCE: . . . because I can appreciate that, because I would have done the same thing. If there was something to be rectified, or if somebody had a problem, I would have done the same thing. I would have wanted to help her. The vehicle that came onto her property.

MILLER: Right.

BOYCE: . . . fits the description of your vehicle.

MILLER: It does.

BOYCE: Yes. Now, that's the fourth point. And when I say fits the description, what I mean, Frank, is it fits the description to a "t," and as we talked about before, how many other vehicles are there like yours in the County right now?

MILLER: There shouldn't be too many, if any . . .

BOYCE: If any . . .

MILLER: Because of the damage on the right-hand side.

BOYCE: Now, what would your conclusion be under those circumstances, if someone told you that?

MILLER: I'd probably, uh, have the same conclusion you got.

BOYCE: Which is what?

MILLER: That I'm the guy that did this.

BOYCE: That did what?

MILLER: Committed this crime.

BOYCE: What crime?

MILLER: Well, you said before the girl was dead, killed, killed this girl.

BOYCE: Who killed this girl?

MILLER: The guy driving this car.

BOYCE: I think the guy driving this car . . . wait, let me, I forgot something. . . . We have a physical description . . .

MILLER: Un huh.

BOYCE: . . . of this individual from another witness. The physical description Frank, . . .

MILLER: Yeah.

BOYCE: . . . fits you and the clothes you were wearing. Frank, I don't think you're a criminal. I don't think you're a criminal. I don't think you have a criminal mind. As a matter of fact, I know you don't have a criminal mind, because we've been talking now for a few hours together, haven't we?

MILLER: Right.

BOYCE: Right?

MILLER: Yeah.

BOYCE: You don't have a criminal mind.

MILLER: No.

BOYCE: I know you don't. But, like I noted before, we all have problems.

MILLER: Right.

BOYCE: Am I right?

MILLER: Yeah, you said this over there at the plant.

BOYCE: And you agree with me?

MILLER: Yes, sir.

BOYCE: I have problems and you have.

MILLER: Right.

BOYCE: Now, how do you solve a problem?

MILLER: That depends on the problem.

BOYCE: Your problem how do we solve it? How are we going to solve it?

MILLER: This I don't know.

BOYCE: Do you want me to help you solve it?

MILLER: Yeah.

BOYCE: You want me to extend all the help I can possibly give you, don't you?

MILLER: Right.

BOYCE: Are you willing to do the same to me?

MILLER: Yeah.

BOYCE: Now, I feel . . .

MILLER: Yeah.

BOYCE: . . . who is ever, whoever is responsible for this act . . .

MILLER: Yeah.

BOYCE: He's not a criminal. Does not have a criminal mind. I think they have a problem.

MILLER: Uh, huh.

BOYCE: Do you agree with me?

MILLER: Yeah.

BOYCE: They have a problem.

MILLER: Right.

BOYCE: A problem, and a good thing about that Frank, is a problem can be rectified.

MILLER: Yeah.

BOYCE: I want to help you. I mean I really want to help you, but you know what they say, God helps those who help themselves, Frank.

MILLER: Right.

BOYCE: We've got to get together on this. You know what I'm talking about, don't you?

MILLER: Yeah, especially if they're trying to say that, you know, that like you say, I'm identified and my car's identified, and uh, we got to get together on this.

BOYCE: Yes we do. Now, that only a few of the items . . .

MILLER: Uh, huh.

BOYCE: . . . that we have now. Your problem, I'm not, let's forget this incident, okay . . .

MILLER: Yeah.

BOYCE: . . . let's forget this incident, let's talk about your problem. This is what, this is what I'm concerned with, Frank, your problem.

MILLER: Right.

BOYCE: If I had a problem like your problem, I would want you to help me with my problem.

MILLER: Uh, huh.

BOYCE: Now, you know what I'm talking about.

MILLER: Yeah.

BOYCE: And I know, and I think that, uh, a lot of other people know. You know what I'm talking about. I don't think you're a criminal, Frank.

MILLER: No, but you're trying to make me one.

BOYCE:	No I'm not, no I'm not, but I want you to talk to me so we can get this thing worked out. This is what I want, this is what I want, Frank. I mean it's all there, it's all there. I'm not saying. . . .
MILLER:	Let me ask you a question.
BOYCE:	Sure.
MILLER:	Now you say this girl's dead, right?
BOYCE:	She died just a few minutes ago. I just got . . . that's what the call was about.
MILLER:	Cause Officer Scott said she was in the hospital and I said well then let's go, you know, go right over there.
BOYCE:	She was in the hospital . . .
MILLER:	And, uh . . .
BOYCE:	. . . the call that Detective Doyle got, that's, that's what that call was.
MILLER:	Cause, I told him . . .
BOYCE:	Are you, do you feel what I feel right now?
MILLER:	I feel pretty bad.
BOYCE:	Do you want to talk to me about it?
MILLER:	There's nothing I can tell . . .
BOYCE:	About how you feel?
MILLER:	. . . there's nothing I can talk, I mean I feel sorry for this girl, I mean, uh, this is something that, you know . . .
BOYCE:	That what?
MILLER:	Well, it's a shame, uh . . .
BOYCE:	What did she say to you?
MILLER:	Beg your pardon?
BOYCE:	What did she say to you?
MILLER:	Who?
BOYCE:	This girl?
MILLER:	I never talked to this girl. If she was to walk in here now, I wouldn't know, know that she was the girl that, uh, you're talking about.
BOYCE:	But you were identified as being there talking to her minutes before she was . . . probably this thing that happened to her. How can you explain that?
MILLER:	I can't.
BOYCE:	Why?
MILLER:	I don't know why, but I, I, you know, how can I explain something that I don't know anything about.

BOYCE: Frank, look, you want, you want help, don't you Frank?

MILLER: Yes, uh huh, yes, but yet I'm, I'm not going to admit to something that, that I wasn't involved in.

BOYCE: We don't want you to, all I want you to do is talk to me, that's all. I'm not talking about admitting to anything, Frank, I want you to talk to me. I want you to tell me what you think. I want you to tell me how you think about this, what you think about this?

MILLER: What I think about it?

BOYCE: Yeah.

MILLER: I think whoever did it really needs help.

BOYCE: And that's what I think and that's what I know. They don't, they don't need punishment, right? Like you said, they need help.

MILLER: Right.

BOYCE: They don't need punishment. They need help, good medical help.

MILLER: That's right.

BOYCE: . . . to rectify their problem. Putting them in, in a prison isn't going to solve it, is it?

MILLER: No sir. I know, I was in there for three and a half years.

BOYCE: That's right. That's the, that's not going to solve your problem is it?

MILLER: No, you get no help down there. The only think you learn is how to, you know . . .

BOYCE: Well, let's say this Frank, suppose you were the person who needed help. What would you want somebody to do for you?

MILLER: Help me.

BOYCE: In what way?

MILLER: In any way that they, they see, you know, fit, that it would help me.

BOYCE: What, what do you think compels somebody to do something like this. What do you think it is, Frank?

MILLER: Well, it could be a number of things.

BOYCE: Give me an example.

MILLER: It could be a person that, that drinks, uh, you know, a lot, and just, you know, don't know what they, what they did once they been drinking. It could be somebody with narcotics that, that don't know what they're, you know, what they're doing once they shot up or took some pills or whatever they do, I don't know, I'm not a drug addict and never intend to be.

BOYCE: What else Frank? What other type of person would do something like this?

MILLER: Somebody with a mental problem.

BOYCE:	Right. Somebody with a . . .
MILLER:	Mental problem . . .
BOYCE:	. . . serious mental problem, and you know what I'm interested in, I'm not, I'm interested in, in preventing this in the future.
MILLER:	Right.
BOYCE:	Now, don't you think it's better if someone knows that he or she has a mental problem to come forward with it and say, look, I've, I've, I've done these acts. I'm responsible for this, but I want to be helped, I couldn't help myself, I had no control of myself and if I'm examined properly you'll find out that's the case. Is that right or wrong?
MILLER:	Yeah, that, they should be examined and, uh, you know, maybe a doctor could find out what's wrong with me.
BOYCE:	Have you ever been examined?
MILLER:	Yes.
BOYCE:	And did you have a problem?
MILLER:	Well, when I come, uh, made parole in, uh, September, the uh stipulation was, uh, that I see a psychiatrist.
BOYCE:	Alright . . .
MILLER:	Dr. Taylor over here at the Medical Center, I seen him, two, maybe three times and last time I was there he gave me a test . . .
BOYCE:	Uh, huh.
MILLER:	. . . uh, it was a bunch of bull shit, in plain English. If the big wheel turns one way, what way does the little wheel turn? So I took that test. He says, alright, he says, I say when do I come back, because this is part of my parole.
BOYCE:	I see.
MILLER:	And he says, uh, I'll call you and let you know, he says I want to get this, work this test out first. He up to this date, the man has never called me, uh . . .
BOYCE:	How do you feel about this?
MILLER:	Well, I think it's wrong.
BOYCE:	Would you, do you, did you feel that after not finding out the results of that test that you might do something that you might not be responsible for?
MILLER:	No.
BOYCE:	Did you feel that you were capable, maybe, of doing something because you didn't get the results of this . . . because they didn't like, help you, did they?
MILLER:	No.

BOYCE: Well, then did you still feel this way that something might happen it
            would be their fault because, as far as I'm concerned if something
            did happen, it's not your fault, it's their fault . . .

MILLER: Right.

BOYCE: . . . because that was a part of your parole . . .

MILLER: Right.

BOYCE: . . . and they didn't live up to it.

MILLER: Right.

BOYCE: You agree with me?

MILLER: Yeah, that . . .

BOYCE: So, therefore, if you did commit an act, actually they're the ones that
            are to blame, in my eyes . . .

MILLER: Right.

BOYCE: . . . not you as an individual. You were there seeking help. You went
            there, they didn't right, you went there voluntarily, right?

MILLER: Right. It was, uh, it was all set up through . . .

BOYCE: It was all set up.

MILLER: . . . the parole board, or well, my parole officer, I believe set it up.
            At that time it was, uh, Gene, uh, DiGennie, I believe his name was.

BOYCE: DiGianni.

MILLER: DiGianni.

BOYCE: Frank, you're very, very nervous. Now, I, I don't, you know, you,
            you're, you understand what I'm saying?

MILLER: Yeah, I know what you're saying.

BOYCE: Now, there's a reason for that, isn't there?

MILLER: Yes.

BOYCE: Do you want to tell me about it?

MILLER: Being involved in something like this is . . .

BOYCE: Is what, does it, does it, does it visibly shake you physically?

MILLER: Yes, it does, because, well, Officer Scott can tell you, it ain't been not
            even a month ago I sat right in the same room . . .

BOYCE: Uh, huh.

MILLER: . . . behind the girl that I really loved, because she was a minor her
            father forced her into making statements, which, she didn't lie on the
            statements. I tried to cover up with Officer Scott until I heard from
            her and she said yes, she says, I did tell him, she says, I had to tell
            him. So, then when I talked to my lawyer, you know, I admitted to
            him, I admitted to my parole officer, I said I'm not making a liar out

of the girl, cause I love her too much and so I admitted, you know, he asked me if we were having sex . . .

BOYCE: Alright. What . . .

MILLER: . . . and, uh, I had no intentions of making a liar out of her.

BOYCE: Now listen to me Frank. This hurts me more than it hurts you, because I love people.

MILLER: It can't hurt you anymore than it hurts me.

BOYCE: Okay, listen Frank, I want you . . .

MILLER: I mean even being involved in something like this.

BOYCE: Okay. listen Frank, if I promise to, you know, do all I can with the psychiatrist and everything, and we get the proper help for you, and get the proper help for you, will you talk to me about it?

MILLER: I can't talk to you about something I'm not . . .

BOYCE: Alright, listen Frank, alright, honest. I know, I know what's going on inside you, Frank. I want to help you, you know, between us right now. I know what going on inside you. Frank, you've got to come forward and tell me that you want to help yourself. You've got to talk to me about it. This is the only way we'll be able to work it out. I mean, you know, listen, I want to help you, because you are in my mind, you are not responsible. You are not responsible, Frank. Frank, what's the matter?

MILLER: I feel bad.

BOYCE: Frank, listen to me, honest to God, I'm, I'm telling you, Frank (inaudible). I know, it's going to bother you. Frank, it's going to bother you. It's there, it's not going to go away, it's there. It's right in front of you, Frank. Am I right or wrong?

MILLER: Yeah.

BOYCE: You can see it Frank, you can feel it, you can feel it but you are not responsible. This is what I'm trying to tell you, but you've got to come forward and tell me. Don't, don't, don't let it eat you up, don't, don't fight it. You've got to rectify it, Frank. We've got to get together on this thing, or I, I mean really, you need help, you need proper help and you know it, my God, you know, in God's name, you, you know it. You are not a criminal, you are not a criminal.

MILLER: Alright. Yes, I was over there and I talked to her about the cow and left. I left in my car and I stopped up on the road where, you know, where the cow had been and she followed me in her car . . .

BOYCE: Right.

MILLER: . . . and the cow wasn't down there and we started walking through the fields and stuff, and you could see where the cow was.

BOYCE: Uh, huh.

MILLER: Now, I don't know . . .

BOYCE: Now, Frank please . . .

MILLER: Wait, wait a minute.

BOYCE: I'm sorry, I'm sorry.

MILLER: Okay, okay.

BOYCE: Go ahead, I'm sorry.

MILLER: I don't know where this guy come from . . .

BOYCE: Tell me about him, I'm sorry, go ahead.

MILLER: But . . .

BOYCE: Tell me about him Frank . . .

MILLER: Alright, he, alright, he grabbed her . . .

BOYCE: Right.

MILLER: . . . that's how I got the cut on my hand, I didn't get cut in the car.

BOYCE: Alright, tell me what happened. Tell me what happened. Let it come out, Frank, let it come out. This is what you need, Frank. I'm, it's you and me, now listen.

MILLER: Alright now, he, you know I, tried to get ahold of him and he cut me in the hand with the knife, and he'd already cut her, and then he ran.

BOYCE: Alright.

MILLER: So first thing I thought, you know, try and help her. I got her in the car and she just, you know, she just fell over and I got scared because, you know, I thought she was dead.

BOYCE: Alright.

MILLER: So, I got down by the bridge, I just, you know, laid her off there and got the hell out of there because I was scared, because, you know . . .

BOYCE: Let it come out, Frank. I'm here, I'm here with you now. I'm on your side, I'm on your side, Frank. I'm your brother, you and I are brothers Frank. We are brothers and I want to help my brother.

MILLER: If I hadn't went down on that road I wouldn't even have been involved in it.

BOYCE: Frank, listen . . .

MILLER: It was a shorter way home from, from the Post Office. I'm not lying about that Post Office or nothing. I came out past that cemetery and up that, up that dirt road . . .

BOYCE: Alright, let's . . .

MILLER: . . . because I could have, you know, swung off at the Whitehall area, I could have swung off and went through the back way to the house.

BOYCE: Let's, Frank, listen. Let's go back to the Post Office, okay? Did you go to the Post Office?

MILLER: Yes.

BOYCE: Okay . . .

MILLER: There was one . . .

BOYCE: Tell me . . .

MILLER: . . . one woman there, I don't, I don't, I couldn't even begin to describe.

BOYCE: Now tell me where you went. Tell me again about this incident, okay?

MILLER: Right.

BOYCE: Alright Frank, tell me what happened.

MILLER: I left the Post Office, you want to go from the Post Office, right?

BOYCE: Uh, huh.

MILLER: Alright. Alright, then I stuck the letter in the mailbox, the out of town mail, and I left there and I could, went up, was gonna go up the back way because it was a shorter way home. Then I seen this cow along the road and there was a farm there so I figured, you know, it must be their cow. So, I went in there, and I started to get out of the car and the dogs barked so I blew the horn . . .

BOYCE: Right.

MILLER: . . . because I wasn't about, I didn't know whether this dog would bite or not. And, I blew the horn two or three times and then this girl come out.

BOYCE: Do you remember what the girl looked like? What she was wearing?

MILLER: She was wearing a two piece bathing suit, like you said.

BOYCE: Go ahead.

MILLER: I told her there was a cow out there and she said, yeah it's probably one that's always getting out. And I said well do you need a help, you got anybody here to help you get it in and she says, uh, I don't need no help, she says I can get it back myself. So, I went out, went up the road there, out the driveway, she was following me in her car. I think a Corvair, or . . . So, I stop up the road there where I, where I had seen the cow and, uh, the cow wasn't there. She pulled up behind me, she got out of the car and I said the cow was here. Well, you can see the marks where the cow had been and we started walking through the, through the field there, uh, it's be on your left-hand side. And, like I say, I don't know where this guy come from.

BOYCE: Tell me what happened.

MILLER: Well, I heard her scream. She, I was walking more or less along the hedgerow there, or trees, whatever you want to call it. I heard her scream and I turned around and I seen a guy there, I'd say he was maybe my height, maybe a little taller, a little smaller, and I don't know, when, when I ran up there he whipped on me, that's how I got this, and . . .

BOYCE: Listen Frank, this guy, do you know him? Do you know where he lives?

MILLER: No, I don't know where he lives. (inaudible)

BOYCE: You killed this girl didn't you?

MILLER: No, I didn't.

BOYCE: Honest, Frank? It's got to come out. You can't leave it in. It's hard for you, I realize that, how hard it is, how difficult it is, I realize that, but you've got to help yourself before anybody else can help you. And we're going to see to it that you get the proper help. This is our job, Frank. This is our job. This is what I want to do.

MILLER: By sending me back down there.

BOYCE: Wait a second now, don't talk about going back down there. First thing we have to do is let it all come out. Don't fight it because it's worse, Frank, it's worse. It's hurting me because I feel it. I feel it wanting to come out, but it's hurting me, Frank. You're my brother, I mean we're brothers. All men on this, all men on the face of this earth are brothers, Frank, but you got to be completely honest with me.

MILLER: I'm trying to be, but you don't want to believe me.

BOYCE: I want to believe you, Frank, but I want you to tell me the truth, Frank, and you know what I'm talking about and I know what you're talking about. You've got to tell me the truth. I can't help you without the truth.

MILLER: I'm telling you the truth. Sure, that's her blood in the car because when I seen the way she was cut I wanted to help her, and then when she fell over I got scared to even be involved in something like this, being on parole and . . .

BOYCE: I realize this, Frank, it may have been an accident. Isn't that possible, Frank? Isn't that possible?

MILLER: Sure, it's possible.

BOYCE: Well, this is what I'm trying to bring out, Frank. It may be something that, that you did that you can't be held accountable for. This, I can help you, I can help you once you tell me the truth. You know what I'm talking about. I want to help you, Frank. I like you. You've been honest with me. You've been sincere and I've been the same way with you. Now this is the kind of relationship we have, but I can't help you unless you tell me the complete truth. I'll listen to you. I understand, Frank. You have to believe that, I understand. I understand how you feel. I understand how much it must hurt you inside. I know how you feel because I feel it too. Because some day I may be in the same situation Frank, but you've got to help yourself. Tell me exactly what happened, tell me the truth, Frank, please.

MILLER: I'm trying to tell you the truth.

BOYCE: Let me help you. It could have been an accident. You, you've got to tell me the truth, Frank. You know what I'm talking about. I can't help you without the truth. Now you know and I know that's, that's, that's all that counts, Frank. You know and I know that's what counts, that's what it's all about. We can't hide it from each other because we both know, but you've got to be willing to help yourself. You know, I don't think you're a criminal. You have this problem like we talked about before, right?

MILLER: Yeah, you, you say this now, but this thing goes to court and everything and you . . .

BOYCE: No. listen to me, Frank, please listen to me. The issue now is what happened. The issue now is truth. Truth is the issue now. You've got to believe this, and the truth prevails in the end, Frank. You have to believe that and I'm sincere when I'm saying it to you. You've got to be truthful with yourself.

MILLER: Yeah, truth, you say in the end, right? That's why I done three and a half years for . . .

BOYCE: Wait, whoa . . .

MILLER: . . . for a crime that I never committed because of one stinkin detective framing me . . .

BOYCE: Frank, Frank.

MILLER: . . . by the name of Rocco.

BOYCE: Frank, you're talking to me now. We have, we have a relationship, don't we? Have I been sincere with you, Frank?

MILLER: Yeah, you . . .

BOYCE: . . . Have I been honest?

MILLER: . . . Yes.

BOYCE: Have I defined your problem, Frank? Have I been willing to help you? Have I stated I'm willing to help you all I can?

MILLER: Yes.

BOYCE: Do I mean it?

MILLER: Yes.

BOYCE: Whenever I talk to anybody I talk the same way, because you have a very, very serious problem, and we want to prevent anything in the future. This is what's important, Frank, not what happened in the past. It's right now, we're living now, Frank, we want to help you now. You've got a lot more, a lot more years to live.

MILLER: No, I don't.

BOYCE: Yes, you do.

MILLER: No, I don't.

BOYCE: Don't say you don't. Now you've got to tell me.

MILLER: Not after all this, because this is going to kill my father.

BOYCE: Listen, Frank. There is where you, the truth comes out. Your father
            will understand. This is what you have to understand, Frank. If the
            truth is out he will understand. That's the most important thing, not,
            not what has happened, Frank. The fact that you were truthful, you
            came forward and you said, look I have a problem. I didn't mean to
            do what I did. I have a problem, this is what's important, Frank. This
            is very important, I got, I, I got to get closer to you, Frank, I got to
            make you believe this and I'm and I'm sincere when I tell you this.
            You got to tell me exactly what happened, Frank. That's very
            important. I know how you feel inside, Frank, it's eating you up, am
            I right? It's eating you up, Frank. You've got to come forward. You've
            got to do it for yourself, for your family, for your father, this is what's
            important Frank. Just tell me. You didn't mean to kill her did you?

MILLER: I thought she was dead or I'd have never dropped her off like that.

BOYCE: Why, Frank? Frank, look at me, okay? I'm lookin at your problem
            now. Just picture this, okay? I'm lookin at your problem, okay? You
            follow me?

MILLER: Uhm.

BOYCE: What made you do this, please tell me. Please tell me now. What
            made you do this?

MILLER: I don't know.

BOYCE: Alright, explain to me, how, exactly how it happened and then we'll
            see, maybe we can find out why it happened, alright? Is that fair?
            Just tell me how it happened and then we'll talk about why it could
            have happened. This is what's important to me.

MILLER: I don't even know.

BOYCE: Well, just tell me what happened, tell me the truth this time. Please,
            I can't help you without the truth.

MILLER: Like I said I went, I went there because the cow was out . . .

BOYCE: I know that and . . .

MILLER: Wait, wait, alright, wait a minute. She followed me out the driveway.

   We stopped up there on the road. The cow wasn't around and we were talkin. She
got in my car. We figured the cow might be down on the other road, or down
further.

BOYCE: You want it to happen.

MILLER: Yes.

BOYCE: Okay. When you got down there, Frank, when you went down there, something happened inside you. This is what I'm interested in, now please tell me, you've got to, you've got to get the proper help, Frank, we want to help you. Please tell me, Frank.

MILLER: I don't know what happened, I really don't.

BOYCE: Alright, but tell me, tell me how it happened, the truth this time, Frank.

MILLER: I can't even tell ya that.

BOYCE: Well, tell me, tell me Frank, (inaudible) . . . have to be completely truthful with me the way I am with you. It's so important, Frank, honest to God, because people believe truth. I mean, Frank, this is hurting me, God listen. I just want you to come out and tell me, so I can help you, that's all. Listen, it's the right way.

MILLER: I, I swear to God, I don't know what happened down there.

BOYCE: Why? Why did you do it?

MILLER: I don't even know that.

BOYCE: What did you, what did you cut the girl with? What did you use, Frank?

MILLER: A penknife

BOYCE: Your penknife?

MILLER: Yes, sir.

BOYCE: Which penknife?

MILLER: The one you have.

BOYCE: The one I have?

MILLER: Yes.

BOYCE: Where did you cut her, Frank?

MILLER: In the throat.

BOYCE: In the throat?

MILLER: Uh, huh.

BOYCE: Now, right before you cut her in the throat, what, why did you cut, did, was she fighting you off?

MILLER: No.

BOYCE: She wasn't fighting you?

MILLER: No.

BOYCE: Why do you think, where were you when you cut her in the throat? Where were you, where were you at, at that moment?

MILLER: Down by the bridge.

BOYCE: Down by the bridge?

MILLER: Yes.

BOYCE: Were you in the vehicle or were you outside the vehicle?

MILLER: In the car.

BOYCE: You were in the car?

MILLER: Yes.

BOYCE: Okay, now, you were in the car, right?

MILLER: Uh, huh.

BOYCE: Did she get in the car voluntarily?

MILLER: Yes.

BOYCE: She did?

MILLER: Yes.

BOYCE: Did you ask her to get into the car?

MILLER: Yes.

BOYCE: What did you say to her, Frank?

MILLER: I said, why don't we go on down the road and see if the cow's down there.

BOYCE: And she got in the car with you?

MILLER: Yes.

BOYCE: Where did she get in the car with you?

MILLER: Up on the main road.

BOYCE: Where she parked her car?

MILLER: Yes.

BOYCE: Alright. Then you drove down by the bridge.

MILLER: Right.

BOYCE: Okay, now. What happened in the car? Where did you have your knife?

MILLER: In my pocket.

BOYCE: In your pocket?

MILLER: Yes.

BOYCE: And, when did you take it out?

MILLER: From there everything's a blank.

BOYCE: Well . . .

MILLER: I didn't, as far as what, you know, what really . . .

BOYCE: Alright, well where did you cut her with the knife?

MILLER: In the car.

BOYCE: Did she fight you in any way?

MILLER: No.

BOYCE: Did you cut any other part of her body, Frank?

MILLER: No, not that I, no, not that I know of.

BOYCE: Did you bite her in any way, Frank?

MILLER: No, not that I know of.

BOYCE: Not that you know of?

MILLER: No.

BOYCE: Did she bleed a lot in the car, Frank?

MILLER: Some, yes.

BOYCE: What happened to the blood that was in the car, Frank? Did you clean the car, Frank? Did you clean the car out after the blood was in the vehicle?

MILLER: There wasn't really, no, I, I just, you know, wiped what little bit was on the seat.

BOYCE: Alright. After you cut her throat, now, what did you do then? After that, after that happened, what did you do then, Frank?

MILLER: I don't know, I, everything just, everything's a blank, really.

BOYCE: Well, try and remember now. What, did you get out of the vehicle?

MILLER: I guess. Yeah, I, I got, I got out of the car and I took her out of the car . . .

BOYCE: Alright, then what did you do?

MILLER: Carried her over the bridge.

BOYCE: Threw her over the bridge?

MILLER: Yes.

BOYCE: Did, then, after you threw her over the bridge, then what did you do, Frank?

MILLER: I didn't do, I don't know.

BOYCE: Did you drag, did you drag her any further after you threw her over the bridge?

MILLER: I don't think so, no.

BOYCE: Try and remember now, it's very important. I'm sure you can understand that, right?

MILLER: Yeah.

BOYCE: Try and remember now. You threw her over the bridge . . .

MILLER: Yeah.

BOYCE: . . . Now, did you go down and look at her again?

MILLER: I don't really know.

BOYCE: Okay. Did you, did you have sexual relations with her, Frank?

MILLER: Not that I know of.

BOYCE: Are you sure now? Think hard. Think hard now, while you were in the car?

MILLER: I don't think so.

BOYCE: Alright. After she, after you threw her out over the bridge?

MILLER: Yeah.

BOYCE: Is that where you had the sexual relations with her?

MILLER: I don't think I did.

BOYCE: Did you remove any of her clothing, Frank?

MILLER: I don't believe so, no. I don't really know.

BOYCE: Alright. Now think about, did you try and drag her body anywhere?

MILLER: I don't think so.

BOYCE: Did you drag the body up towards the water anywhere?

MILLER: I don't think so, no. I say I, I don't know, I . . .

BOYCE: Where, once again now, you're in the car with her right?

MILLER: Uh, huh.

BOYCE: Now, did you pull the knife out right away? What did you say to her, Frank, before you pulled the knife out? Did you ask her anything?

MILLER: I don't know if I did or not.

BOYCE: And you said the pocket knife, what pocket knife were you referring to now, that you used.

MILLER: The one you have.

BOYCE: The one that you gave me at PFD Plastics?

MILLER: Yeah.

BOYCE: And whereabouts did you cut her?

MILLER: In the throat.

BOYCE: In the throat? Is there any reason why you cut her in the throat, Frank?

MILLER: No, not that I know of.

BOYCE: Did you, did you caress her breasts in any way?

MILLER: No.

BOYCE: Was she an attractive girl?

MILLER: Um, I'd say so, yes.

BOYCE: About what time was that, Frank?

MILLER: I'm not sure.

BOYCE: About what time?

MILLER: Well, I was at the Post Office around, I figure 11 o'clock, so it had to be after that.

BOYCE: It happened sometime after that, about, about how long?

MILLER: I'd say maybe five after, ten after, something like this. That's about all the time it would take to go from the Post Office to there.

BOYCE: And what road were you on when this, when you cut her throat in the vehicle, what road were you on?

MILLER: I don't know the road exactly.

BOYCE: Was it a dirt road, Frank?

MILLER: Yes.

BOYCE: It was a dirt road?

MILLER: Yes.

BOYCE: Did you see anybody at the house when you were there?

MILLER: Just her.

BOYCE: Did you see any of her brothers?

MILLER: No.

BOYCE: Did you see anyone else?

MILLER: No. No one came out but her.

BOYCE: Did you cut any other portion of her body, Frank? Just, just think hard, now, take your time, ah. You know, I realize that, you know, that, just take your time and think, did you cut any portion of her body? Did you cut her breasts?

MILLER: No.

BOYCE: Are you sure, Frank?

MILLER: Positive.

BOYCE: Did you bite her in anyway?

MILLER: I don't think . . .

BOYCE: Tell me the truth, Frank. Honest? You've been so honest with me so far, you've been truthful, you've been honest, you've been sincere. Now, after you threw, how did you, which car, which car did you, uh, side of the car did you drag her out of?

MILLER: The driver's side.

BOYCE: Driver's side?

MILLER: Yeah.

BOYCE: I see. Did you clean your car in anyway?

MILLER: Yeah.

BOYCE: Where, where did you clean your car, Frank?

MILLER: I used the hose at home.

BOYCE: At home?

MILLER: Yeah, in the driveway.

BOYCE: And did you enter your house through the front door, Frank?

MILLER: Through the breezeway.

BOYCE: Through the breezeway?

MILLER: Yeah.

BOYCE: Where are the rags? What did you use to clean the car out with?

MILLER: I just used the hose.

BOYCE: The hose?

MILLER: Yeah.

BOYCE: You washed it out?

MILLER: Yes.

BOYCE: Where was the vehicle when you washed it out, Frank?

MILLER: In the driveway.

BOYCE: In the driveway? Did you use any type of rag on the inside of the car?

MILLER: Just a . . . no.

BOYCE: Are you sure, Frank?

MILLER: There was a . . . I had a paper bag, a brown paper bag and the . . . I just wiped some of the water off of the seat and stuff.

BOYCE: Where is the brown paper bag now, Frank? What did you do with it?

MILLER: I threw it away.

BOYCE: Where did you throw it, Frank?

MILLER: Driving along the road on my way up to Flemington.

BOYCE: Where, do you remember on which road you were, or how far you were away from the house when you threw it out the window?

MILLER: No, I don't.

BOYCE: You don't have any idea, Frank?

MILLER: No.

BOYCE: Now, did you actually throw her over the, uh, the fence then the rail?

MILLER: Yes.

BOYCE: You did?

MILLER: Yes.

BOYCE: Did you go, after you threw her over the fence, did you go and look at her again to see if she was dead?

MILLER: I don't believe I did, no.

BOYCE: Was there anyone with you, Frank, when this occurred, or were you alone? You indicated before that you were alone, were you alone with her when this happened?

MILLER: Yeah.

BOYCE: I see. Were you driving your car, Frank?

MILLER: Yeah.

BOYCE: What kind of a car do you drive?

MILLER: A white Mercury.

BOYCE: What year is that Mercury?

MILLER: '69.

BOYCE: '69? Is there any damage, is there any damage to your vehicle?

MILLER: Yes.

BOYCE: Where is the damage?

MILLER: Right-hand side.

BOYCE: Is your trunk tied down?

MILLER: Yes.

BOYCE: Alright. I've indicated before that you would be willing to sit down with me and the Assistant Prosecutor and indicate to him, like you said, that you have a problem.

MILLER: uh, huh.

BOYCE: Would you be willing to sit down with us while we take a statement from you?

MILLER: Yes.

BOYCE: So it can be incorporated, you follow me?

MILLER: Yeah.

BOYCE: In order to help you.

MILLER: Uh, huh.

BOYCE: Would you be willing to do that?

MILLER: Uh, huh.

BOYCE: Now, is there anything I can get you now? You want coffee?

MILLER: No.

BOYCE: You want to just sit here for awhile?

MILLER: Yes.

The time now is 2:45 a.m. Statement concluded at this time. Statement and interrogation concluded at this time.

At the end of this interrogation, Miller collapsed into a catatonic state, whereupon he was hospitalized.

Chapter 20

MIRANDA REVISITED

DICKERSON v. UNITED STATES
530 U.S. 428 (2000)

CHIEF JUSTICE REHNQUIST delivered the opinion of the Court.

In *Miranda v. Arizona*, 384 U.S. 436 (1966), we held that certain warnings must be given before a suspect's statement made during custodial interrogation could be admitted in evidence. In the wake of that decision, Congress enacted 18 U.S.C. § 3501, which in essence laid down a rule that the admissibility of such statements should turn only on whether or not they were voluntarily made. We hold that *Miranda*, being a constitutional decision of this Court, may not be in effect overruled by an Act of Congress, and we decline to overrule *Miranda* ourselves. We therefore hold that *Miranda* and its progeny in this Court govern the admissibility of statements made during custodial interrogation in both state and federal courts.

Petitioner Dickerson was indicted for bank robbery, conspiracy to commit bank robbery, and using a firearm in the course of committing a crime of violence, all in violation of the applicable provisions of Title 18 of the United States Code. Before trial, Dickerson moved to suppress a statement he had made at a Federal Bureau of Investigation field office, on the grounds that he had not received "*Miranda* warnings" before being interrogated. The District Court granted his motion to suppress, and the Government took an interlocutory appeal to the United States Court of Appeals for the Fourth Circuit. That court, by a divided vote, reversed the District Court's suppression order. It agreed with the District Court's conclusion that petitioner had not received *Miranda* warnings before making his statement. But it went on to hold that § 3501, which in effect makes the admissibility of statements such as Dickerson's turn solely on whether they were made voluntarily, was satisfied in this case. It then concluded that our decision in *Miranda* was not a constitutional holding, and that therefore Congress could by statute have the final say on the question of admissibility.

Because of the importance of the questions raised by the Court of Appeals' decision, we granted certiorari, and now reverse.

We begin with a brief historical account of the law governing the admission of confessions. Prior to *Miranda*, we evaluated the admissibility of a suspect's confession under a voluntariness test. The roots of this test developed in the common law, as the courts of England and then the United States recognized that coerced confessions are inherently untrustworthy. Over time, our cases recognized two constitutional bases for the requirement that a confession be voluntary to be admitted into evidence: the Fifth Amendment right against self-incrimination and the Due Process Clause of the Fourteenth Amendment. *See, e.g., Bram v. United States*, 168 U.S. 532, 542 (1897) (stating that the voluntariness test "is controlled by that portion of the Fifth Amendment . . . commanding that no person 'shall be compelled in any criminal case to be a witness against himself' "); *Brown v. Mississippi* (reversing a criminal conviction under the Due Process Clause because it was based on a confession obtained by physical coercion).

While *Bram* was decided before *Brown* and its progeny, for the middle third of the 20th century our cases based the rule against admitting coerced confessions primarily, if not exclusively, on notions of due process. We applied the due process voluntariness test in "some 30 different cases decided during the era that intervened between *Brown* and *Escobedo v. Illinois*." Those cases refined the test into an inquiry that examines "whether a defendant's will was overborne" by the circumstances surrounding the giving of a confession. The due process test takes into consideration "the totality of all the surrounding circumstances — both the characteristics of the accused and the details of the interrogation."

We have never abandoned this due process jurisprudence, and thus continue to exclude confessions that were obtained involuntarily. But our decisions in *Malloy v. Hogan*, 378 U.S. 1 (1964), and *Miranda* changed the focus of much of the inquiry in determining the admissibility of suspects' incriminating statements. In *Malloy*, we held that the Fifth Amendment's Self-Incrimination Clause is incorporated in the Due Process Clause of the Fourteenth Amendment and thus applies to the States. We decided *Miranda* on the heels of *Malloy*.

In *Miranda*, we noted that the advent of modern custodial police interrogation brought with it an increased concern about confessions obtained by coercion. Because custodial police interrogation, by its very nature, isolates and pressures the individual, we stated that "even without employing brutality, the 'third degree' or [other] specific stratagems, . . . custodial interrogation exacts a heavy toll on individual liberty and trades on the weakness of individuals." We concluded that the coercion inherent in custodial interrogation blurs the line between voluntary and involuntary statements, and thus heightens the risk that an individual will not be "accorded his privilege under the Fifth Amendment . . . not to be compelled to incriminate himself." Accordingly, we laid down "concrete constitutional guidelines for law enforcement agencies and courts to follow." Those guidelines established that the admissibility in evidence of any statement given during custodial interrogation of a suspect would depend on whether the police provided the suspect with four warnings. These warnings (which have come to be known colloquially as "*Miranda* rights") are: a suspect "has the right to remain silent, that anything he says can be used against him in a court of law, that he has the right to the presence of an attorney, and that if he cannot afford an attorney one will be appointed for him prior to any questioning if he so desires."

Two years after *Miranda* was decided, Congress enacted § 3501. That section provides, in relevant part:

(a) In any criminal prosecution brought by the United States or by the District of Columbia, a confession . . . shall be admissible in evidence if it is voluntarily given. Before such confession is received in evidence, the trial judge shall, out of the presence of the jury, determine any issue as to voluntariness. If the trial judge determines that the confession was voluntarily made it shall be admitted in evidence and the trial judge shall permit the jury to hear relevant evidence on the issue of voluntariness and shall instruct the jury to give such weight to the confession as the jury feels it deserves under all the circumstances.

(b) The trial judge in determining the issue of voluntariness shall take into consideration all the circumstances surrounding the giving of the confession, including (1) the time elapsing between arrest and arraignment of the defendant making the confession, if it was made after arrest and before arraignment, (2) whether such defendant knew the nature of the offense with which he was charged or of which he was suspected at the time of making the confession, (3) whether or not such defendant was advised or knew that he was not required to make any statement and that any such statement could be used against him, (4) whether or not such defendant had been advised prior to questioning of his right to the assistance of counsel; and (5) whether or not such defendant was without the assistance of counsel when questioned and when giving such confession.

The presence or absence of any of the above-mentioned factors to be taken into consideration by the judge need not be conclusive on the issue of voluntariness of the confession.

Given § 3501's express designation of voluntariness as the touchstone of admissibility, its omission of any warning requirement, and the instruction for trial courts to consider a nonexclusive list of factors relevant to the circumstances of a confession, we agree with the Court of Appeals that Congress intended by its enactment to overrule *Miranda. See also Davis v. United States* (SCALIA, J., concurring) (stating that, prior to *Miranda*, "voluntariness *vel non* was the touchstone of admissibility of confessions"). Because of the obvious conflict between our decision in *Miranda* and § 3501, we must address whether Congress has constitutional authority to thus supersede *Miranda*. If Congress has such authority, § 3501's totality-of-the-circumstances approach must prevail over *Miranda's* requirement of warnings; if not, that section must yield to *Miranda's* more specific requirements.

The law in this area is clear. This Court has supervisory authority over the federal courts, and we may use that authority to prescribe rules of evidence and procedure that are binding in those tribunals. However, the power to judicially create and enforce nonconstitutional "rules of procedure and evidence for the federal courts exists only in the absence of a relevant Act of Congress." Congress retains the ultimate authority to modify or set aside any judicially created rules of evidence and procedure that are not required by the Constitution.

But Congress may not legislatively supersede our decisions interpreting and applying the Constitution. *See, e.g., City of Boerne v. Flores*, 521 U.S. 507, 517–521 (1997). This case therefore turns on whether the *Miranda* Court announced a constitutional rule or merely exercised its supervisory authority to regulate evidence in the absence of congressional direction. Recognizing this point, the Court of Appeals surveyed *Miranda* and its progeny to determine the constitutional status of the *Miranda* decision. Relying on the fact that we have created several exceptions to *Miranda's* warnings requirement and that we have repeatedly referred to the *Miranda* warnings as "prophylactic," *New York v. Quarles,* and "not themselves rights protected by the Constitution," *Michigan v. Tucker,* 417 U.S. 433, 444 (1974),[2] the Court of Appeals concluded that the protections announced in *Miranda* are not constitutionally required.

We disagree with the Court of Appeals' conclusion, although we concede that there is language in some of our opinions that supports the view taken by that court. But first and foremost of the factors on the other side — that *Miranda* is a constitutional decision — is that both *Miranda* and two of its companion cases applied the rule to proceedings in state courts — to wit, Arizona, California, and New York. Since that time, we have consistently applied *Miranda's* rule to prosecutions arising in state courts. *See, e.g., Stansbury v. California; Minnick v. Mississippi; Arizona v. Roberson; Edwards v. Arizona.* It is beyond dispute that we do not hold a supervisory power over the courts of the several States. *Smith v. Phillips,* 455 U.S. 209, 221, 102 S. Ct. 940, 71 L. Ed. 2d 78 (1982) ("Federal courts hold no supervisory authority over state judicial proceedings and may intervene only to correct wrongs of constitutional dimension").[3]

The *Miranda* opinion itself begins by stating that the Court granted certiorari "to explore some facets of the problems . . . of applying the privilege against self-incrimination to in-custody interrogation, *and to give concrete constitutional guidelines for law enforcement agencies and courts to follow.*" (emphasis added). In fact, the majority opinion is replete with statements indicating that the majority thought it was announcing a constitutional rule. Indeed, the Court's ultimate conclusion was that the unwarned confessions obtained in the four cases before the Court in *Miranda* "were obtained from the defendant under circumstances that did not meet constitutional standards for protection of the privilege."[5]

---

[2] *See also Davis v. United States,* 512 U.S. 452, 457–458 (1994); *Withrow v. Williams,* 507 U.S. 680, 690–691 (1993) ("*Miranda's* safeguards are not constitutional in character"); *Duckworth v. Eagan,* 492 U.S. 195, 203 (1989); *Connecticut v. Barrett,* 479 U.S. 523, 528 (1987) ("The *Miranda* Court adopted prophylactic rules designed to insulate the exercise of Fifth Amendment rights"); *Oregon v. Elstad,* 470 U.S. 298, 306 (1985); *Edwards v. Arizona,* 451 U.S. 477, 492 (1981) (Powell, J., concurring in result).

[3] Our conclusion regarding *Miranda's* constitutional basis is further buttressed by the fact that we have allowed prisoners to bring alleged *Miranda* violations before the federal courts in habeas corpus proceedings. *See Thompson v. Keohane,* 516 U.S. 99 (1995); *Withrow.* Habeas corpus proceedings are available only for claims that a person "is in custody in violation of the Constitution or laws or treaties of the United States." 28 U.S.C. § 2254(a). Since the *Miranda* rule is clearly not based on federal laws or treaties, our decision allowing habeas review for *Miranda* claims obviously assumes that *Miranda* is of constitutional origin.

[5] Many of our subsequent cases have also referred to *Miranda's* constitutional underpinnings. *See, e.g., Withrow* (" 'Prophylactic' though it may be, in protecting a defendant's Fifth Amendment privilege against self-incrimination, *Miranda* safeguards a 'fundamental trial right' "); *Illinois v. Perkins* (describing *Miranda's* warning requirement as resting on "the Fifth Amendment privilege against self-incrimination"); *Butler v. McKellar,* 494 U.S. 407, 411 (1990) ("The Fifth Amendment bars police-initiated interrogation following a suspect's request for counsel in the context of a separate

Additional support for our conclusion that *Miranda* is constitutionally based is found in the *Miranda* Court's invitation for legislative action to protect the constitutional right against coerced self-incrimination. After discussing the "compelling pressures" inherent in custodial police interrogation, the *Miranda* Court concluded that, "in order to combat these pressures and to permit a full opportunity to exercise the privilege against self-incrimination, the accused must be adequately and effectively appraised of his rights and the exercise of those rights must be fully honored." However, the Court emphasized that it could not foresee "the potential alternatives for protecting the privilege which might be devised by Congress or the States," and it accordingly opined that the Constitution would not preclude legislative solutions that differed from the prescribed *Miranda* warnings but which were "at least as effective in apprising accused persons of their right of silence and in assuring a continuous opportunity to exercise it."[6]

The Court of Appeals also relied on the fact that we have, after our *Miranda* decision, made exceptions from its rule in cases such as *New York v. Quarles* and *Harris v. New York*. But we have also broadened the application of the *Miranda* doctrine in cases such as *Doyle v. Ohio*, 426 U.S. 610 (1976), and *Arizona v. Roberson*. These decisions illustrate the principle — not that *Miranda* is not a constitutional rule — but that no constitutional rule is immutable. No court laying down a general rule can possibly foresee the various circumstances in which counsel will seek to apply it, and the sort of modifications represented by these cases are as much a normal part of constitutional law as the original decision.

The Court of Appeals also noted that in *Oregon v. Elstad*, we stated that " 'the *Miranda* exclusionary rule . . . serves the Fifth Amendment and sweeps more broadly than the Fifth Amendment itself.' " Our decision in that case — refusing to apply the traditional "fruits" doctrine developed in Fourth Amendment cases — does not prove that *Miranda* is a nonconstitutional decision, but simply recognizes the fact that unreasonable searches under the Fourth Amendment are different from unwarned interrogation under the Fifth Amendment.

As an alternative argument for sustaining the Court of Appeals' decision, the court-invited *amicus curiae*[7] contends that the section complies with the requirement that a legislative alternative to *Miranda* be equally as effective in preventing coerced confessions. We agree with the *amicus'* contention that there are more remedies available for abusive police conduct than there were at the time *Miranda* was decided, *see, e.g., Wilkins v. May*, 872 F.2d 190, 194 (7th Cir. 1989) (applying *Bivens v. Six Unknown Fed. Narcotics Agents*, 403 U.S. 388 (1971), to hold that a

---

investigation"); *Michigan v. Jackson* ("The Fifth Amendment protection against compelled self-incrimination provides the right to counsel at custodial interrogations"); *Moran v. Burbine* (referring to *Miranda* as "our interpretation of the Federal Constitution"); *Edwards*.

[6] The Court of Appeals relied in part on our statement that the *Miranda* decision in no way "creates a 'constitutional straightjacket.' " However, a review of our opinion in *Miranda* clarifies that this disclaimer was intended to indicate that the Constitution does not require police to administer the particular *Miranda* warnings, not that the Constitution does not require a procedure that is effective in securing Fifth Amendment rights.

[7] Because no party to the underlying litigation argued in favor of § 3501's constitutionality in this Court, we invited Professor Paul Cassell to assist our deliberations by arguing in support of the judgment below.

suspect may bring a federal cause of action under the Due Process Clause for police misconduct during custodial interrogation). But we do not agree that these additional measures supplement § 3501's protections sufficiently to meet the constitutional minimum. *Miranda* requires procedures that will warn a suspect in custody of his right to remain silent and which will assure the suspect that the exercise of that right will be honored. As discussed above, § 3501 explicitly eschews a requirement of pre-interrogation warnings in favor of an approach that looks to the administration of such warnings as only one factor in determining the voluntariness of a suspect's confession. The additional remedies cited by *amicus* do not, in our view, render them, together with § 3501 an adequate substitute for the warnings required by *Miranda*.

The dissent argues that it is judicial overreaching for this Court to hold § 3501 unconstitutional unless we hold that the *Miranda* warnings are required by the Constitution, in the sense that nothing else will suffice to satisfy constitutional requirements. But we need not go farther than *Miranda* to decide this case. In *Miranda*, the Court noted that reliance on the traditional totality-of-the-circumstances test raised a risk of overlooking an involuntary custodial confession, risk that the Court found unacceptably great when the confession is offered in the case in chief to prove guilt. The Court therefore concluded that something more than the totality test was necessary. As discussed above, § 3501 reinstates the totality test as sufficient. Section 3501 therefore cannot be sustained if *Miranda* is to remain the law.

Whether or not we would agree with *Miranda's* reasoning and its resulting rule, were we addressing the issue in the first instance, the principles of *stare decisis* weigh heavily against overruling it now.

We do not think there is such justification for overruling *Miranda. Miranda* has become embedded in routine police practice to the point where the warnings have become part of our national culture. *See Mitchell v. United States*, 526 U.S. 314, 331–332 (1999) (SCALIA, J., dissenting) (stating that the fact that a rule has found " 'wide acceptance in the legal culture' " is "adequate reason not to overrule" it). While we have overruled our precedents when subsequent cases have undermined their doctrinal underpinnings, *see, e.g., Patterson v. McLean Credit Union*, 491 U.S. 164, 173 (1989), we do not believe that this has happened to the *Miranda* decision. If anything, our subsequent cases have reduced the impact of the *Miranda* rule on legitimate law enforcement while reaffirming the decision's core ruling that unwarned statements may not be used as evidence in the prosecution's case in chief.

The disadvantage of the *Miranda* rule is that statements which may be by no means involuntary, made by a defendant who is aware of his "rights," may nonetheless be excluded and a guilty defendant go free as a result. But experience suggests that the totality-of-the-circumstances test which § 3501 seeks to revive is more difficult than *Miranda* for law enforcement officers to conform to, and for courts to apply in a consistent manner. The requirement that *Miranda* warnings be given does not, of course, dispense with the voluntariness inquiry. But as we said in *Berkemer v. McCarty*, "cases in which a defendant can make a colorable argument that a self-incriminating statement was 'compelled' despite the fact that the law enforcement authorities adhered to the dictates of *Miranda* are rare."

In sum, we conclude that *Miranda* announced a constitutional rule that Congress may not supersede legislatively. Following the rule of *stare decisis*, we decline to overrule *Miranda* ourselves. The judgment of the Court of Appeals is therefore

Reversed.

JUSTICE SCALIA, with whom JUSTICE THOMAS joins, dissenting.

Those to whom judicial decisions are an unconnected series of judgments that produce either favored or disfavored results will doubtless greet today's decision as a paragon of moderation, since it declines to overrule *Miranda v. Arizona.* Those who understand the judicial process will appreciate that today's decision is not a reaffirmation of *Miranda,* but a radical revision of the most significant element of *Miranda* (as of all cases): the rationale that gives it a permanent place in our jurisprudence.

Marbury v. Madison, 5 U.S. 137, 1 Cranch 137 (1803), held that an Act of Congress will not be enforced by the courts if what it prescribes violates the Constitution of the United States. That was the basis on which *Miranda* was decided. One will search today's opinion in vain, however, for a statement (surely simple enough to make) that what 18 U.S.C. § 3501 prescribes — the use at trial of a voluntary confession, even when a *Miranda* warning or its equivalent has failed to be given — violates the Constitution. The reason the statement does not appear is not only (and perhaps not so much) that it would be absurd, inasmuch as § 3501 excludes from trial precisely what the Constitution excludes from trial, viz., compelled confessions; but also that Justices whose votes are needed to compose today's majority are on record as believing that a violation of *Miranda* is *not* a violation of the Constitution. *See Davis v. United States,* 512 U.S. 452 (1994) (opinion of the Court, in which KENNEDY, J., joined); *Duckworth v. Eagan,* 492 U.S. 195 (1989) (opinion of the Court, in which KENNEDY, J., joined); *Oregon v. Elstad,* 470 U.S. 298 (1985) (opinion of the Court by O'CONNOR, J.); *New York v. Quarles,* 467 U.S. 649 (1984) (opinion of the Court by REHNQUIST, J.). And so, to justify today's agreed-upon result, the Court must adopt a significant *new,* if not entirely comprehensible, principle of constitutional law. As the Court chooses to describe that principle, statutes of Congress can be disregarded, not only when what they prescribe violates the Constitution, but when what they prescribe contradicts a decision of this Court that "announced a constitutional rule." As I shall discuss in some detail, the only thing that can possibly mean in the context of this case is that this Court has the power, not merely to apply the Constitution but to expand it, imposing what it regards as useful "prophylactic" restrictions upon Congress and the States. That is an immense and frightening antidemocratic power, and it does not exist.

It takes only a small step to bring today's opinion out of the realm of power-judging and into the mainstream of legal reasoning: The Court need only go beyond its carefully couched iterations that "*Miranda* is a constitutional decision," that "*Miranda* is constitutionally based," that *Miranda* has "constitutional under-pinnings," and come out and say quite clearly: "We reaffirm today that custodial interrogation that is not preceded by *Miranda* warnings or their equivalent violates the Constitution of the United States." It cannot say that, because a majority of the Court does not believe it. The Court therefore acts in plain violation of the Constitution when it denies effect to this Act of Congress.

I

Early in this Nation's history, this Court established the sound proposition that constitutional government in a system of separated powers requires judges to regard as inoperative any legislative act, even of Congress itself, that is "repugnant to the Constitution."

> So if a law be in opposition to the constitution; if both the law and the constitution apply to a particular case, so that the court must either decide that case conformably to the law, disregarding the constitution; or conformably to the constitution, disregarding the law; the court must determine which of these conflicting rules governs the case.

Marbury. The power we recognized in *Marbury* will thus permit us, indeed require us, to "disregard" § 3501, a duly enacted statute governing the admissibility of evidence in the federal courts, only if it "be in opposition to the constitution" — here, assertedly, the dictates of the Fifth Amendment.

It was once possible to characterize the so-called *Miranda* rule as resting (however implausibly) upon the proposition that what the statute here before us permits — the admission at trial of un-*Mirandized* confessions — violates the Constitution. That is the fairest reading of the *Miranda* case itself. The Court began by announcing that the Fifth Amendment privilege against self-incrimination applied in the context of extrajudicial custodial interrogation, — itself a doubtful proposition as a matter both of history and precedent, see Harlan, J., dissenting (characterizing the Court's conclusion that the Fifth Amendment privilege, rather than the Due Process Clause, governed stationhouse confessions as a *"trompe l'oeil"*). Having extended the privilege into the confines of the station house, the Court liberally sprinkled throughout its sprawling 60-page opinion suggestions that, because of the compulsion inherent in custodial interrogation, the privilege was violated by any statement thus obtained that did not conform to the rules set forth in *Miranda,* or some functional equivalent.

The dissenters, for their part, also understood *Miranda's* holding to be based on the "premise . . . that pressure on the suspect must be eliminated though it be only the subtle influence of the atmosphere and surroundings." And at least one case decided shortly after *Miranda* explicitly confirmed the view. *See Orozco v. Texas* ("The use of these admissions obtained in the absence of the required warnings was a flat violation of the Self-Incrimination Clause of the Fifth Amendment as construed in *Miranda*").

So understood, *Miranda* was objectionable for innumerable reasons, not least the fact that cases spanning more than 70 years had rejected its core premise that, absent the warnings and an effective waiver of the right to remain silent and of the (thitherto unknown) right to have an attorney present, a statement obtained pursuant to custodial interrogation was necessarily the product of compulsion. *See Crooker v. California* (confession not involuntary despite denial of access to counsel); *Cicenia v. Lagay* (same); *Powers v. United States*, 223 U.S. 303 (1912) (lack of warnings and counsel did not render statement before United States Commissioner involuntary); *Wilson v. United States*, 162 U.S. 613 (1896) (same). Moreover, history and precedent aside, the decision in *Miranda*, if read as an explication of what the Constitution *requires*, is preposterous. There is, for example, simply no basis in reason for concluding that a response to the very first question asked, by a suspect who already *knows* all of the rights described in the *Miranda* warning, is anything other than a volitional act. *See Miranda* (White, J., dissenting). And even if one assumes that the elimination of compulsion absolutely requires informing even the most knowledgeable suspect of his right to remain silent, it cannot conceivably require the right to have *counsel* present. There is a world of difference, which the Court recognized under the traditional voluntariness test but ignored in *Miranda*, between compelling a suspect to incriminate himself and preventing him from foolishly doing so of his own accord. Only the latter (which is *not* required by the Constitution) could explain the Court's inclusion of a right to counsel and the requirement that it, too, be knowingly and intelligently waived. Counsel's presence is not required to tell the suspect that he *need* not speak; the interrogators can do that. The only good reason for having counsel there is that he can be counted on to advise the suspect that he *should* not speak. *See Watts v. Indiana* (Jackson, J., concurring in result in part and dissenting in part) ("Any lawyer worth his salt will tell the suspect in no uncertain terms to make no statement to police under any circumstances").

Preventing foolish (rather than compelled) confessions is likewise the only conceivable basis for the rules (suggested in *Miranda*) that courts must exclude any confession elicited by questioning conducted, without interruption, after the suspect has indicated a desire to stand on his right to remain silent, see *Michigan v. Mosley*, or initiated by police after the suspect has expressed a desire to have counsel present, see *Edwards v. Arizona*. Nonthreatening attempts to persuade the suspect to reconsider that initial decision are not, without more, enough to render a change of heart the product of anything other than the suspect's free will. Thus, what is most remarkable about the *Miranda* decision — and what made it unacceptable as a matter of straightforward constitutional interpretation in the *Marbury* tradition — is its palpable hostility toward the act of confession *per se*, rather than toward what the Constitution abhors, *compelled* confession. See *United States v. Washington*, 431 U.S. 181, 187 (1977) ("Far from being prohibited by the Constitution, admissions of guilt by wrongdoers, if not coerced, are inherently desirable"). The Constitution is not, unlike the *Miranda* majority, offended by a criminal's commendable qualm of conscience or fortunate fit of stupidity. *Cf. Minnick v. Mississippi* (SCALIA, J., dissenting).

For these reasons, and others more than adequately developed in the *Miranda* dissents and in the subsequent works of the decision's many critics, any conclusion that a violation of the *Miranda* rules *necessarily* amounts to a violation of the privilege against compelled self-incrimination can claim no support in history, precedent, or common sense, and as a result would at least presumptively be worth reconsidering even at this late date. But that is unnecessary, since the Court has (thankfully) long since abandoned the notion that failure to comply with *Miranda's* rules is itself a violation of the Constitution.

II

As the Court today acknowledges, since *Miranda* we have explicitly, and repeatedly, interpreted that decision as having announced, not the circumstances in which custodial interrogation runs afoul of the Fifth or Fourteenth Amendment, but rather only "prophylactic" rules that go beyond the right against compelled self-incrimination. Of course the seeds of this "prophylactic" interpretation of *Miranda* were present in the decision itself. *See Miranda* (discussing the "necessity for procedures which assure that the [suspect] is accorded his privilege"). In subsequent cases, the seeds have sprouted and borne fruit: The Court has squarely concluded that it is possible — indeed not uncommon — for the police to violate *Miranda* without also violating the Constitution.

Michigan v. Tucker, 417 U.S. 433 (1974), an opinion for the Court written by then-Justice REHNQUIST, rejected the true-to-*Marbury*, failure-to-warn-as-constitutional-violation interpretation of *Miranda*. It held that exclusion of the "fruits" of a *Miranda* violation — the statement of a witness whose identity the defendant had revealed while in custody — was not required. The opinion explained that the question whether the "police conduct complained of directly infringed upon respondent's right against compulsory self-incrimination" was a "separate question" from "whether it instead violated only the prophylactic rules developed to protect that right." The "procedural safeguards" adopted in *Miranda*, the Court said, "were not themselves rights protected by the Constitution but were instead measures to insure that the right against compulsory self-incrimination was protected," and to "provide practical reinforcement for the right." Comparing the particular facts of the custodial interrogation with the "historical circumstances underlying the privilege," the Court concluded, unequivocally, that the defendant's statement could not be termed "involuntary as that term has been defined in the decisions of this Court," and thus that there had been no constitutional violation, notwithstanding the clear violation of the "procedural rules later established in *Miranda*." Lest there be any confusion on the point, the Court reiterated that the "police conduct at issue here did not abridge respondent's constitutional privilege against compulsory self-incrimination, but departed only from the prophylactic standards later laid down by this Court in *Miranda* to safeguard that privilege." It is clear from our cases, of course, that if the statement in *Tucker had* been obtained in violation of the Fifth Amendment, the statement and its fruits would have been excluded. See *Nix v. Williams*.

The next year, in *Oregon v. Hass*, 420 U.S. 714 (1975), the Court held that a defendant's statement taken in violation of *Miranda* that was nonetheless *voluntary* could be used at trial for impeachment purposes. This holding turned upon the recognition that violation of *Miranda* is not unconstitutional compulsion, since statements obtained in actual violation of the privilege against compelled self-incrimination, "as opposed to . . . taken in violation of *Miranda*," quite simply "may not be put to any testimonial use whatever against [the defendant] in a criminal trial," including as impeachment evidence. *New Jersey v. Portash*, 440 U.S. 450, 459 (1979). *See also Mincey v. Arizona* (holding that while statements obtained in violation of *Miranda* may be used for impeachment if otherwise trustworthy, the Constitution prohibits "*any* criminal trial use against a defendant of his *involuntary* statement").

Nearly a decade later, in *New York v. Quarles*, the Court relied upon the fact that "the prophylactic *Miranda* warnings . . . are 'not themselves rights protected by the Constitution,'" to create a "public safety" exception. In that case, police apprehended, after a chase in a grocery store, a rape suspect known to be carrying a gun. After handcuffing and searching him (and finding no gun) — but before reading him his *Miranda* warnings — the police demanded to know where the gun was. The defendant nodded in the direction of some empty cartons and responded that "the gun is over there." The Court held that both the unwarned statement — "the gun is over there" — and the recovered weapon were admissible in the prosecution's case in chief under a "public safety exception" to the "prophylactic rules enunciated in *Miranda*." It explicitly acknowledged that if the *Miranda* warnings were an imperative of the Fifth Amendment itself, such an exigency exception would be impossible, since the Fifth Amendment's bar on compelled self-incrimination is absolute, and its "'strictures, unlike the Fourth's are not removed by showing reasonableness.'"

The next year, the Court again declined to apply the "fruit of the poisonous tree" doctrine to a *Miranda* violation, this time allowing the admission of a suspect's properly warned statement even though it had been preceded (and, arguably, induced) by an earlier inculpatory statement taken in violation of *Miranda*. *Oregon v. Elstad* [Chapter 22, *infra*]. As in *Tucker*, the Court distinguished the case from those holding that a confession obtained as a result of an unconstitutional search is inadmissible, on the ground that the violation of *Miranda* does not involve an "actual infringement of the suspect's constitutional rights." *Miranda*, the Court explained, "sweeps more broadly than the Fifth Amendment itself," and "*Miranda's* preventive medicine provides a remedy even to the defendant who has suffered no identifiable constitutional harm." "Errors [that] are made by law enforcement officers in administering the prophylactic *Miranda* procedures . . . should not breed the same irremediable consequences as police infringement of the Fifth Amendment itself."

In light of these cases, and our statements to the same effect in others, it is simply no longer possible for the Court to conclude, even if it wanted to, that a violation of *Miranda's* rules is a violation of the Constitution. But as I explained at the outset, that is what is required before the Court may disregard a law of Congress governing the admissibility of evidence in federal court. The Court today insists that the *decision* in *Miranda* is a "constitutional" one, that it has "constitutional underpinnings", a "constitutional basis" and a "constitutional origin", that it was "constitutionally based", and that it announced a "constitutional rule." It is fine to play these word games; but what makes a decision "constitutional" in the only sense relevant here — in the sense that renders it impervious to supersession by congressional legislation such as § 3501 — is the determination that the Constitution *requires* the result that the decision announces and the statute ignores. By disregarding congressional action that concededly does not violate the Constitution, the Court flagrantly offends fundamental principles of separation of powers, and arrogates to itself prerogatives reserved to the representatives of the people.

The Court seeks to avoid this conclusion in two ways: First, by misdescribing these post-*Miranda* cases as mere dicta. The Court concedes only "that there is language in some of our opinions that supports the view" that *Miranda's* protections are not "constitutionally required." It is not a matter of *language*; it is a matter of *holdings*. The proposition that failure to comply with *Miranda's* rules does not establish a constitutional violation was central to the *holdings* of *Tucker, Hass, Quarles,* and *Elstad.*

The second way the Court seeks to avoid the impact of these cases is simply to disclaim responsibility for reasoned decisionmaking. It says:

> These decisions illustrate the principle — not that *Miranda* is not a constitutional rule — but that no constitutional rule is immutable. No court laying down a general rule can possibly foresee the various circumstances in which counsel will seek to apply it, and the sort of modifications represented by these cases are as much a normal part of constitutional law as the original decision.

The issue, however, is not whether court rules are "mutable"; they assuredly are. It is not whether, in the light of "various circumstances," they can be "modified"; they assuredly can. The issue is whether, *as mutated and modified,* they must *make sense.* The requirement that they do so is the only thing that prevents this Court from being some sort of nine-headed Caesar, giving thumbs-up or thumbs-down to whatever outcome, case by case, suits or offends its collective fancy. And if confessions procured in violation of *Miranda* are confessions "compelled" in violation of the Constitution, the post-*Miranda* decisions I have discussed do not make sense. The only reasoned basis for their outcome was that a violation of *Miranda* is *not* a violation of the Constitution. If, for example, as the Court acknowledges was the holding of *Elstad,* "the traditional 'fruits' doctrine developed in Fourth Amendment cases" (that the fruits of evidence obtained unconstitutionally must be excluded from trial) does *not* apply to the fruits of *Miranda* violations, and if the reason for the difference is *not* that *Miranda* violations are not constitutional violations (which is plainly and flatly what *Elstad* said); then the Court must come up with some *other* explanation for the difference. (That will take quite a bit of doing, by the way, since it is *not* clear on the face of the Fourth Amendment that evidence obtained in violation of that guarantee must be excluded from trial, whereas it *is* clear on the face of the Fifth Amendment that unconstitutionally compelled confessions cannot be used.) To say simply that "unreasonable searches under the Fourth Amendment are different from unwarned interrogation under the Fifth Amendment," is true but supremely unhelpful.

Finally, the Court asserts that *Miranda* must be a "constitutional decision" announcing a "constitutional rule," and thus immune to congressional modification, because we have since its inception applied it to the States. If this argument is meant as an invocation of *stare decisis,* it fails because, though it is true that our cases applying *Miranda* against the States must be reconsidered if *Miranda* is not required by the Constitution, it is likewise true that our cases (discussed above) based on the principle that *Miranda* is *not* required by the Constitution will have to be reconsidered if it *is.* So the *stare decisis* argument is a wash. If, on the other hand, the argument is meant as an appeal to logic rather than *stare decisis,* it is a classic example of begging the question: Congress's attempt to set aside *Miranda,* since it represents an assertion that violation of *Miranda* is not a violation of the

Constitution, *also* represents an assertion that the Court has no power to impose *Miranda* on the States. To answer this assertion — not by showing why violation of *Miranda is* a violation of the Constitution — but by asserting that *Miranda does* apply against the States, is to assume precisely the point at issue. In my view, our continued application of the *Miranda* code to the States despite our consistent statements that running afoul of its dictates does not necessarily — or even usually — result in an actual constitutional violation, represents not the source of *Miranda's* salvation but rather evidence of its ultimate illegitimacy. As Justice STEVENS has elsewhere explained, "this Court's power to require state courts to exclude probative self-incriminatory statements rests entirely on the premise that the use of such evidence violates the Federal Constitution. . . . If the Court does not accept that premise, it must regard the holding in the *Miranda* case itself, as well as all of the federal jurisprudence that has evolved from that decision, as nothing more than an illegitimate exercise of raw judicial power." *Elstad* (dissenting opinion). Quite so.

III

There was available to the Court a means of reconciling the established proposition that a violation of *Miranda* does not itself offend the Fifth Amendment with the Court's assertion of a right to ignore the present statute. That means of reconciliation was argued strenuously by both petitioner and the United States, who were evidently more concerned than the Court is with maintaining the coherence of our jurisprudence. It is not mentioned in the Court's opinion because, I assume, a majority of the Justices intent on reversing believes that incoherence is the lesser evil. They may be right.

Petitioner and the United States contend that there is nothing at all exceptional, much less unconstitutional, about the Court's adopting prophylactic rules to buttress constitutional rights, and enforcing them against Congress and the States. Indeed, the United States argues that "prophylactic rules are now and have been for many years a feature of this Court's constitutional adjudication." That statement is not wholly inaccurate, if by "many years" one means since the mid-1960's. However, in their zeal to validate what is in my view a lawless practice, the United States and petitioner greatly overstate the frequency with which we have engaged in it. For instance, petitioner cites several cases in which the Court quite simply exercised its traditional judicial power to define the scope of constitutional protections and, relatedly, the circumstances in which they are violated. *See Loretto v. Teleprompter Manhattan CATV Corp.*, 458 U.S. 419, 436–437 (1982) (holding that a permanent physical occupation constitutes a *per se* taking); *Maine v. Moulton*, 474 U.S. 159, 176 (1985) (holding that the Sixth Amendment right to the assistance of counsel is *actually* "violated when the State obtains incriminating statements by knowingly circumventing the accused's right to have counsel present in a confrontation between the accused and a state agent").

Similarly unsupportive of the supposed practice is *Bruton v. United States*, 391 U.S. 123 (1968), where we concluded that the Confrontation Clause of the Sixth Amendment forbids the admission of a nontestifying co-defendant's facially incriminating confession in a joint trial, even where the jury has been given a limiting instruction. That decision was based, not upon the theory that this was desirable protection "beyond" what the Confrontation Clause technically required; but rather upon the self-evident proposition that the inability to cross-examine an available witness whose damaging out-of-court testimony is introduced violates the Confrontation Clause, combined with the conclusion that in these circumstances a mere jury instruction can never be relied upon to prevent the testimony from being damaging, see *Richardson v. Marsh*, 481 U.S. 200, 207–208 (1987).

The United States also relies on our cases involving the question whether a State's procedure for appointed counsel's withdrawal of representation on appeal satisfies the State's constitutional obligation to " 'afford adequate and effective appellate review to indigent defendants.' " *Smith* v. *Robbins*, 528 U.S. 259 (2000) (quoting *Griffin v. Illinois*, 351 U.S. 12, 20 (1956)). In *Anders v. California*, 386 U.S. 738 (1967), we concluded that California's procedure governing withdrawal fell short of the constitutional minimum, and we outlined a procedure that *would* meet that standard. But as we made clear earlier this Term in *Smith*, which upheld a procedure *different* from the one *Anders* suggested, the benchmark of constitutionality is the constitutional requirement of adequate representation, and not some excrescence upon that requirement decreed, for safety's sake, by this Court.

In a footnote, the United States directs our attention to certain overprotective First Amendment rules that we have adopted to ensure "breathing space" for expression. *See Gertz v. Robert Welch, Inc.*, 418 U.S. 323, 340, 342 (1974) (recognizing that in *New York Times Co. v. Sullivan*, 376 U.S. 254 (1964), we "extended a measure of strategic protection to defamatory falsehood" of public officials); *Freedman v. Maryland*, 380 U.S. 51, 58 (1965) (setting forth "procedural safeguards designed to obviate the dangers of a censorship system" with respect to motion picture obscenity). In these cases, and others involving the First Amendment, the Court has acknowledged that in order to guarantee that protected speech is not "chilled" and thus forgone, it is in some instances necessary to incorporate in our substantive rules a "measure of strategic protection." But that is because the Court has viewed the importation of "chill" as *itself* a violation of the First Amendment — not because the Court thought it could go beyond what the First Amendment *demanded* in order to provide some prophylaxis.

Petitioner and the United States are right on target, however, in characterizing the Court's actions in a case decided within a few years of *Miranda*, *North Carolina v. Pearce*, 395 U.S. 711 (1969). There, the Court concluded that due process would be offended were a judge vindictively to resentence with added severity a defendant who had successfully appealed his original conviction. Rather than simply announce that vindictive sentencing violates the Due Process Clause, the Court went on to hold that "in order to assure the absence of such a [vindictive] motivation, . . . the reasons for [imposing the increased sentence] must affirmatively appear" and must "be based upon objective information concerning identifiable conduct on the part of the defendant occurring after the time of the original sentencing proceeding." The Court later explicitly acknowledged *Pearce's* prophylactic character, see *Michigan v. Payne*, 412 U.S. 47, 53 (1973). It is true, therefore, that the case exhibits the same fundamental flaw as does *Miranda* when deprived (as it has been) of its original (implausible) pretension to announcement of what the Constitution itself required. That is, although the Due Process Clause may well prohibit punishment based on judicial vindictiveness, the Constitution by no means vests in the courts "any general power to prescribe particular devices 'in order to assure the absence of such a motivation' " (Black, J., dissenting). Justice Black surely had the right idea when he derided the Court's requirement as "pure legislation if there ever was legislation," although in truth *Pearce's* rule pales as a legislative achievement when compared to the detailed code promulgated in *Miranda*.[1]

The foregoing demonstrates that, petitioner's and the United States' suggestions to the contrary notwithstanding, what the Court did in *Miranda* (assuming, as later cases hold, that *Miranda* went beyond what the Constitution actually requires) is in fact extraordinary. That the Court has, on rare and recent occasion, repeated the mistake does not transform error into truth, but illustrates the potential for future mischief that the error entails. Where the Constitution has wished to lodge in one of the branches of the Federal Government some limited power to supplement its guarantees, it has said so. *See* Amdt. 14, § 5 ("The Congress shall have power to enforce, by appropriate legislation, the provisions of this article"). The power with which the Court would endow itself under a "prophylactic" justification for *Miranda* goes far beyond what it has permitted Congress to do under authority of that text. Whereas we have insisted that congressional action under § 5 of the Fourteenth Amendment must be "congruent" with, and "proportional" to, a *constitutional violation, see City of Boerne v. Flores*, 521 U.S. 507, 520 (1997), the *Miranda* nontextual power to embellish confers authority to prescribe preventive measures against not only constitutionally prohibited compelled confessions, but also (as discussed earlier) foolhardy ones.

I applaud, therefore, the refusal of the Justices in the majority to enunciate this boundless doctrine of judicial empowerment as a means of rendering today's decision rational. In nonetheless joining the Court's judgment, however, they overlook two truisms: that actions speak louder than silence, and that (in judge-made law at least) logic will out. Since there is in fact no other principle that can reconcile today's judgment with the post-*Miranda* cases that the Court refuses to abandon, what today's decision will stand for, whether the Justices can bring themselves to say it or not, is the power of the Supreme Court to write a prophylactic, extraconstitutional Constitution, binding on Congress and the States.

IV

Thus, while I agree with the Court that § 3501 cannot be upheld without also concluding that *Miranda* represents an illegitimate exercise of our authority to review state-court judgments, I do not share the Court's hesitation in reaching that conclusion. For while the Court is also correct that the doctrine of *stare decisis* demands some "special justification" for a departure from longstanding precedent — even precedent of the constitutional variety — that criterion is more than met here. To repeat Justice STEVENS' cogent observation, it is "obviou[s]" that "the

---

[1] As for *Michigan v. Jackson*, upon which petitioner and the United States also rely, in that case we extended to the Sixth Amendment, postindictment, context the *Miranda*-based prophylactic rule of *Edwards v. Arizona*, that the police cannot initiate interrogation after counsel has been requested. I think it less a separate instance of claimed judicial power to impose constitutional prophylaxis than a direct, logic-driven consequence of *Miranda* itself.

Court's power to reverse Miranda's conviction rested *entirely* on the determination that a violation of the Federal Constitution had occurred."(dissenting opinion) (emphasis added). Despite the Court's Orwellian assertion to the contrary, it is undeniable that later cases (discussed above) have "undermined [*Miranda's*] doctrinal underpinnings," denying constitutional violation and thus stripping the holding of its only constitutionally legitimate support. *Miranda's* critics and supporters alike have long made this point.

The Court cites *Patterson v. McLean Credit Union*, 491 U.S. 164, 173 (1989), as accurately reflecting our standard for overruling, — which I am pleased to accept, even though *Patterson* was speaking of overruling statutory cases and the standard for constitutional decisions is somewhat more lenient. What is set forth there reads as though it was written precisely with the current status of *Miranda* in mind:

> In cases where statutory precedents have been overruled, the primary reason for the Court's shift in position has been the intervening development of the law, through either the growth of judicial doctrine or further action taken by Congress. Where such changes have removed or weakened the conceptual underpinnings from the prior decision, . . . or where the later law has rendered the decision irreconcilable with competing legal doctrines or policies, . . . the Court has not hesitated to overrule an earlier decision.

Neither am I persuaded by the argument for retaining *Miranda* that touts its supposed workability as compared with the totality-of-the-circumstances test it purported to replace. *Miranda's* proponents cite *ad nauseam* the fact that the Court was called upon to make difficult and subtle distinctions in applying the "voluntariness" test in some 30-odd due process "coerced confessions" cases in the 30 years between *Brown v. Mississippi* and *Miranda*. It is not immediately apparent, however, that the judicial burden has been eased by the "bright-line" rules adopted in *Miranda*. In fact, in the 34 years since *Miranda* was decided, this Court has been called upon to decide nearly *60* cases involving a host of *Miranda* issues, most of them predicted with remarkable prescience by Justice White in his *Miranda* dissent.

Moreover, it is not clear why the Court thinks that the "totality-of-the-circumstances test . . . is more difficult than *Miranda* for law enforcement officers to conform to, and for courts to apply in a consistent manner." Indeed, I find myself persuaded by Justice O'CONNOR's rejection of this same argument in her opinion in *Williams* (O'CONNOR, J., joined by REHNQUIST, C. J., concurring in part and dissenting in part):

> *Miranda*, for all its alleged brightness, is not without its difficulties; and voluntariness is not without its strengths . . . . *Miranda* creates as many close questions as it resolves. The task of determining whether a defendant is in "custody" has proved to be "a slippery one." And the supposedly "bright" lines that separate interrogation from spontaneous declaration, the exercise of a right from waiver, and the adequate warning from the inadequate, likewise have turned out to be rather dim and ill defined. The totality-of-the-circumstances approach, on the other hand, permits each fact to be taken into account without resort to formal and dispositive labels.

By dispensing with the difficulty of producing a yes-or-no answer to questions that are often better answered in shades and degrees, *the voluntariness inquiry often can make judicial decisionmaking easier rather than more onerous.*

(Emphasis added.)

But even were I to agree that the old totality-of-the-circumstances test was more cumbersome, it is simply not true that *Miranda* has banished it from the law and replaced it with a new test. Under the current regime, which the Court today retains in its entirety, courts are frequently called upon to undertake *both* inquiries. That is because, as explained earlier, voluntariness remains the *constitutional* standard, and as such continues to govern the admissibility for impeachment purposes of statements taken in violation of *Miranda*, the admissibility of the "fruits" of such statements, and the admissibility of statements challenged as unconstitutionally obtained *despite* the interrogator's compliance with *Miranda*, see, e.g., *Colorado v. Connelly*.

Finally, I am not convinced by petitioner's argument that *Miranda* should be preserved because the decision occupies a special place in the "public's consciousness." As far as I am aware, the public is not under the illusion that we are infallible. I see little harm in admitting that we made a mistake in taking away from the people the ability to decide for themselves what protections (beyond those required by the Constitution) are reasonably affordable in the criminal investigatory process. And I see much to be gained by reaffirming for the people the wonderful reality that they govern themselves — which means that "the powers not delegated to the United States by the Constitution" that the people adopted, "nor prohibited . . . to the States" by that Constitution, "are reserved to the States respectively, or to the people," U.S. CONST., Amdt. 10.[2]

Today's judgment converts *Miranda* from a milestone of judicial overreaching into the very Cheops' Pyramid (or perhaps the Sphinx would be a better analogue) of judicial arrogance. In imposing its Court-made code upon the States, the original opinion at least *asserted* that it was demanded by the Constitution. Today's decision does not pretend that it is — and yet *still* asserts the right to impose it against the will of the people's representatives in Congress. Far from believing that *stare decisis* compels this result, I believe we cannot allow to remain on the books even a celebrated decision — *especially* a celebrated decision — that has come to stand for the proposition that the Supreme Court has power to impose extraconstitutional constraints upon Congress and the States. This is not the system that was established by the Framers, or that would be established by any sane supporter of government by the people.

---

[2] The Court cites my dissenting opinion in *Mitchell v. United States*, 526 U.S. 314, 331–332 (1999), for the proposition that "the fact that a rule has found 'wide acceptance in the legal culture' is 'adequate reason not to overrule' it." But the legal culture is not the same as the "public's consciousness"; and unlike the rule at issue in *Mitchell* (prohibiting comment on a defendant's refusal to testify) *Miranda* has been continually criticized by lawyers, law enforcement officials, and scholars since its pronouncement (not to mention by Congress, as § 3501 shows). In *Mitchell*, moreover, the constitutional underpinnings of the earlier rule had not been demolished by subsequent cases.

I dissent from today's decision, and, until § 3501 is repealed, will continue to apply it in all cases where there has been a sustainable finding that the defendant's confession was voluntary.

QUESTIONS AND NOTES

1.   Does Chief Justice Rehnquist appear to have changed his view regarding *Miranda*? Why do you suppose that he wrote the majority opinion?

2.   Does *stare decisis* support the Court's view or is Justice Scalia correct in suggesting that *stare decisis* is a wash? Explain.

3.   What, if anything, does *Dickerson* portend for the future of *Miranda*?

4.   Is a prophylactic rule legitimately a constitutional rule? Why? Why not?

5.   How many other prophylactic rules can you identify?

6.   How much of *Dickerson* is predicated on the Court's rejecting Congress' power to overrule a Constitutional decision? *C.f. City of Boerne v. Flores*, 521 U.S. 507 (1997.)

7.   How relevant to the Court's decision was the Government's decision to defend *Miranda*? Why do you suppose that the Government did that? Didn't it want Dickerson convicted?

8.   Is *Miranda* related to preventing only *compelled* self-incrimination, or also foolish self-incrimination? Is *compelled* self-incrimination self-defining? Explain.

9.   Could (should) *Miranda* be reconceptualized as a Sixth Amendment decision? How, if at all, would that change the law?

10.   What do you think of the last sentence of Justice Scalia's dissent? Is it jurisprudentially sound or unwarranted petulance from the losing side? Explain.

11.   We close this chapter with *Chavez v. Martinez*, a case that tells us a lot about the nature of the Fifth Amendment in general, and *Miranda* in particular.

CHAVEZ v. MARTINEZ
538 U.S. 760 (2003)

JUSTICE THOMAS announced the judgment of the Court and delivered an opinion.

This case involves a § 1983 suit arising out of petitioner Ben Chavez's allegedly coercive interrogation of respondent Oliverio Martinez. The United States Court of Appeals for the Ninth Circuit held that Chavez was not entitled to a defense of qualified immunity because he violated Martinez's clearly established constitutional rights. We conclude that Chavez did not deprive Martinez of a constitutional right.

I

On November 28, 1997, police officers Maria Peã and Andrew Salinas were near a vacant lot in a residential area of Oxnard, California, investigating suspected narcotics activity. While Peã and Salinas were questioning an individual, they heard a bicycle approaching on a darkened path that crossed the lot. They ordered the rider, respondent Martinez, to dismount, spread his legs, and place his hands behind his head. Martinez complied. Salinas then conducted a patdown frisk and discovered a knife in Martinez's waistband. An altercation ensued.[1]

There is some dispute about what occurred during the altercation. The officers claim that Martinez drew Salinas' gun from its holster and pointed it at them; Martinez denies this. Both sides agree, however, that Salinas yelled, " 'He's got my gun!' " Peã then drew her gun and shot Martinez several times, causing severe injuries that left Martinez permanently blinded and paralyzed from the waist down. The officers then placed Martinez under arrest.

Petitioner Chavez, a patrol supervisor, arrived on the scene minutes later with paramedics.

Chavez accompanied Martinez to the hospital and then questioned Martinez there while he was receiving treatment from medical personnel. The interview lasted a total of about 10 minutes, over a 45-minute period, with Chavez leaving the emergency room for periods of time to permit medical personnel to attend to Martinez.

At first, most of Martinez's answers consisted of "I don't know," "I am dying," and "I am choking." Later in the interview, Martinez admitted that he took the gun from the officer's holster and pointed it at the police. He also admitted that he used heroin regularly. At one point, Martinez said "I am not telling you anything until they treat me," yet Chavez continued the interview. At no point during the interview was Martinez given Miranda warnings.

Martinez was never charged with a crime, and his answers were never used against him in any criminal prosecution. Nevertheless, Martinez filed suit under § 1983, maintaining that Chavez's actions violated his Fifth Amendment right not to be "compelled in any criminal case to be a witness against himself," as well as his Fourteenth Amendment substantive due process right to be free from coercive questioning. The District Court granted summary judgment to Martinez as to Chavez's qualified immunity defense on both the Fifth and Fourteenth Amendment claims. Applying *Saucier v. Katz* 533 U.S. 194 (2001), the Ninth Circuit first concluded that Chavez's actions, as alleged by Martinez, deprived Martinez of his rights under the Fifth and Fourteenth Amendments. The Ninth Circuit did not attempt to explain how Martinez had been "compelled in any criminal case to be a witness against himself." Instead, the Ninth Circuit reiterated the holding of an earlier Ninth Circuit case, *Cooper v. Dupnik* 963 F. 2d 120, 129 (C. A. 9 1992) (en banc), that "the Fifth Amendment's purpose is to prevent coercive interrogation practices that are destructive of human dignity," (internal quotation marks omitted), and found that Chavez's "coercive questioning" of Martinez violated his Fifth Amendment rights, "[e]ven though Martinez's statements were not used against him in a criminal proceeding." As to Martinez's due process claim, the Ninth

---

[1] The parties disagree over what triggered the altercation. The officers maintain that Martinez ran away from them and that they tackled him while in pursuit; Martinez asserts that he never attempted to flee and Salinas tackled him without warning.

Circuit held that "a police officer violates the Fourteenth Amendment when he obtains a confession by coercive conduct, regardless of whether the confession is subsequently used at trial."

The Ninth Circuit then concluded that the Fifth and Fourteenth Amendment rights asserted by Martinez were clearly established by federal law, explaining that a reasonable officer "would have known that persistent interrogation of the suspect despite repeated requests to stop violated the suspect's Fifth and Fourteenth Amendment right to be free from coercive interrogation."

We granted certiorari. 535 U.S. 1111 (2002).

II

In deciding whether an officer is entitled to qualified immunity, we must first determine whether the officer's alleged conduct violated a constitutional right. If not, the officer is entitled to qualified immunity, and we need not consider whether the asserted right was "clearly established." We conclude that Martinez's allegations fail to state a violation of his constitutional rights.

A

1

We fail to see how, based on the text of the Fifth Amendment, Martinez can allege a violation of this right, since Martinez was never prosecuted for a crime, let alone compelled to be a witness against himself in a criminal case.

Although Martinez contends that the meaning of "criminal case" should encompass the entire criminal investigatory process, including police interrogations, we disagree. In our view, a "criminal case" at the very least requires the initiation of legal proceedings. We need not decide today the precise moment when a "criminal case" commences; it is enough to say that police questioning does not constitute a "case" any more than a private investigator's precomplaint activities constitute a "civil case." Statements compelled by police interrogations of course may not be used against a defendant at trial, but it is not until their use in a criminal case that a violation of the Self-Incrimination Clause occurs.

Here, Martinez was never made to be a "witness" against himself in violation of the Fifth Amendment's Self-Incrimination Clause because his statements were never admitted as testimony against him in a criminal case. Nor was he ever placed under oath and exposed to " 'the cruel trilemma of self-accusation, perjury or contempt.' " The text of the Self-Incrimination Clause simply cannot support the Ninth Circuit's view that the mere use of compulsive questioning, without more, violates the Constitution.

2

Nor can the Ninth Circuit's approach be reconciled with our case law. It is well established that the government may compel witnesses to testify at trial or before a grand jury, on pain of contempt, so long as the witness is not the target of the criminal case in which he testifies.

We fail to see how Martinez was any more "compelled in any criminal case to be a witness against himself" than an immunized witness forced to testify on pain of contempt. One difference, perhaps, is that the immunized witness *knows* that his statements will not, and may not, be used against him, whereas Martinez likely did not. But this does not make the statements of the immunized witness any less "compelled" and lends no support to the Ninth Circuit's conclusion that coercive police interrogations, absent the use of the involuntary statements in a criminal case, violate the Fifth Amendment's Self-Incrimination Clause. Moreover, our cases provide that those subjected to coercive police interrogations have an *automatic* protection from the use of their involuntary statements (or evidence derived from their statements) in any subsequent criminal trial. This protection is, in fact, coextensive with the use and derivative use immunity mandated by *Kastigar* when the government compels testimony from a reluctant witness. Accordingly, the fact that Martinez did not *know* his statements could not be used against him does not change our view that no violation of Fifth Amendment's Self-Incrimination Clause occurred here.

3

In the Fifth Amendment context, we have created prophylactic rules designed to safeguard the core constitutional right protected by the Self-Incrimination Clause. *See, e.g., Tucker* 417 U.S., at 444 (describing the "procedural safeguards" required by *Miranda* as "not themselves rights protected by the Constitution but . . . measures to insure that the right against compulsory self-incrimination was protected" to "provide practical reinforcement for the right.")

Rules designed to safeguard a constitutional right, however, do not extend the scope of the constitutional right itself, just as violations of judicially crafted prophylactic rules do not violate the constitutional rights of any person. As we explained, we have allowed the Fifth Amendment privilege to be asserted by witnesses in noncriminal cases in order to safeguard the core constitutional right defined by the Self-Incrimination Clause — the right not to be compelled in any criminal case to be a witness against oneself.[2] We have likewise established the *Miranda* exclusionary rule as a prophylactic measure to prevent violations of the right protected by the text of the Self-Incrimination Clause — the admission into evidence in criminal case of confessions obtained through coercive custodial questioning. Because we find that Chavez's alleged conduct did not violate the Self-Incrimination Clause, we reverse the Ninth Circuit's denial of qualified immunity as to Martinez's Fifth Amendment claim.

Our views on the proper scope of the Fifth Amendment's Self-Incrimination Clause do not mean that police torture or other abuse that results in a confession is constitutionally permissible so long as the statements are not used at trial; it simply means that the Fourteenth Amendment's Due Process Clause, rather than

---

[2] That the privilege is a prophylactic one does not alter our penalty cases jurisprudence, which allows such privilege to be asserted prior to, and outside of, criminal proceedings.

the Fifth Amendment's Self-Incrimination Clause, would govern the inquiry in those cases and provide relief in appropriate circumstances.

B

The Fourteenth Amendment provides that no person shall be deprived "of life, liberty, or property, without due process of law." Convictions based on evidence obtained by methods that are "so brutal and so offensive to human dignity" that they "shoc[k] the conscience" violate the Due Process Clause. *Rochin v. California,* 342 U.S. 165, 172, 174 (1952). Although *Rochin* did not establish a civil remedy for abusive police behavior, we recognized in *County of Sacramento v. Lewis,* 532 U.S. 83, 846 (1998), that deprivations of liberty caused by "the most egregious official conduct," may violate the Due Process Clause. While we rejected, in Lewis a § 1983 plaintiff's contention that a police officer's deliberate indifference during a high-speed chase that caused the death of a motorcyclist violated due process, we left open the possibility that unauthorized police behavior in other contexts might "shock the conscience" and give rise to § 1983 liability.

We are satisfied that Chavez's questioning did not violate Martinez's due process rights. Even assuming, *arguendo,* that the persistent questioning of Martinez somehow deprived him of a liberty interest, we cannot agree with Martinez's characterization of Chavez's behavior as "egregious" or "conscience shocking." As we noted in *Lewis* the official conduct "most likely to rise to the conscience-shocking level," is the "conduct intended to injure in some way unjustifiable by any government interest." Here, there is no evidence that Chavez acted with a purpose to harm Martinez by intentionally interfering with his medical treatment. Medical personnel were able to treat Martinez throughout the interview and Chavez ceased his questioning to allow tests and other procedures to be performed. Nor is there evidence that Chavez's conduct exacerbated Martinez's injuries or prolonged his stay in the hospital. Moreover, the need to investigate whether there had been police misconduct constituted a justifiable government interest given the risk that key evidence would have been lost if Martinez had died without the authorities ever hearing his side of the story.

The Court has held that the Due Process Clause also protects certain "fundamental liberty interest[s]" from deprivation by the government, regardless of the procedures provided, unless the infringement is narrowly tailored to serve a compelling state interest.

We therefore must take into account the fact that Martinez was hospitalized and in severe pain during the interview, but also that Martinez was a critical nonpolice witness to an altercation resulting in a shooting by a police officer, and that the situation was urgent given the perceived risk that Martinez might die and crucial evidence might be lost. In these circumstances, we can find no basis in our prior jurisprudence, see, *e.g., Miranda,* 384 U.S., at 47–478 ("It is an act of responsible citizenship for individuals to give whatever information they may have to aid in law enforcement"), or in our Nation's history and traditions to suppose that freedom from unwanted police questioning is a right so fundamental that it cannot be abridged absent a "compelling state interest." We have never required such a justification for a police interrogation, and we decline to do so here. The lack of any "guideposts for responsible decisionmaking" in this area, and our oft-stated reluctance to expand the doctrine of substantive due process, further counsel against recognizing a new "fundamental liberty interest" in this case.

We conclude that Martinez has failed to allege a violation of the Fourteenth Amendment, and it is therefore unnecessary to inquire whether the right asserted by Martinez was clearly established.

III

Because Chavez did not violate Martinez's Fifth and Fourteenth Amendment rights, he was entitled to qualified immunity. The judgment of the Court of Appeals for the Ninth Circuit is therefore reversed and the case is remanded for further proceedings. *It is so ordered.*

JUSTICE SOUTER, delivered an opinion, Part II of which is the opinion of the Court, and Part I of which is an opinion concurring in the judgment.[3]

I

Respondent Martinez's claim under § 1983 for violation of his privilege against compelled self-incrimination should be rejected and his case remanded for further proceedings. I write separately because I believe that our decision requires a degree of discretionary judgment greater than Justice THOMAS acknowledges. As he points out, the text of the Fifth Amendment (applied here under the doctrine of Fourteenth Amendment incorporation) focuses on courtroom use of a criminal defendant's compelled, self-incriminating testimony, and the core of the guarantee against compelled self-incrimination is the exclusion of any such evidence. Justice GINSBURG makes it clear that the present case is very close to Mincey v. Arizona, 437 U.S. 385 (1978), and Martinez's testimony would clearly be inadmissible if offered in evidence against him. But Martinez claims more than evidentiary protection in asking this Court to hold that the questioning alone was a completed violation of the Fifth and Fourteenth Amendments subject to redress by an action for damages under § 1983.

To recognize such a constitutional cause of action for compensation would, of course, be well outside the core of Fifth Amendment protection, but that alone is not a sufficient reason to reject Martinez's claim. As Justice Harlan explained in his dissent in *Miranda* "extension[s]" of the bare guarantee may be warranted, if clearly shown to be desirable means to protect the basic right against the invasive pressures of contemporary society. In this light, we can make sense of a variety of Fifth Amendment holdings: barring compulsion to give testimonial evidence in a civil proceeding; and conditioning admissibility on warnings and waivers to promote intelligent choices and to simplify subsequent inquiry into voluntariness, *see Miranda* All of this law is outside the Fifth Amendment's core, with each case expressing a judgment that the core guarantee, or the judicial capacity to protect

---

[3] Justice BREYER joins this opinion in its entirety. Justice STEVENS, Justice KENNEDY, and Justice GINSBURG join Part II of this opinion.

it, would be placed at some risk in the absence of such complementary protection.

I do not, however, believe that Martinez can make the "powerful showing," subject to a realistic assessment of costs and risks, necessary to expand protection of the privilege against compelled self-incrimination to the point of the civil liability he asks us to recognize here. The most obvious drawback inherent in Martinez's purely Fifth Amendment claim to damages is its risk of global application in every instance of interrogation producing a statement inadmissible under Fifth and Fourteenth Amendment principles, or violating one of the complementary rules we have accepted in aid of the privilege against evidentiary use. If obtaining Martinez's statement is to be treated as a stand-alone violation of the privilege subject to compensation, why should the same not be true whenever the police obtain any involuntary self-incriminating statement, or whenever the government so much as threatens a penalty in derogation of the right to immunity, or whenever the police fail to honor *Miranda*?[4] Martinez offers no limiting principle or reason to foresee a stopping place short of liability in all such cases.

Recognizing an action for damages in every such instance not only would revolutionize Fifth and Fourteenth Amendment law, but would beg the question that must inform every extension or recognition of a complementary rule in service of the core privilege: why is this new rule necessary in aid of the basic guarantee? Martinez has offered no reason to believe that the guarantee has been ineffective in all or many of those circumstances in which its vindication has depended on excluding testimonial admissions or barring penalties. And I have no reason to believe the law has been systemically defective in this respect.

But if there is no failure of efficacy infecting the existing body of Fifth Amendment law, any argument for a damages remedy in this case must depend not on its Fifth Amendment feature but upon the particular charge of outrageous conduct by the police, extending from their initial encounter with Martinez through the questioning by Chavez. That claim, however, if it is to be recognized as a constitutional one that may be raised in an action under § 1983, must sound in substantive due process. *See generally County of Sacramento v. Lewis*, 523 U.S. 833 (1998) ("[C]onduct intended to injure in some way unjustifiable by any government interest is the sort of official action most likely to rise to the conscience-shocking level"). Here, it is enough to say that Justice STEVENS shows that Martinez has a serious argument in support of such a position.

II

Whether Martinez may pursue a claim of liability for a substantive due process violation is thus an issue that should be addressed on remand, along with the scope and merits of any such action that may be found open to him.

---

[4] The question whether the absence of *Miranda* warnings may be a basis for a § 1983 action under any circumstance is not before the Court.

JUSTICE SCALIA, concurring in part in the judgment.

I agree with the Court's rejection of Martinez's Fifth Amendment claim, that is, his claim that Chavez violated his right not to be compelled in any criminal case to be a witness against himself.

My reasons for rejecting Martinez's Fifth Amendment claim are those set forth in Justice THOMAS's opinion. I join Parts I and II of that opinion, including Part II-B, which deals with substantive due process. Consideration and rejection of that constitutional claim is absolutely necessary to support reversal of the Ninth Circuit's judgment. For after discussing (and erroneously deciding) Martinez's Fifth Amendment claim, the Ninth Circuit continued as follows:

> "Likewise, a police officer violates the Fourteenth Amendment when he obtains a confession by coercive conduct, regardless of whether the confession is subsequently used at trial. The due process violation caused by coercive behavior of law-enforcement officers in pursuit of a confession is *complete with the coercive behavior itself.* . . . *The actual use or attempted use of that coerced statement in a court of law is not necessary to complete the affront to the Constitution.' Cooper v. Dupnik*, 963 F. 2d at 1244–45 (emphasis added). Mr. Martinez has thus stated a *prima facie* case that Sergeant Chavez violated his Fifth and Fourteenth Amendment rights to be free from police coercion in pursuit of a confession."

It seems to me impossible to interpret this passage as anything other than an invocation of the doctrine of "substantive due process," which makes unlawful certain government conduct, regardless of whether the procedural guarantees of the Fifth Amendment (or the guarantees of any of the other provisions of the Bill of Rights) have been violated.

I believe that addressing it, and resolving it against respondent, is essential to the Court's disposition, which reverses the Ninth Circuit's judgment in its entirety.

Nowhere did respondent's appellate brief mention the words "substantive due process"; the only rights it asserted were the right against self-incrimination and the right to warnings under *Miranda*. If, as Justice SOUTER apparently believes, the opinion below did not address respondent's "substantive due process" claim, that claim has been forfeited.

JUSTICE STEVENS, concurring in part and dissenting in part.

As a matter of fact, the interrogation of respondent was the functional equivalent of an attempt to obtain an involuntary confession from a prisoner by torturous methods. As a matter of law, that type of brutal police conduct constitutes an immediate deprivation of the prisoner's constitutionally protected interest in liberty. Because these propositions are so clear, the District Court and the Court of Appeals correctly held that petitioner is not entitled to qualified immunity.

I

What follows is an English translation of portions of the tape-recorded questioning in Spanish that occurred in the emergency room of the hospital when, as is evident from the text, both parties believed that respondent was about to die:

"Chavez: What happened? Olivero, tell me what happened. "O[liverio] M[artinez]: I don't know "Chavez: I don't know what happened (sic)?

"O. M.:   Ay! I am dying. Ay! What are you doing to me? No, . . . ! (unintelligible scream). "Chavez: What happened, sir?

"O. M.:   My foot hurts . . .

"Chavez: Olivera. Sir, what happened?

"O. M.:   I am choking.

"Chavez: Tell me what happened.

"O. M.:   I don't know.

"Chavez: 'I don't know.'

"O. M.:   My leg hurts.

"Chavez: I don't know what happened (sic)?

"O. M.:   It hurts . . .

"Chavez: Hey, hey look.

"O. M.:   I am choking.

"Chavez: Can you hear? Look listen, I am Benjamin Chavez with the police here in Oxnard, look.

"O. M.:   I am dying, please.

"Chavez: OK, yes, tell me what happened. If you are going to die, tell me what happened. Look I need to tell (sic) what happened.

"O. M.:   I don't know.

"Chavez: You don't know, I don't know what happened (sic)? Did you talk to the police?

"O. M.:   Yes.

"Chavez: What happened with the police?

"O. M.:   We fought.

"Chavez: Huh? What happened with the police?

"O. M.:   The police shot me.

"Chavez: Why?

"O. M.:   Because I was fighting with him.

"Chavez: Oh, why were you fighting with the police?

"O. M.:   I am dying . . .

"Chavez: OK, yes you are dying, but tell me why you are fighting, were you fighting with the police? . . . .

"O. M.: Doctor, please I want air, I am dying.

"Chavez: OK, OK. I want to know if you pointed the gun [to yourself] at the police.

"O. M.: Yes.

"Chavez: Yes, and you pointed it [to yourself]? (sic) at the police pointed the gun? (sic) Huh?

"O. M.: I am dying, please . . . .

"Chavez: OK, listen, listen I want to know what happened, ok?

"O. M.: I want them to treat me.

"Chavez: OK, they are do it (sic), look when you took out the gun from the tape (sic) of the police . . .

"O. M.: I am dying . . .

"Chavez: Ok, look, what I want to know if you took out (sic) the gun of the police?

"O. M.: I am not telling you anything until they treat me.

"Chavez: Look, tell me what happened, I want to know, look well don't you want the police know (sic) what happened with you?

"O. M.: Uuuggghhh! my belly hurts . . . .

"Chavez: Nothing, why did you run (sic) from the police?

"O. M.: I don't want to say anything anymore.

"Chavez: No?

"O. M.: I want them to treat me, it hurts a lot, please.

"Chavez: You don't want to tell (sic) what happened with you over there?

"O. M.: I don't want to die, I don't want to die.

"Chavez: Well if you are going to die tell me what happened, and right now you think you are going to die?

"O. M.: No.

"Chavez: No, do you think you are going to die?

"O. M.: Aren't you going to treat me or what?

"Chavez: Look, think you are going to die, (sic) that's all I want to know, if you think you are going to die? Right now, do you think you are going to die?

"O. M.: My belly hurts, please treat me. "Chavez: Sir?

"O. M.: If you treat me I tell you everything, if not, no.

"Chavez: Sir, I want to know if you think you are going to die right now?

"O. M.:   I think so.

"Chavez: You think (sic) so? Ok. Look, the doctors are going to help you with all they can do, Ok?. That they can do.

"O. M.:   Get moving, I am dying, can't you see me? come on.

"Chavez: Ah, huh, right now they are giving you medication." App. 8-22.

The sound recording of this interrogation, which has been lodged with the Court, vividly demonstrates that respondent was suffering severe pain and mental anguish throughout petitioner's persistent questioning.

II

The Due Process Clause of the 14th Amendment protects individuals against state action that either " 'shocks the conscience,' *Rochin v. California*, 342 U.S. 165, 172 (1952), or interferes with rights 'implicit in the concept of ordered liberty,' *Palko v. Connecticut*, 302 U.S. 319, 325–326 (1937)." In *Palko* the majority of the Court refused to hold that every violation of the Fifth Amendment satisfied the second standard. In a host of other cases, however, the Court has held that unusually coercive police interrogation procedures do violate that standard.

By its terms, the Fifth Amendment itself has no application to the States. It is, however, one source of the protections against state actions that deprive individuals of rights "implicit in the concept of ordered liberty" that the Fourteenth Amendment guarantees. Indeed, as I pointed out in my dissent in *Oregon v. Elstad* it is the most specific provision in the Bill of Rights "that protects all citizens from the kind of custodial interrogation that was once employed by the Star Chamber, by 'the Germans of the 1930's and early 1940's,' and by some of our own police departments only a few decades ago." Whenever it occurs, as it did here, official interrogation of that character is a classic example of a violation of a constitutional right "implicit in the concept of ordered liberty."[5]

I respectfully dissent, but for the reasons articulated by Justice KENNEDY, concur in Part II of Justice SOUTER's opinion.

JUSTICE KENNEDY, with whom JUSTICE STEVENS joins, and with whom JUSTICE GINSBURG joins as to Parts II and III, concurring in part and dissenting in part.

A single police interrogation now presents us with two issues: first, whether failure to give a required warning under *Miranda*, was itself a completed

---

[5] A person's constitutional right to remain silent is an interest in liberty that is protected against federal impairment by the Fifth Amendment and from state impairment by the Due Process Clause of the Fourteenth Amendment. Justice THOMAS' opinion is fundamentally flawed in two respects. It incorrectly assumes that the claim it rejects is not a Due Process claim, and it incorrectly assumes that coercive interrogation is not unconstitutional when it occurs because it merely violates a judge-made "prophylactic" rule. But the violation in this case is far more serious than a mere failure to advise respondent of his *Miranda* rights; moreover, the Court disavowed the "prophylactic" rule. But the violation in this case is far more serious than a mere failure to advise respondent of his *Miranda* rights; moreover, the Court disavowed the "prophylactic" characterization of *Miranda* in *Dickerson v. United States*, 530 U.S. 428, 437–439 (2000.)

constitutional violation actionable under § 1983; and second, whether an actionable violation arose at once under the Self-Incrimination Clause (applicable to the States through the Fourteenth Amendment) when the police, after failing to warn, used severe compulsion or extraordinary pressure in an attempt to elicit a statement or confession.

I agree with Justice THOMAS that failure to give a *Miranda* warning does not, without more, establish a completed violation when the unwarned interrogation ensues. As to the second aspect of the case, which does not involve the simple failure to give a *Miranda* warning, it is my respectful submission that Justice SOUTER and Justice THOMAS are incorrect. They conclude that a violation of the Self-Incrimination Clause does not arise until a privileged statement is introduced at some later criminal proceeding.

A constitutional right is traduced the moment torture or its close equivalents are brought to bear. Constitutional protection for a tortured suspect is not held in abeyance until some later criminal proceeding takes place. These are the premises of this separate opinion.

I

The *Miranda* warning, as is now well settled, is a constitutional requirement adopted to reduce the risk of a coerced confession and to implement the Self-Incrimination Clause. *Dickerson v. United States. Miranda* mandates a rule of exclusion. It must be so characterized, for it has significant exceptions that can only be assessed and determined in the course of trial. Unwarned custodial interrogation does not in every instance violate *Miranda See, e.g., New York v. Quarles.* Furthermore, statements secured in violation of *Miranda* are admissible in some instances. See, *e.g., Harris v. New York* 401 U.S. 222 (1971) (statement admissible for purposes of impeachment). The identification of a *Miranda* violation and its consequences, then, ought to be determined at trial. The exclusion of unwarned statements, when not within an exception, is a complete and sufficient remedy.

II

Justice SOUTER and Justice THOMAS are wrong, in my view, to maintain that in all instances a violation of the Self-Incrimination Clause simply does not occur unless and until a statement is introduced at trial, no matter how severe the pain or how direct and commanding the official compulsion used to extract it.

It must be remembered that the Self-Incrimination Clause of the Fifth Amendment is applicable to the States in its full text through the Due Process Clause of the Fourteenth Amendment. The question is the proper interpretation of the Self-Incrimination Clause in the context of the present dispute.

The Clause provides both assurance that a person will not be compelled to testify against himself in a criminal proceeding and a continuing right against government conduct intended to bring about self-incrimination. *Lefkowitz v. Turley*, 414 U.S. 70, 77 (1973) ("The Amendment not only protects the individual against being involuntarily called as a witness against himself in a criminal prosecution but also privileges him not to answer official questions put to him in any other proceeding, civil or criminal, formal or informal, where the answers might incriminate him in future criminal proceedings"); accord, *Bram v. United States*, 168 U.S. 532, 542–543 (1897); *Counselman v. Hitchcock*, 142 U.S. 547, 562 (1892). The principle extends to forbid policies which exert official compulsion that might induce a person into forfeiting his rights under the Clause. *Lefkowitz v. Cunningham*, 431 U.S. 801, 806 (1977) ("These cases settle that government cannot penalize assertion of the constitutional privilege against compelled self-incrimination by imposing sanctions to compel testimony which has not been immunized"); Justice SOUTER and Justice THOMAS acknowledge a future privilege. That does not end the matter. A future privilege does not negate a present right.

Their position finds some support in a single statement in United States v. Verdugo-Urquidez, 494 U.S. 259, 264 (1990) ("Although conduct by law enforcement officials prior to trial may ultimately impair that right [against compelled self-incrimination], a constitutional violation occurs only at trial"). That case concerned the application of the Fourth Amendment, and the extent of the right secured under the Self-Incrimination Clause was not then before the Court. Furthermore, *Verdugo-Urquidez* involved a prosecution in the United States arising from a criminal investigation in another country, so there was a special reason for the Court to be concerned about the application of the Clause in that context. In any event, the decision cannot be read to support the proposition that the application of the Clause is limited in the way Justice SOUTER and Justice THOMAS describe today.

A recent case illustrates that a violation of the Self-Incrimination Clause may have immediate consequences. Just last Term, nine Justices all proceeded from the premise that a present, completed violation of the Self-Incrimination Clause could occur if an incarcerated prisoner were required to admit to past crimes on pain of forfeiting certain privileges or being assigned harsher conditions of confinement. *McKune v. Lile* 536 U.S. 24 (2002); *id.* at 48 (O'CONNOR, J., concurring in judgment); *id.* at 54 (STEVENS, J., dissenting). Although there was disagreement over whether a violation occurred in the circumstances of that case, there was no disagreement that a present violation could have taken place. No Member of the Court suggested that the absence of a pending criminal proceeding made the Self-Incrimination Clause inquiry irrelevant.

The conclusion that the Self-Incrimination Clause is not violated until the government seeks to use a statement in some later criminal proceeding strips the Clause of an essential part of its force and meaning. This is no small matter. It should come as an unwelcome surprise to judges, attorneys, and the citizenry as a whole that if a legislative committee or a judge in a civil case demands incriminating testimony without offering immunity, and even imposes sanctions for failure to comply, that the witness and counsel cannot insist the right against compelled self-incrimination is applicable then and there. Justice SOUTER and Justice THOMAS, I submit, should be more respectful of the understanding that has prevailed for generations now. To tell our whole legal system that when conducting a criminal investigation police officials can use severe compulsion or even torture with no present violation of the right against compelled self-incrimination can only diminish a celebrated provision in the Bill of Rights. A Constitution survives over time because the people share a common, historic commitment to certain simple but fundamental principles which preserve their freedom. Today's decision undermines one of those respected precepts.

Dean Griswold explained the place the Self-Incrimination Clause has secured in our legal heritage:

> "The Fifth Amendment has been very nearly a lone sure rock in a time of storm. It has been one thing which has held quite firm, although something like a juggernaut has pushed upon it. It has, thus, through all its vicissitudes, been a symbol of the ultimate moral sense of the community, upholding the best in us, when otherwise there was a good deal of wavering under the pressures of the times." E. Griswold, The Fifth Amendment Today 73 (1955).

It damages the law, and the vocabulary with which we impart our legal tradition from one generation to the next, to downgrade our understanding of what the Fifth Amendment requires.

There is some authority, it must be acknowledged, for the proposition that the act of torturing to obtain a confession is not comprehended within the Self-Incrimination Clause itself. In *Brown v. Mississippi*, 297 U.S. 278 (1936), the Court held that convictions based upon tortured confessions could not stand, but it identified the Due Process Clause, and not the Self-Incrimination Clause, as the source for its ruling. The Court interpreted the Self-Incrimination Clause as limited to "the processes of justice by which the accused may be called as a witness and required to testify. Compulsion by torture to extort a confession is a different matter." The decision in *Brown* antedated the incorporation of the Clause and the ensuing understanding of its fundamental role in our legal system.

III

In my view the Self-Incrimination Clause is applicable at the time and place police use compulsion to extract a statement from a suspect. The Clause forbids that conduct. A majority of the Court has now concluded otherwise, but that should not end this case. It simply implicates the larger definition of liberty under the Due Process Clause of the Fourteenth Amendment.

That brings us to the interrogation in this case. Had the officer inflicted the initial injuries sustained by Martinez (the gunshot wounds) for purposes of extracting a statement, there would be a clear and immediate violation of the Constitution, and no further inquiry would be needed. That is not what happened, however. The initial injuries and anguish suffered by the suspect were not inflicted to aid the interrogation. The wounds arose from events preceding it. True, police officers had caused the injuries, but they had not done so to compel a statement or with the purpose of facilitating some later interrogation. The case can be analyzed, then, as if the wounds had been inflicted by some third person, and the officer came to the hospital to interrogate.

There is no rule against interrogating suspects who are in anguish and pain. The police may have legitimate reasons, borne of exigency, to question a person who is suffering or in distress. Locating the victim of a kidnaping, ascertaining the whereabouts of a dangerous assailant or accomplice, or determining whether there is a rogue police officer at large are some examples. That a suspect is in fear of dying, furthermore, may not show compulsion but just the opposite. The fear may be a motivating factor to volunteer information. The words of a declarant who believes his death is imminent have a special status in the law of evidence. A declarant in Martinez's circumstances may want to tell his story even if it increases his pain and agony to do so. The Constitution does not forbid the police from offering a person an opportunity to volunteer evidence he wishes to reveal.

There are, however, actions police may not take if the prohibition against the use of coercion to elicit a statement is to be respected. The police may not prolong or increase a suspect's suffering against the suspect's will. That conduct would render government officials accountable for the increased pain. The officers must not give the impression that severe pain will be alleviated only if the declarant cooperates, for that, too, uses pain to extract a statement. In a case like this one, recovery should be available under § 1983 if a complainant can demonstrate that an officer exploited his pain and suffering with the purpose and intent of securing an incriminating statement. That showing has been made here.

The transcript of the interrogation set out by Justice STEVENS and other evidence considered by the District Court demonstrate that the suspect thought his treatment would be delayed, and thus his pain and condition worsened, by refusal to answer questions.

It is true that the interrogation was not continuous. Ten minutes of questions and answers were spread over a 45-minute interval. Treatment was apparently administered during those interruptions. The pauses in the interrogation, however, do not indicate any error in the trial court's findings and conclusions.

The District Court found that Martinez "had been shot in the face, both eyes were injured; he was screaming in pain, and coming in and out of consciousness while being repeatedly questioned about details of the encounter with the police." His blinding facial wounds made it impossible for him visually to distinguish the interrogating officer from the attending medical personnel. The officer made no effort to dispel the perception that medical treatment was being withheld until Martinez answered the questions put to him. There was no attempt through *Miranda* warnings or other assurances to advise the suspect that his cooperation should be voluntary. Martinez begged the officer to desist and provide treatment for his wounds, but the questioning persisted despite these pleas and despite Martinez's unequivocal refusal to answer questions. *Cf. Mincey v. Arizona* (Court said of similar circumstances: "It is hard to imagine a situation less conducive to the exercise of a rational intellect and a free will" (internal quotation marks omitted)).

The standards governing the interrogation of suspects and witnesses who suffer severe pain must accommodate the exigencies that law enforcement personnel encounter in circumstances like this case. It is clear enough, however, that the police should take the necessary steps to ensure that there is neither the fact nor the perception that the declarant's pain is being used to induce the statement against his will. In this case no reasonable police officer would believe that the law permitted him to prolong or increase pain to obtain a statement. The record supports the ultimate finding that the officer acted with the intent of exploiting

Martinez's condition for purposes of extracting a statement.

Accordingly, I would affirm the decision of the Court of Appeals that a cause of action under § 1983 has been stated. The other opinions filed today, however, reach different conclusions as to the correct disposition of the case. Were Justice STEVENS, Justice GINSBURG, and I to adhere to our position, there would be no controlling judgment of the Court. In these circumstances, and because a ruling on substantive due process in this case could provide much of the essential protection the Self-Incrimination Clause secures, I join Part II of Justice SOUTER's opinion and would remand the case for further consideration.

JUSTICE GINSBURG, concurring in part and dissenting in part.

I join Parts II and III of Justice KENNEDY's opinion. For reasons well stated therein, I would hold that the Self-Incrimination Clause applies at the time and place police use severe compulsion to extract a statement from a suspect. The evidence in this case, as Justice KENNEDY explains, supports the conclusion "that the suspect thought his treatment would be delayed, and thus his pain and condition worsened, by refusal to answer questions." I write separately to state my view that, even if no finding were made concerning Martinez's belief that refusal to answer would delay his treatment, or Chavez's intent to create such an impression, the interrogation in this case would remain a clear instance of the kind of compulsion no reasonable officer would have thought constitutionally permissible.

In *Mincey v. Arizona*, appropriately referenced by Justice KENNEDY, this Court held involuntary certain statements made during an in-hospital police interrogation[6]. The suspect questioned in *Mincey* had been "seriously wounded just a few hours earlier," and "[a]lthough he had received some treatment, his condition at the time of [the] interrogation was still sufficiently serious that he was in the intensive care unit." He was interrogated while "lying on his back on a hospital bed, encumbered by tubes, needles, and breathing apparatus." Despite the suspect's clear and repeated indications that he did not want to talk, the officer persisted in questioning him as he drifted in and out of consciousness. The Court thought it "apparent" in these circumstances that the suspect's statements "were not the product of his free and rational choice."

Martinez's interrogation strikingly resembles the hospital-bed questioning in *Mincey*. Like the suspect in *Mincey* Martinez was "at the complete mercy of [his interrogator], unable to escape or resist the thrust of [the] interrogation." *Id.* at 399 (internal quotation marks omitted). As Justice KENNEDY notes, Martinez "had been shot in the face, both eyes were injured; he was screaming in pain, and coming in and out of consciousness while being repeatedly questioned about details of the encounter with the police." "In this debilitated and helpless condition, [Martinez] clearly expressed his wish not to be interrogated." Chavez nonetheless continued to question him, "ceas[ing] the interrogation only during intervals when [Martinez] lost consciousness or received medical treatment." Martinez was "weakened by pain and shock"; "barely conscious, . . . his will was simply overborne."

---

[6] While *Mincey* concerned admissibility under the Due Process Clause of the Fourteenth Amendment, its analysis of the coercive nature of the interrogation is nonetheless instructive in this case.

Thus, whatever Martinez might have thought about Chavez's interference with his treatment, I would agree with the District Court that "the totality of the circumstances in this case" establishes "that [Martinez's] statement was not voluntarily given."

In common with the Due Process Clause, the privilege against self-incrimination safeguards "the freedom of the individual from the arbitrary power of governmental authorities." Closely connected "with the struggle to eliminate torture as a governmental practice," the privilege is rightly regarded as "one of the great landmarks in man's struggle to make himself civilized." Its core idea is captured in the Latin maxim, *"Nemo tenetur prodere se ipsum,"* in English, "No one should be required to accuse himself." As an "expression of our view of civilized governmental conduct," the privilege should instruct and control all of officialdom, the police no less than the prosecutor.

Convinced that Chavez's conduct violated Martinez's right to be spared from self-incriminating interrogation, I would affirm the judgment of the Court of Appeals. To assure a controlling judgment of the Court, however, I join Part II of Justice SOUTER's opinion.

QUESTIONS AND NOTES

1. What was the holding of the Court on the Fifth Amendment issue? What was the holding of the Court on the Due Process issue? Explain.

2. With which (if any) Justice did you agree? Why?

3. Was the Due Process issue substantive or procedural? Does it matter? Why? Why not?

4. What does the opinion tell us about the nature of the Fifth Amendment? How does that compare to the Fourth Amendment?

Chapter 21

DUE PROCESS OUTSIDE OF THE CONFESSION CONTEXT

Under current constitutional dogma, virtually all significant provisions of the Bill of Rights concerning criminal procedure are applicable to the states. That was not always the case, however. As you know, prior to 1961, the exclusionary rule of the Fourth Amendment was not applicable to the states, and the privilege against self-incrimination was not applied to the states until 1964.

Before that time, virtually all constitutional criminal procedure applicable to the states had to be justified under the rubric of due process. Today, of course, that is not the case. Nevertheless, as cases like *Fulminante* demonstrate, the due process clause remains one of major import. In terms of strategy, a criminal defense lawyer is generally better off if she can persuade a judge that the complained of procedure violates a specific constitutional prohibition. However, she would be downright incompetent if she fails to raise a due process claim when one is possibly available.

In this Chapter, we will examine due process in two cases decided prior to the applicability of specific provisions of the Bill of Rights to the states (*Rochin* and *Irvine*), one due process plus specific provision case (*Schmerber*) decided after the Fourth, Fifth, and Sixth amendment criminal procedure provisions were held applicable to the states, and one case (*Brathwaite*), where the due process clause has more or less replaced the Sixth Amendment as the primary guarantor of fair identification procedures.

A.   DUE PROCESS AND THE FOURTH OR FIFTH AMENDMENT

ROCHIN v. CALIFORNIA
342 U.S. 165 (1952)

Mr. Justice Frankfurter delivered the opinion of the Court.

Having "some information that [the petitioner here] was selling narcotics," three deputy sheriffs of the County of Los Angeles, on the morning of July 1, 1949, made for the two-story dwelling house in which Rochin lived with his mother, common-law wife, brothers and sisters. Finding the outside door open, they entered and then forced open the door to Rochin's room on the second floor. Inside they found petitioner sitting partly dressed on the side of the bed, upon which his wife was lying. On a "night stand" beside the bed the deputies spied two capsules. When asked "Whose stuff is this?" Rochin seized the capsules and put them in his mouth. A struggle ensued, in the course of which the three officers "jumped upon him" and attempted to extract the capsules. The force they applied proved unavailing against

Rochin's resistance. He was handcuffed and taken to a hospital. At the direction of one of the officers a doctor forced an emetic solution through a tube into Rochin's stomach against his will. This "stomach pumping" produced vomiting. In the vomited matter were found two capsules which proved to contain morphine.

Regard for the requirements of the Due Process Clause "inescapably imposes upon this Court an exercise of judgment upon the whole course of the proceedings [resulting in a conviction] in order to ascertain whether they offend those canons of decency and fairness which express the notions of justice of English-speaking peoples even toward those charged with the most heinous offenses." These standards of justice are not authoritatively formulated anywhere as though they were specifics. Due process of law is a summarized constitutional guarantee of respect for those personal immunities which, as Mr. Justice Cardozo twice wrote for the Court, are "so rooted in the traditions and conscience of our people as to be ranked as fundamental," *Snyder v. Commonwealth of Massachusetts*, 291 U.S. 97, 105, or are "implicit in the concept of ordered liberty." *Palko v. State of Connecticut*, 302 U.S. 319, 325.

The vague contours of the Due Process Clause do not leave judges at large. We may not draw on our merely personal and private notions and disregard the limits that bind judges in their judicial function. Even though the concept of due process of law is not final and fixed, these limits are derived from considerations that are fused in the whole nature of our judicial process. These are considerations deeply rooted in reason and in the compelling traditions of the legal profession. The Due Process Clause places upon this Court the duty of exercising a judgment, within the narrow confines of judicial power in reviewing State convictions, upon interests of society pushing in opposite directions.

To practice the requisite detachment and to achieve sufficient objectivity no doubt demands of judges the habit of self-discipline and self-criticism, incertitude that one's own views are incontestable and alert tolerance toward views not shared. But these are precisely the presuppositions of our judicial process. They are precisely the qualities society has a right to expect from those entrusted with ultimate judicial power.

Applying these general considerations to the circumstances of the present case, we are compelled to conclude that the proceedings by which this conviction was obtained do more than offend some fastidious squeamishness or private sentimentalism about combatting crime too energetically. This is conduct that shocks the conscience. Illegally breaking into the privacy of the petitioner, the struggle to open his mouth and remove what was there, the forcible extraction of his stomach's contents — this course of proceeding by agents of government to obtain evidence is bound to offend even hardened sensibilities. They are methods too close to the rack and the screw to permit of constitutional differentiation.

It has long since ceased to be true that due process of law is heedless of the means by which otherwise relevant and credible evidence is obtained. This was not true even before the series of recent cases enforced the constitutional principle that the States may not base convictions upon confessions, however much verified, obtained by coercion. These decisions are not arbitrary exceptions to the comprehensive right of States to fashion their own rules of evidence for criminal trials.

They are not sports in our constitutional law but applications of a general principle. They are only instances of the general requirement that States in their prosecutions respect certain decencies of civilized conduct. Due process of law, as a historic and generative principle, precludes defining, and thereby confining, these standards of conduct more precisely than to say that convictions cannot be brought about by methods that offend "a sense of justice." See Mr. Chief Justice Hughes, speaking for a unanimous Court in *Brown v. State of Mississippi*. It would be a stultification of the responsibility which the course of constitutional history has cast upon this Court to hold that in order to convict a man the police cannot extract by force what is in his mind but can extract what is in his stomach.

To attempt in this case to distinguish what lawyers call "real evidence" from verbal evidence is to ignore the reasons for excluding coerced confessions. Use of involuntary verbal confessions in State criminal trials is constitutionally obnoxious not only because of their unreliability. They are inadmissible under the Due Process Clause even though statements contained in them may be independently established as true. Coerced confessions offend the community's sense of fair play and decency. So here, to sanction the brutal conduct which naturally enough was condemned by the court whose judgment is before us, would be to afford brutality the cloak of law. Nothing would be more calculated to discredit law and thereby to brutalize the temper of a society.

We are not unmindful that hypothetical situations can be conjured up, standing imperceptibly from the circumstances of this case and by gradations producing practical differences despite seemingly logical extensions. But the Constitution is "intended to preserve practical and substantial rights, not to maintain theories."

On the facts of this case the conviction of the petitioner has been obtained by methods that offend the Due Process Clause. The judgment below must be Reversed.

MR. JUSTICE BLACK, concurring.

In the view of a majority of the Court, the Fifth Amendment imposes no restraint of any kind on the states. They nevertheless hold that California's use of this evidence violated the Due Process Clause of the Fourteenth Amendment. Since they hold as I do in this case, I regret my inability to accept their interpretation without protest. But I believe that faithful adherence to the specific guarantees in the Bill of Rights insures a more permanent protection of individual liberty than that which can be afforded by the nebulous standards stated by the majority.

What the majority hold is that the Due Process Clause empowers this Court to nullify any state law if its application "shocks the conscience," offends "a sense of justice" or runs counter to the "decencies of civilized conduct." The majority emphasize that these statements do not refer to their own consciences or to their senses of justice and decency. For we are told that "we may not draw on our merely personal and private notions"; our judgment must be grounded on "considerations deeply rooted in reason and in the compelling traditions of the legal profession." We are further admonished to measure the validity of state practices, not by our reason, or by the traditions of the legal profession, but by "the community's sense of fair play and decency"; by the "traditions and conscience of our people"; or by "those canons of decency and fairness which express the notions of justice of English-speaking peoples." These canons are made necessary, it is said, because of "interests of society pushing in opposite directions."

If the Due Process Clause does vest this Court with such unlimited power to invalidate laws, I am still in doubt as to why we should consider only the notions of English-speaking peoples to determine what are immutable and fundamental principles of justice. Moreover, one may well ask what avenues of investigation are open to discover "canons" of conduct so universally favored that this Court should write them into the Constitution? All we are told is that the discovery must be made by an "evaluation based on a disinterested inquiry pursued in the spirit of science, on a balanced order of facts."

Some constitutional provisions are stated in absolute and unqualified language such, for illustration, as the First Amendment stating that no law shall be passed prohibiting the free exercise of religion or abridging the freedom of speech or press. Other constitutional provisions do require courts to choose between competing policies, such as the Fourth Amendment which, by its terms, necessitates a judicial decision as to what is an "unreasonable" search or seizure. There is, however, no express constitutional language granting judicial power to invalidate *every* state law of *every* kind deemed "unreasonable" or contrary to the Court's notion of civilized decencies; yet the constitutional philosophy used by the majority has, in the past, been used to deny a state the right to fix the price of gasoline, and even the right to prevent bakers from palming off smaller for larger loaves of bread, *Jay Burns Baking Co. v. Bryan*, 264 U.S. 504. These cases, and others, show the extent to which the evanescent standards of the majority's philosophy have been used to nullify state legislative programs passed to suppress evil economic practices. What paralyzing role this same philosophy will play in the future economic affairs of this country is impossible to predict. Of even graver concern, however, is the use of the philosophy to nullify the Bill of Rights. I long ago concluded that the accordion-like qualities of this philosophy must inevitably imperil all the individual liberty safeguards specifically enumerated in the Bill of Rights. Reflection and recent decisions of this Court sanctioning abridgment of the freedom of speech and press have strengthened this conclusion.

Mr. Justice Douglas, concurring.

The evidence obtained from this accused's stomach would be admissible in the majority of states where the question has been raised. So far as the reported cases reveal, the only states which would probably exclude the evidence would be Arkansas, Iowa, Michigan, and Missouri. Yet the Court now says that the rule which the majority of the states have fashioned violates the "decencies of civilized conduct." To that I cannot agree. It is a rule formulated by responsible courts with judges as sensitive as we are to the proper standards for law administration.

As an original matter it might be debatable whether the provision in the Fifth Amendment that no person "shall be compelled in any criminal case to be a witness against himself" serves the ends of justice. Not all civilized legal procedures recognize it. But the Choice was made by the Framers, a choice which sets a standard for legal trials in this country. The Framers made it a standard of due process for prosecutions by the Federal Government. If it is a requirement of due process for a trial in the federal courthouse, it is impossible for me to say it is not a requirement of due process for a trial in the state courthouse.

QUESTIONS AND NOTES

1.   What was so shocking about the police behavior in *Rochin*? Was it not desirable to remove morphine (which presumably is not good for people) from the defendant's stomach?

2.   Is the *Rochin* problem more nearly analogous to the Fourth or Fifth Amendment?

3.   Was the police "wrong" in *Rochin* obtaining the evidence or using the evidence? If the former, how, if at all, does it differ from a Fourth Amendment violation?

4.   Do you think that judges can (should) achieve the level of objectivity suggested by Frankfurter?

5.   The uncertainty of the *Wolf/Rochin* approach was illustrated in *Irvine*.

IRVINE v. CALIFORNIA
347 U.S. 128 (1954)

MR. JUSTICE JACKSON announced the judgment of the Court and an opinion in which the CHIEF JUSTICE, MR. JUSTICE REED and MR. JUSTICE MINTON join.

This case involves constitutional questions growing out of methods employed to convict petitioner on charges of horserace bookmaking and related offenses against the antigambling laws of California. Petitioner exhausted all avenues to relief under state procedures and then sought review here of duly raised federal issues.

[T]he questions raised by the officers' conduct while investigating this case are serious. The police strongly suspected petitioner of illegal bookmaking but were without proof of it. On December 1, 1951, while Irvine and his wife were absent from their home, an officer arranged to have a locksmith go there and make a door key. Two days later, again in the absence of occupants, officers and a technician made entry into the home by the use of this key and installed a concealed microphone in the hall. A hole was bored in the roof of the house and wires were strung to transmit to a neighboring garage whatever sounds the microphone might pick up. Officers were posted in the garage to listen. On December 8, police again made surreptitious entry and moved the microphone, this time hiding it in the bedroom. Twenty days later they again entered and placed the microphone in a closet, where the device remained until its purpose of enabling the officers to overhear incriminating statements was accomplished.

At the trial, officers were allowed to testify to conversations heard through their listening installations. The snatches of conversation which the prosecution thought useful were received in evidence. They were in the lingo of the race track and need not be recited, but the jury might well have regarded them as incriminating. The testimony was received under objection, properly raising the question that it was constitutionally inadmissible since obtained by methods which violate the Fourteenth Amendment.

Each of these repeated entries of petitioner's home without a search warrant or other process was a trespass, and probably a burglary, for which any unofficial person should be, and probably would be, severely punished. Science has perfected amplifying and recording devices to become frightening instruments of surveillance and invasion of privacy, whether by the policeman, the blackmailer, or the busy-body. That officers of the law would break and enter a home, secrete such a device, even in a bedroom, and listen to the conversation of the occupants for over a month would be almost incredible if it were not admitted. Few police measures have come to our attention that more flagrantly, deliberately, and persistently violated the fundamental principle declared by the Fourth Amendment as a restriction on the Federal Government that "The right of the people to be secure in their persons, houses, papers, and effects, against unreasonable searches and seizures, shall not be violated, and no Warrants shall issue, but upon probable cause, supported by Oath or affirmation, and particularly describing the place to be searched, and the persons or things to be seized." The decision in *Wolf v. Colorado* for the first time established that "[t]he security of one's privacy against arbitrary intrusion by the police" is embodied in the concept of due process found in the Fourteenth Amendment.

But *Wolf*, for reasons set forth therein, declined to make the subsidiary procedural and evidentiary doctrines developed by the federal courts limitations on the states. On the contrary, it declared, "We, hold, therefore, that in a prosecution in a State court for a State crime the Fourteenth Amendment does not forbid the admission of evidence obtained by an unreasonable search and seizure." That holding would seem to control here.

An effort is made, however, to bring this case under the sway of *Rochin*. That case involved, among other things, an illegal search of the defendant's person. But it also presented an element totally lacking here — coercion, applied by a physical assault upon his person to compel submission to the use of a stomach pump. This was the feature which led to a result in *Rochin* contrary to that in *Wolf*. Although *Rochin* raised the search-and-seizure question, this Court studiously avoided it and never once mentioned the *Wolf* case. Obviously, it thought that illegal search and seizure alone did not call for reversal. However obnoxious are the facts in the case before us, they do not involve coercion, violence or brutality to the person, but rather a trespass to property, plus eavesdropping.

It is suggested, however, that although we affirmed the conviction in *Wolf*, we should reverse here because this invasion of privacy is more shocking, more offensive, than the one involved there. The opinions in *Wolf* were written entirely in the abstract and did not disclose the details of the constitutional violation. Actually, the search was offensive to the law in the same respect, if not the same degree, as here. A deputy sheriff and others went to a doctor's office without a warrant and seized his appointment book, searched through it to learn the names of all his patients, looked up and interrogated certain of them, and filed an information against the doctor on the information that the District Attorney had obtained from the books. The books also were introduced in evidence against the doctor at his trial.

We are urged to make inroads upon *Wolf* by holding that it applies only to searches and seizures which produce on our minds a mild shock, while if the shock is more serious, the states must exclude the evidence or we will reverse the conviction. We think that the *Wolf* decision should not be overruled, for the reasons so persuasively stated therein. We think, too, that a distinction of the kind urged would leave the rule so indefinite that no state court could know what it should rule in order to keep its processes on solid constitutional ground.

It appears to the writer, in which view he is supported by the Chief Justice, that there is no lack of remedy if an unconstitutional wrong has been done in this instance without upsetting a justifiable conviction of this common gambler. If the officials have willfully deprived a citizen of the United States of a right or privilege secured to him by the Fourteenth Amendment, that being the right to be secure in his home against unreasonable searches, their conduct may constitute a federal crime under 62 Stat. 696, 18 U.S.C. (Supp. III) § 242. This section provides that whoever, under color of any law, statute, ordinance, regulation or custom, willfully subjects any inhabitant of any state to the deprivation of any rights, privileges or immunities secured or protected by the Constitution of the United States shall be fined or imprisoned. It does not appear that the statute of limitations yet bars prosecutions. We believe the Clerk of this Court should be directed to forward a copy of the record in this case, together with a copy of this opinion, for attention of the Attorney General of the United States. However, Mr. Justice Reed and Mr. Justice Minton do not join in this paragraph.

Judgment affirmed.

Mr. Justice Clark, concurring.

Had I been here in 1949 when *Wolf* was decided I would have applied the doctrine of *Weeks v. United States*, 232 U.S. 383 (1914), to the states. But the Court refused to do so then, and it still refuses today. Thus *Wolf* remains the law and, as such, is entitled to the respect of this Court's membership.

Of course, we could sterilize the rule announced in *Wolf* by adopting a case-by-case approach to due process in which inchoate notions of propriety concerning local police conduct guide our decisions. But this makes for such uncertainty and unpredictability that it would be impossible to foretell — other than by guess-work — just how brazen the invasion of the intimate privacies of one's home must be in order to shock itself into the protective arms of the Constitution. In truth, the practical result of this *ad hoc* approach is simply that when five Justices are sufficiently revolted by local police action a conviction is overturned and a guilty man may go free. *Rochin* bears witness to this. We may thus vindicate the abstract principle of due process, but we do not shape the conduct of local police one whit; unpredictable reversals on dissimilar fact situations are not likely to curb the zeal of those police and prosecutors who may be intent on racking up a high percentage of successful prosecutions. I do not believe that the extension of such a vacillating course beyond the clear cases of physical coercion and brutality, such as *Rochin*, would serve a useful purpose.

In light of the "incredible" activity of the police here it is with great reluctance that I follow *Wolf*. Perhaps strict adherence to the tenor of that decision may produce needed converts for its extinction. Thus I merely concur in the judgment of affirmance.

Mr. Justice Frankfurter, whom Mr. Justice Burton joins, dissenting.

Mere failure to have an appropriate warrant for arrest or search, without aggravating circumstances of misconduct in obtaining evidence, invalidates a federal conviction helped by such an unreasonable search and seizure. But *Wolf* held that the [exclusionary] rule was not to be deemed part of the Due Process Clause of the Fourteenth Amendment and hence was not binding upon the States. Still more recently, however, in *Rochin*, the Court held that "stomach pumping" to obtain morphine capsules, later used as evidence in a trial, was offensive to prevailing notions of fairness in the conduct of a prosecution and therefore invalidated a resulting conviction as contrary to the Due Process Clause.

The comprehending principle of these two cases is at the heart of "due process." The judicial enforcement of the Due Process Clause is the very antithesis of a Procrustean rule. In its first full-dress discussion of the Due Process Clause of the Fourteenth Amendment, the Court defined the nature of the problem as a "gradual process of judicial inclusion and exclusion, as the cases presented for decision shall require, with the reasoning on which such decisions may be founded."

In the *Wolf* case, the Court rejected one absolute. In *Rochin*, it rejected another.

In holding that not all conduct which by federal law is an unreasonable search and seizure vitiates a conviction in connection with which it transpires, *Wolf* did not and could not decide that as long as relevant evidence adequately supports a conviction, it is immaterial how such evidence was acquired.

Rochin decided that the Due Process Clause of the Fourteenth Amendment does not leave States free in their prosecutions for crime. The Clause puts limits on the wide discretion of a State in the process of enforcing its criminal law. The holding of the case is that a State cannot resort to methods that offend civilized standards of decency and fairness. The conviction in the *Rochin* case was found to offend due process not because evidence had been obtained through an unauthorized search and seizure or was the fruit of compulsory self-incrimination. Neither of these concepts, relevant to federal prosecutions, was invoked by the Court in *Rochin*, so of course the *Wolf* case was not mentioned. While there is in the case before us, as there was in *Rochin*, an element of unreasonable search and seizure, what is decisive here, as in *Rochin*, is additional aggravating conduct which the Court finds repulsive.

Thus, the basis on which this case should be adjudicated is laid down in *Rochin*: "Regard for the requirements of the Due Process Clause 'inescapably imposes upon this Court an exercise of judgment upon the whole course of the proceedings [resulting in a conviction] in order to ascertain whether they offend those canons of decency and fairness which express the notions of justice of English-speaking peoples even toward those charged with the most heinous offenses.' "

This brings us to the specific circumstances of this case. This is a summary of the conduct of the police:

(1) They secretly made a key to the Irvines' front door.

(2) By boring a hole in the roof of the house and using the key they had made to enter, they installed a secret microphone in the Irvine house with a listening post in a neighboring garage where officers listened in relays.

(3) Using their key, they entered the house twice again to move the microphone in order to cut out interference from a fluorescent lamp. The first time they moved in into Mr. and Mrs. Irvine's bedroom, and later into their bedroom closet.

(4) Using their key, they entered the house on the night of the arrest and in the course of the arrest made a search for which they had no warrant.

There was lacking here physical violence, even to the restricted extent employed in *Rochin*. We have here, however, a more powerful and offensive control over the Irvines' life than a single, limited physical trespass. Certainly the conduct of the police here went far beyond a bare search and seizure. The police devised means to hear every word that was said in the Irvine household for more than a month. Those affirming the conviction find that this conduct, in its entirety, is "almost incredible if it were not admitted."

The underlying reasoning of *Rochin* rejected the notion that States may secure a conviction by any form of skullduggery so long as it does not involve physical violence. The cases in which coercive or physical infringements of the dignity and privacy of the individual were involved were not deemed "sports in our constitutional law but applications of a general principle. They are only instances of the general requirement that States in their prosecutions respect certain decencies of civilized conduct. Due process of law, as a historic and generative principle, precludes defining, and thereby confining, these standards of conduct more precisely than to say that convictions cannot be brought about by methods that offend 'a sense of justice.' "

"Our people may tolerate many mistakes of both intent and performance, but, with unerring instinct, they know that when any person is intentionally deprived of his constitutional rights those responsible have committed no ordinary offense. A crime of this nature, if subtly encouraged by failure to condemn and punish, certainly leads down the road to totalitarianism."[2]

---

[2] Statement by Director J. Edgar Hoover of the Federal Bureau of Investigation in FBI Law Enforcement Bulletin, September 1952.

[JUSTICE BLACK dissented on Firth Amendment grounds. JUSTICE DOUGLAS dissented on Fourth Amendment grounds.]

QUESTIONS AND NOTES

1.   Why does Frankfurter think that *Rochin* rather than *Wolf* controlled *Irvine*?

2.   Was he saying that the search in *Wolf* was *not* a violation of due process? If not, what was he saying?

3.   Do you see any constitutionally significant difference between *Irvine* and any other Fourth Amendment case?

4.   Given *Wolf* and *Rochin* do you think that *Irvine* was correctly decided?

5.   We now turn to *Schmerber*, a due process plus Fifth Amendment case decided *after* the Fifth Amendment had been held applicable to the states.

SCHMERBER v. CALIFORNIA
384 U.S. 757 (1966)

MR. JUSTICE BRENNAN delivered the opinion of the Court.

Petitioner was convicted in Los Angeles Municipal Court of the criminal offense of driving an automobile while under the influence of intoxicating liquor. He had been arrested at a hospital while receiving treatment for injuries suffered in an accident involving the automobile that he had apparently been driving. At the direction of a police officer, a blood sample was then withdrawn from petitioner's body by a physician at the hospital. The chemical analysis of this sample revealed a percent by weight of alcohol in his blood at the time of the offense which indicated intoxication, and the report of this analysis was admitted in evidence at the trial. Petitioner objected to receipt of this evidence of the analysis on the ground that the blood had been withdrawn despite his refusal, on the advice of his counsel, to consent to the test. He contended that in that circumstance the withdrawal of the blood and the admission of the analysis in evidence denied him due process of law under the Fourteenth Amendment.

I

THE DUE PROCESS CLAUSE CLAIM

Breithaupt [*v. Abram*, 352 U.S. 432 (1957),] was also a case in which police officers caused blood to be withdrawn from the driver of an automobile involved in an accident, and in which there was ample justification for the officer's conclusion that the driver was under the influence of alcohol. There, as here, the extraction was made by a physician in a simple, medically acceptable manner in a hospital environment. There, however, the driver was unconscious at the time the blood was withdrawn and hence had no opportunity to object to the procedure. We affirmed the conviction there resulting from the use of the test in evidence, holding that under such circumstances the withdrawal did not offend "that 'sense of justice' of which we spoke in *Rochin*." *Breithaupt* thus requires the rejection of petitioner's due process argument, and nothing in the circumstances of this case[4] or in supervening events persuades us that this aspect of *Breithaupt* should be over-ruled.

II

THE PRIVILEGE AGAINST SELF-INCRIMINATION CLAIM

Breithaupt summarily rejected an argument that the withdrawal of blood and the admission of the analysis report involved in that state case violated the Fifth Amendment privilege of any person not to "be compelled in any criminal case to be a witness against himself," citing *Twining v. State of New Jersey*, 211 U.S. 78. But that case, holding that the protections of the Fourteenth Amendment do not embrace this Fifth Amendment privilege, has been succeeded by *Malloy v. Hogan*, 378 U.S. 1, 8. We there held that "[t]he Fourteenth Amendment secures against state invasion the same privilege that the Fifth Amendment guarantees against federal infringement — the right of a person to remain silent unless he chooses to speak in the unfettered exercise of his own will, and to suffer no penalty . . . for such silence." We therefore must now decide whether the withdrawal of the blood and admission in evidence of the analysis involved in this case violated petitioner's privilege. We hold that the privilege protects an accused only from being compelled to testify against himself, or otherwise provide the State with evidence of a testimonial or communicative nature,[5] and that the withdrawal of blood and use of the analysis in question in this case did not involve compulsion to these ends.

It could not be denied that in requiring petitioner to submit to the withdrawal and chemical analysis of his blood the State compelled him to submit to an attempt to discover evidence that might be used to prosecute him for a criminal offense. He submitted only after the police officer rejected his objection and directed the physician to proceed. The officer's direction to the physician to administer the test over petitioner's objection constituted compulsion for the purposes of the privilege. The critical question, then, is whether petitioner was thus compelled "to be a witness against himself."

---

[4] We "cannot see that it should make any difference whether one states unequivocally that he objects or resorts to physical violence in protest or is in such condition that he is unable to protest." It would be a different case if the police initiated the violence, refused to respect a reasonable request to undergo a different form of testing, or responded to resistance with inappropriate force.

[5] A dissent suggests that the report of the blood test was "testimonial" or "communicative," because the test was performed in order to obtain the testimony of others, communicating to the jury facts about petitioner's condition. Of course, all evidence received in court is "testimonial" or "communicative" if these words are thus used. But the Fifth Amendment relates only to acts on the part of the person to whom the privilege applies, and we use these words subject to the same limitations. A nod or headshake is as much a "testimonial" or "communicative" act in this sense as are spoken words. But the terms as we use them do not apply to evidence of acts noncommunicative in nature as to the person asserting the privilege, even though, as here, such acts are compelled to obtain the testimony of others.

[T]he privilege has never been given the full scope which the values it helps to protect suggest. History and a long line of authorities in lower courts have consistently limited its protection to situations in which the State seeks to submerge those values by obtaining the evidence against an accused through "the cruel, simple expedient of compelling it from his own mouth. . . . In sum, the privilege is fulfilled only when the person is guaranteed the right 'to remain silent unless he chooses to speak in the unfettered exercise of his own will.' " The leading case in this Court is *Holt v. United States*, 218 U.S. 245. There the question was whether evidence was admissible that the accused, prior to trial and over his protest, put on a blouse that fitted him. It was contended that compelling the accused to submit to the demand that he model the blouse violated the privilege. Mr. Justice Holmes, speaking for the Court, rejected the argument as "based upon an extravagant extension of the Fifth Amendment," and went on to say: "[T]he prohibition of compelling a man in a criminal court to be witness against himself is a prohibition of the use of physical or moral compulsion to extort communications from him, not an exclusion of his body as evidence when it may be material. The objection in principle would forbid a jury to look at a prisoner and compare his features with a photograph in proof."

It is clear that the protection of the privilege reaches an accused's communications, whatever form they might take, and the compulsion of responses which are also communications, for example, compliance with a subpoena to produce one's papers. *Boyd v. United States*, 116 U.S. 616. On the other hand, both federal and state courts have usually held that it offers no protection against compulsion to submit to fingerprinting, photographing, or measurements, to write or speak for identification, to appear in court, to stand, to assume a stance, to walk, or to make a particular gesture. The distinction which has emerged, often expressed in different ways, is that the privilege is a bar against compelling "communications" or "testimony," but that compulsion which makes a suspect or accused the source of "real or physical evidence" does not violate it.

Although we agree that this distinction is a helpful framework for analysis, we are not to be understood to agree with past applications in all instances. There will be many cases in which such a distinction is not readily drawn. Some tests seemingly directed to obtain "physical evidence," for example, lie detector tests measuring changes in body function during interrogation, may actually be directed to eliciting responses which are essentially testimonial. To compel a person to submit to testing in which an effort will be made to determine his guilt or innocence on the basis of physiological responses, whether willed or not, is to evoke the spirit and history of the Fifth Amendment. Such situations call to mind the principle that the protection of the privilege "is as broad as the mischief against which it seeks to guard." *Counselman v. Hitchcock*, 142 U.S. 547, 562.

In the present case, however, no such problem of application is presented. Not even a shadow of testimonial compulsion upon or enforced communication by the accused was involved either in the extraction or in the chemical analysis. Petitioner's testimonial capacities were in no way implicated; indeed, his participation, except as a donor, was irrelevant to the results of the test, which depend on chemical analysis and on that alone.[9] Since the blood test evidence, although an incriminating product of compulsion, was neither petitioner's testimony nor evidence relating to some communicative act or writing by the petitioner, it was not inadmissible on privilege grounds.

III

THE RIGHT TO COUNSEL CLAIM

This conclusion also answers petitioner's claim that, in compelling him to submit to the test in face of the fact that his objection was made on the advice of counsel, he was denied his Sixth Amendment right to the assistance of counsel. Since petitioner was not entitled to assert the privilege, he has no greater right because counsel erroneously advised him that he could assert it. His claim is strictly limited to the failure of the police to respect his wish, reinforced by counsel's advice, to be left inviolate. No issue of counsel's ability to assist petitioner in respect of any rights he did possess is presented. The limited claim thus made must be rejected.

Affirmed.

Mr. Chief Justice Warren, dissenting.

While there are other important constitutional issues in this case, I believe it is sufficient for me to reiterate my dissenting opinion in *Breithaupt* as the basis on which to reverse this conviction.

Mr. Justice Black with whom Mr. Justice Douglas joins, dissenting.

I would reverse petitioner's conviction.

The Court admits that "the State compelled [petitioner] to submit to an attempt to discover evidence [in his blood] that might be [and was] used to prosecute him for

---

[9] This conclusion would not necessarily govern had the State tried to show that the accused had incriminated himself when told that he would have to be tested. Such incriminating evidence may be an unavoidable by-product of the compulsion to take the test, especially for an individual who fears the extraction or opposes it on religious grounds. If it wishes to compel persons to submit to such attempts to discover evidence, the State may have to forgo the advantage of any *testimonial* products of administering the test — products which would fall within the privilege. Indeed, there may be circumstances in which the pain, danger, or severity of an operation would almost inevitably cause a person to prefer confession to undergoing the "search," and nothing we say today should be taken as establishing the permissibility of compulsion in that case. But no such situation is presented in this case.

Petitioner has raised a similar issue in this case, in connection with a police request that he submit to a "Breathalyzer" test of air expelled from his lungs for alcohol content. He refused the request, and evidence of his refusal was admitted in evidence without objection. He argues that the introduction of this evidence and a comment by the prosecutor in closing argument upon his refusal is ground for reversal. Since trial here was conducted after our decision in *Malloy*, making those principles applicable to the States, we think petitioner's contention is foreclosed by his failure to object on this ground to the prosecutor's question and statements. [Several years later the Court held that the procedure described in this paragraph did not violate the privilege against self-incrimination. *South Dakota v. Neville*, 459 U.S. 553 (1983) — Ed.]

a criminal offense." To reach the conclusion that compelling a person to give his blood to help the State convict him is not equivalent to compelling him to be a witness against himself strikes me as quite an extraordinary feat. The Court, however, overcomes what had seemed to me to be an insuperable obstacle to its conclusion by holding that

> . . . the privilege protects an accused only from being compelled to testify against himself, or otherwise provide the State with evidence of a testimonial or communicative nature, and that the withdrawal of blood and use of the analysis in question in this case did not involve compulsion to these ends.

I cannot agree that this distinction and reasoning of the Court justify denying petitioner his Bill of Rights' guarantee that he must not be compelled to be a witness against himself.

In the first place it seems to me that the compulsory extraction of petitioner's blood for analysis so that the person who analyzed it could give evidence to convict him had both a "testimonial" and a "communicative nature." The sole purpose of this project which proved to be successful was to obtain "testimony" from some person to prove that petitioner had alcohol in his blood at the time he was arrested. And the purpose of the project was certainly "communicative" in that the analysis of the blood was to supply information to enable a witness to communicate to the court and jury that petitioner was more or less drunk.

[T]he Court concedes, as it must so long as *Boyd* stands, that the Fifth Amendment bars a State from compelling a person to produce papers he has that might tend to incriminate him. It is a strange hierarchy of values that allows the State to extract a human being's blood to convict him of a crime because of the blood's content but proscribes compelled production of his lifeless papers. Certainly there could be few papers that would have any more "testimonial" value to convict a man of drunken driving than would an analysis of the alcoholic content of a human being's blood introduced in evidence at a trial for driving while under the influence of alcohol. In such a situation blood, of course, is not oral testimony given by an accused but it can certainly "communicate" to a court and jury the fact of guilt.

The Court itself expresses its own doubts, if not fears, of its own shadowy distinction between compelling "physical evidence" like blood which it holds does not amount to compelled self-incrimination, and "eliciting responses which are essentially testimonial." And in explanation of its fears the Court goes on to warn that

> To compel a person to submit to testing [by lie detectors for example] in which an effort will be made to determine his guilt or innocence on the basis of physiological responses, whether willed or not, is to evoke the spirit and history of the Fifth Amendment. Such situations call to mind the principle that the protection of the privilege "is as broad as the mischief against which it seeks to guard."

A basic error in the Court's holding and opinion is its failure to give the Fifth Amendment's protection against compulsory self-incrimination the broad and liberal construction that *Counselman* and other opinions of this Court have declared it ought to have.

> A close and literal construction [of constitutional provisions for the security of persons and property] deprives them of half their efficacy, and leads to gradual depreciation of the right, as if it consisted more in sound than in substance. It is the duty of courts to be watchful for the constitutional rights of the citizen, and against any stealthy encroachments thereon.

Boyd. The Court went on to say that to require "an owner to produce his private books and papers, in order to prove his breach of the laws, and thus to establish the forfeiture of his property, is surely compelling him to furnish evidence against himself." The Court today departs from the teachings of *Boyd*. Petitioner Schmerber has undoubtedly been compelled to give his blood "to furnish evidence against himself," yet the Court holds that this is not forbidden by the Fifth Amendment. With all deference I must say that the Court here gives the Bill of Rights' safeguard against compulsory self-incrimination a construction that would generally be considered too narrow and technical even in the interpretation of an ordinary commercial contract.

I think the interpretive constitutional philosophy used in *Miranda*, unlike that used in this case, gives the Fifth Amendment's prohibition against compelled self-incrimination a broad and liberal construction in line with the wholesome admonitions in the *Boyd* case. The closing sentence in the Fifth Amendment section of the Court's opinion in the present case is enough by itself, I think, to expose the unsoundness of what the Court here holds. That sentence reads:

> Since the blood test evidence, although an incriminating product of compulsion, was neither petitioner's testimony nor evidence relating to some communicative act or writing by the petitioner, it was not inadmissible on privilege grounds.

How can it reasonably be doubted that the blood test evidence was not in all respects the actual equivalent of "testimony" taken from petitioner when the result of the test was offered as testimony, was considered by the jury as testimony, and the jury's verdict of guilt rests in part on that testimony? The refined, subtle reasoning and balancing process used here to narrow the scope of the Bill of Rights' safeguard against self-incrimination provides a handy instrument for further narrowing of that constitutional protection, as well as others, in the future. Believing with the Framers that these constitutional safeguards broadly construed by independent tribunals of justice provide our best hope for keeping our people free from governmental oppression, I deeply regret the Court's holding. I dissent from the Court's holding and opinion in this case.

MR. JUSTICE DOUGLAS, dissenting.

We are dealing with the right of privacy which, since the *Breithaupt* case, we have held to be within the penumbra of some specific guarantees of the Bill of Rights. *Griswold v. Connecticut*, 381 U.S. 479. Thus, the Fifth Amendment marks "a zone of privacy" which the Government may not force a person to surrender. Likewise the Fourth Amendment recognizes that right when it guarantees the right of the people to be secure "in their persons." No clearer invasion of this right of privacy can be imagined than forcible bloodletting of the kind involved here.

Mr. Justice Fortas, dissenting.

I would reverse. In my view, petitioner's privilege against self-incrimination applies. I would add that, under the Due Process Clause, the State, in its role as prosecutor, has no right to extract blood from an accused or anyone else, over his protest. As prosecutor, the State has no right to commit any kind of violence upon the person, or to utilize the results of such a tort, and the extraction of blood, over protest, is an act of violence.

QUESTIONS AND NOTES

1.   Why was the due process standard of *Rochin* not violated in this case? Do you agree?

2.   In an edited portion of the opinion, the Court held that the Fourth Amendment was not violated because there was probable cause to "search" for the blood and insufficient time to obtain a warrant.

3.   However, in *Missouri v. McNeely*, 569 U.S. ___, 133 S. Ct. 1552 (2013), the Supreme Court held that the mere potential of blood alcohol to dissipate was insufficient to justify dispensing with a warrant. *Schmerber* was distinguished as a case where there was in fact insufficient time.

4.   Does the Court intend to construe the Fifth Amendment as broadly as necessary to combat the mischief it was intended to correct?

5.   Is the standard of testimonial or communicative evidence a meaningful way to limit the Fifth Amendment? Is it desirable?

6.   Suppose the police ask a D.U.I. suspect, the date of his sixth birthday and introduce his ignorance of the date to prove his intoxication. Is his ignorance "testimonial?" For the Supreme Court's resolution, see *Pennsylvania v. Muniz*, 496 U.S. 582 (1990).

7.   Is there something wrong with a system that values lifeless papers more than blood?

8.   Even lifeless papers are not protected to the same extent today as they were at the time of *Boyd. See Fisher v. United States*, 425 U.S. 391 (1976).

B.   DUE PROCESS AND IDENTIFICATION

For several years, it appeared as though right to counsel was going to be the constitutional provision that governed the identification process. In 1967, the Supreme Court decided *United States v. Wade*, 388 U.S. 218, which for a time was nearly as prominent as *Miranda*. Specifically *Wade* held (1) on reasoning similar to *Schmerber*, mandatory participation in a lineup (including uttering the words and wearing the clothing of the robber) did *not* violate the Fifth Amendment. However, it also held that (at least) at a post-indictment lineup, the Sixth Amendment required the presence of counsel. Consequently, if an uncounseled defendant was identified at a post-indictment lineup, the State could not introduce that identification at trial. Furthermore, the witness could not identify the defendant at trial unless the State could establish by clear and convincing evidence that the in-court identification was not tainted by the unconstitutional identification obtained in the absence of counsel.

Two cases in the early 1970s stripped *Wade* of much of its potential. First, *Kirby v. Illinois*, 406 U.S. 682 (1972) held that *Wade* did not apply to a pre-indictment lineup.[1] Second, *United States v. Ash*, 413 U.S. 300 (1973), held that a post-indictment pictorial lineup did not require the presence of counsel. Thus, after these two cases, *Wade* became largely irrelevant. If the police wanted to hold a lineup before the onset of formal proceedings (certainly the usual time to hold a lineup if the police aren't sure they have the perpetrator), *Wade* didn't apply. And, if the police or prosecutor wanted to hold a post-indictment lineup, they could simply do it pictorially rather than corporeally. On those rare occasions in which a post-indictment corporeal lineup was necessary, only an extremely incompetent policeman or prosecutor would not alert counsel for defendant, who after all couldn't do anything anyway except observe.

Quite apart from the right to counsel, a lineup identification which was obtained under fundamentally unfair circumstances may not be introduced. In *Manson v. Brathwaite*, the Court explores the various tests considered by the Court and settles on the one it finds most appropriate. As you read *Manson*, consider whether the Court adopted the best possible standard for measuring due process.

MANSON v. BRATHWAITE
432 U.S. 98 (1977)

Mr. Justice Blackmun delivered the opinion of the Court.

This case presents the issue as to whether the Due Process Clause of the Fourteenth Amendment compels the exclusion, in a state criminal trial, apart from any consideration of reliability, of pretrial identification evidence obtained by a police procedure that was both suggestive and unnecessary.

I

Jimmy D. Glover, a full-time trooper of the Connecticut State Police, in 1970 was assigned to the Narcotics Division in an undercover capacity. On May 5 of that year, about 7:45 p.m., e.d.t., and while there was still daylight, Glover and Henry Alton Brown, an informant, went to an apartment building at 201 Westland, in Hartford, for the purpose of purchasing narcotics from "Dickie Boy" Cicero, a known narcotics dealer. Cicero, it was thought, lived on the third floor of that apartment

---

[1] Pre-indictment is a slightly oversimplified term. More accurately, we are speaking of the time frame before the onset of formal judicial proceedings, not necessarily an indictment. *See, e.g., Brewer v. Williams.*

building. Glover and Brown entered the building, observed by back-up Officers D'Onofrio and Gaffey, and proceeded by stairs to the third floor. Glover knocked at the door of one of the two apartments served by the stairway.[2] The area was illuminated by natural light from a window in the third floor hallway. The door was opened 12 to 18 inches in response to the knock. Glover observed a man standing at the door and, behind him, a woman. Brown identified himself. Glover then asked for "two things" of narcotics. The man at the door held out his hand, and Glover gave him two $10 bills. The door closed. Soon the man returned and handed Glover two glassine bags. While the door was open, Glover stood within two feet of the person from whom he made the purchase and observed his face. Five to seven minutes elapsed from the time the door first opened until it closed the second time.

Glover and Brown then left the building. This was about eight minutes after their arrival. Glover drove to headquarters where he described the seller to D'Onofrio and Gaffey. Glover at that time did not know the identity of the seller. He described him as being "a colored man, approximately five feet eleven inches tall, dark complexion, black hair, short Afro style, and having high cheekbones, and of heavy build. He was wearing at the time blue pants and a plaid shirt." D'Onofrio, suspecting from this description that respondent might be the seller, obtained a photograph of respondent from the Records Division of the Hartford Police Department. He left it at Glover's office. D'Onofrio was not acquainted with respondent personally but did know him by sight and had seen him "[s]everal times" prior to May 5. Glover, when alone, viewed the photograph for the first time upon his return to headquarters on May 7; he identified the person shown as the one from whom he had purchased the narcotics.

Respondent was arrested on July 27 while visiting at the apartment of a Mrs. Ramsey on the third floor of 201 Westland. This was the apartment at which the narcotics sale had taken place on May 5.[4]

At his trial in January 1971, the photograph from which Glover had identified respondent was received in evidence without objection on the part of the defense. Glover also testified that, although he had not seen respondent in the eight months that had elapsed since the sale, "there [was] no doubt whatsoever" in his mind that the person shown on the photograph was respondent. Glover also made a positive in-court identification without objection.

No explanation was offered by the prosecution for the failure to utilize a photographic array or to conduct a lineup.

Respondent, who took the stand in his own defense, testified that on May 5, the day in question, he had been ill at his Albany Avenue apartment ("a lot of back pains, muscle spasms . . . a bad heart . . . high blood pressure . . . neuralgia in my

---

[2] It appears that the door on which Glover knocked may not have been that of the Cicero apartment. Petitioner concedes, in any event, that the transaction effected "was with some other person than had been intended."

[4] Respondent testified: "Lots of times I have been there before in that building." He also testified that Mrs. Ramsey was a friend of his wife, that her apartment was the only one in the building he ever visited, and that he and his family, consisting of his wife and five children, did not live there but at 453 Albany Avenue, Hartford.

face, and sinus," and that at no time on that particular day had he been at 201 Westland. His wife testified that she recalled, after her husband had refreshed her memory, that he was home all day on May 5. Doctor Wesley M. Vietzke, an internist and assistant professor of medicine at the University of Connecticut, testified that respondent had consulted him on April 15, 1970, and that he took a medical history from him, heard his complaints about his back and facial pain, and discovered that he had high blood pressure. The physician found respondent, subjectively, "in great discomfort." Respondent in fact underwent surgery for a herniated disc on August 17.

The jury found respondent guilty on both counts of the information. He received a sentence of not less than six nor more than nine years. His conviction was affirmed *per curiam* by the Supreme Court of Connecticut. That court noted the absence of an objection to Glover's in-court identification and concluded that respondent "has not shown that substantial injustice resulted from the admission of this evidence." Under Connecticut law, substantial injustice must be shown before a claim of error not made or passed on by the trial court will be considered on appeal.

Fourteen months later, respondent filed a petition for habeas corpus in the United States District Court for the District of Connecticut. He alleged that the admission of the identification testimony at his state trial deprived him of due process of law to which he was entitled under the Fourteenth Amendment. The District Court, by an unreported written opinion based on the court's review of the state trial transcript, dismissed respondent's petition. On appeal, the United States Court of Appeals for the Second Circuit reversed, with instructions to issue the writ unless the State gave notice of a desire to retry respondent and the new trial occurred within a reasonable time to be fixed by the District Judge.

In brief summary, the court felt that evidence as to the photograph should have been excluded, regardless of reliability, because the examination of the single photograph was unnecessary and suggestive. And, in the court's view, the evidence was unreliable in any event. We granted certiorari.

II

Stovall v. Denno, decided in 1967, concerned a petitioner who had been convicted in a New York court of murder. He was arrested the day following the crime and was taken by the police to a hospital where the victim's wife, also wounded in the assault, was a patient. After observing Stovall and hearing him speak, she identified him as the murderer. She later made an in-court identification. On federal habeas, Stovall claimed the identification testimony violated his Fifth, Sixth, and Fourteenth Amendment rights. The District Court dismissed the petition, and the Court of Appeals, en banc, affirmed. This Court also affirmed. On the identification issue, the Court reviewed the practice of showing a suspect singly for purposes of identification, and the claim that this was so unnecessarily suggestive and conducive to irreparable mistaken identification that it constituted a denial of due process of law. The Court noted that the practice "has been widely condemned," but it concluded that "a claimed violation of due process of law in the conduct of a confrontation depends on the totality of the circumstances surrounding it." In that case, showing Stovall to the victim's spouse "was imperative." The Court then quoted the observations of the Court of Appeals, to the effect that the spouse was the only person who could possibly exonerate the accused; that the hospital was not far from the courthouse and jail; that no one knew how long she might live; that she was not able to visit the jail; and that taking Stovall to the hospital room was the only feasible procedure, and, under the circumstances, "the usual police station line-up . . . was out of the question."

Neil v. Biggers, decided in 1972, concerned a respondent who had been convicted in a Tennessee court of rape, on evidence consisting in part of the victim's visual and voice identification of Biggers at a station-house showup seven months after the crime. The victim had been in her assailant's presence for some time and had directly observed him indoors and under a full moon outdoors. She testified that she had "no doubt" that Biggers was her assailant. She previously had given the police a description of the assailant. She had made no identification of others presented at previous showups, lineups, or through photographs. On federal habeas, the District Court held that the confrontation was so suggestive as to violate due process. The Court of Appeals affirmed. This Court reversed on that issue, and held that the evidence properly had been allowed to go to the jury. The Court reviewed *Stovall* and certain later cases where it had considered the scope of due process protection against the admission of evidence derived from suggestive identification procedures, namely, *Simmons v. United States*, 390 U.S. 377 (1968) [and] *Foster v. California*, 394 U.S. 440 (1969).[8] The Court concluded that general guidelines emerged from these cases "as to the relationship between suggestiveness and misidentification." The "admission of evidence of a showup without more does not violate due process." The Court expressed concern about the lapse of seven months between the crime and the confrontation and observed that this "would be a seriously negative factor in most cases." The "central question," however, was "whether under the 'totality of the circumstances' the identification was reliable even though the confrontation procedure was suggestive." Applying that test, the Court found "no substantial likelihood of misidentification. The evidence was properly allowed to go to the jury."

Biggers well might be seen to provide an unambiguous answer to the question before us: The admission of testimony concerning a suggestive and unnecessary identification procedure does not violate due process so long as the identification possesses sufficient aspects of reliability.[9] In one passage, however, the Court

---

[8] *Simmons* involved photographs, mostly group ones, shown to bank-teller victims who made in-court identifications. The Court discussed the "chance of misidentification," declined to prohibit the procedure "either in the exercise of our supervisory power or, still less, as a matter of constitutional requirement," and held that each case must be considered on its facts and that a conviction would be set aside only if the identification procedure "was so impermissibly suggestive as to give rise to a very substantial likelihood of irreparable misidentification." The out-of-court identification was not offered. Mr. Justice Black would have denied Simmons' due process claim as frivolous.

Foster concerned repeated confrontations between a suspect and the manager of an office that had been robbed. At a second lineup, but not at the first and not at a personal one-to-one confrontation, the manager identified the suspect. At trial he testified as to this and made an in-court identification. The Court reaffirmed the *Stovall* standard and then concluded that the repeated confrontations were so suggestive as to violate due process. The case was remanded for the state courts to consider the question of harmless error.

[9] Mr. Justice Marshall argues in dissent that our cases have "established two different due process

observed that the challenged procedure occurred pre-*Stovall* and that a strict rule would make little sense with regard to a confrontation that preceded the Court's first indication that a suggestive procedure might lead to the exclusion of evidence. One perhaps might argue that, by implication, the Court suggested that a different rule could apply post-*Stovall*. The question before us, then, is simply whether the *Biggers* analysis applies to post-*Stovall* confrontations as well to those pre-*Stovall*.

III

In the present case the District Court observed that the "sole evidence tying Brathwaite to the possession and sale of the heroin consisted in his identifications by the police undercover agent, Jimmy Glover." On the constitutional issue, the court stated that the first inquiry was whether the police used an impermissibly suggestive procedure in obtaining the out-of-court identification. If so, the second inquiry is whether, under all the circumstances, that suggestive procedure gave rise to a substantial likelihood of irreparable misidentification. *Biggers* and *Simmons* were cited. The court noted that in the Second Circuit, its controlling court, it was clear that "this type of identification procedure [display of a single photograph] is impermissibly suggestive," and turned to the second inquiry. The factors *Biggers* specified for consideration were recited and applied. The court concluded that there was no substantial likelihood of irreparable misidentification. It referred to the facts: Glover was within two feet of the seller. The duration of the confrontation was at least a "couple of minutes." There was natural light from a window or skylight and there was adequate light to see clearly in the hall. Glover "certainly was paying attention to identify the seller." He was a trained police officer who realized that later he would have to find and arrest the person with whom he was dealing. He gave a detailed description to D'Onofrio. The reliability of this description was supported by the fact that it enabled D'Onofrio to pick out a single photograph that was thereafter positively identified by Glover. Only two days elapsed between the crime and the photographic identification. Despite the fact that another eight months passed before the in-court identification, Glover had "no doubt" that Brathwaite was the person who had sold him heroin.

The Court of Appeals confirmed that the exhibition of the single photograph to Glover was "impermissibly suggestive," and felt that, in addition, "it was unneces-

---

tests for two very different situations." Pretrial identifications are to be covered by *Stovall*, which is said to require exclusion of evidence concerning unnecessarily suggestive pretrial identifications without regard to reliability. In-court identifications, on the other hand, are to be governed by *Simmons* and admissibility turns on reliability. The Court's cases are sorted into one category or the other. *Biggers*, which clearly adopts the reliability of the identification as the guiding factor in the admissibility of both pretrial and in-court identifications, is condemned for mixing the two lines and for adopting a uniform rule.

Although it must be acknowledged that our cases are not uniform in their emphasis, they hardly suggest the formal structure the dissent would impose on them. If our cases truly established two different rules, one might expect at some point at least passing reference to the fact. There is none. And if *Biggers* departed so grievously from the past cases, it is surprising that there was not at least some mention of the point in Mr. Justice Brennan's dissent. In fact, the cases are not so readily sorted as the dissent suggests. Although *Foster* involved both in-court and out-of-court identifications, the Court seemed to apply only a single standard for both. Thus, *Biggers* is not properly seen as a departure from the past cases, but as a synthesis of them.

sarily so." There was no emergency and little urgency. The court said that prior to the decision in *Biggers*, except in cases of harmless error, "a conviction secured as the result of admitting an identification obtained by impermissibly suggestive and unnecessary measures could not stand." It noted what it felt might be opposing inferences to be drawn from passages in *Biggers*, but concluded that the case preserved the principle "requiring the exclusion of identifications resulting from 'unnecessarily suggestive confrontation'" in post-*Stovall* situations. The court also concluded that for post-*Stovall* identifications, *Biggers* had not changed the existing rule. Thus: "Evidence of an identification unnecessarily obtained by impermissibly suggestive means must be excluded under *Stovall*. . . . No rules less stringent than these can force police administrators and prosecutors to adopt procedures that will give fair assurance against the awful risks of misidentification." Finally, the court said, even if this conclusion were wrong, the writ, nevertheless, should issue. It took judicial notice that on May 5, 1970, sunset at Hartford was at 7:53 p.m. It characterized Glover's duty as an undercover agent as one "to cause arrests to be made," and his description of the suspect as one that "could have applied to hundreds of Hartford black males." The in-court identification had "little meaning," for Brathwaite was at the counsel table. The fact that respondent was arrested in the very apartment where the sale was made was subject to a "not implausible" explanation from the respondent, "although evidently not credited by the jury." And the court was troubled by "the long and unexplained delay" in the arrest. It was too great a danger that the respondent was convicted because he was a man D'Onofrio had previously observed near the scene, was thought to be a likely offender, and was arrested when he was known to be in Mrs. Ramsey's apartment, rather than because Glover "really remembered him as the seller."

IV

Petitioner at the outset acknowledges that "the procedure in the instant case was suggestive [because only one photograph was used] and unnecessary" [because there was no emergency or exigent circumstance]. The respondent, in agreement with the Court of Appeals, proposes a *per se* rule of exclusion that he claims is dictated by the demands of the Fourteenth Amendment's guarantee of due process. He rightly observes that this is the first case in which this Court has had occasion to rule upon strictly post-*Stovall* out-of-court identification evidence of the challenged kind.

Since the decision in *Biggers*, the Courts of Appeals appear to have developed at least two approaches to such evidence. The first, or *per se* approach, employed by the Second Circuit in the present case, focuses on the procedures employed and requires exclusion of the out-of-court identification evidence, without regard to reliability, whenever it has been obtained through unnecessarily suggested confrontation procedures.[10] The justifications advanced are the elimination of evidence

[10] Although the *per se* approach demands the exclusion of testimony concerning unnecessarily suggestive identifications, it does permit the admission of testimony concerning a subsequent identification, including an in-court identification, if the subsequent identification is determined to be reliable. The totality approach, in contrast, is simpler: if the challenged identification is reliable, then testimony as to it and any identification in its wake is admissible.

of uncertain reliability, deterrence of the police and prosecutors, and the stated "fair assurance against the awful risks of misidentification."

The second, or more lenient, approach is one that continues to rely on the totality of the circumstances. It permits the admission of the confrontation evidence if, despite the suggestive aspect, the out-of-court identification possesses certain features of reliability. Its adherents feel that the *per se* approach is not mandated by the Due Process Clause of the Fourteenth Amendment. This second approach, in contrast to the other, is ad hoc and serves to limit the societal costs imposed by a sanction that excludes relevant evidence from consideration and evaluation by the trier of fact.

There are, of course, several interests to be considered and taken into account. The driving force behind *Wade, Gilbert,* and *Stovall,* all decided on the same day, was the Court's concern with the problems of eyewitness identification. Usually the witness must testify about an encounter with a total stranger under circumstances of emergency or emotional stress. The witness' recollection of the stranger can be distorted easily by the circumstances or by later actions of the police. Thus, *Wade* and its companion cases reflect the concern that the jury not hear eyewitness testimony unless that evidence has aspects of reliability. It must be observed that both approaches before us are responsive to this concern. The *per se* rule, however, goes too far since its application automatically and peremptorily, and without consideration of alleviating factors, keeps evidence from the jury that is reliable and relevant.

The second factor is deterrence. Although the *per se* approach has the more significant deterrent effect, the totality approach also has an influence on police behavior. The police will guard against unnecessarily suggestive procedures under the totality rule, as well as the *per se* one, for fear that their actions will lead to the exclusion of identifications as unreliable.[12]

The third factor is the effect on the administration of justice. Here the *per se* approach suffers serious drawbacks. Since it denies the trier reliable evidence, it may result, on occasion, in the guilty going free. Also, because of its rigidity, the *per se* approach may make error by the trial judge more likely than the totality approach. And in those cases in which the admission of identification evidence is error under the *per se* approach but not under the totality approach — cases in which the identification is reliable despite an unnecessarily suggestive identification procedure — reversal is a Draconian sanction.[13] Certainly, inflexible rules of exclusion that may frustrate rather than promote justice have not been viewed recently by this Court with unlimited enthusiasm.

We therefore conclude that reliability is the linchpin in determining the admissibility of identification testimony for both pre- and post-*Stovall* confronta-

---

[12] The interest in obtaining convictions of the guilty also urges the police to adopt procedures that show the resulting identification to be accurate. Suggestive procedures often will vitiate the weight of the evidence at trial and the jury may tend to discount such evidence.

[13] Unlike a warrantless search, a suggestive preindictment identification procedure does not in itself intrude upon a constitutionally protected interest. Thus, considerations urging the exclusion of evidence deriving from a constitutional violation do not bear on the instant problem.

tions. The factors to be considered are set out in *Biggers*. These include the opportunity of the witness to view the criminal at the time of the crime, the witness' degree of attention, the accuracy of his prior description of the criminal, the level of certainty demonstrated at the confrontation, and the time between the crime and the confrontation. Against these factors is to be weighed the corrupting effect of the suggestive identification itself.

V

We turn, then, to the facts of this case and apply the analysis:

1. The opportunity to view. Glover testified that for two to three minutes he stood at the apartment door, within two feet of the respondent. The door opened twice, and each time the man stood at the door. The moments passed, the conversation took place, and payment was made. Glover looked directly at his vendor. It was near sunset, to be sure, but the sun had not yet set, so it was not dark or even dusk or twilight. Natural light from outside entered the hallway through a window. There was natural light, as well, from inside the apartment.

2. The degree of attention. Glover was not a casual or passing observer, as is so often the case with eyewitness identification. Trooper Glover was a trained police officer on duty — and specialized and dangerous duty — when he called at the third floor of 201 Westland in Hartford on May 5, 1970. Glover himself was a Negro and unlikely to perceive only general features of "hundreds of Hartford black males," as the Court of Appeals stated. It is true that Glover's duty was that of ferreting out narcotics offenders and that he would be expected in his work to produce results. But it is also true that, as a specially trained, assigned, and experienced officer, he could be expected to pay scrupulous attention to detail, for he knew that subsequently he would have to find and arrest his vendor. In addition, he knew that his claimed observations would be subject later to close scrutiny and examination at any trial.

3. The accuracy of the description. Glover's description was given to D'Onofrio within minutes after the transaction. It included the vendor's race, his height, his build, the color and style of his hair, and the high cheekbone facial feature. It also included clothing the vendor wore. No claim has been made that respondent did not possess the physical characteristics so described. D'Onofrio reacted positively at once. Two days later, when Glover was alone, he viewed the photograph D'Onofrio produced and identified its subject as the narcotics seller.

4. The witness' level of certainty. There is no dispute that the photograph in question was that of respondent. Glover, in response to a question whether the photograph was that of the person from whom he made the purchase, testified: "There is no question whatsoever." This positive assurance was repeated.

5. The time between the crime and the confrontation. Glover's description of his vendor was given to D'Onofrio within minutes of the crime. The photographic identification took place only two days later. We do not have here the passage of weeks or months between the crime and the viewing of the photograph.

These indicators of Glover's ability to make an accurate identification are hardly outweighed by the corrupting effect of the challenged identification itself. Although identifications arising from single-photograph displays may be viewed in general with suspicion, we find in the instant case little pressure on the witness to acquiesce in the suggestion that such a display entails. D'Onofrio had left the photograph at Glover's office and was not present when Glover first viewed it two days after the event. There thus was little urgency and Glover could view the photograph at his leisure. And since Glover examined the photograph alone, there was no coercive pressure to make an identification arising from the presence of another. The identification was made in circumstances allowing care and reflection.

Although it plays no part in our analysis, all this assurance as to the reliability of the identification is hardly undermined by the facts that respondent was arrested in the very apartment where the sale had taken place, and that he acknowledged his frequent visits to that apartment.

Surely, we cannot say that under all the circumstances of this case there is "a very substantial likelihood of irreparable misidentification." Short of that point, such evidence is for the jury to weigh. We are content to rely upon the good sense and judgment of American juries, for evidence with some element of untrustworthiness is customary grist for the jury mill. Juries are not so susceptible that they cannot measure intelligently the weight of identification testimony that has some questionable feature.

Of course, it would have been better had D'Onofrio presented Glover with a photographic array including "so far as practicable . . . a reasonable number of persons similar to any person then suspected whose likeness is included in the array." Model Code, § 160.2(2). The use of that procedure would have enhanced the force of the identification at trial and would have avoided the risk that the evidence would be excluded as unreliable. But we are not disposed to view D'Onofrio's failure as one of constitutional dimension to be enforced by a rigorous and unbending exclusionary rule. The defect, if there be one, goes to weight and not to substance.

The judgment of the Court of Appeals is reversed.

MR. JUSTICE STEVENS, concurring.

While I join the Court's opinion, I would emphasize two points.

First, as I indicated in my opinion in *United States ex rel. Kirby v. Sturges*, 510 F.2d 397, 405–406 (CA7 1975), the arguments in favor of fashioning new rules to minimize the danger of convicting the innocent on the basis of unreliable eyewitness testimony carry substantial force. Nevertheless, for the reasons stated in that opinion, as well as those stated by the Court today. I am persuaded that this rulemaking function can be performed "more effectively by the legislative process than by a somewhat clumsy judicial fiat," and that the Federal Constitution does not foreclose experimentation by the States in the development of such rules.

Second, in evaluating the admissibility of particular identification testimony it is sometimes difficult to put other evidence of guilt entirely to one side.* Mr. Justice Blackmun's opinion for the Court carefully avoids this pitfall and correctly relies only on appropriate indicia of the reliability of the identification itself. Although I consider the factual question in this case extremely close, I am persuaded that the Court has resolved it properly.

MR. JUSTICE MARSHALL, with whom MR. JUSTICE BRENNAN joins, dissenting.

Today's decision can come as no surprise to those who have been watching the Court dismantle the protections against mistaken eyewitness testimony erected a decade ago in *Wade, Gilbert,* and *Stovall.* But it is still distressing to see the Court virtually ignore the teaching of experience embodied in those decisions and blindly uphold the conviction of a defendant who may well be innocent.

I

Stovall, while holding that the *Wade* prophylactic rules were not retroactive, was decided at the same time and reflects the same concerns about the reliability of identification testimony. *Stovall* recognized that, regardless of Sixth Amendment principles, "the conduct of a confrontation" may be "so unnecessarily suggestive and conducive to irreparable mistaken identification" as to deny due process of law. The pretrial confrontation in *Stovall* was plainly suggestive,[2] and evidence of it was introduced at trial along with the witness' in-court identification. The Court ruled that there had been no violation of due process, however, because the unusual necessity for the procedure[3] outweighed the danger of suggestion.

The development of due process protections against mistaken identification evidence, begun in *Stovall,* was continued in *Simmons v. United States,* 390 U.S. 377 (1968). There, the Court developed a different rule to deal with the admission of in-court identification testimony that the accused claimed had been fatally tainted by a previous suggestive confrontation. In *Simmons,* the exclusionary effect of *Stovall* had already been accomplished, since the prosecution made no use of the suggestive confrontation. *Simmons,* therefore, did not deal with the constitutionality of the pretrial identification procedure. The only question was the impact of the Due Process Clause on an in-court identification that was not itself unnecessarily

---

* In this case, for example, the fact that the defendant was a regular visitor to the apartment where the drug transaction occurred tends to confirm his guilt. In the *Kirby* case, where the conviction was for robbery, the fact that papers from the victim's wallet were found in the possession of the defendant made it difficult to question the reliability of the identification. These facts should not, however, be considered to support the admissibility of eyewitness testimony when applying the criteria identified in *Neil v. Biggers.* Properly analyzed, however, such facts would be relevant to a question whether error, if any, in admitting identification testimony was harmless.

[2] The accused, a Negro, was brought handcuffed by seven white police officers and employees of the District Attorney to the hospital room of the only witness to a murder. As the Court said of this encounter: "It is hard to imagine a situation more clearly conveying the suggestion to the witness that the one presented is believed to be guilty by the police."

[3] The police reasonably feared that the witness might die before any less suggestive confrontation could be arranged.

suggestive. *Simmons* held that due process was violated by the later identification if the pretrial procedure had been "so impermissibly suggestive as to give rise to a very substantial likelihood of irreparable misidentification." This test focused, not on the necessity for the challenged pretrial procedure, but on the degree of suggestiveness that it entailed. In applying this test, the Court understandably considered the circumstances surrounding the witnesses' initial opportunity to view the crime. Finding that any suggestion in the pretrial confrontation had not affected the fairness of the in-court identification, *Simmons* rejected petitioner's due process attack on his conviction.

Thus, *Stovall* and *Simmons* established two different due process tests for two very different situations. Where the prosecution sought to use evidence of a questionable pretrial identification, *Stovall* required its exclusion, because due process had been violated by the confrontation, unless the necessity for the unduly suggestive procedure outweighed its potential for generating an irreparably mistaken identification. The *Simmons* test, on the other hand, was directed to ascertaining due process violations in the introduction of in-court identification testimony that the defendant claimed was tainted by pretrial procedures. In the latter situation, a court could consider the reliability of the identification under all the circumstances.

The Court inexplicably seemed to erase the distinction between *Stovall* and *Simmons* situations in *Neil v. Biggers*. In *Biggers* there was a pretrial confrontation that was clearly both suggestive and unnecessary.[6] Evidence of this, together with an in-court identification, was admitted at trial. *Biggers* was, in short, a case plainly cast in the *Stovall* mold. Yet the Court, without explanation or apparent recognition of the distinction, applied the *Simmons* test. The Court stated: "[T]he primary evil to be avoided is 'a very substantial likelihood of irreparable misidentification.' It is the likelihood of misidentification which violates a defendant's right to due process . . . ." While this statement accurately describes the lesson of *Simmons*, it plainly ignores the teaching of *Stovall* and *Foster* that an unnecessarily suggestive pretrial confrontation itself violates due process.

II

Apparently, the Court does not consider *Biggers* controlling in this case. I entirely agree, since I believe that *Biggers* was wrongly decided. The Court, however, concludes that *Biggers* is distinguishable because it, like the identification decisions that preceded it, involved a pre-*Stovall* confrontation, and because a paragraph in *Biggers* itself, seems to distinguish between pre- and post-*Stovall* confrontations. Accordingly, in determining the admissibility of the post-*Stovall* identification in this case, the Court considers two alternatives, a *per se* exclusionary rule and a totality-of-the circumstances approach. The Court weighs three factors in deciding that the totality approach, which is essentially the test used in

---

[6] "The showup itself consisted of two detectives walking respondent past the victim." The police also ordered respondent to repeat the words used by the criminal. Inadequate efforts were made to secure participants for a lineup, and there was no pressing need to use a showup.

Biggers, should be applied. In my view, the Court wrongly evaluates the impact of these factors.

First, the Court acknowledges that one of the factors, deterrence of police use of unnecessarily suggestive identification procedures, favors the *per se* rule. Indeed, it does so heavily, for such a rule would make it unquestionably clear to the police they must never use a suggestive procedure when a fairer alternative is available. I have no doubt that conduct would quickly conform to the rule.

Second, the Court gives passing consideration to the dangers of eyewitness identification recognized in the *Wade* trilogy. It concludes, however, that the grave risk of error does not justify adoption of the *per se* approach because that would too often result in exclusion of relevant evidence. In my view, this conclusion totally ignores the lessons of *Wade*. The dangers of mistaken identification are, as *Stovall* held, simply too great to permit unnecessarily suggestive identifications. Neither *Biggers* nor the Court's opinion today points to any contrary empirical evidence. Studies since *Wade* have only reinforced the validity of its assessment of the dangers of identification testimony. While the Court is "content to rely on the good sense and judgment of American juries," the impetus for *Stovall* and *Wade* was repeated miscarriages of justice resulting from juries' willingness to credit inaccurate eyewitness testimony.

Finally, the Court errs in its assessment of the relative impact of the two approaches on the administration of justice. The Court relies most heavily on this factor, finding that "reversal is a Draconian sanction" in cases where the identification is reliable despite an unnecessarily suggestive procedure used to obtain it. Relying on little more than a strong distaste for "inflexible rules of exclusion," the Court rejects the *per se* test. In so doing, the Court disregards two significant distinctions between the *per se* rule advocated in this case and the exclusionary remedies for certain other constitutional violations.

First, the *per se* rule here is not "inflexible." Where evidence is suppressed, for example, as the fruit of an unlawful search, it may well be forever lost to the prosecution. Identification evidence, however, can by its very nature be readily and effectively reproduced. The in-court identification, permitted under *Wade* and *Simmons* if it has a source independent of an uncounseled or suggestive procedure, is one example. Similarly, when a prosecuting attorney learns that there has been a suggestive confrontation, he can easily arrange another lineup conducted under scrupulously fair conditions. Since the same factors are evaluated in applying both the Court's totality test and the *Wade-Simmons* independent-source inquiry, any identification which is "reliable" under the Court's test will support admission of evidence concerning such a fairly conducted lineup. The evidence of an additional, properly conducted confrontation will be more persuasive to a jury, thereby increasing the chance of a justified conviction where a reliable identification was tainted by a suggestive confrontation. At the same time, however, the effect of an unnecessarily suggestive identification — which has no value whatsoever in the law enforcement process — will be completely eliminated.

Second, other exclusionary rules have been criticized for preventing jury consideration of relevant and usually reliable evidence in order to serve interest unrelated to guilt or innocence, such as discouraging illegal searches or denial of counsel. Suggestively obtained eyewitness testimony is excluded, in contrast, precisely because of its unreliability and concomitant irrelevance. Its exclusion both protects the integrity of the truth-seeking function of the trial and discourages police use of needlessly inaccurate and ineffective investigatory methods.

Indeed, impermissibly suggestive identifications are not merely worthless law enforcement tools. They pose a grave threat to society at large in a more direct way than most governmental disobedience of the law. For if the police and the public erroneously conclude, on the basis of an unnecessarily suggestive confrontation, that the right man has been caught and convicted, the real outlaw must still remain at large. Law enforcement has failed in its primary function and has left society unprotected from the depredations of an active criminal.

For these reasons, I conclude that adoption of the *per se* rule would enhance, rather than detract from, the effective administration of justice. In my view, the Court's totality test will allow seriously unreliable and misleading evidence to be put before juries. Equally important, it will allow dangerous criminals to remain on the streets while citizens assume that police action has given them protection. According to my calculus, all three of the factors upon which the Court relies point to acceptance of the *per se* approach.

III

Despite my strong disagreement with the Court over the proper standards to be applied in this case, I am pleased that its application of the totality test does recognize the continuing vitality of *Stovall*. In assessing the reliability of the identification, the Court mandates weighing "the corrupting effect of the suggestive identification itself" against the "indicators of [a witness'] ability to make an accurate identification." The Court holds, as *Neil v. Biggers* failed to, that a due process identification inquiry must take account of the suggestiveness of a confrontation and the likelihood that it led to misidentification, as recognized in *Stovall* and *Wade*. Thus, even if a witness did have an otherwise adequate opportunity to view a criminal, the later use of a highly suggestive identification procedure can render his testimony inadmissible. Indeed, it is my view that, assuming applicability of the totality test enunciated by the Court, the facts of the present case require that result.

I consider first the opportunity that Officer Glover had to view the suspect. Careful review of the record shows that he could see the heroin seller only for the time it took to speak three sentences of four or five short words, to hand over some money, and later after the door reopened, to receive the drugs in return. The entire face-to-face transaction could have taken as little as 15 or 20 seconds. But during this time, Glover's attention was not focused exclusively on the seller's face. He observed that the door was opened 12 to 18 inches, that there was a window in the room behind the door, and, most importantly, that there was a woman standing behind the man. Glover was, of course, also concentrating on the details of the transaction he must have looked away from the seller's face to hand him the money and receive the drugs. The observation during the conversation thus may have been as brief as 5 or 10 seconds.

As the Court notes, Glover was a police officer trained in and attentive to the need for making accurate identifications. Nevertheless, both common sense and scholarly study indicate that while a trained observer such as a police officer "is somewhat less likely to make an erroneous identification than the average untrained observer, the mere fact that he has been so trained is no guarantee that he is correct in a specific case. His identification testimony should be scrutinized just as carefully as that of the normal witness." Moreover, "identifications made by policemen in highly competitive activities, such as undercover narcotic agents . . . , should be scrutinized with special care." Yet it is just such a searching inquiry that the Court fails to make here.

Another factor on which the Court relies — the witness' degree of certainty in making the identification — is worthless as an indicator that he is correct. Even if Glover had been unsure initially about his identification of respondent's picture, by the time he was called at trial to present a key piece of evidence for the State that paid his salary, it is impossible to imagine his responding negatively to such questions as "is there any doubt in your mind whatsoever" that the identification was correct. As the Court noted in *Wade*: "It is a matter of common experience that, once a witness has picked out the accused at the [pretrial confrontation], he is not likely to go back on his word later on."

Next, the Court finds that because the identification procedure took place two days after the crime, its reliability is enhanced. While such temporal proximity makes the identification more reliable than one occurring months later, the fact is that the greatest memory loss occurs within hours after an event. After that, the dropoff continues much more slowly. Thus, the reliability of an identification is increased only if it was made within several hours of the crime. If the time gap is any greater, reliability necessarily decreases.

Finally, the Court makes much of the fact that Glover gave a description of the seller to D'Onofrio shortly after the incident. Despite the Court's assertion that because "Glover himself was a Negro and unlikely to perceive only general features of 'hundreds of Hartford black males,' as the Court of Appeals stated," the description given by Glover was actually no more than a general summary of the seller's appearance. We may discount entirely the seller's clothing, for that was of no significance later in the proceeding. Indeed, to the extent that Glover noticed clothes, his attention was diverted from the seller's face. Otherwise, Glover merely described vaguely the seller's height, skin color, hairstyle, and build. He did say that the seller had "high cheekbones," but there is no other mention of facial features, nor even an estimate of age. Conspicuously absent is any indication that the seller was a native of the West Indies, certainly something which a member of the black community could immediately recognize from both appearance and accent.[12]

From all of this, I must conclude that the evidence of Glover's ability to make an accurate identification is far weaker than the Court finds it. In contrast, the

---

[12] Brathwaite had come to the United States from his native Barbados as an adult. It is also noteworthy that the informant who witnessed the transaction and was described by Glover as "trustworthy," disagreed with Glover's recollection of the event. The informant testified that it was a woman in the apartment who took the money from Glover and gave him the drugs in return.

procedure used to identify respondent was both extraordinarily suggestive and strongly conducive to error. In dismissing "the corrupting effect of the suggestive identification" procedure here, the Court virtually grants the police license to convict the innocent. By displaying a single photograph of respondent to the witness Glover under the circumstances in this record almost everything that could have been done wrong was done wrong.

In the first place, there was no need to use a photograph at all. Because photos are static, two-dimensional, and often outdated, they are "clearly inferior in reliability" to corporeal procedures. While the use of photographs is justifiable and often essential where the police have no knowledge of an offender's identity, the poor reliability of photos makes their use inexcusable where any other means of identification is available. Here, since Detective D'Onofrio believed that he knew the seller's identity, further investigation without resort to a photographic showup was easily possible. With little inconvenience, a corporeal lineup including Brathwaite might have been arranged.[13] Properly conducted, such a procedure would have gone far to remove any doubt about the fairness and accuracy of the identification.[14]

The use of a single picture (or the display of a single live suspect, for that matter) is a grave error, of course, because it dramatically suggests to the witness that the person shown must be the culprit. Why else would the police choose the person? And it is deeply ingrained in human nature to agree with the expressed opinions of others — particularly others who should be more knowledgeable — when making a difficult decision. In this case, moreover, the pressure was not limited to that inherent in the display of a single photograph. Glover, the identifying witness, was a state police officer on special assignment. He knew that D'Onofrio, an experienced Hartford narcotics detective, presumably familiar with local drug operations, believed respondent to be the seller. There was at work, then, both loyalty to another police officer and deference to a better-informed colleague.[16] Finally, of course, there was Glover's knowledge that without an identification and arrest, government funds used to buy heroin had been wasted.

The Court discounts this overwhelming evidence of suggestiveness, however. It reasons that because D'Onofrio was not present when Glover viewed the photo-

---

[13] Indeed, the police carefully staged Brathwaite's arrest in the same apartment that was used for the sale, indicating that they were fully capable of keeping track of his whereabouts and using this information in their investigation.

[14] It should be noted that this was not a case where the witness knew the person whom he saw committing a crime, or had an unusually long time to observe the criminal, so that the identification procedure was merely used to confirm the suspect's identity. Cf. Wade (White, J., dissenting). For example, had this been an ongoing narcotics investigation in which Glover had met the seller a number of times, the procedure would have been less objectionable.

[16] In fact, the trial record indicates that D'Onofrio was remarkably ill-informed, although it does not appear that Glover knew this at the time of the identification. While the Court is impressed by D'Onofrio's immediate response to Glover's description, that cannot alter the fact that the detective, who had not witnessed the transaction, acted on a wild guess that respondent was the seller. D'Onofrio had seen respondent only "[s]everal times, mostly in his vehicle." There was no evidence that respondent was even a suspected narcotics dealer, and D'Onofrio thought that the drugs had been purchased at a different apartment from the one Glover actually went to. The identification of respondent provides a perfect example of the investigator and the witness bolstering each other's inadequate knowledge to produce a seemingly accurate but worthless identification.

graph, there was "little pressure on the witness to acquiesce in the suggestion." That conclusion blinks psychological reality. There is no doubt in my mind that even in D'Onofrio's absence, a clear and powerful message was telegraphed to Glover as he looked at respondent's photograph. He was emphatically told that "*this* is the man," and he responded by identifying respondent then and at trial "whether or not he was in fact 'the man.' " *Foster v. California.*[18]

I must conclude that this record presents compelling evidence that there was "a very substantial likelihood of misidentification" of respondent Brathwaite. The suggestive display of respondent's photograph to the witness Glover likely erased any independent memory that Glover had retained of the seller from his barely adequate opportunity to observe the criminal.

IV

Since I agree with the distinguished panel of the Court of Appeals that the legal standard of *Stovall* should govern this case, but that even if it does not, the facts here reveal a substantial likelihood of misidentification in violation of respondent's right to due process of law, I would affirm the grant of habeas corpus relief. Accordingly, I dissent from the Court's reinstatement of respondent's conviction.

QUESTIONS AND NOTES

1. Do you think that the identification procedure in *Brathwaite* was unnecessarily suggestive? If so, why does the Court allow it?

2. Are unnecessarily suggestive procedures necessarily *excessively* suggestive? Was the *Neil v. Biggers* procedure excessively suggestive?

3. Is the dissent correct in asserting that unnecessarily suggestive identifications can be overcome with scrupulously fair identification procedures? Could that have been done in *Foster* (fn. 8)?

4. If Glover had been allowed to identify Brathwaite at trial, but not introduce the arguably tainted identification, how do you suppose that the defense attorney would have cross-examined him?

5. If you answered Question 4 by saying that the attorney would have confronted him with his prior tainted identification, does that not establish the

---

[18] This discussion does not imply any lack of respect for the honesty and dedication of the police. We all share the frailties of human nature that create the problem. Justice Frank O'Connor of the New York Supreme Court decried the dangers of eyewitness testimony in a recent article that began with this caveat:

> From the vantage point of ten years as District Attorney of Queens County (1956–1966) and six years on the trial bench (1969 to (1974)), the writer holds in high regard the professional competence and personal integrity of most policemen. Laudable instances of police efforts to clear a doubtful suspect are legion. Deliberate, willful efforts to frame or railroad an innocent man are totally unknown, at least to me. Yet, once the best-intentioned officer becomes honestly convinced that he has the right man, human nature being what it is, corners may be cut, some of the niceties forgotten, and serious error committed.

wisdom of the Court in allowing the arguably tainted identification to be introduced in the first place?

PROBLEM

Around 3 a.m. on August 15, 2008, Joffre Ullon called the Nashua, New Hampshire, Police Department and reported that an African-American male was trying to break into cars parked in the lot of Ullon's apartment building. Officer Nicole Clay responded to the call. Upon arriving at the parking lot, Clay heard what "sounded like a metal bat hitting the ground." She then saw petitioner Barion Perry standing between two cars. Perry walked toward Clay, holding two car-stereo amplifiers in his hands. A metal bat lay on the ground behind him. Clay asked Perry where the amplifiers came from. "[I] found them on the ground," Perry responded.

Meanwhile, Ullon's wife, Nubia Blandon, woke her neighbor, Alex Clavijo, and told him she had just seen someone break into his car. Clavijo immediately went downstairs to the parking lot to inspect the car. He first observed that one of the rear windows had been shattered. On further inspection, he discovered that the speakers and amplifiers from his car stereo were missing, as were his bat and wrench. Clavijo then approached Clay and told her about Blandon's alert and his own subsequent observations.

By this time, another officer had arrived at the scene. Clay asked Perry to stay in the parking lot with that officer, while she and Clavijo went to talk to Blandon. Clay and Clavijo then entered the apartment building and took the stairs to the fourth floor, where Blandon's and Clavijo's apartments were located. They met Blandon in the hallway just outside the open door to her apartment.

Asked to describe what she had seen, Blandon stated that, around 2:30 a.m., she saw from her kitchen window a tall, African-American man roaming the parking lot and looking into cars. Eventually, the man circled Clavijo's car, opened the trunk, and removed a large box.[1]

Clay asked Blandon for a more specific description of the man. Blandon pointed to her kitchen window and said the person she saw breaking into Clavijo's car was standing in the parking lot, next to the police officer. Perry's arrest followed this identification.

About a month later, the police showed Blandon a photographic array that included a picture of Perry and asked her to point out the man who had broken into Clavijo's car. Blandon was unable to identify Perry.

Should Blandon's pre-trial identification of Perry be admissible? For the Supreme Court's resolution, see *Perry v. New Hampshire*, 565 U.S. ___, 132 S. Ct. 716 (2012).

---

[1] The box, which Clay found on the ground near where she first encountered Perry, contained car-stereo speakers.

Chapter 22

ATTENUATION

A. FOURTH AMENDMENT

WONG SUN v. UNITED STATES
371 U.S. 471 (1963)

MR. JUSTICE BRENNAN delivered the opinion of the Court.

About 2 a.m. on the morning of June 4, 1959, federal narcotics agents in San Francisco, after having had one Hom Way under surveillance for six weeks, arrested him and found heroin in his possession. Hom Way, who had not before been an informant, stated after his arrest that he had bought an ounce of heroin the night before from one known to him only as "Blackie Toy," proprietor of a laundry on Leavenworth Street.

About 6 a.m. that morning six or seven federal agents went to a laundry at 1733 Leavenworth Street. The sign above the door of this establishment said "Oye's Laundry." It was operated by the petitioner James Wah Toy. There is, however, nothing in the record which identifies James Wah Toy and "Blackie Toy" as the same person. The other federal officers remained nearby out of sight while Agent Alton Wong, who was of Chinese ancestry, rang the bell. When petitioner Toy appeared and opened the door, Agent Wong told him that he was calling for laundry and dry cleaning. Toy replied that he didn't open until 8 o'clock and told the agent to come back at that time. Toy started to close the door. Agent Wong thereupon took his badge from his pocket and said, "I am a federal narcotics agent." Toy immediately "slammed the door and started running" down the hallway through the laundry to his living quarters at the back where his wife and child were sleeping in a bedroom. Agent Wong and the other federal officers broke open the door and followed Toy down the hallway to the living quarters and into the bedroom. Toy reached into a nightstand drawer. Agent Wong thereupon drew his pistol, pulled Toy's hand out of the drawer, placed him under arrest and handcuffed him. There was nothing in the drawer and a search of the premises uncovered no narcotics.

One of the agents said to Toy "[Hom Way] says he got narcotics from you." Toy responded, "No, I haven't been selling any narcotics at all. However, I do know somebody who has." When asked who that was, Toy said, "I only know him as Johnny. I don't know his last name." However, Toy described a house on Eleventh Avenue where he said Johnny lived; he also described a bedroom in the house where he said "Johnny kept about a piece"[2] of heroin, and where he and Johnny had smoked some of the drug the night before. The agents left immediately for Eleventh Avenue and located the house. They entered and found one Johnny Yee in the bedroom. After a discussion with the agents, Yee took from a bureau drawer several tubes containing in all just less than one ounce of heroin, and surrendered them. Within the hour Yee and Toy were taken to the Office of the Bureau of Narcotics. Yee there stated that the heroin had been brought to him some four days earlier by petitioner Toy and another Chinese known to him only as "Sea Dog."

Toy was questioned as to the identity of "Sea Dog" and said that "Sea Dog" was Wong Sun. Some agents, including Agent Alton Wong, took Toy to Wong Sun's neighborhood where Toy pointed out a multifamily dwelling where he said Wong Sun lived. Agent Wong rang a downstairs door bell and a buzzer sounded, opening the door. The officer identified himself as a narcotics agent to a woman on the landing and asked for Mr. Wong. The woman was the wife of petitioner Wong Sun. She said that Wong Sun was in the back room sleeping. Alton Wong and some six other officers climbed the stairs and entered the apartment. One of the officers went into the back room and brought petitioner Wong Sun from the bedroom in handcuffs. A thorough search of the apartment followed, but no narcotics were discovered.

Petitioner Toy and Johnny Yee were arraigned before a United States Commissioner on June 4 on a complaint charging a violation of 21 U.S.C. § 174. Later that day, each was released on his own recognizance. Petitioner Wong Sun was arraigned on a similar complaint filed the next day and was also released on his own recognizance. Within a few days, both petitioners and Yee were interrogated at the office of the Narcotics Bureau by Agent William Wong, also of Chinese ancestry. The agent advised each of the three of his right to withhold information which might be used against him, and stated to each that he was entitled to the advice of counsel, though it does not appear that any attorney was present during the questioning of any of the three. The officer also explained to each that no promises or offers of immunity or leniency were being or could be made.

The agent interrogated each of the three separately. After each had been interrogated the agent prepared a statement in English from rough notes. The agent read petitioner Toy's statement to him in English and interpreted certain portions of it for him in Chinese. Toy also read the statement in English aloud to the agent, said there were corrections to be made, and made the corrections in his own hand. Toy would not sign the statement, however; in the agent's words "he wanted to know first if the other persons involved in the case had signed theirs." Wong Sun had considerable difficulty understanding the statement in English and the agent restated its substance in Chinese. Wong Sun refused to sign the statement although he admitted the accuracy of its contents.

The Government's evidence tending to prove the petitioners' possession consisted of four items which the trial court admitted over timely objections that they were inadmissible as "fruits" of unlawful arrests or of attendant searches: (1) the statements made orally by petitioner Toy in his bedroom at the time of his arrest;

---

[2] A "piece" is approximately one ounce.

(2) the heroin surrendered to the agents by Johnny Yee; (3) petitioner Toy's pretrial unsigned statement; and (4) petitioner Wong Sun's similar statement. The dispute below and here has centered around the correctness of the rulings of the trial judge allowing these items in evidence.

The Court of Appeals held that the arrests of both petitioners were illegal because not based on "probable cause" within the meaning of the Fourth Amendment nor reasonable grounds within the meaning of the Narcotic Control Act of 1956. The court said as to Toy's arrest, There is no showing in this case that the agent knew Hom Way to be reliable, and, furthermore, found nothing in the circumstances occurring at Toy's premises that would provide sufficient justification for his arrest without a warrant. As to Wong Sun's arrest, the court said there is no showing that Johnnie Yee was a reliable informer. The Court of Appeals nevertheless held that the four items of proof were not the fruits of the illegal arrests and that they were therefore properly admitted in evidence.

We believe that significant differences between the cases of the two petitioners require separate discussion of each. We shall first consider the case of petitioner Toy.

I

[The Court found that Toy's arrest was unlawful].

II

It is conceded that Toy's declarations in his bedroom are to be excluded if they are held to be fruits of the agents unlawful action.

The exclusionary prohibition extends as well to the indirect as the direct products of such invasions. *Silverthorne Lumber Co.* v. *United States*, 251 U.S. 385. Mr. Justice HOLMES, speaking for the Court in that case, in holding that the Government might not make use of information obtained during an unlawful search to subpoena from the victims the very documents illegally viewed, expressed succinctly the policy of the broad exclusionary rule:

> The essence of a provision forbidding the acquisition of evidence in a certain way is that not merely evidence so acquired shall not be used before the Court but that it shall not be used at all. Of course this does not mean that the facts thus obtained become sacred and inaccessible. If knowledge of them is gained from an independent source they may be proved like any others, but the knowledge gained by the Government's own wrong cannot be used by it in the way proposed.

[V]erbal evidence which derives so immediately from an unlawful entry and an unauthorized arrest as the officers' action in the present case is no less the "fruit" of official illegality than the more common tangible fruits of the unwarranted intrusion.

The Government argues that Toy's statements to the officers in his bedroom, although closely consequent upon the invasion which we hold unlawful, were nevertheless admissible because they resulted from "an intervening independent act of a free will." This contention, however, takes insufficient account of the circumstances. Six or seven officers had broken the door and followed on Toy's heels into the bedroom where his wife and child were sleeping. He had been almost immediately handcuffed and arrested. Under such circumstances it is unreasonable to infer that Toy's response was sufficiently an act of free will to purge the primary taint of the unlawful invasion.[12]

The Government also contends that Toy's declarations should be admissible because they were ostensibly exculpatory rather than incriminating. There are two answers to this argument. First, the statements soon turned out to be incriminating, for they led directly to the evidence which implicated Toy. Second, when circumstances are shown such as those which induced these declarations, it is immaterial whether the declarations be termed "exculpatory." Thus we find no substantial reason to omit Toy's declarations from the protection of the exclusionary rule.

III

We now consider whether the exclusion of Toy's declarations requires also the exclusion of the narcotics taken from Yee, to which those declarations led the police. The prosecutor candidly told the trial court that "we wouldn't have found those drugs except that Mr. Toy helped us to." Hence this is not the case envisioned by this Court where the exclusionary rule has no application because the Government learned of the evidence 'from an independent source, *Silverthorne* nor is this a case in which the connection between the lawless conduct of the police and the discovery of the challenged evidence has become so attenuated as to dissipate the taint. *Nardone* v. *United States*, 308 U.S. 338, 341. We need not hold that all evidence is "fruit of the poisonous tree" simply because it would not have come to light but for the illegal actions of the police. Rather, the more apt question in such a case is' whether, granting establishment of the primary illegality, the evidence to which instant objection is made has been come at by exploitation of that illegality or instead by means sufficiently distinguishable to be purged of the primary taint. We think it clear that the narcotics were come at by the exploitation of that illegality and hence that they may not be used against Toy.

IV

It remains only to consider Toy's unsigned statement. We need not decide whether, in light of the fact that Toy was free on his own recognizance when he made the statement, that statement was a fruit of the illegal arrest. Since we have concluded that his declarations in the bedroom and the narcotics surrendered by Yee should not have been admitted in evidence against him, the only proofs

---

[12] *See* Lord Devlin's comment:

> It is probable that even today, when there is much less ignorance about these matters than formerly, there is still a general belief that you must answer all questions put to you by a policeman, or at least that it will be the worse for you if you do not.

DEVLIN, THE CRIMINAL PROSECUTION IN ENGLAND (1958), 32.

remaining to sustain his conviction are his and Wong Sun's unsigned statements. Without scrutinizing the contents of Toy's ambiguous recitals, we conclude that no reference to Toy in Wong Sun's statement constitutes admissible evidence corroborating any admission by Toy. We arrive at this conclusion upon two clear lines of decisions which converge to require it. One line of our decisions establishes that criminal confessions and admissions of guilt require extrinsic corroboration; the other line of precedents holds that an out-of-court declaration made after arrest may not be used at trial against one of the declarant's partners in crime.

Thus as to Toy the only possible source of corroboration is removed and his conviction must be set aside for lack of competent evidence to support it.

V

We turn now to the case of the other petitioner, Wong Sun. We have no occasion to disagree with the finding of the Court of Appeals that his arrest, also, was without probable cause or reasonable grounds. At all events no evidentiary consequences turn upon that question. For Wong Sun's unsigned confession was not the fruit of that arrest, and was therefore properly admitted at trial. On the evidence that Wong Sun had been released on his own recognizance after a lawful arraignment, and had returned voluntarily several days later to make the statement, we hold that the connection between the arrest and the statement had become so attenuated as to dissipate the taint. *Nardone* v. *United States*, 308 U.S. 338, 341.

We must then consider the admissibility of the narcotics surrendered by Yee. Our holding, supra, that this ounce of heroin was inadmissible against Toy does not compel a like result with respect to Wong Sun. The exclusion of the narcotics as to Toy was required solely by their tainted relationship to information unlawfully obtained from Toy, and not by any official impropriety connected with their surrender by Yee. The seizure of this heroin invaded no right of privacy of person or premises which would entitle Wong Sun to object to its use at his trial.

However, for the reasons that Wong Sun's statement was incompetent to corroborate Toy's admissions contained in Toy's own statement, any references to Wong Sun in Toy's statement were incompetent to corroborate Wong Sun's admissions. Thus, the only competent source of corroboration for Wong Sun's statement was the heroin itself. We cannot be certain, however, on this state of the record, that the trial judge may not also have considered the contents of Toy's statement as a source of corroboration.

We therefore hold that petitioner Wong Sun is also entitled to a new trial.

MR. JUSTICE CLARK, with whom MR. JUSTICE HARLAN, MR. JUSTICE STEWART and MR. JUSTICE WHITE join, dissenting.

[The dissenting opinion believed that the arrest was lawful and consequently the evidence was admissible.]

QUESTIONS AND NOTES

1.   What does the phrase "so attenuated as to dissipate the taint" mean?

2.   Upon which of the evidence was the taint dissipated? Upon which was it not dissipated? Why?

3.   Toy's conviction was apparently reversed outright whereas Wong Sun's case was remanded for a new trial. Why the distinction?

4.   In *Taylor*, we see that sometimes even *Miranda* warnings are insufficient to dissipate the taint.

TAYLOR v. ALABAMA
457 U.S. 687 (1982)

Justice Marshall delivered the opinion of the Court.

This case presents the narrow question whether petitioner's confession should have been suppressed as the fruit of an illegal arrest. The Supreme Court of Alabama held that the evidence was properly admitted. Because the decision below is inconsistent with our decisions in *Dunaway v. New York*, 442 U.S. 200 (1979), and *Brown v. Illinois*, 422 U.S. 590 (1975), we reserve.

I

In 1978, a grocery store in Montgomery, Ala., was robbed. There had been a number of robberies in this area and the police had initiated an intensive manhunt in an effort to apprehend the robbers. An individual who was at that time incarcerated on unrelated charges told a police officer that "he had heard that [petitioner] Omar Taylor was involved in the robbery." This individual had never before given similar information to this officer, did not tell the officer where he had heard this information, and did not provide any details of the crime. This tip was insufficient to give the police probable cause to obtain a warrant or to arrest petitioner.

Nonetheless, on the basis of this information, two officers arrested petitioner without a warrant. They told petitioner that he was being arrested in connection with the grocery-store robbery, searched him, and took him to the station for questioning. Petitioner was given the warnings required by *Miranda*. At the station, he was fingerprinted, readvised of this *Miranda* rights, questioned, and placed in a lineup. The victims of the robbery were unable to identify him in the lineup. The police told petitioner that his fingerprints matched those on some grocery items that had been handled by one of the participants in the robbery. After a short visit with his girlfriend and a male companion, petitioner signed a waiver-of-rights form and executed a written confession. The form and the signed confession were admitted into evidence.

Petitioner objected to the admission of this evidence at this trial. He argued that his warrantless arrest was not supported by probable cause, that he had been involuntarily transported to the police station, and that the confession must be suppressed as the fruit of this illegal arrest. The trial court overruled this objection, and petitioner was convicted.

II

In *Brown* and *Dunaway*, the police arrested suspects without probable cause. The suspects were transplanted to police headquarters, advised of their *Miranda* rights, and interrogated. They confessed within two hours of their arrest. This Court held that the confessions were not admissible at trial, reasoning that a confession obtained through custodial interrogation after an illegal arrest should be excluded unless intervening events break the causal connection between the illegal arrest and the confession so that the confession is " 'sufficiently an act of free will to purge the primary taint.' " *Brown* (quoting *Wong Sun*) *See also Dunaway*. This Court identified several factors that should be considered in determining whether a confession has been purged of the taint of the illegal arrest: "[t]he temporal proximity of the arrest and the confession, the presence of intervening circumstances, . . . and, particularly, the purpose and flagrancy of the official misconduct. "The State bears the burden of proving that a confession is admissible."

In *Brown* and *Dunaway*, this Court firmly established that the fact that the confession may be "voluntary" for purposes of the Fifth Amendment, in the sense that *Miranda* warnings were given and understood, is not by itself sufficient to purge the taint of the illegal arrest. In this situation, a finding of "voluntariness" for purposes of the Fifth Amendment is merely a threshold requirement for Fourth Amendment analysis. The reason for this approach is clear: "[t]he exclusionary rule, . . . when utilized to effectuate the Fourth Amendment, serves interests and policies that are distinct from those it serves under the Fifth" Amendment. If *Miranda* warnings were viewed as a talisman that cured all Fourth Amendment violations, then the constitutional guarantee against unlawful searches and seizures would be reduced to a mere "form of words.' "

This case is a virtual replica of both *Brown* and *Dunaway*. Petitioner was arrested without probable cause in the hope that something would turn up, and he confessed shortly thereafter without any meaningful intervening event. The State's arguments to the contrary are unpersuasive. The State begins by focusing on the temporal proximity of the arrest and the confession. It observes that the length of time between the illegal arrest and the confession was six hours in this case, while in *Brown* and *Dunaway* the incriminating statements were obtained within two hours. However, a difference of a few hours is not significant where, as here, petitioner was in police custody, unrepresented by counsel, and he was questioned on several occasions, finger-printed, and subjected to a lineup. The State has not even demonstrated the amount of this time that was spent in interrogation, arguing only that petitioner "had every opportunity to consider his situation, to organize his thoughts, to contemplate his constitutional rights, and to exercise his free will."

The State points to several intervening events that it argues are sufficient to break the connection between the illegal arrest and petitioner's confession. It observes that petitioner was given *Miranda* warnings three times. As our foregoing discussion of *Brown* and *Dunaway* demonstrates, however, the State's reliance on the giving of *Miranda* warnings is misplaced. The State also observes that petitioner visited with his girlfriend and a male companion before he confessed. This claim fares no better. According to the officer and petitioner, these two visitors were outside the interrogation room where petitioner was being questioned. After petitioner signed a waiver-of-rights form, he was allowed to meet with these visitors. The State fails to explain how this 5- to 10-minute visit, after which petitioner immediately recanted his former statements that he knew nothing about the robbery and signed the confession, could possibly have contributed to his ability to consider carefully and objectively his options and to exercise his free will. This suggestion is particularly dubious in light of petitioner's uncontroverted testimony that his girlfriend was emotionally upset at the time of this visit.[1] If any inference could be drawn, it would be that this visit had just the opposite effect.

The State points to an arrest warrant filed after petitioner had been arrested and while he was being interrogated as another significant "intervening event." While petitioner was in custody, the police determined that the fingerprints on some grocery items matched those that they had taken from petitioner immediately after his arrest. Based on this comparison, an arrest warrant was filed. The filing of this warrant, however, is irrelevant to whether the confession was the fruit of the illegal arrest. This case is not like *Johnson v. Louisiana*, 406 U.S. 356 (1972), where the defendant was brought before a committing Magistrate who advised him of his rights and set bail. Here, the arrest warrant was filed *ex parte*, based on the comparison of the fingerprints found at the scene of the crime and petitioner's fingerprints, which had been taken immediately after his arrest. The initial fingerprints, which were themselves fruit of petitioner's illegal arrest, *see Davis v. Mississippi*, 394 U.S. 721 (1969), and which were used to extract the confession from petitioner, cannot be deemed sufficient "attenuation" to break the connection between the illegal arrest and the confession merely because they also formed the basis for an arrest warrant that was filed while petitioner was being interrogated.

Finally, the State argues that the police conduct here was not flagrant or purposeful, and that we should not follow our decisions in *Brown* and *Dunaway* for that reason. However, we fail to see any relevant distinction between the conduct here and that in *Dunaway*. In this case, as in Dunaway, the police effectuated an investigatory arrest without probable cause, based on an uncorroborated informant's tip, and involuntarily transported petitioner to the station for interrogation in the hope that something would turn up. The fact that the police did not physically abuse petitioner, or that the confession they obtained may have been "voluntary" for purposes of the Fifth Amendment, does not cure the illegality of the initial

---

[1] According to petitioner, his girlfriend became upset upon hearing the officer advise petitioner to cooperate. Contrary to the allegations in the dissent, at no point did the officer contradict petitioner's version of his girlfriend's emotional state or petitioner's statement that his girlfriend's emotional state or petitioner's statement that his girlfriend was present at the time the officer advised him to cooperate. In fact, the testimony from both petitioner and the officer with respect to this visit are consistent. The officer testified only that he advised petitioner to cooperate between the time petitioner signed a rights form at the commencement of this interrogation period and the time that petitioner signed the statement of confession. He also testified that during this same interval, he allowed the short visit between petitioner and his girlfriend. The District Court made no findings of fact with respect to these incidents. In any event, even assuming the accuracy of the dissent's version of the facts, the dissent offers no explanation for its conclusion that this 5- to 10-minute visit should be viewed as an intervening event that purges the taint of the illegal arrest.

arrest. Alternatively, the State contends that the police conduct here argues for adopting a "good faith" exception to the exclusionary rule. To date, we have not recognized such an exception, and we decline to do so here.*

JUSTICE O'CONNOR, with whom THE CHIEF JUSTICE, JUSTICE POWELL, and JUSTICE REHNQUIST join, dissenting.

The Court holds today that Omar Taylor's detailed confession was the fruit of an illegal arrest, and consequently, should be suppressed. Because I conclude that neither the facts nor the law supports the Court's analysis, I respectfully dissent.

II

Although the Court misapprehends the facts of the present case, it has stated correctly the controlling substantive law. In the Court's words, "a confession obtained through custodial interrogation after an illegal arrest should be excluded unless intervening events break the causal connection between the illegal arrest and the confession so that the confession is 'sufficiently an act of free will to purge the primary taint.'"

In *Brown*, this Court emphasized that *"Miranda* warnings are an important factor . . . in determining whether the confession [was] obtained by exploitation of an illegal arrest."[5]

The Court did not discount the significance of other factors, however, noting that *"Miranda* warnings, *alone* and *per se*, cannot always make the act sufficiently a product of free will to break, for Fourth Amendment purposes, the causal connection between the illegality and the confession." *Brown* holds, therefore, that not only *Miranda* warnings, but also "[t]he temporal of intervening circumstances, and, particularly, the purpose and flagrancy of the official misconduct are all relevant."

In light of those factors, the *Brown* Court reviewed the record and found that "Brown's first statement was separated from his illegal arrest by less than two hours, and [that] there was no intervening event of significance whatsoever." Moreover, the police conduct in arresting *Brown* was particularly egregious. The "impropriety of the arrest was obvious," and the "manner in which Brown's arrest was effected gives the appearance of having been calculated to cause surprise, fright, and confusion." The Court held that as a consequence the confession should have been suppressed.

Four Terms later, in *Dunaway*, this Court reaffirmed the *Brown* rule that in order to use at trial statements obtained following an arrest on less than probable cause

---

* [Of course, this case was decided before *Leon.* — Ed.]

[5] The holding in *Brown* was derived from this Court's seminal decision in *Wong Sun*, in which we rejected a "but for" test for determining whether to suppress evidence gathered following a Fourth Amendment violation.

the prosecution must show not only that the statements meet the Fifth Amendment voluntariness standard, but also that the causal connection between the statements and the illegal arrest is broken sufficiently to purge the primary taint of the illegal arrest.

Finding the facts in *Dunaway* to be "virtually a replica of the situation in *Brown*," the Court help that the petitioner's confession should have been suppressed. Critical to the Court's holding was its observation that the petitioner "confessed without any intervening event of significance."

III

Our task is to apply the law as articulated in *Brown* and *Dunaway* to the facts of this case.

The first significant consideration is that following his unlawful arrest, Taylor was warned on three separate occasions that he "had a right to remain silent, [and] anything he said could be used against him in a court of law[;] he had the right to have an attorney present, [and] if he could not afford one, the State would appoint one for him [;] he could answer questions but he could stop answering at any time."

Under *Brown* and *Dunaway*, these warnings must be counted as "an important factor . . . in determining whether the confession [was] obtained by exploitation of an illegal arrest," though they are, standing alone, insufficient to prove that the primary taint of an illegal arrest had been purged.

Second, in contrast to the facts in *Brown*, the facts in the present case show that the petitioner was not subjected to intimidating police misconduct. In *Brown*, police had broken into the petitioner's house and searched it. When the petitioner later came home, two officers pointed their guns at him and arrested him, leading the Court to conclude that "[t]he manner in which [the petitioner's] arrest was effected gives the appearance of having been calculated to cause surprise, fright, and confusion." By contrast, nothing in the record before us indicates that the petitioner's arrest was violent, or designed to "cause surprise, fright, and confusion." Instead, Montgomery officers approached Taylor, asked him his name, and told him that he was under arrest for the Moseley robbery. They then searched him, advised him of his rights, and took him to the police station.

Third, while in both *Brown* and *Dunaway* there was "no intervening event of significance whatsoever," in the present case Taylor's girlfriend and neighbor came to the police station and asked to speak with him. Before meeting with his two friends, the petitioner steadfastly had denied involvement in the Moseley robbery. Immediately following the meeting, the petitioner gave a complete and detailed confession of his participation in the armed robbery. This meeting between the petitioner and his two friends, as described by the police in their testimony at the suppression hearing, plainly constituted an intervening circumstance.

Finally, the record reveals that the petitioner spent most of the time between his arrest and confession by himself. In *Dunaway* and *Brown*, by contrast, the defendants were interrogated continuously before they made incriminating statements.

In sum, when these four factors are considered together,[7] it is obvious that there is not sufficient basis on which to overturn the trials court's finding that "there were enough intervening factors" to overcome the taint of the illegal arrest. In fact, I believe it is clear that the State carried its burden of proof. The petitioner was warned of his rights to remain silent and to have a lawyer present, and there is no dispute that he understood those rights or that the waived them voluntarily and without coercion. After receiving three sets of such warnings, he met with his girlfriend and neighbor, *at his request*. Following that meeting, at which no police officers were present, the petitioner decided to confess to this participation in the robbery. The petitioner's confession was not proximately caused by his illegal arrest, but was the product of a decision based both on knowledge of his constitutional rights and on the discussion with his friends. Accordingly, I respectfully dissent.

QUESTIONS AND NOTES

1.   Given that the very purpose of *Miranda* warnings is to dissipate the inherent coercion of the police station, why aren't they per se sufficient to dissipate the taint of an unlawful arrest in cases like *Brown, Dunaway,* and *Taylor*?

2.   The *Taylor* confession came six hours after the unlawful arrest whereas the *Brown* and *Dunaway* confessions came only two hours after the unlawful arrest? Which way should that distinction cut? Why? Suppose the defendant had been held without interrogation for three days following his unlawful arrest. What result? Why?

3.   Had you been on the Court would you have concurred with Marshall? O'Connor? Neither? Explain.

4.   In *Harris*, the Court found that a *Payton* violation has very little taint to dissipate. As you read the opinion, assess the persuasiveness of that perspective.

NEW YORK v. HARRIS
495 U.S. 14 (1990)

JUSTICE WHITE delivered the opinion of the Court.

On January 11, 1984, New York City police found the body of Ms. Thelma Staton murdered in her apartment. Various facts gave the officers probable cause to believe that the respondent in this case, Bernard Harris, had killed Ms. Staton. As a result, on January 16, 1984, three police officers went to Harris' apartment to take him into custody. They did not first obtain an arrest warrant.

When the police arrived, they knocked on the door, displaying their guns and badges. Harris let them enter. Once inside, the officers read Harris his rights under *Miranda*. Harris acknowledged that he understood the warnings, and agreed to

---

[7]   The Court has taken each circumstance out of context and examined it to see whether it alone would be enough to purge the taint of the illegal arrest. The Court's failure to consider the circumstances of this case as a whole may have contributed to its erroneous conclusion.

answer the officers' questions. At that point, he reportedly admitted that he had killed Ms. Staton.

Harris was arrested, taken to the station house, and again informed of his *Miranda* rights. He then signed a written inculpatory statement. The police subsequently read Harris the *Miranda* warnings a third time and videotaped an incriminating interview between Harris and a district attorney, even though Harris had indicated that he wanted to end the interrogation.

The trial court suppressed Harris' first and third statements; the State does not challenge those rulings. The sole issue in this case is whether Harris' second statement — the written statement made at the station house — should have been suppressed because the police, by entering Harris' home without warrant and without his consent, violated *Payton v. New York*, which held that the Fourth Amendment prohibits the police from effecting a warrantless and nonconsensual entry into a suspect's home in order to make a routine felony arrest.

For present purposes, we accept the finding below that Harris did not consent to the police officer's entry into his home and the conclusion that the police had probable cause to arrest him. It is also evident, in light of *Payton*, that arresting Harris in his home without an arrest warrant violated the Fourth Amendment. [I]n this connect, we have stated that "[t]he penalties visited upon the Government, and in turn upon the public, because its officers have violated the law must bear some relation to the purposes which the law is to serve." In light of these principles, we decline to apply the exclusionary rule in this context because the rule in *Payton* was designed to protect the physical integrity of the home; it was not intended to grant criminal suspects, like Harris, protection for statement made outside their premises where the police have probable cause to arrest the suspect for committing a crime.

Payton itself emphasized that our holding in that case stemmed from the "overriding respect for the sanctity of the home that has been embedded in our traditions since the origins of the Republic." Although it had long been settled that a warrantless arrest in a public place was permissible as long as the arresting officer had probable cause, *Payton* nevertheless drew a line at the entrance to the home. This special solicitude was necessary because "physical entry of the home is the chief evil against which the wording of the Fourth Amendment is directed.' " The arrest warrant was required to "interpose the magistrate's determination of probable cause" to arrest before the officers could enter a house to effect an arrest.

Nothing in the reasoning of that case suggests that an arrest in a home without a warrant but with probable cause somehow renders unlawful continued custody of the suspect once he is removed from the house. There could be no valid claim here that Harris was immune from prosecution because his person was the fruit of an illegal arrest. Nor is there any claim that the warrantless arrest required the police to release Harris or that Harris could not be immediately rearrested if momentarily released. Because the officers had probable cause to arrest Harris for a crime, Harris was not unlawfully in custody when he was removed to the station house, given *Miranda* warnings, and allowed to talk. For Fourth Amendment purposes, the legal issue is the same as it would be had the police arrested Harris on his doorstep, illegally entered his home to search for evidence, and later interrogated Harris at the station house. Similarly, if the police had made a warrantless entry into Harris' home, not found him there, but arrested him on the street when he returned, a later statement made by him after proper warnings would no doubt be admissible.

This case is therefore different from *Brown, Dunaway*, and *Taylor*. In each of those cases, evidence obtained from a criminal defendant following arrest was suppressed because the police lacked probable cause. The three cases sand for the familiar proposition that the indirect fruits of an illegal search or arrest should be suppressed when they bear a sufficiently close relationship to the underlying illegality. *See also Wong Sun*. We have emphasized, however, that attenuation analysis is only appropriate where, as a threshold matter, courts determine that "the challenged evidence is in some sense the product of illegal governmental activity."

Harris's statement taken at the police station was not the product of being in unlawful custody. Neither was it the fruit having been arrested in the home rather than someplace else.

Here, the police had a justification to question Harris prior to his arrest; therefore, his subsequent statement was not an exploitation of the illegal entry into Harris' home.

We do not hold, as the dissent suggests, that a statement taken by the police while a suspect is in custody is always admissible as long as the suspect is in legal custody. Statements taken during legal custody would of course be inadmissible, for example, if they were the product of coercion, if *Miranda* warnings were not given, or if there was violation of *Edwards*. We do hold that the station house statement in this case was admissible because Harris was in legal custody, as the dissent concedes, and because the statement, while the product of an arrest and being in custody, was not the fruit of the fact that the arrest was made in the house rather than someplace else.

To put the matter another way, suppressing the statement taken outside the house would not serve the purpose of the rule that made Harris' in-house arrest illegal. The warrant requirement for an arrest in the home is imposed to protect the home, and anything incriminating the police gathered from arresting Harris in his home, rather than elsewhere, has been excluded, as it should have been; the purpose of the rule has thereby been vindicated. We are not required by the Constitution to go further and suppress statements later made by Harris in order to deter police from violating *Payton*. "As cases considering the use of unlawfully obtained evidence in criminal trials themselves make clear, it does not follow from the emphasis on the exclusionary rule's deterrent value the 'anything which deters illegal searches is thereby commanded by the Fourth Amendment.'" *Leon*. Even though we decline to suppress statements made outside the home following a *Payton* violation, the principal incentive to obey *Payton* still obtains: the police know that a warrantless entry will lead to the suppression of any evidence found, or statements taken, inside the home. If we did suppress statements like Harris', moreover, the incremental deterrent value would be minimal. Given that the police have probable cause to arrest a suspect in Harris' position, they need not violate *Payton* in order to interrogate the suspect. It is doubtful therefore that the desire to secure a statement from a criminal suspect would motivate the police to violate

Payton. As a result, suppressing a station house statement obtained after a *Payton* violation will have little effect on the officers' actions, one way or another.

We hold that, where the police have probable cause to arrest a suspect, the exclusionary rule does not bar the State's use of a statement made by the defendant outside of his home, even though the statement is taken after an arrest made in the home in violation of *Payton*. The judgment of the court below is accordingly.

Reversed.

Justice Marshall, with whom Justice Brennan, Justice Blackmun, and Justice Stevens join, dissenting.

Police officers entered Bernard Harris' home and arrested him there. They did not have an arrest warrant, he did not consent to their entry, and exigent circumstance did not exist. An arrest in such circumstances violates the Fourth Amendment. *See Payton*. About an hour after his arrest, Harris made in incriminating statement, which the government subsequently used at his trial. The majority concedes that the fruits of the illegal entry must be suppressed. The sole question before us is whether Harris's statement falls within that category.

The majority answers this question by adopting a broad and unprecedented principle, holding that "where the police have probable cause to arrest a suspect, the exclusionary rule does not bar the State's use of a statement made by the defendant outside of his home, even though the statement is taken after an arrest made in the home in violation of *Payton*." The majority's conclusion is wrong. Its reasoning amounts to nothing more than an analytical sleight of hand, resting on errors in logic, misreading of our cases, and an apparent blindness to the incentives the Court's ruling creates for knowing and intentional constitutional violations by the police. I dissent.

I

In recent years, this Court has repeatedly stated that the principal purpose of the Fourth Amendment's exclusionary rule is to eliminate incentives for police officers to violate that Amendment. See *e.g., Leon*. A police officer who violates the Constitution usually does so to obtain evidence that he could not secure lawfully. The best way to deter him is to provide that any evidence so obtained will not be admitted at trial. Deterrence of constitutional violations thus requires the suppression not only of evidence seized during an unconstitutional search, but also of "derivative evidence, both tangible and testimonial, that is the product of the primary evidence, or that is otherwise acquired as an indirect result of the unlawful search." Not all evidence connected to a constitutional violation is suppressible, however. Rather, the Court has asked "whether, granting establishment of the primary illegality, the evidence to which instant objection is made has been come at by exploitation of the illegality or instead by means sufficiently distinguishable to be purged of the primary taint.' "

Because deterrence is a principal purpose of the exclusionary rule, our attenuation analysis must be driven by an understanding of how extensive exclusion must be to deter violations of the Fourth Amendment. We have long held that where police have obtained a statement after violating the Fourth Amendment, the interest in deterrence does not disappear simply because the statement was voluntary, as required by the Fifth Amendment. *See, e.g., Brown, Dunaway,* and *Taylor.* Police officers are well aware that simply because a statement is "voluntary" does not mean that it was entirely unaffected by the Fourth Amendment violation.

Attenuation analysis *assumes* that the statement is "voluntary" and asks whether the connection between the illegal police conduct and the statement nevertheless requires suppression to deter Fourth Amendment violations. That question cannot be answered with a set of *per se* rules. An inquiry into whether a suspect's statement is properly treated as attributable to a Fourth Amendment violation or to the suspect's independent act of will has an irreducibly psychological aspect, and irrebuttable presumptions are peculiarly unhelpful in such a context. Accordingly, we have identified several factors as relevant to the issue of attenuation: the length of time between the arrest and the statement, the presence of intervening circumstances, and the "purpose of flagrancy" of violation. *Brown.*

We have identified the last factor as "particularly" important. When a police officer intentionally violates what he knows to be a constitutional command, exclusion is essential to conform police behavior to the law. Such a "flagrant" violations in marked contrast to a violation that is the product of a good-faith misunderstanding of the relevant constitutional requirements. This Court has suggested that excluding evidence that is the product of the latter variety of violation may result in deterrence of legitimate law enforcement efforts. *Leon.* Whatever the truth of the theory, the concern that officers who act in good faith will be overdeterred is non-existent when, based on a cynical calculus of the likely results of a suppression hearing, an officer intentionally decides to violate what he knows to be a constitutional command.

An application of the *Brown* factors to this case compels the conclusion that Harris' statement at the station house must be suppressed. About an hour elapsed between the illegal arrest and Harris' confession, without any intervening factor other than the warnings required by *Miranda*.

As to the flagrancy of the violation, petitioner does not dispute that the officers were aware that the Fourth Amendment prohibited them from arresting Harris in his home without a warrant. Notwithstanding the officers' knowledge that a warrant is required for a routine arrest in the home,

> the police went to defendants apartment to arrest him and, as the police conceded, if defendant refused to talk to them there they intended to take him into custody for questioning. Nevertheless, they made no attempt to obtain a warrant although five days had elapsed between the killing and the arrest and they had developed evidence of probably cause early in their investigation. Indeed, one of the officers testified that it was departmental policy not to get warrants before making arrests in the home. From this statement a reasonable inference can be drawn . . . that the department's policy was a device used to avoid restrictions on questioning a suspect until after the police had strengthened their case with a confession. Thus, the

police illegality was knowing and intentional, in the language of *Brown*, it "had a quality of purposefulness," and the linkage between the illegality and the confession is clearly established.

72 N.Y.2d 614, 622, 532 N.E.2d 1229, 1233–1234 (1988) (citation omitted).[2]

In short, the officers decide, apparently consistent with a "departmental policy," to violate Harris' Fourth Amendment rights so they could get evidence that they could not otherwise obtain. As the trial court held, "No more clear violation of [*Payton*], in my view, could be established." Where, as here, there is a particularly flagrant constitutional violation and little in the way of elapsed time or intervening circumstances, the statement in the police station must be suppressed.

II

Had the Court analyzed this case as our precedents dictate that it should, I could end my discussion here — the dispute would reduce to an application of the *Brown* factors to the constitutional wrong and the inculpatory statement that followed. But the majority chooses no such unremarkable battleground. instead, the Court redrafts our cases in the service of conclusions they straightforwardly and explicitly reject. Specifically, the Court finds suppression unwarranted on the authority of its newly fashioned per se rule. In the majority's view, when police officers make a warrantless home arrest in violation of *Payton*, their physical exit from the suspect's home *necessarily* breaks the causal chain between the illegality and any subsequent statement by the suspect, such that the statement is admissible regardless of the *Brown* factors.

The Court purports to defend its new rule on the basis of the self-evident proposition that the Fourth Amendment does not necessarily require the police to release or to forgo the prosecution of a suspect arrested in violation of *Payton*. To the Court, it follows as a matter of course from this proposition that a Payton violation cannot in any way be the "cause" of a statement obtained from his home and is being lawfully detained. Because an attenuation inquiry presupposes *some* connection between the illegality and the statement, the Court concludes that no such inquiry is necessary here. Neither logic nor precedent supports that conclusion.

---

[2] The "restrictions on questioning" to which the court refers are restrictions imposed by New York law. New York law provides that an arrest warrant may not issue until an "accusatory instrument" has been filed against the suspect. N.Y. CRIM. PROC. LAW § 120.20 (McKinney 1981). The New York courts have held that police officers may not question a suspect in the absence of an attorney once such an accusatory instrument has been filed. *People v. Samuels*, 49 N.Y. 2d 218, 400 N.E.2d 1344 (1980). These two rules operate to prohibit police from questioning a suspect after arresting him in his home unless his lawyer is present. If the police comply with *Payton*, the suspect's lawyer will likely tell him not to say anything, and the police will get nothing. On the other hand, if they violate *Payton* by refusing to obtain a warrant, the suspect's right to counsel will not have attached at the time of the arrest, and the police may be able to question him without interference by a lawyer. The lower court's inference that a departmental policy of violating the Fourth Amendment existed was thus fully justified.

A

The majority's *per se* rule in this case fails to take account of our repeated holdings that violations of privacy in the home are especially invasive. Rather, its rule is necessarily premised on the proposition that the effect of a *Payton* violation magically vanishes once the suspect is dragged from his home. But the concerns that make a warrantless home arrest a violation of the Fourth Amendment are nothing so evanescent. A person who is forcibly separated from his family and home in the dark of night after uniformed officers have broken down his door, handcuffed him, and forced him at gunpoint to accompany them to a police station does not suddenly breathe a sigh of relief at the moment he is dragged across his doorstep. Rather, the suspect is likely to be so frightened and rattled that he will say something incriminating. These effects, of course, extend far beyond the moment the physical occupation of the home ends. The entire focus of the *Brown* factors is to fix the point at which those effects are sufficiently dissipated that deterrence is not meaningfully advance by suppression. The majority's assertion, as though the proposition were axiomatic, that the effects of such an intrusion *must* end when the violation ends is both undefended and indefensible. The Court's saying it may make it law, but does not make it true.

B

The majority's reading of our cases similarly lacks foundation. In the majority's view, our attenuation cases are not concerned with the lingering taint of an illegal arrest; rather, they focus solely on whether a subsequently obtained statement is made during an illegal detention of the suspect. In the Court's view, if (and only if) the detention is illegal at the moment the statement is made will it be suppressed. Unlike an arrest without probable cause, *Payton* violation alone does not make the subsequent detention of the suspect illegal. Thus, the Court argues, no statement made after *Payton* violation has ended is suppressible by reason of the Fourth Amendment violation as long the police have probable cause.

The majority's theory lacks any support in our cases. In each case presenting issues similar to those here, we have asked the same question: whether the invasion of privacy occasioned by the illegal *arrest* taints a statement made after the violation has ended — stated another way, whether the arrest caused the statement.

Indeed, such an approach would render irrelevant the first and second of the *Brown* factors, which focus, respectively, on the passage of time and the existence of intervening factors between the illegality and the subsequently obtained statement. If, as the majority claims, the *Brown* analysis does not even *apply* unless the illegality is ongoing at the time the evidence is secured, no time would ever pass and no circumstance would ever intervene between the illegality and that statement.

C

Perhaps the most alarming aspect of the Court's ruling is its practical consequences for the deterrence of *Payton* violations. Imagine a police officer who has probable cause to arrest a suspect but lacks a warrant. The officer knows if he were to break into the home to make the arrest without first securing a warrant, he would violate the Fourth Amendment and any evidence he finds in the house would be suppressed. Of course, if he does not enter the house, he will not be able to use any evidence inside the house either, for the simple reason that he will never see it. The officer also knows, though, that waiting for the suspect to leave his house before arresting him could entail a lot of waiting, and the time he would spend getting a warrant would be better spend arresting criminals. The officer could leave the scene to obtain a warrant, thus avoiding some of the delay, but that would entail giving the suspect an opportunity to flee.

More important, the officer knows that if he breaks into the house without a warrant and drags the suspect outside, the suspect, shaken by the enormous invasion of privacy he has just undergone, may say something incriminating. Before today's decision, the government would only be able to use that evidence if the Court found that the taint of the arrest had been attenuated; after the decision, the evidence will be admissible regardless of whether it was the product of the unconstitutional arrest.[5] Thus, the officer envisions the following best-case scenario if he chooses to violate the Constitution: He avoids a major expenditure of time and effort, ensures that the suspect will not escape, and procures the most damaging evidence of all, a confession. His worst-case scenario is that he will avoid a major expenditure of effort, ensure that the suspect will not escape, and will see evidence in the house (which would have remained unknown absent the constitutional violation) that cannot be used in the prosecution's case in chief. The Court thus creates powerful incentives for police officers to violate the Fourth Amendment. In the context of our constitutional rights and the sanctity of our homes, we cannot afford to presume that officers will be entirely impervious to those incentives.

I dissent.

QUESTIONS AND NOTES

1.   Is it clear that *Harris'* first and third statements were properly excluded? Why?

2.   Is (should) this case (be) the same as one in which the police arrested Harris outside of his home, entered to make an illegal search, and subsequently obtained a confession from him? Explain. Would it matter if the police found evidence connecting Harris to the murder and confronted him with it? Why? Why not?

3.   If the police had arrested *Harris* in his home, taken him outside, released him, and then rearrested him outside of the home pursuant to the probable cause that they already had, would there be any merit to the dissent's position? Explain.

4.   Do you think that *Harris* is likely to retard adherence to *Payton*? Why? Do

---

[5]   Indeed, if the officer, as here, works in New York State, the Court's assertion that "[i]t is doubtful therefore that the desire to secure a statement from a criminal suspect would motivate the police to violate *Payton*." Takes on singularly ironic cast. The court below found as a matter of fact that the officers in this case had intentionally violated Payton for precisely the reason the Court identifies as "doubtful." *See* n. 2, *supra*, and accompanying text.

you think that the majority (consisting of White and Rehnquist, who dissented in *Payton*, and O'Connor, Scalia, and Kennedy who were not on the Court when *Payton* was decided) really cared?

5.   We conclude this section with *Ceccolini*, a case indicating that some types of evidence can be more easily attenuated than other types of evidence.

UNITED STATES v. CECCOLINI
435 U.S. 268 (1978)

MR. JUSTICE REHNQUIST delivered the opinion of the Court.

In December 1974, Ronald Biro, a uniformed police officer on assignment to patrol school crossings, entered respondent's place of business, the Sleepy Hollow Flower Shop, in North Tarrytown, N. Y. He went behind the customer counter and, in the words of Ichabod Crane, one of Tarrytown's more illustrious inhabitants of days gone past, "tarried," spending his short break engaged in conversation with his friend Lois Hennessey, an employee of the shop. During the course of the conversation he noticed an envelope with money sticking out of it lying on the drawer of the cash register behind the counter. Biro picked up the envelope and, upon examining its contents, discovered that it contained not only money but policy slips. He placed the envelope back on the register and, without telling Hennessey what he had seen, asked her to whom the envelope belonged. She replied that the envelope belonged to respondent Ceccolini, and that he had instructed her to give it to someone.

The next day, Officer Biro mentioned his discovery to North Tarrytown detectives who in turn told Lance Emory, an FBI agent. This very ordinary incident in the lives of Biro and Hennessey requires us, over three years later, to decide whether Hennessey's testimony against respondent Ceccolini should have been suppressed in his trial for perjury. Respondent was charged with that offense because he denied that he knew anything of, or was in any way involved with, gambling operations.

I

During the latter part of 1973, the Federal Bureau of Investigation was exploring suspected gambling operations in North Tarrytown. Among the establishments under surveillance was respondent's place of business, which was a frequent and regular stop of one Francis Millow, himself a suspect in the investigation. While the investigation continued on a reduced scale after December 1973, surveillance of the flower shop was curtailed at that time. It was thus a full year after this discontinuance of FBI surveillance that Biro spent his patrol break behind the counter with Hennessey. When Biro's discovery of the policy slips was reported the following day to Emory, Emory was not fully informed of the manner in which Biro had obtained the information. Four months later, Emory interviewed Hennessey at her home for about half an hour in the presence of her mother and two sisters. He identified himself, indicated that he had learned through the local police department that she worked for respondent, and told her that the Government would appreciate any information regarding respondent's activities that she had acquired in the shop. Emory did not specifically refer to the incident involving Officer Biro. Hennessey told Emory that she was studying police science in college and would be willing to help. She then related the events which had occurred during her visit with Officer Biro.

In May 1975, respondent was summoned before a federal grand jury where he testified that he had never taken policy bets for Francis Millow at the flower shop. The next week Hennessey testified to the contrary, and shortly thereafter respondent was indicted for perjury. Respondent waived a jury, and with the consent of all parties the District Court considered simultaneously with the trial on the merits respondent's motion to suppress both the policy slips and the testimony of Hennessey. At the conclusion of the evidence, the District Court excluded from its consideration "the envelope and the contents of the envelope," but nonetheless found respondent guilty of the offense charged. The court then, granted respondent's motion to suppress the testimony of Hennessey, because she "first came directly to the attention of the government as a result of an illegal search" and the Government had not "sustained its burden of showing that Lois Henness[e]y's testimony definitely would have been obtained without the illegal search."

The Court of Appeals affirmed this ruling on the Government's appeal, reasoning that "the road to Miss Henness[e]y's testimony from Officer Biro's concededly unconstitutional search is both straight and uninterrupted." 542 F.2d at 142. Because we decide that the Court of Appeals was wrong in concluding that there was insufficient attenuation between Officer Biro's search and Hennessey's testimony at the trial, we also do not reach the Government's contention that the exclusionary rule should not be applied when the evidence derived from the search is being used to prove a subsequent crime such as perjury.

II

The "road" to which the Court of Appeals analogized the train of events from Biro's discovery of the policy slips to Hennessey's testimony at respondent's trial for perjury is one of literally thousands of such roads traveled periodically between an original investigative discovery and the ultimate trial of the accused. The constitutional question under the Fourth Amendment was phrased in *Wong Sun* as whether "the connection between the lawless conduct of the police and the discovery of the challenged evidence has "become so attenuated as to dissipate the taint." "The question was in turn derived from the Court's earlier decision in *Nardone v. United States*, 308 U.S. 338, 341 (1939), where Mr. Justice Frankfurter stated for the Court:

> Here, as in the *Silverthorne* case [*Silverthorne Lumber Co. v. United States*], the facts improperly obtained do not "become sacred and inaccessible. If knowledge of them is gained from an independent source they may be proved like any others, but the knowledge gained by the Government's own wrong cannot be used by it" simply because it is used derivatively. 251 U.S. 385, 392, 40 S. Ct. 182, 64 L. Ed. 319.

In practice this generalized statement may conceal concrete complexities. Sophisticated argument may prove a causal connection between information obtained through illicit wire-tapping and the Government's proof. As a matter of good sense, however, such connection may have become so attenuated as to dissipate the taint.

This, of course, makes it perfectly clear, if indeed ever there was any doubt about the matter, that the question of causal connection in this setting, as in so many other questions with which the law concerns itself, is not to be determined solely through the sort of analysis which would be applicable in the physical sciences. The issue cannot be decided on the basis of causation in the logical sense alone, but necessarily includes other elements as well. And our cases subsequent to *Nardone*, have laid out the fundamental tenets of the exclusionary rule, from which the elements that are relevant to the causal inquiry can be divined.

An examination of these cases leads us to reject the Government's suggestion that we adopt what would in practice amount to a per se rule that the testimony of a live witness should not be excluded at trial no matter how close and proximate the connection between it and a violation of the Fourth Amendment. We also reaffirm the holding of *Wong Sun*, that "verbal evidence which derives so immediately from an unlawful entry and an unauthorized arrest as the officers' action in the present case is no less the 'fruit' of official illegality than the more common tangible fruits of the unwarranted intrusion." We are of the view, however, that cases decided since *Wong Sun* significantly qualify its further observation that "the policies underlying the exclusionary rule [do not] invite any logical distinction between physical and verbal evidence." Rather, at least in a case such as this, where not only was the alleged "fruit of the poisonous tree" the testimony of a live witness, but unlike *Wong Sun* the witness was not a putative defendant, an examination of our cases persuades us that the Court of Appeals was simply wrong in concluding that if the road were uninterrupted, its length was immaterial. Its length, we hold, is material, as are certain other factors enumerated below to which the court gave insufficient weight.

Even in situations where the exclusionary rule is plainly applicable, we have declined to adopt a "per se or 'but for' rule" that would make inadmissible any evidence, whether tangible or live-witness testimony, which somehow came to light through a chain of causation that began with an illegal arrest. *Brown v. Illinois*. Evaluating the standards for application of the exclusionary rule to live-witness testimony in light of this balance, we are first impelled to conclude that the degree of free will exercised by the witness is not irrelevant in determining the extent to which the basic purpose of the exclusionary rule will be advanced by its application. This is certainly true when the challenged statements are made by a putative defendant after arrest, *Wong Sun; Brown v. Illinois*, and *a fortiori* is true of testimony given by nondefendants.

The greater the willingness of the witness to freely testify, the greater the likelihood that he or she will be discovered by legal means and, concomitantly, the smaller the incentive to conduct an illegal search to discover the witness.[4] Witnesses are not like guns or documents which remain hidden from view until one turns over a sofa or opens a filing cabinet. Witnesses can, and often do, come forward and offer evidence entirely of their own volition. And evaluated properly, the degree of free will necessary to dissipate the taint will very likely be found more often in the case of live-witness testimony than other kinds of evidence. The time, place and manner of the initial questioning of the witness may be such that any statements are truly the product of detached reflection and a desire to be cooperative on the part of the witness. And the illegality which led to the discovery of the witness very often will not play any meaningful part in the witness' willingness to testify.

> The proffer of a living witness is not to be mechanically equated with the proffer of inanimate evidentiary objects illegally seized. The fact that the name of a potential witness is disclosed to police is of no evidentiary significance, per se, since the living witness is an individual human personality whose attributes of will, perception, memory and volition interact to determine what testimony he will give. The uniqueness of this human process distinguishes the evidentiary character of a witness from the relative immutability of inanimate evidence.

Smith v. United States, 324 F.2d 879, 881–882, 117 U.S. App. D.C. 1, 3–4 (1963) (Burger, J.).

Another factor which not only is relevant in determining the usefulness of the exclusionary rule in a particular context, but also seems to us to differentiate the testimony of all live witnesses — even putative defendants — from the exclusion of the typical documentary evidence, is that such exclusion would perpetually disable a witness from testifying about relevant and material facts, regardless of how unrelated such testimony might be to the purpose of the originally illegal search or the evidence discovered thereby. Rules which disqualify knowledgeable witnesses from testifying at trial are, in the words of Professor McCormick, "serious obstructions to the ascertainment of truth"; accordingly, "[f]or a century the course of legal evolution has been in the direction of sweeping away these obstructions." C. McCormick, Law of Evidence § 71 (1954). Alluding to the enormous cost engendered by such a permanent disability in an analogous context, we have specifically refused to hold that "making a confession under circumstances which preclude its use, perpetually disables the confessor from making a usable one after those conditions have been removed." *United States* v. *Bayer,* 331 U.S. 532, 541 (1947). For many of these same reasons, the Court has also held admissible at trial testimony of a witness whose identity was disclosed by the defendant's statement given after inadequate *Miranda* warnings. *Michigan v. Tucker,* 417 U.S. 433, 450–451 (1974).

> For, when balancing the interests involved, we must weigh the strong interest under any system of justice of making available to the trier of fact all concededly relevant and trustworthy evidence which either party seeks

---

[4] Of course, the analysis might be different where the search was conducted by the police for specific purpose of discovering potential witnesses.

to adduce. . . . Here respondent's own statement, which might have helped the prosecution show respondent's guilty conscience at trial, had already been excised from the prosecution's case. To extend the excision further under the circumstances of this case and exclude relevant testimony of a third-party witness would require far more persuasive arguments than those advanced by respondent.

In short, since the cost of excluding live-witness testimony often will be greater, a closer, more direct link between the illegality and that kind of testimony is required.

This is not to say, of course, that live-witness testimony is always or even usually more reliable or dependable than inanimate evidence. Indeed, just the opposite may be true. But a determination that the discovery of certain evidence is sufficiently unrelated to or independent of the constitutional violation to permit its introduction at trial is not a determination which rests on the comparative reliability of that evidence. Attenuation analysis, appropriately concerned with the differences between live-witness testimony and inanimate evidence, can consistently focus on the factors enumerated above with respect to the former, but on different factors with respect to the latter.

In holding that considerations relating to the exclusionary rule and the constitutional principles which it is designed to protect must play a factor in the attenuation analysis, we do no more than reaffirm an observation made by this Court half a century ago:

A criminal prosecution is more than a game in which the Government may be checkmated and the game lost merely because its officers have not played according to rule.

McGuire v. *United States*, 273 U.S. 95, 99 (1927).

The penalties visited upon the Government, and in turn upon the public, because its officers have violated the law must bear some relation to the purposes which the law is to serve.

III

Viewing this case in the light of the principles just discussed, we hold that the Court of Appeals erred in holding that the degree of attenuation was not sufficient to dissipate the connection between the illegality and the testimony. The evidence indicates overwhelmingly that the testimony given by the witness was an act of her own free will in no way coerced or even induced by official authority as a result of Biro's discovery of the policy slips. Nor were the slips themselves used in questioning Hennessey. Substantial periods of time elapsed between the time of the illegal search and the initial contact with the witness, on the one hand, and between the latter and the testimony at trial on the other. While the particular knowledge to which Hennessey testified at trial can be logically traced back to Biro's discovery of the policy slips both the identity of Hennessey and her relationship with the respondent were well known to those investigating the case. There is, in addition, not the slightest evidence to suggest that Biro entered the shop or picked up the envelope with the intent of finding tangible evidence bearing on an illicit gambling operation, much less any suggestion that he entered the shop and searched with the intent of finding a willing and knowledgeable witness to testify against respondent. Application of the exclusionary rule in this situation could not have the slightest deterrent effect on the behavior of an officer such as Biro. The cost of permanently silencing Hennessey is too great for an evenhanded system of law enforcement to bear in order to secure such a speculative and very likely negligible deterrent effect.

Obviously no mathematical weight can be assigned to any of the factors which we have discussed, but just as obviously they all point to the conclusion that the exclusionary rule should be invoked with much greater reluctance where the claim is based on a causal relationship between a constitutional violation and the discovery of a live witness than when a similar claim is advanced to support suppression of an inanimate object. The judgment of the Court of Appeals is accordingly

Reversed.

Mr. Justice BLACKMUN took no part in the consideration or decision of this case.

MR. CHIEF JUSTICE BURGER, concurring in the judgment.

I agree with the Court's ultimate conclusion that there is a fundamental difference, for purposes of the exclusionary rule, between live-witness testimony and other types of evidence. I perceive this distinction to be so fundamental, however, that I would not prevent a factfinder from hearing and considering the relevant statements of any witness, except perhaps under the most remarkable of circumstances — although none such have ever been postulated that would lead me to exclude the testimony of a live witness.

To appreciate this position, it is essential to bear in mind the purported justification for employing the exclusionary rule in a Fourth Amendment context: deterrence of official misconduct. As an abstract intellectual proposition this can be buttressed by a plausible rationale since there is at least some comprehensible connection — albeit largely and dubiously speculative — between the exclusion of evidence and the deterrence of intentional illegality on the part of a police officer. But if that is the purpose of the rule, it seems to me that the appropriate inquiry in every case in which a defendant seeks the exclusion of otherwise admissible and reliable evidence is whether official conduct in reality will be measurably altered by taking such a course.

On the facts of this case the Court is, of course, correct in holding that the "[a]pplication of the exclusionary rule in this situation could not have the slightest deterrent effect on the behavior of an officer such as Biro." Reaching this result, however, requires no judicial excursion into an area about which "philosophers have been able to argue endlessly," namely, the degree of "free will" exercised by a person when engaging in an act such as speaking.

It can, of course, be argued that the prospect of finding a helpful witness may play some role in a policeman's decision to be indifferent about Fourth Amendment procedures. The answer to this point, however, is that we have never insisted on employing the exclusionary rule whenever there is some possibility, no matter how remote, of deterring police misconduct. Rather, we balance the cost to society of losing perfectly competent evidence against the prospect of incrementally enhancing Fourth Amendment values. *See, e.g., Calandra.*

Using this approach it strikes me as evident that the permanent silencing of a witness — who, after all, is appearing under oath — is not worth the high price the exclusionary rule exacts. Any rule of law which operates to keep an eyewitness to a crime — a murder, for example — from telling the jury what that person saw has a rational basis roughly comparable to the primitive rituals of human sacrifice.

I would, therefore, resolve the case of a living witness on a per se basis, holding that such testimony is always admissible, provided it meets all other traditional evidentiary requirements. At very least this solution would alleviate the burden — now squarely thrust upon courts — of determining in each instance whether the witness possessed that elusive quality characterized by the term "free will."[4]

MR. JUSTICE MARSHALL, with whom MR. JUSTICE BRENNAN joins, dissenting.

While "reaffirm[ing]" the holding of *Wong Sun* that verbal evidence, like physical evidence, may be "fruit of the poisonous tree," the Court today "significantly qualif[ies]" *Wong Sun's* further conclusion, that no " 'logical distinction' " can be drawn between verbal and physical evidence for purposes of the exclusionary rule. In my view, the distinction that the Court attempts to draw cannot withstand close analysis. To extend "a time-worn metaphor," I do not believe that the same tree, having its roots in an unconstitutional search or seizure, can bear two different kinds of fruit, with one kind less susceptible than the other of exclusion on Fourth Amendment grounds. I therefore dissent.

The Court correctly states the question before us: whether the connection between the police officer's concededly unconstitutional search and Hennessey's disputed testimony was "so attenuated as to dissipate the taint." In resolving questions of attenuation, courts typically scrutinize the facts of the individual case, with particular attention to such matters as the "temporal proximity" of the official illegality and the discovery of the evidence, "the presence of intervening circumstances," and "the purpose and flagrancy of the official misconduct." *Brown.* The Court retains this general framework, but states that "[a]ttenuation analysis" should be "concerned with the differences between live-witness testimony and inanimate evidence." The differences noted by the Court, however, have to a large extent already been accommodated by current doctrine. Where they have not been so accommodated, it is because the differences asserted are either illusory or of no relevance to the issue of attenuation.

---

[4] Perhaps a case might arise in which the police conducted a search only for the purposes of obtaining the name of witnesses. In such a circumstance it is possibly arguable that the exclusion of any testimony gained as a result of the search would have an effect on official behavior. This clearly did not occur here, nor can I conceive of many instances in which it would. In any ever, the decision to exclude such testimony should depend on the officers' motivation and not on the "free will" of the witnesses. I would not want to speculate, however, as to whether such an unlikely case would justify modifying a per se approach to this general problem. [Footnote repositioned. — Ed.]

One difference mentioned by the Court is that witnesses, unlike inanimate objects, "can, and often do, come forward and offer evidence entirely of their own volition." Recognition of this obvious fact does nothing to advance the attenuation inquiry. We long ago held that, if knowledge of evidence is gained from a source independent of police illegality, the evidence should be admitted. This "independent source" rule would plainly apply to a witness whose identity is discovered in an illegal search but who later comes to the police for reasons unrelated to the official misconduct. In the instant case, however, as the Court recognizes there is a straight and uninterrupted' " road between the illegal search and the disputed testimony.

Even where the road is uninterrupted, in some cases the Government may be able to show that the illegally discovered evidence would inevitably have come to light in the normal course of a legal police investigation. Assuming such evidence is admissible — a proposition that has been questioned, *Fitzpatrick v. New York*, 414 U.S. 1050 (1973) (White, J., dissenting from denial of certiorari) — this "inevitable discovery" rule would apply to admit the testimony of a witness who, in the absence of police misconduct, would have come forward "entirely of [his or her] own volition." Again, however, no such situation is presented by this case, since the Court accepts the findings of the two lower courts that Hennessey's testimony would not inevitably have been discovered.

Both the independent-source and inevitable-discovery rules, moreover, can apply to physical evidence as well as to verbal evidence. The police may show, for example, that they learned from an independent source, or would inevitably have discovered through legal means, the location of an object that they also knew about as a result of illegal police activity. It may be that verbal evidence is more likely to have an independent source, because live witnesses can indeed come forward of their own volition, but this simply underscores the degree to which the Court's approach involves a form of judicial "double counting." The Court would apparently first determine whether the evidence stemmed from an independent source or would inevitably have been discovered; if neither of these rules was found to apply, as here, the Court would still somehow take into account the fact that, as a general proposition (but not in the particular case), witnesses sometimes do come forward of their own volition.

The Court makes a related point that "[t]he greater the willingness of the witness to freely testify, . . . the smaller the incentive to conduct an illegal search to discover the witness." The somewhat incredible premise of this statement is that the police in fact refrain from illegal behavior in which they would otherwise engage because they know in advance both that a witness will be willing to testify and that he or she "will be discovered by legal means." This reasoning surely reverses the normal sequence of events; the instances must be very few in which a witness' willingness to testify is known before he or she is discovered. In this case, for example, the police did not even know that Hennessey was a potentially valuable witness, much less whether she would be willing to testify, prior to conducting the illegal search. When the police are certain that a witness "will be discovered by legal means," if they ever can be certain about such a fact — they of course have no incentive to find him or her by illegal means, but the same can be said about physical objects that the police know will be discovered legally.

The only other point made by the Court is that exclusion of testimony "perpetually disable[s] a witness from testifying about relevant and material facts." The "perpetual . . . disable[ment]" of which the Court speaks, however, applies as much to physical as to verbal evidence. When excluded, both types of evidence are lost for the duration of the particular trial, despite their being "relevant and material . . . [and] unrelated . . . to the purpose of the originally illegal search." Moreover, while it is true that "often" the exclusion of testimony will be very costly to society, least as often the exclusion of physical evidence — such as heroin in a narcotics possession case or business records in a tax case — will be as costly to the same societal interests. But other, more important societal interests, have led to the rule, which the Court today reaffirms, that "fruits of the poisonous tree" must be excluded despite their probative value, unless the facts of the case justify a finding of sufficient attenuation.

The facts of this case do not justify such a finding. Although, as the Court notes, four months elapsed between the illegal search and the FBI's first contact with Hennessey, the critical evidence was provided at the time and place of the search, when the police officer questioned Hennessey and she identified respondent. The time that elapsed thereafter is of no more relevance than would be a similar time period between the discovery of an object during an illegal search and its later introduction into evidence at trial. In this case, moreover, there were no intervening circumstances between Hennessey's statement at the time of the search and her later testimony. She did not come to the authorities and ask to testify, despite being a student of police science; an FBI agent had to go to her home and interrogate her.

Finally, whatever the police officer's purpose in the flower shop on the day of the search, the search itself was not even of arguable legality, as was conceded by the Government below. It is also undisputed that the shop had been under surveillance as part of an ongoing gambling investigation in which the local police force had actively participated; its participation included interception of at least one of respondent's telephone conversations in the very month of the search. Under all of the circumstances, the connection here between the official illegality and the disputed testimony cannot be deemed "so attenuated as to dissipate the taint." The District Court therefore properly excluded the testimony.

I would affirm the judgment of the Court of Appeals

QUESTIONS AND NOTES

1.   With which, if any, of the three opinions (Rehnquist, Burger, Marshall) did you agree? Why?

2.   Considering the *Brown* factors (temporal proximity, intervening circumstances, and purpose and flagrancy of the illegality) is there anything about a live witness that makes it more likely that the taint will be dissipated as contrasted to (a) tangible evidence, or (b) the witnesses own statements?

3.   When wouldn't the original taint be dissipated in regard to a witness?

4.   As between Hennessy's statement in this case or Wong Sun's statement three days after his arrest in *Wong Sun*, which was the stronger case for finding the

taint dissipated? If you said Hennessey's statement, was Justice Marshall's dissent necessarily wrong?

B. MIRANDA

In *New York v. Quarles*, Chapter 17, Section G, *supra*, a majority of the Court found no violation of *Miranda* because of the "emergency." Consequently, it was unnecessary for the Court to assess the impact of the attenuation doctrine on the admissibility of the gun. For Justice O'Connor, who found a Miranda violation, such an assessment was necessary. We begin this section by examining that aspect of *Quarles*. If you have forgotten the basic fact pattern or the holding, you should, of course, refresh your recollection by rereading the case.

NEW YORK v. QUARLES
467 U.S. 649 (1984)

JUSTICE O'CONNOR, concurring in part in the judgment and dissenting in part.

II

The court below assumed, without discussion, that the privilege against self-incrimination required that the gun derived from respondent's statement also be suppressed, whether or not the State could independently link it to him. That conclusion was, in my view, incorrect.

A

The distinction between testimonial and nontestimonial evidence was explored in some detail in *Schmerber v. California*, a decision this Court handed down within a week of deciding *Miranda*. The defendant in *Schmerber* had argued that the privilege against self-incrimination barred the state from compelling him to submit to a blood test, the results of which would be used to prove his guilt at trial. This Court favored an approach that protected the "accused only from being compelled to testify against himself, or otherwise provide the State with evidence of a testimonial or communicative nature." The blood tests were admissible because they were neither testimonial nor communicative in nature.

In subsequent decisions, the Court relied on *Schmerber* in holding the privilege inapplicable to situations where the accused was compelled to stand in a lineup and utter words that allegedly had been spoken by the robber, *see United States v. Wade*, 388 U.S. 218, 221–223 (1967), to provide handwriting samples, *see Gilbert v. California*, 388 U.S. 263, 265–266, (1967), and to supply voice exemplars. *See United States v. Dionisio*, 410 U.S. 1, 5–7, (1973). "The distinction which . . . emerged [in these cases], often expressed in different ways, [was] that the privilege is a bar against compelling 'communications' or 'testimony,' but that compulsion which makes a suspect or accused the source of 'real or physical evidence' does not violate it." *Schmerber.*

B

The gun respondent was compelled to supply is clearly evidence of the "real or physical" sort. What makes the question of its admissibility difficult is the fact that, in asking respondent to produce the gun, the police also "compelled" him, in the *Miranda* sense, to create an incriminating testimonial response. In other words, the case is problematic because police compelled respondent not only to provide the gun but also to admit that he knew where it was and that it was his.

It is settled that *Miranda* did not itself determine whether physical evidence obtained in this manner would be admissible. See Michigan v. Tucker, 417 U.S., at 445–446, 447, 452, and n. 26. But the Court in *Schmerber*, with *Miranda* fresh on its mind, did address the issue. In concluding that the privilege did not require suppression of compelled blood tests, the Court noted:

> This conclusion would not necessarily govern had the State tried to show that the accused had incriminated himself when told that he would have to be tested. Such incriminating evidence may be an unavoidable by-product of the compulsion to take the test, especially for an individual who fears the extraction or opposes it on religious grounds. If it wishes to compel persons to submit to such attempts to discover evidence, the State may have to forgo the advantage of any testimonial products of administering the test — products which would fall within the privilege.

Thus, *Schmerber* resolved the dilemma by allowing admission of the nontestimonial, but not the testimonial, products of the State's compulsion.

[B]ased on the distinction first articulated in *Schmerber*, "a strong analytical argument can be made for an intermediate rule whereby[,] although [the police] cannot require the suspect to speak by punishment or force, the nontestimonial [evidence derived from] speech that is [itself] excludable for failure to comply with the *Miranda* code could still be used." H. FRIENDLY, BENCHMARKS 280 (1967). To be sure, admission of nontestimonial evidence secured through informal custodial interrogation will reduce the incentives to enforce the *Miranda* code. But that fact simply begs the question of how much enforcement is appropriate. There are some situations, as the Court's struggle to accommodate a "public safety" exception demonstrates, in which the societal cost of administering the *Miranda* warnings is very high indeed.[3] The *Miranda* decision quite practically does not express any societal interest in having those warnings administered for their own sake. Rather, the warnings and waiver are only required to ensure that "testimony" used against the accused at trial is voluntarily given. Therefore, if the testimonial aspects of the accused's custodial communications are suppressed, the failure to administer the *Miranda* warnings should cease to be of concern. *Cf. Weatherford v. Bursey*, 429 U.S. 545 (1977) (where interference with assistance of counsel has no effect on trial, no Sixth Amendment violation lies). The harm caused by failure to administer *Miranda* warnings relates only to admission of testimonial self-incriminations, and

---

[3] The most obvious example, first suggested by Judge Henry Friendly, involves interrogation directed to the discovery and termination of an on-going criminal activity such as kidnapping or extortion. *See* Friendly, *The Bill of Rights as a Code of Criminal Procedure*, 53 CALIF. L. REV. 929, 949 (1965).

the suppression of such incriminations should by itself produce the optimal enforcement of the *Miranda* rule.

C

There are, of course, decisions of this Court which suggest that the privilege against self-incrimination requires suppression of not only compelled statements but also of all evidence derived therefrom. *See, e.g., Maness v. Meyers,* 419 U.S. 449 (1975); *Kastigar v. United States,* 406 U.S. 441 (1972); *McCarthy v. Arndstein,* 266 U.S. 34 (1924); *Counselman v. Hitchcock,* 142 U.S. 547 (1892). In each of these cases, however, the Court was responding to the dilemma that confronts persons asserting their Fifth Amendment privilege to a court or other tribunal vested with the contempt power. In each instance, the tribunal can require witnesses to appear without any showing of probable cause to believe they have committed an offense or that they have relevant information to convey, and require the witnesses to testify even if they have formally and expressly asserted a privilege of silence. Individuals in this situation are faced with what Justice Goldberg once described as "the cruel trilemma of self-accusation, perjury, or contempt." *Murphy v. Waterfront Comm'n,* 378 U.S. 52, 55 (1964). If the witness' invocation of the privilege at trial is not to be defeated by the State's refusal to let him remain silent at an earlier proceeding, the witness has to be protected "against the use of his compelled answers and evidence derived therefrom in any subsequent criminal case . . . ." *Lefkowitz v. Turley,* 414 U.S. 70, 78 (1973).

By contrast, suspects subject to informal custodial police interrogation of the type involved in this case are not in the same position as witnesses required to appear before a court, grand jury, or other such formal tribunal. Where independent evidence leads police to a suspect, and probable cause justifies his arrest, the suspect cannot seriously urge that the police have somehow unfairly infringed on his right "to a private enclave where he may lead a private life." Moreover, when a suspect interjects not the privilege itself but a post hoc complaint that the police failed to administer *Miranda* warnings, he invokes only an irrebuttable presumption that the interrogation was coercive. He does not show that a privilege was raised and that the police actually or overtly coerced him to provide testimony and other evidence to be used against him at trial. *See Johnson v. New Jersey,* 384 U.S. 719, 730 (1966). He could have remained silent and the interrogator could not have punished him for refusing to speak. Indeed, the accused is in the unique position of seeking the protection of the privilege without having timely asserted it. The person in police custody surely may sense that he is in "trouble," but he is in no position to protest that he faced the Hobson's choice of self-accusation, perjury, or contempt. He therefore has a much less sympathetic case for obtaining the benefit of a broad suppression ruling.

Indeed, whatever case can be made for suppression evaporates when the statements themselves are not admitted, given the rationale of the Schmerber line of cases. Certainly interrogation which provides leads to other evidence does not offend the values underlying the Fifth Amendment privilege any more than the compulsory taking of blood samples, fingerprints, or voice exemplars, all of which may be compelled in an "attempt to discover evidence that might be used to prosecute [a defendant] for a criminal offense." Use of a suspect's answers "merely to find other evidence establishing his connection with the crime [simply] differs only by a shade from the permitted use for that purpose of his body or his blood." H. FRIENDLY, BENCHMARKS 280 (1967). The values underlying the privilege may justify exclusion of an unwarned person's out-of-court statements, as perhaps they may justify exclusion of statements and derivative evidence compelled under the threat of contempt. But when the only evidence to be admitted is derivative evidence such as a gun — derived not from actual compulsion but from a statement taken in the absence of *Miranda* warnings — those values simply cannot require suppression, at least no more so than they would for other such nontestimonial evidence.[4]

On the other hand, if a suspect is subject to abusive police practices and actually or overtly compelled to speak, it is reasonable to infer both an unwillingness to speak and a perceptible assertion of the privilege. *See Mincey v. Arizona*, 437 U.S. 385, 396–402 (1978). Thus, when the *Miranda* violation consists of a deliberate and flagrant abuse of the accused's constitutional rights, amounting to a denial of due process, application of a broader exclusionary rule is warranted. Of course, "a defendant raising [such] a coerced-confession claim . . . must first prevail in a voluntariness hearing before his confession and evidence derived from it [will] become inadmissible." *Kastigar v. United States*, 406 U.S. at 462. By contrast, where the accused proves only that the police failed to administer the *Miranda* warnings, exclusion of the statement itself is all that will and should be required.[5] Limitation of the *Miranda* prohibition to testimonial use of the statements themselves adequately serves the purposes of the privilege against self-incrimination.

QUESTIONS AND NOTES

1. Why did Justice O'Connor think that *Schmerber* had any relevance to the admissibility of the gun? Do you agree? Explain.

2. Apart from *Schmerber*, what is the theory behind Justice O'Connor's opinion? Does it make sense?

3. The influence of Justice O'Connor's *Quarles* concurrence can be seen in her opinion for the Court in *Elstad*.

---

[4] In suggesting that *Wong Sun v. United States*, 371 U.S. 471 (1963), requires exclusion of the gun, Justice MARSHALL fails to acknowledge this Court's holding in *Michigan v. Tucker*, 417 U.S. 433, 445–446 (1974). In *Tucker*, the Court very clearly held that *Wong Sun* is inapplicable in cases involving mere departures from *Miranda*. *Wong Sun* and its "fruit of the poisonous tree" analysis lead to exclusion of derivative evidence only where the underlying police misconduct infringes a "core" constitutional right. Failure to administer *Miranda* warnings violates only a nonconstitutional prophylactic.

[5] Respondent has not previously contended that his confession was so blatantly coerced as to constitute a violation of due process. He has argued only that police failed to administer Miranda warnings. He has proved, therefore, only that his statement was presumptively compelled. In any event, that is a question for the trial court on remand to decide in the first instance, not for this Court to decide on certiorari review.

OREGON v. ELSTAD
470 U.S. 298 (1985)

JUSTICE O'CONNOR delivered the opinion of the Court.

This case requires us to decide whether an initial failure of law enforcement officers to administer the warnings required by *Miranda v. Arizona*, 384 U.S. 436, 86 S. Ct. 1602, 16 L. Ed. 2d 694 (1966), without more, "taints" subsequent admissions made after a suspect has been fully advised of and has waived his *Miranda* rights. Respondent, Michael James Elstad, was convicted of burglary by an Oregon trial court. The Oregon Court of Appeals reversed, holding that respondent's signed confession, although voluntary, was rendered inadmissible by a prior remark made in response to questioning without benefit of *Miranda* warnings. We granted certiorari,465 U.S. 1078, 104 S. Ct. 1437, 79 L. Ed. 2d 759 (1984), and we now reverse.

I

In December 1981, the home of Mr. and Mrs. Gilbert Gross, in the town of Salem, Ore., was burglarized. Missing were art objects and furnishings valued at $150,000. A witness to the burglary contacted the Polk County Sheriff's office, implicating respondent Michael Elstad, an 18-year-old neighbor and friend of the Grosses' teenage son. Thereupon, Officers Burke and McAllister went to the home of respondent Elstad, with a warrant for his arrest. Elstad's mother answered the door. She led the officers to her son's room where he lay on his bed, clad in shorts and listening to his stereo. The officers asked him to get dressed and to accompany them into the living room. Officer McAllister asked respondent's mother to step into the kitchen, where he explained that they had a warrant for her son's arrest for the burglary of a neighbor's residence. Officer Burke remained with Elstad in the living room. He later testified: "I sat down with Mr. Elstad and I asked him if he was aware of why Detective McAllister and myself were there to talk with him. He stated no, he had no idea why we were there. I then asked him if he knew a person by the name of Gross, and he said yes, he did, and also added that he heard that there was a robbery at the Gross house. And at that point I told Mr. Elstad that I felt he was involved in that, and he looked at me and stated, 'Yes, I was there.' " The officers then escorted Elstad to the back of the patrol car. As they were about to leave for the Polk County Sheriff's office, Elstad's father arrived home and came to the rear of the patrol car. The officers advised him that his son was a suspect in the burglary. Officer Burke testified that Mr. Elstad became quite agitated, opened the rear door of the car and admonished his son: "I told you that you were going to get into trouble. You wouldn't listen to me. You never learn."

Elstad was transported to the Sheriff's headquarters and approximately one hour later, Officers Burke and McAllister joined him in McAllister's office. McAllister then advised respondent for the first time of his *Miranda* rights, reading from a standard card. Respondent indicated he understood his rights, and, having these rights in mind, wished to speak with the officers. Elstad gave a full statement, explaining that he had known that the Gross family was out of town and had been paid to lead several acquaintances to the Gross residence and show them how to gain entry through a defective sliding glass door. The statement was typed, reviewed by respondent, read back to him for correction, initialed and signed by Elstad and both officers. As an afterthought, Elstad added and initialed the sentence, "After leaving the house Robby & I went back to [the] van & Robby handed me a small bag of grass." Respondent concedes that the officers made no threats or promise either at his residence or at the Sheriff's office.

II

The arguments advanced in favor of suppression of respondent's written confession rely heavily on metaphor. One metaphor, familiar from the Fourth Amendment context, would require that respondent's confession, regardless of its integrity, voluntariness, and probative value, be suppressed as the "tainted fruit of the poisonous tree" of the *Miranda* violation. A second metaphor questions whether a confession can be truly voluntary once the "cat is out of the bag." Taken out of context, each of these metaphors can be misleading. They should not be used to obscure fundamental differences between the role of the Fourth Amendment exclusionary rule and the function of *Miranda* in guarding against the prosecutorial use of compelled statements as prohibited by the Fifth Amendment. The Oregon court assumed and respondent here contends that a failure to administer *Miranda* warnings necessarily breeds the same consequences as police infringement of a constitutional right, so that evidence uncovered following an unwarned statement must be suppressed as "fruit of the poisonous tree." We believe this view misconstrues the nature of the protections afforded by *Miranda* warnings and therefore misreads the consequences of police failure to supply them.

A

Prior to *Miranda*, the admissibility of an accused's in-custody statements was judged solely by whether they were "voluntary" within the meaning of the Due Process Clause. The Court in *Miranda* required suppression of many statements that would have been admissible under traditional due process analysis by presuming that statements made while in custody and without adequate warnings were protected by the Fifth Amendment. The Fifth Amendment, of course, is not concerned with nontestimonial evidence. See *Schmerber*. Nor is it concerned with moral and psychological pressures to confess emanating from sources other than official coercion. *See Innis*. Voluntary statements "remain a proper element in law enforcement." *Miranda* "Indeed, far from being prohibited by the Constitution, admissions of guilt by wrongdoers, if not coerced, are inherently desirable. . . . Absent some officially coerced self-accusation, the Fifth Amendment privilege is not violated by even the most damning admissions." *United States v. Washington*, 431 U.S. 181, 187 (1977).

Respondent's contention that his confession was tainted by the earlier failure of the police to provide *Miranda* warnings and must be excluded as "fruit of the poisonous tree" assumes the existence of a constitutional violation. This figure of speech is drawn from *Wong Sun* in which the Court held that evidence and witnesses discovered as a result of a search in violation of the Fourth Amendment must be excluded from evidence. The *Wong Sun* doctrine applies as well when the fruit of the Fourth Amendment violation is a confession. It is settled law that "a confession obtained through custodial interrogation after an illegal arrest should be excluded unless intervening events break the causal connection between the illegal arrest and the confession so that the confession is 'sufficiently an act of free will to purge the primary taint.' " *Taylor.*

But as we explained in *Quarles* and *Tucker*, a procedural *Miranda* violation differs in significant respects from violations of the Fourth Amendment, which have traditionally mandated a broad application of the "fruits" doctrine. The purpose of the Fourth Amendment exclusionary rule is to deter unreasonable searches, no matter how probative their fruits. "The exclusionary rule, . . . when utilized to effectuate the Fourth Amendment, serves interests and policies that are distinct from those it serves under the Fifth." Where a Fourth Amendment violation "taints" the confession, a finding of voluntariness for the purposes of the Fifth Amendment is merely a threshold requirement in determining whether the confession may be admitted in evidence. *Taylor.* Beyond this, the prosecution must show a sufficient break in events to undermine the inference that the confession was caused by the Fourth Amendment violation.

The *Miranda* exclusionary rule, however, serves the Fifth Amendment and sweeps more broadly than the Fifth Amendment itself. It may be triggered even in the absence of a Fifth Amendment violation.[1] The Fifth Amendment prohibits use by the prosecution in its case in chief only of compelled testimony. Failure to administer *Miranda* warnings creates a presumption of compulsion. Consequently, unwarned statements that are otherwise voluntary within the meaning of the Fifth Amendment must nevertheless be excluded from evidence under *Miranda.* Thus, in the individual case, *Miranda's* preventive medicine provides a remedy even to the defendant who has suffered no identifiable constitutional harm.

In *Michigan v. Tucker*, the Court was asked to extend the *Wong Sun* fruits doctrine to suppress the testimony of a witness for the prosecution whose identity was discovered as the result of a statement taken from the accused without benefit of full *Miranda* warnings. As in respondent's case, the breach of the *Miranda* procedures in Tucker involved no actual compulsion. The Court concluded that the unwarned questioning "did not abridge respondent's constitutional privilege . . . but departed only from the prophylactic standards later laid down by this Court in *Miranda* to safeguard that privilege." Since there was no actual infringement of the suspect's constitutional rights, the case was not controlled by the doctrine expressed in *Wong Sun* that fruits of a constitutional violation must be suppressed. In deciding "how sweeping the judicially imposed consequences" of a failure to administer *Miranda* warnings should be, the Tucker Court noted that neither the

---

[1] Justice STEVENS expresses puzzlement at our statement that a simple failure to administer *Miranda* warnings is not in itself a violation of the Fifth Amendment. Yet the Court so held in *New York v. Quarles*, 467 U.S. 649, 654 (1983), and *Michigan v. Tucker*, 417 U.S. 433, 444 (1974). The *Miranda* Court itself recognized this point when it disclaimed any intent to create a "constitutional straitjacket" and invited Congress and the States to suggest "potential alternatives for protecting the privilege" A *Miranda* violation does not *constitute* coercion but rather affords a bright-line, legal presumption of coercion, requiring suppression of all unwarned statements. It has never been remotely suggested that any statement taken from Mr. Elstad without benefit of *Miranda* warnings would be admissible.

general goal of deterring improper police conduct nor the Fifth Amendment goal of assuring trustworthy evidence would be served by suppression of the witness' testimony. The unwarned confession must, of course, be suppressed, but the Court ruled that introduction of the third-party witness' testimony did not violate Tucker's Fifth Amendment rights.

We believe that this reasoning applies with equal force when the alleged "fruit" of a noncoercive *Miranda* violation is neither a witness nor an article of evidence but the accused's own voluntary testimony. As in *Tucker*, the absence of any coercion or improper tactics undercuts the twin rationales — trustworthiness and deterrence — for a broader rule. Once warned, the suspect is free to exercise his own volition in deciding whether or not to make a statement to the authorities. The Court has often noted: " '[A] living witness is not to be mechanically equated with the proffer of inanimate evidentiary objects illegally seized. . . . [T]he living witness is an individual human personality whose attributes of will, perception, memory and volition interact to determine what testimony he will give.' " *Ceccolini.*

Because *Miranda* warnings may inhibit persons from giving information, this Court has determined that they need be administered only after the person is taken into "custody" or his freedom has otherwise been significantly restrained. Unfortunately, the task of defining "custody" is a slippery one, and "policemen investigating serious crimes [cannot realistically be expected to] make no errors whatsoever." If errors are made by law enforcement officers in administering the prophylactic *Miranda* procedures, they should not breed the same irremediable consequences as police infringement of the Fifth Amendment itself. It is an unwarranted extension of *Miranda* to hold that a simple failure to administer the warnings, unaccompanied by any actual coercion or other circumstances calculated to undermine the suspect's ability to exercise his free will, so taints the investigatory process that a subsequent voluntary and informed waiver is ineffective for some indeterminate period. Though *Miranda* requires that the unwarned admission must be suppressed, the admissibility of any subsequent statement should turn in these circumstances solely on whether it is knowingly and voluntarily made.

B

The Oregon court, however, believed that the unwarned remark compromised the voluntariness of respondent's later confession. It was the court's view that the prior answer and not the unwarned questioning impaired respondent's ability to give a valid waiver and that only lapse of time and change of place could dissipate what it termed the "coercive impact" of the inadmissible statement. When a prior statement is actually coerced, the time that passes between confessions, the change in place of interrogations, and the change in identity of the interrogators all bear on whether that coercion has carried over into the second confession. *See Westover v. United States*, decided together with *Miranda*. The failure of police to administer *Miranda* warnings does not mean that the statements received have actually been coerced, but only that courts will presume the privilege against compulsory self-incrimination has not been intelligently exercised. Of the courts that have considered whether a properly warned confession must be suppressed because it was preceded by an unwarned but clearly voluntary admission, the majority have explicitly or implicitly recognized that Westover 's requirement of a break in the stream of events is inapposite. In these circumstances, a careful and thorough administration of *Miranda* warnings serves to cure the condition that rendered the unwarned statement inadmissible. The warning conveys the relevant information and thereafter the suspect's choice whether to exercise his privilege to remain silent should ordinarily be viewed as an "act of free will."

The Oregon court nevertheless identified a subtle form of lingering compulsion, the psychological impact of the suspect's conviction that he has let the cat out of the bag and, in so doing, has sealed his own fate. But endowing the psychological effects of *voluntary* unwarned admissions with constitutional implications would, practically speaking, disable the police from obtaining the suspect's informed cooperation even when the official coercion proscribed by the Fifth Amendment played no part in either his warned or unwarned confessions. As the Court remarked in Bayer: "[A]fter an accused has once let the cat out of the bag by confessing, no matter what the inducement, he is never thereafter free of the psychological and practical disadvantages of having confessed. He can never get the cat back in the bag. The secret is out for good. In such a sense, a later confession may always be looked upon as fruit of the first. But this Court has never gone so far as to hold that making a confession under circumstances which preclude its use, perpetually disables the confessor from making a usable one after those conditions have been removed."

Even in such extreme cases as *Lyons* v. *Oklahoma*, 322 U.S. (1944), in which police forced a full confession from the accused through unconscionable methods of interrogation, the Court has assumed that the coercive effect of the confession could, with time, be dissipated.

This Court has never held that the psychological impact of voluntary disclosure of a guilty secret qualifies as state compulsion or compromises the voluntariness of a subsequent informed waiver. The Oregon court, by adopting this expansive view of Fifth Amendment compulsion, effectively immunizes a suspect who responds to pre-*Miranda* warning questions from the consequences of his subsequent informed waiver of the privilege of remaining silent. This immunity comes at a high cost to legitimate law enforcement activity, while adding little desirable protection to the individual's interest in not being *compelled* to testify against himself.

There is a vast difference between the direct consequences flowing from coercion of a confession by physical violence or other deliberate means calculated to break the suspect's will and the uncertain consequences of disclosure of a "guilty secret" freely given in response to an unwarned but noncoercive question, as in this case. Justice BRENNAN's contention that it is impossible to perceive any causal distinction between this case and one involving a confession that is coerced by torture is wholly unpersuasive. Certainly, in respondent's case, the causal connection between any psychological disadvantage created by his admission and his ultimate decision to cooperate is speculative and attenuated at best. It is difficult to tell with certainty what motivates a suspect to speak. A suspect's confession may be traced to factors as disparate as "a prearrest event such as a visit with a minister," *Dunaway v. New York*, 442 U.S. at 220, (STEVENS, J., concurring), or an intervening event such as the exchange of words respondent had with his father. We must conclude that, absent deliberately coercive or improper tactics in obtaining the initial statement, the mere fact that a suspect has made an unwarned admission does not warrant a presumption of compulsion. A subsequent administration of *Miranda* warnings to a suspect who has given a voluntary but unwarned statement ordinarily should suffice to remove the conditions that precluded admission of the earlier statement. In such circumstances, the finder of fact may reasonably conclude that the suspect made a rational and intelligent choice whether to waive or invoke his rights.

<h1 style="text-align:center">III</h1>

There is no question that respondent knowingly and voluntarily waived his right to remain silent before he described his participation in the burglary. It is also beyond dispute that respondent's earlier remark was voluntary, within the meaning of the Fifth Amendment. Neither the environment nor the manner of either "interrogation" was coercive. The initial conversation took place at midday, in the living room area of respondent's own home, with his mother in the kitchen area, a few steps away. Although in retrospect the officers testified that respondent was then in custody, at the time he made his statement he had not been informed that he was under arrest. The arresting officers' testimony indicates that the brief stop in the living room before proceeding to the station house was not to interrogate the suspect but to notify his mother of the reason for his arrest.

The State has conceded the issue of custody and thus we must assume that Burke breached *Miranda* procedures in failing to administer *Miranda* warnings before initiating the discussion in the living room. This breach may have been the result of confusion as to whether the brief exchange qualified as "custodial interrogation" or it may simply have reflected Burke's reluctance to initiate an alarming police procedure before McAllister had spoken with respondent's mother. Whatever the reason for Burke's oversight, the incident had none of the earmarks of coercion. Nor did the officers exploit the unwarned admission to pressure respondent into waiving his right to remain silent.

Respondent, however, has argued that he was unable to give a fully informed waiver of his rights because he was unaware that his prior statement could not be used against him. Respondent suggests that Officer McAllister, to cure this deficiency, should have added an additional warning to those given him at the Sheriff's office. Such a requirement is neither practicable nor constitutionally necessary. In many cases, a breach of *Miranda* procedures may not be identified as such until long after full *Miranda* warnings are administered and a valid confession obtained. The standard *Miranda* warnings explicitly inform the suspect of his right to consult a lawyer before speaking. Police officers are ill-equipped to pinch-hit for counsel, construing the murky and difficult questions of when "custody" begins or whether a given unwarned statement will ultimately be held admissible.

This Court has never embraced the theory that a defendant's ignorance of the full consequences of his decisions vitiates their voluntariness. If the prosecution has actually violated the defendant's Fifth Amendment rights by introducing an inadmissible confession at trial, compelling the defendant to testify in rebuttal, the rule announced in *Harrison* v. *United States* 392 U.S. 219 (1968), precludes use of that testimony on retrial. "Having 'released the spring' by using the petitioner's unlawfully obtained confessions against him, the Government must show that its illegal action did not induce his testimony." But the Court has refused to find that a defendant who confesses, after being falsely told that his codefendant has turned State's evidence, does so involuntarily. *Frazier v. Cupp*, 394 U.S. 731, 739, 89 S. Ct. 1420, 1424, 22 L. Ed. 2d 684 (1969). The Court has also rejected the argument that a defendant's ignorance that a prior coerced confession could not be admitted in evidence compromised the voluntariness of his guilty plea. Likewise, in *California v. Beheler*, 463 U.S. 1121 (1983), the Court declined to accept defendant's contention that, because he was unaware of the potential adverse consequences of statements he made to the police, his participation in the interview was involuntary. Thus we have not held that the sine qua non for a knowing and voluntary waiver of the right to remain silent is a full and complete appreciation of all of the consequences flowing from the nature and the quality of the evidence in the case.

IV

When police ask questions of a suspect in custody without administering the required warnings, *Miranda* dictates that the answers received be presumed compelled and that they be excluded from evidence at trial in the State's case in chief. The Court has carefully adhered to this principle, permitting a narrow exception only where pressing public safety concerns demanded. *Quarles.* The Court today in no way retreats from the bright-line rule of *Miranda*. We do not imply that good faith excuses a failure to administer *Miranda* warnings; nor do we condone inherently coercive police tactics or methods offensive to due process that render the initial admission involuntary and undermine the suspect's will to invoke his rights once they are read to him. A handful of courts have, however, applied our precedents relating to confessions obtained under coercive circumstances to situations involving wholly voluntary admissions, requiring a passage of time or break in events before a second, fully warned statement can be deemed voluntary. Far from establishing a rigid rule, we direct courts to avoid one; there is no warrant for presuming coercive effect where the suspect's initial inculpatory statement, though technically in violation of *Miranda*, was voluntary.[5] The relevant inquiry is whether, in fact, the second statement was also voluntarily made. As in any such inquiry, the finder of fact must examine the surrounding circumstances and the entire course of police conduct with respect to the suspect in evaluating the voluntariness of his statements. The fact that a suspect chooses to speak after being informed of his rights is, of course, highly probative. We find that the dictates of *Miranda* and the goals of the Fifth Amendment proscription against use of compelled testimony are fully satisfied in the circumstances of this case by barring use of the unwarned statement in the case in chief. No further purpose is served by imputing "taint" to subsequent statements obtained pursuant to a voluntary and knowing waiver. We hold today that a suspect who has once responded to unwarned yet uncoercive questioning is not thereby disabled from waiving his rights and confessing after he has been given the requisite *Miranda* warnings.

---

[5] Justice BRENNAN, with an apocalyptic tone, heralds this opinion as dealing a "crippling blow to *Miranda*." Justice BRENNAN not only distorts the reasoning and holding of our decision, but, worse, invites trial courts and prosecutors to do the same.

The judgment of the Court of Appeals of Oregon is reversed, and the case is remanded for further proceedings not inconsistent with this opinion.

JUSTICE BRENNAN, with whom JUSTICE MARSHALL joins, dissenting.

The Self-Incrimination Clause of the Fifth Amendment guarantees every individual that, if taken into official custody, he shall be informed of important constitutional rights and be given the opportunity knowingly and voluntarily to waive those rights before being interrogated about suspected wrongdoing. *Miranda*. This guarantee embodies our society's conviction that "no system of criminal justice can, or should, survive if it comes to depend for its continued effectiveness on the citizens' abdication through unawareness of their constitutional rights." *Escobedo*.

Even while purporting to reaffirm these constitutional guarantees, the Court has engaged of late in a studied campaign to strip the *Miranda* decision piecemeal and to undermine the rights *Miranda* sought to secure. Today's decision not only extends this effort a further step, but delivers a potentially crippling blow to *Miranda* and the ability of courts to safeguard the rights of persons accused of crime. For at least with respect to successive confessions, the Court today appears to strip remedies for *Miranda* violations of the "fruit of the poisonous tree" doctrine prohibiting the use of evidence presumptively derived from official illegality.

Two major premises undergird the Court's decision. The Court rejects as nothing more than "speculative" the long-recognized presumption that an illegally extracted confession causes the accused to confess again out of the mistaken belief that he already has sealed his fate, and it condemns as " 'extravagant' " the requirement that the prosecution affirmatively rebut the presumption before the subsequent confession may be admitted. The Court instead adopts a new rule that, so long as the accused is given the usual *Miranda* warnings before further interrogation, the taint of a previous confession obtained in violation of *Miranda* "ordinarily" must be viewed as *automatically* dissipated.

The Court's decision says much about the way the Court currently goes about implementing its agenda. In imposing its new rule, for example, the Court mischaracterizes our precedents, obfuscates the central issues, and altogether ignores the practical realities of custodial interrogation that have led nearly every lower court to reject its simplistic reasoning. Moreover, the Court adopts startling and unprecedented methods of construing constitutional guarantees. Finally the Court reaches out once again to address issues not before us. For example, although the State of Oregon has conceded that the arresting officers broke the law in this case, the Court goes out of its way to suggest that they may have been objectively justified in doing so.

Today's decision, in short, threatens disastrous consequences far beyond the outcome in this case. As the Court has not seen fit to provide a full explanation for this result, I believe it essential to consider in detail the premises, reasoning, and implications of the Court's opinion.

I

The threshold question is this: What effect should an admission or confession of guilt obtained in violation of an accused's *Miranda* rights be presumed to have upon the voluntariness of subsequent confessions that are preceded by *Miranda* warnings? Relying on the "cat out of the bag" analysis of *United States v. Bayer*, the Oregon Court of Appeals held that the first confession presumptively taints subsequent confessions in such circumstances. On the specific facts of this case, the court below found that the prosecution had not rebutted this presumption. Rather, given the temporal proximity of *Elstad's* second confession to his first and the absence of any significant intervening circumstances, the court correctly concluded that there had not been "a sufficient break in the stream of events between [the] inadmissible statement and the written confession to insulate the latter statement from the effect of what went before."

The Court today sweeps aside this common-sense approach as "speculative" reasoning, adopting instead a rule that "the psychological impact of voluntary disclosure of a guilty secret" neither "qualifies as state compulsion" nor "compromises the voluntariness" of subsequent confession. (emphasis added). So long as suspect received the usual *Miranda* warnings before further interrogation, the Court reasons, the fact that he "is free to exercise his own volition in deciding whether or not to make" further confessions "ordinarily" is a sufficient "cure" and serves to break any causal connection between the illegal confession and subsequent statements.

The Court's marble-palace psychoanalysis is tidy, but it flies in the fact of our own precedents, demonstrates a starling unawareness of the realities of police interrogation, and is completely out of tune with the experience of state and federal courts over the last 20 years. Perhaps the Court has grasped some psychology truth that has eluded persons far more experienced in these matters; if so, the Court owes an explanation of how so many could have been so wrong for so many years.

A

1

This Court has had long experience with the problem of confessions obtained after an earlier confession has been illegally secured. Subsequent confessions in these circumstances are not per se inadmissible, but the prosecution must demonstrate facts "sufficient to insulate the [subsequent] statement from the effect of all that went before." *Clewis v. Texas*, 386 U.S. 707, 710 (1967).

One of the factors that can vitiate the voluntariness of a subsequent confession is the hopeless feeling of an accused that he has nothing to lose by repeating his confession, even where the circumstances that rendered his first confession illegal have been removed. As the Court observed in *United States v. Bayer*, 331 U.S. at 540, 67 S. Ct. at 1398: "[A]fter an accused has once let the cat out of the bag by confessing, no matter what the inducement, he is never thereafter free of the psychological and practical disadvantages of having confessed. He can never get the cat back in the bag. The secret is out for good. In such a sense, a later confession always may be looked upon as a fruit of the first."

The Court today decries the "irremediable consequences" of this reasoning, but it has always been clear that even after "let[ting] the cat out of the bag" the accused is not "perpetually disable[d]" from giving an admissible subsequent confession. *Bayer.* Rather, we have held that subsequent confessions in such circumstances may be admitted if the prosecution demonstrates that, "[c]onsidering the 'totality of the circumstances,' " there was a " 'break in the stream of events . . . sufficient to insulate' " the subsequent confession from the damning impact of the first. *Darwin* v. *Connecticut*, 391 U.S. 346, 349 (1968).

2

Our precedents did not develop in a vacuum. They reflect an understanding of the realities of police interrogation and the everyday experience of lower courts. Expert interrogators, far from dismissing a first admission or confession as creating merely a "speculative and attenuated" disadvantage for a suspect, understand that such revelations frequently lead directly to a full confession. Standard interrogation manuals advise that "[t]he securing of the first admission is the biggest stumbling block . . . ." A. AUBRY & R. CAPUTO, CRIMINAL INTERROGATION 290 (3d ed. 1980). If this first admission can be obtained, "there is every reason to expect that the first admission will lead to others, and eventually to the full confession." *Ibid.*

The practical experience of state and federal courts confirms the experts' understanding. From this experience, lower courts have concluded that a first confession obtained without proper *Miranda* warnings, far from creating merely some "speculative and attenuated" disadvantage for the accused, frequently enables the authorities to obtain subsequent confessions on a "silver platter."

One police practice that courts have frequently encountered involves the withholding of *Miranda* warnings until the end of an interrogation session. Specifically, the police escort a suspect into a room, sit him down and, without explaining his Fifth Amendment rights or obtaining a knowing and voluntary waiver of those rights, interrogate him about his suspected criminal activity. If the police obtain a confession, it is then typed up, the police hand the suspect a pen for his signature, and — just before he signs — the police advise him of his *Miranda* rights and ask him to proceed. Alternatively, the police may call a stenographer in after they have obtained the confession, advise the suspect for the first time of his *Miranda* rights, and ask him to repeat what he has just told them. In such circumstances, the process of giving *Miranda* warnings and obtaining the final confession is " 'merely a formalizing, a setting down almost as a scrivener does, [of] what ha[s] already taken [place].' " *People v. Raddatz*, 91 Ill. App. 2d 425, 430, 235 N.E.2d 353, 356 (1968) (quoting trial court). In such situations, where "it was all over except for reading aloud and explaining the written waiver of the *Miranda* safeguards," courts have time and again concluded that "[t]he giving of the *Miranda* warnings before reducing the product of the day's work to written form could not undo what had been done or make legal what was illegal." *People v. Bodner*, 75 App. Div. 2d 440, 448, 430 N.Y.S.2d 433, 438 (1980).

There are numerous variations on this theme. [T]he suspect might be questioned by arresting officers "in the field" and without *Miranda* warnings, as was young Elstad in the instant case. After making incriminating admissions or a confession, the suspect is then brought into the station house and either questioned by the same officers again or asked to repeat his earlier statements to another officer.

For all practical purposes, the prewarning and post-warning questioning are often but stages of one overall interrogation. Whether or not the authorities explicitly confront the suspect with his earlier illegal admissions makes no significant difference, of course, because the suspect knows that the authorities know of his earlier statements and most frequently will believe that those statements already have sealed his fate. Thus a suspect in such circumstances is likely to conclude that "he might as well answer the questions put to him, since the [authorities are] already aware of the earlier answers."

I would have thought that the Court, instead of dismissing the "cat out of the bag" presumption out of hand, would have accounted for these practical realities. *Compare Nardone v. United States*, 308 U.S. at 342 (derivative-evidence rules should be grounded on the "learning, good sense, fairness and courage" of lower-court judges). Expert interrogators and experienced lower-court judges will be startled, to say the least, to learn that the connection between multiple confessions is "speculative" and that a subsequent rendition of *Miranda* warnings "ordinarily" enables the accused in these circumstances to exercise his "free will" and to make "a rational and intelligent choice whether to waive or invoke his rights."

B

The Court's new approach is therefore completely at odds with established dissipation analysis. A comparison of the Court's analysis with the factors most frequently relied on by lower courts in considering the admissibility of subsequent confessions demonstrates the practical and legal flaws of the new rule.

Advice that earlier confession may be inadmissible. The most effective means to ensure the voluntariness of an accused's subsequent confession is to advise the accused that his earlier admissions may not be admissible and therefore that he need not speak solely out of a belief that "the cat is out of the bag." Many courts have required such warnings in the absence of other dissipating factors, and this Court has not uncovered anything to suggest that this approach has not succeeded in the real world. The Court, however, believes that law enforcement authorities could never possibly understand "the murky and difficult questio[n]" of when *Miranda* warnings must be given, and therefore that they are "ill-equipped" to make the decision whether supplementary warnings might be required.

This reasoning is unpersuasive for two reasons. First, the whole point of *Miranda* and its progeny has been to prescribe "bright line" rules for the authorities to follow. Although borderline cases will of course occasionally arise, thus militating against a per se rule requiring supplementary warnings, the experience of the lower courts demonstrates that the vast majority of confrontations implicating this question involve obvious *Miranda* violations. The occasional "murky and difficult" case should not preclude consideration of supplementary warnings in situations where the authorities could not possibly have acted in an objectively reasonable manner in their earlier interrogation of the accused. Second, even where the authorities are not certain that an earlier confession has been illegally obtained, courts and commentators have recognized that a supplementary warning merely advising the accused that his earlier confession may be inadmissible can dispel his belief that he has nothing to lose by repetition.

Proximity in time and place. Courts have frequently concluded that a subsequent confession was so removed in time and place from the first that the accused most likely was able fully to exercise his independent judgment in deciding whether to speak again. As in the instant case, however, a second confession frequently follows immediately on the heels of the first and is obtained by the same officials in the same or similar coercive surroundings. In such situations, it is wholly unreasonable to assume that the mere rendition of *Miranda* warnings will safeguard the accused's freedom of action.

Intervening factors. Some lower courts have found that because of intervening factors — such as consultation with a lawyer or family members, or an independent decision to speak — an accused's subsequent confession could not fairly be attributed to the earlier statement taken in violation of *Miranda*. On the other hand, whereas here an accused has continuously been in custody and there is no legitimate suggestion of an intervening event sufficient to break the impact of the first confession, subsequent confessions are inadmissible. The Court reasons, however, that because "[a] suspect's confession may be traced to . . . an intervening event," it "must [be] conclude[d]" that subsequent *Miranda* warnings presumptively enable the suspect to make "a rational and intelligent choice" whether to repeat his confession. (emphasis added). In applying the intervening-events inquiry, however, "courts must use a surgeon's scalpel and not a meat axe." Cf. 3 W. LaFave, Search and Seizure, § 11.4, p. 624 (1978). The only proper inquiry is whether a meaningful intervening event actually occurred, not whether a court simply chooses to shut its eyes to human nature and the realities of custodial interrogation.

II

Not content merely to ignore the practical realities of police interrogation and the likely effects of its abolition of the derivative-evidence presumption, the Court goes on to assert that nothing in the Fifth Amendment or the general judicial policy of deterring illegal police conduct "ordinarily" requires the suppression of evidence derived proximately from a confession obtained in violation of *Miranda*. The Court does not limit its analysis to successive confessions, but recurrently refers generally to the "fruits" of the illegal confession. Thus the potential impact of the Court's reasoning might extend far beyond the "cat out of the bag" context to include the discovery of physical evidence and other derivative fruits of *Miranda* violations as well.[29]

---

[29] Notwithstanding the sweep of the Court's language, today's opinion surely ought not be read as also foreclosing application of the traditional derivative-evidence presumption to physical evidence obtained as a proximate result of a Miranda violation. The Court relies heavily on individual "volition"

A

Twice in the last 10 years, however, the Court has suggested that the *Miranda* safeguards are not themselves rights guaranteed by the Fifth Amendment. In *Tucker*, the Court stated that *Miranda* had only prescribed "recommended" procedural safeguards "to provide practical reinforcement for the right against compulsory self-incrimination," the violation of which may not necessarily violate the Fifth Amendment itself. And in *Quarles*, the Court last Term disturbingly rejected the argument that a confession "must be presumed compelled because of . . . failure to read [the accused] his *Miranda* warnings." (emphasis in original).

These assertions are erroneous. *Miranda* 's requirement of warnings and an effective waiver was not merely an exercise of supervisory authority over interrogation practices. As Justice Douglas noted in his *Tucker* dissent:

> *Miranda's* purpose was not promulgation of judicially preferred standards for police interrogation, a function we are quite powerless to perform; the decision enunciated *constitutional* standards for protection of the privilege' against self-incrimination.

(emphasis in original). *Miranda* clearly emphasized that warnings and an informed waiver are essential to the Fifth Amendment privilege itself. As noted in *Tucker,* *Miranda* did state that the Constitution does not require " 'adherence to any particular solution' " for providing the required knowledge and obtaining an informed waiver. But to rely solely on this language in concluding that the *Miranda* warnings are not constitutional rights, as did the Court in *Tucker*, ignores the central issue. The Court in *Tucker* omitted to mention that in *Miranda*, after concluding that no "particular solution" is required, we went on to emphasize that "unless we are shown other procedures which are at least as effective in apprising accused persons of their right of silence and in assuring a continuous opportunity to exercise it, the [prescribed] safeguards must be observed." Thus "the use of [any] admissions obtained in the absence of the required warnings [is] a flat violation of the Self-Incrimination Clause of the Fifth Amendment . . . ."

The Court today finally recognizes these flaws in the logic of *Tucker* and *Quarles*. Although disastrous in so many other respects, today's opinion at least has the virtue of rejecting the inaccurate assertion in *Quarles* that confessions extracted in violation of *Miranda* are not presumptively coerced for Fifth Amendment purposes. Instead, the Court holds squarely that there is an "irrebuttable" presumption that such confessions are indeed coerced and are therefore inadmissible under the Fifth Amendment except in narrow circumstances.[31]

---

as an insulating factor in successive-confession cases. Although the Court's reliance on this factor is clearly misplaced the factor is altogether missing in the context of inanimate evidence.

[31] The exceptions are where a confession is used to impeach the defendant's trial testimony, *Harris v. New York*, 401 U.S. 222 (1971), and where *Miranda* warnings were not given because of "pressing public safety concerns," *Quarles.*

B

Unfortunately, the Court takes away with one hand far more than what it has given with the other. Although the Court concedes, as it must, that a confession obtained in violation of *Miranda* is irrebuttably presumed to be coerced and that the Self-Incrimination Clause therefore prevents its use in the prosecution's case in chief, the Court goes on to hold that nothing in the Fifth Amendment prevents the introduction at trial of evidence proximately derived from the illegal confession. It contends, for example, that the Fifth Amendment prohibits introduction "only" of the "compelled testimony," and that this constitutional guarantee "is not concerned with nontestimonial evidence."

This narrow compass of the protection against compelled self-incrimination does not accord with our historic understanding of the Fifth Amendment. Although the Self-Incrimination Clause "protects an accused only from being compelled to testify against himself, or otherwise provide the State with evidence of a testimonial or communicative nature," *Schmerber*, it prohibits the use of such communications "against" the accused in any way. The Fifth Amendment therefore contains a self-executing rule commanding the exclusion of evidence derived from such communications.[32]

D

Not content with its handiwork discussed above, the Court goes on and devotes considerable effort to suggesting that, "[u]nfortunately," *Miranda* is such an inherently "slippery," "murky," and "difficult" concept that the authorities in general, and the police officer conducting the interrogation in this case in particular, cannot be faulted for failing to advise a suspect of his rights and to obtain an informed waiver. *Miranda* will become "murky," however, only because the Court's opinion today threatens to become a self-fulfilling prophecy. Although borderline cases occasionally have arisen respecting the concepts of "custody" and "interrogation," until today there has been nothing "slippery," "murky," or "difficult" about *Miranda* in the overwhelming majority of cases. The whole point of the Court's work in this area has been to prescribe "bright line" rules to give clear guidance to the authorities.

Rather than acknowledge that the police in this case clearly broke the law, the Court bends over backwards to suggest why the officers may have been justified in failing to obey *Miranda*.

First. The Court asserts that "[n]either the environment nor the manner of either 'interrogation' was coercive," noting that the initial interrogation took place in Elstad's "own home." The Court also believes that, "[a]lthough in retrospect the officers testified that respondent was then in custody, at the time he made his statement he had not been informed that he was under arrest." There is no

---

[32] The Court's reliance on *Schmerber* in support of its constricted view of the Fifth Amendment, is wholly inappropriate. *Schmerber* had nothing to do with the derivative-evidence rule, but held only that the evidence compelled in the first instance in that case — blood samples — was nontestimonial in nature.

question, however, that Michael Elstad was in custody and "deprived of his freedom of action in [a] significant way" at the time he was interrogated. Two police officers had entered his bedroom, ordered him to get out of bed and come with them, stood over him while he dressed, taken him downstairs, and separated him from his mother. The officers themselves acknowledged that *Elstad* was then under arrest. Moreover, we have made clear that police interrogation of an accused in custody triggers the *Miranda* safeguard even if he is in the "familiar surroundings" of his own home, precisely because he is no less " 'deprived of his freedom of action' " there than if he were at a police station. *Orozco.*

Thus because *Elstad* was in custody, the circumstances of his interrogation were inherently coercive, and the Court once again flouts settled law in suggesting otherwise.

Second. Without anything in the record to support its speculation, the Court suggests that Officer Burke's violation of *Miranda* "may have been the result of confusion as to whether the brief exchange qualified as 'custodial interrogation' . . . ." There was no confusion on this point until today. Burke made *Elstad* sit down and, standing over him, said "[y]ou know why we're here," asked if he knew the Gross family, and "asked what he knew about the burglary." This questioning obviously constituted interrogation because it was "reasonably likely to evoke an incriminating response" from *Elstad*, as it did. *Innis.*

Third. The Court contends that the interrogation might be excusable because "the brief stop in the living room before proceeding to the station house was not to interrogate the suspect but to notify his mother of the reason for his arrest." Officer Burke's partner did take Elstad's mother into the kitchen to inform her of the charges, but Burke took *Elstad* into another room, sat him down, and interrogated him concerning "what he knew about the burglary."

How can the Court possibly describe this interrogation as merely informing Elstad's mother of his arrest?

Finally. The Court suggests that Burke's violation of *Elstad's* Fifth Amendment rights "may simply have reflected Burke's reluctance to initiate an alarming police procedure before McAllister had spoken with respondent's mother." As the officers themselves acknowledged, however, the fact that they "[took] the young fellow out of bed" had "[o]bviously" already created "tension and stress" for the mother, which surely was not lessened when she learned that her son was under arrest. And if Elstad's mother was in earshot, as the Court assumes, it is difficult to perceive how listening to the *Miranda* warnings would be any more "alarming" to her than what she actually heard — actual interrogation of her son, including Burke's direct accusation that the boy had committed a felony. Most importantly, an individual's constitutional rights should not turn on whether his relatives might be upset. Surely there is no "tender feelings" exception to the Fifth Amendment privilege against self-incrimination.

III

The Court's decision today vividly reflects its impatience with the constitutional rights that the authorities attack as standing in the way of combating crime. But the

States that adopted the Bill of Rights struck that balance and it is not for this Court to balance the Bill of Rights away on a cost/benefit scale "where the 'costs' of excluding illegally obtained evidence loom to exaggerated heights and where the 'benefits' of such exclusion are made to disappear with a mere wave of the hand." *Leon* (BRENNAN, J., dissenting).

The lesson of today's decision is that, at least for now, what the Court decrees are "legitimate" violations by authorities of the rights embodied in *Miranda* shall "ordinarily" go undeterred. It is but the latest of the escalating number of decisions that are making this tribunal increasingly irrelevant in the protection of individual rights, and that are requiring other tribunals to shoulder the burden. "There is hope, however, that in time this or some later Court will restore these precious freedoms to their rightful place as a primary protection for our citizens against overreaching officialdom."

I dissent.

JUSTICE STEVENS, dissenting.

The Court concludes its opinion with a carefully phrased statement of its holding: "We hold today that a suspect who has once responded to unwarned yet uncoercive questioning is not thereby disabled from waiving his rights and confessing after he has been given the requisite *Miranda* warnings."

I find nothing objectionable in such a holding. Moreover, because the Court expressly endorses the "bright-line rule of *Miranda*," which conclusively presumes that incriminating statements obtained from a suspect in custody without administering the required warnings are the product of compulsion, and because the Court places so much emphasis on the special facts of this case, I am persuaded that the Court intends its holding to apply only to a narrow category of cases in which the initial questioning of the suspect was made in a totally uncoercive setting and in which the first confession obviously had no influence on the second. I nevertheless dissent because even such a narrowly confined exception is inconsistent with the Court's prior cases, because the attempt to identify its boundaries in future cases will breed confusion and uncertainty in the administration of criminal justice, and because it denigrates the importance of one of the core constitutional rights that protects every American citizen from the kind of tyranny that has flourished in other societies.

I

The desire to achieve a just result in this particular case has produced an opinion that is somewhat opaque and internally inconsistent. If I read it correctly, its conclusion rests on two untenable premises: (1) that the respondent's first confession was not the product of coercion; and (2) that no constitutional right was violated when respondent was questioned in a tranquil, domestic setting.

Even before *Miranda* it had been recognized that police interrogation of a suspect who has been taken into custody is presumptively coercive. That presumption had its greatest force when the questioning occurred in a police station, when it was prolonged, and when there was evidence that the prisoner had suffered physical injury. To rebut the presumption, the prosecutor had the burden of proving the absence of any actual coercion. Because police officers are generally more credible witnesses than prisoners and because it is always difficult for triers of fact to disregard evidence of guilt when addressing a procedural question, more often than not the presumption of coercion afforded only slight protection to the accused.

Miranda clarified the law in three important respects. First, it provided the prosecutor with a simple method of overcoming the presumption of coercion. If the police interrogation is preceded by the warning specified in that opinion, the usual presumption does not attach. Second, it provided an important protection to the accused by making the presumption of coercion irrebuttable if the prescribed warnings are not given. Third, the decision made it clear that a self-incriminatory statement made in response to custodial interrogation was always to be considered "compelled" within the meaning of the Fifth Amendment to the Federal Constitution if the interrogation had not been preceded by appropriate warnings. Thus the irrebuttable presumption of coercion that applies to such a self-incriminatory statement, like a finding of actual coercion, renders the resulting confession inadmissible as a matter of federal constitutional law.

In my opinion, the Court's attempt to fashion a distinction between actual coercion "by physical violence or other deliberate means calculated to break the suspect's will," and irrebuttably presumed coercion cannot succeed. The presumption is only legitimate if it is assumed that there is always a coercive aspect to custodial interrogation that is not preceded by adequate advice of the constitutional right to remain silent. Although I would not support it, I could understand a rule that refused to apply the presumption unless the interrogation took place in an especially coercive setting — perhaps only in the police station itself — but if the presumption arises whenever the accused has been taken into custody or his freedom has been restrained in any significant way, it will surely be futile to try to develop subcategories of custodial interrogation.[10] Indeed, a major purpose of treating the presumption of coercion as irrebuttable is to avoid the kind of fact-bound inquiry that today's decision will surely engender.

As I read the Court's opinion, it expressly accepts the proposition that routine *Miranda* warnings will not be sufficient to overcome the presumption of coercion and thereby make a second confession admissible when an earlier confession is tainted by coercion "by physical violence or other deliberate means calculated to break the suspect's will." Even in such a case, however, it is not necessary to assume that the earlier confession will always "effectively immunize" a later voluntary confession. But surely the fact that an earlier confession was obtained by unlawful methods should add force to the presumption of coercion that attaches to subsequent custodial interrogation and should require the prosecutor to shoulder a heavier burden of rebuttal than in a routine case. Simple logic, as well as the interest in not providing an affirmative incentive to police misconduct, requires that result. I see no reason why the violation of a rule that is as well recognized and

---

[10] Of course, in *Orozco* this Court rejected the contention that *Miranda* warnings were inapplicable because a defendant "was interrogated on his own bed, in familiar surrounds."

easily administered as the duty to give *Miranda* warnings should not also impose an additional burden on the prosecutor.[13] If we are faithful to the holding in *Miranda* itself, when we are considering the admissibility of evidence in the prosecutor's case in chief, we should not try to fashion a distinction between police misconduct that warrants a finding of actual coercion and police misconduct that establishes an irrebuttable presumption of coercion.

II

For me, the most disturbing aspect of the Court's opinion is its somewhat opaque characterization of the police misconduct in this case. The Court appears ambivalent on the question whether there was any constitutional violation.[14] This ambivalence is either disingenuous or completely lawless. This Court's power to require state courts to exclude probative self-incriminatory statements rests entirely on the premise that the use of such evidence violates the Federal Constitution. The same constitutional analysis applies whether the custodial interrogation is actually coercive or irrebuttably presumed to be coercive. If the Court does not accept that premise, it must regard the holding in the *Miranda* case itself, as well as all of the federal jurisprudence that has evolved from that decision, as nothing more than an illegitimate exercise of raw judicial power. If the Court accepts the proposition that respondent's self-incriminatory statement was inadmissible, it must also acknowledge that the Federal Constitution protected him from custodial police interrogation without first being advised of his right to remain silent.

Indeed, the Court's holding rests on its view that there were no "improper tactics in obtaining the initial statement."

The source of respondent's constitutional protection is the Fifth Amendment's privilege against compelled self-incrimination that is secured against state invasion by the Due Process Clause of the Fourteenth Amendment. Like many other provisions of the Bill of Rights, that provision is merely a procedural safeguard. It is, however, the specific provision that protects all citizens from the kind of custodial interrogation that was once employed by the Star Chamber, by "the Germans of the 1930's and early 1940's," and by some of our own police departments only a few decades ago. Custodial interrogation that violates that provision of the Bill of Rights is a classic example of a violation of a constitutional right.

I respectfully dissent.

---

[13] I am not persuaded that the *Miranda* rule is so "murky," that the law enforcement profession would be unable to identify the cases in which a supplementary warning would be appropriate. *Miranda* was written, in part, "to give concrete constitutional guidelines for law enforcement agencies and courts to follow." Nearly two decades after the disposition, it is undisputed that the *Miranda* rule — now so deeply embedded in our culture that most school children know not only the warnings, but also when they required — has given that clarity.

[14] Indeed, the Court's holding rests on its view that there were no "improper tactics in obtaining the initial statement."

QUESTIONS AND NOTES

1.   Do you believe that Elstad was in custody at the time of his initial confession?

2.   If the answer to Question 1 is even arguably "no," might that have influenced the Court's decision?

3.   Is *Elstad* an unfortunate decision because it blurs *Miranda's* bright lines?

4.   Would (should) *Elstad* have been different if the police had referred to his earlier confession to overcome his reluctance to give a post-*Miranda*-warning confession?

5.   Do Stevens and Brennan differ in their respective readings of the Court's opinion? To the extent that they do, whose reading is more accurate? Why?

6.   Given the opening two sentences of Justice Stevens' opinion, why did he dissent?

7.   According to the dissents, what more should the police have done to render Elstad's second confession admissible? Why wasn't this required by the majority?

8.   Is *Elstad* likely to encourage police to ignore *Miranda*? If so, is that an unmitigated evil?

9.   In *Seibert* and *Patane*, neither of which could garner an opinion of the Court, the Court's center came out right down the middle.

MISSOURI v. SEIBERT
542 U.S. 600 (2004)

JUSTICE SOUTER announced the judgment of the Court and delivered an opinion, in which JUSTICE STEVENS, JUSTICE GINSBURG, and JUSTICE BREYER join.

This case tests a police protocol for custodial interrogation that calls for giving no warnings of the rights to silence and counsel until interrogation has produced a confession. Although such a statement is generally inadmissible, since taken in violation of *Miranda*, the interrogating officer follows it with *Miranda* warnings and then leads the suspect to cover the same ground a second time. The question here is the admissibility of the repeated statement. Because this midstream recitation of warnings after interrogation and unwarned confession could not effectively comply with *Miranda's* constitutional requirement, we hold that a statement repeated after a warning in such circumstances is inadmissible.

I

Respondent Patrice Seibert's 12-year-old son Jonathan had cerebral palsy, and when he died in his sleep she feared charges of neglect because of bedsores on his body. In her presence, two of her teenage sons and two of their friends devised a plan to conceal the facts surrounding Jonathan's death by incinerating his body in the course of burning the family's mobile home, in which they planned to leave Donald Rector, a mentally ill teenager living with the family, to avoid any appearance that Jonathan had been unattended. Seibert's son Darian and a friend set the fire, and Donald died.

Five days later, the police awakened Seibert at 3 a.m. at a hospital where Darian was being treated for burns. In arresting her, Officer Kevin Clinton followed instructions from Rolla, Missouri, officer Richard Hanrahan that he refrain from giving *Miranda* warnings. After Seibert had been taken to the police station and left alone in an interview room for 15 to 20 minutes, Hanrahan questioned her without *Miranda* warnings for 30 to 40 minutes, squeezing her arm and repeating "Donald was also to die in his sleep." After Seibert finally admitted she knew Donald was meant to die in the fire, she was given a 20-minute coffee and cigarette break. Officer Hanrahan then turned on a tape recorder, gave Seibert the *Miranda* warnings, and obtained a signed waiver of rights from her. He resumed the questioning with "Ok, 'trice, we've been talking for a little while about what happened on Wednesday the twelfth, haven't we?," and confronted her with her prewarning statements:

Hanrahan: "Now, in discussion you told us, you told us that there was a[n] understanding about Donald."

Seibert: "Yes."

Hanrahan: "Did that take place earlier that morning?"

Seibert: "Yes."

Hanrahan: "And what was the understanding about Donald?"

Seibert: "If they could get him out of the trailer, to take him out of the trailer."

Hanrahan: "And if they couldn't?"

Seibert: "I, I never even thought about it. I just figured they would."

Hanrahan: " 'Trice, didn't you tell me that he was supposed to die in his sleep?"

Seibert: "If that would happen, 'cause he was on that new medicine, you know . . ."

Hanrahan: "The Prozac? And it makes him sleepy. So he was supposed to die in his sleep?"

Seibert: "Yes."

After being charged with first-degree murder for her role in Donald's death, Seibert sought to exclude both her prewarning and postwarning statements. At the suppression hearing, Officer Hanrahan testified that he made a "conscious decision" to withhold *Miranda* warnings, thus resorting to an interrogation technique he had been taught: question first, then give the warnings, and then repeat the question "until I get the answer that she's already provided once." He acknowledged that Seibert's ultimate statement was "largely a repeat of information . . . obtained" prior to the warning.

The trial court suppressed the prewarning statement but admitted the responses given after the *Miranda* recitation. A jury convicted Seibert of second-degree murder.

II

In *Miranda*, we explained that the "voluntariness doctrine in the state cases . . . encompasses all interrogation practices which are likely to exert such pressure upon an individual as to disable him from making a free and rational choice." We appreciated the difficulty of judicial enquiry post hoc into the circumstances of a police interrogation and recognized that "the coercion inherent in custodial interrogation blurs the line between voluntary and involuntary statements, and thus heightens the risk" that the privilege against self-incrimination will not be observed. Hence our concern that the "traditional totality-of-the-circumstances" test posed an "unacceptably great" risk that involuntary custodial confessions would escape detection.

III

There are those, of course, who preferred the old way of doing things, giving no warnings and litigating the voluntariness of any statement in nearly every instance. In the aftermath of *Miranda*, Congress even passed a statute seeking to restore that old regime, 18 U.S.C. § 3501, although the Act lay dormant for years until finally invoked and challenged in *Dickerson*. *Dickerson* reaffirmed *Miranda* and held that its constitutional character prevailed against the statute.

The technique of interrogating in successive, unwarned and warned phases raises a new challenge to *Miranda*. Although we have no statistics on the frequency of this practice, it is not confined to Rolla, Missouri. An officer of that police department testified that the strategy of withholding Miranda warnings until after interrogating and drawing out a confession was promoted not only by his own department, but by a national police training organization and other departments in which he had worked. Consistently with the officer's testimony, the Police Law Institute, for example, instructs that "officers may conduct a two-stage interrogation . . . . At any point during the pre-*Miranda* interrogation, usually after arrestees have confessed, officers may then read the *Miranda* warnings and ask for a waiver. If the arrestees waive their *Miranda* rights, officers will be able to repeat any subsequent incriminating statements later in court." The upshot of all this advice is a question-first practice of some popularity, as one can see from the reported cases describing its use, sometimes in obedience to departmental policy.

IV

When a confession so obtained is offered and challenged, attention must be paid to the conflicting objects of Miranda and question-first. Miranda addressed "interrogation practices . . . likely . . . to disable [an individual] from making a free and rational choice" about speaking, and held that a suspect must be "adequately and effectively" advised of the choice the Constitution guarantees. The object of question-first is to render *Miranda* warnings ineffective by waiting for a particularly opportune time to give them, after the suspect has already confessed.

"The inquiry is simply whether the warnings reasonably 'conve[y] to [a suspect] his rights as required by *Miranda*.'" *Duckworth v. Eagan*. The threshold issue when interrogators question first and warn later is thus whether it would be reasonable to find that in these circumstances the warnings could function "effectively" as *Miranda* requires. Could the warnings effectively advise the suspect that he had a real choice about giving an admissible statement at that juncture? Could they reasonably convey that he could choose to stop talking even if he had talked earlier? For unless the warnings could place a suspect who has just been interrogated in a position to make such an informed choice, there is no practical justification for accepting the formal warnings as compliance with *Miranda*, or for treating the second stage of interrogation as distinct from the first, unwarned and inadmissible segment.[4]

There is no doubt about the answer that proponents of question-first give to this question about the effectiveness of warnings given only after successful interrogation, and we think their answer is correct. By any objective measure, applied to circumstances exemplified here, it is likely that if the interrogators employ the technique of withholding warnings until after interrogation succeeds in eliciting a confession, the warnings will be ineffective in preparing the suspect for successive interrogation, close in time and similar in content. After all, the reason that question-first is catching on is as obvious as its manifest purpose, which is to get a confession the suspect would not make if he understood his rights at the outset; the sensible underlying assumption is that with one confession in hand before the warnings, the interrogator can count on getting its duplicate, with trifling additional trouble. Upon hearing warnings only in the aftermath of interrogation and just after making a confession, a suspect would hardly think he had a genuine right to remain silent, let alone persist in so believing once the police began to lead him over the same ground again.[5] A more likely reaction on a suspect's part would be perplexity about the reason for discussing rights at that point, bewilderment being an unpromising frame of mind for knowledgeable decision. What is worse, telling a

---

[4] Respondent Seibert argues that her second confession should be excluded from evidence under the doctrine known by the metaphor of the "fruit of the poisonous tree," developed in the Fourth Amendment context in *Wong Sun*: evidence otherwise admissible but discovered as a result of an earlier violation is excluded as tainted, lest the law encourage future violations. But the Court in *Elstad* rejected the *Wong Sun* fruits doctrine for analyzing the admissibility of a subsequent warned confession following "an initial failure . . . to administer the warnings required by *Miranda*. In *Elstad*, "a simple failure to administer the warnings, unaccompanied by any actual coercion or other circumstances calculated to undermine the suspect's ability to exercise his free will" did not "so tain[t] the investigatory process that a subsequent voluntary and informed waiver is ineffective for some indeterminate period. Though *Miranda* requires that the unwarned admission must be suppressed, the admissibility of any subsequent statement should turn in these circumstances solely on whether it is knowingly and voluntarily made." *Elstad* held that "a suspect who has once responded to unwarned yet uncoercive questioning is not thereby disabled from waiving his rights and confessing after he has been given the requisite *Miranda* warnings." In a sequential confession case, clarity is served if the later confession is approached by asking whether in the circumstances the *Miranda* warnings given could reasonably be found effective. If yes, a court can take up the standard issues of voluntary waiver and voluntary statement; if no, the subsequent statement is inadmissible for want of adequate *Miranda* warnings, because the earlier and later statements are realistically seen as parts of a single, unwarned sequence of questioning.

[5] It bears emphasizing that the effectiveness *Miranda* assumes the warnings can have must potentially extend through the repeated interrogation, since a suspect has a right to stop at any time. It seems highly unlikely that a suspect could retain any such understanding when the interrogator leads him a second time through a line of questioning the suspect has already answered fully. The point is not that a later unknowing or involuntary confession cancels out an earlier, adequate warning; the point is that the warning is unlikely to be effective in the question-first sequence we have described.

suspect that "anything you say can and will be used against you," without expressly excepting the statement just given, could lead to an entirely reasonable inference that what he has just said will be used, with subsequent silence being of no avail. Thus, when *Miranda* warnings are inserted in the midst of coordinated and continuing interrogation, they are likely to mislead and "depriv[e] a defendant of knowledge essential to his ability to understand the nature of his rights and the consequences of abandoning them." *Moran v. Burbine*, 475 U.S. 412, 424 (1986). By the same token, it would ordinarily be unrealistic to treat two spates of integrated and proximately conducted questioning as independent interrogations subject to independent evaluation simply because *Miranda* warnings formally punctuate them in the middle.

V

Missouri argues that a confession repeated at the end of an interrogation sequence envisioned in a question-first strategy is admissible on the authority of *Elstad*, but the argument disfigures that case. In *Elstad*, the police went to the young suspect's house to take him into custody on a charge of burglary. Before the arrest, one officer spoke with the suspect's mother, while the other one joined the suspect in a "brief stop in the living room," where the officer said he "felt" the young man was involved in a burglary. The suspect acknowledged he had been at the scene. This Court noted that the pause in the living room "was not to interrogate the suspect but to notify his mother of the reason for his arrest," and described the incident as having "none of the earmarks of coercion." The Court, indeed, took care to mention that the officer's initial failure to warn was an "oversight" that "may have been the result of confusion as to whether the brief exchange qualified as 'custodial interrogation' or . . . may simply have reflected . . . reluctance to initiate an alarming police procedure before [an officer] had spoken with respondent's mother." At the outset of a later and systematic station house interrogation going well beyond the scope of the laconic prior admission, the suspect was given *Miranda* warnings and made a full confession. In holding the second statement admissible and voluntary, *Elstad* rejected the "cat out of the bag" theory that any short, earlier admission, obtained in arguably innocent neglect of *Miranda*, determined the character of the later, warned confession; on the facts of that case, the Court thought any causal connection between the first and second responses to the police was "speculative and attenuated." Although the *Elstad* Court expressed no explicit conclusion about either officer's state of mind, it is fair to read *Elstad* as treating the living room conversation as a good-faith *Miranda* mistake, not only open to correction by careful warnings before systematic questioning in that particular case, but posing no threat to warn-first practice generally.

The contrast between *Elstad* and this case reveals a series of relevant facts that bear on whether *Miranda* warnings delivered midstream could be effective enough to accomplish their object: the completeness and detail of the questions and answers in the first round of interrogation, the overlapping content of the two statements, the timing and setting of the first and the second, the continuity of police personnel, and the degree to which the interrogator's questions treated the second round as continuous with the first. In *Elstad*, it was not unreasonable to see the occasion for questioning at the station house as presenting a markedly different experience from the short conversation at home; since a reasonable person in the suspect's shoes could have seen the station house questioning as a new and distinct experience, the *Miranda* warnings could have made sense as presenting a genuine choice whether to follow up on the earlier admission.

At the opposite extreme are the facts here, which by any objective measure reveal a police strategy adapted to undermine the *Miranda* warnings.[6] The unwarned interrogation was conducted in the station house, and the questioning was systematic, exhaustive, and managed with psychological skill. When the police were finished there was little, if anything, of incriminating potential left unsaid. The warned phase of questioning proceeded after a pause of only 15 to 20 minutes, in the same place as the unwarned segment. When the same officer who had conducted the first phase recited the *Miranda* warnings, he said nothing to counter the probable misimpression that the advice that anything Seibert said could be used against her also applied to the details of the inculpatory statement previously elicited. In particular, the police did not advise that her prior statement could not be used.[7] Nothing was said or done to dispel the oddity of warning about legal rights to silence and counsel right after the police had led her through a systematic interrogation, and any uncertainty on her part about a right to stop talking about matters previously discussed would only have been aggravated by the way Officer Hanrahan set the scene by saying "we've been talking for a little while about what happened on Wednesday the twelfth, haven't we?" The impression that the further questioning was a mere continuation of the earlier questions and responses was fostered by references back to the confession already given. It would have been reasonable to regard the two sessions as parts of a continuum, in which it would have been unnatural to refuse to repeat at the second stage what had been said before. These circumstances must be seen as challenging the comprehensibility and efficacy of the *Miranda* warnings to the point that a reasonable person in the suspect's shoes would not have understood them to convey a message that she retained a choice about continuing to talk.[8]

VI

Strategists dedicated to draining the substance out of *Miranda* cannot accomplish by training instructions what *Dickerson* held Congress could not do by statute. Because the question-first tactic effectively threatens to thwart *Miranda's* purpose of reducing the risk that a coerced confession would be admitted, and because the facts here do not reasonably support a conclusion that the warnings given could have served their purpose, Seibert's postwarning statements are

---

[6] Because the intent of the officer will rarely be as candidly admitted as it was here (even as it is likely to determine the conduct of the interrogation), the focus is on facts apart from intent that show the question-first tactic at work.

[7] We do not hold that a formal addendum warning that a previous statement could not be used would be sufficient to change the character of the question-first procedure to the point of rendering an ensuing statement admissible, but its absence is clearly a factor that blunts the efficacy of the warnings and points to a continuing, not a new, interrogation.

[8] Because we find that the warnings were inadequate, there is no need to assess the actual voluntariness of the statement.

inadmissible. The judgment of the Supreme Court of Missouri is affirmed.

It is so ordered.

JUSTICE BREYER, concurring.

In my view, the following simple rule should apply to the two-stage interrogation technique: Courts should exclude the "fruits" of the initial unwarned questioning unless the failure to warn was in good faith. *Cf. Oregon v. Elstad; United States v. Leon.* I believe this is a sound and workable approach to the problem this case presents. Prosecutors and judges have long understood how to apply the "fruits" approach, which they use in other areas of law. *See Wong Sun v. United States.* And in the workaday world of criminal law enforcement the administrative simplicity of the familiar has significant advantages over a more complex exclusionary rule.

I believe the plurality's approach in practice will function as a "fruits" test. The truly "effective" *Miranda* warnings on which the plurality insists will occur only when certain circumstances — a lapse in time, a change in location or interrogating officer, or a shift in the focus of the questioning — intervene between the unwarned questioning and any postwarning statement. *Cf. Taylor v. Alabama,* (evidence obtained subsequent to a constitutional violation must be suppressed as "fruit of the poisonous tree" unless "intervening events break the causal connection").

I consequently join the plurality's opinion in full. I also agree with Justice KENNEDY's opinion insofar as it is consistent with this approach and makes clear that a good-faith exception applies.

JUSTICE KENNEDY, concurring in the judgment.

The interrogation technique used in this case is designed to circumvent *Miranda.* It undermines the *Miranda* warning and obscures its meaning. The plurality opinion is correct to conclude that statements obtained through the use of this technique are inadmissible. Although I agree with much in the careful and convincing opinion for the plurality, my approach does differ in some respects, requiring this separate statement.

The *Miranda* rule has become an important and accepted element of the criminal justice system. *See Dickerson.* At the same time, not every violation of the rule requires suppression of the evidence obtained. Evidence is admissible when the central concerns of *Miranda* are not likely to be implicated and when other objectives of the criminal justice system are best served by its introduction. Thus, we have held that statements obtained in violation of the rule can be used for impeachment, so that the truth finding function of the trial is not distorted by the defense, *see Harris v. New York,* that there is an exception to protect countervailing concerns of public safety, *see New York v. Quarles*; and that physical evidence obtained in reliance on statements taken in violation of the rule is admissible, *see United States v. Patane.* These cases, in my view, are correct. They recognize that admission of evidence is proper when it would further important objectives without compromising Miranda's central concerns. Under these precedents, the scope of the *Miranda* suppression remedy depends on a consideration of those legitimate interests and on whether admission of the evidence under the circumstances would frustrate *Miranda's* central concerns and objectives.

Elstad reflects this approach. In *Elstad*, a suspect made an initial incriminating statement at his home. The suspect had not received a *Miranda* warning before making the statement, apparently because it was not clear whether the suspect was in custody at the time. The suspect was taken to the station house, where he received a proper warning, waived his *Miranda* rights, and made a second statement. He later argued that the postwarning statement should be suppressed because it was related to the unwarned first statement, and likely induced or caused by it. The Court held that, although a *Miranda* violation made the first statement inadmissible, the postwarning statements could be introduced against the accused because "neither the general goal of deterring improper police conduct nor the Fifth Amendment goal of assuring trustworthy evidence would be served by suppression" given the facts of that case.

In my view, *Elstad* was correct in its reasoning and its result. *Elstad* reflects a balanced and pragmatic approach to enforcement of the *Miranda* warning. An officer may not realize that a suspect is in custody and warnings are required. The officer may not plan to question the suspect or may be waiting for a more appropriate time. Skilled investigators often interview suspects multiple times, and good police work may involve referring to prior statements to test their veracity or to refresh recollection. In light of these realities it would be extravagant to treat the presence of one statement that cannot be admitted under *Miranda* as sufficient reason to prohibit subsequent statements preceded by a proper warning. *See Elstad*, ("It is an unwarranted extension of *Miranda* to hold that a simple failure to administer the warnings . . . so taints the investigatory process that a subsequent voluntary and informed waiver is ineffective for some indeterminate period"). That approach would serve "neither the general goal of deterring improper police conduct nor the Fifth Amendment goal of assuring trustworthy evidence would be served by suppression of the . . . testimony."

This case presents different considerations. The police used a two-step questioning technique based on a deliberate violation of *Miranda*. The *Miranda* warning was withheld to obscure both the practical and legal significance of the admonition when finally given. As Justice SOUTER points out, the two-step technique permits the accused to conclude that the right not to respond did not exist when the earlier incriminating statements were made. The strategy is based on the assumption that *Miranda* warnings will tend to mean less when recited midinterrogation, after inculpatory statements have already been obtained. This tactic relies on an intentional misrepresentation of the protection that *Miranda* offers and does not serve any legitimate objectives that might otherwise justify its use.

Further, the interrogating officer here relied on the defendant's prewarning statement to obtain the postwarning statement used against her at trial. The postwarning interview resembled a cross-examination. The officer confronted the defendant with her inadmissible prewarning statements and pushed her to acknowledge them. (" 'Trice, didn't you tell me that he was supposed to die in his sleep?' "). This shows the temptations for abuse inherent in the two-step technique. Reference to the prewarning statement was an implicit suggestion that the mere repetition of the earlier statement was not independently incriminating. The implicit suggestion was false.

The technique used in this case distorts the meaning of *Miranda* and furthers no legitimate countervailing interest. The *Miranda* rule would be frustrated were we to allow police to undermine its meaning and effect. The technique simply creates too high a risk that postwarning statements will be obtained when a suspect was deprived of "knowledge essential to his ability to understand the nature of his rights and the consequences of abandoning them." When an interrogator uses this deliberate, two-step strategy, predicated upon violating *Miranda* during an extended interview, postwarning statements that are related to the substance of prewarning statements must be excluded absent specific, curative steps.

The plurality concludes that whenever a two-stage interview occurs, admissibility of the postwarning statement should depend on "whether the *Miranda* warnings delivered midstream could have been effective enough to accomplish their object" given the specific facts of the case. This test envisions an objective inquiry from the perspective of the suspect, and applies in the case of both intentional and unintentional two-stage interrogations. In my view, this test cuts too broadly. *Miranda's* clarity is one of its strengths, and a multifactor test that applies to every two-stage interrogation may serve to undermine that clarity. I would apply a narrower test applicable only in the infrequent case, such as we have here, in which the two-step interrogation technique was used in a calculated way to undermine the *Miranda* warning.

The admissibility of postwarning statements should continue to be governed by the principles of Elstad unless the deliberate two-step strategy was employed. If the deliberate two-step strategy has been used, postwarning statements that are related to the substance of prewarning statements must be excluded unless curative measures are taken before the postwarning statement is made. Curative measures should be designed to ensure that a reasonable person in the suspect's situation would understand the import and effect of the *Miranda* warning and of the *Miranda* waiver. For example, a substantial break in time and circumstances between the prewarning statement and the *Miranda* warning may suffice in most circumstances, as it allows the accused to distinguish the two contexts and appreciate that the interrogation has taken a new turn. *Cf. Westover v. United States*, decided with *Miranda*. Alternatively, an additional warning that explains the likely inadmissibility of the prewarning custodial statement may be sufficient. No curative steps were taken in this case, however, so the postwarning statements are inadmissible and the conviction cannot stand. For these reasons, I concur in the judgment of the Court.

JUSTICE O'CONNOR, with whom THE CHIEF JUSTICE, JUSTICE SCALIA, and JUSTICE THOMAS join, dissenting.

The plurality devours *Oregon v. Elstad* even as it accuses petitioner's argument of "disfigur[ing]" that decision. I believe that we are bound by *Elstad* to reach a different result, and I would vacate the judgment of the Supreme Court of Missouri.

I

On two preliminary questions I am in full agreement with the plurality. First, the plurality appropriately follows *Elstad* in concluding that Seibert's statement cannot be held inadmissible under a "fruit of the poisonous tree" theory. Second, the plurality correctly declines to focus its analysis on the subjective intent of the interrogating officer.

A

This Court has made clear that there simply is no place for a robust deterrence doctrine with regard to violations of *Miranda*. Consistent with that view, the Court today refuses to apply the traditional "fruits" analysis to the physical fruit of a claimed *Miranda* violation. *Patane*. The plurality correctly refuses to apply a similar analysis to testimonial fruits.

Although the analysis the plurality ultimately espouses examines the same facts and circumstances that a "fruits" analysis would consider (such as the lapse of time between the two interrogations and change of questioner or location), it does so for entirely different reasons. The fruits analysis would examine those factors because they are relevant to the balance of deterrence value versus the "drastic and socially costly course" of excluding reliable evidence. The plurality, by contrast, looks to those factors to inform the psychological judgment regarding whether the suspect has been informed effectively of her right to remain silent. The analytical underpinnings of the two approaches are thus entirely distinct, and they should not be conflated just because they function similarly in practice.

B

The plurality's rejection of an intent-based test is also, in my view, correct. Freedom from compulsion lies at the heart of the Fifth Amendment, and requires us to assess whether a suspect's decision to speak truly was voluntary. Because voluntariness is a matter of the suspect's state of mind, we focus our analysis on the way in which suspects experience interrogation.

Thoughts kept inside a police officer's head cannot affect that experience. A suspect who experienced the exact same interrogation as Seibert, save for a difference in the undivulged, subjective intent of the interrogating officer when he failed to give *Miranda* warnings, would not experience the interrogation any differently. "[W]hether intentional or inadvertent, the state of mind of the police is irrelevant to the question of the intelligence and voluntariness of respondent's election to abandon his rights. Although highly inappropriate, even deliberate deception of an attorney could not possibly affect a suspect's decision to waive his *Miranda* rights unless he were at least aware of the incident."

Because the isolated fact of Officer Hanrahan's intent could not have had any bearing on Seibert's "capacity to comprehend and knowingly relinquish" her right to remain silent it could not by itself affect the voluntariness of her confession. Moreover, recognizing an exception to *Elstad* for intentional violations would require focusing constitutional analysis on a police officer's subjective intent, an unattractive proposition that we all but uniformly avoid. In general, "we believe that 'sending state and federal courts on an expedition into the minds of police officers would produce a grave and fruitless misallocation of judicial resources.' " This case presents the uncommonly straightforward circumstance of an officer openly admitting that the violation was intentional. But the inquiry will be complicated in other situations probably more likely to occur. For example, different officers involved in an interrogation might claim different states of mind regarding the failure to give *Miranda* warnings. Even in the simple case of a single officer who claims that a failure to give *Miranda* warnings was inadvertent, the likelihood of error will be high.

These evidentiary difficulties have led us to reject an intent-based test in several criminal procedure contexts. For example, in *New York v. Quarles* one of the factors that led us to reject an inquiry into the subjective intent of the police officer in crafting a test for the "public safety" exception to *Miranda* was that officers' motives will be "largely unverifiable." Similarly, our opinion in *Whren v. United States* made clear that "the evidentiary difficulty of establishing subjective intent" was one of the reasons (albeit not the principal one) for refusing to consider intent in Fourth Amendment challenges generally.

For these reasons, I believe that the approach espoused by Justice KENNEDY is ill advised. Justice KENNEDY would extend *Miranda's* exclusionary rule to any case in which the use of the "two-step interrogation technique" was "deliberate" or "calculated." This approach untethers the analysis from facts knowable to, and therefore having any potential directly to affect, the suspect. Far from promoting "clarity," the approach will add a third step to the suppression inquiry. In virtually every two-stage interrogation case, in addition to addressing the standard *Miranda* and voluntariness questions, courts will be forced to conduct the kind of difficult, state-of-mind inquiry that we normally take pains to avoid.

II

The plurality's adherence to *Elstad*, and mine to the plurality, end there. Our decision in *Elstad* rejected two lines of argument advanced in favor of suppression. The first was based on the "fruit of the poisonous tree" doctrine, discussed above. The second was the argument that the "lingering compulsion" inherent in a defendant's having let the "cat out of the bag" required suppression.

The plurality might very well think that we struck the balance between Fifth Amendment rights and law enforcement interests incorrectly in *Elstad*; but that is not normally a sufficient reason for ignoring the dictates of *stare decisis*.

I would analyze the two-step interrogation procedure under the voluntariness standards central to the Fifth Amendment and reiterated in *Elstad*. *Elstad* commands that if Seibert's first statement is shown to have been involuntary, the court must examine whether the taint dissipated through the passing of time or a change in circumstances: "When a prior statement is actually coerced, the time that passes between confessions, the change in place of interrogations, and the change in identity of the interrogators all bear on whether that coercion has carried over into the second confession." In addition, Seibert's second statement should be suppressed if she showed that it was involuntary despite the *Miranda* warnings. Although I would leave this analysis for the Missouri courts to conduct on remand, I note that, unlike the officers in *Elstad*, Officer Hanrahan referred to Seibert's unwarned statement during the second part of the interrogation when she made a statement at odds with her unwarned confession. (" 'Trice, didn't you tell me that he was supposed to die in his sleep?' "); *cf. Elstad* (officers did not "exploit the unwarned admission to pressure respondent into waiving his right to remain silent"). Such a tactic may bear on the voluntariness inquiry.

* * *

Because I believe that the plurality gives insufficient deference to *Elstad* and that Justice KENNEDY places improper weight on subjective intent, I respectfully dissent.

QUESTIONS AND NOTES

1.   According to the plurality, is this case about the adequacy of Seibert's first *Miranda* warning or is it about the fruit of her original unwarned confession? What would Justice Breyer say?

2.   Should it matter whether the officer deliberately conducted custodial interrogation without the benefit of *Miranda*? What would Souter say? What would Kennedy say? What would O'Connor say? What is the law of the case?

3.   Does the majority give insufficient weight to *Elstad*? Explain.

4.   Does the dissent give insufficient weight to *Miranda*? Explain.

5.   Is *Elstad* still good law after *Seibert*? Should it be?

6.   In the companion *Patane* case, the Court considered specifically the issue raised by O'Connor in *Quarles*.

UNITED STATES v. PATANE
542 U.S. 630 (2004)

JUSTICE THOMAS announced the judgment of the Court and delivered an opinion, in which THE CHIEF JUSTICE and JUSTICE SCALIA join.

In this case we must decide whether a failure to give a suspect the warnings prescribed by *Miranda*, requires suppression of the physical fruits of the suspect's unwarned but voluntary statements. Because the *Miranda* rule protects against violations of the Self-Incrimination Clause, which, in turn, is not implicated by the introduction at trial of physical evidence resulting from voluntary statements, we answer the question presented in the negative.

I

In June 2001, respondent, Samuel Francis Patane, was arrested for harassing his ex-girlfriend, Linda O'Donnell. He was released on bond, subject to a temporary restraining order that prohibited him from contacting O'Donnell. Respondent apparently violated the restraining order by attempting to telephone O'Donnell. On June 6, 2001, Officer Tracy Fox of the Colorado Springs Police Department began to investigate the matter. On the same day, a county probation officer informed an agent of the Bureau of Alcohol, Tobacco, and Firearms (ATF), that respondent, a convicted felon, illegally possessed a .40 Glock pistol. The ATF relayed this information to Detective Josh Benner, who worked closely with the ATF. Together, Detective Benner and Officer Fox proceeded to respondent's residence.

After reaching the residence and inquiring into respondent's attempts to contact O'Donnell, Officer Fox arrested respondent for violating the restraining order. Detective Benner attempted to advise respondent of his Miranda rights but got no further than the right to remain silent. At that point, respondent interrupted, asserting that he knew his rights, and neither officer attempted to complete the warning.[9]

Detective Benner then asked respondent about the Glock. Respondent was initially reluctant to discuss the matter, stating: "I am not sure I should tell you anything about the Glock because I don't want you to take it away from me." Detective Benner persisted, and respondent told him that the pistol was in his bedroom. Respondent then gave Detective Benner permission to retrieve the pistol. Detective Benner found the pistol and seized it.

As we explain below, the *Miranda* rule is a prophylactic employed to protect against violations of the Self-Incrimination Clause. The Self-Incrimination Clause, however, is not implicated by the admission into evidence of the physical fruit of a voluntary statement. Accordingly, there is no justification for extending the *Miranda* rule to this context. And just as the Self-Incrimination Clause primarily focuses on the criminal trial, so too does the *Miranda* rule. The *Miranda* rule is not a code of police conduct, and police do not violate the Constitution (or even the *Miranda* rule, for that matter) by mere failures to warn. For this reason, the exclusionary rule articulated in cases such as *Wong Sun* does not apply. Accordingly, we reverse the judgment of the Court of Appeals and remand the case for further proceedings consistent with this opinion.

II

The Self-Incrimination Clause provides: "No person . . . shall be compelled in any criminal case to be a witness against himself." We need not decide here the precise boundaries of the Clause's protection. For present purposes, it suffices to note that the core protection afforded by the Self-Incrimination Clause is a prohibition on compelling a criminal defendant to testify against himself at trial.

To be sure, the Court has recognized and applied several prophylactic rules designed to protect the core privilege against self-incrimination. For example, although the text of the Self-Incrimination Clause at least suggests that "its

---

[9] The Government concedes that respondent's answers to subsequent on-the-scene questioning are inadmissible at trial under *Miranda*, despite the partial warning and respondent's assertions that he knew his rights.

coverage [is limited to] compelled testimony that is used against the defendant in the trial itself," potential suspects may, at times, assert the privilege in proceedings in which answers might be used to incriminate them in a subsequent criminal case.

In *Miranda*, the Court concluded that the possibility of coercion inherent in custodial interrogations unacceptably raises the risk that a suspect's privilege against self-incrimination might be violated. To protect against this danger, the *Miranda* rule creates a presumption of coercion, in the absence of specific warnings, that is generally irrebuttable for purposes of the prosecution's case in chief.

But because these prophylactic rules (including the *Miranda* rule) necessarily sweep beyond the actual protections of the Self-Incrimination Clause, any further extension of these rules must be justified by its necessity for the protection of the actual right against compelled self-incrimination. Indeed, at times the Court has declined to extend *Miranda* even where it has perceived a need to protect the privilege against self-incrimination. *See, e.g., Quarles.*

It is for these reasons that statements taken without *Miranda* warnings (though not actually compelled) can be used to impeach a defendant's testimony at trial, though the fruits of actually compelled testimony cannot. More generally, the *Miranda* rule "does not require that the statements [taken without complying with the rule] and their fruits be discarded as inherently tainted," *Elstad*. Such a blanket suppression rule could not be justified by reference to the "Fifth Amendment goal of assuring trustworthy evidence" or by any deterrence rationale, and would therefore fail our close-fit requirement.

Furthermore, the Self-Incrimination Clause contains its own exclusionary rule. It provides that "[n]o person . . . shall be compelled in any criminal case to be a witness against himself." Unlike the Fourth Amendment's bar on unreasonable searches, the Self-Incrimination Clause is self-executing. We have repeatedly explained "that those subjected to coercive police interrogations have an automatic protection from the use of their involuntary statements (or evidence derived from their statements) in any subsequent criminal trial."

Finally, nothing in *Dickerson*, including its characterization of *Miranda* as announcing a constitutional rule, changes any of these observations. Indeed, in *Dickerson*, the Court specifically noted that the Court's "subsequent cases have reduced the impact of the Miranda rule on legitimate law enforcement while reaffirming [*Miranda*]'s core ruling that unwarned statements may not be used as evidence in the prosecution's case in chief." This description of *Miranda*, especially the emphasis on the use of "unwarned statements . . . in the prosecution's case in chief," makes clear our continued focus on the protections of the Self-Incrimination Clause. The Court's reliance on our *Miranda* precedents, including both *Tucker* and *Elstad*, further demonstrates the continuing validity of those decisions. In short, nothing in *Dickerson* calls into question our continued insistence that the closest possible fit be maintained between the Self-Incrimination Clause and any rule designed to protect it.

III

Our cases also make clear the related point that a mere failure to give *Miranda* warnings does not, by itself, violate a suspect's constitutional rights or even the *Miranda* rule. So much was evident in many of our pre-*Dickerson* cases, and we have adhered to this view since *Dickerson*. *See Chavez*, (plurality opinion) (holding that a failure to read *Miranda* warnings did not violate the respondent's constitutional rights).

It follows that police do not violate a suspect's constitutional rights (or the *Miranda* rule) by negligent or even deliberate failures to provide the suspect with the full panoply of warnings prescribed by *Miranda*. Potential violations occur, if at all, only upon the admission of unwarned statements into evidence at trial. And, at that point, "[t]he exclusion of unwarned statements . . . is a complete and sufficient remedy" for any perceived *Miranda* violation.

Thus, unlike unreasonable searches under the Fourth Amendment or actual violations of the Due Process Clause or the Self-Incrimination Clause, there is, with respect to mere failures to warn, nothing to deter. There is therefore no reason to apply the "fruit of the poisonous tree" doctrine of *Wong Sun*.

IV

Because police cannot violate the Self-Incrimination Clause by taking unwarned though voluntary statements, an exclusionary rule cannot be justified by reference to a deterrence effect on law enforcement, as the Court of Appeals believed. Our decision not to apply *Wong Sun* to mere failures to give *Miranda* warnings was sound at the time *Tucker* and *Elstad* were decided, and we decline to apply *Wong Sun* to such failures now.

The Court of Appeals ascribed significance to the fact that, in this case, there might be "little [practical] difference between [respondent's] confessional statement" and the actual physical evidence. The distinction, the court said, "appears to make little sense as a matter of policy." But, putting policy aside, we have held that "[t]he word 'witness' in the constitutional text limits the" scope of the Self-Incrimination Clause to testimonial evidence. The Constitution itself makes the distinction.[6] And although it is true that the Court requires the exclusion of the physical fruit of actually coerced statements, it must be remembered that statements taken without sufficient Miranda warnings are presumed to have been coerced only for certain purposes and then only when necessary to protect the privilege against self-incrimination. For the reasons discussed above, we decline to extend that presumption further.

Accordingly, we reverse the judgment of the Court of Appeals and remand the case for further proceedings consistent with this opinion.

---

[6] While Fourth Amendment protections extend to "persons, houses, papers, and effects," the Self-Incrimination Clause prohibits only compelling a defendant to be "a witness against himself," Amdt. 5.

JUSTICE KENNEDY, with whom JUSTICE O'CONNOR joins, concurring in the judgment.

In *Elstad*, *Quarles*, and *Harris v. New York*, evidence obtained following an unwarned interrogation was held admissible. This result was based in large part on our recognition that the concerns underlying the *Miranda* rule must be accommodated to other objectives of the criminal justice system. I agree with the plurality that *Dickerson* did not undermine these precedents and, in fact, cited them in support. Here, it is sufficient to note that the Government presents an even stronger case for admitting the evidence obtained as the result of Patane's unwarned statement. Admission of nontestimonial physical fruits (the Glock in this case), even more so than the postwarning statements to the police in *Elstad* and *Tucker*, does not run the risk of admitting into trial an accused's coerced incriminating statements against himself. In light of the important probative value of reliable physical evidence, it is doubtful that exclusion can be justified by a deterrence rationale sensitive to both law enforcement interests and a suspect's rights during an in-custody interrogation. Unlike the plurality, however, I find it unnecessary to decide whether the detective's failure to give Patane the full *Miranda* warnings should be characterized as a violation of the *Miranda* rule itself, or whether there is "[any]thing to deter" so long as the unwarned statements are not later introduced at trial.

With these observations, I concur in the judgment of the Court.

JUSTICE SOUTER, with whom JUSTICE STEVENS and JUSTICE GINSBURG join, dissenting.

The majority repeatedly says that the Fifth Amendment does not address the admissibility of nontestimonial evidence, an overstatement that is beside the point. The issue actually presented today is whether courts should apply the fruit of the poisonous tree doctrine lest we create an incentive for the police to omit *Miranda* warnings, before custodial interrogation.[1] In closing their eyes to the consequences of giving an evidentiary advantage to those who ignore *Miranda*, the majority adds an important inducement for interrogators to ignore the rule in that case.

Miranda rested on insight into the inherently coercive character of custodial interrogation and the inherently difficult exercise of assessing the voluntariness of any confession resulting from it. Unless the police give the prescribed warnings meant to counter the coercive atmosphere, a custodial confession is inadmissible, there being no need for the previous time-consuming and difficult enquiry into voluntariness. That inducement to forestall involuntary statements and troublesome issues of fact can only atrophy if we turn around and recognize an evidentiary benefit when an unwarned statement leads investigators to tangible evidence. There is, of course, a price for excluding evidence, but the Fifth Amendment is worth a price, and in the absence of a very good reason, the logic of *Miranda* should

---

[1] In so saying, we are taking the legal issue as it comes to us, even though the facts give off the scent of a made-up case. If there was a *Miranda* failure, the most immediate reason was that Patane told the police to stop giving the warnings because he already knew his rights. There could easily be an analogy in this case to the bumbling mistake the police committed in *Elstad*.

be followed: a *Miranda* violation raises a presumption of coercion, and the Fifth Amendment privilege against compelled self-incrimination extends to the exclusion of derivative evidence. That should be the end of this case.

The fact that the books contain some exceptions to the *Miranda* exclusionary rule carries no weight here. In *Harris v. New York*, 401 U.S. 222 (1971), it was respect for the integrity of the judicial process that justified the admission of unwarned statements as impeachment evidence. But Patane's suppression motion can hardly be described as seeking to "pervert" *Miranda* "into a license to use perjury" or otherwise handicap the "traditional truth-testing devices of the adversary process." Nor is there any suggestion that the officers' failure to warn Patane was justified or mitigated by a public emergency or other exigent circumstance, as in *Quarles*. And of course the premise of *Elstad* is not on point; although a failure to give *Miranda* warnings before one individual statement does not necessarily bar the admission of a subsequent statement given after adequate warnings, *cf. Missouri v. Seibert*, (plurality opinion), that rule obviously does not apply to physical evidence seized once and for all.[2]

There is no way to read this case except as an unjustifiable invitation to law enforcement officers to flout *Miranda* when there may be physical evidence to be gained. The incentive is an odd one, coming from the Court on the same day it decides *Missouri v. Seibert*. I respectfully dissent.

JUSTICE BREYER, dissenting.

For reasons similar to those set forth in Justice SOUTER's dissent and in my concurring opinion in *Missouri v. Seibert* I would extend to this context the "fruit of the poisonous tree" approach, which I believe the Court has come close to adopting in *Seibert*. Under that approach, courts would exclude physical evidence derived from unwarned questioning unless the failure to provide *Miranda* warnings was in good faith. Because the courts below made no explicit finding as to good or bad faith, I would remand for such a determination.

QUESTIONS AND NOTES

1. Do you think that questioning Patane violated *Miranda*? Why do you suppose that the government conceded the point?

2. If the police did violate *Miranda* do you think that they did so in good faith? Explain.

3. Is the only (primary) purpose of the privilege against self-incrimination to insure trustworthy evidence? If there are other purposes, does Justice Thomas' opinion misweigh the relevant values?

---

[2] To the extent that *Michigan v. Tucker*, 417 U.S. 433, (1974) (admitting the testimony of a witness who was discovered because of an unwarned custodial interrogation), created another exception to *Miranda*, it is off the point here. In *Tucker*, we explicitly declined to lay down a broad rule about the fruits of unwarned statements. Instead, we "place[d] our holding on a narrower ground," relying principally on the fact that the interrogation occurred before *Miranda* was decided and was conducted in good faith according to constitutional standards governing at that time.

4. Do we (should we) care if police officer's flout *Miranda*?

5. Do we (should we) care if the police benefit at the defendant's expense by flouting *Miranda*?

6. Are questions 4 and 5 the same or different questions? Explain

PROBLEM

On Aug. 4, 2009, in San Antonio, Texas, neighbors of Miguel and Rosa Gonzalez heard a loud argument going on at their home. Subsequently the neighbors heard a gunshot. Shortly thereafter, two of the neighbors saw Miguel carrying what appeared to be a dead body, covered with a blanket. Miguel drove off and returned three hours later. The neighbors reported these events to police. After interviewing the neighbors, the police obtained a warrant to arrest Miguel for murder, and another warrant to search his home.

Before entering the Gonzalez home, the two policemen decided among themselves to not give "Miranda" warnings in the hope that an unwarned Gonzalez may be more likely to reveal the location of his wife's body than he would be if he were warned. Thus, they entered his home (after knocking and being greeted by Gonzalez), arrested and handcuffed him. While one policeman guarded the handcuffed Gonzalez on the living room sofa, the other searched the house and found a gun.

About fifteen minutes after the arrest, the following dialogue occurred:

Policeman: Where's your wife's body?

Gonzalez: Do I have to tell you?

Policeman: A good citizen would tell me.

Gonzalez: Ok, I'll show you where it is.

Gonzalez and the officers got in the car, where he led the officers to the body, which was buried near a small obscure lake just south of New Braunfels (about 30 miles north of San Antonio). The officers (and all other relevant state personnel) candidly admitted that they would have never found Rosa Gonzalez's body if Miguel Gonzalez hadn't led them to it.

The State introduced the body at the trial along with the gun, forensic evidence proving that Miguel Gonzalez's gun had fired the fatal shot, and other evidence from the neighbors regarding the day of the shooting. Gonzalez was convicted. His lawyer's contention that the body, and the forensic evidence obtained from it, be excluded as a violation of *Miranda* was rejected. Gonzalez was convicted of murder and sentenced to life imprisonment. The Texas Court of Criminal Appeals affirmed the conviction, and the Supreme Court of the United States granted certiorari on the following question:

"Is the admission of a body, and forensics evidence done on that body, permissible if the body would not have been found but for an intentional violation of *Miranda*"?

Chief Justice Roberts, joined by Justices Scalia, Thomas, and Alito are prepared to answer the certiorari question "yes." Justice Stevens, joined by Justices Ginsburg, Breyer, and Sotomayor are prepared to answer the certiorari question "no." Justice Kennedy is uncertain as to how to vote. He has, however, been told by both Roberts and Stevens that he will be assigned the opinion when he makes up his mind.

Fortunately, he has you for a law clerk. He would like you to advise him as to how he should vote and why. What advice would you give Justice?

PROBLEM
FELLERS v. UNITED STATES

On February 24, 2000, after a grand jury indicted petitioner for conspiracy to distribute methamphetamine, Lincoln Police Sergeant Michael Garnett and Lancaster County Deputy Sheriff Jeff Bliemeister went to petitioner's home in Lincoln, Nebraska, to arrest him. The officers knocked on petitioner's door and, when petitioner answered, identified themselves and asked if they could come in. Petitioner invited the officers into his living room.

The officers advised petitioner they had come to discuss his involvement in methamphetamine distribution. They informed petitioner that they had a federal warrant for his arrest and that a grand jury had indicted him for conspiracy to distribute methamphetamine. The officers told petitioner that the indictment referred to his involvement with certain individuals, four of whom they named. Petitioner then told the officers that he knew the four people and had used methamphetamine during his association with them.

After spending about 15 minutes in petitioner's home, the officers transported petitioner to the Lancaster County jail. There, the officers advised petitioner for the first time of his rights under *Miranda* and *Patterson v. Illinois*. Petitioner and the two officers signed a Miranda waiver form, and petitioner then reiterated the inculpatory statements he had made earlier, admitted to having associated with other individuals implicated in the charged conspiracy and admitted to having loaned money to one of them even though he suspected that she was involved in drug transactions.

Before trial, petitioner moved to suppress the inculpatory statements he made at his home and at the county jail.

Assuming that petitioner's at home statements are inadmissible because of *Massiah* and *Patterson* can his station house statements be admitted? For the Supreme Court's non-answer, see *Fellers v. United States*, 540 U.S. 519 (2004).

Chapter 23

INEVITABLE DISCOVERY

In the preceding Chapter, we focused on the attenuation doctrine. The clearest illustration of attenuation occurs when the source of the evidence is actually and demonstrably independent of the illegality. For example in *Brewer v. Williams*, Chapter 18, *supra*, suppose that when Williams told Detective Leaming where the child's body was buried, Leaming responded: "I know, we found it four hours ago." Under that hypothetical circumstance, the body would, of course, be admissible. In the real world, its admissibility was dependent on whether it would have inevitably been discovered without Williams' post-Christian burial speech statement. In *Nix v. Williams*, the Court resolved that issue:

NIX v. WILLIAMS
467 U.S. 431 (1984)

CHIEF JUSTICE BURGER delivered the opinion of the Court.

We granted certiorari to consider whether, at respondent *Williams'* second murder trial in state court, evidence pertaining to the discovery and condition of the victim's body was properly admitted on the ground that it would ultimately or inevitably have been discovered even if no violation of any constitutional or statutory provision had taken place.

I

Second Trial

At Williams' second trial in 1977 in the Iowa court, the prosecution did not offer Williams' statements into evidence, nor did it seek to show that Williams had directed the police to the child's body. However, evidence of the condition of her body as it was found, articles and photographs of her clothing, and the results of post mortem medical and chemical tests on the body were admitted. The trial court concluded that the State had proved by a preponderance of the evidence that, if the search had not been suspended and Williams had not led the police to the victim, her body would have been discovered "within a short time" in essentially the same condition as it was actually found. The trial court also ruled that if the police had not located the body, "the search would clearly have been taken up again where it left off, given the extreme circumstances of this case and the body would [have] been found in short order." (emphasis added).

In finding that the body would have been discovered in essentially the same condition as it was actually found, the court noted that freezing temperatures had prevailed and tissue deterioration would have been suspended. The challenged evidence was admitted and the jury again found Williams guilty of first-degree murder; he was sentenced to life in prison.

II

A

The Iowa Supreme Court correctly stated that the "vast majority" of all courts, both state and federal, recognize an inevitable discovery exception to the Exclusionary Rule. We are now urged to adopt and apply the so-called ultimate or inevitable discovery exception to the Exclusionary Rule.

Williams contends that evidence of the body's location and condition is "fruit of the poisonous tree," *i.e.*, the "fruit" or product of Detective Leaming's plea to help the child's parents give her "a Christian burial," which this Court had already held equated to interrogation. He contends that admitting the challenged evidence violated the Sixth Amendment whether it would have been inevitably discovered or not. Williams also contends that, if the inevitable discovery doctrine is constitutionally permissible, it must include a threshold showing of police good faith.

B

The doctrine requiring courts to suppress evidence as the tainted "fruit" of unlawful governmental conduct had its genesis in *Silverthorne Lumber Co. v. United States*, 251 U.S. 385, 40 S. Ct. 182, 64 L. Ed. 319 (1920); there, the Court held that the Exclusionary Rule applies not only to the illegally obtained evidence itself, but also to other incriminating evidence derived from the primary evidence. The holding of *Silverthorne* was carefully limited, however, for the Court emphasized that such information does not automatically become "sacred and inaccessible."

> If knowledge of [such facts] is gained from an independent source, they may be proved like any others . . . ." (emphasis added).

Wong Sun extended the Exclusionary Rule to evidence that was the indirect product or "fruit" of unlawful police conduct, but there again the Court emphasized that evidence that has been illegally obtained need not always be suppressed, stating:

> We need not hold that all evidence is "fruit of the poisonous tree" simply because it would not have come to light but for the illegal actions of the police. Rather, the more apt question in such a case is "whether, granting establishment of the primary illegality, the evidence to which instant objection is made has been come at by exploitation of that illegality or instead by means sufficiently distinguishable to be purged of the primary taint."

The Court thus pointedly negated the kind of good-faith requirement advanced by the Court of Appeals in reversing the District Court.

Although *Silverthorne* and *Wong Sun* involved violations of the Fourth Amendment, the "fruit of the poisonous tree" doctrine has not been limited to cases in which there has been a Fourth Amendment violation. The Court has applied the doctrine where the violations were of the Sixth Amendment, *see United States v. Wade*, 388 U.S. 218 (1967), as well as of the Fifth Amendment.

The core rationale consistently advanced by this Court for extending the Exclusionary Rule to evidence that is the fruit of unlawful police conduct has been that this admittedly drastic and socially costly course is needed to deter police from violations of constitutional and statutory protections. This Court has accepted the argument that the way to ensure such protections is to exclude evidence seized as a result of such violations notwithstanding the high social cost of letting persons obviously guilty go unpunished for their crimes. On this rationale, the prosecution is not to be put in a better position than it would have been in if no illegality had transpired.

By contrast, the derivative evidence analysis ensures that the prosecution is not put in a worse position simply because of some earlier police error or misconduct. The independent source doctrine allows admission of evidence that has been discovered by means wholly independent of any constitutional violation. That doctrine, although closely related to the inevitable discovery doctrine, does not apply here; Williams' statements to Leaming indeed led police to the child's body, but that is not the whole story. The independent source doctrine teaches us that the interest of society in deterring unlawful police conduct and the public interest in having juries receive all probative evidence of a crime are properly balanced by putting the police in the same, not a worse, position than they would have been in if no police error or misconduct had occurred. When the challenged evidence has an independent source, exclusion of such evidence would put the police in a worse position than they would have been in absent any error or violation. There is a functional similarity between these two doctrines in that exclusion of evidence that would inevitably have been discovered would also put the government in a worse position, because the police would have obtained that evidence if no misconduct had taken place. Thus, while the independent source exception would not justify admission of evidence in this case, its rationale is wholly consistent with and justifies our adoption of the ultimate or inevitable discovery exception to the Exclusionary Rule.

It is clear that the cases implementing the Exclusionary Rule "begin with the premise that the challenged evidence is in *some sense* the product of illegal governmental activity." *United States v. Crews*, 445 U.S. 463, 471 (1980) (emphasis added). Of course, this does not end the inquiry. If the prosecution can establish by a preponderance of the evidence that the information ultimately or inevitably would have been discovered by lawful means — here the volunteers' search — then the deterrence rationale has so little basis that the evidence should be received. Anything less would reject logic, experience, and common sense.[5]

---

[5] As to the quantum of proof, we have already established some relevant guidelines. In *United States*

The requirement that the prosecution must prove the absence of bad faith, imposed here by the Court of Appeals, would place courts in the position of withholding from juries relevant and undoubted truth that would have been available to police absent any unlawful police activity. Of course, that view would put the police in a *worse* position than they would have been in if no unlawful conduct had transpired. And, of equal importance, it wholly fails to take into account the enormous societal cost of excluding truth in the search for truth in the administration of justice. Nothing in this Court's prior holdings supports any such formalistic, pointless, and punitive approach.

The Court of Appeals concluded, without analysis, that if an absence of bad faith requirement were not imposed, "the temptation to risk deliberate violations of the Sixth Amendment would be too great, and the deterrent effect of the Exclusionary Rule reduced too far." We reject that view. A police officer who is faced with the opportunity to obtain evidence illegally will rarely, if ever, be in a position to calculate whether the evidence sought would inevitably be discovered. Cf. *Ceccolini*: "[T]he concept of effective deterrence assumes that the police officer consciously realizes the probable consequences of a presumably impermissible course of conduct." (Opinion concurring in judgment.) On the other hand, when an officer is aware that the evidence will inevitably be discovered, he will try to avoid engaging in any questionable practice. In that situation, there will be little to gain from taking any dubious "shortcuts" to obtain the evidence. Significant disincentives to obtaining evidence illegally — including the possibility of departmental discipline and civil liability — also lessen the likelihood that the ultimate or inevitable discovery exception will promote police misconduct. In these circumstances, the societal costs of the Exclusionary Rule far outweigh any possible benefits to deterrence that a good-faith requirement might produce.

Williams contends that because he did not waive his right to the assistance of counsel, the Court may not balance competing values in deciding whether the challenged evidence was properly admitted. He argues that, unlike the Exclusionary Rule in the Fourth Amendment context, the essential purpose of which is to deter police misconduct, the Sixth Amendment Exclusionary Rule is designed to

---

v. Matlock, 415 U.S. 164, 178, n. 14, 94 S. Ct. 988, 996, n. 14, 39 L. Ed. 2d 242 (1974) (emphasis added), we stated that "the controlling burden of proof at suppression hearings should impose no greater burden than proof by a preponderance of the evidence." In *Lego v. Twomey*, 404 U.S. 477, 488, 92 S. Ct. 619, 626, 30 L. Ed. 2d 618 (1972), we observed "from our experience [that] no substantial evidence has accumulated that federal rights have suffered from determining admissibility by a preponderance of the evidence" and held that the prosecution must prove by a preponderance of the evidence that a confession sought to be used at trial was voluntary. We are unwilling to impose added burdens on the already difficult task of proving guilt in criminal cases by enlarging the barrier to placing evidence of unquestioned truth before juries. Williams argues that the preponderance of the evidence standard used by the Iowa courts is inconsistent with *United States v. Wade*. In requiring clear and convincing evidence of an independent source for an in-court identification, the Court gave weight to the effect an uncounseled pre-trial identification has in "crystalliz[ing] the witnesses' identification of the defendant for the future reference." The Court noted as well that possible unfairness at the lineup "may be the sole means of attack upon the unequivocal courtroom identification," ibid., and recognized the difficulty of determining whether an in-court identification was based on independent recollection unaided by the lineup identification, id., at 240–241, 87 S. Ct., at 1939–1940. By contrast, inevitable discovery involves no speculative elements but focuses on demonstrated historical facts capable of ready verification or impeachment and does not require a departure from the usual burden of proof at suppression hearings.

protect the right to a fair trial and the integrity of the factfinding process. Williams contends that, when those interests are at stake, the societal costs of excluding evidence obtained from responses presumed involuntary are irrelevant in determining whether such evidence should be excluded. We disagree.

Exclusion of physical evidence that would inevitably have been discovered adds nothing to either the integrity or fairness of a criminal trial. The Sixth Amendment right to counsel protects against unfairness by preserving the adversary process in which the reliability of proffered evidence may be tested in cross-examination. Here, however, Detective Leaming's conduct did nothing to impugn the reliability of the evidence in question — the body of the child and its condition as it was found, articles of clothing found on the body, and the autopsy. No one would seriously contend that the presence of counsel in the police car when Leaming appealed to Williams' decent human instincts would have had any bearing on the reliability of the body as evidence. Suppression, in these circumstances, would do nothing whatever to promote the integrity of the trial process, but would inflict a wholly unacceptable burden on the administration of criminal justice.

More than a half century ago, Judge, later Justice, Cardozo made his seminal observation that under the Exclusionary Rule "[t]he criminal is to go free because the constable has blundered." *People v. Defore*, 242 N.Y. 13, 21, 150 N.E. 585, 587 (1926). Prophetically, he went on to consider "how far-reaching in its effect upon society" the Exclusionary Rule would be when "[t]he pettiest peace officer would have it in his power through overzeal or indiscretion to confer immunity upon an offender for crimes the most flagitious." Someday, Cardozo speculated, some court might press the Exclusionary Rule to the outer limits of its logic — or beyond — and suppress evidence relating to the "body of a murdered" victim because of the means by which it was found. Cardozo's prophecy was fulfilled in *Killough v. United States*, 315 F.2d 241, 245, 114 U.S. App. D.C. 305, 309 (1962) (en banc). But when, as here, the evidence in question would inevitably have been discovered without reference to the police error or misconduct, there is no nexus sufficient to provide a taint and the evidence is admissible.

C

The Court of Appeals did not find it necessary to consider whether the record fairly supported the finding that the volunteer search party would ultimately or inevitably have discovered the victim's body. However, three courts independently reviewing the evidence have found that the body of the child inevitably would have been found by the searchers. Williams challenges these findings, asserting that the record contains only the "*post hoc* rationalization" that the search efforts would have proceeded two and one-half miles into Polk County where Williams had led police to the body.

When that challenge was made at the suppression hearing preceding Williams' second trial, the prosecution offered the testimony of Agent Ruxlow of the Iowa Bureau of Criminal Investigation. Ruxlow had organized and directed some 200 volunteers who were searching for the child's body. The searchers were instructed "to check all the roads, the ditches, any culverts. . . . If they came upon any abandoned farm buildings, they were instructed to go onto the property and search those abandoned farm buildings or any other places where a small child could be secreted." Ruxlow testified that he marked off highway maps of Poweshiek and Jasper Counties in grid fashion, divided the volunteers into teams of four to six persons, and assigned each team to search specific grid areas. Ruxlow also testified that, if the search had not been suspended because of Williams' promised cooperation, it would have continued into Polk County, using the same grid system. Although he had previously marked off into grids only the highway maps of Poweshiek and Jasper Counties, Ruxlow had obtained a map of Polk County, which he said he would have marked off in the same manner had it been necessary for the search to continue.

The search had commenced at approximately 10 a.m. and moved westward through Poweshiek County into Jasper County. At approximately 3 p.m., after Williams had volunteered to cooperate with the police, Officer Leaming, who was in the police car with Williams, sent word to Ruxlow and the other Special Agent directing the search to meet him at the Grinnell truck stop and the search was suspended at that time. Ruxlow also stated that he was "under the impression that there was a possibility" that Williams would lead them to the child's body at that time. The search was not resumed once it was learned that Williams had led the police to the body, id., which was found two and one-half miles from where the search had stopped in what would have been the eastern most grid to be searched in Polk County. There was testimony that it would have taken an additional three to five hours to discover the body if the search had continued, the body was found near a culvert, one of the kinds of places the teams had been specifically directed to search.

On this record it is clear that the search parties were approaching the actual location of the body and we are satisfied, along with three courts earlier, that the volunteer search teams would have resumed the search had Williams not earlier led the police to the body and the body inevitably would have been found.

The judgment of the Court of Appeals is reversed, and the case is remanded for further proceedings consistent with this opinion.

JUSTICE WHITE, concurring.

I join fully in the opinion of the Court. I write separately only to point out that many of Justice Stevens' remarks are beside the point when it is recalled that *Brewer v. Williams* was a 5-4 decision and that four members of the Court, including myself, were of the view that Officer Leaming had done nothing wrong at all, let alone anything unconstitutional. Three of us observed that: "To anyone not lost in the intricacies of the prophylactic rules of *Miranda*, the result in this case seems utterly senseless . . . ." It is thus an unjustified reflection on Officer Leaming to say that he "decided to dispense with the requirements of the law," or that he decided "to take procedural shortcuts instead of complying with the law." He was no doubt acting as many competent police officers would have acted under similar circumstances and in light of the then-existing law. That five Justices later thought he was mistaken does not call for making him out to be a villain or for a lecture on deliberate police misconduct and its resulting costs to society.

JUSTICE STEVENS, concurring in the judgment.

This litigation is exceptional for at least three reasons. The facts are unusually tragic; it involves an unusually clear violation of constitutional rights; and it graphically illustrates the societal costs that may be incurred when police officers decide to dispense with the requirements of law. Because the Court does not adequately discuss any of these aspects of the case, I am unable to join its opinion.

I

There can be no denying that the character of the crime may have an impact on the decisional process. As the Court was required to hold, however, that does not permit any court to condone a violation of constitutional rights.[1] Today's decision is no more an ad hoc response to the pressures engendered by the special facts of the case than was *Williams I*. It was the majority in *Williams I* that recognized that "evidence of where the body was found and of its condition might well be admissible on the theory that the body would have been discovered in any event, even had incriminating statements not been elicited from Williams." It was the author of today's opinion of the Court who characterized this rule of law as a "remarkable" and "unlikely theory." (BURGER, C.J., dissenting). The rule of law that the Court adopts today has an integrity of its own and is not merely the product of the hydraulic pressures associated with hard cases or strong words.

II

The constitutional violation that gave rise to the decision in *Williams I* is neither acknowledged nor fairly explained in the Court's opinion. Yet the propriety of admitting evidence relating to the victims' body can only be evaluated if that constitutional violation is properly identified.

Williams I held that Detective Leaming had violated "the clear rule of *Massiah*" by deliberately eliciting incriminating statements from respondent during the pendency of the adversarial process and outside of that process. *See* 430 U.S. at 399–401, 97 S. Ct. at 1239–1241. The violation was aggravated by the fact that Detective Leaming had breached a promise to counsel, an act which can only undermine the role of counsel in the adversarial process. The Christian burial speech was nothing less than an attempt to substitute an ex parte, inquisitorial process for the clash of adversaries commanded by the Constitution.[5] Thus the

---

[1] As I wrote at the time:

Nothing we write, no matter how well reasoned or forcefully expressed, can bring back the victim of this tragedy or undo the consequences of the official neglect which led to the respondent's escape from a state mental institution. The emotional aspects of the case make it difficult to decide dispassionately, but do not qualify our obligation to apply the law with an eye to the future as well as with concern for the result in the particular case before us.

(concurring opinion).

[5] "The whole point of *Massiah* is the prevention of the state from taking advantage of an uncounseled defendant once sixth amendment rights attach. The Christian burial speech was an attempt to take advantage of Williams. The attempt itself *is* what *Massiah* prohibits. The attempt violates the constitutional mandate that the system proceed, after some point, only in an accusatorial manner."

now-familiar plaint that "[t]he criminal is to go free because the constable has blundered," is entirely beside the point. More pertinent is what The Chief Justice wrote for the Court on another occasion: "This is not a case where, in Justice Cardozo's words, 'the constable . . . blundered,' rather, it is one where the 'constable' planned an impermissible interference with the right to the assistance of counsel." *United States v. Henry*, 447 U.S. 264, 274–275 (1980) (footnote and citation omitted).

III

Once the constitutional violation is properly identified, the answers to the questions presented in this case follow readily. Admission of the victim's body, if it would have been discovered anyway, means that the trial in this case was not the product of an inquisitorial process; that process was untainted by illegality. The good or bad faith of the Detective Leaming is therefore simply irrelevant. If the trial process was not tainted as a result of his conduct, this defendant received the type of trial that the Sixth Amendment envisions. *See Weatherford v. Bursey; United States v. Wade.* Generalizations about the Exclusionary Rule employed by the majority, simply do not address the primary question in the case.

The majority is correct to insist that any rule of exclusion not provide the authorities with an incentive to commit violations of the Constitution. If the inevitable discovery rule provided such an incentive by permitting the prosecution to avoid the uncertainties inherent in its search for evidence, it would undermine the constitutional guarantee itself, and therefore be inconsistent with the deterrent purposes of the Exclusionary Rule. But when the burden of proof on the inevitable discovery question is placed on the prosecution, it must bear the risk of error in the determination made necessary by its constitutional violation. The uncertainty as to whether the body would have been discovered can be resolved in its favor here only because, as the Court explains, petitioner adduced evidence demonstrating that at the time of the constitutional violation an investigation was already under way which, in the natural and probable course of events, would have soon discovered the body. This is not a case in which the prosecution can escape responsibility for a constitutional violation through speculation; to the extent uncertainty was created by the constitutional violation the prosecution was required to resolve that uncertainty through proof.[8] Even if Detective Leaming acted in bad faith in the sense that he deliberately violated the Constitution in order to avoid the possibility that the body would not be discovered, the prosecution ultimately does not avoid that risk; its burden of proof forces it to assume the risk. The need to adduce proof sufficient to discharge its burden, and the difficulty in predicting whether such proof will be available or sufficient, means that the inevitable discovery rule does

---

Grano, Rhode Island v. Innis: *A Need to Reconsider the Constitutional Premises Underlying the Law of Confessions*, 17 AM. CRIM. L. REV. 1, 35 (1979) (emphasis in original).

[8] I agree with the majority's holding that the prosecution must prove that the evidence would have been inevitably discovered by a preponderance of the evidence rather than by clear and convincing evidence. An inevitable discovery finding is based on objective evidence concerning the scope of the ongoing investigation which can be objectively verified or impeached. Hence an extraordinary burden of proof is not needed in order to preserve the defendant's ability to subject the prosecution's case to the meaningful adversarial testing required by the Sixth Amendment.

not permit state officials to avoid the uncertainty they would have faced but for the constitutional violation.

The majority refers to the "societal cost" of excluding probative evidence. In my view, the more relevant cost is that imposed on society by police officers who decide to take procedural shortcuts instead of complying with the law. What is the consequence of the shortcut that Detective Leaming took when he decided to question Williams in this case and not to wait an hour or so until he arrived in Des Moines?[9] The answer is years and years of unnecessary but costly litigation. Instead of having a 1969 conviction affirmed in routine fashion, the case is still alive 15 years later. Thanks to Detective Leaming, the State of Iowa has expended vast sums of money and countless hours of professional labor in his defense. That expenditure surely provides an adequate deterrent to similar violations; the responsibility for that expenditure lies not with the Constitution, but rather with the constable.

Accordingly, I concur in the Court's judgment.

JUSTICE BRENNAN, with whom JUSTICE MARSHALL joins, dissenting.

To the extent that today's decision adopts [the] "inevitable discovery" exception to the exclusionary rule, it simply acknowledges a doctrine that is akin to the "independent source" exception first recognized by the Court in *Silverthorne Lumber Co.* In particular, the Court concludes that unconstitutionally obtained evidence may be admitted at trial if it inevitably would have been discovered in the same condition by an independent line of investigation that was already being pursued when the constitutional violation occurred. As has every federal Court of Appeals previously addressing this issue, I agree that in these circumstances the "inevitable discovery" exception to the exclusionary rule is consistent with the requirements of the Constitution.

In its zealous efforts to emasculate the exclusionary rule, however, the Court loses sight of the crucial difference between the "inevitable discovery" doctrine and the "independent source" exception from which it is derived. When properly applied, the "independent source" exception allows the prosecution to use evidence only if it was, in fact, obtained by fully lawful means. It therefore does no violence to the constitutional protections that the exclusionary rule is meant to enforce. The "inevitable discovery" exception is likewise compatible with the Constitution, though it differs in one key respect from its next of kin: specifically, the evidence sought to be introduced at trial has not actually been obtained from an independent source, but rather would have been discovered as a matter of course if independent investigations were allowed to proceed.

In my view, this distinction should require that the government satisfy a heightened burden of proof before it is allowed to use such evidence. The inevitable

---

[9] In this connection, it is worth noting, as Justice MARSHALL did in *Williams I*, that in light of the assistance that respondent's attorney had provided to the Des Moines police, it seems apparent that the lawyer intended to learn the location of the body from his client and then reveal it to the police. Thus, the need for a shortcut was practically nonexistent.

discovery exception necessarily implicates a hypothetical finding that differs in kind from the factual finding that precedes application of the independent source rule. To ensure that this hypothetical finding is narrowly confined to circumstances that are functionally equivalent to an independent source, and to protect fully the fundamental rights served by the exclusionary rule, I would require clear and convincing evidence before concluding that the government had met its burden of proof on this issue. *See Wade.* Increasing the burden of proof serves to impress the factfinder with the importance of the decision and thereby reduces the risk that illegally obtained evidence will be admitted. *Cf. Addington v. Texas,* 441 U.S. 418, 427, 99 S. Ct. 1804, 1810, 60 L. Ed. 2d 323 (1979); *Santosky v. Kramer,* 455 U.S. 745, 764, 102 S. Ct. 1388, 1399, 71 L. Ed. 2d 599 (1982) ("Raising the standard of proof would have both practical and symbolic consequences"). Because the lower courts did not impose such a requirement, I would remand this case for application of this heightened burden of proof by the lower courts in the first instance. I am therefore unable to join either the Court's opinion or its judgment.

QUESTIONS AND NOTES

1.   The entire Court accepts the inevitable discovery exception to the exclusionary rule. Do you agree? Why? Why not?

2.   The entire Court also seems to agree that "good faith" is irrelevant. Do you agree? Why? Why not?

3.   If it mattered, would you assess Leaming's behavior as "good faith," "bad faith," or neither? Explain.

4.   Did the Court adopt an appropriate burden of proof? Did Justice Brennan?

5.   Linguistically speaking, how can something be "inevitable," if it is only more likely than not?

6.   Assess the following observation of Professor Phillip Johnson, made before the Supreme Court's decision in *Nix v. Williams*:

> The fact that constitutional law is complex and technical suggests to me that it should be enforced with a sense of proportion. Granting that Captain Leaming crossed a certain line that the Supreme Court has drawn, and even granting that he ought to have known better, his misdeed was what we criminal lawyers call malum prohibitum, rather than malum in se. Legalisms aside, what he did was to appeal to the conscience of a suspected murderer to do the only decent and honorable thing: to reveal where he had hidden the body, so the police could recover it and return it to the grieving family for burial. Perhaps the police ought not to be allowed to make such an appeal to a suspect in their custody, but in my opinion somebody ought to do it.

> We have stringent rules governing police interrogation of suspects for good reason. Not so long ago, the "third degree'" was a standard and acknowledged police investigative tool. Suspects were arrested and rearrested on flimsy grounds, kept awake while relays of questioners wore them down, stripped naked and threatened with beatings, pressured,

cajoled, and tricked into confessing. The characteristic vice of dedicated policemen is that they tend to see themselves as fighting a war against the criminal elements of society. From this it is only a short step to the conclusion that the end justifies the means. The courts are entirely right to take strong measures to keep this mentality in check.

But we lawyers, a class which includes judges, also have our characteristic faults. One of these is a tendency to make a fetish of procedure, so that the merits of a dispute become obscured in an endless tangle of arguments about how the dispute ought to have been resolved. Another is a tendency to become captured by our own abstractions, so that we push every principle to the limits of its logic and sometimes beyond. Society has police to protect it from thieves and murderers, and it has lawyers to protect it from the police. No one has yet discovered how to protect society from the lawyers.

Johnson, *The Return of the Christian Burial Speech*, 32 EMORY L.J. 349, 381 (1983).

7.   The separate issue of inevitable discovery, or independent source, as applied to a search warrant obtained after a warrantless search was explored in *Murray*.

MURRAY v. UNITED STATES
487 U.S. 533 (1988)

JUSTICE SCALIA delivered the opinion of the Court.

In *Segura v. United States*, 468 U.S. 796 (1984), we held that police officers' illegal entry upon private premises did not require suppression of evidence subsequently discovered at those premises when executing a search warrant obtained on the basis of information wholly unconnected with the initial entry. In these consolidated cases we are faced with the question whether, again assuming evidence obtained pursuant to an independently obtained search warrant, the portion of such evidence that had been observed in plain view at the time of a prior illegal entry must be suppressed.

I

Both cases arise out of the conviction of petitioner Michael F. Murray, petitioner James D. Carter, and others for conspiracy to possess and distribute illegal drugs. Insofar as relevant for our purposes, the facts are as follows: Based on information received from informants, federal law enforcement agents had been surveilling petitioner Murray and several of his co-conspirators. At about 1:45 p.m. on April 6, 1983, they observed Murray drive a truck and Carter drive a green camper, into a warehouse in South Boston. When the petitioners drove the vehicles out about 20 minutes later, the surveilling agents saw within the warehouse two individuals and a tractor-trailer rig bearing a long, dark container. Murray and Carter later turned over the truck and camper to other drivers, who were in turn followed and ultimately arrested, and the vehicles lawfully seized. Both vehicles were found to contain marijuana.

After receiving this information, several of the agents converged on the South Boston warehouse and forced entry. They found the warehouse unoccupied, but observed in plain view numerous burlap-wrapped bales that were later found to contain marijuana. They left without disturbing the bales, kept the warehouse under surveillance, and did not reenter it until they had a search warrant. In applying for the warrant, the agents did not mention the prior entry, and did not rely on any observations made during that entry. When the warrant was issued — at 10:40 p.m., approximately eight hours after the initial entry — the agents immediately reentered the warehouse and seized 270 bales of marijuana and notebooks listing customers for whom the bales were destined.

II

The exclusionary rule prohibits introduction into evidence of tangible materials seized during an unlawful search, and of testimony concerning knowledge acquired during an unlawful search, *Silverman v. United States*, 365 U.S. 505, 81 S. Ct. 679, 5 L. Ed. 2d 734 (1961). Beyond that, the exclusionary rule also prohibits the introduction of derivative evidence, both tangible and testimonial, that is the product of the primary evidence, or that is otherwise acquired as an indirect result of the unlawful search, up to the point at which the connection with the unlawful search becomes "so attenuated as to dissipate the taint," *Nardone. See Wong Sun.*

Almost simultaneously with our development of the exclusionary rule, in the first quarter of this century, we also announced what has come to be known as the "independent source" doctrine. *See Silverthorne Lumber Co.* That doctrine, which has been applied to evidence acquired not only through Fourth Amendment violations but also through Fifth and Sixth Amendment violations, has recently been described as follows: "[T]he interest of society in deterring unlawful police conduct and the public interest in having juries receive all probative evidence of a crime are properly balanced by putting the police in the same, not a worse, position that they would have been in if no police error or misconduct had occurred. . . . When the challenged evidence has an independent source, exclusion of such evidence would put the police in a worse position than they would have been in absent any error or violation."

The dispute here is over the scope of this doctrine. Petitioners contend that it applies only to evidence obtained for the first time during an independent lawful search. The Government argues that it applies also to evidence initially discovered during, or as a consequence of, an unlawful search, but later obtained independently from activities untainted by the initial illegality. We think the Government's view has better support in both precedent and policy.

Our cases have used the concept of "independent source" in a more general and a more specific sense. The more general sense identifies all evidence acquired in a fashion untainted by the illegal evidence-gathering activity. Thus, where an unlawful entry has given investigators knowledge of facts x and y, but fact z has been learned by other means, fact z can be said to be admissible because derived from an "independent source." This is how we used the term in *Segura v. United States*. In that case, agents unlawfully entered the defendant's apartment and remained there until a search warrant was obtained. The admissibility of what they discovered while waiting in the apartment was not before us, but we held that the evidence found for the first time during the execution of the valid and untainted search warrant was admissible because it was discovered pursuant to an "independent source."

The original use of the term, however, and its more important use for purposes of these cases, was more specific. It was originally applied in the exclusionary rule context, by Justice HOLMES, with reference to that particular category of evidence acquired by an untainted search *which is identical to the evidence unlawfully acquired* — that is, in the example just given, to knowledge of facts x and y derived from an independent source: "The essence of a provision forbidding the acquisition of evidence in a certain way is that not merely evidence so acquired shall not be used before the Court but that it shall not be used at all. Of course this does not mean that the facts thus obtained become sacred and inaccessible. If knowledge of them is gained from an independent source they may be proved like any others."

We recently assumed this application of the independent source doctrine (in the Sixth Amendment context) in *Nix v. Williams*.

Petitioners' asserted policy basis for excluding evidence which is initially discovered during an illegal search, but is subsequently acquired through an independent and lawful source, is that a contrary rule will remove all deterrence to, and indeed positively encourage, unlawful police searches. As petitioners see the incentives, law enforcement officers will routinely enter without a warrant to make sure that what they expect to be on the premises is in fact there. If it is not, they will have spared themselves the time and trouble of getting a warrant; if it is, they can get the warrant and use the evidence despite the unlawful entry. Brief for Petitioners 42. We see the incentives differently. An officer with probable cause sufficient to obtain a search warrant would be foolish to enter the premises first in an unlawful manner. By doing so, he would risk suppression of all evidence on the premises, both seen and unseen, since his action would add to the normal burden of convincing a magistrate that there is probable cause the much more onerous burden of convincing a trial court that no information gained from the illegal entry affected either the law enforcement officers' decision to seek a warrant or the magistrate's decision to grant it. *See* Part III, *infra*. Nor would the officer without sufficient probable cause to obtain a search warrant have any added incentive to conduct an unlawful entry, since whatever he finds cannot be used to establish probable cause before a magistrate.[2]

---

[2] Justice MARSHALL argues, in effect, that where the police cannot point to some historically verifiable fact demonstrating that the subsequent search pursuant to a warrant was wholly unaffected by the prior illegal search — *e.g.*, that they had already sought the warrant before entering the premises — we should adopt a *per se* rule of inadmissibility. We do not believe that such a prophylactic exception to the independent source rule is necessary. To say that a district court must be satisfied that a warrant would have been sought without the illegal entry is not to give dispositive effect to police officer's assurances on the point. Where the facts render those assurances implausible, the independent source doctrine will not apply.

We might note that there is no basis for pointing to the present cases as an example of a "search first, warrant later" mentality. The District Court found that the agents entered the warehouse "in an effort to apprehend any participants who might have remained inside and to guard against the destruction of possibly critical evidence. While they may have misjudged the existence of sufficient exigent circum-

III

To apply what we have said to the present cases: Knowledge that the marijuana was in the warehouse was assuredly acquired at the time of the unlawful entry. But it was also acquired at the time of entry pursuant to the warrant, and if that later acquisition was not the result of the earlier entry there is no reason why the independent source doctrine should not apply. Invoking the exclusionary rule would put the police (and society) not in the same position they would have occupied if no violation occurred, but in a worse one. *See Nix v. Williams.*

The ultimate question, therefore, is whether the search pursuant to warrant was in fact a genuinely independent source of the information and tangible evidence at issue here. This would not have been the case if the agents' decision to seek the warrant was prompted by what they had seen during the initial entry,[3] or if information obtained during that entry was presented to the Magistrate and affected his decision to issue the warrant. On this point the Court of Appeals said the following:

> [W]e can be absolutely certain that the warrantless entry in no way contributed in the slightest either to the issuance of a warrant or to the discovery of the evidence during the lawful search that occurred pursuant to the warrant.

> This is as clear a case as can be imagined where the discovery of the contraband in plain view was totally irrelevant to the later securing of a warrant and the successful search that ensued. As there was no causal link whatever between the illegal entry and the discovery of the challenged evidence, we find no error in the court's refusal to suppress.

United States v. Moscatiello, 771 F.2d at 603, 604.

Although these statements can be read to provide emphatic support for the Government's position, it is the function of the District Court rather than the Court of Appeals to determine the facts, and we do not think the Court of Appeals' conclusions are supported by adequate findings. The District Court found that the agents did not reveal their warrantless entry to the Magistrate, and that they did not include in their application for a warrant any recitation of their observations in the warehouse. It did not, however, explicitly find that the agents would have sought a warrant if they had not earlier entered the warehouse. The Government concedes this in its brief. To be sure, the District Court did determine that the purpose of the

---

stances to justify the warrantless entry (the Court of Appeals did not reach that issue and neither do we), there is nothing to suggest that they went in merely to see if there was anything worth getting a warrant for.

[3] Justice MARSHALL argues that "the relevant question [is] whether, even if the initial entry uncovered no evidence, the officers would return immediately with a warrant to conduct a second search." We do not see how this is "relevant" at all. To determine whether the warrant was independent of the illegal entry, one must ask whether it would have been sought even if what actually happened had not occurred — not whether it would have been sought if something else had happened. That is to say, what counts is whether the actual illegal search had any effect in producing the warrant, no whether some hypothetical illegal search would have aborted the warrant. Only that much is needed to assure that what comes before the court is not the product of illegality; to go further than that would be to expand our existing exclusionary rule.

warrantless entry was in part "to guard against the destruction of possibly critical evidence," and one could perhaps infer from this that the agents who made the entry already planned to obtain that "critical evidence" through a warrant-authorized search. That inference is not, however, clear enough to justify the conclusion that the District Court's findings amounted to a determination of independent source.

Accordingly, we vacate the judgment and remand these cases to the Court of Appeals with instructions that it remand to the District Court for determination whether the warrant-authorized search of the warehouse was an independent source of the challenged evidence in the sense we have described.

Justice BRENNAN and Justice KENNEDY took no part in the consideration or decision of these cases.

Justice MARSHALL, with whom Justice STEVENS and Justice O'CONNOR join, dissenting.

The Court today holds that the "independent source" exception to the exclusionary rule may justify admitting evidence discovered during an illegal warrantless search that is later "rediscovered" by the same team of investigators during a search pursuant to a warrant obtained immediately after the illegal search. I believe the Court's decision, by failing to provide sufficient guarantees that the subsequent search was, in fact, independent of the illegal search, emasculates the Warrant Clause and undermines the deterrence function of the exclusionary rule. I therefore dissent.

This Court has stated frequently that the exclusionary rule is principally designed to deter violations of the Fourth Amendment. By excluding evidence discovered in violation of the Fourth Amendment, the rule "compel[s] respect for the constitutional guaranty in the only effectively available way, by removing the incentive to disregard it." The Court has crafted exceptions to the exclusionary rule when the purposes of the rule are not furthered by the exclusion. As the Court today recognizes, the independent source exception to the exclusionary rule "allows admission of evidence that has been discovered by means wholly independent of any constitutional violation." The independent source exception, like the inevitable discovery exception, is primarily based on a practical view that under certain circumstances the beneficial deterrent effect that exclusion will have on future constitutional violations is too slight to justify the social cost of excluding probative evidence from a criminal trial. When the seizure of the evidence at issue is "wholly independent of" the constitutional violation, then exclusion arguably will have no effect on a law enforcement officer's incentive to commit an unlawful search.[1]

---

[1] The clearest case for the application of the independent course exception is when a wholly separate line of investigation, shielded from information gathered in an illegal search, turns up the same evidence through a separate, lawful search. Under these circumstance, there is little doubt that the lawful search was not connected to the constitutional violation. The exclusion of such evidence would not significantly add to the deterrence facing the law enforcement officers conducting the illegal search, because they would have little reason to anticipate the separate investigation leading to the same evidence.

Given the underlying justification for the independent source exception, any inquiry into the exception's application must keep sight of the practical effect admission will have on the incentives facing law enforcement officers to engage in unlawful conduct. The proper scope of the independent source exception, and guidelines for its application, cannot be divined in a factual vacuum; instead, they must be informed by the nature of the constitutional violation and the deterrent effect of exclusion in particular circumstances. In holding that the independent source exception may apply to the facts of these cases, I believe the Court loses sight of the practical moorings of the independent source exception and creates an affirmative incentive for unconstitutional searches. This holding can find no justification in the purposes underlying both the exclusionary rule and the independent source exception.

The factual setting of the instant case is straightforward. Federal Bureau of Investigation (FBI) and Drug Enforcement Agency (DEA) agents stopped two vehicles after they left a warehouse and discovered bales of marijuana. DEA Supervisor Garibotto and an assistant United States attorney then returned to the warehouse, which had been under surveillance for several hours. After demands that the warehouse door be opened went unanswered, Supervisor Garibotto forced open the door with a tire iron. A number of agents entered the warehouse. No persons were found inside, but the agents saw numerous bales of marijuana in plain view. Supervisor Garibotto then ordered everyone out of the warehouse. Agents did not reenter the warehouse until a warrant was obtained some eight hours later. The warehouse was kept under surveillance during the interim.

It is undisputed that the agents made no effort to obtain a warrant prior to the initial entry. The agents had not begun to prepare a warrant affidavit, and according to FBI Agent Cleary, who supervised the FBI's involvement, they had not even engaged in any discussions of obtaining a warrant. The affidavit in support of the warrant obtained after the initial search was prepared by DEA Agent Keaney, who had tactical control over the DEA agents, and who had participated in the initial search of the warehouse. The affidavit did not mention the warrantless search of the warehouse, nor did it cite information obtained from that search. In determining that the challenged evidence was admissible, the Court of Appeals assumed that the initial warrantless entry was not justified by exigent circumstances and that the search therefore violated the Warrant Clause of the Fourth Amendment.

Under the circumstances of these cases, the admission of the evidence "reseized" during the second search severely undermines the deterrence function of the exclusionary rule. Indeed, admission in these cases affirmatively encourages illegal searches. The incentives for such illegal conduct are clear. Obtaining a warrant is inconvenient and time consuming. Even when officers have probable cause to support a warrant application, therefore, they have an incentive first to determine whether it is worthwhile to obtain a warrant. Probable cause is much less than certainty, and many "confirmatory" searches will result in the discovery that no evidence is present, thus saving the police the time and trouble of getting a warrant. If contraband is discovered, however, the officers may later seek a warrant to shield the evidence from the taint of the illegal search. The police thus know in advance that they have little to lose and much to gain by forgoing the bother of obtaining a warrant and undertaking an illegal search.

The Court, however, "see[s] the incentives differently." Under the Court's view, today's decision does not provide an incentive for unlawful searches, because the officer undertaking the search would know that "his action would add to the normal burden of convincing a magistrate that there is probable cause the much more onerous burden of convincing a trial court that no information gained from the illegal entry affected either the law enforcement officers' decision to seek a warrant or the magistrate's decision to grant it." The Court, however, provides no hint of why this risk would actually seem significant to the officers. Under the circumstances of these cases, the officers committing the illegal search have both knowledge and control of the factors central to the trial court's determination. First, it is a simple matter, as was done in these cases, to exclude from the warrant application any information gained from the initial entry so that the magistrate's determination of probable cause is not influenced by the prior illegal search. Second, today's decision makes the application of the independent source exception turn entirely on an evaluation of the officers' intent. It normally will be difficult for the trial court to verify, or the defendant to rebut, an assertion by officers that they always intended to obtain a warrant, regardless of the results of the illegal search.[2] The testimony of the officers conducting the illegal search is the only direct evidence of intent, and the defendant will be relegated simply to arguing that the officers should not be believed. Under these circumstances, the litigation risk described by the Court seems hardly a risk at all; it does not significantly dampen the incentive to conduct the initial illegal search.[3]

The strong Fourth Amendment interest in eliminating these incentives for illegal entry should cause this Court to scrutinize closely the application of the independent source exception to evidence obtained under the circumstances of the instant cases; respect for the constitutional guarantee requires a rule that does not undermine the deterrence function of the exclusionary rule. When, as here, the same team of investigators is involved in both the first and second search, there is a significant danger that the "independence" of the source will in fact be illusory, and that the initial search will have affected the decision to obtain a warrant

---

[2] Such an intent-based rule is of dubious value for other reasons as well. First, the intent of the officers prior to the illegal entry often will be of little significance to the relevant question: whether, even if the initial entry uncovered no evidence, the officers would return immediately with a warrant to conduct a second search. Officers who have probable cause to believe contraband is present genuinely might intend later to obtain a warrant, but after the illegal search uncovers no such contraband, those same offices might decide their time is better spend than to return with a warrant. In additional, such an intent rule will be difficult to apply. The Court fails to describe how a trial court will properly evaluate whether the law enforcement officers fully intended to obtain a warrant regardless safe what they discovered during the illegal search. The obvious question is whose intent is relevant? Intentions clearly may differ both among supervisory officers and among officers who initiate the illegal search.

[3] The litigation risk facing these law enforcement officers may be contrasted with the risk faced by the officer in *Nix v. Williams. Nix* involved an application of the inevitable discovery exception to the exclusionary rule. In that case, the Court stressed that an officer "who is faced with the opportunity to obtain evidence illegally will rarely, if ever, be in a position to calculate whether the evidence sought would inevitably be discovered." Unlike the officer in *Nix*, who had no way of knowing about the progress of a wholly separate line of investigation that already had begun at the time of his unconstitutional conduct, the officers in the instant cases, at least under the Court's analysis, have complete knowledge and control over the factors relevant to the determination of "independence."

notwithstanding the officers' subsequent assertions to the contrary. It is therefore crucial that the factual premise of the exception — complete independence — be clearly established before the exception can justify admission of the evidence. I believe the Court's reliance on the intent of the law enforcement officers who conducted the warrantless search provides insufficient guarantees that the subsequent legal search was unaffected by the prior illegal search.

In the instant cases, there are no "demonstrated historical facts" capable of supporting a finding that the subsequent warrant search was wholly unaffected by the prior illegal search. The same team of investigators was involved in both searches. The warrant was obtained immediately after the illegal search, and no effort was made to obtain a warrant prior to the discovery of the marijuana during the illegal search. The only evidence available that the warrant search was wholly independent is the testimony of the agents who conducted the illegal search. Under these circumstances, the threat that the subsequent search was tainted by the illegal search is too great to allow for the application of the independent source exception.[4] The Court's contrary holding lends itself to easy abuse, and offers an incentive to bypass the constitutional requirement that probable cause be assessed by a neutral and detached magistrate before the police invade an individual's privacy.[5]

The decision in *Segura* is not to the contrary. In *Segura*, the Court expressly distinguished between evidence discovered during an initial warrantless entry and evidence that was not discovered until a subsequent legal search. The Court held that under those circumstances, when no information from an illegal search was used in a subsequent warrant application, the warrant provided an independent source for the evidence first uncovered in the second, lawful search.

Segura is readily distinguished from the present cases. The admission of evidence first discovered during a legal search does not significantly lessen the deterrence facing the law enforcement officers contemplating an illegal entry so long as the evidence that is seen is excluded. This was clearly the view of Chief Justice BURGER, joined by Justice O'CONNOR, when he stated that the Court's ruling would not significantly detract from the deterrent effects of the exclusionary rule because "officers who enter illegally will recognize that whatever evidence they discover as a direct result of the entry may be suppressed, as it was by the Court of Appeals in this case." As I argue above, extending *Segura* to cover evidence discovered during an initial illegal search will eradicate this remaining deterrence

---

[4] To conclude that the initial search had no effect on the decision to obtain a warrant, and thus that the warrant search was an "independent source" of the challenge evidence, one would have to assume that even if the officers entered the premises and discovered no contraband, they nonetheless would have gone to the Magistrate, sworn that they had probable cause to believe that contraband was in the building, and then returned to conduct another search. Although such a scenario is possible, I believe is more plausible to believe that the officers would not have chosen to return immediately to the premises with a warrant to search for evidence had they not discovered evidence during the initial search.

[5] Given that the law enforcement officers in these cases made no movement to obtain a warrant prior to the illegal search, these case d do not present the more difficult issue whether, in light of the strong interest in deterring illegal warrantless searches, the evidence discovered during an illegal search ever may be admitted under the independent source exception when the second legal search is conducted by the same investigative team pursuing the same line of investigation.

to illegal entry. Moreover, there is less reason to believe that an initial illegal entry was prompted by a desire to determine whether to bother to get a warrant in the first place, and thus was not wholly independent of the second search, if officers understand that evidence they discover during the illegal search will be excluded even if they subsequently return with a warrant.

In sum, under circumstances as are presented in these cases, when the very law enforcement officers who participate in an illegal search immediately thereafter obtain a warrant to search the same premises, I believe the evidence discovered during the initial illegal entry must be suppressed. Any other result emasculates the Warrant Clause and provides an intolerable incentive for warrantless searches. I respectfully dissent.

JUSTICE STEVENS, dissenting.

While I join Justice MARSHALL's opinion explaining why the majority's extension of the Court's holding in *Segura* "emasculates the Warrant Clause and provides an intolerable incentive for warrantless searches," I remain convinced that the *Segura* decision itself was unacceptable because, even then, it was obvious that it would "provide government agents with an affirmative incentive to engage in unconstitutional violations of the privacy of the home." I fear that the Court has taken another unfortunate step down the path to a system of "law enforcement unfettered by process concerns." In due course, I trust it will pause long enough to remember that "the efforts of the courts and their officials to bring the guilty to punishment, praiseworthy as they are, are not to be aided by the sacrifice of those great principles established by years of endeavor and suffering which have resulted in their embodiment in the fundamental law of the land." *Weeks v. United States*, 232 U.S. 383 652 (1914).

QUESTIONS AND NOTES

1. Does *Murray* create an incentive for the police to enter a home without a warrant?

2. If your answer to Question 1 was "yes," was the decision necessarily incorrect?

3. Does the Court's requirement that the police establish that they would have obtained a warrant regardless of their discovery eliminate the concern expressed in Question 1? Does it reduce it?

4. If you disagree with the Court in *Murray*, do you also support Justice Stevens' rejection of *Segura*? Explain.

5. Is it relevant that the purpose of the warrant requirement is to prevent the intrusion in the first place?

Chapter 24

ENTRAPMENT

We close our study of police practices by looking at entrapment, a classic hybrid between substantive criminal law and criminal procedure (police practices). Whether this subject belongs in criminal law or criminal procedure depends in significant part on one's theory of entrapment. To the extent that an entrapped defendant is less culpable than a similarly-situated non-entrapped defendant, the subject is a species of substantive criminal law. On the other hand, if entrapment is designed to control police excesses in ferreting out crime, one can view it as a relative (however distant) of unreasonable searches and seizures, coerced confessions, and due process violations.

For the most part, Supreme Court doctrine focuses on the predisposition of the defendant, thereby rendering the doctrine a species of substantive criminal law. However, that perspective of entrapment has not been historically shared by all of the Supreme Court Justices, and has been clearly rejected by some state courts [*see, e.g., State v. Powell*, 726 P.2d 266 (Haw. 1986)], and condemned by some thoughtful commentators [*see, e.g.*, Webster, *Building a Better Mousetrap: Reconstructing Federal Entrapment Theory from* Sorrells *to* Mathews, 32 ARIZ. L. REV. 605 (1990)]. Because entrapment doctrine, for the most part, does not emanate from the Constitution, states are free to develop their own law on the subject.

In Section A of this Chapter, we focus on the Supreme Court's debate on and treatment of the concept of predisposition. In Section B, our focus is on the emerging due process defense against government overreaching.

A. THE RELEVANCE OF PREDISPOSITION

SHERMAN v. UNITED STATES
356 U.S. 369 (1958)

MR. CHIEF JUSTICE WARREN delivered the opinion of the Court.

The issue before us is whether petitioner's conviction should be set aside on the ground that as a matter of law the defense of entrapment was established. Petitioner was convicted under an indictment charging three sales of narcotics in violation of 21 U.S.C. § 174.

In late August 1951, Kalchinian, a government informer, first met petitioner at a doctor's office where apparently both were being treated to be cured of narcotics addiction. Several accidental meetings followed, either at the doctor's office or at the pharmacy where both filled their prescriptions from the doctor. From mere greetings, conversation progressed to a discussion of mutual experiences and problems, including their attempts to overcome addiction to narcotics. Finally Kalchinian asked petitioner if he knew of a good source of narcotics. He asked petitioner to supply him with a source because he was not responding to treatment. From the first, petitioner tried to avoid the issue. Not until after a number of repetitions of the request, predicated on Kalchinian's presumed suffering, did petitioner finally acquiesce. Several times thereafter he obtained a quantity of narcotics which he shared with Kalchinian. Each time petitioner told Kalchinian that the total cost of narcotics he obtained was twenty-five dollars and that Kalchinian owed him fifteen dollars. The informer thus bore the cost of his share of the narcotics plus the taxi and other expenses necessary to obtain the drug. After several such sales Kalchinian informed agents of the Bureau of Narcotics that he had another seller for them. On three occasions during November 1951, government agents observed petitioner give narcotics to Kalchinian in return for money supplied by the Government.

At the trial the factual issue was whether the informer had convinced an otherwise unwilling person to commit a criminal act or whether petitioner was already predisposed to commit the act and exhibited only the natural hesitancy of one acquainted with the narcotics trade. The issue of entrapment went to the jury, and a conviction resulted. Petitioner was sentenced to imprisonment for ten years.

In *Sorrells v. United States*, 287 U.S. 435 (1932), this Court firmly recognized the defense of entrapment in the federal courts. The intervening years have in no way detracted from the principles underlying that decision. The function of law enforcement is the prevention of crime and the apprehension of criminals. Manifestly, that function does not include the manufacturing of crime. Criminal activity is such that stealth and strategy are necessary weapons in the arsenal of the police officer. However, "a different question is presented when the criminal design originates with the officials of the Government, and they implant in the mind of an innocent person the disposition to commit the alleged offense and induce its commission in order that they may prosecute." Then stealth and strategy become as objectionable police methods as the coerced confession and the unlawful search. Congress could not have intended that its statutes were to be enforced by tempting innocent persons into violations.

However, the fact that government agents "merely afford opportunities or facilities for the commission of the offense does not" constitute entrapment. Entrapment occurs only when the criminal conduct was "the product of the *creative* activity" of law-enforcement officials. (Emphasis supplied.) To determine whether entrapment has been established, a line must be drawn between the trap for the unwary innocent and the trap for the unwary criminal. The principles by which the courts are to make this determination were outlined in *Sorrells*. On the one hand, at trial the accused may examine the conduct of the government agent; and on the other hand, the accused will be subjected to an "appropriate and searching inquiry into his own conduct and predisposition" as bearing on his claim of innocence.

We conclude from the evidence that entrapment was established as a matter of law. In so holding, we are not choosing between conflicting witnesses, nor judging credibility. Aside from recalling Kalchinian, who was the Government's witness, the defense called no witnesses. We reach our conclusion from the undisputed testimony of the prosecution's witnesses.

It is patently clear that petitioner was induced by Kalchinian. The informer himself testified that, believing petitioner to be undergoing a cure for narcotics addiction, he nonetheless sought to persuade petitioner to obtain for him a source of narcotics. In Kalchinian's own words we are told of the accidental, yet recurring, meetings, the ensuing conversations concerning mutual experiences in regard to narcotics addiction, and then of Kalchinian's resort to sympathy. One request was not enough, for Kalchinian tells us that additional ones were necessary to overcome, first, petitioner's refusal, then his evasiveness, and then his hesitancy in order to achieve capitulation. Kalchinian not only procured a source of narcotics but apparently also induced petitioner to return to the habit. Finally, assured of a catch, Kalchinian informed the authorities so that they could close the net. The Government cannot disown Kalchinian and insist it is not responsible for his actions. Although he was not being paid, Kalchinian was an active government informer who had but recently been the instigator of at least two other prosecutions. Undoubtedly the impetus for such achievements was the fact that in 1951 Kalchinian was himself under criminal charges for illegally selling narcotics and had not yet been sentenced.[3] It makes no difference that the sales for which petitioner was convicted occurred after a series of sales. They were not independent acts subsequent to the inducement but part of a course of conduct which was the product of the inducement. In his testimony the federal agent in charge of the case admitted that he never bothered to question Kalchinian about the way he had made contact with petitioner. The Government cannot make such use of an informer and then claim disassociation through ignorance.

The Government sought to overcome the defense of entrapment by claiming that petitioner evinced a "ready complaisance" to accede to Kalchinian's request. Aside from a record of past convictions, which we discuss in the following paragraph, the Government's case is unsupported. There is no evidence that petitioner himself was in the trade. When his apartment was searched after arrest, no narcotics were found. There is no significant evidence that petitioner even made a profit on any sale to Kalchinian. The Government's characterization of petitioner's hesitancy to Kalchinian's request as the natural wariness of the criminal cannot fill the evidentiary void.

The Government's additional evidence in the second trial to show that petitioner was ready and willing to sell narcotics should the opportunity present itself was petitioner's record of two past narcotics convictions. In 1942 petitioner was convicted of illegally selling narcotics; in 1946 he was convicted of illegally possessing them. However, a nine-year-old sales conviction and a five-year-old possession conviction are insufficient to prove petitioner had a readiness to sell narcotics at the time Kalchinian approached him, particularly when we must assume from the record he was trying to overcome the narcotics habit at the time.

---

[3] Kalchinian received a suspended sentence in 1952 after a statement by the United States Attorney to the Judge that he had been cooperative with the Government.

The case at bar illustrates an evil which the defense of entrapment is designed to overcome. The government informer entices someone attempting to avoid narcotics not only into carrying out an illegal sale but also into returning to the habit of use. Selecting the proper time, the informer then tells the government agent. The set-up is accepted by the agent without even a question as to the manner in which the informer encountered the seller. Thus the Government plays on the weaknesses of an innocent party and beguiles him into committing crimes which he otherwise would not have attempted. Law enforcement does not require methods such as this.

It has been suggested that in overturning this conviction we should reassess the doctrine of entrapment according to principles announced in the separate opinion of Mr. Justice Roberts in *Sorrells*, 287 U.S. at 453. To do so would be to decide the case on grounds rejected by the majority in *Sorrells* and, so far as the record shows, not raised here or below by the parties before us.

At least two important issues of law enforcement and trial procedure would have to be decided without the benefit of argument by the parties, one party being the Government. Mr. Justice Roberts asserted that although the defendant could claim that the Government had induced him to commit the crime, the Government could not reply by showing that the defendant's criminal conduct was due to his own readiness and not to the persuasion of government agents. The handicap thus placed on the prosecution is obvious. Furthermore, it was the position of Mr. Justice Roberts that the factual issue of entrapment — now limited to the question of what the government agents did — should be decided by the judge, not the jury. Not only was this rejected by the Court in *Sorrells*, but where the issue has been presented to them, the Courts of Appeals have since *Sorrells* unanimously concluded that unless it can be decided as a matter of law, the issue of whether a defendant has been entrapped is for the jury as part of its function of determining the guilt or innocence of the accused.

To dispose of this case on the ground suggested would entail both overruling a leading decision of this Court and brushing aside the possibility that we would be creating more problems than we would supposedly be solving.

The judgment of the Court of Appeals is reversed and the case is remanded to the District Court with instructions to dismiss the indictment.

Mr. Justice Frankfurter, whom Mr. Justice Douglas, Mr. Justice Harlan, and Mr. Justice Brennan join, concurring in the result.

Although agreeing with the Court that the undisputed facts show entrapment as a matter of law, I reach this result by a route different from the Court's.

It is surely sheer fiction to suggest that a conviction cannot be had when a defendant has been entrapped by government officers or informers because "Congress could not have intended that its statutes were to be enforced by tempting innocent persons into violations." In these cases raising claims of entrapment, the only legislative intention that can with any show of reason be extracted from the statute is the intention to make criminal precisely the conduct in which the defendant has engaged. That conduct includes all the elements necessary to constitute criminality. Without compulsion and "knowingly," where that is requisite, the defendant has violated the statutory command. If he is to be relieved from the usual punitive consequences, it is on no account because he is innocent of the offense described. In these circumstances, conduct is not less criminal because the result of temptation, whether the tempter is a private person or a government agent or informer.

The courts refuse to convict an entrapped defendant, not because his conduct falls outside the proscription of the statute, but because, even if his guilt be admitted, the methods employed on behalf of the Government to bring about conviction cannot be countenanced. As Mr. Justice Holmes said in *Olmstead v. United States*, 277 U.S. 438, 470 (dissenting), in another connection, "It is desirable that criminals should be detected, and to that end that all available evidence should be used. It also is desirable that the Government should not itself foster and pay for other crimes, when they are the means by which the evidence is to be obtained. . . . [F]or my part I think it a less evil that some criminals should escape than that the Government should play an ignoble part." Insofar as they are used as instrumentalities in the administration of criminal justice, the federal courts have an obligation to set their face against enforcement of the law by lawless means or means that violate rationally vindicated standards of justice, and to refuse to sustain such methods by effectuating them. They do this in the exercise of a recognized jurisdiction to formulate and apply "proper standards for the enforcement of the federal criminal law in the federal courts," *McNabb v. United States*, 318 U.S. 332, 341, an obligation that goes beyond the conviction of the particular defendant before the court. Public confidence in the fair and honorable administration of justice, upon which ultimately depends the rule of law, is the transcending value at stake.

The formulation of these standards does not in any way conflict with the statute the defendant has violated, or involve the initiation of a judicial policy disregarding or qualifying that framed by Congress. A false choice is put when it is said that either the defendant's conduct does not fall within the statute or he must be convicted. The statute is wholly directed to defining and prohibiting the substantive offense concerned and expresses no purpose, either permissive or prohibitory, regarding the police conduct that will be tolerated in the detection of crime. A statute prohibiting the sale of narcotics is as silent on the question of entrapment as it is on the admissibility of illegally obtained evidence. It is enacted, however, on the basis of certain presuppositions concerning the established legal order and the role of the courts within that system in formulating standards for the administration of criminal justice when Congress itself has not specifically legislated to that end. Specific statutes are to be fitted into an antecedent legal system.

It might be thought that it is largely an academic question whether the court's finding a bar to conviction derives from the statute or from a supervisory jurisdiction over the administration of criminal justice; under either theory substantially the same considerations will determine whether the defense of entrapment is sustained. But to look to a statute for guidance in the application of a policy not remotely within the contemplation of Congress at the time of its enactment is to distort analysis. It is to run the risk, furthermore, that the court will shirk the responsibility that is necessarily in its keeping, if Congress is truly silent, to accommodate the dangers of overzealous law enforcement and civilized methods adequate to counter the ingenuity of modern criminals. The reasons that actually underlie the defense of entrapment can too easily be lost sight of in the pursuit of a wholly fictitious congressional intent.

The crucial question, not easy of answer, to which the court must direct itself is whether the police conduct revealed in the particular case falls below standards, to which common feelings respond, for the proper use of governmental power. For answer it is wholly irrelevant to ask if the "intention" to commit the crime originated with the defendant or government officers, or if the criminal conduct was the product of "the creative activity" of law-enforcement officials. Yet in the present case the Court repeats and purports to apply these unrevealing tests. Of course in every case of this kind the intention that the particular crime be committed originates with the police, and without their inducement the crime would not have occurred. But it is perfectly clear from such decisions as the decoy letter cases in this Court, *e.g.*, *Grimm v. United States*, 156 U.S. 604, where the police in effect simply furnished the opportunity for the commission of the crime, that this is not enough to enable the defendant to escape conviction.

The intention referred to, therefore, must be a general intention or predisposition to commit, whenever the opportunity should arise, crimes of the kind solicited, and in proof of such a predisposition evidence has often been admitted to show the defendant's reputation, criminal activities, and prior disposition. The danger of prejudice in such a situation, particularly if the issue of entrapment must be submitted to the jury and disposed of by a general verdict of guilty or innocent, is evident. The defendant must either forego the claim of entrapment or run the substantial risk that, in spite of instructions, the jury will allow a criminal record or bad reputation to weigh in its determination of guilt of the specific offense of which he stands charged. Furthermore, a test that looks to the character and predisposition of the defendant rather than the conduct of the police loses sight of the underlying reason for the defense of entrapment. No matter what the defendant's past record and present inclinations to criminality, or the depths to which he has sunk in the estimation of society, certain police conduct to ensnare him into further crime is not to be tolerated by an advanced society. And in the present case it is clear that the Court in fact reverses the conviction because of the conduct of the informer Kalchinian, and not because the Government has failed to draw a convincing picture of petitioner's past criminal conduct. Permissible police activity does not vary according to the particular defendant concerned; surely if two suspects have been solicited at the same time in the same manner, one should not go to jail simply because he has been convicted before and is said to have a criminal disposition. No more does it vary according to the suspicions, reasonable or unreasonable, of the police concerning the defendant's activities. Appeals to sympathy, friendship, the possibility of exorbitant gain, and so forth, can no more be tolerated when directed against a past offender than against an ordinary law-abiding citizen. A contrary view runs afoul of fundamental principles of equality under law, and would espouse the notion that when dealing with the criminal classes anything goes. The possibility that no matter what his past crimes and general disposition the defendant might not have committed the particular crime unless confronted with inordinate inducements, must not be ignored. Past crimes do not forever outlaw the criminal and open him to police practices, aimed at securing his repeated conviction, from which the ordinary citizen is protected. The whole ameliorative hopes of modern penology and prison administration strongly counsel against such a view.

This does not mean that the police may not act so as to detect those engaged in criminal conduct and ready and willing to commit further crimes should the occasion arise. Such indeed is their obligation. It does mean that in holding out inducements they should act in such a manner as is likely to induce to the commission of crime only these persons and not others who would normally avoid crime and through self-struggle resist ordinary temptations. This test shifts attention from the record and predisposition of the particular defendant to the conduct of the police and the likelihood, objectively considered, that it would entrap only those ready and willing to commit crime. It is as objective a test as the subject matter permits, and will give guidance in regulating police conduct that is lacking when the reasonableness of police suspicions must be judged or the criminal disposition of the defendant retrospectively appraised. It draws directly on the fundamental intuition that led in the first instance to the outlawing of "entrapment" as a prosecutorial instrument. The power of government is abused and directed to an end for which it was not constituted when employed to promote rather than detect crime and to bring about the downfall of those who, left to themselves, might well have obeyed the law. Human nature is weak enough and sufficiently beset by temptations without government adding to them and generating crime.

What police conduct is to be condemned, because likely to induce those not otherwise ready and willing to commit crime, must be picked out from case to case as new situations arise involving different crimes and new methods of detection. The *Sorrells* case involved persistent solicitation in the face of obvious reluctance, and appeals to sentiments aroused by reminiscences of experiences as companions in arms in the World War. Particularly reprehensible in the present case was the use of repeated requests to overcome petitioner's hesitancy, coupled with appeals to sympathy based on mutual experiences with narcotics addiction. Evidence of the setting in which the inducement took place is of course highly relevant in judging its likely effect, and the court should also consider the nature of the crime involved, its secrecy and difficulty of detection, and the manner in which the particular criminal business is usually carried on.

As Mr. Justice Roberts convincingly urged in the *Sorrells* case, such a judgment, aimed at blocking off areas of impermissible police conduct, is appropriate for the court and not the jury. "The protection of its own functions and the preservation of the purity of its own temple belongs only to the court. It is the province of the court and of the court alone to protect itself and the government from such prostitution of the criminal law. The violation of the principles of justice by the entrapment of the unwary into crime should be dealt with by the court no matter by whom or at what stage of the proceedings the facts are brought to its attention." 287 U.S. at 457 (separate opinion). Equally important is the consideration that a jury verdict, although it may settle the issue of entrapment in the particular case, cannot give significant guidance for official conduct for the future. Only the court, through the gradual evolution of explicit standards in accumulated precedents, can do this with the degree of certainty that the wise administration of criminal justice demands.

QUESTIONS AND NOTES

1. Do you think that the Supreme Court reversed Sherman's conviction because he was basically innocent or because it disapproved of the police practices in this case? Explain.

2. Do you think Sherman was less culpable than the average drug dealer? If so, should he have been released even if Kalchinian did not work for the government?

3. Do you disapprove of the police practices employed in *Sherman*? Why? Why not?

4. In an ideal system of jurisprudence, would the entrapment issue be resolved by a judge or a jury? Why?

5. In *Sherman*, the Court noted that the issue was not Sherman's predisposition when he made the *last* sale to Kalchinian, but his predisposition when he made the *first* sale? In *Jacobson*, the Court considered the extent to which the government could create a predisposition to criminality by non-criminal entreaties designed to play on the susceptibilities of the ultimate defendant.

JACOBSON v. UNITED STATES
503 U.S. 540 (1992)

JUSTICE WHITE delivered the opinion of the Court.

On September 24, 1987, petitioner Keith Jacobson was indicted for violating a provision of the Child Protection Act of 1984, which criminalizes the knowing receipt through the mails of a "visual depiction [that] involves the use of a minor engaging in sexually explicit conduct . . . ." Petitioner defended on the ground that the Government entrapped him into committing the crime through a series of communications from undercover agents that spanned the 26 months preceding his arrest. Petitioner was found guilty after a jury trial. The Court of Appeals affirmed his conviction, holding that the Government had carried its burden of proving beyond reasonable doubt that petitioner was predisposed to break the law and hence was not entrapped.

Because the Government overstepped the line between setting a trap for the "unwary innocent" and the "unwary criminal," *Sherman*, and as a matter of law failed to establish that petitioner was independently predisposed to commit the crime for which he was arrested, we reverse the Court of Appeals' judgment affirming his conviction.

I

In February 1984, petitioner, a 56-year-old veteran-turned-farmer who supported his elderly father in Nebraska, ordered two magazines and a brochure from a California adult bookstore. The magazines, entitled Bare Boys I and Bare Boys II, contained photographs of nude preteen and teenage boys. The contents of the magazines startled petitioner, who testified that he had expected to receive photographs of "young men 18 years or older." On cross-examination, he explained his response to the magazines:

PROSECUTOR: You were shocked and surprised that there were pictures of very young boys without clothes on, is that correct?

JACOBSON: Yes, I was.

PROSECUTOR: Were you offended?

. . .

JACOBSON: I was not offended because I thought these were a nudist type publication. Many of the pictures were out in a rural or outdoor setting. There was — I didn't draw any sexual connotation or connection with that.

The young men depicted in the magazines were not engaged in sexual activity, and petitioner's receipt of the magazines was legal under both federal and Nebraska law. Within three months, the law with respect to child pornography changed; Congress passed the Act illegalizing the receipt through the mails of sexually explicit depictions of children. In the very month that the new provision became law, postal inspectors found petitioner's name on the mailing list of the California bookstore that had mailed him Bare Boys I and II. There followed over the next 21/2 years, repeated efforts by two Government agencies, through five fictitious organizations and a bogus pen pal, to explore petitioner's willingness to break the new law by ordering sexually explicit photographs of children through the mail.

The Government began its efforts in January 1985 when a postal inspector sent petitioner a letter supposedly from the American Hedonist Society, which in fact was a fictitious organization. The letter included a membership application and stated the Society's doctrine: that members had the right to read what we desire, the right to discuss similar interests with those who share our philosophy, and finally that we have the "right to seek pleasure without restrictions being placed on us by outdated puritan morality." Petitioner enrolled in the organization and returned a sexual attitude questionnaire that asked him to rank on a scale of one to four his enjoyment of various sexual materials, with one being "really enjoy," two being "enjoy," three being "somewhat enjoy," and four being "do not enjoy." Petitioner ranked the entry "pre-teen sex" as a two, but indicated that he was opposed to pedophilia.

For a time, the Government left petitioner alone. But then a new "prohibited mail specialist" in the Postal Service found petitioner's name in a file, and in May 1986, petitioner received a solicitation from a second fictitious consumer research company, "Midlands Data Research," seeking a response from those who "believe in the joys of sex and the complete awareness of those lusty and youthful lads and lasses of the neophite [sic] age." The letter never explained whether "neophite" referred to minors or young adults. Petitioner responded: "Please feel free to send me more information, I am interested in teenage sexuality. Please keep my name confidential."

Petitioner then heard from yet another Government creation, "Heartland Institute for a New Tomorrow" (HINT), which proclaimed that it was "an organization founded to protect and promote sexual freedom and freedom of choice. We believe that arbitrarily imposed legislative sanctions restricting your sexual freedom should be rescinded through the legislative process." The letter also enclosed a second survey. Petitioner indicated that his interest in "preteen sex-homosexual" material was above average, but not high. In response to another question, petitioner wrote: "Not only sexual expression but freedom of the press is under attack. We must be ever vigilant to counter attack right wing fundamentalists who are determined to curtail our freedoms."

"HINT" replied, portraying itself as a lobbying organization seeking to repeal "all statutes which regulate sexual activities, except those laws which deal with violent behavior, such as rape. HINT is also lobbying to eliminate any legal definition of the age of consent." These lobbying efforts were to be funded by sales from a catalog to be published in the future "offering the sale of various items which we believe you will find to be both interesting and stimulating." HINT also provided computer matching of group members with similar survey responses; and, although petitioner was supplied with a list of potential "pen pals," he did not initiate any correspondence.

Nevertheless, the Government's "prohibited mail specialist" began writing to petitioner, using the pseudonym "Carl Long." The letters employed a tactic known as "mirroring," which the inspector described as "reflecting whatever the interests are of the person we are writing to." Petitioner responded at first, indicating that his interest was primarily in "male-male items." Inspector "Long" wrote back:

> My interests too are primarily male-male items. Are you satisfied with the type of VCR tapes available? Personally, I like the amateur stuff better if its [sic] well produced as it can get more kinky and also seems more real. I think the actors enjoy it more.

Petitioner responded:

> As far as my likes are concerned, I like good looking young guys (in their late teens and early 20's) doing their thing together.

Petitioner's letters to "Long" made no reference to child pornography. After writing two letters, petitioner discontinued the correspondence.

By March 1987, 34 months had passed since the Government obtained petitioner's name from the mailing list of the California bookstore, and 26 months had passed since the Postal Service had commenced its mailings to petitioner. Although petitioner had responded to surveys and letters, the Government had no evidence that petitioner had ever intentionally possessed or been exposed to child pornography. The Postal Service had not checked petitioner's mail to determine whether he was receiving questionable mailings from persons — other than the Government — involved in the child pornography industry.

At this point, a second Government agency, the Customs Service, included petitioner in its own child pornography sting, "Operation Borderline," after receiving his name on lists submitted by the Postal Service. Using the name of a fictitious Canadian company called "Produit Outaouais," the Customs Service mailed petitioner a brochure advertising photographs of young boys engaging in sex. Petitioner placed an order that was never filled.

The Postal Service also continued its efforts in the *Jacobson* case, writing to petitioner as the "Far Eastern Trading Company Ltd." The letter began:

> As many of you know, much hysterical nonsense has appeared in the American media concerning pornography and what must be done to stop it from coming across your borders. This brief letter does not allow us to give much comments; however, why is your government spending millions of dollars to exercise international censorship while tons of drugs, which makes yours the world's most crime ridden country are passed through easily.

The letter went on to say:

> We have devised a method of getting these to you without prying eyes of U.S. Customs seizing your mail. . . . After consultations with American solicitors, we have been advised that once we have posted our material through your system, it cannot be opened for any inspection without authorization of a judge.

The letter invited petitioner to send for more information. It also asked petitioner to sign an affirmation that he was "not a law enforcement officer or agent of the U.S. Government acting in an undercover capacity for the purpose of entrapping Far Eastern Trading Company, its agents or customers." Petitioner responded. A catalogue was sent, and petitioner ordered Boys Who Love Boys, a pornographic magazine depicting young boys engaged in various sexual activities. Petitioner was arrested after a controlled delivery of a photocopy of the magazine.

When petitioner was asked at trial why he placed such an order, he explained that the Government had succeeded in piquing his curiosity:

> Well, the statement was made of all the trouble and the hysteria over pornography and I wanted to see what the material was. It didn't describe the — I didn't know for sure what kind of sexual action they were referring to in the Canadian letter. . . .

In petitioner's home, the Government found the Bare Boys magazines and materials that the Government had sent to him in the course of its protracted investigation, but no other materials that would indicate that petitioner collected or was actively interested in child pornography.

The trial court instructed the jury on the petitioner's entrapment defense,[1] petitioner was convicted.

---

[1] The jury was instructed:

> As mentioned, one of the issues in this case is whether the defendant was entrapped. If the defendant was entrapped he must be found not guilty. The government has the burden of proving beyond a reasonable doubt that the defendant was not entrapped.

> If the defendant before contact with law-enforcement officers or their agents did not have any intent or disposition to commit the crime charged and was induced or persuaded by

II

There can be no dispute about the evils of child pornography or the difficulties that laws and law enforcement have encountered in eliminating it. Likewise, there can be no dispute that the Government may use undercover agents to enforce the law. "It is well settled that the fact that officers or employees of the Government merely afford opportunities or facilities for the commission of the offense does not defeat the prosecution. Artifice and stratagem may be employed to catch those engaged in criminal enterprises."

In their zeal to enforce the law, however, Government agents may not originate a criminal design, implant in an innocent person's mind the disposition to commit a criminal act, and then induce commission of the crime so that the Government may prosecute. *Sherman.* Where the Government has induced an individual to break the law and the defense of entrapment is at issue, as it was in this case, the prosecution must prove beyond reasonable doubt that the defendant was disposed to commit the criminal act prior to first being approached by Government agents.[2]

Thus, an agent deployed to stop the traffic in illegal drugs may offer the opportunity to buy or sell drugs, and, if the offer is accepted, make an arrest on the spot or later. In such a typical case, or in a more elaborate "sting" operation involving government-sponsored fencing where the defendant is simply provided with the opportunity to commit a crime, the entrapment defense is of little use because the ready commission of the criminal act amply demonstrates the defendant's predisposition. Had the agents in this case simply offered petitioner the opportunity to order child pornography through the mails, and petitioner — who

---

law-enforcement officers or their agents to commit that crime, then he was entrapped. On the other hand, if the defendant before contact with law-enforcement officers or their agents did have an intent or disposition to commit the crime charged, then he was not entrapped even though law-enforcement officers or their agents provided a favorable opportunity to commit the crime or made committing the crime easier or even participated in acts essential to the crime.

[2] Inducement is not at issue in this case. The Government does not dispute that it induced petitioner to commit the crime. The sole issue is whether the Government carried its burden of proving that petitioner was predisposed to violate the law before the Government intervened. The dissent is mistaken in claiming that this is an innovation in entrapment law and in suggesting that the Government's conduct prior to the moment of solicitation is irrelevant. The Court rejected these arguments five decades ago in *Sorrells*, when the Court wrote that the Government may not punish an individual "for an alleged offense which is the product of the creative activity of its own officials" and that in such a case the Government "is in no position to object to evidence of the activities of its representatives in relation to the accused . . . ." Indeed, the proposition that the accused must be predisposed prior to contact with law enforcement officers is so firmly established that the Government conceded the point at oral argument, submitting that the evidence it developed during the course of its investigation was probative because it indicated petitioner's state of mind prior to the commencement of the Government's investigation.

This long-established standard in no way encroaches upon Government investigatory activities. Indeed, the Government's internal guidelines for undercover operations provide that an inducement to commit a crime should not be offered unless:

(a) there is a reasonable indication, based on information developed through informants or other means, that the subject is engaging, has engaged, or is likely to engage in illegal activity of a similar type; or (b) the opportunity for illegal activity has been structured so that there is reason for believing that persons drawn to the opportunity, or brought to it, are predisposed to engage in the contemplated illegal activity.

Attorney General's Guidelines on FBI Undercover Operations (Dec. 31, 1980).

must be presumed to know the law — had promptly availed himself of this criminal opportunity, it is unlikely that his entrapment defense would have warranted a jury instruction.

But that is not what happened here. By the time petitioner finally placed his order, he had already been the target of 26 months of repeated mailings and communications from Government agents and fictitious organizations. Therefore, although he had become predisposed to break the law by May 1987, it is our view that the Government did not prove that this predisposition was independent and not the product of the attention that the Government had directed at petitioner since January 1985. *Sorrells; Sherman.*

The prosecution's evidence of predisposition falls into two categories: evidence developed prior to the Postal Service's mail campaign, and that developed during the course of the investigation. The sole piece of preinvestigation evidence is petitioner's 1984 order and receipt of the Bare Boys magazines. But this is scant if any proof of petitioner's predisposition to commit an illegal act, the criminal character of which a defendant is presumed to know. It may indicate a predisposition to view sexually-oriented photographs that are responsive to his sexual tastes; but evidence that merely indicates a generic inclination to act within a broad range, not all of which is criminal, is of little probative value in establishing predisposition.

Furthermore, petitioner was acting within the law at the time he received these magazines. Receipt through the mails of sexually explicit depictions of children for noncommercial use did not become illegal under federal law until May 1984, and Nebraska had no law that forbade petitioner's possession of such material until 1988. Evidence of predisposition to do what once was lawful is not, by itself, sufficient to show predisposition to do what is now illegal, for there is a common understanding that most people obey the law even when they disapprove of it. This obedience may reflect a generalized respect for legality or the fear of prosecution, but for whatever reason, the law's prohibitions are matters of consequence. Hence, the fact that petitioner legally ordered and received the Bare Boys magazines does little to further the Government's burden of proving that petitioner was predisposed to commit a criminal act. This is particularly true given petitioner's unchallenged testimony was that he did not know until they arrived that the magazines would depict minors.

The prosecution's evidence gathered during the investigation also fails to carry the Government's burden. Petitioner's responses to the many communications prior to the ultimate criminal act were at most indicative of certain personal inclinations, including a predisposition to view photographs of preteen sex and a willingness to promote a given agenda by supporting lobbying organizations. Even so, petitioner's responses hardly support an inference that he would commit the crime of receiving child pornography through the mails.[3] Furthermore, a person's inclinations and

---

[3] We do not hold, as the dissent suggests, that the Government was required to prove that petitioner knowingly violated the law. We simply conclude that proof that petitioner engaged in legal conduct and possessed certain generalized personal inclinations is not sufficient evidence to prove beyond a reasonable doubt that he would have been predisposed to commit the crime charged independent of the Government's coaxing.

"fantasies . . . are his own and beyond the reach of government . . . ."

On the other hand, the strong arguable inference is that, by waving the banner of individual rights and disparaging the legitimacy and constitutionality of efforts to restrict the availability of sexually explicit materials, the Government not only excited petitioner's interest in sexually explicit materials banned by law but also exerted substantial pressure on petitioner to obtain and read such material as part of a fight against censorship and the infringement of individual rights. For instance, HINT described itself as "an organization founded to protect and promote sexual freedom and freedom of choice" and stated that "the most appropriate means to accomplish [its] objectives is to promote honest dialogue among concerned individuals and to continue its lobbying efforts with State Legislators." These lobbying efforts were to be financed through catalogue sales. Mailings from the equally fictitious American Hedonist Society, and the correspondence from the non-existent Carl Long, endorsed these themes.

Similarly, the two solicitations in the spring of 1987 raised the spectre of censorship while suggesting that petitioner ought to be allowed to do what he had been solicited to do. The mailing from the Customs Service referred to "the worldwide ban and intense enforcement on this type of material," observed that "what was legal and commonplace is now an underground and secretive service," and emphasized that "this environment forces us to take extreme measures" to insure delivery. The Postal Service solicitation described the concern about child pornography as "hysterical nonsense," decried "international censorship," and assured petitioner, based on consultation with "American solicitors" that an order that had been posted could not be opened for inspection without authorization of a judge. It further asked petitioner to affirm that he was not a government agent attempting to entrap the mail order company or its customers. In these particulars, both government solicitations suggested that receiving this material was something that petitioner ought to be allowed to do.

Petitioner's ready response to these solicitations cannot be enough to establish beyond reasonable doubt that he was predisposed, prior to the Government acts intended to create predisposition, to commit the crime of receiving child pornography through the mails. The evidence that petitioner was ready and willing to commit the offense came only after the Government had devoted 2 1/2 years to convincing him that he had or should have the right to engage in the very behavior proscribed by law. Rational jurors could not say beyond a reasonable doubt that petitioner possessed the requisite predisposition prior to the Government's investigation and that it existed independent of the Government's many and varied approaches to petitioner. As was explained in *Sherman*, where entrapment was found as a matter of law, "the Government [may not] play on the weaknesses of an innocent party and beguile him into committing crimes which he otherwise would not have attempted."

Law enforcement officials go too far when they "implant in the mind of an innocent person the disposition to commit the alleged offense and induce its commission in order that they may prosecute." Like the *Sorrells* court, we are "unable to conclude that it was the intention of the Congress in enacting this statute that its processes of detection and enforcement should be abused by the instigation by government officials of an act on the part of persons otherwise innocent in order to lure them to its commission and to punish them." When the Government's quest for convictions leads to the apprehension of an otherwise law-abiding citizen who, if left to his own devices, likely would have never run afoul of the law, the courts should intervene.

Because we conclude that this is such a case and that the prosecution failed, as a matter of law, to adduce evidence to support the jury verdict that petitioner was predisposed, independent of the Government's acts and beyond a reasonable doubt, to violate the law by receiving child pornography through the mails, we reverse the Court of Appeals' judgment affirming the conviction of Keith Jacobson.

JUSTICE O'CONNOR, with whom THE CHIEF JUSTICE and JUSTICE KENNEDY join, and with whom JUSTICE SCALIA joins except as to Part II, dissenting.

Keith Jacobson was offered only two opportunities to buy child pornography through the mail. Both times, he ordered. Both times, he asked for opportunities to buy more. He needed no Government agent to coax, threaten, or persuade him; no one played on his sympathies, friendship, or suggested that his committing the crime would further a greater good. In fact, no Government agent even contacted him face-to-face. The Government contends that from the enthusiasm with which Mr. Jacobson responded to the chance to commit a crime, a reasonable jury could permissibly infer beyond a reasonable doubt that he was predisposed to commit the crime. I agree.

The first time the Government sent Mr. Jacobson a catalog of illegal materials, he ordered a set of photographs advertised as picturing "young boys in sex action fun." He enclosed the following note with his order: "I received your brochure and decided to place an order. If I like your product, I will order more later." For reasons undisclosed in the record, Mr. Jacobson's order was never delivered.

The second time the Government sent a catalog of illegal materials, Mr. Jacobson ordered a magazine called "Boys Who Love Boys," described as: "11 year old and 14 year old boys get it on in every way possible. Oral, anal sex and heavy masturbation. If you love boys, you will be delighted with this." Along with his order, Mr. Jacobson sent the following note: "Will order other items later. I want to be discreet in order to protect you and me."

Government agents admittedly did not offer Mr. Jacobson the chance to buy child pornography right away. Instead, they first sent questionnaires in order to make sure that he was generally interested in the subject matter. Indeed, a "cold call" in such a business would not only risk rebuff and suspicion, but might also shock and offend the uninitiated, or expose minors to suggestive materials. Mr. Jacobson's responses to the questionnaires gave the investigators reason to think he would be interested in photographs depicting preteen sex.

The Court, however, concludes that a reasonable jury could not have found Mr. Jacobson to be predisposed beyond a reasonable doubt on the basis of his responses to the Government's catalogs, even though it admits that, by that time, he was predisposed to commit the crime. The Government, the Court holds, failed to provide evidence that Mr. Jacobson's obvious predisposition at the time of the crime "was independent and not the product of the attention that the Government had directed at petitioner." In so holding, I believe the Court fails to acknowledge the reasonableness of the jury's inference from the evidence, redefines "predisposition," and introduces a new requirement that Government sting operations have a reasonable suspicion of illegal activity before contacting a suspect.

I

This Court has held previously that a defendant's predisposition is to be assessed as of the time the Government agent first suggested the crime, not when the Government agent first became involved. *Sherman*. Until the Government actually makes a suggestion of criminal conduct, it could not be said to have "implanted in the mind of an innocent person the disposition to commit the alleged offense and induce its commission . . . ." *Sorrells*. Even in *Sherman*, in which the Court held that the defendant had been entrapped as a matter of law, the Government agent had repeatedly and unsuccessfully coaxed the defendant to buy drugs, ultimately succeeding only by playing on the defendant's sympathy. The Court found lack of predisposition based on the Government's numerous unsuccessful attempts to induce the crime, not on the basis of preliminary contacts with the defendant.

Today, the Court holds that Government conduct may be considered to create a predisposition to commit a crime, even before any Government action to induce the commission of the crime. In my view, this holding changes entrapment doctrine. Generally, the inquiry is whether a suspect is predisposed before the Government induces the commission of the crime, not before the Government makes initial contact with him. There is no dispute here that the Government's questionnaires and letters were not sufficient to establish inducement; they did not even suggest that Mr. Jacobson should engage in any illegal activity. If all the Government had done was to send these materials, Mr. Jacobson's entrapment defense would fail. Yet the Court holds that the Government must prove not only that a suspect was predisposed to commit the crime before the opportunity to commit it arose, but also before the Government came on the scene.

The rule that preliminary Government contact can create a predisposition has the potential to be misread by lower courts as well as criminal investigators as requiring that the Government must have sufficient evidence of a defendant's predisposition before it ever seeks to contact him. Surely the Court cannot intend to impose such a requirement, for it would mean that the Government must have a reasonable suspicion of criminal activity before it begins an investigation, a condition that we have never before imposed. The Court denies that its new rule will affect run-of-the-mill sting operations, and one hopes that it means what it says. Nonetheless, after this case, every defendant will claim that something the Government agent did before soliciting the crime "created" a predisposition that was not there before. For example, a bribe taker will claim that the description of the amount of money available was so enticing that it implanted a disposition to accept the bribe later offered. A drug buyer will claim that the description of the drug's purity and effects was so tempting that it created the urge to try it for the first time. In short, the Court's opinion could be read to prohibit the Government from advertising the seductions of criminal activity as part of its sting operation, for fear of creating a predisposition in its suspects. That limitation would be especially likely to hamper sting operations such as this one, which mimic the advertising done by genuine purveyors of pornography. No doubt the Court would protest that its opinion does not stand for so broad a proposition, but the apparent lack of a principled basis for distinguishing these scenarios exposes a flaw in the more limited rule the Court today adopts.

The Court's rule is all the more troubling because it does not distinguish between Government conduct that merely highlights the temptation of the crime itself, and Government conduct that threatens, coerces, or leads a suspect to commit a crime in order to fulfill some other obligation. For example, in *Sorrells*, the Government agent repeatedly asked for illegal liquor, coaxing the defendant to accede on the ground that "one former war buddy would get liquor for another." In *Sherman*, the Government agent played on the defendant's sympathies, pretending to be going through drug withdrawal and begging the defendant to relieve his distress by helping him buy drugs.

The Government conduct in this case is not comparable. While the Court states that the Government "exerted substantial pressure on petitioner to obtain and read such material as part of a fight against censorship and the infringement of individual rights," one looks at the record in vain for evidence of such "substantial pressure." The most one finds is letters advocating legislative action to liberalize obscenity laws, letters which could easily be ignored or thrown away. Much later, the Government sent separate mailings of catalogs of illegal materials. Nowhere did the Government suggest that the proceeds of the sale of the illegal materials would be used to support legislative reforms. While one of the HINT letters suggested that lobbying efforts would be funded by sales from a catalog, the catalogs actually sent, nearly a year later, were from different fictitious entities (Produit Outaouais and Far Eastern Trading Company), and gave no suggestion that money would be used for any political purposes. Nor did the Government claim to be organizing a civil disobedience movement, which would protest the pornography laws by breaking them. Contrary to the gloss given the evidence by the Court, the Government's suggestions of illegality may also have made buyers beware, and increased the mystique of the materials offered: "[f]or those of you who have enjoyed youthful material . . . we have devised a method of getting these to you without prying eyes of U.S. Customs seizing your mail." Mr. Jacobson's curiosity to see what "all the trouble and the hysteria" was about, is certainly susceptible of more than one interpretation. And it is the jury that is charged with the obligation of interpreting it. In sum, the Court fails to construe the evidence in the light most favorable to the Government, and fails to draw all reasonable inferences in the Government's favor. It was surely reasonable for the jury to infer that Mr. Jacobson was predisposed beyond a reasonable doubt, even if other inferences from the evidence were also possible.

II

The second puzzling thing about the Court's opinion is its redefinition of predisposition. The Court acknowledges that "petitioner's responses to the many communications prior to the ultimate criminal act were . . . indicative of certain personal inclinations, including a predisposition to view photographs of preteen sex . . . ." If true, this should have settled the matter; Mr. Jacobson was predisposed to engage in the illegal conduct. Yet, the Court concludes, "petitioner's responses hardly support an inference that he would commit the crime of receiving child pornography through the mails."

The Court seems to add something new to the burden of proving predisposition. Not only must the Government show that a defendant was predisposed to engage in the illegal conduct, here, receiving photographs of minors engaged in sex, but also that the defendant was predisposed to break the law knowingly in order to do so. The statute violated here, however, does not require proof of specific intent to break the law; it requires only knowing receipt of visual depictions produced by using minors engaged in sexually explicit conduct. Under the Court's analysis, however, the Government must prove more to show predisposition than it need prove in order to convict.

The Court ignores the judgment of Congress that specific intent is not an element of the crime of receiving sexually explicit photographs of minors. The elements of predisposition should track the elements of the crime. The predisposition requirement is meant to eliminate the entrapment defense for those defendants who would have committed the crime anyway, even absent Government inducement. Because a defendant might very well be convicted of the crime here absent Government inducement even though he did not know his conduct was illegal, a specific intent requirement does little to distinguish between those who would commit the crime without the inducement and those who would not. In sum, although the fact that Mr. Jacobson's purchases of Bare Boys I and Bare Boys II were legal at the time may have some relevance to the question of predisposition, it is not, as the Court suggests, dispositive.

The crux of the Court's concern in this case is that the Government went too far and "abused" the "processes of detection and enforcement" by luring an innocent person to violate the law. Consequently, the Court holds that the Government failed to prove beyond a reasonable doubt that Mr. Jacobson was predisposed to commit the crime. It was, however, the jury's task, as the conscience of the community, to decide whether or not Mr. Jacobson was a willing participant in the criminal activity here or an innocent dupe. The jury is the traditional "defense against arbitrary law enforcement." *Duncan v. Louisiana*, 391 U.S. 145 (1968). Indeed, in *Sorrells*, in which the Court was also concerned about overzealous law enforcement, the Court did not decide itself that the Government conduct constituted entrapment, but left the issue to the jury. There is no dispute that the jury in this case was fully and accurately instructed on the law of entrapment, and nonetheless found Mr. Jacobson guilty. Because I believe there was sufficient evidence to uphold the jury's verdict, I respectfully dissent.

QUESTIONS AND NOTES

1.　Unlike in *Sherman*, both the majority and the dissent in *Jacobson* appear content with the "predisposition" prerequisite required by the majority in *Sherman* and *Sorrells*. On what point do the majority and dissent differ? Who, in your judgment, got it right?

2. Does the majority require some form of reasonable suspicion prior to targeting a potential criminal (such as a purchaser of child pornography)? Should reasonable suspicion be required? Why? Why not?

3. If reasonable suspicion were required, would (should) predisposition be irrelevant?

4. Did the government do anything in *Jacobson* to render it likely that a nonpredisposed person would commit the crime?

5. Was the essential wrong in *Jacobson* the inefficient use of government resources? Should that be the concern of the entrapment defense? *See* Posner, *An Economic Theory of the Criminal Law*, 85 COLUM. L. REV. 1193, 1220 (1985).

B. THE DUE PROCESS DEFENSE

UNITED STATES v. GAMBLE
737 F.2d 853 (10th Cir. 1984)

LOGAN, CIRCUIT JUDGE

Defendant, John Gamble, a physician practicing in Kansas City, Kansas, was convicted on four counts of mail fraud. The charges against defendant resulted from an elaborate undercover investigation by United States postal inspectors.

United States postal inspectors concocted two schemes that ultimately involved defendant. In each scheme United States postal inspectors used fictitious names to obtain Missouri driver's licenses. The inspectors then registered automobiles they did not own and obtained insurance for the automobiles under those names. In cooperation with the Kansas City, Missouri, Police Department, the postal inspectors obtained accident reports for collisions that never occurred. The police officer who filled out the fictitious accident reports testified at trial that normally he would face severe sanctions for filling out false reports.

In each of the schemes the police issued a ticket to one of the inspectors and described the accidents in such a way that the inspector cited would be liable for any damages. After receiving the citations, the inspectors appeared in Municipal Court in Kansas City, Missouri, and pleaded guilty before prosecutors and judges who were unaware that the tickets were shams.

The first fictitious accident report, which was filed on May 6, 1980, described a one-car accident in which the driver of the vehicle, in an attempt to miss a stopped vehicle, swerved and struck a post. Postal Inspectors Armstrong and Gillis posed as passengers in the vehicle. Following this fictitious accident the inspectors visited defendant's office, asking him to help them perpetrate a fraud on the insurance company.

Posing as husband and wife, Armstrong and Gillis visited defendant's office seven times. On their first visit the inspectors' temperatures, weights, and blood pressures were checked. They filled out medical information forms, writing "traffic accident" in the blank for type of injury. When Inspector Armstrong met defendant, he told defendant that he had broken his glasses but had suffered no injuries and that he wanted to obtain some funds from the insurance company. Defendant described the procedure for filing claims with the insurance company and then conducted a routine physical examination of each inspector. On each subsequent visit the inspectors' weights, blood pressures, and temperatures apparently were checked. During the second visit defendant asked if he needed to do anything. Inspector Armstrong said no and stated that he had not yet contacted the insurance company. Subsequently, Inspector Armstrong told Jim Amen, an adjuster for State Farm Insurance Company, about injuries in his back and neck.

On the fourth visit the inspectors informed defendant that they had contacted State Farm Insurance Company. Later, Inspector Armstrong spoke with defendant's assistant, who prepared an insurance form and asked several questions. Armstrong told the assistant to write down that he had been unable to work for almost two months. When Inspectors Armstrong and Gillis visited defendant for the last time, they brought a draft from State Farm Insurance Company for $180, the total medical expense reported to the insurer. Defendant calculated that since they had already paid him $104, they owed him $66. (Correctly subtracted the figure was $76. Defendant had previously made the inspectors pay $10 or $12 apiece at each office visit when they saw defendant.) The inspectors gave defendant a $66 money order and kept the draft.

The second undercover operation began with a false accident report filed on July 9, 1980, which described a rear-end collision. Postal Inspectors Robert Bush and Donjette Gilmore posed as husband and wife and claimed to have been in the car that was hit. They visited defendant's office five times. Apparently at each visit the inspectors were given routine tests. When the inspectors first saw defendant, he asked what was wrong. Bush indicated that nothing was wrong but that the person who was responsible was insured and that there was a chance to make some money. Bush affirmed the doctor's stated assumption that they wanted to take advantage of the situation. Defendant then said, "You'll just have to play it up. You can't go out there tell that man ah, I wasn't hurt." Defendant also said, "You gotta have a back injury and you gotta have a neck injury or something. . . . We have to write it up to that effect and you'll make some money out of the deal." Defendant suggested neck and back injuries would be best because they are hard to prove and told them to come back in a few weeks to fill out the insurance papers.

Several weeks later the inspectors informed defendant that they had contacted the insurance company, and they discussed with defendant the insurer's method of handling claims. At a later visit defendant filled out a handwritten bill and put it in an envelope provided by the inspectors that was addressed to Farmers Insurance Group. Defendant handed the envelope back to Inspector Bush and asked him to take care of it. On December 11, 1980, the inspectors brought a draft for $160 from Farmers Insurance Group to defendant's office. A secretary reimbursed them for the $50 they had paid during previous office visits, and the inspectors signed the draft over to defendant.

II

Defendant contends that the government's conduct in formulating, carrying out, and enmeshing defendant in the mail fraud scheme was so outrageous that defendant's conviction should be overturned as a violation of due process of law. The Supreme Court recognized this defense in *United States v. Russell*, 411 U.S. 423 (1973), when it stated, "[W]e may someday be presented with a situation in which the conduct of law enforcement agents is so outrageous that due process principles would absolutely bar the government from invoking judicial processes to obtain a conviction, *cf. Rochin*."

When the Supreme Court considered the due process defense three years later in *Hampton v. United States*, 425 U.S. 484 (1976), the eight Justices who participated divided into three groups. The plurality opinion, written by Justice Rehnquist, stated that absent a violation of some protected right of the defendant, the Due Process Clause cannot be invoked to overturn a conviction because of governmental misconduct. Justice Rehnquist wrote, "The remedy of the criminal defendant with respect to the acts of Government agents . . . lies solely in the defense of entrapment." The due process defense survives, however, because a majority of the Justices, two who concurred in the result of the case and three who dissented, rejected the position "that the concept of fundamental fairness inherent in the guarantee of due process would never prevent the conviction of a predisposed defendant, regardless of the outrageousness of police behavior in light of the surrounding circumstances." (Powell, J., concurring). (Brennan, J., dissenting). Justice Powell added, "I emphasize that the cases, if any, in which proof of predisposition is not dispositive will be rare. Police overinvolvement in crime would have to reach a demonstrable level of outrageousness before it could bar conviction."

The defense that the government's conduct was so outrageous as to require reversal on due process grounds is often raised but is almost never successful. No Supreme Court case and only two circuit court opinions have set aside convictions on that basis. In *United States v. Twigg*, 588 F.2d 373 (3d Cir. 1978), a Drug Enforcement Agency (DEA) informant, as part of a plea bargain, involved defendant Neville in establishing a laboratory for the production of a controlled substance, methamphetamine hydrochloride (speed). The government gratuitously supplied about twenty percent of the glassware and an indispensable ingredient, phenyl-2-propanone. The DEA made arrangements with chemical supply houses to facilitate the purchase of the rest of the materials, and the DEA informant, operating under a business name supplied by the DEA, purchased all of the equipment and chemicals with the exception of a separatory funnel. When the participants encountered problems in locating an adequate production site, the government solved the problem by providing an isolated farmhouse. The DEA informant provided the expertise to run the laboratory. Neither Twigg nor Neville knew how to manufacture speed, and each provided only minimal assistance at the specific direction of the informant. The Third Circuit stated, "[W]e are not only concerned with the supply by government agents of necessary ingredients for manufacture, but we also have before us a crime . . . conceived and contrived by government agents." It reversed both convictions. In discussing the government's conduct the court noted in regard to Neville,

They [the government] set him up, encouraged him, provided the essential supplies and technical expertise, and when he and Kubica encountered difficulties in consummating the crime, they assisted in finding solutions. This egregious conduct on the part of government agents generated new crimes by the defendant merely for the sake of pressing criminal charges against him when, as far as the record reveals, he was lawfully and peacefully minding his own affairs. Fundamental fairness does not permit us to countenance such actions by law enforcement officials and prosecution for a crime so fomented by them will be barred.

It is important to note that the entrapment defense, which requires an absence of predisposition to commit the crime, is not involved in the instant case. Nevertheless, in a sense, entrapment and the due process defense are on a continuum, because both are based on the principle "that courts must be closed to the trial of a crime instigated by the government's own agents. No other issue, no comparison of equities as between the guilty official and the guilty defendant, has any place in the enforcement of this overruling principle of public policy." In stating that until the government provided the means to manufacture speed the *Twigg* defendant Neville was "minding his own affairs," the court notes precisely the point on the entrapment-due process continuum that the two concepts begin to merge. Although the due process defense purportedly ignores the defendant's predisposition to commit the crime charged, the defense nevertheless is concerned with the extent of government involvement in crime and the type of opportunity to become involved with crime that this conduct provides to the unwitting defendant. "[W]hen the government permits itself to become enmeshed in criminal activity, from beginning to end . . . the same underlying objections which render entrapment repugnant to American criminal justice are operative."

In the case at bar the government conceived and directed a crime in which defendant participated. The government used fictitious names to obtain driver's licenses, obtained insurance under those names for automobiles they did not own, orchestrated the production of false accident reports, appeared in court and pleaded guilty to traffic violations, and solicited defendant's aid in making false claims against insurance companies. Of the government agencies involved only the Kansas City, Missouri, Police Department knew of the operation. Involved without their knowledge were judges, prosecutors, state licensing authorities, and insurance companies. The government agents submitted the false claims to the insurance companies and lied to the companies about their injuries.

The government agents in the case before us displayed shocking disregard for the legal system. But these actions did not directly induce defendant to participate in the fraudulent scheme. Perhaps the false statements to state agents and the courts helped the inspectors obtain the medical forms defendant filled out and ultimately secure the settlement check. But defendant did not rely on any display of fictitious credentials or falsified documents; apparently he relied entirely upon what his "patients" told him. Therefore, we must ignore these acts of the government agents in evaluating defendant's due process claim.

Some of the artifices that the government inspectors used in the scheme, however, did directly contribute to defendant's decision to participate. The postal inspectors, with their elaborate machinations, sowed the seeds of criminality and brought defendant into their scheme. This brings the case closer to government manufacture of crime than the sting, Abscam, and other operations in which undercover agents set themselves up as amenable to law-breaking schemes brought to them by others. But did the action of the government agents cross the due process line? We recognize that "because the difficulties in detecting covert crime often warrant secretive investigations, involvement of Government agents must be of the tenor to shock the conscience before a violation of the due process clause will be found." In common with other courts we have struggled to draw the line that defines and identifies what is governmental involvement so outrageous as to warrant finding a due process violation.

The government here enmeshed in criminal schemes fabricated entirely by government agents a black doctor who had no criminal record and with respect to whom the agents had no apparent hint of a predisposition to criminal activity. The government sent agents apparently posing as poor people to a doctor serving a ghetto community to seek to have the doctor help them out financially in appealing circumstances, circumstances in which the doctor might appear callous if he did not cooperate. The record implies that the inspectors pretended to be economically disadvantaged people typical of defendant's patient population. Sympathy based upon economic disadvantage or race may have been played upon as a factor in inducing defendant to join what he informed the inspectors was "the white boys' game." Defendant sought very little profit from his participation, apparently charging only normal office rates for the time he spent with the inspectors.

We must conclude, however, that the government's conduct was insufficient to violate defendant's right to due process. Insurance fraud on a small scale no doubt is very widespread in this country. Many professional or business people may not regard it a serious infraction of society's rules to assist customers or patients in the small scale cheating of insurance companies. Yet, like the Second Circuit in *Myers*, which said it could not accept an "inducement" argument that a proffered bribe was so large a congressman could not be expected to resist, we cannot accept the notion that insurance cheating is so commonplace that it is improper for the government to try to catch and convict citizens who engage in it. We have held that the government need not have a reasonable suspicion of wrongdoing in order to conduct an undercover investigation of a particular person. No issue of impermissible selective prosecution was raised in the instant case. *See Yick Wo v. Hopkins*, 118 U.S. 356 (1886).

III

We have also considered defendant's conviction and the government agents' conduct in light of our supervisory power over the administration of criminal justice. But the breadth of the Supreme Court's language in *United States v. Payner*, requires us to conclude, despite the differences between *Payner* and the case at bar, that we may not fashion a "sub-constitutional" rule to permit dismissal of this case because of the government agents' conduct. In *Payner* government agents sought to examine materials in a third party's briefcase that they thought might incriminate defendant. To gain access to the briefcase a government agent introduced the owner of the briefcase, Michael Wolstencroft, to Sybol Kennedy, a female private investigator who worked for the agent. Wolstencroft and Kennedy spent time together in Kennedy's apartment, where Wolstencroft left his locked briefcase while the two went out to eat at a restaurant. While one government agent acted as a "lookout" at the restaurant, other agents entered the apartment with a key furnished by Kennedy, took the briefcase to a locksmith who made a key for it, opened the briefcase and photographed documents in it that led to evidence used to convict Payner. Payner, of course, did not have standing to object to the search. The district court found that the United States "knowingly and willfully participated" in the illegal search. Nonetheless, the Supreme Court refused to affirm the use of the courts' supervisory power to suppress the evidence. It agreed with a government argument that even though the evidence was tainted with gross illegalities, "such an extension of the supervisory power would enable federal courts to exercise a standardless discretion."

Affirmed.

QUESTIONS AND NOTES

1. Do you think that the government did anything wrong in *Gamble*? If so what was it? If not, why not?

2. Do you think that the government did anything wrong in *Twigg*? If so what? If not, why not?

3. Should the government be required to have reasonable suspicion (or probable cause) (or a warrant) before it engages in practices such as those described in *Gamble* or *Twigg*?

4. When the government is excessively involved, predisposition is irrelevant. Does this comport with your notion of sound jurisprudence? Explain.

5. Arguably, it is not even necessary that the inducement be of the type likely to tempt a hypothetically nonpredisposed person (for example, in *Twigg*, it is doubtful that a totally nonpredisposed person would go into the drug business simply because it was there). Is there a good reason for not even requiring at least that much?

TABLE OF CASES

[References are to pages]

A

Abel v. United States, 362 U.S. 217 (1960).175; 611

Adams v. United States, 317 U.S. 269 (1942). .1144

Adams v. Williams, 407 U.S. 143 (1972). .328; 343; 375; 443

Addington v. Texas, 441 U.S. 418 (1979). . . .1356

Agnello v. United States, 269 U.S. 20 (1925) . . 168

Aguilar v. Texas, 378 U.S. 108 (1964). 18

Air Pollution Variance Board v. Western Alfalfa Corp., 416 U.S. 861 (1974). 528, 529; 553

Alabama v. White, 496 U.S. 325 (1990) 371

Albernaz v. United States, 450 U.S. 333 (1981).1122

Alberty v. United States, 162 U.S. 499 (1896) . .395

Alderman v. United States, 394 U.S. 165 (1969) 561; 567; 785

Almeida-Sanchez v. United States, 413 U.S. 266 (1973) 259; 718; 795

Anders v. California, 386 U.S. 738 (1967) . . . 1224

Anderson v. Creighton, 483 U.S. 635 (1987). . .644

Arizona v. Evans, 514 U.S. 1 (1995) . 710; 747; 760; 761; 767, 768; 775, 776; 782

Arizona v. Fulminante, 499 U.S. 279 (1991) . . 1174

Arizona v. Gant, 556 U.S. 332 (2009). . . .228; 684

Arizona v. Hicks, 480 U.S. 321 (1987) . . . 194; 201

Arizona v. Johnson, 555 U.S. 323 (2009). 489

Arizona v. Roberson, 486 U.S. 675 (1988).935; 991; 1024

Arkansas v. Sanders, 442 U.S. 753 (1979) 212

Arkansas v. Sullivan, 532 U.S. 769 (2001). . . .648

Arvizu; United States v., 534 U.S. 266 (2002) . .408

Ash; United States v., 413 U.S. 300 (1973). . .1261

Ashcraft v. Tennessee, 322 U.S. 143 (1944). . .843; 856

Atwater v. City of Lago Vista, 532 U.S. 318 (2001). 630

B

Badgett; State v., 512 A.2d 160 (Conn. 1986) . . 233

Bailey v. United States, 134 S. Ct. 484 (2013). .167

Banks; United States v., 540 U.S. 31 (2003) . . .702

Barron v. Mayor of Baltimore, 7 Pet. 243 (1833). 634

Bayer; United States v., 331 U.S. 532 (1947) . 1300; 1318

Beckwith v. United States, 425 U.S. 341 (1977) .997

Bell v. Wolfish, 441 U.S. 520 (1979). 674

Bellotti v. Baird, 443 U.S. 622 (1979). 1007

Berger v. New York, 388 U.S. 41 (1967). 718

Berghuis v. Thompkins, 560 U.S. 370 (2010) . . 981

Berkemer v. McCarty, 468 U.S. 420 (1984). . . .444, 445; 637; 642; 1008; 1013; 1019

Biswell; United States v., 406 U.S. 311 (1972). .685

Bivens v. Six Unknown Named Agents of Federal Bureau of Narcotics, 403 U.S. 388 (1971) . . 696; 705; 1215

Black v. State, 810 N.E.2d 713 (Ind. 2004). . . .233

Blackburn v. Alabama, 361 U.S. 199 (1960). . .868; 1162; 1166

Blockburger v. United States, 284 U.S. 299 (1932). 1116; 1119

Board of Comm'rs of Bryan Cty. v. Brown, 520 U.S. 397 (1996). 624

Board of Education of Pottawatomie County v. Earls, 536 U.S. 822 (2002) 685

Bodner; People v., 75 A.D.2d 440 (1980). . . .1319

Boerne, City of v. Flores, 521 U.S. 507 (1997) 1213; 1225; 1228

Bolinski; People v., 260 Cal.App.2d 705 (1968) . 908

Bond v. United States, 529 U.S. 334 (2000) . . . 542

Boyd v. United States, 116 U.S. 616 (1886).98; 712; 1256

Bram v. United States, 168 U.S. 532 (1897). . .857; 888; 1170; 1176; 1212; 1240

Breard v. Alexandria, 341 U.S. 622 (1951). . . .574

Brendlin v. California, 551 U.S. 249 (2007) . . . 482

Brewer v. Williams, 430 U.S. 387 (1977). . . .1067; 1088; 1353

Bridger v. State, 503 S.W.2d 801 (Tex. Crim. App. 1974). .32

Brignoni-Ponce; United States v., 422 U.S. 873 (1975) 351; 391; 625

Brinegar v. United States, 338 U.S. 160 (1949).2; 5; 336; 731; 754

Brower v. Inyo County, 489 U.S. 593 (1989) . . 475; 483

Brown v. Illinois, 422 U.S. 590 (1975) . . 762; 1284

Brown v. Mississippi, 297 U.S. 278 (1936). . . .586; 825; 1241

Brown v. Texas, 443 U.S. 47 (1979) . 251; 276; 391; 442; 451

Bruner v. People, 156 P.2d 111 (Colo. 1945). . .867

Bruton v. United States, 391 U.S. 123 (1968). .1223

Bumper v. North Carolina, 391 U.S. 543 (1968).589; 817

Burdeau v. McDowell, 256 U.S. 465 (1921) . . 1167

Burnet v. Coronado Oil & Gas Co., 285 U.S. 393 (1932). 650

Butler v. McKellar, 494 U.S. 407 (1990) 1214

Byars v. United States, 273 U.S. 28 (1927). . . .689

C

Cady v. Dombrowski, 413 U.S. 433 (1973).285; 433

Cahan; People v., 282 P.2d 905 (1955). 690

Calandra; United States v., 414 U.S. 338 (1973).693; 710; 740; 766; 772; 777; 1167

California v. Acevedo, 500 U.S. 565 (1991) . . . 212

California v. Beheler, 463 U.S. 1121 (1983) . . 1013; 1014; 1316

California v. Carney, 471 U.S. 386 (1985). . . . 203

California v. Ciraolo, 476 U.S. 207 (1986).533; 547; 550

California v. Greenwood, 486 U.S. 35 (1988). . .542; 652

California v. Hodari D., 499 U.S. 621 (1991). . .394; 472

California v. Prysock, 453 U.S. 355 (1981). . . .904

Camara v. Municipal Court, 387 U.S. 523 (1967).79; 265; 685

Cardwell v. Lewis, 417 U.S. 583 (1974). 205

Carnley v. Cochran, 369 U.S. 506 (1962). 876

Carroll v. United States, 267 U.S. 132 (1925). 6; 72; 637; 796

Caseres; United States v., 533 F.3d 1064 (9th Cir. 2008) 233

Ceccolini; United States v., 435 U.S. 268 (1978). 1297

Ceccolini; United States v., 542 F.2d 136 (2d Cir. 1976). .1298

Chadwick; United States v., 433 U.S. 1 (1977). .76; 521

Chambers v. Florida, 309 U.S. 227 (1940) . 868; 878

Chambers v. Maroney, 399 U.S. 42 (1970). 71

Chandler v. Miller, 520 U.S. 305 (1997). 685

Chapman v. California, 386 U.S. 18 (1967) . . 1177; 1182

Chapman v. United States, 365 U.S. 610 (1961).817

Chavez v. Martinez, 538 U.S. 760 (2003). . . . 1228

Chimel v. California, 395 U.S. 752 (1969).167; 294; 777

Cicenia v. Lagay, 357 U.S. 504 (1958). 860

City and County of (see name of city and county)

City of (see name of city)

Clewis v. Texas, 386 U.S. 707 (1967). 1318

Cohens v. Virginia, 6 Wheat. 264 (1821). 866

Colonnade Catering Corp. v. United States, 397 U.S. 72 (1970). 685

Colorado v. Bannister, 449 U.S. 1 (1980). 609

Colorado v. Bertine, 479 U.S. 367 (1987). .269; 278

Colorado v. Connelly, 479 U.S. 157 (1986) . . . 985; 991; 1165

Colorado v. Spring, 479 U.S. 564 (1987). 911

Commissioner v. (see name of defendant)

Commonwealth v. (see name of defendant)

Commonwealth of (see name of commonwealth)

Connally v. Georgia, 429 U.S. 245 (1977). 88

Connecticut v. Barrett, 479 U.S. 523 (1987). . .977; 1214

Conner; Commonwealth v., 452 Pa. 333 (1973).736, 737

Coolidge v. New Hampshire, 403 U.S. 443 (1971). 43; 88; 104; 1167

Cooper v. California, 386 U.S. 58 (1967). 652

Cooper v. Dupnik, 963 F.2d 1220 (9th Cir. 1992). 967; 1235

Cooper; United States v., 428 F. Supp. 652 (S.D. Ohio 1977) 286

Correctional Services Corp. v. Malesko, 534 U.S. 61 (2001). .705

Cortez; United States v., 449 U.S. 411 (1981) . . 31; 349

Counselman v. Hitchcock, 142 U.S. 547 (1892). 1001; 1240; 1256; 1308

County of (see name of county)

Crews; United States v., 445 U.S. 463 (1980). .1349

Crooker v. California, 357 U.S. 433 (1958). . . .834

Culombe v. Connecticut, 367 U.S. 568 (1961). .915; 1170

D

Dalia v. United States, 441 U.S. 238 (1979) . . . 115

Dana; Commonwealth v., 2 Met. 329 (1841). . . .52

Darwin v. Connecticut, 391 U.S. 346 (1968) . . 1319

Davis v. Mississippi, 394 U.S. 721 (1969) . . . 1286

Davis v. United States, 328 U.S. 582 . . . . 588; 592

Davis v. United States, 512 U.S. 452 (1994). . .962; 1214; 1217

Davis v. United States, 131 S. Ct. 2419 (2011). .770

Defore v. New York, 270 U.S. 657 (1926). 691

Defore; People v., 242 N.Y. 13 (1926) . . 763; 1076; 1351

Delaware v. Prouse, 440 U.S. 648 (1979). .244; 625

Delaware v. Van Arsdall, 475 U.S. 673 (1986) . 1167

Di Re; United States v., 332 U.S. 581 (1948). .652; 655

Dickerson v. State, 257 Ind. 562 (1972) 907

Dickerson v. United States, 530 U.S. 428 (2000). 235; 1211; 1238

Dionisio; United States v., 410 U.S. 1 (1973). .1306

Doe v. Renfrow, 451 U.S. 1022 (1981). 495

[References are to pages]

Doe v. Renfrow, 475 F. Supp. 1012 (N.D. Ind. 1979) 493

Doran; State v., 563 N.W.2d 620 (Iowa 1997) . . 628

Dorman v. United States, 435 F.2d 385 (D.C. Cir. 1970) 98

Douglas v. California, 372 U.S. 353 (1963) . . . 875

Douglas v. Jeannette, 319 U.S. 157 (1943) . . . 1108; 1150

Dow Chemical Co. v. United States, 476 U.S. 227 (1986) 553

Doward; United States v., 41 F.3d 789 (1st Cir. 1994) 233

Doyle v. Ohio, 426 U.S. 610 (1976) 1215

Draper v. United States, 358 U.S. 307 (1959) . . 3; 13

Duberstein; Commissioner v., 363 U.S. 278 (1960) 406

Duckworth v. Eagan, 492 U.S. 195 (1989) 901; 1214; 1217

Dunaway v. New York, 442 U.S. 200 (1979) . . . 357; 443; 640; 642; 1284; 1314

Duncan v. Louisiana, 391 U.S. 145 (1968) . . . 1384

Dunn; United States v., 480 U.S. 294 (1987) . . .532

E

Edmunds; Commonwealth v., 586 A.2d 887 (Pa. 1991) 736

Edwards v. Arizona, 451 U.S. 477 (1981) . 930; 951; 1024; 1214

Ekstrom, State ex rel. v. Justice Court, 136 Ariz. 1 (1983) 467

Elkins v. United States, 364 U.S. 206 (1960) . . 654; 691; 693; 766

Entick v. Carrington, 95 Eng. Rep. 807 (C.P. 1765) 559

Escobedo v. Illinois, 378 U.S. 478 (1964) . .586; 854

Ex parte (see name of relator)

Ex rel. (see name of relator)

F

Faretta v. California, 422 U.S. 806 (1975) 1132

Fellers v. United States, 540 U.S. 519 (2004) . 1134; 1346

Ferguson v. City of Charleston, 532 U.S. 67 (2001) 685; 1232

Fernandez v. California, 134 S. Ct. 1126 (2014) . 605

Fisher v. United States, 425 U.S. 391 (1976) . . 1260

Fitzpatrick v. New York, 414 U.S. 1050 (1973) . 1304

Flores-Lopez; United States v., 670 F.3d 803 (7th Cir. 2012) 302

Flores-Montano; United States v., 541 U.S. 149 (2004) 685

Florida v. Bostick, 501 U.S. 429 (1991) . . .391; 461

Florida v. Brady, 406 So.2d 1093 (Fla. 1981) . . 530

Florida v. Harris, 133 S. Ct. 1050 (2013) 59

Florida v. J.L., 529 U.S. 266 (2000) 375

Florida v. Jardines, 133 S. Ct. 1409 (2013) 571

Florida v. Jimeno, 500 U.S. 248 (1991) . . .596; 617

Florida v. Powell, 559 U.S. 50 (2010) 911

Florida v. Riley, 484 U.S. 1058 (1988) 533

Florida v. Riley, 488 U.S. 445 (1989) 533

Florida v. Rodriguez, 469 U.S. 1 (1984) . .370; 378; 391

Florida v. Royer, 460 U.S. 491 (1983) . 44; 355; 414; 456; 463; 585

Florida v. Wells, 495 U.S. 1 (1990) 288

Foster v. California, 394 U.S. 440 (1969) 1264

Franks v. Delaware, 438 U.S. 154 (1978) . .719; 722

Frazier v. Cupp, 394 U.S. 731 (1969) 1316

Freedman v. Maryland, 380 U.S. 51 (1965) . . .1224

G

G. M. Leasing Corp. v. United States, 429 U.S. 338 (1977) 98

Gallegos v. Colorado, 370 U.S. 49 (1962) 1012

Gamble; United States v., 737 F.2d 853 (10th Cir. 1984) 1385

Garcia; United States v., 431 F.2d 134 (CA9 1970) 908

Garcia; United States v., 897 F.2d 1413 (1990) . .401

Georgia v. Randolph, 547 U.S. 103 (2006) 712

Gerstein v. Pugh, 420 U.S. 103 (1975) 956

Gertz v. Robert Welch, Inc., 418 U.S. 323 (1974) 1224

Gideon v. Wainwright, 372 U.S. 335 (1963) . . .854; 858; 859; 875; 895; 1118; 1123

Gilbert v. California, 388 U.S. 263 (1967) . . . 1306

Go-Bart Importing Co. v. United States, 282 U.S. 344 (1931) 168; 641; 696

Goldman v. United States, 316 U.S. 129 (1942) . 566

Gonzalez; United States v., 71 F.3d 819 (11th Cir. 1996) 778

Gould v. Davis, 165 F.3d 265 (CA4 1998) 705

Gouled v. United States, 255 U.S. 298 (1921) . .510; 513

Graham v. Connor, 490 U.S. 386 (1989) 139

Green v. Butler, 420 F.3d 689 (CA7 2005) 705

Griffin v. California, 380 U.S. 609 (1965) 873

Griffin v. Illinois, 351 U.S. 12 (1956) 1224

Griffin v. Wisconsin, 483 U.S. 868 (1987) 686

Grimm v. United States, 156 U.S. 604 (1895) . .1372

Griswold v. Connecticut, 381 U.S. 479 (1965) . 1259

Groh v. Ramirez, 540 U.S. 551 (2004). 80; 735

Gustafson v. Florida, 414 U.S. 260 (1973) . 609; 641

H

Haley v. Ohio, 332 U.S. 596 (1948). 1012

Hamilton v. Alabama, 368 U.S. 52 (1961) 857

Hamilton; Commonwealth v., 445 Pa. 292 (1971). .1043

Hampton v. United States, 425 U.S. 484 (1976). .1387

Harlow v. Fitzgerald, 457 U.S. 800 (1982) . 638; 768

Harper; People v., 418 N.E.2d 894 (Ill. App. Ct. 1981). 967

Harris v. Coweta County, 433 F.3d 807 (11th Cir. 2005). 145

Harris v. New York, 401 U.S. 222 (1971) . . . 1137; 1160; 1239; 1322; 1344

Harris v. South Carolina, 338 U.S. 68 (1949). . .831

Harris v. State, 71 So. 3d 756 (Fla. 2011). 62

Harris v. United States, 331 U.S. 145 (1947) . . 157; 169; 241; 734; 777; 811

Harris; People v., 72 N.Y.2d 614 (1988). 1294

Harrison v. United States, 392 U.S. 219 (1968).1315

Havens; United States v., 446 U.S. 620 (1980) . 1167

Hayes v. Florida, 470 U.S. 811 (1985). 443

Haynes v. Washington, 373 U.S. 503 (1963). . .856; 885; 888

Hebert v. Louisiana, 272 U.S. 312 (1926) 828

Henry; United States v., 447 U.S. 264 (1980) . 1083; 1087; 1354

Hensley; United States v., 469 U.S. 221 (1985). 383; 443; 749

Herring v. United States, 555 U.S. 135 (2009). .758; 772

Hester v. United States, 265 U.S. 57 (1924). . .475; 516; 519; 520; 562; 573; 790

Hickory v. United States, 160 U.S. 408 (1896). .397

Hiibel v. Sixth Judicial Dist. Court, 118 Nev. 868 (2002). .442

Hiibel v. Sixth Judicial Dist. Court, 542 U.S. 177 (2004). .440

Hill v. California, 401 U.S. 797 (1971). 599

Hoay v. State, 348 Ark. 80 (2002) 759

Hoffa v. United States, 385 U.S. 293 (1966). . .512

Holt v. United States, 218 U.S. 245 (1910). . .1256

Horton v. California, 496 U.S. 128 (1990). . . . 185

House v. Mayo, 324 U.S. 42 (1945) 837

Howes v. Fields, 132 S. Ct. 1181 (2012) 1032

Hudson v. Michigan, 547 U.S. 586 (2006).701; 768; 771; 773

I

I.N.S. v. Lopez-Mendoza, 468 U.S. 1032 (1984). 701; 710

Illinois v. Andreas, 463 U.S. 765 (1983). 193

Illinois v. Caballes, 543 U.S. 405 (2005). 501

Illinois v. Gates, 462 U.S. 213 (1983). . 28; 83; 717

Illinois v. Krull, 480 U.S. 340 (1987).735; 769; 773; 775

Illinois v. Lafayette, 462 U.S. 640 (1983). .220; 279

Illinois v. Lidster, 540 U.S. 419 (2004). 274

Illinois v. McArthur, 531 U.S. 326 (2001). .71; 296; 298

Illinois v. Perkins, 496 U.S. 292 (1990) . 1021; 1034

Illinois v. Rodriguez, 497 U.S. 177 (1990). . . .597

Illinois v. Wardlow, 528 U.S. 119 (2000). . 390; 445

In re (see name of party)

Indianapolis, City of v. Edmond, 531 U.S. 32 (2000). .263

INS v. Delgado, 466 U.S. 210 (1984) . 443; 460, 461

Irvine v. California, 347 U.S. 128 (1954). . . . 1249

J

J. D. B. v. North Carolina, 131 S. Ct. 2394 (2011). .1003

J. D. B., In re, 686 S. E. 2d 135 (N.C. 2009). .1004

Jacobsen; United States v., 466 U.S. 109 (1984).478; 496

Jacobson v. United States, 503 U.S. 540 (1992).1374

Janis; United States v., 428 U.S. 433 (1976). . .701; 709, 710; 771; 1167

Jay Burns Baking Co. v. Bryan, 264 U.S. 504 (1924). .1248

Jeffers; United States v., 342 U.S. 48 (1951). . .513; 548; 802; 809

Johns; United States v., 469 U.S. 478 (1985). . .215

Johnson v. Glick, 481 F.2d 1028 (2d Cir. 1973) . 141

Johnson v. Louisiana, 406 U.S. 356 (1972). . .1286

Johnson v. New Jersey, 384 U.S. 719 (1966) . .1308

Johnson v. State, 114 S.W.2d 819 (Tenn. 1938) . 129; 135

Johnson v. United States, 333 U.S. 10 (1948).79; 86; 293

Johnson v. Zerbst, 304 U.S. 458 (1938) . . 589; 876; 976; 990

Johnson; United States v., 457 U.S. 537 (1982).719; 775; 778

Jones v. United States, 357 U.S. 493 (1958) . . .104

Jones v. United States, 362 U.S. 257 (1960).27; 785; 790

[References are to pages]

Jones; United States v., 132 S. Ct. 945 (2012). . 558

Joseph E. Seagram & Sons, Inc. v. Hostetter, 384 U.S. 35 (1966). 1232

Julius; United States v., 610 F.3d 60 (2d Cir. 2010) 782

K

Kaiser Aetna v. United States, 444 U.S. 164 (1979). 808

Kansas v. Ventris, 556 U.S. 586 (2009) 1135

Karo; United States v., 468 U.S. 705 (1984). . .550; 561; 570

Kastigar v. United States, 406 U.S. 441 (1972).1308, 1309

Katz v. United States, 389 U.S. 347 (1967) . 78; 306; 515; 520; 560; 567; 788; 790

Kelly; United States v., 55 F.2d 67 (C.A.2 1932).673

Kelsey; State v., 592 S.W.2d 509 (Mo. App. 1979) 193

Kendricks; People v., 121 Ill. App. 3d 442 (1984). 968

Kentucky v. King, 131 S. Ct. 1849 (2011) 128

Kier v. State, 132 A.2d 494 (Md. 1957) 867

Killough v. United States, 114 U.S. App. D.C. 305 (1962) 1351

Killough v. United States, 119 U.S. App. D.C. 10 (1964) 1072

Kirby v. Illinois, 406 U.S. 682 (1972). . 1118; 1131; 1261

Kirschenblatt; United States v., 16 F.2d 202 (2d Cir. 1926). 173; 300

Knights; United States v., 534 U.S. 112 (2002). .686

Knotts; United States v., 103 S. Ct. 1081 (1983). 495; 570

Knowles v. Iowa, 525 U.S. 113 (1998) 627

Kolender v. Lawson, 461 U.S. 352 (1983) . 442; 445

Kuhlmann v. Wilson, 477 U.S. 436 (1986) . . . 1090

Kyllo v. United States, 533 U.S. 27 (2001).546; 577

L

Lace; United States v., 669 F.2d 46 (CA2 1982).530

Lankford v. Gelston, 364 F.2d 197 (CA4 1966) . 112

Lee; United States v., 274 U.S. 559 (1927). . . .790

Lefkowitz v. Cunningham, 431 U.S. 801 (1977) 1240

Lefkowitz v. Turley, 414 U.S. 70 (1973).1239; 1308

Lefkowitz; United States v., 285 U.S. 452 (1932). 168

Lego v. Twomey, 404 U.S. 477 (1972) 1349

Leon; United States v., 468 U.S. 897 (1984). . .710; 715; 749; 761; 769; 771–773; 775; 782; 1149

Lewis v. United States, 385 U.S. 206 (1966) . . 509; 790

Leyra v. Denno, 347 U.S. 556 (1954). 868

Linkletter v. Walker, 381 U.S. 618 (1965). .693; 698

Lisenba v. California, 314 U.S. 219 (1941) . . .1168

Locke v. United States, 7 Cranch 339 (1813) . 7; 32; 57

Lo-Ji Sales, Inc. v. New York, 442 U.S. 319 (1979) 720; 722

Lopez v. United States, 373 U.S. 427 (1963). . .514

Loretto v. Teleprompter Manhattan CATV Corp., 458 U.S. 419 (1982) 1223

Lugo; United States v., 978 F.2d 631 (10th Cir. 1992) 233

Lynumn v. Illinois, 372 U.S. 528 (1963) 916

M

Mackey; United States v., 387 F. Supp. 1121 (Nev. 1975) 756

Maine v. Moulton, 474 U.S. 159 (1985) . 1080; 1223

Malinski v. New York, 324 U.S. 401 (1945). . .870

Malloy v. Hogan, 378 U.S. 1 (1964) . . . 862; 1171; 1212; 1255

Mancusi v. DeForte, 392 U.S. 364 (1968) 788

Maness v. Meyers, 419 U.S. 449 (1975). 1308

Manson v. Brathwaite, 432 U.S. 98 (1977) . . .1261

Mapp v. Ohio, 367 U.S. 643 (1961). .687; 698; 894

Marbury v. Madison, 5 U.S. 137 (1803). 1217

Marron v. United States, 275 U.S. 192 (1927). .168

Martinez-Fuerte; United States v., 428 U.S. 543 (1976). 252; 270; 421; 433

Maryland v. Buie, 494 U.S. 325 (1990). 176

Maryland v. Garrison, 480 U.S. 79 (1987) 599

Maryland v. King, 133 S. Ct. 1958 (2013) . 298; 666

Maryland v. Pringle, 540 U.S. 366 (2003). 56

Maryland v. Shatzer, 559 U.S. 98 (2010).951; 1013; 1029

Maryland v. Wilson, 519 U.S. 408 (1997). .485; 619

Massachusetts v. Sheppard, 468 U.S. 981 (1984).82; 83; 85; 735; 761; 769; 776

Massachusetts v. Upton, 466 U.S. 727 (1984). . .47

Massiah v. United States, 377 U.S. 201 (1964) . 847; 1143

Master; United States v., 614 F.3d 236 (6th Cir. 2010) 782

Mathis v. United States, 391 U.S. 1 (1968) . . . 997; 1031; 1033

Matlock; People v., 336 P.2d 505 (Cal. 1959) . . 867

Matlock; United States v., 415 U.S. 164 (1974).597; 1349

McCarthy v. Arndstein, 266 U.S. 34 (1924). . .1308

[References are to pages]

McCray v. Illinois, 386 U.S. 300 (1967). 18

McCulloch v. Maryland, 17 U.S. 316 (1819) . . .525; 726

McDonald v. Lucas, 677 F.2d 518 (CA5 1982). .992

McDonald v. United States, 335 U.S. 451 (1948).82; 120; 170; 797

McGuire v. United States, 273 U.S. 95 (1927) . 1301

McKune v. Lile, 536 U.S. 24 (2002). 1240

McLaughlin; United States v., 170 F.3d 889 (9th Cir. 1998) 233

McMann v. Richardson, 397 U.S. 759 (1970). .1139

McNabb v. United States, 318 U.S. 332 (1943) . 837; 1371

McNeil v. Wisconsin, 498 U.S. 1065 (1991) . . 1120

McNeil v. Wisconsin, 501 U.S. 171 (1991) . . . 955; 1103

Melilli; Commonwealth v., 521 Pa. 405 (1989) . 740; 746

Mena v. Simi Valley, 226 F.3d 1031 (CA9 2000) 705

Mendenhall; United States v., 446 U.S. 544 (1980) 44; 362; 403; 424; 447

Michigan v. Chesternut, 486 U.S. 567 (1988) . .475; 486; 615, 616

Michigan v. DeFillippo, 443 U.S. 31 (1979) . . .718

Michigan v. Harvey, 494 U.S. 344 (1990). . . .1136

Michigan v. Jackson, 475 U.S. 625 (1986) . . . 1097

Michigan v. Long, 463 U.S. 1032 (1983). .236; 326; 748

Michigan v. Mosley, 423 U.S. 96 (1975) . 920; 1024

Michigan v. Payne, 412 U.S. 47 (1973) 1224

Michigan v. Summers, 452 U.S. 692 (1981) . . .153

Michigan v. Tucker, 417 U.S. 433 (1974).904; 1214; 1220; 1231; 1300; 1307; 1309; 1312; 1344

Michigan v. Tyler, 436 U.S. 499 (1978). 265

Michigan Dep't of State Police v. Sitz, 496 U.S. 444 (1990) 250

Miller v. Fenton, 474 U.S. 104 (1985) 403

Miller v. Fenton, 796 F.2d 598 (3d Cir. 1986). .1183

Miller v. United States, 357 U.S. 301 (1958). . .101

Miller; Commonwealth v., 513 Pa. 118 (1986). .746

Miller; United States v., 425 U.S. 435 (1976). .564; 740

Milliken; Commonwealth v., 450 Pa. 310 (1973).742

Mincey v. Arizona, 437 U.S. 385 (1978) . 195; 1159; 1233; 1309

Minnesota v. Carter, 525 U.S. 83 (1998). .548; 561; 584; 812

Minnesota v. Dickerson, 508 U.S. 366 (1993) . . 326

Minnesota v. Murphy, 465 U.S. 420 (1984). . .1002

Minnesota v. Olson, 495 U.S. 91 (1990) . .124; 813, 814

Minnick v. Mississippi, 498 U.S. 146 (1990). . .941

Miranda v. Arizona, 384 U.S. 436 (1966) . . 56; 444; 588; 645; 865; 911; 958; 990; 1005; 1010; 1032; 1211; 1310

Missouri v. McNeely, 133 S. Ct. 1552 (2013). .1260

Missouri v. Seibert, 542 U.S. 600 (2004) 1328

Mitchell v. United States, 526 U.S. 314 (1999).1216; 1227

Monell v. Dep't of Soc. Servs., 436 U.S. 658 (1978) 705; 768; 777

Monroe v. Pape, 365 U.S. 167 (1961). . . .705; 786

Montejo v. Louisiana, 556 U.S. 778 (2009). . .1140

Montoya v. Collins, 955 F.2d 279 (1992) 1141

Montoya de Hernandez; United States v., 473 U.S. 531 (1985) 685

Mooney v. Holohan, 294 U.S. 103 (1935) 828

Moran v. Burbine, 475 U.S. 412 (1986) . . 915, 916; 918; 955; 1024; 1135; 1332

Moscatiello; United States v., 771 F.2d 589 (1st Cir. 1985). 1360

Muehler v. Mena, 544 U.S. 93 (2005) 158

Murphy v. Waterfront Comm'n, 378 U.S. 52 (1964) 1308

Murray v. United States, 487 U.S. 533 (1988) . 1357

N

Nardone v. United States, 308 U.S. 338 (1939). 1282, 1283; 1298; 1320

Nathanson v. United States, 290 U.S. 41 (1933). .34

Navarette v. California, 134 S. Ct. 1683 (2014) . 380

New Jersey v. Portash, 440 U.S. 450 (1979) . .1136; 1220

New Jersey v. T.L.O., 469 U.S. 325 (1985).378; 686

New State Ice Co. v. Liebmann, 285 U.S. 262 (1932). 757

New York v. Belton, 453 U.S. 454 (1981) . 228; 684

New York v. Burger, 482 U.S. 691 (1987) . 265; 608; 685

New York v. Harris, 495 U.S. 14 (1990) 1289

New York v. Quarles, 467 U.S. 649 (1984). . .1013, 1014; 1052; 1217; 1306; 1312

New York Times Co. v. Sullivan, 376 U.S. 254 (1964) 1224

Nix v. Williams, 467 U.S. 431 (1984). 1347

North v. Superior Court, 502 P.2d 1305 (1972). .186

North Carolina v. Butler, 441 U.S. 369 (1979). .971

North Carolina v. Pearce, 395 U.S. 711 (1969) . 1224

[References are to pages]

O

O'Connor v. Ortega, 480 U.S. 709 (1987) . 219; 815

Ohio v. Robinette, 519 U.S. 33 (1996) 613

Oliver v. United States, 466 U.S. 170 (1984) . . 519; 567

Olmstead v. United States, 277 U.S. 438 (1928).530; 560; 689; 691; 697; 734; 772; 879; 1371

Oregon v. Bradshaw, 462 U.S. 1039 (1983) . . . 935

Oregon v. Elstad, 470 U.S. 298 (1985) . 1214; 1217; 1310

Oregon v. Hass, 420 U.S. 714 (1975). . . .649; 967; 1160; 1220

Oregon v. Mathiason, 429 U.S. 492 (1977) . . . 998; 1000; 1013

Ornelas v. United States, 517 U.S. 690 (1996). .400

Orozco v. Texas, 394 U.S. 324 (1969) . . 997; 1015; 1031

Ortiz; United States v., 422 U.S. 891 (1975). . .258; 795

Overdorff, Holland ex rel. v. Harrington, 268 F.3d 1179 (CA10 2001) 705

Oystead v. Shed, 13 Mass. 520 (1816) 817

P

Palko v. Connecticut, 302 U.S. 319 (1937). . . .1238; 1243; 1246

Papachristou v. Jacksonville, 405 U.S. 156 (1972). .442

Patane; United States v., 542 U.S. 630 (2004) . 1339

Patrick; United States v., 899 F.2d 169 (2d Cir. 1990) 402

Patterson v. Illinois, 487 U.S. 285 (1988). . . .1124

Patterson v. McLean Credit Union, 491 U.S. 164 (1989). 1216; 1226

Paul v. Davis, 424 U.S. 693 (1976). 643

Payne v. Arkansas, 356 U.S. 560 (1958). 1177

Payner; United States v., 447 U.S. 727 (1980). .706; 824

Payton v. New York, 445 U.S. 573 (1980). 96

Pennsylvania v. Mimms, 434 U.S. 106 (1977). .328; 485; 608; 614; 619; 794

Pennsylvania v. Muniz, 496 U.S. 582 (1990) . . 1260

Pennsylvania Board of Probation & Parole v. Scott, 524 U.S. 357 (1998). 701; 710; 771

People v. (see name of defendant)

Perry v. New Hampshire, 132 S. Ct. 716 (2012) 1277

Pierce v. Underwood, 487 U.S. 552 (1988). . . .406

Place; United States v., 462 U.S. 696 (1983) . . 266; 272; 421; 494

Portelli; People v., 15 N.Y.2d 235 (1965). 867

Powell v. Alabama, 287 U.S. 45 (1932) . . 839; 857; 1118

Powell v. Nevada, 511 U.S. 79 (1994) 774

Powell; State v., 726 P.2d 266 (Haw. 1986). . . .1367

Powers v. United States, 223 U.S. 303 (1912) . 1219

Preston v. United States, 376 U.S. 364 (1964) . . 69; 796

PruneYard Shopping Center v. Robins, 447 U.S. 74 (1980) .737

Puerta; United States v., 982 F.2d 1297 (9th Cir. 1992) 402

R

Rabinowitz; United States v., 339 U.S. 56 (1950). 170; 241; 335; 539; 732; 777

Raddatz; People v., 91 Ill.App.2d 425 (1968). .1319

Rainey v. Commonwealth, 197 S.W.3d 89 (Ky. 2006). 233

Rakas v. Illinois, 439 U.S. 128 (1978) 784

Ramirez v. Butte-Silver Bow County, 298 F.3d 1022 (C.A.9 2002). 84

Ramos; United States v., 933 F.2d 968 (11th Cir. 1991) 402

Rawlings v. Kentucky, 448 U.S. 98 (1980). . . .804

Reid v. Georgia, 448 U.S. 438 (1980). 362; 366; 403

Rembert; United States v., 694 F. Supp. 163 (W.D.N.C. 1988). 467

Retherford; State v., 69 Ohio St. 3d 1488 (1994).617

Retherford; State v., 93 Ohio App. 3d 586 (1994). .617

Rhode Island v. Innis, 446 U.S. 291 (1980). . .1040

Richards v. Wisconsin, 520 U.S. 385 (1997). . .377; 627

Richardson v. Marsh, 481 U.S. 200 (1987). . . .1224

Riley v. California, 134 S. Ct. 2473 (2014). . . .291

Rios v. United States, 364 U.S. 253 (1960). . . .792

Rivera; People v., 201 N.E.2d 32 (N.Y. 1964) . . 324

Riverside, County of v. McLaughlin, 500 U.S. 44 (1991). 636; 639; 643; 956

Robinson; United States v., 414 U.S. 218 (1973). .176; 243; 332; 609; 627; 628; 636; 641; 649; 654

Rochin v. California, 342 U.S. 165 (1952). . . .1232; 1238; 1245

Rodriguez-Diaz; United States v., 161 F. Supp. 2d 627 (Md. 2001) 485

Rogan v. Los Angeles, 668 F. Supp. 1384 (CD Cal. 1987) 756

Rogers v. Richmond, 365 U.S. 534 (1961). . . .691

Roper v. Simmons, 543 U.S. 551 (2005) 1007

Ross; United States v., 456 U.S. 798 (1982). 46; 212

Roth; People v., 85 P. 3d 571 (Colo. App. 2003).485
Routhier; State v., 137 Ariz. 90 (1983) 935
Russell; United States v., 411 U.S. 423 (1973) . 1387

S

Sacramento, County of v. Lewis, 523 U.S. 833
 (1998). 142; 483; 1234
Safford Unified School District v. Redding, 557 U.S.
 364 (2009). 686
Salinas v. State, 369 S.W.3d 176 (Tex. Crim. App.
 2012). 1173
Salinas v. Texas, 133 S. Ct. 2174 (2013) 1173
Salvucci; United States v., 448 U.S. 83 (1980). .800
Samuel v. Payne, 1 Doug. 359 (K.B. 1780). . . .103
Samuels; People v., 49 N.Y. 2d 218 (1980). . . .1294
Santana; United States v., 427 U.S. 38 (1976). . .94
Santiago; People v., 133 App.Div.2d 429 (N.Y. App.
 Div. 1987). 968
Santosky v. Kramer, 455 U.S. 745 (1982). . . .1356
Saucier v. Katz, 533 U.S. 194 (2001) . . . 142; 1229
Schmerber v. California, 384 U.S. 757 (1966) . 1254
Schneckloth v. Bustamonte, 412 U.S. 218
 (1973). 585
Scott v. Harris, 550 U.S. 372 (2007) 142
Scott v. United States, 436 U.S. 128 (1978) . . . 609
Segura v. United States, 468 U.S. 796 (1984). .1357
Shadwick v. Tampa, 407 U.S. 345 (1972). 88
Sharpe; United States v., 470 U.S. 675 (1985). .429
Sherman v. United States, 356 U.S. 369 (1958).1367
Sibron v. New York, 392 U.S. 40 (1968) . . 323; 718
Silverman v. United States, 365 U.S. 505
 (1960). 513; 566; 1358
Silverthorne Lumber Co. v. United States, 251 U.S.
 385 (1920) . . . 689; 762; 866; 1281; 1298; 1348
Simmons v. United States, 390 U.S. 377 (1968).802;
 1264; 1270
Skinner v. Railway Labor Executives' Ass'n, 489 U.S.
 602 (1989). 264; 638; 685
Smith v. Illinois, 469 U.S. 91 (1984) . 963; 968; 971;
 990
Smith v. Maryland, 442 U.S. 735 (1979). 519
Smith v. Phillips, 455 U.S. 209 (1982) 1214
Smith v. Robbins, 528 U.S. 259 (2000). 1224
Smith v. United States, 117 U.S. App. D.C. 1
 (1963). 1300
Smith; United States v., 218 F.3d 777 (CA7
 2000) .992
Snook; United States v., 88 F.3d 605 (8th Cir.
 1996) .233
Snyder v. Massachusetts, 291 U.S. 97 (1934) . .828;
 1246

Soffar v. Cockrell, 300 F.3d 588 (CA5 2002). . .995
Sokolow; United States v., 490 U.S. 1 (1989) . . 363
Soldal v. Cook County, 506 U.S. 56 (1992).561; 567
Sorrells v. United States, 287 U.S. 435 (1932).1368;
 1370
Sotelo v. State, 342 N.E.2d 844 (Ind. 1976) . . . 908
South Dakota v. Neville, 459 U.S. 553 (1983) . 1257
South Dakota v. Opperman, 428 U.S. 364
 (1976). 205; 279
Spano v. New York, 358 U.S. 919 (1958) 842
Spano v. New York, 360 U.S. 315 (1959) . 840; 856;
 916
Spears; United States v., 965 F.2d 262 (7th Cir.
 1992). 402
Spinelli v. United States, 393 U.S. 410 (1969). . .18
Stanley v. Georgia, 394 U.S. 557 (1969) 201
Stanley v. State, 313 A.2d 847 (Md. Ct. Spec. App.
 1974). .30
Stansbury v. California, 511 U.S. 318 (1994). .1008;
 1021
State v. (see name of defendant)
State ex rel. (see name of relator)
State of (see name of state)
Steagald v. United States, 451 U.S. 204 (1981) . 109
Stefonek; United States v., 179 F.3d 1030 (7th Cir.
 1999). .84
Stein v. New York, 346 U.S. 156 (1953) 1172
Stone v. Powell, 428 U.S. 465 (1976).710; 718; 721;
 773; 777; 794
Stoner v. California, 376 U.S. 483 (1964) 600
Strickland v. Washington, 466 U.S. 668 (1984).1139
Stroble v. California, 343 U.S. 181 (1952). . . . 888
Sturges; United States ex rel. v., 510 F.2d 397 (CA7
 1975). 1269
Sullivan, Ex parte, 107 F. Supp. 514 (D. Utah
 1952) .858
Sullivan; State v., 340 Ark. 315 (2000). 648

T

Tague v. Louisiana, 444 U.S. 469 (1980). 975
Taylor v. Alabama, 457 U.S. 687 (1982) 1284
Tejada; United States v., 524 F.3d 809 (CA7
 2008) .241
Tennessee v. Garner, 471 U.S. 1 (1985) . . 128; 145;
 636
Terry v. Ohio, 392 U.S. 1 (1968) . 75; 309; 698; 766
Texas v. Brown, 460 U.S. 730 (1983). . . . 185; 545
Texas v. Cobb, 532 U.S. 162 (2001). 1111
Thompson v. Keohane, 516 U.S. 99 (1995). . .1214

Thornton v. United States, 541 U.S. 615 (2004).228; 232; 234; 237

Three Affiliated Tribes of Fort Berthold Reservation v. Wold Engineering, P. C., 467 U.S. 138 (1984). 993

Torres v. Puerto Rico, 442 U.S. 465 (1979). . . .718

Townsend v. Sain, 372 U.S. 293 (1963) . 1162; 1166

Treasury Employees v. Von Raab, 109 S. Ct. 1384 (1989) 262; 264; 685

Trupiano v. United States, 334 U.S. 699 (1948) . 169

Turner v. Pennsylvania, 338 U.S. 62 (1949) . . . 831

Twigg; United States v., 588 F.2d 373 (3d Cir. 1978). .1387

Twining v. New Jersey, 211 U.S. 78 (1908). . .828; 1255

U

U.S. v. (see name of defendant)

United States v. (see name of defendant)

Upton; Commonwealth v., 476 N.E.2d 548 (Mass. 1985). 52

V

Vale v. Louisiana, 399 U.S. 30 (1970) 67

Van Camp v. AT&T Info. Sys., 963 F.2d 119 (C. A. 9 1992). .1229

Vasquez v. Hillery, 474 U.S. 254 (1986) 650

Vaughan v. Cox, 343 F.3d 1323 (CA11 2003) . . 146

Verdugo-Urquidez; United States v., 494 U.S. 259 (1990) 685; 1240

Villamonte-Marquez; United States v., 462 U.S. 579 (1983). .609

Virginia v. Moore, 553 U.S. 164 (2008) 650

W

Wade; United States v., 388 U.S. 218 (1967). .1155; 1260; 1306; 1349

Wakat v. Harlib, 253 F.2d 59 (7th Cir. 1958). . .867

Wakat; People v., 114 N.E.2d 706 (Ill. 1953). . .867

Walder v. United States, 347 U.S. 62 (1954). . .710; 1136

Walter v. United States, 447 U.S. 649 (1980). .1167

Warden v. Hayden, 387 U.S. 294 (1967). . .95; 113; 516; 592

Washington v. Washington State Commercial Passenger Fishing Vessel Ass'n, 443 U.S. 658 (1979). .920

Washington; United States v., 431 U.S. 181 (1977). 1219; 1311

Waterman; People v., 9 N.Y.2d 561 849

Watson; United States v., 423 U.S. 411 (1976) . . 93; 522

Watts v. Indiana, 338 U.S. 49 (1949) 829; 888

Weatherford v. Bursey, 429 U.S. 545 (1977). . .853; 1307

Weeks v. United States, 232 U.S. 383 (1914) . . 168; 219; 293; 516; 688; 697; 1251; 1365

Welsh v. Wisconsin, 466 U.S. 740 (1984). 119

White v. Maryland, 373 U.S. 59 (1963). 857

White; United States v., 401 U.S. 745 (1971) . . 519

Whiteley v. Warden, 401 U.S. 560 (1971) . 722; 750; 763

Whithead v. Keyes, 85 Mass. 495 (1862). 473

Whren v. United States, 517 U.S. 806 (1996) . . 268; 271; 607; 768

Wilkins v. May, 872 F.2d 190 (7th Cir. 1989). .1215

Williams v. Adams, 436 F.2d 30 (2d Cir. 1970) . 345

Wilson v. Arkansas, 514 U.S. 927 (1995). .612; 631; 632; 640; 702

Wilson v. United States, 162 U.S. 613 (1896). .1219

Winston v. Lee, 470 U.S. 753 (1985) 640; 659

Withrow v. Williams, 507 U.S. 680 (1993) . . . 909; 1214

Wolf v. Colorado, 338 U.S. 25 (1949). . . .688; 894

Wong Sun v. United States, 371 U.S. 471 (1963). 655; 1279; 1309

Wurie; United States v., 728 F.3d 1 (1st Cir. 2013) 304

Wyoming v. Houghton, 526 U.S. 295 (1999).58; 227

Y

Ybarra v. Illinois, 444 U.S. 85 (1979).154; 336; 718

Yick Wo v. Hopkins, 118 U.S. 356 (1886) . . . 1389

INDEX

[References are to sections.]

A

ADMINISTRATIVE SEARCHES
Generally . . . 13[D]

ARRESTS
Automobiles, searches incident to arrests in
 . . . 6[C]
Detention of persons pursuant to search warrants
 . . . 4[C]
Force in effectuating . . . 4[B]
Homes, in . . . 4[A]
Searches incident to
 Generally . . . 4[D]
 Automobiles, arrest in . . . 6[C]
Search warrants, detention of persons pursuant to
 . . . 4[C]

ATTENUATION
Fourth Amendment . . . 22[A]
Miranda . . . 22[B]

ATTORNEYS
Miranda invoking right to . . . 17[C][2]
Right to (See RIGHT TO COUNSEL)

AUTOMOBILES
Arrests in, searches incident to . . . 6[C]
Cars and containers . . . 6[B]
Containers . . . 6[B]
Highway stops without suspicions . . . 6[D]
Inventory searches . . . 6[E]
Open season on . . . Ch.12
Rule and rationale . . . 6[A]
Suspicionless highway stops . . . 6[D]

B

BORDER SEARCHES
Generally . . . 13[C]

C

CARS
Automobiles, in . . . 6[B]

CELL PHONES
Searches . . . Ch.7

COMPUTERS
Searches . . . Ch.7

CONFESSIONS
Due process (See DUE PROCESS)
Outside confession context (See DUE PROCESS)
Right to counsel (See RIGHT TO COUNSEL)
Voluntariness . . . Ch.15; Ch.19

CONSENT SEARCHES
Generally . . . Ch.11

CONTAINERS
Automobiles, in . . . 6[B]

COUNSEL
Miranda invoking right to . . . 17[C][2]
Right to (See RIGHT TO COUNSEL)

CUSTODY
Miranda . . . 17[E]

D

DISCOVERY
Inevitable discovery . . . Ch.23

DUE PROCESS
Entrapment . . . 24[B]
Fourth or Fifth Amendment considerations
 . . . 21[A]
Identification . . . 21[B]

E

ENTRAPMENT
Due process defense . . . 24[B]
Predisposition, relevance of . . . 24[A]

EXCLUSIONARY RULE
Good faith exception to . . . 14[B]
Rationale for . . . 14[A]
Standing requirement . . . 14[C]

F

FIFTH AMENDMENT
Confessions
 Due process (See DUE PROCESS)
 Right to counsel (See RIGHT TO COUNSEL)
 Voluntariness . . . Ch.15; Ch.19
Due process (See DUE PROCESS)
Miranda (See *MIRANDA*)
Voluntariness . . . Ch.15; Ch.19

FOURTH AMENDMENT
Arrests (See ARRESTS)
Attenuation . . . 22[A]
Automobiles (See AUTOMOBILES)
Consent searches . . . Ch.11
Divining Rod Theory of . . . 10[A]
Due process (See DUE PROCESS)
Exclusionary rule (See EXCLUSIONARY RULE)
Plain view . . . Ch.5
Probable cause (See PROBABLE CAUSE)
Protections of and rationale for . . . Ch.1
Searches (See SEARCHES)
Seizures . . . Ch.9
Warrants (See WARRANTS)

[References are to sections.]

G

GOOD FAITH
Exclusionary rule, exception to . . . 14[B]

H

HIGHWAY STOPS
Suspicionless . . . 6[D]

I

INEVITABLE DISCOVERY
Generally . . . Ch.23

INTERNATIONAL SEARCHES
Generally . . . 13[C]

INTERROGATION
Miranda . . . 17[F]

INVENTORY SEARCHES
Automobiles . . . 6[E]

M

MASSIAH
Miranda contrasted . . . 18[B]
Revisited . . . 18[A]

MIRANDA
Attenuation . . . 22[B]
Case itself . . . 17[A]
Counsel, invoking right to . . . 17[C][2]
Custody . . . 17[E]
Interrogation . . . 17[F]
Invoking
    Generally . . . 17[C]
    Counsel, right to . . . 17[C][2]
    Silence . . . 17[C][1]
Massiah contrasted . . . 18[B]
Nature of warnings . . . 17[B]
Public safety exception . . . 17[G]
Revisited . . . Ch.20
Silence, invoking right to . . . 17[C][1]
Waiver of rights . . . 17[D]
Warnings, nature of . . . 17[B]

P

PLAIN VIEW
Generally . . . Ch.5

PRIVACY
Reasonable expectation of . . . 10[B]

PROBABLE CAUSE
Generally . . . Ch.2
Limited searches on less than probable cause
    Protection of officer . . . 8[A]
    Reasonable suspicion and probable cause distinguished . . . 8[B]
    Terry-type stops, limits on . . . 8[C]
Reasonable suspicion distinguished . . . 8[B]

PUBLIC SAFETY EXCEPTION
Miranda . . . 17[G]

R

RIGHT TO COUNSEL
Generally . . . Ch.16
Confessions and
    Changes under Roberts Court decisions
        . . . 18[C]
    Massiah
        Miranda contrasted, and . . . 18[B]
        Revisited . . . 18[A]
    Miranda and *Massiah* contrasted . . . 18[B]
    Roberts Court decisions . . . 18[C]
    Sixth Amendment . . . 18[C]

ROBERTS COURT
Sixth Amendment decisions . . . 18[C]

S

SEARCHES
Administrative and other noncriminal searches
    . . . 13[D]
Arrests, incident to
    Generally . . . 4[D]
    Automobiles, arrests in . . . 6[C]
Automobile searches (See AUTOMOBILES)
Border searches . . . 13[C]
Cell phones . . . Ch.7
Computers . . . Ch.7
Consent searches . . . Ch.11
Divining Rod Theory of Fourth Amendment
    . . . 10[A]
DNA sample . . . 13[B]
Especially intrusive searches . . . 13[A]
International searches . . . 13[C]
Inventory searches in automobiles . . . 6[E]
Limited searches on less than probable cause (See
    PROBABLE CAUSE, subhead: Limited searches
    on less than probable cause)
Probable cause (See PROBABLE CAUSE)
Reasonable expectation of privacy . . . 10[B]

SEIZURES
Generally . . . Ch.9

SIXTH AMENDMENT
Right to counsel (See RIGHT TO COUNSEL)
Roberts Court decisions . . . 18[C]

STANDING
Exclusionary rule, standing to assert . . . 14[C]

V

VOLUNTARINESS
Generally . . . Ch.15
Revisited . . . Ch.19

[References are to sections.]

W

WAIVERS
Miranda . . . 17[D]

WARRANTS
Anatomy of . . . 3[B]
Detention of persons pursuant to search warrant
    . . . 4[C]
Issuing authority, persons with . . . 3[C]

WARRANTS—Cont.
Need for
    Anatomy of warrant . . . 3[B]
    Issuing authority, persons with . . . 3[C]
    Warrant requirement as exception or rule
        . . . 3[A]
Requirement as exception or rule . . . 3[A]
Search warrants, detention of persons pursuant to
    . . . 4[C]